Oxford Guide to British and American Culture

for learners of English

Editor **Jonathan Crowther**

Assistant Editor **Kathryn Kavanagh**

OXFORD
UNIVERSITY PRESS
Great Clarendon Street, Oxford OX2 6DP

Oxford University Press is a department of the University of Oxford.
It furthers the University's objective of excellence in research,
scholarship, and education by publishing worldwide in

Oxford New York

Athens Auckland Bangkok Bogotá Buenos Aires Cape Town Chennai
Dar es Salaam Delhi Florence Hong Kong Istanbul Karachi Kolkata
Kuala Lumpur Madrid Melbourne Mexico City Mumbai Nairobi
Paris São Paulo Singapore Taipei Tokyo Toronto Warsaw

with associated companies in Berlin Ibadan

Second impression (paperback) 2000

ISBN 0 19 431333 6 (hardback)
ISBN 0 19 431332 8 (paperback)

Cover illustrations *Front (left to right)*: the Statue of Liberty,
a US dollar bill, the Beatles, Concorde, Queen Elizabeth I.
Back (left to right): the Notting Hill Carnival, American Football.

Designed by Holdsworth Associates, Isle of Wight
Text capture and processing by Oxford University Press
Printed in China

Labels
used in the Guide

approv	showing that the user feels approval or admiration
disapprov	showing that the user feels disapproval or scorn
fig	(figurative) used before examples indicating non-literal or metaphorical usage
fml	(formal) usually used in serious or official, especially written, language
humor	(humorous) used with the intention of being funny
infml	(informal) used in a relaxed or unofficial context, especially in spoken English
ironic	used to mean the opposite of, or something very different from, the apparent meaning
less frequent	becoming less commonly used
offensive	used to address or refer to people in a very insulting way
old-fash	(old-fashioned) passing out of current use and seen as dated
old use	no longer in current use
rare	not often used
sl	(slang) very informal, mainly used in speech and sometimes restricted to a particular group of people
spoken	used only in spoken English
written	used only in written English

Noun and adjective types

[C]	countable noun, used in singular and plural forms with *is/are*, etc.; must have a determiner in the singular
[U]	uncountable noun, used in the singular only; can be used without a determiner
[C, U]	noun that can be countable or uncountable
[sing]	singular noun, agreeing with a singular verb
[pl]	plural noun, agreeing with a plural verb
[usu sing]	countable noun, usually singular
[usu pl]	countable noun, usually plural
[C + sing/pl *v*]	countable noun, used in both singular and plural forms but the singular form may also agree with a plural verb
[sing + sing/pl *v*]	singular noun, used with either a singular or plural verb
[not before *n*]	(of adjectives) not used before a noun
[only before *n*]	(of adjectives) only used before a noun
[usu before *n*]	(of adjectives or nouns) usually used before a noun

Verb types

[I] intransitive

[T] transitive

Contents

The Guide 1–599

Articles and lists (at or near their alphabetical positions)

Colour pages (between pages 280 and 281)

Advisory Board

Dr Keith Brown **Ms Moira Runcie** **Dr Norman Whitney**
Dr Alan Cruse **Prof Gabriele Stein** **Prof Henry Widdowson**

Phonetics consultant **Michael Ashby**

Foreword

Who are or were the *Princes in the Tower*, *Beavis and Butt-head*, *Mo Mowlam* and *Mark McGwire*? What is or was *Sojourner*, *Marmite*, *Groundhog Day* and *Blind Date*? What is the difference between *Soho* and *SoHo*? And *Who Killed Cock Robin?* Students of English regularly come across references like these to aspects of British and American life and traditions which are not adequately explained, or not given at all, in standard language dictionaries.

This new dictionary has been written as a guide to a better understanding of such references, and thus as a starting-point to help more advanced students and teachers of English to explore the language through its culture. As such it can be seen as a companion volume to the **Oxford Advanced Learner's Dictionary** (**OALD**), a reader's encyclopedia of Britain and the US covering most aspects of life in the two countries as well as their historical heritage. Acting on the advice of teachers, we have interpreted 'culture' in its broadest sense, from 'high art' – literature, music, architecture, etc. – on the one hand, to popular culture on the other. So readers will find entries on poets, painters and politicians alongside pop stars, media personalities and sportspeople; and famous buildings, institutions and historical events as well as household brand names, food dishes, children's rhymes, and much more besides.

An important feature of the dictionary is the inclusion where appropriate of information on the special connotation that items have for British and American people, in addition to the purely factual details given about them. This can be seen especially in the 'notes' and 'articles', longer entries on broad thematic topics such as *education*, *humour* and *class*.

As in the OALD, the dictionary entries have been written within a limited vocabulary, to make them easier to understand. When more difficult or technical words have had to be used they are usually explained by glosses in the text. Key items of vocabulary are also highlighted in the notes and articles in **dark type**.

In choosing the entries for the **Guide**, we have tried to include the most important or currently significant items and cultural topics that advanced students of English are likely to encounter, though in a rapidly changing world some of these will of course date more quickly than others. We look forward to hearing what users think of the choices we have made, and we welcome any suggestions for future editions.

I am very grateful to the following members of the writing team who helped to create the dictionary: D'Arcy Adrian-Vallance, Gary Dexter, David Hallworth, Mark Harrison, Fiona McIntosh, Diane E Pecorari, David Pickering and John Wright. In addition I must thank Michael Ashby of University College, London, for his advice on the treatment of punctuation and stress, and Susan Wilkin for editing this aspect of the dictionary. Fran Holdsworth must take full credit for the overall design of the dictionary, and the choice of illustrations owes a great deal to the painstaking picture research done by Suzanne Williams. Special thanks are due to my colleague Kathy Kavanagh for her work on the notes, articles and colour pages.

Jonathan Crowther
February 1999

Key to entries

ba'roque *adj* in a highly decorated style of art that was fashionable in Europe in the 17th and early 18th centuries after developing in Italy. Examples of the British baroque style include buildings designed by the architects *Wren and *Vanbrugh, and the music of *Purcell and *Handel.

▶ **baroque** (*often* **the baroque**) *n* [U] the baroque style or baroque art.

ˌBattery 'Park /ˌbætəri/ a park at the southern end of *Manhattan(1) Island, New York, opposite the *Statue of Liberty. Boats take tourists, etc. from the park to the statue, *Ellis Island and *Staten Island.

beer

In Britain, beer is the most popular alcoholic drink which is drunk in *pubs. Many people drink **bitter**, a brown-coloured beer. It is sold **on draught**, if it is drawn for each customer from a large container, usually a **keg** or **barrel**, or **bottled**, if it has been put in small bottles at a factory.

ˌElmer '**Bernstein**[1] /ˌelmə 'bɜːnstaɪn; *AmE* ˌelmər 'bɜːrnstaɪn/ (1922–) a US composer, especially of music for films. His successes include *The Magnificent Seven* (1960), *To Kill A Mockingbird* (1962) and *The Age of Innocence* (1993).

ˌLeonard '**Bernstein**[2] /'bɜːnstaɪn; *AmE* 'bɜːrnstaɪn/ (1918–90) a US conductor, composer and piano player. He wrote several popular *musicals. The most successful was *West Side Story* (1957) which became a film in 1961.

ˌblood 'sausage ⇨ BLACK PUDDING.

the '**Borscht Belt** /'bɔːʃt; *AmE* 'bɔːrʃt/ (*also* the '**Borscht ˌcircuit**) (*AmE humor*) a holiday area in the *Catskill Mountains in New York State.

'Boston ˌbaked 'beans /'bɒstən; *AmE* 'bɔːstən/ (*also* **baked beans**) *n* [pl] (in the US) white haricot beans baked with pork and brown sugar or molasses (= a dark, sweet, thick liquid obtained from sugar).

The '***Brains Trust*** a *BBC radio programme in the 1940s which became a television programme in the 1950s In it a group of well-known intellectuals discussed a wide range of topics.

'Bramley /'bræmli/ (*also* **Bramley apple**, **Bramley's seedling**) *n* a type of large green apple that is suitable for cooking rather than for eating raw. Bramleys are especially popular in Britain.

the '**brat pack** *n* [usu sing] (*infml*) a group of well-known or successful young people, especially actors, who enjoy being famous and sometimes behave badly: *Tom Cruise was a member of the Hollywood brat pack.*

the ˌ**Bridge of 'Sighs** **1** an attractive old bridge over the river Cam in *Cambridge, England. It belongs to St John's College, part of Cambridge University, and looks like the famous Bridge of Sighs in Venice. **2** a similar bridge between two buildings of Hertford College, part of *Oxford University.

the ˌ**British Ath'letic Fedeˌration** the organization that controls British athletics and is responsible for British athletes taking part in international events. Compare AAA.

the '**British 'Board of 'Film Classifiˌcation** the organization that decides which films and videos can be seen by people of different ages in Britain. See also FILM CERTIFICATE.

British English ⇨ article.

Labels (left):
- entry word/phrase in **dark type**
- ▶ derivatives section with special symbol
- * indicates an item with its own entry
- special note
- raised numbers distinguish separate entries for people, places, etc. with the same name
- labels giving information about usage and geographical restriction (*see inside front cover*)
- explanation of uncommon word used in entry
- entry phrase/word in ***dark italic type*** indicating a title
- information on grammar (*see inside front cover*)
- separate numbered parts of entry when entry phrase/word refers to more than one thing
- cross-reference to related entry

Labels (right):
- part of speech, where appropriate (*see inside front cover*)
- indicates numbered part of entry referred to
- key vocabulary highlighted in **dark type**
- indicates date of birth of a living person
- 'dummy' entry referring to main entry elsewhere
- British and American English pronunciation of proper names (*see inside back cover*)
- variants of entry word/phrase
- example in *italic type* showing typical usage
- stress pattern indicated on entry phrase/word (*see inside back cover*)
- cross-reference to contrasted entry
- 'dummy' entry referring to special article nearby

Acknowledgements

We are grateful to the following for permission to reproduce illustrations:

b = bottom c = centre l = left r = right t = top

AA Photo Library *402l, 433* ™**Aardman/Wallace & Gromit Ltd 1993** *567* **Action-Plus Photographic** *135, 591*; C Barry *373l*; R Francis *295*; N Haynes *374*; C Jarman *137b*; G Kirk *105, 316*; G Tiederman *268* ©**The New Yorker Collection 1947 Charles Addams** from cartoonbank.com All Rights Reserved. *5* **Aga-Rayburn** APR Studio & Location Photography *7* **AKG London** E Lessing *43b, 61r* **Bryan and Cherry Alexander Photography** *271* **Allsport** A Bello *41*; M Hewitt *537l* **Arcaid** R Bryant *390b* **Ashmolean Museum, University of Oxford** M Beerbohm © by kind permission of Mrs Reichmann *47* **Assay Office, London** *240* **Associated Press** *170l, 257*; J Scott Applewhite *396r*; S Katzendobler *281tl* **The Automobile Association of Great Britain** *1* **Clive Barda** *162r, 342, 445* **BBC** *228, 261, 531r* **BBC Natural History Unit** B Osborne *30* **BBC Proms Office** C Faulds *298tl* **Catherine Blackie** *36r* **The Enid Blyton signature and the Famous Five are trademarks of Enid Blyton Ltd. (All rights reserved)** ©Enid Blyton 'Five on a Treasure Island' 1942 illustrated by Eileen A Soper. Reproduced by permission of Hodder and Stoughton *60tr* **The Bridgeman Art Library, London and New York** Alecto Historical Editions, London *156tr*; English School, 'John Tradescant the Elder and his wife Elizabeth', 1656 The Ashmolean Museum, University of Oxford *C28b*; Belvoir Castle, Leicestershire *C19tl*; F Madox Brown 'The Last of England' 1852–55 ©Birmingham Museum and Art Gallery *298bl*; British Library, London *310t*; Christie's Images *C29t*; W Blake Plate 1 from 'Songs of Innocence and of Experience' (copy AA) c.1815–26 (etching, ink and watercolour) Fitzwilliam Museum, University of Cambridge, UK *58t*; Guildhall Art Gallery, Corporation of London *462*; Guildhall Library, Corporation of London *10b*; Paul Nash 'The Mule Track' 1917, Imperial War Museum, London *366*; Museum of the North American Indian, New York *221l*; The National Gallery, London *214*; National Library of Scotland, Edinburgh *C28tl*; Private Collections *93, 101b, 137t, 356t, 575b*; Private Collection Jean Leon Jerome Ferris (1863–1930) 'The Drafting of the Declaration of Independence in 1776', by kind permission of the artist's estate *208r*; Private Collection J S Sargent 'Mrs Carl Meyer and her two children', 1896 *474*; A Warhol 'Self Portrait', 1967, Private Collection ©The Andy Warhol Foundation for the Visual Arts Inc/ARS, New York & DACS, London 1999 *568*; W Larkin 'Portrait of Richard Sackville', 1613, Ranger's House, Blackheath *C28tr*; By kind permission of Mrs Carol A Danes/Needham & Grant Solicitors, Rochdale Art Gallery, Lancashire *321*; Scottish National Portrait Gallery, Edinburgh *81l*; Victoria & Albert Museum, London *31, 152r*; Watlington Hall, Northumberland *C19tr*; Woburn Abbey, Bedfordshire *171* **British Airways** *cover/Concorde* ©**The British Library Board** *71l* ©**BSI** *77* ©**Camelot** *320* **Camera Press London** Sir Cecil Beaton *45r*; Sunday Times/M Ellidge *212*; T Spencer *51* **Carlton Television** *270* **J Allan Cash Photolibrary** *35r, 37l, 57t, 65r, 86b, 88b, 92r, 101t, 107, 312l, 387, 407b, 569l, 575t, 579l, 595* **Centre for the Study of Cartoons and Caricature, University of Kent, Canterbury** Mirror Group/R Smythe *18* **Christie's Images** *118, 531l, 539r*; Burt Sugarman Collection *25t, 103* **Collections** J D Beldom *C20tl*; A Cooper *C10b (also C8)*; R Davis *C21tr*; R Hallmann *C10t (also C9)*; G Howard *146*; C Inch *C13b (also C9)*; M Kipling *C13cb*; A Le Garsmeur *194r*; Select *C12tr*; B Shuel *C32tl, 347t*; A Sieveking *508*; M St Maur Sheil *241b*; R Weaver *C13bl (also C9)* **Colorsport** *39t* **Beryl Cook** 'The Ladies Match' published in 'Bouncers' 1991 by Victor Gollancz. Copyright ©1991 Beryl Cook. Reproduced by arrangement with the artist c/o Rogers, Coleridge & White Ltd, 20 Powis Mews, London W11 1JN *126r* **Donald Cooper/Photostage** *64, 69, 142b, 142t, 186b, 225, 401r* **Corbis-Bettmann** *C16tr, C17tl, 162l, 164, 174l, 198, 204, 287l, 300, 347b, 470b, 492*; Reuter/J Christensen *163r*; Springer *247b*; UPI *156br, 213, 286r*; Grant Wood 'American Gothic', 1930. The Art Institute of Chicago, Illinois. Friends of America Art Collection *14* **Corbis Images** *140*; T Aruzza *C21tl*; J P Blair *354tl*; Chromo-Sohn Inc/J Sohn *244*; R A Cooke *258, 358l*; Cordaiy Photo Library Ltd/G Taunton *331tl*; Everett *97, 286l, 335*; K Fleming *C1t, 337t*; O Franken *C5ct*; L Goldsmith *C32b*; A Griffiths Belt *280*; J Heseltine *328*; Hulton Getty Collection *539l*; J Hurst *165t*; Krist *C7t (also C3)*; C & J Lenars *cover/carnival 343*; Library of Congress *507t, 583*; ©Estate of Roy Lichtenstein/DACS, London 1999 *308*; The National Archives *553*; The National Gallery, London *126l, 549*; B May *C32tr*; D Muench *315t*; M Nicholson *81r*; D Peebles *298r*; S Raymer *C5b*; R Ressmeyer *C5cb*; Reuter/G Hershorn *306*; Sean Sexton Collection *409l*; L Skoogfors *307*; T Spiegel *134, 267*; UPI *511*; US Dept of Defence/Cdr J Leenhouts *409r*; P Ward *435l, 435r, 526*; A Woolfitt *517* **Julian Cotton** *(also C9)* **Photo Library** J Hawkes *C15 (also C9)* **Country Life Picture Library** J Gibson *322l* ©**Crown Copyright** Historic Royal Palaces *37r*; The Queen's Awards Office *439*; The Royal Mint *466t* ©**Digital Vision** *cover/Statue of Liberty/yellow cab* ©**Disney Enterprises, Inc. The Walt Disney Company/Mickey Mouse Magazine** *345* **The D'Oyly Carte Opera Company** R Workman *346* **The Board of Trinity College, Dublin** *63* **Dulux, ICI** *161* **e.t.archive** *133, 233*; British Museum *C18l*; Greater London Record Office *380*; Hereford Cathedral Library *329* **Walker Evans** 'Sharecropper's Family' 1936, gelatin-silver print 7¾×9⅝ inches (19.7×24.4 cm) The Museum of Modern Art, New York. Gift of the Farm Security Administration. Copyright ©1998 The Museum of Modern Art, New York *181* **Elisabeth Frink DBE CH RA. By kind permission of the artist's estate** *212* **John Frost Historical Newspaper Service/The New Yorker** *5* **S Gamester** *163l* **Genesis Space Photo Library/NASA** *322r* **The Glasgow Picture Library** *324* **Sally & Richard Greenhill** *597*; S Greenhill *C5tr, C13t* **Robert Harding Picture Library** *C25tl, 42, 49, 74, 102, 220, 237t, 262, 294, 413r, 414, 444r, 463, 488, 514*; C Bowman *436, 456*; F & D Caldwell *C7b (also C2)*; P Craven *207*; N Francis *33, 230, 467c, 487*; R Francis *35l, 158*; I Griffiths *156l*; S Harris *473b, 538*; M J Howell *447*; D Hughes *12r, 44*; D Jacobs *390t*; M Jenner *4, 94l*; R Kamal *467b*; M Mawson *78*; J Miller *87*; R Rainford *C20tr, C31b, 10t, 239, 379, 586t*; W Rawlings *485*; P van Reil *309*; C Rennie *391r*; R Richardson *12l, 221r, 315b*; A Robinson *186t*; R Scagell *82t*; Schuster *566r*; T Waltham *206*; Van der Larst *499*; A Woolfitt *32, 96l, 129t, 354b, 356b, 512, 555b*; E Young *C20b* **Hasbro UK Ltd** *2t* **Edward Hopper** 'Gas' 1940 oil on canvas 26½×40¼ inches (66.7×102.2 cm) The Museum of Modern Art, New York. Mrs Simon Guggenheim Fund. Photograph ©1998 The Museum of Modern Art, New York *260b* **House of Commons Education Unit** G Quin ©1995 Parliamentary copyright *323, 405, 504* **Hulton Getty** *C16tl, 36l, 43t, 48bl, 57b, 67b, 71r, 88c, 96r, 106r, 130, 179, 201, 219, 224b, 252, 289r, 331tr, 357, 401l, 432, 457, 470t, 493, 529, 535, 537r, 551, 588* **The Image Bank** G Cralle *C6t (also C3)*; P McConcille *C23tr*; M Melford *C4l (also C3), C30bl*; C Molyneux *C24r*; G Rossi *C14 (also C3)*; *C22b*; E L Simmons *C22t (also C3)*; H Sund *C4r*; S Wilkinson *C5tl (also C2)* **Impact Photos** P Achache *60l*; T Bouzac *C11c (also C8)*; J Calder *281tr*; P Cavendish *180, 502*; C Cormack *C25b, C30tl, 90, 464*; N Davies *106l*; S Fear *237b*; P Gordon *C13ct*; M Hicks *562*; C Jones *86t*; A MacNaughton *C1b*; Material World/P Ginter & P Menzel *C26*; D Reed *C27*; P Menzel *C23c*; T Page *C30c*; B Rybolt *C23tl*; S Shepheard *521*; H Sykes *132* **A F Kersting** *410* **Knight Features ©1996 United Feature Syndicate, Inc** *407c* **The Kobal Collection** *25b, 50, 66, 145b, 165b, 217, 227, 231, 285, 289l, 299c, 443, 476, 571, 587*; F Albertson *334*; ©1996 Castle Rock Entertainment/K Hayes *354tr*; K Hamshere *260t*; M Little *148*; National Film Archive *290*; Olivier Prods/London Films/Big Ben Films *392b*; Pathe/H Roach *313*; Sony Pictures Entertainment Co *138*; Spelling/ABC *119*; Twentieth Century Fox *145t*; Universal *208l* **Magnum Photos** E Arnold *C6b*; S Franklin *C11t*; M Parr *C31t*; F Scianna *C21bl* **Mary Evans Picture Library** *45l, 392t, 541t*, H Grant *452*, J Hassall *11, 281bl*; Illustrated London News *C19b* **Donald McGill** ©Pharos International Ltd & ©Elfreda Buckland. From E Buckland 'The World of Donald McGill', Blandford Press, 1984. Photo J M Dudley *339* **Meccano® Toys Ltd** *340* **MTV Networks ©1996. All rights reserved** *46* **The Muppets ©Jim Henson Company** *361* **The Trustees of the National Maritime Museum** *467t* **National Motor Museum, Beaulieu** *48tl*; ©British Motor Industry Heritage Trust *348* **National Portrait Gallery, London** *82b*; M Droeshout *486* **New Millennium Experience Company** A Putler *C21br (also C9)* **Peter Newark's Pictures** *13, 21, 54, 79, 92l, 124, 139, 229, 291, 312br, 406, 451, 458l, 548*; L Hine *C16c, C17tr, C29b, C29c, 569r* **Map and symbols reproduced from Ordnance Survey Landranger 1:50 000 scale mapping map with the permission of The Controller of Her Majesty's Stationery Office ©Crown copyright, Licence number 399612** *395* **Oxford Scientific Films** M Cordano *425b* **Oxford University Press** K Baxendale *242*; B Brecken *174r*; J M Dudley *39b, 129b, 399, 498, 584*; R Judges *185, 194l, 197, 199, 373r*; *518b, 530*; J Richards *40t*; Technical Graphics Dept *C2/3, C8/9, 89*; Thomas-Photos Oxford *362* **'PA' Weather Centre Ltd** The Independent *572* **Images® copyright 1999 PhotoDisc, Inc** *cover/football, London taxi* **The Photolibrary Wales** D Williams *C12tl*; J Moore *C11b* **Pictorial Press** *cover/Beatles* ©**Lawrence Pollinger Ltd and the Estate of Mrs J C Robinson** *247t* **Jackson Pollock, Springs, New York, 1950 ©ARS, New York and DACS, London 1999.** Photo ©Hans Namuth *2b* **Pooh** ©E H Shepard. Reproduced by kind permission of Curtis Brown Ltd. From 'Winnie-the-Pooh' by A A Milne ©copyright 1926. Reprinted by arrangement with Dutton Children's Books a Division of Penguin Putnam Inc *422* **Popperfoto** S G Forster *C17b, 541b, 561*; Reuters/C Rodwell *384*; Reuters/J Skipper *154* **Beatrix Potter** 'The Tale of Peter Rabbit' copyright ©Frederick Warne & Co, 1902, 1987. Reproduced by kind permission of Frederick Warne & Co *425c* **Redferns** P Ford *516*; W P Gottlieb/Library of Congress *278*; D Redfern *131* **Rex Features** *48br, 65l, 67t, 287r, 310b, 318, 325, 337b, 358r, 438, 442, 473c, 481, 491, 513bl*; B Armstrong *389*; S Barker *507b*; P Brookes *224t*; P Brown *241t*; R Collins *506t*; N Cornish *465*; C Dixon *62*; C Harris *385*; A Pullen *299b*; T Rooke *152l*; D Store *183*; The Times/C Harris *466b*; Today *299t, 480*; R Young *402r, 579r* **Rover Group Product Communications** *444l* **Royal Geographical Society, London** Ponting *479* **The Salvation Army** R Bryant *472* **Science Photo Library** C Butler *263*; NASA *22t, 501* **The Scotch House** *22b* ©**The Trustees of the National Museums of Scotland 1999** *95* **Frank Spooner Pictures** K Bernstein FSP *59*; Gamma/Arkell *60br*; Gamma/C Ducasse *333*; Gamma/I Jones FSP *58b, 506c*; Gamma/Parker *94tr*; Gamma/Photo-News *425t*; Gamma/J Prayer *222*; Gaywood *534*; Liaison/Barr *396l*; Liaison/Gamma/Agostini *596*; Liaison/Narkel *113b*; Liaison/D Walker *513tl*; MC-Liaison *586c* **Still Moving Picture Library** D Corrance *166* **By courtesy of the Marquess of Tavistock and the Trustees of the Bedford Estates Armada Portrait of Queen Elizabeth I by George Gower in Woburn Abbey** *cover* **Thomas-Photos Oxford** *61l* ©**D C Thomson & Co Ltd 1997** *40b* **Tony Stone Images** D Armand *378t*; O Benn *113t*; T Brase *391l, 547*; G Brettnacher *458r*; C Davidson *555t*; P Degginger *411*; R Elliott *94br*; S & N Geary *580*; S Grandadam *17*; A Hicks *515*; P Ingrand *413l*; R Jack *469*; J Lamb *288*; J Lawrence *398*; I Murphy *518t*; E Pritchard *542*; A & L Sinibaldi *513br*; B Stablyk *471*; B Thomas *574*; *473c*; R Wells *88t, 331br* **Alfred Wainwright** one map from 'Ascent from Wrynose' (Cold Pike 2) from 'A Pictorial Guide to the Lakeland Fells' by A Wainwright (Michael Joseph, 1992) ©copyright 1992 Michael Joseph Ltd. Reproduced by permission of Penguin Books Ltd. *566l* **Wales Tourist Board** *170r* **John Walmsley Photo-Library** *C24l* **Trustees of the Wedgwood Museum, Barlaston, Stoke-on-Trent** *573* **Elizabeth Whiting & Associates** *C25tr* **Wind in the Willows** ©E H Shepard. Reproduced by kind permission of Curtis Brown Ltd. Reprinted with the permission of Atheneum Books for Young Readers, an imprint of Simon & Schuster Children's Publishing Division from 'The Wind in the Willows' by Kenneth Grahame, illustrated by Ernest H Shepard. Copyright 1933 Charles Scribner's Sons, copyright renewed ©1961 Ernest H Shepard *585*

Aa

AA /ˌeɪ ˈeɪ/ **1** ⇨ ALCOHOLICS ANONYMOUS. **2** (the **AA**) (in Britain) an organization for drivers that provides help when their cars break down. The AA also offers other services to its members, such as travel advice and insurance: *Are you in the AA?*

an AA man helping a motorist

AAA /ˌeɪ eɪ ˈeɪ, ˌθriː ˈeɪz/ ⇨ AMATEUR ATHLETIC ASSOCIATION, AMERICAN AUTOMOBILE ASSOCIATION.

A and P /ˌeɪ ənd ˈpiː/ (*in full* the **Great Atlantic and Pacific Tea Company**) a popular US supermarket with branches in all the states. It began in 1859 in New York City and became successful as one of the first companies to buy large numbers of items at a cheap rate and offer them for sale at low prices.

ˌHank ˈ**Aaron** /ˈeərən; *AmE* ˈerən, ˈærən/ (1934–) a famous US *African-American *baseball player who hit more home runs (755) during his career than any other player. His popular name was 'Hammerin' Hank'. He played for 23 years (1954–74) with the Braves in *Milwaukee and then in *Atlanta. He was chosen for the Baseball *Hall of Fame in 1982.

AAU ⇨ AMATEUR ATHLETIC UNION.

the ˌ**Abbey** ˈ**National** a British bank with branches in many towns and cities. It was formerly the second largest *building society in Britain and became a bank in 1989, the first building society to do so. ⇨ note at BUILDING SOCIETIES.

ˈ**Abbotsford** /ˈæbətsfəd; *AmE* ˈæbətsfɔːrd/ a large house built near the river Tweed in Scotland for Walter *Scott in 1822–4. It was Scott's final home. The style of its architecture is like a romantic castle in one of his novels. It now contains some of his possessions and other Scottish historical objects.

ˌGeorge ˈ**Abbott** /ˈæbət/ (1887–1995) a US writer of plays and director and producer of Broadway shows, mostly *musicals. He wrote nearly 50 plays, including *The Boys from Syracuse* (1938) and *Damn Yankees* (1955). The George Abbott Theater on Broadway is named after him. He lived to be 108 and was still writing at the age of 100.

ˌ**Abbott and Co**ˈ**stello** /ˌæbət, kɒˈsteləʊ; *AmE* kɑːˈsteloʊ/ the US comic actors **Bud Abbott** (1895–1974), who was thin and angry, and **Lou Costello** (1906–59), who was fat and funny. They were most popular as a team in films during the 1940s, making such successes as *Buck Privates* (1941) and *Abbott and Costello Meet Frankenstein* (1948).

ABC /ˌeɪ biː ˈsiː/ (*in full* the **American Broadcasting Company**) one of the original three major television networks in America. It began in 1943 as the 'Blue Network' of six radio stations. Popular television shows on ABC have included **NYPD Blue* and **Roseanne*. ABC is now owned by the Walt *Disney Company. See also CBS, NBC.

the ˌ**abdi**ˈ**cation** ˌ**crisis** *n* [sing] (in British history) a series of events in 1936, following King *Edward VIII's decision to marry a divorced American woman, Wallis *Simpson. It was thought that the British public would not accept a queen who had been divorced, and Edward was advised by the *Prime Minister to abdicate (= give up his position as king). The couple were married in France in 1937, and Edward's brother (as *George VI) became king in his place.

ˌ**Aber**ˈ**deen** /ˌæbəˈdiːn; *AmE* ˌæbərˈdiːn/ a city and port in north-east Scotland. It is an important fishing port, and the main centre of the *North Sea oil and gas industries. Many of its buildings are made of granite, a hard grey stone, and for this reason it is often called the 'granite city'.

ˌ**Aberdeen** ˈ**Angus** /ˌæbədiːn ˈæŋgəs; *AmE* ˌæbərdiːn/ a breed of black cattle without horns, originally bred in Scotland. They are known for the quality of their meat.

ˌ**Aber**ˈ**donian** /ˌæbəˈdəʊniən; *AmE* ˌæbərˈdoʊniən/ *n* a person from *Aberdeen.
▶ **Aberdonian** *adj* of or from Aberdeen.

ˌ**Aber**ˈ**fan** /ˌæbəˈvæn; *AmE* ˌæbərˈvæn/ a small *coal-mining town in South Wales. In 1966 a large pile of coal waste fell onto the school there, killing 116 children and 28 adults.

Aˌ***bide With*** ˈ***Me*** a Christian hymn, written in the 18th century. It is sometimes sung at funerals, and English football supporters traditionally sing it at the *FA *Cup Final.

ˈ**Abilene** /ˈæbəliːn/ a city in the US state of *Kansas. It was first settled in 1856 and became in the 1860s a major rail centre for transporting cattle driven up the *Chisholm Trail from *Texas. Today it is a centre for agricultural products and makes aircraft parts. President Dwight *Eisenhower, who lived in Abilene as a boy, is buried there, and the city has an Eisenhower museum.

ˌ**abo**ˈ**litionism** *n* [U] the American campaign in the 1800s to free the slaves in the southern states. Its members were called **abolitionists**, and many hid slaves who were escaping on the *Underground Railroad. Famous abolitionists included the poet John Greenleaf *Whittier and the author Harriet Beecher *Stowe.

ˌ***Absolutely*** ˈ***Fabulous*** a British television comedy series that was very popular in the early 1990s. It was written by Jennifer *Saunders, who also acted in it. It is about two women, Patsy and Edina, who work in the fashion business. They spend most of their time drinking, smoking and taking drugs, and arguing with Edina's daughter, who is very serious and disapproves of them.

ˌ**abstract ex**ˈ**pressionism** *n* [U] a style of painting that was developed in the 1940s by US artists such as Jackson *Pollock and Mark *Rothko. In their paintings they use shapes and colours to express their

A

feelings instead of representing objects or scenes. ▶ **abstract expressionist** *n, adj: an abstract expressionist painting.*

ABTA /ˈæbtə/ (*in full* the **Association of British Travel Agents**) a British organization that protects the customers of travel agents, e.g. by giving people back the money for their tickets if the travel company goes bankrupt.

Aˈcademy Aˌward *n* any of the famous *Oscar film awards. They are presented every March in *Los Angeles by the *Academy of Motion Picture Arts and Sciences. The awards were first presented in 1929 by Douglas *Fairbanks[1]. Winners receive a small metal statue, and the most important ones are for 'Best Actor', 'Best Actress', and 'Best Picture'. Walt *Disney has won the most Oscars (32), and the films winning the most (11) have been **Ben-Hur* in 1959 and **Titanic* in 1998.

the **Aˈcademy of ˈMotion ˌPicture ˈArts and ˈSciences** the US film organization in *Los Angeles that presents the *Academy Awards. It was created in 1927 by Louis B *Mayer and now has 4 000 members who are actors, directors, producers and technical workers. The Academy also decides on technical standards for the film industry.

the **Aˈcademy of St ˈMartin-in-the-ˈFields** a small British orchestra, formed in 1959. At first, it played only *baroque music, and all its concerts took place in the church of St Martin-in-the-Fields in *Trafalgar Square, London. Now it is one of London's most famous small orchestras, playing a wide variety of music.

ACAS /ˈeɪkæs/ (*in full* the **Advisory, Conciliation and Arbitration Service**) an independent British organization which brings together workers and their employers when the usual methods of dealing with arguments about pay and working conditions have failed. It was set up by the government in 1975: *Eventually ACAS was called in to mediate.*

Accent and dialect ⇨ article.

ˈaccess course *n* (in Britain) an adult education course that prepares especially older students who do not have *A levels for study at a university or college of higher education. ⇨ note at ADULT EDUCATION.

Ace™ /eɪs / *n* a US make of elastic bandage. It is often used by runners for muscle pain.

ˌDean ˈ**Acheson** /ˈætʃɪsn/ (1893–1971) a US diplomat. He directed the *Marshall Plan to help Europe after World War II and, as *Secretary of State under President *Truman, helped in 1949 to create the *North Atlantic Treaty Organization. He received a *Pulitzer Prize in 1970 for his book *Present at the Creation: My Years in the State Department.*

ˈacid drop *n* (*BrE*) a type of hard sweet with a slightly bitter taste. Acid drops are often sold in paper bags by weight, and are popular with children.

ˌacid ˈhouse *n* [U] (*becoming less frequent*) a type of fast electronic pop music with few words (a form of *house) that first became popular in the US in the mid 1980s, and later in Britain. It was played especially at *raves or **acid house parties**, which were often held illegally in large buildings or outdoors, and where drugs such as Ecstasy were often used.

ˌacid ˈjazz *n* [U] a type of dance music, popular in the 1990s. It is a mixture of *soul, *jazz and *hip hop styles. Groups such as Incognito and the Brand New Heavies are typical of the style, using jazz instruments, *rap singers and a fast rhythm.

ˌacid ˈrock *n* [U] a type of *rock music that was popular in the 1960s when many groups and their audiences used acid (a slang name for the drug LSD). US groups such as the *Grateful Dead and Jefferson Airplane were typical of this style. Their mysterious songs, played on electronic guitars, were much influenced by drugs.

ACT /ˌeɪ siː ˈtiː/ (*in full* **American College Test**) a standard test that a person must take to become a student at most American colleges. It tests knowledge of English, mathematics, sciences, and other subjects.

ˈAction Man™ *n* a toy in the form of a man, with different clothes and equipment that can be bought separately. When it was first sold in the 1960s as a doll for boys, Action Man was a soldier. Later, it was possible to dress the doll for other activities, including some sports. Some people in Britain have said that these toys should be forbidden because they encourage boys to be violent.

Action Man

ˈAction on ˈSmoking and ˈHealth ⇨ ASH.

ˈaction ˌpainting *n* [U] a method of painting used by Jackson *Pollock and other *abstract expressionist artists. Instead of using a brush, the artist throws or pours paint onto the painting as a way of expressing his or her unconscious feelings more directly.

Jackson Pollock at work

Act of Parliament ⇨ article.

the **ˌAct of ˈSettlement** (in Britain) an *Act of Parliament in 1701, saying that the children of *James I's granddaughter Sophia would be the future kings and queens. The government made this law because the king at that time, *William III, had no children, and they wanted to stop the *Catholic *Stuarts from becoming kings and queens. Sophia was a *Protestant. She was married to the Elector (= a type of prince) of *Hanover. Their son became King *George I, the first king of the House of Hanover. ⇨ table at KINGS AND QUEENS.

the **ˌAct of Suˈpremacy** (in Britain) an *Act of Parliament in 1534 that made King *Henry VIII the head of the *Church of England. This left the Pope with no power in England.

the **ˌAct of ˈUnion** (in Britain) either of two *Acts

Accent and dialect

Accent refers to the way a language is spoken. Most foreign speakers of English have accents which are influenced by their first language. Native speakers may have an accent associated with the region they come from. *Accent* includes both **pronunciation** (= the way sounds and words are spoken) and **intonation** (= the sound patterns of sentences). Each regional accent has its own mixture of sounds and intonation. The way in which individuals speak is also influenced by other factors, such as social background, age and level of education, and whether they have moved away from their home area.

The terms **variety** and **dialect** overlap. A *variety* may be a form of English associated with a group of people, e.g. *Black English, with a particular region, e.g. *British English and *American English, or with an activity or function, e.g. legal English. A *dialect* is a variety that is usually associated with a geographical region. Dialects have a distinctive vocabulary and grammar, and when people **speak in dialect** they use an associated local accent.

Authors such as Charles *Dickens, Thomas *Hardy, D H *Lawrence, Mark *Twain and Joel Chandler Harris (*Uncle Remus) have used dialect very effectively in their books, but relatively little is now written in dialect.

Dialect or standard?

The word *variety* usually arouses fewer emotions than *dialect*. This is because dialects are often considered inferior to standard forms of English. In Britain, people may assume that somebody speaking in dialect has a lower-class background or has had little education. In the US, a dialect suggests where a person comes from but not their social status. Use of **non-standard forms**, such as *ain't* for 'isn't', 'aren't' or 'am not', which are found in many British and American dialects, is seen as a sign of a low level of education in both countries.

In Britain some dialects differ greatly from **standard English**, but many dialect speakers use standard English when speaking to people from another region. The accent called **RP** (***Received Pronunciation**) has been the one most closely associated in the past with educated speakers and is still used as a standard for foreign learners of English. The **marked** (= extreme) form of RP is restricted to the *upper classes, but an ordinary, **unmarked** form is associated with standard English as traditionally used by the ***BBC**. In fact the term is unknown to most British people, schools now pay much less attention to teaching it, and most people's speech has traces of a regional accent.

In the US ***General American English** is the closest to a standard form and is heard on national television. Regional dialects have some differences in vocabulary, and their accents are distinctive, but it is uncommon for Americans from different parts of the country to have difficulty understanding each other. Vocabulary and accent are influenced as much by social contact, ethnic background, age, class and occupation as by regional boundaries. Varieties such as Black English, Jewish English, Hispanic English and *Cajun English are based on ethnic background, but many of their features have become more widely known through the media. The accent that is closest to being a standard, and which is associated with General American English, is the **Midwestern** accent, which is spoken in most of the northern states and by many people throughout the country.

Accent and social status

In Britain attitudes towards accents and dialects are linked with regional and social prejudices, e.g. between the north and south. Standard English and RP originated in the south, in and around London, the capital and main cultural centre of the country. Anything northern can be seen as unsophisticated and inferior by some southerners and they may, however unfairly, consider people speaking with a northern accent to be less well educated. The **broader** (= stronger) the accent, the greater the prejudice against the person using it, especially if the accent is so **thick** (= strong) that others have difficulty understanding it. Urban accents such as *Cockney, *Scouse, Glaswegian and the *Brummie accent are least favoured. Accents were for a long time used by comedians to make fun of people from a particular region or social group, but this is now less acceptable.

Although RP is still widely used by professional people, its status, especially among younger people, is not as high as it was. Many public figures, such as politicians and broadcasters, now emphasize their regional accents rather than trying to lose them. And the development in the the 1990s of ***Estuary English**, a combination of Cockney and RP, can be seen as an attempt to reduce class difference. This trend away from RP seems likely to continue.

In the US accents provide much less information about people. It can be hard to identify where a person comes from by their accent, harder still to learn anything about their social position. The South is not as rich as the North, and African Americans are more likely to be poor than white people, but that says little about an individual with a particular accent. But at a local level, New Yorkers use accent as the basis for making judgements about their fellow citizens, and a Bostonian accent, the American equivalent of marked RP, helps identify the old, rich families of *New England.

Attitudes to accents vary in different parts of the US. In big cities people barely notice accents, but in small towns and country areas people may be much more sensitive. The accent which is most widely criticized is the **southern drawl**. Many southerners feel embarrassed about their accent and try to modify it. There is some feeling in the US now that professional people should lose an accent which is considered less socially acceptable.

of Parliament. The first Act of Union, in 1707, officially joined England and Scotland as one kingdom, called Great Britain, ruled by the parliament in London. The second Act of Union, in 1800, added Ireland to this group of countries, which was then called the *United Kingdom of Great Britain and Ireland.

the ˌ**Actors' ˈStudio** a school in New York for professional actors. It was begun in 1947 by Elia *Kazan, Robert Lewis, and Cheryl Crawford. It became the

A

Act of Parliament

Statute law

In Britain a proposal for a new law goes through a long process of discussion in *Parliament. It is debated in both the ***House of Commons** and the ***House of Lords** and must also be approved by the King or Queen before it becomes an **Act of Parliament**.

All Acts of Parliament together form **statute law**. New laws are sometimes said to **go on the statute book**. Two copies of each Act are made on vellum (= very smooth, high-quality material made from animal skin) and are kept in the House of Lords and in the *Public Record Office. Copies of all the Acts passed in a particular year are issued in book form, but there is no such thing as 'the statute book'. *Parliament has the power to **repeal a statute** if it is no longer appropriate.

Bills

Most laws begin as **proposals** which are discussed widely before they start their formal progress through Parliament. Members of appropriate professional organizations and *pressure groups may be asked for their advice and opinions. Sometimes the government produces a **Green Paper**, a document that is circulated to members of the public asking for their comments. Proposals may also be **set out** in a government ***White Paper** to be debated in Parliament.

After the discussion period lawyers draft the proposals into a **bill**. Bills relating to the powers of particular organizations, e.g. local councils, or to the rights of individuals, are called ***private bills**. The majority of bills change the general law and are called ***public bills**.

Public bills may be introduced first in either the House of Commons or the House of Lords. Most public bills that become Acts of Parliament are introduced by a government minister and are called **government bills**. Bills introduced by other *Members of Parliament (MPs) are called ***private members' bills**. The bills that form part of the government's legislative (= law-making) programme are announced in the *Queen's speech at the *State Opening of Parliament.

On some Fridays, private members' bills have priority over government business. MPs also have a chance to introduce a bill under the 'ten minute rule', when they can make a short speech in support of it. Only a few of of these bills ever become law. Private members' bills may also be introduced in the House of Lords. The time available for debating such a bill may be restricted by a **timetable motion**, often called a 'guillotine'.

The progress of a bill

Most bills start in the House of Commons where they go through a number of stages: the ***first reading** is a formal announcement only, without a debate. The bill is then printed. The ***second reading** may take place several weeks later. The House debates the general principles of the bill and takes a vote. This is followed by the ***committee stage**: a committee of MPs examines the details of the bill and votes on **amendments** (= changes) to parts of it. Sometimes, all MPs take part in the committee stage and form a **Committee of the Whole House**. At the ***report stage** the House considers the amendments and may propose further changes. At the ***third reading** the amended bill is debated as a whole.

The bill is then sent to the House of Lords, where it goes through all the same stages. If the Lords make new amendments, these will be considered later by the Commons. By tradition, the Lords pass bills authorizing taxation or national expenditure without amendment. When both Houses have reached agreement the bill must **go for *royal assent** (= be approved by the king or queen). It then becomes an **Act of Parliament** which can be applied as part of the law. Royal assent is in the form of an announcement, not a signature on a bill. It has not been refused since 1707.

---

centre of *method acting under its artistic director Lee *Strasberg, and its many famous students included Marlon *Brando and Rod Steiger.

ˌRoy ˈ**Acuff** /ˈeɪkʌf/ (1903–92) a US singer known as the 'King of Country Music'. He was the first singer chosen (in 1962) for the Country Music *Hall of Fame. Acuff joined the *Grand Ole Opry in *Nashville in 1938, and his best-known songs included *The Great Speckled Bird*, *Wabash Cannonball*, and *Night Train to Memphis*.

ˌRobert ˈ**Adam** /ˈædəm/ (1728–92) a Scottish architect who, with his brother James (1730–94), started a new *neoclassical style (= one influenced by the styles of ancient Greece and Rome) in British building and furniture design. They designed many famous houses, including *Kenwood House and the main building of *Edinburgh University.

▶ **Adam** *adj* [usu before noun] designed or influenced by Robert Adam: *an Adam ceiling/fireplace.*

ˌ***Adam*** ˈ***Bede*** /ˈbiːd/ the first novel (1859) by George *Eliot. Adam Bede, a carpenter in a village in the English *Midlands, falls in love with a beautiful young woman, but she has a tragic affair with another man. Later, Adam falls in love with and marries her cousin, a good, calm and religious person.

ˌAnsel ˈ**Adams**[1] /ˌænsəl ˈædəmz/ (1902–85) a US photographer who took black and white photographs of the US South-West. One of his best-known books was *Taos Pueblo* (1930). He helped to create the department of photography at the *Museum of Modern Art

the hall of Osterley Park House, designed by Robert Adam

in New York in 1940, and was director of the *Sierra Club, an organization to protect nature, for 37 years.

ˌDouglas ˈ**Adams**[2] /ˈædəmz/ (1952–) an English writer of comic science fiction. His best known book is *The *Hitch Hiker's Guide to the Galaxy*.

ˌGerry ˈ**Adams**[3] /ˈædəmz/ (1948–) a Northern Ireland politician. He has been the leader of *Sinn Fein since 1978. He was elected *MP for West *Belfast in 1983 and 1987, but did not take his seat in Parliament because he refused to recognize the authority of *Westminster(2) in Northern Ireland. He has been critized for being involved with terrorists, and for a time his voice was banned from broadcasts in Britain.

ˌJohn ˈ**Adams**[4] /ˈædəmz/ (1735–1826) the second *President of the US after being the country's first Vice-president. He was a leader in forming the *Declaration of Independence. He was not a very popular president because of arguments within his government and problems in foreign relations, especially with France.

ˈJohn ˈQuincy ˈ**Adams**[5] /ˈædəmz/ (1767–1848) the sixth *President of the US. He was not a popular president because his government passed a tariff act (= a tax on imports). He had had more success earlier as *Secretary of State, helping to write the *Monroe Doctrine and adding *Florida as a state. He was the son of John *Adams.

the ˌ**Adam** ˈ**Smith** ˌ**Institute** /ˈsmɪθ/ a British organization formed in 1977 which gives economic advice to the British government, foreign governments and other groups. It is named after the 18th-century economist Adam *Smith, and shares many of his ideas (e.g. about the importance of reducing the extent to which the state is involved in social and commercial affairs). It was associated particularly with the *Conservative governments of the 1980s and 1990s in Britain.

ADAS /ˈeɪdæs/ ⇨ AGRICULTURAL DEVELOPMENT AND ADVISORY SERVICE.

ˌJane ˈ**Addams** /ˈædəmz/ (1860–1935) an American who worked to improve social conditions and shared the 1931 *Nobel Prize for peace. She and Ellen Gates Starr began the Hull House in *Chicago in 1889 to help poor people. From 1915 to 1929, Addams was President of the Women's International League for Peace and Freedom.

the ˈ**Addams** ˌ**Family** /ˈædəmz/ a family of strange but funny cartoon characters who live in a large dark house and behave in an unusual way that suggests evil and death. They were created in 1935 in the **New Yorker* magazine by Charles Addams. The characters were used for a popular television comedy series (1964–6) and a film (1991).

ˌJoseph ˈ**Addison** /ˈædɪsən/ (1672–1719) an English writer and poet who was also active in politics. With his friend Richard *Steele he started the **Spectator*. He wrote many poems and a tragic play, *Cato* (1713), but he is remembered mainly for his essays in the **Spectator* and the **Tatler*, written in a simple, direct style.

Aˌdeste Fiˈdeles /æˌdesteɪ fɪˈdeɪleɪz/ the Latin title and first line of a popular Christmas *carol. The English version is called *O Come, All Ye Faithful*.

the ˌ**Adiˈrondack** ˈ**Mountains** /ˌædɪˈrɒndæk; *AmE* ˌædɪˈrɑːndæk/ (*also* the **Adirondacks**) a mountain range in the US state of New York, where the *Hudson River begins. Tourists are attracted to its lakes and forests, including the **Adirondack Forest Preserve**.

ˌLarry ˈ**Adler** /ˈædlə(r)/ (1914–) a US musician who plays the harmonica (= a small instrument held against the mouth). He moved to Britain in the 1950s. Several composers, including Malcolm *Arnold and Ralph *Vaughan Williams, have written music specially for him. Adler has written and played music for a number of films, including *Genevieve* (1954), *A High Wind in Jamaica* (1965) and *My Life* (1992).

the Addams family in The New Yorker, *1947*

the ˌ**Admiral's** ˈ**Cup** the prize given to the winner of a series of yacht races off the south coast of England. The last race in the series is the *Fastnet Race.

the ˈ**Admiralty** /ˈædmərəlti/ **1** the British government department that was responsible for the *Royal Navy until 1964, when it became part of the *Ministry of Defence. **2** the building in *Whitehall, London, that used to be the headquarters of the Admirality. Now it is the headquarters of the *Civil Service.

ˌ**Admiralty** ˈ**Arch** /ˌædmərəlti/ a large, grand arch at the end of The *Mall in central London, England. It was built in 1906–10 in memory of Queen *Victoria and is next to the *Admiralty(2) building.

adult education

Adult education, sometimes called **continuing education**, includes courses of general interest at all levels, *vocational training for jobs in industry, and academic study for a degree.

In Britain most general interest courses are part-time and commonly consist of **evening classes** held once a week at local colleges, schools and community centres. Some classes are also held during the day. Courses offered include both academic and recreational subjects, e.g. Spanish, local history, yoga and pottery. Students have to pay, but people who are unemployed may get a reduction or go free. Most classes are organized by local **adult education institutes** or by the ***Workers' Educational Association**. There are about 1 500 centres for adult education in Britain. Some universities also have a **department of continuing education**, which runs courses and organizes residential summer schools. In the mid 1990s about 1.6 million people, of whom 70% were women, attended evening classes.

Some people return to college as **mature students** and take full- or part-time training courses in a skill

that will help them to get a job. The development of *open learning, the opportunity to study when it is convenient for the student, has increased the opportunities available to many people. This type of study was formerly restricted to book-based learning and **correspondence courses** but now includes courses on television, CD-ROM or the Internet, and **self-access courses** at language or computer centres.

Americans believe that education is important at all stages of life and does not always stop when people get their first job. About 40% of adults take part in some kind of formal education. About half of them are trying to get qualifications and skills to help them with their jobs, the rest are taking recreational subjects for personal satisfaction. Schools and *community colleges arrange evening classes, and a **catalog** of courses is published by local boards of education.

Many US universities have a department of continuing education. State universities often allow anyone who wants to attend classes to do so, whether or not they are working towards a degree. Adults who never completed secondary school have a chance to take an **equivalency exam**, and if they pass they get a certificate saying that they have the same level of education as somebody who has finished *high school.

ˈAdvent (in the Christian religion) the period of time before *Christmas, from the Sunday closest to 30 November (**Advent Sunday**) to Christmas Day. It is called Advent, which means 'coming' in Latin, because it is the time just before Jesus Christ came into the world.

ˈAdvent ˌcalendar *n* a cardboard picture with tiny doors in it, given to children as a present for *Advent. They open one door for each day in Advent, usually from 1 December to 24 December. Behind each one is a picture, and sometimes a small gift.

advertising

Most companies in Britain and the US have to work hard to **promote** and **market** their goods in order to sell them. *Political parties, *charities and other organizations also use advertising. Many pages in *newspapers and *magazines are filled with advertisements (also called **ads** or, in Britain, **adverts**) and there are also advertisements, usually called **commercials**, on radio and television.

Advertisements in newspapers and magazines are expensive and only the largest companies can afford to advertise their products in this way. Many organizations, however, use newspapers to advertise jobs and these are generally grouped together in the **situations vacant** section. Small companies, such as travel agents, advertise in the **small ads** columns, where each advertisement consists of a few lines of text only. Shops and businesses, and individuals wanting to buy or sell second-hand household goods advertise in local papers.

The wealthiest companies buy advertising time on television. There is no advertising on the *BBC, but programmes broadcast by US and British commercial stations are interrupted by a **commercial break** about every 15 minutes. Famous actors or singers are sometimes associated with advertisements for a particular product. Some advertising **slogans** are known by everyone, e.g. 'Have a break – have a *KitKat'. Some advertisements are like very brief episodes of a story. Tobacco advertising is now banned (= forbidden) on British radio and television and on television in the US. Advertisers have no influence over the people who make programmes, even if they help pay for them through sponsorship. In the US some commercials are national, others are shown only in a particular area. National commercials are often fun to watch, but local ones have the reputation of being badly made. Some products are sold on smaller channels by an **infomercial**, a commercial that lasts half an hour or more and tries to look like an entertainment programme.

Other ways of advertising include displaying large posters on **hoardings** or **billboards** by the side of roads. **Flyers** (= small posters) advertising local events or special offers given to people in the street. Restaurants advertise in theatre programmes, and shops advertise in their own magazines or on their shopping trolleys (*AmE* carts). Many companies now also advertise on the Internet.

The biggest US **ad agencies** have offices in New York on *Madison Avenue, so **Madison Avenue** has come to mean the advertising industry. The most famous agency in Britain is *Saatchi & Saatchi. In Britain, the advertising industry is controlled by the ***Advertising Standards Authority**, the ***Independent Television Commission** and the ***Radio Authority**. All advertisements must be 'legal, decent, honest and truthful'. In the US the ***Federal Communications Commission** makes rules about advertising. Television and radio stations are required to do some **public service announcements** (= commercials that give information to the community) free of charge.

Many people are against advertising, partly because it adds to the cost of a product. People also say that the influence of advertising is too great, and that children especially want every product they see advertised. However, many Americans buy newspapers on Sundays only because they advertise **special offers** and contain **coupons** (= pieces of paper enabling people to buy products at a reduced price).

the **ˌAdvertising ˈStandards Auˌthority** (*abbr* **ASA**) an independent organization which checks that advertisements do not lie or make false claims about a product. Anyone can ask the Advertising Standards Authority to investigate an advertisement. If there is a problem with it, the Authority may then tell the company to change or remove it.

the **Adˈvisory, Conˌciliˈation and Arbiˈtration ˌService** ⇨ ACAS.

ˈadvocate *n* [C] **1** (in England and Wales) any lawyer who presents a client's case in a court of law. **2** (in Scotland) a lawyer who has the right to speak in the higher courts of law. See also FACULTY OF ADVOCATES, LORD ADVOCATE.

AEC /ˌeɪ iː ˈsiː/ ⇨ ATOMIC ENERGY COMMISSION.

the **AEEU** /ˌeɪ iː iː ˈjuː/ (*in full* the **Amalgamated Engineering and Electrical Union**) one of the biggest trade unions in Britain, formed in 1992 when two separate unions combined.

ˌAesop's ˈFables /ˌiːsɒps ˈfeɪblz; *AmE* ˌiːsɑːps/ a collection of short stories about animals which behave in a human way. Each story teaches a moral lesson. They are said to be by a Greek called Aesop who lived in the 6th century BC, but many of them are much older. Well-known stories include *The *Tortoise and the Hare* and *The Fox and the Grapes*.

the **Aesˈthetic ˌMovement** a movement that developed in England in the late 1880s. It was based on the belief that art should exist as an independent idea, and not in order to support religion, the state, etc. This principle is most clearly expressed in the phrase 'art for art's sake'. The movement was influenced by the *Pre-Raphaelites and John *Ruskin. Its supporters included Samuel Taylor *Coleridge, William *Morris, Oscar *Wilde and Aubrey *Beardsley. See also ARTS AND CRAFTS MOVEMENT.

af,firmative 'action *n* [U] a US government policy requiring that minorities (including women) should be favoured when people are chosen for jobs or entry to college. Americans are divided about this practice and often say it is 'reverse discrimination'. It has existed since the 1960s, but the *Supreme Court has since decided against strict quotas (= numbers of people) and forcing affirmative action on private businesses. The more informal practice in Britain is sometimes known as 'positive discrimination'. See also EQUAL EMPLOYMENT OPPORTUNITY COMMISSION, EQUAL OPPORTUNITIES COMMISSION.

the **AFL-CIO** /ˌeɪ ef ˈel ˌsiː aɪ ˈəʊ/ (*in full* the **American Federation of Labor and Congress Industrial Organizations**) the largest organization for workers in America, with almost 14 million members from 78 *trade unions. It was created in 1955 when the AFL and CIO joined together. It usually gives its powerful political support to the *Democratic Party.

ˌAfrican Aˈmerican *n* a recent US name for black Americans descended from Africans, especially those descended from American slaves. In the 1990s, the name has become more popular and politically correct (= avoiding language that may be offend a particular group) than 'black'. About 12% of the US population are African Americans. ▶ **African-American** *adj*.

ˌAfro-Caribˈbean /ˌæfrəʊ kærɪˈbɪən; *AmE* ˌæfroʊ/ *n* [C] (in Britain) a black person whose family comes from the *Caribbean.
▶ **Afro-Caribbean** *adj* of Afro-Caribbeans or their culture: *Only 1 in 40 students come from the Afro-Caribbean community.*

AFTRA /ˈæftrə/ (*in full* the **American Federation of Television and Radio Artists**) a *trade union for US actors and other people working in television and radio. AFTRA works with the *Screen Actors Guild to gain better contracts and conditions of work for the members of both organizations.

ˈAga™ /ˈɑːɡə/ *n* (*pl* **Agas**) a cooker that is made of solid iron. It has a traditional design, but is now very fashionable in Britain. Agas use oil, gas or electricity and are usually left on once they have been lit. They can also be used to provide hot water and central heating. The phrase **Aga saga** is a humorous name for a novel about the lives of rich *middle-class British people: *Like some women want mink coats, Roberta wanted an Aga.*

an Aga

ˈAge Conˌcern a British charity that looks after the interests of old people. It was begun in 1940 and provides meals, places for them to meet, etc.

the **ˈAgency for Interˈnational Deˈvelopment** (*abbr* **AID**) a US government organization that sends foreign aid (= money and other economic help) to other nations, especially for agricultural, educational and health programmes. It also sends help after natural disasters, such as floods.

ˌAgent ˈOrange *n* [U] a poisonous chemical used by US soldiers during the Vietnam War to remove the leaves from forests so that they could see the enemy. It caused birth defects in many Vietnamese children, and after the war about 60 000 former US soldiers complained of illnesses. In 1984, the seven companies that had made Agent Orange gave $180 million to help such people.

the **ˌage of conˈsent** *n* [sing] the age at which a young person can legally agree to have sex with someone. In Britain it is 16 for people who want to have sex with people of the opposite sex. The age of consent for men who want to have sex with other men was lowered from 21 to 18 in 1994. In the US the age of consent varies in different states, but it is usually between 16 and 18.

the **ˌage of diˈscretion** *n* [sing] the age at which young people are considered able to deal with their own affairs, e.g. to own property, to make a contract with someone, or to make a will (= sign a document saying what will happen to their possessions when they die). The age of discretion in Britain is now 14. In the US it varies in different states.

the **ˌAge of Enˈlightenment** (*also* **Age of Reason**) a period in Europe in the 18th century when many writers and thinkers began to question established beliefs, e.g. in the authority of kings or of the Church, in favour of reason and scientific proof. The idea developed that everyone was of equal value and had equal rights.

the **ˌage of ˈsteam** a phrase sometimes used to refer to the 18th and 19th centuries in Britain, when different types of steam engine were being invented and developed by people such as James *Watt and George *Stephenson. Steam engines were used as the power for factories, ships and trains. Some people in Britain speak of the age of steam with feelings of sadness because they imagine that life was more pleasant and relaxed then.

ˈAgincourt /ˈædʒɪnkɔː(r)/ a battle fought in northern France in 1415, between the French and the English under King *Henry V. The English won, even though there were many more French soldiers, and were then in a strong position to take much of France. Agincourt is especially remembered because it forms an important part of Shakespeare's play **Henry V*.

the **ˌAgriˈcultural Deˈvelopment and Adˈvisory ˌService** (*abbr* **ADAS**) a British government organization that carries out research in agriculture and advises the government on policy.

Agriculture and fishing ⇨ article.

ˌCaptain **ˈAhab** /ˈeɪhæb/ the main character in the novel **Moby-Dick* by Herman *Melville. Captain Ahab, who hunts a white whale, is an example of a person who becomes crazy and puts others in danger by having only one aim in life.

Agriculture and fishing

Agriculture in Britain

About 75% of Britain is **farmed**, and British farms supply over half the country's food. **Arable farms** are mainly in the east and south of England and in eastern Scotland. The main crops are **cereals**, e.g. wheat and barley, and potatoes, sugar beet and oilseed rape. **Livestock**, mainly sheep and cattle, are reared in hilly areas, though **dairy cows** (= cows bred for their milk) are kept on the richer grass of the lowlands. Many cattle farmers have had a difficult time recently because of the *BSE crisis. *Kent, often called 'the *garden of England', and the Vale of Evesham are famous for **horticultural** produce (= fruit and flowers).

The average size of a British farm is 173 acres (70 hectares). Most farms are managed like other modern businesses. The word **agribusiness** describes the commercial aspects of farming. It is also used to refer to all the industries, including farming, which are associated with food production.

The ***Ministry of Agriculture, Fisheries and Food** is the government department responsible for agriculture. Farmers' interests are represented by the *National Farmers' Union. Agriculture only employs about 2% of the British workforce, though this figure rises to 25% when food processing industries are included.

In 1973, Britain's entry into the *European Community led to many changes in farming. The ***Common Agricultural Policy** (CAP) provides help for farmers through **subsidies** (= financial support). Originally, farmers were encouraged to produce as much as they could, and any **surplus** was put into storage. The cost of this policy was passed on to customers, who had to pay higher prices for food. Many people are still unhappy about the CAP. Farmers complain that their work is made more difficult by rules and regulations that have been introduced. They also claim that **quota systems**, which limit the amount of produce they can sell, make it impossible to make a profit. In recent years many farmers have tried to find additional ways of making money, e.g. by letting farm cottages, offering *bed and breakfast, or growing strawberries.

But farmers do not get much sympathy from other people, mainly because of the money they receive in subsidies. The CAP's **set-aside** policy, which pays farmers to leave some fields uncultivated, is seen by some people as helping farmers get rich for doing nothing. Farmers are sometimes called 'custodians of the countryside', but they are often criticized for destroying woods and hedges and for poisoning the environment with fertilizers and pesticides. Some farmers practise **organic farming** without chemicals, but although people approve of this most are unwilling to pay higher prices for organic produce. Farmers may also be accused of cruelty towards their animals: in **battery farming**, for instance, chickens are reared in crowded cages.

Agriculture in the US

Agribusiness in the US employs more people than any other industry, over 22 million, but only about 2.5% of the American workforce are farmers. Many people got into debt and left their farms in the 1950s, and in the 1980s many more farmers **sold out** and moved to the cities. The average size of a farm is now 470 acres (190 hectares), compared with 174 acres (70 hectares) in 1940. In 1996 farm income was more than $51 billion, the highest ever, but despite this many farmers had large debts.

Many farmers live in the ***Corn Belt** of the Midwest where corn (= maize) and soya beans (*AmE* soybeans) are grown. The US grows 36% of the world's corn and 47% of its soya beans. Others live on the **prairies** of the *Great Plains, in what is known as the ***Wheat Belt**, which stretches from Canada to southern Texas on the eastern side of the *Rocky Mountains. Most livestock farmers live around the *Great Lakes in the **Dairy Belt**, or further south in states like Texas where cattle are bred for meat on **ranches**. In the *South many live in the ***Cotton Belt**. Citrus fruits, e.g. oranges, are grown in Florida, Southern California and Hawaii, and tobacco is grown in the south-east. In 1996 the total value of agricultural products was $200 billion, of which $60 billion-worth, mostly grain and soya beans, was exported. Farmers and **ranchers** are usually well respected by other people.

The US ***Department of Agriculture** spends a lot of its budget on buying surpluses and paying subsidies (in this case, money for *not* growing certain crops) to farmers, though in 1996 Congress passed a 'freedom to farm' law that will gradually end these subsidies and give farmers more freedom to respond to public demand and grow what they want.

Farmers are represented by the American Farm Bureau Federation and county farm organizations called **farm bureaus**. The Federation is involved in agricultural research, but it also protects farmers' rights and tries to influence government policy. Agricultural colleges attached to universities are highly respected. **Extension officers** act as a link between research departments and farmers.

As in Britain, many people think **factory farming** is bad and are in favour of organic produce, but they are unwilling to pay the extra cost.

Fishing

Like agriculture, Britain's fishing industry has experienced problems in recent years. The formerly large **fishing fleet** has been much reduced, but British **fishermen** still provide about 60% of all the fish eaten in Britain. About half of the **catch** consists of deep-sea fish such as haddock and cod. Britain's busiest fishing port is Peterhead in Scotland.

The *European Union's (EU) **Common Fisheries Policy** is unpopular with Britain's fishermen. The policy allows only British ships to fish within six miles of the British mainland, but **trawlers** (= fishing boats) from other EU countries can fish between 6 and 12 miles away.

The US fishing industry is very large, especially for sea fish, and in 1996 $3.4 billion-worth of fish were caught in US waters. The government supports the industry through the **Fish and Wildlife Service,** but states are responsible for the fish industry off their own shores. More than 60 types of fish are reared at national **fish hatcheries**, so that each year there are about 200 million new fish available.

A

aid

Most aid (= money, food and equipment) is given to the world's poorest countries to help reduce poverty. Projects paid for by aid money are often aimed at improving local housing and water supply, agriculture, health and education. Training local people is also a central part of many programmes. A lot of **aid money** comes from governments, but many **development projects** are run with the help of **non-governmental organizations (NGOs)**, such as *charities. Some charities, for example *Oxfam, the *Red Cross and the *Save the Children Fund, run their own aid programmes with money given by the general public. Additional emergency aid is given after natural disasters.

The British government gives over £2 000 million in aid each year to **developing countries**, especially those which belong to the *Commonwealth. British aid is distributed by the ***Department for International Development**. Until 1997, this was the responsibility of the **Overseas Development Administration**. Some aid is given direct to individual countries; the rest is distributed through international organizations such as the *European Union, the *United Nations and the World Bank. Money is also invested in businesses in developing countries by the **Commonwealth Development Corporation**. Britain, together with other countries, is helping to reduce the debts of poorer countries and may under certain circumstances cancel debts from Commonwealth countries.

The US began giving foreign aid during *World War II, when the *Lend-Lease Act made it possible to give military equipment to foreign countries. After the war the US created the *Marshall Plan, a $15 billion programme to help European countries rebuild their economies. The US has continued to spend large amounts of money on foreign aid, but has often been criticized for the way it decides who to help. In general, money goes to poor countries that are important to the US for commercial or military reasons. Formerly, the US gave money to countries in Africa, Asia and Latin America so that they would not accept money from the Soviet Union. ***USAID** distributes US foreign aid. In 1998 its budget was over $7 billion. Much of this was spent on US equipment, food and services to be sent abroad.

Two organizations are particularly concerned with training local people. In Britain ***Voluntary Service Overseas (VSO)** arranges for skilled people to work abroad for a few years so that they can pass on their skills. They are paid at local rates by the government of the country they are working in. The ***Peace Corps**, a US government agency, does similar work but pays volunteers living expenses and gives them a small allowance.

ˈAintree /ˈeɪntriː/ a course near *Liverpool, England, where horse races are held. The most famous of these is the *Grand National.

ˈAiredale /ˈeədeɪl; *AmE* ˈerdeɪl/ *n* (*also* **Airedale terrier**) a breed of dog, the largest of the English *terriers, originally bred in *Yorkshire. It has a black body and a yellowish-brown head and legs.

air force ⇨ articles at ARMED FORCES.

ˌAir Force ˈOne the plane used by the US President. The first such plane was provided in 1944 for Franklin D *Roosevelt, but the first to be called Air Force One was the one provided for John F *Kennedy in 1961. The plane is now a US Air Force VC-25A.

ˈAir Miles™ *n* [pl] a scheme to encourage air travel, run by *British Airways. People get points when they spend money on particular goods, hotels, etc. They can then travel an equivalent number of miles free on *British Airways flights: *I've nearly got enough Air Miles for that trip to Florida.*

ˈAjax™ /ˈeɪdʒæks/ *n* [U] a cleaning substance used to remove dirt from floors, baths, etc.: *Where's the Ajax?*

AKC ⇨ AMERICAN KENNEL CLUB.

ˌAlaˈbama /ˌæləˈbæmə/ a southern US state, also called the Cotton State and the Heart of *Dixie. The capital city is *Montgomery and the largest city is *Birmingham.

Aˈladdin /əˈlædɪn/ a poor young Chinese boy in a story in *The *Arabian Nights*. A magician (= a person who does magic tricks) asks him to go down into a deep cave full of gold and jewels, but to bring up only an old lamp. Aladdin will not give the magician the lamp until he helps him out of the cave, so the magician shuts him in. Aladdin discovers that when he rubs the lamp, a genie (= a spirit with magic powers) comes out of it. He uses the power of the genie to become rich, defeat the magician and marry a princess. The story of Aladdin is often performed as a *pantomine in Britain. The phrase *an Aladdin's cave* is sometimes used to mean a place full of wonderful things: *The shop is a real Aladdin's cave of unusual gift ideas.*

ˈAlamein ⇨ EL ALAMEIN.

the **ˈAlamo** /ˈæləməʊ; *AmE* ˈæləmoʊ/ the fort (now in *San Antonio, *Texas) where an army of about 4 000 Mexican soldiers killed all 187 Texans defending it in 1836. Davy *Crockett and James *Bowie died there. 'Remember the Alamo!' became a famous cry for Texas independence from Mexico. John *Wayne directed and acted in a film about the battle, *The Alamo* (1960).

Aˈlaska /əˈlæskə/ the largest and most northern state of the US, connected to the other states to the south by the **Alaska Highway** through Canada. It is sometimes called 'the last frontier' and produces a lot of oil, which is sent through the *Alaska pipeline. The capital city is Juneau, and the largest city is Anchorage.

the **Aˌlaska ˈpipeline** /əˌlæskə/ the pipeline completed in 1977 to send oil from Pruehoe Bay on the north coast of *Alaska to its southern port of Valdez. It is 795 miles/1 270 kilometres long, and many people were opposed to it because of possible damage to the environment.

ˈAlbany /ˈɔːlbəni/ **1** the capital city of New York State, 145 miles/230 kilometres north of New York City. **2** (*also* **the Albany**) a very expensive block of flats/apartments in west London, built in the late 18th century.

ˌEdward **ˈAlbee** /ˈɔːlbiː/ (1928–) a US writer of plays who became famous for *Who's Afraid of Virginia Woolf?* (1962). He later won the *Pulitzer Prize twice, for *A Delicate Balance* (1966) and *Seascape* (1975).

ˌPrince **ˈAlbert** (1819–61) the husband (and also cousin) of Queen *Victoria. The son of a German *duke, Albert married Victoria in 1840, and in 1857 he was given the title of *Prince Consort. He took great interest in the arts, as well as business, science and technology, and was a strong influence behind the *Great Exhibition of 1851. Albert died suddenly when he was only 42, and the Queen wore black clothes for the next 40 years as a sign of her great sadness.

the **ˌAlbert ˈHall** (*also* the **Royal Albert Hall**) a large round concert hall in west London, England, which holds 8 000 people. It was built in 1868–71 in memory of Prince *Albert. Various musical and

A

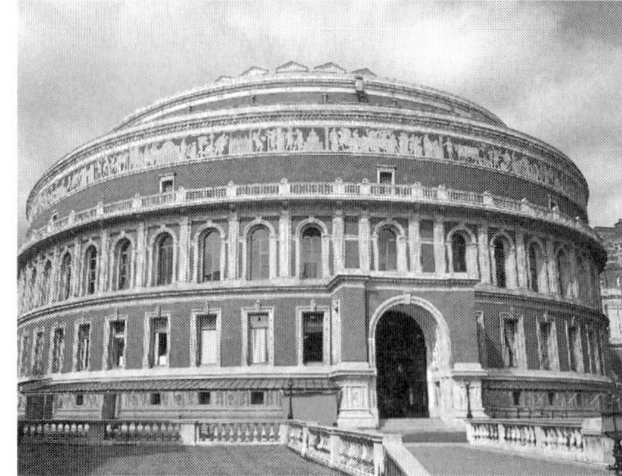

the Albert Hall

sporting events take place in it, but it is best known as the main hall where the *Proms are held.

the ˌ**Albert Me'morial** a monument opposite the *Albert Hall in London, England, built in the 1860s in memory of Prince *Albert.

ˌ**Albert 'Square** ⇨ EASTENDERS.

'**Albion** /'ælbiən/ an ancient name for Britain or England. It may be connected with the Latin word *albus*, meaning 'white', and refer to the *white cliffs of Dover, often the first thing seen by anyone crossing the *English Channel to land in Britain. The word 'Albion' is now used only in poetry or in names, especially those of streets and football clubs. The expression *perfidious Albion*, meaning that England cannot be trusted, was often used by the French about the English in the time of Napoleon.

ˌMadeleine '**Albright** /'ɔːlbraɪt/ (1936–) the first woman US *Secretary of State. She was born in Prague, Czechoslovakia, but her family moved to the US in 1948. Albright was the US representative to the *United Nations for four years before replacing Warren Christopher as Secretary of State in 1997.

'**Alcatraz** /'ælkətræz/ a small island with a famous prison on it in *San Francisco Bay, *California. The island was known as 'the Rock'. The prison was used from 1933 to 1963 for the country's most dangerous prisoners, including Al *Capone. It is now a popular tourist attraction.

The '***Alchemist*** a comedy play (1610) by Ben *Jonson about a man who pretends to be an alchemist (= a person who was thought to be able to turn ordinary metal into gold) in order to cheat people out of their money. Many people consider it to be Jonson's greatest play.

ˌJohn '**Alcock** /'ɔːlkɒk; *AmE* 'ɔːlkɑːk/ (1892–1919) an English pilot. In 1919 he and Arthur *Brown were the first people to fly across the Atlantic Ocean, from Newfoundland in Canada to the west coast of Ireland. Alcock was made a *knight in 1919.

ˌ**Alcoholics A'nonymous** (*abbr* **AA**) an international organization, begun in *Chicago in 1935, for alcoholics who are trying to stop drinking. They have regular meetings at which people help each other by talking about their problem.

'**alcopop** /'ælkəʊpɒp; *AmE* 'ælkoʊpɑːp/ *n* [C, U] (*BrE*) a type of sweet alcoholic drink, usually sold in small bottles. Alcopops have been criticized in Britain because they are attractive to children, and some makes are now no longer sold.

Lou'isa 'May '**Alcott** /'meɪ 'ɔːlkɒt; *AmE* 'ɔːlkɑːt/ (1832–88) the US author who wrote **Little Women*. She was also a nurse in the US Army during the American *Civil War and wrote about her experiences at the time.

the ˌ**Aldeburgh 'Festival** /ˌɔːldbərə/ a music festival that takes place every summer in Aldeburgh, a small town in *Suffolk, England. The festival was created by Benjamin *Britten, who lived in Aldeburgh.

'**alderman** *n* (*pl* **aldermen**) **1** (in the US) a local government officer, usually a member of a city council, responsible for part of the city. **2** (formerly in Britain) a senior member of a local council. The system of local government changed in 1974 in most of Britain, and the only aldermen left now are in the *City of London.

'**Aldermaston** /'ɔːldəmɑːstən; *AmE* 'ɔːldərmæstən/ a small town in *Berkshire, England, close to an important nuclear weapons research centre. In the 1950s and 1960s there were large organized marches once a year from London to Aldermaston to protest against nuclear weapons: *Many young poets went on the Aldermaston marches.*

'**Alderney** /'ɔːldəni; *AmE* 'ɔːldərni/ the furthest north of the *Channel Islands.

'**Aldershot** /'ɔːldəʃɒt; *AmE* 'ɔːldərʃɑːt/ a town in *Hampshire, England, which is one of the main centres for the army. People tend to think of it as an army town.

ˈ'Buzz' '**Aldrin** /ˌbʌz 'ɔːldrɪn/ (1930–) the second US astronaut to walk on the moon (15 minutes after Neil *Armstrong), in 1966. Six years later, Aldrin had a nervous breakdown and left the US Air Force.

the ˌ**Aldwych 'Theatre** /ˌɔːldwɪtʃ/ a theatre in the *West End of London, famous for the **Aldwych farces**, comedy plays by Ben *Travers which were performed there in the 1920s and 1930s.

the **A'leutian ˌIslands** /ə'luːʃn/ about 150 islands spread over 1 200 miles (1 920 kilometres) from the Alaskan Peninsula to Russia. About 8 000 people, mostly fishermen, live on the islands. See also BERING STRAIT. ⇨ note at INUITS.

'**A ˌlevel** /'eɪ/ (*in full* **Advanced level**) *n* [U, C] (in Britain) a school leaving examination in a particular subject, normally taken at the age of 18 in England and Wales. Students usually take three or four A levels, which they need to pass with good marks in order to go to university: *When do you take A level?* ○ *She's got three A levels.* ○ *I'm studying A level maths.* ⇨ article at EDUCATION IN BRITAIN.

ˌ***Ale'xander's 'Ragtime 'Band*** /ˌælɪg'zɑːndəz; *AmE* ˌælɪg'zændərz/ the song that made Irving *Berlin famous. He wrote the quick, happy *ragtime tune in 1911. It was also sung in a 1938 film of the same name.

ˌ**Alexandra 'Palace** a large building in Alexandra park in north London, England. It was first built for an international exhibition in central London in 1862, and later moved. It is best known for having been the *BBC's main television centre when the first public broadcasts were made in the 1930s.

a lithograph made in 1873 of Alexandra Palace

*The ˌ**Ale'xandria Quar'tet*** /ˌælɪɡˈzɑːndriə; *AmE* ˌælɪɡˈzændriə/ a series of four novels by Lawrence *Durrell about the complicated love affairs of a group of friends in Alexandria, Egypt, in the 1930s. The four books are *Justine* (1957), *Balthazar* (1958), *Mountolive* (1958) and *Clea* (1960). The series forms Durrell's best-known work.

Moˌhamed **al-'Fayed** /məˌhæməd æl ˈfaɪəd/ (1933–) a businessman, born in Egypt and now living in Britain. He owns several companies, including *Harrods Ltd and the Ritz Hotel in Paris, and is the owner of **Punch* magazine. His son Dodi Fayed (1956–97) became a close friend of Princess *Diana and was killed with her in a car crash in 1997.

ˌ**Alfred the 'Great** (849–899) king of *Wessex (871–99). He is remembered for defending England against Danish attacks, for establishing the English navy, and for encouraging education and the use of the English language. There is a popular story of King Alfred and the cakes. After a battle he was hiding in a woman's house. Not knowing who he was, she told him to look after her cakes which were cooking by the fire, and then became very angry when he let them burn.

Hoˌratio **'Alger** /həˌreɪʃiəʊ ˈældʒə(r)/ (1834–99) a US author of more than 100 books for boys. Most were about poor boys who became rich and successful by their hard work and good behaviour. Readers believed that these 'rags-to-riches' stories illustrated the opportunities for success in America.

the **Al'gonquin ˌRound 'Table** /ælˈɡɒŋkwɪn; *AmE* ælˈɡɑːŋkwɪn/ the informal name for a group of Americans known for their humour. They met regularly in the 1920s and 1930s at the Algonquin Hotel in New York, and the group included the writers Dorothy *Parker and Robert Benchley.

Muˌhammad **'Ali** /məˌhæmɪd ˈɑːli, ɑːˈliː/ (1942–) a famous US boxer. He was the world heavyweight champion from 1964 to 1967 and from 1974 to 1978. His original name was Cassius Clay, but he changed this in 1964 after joining the *Black Muslims. He had a very strong and confident personality, calling himself 'the greatest' and writing poetry about his victories. His title as champion was taken away in 1967 because he avoided the *Vietnam War. He has gradually become ill with a disease of the muscles.

ˌ**Ali 'Baba** /ˌæli ˈbɑːbɑː/ a character in an old Arabian story who hears some thieves say 'Open Sesame!', the magic words that open the door of the cave where they keep everything they have stolen. He steals their gold and they try to kill him, but he is saved by his servant Morgiana. The story is popular as a *pantomime in Britain: *The new shop is an Ali Baba's cave of designer jewellery.*

ˌ***Alice in 'Wonderland*** a children's book (1865) by Lewis *Carroll. Its full title is *Alice's Adventures in Wonderland*. Alice, a young girl, dreams that she follows a white rabbit down its hole and has a series of adventures with imaginary creatures. Some of the characters, such as the *Mad Hatter and the *Cheshire Cat, are referred to in informal English expressions.

ˌ**Alka-'Seltzer**™ /ˌælkə ˈseltsə(r); *AmE* ˈælkə ˌseltsər/ a medicine which is mixed with water to make a fizzy drink that people take when they have indigestion (= stomach pain caused by difficulty in digesting food or drink): *He took an Alka Seltzer and went to bed.*

ˌ**all-A'merican** *n* a US player of a sport in college who is one of the best in the country. To be called an all-American, a player must be chosen for a national team, the best-known teams being for football and *basketball.

Alice in Wonderland: *The Mad Tea-Party, illustrated by John Tenniel*

▶ **all-American** *adj* **1** of an American player who is one of the best in his or her sport: *an All-American quarterback on the All-American team.* **2** representing typical American characteristics, physical appearance, etc.: *an all-American boy.*

'All-Bran™ *n* [U] a breakfast food made mainly of bran (= the outer skin of grain such as wheat, oats, etc.), which helps to make the bowels work properly. It is usually eaten with milk and sugar.

the ˌ**Alle'gheny 'Mountains** /ˌælɪˈɡeɪni/ (*also* the **Alleghenies**) /ˌælɪˈɡeɪniz/ a range of mountains that runs from south-west *Virginia to central *Pennsylvania. They are part of the central *Appalachian Mountains.

ˌGracie **'Allen**[1] /ˈælən/ (1906–64) a US comic actor who was married to and regularly acted with George *Burns. She played a humorous wife who mostly talked nonsense in their popular programmes on radio and television.

ˌWoody **'Allen**[2] /ˌwʊdi ˈælən/ (1935–) a US comic actor, director and writer of films. His films often make fun of the worries of modern life in big US cities. He has won three *Oscars, for writing and directing *Annie Hall* (1977), and for writing *Hannah and Her Sisters* (1986). He and his former partner, the actor Mia *Farrow, were involved in a legal contest in 1993 because he had a love affair with her adopted daughter.

the ˌ**All 'England Club** (*in full* the **All England Lawn Tennis and Croquet**) the tennis club in *Wimbledon, London, where the famous tennis competition is held every year. It started as a *croquet club in 1868.

ˌEdward **'Alleyn** /ˈæleɪn/ (1566–1626) an English actor, famous for his performances in plays by *Marlowe, while his great rival Richard Burbage (*c.* 1567–1619) acted in Shakespeare's plays. He owned the *Rose Theatre, and provided the money to establish *Dulwich College.

'All ˌHallows 'Eve /ˌhæləʊz; *AmE* ˌhæloʊz/ ⇨ HALLOWE'EN.

the **Alˌliance and 'Leicester** /ˈlestə(r)/ a British bank with branches in many towns and cities. It used to be a *building society, and became a bank in 1997. In 1990 it took over the *Girobank.

the **Alˌliance for 'Progress** a financial and social programme of help for Latin American countries. It was suggested by US President John F *Kennedy and started in 1961. The *Organization of American States (OAS) is in charge of the money given by the US and also directs the programmes.

the **Al'liance ˌParty** (*in full* the **Alliance Party of**

A

Northern Ireland) a political party formed in *Northern Ireland in 1970 by people who disagreed with the extreme views of both Catholics and Protestants. The party aims to end the *Troubles by uniting the moderate people from both sides.

the ˈ**Allies** /ˈælaɪz/ *n* [pl] **1** the group of countries that fought together against Germany, Austria-Hungary, Turkey and Bulgaria in *World War I, including Britain, France, Italy, Russia, the US and the *Commonwealth countries. **2** the group of countries that fought together against Germany, Italy and Japan (the Axis powers) in *World War II. They included Britain, France, the US, the USSR and the *Commonwealth countries.

alˈlotment /əˈlɒtmənt; *AmE* əˈlɑːtmənt/ *n* (in Britain) a small piece of land that a person can rent from the local *council for growing vegetables, flowers, etc. Allotments are usually grouped together in a large field in a town or city. In the 19th century and during the two world wars, many people used their allotments to feed their families. Working on an allotment is now a popular way of relaxing.

a group of allotments

ˌ**all points ˈbulletin** *n* ⇨ APB.

ˌ**All ˈSaints Day** (*also* **All Hallows**) 1 November, when members of some Christian Churches traditionally say prayers to all the saints. The previous night, known as All Hallows Eve, is now usually called *Hallowe'en.

ˌ**All ˈSouls' Day** 2 November, the special day in the Catholic Church when people say prayers for the souls of the dead.

ˌ**all-star ˈgame** *n* (*AmE*) a game played between the best players in their sport. The 'all-stars' are often divided into teams that represent different sections of a league (= a group of sports clubs) or different parts of the country: *the NBA All-Star Game* ○ *the East-West All-Star Game.*

ˌ***All's Well That ˈEnds Well*** a comedy play by Shakespeare, written about 1603. Bertram is ordered by the king to marry Helena, who loves him, but under the bad influence of Parolles, he runs away to Florence. Helena follows him there, and tricks him into accepting her as his wife.

ˈ***All Things ˈBright and ˈBeautiful*** a hymn sung especially by children. Many British and US people remember singing the first verse as children:

All things bright and beautiful,
All creatures great and small.
All things wise and wonderful,
The Lord God made them all.

ˌ**Ally ˈPally** /ˌæli ˈpæli/ (*infml*) a popular name for *Alexandra Palace.

ˌ**alma ˈmater** /ˌælmə ˈmɑːtə(r)/ *n* **1** (*also* **Alma Mater**) a person's old school or university. The words mean 'generous mother' in Latin. The *alma mater* is an especially important idea to Americans: *He's taking a post in the history department at his alma mater.* See also ALUMNI ASSOCIATION. **2** (in the US) the official song of a school.

almshouses

ˈLawrence ˌ**Alma-ˈTadema** /ˌælmə ˈtædɪmə/ (1836–1912) an artist who was born in Holland but in 1873 became a British citizen. Many of his paintings represent life in ancient Greece and Rome. He painted an very accurate and detailed style that was very popular at the time. He was made a *knight in 1899.

ˈ**almshouse** *n* (in Britain) a house provided by the Church or a charity for old poor people. Almshouses were mostly built between the 16th and 19th centuries by rich local men, often in a row and in a grand style. Many older British towns have almshouses.

ˌRobert ˈ**Altman** /ˈɔːltmən / (1920–) a US film director. His films usually give a sad or funny picture of US life.

ˌ**Alton ˈTowers** /ˌɔːltən/ an amusement park near *Derby, England. It has some of the biggest rides in Britain.

aˈlumni associˌation /əˈlʌmnaɪ/ *n* (in the US) an organization of people who have all been to a particular school or university. See also ALMA MATER.

the ˌ**Amateur Athˈletic Associˌation** (*also* the **AAA**, the **Three As**) the organization that controls amateur athletics in Britain. It began in 1880, when it was for men only, but in 1991 it combined with the Women's Amateur Athletic Association.

the **Amateur Athletic Union** (*abbr* the **AAU**) an organization that supports amateur sports in the US. It was established in 1888. Each year it gives the James E Sullivan Award to the Outstanding Amateur Athlete in the US.

ˌ**amateur draˈmatics** (*also infml* **am-dram**) *n* [U] the activity of people who perform plays, etc. as a hobby and not for money. It is very popular in Britain, where there are many amateur dramatics clubs for people to join, even in small towns and villages. They perform plays for local people, charging them a small amount in order to pay for the costumes, hall, etc. People who do amateur dramatics are often very enthusiastic, but not always very good actors.

Aˌmazing ˈGrace /əˌmeɪzɪŋ ˈɡreɪs/ a popular 18th-century Christian hymn. It begins:

Amazing Grace, how sweet the sound
That saved a wretch like me.
I once was lost, but now am found,
Was blind, but now I see.

ˈ**Ambridge** /ˈæmbrɪdʒ/ the village in the British radio programme *The *Archers* where all the main characters live. It has come to represent a safe, protected corner of England where the old social values still exist.

A

ˌam-ˈdram /ˌæm ˈdræm/ ⇨ AMATEUR DRAMATICS.

aˈmendment /əˈmendmənt/ *n* an addition or change to a law or official document. In the US the first ten amendments to the Constitution are called the *Bill of Rights. Each amendment to the US Constitution must have the approval of 75% of the states.

ˌAmeˈrasian /ˌæməˈreɪʒn/ *n* a person born to an American and an Asian. The word is mostly used for a child of a US soldier and an Asian woman. Many Amerasian children were born as a result of the *Vietnam War.

Aˈmerica a popular national song in the US, first sung in 1831. It has the same tune as the British *national anthem **God Save the Queen/King* and begins with these lines:

My country, 'tis of thee,
Sweet land of liberty,
Of thee I sing.

America

The **United States of America** is called by several different names, both by the people who live there and by people in other countries. These names include **the USA**, **the United States**, **the US**, **the States** and **America**. The official name, the United States of America, first appears in the *Declaration of Independence of 1776, when the country was called 'the thirteen united States of America'. *America* is widely used as a name for the US, though this seems unfair on all the other nations in **the Americas** (= the continents of North and South America). Songs like **America* and **America the Beautiful* are about the US. Americans also use informal names like **the US of A** and **Stateside**, especially when they are out of the country. Other names, e.g. 'the land of the free', 'the land of liberty', 'God's country', 'the *melting pot' and 'the greatest nation on earth', show their pride in their country. British people sometimes refer humorously to America as 'the other side of the pond', i.e. the other side of the Atlantic Ocean.

North America refers to a continent and region, and includes Canada and Mexico as well as the US. Between the US and South America is the region of **Central America**. Sometimes the countries of Central and South America are together referred to as **Latin America**.

America and the Americas are said to have been named after Amerigo *Vespucci, an Italian explorer who sailed to South America in 1499, visiting the area that later became known as Brazil, and also the *Bahamas. Vespucci believed that the land he had discovered was a new continent, not part of Asia as *Columbus had thought. By 1538, the famous mapmaker Gerhardus Mercator was using the name 'America', the Latin form of Vespucci's name, for the **New World** (= North and South America, as opposed to Europe).

People from the US are called **Americans**, though British people may, rather rudely, call them 'Yanks'. People from other countries in the Americas are called by national names derived from the name of their country, e.g. Canadians. The adjective used to describe things from the US is **American**. The US is always referred to in organizations such as the *American Legion and in expressions like 'the *American dream'. **US** is also used as an adjective, as in the US Olympic team. Official names of government organizations may use **United States**, e.g. the United States Military Academy.

the **Aˈmerican Aˈcademy of Draˌmatic ˈArts** a school for actors in New York City. It began in 1884 and is the oldest dramatic school in America.

the **Aˈmerican Assoc'iation of Reˈtired ˌPersons** (*abbr* **AARP**) an organization in Washington, DC, for Americans who are at least 50 years old. It began in 1958 and offers its members medical insurance, a *credit union and other advantages.

the **Aˈmerican ˈAutomobile Associˌation** (*abbr* **AAA**) (*also* the **Triple A**) an organization for US and Canadian drivers. It helps travellers to plan their trips and rescues drivers in emergencies on the road. It began in 1902 and now has about 25 million members.

Aˌmerican ˈBandstand a US television programme of pop music and dance. It celebrated its 40th anniversary in 1996. For more than 40 years it was presented by Dick Clark, called 'the world's oldest teenager'.

the **Aˌmerican ˈBar Associˌation** (*abbr* **ABA**) a professional organization for US lawyers. It began in 1878 and has its main office in *Chicago. The ABA encourages legal standards, the study of law, and improvements in the US system of justice.

Aˌmerican ˈbreakfast *n* a large morning meal in America. It usually includes several choices from such items as juice, cereal, eggs with ham or bacon, *pancakes, toast, and *hash browns or, in the southern states, *grits.

the **Aˌmerican ˈBroadcasting ˌCompany** ⇨ ABC.

Aˌmerican ˈcheese *n* [U] a mild processed US cheese, similar to *Cheddar and yellow or orange in colour. It is often sold in separately wrapped slices.

the **Aˈmerican ˌCivil ˈLiberties ˌUnion** (*abbr* the **ACLU**) a US organization that defends the rights of people under the US Constitution. It was involved in the legal case in 1954 that ended the system of separate schools for African-Americans. The ACLU has sometimes been criticized for defending freedoms for everyone, as in 1978 when it supported the right of the Nazi Party in America to march.

Aˌmerican ˈCollege Test ⇨ ACT.

the **Aˌmerican ˈdream** the belief of Americans that their country offers opportunities for a good and successful life. For minorities and people coming from abroad to live in America, the dream also includes freedom and equal rights.

the **Aˌmerican ˈeagle** the national symbol of the United States. It is also called the 'bald eagle', and it appears on the Great Seal of the United States and on coins. In its mouth, the eagle holds the words *e pluribus unum* ('one out of many'). It holds arrows (a symbol of war) in its left foot and an olive branch (a symbol of peace) in its right foot.

the American eagle on the Great Seal of the US

American English ⇨ article.

Aˌmerican Exˈpress™ (*abbr* **AmEx**) an international US company best known for its traveller's cheques (= cheques for various fixed amounts which can be exchanged for cash in foreign countries) and charge cards. Established in 1850, the company also now has the largest travel agency in the world and offers many financial services.

the **Aˌmerican ˈFootball ˌConference** (*abbr* the **AFC**) one of the two divisions of the *National Football League of professional football in the US. It has 15 teams, and the winner goes to the *Super Bowl to

A

play the team that wins the *National Football Conference.

the **A'merican 'Forces 'Network** /'fɔːsɪz; *AmE* 'fɔːrsɪz/ (*abbr* the **AFN**) the television and radio stations run by the US armed forces for their members in foreign countries.

A,merican 'Gothic a painting (1930) by the US artist Grant Wood. It shows a farmer holding a pitchfork (= a farm implement with two sharp metal points) and standing next to a woman in front of a farm building. Both look sad, and the picture is often used for humorous advertisements.

American Gothic *by Grant Wood*

the 'War of **A'merican Inde'pendence** the usual British name for the *American Revolution.

A,merican 'Indian *n* any of the native people of North and South America and the Caribbean, but especially North America. They lived in tribes until Europeans settling in America fought them and forced them to move west. Today many Indians still live on reservations (= land given and protected by the US government). The name for American Indians now preferred in the United States is 'Native Americans'.

the **A,merican 'Kennel Club** (*abbr* the **AKC**) a US organization that holds the official records relating to dog breeding in the US, proving that individual dogs are of a pure breed. It was established in 1884 and has more than 500 local clubs which organize about 13 000 dog shows each year. The AKC also encourages responsible dog ownership and has a service to find lost dogs and a Canine Health Foundation for research to improve the health of dogs. Compare KENNEL CLUB.

the **A'merican League** one of the two organizations of professional *baseball in the United States. It has 14 teams and the winning team plays the winner of the *National League in the *World Series.

the **A,merican 'Legion** the largest organization for former members of the US armed forces. It began in 1919 and now has about 3 million members. From its main office in *Indianapolis, Indiana, it supports benefits for former US soldiers, etc. and a strong national defence. Compare VETERANS OF FOREIGN WARS.

the **A,merican 'Medical Associ,ation** (*abbr* the **AMA**) the largest professional organization for US doctors. It began in 1847 and has its main office in *Chicago. The AMA supports high standards in medical education, research and work, and it has great political influence.

the **A'merican 'National 'Standards ,Institute** (*abbr* the **ANSI**) an organization that works to develop standards for measurements and products in the United States, and to help US businesses compete internationally. It began in 1921, and its members now include more than 1 300 companies. Its main office is in New York.

the **A'merican plan** *n* [sing] (*AmE*) a system of hotel prices that includes the cost of a room, all meals and service. Compare EUROPEAN PLAN.

The American Revolution ⇨ article.

the **A'merican So'ciety of Comp'osers, 'Authors and 'Publishers** (*abbr* **ASCAP**) an organization in America that protects the rights of writers of music. It collects money for its members from anyone who plays or sings in a professional performance.

*the **A'merican 'Standard 'Version** (abbr the **ASV**)* a new version by US scholars of the **King James Version* of the Bible. It is sometimes called the *American Revised Version*. It was published in 1901 after the same Americans had helped to write the **Revised Version* (1881–5) in England.

the **A,merican 'Stock Ex,change** (*abbr* **AMEX**) the second largest financial market in the US. It began in 1911 and is in the financial district of *New York. More than 700 companies are members. See also NEW YORK STOCK EXCHANGE.

the **A,merica's 'Cup** an international sailing contest, first held in 1851. It is usually held every three or four years, and a US crew has won it every time except twice. Australia won in 1983 and New Zealand in 1995.

A,merica the 'Beautiful a popular US song in praise of America, written in 1893. The first verse is

O beautiful for spacious skies,
For amber waves of grain,
For purple mountain majesties
Above the fruited plain.
America! America!
God shed His grace on thee,
And crown thy good with brotherhood
From sea to shining sea.

A'meriCorps /ə'merɪkɔː(r)/a US organization for community service established in 1995. By 1996, it had about 23 000 members of all ages active in over 1 200 communities. They help to build and repair homes, clean parks and other areas, prevent crime and take part in other projects. For this work, they receive money to attend college.

,Amer'indian *n* (*old-fash*) an *American Indian ▶ **Amerindian** *adj*.

,Hardy **'Amies** /,hɑːdi 'eɪmɪs; *AmE* 'hɑːrdi/ (1909–) a leading British fashion designer. He began designing dresses for Queen *Elizabeth II in 1955 and was made a *knight in 1989.

,Kingsley **'Amis¹** /,kɪŋzli 'eɪmɪs/ (1922–95) an English writer and poet. His most famous book is the comic novel *Lucky Jim* (1954). In 1986 he won the *Booker Prize with *The Old Devils*. Most of his novels are angry but humorous attacks on aspects of modern life. He was the father of Martin *Amis and was made a *knight in 1990.

American English

There are about twice as many speakers of American English as of other **varieties** of English, and four times as many as speakers of *British English. The leading position of the US in world affairs is partly responsible for this. **Americanisms** have also been spread through advertising, tourism, telecommunications and the cinema.

As a result, forms of English used in Britain, Australia, etc. have become less distinct. But there remain many differences in idiom and vocabulary, especially between British and American English. For most people, however, the most distinctive feature of American English is its ***accent**.

The development of American English

British people who went to the US in the 17th century spoke a variety of ***dialects**. After they reached the US their language developed independently of British English. New words were added for food, plants, animals, etc. not found in Britain. Many were taken from the Indian languages of *Native Americans. The languages of Dutch and French settlers, and of the huge numbers of *immigrants entering the US in the 19th and 20th centuries, also contributed to the development of American English. Inventions such as electric lighting, the typewriter, telephone and television added large numbers of words to the language and these, with the inventions, soon spread to Britain.

Spelling, grammar and pronunciation

In written English, spelling shows whether the writer is American or British. Americans use *-or* instead of *-our* in words like *color* and *flavor*, and *-er* instead of *-re* in words like *center*. Other variants include *-x-* for *-ct-* (*connexion*) and *-l-* for *-ll-* (*traveler*). British people consider such spellings to be wrong. American spellings which may be used in British English include using *-z-* instead of *-s-* in words like *realize*, and writing the past tense of some verbs with *-ed* instead of *-t*, e.g. *learned*, *dreamed*.

There are various differences in grammar and idiom. For instance, *gotten*, an old form of the past participle of *get*, is often used in American English in the sense of 'received', e.g. 'I've gotten 16 Christmas cards so far.' Americans say 'He's in *the* hospital' while British people say 'He's in hospital'. The subjunctive is also common in American English, e.g. 'They insisted that *she remain* behind.'

Several features of pronunciation contribute to the American accent. Any 'r' is usually pronounced, e.g. card /kɑːrd/, dinner /ˈdɪnər/. A 't' between vowels may be flapped (= pronounced like a 'd'), so that *latter* sounds like *ladder*. The vowel /æ/ rather than /ɑː/ is used in words like *path*, *cot* and *caught* are usually both pronounced /kɑːt/, and 'o' as in *go* (/goʊ/) is more rounded than in Britain. *Tune* is pronounced /tuːn/ not /tjuːn/. Stress patterns and syllable length are often also different, as in *laboratory* (/ˈlæbrətɔːri/, *BrE* /ləˈbɒrətri/) and *missile* (/ˈmɪsl/, *BrE* /ˈmɪsaɪl/).

Americans tend to use very direct language, and polite forms which occur in British English, such as 'Would you mind if I …' or 'I'm afraid that …' sound formal and unnatural to them.

Regional differences

***General American English** (GAE) is the dialect that is closest to being a standard. It is especially common in the *Midwest but is used in many parts of the US. The associated **Midwestern** accent is spoken across most of the northern states, and by many people elsewhere.

The main dialect groups are the **Northern**, the **Coastal Southern**, the **Midland**, from which GAE is derived, and the **Western**. The main differences between them are in accent, but some words are restricted to particular dialects because the item they refer to is not found elsewhere: **grits*, for example, is eaten mainly in the *South and is considered to be a Southern word.

Northern dialects spread west from New York and *Boston. *New England has its own accent, though many people there have a Midwestern accent. The old, rich families of Boston speak with a distinctive **Bostonian** accent which is similar to Britain's *RP.

Midland dialects developed after settlers moved west from *Philadelphia. Both Midland and Western dialects contain features from the Northern and Southern groups. There are increasing differences within the Western group, as south-western dialects have been influenced by Mexican Spanish.

The Southern dialects are most distinctive. They contain old words no longer used in other American dialects, e.g. *kinfolk* for 'relatives' and *hand* for 'farmworker'. French, Spanish and Native-American languages also contributed to Southern dialects. Since black slaves were taken mainly to the South and most *African Americans still live there, ***Black English** and Southern dialects have much in common. The accent is a **southern drawl** which even foreigners recognize. An 'r' at the end of a word is often omitted, so that *door* is pronounced /doʊ/, and diphthongs are replaced with simple vowels, so that *hide* is pronounced /hɑːd/. Some people use *y'all* as a plural form of 'you'. This is more common in speech than in writing.

Southern dialects and accents are often thought by other Americans to be inferior. Black English and *Cajun English may also be less acceptable. Both varieties are restricted to particular ethnic or social groups, and the attitude probably reflects more general feelings about those groups.

An official language?

For a long time English helped to unite immigrants who had come from many countries. Now, Hispanic immigrants, especially in south-western states, want to continue to use their own language, and many Americans are afraid that this will divide the country. The Hispanic population is growing and will reach 80 million by 2050.

This situation led to the founding of the ***English Only Movement**, which wants to make English the official language of the US. Supporters believe that this will help keep states and people together, and that money spent on printing forms, etc. in both English and Spanish would be better spent on teaching the immigrants English. Others think that an official language is unnecesary. They argue that children of immigrants, and *their* children, will want to speak English anyway, and that a common language does not always lead to social harmony.

The American Revolution

The War of Revolution between America and Britain began in April 1775 in *Lexington, Massachusetts, when soldiers from each side met and somebody fired a shot. It was called the 'shot heard round the world' because the war that followed changed the future of the *British Empire and America. But the American Revolution, the movement to make an independent nation, began many years earlier.

The causes of revolution

The desire of Americans to be independent from Britain arose out of a long series of disagreements about money and political control. Britain had had **colonies** (= places taken over by people from a foreign country) in North America since 1607 and kept soldiers there to defend them from attack by the French and Spanish, and by *Native Americans. In order to raise money for this, the British *Parliament tried to make the **colonists** (= people who had gone to settle in America) pay taxes.

From 1651, Britain passed a series of laws called **Navigation Acts**, which said that the colonists should trade only with Britain. These laws were frequently broken and were a continuing source of tension. Taxes imposed in the 18th century increased ill feeling towards Britain. In 1764 the **Sugar Act** made colonists pay tax on sugar, and in 1765 the ***Stamp Act** put a tax on newspapers and official documents. Opposition to this was strong and the following year Parliament had to remove the tax. By then, people in both America and Britain were arguing about who had the power to tax the colonies. The 13 colonies each had an **assembly** of elected representatives, and the colonists wanted these assemblies to decide what taxes they should pay, not Parliament. Some colonists, called **patriots**, began to want independence from Britain. They expressed their feelings in the slogan 'no taxation without representation'.

In 1767 there was a disagreement in New York about whether Britain could ask people to give soldiers accommodation in their houses. The local assembly agreed, eventually, but became involved in a dispute with Parliament over who had the right to decide such matters. In the same year the **Townshend Acts** put taxes on certain products including tea. The assemblies refused to help collect the money and Parliament responded by closing them down. All this caused many more people to want independence. *Boston, especially, had many patriots, including those who called themselves the ***Sons of Liberty**. On 5 March 1770 there was a riot in Boston and British soldiers killed five people. This incident became known as the ***Boston Massacre**.

The **Tea Act** gave a British company the right to sell tea to the colonists and actually lowered the price for legally imported tea. But most colonists bought cheaper tea that had been smuggled into the country. On 16 December 1773, when ships arrived in Boston Harbour carrying the tea, a group of patriots dressed up as Native Americans went onto the ships and threw the tea into the water. After the ***Boston Tea Party**, as the event was later called, Britain passed the **Intolerable Acts**, laws to increase her control over the colonies.

As more Americans began to support revolution, Britain sent yet more soldiers. On 5 September 1774 representatives of all the colonies except *Georgia met in *Philadelphia, calling themselves the ***Continental Congress**. The Congress decided that the colonies needed soldiers of their own, and agreed to start training **militiamen** who could leave their jobs and be used as soldiers if necessary. Since the militiamen had to be ready to fight at short notice, they were called ***minutemen**.

On 18 April 1775 British soldiers marched out of Boston into the countryside to search for weapons that the colonists had hidden. **Paul *Revere**, a patriot from Boston, rode ahead to warn people that the British were coming. The minutemen got ready, and when they and the British met, the 'shot heard round the world' was fired.

The Revolutionary War

The Americans had the advantage of fighting at home, but Britain was a much stronger military power. There were victories and defeats on both sides during the seven years of war.

The first aim of the American army led by George *Washington was to force the British, called ***Redcoats** because of the colour of their uniform, to leave Boston. On 17 June 1775 the British fought and won the **Battle of *Bunker Hill**, but they lost so many soldiers that their position in Boston was weak and in March 1776 they were forced to leave. The Continental Congress suggested that Britain and America should make an agreement, but Britain refused and so, on 4 July 1776, members of the Congress signed the ***Declaration of Independence**. This document, written by the future President Thomas *Jefferson, gave the Americans' reasons for wanting to be independent. It included ideas that were rather new, e.g. that ordinary people had certain rights that governments should respect. Since the British king *George III refused to accept this, Americans had the right, and the duty, to form their own government.

Later in the same year the British took control of *New York and *Rhode Island, and Washington's army moved away into *Pennsylvania. The defeats discouraged many Americans, but at Christmas, when soldiers were not expecting an attack, Washington surprised the British by taking his army across the Delaware River to Trenton, *New Jersey, and defeating the **Hessians**, German soldiers paid by the British to fight for them. A story often told is that, before crossing the river, Washington threw down a silver dollar, thinking that if any guards were near they would hear the noise and come. Since nobody came, he knew it was safe to attack.

Washington's army spent the winter at *Valley Forge, Pennsylvania. It was very cold and the new government of the United States did not have money to provide soldiers with warm clothes and food. Many became ill, and many more lost their enthusiasm for the war. But in the spring of 1777 they received help from two different sources. A German, General von Steuben, came to train the American soldiers, and the Marquis de *Lafayette brought French soldiers to fight on the American side. With this help, the Americans won a victory at *Saratoga, New York. France and also Spain

A

supported the United States because they thought that if Britain became weaker in North America, it would also be weaker in Europe.

Over the next few years, neither side was strong enough to defeat the other completely. But in 1781 Washington saw a perfect opportunity to win. The British General *Cornwallis had taken his army to *Yorktown, Virginia, where he was too far away to get supplies or help. Washington marched south to meet him, while French ships made sure that the British could not receive help by sea. Cornwallis realized how bad his position was and surrendered.

In 1783, after a period of talks, Britain recognized the **United States of America**, making the US completely independent and giving it the western parts of North America.

Modern American attitudes to the Revolution

The Revolution is remembered by Americans in many ways. *Freedom, and the right of ordinary people to take part in their own government, the main reasons why Americans fought the War of Revolution, are values that almost all Americans still support strongly. The *Fourth of July, the day on which the Declaration of Independence was signed, is a national holiday, ***Independence Day**.

Places, like Boston Harbour and *Independence Hall in Philadelphia, where the Declaration of Independence was signed, are visited by millions of Americans every year. The names of people involved in the Revolution are known to everyone. George Washington's birthday is celebrated as a national holiday. John *Hancock's signature on the Declaration of Independence was the largest, so today *John Hancock* means 'signature'. Patrick *Henry is remembered for his speeches, especially for saying, 'Give me liberty or give me death'.

But if Americans remember the Revolution as a great victory, they seem to forget that the British were the enemy. The governments and people of the two countries have always had a special relationship, and for many Americans, even those whose ancestors were not British, Britain is still the 'mother country'.

ˌMartin '**Amis²** /'eɪmɪs/ (1949–) an English writer and journalist. His books include *Dead Babies* (1975) and *Money* (1984). He is the son of Kingsley *Amis.

the '**Amish** /'ɑːmɪʃ/ a strict Christian group in America who were once part of the *Mennonites. They are mostly farmers in the states of Pennsylvania, Ohio and Indiana. Because of their many religious rules, they do not have cars, telephones or electricity, and they wear old-fashioned clothes. See also PENNSYLVANIA DUTCH 1.

an Amish family

ˌ**Amnesty Inter'national** an international organization that works to help people who have been put in prison for their beliefs or because of their colour, race or religion (but only if these people do not believe in using violence). It is also opposed to torture and *capital punishment. It was established in Britain in 1961, and now has members in over 70 countries.

ˌ**Ampleforth 'College** /ˌæmplfɔːθ; *AmE* ˌæmplfɔːrθ/ a Roman Catholic *public school for boys in *Yorkshire in the north of England. It was set up in 1802.

'**Amtrak**™ /'æmtræk/ the public company, set up by *Congress in 1970, which runs trains for passengers in the US. Its formal name is the National Railroad Passenger Corporation. Only 1% of Americans using public transport travel by Amtrak. It has lost money every year, and in 1997 the service was greatly reduced.

'**Amway**™ /'æmweɪ/ a US company which employs people to sell its products in their spare time, often at special parties in their own homes. The items they sell include cosmetics and cleaning products, and the more they sell the more money they are paid by the company.

ˌ**Ana'baptist** /ˌænə'bæptɪst/ *n* a member of any of several strict religious groups in the 16th century, during the *Reformation. They believed in following the Bible's teachings exactly, separating the Church from the State, and shared ownership of goods. They also believed that only adults should be baptized Their views were considered extreme by both *Protestants and *Catholics. They were strongest in Germany and the Netherlands, but later the movement spread to the US. They influenced the beliefs of the later *Baptist movement and of other groups such as the *Hutterites and the *Mennonites.

'**Anacin**™ /'ænæsɪn/ *n* [C, U] (in the US) a medicine taken to relieve minor pains, invented in 1918.

'**Anadin**™ /'ænædɪn/ *n* [C, U] the British name for the medicine called *Anacin in the US.

'**Anchorage** /'æŋkərɪdʒ/ the largest city in *Alaska. It is on a port in the southern part of the state. An earthquake badly damaged the city in 1964 and killed 131 people.

ˌ**ancient 'lights** *n* [U] (in English law) the principle that you have the right to receive light through any window that has been there for 20 years or more. It may be used in cases where a person wants to build something in front of your house, etc.

The ˌ***Ancient 'Mariner*** /'mærɪnə(r)/ (*in full* **The Rime of the Ancient Mariner**) a long poem (1798) by Samuel Taylor * Coleridge. In it an old sailor tells a wedding guest how he once shot an albatross (= a large sea bird considered lucky by sailors). His friends hung the bird around his neck as a punishment. They all died of thirst, and he was left alive to tell his story to anyone who would listen. The best-known lines from the poem are these:

Water, water, everywhere
Nor any drop to drink.

ˌ**ancient 'monument** *n* (in Britain) a building or place officially protected by law from being damaged or destroyed. *Stonehenge is an example of an ancient monument. See also ENGLISH HERITAGE, LISTED BUILDINGS.

E'lizabeth 'Garrett '**Anderson¹** /'gærət 'ændəsən;

AmE ˈɡærət ˈændərsən/ (1836–1917) the first British woman doctor, who fought for the right of other women to become doctors after struggling to get her own medical qualifications in 1865. Later she set up a hospital where women could be treated by women. In 1908 she also became the first woman *mayor of an English town.

ˌMarian ˈ**Anderson²** /ˈændəsən; *AmE* ˈændərsən/ (1902–1993) a US singer. In 1939 she was prevented from entering a hall to give a concert by the *Daughters of the American Revolution because she was black, so she gave a free concert from the steps of the *Lincoln Memorial. In 1955, she became the first black singer to perform at the *Metropolitan Opera in New York.

ˌSherwood ˈ**Anderson³** /ˌʃɜːwʊd ˈændəsən; *AmE* ˌʃɜːrwʊd ˈændərsən/ (1876–1941) a US writer. His most successful collection of short stories was *Winesburg, Ohio* (1919) about the dull life of a small town. His novels included *Poor White* (1920) and *Dark Laughter* (1925).

ˈ**Anderson ˌshelter** /ˈændəsən; *AmE* ˈændərsən/ *n* a small hut made of metal that British people put up in their gardens during *World War II. The huts were used for shelter when bombs were dropped on their homes by the Germans, during the *Blitz. They were named after the *Home Secretary in 1939–40, Sir John Anderson.

ˌMario **Anˈdretti** /ˌmæriəʊ ænˈdreti/ (1940–) a US driver of racing cars, born in Italy. He has won the national championship of the United States Auto Club three times (1965–6 and 1969). He also won the Grand Prix championship in 1978 and the *Indianapolis 500 in 1969.

ˌPrince ˈ**Andrew¹** ⇨ YORK³(1).

St ˈ**Andrew²** (1st century AD) the patron saint of Scotland. He was one of the 12 apostles, the brother of St Peter. He became the patron saint of the *Picts in the 8th century, when, it is thought, his bones were brought to a town on the east coast of Scotland, later called *St Andrews. According to tradition, he was killed in Greece on an cross in the shape of an X, and so this cross is on the Scottish flag.

ˌJulie ˈ**Andrews** /ˈændruːz/ (1935–) an English actor, best known for her film roles in **Mary Poppins* (1964), for which she won an *Oscar, and *The *Sound of Music* (1965). Because of these roles, people tend to see her as a healthy, cheerful, moral person, although she has tried to change this impression in later films. She is married to the US film producer Blake *Edwards.

the ˈ**Andrews ˌSisters** /ˈændruːz / three US sisters who sang together with great success, especially during *World War II. They were Patty (1920–), Maxene (1918–95) and LaVerne (1913–67). Their most popular songs included *Bei Mir Bist Du Schon* (1937) and *Don't Sit Under the Apple Tree* (1942).

ˈ**Andrex**™ /ˈændreks/ a make of toilet paper. Its popular advertisements have often used a Labrador puppy (= young dog).

ˌ**Andy ˈCapp** /ˈkæp/ a humorous character in a British strip cartoon in *The *Mirror*. He drinks a lot, is very lazy, and is unfair to his wife Flo. He always wears a flat cap, which was a traditional working man's piece of clothing, and has a cigarette hanging from his mouth: *She's got a real Andy Capp of a husband – he's utterly selfish!*

ˈ**Anfield** /ˈænfiːld/ (*also* **Anfield Road**) the football ground of *Liverpool Football Club.

The ˌ**Angel, ˈIslington** /ˈɪzlɪŋtən/ a busy place where several roads meet in Islington, an area of north London. It is called after a pub for travellers which existed there in the 17th century.

ˌ**Angeˈleno** /ˌændʒəˈliːnəʊ; *AmE* ˌændʒəˈliːnoʊ/ *n* (*pl* **-nos**) (*AmE, infml*) a person who lives in Los Angeles.

ˈ**angel food cake** (*also* **angel cake**) *n* a soft white cake with a light texture, made with sugar, flour and the white parts of eggs beaten until they are stiff.

ˌMaya ˈ**Angelou** /ˌmaɪə ˈændʒəluː/ (1928–) an African-American writer, singer and teacher. Her best-known book is *I Know Why the Caged Bird Sings* (1970), a true story of her difficult but successful life. In 1997 she directed her first film for television, *Down in the Delta*.

ˈ**Anglepoise**™ /ˈæŋɡlpɔɪz/ *n* a make of lamp, used especially on a desk, that can be easily moved into different positions so that the light shines where it is needed.

ˈ**Anglesey** /ˈæŋɡlsi/ a large island off the north-west coast of *Wales, a part of *Gwynedd. It is joined to the mainland by both road and rail bridges, and passenger boats sail regularly between Holyhead on Anglesey and Ireland.

ˌ**Anglia TˈV** /ˌæŋɡliə/ one of the *ITV television companies that supply programmes to the regions of Britain. It broadcasts mainly to *East Anglia.

ˈ**Anglican** *n* a member of one of the churches in the *Anglican Communion. In Britain these are the *Church of England, the *Church in Wales, the Episcopal Church in Scotland, and the *Church of Ireland. In the US, the Anglican Communion is represented by the *Protestant Episcopal Church. Many people in Britain call themselves Anglican, even though they may never attend church. See also CHURCH OF SCOTLAND. ⇨ article at RELIGION. ▶ **Anglican** *adj*.

the ˌ**Anglican Comˈmunion** an organization consisting of the *Church of England and other churches in Britain and abroad that have historical links with the Church of England. Its leader is the *Archbishop of Canterbury. Every ten years all the bishops of the Anglican Communion attend the *Lambeth Conference.

ˈ**angling** /ˈæŋɡlɪŋ/ *n* [U] the sport of fishing with a line and a hook, usually in rivers and lakes, etc. rather than in the sea. It is one of the most popular leisure activities in Britain.

ˌ**Anglo-Aˈmerican** *n* an American, especially of the US, who is descended from an English family.
▶ **Anglo-American** *adj* involving Britain and America, especially the US: *the history of Anglo-American relations.*

ˌ**Anglo-Caˈtholicism** *n* [U] a movement within the *Church of England that emphasizes its connections

Andy Capp

with the *Roman Catholic Church. **Anglo-Catholic** ideas were strongly expressed in the *Oxford Movement of the 1830s. In recent years many **Anglo-Catholics** have considered leaving the Church of England because it has accepted women as priests. See also ORDINATION OF WOMEN.

the ˌ**Anglo-Dutch** ˈ**Wars** three wars fought by the English against the Dutch between 1652 and 1674, at a time when the two countries were competing strongly for trade around the world. One important result was that the town of *New Amsterdam was given to the English in 1667. They gave it the new name of New York.

the ˈ**Anglo-ˈIrish Aˈgreement** an agreement reached in November 1985 between the UK and Ireland, allowing the Irish government to take part in discussions about *Northern Ireland. Many *Unionists do not like it.

the ˈ**Anglo-ˈIrish ˈTreaty** the agreement that formally ended the *Troubles in *Northern Ireland in 1921.

the ˈ**Anglo-ˈIrish ˈWar** the formal name for the *Troubles in *Northern Ireland between 1919 and 1921. It involved violent fighting between the *IRA and the *Black and Tans and was brought to an end by the *Anglo-Irish Treaty, which recognized the establishment of the independent republic of Ireland. ⇨ article at NORTHERN IRELAND.

ˌ**Anglo-ˈSaxon** *n* **1** [C] an English person of the period between the time when the Romans left Britain in the 5th century AD and the *Norman Conquest in 1066. The name is formed from the names of two of the tribes that occupied England after the Romans left, the Angles and the *Saxons. **2** (*also* **Old English**) [U] the English language of the period before the *Norman Conquest. Compare MIDDLE ENGLISH. **3** [U] (*AmE*) the modern English language. **4** [C] a white person whose native language is English. See also WASP. ▶ **Anglo-Saxon** *adj*.

The ˈ***Anglo-ˈSaxon*** ˈ***Chronicle*** an early history of England, written in *Old English. It ends in the 12th century, but mostly covers the period from the time when the Romans came to Britain until the *Norman Conquest in 1066.

ˌ**angry young** ˈ**man** *n* (*pl* **angry young men**) (*esp BrE*) a young person who strongly criticizes political and social institutions. The phrase was originally used by British newspapers in the late 1950s, after the success of the play **Look Back in Anger* by John *Osborne, to describe young British writers like Osborne, Kingsley *Amis, and Kenneth *Tynan: *You don't have to be an angry young man to feel disgusted by what's happening in the country today.*

ˌ**animal** ˈ**crackers** *n* [pl] small, sweet American biscuits shaped like different animals. They are sold together in boxes and are popular with children.

ˌ***Animal*** ˈ***Farm*** a book (1945) by George *Orwell in which some farm animals start a revolution against the farmer but are betrayed by their leaders, the pigs, and suffer even more than before. *Animal Farm* is a satire on the Russian Revolution and the struggle for power between Stalin and Trotsky, represented by the pigs Napoleon and Snowball. The most often quoted and adapted line from the book is 'All animals are equal, but some animals are more equal than others.'

the ˈ**Animal Libeˈration** ˈ**Front** a British group, formed in the early 1970s, that believes in attacking any organization which they feel is cruel to animals. They use public protest and even violence to do this. For example, they sometimes steal animals that a company's scientists are using in their experiments, and damage the company's property.

Animals ⇨ article.

Anˈnapolis /əˈnæpəlɪs/ the capital city of the US state of *Maryland. The United States Naval Academy, where officers are trained, is there. The Academy is usually called Annapolis: *He's a senior at Annapolis.*

ˌPrincess ˈ**Anne¹** (1950–) a British princess, the only daughter of Queen *Elizabeth II and Prince *Philip. She has a strong interest in horse-riding, and represented Britain in the *three-day event at the 1976 Olympic Games. She is also known for her work as the President of the *Save the Children Fund. In 1973 she married Captain Mark Phillips, and had two children, Peter (1977–) and Zara (1981–). In 1992 she was divorced from her husband, and in the same year married Timothy Laurence (1955–), a Royal Navy Commander. She was given the title of *Princess Royal in 1987. ⇨ article at ROYAL FAMILY.

ˌQueen ˈ**Anne²** (1665–1714) the queen of Britain from 1702–14. She was the daughter of King *James II and the last of the House of *Stuart. None of her 18 children lived beyond the age of 11, so when she died her cousin George from Hanover in Germany became King *George I. Queen Anne was the last British ruler to be able to prevent parliament from passing a law by using her power to veto (= reject) it. See also QUEEN ANNE.

ˌ**Anne of** ˈ**Cleves** /ˈkliːvz/ (1515–57) a German princess who in 1540 became the fourth wife of King *Henry VIII. They were divorced after six months.

ˌ***Annie Get Your*** ˈ***Gun*** a US musical play (1946) by Irving *Berlin. It is a story about Annie *Oakley, and a film version was made in 1950. One of its songs, *There's No Business Like Show Business*, has a special meaning for entertainers.

ˌ***Annie*** ˈ***Hall*** /ˈhɔːl/ a successful US film (1977), written and directed by Woody *Allen. It is a romantic comedy and won *Oscars for Best Picture, Best Director and Best Actress (Diane *Keaton).

ˌ**Annie** ˈ**Oakley** /ˈəʊkli; *AmE* ˈoʊkli/ *n* (*AmE infml*) a free ticket or pass, e.g. for a theatre performance. It is called this because it has holes in it (so that it cannot be used again) and looks like one of the cards shot by Annie *Oakley as part of her act.

ˈ**annual perˈcentage** ˈ**rate** *n* ⇨ APR.

ˌ**annus horˈribilis** /ˌænəs hɒˈriːbɪlɪs; *AmE* hɔːˈriːbɪlɪs/ *n* [sing] the Latin for 'horrible year'. Queen *Elizabeth II used this expression in a speech in November 1992 to describe how she felt about that year, during which the British royal family had had a very difficult time. The *Princess Royal got divorced, the Duke of *York(1) separated from his wife, the *Prince of Wales had marriage problems, and there was a serious fire at *Windsor Castle.

ˌ**annus miˈrabilis** /ˌænəs mɪˈrɑːbɪlɪs/ *n* [sing] the Latin for 'remarkable year'. John *Dryden's poem *Annus Mirabilis* (1667) describes the year 1666 when the *Great Fire of London happened and the English defeated the Dutch: *The year 1996 was something of an annus mirabilis for British racing drivers.*

aˌnother ˈ**place** an expression used in the *House of Commons to refer to the *House of Lords or in the House of Lords to refer to the House of Commons.

ˌ**anteˈbellum** /ˌæntiˈbeləm/ *adj* [only before *n*] of the years before a war. The word is mainly used in the US to describe grand houses built in the southern states before the American *Civil War.

ˌSusan B ˈ**Anthony** /ˈænθəni/ (Susan Brownell Anthony 1820–1906) a US teacher who was a leader of the campaign for women's right to vote. In 1869 she

A

Animals

The British are famous for being a nation of animal lovers, and many families have at least one *__pet__. Americans also like animals, and about 60% of families have a pet. People from other countries think British and American people are sentimental about animals, and say that they fuss over them and treat them as well as people. But though most people love their pets they generally put people's interests before those of animals.

At weekends people have opportunities to see other animals. Many towns have a river with ducks to feed. In Britain people visit **farm parks**, **safari parks** (= parks where people can drive close to lions, zebras, etc.), **zoos**, **bird parks**, and **sealife centres**. In the US there are zoos and **aquaria** (= large tanks of fish), which are educational, and also amusement parks with animals, like Busch Gardens and *Disney's Animal Kingdom.

Television programmes about animals are very popular. These range from factual programmes to films and *cartoons starring fictional animals such as *Lassie and *Tom and Jerry. Children get interested in animals from an early age when they are given cuddly toy animals and picture books. Children's literature has created many famous animal characters, such as *Black Beauty, *Brer Rabbit, *Pooh, and Ratty, Mole and Toad in *The *Wind in the Willows*. Many animals in books have their own distinctive character: lions are typically brave, foxes are cunning, and cats are proud.

News stories about animals appear regularly in the media. When in 1998 two pigs being taken to slaughter escaped into the countryside, their adventures appeared on the front pages of British national newspapers. In the US many newspapers regularly feature a photograph of an animal being cared for by an animal *charity in order to find somebody who will adopt it.

America's fondness for animals has also led to names of animals being used for sports teams, e.g. the Chicago Bears and Philadelphia Eagles.

Animal welfare

People get very upset when others are cruel to animals. Such cruelty is illegal in Britain and the US, and anyone found guilty of treating animals badly may be forbidden to keep any in the future and fined or even put in prison.

People give generously to animal charities, and this money helps them set up **animal hospitals** and **rescue centres** for injured and abandoned animals. Each spring US charities celebrate a 'be kind to animals week'. The American Society for the Prevention of Cruelty to Animals runs a pet adoption programme in many cities.

There has been concern over the way animals are treated in zoos, and people have campaigned for poorly run zoos throughout the world to be closed down. Most British and American zoos are fairly modern, and many animals live in a large **enclosure** similar to their natural **habitat**, rather than in a **cage**. Many zoos now also keep only animals that cannot survive in the wild or which were born **in captivity**. Some breed animals to put back into the wild, and try to raise public awareness about the need for **conservation**.

Protecting wild animals

Caring about wild animals is a common middle-class attitude. Many people feed wild birds in the winter. In the US the National Wildlife Federation (NWF) helps people to create their own 'backyard wildlife habitat'. Some people have bumper stickers on their cars saying 'Warning – I brake for animals'.

Reports that a species is **endangered** (= may become extinct) inspire campaigns to save them. There have been international campaigns to save the whale, the tiger and the rhino. In the US the NWF is fighting to save wolves and buffalo. In Britain there have been attempts to increase the numbers of red squirrels and hedgehogs. But there is a lot of inconsistency in people's attitudes to wild animals. More people are concerned about baby seals being clubbed to death than about the killing of alligators because seals are seen as more attractive creatures.

In rural areas people generally have much less romantic ideas about animals. In Britain foxes steal chickens, and in the US bears and wolves kill livestock. Road signs that say 'Deer Crossing' are for the driver's protection not the animal's. In Britain hunting arouses hostile feelings, especially among people living in towns, and there are frequent attempts to disrupt hunts and to have hunting stopped. But many country people say that this is a traditional sport which serve a useful purpose.

Animal rights

In Britain many people are worried about the use of animals in scientific research. Public pressure has forced many cosmetics manufacturers to stop testing products on animals. Stopping the use of animals for medical research is more difficult, as people want the medical advances that may be achieved through animal experiments. Several groups, including the *Animal Liberation Front, strongly oppose **vivisection** (= the use of live animals in experiments) and **animal rights activists** organize protests at laboratories.

There are several animal rights groups in the US, but most Americans accept the need for animal research. Products labelled 'cruelty-free' are less common in the US than in Britain.

Some people oppose the use of animals in circuses and other entertainment. Many do not believe people should wear furs, and in New York and some other cities people may throw paint at those wearing furs.

Factory farming

Many people are against farming methods in which animals are fattened as quickly as possible in artificial conditions. But meat from these animals costs less than that from animals that have not been intensely reared and people are not prepared to pay the higher price. Eggs and chickens from a **battery farm**, where hens are kept in small cages, are cheaper than free-range eggs and chickens.

In Britain people are concerned about the way farm animals are transported, and regulations now say how often they must be given food and water on a journey. There has been particular concern over **veal lorries** (= lorries carrying calves for veal) travelling to Europe, and people have lain down in protest in front of the lorries.

and Elizabeth Cady Stanton established the National Woman Suffrage Association. Anthony also organized the International Council of Women in 1888 and was President of the National American Woman Suffrage Association from 1892 to 1900. Her image is on the *Anthony dollar.

ˌAnthony ˈdollar /ˌænθəni/ *n* a US dollar coin with the image of Susan B *Anthony on it. These coins were produced in memory of her between 1979 and 1981, and she is the first American woman to be honoured in this way. Some people like to collect and keep Anthony dollars.

AnˌtiguaandBarˈbuda /ænˌtiːɡə, bɑːˈbjuːdə; *AmE* bɑːrˈbjuːdə/ the official name of a country consisting of three small islands in the Caribbean. Antigua and Barbuda were British colonies from the early 17th century until they became fully independent and a member of the *Commonwealth in 1981. Most of the country's population live on Antigua. ▶ **Antiguan** *adj, n*; **Barbudan** *adj, n*.

antiques

Some people say that anything over 50 years old can be called an **antique**, while others say an antique must be over 100 years old. The term is usually applied to objects that are valuable because they are rare or are of high quality. In the US the word *antique* can also describe any object that is old enough to be interesting and unusual, or was made by hand in the days before factories. Antiques include furniture, carpets, clocks, china, glass, silver, jewellery, embroidery and even toys. Any extra information about an antique, such as the maker's bill or a **letter of provenance** (= a letter referring to an object's history and origin) increases its value. Other items that people may collect are called **collectibles**. They may be of any age and include old picture cards, metal signs and beer mats.

Many people in Britain are interested in antiques, even if they do not own any. Antique-collecting became popular in the late 1980s and 1990s, and towns such as *Warwick and *Hungerford are famous for their **antique shops**. People also look in **junk shops** and **second-hand shops** in the hope of finding a bargain. **Antiques fairs** are held occasionally in hotels or conference centres. **Auction houses**, such as *Christie's and *Sotheby's, hold sales which are attended by members of the public and **dealers**.

In the US antiques are especially popular with older people. Antiques can be bought in antique shops in large cities, in small shops in the country, in **flea markets** (= markets selling old and used goods cheaply) or at ***garage sales**. *New England is a popular area for **hunting antiques** (*AmE*), and many people spend weekends driving through small towns hoping to find something special. Among antiques that originate in the US is ***Shaker furniture**, made in a very simple style. Some people are interested in **Americana**, objects associated with US history such as letters written by George *Washington, silver objects made by Paul *Revere, or early versions of the American flag.

*The *Antiques Roadshow*, a popular television programme, has encouraged many people in Britain and the US to take an interest in antiques.

The ***ˌAntiques ˈRoadshow*** /ˈrəʊdʃəʊ; *AmE* ˈroʊdʃoʊ/ a popular *BBC television programme in which members of the public bring interesting old possessions, e.g. furniture or pottery, for experts to examine and talk about their history and value. It began in 1979. A similar programme with the same name began on US television in 1996.

ˌantiˈtrust legisˌlation /ˌæntiˈtrʌst/ *n* [U] laws introduced in the US to encourage competition in business. Their main aim has been to prevent or control monopolies (= companies which are so large that no others can compete with them). The most important early antitrust laws passed by the United States Congress were the Sherman Antitrust Act (1890) and the Clayton Antitrust Act (1914). See also TAFT-HARTLEY ACT.

the **ˌAntonine ˈWall** /ˌæntənaɪn/ a wall built in 142 AD across southern Scotland during the reign of the Roman emperor Antoninus Pius. It was about 37 miles (59 kilometres) long and was intended to replace *Hadrian's Wall further south as the northern frontier of the Roman Empire, but it had to be abandoned by 197 AD. Little of the wall now remains.

ˌAntony and Cleoˈpatra /kliːəˈpætrə/ a play (*c.* 1607) by William *Shakespeare about the true story of the great love between the Roman general Mark Antony and Cleopatra, the queen of Egypt. At the end, when Mark Antony has been defeated in battle, they both kill themselves, Antony by falling on his sword and Cleopatra by letting a poisonous snake bite her.

ˌAny ˈQuestions? a British radio programme in which members of the public can ask politicians and other well-known people for their opinions about issues that are in the news. It is broadcast every week from a different town, and has been running since 1948. People can also telephone the *BBC to give their response to what the politicians, etc. have said in a programme called *Any Answers?* Since 1979 there has been a similar programme to *Any Questions?* on BBC television, called **Question Time*.

AP /ˌeɪ ˈpiː/ ⇨ ASSOCIATED PRESS.

Aˈpache /əˈpætʃi/ *n* (*pl* **Apaches** *or* **Apache**) a member of a Native American group in the southwestern US. In the late 19th century the Apaches, under such leaders as *Cochise and *Geronimo, were the last Native Americans to be defeated by the US Cavalry. Today many Apaches live on reservations (= areas of land given and protected by the US government) in the states of Arizona, Oklahoma and New Mexico.

an Apache chief

APB /ˌeɪ piː ˈbiː/ (*in full* **all points bulletin**) *n* a US police radio message telling all officers on duty to look for a particular person: *There's an APB out for him.*

APO /ˌeɪ piː ˈəʊ; *AmE* ˌeɪ piː ˈoʊ/ (*in full* **Army Post Office**) the special post office system of the US

A

Army. Mail can be sent between army bases in the US and abroad quickly and cheaply. Compare FPO.

the **A'pollo ˌprogram** /ə'pɒləʊ; *AmE* ə'pɑːloʊ/ the US space programme to put men on the moon. It was begun in 1961 by President John F *Kennedy and achieved its aim on 20 July 1969 when Neil *Armstrong and Buzz *Aldrin landed on the moon during the *Apollo 11* flight.

the crew of Apollo 11: Neil Armstrong, Michael Collins and Buzz Aldrin

ˌAppa'lachia /ˌæpə'leɪʃə/ a region of the *Appalachian Mountains in the southern US. It includes parts of 13 states and is known for the poverty of its mostly white population. The local people are famous for their traditional arts.

the **ˌAppa'lachian 'Mountains** /ˌæpə'leɪʃn/ a range of mountains in eastern North America. It runs 1 800 miles (2 900 kilometres) from Newfoundland in Canada to central Alabama in the US. This includes the region of *Appalachia and the *Allegheny Mountains, the *Great Smoky Mountains and the Blue Ridge Mountains. The Appalachian National Scenic Trail is the longest in the world with signs for hikers (= people walking for pleasure).

ap'peasement /ə'piːzmənt/ *n* [U] (*usu disapprov*) doing what somebody else wants you to do in order to keep them from attacking you. The word was used to describe the British government's policy of trying to remain on friendly terms with Hitler and Mussolini, despite their aggressive actions, before World War II. Many people thought that this policy was too weak. See also CHAMBERLAIN, MUNICH AGREEMENT.

'Apple (*also* **Apple Mac** /mæk/, **Mac**) the popular name for the Macintosh computer produced by the US company Apple Computer, Inc. It is the only major computer that is not designed to exchange information with an *IBM computer. The company was begun in 1976 by two engineers, Steven Jobs and Stephen Wozniak, and has always made small, simple computers that are easy to use. Its main office is in *Silicon Valley, *California.

'applejack /'æpldʒæk/ *n* [U] (*AmE*) a very strong alcoholic drink made from apples. It is stronger than cider. Compare SCRUMPY.

ˌapple 'pie *n* [U, C] a sweet dish popular in America and Britain. It is made with apples, sugar and spices cooked in pastry. The phrase *in apple-pie order* means 'in excellent or perfect order'. People say that something is *as American as apple pie* because it is a favourite dish in the US. Americans also say that nothing is better than *mom and apple pie*.

ˌJohnny **'Appleseed** /'æplsiːd/ (1774–1845) the popular name for John Chapman, an American who planted apple seeds for 40 years in the Ohio River valley. He began planting in 1806, and his work made him an American legend. He had long hair and travelled around in torn clothes and without shoes.

ˌAppo'mattox 'Court House /ˌæpə'mætəks/ a former small community in the US state of Virginia where the American *Civil War ended. General Robert E *Lee of the *Confederate States surrendered on 9 April 1865 to General Ulysses S *Grant in a private house. The area is now a national historical park.

ap'portionment /ə'pɔːʃnmənt; *AmE* ə'pɔːrʃnmənt/ *n* [C, U] (in the US) the way in which the number of seats (= places for members) is decided in a law-making assembly, especially the *House of Representatives, where the apportionment of seats is based on how many people live in each state: *a change in party rules to tie delegate apportionment more directly to primary election results.*

the **Apˌprentice Boys' Pa'rade** an occasion on 12 August every year when some of the Protestant citizens of *Northern Ireland march through the streets of *Londonderry(1), in memory of the day in 1689 when the army of the Roman Catholic King *James II was forced to give up attacking the town. The march creates a lot of tension between Protestants and Catholics, and this sometimes leads to violence. See also ORANGEMEN. ⇨ article at NORTHERN IRELAND.

APR (*in full* **annual percentage rate**) the rate of interest that you pay to an organization from which you borrow money in order to buy something over a period of time. The APR can vary during the time the money is being paid back: *The APR on your loan is 27.8% (variable).*

ˌApril 'Fool's Day (*also* **April Fools' Day**) 1 April, the day when people in many countries play tricks or jokes on each other. The victim of the joke is called the **April Fool**. A typical trick is to make somebody believe something that is not true, e.g. that the clocks have changed and everything is an hour later, or that the government has announced an election. Newspapers, television and radio stations often join in with imaginary news stories.

ˌApsley 'House /ˌæpsli/ a large elegant house near *Hyde Park(1) in London, sometimes called 'No. 1, London'. It was built by Robert *Adam in the 18th century, and later belonged to the Duke of *Wellington. It is now the Wellington Museum.

The ***Aˌrabian 'Nights*** the name often given to the *Thousand and One Nights*, a collection of folk (= traditional) stories from the Middle East, originally written in Arabic. Scheherezade marries a king who kills his wives after their first night together. She survives by telling him a different story every night. Many popular films, songs and *pantomimes are based on some of these stories, such as **Aladdin* and **Sindbad*.

'Araldite™ /'ærəldaɪt/ *n* [U] a make of very strong glue: *She mended the vase with Araldite.*

the **'Aran ˌIslands** /'ærən/ *n* [pl] a group of three islands off the west coast of Ireland.

ˌAran 'jumper /ˌærən/ (*also* **Aran sweater**) *n* a sweater (= a piece of clothing for the upper body) made of thick wool knitted in the traditional raised patterns of the *Aran Islands.

an Aran jumper

A'rapaho /ə'ræpəhəʊ; *AmE* ə'ræpəhoʊ/ *n* (*pl* **Arapahos** *or* **Arapaho**) a member of a Native-American group. They lived on the *Great Plains, where they hunted buffalo. Today most Arapahos live on reservations (= areas of land given and protected by the US government) in Oklahoma and Wyoming, and earn money by renting their land for the discovery of oil and gas.

ˈ**Arbor Day** /ˈɑːbə; *AmE* ˈɑːrbər/ a special day in America when people plant trees. Each state chooses its own day, usually in the spring, but some southern states have it in the winter.

ˌFatty' ˈ**Arbuckle** /ˈɑːbʌkl; *AmE* ˈɑːrbʌkl/ (1887–1933) a US comic actor in silent films. He was one of the *Keystone Kops before becoming a star of popular films. In 1921 he was suspected of causing the death of an actress during a party. Although a court of law found him not guilty, his career was ruined.

archˈbishop *n* (in some Christian Churches) a *bishop of the highest rank, responsible for a large church district. In the *Church of England there are two archbishops, the *Archbishop of Canterbury and the *Archbishop of York, who both have a place in the *House of Lords. The *Archbishop of Westminster is the *Roman Catholic bishop of the highest rank in Britain. The title 'Your Grace' is used when talking to an archbishop and 'His Grace' when referring to one.

the **Archˌbishop of ˈCanterbury** /ˈkæntəbəri; *AmE* ˈkæntərberi/ the spiritual head of the *Church of England, who is also the *bishop of *Canterbury. His official title is 'Primate of All England'.

the **Archˌbishop of ˈWestminster** /ˈwestmɪnstə(r)/ the head of the *Roman Catholic Church in Britain.

the **Archˌbishop of ˈYork** /ˈjɔːk; *AmE* ˈjɔːrk/ the second most senior religious leader of the *Church of England, who is also the *bishop of *York. His official title is 'Primate of England'.

ˌJeffrey ˈ**Archer** /ˈɑːtʃə(r); *AmE* ˈɑːrtʃər/ (1940–) a former British *Conservative *Member of Parliament and a writer of popular novels. In 1985 he became Deputy Chairman of the Conservative Party, an important political position, but he had to leave the job in 1986 after the **News of the World* reported that he had sent £2 000 to a prostitute. He continues to be a successful politician and writer, and in 1992 he was made a *life peer.

*The ˈ**Archers*** /ˈɑːtʃəz; *AmE* ˈɑːrtʃərz/ a popular British radio programme presenting a continuing story about the lives of ordinary people. The Archers are a family in the imaginary village of *Ambridge, a small farming community somewhere in the middle of England. The programme has been broadcast five days a week by the *BBC since 1951, longer than any other programme of its kind in the world. Many famous people admit that they listen to it regularly: *Don't ring her up when she's listening to the Archers.*

the ˌForest of ˈ**Arden** /ˈɑːdn; *AmE* ˈɑːrdn/ a large forest that once existed in *Warwickshire, England. Shakespeare's play **As You Like It* is set in it.

ˈ**area code** (in the US) the first three numbers of a telephone number, usually shown in brackets. They identify the area of the country. Some states have one code but larger states and cities have several.

ARELS /ˈærəlz/ a British organization of independent English language schools. Most British language schools that have been approved of officially by the *British Council are members of ARELS.

ˌHannah ˈ**Arendt** /ˈærənt; *also* ˈeərənt/ (1906–75) a US political writer, philosopher and teacher. She was born in Germany and, being Jewish, escaped from the Nazis by going in 1933 to Paris and in 1941 to the US. Her major books included *The Human Condition* (1958) and *The Life of the Mind* (1977).

ˈ**Argos**™ /ˈɑːgɒs; *AmE* ˈɑːrgɑːs/ any of a chain of large shops in Britain selling electrical and other goods, usually at low prices. Only a small number of the goods on sale are displayed. People order in the shop from a catalogue containing illustrations of every item available.

the **Arˈgyll Group** /ɑːˈgaɪl; *AmE* ɑːrˈgaɪl/ a large British company that owns the Safeway chain of supermarket and other food businesses in Britain. The Argyll Group was the company competing with *Guinness in the *Guinness Affair.

ˈ**Ariel**™ /ˈeəriəl; *AmE* ˈeriəl/ *n* [U] a make of washing powder that is popular in Britain.

the **aristocracy**

British society still has quite a strong *class system which is based on birth and social position. The upper class consists mainly of members of the aristocracy. The most senior are the ***royal family** and members of the ***peerage**. Next below them are ***baronets**. Baronets have hereditary titles (= ranks passed on in the family from one generation to the next) but, unlike peers, are not allowed to sit in the *House of Lords. Below this there are various **orders of knighthood**.

***Knights** are appointed by the king or queen. In *medieval times soldiers were made knights in recognition of military service for their local lord. Today, knighthoods and other *honours are announced at *New Year or on the king's or queen's birthday and are given in recognition of distinguished public service or achievement. New knights receive their title at a special ceremony, during which they kneel before the king or queen, who taps them once on each shoulder with a sword. Knights may put **Sir** (for men) or **Dame** (for women) before their first name, and are allowed to have their own **coat of arms** (= a family symbol, usually a design on a shield).

The oldest order of knighthood in England, which is also the oldest **order of chivalry** in Europe, is the ***Order of the Garter**. There are 25 Knights of the Garter, in addition to the king or queen and the *Prince of Wales. Other senior orders of knighthood include the *Order of the Thistle, the *Order of the Bath, the *Order of the British Empire and the Royal Victorian Order. Letters after a person's name indicate which order he or she belongs to. Other knights are known as **knights bachelor**.

People who have an upper-class family background may be considered as part of the local aristocracy even if they do not have a title. They often have an upper-class *accent and *Conservative social and political views and are referred to as **the county set**. Members of the aristocracy are sometimes described as 'blue-blooded', because in former times their veins showed blue through their skin which was pale from not having to work in the fields. They are also referred to informally as 'the upper crust', or more rudely as 'toffs'. Formerly, members of the aristocracy could command respect because of their noble birth. Nowadays, people are much more critical of those who inherit honours but who from their behaviour do not appear to deserve them.

The US has no formal aristocracy in that there are no families who have been given titles by the head of state. In fact, the *Constitution forbids an aristocracy, saying 'No title of nobility shall be granted by the United States'. Perhaps because of this, Americans are very interested in Britain's royal family and nobility. There is, however, respect for US families who, though they do not have titles, have wealth and a social position similar to the British aristocracy. Class in the US is, to a large extent, based on

money, but some people have more respect for **old money** (= money, land, etc. that has belonged to a family for many years) than **new money** (= money that a person has earned by working). The ***Boston Brahmins** are the old, traditional families of *Boston and they, together with groups of old families from other parts of the US, make up a type of American aristocracy.

ˌAriˈzona /ˌærɪˈzəʊnə; *AmE* ˌærɪˈzoʊnə/ a state in the south-western US. The capital city is *Phoenix[1](1). Arizona's natural features include the *Grand Canyon, the *Painted Desert and the *Petrified Forest. It was the home of the Apaches in the 19th century, and today Native Americans have 19 reservations (= areas of land given and protected by the US government) in the state.

ˈArkansas /ˈɑːkənsɔː; *AmE* ˈɑːrkənsɔː/ a state in the central southern US. Its popular name is the Land of Opportunity. Its natural features include Hot Springs National Park and the only diamond mine in America. Bill *Clinton was governor of Arkansas before becoming US President. See also ARKY, LITTLE ROCK.

the ***ˌArk ˈRoyal*** a British aircraft carrier (= a large ship with an area where aircraft can take off and land). There is a tradition in the *Royal Navy of naming important ships *Ark Royal*. The first one was the leading British ship that fought the Spanish *Armada. Another famous *Ark Royal* was sunk in *World War II.

ˌRichard **ˈArkwright** /ˈɑːkraɪt; *AmE* ˈɑːrkraɪt/ (1732–92) an English businessman who invented a machine using water power for spinning cotton, which had been spun by hand until then. He built his own factory, and became one of the early leaders of the *Industrial Revolution. He was made a *knight in 1786.

ˈArky /ˈɑːki; *AmE* ˈɑːrki/ *n* (*infml*) a person from *Arkansas.

ˈArlington ˈNational ˈCemetery /ˈɑːlɪŋtən; *AmE* ˈɑːrlɪŋtən/ the most famous national cemetery in the US. It contains the *Tomb of the Unknown Soldier and the grave of President John F *Kennedy. More than 160 000 Americans who were killed in wars, as well as politicians and other well-known people, are also buried there. It is in Arlington, Virginia, outside Washington, DC, and was begun in 1864. In 1997 a Women in Military Service for America Memorial was put up at the entrance to the cemetery.

ˌJohn **ˈArlott** /ˈɑːlət; *AmE* ˈɑːrlət/ (1914–91) a popular English *cricket commentator who described cricket matches on *BBC radio and television regularly from 1947 to 1980. Many people in Britain associated the sound of his voice with cricket, or with the summer in general.

the **Arˈmada** /ɑːˈmɑːdə; *AmE* ɑːrˈmɑːdə/ (*also* **the Spanish Armada**) *n* the group of 129 ships sent by Spain in 1588 to attack England. A group of British ships, led by Lord Howard of Effingham's **Ark Royal* and Francis *Drake's **Revenge*, defeated the Armada in the *English Channel. It was the first sea battle in history involving large numbers of ships, and was seen by the English as a great victory. The word *armada* is now often used to mean any large group of ships: *A small armada of fishing boats blocked the port in protest against the new regulations.*

The armed forces in Britain ⇨ article.

The armed forces in the US ⇨ article.

Arˈmagh /ɑːˈmɑː; *AmE* ɑːrˈmɑː/ **1** one of the former *Six Counties of Ulster, in the southern part of *Northern Ireland. **2** a town in the south of *Northern Ireland. It is the religious centre of Northern Ireland and the Republic of Ireland, and has both a Roman Catholic and a Protestant *archbishop.

ˈArmistice Day 11 November, the anniversary of the end of *World War I, also called *Poppy Day. People used to stop what they were doing at 11 a.m. on Armistice Day and stand in silence for two minutes to remember the dead. After *World War II it was replaced by *Remembrance Sunday in Britain and *Veterans' Day in America.

ˌLouis **ˈArmstrong[1]** /ˈɑːmstrɒŋ; *AmE* ˈɑːrmstrɔːŋ/ (1900–71) a famous US *jazz musician and leader of a band. His popular name was 'Satchmo', a short form of 'Satchelmouth', because of his large mouth. He played the trumpet and sang with a rough voice. He appeared in more than 50 films and performed around the world as a special representative of the US *State Department. Many people think he was the greatest of all jazz musicians.

ˌNeil **ˈArmstrong[2]** /ˈɑːmstrɒŋ; *AmE* ˈɑːrmstrɔːŋ/ (1930–) the US astronaut who was the first man to walk on the moon, on 20 July 1969. As he stepped onto the surface of the moon, he said, 'That's one small step for man, one giant leap for mankind.' He later taught at Cincinnati University in the 1970s. See also ALDRIN, APOLLO PROJECT.

army ⇨ articles at ARMED FORCES.

ˈArnhem /ˈɑːnəm; *AmE* ˈɑːrnəm/ a town in the Netherlands, on the River Rhine. A famous *World War II battle took place there in 1944, when Allied forces tried, and failed, to capture a bridge over the Rhine. Thousands of people were killed. The battle was the subject of the film *A Bridge Too Far*. See also ALLIES.

ˌBenedict **ˈArnold[1]** /ˌbenədɪkt ˈɑːnəld; *AmE* ˈɑːrnəld/ (1741–1801) an American general who betrayed his country in the *American Revolution. Although at first he fought bravely and won battles for the Americans, he tried in 1780 to give the fort at *West Point, which he commanded, to the British. He failed and escaped to London. His name is still used by Americans to mean somebody who betrays their country.

ˌMalcolm **ˈArnold[2]** /ˈɑːnəld; *AmE* ˈɑːrnəld/ (1921–) a British composer who has written several symphonies, as well as music for ballets and films. He was made a *knight in 1993.

ˌMatthew **ˈArnold[3]** /ˈɑːnəld; *AmE* ˈɑːrnəld/ (1822–88) a English poet and critic, son of Thomas *Arnold. He wrote several collections of poetry, and important essays about education and social and political life in Britain. His best-known poems are *Dover Beach* and *The Scholar-Gypsy*.

ˌThomas **ˈArnold[4]** /ˈɑːnəld; *AmE* ˈɑːrnəld/ (1795–1842) headmaster of *Rugby School (1828–42). He introduced many changes that influenced the development of *public school(1) education in Britain. See also *TOM BROWN'S SCHOOLDAYS*.

ˈArsenal a *football club in North London. The name *Arsenal* and the *nickname of the club, 'the Gunners', come from the club's origin in the 1880s, when the players worked at the Royal Arsenal, the place where army weapons were stored. The club has been quite successful in English and European competitions since the 1930s.

ˈArsenic and Old ˈLace a humorous US play (1941) by Joseph Kasselring. The story is about two old women who murder their visitors. It had 1 444 performances on Broadway and a film version was made in 1944. It is still regularly performed by amateur actors, especially in Britain.

ˌart ˈdeco /ˈdekəʊ; *AmE* ˈdekoʊ/ (*also* **deco**) *n* [U] a style of art, design and architecture, popular in the 1920s and 1930s, using simple shapes, bright colours, and modern materials such as chrome and plastic. Many of New York's famous buildings are influenced by art deco: *I bought some art deco lamps in a local antique shop.*

an art deco lamp

the ˌ**Artful** ˈ**Dodger** /ˈdɒdʒə(r); *AmE* ˈdɑːdʒər/ a character in **Oliver Twist* by Charles *Dickens. He is a young thief who steals from people's pockets, and is one of the group of thieves that Oliver joins.

art galleries and art museums

In Britain, works of art are displayed in art galleries and, especially outside London, in *museums. Shops that sell paintings are also called galleries. In the US public **art collections** are displayed in **art museums**, and a **gallery** is a place where people go to buy works of art.

Many galleries and museums in Britain and the US receive limited financial support from national or local government. Other money is raised through admission fees and the sale of postcards, calendars, etc. Some galleries obtain money through sponsorship. Works of art are often expensive and galleries can rarely buy them without organizing a public appeal or, in Britain, asking for money from the *National Art Collections Fund.

Visiting an art gallery is a popular leisure activity for a large number of British people. Galleries and museums are friendlier places than they used to be. Many try to encourage children's interest in art by arranging school visits. Most Americans make their first trip to an art museum with their school class, but when they are older, they usually only visit museums when they travel on vacation.

The most popular galleries in Britain, all in London, are the *National Gallery, which receives over 4 million visitors a year, the *National Portrait Gallery, and the *Tate Gallery, which specializes in the work of British artists. The Royal Academy's Summer Exhibition of paintings sent in by the general public also receives a lot of visitors. Sculpture attracts less attention, and though the names of Henry *Moore and Barbara *Hepworth are known to many people, few could describe any of their works. Well-known galleries outside London include the *National Gallery of Scotland in Edinburgh and the Birmingham Museum and Art Gallery.

Important art museums in the US include the *Metropolitan Museum of Art, the Museum of Modern Art and the *Guggenheim Museum, all in New York, and the *Smithsonian Institution in Washington, DC. Most US cities and many smaller towns have art museums.

Galleries sometimes **mount exhibitions** of the paintings of one artist, e.g. *Turner, that are brought together from all over the world. People are prepared to queue for a long time to see them. Many people admire **old masters**, famous works by great artists, but have little interest in modern art. New works receive publicity in the media only when they are unusual or likely to shock people. Galleries and museums try to encourage a more positive attitude to modern art but many people remain doubtful.

ˈ**art house** *n* (*pl* **houses**) (*AmE*) a small, usually independent cinema showing films which are made more for artistic reasons than for commercial profit: *It makes a change to go to an art-house movie instead of another Hollywood blockbuster.*

ˌKing ˈ**Arthur** (5th or 6th century) a king of England who led the Britons in battles against the *Saxons. There are many stories about King Arthur, e.g. that he pulled his sword *Excalibur from a stone, and that he sat with his *knights at a *Round Table(1). Nobody knows if the stories are true, but they are very popular and have been used in poems, plays and films. ⇨ article at ARTHURIAN LEGEND.

Arthurian Legend ⇨ article.

the ˈ**Articles of Con**ˌ**fede**ˈ**ration** the first written American laws of government. The *thirteen colonies agreed to the articles in 1781 and used them until the US Constitution replaced them in 1789.

ˌ**Art Nou**ˈ**veau** /ˌɑː nuːˈvəʊ; *AmE* ˌɑːr nuːˈvoʊ/ *n* [U] a style of art, design and architecture, popular at the end of the 19th century. It uses long curving lines influenced by the shapes of leaves and flowers. The most famous British artists and designers working in this style were Aubrey *Beardsley and Charles Rennie *Mackintosh.

the ˌ**Arts and** ˈ**Crafts** ˌ**Movement** a social and artistic movement in Britain in the second half of the 19th century, led by William *Morris and John *Ruskin. During the *Industrial Revolution, when more and more things were made by machines, the aim of the Arts and Crafts Movement was to make objects by hand that were beautiful as well as useful.

ˈ**Arts** ˌ**Council** *n* any of four organizations in Britain (one each for England, Scotland, Wales and Northern Ireland) that give government money to artistic projects with the aim of encouraging the arts and making them more popular. For example, if a theatre company receives money from the Arts Council, it may help the company to reduce the price of tickets.

the **ASA** /ˌeɪ es ˈeɪ/ ⇨ ADVERTISING STANDARDS AUTHORITY.

ASCAP /ˈæskæp/ ⇨ AMERICAN SOCIETY OF COMPOSERS, AUTHORS AND PUBLISHERS.

Asˈ**cension Day** (*also* **Holy Thursday**) the 40th day after Easter, a Christian holy day celebrating **Ascension** (= Christ's rising to heaven).

ˈ**Ascot** /ˈæskət/ a course for horse races near *Windsor(1) in *Berkshire, England. See also ROYAL ASCOT.

ˈ**Asda**™ /ˈæzdə/ any of a chain of large supermarkets in Britain, selling food, clothes and household goods at low prices.

ASH /æʃ/ (*in full* **Action on Smoking and Health**) a 7ple stop smoking, mainly through advertisements showing the dangers of smoking.

ˌPeggy ˈ**Ashcroft** /ˈæʃkrɒft; *AmE* ˈæʃkrɑːft/ (1907–91) an English actor who had a long and impressive career, playing many different parts. In the 1960s and 1970s she worked with the *English Stage Company and the *Royal Shakespeare Company, and in the 1980s she became a popular film and television actor, appearing in the **Jewel in the Crown* and *A *Passage to India*. She was made a *dame(2) in 1956.

Peggy Ashcroft in A Passage to India

The armed forces in Britain

The British armed forces, sometimes called **the services**, consist of the **Army**, the **Royal Navy** and the **Royal Air Force** (**RAF**) The Queen is **Commander-in-Chief** of all three services, but responsibility for their management lies with the ***Ministry of Defence** (**MOD**), which is headed by the **Secretary of State for Defence**.

British armed forces fight alongside other *NATO forces when necessary and are used in *United Nations' peacekeeping activities. The size of the armed forces today is very small, only about 210 000 people. *National service, also called **conscription**, was ended in 1957 and the services now attract **recruits** through advertisements.

Changes in the structure of the services have meant increased opportunities for women. Since 1992 women have been allowed to take on roles previously restricted to men, and they now have more opportunity to reach the higher **ranks**. The services have always been seen as part of the British *Establishment, and most **officers** used to be men from the *upper classes. They entered the army with a **commission** and held an officer's rank from the beginning. Now, more people have the opportunity to **rise through the ranks** (= become officers after serving as ordinary soldiers).

The issue is of homosexuality in the services is sometimes discussed in the press. There is still a ban on homosexuals serving in the armed forces, despite several campaigns to lift it, and practising homosexuals, if discovered, may be **discharged**.

The Army

The Army is the largest of the three services, with around 108 000 personnel. This is compared with 4 million in *World War I and 3 million in *World War II. The ***Territorial Army**, formed from members of the public who do military training in their spare time, provides additional troops in an emergency. Army officers train at the Royal Military Academy, usually known as ***Sandhurst**. Although small, the army is one of the most highly trained in the world.

The Army is based on a system of **divisions** which include the *Guards Division, the *Parachute Regiment, and the Special Air Service Regiment (*SAS). These are supported by specialist **corps** concerned with, for example, artillery (= large guns) or intelligence (= military information). Each division consists of several **regiments**, some of which can trace their history back many years. Old regimental **colours** (= flags) are commonly preserved in churches and museums. Among the most famous regiments are the *Coldstream Guards, the *Black Watch and the Duke of Wellington's Regiment. Cuts in finance have resulted in a lot of reorganization, with several regiments being combined.

British army units are **stationed** (= have a base) in several countries throughout the world, including *Belize, *Brunei, *Cyprus, Germany and *Gibraltar.

The Royal Navy

The Royal Navy is the oldest of the three services and is often described as **the senior service**. It dates back to the time of *Alfred the Great and has a long history of famous victories, especially the defeat of the Spanish *Armada in 1588.

The Navy has only around 45 000 personnel, but is supported by the **Royal Naval Reserve**. Women formerly belonged to the **Women's Royal Naval Service** (*WRNS) and were known as **Wrens**. They were limited to **shore duties**. In 1993 the WRNS was disbanded (= closed down) and now women serve with men in the Royal Navy.

The most important branch of the Navy is the **Fleet**, which includes nuclear submarines (= ships that go under water) carrying *Trident missiles. Other branches include the **Royal Fleet Auxiliary**, which provides support for fighting ships, and the ***Fleet Air Arm**, which is responsible for the planes used on aircraft carriers like **Ark Royal*. The ***Royal Marines** are also part of the Navy. They are trained to fight on land as well as to serve at sea, and include the highly skilled *Commando Brigade.

The Royal Navy was formerly run by the ***Admiralty** but is now managed by the Ministry of Defence. Famous naval towns include *Dartmouth, where the *Britannia Royal Naval College is situated, *Chatham and *Portsmouth.

The Royal Air Force

The Royal Air Force is the most recently established of the services. Its greatest moment came when defending Britain in 1940 during the *Battle of Britain. It has around 56 000 personnel divided into three **commands**: **Strike Command**, which undertakes attack and defence tasks, **Logistics Command**, which provides support and maintenance, and **Personnel and Training Command**. Since 1994, when the **Women's Royal Air Force** (*WRAF) was disbanded, women have joined the RAF and taken on many new roles, including flying aircraft. Additional personnel are trained by the **Royal Auxiliary Air Force** and the **Royal Air Force Volunteer Reserve**. RAF officers train at *Cranwell.

RAF **stations** abroad include those in Cyprus and the *Falkland Islands. The skies over less densely populated parts of Britain are used for training purposes, and people living in these areas have become used to hearing the roar of low-flying aircraft. Other members of the public are more familiar with the sight of the *Red Arrows, the red jets of the RAF's aerobatic display team.

Public attitudes to the services

Many older people served **in the forces** during World War II and, especially formerly, retired soldiers were treated with respect. Relatively few young people have much contact with the services, though some join an **Officers' Training Corps** at school or university. Press reports of **squaddies** (= young soldiers) getting drunk and fighting give a bad impression of the services.

The armed forces are generally well supported by the public when **on active service**, as in the *Falklands War or during the *Gulf War, but the **deployment** (= use) of soldiers in *Northern Ireland caused a lot of disagreement.

Members of the public are most likely to see the armed forces at ceremonies such as *Trooping the Colour and on *Remembrance Sunday. Military **tattoos** (= displays of marching), like that at *Edinburgh, and displays of acrobatics are popular entertainment.

The armed forces in the US

In 1997 the US armed forces had a total of nearly 1.5 million men and women **on active service.** This compares with a force of more than 12 million during *World War II and over 3 million during the *Vietnam War. In 1973 *national service, known as the ***draft**, was ended and by 1989, at the end of the *Cold War, US military **bases** in other countries were closed. The US has about 25 000 **veterans** (= former soldiers) still alive.

The **commander-in-chief** of the armed forces is the President. Below him is the **Secretary of Defense**, then a civilian **Secretary** for each service, and then the ***Joint Chiefs of Staff**, the military leaders of the four major **services**, the **Army**, **Navy**, **Air Force** and **Marine Corps**. The fifth service, the **US Coast Guard** is part of the Navy during wartime but is otherwise part of the US Department of Transportation.

The US armed forces have tried to set a good example in the ethnic balance of their personnel. *African Americans generally receive equal treatment with others and may advance to higher **ranks**. The first black Chairman of the Joint Chiefs of Staff, the nation's highest military job, was Colin *Powell, who served during the *Gulf War. Women comprise about 13% of the armed forces, and more than 80% of all military jobs are open to them. Homosexuals are allowed to join the services, but President *Clinton advised them not to reveal that they were homosexual, and he also told the military authorities that they should not ask.

Americans have traditionally given their armed forces great support and were proud to say the US had never lost a war. This changed in the 1960s when many young people protested against the Vietnam War and some even exploded bombs at ***ROTC** (Reserve Officers' Training Corps) buildings in colleges. Veterans of the Vietnam War were often publicly ignored or criticized. But after Vietnam and the end of the draft the military services became popular again.

Members of the US armed forces, together with those of other countries, take part in *NATO and *United Nations military activities.

The US Army

Most of America's military history is that of the US Army and its leaders. They have included famous men like George *Washington in the *American Revolution, Andrew *Jackson in the *War of 1812, George *Custer in the *Indian wars, Ulysses S *Grant during the *Civil War, John *Pershing in *World War I, and Dwight *Eisenhower, Douglas *MacArthur and George *Patton in World War II. America's pride in its military leaders shows in the fact that Washington, Jackson, Grant and Eisenhower all became US presidents.

The Army has nearly half a million men and women and is supported by the **US Army Reserve** and the **Army National Guard**. Both organizations fought in the Gulf War.

Like the other services, the Army is led by a civilian, the **Secretary of the Army**. The **Army Chief of Staff** is the service's highest military officer. Many Army officers attend the *United States Military Academy at West Point, New York. The Army is organized into field armies, army corps, divisions, brigades, battalions, companies, platoons and (smallest of all) squads. Special forces have included the *Green Berets, who fought in Vietnam.

The US Navy

The US Navy played a small part in the American Revolution, and John Paul *Jones became the country's first Navy hero. During the Civil War, the Navy closed southern ports and Admiral David Farragut gave his famous order: '*Damn the torpedoes! Full speed ahead!' In World War II, after *Pearl Harbor, the US Navy became a major sea power.

The US Navy consists of about 400 000 men and women, with an additional 200 000 in the **Navy Reserve**. The head of the Navy is the **Secretary of the Navy**, who is senior to the **Chief of Naval Operations**. The service has 350 ships and, perhaps surprisingly, nearly 5 000 aircraft. To many people the most impressive ships are the nuclear aircraft carriers, the *USS Nimitz*, *USS Enterprise* and *USS Constellation*, which are the largest ships in the world. Nuclear submarines (= ships that go under water) are equipped with *Trident missiles.

Ships and sailors are divided between different **fleets**. For example, the US Sixth Fleet is based in the Mediterranean. Special forces include the Seals and the Seabees. Officers are trained at the *United States Naval Academy at *Annapolis, *Maryland.

The US Air Force

The US Air Force, America's youngest service, has nearly 400 000 staff. The US Air Force National Guard consists of 88 **flying units** based at more than 170 centres throughout the country. Its officers are educated at the Air Force Academy in Colorado Springs, *Colorado. The service is organized into numbered Air Forces that are each divided into **wings**, **squadrons** and **flights**. The Air Force has a reputation among the services of providing its members with the best homes, clubs, food and other comforts.

Until 1947, the Air Force was the **Army Air Corps**, part of the US Army. During World War II, its planes supported British aircraft. The service was responsible for dropping the first atomic bomb, which was dropped by the plane **Enola Gay* on *Hiroshima. The service was also active in the Vietnam and Gulf Wars.

The US Marine Corps

The US Marines Corps is a separate military service though it is managed by the Department of the Navy. It is led by the **Commandant of the Marine Corps**. The service has over 150 000 men and women. It was established in 1775 and has fought in all American wars. Marines take part in land, sea and air operations and are proud that their service is known as the most physically tough. The service is famous for its beach attacks during World War II to capture Wake Island, *Guam and *Guadalcanal from the Japanese. Marine Corps officers are educated at the United States Naval Academy. Other Marines take a difficult basic training programme at Quantico, *Virginia.

ˌPaddy ˈ**Ashdown** /ˈæʃdaʊn/ (1941–) a British politician, and leader of the *Liberal Democratic Party 1988–99. He is sometimes referred to in the press as 'Paddy Pantsdown' because in 1992 he admitted that he had once had a love affair with his secretary.

ˌArthur ˈ**Ashe** /æʃ/ (1943–93) a US *tennis player. He was the first African American to win the *US Open(2) (1968) and *Wimbledon (1975). He became captain of the US *Davis Cup team in 1983.

the **Ashes** an imaginary prize that goes to the winner of each series of international *cricket matches between England and Australia. The name comes from a humorous newspaper article written when Australia beat England at cricket in 1882, saying that English cricket had died, that it would be cremated (= burnt after death), and that its ashes would be taken to Australia: *With this victory Australia have retained the Ashes.*

The ˈ***Ash Grove*** a traditional Welsh song about a beautiful young woman who has died and is buried under a group of ash trees.

ˌLaura ˈ**Ashley** ⇨ LAURA ASHLEY.

the **Ashˌmolean Muˈseum** /æʃˌməʊliən; *AmE* æʃˌmoʊliən/ (*infml* the **Ashmolean**) a museum in *Oxford, England. It is the oldest public museum in Britain, and was opened by Elias Ashmole in 1683. It has important collections of paintings and archaeological objects such as ancient Greek sculptures and coins.

ˌFrederick ˈ**Ashton** /ˈæʃtən/ (1904–88) a British ballet dancer and choreographer. He was the first choreographer of the *Royal Ballet, and later its director (1963–70). His best-known ballets are *Façade, La Fille Mal Gardée* and *A Month in the Country*. He was made a *knight in 1962.

ˌ**Ash ˈWednesday** (in the Christian Church) the first day of *Lent. Traditionally, *Roman Catholics go to church on Ash Wednesday and their foreheads are marked with ashes as a sign that they are sorry for their sins (= offences against religious or moral laws). In the US this tradition is still widely followed. They ashes are not washed off but left to go away on their own. It is not polite to make a comment on such marks on a person's forehead.

ˌ**Asian Aˈmerican** *n* an American who was born in an Asian country or who is descended from Asians. Asian Americans live mostly on the west coast of the US, and include Chinese, Japanese and Vietnamese. ▶ **Asian-American** *adj.*

ˌ**Asian ˈDub Founˌdation** /ˈdʌb/ a British pop group, formed in 1994, who mix Asian music with *jungle, *dub and other styles. Their albums include *Facts and Fictions* (1995) and *Rafi's Revenge* (1998).

ˌ***Asian ˈTimes*** a British newspaper published every week, which contains articles on politics, culture, sport and other subjects of interest to people in Britain's Asian community. It first appeared in 1983.

ˌIsaac ˈ**Asimov** /ˈæzɪmɒf; *AmE* ˈæzɪmɑːf/ (1920–92) a US writer of science fiction who invented the word 'robotics'.His books include *Foundation* (1951) and the short story collection *I, Robot* (1950).

ASLEF /ˈæzlef/ (*in full* the **Associated Society of Locomotive Engineers and Firemen**) a British *trade union that represents railway workers. See also RMT.

ˌ**AˈS ˌlevel** /ˌeɪ ˈes/ (*in full* **Advanced Supplementary level**) *n* [U, C] (in England and Wales) a examination in a particular subject at a level between *GCSE and *A level, for students who want to study more subjects than they would at A level. An AS level is worth half as many points as an A level for university entry. Many students take a combination of the two.

ˈ**Aspen** /ˈæspən/ a town that is famous as a centre for skiing, in the US state of Colorado. It is in the *Rocky Mountains and is often visited by rich and well-known people. It also has a cultural festival in the summer.

ˈHerbert ˈHenry ˈ**Asquith** /ˈæskwɪθ/ (1852–1928) a British Liberal *prime minister (1908–16). His government introduced the first benefits of the *welfare state, such as *pensions for old people. He was also responsible for reducing the powers of the *House of Lords and for leading Britain into *World War I. He was made an *earl(1) in 1925.

Asˈsay ˌOffice *n* (in Britain) any of the offices where gold, silver and platinum are tested and given *hallmarks (= small marks showing the quality of the metal). There are four such offices in Britain: in London, *Birmingham, *Sheffield and *Edinburgh.

Asˌsemblies of ˈGod the largest Pentecostal Church in America. It began in 1914 and has more than a million members. They believe illness can be cured by faith. The main office of the church is in Springfield, Missouri. See also PENTECOSTALIST.

asˌsisted ˈarea *n* (in Britain) a part of the country in which there are many unemployed people, and the government tries to encourage business and industry to employ more people, e.g. by lending money to companies at low interest: *When the mines closed down the region was granted assisted area status.*

the **Asˌsisted ˈPlaces Scheme** a British government plan that helps clever pupils from poorer families to pay for their places at *independent schools. It was introduced in 1980.

Asˌsociated ˈPress (*abbr* **AP**) the oldest and largest US news service, with offices all over the world. Its members include newspapers and television and radio stations. They collect the news and AP sends it to all members. The service began in 1848 and is a non-profit company.

the **Asˌsociˈation of ˈBritish ˈTravel ˌAgents** ⇨ ABTA.

the **Asˌsociˈation of ˈRecognized ˈEnglish ˈLanguage Schools** ⇨ ARELS.

ˌFred **Aˈstaire** /əˈsteə(r); *AmE* əˈster/ (1899–1987) a US dancer, singer and actor. His many musical films included *Top Hat* (1935), *Easter Parade* (1948) and *Silk Stockings* (1957). He danced mostly with Ginger *Rogers but also with Audrey *Hepburn, Cyd Charisse and others.

ˌ**Aston ˈMartin**™ /ˌæstən ˈmɑːtɪn; *AmE* ˈmɑːrtn/ *n* an expensive and fashionable British make of sports car. It is the make driven by James *Bond in several films.

ˌ**Aston Uniˈversity** /ˌæstən/ a university in *Birmingham, England, formed in 1966.

ˌ**Aston ˈVilla** /ˌæstən ˈvɪlə/ a *football club in *Birmingham, England, having its ground at Villa Park in the Aston area of the city. The club was very successful at the end of the 19th century, and in the 1970s and 80s, winning the *European Cup in 1982.

ˌNancy ˈ**Astor** /ˈæstə(r)/ (1879–1964) a British politician, born in the US. In 1919 she became the first woman Member of Parliament in the *House of Commons.

Aˌstronomer ˈRoyal an honorary title given to an important British astronomer. Until 1972 it was the title of the director of the *Royal Greenwich Observatory.

ˈ**Astroturf**™ /ˈæstrəʊtɜːf; *AmE* ˈæstroʊtɜːrf/ *n* [U] a make of artificial grass used as a surface on which

A

Arthurian legend

The legends of **King *Arthur** and the ***Knights of the Round Table** are familiar to many British people. They are the subject of several poems and stories of the *Middle Ages (11th–15th centuries), as well as of later novels, musical plays and films, and are a central part of British tradition and folklore. The most important **Arthurian** works include Sir Thomas *Malory's *Le *Morte D'Arthur*, a set of long prose romances (= stories of love and adventure) written in the 15th century, Alfred Lord *Tennyson's **Idylls of the King*, a series of 12 poems dating from the 19th century, and T H *White's novel *The Once and Future King* (1958). The legends continue to be retold in new ways, for instance in the musical *Camelot* and the *Disney film of T H White's *The *Sword in the Stone*.

Historical origins

The real King Arthur lived in the late 5th and early 6th century. He was a *Celtic warrior chief who fought against the *Anglo-Saxons and probably defeated them at the Battle of Badon. He is said to have died in the battle of Camlan. Stories about him were collected in the 12th century by the historian *Geoffrey of Monmouth. They were added to and developed by French writers such as Chrétien de Troyes, who wrote during the period 1170–90, and also became the centre of a group of legends in German. As a result, other characters such as ***Lancelot**, **Tristram** (Tristan) and **Perceval** (Parzival) became associated with Arthur and were included by Malory in *Le Morte D'Arthur*, the version of the legends which became most widely known in Britain. Arthur is the central character in the stories of his early life and the battle that led to his death, but much of the rest of the work describes the adventures of his knights.

The stories of Arthur and his knights celebrate the **age of chivalry**, when knights aimed to live according to the highest Christian principles. Their character and courage are constantly tested by meetings with giants, dragons and sorcerers, and by their own human weaknesses, such as pride or forbidden love. The love affairs of Tristram and Isoud (Iseult) and Lancelot and Guinevere are part of the tradition of **courtly love** which was a central theme in European poetry of the Middle Ages. The passionate love of a nobleman for his lady was worthy and uplifting but unfulfilled because one of the lovers was married or committed to somebody else, and the love often ended tragically.

King Arthur and his knights

According to most versions of the legends, Arthur was born at ***Tintagel** in *Cornwall, the son of Uther Pendragon, King of all England. One version says that at a young age he was put under a spell by the magician *Merlin so that he grew up not knowing he was heir to the English throne. He became King at the age of 15 after he pulled the magic sword ***Excalibur** out of a stone when all the knights of the kingdom had failed to do so. Another version of the legend says that he received the sword from the ***Lady of the Lake**, and this fits in with the story that, as he was dying, he ordered the sword to be thrown back into the lake and it was caught by a hand that rose from the water. After becoming King, Arthur gathered round him the most worthy knights in the land, including Sir Lancelot, Lancelot's son **Sir *Galahad**, **Sir Bedivere** and **Sir *Gawain**, and established his court at ***Camelot**. On Arthur's orders the knights all sat at the *Round Table, so nobody could sit at the head of the table and claim to be more important than the rest. They promised to defend the principles of chivalry and romantic love, and many of the stories are about their adventures.

Arthur won many victories in battle and married the beautiful ***Guinevere**. Later, Arthur's half-sister, the sorceress **Morgan le Fay**, attempted to kill him, and Arthur's discovery of a love affair between his wife and Sir Lancelot further threatened his court. The knights went off in search of the ***Holy Grail**, the wine cup used to catch Christ's blood at the Crucifixion and a symbol of perfection. Lancelot saw but failed to obtain it because he was not sufficiently pure, and it was eventually found by Sir Galahad. Arthur went to fight against Rome with Sir Gawain but while he was abroad, his nephew ***Mordred** seized the kingdom and made Guinevere his prisoner. Arthur returned to England to defeat and kill Mordred at the Battle of Camlan, but was himself seriously wounded. He told Sir Bedivere to throw Excalibur into an enchanted lake where it was caught by the hand of the Lady of the Lake. Morgan le Fay, or in some versions three women, then appeared in a boat to take Arthur to *Avalon, the Celtic paradise. According to some versions Arthur and his knights now lie asleep underground, waiting for the day they are needed to wake and save England from danger.

In search of Arthur

Many people now visit Tintagel Castle high above the sea, the place where Arthur was born and later the home of Mark, the husband of Iseult, Tristram's lover. Several attempts have been made to identify where Arthur's Camelot was. The most popular suggestions include Caerleon in South Wales, Camelford and South Cadbury, both in Somerset, and *Winchester. The town of *Glastonbury is said to be Avalon because in the 12th century some monks there claimed to have found the graves of Arthur and Guinevere. It has been suggested that the bones were 'found' in the time of *Henry II in order to end the tradition that Arthur would one day return to claim the kingdom. For centuries it was believed that a huge round table in Winchester Cathedral was Arthur's Round Table, but recent scientific tests have proved that it was made in the 14th century.

sports are played: *We can play football all year round now they've installed an Astroturf pitch.*

ˌAs You ˈLike It a comedy play (1599) by William Shakespeare about the family and friends of a *duke who are forced to live in the Forest of *Arden when the duke's brother, Frederick, takes his land. Rosalind, the duke's daughter, disguises herself as a boy to be with the man she loves, Orlando. Her friend, Frederick's daughter, falls in love with Orlando's brother. They reveal who they really are, and the two couples get married. As well as the love story between the central characters, much of the

A

comedy in the play comes from minor characters, including Touchstone and Jaques.

AT&T /ˌeɪ tiː ənd ˈtiː/ (*in full* **American Telephone and Telegraph**) the largest telephone and communications company in the US, providing many international services. It began in 1885 by running a telephone line from New York to *Philadelphia. In 1998 AT&T joined with *BT to form a new international communications company.

the ˌ**Atheˈnaeum** /ˌæθɪˈniːəm/ a London men's club formed in 1824 for people in the fields of literature, art and science. It is named after an Ancient Greek temple where people met to discuss academic matters. ⇨ note at GENTLEMEN'S CLUBS.

ˌChet ˈ**Atkins**[1] /ˌtʃet ˈætkɪnz/ (1924–) a US guitar player who helped to create the 'Nashville Sound'. In 1973, he was chosen for the Country Music *Hall of Fame. The Country Music Association has named him 'Musician of the Year' nine times. See also NASHVILLE.

ˌTommy ˈ**Atkins**[2] /ˈætkɪnz/ the name used by people to refer to the average British soldier in the 19th and early 20th centuries: *While the officers had comfortable beds Tommy Atkins slept in the trenches.*

ˌRowan ˈ**Atkinson** /ˌrəʊən ˈætkɪnsən; *AmE* ˌroʊən/ (1955–) an English comedy actor, well known for his ability to show amusing expressions on his face. He has acted in many popular films and television programmes, including **Blackadder* and **Mr Bean.*

Atˈlanta /ətˈlæntə/ the capital city of the US state of *Georgia. It is a major commercial centre for the south-eastern US. Martin Luther *King led the *civil rights movement from Atlanta. The 1996 Olympic Games were also held there.

the **Atˌlantic ˈCharter** /ətˌlæntɪk/ an agreement signed by Winston *Churchill, the British Prime Minister, and Franklin D *Roosevelt, the US President, in 1941 about the rights of nations and international relations. Its main purpose was to condemn the actions of Germany. In 1942 statements of the Atlantic Charter became part of the Declaration of the United Nations. See also WORLD WAR II.

Atˌlantic ˈCity /ətˌlæntɪk/ a city on the coast in the American state of *New Jersey. It is popular with tourists and contains many casinos (= gambling clubs) where people can gamble legally. The 'Miss America' competition is held there each year. The city has a famous Boardwalk (= a wide path made of wood) along the edge of the sea.

The ***Atˌlantic ˈMonthly*** /ətˌlæntɪk ˈmʌnθli/ a US magazine known for its intelligent writing on culture and modern life. It is published in *Boston, where it began in 1857 as a 'journal of literature, politics, science, and the arts'. It became famous for its reports on the American *Civil War. Ernest *Hemingway sold his first short story to the magazine in 1927.

ˌCharles ˈ**Atlas** /ˈætləs/ (1894–1974) an American who had great success selling courses on how to develop muscles and a stronger body, using a method which he called 'dynamic tension'. The advertisements for his courses showed a thin man ('a seven-stone weakling') on the beach having sand kicked in his face by a strong man who was popular with the girls. Atlas's name is sometimes used to refer to somebody who is very strong: *OK, Charles Atlas, let's see you lift this!*

ATM /ˌeɪ tiː ˈem/ (*in full* **automated teller machine**) *n* (*AmE*) a machine, usually outside a bank, that allows a customer to receive money by using a plastic card. It can also provide other services, e.g. putting money into a bank account and moving it to another account.

the **Aˌtomic ˈEnergy Comˌmission** (*abbr* **AEC**) the US government department responsible for nuclear energy.

ˌDavid ˈ**Attenborough**[1] /ˈætənbrə/ (1926–) a British television presenter and programme maker who has made many programmes about nature, including the series **Life on Earth.* He is well known for getting very close to the animals he films, and describing them in a voice that is very quiet but very enthusiastic. He was made a *knight in 1985. Richard *Attenborough is his brother.

David Attenborough with penguins

ˌRichard ˈ**Attenborough**[2] /ˈætənbrə/ (1923–) a English film actor, producer and director. He has acted in many famous British films, including *Brighton Rock* (1947). His most successful film as director and producer was *Gandhi* (1982), which won eight *Oscars. He is well known for becoming very emotional in his work. He was made a *knight in 1976 and a *life peer in 1993.

atˈtendance ˌcentre (in Britain) a place where young people aged 17–21 are sent if they break the law but their crimes are not serious enough for them to be sent to a *young offender institution. They have to go to an attendance centre for a particular number of hours, usually in the evenings and at weekends: *He went to the youth court and got 24 hours at an attendance centre.*

ˌClement ˈ**Attlee** /ˈætli/ (1883–1967) a British *Labour politician who became Prime Minister (1945–51), defeating Winston *Churchill in the 1945 election. His government introduced the *National Health Service, nationalized important industries such as coal, gas, electricity and railways, and gave independence to India, Pakistan, Burma (now Myanmar) and Ceylon (now Sri Lanka).

Atˌtorney ˈGeneral 1 the most senior legal officer in England, Wales and Northern Ireland. The Attorney General is a *Member of Parliament belonging to the party in power who advises the government on legal matters and represents it in law courts. **2** the head of the US Department of Justice, who is chosen by the President to represent the government in legal matters. **3** the most senior legal officer in any state of the US.

ˌJohn ˈ**Aubrey** /ˈɔːbri/ (1626–97) an English writer and archaeologist. He studied *Stonehenge and *Avebury and suggested the idea, which many people still believe today, that Stonehenge was built by *Druids. He is now mainly remembered for his book **Brief Lives*.

ˌW H ˈ**Auden** /ˈɔːdn/ (Wystan Hugh Auden 1907–73) an English poet who wrote poems of many different types, often using traditional forms of verse but with modern language. He also wrote the words for operas and a famous publicity film for the *Post Office. In the 1930s, when he wrote some of his best poems, he was a leading member of a group of left-wing writers. Many of his most famous poems are in the collection *Another Time* (1940). In 1946 he became a US citizen and his later poetry became more religious. His work has had a strong influence on later 20th-century poetry.

ˈJohn ˈJames ˈ**Audubon** /ˈɔːdəbən/ (1785–1851) a US naturalist, born in Haiti. He painted every bird that was then known in North America and collected over 1 000 paintings in his book *Birds of America* (1827–38). See also AUDUBON SOCIETY.

passenger pigeons from Audubon's Birds of America

the ˈ**Audubon Soˌciety** /ˈɔːdəbən/ a non-profit US organization that works to protect birds and wild animals, and the places where they live and breed. The society began in 1905 and the main office is in New York City. It is named in memory of John James *Audubon.

the **Auˈgustan Age** /ɔːˈɡʌstən/ the period of English literature in the early 18th century, when writers such as *Swift and *Pope were active. The name comes from that of the Roman emperor Augustus, who ruled when Virgil, Horace and Ovid were writing, and suggests a classical period of elegant literature.

ˌ**August Bank ˈHoliday** (*also* **Summer Bank Holiday**) *n* [usu sing] (in England, Wales and Northern Ireland) a *bank holiday on the last Monday in August, when many people go to the coast, or to events such as the *Edinburgh Festival or the *Notting Hill Carnival: *We got stuck in the August Bank Holiday traffic on the way back.*

St **Auˈgustine** /ɔːˈɡʌstɪn/ (*died* 604) a Christian saint who was sent from Rome to England with 40 monks to teach Christianity to the *Anglo-Saxons. The king of *Kent, Ethelbert, was converted by him and became a Christian. Augustine built a church in his capital city, *Canterbury, and became the first *Archbishop of Canterbury.

ˌ***Auld Lang ˈSyne*** /ˌɔːld læŋ ˈzaɪn/ an old Scottish song about friendship and remembering good times in the past. The title means 'old long since'. Traditionally, people in Britain hold hands and sing it at midnight on *New Year's Eve. It was already a traditional song when Robert *Burns wrote the version that most people sing now. Many people know the beginning of the song:

Should auld acquaintance be forgot,
And never brought to min' (= mind)?
Should auld acquaintance be forgot,
And auld lang syne!

ˌ**Auld ˈReekie** /ˌɔːld ˈriːki/ a popular name for *Edinburgh. It means 'old smoky' and refers to the smoke from the city's many chimneys.

ˌ**Aunt JeˈmimaTM** /dʒəˈmaɪmə/ *n* [C, U] a US food product that is mixed with milk and eggs to make pancakes (= flat round cakes). The box originally had a picture of an African-American woman wearing a piece of material on her head like a servant. This came to be seen as offensive, and the name Aunt Jemima was sometimes used to mean an African-American woman who liked to serve white people. The picture was changed in the 1970s to show a modern African-American woman.

ˌ**Aunt ˈSally** *n* (*esp BrE*) **1** a model of a person's head that people throw balls at to win prizes, usually at *fairs and other outdoor social events. The aim is to hit the head or knock it down. **2** a person or thing that everyone criticizes or laughs at: *His handling of the crisis has made him the Aunt Sally of politics.*

ˌJane ˈ**Austen** /ˈɒstɪn; *AmE* ˈɔːstɪn/ (1775–1817) an English writer whose novels have had a strong influence on the development of English literature. In them she describes the personal relationships and social life of the English *upper middle class of her time with gentle humour. She herself never married. Her best-known books are **Sense and Sensibility* (1811), **Pride and Prejudice* (1813), **Emma* (1816) and **Persuasion* (1818).

ˈ**Austin**[1] /ˈɒstɪn; *AmE* ˈɔːstɪn/ the capital city of the US state of *Texas, on the Colorado river.

ˈ**Austin**TM[2] /ˈɒstɪn; *AmE* ˈɔːstɪn/ *n* a popular make of British car. The company making it became part of *British Leyland in 1968. The name *Austin* was still used on some British cars until the 1980s: *Are you still driving that old Austin Allegro?*

ˌ**Austin ˈReed**TM /ˌɒstɪn ˈriːd; *AmE* ˌɔːstɪn/ any of a chain of shops in Britain selling expensive men's clothes of good quality.

Australia a large island country and continent in the south-west Pacific Ocean. Its capital city is Canberra and its official language is English. The first inhabitants of Australia were the Aborigines, who now form only about 1.5% of the population. In 1770 the country was visited by Captain James *Cook, and in the 18th and 19th centuries it was used by the British as a place to send criminals because the prisons in Britain were so crowded. Many of Australia's present inhabitants are descended from British people. It is now independent from Britain, although it remains a member of the *Commonwealth. Most of the population live on or near the

coast in the east and south of the country, and there are large areas in the west, north and centre of the country that have very few inhabitants. The climate is generally warm. Australian culture is popular in Britain. A number of Australian programmes, including *soap operas such as *Neighbours*, appear regularly on British television. A popular informal name for Australia is 'Down Under'. See also BOTANY BAY. ▶ **Australian** *adj, n.*

the ˌ**Authorized** ˈ**Version** (*abbr* the **AV**) (*also* the **King James Version**) an English translation of the Bible that was ordered by King *James I for use in churches. It was first published in 1611 and became the main English version of the Bible. In the 20th century more modern translations were made, but many *Anglican churches continue to use the Authorized Version, and many people still prefer its old-fashioned language.

the ˈ**Automobile Associˌation** ⇨ AA 2.

ˌGene ˈ**Autry** /ˈɔːtri/ (1907–98) a US actor and singer in *western films in the 1930s and 1940s. He was known as the 'singing cowboy' and made more than 90 films. His horse was called Champion. Autry also had a popular radio programme. His best-known songs included *Tumblin' Tumbleweeds* (1935) and *Rudolph the Red-nosed Reindeer* (1950). He was later very successful in business and owned the California Angels baseball team.

ˌ**autumn** ˈ**statement** *n* a British government statement made every year in the autumn about the economy and the government's future economic plans: *The Chancellor announced in his autumn statement that he would lower income tax.*

AV /ˌeɪ ˈviː/ ⇨ AUTHORIZED VERSION.

ˈ**Avalon** /ˈævəlɒn; *AmE* ˈævəlɑːn/ (in ancient Welsh stories) a beautiful island where dead heroes go. In *Arthurian legend, it is the place where King *Arthur's body was taken after his last battle. Some people believe Avalon to be in or near what is now *Glastonbury.

ˈ**Avebury** /ˈeɪvbri/ a village in *Wiltshire, England, where there is an important prehistoric monument. This consists of *Silbury Hill and a circle of standing stones that is much larger than *Stonehenge. Avebury was made a *World Heritage Site in 1986.

Avebury

The ***A*ˈ*vengers*** /əˈvendʒəz; *AmE* əˈvendʒərz/ a popular British television series, made in the 1960s, in which John Steed, an English *gentleman(3), and his friend Emma Peel, an expert in judo, had slightly comic adventures fighting crime. Many people remember *The Avengers* for Emma Peel's leather suits and Steed's bowler hat and rolled umbrella.

ˌTex ˈ**Avery** /ˌteks ˈeɪvəri/ (1918–80) a US cartoonist. He created the characters of *Daffy Duck (1937), *Bugs Bunny (1940) and Droopy (1943). He later joined *Hanna and Barbera for the television series *The *Flintstones*.

ˈ**Avis**™ /ˈeɪvɪs/ a large car hire company with offices in many countries.

ˈ**Avon**[1] /ˈeɪvn/ any of three rivers with the same name in south-west England. The longest of these flows through *Warwick and *Stratford-upon-Avon. Shakespeare, who was born at Stratford, is sometimes called the 'Bard of Avon'.

ˈ**Avon**™[2] /ˈeɪvɒn; *AmE* ˈeɪvɑːn/ an international company selling beauty products, soap, etc. Avon representatives, usually women (called **Avon ladies**), sell these products by going to people's homes with them.

AWACS /ˈeɪwæks/ (*in full* **airborne warning and control system**) a US system of radar used in military planes to find and follow enemy planes and missiles. An AWACS plane can fly very high and for 10 hours without making a stop. It is easily recognized by the large disc above its wings.

A*ˌ*way in a* ˈ*Manger a *carol sung especially by children at church services at *Christmas. The first verse is:

Away in a manger, no crib for a bed,
The little Lord Jesus laid down his sweet head.
The stars in the bright sky looked down where
he lay,
The little Lord Jesus asleep on the hay.

ˌRev W ˈ**Awdry** /ˈɔːdri/ (Wilbert Awdry 1911–97) an English vicar (= *Church of England priest) and writer of children's books. He is best known for having created *Thomas, the Tank Engine*.

ˈ**Axminster** /ˈæksmɪnstə(r)/ *n* [C, U] a type of thick carpet made by a special factory process so that it looks as if it has been made by hand. These carpets were originally made in Axminster, a town in *Devon, England: *The hall is carpeted in good-quality Axminster.*

ˌAlan ˈ**Ayckbourn** /ˈeɪkbɔːn; *AmE* ˈeɪkbɔːrn/ (1939–) an English writer of many plays for the theatre and television, well known for his cleverly written and often disturbing comedies about English *middle-class behaviour, including *Absurd Person Singular* (1973) and the series of three plays called *The Norman Conquests* (1974). He usually gives the first performances of his plays in *Scarborough, where he is the artistic director of a theatre company. He was made a *knight in 1997.

ˌA J ˈ**Ayer** /ˈeə(r); *AmE* ˈer/ (Alfred Jules Ayer 1910–89) a British philosopher. His best-known work, *Language, Truth and Logic* (1936), develops the philosophy of 'logical positivism', the idea that a statement only has meaning if it can be proved to be true or false. He was made a *knight in 1970.

ˈ**Ayrshire** /ˈeəʃə(r); *AmE* ˈerʃər/ **1** a former county in south-west Scotland. In 1975 it became part of the Strathclyde region. **2** *n* a brown and white breed of cow, originally bred in Ayrshire and now used in many countries for its milk.

Bb

BA /ˌbiː ˈeɪ/ ⇨ BRITISH AIRWAYS.

BAA /ˌbiː eɪ ˈeɪ/ the private company that owns and runs most of Britain's major airports. Until 1987 it belonged to the state and was called *British Airports Authority.

ˌ***Baa, Baa, ˈBlack Sheep*** a traditional *nursery rhyme, which may refer to a tax put on wool in England in 1275. The full song is:

Baa, baa, black sheep,
Have you any wool?
Yes sir, yes sir,
Three bags full.
One for the master,
And one for the dame,
And one for the little boy
Who lives down the lane.

the ˈ**Baa-baas** /ˈbɑː bɑːz/ ⇨ BARBARIANS.

ˈ**Babbitt** /ˈbæbɪt/ *n* (*AmE*) a man who is too satisfied with a narrow set of values and thinks mainly about possessions and making money. Babbitt is a character in a novel of that name by Sinclair *Lewis.

ˌ***Babes in the ˈWood*** a traditional story about a boy and girl who go to live with their wicked uncle after their father dies. He pays two men to kill them, so that he can steal their property. However, one of the men feels sorry for the children, so he kills his partner and leaves them in a wood. They die and a bird covers them with leaves. Soon afterwards, the uncle's sons also die, and then he loses his property and dies himself, in prison. The story is often performed as a *pantomime, when it is given a happy ending.

Babies ⇨ article.

ˈ**Babycham**™ /ˈbeɪbiʃæm/ *n* [C, U] a sweet British fizzy alcoholic drink. It is sold in small bottles and drunk mainly by women.

ˌ**Baby ˈRuth**™ a popular make of US chocolate bar that is filled with peanuts.

ˌLauren **Baˈcall** /ˌlɔːrən bəˈkɔːl/ (1924–) a US actor well known for her deep voice. She was formerly married to Humphrey *Bogart, with whom she acted in several films, including *The Big Sleep* (1946) and *Key Largo* (1948). At the age of 72, she was nominated for an *Oscar as Best Supporting Actress for her role in *The Mirror Has Two Faces* (1996).

ˌBurt ˈ**Bacharach** /ˌbɜːt ˈbækəræk; *AmE* ˌbɜːrt/ (1928–) a US composer of popular songs, often with Hal David as his partner. Their songs include *Walk on By* (1964) and *Raindrops Keep Fallin' on My Head*, which won an *Oscar in 1969.

ˈ**bachelor's degree** *n* (*fml*) the first degree that you get when you study at a university. Compare MASTER'S DEGREE.

backˈbencher /bækˈbentʃə(r)/ *n* (in Britain) a *Member of Parliament who does not hold a senior position in the government or in the opposition. Backbenchers sit on the **backbenches**, the seats behind ministers or members of the *Shadow Cabinet. They are expected to vote as the party *Whip tells them to: *Mrs Pearson, a senior Tory backbencher, denied the reports.* ⇨ article at PARLIAMENT.

the ˈ**Backs** *n* [pl] the attractive area at the back of some of the colleges of *Cambridge University in England, between the colleges and the River Cam.

the Backs

ˌ**back-to-ˈback** *n* a house that is part of a row and has its back against the back of a house in another row facing in the opposite direction. Back-to-back houses are mostly found in towns in the *Midlands and north of Britain and were built for workers during the *Industrial Revolution.

ˌ**back to basics** a phrase used by politicians and others who are concerned about standards in people's private and public life. The British Prime Minister John *Major used it in the early 1990s when he was trying to encourage people to have strong moral principles, to obey the law, to have respect for each other, and to take responsibility for themselves and their families. However, soon afterwards some Conservative politicians were accused of immoral behaviour, and it was suggested that they should have given people a better example to follow. The phrase has also been used in the US by people who want to stop standards of education falling.

ˌ***Back to the ˈFuture*** a US comedy science fiction film (1985) that made a star of Michael J *Fox. He plays a boy in *high school who, helped by a funny scientist, travels back in time from 1985 to 1955 to meet his parents when they were young. Fox also appeared in *Back to the Future II* (1989), about a trip to the year 2015, and *Back to the Future III* (1990), in which he returns to the *Wild West of 1885. All three films were directed by Robert *Zemeckis.

ˌFrancis ˈ**Bacon¹** /ˈbeɪkən/ (1561–1626) an English lawyer, politician and philosopher. He was very successful in his early career and became *Lord Chancellor to King *James I in 1618, but he was later accused of accepting money illegally and sent to prison. He was released after only four days, but never returned to public service. Bacon's books, including *The Advancement of Learning* (1605), show a scientific interest in the world which was new at that time.

Since 1856 some people have claimed that Francis Bacon is the real author of the plays of William *Shakespeare, because they feel that Shakespeare's

B

Babies

Around 730 000 babies are born in Britain each year, though the **birth rate** has fallen since the **baby boom** of the 1960s and 1970s. The average number of children in a British family is 2.4.

In the US about 4 million babies are born each year. The **infant mortality rate** (= the number of babies who die) is 7.2 per 1 000 live births, which is very high compared to Britain and most other developed countries, though the rate is lower than it has ever been. The situation is explained by the fact that in the US good medical care is too expensive for poorer people to afford. The infant mortality rate for whites is 6 per 1 000, the same as in Britain, but for *African Americans, who are generally poorer than whites, it is 14.2 per 1 000.

Choosing to have a baby

For many women in Britain and the US, getting **pregnant** is now a matter of individual choice. **Contraception** (= practices that prevent women from becoming pregnant) is widely used to help with **family planning**. About 10 million women use the **birth-control pill**, often called the **pill**, and almost 8 million depend on their partner using **condoms**. Only about 10% of babies born in the US are not wanted or planned by their parents.

Many couples now choose to have children later in life. Some women wait to **start a family** until they can 'hear their biological clocks ticking' (= they are nearly too old). In the US more than a third of babies are born to mothers over 30. In Britain the figure is 15%. Couples who have difficulty **conceiving** (= starting a baby) may try to get **fertility treatment**. Advances in medical techniques mean that it is now possible for women who are too old to conceive naturally to have a baby. This raises many ethical (= moral) and practical questions, including whether it is a good thing for a child to be born to an elderly mother.

Giving birth

During **pregnancy** women go to **antenatal** (*AmE* **prenatal**) classes to prepare for the birth. Fathers are encouraged to attend. British and American women often have strong feelings about where and how they want to **give birth**. In Britain mothers can choose between giving birth in the **maternity wing** of a hospital or having their baby at home. Most Americans have their babies in a hospital **birthing centre** that is made to feel like home. Americans can choose whether they want the baby to be **delivered** by an **obstetrician** (= a specialist doctor) or a **midwife** (= a nurse with special training). Fathers are often present and help at the birth.

Some women want to experience a **natural birth**, without pain-relieving drugs; others want drugs that will help reduce the pain. In the US doctors give mothers as much control over the birth as possible but take over when it seems necessary. There is a high rate of **litigation** (= court cases) resulting from difficult births and doctors want to avoid this. This may also explain why one baby in five in the US is born by **caesarean section** (= a surgical operation to remove the baby from the mother).

A new baby is a cause for celebration. Relatives and friends visit the mother and baby in hospital and take cards and gifts. Many women are sentimental (= emotional) about babies and coo over them (= talk lovingly in a soft voice) and want to hold them. The parents choose a name for the baby and may send out a printed card giving the baby's name, weight and date of birth or put a notice in the local newspaper. Later, there may be a *Christening service in a church. In Britain the parents must report the birth to the local **registrar** (= a council officer) and obtain a **birth certificate** for the baby. In the US births are registered at the local courthouse (= administrative offices of a county).

Looking after the baby

Most people now believe that **breastfeeding** a baby (= letting it take milk from the mother's breasts) is better than **bottle-feeding** with **formula**, a product made from cow's milk mixed with water, though for a long time bottle-feeding was fashionable. Now, about 55% of American babies are breastfed, more among better educated and older women, and women who want to bottle-feed may be made to feel guilty. **Nursing** (= breastfeeding) in public is now accepted and only a few older people are embarrassed to see it.

Fathers are encouraged to help with baby care as this is thought to help them **bond** (= form a close emotional relationship) with their children. In practice, women still do most of the work. This is partly because men cannot usually stay at home very long after a baby is born.

In Britain most women who work are entitled to **maternity leave**, about 18 weeks off work with reduced pay, though many employers offer more money and longer leave. Women's jobs have to be kept open for them to return to after their maternity leave. In the US the right to take any time off work depends on individual employers. There is some limited financial help for poor mothers, but many Americans believe that people who cannot afford to support a baby should not have one.

Some women give up their jobs to look after their baby; others return to work and must find somebody to care for it. In the US people get a **babysitter** or take the baby to a **daycare centre** where there are other children. In Britain parents may take the baby to a **childminder** or to a **day nursery**. People do not generally expect their families to look after the baby.

The abortion issue

In Britain **abortion** (= the deliberate ending of a pregnancy before a baby is old enough to live) has been legal since 1967. There are about 150 000 abortions each year. In 1973 abortion became legal all over the US through the *Supreme Court decision **Roe v Wade*. Since then, there has been much debate in both Britain and the US between people on the **pro-choice** side, who think that women have the right to decide what happens to their bodies, and **pro-life** or **right-to-life** supporters, who believe that abortion is murder. Pro-life groups in the US have drawn attention to their views by putting bombs in clinics where abortions are done and killing doctors who perform them. The Supreme Court has recently changed its opinion slightly, and now some states have laws limiting abortion.

education and social background were not good enough to have produced such great literature.

ˌFrancis ˈ**Bacon**[2] /ˈbeɪkən/ (1909–92) an Irish painter who lived in England from 1928. He often painted people who were in pain or who were being treated in a cruel way, making their bodies look ugly and twisted in order to emphasize their pain. He destroyed any of his paintings that he was not satisfied with.

ˌRoger ˈ**Bacon**[3] (*c.* 1214–92) a Franciscan monk and philosopher who became known as 'Doctor Mirabilis', or 'the Admirable Doctor'. He was unusual for his time in regarding mathematics and science as very important. His writings show that he was particularly interested in chemistry, optics (= the scientific study of sight and light) and astrology, and he seems to have understood the possibilities of gunpowder (= an explosive powder), the telescope, glasses and flying. In 1278 his work was declared to be heretical (= opposed to religious beliefs) and he was put in prison until just before his death.

ˌ**bacon and** ˈ**eggs** *n* [U] a dish consisting of fried slices of bacon and one or more fried eggs, eaten especially as part of a traditional English breakfast: *I had bacon and eggs for breakfast.*

ˈ**Bactine**™ /ˈbæktiːn/ *n* [U] a US product name for a substance that helps to prevent infection in small cuts and wounds. It can be bought without a doctor's permission and is made by Miles Laboratories.

Lord ˌ**Baden-**ˈ**Powell** /ˌbeɪdn ˈpəʊəl; *AmE* ˈpoʊəl *also* ˈpaʊəl/ (Robert Stephenson Smyth Baden-Powell 1857–1951) a British soldier who became famous for defending the South African town of Mafeking in the *Boer War. He later left the army to start the Boy Scout organization (now called the *Scouts or the Scout Association) in 1908 and, with his sister Agnes, the Girl Guides (now called the *Guides or, in the US, the Girl Scouts) in 1910.

ˌDouglas ˈ**Bader** /ˈbɑːdə(r)/ (1910–82) a member of the *Royal Air Force who lost both his legs after an aircraft accident in 1931. He returned to the Air Force in 1939 and fought for Britain in World War II until he was captured by the Germans and put in Colditz prison. After the war he did a lot of work for disabled people, and he was made a *knight in 1976.

ˈ**badlands** /ˈbædlændz/ *n* [pl] (*esp AmE*) a dry bare area of land with deep channels worn away by water. The **Badlands National Park** is in the US state of *South Dakota.

Badlands, South Dakota

ˈ**Badminton** /ˈbædmɪntən/ (*also fml* the **Badminton Horse Trials**) a riding contest held every year on land around Badminton House, a large house near *Bath, England. Riders compete in riding across fields, water etc, in jumping fences around a course, and in showing that their horses will obey them in various exercises. See also THREE-DAY EVENT.

ˌJoan ˈ**Baez** /ˈbaɪez/ (1941–) a US *rock and folk singer who also plays the guitar and writes songs. She is known especially for her protest songs and her strong, clear voice.

BAFTA /ˈbæftə/ (*in full* the **British Academy of Film and Television Arts**) a British organization which gives awards every year to film and television actors, producers, etc. It was formed in 1959. See also EMMY.

ˈ**bagel** /ˈbeɪgl/ *n* a hard bread roll in the shape of a ring. Bagels first became popular in New York City as a Jewish bread. They are often eaten there with cream cheese and smoked salmon.

ˈ**Baggies**™ /ˈbægiz/ a US make of plastic bags for storing food in.

ˈ**bagpipes** (*also infml* **pipes**) *n* [pl] a musical instrument played by blowing air into a bag held under the arm, and pressing it out through pipes. Similar instruments are played in many countries, including Ireland, but in Britain the bagpipes are mainly associated with Scotland. The sound they make is unusual, but their music is suitable both for dancing and for serious occasions such as funerals. A person who plays the bagpipes is called a *piper*: *the wail of the bagpipes.*

a piper playing the bagpipes

the **Ba**ˈ**hamas** /bəˈhɑːməz/ a group of about 700 small islands that form an independent state in the *West Indies. The two main islands are New Providence, where the capital city of Nassau is and where 75% of the population of 250 000 live, and Grand Bahama. The Bahamas is a member of the Commonwealth, and its official language is English. It is very popular with tourists. ▶ **Bahamian** *adj, n.*

ˈ**bailiff** /ˈbeɪlɪf/ *n* **1** (in Britain) an officer who works for the county court. The bailiff's job is to make sure that the court's orders are obeyed. Bailiffs can come into a person's home to take goods in payment of a debt, to collect money owed for rent or taxes, to remove somebody who has no right to be there, etc. The police sometimes help them. There are also private companies of bailiffs, who have more limited powers. See also LAW ENFORCEMENT. **2** (in the US) an official who keeps order in a court of law. **3** (especially in Britain) a person whose job is to look after land for its owner.

ˌBeryl ˈ**Bainbridge** /ˈbeɪnbrɪdʒ/ (1934–) an English writer of novels. Her books include *The Bottle Factory Outing* (1974) and *An Awfully Big Adventure* (1989).

ˈJohn ˈLogie ˈ**Baird** /ˈdʒɒn ˈləʊgi ˈbeəd; *AmE* ˈloʊgi ˈberd/ (1888–1946) a Sottish inventor who is remembered mainly for his work on early forms of television in the 1920s and 1930s. The *BBC began using Baird's system in 1929, but by 1937 Marconi-EMI had replaced his mechanical system by a much more efficient electronic one.

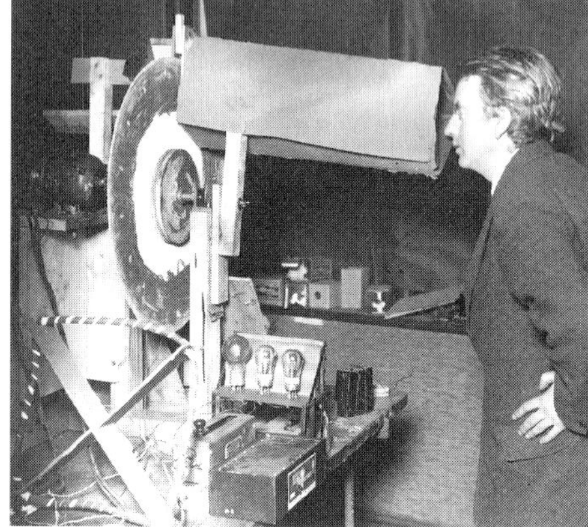

John Logie Baird with his first television apparatus

ˌ**baked Aˈlaska** /əˈlæskə/ *n* [C, U] a sweet dish consisting of cake and ice cream covered in meringue (= a mixture of egg whites and sugar) and cooked quickly in a very hot oven.

ˌ**baked ˈbeans** *n* [pl] **1** (in Britain) small white beans that are baked and sold in tins with tomato sauce, which gives them an orange colour: *I gave the children baked beans on toast for tea.* **2** ⇨ BOSTON BAKED BEANS.

ˈ**Bakelite**™ /ˈbeɪkəlaɪt/ *n* [U] a type of hard plastic that was widely used in the radio and electrical industry in the first half of the 20th century. It was invented by the Belgian-American chemist Leo Hendrik Baekeland: *an old Bakelite telephone.*

ˌJanet ˈ**Baker**¹ /ˈbeɪkə(r)/ (1933–) an English singer who is well known for her performances of *baroque music as well as that of modern British composers, especially *Elgar and *Britten. She was made a *dame(2) in 1976.

ˈSamuel ˈWhite ˈ**Baker**² /ˌwaɪt ˈbeɪkə(r)/ (1812–93) a British explorer who in 1864 discovered Lake Albert as one of the sources of the River Nile. He was made a *knight in 1866.

ˌ**Baker's ˈChocolate**™ /ˌbeɪkəz; *AmE* ˌbeɪkərz/ *n* [U] a US make of chocolate mostly used for making cakes and sweets/candy. It is not very sweet and is sold in small squares. The original Baker's Chocolate Company started in 1780. It is now owned by *Kraft.

a ˌ**baker's ˈdozen** a phrase meaning 13. It comes from the fact that in the past people who sold bread always added an extra loaf when somebody ordered a dozen (= 12) loaves, in case they might be punished for supplying too few.

ˈ**Baker Street** /ˈbeɪkə; *AmE* ˈbeɪkər/ a street in central London. It is perhaps best known as the place where Sherlock *Holmes, the *detective created by Sir Arthur *Conan Doyle, lived. His address was number 221B Baker Street, which is now part of a bank. In the stories, Holmes sometimes uses a group of local children he calls the **Baker Street irregulars** to get information for him.

ˌ**Bakewell ˈtart** /ˌbeɪkwel/ *n* [C, U] an open pastry case filled with sponge cake flavoured with almonds over a layer of jam. It was originally made in Bakewell, a town in *Derbyshire, England.

ˈ**Bakke deˌcision** /ˈbæki/ an important ruling made by the US *Supreme Court in 1978. A white man called Allan Bakke claimed that he had been illegally refused a job because of his colour. The Court decided that the employers had acted illegally in not offering him a job, but that employers had a right to consider somebody's race when deciding whether to give them a job. See also AFFIRMATIVE ACTION.

ˌJim ˈ**Bakker** /ˈbeɪkə(r)/ (1941–) an American religious leader who, with his wife Tammy Faye, had a popular national television programme. In 1989 he was sent to prison for 45 years for illegally taking money that people gave to support his work. He was released early from prison in 1994.

ˌ**Balaˈclava** /ˌbæləˈklɑːvə/ (*also* the **Battle of Balaclava**) a battle in the *Crimean War, fought in 1854 near the small town of Balaclava in the Ukraine. It is remembered for the *Charge of the Light Brigade, in which the British army suffered heavy losses.

ˌ**balaˈclava** /ˌbæləˈklɑːvə/ (*fml* **balaclava helmet**) *n* a woollen hat that fits closely over the head and neck, with an opening for the face. It was originally worn by soldiers in the *Crimean War.

a balaclava

ˌGeorge ˈ**Balanchine** /ˈbæləntʃiːn/ (1904–83) a US choreographer, born in Russia. After working with Diaghilev he went to the US and started the New York City Ballet.

ˌ**bald ˈeagle** *n* ⇨ AMERICAN EAGLE.

ˌJames ˈ**Baldwin**¹ /ˈbɔːldwɪn/ (1924–87) an African-American writer of novels and plays. He had immediate success with his first novel *Go, Tell It on the Mountain* (1954), which, like much of his later work, deals with the condition of black people in the US.

ˌStanley ˈ**Baldwin**² /ˈbɔːldwɪn/ (1867–1947) a British Conservative politician who was *prime minister three times in the 1920s and 1930s. His government created a law that defeated the *General Strike of 1926. He also dealt skilfully with the difficult matter of the abdication of King *Edward VIII. He was made an *earl(1) in 1937.

ˌA J ˈ**Balfour** /ˈbælfə(r)/ (Arthur James Balfour 1848–1930) a British Conservative politician, the nephew of Lord *Salisbury. He was Prime Minister from 1902 to 1905 and Foreign Secretary from 1916 to 1919, during World War I. He was made an *earl in 1922.

the ˌ**Balfour Declaˈration** /ˌbælfə; *AmE* ˌbælfər/ a letter of 2 November 1917 in which A J *Balfour, the British Foreign Secretary, wrote that the British government was in favour of establishing Palestine as a national home for the Jewish people. The other *Allies(1) soon said that they agreed with this.

ˌLucille ˈ**Ball** /ˌluːsiːl ˈbɔːl/ (1911–89) a US comedy actor, especially on television where she was the star of the 1950s comedy series *I Love Lucy*. She received three *Emmy awards.

The **'Ballad of 'Reading 'Gaol** /ˈredɪŋ/ a long poem by Oscar *Wilde, written in 1898 after he had been in prison, about the horror of prison life.

ˌJ G **'Ballard** /ˈbælɑːd; *AmE* ˈbælɑːrd/ (James Graham Ballard 1930–) a British author who is best known for his science fiction novels and short stories, and for *Empire of the Sun* (1984), about a boy's experiences in a Japanese prison camp during *World War II.

the **ˌBallet 'Rambert** /ˈrɒmbeə(r); *AmE* ˈrɑːmber/ the former name of the *Rambert Dance Company.

Bal'moral /bælˈmɒrəl; *AmE* bælˈmɔːrəl/ a castle near *Aberdeen, Scotland, which the British *royal family used as a private holiday home. It was built for Queen *Victoria in 1853–6.

Balmoral

'Balti /ˈbɔːlti, ˈbælti/ *n* [U, C] a type of hot and spicy food from *Pakistan that is popular in Britain. It is cooked and served in a round shallow dish: *a Balti house* (= a restaurant that serves Balti meals).

'Baltimore /ˈbɔːltəmɔː(r)/ the largest city in the US state of *Maryland. It is a busy port on the Atlantic Ocean and contains Fort McHenry which caused Francis Scott *Key to write *The *Star-Spangled Banner*. The famous Preakness horse race takes place in Baltimore.

'Bambi /ˈbæmbi/ a young deer in a Walt *Disney cartoon film (1942) of the same name. Bambi is a gentle and innocent animal. The film is remembered particularly for its sad moments.

'Banbury /ˈbænbri/ a town in the county of *Oxfordshire, England, once famous for its cakes. There is a stone cross in the town's centre, which is mentioned in the old children's *nursery rhyme **Ride a Cock-horse to Banbury Cross.*

'Band Aid a large group of pop stars brought together by Bob *Geldof in 1984 to help people without food in Ethiopia. The song that they recorded, *Do They Know It's Christmas?*, was bought by millions of people, and the profits were sent to Ethiopia. See also LIVE AID.

'Band-Aid™ *n* [C, U] a US make of sticking-plaster (= a strip of fabric that can be stuck to the skin to protect a small wound or cut), made by *Johnson & Johnson. They were first made in 1921 and are now so common that Americans use the name for any plaster/bandage.

ˌbangers and 'mash *n* [U] (*BrE infml*) sausages and mashed potatoes (= boiled potatoes that have been crushed into a soft mass). The phrase is often used as an example of a simple, solid and very British meal: *I'd rather eat bangers and mash than an expensive meal in a French restaurant.*

ˌBangla'desh /ˌbæŋgləˈdeʃ/ a country which was part of *Pakistan until it became an independent member of the Commonwealth in 1971. Its capital city is Dhaka. About 170 000 people from Bangladesh now live in Britain. ▶ **Bangladeshi** *adj, n.*

B

ˌbank 'holiday *n* **1** (in Britain) an official public holiday (on a day other than Saturday or Sunday) when all banks and post offices are closed, as well as most factories, offices and shops. **2** (in the US) a period when banks are closed to prevent a financial problem, usually on special instructions from the government.

'Bank of 'Credit and 'Commerce Inter'national ⇨ BCCI.

the **ˌBank of 'England** the central bank of the United Kingdom, in London. It is the official source of all paper money in Britain, it advises the government on financial matters, and it acts as banker to the government and to other banks. It was privately owned until 1946, when it came under government control. ⇨ article at BANKS AND BANKING.

the **ˌBank of 'Scotland** /ˈskɒtlənd/ one of the three largest banks in Scotland. The largest is the *Royal Bank of Scotland and the other is the *Clydesdale Bank. Although they are private commercial banks, all three print their own paper money, which has no legal status but is accepted in Scotland and usually in England.

ˌJoseph **'Banks** /ˈbæŋks/ (1743–1820) an English naturalist who sailed with Captain *Cook on his first journey round the world. He discovered and collected many unknown plants, especially in Australia, and helped to start the famous collection of plants at *Kew Gardens. He was President of the *Royal Society for over 40 years and was made a *knight in 1781.

Banks and banking ⇨ article.

ˌRoger **'Bannister** /ˈbænɪstə(r)/ (1929–) the first person to run a mile in under four minutes. He achieved this in 1954 while he was a medical student at *Oxford University. He later had an impressive medical career. He was made a *knight in 1975.

the ˌBattle of **'Bannockburn** /ˈbænəkbɜːn; *AmE* ˈbænəkbɜːrn/ a victory for the army of the Scottish king *Robert the Bruce over the army of the English king *Edward II in 1314. The battle was fought in central Scotland and it allowed Scotland to remain independent from England.

the **'Banqueting House** /ˈbæŋkwɪtɪŋ/ one of the most famous buildings in *Whitehall, London, designed by Inigo *Jones in 1622. Today it is used for formal social events.

the Banqueting House

'Baptist *n* a member of the largest group of Protestant Christians in the US, with over 38 million members around the world, including a small number in

B

Banks and banking

In Britain, the **central bank**, which acts as banker for the state and for commercial banks, is the ***Bank of England**. The Governor of the Bank of England advises the government on financial matters. Since 1997, the Bank has set national interest rates (= the cost of borrowing money). It is also responsible for issuing **banknotes**.

The main commercial banks, called **clearing banks** or **high-street banks**, are the *National Westminster (NatWest), *Barclays, *Lloyds and the *Midland. These are known as the 'big four' and have branches in most towns. Former *building societies that became banks in the mid 1990s, such as the *Abbey National and the *Halifax, now compete with them for customers.

In the US there are over 14 000 different commercial banks. This is because banks are prevented by law from operating in more than one state. Some banks get round this rule by forming **holding companies** which own banks with the same names in different states. Unlike British banks, American banks are banks of **deposit** and **credit** and do not build up **capital**. Banking is dominated by large **money center** banks, such as *Chase Manhattan, which raise money by dealing in the international money markets and lend it to businesses and other banks.

The US central bank is the ***Federal Reserve Bank**, often called the **Fed**. In addition to the national Fed, there are 12 regional ones. The Fed tells commercial banks how much money they must keep in reserve and decides what rate of interest to charge when lending them money. This affects the rate of interest the commercial banks charge their customers. The Fed does not issue money: dollar **bills** (= banknotes) and coins are issued by the *Department of the Treasury.

Using a bank account in Britain

Most adults in Britain have a bank account. People use a **current account** for their general expenses. Current account holders are given a **cheque book** containing a number of **crossed cheques**, cheques with two vertical lines down the middle. These cheques can only be paid into the bank account of the person to whom they are **made payable**. Some cheque books have cheques with **stubs** on which to write the name of the person the cheque was paid to; others have a list at the back. It is possible to **withdraw** money from an account by cheque, but most people use a **cash dispenser**, a machine set in the wall outside a bank or supermarket.

Many people receive their salaries by automated transfer direct from their employer's account into their own. Similarly, customers can ask their bank to pay bills by **standing order** or **direct debit**. Banks send their customers regular **statements**. Cash dispensers can supply a **ministatement**, a record of the most recent **transactions**, or a note stating the **balance** (= the amount of money in an account). People who **have an overdraft** (= have spent more money than was in their account) pay **bank charges**, but otherwise banking is free.

Some people also have a **deposit account** in which they put money they want to save and on which they receive **interest**. Some types of deposit account have restrictions on how often money can be taken out of them.

Banks issue a variety of plastic cards. These include **cashcards** for getting money out of a cash dispenser, **cheque cards** to guarantee that cheques will be **honoured**, ***debit cards**, such as *Switch and *Delta, and ***credit cards** which allow goods to be paid for at a later date.

The high-street banks offer **bank loans** for individuals and small businesses. **Merchant banks** deal with company finance on a larger scale. Recently, banks have also begun to offer services such as *mortgages, insurance, and buying and selling shares. They also buy and sell **traveller's cheques** and foreign currency.

Banks used to open late (9.30 a.m.) and close early (3.30 p.m.), but due to customer pressure they now open and close at the same time as shops. Bank customers are being encouraged to use **telephone banking**, or **telebanking**, and to check their accounts and give instructions over the telephone. Computer banking is being developed.

Although the **bank manager** was once an important and respected person in society, banks have in recent years become unpopular because of high charges on overdrafts and poor interest rates for savers. Some banks invested badly and lost money, so people are less willing to trust them with their money. Complaints to the banking ***ombudsman** (= a person appointed by the government to investigate complaints) have increased.

Bank accounts in the US

Ordinary people keep their accounts in commercial banks which must have a charter (= permission to operate) from the US or a state government. Each state decides whether to allow **branch banking**, i.e. to allow customers to do business at any branch of a bank, not just the one where they have their account. People also keep money in *savings and loans organizations.

The most common accounts are **checking** and **savings** accounts. US banks issue **checkbooks** and offer similar **card services** to British banks. Many banks offer free banking, but some make customers pay a service charge for a checking account. This may be a few dollars a month or a few cents for each **check**. Customers get a monthly statement from the bank, and the bank **cancels** and returns any checks they have written.

To **deposit** a check in a bank account, the person it is **made out to** must **endorse** it by signing their name on the back. If they want to get cash they have to go to the bank which issued the check. The **teller** there makes sure that there is enough money in the account before paying the cash. US banks do not use crossed checks.

Credit cards are widely used and debit cards are becoming more common, but checks are used to pay for many goods. Every year shops lose money from checks that **bounce** (= are not paid because there is not enough money in the account).

As in Britain, banks used to have short working hours, and if a person is said to 'work banker's hours' they work just a few hours each day. Now, banks open at more convenient times, and when they are closed many transactions can be done through an ***ATM** (**Automated Teller Machine**).

Britain. The group was formed in England in the early 17th century by people who disagreed with other Protestants about the ceremony of baptism. Baptists believe in putting a new member of the Church completely under water during baptism. They also believe that baptism should be for adults and not for children, because they think that children are not old enough to understand what the ceremony means. ⇨ article at RELIGION.

B & Q™ /ˌbiː ənd ˈkjuː/ any of a chain of large shops in Britain where people can buy materials to decorate or repair their homes, usually at low cost. The shops also sell tools, furniture, etc. for the garden. They are named after Richard Block and David Quayle, who started the company: *I got the paint from B & Q.*

the ˈ**Bar** the profession of *barrister. To be *called to the Bar* is to be received into the profession after *training for the Bar*. The Bar is governed by the *Bar Council. The head of the Bar of England and Wales and the Bar of Northern Ireland is called the *Attorney General, and the head of the Scottish Bar is called the Dean of Faculty.

Barˈbados /bɑːˈbeɪdɒs; *AmE* bɑːrˈbeɪdɑːs/ an island in the *Caribbean and an independent member of the Commonwealth since 1966. Its capital city is Bridgetown. ▶ **Barbadian** *adj, n.*

the **Barˈbarians** /bɑːˈbeəriənz; *AmE* bɑːrˈberiənz/ (*also infml* the **Baa-baas**) a *Rugby Union club which many of the best players from Britain, France and the Commonwealth are invited to join. It has no ground of its own but plays six games a year against English and Welsh clubs as well as games against foreign teams visiting Britain.

ˌSamuel ˈ**Barber** /ˈbɑːbə(r); *AmE* ˈbɑːrbər/ (1910–81) a US composer whose music is traditional in style. His best-known works are the *Adagio for Strings* (1936) and the opera *Vanessa* (1958).

the ˈ**Barber** ˈ**Institute of** ˈ**Fine** ˈ**Arts** /ˈbɑːbə(r)/ an institution for the study of art history at the University of *Birmingham, England. Since it began in 1932 it has built up a fine collection of paintings from all periods.

ˈ**barber-shop** *n* [U] a type of singing performed by four men (or less often women) in close harmony, without instruments. It is especially popular in the US where many towns have **barber-shop quartets**. Barber-shop songs are often sentimental, and well-known favourites include *Sweet Adeline* (1903) and *Down by the Old Mill Stream* (1910).

the ˈ**Barbican** ˌ**Centre** /ˈbɑːbɪkən; *AmE* ˈbɑːrbɪkən/ a large cultural centre in the **Barbican**, an area of modern buildings in the *City of London, north of *St Paul's Cathedral. The Centre includes a concert hall which is the home of the *London Symphony Orchestra, three cinemas, a theatre which is the London home of the *Royal Shakespeare Company, and a smaller theatre, an art gallery, a public library and two exhibition halls, as well as a conference hall, bar and restaurants.

ˈ**Barbie doll** /ˈbɑːbi; *AmE* ˈbɑːrbi/ *n* a child's toy doll in the form of an attractive young woman with a wide choice of fashionable clothes. In the US a woman who is attractive and well dressed but not intelligent is sometimes described as a Barbie doll.

a Barbie doll

bar billiards

ˌ**bar** ˈ**billiards** *n* [U] (*BrE*) a game played mainly in *pubs on a special table. Players use cues (= long wooden rods) to try to hit balls into holes on the surface of the table.

ˌJohn **Barbiˈrolli** /bɑːbiˈrɒli; *AmE* bɑːrbəˈrɑːli/ (1899–1970) an English musician and conductor whose family came originally from Italy. He was conductor of the *New York Phiharmonic Orchestra from 1937 to 1943 and then conductor of the *Hallé Orchestra, Manchester, until his death. He was made a *knight in 1949.

ˈ**Barbour**™ /ˈbɑːbə(r); *AmE* ˈbɑːrbər/ *n* an English company that makes expensive coats of specially treated cotton that keeps out the rain and wind. Barbours are worn especially by people who live or spend time in the country, but they are also fashionable with city people. They are usually dark green in colour and often worn with green wellington boots. See also GREEN WELLY BRIGADE.

Barˈbuda /bɑːˈbjuːdə; *AmE* bɑːrˈbjuːdə/ ⇨ ANTIGUA AND BARBUDA.

ˌ***Barchester*** ˈ***Towers*** /ˌbɑːtʃɪstə; *AmE* ˌbɑːrtʃɪstər/ a novel (1857) by Anthony *Trollope. It is the second of his six *Barsetshire novels and is about a struggle for power among the people associated with the cathedral in Barchester, an imaginary town in England.

ˈ**Barclaycard** /ˈbɑːklikɑːd; *AmE* ˈbɑːrklikɑːrd/ *n* the name of one of the most widely used British *credit cards and of the organization, owned by *Barclays Bank, from which these cards are available.

ˌ**Barclays** ˈ**Bank** /ˌbɑːkliz; *AmE* ˌbɑːrkliz/ (*also* **Barclays**) one of the four main English banks. It was established in 1896 and has branches in most towns and cities in Britain.

the ˌ**Bar** ˈ**Council** (in Britain) the group of senior *barristers that governs the *Bar and the *Inns of Court. Its full name is the General Council of the Bar and of the Inns of Court.

bard /bɑːd; *AmE* bɑːrd/ *n* an old-fashioned word for a poet. Shakespeare is sometimes called the **Bard of Avon** after the river near his place of birth. The word is also used as the title of a poet who wins a competition at an *eisteddfod.

ˈ**Baring** ˌ**brothers** /ˈbeərɪŋ; *AmE* ˈberɪŋ/ the oldest merchant bank (= bank that lends money to large companies) in London, England. It stopped trading in February 1995 after an employee, Nick Leeson, lost £250 million while trading illegally in Singapore. The bank was bought by a Dutch company a month later and began trading again. Leeson was sent to prison.

ˌClive ˈ**Barker**[1] /ˈbɑːkə(r); *AmE* ˈbɑːrkər/ (1952–) an English writer of horror stories, including the novels *Weaveworld* (1987) and *Sacrament* (1996). He has also worked as a film director, and his best-known films include *Hellraiser* (1987) and *Lord of Illusions* (1995).

B

ˌRonnie ˈ**Barker²** /ˈbɑːkə(r); *AmE* ˈbɑːrkər/ (1929–) a popular English actor and comedian, especially on television. He is best known for *The Two Ronnies*, a regular show in which he appeared with Ronnie *Corbett, and *Porridge*, a comedy series about life in prison. He has now retired.

ˌSue ˈ**Barker³** /ˈbɑːkə(r); *AmE* ˈbɑːrkər/ (1956–) an English presenter of sports programmes on television, including **Grandstand* (from 1994) and the quiz show *A *Question of Sport* (from 1997). She earlier had a successful career as a tennis player.

ˌ**barley** ˈ**wine** *n* [U] (*esp BrE*) a type of strong beer.

ˈ**barmaid** *n* (*esp BrE*) a woman who serves drinks from behind the bar in a *pub. In jokes, cartoons, etc. the typical British barmaid is a cheerful, friendly woman with a lot of make-up and large breasts.

Barˈnardo's /bəˈnɑːdəʊz; *AmE* bərˈnɑːrdoʊz/ a British charity that helps children with social, physical or mental problems. It began in 1870 when an Irish man, Dr Thomas Barnardo, started a home in London for poor children without parents.

ˌP T ˈ**Barnum** /ˈbɑːnəm; *AmE* ˈbɑːrnəm/ (Phineas Taylor Barnum 1810–91) a US showman who was famous for his exaggerated claims. He owned a travelling circus, called the Greatest Show on Earth, and later joined his great rival J A Bailey to form Barnum and Bailey's Circus. His circus acts included *Tom Thumb and the elephant Jumbo.

ˈ**baron** *n* a man who has the fifth rank in the British *peerage. He has the title 'Lord' and is a member of the *House of Lords. ⇨ note at PEERAGE.

ˈ**baroness** *n* **1** (in Britain) a woman who has the rank of *baron and the title 'Lady' or sometimes 'Baroness'. **2** the wife of a *baron, having the title 'Lady'. ⇨ note at PEERAGE.

ˈ**baronet** *n* (*abbrs* **Bart**, **Bt**) (in Britain) a man who has rank of honour below a *baron but above a *knight. He is not a member of the *House of Lords but has the title 'Sir' and his wife the title 'Lady'.

baˈroque *adj* in a highly decorated style of art that was fashionable in Europe in the 17th and early 18th centuries after developing in Italy. Examples of the British baroque style include buildings designed by the architects *Wren and *Vanbrugh, and the music of *Purcell and *Handel.

▶ **baroque** (*often* **the baroque**) *n* [U] the baroque style or baroque art.

ˌRoseanne ˈ**Barr** /ˌrəʊzæn ˈbɑː(r); *AmE* ˌroʊzæn ˈbɑːr/ ⇨ ROSEANNE.

Eˈlizabeth ˈ**Barrett** ˈ**Browning** /ˈbærət ˈbraʊnɪŋ/ (*born* Elizabeth Barrett 1806–61) an English poet and the wife of Robert *Browning. Although her poetry was more popular than his during their life, she is now remembered more for the story of their secret love affair and marriage, which enabled her to escape from her harsh and selfish father to a new life in Italy.

ˌJ M ˈ**Barrie** /ˈbæri/ (James Matthew Barrie 1860–1937) a Scottish writer of plays and novels. His best-known works are the plays **Peter Pan* (1904) and *The Admirable Crichton* (1902).

ˈ**barrister** *n* (in England and Wales) a lawyer who has the right to represent people in the higher courts. It is possible that in future this right will be given to other lawyers, e.g. solicitors. The Scottish equivalent of a barrister is called an *advocate*. ⇨ article at LEGAL SYSTEM IN BRITAIN.

ˈ**barrow** *n* (*esp BrE*) a large pile of earth built in ancient times to cover a grave. In Britain *long barrows* date mainly from the later *Stone Age (4000–2100 BC), and *round barrows* date from the *Bronze Age (2100–700 BC).

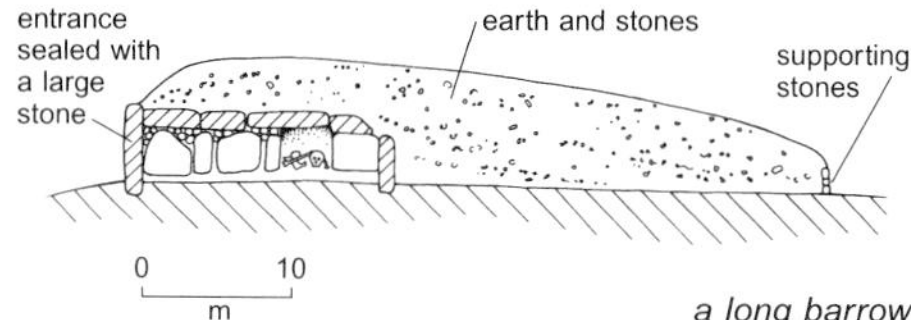

a long barrow

ˌCharles ˈ**Barry** /ˈbæri/ (1795–1860) an English architect who designed the *Houses of Parliament(2) in London, built in the style of the *Gothic Revival. He was made a *knight in 1852.

ˈ**Barrymore** /ˈbærimɔː(r)/ a family of US stage and (later) film actors, Lionel (1878–1954), his sister Ethel (1879–1959) and his brother John (1882–1942)). John was the grandfather of the actor Drew Barrymore (1975–).

ˈ**Barsetshire** /ˈbɑːsɪtʃə(r) *AmE* ˈbɑːrsɪtʃər/ an imaginary English county in a series of six novels by Anthony *Trollope.

ˈ**bar snack** *n* [usu pl] (*BrE*) a light meal that can be bought and eaten in a pub. Bar snacks might include sandwiches, salads and pies. See also PLOUGHMAN'S LUNCH.

BART /bɑːt; *AmE* bɑːrt/ (*in full* **Bay Area Rapid Transit**) the underground transport system in the US city of *San Francisco. The trains also go across San Francisco Bay to *Oakland and *Berkeley.

ˌJohn ˈ**Barth** /ˈbɑːθ; *AmE* ˈbɑːrθ/ (1930–) a US writer, formerly a teacher. His long and often complicated novels show the humorous aspect of modern life in the US. They include *The Sot-Weed Factor* (1960), *Giles Goat-Boy* (1966) and *Tidewater Tales* (1988).

ˈ***Bartlett's Famˈiliar Quoˈtations*** /ˈbɑːtləts; *AmE* ˈbɑːrtləts/ a popular US book of quotations (= passages from books, poems, plays, etc). It was first published in 1855 by John Bartlett (1820–1905) and now contains more than 22 000 quotations.

ˌClara ˈ**Barton** /ˌkleərə ˈbɑːtn; *AmE* ˌklerə ˈbɑːrtn/ (1821–1912) a US nurse who started the American Red Cross in 1881. She was its first president until 1904. Barton, who had earlier been a teacher, became a nurse for Union soldiers during the *Civil War and was known as 'the Angel of the Battlefield'.

Bart's /bɑːts; *AmE* bɑːrts/ the popular name for St Bartholomew's Hospital, a well-known teaching hospital in London, England. It has a long history going back to the 12th century, and recent proposals to close the hospital were strongly opposed by the medical profession.

Baseball ⇨ article.

the ˈ**Bash Street Kids** /ˈbæʃ/ a group of children in *The *Beano*, a British *comic published every week. They are always playing tricks on their teacher and getting into trouble.

the Bash Street Kids

Baseball

Baseball is America's national sport, played mainly by men. It developed in the mid 19th century from the British games of *rounders and *cricket. Baseball is also popular in Japan and several Latin American countries, and has been an Olympic sport since 1992. *Softball is similar but uses a larger, softer ball and is popular with women.

Many Americans play baseball for fun because players do not have to be strong like *football players or tall like *basketball players. Some people think baseball is too slow, but the team **managers** often change their players and plans during the game, and there are many exciting **plays**. Many American families enjoy going to a Sunday afternoon **double-header** (= two games between the same two teams in one day).

The game

Baseball is played with long wooden **bats** and a small, hard ball, by two teams of nine players each. The **infield** has three **bases** (= bags filled with sand) and a **home plate**, also called **home**, arranged in a **diamond**. The distance between each base is 90 feet (27.4 metres). The **pitcher**, who throws the ball to the **batter** at the home plate, stands in the centre of the diamond. The distance from the **pitcher's mound** to the home plate is 60.5 feet (18.4 metres). The team that scores the most **runs** as its players move round the bases is the winner.

Each game lasts nine **innings**. In each inning the **visiting team** is first to **bat** (= hit the ball), while the **home team** plays defense. Players bat in turn but when a team has three **outs**, it must let the other side bat. If a batter hits the ball and it is not caught in the air for **an out**, he runs to **first base**. If the ball is thrown to first base before the batter gets there, he is out. If not, he then tries to advance to **second base**, **third base** and back to home for a run while other players bat. A **base runner** is out if another player in his team hits the ball and it is thrown to second or third base before he gets there. The most exciting play is when the batter hits a ball very far and can go round all the bases for a **home run**, also called a **homer**.

An **umpire** judges the throws. If a **pitch** (= ball that is thrown) is not hit, the ball is caught by the **catcher** behind the batter and returned to the pitcher. A batter **strikes out** (= is out) if the pitcher throws three balls within the **strike zone** (= the area between the batter's shoulders and knees) and he misses them or does not try to hit them. A batter can go to first base on a **walk** if the pitcher throws four balls outside the strike zone. As well as the pitcher and the catcher, the defense has four other players in the infield and three in the **outfield**.

Competitions

The professional season lasts from April to October. **Major league** baseball is organized into the *American League and the *National League. At the end of the season the four best teams in each league play to decide which two will go forward to the ***World Series**. The team that wins four games in this competition are the World Champions. The New York *Yankees have won the World Series the most times. Other well-known teams include the Boston Red Sox, the Cleveland Indians, the Detroit Tigers, the Chicago Cubs, the St Louis Cardinals and the Los Angeles Dodgers. There are also several minor leagues around the country.

Amateur competitions include the *NCAA College World Series, won most often by the University of Southern California. Both American and foreign teams play in the Little League, and young people play in the Little League or Babe Ruth League.

Famous baseball players have included Ty *Cobb, 'Cy' *Young, 'Babe' *Ruth, Lou *Gehrig, Jackie *Robinson, Joe *DiMaggio, Mickey *Mantle, Willie *Mays, Ted *Williams, and Hank *Aaron. All have been chosen for the **Baseball Hall of Fame**.

Language and culture

Baseball has its own colourful language, such as an **Annie Oakley** (a free walk to first base), a **Texas Leaguer** (a weak hit just over the infield) and a **grand slam** (a home run with three runners on bases). Some expressions are more widely used. *To strike out* means to fail, *to throw somebody a curve* means to trick them (because a **curve ball** deceives the batter), *not get to first base* means to get nothing done, and *to take a rain check* is to delay an event (a free **rain check** to a later game is given if a game is stopped by rain).

Baseball has entered the national culture in other ways. It is the subject of an old popular song, *Take Me Out to the Ballgame*, novels such as *Shoeless Joe* (1982) which became the film *Field of Dreams* (1989), and other films like *The Pride of the Yankees* (1942) and *The Babe* (1992). Baseball caps and shirts are fashionable in many countries.

baseball: the pitcher pitches to the batter while the catcher crouches behind and the umpire watches

B

ˌbasic 'English a simple form of international English suggested by two *Cambridge University teachers in the 1920s. It used only 850 words and was intended for teachers and learners of English as a foreign language.

ˈˌCount' **'Basie** /ˌkaʊnt 'beɪsi/ (1904–84) a US *jazz musician. He formed his own orchestra in 1935, leading it from the piano. It became famous for its 'big band' sound.

ˌKim **'Basinger** /'bæsɪndʒə(r)/ (1953–) a US actor who was a sex symbol in the 1980s. She became famous for the film *9½ Weeks* (1985) but was later made bankrupt after losing a legal case when she left the film *Boxing Helena* (1993).

'Basin Street /'beɪsn/ a street in the US city of *New Orleans which is especially associated with the playing of *jazz music. There is a well-known song called *The Basin Street Blues*.

basketball

Basketball is the most popular sport played indoors in the US. It was invented in 1891 in Springfield, *Massachusetts by Dr James Naismith. He used fruit baskets for the hoops and baskets, and a *soccer ball. The first professional organization for male players was established in 1898, and the ***NBA (National Basketball Association)** was set up in 1949. Games are now played by rich basketball stars before audiences of over 20 000 people. The team seen most outside the US is the *Harlem Globetrotters. By contrast, the sport is played with just as much enthusiasm by young people on the streets of US cities.

Basketball is played by two teams of five players, but seven other players can be brought on to replace them during the game. The **court** is up to 94 feet (29.7 metres) long and 50 feet (15 metres) wide. At each end is a **hoop** (= a metal ring) 10 feet (3 metres) above the floor. The hoop is attached to a backboard and has a net without a bottom hanging from it. Players score two points when they throw the ball through the hoop from an area near the basket, and three points if they are further away. The team that scores the most points wins. The most exciting score is a **slam dunk** when a tall player jumps up high and pushes the ball down through the hoop. The ball is moved between players by a **pass**, or a **dribble** if a player bounces it on the floor. Players are not allowed to push an opponent, but this often happens. When a **foul** is committed against a player, he can have one or two **free throws**, also called **foul shots**, that count one point each. If the **referee** calls five illegal plays on a player, **he fouls out** and cannot play the rest of the game.

The NBA has 29 teams which play between November and June. The season ends when the best eight teams in the **Eastern Conference** and the best eight in the **Western Conference** compete to play in the **NBA Championship**. The Boston Celtics have won this most often, a total of 16 times. The best team recently has been the Chicago Bulls, with five championships since 1991. Women players take part in the **American Basketball League** and the **Women's National Basketball Association** league. Colleges and universities have teams that play in the *NCAA (National Collegiate Athletic Association) Basketball Championships. Basketball is also popular in *high schools.

NBA players are among the highest paid sports people in the world. Michael *Jordan of the Chicago Bulls, the richest of all sports players, was paid more than $33 million for the 1996–7 season and earned another $47 million from advertisements and other deals. Famous players in basketball history include Wilt 'the Stilt' *Chamberlain and Julius Erving. Together with many others, they are in the Basketball *Hall of Fame.

Basketball is also played in Britain, where there are national leagues for both men and women. But the sport receives less attention than in the US and, in contrast to football, the names of the leading teams and players are unfamiliar to most people.

Bass[1] /bæs/ a large British company that makes beer. It also owns many pubs in Britain and hotels around the world.

ˌSam **'Bass[2]** /'bæs/ (1851–78) an US outlaw (= criminal) who was called 'the Robin Hood of Texas'. He was a *cowboy before becoming an outlaw. In 1877, his gang stole $60 000 from a train in *Nebraska, the largest train robbery in history at that time. Bass died the following year after being shot.

ˌShirley **'Bassey** /'bæsi/ (1937–) a British singer of popular music, born in Wales. She is famous for her strong voice and personality. Her most successful songs include *Hey, Big Spender* and the theme songs for two James *Bond films, *Goldfinger* (1964) and *Diamonds are Forever* (1971).

ˌH M **'Bateman** /'beɪtmən/ (Henry Mayo Bateman 1887–1970) a British cartoonist, born in Australia. His cartoons often show an embarrassed person who has just shocked everyone by accidentally breaking a rule of social behaviour.

ˌAlan **'Bates[1]** /'beɪts/ (1934–) an English actor in theatre, films and television. He appeared in the first theatre performance of **Look Back in Anger* and his films have included *A Kind of Loving* (1962), *Women in Love* (1969) and **Hamlet* (1990).

ˌH E **'Bates[2]** /'beɪts/ (Herbert Ernest Bates 1905–74) an English writer of novels and short stories, many of which are about life in the English countryside. His best-known novel is *The Darling Buds of May* (1958).

ˌNorman **'Bates[3]** /'beɪts/ ⇨ PSYCHO.

Bath /bɑːθ; *AmE* bæθ/ a city in the county of *Avon in south-west England, famous for its healthy mineral water and hot springs, its ancient Roman baths and beautiful *Georgian buildings. The **Bath Festival** is a festival of classical music held every year in May and June. In 1987 Bath was one of the first places in Britain to become a *World Heritage Site.

Bath: the abbey and Roman baths

ˌ**Bath ˈbun** /ˌbɑːθ ; *AmE* ˌbæθ/ *n* a small round sweet cake that contains dried fruit and has crisp melted sugar on top. Bath buns were originally made in *Bath.

ˈ**bathing machine** *n* a beach hut on wheels, used in the 18th and 19th centuries. People changed their clothes privately inside it and it was then pulled into the sea so that they could bathe from it.

bathing machines

ˌ**Bath ˈOliver** /ˌbɑːθ ˈɒlɪvə(r); *AmE* ˌbæθ ˈɑːlɪvər/ *n* a type of thin hard biscuit that is made without sugar and is eaten especially with cheese. It was invented in *Bath by Dr William Oliver (1695–1764), who wanted his patients to eat simple, healthy food.

ˈ**Batman** /ˈbætmæn/ a character in US *comics, on television and in films who wears a costume like a bat (= a small animal like a mouse with wings), and has special powers of intelligence. With his friend Robin he spends his time helping ordinary people in trouble and fighting crime. He drives a vehicle called the **Batmobile** and is sometimes referred to as the 'caped crusader'. His regular enemies include the Penguin and the Joker.

ˈ**Battenberg** /ˈbætnbɜːg; *AmE* ˈbætnbɜːrg/ (*also* **Battenberg cake**) *n* [C, U] (*BrE*) a cake with a long square shape, covered with marzipan (= a mixture of almonds, sugar and eggs). When cut, each slice shows four squares of cake, two pink and two yellow.

ˌ**Battersea ˈDog's Home** /ˌbætəsiː; *AmE* ˌbætərsiː/ a temporary home for dogs in Battersea, London. Every year it finds new homes for about 12 000 dogs whose owners do not want them, and returns about 3 000 lost dogs to their owners.

ˌ**Battersea ˈPower ˌStation** /ˌbætəsiː; *AmE* ˌbætərsiː/ a very large building in Battersea, London, with four tall chimneys. It was built in 1937 to produce electricity for south London, but since it was closed down in the 1980s it has been completely empty. There are now plans to convert it into a very large cinema with many separate screens.

ˌ**Battery ˈPark** /ˌbætəri/ a park at the southern end of *Manhattan(1) Island, New York, opposite the *Statue of Liberty. Boats take tourists, etc. from the park to the statue, *Ellis Island and *Staten Island.

ˌ**Battle ˈCreek** /ˌbætl ˈkriːk/ a town in southern *Michigan, US, which is the centre of the breakfast cereal industry. The Kellogg Company has its main office there. See also KELLOGG'S.

The ˌ***Battle Hymn of the Reˈpublic*** an American religious song, written by Julia Ward *Howe for the North during the American *Civil War. It is sung to the tune of **John Brown's Body*. It was also used during marches for *civil rights in the 1960s and 1970s.

the ˌ**Battle of ˈBritain** the fighting between British and German planes over the south of England in the autumn of 1940. It was a very important battle in *World War II, because the British prevented the Germans from controlling the skies over Britain and the English Channel, and so stopped the German army from invading Britain. In a famous speech, Winston *Churchill said that 'never in the field of human conflict was so much owed by so many to so few'. The battle is remembered each year on **Battle of Britain Day** (15 September).

the ˌ**Battle of the Atˈlantic** /ətˈlæntɪk/ the long struggle for control of the Atlantic between the navies of Germany and the *Allies. The phrase can refer to this struggle in either of the two World Wars. In both wars, submarines and ships in the German navy attacked cargo ships bringing food and equipment from the US to Britain but, after some early successes, failed to stop the supplies getting through.

the ˌ**Battle of the ˈBoyne** /ˈbɔɪn/ a victory in Ireland in 1690 for the English king *William III over the *Jacobite armies of the former King *James II. About 35 000 Protestants under William defeated about 25 000 Irish and French Catholics near the Boyne river. The event is celebrated by Protestants in Northern Ireland on 12 July every year.

the ˌ**Battle of the ˈBulge** /ˈbʌldʒ/ a strong but unsuccessful attack by German forces against the *Allies in southern Belgium in 1944. The word *bulge* means a swelling, so the phrase is also used in a humorous way to mean a struggle to lose weight, e.g. by going on a diet: *I'm fighting the battle of the bulge.*

ˈ**battles** See also AGINCOURT, ARNHEM, BALACLAVA, BANNOCKBURN, BLENHEIM, BOSWORTH FIELD, BULL RUN, BUNKER HILL, CHANCELLORSVILLE, CONCORD, COPENHAGEN, CRÉCY, CULLODEN, EDGEHILL, EL ALAMEIN, FLODDEN, GETTYSBURG, GUADALCANAL, HASTINGS[1], LEXINGTON AND CONCORD, LITTLE BIGHORN, MARNE, MARSTON MOOR, MIDWAY, MOBILE BAY, MONS, NASEBY, NILE, PASSCHENDAELE, PLASSEY, PRESTONPANS, SAN JACINTO, SARATOGA, SEDGEMOOR, SHILOH, SOMME, STAMFORD BRIDGE 1, TRAFALGAR, VERDUN, WATERLOO[2], WORCESTER[2], YPRES.

ˌNora ˈ**Batty** /ˈbæti/ a female character in the humorous *BBC television series **Last of the Summer Wine*. People sometimes use her name to refer to a woman of middle age who is bad-tempered and rather ugly.

ˌ**Bay ˈCity** a popular name for *San Francisco.

the ˌ**Bayeux ˈTapestry** /ˌbaɪjɜː/ a finely decorated cloth wall covering made in the 11th century. It shows the events that led to the Battle of *Hastings (1066) between the *Normans under *William the Conqueror and the English under King *Harold II, and the death of King Harold. It is 74 yards (68

the Bayeux Tapestry: English foot soldiers facing a Norman attack metres) long and is kept in a museum at Bayeux in northern France.

ˌLilian ˈ**Baylis** /ˈbeɪlɪs/ (1874–1937) an English theatre manager. She ran the *Old Vic, famous for its *Shakespeare productions, and *Sadler's Wells, the home of the companies that later became the *Royal Ballet and the *English National Opera.

the ˌ**Bay of** ˈ**Pigs** a bay on the south-west coast of Cuba, where in 1961 about 1 500 Cuban exiles, supported by the US *CIA, landed in an attempt to end the rule of Fidel Castro. The attempt failed, causing great embarrassment to the US President John F *Kennedy and making Castro's position stronger than ever. See also CUBAN MISSILE CRISIS.

ˈ**Bayswater** /ˈbeɪzwɔːtə(r)/ a district in west London, England. It is between *Paddington and *Kensington Gardens and has many hotels.

ˈ***Baywatch*** /ˈbeɪwɒtʃ; *AmE* ˈbeɪwɑːtʃ/ a popular US television series about lifeguards (= people employed to rescue people who get into difficulty while swimming) on the coast of *California. People sometimes make fun of the series because they think the actors are chosen more for their attractive bodies than because they can act well. One of the best-known of these was Pamela Anderson (1967–).

Baˈ**zooka**™ *n* [U] a popular US make of bubble gum. Packets contain cards with pictures of baseball or other sports players on them, and these are collected and exchanged by young people. The older cards are becoming valuable. Bazooka was originally sold with a small *comic about a character called Bazooka Joe.

the **BBC** /ˌbiː biː ˈsiː / (*in full* the **British Broadcasting Corporation**) one of the main television and radio broadcasting organizations in Britain, paid for by the government since 1927 but free to choose the contents of its programmes. The head of the BBC has the title of 'director general'. ⇨ note at RADIO.

ˌ**BBC** ˈ**English** *n* [U] a form of English pronunciation that was traditionally associated with that used by *BBC news readers.

BBC1 /ˌbiː biː siː ˈwʌn/ the main television channel of the *BBC. Its programmes are mostly of general interest, e.g. light entertainment, news, sport, films and children's programmes.

Beachy Head before 1999

the ˈ**BBC** ˈ**Philharmonic** ˈ**Orchestra** the *BBC's main orchestra in the north of England. It has a strong reputation for its performances of 20th-century British music, which can often be heard on *Radio 3.

the ˌ**BBC** ˈ**Symphony** ˌ**Orchestra** the *BBC's main orchestra, whose concerts are broadcast on *Radio 3. It is well known as the orchestra that plays at the *Last Night of the Proms.

BBC2 /ˌbiː biː si ˈtuː/ the second television channel of the *BBC. Some of its programmes are more serious than those of *BBC1 and include plays, concerts and *Open University programmes.

ˌ**BBC** ˈ**World** an international news programme broadcast by the *BBC on satellite television.

the ˌ**BBC** ˈ**World** ˈ**Service** the service of English and foreign language radio programmes broadcast 24 hours a day to countries around the world by the *BBC from *Bush House in London. It began in 1932 and is highly regarded for its honesty and accuracy, especially in countries where broadcast news is controlled by the government.

BB gun /ˈbiːbiː/ *n* (*AmE*) a long, light gun that uses air power to fire small round metal balls. BB guns are usually the first guns given to older children when they are learning to shoot. They use them to fire at targets and to shoot small animals.

BCCI /ˌbiː siː siː ˈaɪ/ (*in full* **Bank of Credit and Commerce International**) a large private international bank, owned by Asians and with its head office in London, which had to close in 1991 with very large debts. It became clear that the bank had been run as a criminal activity, and many local government *councils and small Asian businesses in Britain lost most of the money that they had invested in the bank.

the ˈ**Beach Boys** a popular US pop group in the 1960s, many of whose songs were about enjoying life on the coast of *California, surfing and swimming in the sea. Their most successful songs included *I Get Around* (1964) and *Good Vibrations* (1966). They still sing and perform on stage, though one member of the original group, Carl Wilson, died in 1998.

ˌ**Beachy** ˈ**Head** /ˌbiːtʃi/ a high piece of land with steep white cliffs that sticks out into the sea on the south coast of England, between Eastbourne and *Brighton. In early 1999 a large part of it broke off and fell into the sea.

ˌ**Beacon** ˈ**Hill** an old, fashionable area of *Boston, *Massachusetts, US, where many rich families and politicians live.

ˌJeremy ˈ**Beadle** /ˈbiːdl/ (1948–) a British television entertainer who presents a programme in which people are shown in embarrassing or ridiculous situations. The programme often uses videos made by members of the public.

ˌ*HMS* ˈ***Beagle*** /ˈbiːgl/ the ship in which Charles *Darwin sailed to South America and the Galapagos Islands in 1831–6.

ˈ**Beale Street** /ˈbiːl/ a street in the US town of *Memphis, *Tennessee, famous for its African-American *blues music. There is a popular song called *The Beale Street Blues*.

ˌJudge Roy ˈ**Bean** /ˈbiːn/ (1825–1903) a US judge of the *Wild West known as 'the hanging judge' because he ordered many people to be hanged. He called himself 'the only law west of the Pecos (river)' and ran a careless and often humorous court of law in the town of Langtry, Texas.

The ˈ**Beano** /ˈbiːnəʊ; *AmE* ˈbiːnoʊ/ a popular British children's *comic which has been published every week since 1938. Its characters include The *Bash Street Kids, *Dennis the Menace, Ivy the Terrible and Minnie the Minx.

ˈ**Bean Town** a popular name for the US town of *Boston, *Massachusetts, because of its famous *Boston baked beans.

ˌJames ˈ**Beard** /ˈbɪəd; *AmE* ˈbɪrd/ (1903–85) a well-known US cook and writer of books and newspaper articles on food and cooking. In 1945 he became the first person to present a programme about cooking on American national television.

ˌAubrey ˈ**Beardsley** /ˈbɪədzli; *AmE* ˈbɪrdzli/ (1872–98) an English artist, best known for his book illustrations, mostly black and white, which were much influenced by the *Pre-Raphaelites and Japanese prints. His style, using long curved lines and a strong sense of visual design, was often openly erotic (= sexual) and considered shocking by many people. His best-known works are the illustrations for Oscar *Wilde's *Salome* and Thomas *Malory's **Morte d'Arthur*.

the Peacock Skirt, from Salome, *illustrated by Aubrey Beardsley*

ˈ**bear** ˌ**market** /ˈbeə; *AmE* ˈber/ *n* a situation at the stock exchange in which company share prices are falling rapidly. People who sell their shares, hoping to buy them back later at a lower price, are called **bears**. Compare BULL MARKET.

the ˌ**Beast of** ˈ**Bodmin** /ˈbɒdmɪn; *AmE* ˈbɑːdmɪn/ an animal that was seen occasionally on *Bodmin Moor in south-west England in the 1990s. Some people thought it was a big cat, such as a lion, that had escaped from a zoo. Others think that there was no Beast of Bodmin, and that people have simply seen large dogs in the fog.

the ˈ**beat gene**ˌ**ration** *n* [sing+ sing/pl *v*] a group of young people in the 1950s and early 1960s, especially writers and artists, who rejected the social values of their time. They tried to find a different style of living, becoming interested in eastern religions and new forms of writing. The movement began in the US and included such writers as Jack *Kerouac and Allen *Ginsberg: *The hippies just carried on where the beat generation left off.*

Audrey Hepburn, photographed by Cecil Beaton

ˌ**beating the** ˈ**bounds** an old custom, still kept in some parts of Britain, of marking the boundaries of a church *parish(1) by marching round them and hitting the ground, or certain boundary marks, with long sticks. The ceremony is performed once a year, usually on *Ascension Day or before *Easter.

ˌ**Beatle**ˈ**mania** /ˌbiːtlˈmeɪniə/ *n* [U] a word that was invented to describe the wild enthusiasm of the *Beatles' fans when they were very popular in the 1960s.

the ˈ**Beatles** /ˈbiːtlz/ an internationally famous British pop group whose members during their most successful period in the 1960s were John *Lennon, Paul *McCartney, George Harrison and Ringo Starr. The group, sometimes called the 'Fab Four' in the press, all came from *Liverpool, England. Most of their songs were written by Lennon and McCartney. After their first great success with *Please Please Me* in 1962, their records were regularly No. 1 hits in Britain and the US. In the late 1960s they became interested in eastern religions and drugs, and these influences appeared in their music. They separated in 1970 to follow individual careers. They have had more influence on the development of pop music than any other group. They also made several successful films.

ˌCecil ˈ**Beaton** /ˈbiːtn/ (1904–80) an English photographer and dress designer. He is best known for his photographs of famous people, especially the *royal family, and of fashion models, and for his costumes for films and the theatre. He was made a *knight in 1972.

ˌWarren ˈ**Beatty** /ˈbeɪti/ (1937–) a US film actor and director whose many films include *Bonnie and Clyde* (1967) and *McCabe and Mrs Miller* (1971). He received an *Oscar as 'Best Director' for *Reds* (1981). Beatty is

B

famous for having had affairs with many beautiful women. His sister is the actor Shirley *MacLaine.

ˌ**Beaujolais Nouˈveau** /ˌbəʊʒəleɪ nuːˈvəʊ; *AmE* ˌboʊʒəleɪ nuːˈvoʊ/ (*AmE also* ˌ**Beaujolais Priˈmeur** /ˌbəʊʒəleɪ priːˈmɜː(r); *AmE* ˌboʊʒəleɪ priːˈmɜːr/) *n* [U] standard Beaujolais wine that is exported from France each year just after it has been put in bottles. In Britain it is sold in *pubs, shops, etc. as a commercial attraction.

ˈ**Beaulieu** /ˈbjuːli/ a village in *Hampshire, England, which many tourists visit to see the *National Motor Museum. The museum has examples of all the important cars and motorcycles ever made in Britain, as well as rare vehicles such as **Bluebird*.

ˌFrancis ˈ**Beaumont** /ˈbəʊmɒnt; *AmE* ˈboʊmɑːnt/ (1584–1616) an English writer of plays, many of which he wrote with John *Fletcher. His best-known play is *The Knight of the Burning Pestle* (1607), which he probably wrote alone. He also helped Ben *Jonson to write several of his plays.

ˌ***Beauty and the ˈBeast*** a traditional story about a young girl who manages to save a monster from a magic spell by her love. He turns into a handsome prince and they get married. The phrase *beauty and the beast* is sometimes used to describe partners when one of them is much more attractive than the other.

ˌLord ˈ**Beaverbrook** /ˈbiːvəbrʊk; *AmE* ˈbiːvərbrʊk/ (*born* William Maxwell Aitken 1874–1964) a British newspaper owner and politician. He was born in Canada, but settled in Britain and became a *Member of Parliament in 1910. He was a *Cabinet minister in both World Wars. He bought the **Daily Express* and the **Evening Standard* and started the **Sunday Express*. He strongly influenced the policy and style of writing in these newspapers, introducing campaigns in them to try to make various ideas popular, such as his desire to preserve the *British Empire.

ˈ**Beaver Scout** (*also* **Beaver**) *n* a boy between six and eight years old who is a member of the most junior branch of the *Scouts.

ˌ**Beavis and ˈButt-head** /ˌbiːvɪs, ˈbʌthed/ a pair of US television cartoon characters who are very stupid and always behave in an unpleasant way.

Beavis and Butt-head

ˈ**bebop** /ˈbiːbɒp; *AmE* ˈbiːbɑːp/ (*also* **bop**) *n* [U] a type of *jazz music that was especially popular in the 1940s and 1950s. It emphasizes the creative playing of individual musicians in small groups. Famous players include 'Dizzy' *Gillespie, Charlie 'Bird' *Parker and Thelonious *Monk. The music became popular again in the 1990s because of musicians like the trumpet player Wynton *Marsalis.

ˌ**Becher's ˈBrook** /ˌbiːtʃəz ˈbrʊk; *AmE* ˌbiːtʃərz/ the most famous and one of the most difficult jumps on the *Grand National course, where many horses fall.

ˌSidney ˈ**Bechet** /ˈbeʃeɪ/ (1897–1959) a US *jazz musician who played the saxophone and the clarinet.

St ˌThomas ˈ**Becket** /ˈbekɪt/ (*also called* ˌ**Thomas à ˈBecket**) (*c.* 1118–70) an English saint. He was a close friend of King *Henry II, who made him chancellor (= senior law official) and later *Archbishop of Canterbury, hoping by doing this to be able to control the English Church. When Thomas resisted they quarrelled. According to tradition, Henry said, 'Who will rid me of this turbulent priest?' As a result four *knights murdered Becket in *Canterbury Cathedral, which became a place of pilgrimage where people travelled to show respect for the saint. His story was made into a play, *Murder in the Cathedral* (1935) by T S *Eliot.

ˌMargaret ˈ**Beckett**[1] /ˈbekɪt/ (1943–) a British *Labour politician. She became a *Member of Parliament in 1974 and held several important positions in the Labour *Shadow Cabinet, including a brief period as the acting leader of the party in 1994 after the death of John *Smith[8]. She lost the position after being defeated by Tony *Blair in an election later that year. In 1997 she became President of the Board of Trade and later Leader of the House of Commons.

ˌSamuel ˈ**Beckett**[2] /ˈbekɪt/ (1906–89) an Irish writer of plays, novels and poetry. He is best known for his plays, including **Waiting for Godot* (1952) and *Endgame* (1957). He settled in France early in his career and much of his work was written in French. He was given the *Nobel Prize for literature in 1969.

ˈ**Bedales** /ˈbiːdeɪlz/ Britain's oldest boarding school (= a school where the pupils live) for boys and girls, in *Hampshire, England. It began as a school for boys in 1893 and started to take girls in 1898.

ˌ**bed and ˈbreakfast 1** *n* [U] a bed for the night and breakfast the next morning in a hotel, pub or private house, paid for as a single service by the guest: *It's £50 for bed and breakfast or £80 for bed, breakfast and evening meal.* **2** *n* [C] (in Britain) a private house that provides bed and breakfast to paying guests. Bed and breakfasts are common throughout Britain and especially near the coast. They are cheaper than hotels and usually have a friendly atmosphere and provide a cooked *English breakfast: *We went to Cornwall for a week and stayed in a funny little bed and breakfast.*

Bede /biːd/ (*also called* **the** ˌ**Venerable** ˈ**Bede**) (*c.* 673–735) an English monk and historian. At his monastery in *Jarrow in north-east England, he wrote many books, the most important of which, *Ecclesiastical History of the English People*, written in Latin, was the first serious work of English history.

ˈ**Bedfordshire** /ˈbedfədʃə(r); *AmE* ˈbedfərdʃər/ (*written abbr* **Beds**) a county in southern central England. Its administrative centre is Bedford.

ˈ**Bedlam** /ˈbedləm/ (formerly) a popular name for the Hospital of St Mary of Bethlehem in London. It was established as a priory (= a small Christian religious community) in 1274, and in the 14th century it became a place for mentally ill people, who were then called 'lunatics'. People used to come and watch the patients and be entertained by their disturbed condition. From this the word *bedlam* has come to mean a scene of noisy confusion: *The teacher's whistle could not be heard above the bedlam in the playground.*

ˈ**bedsit** (*also* ˌ**bedˈsitter**) *n* (in Britain) a flat consisting of one room, used for living and sleeping in. Bedsits are usually rooms in large old houses that have been divided into flats, and are rented mainly by people who live alone, such as students. An area of a town where many houses have been made into bedsits is sometimes called **bedsit-land** or **bedsitter-land**: *He learned to cook in his first bedsit.*

the **Beeb** /biːb/ (*BrE*) an informal name for the *BBC.

ˌThomas ˈ**Beecham** /ˈbiːtʃəm/ (1879–1961) an English conductor who established two of the great London orchestras, the *London Philharmonic and the *Royal Philharmonic, and helped to make the British music of his time, especially the music of his friend *Delius, more popular. He was also famous for making intelligent, funny and sometimes unkind remarks. He was made a *knight in 1916.

ˌ**Beecham's ˈpills**™ /ˌbiːtʃəmz/ *n* [pl] a popular British medicine for minor illnesses like colds, headaches, etc. They were first produced in 1847 by the grandfather of Sir Thomas *Beecham. The medicine is also available in powder form, called **Beecham's powders**.

ˈ**beefeater** *n* a popular name for a *Yeoman Warder of the *Tower of London.

ˌ**beef ˈolives** *n* [pl] a traditional British dish consisting of thin slices of beef wrapped around a herb stuffing and baked.

the ˈ**beef war** *n* an informal name, used especially in the press, for the discussions and arguments about beef between Britain and its partners in the *European Union in the 1990s, when the European Union countries refused to buy beef or any other products of British cows after many of them were found to have the disease *BSE.

the ˈ**Bee Gees** /ˈbiː dʒiːz/ a British pop group consisting of three brothers, Barry, Robin and Maurice Gibb. Their most successful records have included *Massachusetts* (1967), *I've Gotta Get a Message to You* (1968), *How Deep is Your Love* (1977) and *You Win Again* (1987). They also wrote and performed the music for the film *Saturday Night Fever* (1978).

beer

In Britain, beer is the most popular alcoholic drink which is drunk in *pubs. Many people drink **bitter**, a brown-coloured beer. It is sold **on draught**, if it is drawn for each customer from a large container, usually a **keg** or **barrel**, or **bottled**, if it has been put in small bottles at a factory. Bottled beer is sometimes called **ale**. Bitter is usually drunk at room temperature. **Lager**, which is yellow in colour, has more gas in it and is usually drunk cold. Many pubs sell a selection of French, German and Australian lagers. **Stout** is a strong, dark brown beer which forms a thick white froth, or 'head', on top when poured into a glass. Two of the most popular makes are *Guinness and Murphy's. **Mild** is a sweeter, darker form of bitter but is less popular. **Shandy** is a mixture of beer and lemonade or ginger beer. Draught beer or lager is sold in **pints** or **half-pints**. Some people drink **low-alcohol** beers and lagers in order to reduce the risk of **drink-driving** (= driving a car while under the influence of alcohol), which is against the law. Many people like to drink **real ale**, which is often stronger than keg beer and made by smaller **breweries** (= companies that make beer). The interests of real ale drinkers are defended by ***CAMRA**, the Campaign for Real Ale, which publishes a list of **real-ale pubs**.

At home some people drink **homebrew**, beer they have made themselves using a special **beer kit**. Many people buy bottled beer or **six-packs** (= packs of six) from supermarkets and **off-licences** (= shops officially allowed to sell alcohol).

Originally, beer was a drink of the lower classes in Britain. Today, although beer has fewer class associations, it is still unusual for it to be drunk in smart restaurants. There, people generally drink wine or spirits. Lager is popular with young people and this gave rise to the term **lager lout**, a young man who behaves badly when drunk. Until relatively recently few women drank beer, or even went in to pubs, but attitudes have changed over the years, and now many women drink lager or bitter.

The US **brewing** industry was begun by Germans who moved to the US, and so the typical US beer has always been like German beer, light in colour, similar to what the British call lager, although Americans do not use that word. Until the beginning of the 20th century there were many small, family-run breweries in the US, but then ***Prohibition** came into effect and it became illegal to sell alcohol. By the time Prohibition was cancelled most of the small breweries had gone out of business. Today, most beer is produced by a few large breweries, all of whom make similar products. Recently, however, Americans have begun to appreciate different sorts of beer and many **microbreweries** have opened. These brew and serve high quality beer made in traditional ways. This movement has even led some of the large breweries to return to traditional methods and materials. The microbrewery movement has been supported largely by professional people with a high income but, in general, beer is seen as a drink for people with less money, or for informal occasions. People drink beer after playing sports or while watching them, but wine is considered more appropriate to drink with a meal.

Many makes of beer in the US are sold in both bottles and cans, though microbrewery beers come only in bottles. Restaurants always serve bottled beer. In some states beer can be sold in supermarkets, gas stations and local convenience stores (= shops that are open for many hours each day). In other states it can be sold only in specially licensed **liquor stores** or **bottle shops**. This can be confusing and even embarrassing for Americans when they travel to a different state, as well as for foreign visitors.

ˌMax ˈ**Beerbohm** /ˈbɪəbəʊm; *AmE* ˈbɪrboʊm/ (1872–1956) a British humorous writer who also drew caricatures (= exaggerated comic pictures) of well-known people in the artistic world. His best-known novel is *Zuleika Dobson* (1911), set in *Oxford during the 1890s. He was made a *knight in 1939.

Max Beerbohm: self-portrait

ˈ**beer ˌgarden** *n* **1** (in Britain) the garden of a pub where customers can sit in fine weather to eat the food and drink the beer, etc. that they have bought in the pub. **2** (in the US) a place where beer, etc. is served at outdoor events such as county fairs. ⇨ article at PUBS.

ˈ**Beer Nuts**™ *n* [pl] a product name for a popular US snack food (= one eaten quickly between meals). They are peanuts in their skins, treated to make them 'slightly sweet, slightly salty', according to the advertisements for them.

ˈ**beer tent** *n* (*BrE*) a large tent, often open at one side, where drinks are served at an outdoor sporting event or entertainment such as a *cricket match.

ˈ**Beetle**™ /ˈbiːtl/ *n* the English name for the original Volkswagen small car with a rounded design. In the US it is also called the **bug**: *Her first car was a Beetle.*

ˌMrs ˈ**Beeton** /ˈbiːtn/ (Isabella Mary Mayson Beeton 1836–65) the British writer of *the Book of Household Management* (1861), a famous book on cooking and running a household, which gives much information

a Beetle

about 19th-century life in the home: *According to Mrs Beeton, we should cook it with cream.*

BEF /ˌbiː iː ˈef/ ⇨ BRITISH EXPEDITIONARY FORCE.

*The ˌ**Beggar's** ˈ**Opera*** an opera (1728) by John *Gay, in which the songs are set to the popular tunes of the time. The main character is Macheath, a highwayman (= a person who robs travellers), and many of the other characters are criminals. The opera was written as a humorous comment on the dishonest government of the day. *The Threepenny Opera* (1928) by Bertold Brecht and Kurt Weill was based on *The Beggar's Opera*.

ˈˌBix' ˈ**Beiderbecke** /ˌbɪks ˈbaɪdəbek; *AmE* ˈbaɪdərbek/ (1903–31) a US *jazz musician and composer who played the cornet (= a type of small trumpet) and the piano. He was chosen for the Jazz *Hall of Fame in 1962.

ˌHarry **Belaˈfonte** /beləˈfɒnti; *AmE* beləˈfɑːnti/ (1927–) an African-American singer and actor who became famous in the 1950s singing calypso songs (= West Indian songs in African rhythm, often about subjects of current interest). His most successful song was *The Banana Boat Song* (1956). He was a star of the film *Island in the Sun* (1957) and in 1960 he became the first African-American to win an *Emmy award.

Alexander Graham Bell making the first telephone call from New York to Chicago, 1892

Belˈfast /belˈfɑːst, ˈbelfɑːst; *AmE* belˈfæst, ˈbelfæst/ the capital city of Northern Ireland. Its main industries are making ships and aircraft, but many people are unemployed and the city has suffered greatly in recent times from the *Troubles. Two streets are often mentioned in the news, the Falls Road where mainly *Roman Catholic people live, and the *Shankhill Road, which is mainly Protestant.

the ˌ*General **Belˈgrano*** /belˈgrɑːnəʊ; *AmE* belˈgrɑːnoʊ/ an Argentinian ship that was attacked and sunk by the British during the *Falklands War. The British government was widely criticized for ordering the attack because the *Belgrano* was sailing away from the Falklands when it happened.

Belˈgravia /belˈgreɪviə/ a fashionable and expensive area of London, near *Buckingham Palace and around Belgrave Square.

Beˌlisha ˈbeacon /bəˌliːʃə/ *n* (in Britain) a black and white post with an orange flashing light on top, marking a *zebra crossing (= a place in a street where people may walk across the road). Belisha beacons are named after Leslie Hore-Belisha, the Minister of Transport when they were introduced.

Beˈlize /beˈliːz/ a country in Central America, on the Caribbean Sea, that used to be a British colony called **British Honduras**. It became independent and joined the Commonwealth in 1981. Its main industries are sugar and wood production, and it has an important tourist industry. ▶ **Belizian** *adj*, *n*.

Aleˈxander ˈGraham ˈ**Bell**[1] /ˈbel/ (1847–1922) a scientist and inventor who is best known for inventing the telephone. He was born in Scotland but from 1872 lived in the US, where he later started the **Bell Telephone Company** which became one of the largest companies in America.

ˌMartin ˈ**Bell**[2] /ˈbel/ (1938–) an English journalist and politician. He joined the *BBC as a television news reporter in 1965 and is remembered especially for his reports during the wars in Yugoslavia and elsewhere. In 1997 he was elected as an independent *Member of Parliament for Tatton in Cheshire. His opponent in the election was the *Conservative candidate, Neil Hamilton, who had been accused of dishonestly taking money to ask questions in the *House of Commons. See also CASH FOR QUESTIONS.

ˈ***Bella*** /ˈbelə/ a British magazine for women that contains articles on health, beauty, fashion, food and other subjects. It first appeared in 1987 and is published every week.

ˌDavid ˈ**Bellamy** /ˈbeləmi/ (1933–) an English scientist who appears regularly on television in programmes of popular science. He is particularly interested in the protection of the environment and in preserving wild life of all kinds.

David Bellamy

*La ˈ**Belle** ˈ**Dame Sans Merˈci*** /ˈbel ˈdæm sɑ̃ː meəˈsiː; *AmE* merˈsiː/ one of the best-known poems by John *Keats about a *knight who falls in love with a beautiful woman with magic powers. He dreams that he is with her in the countryside, but wakes up alone and sad.

ˌHilaire ˈ**Belloc** /ˌhɪleə ˈbelɒk; *AmE* ˌhɪler ˈbelɑːk/ (1870–1953) a British author, born in France. He wrote books of various different kinds, including biographies and travel books, but he is mainly remembered for his humorous poetry, especially *The*

Bad Child's Book Of Beasts (1896) and *Cautionary Tales* (1907).

ˌSaul ˈ**Bellow** /ˌsɔːl ˈbeləʊ; *AmE* ˈbeloʊ/ (1915–) a US writer of novels, born in Canada. His books often relate to his Jewish background and many are very humorous. They include *The Adventures of Augie March* (1953), *Herzog* (1964) and *The Actual* (1997). He was given the *Nobel Prize for literature in 1976.

bells and bell-ringing

Bells hung high in the towers of *churches are rung to announce church services. In Britain the sound of church bells from a **belfry** is associated with Sunday mornings and with *weddings. Bells throughout the country may also be rung at times of national celebration. Before minor services or to announce a funeral (= a service for a dead person), a single bell is usually sounded repeatedly for five or ten minutes. The blessing of the bread and wine at a Communion service may also be indicated by the sounding of a bell.

Churches usually have between 5 and 12 bells, which are rung by teams of **bell-ringers**. The ringers stand far below the bells and each pulls on a long rope attached to a bell in such a way that the bell swings over in a circle, causing the **clapper** inside the bell to strike the side. In a peal each of the bells is rung in turn, and the order in which they are rung changes according to a pattern. This is called **change-ringing**. Complicated tunes can be played and many **changes** have their own name, e.g. *Grandsire Triples* and *Oxford Treble Bob*.

Other types of institution also use bells: Great Tom, the big bell at Christ Church College, Oxford, is rung 101 times each night, indicating the original number of scholars at the college. The most famous bell in Britain is Big Ben, the large bell in the clock tower next to the *Houses of Parliament in London, which **chimes** the hours and which has traditionally been heard on radio and television.

Bell-ringing used to be a popular hobby though it is now sometimes necessary to use a recording of bells before church services because of a shortage of bell-ringers. Some people complain about the noise of bells but most people like the sound.

America's experience with bells did not begin well, since the nation's *Liberty Bell cracked in 1752. Bells are heard in churches and at colleges and universities. Some communities, especially in *New England, ring bells as a celebration. In 1997, however, police arrested six people in Brookline, *New Hampshire, after they rang church bells at midnight before *Independence Day. Though this is a New England tradition, some people in Brookline had complained about the noise. Bells are also used to announce the time, mostly using the eight notes of Big Ben.

bell-ringers in a church

The US has no traditional bell-ringers as in Britain. Instead, many institutions have **carillon bells**, a group of up to 70 bells controlled from a keyboard like that of an organ. Carillon bells can play tunes and simple harmonies. The 50 bells of the Allen & Perkins Carillon at Duke University in *North Carolina were first used to play songs in 1932. Other well-known carillons include the Sather Tower Carillon at the University of California at *Berkeley. Few of the bells are made in the US and most are imported from Britain.

the ˌ**Belmont** ˈ**Stakes** /ˌbelmɒnt; *AmE* ˌbelmɑːnt/ a horse race run at Belmont Park near New York City. It was first run in 1867 and is one of the races that form the US *triple crown. The horses in the race must be three years old.

ˈ**beltway** *n* (*AmE*) a ring road (= a road built around a town to reduce traffic in the centre). The expression *inside the beltway* is used to describe affairs at the centre of Washington politics.

the **Bench** the place where the judge sits in a court of law. It is also used to refer to the judge in a court, or to judges in general: *The prisoner was told to address his remarks to the Bench.*

the ˈ**Benefits** ˌ**Agency** (in Britain) the organization within the *Department of Social Security responsible for paying money from the State to people who are unemployed, old, sick, etc. from its many offices around the country.

ˈ**benefit so**ˌ**ciety** ⇨ FRIENDLY SOCIETY.

ˈStephen ˈVincent **Beˈnét** /bəˈneɪ/ (1898–1943) a US writer of poems and novels. He received a *Pulitzer Prize for his best-known poem *John Brown's Body* (1928), about the American Civil War. His brother, William Benét (1886–1950) was also a successful poet.

BenˈGay™ /benˈɡeɪ/ *n* [U] a US make of ointment put on the body to help relieve pain in the muscles and joints. It can be bought without a doctor's permission and is produced by Pfizer Inc.

ˌ***Ben-ˈHur*** /ˌben ˈhɜː(r)/ a novel (1880) by Lew *Wallace about the early days of Christianity. It has twice been made into a film. The second of these, made in 1959 with Charlton *Heston, won 11 *Oscars. The story is about Ben-Hur, a young Jew who meets Jesus and is converted to Christianity after many adventures.

ˌTony ˈ**Benn** /ˈben/ (1925–) a British *Labour politician, famous for his left-wing views, who has had important positions in two Labour governments. He first became a *Member of Parliament in 1950. He is the son of a *viscount(1) and when his father died the title legally passed to him, so he was unable to continue in the *House of Commons. He refused to accept the title and started a campaign to introduce a law allowing people with such titles to give them up if they wished. It was made a law in 1963, and Benn returned to the House of Commons. His full name is Anthony Wedgwood Benn but he has chosen the shorter form, preferring to be seen as a man of the people.

ˌAlan ˈ**Bennett**[1] /ˈbenɪt/ (1934–) an writer and actor, well known for his humorous yet sympathetic plays, especially on television, about the lives of ordinary people. He first made his name in **Beyond the Fringe*. His best-known work is probably the series of television monologues (= plays written for one character) called *Talking Heads* (1988 and 1998).

ˌArnold ˈ**Bennett**[2] /ˈbenɪt/ (1867–1931) an English writer of novels, most of which are set in the *Potteries and describe the life of working people in great detail. His best-known works are *Anna of the Five Towns* (1902) and the *Clayhanger* series (1902–8).

B

ˈRichard ˈRodney **ˈBennett**[3] /ˈbenɪt/ (1936–) an English composer, best known for his operas *The Mines of Sulphur* (1965) and *Victory* (1970). He was made a *knight in 1998.

ˌTony **ˈBennett**[4] /ˈbenɪt / (1926–) a US singer with an easy style whose career began in the 1940s. He received a *Grammy award in 1962 for his famous song *I Left My Heart in San Francisco*. He has won a total of four Grammy awards, two of them in 1994 (at the age of 68) for his album *MTV Unplugged*.

ˌJack **ˈBenny** /ˈbeni/ (1894–1974) a popular US comedian who appeared mainly on television and radio. Many of his jokes were based on the idea that he was very mean. He also made people laugh by pretending to play the violin very badly.

ˌ**Benson and ˈHedges**™ /ˌbensən, ˈhedʒɪz/ a British company that makes cigarettes and sponsors (= pays for) certain sports events such as *cricket and *snooker competitions: *Once again Lancashire are through to the Benson and Hedges Cup final.*

ˌJeremy **ˈBentham** /ˈbenθəm, *also* ˈbentəm/ (1748–1832) a English philosopher who believed that society's aim should be 'the greatest happiness for the greatest number' and argued that laws should be changed to produce this. His ideas had a great influence on 19th-century thought.

▶ **Benthamism** *n* [U] the philosophy of Jeremy Bentham. **Benthamite** *n, adj.*

ˈBentley[1] /ˈbentli/ *n* an expensive British make of car, made by the *Rolls-Royce company: *The chauffeur was waiting in the Bentley.*

ˈEdmund ˈClerihew **ˈBentley**[2] /ˈklerɪhju: ˈbentli/ (1875–1956) a English journalist who wrote *detective stories and invented a form of comic verse with four lines, now called a **clerihew** after his middle name. Clerihews are usually about well-known people. A typical example is

John Stuart Mill
By a mighty effort of will
Overcame his natural bonhomie
And wrote 'Principles of Political Economy'.

ˌ**Bentley and ˈCraig** /ˌbentli, ˈkreɪg/ a famous British legal case. In 1952 two young men, Derek Bentley and Christopher Craig, were caught on a roof in south London by the police, who believed they were involved in a crime. Craig shot and killed a policeman after Bentley had shouted, 'Let him have it!' (which could mean either 'Give him the gun!' or 'Shoot him!'). Britain still had *capital punishment at the time, and Bentley, who was 19 but had a mental age of 11, was hanged. Craig, who was 16, was sent to prison. Bentley's family continued to argue that he should not have been executed, and in 1998 the *Court of Appeal finally pardoned him.

ˈBenzedrine™ /ˈbenzədri:n/ *n* [U] (*also infml* **benny** [U, C]) a make of amphetamine (= a drug that makes people feel lively and excited) that is sometimes taken illegally. It was very popular with the *beat generation.

ˈ*Beowulf* /ˈbeɪəwʊlf/ a long poem in *Old English, probably written in the 8th century. It tells how the hero Beowulf kills two monsters and finally dies killing a third. It was the first major European poem that was not written in Latin or Greek.

Beˈretta /bəˈretə/ a US make of small gun that is held in the hand.

ˌIngrid **ˈBergman** /ˈbɜ:gmən; *AmE* ˈbɜ:rgmən/ (1915–82) a Swedish actor who went to America and appeared in many *Hollywood films, including **Casablanca* (1942). She shocked US society by leaving her husband to have a child with the Italian film director Roberto Rossellini, and made most of her later films in Europe.

the ˌ**Bering ˈStrait** /ˌbeərɪŋ; *AmE* ˌberɪŋ/ the narrow passage of water between *Alaska and Russia. It connects the **Bering Sea**, the most northern part of the Pacific Ocean, with the Arctic Ocean. The Bering Strait and the Bering Sea are named after the Danish explorer Vitus Jonassen Bering (1681–1741).

ˈBerkeley[1] /ˈbɜ:kli; *AmE* ˈbɜ:rkli/ a city on *San Francisco Bay in *California, US. It has the largest branch of the University of California. In the 1960s and 1970s protests by students at Berkeley influenced other student movements in America.

ˌBusby **ˈBerkeley**[2] /ˌbʌzbi ˈbɜ:kli; *AmE* ˈbɜ:rkli/ (1895–1976) a US film and stage director and choreographer. He is best remembered for his grand music and dance sequences involving many actors, in such films as *42nd Street* (1933).

Busby Berkeley with dancers in 42nd Street

ˌLennox **ˈBerkeley**[3] /ˌlenəks ˈbɑ:kli; *AmE* ˈbɑ:rkli/ (1903–89) an English composer whose work was much influenced by Benjamin *Britten. He wrote a wide variety of music, but is best known for his chamber works (= music for a small orchestra) and some fine modern religious pieces. He was made a *knight in 1974.

ˌ**Berkeley ˈSquare** /ˌbɑ:kli; *AmE* ˈbɑ:rkli/ a square in west central London that still has several of its original 18th-century buildings. It is mentioned in the song *A Nightingale Sang in Berkeley Square*, written in 1940 and still popular.

the **Berkshires** /ˈbɜ:kʃəz; *AmE* ˈbɜ:rkʃərz/ (*also* the **Berkshire Hills**) a range of hills in the western part of the US state of *Massachusetts. It is an area of beautiful woods that are popular with tourists.

ˌMilton **ˈBerle** /ˌmɪltən ˈbɜ:l; *AmE* ˈbɜ:rl/ (1908–) a US comedian known as 'Mister Television'. He became the first national television star in the 1950s with his programme *Texaco Star Theater.*

ˌIrving **Berˈlin**[1] /ˌɜ:vɪŋ bɜ:ˈlɪn; *AmE* ˌɜ:rvɪŋ bɜ:rˈlɪn/ (1888–1989) a US writer of popular songs, born in Russia. Although he had little technical skill, he wrote over 100 songs. Many of his greatest successes, like *White Christmas* (1942), were written for *Hollywood films. He also wrote **God Bless America* (1918).

Iˌsaiah **Berˈlin**[2] /aɪˌzaɪə bɜ:ˈlɪn; *AmE* bɜ:rˈlɪn/ (1909–97) a British writer and philosopher, born in Russia. He is best known for his books about Russian literature and thought, such as *The Hedgehog and the Fox* (1953) about Tolstoy. He was made a *knight in 1957 and a member of the *Order of Merit in 1971.

ˈ**Bermondsey** /ˈbɜːmənzi; *AmE* ˈbɜːrmənzi/ a traditional *working-class area of south-east London, on the south bank of the *Thames near *Tower Bridge. Formerly, many people living in Bermondsey worked in the docks, loading and unloading ships. It now has a reputation for poverty and racial tension, though attempts are being made to change the character of the area by building expensive flats, restaurants, etc.

Berˈmuda /bəˈmjuːdə; *AmE* bərˈmjuːdə/ a British colony in the west Atlantic, consisting of a large number of small islands. It has an important tourist industry. The capital city is Hamilton. ▶ **Bermudian** *adj, n.*

Berˌmuda ˈshorts /bəˌmjuːdə; *AmE* bərˌmjuːdə/ (*also* **Bermudas**) *n* [pl] short trousers, usually with a colourful design, that reach down to the knees. They are usually worn in warm weather: *He wore sunglasses, a red shirt and flowered Bermuda shorts.*

the **Berˌmuda ˈTriangle** /bəˌmjuːdə; *AmE* bərˌmjuːdə/ an area of the Atlantic Ocean between *Bermuda and *Florida that is thought to be dangerous because of the number of ships and planes that have disappeared there in a mysterious way.

ˌElmer ˈ**Bernstein[1]** /ˌelmə ˈbɜːnstaɪn; *AmE* ˌelmər ˈbɜːrnstaɪn/ (1922–) a US composer, especially of music for films. His successes include *The Magnificent Seven* (1960), *To Kill A Mockingbird* (1962) and *The Age of Innocence* (1993).

ˌLeonard ˈ**Bernstein[2]** /ˈbɜːnstaɪn; *AmE* ˈbɜːrnstaɪn/ (1918–90) a US conductor, composer and piano player. He wrote several popular *musicals. The most successful was *West Side Story* (1957) which became a film in 1961. He also wrote more serious works for orchestras and choirs.

ˈˌYogi' ˈ**Berra** /ˌjəʊgi ˈberə; *AmE* ˌjoʊgi/ (1925–) a US baseball player and manager. He played in 14 *World Series. He is famous for saying things which make no sense or use language in a ridiculous way, e.g. 'No wonder nobody comes here – it's too crowded.'

ˈˌChuck' ˈ**Berry** /ˌtʃʌk ˈberi/ (1926–) an African-American *rock and roll singer and writer of songs whose style has influenced many other musicians, including the *Beatles and Bob *Dylan.

ˌ**Bertram** ˈ**Mills** /ˌbɜːtrəm ˈmɪlz; *AmE* ˌbɜːrtrəm/ a popular British circus which regularly travelled round the country between 1920 and 1966. One of its most famous attractions was Coco the clown.

ˌ**Beryl the** ˈ**Peril** a character in a British children's *comic, *The *Dandy*. She often gets into trouble.

ˌHenry ˈ**Bessemer** /ˈbesɪmə(r)/ (1813–98) an English engineer and inventor, best known for inventing the **Bessemer process**, a way of making steel by blowing air through melted iron to remove the other substances from it. He was made a *knight in 1879.

Best /best/ a British magazine for women that contains articles on health, fashion, sex, food and other subjects. It first appeared in 1987 and is published every week.

ˌGeorge ˈ**Best** /ˈbest/ (1946–) a football player from Northern Ireland who played for *Manchester United (1963–73) and Northern Ireland. He was a skilful and exciting attacking player, and many people think that he was one of the best players of all time. During his career he was also well known for going to nightclubs with beautiful women, and for drinking too much: *After Giggs's first few games they were already calling him 'the new George Best'.*

ˌ**Bethnal** ˈ**Green** /ˌbeθnəl/ an area of east London, at the centre of the *East End. It was once a traditional *cockney area but it is now the home of one of the largest Bengali communities in Britain.

ˌJohn ˈ**Betjeman** /ˈbetʃəmən/ (1906–84) an English poet who wrote humorous popular verse about ordinary people and social situations. He was also well known for his interest in *Victorian(1) architecture and his campaigns to preserve Victorian buildings. His best-known work is *Summoned by Bells* (1960), a long poem about his own life. He was made a *knight in 1969 and *Poet Laureate in 1972.

John Betjeman

ˈ***Better*** ˌ***Homes and*** ˈ***Gardens*** a US magazine that gives advice on how to decorate homes and create beautiful gardens. It also includes articles about food, health and other information for families.

betting and gambling

About £13 billion is spent in Britain each year on **betting** and **gambling** and about £1 billion of this goes in tax to the government. Half of the £13 billion is bet on horse and *greyhound races. The *Grand National attracts millions of pounds in bets, as people who otherwise never bet **have a flutter** of a few pounds on this race. People who go to the races bet at the course but many bets are placed by telephone or in person at licensed high-street betting shops called **bookmakers** or **turf accountants** or, informally, **bookies**. Bookmakers accept bets on a wide range of sports, and also on many other events such as the results of an election. It is a tradition to bet on the chances of there being a white *Christmas, i.e. whether any snow will fall in London on Christmas Day.

A popular form of betting in Britain used to be the **football pools**. **Doing the *pools** involves trying to predict the results of football matches and what the scores will be. The amount of money bet on the pools has fallen considerably since the ***National Lottery** started. About 70% of the population buys lottery tickets and watches the Wednesday and Saturday lottery **draws** on television to see if they have won the **jackpot** (= a big prize). Many people also buy **Instants**, ***scratchcards** which, when the surface is scratched off, show if the buyer has won a prize. Relatively few British people go to **casinos** or play cards for money. Many more play on **gaming machines** and **fruit machines** in *pubs or amusement arcades. ***Bingo** clubs are also popular, especially with older women.

Betting was first taken to America by European settlers. They bet on sports events, the weather, politics, *billiards and card games, and betting was a major activity by both armies during the *Civil War. *Louisiana formally passed laws making gambling legal in 1812 and *Nevada in 1931. This allowed *Las Vegas to become the gambling centre of the US, and more than 40% of Nevada's taxes now come from gambling. The state of *New Jersey made casinos legal in 1977, and *Atlantic City has become America's second city for gambling. Many casinos are operated by *Native Americans on reservations and there are many in *Wisconsin. Casino bets can be placed on games like keno, bingo, roulette and card games like baccarat. Slot machines are also very popular, as well as video poker.

Gambling is legal in only 37 states but in 1995 Americans spent a total of $40 billion on bets. Most of this was spent on lotteries supported by state governments. About 125 million Americans also visited casinos. It is estimated that in 1994 about $40 billion was spent on illegal bets, and 18 000 people were arrested for this. In 1998 the *FBI arrested managers of companies which take bets over the Internet, because **cyberspace gambling** is also illegal. A 1996 *Gallup Poll found that, although 75% of Americans approved of lotteries, only 40% wanted casinos.

Americans also bet on sports. Horse racing is popular and, as in Britain, bets are taken at the track and, in some states, off-track by bookmakers. There are many types of bet: a **side bet**, for instance, is one that predicts which team will win. This is placed **against the spread**, which is the number of points the **odds makers** believe one team will win by. Another type of bet is the **total bet**, also called the **over/under** bet, that predicts the total number of points both teams will score.

Betting and gambling are fiercely opposed by some religious groups and by people who believe that they cause people to get into debt. Many British people were worried that the introduction of the National Lottery would make gambling much more widespread and this seems to have happened. In 1996–7 £4.7 billion was spent on the lottery. In America those against gambling include the National Council of Churches and the *Mormons. A study in *Minnesota estimated that **compulsive gamblers** cost the state $200 million a year in lost income, bad debts and crime. Gamblers Anonymous was established in the US in 1957 to help people addicted to gambling, and a British branch was founded in 1964.

ˌ**Betty** ˈ**Boop** /ˈbuːp/ a popular US cartoon character created by Max Fleischer. She was often shown wearing a very short skirt. The cartoon began in 1915 and was based on Helen Kane, who was called the 'boop-a-doop' singer.

ˌ**Betty** ˈ**Crocker**™ /ˈkrɒkə(r); *AmE* ˈkrɑːkər/ the name of an imaginary woman used since 1922 for a popular US book on cooking. *Betty Crocker's New Cookbook* was published in 1997. Several Betty Crocker food products are also made by the General Mills Company.

Aˌneurinˈ**Bevan** /əˌnaɪrɪn ˈbevn/ (1897–1960) a British *Labour politician, born in Wales. He started work as a coal miner before becoming a trade unionist and politician. As minister of health (1945–51) he was responsible for introducing the *National Health Service. He was well known for his left-wing views and for his skill as a public speaker.

the ˈ**Beveridge Re**ˌ**port** /ˈbevərɪdʒ/ a report about social conditions in Britain produced in 1942 by a committee led by the economist William Beveridge (1879–1963). It led to the *welfare state being created.

The ˌ***Beverly*** ˈ***Hillbillies*** /ˌbevəli ˈhɪlbɪliz; *AmE* ˌbevərli/ a successful US comedy television programme in the 1960s. It was about a poor family that become rich and go to live in fashionable *Beverly Hills The characters were Jed Clampett, 'Granny' Moses, Jethro Bodine and Elly May Clampett.

ˌ**Beverly** ˈ**Hills** /ˌbevəli; *AmE* ˌbevərli/ a fashionable town in the US state of *California. It is surrounded by *Los Angeles but is not part of it. It is expensive and many people living there are film stars. Its most famous street for shopping is *Rodeo Drive.

ˌErnest ˈ**Bevin** /ˈbevɪn/ (1881–1951) a British *trade union leader and *Labour politician. He established the *TGWU and became its leader. During *World War II he was minister of labour and national service. Later, as foreign secretary (1945–51), he played an important part in creating *NATO.

ˈ**Bevin boys** /ˈbevɪn/ *n* [pl] (*infml*) the young British men who were sent to work in coal mines instead of joining the armed forces during *World War II, when Ernest *Bevin was minister of labour and national service.

ˌThomas ˈ**Bewick** /ˈbjuːɪk/ (1753–1828) an English artist who worked mainly in book illustrations. He brought a new realistic style to the art of engraving (= cutting or carving designs on metal, stone, etc). He is especially famous for his pictures of animals and birds. His best-known works are *A General History of Quadrupeds* (1790) and the *History of British Birds* in two volumes (1797–1804).

the coal tit, a woodcut by Thomas Bewick

Beˌ***yond the*** ˈ***Fringe*** a British satirical comedy show, written and performed by Alan *Bennett, Peter *Cook, Jonathan *Miller and Dudley *Moore. It was first performed at the *Edinburgh Festival in 1960, and then moved successfully to the *West End and *Broadway. It had a strong influence on later British comedy.

the **BFI** /ˌbiː ef ˈaɪ/ (*in full* the **British Film Institute**) an organization established in 1933 to encourage people to make films in Britain. It gives government money to people making films, and has a large library of film scripts and books about films. It also runs the *National Film Theatre.

BhS /ˌbiː eɪtʃ ˈes/ any of a group of shops in Britain selling clothes and goods for the home, such as lights, curtains, etc. The shops used to be called British Home Stores, but the name was changed in 1986.

the ˈ**Bible Belt** a name sometimes used to describe the US *Deep South and parts of the Midwest because many people there are religious Protestants who follow the words of the Bible very closely.

ˈ**bicycle shed** (*also infml* ˈ**bike shed**) *n* a small building, open on one side, where bicycles are kept in a school or park. In Britain, people sometimes refer humorously to things that happen *behind the bike shed*, since this is an area of many schools where students do things secretly, such as smoking or sexual behaviour.

ˌAmbrose ˈ**Bierce** /ˌæmbrəʊz ˈbɪəs; *AmE* ˌæmbroʊz ˈbɪrs/ (1842–*c*. 1914) a US journalist who wrote realistic but satirical short stories. They were collected in *In the Midst of Life* (1892). He also wrote a humorous dictionary, *The Devil's Dictionary* (1906). Bierce disappeared in Mexico in 1914 and was never found.

the ˌ**Big** ˈ**Apple** (*AmE infml*) a popular name for New York City. The name was first used by *jazz musicians to mean the 'big time', or success: *She dreamed of finding wealth and fame in the Big Apple.*

the ˌ**Big Bad** ˈ**Wolf** a frightening wolf that appears in several children's stories, e.g. **Little Red Riding Hood.* In the story of the **Three Little Pigs* the pigs sing the popular children's song *Who's Afraid of the Big Bad Wolf?* when the wolf threatens to blow their houses down. The phrase 'big bad wolf' is sometimes used to describe a person who is regarded as a dangerous enemy.

ˈ**big band** a large band of musicians playing *jazz and other forms of dance music. Big bands were especially popular in the 1940s and produced what was called the **big band sound**. The most famous were led by Glenn *Miller, Benny *Goodman, 'Duke' *Ellington, 'Count' *Basie, and Jimmy and Tommy *Dorsey.

ˌ**Big** ˈ**Bang** (*infml*) (in Britain) the name given to the introduction of important changes to the *London Stock Exchange rules on 27 October 1986, when some controls were removed and new ways of trading allowed: *Some investors benefited from lower commissions after Big Bang.*

ˌ**Big** ˈ**Ben** the bell in the clock tower of the British *Houses of Parliament(2). Its sound is well known because it has often been used in films, and British television and radio companies use it to introduce news broadcasts. Many people think that Big Ben is the name of the clock, or of the tower itself.

the ˌ**big** ˈ**board** (*AmE infml*) a popular name for the *New York Stock Exchange because of its large sign showing the prices of shares of companies.

ˌ**Big** ˈ**Brother** a character in George *Orwell's **Nineteen Eighty-Four*. He is the ruler of the state, who watches people all the time and controls everything they do, allowing them no freedom. Heads of state or government departments who act in this way are sometimes referred to as 'Big Brother': *They are putting these Big Brother surveillance cameras up all over the place.*

the ˌ**big** ˈ**C** /ˈsiː/ an informal name for cancer.

ˌ**big** ˈ**daddy** (*AmE infml*) a man who is powerful, important or rich, or all of these. He is usually a man who acts like a father to people who work for him or depend on him. Big Daddy is the name of the frightening head of the family in the play *Cat on a Hot Tin Roof* (1955) by Tennessee *Williams.

ˌ**Big** ˈ**Easy** (*AmE infml*) a popular name for the American city of *New Orleans because of the relaxed atmosphere there.

ˈ**Bigfoot** /ˈbɪgfʊt/ *n* (*pl* **Bigfeet**) ⇨ SASQUATCH.

ˈ**Biggles** /ˈbɪglz/ the main character in a series of children's books by Captain W E Johns (1893–1968). He is a pilot in *World War I who wins many air battles against the Germans. His adventures have been popular with British children since the 1930s, but many people now do not approve of his attitude that British people are better than foreigners.

the ˌ***Big*** ˈ***Issue*** a British magazine, started in 1991. It is sold on the street by homeless people, who are allowed to keep most of the money they make from selling it. It consists mainly of news of the music, films, plays, etc. that are on in the city where it is sold, as well as articles about homelessness and unemployment. The aim is for homeless people to earn money without begging, and to inform other people about their situation.

ˌ**Big** ˈ**Mac**™ *n* a type of hamburger made by *McDonalds which contains more meat than their standard hamburgers.

ˌ**Big Man on** ˈ**Campus** (*abbr* **BMOC**) (*AmE infml*) a successful, usually popular, male student at a college or university. He is often the president of the Student Government Association or a well-known football or *basketball player.

ˌ**Big** ˈ**Muddy** /ˈmʌdi/ (*AmE infml*) **1** the *Mississippi River. **2** a name for Vietnam used by US soldiers who fought there.

the ˌ**Big** ˈ**Smoke** (*old-fash*) a popular name for London, England, because of the clouds of smoke from its factories. Compare AULD REEKIE.

ˌ**big** ˈ**stick** *n* [sing] the use of military or political power to influence or threaten other countries. The phrase was made popular by President Theodore *Roosevelt, who said that the US government should 'speak softly and carry a big stick'.

ˌ**Big** ˈ**Sur** /ˈsɜː(r)/ a town on the coast of *California 100 miles/160 kilometres south of *San Francisco. The area is famous for its high cliffs and grand scenery. The writer Henry Miller lived in Big Sur and the actor Orson *Welles had a small house there.

ˌSergeant ˈ**Bilko** /ˈbɪlkəʊ; *AmE* ˈbɪlkoʊ/ the main character in a US comedy television series (1955–9) *You'll Never Get Rich*, later called *Sergeant Bilko* and then *The Phil Silvers Show*. Ernie Bilko, played by Phil Silvers, is an army sergeant who talks fast and is dishonest but has great charm and usually tricks his senior officers.

The ˈ***Bill*** /ˈbɪl/ a British television series of the 1980s and 1990s about the officers of a police station in an imaginary area of London. It is very realistic in the way it shows the problems faced by the police in British cities. *The Bill* and *the Old Bill* are British slang names for the police.

bill *n* **1** (in Britain) a written proposal for a new law, which must be discussed in the *House of Commons and the *House of Lords before it can become a law: *Thousands of people marched through London to protest against the Criminal Justice Bill.* ⇨ article at ACT OF PARLIAMENT. **2** (in the US) a proposal for a new law which must be discussed either in the *House of Representatives or the *Senate. If enough people vote for it there, it is discussed in *Congress, and if it is passed it goes to the President, who decides whether or not it should become a law.

ˈ***Billboard*** a US magazine about the music industry. Each week it publishes lists ('the charts') of the most popular single songs, albums and videos.

ˈ**billiards** *n* [U] a game for two people, played by hitting three balls with long rods called *cues*, on a large table covered with cloth. The aim is to score points by hitting one ball against another in a particular way, or into one of the six pockets around the table.

ˈ**Billingsgate** /ˈbɪlɪŋzgeɪt/ a famous old London fish market that used to be on the north bank of the *Thames in the *City. It was well known for the bad language of the people who worked there. In 1982 it was moved to the Isle of Dogs, an area of London's *Docklands: *swearing like a Billingsgate fishwife.*

the Bill of Rights

The name 'Bill of Rights' is used of two completely different documents.

In the US the Bill of Rights consists of the first ten **amendments**, or changes, to the US *Constitution. All of the amendments were agreed in 1791, two years after the Constitution was signed. They give Americans rights which are now considered basic, but which were unusual at the time. The government cannot limit these rights.

Some of the amendments apply to all Americans. The First Amendment promises ***freedom of religion** and also **free speech** and ***freedom of the press**, which means that ordinary people and journalists can speak or write what they want, without restriction by the government. The Second Amendment, which gives people the right to own guns, is now the subject of much debate. The Fourth Amendment says that people cannot be arrested and their houses may not be searched, unless the police have a good reason for doing so. The Ninth and Tenth Amendments say that people and states have other rights beside those mentioned in the Constitution, but that the US government has only the powers that are listed there.

Other amendments give rights to people who are accused of a crime. The Fifth Amendment says that people do not have to give evidence against themselves. Somebody who wants to use this right says, '**I take the Fifth**', and this is often thought to mean that they are afraid to answer questions in case they get into trouble. The Sixth Amendment promises that people who have been accused of a crime will get a trial quickly. In fact, US courts are so busy that people often have to wait a long time, but the government cannot make them wait any additional time. The Seventh Amendment gives people who are accused of a serious crime the right to have their case heard by a jury, so that 12 ordinary citizens, not just a judge, decide whether they are innocent or guilty. The Eighth Amendment says that people who are found guilty of a crime cannot be given 'cruel and unusual punishments'. There has been a lot of discussion about exactly what this means. This amendment was once used as an argument against *capital punishment but it was decided later that the death sentence was not a cruel and unusual punishment.

In Britain the Bill of Rights is the informal name of the Act Declaring the Rights and Liberties of the Subject, which was passed by *Parliament in 1689. This Act dealt with the relationship between the king or queen and Parliament, not with the rights of individuals. The earlier Declaration of Right had greatly reduced the power of the king or queen, and the new Act helped make Britain a ***constitutional monarchy**, in which real power lies with Parliament, not the monarch. The Act also prevented a *Roman Catholic from becoming king or queen.

ˌBilly the ˈKid (1859–81) the popular name for William H Bonney, also known as William Wright, a US outlaw (= criminal) in the *Wild West. By the age of 12 he had murdered a man, and by 18 he had killed 21 more. Bonney was shot dead by Sheriff Pat *Garrett. He was later turned into a romantic character in *dime novels and films, such as *Billy the Kid* (1930) and *The Kid from Texas* (1950). Aaron *Copland also wrote the music for the ballet *Billy the Kid* (1938).

ˈbingo *n* [U] a game of chance for any number of players. Each player is given a card with numbers on it. Players mark their cards as numbers are called out, and the first person to have all their numbers called wins a prize or an amount of money. In Britain it is thought of as a game for older people. In the 1970s it became so popular that many large buildings such as cinemas were converted into **bingo halls**. It was traditional to have special names for numbers as they were read out. For example, 66 was 'clickety-click' and 88 was 'two fat ladies'. Now the numbers are produced by a computer and the old names are rarely used: *Auntie Norma goes to bingo three or four times a week.*

ˈBirdseye™ /ˈbɜːdzaɪ; *AmE* ˈbɜːrdzaɪ/ a US make of frozen food sold in many countries. It is named after Clarence Birdseye (1886–1956) who in the 1920s developed a method of freezing fresh fish quickly to preserve their flavour.

Lord **ˌBirkenˈhead** /ˌbɜːkənˈhed; *AmE* ˌbɜːrkənˈhed/ (*born* Frederick Edwin Smith 1872–1930) a British lawyer and *Conservative politician who was well known for the humorous things he said. He was *Attorney General (1915–8) and then *Lord Chancellor (1919–22), when he improved the laws of land and property.

ˈBirmingham /ˈbɜːmɪŋəm; *AmE* ˈbɜːrmɪŋəm, ˈbɜːrmɪŋhæm/ **1** an industrial city in the *West Midlands of England. It is the second largest city in Britain. Since the late 18th century it has been well known as a centre for business and engineering. In the late 20th century it began to be known also as a centre for the arts, though much of the architecture in the city centre was destroyed in order to build roads in the 1950s and 1960s. **2** the largest city in the US state of *Alabama, sometimes called 'the Magic City'. It is a centre of iron and steel production, which is why it was named after Birmingham, England. In the 1960s it was the scene of many protests by *African Americans and other members of the *civil rights movement, some of which led to fighting in the streets. Martin Luther *King was arrested there in 1963 and wrote his *Letter from the Birmingham Jail* to explain why he did not obey unfair laws.

The **ˌBirmingham ˌPost** /ˌbɜːmɪŋəm; *AmE* ˈbɜːrmɪŋəm/ an English daily newspaper for the Birmingham area, first published in 1857. It is the main newspaper of the *Midlands.

the **ˌBirmingham ˈSix** /ˌbɜːmɪŋəm; *AmE* ˈbɜːrmɪŋəm/ six Irishmen who were sent to prison for life in England for putting *IRA bombs in two *pubs in *Birmingham, England in 1974. The bombs had

a poster advertising a reward for the capture of Billy the Kid killed 21 people, but the six men protested that they were innocent. In the 1980s new scientific tests proved that the evidence against them was not reliable, and that the police had changed their notes. In 1991 the Six were set free. The police officers responsible for their being sent to prison were never punished. This is one of several cases at around the same time that have made the British public doubt the honesty of the police, particularly when dealing with Irish or black people. See also BRIDGEWATER, GUILDFORD FOUR, MAGUIRE SEVEN, TOTTENHAM THREE.

ˌ**Birnam ˈWood** /ˌbɜːnəm; *AmE* ˌbɜːrnəm/ a wood in central Scotland. In *Shakespeare's play **Macbeth*, the witches tell Macbeth that he will not be defeated until Birnam Wood comes to Dunsinane. Later, Macduff's army hide themselves behind branches cut from the wood as they advance to attack Macbeth's castle at Dunsinane, so it appears as though the wood is moving.

ˌJohn ˈ**Birt** /ˈbɜːt; *AmE* ˈbɜːrt/ (1944–) the head of the *BBC since 1993. He has been criticized for changing the organization of the BBC so that different departments have to deal with each other as if they were separate businesses. He was made a *knight in 1998.

ˌ**Birthday ˈHonours** (in Britain) the honorary titles and other awards given to people by the queen on her *Official Birthday each year: *She got an OBE in the Birthday Honours List.* Compare NEW YEAR HONOURS. ⇨ note at HONOURS.

birthdays

Birthdays are especially important to the very young and the very old. On their birthday, people receive **birthday cards** and **birthday presents** from their family and friends. Children's cards often have a large number on them showing how old they are. Cards for adults have pictures of flowers or scenery, or humorous or rude cartoons. Inside there is usually a simple greeting, such as 'Happy Birthday' or 'Many Happy Returns of the Day'. Children expect to receive a special birthday present from their parents. As they get older, many expect larger, more expensive presents, such as a music system or a television.

In the US children who have their birthdays during the school year take a cake to school and have a small party with their class. In Britain children sometimes get **bumped** by their friends (= lifted off the ground horizontally and put down again sharply), the same number of times as their age. Some US parents have the custom of **spanking** their child, once for each year of their age.

Many younger children invite their friends to a **birthday party** at their home. Balloons are often tied to the gate of the house where the party is being held. Children wear their **party clothes** and take a present. They play **party games** such as 'pin the tail on the donkey' or 'musical chairs'. Sometimes parents arrange for a magician to visit the house. After the games there is a special tea with a **birthday cake**. The cake is covered with sugar icing (*AmE* frosting), and has small candles on top, the same number of candles as the child's age. As the cake is carried into the room with the candles lit, everyone sings '*Happy Birthday To You!*' and then the **birthday boy** or **birthday girl** tries to blow out all the candles with one breath and makes a secret wish.

In the US the 16th birthday is called **sweet sixteen**. It is the age at which a person can get a US driver's licence, and some wealthier parents give their children a car as a present. At 18, in Britain and in the US, young people become adults and many have a big party. In most parts of the US 21 is the age at which people can drink alcohol legally. In Britain people celebrate 21st birthdays less than when 21 was the age at which they became adults.

Many adults dislike getting older and a few lie about their age, saying they are younger than they really are. But in general older people are now much more willing to tell others their age. You may see a sign by the side of a road saying: 'Dave Ellis 40 today!', put there by Dave's friends. At about 65 people retire, and those who have reached this age are called 'senior citizens'. Few people live to be 100, so a 100th birthday is very special. In Britain people reaching this age may receive a card containing a printed message from the Queen.

The ˌ***Birth of a ˈNation*** a US silent film (1915) by D W *Griffith. It tells the story of the American *Civil War and the period of *Reconstruction after it. Although it was a great success and influenced later films, it made the *Ku Klux Klan seem good, and there was violence in several US cities when it was shown.

ˌHarrison ˈ**Birtwistle** /ˌhærɪsən ˈbɜːtwɪsl; *AmE* ˈbɜːrtwɪsl/ (1934–) an English composer who has written classical music for large and small orchestras, and is well known for his music for the theatre and opera. He has been responsible for the music at the *National Theatre since 1975. His operas include *Punch and Judy* (1967) and *Sir Gawain and the Green Knight* (1991). He was made a *knight in 1988.

ˈ**bishop** *n* a senior priest in the Anglican, Roman Catholic, Episcopal or Eastern Orthodox churches. Bishops are in charge of the work of other priests in a diocese (= a city or district). On ceremonial occasions a bishop wears a tall pointed hat, called a *mitre*, and carries a long decorated stick, or *staff*. When talked about, a bishop has the title 'the Right Reverend' or, in the Roman Catholic Church, 'the Most Reverend'. A bishop is usually addressed as 'Your Grace'. Only an *archbishop is higher in rank within the Church, and in Britain only some senior bishops are members of the *House of Lords. In 1989, the first female bishop was appointed, in the Episcopal Church of the United States. In the Anglican church, women cannot be bishops or archbishops.

ˈ**Bisquick**™ /ˈbɪskwɪk/ *n* [U] a US make of biscuit mixture with which it is possible to cook biscuits quickly. It is made by General Mills.

ˈ**Bisto**™ /ˈbɪstəʊ; *AmE* ˈbɪstoʊ/ *n* [U] a British make of gravy powder which has been sold since 1910. Bisto is well known for the advertisement in which two children, called the **Bisto kids**, are seen enjoying the smell of a pie cooked with Bisto in, and saying 'Ah, Bisto!'

ˈ**bitter** *n* [U, C] (*BrE*) a type of strong *draught beer with a bitter taste. ⇨ note at BEER.

ˌCilla ˈ**Black** /ˈblæk/ (1943–) a well-known English singer of the 1960s, born in *Liverpool. She later became the presenter of several popular entertainment shows on British television, including **Blind Date* and *Surprise, Surprise*. She is known for her cheerful and friendly personality.

ˈ**Blackadder** /ˈblækædə(r)/ the main character, played by Rowan *Atkinson, in several *BBC comedy television series. Each series was set in a different historical period, the last one being during *World War I. The other character best remembered from *Blackadder* is Baldrick, Blackadder's dirty servant, who remains loyal to his master although he is often badly treated.

the ˌ**Black and ˈTans** (*disapprov*) a popular name for the extra police force sent from England to Ireland in 1920, during the *Troubles, to help the police there against *Sinn Fein. As there were not enough

B

police uniforms, they were given a mixture of police and army clothing: dark green caps and tan (= light brown) uniforms. The name 'Black and Tans' was also a reference to their cruel methods, as it was the name of a pack of dogs used for hunting in County Limerick.

the ˌ**Black and White** ˈ**Minstrels** a British group of men and women who sang and danced on the stage and in a popular *BBC television show (1958–78). The men had black make-up on their faces. This type of entertainment had been popular in 19th-century America, and Al *Jolson had used similar make-up in his films in the 1930s, but by 1978 this had become unacceptable to audiences and the show never returned to television.

ˈ**Blackbeard** /ˈblækbɪəd; *AmE* ˈblækbɪrd/ (*died* 1718) the name by which the English pirate Edward Teach was known. He was active in the *Caribbean and along the eastern coast of North America during 1717 and 1718, until he was killed during a battle at sea with two ships of the English navy.

ˌ**Black** ˈ**Beauty** a black horse which is the main character in a novel (1877) of the same name written for children by Anna Sewell (1820–78). The story is about the horse's experiences with a series of different owners. There have been several films and television programmes made of it.

ˌ**black** ˈ**bottom** *n* [sing] a lively dance popular in America in the 1920s. It involved a lot of movement of the hips.

the ˈ**Black** ˌ**Country** a large industrial area in Britain whose centre is the town of Dudley in the *Midlands. In the 18th century there were many factories here, producing a lot of black smoke, and this gave the area its name: *industrial expansion in Birmingham and the Black Country.*

the ˌ**Black** ˈ**Death** the name given to the major outbreak in Europe in 1348–51 of bubonic plague (= a serious disease spread by rats). People with the disease coughed up blood and got large painful black spots on their bodies, and usually died. It is thought that the Black Death killed about one third of the population of Europe. See also GREAT PLAGUE.

Black English

The forms of English spoken by black and white Americans have always been different. At one time, the speech of white Americans was believed to be correct, and that of *African Americans to be wrong. More recently, the way African Americans speak has been treated with more respect. Black English is considered to be a *dialect. It is called **Black English Vernacular (BEV)** or **African-American Vernacular English (AAVE)**. The study of Black English has been called **ebonics**. Not all African Americans speak BEV, and some only speak it when talking to other African Americans. There are variations within Black English, and some forms overlap with regional dialects of *American English.

Black English developed at the time when black people were brought as *slaves to the US. They came from different parts of Africa and spoke different languages, so they used **pidgin**, a method of communication based on their own languages and English, in order to talk to each other. Over time, this developed into a **creole** (= a language that has developed from a European and an African language). Black English developed further as a result of contact with other American English dialects, but since African Americans have traditionally led very separate lives from white Americans, differences in language have remained.

There are many differences between BEV and standard English in vocabulary, grammar and pronunciation. Black English contains many words from West Africa, e.g. *yam* for 'sweet potato' and *tote* for 'carry'. There are a lot of *slang expressions: for instance, the word *bad* may be used to mean its opposite, 'good', and *cool* and *hot* both mean 'excellent'. Differences of grammar include sometimes leaving out the verb 'to be', and the use of several negatives in one sentence. Inflected endings for plural and possessive forms are often omitted. The 'l' is left out of words like *help* and *self* which are pronounced /hep/ and /sef/. Consonant groups may be reduced, e.g. *desk* is said as /des/ and *test* as /tes/. A final or middle 'r' is not pronounced. Words like *this* and *that* are pronounced with a /d/ instead of /ð/ sound, as /dɪs/ and /dæt/. Words with two syllables usually have heavy stress on the first syllable.

BEV has influenced the language of white Americans, and has much in common with the way white people from the *South speak. *Homies*, a word first used by African Americans to refer to people from their own village or in Africa, is now used as an informal word for 'friends' by some white Americans. Features of pronunciation are also shared by African Americans and southern white Americans.

Special features of Black English are **the dozens** (= verbal insults towards an opponent's mother), **sounding** (= having verbal contests), **shucking** and **jiving** (= deceiving white people) and **rapping** (= language used for seduction and in the words of songs). These are based on traditions brought from Africa and influenced by the Bible.

There has been much debate in the US about the use of BEV in *schools. Some people believe that BEV is not as good as other forms of English, and should not be used in school. This is linked to an idea that speaking Black English is a sign of ignorance and lack of education. Although the number of people who think this is decreasing, they still have influence. BEV had first to be taken account of in schools as a result of the *civil rights protests of the 1960s. Some people now believe that students learn best if they use a language they know well, and that teachers who respect BEV are more likely to help African-American students learn. Others say African Americans need to speak the form of English used by white people if they are to find jobs and succeed, and that schools should help them.

In Britain the term *Black English* is used to refer to the English of West Indian communities, and is the dialect used by *immigrants to Britain from the *Caribbean in the 1950s. The children of these immigrants, and their children, often now use a regional British dialect or speak a modified version of their parents' creole, or switch between the two.

ˌ**black-eyed** ˈ**pea** *n* [usu pl] (*AmE*) (*BrE* **cowpea**, **black-eyed bean**) a small white bean with a black spot on it, eaten a lot in the US. A dish called **hopping John** (black-eyed peas and rice) is eaten in the southern US states on *New Year's Day because it is thought to bring good luck in the new year.

ˈ**Blackfoot** /ˈblækfʊt/ *n* (*pl* **Blackfeet** *or* **Blackfoot**) a member of a Native-American tribe. They had this name because they wore black moccasins (= shoes made of soft leather). They grew tobacco and had more horses than most tribes. Today many of their people live on reservations (= land given and protected by the government) in the state of *Montana and in Canada in the province of Alberta.

ˈ**Black** ˌ**Forest** ˈ**gâteau** *n* [U, C] (*pl* **gâteaux**) a rich chocolate cake with cherries and cream in the middle of it. In Britain it is often eaten in restaurants as the sweet course of a meal.

Blackpool Tower and beach

ˌ**Blackˈheath** /ˌblækˈhiːθ/ an area of open land in south-east London, England. It was the place where people gathered to support Wat *Tyler in 1381 and Jack *Cade in 1450, and where they greeted King *Henry VII after the Battle of *Agincourt and King *Charles II at the *Restoration. The name Blackheath is now most commonly used to refer to the area where people live, around the open land.

the ˌ**Black ˈHills** a US mountain range in western *South Dakota and eastern *Wyoming. They are covered with forests which look dark from a distance, and this explains their name. The mountains contain many minerals, including gold. The highest part is Harney Peak (7 242 feet/2 209 metres). Mount *Rushmore is also there.

the ˈ**Black Hole of Calˈcutta** /kælˈkʌtə/ the name later given to the tiny room in Calcutta, India, in which 146 British prisoners, including one woman, were put by the Indian leader who captured them on 20 June 1756. The next morning only 22 men and the woman were still alive, though some Indian sources of information say that far fewer people were involved. People sometimes talk about a small dark room without fresh air as being 'like the Black Hole of Calcutta'.

ˌ**Black ˈMagic**™ *n* [U] a popular British make of dark chocolates, sold in a black box: *Get her some Black Magic.*

ˌ**Black ˈMonday** Monday 19 October 1987, when prices on stock exchanges all over the world suddenly began to fall. Over the next four days, for example, the Financial Times Index in London fell by 25%, and the *Dow-Jones Index in New York fell by 33%. See also FINANCIAL TIMES INDICES.

the ˌ**Black ˈMountains** a range of mountains in the *Brecon Beacons in south Wales.

ˌ**Black ˈMuslim** *n* a member of an organization of African Americans, formed in 1930, who want their own separate nation within the US. They believe in the religion of Islam and are officially named the Nation of Islam. Well-known members have included *Malcolm X and Muhammad *Ali. A new group, the Lost-Found Nation of Islam, was organized in 1977 by Louis *Farrakhan. See also BLACK PANTHERS, BLACK POWER.

ˌ**Black ˈPanther** *n* a member of the Black Panther Party, an organization of *African Americans with extreme views formed in 1966. They supported legal action and even violence to gain better conditions for black people. One of the leaders was Eldridge *Cleaver. See also BLACK MUSLIM, BLACK POWER.

ˈ**Blackpool** /ˈblækpuːl/ a town on the coast of *Lancashire in north-west England. It is popular with British people wanting a holiday by the sea with a lot of amusements. Its famous beach is 7 miles/11 kilometres long, and the town offers a lot of entertainment. The **Blackpool Tower** is a famous landmark in the area. It was built in 1894 out of metal, like the Eiffel Tower in Paris, and is 520 feet/158 metres high. Blackpool is also famous for the **Blackpool Illuminations**, an event in the autumn when the Tower and the streets are lit up every night for several weeks with thousands of coloured lights.

ˌ**black ˈpower** *n* [U] a movement among *African Americans in the 1960s and 1970s which supported the rights and political power of black people. The expression was used officially by the *Black Panthers. A **black power salute** was made by holding up a fist. Two African-American competitors did this after winning medals at the 1968 Olympic Games. See also BLACK MUSLIMS.

the ˌ**Black ˈPrince** (1330–76) the name by which Prince Edward, the eldest son of King *Edward III of England, is usually known, though the reason for the name is not known. He showed that he was an excellent soldier at the Battle of *Crécy when he was only 16. He died before his father, so his son Richard became the next king.

ˌ**black ˈpudding** (*esp BrE*) (*AmE also* **blood sausage**) *n* [U, C] a type of large dark sausage made from dried pig's blood, fat and grain and cooked by boiling or frying. In Britain, it is associated with the North of England, where it is a popular dish.

ˌ**Black ˈRod** (*in full* **Gentleman Usher of the Black Rod**) an official who is responsible for keeping order in the British *House of Lords. He is known to the public because he has an important part in the ceremony of the *State Opening of Parliament. When he goes to the *House of Commons to call its members to the *House of Lords to hear the *Queen's Speech, they close the door and he has to knock three times with his rod (a black stick) and announce who he is. They let him in and he gives the

Black Rod knocking on the door of the House of Commons

message that 'The Queen commands the presence of the honourable House.' Then they all go to the House of Lords. This ceremony started after 1642, when King *Charles I tried to arrest five Members of Parliament in the House of Commons. It shows that the queen or king has no right to interfere in the business of the House of Commons.

ˈ**blackshirt** /ˈblækʃɜːt; *AmE* ˈblækʃɜːrt/ *n* [usu pl] the name people gave to any member of the British Union of Fascists, a political party started by Oswald *Mosley in 1932. Members wore black uniforms, like the members of other Fascist parties in Europe. In 1936, after a lot of disturbances in Jewish areas of London, the wearing of uniforms by political groups was made illegal under a new Public Order Act.

ˌ**Black** ˈ**Tuesday** (in the US) the name given to 29 October 1929, the day on which the *New York Stock Exchange lost $9 billion. It was the beginning of the *Great Depression. When another large loss occurred on 19 October 1987, the day was called Black Monday.

the ˌ**Black** ˈ**Watch** the popular name for the *Royal Highland Regiment in the British army, given to them because of the dark *tartan that they wear.

ˌ**Black** ˈ**Wednesday** Wednesday 14 September 1992, when the British *Chancellor of the Exchequer, Norman Lamont, raised interest rates by 5% in one day in an unsuccessful attempt to improve the value of the British currency within the *exchange-rate mechanism.

ˌTony ˈ**Blair** /ˈbleə(r); *AmE* ˈbler/ (1953–) a British *Labour politician who became *Prime Minister after the election of 1 May 1997, with a very large Labour majority in parliament. After becoming the leader of the Labour Party in 1994, he had made major changes to its organization, calling it *New Labour. He got rid of the old image of Labour as a party controlled by the trade unions, and one which rejected the idea of individuals getting more private wealth, having more personal choices about education, health care, etc.

Tony and Cherie Blair with Bill and Hillary Clinton outside 10 Downing Street

ˌEubie ˈ**Blake**[1] /ˌjuːbi ˈbleɪk/ (1883–1983) an African-American piano player and composer. Both his parents had been slaves. He began playing *ragtime music and continued performing on stage until he was 99 years old. His successful songs include *I'm Just Wild About Harry* (used by President *Truman as his political song) and *Memories of You*. Blake received the *Presidential Medal of Freedom in 1981.

ˌWilliam ˈ**Blake**[2] /ˈbleɪk/ (1757–1827) an English artist and poet who from childhood claimed to have visions (= religious experiences like dreams) and talk to beings from heaven. He had a very personal style, full of religious symbols. He produced 'illuminated books' of his work, containing his poems and paintings to illustrate them, done by hand. The most famous of these is **Songs of Innocence and of Experience* (1794). His best-known poems are **Jerusalem* and *The Tyger*. He was very poor all his life, and is buried in London in a common grave. The biggest collection of his paintings is in the *Tate Gallery.

William Blake: etching for the title page of Songs of Innocence and of Experience

ˌArt ˈ**Blakey** /ˌɑːt ˈbleɪki; *AmE* ˌɑːrt/ (1919–90) (*also called* **Abdulla Ibn Buhaina**) a US *jazz musician who played the drums. From 1954 he led a small group, the Jazz Messengers, and one of their most successful records was *Buhaina's Delight* (1961). He was chosen for the Jazz *Hall of Fame in 1981.

the ˈ**Blarney Stone** /ˈblɑːni; *AmE* ˈblɑːrni/ a famous stone on the outside wall of Blarney Castle in County Cork, Ireland. It is supposed to give any person who kisses it the ability to speak well and skilfully, and the power to persuade people.

ˌ***Bleak*** ˈ***House*** a novel (1853) by Charles *Dickens in which he attacks the ridiculous procedures of English law at the time. One of the many colourful characters in the book is Mrs Jellyby, an old woman who is concerned for the welfare of poor people in foreign countries and offers them help, but ignores the needs of the people around her, including her own children.

ˈ**Blenheim** /ˈblenɪm/ **1** (*also* the ˌ**Battle of** ˈ**Blenheim**) a battle fought in 1704 near the small town of Blenheim in Bavaria, at which the British, led by the first Duke of *Marlborough, defeated the army of the French king Louis XIV. **2** (*also* ˌ**Blenheim** ˈ**Palace**) a grand house in large grounds near *Oxford, England, the home of the Duke of *Marlborough. It was designed by Sir John *Vanbrugh between 1705 and 1724. Sir Winston *Churchill was born there in 1874. It was made a *World Heritage Site in 1987.

ˈCaptain ˈWilliam ˈ**Bligh** /ˈblaɪ/ (1754–1817) an officer in the British navy who is remembered because his men turned against him when he was the captain of a ship called *HMS *Bounty* in the Pacific Ocean in 1789. Bligh was put in an open boat with 18 of his men and a few supplies. They reached land seven weeks later. In 1805 Bligh became the Governor of New South Wales in Australia, and in 1808 the soldiers there also turned against him, putting him in prison for two years. He was not blamed by the British government, however, and was made an admiral in 1811. See also MUTINY ON THE BOUNTY.

B

ˌColonel ˈ**Blimp** /ˈblɪmp / *n* [usu sing] a man who is very traditional in his attitudes and values, and will not accept any change, especially one who believes that Britain is best. Originally, Colonel Blimp was a cartoon character created by David Low (1891–1963) in the 1930s. He was an old, bald, fat man who had been an army officer. He was not very intelligent and considered his own opinions to be more important than anyone else's: *The club is full of retired military officers of the Colonel Blimp type.*

ˌ***Blind*** ˈ***Date*** a popular British television programme. In it, one person asks three questions to each of three people of the opposite sex who are hidden behind a screen. He or she chooses the person whose answers he or she likes best, and the two then go away to spend a few days together. Then they both come back on the programme to tell the audience what they think about each other. *Blind Date* started in 1985, and is presented by Cilla *Black. It is based on an earlier US television programme of the same name (1949–53).

Blind Date

ˌ**blind man's** ˈ**buff** (*AmE also* **blindman's bluff**) *n* [U] a children's game, played at parties, in which a player whose eyes have been covered tries to catch and identify the other players. ⇨ note at TOYS AND GAMES.

ˌArthur ˈ**Bliss** /ˈblɪs/ (1891–1975) an English composer. He studied under *Holst and *Vaughan Williams at the *Royal College of Music, and went on to write a wide variety of music, including ballets and film music. He was made a *knight in 1950, and *Master of the Queen's Music in 1953.

the ˈ**Blitz** the period of intense bomb attacks by German planes on British cities in *World War II. Whole areas of cities were destroyed, and many people died, but some British people have fond memories of this time because of the friendly atmosphere, e.g. among people sheltering in *London Underground stations.

ˌJoe ˈ**Bloggs** ⇨ JOE BLOGGS.

ˈ**Blondie** /ˈblɒndi; *AmE* ˈblɑːndi/ a US pop group, formed in 1974, whose singer was Deborah Harry. Their most successful records included *Heart of Glass* (1978), *Call Me* (1980) and *The Tide Is High* (1980).

ˈ***Blondie*** /ˈblɒndi; *AmE* ˈblɑːndi/ a popular US *comic strip which first appeared in 1930. The main characters are clever Blondie and her often confused husband Dagwood Bumstead. The characters have also been used for radio and television programmes and for a series of films.

the ˌ**Bloodless Revo**ˈ**lution** the events in Britain in 1688 when the *Roman Catholic *James II was removed as king and replaced by his daughter *Mary and her husband *William III (William of Orange). So many of James's *Protestant officers joined William's side that there was no fighting, and James escaped to France with his family. These events are also called the **Glorious Revolution** because *constitutional monarchy was introduced at the same time.

ˌ**blood** ˈ**sausage** ⇨ BLACK PUDDING.

the ˌ**Bloody As**ˈ**sizes** /əˈsaɪzɪz/ a series of assizes (= courts of law) in the west of England in 1685 at which Judge *Jeffreys condemned 300 people to death, and 1 000 to be sent as slaves to America, for supporting the Duke of *Monmouth against King *James II.

ˌ**Bloody** ˈ**Mary 1** a *nickname for the British queen *Mary I because of the many people who were killed for religious reasons when she was queen. **2** (*also* **bloody mary**) *n* a drink consisting of vodka (= a strong, colourless, alcoholic drink) and tomato juice, often with *Worcester sauce.

ˌ**Bloody** ˈ**Sunday** the day (30 January 1972) when British soldiers shot and killed 13 people taking part in a march in *Londonderry(1), Northern Ireland, to protest against *internment. This event, and the fact that the soldiers were not punished, caused more violence in Northern Ireland, and this led to *direct rule. ⇨ article at NORTHERN IRELAND.

the ˌ**Bloody** ˈ**Tower** the name given to one of the towers of the *Tower of London, built in the 14th century. It is called this because it is the place where the *Princes in the Tower were kept prisoner and probably murdered in the late 15th century.

ˈ**Bloomingdale's** /ˈbluːmɪŋdeɪlz/ a large, expensive department store in New York City. It began in 1872 and is known for selling excellent clothes, furniture and foods. It is owned by Federated Department Stores, which also owns *Macy's. Bloomingdale's has stores in several other major US cities, including *Chicago, *Boston and *Los Angeles.

ˈ**Bloomsbury** /ˈbluːmzbri/ an area of central London, England. The *British Museum and the main buildings of *London University are in Bloomsbury, and many famous people have lived there, including the *Bloomsbury Group.

the ˈ**Bloomsbury Group** /ˈbluːmzbri/ a group of artists and writers who met regularly as friends in *Bloomsbury, London, in the early 20th century. They rejected *Victorian(2) attitudes and believed in art, friendship and social progress. They included many of the leading figures of the time, such as Virginia *Woolf, E M *Forster, Maynard *Keynes and Lytton *Strachey.

BLT /ˌbiː el ˈtiː/ an abbreviation for bacon, lettuce and tomato, a popular mixture of food used for filling *sandwiches in Britain and the US.

ˈ***Bluebird*** /ˈbluːbɜːd; *AmE* ˈbluːbɜːrd/ the name of any one of a series of very fast cars and boats that were built and driven by Malcolm *Campbell and his son Donald *Campbell to travel at faster speeds than anybody had ever gone before.

ˈ**blue book** *n* **1** (in Britain) an official report published by Parliament, usually from a government committee or a *Royal Commission. It is bound in a blue cover. Compare WHITE PAPER. **2** (in the US) a book that gives details of people who have an important position in society.

The ˈ***Blue Boy*** a famous painting (1779) by Thomas *Gainsborough. It is one of his best-known works, and is a portrait of a boy dressed in blue.

ˌ**Blue** ˈ**Cross 1** the largest private health insurance company in the US. In 1997 about 66 million Ameri-

B

cans were members. It was formed in 1929 and in 1982 joined with its rival Blue Shield, which began in 1917. The main office of the Blue Cross and Blue Shield Association is in *Chicago. **2 the Blue Cross** a British charity organization that treats sick animals.

ˌ**blue** ˈ**ensign** *n* a blue flag with a *Union Jack in the top left quarter. It is displayed on ships to show that they are being used by the British government.

ˈ**bluegrass** *n* [U] **1** a type of grass that is bluish-green in colour. It is common in parts of the US, especially *Kentucky, which is sometimes called the Bluegrass State. **2** a type of country music of the southern US. It has fast strong rhythms and is played on instruments with strings, especially guitars and banjos.

ˈ**blue law** *n* [often pl] (*AmE*) a law that forbids business and certain other activities, such as dancing or sport, on Sundays. Blue laws were first introduced in colonial *New England and were originally printed on blue paper. Now they vary widely in different parts of the US. Although many shops open on Sundays, they often do not sell alcohol on that day because of a blue law.

ˌ***Blue*** ˈ***Peter*** a British children's television programme that has been broadcast by the *BBC since 1958. It is well known for teaching children how to make things from objects that they can find at home, and for organizing events to collect money for charities.

ˌ**blue** ˈ**plaque** *n* any of the round blue notices that are attached to the front walls of houses in London, England to show that a famous person once lived there.

a blue plaque

ˌ**Blue** ˈ**Riband** /ˈrɪbənd/ the title given to the ship that crosses the Atlantic in the fastest time. The phrase *blue riband* or *blue ribbon* is also used to refer to anything that is the best in its field: *He has never won the Greyhound Derby, the sport's blue riband event.*

ˌ**blue** ˈ**rinse** *n* [C, U] a light blue dye for colouring the hair, used especially by older women. Blue rinses are thought to be typical of old-fashioned *Conservative women: *The blue rinse brigade are calling for sex education in schools to be banned.*

the ˈ**blues** *n* [U+sing/pl *v*] a type of US *jazz music with a slow, sad sound. *African Americans created it in the southern states to express the sadness of their experience. The music developed into *rhythm and blues and then *rock and roll and *soul.

ˌ***Blue Tail*** ˈ***Fly*** a lively American song sometimes called 'Jimmy Crack Corn'. It was written before the American *Civil War by Daniel Emmett who also wrote *Dixie*. It became popular among slaves, because it was about the death of an owner of slaves.

ˌDavid ˈ**Blunkett** /ˈblʌnkɪt/ (1947–) a British *Labour politician who is Britain's only blind member of parliament. He became *Secretary of State for Education and Employment in 1997.

ˌAnthony ˈ**Blunt** /ˈblʌnt/ (1907–83) a British spy who gave British secrets to the Soviet Union. He was a member of the group called the *Cambridge spies, which also included *Burgess[2], *Maclean[2] and *Philby. He was a successful art historian, working for the Queen, who made him a *knight. When in 1979 it was discovered that he was a spy, his knighthood was taken away from him.

Blur /blɜː(r)/ a British pop group, one of the most popular of the *Britpop groups of the 1990s. Their best-known album, *Parklife* (1994), consists of songs about the life of ordinary working people in London.

ˌEnid ˈ**Blyton** /ˌiːnɪd ˈblaɪtn/ (1897–1968) a very successful English writer of children's books. She wrote over 700 books, including the *Famous Five, Secret Seven and *Noddy series, which are still very popular with children.

the cover of one of Enid Blyton's 'Famous Five' novels

the **BMA** /ˌbiː em ˈeɪ/ (*in full* the **British Medical Association**) a professional association like a *trade union that represents British doctors. It also organizes discussions on medical and moral questions, and acts as a *pressure group: *The BMA has called for an inquiry into the sale of human organs for transplants.*

BMJ /ˌbiː em ˈdʒeɪ/ ⇨ BRITISH MEDICAL JOURNAL.

BMX /ˌbiː em ˈeks/ (*in full* **bicycle moto-cross**) *n* **1** [C] a type of strong bicycle with small wheels, designed for riding on rough ground. They are popular with young people, who use them to perform jumps and other tricks. **2** [U] the sport of riding or racing BMX bicycles on rough ground.

ˌ**B'nai** ˈ**B'rith** /ˌbəneɪ ˈbrɪθ/ *n* the oldest and largest Jewish organization in the world. In 1997 it had associations in 56 countries. It began in 1843 in New York and has its main office in Washington, DC. It is a cultural, social and educational organization that also supports hospitals and gives help after disasters. In 1913 it created the Anti-Defamation League to fight unfair treatment of Jews and others. B'nai B'rith means 'Sons of the Covenant'.

BNFL /ˌbiː en ef ˈel/ ⇨ BRITISH NUCLEAR FUELS.

BNP /ˌbiː en ˈpiː/ ⇨ BRITISH NATIONAL PARTY.

ˌ**Boadi**ˈ**cea** /ˌbəʊədɪˈsiːə; *AmE* ˌboʊədɪˈsiːə/ ⇨ BOUDICCA.

ˌChris ˈ**Boardman** /ˈbɔːdmən; *AmE* ˈbɔːrdmən/ (1969–) an English cyclist who won a gold medal at the 1992 Olympic Games on a new design of bicycle that looked very different from the traditional style. Since then, he has taken part in the Tour de France bicycle race.

the ˈ**Boat Race** a race that takes place each year on the River *Thames in west London, England, between rowing teams from the universities of *Oxford

BMX World Championships

and *Cambridge. Unlike other sports contests between the two universities, it is seen as a national event and is watched by many people on television. The first Boat Race was in 1829.

ˌ**Bob-a-ˈjob** /ˌbɒb ə ˈdʒɒb; *AmE* ˌbɑːb ə ˈdʒɑːb/ a phrase used by British children when they go to people's houses and offer to do small jobs, such as gardening, for money. Traditionally, this happened during **Bob-a-job week**, a week when British *Scouts earned money in this way. For each job they were paid a *bob*, an informal name for a shilling, the British coin that was replaced by 5p in 1971.

ˌ***Bobby ˈShafto*** /ˈʃæftəʊ; *AmE* ˈʃæftoʊ/ an old children's song, which may have been sung in support of Robert Shafto, a candidate in the British general election in 1761. Many British people know the first verse:

Bobby Shafto's gone to sea,
Silver buckles at his knee,
He'll come back and marry me,
Bonny Bobby Shafto!

the ˌ**Bodleian ˈLibrary** /ˌbɒdliən; *AmE* ˌbɑːdliən/ the main library of *Oxford University. It has one of the largest collections in the world of books and papers, many of them written by hand. It is one of the six British *copyright libraries.

the Bodleian Library

ˌ**Bodmin ˈMoor** /ˌbɒdmɪn; *AmE* ˌbɑːdmɪn/ a moor in *Cornwall, England.

ˈ**bodyline** /ˈbɒdilaɪn; *AmE* ˈbɑːdilaɪn/ *n* [U] a type of very fast bowling (= delivering the ball) in *cricket, in which the ball is aimed at the batsman's body rather than at the wicket. It was first used by the English team in Australia in 1932, and shocked many people, who thought it was unfair.

the ˈ**Body Shop** any of a chain of shops selling products for cleaning and caring for the skin and hair. The shops are well known for only selling natural products that have not been tested on animals. The business was started in Britain by Anita *Roddick, but there are now shops in many countries around the world: *She gets all her make-up and stuff from the Body Shop.*

ˈ**Boeing** /ˈbəʊɪŋ; *AmE* ˈboʊɪŋ/ a US company that makes aircraft. Its well-known passenger planes include the Boeing 707, Boeing *737 and Boeing *747 (the 'jumbo jet'). In 1997 it joined other companies to create a new satellite for the *Internet. William Boeing (1881–1956) began the company in 1917, and its main offices are in *Seattle.

Humphrey Bogart with Lauren Bacall in The Big Sleep

the ˌ**Boer ˈWar** /ˌbɔː(r)/ (*BrE*) (*also* the **South African War**) a war (1899–1902) between the British and the Boers, Dutch farmers who had settled in southern Africa. The Boers had established two independent republics (Transvaal and Orange Free State) in what is now *South Africa, and the British wanted to control the whole region. The British won, but only after much bitter fighting.

ˌDirk ˈ**Bogarde** /ˈbəʊgɑːd; *AmE* ˈboʊgɑːrd/ (1920–99) an English actor. He first became well known in the 1950s in a series of British comedy films about medical students, and later worked in more serious films, many of them in Europe, such as *The Damned* 1969 and *Death in Venice* (1971). He also wrote an autobiography and several novels. He was made a *knight in 1992.

ˌHumphrey ˈ**Bogart** /ˈbəʊgɑːt; *AmE* ˈboʊgɑːrt/ (1899–1957) a US film actor. His popular name was Bogey. He often played criminals or violent characters. His successful films include *The *Maltese Falcon* (1941), *Casablanca (1942) and *The African Queen* (1951) for which he received his only *Oscar. He was married to Lauren *Bacall, and they made several films together.

ˈ**Bogside** /ˈbɒgsaɪd; *AmE* ˈbɔːgsaɪd/ an area of *Londonderry(1), Northern Ireland, where mainly *Roman Catholic people live. There have been many violent incidents between the two religious communities there during the *Troubles.

Bold™ /bəʊld; *AmE* boʊld/ *n* [U] a make of soap powder for washing clothes. It is made by *Procter and Gamble.

ˌAnne **Boˈleyn** /bəˈlɪn/ (1507–36) the second wife of King *Henry VIII and the mother of Queen *Elizabeth I. Her marriage to Henry against the wishes of the Pope led to England's break from the *Roman Catholic Church and the start of the *Church of England. However, when she failed to produce a son, Henry lost interest in her. She was accused of having affairs with other men, and her head was cut off.

ˌRobert ˈ**Bolt** /ˈbəʊlt; *AmE* ˈboʊlt/ (1924–95) an English writer of plays and films. He first achieved fame with his play about Thomas *More, *A Man for All Seasons* (1960). He also wrote the script for the film *Lawrence of Arabia* (1962). Two of his film scripts won *Oscars: *Dr Zhivago* (1965) and *A Man for All Seasons* (1967).

ˌ**Bomber Comˈmand** the section of the British *Royal Air Force in World War II which was responsible for dropping bombs on enemy cities and military targets.

Bo'nanza a popular Western series on US television between 1959 and 1972. It was about a father and his three sons living on the Ponderosa Ranch in the *Wild West. Lorne Greene played the father Ben Cartwright, Pernell Roberts was Adam, Dan Blocker was Hoss and Michael Landon was Little Joe.

ˌEdward '**Bond**[1] /'bɒnd; *AmE* 'bɑ:nd/ (1934–) an English writer of plays. Many people were shocked by the violence in his early plays, and his *Early Morning* (1968) was the last play to be banned in the UK by the *Lord Chamberlain.

ˌJames '**Bond**[2] /'bɒnd; *AmE* 'bɑ:nd/ the main character in a series of novels by Ian *Fleming. James Bond is a daring and attractive British secret agent, who is also known as '007'. The first James Bond book was *Casino Royale* (1953). Many of the books have been made into exciting and often humorous adventure films.

Bond Street /'bɒnd; *AmE* 'bɑ:nd/ a street in the *West End of London, England, known for its expensive shops and art galleries.

Bonfire Night

British people celebrate Bonfire Night every year on 5 November in memory of a famous event in British history, the ***Gunpowder Plot**. On 5 November 1605 a group of *Roman Catholics planned to blow up the *Houses of Parliament while King *James I was inside. On the evening before, one of them, Guy *Fawkes, was caught in the cellars with gunpowder (= an explosive), and the plot was discovered. He and all the other conspirators were put to death. Bonfire Night is sometimes called **Guy Fawkes Night**.

Originally, Bonfire Night was celebrated as a victory for *Protestants over Catholics, but the festival is now enjoyed by everyone. Some children make a **guy**, a figure of a man made of old clothes stuffed with newspaper or straw to represent Guy Fawkes. The guy is then burned on top of a **bonfire** on Bonfire Night. A few weeks before, children take their guy into the street and ask for a 'penny for the guy'. They use the money to buy **fireworks** (= small packets of explosives which, when lit, make a bang or send a shower of coloured light into the air). Only adults are legally allowed to buy fireworks.

Bonfire Night: 'penny for the guy'

Some people hold private **bonfire parties** in their gardens, while others attend larger public events organized by local councils or *charities. Chestnuts or potatoes are often put in the bonfire so that they will cook as it burns. Fireworks such as Roman Candles, Catherine Wheels, bangers and rockets are put in the ground and are let off one by one. Children hold lighted **sparklers** (= metal sticks covered in a hard chemical substance that burns brightly when lit) in their hands and wave them around to make patterns. Unfortunately, there are sometimes accidents involving fireworks and there are now restrictions on the type of fireworks that can be used by the general public.

The events of 5 November 1605 are celebrated in a nursery rhyme:

Please to remember,
The fifth of November,
Gunpowder, treason and plot;
I know no reason
Why gunpowder treason
Should ever be forgot.

ˌChris '**Bonington** /'bɒnɪŋtən; *AmE* 'bɑ:nɪŋtən/ (1934–) an English mountaineer who led a team of British climbers up Mount Everest in 1975 and again in 1985 and 1997. He was made a *knight in 1996.

ˌ**Bonnie and 'Clyde** /ˌbɒni, 'klaɪd; *AmE* ˌbɑni/ a pair of young US criminals, **Bonnie Parker** (1911–34) and **Clyde Barrow** (1909–34). They met in 1932 and robbed banks and murdered 12 people in the south-western US before being shot dead by police in *Louisiana. Their story was made romantic in the film *Bonnie and Clyde* (1967) with Faye Dunaway and Warren *Beatty in the main parts.

ˌ**Bonny Prince 'Charlie** (1720–88) the popular name of Prince Charles Edward Stuart, also sometimes called the *Young Pretender. His father was the son of *James II, the king of England, Scotland and Ireland, and Charles therefore believed that his father should be king. Many people in Scotland supported the Stuarts, and in 1745 Charles led a Scottish army against King *George II. After some successes, Charles's army was defeated at the battle of *Culloden. He then spent five months hiding from government soldiers in Scotland before escaping to France. He never returned to Britain. See also SKYE, MACDONALD.

boogie /'bu:gi/ (*also* **boogie-woogie**) /ˌbu:gi 'wu:gi/ *n* [U] a type of US *blues music with a strong beat, played on the piano. It was especially popular in the 1930s. Musicians who helped to make it popular included 'Cow Cow' Davenport and 'Pine Top' Smith, who recorded *Pine Top's Boogie-Woogie* in 1928. The 'boogie-woogie' was also an early name for the *jitterbug dance.

the '**Booker Prize** /'bʊkə; *AmE* 'bʊkər/ a prize that is given each autumn to the writer of the best novel published in Britain that year. The judging is organized by Book Trust, and the prize money, £20 000, is given by Booker, a large food company.

the '***Book of ˌCommon 'Prayer*** the name of the prayer book most commonly used in the *Church of England. It was first published in 1549, with a new version appearing in 1622. The beauty of its language is widely admired, but many people now prefer the modern *Alternative Service Book*.

the ˌ**Book of 'Kells** /'kelz/ a copy of the four Gospels of the Bible made in the 8th century at a religious community in the town of Kells in Ireland. It has many beautiful illustrations, and can be seen in the library of Trinity College, *Dublin.

a page from the Book of Kells

the ˌ**Book of the** ˈ**Month Club** a US company that sells books at reduced prices through the post. It began in 1926 and now has an International Book of the Month Club on the *Internet. Customers can order books each month from the club's magazine.

ˌDaniel ˈ**Boone**[1] /ˈbuːn/ (1734–1820) a famous American *frontiersman. He crossed the *Appalachian Mountains to explore and help in settling land that became *Kentucky. He fought the Native Americans and was twice captured by them. Later he was elected a representative to the Kentucky government. He became an American legend and is even mentioned in *Byron's poem *Don Juan*.

ˌPat ˈ**Boone**[2] /ˈbuːn/ (1934–) a US singer and actor who was especially popular in the late 1950s. He began with *rock and roll songs, such as *Ain't That a Shame* (1955). He was attractive to many people because he was religious and did not behave badly. In 1997, however, he changed his image at the age of 62 and recorded *heavy metal music.

ˌJohn ˈ**Boorman** /ˈbɔːmən; *AmE* ˈbɔːrmən/ (1933–) an English film director. After working in television in Britain, he moved to the US to make *Point Blank* in 1967. His best-known films since then have included *Deliverance* (1972), *Excalibur* (1981) and *Beyond Rangoon* (1995).

ˌJohn Wilkes ˈ**Booth** /wɪlks ˈbuːð/ (1838–65) the US actor who shot and killed President Abraham *Lincoln on 14 April 1865 in Ford's Theater, Washington, DC, while the President was watching a play. Booth had sympathy for the *Confederate States and was angry at their defeat by Lincoln's government. After shooting the President, he jumped onto the stage and broke his leg but escaped. He was later found in a barn and died when he either shot himself or was shot.

ˌ**Boot** ˈ**Hill** (*AmE infml*) a humorous name for a cemetery in the *Wild West. One of the best known is at *Tombstone, *Arizona. The name comes from the idea that many people were buried in the boots they were wearing when they were killed.

ˌBetty ˈ**Boothroyd** /ˈbuːθrɔɪd/ (1929–) a British *Labour politician who in 1992 became the first woman to be elected *Speaker of the *House of Commons.

Boots /buːts/ a company with shops in almost every town in Britain. The shops sell medicines and many other items for personal use, as well as some food.

ˌ**Bo-**ˈ**peep** /ˌbəʊ ˈpiːp; *AmE* ˌboʊ/ a character in a *nursery rhyme. She is a little girl who has lost her sheep. The full nursery rhyme is:

Little Bo-peep has lost her sheep
And doesn't know where to find them.
Leave them alone, and they'll come home
Bringing their tails behind them.

ˌLizzy ˈ**Borden** /ˈbɔːdn; *AmE* ˈbɔːrdn/ (1860–1927) an American woman who was accused of murdering her rich father and stepmother with an axe on 4 August 1892. Her trial was a famous event. She was judged to be innocent, but many people still believed her guilty. Her name is remembered in a popular children's rhyme that begins:

Lizzy Borden took an axe
And gave her mother 40 whacks.

ˈ**Borders** /ˈbɔːdəz; *AmE* ˈbɔːrdərz/ an administrative *region in south-east Scotland near the border with England.

ˌ**Border** ˈ**Television** /ˌbɔːdə; *AmE* ˌbɔːrdər/ one of the British *ITV companies. It broadcasts programmes to northern England and southern Scotland.

ˈ**borough** *n* a district, town or part of a large city that has some powers of local government. London, England, has 32 boroughs, which make up the area known as *Greater London. The five boroughs of New York City are *Manhattan(1), *Brooklyn, *Queens, the *Bronx and *Staten Island. See also LOCAL GOVERNMENT.

the ˈ**Borscht Belt** /ˈbɔːʃt; *AmE* ˈbɔːrʃt/ (*also* the ˈ**Borscht** ˌ**circuit**) (*AmE humor*) a holiday area in the *Catskill Mountains in New York State. It is known for attracting Jewish visitors and many American Jewish performers began their careers there. Borscht is a soup that is popular with Jewish people.

ˈ**Borstal** /ˈbɔːstl; *AmE* ˈbɔːrstl/ *n* [C, U] a British prison school for young offenders (= people who commit crimes) which opened in 1902 in Borstal, Kent. Similar institutions became known as 'borstals', and later as 'detention centres'. They are now called *young offender institutions.

ˈ**Boston** /ˈbɒstən; *AmE* ˈbɔːstən/ the capital and largest city in the US state of *Massachusetts. It is a major port and cultural centre, having 30 colleges and universities. It also has the oldest underground railway in the US. Boston was settled in 1630 and played an important part in the *American Revolution. It became a centre for Irish immigrants in the second half of the 19th century. International runners compete each year in the **Boston Marathon** race, first run in 1897. See also BOSTON MASSACRE, BOSTON TEA PARTY.

ˈ**Boston** ˌ**baked** ˈ**beans** /ˈbɒstən; *AmE* ˈbɔːstən/ (*also* **baked beans**) *n* [pl] (in the US) white haricot beans baked with pork and brown sugar or molasses (= a dark, sweet, thick liquid obtained from sugar). It was originally popular in *Boston, US.

ˌ**Boston** ˈ**Brahmin** /ˌbɒstən; *AmE* ˌbɔːstən/ *n* (*AmE*) a member of one of the old families with high social and cultural status in *Boston, US. The Brahmins have traditionally lived in the city's best area, *Beacon Hill and had the most money and power. This has slowly changed as Boston has become larger and new groups have become more rich and powerful.

the ˌ**Boston** ˈ**Massacre** /ˌbɒstən; *AmE* ˌbɔːstən/ an incident on 5 March 1770 when British soldiers shot at American colonists and killed five of them. It was called a *massacre* (= the killing of many people) to increase hatred for the British, and was one of the events that led to the *American Revolution.

the ˌ**Boston** ˈ**Pops** /ˌbɒstən; *AmE* ˌbɔːstən/ a US orchestra that plays popular classical and other music. It was led for almost 50 years by Arthur *Fiedler. Its musicians are members of the Boston Symphony Orchestra.

the ˌ**Boston** ˈ**Strangler** /ˌbɒstən; *AmE* bɔːstən/ the name given by newspapers, etc. to Albert DeSalvo, a

B

US man who attacked and killed 13 women in *Boston, Massachusetts, between 1962 and 1964. He killed the women by strangling them (= squeezing their throat tightly). He was sent to prison for his crimes and was killed by another prisoner.

the ˌ**Boston** ˈ**Stump** /ˌbɒstən; *AmE* ˌbɔːstən/ the popular name for the very tall 15th-century church tower in the English town of Boston, *Lincolnshire. The tower can be seen easily from the sea and this was helpful to sailors when Boston was an important port. The US city of *Boston is named after this port because many of the *Pilgrim Fathers began their journey from there in 1608.

the ˌ**Boston** ˈ**Tea** ˌ**Party** /ˌbɒstən; *AmE* ˌbɔːstən/ an incident in American history. It occurred on 16 December 1773, two years before the *American Revolution. In order to protest about the British tax on tea, a group of Americans dressed as Mohawk Indians went onto three British ships in *Boston harbour and threw 342 large boxes of tea into the sea.

ˌJames ˈ**Boswell** /ˈbɒzwel; *AmE* ˈbɑːzwel/ (1740–95) a Scottish writer. He is best known for his book about his famous friend Dr *Johnson[6], *The Life of Samuel Johnson* (1791) and for his personal diaries, which were discovered in the 1920s.

the ˈBattle of ˈ**Bosworth** ˈ**Field** /ˈbɒzwəθ; *AmE* ˈbɑːzwərθ/ the last battle (1585) in the *Wars of the Roses. It was fought near Market Bosworth in Leicestershire between King *Richard III of England and Henry Tudor. Richard died in the battle and Henry became King *Henry VII. There is a dramatic version of the battle at the end of Shakespeare's play *Richard III*.

ˌ**Botany** ˈ**Bay** /ˌbɒtəni; *AmE* ˌbɑːtəni/ the place on the east coast of Australia where Captain *Cook landed in 1770. The British government decided in 1787 to send criminals there from British prisons. After that the name Botany Bay was often used to mean any place in Australia where criminals were sent from Britain.

ˌIan ˈ**Botham** /ˈbəʊθəm; *AmE* ˈboʊθəm/ (1955–) an English *cricket player who played for England between 1977 and 1992, including a short period as captain. He was one of the most successful players of all time, both as a batsman and as a bowler. He has also raised a lot of money for charity and often appears on television.

the ˌEarl of ˈ**Bothwell** /ˈbɒθwel; *AmE* ˈbɑːθwel/ (*c.* 1536–78) the third husband of *Mary Queen of Scots. He was probably involved with her in the murder of her second husband, the Earl of *Darnley, in 1567. When they got married three months after the murder, they were forced to leave the country and finally became prisoners until their deaths. Bothwell died in prison in Denmark.

Botˈ**swana** /bɒtˈswɑːnə; *AmE* bɑːtˈswɑːnə/ a country in southern Africa and an independent member of the Commonwealth since 1966. Its capital city is Gaborone.

ˈ**Bottom** /ˈbɒtəm; *AmE* ˈbɑːtəm/ a comic character in Shakespeare's play *A *Midsummer Night's Dream*. For most of the play, Bottom has the head of an ass because of a magic trick played by *Oberon.

ˈ**Boudicca** /ˈbuːdɪkə/ (*also* **Boadicea**) (*died* AD 62) the queen of the Iceni tribe of eastern Britain when it was part of the Roman Empire. She led the Iceni against the Romans and destroyed several of their camps. When she was defeated she killed herself. She is often shown in pictures driving a chariot (= an open carriage pulled by a horse) with blades attached to the wheels.

ˌAdrian ˈ**Boult** /ˈbəʊlt; *AmE* ˈboʊlt/ (1889–1983) a English conductor who worked with many orchestras, including the Birmingham Symphony Orchestra (1924–30), the *BBC Symphony Orchestra (1931–50) and the *London Philharmonic Orchestra (1951–7). He was made a *knight in 1937.

Titania (Serena Evans) with Bottom (Ian Talbot) in A Midsummer Night's Dream

the ˈ**Boulting** ˌ**brothers** /ˈbəʊltɪŋ; *AmE* ˈboʊltɪŋ/ **John Boulting** (1913–85) and **Roy Boulting** (1913–), twin brothers who produced films together. Their films, mostly about life in Britain in the years after *World War II, include *Brighton Rock* (1947), **Lucky Jim* (1957) and *I'm All Right Jack* (1959).

the ˈ**Boundary Com**ˌ**missions** the four British government organizations (one each for England, Scotland, Wales and Northern Ireland) which decide the boundaries of *constituencies. They recommend changes to the boundaries so that the average population of constituencies (about 70 000) remains the same in spite of population movements.

ˌ*HMS* ˈ***Bounty*** (*also* ***The Bounty***) a British ship on which a famous mutiny took place in 1789. The ship was returning from Tahiti in the Pacific Ocean when one of the officers, Fletcher *Christian, led the crew against their harsh captain, William *Bligh. Captain Bligh and some men who supported him were left in a small open boat while Christian and the crew returned on *HMS Bounty* to Tahiti and then settled in the *Pitcairn Islands. See also *MUTINY ON THE BOUNTY*.

ˈ**Bounty**™ *n* a chocolate bar with sweet coconut inside, sold in Britain.

Bournemouth a town on the south coast of England, in *Dorset. Many British people go there on holiday, and it is also a place where foreign students of English go to study. The **Bournemouth Symphony Orchestra** is well known for encouraging young British composers.

ˈ**Bournville** /ˈbɔːnvɪl; *AmE* ˈbɔːrnvɪl/ a suburb of Birmingham, England. It was built by the brothers George and Richard Cadbury to provide houses for the workers at the chocolate factory which they opened there in 1879. The Cadburys were * Quakers and believed that social problems were often the result of bad homes. The houses at Bournville were well designed, with gardens, and they had an important influence on the planning of other suburbs in Britain. See also CADBURY SCHWEPPES.

ˈ**Bovril**™ /ˈbɒvrɪl; *AmE* ˈbɑːvrɪl/ *n* [U] a dark brown substance made from beef. It is sold in jars, especially in Britain, and can be mixed with hot water to make a drink, added to food to give it a stronger taste of meat, or spread on bread.

ˌClara ˈ**Bow** /ˌklærə ˈbəʊ; *AmE* ˈboʊ/ (1905–65) a US actor known as the 'It Girl'. She was in both silent and talking films and usually played a lively *flapper of the *Roaring Twenties. Her best films included *Wings* (1927) and *It* (1927), from which she got her special name. 'It' means the quality that makes women attractive to men.

ˌ**Bow ˈBells** /ˌbəʊ; *AmE* ˌboʊ/ the bells of the church of St Mary-le-Bow in the *East End of London, England. Traditionally, a true *cockney is somebody who was born within the sound of Bow Bells. The bells are also important in the story of Dick *Whittington. See also *ORANGES AND LEMONS*.

the ˈ**Bowery** /ˈbaʊəri/ a poor area of south-east *Manhattan(1) in New York City where many people without homes or jobs live. It is also a centre for young musicians. One of the streets there is also called the Bowery.

the ˈ**Bow Group** /ˈbəʊ; *AmE* ˈboʊ/ a political group within the *Conservative Party. It was started after *World War II by young Conservatives who wanted to encourage new ideas in the party, including a freer economy and independence for the countries in the *British Empire. The group publishes a magazine called *Crossbow*. Compare MONDAY CLUB.

ˌDavid ˈ**Bowie**[1] /ˈbəʊi; *AmE* ˈboʊi/ (1947–) an English pop singer, writer of songs and actor. He is especially known for introducing fresh combinations of music and images, and for the characters that he has created. These have included Major Tom, in his first hit song *Space Oddity* (1969), and Ziggy Stardust in songs and performances in the 1970s. Through the character of Ziggy, Bowie created the style known as 'glam rock' or 'glitter rock'. Bowie has also acted in plays and films.

David Bowie

ˌJames ˈ**Bowie**[2] /ˈbuːi; *also* ˈbəʊi, *AmE* ˈboʊi/ (*c.* 1796–1836) a famous American *frontiersman and soldier. The large, heavy knife called a **bowie knife** was named after him. He was killed at the *Alamo with Davy *Crockett.

ˈ**bowl game** (*also* **bowl**) *n* (*AmE*) a US college football game played in December or January at the end of the football season. The best teams meet in several bowl games (so called because the stadiums in which they are played are bowl-shaped). The most famous are the *Rose Bowl in Pasadena, *California, the Sugar Bowl in *New Orleans, the Orange Bowl in *Miami and the Cotton Bowl in *Dallas.

bowls *n* [U] a game, played on a smooth grass area called a **bowling green**, in which two to eight players take turns to roll large black balls as near as possible to a small white ball. The balls are heavier on one side so they travel in a curve. Bowls has been popular in Britain for about 600 years and there is a famous story from 1588 about Sir Francis *Drake

bowls

and a game of bowls. According to the story, he was told during the game that the Spanish *Armada was coming, but he said, 'There is time to win this game and beat the Spaniards, too.' Bowls is now usually played by older people.

ˈ**Bow Street** /ˈbəʊ; *AmE* ˈboʊ/ the main police court in London, which was in the street of this name until the early 1990s. It is now at *Charing Cross. When Henry *Fielding was a magistrate at Bow Street in the 1740s, he formed the **Bow Street Runners**, a group of people trained to catch thieves. This was the first step towards the creation of the *Metropolitan Police in 1829.

ˈ**Boxing Day** (in Britain) 26 December, the day after *Christmas Day. It is a *bank holiday. Traditionally it was the day when people gave **Christmas boxes** (small gifts of money) to their employees or servants. Now most people relax, digest the food and drink of the day before, and perhaps visit friends or relatives.

ˌGeoffrey ˈ**Boycott** /ˈbɔɪkɒt; *AmE* ˈbɔɪkɑːt/ (1940–) an English *cricket player who played for *Yorkshire (1962–86) and England (1964–82). He is well known for having scored a very large number of runs (= points) during his career as a player, and for saying what he thinks in plain language. He still comments regularly on the game.

ˌRobert ˈ**Boyle** /ˈbɔɪl/ (1627–91) a British scientist whose experiments and the way he wrote about them were ahead of his time. Before chemical elements were discovered, he suggested a theory of atoms, saying that things were made of 'corpuscles'. He is best remembered for **Boyle's Law**, which explains the relationship between the pressure and volume of gases.

the ˈ**Boys' Brigade** a British Christian organization for boys. It was set up in 1883 with the aim of teaching boys discipline and respect for themselves and others.

ˈ**Boys' Clubs** (in Britain) clubs for boys and young men which organize sports and outdoor activities such as sailing and climbing. There are more than 2 000 of them around the country, usually in cities, where the boys would not normally be able to take part in such activities. Many of them now also accept girls.

ˌ**Boy ˈScouts of Aˈmerica** the US branch of the *Scouts. It was formed in 1910 and was based on the British organization. In 1998 there were about 5.6 million members. The US Scouts have kept the traditional camps and skills and also learn about different careers. The main groups are Tiger Cubs (age 6), Cub Scouts (7 to 10), Boy Scouts (11 to 18) and Explorers (15 to 20). See also EAGLE SCOUT.

ˌ***Boy's Own ˈPaper*** a British magazine for boys that was published from 1879 to 1967. It contained many exciting adventure stories. British people sometimes use the phrase *Boy's Own* to describe brave or exciting things that people have done: *His escape from the rebels' camp was pure Boy's Own stuff.*

Boz /bɒz; *AmE* bɑːz/ a name used by Charles *Dickens instead of his own name for some of his early work.

BP /ˌbiː ˈpiː/ (*in full* **British Petroleum**) a large international company that produces oil, petrol/gasoline, gas and chemicals. It owns many petrol stations in Britain, and is the largest producer of *North Sea oil and gas. The British government used to own more than half of the shares in the company, but they were sold in the 1980s.

ˌJack ˈ**Brabham** /ˈbræbəm/ (1926–) an Australian driver of racing cars, based in Britain. He won the world championship three times in the 1950s and 1960s, once in a **Brabham**, a car made by the company he had set up. The company continued to be successful in the sport after he stopped racing.

ˌLady ˈ**Bracknell** /ˈbræknəl/ a character in Oscar *Wilde's play *The *Importance of Being Earnest*. She is a severe *upper-class Englishwoman who speaks some of Wilde's most humorous lines. Jack, the main character, is in love with her daughter: *The tea shop was full of Lady Bracknell types with hilarious hats and accents to match.*

ˌMalcolm ˈ**Bradbury** /ˈbrædbri/ (1932–) an English writer and university teacher who writes mainly comic novels about university life. His best-known book, *The History Man* (1975), was made into a television series in 1981.

ˈ**Bradford**[1] /ˈbrædfəd; *AmE* ˈbrædfərd/ an industrial city in *Yorkshire, England. Since the Middle Ages it has been an important centre for the wool trade and for textile production. It now has a large Asian community and is the home of the National Museum of Photography, Film and Television.

ˈBarbara ˈTaylor ˈ**Bradford**[2] /ˈteɪlə ˈbrædfəd; *AmE* ˈteɪlər ˈbrædfərd/ (1933–) one of the world's most popular writers of fiction. By 1997 her books had sold 56 million copies. The stories are usually about modern, successful women who fall in love. They include *A Woman of Substance* (1979), and *Power of a Woman* (1997). Bradford was born in England, where she was a journalist, and now lives in the US.

ˌOmar ˈ**Bradley** /ˌəʊmɑː ˈbrædli; *AmE* ˌoʊmɑːr/ (1893–1981) a US general in *World War II. He led the Allied forces at Normandy on D-Day in 1944 and into Germany. He then became the first Chairman of the *Joint Chiefs of Staff from 1949 to 1953. Bradley was named General of the Army in 1950. His many medals included the *Presidential Medal of Freedom.

Marlon Brando in The Wild One

ˈ**Bradshaw** /ˈbrædʃɔː/ an informal name for *Bradshaw's Railway Guide*, a book published each year from 1839 to 1961 giving details of all the railway services in Britain.

ˌMelvyn ˈ**Bragg** /ˌmelvɪn ˈbræg/ (1939–) an English writer and presenter of television and radio programmes. He is best known for presenting *The *South Bank Show*, in which he introduced the British television audience to serious art, literature, drama, etc. He has also written several novels, mostly set in the *Lake District. He was made a *life peer in 1998.

ˌDennis ˈ**Brain** /ˈbreɪn/ (1921–57) an English musician who played the French horn and the German double horn. He was considered one of the greatest players of these instruments. His best-known recordings are of Mozart's music. He was killed in a car crash.

ˌJohn ˈ**Braine** /ˈbreɪn/ (1922–86) an English writer of realistic novels, the best known of which is **Room at the Top* (1957). He is usually considered one of the *angry young men.

ˌ***Brain of ˈBritain*** a British radio quiz programme which has been broadcast regularly on the *BBC since 1967. The winner of each series of programmes is named *Brain of Britain* for that year: *You don't need to be Brain of Britain to see what's going on.*

*The ˈ**Brains Trust*** a *BBC radio programme in the 1940s which became a television programme in the 1950s In it a group of well-known intellectuals discussed a wide range of topics.

ˈ**Bramley** /ˈbræmli/ (*also* **Bramley apple**, **Bramley's seedling**) *n* a type of large green apple that is suitable for cooking rather than for eating raw. Bramleys are especially popular in Britain.

ˌKenneth ˈ**Branagh** /ˈbrænə/ (1960–) a British actor and director who has worked successfully both in the theatre and in films. He is especially well known for his versions of Shakespeare's plays. He was married to Emma *Thompson and they appeared together in several films. His best-known films (as both actor and director) include **Henry V* (1989), **Much Ado About Nothing* (1993) and **Hamlet* (1997).

ˌ**Branch Da'vidians** /ˌbrɑːntʃ də'vɪdiənz/ a US religious group, based in Waco, *Texas which believed that Christ would soon return to earth. Their leader was David *Koresh. In 1993 members of the group killed four US government officers who were trying to enter their building. The building was then surrounded for 51 days until the Branch Davidians began a fire in which 82 of them died (33 from Britain).

ˌMax '**Brand** /'brænd/ (1892–1944) a popular US writer of novels about the *Wild West. He also created the character of Dr Kildare for several books and then wrote a series of Dr Kildare films.

ˌMarlon '**Brando** /ˌmɑːlən 'brændəʊ; *AmE* ˌmɑːrlən 'brændoʊ/ (1924–) a US actor known for using for playing characters with strong moods. He began on the stage in *A Streetcar Named Desire* (1947) and acted in the film version four years later. He received *Oscars as Best Actor for *On the Waterfront* (1954) and *Last Tango in Paris* (1972).

ˌ**Brand's 'Hatch** /ˌbrændz 'hætʃ/ a motor racing track in *Kent, England, where many *British Grand Prix races took place until 1986.

ˌ**brandy 'butter** *n* [U] (*BrE*) a thick sauce made by mixing brandy, butter and sugar. It is traditionally served with Christmas pudding.

ˌRichard '**Branson** /'brænsn/ (1950–) an English businessman who became very rich through the successful *Virgin companies he created. He set up the Virgin record company in 1970 and sold it to *Thorn-EMI in 1992. In 1984 He started the airline Virgin Atlantic. He is also well known for being the first person to cross the Atlantic (1987) and the Pacific (1991) by balloon.

ˌ**Branston 'Pickle**™ /ˌbrænstən/ *n* [U] a make of pickle (= a mixture of fruit and vegetables preserved in vinegar) which is popular in Britain. It is usually eaten with cold meat or cheese. A phrase often used in advertising it is 'Bring on the Branston'.

ˌ**brass 'band** *n* a band that plays mainly brass instruments such as trumpets, trombones and tubas. In Britain brass bands are traditionally associated with northern England, where many bands were started by groups of workers in a particular factory or coal mine.

a brass band

'**Brasso**™ /'brɑːsəʊ; *AmE* 'bræsoʊ/ *n* [U] a British make of polish for polishing things made of brass.

'**brass-ˌrubbing** *n* [U] the British hobby of making copies of church brasses. These are large flat pieces of decorated brass which have been put in the walls and floors of churches in memory of dead people. Most brasses were put into churches from the 13th century to the 17th century, and usually have designs cut into them representing the dead person. People make their own copies by covering the brass with paper and rubbing the paper with coloured chalk or wax.

Richard Branson

the '**brat pack** *n* [usu sing] (*infml*) a group of well-known or successful young people, especially actors, who enjoy being famous and sometimes behave badly: *Tom Cruise was a member of the Hollywood brat pack.*

ˌWernher von '**Braun** ⇨ VON BRAUN.

ˌ***Brave New 'World*** a novel (1932) by Aldous *Huxley. It is set in the future, when there have been many scientific advances but people have no personal freedom. People sometimes use the phrase *brave new world* to refer to present societies like this, or to refer humorously to something new and unknown: *I'm a bit sceptical about the brave new world of social care promised by the government.*

ˌAngela **Bra'zil** /brə'zɪl/ (1868–1947) an English writer of books for girls, mainly set in girls' schools.

ˌ**bread-and-butter 'pudding** *n* [U] (*BrE*) a traditional British sweet dish, made of slices of bread and butter mixed with raisins and sugar and baked in a mixture of milk and eggs.

ˌ**bread 'sauce** *n* [U] (*BrE*) a sauce made with milk, onion, breadcrumbs and spices. It is usually served hot with chicken or turkey.

ˌ**breakfast 'television** *n* [U] (*BrE*) television programmes shown early in the morning. The most popular breakfast television programmes in Britain are *Breakfast News*, a serious news programme on *BBC1, *GMTV*, a mixture of news and interviews with people such as television actors and sports stars on *ITV, and *The Big Breakfast* on *Channel Four, which consists mostly of comedy and interviews with pop stars. The phrase 'breakfast television' is not used in the US, where television all through the day has been common for many years.

ˌJulian '**Bream** /'briːm/ (1933–) an English musician, well known for playing classical music on the guitar and the lute, an ancient instrument like a guitar. Composers such as *Britten and *Walton have written music especially for him.

B

the ˌ**Brecon** ˈ**Beacons** /ˌbrekən ˈbiːkənz/ an area of mountains in south Wales. It is popular with tourists who like walking and enjoying the attractive scenery.

ˌRory ˈ**Bremner** /ˈbremnə(r)/ (1961–) an English entertainer who makes fun of well-known people, especially politicians, by copying the way they behave and speak.

ˌSt ˈ**Brendan** /ˈbrendən/ (*c.* 485–*c.* 578) an Irish monk who travelled around Ireland and Scotland. According to legends he was also the first European to sail to America. In 1977 a group of people sailed from Ireland to America in a leather boat like the ones used in the 6th century, to prove that it was possible.

ˈWilliam J ˈ**Brennan** ˈJunior /ˈbrenən/ (William Joseph Brennan 1906–97) a US *Supreme Court judge (1956–90) who was known for his liberal views and for his strong support for personal freedom and the rights of minorities. In 1990 he was responsible for a court decision which stated that the government could not stop people who insulted or destroyed the US flag, because that would restrict their freedom.

Brer Rabbit and Brer Fox

ˌ**Brer** ˈ**Rabbit** /ˌbreə; *AmE* ˌbrer/ the main animal character in the *Uncle Remus books by the US writer Joel Chandler Harris. 'Brer' is how some people in the southern US say 'brother'.

the ˈ**Brethren** ⇨ PLYMOUTH BRETHREN.

ˌ**Bretton** ˈ**Woods** /ˈbretn/ a holiday town in the White Mountains in the US state of *New Hampshire. The *International Monetary Fund and the World Bank were created there in 1944 during an international financial meeting.

ˈ***Brewer's*** ˈ***Dictionary of*** ˈ***Phrase and*** ˈ***Fable*** /ˈbruːəz; *AmE* ˈbruːərz/ (*also* ***Brewer***) a dictionary that gives information about the origins of many English words and phrases by referring to history, religion, art, etc. It was first published in 1870 and the original author was Dr E Cobham Brewer. It has been regularly revised, and there is now *Brewer's Dictionary of 20th Century Phrase and Fable*, as well as versions dealing with areas such as film and politics: *Look it up in Brewer.*

ˌFanny ˈ**Brice** /ˌfæni ˈbraɪs/ (1891–1951) a US comedy actor who sang humorous songs and told Jewish jokes. She was a success in the *Ziegfeld Follies on *Broadway before becoming popular on radio. Her story was told in the films *Funny Girl* (1968) and *Funny Lady* (1975).

ˌ***Brideshead Re***ˈ***visited*** /ˌbraɪdzhed/ a novel (1945) by Evelyn *Waugh. It is the story of an Oxford student who becomes involved with a rich but tragic Catholic family in England. The family's large country home is called Brideshead. The book was made into a successful television series in the 1980s. The British public enjoyed watching how the *upper classes of a period in the past dressed, spoke and behaved towards each other, and the series influenced fashions and other television programmes.

the ˌ**Bridge of** ˈ**Sighs** **1** an attractive old bridge over the river Cam in *Cambridge, England. It belongs to St John's College, part of Cambridge University, and looks like the famous Bridge of Sighs in Venice. **2** a similar bridge between two buildings of Hertford College, part of *Oxford University. It is built across a street, not a river.

ˌJim ˈ**Bridger** /ˈbrɪdʒə(r)/ (1804–81) a *mountain man in the American West who discovered the *Great Salt Lake in 1824. He trapped animals and sold their furs, and worked for the army as a scout (= a person who goes first to watch for danger). He began the town of Fort Bridger in *Wyoming. One of his friends said Bridger had 'little fear of God and none of the devil'.

ˌRobert ˈ**Bridges** /ˈbrɪdʒɪz/ (1844–1930) an English poet, best known for his short poems. He was more popular during his life than he is now. He was made *Poet Laureate in 1913. He was also responsible for publishing the poetry of his friend Gerard Manley *Hopkins.

ˌCarl ˈ**Bridgewater** /ˈbrɪdʒwɔːtə(r)/ (1965–78) a British boy who was murdered in 1978. He was delivering newspapers to a farm in Staffordshire and was shot by thieves who were robbing the house. Four men were arrested and sent to prison because one of them, Patrick Molloy, admitted the murder to a policeman who has since been proved dishonest. Molloy died in prison. The others, who became known as the **Bridgewater Three**, protested that they were innocent. In late 1996 they were set free. This is one of several cases at around the same time that have made the British public doubt the honesty of the police. See also BIRMINGHAM SIX, GUILDFORD FOUR, TOTTENHAM THREE.

ˌ***Brief En***ˈ***counter*** a British film (1945) made by David *Lean, based on a play by Noel *Coward. It is about a married woman and a doctor who meet in a railway station and fall in love. After a short relationship they decide to separate, although they love each other. The film is well known for its beautiful photography and for the typically British *middle-class way the couple feel strong emotions without showing them.

ˌ***Brief*** ˈ***Lives*** a book written in the 17th century by John *Aubrey. It consists of the stories of the lives of famous people from that time. Each person's story is short but full of interesting information, and written in a relaxed, amusing style.

ˌRaymond ˈ**Briggs** /ˈbrɪgz/ (1934–) an English writer and illustrator of children's books, mostly in *comic strip form. His original characters and strong, clear illustrations show great understanding of children's imagination. *The *Snowman* and *Fungus the Bogeyman* (1977) are among British children's favourites. Another book, *When the Wind Blows* (1982), is a warning about nuclear weapons. Some of his books have been made into successful cartoon films.

ˈ**Brighton** /ˈbraɪtn/ a large town on the coast of *East Sussex in southern England. In the 18th century it became a fashionable place for people to swim, and it is still a popular place for people to spend their holidays. Its well-known buildings include the *Royal Pavilion and the Palace Pier, and it is also famous for its *Regency architecture. The Grand Hotel was the scene of the **Brighton bombing** in 1984, when five people died after the *IRA tried to kill members of the *Conservative government who were staying there. See also BRIGHTON CAR RALLY.

the ˌ**Brighton** ˈ**car** ˌ**rally** /ˌbraɪtn/ (*also* the **Brighton run**, the **London to Brighton Veteran Car Run**) *n* an event in which many veteran cars (= ones made before 1905) drive from London to *Brighton, England. It takes place in November every year and is an important social event for the owners of the old cars. Many people go to Brighton to watch them arrive. Recently, other groups of car owners have organized their own London-to-Brighton runs at different times of the year.

ˌ**Brighton Pa**ˈ**vilion** /ˌbraɪtn/ ⇨ ROYAL PAVILION.

ˌ**bright young** ˈ**things** *n* [pl] (*sometimes disapprov, often ironic*) a phrase originally used to describe certain rich young people in the 1920s who went to many parties and behaved in a way that older people found shocking. The phrase is now used to refer to any group of clever, ambitious young people: *The club was full of TV researchers and politician's assistants, all bright young things on their way up.*

ˈ**Brillo pad**™ /ˈbrɪləʊ; *AmE* ˈbrɪloʊ/ *n* a British product for cleaning kitchen pans, etc., consisting of a pad of very fine wire with soap inside: *His hair was thick and wiry like a Brillo pad.*

ˌDavid ˈ**Brinkley** /ˈbrɪŋkli/ (1920–) a US television journalist. He and Chet Huntley (1911–74) presented the popular *The Huntley-Brinkley Report* (1955–71) on *NBC. He now has a news programme on *ABC, *This Week with David Brinkley*.

ˌ**Brink's** ˈ**Mat** /ˌbrɪŋks ˈmæt/ a British company that owns a building for storing valuable things at *Heathrow Airport. In 1983 thieves stole gold worth £26 million from the building. At that time it was Britain's largest robbery. The police spent many years investigating the crime, but it is still not certain that they have caught all the criminals. It is one of those crimes, like the *Great Train Robbery, that the British public and press like to talk about.

ˈ**Bristol** /ˈbrɪstl/ a large port and industrial city in south-west England, on the river *Avon. It was an important port in the slave trade in the 17th and 18th centuries. In the 1990s it became one of Britain's most fashionable cities. Local pop groups such as *Massive Attack and *Portishead became famous all over the world and their style of music, trip-hop, is sometimes called the 'Bristol sound'.

the ˌ**Bristol** ˈ**Channel** /ˌbrɪstl/ a long area of water between south-east England and the south coast of Wales. The *Severn and *Avon rivers flow into it.

ˌ**Bristol** ˈ**Cream**™ /ˌbrɪstl/ *n* [U, C] a type of rich, sweet sherry sold by *Harvey's. It is one of the best-known sherries in Britain, where bottles of it are often given as presents, e.g. at Christmas.

ˌ**Bristol Old** ˈ**Vic** /ˌbrɪstl, ˈvɪk/ a British theatre company. It was formed in 1946 as a branch of the London *Old Vic and has been based since then at the Theatre Royal, Bristol. It is Britain's oldest theatre in continuous use.

Britain and the US

The relationship between Britain and the US has always been a close one. Like all close relationships it has had difficult times. The US was first a British colony, but between 1775 and 1783 the US fought a war to become independent. The US fought the British again in the *War of 1812.

In general, however, the two countries have felt closer to each other than to any other country, and their foreign policies have shown this. During *World War I and *World War II, and more recently in the *Falklands War and the *Gulf War, Britain and the US supported each other. When the US looks for foreign support, Britain is usually the first country to come forward and it is sometimes called 'the 51st state of the union'.

But the **special relationship** that developed after 1945 is not explained only by shared political interests. An important reason for the friendship is that the people of the two countries are very similar. They share the same language and enjoy each other's literature, films and television. Many Americans have British ancestors, or relatives still living in Britain. The US government and political system is based on Britain's, and there are many Anglo-American businesses operating on both sides of the Atlantic. In Britain some people are worried about the extent of US influence, and there is some jealousy of its current power.

The special relationship was strongest in the early 1980s when Margaret *Thatcher was Prime Minister in Britain and Ronald *Reagan was President of the US. Now, Britain is part of the *European Union and the US belongs to the trade association *NAFTA, and some people wonder if these new relationships will replace the old one.

Briˈ**tannia** /brɪˈtænjə/ a figure of a woman representing Britain on many coins. She is shown sitting down wearing a helmet and holding a trident (= a long weapon with three points). Britannia was the Roman name for Britain. See also *RULE, BRITANNIA!*

Jane Carr as Britannia in the musical Poppy *by Peter Nichols*

Briˈ***tannia*** /brɪˈtænjə/ the last British *royal yacht. Its permanent home is now in the port of Leith, in *Edinburgh, where it has been turned into a tourist attraction.

the **Bri**ˈ**tannia** ˌ**Royal** ˈ**Naval** ˌ**College** /brɪˈtænjə/ (*also* the **Royal Naval College**) a military college in *Dartmouth, south-west England, where people train to be officers in the *Royal Navy.

the ˈ**Brit Awards** /ˈbrɪt/ a ceremony at which pop groups and singers are given prizes such as 'best record' or 'best new group' of the year. It takes place in London every year and many people watch it on television.

the ˌ**British A**ˈ**cademy** a society of leading academic people in Britain that was established in 1901 to encourage the study of history, philosophy and language. It is responsible for deciding which university research projects should receive money from the government. Its full name is the British Academy for the Promotion of Historical, Philosophical and Philological Studies. Compare ROYAL SOCIETY.

the ˈ**British A**ˈ**cademy of** ˈ**Film and** ˈ**Television** ˈ**Arts** ⇨ BAFTA.

ˌ**British** ˈ**Aerospace** (*abbr* **BAe**) the largest British aircraft company, making civil and military aircraft as well as weapons and space communication systems. It was formed as a nationalized industry in 1977 and then sold to private owners in 1981.

ˌ**British** ˈ**Airports Au**ˌ**thority** the former name of the company that owns most of Britain's major airports, when it was owned by the state. It changed its name to *BAA when it was sold to private owners in 1987.

ˌ**British** ˈ**Airways** (*abbr* **BA**) Britain's largest airline. The company was originally owned by the state and formed by combining smaller airlines in 1974. It

B

was then sold to private owners in 1987. Although it advertises itself as 'the world's favourite airline', it has a reputation for dishonest behaviour. In recent years *Virgin and Laker Airways have both won legal cases against British Airways for unfair business practice.

the **ˈBritish Asˌsociˈation** (the British Association for the Advancement of Science) a British organization established in 1831 to encourage people to be interested in science. It organizes talks and exhibitions and publishes small books. It aims particularly to encourage science in schools.

the **ˌBritish Athˈletic Fedeˌration** the organization that controls British athletics and is responsible for British athletes taking part in international events. Compare AAA.

the **ˈBritish ˈBoard of ˈFilm Classifiˌcation** the organization that decides which films and videos can be seen by people of different ages in Britain. See also FILM CERTIFICATE.

the **ˌBritish ˈBroadcasting Corpoˌration** ⇨ BBC.

ˌBritish ˈCoal the state organization that formerly managed most of Britain's coal mines. When coal mining became a nationalized industry in 1947, the company in charge of the mines was called the **National Coal Board**. Its name was changed to British Coal in the 1980s, when the government began to close many mines. It was sold to smaller private companies in 1994.

the **British Constitution**

Britain is a **constitutional monarchy**: it is ruled by a king or queen who accepts the advice of ***Parliament**. It is also a **parliamentary democracy**, a country whose government is controlled by a parliament that has been elected by the people. The highest positions in government are taken by elected *Members of Parliament, also called MPs. The king or queen now has little real power.

The principles and procedures by which Britain is governed have developed over many centuries. They are not written down in a single document that can be referred to in a dispute. The British Constitution is made up of **statute law** (= laws agreed by Parliament), **common law** (= judges' decisions made in court and then written down) and **conventions** (= rules and practices that people cannot be forced to obey but which are considered necessary for efficient government). The Constitution can be altered by *Acts of Parliament, or by general agreement.

Similarly, there is no single document that lists people's rights. Some rights have been formally recognized by Parliament through laws, e.g. the right of a person not to be discriminated against (= treated differently) because of his or her sex. Other rights, such as the right not to be discriminated against on the grounds of religion, are not formally written down. It is generally understood that these rights are part of the Constitution.

---

the **ˌBritish ˈCouncil** a British government organization that was set up in 1934 to develop a better understanding of Britain, British culture and the English language in other countries. It has libraries and cultural centres in many countries, and organizes films, exhibitions, visits by British writers and artists, student exchanges and language lessons.

the **British Empire** ⇨ article.

the **ˈBritish ˈEmpire ˈMedal** (*abbr* **BEM**) a former British *honour given to people as a title for good work done in fields such as entertainment, art, business or charity. It was the lowest of the honours and was combined in 1993 with the *MBE.

British English ⇨ article.

the **ˌBritish Expeˈditionary Force** (*abbr* the **BEF**) the name used for the first groups of British soldiers sent to fight on the continent of Europe in *World War I and *World War II. They were professional soldiers, trained to deal quickly with dangerous situations. They were joined later by people who had been taken into the armed forces because of the war.

the **ˌBritish ˈFilm ˌInstitute** ⇨ BFI.

ˌBritish ˈGas the largest company supplying gas to homes and businesses in Britain. It used to be a nationalized industry but was sold to private owners in 1986.

the **ˈBritish ˌGrand ˈPrix 1** an international motor race for very fast cars that takes place every year at *Silverstone. It is one of a series of races around the world at this level. The driver who wins most points in the series in a particular year becomes the world champion. **2** an important international motorcycle race that takes place in England every year at Donington Park, near Derby.

the **ˌBritish ˈIsles** the name for the group of islands that includes Great Britain, Ireland and all the smaller islands around them, including the *Shetlands, the *Isle of Man and the *Channel Islands. Compare GREAT BRITAIN, UNITED KINGDOM.

the **ˌBritish ˈLegion** (*also* the **Royal British Legion**) a charity organization that helps former members of the British armed forces by giving them money and other things that they may need, and by providing clubs where they can meet. Most British towns have a **British Legion Club**. The charity collects most of its money on *Poppy Day.

ˌBritish ˈLeyland /ˈleɪlənd/ a large British company that made cars, buses and lorries/trucks in the 1970s and 80s. It was formed in 1968 when several large companies including *Austin, *Morris, *Rover and *Jaguar combined, but continued to use the original names for the cars they produced. The company was losing money in the 1970s and became a nationalized industry. It continued to lose money and in the 1980s it was separated into smaller companies and sold to private owners.

the **ˌBritish ˈLibrary** the library of Britain and the most important of the *copyright libraries. It used to be part of the *British Museum but in the 1990s a new library was built in north London. Many people in Britain dislike the architecture of the new library, in the shape of a ship, and were unhappy at how much it cost to build and the many delays before it opened. Although it is much larger than the old library, it is still not big enough for all the books and documents that need to be kept.

the **ˌBritish ˈLions** (*also* the **Lions**) *n* [pl] a *Rugby Union team consisting of the best players from England, Ireland, Scotland and Wales. The team is chosen to play on tours abroad.

the **ˌBritish ˈMedical Associˌation** ⇨ BMA.

The ***ˌBritish ˈMedical ˌJournal*** (*abbr The* ***BMJ***) a British magazine, the official magazine of the *British Medical Association, which contains news and information about medicine and matters of interest to doctors. It first appeared in 1857 and is published every week.

the **ˌBritish Muˈseum** the museum of Britain, established in 1753. The main building is in *Bloomsbury, London, and includes the famous reading room, a large round room that used to be part of the *British Library. Many well-known writers have studied and written their books there. The museum has one of the world's finest collections of art and

The British Library reading room at the British Museum

ancient objects, including the *Elgin marbles and the *Rosetta Stone.

the ˌ**British** ˈ**National** ˌ**Party** (*abbr* the **BNP**) a small, extreme right-wing British political party. Its members are mostly white people who have a strong fear or dislike of other races. It has no *Members of Parliament, but in 1993 its first councillor was elected to represent it on a local *council in an area of east London where many Asian people live.

ˈ**British** ˈ**Nuclear** ˈ**Fuels** (*abbr* **BNFL**) a British company, owned by the state, that produces nuclear fuel and processes nuclear waste so that it can be used again. It is based at *Sellafield in north-west England. The company often advertises on British television to try to persuade people that what it does is safe, but many people believe that it is dangerous.

the ˌ**British** ˈ**Open** (*also* the **Open**) the British Open Golf Championship, the most important golf contest in Britain, which takes place once a year at one of several British golf courses. It is the oldest international golf event in the world, and both professional and amateur players take part.

ˌ**British Pe**ˈ**troleum** ⇨ BP.

ˌ**British** ˈ**Rail** the company, owned by the state, which ran the rail transport system in Britain until the 1990s, when it was separated into several smaller companies and sold to private owners.

the ˌ**British** ˈ**Raj** ⇨ RAJ.

ˈ**British** ˈ**Sky** ˈ**Broadcasting** ⇨ BSKYB.

the ˌ**British** ˈ**Standards Insti**ˌ**tution** ⇨ BSI.

ˌ**British** ˈ**Steel** the state company that formerly manufactured most of the iron and steel produced in Britain. It was sold to private owners in 1988.

ˌ**British** ˈ**Summer Time** (*abbr* **BST**) *n* [U] the time shown on clocks, etc. in Britain from March to October each year. It is one hour ahead of *GMT, giving an hour more light each evening.

ˌ**British** ˈ**Telecom** /ˈtelɪkɒm; *AmE* ˈtelɪkɑːm/ the former name of *BT.

the ˌ**British** ˈ**Tourist Au**ˌ**thority** ⇨ BTA.

ˈ**British U**ˈ**nited** ˈ**Provident As**ˌ**soci**ˈ**ation** ⇨ BUPA.

ˈ**Briton** *n* **1** (*also infml, sometimes disapprov* **Brit**) a British person: *More and more Britons are taking their holidays abroad.* **2** (*also* **Ancient Briton**) one of the Celtic people who lived in Britain before the Romans arrived. ⇨ article at CELTS AND CELTIC CULTURE.

ˈ**Britpop** /ˈbrɪtpɒp; *AmE* ˈbrɪtpɑːp/ *n* [U] a type of pop music played in the 1990s by white British groups such as *Blur, *Oasis and *Pulp. They have been influenced by British groups from the 1960s like the *Beatles and the *Kinks, and play short, simple songs with strong tunes and words full of clever humour: *They aim to be the first Britpop band to crack the US market.*

ˌLeon ˈ**Brittan** /ˌliːɒn ˈbrɪtn; *AmE* ˌliːɑːn/ (1939–) a British *Conservative politician. He was *Home Secretary (1983–5) and *Secretary of State for trade and industry (1985–6). He resigned in 1986 because he had been involved in the *Westland affair. He became a *European Commissioner in 1988, and was made a *knight in 1989.

ˌBenjamin ˈ**Britten** /ˈbrɪtn/ (1913–76) an composer who wrote some of the best and most popular British classical music of the 20th century. His best-known music was written for voices, including the operas *Peter Grimes* (1945) and *Billy Budd* (1951) Many of his pieces were written to be sung by his friend Peter *Pears, and many others were written for children. He lived the second half of his life in Aldeburgh, and established the music festival there. He was made a *life peer in 1976. See also ALDEBURGH FESTIVAL.

Peter Pears (singing) and Benjamin Britten (playing the piano)

ˈ**Brixton** /ˈbrɪkstən/ a district of south London, England. It is well known as one of the most multicultural parts of London, with large communities of Irish and *Afro-Caribbean people, and smaller communities from many European, African and Asian countries. In the early 1980s there were violent protests on the streets of Brixton, called the **Brixton riots**, against the lack of jobs and houses, and the prejudice of some members of the police against people of other races. As a result the government started to spend money on improving the houses, the sports centre and the opportunities for young people in Brixton. Some people think of it as a dangerous area, but many others go there to enjoy the shops, restaurants and clubs of many different cultures: *Karen buys all her clothes in Brixton market.*

the ˌ**Broadcasting Com**ˈ**plaints Com**ˌ**mission** a group of people whose job is to deal with complaints made by the public about radio and television programmes in Britain.

ˌ**Broadcasting** ˈ**House** the main building of the *BBC, in central London. It contains most of the BBC's administrative offices, and many studios where radio programmes are made.

the ˌ**Broadcasting** ˈ**Standards** ˌ**Council** a group of people whose job is to watch television programmes and listen to radio programmes that people have complained about in Britain, and decide if they are offensive to anybody, or contain too much sex or violence.

ˈ**Broadmoor** /ˈbrɔːdmɔː(r)/ a hospital in *Berkshire, southern England, for people who are mentally ill. It is well known to British people as a place to which criminals are sent if they cannot go to an ordinary prison because of mental illness: *He was sent to Broadmoor in 1985 and may never be released.*

The British Empire

The British Empire was at its largest and most powerful around 1920, when about 25% of the world's population lived under British rule and over a quarter of the land in the world belonged to Britain. It was said that it was an empire 'on which the sun never sets'.

The building of the Empire

The growth of the British Empire was at first the result of competition among European nations, especially Britain, France, Spain and the Netherlands, for new areas in which to trade and new sources of raw materials. Explorers visited the Americas and the Far East, and in the 16th century trading companies, such as the Dutch and English *East India Companies, were set up. Many **colonies** (= places taken over by a foreign country and settled by people from that country) began as trading centres, or were founded to protect a trade route, and were run for the profit of the **mother country**. Some colonies were founded by people trying to make a new life for themselves, others were originally **penal colonies** (= places where people were sent as a punishment).

Britain gained its first foreign possessions in the late 15th century. **Newfoundland**, now part of *Canada, was claimed for England in 1497. Canada itself was won in 1763 after war with the French. During the 17th and 18th centuries colonies were established on the east coast of North America, including ***Plymouth Colony** founded by the ***Pilgrim Fathers**. In the 1770s people in the American colonies became angry with Britain, mainly because of taxes they had to pay. This resulted in the *American Revolution and later the independence of the United States.

The wealthiest area in the early days of empire was the ***West Indies** because of money made from sugar cane and tobacco. Britain's colonies included *Barbados, *Antigua and *Montserrat and *Jamaica. Later, other islands were added. *Slaves were brought to the West Indies from Africa to work in the plantations. The slave trade was abolished (= ended) in the British Empire in 1807, though slavery did not end in the West Indies until 1838.

***India** was controlled for many years by the wealthy English East India Company. After the Company expanded into Bengal, the British Government began to see India as important politically and took a greater interest in the territory. Roads and railways were built to make trade easier and improve contact with more remote districts, a **Governor-General** was put in charge, and British *civil servants and troops were sent to the region.

***Australia**, discovered for Britain by Captain *Cook, was first settled as a penal colony. The first prisoners and their guards reached *Botany Bay in 1788. Originally there were six colonies, including New South Wales and Tasmania, but in 1901 these joined together and became a federation. ***New Zealand** became a colony in 1840.

From 1801 the expanding empire was managed from London by the **Colonial Office**. District officers and civil servants were sent out to administer the colonies on behalf of Britain. Regular **imperial conferences** were held in Britain to discuss matters of general concern, such as trade, defence and foreign policy.

Expansion

The second period of empire-building took place in the late 19th century. At that time Britain was one of the leading economic and political powers in the world, and wanted to protect her interests and also increase her international influence by obtaining new lands. It was also thought by some people to be a matter of moral obligation and destiny to run poorer, less advanced countries and to pass on European culture to the native inhabitants. This was what Rudyard *Kipling called 'the *white man's burden'.

***Hong Kong** was important both for trade with China and for strategic (= political and military) reasons, and became a British colony in 1842. It later became an important business centre.

In 1858, following the *Indian Mutiny, India was placed under the direct control of the British Government and a **viceroy** replaced the Governor-General. British influence in India had expanded from a few trading stations into the ***Raj** (= British rule). India brought Britain great wealth and strategic advantage, and was called 'the *jewel in the crown' of the Empire. Local Indian rulers were allowed to remain in power provided they were loyal to the viceroy. Many British people spent years working in India as civil servants, engineers, police officers, etc. and took their families with them. By about 1880 the British in India had developed a distinct lifestyle which is described in E M *Forster's *A *Passage to India* and Paul *Scott's *The *Raj Quartet*.

In Africa, the **Cape of Good Hope** was important to Britain because it was on the sea route to India. It was bought from the Boers in 1815, and British settlers went out to live there alongside the Boers. There were many problems between them and in 1836 the Boers left to found the Orange Free State, Transvaal and Natal. In 1889 Cecil *Rhodes formed the British South Africa Company which took over land further north in what came to be called Rhodesia. In 1910, after the second *Boer War, the Cape, Natal, the Transvaal and Orange Free State formed the Union of South Africa.

Between about 1870 and 1900 Britain, Belgium, France, Italy and Germany took part in what came to be called **the scramble for Africa**. The journeys of explorers and missionaries (= religious teachers) like David *Livingstone encouraged interest in the interior of Africa, and gaining control of these areas became important for national pride as well as providing new opportunities for trade. In 1884 the European nations, in an attempt at cooperation, agreed **spheres of influence**. Britain's colonies in West Africa were the Gold Coast (now *Ghana), *Nigeria, *Sierra Leone and *Gambia. In East Africa, countries that were acquired as **protectorates** (= states controlled and protected by Britain) included the East African Protectorate (now *Kenya), *Uganda, Somaliland, Zanzibar, Northern and Southern Rhodesia (now *Zambia and *Zimbabwe) and Nyasaland (now *Malawi). After *World War I Britain also administered the former German colony of Tanganyika which later joined with Zanzibar to form *Tanzania.

B

Independence

In the 19th century the Empire was a source of pride for Britain. During the 20th century it became expensive to run and also an embarrassment. The middle of the century was a time of changing values and it was morally no longer acceptable to take over other countries and cultures and to exploit them. Many colonies had growing nationalist movements for independence.

Canada, Australia and New Zealand had already become **dominions** (= self-governing regions) in 1907 and South Africa in 1910. Each had a British governor advised by local ministers. They gained full independence in 1931.

The Indian National Congress under Mahatma Gandhi led the movement for independence in India, but the situation was complicated by hostility between Hindus and Moslems. When India was given independence in 1947 parts of the north-west and north-east became West and East Pakistan. After a civil war in 1971 they became separate countries, *Pakistan and *Bangladesh.

Most other countries of the Empire became independent in the 1950s and 1960s, beginning with Ghana in 1957. When Hong Kong was returned to China in 1997 many people described this as the final part in the story of the Empire. Many countries, including India and Ghana, became republics after independence, but others still recognize the British King or Queen as their head of state. Countries such as *Bermuda and *St Helena, which are not independent, have chosen to remain British.

The legacy of the Empire

The loss of the Empire inevitably meant loss of power and status, but Britain's world influence has been partly maintained through the ***Commonwealth**, which was founded in 1931. When countries became independent most chose to join the Commonwealth and to keep their links with Britain. Britain is closely involved with Commonwealth countries, both politically and economically, and has friendly relations with most of them. From the early 1950s a growing number of immigrants from the *Caribbean and South Asia came to settle in Britain. Until 1962 Commonwealth citizens were freely admitted to Britain, and some areas of Britain now have large Asian or West Indian communities.

The Empire has had both a positive and a negative influence on the cultures of the countries that were part of it. British rule influenced local systems of government, and most countries have a civil service, army and legal system organized in a similar way to those in Britain. Many roads and railways were also started under British rule, and schools were established. On the other hand much of British foreign policy was based on racial prejudice and contempt for native cultures. Most British people sent to India, for example, showed little understanding of Indian history, character or culture. Many people believed that they had a moral duty to convert local people to Christianity, and did not sufficiently respect local religions. Native people everywhere were usually considered inferior to white people and to have few rights.

Perhaps the most important and lasting cultural influence of the British Empire has been the spread of the *English language. After independence, English remained an official language in many countries and is taught as a second language in schools. The ability to speak English as well as local languages was useful for establishing a position in international politics, trade and finance. The English language has in turn become richer with words borrowed from many of the cultures with which it came into contact.

the '**Broads** /'brɔːdz/ (*also* the **Norfolk Broads**) *n* [pl] a *national park in *East Anglia, England, where there are many small lakes connected to each other by rivers and canals. It is a very popular area for people who go on holiday/vacation in boats.

'**broadsheet** *n* (in Britain) a newspaper with large pages. The more serious newspapers such as *The *Guardian*, *The *Independent* and *The *Times* are often referred to as 'the broadsheets'. Compare TABLOID. ⇨ article at NEWSPAPERS.

'**Broadwater 'Farm E'state** /'brɔːdwɔːtə; *AmE* 'brɔːdwɔːtər/ a group of flats and houses in Tottenham, north London, where a violent protest took place in 1985. An *Afro-Caribbean woman died while the police were searching her house, and a group of angry young people started burning buildings and cars and fighting the police. A police officer called Keith Blakelock was killed by a group of people who the police never caught. Three men, the *Tottenham Three, were arrested and sent to prison for the murder but they were released in 1991 after they had been proved innocent.

Broadway

Broadway is the name of a street in New York that is closely associated with the theatre and is often used to mean US theatre in general. The street runs the whole length of *Manhattan, but its 36 theatres are in the **Theater District** between West 41st Street and West 57th Street. The most famous are between 44th and 45th Streets, near *Times Square. This part is called the *Great White Way because of its many bright lights. The first theatres were built there in 1894 and New York's subway system was extended north shortly afterwards to help audiences get to them. Other theatres in New York, usually smaller, are said to be **off-Broadway**, and there are even **off-off-Broadway** theatres, which are less commercial.

Before the rise of the film industry, Broadway was the place where actors could become famous. Broadway's best years were in the 1920s when there were about 80 theatres. Most of the longest running plays on Broadway have been *musicals such as **South Pacific*, **Guys and Dolls*, **My Fair Lady* and *A *Chorus Line*. Andrew *Lloyd Webber's **Cats* has had the longest run. Serious plays that have won *Tony awards include **Death of a Salesman*, **Long Day's Journey into Night* and **Who's Afraid of Virginia Woolf?* Famous actors who have appeared on Broadway include Dustin *Hoffman, Robert *Redford, Elizabeth *Taylor, Liza *Minnelli and, from Britain, Richard *Burton, Jeremy *Irons, Maggie *Smith and Ralph *Fiennes.

Since the early 1970s the high cost of producing plays has forced many theatres to close or to become cinemas/movie theaters, and Broadway is not as important as it once was. It has had fewer successful new plays and has tried to attract audiences with **revivals** or with successful British productions. A bad **review** by the drama critic of the **New York Times* can close a play. Paul *Simon's $11-million musical, *The Capeman*, for instance, ran for only two months after bad reviews. Recently, there have been signs that Broadway is attracting larger audiences again with new musicals such as *Titanic*, but most new avant-garde (= experimental) works are produced off-Broadway, or off-off-Broadway in the **lofts** (= old warehouses) of *SoHo.

ˈ**Broadwood** /ˈbrɔːdwʊd/ a British company that has produced pianos since 1728, and became famous by making one for Beethoven in 1817. Many people consider Broadwoods the best pianos in the world.

ˈ**Brobdingnag** /ˈbrɒbdɪŋnæg; *AmE* ˈbrɑːbdɪŋnæg/ an imaginary country visited by Gulliver in Jonathan *Swift's **Gulliver's Travels*. The people there are much bigger than Gulliver, and they are disgusted by his descriptions of life in Europe.

ˌTom ˈ**Brokaw** /ˈbrəʊkɔː; *AmE* ˈbroʊkɔː/ (1940–) a US journalist who has presented the *NBC Nightly News* on television since 1982. He began his career with *NBC in 1973 as their journalist for the *White House, and has also presented the **Today* show (1976–81). Compare RATHER.

ˌ**Brompton** ˈ**Oratory** /ˌbrɒmptən; *AmE* ˈbrɑːmptən/ a large *Roman Catholic church in central London, England, built in the late 19th century in the highly decorated *baroque style. It was London's main Catholic church until *Westminster Cathedral was built.

the ˈ**Brontë** ˌ**sisters** /ˈbrɒnteɪ; *AmE* ˈbrɑːnteɪ/ **Charlotte Brontë** (1816–55), **Emily Brontë** (1818–48) and **Anne Brontë** (1820–49), three British writers who lived most of their lives in *Haworth, a small village in *Yorkshire, England, where their father was the local *Anglican priest. They began to write poetry and novels when they were very young, creating imaginary worlds when they were alone in the Yorkshire countryside. They died before their best-known books, including Charlotte's **Jane Eyre*, Emily's **Wuthering Heights* and Anne's *Tenant of Wildfell Hall* (1848), became the famous works of English literature that they are today.

the ˈ**Bronx** /ˈbrɒŋks; *AmE* ˈbrɑːŋks/ one of the five *boroughs of New York City, north of *Harlem. It is a poor area and in its southern part there is a lot of crime and drug dealing. It contains Yankee Stadium and the Bronx Zoo. See also YANKEES.

ˌ**Bronx** ˈ**cheer** /ˌbrɒŋks; *AmE* ˌbrɑːŋks/ *n* (*AmE infml*) a rude noise made with the lips and tongue, sometimes directed at a rival team in *baseball or some other sport.

Bronze Age Britain

In Britain the *Stone Age changed slowly into the Bronze Age from about 2100 BC. Metal started to be used for the first time instead of stone to make tools. The skill to make things with metal may have been brought to Britain soon after 2000 BC by the Beaker Folk who were named after the bell-shaped beakers (= cups with wide mouths) found in their tombs. Copper was used at first, then bronze, a mixture of copper and tin. Tools were made by pouring the metal into a mould. In the latter part of the Bronze Age most **settlements** (= villages) had their own **smiths** or skilled craftsmen.

Bronze Age people built the impressive **stone circles** still to be seen at ***Stonehenge** and other places. The double circle of **standing stones** at Stonehenge dates from about 2100 BC. Several pairs of stones still have a large, thick horizontal stone across the top of them. The upright sandstone boulders, called *sarsens*, are thought to have been dug from the ground about 20 miles (32 kilometres) away, but the smaller blue-coloured stones laid across the top come from Wales. It is not known whether they were transported by people using rollers or whether they were left near the site of Stonehenge by glaciers during the Ice Age. In either case, many people would have been involved in building the monument. Stonehenge now attracts a lot of visitors and is a source of wonder and pride. Some people believe that it has a special religious or astronomical meaning and was originally used to calculate when the seasons began and ended.

On *Dartmoor many **stone rows** extend in lines for distances up to two miles (3 kilometres). There are few traces of Bronze Age houses, though **pounds** (= areas surrounded by stone walls) on the edge of the moor may have contained groups of houses.

In the Bronze Age important people were buried in round ***barrows** (= piles of earth) made near the top of a hill. Over 20 000 round barrows are known. There was usually only one person buried in each, together with metal goods and pottery.

In about 500 BC iron began to be used instead of bronze for making tools, and the period after this became known as the *Iron Age.

ˌPeter ˈ**Brook** /ˈbrʊk/ (1925–) a British theatre director who became famous in the 1960s and 1970s for presenting plays in new and interesting ways. In 1970 he moved to France and set up an experimental theatre company in Paris which became internationally famous for its new versions of works such as the ancient Indian story *The Mahabharata*.

ˌRupert ˈ**Brooke** /ˈbrʊk/ (1897–1915) a English poet who fought and died in *World War I. His best-known poems are about the war, such as *The Soldier* (1915), which includes the famous lines:

If I should die, think only this of me:
That there's some corner of a foreign field
That is forever England.

ˌ**Brooke** ˈ**Bond**™ /ˌbrʊk/ a British company that produces several types of food and drink, including **Brooke Bond PG Tips**, one of the most popular makes of *tea(1) in Britain. It is well known for its television advertisements, which show a group of chimpanzees dressed as people drinking tea.

ˈ**Brooklyn** /ˈbrʊklɪn/ one of the five *boroughs of New York City, south of *Manhattan(1) and connected to it by the *Brooklyn Bridge. It is an industrial port, but the area in it called **Brooklyn Heights** is one of the most beautiful in the city. Atlantic Avenue in Brooklyn is famous for its Middle-Eastern restaurants and shops.

the ˌ**Brooklyn** ˈ**Bridge** /ˌbrʊklɪn/ the bridge over the East River in New York City that connects *Manhattan(1) with *Brooklyn. It was opened in 1883 and has a length of 1 595 feet (486 metres). The expression

the Brooklyn Bridge

British English

The term *British English* is used by linguists to contrast the form of *English used in Britain with *American English, and also with Australian English, South African English, etc. In broad terms, British English is English as used throughout the United Kingdom, but it is often more narrowly understood as the English of England, especially that of south-east England as used by the upper and middle classes. English people are rather possessive about their language and to them it is simply *English*. Other varieties are seen as modified, usually less acceptable forms.

Standard English

From the 15th century onwards standards of pronunciation and vocabulary gradually became established. In the 18th century there was a lot of discussion about 'correct' English, and Samuel *Johnson's dictionary, published in 1755, came to be considered an authority on the correct use of words. ***Dialects** (= forms of a language used in a particular region) were considered inferior to **standard English**, also called **the *Queen's/King's English** or ***BBC English**. Today, standard English is used by educated speakers and is taught in schools and to foreign students.

Standard English used to be associated with the ***accent** (= way of speaking) known as ***Received Pronunciation** (**RP**). It is often assumed to require RP, but it can be spoken with a variety of accents. Phonetic transcriptions of British English in dictionaries are usually based on RP. It used to be thought necessary for a person to get rid of their regional accent and speak RP in order to get a good job. Now, though many educated people use RP, others are proud to keep their regional accent.

Regional English

Modern dialects have their roots in *Old English or *Middle English. The old East Midlands dialect developed into standard English, while others became the many regional dialects spoken today. Dialects are often characterized by use of **non-standard** forms such as double negative structures, e.g. *I don't want none*, dropped prepositions as in *He's gone down the pub*, or variant pronouns such as *hisself* and *theirselves*. Dialects are usually spoken with a regional accent.

Most British people can recognize ***Cockney**, a London dialect of the *working class. Grammatical variations include *them as* for 'those who' and double negatives. Characteristics of a Cockney accent include dropping the letter 'h', e.g. *'ouse* for *house*, a feature shared by many urban accents, and pronouncing 'th' in words like *think* as /f/ not /θ/. A glottal stop /ʔ/ replaces the /t/ in words like *water*, and the /eɪ/ in *mate* is replaced by /aɪ/.

The northern ***Geordie** dialect shares many features with Scottish English. Speakers of ***Scouse**, a Liverpool dialect, tend to **slur** (= join) their words, as in *gorra* for 'got a' or 'got to'. Words unique to the north include *gradely* (= excellent) and *mardy* (= spoilt). A feature which usually identifies somebody as coming from the north is the use of /æ/ instead of /ɑː/ in words like *castle* and *bath*. Urban dialects of the Midlands, e.g. ***Brummie**, share features with northern dialects.

The *West Country is known for its distinctive rural dialects. Non-standard usages include *I be* for 'I am' and *her says* for 'she says'. Accents have **burred** (= rolled) 'r's, and 's' is pronounced more like 'z', as in *Zummerzet* for 'Somerset'.

Scottish dialect expressions that are well known to English people are *aye* for 'yes', *wee* for 'little', *bairns* for 'children' and *I dinna ken* for 'I don't know'. Scottish pronunication is noted for its burred 'r's and distinctive vowel sounds. Words like *rice* or *tide* are pronounced more like /reɪs/ or /teɪd/ than the standard /raɪs/ or /taɪd/ sound. Educated Scottish accents have features in common with RP.

In Wales, dialect usages include *boyo* for 'man' and *look you* for 'you see'. Well-known Irish dialect forms include *would you be after wanting* for 'do you want', and the repetition of a phrase at the end of a sentence, such as *at all, at all*. Welsh, Irish and some Scottish accents often have an attractive **lilt** (= rising and falling intonation pattern). These dialects and accents are sometimes made fun of.

In Britain there are many people whose families came from South Asia or the *Caribbean. Younger people from these groups speak English as their first language, while some older people use it as a second language. Many have dialects and accents which are influenced both by their first language and by the dialect of the area where they now live.

The changing language

In the 1990s a new dialect, ***Estuary English**, spread through south-east England. It developed from a combination of Cockney and RP, and was the result of the upward social movement of some Cockney speakers and a downward trend from RP by some middle-class speakers. Estuary English was adopted by some people as a feature of a new classless society. It can be heard in Parliament and on television though it seems less popular than originally, perhaps because many people find its accent unattractive. It has some of the glottal stops found in Cockney, and in words like *hill* the /l/ is replaced by /ʊ/, so *hill* is pronounced /hɪʊ/. Non-standard forms include the use of *was* for *were*, as in 'We was walking home', and variant prepositions such as *off of*, as in 'She got off of the bus'.

The spread of Estuary English provoked a strong reaction among people who believed that the standard of English was falling. Previously, there was a distinction between written English and the more informal spoken language. This has been reduced in recent years, with many books and newspapers using easier, more informal English to reach a wider group of readers.

Some people are also worried about the increasing influence of American English. Both written and spoken British English are today more aggressive and direct. But one development which most people welcome is the campaign to replace the difficult and obscure language used on official forms with **plain English**.

Britain has no language academy to set and enforce standards, though recently there have been calls for one to be set up. Others argue that rules laid down by such an organization would hinder the natural development of the language and would in any case probably be resisted by the public.

B

selling the Brooklyn Bridge to somebody means tricking them in a deal.

ˌ**Brooklyn'ese** /ˌbrʊklɪn'iːz/ *n* [U] the pronunciation and words used by many people living in *Brooklyn in New York City. 'You' becomes 'youse', 'them' is 'dem' and 'thirty-third' is 'toidy-toid'. This way of speaking is also heard in other parts of the city, so many Americans believe that all people from New York speak Brooklynese.

Aˌnita '**Brookner** /'brʊknə(r)/ (1928–) an English writer who had a successful career writing about the history of art before she began writing novels in the 1980s. She writes about *middle-class people with intelligence and humour. Her best-known book, *Hotel du Lac* (1984), won the *Booker Prize.

ˌGarth '**Brooks**[1] /ˌgɑːθ 'brʊks; *AmE* ˌgɑːrθ/ (1956–) a US singer of *country music. His shows on stage are exciting, with Brooks sometimes 'flying' on wires over the audience as he sings. His album *No Fences* sold 13 million copies. He won *Grammy awards for *Ropin' the Wind* (1991) and *In Another's Eyes* (1998).

ˌMel '**Brooks**[2] /ˌmel 'brʊks/ (1926–) a US comic actor who also directs, writes and produces films. He is known for his wild humour. He began in the 1950s as a television writer for Sid *Caesar. His films have included *The Producers* (1968), the comic Western *Blazing Saddles* (1973), *Young Frankenstein* (1974), and *Robin Hood: Men in Tights* (1993). Brooks is married to the actor Anne Bancroft.

'***Brookside*** /'brʊksaɪd/ a British television *soap opera about the lives of a group of families living on the same street in *Liverpool. It has been broadcast since 1982 three times a week by *Channel Four and is one of the most serious soap operas, dealing with subjects such as death, disability, drugs and child abuse.

ˌDavid '**Broome** /'bruːm/ (1940–) the most successful British showjumper (= a person who rides horses over difficult barriers as a sport) of all time. His many successes included gold medals in the world championships (1970 and 1978) and bronze medals at the Olympic Games (1960 and 1968).

'Arthur 'Whitten '**Brown**[1] /'wɪtn 'braʊn/ (1886–1948) a Scottish pilot. In 1919 he and John *Alcock were the first people to fly across the Atlantic Ocean, from Newfoundland in Canada to the west coast of Ireland. Brown was made a *knight in 1919.

'ˌCapa'bility' '**Brown**[2] /'braʊn/ (*real name* Lancelot Brown 1716–83) a British gardener and architect who designed the gardens of many great houses and parks, including *Blenheim Palace and *Chatsworth. He is famous for designing gardens to look natural rather than formal. He was known as 'Capability' Brown because he told people that their gardens had 'great capabilities', meaning that they were capable of being greatly improved in design.

ˌCharlie '**Brown**[3] /'braʊn/ the main character in the US *comic strip **Peanuts*. He is a child who has bad luck with the important things in life (such as baseball), worries that his friends do not respect him and is too shy to speak to the girl he loves.

'Ford 'Madox '**Brown**[4] /'fɔːd 'mædəks 'braʊn; *AmE* 'fɔːrd/ (1821–93) a British artist. He was a friend of the *Pre-Raphaelites and his style of painting was similar to theirs. His best-known works are *The *Last of England* (1852–5) and *Work* (1852–65), which is full of realistic details.

ˌGeorge '**Brown**[5] /'braʊn/ (1914–85) a British *Labour politician. He was *Secretary of State for economic affairs (1964–6) and *Foreign Secretary (1966–8). He had a reputation as a very intelligent politician, but many people made jokes about the amount of alcohol he drank. He was made a *life peer in 1970.

ˌGordon '**Brown**[6] /'braʊn/ (1951–) a British *Labour politician. He became a *Member of Parliament in 1983 and held several important positions in the Labour *Shadow Cabinet before becoming *Chancellor of the Exchequer in the Labour government of 1997.

'Helen 'Gurley '**Brown**[7] /'gɜːli 'braʊn; *AmE* 'gɜːrli/ (1922–) a US writer and journalist. She became editor of the magazine *Cosmopolitan* in 1965 and changed it from a general magazine into one for women with articles about 'the new woman', love and sex. Although she was criticized for this, *Cosmopolitan* became more popular and other women's magazines copied it. Brown also wrote the books *Sex and the Single Girl* (1962) and *Having It All* (1982).

ˌJames '**Brown**[8] /'braʊn/ (1928–) an African-American singer and writer of *soul music. He is known for his great energy on stage. He received *Grammy awards for the songs *Papa's Got A Brand New Bag* (1965) and *Living in America* (1986). He spent some time in prison (1988–91) for violence and having a gun.

ˌJim '**Brown**[9] /'braʊn/ (1936–) an African-American football player and actor. He played for the Cleveland Browns, and scored more touchdowns (= taking the ball across the opponents' line) during his career (1957–66) than any player had ever done. He was chosen for the Pro Football *Hall of Fame in 1971. His films include *The Dirty Dozen* (1967).

ˌJohn '**Brown**[10] /'braʊn/ (1800–59) an American *abolitionist. On 16 October 1859 he led a group of his supporters to occupy a building containing military weapons in Harpers Ferry, Virginia. He was captured, put on trial and hanged. During the American Civil War, northern soldiers sang a song called *John Brown's Body* to the tune of *The *Battle Hymn of the Republic*. It is still sung in the US and contains the lines:

John Brown's body lies a-mouldering in the grave,
But his soul goes marching on.

the ˌ**Brown** '**Bomber** the popular US name for the boxer Joe *Louis.

'**Brownie** (*also* **Brownie Guide**) *n* a member of the junior branch of the *Guides, for girls between the ages of 7 and 11. Many British girls join their local group of Brownies. Each group is led by a woman who is called Brown Owl, and there are regular group meetings at which the girls play games and learn to do useful things. In the US Brownies are called **Brownie Girl Scouts** and are between 6 and 8 years old.

ˌRobert '**Browning** /'braʊnɪŋ/ (1812–89) an English poet. His early work was written to be performed in the theatre, and most of his poetry is easy to read, but full of meaning. In 1846 he secretly married Elizabeth Barrett and they went to live in Italy. They were friends of many other important British writers, including *Carlyle and *Tennyson. Browning is probably best remembered for his poems *The Pied Piper of Hamelin* (1842) and *Home Thoughts from Abroad* (1845).

'***Brown v 'Board of Edu'cation*** an important US Supreme Court case (1954) which made *segregation in public schools illegal. It was held after a school for white children in Topeka, *Kansas, refused to accept a black girl called Linda Brown. The court's decision ended the idea of 'separate but equal' schools for whites and *African Americans, and encouraged the *civil rights movement. Compare *PLESSY V FERGUSON*.

ˌDave '**Brubeck** /'bruːbek/ (1920–) a US *jazz musician who plays the piano and writes music. He became famous in the 1950s leading his Dave Brubeck Quartet. They were the first to sell over a million copies of a record that used only jazz musical instruments, *Take Five* (1959).

ˌLenny ˈ**Bruce**[1] /ˈbruːs/ (1926–66) a US performer of comedy who used rude language and told jokes about subjects that are usually avoided, such as sex, religion and race. He was sent to prison for this in 1961 and two years later was refused permission to enter Britain. He died after taking too much of the drug heroin. His story was told in the film *Lenny* (1974) with Dustin *Hoffman as Bruce.

ˌRobert the ˈ**Bruce**[2] ⇨ ROBERT THE BRUCE.

Brum /brʌm/ (*BrE*) an informal name for *Birmingham, England, used especially by people living there. See also BRUMMIE.

ˌBeau ˈ**Brummel** /ˌbəʊ ˈbrʌməl; *AmE* ˌboʊ/ (*real name* George Bryan Brummel 1778–1840) the best-known dandy (= man who cares very much about the way he looks) in British history. He was a friend of the *Prince of Wales and his choice of clothes had a strong influence on the fashions of the *Regency period.

ˈ**Brummie** /ˈbrʌmi/ *n* (*BrE infml*) a person who lives in or comes from *Birmingham, England.
▶ **Brummie** *adj* (*BrE infml*) of or from Birmingham: *He spoke with a broad Brummie accent.*

ˈ**Brunei** /ˈbruːnaɪ/ a small country in south-east Asia, on the north coast of Borneo. It has been influenced and protected by Britain since 1888, and became a member of the *Commonwealth in 1984. It produces large amounts of oil and gas, and its ruler, the Sultan of Brunei, is one of the richest people in the world. ▶ **Bruˈneian** *adj, n.*

ˈIsambard ˈKingdom **Bruˈnel** /ˈɪzəmbɑːd ˈkɪŋdəm bruˈnel; *AmE* ˈɪzəmbɑːrd/ (1806–69) an English engineer, famous for his ambitious designs for ships, bridges and railways. He designed the *Clifton Suspension Bridge and the largest ships that had ever been built at the time, including the *Great Western*, the first steamship designed to cross the Atlantic.

ˌFrank ˈ**Bruno** /ˈbruːnəʊ; *AmE* ˈbruːnoʊ/ (1961–) an English boxer. He became the European heavyweight champion in 1985, but always lost his fights when trying to become the world heavyweight champion. He became well known to British television audiences for joking with the commentator Harry Carpenter after his fights, and for saying 'Know what I mean, Harry?' after each joke. His easy humour and natural good nature made him a popular television personality in the 1990s.

ˈWilliam ˈJennings ˈ**Bryan** /ˈdʒenɪŋz ˈbraɪən/ (1860–1925) a US politician known for his skill as a public speaker. His famous 'Cross of Gold' speech in 1896 supported the idea that US coins should be made of silver. Bryan was very religious and at the *Scopes trial he spoke against the teaching of evolution. He was the US Secretary of State from 1913 to 1915.

ˈ**Brylcreem**™ /ˈbrɪlkriːm/ *n* [U] a make of hair cream used mainly by men to fix their hair in a particular style. It was fashionable in the 1950s, and is now used mainly by older men, or by people who want to copy the hair styles of the 1950s.

ˌBill ˈ**Bryson** /ˈbraɪsn/ (1951–) a US writer, best known for his humorous travel books. He lived in England from 1977 to 1997 and then moved to *New England. His books include *The Lost Continent* (1989), about his visits to small US towns, *Neither Here Nor There* (1991), about his travels in Europe, *Notes from a Small Island* (1995), about Britain, and *A Walk in the Woods* (1998), about his walk along the Appalachian Trail.

BSA /ˌbiː es ˈeɪ/ (*in full* **Birmingham Small Arms**) a British company that produces motorcycles. It originally made weapons but began making motorcycles in the early 20th century. In the middle of the 20th century BSA motorcycles were popular all around the world, but by the 1960s they were less successful than Japanese ones, and no more were made after 1971. In the 1980s a new British company began making motorcycles using the old name.

BSE /ˌbiː es ˈiː/ (*in full* ˈ**bovine** ˈ**spongiform enˌcephaˈlopathy** /ˈspʌndʒɪfɔːm enˌsefəˈlɒpəθi; *AmE* ˈspʌndʒɪfɔːrm enˌsefəˈlɑːpəθi/) (*also infml* **mad cow disease**) *n* [U] a disease that affects the brains of cows and kills them. In the 1980s many British cows were found to have the disease, and thousands of them were destroyed. Scientists believe it is caused by feeding the cows with parts of sheep that had a similar disease (called *scrapie*), and that people can catch another similar disease, Creutzfeldt-Jakob disease (CJD), by eating the meat of cows with BSE. In the 1990s many people stopped eating British beef, and many countries refused to import it.

BSI /ˌbiː es ˈaɪ/ (*in full* the **British Standards Institution**) the organization responsible for establishing the standard sizes for goods produced in Britain, such as clothes, tools and containers. It is also responsible for making sure that things such as electrical goods and children's toys are not dangerous. Goods that have been tested by BSI and found acceptable are given a label in the shape of a triangle, called a **Kitemark**.

the Kitemark of BSI

BSkyB /ˌbiːskaɪˈbiː/ (*in full* **British Sky Broadcasting**) (*also* **Sky**) a company formed in 1990 that uses satellites to broadcast television programmes. It is partly owned by Rupert *Murdoch's News International company, and was formed by joining British Satellite Broadcasting and *Sky TV. People in Britain can receive the programmes by paying for the service and using a small satellite dish (= a device for receiving signals from a satellite) which is usually fixed to the outside of their homes. Programmes include films, sport and news. Some sports events can only be seen on BSkyB.

BST /ˌbiː es ˈtiː/ ⇨ BRITISH SUMMER TIME.

BT /ˌbiː ˈtiː/ the largest telephone company in Britain. The British telephone service used to be run by the *Post Office but in 1984 it was sold to private owners as a company called *British Telecom. It was the first of Britain's public services to become a private company. Many people bought shares in the new company and made a profit by selling them again at a higher price. In 1991 it changed its name to BT. Compare CABLE AND WIRELESS, MERCURY.

the **BTA** /ˌbiː tiː ˈeɪ/ (*in full* the **British Tourist Authority**) an organization that works with the English, Scottish and Welsh Tourist Boards to encourage tourists from other countries to visit Britain. See also ENGLISH TOURIST BOARD.

BTEC /ˈbiːtek/ (*in full* the **Business and Technology Education Council**) a British organization that runs courses and awards qualifications at various levels in a wide range of areas relating to work, such as business, design, engineering and public administration. BTEC courses are offered by schools, colleges and universities.

BTU (*also* **Btu**) /ˌbiː tiː ˈjuː/ (*in full* **British Thermal Unit**) *n* a unit for measuring a quantity of heat. It represents the heat needed to raise the temperature of a pound of water by one degree Fahrenheit. It is now more common to measure heat in calories.

B

ˌ**bubble and ˈsqueak** *n* [U] (*BrE*) a British dish consisting of potatoes and cabbage that have already been cooked. They are mixed together and fried. It is a popular way of using food that is left from an earlier meal, and is sometimes eaten as part of an *English breakfast. Its name comes from the noise it makes as it is being fried.

ˈ**bubblegum** *n* [U] (*infml disapprov*) a very simple type of pop music made for children. It was popular in America and Britain in the 1960s and 1970s. The name comes from a type of chewing gum that can be blown into bubbles and is popular with children.

ˈ***Bubbles*** a painting (1886) by *Millais of his young grandson blowing soap bubbles. It is especially well known in Britain because it was bought by Pears, a soap company, who used it in their advertisements.

ˌJohn ˈ**Buchan** /ˈbʌkn/ (1875–1940) a Scottish writer and politician, best known for his adventure stories, many of which involved the character Richard Hannay, including *The Thirty-Nine Steps* (1915). He was made a *baron in 1935, and was Governor-General of Canada from 1935 to 1940.

ˌPearl S ˈ**Buck** /ˈbʌk/ (Pearl Sydenstricker Buck 1892–73) a US author who won the 1938 *Nobel Prize for Literature. She wrote mainly about China, where she lived for many years as a Christian teacher. It was the subject of her best-known novel, *The Good Earth*, for which she received the 1932 *Pulitzer Prize. Her other books include *East Wind; West Wind* (1930), *A House Divided* (1935) and *Dragon Seed* (1942).

ˌ**Buck ˈHouse** (*BrE often ironic*) an informal name for *Buckingham Palace: *We stayed at Thomas's place. It isn't exactly Buck House, but it's comfortable enough.*

ˌ**Buckingham ˈPalace** /ˌbʌkɪŋəm/ the official home of the British *royal family in central London. It is a very large house, originally built in 1703 for the Duke of Buckingham, though the part that can be seen from the road was built in 1913. Many tourists stand outside the Palace to watch the ceremony of *Changing the Guard, and in 1993 parts of the inside of the house were opened to tourists.

Buckingham Palace

ˈ**Buckinghamshire** /ˈbʌkɪŋəmʃə(r)/ (*abbr* **Bucks**) a *county in central southern England. Its main town and administrative centre is Aylesbury.

ˌ**Buck's ˈFizz** *n* [U, C] (*BrE*) a drink consisting of champagne mixed with orange juice. It is usually drunk at special events such as weddings or important parties. It is named after Buck's, a London club.

the **budget**

To people in Britain the budget means an announcement made each year by the ***Chancellor of the Exchequer**, the minister in charge of finance, about the government's plans concerning **taxation** and **public spending** (= money to be spent by the government).

Budget Day used to be in March each year, with an additional **autumn statement** by the Chancellor in November. The budget itself was then moved to November/December and linked to the ***public spending round**, the negotiation between ministers in charge of government *departments about how much money they will have to spend during the next year. From 1997 Budget Day was moved back to April. A **pre-budget report** each autumn is intended to introduce ideas on which the following year's budget will be based.

On Budget Day the Chancellor explains, in a long speech to the *House of Commons, the financial policy of the ***Treasury**, plans for government spending, and how the money for this will be raised through taxation. There is then a debate on the budget, which lasts for several days, followed by a vote to accept or reject it. The contents of the budget speech are kept secret until the last moment, and any leak of information is a serious embarrassment. The speech is broadcast on national radio and television and is much discussed by financial and political experts. Photographs of the Chancellor on Budget Day usually show him holding up the red leather case in which the speech is contained. The word *budget* originally meant a small leather bag. Until 1997 the same case had been used for many years.

Many people fear budget changes, because they usually mean tax increases rather than reductions, particularly on alcohol, tobacco and petrol. Some of these increases become effective immediately and car drivers may rush to buy petrol just before the budget. Budgets announced close to general elections usually contain fewer tax increases to avoid making the government unpopular.

In the US the budget is a document describing how much money the government expects to have, and how it will use that money. *Congress spends a lot of time discussing how much money each part of the government needs. Each member of Congress tries to make sure that as much money as possible will be spent in the area he or she represents. This is called **pork-barrel politics**, and money spent to benefit a particular place is called **pork**. When Congress has decided on a budget the President considers it. In the past the President had to approve or veto the whole budget, but now he has a **line-item veto** and can veto an individual item. The ***Office of Management and Budget** helps prepare the budget and checks how the money is spent.

The US budget includes **revenues** (= sources of money) and **spending**. In 1997 the revenue was $1 579 billion, while spending was $1 601 billion. The government's largest source of money is ***income tax**. Since the government's revenues are smaller than its spending, the US has a **budget deficit**.

Individual states also make budgets, and the laws of a state may say that it must not have a deficit.

ˈ**Budweiser**™ /ˈbʌdwaɪzə(r)/ (*infml* **Bud**) *n* [U, C] a US beer produced by the Anheuser-Busch Company.

ˌ**Buffalo ˈBill** the popular name of William Cody (1846–1917), an American *frontiersman and (later) entertainer. He killed many buffalo to provide meat for workers on the Kansas Pacific Railroad. He was also a rider for the *Pony Express in 1860. Ned *Buntline made him famous by writing stories about his life in his *dime novels. In the 1870s Buffalo Bill organized his own Wild West Show to entertain audiences in the US and Europe.

ˌ**Bugs ˈBunny** /ˌbʌgz/ an American rabbit cartoon character. He was created in 1940 by Tex *Avery for *Warner Brothers. Bugs likes carrots (= long orange vegetables), often asks 'What's up, Doc?' and always

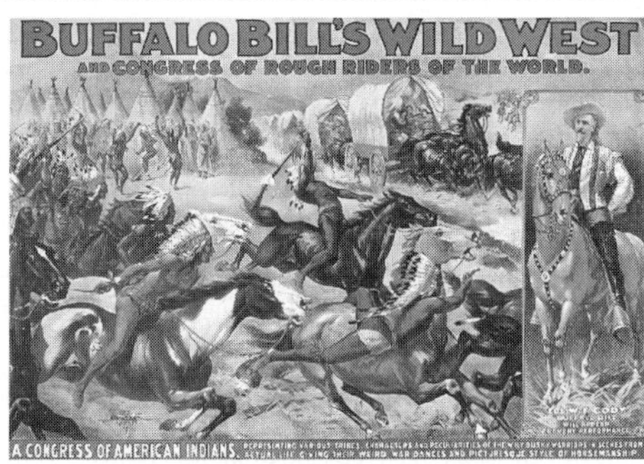

a poster for Buffalo Bill's Wild West Show, 1899

tricks the hunter Elmer Fudd. In 1997 he became the first cartoon character to appear on a US stamp.

'Buick™ /ˈbjuːɪk/ *n* a US make of car produced by the *General Motors Corporation.

building societies and savings and loan associations

Building societies are British financial institutions that give ***mortgages** (= a type of loan) to people to help them buy a house. They also offer a range of **savings accounts** for those who want to save money. In the US savings and loan associations provide a similar service. Mortgages are paid for out of interest paid by people borrowing money and out of money placed by the public in savings accounts, which is then invested by the society at a profit.

Traditionally, building societies operated as **mutual organizations** which shared profits with their members. The first building societies had a few members who paid subscriptions towards their own home. When homes had been built for all of them the societies were closed. In the 19th century hundreds of permanent societies were created throughout Britain. Names such as The Coventry Building Society showed their local origins. People investing money in these societies did so in order to obtain interest on their savings, not necessarily because they wanted a loan for a house. Many building societies later joined together to form larger, national organizations, each with hundreds of **branches**.

In the 1980s and 1990s, building societies had to compete for customers with high-street banks, which also offered mortgages, and they began to offer banking facilities themselves. After 1986, many of the larger building societies including the *Abbey National, the Halifax and the *Woolwich became banks. This meant that they could offer a full range of banking services, and also increase their profits by having their shares sold on the stock market. Many savers with these societies received **windfalls** (= large additional payments) when they became banks. The country's largest surviving building society, the Nationwide, decided not to become a bank because it believed that it could defend customers' interests more effectively as a building society.

In the US savings and loan associations, also called **S & Ls** or **thrifts**, were created for people who wanted get a mortgage or save money. Originally, they operated under different rules from banks and had limits on the services they could provide. In the 1980s, as in Britain, the rules changed and now S & Ls and banks offer similar kinds of accounts.

In the late 1980s S & Ls got a bad reputation when many failed. This was partly because they had taken risks in investing money in an attempt to compete with banks, and partly because many were dishonestly run. The US government gave back to people the money they had invested, but many Americans still associate S & Ls with this problem. The S & Ls that exist now are run under tighter controls and are regarded as safe places to keep money.

ˌJames **'Bulger** /ˈbʊldʒə(r)/ (1990–3) a boy who was murdered in *Merseyside, England, when he was two years old. The murder was particularly shocking because he was killed by two boys who were only ten years old. Many people believe that they were influenced by a violent video, and this caused some people to argue that such videos should not be allowed in Britain.

the ˌ**bulldog 'breed** *n* [sing + sing/pl *v*] a phrase used to refer to British people in general, and especially to British soldiers. The bulldog, a strong British dog with a large head and short thick neck and legs, is traditionally used to represent qualities that were considered typically British, such as courage, loyalty and determination. See also JOHN BULL.

ˌ**Bulldog 'Drummond** /ˈdrʌmənd/ a character in a series of novels by the English writer 'Sapper' (Herman Cyril McNeile 1888–1937). He is a former British soldier who becomes a secret agent. He is not very attractive or intelligent but he has the qualities of the *bulldog breed such as courage and loyalty. The books were very popular in the first half of the 20th century, and many were made into films.

'bull ˌmarket *n* a situation at the stock exchange in which the prices of shares are rising and people known as **bulls** buy shares in order to make a profit by selling them soon afterwards at a higher price.

the **'Bull Ring** a large shopping centre in *Birmingham, England. It was built in the 1960s on an old market where bulls used to be sold. For some people it represents a mistake of 20th-century architecture, destroying historical areas and replacing them with buildings that have no interesting features or beauty.

the 'Battles of ˌ**Bull 'Run** (*also* **Ma'nassas**) /məˈnæsəs/ two battles of the American *Civil War, both won by the South. They were fought near Bull Run Creek at Manassas Junction, *Virginia. The first, on 21 July 1861, was the first major battle of the war. The second was on 29–30 August 1862. The area can now be visited in the Manassas National Battlefield Park. See also JACKSON[7].

'bullying /ˈbʊliɪŋ/ *n* [U] a problem that is common in schools where some children use their strength or important positions to hurt or frighten smaller or weaker children. The people who do this are called **bullies**. There are many books about British schools that describe how bullies make other children unhappy in this way. The most famous bully in English literature is *Flashman in **Tom Brown's Schooldays*.

ˌClaus von **'Bulow** ⇨ VON BULOW.

'Bundt pan /ˈbʌnt/ *n* a US type of heavy metal pan in the shape of a ring, made by Nordic Ware. Bundt pans are mostly used to shape and bake cakes but also for bread and salads. They were first made in the 1970s.

'bungalow *n* a small house in which all the rooms are on ground level. Many old people live in bungalows because there are no stairs to climb. In Britain, large groups of bungalows are often built together on the edges of towns, or in places were people go to live when they have retired from work, such as the south coast. Many people find these groups of bungalows boring to look at.

ˌArchie **'Bunker** /ˈbʌŋkə(r)/ the main character in the popular US television comedy series *All in the Family* (1971–6). He is often bad-tempered and has very old-fashioned opinions, especially about people of a different race or social class to his own. The series aimed to make fun of the typical attitudes of white *working-class Americans. The character of

Bunker was copied from the British television character Alf *Garnett.

the ˈBattle of ˌ**Bunker ˈHill** /ˌbʌŋkə; *AmE* ˌbʌŋkər/ the first major battle of the *American Revolution. It is named wrongly because the battle was actually fought on Breed's Hill. It was on 17 June 1775 near *Boston. Although the British won, the Americans were encouraged because they fought well and killed many British soldiers until they had used all their bullets.

ˌBilly ˈ**Bunter** /ˈbʌntə(r)/ the main character in a series of children's stories by Frank Richards. He is a greedy fat boy at a British *public school called Greyfriars who often gets into trouble. There have been several television series based on the Bunter stories.

ˌNed ˈ**Buntline** /ˈbʌntlaɪn / (1823–86) a US writer of cheap novels of action and adventure. He wrote more than 400 of these, many of them based on his own experiences, and created *Buntline's Own*, a magazine containing similar stories. His style was later copied by writers of *dime novels.

ˌJohn ˈ**Bunyan**[1] /ˈbʌnjən/ (1628–88) an English writer of religious books, who also made religious speeches in public places. He fought on the side of *Parliament in the *English Civil War and later spent 11 years in prison for making *Nonconformist religious speeches. While in prison, he began his most famous book, *The *Pilgrim's Progress*.

ˌPaul ˈ**Bunyan**[2] /ˈbʌnjən/ a character in American legends. He is said to be a very large and strong lumberjack (= a person whose job is cutting down trees). He has a blue ox called Babe. Wild stories were told about him. In one of these the British navy built seven ships with the wood from his baby bed. Another said that Babe was so big that a new iron mine had to be opened each time he needed shoes.

BUPA /ˈbuːpə/ (*in full* **British United Provident Association**) a British company that sells insurance to people who want to have private medical treatment instead of using the *National Health Service. It also owns several private hospitals: *I had the operation on BUPA.*

ˈ**Burberry**™ /ˈbɜːbəri; *AmE* ˈbɜːrbəri/ *n* a British make of raincoat that is well known for being expensive and of very good quality: *He was wearing a grey Burberry and carried an umbrella.*

the ˌ**Bureau of ˈAlcohol, Toˈbacco and ˈFirearms** the division of the US Department of the Treasury that is responsible for laws relating to alcohol, tobacco, guns and explosives. It also collects taxes from companies that make such products. The Bureau was established in 1972 and has officers in all regions of the US.

ˌWarren ˈ**Burger** /ˈbɜːgə(r); *AmE* ˈbɜːrgər/ (1907–95) a Chief Justice of the US *Supreme Court for longer than any other in the 20th century (1969–86). He was appointed by President Richard *Nixon, but the Supreme Court under him ordered Nixon to give his telephone tapes relating to *Watergate to the House Judiciary Committee.

ˈ**Burger King** a well-known group of restaurants selling hamburgers and other types of *fast food. The group began in the US in 1954 and now has more than 8 000 restaurants around the world. Its most famous hamburger is called the Whopper. Burger King has been owned by the British company *Grand Metropolitan since 1989.

ˌAnthony ˈ**Burgess**[1] /ˈbɜːdʒɪs; *AmE* ˈbɜːrdʒɪs/ (1917–93) an English writer, best known for his short novel *A Clockwork Orange* (1962). He wrote many different types of novel, including *Earthly Powers* (1980), a description of the main events of the 20th century from the point of view of an imaginary character. He also wrote books and newspaper articles about literature and music, and several pieces of classical music.

ˌGuy ˈ**Burgess**[2] /ˈbɜːdʒɪs; *AmE* ˈbɜːrdʒɪs/ (1911–63) a British spy who sold government secrets to the former Soviet Union. He was one of the famous *Cambridge spies and escaped to Moscow with Donald *Maclean in 1951.

ˌLord ˈ**Burghley** /ˈbɜːli; *AmE* ˈbɜːrli/ (William Cecil 1520–98) a British politician. He was one of the most important members of Queen *Elizabeth I's government, working as *Secretary of State (1558–72) and Lord Treasurer (1572–98). He was responsible for making England a strong military and economic power. He was also responsible for many grand buildings, including *Burghley House. He was made a *knight in 1551 and a *baron in 1571.

ˌ**Burghley ˈHouse** /ˌbɜːli; *AmE* ˈbɜːrli/ a large and grand house near Peterborough in eastern England, built in the *Elizabethan style in the 16th century. The inside of the house was decorated in the *baroque style 100 years later, and in the 18th century the gardens were designed by 'Capability' *Brown. Each autumn an important *three-day event, the **Burghley Horse Trials**, takes place in the grounds.

ˌEdmund ˈ**Burke** /ˈbɜːk; *AmE* ˈbɜːrk/ (1729–97) a British *Whig(1) politician and writer, born in Ireland. He was a *Member of Parliament (1765–94) but is best remembered for speaking and writing in favour of American independence and the rights of Irish Catholics. In his best-known book, *Reflections of the Revolution in France* (1790), he argued against the more extreme acts of the French Revolution.

ˌ**Burke and ˈHare** /ˌbɜːk ənd ˈheə(r); *AmE* ˌbɜːrk/ two Irish criminals who lived in *Edinburgh in the early 19th century. They stole bodies from graves and sold them to medical students for their experiments. They also killed people in order to sell their bodies, but they are best known to most British people as grave robbers: *Some say that the archaeologists in the pyramids are no better than Burke and Hare.*

ˈ***Burke's ˈLanded ˈGentry*** /ˈbɜːks ˈlændɪd; *AmE* ˈbɜːrks/ a book published regularly in Britain that gives details of many families with high social positions who own land in Britain but do not belong to the *aristocracy. Compare BURKE'S PEERAGE.

ˌ***Burke's ˈPeerage*** /ˌbɜːks; *AmE* ˌbɜːrks/ a book published regularly in Britain that gives details and short family histories of the members of the British *aristocracy and other people with titles. Its full title is *Burke's Peerage, Baronetage and Knightage*. Compare DEBRETT. ⇨ note at PEERAGE.

burˈlesque (*also* **burlesk**) *n* [U, C] (*AmE*) a type of stage variety show once popular in the US. It began as family entertainment in the 1860s with singers, dancers, performers of comedy, etc. It started to include striptease (= women taking their clothes off) in the 1920s when films began to reduce the audiences. Performers who began in burlesque included W C *Fields, Fanny *Brice and Al *Jolson.

ˌ**Burlington ˈHouse** /ˌbɜːlɪŋtən ˈhaʊs; *AmE* ˌbɜːrlɪŋtən/ a large building in *Piccadilly, London, that is the home of the *Royal Academy. It consists of four buildings combined to form a square. The main part was built in the 17th century and the other three sides were added in the 19th century for other artistic and scientific organizations.

the ˌ**Burma ˈrailway** /ˌbɜːmə; *AmE* ˌbɜːrmə/ a railway built by the Japanese in Burma during *World War II. They used prisoners of war to build the railway, and many of them died. The film *Bridge on the River Kwai* (1957) is about a group of British prisoners who have to build a bridge for the railway.

ˈ**Burma Shave**™ /ˈbɜːmə; *AmE* ˈbɜːrmə/ a US make of cream used on the face when shaving. Between 1926 and 1963 the Burma-Vita Company advertised it on a series of small red and white signs along roads. Each sign in a group had a few words printed on it, and the whole group, read by a driver in sequence, formed a short humorous poem. At one time, there were 35 000 of these. One was:

Noah had whiskers
In the ark
But he wouldn't get by
On a bench
In the park.
Burma-Shave.

ˈEdward ˈ**Burne-ˈJones** /ˈbɜːn ˈdʒəʊnz; *AmE* ˈbɜːrn ˈdʒoʊnz/ (1833–98) an English *Pre-Raphaelite painter. He was influenced by Dante Gabriel *Rossetti and painted many scenes from old legends. He also created designs for his friend William *Morris. He was made a *baronet in 1894.

ˈFrances ˈHodgson **Burˈnett** /ˈhɒdʒsən bɜːˈnet; *AmE* ˈhɑːdʒsən bɜːrˈnet/ (1849–1924) a US writer, born in Britain. She is best remembered for her children's books, especially **Little Lord Fauntleroy* and *The Secret Garden* (1911).

ˌGeorge ˈ**Burns¹** /ˈbɜːnz; *AmE* ˈbɜːrnz/ (1896–1996) a US comedian who continued to perform until he was nearly 100. He was known for his large cigar, slow talk and humorous singing. He joined his wife, Gracie Allen (1906–64), on stage, in films and on radio and television. After she died, he received an *Oscar as 'Best Supporting Actor' for *The Sunshine Boys* (1975) and played God in *Oh, God!* (1977) and two later films.

ˌRobert ˈ**Burns²** /ˈbɜːnz; *AmE* ˈbɜːrnz/ (1759–96) a Scottish poet, often referred to as Robbie (or Rabbie) Burns. He wrote many poems and songs in English, and in the *dialect of Lowland Scotland, about love, the countryside, the life of working people, and his love of Scotland. He is regarded as Scotland's national poet and his poems and songs, such as **Tam o' Shanter* and **Auld Lang Syne*, are popular even among people who normally read little poetry.

Robert Burns, painted by Alexander Nasmyth

ˈ**Burns Night** /ˈbɜːnz; *AmE* ˈbɜːrnz/ 25 January, the birthday of Robert *Burns. It is celebrated every year in Scotland, and by Scottish people all around the world, in an evening of music, poetry, food and drink. People drink *whisky and eat typical Scottish food such as *haggis while *bagpipes music is played and some of Burns's most popular poems are read aloud.

ˈEdgar ˈRice ˈ**Burroughs¹** /ˈraɪs ˈbʌrəʊz; *AmE* ˈbɜːroʊz/ (1875–1950) a US writer who created the character of *Tarzan. The first book in the series was *Tarzan of the Apes* (1914) and 23 more followed. Many Tarzan films have been made. Burroughs also wrote science fiction novels, including *The Gods of Mars* (1913).

ˌWilliam ˈ**Burroughs²** /ˈbʌrəʊz; *AmE* ˈbɜːroʊz/ (1914–97) a US writer of the *beat generation. His experiences as a homosexual and drug user are often reflected in his books. His best-known novel is *The Naked Lunch* (1959).

ˈ**Burton¹** /ˈbɜːtn; *AmE* ˈbɜːrtn/ any of a group of British *high-street shops selling men's clothes which are not very expensive. There are Burton shops in most British towns.

ˌRichard ˈ**Burton²** /ˈbɜːtn; *AmE* ˈbɜːrtn/ (1821–90) an English writer and explorer. He travelled to India, Arabia and several African countries, and learnt many languages so that he could talk to local people and write about their cultures and traditions. He is also well known for his translation of the *Arabian Nights. He was made a *knight in 1886.

ˌRichard ˈ**Burton³** /ˈbɜːtn; *AmE* ˈbɜːrtn/ (1925–84) a Welsh actor. He first became famous for his performances of Shakespearian roles in the theatre, and in the 1960s and 1970s he acted in many major British and US films. He was also well known for his relationship with Elizabeth *Taylor. They were married and divorced twice, and acted in several successful films together, including **Cleopatra* and **Who's Afraid of Virginia Woolf?*

bus *n* a large vehicle carrying passengers along a fixed route with places for stopping on the way. London and many other British cities and towns still have some traditional double-deckers (= buses with two floors). Passengers get on and off these through the open door at the back, and a conductor walks around inside the bus selling tickets. The more modern buses have no conductor. Passengers pay the driver when they get on. The door is at the front, and only opens at official bus stops.

Buses used for long distances or tours are called *coaches* in Britain but *buses* in the US. Yellow school buses are a tradition in the US and parts of Britain.

ˌMatt ˈ**Busby** /ˈbʌzbi/ (1909–94) a British football player and manager. He was a successful player for *Manchester City and *Liverpool in the 1930s but is best remembered as the manager of *Manchester United (1945–69). Several members of the team died in a plane crash in 1958 and Busby introduced many new young players, who were called the **Busby babes**. They became the most successful team in England, winning the *European Cup in 1968. Busby was made a *knight in 1968.

ˌGeorge ˈ**Bush** /ˈbʊʃ/ (1924–) the 41st US *President (1989–93) and a member of the *Republican Party. He was twice the Vice-president under Ronald *Reagan (1981–89). Bush was especially popular after the *Gulf War was won in 1991, but lost support during America's later economic problems. He was defeated by Bill *Clinton in the election of 1992.

ˌ**Bush ˈHouse** /ˌbʊʃ/ the main centre of the *BBC

Bush House

World Service. It is a large building in central London containing the administrative offices and the studios where World Service programmes are recorded.

B

the '**Business and Tech'nology Edu'cation ˌCouncil** ⇨ BTEC.

'**busking** /'bʌskɪŋ/ *n* [U] (*BrE infml*) a way of earning money by entertaining people in a public place, usually by playing music. In Britain, some places, such as *Covent Garden in London, have special areas for **buskers** to perform in. Many buskers also perform in London's *Underground stations, where busking is not allowed and the police often make them move.

a busker

'**bus pass** *n* (*BrE*) (in Britain) a special ticket that allows a *senior citizen to travel free on a bus. If you say that somebody has got their bus pass, it is a humorous way of saying that they have become a senior citizen.

ˌDarcey '**Bussell** /ˌdɑːsi 'bʌsl; *AmE* ˌdɑːrsi/ (1969–) an English dancer. She became Principal Ballerina of the *Royal Ballet in 1989.

'**bussing** (*AmE also* **busing**) /'bʌsɪŋ/ *n* [U] (in the US) the system of transporting children in buses from their homes to schools in a different area, in order to achieve a greater mixture of races in schools. Usually African-American children travel to better white schools. This began in 1954 and was approved by the US *Supreme Court in 1971. Many white parents have moved out of cities to avoid bussing.

R A ('Rab') **Butler**[1] /ˌræb 'bʌtlə(r)/ (Richard Austen Butler 1902–82) a English *Conservative politician who held every important position in government except that of *prime minister. He was *Chancellor of the Exchequer (1951–5), *Home Secretary (1957–62) and *Foreign Secretary (1963–4). He was made a *life peer in 1965.

ˌRhett '**Butler**[2] /ˌret 'bʌtlə(r)/ one of the main characters in the novel **Gone with the Wind*. Clark *Gable played the role in the 1939 film version. Butler marries Scarlett *O'Hara but leaves her at the end with the words, 'Frankly, my dear, I don't give a damn!'

ˌSamuel '**Butler**[3] /'bʌtlə(r)/ (1835–1902) an English writer who escaped from his extremely religious English family to become a farmer in New Zealand. He wrote about this experience in his novel *The Way of All Flesh* (1903). His other famous book, **Erewhon*, makes fun of religion and other human ideas.

'**Butlin's** /'bʌtlɪnz/ any of a group of British holiday camps, where families can sleep, eat and be entertained without leaving the centre. The first one was opened in Skegness, on the east coast of England, in 1936 by Billy Butlin (1899–1980). They were very popular in the 1950s before travel abroad became cheap, and they still attract many British families who want to enjoy a wide range of entertainments that are not too expensive: *We always went to Butlin's for our summer holiday when I was young.*

'**Buttons** /'bʌtnz/ a character in the *pantomime **Cinderella*. He is Cinderella's friend, and usually wears a suit with many buttons.

ˌA S '**Byatt** /ˌeɪ es 'baɪət/ (Antonia Susan Byatt 1936–) an English writer and university teacher of English literature. Her novels contain many references to other works of literature. She won the *Booker Prize for her novel *Possession* (1990). The author Margaret Drabble (1939–) is her sister.

'**by-eˌlection** *n* (in Britain) the election of a single *Member of Parliament to the *House of Commons at any time other than a general election, usually when another MP has died or resigned.

'**by-law** (*also* **bye-law**) *n* **1** (in Britain) a law made by a local authority, such as a town *council, which only applies in that area, rather than a law made by the central government. **2** (in the US) a rule made by a particular organization, such as a club or company, which only applies to the members of that organization.

ˌRichard E '**Byrd**[1] /'bɜːd; *AmE* 'bɜːrd/ (Richard Evelyn Byrd 1888–1957) a US explorer and navy pilot. In 1926, he and Floyd Bennett made the first flight over the North Pole. Byrd also flew over the South Pole in 1929 and went on several journeys to Antarctica.

ˌWilliam '**Byrd**[2] /'bɜːd; *AmE* 'bɜːrd/ (1543–1623) an English composer, best known for his religious music. He was a student of Thomas *Tallis, and one of the greatest musicians of the *Tudor(1) period. Although he was a *Roman Catholic, he also wrote many pieces of music for the *Church of England.

ˌLord '**Byron** /'baɪrən/ (George Gordon Byron 1788–1824) an English poet whose life is as well known as his poetry. He had many love affairs, and probably had a child by his half-sister (= sister by a different mother). He was a leading figure in the *Romantic Movement and himself lived the life of a romantic hero, often unhappy about a love affair and angry about the unfair political and social situations he saw around him. His work, including **Childe Harold's Pilgrimage* (1812–18) and *Don Juan* (1818–20), often expresses the same feelings. Rejected by British society, he spent much of his life abroad, and he died helping the Greek struggle against Turkish rule.

Lord Byron, painted by Thomas Phillips

Cc

the **CAA** /ˌsiː eɪ ˈeɪ/ ⇨ CIVIL AVIATION AUTHORITY.

the **CAB** /ˌsiː eɪ ˈbiː/ ⇨ CITIZENS ADVICE BUREAU.

the **Cabinet**

In Britain, the Cabinet is a committee responsible for deciding government policy and for coordinating the work of government *departments. It consists of about 20 *ministers chosen by the *Prime Minister and meets for a few hours each week at *Downing Street. Its members are bound by oath not to talk about the meetings. Reports are sent to government departments but these give only summaries of the topics discussed and decisions taken. They do not mention who agreed or disagreed. The principle of **collective responsibility** means that the Cabinet acts unanimously (= all together), even if some ministers do not agree. When a policy has been decided, each minister is expected to support it publicly or resign. In recent years, prime ministers have changed the members of their Cabinet quite often in Cabinet **reshuffles**. Some members are dropped, new ones are brought in, and the rest are given new departmental responsibilities.

The leader of the main opposition party forms a **shadow cabinet** of **shadow ministers**, each with their own area of responsibility, so that there is a team ready to take over immediately if the party in power should be defeated.

Committees are appointed by the Cabinet to examine issues in more detail than the Cabinet has time for. Members of these committees are not necessarily politicians. The ***Cabinet Office** led by the Secretary to the Cabinet, the most senior *civil servant in Britain, prepares agendas for Cabinet meetings and committees.

In the US the Cabinet consists of the heads of the 14 departments that make up the **executive branch** of the *federal government. Each president appoints the department heads, called **secretaries**, from his or her own party, and they advise him or her on policy. Since the Cabinet was not established by the *Constitution, the President may add, remove or combine government departments, and can decide when to ask the Cabinet for advice, and whether or not to follow it.

State governments are usually organized in a similar way to the national government, and most have a cabinet.

the **ˈCabinet ˌOffice** a British government department that is responsible for the administrative work of the *Cabinet, and for managing the *Civil Service.

ˌCable and ˈWireless a large international telecommunications company. It owns several smaller companies, including **Cable and Wireless Communications**, Britain's second largest telephone company, which used to be called *Mercury, and Videotron, one of Britain's main cable telephone and television companies.

ˌCable ˈNews ˌNetwork ⇨ CNN.

ˌJohn **ˈCabot** /ˈkæbət/ (*c.* 1450–*c.* 1498) an Italian explorer. With his son Sebastian he sailed across the Atlantic in 1498 on behalf of the English king, *Henry VII, and reached North America (which he thought was China) before *Columbus.

ˌMother **Caˈbrini** /kəˈbriːni/ (1850–1917) the first US citizen to become a Roman Catholic saint. She was born Francesca Cabrini in Lombardy, Italy. She became a nun, began the Missionary Sisters of the Sacred Heart and went to the US in 1889 to continue her good work. She was named a saint in 1946.

ˌCadbury ˈSchweppes /ˌkædbri ˈʃweps/ a large British food and drinks company. It was formed in 1969 when Cadbury's, Britain's leading chocolate producer, combined with Schweppes, which makes soft drinks (= drinks containing no alcohol) such as tonic water and lemonade.

ˌJack **ˈCade** /ˈkeɪd/ (*died* 1450) the leader in 1450 of a violent protest in *Kent, England, against *Henry VI's high taxes and bad government. His army defeated the royal forces and entered London. After receiving certain promises, Cade's army went back to their homes but Cade himself was later caught and killed.

ˈCadillac™ /ˈkædɪlæk/ *n* an large and expensive US make of car. Owning a Cadillac is seen by Americans as a sign of wealth and success. Cadillacs were first produced in 1903 in *Detroit by the Cadillac Motor Car Company and are now made by the *General Motors Corporation.

ˈCaedmon /ˈkædmən/ (7th century) the first English poet. According to *Bede, he worked for a monastery, looking after the cows. One day he woke up after having a dream and was able to write religious poetry in English. Only a small part of his work survives.

Caerˈnarfon /kəˈnɑːvn; *AmE* kərˈnɑːrvn/ a town in *Gwynedd, Wales. It is famous for its 13th-century castle where, at a special ceremony in 1969, Prince *Charles became officially the *Prince of Wales.

Caerˈphilly /keəˈfɪli; *AmE* kerˈfɪli/ *n* [U] a type of mild white cheese, originally made in Caerphilly, a town in *Mid Glamorgan, Wales.

ˌJulius **ˈCaesar**[1] ⇨ JULIUS CAESAR.

ˌSid **ˈCaesar**[2] /ˈsiːzə(r)/ (1922–) a very popular comedian on early US television. His programme was *Your Show of Shows* (1950–55) with Imogene Coca, and Caesar won two *Emmy awards. The show's writers included Woody *Allen, Neil *Simon and Mel *Brooks.

ˌCaesar ˈsalad /ˌsiːzə; *AmE* ˌsiːzər/ *n* [C, U] an American cold dish made mainly with lettuce, cheese and eggs. It was created about 1903 by an Italian-American cook in *Chicago, who named it after Julius Caesar.

the **ˌCafé ˈRoyal** a famous restaurant in *Regent Street, London, England. In the 19th century it was a fashionable place for artists and writers to meet.

CAFOD /ˈkæfɒd; *AmE* ˈkæfɑːd/ (*in full* **Catholic Fund for Overseas Development**) a charity organization run by the *Roman Catholic Church in Britain. Its aims are to help development projects in poor countries, and to educate people in Britain about these countries.

ˌJohn **ˈCage**[1] /ˈkeɪdʒ/ (1912–) a US composer of modern and unusual music. He has used ordinary noises and a 'prepared piano' with items attached to its strings to produce different sounds. His works include the silent *Four Minutes 33 Seconds* (1952), during which a person sits at a closed piano for that length of time without making a sound.

C

ˌNicolas ˈ**Cage²** /ˈkeɪdʒ/ (1964–) a US film actor who won an *Oscar and *Golden Globe Award for his part in *Leaving Las Vegas* (1995). His uncle is the director Francis Ford *Coppola. Cage's other films include *Raising Arizona* (1987), *Wild at Heart* (1990), *The Rock* (1996) and *Con Air* (1997).

ˌJames ˈ**Cagney** /ˈkæɡni/ (1899–1986) a US film actor who usually played tough characters and criminals, as in the films *The Public Enemy* (1931) and *Angels with Dirty Faces* (1938). He won his *Oscar, however, as a dancer and singer in *Yankee Doodle Dandy* (1942).

ˌSammy ˈ**Cahn** /ˈkɑːn/ (1913–93) a US writer of songs, especially for films. He won *Oscars for *Three Coins in the Fountain* (1954), *All the Way* (1957) and *High Hopes* (1959). Many of his songs were sung by Frank *Sinatra.

ˌMichael ˈ**Caine** /ˈkeɪn/ (1933–) a English film actor, well known for his *cockney *accent. He first became famous in the 1960s when he was the main actor in films such as *The Ipcress File* (1965) and *Alfie* (1966). Since then he has acted in many British and US films, including *Hannah and her Sisters* (1986) for which he won an *Oscar.

the ˈ**Cairngorms** /ˈkeəŋɡɔːmz; *AmE* ˈkernɡɔːrmz/ a mountain range in central Scotland which is popular for climbing, walking and skiing. A valuable stone, called **cairngorm**, is found in the mountains.

ˌ**cairn** ˈ**terrier** (*also* **cairn**) *n* a small breed of *terrier with rough hair, originally bred in Scotland for hunting.

ˈ**Cajun** /ˈkeɪdʒən/ *n* a member of the people in the US state of *Louisiana who are descended from French Canadians called Acadians. They moved to Louisiana after the British forced them in 1755 to leave Acadia (Nova Scotia) in Canada. They speak a form of French, and are known for their lively music and hot, spicy food. Compare CREOLE. ▶ **Cajun** *adj*: *Cajun food/music.*

ˈ**Calais** /ˈkæleɪ/ a town in northern France. It is the nearest port to England, across the *English Channel from *Dover. It was captured by the British in 1347 during the *Hundred Years War, and remained a British town in France until 1558. Now it is the main port for passenger ships from Dover, and many British people go there to buy things such as alcohol and cigarettes, which have lower tax in France than in Britain.

Caˌlamity ˈJane (*c.* 1852–1903) the popular name of Martha Jane Burke, a woman who became famous in America's *Wild West for her skill at riding and shooting. She dressed like a man and said she would bring calamity (= great harm) to anyone who made her angry or tried to love her. She was well known in Deadwood, South Dakota, in the 1870s and was a friend or lover of Wild Bill *Hickok.

the **Calˌcutta ˈCup** /kælˌkʌtə/ the prize given to the winner of a *Rugby Union match played once a year between the teams of England and Scotland.

the ˌ**Caleˈdonian Caˈnal** /ˌkælɪˈdəʊniən; *AmE* ˌkælɪˈdoʊniən/ a system of canals and lakes, including *Loch Ness, that crosses Scotland from the Atlantic Ocean to the *North Sea. It was built in the 18th century for industrial and business transport, but is now used mainly by tourists.

the **calendar**

Britain and the US follow the Gregorian calendar, which replaced the Roman Julian calendar in 1752. The year is divided into 12 months, with 30 or 31 days in each month, except February, which has 28 days. An extra day is added to February every fourth year, called a **leap year**, to keep the calendar in time with the moon. A well-known verse helps people remember how many days there are in each month:

Thirty days hath September,
April, June and November.
All the rest have thirty-one,
Excepting February alone,
Which hath twenty-eight days clear,
and twenty-nine in each leap year.

The **calendar year** starts on 1 January, *New Year's Day. The number of each year (1998, 1999, etc.) represents the number of years that have passed since the birth of Jesus Christ. The year 2000 will mark the end of the second millennium (= a period of 1000 years) since Christ was born. The years before Christ are now described as **BC** (= before Christ), e.g. 55 BC. The abbreviation **AD** (Latin *anno Domini*, meaning 'in the year of the Lord') is put before or after the date for the years after Christ's birth, e.g. AD 44 or 44 AD, but it is not used with years after about 200 AD. Some cultural and religious groups use different calendars: the year 2000 in the Gregorian calendar will begin during the year 5760 in the Jewish calendar, 1420 in the Islamic calendar and 1921 in the Hindu calendar.

The **academic year** used by schools and colleges runs from September to July, with short holidays at *Christmas and *Easter and a long summer vacation. Many business companies have a **financial year** (= a period of accounting) that runs from April to the following March. The **tax year** in Britain begins on 5 April. The reason is that in *medieval times the calendar year began on 25 March, not 1 January. When the Gregorian Calendar was introduced, an adjustment was needed and 11 days were removed from September 1752. To avoid being accused of collecting a full year's taxes in a short year, the government extended the end of the tax year 1752–3 to 4 April.

Many festivals are celebrated during the year. Christmas and Easter are the main Christian festivals, and are widely celebrated by people who are not Christians. Jews remember Passover and Yom Kippur. Ramadan, a month of fasting, and Eid ul-Fitr are celebrated by Muslims. Diwali, the Hindu festival of light, takes place in October or November, and the Chinese celebrate their new year in January or February. Special occasions such as *Bonfire Night in Britain and *Thanksgiving in the US are enjoyed by almost everyone.

ˌ**Caliˈfornia** /ˌkælɪˈfɔːniə; *AmE* ˌkælɪˈfɔːrniə/ a US state on the Pacific Ocean, also called the Golden State. California has the largest population of all the states and its largest city is *Los Angeles. It is known for *Hollywood, *Disneyland, the *Silicon Valley (computers) and for its agricultural and wine products. Its history has included the *Gold Rush of 1849 and the *San Francisco earthquake of 1906. Ronald *Reagan was the governor of California from 1966 to 1974.

ˌJames ˈ**Callaghan** (1912–) a British *Labour politician and *Prime Minister (1976–9). He was Harold *Wilson's *Foreign Secretary, and became Prime Minister when Wilson resigned. At this time there were many strikes in Britain, including the *winter of discontent, and Labour lost the next general election. Callaghan was made a *life peer in 1987.

Ma,ria '**Callas** /ˈkæləs/ (1923–77) a US opera singer, with Greek parents. Her strong voice and personality (and her habit of becoming angry easily) helped to make opera more popular in the US. She had a long romantic friendship with Aristotle Onassis, who later married Jackie *Kennedy.

,**call 'waiting** *n* [C, U] a telephone device, popular in the US, which allows a person to receive two calls on one line at the same time. The machine makes a soft sound for the second call, and the person receiving the calls can temporarily interrupt the first one to answer the second: *So many people ring me at home I think I'll get a call waiting.*

'**Cambridge** /ˈkeɪmbrɪdʒ/ **1** the main city and administrative centre of *Cambridgeshire, England, on the River Cam. It is famous for its university, the second oldest in Britain, and is visited by many tourists. ⇨ note at OXBRIDGE. **2** a city in the US state of *Massachusetts, across the Charles River from *Boston. It is famous for its universities, *Harvard and the *Massachusetts Institute of Technology.

the ,**Cambridge Cer'tificate** /ˌkeɪmbrɪdʒ/ either of two qualifications in English for speakers of other languages who are successful in examinations set by *Cambridge University. The full name of the lower one is the First Certificate in English and the higher one is the Certificate of Proficiency in English.

the ,**Cambridge 'Footlights** /ˌkeɪmbrɪdʒ/ a club for students at *Cambridge University which performs regular comedy shows. Many famous British comedians, including several members of **Monty Python's Flying Circus*, were originally members of the Cambridge Footlights.

the ,**Cambridge 'mafia** /ˌkeɪmbrɪdʒ/ (*humor*) a name given by the British press to a group of senior *Conservative politicians who were at *Cambridge University together in the 1960s. The group includes five members of the 1992 *Cabinet.

'**Cambridgeshire** /ˈkeɪmbrɪdʒʃə(r)/ (*written abbr* **Cambs**) a county in south-east England. Its administrative centre is *Cambridge.

the ,**Cambridge 'spies** /ˌkeɪmbrɪdʒ/ *n* [pl] a group of British spies who gave British secrets to the Soviet Union. They were at *Cambridge University together in the 1930s, and believed that Communism was the only way of fighting Fascism. People first knew about the group when two of them, Guy *Burgess and Donald *Maclean went to live in the Soviet Union in 1951. A third man, Kim *Philby, joined them in 1963, and in 1979 the fourth man was named as Anthony *Blunt. Some people believe that there was a fifth member of the group who was never discovered.

,**Cambridge Uni'versity** /ˌkeɪmbrɪdʒ/ Britain's second oldest university, in the town of *Cambridge in eastern England. It has a high reputation for academic achievement. The university consists of a number of independent colleges, the oldest of which is Peterhouse (established 1284). Other famous colleges include Corpus Christi, King's, Magdalene, Queen's and Trinity. Most take both male and female students. Among the university's famous buildings are *King's College chapel, the *Bridge of Sighs and the *Fitzwilliam Museum. Since the 19th century the university has been a major centre of scientific research, particularly at the *Cavendish Laboratory. See also BACKS, TRIPOS. Compare OXFORD UNIVERSITY. ⇨ note at OXBRIDGE.

'**Cambridge Uni'versity 'Press** /ˈkeɪmbrɪdʒ/ a publishing company belonging to *Cambridge University. Its offices are in *Cambridge, England, and it produces mainly educational books. It started printing in 1534, and is the oldest printing company in the world.

'**Camden** /ˈkæmdən/ (*also* ,**Camden 'Town**) an area of north London, England. It was once a *working-class area but is now a fashionable place to live. It has a lively market that is particularly popular with young tourists.

the ,**Camden 'Town Group** /ˌkæmdən/ a group of British artists based in London in the early 20th century, including Walter *Sickert and Augustus *John. They organized exhibitions together of their paintings of the ordinary scenes, objects and people of London.

'**Camel**™ /ˈkæml/ *n* a US make of cigarette produced by the R J Reynolds Tobacco Company. It was one of the first popular cigarettes in the US and a well-known advertisement included the line, 'I'd walk a mile for a Camel.'

'**Camelot** /ˈkæməlɒt; *AmE* ˈkæməlɑːt/ **1** according to tradition, the wonderful and magic place where King *Arthur lived with his family and the *Knights of the Round Table. Some people believe Camelot was in what is now *Winchester(1). Others think it was in *Somerset, *Cornwall or Caerleon in south-east Wales. ⇨ article at ARTHURIAN LEGEND. **2** the name of the company that runs Britain's *National Lottery.

Ca'millagate /kəˈmɪləgeɪt/ the name used by some British newspapers to describe events in 1993 involving the *Prince of Wales and his friend Camilla Parker-Bowles. The newspapers claimed to have recordings of a telephone conversation between the prince and Mrs Parker-Bowles which suggested that they were having a sexual relationship. The recordings were called the **Camillagate tapes** to make a humorous comparison with *Watergate.

the **Cam'paign for 'Nuclear Dis'armament** ⇨ CND.

the **Cam'paign for 'Real 'Ale** ⇨ CAMRA.

,Donald '**Campbell**[1] /ˈkæmbl/ (1921–67) an English sports driver whose aim was to travel faster than anybody had ever done before. In the 1950s and 1960s he held the world records for speed on land and water. He died in 1967 when his boat **Bluebird* crashed while he was trying to break another speed record. Malcolm *Campbell was his father.

,Glen '**Campbell**[2] /ˈkæmbl / (1936–) a US singer of *country music. He received *Emmy awards for the song *Gentle on My Mind* (1967) and the album *By the Time I Get to Phoenix* (1968). His other successes include *Rhinestone Cowboy* (1975).

,Malcolm '**Campbell**[3] /ˈkæmbl/ (1885–1948) a British motor racing driver who held the world records for speed on land and water in the 1920s and 1930s. Many of his cars and boats were called **Bluebird* and his son Donald continued this tradition. He was made a *knight in 1931.

'Mrs 'Patrick '**Campbell**[4] /ˈkæmbl/ (1865–1940) An English actor who was well known for her intelligent and humorous remarks. Her name before her marriage to Patrick Campbell was Beatrice Tanner. Her best-known role was as Eliza in George Bernard *Shaw's **Pygmalion.*

,Naomi '**Campbell**[5] /ˈkæmbl/ (1970–) an English fashion model whose photographs appear in magazines and advertisements all over the world.

,**Campbell's 'soups**™ /ˌkæmblz/ a range of soups produced by the US Campbell Soup Company and sold especially in cans. They were first made in 1897 and were advertised for a long time by two children with round faces called the Campbell Kids. The company's main office is in Camden, New Jersey,

C

and it also now makes spaghetti (= Italian food consisting of many long thin pieces that become soft when cooked), frozen dinners and many other food products.

ˌ**Camp ˈDavid** the special home, office and camp for the US President in the Catoctin Mountains in the state of *Maryland. It was called Shangri-La when first used in 1942 by President Franklin D *Roosevelt but in 1953 President *Eisenhower named it after his grandson David. Meetings there in 1978 led to the **Camp David Agreement** for peace between Egypt and Israel. Compare CHEQUERS.

ˌEdmund ˈ**Campion** /ˈkæmpiən/ (1540–81) a English Catholic martyr (= a person who is killed because of his or her religious beliefs) in the time of Queen *Elizabeth I. He joined the Jesuits, a branch of the *Roman Catholic Church, and performed secret religious services for Catholics in Britain. He was caught and hanged for treason. He was made a saint in 1970.

ˌ***Camptown ˈRaces*** /ˌkæmptaʊn/ an old popular US song. It was written by Stephen *Foster in 1850 and has the line of nonsense, 'Oh dee doo dah day'.

CAMRA /ˈkæmrə/ (*in full* the **Campaign for Real Ale**) a British organization whose aim is to persuade beer companies to produce traditional beer, and to encourage people to drink it. It was started in the 1970s by a group of people who felt that beer made in industrial processes by large companies was losing its flavour. CAMRA publishes books about beer and pubs, and organizes beer festivals. ⇨ note at BEER.

Canada a large country in the northern half of North America. Its climate is generally cold, and much of it is covered with forests and lakes. Canada was formerly owned by Britain and France, and is now an independent member of the *Commonwealth. Its capital city is Ottawa, and its official languages are English and French. Today there are still some tensions between English and French speakers, especially in Quebec, where many of the French speakers wish to form a separate country. See also CABOT, HUDSON'S BAY COMPANY, WOLFE. ▶ **Canadian** *adj, n.*

ˈ**Canada-UˌnitedˈStates ˌFree ˈTrade Aˌgreement** a 1989 agreement to end barriers to trade between the US and Canada. It received the approval of the US Congress in 1991 and the following year Mexico was included in the new *North American Free Trade Agreement.

canals

Britain's canals (= man-made channels of water for boats to travel along) were built in the late 18th and early 19th centuries, at the start of the *Industrial Revolution. They provided a cheap and convenient means of transport for heavy goods, especially between the mining and industrial centres of the Midlands and north-west England. Coal, grain, clay and other materials were transported on **narrow boats**, also called **barges**, that were pulled along by horses walking along a **towpath** beside the canal. Many miles of channel had to be dug, with some sections passing through tunnels or over **aqueducts**. Hundreds of **locks** were built to enable boats to go up or down a hill. A **flight** (= series) of 20 or 30 locks was needed on some steep sections.

In the US canals were used for a short period to transport goods to areas where there were no large rivers. The most famous, the *Erie Canal in New York State, ran from Buffalo on Lake *Erie to Albany on the *Hudson River and connected New York City with *Ohio, *Michigan and *Pennsylvania. Mules, not horses, were used to pull the barges. The growth

canal boats going through a flight of locks

of the railway in the 1840s soon took business away from the canals, but the canal system played an important role in expanding trade and encouraging people to move west.

After the railways were built, many canals were filled in. In Britain especially, canals that still exist have become popular with people wanting a quiet country holiday away from traffic. Old narrow boats have been fitted with motors and converted into attractive self-contained accommodation. Speed is restricted on canals so the pace is slow and restful. Some locks are operated by **lock-keepers**, but many are **worked** (= opened and closed) by people on the boats. Going through a flight of locks is seen as part of the fun. At night, people moor their boats at the side of the canal. Canals are also popular with fishermen, and with walkers using the towpath. Many pubs are built beside canals and attract people enjoying a canal holiday or having a day out.

In Britain, some people live in narrow boats and stay most of the time on a particular stretch of canal. These **houseboats** are often painted in bright colours, with pictures of flowers on the side. On the flat roof there are sometimes traditional jugs and pots painted with similar designs.

CaˌnaryˈWharf part of the *Docklands area of east London, England, where modern offices were built in the 1980s. The **Canary Wharf tower**, where several newspapers have their offices, is the highest building in Britain. Many offices in Canary Wharf were damaged, though no one was killed, when an *IRA bomb exploded there in February 1996.

Canary Wharf

C & A /ˌsiː ənd ˈeɪ/ any of a chain of large shops in Britain and many other European countries selling clothes, usually at low prices. The shops get their name from the first letters of the names of the two brothers, Clemens and August Brenninkmeyer, who started the business in the Netherlands in 1841.

ˌ***Candid*** ˈ***Camera*** a television programme that was popular in Britain and the US in the 1950s and 1960s. It showed members of the public who had been secretly filmed in funny or embarrassing situations. At the end of each section the person being filmed was told, 'Smile, you're on Candid Camera!': *They were so rude in that shop, I thought we were on Candid Camera.*

ˌGeorge ˈ**Canning** /ˈkænɪŋ/ (1770–1827) a British *Tory prime minister (1827). He died soon after becoming Prime Minister, and is better remembered for his period as *Foreign Secretary (1822–7), when he gave British support to many independence movements in Europe and South America. He is also well known for fighting a duel with his rival, Lord *Castlereagh.

ˈ**Canterbury** /ˈkæntəbri; *AmE* ˈkæntərberi/ a city in *Kent, England, with many fine old buildings, including the famous cathedral, the central church of the *Church of England. It became a special place for Christians to visit after Thomas *Becket was killed there in 1170. It is now a popular tourist centre. Canterbury Cathedral was made a *World Heritage Site in 1988. See also ARCHBISHOP OF CANTERBURY. ⇨ article at CHURCH OF ENGLAND.

Canterbury Cathedral

The ˌ***Canterbury*** ˈ***Tales*** /ˌkæntəbri; *AmE* ˌkæntərberi/ a long poem by Geoffrey *Chaucer, begun in 1387. It consists of the stories told by a varied group of pilgrims, people travelling from London to Canterbury to show respect for St Thomas *Becket. It is one of the first great poems in English, and is also well known for referring to sex in humorous ways.

ˌEddie ˈ**Cantor** /ˈkæntə(r)/ (1892–1964) a US comedian and singer who performed in films and on stage, radio and television. He was known for his cheerful personality, big eyes and high voice. He began in 1917 with the *Ziegfeld Follies and his best-known songs were *Making Whoopee* and *If You Knew Susie*. In 1956 he received a special *Oscar.

Caˈ**nute** /kəˈnjuːt/ (*also* **Cnut** /knʊt/) (*c.* 994–1035) a king of England (1017–35) who was born in Denmark and was also king of Denmark and Norway. He is best remembered for the story of how he proved to his companions that not everything in the world obeyed him. He took them to the sea and ordered it to stop rising, but it continued to rise. Canute's name is now sometimes used when describing somebody who foolishly tries to do something impossible: *He is the King Canute of Parliament, trying to turn back the tide of reform.*

CAP /ˌsiː eɪ ˈpiː/ ⇨ COMMON AGRICULTURAL POLICY.

ˌ**Cape Ca**ˈ**naveral** /kəˈnævərəl/ the US base in *Florida on the Atlantic coast where spacecraft and rockets are launched by *NASA. It has been used for this since 1947 and was named **Cape Kennedy** between 1963 and 1973.

ˌ**Cape** ˈ**Cod** /ˈkɒd; *AmE* ˈkɑːd/ a summer holiday area in the US state of *Massachusetts, on the Atlantic coast. The most popular towns are Hyannis and Provincetown. Cape Cod is also known for growing cranberries (= red berries eaten especially at Thanksgiving). The *Pilgrim Fathers landed there in 1620.

the ˌ**caped cru**ˈ**sader** ⇨ BATMAN.

ˌ**capital** ˈ**gains tax** *n* [C, U] (in Britain) a tax on the profits people make from selling investments (= things in which they have invested money), such as shares or property.

capital punishment

Capital punishment is the legal killing of a person for a crime they have been proved in a court of law to have committed. In the US the **death penalty** is used in 38 states. In 1972 the *Supreme Court decided that it was 'cruel and unusual punishment', which the *Constitution does not allow, and it became illegal until 1977, when the Court changed its mind.

Each state decides what methods of **execution** (= killing) will be used. These include **hanging**, a **firing squad** (= a group of soldiers who shoot the prisoner), the **gas chamber** (= a room that is filled with poisonous gas when the prisoner is inside), the **electric chair** (= a chair which sends a strong electric current through the prisoner's body), and a **lethal injection** (= an injection of a poisonous chemical).

In the US the death penalty is passed on people found guilty of murder. Although there are about 24 000 murders each year, since 1977 only 5 000 people have been given the death penalty, and under 400 have been executed. Most people who receive the **death sentence** appeal to higher courts, and the sentence may be changed. The legal system moves slowly, so that a long time passes between the sentence being given and the execution taking place. The result is that there are over 3 000 prisoners **on death row**, i.e. waiting to be executed. The state governor can give a **stay of execution** (= a delay so that the prisoner has time to appeal to another court) or a **pardon**. This can happen at any time until the execution takes place.

Another reason why so few death sentences are carried out is that there is strong opposition to capital punishment. People argue that it is immoral, and that if a mistake is made it cannot be put right. They also say that the death penalty does not prevent people from committing murder. Another strong argument is that more African Americans are sentenced to death than other racial groups and this is unfair.

In Britain the death penalty for murder was abolished in 1965, but it can still be passed on anyone found guilty of treason (= crimes against the state). Many British people think that the death penalty should be brought back for crimes such as terrorism (= the use of violence for political aims) or the murder of a police officer, but Parliament has voted several times against this. In former times about 200 crimes were **capital offences**, punishable by **hanging**. The wooden **gallows** or **gibbet** on which criminals were hanged can still be seen in some places. Many criminals were hanged in public at *Tyburn in London, and later at *Newgate prison. Traitors were **hanged, drawn and quartered**, i.e. hanged on the gallows, then taken down whilst still alive and their intestines cut out. Their heads were cut off and their bodies cut into four pieces.

C

the Capitol

ˌ**Capital ˈRadio** a commercial radio station in London, England, which plays pop music and has advertisements. The company that owns it also owns several other local radio stations in southern England and **Capital Gold**, a station that plays pop music of the 1960s and 1970s.

the ˈ**Capitol** /ˈkæpɪtl/ the building where the US Congress meets, on *Capitol Hill in Washington, DC. The *Senate meets in the north side and the *House of Representatives in the south side. The building was begun in 1793, burnt by the British army in 1814 and built again in 1863.

ˌ**Capitol ˈHill** /ˌkæpɪtl/ **1** the hill in Washington, DC, on which the US *Capitol stands. **2** (*also* **the Hill**) (*infml*) the US Congress: *Capitol Hill decided to lower taxes.*

ˌAl **Caˈpone** /kəˈpəʊn / (1898–1947) a powerful leader of organized crime in *Chicago, US, during the period of *Prohibition. His nickname was Scarface. He had seven rival criminals murdered in the *St Valentine's Day Massacre, but the police could not find enough evidence on which to arrest him. He was finally sent to prison in 1931 for not paying enough income tax.

Al Capone

ˌTruman **Caˈpote** /ˌtruːmən kəˈpəʊti; *AmE* kəˈpoʊti/ (1924–84) a US writer. His best-known works are *Breakfast at Tiffany's* (1958) and the 'non-fiction novel' *In Cold Blood* (1966). Film versions were made of both books. Capote became popular with members of New York society but was later rejected after writing unpleasant things about them.

ˌFrank ˈ**Capra** /ˈkæprə/ (1897–1991) a US film director known especially for his comedies. His best films show an ordinary, good person fighting against evil people in business or government. Capra received *Oscars for *It Happened One Night* (1934), *Mr Deeds Goes to Town* (1936) and *You Can't Take It With You* (1938).

ˌ**Captain ˈBeefheart** /ˈbiːfhɑːt; *AmE* ˈbiːfhɑːrt/ (1941–) a US *rock musician with a harsh voice, who also played the saxophone and who had a great influence on *punk(1) rock music. He was born Don Van Vliet and began his recording career in 1964. Albums recorded by him and his Magic Band included *Safe as Milk* (1967), *Trout Mask Replica* (1969) and *Ice Cream for Crow* (1982). Captain Beefheart himself gave up performing in 1982 to become a painter.

ˌ**Captain ˈBob** (*humor*) a name used by some British newspapers, etc. to refer to Robert *Maxwell.

ˌ**Captain ˈHook** a character in J M *Barrie's play *Peter Pan*. He is the leader of the pirates and has a metal hook instead of one of his hands.

ˌ***Captain Kangaˈroo*** a US children's television programme. It began in 1953 and continued for nearly 30 years, longer than any other programme of its kind. It won an *Emmy award in 1978. A new series was started in 1997.

ˌ**Captain ˈKidd** /ˈkɪd/ ⇨ KIDD.

ˌ**Captain ˈMarvel** a US comic book character. He began in 1940 in Whiz Comics and has also appeared in Marvel Comics and DC Comics. He was an ordinary man who changed into a 'super hero' by saying 'Shazam'. Other characters were Mary Marvel and Captain Marvel, Junior. The stories had unusual titles, such as 'The Mad Master of the Murder Maze'. ⇨ note at COMICS AND COMIC STRIPS.

ˌ**car ˈboot sale** *n* (*BrE*) an informal market, often in a field, where people sell things from the backs of their cars or from tables. People usually sell books, clothes, children's toys, etc. which they no longer want, but some people use the sales to sell stolen goods or illegally copied music, videos or computer programs. Car boot sales are very popular in Britain and take place regularly in many parts of the country: *The tools didn't cost much – I got them at a car boot sale.*

ˌ**cardboard ˈcity** *n* a place in a city where many people with nowhere to live sleep, often using pieces of cardboard as beds or shelters. There is a well-known cardboard city under a bridge on the *South Bank in London, England: *John's new place isn't very luxurious, but it's better than living in cardboard city.*

ˈ**Cardiff** /ˈkɑːdɪf; *AmE* ˈkɑːrdɪf/ the capital city of Wales, in the south-east of the country. It is an important industrial city and port, and a major cultural centre.

ˌ**Cardiff Arms ˈPark** /ˌkɑːdɪf; *AmE* ˌkɑːrdɪf/ the Welsh national *Rugby Union stadium, in *Cardiff. It is well known for its emotional atmosphere, and the enthusiastic singing of the Welsh supporters. From 1999 it will be called the Millennium Stadium.

ˌLord ˈ**Cardigan** /ˈkɑːdɪgən; *AmE* ˈkɑːrdɪgən/ (James Brudenell 1797–1868) a British army officer, well known for leading the *Charge of the Light Brigade during the *Crimean War.

CARE /ˈkeə(r); *AmE* ˈker/ (*in full* the **Cooperative for American Relief Everywhere**) a private US charity. It was established as the Cooperative for American Remittances to Europe in 1945, to help Europeans after the *World War II by sending **CARE packages** of food and other items. Today these are sent to refugees (= people forced from their homes by war or other events) and people who have sur-

a car boot sale

vived natural disasters. The phrase 'CARE package' is sometimes also used in a humorous way to mean a parcel of items sent by US parents to children who are away from home.

ˌ**care in the comˈmunity** *n* [U] (in Britain) the policy of taking people out of institutions such as special hospitals for the mentally ill, and letting them live in their own homes with some help from the local social services. Care in the community, which started in the 1980s, has been criticized because many of the people involved have been unable to look after themselves, and some have committed crimes such as murder.

ˌGeorge ˈ**Carey** /ˈkeəri; *AmE* ˈkeri/ (1935–) the *Archbishop of Canterbury since 1991. He grew up in the *East End of London and has modern views on religious matters. During his time as archbishop, Britain's first women priests were ordained.

the ˌ**Caribˈbean** /ˌkærəˈbiːən/ the area of the **Caribbean Sea**, to the east of Central America, that includes islands such as Cuba, Jamaica, Puerto Rico, Trinidad, Tobago and Barbados. Many of these islands, sometimes called the **West Indies**, are members of the British *Commonwealth. Most of the people living in the Caribbean are descended from African slaves taken there by Britain and other European countries in the 16th and 17th centuries. Since the 1950s, many people from these islands have come to live and work in Britain, and refer to themselves as **West Indians** or **Afro-Caribbeans**.

ˌ***Caribbean ˈTimes*** /ˌkærɪbiːən/ a British newspaper, published every week, which contains articles on politics, culture, sport and other subjects of interest to people in Britain's African-Caribbean community. It first appeared in 1981.

ˌWill ˈ**Carling** /ˈkɑːlɪŋ; *AmE* ˈkɑːrlɪŋ/ (1965–) a British *Rugby Union player who played for the *Harlequins club and was captain of the England team during one of their most successful periods (1988–96). His troubled private life has received a lot of publicity.

ˌ**Carling Black ˈLabel**™ /ˌkɑːlɪŋ; *AmE* ˌkɑːrlɪŋ/ *n* [U] a British make of lager, a type of pale light *beer. A series of amusing advertisements for it appeared in the 1980s and 1990s. They showed a man doing something very unusual or surprising, usually requiring special skill or strength, and somebody else saying, 'I bet *he* drinks Carling Black Label.'

Carˈlisle /kɑːˈlaɪl; *AmE* kɑːrˈlaɪl/ a city in *Cumbria, England. It has been a border town between England and Scotland since the time when the Romans were in Britain, and as a result it has an interesting military history and many fine buildings.

ˌ**Carlsbad ˈCaverns** /ˌkɑːlzbæd; *AmE* ˌkɑːrlzbæd/ a series of beautiful underground caves in the US state of *New Mexico. They were discovered in 1901 and are more than 40 miles (64 kilometres) long. The **Carlsbad Caverns National Park** was made a *World Heritage Site in 1995.

the ˈ**Carlton Club** /ˈkɑːltən; *AmE* ˈkɑːrltən/ a club in London, England, which is closely connected with the *Conservative Party. It was established by the *Tories in 1832. In 1922 the *1922 Committee was formed there. ⇨ article at CLUBS AND SOCIETIES.

ˌ**Carlton House ˈTerrace** /ˌkɑːltən; *AmE* ˌkɑːrltən/ a fashionable street of large houses in central London, England, near *St James's Park. It contains the official home of the *Foreign Secretary.

Carlton TV /ˌkɑːltən tiː ˈviː; *AmE* ˌkɑːrltən/ a British independent television company, formed in 1993, which broadcasts to the London area from Monday to Friday as part of *ITV. *London Weekend Television broadcasts to the same area on Friday night, Saturday and Sunday.

ˌThomas **Carˈlyle** /kɑːˈlaɪl; *AmE* kɑːrˈlaɪl/ (1795–1881) a Scottish writer of books and essays about history and philosophy, who attacked the social injustice that resulted from the *Industrial Revolution. His best-known work is *The French Revolution* (1837). He was also famous for his public talks.

ˈ**Carmel** /ˈkɑːmel; *AmE* ˈkɑːrmel/ (*in full* **Carmel-by-the-Sea**) a small US town on the coast of central *California. Many rich people live there and it is a popular holiday town. The actor Clint *Eastwood was *mayor of Carmel from 1986 to 1988.

ˌHoagy ˈ**Carmichael**[1] /ˌhəʊgi ˈkɑːmaɪkl; *AmE* ˌhoʊgi ˈkɑːrmaɪkl/ (1899–1981) a US song writer, piano player and singer. His songs were usually slow and beautiful. The best known is *Stardust* (1927) and others

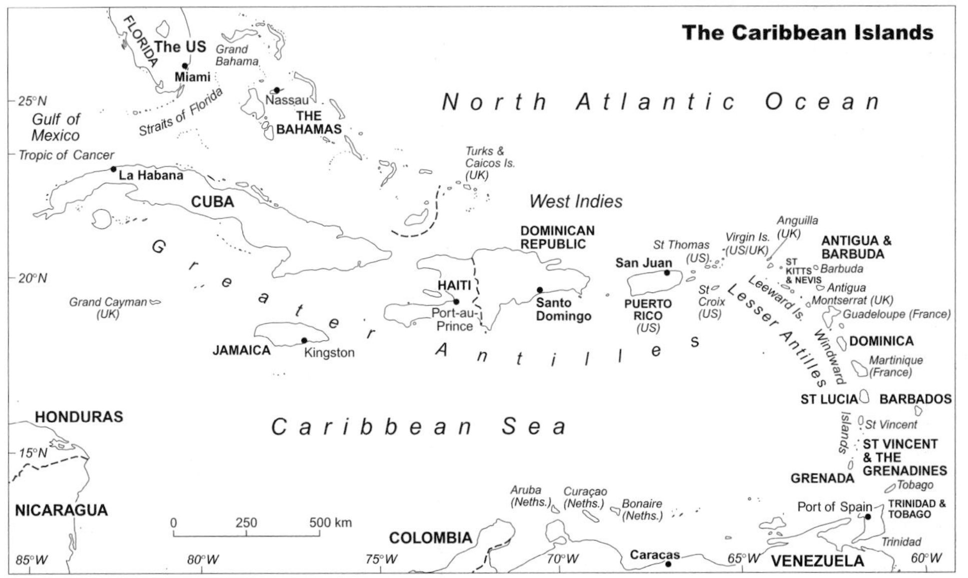

include *Lazy River* (1931) and *In the Cool, Cool, Cool of the Evening* (1951) which won an *Oscar. Carmichael was chosen for the Songwriters' *Hall of Fame in 1971.

ˌStokely ˈ**Carmichael**[2] /ˌstəʊkli ˈkɑːmaɪkl; *AmE* ˌstoʊkli ˈkɑːrmaɪkl/ (1941–98) an African-American leader of the 1960s who introduced the idea of 'black power'. He led the *Student Nonviolent Coordinating Committee in 1966 and was later a member of the *Black Panthers. In 1969 he moved to Guinea and changed his name to Kwame Toure.

ˈ**Carnaby Street** /ˈkɑːnəbi; *AmE* ˈkɑːrnəbi/ a small street in central London, England, which was famous in the 1960s for its shops selling fashionable clothes: *In the 60s all the pop stars came to Carnaby Street. Now it's full of tourists buying souvenirs.*

ˌAndrew **Carˈnegie**[1] /kɑːˈneɪgi; *AmE* kɑːrˈneɪgi/ (1835–1919) a rich American who gave about $350 million to help good projects. He was born in Scotland and made his wealth in the steel industry. He gave money to organizations working for world peace and to build many libraries and other buildings, such as *Carnegie Hall.

ˌDale **Carˈnegie**[2] /kɑːˈneɪgi; *AmE* kɑːrˈneɪgi/ (1888–1955) a US author and public speaker. He is best known for his book *How to Win Friends and Influence People* (1936), a guide on how to achieve success in life. It is still in print and is probably the most successful book of its kind ever written. Carnegie also wrote *How to Stop Worrying and Start Living* (1948), and established the Carnegie Institute for Effective Speaking and Human Relations.

ˌ**Carnegie ˈHall** /ˌkɑːnəgi; *AmE* ˌkɑːrnəgi/ a large concert hall in New York, used for all types of music. When it first opened in 1891 it was called the Music Hall, but in 1898 it was named after Andrew *Carnegie. Performers there have included Yehudi *Menuhin and the *Beatles. There were plans to destroy it in the late 1950s but a campaign by well-known musicians saved it.

the **Carˌnegie ˈMedal** /kɑːˌneɪgi; *AmE* kɑːrˌneɪgi/ (in Britain) an award for the best children's book published each year, made by the Library Association and named after Andrew *Carnegie. The first book to win the award was Arthur *Ransome's *Pigeon Post* (1936).

carols and carol-singing

Carols are traditional songs that are sung just before *Christmas. Many of them celebrate the birth of Jesus Christ.

Carols were first sung in the 14th century. They were popular songs with a lively tune, and contained references to the celebrations and feeling of goodwill associated with Christmas, as well as to Christ's birth. One of the oldest printed carols, dating from 1521, is the *Boar's Head Carol*, which was sung in Queen's College, *Oxford, as Christmas lunch was carried in. Other traditional carols that are thought to have originated at this time include **God Rest You Merry, Gentlemen* and **While Shepherds Watched Their Flocks by Night*.

In England during the 16th century, the *Puritans tried to stop people singing carols, but the words continued to be handed down from one generation to the next. In the 19th century many of these carols were collected and printed. Some tunes were taken from *folk songs, others were specially written. Many of the most popular carols heard today date from this time. They include **O Come, All Ye Faithful*, **Hark! the Herald Angels Sing*, **Good King Wenceslas*, **Away in a Manger* and **O Little Town of Bethlehem*.

Traditional carols are very popular in Britain and America, but children also like more modern songs, such as **Rudolph, the Red-nosed Reindeer*, about how a reindeer's bright red nose lights the way for *Santa Claus to take toys to children during a storm, and *Frosty the Snowman*, which tells the story of a figure made of snow who comes to life.

carol-singing

In the 19th century groups of **carol-singers**, called *waits*, used to gather in the streets to play and sing for local people, who thanked them by offering drinks or mince pies (= small round pies containing dried fruit, apples and sugar). This custom became known as **wassailing** and still continues in Britain, with people meeting to sing carols in most town and village centres. Any money that is collected is given to *charity. Some singers walk from street to street, singing carols outside each house. In the US door-to-door carol-singing is not common, except in a few small communities. Families sing carols when they decorate the Christmas tree.

Carols are also sung in churches and schools, in special Christmas services. One of the most famous **carol services** is the *Festival of Nine Lessons and Carols, which is performed at *King's College, Cambridge, and broadcast on *BBC radio on Christmas Eve.

ˌJim ˈ**Carrey** / ˈkæri / (1962–) a US comic actor, born in Canada. His best-known film is *Ace Ventura: Pet Detective* (1994). He was paid $20 million to act in *Cable Guy* (1997), the most ever paid to a comic actor at the time.

ˌLord ˈ**Carrington** / ˈkærɪŋtən/ (Peter Carrington 1919–) a British *Conservative politician, best known for his period as *Foreign Secretary (1979–82) when he played an important role in Zimbabwe's independence. He gave up this position at the start of the *Falklands War, and later became secretary general of *NATO.

ˌLewis ˈ**Carroll** /ˈkærəl/ (1832–98) an English writer, best known for his children's books **Alice in Wonderland* and **Through the Looking Glass*. He also wrote nonsense verse and taught mathematics at *Oxford University. His real name was Charles Dodgson.

ˌ**Carry ˈOn film** *n* any in a series of popular British comedy films made mostly in the 1960s and 1970s with the same group of actors, including Sid *James, Kenneth *Williams and Hattie *Jacques. The films had titles like *Carry On Nurse* and *Carry On up the Khyber*, and were full of rude jokes about sex and parts of the body.

ˌEdward ˈ**Carson**[1] /ˈkɑːsn; *AmE* ˈkɑːrsn/ (1854–1935) an Irish politician and lawyer, well known as the lawyer who questioned Oscar *Wilde at his trial in 1895. He was against *Home Rule in Ireland, and led the Northern Irish opposition to it. He was made a *knight in 1900 and a *life peer in 1921.

ˌJohnny ˈ**Carson**[2] /ˈkɑːsn; *AmE* ˈkɑːrsn/ (1925–) a US television star who presented *The *Tonight Show* for 30 years (1962–92). He was known for his friendly personality and easy style. Each programme was introduced with the words 'Here's Johnny!'

ˌKit ˈ**Carson**[3] /ˈkɑːsn; *AmE* ˈkɑːrsn/ (1809–68) a US explorer, guide and army officer in the American *Wild West. He was an Indian agent (= a government official dealing with Native Americans) in 1853 and was in the Union army during the American *Civil War. Carson City, *Nevada, is named after him.

ˌRachel ˈ**Carson**[4] / ˈkɑːsn; *AmE* ˈkɑːrsn/ (1907–64) a US scientist and author. Her book *The Silent Spring* (1963), about the threat to animals from farm chemicals, helped to change the way such chemicals are used. She also wrote *The Sea Around Us* (1951).

ˌWillie ˈ**Carson**[5] /ˈkɑːsn; *AmE* ˈkɑːrsn/ (1942–) a British jockey, born in Scotland. He is one of the most successful jockeys of all time, winning most of the important British races.

ˈ**car tax** (*also* **road tax**) *n* [U, C] (in Britain) tax paid by the owners of motor vehicles. People who pay the tax receive a **tax disc** (also called a **road fund licence**) which they must display, usually in a corner of the front window of their vehicle. It is illegal to have a vehicle on a public road without a tax disc.

ˌAngela ˈ**Carter**[1] /ˈkɑːtə(r); *AmE* ˈkɑːrtər/ (1940–92) an English writer of fiction. She was especially known for describing magical or impossible situations in a realistic way. Her best-known novels are *Nights at the Circus* (1984) and *Wise Children* (1991). She also wrote the film *The Company of Wolves* (1984), which was based on one of her stories.

ˌJimmy ˈ**Carter**[2] /ˈkɑːtə(r); *AmE* ˈkɑːrtər/ (1924–) the 39th US *President (1977–81), a member of the *Democratic Party and known for his strong moral principles. He arranged for the *Camp David peace agreement in 1979 between Egypt and Israel. In the same year, he failed to end the *Iranian embassy siege and lost the next election to Ronald *Reagan. He has since represented the US in international disputes.

ˌNick ˈ**Carter**[3] /ˈkɑːtə(r); *AmE* ˈkɑːrtər/ a US detective character in more than 500 *dime novels, a magazine, radio and television series, and films. He was created in 1886 by John Russell Coryell and Ormond G Smith, and the later stories were by many different writers.

the ˈ**Carter ˌFamily** /ˈkɑːtə; *AmE* ˈkɑːrtər/ a US family of *folk music singers. The original Carter Family performed from 1927 to 1941 and included A P Carter, his wife Sara and his brother's sister Maybelle. Their successful songs included *Wabash Cannonball* and *Will the Circle Be Unbroken?* 'Mother' Maybelle later formed a second Carter Family with her three daughters. In 1970 the original Carter Family was the first group chosen for the Country Music *Hall of Fame.

ˌBarbara ˈ**Cartland** /ˈkɑːtlənd; *AmE* ˈkɑːrtlənd/ (1900–) an English writer of popular romantic fiction. She has written over 600 books, and sold more copies than any other living writer. She is also well known for encouraging people to eat healthy food, and for wearing very colourful (especially pink) dresses. She was made a *dame(2) in 1991: *They walked into the sunset, hand-in-hand, just like in a Barbara Cartland novel.*

ˌRaymond ˈ**Carver** /ˈkɑːvə(r); *AmE* ˈkɑːrvər/ (1938–88) a US writer of short stories and poetry. He used short, simple sentences and wrote about poor American workers. His works were collected in several books, including *Cathedral* (1983) and *Ultramarine* (1985).

ˌ***Casaˈblanca*** /ˌkæsəˈblæŋkə/ a popular romantic film (1942) set in the North African town of Casablanca during World War II, with Humphrey *Bogart and Ingrid *Bergman. The film includes the song *As Time Goes By*. It won three *Oscars, including 'Best Picture'.

Caˈscades /kæˈskeɪdz/ a mountain range that runs from northern *California in the US to British Columbia in Canada. The range include Mount *Rainier and Mount *St Helens.

ˌ***Casey at the ˈBat*** /ˌkeɪsi/ a popular US poem (1888) by Ernest Lawrence Thayer, about a great baseball player who fails. Casey has a chance to win the game but he strikes out (= fails to hit the ball three times and is dismissed). The poem ends:

And somewhere men are laughing, and somewhere children shout;
But there is no joy in Mudville – Mighty Casey has struck out.

ˌ***Casey ˈJones*** /ˌkeɪsi ˈdʒəʊnz; *AmE* ˈdʒoʊnz/ a popular US song about a brave railway engineer called John Luther ('Casey') Jones (1864–1900). When the train he was driving was about to crash, Jones stayed on it to slow it down. The passengers survived the crash but Jones was killed. The song has the lines:

Casey said just before he died,
'There's two more roads that I'd like to ride.'
The fireman said what could they be?
'The Southern Pacific and the Sante Fe.'

ˌJohnny ˈ**Cash** /ˈkæʃ/ (1932–) a US singer and writer of *country music. He is called 'The Man in Black' because he often wears black clothes. His successful songs include *I Walk the Line* (1956) and *A Boy Named Sue* (1969). He has received many *Grammy awards, including one in 1994 for the album *American Recordings*. His wife June Carter and daughter Roseanne Carter are both country music singers.

ˌ**cash for ˈquestions** (in Britain) the name given to events in 1996 when some *Conservative *Members of Parliament were accused of accepting money from business people in order to ask questions for them in *Parliament. Because of this, many people stopped trusting the government. The 'cash for questions affair' was one of the reasons why the *Conservatives lost the 1997 general election so heavily.

Casˈsandra /kəˈsændrə/ (*real name* William Connor 1909–67) a British journalist who wrote a regular popular column in the *Daily Mirror*. He was made a *knight in 1966.

ˌButch ˈ**Cassidy**[1] /ˌbʊtʃ ˈkæsədi/ (1869–*c.* 1908) the leader of a group of criminals in the American *Wild West called the 'Wild Bunch' or the 'Hole-in-the-Wall Gang'. Another member of the group was Harry Longbaugh, also called the 'Sundance Kid'. They robbed trains in *Wyoming. Both Cassidy and Longbaugh disappeared to Bolivia and may have died there. Their story was told in the 1969 film *Butch Cassidy and the Sundance Kid* with Paul *Newman and Robert *Redford.

C

Butch Cassidy (front right) with Harry Longbaugh (front left) and the Wild Bunch

ˌHopalong ˈ**Cassidy**[2] /ˌhɒpəlɒŋ ˈkæsədi; *AmE* ˌhɑːpəlɔːŋ/ a character in a series of US Western books, films and television programmes. He was created by the writer Clarence E Mulford and used in 26 books written between 1912 and 1956. William Boyd (1898–1972) played him in 66 films, beginning in 1935. Hopalong, also called 'Hoppy' by his friends, wore black and was very polite.

ˌBarbara ˈ**Castle** /ˈkɑːsl; *AmE* ˈkæsl/ (1911–) a British *Labour politician. She was a government minister in the 1960s and 1970s and the leader of the Labour group in the *European Parliament (1979–89). She was made a *life peer in 1990.

ˌ**Castle** ˈ**Howard** /ˈhaʊəd; *AmE* ˈhaʊərd/ a large and grand house in *Yorkshire, England, designed by *Vanbrugh and *Hawksmoor in the early 18th century. It is well known for its *baroque style and decoration.

Castlemaine XXXX™ /ˈkɑːslmeɪn ˌfɔːr ˈeks/ an Australian make of lager (= a type of pale light *beer) which is popular in Britain. Many people remember the series of amusing advertisements for it which always ended with the phrase, 'Australians wouldn't give a Castlemaine XXXX for anything else.' XXXX is sometimes used in written English instead of a rude word: *The landlord clearly couldn't give a Castlemaine XXXX for customer relations.*

ˌLord ˈ**Castlereagh** / ˈkɑːslreɪ/ (*born* Robert Stewart 1769–1822) a British *Tory politician who was responsible for the *Act of Union with Ireland (1800). In 1809 he fought a duel with his rival, Canning, and left the government. He returned as *Foreign Secretary (1812–22). After the *Napoleonic Wars he tried to keep the balance of power between European states.

castles

Thick walls and strong towers are characteristic features of Britain's castles. When built, they were were solid buildings with few comforts, designed for the defence of a town or region. About 1 200 castles were built in the 11th and 12th centuries, but the grandest were built in *Edward I's reign (1272–1307). These include the castles of *Caernarfon, Conwy and *Harlech, all in Wales, which were built by Edward after he defeated the Welsh leader Llewelyn ap Gruffydd. Many Scottish castles were built between the 13th and 17th centuries. They were **tower houses**, square buildings five or six floors high with towers on top.

Few castles are now lived in. Some are museums and contain valuable old furniture and weapons; others are ruins. Many are open to the public and are popular tourist attractions.

The site for a castle was very important. It needed to be on top of a hill or steep cliff, and to have a reliable source of water. The earliest **fortifications**, dating from the 9th century, consisted of earthen **ramparts** (= high banks of soil) and a **stockade** (= wooden fence).

In the 11th century, the *Normans built **motte and bailey** castles. On top of a **motte**, a bank of earth, they built a wooden tower surrounded by a **palisade** (= fence). Around this was a **bailey** (= courtyard) which was surrounded by another palisade and a ditch. Later, wooden towers were replaced with stone towers, called **keeps**. The tower contained accommodation for people living in the castle, a **great hall** where they ate meals, and often a **dungeon**, a room under the ground where prisoners could be kept. The Great Tower at the *Tower of London, begun in 1078, is one of the earliest stone keeps.

In the 13th century, wooden fences were replaced by long, high **curtain walls** made of stone, with **battlements** (= a wall with gaps in it at intervals) along the top. Walls might be 10 feet (3 metres) thick. Towers often projected outwards at the base so that people attacking could easily be seen from above.

Harlech Castle

Many castles had a strong **gatehouse** or a **moat** (= a deep, wide channel of water) which was crossed by a **drawbridge** that was raised and lowered by chains operated from inside the gatehouse. There was also a thick door and a **portcullis**, a heavy metal grating that slid down to block the entrance.

The main method of attacking a castle was to fill the moat with stones and to attack the walls with **battering rams** (= wooden beams). Stones and balls of fire were thrown into the castle by **siege engines**. Attackers also dug tunnels under the walls. Defenders shot arrows from the battlements or through **slit windows** (= narrow openings), or poured hot oil onto the attackers. In later times **cannon** were used. If the castle was strong and could not be captured, the attackers would **besiege** it until the defenders had no more food and were forced to surrender.

ˈ***Casualty*** a popular British television *soap opera, set in a hospital. It has been broadcast regularly by the *BBC since 1986.

ˌ***Catcher in the*** ˈ***Rye*** a US novel (1951) by J D *Salinger. The story is about Holden Caulfield, a young man who runs away from school and finds the adult world to be false and unfair. The book was very popular with students in the 1950s, and is widely regarded as a major novel about the problems of growing up.

Catch-22 /ˌkætʃ twentiˈtuː/ a comic but serious US novel (1961) about the madness of war. It was written by Joseph Heller (1923–99), and a film version was made in 1970. The story is about a US Air Force pilot during the Second World War. He hates the war and tries to avoid having to fly planes. The book was a great success with US students in the 1960s. The expression *Catch-22* has now entered the English language, meaning an unpleasant situation from which you cannot escape because all possible courses of action are equally bad: *We're in a Catch-22 situation.*

ˌWilla ˈ**Cather** /ˌwɪlə ˈkæðə(r); *also* ˈkæθə(r)/ (1876–1947) a US writer of novels, short stories and poetry. She began as a teacher and journalist. Her stories were often about the US West, and they include *O Pioneers!* (1913), *A Lost Lady* (1923) and *Death Comes for the Archbishop* (1927).

ˌ**Catherine of ˈAragon** /ˈærəgən/ (1485–1536) a Spanish princess who in 1509 became the first wife of King *Henry VIII of England. They had six children, all of whom died soon after being born except for *Mary I. Henry wanted a son to be the next king, and had the marriage annulled in 1533. The Pope did not agree with this, and the *Reformation was a result of the divorce.

ˈ**Catholic** ⇨ ROMAN CATHOLIC.

the ˈ**Catholic ˈFund for ˈOverseas Deˈvelopment** ⇨ CAFOD.

the ˌ***Catholic ˈHerald*** a British religious newspaper, published once a week. Most of the writing is about *Roman Catholic matters, but the newspaper is independent, and often disagrees with the ideas of the Church.

ˌ***Cathy Come ˈHome*** a British television play about a young mother who has nowhere to live. It was directed by Ken Loach and first broadcast by the *BBC in 1966. It had a strong effect on the British public, who did not know about the problems of homelessness until they saw it.

Cats a musical show (1981) by Andrew *Lloyd Webber, based on *Old Possum's Book of Practical Cats*, a book of poems by T S *Eliot. It has been very successful in many cities around the world and has been running in New York longer than any other musical show in history.

the ˌ**Catskill ˈMountains** /ˌkætskɪl/ (*also* the **Catskills**) a range of low mountains in the US in south-east New York State. They are part of the *Appalachian Mountains and a popular holiday region. See also BORSCHT BELT.

ˈ**catsup** /ˈkætsʌp/ ⇨ KETCHUP.

CATV /ˌsiː eɪ tiː ˈviː/ (*in full* **Community Antenna Television**) the oldest US company supplying cable television. It serves areas that cannot receive normal signals or receive them badly. The name is still sometimes used for all cable television.

caucus

In US politics the word *caucus* is used to refer to several different types of meeting, usually held by a group of people in private.

Leaders and important people in *political parties may hold a caucus in order to choose and agree privately on candidates for public office. Until the early 1800s, caucuses decided who would be candidates for President. Now, they mostly choose candidates for local offices. Candidates for important positions are openly elected by party members through elections.

A *caucus* can also refer to a meeting of the members of each party in *Congress or in a state legislature (= government) to decide what political action the party will take. In a majority party a caucus also decides which people will hold important positions, e.g. be in charge of committees. In Congress the word *conference* is sometimes used instead of *caucus*.

More generally, *caucus* can be used to describe any private meeting of politicians to decide something between themselves. Americans have a strong belief that political processes and institutions should be public and open, and so the word *caucus*, since it refers to a secret and private activity, is often used in a negative or disapproving way.

ˌHolden ˈ**Caulfield** /ˌhəʊldən ˈkɔːlfiːld; *AmE* ˌhoʊldən/ ⇨ *CATCHER IN THE RYE*.

ˌSteve ˈ**Cauthen** /ˈkɔːθən/ (1960–) a US jockey. He moved to Britain in 1979 and became the first person to win both the *Kentucky Derby (1978) and the British *Derby (1985 and 1987).

ˌ**Cavaˈlier** *n* [often pl] a supporter of King *Charles I in the *English Civil War. The name Cavaliers, which originally meant soldiers on horses, was first used by their enemies, the *Roundheads, to show their disapproval of the Cavaliers' enthusiasm for war: *The children play war games like Roundheads and Cavaliers in the playground.*

ˌEdith ˈ**Cavell** /ˈkævl/ (1865–1915) an English nurse who became a national heroine in *World War I. From the *Red Cross hospital where she worked in Belgium she helped many Allied soldiers to escape to Holland, before being caught and shot by the Germans.

the ˈ**Cavendish Laˌboratory** /ˈkævəndɪʃ/ a centre for scientific experiments in *Cambridge, England. Since it was set up in 1871 many famous discoveries have been made there, including parts of the atom and the structure of DNA (= the substance in the human body that passes from parents to children and makes it possible to identify every individual human being).

the ˈ**Cavern Club** a nightclub in *Liverpool, England. It is famous as the place where the *Beatles first performed in the early 1960s.

ˌWilliam ˈ**Caxton** /ˈkækstən/ (*c.* 1422–91) the man who set up the first printing firm in Britain. He printed his first book in 1474. By printing books in English, Caxton had a strong influence on the spelling and development of the language. Many of the books he published were French stories which he translated himself.

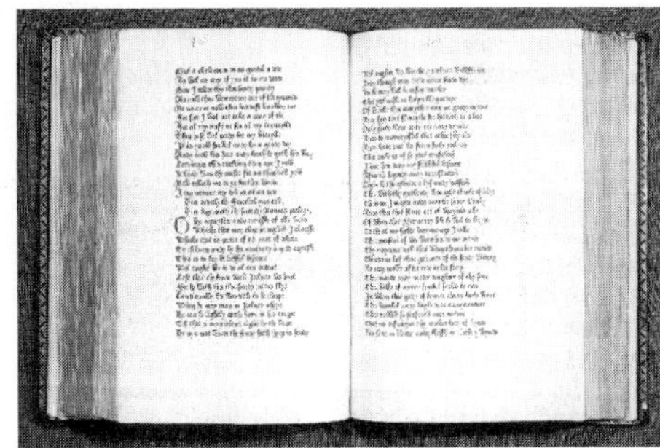

a book printed by William Caxton

the ˈ**Cayman ˌIslands** /ˈkeɪmən/ a group of three islands in the *Caribbean Sea, north-west of *Jamaica. The islands were a British colony from the 17th century until they became independent in 1962, when they voted to remain under British control. Their main industries are banking and tourism.

CB /ˌsiː ˈbiː/ ⇨ CITIZEN'S BAND.

the **CBI** /ˌsiː biː ˈaɪ/ (*in full* the **Confederation of British Industry**) the employers' organization in Britain, started in 1965 and paid for by member companies. It aims to keep the government and the public informed about the needs and problems of industry.

CBS /ˌsiː biː ˈes/ (*in full* **Columbia Broadcasting System**) one of the original three US national broadcasting companies. It began as a national radio company in 1927 and added television in the 1950s. The company also has branches in the recording and entertainment business. Compare ABC, NBC.

the **CBSO** /ˌsiː biː es ˈəʊ; *AmE* ˌsiː biː es ˈoʊ/ ⇨ CITY OF BIRMINGHAM SYMPHONY ORCHESTRA.

CDT /ˌsiː diː ˈtiː/ **1** (*in full* **Craft, Design and Technology**) a subject taught in British secondary schools. In it, pupils learn how to design and make objects, usually in metal or wood. **2** ⇨ CENTRAL DAYLIGHT TIME.

ˌRobert ˈ**Cecil** /ˈsesl/ (1563–1612) a British politician who became Queen *Elizabeth I's most important minister after the death of his father, Lord *Burghley. He was made a *knight in 1591 and *Secretary of State in 1596. He remained an important politician when *James I became king.

ˈ**Ceefax**™ /ˈsiːfæks/ *n* [U] a British television information service provided by the *BBC. It offers many different types of information, e.g. weather reports, sports results and financial news, and the information is shown without sound on special channels: *According to Ceefax there are road works causing delays on the M6 near Preston.* See also TELETEXT.

CEGB /ˌsiː iː dʒiː ˈbiː/ (*in full* the **Central Electricity Generating Board**) the main organization responsible for the nationalized electricity industry in England and Wales. In 1991 it was divided into smaller, mostly private companies.

ˈ**Celtic** /ˈseltɪk/ a Scottish football team, based in *Glasgow. Traditionally, Celtic's supporters are from Glasgow's *Roman Catholic community, and their rivals *Rangers are supported by the *Protestants. Celtic and Rangers are the two most successful teams in the history of Scottish football. In 1967 Celtic became the first British team to win the *European Cup.

ˌ**Celtic** ˈ**cross** /ˌkeltɪk/ *n* a version of the Christian symbol of the cross, found mainly in Britain. It has a circle at the point where the two parts cross. The most famous crosses of this type are the ancient carved stone crosses found in Ireland.

a Celtic cross

the ˌ**Celtic** ˈ**fringe** /ˌkeltɪk/ *n* [sing] (*sometimes disapprov*) a name for the parts of the Britain where the people are descended from *Celts, such as Scotland, Ireland, Wales and *Cornwall. The phrase is used mainly by people in England, who feel that they have a different way of life.

ˌ**Celtic** ˈ**twilight** /ˌkeltɪk/ *n* [U] (*sometimes ironic*) the romantic and mysterious atmosphere that many people associate with the Irish people and their literature, including their belief in fairies, ghosts, etc. *The Celtic Twilight* is the title of a collection of stories (1893) by W B *Yeats.

Celts and Celtic culture ⇨ article.

the ˈ**Cenotaph** a stone monument in the middle of *Whitehall, London, built in memory of the members of the armed forces who died in the two *World Wars. Every year, on *Remembrance Sunday, the Queen and the leaders of the main political parties place wreaths (= arrangements of flowers) there as part of a special ceremony. The word *cenotaph* means 'empty tomb'.

Remembrance Sunday at the Cenotaph

ˈ**Centers for Diˈsease Conˌtrol and Preˈvention** (*abbr* **CDC**) the US government office in *Atlanta, *Georgia, that works to protect Americans from infectious diseases. It counts the numbers of cases, does medical research and sends out health information to the public. CDC was established in 1946 and is part of the US Department of Health and Human Services.

Central a *region of central Scotland. Its administrative centre is *Stirling.

the ˌ**Central** ˈ**Criminal Court** ⇨ OLD BAILEY.

ˌ**Central** ˈ**Daylight Time** (*abbr* **CDT**) (in the US) the time used between early April and late October in the central states. It is an hour earlier than *Central Standard Time.

the ˈ**Central Elecˈtricity** ˈ**Generating Board** ⇨ CEGB.

the ˌ**Central Inˈtelligence** ˌ**Agency** ⇨ CIA.

the ˈ**Central** ˈ**Office of Inforˈmation** (*abbr* **COI**) a British government office that writes and publishes most official information about Britain, including advertisements and information for the press.

ˌ**Central** ˈ**Park** the large park in the middle of *Manhattan(1) in New York City. It is very popular but is known to be a dangerous place at night. Concerts are given on the Sheep Meadow in the summer. The park also contains *Cleopatra's Needle and a zoo.

the ˈ**Central** ˌ**School of** ˈ**Speech and** ˈ**Drama** a leading school for actors in central London, England.

ˌ**Central** ˈ**Standard Time** (*abbr* **CST**) (*also* **Central Time**) (in the US) the time used between late Oc-

Central Park

Celts and Celtic culture

Who were the Celts?

During the late *Bronze Age and the *Iron Age, Celtic influence gradually spread north and west from Austria and Switzerland to Britain and Ireland. Celtic culture became established in Britain and continued during the *Roman occupation. In the south and east it was combined with Roman culture but it remained separate in Scotland, Ireland and parts of Wales and south-west England. These areas have kept strong Celtic traditions to the present day. Early in the 5th century the Romans left and *Anglo-Saxons moved west through Britain, This was the time when the legendary King *Arthur fought on the side of the Romano-British Celts against the Anglo-Saxons. It was also the beginning of the so-called *Dark Ages. By the 7th century there were Anglo-Saxon kingdoms in the south and east and Celtic kingdoms elsewhere. This was the most important period of Celtic culture in Scotland and Ireland, before the *Vikings came from Scandinavia in the late 8th century.

Celtic society was organized in tribes, each of which had a king or chief. There were three social orders: warriors and noblemen, **druids** (= learned people), and ordinary people. The druids included priests, doctors, musicians and the most highly skilled craftsmen. The priests are particularly known for having taken part in sacrifices, including sacrifices of people, in order to know the future. In the Dark Ages, the druids also included Christian priests. The ordinary people were farmers or craftsmen.

Celtic languages

Different forms of the Celtic language developed over time and still survive in Scotland, Ireland, Wales and Cornwall. The forms spoken today in Ireland and Scotland are known as ***Gaelic** or Erse. Irish literature began to be written down in the 6th century and contains stories of earlier heroes. At this time the language spread from Ireland to Scotland, where it developed independently. The Welsh and Cornish languages are similar to Breton, the Celtic language of north-west France. The Celtic language also survives in England in the names of many places and rivers. *Dover* and *Kent* and the rivers *Thames* and *Severn* are all names derived from Celtic words.

Celtic art

The Celts are best known for their art. Many bronze objects including swords, daggers and parts of shields have been found in the graves of Iron Age chiefs and warriors. Bowls, brooches, pins and mirrors were also buried with the dead. The beauty of these objects lies in the elaborate designs engraved in the metal or created with enamel (= a hard, coloured substance like glass). A large number of torcs (= necklaces made of a length of twisted metal with a knob at each end) have been found. At Snettisham in East Anglia, about 200 gold torcs were buried at about the time of the Roman conquest. They were made from gold coins that had been melted down.

In the 6th century Christian missionaries went from Ireland to Scotland and northern England.

the Hunterston brooch

St Columba founded a monastery on the island of *Iona and introduced there the artistic tradition of illumination. This involves decorating texts of the psalms and gospels from the Bible with patterns and pictures. The most famous manuscript of this kind is the *Book of Kells which was created by several artists. It has three illuminated pages at the beginning of each gospel and additional pages for important events, as well as many smaller decorations (⇨ picture at BOOK OF KELLS). It is likely that it was begun on Iona and taken to Kells in Ireland when the monks left Iona because of Viking raids. The 7th century *Lindisfarne Gospels are also famous. Designs were laid out using grids, and compass patterns and guide marks can still be seen on some pages. Colours were made from plants and minerals.

In Ireland in the 7th and 8th centuries, an important period for Celtic culture, brooches were used to indicate status. Brooches in the shape of an omega (Ω) with a pin laid across them date from the 5th century. They were originally simple in design, sometimes showing stylized animal heads. In the 7th and 8th centuries designs became more elaborate and brooches were decorated with **filigree work** (= fine gold or silver wire curving round and crossing over itself in patterns). The beautiful 8th-century Hunterston brooch, perhaps from Iona, is 5 inches (12 centimetres) in diameter and made of silver, amber and gold decorated with gold filigree birds and animals (⇨ picture). Jewellery and ornaments inspired by Celtic designs are now made for sale to tourists.

Celtic stone crosses from the 8th to 10th centuries can still be seen in western Scotland, Ireland, Wales and Cornwall (⇨ picture at CELTIC CROSS). They are usually carved from a single block of stone. Crosses were often carved with patterns or scenes from the Bible. The pattern was drawn on the stone, then covered over while the background was cut out. Figures were carved last and then the carving was painted. The crosses may have been erected to mark a grave or a boundary.

tober and early April in the central states. It is six hours earlier than *Greenwich Mean Time.

the ˌ**Central Staˈtistical ˌOffice** (*abbr* the **CSO**) a British government office that does research into many areas of social and economic life in Britain, and provides official statistics (= facts and figures). It publishes many of these in *Economic Trends*, which appears each month.

ˌ**Central ˈTelevision** a British commercial television company, based in *Birmingham. It broadcasts *ITV programmes to the *Midlands and produces its own programmes, some of which are sold to other ITV companies or to *Channel Four.

ˈ**Central Time** ⇨ CENTRAL STANDARD TIME.

ˌ**Centre ˈPoint** a tall office building at the end of *Oxford Street in central London, England. It was built in the 1960s but remained empty for several years. In the 1970s some people occupied it to protest against such a large building staying empty when so many people in London had nowhere to live. It is now a *listed building, and a charity for people without homes has been named after it.

the ˌ**Ceremony of the ˈKeys** a ceremony that takes place at 10 p.m. every night at the *Tower of London, when a *beefeater closes the gates, exchanges secret passwords with a guard, and gives him the keys.

the ˌ**Cerne ˈGiant** /ˌsɜːn; *AmE* ˌsɜːrn/ a very large figure of a naked man holding a heavy stick as a weapon, cut in ancient times in the side of a hill near Cerne Abbas in Dorset, England. The ground is chalk, so the figure appears white against the green grass.

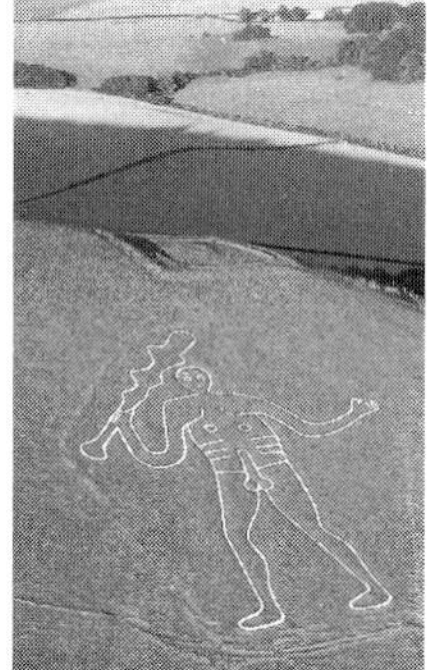

the Cerne Giant

Ceyˈlon /sɪˈlɒn; *AmE* sɪˈlɑːn/ the former name of *Sri Lanka.

ˈ**chain gang** *n* (especially in the US) a group of prisoners who are made to work together joined by chains on their legs. The practice was considered cruel and was stopped in the 1960s, but it began again in 1996 in *Alabama and then in some other southern states.

ˈ***Challenger*** /ˈtʃælɪndʒə(r)/ the name of the US space shuttle (= spacecraft that can be used again) which exploded in the air on 28 January 1986 and killed all seven astronauts in it. This disaster was seen on television by millions of people and resulted in flights with astronauts being stopped for two years. There were other *Challenger* spacecraft.

ˌAusten ˈ**Chamberlain**[1] /ˌɒstɪn ˈtʃeɪmbəlɪn; *AmE* ˌɔːstɪn ˈtʃeɪmbərlɪn/ (1863–1937) a British *Conservative politician and son of Joseph *Chamberlain. He was the leader of the Conservative Party (1921–2) and *Foreign Secretary (1924–9). He was given the *Nobel Prize for peace in 1925 for his work on fixing Germany's borders after *World War I.

ˌJoseph ˈ**Chamberlain**[2] /ˈtʃeɪmbəlɪn; *AmE* ˈtʃeɪmbərlɪn/ (1836–1914) a British *Liberal politician. He first became well known as the *mayor(1) of *Birmingham, where he was responsible for many improvements to the city's houses and services. He became a Member of Parliament in 1876, and was soon a *Cabinet minister. He left the Cabinet in 1886 because he disagreed with *Gladstone's policy of *Home Rule for Ireland.

Neville Chamberlain holding the Munich Agreement

ˌNeville ˈ**Chamberlain**[3] /ˌnevɪl ˈtʃeɪmbəlɪn; *AmE* ˈtʃeɪmbərlɪn/ (1869–1940) a British *Conservative *prime minister (1937–40) and son of Joseph *Chamberlain. He is mainly remembered for his policy of *appeasement. He signed the *Munich Agreement in 1938, trying to avoid a war against Germany and Italy and using the famous phrase, 'Peace in our time', but said that Britain would defend Poland if Germany attacked it. This led to the start of *World War II. He left the government soon after Britain entered the war, when British forces were defeated in Norway.

ˌWilt ˈ**Chamberlain**[4] /ˌwɪlt ˈtʃeɪmbəlɪn; *AmE* ˈtʃeɪmbərlɪn/ (1936–99) a famous US *basketball player. His popular name was 'Wilt the Stilt' because he was very tall and thin. Stilts are poles used for walking high above the ground. Chamberlain played for the University of Kansas and then was a professional from 1959 to 1973 with teams in *Philadelphia, *San Francisco and *Los Angeles. During his professional career he scored 31 419 points, and he was chosen for the Basketball *Hall of Fame in 1978.

ˈ**Chamberlain's Men** /ˈtʃeɪmbəlɪnz; *AmE* ˈtʃeɪmbərlɪnz/ the most famous company of actors in *Elizabethan England. *Shakespeare joined them in 1594, and wrote most of his plays for the company.

ˌ**chamber of ˈcommerce** *n* an organization of local business people in a particular town or city formed to encourage, protect and improve their businesses.

the ˌ**Chamber of ˈHorrors** a special part of *Madame Tussaud's waxworks museum in London, containing wax models of famous criminals and murder scenes: *His kitchen looked like something out of the Chamber of Horrors.*

ˌ**champion ˈjockey** *n* (in Britain) the jockey who has won the most horse races in a season. There are two champion jockeys each year, the one who wins the most steeplechases (= races with jumps) in the winter, and the one who wins the most flat races (= ones without jumps) in the summer.

ˌCharlie ˈ**Chan** /ˈtʃæn/ an American Chinese *detective character in books, in films and on television, who regularly solved crimes which the police had failed to solve. He was created in 1925 by the author Earl Derr Biggers who based him on the real detective Chang Apana. More than 40 films were made with different actors playing Chan, including Peter *Ustinov in 1980. Chan was very polite and was often helped by his 'Number One Son'.

the ˈ**Chancellor of the ˈDuchy of ˈLancaster** /ˈlæŋkəstə(r)/ a British *Cabinet minister who has almost no official duties, and so is free to work on any special jobs given to him by the *Prime Minister. The title remains from the 15th century, when the royal family came from *Lancashire(1), and owned land there.

the ˌ**Chancellor of the** ˈ**Exchequer** (*also* the **Chancellor**) the British government minister who is responsible for financial affairs. The Chancellor decides the government's economic policy with the *Prime Minister and makes decisions about taxes and government spending.

the ˌBattle of ˈ**Chancellorsville** /ˈtʃɑːnsələzvɪl; *AmE* ˈtʃænsələrzvɪl/ a major battle (1–5 May 1863) fought in *Virginia during the American *Civil War The South, led by Robert E *Lee and Thomas 'Stonewall' *Jackson, defeated a large northern army. More than 30 000 soldiers died in the battle, including Jackson himself.

ˈ**Chancery Di**ˌ**vision** (*also* **Chancery**) (in Britain) the *Lord Chancellor's section of the *High Court of Justice, which deals mainly with commercial cases such as company law, patents (= official documents that give people the right to make, use or sell an invention, and stop other people from copying them) and bankruptcy. ⇨ article at LEGAL SYSTEM IN BRITAIN.

ˌRaymond ˈ**Chandler** /ˈtʃɑːndlə(r)/ (1888–1959) a US writer of crime novels. He created the tough *detective character Philip *Marlowe who appears in several books, including *The Big Sleep* (1939). Chandler also wrote several films, including *Double Indemnity* (1944).

ˌLon ˈ**Chaney** /ˌlɒn ˈtʃeɪni; *AmE* ˌlɑːn/ (1883–1930) a US actor in silent films who often played ugly and frightening characters. He was known as the 'Man of a Thousand Faces' because he used make-up to change his appearance in many different parts. His best films include *The Hunchback of Notre Dame* (1923) and *The Phantom of the Opera* (1925). His son, Lon Chaney Junior (1906–73), also played similar characters in films.

ˈ**Changing the** ˈ**Guard** a traditional and formal ceremony that takes place in London, England, when one set of soldiers guarding a royal building replaces another on duty. It takes place every day in summer, and every two days in winter outside *Buckingham Palace and outside the *Horse Guards(1) building on *Whitehall, and is very popular with tourists.

the ˈ**Channel** ⇨ ENGLISH CHANNEL.

ˌ**Channel** ˈ**Five** a British commercial television station that started broadcasting in 1997 and can be seen on normal televisions in most of Britain. It broadcasts mainly popular programmes such as games, comedies and films.

ˌ**Channel** ˈ**Four** a British commercial television station that started broadcasting in 1982 and can be seen on normal televisions all over Britain, except Wales, which has *S4C. It broadcasts many cultural programmes, such as operas and foreign films, as well as documentaries (= films presenting facts about real life) and programmes for minorities such as *Afro-Caribbeans and gays (= people who are sexually attracted to others of their own sex). Channel Four is also an important producer of British films.

the ˈ**Channel** ˌ**Islands** *n* [pl] a group of islands in the *English Channel near the north-western coast of France. They have belonged to Britain since the *Normans arrived in the 11th century, although they are not officially part of the *United Kingdom. Each island has its own parliament and laws. The main islands are *Jersey(1), *Guernsey, *Alderney and *Sark. They are popular with British tourists because of their pleasant climate. They are also popular with people who want to invest money or avoid British taxes, since their taxes are lower than in Britain.

the ˌ**Channel** ˈ**Tunnel** (*also infml* the **Chunnel**) a rail tunnel under the *English Channel between England and France. There had been proposals for a tunnel since the 19th century, but political and practical problems prevented any progress being made until the 1980s. It was opened in 1994 and is used by the *Eurostar passenger train service and the *Shuttle trains which carry cars: *Cross-Channel ferry prices are lower than ever, thanks to competition from the Channel Tunnel.*

ˈ**chapel** *n* (in Britain) a place where *Nonconformists have their Christian religious services.

▶ **chapel** *adj* [not before noun] (*old-fash*) (in England and Wales) belonging to a *Nonconformist group: *Were your family church* (= *Anglican) *or chapel?*

ˌ**chapel of** ˈ**rest** *n* (*BrE*) a room in an undertaker's offices where the body of a dead person is kept before being buried, so that friends and relatives can come to see him or her. Although called a chapel, it is not a religious place.

ˌCharlie ˈ**Chaplin** /ˈtʃæplɪn/ (1889–1977) an English film actor and director who did most of his work in the US. Most people consider him the greatest comic actor of the silent cinema. He appeared in many of his films as the best-known character he created, a poor man with a small round hat, a small moustache and trousers and shoes that are too big for him, causing him to walk in a funny way. He made many short comic films, such as *The Kid* (1921), and several longer films, such as *City Lights* (1931) and *Modern Times* (1936), which combined comedy with social and political comments. He was made a *knight in 1975.

Charlie Chaplin in Modern Times

ˌ**Chappa**ˈ**quiddick** /ˌtʃæpəˈkwɪdɪk/ an island off the coast of *Massachusetts in the US. Edward *Kennedy, the brother of President John F *Kennedy, had a car accident there in 1969. His car went off a bridge and sank. Kennedy managed to swim away but his female passenger was killed. Chappaquiddick is sometimes mentioned as the reason why Kennedy, now a Senator, did not try to become President.

ˈ**Chap Stick**™ *n* a stick of a substance like soft wax which is put on the lips to make them less sore. Chap Sticks were first made in the US more than 100 years ago, and they are now available in various flavours.

Character and characteristics ⇨ article.

the ˌ**Charge of the** ˈ**Light Brigade** a famous attack by British cavalry (= soldiers on horses) during the *Crimean War in 1854. An order was understood wrongly, and the soldiers, armed only with swords, were sent in the wrong direction. They went into a valley with heavy guns on both sides of them and 247 out of 637 men were killed. The courage of the men is celebrated in *Tennyson's poem *The Charge of the Light Brigade*. Its most famous lines are

Their's not to reason why,
Their's but to do and die:
Into the valley of Death
Rode the six hundred.

Character and characteristics: a humorous look at stereotypes

What the British think of Americans ...

British people have mixed opinions about the Americans, reflecting the close but sometimes troubled relationship between the two nations. When people get to know Americans as individuals they have a lot more respect and affection for them than the popular, rather negative, stereotype (= fixed idea of a person's character) based on a casual meeting or on television programmes might suggest.

For many British people the US is associated with power in international politics, *Hollywood, money and violence. The British are a little jealous of America's power. But although Americans believe they rule the world, few of them know much about anything outside the US. The British think that money matters more than anything else to Americans, and they do not really approve of this and do not like brash (= too public) displays of wealth. They also believe that the US is a dangerous place where you cannot walk in the streets or subways without fear of being attacked. Despite this, many want to go there for their holidays. Young people generally have a much more positive attitude and love everything that comes out of America.

Many people see and hear American tourists in Britain and this influences their opinion of Americans in general. The average American man visiting Britain appears to be middle-aged or old, wealthy, and wearing a colourful shirt or check 'pants'. He is fat, because of the unhealthy foods that Americans eat, and friendly, but can easily become excited and rude. His wife has permed hair and wears little white socks, trainers and 'pants', and has a *Burberry in case it rains. She finds everything British 'cute' or 'quaint', especially anything to do with the *royal family. They both talk loudly with strong accents. British people make fun of Americanisms like 'Gee, honey!' and 'Have a nice day!' They think names ending with numbers, like William D Hancock III, are rather silly and pretentious (= suggesting importance without good reason).

British people believe that Americans have no culture, and that except for a few intellectuals Americans are not very interested in culture. Americans spend their free time watching baseball and football, often on television. If they want culture they get television programmes from the *BBC.

Seriously, however, there are, many more positive aspects of the American character. British people who visit Americans in their own country find them friendly and welcoming to visitors. They have no worries about *class, they work hard, they enjoy the best living standards and the most advanced technology in the world, and they have an open attitude to life that is refreshing. The popular stereotype of white Americans is created by white Britons, but these people know that the US, like Britain, is a multiracial, multicultural society and are aware of the great variety of attitudes and lifestyles, as well as the problems, which that brings.

What Americans think of the British ...

The US once belonged to Britain, and many Americans have British ancestors, so when Americans think of Britain, they think of a place that seems very familiar. Americans watch British television programmes, especially period dramas (= plays set in a historical period), see James *Bond films, and read detective stories by Agatha *Christie. As children, they read British books like **Winnie-the-Pooh*. On the basis of these experiences, which are common even to people who are not of British origin, most Americans know more about Britain than about any other country. Although only a few Americans travel to Britain, almost all have an opinion of the British.

Many Americans would have difficulty drawing a map of Britain. They think the country consists of London and a village in Scotland where one of their ancestors came from. London itself is covered in fog. The average British man wears a bowler hat and carries an umbrella. He waits in a queue for the bus, eats fish and chips, and drinks a lot of tea. He has a servant – everyone in Britain does – and he has great respect for the Queen.

Americans admire the behaviour of the British, although they themselves would never want all their social rules. Americans think of the British as being perfectly polite and proper, always knowing which knife and fork to use, always saying 'please', 'thank you' and 'excuse me'. The violence associated with football matches is not widely known about in the US. Britons are also famous for their reserve and their 'stiff upper lip', i.e. for not giving their opinion or showing their feelings in public, which makes them seem formal and distant.

Americans often say that the British are 'quaint', a word which means old-fashioned, but in a nice way. This impression comes partly from differences in how the two countries speak English. *British English has words and structures that have not been used in the US for a long time, and so it sounds old-fashioned or formal. A favourite British adjective is *lovely*, which is used to describe anything, including the weather. Other British words, like *holiday*, *smashing* and *brilliant* make Americans smile.

The view of Britain as a country where everyone behaves in a strange but nice way is not realistic, and Americans who have been to Britain have some negative impressions to add to the positive. The British are snobbish and do not seem very friendly. The famous British reserve seems cold to Americans who are more used to an open, enthusiastic way of communicating. British people cause confusion by not saying what they mean. They say: 'That's no problem' when they know that it will be a big problem, and get upset when Americans fail to understand. Overcooked food, the smallness of the houses, baths instead of showers, and the weather which is always dull or rainy, are other favourite complaints of Americans visiting 'the old country'. But in spite of these negative things, the view of Britain from the US is, in general, very positive and for many Americans, going to Britain is almost like going home.

ˌ**Charing ˈCross** /ˌtʃærɪŋ/ an area of central London, England, where *Whitehall joins *Trafalgar Square. Its name comes from one of the stone crosses left at each place where the body of Queen *Eleanor of Castile spent a night on its way to be buried at *Westminster Abbey in 1290. The original cross was close to what is now Charing Cross Station, one of London's main train stations, for trains to and from south and south-east England, which also has a station on the *London Underground. A copy of the cross stands in front of the station. Charing Cross is considered to be the exact centre of London when measuring distances to other towns.

ˌ**Charing Cross ˈRoad** /ˌtʃærɪŋ/ a street in central London, England, which is famous for its second-hand bookshops. Many of London's most important shops selling new books are also on Charing Cross Road.

ˌ***Chariots of ˈFire*** a film (1981) about the 1924 Olympic Games, in which Harold Abrahams, a British runner, won the gold medal for the 100 metres race. The film won several *Oscars and was very popular in Britain, where it made people feel proud to be British. Its title is a phrase from the poem **Jerusalem* by William *Blake: *It was only the school sports day and he was acting as if it was Chariots of Fire.*

Charities ⇨ article.

the ˈ**Charity Comˌmission** the British organization responsible for controlling all the charities in Britain. It is made up of five **Charity Commissioners**, who keep a list of all the charities, check that they are run properly, and make decisions about new groups that apply to become charities.

ˌPrince ˈ**Charles**[1] (1948–) the present *Prince of Wales. He is the first son of Queen *Elizabeth II and is expected to become the next British king. In 1981 he married Lady Diana Spencer, who became *Diana, Princess of Wales. They had two children but separated in 1992. Prince Charles is well known for his interest in architecture and his concern for the environment. He is also a keen painter and has written a successful children's book, *The Old Man of Lochnagar* (1980). ⇨ article at ROYAL FAMILY.

ˌRay ˈ**Charles**[2] (1930–) a blind African-American singer who writes songs and plays the piano. He has recorded many kinds of music, including the *blues, *country music, *gospel and *jazz. His best-known songs include *I've Got a Woman* (1955) and *Georgia on My Mind* (1960). Charles has received several *Grammy awards, including those for *Crying Time* (1966) and *A Song for You* (1993).

Charles I /ˌtʃɑːlz ðə ˈfɜːst; *AmE* ˌtʃɑːrlz/ (1600–49) king of England, Scotland and Ireland (1625–49). He often disagreed with *Parliament, and in 1629 he stopped it meeting and tried to rule the country without it until 1640, when he needed parliament to help raise money for a war against Scotland. The *Long Parliament refused to help him, and this led to the *English Civil War. Charles was arrested in 1647 and two years later he was killed by having his head cut off.

Charles II /ˌtʃɑːlz ðə ˈsekənd; *AmE* ˌtʃɑːrlz/ (1630–85) king of England, Scotland and Ireland (1660–85). He was the son of *Charles I. He spent most of the *English Civil War living abroad until *Parliament invited him to return to be king after the death of Oliver *Cromwell. He enjoyed the pleasures of life and was well known for having affairs with many women, including Nell *Gwyn. See also RESTORATION.

ˈ**Charleston** /ˈtʃɑːlstən; *AmE* ˈtʃɑːrlstən/ **1** a beautiful US city on the coast of *South Carolina. The American *Civil War began here in 1861 when the South captured *Fort Sumter. **2 the Charleston** *n* [sing] a lively dance, popular in the 1920s. It was named after the city of Charleston.

ˌ***Charley's ˈAunt*** /ˌtʃɑːliz; *AmE* ˌtʃɑːrliz/ a British comedy play (1892) by Brandon Thomas (1856–1914) which is still often performed, especially by amateur actors. It is about a man who pretends to be his friend's rich aunt from Brazil. Amusing and ridiculous things happen when the real aunt arrives.

ˌ**Charlie ˈBrown** ⇨ *PEANUTS*.

ˌBobby ˈ**Charlton**[1] /ˈtʃɑːltən; *AmE* ˈtʃɑːrltən/ (1937–) an English football player who played for *Manchester United (1954–73) and England. He scored 49 goals for England, more than any other player, although his usual position was in midfield, between the attack and defence. He is best remembered for the exciting goals he scored by kicking the ball very hard from a long distance outside the goal area. He was made a *knight in 1994.

ˌJack ˈ**Charlton**[2] /ˈtʃɑːltən; *AmE* ˈtʃɑːrltən/ (1935–) an English football player who played for Leeds United (1952–73) and England. He often played in the England defence in the same team as his younger brother Bobby *Charlton. After he stopped playing football, he became a successful football manager, taking the Republic of Ireland team to the final rounds of the World Cup in 1990 and 1994.

ˈ**Charmin**™ /ˈʃɑːmɪn; *AmE* ˈʃɑːrmɪn/ *n* [U] the name of a range of US paper products made by *Procter and Gamble. For many years television advertisements for soft Charmin toilet paper showed Mr Whipple, a supermarket employee, telling customers: 'Please don't squeeze the Charmin!'

ˈ**Charterhouse** /ˈtʃɑːtəhaʊs; *AmE* ˈtʃɑːrtərhaʊs/ (*also* **Charterhouse School**) a British *public school which was built in 1611 at a place in London where a Carthusian monastery used to be. The pupils are still called **Carthusians**. In 1872 it moved to new buildings in *Surrey. It was a school for boys only until 1972, when girls were allowed into the *sixth form.

ˈ**Chartist** /ˈtʃɑːtɪst; *AmE* ˈtʃɑːrtɪst/ *n* [usu pl] a member of a group of people in Britain in the 1830s and 1840s who supported the *People's Charter*. This document demanded improvements to the political system, such as the right to vote for all adult men, the right to vote in secret, and the right to become a Member of Parliament without owning land. Over three million people signed the Charter, and some Chartists took part in political violence, but most of the changes they demanded were not made until much later.

ˈ**Chartwell** /ˈtʃɑːtwel; *AmE* ˈtʃɑːrtwel/ a large house in *Kent, England, where Winston *Churchill lived from 1922 until he died. The house and gardens, which contain many objects from his life, are now open to the public as a museum.

ˈ**Chase Manˈhattan ˈBank** /ˈtʃeɪs mænˈhætn/ (*also infml* **Chase**) one of largest banks in the US, operating in many countries and with its main office in New York. It is nearly 200 years old.

ˈ**Chatham**[1] /ˈtʃætəm/ a town in *Kent, England, on the River *Medway. *Henry VIII established a royal dockyard for building ships there, and some of Britain's most important military ships were built there until 1984, when it became a museum.

the ˌEarl of ˈ**Chatham**[2] /ˈtʃætəm/ (William Pitt, *also called* Pitt the Elder 1708–78) a British *Whig(1) *prime minister (1756–61 and 1766–86) who was called the Great Commoner because he was so popular in the country. He was also known as a great speaker in *Parliament, and successfully led Britain

Charities

Charities are independent organizations that help the poor, the homeless, children, old people and animals. They are involved with human rights, education, medical research and conservation of the environment. Many of them began in the time before governments provided any social services, when poor people had to turn to charitable organizations for help. Charities rely on money given by the public, and on help from volunteers in fund-raising and carrying out their activities.

In 1997 there were about 180 000 charities in Britain, with a total income of £18 billion. Many charities that are now well known throughout the world, such as *Oxfam and *Amnesty International, began in Britain. Americans are also enthusiastic supporters of charities. In 1995 they gave over $116 billion, about $446 for each person.

Charitable status

In Britain organizations qualify for **charitable status** if they are established for the relief of poverty, the promotion of education or religion, or other activities of public benefit, such as good community relations. Many charities ask well-known people, including members of the royal family, to become their **patrons**, which may encourage people to give money to the charity. Charities do not pay tax on the money they receive, but they are not allowed to make a profit. In the US charities are **non-profit organizations**, and people do not have to pay taxes on charitable contributions.

Charities in Britain are not allowed to take part in political activity, so some set up a separate *pressure group which campaigns on related issues. The *Charity Commission keeps a list of charities and advises them. The Charities Aid Foundation helps charities raise money from individuals and companies.

Charity work

Oxfam has aid programmes to help poor people overseas, especially those who are victims of a natural disaster. In the US, people give money to the *Red Cross to provide similar help in an emergency. *Save the Children is internationally famous for its work with children.

Well-known charities working in Britain include *Barnardo's, which helps children, and *Age Concern and *Help the Aged, which support old people. *Shelter provides food and a place to stay for people who have no home. Several charities are associated with a religious group, for example the *Salvation Army, *Christian Aid and *CAFOD. Some charities support people who have a particular disease, such as Aids or cystic fibrosis, and are involved in medical research to find a cure. The *Samaritans give support and counselling over the telephone to people in despair. Several popular charities are concerned with animals, including the Royal Society for the Prevention of Cruelty to Animals.

In the US religious organizations receive most money from the public, followed by those concerned with social services, education and health. Well-known charities include the Salvation Army, the *United Negro College Fund, which helps *African Americans get an education, and the American Cancer Society. Local charities operate shelters for the homeless and soup kitchens where poor people can eat free.

A lot of the work done by charities in the US, such as caring for the poor or providing education, is done in other countries by the government. Americans have a strong belief that, if possible, private groups, not the government, should do this work. Many Americans want to be generous and are happy to give money to charity, but they want it to be from personal choice.

Fund-raising methods

The traditional method of raising money is to organize a **flag day**. Volunteers stand in busy streets asking members of the public to put money in a **collecting tin**. In exchange, they are given a paper **sticker**, formerly a small paper flag with a pin through it, with the charity's name on it. This is sometimes called 'tin-rattling'. The *British Legion's flag day, called *Poppy Day, has become a feature of British life.

Nearly every town in Britain has at least one **charity shop**. These are run by volunteer staff and sell second-hand clothes, books and household goods at low prices in aid of charity. Some shops, e.g. Oxfam shops, also sell goods made by people who are benefiting from the charity's work. At *Christmas, people often buy **charity cards**, Christmas cards sold in aid of charity. Charity shops are less common in the US, but the Salvation Army and *Goodwill run shops selling second-hand clothes.

In recent years, the **telethon** has proved an effective method of fund-raising. During an evening of popular television programmes, television stars ask the public to telephone and **pledge** (= promise) money to the charities involved. The *Comic Relief evening in Britain and the muscular dystrophy telethon in the US are the most famous. Other fund-raising activities include **fêtes** (= outdoor sales of craftwork, plants, etc.) and **jumble sales** (= sales of second-hand goods). Sponsored walks, cycle rides, even parachute jumps, are also popular. At Christmas or *Thanksgiving, schools and churches organize collections of food, called **food drives** in the US, for old people and the poor. In America, the custom on *Hallowe'en of children asking for sweets has changed, and now some children ask for money to give to UNICEF, a charity for children run by the *United Nations.

A recent source of funds for charities in Britain is the *National Lottery. Well over £2 billion of lottery money has been distributed among a large number of charities. However, some people believe that the introduction of the lottery has resulted in less money being given directly to charity.

In the US many workers have money taken from their pay and sent to charity. Some companies hold **fund-raising drives**, in which different parts of the company compete to see which of them **pledges** the most money. The *United Way, a national organization that collects money to give to small local charities, benefits from this. As in Britain, many people leave money to charity in their will. It is also common, when somebody dies, to send a contribution to a charity instead of sending flowers to the funeral.

in the *Seven Years War against France. See also PITT.

ˈ**chat show** (*BrE*) (*also esp AmE* **talk show**) *n* a television or radio programme in which people, especially famous people, are invited to talk in an informal way about various topics.

ˈ**Chatsworth** /ˈtʃætswəθ; *AmE* ˈtʃætswərθ/ a large and grand house in *Derbyshire, England, built in the 17th century. It is now open to the public, and attracts many tourists. Its beautiful gardens were originally designed by 'Capability' *Brown and Joseph Paxton (1801–65).

Chatsworth

ˌ**Chattaˈnooga** /ˌtʃætəˈnuːɡə/ a US city in the state of *Tennessee. It is on the Tennessee River and next to Lookout Mountain. During the American *Civil War, Union soldiers climbed the mountain to defeat the Southern army at the Battle of Chattanooga (1863). The city is also well known because of the song *Chattanooga Choo Choo*.

ˌLady ˈ**Chatterley** /ˈtʃætəli; *AmE* ˈtʃætərli/ a character in the novel **Lady Chatterley's Lover* by D H *Lawrence. She is an *upper-class Englishwoman who has an affair with her gamekeeper, a man whose job is to look after the animals on her land.

ˌThomas ˈ**Chatterton** /ˈtʃætətən; *AmE* ˈtʃætərtən/ (1752–70) an English poet. He wrote poetry in an old-fashioned style, and pretended it was the work of a 15th-century priest called Thomas Rowley, who never existed. In 1770 he came to London to produce an opera he had written. He was not very successful, and killed himself at the age of 17. His poetry and his death influenced the Romantic poets and the *Pre-Raphaelites. See also ROMANTICISM.

ˌGeoffrey ˈ**Chaucer** /ˈtʃɔːsə(r)/ (*c.* 1343–1400) an English poet. He is often called 'the father of English poetry' because he was the first major poet to write in English rather than Latin or French. His best-known work is *The *Canterbury Tales*.

Geoffrey Chaucer pictured on a manuscript of The Canterbury Tales

Céˌsar ˈ**Chávez** /seɪˌzɑː ˈtʃɑːvez; *AmE* seɪˌzɑːr/ (1927–93) a Mexican-American trade union leader. In 1962, he organized the United Farm Workers Association. He also led several strikes which resulted in better pay and conditions for workers picking fruit and vegetables.

ˌChubby' ˈ**Checker** /ˌtʃʌbi ˈtʃekə(r)/ (1941–) a US singer who was popular in the 1960s. He is mainly remembered for *The Twist* (1960) which created a craze (= something that is suddenly very popular or fashionable) for the dance of that name. He was born Ernest Evans and chose his new name as a humorous variation of the name Fats *Domino. (A checker and a domino are pieces used in different board games.)

ˈ**Checkers** /ˈtʃekəz; *AmE* ˈtʃekərz/ the name of a dog that belonged to Richard *Nixon. Nixon was accused of accepting money illegally when he was a candidate for Vice-president in 1952. He made an emotional speech on television and said the only gift he had accepted was his dog. This **Checkers speech** was a great success and made Nixon more popular. He was elected with President *Eisenhower.

ˌ**Checkpoint ˈCharlie** an official place at which people crossed the border between East Berlin and West Berlin during the time when the city was divided by the Berlin Wall. It was opened in 1961. The East Germans often caused delays before allowing people through. Checkpoint Charlie was removed in 1990 to a museum, and this was seen as a symbol of the end of the *Cold War.

ˌ**checks and ˈbalances** a phrase that expresses one of the basic principles of government in the US. It means a system in which each branch of government has a certain amount of control over the other branches, creating a balance of power. For example, the President can veto (= reject) laws passed by *Congress, but Congress can overcome this veto and even investigate the President and dismiss him from his job.

ˈ**Cheddar** /ˈtʃedə(r)/ (*also* **Cheddar cheese**) *n* [U] a type of firm yellow cheese, originally made in Cheddar, a small town in *Somerset, England. It is Britain's best-known cheese, and is now made in many countries around the world. Most Cheddar has a mild flavour, but **farmhouse Cheddar**, which is still made in the traditional way, can be very strong.

ˌ**Cheddar ˈGorge** /ˌtʃedə; *AmE* ˌtʃedər/ a long deep valley in *Somerset, England. It is known for its attractive scenery and many caves in the cliffs around the valley, where people lived in prehistoric times.

ˈ**Cheerios**™ /ˈtʃɪəriəʊz/ *n* [pl] a popular US cereal made of oats, usually eaten with milk at breakfast. Each piece is round with a hole in the middle.

Cheers a popular US comedy television programme of the 1980s and 1990s. It involved characters in a bar in *Boston and won several *Emmy awards.

ˌJohn ˈ**Cheever** (1912–82) a US author. His books are often about the private problems of families who seem to be successful. They include *The Wapshot Chronicle* (1957), *The Wapshot Scandal* (1964) and *Falconer* (1977). He also wrote short stories, many of which appeared in *The *New Yorker*. Some were collected in *The Stories of John Cheever* (1978), which received the *Pulitzer Prize and other awards.

ˌ**Cheeze ˈWhiz**™ /ˌtʃiːz ˈwɪz/ *n* [U] a make of US processed cheese, produced by *Kraft. It is soft and can be easily spread on bread, biscuits, etc.

ˌ**chef's ˈsalad** a US salad that contains meat, lettuce and sometimes eggs, cheese or potatoes. A chef's salad is often large and eaten as a meal in itself.

ˈ**Chelsea** /ˈtʃelsi/ **1** a district of London, England, on the north bank of the *Thames west of *Westminster(1). In the 19th and early 20th centuries many artists lived there and it had a reputation as an artistic area. Now it is one of the most fashionable and expensive parts of London to live in. **2** an English football club, based in *Fulham(1), West London, which has had moderate success in Britain and Europe since the 1950s.

ˌ**Chelsea ˈArts Club** /ˌtʃelsi/ a London club which was established in 1891 by a group of artists living in *Chelsea. It was well known for the **Chelsea Arts Ball**, a party held every year from 1910 to 1958 at the *Albert Hall, for which art students in London made special costumes and decorations. ⇨ article at CLUBS AND SOCIETIES.

C

the ˌ**Chelsea ˈFlower Show** /ˌtʃelsi/ an exhibition of flowers, plants and garden design that takes place every year in the gardens of the *Chelsea Hospital, London. It is the most important garden exhibition in Britain, and a major social event.

ˌ**Chelsea ˈHospital** /ˌtʃelsi/ (*also* **Chelsea Royal Hospital**) a large building in *Chelsea, London, built in the 1680s by *Charles II as a home for 440 old or injured soldiers, who became known as the *Chelsea Pensioners. It was designed by Christopher *Wren.

ˌ**Chelsea ˈPensioner** /ˌtʃelsi/ *n* [often pl] any of the former soldiers who live at *Chelsea Hospital, London. They can often be seen in the *Chelsea area wearing their traditional uniform, long red coats in summer and long blue coats in winter.

Chelsea Pensioners

ˈ**Cheltenham** /ˈtʃeltnəm/ a town in *Gloucestershire, England. In the 18th century it was an important spa town, where people came to drink the spring water for their health. Now it is well known for its elegant architecture and the two **Cheltenham Festivals**. The music festival takes place every summer and is an important event in modern British music. The literature festival takes place every autumn, and attracts writers and visitors from all over Britain.

the ˈ**Cheltenham ˌGold ˈCup** /ˈtʃeltnəm/ a horse race with jumps that takes place in March each year in *Cheltenham, England. It is one of the most famous British races, and many people gamble on it.

ˌ**Cheltenham ˈLadies' ˌCollege** /ˈtʃeltnəm/ one of the best-known British *public schools for girls, established in *Cheltenham, England, in 1853.

The ˈ**Chemical ˌBrothers** a British pop group, formed in 1992 and known for their electronic dance music. The group's best-known albums include *Exit Planet Dust* (1995) and *Dig Your Own Hole* (1997).

ˈ**Chequers** /ˈtʃekəz; *AmE* ˈtʃekərz/ a large house in the country in *Buckinghamshire, England, built in the 16th century. It is the official country home of the British *prime minister. Compare DOWNING STREET.

Cher /ʃeə(r); *AmE* ʃer/ (1946–) a US singer and actor. Her original name was Cherilyn Sarkisian La Piere. She was married to the singer Sonny Bono and, as Sonny and Cher, they made a number of successful records, including *I've Got You, Babe* (1965) and *The Beat Goes On* (1967). Cher won an *Oscar for her part in the film *Moonstruck* (1987) and her other films have included *Silkwood* (1983) and, for television, *If These Walls Could Talk* (1996).

ˈ**Cherokee** /ˈtʃerəkiː/ *n* (*pl* **-kees** *or* **-kee**) a member of a *Native-American people who lived by farming and trading. Their language was written in 1826 by *Sequoyah, and they had a form of government called the **Cherokee Nation**. The US government moved them in 1838 from *Georgia to *Oklahoma, and many died on the journey, called the *Trail of Tears. Some Cherokees still live in the eastern US in the *Great Smoky Mountains.

ˈ**Cheshire**[1] /ˈtʃeʃə(r)/ (*written abbr* **Ches**) a county in north-west England. Its administrative centre is *Chester.

ˌLeonard ˈ**Cheshire**[2] /ˈtʃeʃə(r)/ (1917–92) a British pilot, well known for his courage in *World War II. He took part in many dangerous flights, many of them with the *Dam Busters, and was given the *Victoria Cross. After the war he set up the first of the **Cheshire Homes**, large houses where people can be cared for when they are very sick and are probably not going to get better. There are now many Cheshire Homes around the world. Cheshire himself was made a *life peer in 1991.

the ˌ**Cheshire ˈCat** /ˌtʃeʃə; *AmE* ˌtʃeʃər/ a character in Lewis *Carroll's novel **Alice in Wonderland*. It is a cat that disappears, leaving only its smile behind. If a person is described as smiling *like a Cheshire cat*, it means that they have a broad, fixed smile: *He just sat there, grinning like a Cheshire cat and saying nothing.*

ˌ**Cheshire ˈcheese** /ˌtʃeʃə; *AmE* ˌtʃeʃər/ (*also* **Cheshire**) *n* [U] a type of mild white cheese that breaks easily into small pieces. It was originally made in Cheshire, a county in north-west England.

ˈ**Chester** /ˈtʃestə(r)/ a city in Cheshire, north-west England, and its administrative centre. It was an important military centre in *Roman Britain, and is best known now for its 15th- and 16th-century buildings and for the city wall, originally built all round the town to protect it from attack, which still stands.

ˌG K ˈ**Chesterton** /ˈtʃestətən; *AmE* ˈtʃestərtən/ (Gilbert Keith Chesterton 1874–1936) an English writer of essays, novels and poetry. He is best remembered for his short stories about *Father Brown, a *Roman Catholic priest who solves *detective mysteries.

ˌAlbert **Cheˈvalier** /ʃəˈvælieɪ/ (1861–1923) a British *music-hall(1) entertainer, well known for singing *cockney songs, including *My Old Dutch*.

the ˈ**Cheviots** /ˈtʃiːviəts/ (*also* the **Cheviot Hills**) a range of hills that forms part of the border between England and Scotland. **Cheviot sheep**, which were originally bred there, are famous for the quality of their wool.

ˈ**Chevrolet**™ /ˈʃevrəleɪ/ (*also infml* **Chevy**) a well-known US make of car produced by *General Motors Corporation since 1915. It was first made in 1911 by Louis Chevrolet and William Durant. One successful advertisement for it included the phrase 'See the USA in your Chevrolet.' It is a large car and therefore a favourite with US families. See also CORVETTE.

ˈ**Chevy** /ˈʃevi/ ⇨ CHEVROLET.

Chex™ /tʃeks/ *n* [U] the name of a range of US breakfast cereals, made by General Mills Inc. Different varieties are made with corn, rice and wheat.

Cheˈyenne /ʃaɪˈæn/ (*pl* **Cheyennes** *or* **Cheyenne**) a member of a *Native-American people of the *Great Plains. They had wars against other Native-American groups and helped the *Sioux to defeat General *Custer at the Battle of *Little Bighorn.

They were then forced to live on reservations (= land given and protected by the US government) in *Oklahoma and *Montana.

Chi'antishire /ki'æntiʃə(r)/ (*BrE ironic*) a humorous name for Tuscany, an area of Italy which is very fashionable among *upper-middle-class British people. Many British people live there, and many more spend their summer holidays there. Chianti is the name of a wine produced in Tuscany: *They've invited us to stay at their villa in Chiantishire.*

Chi'cago /ʃɪ'kɑːgəʊ; *AmE* ʃɪ'kɑːgoʊ/ the third largest US city. It is in the state of *Illinois on Lake *Michigan and is sometimes called the 'Windy City'. It had the world's first *skyscrapers, and the *Sears Tower is now the tallest building in the US. Chicago is the centre of the American *Middle West and has the busiest airport in the world. The *El train runs around the business district, called the *Loop. During *Prohibition, Chicago was known for its gangsters (= criminals), especially Al *Capone.

the **Chi,cago 'Seven** /ʃɪˌkɑːgəʊ ; *AmE* ʃɪˌkɑːgoʊ/ a group of seven people who protested violently against the *Vietnam War in Chicago during the 1968 *Democratic Party convention (= national meeting to select a candidate for President). Their leaders were Abbie Hoffman and Jerry Rubin. They were arrested and put on trial, and five of them, including Hoffman and Rubin, were found guilty. A judge later said that the trial had been unfair, and they did not go to prison.

Chi'cana /tʃɪ'kɑːnə/ *n* (*pl* **-nas**) a female Mexican American. See also CHICANO.

Chi'cano /tʃɪ'kɑːnəʊ; *AmE* tʃɪ'kɑːnoʊ/ *n* (*pl* **-nos**) a Mexican American, i.e. a Mexican person now living in the US or an American descended from Mexicans. The word Chicano was originally a name used by others as an insult but is now preferred by Mexican Americans themselves.

'Chichester[1] /'tʃɪtʃɪstə(r)/ the main town of *West Sussex, England. It is famous for its 18th-century architecture and for the **Chichester Festival**, a theatre festival that takes place every summer.

,Francis **'Chichester[2]** /'tʃɪtʃɪstə(r)/ (1901–72) an English yachtsman. In 1960 he won the first race across the Atlantic for people sailing alone in yachts. He is best remembered for sailing alone round the world in 1966–7 at the age of 65. He was made a *knight in 1967.

,Chief E'xecutive *n* the US President in his position as head of government.

,Chief 'Joseph ⇨ JOSEPH.

,Chief of 'Air Staff *n* the officer in charge of the *Royal Air Force.

,Chief of De'fence Staff *n* the military officer in charge of all of Britain's armed forces.

,Chief of 'Naval Staff *n* the officer in charge of the *Royal Navy.

,Chief 'Rabbi *n* the main Jewish religious leader in a particular country. The British Chief Rabbi is usually considered a representative of all the Jews in Britain, although he is only officially responsible for the Orthodox branch of the Jewish religion. There is no Chief Rabbi in the US.

'Chief 'Secretary to the 'Treasury *n* the title of a member of the British *Cabinet. He works under the *Chancellor of the Exchequer and is in control of the money the state spends on health, education, etc.

,Chief 'Whip *n* (in Britain) a member of a political party who is in charge of the other *Whips in the party. The Chief Whips are among the most powerful people in *Parliament, with responsibilities for keeping discipline among the party's *MPs, making sure that they go to debates, and advising them how to vote.

'child ,benefit *n* [U] (in Britain) payments made by the government to the parents of all children under 16. Child benefit is also paid for older children if they are still at school.

C

,Childe 'Harold's 'Pilgrimage /ˌtʃaɪld/ a long poem (1812–18) by Lord *Byron. It tells the story of a young Englishman travelling through several European countries, and of the romantic ideas and historical events that these places make him think of. It is one of Byron's best-known poems, and describes many of his own feelings and experiences.

'ChildLine /'tʃaɪldlaɪn/ a British charity that provides a special telephone service for children to call for advice and help with their problems. It is aimed especially at children who are being treated violently or sexually abused by adults. See also RANTZEN.

Children ⇨ article.

,Children in 'Need a British charity, set up by the *BBC. Once a year it organizes a special evening of television and radio entertainment to persuade people to send money, which it gives to other children's charities in Britain.

'Children's Hour a *BBC radio programme for children that was broadcast in Britain early every evening from 1922 to 1964. It was very popular in the years before children's television.

the **,Child Sup'port ,Agency** the British government department that is responsible for finding parents, usually divorced fathers, who do not live with their children, and making them pay the other parent regular amounts to look after the children.

the **'Chilterns** /'tʃɪltənz; *AmE* 'tʃɪltərnz/ (*also* the **Chiltern Hills**) a range of hills in southern England, between London and *Oxford, well known for their attractive scenery. It is a fashionable and expensive area to live in, and has been made an *area of outstanding natural beauty.

'Chinatown /'tʃaɪnətaʊn/ *n* [U, C, usu sing] the area of a city where many Chinese people live and there are Chinese shops, restaurants, etc. In cities such as *San Francisco, New York and London the Chinatown street signs are in Chinese as well as English.

,Chinese 'whispers /ˌtʃaɪniːz/ *n* [U] a game in which one person in a circle of people whispers a message (= says it very quietly) to the next person, who whispers it to the next, and so on until it comes back to the first person. The words have usually changed completely on their way around the circle, and this makes everyone laugh: *It's like Chinese Whispers in the office at the moment – all sorts of rumours are going around.*

'Chippawa (*also* **Chippaway**) ⇨ OJIBWA.

'Chippendale[1] /'tʃɪpəndeɪl/ *n* [U] a style of 18th-century furniture, based on the designs of Thomas *Chippendale. His book of designs, *The Gentleman and Cabinet-Maker's Director* (1754), spread the English rococo (= highly decorated) style to furniture makers outside Britain. A lot of the furniture made in America between 1755 and 1790 became known as Chippendale: *a set of Chippendale chairs.*

a Chippendale chair

Children

A child's life

Most American and British families put their children at the centre of their plans and activities. Many children have a happy **childhood** and are encouraged to have hobbies and to develop their own personalities. Parents also try to bring children up to be caring and responsible. Many families have *pets, and children usually have some responsibility for looking after them. Children are also expected to do **chores**, little jobs around the house like washing dishes. Most receive regular **pocket money** or an **allowance** to spend as they wish. From an early age children are encouraged to make friends with other children. Then they go through **fads** or **crazes** when they want to have the same clothes and toys as their friends.

Some children have lots of *toys, games and books, and even their own televisions and computers. Young children are given soft cuddly toys, including a *teddy bear. Later, they accumulate building blocks, dolls, toy cars, balls, paints and model-making kits. Most children spend part of each day watching television. There are special programmes for children during the day and in the early evening. Parents often use the television to keep children amused while they are busy.

Young children go to a local playground where there are swings and slides. Older ones like to play on bikes, skateboards or Rollerblades, or just to mess around with their friends. Some hang around in the local shopping centre or mall. Sports are popular, especially football and basketball. In cities children play on car parks or waste ground. In the past children regularly went out alone, but now parents worry about danger from traffic or that their children might get involved in drugs or crime. Many families find it difficult to strike a balance between encouraging their children to be responsible and independent and trying to protect them.

Some children, usually from wealthier families, take part in lots of organized activities. Some go to *Cubs or *Brownies. Many have music lessons. At weekends and in school holidays, they are taken to theme parks, zoos and wildlife parks, castles and museums, and to the beach. Other children have few of these opportunities, and for some it is a treat to visit the local hamburger restaurant.

Many children do not have a happy and secure family life. Some suffer emotionally because of family problems. Some do not receive enough attention and grow up lacking in confidence or get into trouble with the police. Some beg in the streets. A few suffer physical or sexual abuse. In Britain, children may be taken into care (= put into a children's home) by the social services department if there is nobody to look after them or if they have been abused. In the US, and often also in Britain, they are put into foster care (= looked after by another family for a period of time).

Education and discipline

Children aged five to sixteen have to attend *school, and some go on to a college or university (⇨ articles at EDUCATION IN BRITAIN, EDUCATION IN THE US). Most children go to a day school, but a few go to boarding school and live away from home during school terms. Children from some families have little help and encouragement from their parents. Other parents put pressure on their children to do well, especially when they get older and start taking exams. Children from families whose first language is not English have special difficulties.

In the past, children were smacked or beaten when they were naughty. Today, fewer parents hit their children but use other forms of punishment, such as reducing their pocket money or grounding them (= not allowing them to be out with their friends). Children are now believed to have certain rights, such as the right to be treated with consideration and not be abused, and to have their opinions taken into account.

Childcare

Traditionally, mothers stayed at home with young children and were there waiting when older children returned from school. This is now far less common. Sometimes it is the father who stays at home. But there are many families in which both parents have jobs, often because the family needs extra money. As the divorce rate has increased, there are also more single-parent families. In Britain, the government provides limited financial support for families through **child benefit**, but this is less than £15 a week for each child.

Finding good, affordable childcare is a problem. Some wealthier parents employ ***nannies** who live in the family home, while others use **childminders** (*AmE* **daycare providers**) who take care of a group of children. Others send their children to a **day nursery** (*AmE* **daycare center**) or **nursery school**. Childcare may take a large proportion of a parent's income. Older children often go home to an empty house. These **latchkey kids** have to behave responsibly and get on with their homework by themselves. Many working parents try to spend **quality time** (= a period of time in which children get their parents' full attention) with their children each day and have a family meal with them at least once a week.

Growing up

Teenagers cannot be called children, though they are still **minors** (= not adults) in law until they are 18. When they reach **adolescence** (= the period during which children develop into adults) some become rebellious and difficult. They develop tastes and opinions that are different from those of their parents and there are often **run-ins** (= arguments) in the family. At 13 or 14 some teenagers get part-time jobs such as delivering newspapers. Later, they may work in shops or fast-food restaurants. Most want to earn extra money and are encouraged to do so by their parents.

Most teenagers love pop music. They spend money on CDs and on going to discos and concerts. Teenagers also become interested in fashion and many have a clothing allowance to buy their own clothes. Girls start using make-up and worry about their weight and figure. By 14 or 15 many teenagers are interested in the opposite sex, and some have regular boyfriends or girlfriends. On their 18th birthday they usually have a party. Although they are now adults, some continue to live at home for a few more years.

ˌThomas ˈ**Chippendale²** /ˈtʃɪpəndeɪl/ (1718–79) an English designer of strong but elegant furniture, often with flowing lines and carved decoration. Chippendale's work influenced many others, including George *Hepplewhite and Thomas *Sheraton. His son, also called Thomas, continued his business until 1813.

the ˈ**Chippendales** /ˈtʃɪpəndeɪlz/ a group of male entertainers. They are attractive young men with good bodies who do stage shows in which they take most of their clothes off. Their audiences consist mainly of women. The group started in the US, but now there are British Chippendales too: *My brothers seem to think they're Glasgow's answer to the Chippendales!*

ˌ**Chips Aˈhoy!**™ a popular US make of chocolate-chip cookies (= sweet biscuits with small pieces of chocolate in them). They have been made since 1963 by *Nabisco, which now produces about 475 000 million of them each year.

the ˌ**Chisholm ˈTrail** /ˌtʃɪzəm/ (in the American West) a route along which cows were driven to eastern markets in the late 19th century. It was also called 'the long drive'. About 2 million cattle went along the Trail, from south *Texas to *Abilene, *Kansas, where they were put on trains to *Chicago. The trail was named after Jesse Chisholm (1806–68), a scout (= a person who goes ahead to check the route and look for dangers).

ˈ**Choctaw** /ˈtʃɒktɔː; *AmE* ˈtʃɑːktɔː/ *n* (*pl* **Choctaws** *or* **Choctaw**) a member of a peaceful *Native-American people. They were farmers who lived mostly in an area that became the state of *Mississippi. They were moved west by the US government in 1832 and most of them now live in *Oklahoma.

ˌNoam ˈ**Chomsky** /ˌnəʊəm ˈtʃɒmski; *AmE* ˌnoʊəm ˈtʃɑːmski/ (1927–) a US linguist (= expert on language). In his theory of 'transformational generative grammar' he developed the idea that language and the understanding of grammar result from an ability that everyone has when they are born. He explained this in his book *Syntactic Structures* (1957). Chomsky is also interested in politics and strongly criticized US government policy during the *Vietnam War and the *Gulf War.

ˈ***Chopsticks*** a simple, cheerful piano tune for one or two players. Even people who have never properly learnt to play the piano often know how to play *Chopsticks*.

A ˈ***Chorus Line*** a very successful US musical play (1975) and film (1985) about dancers trying to get a part in a *Broadway show. The play won a *Pulitzer Prize and a *Tony Award. The music was written by Marvin Hamlisch and the words by Edward Kleban. The show ran for 6 137 performances on Broadway between 1975 and 1990, at that time more than any other show in history.

ˈ**chowder** *n* [U] a thick US soup usually made with fish, potatoes, onions and other vegetables. Clam chowder, made with a type of shellfish, is especially popular in *New England.

ˈ**christening** *n* a ceremony at which a person officially becomes a member of the Christian Church, usually while still a baby. The priest puts water from the font (= a special bowl) on the child's head and gives it a name. Promises are made on behalf of the child by three adults, its godparents. Two of them must be of the same sex as the child. A christening is a special occasion for a family, although fewer people have one now than in the past. The baby wears a special dress, or **christening robe**, and receives **christening presents**, which are often things made of silver.

ˈ**Christian¹** the main character in *The *Pilgrim's Progress* by John *Bunyan.

ˌFletcher ˈ**Christian²** /ˌfletʃə ˈkrɪstʃən; *AmE* ˌfletʃər/ (*c.* 1764–*c.* 1794) the leader of the mutiny on *HMS *Bounty* against Captain *Bligh, of whom he had originally been a close friend. Christian took the *Bounty* to Tahiti, and later moved on with some of the other sailors and some Tahitians to the *Pitcairn Islands, where he probably died. His brother Edward was a professor of law at *Cambridge University.

ˌ**Christian ˈAid** a British charity supported by most of the Churches in Britain. It was established in 1949 and provides help and money all over the world, especially in poorer countries.

ˈ***Christian ˈScience ˈMonitor*** a national US newspaper published every day by the *Christian Scientists. It was started in 1908.

ˌ**Christian ˈScientist** *n* a person who believes in **Christian Science**, a form of Christianity started by Mary Baker *Eddy in *Boston, US, in 1879. She said that the mind is the only thing that is real, that the physical world is just an illusion (= false idea), and that suffering and death can be overcome by prayer alone. Christian Scientists do not take medicine or go into hospital, but talk to a **Christian Science Practitioner** who helps them deal with their illness. They have no priests, and their services are very simple, consisting of readings from the Bible and the works of Mary Baker Eddy, religious songs, and accounts from people who have been cured.

ˌAgatha ˈ**Christie¹** /ˌæɡəθə ˈkrɪsti/ (1890–1976) one of the most successful English authors of *detective stories. Her 67 books and 16 plays have been translated into many different languages. They include *The Mysterious Affair at Styles* (1920), *The Murder of Roger Ackroyd* (1926), *Murder on the Orient Express* (1934), *Death on the Nile* (1937) and *A Murder is Announced* (1950). She created the detectives Hercule *Poirot and Miss *Marple. Agatha Christie's play *The *Mousetrap* has been running in the *West End continuously since 1952. Christie also wrote under the name of Mary Westmacott. In 1971, she was made a *dame(2). A film has been made about a strange incident in her life, when she could not be found for nine days in 1926. She was suffering from loss of memory.

ˌLinford ˈ**Christie²** /ˌlɪnfəd ˈkrɪsti/ (1960–) one of Britain's finest athletes. He won the gold medal for the 100 metres race at the Olympic Games in Barcelona in 1992, and was also world, Commonwealth and European champion at this distance.

Linford Christie in Barcelona, 1992

ˈ**Christie's** /ˈkrɪstiz/ a well-known firm of London auctioneers, with a branch also in New York. It was started by James Christie in London in 1776 and now deals mainly with fine paintings, sculpture, furniture, etc.

Its full name is Christie, Manson and Woods. See also SOTHEBY'S.

*A ˌ**Christmas** ˈ**Carol*** a short novel (1843) by Charles *Dickens. It is about Ebenezer *Scrooge, a mean old man, who on the night before Christmas sees ghosts of Christmasses past, present and future. He realizes that he has been very unpleasant to people and that no one likes him. He immediately changes and sends gifts to his poor employee, Bob Cratchit, and to Cratchit's family, including his little lame son, *Tiny Tim.

ˌ**Christopher** ˈ**Robin** a small boy who is the main character in the books of A A *Milne, including the *Winnie-the-Pooh stories. He was based on the author's only son, Christopher Robin Milne.

ˌ**Christ's** ˈ**Hospital** an English independent school for boys and girls, started by King *Edward VI in 1533 to help poor children in London. Later it split into two schools, one for boys and one for girls, but since 1985 it has been a single school for both again, in Horsham, *Sussex. Christ's Hospital is sometimes called 'the Blue-Coat School', because of the traditional long blue coats sometimes worn by the boys as part of their uniform.

ˈ**Chrysler** /ˈkraɪzlə(r)/ *n* a large US car made by the Chrysler Corporation, a company begun by Walter Chrysler (1875–1940) in 1925. Chryslers are expensive and owning one is seen as a symbol of success in the US. Popular models have included the New Yorker and the Le Baron. In 1998 Chrysler joined with the German car company Daimler-Benz to form DaimlerChrysler.

the ˈ**Chrysler** ˌ**Building** /ˈkraɪzlə; *AmE* ˈkraɪzlər/ a *skyscraper on East 42nd Street in New York. It was completed in 1930 and was then the tallest building in the world. Its design has been greatly admired.

Chubb™ /tʃʌb/ *n* a type of lock that is very difficult to open without a key. It is named after Charles Chubb, the Englishman who invented it in 1818.

the Chrysler Building

the ˈ**Chunnel** /ˈtʃʌnl/ (*infml*) a popular name, used mainly in the press, for the *Channel Tunnel.

the ˌ**Church** ˈ**Army** an Christian organization within the *Church of England that gives help to those who need it, such as poor people, old people and people without a home. It was started by Wilson Carlile in London in 1882. Compare SALVATION ARMY.

the ˌ**Church Com**ˈ**missioners** an organization set up by the British government in 1948 to deal with the money and lands of the *Church of England. It is based in London.

Churches and cathedrals ⇨ article.

Winston Churchill (left) looking at war damage

ˌWinston ˈ**Churchill** /ˌwɪnstən ˈtʃɜːtʃɪl; *AmE* ˈtʃɜːrtʃɪl/ (1874–1965) a politician who is remembered as one of Britain's greatest statesmen. He was the son of the *Conservative politician Lord Randolph Churchill and his American wife Jennie. As a young man he served as a soldier in India and Egypt, and as a journalist in South Africa, before entering politics. He was a *Member of Parliament from 1900 to 1965, for five different *constituencies. Between 1906 and 1929 he held many important positions in government, but went against the general feeling of his day in opposing Hitler's moves to increase Germany's supplies of weapons. When Neville *Chamberlain was forced to resign in 1940, Churchill became Prime Minister and Minister of Defence. His radio speeches during *World War II gave the British people a strong determination to win the war, especially at times of great crisis. Examples of Churchill's phrases still often quoted today are 'I have nothing to offer but blood, toil, tears and sweat', when he became Prime Minister, and 'This was their finest hour', about *Dunkirk. The Conservative Party, led by Churchill, lost the election of 1945, but he became Prime Minister again from 1951 to 1955 when he retired, aged 80. He was made a *knight in 1953, the same year in which he won the *Nobel Prize for literature. Churchill was also a skilled painter. He was famous for smoking a large cigar, and making a *V-sign for 'victory'. He was often referred to simply as 'Winnie' and is remembered with great affection in both Britain and the US. In 1963 Congress made him an honorary US citizen. When he died in January 1965, he was given a state funeral. He is buried in the village of Bladon, near *Blenheim in *Oxfordshire.

the ˌ**Church in** ˈ**Wales** /ˈweɪlz/ the Welsh branch of the *Church of England. It became the main Welsh Church in the 16th century, although in the 18th and 19th centuries the majority of people in Wales left it and joined *Nonconformist Churches such as the *Baptists and the *Methodists. The Church in Wales

Churches and cathedrals

Churches are landmarks in every town and village. Their tower or spire (= a cone-shaped structure on top of a small tower) can be seen from a long distance away. Churches are used for worship by the *Church of England. *Methodists, *Roman Catholics and other religious groups use chapels or halls. The church and **church hall**, a building used for meetings and *Sunday School, were formerly the centre of the community. Now, far fewer people attend church and this has resulted in some churches being closed.

Cathedrals may belong to either the Church of England or the Roman Catholic Church. Some are called **minsters**, e.g. *York Minster, and were originally centres for teaching Christianity in the surrounding countryside. A cathedral is the headquarters of a ***bishop** or ***archbishop**. Canterbury Cathedral is the headquarters of the *Archbishop of Canterbury, who is head of the Church of England.

Many people visit churches and cathedrals to admire their architecture. The atmosphere inside makes everyone talk quietly, even if they are not religious.

Church architecture

As the 'house of God', a church had to be an impressive building. It is usually built of stone, with a **tower** or **spire** at the west end. ***Bells** are placed high up in the tower and rung by long ropes before services. Roofs are made of wood or stone and are often very elaborate. The church is approached through a gate, sometimes a **lych-gate** (= a gate with a roof over it), which leads into the **churchyard** where people are buried. The main entrance is usually on the south side. The church **porch** has a noticeboard and often a seat in it. Cathedrals are large churches, usually built in the shape of a long cross with a central tower. Older cathedrals stand in a quiet grassy **cathedral close**.

Many churches and cathedrals have been rebuilt over time and contain a mixture of architectural styles. The earliest stone churches date from the *Anglo-Saxon period (6th–11th centuries). *Norman churches, from the 11th and 12th centuries, are massive structures. **Buttresses**, pillars of stone built against the walls, support the roof and take the pressure of the **vault** (= arched stone ceiling). Rounded arches over doorways and windows are a distinctive feature of Norman architecture. Examples of Norman cathedrals are those at Durham and Ely.

The English *Gothic style of the 13th–15th centuries is characterized by pointed arches and increasingly ornate designs for the vault. Windows were tall and narrow in the *Early English period (13th century), and later, in the *Decorated period, had **tracery** (= lace-like patterns) at the top. In the *Perpendicular period (15th century), they were greatly increased in size and filled with **stained glass** (= small pieces of coloured glass in a lead frame) showing pictures of saints. Ceilings with elaborate fan vaults (= curved strips of stone spreading out from a point, with patterns between them) were supported by **flying buttresses** that leaned at an angle from the wall and formed an arch. Salisbury Cathedral is a characteristic Early English building, Exeter Cathedral dates mainly

a village church with a lych-gate

from the Decorated period and Gloucester Cathedral with its fan vaults is typical of the Perpendicular period.

Some later buildings, such as *St Paul's Cathedral designed by Christopher *Wren, are more like classical temples, with a central dome and spire added. Wren and James Gibbs, designer of *St Martin-in-the-Fields, influenced architects in America: Christ Church in *Philadelphia is a copy of St Martin. But the new Coventry Cathedral, designed by Basil Spence in the 1950s, is a hall-like church with narrow stained-glass windows. By contrast, the Roman Catholic cathedral in Liverpool, built in the 1960s, is shaped like a crown.

Churches in the US

The traditional church dating from early in US history was a one-room building made of wood and used also as a school. It had a tall, thin **steeple** at one end, which held the bell. Most communities now have several churches in varying styles. Some are made of stone in order to look like old English churches, some are small, plain buildings made of brick or wood, and others are modern buildings with glass walls. Storefront churches look like a shop/store.

Inside a church

The main focus inside a church is the **altar**, a table at the eastern end, with a cloth, a cross and candles on it. In the Holy Communion service, people go to the **communion rail** at the foot of the altar steps to receive bread and wine. Below the altar are the **choir stalls**, seats facing across the church, where the choir sits. Sometimes, between the choir and the congregation (= ordinary people at a service) there is a carved **choir screen** with an organ above it.

In the main part of a church, the **nave**, there are **pews** (= long benches with backs) for the congregation. In front of each pew are **kneelers** (= cushions) for people to kneel on when they pray. Pews face the altar on both sides of a central **aisle**. In cathedrals there are **side aisles** and, sometimes, small **side chapels**. In front of the pews is a raised **pulpit** where the vicar stands to give his sermon (= religious talk). Near the west end is a stone **font** where babies are *christened. Larger churches often have an underground **crypt** which was originally used as a burial place. Attached to a church is a **vestry** where the vicar prepares for the service. On special occasions such as *Easter churches are decorated with flowers.

C

The Church of England

The Church of England is the official *__Protestant__ church in England. It became independent of the *Roman Catholic Church in the 16th century, in the time of *Henry VIII. By the *Act of Supremacy (1534), the king replaced the Pope as head of the English, or **Anglican**, Church and personally chose senior members of the **clergy** (= people allowed to perform religious ceremonies). The king or queen is still the **Supreme Governor** of the Church of England but *archibishops and *bishops are now appointed on the recommendation of the *prime minister. The Church is led by the *__Archbishop of Canterbury__ and governed by the *__General Synod__ of bishops, clergy and laity (= ordinary church members).

England is divided into 13 500 **parishes**, each based around a parish *church. Every parish has a **vicar** or **rector** in charge who, in many towns and villages, continues to be an important and respected member of the community. Parishes are grouped geographically into **dioceses**, each led by a bishop. In 1992, the General Synod decided to allow women to become priests, and the first women were ordained in 1994. This caused a lot of disagreement among both clergy and laity and some people left the Church. Church of England priests are allowed to marry, and a vicar's wife or husband is expected to take part in parish activities. Members of the clergy usually wear a white circular collar, informally called a **dog-collar**.

Church services

Services are in English, and forms of service were originally given in the *__Book of Common Prayer__ (1549). This is still used but there are now also services in modern English. The most important service is **Holy Communion**, often called simply **Communion**, at which people **take Communion** (= share bread and wine in memory of Christ). Many churches also have a Family Communion service with hymns and a **sermon** (= a religious talk). A morning service with hymns, prayers and a sermon, but no communion, is called **Matins**; an evening service is called **Evensong**. A special *__Sunday School__ is held for children at which they are taught stories from the Bible and learn about Jesus Christ and the beliefs of the Church.

There is a broad range of religious belief and practice within the Church. Vicars and people who are *__High Church__, or *__Anglo-Catholic__, are closest to the Roman Catholic Church and put a lot of emphasis on the authority of the clergy, the power of the sacraments and on ritual (= ceremonies always performed in the same way). Those who are *__Low Church__ prefer simpler, less formal services, with more emphasis on the teachings of the Bible and on personal faith as the means of salvation.

Membership of the Church

People become members of the Church at a *__christening__ ceremony, usually held when they are babies. Later, when they are old enough to understand and accept the Church's teachings, they are **confirmed** and are allowed to take Communion. Many people are christened but not confirmed, and the number of people going to church has fallen in recent years. Only about a million now go regularly. Despite this, a lot of people still claim to be 'C of E', and use the Church at important times in their lives. Many get married in church, or give their relations a Christian funeral. Christian values such as honesty, generosity and care for others form the basis of most people's moral code, whether they are religious or not.

The Church of England is one of the most powerful institutions in the country, and many people think it should be more active politically and speak out for social justice.

The Anglican Communion

There are about 70 million Anglicans throughout the world, all of whom recognize the Archbishop of Canterbury as their head. Every ten years the heads of all the Anglican churches meet in Britain for the *Lambeth Conference. The **Episcopal Church of Scotland** (not the presbyterian *Church of Scotland), the **Church of Ireland**, the **Church in Wales** and the **Episcopal Church** in the US are all part of the **Anglican Communion**.

The Episcopal Church reached the US in 1607 with the first English people to settle in North America and is the oldest Christian religion there. There are now about 2.5 million **Episcopalians** in the US. Anyone can become a member of the Church, but because of its long history some people associate it with high social status. In the 1970s, a few people left the Church because it began to use a new Book of Common Prayer and to ordain women, but both changes are now widely accepted.

---

is now a 'disestablished' church, i.e. the British king or queen is no longer its Supreme Governor and it has no connections with the British State.

the ˌ**Church** ˈ**Missionary So**ˌ**ciety** a *Church of England organization that sends missionaries all over the world to teach people about Christianity. It was started in 1799.

The ˌ**Church of** ˈ**England** ⇨ article.

the ˈ**Church of** ˈ**Jesus** ˈ**Christ of** ˈ**Latter-Day** ˈ**Saints** /ˈlætə deɪ; *AmE* ˈlætərdeɪ/ the official name of the Church to which *Mormons belong. It is more correct to call Mormons 'latter-day saints'. 'Latter-day' means 'recent' or 'modern', because Mormons believe that the Church did not survive in the form that Jesus intended and was started again by Joseph *Smith in 1830. 'Saint' here means, as in the Bible, 'a member of Jesus Christ's church'.

the ˌ**Church of** ˈ**Scotland** the official Church in Scotland, started by John *Knox and Andrew Melville in 1560, and officially accepted in 1690. It does not have *bishops like the *Church of England, and the members of its clergy are called *ministers*, rather than *priests*. Both men and women can be ministers. The churches of the Church of Scotland are run by a minister and a group of senior church members called *elders*. This system is known as *Presbyterianism. See also EPISCOPAL CHURCH, FREE CHURCH OF SCOTLAND, MODERATOR OF THE CHURCH OF SCOTLAND.

the **CIA** /ˌsiː aɪ ˈeɪ/ (*in full* the **Central Intelligence Agency**) the US government organization that gathers information and does research on foreign governments and operations. In the 1960s and later, it changed its methods of operating, after being criticized in the US for trying to influence or remove foreign governments. It was established in 1947 and is based in Langley, *Virginia.

the **CID** /ˌsiː aɪ ˈdiː/ (*in full* the **Criminal Investigation Department**) (in Britain) a branch of the *Metropolitan Police, consisting of detectives who investigate serious crimes. It is based at *New Scotland Yard in London. There are several departments of the CID that are well known to the British public, including the *Special Branch and the *Fraud Squad. See also FLYING SQUAD.

ˌ***Cindeˈrella*** /ˌsɪndəˈrelə/ a traditional story about a young girl called Cinderella who has to work very hard for her stepmother (= the woman who married her father after her mother died) and her two ugly older sisters. One day the sisters go to a ball (= a grand event at which people dance) at the royal palace, and Cinderella wishes she could go too. Suddenly her fairy godmother appears and says, 'You *shall* go to the ball!' She uses her magic powers to produce a wonderful dress and glass slippers (= shoes) for Cinderella, and makes a coach and horses for her from a pumpkin and four white mice. But she warns Cinderella that she must leave the ball at midnight. Cinderella is so beautiful that the prince dances with her all the time, but at midnight she suddenly runs from the palace, leaving one of her glass slippers behind. The prince sends his servants all over the country to find her by trying the slipper on every young woman's foot. When at last they find Cinderella the prince marries her.

The story of Cinderella is a favourite one for British *pantomimes. The Ugly Sisters are played by men dressed as women. The prince is called Prince Charming, and Cinderella (or 'Cinders') has a male friend called *Buttons who works with her and secretly loves her. The word *Cinderella* is also used to refer to things that have not been given enough attention in the past: *The railways are the Cinderella of public transport services.*

the ˌ**Cinque ˈPorts** /ˌsɪŋk/ a group of towns on the south-east coast of England that had the responsibility of protecting the coast and providing most of the English navy from the 11th to the 14th centuries. 'Cinque' is an old French word meaning 'five'. The original five towns were Dover, Hastings, Hythe, Romney and Sandwich. Later Rye and Winchelsea were added to the group.

ˌ**circle the ˈwagons** a call of warning in the American *Wild West, used by people travelling together in a line of wagons. When they were in a dangerous situation, such as an attack by *Native Americans, they formed a circle with the wagons as a protective barrier. The expression is now sometimes used in a humorous way when problems occur.

the ˈ**Citadel** a well-known US military college in *Charleston, *South Carolina. It began in 1842. The Citadel refused to have women students until pressure from the US government forced them to accept the first four in 1996.

ˌ***Citizen ˈKane*** /ˈkeɪn/ a US film (1941), which many people think is one of the best ever made. Orson *Welles wrote, produced and directed it and played the main character. He received *Oscars as 'Best Director' and 'Best Actor', and the film itself was named 'Best Film'. The story was based on the life of the rich US newspaper owner William Randolph *Hearst, who tried to stop it being filmed. It showed Kane as a rich but immoral person who becomes sad and lonely in his old age.

the ˌ**Citizens Adˈvice ˌBureau** (*abbr* **CAB**) a British organization with offices in many towns to which people can go for free advice about the law, money problems, the government services available to help them, etc. The Citizens Advice Bureau is mostly paid for by local authorities. It started in 1939, when people needed information about the arrangements during World War II.

ˈ**Citizen's Band** (*abbr* **CB**) a radio system used for communicating over short distances, especially by drivers of lorries and cars. It first became popular in the US in the 1970s as a way of exchanging warnings about traffic problems and police. It was illegal in Britain until 1981. CB users give themselves unusual radio names, such as 'Hound Dog' and 'Sweet Mama'.

the ˌ**Citizen's ˈCharter** a social programme introduced by the British Prime Minister John *Major in 1991. Its aim was to improve the standard of public services and to make government departments explain their actions more clearly to the public. A new department, the Office of Public Service and Science, was set up to see that the aims of the Charter were carried out. There are now over 40 individual charters related to the programme, e.g. The Taxpayer's Charter, The Charter for Court Users, and The Patient's Charter.

the **City**

The business and financial centre of London is called **the City** or **the City of London**. It covers an area in east central London north of the River Thames, between Blackfriars Bridge and *Tower Bridge. It is only about one square mile (2.5 square kilometres) in size and is often referred to as **the Square Mile**.

Many financial institutions have their head offices in the City, including the *Bank of England in Threadneedle Street, the *London Stock Exchange in Old Broad Street and *Lloyd's of London in Lime Street. Many banks, insurance companies and **stockbrokers** (= companies that buy and sell shares for others) have been in the City many years. When journalists talk about 'the City' they are usually not referring to the place but to the people involved in business and commerce, as in: *The City had been expecting poor results from the company.* (Compare WALL STREET.)

In the City old and new buildings stand next to each other. The most famous older buildings include *St Paul's Cathedral, the *Guildhall and the *Mansion House, where the *Lord Mayor of London lives. At 600 feet (183 metres) high, the National Westminster Tower is one of the City's more recent landmarks. The new *Barbican Centre includes an art gallery, a theatre and a concert hall, and has flats/apartments built above it.

Few people live in the City and at night the population is less than 8 000. During the day it rises to about half a million, as business people ***commute** to the City by car, bus and train. The traditional image of the **City gent** is of a businessman in a dark suit and bowler hat, who carries a briefcase and a newspaper or an umbrella. The expression *He's something in the City* means 'He has an important job with a bank or firm of stockbrokers', and suggests wealth and high social status. The image is now rather dated as an increasing number of women hold senior positions in City companies.

the ˌ**City and ˌGuilds ˈInstitute** a British organization that gives qualifications in technical subjects and in skills that require practical ability, such as hairdressing or cooking. It was started in 1868: (*infml*) *She's doing her City and Guilds* (= the City and Guilds Institute course) *in engineering.*

ˌ**City ˈChallenge** a new approach to making areas of Britain's inner cities more pleasant to live and work

The Civil War

Causes of the war

The American Civil War was fought between the northern and southern states from 1861 to 1865. There were two main causes of the war. The first was the issue of *__slavery__: should Africans who had been brought by force to the US be used as slaves. The second was the issue of **states' rights**: should the US federal government be more powerful than the governments of individual states.

The North and South were very different in character. The economy of the South was based on agriculture, especially cotton. Picking cotton was hard work, and the South depended on slaves for this. The North was more industrial, with a larger population and greater wealth. Slavery, and opposition to it, had existed since before independence (1776) but, in the 19th century, the **abolitionists**, people who wanted to make slavery illegal, gradually increased in number. The South's attitude was that each state had the right to make any law it wanted, and if southern states wanted slavery, the US government could not prevent it. Many southerners became **secessionists**, believing that southern states should **secede from the Union** (= become independent from the US).

In 1860, Abraham *Lincoln was elected President. He and his party, the *Republicans, were against slavery, but said that they would not end it. The southern states did not believe this, and began to leave the Union. In 1860 there were 34 states in the US. Eleven of them (South Carolina, Mississippi, Florida, Alabama, Georgia, Louisiana, Texas, Virginia, Arkansas, Tennessee and North Carolina) left the Union and formed the *__Confederate States of America__, often called the **Confederacy**. Jefferson *Davis became its President, and for most of the war *Richmond, Virginia, was the capital.

Four years of fighting

The US government did not want a war but, on 12 April 1861, the Confederate Army attacked *Fort Sumter, which was in the Confederate state of South Carolina but still occupied by the Union army. President Lincoln could not ignore the attack and so the Civil War began.

Over the next four years the Union army tried to take control of the South. The battles that followed, *Shiloh, Antietam, *Bull Run and Chicamauga, have become part of America's national memory. After the battle of *Gettysburg in 1863, in a speech known as the *__Gettysburg Address__, President Lincoln said that the North was fighting the war to keep the Union together so that '... government of the people, by the people, for the people, shall not perish from the earth'. In the same year he issued the *__Emancipation Proclamation__ which made slavery illegal, but only in the Confederacy.

Slaves and former slaves played an important part in the war. Some gave information to Union soldiers, because they knew that their best chance of freedom was for the North to win the war. Many former slaves wanted to become Union soldiers, but this was not very popular among white northerners. In spite of this opposition about 185 000 former slaves served in the Union army.

Women on both sides worked as spies, taking information, and sometimes even people, across borders by hiding them under their large skirts.

In the South especially, people suffered greatly and had little to eat. On 9 April 1865, when the South could fight no more, General Robert E *Lee surrendered to General Ulysses S *Grant at *Appomattox Court House in Virginia. A total of 620 000 people had been killed and many more wounded.

The war was over but feelings of hostility against the North remained strong. John Wilkes *Booth, an actor who supported the South, decided to kill President Lincoln. On 14 April 1865 he approached the President in Ford's Theatre in Washington and shot him. Lincoln died the next morning.

The killing of President Lincoln showed how bitter many people felt. The South had been beaten, but its people had not changed their opinions about slavery or about states' rights. During the war, the differences between North and South had become even greater. The North had become richer. In the South, cities had been destroyed and the economy ruined.

Reconstruction

After the war the South became part of the United States again. This long, difficult period was called Reconstruction. The issues that had caused the war, slavery and states' rights, still had to be dealt with. The issue of slavery was difficult, because many people even in the North had prejudices against Blacks. The new state governments in the South wanted to make laws limiting the rights of Blacks, and the US government tried to stop them. Between 1865 and 1870 the 13th, 14th and 15th *Amendments to the *Constitution were passed, giving Blacks freedom, making them citizens of the US and the state where they lived, and giving them, in theory, the same rights as white Americans.

Many northern politicians went to the South where they thought they could get power easily. These northerners were called *carpet-baggers. Both carpet-baggers and southern politicians were dishonest and stole money from the new governments, which hurt the South even more.

In 1870 the last three southern states were admitted to the Union again, and in 1877 the northern army finally left the South. The war lasted four years, but efforts to reunite the country took three times as long.

Effects of the Civil War

Differences between North and South are still strong. In the South the Confederate flag is still often used, and the state flags of *Georgia and *Mississippi were made to look similar to it. The state motto is *Audemus jura nostra defendere*, which is Latin for 'We dare to defend our rights'. The Civil War helped to end slavery, but long afterwards Blacks were still being treated badly, and race relations continue to be a problem. The South was so angry with the *Republicans, the party of Lincoln and Reconstruction, that southerners voted *Democratic for a century. The war showed strong differences between parts of the US, but many people believe that the most important thing it did was to prove that the US is one country.

in. Local authorities join with companies,voluntary organizations and other groups to plan new schemes for their area. The government then decides which authorities should receive the money to carry out their ideas. City Challenge started in 1991.

the **ˈCity of ˈBirmingham ˈSymphony ˌOrchestra** /ˈbɜːmɪŋəm; *AmE* ˈbɜːrmɪŋəm/ (*abbr* **CBSO**) the orchestra of the city of Birmingham, in England, which was started in 1920 and now has an international reputation. Simon *Rattle was its conductor for several years.

ˌCity Techˈnology ˌCollege (*abbr* **CTC**) *n* (in Britain) a type of secondary school in a town or city that puts a special emphasis on teaching mathematics, technology and science. It has no connection with the *Local Education Authority, getting its money directly from the government and from business companies. The first City Technology College opened in 1988 near *Birmingham, and there are now 15 of them, with over 11 000 students.

the **ˌCivic ˈTrust** a British organization that aims to preserve and improve the environment, for example by giving awards to good modern architecture. It was started in 1957.

the **ˌCivil Aviˈation Auˌthority** (*abbr* the **CAA**) the organization that controls air traffic in Britain.

the **ˌCivil ˈList** (in Britain) the amount of money that parliament agrees to give every year to the king or queen, and to some members of the *royal family, to meet their official expenses, such as wages for the *royal household. See also PRIVY PURSE.

the **Civil Rights Act of 1964** /ˌsɪvl ˈraɪts ækt əv ˈnaɪntiːn sɪksti ˈfɔː(r)/ the US law that forced the southern states to allow *African Americans to enter restaurants, hotels, etc. which had been reserved for white people only, and to end the practice of having separate areas for black and white people in theatres, train stations, buses, etc. The act was mostly the result of the *civil rights movement and was strongly supported by President Lyndon *Johnson. It was followed the next year by the *Voting Rights Act.

the **ˌcivil ˈrights ˌmovement** (in the US) the national campaign by *African Americans for equal rights, especially in the 1950s and 1960s. The campaign included boycotts (= refusals to buy particular products), the actions of *freedom riders, and in 1963 a march to Washington led by Martin Luther *King. It succeeded in causing the introduction of *bussing and *affirmative action. The Civil Rights Act of 1964 and the Voting Rights Act of 1965 were also introduced as a result of the civil rights movement, which has helped to change the attitudes of many white Americans.

the **Civil Service**

British **civil servants** are servants of the **Crown**, which in practice means the government. Responsibility for the Civil Service is divided between the *Cabinet Office and the *Treasury. The Prime Minister is Minister for the Civil Service.

Some civil servants work in government *departments. They are expected to work with a government formed by any *political party and to remain fair and impartial, whatever their personal opinions. A change of government, or the appointment of a new minister in charge of a department, does not involve a change of its civil servants. This is very useful to ministers who are new to an area of responsibility and have little time to learn about it. The most senior civil servant in a department is called the **Permanent Secretary**.

Ministers are not allowed to ask civil servants to do work that is intended to promote a political party. In the past ministers relied almost entirely on the advice of their civil servants when making decisions and the power that senior civil servants had over politicians has been humorously shown in the television series **Yes, Minister*. More recently, party politics and pressure from *Members of Parliament and commercial organizations may have had greater influence on decision-making.

Most civil servants are not directly involved in government. They have technical or administrative jobs outside London, e.g. calculating and collecting taxes, paying *social security benefits or running *Jobcentres. In 1996 there were about 500 000 civil servants, a quarter of whom were employed in the *Ministry of Defence.

In the US civil servants are government employees who get their jobs on the basis of ability and experience, not political favour. The US Civil Service was created so that government employees would not lose their jobs every time a new president was elected. Although the President can appoint people to important jobs, the majority of the three million government employees are civil servants. People wanting a government job take the **Civil Service Exam**. Civil servants are expected to be loyal to the government, and not to any political party. Some people believe that, because it is difficult to dismiss civil servants, they do not work very hard or efficiently. Each individual state also has its own civil service which works in a similar way.

The **ˌCivil ˈWar** ⇨ article. See also ENGLISH CIVIL WAR.

ˌTom ˈClancy /ˈklænsi/ (1947–) a popular US writer of novels about spies and military operations by the US government. Many have Jack Ryan of the *CIA as the main character. Clancy's books are known for their technical details. They include *The Hunt for Red October* (1984), *Patriot Games* (1987), *Clear and Present Danger* (1989) and *Executive Orders* (1996). Several have been made into films.

clans

A clan is a Scottish social group whose members usually claim to be descended from the same family. In the 11th century, tribes living in Scotland divided into small clans that settled round lochs (= lakes) and glens (= valleys), and on the islands. Among the most powerful were the Campbells and the MacGregors of Argyll, the MacLeods and the MacDonalds of the Western Isles, the MacKays of Caithness and the Stewarts of Appin. The **chief** of each clan had complete authority. **Clansmen** were known by the name of their father, and this was shown by the prefix *Mac-* added to the father's name. Many Scottish surnames begin with *Mac-*. Clan membership did not in fact depend on sharing the same name, and many clan members were not related to the chief, but were admitted to the clan as loyal supporters.

The clans often fought one another. The most famous argument was between the Campbells and the MacDonalds. After *William III became king in 1688, many clans joined the *Jacobites who supported the former Roman Catholic king, *James II. When William ordered all the clans to swear allegiance (= swear that they would be loyal) to himself the MacDonalds of *Glencoe failed to so. The Campbells were sent to punish them, resulting in the Massacre of Glencoe (1692), in which many MacDonalds were murdered.

The clans fought with the Jacobites against the English in 1715 and again, under *Bonny Prince Charlie, in 1745, but they were finally defeated at the Battle of *Culloden (1746). Many clansmen were killed or put in prison. Shortly afterwards, the *Highland Clearances, in which the crofts (= small farms) of many Scots were destroyed to make way for sheep farming, further reduced the influence of the clans.

After Culloden, the clans were forbidden to wear ***tartan** because it was thought to be a symbol of the desire for an independent Scotland. A tartan **kilt** (= man's knee-length pleated skirt) was an important part of a clansman's traditional clothing, but individual tartan patterns were not associated with a particular clan until *Victorian times. Today, Scotsmen generally only wear kilts on special occasions.

Clans are still important in Scotland, especially in the *Highlands. Many people outside Scotland, especially in the US, also take pride in having Scottish ancestors and being members of a clan.

ˌ**Clapham ˈJunction** /ˌklæpəm/ a railway station in south London, England. It is the busiest station in Britain, with about 2 200 trains passing through it each day. Thirty-five people were killed in a train crash there in 1988. People sometimes use 'Clapham Junction' to describe a place that is crowded and busy: *We've got builders in this week and the house is like Clapham Junction.*

the man on the ˌ**Clapham ˈomnibus** /ˌklæpəm/ (*BrE*) a phrase like *the man in the street*, which means the average ordinary English person (of either sex). The phrase has been in use since the 1890s when the word 'bus' was already replacing 'omnibus'. The choice of the bus from Clapham, an area of south-west London, has no special meaning; it is just a typical bus from a fairly ordinary place: *What will the man on the Clapham omnibus think of this new tax?*

ˌEric ˈ**Clapton** /ˈklæptən/ (1945–) a English *rock guitarist and singer known for his great skill on the guitar. He played with The Yardbirds (1963–65) and with Cream (1966–68), one of the first heavy rock bands. Since then he has recorded many successful songs with other bands and alone. In recent years he has performed regularly at the *Albert Hall.

ˌJohn ˈ**Clare** /ˈkleə(r); *AmE* ˈkler/ (1793–1864) an English poet who wrote poems about the English countryside, including *Shepherd's Calendar* (1827). He was a farm worker for much of his life but he became mentally ill and spent the last part of his life in an institution, where he continued to write poetry.

ˌ**Clarence ˈHouse** /ˌklærəns/ a large house in London, England, next to *St James's Palace. It was built in 1829 for the Duke of Clarence (later King *William IV). Queen *Elizabeth II lived there before she was Queen, and then in 1953 it became the home of the *Queen Mother(2).

the ˌEarl of ˈ**Clarendon** /ˈklærəndən/ (*born* Edward Hyde 1609–74) an English politician and historian who was the chief adviser of King *Charles II. He was *Lord Chancellor from 1660 to 1667 when he lost his influence over the king and had to leave the country. He then wrote his *Life* and the *History of the Rebellion and Civil Wars in England.*

ˈ**Claridge's** /ˈklærɪdʒɪz/ a famous hotel in *Mayfair in the *West End of London, England. It has been fashionable since the 1800s among rich people, including various kings and queens.

ˌAlan ˈ**Clark**[1] /ˈklɑːk; *AmE* ˈklɑːrk/ (1928–99) a British politician who was also known for his sexual adventures and patient wife. His father was Kenneth *Clark. He was a member of Margaret *Thatcher's government and came to the public's attention through the *Matrix Churchill affair and through his diary of the Thatcher years, which was very successful when it was published in 1993.

ˌKenneth ˈ**Clark**[3] /ˈklɑːk; *AmE* ˈklɑːrk/ (1903–83) an expert on the history of art who wrote many books. He is best known for his very successful television series and book *Civilisation* (1969) about the history of Western European art and culture. He was made a *knight in 1938 and a *life peer in 1969.

ˌArthur C ˈ**Clarke**[1] /ˈklɑːk; *AmE* ˈklɑːrk/ (Arthur Charles Clarke 1917–) an Engish writer of science-fiction novels and books about space travel. He is best known for the very successful Stanley *Kubrick film *2001: A Space Odyssey* (1968) which was made from his story *The Sentinel* (1951). Clarke has lived for many years in Sri Lanka. He was made a *knight in 1998.

ˌKenneth ˈ**Clarke**[2] /ˈklɑːk; *AmE* ˈklɑːrk/ (1940–) a British politician in the *Conservative Party. He earned a reputation for strength of purpose as *Secretary of State for health (1988–90) and for education (1990–92). He became *Home Secretary in 1992 and *Chancellor of the Exchequer in 1993.

Clarks™ /klɑːks; *AmE* klɑːrks/ the name of a British company that makes and sells shoes, or any of the shops owned by the company. Clarks are well known for making children's shoes in different widths.

The **Clash** /klæʃ/ a British *punk group (1976–85). Their best-known songs included *White Riot* (1977), *Tommy Gun* (1978) and *Should I Stay or Should I Go?* (1982).

Class ⇨ article.

ˌ**Classic FˈM** /ef ˈem/ a British national commercial radio station, begun in 1992, which broadcasts popular classical music.

Clause 4 /ˌklɔːz ˈfɔː(r)/ (in Britain) a part of the original constitution of the *Labour Party. It states that the Party will try to increase the number of nationalized industries. Many members of the Labour Party no longer believe this is a good idea, and it has been quietly dropped in recent years.

Clause 28 /ˌklɔːz twentiˈeɪt/ (in British law) section 28 of the Local Government Act (1988), which makes it illegal for local government authorities to present homosexuality in a favourable way. There was strong opposition to this law when it was introduced.

ˌCassius ˈ**Clay** /ˌkæsiəs ˈkleɪ/ ⇨ ALI.

the ˌ**Clean ˈAir Act** (in Britain) any of a series of laws passed between 1956 and 1968 with the aim of making the air cleaner, especially by forbidding the burning of any fuel that produces smoke in certain areas. Before the first Clean Air Act of 1956, a mixture of smoke from coal fires and damp winter air produced the famous London smog (= smoke mixed with fog), which in some years caused the deaths of thousands of people.

the ˈ**Clearances** ⇨ HIGHLAND CLEARANCES.

ˈ**clear and ˈpresent ˈdanger** the expression used by the US Supreme Court to indicate a situation in which complete freedom of speech is not a person's legal right. No one has a right to say something that would cause a clear (= obvious) and present (= immediate) danger to other people. As an example, the freedom of speech protected by the *First Amendment does not allow a person to shout 'Fire' in a crowded theatre.

ˈ**clearing bank** *n* (*BrE*) a bank which provides cheque books and other services to members of the public (unlike **merchant banks**, which provide services only to businesses). The clearing banks are the English 'big four' (*Barclays Bank, *Lloyds Bank, the *Midland Bank and the *National Westminster

Bank), three Scottish banks and a number of smaller English banks. The name 'clearing bank' is used because these banks are members of a **clearing house**, a place where cheques from various banks are balanced against each other so that banks can pay the amount that they owe to each other at the end of each day.

ˌEldridge ˈ**Cleaver** /ˌeldrɪdʒ ˈkliːvə(r)/ (1935–98) an *African-American leader and writer in the 1960s. After being in prison for different crimes, he joined the *Black Panthers and collected his writings in *Soul on Ice* (1968). After more trouble with the police, he went to Cuba and Algeria, but then returned to the US as a 'born-again' Christian.

ˌJohn ˈ**Cleese** /ˈkliːz/ (1939–) a popular English comedy actor and writer. He became famous through two very successful television series, **Monty Python's Flying Circus* and **Fawlty Towers*, both of which are widely remembered in Britain. He has also appeared in several films, including *The Life of Brian* (1978) and *A Fish Called Wanda* (1988).

ˌSamuel ˈ**Clemens** /ˈklemənz/ ⇨ TWAIN.

ˈ***Clementine*** /ˈkleməntaɪn/ a popular old US song about Clementine, a girl who drowns. It is usually sung with a false sadness that makes it humorous. It includes the lines

Oh my darling, oh my darling,
Oh my darling, Clementine;
You are lost and gone forever,
Dreadful sorry, Clementine.

ˌ***Cleoˈpatra*** /ˌkliːəˈpætrə/ a US film (1963), directed by Joseph L Mankiewicz. Elizabeth *Taylor played the part of the Egyptian queen Cleopatra and Richard *Burton[3] played her lover Mark Antony. These actors also had a romantic relationship and later married. *Cleopatra* cost $44 million to make and was at the time the most expensive film ever made.

Cleopatra's Needle /kliːəˌpætrəz/ the popular name of either of two stone obelisks (= tall stone columns with four sides and pointed tops), originally from Egypt, one of which stands on the bank of the River Thames in London and the other in *Central Park, New York. They were given by the ruler of Egypt in 1819.

ˈ**clerihew** /ˈklerɪhjuː/ *n* ⇨ BENTLEY.

ˈ**Cleveland[1]** /ˈkliːvlənd/ **1** a county in north-east England, formed in 1974 from parts of Durham and North Yorkshire. Its administrative centre is Middlesbrough. **2** the largest city in the US state of *Ohio. It is on Lake *Erie and is a major port. John D *Rockefeller began *Standard Oil there in 1870. Cleveland was the first large US city to have an *African-American *mayor.

ˌGrover ˈ**Cleveland[2]** /ˌɡrəʊvə ˈkliːvlənd; *AmE* ˌɡrəʊvər/ (1837–1908) a US *Democratic Party politician who was also *President for two separate periods (1885–9 and 1893–7). He was known for his honest government, but the country had economic problems while he was President.

ˌVan ˈ**Cliburn** /ˌvæn ˈklaɪbɜːn; *AmE* ˈklaɪbɜːrn/ (1934–) a US piano player of classical music. He first became famous in 1958 when he won the International Tchaikovsky Competition in Moscow, the first time it had been won by someobody who was not Russian.

the ˌ**Clifton Suˈspension Bridge** /ˌklɪftən/ a very high road bridge over the river *Avon near *Bristol in the west of England. It was designed by Isambard Kingdom *Brunel, and when it was completed in 1864 it was the longest and highest bridge in the world. People regularly kill themselves by jumping off the bridge.

the Clifton Suspension Bridge

ˌPatsy ˈ**Cline** /ˌpætsi ˈklaɪn/ (1932–63) a US singer of *country music. Her most popular songs were *I Fall to Pieces* (1961) and *Crazy* (1961). She was killed in a plane crash. The film *Sweet Dreams* (1985) is the story of her life.

ˌBill ˈ**Clinton[1]** /ˈklɪntən/ (1946–) the 42nd US *President, elected in 1992 and 1996. He is a Democrat and was previously the governor of *Arkansas. The US economy has improved under Clinton, and the *North American Free Trade Agreement has been signed. His successes in helping to achieve world peace include the *Camp David Agreement for the Near East and the Dayton Agreement to end the war in Bosnia and Herzegovina. His wife Hillary (1947–) has tried without success to improve the US health system. In 1998 President Clinton admitted that he had had a sexual relationship with Monica Lewinsky, a junior member of the *White House staff, after denying it earlier. He was *impeached (= charged with acting illegally) for lying under oath and obstructing justice, but the Senate judged him not guilty. See also WHITEWATER AFFAIR.

Bill Clinton

ˌGeorge ˈ**Clinton[2]** /ˈklɪntən/ (1940–) a US singer who also produces records and helped to establish funk music in the 1970s. With his group, Funkadelic, he produced such successful albums as *Funkadelic* (1970) and *One Nation Under a Groove* (1978). At the same time, Clinton also sang with the bands Parliament and the P Funk All Stars.

ˌRobert ˈ**Clive** /ˈklaɪv/ (1725–74) an English soldier and administrator. He is also known as 'Clive of India' because he played a major part in making India part of the *British Empire. While working for the *East India Company, he fought against the French and broke their power in India. Then at the battle of *Plassey (1757) Clive defeated the ruler of Bengal (a part of India) and replaced him with a

C

Class

Class in Britain

British society has historically been divided into three main classes, the upper class, the middle class and the lower (or working) class, with further divisions within these groups. But although much has been written and said about class differences, they mean less today to most British people than they used to as society changes. It is also increasingly difficult to decide what factors determine a person's class. For some people it is money (or lack of it), for others it is family background or the job a person does. But although most rich people are generally regarded as belonging to the upper or middle classes, and poorer people to the lower class, class is not simply a matter of wealth. People may have very little money yet still belong to the upper class, or be very rich and still think of themselves as working-class.

Members of the upper class are sometimes accused of **snobbery** (= being too concerned with social status and showing contempt for people of lower status). At the same time people who criticize anything associated with high social status are said to be guilty of **inverted snobbery**. The fact is that although **social climbing** (trying to gain a higher social status) is quite common, most people are proud of their background and see no need to change. And while the idea of what is meant by 'working class' and 'middle class' is different to what it was, say, fifty years ago, more people now claim to be working-class than did so then.

The classes

The **upper class** was traditionally composed of the *aristocracy, with its close links with the monarchy, and owners of country houses and estates. These people were the richest members of society and passed on their wealth and social status to their children. Today, the increased cost of maintaining large houses has meant that many landowners are no longer rich and, in some cases, have had to sell their estates. They still keep their upper-class status because of their family history and the social circle they move in. Judges, who were formerly always members of the aristocracy, still have upper-class status although they now come from a wider social background. Some members of the upper class can be identified by the way they speak, described as *Oxford English or as marked RP (= an extreme form of *Received Pronunciation).

A typical view of the upper class is that they send their children to *public schools such as *Eton, and then to *Oxford or *Cambridge University. They traditionally enjoy *field sports and horse-racing, go to fashionable social events like *Henley, and tend to support the *Conservative Party. Today, the upper class also includes many top professional people and wealthy business people. The upper class as a whole is sometimes accused of being concerned only with their own interests and not with the rest of society.

The middle class is the newest and largest of the three main classes and is sometimes divided into the **upper middle class** and the **lower middle class** according to income and seniority. The middle class has its origins in the 18th-century *Industrial Revolution when entrepreneurs (= people with money who are willing to take risks to make more money) changed Britain from a village-based society in which goods were made by hand to an urban economy in which goods were made in large quantities in factories by machines. This led to a new class of factory managers and traders who became increasingly rich and important.

The middle class grew rapidly in the 20th century with the spread of education, giving more people access to colleges and universities. These people became doctors, teachers, etc. or **white-collar workers** (= people working in an office rather than operating machines in a factory), and formed a professional middle class based on education and money rather than on birth. More recently there has developed the idea of a **meritocracy**, a society in which people can succeed through their own abilities and efforts rather than because of their birth or background. Most middle-class people now own their own house and car, have a comfortable lifestyle, and encourage their children to go to university. They are sometimes called 'bourgeois', suggesting that they are too conventional and interested only in possessions and helping their own family, though many care deeply about the problems and injustices of society, and would like social conditions to be improved for everyone whose quality of life is not as good as theirs. For this reason many of them vote *Labour or *Liberal Democrat.

The **lower class** (now usually called the **working class**) consisted historically of poor people of low birth who became servants, farm labourers or market traders. Today it is generally understood to include factory workers, builders, cleaners and other **blue-collar workers** (= people doing practical work or work that requires physical strength). But although many people take pride in their working-class origins, the term 'working class' has less relevance today than it did, especially among younger people who see less need to distinguish between manual work and other types of work. And because of increased **social mobility** (= changing one's social status), most 'working-class' people enjoy what might have been regarded as a middle-class consumer lifestyle only a few years ago. It is still true, however, that unemployment is highest among 'working-class' people who have left school at 16 and may not have the educational qualifications to enable them to get skilled work. Working-class people have traditionally tended to vote Labour, though this is less true today.

In addition to the three main classes people also now recognize an **underclass** in British society. This consists of people who are very poor, unemployed, often without a home, and unable to live without money and other help from the state.

Social grading

A different, alphabetical grading system is used by economists and sociologists to describe the layers of British society. The upper middle class (3% of the population) forms the *A* group, and the middle class (16%) the *B* group. *C1* is the lower middle class (26%), and *C2* the skilled lower class (26%). The semi-skilled and unskilled working class (17%) is group *D*, and occasional workers and people who do not work (13%) are group *E*. The letter *Z* is used to refer to the underclass.

The breakdown of the class system

Class differences in Britain today are less important than they once were. Because of social mobility people are less **class-conscious** and move easily in and out of groups with different social backgrounds. But although much is said, especially by politicians, about creating a **classless society**, there is strong evidence that most people think that this will never happen, though the majority do not see themselves as belonging to a particular class. The gap between rich and poor in Britain is still great – wider than it was and wider than in most other European countries – and many people see this as a force that divides society. The government intends to reform the *House of Lords and reduce the power and influence of hereditary peers, but the privileges that wealth brings can still be seen. Richer people may still choose to send their children to fee-paying schools because they see them as offering academic and other advantages, and private healthcare is also available to those who can afford it. Many people feel that society would be fairer if these choices were not there for them to make.

It is sometimes said that Britain is moving towards being a completely middle-class society. Old attitudes and old labels still persist, however. In 1995 John *Prescott, the Deputy Leader of the Labour Party who is the son of a railway worker and left school at 15, told an interviewer: 'My roots, my background and the way I act are working-class, but it would be hypocritical to say that I'm anything else than middle-class now.' But his 78-year-old mother disagreed. She told a journalist: 'John ... is a working-class man at heart and always will be.'

Class in the US – no class at all?

Many Americans say with pride that there are no class differences in the US, but this is not really true. Class differences exist, but social mobility is possible with hard work. The ***American dream** is based on people's ability, provided they use enough effort, to reach any goal. But the goal is not to reach the upper classes, and most Americans like to think that they are middle-class.

The key to the American class system is money. Anyone can live in a pleasant house in a good area of town and send their children to a top university if they have enough money. Money is obtained through hard work, and so a high social class is seen as a reward for effort, not something that depends on family history. People who improve their social position are proud of being **self-made men** or **women**, but those who come from rich families are thought to have an unfair advantage.

It can be difficult to know what social class an American belongs to. A person's accent does not usually indicate class, merely the part of the country they come from. Even people with a lot of money send their children to state-run schools, and people who do blue-collar jobs encourage their children to get a good education and to become lawyers, doctors, etc. During the 1980s differences between rich and poor became greater, and in some very poor areas the quality of education is low, making it more difficult for people to move into a higher class. Social mobility is easiest for whites of Northern European origin. These people are called ***WASPs** (= White Anglo-Saxon Protestants). People of other ethnic origins, particularly *African Americans and *Hispanics, still experience strong discrimination, and are treated worse and given fewer opportunities than other people of similar ability.

Old money

A few Americans belong to a more restricted class system. These people live mostly in the large cities of the East Coast and have 'old money', i.e. they inherited it from their families instead of earning it. Those who live in Boston are called *Boston Brahmins. Many are proud of having ancestors who came over on the **Mayflower*, the ship that brought the first permanent European settlers to North America. They support institutions such as the **social register**, a list of important people in certain cities, and the *Daughters of the American Revolution. Their children go to expensive secondary schools, called prep schools, and then to *Ivy League universities like *Harvard or *Yale. When their daughters are old enough to take part in formal social events, they may become **debutantes** and have **coming-out parties**.

ruler who allowed the British to govern Bengal through him. This was the beginning of a system that later spread through most of India.

ˌGlenn **ˈClose** /ˌglen ˈkləʊs; *AmE* ˈkloʊs/(1948–) a US actor best known for her film roles as a dangerous woman in *Fatal Attraction* (1987) and *Dangerous Liaisons* (1988). Her other films include *The World According to Garp* (1982), *Reversal of Fortune* (1990) and *Mars Attacks!* (1996). Close has also had a successful stage career. She has won three *Tony awards as Best Actress for *The Real Thing* (1984), *Death and the Maiden* (1992) and *Sunset Boulevard* (1995).

ˌ**closed ˈshop** *n* a factory, business, etc. whose employees must be members of a particular trade union. Closed shops were made illegal in Britain in the 1980s. In the US they were made illegal by the *Taft-Hartley Act of 1947, but they became legal again in 1951: *support the closed shop* (= the practice of having closed shops) ○ *a closed-shop agreement*. ⇨ article at TRADE UNIONS AND LABOR UNIONS.

ˈ**close season** (*BrE*) (*AmE* **closed season**) *n* [usu sing] a time of the year when it is illegal to kill certain animals, birds and fish because they are breeding. Most of these times are during the spring and summer, but for fish they are during the winter.

ˌ**clotted ˈcream** /ˌklɒtɪd; *AmE* ˌklɑːtɪd/ *n* [U] (*esp BrE*) thick cream that is made by slowly heating milk and taking the solid layers of cream that form on the top. It is common in the south-west of England where the cows produce milk with a lot of cream in it. Clotted cream is often eaten with jam on *scones or with fruit such as strawberries. See also CREAM TEA, DEVONSHIRE CREAM.

ˌBrian **ˈClough** (1935–) an English football player and team manager. While he was manager of *Nottingham Forest (1975–93), the club won the *Football

League, the League Cup four times and the European Cup twice.

In,spector 'Clouseau /'klu:zəʊ; *AmE* 'klu:zoʊ/ a humorous character played by the English actor Peter *Sellers in the *Pink Panther films. He is a French policeman who is very serious, usually wrong, but finally successful by accident.

C

Clubs and societies ⇨ article.

'Cluedo™ /'klu:dəʊ; *AmE* 'klu:doʊ/ (*AmE* **Clue**™) a board game in which each player is one of the characters in a murder mystery and tries to discover who committed the murder, with what instrument and where.

'Clwyd /'klu:ɪd/ a county in north-east Wales, created in 1974.

the **'Clyde** a river in south-west Scotland, flowing through *Glasgow and into the *Irish Sea. It is 106 miles (170 kilometres) long. There were once several yards for building ships along its banks but this industry has now almost disappeared in Britain.

'Clydesdale /'klaɪdzdeɪl/ *n* a breed of large, strong horse, usually reddish-brown in colour and originally from the valley of the river *Clyde in Scotland. In the past Clydesdales were used on farms and for pulling heavy loads.

the **,Clydesdale 'Bank** /,klaɪdzdeɪl/ one of the three main Scottish banks. It started in 1838 and has its head office in *Glasgow, which is in Clydesdale, the broad valley of the river *Clyde.

CND /,si: en 'di:/ (*in full* the **Campaign for Nuclear Disarmament**) a British organization started in 1958 to protest against nuclear weapons. It was originally best known for organizing the *Aldermaston marches in the 1960s, but it became very active again in the 1980s organizing concerts, marches and other events to protest against US nuclear bases in Britain.

CNN /,si: en 'en/ (*in full* **Cable News Network**) a US television company that broadcasts news and special information programmes all round the world by satellite, 24 hours a day. It was begun in 1980 by Ted Turner and is based in *Atlanta, Georgia. It became especially known in 1991 as the main news source for the *Gulf War.

'Coalite™ /'kəʊlaɪt; *AmE* 'koʊlaɪt/ *n* [U] (*BrE*) a fuel like coal that burns without producing smoke, for use on fires in areas where people are not allowed to burn coal. See also CLEAN AIR ACT.

coal mining

Coal was very important in the economic development of Britain. It was used as fuel in the factories built during the *Industrial Revolution and continued to be important until the 1980s. The main **coalfields** are in north-east England, the north Midlands and the valleys of south Wales, especially the *Rhondda Valley. Towns and villages grew around the **collieries** or **pits** (= coal mines), and their inhabitants were dependent on mining for their living. The towns were dominated by the **pithead** where the lifting machinery was, and by large black **slag heaps** (= piles of waste material).

Work in the mines was hard, and there was a risk of being trapped or killed when tunnels collapsed, but there was often no other work, so men had to 'go down the pit'. Poor conditions and low pay led to a long history of industrial trouble and caused miners to play a leading role in the development of the *trade union movement.

In 1913 Britain produced 292 million tons of coal and employed over a million miners. In 1947, when the mines were nationalized (= brought under government control), there were still about a 1 000 collieries and 700 000 miners. Increased use of *North Sea oil and gas in the 1970s led to a lower demand for coal. Coal gas, once widely used for domestic heating and cooking, was replaced by natural gas. By the mid 1980s there were only 160 collieries and 200 000 miners. Fear of further job losses led to the long and violent *miners' strike of 1984–5, which is still widely remembered. In the 1990s there were more **pit closures**, leaving only 16 working collieries operated by 7 000 miners. Coal mining has now almost completely ended in south Wales. Mining communities throughout Britain have been much affected, with thousands of unemployed men struggling to find new jobs and local shops and businesses having to close. Collieries were returned to private ownership in 1994, and most coal now produced in Britain is sold to the electricity-generating industry.

Coal mining is also important in the US. In 1988 the US produced nearly a fifth of the world's coal. Most is mined in the *Appalachian Mountains. Modern mining techniques used in *West Virginia have removed whole mountain tops and destroyed large areas of forest. Coal is used especially in the electricity-generating industry and in the manufacture of steel. In 1995 the US coal mining industry employed about 85 000 workers.

,Kurt **'Cobain** /,kɜ:t 'kəʊbeɪn; *AmE* ,kɜ:rt 'koʊbeɪn/ (1967–94) a US singer and writer of *rock music, married to the singer Courtney Love. He played the guitar and was the leader of the *grunge(1) band *Nirvana. Cobain had problems with drugs and shot himself.

,John **'Cobb**[1] /'kɒb; *AmE* 'kɑ:b/ (1899–1952) an English driver who held the world speed record on land from 1947 until 1964 when the record was broken by Donald *Campbell. Cobb died trying to break the water speed record on *Loch Ness in Scotland.

,William **'Cobbett** /'kɒbɪt; *AmE* 'kɑ:bɪt/ (1763–1835) an English political journalist who became a leader of the movement towards modern democracy in Britain. He published most of his work in his own magazine *Political Register*, which in addition contained summaries of debates in parliament and later developed into the modern *Hansard. His frequent attacks on authority often got him into trouble, including two years in prison. He was the son of a farmer and he is best known today for his book *Rural Rides* (1830) which describes life in the English countryside and the conditions of poor farm workers before the *Reform Act of 1832.

'cobbler *n* **1** (*esp AmE*) a fruit pie with thick pastry on top. It is usually served in a bowl. **2** a cold drink made with wine, *whisky or rum, lemon or other fruit, sugar and ice.

,Coca-'Cola™ (*also infml* **Coke**™) *n* [C, U] a US sweet fizzy drink (= one containing many bubbles). It was invented in 1886 by Dr John S Pemberton, a pharmacist (= a person trained to prepare medicines) in *Atlanta, who said it would cure feelings of sickness in the stomach or the head. Coca-Cola was originally made with cocaine, but this was replaced by caffeine in 1906. It is sold in cans and bottles and is bought more than any other product in the world.

Co'chise /kəʊ'tʃi:s; *AmE* koʊ'tʃi:s/ (*c.* 1823–74) a leader of the *Apache people. In 1861 he began to lead about 200 Apaches in attacks on US soldiers in *Arizona, but in 1871 he agreed to live with his people on a reservation (= land given and protected by the US government).

,Eddie **'Cochran** /'kɒkrən; *AmE* 'kɑ:krən/ (1938–60) a US singer of *rock and roll music whose career began in 1956. He played the guitar, and his most popular songs were *C'mon Everybody* (1958) and *Summertime Blues* (1958). He died in a car crash, but

Clubs and societies

Many people in Britain and the US belong to at least one club or society. *Club* is often used to refer to a group of people who regularly meet together socially or take part in sports. Most young people's groups are called *clubs*. A *society* is usually concerned with a special interest, e.g. birdwatching or local history, and sends newsletters or magazines to its members. National societies, such as the *Royal Society for the Protection of Birds, usually have local **branches**. Some have a children's section. People usually have to pay an annual **subscription** or **membership fee** to join a club or society, and in return receive regular newsletters or can use club facilities and attend club events.

Social clubs

Social clubs have a bar where members can sit and talk to each other. Since people like to feel comfortable with those they see regularly, members of a club often come from the same social background. Members of the upper class or business people may belong to a ***gentlemen's club**. Most of these are in London and only a very few allow women to be members. They are places to relax in, but also to make business contacts and take clients. Some business and professional men become *Freemasons, and join a lodge (= branch) in their home town. Masons are sometimes accused of giving unfair advantages to other Masons in business.

Some clubs combine social events with community service. Members of the *Rotary Club, the *Round Table, the *Kiwanians and the *Lions Club are usually professional or business people. In the US these organizations are called **service clubs**. They are mostly open only to men. Professional women and wives of members may join similar women-only clubs, such as the *Inner Wheel. They hold events to raise money for good causes, e.g. to provide scholarships for university students or to raise money for a hospital.

In Britain, **working men's clubs** were set up for men doing manual jobs. The clubs, mainly in central and northern England, offer a range of entertainment, such as comedians or *darts matches, as well as a bar. In recent years some clubs have decided to admit women. In the US men who are not rich are most likely to join clubs based on ethnic origin, religion or military background. For example, the *Knights of Columbus is a club for Roman Catholic men. People who have served in the armed forces join the *Veterans of Foreign Wars or the *American Legion. The *British Legion is a similar organization for former British servicemen.

Until recently, there were few clubs open to women. In Britain, the *WI and the Townswomen's Guild, began with the aim of improving women's education. Both now organize social and cultural activities. Every town has clubs which attract different groups of people: for instance, there are clubs for older people such as *Darby and Joan clubs, mother and toddler groups, and singles clubs for people without a partner.

Nightclubs, often called simply **clubs**, are places where mainly young people meet to drink and dance. They charge **admission fees** rather than a subscription. Fees are higher at weekends and in large cities, especially London.

Sports clubs

Many sports clubs hold parties and arrange social events, as well as providing facilities for various sports. *Golf clubs are among the most expensive to join, and there is often a long waiting list. Other sports clubs include those for squash, tennis, cricket, bowls, snooker and cycling. Many clubs own their own sports ground and **clubhouse**. Most towns also have gym or fitness clubs. In Britain, **sports and social clubs** are run by some big companies for their employees. In the US most sports clubs are associated with companies. *Softball and *basketball teams play against teams from other companies in the same city.

Country clubs are found in green areas near cities all over the US. They offer sports like swimming, golf and tennis, and hold dances and other social events in the restaurants and bars. The oldest and most famous country club was established in Brookline, Massachusetts in 1882. New members must be proposed (= suggested) by existing members, and membership fees are high.

Alumni clubs

Many Americans belong to the **alumni club** of the college or university they attended. Members take part in social activities and raise money for the university. A state university, which anyone can attend, usually has a large alumni club. Fewer people can afford to attend private universities like *Harvard, so being a member of the Harvard Club is associated with wealth and social position.

Some students, join **Greek societies**, societies named with Greek letters, e.g. Alpha Epsilon Pi. **Fraternities** are for men, and **sororities** are for women. Members of academic fraternities and sororities study the same subject or are the university's most outstanding students. *Phi Beta Kappa is the most famous of these. Most Greek societies are social organizations and their members, who usually come from rich families, live in a fraternity or sorority house. After they leave university, many members continue to be active in the organization. Schools, colleges and universities in Britain also have societies for former students, generally called **old boys'** or **old girls' associations**.

Special interest societies

In most towns there are local societies for almost every interest or *hobby, including singing, drama, film, folk music, archaeology, natural history and photography. Societies organize concerts, put on plays, run courses or do fieldwork. Local branches of national societies, such as the *National Trust in Britain and the *Audubon Society in the US, organize events in their area. Only a small proportion of members attend local events, and most people join these societies because they support their aims.

Clubs are an important feature of school life, especially in the US. They include clubs for chess, stamp-collecting and the game of *Dungeons and Dragons*, as well as language clubs. Outside school, children can join a local **youth club**, *Scouts or *Guides, or another *youth organization.

his passenger, the singer Gene Vincent, survived. Cochran had recorded *Three Steps to Heaven* (1960) just before his death.

ˌ**cock-a-ˈleekie** /ˌkɒk ə ˈliːki; *AmE* ˌkɑːk ə ˈliːki/ *n* [U] a Scottish soup made from chicken boiled with vegetables, including leeks.

C

ˌJoe ˈ**Cocker** /ˈkɒkə(r); *AmE* ˈkɑːkər/ (1944–) an English pop singer with a very rough voice. His most successful record was *With a Little Help from my Friends* (1968), since when heavy drinking and drugs have badly affected his career.

ˌ**cocker ˈspaniel** (*also* **cocker**) *n* a small dog with thick golden-brown hair and long ears.

ˈ**cockney** *n* **1** [C] a person born in the *East End of London, England. Traditionally, a true cockney was somebody born within the sound of *Bow Bells, but the word is often used of any Londoner who speaks with a local *accent. Cockneys are thought of as quick, cheerful people with a good sense of humour. **2** [U] the type of English that is spoken by cockneys. One famous feature of cockney is its use of *rhyming slang.

▶ **cockney** *adj* of, belonging to or typical of the cockneys or their way of speaking: *a cockney accent/woman* ○ *cockney humour* ○ *He's always cheeky and full of jokes – a true cockney sparrow* (= person).

ˌJohn ˈ**Cockroft** /ˈkɒkrɒft; *AmE* ˈkɑːkrɑːft/ (1897–1967) the English scientist who, with Ernest Walton, succeeded in splitting the atom at the *Cavendish Laboratory in 1932. He was later closely involved with Britain's nuclear energy programme and was the first director of the research centre at *Harwell. He was made a *knight in 1948 and he and Walton shared the *Nobel Prize for physics in 1951.

ˌWilliam ˈ**Cody** /ˈkəʊdi; *AmE* ˈkoʊdi/ ⇨ BUFFALO BILL.

Seˌbastian ˈ**Coe** /ˈkəʊ; *AmE* ˈkoʊ/ (1956–) a successful English athlete and later a politician. He broke three world records in 1979 and won the 1 500 metres race in the Olympic Games in 1980 and 1984. When he retired in 1990 to start a career in politics, he had broken a total of twelve world records. He became a *Conservative *MP in 1992, but lost his seat in the 1997 general election.

ˌ**Coeur de ˈLion** /ˌkɜː də ˈliːɒn; *AmE* ˌkɜːr, ˈliːɑːn/ ⇨ RICHARD I.

ˈ**coffeecake** /ˈkɒfikeɪk; *AmE* ˈkɑːfikeɪk/ *n* (*AmE*) any of several types of small cake or sweet bread often served with coffee. The cakes usually contain nuts and raisins and are covered with melted sugar.

ˌGeorge M ˈ**Cohan** /ˈkəʊhæn; *AmE* ˈkoʊhæn/ (George Michael Cohan 1878–1942) a US actor and writer of musical plays that praised America. His best-known songs include *Give My Regards to Broadway* (1904), *You're A Grand Old Flag* (1904) and the *World War I song *Over There* (1917) for which he received a special medal from *Congress. The film *Yankee Doodle Dandy* (1942) was the story of his life, with James *Cagney playing Cohan.

COHSE /ˈkəʊzi; *AmE* ˈkoʊzi/ (*in full* **Confederation Of Health Service Employees**) ⇨ UNISON.

the **COI** /ˌsiː əʊ ˈaɪ; *AmE* oʊ/ ⇨ CENTRAL OFFICE OF INFORMATION.

Coke™ ⇨ COCA-COLA.

ˈ**Colchester** /ˈkəʊltʃəstə(r); *AmE* ˈkoʊltʃestər/ a town in *Essex, England. It is probably the oldest town in Britain and was one of the richest towns in *Roman Britain. It has a castle built by the *Normans in the 11th century, and some good museums.

ˈ***Cold*** ˈ***Comfort*** ˈ***Farm*** a humorous novel (1932) by the English author Stella Gibbons (1902–89), about a lonely farm and the strange people who live there.

ˌ**cold ˈduck** *n* [U] (*AmE*) a drink made by mixing red wine and champagne, sometimes with lemon juice and sugar added.

the ˌ**Coldstream ˈGuards** /ˌkəʊldstriːm; *AmE* ˌkəʊldstriːm/ the second regiment of *Foot Guards, the personal guards of the British king or queen. It was formed in 1650 and is one of the oldest and most respected regiments in the British army.

ˌ**cold ˈturkey** *n* [U] (*slang*) a phrase that is used about drug addicts. To *go cold turkey* means to stop using a drug suddenly and to experience the unpleasant fever and sick feeling that results from this.

the ˌ**Cold ˈWar** *n* [sing] the political conflict between the capitalist countries of the West (the US and western Europe) and the Communist countries of the East (the Soviet Union and eastern Europe) that began after *World War II. Both sides had large military forces which were kept ready for war, and threatened each other with nuclear weapons. They also tried to find out each other's secrets using spies. There was no actual fighting, except where the US and the Soviet Union supported different sides in conflicts such as the *Korean War. The Cold War ended in the early 1990s after the Soviet Union had begun to break up, and agreements were made to reduce military forces on both sides. See also CUBAN MISSILE CRISIS, IRON CURTAIN, NORTH ATLANTIC TREATY ORGANIZATION.

ˌNat 'King' ˈ**Cole** /ˈkəʊl; *AmE* ˈkoʊl/ (1919–65) a US singer, especially of love songs, with a soft and pleasant voice. He was also an excellent piano player. He was the first *African American to have a programme on radio (1948–9) and television (1956–7). His most successful songs included *Mona Lisa* (1950) and *Rambling Rose* (1962). His daughter, Natalie Cole (1949–), is a singer who received a *Grammy award for *Unforgettable* (1991) in which she added her voice to her father's old recording.

ˌDavid ˈ**Coleman** /ˈkəʊlmən; *AmE* ˈkoʊlmən/ (1926–) a British sports commentator well known for his great enthusiasm, especially on the *BBC television programmes **Grandstand* and *Sportsnight*. He also presented the BBC television quiz show *A *Question of Sport* for many years.

ˈSamuel ˈTaylor ˈ**Coleridge** /ˈteɪlə ˈkəʊlərɪdʒ; *AmE* ˈteɪlər ˈkoʊlərɪdʒ/ (1772–1834) an English poet. One of his most famous poems is *The *Ancient Mariner*. This was published in *Lyrical Ballads* (1798), a collection of poems by Coleridge and William *Wordsworth which marked the beginning of *Romanticism in Britain. His other well-known poem is **Kubla Khan*, which was written under the influence of the drug opium.

the ˌ**Coliˈseum** /ˌkɒləˈsiːəm; *AmE* ˌkɑːləˈsiːəm/ the largest theatre in the *West End of London, England, and the home of the *English National Opera.

the ˌ**College of ˈArms** (*also* the ˌ**College of ˈHeralds**) an organization in London that is responsible for giving coats of arms to families and institutions in England and Wales. It was formed in the 15th century and its head is the Earl Marshal, who is responsible for organizing state ceremonies in Britain.

a coat of arms

ˈ**college of ˈfurther eduˈcation** (*also* **CFE**) *n* (*BrE*) a college for students over the age of 16, providing courses that lead to *A levels, *GNVQs and other qualifications. Many further education courses prepare people for jobs. ⇨ note at FURTHER EDUCATION.

ˈcollege of ˈhigher eduˈcation *n* (*BrE*) a college that provides courses mostly at university level. In Britain some of the largest of these colleges became universities during a reorganization of higher education in 1992.

ˌJackie **ˈCollins¹** /ˈkɒlɪnz; *AmE* ˈkɑːlɪnz/ (1941–) an English writer of popular novels, often about rich people. She is the sister of Joan *Collins.

ˌJoan **ˈCollins²** /ˈkɒlɪnz; *AmE* ˈkɑːlɪnz/ (1933–) an English actor who has been in many films but is best known for playing the part of Alexis in the US television series **Dynasty*.

Joan Collins in Dynasty

ˌJudy **ˈCollins³** /ˈkɒlɪnz; *AmE* ˈkɑːlɪnz/ (1939–) a US singer and writer of *folk music. She has a very clear voice. In the 1960s she protested against the *Vietnam War and supported the *civil rights movement. Her most successful songs include *Amazing Grace* (1970) and *Send in the Clowns* (1975). She has also written a novel, *Shameless* (1995). President *Clinton named his daughter Chelsea after Judy Collins's song *Chelsea Morning* (1972).

ˌMichael **ˈCollins⁴** /ˈkɒlɪnz; *AmE* ˈkɑːlɪnz/ (1890–1922) a leader in the fight against British rule in Ireland. He fought in the *Easter Rising in Dublin in 1916, joined *Sinn Fein and helped to form the *Irish Republican Army. After helping to create the Irish Free State in 1921, he commanded the Irish Free State forces and was head of the state for ten days before being killed by Irishmen who disagreed with him.

ˌWilkie **ˈCollins⁵** /ˌwɪlki ˈkɒlɪnz; *AmE* ˈkɑːlɪnz/ (1824–89) an English writer of novels. His most famous novels are *The Woman in White* (1860) and *The *Moonstone* (1868), which is regarded as the first real *detective novel in English.

ˌColonel ˈBogey /ˈbəʊgi; *AmE* ˈboʊgi/ a march tune which was written at the beginning of World War I and remained popular during World War II. It was also later used in the film *The Bridge on the River Kwai*. In World War II, British soldiers sang the tune with these words:

Hitler has only got one ball,
Goering has two but very small,
Himmler is somewhat similar,
But poor old Goebbels has no balls at all.

ˌColonel ˈSanders ⇨ SANDERS.

ˌColoˈrado /ˌkɒləˈrɑːdəʊ; *AmE* ˌkɑːləˈrædoʊ/ a western US state whose capital city is *Denver. It is popular with tourists and is famous for *Aspen and other towns in the *Rocky Mountains where people ski. The state's history includes the discovery of gold in 1858 and the cultural influences of *Native Americans and Mexicans. See also PIKE'S PEAK.

the **ˈColoˈrado ˈRiver** /ˈkɒləˈrɑːdəʊ; *AmE* ˈkɑːləˈrædoʊ/ **1** a major US river that runs through the *Grand Canyon. It begins in the *Rocky Mountains in northern *Colorado and flows 1 450 miles/2 333 kilometres to the Gulf of California. For 90 miles/145 kilometres it is in Mexico. See also HOOVER DAM. **2** a US river in *Texas that flows 894 miles/1 438 kilometres from the north-western part of the state to the *Gulf of Mexico.

Colours ⇨ article.

ˈcolour ˌsupplement *n* (*BrE*) a magazine, printed all or partly in colour, that is part of a newspaper, especially a Sunday newspaper. The phrase is also used to describe something that looks like an advertisement in a colour supplement. For example, *a colour supplement kitchen* is very tidy, modern and well equipped.

ˌSamuel **ˈColt** /ˈkəʊlt; *AmE* ˈkoʊlt/ (1814–62) an American who invented the revolver (= gun with a container for bullets that turns) in 1835. It was sometimes called the Colt 'six shooter' because it could hold six bullets. Another name for it was the 'Great Equalizer'. It was first used by the US Army in the *Mexican War. Colt built the world's largest gun factory in 1855 at Hartford, *Connecticut, where the Colt company is still based.

ˌJohn **Colˈtrane** /kɒlˈtreɪn; *AmE* kɔːlˈtreɪn/ (1926–67) an *African-American *jazz musician who played the saxophone. He became well known in the Miles *Davis Quintet in the 1950s and then formed his own group in 1960. He helped to develop 'free jazz'. One of his best recordings was *Giant Steps* (1959). He was chosen for the Jazz *Hall of Fame in 1965.

Coˈlumbia the first US space shuttle (= spacecraft that can be used again). Its first flight was in 1981 with two astronauts, John Young and Robert Crippen. By 1996 Columbia had made 20 flights and that year made the longest one (more than 405 hours).

the **Coˌlumbia ˈBroadcasting ˌSystem** /kəˌlʌmbiə/ ⇨ CBS.

Coˌlumbia ˈPictures /kəˌlʌmbiə/ a large *Hollywood film company, producing films for the cinema and television. It was established in 1924 and its first big success was *It Happened One Night* (1934). Others have included *Lawrence of Arabia* (1962), *Easy Rider* (1969), *Kramer vs Kramer* (1979) and *The Last Emperor* (1987). Frank *Capra directed several films for Columbia, and one of the company's first stars was Rita *Hayworth.

Coˌlumbia Uniˈversity /kəˌlʌmbiə/ (*also* **Columbia**) a large private university in New York City. It was established in 1754 as King's College and became Columbia University in 1896. It has a high reputation for training students to become doctors, journalists and teachers. See also IVY LEAGUE.

Coˈlumbo /kəˈlʌmbəʊ; *AmE* kəˈlʌmboʊ/ a US television series (1971–93) in which the main character is Lieutenant Columbo (whose first name was never revealed), played by Peter Falk. Columbo is a *Los Angeles police *detective who wears an untidy old coat and drives an old car. His murder cases often seem to confuse him.

ˌChristopher **Coˈlumbus** /kəˈlʌmbəs/ (1451–1506) the Italian explorer who was the first European to discover America, in 1492. He had persuaded King Ferdinand and Queen Isabella of Spain to pay for his attempt to find a new route to Asia by crossing the Atlantic Ocean. When he arrived at one of the Caribbean islands, he thought he had found the coast of Asia and continued to believe this for the rest of his life. He made three more journeys to America, but because they were not commercially successful he lost favour and died in poverty.

Coˈlumbus Day /kəˈlʌmbəs/ a US holiday that celebrates the discovery of America by Christopher *Columbus. It is sometimes also called Discovery

C

Colours

Colours (*AmE* colors) have cultural associations which are understood by everyone. Many words describing shades of colours are the same in Britain and the US. Some are taken from nature, e.g. *coal-black*, *emerald*, *duck-egg blue* (called *robin's-egg blue* in the US) and *violet*. Food is the inspiration for other colour names: *cream*, *lime green*, *chocolate* and *wine*. Some shades are named after an object that has traditionally been painted that colour, e.g. in Britain *pillar-box red*, and in the US *fire-engine red*.

Similes (= comparisons) relate colours to natural features or familiar objects. A dark place may be 'as black as night' or 'as black as ink'. A person may be 'white as the driven snow' (= innocent), but if they turn 'as white as a ghost' or 'as white as a sheet' their face becomes pale from fear or shock.

Skin colour

People are often described according to their colour, and this is a sensitive issue. A person who appears not to worry about skin colour is sometimes called 'colour-blind'. *Black* refers to people whose ancestors came from Africa. The word *coloured* is not acceptable as it offends many people. Pale-skinned people are described as *white*, though their colouring varies greatly.

A white person with a suntan is said to be *bronzed* or *brown*, both complimentary words. Rosy (= pink) cheeks are a sign of health, and if someone is 'in the pink' they are very well. People who are ill may be *grey (AmE* gray*)* or *ashen*. A *blue-blooded* person, or a *blue blood*, belongs to the upper class. This is because veins appear blue through the pale skin of people who do not spend much time in the open air. In the past, these people were from the upper class. A *red-blooded* person is strong and passionate.

Redheads have hair that is a shade of red or orange and are thought to have a quick temper. Blond women are considered attractive, but are sometimes presented in jokes, cartoons, etc. as not very intelligent (as in the phrase *a dumb blond*). The most handsome men are, traditionally, tall and dark.

Emotions

The colour *red*, suggesting heat or fire, is associated with anger. A person may 'see red' (= lose their temper). An action likely to make somebody angry is 'a red rag to a bull'. Red is also associated with love, and red roses are given to lovers. People go as 'red as a beetroot' or (*AmE*) 'red as a beet', when they are embarrassed.

Purple and *blue* also suggest anger, and a person may 'turn purple with rage' or 'argue till they are blue in the face'. Somebody who swears a lot uses 'colourful language', and, in the US, may 'swear a blue streak'. Blue suggests unhappiness, and somebody who is sad may be 'feeling blue' or 'have the blues'. But if they are 'in a blue funk' they are in a state of terror or panic. Blue also represents loyalty, and people who are described as 'true blue' are faithful and reliable.

A person who is *green* is very innocent about the world. Green also represents jealousy, and a person 'turns green with envy'. Jealousy itself is called the 'green-eyed monster'. *Yellow* is associated with fear. Cowards have 'yellow streaks' and may be called 'yellow-bellies'. *Brown* represents thoughtfulness when a person falls into a 'brown study' (= a thoughtful silence). But if somebody is 'browned off' they are bored.

Clothes

Black is associated with death and is worn at funerals. Invitations to formal events often say 'black tie', which means that men should wear a dinner jacket and black bow tie. For women, wearing a black dress or (*AmE*) wearing 'basic black' for evening social occasions is thought to be smart. *White* is the colour of innocence and is usually worn by a bride at her wedding.

Baby girls traditionally wear *pink*, while boys are dressed in *baby blue*. Blue is the colour of the Virgin Mary and it was once thought that dressing a boy in blue gave him the protection of heaven. Men rarely wear pink clothes except as fashion items, whereas women regularly wear blue.

Traditions and superstitions

Red is associated with danger or trouble. In traffic lights, red means 'stop'. 'Red tape' is a complicated and annoying set of rules. A person found doing something wrong is said to have been 'caught red-handed'. If someone is 'in the red' they owe the bank money. Red also suggests excitement. 'Red-letter days' are days when something special happens, and something that is 'red-hot' is very fashionable or desirable. Because red attracts the eye, it was traditionally used in Britain for postboxes and telephone kiosks.

Black is often associated with bad things. A 'black day' is a day on which a disaster takes place, e.g. *Black Monday. A 'black look' shows anger or hatred. But seeing a black cat is said to bring luck. Somebody who 'sees things in black and white' thinks everything is either bad or good. People tell 'white lies', which are harmless, or try to hide a mistake with 'whitewash'. Something that is unclear is described as a 'grey area'.

Green in traffic lights means 'go', and if a person is 'given the green light' they have permission to do something. Green is associated with nature, and people who are good at growing plants are said to have 'a green thumb' (*AmE*) or 'green fingers' (*BrE*). Green is now widely used to describe people who care for, or things that are good for, the environment. Green is also unlucky, so some people avoid having green at weddings.

Yellow is a warning colour. In the US school buses are also yellow. Americans tie a yellow ribbon round a tree in their garden to remember somebody who has gone to fight in a war.

Blue is associated with value: a blue chip (= counter) has a high value in poker, and 'blue-chip' stocks are a good place to invest money. A blue ribbon is given for first prize in a show. Something that happens 'once in a blue moon' is very rare.

Colours are associated with particular festivals. *Christmas colours are red and green, but a 'white Christmas' is a Christmas with snow. *Hallowe'en is celebrated with black and orange, and pink and red are associated with *St Valentine's Day. On *Independence Day, everything is red, white and blue, the colours of the American flag.

Day. It is the second Monday in October in most states. The day was first celebrated in 1792 in New York City.

Co'manche /kə'mæntʃi/ *n* (*pl* **Comanche** *or* **Comanches**) a member of a *Native-American people of the *Great Plains in the south-western US. They are related to the *Shoshone people. The Comanches were excellent riders who fought hard and kept white people out of western *Texas until the 1870s. Most now live in western *Oklahoma.

ˌ*Come 'Dancing* a popular British television programme in which couples and teams compete in ballroom dancing competitions.

The **ˌ*Comedy of 'Errors*** the first of *Shakespeare's comedy plays (*c*. 1593). It is about two sets of twins (= children of the same mother born at the same time), both called Antipholus, who employ another pair of twins, both called Dromio. None of the twins know of their twin brothers because they were separated at birth, so there is great confusion when they all come by chance to the same city.

'Comet[1] /'kɒmɪt/ the world's first commercial jet plane, operated by BOAC (British Overseas Airways Corporation) from 1952. Comets were almost twice as fast as earlier planes, but three of them crashed in 1953–4 because of problems in the metal from which they were made. They stopped flying until 1958 when an improved type of Comet offered the first jet service across the Atlantic.

'Comet™[2] /'kɒmɪt/ any of a chain of large shops found in many towns in Britain. They sell household electrical goods such as televisions and cookers.

ˌComic Re'lief a British charity organization that was started by a group of comedy actors to raise money for poor people and people with special disadvantages. Once every two years in March there are comedy programmes on television in which the actors and presenters ask people to send money for various charities. On the same day, also called *Red Nose Day, ordinary people buy and wear red noses and do crazy or amusing things to raise money.

the **'comics** ⇨ FUNNIES.

comics and comic strips

A comic in the US means a **comic strip** or **strip cartoon**. Comic strips are a series of small drawings, called **frames**, with words that tell a story. Most US newspapers contain comic strips that are read by both adults and children. On weekdays they are usually four frames long, printed in black and white. On Sundays they are longer and in colour. Comic strips are also popular in British newspapers. Some can be found on the Internet.

Most comic strips make jokes about the characters in them and the things that happen to them. For instance, in the **Peanuts* strips many of the jokes are about Charlie *Brown, who has very bad luck, and his sister Lucy, who is unkind to him. In *Calvin and Hobbes*, the humour comes from the relationship between a boy and his imaginary friend, a toy tiger. Comic strips in British newspapers include **Andy Capp*, **Garfield* and *The Perishers*. Other comic strips, such as *Li'l Orphan Annie*, tell a long story with a new part each day. *The *Dilbert Zone* is about life in the office. *Doonesbury* comments on political situations through its characters. Most newspapers also print single frames that comment humorously on politicians and other people in the news.

In Britain a *comic* is a picture magazine, usually for children. Comics contain short stories written as comic strips, and sometimes also competitions and articles. Some parents do not approve of comics, but others argue that they encourage children to read. Comics intended for boys, e.g. *2000 AD*, contain adventure stories and stories about football or aliens from space. Girls' comics, such as *Bunty*, contain school adventures and stories about horses. At the end of a story something exciting happens, so that children want to buy the comic again the following week. Comics for younger children include *Buster*, *Sonic the Comic* and, for the very small, *Fireman Sam* and *Ragdoll and Friends*. Adult comics, such as *Viz*, are usually very rude.

*The *Beano*, which started in 1938, is still popular. Its most famous character is *Dennis the Menace, a boy who, with his dog Gnasher, plays tricks on people. Another favourite comic is **Dandy*. Some of the characters in *The Beano* and *Dandy* have not changed much over the years and now look old-fashioned. Teachers, for instance, still wear mortarboards (= stiff black hats with a square top), though real teachers stopped wearing them long ago. Many of the most popular comics appear in the form of books, called **annuals**, around Christmas each year.

Comic books are similar to comics. Each book has a set of characters who have adventures. Many of the characters, such as *Spider-Man, *Superman and Wonder Woman, have powers that ordinary people do not have.

Pictures of the most famous characters from comic strips and comic books are used on a range of products. For instance, Gnasher and *Snoopy, a character from the *Peanuts* strip, are printed on bed covers, T-shirts, lunch boxes and birthday cards.

ˌ*Coming through the 'Rye* the title of a well-known Scottish song. The words were written by the Scottish poet Robert *Burns.

the **Com'mandos** a British military unit. They are part of the *Royal Marines and are specially trained to make quick attacks on difficult targets inside enemy areas. The word *commando* is also used to mean soldiers of this type in other countries.

the **Com'mission for 'Racial E'quality** a British government organization formed by the third of the *Race Relations Acts in 1976 to make sure that people of all races receive equal opportunities from employers, schools, etc.

the **Com'mission on ˌCivil 'Rights** an independent US government organization which works to achieve equal rights for all Americans. It investigates complaints, informs the President and *Congress, and sends information to the public. An original Commission was established by the Civil Rights Act of 1957 and the present one by the Civil Rights Act of 1983. Compare COMMISSION FOR RACIAL EQUALITY.

com'mittee stage *n* [sing] (*BrE*) the stage between the second and third reading of a *bill(1) (= suggested new law) in the *Houses of Parliament(1). At this stage the bill is closely examined by a small committee of *MPs.

the **ˌCommon Agri'cultural ˌPolicy** (*also* the **CAP**) the policy introduced in 1962 by the European Community, now the *European Union, to protect European farmers. Under the new system, farmers were paid even if they produced food that was not needed. Too much food was produced as a result, and this was given names such as the 'butter mountain' and the 'wine lake'. This great waste of money caused much argument about how to improve the system, and in the 1980s some changes were made. One of the solutions was to pay farmers not to produce food in some of their fields.

ˌCommon 'Entrance the entrance examination for British *public schools. Boys whose parents want them to go to a public school take this examination

C

at the age of 12 or 13, usually at a *preparatory school(1). Girls usually take it at the age of 10. ⇨ article at EDUCATION IN BRITAIN.

ˈ**common land** *n* [U] (in Britain) land that belongs to or may be used by the whole community, especially in a village. Most areas of common land have been used for keeping sheep or cows on or for other purposes for many centuries, and they have been protected by law since 1852.

C

ˌ**common ˈlaw** (*also* **case law**) *n* [U] (in England) law which has developed from old customs and from past decisions made by judges, i.e. not created by Parliament. A **common law wife/husband** is a person with whom a man or woman has lived for some time and who is recognized as a wife or husband under common law, although the couple are not legally married.

the ˌ**Common ˈMarket** an old name for the *European Union.

The **Commonwealth[1]** ⇨ article.

the ˈ**Commonwealth[2]** a period (1649–60) in English history when the country was governed without a king or queen. For the first four years after the death of King *Charles I, the country was governed by the *House of Commons. Then in 1653 the army gave power to Oliver *Cromwell with the title of Lord Protector. The years 1653–9 are therefore known as the *Protectorate. The Commonwealth ended with the *Restoration of King *Charles II.

the ˌ**Commonwealth ˈConference** a meeting of the *prime ministers of all the countries in the *Commonwealth[1], which takes place every two years.

ˈ**Commonwealth Day** a public holiday in some parts of the *Commonwealth[1] (but not Britain), celebrated every year on Queen *Elizabeth II's *Official Birthday. Until 1966 it was celebrated on Queen *Victoria's birthday (24 May). Before 1958 it was called Empire Day.

the ˌ**Commonwealth ˈGames** a sports contest for competitors from *Commonwealth[1] countries. It has taken place every four years since the first Games in Hamilton, Canada, in 1930. The event was called the British Empire Games until 1970.

the ˌ**Commonwealth ˈInstitute** the educational and cultural centre of the *Commonwealth[1]. The Institute organizes events and exhibitions, and its building in London, England, has permanent exhibitions from each member country.

the ˈ**Communist ˈParty of ˌGreat ˈBritain** a very small political party whose members believe that the ideas of Karl Marx should form the basis of government in Britain. The party was formed in 1920 but never achieved more than two seats in *Parliament. In the 1960s and 1970s the party received large payments from Moscow to help them cause problems in British industry. In 1991 the majority of the 5 000 members decided to change the party's name to the Democratic Left.

the ˈ**Communist ˈParty of the ˌUnited ˈStates** a small US political party which believes in the principles of Communism. It was established in 1921 and was called the Workers' Party of America before it changed to the present name in 1929. *Congress took away many of its rights in 1954, but the party began open activities again in 1966.

the **comˈmunity charge** (*also infml* the **poll tax**) *n* [sing] (in Britain) a local tax introduced by the *Conservative government in 1990 to replace the *rates. It was very unpopular because poor people had to pay the same as rich people. There were serious protests, and many people refused to pay the tax. It was replaced in 1993 by the *council tax.

comˈmunity ˌcollege *n* (in the US) a junior college for local students in a particular area. There is an emphasis on practical career courses, and many adult students attend. Community colleges usually receive money from the local government.

comˈmunity home *n* (in Britain) a centre where young people who have broken the law or need special care are sent to live and receive training.

comˌmunity poˈlicing /pəˈliːsɪŋ/ *n* [U] a system for developing trust and understanding between the people who live in a particular area and the local police, in order to reduce crime in that area. The system involves regular contact between the public and individual police officers.

comˌmunity ˈservice *n* [U] (in Britain) work done for no pay in a local community, such as helping old people or repairing community buildings. People can do community service through various local organizations. Many young people do it as part of the *Duke of Edinburgh's Award Scheme. Some types of community service are also performed as a punishment for small crimes following a **community service order** from a court: *He was given a 150-hour community service order.*

commuting

Commuting is the practice of travelling a long distance to a town or city to work each day, and then travelling home again in the evening. The word *commuting* comes from **commutation ticket**, a US rail ticket for repeated journeys, called a **season ticket** in Britain. Regular travellers are called **commuters**.

The US has many commuters. A few, mostly on the East Coast, commute by train or subway, but most depend on the car. Some leave home very early to avoid the **traffic jams**, and sleep in their cars until their office opens. Many people accept a long trip to work so that they can live in quiet **bedroom communities** away from the city, but another reason is '**white flight**'. In the 1960s most cities began to desegregate their schools, so that there were no longer separate schools for white and black children. Many white families did not want to send their children to desegregated schools, so they moved to the suburbs, which have their own schools, and where, for various reasons, few black people live.

Millions of people in Britain commute by car or train. Some spend two or three hours a day travelling, so that they and their families can live in **suburbia** or in the countryside. Cities are surrounded by **commuter belts**. Part of the commuter belt around London is called the **stockbroker belt** because it contains houses where rich business people live. Some places are becoming **dormitory towns**, because people sleep there but take little part in local activities.

Most commuters travel to and from work at the same time, causing the morning and evening **rush hours**, when buses and trains are crowded and there are traffic jams on the roads. Commuters on trains rarely talk to each other and spend their journey reading, sleeping or using their mobile phones, though this is not popular with other passengers. Increasing numbers of people now work at home some days of the week, linked to their offices by computer, a practice called **telecommuting**.

Cities in both Britain and the US are trying to reduce the number of cars coming into town each day. Some companies encourage **car pooling** (called **car sharing** in Britain), an arrangement for people who live and work near each other to travel together. Some US cities have a public service that helps such people to contact each other, and traffic lanes are reserved for car-pool vehicles. But cars and petrol/gas

C

The Commonwealth

The Commonwealth is an association of 53 independent nations, plus several British dependencies such as *Bermuda, the *Falkland Islands and *Gibraltar. Most members used to be part of the *British Empire, from which the Commonwealth developed. The **British Commonwealth of Nations** was set up in 1931 by the Statute of Westminster, based on decisions made at the 1926 Imperial Conference. Since 1949 it has been known simply as the **Commonwealth**. Any nation wishing to join must be independent, and its application must be acceptable to existing members. All member states recognize the British king or queen as head of the Commonwealth, though he or she is not necessarily the head of each individual state.

Members of the Commonwealth have special links with the United Kingdom and with each other. All members are equal and agree to work together towards world peace, the encouragement of trade, the defence of democracy and improvements in human rights, health and education. During World War II, Commonwealth forces played an important role in the war effort. More recently, Commonwealth nations united to oppose apartheid in South Africa. The Commonwealth also encourages joint cultural activities and sports events, particularly the *Commonwealth Games which are held every four years.

The ***Commonwealth Conference**, a meeting of the heads of government of all Commonwealth states, is held every two years. It is organized by the **Commonwealth Secretariat** which is based in London. The Secretariat also gives out information to member states and administers joint activities. The senior official of the Commonwealth is the **Secretary-General**. Since 1990, the post has been held by Emeka Anyaoku of Nigeria. The ***Commonwealth Institute** in London is the educational and cultural centre of the Commonwealth.

The second Monday in March is celebrated as ***Commonwealth Day**, though most British people are not aware of this, and a special message is broadcast to the Commonwealth by the Queen.

Members of the Commonwealth

Nation	Year joined	Nation	Year joined	Nation	Year joined
Antigua and Barbuda	1981	Kenya	1963	St Vincent and the Grenadines	1979
Australia	1931	Kiribati	1979	Seychelles	1976
Bahamas	1973	Lesotho	1966	Sierra Leone	1961
Bangladesh	1972	Malawi	1964	Singapore	1965
Barbados	1966	Malaysia	1957	Solomon Islands	1978
Belize	1981	Maldives	1982	South Africa	1931–61, 1994
Botswana	1966	Malta	1964	Sri Lanka	1948
Brunei Darussalam	1984	Mauritius	1968	Swaziland	1968
Cameroon	1995	Mozambique	1995	Tanzania	1961
Canada	1931	Namibia	1990	Tonga	1970
Cyprus	1961	Nauru†	1968	Trinidad and Tobago	1962
Dominica	1978	New Zealand	1931	Tuvalu†	1978
Fiji	1970–87, 1997	Nigeria	1960 (suspended 1995)	Uganda	1962
The Gambia	1965	Pakistan	1947–72, 1989	United Kingdom	1931
Ghana	1957	Papua New Guinea	1975	Vanuatu	1980
Grenada	1974	St Kitts and Nevis	1983	Western Samoa	1970
Guyana	1966	St Lucia	1979	Zambia	1964
India	1947			Zimbabwe	1980
Jamaica	1962				

† special member, not entitled to attend Commonwealth Conferences

are cheap in the US, and many people prefer to drive alone because it gives them more freedom. In Britain many cities have **park-and-ride** schemes, car parks on the edge of the city from which buses take drivers into the centre.

ˌPerry **ˈComo** /ˌperi ˈkəʊməʊ; *AmE* ˈkoʊmoʊ/ (1912–) a US singer of popular songs. He had a very relaxed style and pleasant voice. Most of his successful records were made in the 1950s when *The Perry Como Show* was on television. They include *No Other Love* (1953) and *Catch A Falling Star* (1958), for which he received a *Grammy award.

companies

There are several types of business company in Britain. A **chartered company** is established by *royal charter and is usually a non-commercial **corporation**, such as a local council. A **statutory company** is set up by an *Act of Parliament. Many former statutory companies that were managed by the government, such as those responsible for Britain's railway system and coal industry, have now been privatized (= sold and made into privately-run companies operating for profit), because these are thought to be more efficient.

Most commercial businesses in Britain are **registered companies**. Lists of these are kept by the Registrar of Companies, and company information and accounts are kept at *Companies House. Registered companies may be either **private companies** or **public companies**. Private Companies have a limited number of **shareholders**, and their shares are not available to the general public. Shares in public companies can be bought and sold by the public on the stock exchange.

A **limited company**, sometimes called a **limited liability company** or a **joint-stock company**, can be either private or public. The liability (= responsibility) of shareholders for any losses is limited to the value of their shares. Private limited companies have the letters **Ltd** after their name. A **public limited company (plc)** must be worth more than £50 000 and must offer its shares for sale to the pub-

C

lic. Most large companies in Britain, such as *BT and *Marks & Spencer are public limited companies.

Most businesses in the US are **corporations**, which are similar to British limited companies. People who invest money in them are liable for (= risk losing) only the amount they have invested. Some corporations sell their shares on the stock exchange, but others do not. Small corporations, e.g. family businesses, may be called **close corporations**. Corporations have the letters **inc.** (short for 'incorporated') after their name. The laws about how corporations are formed and should operate vary from state to state.

In both Britain and the US, professional businesses like law firms are often **partnerships**. In the US there are two kinds of partnership. **General partnerships** consist of two or more people who own a business, and who are together responsible for its debts. A **limited partnership** has general partners who run the business, and limited partners, people who have invested money but do not take part in the operation of the business. Only general partners are liable for the business's debts.

A **sole proprietorship** is run by one person only. Many small businesses in the US operate in this way because the rules are much simpler than those for corporations. Sole proprietorships do not have limited liability. If the name of the business is not the same as the name of the person who runs it, the letters **d.b.a.** are used, short for **doing business as**, e.g. Ted Smith, d.b.a. Ted's Book Store.

ˌ**Companies ˈHouse** the building in London, England, where records of companies are kept. Companies must send certain information to Companies House, and most of this information is available to the public.

ComˌpanionofˈHonour *n* (*pl* **Companions of Honour**) any of the 65 members of a British *order of chivalry which was started by King *George V in 1917. This honour is given to men and women who have performed a special service of national importance, often in politics or the arts. Members receive no title with the honour but may place the letters **CH** after their name.

The ˈ**Company** an informal name for the *CIA.

ˌ**compreˈhensive school** (*also infml* **comprehensive**) *n* (in Britain) a large state secondary school for boys and girls of all abilities aged 11 or over. Comprehensive schools were introduced in the 1960s to replace the system of dividing children between more academic *grammar schools and less academic *secondary modern schools.

ˌDenis ˈ**Compton** /ˈkɒmptən; *AmE* ˈkɑːmptən/ (1918–97) an English *cricket player who scored more runs (= points) in a single cricket season than any other English player (3 816 runs in 1947). He played for England from 1937 to 1957. He also played football for England.

ˈArthur ˈ**Conan** ˈ**Doyle** /ˈkəʊnən ˈdɔɪl, *also* ˈkɒnən; *AmE* ˈkoʊnən, *also* ˈkɑːnən/ (1859–1930) a Scottish writer. He is best known as the creator of the famous *detective Sherlock *Holmes, but he also wrote historical novels and science fiction. He began his working life as a doctor but gave this up after the success of his first Holmes story, *A Study in Scarlet* (1887). He was made a *knight in 1902.

ˈ**Concord** /ˈkɒŋkɔːd; *AmE* ˈkɑːŋkɔːrd/ a small town in the US state of *Massachusetts about 12 miles (19 kilometres) north-west of *Boston. The Battle of Concord was the second battle of the *American Revolution. The town is remarkable for the number of famous writers who lived there, including Nathaniel *Hawthorne, Ralph Waldo *Emerson, Henry David *Thoreau and Louisa May *Alcott. See also LEXINGTON AND CONCORD.

ˈ**Concorde** /ˈkɒŋkɔːd; *AmE* ˈkɑːŋkɔːrd/ the first passenger plane to fly faster than the speed of sound. It was designed and built by the British and the French together, and its first test flight was in 1969. The plane has been in service since 1976. It flies between London and Paris and New York, and between London and *Barbados. Flying on Concorde is expensive, so most people regard it as a very special experience.

ˌ**Coneˈstogaˌwagon** /ˌkɒnəˈstəʊgə; *AmE* ˌkɒnəˈstəʊgə/ (*also* **Conestoga**) *n* a large *covered wagon used by Americans who moved west between 1725 and 1850. The wagons were first made in the Conestoga Valley of eastern *Pennsylvania.

a Conestoga wagon

ˌ**Coney ˈIsland** /ˌkəʊni; *AmE* ˌkoʊni/ a famous beach and amusement park of south *Brooklyn in New York City. It is not an island. The beach has been popular since 1881 and is often very crowded. The *hot dog(1) was invented there, and so is sometimes called a 'coney'.

the **ConˌfederateˈStates** (*also* the **Conˈfederacy**) the 11 southern states that left the US in 1861 to form a new nation. This caused the American *Civil War. The President of the Confederate States was Jefferson *Davis and their capital city was first *Montgomery, *Alabama and later *Richmond, *Virginia. The Confederate States, in their order of leaving the Union, were *South Carolina, *Mississippi, *Florida, Alabama, *Georgia, *Louisiana, *Texas, Virginia, *Arkansas, *Tennessee and *North Carolina.

the **Conˌfedeˈration of ˈBritish ˈIndustry** ⇨ CBI.

ˌ**CongreˈgationaIist** /ˌkɒŋgrɪˈgeɪʃənəlɪst; *AmE* ˌkɑːŋgrɪˈgeɪʃənəlɪst/ *n* a member of the **Congregational Church**, which is one of the *Protestant branches of the Christian Church and has its origins in 16th-century England. It spread to America in the early 17th century with the first English settlers, the *Pilgrim Fathers, who came from a group of Congregationalists. Congregationalists were also known as Independents because of their belief that each local group should be independent of any central control. They had most influence during the *Puritan period in England when the country was ruled by one of their members, Oliver *Cromwell. English and Welsh Congregationalists have now joined with the *Presbyterians to form a new Church, the *United Reformed Church. ⇨ article at RELIGION.

the **Congress**

The Congress is one of the three branches of the US *federal government, the **legislative branch**. Congress is **bicameral**, i.e. it has two **houses**, the ***Senate** and the ***House of Representatives**. The main job of Congress is making laws. Before a new law can be made, both houses have to pass it, and it must then have the approval of the *President. In a system of government based on a series of **checks and balances**, the two houses of Congress act as an check on each other, as well as together forming a check on the powers of the **executive branch**, especially the President.

ˌ**Congress ˈHouse** the headquarters of the British *Trades Union Congress in London, England.

the **Congressional Gold Medal** the highest award given by *Congress to US civilians. It is presented to men and women who have done something special for the nation. The first was given to George *Washington in 1776, and the singer Frank *Sinatra received the 258th award in 1998. Others who have received it include John *Wayne, Bob *Hope, Walt *Disney, George and Ira *Gershwin, Irving *Berlin, Marian *Anderson and Aaron *Copland.

the **Conˈgressional ˈMedal of ˈHonor** (*also* the **Medal of Honor**) the highest military award in the US. It was established in 1862 and is given by the US *Congress for special personal courage. A total of 125 were given in *World War I, 433 in the *World War II, 131 in the *Korean War and 239 in the *Vietnam War. Compare PURPLE HEART.

the ***Conˌgressional ˈRecord*** a printed record, published every day, of all the speeches and votes in the US *Congress. It has been published since 1873 by the Government Printing Office. Members of Congress can add extra comments or even newspaper articles in the 'Extensions of Remarks' section at the end. Compare HANSARD.

the ˈ**Congress of ˈRacial Eˈquality** (*abbr* **CORE**) a US organization that supports equal rights for *African Americans by peaceful actions. It was established in 1942 in *Chicago by James Farmer. It became well known in the 1960s for encouraging African Americans to vote and for leading *freedom riders into the southern states.

ˌWilliam ˈ**Congreve** /ˈkɒŋɡriːv; *AmE* ˈkɑːŋɡriːv/ (1670–1729) an English writer of plays, which are fine examples of *Restoration comedy. His best-known play is *The Way of the World* (1700).

ˈ**Coniston ˌWater** /ˈkɒnɪstən; *AmE* ˈkɑːnɪstən/ a long, narrow lake in the English *Lake District. It is famous as the place where Malcolm *Campbell and Donald *Campbell achieved the highest speeds on water in their boat **Bluebird*. At the northern end of the lake there is a mountain called Coniston Old Man.

Conˈnecticut /kəˈnetɪkət/ a small US state forming part of *New England. It was one of the 13 original states. Its nickname is the Constitution State and the state song is **Yankee Doodle*. Connecticut has many industries but also large forests. The capital city is Hartford, which is the centre for US insurance companies. Many people living in south-western Connecticut travel to work each day in New York City. See also YALE UNIVERSITY.

ˌSean ˈ**Connery** /ˈkɒnəri; *AmE* ˈkɑːnəri/ (1930–) a Scottish actor who is best known for his role as James *Bond in many of the Bond films, including the first one, *Dr No* (1962). He has made many other films, including *The Name of the Rose* (1986), *The Russia House* (1990), *Rising Sun* (1993) and *The Rock* (1996). He was over 60 years old when the readers of a popular women's magazine voted him the world's sexiest man (= the man most attractive to women).

ˈHarry ˈ**Connick** ˈJr /ˈkɒnɪk; *AmE* ˈkɑːnɪk/ (1967–) a US singer and actor. His best-known song is *It Had to Be You* and his albums have included *When Harry Met Sally* (1989) and *To See You* (1997). His films include *Memphis Belle* (1990), *Independence Day* (1996) and *Hope Floats* (1998).

ˌBilly ˈ**Connolly**[1] /ˈkɒnəli; *AmE* ˈkɑːnəli/ (1942–) a Scottish comedian and actor, known for his rude stories and jokes, which he tells in a strong Scottish *accent. He is sometimes called the 'Big Yin' (which means the 'big one') because of his size and loud voice.

C

ˌCyril ˈ**Connolly**[2] /ˈkɒnəli; *AmE* ˈkɑːnəli/ (1903–74) an English author and literary critic. His best-known book is *The Rock Pool* (1935), a novel about artists living in the south of France. He started a literary magazine called *Horizon*, through which his ideas influenced many writers between 1930 and 1950.

ˌMaureen ˈ**Connolly**[3] /ˈkɒnəli; *AmE* ˈkɑːnəli/ (1934–69) a US tennis player who had the popular name of 'Little Mo' because of her small size. She won the US Open from 1951 to 1953 (the first when she was only 16) and *Wimbledon from 1952 to 1954. In 1953 she became the first woman to win the *grand slam(1). Connolly ended her tennis career in 1954 after she broke her leg in an accident while riding.

ˌJimmy ˈ**Connors** /ˈkɒnəz; *AmE* ˈkɑːnərz/ (1952–) a US tennis player. He won the US Open five times between 1974 and 1983, and *Wimbledon in 1974 and 1982. He was known for his great enthusiasm while playing but also for his bad temper and behaviour. In 1998 he was chosen for the International Tennis *Hall of Fame.

the ˈ**Conqueror** ⇨ WILLIAM I.

the ˈ**Conquest** (*also* the **Norman Conquest**) the events of 1066, the most famous date in English history, when the *Normans defeated the English and took control of England. William, Duke of Normandy, landed with his army at Pevensey in south-east England and defeated the English under King *Harold II at the Battle of *Hastings. King Harold was killed, and William became King *William I of England. By 1070, the Normans had firm control of the whole country.

ˌJoseph ˈ**Conrad** /ˈkɒnræd; *AmE* ˈkɑːnræd/ (1857–1924) a British novelist who was born Teodor Josef Konrad Korzeniowski in a part of Poland under Russian rule. He left home at 17 to go to sea and, after many adventures, he joined the crew of a British ship. He changed his name and became a British citizen in 1886. He used his experiences around the world as the background to many of his novels, such as **Lord Jim*, **Heart of Darkness* and *Nostromo* (1904). He is considered by many people to be one of the greatest novelists in the English language.

ˌShirley ˈ**Conran**[1] /ˈkɒnrən; *AmE* ˈkɑːnrən/ (1932–) an English designer, journalist and author, formerly married to Terence *Conran. Her books include *Superwoman* (1982), *Action Woman* (1979) and the novels *Lace* (1982) and *Savages* (1987).

ˌTerence ˈ**Conran**[2] /ˈkɒnrən; *AmE* ˈkɑːnrən/ (1931–) an English designer and businessman who started the *Habitat chain of furniture shops in 1964. The influence of his style on modern furniture increased as his shops spread throughout Britain and then to the US and France. Conran also owns several restaurants. He was made a *knight in 1983.

ˈ**Consequences** *n* [U] (*BrE*) a game in which each player writes the first line of a story on a piece of paper and then passes it to the next player who writes the second line, and so on. Each player folds the paper so that the next player cannot see what is already written. The result is a number of crazy and often funny stories. The stories follow a pattern that always begins with the names of two people and ends with the sentence 'And the consequence was ...'.

C

ˌ**conserˈvation ˌarea** *n* (in Britain) an area of special natural or historical value which is protected by law from any new building or other changes that would damage its character.

the **Conˈservative ˌParty** (*also* the **Conservatives**, the **Tories**) one of the main British political parties. It developed from the old **Tory Party** in the 1830s and is still sometimes called by this name. It is a right-wing party, supporting capitalism and free enterprise (= an economic system in which there is open competition in business and trade, and no government control). It formed the government in Britain from 1979 to 1997, during which time its leaders were Margaret *Thatcher and then John *Major. ⇨ article at POLITICAL PARTIES IN BRITAIN.

▶ **Conservative** (*also* **Tory**) *n* a member or supporter of the Conservative Party. **Conservative** (*also* **Tory**) *adj*.

ˌJohn ˈ**Constable** /ˈkʌnstəbl/ (1776–1837) an English painter who is considered to be one of the greatest English landscape artists. He often painted scenes from the countryside of *East Anglia, especially along the River Stour, an area that is now described in tourist advertisements as **Constable Country**. One of the most famous of these paintings is *The *Hay Wain*. A large collection of his work was given by his daughter to the *Victoria and Albert Museum in London.

The Hay Wain *by John Constable*

conˈstituency *n* one of the 659 administrative districts into which Britain is divided for the purpose of electing *Members of Parliament or one of the 81 larger divisions for electing *Euro-MPs. ⇨ article at ELECTIONS TO PARLIAMENT.

The **Constitution** ⇨ article.

ˈ*USˌS* ***Constiˈtution*** a famous US Navy ship. Its popular name is 'Old Ironsides'. It was completed in 1797 in *Boston and used in the *War of 1812. When the ship was old there were plans to destroy it, but Oliver Wendell *Holmes's poem *Old Ironsides* (1828) created strong public feeling against the decision and it was saved. The *Constitution* has been open to the public in Boston since 1934. In 1997 it sailed for the first time in 116 years, to celebrate its 200th birthday.

ˌ**constiˈtutional ˈmonarchy** *n* government by a king or queen within laws which limit his or her power. Britain is governed in this way, with the Queen as head of state and with *Parliament and the elected government holding almost all real power. This system began to develop slowly in the 17th century, when the *Bill of Rights became law, and then developed more quickly after the *Reform Act of 1832.

Conˌsumer Reˈports a US magazine, published each month, which tests products and writes about their quality and value. It is published by the independent Consumers Union that does not make a profit. There are no advertisements in the magazine. Compare *WHICH?*.

the **Conˈsumers' Asˌsociˈation** a British organization that tests the quality of products and publishes the results each month in its magazine called **Which?* This helps people to choose the best products and also gives the Association influence, which it uses to protect the interests of consumers (= people who buy goods or use services). The Association was formed in 1956 and now has nearly one million members. It also publishes books, including *The *Good Food Guide*.

ˈ**Con-Tact**™ /ˈkɒntækt; *AmE* ˈkɑːntækt/ *n* [U] a make of paper covered with transparent or coloured plastic on one side and sticky on the other. It is used for covering shelves, desk tops, books, etc.

ˌ**continental ˈbreakfast** *n* a light breakfast of the type eaten in some European countries, including Britain. The phrase is used mainly by hotels and restaurants and not by people in their own homes. A continental breakfast consists typically of bread rolls or croissants with butter and jam, and coffee to drink. Compare ENGLISH BREAKFAST.

the ˌ**Continental ˈCongress** the first governing body (1774–89) of the *thirteen colonies which later became the US. It met in *Philadelphia. The First Continental Congress was in 1774 and made demands for more rights from Britain. The Second Continental Congress began in 1775 and passed the *Declaration of Independence and the *Articles of Confederation.

the ˌ**Contiˈnental Diˈvide** (*also* the **Great Divide**) the range of *Rocky Mountains in North America. It is called this because it divides the flow of rivers on the continent, some going east and others going west.

ˌ**Continental ˈTrailways**™ (*also* **Trailways**) one of the two biggest US bus companies. Its buses travel to all parts of the country. *Continental Trailways Blues* (1983) was a popular song by Steve Earle, a singer of *country music. Compare GREYHOUND BUS.

conˌtinuing eduˈcation (*AmE also* **continued education**) *n* [U] education at any time during a person's adult life. In Britain it is usually provided by *Local Education Authorities and includes a great variety of courses in many different places. Courses are usually part-time and often take place in the evenings. They include cultural subjects, training in new technology, and skills for people with special needs. In the US, many colleges and universities have a department for adult education, often called the School of Continuing Education.

ˌBeryl ˈ**Cook**[1] /ˈkʊk/ (1926–) an English artist who paints humorous pictures of ordinary British people doing everyday things: *She sent me a Beryl Cook postcard of two fat ladies hanging out their washing.*

Ladies' Match *by Beryl Cook*

ˌCaptain ˈ**Cook**[2] /ˈkʊk/ (James Cook 1728–79) an English sailor and explorer who made three journeys by sea to the Pacific Ocean. He was the first European to arrive on the east coast of Australia. He drew maps of the coasts of Australia, New Zealand and New Guinea. He was also the first European to arrive at *Hawaii, where he was killed in a fight with the local people.

The Constitution

The history of the Constitution

One of the reasons why the colonists in North America began the *American Revolution was that the British government had not respected rights that people in America thought important. As a result, when the colonists had won the war and were forming a new government, they wanted to limit its powers. They therefore wrote a document, called the Constitution, describing the new system of government and how it would work.

Leaders from each state met in *Philadelphia in 1787 to write the Constitution. This meeting is known as the **Constitutional Convention**. There was a lot of discussion and compromise, and it was especially difficult to get agreement between large states and smaller ones, and between states with and without *slaves. Finally, the Convention agreed on a document, but it could not be put into effect until nine states had ratified (= formally agreed to) it. People living in each state discussed whether the Constitution would benefit or harm them. In some states the decision was made quickly, but in others, such as *New York and *Virginia, the debate lasted longer. In the end, all 13 states of which the United States was then composed ratified the Constitution. It was signed in 1789 by representatives from each state, including some of the most important figures in early American history, George *Washington, Alexander *Hamilton, Benjamin *Franklin and James *Madison.

What does the Constitution say?

The original document established the **three branches of government**: the legislative, the judicial and the executive. The legislative branch consists of *Congress, the judicial branch is the *Supreme Court and lower courts created by Congress, and the executive branch consists of the *president, vice-president and government *departments (⇨ article at FEDERAL GOVERNMENT IN THE US). The Constitution defined the responsibilities of each branch and dealt with details such as who could be elected to Congress and when Congress should meet. The **separation of powers** between the three branches was designed to provide a series of **checks and balances**, so that no branch would become too powerful.

The Constitution said that it was a responsibility of the US government to protect individual states. It also set a rather difficult process by which it could be **amended** (= changed).

Amendments to the Constitution

Since 1789 the Constitution has been amended 27 times, most recently in 1992. The first ten **amendments** were made in 1791, and list basic rights that many people had wanted to include in the original Constitution, but had left out in order to persuade all the states to ratify it. These amendments are together known as the ***Bill of Rights**. Among other things, the Bill of Rights promises citizens the right to free speech (= the right to say what they want without the government trying to stop them), freedom of religion, the right not to be arrested or searched without a good reason, and the right of anyone accused of a crime to have a fair trial.

Some changes to the Constitution have been more successful than others. The *First Amendment's guarantee of freedom of speech and religion is an essential principle of American life. The Second Amendment, which gives people the right to carry guns, is now the subject of public debate and many people are opposed to it. The 18th Amendment, **passed** in 1919, created *Prohibition, making it illegal for people to make or buy alcoholic drinks. However, this measure was not successful, and in 1933 the 21st Amendment **repealed** the 18th, so that alcohol became legal again.

Some amendments reflect changes in American society. The Constitution was written by white men, mainly to protect their rights. Following the *Civil War, the 13th Amendment (1865) and the 15th Amendment (1870) gave the same rights to people of all races. In 1920 the 19th Amendment gave women the right to vote.

Changing the Constitution requires wide support of people elected to public offices. In the 1970s the *Equal Rights Amendment, which said that women had the same rights as men, was passed by Congress but failed to be ratified by the required number of states and so was defeated.

Interpreting the Constitution

In 1803 the Supreme Court made a very important decision in the case **Marbury v Madison*. The Court said that a law that was relevant to the case went against what was contained in the Constitution. In this way the Supreme Court gave itself the power to decide on the **constitutionality** of any law. If the Court decides that a law is **unconstitutional**, it cannot be used any more.

Experts have different opinions about how to decide whether a law is **constitutional** or not. Some believe it is better to follow exactly what the Constitution says. Others think that it is necessary to consider what was in the minds of the people who wrote it. For instance, the Second Amendment gives people the right to carry guns, and some people say that laws that limit this right are unconstitutional. Others believe that the Amendment was written so that Americans could defend themselves against a possible attack by the British, and since that is not likely to happen today, laws controlling guns would not go against the intentions of the people who wrote the Constitution.

ˌPeter ˈ**Cook**[3] /ˈkʊk/ (1937–95) an English comedy actor and writer who first became famous in the stage show **Beyond the Fringe* in the 1960s. He is best remembered for his performances with Dudley *Moore as Dud and Pete, two ridiculous men who think that they are being philosophical, but are talking nonsense. He helped to start the magazine **Private Eye*, and remained one of its main owners until his death.

ˌRobin ˈ**Cook**[4] /ˈkʊk/ (1946–) a British *Labour politician. He became a *Member of Parliament in 1983 and held several important positions in the Labour *Shadow Cabinet before becoming *Foreign Secretary in the Labour government of 1997.

ˌThomas ˈ**Cook**[5] /ˈkʊk/ (1808–92) an English travel agent who set up the world's first package tours (= holidays for which hotels, meals, etc. are organized in advance) after hiring a train to take people to a meeting of the *temperance movement. **Thomas Cook** is now one of the world's largest travel companies: *They had a little of the local currency and a few Thomas Cook traveller's cheques.*

ˌAlistair ˈ**Cooke¹** /ˈkʊk/ (1908–) a US broadcaster and journalist, born in Britain. He is well known for his *BBC radio series **Letter from America*, in which he describes US life to the British. The series has been running since 1946. He also appears on US television to talk about British life, and to introduce British plays in the **Masterpiece Theater* series.

C

ˌSam ˈ**Cooke²** /ˈkʊk/ (1935–64) an *African-American singer and writer of *soul music. His best-known song was *You Send Me* (1957). Cooke was killed by a woman who was judged innocent because she was defending herself from him.

ˌCatherine ˈ**Cookson** /ˈkʊksən/ (1906–98) an English writer of romantic novels about life in the north-east of England. She was one of Britain's most popular authors, and was made a *dame(2) in 1993.

ˌ**Cool Briˈtannia** /brɪˈtænjə/ (*infml*) a phrase used to describe Britain, showing approval of the new British pop groups, artists and fashions of the late 1990s. It became a popular phrase partly because it sounds like **Rule, Britannia!*, a well-known song.

ˌCalvin ˈ**Coolidge** /ˌkælvɪn ˈkuːlɪdʒ/ (1872–1933) the 30th US *President (1923–9). He was known for his honesty and called 'Silent Cal' because he used few words when speaking. He was a *Republican(1), and had previously been Governor of *Massachusetts (1919–20) and US Vice-president (1921–3). The US economy did well under Coolidge, and he signed the *Kellogg-Briand Pact to encourage international peace.

the ˈ**Co-op** (in Britain) a shop run by the *Co-operative Wholesale Society. There is a Co-op in most British towns and cities. It is usually either a *corner shop, or a department store selling food, furniture, electrical goods and household products: *I bought it at the local Co-op.* See also CO-OPERATIVE MOVEMENT.

ˈ**Cooper¹** /ˈkuːpə(r)/ a British company that made successful racing cars in the 1950s and 1960s. It is best known for making the Mini Cooper, a sports-car version of the *Mini.

ˌGary ˈ**Cooper²** /ˈkuːpə(r)/ (1901–62) a US film actor who is most remembered for his roles in *westerns as a strong, silent hero. These included **High Noon* (1952) for which he received an *Oscar. He received another for playing a soldier in *Sergeant York* (1940). He also had comic roles, as in *Mr Deeds Goes to Town* (1936). Cooper was given a special Oscar in 1961.

ˌHenry ˈ**Cooper³** /ˈkuːpə(r)/ (1934–) a popular English boxer who was twice the British heavyweight champion (1959–69 and 1970–71). He is remembered in Britain for having knocked down Muhammad *Ali, although he lost the contest and never became world champion.

ˈJames ˈFenimore ˈ**Cooper⁴** /ˈfenɪmɔː ˈkuːpə(r); *AmE* ˈfenɪmɔːr ˈkuːpər/ (1789–1851) the first major US writer of novels. He wrote mostly about *frontiersmen and Native Americans. His best-known books include *The *Last of the Mohicans* (1826) and *The Deerslayer* (1841). He also wrote novels about sailors and histories of the US Navy.

ˌTommy ˈ**Cooper⁵** /ˈkuːpə(r)/ (1921–84) an English comedian who performed magic tricks as part of his act. He was well known for wearing a fez (= a small red traditional Turkish hat) and saying 'Just like that' when his tricks went wrong, as they often did.

the **Coˈoperative for ˈAmerican Reˈlief ˈEverywhere** ⇨ CARE.

the **Co-ˈoperative ˌMovement** an international movement that aims to encourage people to produce, buy and sell things together, and to share the profits. The movement started in northern England in the 19th century when poor working people started giving regular small amounts of money so that, as a group, they could buy food, clothes, etc. for less than a single person could. Some members worked for the Movement making these goods.

the **Co-ˌoperative ˈWholesale Soˌciety** (*also* the **Co-op**) (*abbr* **CWS**) a company set up in 1863 by members of the *Co-operative Movement to produce and buy goods, and sell them in special shops. It now has supermarkets all over Britain, and several other businesses, including the **Co-operative Bank**. Members still receive a share of the profits.

Coors™ /kʊəz; *AmE* kʊrz/ an expensive US beer produced by the Adolph Coors Company of *Denver, *Colorado. It is advertised as special because it is made with water from the *Rocky Mountains. The company also makes many other products, including Killian's Irish Brown Ale.

the ˌBattle of **Copenˈhagen** /kəʊpənˈheɪgən; *AmE* koʊpənˈheɪgən/ a sea battle (1801) between the navies of Britain and Denmark during the *Napoleonic Wars. *Nelson was in charge of a group of ships attacking the Danish ships in Copenhagen harbour. It is a well-known story in Britain that Nelson was sent a signal ordering him to leave the battle, but he put his telescope to his blind eye and pretended not to see the signal. His ships stayed where they were, and won the battle.

ˌAaron ˈ**Copland** /ˌeərən ˈkəʊplənd; *AmE* ˌerən ˈkoʊplənd/ (1900–1990) a US composer of modern classical music, much of which uses traditional folk songs. His best-known works include the ballets *Appalachian Spring* (1944), for which he won the *Pulitzer Prize, and *Billy the Kid* (1939). He also wrote music for eight films and received an *Oscar for *The Heiress* (1949).

ˌDavid ˈ**Copperfield¹** ⇨ *DAVID COPPERFIELD.*

ˌDavid ˈ**Copperfield²** /ˈkɒpəfiːld; *AmE* ˈkɑːpərfiːld/ (1956–) a US magician who does magic tricks on a grand scale. He has made the *Statue of Liberty 'disappear' and has 'walked through' the Great Wall of China.

ˈFrancis ˈFord ˈ**Coppola** /ˈfɔːd ˈkɒpələ; *AmE* ˈfɔːrd ˈkɑːpələ/ (1939–) an American who writes, produces and directs films. He is best known for three films about the same criminal family, *The *Godfather* Parts I–III (1972, 1974, 1990). He received three *Oscars for these and another for writing *Patton* (1970). He directed the expensive *Apocalypse Now* (1984) about the *Vietnam War and produced *Mary Shelley's Frankenstein* (1994). Coppola is the uncle of the actor Nicholas *Cage.

ˈ**copyright ˌlibrary** *n* any of six British libraries that have the right to ask for a free copy of any work published in Britain. They are the *British Library, the *Bodleian Library, the *Cambridge University Library, the national libraries of Scotland and Wales and Trinity College Library, *Dublin.

ˈˈGentleman ˈJimˈ ˈ**Corbett¹** /ˈkɔːbɪt; *AmE* ˈkɔːrbɪt/ (1866–1933) a US boxer. He became World Heavyweight Champion (1892–7) when he defeated John L *Sullivan in the first contest fought with gloves and under the *Queensberry Rules. He lost his title to Bob Fitzsimmons in the first filmed fight, and then became an actor. He was born James John Corbett and was called 'Gentleman Jim' because of his elegant manner.

ˌRonnie ˈ**Corbett²** /ˈkɔːbɪt; *AmE* ˈkɔːrbɪt/ (1930–) a

corn circles

British comedian, best known as the very small partner of the much larger Ronnie *Barker in the *BBC television series *The Two Ronnies*.

CORE /kɔː(r)/ ⇨ CONGRESS OF RACIAL EQUALITY.

ˈ**corgi** *n* (*pl* **-gis**) a breed of small dog with smooth hair, a long body and short legs, originally bred in Wales. Corgis are well known in Britain because Queen *Elizabeth II keeps them as pets.

ˌ***Corio*ˈ*lanus*** /ˌkɒriəˈleɪnəs; *AmE* ˌkɔːriəˈleɪnəs/ a play (*c.* 1608) by *Shakespeare about Caius Martius Coriolanus, a successful military leader in ancient Rome. He is sent away from Rome because he is too proud, and joins the enemy, bringing an army to attack Rome. The Romans send his mother, wife and son to persuade him not to the attack, and Caius Martius is killed by the enemy.

ˌRoger ˈ**Corman** /ˈkɔːmən; *AmE* ˈkɔːrmən/ (1926–) a US director of cheap horror and crime films. He is best known for directing several films based on stories by Edgar Allan *Poe. These include *The Pit and the Pendulum* (1961) and *The Raven* (1963). Corman's other films include *Bloody Mama* (1969) and *Frankenstein Unbound* (1990).

the ˈ**Corn Belt** the popular name for the US states of the Midwest, the area that grows most of the nation's corn. The main corn states are *Iowa, *Illinois and *Indiana.

ˈ**corn** ˌ**circle** (*also* **crop circle**) *n* [often pl] an area in a field of corn where parts of the crop have been made flat. The area is round or in other shapes and patterns. Corn circles began to appear in Britain in the 1980s. Some people think that they are made by beings from other planets or by unusual winds, while others think that they are made by local people as a joke.

ˈ**corn** ˌ**dolly** *n* (*BrE*) a small figure made from pieces of corn or dried grass twisted together. Originally corn dollies were made as symbols for the gathering of crops, but now they are mostly for decoration.

corn dollies

ˌ**corner** ˈ**shop** (*BrE*) (*AmE* **convenience store**) *n* a small shop, often on a street corner, that sells food, drinks, cigarettes and small household goods, and usually stays open later than other shops. In Britain many corner shops are run by families of Indian or Pakistani origin: *I'm just going down to the corner shop for some milk.*

Corˈ**netto**™ /kɔːˈnetəʊ; *AmE* kɔːrˈnetoʊ/ *n* (*pl* **-ttos**) a type of ice cream that is popular in Britain. It is a long piece of biscuit in the shape of a cone, filled with ice cream of different flavours, chocolate and nuts.

ˈ**Corning Ware**™ /ˈkɔːnɪŋ; *AmE* ˈkɔːrnɪŋ/ *n* [U] a US make of ceramic (= hard clay) dishes used for baking food in. They have been made since 1958 by Corning Inc, which also makes Pyrex glass bowls, etc.

ˈ**Cornish** /ˈkɔːnɪʃ; *AmE* ˈkɔːrnɪʃ/ *n* [U] the *Celtic language that used to be spoken in *Cornwall, England. There are no people left who speak it as their first language, but there is a political party, Mebyon Kernow ('Sons of Cornwall'), that tries to encourage its use.

the ˈ**Corn Laws** *n* [pl] a set of British laws, first introduced in the *Middle Ages, which controlled the import and export of corn in order to make sure that there was enough British corn. They were unpopular in the 19th century when there was a lack of corn, and the laws were keeping the prices high. Many Members of Parliament owned agricultural land and made large profits from these high prices. In 1846, under pressure from the Anti-Corn Law League, the government changed the laws.

ˈ**corn pone** /pəʊn; *AmE* poʊn/ *n* [C, U] (*AmE*) a simple type of bread made of corn, especially in the southern US. Each is baked or fried as a small piece ('pone') shaped like a slightly flat lemon. It is sometimes called by other names, including 'hoe cake', 'johnny cake' and 'ash cake'.

ˈ**Cornwall**[1] /ˈkɔːnwɔːl; *AmE* ˈkɔːrnwɑːl/ the county at the south-west tip of England. It used to produce a lot of tin, but there are now very few tin mines left. Its scenery and mild climate make it popular with tourists. The administrative centre is Truro.

ˌDuke of ˈ**Cornwall**[2] /ˈkɔːnwɔːl; *AmE* ˈkɔːrnwɑːl/ another title of the *Prince of Wales, who owns land in the county of *Cornwall in south-west England. See also DUCHY OF CORNWALL. ⇨ note at ARISTOCRACY. ⇨ article at ROYAL FAMILY.

ˌLord ˈCharles **Corn**ˈ**wallis** /kɔːnˈwɒlɪs; *AmE* kɔːrnˈwɑːlɪs/ (1738–1805) a general in charge of British forces during the *American Revolution. When he admitted defeat to George *Washington at the Battle of *Yorktown the war was ended. Cornwallis was later made Governor-General of India.

the ˌ**Coro**ˈ**nation** the ceremony that takes place at *Westminster Abbey when a new British king or queen is crowned. After a religious ceremony, they are given the crown and other items that represent power and wealth, and become officially king or queen. The Coronation is always marked by a public holiday and celebrations all over the country: *We had a street party for the Queen's Coronation.*

the ˌ**Coronation** ˈ**Chair** a special chair in *Westminster Abbey where the king or queen sits during the *Coronation ceremony. It was made for King *Edward I and used to have the *Stone of Scone under it.

ˌ***Coro*ˈ*nation Street*** a British television *soap opera about the lives of the people who live on Coronation Street, a street in a typical *working-class area of *Manchester. It is one of Britain's most popular programmes and one of the world's oldest soap operas. It started in 1960, and since 1989 has been broadcast three times a week: *He thinks northerners all speak like Coronation Street characters.*

ˌ**corpo**ˈ**ration tax** *n* [U] a tax paid by companies on their profits. British companies pay between 25% and 33% corporation tax, depending on the size of their profits.

ˌ**corre**ˈ**spondence** ˌ**college** *n* a college that sends its students books, exercises, etc. by post. The students

C

the Coronation of Elizabeth II

work at home and post their work to the college to be marked.

Corˈvette /kɔːˈvet; *AmE* kɔːrˈvet/ (*also infml* **Vette**) *n* a low, fast US sports car produced by the *Chevrolet section of *General Motors Corporation. It was first sold in 1953, and one of its most popular models was the Stingray. There are about 700 clubs of Corvette owners, and the National Corvette Museum opened in 1994 in Bowling Green, *Kentucky.

ˌ**Cosa ˈNostra** /ˌkəʊzə ˈnɒstrə; *AmE* ˌkoʊzə ˈnɑːstrə/ another name for the US *Mafia(1). *Cosa nostra* is Italian for 'our thing'.

ˌBill ˈ**Cosby** /ˈkɒzbi; *AmE* ˈkɑːzbi/ (1937–) an African-American comic actor known for his easy style. He is one of the most highly paid performers on US television. The two most successful series in which he has appeared are *I Spy* (1965–68) and *The Cosby Show* (1984–92). He has received several *Emmy awards and also written a successful book, *Fatherhood* (1986). His son Ennis was murdered in 1997 in *Los Angeles.

ˌ***Cosmoˈpolitan*** a magazine for young women, published each month in the US and Britain. It first appeared in 1972 and was one of the first women's magazines to discuss sex openly. It still contains many articles about sex, but many people now find its views old-fashioned.

the ˌ**Costa del ˈCrime** /ˌkɒstə del ˈkraɪm; *AmE* ˌkɑːstə/ a humorous name, often used by British *tabloid newspapers, for the Costa del Sol, part of the Mediterranean coast of southern Spain. It is a popular area with British tourists, and it is well known that British criminals used to go to live there before the British and Spanish governments agreed to send each other's criminals back for trial.

ˌLou **Coˈstello** /kɒˈsteləʊ; *AmE* kɑːˈsteloʊ/ ⇨ ABBOTT AND COSTELLO.

ˌKevin ˈ**Costner** /ˈkɒstnə(r); *AmE* ˈkɑːstnər/ (1955–) a US actor who also directs films. He usually plays characters who are serious and morally good. His films have included *Field of Dreams* (1989) about *baseball, *Dances with Wolves* (1990) about *Native Americans, for which he won an *Oscar as Best Director, *Waterworld* (1995) and *The Postman* (1997).

the ˈ**Cotswolds** /ˈkɒtswəʊldz; *AmE* ˈkɑːtswoʊldz/ a range of hills in south-west England. It was once a major centre for sheep farming and the wool trade. Now it is a popular tourist area, famous for its beautiful scenery and pretty towns. Many houses in the area are built with the local **Cotswold stone**, which has an attractive pale greyish-yellow colour: *We've rented a cottage in the Cotswolds for the summer.*

ˌ**cottage ˈloaf** *n* (*pl* **loaves**) (*BrE*) a type of traditional British bread consisting of a large round loaf baked with a smaller round piece on top.

ˌ**cottage ˈpie** ⇨ SHEPHERD'S PIE.

the ˈ**Cotton Belt** a popular name for the southern US states, in which most of the country's cotton is grown. The 10 cotton states are *Texas, *Oklahoma, *Louisiana, *Arkansas, *Tennessee, *Mississippi, *Alabama, *Georgia, *South Carolina and *North Carolina.

the ˈ**Cotton Club** a famous US *jazz club in *Harlem, New York City, popular with both black and white people. Its best years were in the late 1920s when 'Duke' *Ellington and his band played there. The club provided the idea for the film *The Cotton Club* (1984), directed by Francis Ford *Coppola.

ˈ**council** *n* [C + sing/pl *v*] (in Britain) a group of people elected to form the local government of an area. Councils represent counties, towns, or parts of a large city. They make local laws and are responsible for roads, parks, cultural services, *council houses, etc: *The neighbours made so much noise he complained to the council.* ⇨ article at LOCAL GOVERNMENT IN BRITAIN.

▶ **councillor** *n* a person who is a member of a council.

the ˈ**Council for the Proˈtection of ˌRural ˈEngland** (*abbr* **CPRE**) a *pressure group that aims to preserve the English countryside in its natural state and prevent people from building on the land.

ˈ**council house** *n* (in Britain) a house provided by a local council at a low rent. Council houses and **council flats** are mainly occupied by people with lower incomes. They are often on **council estates**, groups of buildings containing many flats/apartments. Many people still rent council houses and council flats, but some have bought them from the council since they were given the right to do this in 1980.

the ˌ**Council of ˈEurope** an organization that aims to protect human rights and encourage European countries to work together in areas such as culture, education, sport, health, crime and the environment. It is based in Strasbourg, France, and has 39 European countries as its members. It is responsible for the *European Court of Human Rights.

the ˌ**Council of ˈMinisters** (the Council of Ministers of the European Communities) the most powerful organization of the *European Union, consisting of one government minister from each *European Union member country. Governments can send different ministers to the Council, depending on the subject being discussed. It is based in Brussels and is responsible for most EU decisions.

ˈ**council tax** *n* [C, U] (in Britain) a local tax paid by every household, according to the value of their house or flat/apartment. It replaced the *poll tax, a tax paid by every adult, in 1993: *This year's council tax bills will be the highest ever.*

ˈ***Countdown*** a popular British television show (1982–) in which competitors play games with words and numbers. It is presented by Richard Whiteley and Carol *Vorderman, and was the first programme to be shown on *Channel Four. It is broadcast every afternoon except Saturday and Sunday.

counties

Britain is divided into small administrative regions, many of which are called **counties**. Three counties, *Essex, *Kent and *Sussex, have the same names and cover almost the same areas as three of the former *Anglo-Saxon kingdoms. Other counties, e.g. *Dorset, are probably based on areas where particular tribes once lived.

Counties were previously called **shires**. The original shires were the counties of the English *Midlands and the word became part of their name, e.g. *Northamptonshire. Administrative and legal affairs were dealt with by shire courts presided over by shire-reeves, later called sheriffs. Many shires were divided into smaller districts called **hundreds**. *Yorkshire, the largest county in Britain, was until 1974 divided into **ridings**, North Riding, East Riding and West Riding, named after the three divisions of the 9th century *Viking kingdom of *York.

The families of people who own land in the **shire counties**, are sometimes described as **county**, as in *a county family* and *She's very county*, or said to belong to the **county set**. County people have a high social status and are thought to have a way of life that is typical of the *upper class.

Counties were for a long time the basis for ***local government**. Since 1972 there have been many changes to their boundaries and names, and to the structure of local government. Most recently, some parts of Britain chose to become **unitary authorities**. The main difference is that counties have two tiers (= levels) of local government, at county and at district level, and unitary authorities have only one level. Some towns that were previously part of counties, e.g. *Southampton, are now separate unitary authorities. Many people are confused by all the changes and continue to use the old county names. People do not like to have changes forced upon them, and in 1974 local people were unhappy when the small county of *Rutland was abolished and became part of *Leicestershire. In 1996, when they had the opportunity to change, the people of Rutland chose to have their own separate unitary authority.

In the US most states are divided into counties, which are the largest units of local government. There are over 3 000 counties in the US; Delaware has just three, while Texas has 254. *Connecticut and *Rhode Island have none. In *Louisiana, similar units of local government are called **parishes**, and in *Alaska they are called **boroughs**. In some urban areas, such as *Philadelphia and *Boston, the city takes up almost the entire county. ⇨ article at STATE AND LOCAL GOVERNMENT IN THE US.

the ˌ**Country** ˈ**Code** (in Britain) a set of rules to prevent people from harming the environment when they are in the countryside. They must keep dogs under control, for example, and leave no rubbish/garbage behind.

ˌ***Country*** ˈ***Life*** a British magazine, published every month, about houses, gardens, country sports and social life in the country. Many people associate it with rich people who own large houses in the country. It was first published in 1897.

ˈ**country** ˌ**music** (*also* **country and western music**) *n* [U] a type of popular American music that combines the traditional music of the US West and the South. These two types included *cowboy songs and *hillbilly music. There are more US radio stations playing country music than for any other type of music. The home of country music is *Nashville, *Tennessee, with its *Grand Ole Opry. See also BLUEGRASS, ROCKABILLY.

ˌ**country** ˈ**park** *n* (in Britain) any of the areas of countryside that have been preserved by the *Countryside Commission for the public to enjoy. Many of them have picnic areas and nature trails, special paths where people can see interesting animals and plants.

a country music band

the countryside

The countryside of Britain is well known for its beauty and many contrasts: its bare mountains and moorland, its lakes, rivers and woods, and its long, often wild coastline. Many of the most beautiful areas are ***national parks** and are protected from development. When British people think of the countryside they think of farm land, as well as open spaces. They imagine cows or sheep in green fields enclosed by hedges or stone walls, and fields of wheat and barley. Most farmland is privately owned but is crossed by a network of *public footpaths.

Many people associate the countryside with peace and relaxation. They spend their free time walking or cycling there, or go to the country for a picnic or a pub lunch. In summer people go to fruit farms and pick strawberries and other fruit. Only a few people who live in the country work on farms. Many *commute to work in towns. Many others dream of living in the country, where they believe they would have a better and healthier lifestyle.

The countryside faces many threats. Some are associated with modern farming practices, and the use of chemicals harmful to plants and wildlife. Land is also needed for new houses. The ***green belt**, an area of land around many cities, is under increasing pressure. Plans to build new roads are strongly opposed by organizations trying to protect the countryside. Protesters set up camps to prevent, or at least delay, the building work.

America has many areas of wild and beautiful scenery, and there are many areas, especially in the West in states like *Montana and *Wyoming, where few people live. In the *New England states, such as *Vermont and *New Hampshire, it is common to see small farms surrounded by hills and green areas. In *Ohio, *Indiana, *Illinois and other Midwestern states, fields of corn or wheat reach to the horizon and there are many miles between towns.

Only about 20% of Americans live outside cities and towns. Life may be difficult for people who live in the country. Services like hospitals and schools may be further away, and going shopping can mean driving long distances. Some people even have to drive from their homes to the main road where their mail is left in a box. In spite of the disadvantages, many people who live in the country say that they like the safe, clean, attractive environment. But their children often move to a town or city as soon as they can.

As in Britain, Americans like to go out to the country at weekends. Some people go on camping or fishing trips, others go hiking in national parks.

the ˈ**Countryside Comˌmission** the British government organization responsible for preserving the countryside in England. It encourages local authorities to provide parks, and sets up and runs *national parks and *country parks. Scotland and Wales have their own organizations, **Scottish Natural Heritage** and the **Countryside Commission for Wales**.

C

the ˌ**county ˈchampionship** /ˈtʃæmpiənʃɪp/ (in Britain) a *cricket competition that takes place each year between teams representing *counties. **County cricket** matches last four days each and it is considered the most important British cricket competition. The **county champions** are the team that wins. Compare ONE-DAY CRICKET.

ˌ**county ˈcourt** *n* **1** (in England and Wales) a local court of law for minor civil cases (= ones concerned with the private rights of citizens rather than crimes), e.g. disputes about the ownership of land. Such cases are dealt with by a judge without a jury. See also CROWN COURT, MAGISTRATES' COURT. **2** (in some US states) a court of law in a county, where small civil cases or criminal cases are dealt with. ⇨ article at LEGAL SYSTEM IN THE US.

ˌ**County ˈDurham** /ˈdʌrəm/ the county of *Durham in north-east England. Its administrative centre is the city of *Durham.

ˌ**county ˈschool** *n* (in Britain) a school that is run by the *LEA of a particular *county. Compare VOLUNTARY SCHOOL. ⇨ article at SCHOOLS IN BRITAIN.

ˌ**county ˈtown** (*BrE*) (*AmE* **county seat**) the main town of a *county, where its local government and administration is based.

ˈ**Courage**™ a large British company that makes several types of *beer and owns many *pubs.

the ˌ**Courtauld ˈInstitute** /ˌkɔːtəʊld; *AmE* ˌkɔːrtoʊld/ an art gallery in London, England, famous for its collection of Impressionist paintings. It is also part of *London University, where people study the history of art and architecture.

ˈ**Courtaulds** /ˈkɔːtəʊldz; *AmE* ˈkɔːrtoʊldz/ a British company that makes natural and artificial fabrics. In the early 20th century it was one of the first companies to make artificial fabrics. The company was started in 1816 by Samuel Courtauld (1867–1947), who also gave money to set up the *Courtauld Institute.

ˈ**courtesy ˌtitle** *n* (in Britain) any title used by a member of the *peerage which is not legally valid but is given as a form of politeness, especially to the sons of *dukes.

the ˌ**Court of Apˈpeal** the highest court of law in England and Wales, apart from the *House of Lords. If somebody is found guilty in a court of law, they may apply for their case to be considered again at the Court of Appeal. ⇨ article at LEGAL SYSTEM IN BRITAIN.

the ˌ**Court of ˈSession** the highest civil (= not criminal) court of law in Scotland, apart from the *House of Lords. If somebody is found guilty in a *sheriff court, they may apply for their case to be considered again at the Court of Session.

the ˌ**Court of St ˈJames's** /snt ˈdʒeɪmzɪz/ the official name for the British royal court. Ambassadors in Britain are officially called ambassadors to the Court of St James's.

Coutts /kuːts/ a small and very old British bank, with mainly very rich customers. Queen *Elizabeth II has an account there. Its main office is in London.

ˈ**Covenanter** /ˈkʌvənəntə(r)/ *n* any of a group of 17th-century Scottish *Presbyterians who supported two **Covenants** (1638 and 1643). These were formal statements defending *Presbyterianism and protesting against the religious policies of *Charles I, who wanted to set up a Scottish Church with bishops, like the *Church of England. The Covenanters supported *Parliament in the *English Civil War.

ˌ**Covent ˈGarden** /ˌkɒvənt; *AmE* ˌkɑːvənt/ **1** a fashionable area in central London, England, that used to be London's main market for flowers, fruit and vegetables. In 1974 the market moved to *New Covent Garden and the market square was filled with small shops and restaurants. It is a popular area with tourists, and the street performers who come to entertain them: *We spent all day shopping and sitting around in cafés in Soho and Covent Garden.* **2** another name for the *Royal Opera House, which is next to the old Covent Garden market: *We've got two tickets for Cosi Fan Tutte at Covent Garden.*

street entertainment at Covent Garden

ˈ**Coventry** /ˈkɒvəntri; *AmE* ˈkɑːvəntri/ an industrial city in the English *Midlands, where cars have been made since the end of the 19th century. Many of its buildings were destroyed by bombs in *World War II, including its cathedral. A new cathedral was built after the war.

ˌ**covered ˈwagon** a form of transport used by American pioneers (= people moving west to settle there). The wagons were covered with canvas (= rough cloth) supported by iron hoops. Groups of horses usually pulled the wagons, but sometimes mules or oxen were used.

ˌ**Cow and ˈGate**™ a company that produces milk products and food for babies.

ˌNoel ˈ**Coward** /ˈkaʊəd; *AmE* ˈkaʊərd/ (1899–1973) an English writer and actor, well known for his elegant appearance and intelligent humour. He wrote several successful plays, including *The Vortex* (1924), *Hay Fever* (1925) and *Private Lives* (1930), and film scripts such as **Brief Encounter* (1945). He was also well known for writing and performing comic and romantic songs, such as *Mad Dogs and Englishmen*. He was made a *knight in 1970.

ˈ**cowboy** *n* **1** (*also infml* ˈ**cowpoke** /ˈkaʊpəʊk/ ˈ**cowpuncher** /ˈkaʊpʌntʃə(r)/) a man who looks after cattle in the US West. He usually rides a horse to move and control them. Cowboys were especially important during the late 19th century, when they were needed to drive cattle over long distances. They were given a good public image in books and *westerns, and Americans greatly admire their tough outdoor life and independent spirit. They still exist in the western US, and some compete in *rodeos. See also COWBOYS AND INDIANS. **2** (*BrE infml disapprov*) a dishonest or careless person in business, especially one who has no qualifications: *The house builders were just a bunch of cowboys.*

ˌ**cowboys and ˈIndians** *n* [U] a children's game in which some children pretend to be *cowboys and others pretend to be Indians (Native Americans). They have imaginary fights, sometimes wearing special clothes, based on what they have seen in *westerns: *The kids were playing cowboys and Indians in the back garden.*

ˌColin ˈ**Cowdrey** /ˈkaʊdri/ (1932–) an English cricketer, well known for scoring many runs (= points). He played for *Kent and was the captain of England in the 1960s. He was made a *knight in 1992 and a *life peer in 1997.

Cowes /kaʊz/ a port on the *Isle of Wight. Once a year a series of international yacht races (= for boats with sails) takes place there, called **Cowes Week**. This is an important social event, and is usually attended by members of the *royal family.

ˌWilliam ˈ**Cowper** /ˈkuːpə(r)/ (1731–1800) an English poet whose work is simpler and more natural than most 18th-century English poetry. He was very unhappy for most of his life, and much of his work is sad. His best-known works are hymns, such as *God Moves in a Mysterious Way*.

ˈ**Cox's ˌorange ˈpippin** /ˈkɒksɪz; *AmE* ˈkɑːksɪz/ (*also* **Cox**) *n* (*pl* **Coxes**) a type of English apple with a sweet flavour and greenish-yellow and red skin. Many people think it is the best apple for eating.

the **CPRE** /ˌsiː piː ɑːr ˈiː/ ⇨ COUNCIL FOR THE PROTECTION OF RURAL ENGLAND.

the **CPS** /ˌsiː piː ˈes/ ⇨ CROWN PROSECUTION SERVICE.

ˌ**cracker-barrel phiˈlosophy** *n* (*AmE infml*) honest, simple or direct opinions such as those expressed during a friendly conversation or argument. The phrase was originally used for discussions around the large barrel of crackers (= thin, dry biscuits) once kept in most large US food shops.

ˈ**Cracker Jack**™ a sticky US sweet/candy, popular with children, made of caramel, popcorn and peanuts. It is sold in a box that contains a small gift.

ˈ**Craft, DeˈsIgn and Techˈnology** ⇨ CDT.

ˌSteve ˈ**Cram** /ˈkræm/ (1960–) an English runner who won many races in the 1980s. In 1985 he held the world records for running 1 500 metres, 2 000 metres and one mile.

ˌStephen ˈ**Crane**[1] /ˈkreɪn/ (1871–1900) a US journalist who wrote poems and realistic novels. His most famous novel is *The Red Badge of Courage* (1895) about a frightened soldier who finds courage in the American *Civil War. Crane went to live in England in 1897 but died three years later at the age of 28.

ˌWalter ˈ**Crane**[2] (1845–1915) an English artist and member of the *Arts and Crafts Movement. His colourful book illustrations had a strong influence on the development of children's books.

ˌThomas ˈ**Cranmer** /ˈkrænmə(r)/ (1489–1556) the first *Anglican *Archbishop of Canterbury. He was influenced by the ideas of Martin Luther, and supported King *Henry VIII over the ending of his marriage to *Catherine of Aragon and in establishing the *Church of England. He was responsible for the *Book of Common Prayer and had a strong influence on the *Reformation. He was killed by burning when the *Roman Catholic *Mary I became Queen.

ˈ**Cranwell** /ˈkrænwel/ a military college in *Lincolnshire, where people are trained to be officers in the *RAF.

Walter Crane's illustration of the nursery rhyme Mary, Mary, Quite Contrary

ˌJoan ˈ**Crawford**[1] /ˈkrɔːfəd; *AmE* ˈkrɔːfərd/ (1908–77) a US film actor who was a *Hollywood star for more than 40 years. She won an *Oscar for *Mildred Pierce* (1945) and acted with Bette *Davis in *Whatever Happened to Baby Jane?* (1962). Her daughter Christina wrote a book, *Mommie Dearest* (1978), about how unpleasant Crawford was as a mother, and there was a film version in 1981 in which Faye Dunaway played Crawford.

ˌMichael ˈ**Crawford**[2] /ˈkrɔːfəd; *AmE* ˈkrɔːfərd/ (1942–) an English comedy actor, especially on television where he played the part of Frank Spencer in *Some Mothers Do 'Ave 'Em* (1973–8). He later had international success in musical stage shows, especially *Barnum* (1981) and *The Phantom of the Opera* (1986).

Crayˈola™ /kreɪˈəʊlə; *AmE* kreɪˈoʊlə/ a US make of crayons (= coloured pencils or sticks of soft coloured chalk or wax) which have been popular with children for many years and are sold in boxes of different sizes in many countries. Binney & Smith of Easton, *Pennsylvania have produced them since 1903 and had made 100 000 million by 1996.

the ˈ**Crazy Gang** a group of British comedians who first gave a *music-hall(1) show together in 1932, and continued to perform as a team for the next 30 years. See also FLANAGAN.

ˈ**Crazy Horse** (*c.* 1849–77) a *Native-American leader of the *Sioux people. In 1876 he and *Sitting Bull defeated General *Custer and his soldiers at the Battle of *Little Bighorn. He was captured and put in prison the following year, and was killed while trying to escape. A large **Crazy Horse Memorial**, showing him riding a horse, is being carved into Thunderhead Mountain in *South Dakota.

ˌ**Cream of ˈWheat**™ *n* [U] a US wheat cereal which is cooked and eaten hot. It was first produced in 1893 and is now made by *Nabisco.

ˌ**cream ˈpuff** *n* a type of cake made of very light pastry filled with cream or custard.

ˌ**cream ˈsoda** *n* [U, C] a sweet fizzy drink, flavoured with vanilla: *a glass of cream soda.*

ˌ**cream ˈtea** *n* (*BrE*) an afternoon meal consisting of tea and *scones (= small cakes made with flour, fat and milk) eaten with *clotted cream and jam. Cream teas are traditional in *Devon and *Cornwall in south-west England, and are popular with visitors and tourists.

C

credit cards

Credit cards are increasingly used instead of cash or cheques to pay for goods and services. When the **cardholder** is present, for example in a shop, the card is **swiped** and a bill is printed which the cardholder has to sign. Purchases by credit card can also be made by mail, over the telephone or on the Internet. Credit cards can be used to get money from a cash dispenser. Cards linked to organizations such as ***Visa** and **MasterCard** can be used in many countries. People with good **credit ratings**, i.e. who earn a good salary and have no debts, may get a **gold card** with a higher **credit limit**. Credit card holders receive a monthly **statement** of all their purchases and must pay part of the bill each month. They are charged interest on the amount they do not pay.

The term *credit card* is sometimes used to include **charge cards**, though the whole amount owed on a charge card account must be paid each month. One of the most famous charge cards is ***American Express**. Some people have an **affinity card**, a credit card that is linked to a *charity. Each time the card is used the card company pays a small amount of money to the charity. Credit cards from shops, called **store cards** or sometimes charge cards, can be used only in branches of the shop concerned. **Debit cards** or **banker's cards**, such as ***Switch** and ***Delta**, can be used to pay for goods but the whole amount is automatically deducted from the user's bank account within a few days.

Most Americans have a variety of **plastic money**, including Visa and MasterCard (often more than one of each), American Express and ***Diners Club**, as well as store cards. People decide which cards to have depending on the way they plan to use them. For example, some cards are free but have a high rate of interest, called the **annual percentage rate** or **APR**; others have an **annual fee**, but charge lower interest rates, and so are good for people who do not pay the whole bill every month. Americans use credit cards to pay for everything from a meal in a fast-food restaurant to university fees. Some companies give **incentives** to cardholders to persuade them to use their cards. For instance, at the end of each year, the Discover card gives people back a small proportion of the money that they spent. Many Americans 'max out' their cards, spending up to the credit limit on each.

In Britain credits cards are commonly used in petrol stations, shops, hotels, restaurants, theatres and travel agents. Using them is safer than carrying a lot of cash and more convenient than writing a cheque. However, if a card is stolen and used by the thief the cardholder may have to pay the bill unless the card company is told immediately.

ˈcredit ˌunion (*also* **co-operative credit union**) *n* (*AmE*) a type of US co-operative bank. Members buy shares, and the bank lends money to them at a low rate. Most credit unions are for people who work together, as in a hospital or a university.

Cree /kriː/ *n* (*pl* **Crees** *or* **Cree**) a member of a *Native-American people. They were hunters, originally from Canada where most Crees still live, but one group moved south to land that is now the US state of *Montana.

Creek /kriːk/ *n* (*pl* **Creeks** *or* **Creek**) a member of a *Native-American people. They were mostly farmers, originally in the states of *Alabama and *Georgia. They were one of the *Five Civilized Tribes. Under their leader *Tecumseh they were defeated by General Andrew *Jackson at the Battle of Horseshoe Bend (1814) in Alabama. They were then moved to the West.

ˈCreole *n* **1** [C] (in the US) a person descended from French or Spanish people who settled in the southern states, especially around *New Orleans. Creoles speak a mixed language of their own and are known for their spicy food. **2** [U] the language of the Creoles. Compare CAJUN.

Crewe /kruː/ a town in *Cheshire, England, which became an important railway junction (= a place where several lines meet) during the 19th century.

ˌMichael **ˈCrichton** /ˈkraɪtən/ (1942–) a popular US writer of novels and films, mostly involving science and medicine. His books include *The Andromeda Strain* (1969), *Jurassic Park* (1988) and *The Lost World* (1996), all of which he adapted for films.

ˌFrancis **ˈCrick** /ˈkrɪk/ (1916–) an English scientist. His work with James *Watson at the *Cavendish Laboratory led to the discovery of the structure of DNA in 1953. Crick, Watson and another scientist shared the *Nobel Prize for this work in 1962. Crick's later career has involved work on the visual system and the brain, and he published a book, *The Astonishing Hypothesis*, on this subject in 1994. He became a member of the *Order of Merit in 1992.

Francis Crick and James Watson

Cricket ⇨ article.

Crime ⇨ article.

the **Criˌmean ˈWar** /kraɪˌmiːən/ a war fought by Britain, France and Turkey against Russia between 1853 and 1856 in the Crimea, a part of the Ukraine. Russia wanted power over Turkey, and Britain and France wanted to end Russia's power in the Black Sea. Most of the military action was around Sebastopol, the Russian navy base. It was the first war during which the European public were able to follow events as they happened, because of the invention of the telegraph (= a device for sending messages along wires by the use of electric current). See also CHARGE OF THE LIGHT BRIGADE, NIGHTINGALE.

ˈCrimewatch /ˈkraɪmwɒtʃ; *AmE* ˈkraɪmwɑːtʃ/ a British television programme on *BBC1. It describes serious crimes that the police need help with. Members of the public call the programme if they have any information about the crimes. *Crimewatch* began in 1984.

the **ˈCriminal Inˌvestiˈgation Deˌpartment** ⇨ CID.

the **ˈCriminal ˈJustice and ˌPublic ˈOrder Act** a British law passed in 1994 dealing with a number of social and legal issues. It gave the police new powers to prevent people gathering in large groups, especially *New Age travellers and people attending outdoor *rave parties. It also introduced new laws to deal with terrorism, and allowed *secure training centres to be established for children who repeatedly break the law. The Act was opposed by many people

Cricket

Cricket is a summer sport particularly associated with England and some other *Commonwealth countries. It was traditionally played by men, though there are now several women's teams. In England the game is played between April and September. A game of cricket being played on a village green by players dressed in white is a traditional English summer scene.

The game

Cricket is a complicated game played with **bats** and a leather ball between two teams of 11 players on a grass **pitch**. Each team **bats** (= hits the ball) for an **innings**, trying to score **runs**. Members of the opposing team **bowl** (= throw the ball with a straight arm) and **field** (= try to catch or stop the ball after it has been hit). Their aim is to get the **batsmen out** for as few runs as possible.

Two batsmen are **in** (= on the pitch) at the same time, each defending a **wicket**. A wicket is a set of three upright wooden posts, called *stumps*, with two short pieces of wood, called *bails*, resting on top of them. The two wickets are 22 yards apart, and runs are scored as the batsmen run between them. There is a **boundary** round the edge of the ground. A batsman scores four runs if a ball he or she has hit runs over the boundary, and six runs if it goes over the boundary before it hits the ground. A **bowler** from the opposing team bowls six times (an *over*) from one end, and then a different bowler bowls the next over from the other end. Batsmen can be out for a variety of reasons. An innings usually ends when all but one of the batting team are out. In many matches there are two innings for each team.

Most spectators like to see good hitting and a lot of runs being scored, but play can be very slow and people who do not like or understand cricket usually find it boring compared with other sports. Matches may last for several days, though shorter **one-day**, **single-innings** or **limited-over** matches are popular. Until 1969, the rules of the game were decided by *Marylebone Cricket Club (the MCC) in London. Since then, the Cricket Council has governed the game.

Competitions

Cricket is played at many levels, from informal games on the beach to matches between schools, villages and professional county sides. In England and Wales 18 counties compete each year in the *county championship. Yorkshire has been the most successful and has won it 29 times. Coloured clothing now sometimes replaces the traditional white. People who do not approve of this development call it 'pyjama cricket'.

cricket: a bowler bowls to a batsman while the wicket-keeper and fielders wait and the umpire watches

The English national team plays **test matches** against other national sides, including those of Australia, India, New Zealand, Pakistan, Sri Lanka, the West Indies and Zimbabwe. England and Australia compete for the *Ashes. Test matches last up to five days. Those played in England are broadcast on British radio and television.

The most famous cricket grounds in England, where test matches are played, are Lord's and the Oval (both in London), Old Trafford (Manchester), Headingley (Leeds), Trent Bridge (Nottingham) and Edgbaston (Birmingham). Famous English players have included Dr W G *Grace, Jack *Hobbs, Len *Hutton, Denis *Compton, Geoffrey *Boycott, Freddy *Trueman and Ian *Botham.

'Not cricket'

Some words and phrases used in cricket have become idioms with a wider use. Any unfair action on or off the pitch may be described as *not cricket*, because cricket used to be thought of as a *gentleman's sport and high standards of behaviour were expected from players. Crowds at cricket matches traditionally stayed calm and applauded politely when opponents played well. This is not always true now. The idiom is rather old-fashioned, but is still used humorously.

If somebody is *batting on a sticky wicket* they probably do not have enough evidence to support their theories or are finding it difficult to defend themselves against criticism. In cricket, balls do not bounce very well if the wicket is 'sticky' (= wet and muddy). And when it is said that somebody has *had a good innings*, it means that they have had a long life or career.

---

who thought it gave the police too much power and restricted people's freedom unfairly.

ˌDr ˈ**Crippen** /ˈkrɪpən/ (Hawley Harvey Crippen 1862–1910) a US doctor who came to London in 1896. He fell in love with his secretary Ethel le Neve, murdered his wife and hid her body in the cellar of his house. Crippen and Ethel tried to escape on a ship to New York, with Ethel dressed as a boy, but the captain became suspicious and used the ship's radio to tell the British police. Crippen was hanged for the murder, but Ethel was found not guilty and lived until 1967.

ˌStafford ˈ**Cripps** /ˌstæfəd ˈkrɪps; *AmE* ˌstæfərd/ (1889–1952) a British *Labour politician who is best remembered for his policy of 'austerity' after *World War II, when as *Chancellor of the Exchequer he kept a tight control over Britain's economy. He was the nephew of Beatrice *Webb, and was made a *knight in 1930.

ˈ**Crisco**™ /ˈkrɪskəʊ; *AmE* ˈkrɪskoʊ/ a US make of vegetable shortening (= fat used to make pastry crisp), produced by *Procter & Gamble. It is mostly used for making cakes, sweet biscuits, etc. It was first sold in 1911.

Crime

Crime in Britain

Crime has increased in Britain, as in many countries, since the early 1950s, though recently the number of crimes reported to the *police has fallen. In 1996 there were 9 700 crimes for every 100 000 people, of which the police solved 27%. Over 60 000 people are in *prison for crimes they have committed.

People living in inner city and urban areas are the ones most likely to be victims of crime. **Burglary** (= stealing from a house) is twice as likely there as elsewhere. **Theft** (= stealing goods or property) is the commonest crime, though it fell by 14% in the period 1992–5. **Car theft** is relatively common: in 1995 almost one in five car owners had their car stolen, or had property stolen from inside it. **Criminal damage** or vandalism is an increasing problem. Offences that involve loss or damage to property account for 92% of all crime.

The number of violent crimes is increasing. **Murders** and different types of **assault** (= violent attack) are usually widely reported by the media. The number of **rape** cases reported to the police went up by 50% between 1988 and 1992. **Robbery** (= taking property from a person by force) and **mugging** (= attacking someone in the street and stealing their property) also increased significantly. Racially-motivated attacks and crimes against children, especially sexual abuse and paedophilia (= sexual acts on children), arouse public anger and concern about moral standards.

In 1995 guns were used in 13 000 crimes in England and Wales. The killing of a class of school-children at *Dunblane, Scotland in 1996 greatly increased public feeling against people being allowed to own guns and resulted in two *Acts of Parliament banning public ownership of handguns. Since 1996 there have also been restrictions on the manufacture of some types of knives. It is now illegal to sell sharp-bladed knives to people under 16.

Crime in the US

The US has a reputation for having a lot of crime, especially violent crime. For every 100 000 people, there were 597 violent crimes in 1980 rising to 746 in 1994, nine of which were murders. **Larceny** (= theft) is also common. Many people believe that the increase in crime is linked to the use of drugs. Guns are easy to buy in the US and are often used in crime. A new crime that began in the 1990s is **carjacking**: criminals with guns enter cars that have stopped at traffic lights and make the driver leave the car, or drive to a place where there are not many people around. They take the car, and any money or jewellery, but usually leave the driver unharmed.

The increase in crime does not affect people equally. Crime is worse in cities, especially in the inner cities where poorer people live. African Americans are more likely to be victims of violent crime than whites.

Crime prevention

At a local level, many British people have joined *Neighbourhood Watch schemes, which encourage people to report anything suspicious happening near their houses. There are more policemen **on the beat** (= walking round an area, not driving in cars) to prevent trouble. Community policemen go into schools to talk to children and teenagers to try to stop them from taking part in crime. In 1995, almost four out of ten offenders were aged 14–20. Young people are responsible for a lot of **petty crime** (= less serious offences) such as **shoplifting**, stealing from shops, as well as more serious crimes such as **arson** (= deliberately setting fire to a building), **drug-dealing** and **joyriding** (= stealing a car and driving it round the town very fast).

Closed-circuit television (= video cameras linked to special television screens in police stations) has been installed in many city centres to deter violence and prevent crimes such as **ram-raiding** (= driving a stolen car through a shop window and stealing the goods inside). Some people think that, because video cameras record the activities of innocent people as well as criminals, they are a threat to personal freedom. Nationally, there are repeated calls for harsher penalties and, sometimes, for the return of *capital punishment to deter criminals.

Fear and fascination

Fear of becoming a victim of crime has increased, and people are particularly afraid of being burgled. Some people, especially women and old people, are scared to go out alone in the evening for fear of rape or mugging. In some areas, parents do not allow their children to walk to school alone in case they are attacked or abducted (= taken away). Many people now hesitate to go and help someone being attacked in case they are attacked themselves, but those who do go to help are seen as heroes.

Despite this fear, many people enjoy stories about real and imagined crimes, especially murder. One of the most popular programmes on British television is **Crimewatch*, which asks the public for their help in solving real crimes. Other favourite television programmes include *The *Bill* and **NYPD Blue*, and films of the **Inspector Morse* stories and novels by Agatha *Christie. From time to time there is anxiety about the amount of violence shown on television and fear that it influences people's behaviour in real life.

ˈ**Crisis** /ˈkraɪsɪs/ a British charity that each year gives poor people in large cities food, clothing and shelter in the weeks just before Christmas.

ˌDavy ˈ**Crockett** /ˌdeɪvi ˈkrɒkɪt; *AmE* ˈkrɑːkɪt/ (1786–1836) a famous American *frontiersman from *Tennessee. He was also a soldier with General Andrew *Jackson and a politician, being elected to the US *Congress (1827–31 and 1833–5). He was killed at the *Alamo. Many stories are told of his life. Walt *Disney made a television series about him in the 1950s and the film *Davy Crockett* (1955).

ˈ**Crockford's** /ˈkrɒkfədz; *AmE* ˈkrɑːkfərdz/ (Crockford's Clerical Directory) a book that gives details of all living *Anglican priests and ministers of the Church. It is published every two years and was first published in 1860.

ˈ**Crockpot**™ /ˈkrɒkpɒt; *AmE* ˈkrɑːkpɑːt/ *n* a US make of electric pot that cooks food slowly at low temperatures.

ˌRichmal ˈ**Crompton** /ˌrɪtʃməl ˈkrɒmptən; *AmE* ˈkrɑːmptən/ (1890–1969) a female English teacher who wrote the *William books.

detail from Samuel Cooper's painting of Oliver Cromwell

ˌOliver ˈ**Cromwell**[1] /ˈkrɒmwel; *AmE* ˈkrɑːmwel/ (1599–1658) an English general and politician who for a short time ruled England, Scotland and Ireland. Cromwell was a *Puritan who began his political career as the *Member of Parliament for Huntingdon in 1628. When the *English Civil War started in 1642, he gathered soldiers in his area to fight for Parliament and soon became the leader of the *New Model Army and the greatest soldier in England. He was one of those who signed the death warrant of King *Charles I in 1649. As a leader of the *Commonwealth, he was responsible for the very cruel treatment of those who were opposed to the *Puritans in Ireland and Scotland. In 1653 Cromwell dismissed parliament and became the *Lord Protector of England, Scotland and Ireland, with almost the same power as a king. He was even offered the crown, but refused it. In 1658, he died of malaria and was buried in *Westminster Abbey. Cromwell's son Richard took his place as Lord Protector for a short time after his death, but he did not have his father's gifts as a leader, and in 1660 *Charles II became king at the *Restoration. Oliver Cromwell's body was dug up and his head was put on a pole on the roof of one of the buildings in *Westminster(1) for 24 years.

Cromwell is also remembered for a famous remark he made to the artist Peter Lely (1618–80). He said, 'Mr Lely, I desire you would use all your skill to paint my picture truly like me, and not flatter me at all; but remark (= take notice of) all these roughnesses, pimples, warts, and everything as you see me, otherwise I will never pay a farthing for it.' People often say that something or somebody should be shown *warts and all*, meaning that faults or unpleasant features should not be left out.

ˌThomas ˈ**Cromwell**[2] /ˈkrɒmwel; *AmE* ˈkrɑːmwel/ (*c.* 1485–1540) the chief minister to King *Henry VIII during the 1530s. After the fall of Thomas *Wolsey, Cromwell arranged the king's divorce from *Catherine of Aragon and later organized the *Dissolution of the Monasteries. In 1540, Cromwell was made the Earl of Essex, but four months later the King accused him of treason and had his head cut off. Cromwell said at his execution that he died a Catholic.

ˌWalter ˈ**Cronkite** /ˈkrɒŋkaɪt; *AmE* ˈkrɑːŋkaɪt/ (1916–) a US television journalist who presented the national CBS Evening News programme from 1962 to 1981. He ended each programme by saying, 'And that's the way it is.' Cronkite was known for his honesty and in 1973 was chosen as the 'Most Trusted Man in America'.

ˈ**crop** ˌ**circle** ⇨ CORN CIRCLE.

ˈ**croquet** *n* [U] a game played on grass in which the players hit balls through a series of hoops, using a mallet (= a wooden hammer with a long handle). Croquet became popular among the *upper classes in Britain in the 1850s, and is still often regarded often as an upper-class game today. The All England Croquet Club began at *Wimbledon in 1868. The four countries where croquet is most played (Britain, Australia, New Zealand and the US) compete every three or four years for the MacRobertson Shield.

ˌBing ˈ**Crosby** /ˌbɪŋ ˈkrɒzbi; *AmE* ˈkrɑːzbi/ (1904–77) a US singer and film actor. He was called 'the old crooner' because of his fine voice and relaxed style. His recording of *White Christmas* (1942) has sold more copies than any other record ever made. He won an *Oscar for the film *Going My Way* (1944) and made a series of seven comedy films (1940–47) with Bob *Hope, all with 'road' in the title, including *Road to Morocco* (1942).

ˌ**Crosse and** ˈ**Blackwell** /ˌkrɒs, ˈblækwel; *AmE* ˌkrɑːs/ a British company that makes a lot of different food products.

crosswords

Crosswords, or **crossword puzzles**, first appeared in the US in the early 20th century. Today, many people in the US and in Britain regularly **do crosswords**, sometimes on the bus or train on their way to work. Most newspapers and magazines contain at least one crossword and there are often prizes for people who send in the correct **solution**. Books of crosswords are also popular.

Solving a crossword involves answering a set of **clues**. The answers are words or phrases which fit together in a patterned grid or **diagram**. The clues are usually numbered and listed as **across** and **down**, according to whether the answer reads across the grid or from top to bottom.

There are two basic types of crossword, called in Britain **quick crosswords** and **cryptic crosswords**. In quick crosswords the clues are usually definitions of the answers. This is much the most common type of crossword in the US, where the grids are usually a lot bigger and contain many more words. These crosswords are not necessarily easy, and the one in the Sunday issue of the *New York Times* is considered very difficult.

Cryptic crosswords, which began in Britain and are much more popular there than in any other country, have clues which contain both a definition of the answer and a word puzzle involving the letters in it. One common type of word puzzle is an **anagram**, in which the letters of the answer word are rearranged in the clue to form another word or phrase. For example, CARTHORSE and SHORT RACE are both anagrams of the word ORCHESTRA.

Crow /krəʊ; *AmE* kroʊ/ *n* (*pl* **Crows** *or* **Crow**) a member of a *Native-American people who lived on land that is now *Montana and *Wyoming. They were hunters and grew tobacco. They helped the US Army against the *Sioux people. Most Crows now live on a reservation (= land given and protected by the US government) in southern Montana.

ˌSheryl ˈ**Crow** /ˌʃerəl ˈkrəʊ; *AmE* ˈkroʊ/ (1963–) a US singer who also writes songs. Her first album was *Tuesday Night Music Club* (1994), and that year she won three *Grammy awards, one as Best New Artist and two for the song *All I Wanna Do*. She has also received a Grammy for the song *If It Makes You Happy* (1996).

croquet

ˌthe ˈ**Crown** *n* [sing] (in Britain) the power and authority of the State, as represented by the King or Queen. It is used in phrases such as *Crown Estate, although most things are now the responsibility of the government rather than the King or Queen. ⇨ note at BRITISH CONSTITUTION.

ˌ**Crown ˈAgent** a member of an organization, started in 1833 by the British government, which provides financial and commercial services for foreign governments and international organizations. Crown agents are professional people appointed by the government. Their full official title is Crown Agents for Overseas Governments and Administrations.

ˌ**Crown ˈColony** ⇨ OVERSEAS TERRITORY.

ˌ**Crown ˈCourt** *n* (in England and Wales) a local court in larger towns and cities where serious criminal cases are tried by a judge and jury. Cases may come to the Crown Court when a magistrates' court decides that they are too serious for it to deal with. If a decision of the Crown Court is questioned, the case goes to the *Court of Appeal. See also COUNTY COURT. ⇨ article at LEGAL SYSTEM IN BRITAIN.

ˌ**Crown ˈDependency** *n* a term applied to either of two places close to the British mainland: the *Channel Islands and the *Isle of Man. These have their own governments, which make decisions about the law, police, education and other matters, but rely on the British *Crown for their defence and foreign policy. Compare OVERSEAS TERRITORY.

ˌ**Crown ˈDerby** /ˈdɑːbi; *AmE* ˈdɑːrbi/ *n* [U] a type of china (= fine pottery) made in *Derby, England, in the 18th and 19th centuries. Objects made of Crown Derby are marked with a crown over the letter D.

the ˌ**Crown Eˈstate** all the lands owned by the British king or queen and the money that is made through them. In 1760, King *George III gave up the monarch's rights to these in return for the *Civil List, a payment made to the King or Queen every year by Parliament. As a result the money from the Crown Estate, which is managed by the **Crown Estate Commissioners**, is now collected by the government on behalf of the British people.

ˌ**crown green ˈbowls** *n* [U] a form of the game of *bowls that is played on an area of grass with a slightly raised centre, instead of on a flat surface. It is played especially in the north of England.

the ˌ**Crown ˈJewels** the jewels and other precious objects worn or carried by the British king or queen on official occasions. They are kept for the public to see in the *Tower of London and include several crowns, sceptres and swords. Only two small items are from before 1660, as the original Crown Jewels were destroyed during the *Commonwealth under Oliver *Cromwell. See also KOHINOOR.

the ˌ**Crown Proseˈcution ˌService** (*abbr* **CPS**) an independent organization started in 1986 that decides whether a person should be charged with a crime in a court of law in England or Wales. Before 1986, the police had made this decision themselves. The person in charge of the Crown Prosecution Service is the * Director of Public Prosecutions.

the ˌ**Crucible ˈTheatre** a theatre, opened in 1971, in *Sheffield, England. As well as showing plays, the theatre is well known as the place where major *snooker competitions are held.

Crufts /krʌfts/ the most important dog show in Britain, held for four days every January at the *National Exhibition Centre in *Birmingham. It is run by the *Kennel Club. The show is named after Charles Cruft, who started it in London in 1886: *One of her dogs was Best of Breed at Crufts in 1998.*

ˌGeorge ˈ**Cruickshank** /ˈkrʊkʃænk/ (1792–1878) an English artist who was famous for his political cartoons. He also drew illustrations for the books of many famous authors, including Charles *Dickens and Walter *Scott.

ˌTom ˈ**Cruise** /ˈkruːz / (1962–) a US actor. He won a *Golden Globe Award for *Born on the Fourth of July* (1990) but is probably best remembered for playing a US Navy pilot in *Top Gun* (1986). His more recent films have included *Mission Impossible* (1996) and *Jerry McGuire* (1997). Cruise is married to the actor Nicole Kidman.

Tom Cruise in Jerry McGuire

the **Cruˈsades** a series of military expeditions between the 11th and 14th centuries, in which armies from the Christian countries of Europe tried to get back the Holy Land (= what is now Israel, Palestine, Jordan and Egypt) from the Muslims. The soldiers who took part in the Crusades were called **Crusaders**. The best known British Crusader was King *Richard I. The Crusades achieved very little, but as a result of them new ideas were exchanged, trade was improved, and new goods such as sugar and cotton came to Europe for the first time.

Cruse /kruːz/ a British charity formed in 1959 that gives help and advice to people when a relative or friend has died. Its full name is Cruse – Bereavement Care.

ˌ**Crystal ˈPalace 1 the Crystal Palace** a very large building made of glass and metal, designed in nine days by Joseph Paxton (1801–65) for the *Great Exhibition of 1851. It took six months to put up in *Hyde Park in London. After the Exhibition, it was taken to a new park in south London. In 1936 it burned down. Its name was given to it by the humorous magazine *Punch*. **2** a football club in south London: *He plays for Crystal Palace.* **3** a stadium where sports contests are held in south London.

CST /ˌsiː es ˈtiː/ ⇨ CENTRAL STANDARD TIME.

CTC /ˌsiː tiː ˈsiː/ ⇨ CITY TECHNOLOGY COLLEGE.

the ˌ**Cuban ˈmissile ˌcrisis** /ˌkjuːbən/ a dangerous political situation that developed in 1962 between the US and USSR. President *Kennedy became aware that there were Soviet nuclear weapons in Cuba and sent the US Navy to stop Soviet ships from bringing more. It seemed possible that there would be a nuclear war between the two countries, but the Soviet leader Nikita Khrushchev ordered the Russian ships to turn back and later removed all of the weapons.

ˈ**Cub Scout** (*also* **Cub**) *n* (in Britain) a member of the junior branch of the *Scouts, for boys aged between 8 and 10. Since 1992 girls have been able to join the British Cub Scouts, but only in areas where the local group has agreed to accept them. The adult in charge of a group (or 'pack') of Cubs, is known as *Akela*, from a character in *The *Jungle Book*.

ˌGeorge **ˈCukor** /ˈkjuːkɔː(r)/ (1899–1983) a US film director. He is best remembered for his film comedies, including *The Philadelphia Story* (1940), *Pat and Mike* (1952) and **My Fair Lady* (1964), for which he received an *Oscar. He was 82 when he directed his last film.

the **ˈCullinan ˌdiamond** /ˈkʌlɪnən/ the largest diamond ever found, weighing about 620 grams. It was named after Thomas Cullinan, the head of the Transvaal mine in which it was found in 1905. Two years later the Transvaal government bought it for $1 000 000 and presented it to King *Edward VII. It was then cut into nine large stones and 96 small ones and used in the *Crown Jewels. Compare KOHINOOR.

the ˌBattle of **Culˈloden** /kəˈlɒdn/ a battle (1746) fought on Culloden Moor near Inverness in Scotland between the mainly English soldiers led by the Duke of *Cumberland (the second son of King *George II) and the Scottish army of Charles Edward *Stuart (*Bonny Prince Charlie). Charles was defeated and most of his soldiers killed. Culloden was the last battle to be fought in Britain, and it brought the *Jacobite rebellions to an end.

ˈCumberland¹ /ˈkʌmbələnd; *AmE* ˈkʌmbərlənd/ a former county in north-west England. In 1974 it was joined with *Westmorland and part of *Lancashire(1) to form *Cumbria.

the ˌDuke of **ˈCumberland²** /ˈkʌmbələnd; *AmE* ˈkʌmbərlənd/ (1721–65) an English general, the second son of King *George II. He defeated the Scottish army at the Battle of *Culloden and then treated them so severely that he was given the nickname 'Butcher Cumberland'.

the **ˌCumberland ˈGap** /ˌkʌmbələnd; *AmE* ˈkʌmbərlənd/ a way through the Cumberland Mountains between the US states of *Virginia and *Kentucky. It was used by Daniel *Boone and the early settlers of Kentucky.

ˌCumberland ˈsausage /ˌkʌmbələnd; *AmE* ˈkʌmbərlənd/ *n* [U, C] a very long, spicy pork sausage traditionally made in the north of England. It is twisted into a spiral before cooking.

ˈCumbria a county in north-west England, on the border with Scotland. It consists of the former counties of *Cumberland and *Westmorland and part of *Lancashire. It contains the *Lake District and *Scafell Pike, the highest mountain in England.

ˌcum ˈlaude /ˌkʊm ˈlaʊdeɪ/ (in the US) the Latin expression, meaning 'with praise', used to indicate a high academic achievement of a college or university student who has completed his or her studies. It is the lowest of the three highest grades and is shown on the diploma (= document awarded for completing a course of study). Compare MAGNA CUM LAUDE, SUMMA CUM LAUDE.

ˌE E **ˈCummings** /ˌiː iː ˈkʌmɪŋz/ (Edward Estlin Cummings 1894–1962) a US writer of poetry and novels. His poems contain highly original language and were often printed in an unusual style, e.g. using only small letters. His poetry collections include *Tulips and Chimneys* (1923). His best-known novel is *The Enormous Room* (1922).

ˌSamuel **Cuˈnard** /kjuːˈnɑːd; *AmE* kjuːˈnɑːrd/ (1787–1865) a Canadian ship owner who in 1839 started a service carrying passengers across the Atlantic between Britain and North America. The journey then took about two weeks. The company became known as the **Cunard Line** and had many famous ships, among them the *Mauretania* and the **Lusitania* from 1907, the **Queen Mary* (1936), the **Queen Elizabeth* (1940) and the **QE2* (1967).

ˌJack **ˈCunningham** /ˈkʌnɪŋəm/ (1939–) a British *Labour politician. He became a *Member of Parliament in 1970 and held several important positions in the Labour *Shadow Cabinet before becoming *Secretary of State for Agriculture, Fisheries and Food in the Labour government of 1997. In this position he had special responsibility for dealing with the problem of *BSE.

the **ˈCup ˌFinal** an important football event in England every year. The two teams that remain after playing in the *FA Cup competition play against each other at *Wembley in the Cup Final. There is a separate Scottish Cup Final.

ˌcurate's ˈegg *n* [sing] a thing that is partly good and partly bad. The phrase comes from a cartoon in the British magazine **Punch* in 1895, in which a nervous young curate (= priest) is having breakfast with a *bishop. He is asked if his egg is bad and, not wanting to upset the bishop, replies, 'Oh no, my Lord! ... Parts of it are excellent!': *Their investment plan shows the familiar curate's egg pattern of some bits doing well and some bits doing badly.*

Edˌwina **ˈCurrie** /edˌwiːnə ˈkʌri/ (1946–) a former British *Conservative politician who is known for saying what she thinks in a very direct way. A famous example was when in 1988 as a health minister she caused a lot of problems for the egg industry by saying that most eggs produced in Britain were infected with salmonella (= a germ that can cause food poisoning). Currie has also written some novels.

ˌCurrier and ˈIves /ˌkʌriər ənd ˈaɪvz/ a US company (1835–1907) that produced more than 7 000 different coloured lithographs (= prints made from metal plates) of US life in the 19th century. The pictures are still popular and often used on greetings cards.

On the Mississippi,
a lithograph by Currier and Ives, 1869

ˈCurrys /ˈkʌriz/ (in Britain) a chain of shops that sell electrical goods: *You can buy it at your local Currys.*

ˌTony **ˈCurtis** /ˈkɜːtɪs; *AmE* ˈkɜːrtɪs/ (1925–) a US film actor who has appeared in a wide variety of films, including *Some Like It Hot* (1959) and *The Boston Strangler* (1968). His former wife Janet Leigh (1927–) and their daughter Jamie Lee Curtis (1958–) are also film actors (1995).

the **ˌCurtis ˈCup** /ˌkɜːtɪs; *AmE* ˌkɜːrtɪs/ a woman's golf competition held every two years, in which the British and Irish play against the Americans. It was started by two sisters, Margaret and Harriet Curtis, in 1932. See also WALKER CUP.

ˌLord **ˈCurzon** /ˈkɜːzən; *AmE* ˈkɜːrzən/ (George Nathaniel Curzon 1859–1925) a British diplomat and politician. He became Viceroy of India at the age of only 39. Later (1919–24) he was *Foreign Secretary. Curzon had a strong personality and many people thought he was too proud. There was a popular rhyme about him:

My name is George Nathaniel Curzon,
I am a most superior person.

C

the Cutty Sark

ˈ**custard** *n* [U] (*esp BrE*) a thick yellow liquid that is eaten hot or cold with various sweet dishes. It is made with milk, eggs, flour and sugar. It can also be bought in tins, or in powder form. Some British people associate custard with school meals: *For pudding we had apple crumble with lumpy custard.*

ˈGeneral ˌGeorge ˈ**Custer** (1839–76) a US general who first became famous for his wild courage fighting for the Union during the American *Civil War. He was proud of his appearance and his long fair hair. From 1984, he fought the *Cheyenne and the *Sioux, until he and all his soldiers were killed by them at the Battle of *Little Bighorn. This battle is sometimes called **Custer's last stand**.

ˌ**Customs and ˈExcise** (*also fml* **Her Majesty's Customs and Excise**) the British government department responsible for collecting **customs duties**, taxes charged on imports from outside the European Union, and **excise duties**, taxes charged on certain goods produced in Britain, such as wine and beer, petrol and tobacco products. The Department of Customs and Excise also now collects *VAT, a tax charged on the price of some goods and services in Britain: *A large quantity of drugs has been seized by Customs and Excise officials today.*

the ˌ***Cutty ˈSark*** /ˌkʌti ˈsɑːk; *AmE* ˈsɑːrk/ a famous British sailing ship, built in 1869, which carried tea from China and then, after 1879, wool from Australia. From 1895 until 1922, the *Cutty Sark* was owned by the Portuguese, and then she became a training ship for British sailors. Since 1957 she has been open to visitors at *Greenwich. Her name comes from the 'cutty sark' (short shirt) worn by one of the witches in the poem **Tam o' Shanter* by Robert *Burns.

the ˈ**Cybermen** /ˈsaɪbəmen; *AmE* ˈsaɪbərmen/ *n* [pl] ⇨ DOCTOR WHO.

ˈ**Cyclone**™ /ˈsaɪkləʊn; *AmE* ˈsaɪkloʊn/ *n* a US type of fence made of connected steel links. Cyclone fences are especially strong and often used to protect people's homes.

ˈ***Cymbeline*** /ˈsɪmbəliːn/ a play (*c.* 1610) by William *Shakespeare. It tells how the love of a faithful wife, Imogen, survives a series of terrible experiences, and the play ends happily. Cymbeline, Imogen's father, is based on Cunobelin, a British king of the 1st century.

ˈ**Cymru** /ˈkʌmri/ the Welsh word for 'Wales'. See also PLAID CYMRU.

ˈ**Cyprus** /ˈsaɪprəs/ an island in the Mediterranean Sea which became a colony of Britain in 1914. There has been a lot of tension and violence between the Greek and Turkish communities on the island, and United Nations soldiers have been there since 1964 to keep the peace. ▶ **Cypriot** *adj*, *n*.

Dd

DA /ˌdiː ˈeɪ/ ⇨ DISTRICT ATTORNEY.

ˈDacron™ /ˈdeɪkrɒn, ˈdækrɒn; *AmE* ˈdeɪkrɑːn, ˈdækrɑːn/ *n* [U] an artificial cloth, invented in the US, which can be washed and stays smooth. Many younger people think that clothes made of Dacron are uncomfortable and not fashionable: *He was wearing these awful blue Dacron trousers.*

ˌDad's ˈArmy a popular *BBC television comedy series (1968–77) about an inefficient group of soldiers in the *Home Guard whose job is to defend Warmington-on-Sea, an imaginary village on the south coast of England, during *World War II. The phrase 'dad's army' is now sometimes used in British English to refer to any group of old soldiers.

ˈdaffodil *n* a tall yellow flower that comes out in Britain between February and April. Since the early 20th century the daffodil has been one of the national emblems of Wales, and many Welsh people wear the flowers on their clothes on *St David's Day. See also LEEK.

ˈDaffodils a famous poem (1807) by William *Wordsworth. Its first lines are:

I wandered lonely as a cloud
That floats on high o'er vales and hills,
When all at once I saw a crowd,
A host, of golden daffodils;
Beside the lake, beneath the trees,
Fluttering and dancing in the breeze.

It is remembered by older British people as a poem studied at school, and is considered to be a typical example of *Romantic poetry.

ˌDaffy ˈDuck /ˌdæfi/ a character in the **Looney Tunes* and *Merry Melodies* cartoon series. He first appeared in 1937. Daffy behaves in a crazy way and spits when he says the 's' sound. See also AVERY.

ˈDagwood /ˈdæɡwʊd/ **1** a character in the US strip cartoon **Blondie*. Dagwood Bumstead is the lazy husband of Blondie. He makes and eats very large sandwiches. **2** (*also* **Dagwood sandwich**) *n* (*AmE humor*) a large sandwich filled with a variety of meat, cheese, etc.

ˌRoald **ˈDahl** /ˌrəʊəld ˈdɑːl; *AmE* ˌroʊəld/ (1916–90) a British author best known for his very popular children's books. These include *James and the Giant Peach* (1962), *Charlie and the Chocolate Factory* (1964), *The BFG* (1982) and *Matilda* (1988), all of which have been made into films. Dahl is possibly the most popular children's author ever, though some adults are worried by the cruel aspects of many of his stories. He was born in Wales, of Norwegian parents.

the **Dáil** /dɔɪl/ *also* the **ˌDáil ˈÉireann**) /ˌdɔɪl ˈeərən; *AmE* ˈerən/ the lower house, or House of Representatives, of the National Parliament of Ireland, in Dublin. It has 166 members and its proceedings (= debates and other business) are in Irish or English. The Upper House, or Senate, is called the Seanad.

the ***ˌDaily Exˈpress*** ⇨ *EXPRESS*.

the ***ˌDaily ˈMail*** (*also infml* the ***Mail***) one of Britain's national daily newspapers, started in 1896 by Alfred *Harmsworth, who later became Lord *Northcliffe. It presents political views that are generally right-wing. It has a *tabloid format (= size of page) and is considered to be part of the 'popular press', not one of the 'quality papers': *Could you get me a copy of the Daily Mail?* See also *MAIL ON SUNDAY*. ⇨ article at NEWSPAPERS.

the ***ˌDaily ˈMirror*** ⇨ *MIRROR*.

the ***ˌDaily ˈNews*** a popular New York *tabloid newspaper, established in 1919. Robert *Maxwell owned it for a short time in 1991.

the ***ˌDaily ˈSport*** one of Britain's national daily *tabloid newspapers, started in 1988. It includes articles about sport and sex, and has a lot of pictures.

the ***ˌDaily ˈStar*** (*also infml* the ***Star***) one of Britain's daily *tabloid newspapers. It was started in 1978 as a paper for the North but became a national newspaper the following year. ⇨ article at NEWSPAPERS.

the ***ˌDaily ˈTelegraph*** (*also infml* the ***Telegraph***) one of Britain's national daily newspapers, started in 1855. It is traditionally right-wing in its views and supports the *Conservative Party, though it sometimes criticizes its policies. The *Daily Telegraph* is considered to be one of the 'quality papers' and to be especially good in its writing about sport: *She writes for The Daily Telegraph.* See also *SUNDAY TELEGRAPH*. ⇨ article at NEWSPAPERS.

the ***ˌDaily ˈWorker*** the official newspaper of the *Communist Party of Great Britain, started in 1930. Between 1966 and 1992 it was called the *Morning Star*. See also *SOCIALIST WORKER*. ⇨ article at NEWSPAPERS.

ˈDaimler™ /ˈdeɪmlə(r)/ *n* an expensive make of car produced by the *Rover company in *Coventry, England. It was named after the German designer of the original engine, Gottfried Daimler. Daimlers are typically associated with rich *upper-class people in Britain, and with the British royal family, who have owned several.

ˌDairy ˈQueen™ a large group of US shops that sell soft ice cream, hamburgers, pizzas and other food. Dairy Queen is especially popular with young people.

Daˈkota /dəˈkəʊtə; *AmE* dəˈkoʊtə/ *n* the British name for a US aircraft, the Douglas DC-3. About 11 000 were built between 1935 and 1946. They were popular with airlines, and a military version was built during *World War II: *The plane was an old Dakota.* ○ *He flew Dakotas in the war.*

the **Daˈkotas** /dəˈkəʊtəz; *AmE* dəˈkoʊtəz/ the US states of *North Dakota and *South Dakota. The original **Dakota Territory** (1861–89) included these states, most of *Montana and *Wyoming, and a small part of *Nebraska. It was named after a Native-American people, also called the *Sioux.

ˈDalek /ˈdɑːlek/ *n* a strange and frightening metal creature in the British television series **Doctor Who*. The Daleks are Doctor Who's enemies. When they shoot at people they say, 'Exterminate, exterminate!' in harsh electronic voices. They helped to make the series popular, especially with children.

ˌArthur **ˈDaley[1]** /ˈdeɪli/ a character in the British *ITV television series **Minder*. He sells used cars and other goods, and is always interested in making money, not necessarily in an honest way, but is usually unsuccessful. His name is often used to refer to someone like this. Some of the expressions Arthur Daley uses have also become part of the language. For example, he sometimes describes a business deal as 'a nice little earner', meaning that it will make him a lot of money easily. He also talks about his wife (who is never seen) as ''er indoors'. People sometimes still use both these expressions.

D

ˌRichard J ˈ**Daley**[2] /ˈdeɪli/ (Richard Joseph Daley 1902–76) the mayor of *Chicago from 1955 to 1976, well known for his strong methods. In 1968 he ordered the Chicago police to attack a group of demonstrators (= people taking part in a public protest) and this was embarrassing to the *Democratic Party which was meeting there to choose a candidate for President. Daley's son, Richard M Daley (1942–), was elected mayor of Chicago in 1989.

ˌKenny ˈ**Dalglish** /dælˈgliːʃ/ (1951–) a Scottish football player and club manager. He played for *Celtic (1970–77), for *Liverpool, where he was also manager (1977–90), and for Scotland more times than any other player, between 1971 and 1986.

ˈ**Dallas** /ˈdæləs/ the second largest city in the US state of *Texas. It was established in 1856 and is now a major business centre. President *Kennedy was murdered there in 1963. ⇨ note at FOOTBALL – AMERICAN STYLE.

ˈ***Dallas*** /ˈdæləs/ a popular US television series (1978–88) which has been shown in many countries. The stories were about rich people in the oil industry and their love of money and sex. The main characters were the *Ewing family who owned the Southfork ranch (= large farm).

ˌHugh ˈ**Dalton** /ˈdɔːltən/ (1887–1962) a British *Labour politician who became *Chancellor of the Exchequer in 1945. He had to resign in 1947 because he had given some information to a journalist before he had told the *House of Commons. He soon returned to politics and was made a *life peer in 1960.

ˌCahal ˈ**Daly** /ˌkæhəl ˈdeɪli/ (1917–) the Roman Catholic *bishop of *Armagh since 1990. He was made a cardinal (= one of the senior Roman Catholic priests who elect the Pope) in 1991, and is known for his strong criticism of the violent acts of the *IRA.

the ˈ**Dam** ˌ**Busters** the popular name for the men of 617 Squadron, part of Britain's *Royal Air Force, who on the night of 16 May 1943 dropped the special 'bouncing bombs' designed to destroy the Möhne and Eder dams in Germany. They were successful, but only 11 of the 19 planes returned to Britain. A film was made of the story in 1954, and its title music, the *Dam Busters March* by Eric Coates, is well known.

dame *n* **1** (*also* **pantomime dame**) one of the main characters in a British *pantomime. The dame is an ugly old woman who has a strong comic role, and is almost always played by a man. **2** (*also* **Dame**) (in Britain) the title of a woman who has been given the *OBE or any of certain other awards by the King or Queen: *Dame Judi Dench* ○ *She was made a dame in the Birthday Honours List.* ⇨ note at HONOURS.

ˌ**Dame Com**ˈ**mander** (in Britain) the title of a woman who has been given one of a particular set of honours by the King or Queen. Compare KNIGHT COMMANDER. ⇨ note at HONOURS.

ˌ**Dame** ˈ**Edna** ⇨ EVERAGE.

ˌ**Dame Grand** ˈ**Cross** (in Britain) the title of a woman who has been given one of a particular set of honours by the King or Queen. Compare KNIGHT GRAND CROSS. ⇨ note at HONOURS.

a pantomime dame

ˌWilliam ˈ**Dampier** /ˈdæmpɪə(r)/ (1652–1715) an English sailor and explorer who sailed all over the world. He was a pirate along the South American coast for a few years, and then in 1693 was sent by the *Admiralty to explore around New Guinea and Australia, where he gave his name to the Dampier Strait and Archipelago. He was later the pilot of the ship that rescued Alexander *Selkirk, the man on whom the book *Robinson Crusoe* is based.

ˌ**dancehall** ˈ**reggae** ⇨ RAGGA.

the ˈ**Dance** ˌ**Theater of** ˈ**Harlem** /ˈhɑːləm; *AmE* ˈhɑːrləm/ a US dance group with mostly *African-American dancers. It was established in 1971 in *Harlem in New York and has performed many works by George *Balanchine.

the Dance Theater of Harlem

A ˈ***Dance to the*** ˈ***Music of*** ˈ***Time*** a sequence of twelve novels by the English author Anthony Powell (1905–), published between 1951 and 1975. The novels present a broad picture of the British upper and middle classes during those years and are known for their very large range of characters, including the very ambitious Kenneth Widmerpool. A television version of the series was broadcast in 1997.

ˌ**Dan** ˈ**Dare** /ˈdeə(r); *AmE* ˈder/ a popular character in the British boys' *comic *Eagle*. Colonel Dan Dare was the 'Pilot of the Future', a traveller in space. His main enemy was the Mekon, a small green space creature with a big head.

ˌ**Dandie** ˈ**Dinmont** /ˌdændi ˈdɪnmɒnt/ *n* [C] a type of *terrier with short legs, a long body and tail, and long ears. Its hair is greyish or yellowish. Dandie Dinmonts came originally from Scotland and are named after a Scottish character in a novel by Walter *Scott.

The ˈ**Dandy** /ˈdændi/ a popular British weekly *comic for children, first published in 1937. One of its most popular characters is *Desperate Dan.

ˈ**Danegeld** /ˈdeɪngeld/ *n* [U] a land tax that was introduced in *Anglo-Saxon England in 991 in order to raise money to pay the *Danes not to attack southern England. The payments of Danegeld only delayed the attack until 1013 when the Danish king Sweyn I brought England under Danish control. The tax was introduced again by the *Normans in the 11th century to pay for national defence.

ˈ**Danelaw** /ˈdeɪnlɔː/ the part of north-eastern England that was ruled by the *Danes from 878 until the whole of England came under Danish rule in 1013. The line between Danelaw and the rest of *Anglo-Saxon England ran roughly between London and *Chester. Many places in the north-east of England still have Danish names. For example, Denby means Dane Village.

the **Danes** /deɪnz/ *n* [pl] the name used in English history for those *Vikings who attacked and settled in the eastern and northern parts of England in the 9th century, and whose kings ruled the whole of England from 1013 to 1042.

ˌPaul ˈ**Daniels** /ˈdænjəlz/ (1938–) a popular English television entertainer best known for his magic tricks on *The Paul Daniels Magic Show*.

ˌ**Danish ˈpastry** /ˌdeɪnɪʃ/ (*also* **Danish**, *AmE* **sweet roll**) *n* a sweet cake, round and flat in shape, made with rich pastry and fruit, nuts, cheese, etc.

ˌJohn ˈ**Dankworth** /ˈdæŋkwɜːθ; *AmE* ˈdæŋkwɜːrθ/ (1927–) an English saxophone player, writer of *jazz music and leader of his own jazz orchestra. In 1985 he became the Pops Music Director of the *London Symphony Orchestra. He is married to the jazz singer Cleo *Laine.

ˌ**Darby and ˈJoan** /ˌdɑːbi; *AmE* ˌdɑːrbi/ a typical old couple who are happily married. The names come from an 18th-century poem about such a couple. In Britain, **Darby and Joan clubs** are social clubs for old people, usually run by charity workers.

the ˌ**Dardaˈnelles** /ˌdɑːdəˈnelz; *AmE* ˌdɑːrdəˈnelz/ the narrow piece of water that separates European Turkey from Asian Turkey. In 1915 Australian and New Zealand soldiers landed in *Gallipoli on the western shore of the Dardanelles to attack Turkey, which had entered the war on Germany's side. At the same time, British ships tried to fight their way through the Dardanelles in order to get supplies to southern Russia. Both attacks failed and more than 200 000 men were killed.

the ˈ**dark ˈlady of the ˈsonnets** the woman to whom Shakespeare wrote most of his last *sonnets. Her identity is not known but many guesses have been made about it. She is described as dark because of the colour of her skin and hair and because of the dark thoughts and feelings of guilt that she caused.

ˌGrace ˈ**Darling** /ˈdɑːlɪŋ; *AmE* ˈdɑːrlɪŋ/ (1815–42) a young English woman who helped her father to rescue nine sailors during a storm off the coast of *Northumberland in 1838. Her name is still remembered in that part of Britain, and her father's boat is now in a museum in the village of Bamburgh, where she was born.

ˌLord ˈ**Darnley** /ˈdɑːnli; *AmE* ˈdɑːrnli/ (Henry Stuart 1545–67) the second husband of *Mary Queen of Scots and the father of King *James I of England (James VI of Scotland). Darnley is best known for his murder of Mary's secretary, David Rizzio, in 1566. Darnley was himself murdered the following year, probably by the Earl of *Bothwell, who then took Darnley's place as Mary's third husband.

ˌClarence ˈ**Darrow** /ˈdærəʊ; *AmE* ˈdæroʊ/ (1857–1938) a US lawyer who became famous for defending people on trial. These included *Leopold and Loeb and John T Scopes, the teacher who was taken to court for teaching the theory of evolution to his students. See also SCOPES TRIAL.

ˌ**Darth ˈVader** /ˌdɑːθ ˈveɪdə(r); *AmE* ˌdɑːrθ ˈveɪdər/ an evil and frightening character in the **Star Wars* films. He breathes loudly and has a black costume and a black protective covering over his face and head.

ˈ**Dartington** /ˈdɑːtɪŋtən; *AmE* ˈdɑːrtɪŋtən/ a centre for arts and country crafts in and around Dartington Hall, a large 14th-century house in Devon in south-west England. It was started in the 1920s. Until 1987 there was also a school there, which was known for its freedom and new ideas on methods of education.

ˈ**Dartmoor** /ˈdɑːtmɔː(r); *AmE* ˈdɑːrtmʊr/ a wild, open and hilly part of *Devon in south-west England, 365 square miles (945 square kilometres) in area. It is a *national park and a popular place for walking and horse riding. **Dartmoor ponies** are small, dark brown horses with long hair that live wild on Dartmoor. Parts of Dartmoor are also used for military exercises. **Dartmoor prison** is a men's prison in the middle of Dartmoor, well known because it is difficult to escape from.

ˈ**Dartmouth** /ˈdɑːtməθ; *AmE* ˈdɑːrtməθ/ an old port in Devon, south-west England, and now a popular place for people who enjoy sailing. The *Britannia Royal Naval College at Dartmouth trains people to become officers in the British *Royal Navy.

darts

Darts is a popular indoor game, often played in British *pubs and working men's *clubs. Players throw small steel **darts** with feathers or plastic flights attached at a round **dartboard** fixed to a wall. The dartboard is divided into 20 numbered areas, each of which has a particular score, and an outer, middle and inner ring. Double points are scored if a dart lands in the outer ring around the edge of the board and treble points if it lands in the inner ring. If a dart lands in the small centre circle, called the **bull's-eye**, 50 points are scored.

Two or four players play against each other. They take turns to throw three darts each at the board, standing behind a line on the floor called the oche (pronounced /ˈɒki/). Each player starts with 301, or sometimes 501, and scores are deducted from this. The game is won when one of the players reduces his or her score to zero. The last throw must land in the outer ring or in the bull's-eye.

The game is thought to have developed out of archery several hundred years ago and is said to have been played by the *Pilgrim Fathers on the **Mayflower*. Today, pubs have teams that play in local darts leagues and a few players have been able to turn professional. Major darts matches are sometimes shown on television, though they are not especially popular and some people do not like the association between darts and beer-drinking.

In the US darts is a popular game in bars. The teams sometimes have humorous names, such as The Good, The Bad, The Ugly, and The Flying Syringes. US **dart teams** are organized into **leagues** that play for money. Competitions include the Bluebonnet Classic and the Treasure Island Open.

ˌCharles ˈ**Darwin** /ˈdɑːwɪn; *AmE* ˈdɑːrwɪn/ (1809–82) the English naturalist who developed the theory of evolution by natural selection. As a young man he spent five years on a British ship, *HMS *Beagle*, visiting coasts and islands in the southern part of

D

the world. The different types of animals and plants that he found, especially on the Galapagos Islands in the Pacific, led him to believe that living things develop differently in different places over a long period of time. At that time, most western people believed that all things were created by God in seven days. Darwin returned to England in 1836 and spent the next 23 years collecting evidence to support his theory. When he published *On the Origin of Species by means of Natural Selection* (1859) it caused much argument and anger because it seemed to disagree with the story of creation in the Bible. Most educated people now accept the main points of Darwin's theory, and see it and the Bible as two ways of saying the same thing.

▶ **Darwinian** *adj* of or relating to the theories of Charles Darwin. **Darwinism** *n* [U] Charles Darwin's theory of evolution.

the ˌ**Data Pro**ˈ**tection Act** a British law which limits the use of personal information stored in computers. Organizations that keep this kind of information about other people must inform an authority. They must also make sure that the information is accurate and they must use it only for specific purposes. The law also gives people the right to see most of the information that is kept about them in this way and to have any mistakes corrected.

ˈ**Daughters of the A**ˈ**merican Revo**ˈ**lution** a US organization for women who are descended from people who fought or helped in the *American Revolution. The group was established in 1890. It is very conservative and supports anything it believes is good for America.

Eˌlizabeth ˈ**David**[1] /ˈdeɪvɪd/ (1913–92) an English writer of cookery books, especially about French and Italian cooking. She was a major influence on the quality of English cooking from the 1950s.

St ˈ**David**[2] (*c.* 520–600) the patron saint of Wales. Little is known about him except that he started several religious houses in Wales and he lived in the place now called *St David's. *St David's day (1 March) is Wales's national day.

ˌ***David*** ˈ***Copperfield*** /ˈkɒpəfiːld; *AmE* ˈkɑːpərfiːld/ a novel (1850) by Charles *Dickens. David, a boy in *Victorian(1) England, is sent to London for a life of hard work and poverty. He becomes a successful writer, but marries a silly girl, Dora, without realizing that another woman, Agnes, really loves him. Agnes's father is cheated out of his money by his employee, Uriah *Heep, but in the end they are saved by David's friend Mr *Micawber. Dora dies, and David marries Agnes. The novel is partly based on Dickens's own life.

ˌBette ˈ**Davis**[1] /ˌbeti ˈdeɪvɪs/ (1908–89) a US film actor for more than 50 years. She was famous for playing strong emotional parts and for smoking a lot. She received *Oscars for *Dangerous* (1935) and *Jezebel* (1938). Her other films included *All About Eve* (1950) and *Whatever Happened to Baby Jane?* (1962).

ˌColin ˈ**Davis**[2] /ˈdeɪvɪs/ (1927–) an English conductor who worked with the *English National Opera in the 1960s and at the *Royal Opera House in the 1970s and 1980s. He has also conducted the Boston Symphony Orchestra and is now the main conductor of the *London Symphony Orchestra. He was made a *knight in 1980.

ˌJefferson ˈ**Davis**[3] /ˌdʒefəsən ˈdeɪvɪs; *AmE* ˌdʒefərsən/ (1808–89) the only President of the *Confederate States (1861–5). He had earlier been a US Senator and Secretary of War. After the South lost the American *Civil War, Davis was kept in prison by the US government for two years before being released without a trial.

ˌJoe ˈ**Davis**[4] /ˈdeɪvɪs/ (1901–78) an English *snooker player who won the World Professional Championship every year for 20 years from 1927 until 1946. He was also the first player to achieve on television the maximum score in a single game of 147. The only man who could ever beat him was his younger brother, Fred Davis (1913–).

ˌMiles ˈ**Davis**[5] /ˈdeɪvɪs/ (1926–91) an *African-American trumpet player who led a *jazz band. He played with Charlie 'Bird' *Parker in the 1930s, then helped to develop *bebop in the 1940s, 'cool' jazz in the 1950s (with John *Coltrane in his group) and modern jazz with an electronic trumpet in the 1960s.

ˈSammy ˈ**Davis**[6] ˈJr /ˈdeɪvɪs/ (1925–90) an *African-American singer, dancer and actor. He was known for his energy and cheerful manner on stage. His successes included the film *Porgy and Bess* (1959), the *Broadway show *Golden Boy* (1964) and the song *Candy Man* (1972).

ˌSteve ˈ**Davis**[7] / ˈdeɪvɪs/ (1957–) an English *snooker player who has won more titles than any other player in the world. In the 1980s he won the World Professional Championship six times. He is not related to the first holder of the world title, Joe *Davis.

the ˌ**Davis** ˈ**Cup** an international tennis competition for teams of men representing different countries, or the cup which is presented every year to the country whose team wins this competition. It began in 1900 and is named after Dwight F Davis, who gave the cup.

ˌHumphrey ˈ**Davy** /ˈdeɪvi/ (1778–1829) an English chemist who was one of the first scientists to make use of electricity to break chemical compounds into their separate elements. Between 1807 and 1808 he discovered six chemical elements, including calcium, potassium and sodium. However, he is better known for a practical invention that saved many lives: the **Davy lamp**, a safe lamp for use in coal mines. This was widely used for many years until it was replaced by the electric lamp in the 20th century.

ˈ**Davy** ˈ**Jones's** ˈ**locker** /ˈdeɪvi ˈdʒəʊnzɪz; *AmE* ˈdʒoʊnzɪz/ (*infml often humor*) the bottom of the sea, as the place where people who have died at sea lie dead. The origin of the expression is not known: *The crew are all in Davy Jones's locker.*

ˈCharles ˈGates ˈ**Dawes** /ˈgeɪts ˈdɔːz/ (1865–1951) a US Vice-president (1925–9) under President Herbert *Hoover. Dawes led the international committee that created the **Dawes Plan** (1924) to lend Germany $200 million to help it pay for damages to other countries after *World War I. He received the 1925 *Nobel Prize for peace.

ˌDoris ˈ**Day**[1] /ˈdeɪ/ (1924–) a US singer and actor known for her healthy and happy image. She made several popular film comedies with Rock *Hudson, including *Pillow Talk* (1959). Her songs included *Whatever Will Be, Will Be (Que Sera Sera)* (1956), which won an *Oscar.

ˌRobin ˈ**Day**[2] / ˈdeɪ/ (1923–) a British television and radio broadcaster who is famous for his interviews with politicians. He is a very clever interviewer with an aggressive style that forces politicians to answer questions they would prefer to avoid. He was made a *knight in 1981.

ˈCecil ˌ**Day-**ˈ**Lewis**[1] /ˈdeɪ ˈluːɪs/ (1904–72) an English poet and author, born in Ireland. In the 1930s he was a member of the left-wing group of poets led by W H *Auden. He also wrote detective stories under the name Nicholas Blake. He was made *Poet Laureate in 1968.

Daniel Day-Lewis in The Crucible

ˈDaniel ˌ**Day-ˈLewis²** /ˈdeɪ ˈluːɪs/ (1958–) an English actor who became well known in 1985 for his parts in the films *My Beautiful Laundrette* and *A Room with a View*. He won an *Oscar for his performance in *My Left Foot* (1989) and his films since then have included *The Last of the Mohicans* (1992) and *The Crucible* (1996). He is the son of Cecil *Day-Lewis.

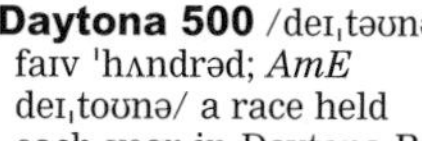

Daytona 500 /deɪˌtəʊnə faɪv ˈhʌndrəd; *AmE* deɪˌtoʊnə/ a race held each year in Daytona Beach, *Florida for stock cars (= ordinary cars fitted with very powerful engines). Compare INDIANAPOLIS 500.

ˈ**D-Day** /ˈdiː/ **1** 6 June 1944, the day on which the *Allies landed in Normandy, northern France, during *World War II. They were led by General *Eisenhower, and defeated the German forces defending the beaches. The secret name of the landings was 'Overlord'. They are often also called the *Normandy landings. See also MULBERRY HARBOURS. **2** a date on which something important is planned to happen: *As D-Day approached we had barely started packing.*

DEA /ˌdiː iː ˈeɪ/ ⇨ DRUG ENFORCEMENT ADMINISTRATION.

the ˌ**dead ˈparrot sketch** a widely remembered, very funny sketch (= short comic play) from *Monty Python's Flying Circus* on British television. John *Cleese plays a man who goes into a pet shop to complain about a parrot (= a large colourful bird) which he has just bought there. Although the bird is obviously dead, the pet shop owner, played by Michael *Palin, argues that it is just 'resting', while Cleese tries harder and harder to prove that it is dead.

ˈˌDizzy' ˈ**Dean¹** /ˌdɪzi ˈdiːn/ (Jay Hanna Dean 1911–74) a famous US baseball pitcher (= player who throws the ball to be hit). He was chosen for the National Baseball *Hall of Fame in 1953. His best years (1930–37) were with the St Louis Cardinals. He was named the Most Valuable Player in 1934.the ˌForest of ˈ**Dean²** ⇨ FOREST OF DEAN.

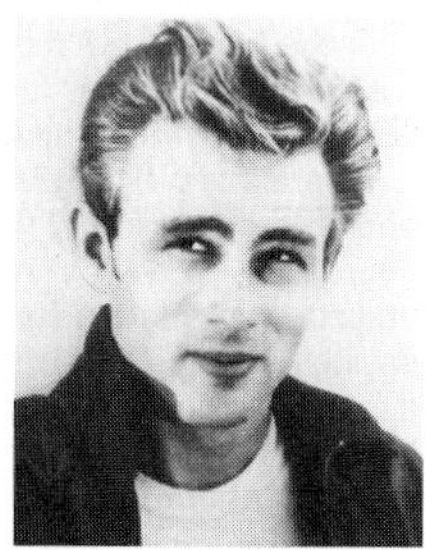

James Dean in Rebel Without a Cause

ˌJames ˈ**Dean³** /ˈdiːn/ (1931–55) a US actor who has come to represent the popular image of a young person resisting authority. He appeared in only three films, *East of Eden* (1955), *Rebel Without a Cause* (1955) and *Giant* (1956), before being killed in a car accident. Posters of him are still popular, especially with young people.

ˌ**dean's ˈlist** *n* a list produced each year at most US colleges and universities of students who have achieved the highest grades in their courses of study. The list is published in local newspapers. A dean is an administrative officer at a school or college.

ˌ***Dear ˈAbby*** /ˈæbi/ a regular newspaper column, appearing in several US newspapers, which answers readers' questions about love and family problems. It began in 1956 and is written by Abigail Van Buren (1918–), the twin sister of Ann *Landers who writes a similar column.

ˌ**Dear ˈJohn ˌletter** (*also* **Dear John**) *n* (*AmE infml*) a letter sent by a woman to a man to say that she wants to stop their relationship. This is usually because she now loves someone else.

Death and funerals ⇨ article.

ˌ***Death of a ˈSalesman*** a play (1949) by Arthur *Miller that won the *Pulitzer Prize. It is about an ordinary man, Willie Loman, who kills himself because his life has been a failure. A film version was made in 1951.

ˌ***Death on the ˈRock*** a British television programme made in 1988 about the death of three suspected *IRA terrorists earlier that year. The three were shot in a street in *Gibraltar by soldiers of the British *SAS. The programme accused the SAS soldiers of shooting them without trying to arrest them first. The British government tried without success to prevent the programme being shown. In 1994 the European Commission of Human Rights decided that the soldiers had acted correctly, but the incident still rouses strong feelings.

ˌ**Death ˈValley** a desert covering part of the US states of *California and *Nevada. It is the lowest land in the western hemisphere, being 282 feet/86 metres below sea level, with very high temperatures (up to 50° Celsius). The desert was a source of the mineral borax in the late 19th century. In 1933 the area became the **Death Valley National Monument**.

ˈ**Debenhams**™ /ˈdebənəmz/ any one of a chain of large shops in Britain. Each shop has various departments selling clothes and household goods.

ˈ**debit card** *n* a small plastic card which is given by banks to their customers to enable them to pay for things without having to write a cheque. When somebody uses a debit card, such as a *Switch card, money is taken directly from their bank account. ⇨ note at CREDIT CARDS.

ˌEdward **de ˈBono** /də ˈbəʊnəʊ; *AmE* də ˈboʊnoʊ/ (1933–) a British doctor and psychologist who wrote *The Use of Lateral Thinking* (1967). This explained how to solve problems by thinking round them instead of thinking directly about them. Since then de Bono has written more books on this subject, and the phrase *lateral thinking* has become part of the English language.

Deˈbrett /dəˈbret/ (*also* ***Deˈbrett's*** /dəˈbrets/) the popular name for *Debrett's Peerage*, a book containing lists and information about the *royal family, the *peerage and other people in Britain who hold titles of rank. The name is also used to refer to other books from the same publisher, such as a guide to polite social behaviour.

ˌEugene V ˈ**Debs** /ˈdebz/ (Eugene Victor Debs 1855–1926) a US socialist politician and trade union leader. In 1893 he established the American Railway Union. He helped organize the Social Democratic Party of America in 1897 and was its candidate for US president five times from 1900 to 1920, even while in prison for opposing the government's decision to enter *World War I.

ˈ**Decca**™ /ˈdekə/ an international record company which was formed in Britain in 1929 and became the second largest record group in the world after *EMI. Decca was bought by Polygram in 1980.

ˌ**decimaliˈzation** *n* [U] the change of the British currency to the present decimal system of 100 pence to the pound, which happened on 15 February 1971. Before then, the pound was divided into 20 shillings with 12 pence in each shilling. ⇨ article at MONEY.

the ˌ**Declaˈration of Indeˈpendence** the document in which the *thirteen colonies declared that they were independent of Britain and stated the

D

Death and funerals

Attitudes to death

People generally avoid talking about death. If they need to mention somebody who has recently died they tend to talk softly and use expressions like *pass away* or *pass on* rather than *die*. Most people in Britain and the US live a long time. Men can expect to live about 73 years and women about 79. The main causes of death are heart disease, cancer and strokes.

When somebody dies, people's reactions depend on the age and health of the person who has died, as well as on how well they knew them. If the person was old, the **bereaved** (= their relations and friends) may comfort each other with phrases such as 'she was a good age'. If the person was still young, or died as the result of an accident, their death is seen as a tragedy. In Britain especially, many people are not religious and do not find comfort in a belief that the dead person's soul has 'gone to heaven'. People are particularly shocked and upset if somebody **commits suicide** (= kills herself/himself).

Some people with **terminal illnesses** (= illnesses that will cause them to die) think about ending their lives to avoid suffering for themselves and their family. There is a debate in both Britain and the US about whether people in this situation should be allowed to kill themselves, and whether doctors or family members should be allowed to help them. The **right to die** debate raises strong feelings, and has been encouraged in the US by **Dr Jack *Kevorkian**, who, in the 1990s, was arrested for helping several people to die. So far, only the state of *Oregon allows **assisted suicide**. In Britain assisted suicide, or **euthanasia**, is illegal.

Funerals

When a person dies their family has to obtain a **death certificate** (= an official document describing the circumstances of death) from a doctor before the **funeral** can take place. This is a formal ceremony during which the **body** of the dead person is **buried** (= put in the ground) or **cremated** (= burned). **Funeral directors**, in Britain sometimes called **undertakers**, help with the funeral arrangements. They collect the body of **the deceased** (= the person who has died) and put it in a **coffin** or **casket** (= a wooden box). Before the lid is closed, there may be a **viewing**, a last chance for family and friends to see the dead person.

In Britain and the US there are different types of funeral, just as there are different cultural groups with their own traditions and practices. The **funeral service** is often a religious ceremony, which is attended by **mourners**, family and friends of the dead person. It takes place in a church, chapel, temple or, in the US, in a **funeral home** (= a place belonging to the funeral directors). Traditionally, mourners wear black and bring **wreaths** of flowers which are put on the coffin. Some people send money to a *charity instead of buying flowers. Most people **grieve** (= feel sad and cry) quietly.

In a church funeral the coffin is carried into a church on the shoulders of **pall-bearers** and put down in front of the mourners. During the service a priest, relation or friend gives a **eulogy**, a talk about the dead person. There are also hymns or songs, and sometimes poetry and music. Afterwards, the coffin is carried out by the pall-bearers and taken in a **hearse** (= a large black car) to the **cemetery** (= a place where people are buried). If the funeral takes place at a **crematorium** (= a place where bodies are burned) the coffin remains in the chapel behind closed curtains.

pall-bearers carrying a coffin from church

If the body is to be buried there is a short service when the body is lowered into the **grave** that has been dug for it. Afterwards, the earth is replaced and the wreaths are put on top. A **headstone**, a piece of stone with information about the dead person, is later placed over the grave. **Family plots** have space for many people to be buried, and some rich families have a **mausoleum**, where all the members of the family are placed after death.

Many people now are cremated and have their **ashes** scattered in a favourite place, such as a garden. Other families keep the ashes in an **urn**. People can generally choose whether they or their relative will be buried or cremated.

After the funeral, mourners are usually invited to the family home or to a hotel for something to eat. Irish-Americans and some other people call this a **wake**, and make it a happy occasion celebrating the dead person's life. It used to be traditional to read the **will** (= a legal document that describes how a dead person's property is to be distributed) after the funeral, but this is now less common. If the dead person was famous there may be a **memorial service** a few weeks later.

Funerals are expensive and many people worry about how their family will pay for their funeral. One way is to pay for the ceremony in advance by putting money into a **funeral plan** (= a type of savings scheme). Many people dislike the idea of a lot of fuss following their death. Others think it is important to give a relation 'a good send-off' and spend a lot of money on the funeral arrangements.

Expressing sympathy

When somebody dies it is polite to offer **condolences** (= sympathy) to their family. People often say, for example, 'I was sorry to hear about your mother', and follow it up with something nice that they remember about her.

An announcement of a person's death and information about their funeral is often printed in the local paper. People do not normally need an invitation to go to a funeral in order to **pay their last respects**. Those who cannot attend may send a card to the family expressing their sympathy.

principles of the new government. One of its most famous sentences is this: 'We hold these truths to be self-evident: that all men are created equal; that they are endowed by their creator with certain inalienable rights; that among these are life, liberty, and the pursuit of happiness.' The document was mostly written by Thomas *Jefferson and received the approval of the *Continental Congress on 4 July 1776. Those signing it included Benjamin *Franklin, John *Adams and John *Hancock. ⇨ INDEPENDENCE DAY.

De,cline and 'Fall the first novel by the English writer Evelyn *Waugh. It was written in 1928 and is about the comic troubles of a quiet young man who has to leave *Oxford University and gets a job at a very bad *public school. The rich mother of one of his pupils brings him into her social circle and he gets put in prison, before finally returning to his religious studies at Oxford. The novel was an immediate success and established Waugh's career as a writer of satire.

The ***De'cline and 'Fall of the ,Roman 'Empire*** a historical work in six books (1776–88) written by the English historian Edward *Gibbon. It covers the history of Europe from Rome in the first century AD to the fall of Constantinople in 1453. Its full title is *The History of the Decline and Fall of the Roman Empire*, but it is usually referred to simply as Gibbon's *Decline and Fall*.

'Decorated style a style of *Gothic architecture that was common in England from about 1290 to about 1350. Its main feature was the ornamental stone carving around windows and doors. ⇨ article at CHURCHES AND CATHEDRALS.

,Deep 'Blue the name of a computer program that plays chess. In one second, it can analyse 100 million possible positions on the board. It was invented in 1985 by two students at Carnegie Mellon University in the US. In 1989 Garry Kasparov, the World Chess Champion, defeated the computer in two matches. The program was later improved and in 1997 it defeated Kasparov in a match of six games.

,Deep 'Purple a British *rock group, formed in 1968. The group broke up in 1976 but came together again in 1984. Two of their best-known albums are *Deep Purple in Rock* (1970) and *Deepest Purple* (1980).

the **,Deep 'South** (*often disapprov*) the most southern states of the south-east US: *Alabama, *Florida, *Georgia, *Louisiana, *Mississippi, *South Carolina and eastern *Texas. They are among the states that once had slaves and left the *Union during the *Civil War. They still have racial problems and the people there are mostly conservative in their politics and religion.

,Deep 'Throat the humorous name taken from the title of a sex film and used by two **Washington Post* journalists, Carl Bernstein and Bob Woodward, to refer to the person who gave them a lot of information about *Watergate. They never revealed the person's real name.

The ***'Deer ,Hunter*** a US film (1978), directed by Michael Cimino, which received three *Oscars, including the one for 'Best Picture'. The story is about a group of friends who hunt deer together and later join the US forces fighting in Vietnam, where they have terrible experiences.

the **De,fence of the 'Realm Act** (*abbr* **DORA**) a law introduced by the British government in 1914 to give special powers to the authorities in Ireland. At that time, after the beginning of the war between Britain and Germany, the British government feared a revolution in Ireland with German support. After the *Easter Rising (1917) against British rule in Ireland, the Act was used to arrest and put in prison many people who had supported the rising.

De,fender of the 'Faith a title used by all kings and queens of England since the 16th century. The abbreviation of the title's Latin form, *Fidei Defensor*, is FD or FID DEF, and this appears on every British coin. The title was first given to King *Henry VIII by Pope Leo X after Henry's defence of the *Roman Catholic faith against the teachings of Martin Luther. But the title was taken away when England left the Roman Catholic Church. King Henry then asked the English *Parliament to give him the same title with a different meaning: defender of the *Church of England.

D

,Daniel **De'foe** /dɪˈfəʊ; *AmE* dɪˈfoʊ/ (1660–1731) an English writer who is considered to be the first English writer of novels. His most famous novel, **Robinson Crusoe* (1719) was followed by **Moll Flanders* (1722), *A Journal of the Plague Year* (1722) set during the *Great Plague of London, and *Roxana* (1724). For most of his life Defoe worked as a political journalist, and he did not begin writing his novels until he was nearly 60.

,Geoffrey **de 'Havilland** /də ˈhævələnd/ (1882–1965) a British aircraft designer whose company produced many of Britain's best-known aircraft. He started the company after designing planes in *World War I, and it produced the *Mosquito during *World War II and then the *Comet, the world's first passenger jet plane. He was made a *knight in 1944. His company is now part of *British Aerospace.

,Len **'Deighton** /ˈdeɪtn/ (1929–) an English writer of novels, especially spy stories (= ones about people employed to find out secret information). These include *The Ipcress File* (1962) and *Funeral in Berlin*. Deighton has also written war novels, such as *Bomber* (1970), and a history of *World War II, *Blood Tears and Folly* (1996).

,Willem **de 'Kooning** /ˌwɪləm də ˈkuːnɪŋ/ (1904–97) a US artist, born in the Netherlands. He went to the US in 1926 and soon became a leader in the *abstract expressionism movement. He painted large pictures with bright colours and great energy. He was also interested in painting the human form, as in his series *Woman I–V* (1952–3). See also ACTION PAINTING.

,Walter **de la 'Mare** /də lɑː ˈmeə(r); *AmE* də lɑː ˈmer/ (1873–1956) an English writer of poems, novels and short stories for adults and children. His best-known works are the poems *Songs of Childhood* (1902) and the novel *Memoirs of a Midget* (1921).

'Delaware /ˈdeləweə(r); *AmE* ˈdeləwer/ a small eastern state in the US, named after a *Native-American people. Its capital city is Dover and its largest city is Wilmington. The northern part of the state is industrial and the southern part agricultural. Delaware was one of the original *thirteen colonies and is sometimes called the First State because it was the first to accept the US *Constitution.

'Del Boy /ˈdel/ the nickname of Derek Trotter, a character played by the English actor David *Jason in the *BBC television comedy series **Only Fools and Horses*. Del Boy makes a living by selling things like cheap watches and is not completely honest, but he is friendly, cheerful and warm-hearted.

,Frederick **'Delius** /ˈdiːliəs/ (1862–1934) an English composer who wrote operas, works for the orchestra, and songs. His parents were originally from Germany. Delius spent much of his adult life in France, but his work often celebrated his love of the English countryside. Two of his best-known works are the opera *A Village Romeo and Juliet* (1907) and a short piece for orchestra *On Hearing the First Cuckoo in Spring* (1912).

D

ˌ**Del ˈMonte** /ˌdel ˈmɒnteɪ; *AmE* ˈmɑːnteɪ/ a US company known for selling fruit and vegetables in cans, and fruit juice. Its best-known advertising character is the 'Man from Del Monte' who visits farmers to judge whether their fruit is good enough to be sold by the company.

ˈ**Delta** /ˈdeltə/ *n* a type of British *debit card. ⇨ note at CREDIT CARDS.

ˈ**Delta Force** /ˈdeltə/ (Special Forces Operational Detachment Delta) a special unit in the US Army that fights against terrorists and guerrillas. Its base is at Fort Bragg, *North Carolina, and it has been active in Vietnam, Iran and other dangerous areas. Delta Force was organized like the British *SAS, and many of its members have trained with that unit.

ˌAgnes **De ˈMille**[1] /də ˈmɪl/ (1905–93) a US dancer and choreographer. She created a new type of dance for *Broadway musical shows when she combined ballet with popular music for *Oklahoma!* (1943) and later for *Carousel* (1945) and *Paint Your Wagon* (1951). Her ballets included *Rodeo* (1942) and *Fall River Legend* (1948). In the early part of her career she danced in London with the *Ballet Rambert. Her uncle was Cecil B *De Mille.

ˌCecil B **De ˈMille**[2] /də ˈmɪl/ (Cecil Blount De Mille 1881–1959) a US film director and producer. He had a strong personality and was famous for making actors do exactly what he wanted. He is remembered for directing expensive films on a large scale, including *Samson and Delilah* (1949) and (twice) *The Ten Commandments* (1923 and 1956).

ˈ**Democrat** *n* a member or supporter of the *Democratic Party of the US.

the ˌ**Demoˈcratic ˌParty** (*also* the ˈ**Democrats**) one of the two major political parties in the US. Compared with their rivals, the *Republican Party, the Democrats are more liberal and have strong support from minorities and the trade/labor unions. The party began in 1792 as the **Democratic Republican Party**. Presidents have included Thomas *Jefferson, Andrew *Jackson, Woodrow *Wilson, Franklin D *Roosevelt, Harry S *Truman, John F *Kennedy, Jimmy *Carter and Bill *Clinton.

ˌJack ˈ**Dempsey** /ˈdempsi/ (1895–1983) a US boxer who was the World Heavyweight Champion from 1919 to 1926. His popular name was the 'Manassa Mauler' because he was from Manassa, *Colorado, and mauled his opponents (= treated them very roughly). Dempsey was involved in the famous 'long count' when he knocked down Gene *Tunney in a 1927 fight. The referee delayed before he began counting. Tunney got up just before he had counted to ten and went on to win the fight.

Deˈnali /dəˈnɑːli/ a US national park in *Alaska which includes Mount *McKinley, the highest mountain in North America. Denali is the local Native-American name for the mountain. The park has glaciers (= masses of ice) and many wild animals, including bears and moose.

ˌJudi ˈ**Dench** /ˌdʒuːdi ˈdentʃ/ (1934–) an English actor who has played many leading roles in the plays of Shakespeare, especially with the *Royal Shakespeare Company. She has also appeared in several television series and films, including *A Room with a View* (1986) and *Mrs Brown* (1997) in which she played the part of Queen *Victoria. She was made a *dame(2) in 1988.

Judi Dench in Mrs Brown

ˌRobert **De ˈNiro** /də ˈnɪərəʊ; *AmE* də ˈnɪroʊ/ (1945–) a US film actor known for his intense style of acting in a wide range of parts. He won *Oscars for *The Godfather Part II* (1974) and *Raging Bull* (1979).

ˌLord ˈ**Denning** (Alfred Denning) /ˈdenɪŋ/ (1899–1999) a British judge who was *Master of the Rolls for twenty years (1962–82). He believed in defending the rights of individual people against powerful groups and he often gave judgements or opinions which caused disagreement. He became a *knight in 1944 and a *life peer in 1957. He was chosen to head the investigation into the *Profumo affair and produced the **Denning Report** on it in 1963.

ˌ**Dennis the ˈMenace 1** a character in the British *comic *The *Beano*. He is a small boy with untidy hair who is always playing tricks on people and getting into trouble. He has a dog called Gnasher that regularly bites people. **2** a US cartoon character created in the early 1950s. He is a small boy who behaves badly and especially annoys his neighbour, Mr Wilson. Dennis has also appeared in a television series (1959–63) and a film (1993).

ˈ**Denny's** /ˈdeniz/ any of a chain of *fast-food restaurants in the US. In 1994 the company was accused of refusing to serve *African Americans and was made to pay $46 million as a result. Denny's now serves everyone and even produced humorous advertisements in 1997 which said that its food is so good that even African Americans eat there.

ˈ**Denver**[1] /ˈdenvə(r)/ the capital and largest city of the US state of *Colorado. It is close to the *Rocky Mountains, and its popular name is the 'Mile High City'. Many people moved to the city in the 1870s and 1880s to work in the local gold and silver mines. In 1995 the city opened the largest airport (in area of land) in North America.

ˌJohn ˈ**Denver**[2] /ˈdenvə(r)/ (1943–97) a US singer and writer of *folk music and *country music. His public image as a nice country boy made him especially popular in the 1970s. His songs included *Take Me Home, Country Roads* (1971), *Back Home Again* (1975) and *Thank God I'm A Country Boy* (1975). He was killed in a plane crash.

ˌ**Denver ˈboot** /ˌdenvə; *AmE* ˌdenvər/ *n* (*AmE*) a heavy metal device for attaching to the wheel of a car that is illegally parked, so that it cannot be driven away. The driver must wait for somebody to remove it and usually has to pay for this to be done. *Denver was one of the first US cities to introduce the device.

the **Deˈpartment for Eduˈcation and Emˈployment** (*abbr* the **DFEE**) the British government department responsible for all levels of education in England and Wales and for job training. (The *Scottish Office until recently dealt with these responsibilities in Scotland.) Education used to be covered by the Department of Education and Science (DES), but in 1992 this department was split into the Office of Public Service and Science and the Department for Education. The Department of Employment and the Department for Education were then brought together to form the present DFEE.

the **Deˈpartment for Interˈnational Deˈvelopment** a British government department that gives help to poorer countries by sending money, food, equipment, etc. ⇨ note at AID.

the **Deˌpartment of ˈAgriculture** the US government department that helps farmers and controls agricultural practices. It is in charge of research into such problems as plant diseases and better ways to use the land. The Department also helps the public through programmes like its approval marks on meat and information concerning food safety.

the **De,partment of 'Commerce** the US government department in charge of trade within the country and with other nations. Its divisions include the Economic Development Administration, the Minority Business Development Agency, the Patent and Trademark Office and the Bureau of the Census.

the **De,partment of De'fense** (*abbr* the **DOD**) the US government department in charge of military forces. It is the government's largest department and receives the most money. The Secretary of Defense is never a military person. His assistants include the military *Joint Chiefs of Staff and three not in the armed forces, the Secretary of the Army, the Secretary of the Nav, and the Secretary of the Air Force.

the **De,partment of Edu'cation** the US government department that establishes policies for the country's schools and is in charge of national programmes for education, including financial help.

the **De,partment of 'Energy** the US government department that plans and controls the development of the country's sources of energy. It is particularly concerned with ways of saving energy sources and of producing more energy. It does research into the dangers of nuclear energy and also is in charge of the US nuclear weapons programme.

the **De,partment of 'Health** the British government department responsible for health. Its main duty is to manage the *National Health Service, and it is also in charge of social services to old people, children, the mentally ill and others in need, though decisions on spending in these areas are made by local authorities.

the **De'partment of 'Health and 'Human 'Services** (*abbr* the **HHS**) the US government department responsible for national health programmes and the *Social Services Administration.

the **De'partment of 'Housing and 'Urban De'velopment** (*abbr* **HUD**) the US government department in charge of financial programmes to build houses and to help people buy their own homes. It provides insurance for mortgages and helps pay for houses for poor and old people. It also plans the development of cities.

the **De,partment of 'Justice** the US government department responsible for making sure that national laws are obeyed. It is also in charge of prisons. The Department represents the government in legal cases and gives advice on legal matters to the *President. See also ATTORNEY GENERAL.

the **De,partment of 'Labor** the US government department responsible for national laws concerning workers. This includes working conditions, such as safety and the hours worked, as well as the pay workers receive. It is also in charge of job training programmes.

the **De'partment of 'Social Se'curity** (*abbr* the **DSS**) the British government department responsible for paying regular amounts of money from the state to people who are retired, ill or very poor, or who have young children.

the **De,partment of the In'terior** the US government department responsible for protecting the country's environment. Its divisions include the National Park Service, the Bureau of Land Management, the Fish and Wildlife Service and the Geological Survey. It is also in charge of government programmes for *Native Americans.

the **De,partment of the 'Treasury** the US government department responsible for national policies to do with money, including the collection of taxes through the *Internal Revenue Service. Other divisions include the US Customs, the US Mint, the *Bureau of Alcohol, Tobacco and Firearms, and the *Secret Service, which protects the *President.

the **De'partment of 'Trade and 'Industry** (*abbr* the **DTI**) the British government department responsible for trade policy, research and development in industry, and company law.

the **De,partment of Transpor'tation** the US government department in charge of national policy on transport. Its divisions include the *Federal Aviation Administration, the Federal Highway Administration, the National Transportation Safety Board, and, when there is no war, the *United States Coast Guard.

the **De'partment of 'Veterans Af'fairs** (*abbr* the **VA**) the US government department in charge of assistance for Americans who have served in the armed forces and for their families. This includes programmes that help to pay for education and houses, and payments after death or serious injury caused by military service. The Department also runs special hospitals.

departments of government

The government of the United Kingdom, formally called **Her Majesty's Government**, consists of a group of **ministers** led by the ***Prime Minister**. Ministers are attached to specialist **departments** which carry out government policy. **Ministers of the Crown**, the most senior ministers, are appointed by the Queen or King on the recommendation of the Prime Minister. Other ministers are appointed directly by the Prime Minister. All ministers sit in *Parliament, and most in the *House of Commons.

The senior minister in each department is generally called the **Secretary of State**, e.g. the Secretary of State for the Environment. The minister in charge of the ***Foreign and Commonwealth Office** is called the ***Foreign Secretary**. The ***Home Secretary** is in charge of the ***Home Office**. The finance minister is known as the ***Chancellor of the Exchequer** and is head of the ***Treasury**. Ministers in charge of departments are usually members of the *Cabinet. The Prime Minister may also appoint a **Minister without Portfolio** (= without departmental responsibilities) to take on special duties.

A Secretary of State is usually supported by several **Ministers of State**, who each have a specific area of responsibility, and **Parliamentary Under-Secretaries of State**, often called **junior ministers**.

Departments are run by ***civil servants** who are not allowed to show favour to any political party. Unlike ministers, they do not have to leave their jobs when the government changes. A change of government does not necessarily affect the number and organization of departments. A new government may, however, create new departments or change the structure of existing ones.

Some departments, e.g. the *Ministry of Defence, have responsibility for the whole of the United Kingdom. Others cover only part, e.g. the *Department for Education and Employment, which operates only in England and Wales. Scotland and Wales each have special departments, called the ***Scottish Office** and the ***Welsh Office**, but both countries are in process of setting up their own political assemblies (⇨ note at DEVOLUTION.).

The leader of the main opposition party appoints a **shadow cabinet** of **shadow ministers**. Each is responsible for knowing and speaking about an area of government.

In the US the *__federal government__ has 14 departments. These, together with the *President and various government **agencies**, make up the **executive branch** of the government and are responsible for its day-to-day operation.

The people in charge of government departments are called **Secretaries**. For example, the *Department of Agriculture is led by the Secretary of Agriculture. The head of the *__State Department__, the department that deals with US foreign policy, is called the *__Secretary of State__. The President decides who will be the head of each department. Not all secretaries are well known: many people know the name of the Secretary of State, but few know the Secretary of Agriculture.

Most of the people working in US government departments are civil servants whose jobs do not depend on political influence. In this way each department has a base of employees with a lot of knowledge and experience, whose careers last longer than a single political administration. Departments may be reorganized according to what issues seem important at a particular time but this kind of change does not happen often.

The heads of departments form a group called the Cabinet, which meets regularly with the President. The President is not required to accept their advice, but may choose to do.

---

deˌpendent ˈterritory ⇨ OVERSEAS TERRITORY.

ˌJohnny **ˈDepp** /dep/ (1963–) a US actor who often plays strange characters. He began his career as a member of The Kids pop group and now plays with the P band. His films include *A Nightmare on Elm Street* (1984), *Edward Scissorhands* (1990), *What's Eating Gilbert Grape?* (1993) and *Ed Wood* (1994).

the **Deˈpression** ⇨ GREAT DEPRESSION.

ˌ***De Proˈfundis*** /ˌdeɪ prəˈfʊndiːs/ a long letter written by Oscar *Wilde in 1897 and published in 1905. It was written to his lover, Lord Alfred *Douglas, when Wilde was in prison. The Latin title means *from the depths*, and the serious tone of the letter makes a strong contrast with the clever humour of his earlier works.

ˌThomas **De ˈQuincey** /də ˈkwɪnsi/ (1785–1859) an English writer who regularly took the drug opium and described its effects on him in his book, *Confessions of an English Opium-Eater* (1821). He was a friend of the poets *Wordsworth and *Coleridge.

ˈDerby[1] /ˈdɑːbi; *AmE* ˈdɑːrbi/ a city in central England famous for its fine *Crown Derby china and for *Rolls-Royce cars, aircraft engines and other engineering products.

the **ˈDerby**[2] /ˈdɑːbi; *AmE* ˈdɑːrbi/ a famous English horse race without jumps which is run every year at Epsom, near London, in May or June. Although **Derby Day** is always a Wednesday, the race is attended by large crowds, and there is a holiday atmosphere. The Derby was first run in 1780 and takes its name from the 12th *earl(1) of Derby, who was one of the original organizers of the event.

ˈDerbyshire /ˈdɑːbiʃə(r); *AmE* ˈdɑːrbiʃər/ a county in north central England. It contains the *Peak District national park. Its administrative centre is the town of Matlock.

ˈderringer /ˈderɪndʒə(r)/ a small US gun held in the hand. It was invented in 1825 by Henry Deringer and was popular in the *Wild West because a person could hide it easily, even in the hand. Derringers are still popular today and often kept by Americans in their homes for protection.

ˈDerry /ˈderi/ the second largest city in Northern Ireland. In 1611 the *Roman Catholic city of Derry, a port on the north coast, was settled by large numbers of *Protestants from England who gave it the new name of *Londonderry(1). This was the city's name until 1984 when it was officially changed back to Derry.

ˈDerwentwater /ˈdɜːwəntwɔːtə(r); *AmE* ˈdɜːrwəntwɔːtər/ one of the most beautiful lakes in the English *Lake District. The lake is surrounded by hills and mountains and has several small islands.

ˈDesert ˌIsland ˈDiscs a popular *BBC radio programme in which famous people choose the eight records they would most like to have with them if they were alone on an island. It has been broadcast regularly since the 1940s.

ˌ**Desert ˈRat** *n* [usu pl] (*infml*) a soldier in the British 7th Armoured Division, which fought in North Africa in *World War II. The Desert Rats were later among the soldiers sent to Kuwait in 1991 during the *Gulf War.

ˈOperation ˌ**Desert ˈShield** the name used for the military operation in which international armed forces, including British and US troops, were sent to protect Saudi Arabia after Iraq attacked Kuwait in 1990. The operation was announced by the US President George *Bush, and it developed into the *Gulf War.

ˈOperation ˌ**Desert ˈStorm** the name used for the military operation in which international armed forces, including British and US troops, attacked Iraq in the *Gulf War. It began on 16 January 1991 and lasted 100 days.

the **Deˈsign ˌCouncil** a British organization set up in 1944 to improve design in British industry. Its offices are in the *Haymarket, London, where it puts on exhibitions that are open to the public.

ˌ**Des ˈMoines** /ˌdə ˈmɔɪn/ the capital and largest city of the US state of *Iowa. It began as Fort Des Moines in 1843 and developed into a centre of the *Corn Belt. The city also grew because of coal mines in the area. It was named after the Des Moines River which runs through it.

ˌ**Desperate ˈDan** a character in the British *comic, *The *Dandy*. He is a very strong *cowboy with a big jaw who is not very intelligent but has a gentle nature. His favourite meal is 'cow pie'. In 1997 he was dropped from the comic but so many readers protested that he was brought back immediately.

deˈtective ˌstory (*also* **deˈtective ˌnovel**) *n* a story in which there is a murder or other crime and a detective who tries to solve it. The best-known British writers of detective stories include Arthur *Conan Doyle, Agatha *Christie and Ruth *Rendell. The older type of British detective story is often set in a large country house, and typically includes the discovery of a murder at the beginning, a small group of characters who are all suspected of having committed the murder, and a surprising solution at the end. In the US, detective stories more often involve the police or the adventures of a 'private eye' (= private detective), and are more violent and realistic. Famous US writers of such stories include Raymond *Chandler and Elmore *Leonard. Detective stories are also known as 'detective fiction' or 'crime fiction' and informally as 'whodunnits' (or 'whodunits').

Deˈtroit /dɪˈtrɔɪt/ **1** the largest city in the US state of *Michigan. It began in 1701 as a French trading post. It is on the Detroit River and connected by a bridge to Windsor, Canada. Detroit is the centre of the US car industry and often has many unemployed workers. It also has a music industry and produces salt from local mines, steel and chemicals. See also MOTOWN. **2** *n* [U] the US car industry: *What will Detroit do about Japanese imports?*

ˈ**Dettol**™ /ˈdetɒl; *AmE* ˈdetɑːl/ *n* [U] a strong liquid for killing bacteria, used especially for treating skin problems such as cuts, stings and spots.

ˌEamon **de Vaˈlera** /ˌeɪmən də vəˈleərə; *AmE* də vəˈlerə/ (1882–1975) an Irish political leader. He was put in prison by the British on various occasions and took part in the *Easter Rising against the British in 1916. He was leader of the *Sinn Fein party from 1917 until 1926 when he formed the *Fianna Fáil party. He directed the talks with Britain which led to southern Ireland's independence from Britain in 1921. He was *Prime Minister of the Irish republic three times and its President from 1959 to 1973.

Niˌnette **de ˈValois** /niːˌnet də ˈvælwɑː/ (1898–) the stage name of Edris Stannus, an Irish dancer and choreographer who had a great influence on the development of British ballet. After appearing in London and Paris in the early 1920s, she opened a ballet school in London with Lilian *Baylis. In 1931, she started the Vic–Wells ballet, which performed at *Sadler's Wells and later became the *Royal Ballet, which she directed until 1963. Among her works are *The Rake's Progress* (1935) and *Checkmate* (1937) with music by Arthur *Bliss. She was made a *dame(2) in 1951.

ˌ**devils-on-ˈhorseback** *n* [pl] **1** (*BrE*) a dish made with prunes wrapped in bacon and then cooked. It is often served at the end of a meal. **2** (*AmE*) a dish made with oysters wrapped in bacon and then cooked and served on toast with a spicy sauce, usually before a meal.

ˌDanny **DeˈVito** /dəˈviːtəʊ; *AmE* dəˈviːtoʊ/ (1944–) a US comic actor who also directs and produces films. Devito, who is short and fat, played the loud character Louis in the television series *Taxi* (1978–83). His film roles include being the twin brother of Arnold *Schwarzenegger in *Twins* (1987) and the evil Penguin in *Batman Returns* (1992). He also directed the films *The War of the Roses* (1989) and *Matilda* (1996).

devolution

Devolution involves the transfer of political power from a central government to a regional government. Scotland and Wales, mainly through their **nationalist** parties, the *Scottish National Party and *Plaid Cymru, both fought to have power **devolved** from the *Parliament of the United Kingdom to their own **political assemblies**. Both parties had only a few MPs in the British parliament.

Scotland has for a long time had its own system of law and a lot of control over its affairs, and the Secretary of State at the ***Scottish Office** had wide powers. Resentment in Scotland about the way it was treated by central government increased during the early 1990s, mainly because the *Conservative government had little support in Scotland. In response, the range of business handled by the **Scottish Grand Committee**, consisting of all 72 Scottish MPs, was widened. But opinion polls suggested that over 50% of people in Scotland wanted either **home rule** (= full control of Scottish affairs) within Britain, or complete independence.

Wales has always been concerned about its cultural as well as its political identity. The *Welsh language is spoken in many homes, especially in north and central Wales, and is taught in schools. Signs and public notices are written in both Welsh and English. The ***Welsh Office** in *Cardiff had responsibilities for the local economy, education and social welfare. As in Scotland, many people in Wales had for a long time wanted greater control over Welsh affairs, and in 1997 Tony *Blair promised to set up a ***Welsh Assembly** if *Labour won the 1997 general election. Labour did win the election, and soon after the new government held a **referendum** in both Scotland and Wales on the issue of devolution.

A large majority of Scottish people voted in favour of having their own ***Scottish Parliament** and it was officially opened on 1 July 1999. The Parliament consists of 129 **MSPs** (**Members of the Scottish Parliament**) some elected by *proportional representation. Elections will be held every four years. The Parliament is led by a **First Minister**. It has power to make laws on most matters affecting Scotland, including health, education, transport, local government and the environment. It also has limited powers to vary the basic rate of *income tax. The British government in London still has control of foreign policy, defence, economic policy, employment law and European matters. From 2001 the Assembly will be based in a building close to *Holyrood House in *Edinburgh.

Support for devolution was always less strong in Wales, and the people voted in favour of a Welsh parliament by only a very small majority. The Welsh Assembly, based in Cardiff, has 60 MPs led by a **First Secretary**. Unlike the Scottish Parliament it cannot vary taxes. The relatively small majority in favour of devolution in Wales persuaded the government to drop plans for similar referendums on devolution for other parts of Britain.

Scotland and Wales continue to have MPs in the British parliament in London, and people may be members of both parliaments. The roles of the Welsh Office and the Scottish Office are being revised. Some people feel that it is wrong that Welsh and Scottish MPs continue to discuss English affairs in the British parliament. See also NORTHERN IRELAND.

ˈ**Devon** /ˈdevən/ (*also* ˈ**Devonshire** /ˈdevənʃə(r)/) a *county in south-west England. With two national parks, *Dartmoor and *Exmoor, and two coasts, north and south, it is a popular area for holidays. The administrative centre is *Exeter.

ˌDonald ˈ**Dewar** /ˈdjuːə(r)/ (1937–) a British *Labour politician. He became a *Member of Parliament in 1966, and held several important positions in the Labour *Shadow Cabinet before becoming *Secretary of State for Scotland in 1997.

the ˌ**Dewey ˈdecimal ˌsystem** /ˌdjuːi/ the most commonly used system for organizing books in public libraries. It was invented by Melvil Dewey (1851–1931), a US librarian. Dewey gave every subject a number between 0 and 999. Every book in a library is given one of these numbers so that books on a particular subject are easy to find. New subjects have been added to Dewey's original list by using decimal numbers, e.g. 331.1, 331.2, etc.

DFC /ˌdiː ef ˈsiː/ ⇨ DISTINGUISHED FLYING CROSS.

DFEE /ˌdiː ef iː ˈiː/ ⇨ DEPARTMENT FOR EDUCATION AND EMPLOYMENT.

DFM /ˌdiː ef ˈem/ ⇨ DISTINGUISHED FLYING MEDAL.

ˈJack "Legs' ˈ**Diamond**[1] /ˈdaɪəmənd/ (1896–1931) a US leader of a crime organization in New York in the 1920s. He was called 'Legs' because, when young, he was a fast runner and could run away quickly after stealing something. During *Prohibition, he sold illegal alcohol and drugs. He killed a number of other criminal leaders but was himself murdered after he opposed a powerful one, 'Dutch' Schultz.

ˌNeil ˈ**Diamond**[2] /ˈdaɪəmənd/ (1941–) a popular US singer and writer of songs. These have included *Sweet Caroline* (1969), *I Am, I Said* (1971) and *Forever in Blue Jeans* (1979).

the ˌ**Diamond** ˈ**Sculls** a rowing race for sculls (= boats rowed by a single person) that takes place every year at *Henley in early June. The first of these races was in 1844 and it is now the most important international contest of its type.

Diˈana, ˈPrincess of ˈWales (*also* **Princess Diana**) (1961–1997) the former wife of Prince *Charles and the mother of Prince William and Prince Henry (Harry). Her name before she married was Lady Diana Spencer. The Spencer family are descended from the English kings *Charles II and *James II, and Diana's father became the 8th Earl Spencer. She was married to Prince Charles in *St Paul's Cathedral in 1981 and soon became the most popular member of the *royal family, often referred to informally as Di. However, the marriage failed and in 1992 the prince and princess separated. Although Princess Diana gave up her public duties and was divorced in 1996, she continued some of her work with charities and remained an object of intense interest to the press and the public. She died in a car accident in Paris while trying to escape from photographers, and her funeral, like her wedding, was watched by almost a fifth of the world's population.

Diana, Princess of Wales in Angola, 1997

The ˈ***Diary of a*** ˌ***Country*** ˈ***Parson*** the diary of James *Woodforde (1740–1803), which was published in five volumes (1924–31) more than a hundred years after his death. It describes Woodforde's life as a parson (= priest) in the country village of Weston Longeville in *Norfolk, and is full of enthusiasm for the ordinary pleasures of life, especially food.

The ˌ***Diary of a*** ˈ***Nobody*** the diary of Mr Charles *Pooter published in London in 1892. Pooter was not a real person; the diary was written by George and Weedon *Grossmith as a comic story of life in *suburbia and the type of person who lives there. It begins when the good but boring Mr Pooter and his wife move into their new house. Pooter describes the pleasures of home improvements, polite parties, his fear of social embarrassment and his many other small pleasures, problems and accidents.

Leoˌnardo **DiˈCaprio** /liːəˌnɑːdəʊ dɪˈkæpriəʊ; *AmE* liːəˌnɑːrdoʊ dɪˈkæprioʊ/ (1974–) a US actor who became an international star after his performance in the film *Titanic* (1998). He has a German mother and an Italian father. He began his career in television advertisements and small parts in television series. His other films include *This Boy's Life* (1993) and *The Man in the Iron Mask* (1998).

ˌCharles ˈ**Dickens** /ˈdɪkɪnz/ (1812–70) an English writer of novels who combined great writing with the ability to write popular stories full of interesting characters, such as *Scrooge, *Fagin and the *Artful Dodger. His many books are mostly about life in *Victorian(1) England and often describe the harsh conditions in which poor people lived. His early novels, which include **Pickwick Papers* and **Oliver Twist*, were written in parts for magazines. His later books include **David Copperfield, A *Tale of Two Cities* and **Great Expectations.*

Charles Dickens, painted by William Frith

ˌ***Dick*** ˈ***Tracy*** /ˈtreɪsi/ a US comic strip about a police detective. It began in 1931 and is still published. Tracy has a famous square chin and has fought criminals with colourful names such as Mumbles, Flattop and the Mole. There have been radio and television versions and several films, including *Dick Tracy* (1990) with Warren *Beatty.

A ˈ***Dictionary of*** ˈ***Modern*** ˈ***English*** ˈ***Usage*** a guide to the rules of good written British English, written by Henry Fowler (1858–1933). It was first published in 1926 and has become one of the standard reference books on the English language. It is often referred to as *Modern English Usage*, or simply 'Fowler': *Look it up in Fowler.*

The ˈ***Dictionary of*** ˈ***National Bi***ˈ***ography*** (*abbr* the **DNB**) a book in many volumes containing the life stories of famous British people from the earliest historical period to the present time. It is published by the *Oxford University Press and was first completed in 1900. A new DNB is published every few years to include people who have died recently.

ˌBo ˈ**Diddley** /ˌbəʊ ˈdɪdli; *AmE* ˌboʊ/ (1928–) an *African-American singer and writer of *rock music and the *blues. He also plays the guitar. The titles of his songs often include his own name, e.g. *Hey Bo Diddley* (1955). His music influenced the *Rolling Stones who have recorded several of his songs.

ˈˌBabe' ˈ**Didrikson** /ˈdɪdrɪksn/ (Mildred Didrikson 1913–56) an American woman who was famous in many sports, including *baseball, *basketball, *golf and *tennis. She has been called 'the greatest woman athlete in history'. In the 1932 Olympic Games she won the javelin and 80-metre hurdles race with world records. In 1938 Didrikson married George Zaharias, a wrestler, and began competing as 'Babe' Zaharias. She began playing professional golf in 1947 and won the US Women's Open three times.

Marˌlene ˈ**Dietrich** /mɑːˌleɪnə ˈdiːtrɪk; *AmE* mɑːrˈleɪnə/ (1901–92) a US film actress and singer, born in Germany. She was known for her deep voice and beautiful legs. She first became famous in Germany in *The Blue Angel* (1930), directed by Josef von Sternberg. They both went to *Hollywood where he directed her in such films as *Blonde Venus* (1932) and *The Scarlet Empress* (1934). Her later films included *Wit-*

ness for the Prosecution (1957) and *Judgment at Nuremberg* (1961).

ˌ**Dieu et mon ˈdroit** /ˌdjɜː eɪ mɒn ˈdrwɑː; *AmE* mɑːn/ a French phrase meaning *God and my right* which has been the motto of the English kings and queens since the 14th century.

ˈ**Dilbert** /ˈdɪlbət; *AmE* ˈdɪlbərt/ a US cartoon character created in 1989 by Scott Adams. Dilbert is an electrical engineer who works with computers in an office. He is polite and honest but often confused by the company's policies. The *Dilbert* cartoon makes fun of boring and stupid office jobs. It now appears in about 1 700 newspapers around the world and a television series began in 1998.

ˌJohn ˈ**Dillinger** /ˈdɪlɪndʒə(r)/ (1903–34) a US criminal who killed 16 people and robbed 20 banks in the *Midwest during the *Great Depression. The *FBI named him 'Public Enemy Number One'. Although he was violent, many Americans regarded Dillinger as an exciting person. He was killed by FBI men in *Chicago as he was leaving a cinema.

ˌJoe **Diˈ Maggio** /dɪˈmædʒiəʊ; *AmE* dɪˈmædʒioʊ/ (1914–99) one of America's most famous *baseball players. His popular name was 'Joltin' Joe'. He played for the New York *Yankees (1936–51) and helped them to win nine *World Series. He was named *Most Valuable Player in the *American League three times and was chosen for the Baseball *Hall of Fame in 1955. DiMaggio married the actor Marilyn *Monroe in 1954 but the marriage lasted only nine months.

ˌDavid ˈ**Dimbleby¹** /ˈdɪmblbi/ (1938–) a British television broadcaster who presents the *BBC's political programmes **Panorama* and **Question Time*, and programmes on national occasions, such royal weddings and funerals. He is the older son of Richard *Dimbleby.

ˌJonathan ˈ**Dimbleby²** /ˈdɪmblbi/ (1944–) a British radio and television broadcaster who presents the weekly *BBC radio programme **Any Questions?*. In 1994 he presented an important *ITV programme about Prince *Charles and he has also written newspaper articles about the prince. He is the younger son of Richard *Dimbleby.

ˌRichard ˈ**Dimbleby³** /ˈdɪmblbi/ (1913–65) a British radio and television broadcaster who presented Britain's first major political television programme, **Panorama*. He is also widely remembered among older people as the television presenter on the day of the *Coronation of Queen *Elizabeth II in 1953 and on other important occasions.

ˈ**dime ˌnovel** *n* (in the US) a type of cheap novel popular in the late 19th century and again from the 1920s to the 1940s. The writing in dime novels was often bad, but the action was fast. The original ones were usually about American *frontiersmen, such as *Buffalo Bill, and soldiers in US wars. The later ones were often about love, crime or horror.

ˌJim ˈ**Dine** /ˈdaɪn/ (1935–) a leading US artist in the *pop art movement. He used ordinary objects that he found and attached them to his paintings. He also created art 'happenings' (events and performances). Dine's recent work has been more traditional in style.

ˈ**Diners Club**™ /ˈdaɪnəz / the international company, based in Britain, that operates **Diners Club cards**, also known as **Diners cards**. These are charge cards, which allow members of Diners Club to pay for things using their card and settle their account at the end of each month. ⇨ note at CREDIT CARDS.

ˌDavid ˈ**Dinkins** /ˈdɪŋkɪnz/ (1927–) the first *African American to be elected *mayor of New York (1990–94). He is from the *Democratic Party. Dinkins was politically moderate and tried to bring people together. He was unable to solve the city's financial and racial problems, however, and was defeated in the next election by Rudolph Guiliani of the *Republican Party.

ˈ**Dinky Toy** ™ /ˈdɪŋki/ (*also* **Dinky**) *n* a British make of small toy vehicle. Dinky Toys have been popular since the 1930s and include a wide range of model cars and other vehicles. Old Dinky Toys are now collected by adults as a hobby and are very valuable.

dinner *n* [C, U] the main meal of the day, eaten either at midday or in the evening. In Britain the word *dinner* is used differently according to a person's social class or the place they come from. A **dinner party** is a private social occasion in the evening, to which guests are invited for dinner. See also TV DINNER. ⇨ note at MEALS.

ˈ**Diplock court** *n* a special court of law in *Northern Ireland for people accused of terrorist offences. Diplock courts were set up in 1972 under the British judge Lord Diplock (1907–85) when the normal system of trial by jury had become impossible because jury members were being threatened and even murdered. In Diplock courts, each case is heard by a single judge. The absence of a jury has been criticized as unfair, although the accused person has certain extra rights in these courts and there are independent checks on them.

Diˈploma of ˈHigher Eduˈcation *n* (in Britain) one of the qualifications that can be obtained from a British *college of higher education. A Diploma is higher than a Certificate but below a degree.

the ˌ**Diploˈmatic ˌService** the department of the British *Civil Service that provides staff to work in British embassies around the world for the *Foreign and Commonwealth Office.

Diˈrector of ˈPublic Proseˈcutions (*abbr* the **DPP**) the head of the *Crown Prosecution Service, which is responsible in England and Wales for deciding whether a case should be tried in a court of law. He or she is appointed by the *Attorney General.

diˌrect ˈrule *n* [U] (formerly) the control of law and order in *Northern Ireland by the British government instead of by the local government in *Belfast. Direct rule ended in 1998 when a new *Northern Ireland Assembly was elected.

ˌ**Dire ˈStraits** a British pop group formed in 1977. Their best-known albums were *Dire Straits* (1978) and *Brothers in Arms* (1985), which became the most successful album of all time in Britain with sales of more than 3 million copies.

ˌ***Dirty ˈHarry*** a US film (1971), directed by Don Siegel, about a tough *San Francisco police detective called Harry Callahan. The film was popular because at the time ordinary people felt threatened by the increase of violent crime in the US. Clint Eastwood played the part of Harry in this and two later films, *Magnum Force* (1973) and *The Enforcer* (1976).

the ***Disˈcovery*** the name of two famous British ships. The first was the ship in which Henry *Hudson sailed in 1610 to Hudson Bay, which he had discovered the previous year. The second *Discovery* was the ship in which Captain *Scott sailed on his first journey to the Antarctic (1901–4). This ship became a museum on the River *Thames in London until it was moved to the River *Tay in *Dundee, Scotland, where it was built.

the **Disˈcovery ˌChannel** a major US cable television channel, which offers programmes on history, technology, nature and adventure. The Discovery

Channel and *ABC together present a regular science news programme.

Dis'gusted, ˌTunbridge 'Wells /ˌtʌnbrɪdʒ 'welz/ (*BrE*) a humorous name for an angry *middle-class older person who writes strong letters of complaint to newspapers about modern behaviour. The name comes from the signature that such a person might put at the end of the letter instead of writing his or her name. *Tunbridge Wells is a town in *Kent where many such people are supposed to live.

D

ˌWalt **'Disney** /ˌwɒlt 'dɪzni; *AmE* ˌwɑːlt/ (1901–66) a US producer of films, especially cartoons. He created *Mickey Mouse and *Donald Duck, and made the first long cartoon films, which included **Snow White and the Seven Dwarfs* (1937), **Fantasia* (1940) and **Bambi* (1942). He also produced many successful nature films, the first of which was *The Living Desert* (1953), and films with live actors, such as *Treasure Island* (1950) and *Mary Poppins* (1964). Disney won 39 *Oscars for his work and people remember him as one of the greatest producers of family entertainment. He also had a television programme and created *Disneyland.

Mickey Mouse and Minnie Mouse lead celebrations on Main Street USA for 25 years of Walt Disney World

'Disneyland /'dɪznilænd/ the original US amusement park opened by Walt *Disney in 1955 at Anaheim, *California. It is divided into several different 'lands' including Adventureland, Frontierland and Tomorrowland, and also has hotels, restaurants and theatres. Similar parks built later are *Disney World in 1971, Tokyo Disneyland in 1983 and Disneyland Paris (Euro Disney) in 1992.

'Disney World /'dɪzni/ the popular name for Walt Disney World, the famous US amusement park near *Orlando, *Florida. It was opened in 1971 and is much larger than *Disneyland although it has similar features, such as live Disney characters, Main Street USA, Frontierland and Adventureland. It is the largest entertainment area in the world (about twice the size of *Manhattan(1)) and is being continuously developed. It includes Disney's newer attractions Magic Kingdom, Animal Kingdom, the EPCOT Center and the Disney–MGM Studios.

di'spatch box *n* **1** (in British political life) a red leather case in which important papers are delivered to senior government ministers. It is traditional for the *Chancellor of the Exchequer to hold his dispatch box up in the air for photographers and tourists to see when he goes to the *House of Commons to make his speech about the *budget each year. **2** [usu sing] either of the two wooden boxes which are permanently kept near the *mace on the table between the two front rows of seats in the *House of Commons. Government and Opposition ministers stand beside the dispatch box on their side of the table when speaking: *The Prime Minister made a lengthy statement from the dispatch box.* ⇨ picture at MACE.

'Disprin™ /'dɪsprɪn/ *n* [C, U] a mild medicine for relieving pain, such as headaches, etc. It is sold in tablets which can be dissolved in water.

ˌBenjamin **Dis'raeli** /dɪz'reɪli/ (1804–81) a British *Conservative politician who was twice *Prime Minister (1868 and 1874–80). He also wrote a number of popular novels which showed his interest in social change. He became leader of the *Conservative Party in 1846 and created its modern central organization. As Prime Minister, he increased Britain's influence abroad and he bought half of the Suez Canal for Britain. He also introduced improvements in housing for poor people in the cities and increased the number of people who could vote at elections. He became a close friend of Queen *Victoria, and she made him an *earl (the Earl of Beaconsfield) in 1876.

the **ˌDisso'lution of the 'Monasteries** /'mɒnəstriz; *AmE* 'mɑːnəstriz/ the destruction or sale of buildings and land belonging to religious communities in England by King *Henry VIII between 1536 and 1541 after he became head of the *Church of England. Henry wanted to make the Church less powerful and he needed money. Many people at the time felt that the Church was too rich and wasted its great wealth, so Henry had little difficulty in taking the Church's wealth for himself, although many fine old buildings were destroyed.

the **Diˌstinguished 'Flying Cross** (*abbr* the **DFC**) a medal for brave actions in battle which is given to officers in the *Royal Air Force.

the **Diˌstinguished 'Flying Medal** (*abbr* the **DFM**) a medal for brave actions in battle which is given to men below officer rank in the *Royal Air Force.

the **Diˌstinguished 'Service Cross** (*abbr* the **DSC**) *n* a British medal for brave actions, given to officers in the *Royal Navy since 1914 and in the *merchant navy (= the country's commercial ships) since 1942.

the **Diˌstinguished 'Service Order** (*abbr* the **DSO**) *n* a British medal for brave actions, given since 1886 to officers in the *Royal Navy and the Army and now also to officers in the *Royal Air Force and the *merchant navy (= the country's commercial ships).

ˌdistrict at'torney *n* (*AmE*) (*abbr* **DA**) a lawyer in a particular district who is responsible for bringing legal charges against people. He or she represents a state government or the US government. Successful district attorneys often become politicians. Compare CROWN PROSECUTION SERVICE.

ˌdistrict 'council *n* (in Britain) the *local government for a district, which may be a town, part of a large city or part of a *county. The members of a district council are elected for four years by the people living in the district and are responsible for local services such as local roads, buses, parks and libraries.

ˌDistrict of Co'lumbia /'kəlʌmbiə/ (*abbr* **DC**) the district of the US capital city of *Washington, DC. The city covers all of the land. It is on the east side of the *Potomac River and belongs to the US government. It was established by *Congress in 1790 and contains many government buildings. The land was originally given by the states of *Virginia and *Maryland, though Virginia later took back its gift. People who live in the district were not allowed to vote for US President until 1961.

the **di'vine 'right of 'kings** *n* [sing] the idea that kings and queens are given their right to rule by God and that therefore nobody should question that right. The last king in Britain to rule completely according to this belief was *Charles I. After the *English Civil War the idea was gradually replaced by *constitutional monarchy.

ˈ**Dixie** /ˈdɪksi/ (*also* ˈ**Dixieland** /ˈdɪksilænd/) an informal US name for the south-eastern states. It came from the song **Dixie* but has never been fully explained. It may refer to the imaginary *Mason-Dixon line that separates the North from the South.

ˈ***Dixie*** /ˈdɪksi/ the battle song of the *Confederate States. It was written in 1859 in New York as *Dixie's Land* by Daniel Emmett, who was later upset that it became the 'Confederate national anthem'. *Dixie* was, however, a favourite song of Abraham *Lincoln. It begins

I wish I was in the land of cotton,
Old times there are not forgotten;
Look away, look away, look away,
Dixie land!

the ˈ**Dixiecrats** /ˈdɪksikræts/ (in US politics), the popular name for the States' Rights Party, a 'third party' that competed in the 1948 election for US President against the *Democratic Party and *Republican Party. It was formed to support *states' rights. The candidate was J Strom *Thurmond, who won five states in the *South with 39 votes in the *Electoral College.

ˈ**Dixie Cup**™ *n* a US make of small paper cup. People usually buy a quantity of them in a plastic container which can be kept in the kitchen or bathroom.

ˈ**Dixieland** /ˈdɪksilænd/ (*also* ˌ**Dixieland** ˈ**jazz** /ˌdɪksilænd/) **1** *n* [U] a type of US *jazz music played by a small band. It has a strong, happy rhythm, and the musicians also play individually during a song. Dixieland began in the South at the end of the 19th century and is still popular, especially in *New Orleans. The best known Dixieland song is *When the Saints Go Marching In.* **2** ⇨ DIXIE.

ˈ***Dixon of*** ˌ***Dock*** ˈ***Green*** /ˈdɪksn/ the first police series on *BBC television (1955–76). The main character was a London policeman, Sergeant Dixon of Dock Green police station, played by the actor Jack Warner, who always introduced the programme with the words 'Evening all' (meaning 'Good evening, everybody'). Dixon represented many people's idea of the traditional British policeman: friendly, helpful and completely honest.

ˈ**Dixons**™ /ˈdɪksnz/ any of a group of shops in Britain that sell electronic equipment such as televisions, cameras and computers. The group, which also owns *Currys, is the largest group of this type in Britain.

DIY /ˌdiː aɪ ˈwaɪ/ (*in full* **do-it-yourself**) *n* [U] (*esp BrE*) repairing, painting, improving or adding to your own house without the help of professional workmen. This is one of the most popular free time activities in Britain and almost every town has at least one large DIY shop, where all the necessary materials and equipment are sold.

DMs /ˌdiː ˈemz/ ⇨ DOC MARTENS.

D-notice /ˈdiː ˌnəʊtɪs; *AmE* ˌnoʊtɪs/ *n* an official notice from the British government advising the press not to publish certain information because it would harm the country if it were to be made public. The 'D' in 'D-notice' stands for 'Defence'.

ˌFrank ˈ**Dobson** /ˈdɒbsn; *AmE* ˈdɑːbsn/ (1940–) a British *Labour politician. He became a *Member of Parliament in 1979 and held several important positions in the Labour *Shadow Cabinet before becoming *Secretary of State for Health in 1997.

ˈ**Dockers**™ /ˈdɒkəz; *AmE* ˈdɑːkərz/ a popular US make of trousers/pants. They are made of khaki (= a strong cloth of a brownish yellow colour) by the Levi Strauss Company. Styles include long and short lengths and golf trousers. Compare LEVI'S.

ˈ**Docklands** /ˈdɒkləndz; *AmE* ˈdɑːkləndz/ an area of new houses and offices in east London, England, on the north side of the River *Thames where London's commercial docks used to be. The old docks were too shallow for large modern ships and this had become a poor area, so the London Docklands *Urban Development Corporation was set up by the government in 1979 to develop it. The project had many problems, but the area now has a new life and includes one of Europe's tallest buildings, the *Canary Wharf tower. Some people have criticized the development because only rich people and yuppies have enough money to buy the expensive new Docklands houses.

ˌ**Doc** ˈ**Martens** /ˌdɒk ˈmɑːtɪnz; *AmE* ˌdɑːk ˈmɑːrtɪnz/ (*abbr* **DMs**) *n* [pl] a popular British make of strong shoes and boots. A special feature of them is a 'cushion of air' under the foot to make them more comfortable to wear. DMs were part of the uniform of the *skinheads in the 1960s and the *punks in the late 1970s, after which they became more widely fashionable among young and older people.

Doctor In some entries the word **Doctor** is replaced by its normal written abbreviation, **Dr**, e.g. **Dr Scholl's, Dr Seuss**.

ˈ**doctorate** *n* the highest type of university degree, e.g. a PhD (Doctor of Philosophy). A person with a doctorate has the title of 'Doctor' and can write 'Dr' before his or her name. Doctorates are sometimes given as an honour, e.g. to politicians.

ˌ**Doctor** ˈ**Dolittle** /ˈduːlɪtl/ the main character in a series of children's books by the English author Hugh Lofting (1886–1947). Dr Dolittle is an expert in animal languages and has many animal friends who he defends against humans when necessary. One is a strange animal called a Push-me-pull-you, with a head at each end of its body. The doctor first appeared in *The Story of Doctor Dolittle* (1920).

ˌ***Doctor*** ˈ***Faustus*** /ˈfaʊstəs/ one of the greatest plays of Christopher *Marlowe, written in about 1590. Its full title is *The Tragical History of Dr Faustus*. It is about a man who has studied all sciences and arts and finds nothing more in the world to study, so he turns to magic. He sells his soul to the Devil in return for 24 years of power and pleasure. He enjoys his 24 years but is finally dragged away by the Devil.

ˌ***Doctor*** ˈ***Foster*** /ˈfɒstə(r); *AmE* ˈfɑːstər/ a character in a short children's poem from the mid 19th century. Nobody knows whether the doctor was a real person or not. These are the words of the poem:

Doctor Foster went to Gloucester
In a shower of rain.
He stepped in a puddle
Right up to his middle,
And never went there again.

ˌE L ˈ**Doctorow** /ˈdɒktərəʊ; *AmE* ˈdɑːktəroʊ/ (Edgar Laurence Doctorow 1931–) a US writer of novels in which fiction is often combined with historical facts. His books include *Ragtime* (1975) and *Billy Bathgate* (1989).

ˌ***Doctor*** ˈ***Who*** /ˈhuː/ a *BBC television science-fiction series (1963–89) made for older children and also popular with many adults. The main character was Doctor Who himself, who travelled through time and space in a machine called the *Tardis. In his adventures he had to fight many strange enemies, including the *Daleks and the Cybermen.

DOD ⇨ DEPARTMENT OF DEFENSE.

ˌKen ˈ**Dodd** /ˈdɒd; *AmE* ˈdɑːd/ (1931–) an English

comedian and singer from *Liverpool with untidy hair and big teeth that stick out. His type of comedy continues many of the old traditions of the *music-hall. In 1989 he was tried for tax offences but the court found him innocent.

Dodge™ /dɒdʒ; *AmE* dɑːdʒ/ a make of US car produced by the Chrysler Corporation.

ˌ**Dodge** ˈ**City** /ˌdɒdʒ; *AmE* ˌdɑːdʒ/ a city in the US state of *Kansas. Originally called Buffalo City, it was important in the 19th century as a centre for cattle at the end of the *Santa Fe Trail. At that time it had a reputation for violence and was known as 'the wickedest little city in America'. See also EARP.

ˈ**dodgems** (*also* ˈ**dodgem cars**, ˈ**bumper cars**) *n* [pl] electric cars for two people at fairgrounds. A ride on the dodgems involves driving around within an enclosed area, either bumping into (= hitting) or dodging (= trying to avoid) the other cars. ⇨ note at FAIRS.

on the dodgems

ˈCharles ˈLutwidge ˈ**Dodgson** /ˈlʌtwɪdʒ ˈdɒdʒsn; *AmE* ˈdɑːdʒsn/ (1832–98) the real name of the English children's author Lewis *Carroll.

ˌSamuel ˈ**Dodsworth** /ˈdɒdswɜːθ; *AmE* ˈdɑːdswɜːrθ/ a character in the novel *Dodsworth* (1929) by Sinclair *Lewis. Dodsworth has retired from his job and travels to Europe with his wife. Lewis uses him to show the different values and behaviour of Americans and Europeans. He is also seen as an example of a typical rich man who cannot communicate well with his wife.

ˈ**Dog Chow**™ *n* [U] a popular US make of dry dog food, made by Ralston Purina. The company also makes Puppy Chow, Cat Chow and Kitten Chow.

ˈ**Doggett's** ˈ**Coat and** ˈ**Badge** /ˈdɒgɪts; *AmE* ˈdɑːgɪts/ a rowing race that has been held every year since 1715 on the River *Thames between *London Bridge and *Chelsea. The winner receives a red coat in 18th-century style and a silver badge. It was started by the Irish comedian Thomas Doggett (*c.* 1670–1721), and is the oldest regular sporting contest in Britain.

ˈ**doggy bag** *n* a paper or plastic bag provided by a restaurant at the end of a meal for customers who want to take home any of their food that they have not eaten. This is normal practice in the US but not in Britain, where guests are sometimes given doggy bags after a party.

ˌ**do-it-your**ˈ**self** ⇨ DIY.

ˈ**Dolby**™ *n* [U] /ˈdɒlbi; *AmE* ˈdɑːlbi/ an electronic system that reduces noise to improve the sound of tape recordings, films, etc. It was invented in London by Ray Dolby (1933–), a recording engineer born in the US: *The new cinema has a Dolby sound system.*

ˌBob ˈ**Dole** /ˈdəʊl; *AmE* ˈdoʊl/ (1923–) the *Republican Party candidate for *President who lost the 1996 election to President Bill *Clinton. He also lost as a candidate for Vice-president in 1976. Dole was a lawyer who became a member of the US *Senate from *Kansas in 1968 and the Senate Majority Leader in 1985.

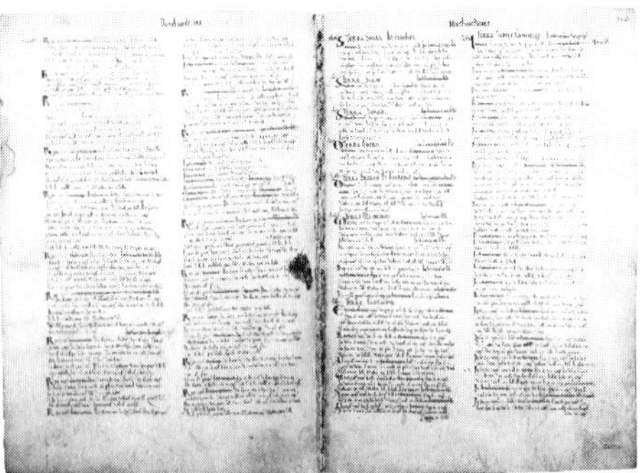

the Domesday Book

ˌAnton ˈ**Dolin** /ˌæntɒn ˈdɒlɪn; *AmE* ˌæntɑːn ˈdɔːlɪn/ (1904–83) an English dancer and choreographer. He began his career with Diaghilev's Ballets Russes in Paris and later formed several ballet companies with Alicia *Markova, including the one which became the *English National Ballet. He was made a *knight in 1981.

ˈ**dolly** ˌ**mixture** *n* [U] (*BrE*) small brightly coloured sweets, bought especially by children.

the ˈ***Domesday Book*** /ˈduːmzdeɪ/ a written record of the ownership and value of land in England in 1086. It was made for *William the Conqueror in order to calculate the size and value of the king's property and the tax value of other land in the country. The book is of great historical importance because it tells us a lot about England at that time. It can be seen at the *Public Record Office in London.

ˌ**Domi**ˈ**nica** /ˌdɒmɪˈniːkə; *AmE* ˌdɑːmɪˈniːkə/ a island with many mountains in the eastern *Caribbean which has been a member of the *Commonwealth since it became independent in 1978. It has a population of about 100 000 and its capital city is Roseau. ▶ **Dominican** *adj*, *n*.

ˈˌFats' ˈ**Domino** /ˌfæts ˈdɒmɪnəʊ; *AmE* ˈdɑːmɪnoʊ/ (*born* Antoine Domino 1928–) an *African American *rock musician who plays the piano and sings in a happy, easy style. He was especially popular in the 1950s, when his most successful songs included *Ain't That A Shame* (1955) and *Blueberry Hill* (1956). Domino was chosen in 1986 for the Rock and Roll *Hall of Fame.

'Fats' Domino

ˌ**Domino's** ˈ**Pizza** /ˌdɒmɪnəʊz; *AmE* ˌdɑːmɪnoʊz/ the largest company in the world delivering pizzas to people's homes. It was started in 1960 and by 1998 it had more than 6 000 shops in the US and in 53 other countries. The company's policy is not to charge for its pizzas if they are delivered late or the customer is not satisfied.

ˌ**Donald** ˈ**Duck** a popular cartoon character created by Walt *Disney. Donald first appeared in *The Wise Little Hen* (1934) He is a lively and sometimes bad-tempered duck, with a voice that is difficult to understand. He has a female friend called Daisy, and three young nephews, Huey, Dewey and Louie. Compare MICKEY MOUSE, BUGS BUNNY.

ˈ**Doncaster** /ˈdɒŋkəstə(r); *AmE* ˈdɑːŋkəstər/ an industrial town in south *Yorkshire in the north of England. It is famous for the *St Leger, a horse race that has been run there every year since 1776.

*The ˈ**Dong with a ˈLuminous ˈNose*** /ˈdɒŋ; *AmE* ˈdɑŋ/ a nonsense poem (1877) by Edward *Lear about an imaginary creature with a light on his nose to help him search at night for his lost love, a 'Jumbly Girl' with blue hands and green hair.

ˈ**donkey ˌderby** *n* (*BrE*) a race on donkeys (= animals of the horse family), usually ridden by children on the beach or at a *fête.

ˌJohn ˈ**Donne** /ˈdʌn/ (*c.* 1572–1631) an English poet who is now regarded as the greatest of the *metaphysical poets. In his youth he was a law student, soldier, drinker, lover and writer of love poems which are famous for their original and surprising comparisons. In one, for example, he compares a woman to a newly discovered continent: 'Oh, my America! my new-found land!' In 1615 he became an *Anglican priest, and six years later Dean of *St Paul's Cathedral. He became famous as a religious speaker and writer, putting the same powerful emotion and imagination into his religious poetry as he had put into his love poems.

ˈ**doodle-bug** /ˈduːdlbʌg/ *n* ⇨ V1.

Eˌliza ˈ**Doolittle[1]** /ˈduːlɪtl/ a character in *Pygmalion*, a comedy play by George Bernard *Shaw, and in *My Fair Lady*, the musical comedy based on it. She is a London *flower girl(2) with a strong *cockney *accent who is taught by a language expert, Professor Henry Higgins, to speak like an *upper-class woman.

ˌHilda ˈ**Doolittle[2]** /ˈduːlɪtl/ (1886–1961) a US poet who also wrote plays, novels and children's stories. She usually wrote as 'H D'. From 1911 to 1937 she lived in Europe, where she was influenced by Ezra *Pound and married the poet Richard Aldington (1913–37). Her collections of poetry include *Sea Garden* (1916) and *The Walls Do Not Fall* (1944).

ˈ***Doonesbury*** /ˈduːnzbri/ a US *comic strip by Gary Trudeau (1948–) which appears in many newspapers and which won the *Pulitzer Prize in 1975. It makes fun of the politics and personal lives of a group of Americans who were once *hippies.

The **Doors** /dɔːz; *AmE* dɔːrz/ a US *rock group formed in 1965. The singer was Jim *Morrison. He and the band were regularly in trouble for bad behaviour, and their songs were criticized for emphasizing drugs and sex. These included *Light My Fire* (1967) and *Touch Me* (1969). After Morrison died, the band continued into the early 1980s. Their story was told in the film *The Doors* (1991).

ˈ**doo-wop** /ˈduː wɒp; *AmE* ˈduː wɑːp/ *n* [U] an African-American style of singing popular in the 1950s. It involved groups singing in harmony, and nonsense phrases like 'doo-wop' and 'sha-boom' regularly repeated. Early doo-wop groups included the Drifters and the Platters.

DORA /ˈdɔːrə/ ⇨ DEFENCE OF THE REALM ACT.

ˈ**Dorchester[1]** /ˈdɔːtʃəstə(r); *AmE* ˈdɔːrtʃəstər/ a town in *Dorset in southern England with a long history. Nearby *Maiden Castle was occupied at least 4 000 years ago, and there was a Roman town, Durnovaria, where Dorchester now stands. In the 19th century, the *Tolpuddle Martyrs were put on trial in Dorchester and the author Thomas *Hardy was born there. In his novels the town is called Casterbridge.

The ˈ**Dorchester[2]** /ˈdɔːtʃəstə(r); *AmE* ˈdɔːrtʃəstər/ a well-known expensive hotel in London's *Park Lane. It first opened in 1931.

Dorset a *county on the coast of south-west England. Its administrative centre is *Dorchester. The author Thomas *Hardy set many of his stories in Dorset.

ˈTommy and ˈJimmy ˈ**Dorsey** /ˈdɔːsi; *AmE* ˈdɔːrsi/ Two US brothers who, together and separately, led a number of popular dance bands in the 1930s and 1940s. Tommy played the trombone and Jimmy played the clarinet. They appeared together in the film *The Fabulous Dorseys* (1947) and then formed another band together in 1953.

D

ˌJohn **Dos ˈPassos** /dɒs ˈpæsɒs; *AmE* dɑːs ˈpæsɑːs/ (1896–1970) a US author who wrote about the problems of 20th century American life. He is best known for *USA*, a series of three related novels called *42nd Parallel* (1930), *1919* (1932) and *The Big Money* (1936). Dos Passos used fictional characters and real events in describing the failures of modern society.

ˌ**Dotheboys ˈHall** /ˌduːðəbɔɪz/ ⇨ *NICHOLAS NICKLEBY*.

ˌAbner ˈ**Doubleday** /ˌæbnə ˈdʌbldeɪ; *AmE* ˌæbnər/ (1819–93) a US general in the American *Civil War. He was in *Fort Sumter when it was attacked by the South. According to a story that is probably not true, he invented the game of baseball (in 1839).

ˌ**double ˈGloucester** /ˈglɒstə(r); *AmE* ˈglɑːstər/ *n* [U] a type of hard English cheese first made in *Gloucestershire. It is orange in colour and has a mild taste.

ˌ**double-ˈheader** *n* [C] (*AmE*) (in baseball) two games played on the same day, usually by the same two teams, with a short interval in between. Double-headers are traditionally played on Sundays.

ˌ**double ˈjeopardy** *n* [U] (in US law) putting somebody on trial or punishing them for something for which they have already been tried or punished. This is not allowed under the *Fifth Amendment of the US Constitution: *Even though the police had new evidence, they could not put him in double jeopardy.*

ˈ**Douglas[1]** /ˈdʌgləs/ the capital of the *Isle of Man. It is a port, mainly for boats from *Liverpool, and a holiday town. See also TYNWALD.

ˌKirk ˈ**Douglas[2]** /ˈdʌgləs/ (1916–) a US film actor well known for playing tough characters. His films include *Lust for Life* (1956), *Gunfight at the O.K. Corral* (1957) and *Spartacus* (1960). He has also written several novels.

ˌLord ˈAlfred ˈ**Douglas[3]** /ˈdʌgləs/ (1870–1945) the young English aristocrat who was Oscar *Wilde's lover when Wilde was arrested and sent to prison for homosexuality, which was illegal at that time. The long letter that Wilde wrote in prison, published later as *De Profundis* (1897), was addressed to Douglas.

ˌMichael ˈ**Douglas[4]** /ˈdʌgləs/ (1944–) a US film actor well known for playing strong, emotional characters. He received an *Oscar for his role as a tough financial expert in *Wall Street* (1987). His other films have included *Fatal Attraction* (1987), *The War of the Roses* (1989), *Basic Instinct* (1992) and *The Game* (1997). He is the son of the actor Kirk *Douglas.

ˌStephen ˈ**Douglas[5]** /ˈdʌgləs/ (1813–61) a US politician who defeated Abraham *Lincoln in 1858 for the US *Senate but lost to him in the 1860 election for US *President. The Lincoln-Douglas debates are famous in US history. Douglas's *Kansas-Nebraska Act allowed new states to choose whether they wanted slaves. He had the popular name of the 'Little Giant'.

ˈAlec ˈ**Douglas-ˈHome** /ˈdʌgləs ˈhjuːm/ (1903–95) a British *Conservative politician and *prime minister (1963–4). He was an *MP when he became Lord

Home on the death of his father in 1951 and moved to the *House of Lords. But in 1963 he gave up his title so that he could return to the *House of Commons as Sir Alec Douglas-Home and become *Prime Minister. Later that year the Conservatives lost the election, and Edward *Heath became the party leader. In the next Conservative government Douglas-Home was *Foreign Secretary (1970–4) under Heath. In 1974 he was made a *life peer and returned to the House of Lords as Lord Home.

D

ˌFrederick **ˈDouglass** /ˈdʌgləs/ (1817–95) a US slave who escaped in 1838, wrote the story of his life as a slave and later went to England, where friends gave him enough money to return to America and buy his freedom. He became the leading African American working to end the system of *slavery and was the US government's representative to Haiti from 1889 to 1891. He also established the *North Star* newspaper in Rochester, New York.

ˌDove ˈCottage /ˌdʌv/ a house in the village of *Grasmere in the English *Lake District where the poet William *Wordsworth lived with his sister Dorothy from 1799 to 1808, after which it became the home of another poet, Thomas *De Quincey.

ˈDover /ˈdəʊvə(r); *AmE* ˈdoʊvər/ a port in *Kent, south-east England, and the nearest English town to France. The part of the *Channel between Dover and Calais (called the **Strait of Dover)** is 21 miles/34 kilometres wide and is one of the busiest sea routes in the world. The high *white cliffs of Dover, which can be seen from a distance, have a special meaning to British people returning home by this route. Dover has a long history. It was a town in Roman times, and its castle, which was the administrative centre of the *Cinque Ports, was an important part of the country's defences.

the port and white cliffs of Dover

ˌLord **ˈDowding** /ˈdaʊdɪŋ/ (*born* Hugh Dowding 1882–1970) the British *Royal Air Force officer in charge of *Fighter Command from 1936 and during *World War II. He was made a *knight in 1933 and a *life peer in 1943. There is a statue of him in front of the church of *St Clement Danes in London.

ˌAnthony **ˈDowell** /ˈdaʊwl/ (1943–) the director of the British *Royal Ballet since 1988. He joined the Royal Ballet as a dancer in 1961 and often danced with Antoinette Sibley in roles created for them by Frederick *Ashton. In the 1970s he also worked with the American Ballet Theatre in New York. He was made a *knight in 1995.

the **ˌDow-Jones ˈAverage** /ˌdaʊ dʒəʊnz; *AmE* ˌdaʊ dʒoʊnz/ (*also* the **ˌDow-Jones ˈIndex**, *infml* the **Dow**) any of several numbers produced on each day of trade by the *New York Stock Exchange. They each represent the total average price of the shares of certain specific companies. The Dow began in 1884 and is used to measure the strength of the US stock market. The numbers are in points, not dollars. Four separate averages are given, and the most important is the Dow-Jones Industrial Average, based on 30 major companies. Compare FINANCIAL TIMES INDICES.

ˈDowning Street /ˈdaʊnɪŋ/ a short street in *Westminster(1), London, which contains the official London home of the British *Prime Minister at number 10. In fact, the words 'Downing Street' and '*Number Ten' are often used to mean the Prime Minister's office or the British government. In the same street is the official home of the *Chancellor of the Exchequer at Number 11 and the office of the Chief *Whip at Number 12. The street was built in about 1680 by an *MP, George Downing.

the **ˈDowning Street ˌDeclaˈration** /ˈdaʊnɪŋ/ a statement about *Northern Ireland made by the British and Irish *prime ministers, John *Major and Albert Reynolds, in London in December 1993. The Declaration tried to push forward the peace process in Northern Ireland by offering something to all the opposing groups. For the first time the British government agreed to include *Sinn Fein in discussions if they and the *IRA promised not to use violence in future. In the following year the IRA stopped their bombing campaign, but refused to make any promises about the use of violence.

ˌDown in the ˈValley a US *folk song about a man who asks a woman if she loves him. Kurt *Weill wrote an opera (1948) with the same name, based on the song. It begins

Down in the valley, the valley so low,
Hang your head over, hear the winds blow.
Hear the winds blow, Dear, hear the winds blow.
Hang your head over, hear the winds blow.

the **Downs** the general name for a number of ranges of low chalk hills, covered with grass but no trees, in southern England. The different ranges have different names, including the North Downs, the *South Downs and the Berkshire Downs.

ˌDownside ˈSchool /ˌdaʊnsaɪd/ an English *Roman Catholic *public school(1) for boys at Downside, near *Bath. The school was started in France in 1606 because at that time Roman Catholic schools were not allowed in England. However, the school moved to England after the French Revolution and has been at Downside since 1814. Its history is therefore similar to that of *Ampleforth College.

ˈDowntown /ˈdaʊntaʊn/ **1** the area of *Manhattan(1) in New York City that is south of 34th Street. It includes *Wall Street, the *Chase Manhattan Bank, the *World Trade Center, *Greenwich Village and *SoHo. Compare UPTOWN 1. **2 ˈdowntown** *n* (*AmE*) the central business area of any large town or city.
▶ **downˈtown** *adj*, *adv* (*AmE*) to or in the centre of a town or city, especially the main business area: *a downtown store* ○ *Let's go downtown and see a movie.*

ˌDown Your ˈWay a *BBC radio programme in which the presenter visited a different place in Britain each week to talk to local people. It was broadcast on Sunday afternoons for more than 40 years (1946–87).

ˈArthur ˈConan **ˈDoyle** ⇨ CONAN DOYLE.

ˈRichard **ˈD'Oyly ˈCarte** /ˈdɔɪli ˈkɑːt; *AmE* ˈkɑːrt/ (1844–1901) the man who brought W S *Gilbert and Sir Arthur *Sullivan together to write their very successful series of operas, called the *Savoy Operas because they were performed after 1881 at D'Oyly Carte's new Savoy Theatre in London. D'Oyly Carte also built the *Savoy Hotel.

DPP /ˌdiː piː ˈpiː/ ⇨ DIRECTOR OF PUBLIC PROSECUTIONS.

ˈDracula a character in many horror films who is a vampire (= a dead person who comes alive at night to suck the blood of living people). He was created by the Irish writer Bram Stoker (1847–1912) in his novel *Dracula* (1897).

the **draft** *n* [sing] (*AmE*) the US government's Selective Service system, in which young people were required by law to serve in the armed forces. It was replaced in 1973 by a system in which people may join the forces only if they wish to. However, young men must still add their names to the **draft list** when they are 18, in case of a future military emergency. People who tried to avoid the draft, especially during the *Vietnam War, were known as **draft dodgers**. ⇨ note at NATIONAL SERVICE.

ˈ***Dragnet*** /ˈdræɡnet/ a US television police series in the early 1950s and again in the 1960s on *NBC. It received three *Emmy awards (1952–4). Jack Webb wrote and produced it and played the main character, Sergeant Joe Friday. *Dragnet* had earlier been a radio series, and was based on cases of the Los Angeles Police Department. It was the first US programme of its type to be shown on British television (in 1955).

ˌFrancis ˈ**Drake** /ˈdreɪk/ (*c.* 1540–96) an English sailor who fought against the Spanish and was the first Englishman to sail around the world. After a successful career attacking and robbing Spanish ships in the *Caribbean, he was given five ships by Queen *Elizabeth I to sail around the world, attacking Spanish ships along the way. When he returned three years later (1580) in the only surviving ship, the **Golden Hind*, Queen Elizabeth made him a *knight.

In 1587 the Spanish were preparing to attack England, but Drake led a surprise attack on the port of Cadiz and burnt the Spanish ships. When the Spanish attack, known as the *Armada, finally came in 1588, Drake was one of the leaders who defeated it. There is a popular belief that he was playing *bowls when the Armada was first seen and that he calmly finished his game before turning his attention to the enemy.

Dramˈbuie™ /dræmˈbjuːi/ *n* [U, C] a very strong alcoholic drink made from Scotch *whisky and drunk in a small glass, usually after a meal. The name comes from a *Gaelic phrase meaning 'the drink that pleases'.

ˈ**draught beer** (*BrE*) (*AmE* **draft beer**) *n* [C, U] beer that is stored in and served from a large container, usually a barrel. Many people who know a lot about beer think draught beer is better than beer sold in bottles or tins: *They do some good draught beers at the local pub.* ⇨ note at BEER.

*The ˌ**Dream of Geˈrontius*** /dʒəˈrɒntiəs; *AmE* dʒəˈrɑːntiəs/ a religious poem 1865 by Cardinal *Newman which was made into a musical work for voices and orchestra by Edward *Elgar in 1900.

ˌ**DreamWorks SKˈG** /ˌdriːmwɜːks es keɪ ˈdʒiː; *AmE* ˌdriːmwɜːrks/ a US film company established in *Hollywood in 1994 by Steven *Spielberg, Jeffrey Katzenberg and David Geffen. Its films have included *The Peacemaker* (1997) and *The Lost World: Jurassic Park* (1997).

the ˌ**Dred ˈScott Case** /ˌdred ˈskɒt; *AmE* ˈskɑːt/ (*also* the ˌ**Dred ˈScott deˌcision**) a US *Supreme Court decision in 1857 that a slave was not a citizen and could not begin a legal case against anyone. Dred Scott was a slave who wanted a court to say he was free because his owner took him to a free state. The Supreme Court also decided that *Congress had no power to prevent *slavery in new states. The case divided the nation and led indirectly to the *Civil War.

the ˌ**Dresden ˈbombing** /ˌdrezdən/ the destruction of the East German city of Dresden in 1945 by British planes of *Bomber Command. On the night of 13 February about 1 300 planes dropped more than 3 000 tons of bombs on the city, killing tens of thousands of men, women and children. The attack has been much criticized because it caused the deaths of ordinary people, not soldiers. See also HARRIS.

ˌNancy ˈ**Drew** /ˈdruː/ the main character in a series of US children's books written by Carolyn Keene, a name used by Mildred Augustine Wirt. Nancy is a young amateur *detective who solves mysteries. The series began in 1929 with *The Secret of the Old Clock* and is still being published. In 1997 40 million copies had been sold in the US. There were also brief film and television series.

ˈ**drive-in** *n* [C] (*esp AmE*) a service that people can use or enjoy without leaving their cars. The idea began in the US with cinemas in 1933 and was followed there by restaurants and banks that serve customers in their cars outside. ▶ **drive-in** *adj* [only before *n*]: *a drive-in movie/bank.*

ˈ**Driver and ˈVehicle ˈLicensing ˌCentre** ⇨ DVLC.

driving

Americans have long had a 'love affair' with the automobile (*BrE* car), and are surprised when they meet somebody who cannot drive. In 1996 there were about 177 million qualified drivers, about 67% of the total population. American life is arranged so that people can do most things from their cars. There are **drive-in** banks, post offices, restaurants, movie theatres and even churches.

In Britain there are around 35 million qualified drivers, and 75% of all British households have a car. As in the US, many people prefer to use their car rather than public transport, because it is more convenient and because they like to be independent. In order to reduce pollution the government tries, not very successfully, to discourage car ownership by making driving expensive. In particular, it puts a heavy tax on petrol and regularly increases the annual **road tax**.

To some British people the make and quality of their car reflects their status in society, and it is important to them to get a smart new car every few years. A **personalized number plate** (= a registration number that spells out the owner's name or initials) may also suggest status. Many people, however, prefer to buy a small, economical car, or get a second-hand one. Cars in the US are often larger than those in Britain and though petrol/gas is cheaper, insurance is expensive. In the US car **license plates**, commonly called **tags**, are given by the states. New ones must be bought every two or three years, or when a driver moves to another state. The states use the plates to advertise themselves: *Alabama plates say 'The heart of Dixie' and have a small heart on them, and *Illinois has 'The land of Lincoln'.

In Britain, before a person can get a **driving licence** he or she must pass an official **driving test**, which includes a written test of the ***Highway Code** and a practical driving exam. Only people aged 17 or over are allowed to drive. **Learner drivers** who have a **provisional driving licence** must display an **L-plate**, a large red 'L', on their car, and be supervised by a qualified driver. The US has no national **driver's license** (*AmE*), but instead licences are issued by each state. Most require written tests, an eye test and a short practical test. Some states give **juvenile licenses** to drivers as young as 14, or even 13 in *Montana. Normal licences are given at the age of 16. Americans have to get a new driver's license if they move to another state. US licences have on them a picture of the holder and are important as a means of identity.

In Britain people drive on the left and in the US they drive on the right. British and US drivers are relatively careful and courteous, though in Britain recently there have been several widely publicized cases of **road rage** (= violent attacks on other drivers). In the US there were over 43 000 deaths due to **traffic accidents** in 1996, a rate of 16 deaths for every 100 000 Americans. About 40% of these accidents were caused by drivers who had drunk alcohol. **Drink-driving** (= driving a car after drinking alcohol) is also a serious problem in Britain. **Speeding** (= going faster than is allowed) is also a problem and in some British towns special cameras have been set up to catch drivers who go too fast. In the US the main job of state **highway patrols** is to control drivers' speeds.

Many drivers belong to a motoring organization in case their car breaks down. In Britain the main ones are the *AA (Automobile Association) and the *RAC (Royal Automobile Club), and in the US the largest is the *American Automobile Association.

ˌDr ˈJekyll and ˌMr ˈHyde /ˈdʒekl, ˈhaɪd/ a novel (1886) by the Scottish author Robert Louis *Stevenson. It is about a doctor who is interested in the good and evil parts of human nature and invents a drug that can separate them. When he tries the drug himself, he temporarily becomes an evil version of himself, whom he calls Mr Hyde. Further experiments lead to disaster because he finds it more and more difficult to return to his original self. There have been several film versions of the story.

ˈdrop scone (*also* **Scotch pancake**) *n* (*BrE*) a small flat cake eaten at *tea(2) with butter and jam. It is made from a mixture of flour, eggs and milk dropped in small amounts onto a hot pan. It is more like a small thick *pancake than a *scone.

ˌDr ˈScholl's™ /ˈʃɒlz; *AmE* ˈʃɑːlz/ a type of open shoes with wooden soles and leather straps invented by Dr William Scholl in 1961 and originally sold mainly in medical shops. They are now regarded as fashionable and sold in shoe shops.

ˌDr ˈSeuss /ˈsuːs/ the name used by the US writer and artist Theodor Seuss Geisel (1904–91) for his popular series of children's books. They are long, funny poems that have been praised as a good way to teach children to read. They include *Horton Hears a Who* (1954), *How the Grinch Stole Christmas* (1957) and *The Cat in the Hat* (1957). Several were made into television cartoon films.

the **ˌDrug Enˈforcement Adminiˈstration** (*abbr* the **DEA**) an organization established in 1973 to see that US drug laws are obeyed. It is part of the US Department of Justice. The DEA especially tries to stop drugs entering the country. It works closely with the *FBI, which was given a similar task in 1982, and with the US Customs Service and the *United States Coast Guard.

drugs

The problem of **drug abuse**, the use of drugs for pleasure, is common in Britain and the US, especially among young people, but using drugs is illegal in both countries. Most teenagers try drugs before they leave school, and many use drugs regularly. There is also concern that younger children are being offered drugs. Drugs are much more widely available today than they were 20 years ago and may be easily obtained from **pushers** on the streets, in schools, at nightclubs and elsewhere.

Many different drugs are available, each known by a variety of slang names. They include **amphetamines** (**uppers** or **speed**), **barbiturates** (**barbs** or **downers**), **cocaine** (**coke**, **crack**, **ice** or **snow**), **heroin** (**junk** or **smack**), **cannabis** (**marijuana**, **dope**, **grass**, **pot** or **weed**), **LSD** (**acid**) and also **benzodiazepines** which are sometimes prescribed by doctors as **tranquillizers**. Other drugs include **mescaline**, **methadone**, **morphine**, **nitrates** (**poppers**) and **phencyclidine** (**angel dust** or **PCP**). Some children experiment with **glue-sniffing** (= breathing in the gas given off by strong glue). One of the most fashionable drugs of the 1990s has been **MDMA**, better known as **Ecstasy** or **E**. Using Ecstasy has led to several highly publicized accidental deaths.

Many people are concerned about the problems associated with drug-taking. The main worry is that using drugs often leads to **addiction**, poor health, and even death. Reflecting public concern, the courts have taken a tough attitude towards pushers and **drugs barons**, the people who supply drugs to the pushers. **Addicts** are less severely punished but are encouraged to get medical treatment and attend **rehabilitation centres**.

Drug-taking is blamed for a lot of *crimes, as **addicts** sometimes steal in order to get money to buy drugs. Also, criminal organizations that sell drugs use violence to prevent others selling them. In the 1980s these problems caused the US government to begin the **War on Drugs**. But not everyone supports the programme: many young people say that they can use drugs without becoming addicted. They also say that it is wrong for alcohol, also an addictive drug, to be legal, while the drugs they enjoy are not. In Britain there have been many campaigns to try to reduce drug use, and in 1998 the government appointed a **drugs czar** to lead the fight against drugs.

There are often calls in both Britain and the US for **soft drugs**, the less harmful drugs such as cannabis, to be made legal, but this is resisted by many experts on the grounds that people taking them are likely to go on eventually to **hard drugs**, the more dangerous drugs such as heroin. People who want drug-taking to be legalized say that making tougher laws against using drugs has not worked, and that many of the problems associated with drugs would be solved if it were legal to use them. For instance, the government would be able to control the supply of drugs, and their quality and price. Criminal organizations would no longer be involved, and that would help reduce violence. The government could put a tax on drugs, as is the case with tobacco and alcohol, and the money could be used to pay for medical treatment for people who become addicted. But many people are scared by the increasing use of drugs and do not believe that legalizing them is a solution.

ˈDruid a priest in the religion of the ancient *Celts in Britain, France and Ireland. This religion was destroyed by the Romans in France and Britain but continued in Scotland and Ireland until Christianity replaced it. Today some people who want to bring this ancient religion back to life call themselves Druids. They sometimes try to hold ceremonies at *Stonehenge.

ˌdrum ’n’ ˈbass *n* [U] a type of pop music that developed from *jungle in Britain in the mid 1990s, with the same very fast drum beats, loud bass and electronic sound effects.

ˌDrury ˈLane /ˌdrʊəri; *AmE* ˌdrʊri/ a street in central London, near *Covent Garden, which contains the *Theatre Royal.

ˌJohn **ˈDryden** /ˈdraɪdn/ (1631–1700) an English poet and writer of plays. He was made *Poet Laureate by King *Charles II in 1668, and most of his poems are about national events of his time. *Absolem and*

Achitophel (1681), for example, is about the Duke of *Monmouth's attempt to become king. His best-remembered play is *All For Love*, a new version of Shakespeare's *Anthony and Cleopatra*.

DSC /ˌdiː es ˈsiː/ ⇨ DISTINGUISHED SERVICE CROSS.

DSO /ˌdiː es ˈəʊ; *AmE* ˈoʊ/ ⇨ DISTINGUISHED SERVICE ORDER.

DSS /ˌdiː es ˈes/ ⇨ DEPARTMENT OF SOCIAL SECURITY.

DTI /ˌdiː tiː ˈaɪ/ ⇨ DEPARTMENT OF TRADE AND INDUSTRY.

dub /dʌb/ *n* [U] a type of *reggae music. In dub recordings emphasis is given to drum and bass sounds. There are usually few words, and unusual sound effects are often added. Dub records are often remixes of existing reggae songs.

ˈ**Dublin** /ˈdʌblɪn/ the capital city of the Republic of Ireland, situated on its east coast on the River Liffey. Dublin was the scene of the 1916 *Easter Rising against the British, who ruled Ireland from Dublin's 13th-century castle until the south of Ireland became an independent state in 1922. Many great writers and poets have come from Dublin, including Jonathan *Swift, Oscar *Wilde, George Bernard *Shaw, W B *Yeats and James *Joyce.

ˌW E B **Du** ˈ**Bois** /duː ˈbɔɪs/ (William Edward Burghardt Du Bois 1868–1963) an *African-American writer who helped to establish the *NAACP. His books include *The Souls of Black Folk* (1903), and he was the editor of the NAACP magazine *Crisis* (1910–34). He was the first African American to receive a PhD degree from *Harvard University and taught economics and history at Atlanta University (1897–1910 and 1932–44). In 1961 Du Bois became a Communist and moved to Ghana, where he died.

Duˈ**buque** /dəˈbjʊk/ a US town on the *Mississippi River in the state of *Iowa. It is sometimes referred to as the typical example of a small, boring US community. A writer in the **New Yorker* once said that it was not the magazine for 'the old lady from Dubuque'.

The ˌ***Duchess of*** ˈ***Malfi*** /ˈmælfi/ a play (1613) by the English writer John Webster about a woman who marries against the wishes of her two powerful and cruel brothers. It is a dark story of evil and guilt, expressed in great poetry. All the main characters die in the end.

the ˌ**Duchy of** ˈ**Cornwall** /ˈkɔːnwəl; *AmE* ˈkɔːrnwəl/ the areas of land in the English county of *Cornwall owned by the Duke of Cornwall. These were first given by King *Edward III to his eldest son Edward the *Black Prince in 1337. Since then the Duchy has always passed to the eldest son of the King or Queen.

the ˌ**Duchy of** ˈ**Lancaster** /ˈlæŋkəstə(r)/ the areas of land in the English county of *Lancashire(1) which have been owned by the King or Queen since 1399 and which now provide the money for the payments from the *Privy Purse each year.

ˈ**duct tape** *n* [U] (*AmE*) a strong type of tape used for repairing many things. It keeps out water and was originally designed to repair ducts (= tubes carrying wires, liquids, etc.).

ˈ**dude ranch** (in the western US) a ranch (= large farm) which is used as a holiday centre. Visitors can ride horses, do ranch work and camp outdoors. A *dude* is a person from a city, especially from the eastern US states.

ˈ**due** ˈ**process of** ˈ**law** *n* [U] a legal right in the US. The *Fifth Amendment to the US Constitution states that a person cannot be 'deprived of life, liberty or property without due process of law'. This includes a fair trial and informing people of their rights if they are suspected of a crime. Due process is an important part of the US legal system and is used by the US *Supreme Court to declare some laws 'unconstitutional'.

ˈ**Duesenberg** /ˈduːzənbɜːg; *AmE* ˈduːzənbɜːrg/ *n* a large, fast and expensive car made in the US between 1920 and 1937 during the *Jazz Age. Its popular name was a 'Duesie', and Americans still use the informal word 'doozy' or 'doozie' to mean something that is special. It was the first US car to win the Grand Prix at Le Mans, France, in 1921.

duke *n* a member of the British *peerage with the highest rank. The wife of a duke is called a **duchess**. Dukes who are members of the royal family are known as **royal dukes** and include the Duke of *Cornwall, the Duke of *Edinburgh and the Duke of *York. The land owned by a duke is called a **duchy**. ⇨ note at ARISTOCRACY.

the ˌ**Duke of** ˈ**Cornwall** ⇨ CORNWALL[2].

the ˌ**Duke of** ˈ**Edinburgh** ⇨ EDINBURGH[2].

the ˌ**Duke of** ˈ**Edinburgh's** ˈ**Award Scheme** a programme of activities for young people between the ages of 14 and 23. It was started in Britain in 1956 by the *Duke of Edinburgh and others. The Award Scheme has become international and is known by different names in some countries, such as the **Congressional Award** in the US. Young people choose a personal interest to develop and also do community service and outdoor activities. Awards for achievement are given at three levels: bronze, silver and gold. The Scheme is operated mainly by schools and youth organizations.

ˈJohn ˈFoster ˈ**Dulles** /ˈfɒstə ˈdʌlɪs; *AmE* ˈfɑːstər/ (1888–1959) a US lawyer who became *Secretary of State (1953–9) under President *Eisenhower. He developed a US foreign policy that was strongly opposed to the former USSR and to Communism, which he considered to be morally evil. He was the brother of Allen *Dulles.

ˈ**Dulux**™ /ˈdjuːlʌks/ a British company that makes paint. Its advertisements use an *Old English sheepdog, which people now sometimes call a 'Dulux dog'.

the Dulux dog

ˌ**Dulwich** ˈ**College** /ˌdʌlɪdʒ/ a large *public school for boys in Dulwich, an area of south-east London. It was started in 1619 by the actor Edward *Alleyn. The writer P G *Wodehouse was a student there.

ˌDaphne **du** ˈ**Maurier**¹ /dju ˈmɒrieɪ; *AmE* djuː ˈmɔːrieɪ/ (1907–89) a popular English writer of exciting and romantic novels set in the south-west of England. Her most famous novel is *Rebecca* (1938). One of her short stories, *The Birds*, was filmed in 1963 by Alfred *Hitchcock.

ˌGeorge **du** ˈ**Maurier**² /dju ˈmɒrieɪ; *AmE* djuː ˈmɔːrieɪ/ (1834–96) a cartoonist and writer of novels, the son of English and French parents. He is best known for his cartoons (= humorous drawings) in *Punch about the social life of rich people. His novels were also very successful, and the name of one of his characters, *Svengali in the novel *Trilby*, has become part of the English language. He was the grandfather of Daphne *du Maurier.

Dumˌ**barton** ˈ**Oaks** /dʌmˌbɑːtn; *AmE* dʌmˌbɑːrtn/

a large house in the Georgetown area of *Washington, DC, in which the **Dumbarton Oaks Conference** was held in 1944 to discuss the idea of forming the *United Nations. The four countries with representatives at the conference were the US, Britain, the USSR and China.

ˌ**dumb** ˈ**Dora** *n* (*AmE disapprov*) a woman who behaves in a silly or stupid way. The name comes from the title of a US *comic strip of the 1920s.

Dumˈ**fries** /dʌmˈfriːs/ a town in south-west Scotland, sometimes called 'Queen of the South'. It is the administrative centre of the Scottish region of **Dumfries and Galloway**. Robert *Burns is buried there.

ˈ**Dumpster**™ /ˈdʌmpstə(r)/ *n* a US make of very large metal container for rubbish, left in the street or near a place where there is building work.

ˌ**Dun and** ˈ**Bradstreet** /ˌdʌn, ˈbrædstriːt/ a US company that is the largest source of business information in the world. It publishes several books each year and regular news about the financial situation and organization of companies. In 1997, it could provide information on 45 million companies in 200 countries. The company's main office is in Wilton, *Connecticut.

Dunˈ**blane** /dʌnˈbleɪn/ a town in central Scotland. In March 1996 a local man called Thomas Hamilton shot and killed 16 children and a teacher in a Dunblane *nursery school, before killing himself. Public feeling was so great that by the middle of 1997 the British government had passed a law making it illegal to own most types of handgun: *the Dunblane massacre*.

ˌIsadora ˈ**Duncan** /ˌɪzədɔːrə ˈdʌŋkən/ (1878–1927) a US dancer who helped to develop modern dance. She was influenced especially by ancient Greek art and often danced in bare feet, wearing a loose tunic. She worked mostly in Europe, and started schools of dance in Berlin, Moscow, Vienna and Salzburg. Her life was very tragic: her Russian husband killed himself, her children were killed in a car accident, and she herself died when her long shawl got caught in the wheel of her car and strangled her.

Isadora Duncan

ˌ**Duncan** ˈ**Hinds**™ /ˌdʌŋkən ˈhaɪndz/ a name for a US range of mixtures for baking different types of cakes. They are produced by *Procter and Gamble and were named after a US food expert who used to travel around the country finding and recommending the best restaurants.

The ˈ***Dunciad*** /ˈdʌnsiæd/ a long and very clever poem by Alexander *Pope, in which he attacked everyone who had criticized his work. Books 1–3 were published in 1728 and Book 4 in 1742.

Dunˈ**dee** /dʌnˈdiː/ a large city in Scotland on the Firth of Tay. It is an important port. Dundee is known for its marmalade (= jam made with oranges and similar fruit) and as a centre for making cloth.

Dunˈ**dee cake** /dʌnˈdiː/ *n* [C, U] (*esp BrE*) a large rich cake containing dried fruit and usually decorated on the top with almonds.

ˈ**Dunhill**™ /ˈdʌnhɪl/ a British company that makes tobacco products: *Twenty Dunhill* (= Dunhill cigarettes)*, please.*

ˌ**Dunkin'** ˈ**Donuts**™ /ˌdʌŋkɪn ˈdəʊnʌts; *AmE* ˈdoʊnʌts/ the largest group of shops in the world selling doughnuts (= small, sweet, ring-shaped cakes) and coffee. They also sell other baked products. In 1997, there were more than 4 000 Dunkin' Donuts shops in 21 countries, including one opened that year in Beijing, China. The US company began in 1950, and its main office is in Randolph, *Massachusetts.

Dunˈ**kirk** /dʌnˈkɜːk; *AmE* dʌnˈkɜːrk/ a port in northern France. During *World War II about 220 ships of the *Royal Navy and 660 small private boats sailed across the *Channel between 26 May and 4 June 1940 to bring back to England many British, French and Belgian soldiers who were trapped in Dunkirk by the advancing German army. More than 330 000 soldiers were rescued, and the expression *the Dunkirk spirit* is now sometimes used in referring to occasions when people show great determination and courage: *He was wounded at Dunkirk.* ○ *The Prime Minister praised the Dunkirk spirit shown by the organizers of the event.*

ˈ**Dunlop** /ˈdʌnlɒp; *AmE* ˈdʌnlɑːp/ **1** a British company that makes tyres and other rubber goods. It is named after John Dunlop, the Scottish inventor of the pneumatic tyre (= one that contains a rubber tube filled with air). **2** a soft cheese similar to *Cheddar, first made at Dunlop in *Ayrshire, Scotland.

the ˌ**Dunmow** ˈ**Flitch** /ˌdʌnməʊ ˈflɪtʃ; *AmE* ˌdʌnmoʊ/ a very large piece of bacon which is regularly given in the *Essex village of Great Dunmow as a prize to a man and woman who can prove that, after being married for at least a year and a day, they have never once wished that they were not married. The ceremony is at least 600 years old, and is mentioned by *Chaucer in *The *Canterbury Tales*. Now it is regarded as just a bit of fun.

ˌ**Dunnet** ˈ**Head** /ˌdʌnɪt/ a place in Scotland which is the most northern part of the British mainland. The most northern point in the whole of Britain, including its islands, is a rock called Muckle Flugga, a mile off the coast of the island of Unst in the *Shetlands. See also JOHN O'GROATS.

Duˈ**Pont** /djuˈpɒnt; *AmE* duˈpɑːnt/ a large US chemical company. It also sells petroleum, fibres, plastics and other products. It began in 1802 as a small family company producing gunpowder (= an explosive powder) in Wilmington, Delaware, and the main office is still there.

ˌJacqueline **du** ˈ**Pré** /dju ˈpreɪ/ (1945–87) an English cellist who had an international concert career before she was 20 years old and was especially famous for her performances and recordings of *Elgar's *Cello Concerto*. She was only 22 when she became seriously ill, and her career ended five years later in 1972. She was married to the Israeli pianist Daniel Barenboim.

Jacqueline du Pré

ˈ**Duracell**™ /ˈdjʊərəsel; *AmE* ˈdjʊrəsel/ a company that makes *batteries. Duracell batteries are said to last longer than most others.

ˌJimmy **Duˈrante** /djʊˈrænti/ (1893–1980) a US comic actor and singer with a harsh voice who was called 'Schnozzola' because of his large nose. He was a star of *vaudeville, radio and television, and ended each show by saying 'Goodnight, Mrs Calabash, wherever you are,' although he never revealed who she was. Durante also appeared in many films.

ˈ**Durex**™ /ˈdjʊəreks; *AmE* ˈdʊreks/ *n* (*pl* **Durex** *or* **Durexes**) (in Britain) a make of rubber contraceptive worn on the penis (= male sex organ) during sex: *a packet of Durex.*

ˈ**Durham** /ˈdʌrəm/ **1** (*abbr* **Dur**) (*also* ˌ**County** ˈ**Durham**) a county in north-east England that used to be a major centre of coal mining, shipbuilding and steel-making. **2** (*also* ˌ**Durham** ˈ**City**) a city in the county of Durham and its administrative centre. It has a castle, now the home of the Durham University, and a beautiful *Norman cathedral, one of the best examples of *Romanesque architecture in Europe. Durham Castle and Durham Cathedral were made a *World Heritage Site in 1986.

the ˈ**Durham** ˈ**Miners'** ˈ**Gala** /ˈdʌrəm, ˈgeɪlə/ an occasion every year when the miners of *Durham, England, parade through the streets of the town. There are colourful displays, traditional *brass bands, etc. The procession is led by leading members of the *Labour Party and of the *National Union of Mineworkers. It is held on the second Saturday in July.

Durham Miners' Gala, 1997

ˌGerald ˈ**Durrell**¹ /ˈdʌrəl/ (1925–95) an English zoologist (= person who studies animals) and author of books about his life studying and collecting animals. These include *My Family and Other Animals* (1956) and *A Zoo in my Luggage* (1960). He was the younger brother of Lawrence *Durrell.

ˌLawrence ˈ**Durrell**² /ˈdʌrəl/ (1912–90) an English author and poet, best known for his sequence of four novels *The *Alexandria Quartet*. Born in India, Durrell lived most of his life in the eastern Mediterranean, where many of his books are set. He was the older brother of Gerald *Durrell and a close friend of the US author Henry *Miller.

the ˈ**Dust Bowl** an area in the western central US where there were terrible dust storms in the 1930s. These were caused by strong winds blowing the dry earth off the fields and made it difficult to grow crops. Many farmers became poor and moved with their families to other areas. This was especially bad because it happened during the *Great Depression. See also *Grapes of Wrath.*

ˈ**Dustbuster**™ /ˈdʌstbʌstə(r)/ *n* a US make of small vacuum cleaner (= a machine that sucks up dust, dirt, etc.), held in the hand. It is used especially to clean in people's homes and inside cars. It has been made since 1978 by the Black and Decker Corporation who developed it from technology needed for the spacecraft of the *Apollo program.

ˌ**Dutch** ˈ**elm disease** *n* [U] a disease that kills elm trees. It is caused by a fungus carried by a type of insect. It seriously affected elm trees in Britain in the 1970s and 1980s, killing about 20 million of them.

ˌRobert **Duˈvall** /djuˈvæl/ (1931–) a US film actor who has played a wide range of unusual characters. He won an *Oscar in the role of a singer of *country music in *Tender Mercies* (1983). His other films have included *The *Godfather*, *Falling Down* (1993), *Geronimo: An American Legend* (1994) and *Apostle* (1998), which he also wrote and directed.

DVLC /ˌdiː viː el ˈsiː/ (*in full* **Driver and Vehicle Licensing Centre**) a British government centre responsible for collecting road tax and sending people their driving licences and vehicle licences. It is in *Swansea, Wales.

ˌAndrea ˈ**Dworkin** /ˌændriə ˈdwɔːkɪn; *AmE* ˈdwɔːrkɪn/ (1946–) an extreme US feminist (= person who believes strongly that women should have the same rights and opportunities as men). She has written many books expressing her views, including *Pornography: Man Possessing Women* (1981), *Intercourse* (1987) and *Life and Death* (1997).

ˌAnthony van ˈ**Dyck** /væn ˈdaɪk/ (1599–1641) a Dutch portrait painter who went to live in London in 1632. He was immediately made a *knight and became the official painter for the court of King *Charles I. One of his most famous paintings is of the king on his horse. His style of painting had a great influence on later British artists, including *Gainsborough.

D'ye* ˌ*Ken John* ˈ*Peel? /djə ˌken, ˈpiːl/ a popular British song written in about 1829 by John Graves, a friend of a farmer called John Peel who for fifty years had a pack of hunting dogs in *Cumberland. It is sung to an old folk tune, *Bonnie Annie.*

ˈ**Dyfed** /ˈdʌvɪd/ a county in Wales since 1974. It was formed from three former counties, Carmarthenshire, Pembrokeshire and Cardiganshire.

ˌBob ˈ**Dylan** /ˈdɪlən/ (1941–) a famous US singer and writer of *folk and rock music, whose unusual voice and sometimes mysterious way of life made him even more popular. His songs of political and social protest greatly influenced young people in the 1960s. They include *Blowin' in the Wind* (1963) and *The Times They Are A-Changin'* (1964). Among his other successful songs are *Mr Tambourine Man* (1965), *Lay Lady Lay* (1969) and *Knocking on Heaven's Door* (1973).

Bob Dylan

ˈ***Dynasty*** /ˈdɪnəsti/ a US television *soap opera which was also shown in many countries round the world. It was about a rich family in the oil business in *Denver, and was famous for the very large amounts of money spent on the actors' costumes. The actors included Joan *Collins as Alexis Carrington and John Forsythe as her former husband, Blake Carrington.

Ee

ˈ***Eagle*** a British *comic for boys started in 1950 by a priest, Marcus Morris. Its most famous character was *Dan Dare. *Eagle* stopped being published in 1969, but started again in 1982 in a different form.

ˈ**Eagle Scout** a boy who has achieved the highest rank in the *Boy Scouts of America and can wear the **Eagle Scout badge**.

the ˌ**Ealing** ˈ**comedies** /ˌiːlɪŋ/ the comedy films produced between 1948 and 1950 by the **Ealing Studios** in west London, England. They are famous for being well written and for their clever stories. They include *Kind Hearts and Coronets* (1949), *The Lavender Hill Mob* (1951) and *Passport to Pimlico* (1949).

AˌmeliaˈEarhart /əˌmiːliə ˈeəhɑːt; *AmE* ˈerhɑːrt/ (1898–1937) a US pilot who in 1932 became the first woman to fly across the Atlantic alone. She and Fred Noonan, another pilot, disappeared in their plane somewhere in the Pacific while trying to fly around the world. What happened to them is still a mystery. In 1997 Linda Finch successfully flew around the world using Earhart's route and the same model of plane that she flew in.

Amelia Earhart beside her plane

earl *n* **1** a member of the British *peerage, with a rank above a *viscount(1) and below a *marquess. The wife of an earl, or a woman with a similar rank, is called a *countess*. **2** a *courtesy title given to the eldest son of a *duke or *marquess. ⇨ note at ARISTOCRACY.

ˌ**Earl** ˈ**Grey** *n* [U] a popular type of Chinese tea with a special flavour. It was introduced into Britain by Earl Grey (1764–1845), an English political leader, after he received some as a gift from the Chinese: *a cup of Earl Grey.*

ˌ**Earl's** ˈ**Court** **1** a large exhibition hall in west London, England, in which many important events are held, e.g. the Boat Show and the *Royal Tournament: *a show at Earl's Court.* **2** an area of west London, part of the *borough of *Kensington: *a small hotel in Earl's Court.*

ˌ**Early** ˈ**English** an early style of *Gothic architecture which developed in England in the 13th century. Its main characteristics are tall, narrow, pointed windows without decorative stonework, and thick walls. The cathedrals of *Salisbury and *Wells are typical examples of the Early English style. See also DECORATED STYLE.

the ˌ**Early** ˈ**Learning** ˌ**Centre** a company with shops in many British towns, selling things that help young children to learn about numbers, letters, materials, etc. in an interesting and exciting way: *Is there an Early Learning Centre in Stratford?*

ˌWyatt ˈ**Earp** /ˌwaɪət ˈɜːp; *AmE* ˈɜːrp/ (1848–1929) a US law officer in the *Wild West, first in Wichita and then in *Dodge City. He is best remembered for being involved in the gun fight at the *OK Corral in *Tombstone in 1881. The story of this and of Earp's life have been told in many books and films, and in a television series in the 1950s and 1960s.

ˈ**Earth,** ˈ**Wind and** ˈ**Fire** a US *jazz funk group who were especially popular in the 1970s. Their album *That's the Way of the World* (1975) included the song *Shining Star*, which won a *Grammy award. Other albums included *I Am* (1979) and *Let's Groove* (1981). The group split up in 1984 but came together again in 1987.

ˌ**East** ˈ**Anglia** /ˈæŋgliə/ a region of eastern England that includes *Norfolk, *Suffolk and parts of *Cambridgeshire and *Essex. It is an agricultural area, producing a lot of grain.

the ˌ**East** ˈ**End** an area to the east of the *City of London, from the *Tower of London along the north bank of the River *Thames. It contains most of the old docks, where many of the local people used to work. The people living in the East End were mostly poor but well known for their friendly and lively nature. With recent new housing developments, the character of the area has completely changed. See also COCKNEY, DOCKLANDS. Compare WEST END.
▶ **East Ender** *n* a person living in the East End.

ˌ***East***ˈ***Enders*** /ˌiːstˈendəz/ a popular British *soap opera on *BBC1. It is about the lives of the people who live in Albert Square in the *borough of Walford, an imaginary place in the *East End of London. Its best-known families are the Fowlers and the Mitchells, who run the local pub, the Queen Vic.

Easter

Easter is a holiday in late March or early April. Many people spend it with their family or have a short holiday/vacation. It is also an important Christian festival. **Easter Sunday**, the day of the Resurrection, is the end of *Lent and the most important date in the Christian year. Many people who do not go to church at other times go on Easter Sunday. It was once common for people to wear new clothes to church on this day. Women wore new hats, called **Easter bonnets**. Today, people sometimes make elaborately decorated Easter bonnets for fun. A few people send **Easter cards** with religious symbols on them or pictures of small chickens, lambs and spring flowers, all traditionally associated with Easter.

The Friday before Easter Sunday is called ***Good Friday** and is remembered as the day Christ was crucified (= hanged on a cross to die). On Good Friday many people eat **hot cross buns** (= fruit buns decorated with a simple cross). The Monday after Easter is called **Easter Monday**. In Britain, Good Friday and Easter Monday are both *bank holidays. In the US, each company decides for itself whether to close or remain open on those days.

Children look forward to Easter Sunday because they are given chocolate **Easter eggs**. These are also popular with adults and millions are sold in the weeks before Easter. Many are packed in coloured foil in brightly-coloured boxes decorated with pictures of cartoon characters. Others are decorated

Easter eggs and Easter bunnies

with sugar flowers and wrapped in clear paper tied with a ribbon. Some shops write the person's name on the egg with icing (*AmE* frosting). Inside each egg are sweets or chocolates. Smaller eggs with a sweet cream inside are also popular. Eggs represent new life and the start of spring, and children sometimes paint the shells of real eggs at home. In some parts of Britain Easter is a time for traditional events such as ***egg-rolling**.

When American children wake up on Easter morning, they hope that the **Easter Bunny** has been. The Easter Bunny is an imaginary rabbit, and parents tell their children that it goes from house to house while they are sleeping. The Easter Bunny hides Easter eggs in each house, small plastic eggs filled with sweets or little presents. When they wake up all the children run about trying to find the eggs. The Easter Bunny also often brings chocolate in the shape of a rabbit. In Britain some families now organize an Easter egg hunt, and people buy chocolate rabbits as well as eggs.

ˌ**Eastern ˈDaylight Time** (*abbr* **EDT**) (in the US) the time used between early April and late October in the eastern states. It is an hour earlier than *Eastern Standard Time.

the ˌ**Eastern Eˈstablishment** (*sometimes disapprov*) the people and institutions in the north-eastern US that have traditionally had great economic and political power in the country. These include the old, rich families in cities like *Boston, *Philadelphia and New York, and institutions like the *Ivy League and the *New York Stock Exchange.

ˌ**Eastern ˈStandard Time** (*abbr* **EST**) (*also* **Eastern Time**) (in the US) the time used between late October and early April in the eastern states. It is five hours earlier than *Greenwich Mean Time.

the ˌ**Easter ˈRising** the rebellion against British rule in Dublin, which took place at Easter in 1916. A hundred British soldiers and 450 of the Irish were killed in the four days of fighting. Several leaders of the rebellion were later executed. See also ANGLO-IRISH WAR.

the ˌ**East ˈIndia ˌCompany** /ˈɪndiə/ an English company started in 1600 to develop trade in the **East Indies** (= the islands off the south-east coast of Asia, including Java and Borneo). By the 18th century it had its own army and political service, and was responsible for the administration of British India. In the early 19th century the company founded the modern *Singapore, which became a British colony in 1826. The East India Company continued to increase its power in India, but after the *Indian Mutiny in 1858 the British government took over its work there, and the company ceased to exist.

ˌGeorge ˈ**Eastman** /ˈiːstmən/ (1854–1932) the American who invented a camera small enough to carry and film in a flexible roll. He started a company in 1884 that later became the Eastman Kodak Company. His *Kodak box camera was first sold in 1888 and the Brownie camera in 1900. This made photography available to many ordinary people for the first time.

ˌ***East of ˈEden*** a novel (1952) by the US author John *Steinbeck. It is about a farmer and his family in the Salinas Valley of California during the early years of the 20th century. A film version (1955) used mostly the second half of the book, in which one of the farmer's sons discovers that his mother owns a brothel. This was James *Dean's first major role.

the ˌ**East ˈSide** the area in New York City between *Fifth Avenue and the East River. See also LOWER EAST SIDE.

ˌ**East ˈSussex** /ˈsʌsɪks/ a county in south-east England, formed in 1974 from part of *Sussex. Its administrative centre is Lewes.

ˌClint ˈ**Eastwood** /ˈiːstwʊd/ (1930–) a US film actor who also directs and produces films. He began in television but then became internationally famous through a series of *spaghetti westerns, including *A Fistful of Dollars* (1964). He often plays strong and good but violent characters, as in **Dirty Harry*. He won an *Oscar in 1992 for directing the Western *Unforgiven* and a special Oscar in 1995. His more recent films include *The Bridges of Madison County* (1995) and *Absolute Power* (1997).

ˌ***Easy ˈRider*** a 1969 US film. It was especially popular with young people, because it showed the freedom from responsibility that many of them wanted in the 1960s. It made stars of Jack *Nicholson, Peter *Fonda and Dennis Hopper (who directed it). The story is about *hippies riding their motorcycles from *Los Angeles to *New Orleans.

Dennis Hopper and Peter Fonda in Easy Rider

Eˈbonics *n* [U] the type of English spoken by many *African Americans. Language teachers call it African American Vernacular English (AAVE). It became a political issue in 1996 when school officials in *Oakland, *California, recognized it as a special language and accepted it in students' written work. Some other schools did the same, but by 1998 many had stopped doing so because of the need for students to speak and write correct English in order to get the best jobs. Compare ENGLISH ONLY MOVEMENT.

ˈ***Ebony*** /ˈebəni/ a US magazine of general interest with many photographs, which is mostly for and about *African Americans. It was first published in 1945 and in 1997 more than 1.8 million people paid to receive it regularly.

EC /ˌiː ˈsiː/ ⇨ EUROPEAN COMMUNITY.

ˈ**Eccles cake** /ˈeklz/ *n* a small round cake made of pastry covered with sugar, and filled with currants

(= dried grapes). They were originally made in Eccles, in *Lancashire (now *Greater Manchester).

ˌBilly ˈ**Eckstine** /ˈekstaɪn/ (1914–93) a US singer of *jazz music who led a band and played the trumpet. His best-known song was *That Old Black Magic*. His band (1944–7) helped to develop *bebop. Its main singers were Eckstine and Sarah *Vaughan, and the musicians included Charlie 'Bird' *Parker and Miles *Davis.

ˌ**Ecoˈnomic and ˈMonetary ˈUnion** (*also* **European Monetary Union**) (*abbr* **EMU**) the plan that there should be completely free movement of people, goods and money between the countries of the *European Union. From 1 January 1993 many controls on the movement of goods and people between the EU countries were removed. There are plans for a European Central Bank and a *single European currency.

The ***Eˈconomist*** a British political and economic magazine that is published every week. It was started in 1843.

ˈ**ecu** /ˈekjuː/ (*in full* **European Currency Unit**) *n* a currency established by the *European Monetary System in 1979, formerly used to make payments between member countries of the *European Union. It was replaced in 1999 by the *euro. See also SINGLE EUROPEAN CURRENCY.

ˌPat ˈ**Eddery** /ˈedəri/ (1952–) an Irish flat-racing jockey who has been the British champion eight times since 1973. In 1990 he rode more than 200 winners in one season, the first time this had been done since Gordon *Richards did it in 1947.

ˈMary ˈBaker ˈ**Eddy**[1] /ˈbeɪkər ˈedi/ (1821–1910) the American woman who in 1879 began the Church of Christ, Scientist. She first presented her idea that religious belief can cure illness in her book *Science and Health* (1875). She also began the **Christian Science Monitor* newspaper in 1908. See also CHRISTIAN SCIENTIST.

ˌNelson ˈ**Eddy**[2] /ˌnelsn ˈedi/ (1901–67) a US singer who appeared in eight romantic films in the 1930s with Jeanette MacDonald (1907–65). These were operettas (= light comic operas) and included *Naughty Marietta* (1935) and *Sweethearts* (1938).

the ˌ**Eddystone ˈlighthouse** /ˌedistən; *AmE* ˌedistoʊn/ a lighthouse (= tower containing a strong light to warn or guide ships) in the *English Channel about 9 miles/14 kilometres from the coast of *Cornwall. It rises 133 feet/41 metres above the water and can be seen for 17 miles/28 kilometres. There has been a light there since 1696.

ˌAnthony ˈ**Eden** /ˈiːdn/ (1897–1977) a *Conservative politician who had a long and successful career, mostly in foreign affairs, and became *Prime Minister in 1955 when Winston *Churchill retired. However, the next year the *Suez Crisis occurred, and in January 1957 Eden resigned because it had affected his health badly. He was made a *knight in 1954 and an *earl(1) in 1961.

ˈ**Edgbaston** /ˈedʒbəstən/ an area of *Birmingham, England, where there is an international cricket ground with the same name. Birmingham University is also in Edgbaston.

the ˌBattle of **Edgeˈhill** /edʒˈhɪl/ the first important battle of the *English Civil War, fought in *Warwickshire in 1642. Neither side really won.

ˈ**Edinburgh**[1] /ˈedɪnbrə/ the capital city of Scotland and a popular tourist centre. It has a famous castle, a zoo, two universities and many museums and art galleries. Other famous features of the city include the *Royal Mile and *Princes Street. In the 18th century Edinburgh was known as 'the Athens of the north'. The name *Edinburgh* means 'Edwin's fort'. The city was made a *World Heritage Site in 1995. See also AULD REEKIE, DUKE OF EDINBURGH, EDINBURGH FESTIVAL, MILITARY TATTOO.

Edinburgh from Calton Hill

the ˌDuke of ˈ**Edinburgh**[2] /ˈedɪnbrə/ (1921–) the title by which Prince *Philip, the husband of Queen *Elizabeth II, is usually known. His father was Prince Andrew of Greece and his mother was Princess Alice of Battenberg, sister of Lord *Mountbatten. He was educated in Britain and was in the *Royal Navy in *World War II. In 1947 he married Princess Elizabeth, who later became Queen *Elizabeth II. Among his many interests are British industry, projects for young people, wild animals and various sports.

the ˌ**Edinburgh ˈFestival** /ˌedɪnbrə/ a festival of music and drama that has been held in *Edinburgh for three weeks every summer since 1947. Many tourists come to see the shows and concerts, including hundreds that are not part of the official Festival. These are known as **the Edinburgh Fringe**, and are now considered as important as the Festival itself because of the many new and exciting ideas they contain.

ˌ**Edinburgh ˈrock** /ˌedɪnbrə/ *n* [U] a sweet in the form of short sticks of sugar, like chalk in texture and tasting of peppermint, sold in different colours. It was first made in *Edinburgh in 1822.

ˌThomas ˈ**Edison** /ˈedɪsn/ (1847–1931) a famous US inventor. His inventions included a machine for reproducing sound, the electric light bulb and the 'kinescopic camera', later used in cinemas. He produced the first talking films in 1912. His statement that 'genius is one per cent inspiration and 99 per cent perspiration' is still often quoted.

ˌNoel ˈ**Edmonds** (1948–) a British television personality who started his career as a disc jockey. His programmes offer light entertainment, in which guests are asked to do silly things and play funny games.

ˌSt ˈ**Edmund** (849–870) a king of *East Anglia, a region of eastern England, who was killed fighting the Danes. It was known all over Europe that he was very holy, and his shrine at Bury St Edmunds in *Suffolk was famous.

ˈ**Edsel**™ /ˈedsəl/ a Ford car model that was a famous failure. It was named after the son of Henry *Ford. Fewer than 100 000 were sold during in its two years from (1957–9). It became a popular US joke, and other unsuccessful products are still sometimes referred to in a humorous way as Edsels: *The movie was Hollywood's Edsel of the year.*

EDT /ˌiː diː ˈtiː/ ⇨ EASTERN DAYLIGHT TIME.

Education in Britain ⇨ article.

Education in the US ⇨ article.

ˌPrince ˈ**Edward** (1964–) the fourth child of Queen

*Elizabeth II. He was educated at *Gordonstoun in Scotland and at *Cambridge University, where he studied history. He joined the *Royal Marines in 1986, but left the next year to begin a career producing plays for the theatre and films for television.

Edward I /ˌedwəd ðə ˈfɜːst; *AmE* ˌedwərd, ˈfɜːrst/ (1239–1307) the king of England from 1272 to 1307, the oldest son of *Henry III. He spent a lot of time trying to control Wales and Scotland, fighting, among others, William *Wallace and *Robert the Bruce. As a result he was called the 'Hammer of the Scots'. In 1296 he brought the *Stone of Scone to England.

Edward II /ˌedwəd ðə ˈsekənd; *AmE* ˌedwərd/ (1284–1327) the king of England from 1307 to 1327, the son of *Edward I and the first *Prince of Wales. He took his armies to Scotland, but was defeated at the Battle of *Bannockburn (1314) by *Robert the Bruce. He was a weak king who upset the English *barons, and in 1327 his son *Edward III replaced him. Later that year he was murdered.

Edward III /ˌedwəd ðə ˈθɜːd; *AmE* ˌedwərd, ˈθɜːrd/ (1312–77) the king of England from 1327 to 1377, the son of *Edward II. He had continuing problems with the Scots, but had some success in his attempts to become the king of France, for example at the battles of *Crécy (1346) and *Poitiers (1355). After his death his grandson became King of England as *Richard II, because his son Edward, the *Black Prince, had died the year before. See also HUNDRED YEARS WAR.

Edward IV /ˌedwəd ðə ˈfɔːθ; *AmE* ˌedwərd, ˈfɔːrθ/ (1442–83) the king of England from 1461 to 1470 and from 1471 to 1483. He was the son of Richard, Duke of *York[3](3). In 1461 his army defeated the soldiers of *Henry VI of the House of *Lancaster. Edward had the support of the powerful Earl of Warwick, known as Warwick the Kingmaker, to whom he was related, but in 1470 he lost this support and also for a short time his throne (to *Henry VI). After the defeat of Warwick and Henry in 1471, England had a period of great stability under Edward, who encouraged the development of art, music, etc. as well as the new science of printing. See also WARS OF THE ROSES.

Edward V /ˌedwəd ðə ˈfɪfθ; *AmE* ˌedwərd/ (1470–83) the king of England for three months in 1483, a son of *Edward IV. It is generally believed that his uncle, who took the throne by force to become King *Richard III, murdered Edward V and his younger brother. See also PRINCES IN THE TOWER.

Edward VI /ˌedwəd ðə ˈsɪksθ; *AmE* ˌedwərd/ (1537–53) the king of England from 1547 to 1553. He was the son of King *Henry VIII and his third wife Jane *Seymour, and the half-brother (= brother by a different mother) of *Mary I and *Elizabeth I. He became king at the age of ten, so other people, called *regents* governed on his behalf. One of them persuaded him to change his will, giving the throne to Lady Jane *Grey, but the plan failed and Mary became queen when Edward died. During this period, with Edward's support, England became much more strongly Protestant, so that Mary was unable to change it back to Catholicism.

Edward VII /ˌedwəd ðə ˈsevənθ; *AmE* ˌedwərd/ (1841–1910) the king of Great Britain and Ireland from 1901 to 1910, the son of Queen *Victoria and Prince *Albert. He was the *Prince of Wales for most of his life, while his mother ruled. Victoria did not let him play much part in state affairs, so he spent most of his time at social events, such as parties, horse-racing, etc. When she died in 1901, he became a popular king. His reign was a pleasant period of peace and economic success before *World War I.

Edward VIII /ˌedwəd ði ˈeɪtθ; *AmE* ˌedwərd/ (1894–1972) the eldest son of King *George V. He became the king of Great Britain and Ireland when his father died in January 1936, but never had the crown officially placed on his head. He had fallen in love with Mrs *Simpson, an American who was divorced, and it was not acceptable at that time that he should marry her and remain king. So in December 1936, he abdicated (= gave up his position as king) and his brother became King *George VI, giving Edward the title of Duke of *Windsor. Edward married Mrs Simpson in June 1937, and they lived in France for many years. See also ABDICATION CRISIS.

Edˈwardian /edˈwɔːdiən; *AmE* edˈwɔːrdiən/ *n* a person who lived during the time of King *Edward VII. ▶ **Edwardian** *adj* of the time of King *Edward VII, especially in relation to the fashions and social customs of that period: *an Edwardian house* ○ *the Edwardian era.*

ˌBlake **ˈEdwards[1]** /ˌbleɪk ˈedwədz; *AmE* ˈedwərdz/ (1922–) an American who directs, writes and produces films. He became well known for the series of **Pink Panther* comedy films which he wrote and directed. He also directed *Breakfast at Tiffany's* (1961) and *Victor/Victoria* (1982) in which his wife Julie *Andrews appeared.

ˌGareth **ˈEdwards[2]** /ˌgærəθ ˈedwədz/ (1947–) a Welsh *Rugby player who was made captain of Wales before he was 21. He played 63 matches for Wales. He helped the teams of *Cardiff, Wales and the *British Lions to win many victories.

ˌJonathan **ˈEdwards[3]** /ˈedwədz; *AmE* ˈedwərdz/ (1703–58) a US clergyman whose powerful sermons (= religious talks) on the power of God helped to create a major religious movement, called the Great Awakening, in *New England (1734–5). Edwards became President of the College of New Jersey (now *Princeton University) in 1757.

ˌEdward the Conˈfessor /ˌedwəd ðə kənˈfesə(r); *AmE* ˌedwərd/ (*c.* 1003–66) the king of England from 1042 to 1066, a son of *Ethelred the Unready. He was considered a very holy man, and in 1161 the Pope made him a saint and gave him the title of 'Confessor'. However, he does not seem to have been very interested in government, and there was great confusion when he died over who had been promised the throne of England. His brother-in-law *Harold Godwin became king, but was soon removed by William of Normandy in the *Norman Conquest of 1066.

EEC /ˌiː iː ˈsiː/ ⇨ EUROPEAN ECONOMIC COMMUNITY.

ˈEeny ˈMeeny ˈMiney ˈMo /ˈiːni ˈmiːni ˈmaɪni ˈməʊ; *AmE* ˈmoʊ/ a children's rhyme used for choosing a person or thing. The words are:

Eeny meeny miney mo,
Catch a tigger (= tiger) by his toe;
If he hollers (= shouts), let him go,
Eeny meeny miney mo.

The child saying the rhyme points to each person or thing in turn on each beat of the rhyme and the person or thing pointed to on the last 'mo' is chosen. Different words are sometimes used instead of *tigger* and *hollers*.

EEOC /ˌiː iː əʊ ˈsiː; *AmE* oʊ/ ⇨ EQUAL EMPLOYMENT OPPORTUNITY COMMISSION.

ˈEeyore /ˈiːɔː(r)/ the donkey in the *Winnie-the-Pooh books by A A *Milne. He is always complaining about things in a very sad way. His name comes from the sound a donkey makes.

ˌegg-and-ˈspoon race *n* a race in which each runner has to carry an egg on a spoon without dropping it. Egg-and-spoon races are especially popular with children, and often run at school *sports days.

ˈegg-nog (*BrE also* **egg-flip**) *n* [C, U] a drink made with beaten eggs, milk, sugar, nutmeg (= a type of

Education in Britain

Education is a subject about which many British people care deeply. Most believe that the state should provide education free of charge and to a high standard. At election time, politicians who promise to spend more on education are popular with voters. Recently, there has been a lot of debate about students having to pay their own fees at *university, as well as their living expenses. Some people are afraid that poorer students will not receive enough financial help and will be discouraged from going on to **higher education**.

The education system

An increasing number of children under 5 receive **pre-school education**. Some go to **playgroups** several times a week and take part in **structured play** (= play with some educational purpose) with other children of the same age. Others go to a **nursery school** or to the **nursery department** or **kindergarten** of a *school. The availability of pre-school education varies from area to area, and parents often have to pay for it.

Children are required to be in full-time education between the ages of 5 and 16. Different areas of Britain have different school systems. In some areas children receive their **primary education** at an ***infant school** and then a ***junior school**, or at a ***primary school** that combines the two. At about 11 they begin their **secondary education** at a ***comprehensive school**, a ***grammar school** or a ***high school**. In other areas children go to a ***first school** at age 5, a ***middle school** at 8 and an ***upper school** from 13 onwards. Some pupils, especially those hoping to go to university, stay at school for the ***sixth form** or go to a **sixth-form college**.

Most children go to *state schools. Until 1988 these were all responsible to a ***Local Education Authority** (LEA). LEAs obtain their funding from central government and the *council tax. In 1988 secondary schools and larger primary schools were encouraged to ***opt out** of LEA control and become ***grant-maintained**. These schools receive money direct from central government are run by a **board of governors** consisting of parents and members of the public. In Scotland and Northern Ireland most schools are still managed by local authorities.

Some children go to ***independent schools** run by private organizations, for which their parents have to pay fees. A few go to ***public schools**, such as *Eton and *Harrow. Younger children may attend a private ***preparatory school** (or **prep school**) until the age of 13. Some parents may send their children to private schools, even if this is against their principles, because they think that their children will receive a better education.

Young people are expected to show respect for their teachers and obey school rules. Pupils who misbehave may be punished, e.g. by having to stay behind after school. **Corporal punishment**, being smacked or caned, was ended many years ago. Sometimes students get into more serious trouble, e.g. by being violent or through using *drugs, and risk being **expelled** (= told to leave permanently).

The British education system aims to educate the whole person, so that each child develops his or her personality as well as gaining academic knowledge. Most primary and secondary schools offer a range of **extra-curricular activities** (= activities outside normal lessons), including sports, music, community service and trips to places of interest. Secondary schools also give **careers advice** and help students to prepare for having a job by arranging short periods of **work experience** with local businesses.

Standards in education

Since 1988 the subjects to be taught in state schools have been laid down in the ***National Curriculum**, which also sets the standards to be achieved. Children have to study the **core subjects** of English, mathematics and science, and also the **foundation subjects** of technology, geography, history, art, music and physical education. Older children take a foreign language. The National Curriculum does not apply in Scotland, and schools there are free to decide how much time they devote to each subject. Children do **standard assessment tests** (SATs) at ages 7, 11 and 14. At 16 students take *exams for the **General Certificate of Secondary Education** (***GCSE**) or the ***Scottish Certificate of Education**. Some may take ***GNVQs** (General National Vocational Qualifications) in work-related subjects. Some students go on to study for ***A levels** in three or four subjects.

Many people worry that the education system fails to make sure that all children reach minimum standards of **literacy** (= reading and writing) and **numeracy** (= number skills), and there are often demands for more attention to be paid to **the three R's** (*r*eading, w*r*iting and a*r*ithmetic). Standards at individual schools are watched closely by parents and the government. Schools are visited regularly by ***OFSTED** inspectors, and schools whose pupils are not making adequate progress or in which discipline is poor risk being closed down. **School performance tables** are published annually to show how well students in individual schools have done in tests and exams. These 'league tables' enable parents to compare one school with another, but many people feel that it is unfair to base a comparison on exam results alone.

Educational standards are often said to be falling. This usually happens after GCSE and A level results are announced: if there are a lot of students with high grades people say that the exams are too easy. Others think that standards are rising and that it is now much harder to achieve good grades.

Further and higher education

A smaller percentage of British students go on to *further or higher education than in any other European country. Many students go to university and study for a ***bachelor's degree**. Others study for a certificate or diploma at a college of further education. Most courses at these colleges train people in a particular skill and combine periods of study with work experience.

Some people return to education later in life and attend **evening classes** run by *adult education institutes. ***Open learning** schemes enable people to obtain recognized qualifications, such as a degree from the *Open University or a qualification in accountancy, without having to leave their job.

Education in the US

The government and education

Although in general Americans prefer to limit the influence of government, this is not so where education is concerned. All levels of government are involved in education and it is considered to be one of their most important responsibilities.

The *federal government provides some money for education through the ***Department of Education**. But *state and local governments have direct control and are responsible for the education of students between the ages of 5 and 18, or the years of *school called **kindergarten**, **first grade**, **second grade**, etc. to **twelfth grade**. These years are together referred to as ***K–12**. Individual states have their own **Boards of Education**, which decide the **curriculum** (= subjects to be studied) and what students must have achieved before they can **graduate** from high school at the age of 18. States are also concerned with **certification standards**, general standards of education including the qualifications needed by teachers.

Most of the money for education comes from taxes that people pay to their local government. Local governments appoint **school boards**, which have control over how individual schools are run. A school board hires a **superintendent**, the person in charge of all the schools in a **school district**, **principals** for each school, and **teachers**. It also decides how the rest of the money available should be spent. School boards are usually made up of people who live in the area, often parents of children in the schools.

At the primary and secondary levels, most school districts have **a Parent-Teacher Association** (**PTA**) which gives all parents a chance to take part in making decisions about how the school is run. Parents regularly visit schools to meet their children's teachers and discuss their progress. Many volunteer (= work without pay) in their children's schools to teach the children a skill, take them on trips, or work in the school library.

The school system

Although many Americans attend **nursery school**, **day care** or **pre-school** from an early age, formal education is usually considered to begin at the age of 5 when children go to kindergarten, the first step in the K–12 education. Kindergarten and the next five or six years of education, first grade, second grade, etc., are together usually called **elementary school** (the term *primary school* is less common in the US than in Britain). Grades seven to twelve are part of **secondary school**, and may be divided in different ways. In some places grades seven and eight are called ***junior high school**. Other school systems have **middle school**, which lasts for three years. ***High school** usually covers four years, from the ninth to the twelfth grades.

Post-secondary education, after twelfth grade, is not free though state governments which run most of the educational institutions subsidize the cost for people who live in the state.

The quality of education

By some standards, American education seems very successful. Although young people must attend school until they are 16, over 80% continue until they are 18. About 45% of Americans have some post-secondary or ***further education**, and over 20% graduate from a college or *university.

However, 20% of adults, about 40 million people, have very limited skills in reading and writing, and 4%, about 8 million, are illiterate (= cannot read or write). Since control over education is mostly at local level, its quality varies greatly from place to place. There are many reasons for this but the most important is money. In general, the people who live in city centres tend to be very poor. Those with more money prefer to live in the suburbs. People in the suburbs pay higher taxes, and so the schools there have more money to spend. Crime and violence are also serious problems in the inner cities, with some students taking weapons to school. In such a situation it is hard to create a good atmosphere for learning.

Public or private education

Most educational institutions in the US are **public** (= run by the government) but there are some **private** schools which students pay a lot of money to attend. Many private schools have a high reputation and parents send their children there so that they will have advantages later in life. Opposition to private schools is not as strong as it is in Britain: individual choice is important in the US, and so the right of people to buy a different education for their children is not questioned. Public or private education is much less of an issue than the difference in quality between inner city and suburban schools. Most parents who have money are likely to spend it not by sending their children to private schools but by moving to a suburb where the public schools are good.

Points of conflict

Americans agree on the importance of education being available to all, but there is disagreement about what should be taught. The greatest area of conflict is the place of religious or moral education. Commonly debated topics include whether teachers should be allowed to say prayers, whether students should learn about sex, and whether it is right to hit students as a punishment. Sometimes the debate ends up in court, and courts usually say that no student should be forced to do something that is against his or her beliefs.

Education for people who come to the US from other countries is also much discussed. In states like *California where there are many people whose first language is not English, there is debate over what language should be used in schools. Some people believe that children have the right to an education in their own language; others say that people who come to the US have a responsibility to learn English and cannot expect special treatment. At university level some people object to the high numbers of foreign students, especially in science and related fields. But since relatively few Americans study these subjects the universities are glad to take international students.

In spite of occasional conflict, most Americans agree that a good education gives people the best chance of getting a good job and of improving their social position.

spice) and usually alcohol (often rum or *whisky). In the US it is traditionally drunk at Christmas and sometimes New Year.

ˈ**egg-rolling** *n* [U] a traditional *Easter custom in northern England, Scotland, Northern Ireland and the *Isle of Man. Each person taking part rolls a hard-boiled egg down a slope, and if it is not damaged at the bottom they will be lucky in various ways. Egg-rolling was introduced into the US in 1877 by Dolly Madison, the wife of President James *Madison. It was originally done at Easter on *Capitol Hill in *Washington, DC, and later in the grounds of the *White House(1), where it still happens every year, except in time of war. It also takes place in many local communities.

ˌ**eggs** ˈ**Benedict** /ˈbenədɪkt/ *n* [U] a US dish of ham on toast or an English *muffin, with poached eggs on top, covered with a rich sauce.

the ˌ**Eighth** ˈ**Army** a branch of the British army, formed to fight in North Africa during *World War II. After 1942 it was led by Field Marshal *Montgomery, and took part in the battles at *El Alamein and Tobruk. It later fought in Italy. Compare DESERT RAT.

800 number /eɪt ˈhʌndrəd ˌnʌmbə(r)/ (*also* **888 number** /ˌeɪteɪtˈeɪt ˌnʌmbə(r)/) *n* (in the US) a telephone number beginning with 800 or 888, which can be called free of charge. They are provided by companies so that customers can telephone them to order their products, etc. In Britain such free numbers begin with 0800.

ˌAlbert ˈ**Einstein** /ˈaɪnstaɪn/ (1879–1955) a physicist, born in Germany, who was possibly the greatest scientist of the 20th century. In 1905 he published his theory of relativity. This led to the equation giving the relationship between mass and energy, $E=mc^2$, which is the basis of atomic energy. Einstein suggested how it could be used for making weapons, but after *World War II he spoke publicly against nuclear weapons. By 1917, he had become famous all over the world. He was given the Nobel Prize for physics in 1921. When Hitler came to power, Einstein, who was Jewish, went to live in the US, becoming a US citizen in 1940. In 1933 he wrote a book called *Why War?* with Sigmund Freud. He became a professor at *Princeton University in 1934, and he spent the rest of his life looking, without success, for a theory that combined those of gravitation and electromagnetism. In 1952 he was offered the presidency (= the position of president) of the state of Israel, but did not accept it.

Albert Einstein writing an equation for the density of the Milky Way, 1931

ˈ**Eire** /ˈeərə; *AmE* ˈerə/ the official name for Ireland between 1937 and 1949, when it became the Republic of Ireland. The name Eire is still sometimes used outside Ireland.

ˌDwight D ˈ**Eisenhower** /ˌdwaɪt diː ˈaɪznhaʊə(r)/ (Dwight David Eisenhower 1890–1969) the 34th *President of the US (1953–61) and a famous general. His popular name was Ike. He was the Supreme Commander of the Allied Forces in *World War II and directed the Allies' plans for D-Day. As a *Republican(1), Eisenhower was strongly against Communism but he ended the *Korean War. He is also remembered for sending US soldiers into *Little Rock, *Arkansas, to protect *African-American children in white schools. He was a popular president, known for his friendly smile and mild manner.

eiˈ**steddfod** /aɪˈsteðvɒd; *AmE* aɪˈsteðvɑːd/ *n* any of several cultural events held every year in Wales at which there are competitions for poets (called *bards*) and musicians. The biggest of these is the Royal National Eisteddfod of Wales. Eisteddfods started in the 12th century. The word *eisteddfod* means 'chairing', from the custom of putting the winning bard in a special chair.

crowning the bard at the Royal National Eisteddfod

the **El** /el/ the popular name for the elevated (= raised) railway in *Chicago. It was built in 1897 by Charles Tyson Yerkes. The city's central business district is called the Loop because the railway makes a loop around the area.

ˌ**El** ˈ**Alamein** /ˌel ˈæləmeɪn/ a village on the north coast of Egypt where two important battles were fought in *World War II. In July 1942 the advance of the German army (under Rommel) towards Cairo was stopped here by the British under Auchinleck, and in October the British, now under *Montgomery[2], forced Rommel back into Tunisia. Soon afterwards the Germans were forced out of North Africa.

ˌ**Eleanor of** ˈ**Aquitaine** /ˈækwɪteɪn/ (1122–1204) a queen of France from 1137 until 1152, when it was officially declared that her marriage to King Louis VII was not valid. Soon afterwards Eleanor married Henry of Anjou, who in 1154 became King *Henry II of England. She supported their sons when they fought against Henry in 1173, and was put in prison until 1189. Henry died in that year and their son Richard then became King *Richard I. Eleanor was a remarkable woman who even led her own soldiers on the second *Crusade.

ˌ**Eleanor of Ca**ˈ**stile** /kæˈstiːl/ (*c.* 1245–90) the Spanish wife of King *Edward I of England. When she died, the king placed nine crosses along the route of her funeral procession, and three still survive at *Northampton, Geddington and Waltham Cross. Another was at *Charing Cross in London.

Elections in the US ⇨ article.

Elections to Parliament ⇨ article.

the **E**ˌ**lectoral** ˈ**College** the system for electing the US *President and Vice-president. People do not vote directly for them. In each state, they vote for 'electors' who vote for a particular candidate. All the electoral votes of a state go to one candidate. It is therefore possible for the President to be elected without getting a majority of the US people's votes. Many Americans think that the system is old-fashioned and should be changed.

the **E**ˌ**lectoral Re**ˈ**form So**ˌ**ciety** a group formed in 1884 to work for a change in the way British elections are decided, and to persuade parliament that a system of *proportional representation should be used.

the **e,lectric 'chair** *n* [usu sing] a chair used in certain US states for executing criminals who have been condemned to death. The person is held in the chair by straps and killed with a powerful electric current. The electric chair was first used in 1890, at Auburn Prison in New York State, and is still used in nine states.

'*Elegy 'Written in a 'Country 'Church Yard* ⇨ GRAY'S ELEGY.

,ele'mentary school (*also* **primary school**, **grammar school**, **grade school**) *n* (in US education), the lowest school at which children receive formal teaching, from the age of six. This usually lasts for six or eight years.

the **,Elephant and 'Castle** the name of a place where several major roads meet in London, south of the River *Thames. It was the name of an inn (= a pub) that once stood there.

the **e,leven-'plus** *n* an examination that used to be taken in England and Wales at the age of 11 in order to decide whether a child would go on to a *grammar school(1) or a *secondary modern school. It was stopped almost everywhere when *comprehensive schools were introduced in the late 1960s: *He failed his eleven-plus.* ⇨ article at EDUCATION IN BRITAIN.

,Edward **'Elgar** /'elgɑː(r)/ (1857–1934) an English composer. His **Enigma Variations* (1899) and *The *Dream of Gerontius* (1900) established him as the leading figure in British music at the time. One of the tunes from his **Pomp and Circumstance* marches was turned into the song **Land of Hope and Glory* (1902), which is now always sung at the last night of the *Proms. Elgar's work encouraged people to take more interest in English music. He was made a *knight in 1904.

the **,Elgin 'marbles** /,elgɪn/ a set of marble sculptures of the 5th century BC from the outside of the Parthenon in Athens which are now in the *British Museum. They were bought in 1801 by Lord Elgin from the Turkish authorities who were governing Greece at that time. Elgin sold them to the British government in 1816. The Greek government has asked Britain to return them to Greece many times.

the **'Elim ,Pente'costal 'Church** /'iːlɪm/ one of the two main *Pentecostal Churches in Britain. Many of its members are of West Indian origin.

,George **'Eliot¹** /'eliət/ (1819–80) the male name that the female English author Mary Ann Evans used on her books. Her works include **Adam Bede* (1859), *The *Mill on the Floss* (1860), *Silas Marner* (1861) and **Middlemarch* (1872). Her books give a remarkable picture of Victorian social and domestic life. She was unusual for her time in living for many years with a man, George Henry Lewes, without getting married. Two years after his death in 1878, she caused another scandal by marrying a man 20 years younger than her.

,T S **'Eliot²** /'eliət/ (Thomas Stearns Eliot 1888–1965) a British poet, writer of plays, and literary critic, born in the US. Ezra *Pound encouraged him to go to England, where from 1914 he made his home. Eliot's poems have had a great influence on other poets, particularly *The *Waste Land* (1922) and **Four Quartets* (1944). One of his most important new ideas was to use the natural rhythms of speech in his poetry. His best-known plays are *Murder in the Cathedral* (1935) and *The Cocktail Party* (1951). In 1948 he was given the *Nobel Prize for literature. See also *OLD POSSUM'S BOOK OF PRACTICAL CATS.*

Elizabeth I /ɪ,lɪzəbəθ ðə 'fɜːst; *AmE* 'fɜːrst/ (1533–1603) the queen of England and Ireland from 1558, after the death of her sister *Mary I. She is regarded as one of England's greatest rulers. The daughter of King *Henry VIII and Anne *Boleyn, Elizabeth was an extremely strong and clever woman who controlled the difficult political and religious situation of the time with great skill. She once said to her soldiers before a battle, 'I know I have the body of a weak and feeble woman, but I have the heart and stomach of a King, and of a King of England, too.' During her reign the country's economy grew very strong, the arts were very active, and England became firmly Protestant and confident in world affairs. However, Elizabeth is often seen as a very lonely figure and is known as the 'Virgin Queen' because she never married, although she is known to have had relationships with the Earl of *Leicester and, late in life, the Earl of *Essex. See also ARMADA, MARY QUEEN OF SCOTS.

Elizabeth I, painted by George Gower

Elizabeth II /ɪ,lɪzəbəθ ðə 'sekənd/ (1926–) the queen of the United Kingdom since 1952. She is the daughter of King *George VI and his wife Queen Elizabeth. She has one sister, Princess *Margaret. In 1947 she married Prince Philip of Greece, who had just been made the *Duke of Edinburgh, in *Westminster Abbey. In February 1952 they were visiting *Kenya when the news came of the death of her father. Elizabeth was crowned on 2 June 1953. She is a highly respected and much loved monarch with a great interest in the *Commonwealth. The Queen and Prince Philip have four children, Charles, Anne, Andrew, and Edward. ⇨ article at ROYAL FAMILY.

E,liza'bethan *n* a person who lived during the time of Queen *Elizabeth I. People of the time of *Elizabeth II are sometimes called the 'New Elizabethans'. ▶ **Elizabethan** *adj* of a style of architecture used during the time of *Elizabeth I. Its features included large windows, wooden panels on the walls, and decorative effects in plaster. Houses in the Elizabethan style are often in the shape of an E or an H. *Longleat House is a good example.

,Queen **E'lizabeth, the ,Queen 'Mother** /ɪ'lɪzəbəθ ðə ,kwiːn 'mʌðə(r)/ ⇨ QUEEN MOTHER 2.

the **Elks** /elks/ a US organization for men, started in 1868 and now international. Its full name is the Benevolent and Protective Order of Elks. Members are called Elks, and they have meetings in **Elk Lodges**. In 1996 the organization gave $133 million to charities and had 1.5 million members.

Elle /el/ a magazine for women, published each month and aimed especially at readers who are interested in fashion and socially aware. It first appeared

E

Elections in the US

Running for office

Elections are held regularly for *President of the US, for both houses of *Congress and for state and local government offices. **Candidates** usually **run for office** with the support of one of the two main *political parties, the ***Republicans** or the ***Democrats**. Anyone who wants to run as an **independent** can organize a **petition** and ask people to sign it. Some people run as ***write-in candidates**: they ask **voters** to add their name to the **ballot** (= list of candidates) when they vote.

During an **election campaign** candidates try to achieve **name recognition** (= making their names widely known) by advertising on television, in newspapers, and on posters in public places. They take part in **debates** and hold **rallies** where they give speeches and go round '**pressing the flesh**', shaking hands with as many voters as possible. A candidate is helped by **campaign workers**. In the last few weeks before an election, these workers concentrate on '**GOTV**' (**get out to vote)**, which involves reminding members of their party to vote.

Election campaigning is very expensive, and the candidate with most money has a big advantage. There are laws limiting the amount of money candidates may take from any one person or group but, except in presidential campaigns, there is no limit to the total that can be spent. In a medium-sized state, a candidate for the *Senate might spend ten million dollars on the campaign.

Electing the President

Only a person over 35 who was born in the US can **run for President**. These are the only restrictions but, in practice, presidents have always come from a narrower group of people. They have all been white, and no woman has ever been President, although Geraldine *Ferraro ran for Vice-president on Walter Mondale's **ticket** (= in association with Mondale when he was trying to become President) in 1984. John F *Kennedy was the first Roman Catholic president. Candidates are usually well-known political figures, such as the governors of large states or members of Congress. Americans believe that a president should be not only a good leader, but also a kind and honest person, so candidates are usually people who know how to seem warm and friendly, especially on television.

Presidential elections are held every four years. Early in election year, the political parties choose their candidates through a series of ***primary elections** held in every state. Voters register to vote in either the Republican or the Democratic primary. States hold both primaries on the same day but voters are given different ballots depending on the party they choose. As these **races** take place it gradually becomes clear which candidates are the strongest.

In the summer each party holds a **convention** to make the final choice of candidates for President and Vice-president. Each state sends **delegates** to the conventions but they do not have to vote for the candidates who won the state's primary. The **platform** of ideas that candidates will emphasize during the campaign is decided at the conventions.

Presidential candidates spend tens of millions of dollars on campaigning. In order to prevent rich candidates from always winning, the *federal government offers an equal sum of money to the candidates of both parties. Those who receive **federal funding** cannot accept money from other sources. Candidates travel round the US giving speeches and meeting voters. A popular candidate may help others from the same party running for lower offices. This is called the **coat-tail effect**.

In November the people go to vote. Although the President is said to be directly elected, the official vote is made by an **electoral college**. Each state has a certain number of **electors** in the college, based on the state's population. All the electors from a state must vote for the candidate who got the most votes in the state, and the candidate with at least 270 votes out of a total of 538 becomes President. This system makes states with a large population, such as California, very important.

After the election, the new President goes to Washington for the ***inauguration** on 20 January, and takes the **oath of office**. Between the election and the inauguration, the old President has little power and is called informally a **lame duck**.

Voting procedures

US elections are held on the Tuesday following the first Monday of November. This date was selected long ago when most Americans lived in the country, because in early November there was little work on the farms and the weather was good enough to allow people to travel into the city to vote.

Americans over the age of 18 have the right to vote, but only about half of them take part in presidential elections, even fewer in other elections. One explanation for low **voter turnout** is the need to **register** to vote. People who move to another state have to register again after they move. In some places registrations forms are now available in fast-food restaurants.

A few weeks before **election day** registered voters receive a card telling them the address of the **polling station** where they should go to vote, usually a school or church hall. People who will be away on election day, or who are ill, may use an **absentee ballot** and post it to election officials.

Polling stations are open from early morning until night. Voters first have to sign their name in a book that lists all the voters in the **precinct** (= area) and then **cast a vote**. Some states use computerized systems, but the most common method is to use a **voting booth**. This has three sides and a curtain that closes the fourth side. In the booth are lists of candidates for each office. Voters pull down a metal lever beside the name of the person they want to vote for. The levers operate mechanical counters which record the total number of votes for each candidate. It is possible to select all the candidates from one party, and this is called **voting a straight ticket**. But many voters choose candidates from both parties and **vote a split ticket**.

Journalists and **pollsters** are allowed to ask people how they voted and these **exit polls** help predict election results. However, the results of exit polls may not be announced until polling stations everywhere have closed, in case they influence or change the result.

Elections to Parliament

The electoral system

Each of the 659 ***Members of Parliament**, or **MPs**, in the ***House of Commons** represents a particular part of the United Kingdom called a **constituency**. The country is divided into areas of roughly equal population (about 90 000 people). Cities have several constituencies. MPs are expected to be interested in the affairs of their constituency and to represent the interests of local people, their **constituents**, in *Parliament. Many hold regular **surgeries**, sessions at which they are available for local people to talk to them. People may also write to their MP if they want to protest about something.

Anyone who wants to become an MP must be elected by the people of a constituency. Before an election one person is chosen by each of the main *political parties to **stand for election** in each constituency. People usually vote for the **candidate** who belongs to the party they support, rather than because of his or her personal qualities or opinions. Only the candidate who gets the most votes in each constituency is elected. This system is called ***first past the post**.

In a **general election**, when elections are held in all constituencies, the winning party, which forms the next **government**, is the one that wins most **seats** in Parliament (= has the most MPs), even though it may have received fewer votes overall than the opposition parties. In 1992, for example, the *Conservative Party gained more than half the total number of seats but fewer than half of all the votes cast. A proposal that Britain should use a system of ***proportional representation**, whereby seats in Parliament would be allocated according to the total number of votes cast for each party, has been put forward on various occasions.

General elections

By law, a **general election** must take place every five years. The government decides when to hold an election, and the *Prime Minister may decide to **go to the country** earlier than is legally necessary if there seems to be a good chance of winning.

General elections are always held on Thursdays. After the date has been fixed, anyone who wants to **stand for Parliament** (= be a candidate for election) has to leave a **deposit** of £500 with the ***Returning Officer**, the person in each constituency responsible for managing the election. The local offices of the major parties pay the deposit for their own candidates. If a candidate wins more than 5% of the votes, he or she gets the deposit back. Otherwise candidates **lose their deposit**. This is intended to stop people who do not seriously want to be MPs from taking part in the election. Sometimes people who feel very strongly about an issue, e.g. protecting the lives of unborn babies, become candidates and **campaign** specifically about that issue. A few people become candidates for a joke, especially in the constituency which the Prime Minister is defending, because they know that they will get a lot of publicity. One candidate, 'Lord' David *Sutch, has stood against the Prime Minister in most elections since 1966.

Before an election takes place candidates campaign for support in the constituency. The amount of money that candidates are allowed to spend on their campaign is strictly limited. Leading members of the government and the opposition parties travel throughout the country addressing meetings and 'meeting the people', especially in **marginals**, constituencies where only a slight shift of opinion would change the outcome of the voting. Local **party workers** spend their time **canvassing**, going from house to house to ask people about how they intend to vote. At national level the parties spend a lot of money on advertising and media coverage. They cannot buy television time: each party is allowed a number of strictly timed ***party political broadcasts**. Each also holds a daily televised **news conference**.

By-elections

If an MP dies or resigns, a ***by-election** is held in the constituency which he or she represented. By-elections are closely watched by the media as they are thought to indicate the current state of public opinion and the government's popularity.

Voting

Anyone over the age of 18 has the right to vote at elections, provided that they are **on the electoral register**. This is a list of all the adults living in a constituency. A new, revised list is compiled each year. Copies are available for people to look at in local public libraries. Voting is not compulsory but the **turnout** (= the number of people voting) at general elections is usually high, about 75%.

About a week in advance of an election everyone on the electoral register receives a **polling card**. This tells them where their **polling station** is, i.e. where they must go to vote. On the day of the election, **polling day**, voters go to the polling station and are given a **ballot paper**. This lists the names of all the candidates for that constituency, together with the names of the parties they represent. Each voter then goes into a **polling booth** where nobody can see what they are writing, and puts a cross next to the name of one candidate only, the one they want to elect. Polling stations, often local schools or church halls, are open from 7 a.m. to 10 p.m. to give everyone an opportunity to vote. During a general election, people leaving the polling station may be asked by professional analysts called **pollsters** how they voted. Similar **exit polls** taken all over the country are used to predict the overall election result.

After **the polls** close, the ballot papers from all the polling stations in a constituency are taken to a central place to be counted. In most constituencies **counting** takes place the same evening, continuing for as long as necessary through the night. If the number of votes for two candidates is very close, the candidates may **demand a recount**. Several recounts may take place until all the candidates are satisfied that the count is accurate. Finally, the Returning Officer makes a public announcement giving the number of votes cast for each candidate and declaring the winner to be the MP for the constituency. On general election night, television and radio keep everyone informed of the results throughout Britain and make predictions about the overall result and the size of the winning party's majority in Parliament.

in France in 1985 but there are now versions published in Britain, the US and other countries.

ˌDuke' **ˈEllington** /ˈelɪŋtən/ (1899–1974) an *African-American *jazz musician who played the piano and wrote music for the band he led. It became well known at the *Cotton Club in *Harlem (1927–31) and played a concert at *Carnegie Hall (1943). Ellington wrote more than 2 000 pieces, including *Mood Indigo* (1930), *It Don't Mean a Thing If It Ain't Got That Swing* (1932) and *Sophisticated Lady* (1933). He received the *Presidential Medal of Freedom in 1969.

immigrants leaving Ellis Island for New York, c. 1900

ˈEllis ˌIsland /ˈelɪs/ a small island off *Manhattan(1) which was the official place of entry to the US for most immigrants between 1891 and 1943. About 20 million people entered the US there, but it was called the 'island of tears' because some were refused entry. It is now the Ellis Island Museum of Immigration.

ˌRalph **ˈEllison** /ˈelɪsn/ (1914–94) an *African-American author who is best known for his novel *Invisible Man* (1952), which won the *National Book Award. It tells, with sadness and humour, the story of an African American's search for identity in a white world.

ˌElmer ˈGantry /ˈgæntri/ a novel (1927) by Sinclair *Lewis. Elmer Gantry is a successful preacher who holds religious meetings in the *Middle West, but does many of the bad things he warns people not to do. The book turned some Americans against this type of religion but made others angry at the author. In a 1960 film version, Burt *Lancaster played Gantry and won an *Oscar.

ˌElmer's ˈglue™ /ˌelməz; *AmE* ˌelmərz/ *n* [U] a US make of white glue which has for many years been a standard item in the art classes of American schools.

ˌElstree ˈStudios /ˌelstriː/ a place in north London where many British films are made. The studios began producing films in the 1920s.

ˌBen **ˈElton** /ˈeltən/ (1962–) an English comedian and writer of humorous books and plays. He has appeared regularly on television.

ˈEly /ˈiːli/ a town in *Cambridgeshire, England, with a famous cathedral. In the past, the town was on an island in the *Fens called the **Isle of Ely**, from which *Hereward the Wake fought the *Normans.

the **Eˌmanciˈpation Act** the British law of 1829 which made it possible for Roman Catholics to hold public positions of power, including being *Members of Parliament, for the first time since 1678.

the **Eˌmanciˈpation Proclaˈmation** the statement made by President Abraham *Lincoln on 1 January 1863 that all slaves in the *Confederate States were 'forever free'. It had no actual power to make them free, but people talk about Lincoln 'freeing the slaves' because of this proclamation (= announcement). It helped the North in the American *Civil War as well, by allowing black people to serve in the army and navy, and by changing the war into a fight against *slavery, which caused many people in England and France to gave their support to the North. The Proclamation led in 1865 to the Thirteenth Amendment to the *American Constitution, which officially ended slavery in all parts of the US.

the **Emˈbankment** (*in full* the **Victoria Embankment**) a street that runs along the north bank of the River *Thames: *a walk along the Embankment.*

emblems

Emblems, **logos** and other **symbols** are widely used as a simple way of identifying countries, states, organizations, companies and sports teams.

Emblems of Great Britain include the figure of ***Britannia**, a woman in long robes carrying a shield with a *Union Jack pattern. Each country within the United Kingdom has a national emblem, as well as its own *flag. England's official emblem is a **red rose**. Red and white roses were chosen as emblems during the *Wars of the Roses. Afterwards, the two were combined in the *Tudor rose. Other emblems include a **bulldog**, often wearing a Union Jack waistcoat, and ***John Bull**, an old-fashioned, fat country gentleman. Wales has two plants, the ***leek** and the ***daffodil**, as its emblems, and also uses the figure of a Welsh woman dressed in traditional costume. Welsh people often wear a daffodil on St *David's Day. Scotland has the **thistle** (= a prickly weed) as its official emblem, but a ***tartan** pattern is used on many products made in Scotland. The national symbol of Northern Ireland is the *Red Hand of Ulster, which appears on its flag. The ***shamrock** and ***harp** are also associated with Ireland and the shamrock is the emblem of the Republic of Ireland.

the red rose, the leek and the daffodil, the thistle, the shamrock

Members of the British *royal family and the aristocracy have **coats of arms**. The *royal arms are placed behind judges and magistrates in law courts as a symbol of authority. Below the arms is the **motto** *Dieu et mon droit*, French for 'God and my right'. Some commercial organizations whose products have royal approval are granted special permission to show the royal arms on their products.

The best-known emblem of the British government is the **portcullis** (= a barred, chained gate) that appears on official government papers. The ***Great Seal of the United States**, which appears on US money and government documents, shows a ***bald eagle**, a very large bird which is itself a symbol of the US, and the Latin motto **e pluribus unum* which refers to the fact that the US is one country made up from many individual states.

Each US state has a variety of emblems, including animals and plants which are commonly found in that state. For example, *Michigan has a state bird (the robin), a state fish (the trout), a state flower (the apple blossom), a state insect (the dragonfly) and a state stone (the Petoskey stone). These symbols may appear on the state flag and on official documents.

Most commercial organizations, *charities, *political parties, sports clubs, etc. have an emblem that they put on flags, notepaper, badges and vehicles, sometimes together with their initials. These emblems are often so well known that there is no need for the organization's name to be added. They may involve a picture that suggests the name, e.g. a picture of an apple for *Apple computers, or the name written in a particular way. Such commercial emblems can be very valuable and may be registered as **trademarks**, to prevent anyone else using them.

---

the ˌ**Emerald** ˈ**Isle** a name for Ireland, referring to the strong green colour of its countryside.

ˈRalph ˈWaldo ˈ**Emerson** /ˈrælf ˈwɔːldəʊ ˈeməsn; *AmE* ˈwɑːldoʊ ˈemərsn/ (1803–82) a US writer of essays and poems. He greatly influenced religion and philosophy, especially with his idea of Transcendentalism, which said that God's nature was in every person and thing. After being a Unitarian minister (= church leader) in *New England, he settled in 1834 in *Concord, *Massachusetts, where he worked closely with Henry David *Thoreau and others. Emerson's essay *Nature* (1836) explained Transcendentalism as the unity of nature.

EMI /ˌiː em ˈaɪ/ (*in full* **Electric and Musical Industries**) a large international music company started in 1931 when two other big companies joined together. The new company included many of the most famous recording labels, such as Columbia, *HMV and Parlophone, and the recording studios at Abbey Road in London. EMI is now part of *Thorn-EMI.

ˌ**eminent doˈmain** *n* [U] (in US law) the right of the government to take private property for public use. The Fifth Amendment to the US Constitution states that 'just compensation' (= fair payment) must be given to the owner when this happens. Eminent domain is used, for example, when houses must be destroyed to build a new motorway/freeway.

ˌ***Eminent Vicˈtorians*** a book (1918) by Lytton *Strachey about the lives of four famous *Victorians. It was important because, with his other books, it changed the art of biography, by giving real opinions instead of simply praise.

ˈ***Emma*** a novel (1816) by Jane *Austen. The main character, a young woman called Miss Emma Woodhouse, believes that she knows what is best for everyone around her, particularly her friend Harriet Smith. Emma comes to realize how foolish she has been, when Harriet seems to be falling in love with the man Emma herself loves, and in the end both women marry happily.

ˈ***Emmerdale*** /ˈemədeɪl; *AmE* ˈemərdeɪl/ a popular British *soap opera on *ITV. It is about the people who live in an imaginary *Yorkshire village called Emmerdale.

ˈ**Emmy** /ˈemi/ *n* (*pl* **Emmys**) a US television award in the form of a small statue about the size of an *Oscar. Emmys are given each year by the Academy of Television Arts and Sciences to the best shows and actors. This began in 1949 and so many are now presented that there are two separate ceremonies. The word Emmy comes from 'immy', an informal name for 'image orthicon tube'.

the ˌ**Empire** ˈ**State** ˌ**Building** an office building in *Manhattan(1), New York City, which for over 40 years after it was built (in 1931) was the tallest in the world. It is 1 250 feet (381 metres) high and has 102 floors. See also *King Kong*.

Employment ⇨ article.

the **Emˈployment** ˌ**Service** a part of the *Department for Education and Employment in Britain which from 1991 has been responsible for *unemployment benefits and *Jobcentres.

the **EMS** /ˌiː em ˈes/ ⇨ European Monetary System.

EMU /ˌiː em ˈjuː/ ⇨ Economic and Monetary Union.

the ***Enˌcycloˈpaedia Briˈtannica*** /ɪnˌsaɪkləˈpiːdiə brɪˈtænɪkə/ the most famous encyclopedia in English, printed in many volumes and regularly revised. It was begun in 1768 by a 'society of Gentlemen in Scotland' and has been mostly American since 1928. Its present owner is William Benton, and it is published from offices at the University of Chicago. Many British and US families regard owning a set of the *Encyclopaedia Britannica* as a status symbol.

The ***Enˌcycloˈpedia Aˌmeriˈcana*** /ɪnˌsaɪkləˈpiːdiə əˌmerɪˈkɑːnə/ a large US encyclopedia, regularly revised. The first edition, in 13 volumes (1827–33), was created by Francis Lieber (1798–1972), a German teacher of politics who settled in the US in 1827. The 1997 *Encyclopedia Americana* contains 45 000 articles.

Enˈdeavor the name of a US space shuttle (= spacecraft that can be used again) used by *NASA. It first flew in 1992 and was used by astronauts in 1993 to repair the *Hubble Space Telescope.

ˌHarry ˈ**Enfield** /ˈenfiːld/ (1961–) an English comedian who appears regularly on television. He makes fun of stupid or unpleasant people by appearing as a range of exaggerated characters, such as Tim Nice-but-Dim and Wayne and Waynetta Slob.

the ˈ**England and** ˈ**Wales** ˈ**Cricket Board** the organization that governs the sport of professional cricket in England and Wales, based at *Lord's in London. Until 1997 it was called the Test and County Cricket Board. ⇨ article at Cricket.

ˌ**England exˈpects** the first words of a famous signal sent by Admiral *Nelson to the ships he commanded, before the Battle of *Trafalgar in 1805. The full signal was 'England expects that every man will do his duty.' The phrase 'England expects' is sometimes used in a humorous way today: *England expects nothing less than a win in today's match.*

ˌ**English** ˈ**breakfast** *n* a large breakfast consisting of fruit juice, cereal, a cooked dish (usually bacon and eggs), toast with butter and jam, and tea or coffee to drink. Only hotels serve English breakfasts and use the expression. Few British people eat so much for breakfast in their own homes. Compare continental breakfast.

the ˌ**English** ˈ**Channel** (*also* the **Channel**) the area of sea between southern England and northern France. Although it is so narrow at one point (20 miles/32 kilometres) that some people can swim across it, it has always formed a physical and cultural barrier between Britain and the rest of Europe.

the ˈ**English** ˌ**Civil** ˈ**War** a war (1642–51) between the King of England, *Charles I, and his parliament. Its causes were both political and religious. It divided the people of England and caused great suffering. Charles I's soldiers (the *Cavaliers) were defeated by those of parliament (the *Roundheads) at the battles of *Marston Moor (1644) and *Naseby (1645). The Roundhead soldiers were very well organized, in the *New Model Army, under Thomas *Fairfax and Oliver *Cromwell. Charles I was held prisoner for more than two years, and was then executed, in January 1649. The *Commonwealth[2] was declared. For 11 years England had no king or queen, although for much of this time it had a strong leader in Oliver Cromwell. The Commonwealth did not last long after Cromwell's death, however, and in 1660 Charles's son took his place as King *Charles II at the *Restoration.

the ˌ**English diˈsease** an expression that has been used by people in Europe about various different aspects of English life. In the 1960s and 1970s it meant the poor performance of English workers and the many strikes in factories, etc. In the 1980s it was used to refer to the bad behaviour of English football supporters.

E

Employment

Going to work

In Britain and the US young people often have a **part-time job** but do not start work properly until they are 16, or older if they take some form of *further education. The usual age for **retirement** is now 65.

Americans share with the British the **Protestant work ethic**, a belief that working hard is good for a person. In the US people who cannot find work often feel that they have no value, and parents believe that the best way to help their children become responsible adults is to encourage them to work hard. In Britain, people who complain about having to work may be accused of **sponging** (= living on money from the state). But the work ethic is less strong now in Britain, perhaps because jobs are less secure and many people feel less committed to a particular company.

The labour market

About 131 million Americans have jobs, and around 5% of these **moonlight** (= have a second job). The British **labour force** is about 27 million, over half of which are **white-collar workers** (= people with office jobs) or **professionals**. **Blue-collar workers**, workers in factories, on building sites, etc., often have difficulty staying in work.

In many American families, the man is still the **breadwinner** (= the person who supports the family), but the number of women in employment has doubled since the 1960s. In about half of all families both the mother and the father work. In Britain, women are nearly 50% of the **workforce**, and form the majority of part-time workers. Some jobs traditionally done by women, such as secretarial work and nursing, still attract more women than men, though discrimination (= different treatment on grounds of sex, race, etc.) is illegal. Most top jobs still go to men. Some women complain of having to do the **second shift**, to spend the evening cooking and cleaning, even though many men believe in principle in sharing the housework.

Most people find jobs through advertisements in newspapers or, in Britain, at ***Jobcentres**. Some register with an **employment agency**. Companies looking for senior staff may approach people working for another company, a practice known as **headhunting**. Many people choose to be **self-employed** (= to have their own business) or to **work freelance** for several employers.

Pay and conditions

People who work in offices have a five-day week and are often said to have **a nine-to-five job**. In fact many office workers begin work earlier or finish later. Many work **flexitime**, a system that lets them decide their own hours. In the US people are expected to work 40 hours, often more, and are not usually paid for the 30 minutes or so they spend eating lunch. People in senior positions often work much longer hours. In Britain, many people with a nine-to-five job work only a 35-hour week and their 8-hour day includes a lunch break. In shops and factories the average working week, including **overtime** (= extra work), is about 45 hours. Factory workers and those in the **service sector** (= shops, public transport, etc.) usually do **shift work**, and their working hours vary from week to week.

Most blue-collar workers are paid **by the hour**. Their **pay** (*BrE* **wages**) may be higher if they work at night or on public holidays: night work, for instance, may pay **time and a half** (= one and a half times the normal hourly rate). White-collar workers and professionals usually get a **salary**. In most industries there is a big gap between the pay of senior managers and that of the workers. An increasing number of people are unhappy with this situation. In the US there has for a long time been a **minimum wage**, and this has recently been introduced in Britain.

Benefits add to the value of a job. These include ***pension plans**, **childcare allowances**, **discounts** on goods produced by the company, and **profit-sharing schemes** which pay employees more money when the business does well. In the US the most important benefit is a **health plan** (= health insurance).

Americans typically get a two-week **vacation**, and around 10 ***holidays** during the year. Employees who have worked for a company for a long time may get more vacation. Those in low-paid jobs may get none at all. Most British people get three or four weeks paid **leave** a year, plus ***bank holidays**.

There are strict laws in Britain and the US about **working conditions**, the number of hours that employees can be required to work, how often they must take a **break**, and what must be done to protect their safety. Many workers belong to ***trade unions** (*AmE* **labor unions**), which provide support for workers in disputes with employers.

Job security

The US labour market is very flexible. It is easy to **hire and fire** people, and so companies can react quickly to economic problems by **downsizing** (= getting smaller) and **laying off** employees (= taking away their jobs). Americans believe that the government should be involved as little as possible in business, and that this will make the economy strong. But this idea has made it hard to get laws passed that would protect workers' jobs.

In Britain people rarely stay in the same job for more than a few years. Many office workers and professionals expect to have **job satisfaction** (= to enjoy their job and feel it is worth doing) and often change jobs in search of something better. Other people, however, are forced to look for a new job because they have been **made redundant** (= told that they are no longer required). For them, finding a new job may be difficult and as a result many people become **unemployed**.

Unemployment figures are an indication of the state of a country's economy and are a politically sensitive issue. In the mid-1990s Britain's **jobless total** was around two million, approximately 8% of the workforce. Of these, 46% of men and 28% of women were **long-term unemployed** (= out of work for more than a year).

The rate of unemployment in the US is around 6%. The flexible labour market means that many people who lose their job get another within about 15 weeks. But *African Americans and *Hispanics have much higher rates of unemployment, and may stay unemployed for longer.

ˌ**English ˈHeritage** another name for the Historic Buildings and Monuments Commission for England, a government organization started in 1984 to look after about 400 important places and buildings in England. It encourages people to visit these places to understand and enjoy their history. *Stonehenge is one example of an English Heritage site. English Heritage also has responsibility for *listed buildings in England. Compare NATIONAL TRUST, WORLD HERITAGE SITE.

The **English Language** ⇨ article.

the ˈ**English ˈNational ˈBallet** a ballet company started in 1950 by Alicia *Markova and Anton *Dolin. It was first called Festival Ballet, and from 1969 to 1989 the London Festival Ballet. It performs both traditional and modern pieces at many theatres around Britain.

the ˈ**English ˈNational ˈOpera** (*abbr* the **ENO**) an opera company started in London in 1931, and known until 1974 as Sadler's Wells Opera. It performs operas in English and often takes them on tour to different parts of England. See also COLISEUM.

ˌ**English ˈNature** (*also* the **Nature Conservancy Council for England**) a British government organization established in 1991 to protect wild animals, plants and natural features in England, and to identify *sites of special scientific interest.

ˌ**English ˈOnly ˌMovement** a campaign by some US groups to make English the official language of the country. It is mainly supported by two organizations, English First and US English. An English Language Amendment to the *American Constitution was introduced in *Congress in 1981, but its members have never voted on it. However, 21 states have passed their own official English Only laws.

The ˈ***English ˌPatient*** a popular and successful film (1996), directed by Anthony Minghella. It is set mainly in *World War II, and is about a dying Hungarian man who remembers a love affair he had with an English woman. The film was based on a book of the same name (1991) by Michael Ondaatje (1943–), and won seven *Oscars. The main actors are Ralph Fiennes, Juliette Binoche and Kristin Scott Thomas.

ˌ**English ˈrose** *n* [usu sing] an expression that people sometimes use to describe any lovely young English woman who looks attractive in a traditional way and has a sweet nature: *Wear the white dress, and you'll look a proper English rose.*

ˌ**English ˈsetter** *n* a British breed of large dog with a long, soft coat, usually black and white or brown and white in colour. It is sometimes used in hunting birds.

the ˌ**English-Speaking ˈUnion** (*abbr* the **ESU**) an independent organization started in 1918. At first its aim was to help the peoples of Britain and the US to become closer, but it soon decided to include people of other countries that speak English in the *Commonwealth, and now around the world. The English-Speaking Union organizes social events, lectures, etc., and helps young people to travel and study.

the ˌ**English ˈStage ˌCompany** an English theatre company started in 1956 to perform modern plays by new young writers. One of its first plays was **Look Back in Anger* by John *Osborne. The company has its base at the *Royal Court Theatre in London.

the ˌ**English ˈTourist Board** a government organization that works to encourage people to visit England, along with the *British Tourist Authority and the local tourist organizations of the regions of England. It also gives different symbols to hotels, etc. to show what standard of accommodation they offer.

the ***EˌnigmaVariˈations*** the name usually given to a popular piece of music by Edward *Elgar called *Variations on an Original Theme*, written in 1899. An enigma is a mystery, and Elgar said that the music had a secret connection with another well-known tune, though no one has discovered for certain which tune it is. Some people think it may be **Auld Lang Syne*, while others argue that it is **Rule, Britannia!* The *Variations* also contained another mystery, as each of the 13 parts was intended to represent one of Elgar's friends, but there were clues to them and they have all been identified.

ˌ**Ennisˈkillen** /ˌenɪsˈkɪlən/ a mainly Protestant town in *Fermanagh in Northern Ireland. In November 1987 the *IRA left a bomb at a service to remember people who died for Britain in the two *World Wars. It exploded, killing 11 people and injuring many more.

ENO /ˌiː en ˈəʊ; *AmE* ˈoʊ/ ⇨ ENGLISH NATIONAL OPERA.

ˌBrian ˈ**Eno** /ˈiːnəʊ; *AmE* ˈiːnoʊ/ (1948–) a British pop musician. He played electronic keyboards for the group Roxy Music (1971–3), and is noted for his work with other musicians, including David *Bowie and David Byrne (1952–) (e.g. the album *My Life in the Bush of Ghosts*, 1981, with David Byrne).

Eˌnola ˈGay /eˌnəʊlə ˈɡeɪ; *AmE* eˌnoʊlə/ the name of the US plane that dropped the first atomic bomb on *Hiroshima in 1945 at the end of *World War II.

ENSA /ˈensə/ (*in full* the **Entertainments National Service Association**) an organization that provided concerts and other forms of entertainment for British soldiers serving abroad during *World War II, and for workers in Britain. Many famous performers took part in these concerts.

the ˌ**Entente Cordiˈale** /ˌɒntɒnt kɔːdiˈɑːl; *AmE* ˌɑːntɑːnt kɔːrdiˈɑːl/ the friendly understanding reached between the British and French governments in 1904, mainly about issues relating to their colonies around the world.

ˌ**Enterprise ˈNeptune** a campaign started by the *National Trust in Britain in 1965. Its aim was to save some of the most beautiful parts of Britain's coast for everyone to enjoy. The National Trust now owns more than 520 miles/850 kilometres of coast.

ˈ**enterprise zone** *n* (in Britain) an area where the government encourages companies to open new offices and factories, for example by offering them money and tax advantages. Enterprise zones are usually city areas which have serious economic problems and where more jobs are badly needed: *The government is to create 24 more enterprise zones in depressed areas.*

Enˌvironmental ˈHealth ˌOfficer *n* (in Britain) a person who is trained in the ways that the environment can affect people's health. Environmental Health Officers work mainly for *district councils, examining places where food is prepared, teaching children about their health, helping people who are disturbed by their neighbours, etc.

the **EnˌvironmentalProˈtection ˌAgency** (*abbr* the **EPA**) a US government organization that establishes rules and standards for protecting the environment, e.g against pollution. It was started in 1970.

the **Eˌpiscopal ˈChurch** (*also* the **Protestant Episcopal Church**) the US Church that is part of the *Anglican Communion. It separated from the *Church of England during the *American Revolution. It has the reputation of having many rich and socially important people as members. A member of the church is called an **Episcopalian**.

the **Eˈpiscopal ˈChurch in ˈScotland** the Scottish branch of the *Church of England, established in the

E

E

The English language

The roots of English

English began as a west Germanic language which was brought to England by the *Saxons around 400 AD. ***Old English** was the spoken and written language of England between 400 and 1100 AD. Many words used today come from Old English, including *man*, *woman*, *king*, *mother*, *give* and *wash*, as do many *slang expressions and *swear words. But Old English was very different from modern English and only a few words can be easily recognized. In the 9th and 10th centuries, when *Vikings invaded England, Old Norse words, e.g. *sky*, *take* and *get* and many *place names, entered the language.

From the *Norman Conquest (1066) until the late 12th century English was replaced as the official language by Norman French, though English was still used by the lower classes. English from about 1300 to 1500 is known as ***Middle English**. It was influenced by French and also Latin in vocabulary and pronunciation. French brought many words connected with government, e.g. *sovereign*, *royal*, *court*, *legal*, and *government* itself. Latin was the language of religion and learning and gave to English words such as *minister*, *angel*, *master*, *school* and *grammar*. Literature began again to be written in English. One of the most famous Middle English works is *Chaucer's *The *Canterbury Tales*.

The development of Modern English

Modern English developed from the Middle English *dialect of the East Midlands and was influenced by the English used in London, where a printing press was set up by William *Caxton in 1476. English changed a great deal from this time until the end of the 18th century. During the Renaissance, many words were introduced from Greek and Latin to express new ideas, especially in science, medicine and philosophy. They included *physics*, *species*, *architecture*, *encyclopedia* and *hypothesis*. In the 16th century several versions of the Bible helped bring written English to ordinary people. The *Elizabethan period is also famous for its drama, and the plays of *Marlowe and *Shakespeare were seen by many people.

The development of printing helped establish standards of spelling and grammar, but there remained a lot of variation. Samuel *Johnson's *A Dictionary of the English Language* (1755), was the first authoritative treatment of English. It defined about 40 000 words and gave examples of their use. Soon afterwards, people tried to establish grammatical rules, like the use of *me*, not *I*, after a preposition, and that *different* should be followed by *from*, not *to* or *than*. The idea of having an English academy to protect agreed standards has been suggested several times, including most recently in the 1990s, but has never found enough support.

By the 18th century ***American English** was well-established and developing independently from ***British English**. After colonists arrived in the US new words began to be added from *Native-American languages, and from French and Spanish. In 1783, soon after Johnson's dictionary was published, Noah *Webster's *The Elementary Spelling Book* was published in the US. At first it used Johnson's spellings, but later editions contained many of what have come to be known as American spellings, e.g. *harbor* and *favorite*. In 1806 Webster's *A Compendious Dictionary of the English Language* contained more spelling changes and became the basis of an American standard.

Americans believed that having their own language was part of their national identity, and Webster's dictionary reinforced the independent status of American English. In the 19th century, more words were added from the languages of the many *immigrants to the US. *Black English also greatly extended the language.

The development of standard forms of English in both Britain and the US led to suggestions that other dialects were inferior. In Britain especially, use of dialect forms was thought to indicate a lack of education and lower social status.

20th-century English

During the 19th and early 20th centuries many dictionaries and books about language were published including, in Britain, the **Oxford English Dictionary*, which was begun in 1858. In 1926 Fowler's *A *Dictionary of Modern English Usage* presented a traditional view of grammar but rejected the more extreme rules, and was held in great respect for a long time. The development of *radio promoted standard English and *Received Pronunciation (RP), which became known as *BBC English. Many older British people still consider this to be 'correct' English, and complain about falling standards in schools and the media.

At the end of the 20th century English tends to be much less formal. Few British people know much about grammar, since it is not usually taught in schools, but a person who cannot speak and write grammatically is likely to be at a disadvantage. An RP accent is now associated mainly with the upper classes, and many younger educated people have a modified regional accent.

In the US, ***General American English** spoken with a Midwestern accent is the standard. In the past English helped to unite immigrants from many countries, but now some people are worried that recent *Hispanic immigrants are continuing to use Spanish. There have been attempts to prevent this by making English the only official language. In the 1980s the *political correctness movement had a lasting influence on American English by trying to get rid of words with negative associations, e.g. those describing disabled people, and to replace them with positive-sounding expressions.

New words are still being added to English from other languages, including Italian (*tiramisu*), Chinese (*feng shui*) and Japanese (*karaoke*). Existing words gain new senses, and many slang terms become part of the standard language. New expressions spread quickly through television and the Internet.

English is now an international language and is used as a means of communication between people from many countries. As a result the influences on the English language are wider than ever and it is possible that ***World English** will move away from using a British or American standard and establish its own international identity.

16th century. It is smaller than the Scottish national Church, the *Church of Scotland.

ˌ**e ˈpluribus ˈunum** /ˌeɪ ˈplʊərɪbəs ˈuːnəm; *AmE* ˈplʊrɪbəs/ a Latin phrase, meaning 'one from many', which was chosen for the *Continental Congress when a single country was created from the *thirteen colonies. The phrase appears on the *Great Seal of the United States and on many US coins.

ˌ**Epping ˈForest** /ˌepɪŋ/ a large forest in *Essex, just north of London, which is a popular place for walking, riding, etc.

ˈ**Epsom** /ˈepsəm/ a town in *Surrey, England, which is famous as a place where horse races are run. The most famous of these are the *Derby and the *Oaks.

ˌJacob ˈ**Epstein** /ˈepstaɪn/ (1880–1959) a sculptor who was born in New York and from 1905 lived mainly in England. His early works, especially his naked figures, shocked many people, but his later work is greatly admired. It includes *Christ in Majesty* in *Coventry Crthedral. In 1954 Epstein was made a *knight.

Jacob Epstein

the ˈ**Equal Emˈployment Opporˈtunity Comˌmission** (*abbr* the **EEOC**) the US government organization that investigates unfair employment practices. It was established by the *Civil Rights Act of 1964. The Commission uses laws that forbid prejudice by employers against a person's race, sex, age, religion or country of origin. It can do this by taking employers to a court of law. Compare EQUAL OPPORTUNITIES COMMISSION.

the ˌ**Equal Opporˈtunities Comˌmission** a British government organization, started in 1975, which encourages companies, colleges, etc. to give the same opportunities to men and women. It also tries to make sure that men and women receive the same pay for the same work. It has the power to enforce (= force people to obey) parts of the *Sex Discrimination Act and the *Equal Pay Act.

the ˌ**Equal ˈPay Act** a British law (1970) which says that men and women should receive the same pay for the same work. Previously many people, especially women, were not being treated fairly.

the ˌ**Equal ˈRights Aˌmendment** /əˌmendmənt/ (*abbr* the **ERA**) a proposal for an *amendment to the US *Constitution which would give women equal rights with men. The proposal began in *Congress in 1923 and was finally passed in 1972. A total of 38 of the 50 states had to give their approval by 1982 for it to become law, but only 35 did, so it failed.

ˈ**Equity 1** (*also* **British Actors' Equity Association**) the trade union to which most professional actors in Britain belong. Any actor who wants to act for pay must have an **Equity card** to show that he or she is a member. **2** (*also* **Actors' Equity Association**) a US trade union for actors who work in the theatre. Compare AFTRA, SCREEN ACTORS GUILD.

ER /ˌiː ˈɑː(r)/ a US television medical series that began in 1994. ER is the abbreviation for Emergency Room, and the programme is set in a *Chicago hospital. It was the most popular series in the US in 1996 when it won the *Emmy award as the 'Outstanding Drama Series'.

ERA /ˌiː ɑːr ˈeɪ/ ⇨ EQUAL RIGHTS AMENDMENT.

ˈ***Erewhon*** /ˈeriwɒn; *AmE* ˈeriwɑːn/ a novel (1872) by Samuel *Butler about an imaginary place called Erewhon. It is an attack on British attitudes of the time towards religion, science, the law, etc., using satire. The word 'Erewhon' is made up of the letters of the word 'nowhere'.

ˌLake ˈ**Erie** /ˈɪəri; *AmE* ˈɪri/ one of the *Great Lakes on the border between the US and Canada, named after the Eriez, a *Native-American people. It has an area of 9 907 square miles (25 667 square kilometres). It is linked to Lake *Huron and Lake *Ontario. Cities on Lake Erie include Buffalo, *Cleveland and Toledo.

the ˌ**Erie Caˈnal** /ˌɪəri; *AmE* ˌɪri/ a US canal completed in 1825. It was built to connect Lake *Erie with the *Hudson River, so that goods from New York City could be sent by water to the states in the *Midwest. The canal was 365 miles (585 kilometres) long. The New York State Barge Canal replaced it in 1918 and goes along some of the old route.

the **ERM** /ˌiː ɑːr ˈem/ (*in full* the **exchange-rate mechanism**) an agreement reached between member countries of the *European Union in 1979 to stop their currencies changing too much in value in relation to each other. The currencies are linked to the *ecu, although their value is usually expressed in relation to the German mark. Britain only joined the ERM in 1990, but left it in September 1992 after the pound fell below the lowest level allowed. See also BLACK WEDNESDAY.

ˈ**Ermine Street** /ˈɜːmɪn; *AmE* ˈɜːrmɪn/ the name given to one of the main Roman roads in Britain, from London to *York.

ˈ**Ernie** /ˈɜːni; *AmE* ˈɜːrni/ the computer that chooses the numbers of winning *Premium Bonds. Its name is made up of the first letters of the words 'electronic random number indicator equipment'.

ˈ**Eros** /ˈɪərɒs; *AmE* ˈɪrɑːs/ the popular name for the statue of a figure with wings that stands in the centre of *Piccadilly Circus in London, a place where people often arrange to meet. Eros was the Greek god of love, often represented as a boy with wings and a bow and arrow. However, the figure on the statue was not meant to represent him, but the idea of Christian charity.

Eskimo *n* ⇨ note at INUITS.

ESPN /ˌiː es piː ˈen/ a US cable television sports network that shows US and international sports events and certain other special programmes. It began as a local television channel in *Connecticut in 1979 and is now owned by *ABC.

Esq (especially in Britain) the short form of the word 'Esquire', sometimes still written after a man's name on an envelope, e.g 'Peter Lewis, Esq'. This used to be the polite way to address something written to a man, but it is now very old-fashioned. Most people now write 'Mr Peter Lewis' or simply 'Peter Lewis'.

E'squire /ɪ'skwaɪə(r)/ an international magazine for men aged between about 20 and 40. It contains articles on the arts, sport, fashion, business and other topics. It began in the US in 1933 and one of its best-known features was the series of drawings of attractive girls done by Alberto Vargas.

'Essex[1] /'esɪks/ a *county in eastern England. Its administrative centre is Chelmsford.

the ˌEarl of **'Essex[2]** /'esɪks/ (Robert Devereux, second Earl of Essex 1566–1601) an English soldier born to an important family who was for some years a favourite of Queen *Elizabeth I. Some people think that she may have had a romantic interest in him. In 1601 he tried without success to make the people of London turn against Elizabeth. He was condemned to death and had his head cut off.

'Essex girl /'esɪks/ *n* (*BrE humor disapprov*) the name used by some people in jokes, etc. to refer to a type of young English woman who is rather stupid, dresses badly, talks in a loud and unpleasant way, and is too willing to have sex. Such women are supposed to be especially common in *Essex: *The salesmen were all telling Essex girl jokes.*

ˌEssex 'man /ˌesɪks/ *n* [usu sing] (*pl* **Essex men**) (*BrE humor disapprov*) the name used by some people in jokes, etc. to refer to a type of modern Englishman who speaks in a loud and unpleasant way, drinks a lot of beer, knows nothing about art, is only concerned with his own interests, and always votes for the *Conservative Party. Such men are supposed to be especially common in *Essex.

'Esso /'esəʊ; *AmE* 'esoʊ/ the original name of the US oil company *Exxon, and the name still used by the branches of the company outside the US.

EST /ˌiː es 'tiː/ ⇨ EASTERN STANDARD TIME..

the **E'stablishment** *n* [sing] (*esp BrE usu disapprov*) the group of powerful people who influence or control policies, ideas, taste, etc. and usually support what has traditionally been accepted: *She criticized the Establishment for refusing to accept the need for change.*

the **E'stablishment Clause** the article in the *First Amendment to the *American Constitution which created the separation of church and state in the US by forbidding the government to establish a state religion. The US Supreme Court used it in 1962 for a decision that stopped prayers in schools, and this upset many US Christians. However, 'In God We Trust' is still the *National Motto and is on US coins.

ˌEstuary 'English *n* [U] (*sometimes disapprov*) a type of spoken English, especially common among younger people in Britain, that mixes *Received Pronunciation and *cockney. It began in the area around the estuary of the River *Thames (= the wide part of the river where it joins the sea), but has now spread to other parts of the country. Some people have criticized it as a lazy and ugly way of speaking the language.

the **ESU** /ˌiː es 'juː/ ⇨ ENGLISH-SPEAKING UNION.

ET /ˌiː 'tiː/ a film (1992) directed and produced by Steven *Spielberg. ET is an 'extraterrestrial' (= a visitor from space) who has been left on earth by mistake. Three children protect him until he can return to his planet. The film was then the most successful ever made and won several *Oscars.

Eˌternal 'Father, ˌStrong to 'Save the title and first line of a Christian hymn written in 1860 by William Whiting. It is especially associated with sailors, as it asks God to help 'those in peril on the sea'. It is the official hymn of the US Navy.

ˌEthelred the Un'ready (*c.* 969–1016) the king of England from 978 to 1016. His name 'the Unready' comes from an old English word and means that he received bad advice. During his rule the Danes attacked England repeatedly, and after his death the Dane *Canute became king of England.

'Eton /'iːtn/ (*also fml* **ˌEton 'College** /ˌiːtn/) an English *public school(1) for boys near *Windsor[1](1) in *Berkshire, started in 1440 by King *Henry VI. Its students are mainly from rich families, and many of Britain's public figures were educated there. Its former students are known as **Old Etonians**. There is a strong sense of competition between Eton and *Harrow, another boys' public school: *He went to Eton.*

students at Eton

'E-type™ /'iː taɪp/ *n* a make of sports car produced in Britain by *Jaguar between 1961 and 1975. People who drove an E-type were considered to be very modern and successful.

EU /ˌiː 'juː/ ⇨ EUROPEAN UNION.

EURATOM /jʊər'ætəm; *AmE* jʊr'ætəm/ ⇨ EUROPEAN ATOMIC ENERGY COMMISSION.

'euro /'jʊərəʊ; *AmE* 'jʊroʊ/ *n* (*pl* **euro** *or* **euros**) the unit of currency of the *European Union, formerly known as the *ecu. It became Europe's official currency on 1 January 1999 as part of *European Monetary Union. Euros will be issued as coins and paper money from 1 January 2002, and will be used together with the existing national currencies of some European countries for a period of six months. After this, the national currencies will no longer be used. The British government does not wish to be among the first countries to use the euro, and has a policy of waiting to see if the currency is successful before joining it.

'Euro-MP /'jʊərəʊ em piː; *AmE* 'jʊroʊ/ *n* (*infml*) a *Member of the European Parliament.

The ***ˌEuro'pean*** a British newspaper that contains news about the whole of Europe, and is available in many European countries. It appears every week and is written in English. It was first published by Robert *Maxwell in 1990.

the **'European A'tomic 'Energy Comˌmission** (*abbr* **EURATOM**) an organization started in 1957 with the aim of developing the use of nuclear energy in a way that helps countries within the *European Community. The different member countries share their knowledge. The Commission has no control over nuclear materials used for military purposes.

the **ˌEuropean Com'mission** one of the main institutions of the *European Union. It consists of 20 members (*European Commissioners) who make proposals for new laws, deal with the administrative work of the European Union and make sure that agreements are kept. It is based in Brussels.

ˌEuropean Com'missioner *n* any of 20 members of

the *European Commission. They are appointed for five years, and each Commissioner is in charge of a particular department (e.g. Transport or Agriculture).

the ˌ**European Comˈmunity** (*abbr* the **EC**) the former name (1967–1993) of the *European Union.

the ˈ**European ˈCourt of ˈHuman ˈRights** the court of law of the *Council of Europe, started in 1950. It decides whether the agreed Convention for the Protection of Human Rights and Fundamental Freedoms has not been obeyed.

the ˈ**European ˈCourt of ˈJustice** (*also* the **Court of Justice of the European Communities**) the court of law of the *European Community since 1958. Its base is in Luxembourg, with judges from each of the member countries. It interprets European Community law and decides when individual member countries have broken that law.

the ˌ**European ˈCup 1** a football competition held every year between major European teams that have won the equivalent of the *Football League in their own countries. **2** the large silver cup given to the winners of this competition.

the ˌ**European ˈCup-Winners' Cup 1** a football competition held every year between European teams that have won their own national football competitions. **2** the large silver cup given to the winners of this competition.

ˌ**European ˈCurrency ˌUnit** ⇨ ECU.

the ˈ**European Ecoˈnomic Comˈmunity** (*abbr* the **EEC**) a former organization, started in 1957, to encourage trade within Europe. In Britain it was also known as the *Common Market. It became a part of the *European Community (now the *European Union) in 1967.

the ˌ**European ˈMonetary ˌSystem** (*abbr* the **EMS**) a system, started in 1979, that helps the member countries of the *European Union to keep a steady economic balance in Europe. It has been responsible for introducing the *ecu and the *ERM.

ˈ**European ˈMonetary ˈUnion** See also ECONOMIC AND MONETARY UNION.

the ˌ**European ˈParliament** the parliament of the *European Union. Between 1958 and 1979, its members were chosen from the parliaments of the member countries, but they are now directly elected every five years by the people in those countries. Its base is in Strasbourg in northern France, but its committees meet in Brussels and its administrative department is in Luxembourg. See also MEMBER OF THE EUROPEAN PARLIAMENT.

Euroˈpean plan *n* [sing] (*AmE*) a system of charging for a hotel room only, without meals.

the ˌ**European ˈSpace ˌAgency** a European organization of European countries, including Britain, for research into space technology, started in 1975. Its base is in Paris. It has worked with *NASA on many projects.

The **European Union** ⇨ article.

ˌ**Euroˈsceptic** /ˌjʊərəʊˈskeptɪk; *AmE* ˌjʊroʊˈskeptɪk/ *n* a person, especially a politician, who is not enthusiastic about increasing the powers of the European Union: *Eurosceptic Conservative backbenchers.*

ˈ**Eurostar** /ˈjʊərəʊstɑː(r); *AmE* ˈjʊroʊstɑːr/ a train that takes people through the *Channel Tunnel between Britain and France or Belgium: *the daily Eurostar service from Edinburgh.* See also SHUTTLE.

ˈ**Eurotunnel** /ˈjʊərəʊtʌnl; *AmE* ˈjʊroʊtʌnl/ a company formed in 1986 that built the *Channel Tunnel and now operates the *Shuttle train service. It is made up of companies from Britain and France.

the ˌ**Eurovision ˈSong ˌContest** /ˌjʊərəʊvɪʒn; *AmE* ˌjʊroʊvɪʒn/ a competition, taking place every year, in which a singers or groups of singers from many European countries sing songs specially written for the occasion. Groups of judges from each country then choose the winner by a system of points. The British song has won five times.

Euˈrythmics /juˈrɪðmɪks/ a British pop group formed in 1980, whose successful songs include *Sweet Dreams* (1983) and *There Must Be an Angel* (1985). The group's singer, Annie Lennox, began a career as a singer on her own in 1992.

ˈ**Euston** /ˈjuːstən/ (*also* **Euston Station**) a major train station in north London for trains to and from the *Midlands, northern England and Scotland. It also has a station on the *London Underground.

E

ˌ**evanˈgelical** *n* a member of a *Protestant Christian movement who believes that people come to God through their own faith and by reading the Bible, and that Christians should bring others to God. There are many evangelical Churches in the US, where they greatly increased in the 1970s. They include the Evangelical Free Church of America and the Evangelical Covenant Church. ▶ **evangelical** *adj.*

eˈvangelist *n* a Protestant Christian who travels to different places and holds religious meetings to persuade people to become Christians or better Christians. See also TELEVANGELIST.

ˌChris ˈ**Evans**[1] /ˈevnz/ (1966–) an English radio and television presenter who first became well known when he introduced the morning television programme *The Big Breakfast* from 1992, and *Don't Forget Your Toothbrush* on *Channel Four. He is very popular with young people, though his behaviour and remarks sometimes shock people and cause a lot of public argument.

ˌEdith ˈ**Evans**[2] /ˈevnz/ (1888–1976) a English actor who appeared in a wide variety of plays and films and continued acting until she was over 80. Her most famous role was as Lady *Bracknell in Oscar *Wilde's *The *Importance of Being Earnest.* She was made a *dame(2) in 1946.

ˌWalker ˈ**Evans**[3] /ˌwɔːkər ˈevnz/ (1903–75) a US photographer. His best-known photographs were of poor people in the southern states during the *Great Depression. These were published in *American Photographs* (1938) and *Let Us Now Praise Famous Men* (1941).

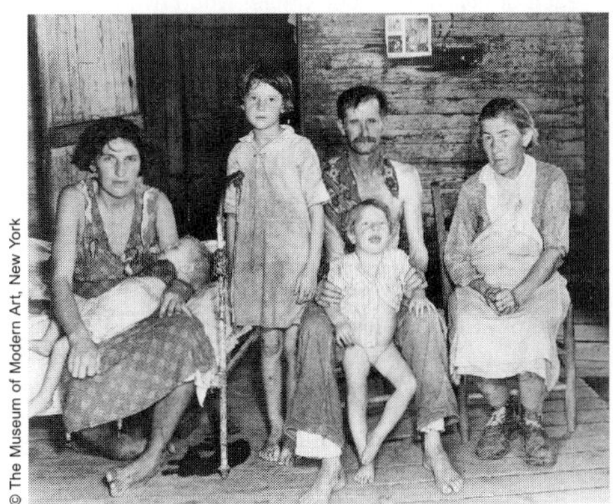

Sharecropper's Family *by Walker Evans, 1936*

ˌJohn ˈ**Evelyn** /ˈiːvlɪn/ (1620–1706) an English writer and traveller, best known for his diary, which was first published in 1818. This tells us a lot about his busy life and many interests. He spent a lot of time at court, was one of the original members of the

The European Union

Britain and the European Union

The *European Economic Community (EEC) was established under the Treaty of Rome in 1957. It was intended that those who signed the treaty would cooperate more closely on economic policies, remove customs duties, and allow people to travel freely from one country to another. In 1967 the EEC joined with two other organizations to become the *European Community (EC).

Britain began negotiations to join the EEC in 1961 but the application was unsuccessful. New negotiations began in 1970 and Britain finally became a member of the EC on 1 January 1973. At that time the EC was often referred to in Britain as **the *Common Market**. In 1974–5 the *Labour government renegotiated the terms of entry and held a **referendum** (= a special vote) to find out whether the people still wanted Britain to be a member. The result was a 2:1 majority in favour. In 1987 the **Single European Act** helped increase cooperation between member states in areas of environmental and foreign policy.

The ***Maastricht Treaty** of 1992 further amended (= changed) the Treaty of Rome. It established the **European Union** (**EU**) and the concept of EU citizenship in addition to national citizenship. At Maastricht, the *Conservative government **opted out of** (= refused to agree to) the ***Social Chapter** on the grounds that responsibility for social policy should remain with individual member states. A **social protocol** allowed other states to agree social legislation that was not applicable in Britain. The Labour Party had always been in favour of the Social Chapter, and after it won the 1997 general election it signed the agreement for Britain.

EU institutions

Britain provides two of the twenty members, called **Commissioners**, of the ***European Commission**. The Commission puts forward policy proposals and carries out decisions of the ***Council of Ministers**. A Council meeting consists of ministers from each of the 15 member states, who have national responsibility for the subject under discussion. When a state holds the **presidency of the Union** its ministers are responsible for chairing Council meetings. The presidency changes every six months. The Commission and the Council meet in Brussels.

Heads of state and foreign ministers form the **European Council**, which meets twice a year.

The ***European Parliament**, which meets in Strasbourg, has 626 elected members, 87 of whom are from Britain. They are called in Britain **Euro-MPs**. Euro-MPs belong to British political parties. They represent **constituencies** (= areas of Britain) which are larger than those used for the British *Parliament. The European Parliament is consulted by the Council of Ministers on major issues.

The ***European Court of Justice** is the authority on EU law. Its rulings must be applied by member states and sanctions (= penalties) can be imposed if they fail to do this. Each member state provides one judge to the Court. It meets in Luxembourg for five days each month, with additional shorter sessions in Brussels.

Economic and Monetary Union

The Maastricht Treaty encouraged progress towards ***Economic and Monetary Union** (**EMU**). Originally, the **European Monetary System** consisted of an **exchange-rate mechanism** (***ERM**), the ***ecu** (**European Currency Unit**) and credit facilities. It was intended that a single European currency would be introduced in 1999. Before that, member states had to satisfy conditions relating to their rates of inflation, interest rates and balance of payments.

At the time, the British government would not commit Britain to joining in a single monetary policy, and there was disagreement throughout the 1990s, both in Parliament and among the British public, about whether Britain should join EMU. In 1997 the Labour government decided that Britain would not join before 2002, and then only if the economic benefits were clear and the public voted for it in a referendum.

On 1 January 1999 the ***euro**, which replaced the ecu, was introduced in the 11 countries which had supported monetary union. In 'Euroland' all business going through banks is now transacted in euros. Euro banknotes and coins will not be introduced until 2002, but euro prices will be shown in shops alongside prices in national currencies before then.

Britain and 'Europe'

Attitudes to the European Union, or to 'Europe' as it is often called, vary a great deal. In Parliament each party has *MPs who are in favour of Britain's membership of the EU (**pro-Europeans**) and want Britain to be 'at the heart of Europe' and involved at all levels of decision-making, and MPs who are suspicious of Europe (**Euro-sceptics**) and afraid that Britain will lose control of her affairs and be part of a federal Europe. Political parties do not like to raise European issues because when they do it exposes disagreements within the party.

There is a similar division of opinion among the general public, much of it based on ignorance of EU affairs. Some people support a close political, economic and social relationship with other member states. Others support the idea of cooperation and closer commercial links but are afraid that Britain's independence will gradually be lost. It is a common attitude that Britain is special and different from the rest of Europe, and that by becoming too involved in the EU it will lose its national identity and individuality. There is suspicion and hostility when European regulations involve changing something particularly British, for example replacing the dark blue British passports with maroon European-style ones. Many people do not want to join EMU because it would mean that Britain no longer had its own currency, the pound. The British do not much like being told what to do by 'Brussels'.

Farmers and fishermen have been particularly affected by EU regulations. Despite the existence of the ***Common Agricultural Policy** (**CAP**), tensions have arisen over trade in agricultural products and the management of fish stocks, sometimes resulting in violence.

Despite the problems and negative feelings, most British people do think that Britain should be part of 'Europe', and would like to see the country playing a leading role in its future development.

*Royal Society, and was active in the building of *St Paul's Cathedral after the *Great Fire of London. He was also a close friend of Samuel *Pepys.

the ˌ**Evening** ˈ**Standard** (*also infml* the **Standard**) London's only evening newspaper, started in 1827. It has stories on both local and national issues. Once a month it has a *colour supplement, called *ES – The Evening Standard Magazine*.

ˌEdna ˈ**Everage** /ˈevərɪdʒ/ a popular female character created and played on stage and television by the male Australian comedian Barry *Humphries. 'Dame' Edna Everage is a middle-aged housewife from Melbourne, Australia, who wears wildly unusual clothes and many different pairs of glasses. She behaves as though she is an international star and is rude to everyone in a loud and funny way.

Dame Edna Everage

ˌ**Eveˈready**™ /ˌevəˈredi/ an international company that makes electrical batteries. The main names of its products are Eveready and Energizer, and its most popular advertising character is a toy rabbit which is driven by a battery and plays a drum.

the ˈ**Everglades** /ˈevəgleɪdz; *AmE* ˈevərgleɪdz/ a large, low, wet region in the southern part of the US state of *Florida. Some *Seminole *Native Americans still live there and it also has alligators and many varieties of birds and snakes. Its area is about 5 000 square miles (12 950 square kilometres). Dry weather has recently damaged parts of the Everglades, and there is concern about the region's future. The **Everglades National Park** was created in 1947 and made a *World Heritage Site in 1979.

the ˈ**Everly** ˌ**Brothers** /ˈevəli; *AmE* ˈevərli/ (*also* the ˈ**Everlys** /ˈevəliz; *AmE* ˈevərliz/) **Don Everly** (1937–) and **Phil Everly** (1939–), two US brothers who sing together and were especially popular in the 1950s and 1960s. They became successful with songs that combined *country music and *rock and roll, such as *Bye Bye Love* (1957) and *Wake Up Little Susie* (1957). The brothers separated in 1973 but are now singing together again.

the ˈ**Evers** ˌ**brothers** /ˈevəz; *AmE* ˈevərz/ two *African-American brothers who led the US *civil rights movement in the state of *Mississippi. **Medgar Evers** (1925–63) was the first Mississippi Field Secretary for the *NAACP and was murdered in 1963. It took 31 years before the person who killed him was sent to prison. **Charles Evers** (1922–) took his brother's NAACP job and then in 1969 became the first African-American *mayor of Fayette, *Mississippi. He published his autobiography, *Have No Fear*, in 1997.

ˌChris ˈ**Evert** /ˈevət; *AmE* ˈevərt/ (1954–) a US tennis player who was the first woman to win $1 million in prize money. She won *Wimbledon three times (1974, 1976 and 1981), the *US Open(2) six times (1975–8, 1980 and 1982), and the French Open seven times (1974–5, 1979–80, 1983 and 1985-6). She was married to the English tennis player John Lloyd for several years and was then known as Chris Evert Lloyd.

ˈ**Everton** /ˈevətən; *AmE* ˈevərtən/ one of the two major football clubs in *Liverpool, England. Its ground is called Goodison Park.

ˌJ R ˈ**Ewing**[1] /ˈjuːɪŋ/ (*also* **JR**) the main character, played by Larry Hagman, in *Dallas*, the US *soap opera. JR was the rich owner of an oil company who had great charm but often behaved badly. He had many love affairs and made many enemies. One of the programmes in the series, called *Who Shot JR?* and first broadcast in November 1980, was the second most popular programme in the history of US television.

exams

Greater emphasis is placed on examination results in Britain than in many other countries. Most universities and employers still rely mainly on exam results for evidence of a person's academic ability.

Children in England and Wales complete **standard assessment tasks (SATs)** at ages 7, 11 and 14 as part of the *National Curriculum. These tests are set nationally and results can be compared across the country. In some areas children take an ***eleven-plus** exam to decide where they will go for their secondary education.

In secondary schools exams are usually held at the end of each school year to assess students' progress. The most important exams are the national ***GCSE** exams that children take at 16. GCSEs replaced the former **O level** and **CSE** examinations in 1988. Schools are free to choose which of several **examination boards** they use to set and mark GCSE exams. Exams are marked on a seven-point scale, A to G, with an additional grade, A*, being awarded to those who reach the highest standard. Final grades are now based on **continuous assessment**, i.e. marks gained for essays and project work during the course, as well as on a student's performance in the exam. Many students take GCSE exams in seven or eight subjects, sometimes more. Those who are less good at academic subjects can take ***GNVQs** as an introduction to *vocational training.

Students who do well in their GCEs often go on to take ***A level** exams two years later. Most take three and must achieve reasonably high grades in order to be offered a place at university. Some students also take **S level** (Special or Scholarship level) exams.

In Scotland students sit ***Scottish Certificate of Education** exams which, at standard grade, are the equivalent of GCSEs. The highest grade is 1. A year later students take the higher grade, **Highers**. After a further year some students take a **Certificate of Sixth Year Studies**.

At university students work towards a **degree**, and most courses end in a series of exams called **finals**. Many take an **honours degree** which is awarded in one of several **classes**. The highest class is a first. The second class is often split between upper second and lower second, and below that is the third class. If a student does not meet the standard for an honours degree he or she may be awarded a **pass degree**.

In the US there are no national exams like those in Britain. Students at school and university usually take one or more exams as part of their **grade assessment** (= a mark from A to E or F showing how well they have done) for each class. At colleges and universities these exams are often called **midterms** or **finals**, and during the year students have exams in all or most of their classes.

People who wish to study at a US university usually have to take one of several **standardized tests**. Students going to university for the first time may take the ***SAT (Scholastic Aptitude Test)** or the ***ACT (American College Test)**. People who want to do a higher degree may take the ***GRE (Graduate Record Examination)**, ***LSAT (Law School Admission Test)** or ***MCAT (Medical College Admission Test)**, depending on what they want to study. Students from other countries must usually show a knowledge of English and the most common test for this purpose is the *__TOEFL (Test of English as a Foreign Language)__. Standardized tests often do not test how much people know about a subject, but how strong their skills are in areas like reading and solving problems. People do not pass or fail but instead each college or university decides on the lowest score it will accept. Test scores are never the only factor to be considered in deciding whether to offer a place to a student.

Some professions require people to pass special exams before they are qualified to practise. Lawyers in the US, for example, must pass the **bar exam** in the state in which they wish to work, to show that they know the laws of that state.

E

Ex'calibur /ek'skælɪbə(r)/ the magic sword of King *Arthur. As a boy, he pulled it from a stone when no one else could move it. At the end of his life he told one of his men to throw it into a lake, where it was caught by the hand of the *Lady of the Lake coming out of the water. According to another version of the story Arthur also received Excalibur from the Lady of the Lake. See also ARTHURIAN LEGEND.

Ex,change and 'Mart /'mɑːt; *AmE* 'mɑːrt/ a British magazine that consists entirely of advertisements, mostly put in by individual people or small businesses. It is published every week and was started in 1868.

the **'exchange-rate ,mechanism** ⇨ ERM.

the **Ex'chequer** (formerly) the British government department in charge of public money. This is now the responsibility of the *Treasury. See also CHANCELLOR OF THE EXCHEQUER.

the **e'xecutive branch** *n* [sing] the division of the US government under the President, who is called the Chief Executive. It carries out the decisions of *Congress, because the *American Constitution says the President must 'take care that the laws be faithfully executed'. The executive branch includes the Vice-president, the President's Cabinet, ambassadors (= senior government representatives in foreign countries), all departments (such as the Department of State and Department of Defense) and many other smaller government organizations. ⇨ article at FEDERAL GOVERNMENT IN THE US.

e,xecutive 'privilege *n* [U] the right of the US President to keep official information from *Congress or special investigations, in order to protect important discussions. President *Nixon used this during *Watergate, but the Supreme Court decided that some items, such as tapes of telephone calls, were not protected. The last president to have total executive privilege was *Eisenhower.

'Exeter /'eksɪtə(r)/ a city in south-west England. It is the administrative centre of the *county of *Devon.

'Exit /'eksɪt/ a British organization whose aim is to change the law to make it legal to help very ill people who want to die to do so. It was started by a group of doctors in 1935. Its formal name is the Voluntary Euthanasia Society.

'Exmoor /'eksmʊə(r); *AmE* 'eksmʊr/ an area of moorland (= high land that is not cultivated) in *Somerset and *Devon in England. It is a *national park 265 square miles (686 square kilometres) in extent. The **Exmoor pony** is a small but strong breed of horse, originally from Exmoor and often trained for children to ride.

ex'pat /eks'pæt/ *n* (*infml sometimes disapprov*) a person living outside his or her own country (a short form of *expatriate*). Many people in Britain think of typical British expats as people who live an easy relaxed life in some warm country, meeting each other often for drinks and other social events, and having little contact with local people.

Explorer I /ɪk,splɔːrə 'wʌn; *AmE* ɪk'splɔːrər/ the first US artificial satellite in space. It was sent up on 31 January 1958 from *Cape Canaveral, *Florida, by the US Army. *Explorer I*, which weighed 30 pounds (13.5 kilograms), discovered the Van Allen radiation belt. Several other *Explorers* were later sent up to study radiation and 'wind' from the sun.

the **'Export 'Credit Guaran'tee De,partment** a British government department that provides insurance for British companies when they sell their goods abroad. The department pays companies for their goods, for example, if their foreign customers do not pay them.

the ***Ex'press*** one of Britain's national daily newspapers, started in 1900 by Arthur Pearson and bought in 1914 by Lord *Beaverbrook. It is a *tabloid, formerly called the *Daily Express*, and its political views are generally right-wing. See also *SUNDAY EXPRESS*. ⇨ article at NEWSPAPERS.

ex'pressway (*also* **'freeway**, **,super'highway**) *n* (*AmE*) a major road for fast travel between towns and cities, with two lanes (= sections for single lines of traffic) in each direction, divided in the middle. Traffic can only enter and leave at certain special places. Other roads cross expressways on bridges or pass under them through tunnels. Compare INTERSTATE, MOTORWAY. ⇨ note at ROADS AND ROAD SIGNS.

'Extel /'ekstel/ (*in full* **Ex,change 'Telegraph ,Company**) a British company that provides financial news (e.g. share prices) and sports news (e.g. horse-racing results) to the press and the public.

'Exxon™ /'eksɒn; *AmE* 'eksɑːn/ the largest oil company in the US. It was originally called Esso, and its divisions in other countries, including Britain, still use the name Esso.

,Exxon Val'dez /,eksɒn væl'diːz; *AmE* ,eksɑːn/ the ship owned by the *Exxon company that caused the worst oil disaster in US history. It was badly damaged when it hit rocks off the coast of *Alaska in March 1989 and lost more than 10 million gallons (40 million litres) of oil into the sea. This killed many birds and animals and ruined the shores. Exxon spent a lot of money to clean up the oil, and also agreed to pay $1 billion to the US and Alaska by the year 2000, but cases against the company are still being brought to court for the damage caused.

,Richard **'Eyre** /'eə(r); *AmE* 'er/ (1943–) an English theatre, film and television director. His work includes the film *The Ploughman's Lunch* (1983) and successful stage productions of **Guys and Dolls* (1982) and **Richard III* (1990). He was artistic director of the *National Theatre from 1988 to 1997, and was made a *knight in 1997.

Ff

FA /ˌef ˈeɪ/ ⇨ FOOTBALL ASSOCIATION.

the **FAA** /ˌef eɪ ˈeɪ/ (*in full* the **Federal Aviation Administration**) the US government organization that controls air transport. This includes air traffic, aircraft safety and noise, and standards for pilots and airports. The FAA is part of the US Department of Transportation. It was established in 1958 and by 1985 had replaced the Civil Aeronautics Board.

the **ˈFabian Soˌciety** /ˈfeɪbiən/ a British political organization that was formed in 1884 with the aim of gradually changing Britain into a socialist society. Many famous left-wing politicians and writers have been members, including George Bernard *Shaw. The Fabian Society was one of the groups responsible for creating the *Labour Party. It still has many important members, but its influence on the Labour Party is not as strong as it used to be.

ˌFace to ˈFace a British television series broadcast by the *BBC from 1958 to 1960. In each programme, a famous person was asked questions about their thoughts, opinions and personal lives. The series was well known for its wide range of guests, including Carl Jung and Bertrand *Russell, and for the very direct and often difficult questions which they had to answer. A new series was broadcast in the 1990s but it was not as popular as the original one.

the **ˈFactory Acts** *n* [pl] a series of British laws concerning safety and working conditions in factories. During the *Industrial Revolution British factories were dangerous places to work in, and most of them made young children work for long hours. People working for social change fought hard campaigns to force the government to make these laws. The most important Factory Acts were those passed in the first half of the 19th century. They limited the number of hours that children could work, and made it illegal to employ very young children.

the **ˌFA ˈCup** /ˌef eɪ/ (*in full* the **Football Association Challenge Cup**) an English football competition that takes place every year. Teams from the *Premier League and the *Football League take part, as well as teams which are not professional and not part of the league. The winner of each match goes into the next round and the team that loses no longer takes part. It is England's oldest football competition, and one of the most important. It is often very exciting when teams from small towns play against famous teams from the Premier League. The winner of the FA Cup each year enters one of the major European competitions in the following season. See also CUP FINAL. ⇨ note at FOOTBALL – BRITISH STYLE.

The ***ˌFaerie ˈQueene*** /ˌfeəri ˈkwiːn; *AmE* ˌferi/ a long poem (1590–6) by Edmund *Spenser. It was written in praise of Queen *Elizabeth I and its imaginary characters and events represent moral values. It is Spenser's best-known poem. The style of writing had a strong influence on the development of English poetry, and the pattern of rhymes in each verse was used by many later poets.

ˈFagin /ˈfeɪɡɪn/ a character in Charles *Dickens's novel, **Oliver Twist*. He is an ugly, evil old man who receives stolen goods and controls the group of young thieves that Oliver joins.

ˌDouglas **ˈFairbanks[1]** /ˈfeəbæŋks; *AmE* ˈferbæŋks/ (1883–1939) one of the most popular stars of US silent adventure films and one of the people who established *United Artists. He was married to the actor Mary *Pickford. His films included *The Mark of Zorro* (1920) and *Robin Hood* (1922). He made a few films with sound that were not great successes. After he died, Fairbanks was awarded an *Oscar for his life's work in films. His son Douglas, usually called Douglas Fairbanks Junior, was also a film actor.

ˌDouglas **ˈFairbanks[2]** /ˈfeəbæŋks; *AmE* ˈferbæŋks/ (1909–) a US actor who is the son of Douglas *Fairbanks[1]. His films include *The Prisoner of Zenda* (1937), *Gunga Din* (1939) and *Ghost Story* (1981). He was in the US Navy during the *World War II and won many medals. He settled in London in the early 1950s and produced films and television shows. Fairbanks was married to the actor Joan *Crawford.

the **ˌFair ˈDeal** the name used by US President Harry S *Truman in 1949 for his domestic (= national) programme. *Congress passed much of it, which continued the *New Deal programme of President Franklin D *Roosevelt. The Fair Deal brought improvements in employment, education, *civil rights, health services and many other areas.

ˌThomas **ˈFairfax** /ˈfeəfæks; *AmE* ˈferfæks/ (1612–71) an English soldier, the most important general on the side of *Parliament in the *English Civil War. He was responsible for forming the *New Model Army and was its first leader. He was made a *knight in 1640 and a *baron in 1648.

ˈFair Isle *n* [U] a style of knitting clothes using different colours and designs which are repeated in rows. It was originally developed on Fair Isle, one of the *Shetland Islands: *a Fair Isle sweater*.

a Fair Isle sweater

ˌFairport Conˈvention /ˌfeəpɔːt; *AmE* ˌferpɔːrt/ a British *folk rock group formed in 1967. Their best-known albums include *Full House* (1970) and *Angel Delight* (1971).

fairs

Some British fairs, such as St Giles Fair in *Oxford and the Goose Fair in *Nottingham, date back hundreds of years. They are travelling fairs that occupy part of a town centre for a few days each year. The people who run the fairs usually live in caravans.

a funfair

Originally, animals were sold at these fairs and people could change employers there. The Appleby Horse Fair in *Cumbria still has animals, but most fairs now consist only of **mechanical rides** and **amusements**. They are especially popular with children and young people.

British fairs typically include rides such as **merry-go-rounds** or **carousels**, **shooting galleries**, where people can win small prizes by shooting at targets, and stalls selling traditional food such as **candy floss** (= pink spun sugar on a stick), **toffee apples** (= apples coated in a boiled sugar mixture) and **hot dogs** (= sausages in bread rolls). Many fairs have a **Ferris wheel**, also called a **big wheel**, **dodgems** (= small cars in which people crash into each other), a **helter-skelter** (= a tall, circular slide), and a **roller coaster** or **big dipper** (= a steep track on which people ride in special cars). There is often a 'dark ride' or **ghost train** (= a ride in the dark past things that jump out or make a frightening noise). Sometimes there is also a **fortune-teller**. Most British people enjoy such **funfairs** and holiday towns like Blackpool have a permanent **fairground**. In recent years a number of **theme parks**, such as *Alton Towers, have been developed, in which all the rides are based on a single theme or idea.

Some fairs in the US also have long histories. **State** and **county fairs** held at the end of summer were important in the days when transport was limited and most Americans were farmers living far from the nearest town. They provided an opportunity to see friends, buy supplies and look at the latest farm equipment. People entered their best animals in competitions and afterwards sold them. Today there are also competitions for crops, e.g. the sweetest corn, and for home crafts like baking and sewing. The winner of the first prize gets a **blue ribbon**. In Britain, competitions like these take place at **village horticultural shows** and **agricultural shows**, such as the *Royal Show. Many Americans who are not farmers go to fairs for other kinds of entertainment. There is a **midway**, a large area with different kinds of rides and games, and an area where ice cream, pies and candy (*BrE* sweets) are sold. The US also has permanent **amusement parks** or theme parks, which have rides like those at fairs. Many beaches have a **boardwalk**, a raised path above the beach where people can play game machines.

In Britain and the US other events are sometimes called *fairs*. At **craft fairs** (*AmE* **crafts fairs** or **arts fairs**) people sell things they have made, e.g. pottery, jewellery, candles and leather goods. But **trade fairs** are large events where business companies show their products and make new contacts.

ˌFairy ˈLiquid™ *n* [U] a British make of liquid soap used for washing dishes, etc. It is often advertised as being 'kind to your hands'.

ˌNick **ˈFaldo** /ˈfældəʊ; *AmE* ˈfældoʊ/ (1957) an English golfer. In the early 1990s he was one of the most successful golfers in the world, winning many major competitions including the *British Open three times (1987, 1990 and 1992) and the *US Masters Tournament twice (1989 and 1990).

the **ˈFalkland ˌIslands** /ˈfɔːlklənd/ (*also* **the ˈFalklands** /ˈfɔːlkləndz/) a group of small islands in the south Atlantic Ocean. A few British people live there, mainly as sheep farmers. The islands belong to Britain, but they are claimed by Argentina, where they are called the Malvinas. In 1982 Britain and Argentina fought the *Falklands War there.

the **ˌFalklands ˈWar** /ˌfɔːlkləndz/ a war between Britain and Argentina that took place in the *Falkland Islands in 1982. The two countries had disagreed about who the islands belonged to since the early 19th century, and when Argentinian armed forces moved there in 1982, Britain declared war. Less than two months later, British forces captured the islands again. These events made many British people feel very proud, and they probably helped the Prime Minister, Margaret *Thatcher, to win the election the next year. Many people, however, thought it was a cruel and unnecessary war. Nearly 1 000 soldiers were killed.

the **ˌFalls ˈRoad** /ˌfɔːlz/ a street in *Belfast, Northern Ireland. It is in a *Roman Catholic area of the town and is known for the many violent conflicts that have taken place there between Catholics and *Protestants during the *Troubles.

ˈfalsely ˈshouting ˈfire in a ˈcrowded ˈtheatre the example used in 1919 by the US Supreme Court judge Oliver Wendell *Holmes to show that in certain circumstances free speech should be limited. Although he greatly supported free speech, Holmes said that 'the most stringent protection of free speech would not protect a man in falsely shouting fire in a theatre and causing a panic'.

Sir ˌJohn **ˈFalstaff** /ˈfɔːlstɑːf; *AmE* ˈfɔːlstæf/ a character who appears in three of *Shakespeare's plays, **Henry IV Parts 1 and 2*, and *The *Merry Wives of Windsor*. He is fat, greedy, dishonest, often drunk, but always humorous and entertaining. He is one of Shakespeare's most popular characters, best known

Falstaff played by Donald Maxwell in Verdi's opera Falstaff

as the friend of young Prince Hal in *Henry IV Part 1*. He is also a main character in Verdi's opera *Falstaff*.

ˌJerry ˈ**Falwell** /ˈfɔːlwel/ (1933–) the US *evangelist who in 1979 established the Moral Majority to help elect conservative politicians (= those that are opposed to much political and social change). His group worked to elect Ronald *Reagan as President. He also has a church and national television programme in Lynchburg, *Virginia, and started the Liberty Baptist College there in 1971.

Families and family life ⇨ article.

ˌ**family ˈcredit** *n* [U] (in Britain) payments made by the government to working people on low incomes with children. The amount paid depends on how many children there are, and how much money a family has. People may receive other payments such as *child benefit and still get some family credit. Compare INCOME SUPPORT.

the ˈ**Family DiˌVision** one of the three parts of the English *High Court of Justice. The Family Division deals with cases such as divorces and disagreements about who keeps the children when parents separate. Compare CHANCERY DIVISION, QUEEN'S BENCH. ⇨ article at LEGAL SYSTEM IN BRITAIN.

the ˌ**Family ˈLaw Act** a British *Act of Parliament (1996) dealing with subjects such as divorce and domestic violence (= violence between a husband and wife). Some people criticized the Act for making it too easy to get divorced.

the ˌ**Family ˈPlanning AssociˌAtion** a British organization that gives people free advice about contraception (= ways of preventing a woman from becoming pregnant), and often gives people free contraceptives.

the ˌ**Famous ˈFive** the main characters in a series of children's books by Enid *Blyton. They are four children and a dog who have exciting adventures, often preventing criminals from doing evil things. Although written between 1942 and 1963, the books are still popular with British children.

ˌ**Faneuil ˈHall** /ˌfænəl/ a building in *Boston, *Massachusetts, which is called the 'Cradle of Liberty'. It was built in 1742 and again in 1763 after a fire. It was a place for markets with a large room for meetings above, where people met to plan the *American Revolution. It is still used for markets and meetings.

ˌ***Fanny ˈHill*** /ˌfæni / a novel (1749) by John Cleland (1707–89) about the sexual adventures of a young woman in 18th-century London. Its original title was *Memoirs of a Woman of Pleasure*. The book was banned in Britain when a company tried to publish it in 1963, and became very popular when it was finally published in 1970.

Fanˈtasia /fænˈteɪziə/ a film made by Walt *Disney in 1940. It uses cartoon characters, including *Mickey Mouse, to illustrate classical music. Although many people felt that this was not an appropriate way to present serious music, the film has remained popular with the public ever since and is still shown in cinemas today.

FAO /ˌef eɪ ˈəʊ; *AmE* ˈoʊ/ ⇨ FOOD AND AGRICULTURE ORGANIZATION.

ˌ**F A O ˈSchwarz** /ˌef eɪ əʊ ˈʃwɔːts; *AmE* oʊ, ˈʃwɔːrts/ a famous toy shop/store in Manhattan, New York City. It is one of the largest in the world.

ˌMichael ˈ**Faraday** /ˈfærədeɪ/ (1791–1867) an English scientist. His family was very poor and he had to teach himself about science, before becoming the assistant of Humphrey *Davy. His early work was in chemistry, but his most famous work was in physics. He discovered electromagnetic induction, the condition under which a magnet can produce electricity. This led to the development of the electric dynamo and motor. His discoveries in the field of electrolysis are still known as **Faraday's Laws**.

the ˌ**Farewell Adˈdress** the speech made by President George *Washington to the US people when he retired. It was not spoken publicly by Washington but published in the *American Daily Advertiser*, a *Philadelphia newspaper, on 19 September 1796. Alexander *Hamilton helped Washington to write the speech, in which he told the nation to have 'as little political connection as possible' with other countries, and also warned about the dangers of political parties because they divide the people.

ˈ***Far from the ˈMadding ˈCrowd*** /ˈmædɪŋ/ a novel (1874) by Thomas *Hardy. It is a love story about a farm worker, Gabriel Oak, and the woman who owns the farm where he works. He wants to marry her but she has relationships with several other men who seem more exciting to her. In the end she agrees to marry Gabriel.

ˌ**Farley's ˈRusks**™ /ˌfɑːliz/ *n* [pl] a British make of hard, dry biscuits for babies. They are often dissolved in milk before eating.

ˌFannie ˈ**Farmer** /ˌfæni ˈfɑːmə(r); *AmE* ˈfɑːrmər/ (1857–1915) a US writer of books on cooking which have been popular for more than a century. Her *Boston Cooking School Cook Book* (1896) was the first one to use standard measurements and instructions. It developed into *Fanny Farmer's Cookbook* which is still sold today. Compare BEETON.

ˌ**Farmer ˈGeorge** a popular name for King *George III in the drawings of the political cartoonist James *Gillray. His pictures showing the king as a rude, uneducated farmer were very popular at the time, and many people referred to the king as Farmer George. George is now often thought of as a typical name for any farmer.

the ˌ**Farnborough ˈAir Show** /ˌfɑːnbrə; *AmE* ˌfɑːrnbrə/ an international exhibition of aircraft that takes place every two years in Farnborough, southern England. Companies show new aircraft to their customers at the show, which is open to the public, and there are flying displays by groups such as the *Red Arrows.

the ˈ**Farne ˌIslands** /ˈfɑːn; *AmE* ˈfɑːrn/ a group of small islands off the coast of north-east England. Nobody lives there, and the many birds and seals (= large sea animals) that go there are protected by law. The islands are perhaps best known because Grace *Darling lived in a lighthouse (= a tower containing a strong light to warn or guide ships) on one of them.

ˌLouis ˈ**Farrakhan** /ˌluːɪs ˈfærəkæn/ (1934–) the *African-American leader since 1977 of the Nation of Islam, the *Black Muslim organization. In 1995 he led about 500 000 African-American men on the 'Million Man March' to Washington, DC, to encourage support for their families and communities. Farrakhan has been criticized as a person who hates white people and Jews.

ˌJames T ˈ**Farrell** /ˈfærəl/ (James Thomas Farrell 1904–79) a US writer of novels, short stories and poems. His realistic novels were about the Irish in the poor section of *Chicago. He wrote three novels between 1932 and 1935 about the character Studs *Lonigan and five between 1936 and 1953 about Danny O'Neill.

ˌMia ˈ**Farrow** /ˌmiːə ˈfærəʊ; *AmE* ˈfæroʊ/ (1945–) a US film actor, formerly married to Frank *Sinatra and then André *Previn. She has 17 children, 12 of them adopted. Her films include *Rosemary's Baby* (1968) and *Hannah and Her Sisters* (1986), one of sev-

Families and family life

A family may include parents and their *children, grandparents, aunts, uncles and cousins, as well as more distant **relatives**. But when British and American people use the word *family* they often mean only a mother, father and their children. In a general social context 'the family' is usually taken to mean this **nuclear family**.

The family unit

*Society in Britain and the US is traditionally based on a nuclear family living in the same house and closely involved in each other's lives. Fifty years ago, the typical family was a husband and wife, and two or three children. The father spent all day at work and made most of the decisions about how the money he earned was spent. The mother stayed at home to manage the house and look after the children. Children were expected to obey their parents.

Many modern families live rather differently, and because of this some people think that the family unit is dying and society is being weakened. Many couples still **get married**, but others **live together** without getting married. A few years ago, couples living together usually got married when they wanted to **start a family** (= have children), but this happens less now. Another trend is for people to get married later in life and to have fewer children, so the size of the average family is shrinking.

Many families are disturbed each year as a result of **divorce**. In the US about half of all married couples **get divorced**. In Britain the divorce rate has more than doubled since the early 1980s. Many children are brought up in **single-parent families** (= families in which children are looked after by their mother or father, not both) and only see the other parent occasionally. Other children have two homes and divide their time between them. If their parents **remarry** (= each marry other people) the children may have to fit into a **step-family** (= a family in which the parents have been married before and have children from their previous marriages). They may later have **half-brothers** or **half-sisters** from the new marriage. Families in which some children are **adopted** (= legally and permanently made part of another family) or **fostered** (= looked after by another family for a period of time) because their own parents cannot take care of them are not uncommon.

An increasing number of organizations are recognizing that there are different family structures. For instance, family tickets to amusement parks, etc. used to be based on two adults and their children, but now there are special deals for families with only one adult and children.

Many mothers now have jobs, and young children spend part of the day being cared for by a child-minder or at a daycare centre. Some politicians and religious leaders, and many ordinary people, still believe that the traditional family in which the mother stays at home is best and criticize mothers who work. But most people accept that this is often not possible, and that other types of families can be loving and caring. In recent years fathers have become more involved in childcare, though the mother is still mainly responsible.

The extended family

Americans often move from city to city, so it is common for members of the **extended family** (= grandparents, aunts, uncles, etc.) to live far away. Some grandparents see very little of their grandchildren. Families try to stay in contact with each other by writing and telephoning, by visiting occasionally, and sometimes by holding big **family reunions**. In Britain members of the same family may live close to each other and see each other regularly, but many do not.

Family loyalty is still important, and many people feel they have a duty to care for members of their family when they need it. But it is not part of British or American culture for old people to live with younger members of their family. Most elderly people live in their own homes and, when they cannot care for themselves, move into an **old people's home** or a **nursing home**.

*Indian, *Pakistani and *Bangladeshi families in Britain often have closer contact with their relatives and may live with them in the same house. In some of these families women play a more traditional role of mother and homemaker, though many have jobs.

Family life

Some families are very **child-centred** (= put the children's interests first). The closest families eat *meals at the same time and spend their free time together. Some families, however, only see each other for a short time in the evening, and though the children are still considered important, they have to fit in with the lives of their parents.

The average day for many families begins with getting the children up and ready for *school. There is usually a rush for everyone to use the bathroom, find clean clothes, eat breakfast, and catch the bus. In the meantime the parents have to get ready for work themselves. Early mornings are a scramble for many families.

The school day usually ends at about 3 p.m. in the US and 4 p.m. in Britain, and the working day at 5 p.m. or later, so many parents have to make arrangements for younger children to be cared for after school. They may go to an **after-school club** (*AmE* **after-school centre**) or stay with a neighbour's children. Older children often do activities like sports or music at their school, or go home and do their homework. Children often also have to do **chores** (= small jobs around the house).

In many families, the children eat when they get home and their parents eat later. In the evenings the children play or go and see friends. If everyone is staying in they may watch television together. Many parents make an effort to spend **quality time** with their children, an hour or so each day when they give them their full attention.

At the weekend families may go to sports games together, go shopping or go on trips to museums, parks, etc. In school holidays/vacations they may visit other family members or go to the beach.

American families are often criticized for they way they do things separately, though many people believe that it is good for children to learn to be independent. From an early age children are encouraged to decide what they want to do, eat or wear, and their parents try to respect their opinions.

eral she made with Woody *Allen, with whom she had a love relationship.

The ˈ***Far Side*** the general name for one or more of the cartoons drawn by the US artist Gary Larson (1950–). He is known for his unusual humour, which includes cows, dogs and other animals talking and acting like humans. Larson stopped drawing the cartoons in 1995, but the old ones still appear in newspapers and books and on cards, calendars, etc.

the ˌ**Far ˈWest** the most western states of the US. This usually means those on the Pacific Ocean (*California, *Oregon and *Washington), but some Americans say the Far West begins with the *Rocky Mountain States.

Fashion ⇨ article.

ˌ**fast ˈfood** *n* [U] food such as hamburgers, fried chicken, etc, that can be cooked easily and quickly, and is sold by restaurants to be eaten quickly or taken away: *fast-food chains like McDonald's and Burger King.*

the ˈ**Fastnet Race** /ˈfɑːstnet; *AmE* ˈfæstnet/ a race for sailing boats that takes place every two years. The boats start at *Cowes on the *Isle of Wight and sail to the Fastnet Rock, off south-west Ireland, and back to *Plymouth in south-west England. It is one of the most famous races in the sailing world, and the final event of the *Admiral's Cup.

ˌ**Father ˈBrown** the main character in a series of stories by G K *Chesterton. He is a *Roman Catholic priest who solves *detective mysteries.

ˌ**Father ˈChristmas** ⇨ note at SANTA CLAUS.

ˌ**father of the ˈchapel** *n* the title of the person in charge of a branch of any of several British *trade unions. Some unions, particularly in newspapers or publishing companies, call their branches 'chapels'.

ˌ**Father of the Constiˈtution** the popular US name for James *Madison, a leading member of the group who planned and wrote the *American Constitution. He also later suggested the *amendments to the Constitution which formed the *Bill of Rights.

the ˌ**Father of the ˈHouse** the title given to the *Member of Parliament who has been a member of the *House of Commons for the longest time without interruption, and to the peer who has been a member of the *House of Lords for the longest time.

ˈ**Father's Day** the third Sunday in June, when it is traditional for people to give cards and sometimes presents to their fathers. In Britain it is not regarded as important as *Mother's Day(1), and many British people ignore the tradition, which began in America in the 20th century.

ˌWilliam ˈ**Faulkner** /ˈfɔːknə(r)/ (1897–1962) one of the most important US writers of novels and short stories in the 20th century. He won the *Nobel Prize for literature in 1949. He wrote about people in the imaginary Yoknapatawpha County in the state of *Mississippi. Most of his stories are about families that were once rich and powerful but have lost their wealth. The writing is excellent but complicated, and many people find it difficult to read. The novels include *The Sound and the Fury* (1929), *Sanctuary* (1931), *A Fable* (1954) and *The Reivers* (1962). The last two won the *Pulitzer Prize.

ˌ**favourite ˈson** (*AmE* **favorite son**) *n* (in US politics) a person supported by his state to be a political party's candidate for President. This happens every four years at the large national conventions (= meetings) of the *Democratic Party and the *Republican Party. A favourite son is usually not an important candidate. His state supports him only for a short time, either to honour him or because they have not yet decided which major candidate to support.

ˌGuy ˈ**Fawkes** /ˈfɔːks/ (1570–1606) one of the people involved in the *Gunpowder Plot to blow up the British *Houses of Parliament(2). He is the most famous of the conspirators (= people involved in the plan) because he was caught with the gunpowder (= explosive powder), tortured until he gave the names of the others, and later killed. There is a tradition in Britain of burning 'guys' representing him every year on *Guy Fawkes Night.

ˌ***Fawlty ˈTowers*** /ˌfɔːlti/ a British comedy television series made in the 1970s and still regularly repeated. The programmes are set in a hotel called Fawlty Towers, where things are always going wrong. The owner, Basil Fawlty, played by John *Cleese, always makes the situation worse in his wild and amusing attempts to hide the problem: *The food was awful and the service was straight out of Fawlty Towers.*

F

the **FBI** /ˌef biː ˈaɪ/ (*in full* the **Federal Bureau of Investigation**) a US government police organization that investigates national crimes. It is also responsible for the safety of the country from international enemies. It publishes a '10 Most Wanted List' of the most dangerous criminals. The FBI, which is part of the US Department of Justice, was created in 1908 as the Bureau of Investigation, and took its present name in 1935. J Edgar *Hoover directed it from 1924 to 1972 and was criticized during his last years for illegally gathering information on ordinary citizens.

the **FCC** /ˌef siː ˈsiː/ (*in full* the **Federal Communications Commission**) an independent US government organization, created in 1934, which makes decisions about communications. This includes the use of television, radio, wires and satellites. The FCC gives stations their licences and the wave ranges on which they can broadcast. It also puts pressure on stations to avoid offensive programmes.

the **FDA** /ˌef diː ˈeɪ/ (*in full* the **Food and Drug Administration**) a US government organization, begun in 1928, that establishes standards for food and drugs and tests their safety. It also stops the false advertising of such products. It is part of the Department of Health and Human Services.

FDIC /ˌef diː aɪ ˈsiː/ ⇨ FEDERAL DEPOSIT INSURANCE CORPORATION.

FDR /ˌef diː ˈɑː(r)/ ⇨ ROOSEVELT².

the **Fed** /fed/ ⇨ FEDERAL RESERVE SYSTEM.

the ˌ**Federal Aviˈation Adminiˌstration** ⇨ FAA.

the ˈ**Federal ˈBureau of Investiˈgation** ⇨ FBI.

the ˌ**Federal Communiˈcations Comˈmission** ⇨ FCC.

the ˈ**Federal Deˈposit Inˈsurance Corpoˌration** (*abbr* the **FDIC**) an independent US government organization that provides insurance for bank accounts. It was created in 1933, and all *Federal Reserve Banks are covered by its insurance. If a bank fails, the FDIC can give each customer up to $100 000. Since 1989 it has also controlled the Savings Association Insurance Fund after *savings and loan associations failed in the 1980s.

ˌ**Federal Exˈpress** a US mail company that delivers parcels all around the world. It began in 1973 and now calls itself the 'world's largest express transportation company'. In 1996 it transported 2 million items each day. The main office is in *Memphis, *Tennessee.

Federal government in the US ⇨ article.

the ˌ**Federal ˈHousing Adminiˌstration** (*abbr* the **FHA**) the US government organization that provides houses for poor families and minority groups. It also

F

Fashion

Haute couture

Fashion begins in the international world of **haute couture** (= high fashion), led by top **fashion designers** and **fashion houses**. There is great public interest in **fashion shows**, when the latest styles are worn **on the catwalk** by highly-paid **supermodels**, even though few ordinary people expect to wear such clothes. Fashion magazines such as **Vogue* and television programmes such as *The Clothes Show* show the latest styles.

Only a few people can afford to buy **designer label** clothing (= clothes by famous designers) even though here are now more young designers and less expensive labels. The most popular designers include Giorgio Armani, Hugo Boss, Donna Karan, Calvin *Klein, Karl Lagerfeld, Ralph *Lauren and Yves Saint-Laurent. Famous British designers include John *Galliano and Vivienne *Westwood.

High-street fashion

Design ideas from fashion shows are quickly copied at more affordable prices. New ranges of clothing reach British shops in time for each new season. As well as department stores and fashion stores such as Dorothy Perkins, Etam and Oasis, people buy clothes in markets and from mail-order catalogues. Many people, men as well as women, spend a lot of time shopping for clothes.

High-street fashion is aimed mainly at young women because they are most **fashion-conscious** (= wanting to wear the latest fashions). New colours, designs and fabrics create the latest **look** or style. Recently, shiny fabrics and clingy, Lycra-based materials in black, grey and dark red have been used for strappy party dresses and close-fitting tops. Black is a fashion colour, and many young women wear black most of the time. Long plain black dresses are especially popular.

Hemlines (= the length of skirts) vary from year to year. Skirts below the knee were fashionable in the 1990s, though miniskirts, popular in the 1960s, also reappeared. Smart shoes have high heels and wedges, but many people wear more practical shoes such as trainers or *Doc Marten's if they have to walk far. The season's colours, fabrics and hemline are used in clothes for women over about 25 in shops like *Laura Ashley and Hobbs.

Grunge, a style of the early 1990s, was based on loose-fitting layers of clothes, often torn or with holes in, and heavy shoes. Second-hand shops were a popular source of clothes. The **ethnic** look, characterized by long flowing dresses and trousers in Indian patterns, has also been fashionable. But in the 1990s individualism was strong and no single look dominated the fashion scene.

Women of all ages wear tight stretchy leggings with a T-shirt. *Jeans remain popular with both men and women. Changes in men's fashion are most noticeable in ties, the style and colour of shirts, and the design of jackets and trousers. Children's clothes are often small versions of adult fashions. Most people dress up to go to a party, and some wear smart clothes for work, but many wear casual clothes most of the time (⇨ note at FORMAL AND INFORMAL DRESS).

US fashions

Americans are not adventurous in the way they dress and prefer practical, comfortable clothes. Simple styles that do not quickly **go out of fashion** are most popular. The **western** or **cowboy** look is no longer fashionable but, because it was very practical, parts of it are still common, especially jeans, heavy cotton or denim shirts, wide leather belts, and boots. In the early 1980s the **preppy** style became popular. Preppy clothes such as chinos (= cotton trousers) and Oxford cloth shirts with button-down collars are still easy to buy.

Clothes may be brightly coloured, but people must follow rules about what colours **match**. Blue and red match, and red matches orange, but an orange shirt should not be worn with a blue sweater. Although it looks strange, people wearing suits or dresses go to work in running shoes because they are more comfortable, and change into smarter shoes at the office.

The **outlet** store is a popular place to buy clothes. Outlets sell clothing that was in stores the previous season but was not sold. Many Americans prefer to buy clothing at a low price, and do not care whether it is fashionable.

For many younger Americans, the world of sport sets fashions. Some try to wear the same kind of basketball shoes that their favourite players wear. They may also buy T-shirts, pants and jackets with the names of sports teams on them. This type of clothing can be expensive.

The total look

Fashion is not just about clothes. A person's **figure** is important, as well as their hairstyle, make-up and **accessories**. Fashion models are usually thin, and it is often difficult for overweight people to buy fashionable clothes, so many people try to diet to improve their figure.

In the 1990s men and women had short hair, compared with the long styles of the 1960s and 1970s. Some people dye their hair, or have a pink or green streak; others have coloured cords plaited in. Styles may be influenced by television characters, e.g. the 'Rachel cut' from **Friends*.

Make-up colours change to match the season's clothes. **Tattoos**, designs pricked on the skin and then coloured, are still common among men. Some people have less permanent designs painted on their skin with henna. Jewellery is now less chunky and obvious. Some men wear a single earring. Younger people may wear several earrings in one ear, or try **body piercing** and wear rings in the nose or navel.

No fashion look is complete without the right accessories. Top designers are now expanding their ranges to include cosmetics, glasses and sunglasses, as well as scarves and bags.

Fashion vocabulary

Britain	US	Britain	US
waistcoat	vest	pinafore dress	jumper
vest	undershirt	jumper	sweater
trousers	pants	dinner jacket	tuxedo
pants	underwear	dressing gown	bathrobe
tights	pantyhose	trainers	running shoes

Federal government in the US

A system of checks and balances

When the *__Founding Fathers__ were deciding what form the federal (= national) government should take, they wanted everyone to have an opportunity to express their opinion, but also to prevent any person or group from having too much influence. The result was the system of government defined in the *__Constitution__, which is based on the **separation of powers** among three branches: the **executive**, the **legislative** and the **judicial**. This system provides a series of *__checks and balances__ because each branch is able to limit the power of the others. Before major changes can be made there must be agreement between all the branches.

The executive branch

The executive branch consists of the *__President__, the **Vice-president** and government *departments and agencies. The President works in the *__White House__, at 1600 Pennsylvania Avenue, Washington, DC. The President has a powerful role: he or she can approve or stop laws proposed by *Congress and can also suggest laws to Congress. In addition, the President appoints senior officials, such as heads of government departments and federal judges, though the appointments must be approved by the *Senate. The President is also Commander-in-Chief of the military forces.

If the President dies or is unable to continue in office, the job passes to the Vice-president. The Vice-president otherwise has little power.

There are 14 departments of government. The heads of these departments make up the *__Cabinet__, a group which meets regularly to discuss current affairs and to advise the President. Each department has its own area of activity. The *Department of Defense, for example, runs the military services. The *Department of Health and Human Services is perhaps the most important department to ordinary Americans. It runs several programmes including *Social Security, *Medicare and *Medicaid. The *State Department advises the President on foreign affairs and runs embassies abroad.

In addition to the 14 cabinet-level departments, various agencies and independent bodies belong to the executive branch of government. These range from the US Postal Service to the *CIA.

The legislative branch

The legislative branch of government is the *__Congress__. This has two **houses**, the **Senate** and the *__House of Representatives__, sometimes called the upper and lower houses. Both meet in the *Capitol Building in Washington, DC. Each has a large room with a circular arrangement of seats, one seat being reserved for each member.

The main job of Congress is to make laws, but its other responsibilities include establishing federal courts, setting taxes and, if necessary, declaring war. Although the Senate and the House of Representatives have similar powers, some jobs belong only to the Senate. These include approving treaties with other countries and confirming appointments made by the President. The process of **impeaching** (= removing from office) a federal official, including the President, because he or she has committed a serious crime can only begin in the House of Representatives, which has the power to decide whether the official should be charged. The Senate has the power to try the official and to decide whether he or she should be impeached.

Daily events in Congress are reported in the **Congressional Record**. The most important responsibility for members of Congress is to represent their **constituents**. When deciding whether to vote for or against a new law, they are expected to put the interests of their state before those of their party. Members of Congress are also expected to help their constituents directly. If, for example, somebody needs a passport urgently they may contact the office of one of their representatives in Congress. A worker in that office, known as a **constituent aid**, will then help them obtain it.

The President and members of Congress are chosen in separate elections. This may mean that the President's party does not have power in Congress. This can have the effect of slowing down the process of government.

The Senate has 100 members, two from each state, both of whom represent the whole state. **Senators** must be over 30 and have been US citizens for at least nine years, They are elected for six years, and every two years two-thirds of the **seats** in the Senate are **up for re-election**. The Vice-president is the **President of the Senate**. The Senate elects a **president pro tempore** when the Vice-president is not available.

The House of Representatives, also known as the House, has 435 members, called **Representatives**, **Congressmen** or **Congresswomen**. The number elected by each state depends on its population: a few states have only one Representative, while California has 45. Larger states are divided into **districts**, each with one Representative. Members of the House must be over 25 and have been US citizens for seven years. Elections are held every two years for every seat in the House. A *__Speaker of the House__ is elected from the majority party to lead discussions.

Both the Senate and the House have many committees. These play an important part in the process of *law-making. Each deals with a certain subject, e.g. small businesses.

The judicial branch

The judicial branch of government has three levels. The Constitution created the *Supreme Court; below it are 13 courts of appeal, and below them are many federal district courts and special courts such as the Court of International Trade.

The Supreme Court has nine members, called **justices**, who are appointed by the President. They are often referred to informally as the **nine old men**. The head of the court is the **Chief Justice**. The Supreme Court has the power to influence the law through a process called **judicial review**. If it decides that a law is **unconstitutional** (= goes against the principles of the Constitution), it must not be applied.

The President appoints federal judges, and they then keep their jobs for the rest of their lives. This is so that they can remain independent, and not be afraid of losing their jobs if the government does not like their decisions.

helps pay for them. The FHA insures *mortgages and was created in 1934 to help build more houses.

the ˈ**Federal Inˈsurance Contriˈbutions Act** (*abbr* **FICA**) the US law by which money is automatically taken from an employee's regular pay as a tax for *Social Security.

*The ˌ**Federalist ˈPapers*** a collection of American essays published as a series in newspapers in 1787–8. Their aim was to persuade citizens in New York State to support the proposal for the *American Constitution. The papers give a complete explanation of the US system of government. They were signed 'Publius' and written mostly by Alexander *Hamilton, James *Madison and John Jay.

F

the ˈ**Federalist ˌParty** the first real political party in the US. It was established in 1789 by Alexander *Hamilton and included John *Adams, the only *president elected by the party. The **Federalists** held power for six years (1794–1800), creating a strong central government. They favoured friendship with Britain and opposed the *War of 1812. They lost power as a national party in 1816 after Hamilton and Adams became enemies.

ˈ**Federal Reˈserve ˈBank** *n* any of the 12 banks in different regions of the US that are part of the *Federal Reserve System.

the ˌ**Federal Reˈserve ˌSystem** (*abbr* the **FRS**) (*also infml* the **Fed**) the central bank system of the US government that controls the supply of money and therefore the nation's economy. It was established by the Federal Reserve Act of 1913. Its *Federal Reserve Banks deal with commercial banks in their regions. All national banks must join the system and state banks, *savings and loan associations and *credit unions may join with the Fed's approval. The system is directed by seven people appointed by the US *President, and their chairman is extremely powerful. Alan Greenspan (1926–) has had this job since 1987.

the ˌ**Federal ˈTrade Comˌmission** ⇨ FTC.

feelings

British and American people are similar in many ways, but in **expressing feelings** they have little in common. Americans believe, at least in principle, that it is better to share what they think and feel. Relatives and friends are expected to say, 'I love you', 'I care for you', or 'I'm glad to have a friend like you'. When people are upset they cry, even in a public place. It is even considered good to show you are angry, to **let it all out** and say what you feel. **Bottling it up inside** is thought to make matters worse.

In contrast to this is the traditional **British reserve**, a national tendency to avoid showing strong emotion of any kind. Many visitors to Britain think that because the British do not express their feelings easily they are cold and uncaring. **Keeping a stiff upper lip**, not showing or talking about your feelings, was formerly a sign of strong character, and people who revealed their feelings were thought to be weak or bad-mannered. This attitude is far less common today and people are now encouraged to show or talk about their feelings.

Older people and men of all ages often find it especially difficult to express their feelings. Recently, some US men have come to believe that they should 'get in touch with their feelings'. These men are sometimes humorously called **sensitive new-age guys (SNAGs)**, and they take **sensitivity training** courses that help them to learn to express what they feel without being embarrassed. But these people are a small proportion of Americans and are often treated as a joke, not as 'real men'.

Most British men, and some women, are embarrassed to be seen crying in public. People are also embarrassed when they see somebody crying, and do not know whether it is better to pretend they have not noticed or to try and comfort them. Women are more likely to respond than men and will put their arm round the person or touch their shoulder.

Many people now show feelings of affection in public. Women sometimes kiss each other on the cheek as a greeting and people may greet or say goodbye to each other with a hug. Lovers hold hands in public, and sometimes embrace and kiss each other, but many older people do not like to see this. The British are also embarrassed about showing anger. If somebody starts to complain in public, e.g. about being kept waiting in a restaurant, people around them may pretend not to hear and avoid getting involved.

When British people are part of a crowd they are less worried about expressing their emotions. Football crowds sing and they cheer when their side scores a goal. Players now hug each other when they score. Even cricket supporters, who had a reputation for being much quieter, cheer as well as giving the traditional polite applause.

ˌ**Felix the ˈCat** a US cartoon character created in the early 1920s by Otto Messmer. Felix is a black-and-white cat who has big eyes and is innocent and happy. He first appeared in silent films in 1921. Charles *Lindbergh carried a Felix doll for good luck during his famous flight over the Atlantic. There are now Felix Comics and a Felix television series.

ˈ**Fellow of the ˌRoyal Soˈciety** (*abbr* **FRS**) the title of a member of the *Royal Society. People are usually made members after doing some original scientific work: *Sir John Randall FRS* ○ *He was elected FRS in 1953.*

feminism

The issue of **equality** for women in British society first attracted national attention in the early 20th century, when the ***suffragettes** won for women the right to vote. In the 1960s **feminism** (= the belief that women and men are equal in abilities and should have equal rights and opportunities) became the subject of intense debate when the ***women's lib** movement encouraged women to 'burn their bras', to reject their traditional supporting role and to demand equal status and equal rights with men in areas such as employment and pay.

Since then, the **gender gap** between the sexes has been reduced. The *Equal Pay Act of 1970, for instance, made it illegal for women to be paid less than men for doing the same work, and in 1975 the *Sex Discrimination Act aimed to prevent either sex having an unfair advantage when applying for jobs. Women now have much better employment opportunities than formerly, though they still tend to get less well-paid jobs than men, and very few are appointed to top jobs in industry.

Many feminists believe that there is still a long way to go before women are treated as equals. Some men, however, believe that the balance has already swung too far in favour of women. The *Equal Opportunities Commission, to which people can appeal if they think they have been unfairly treated, now gets nearly as many complaints from men as from women.

The battle between feminist and traditional views of a woman's role continues. It is widely accepted by younger people that women should, if they wish, be allowed to develop their careers and not give up work when they have a family. But others, particularly among the older generation, complain that women today do not place enough importance on the roles of mother and homemaker and blame them for the breakdown of family life.

In the US the movement that is often called the 'first wave of feminism' began in the mid 1800s. Susan B *Anthony worked for the right to vote, Margaret Sanger wanted to provide women with the means of contraception so that they could decide whether or not to have children, and Elizabeth Blackwell, who had to fight for the chance to become a doctor, wanted women to have greater opportunities to study. Many **feminists** were interested in other social issues.

The second wave of feminism began in the 1960s. Women like Betty *Friedan and Gloria Steinem became associated with the fight to get equal rights and opportunities for women under the law. An important issue was the ***Equal Rights Amendment (ERA)**, which was intended to change the *Constitution. Although the ERA was not passed there was progress in other areas. It became illegal for employers, schools, clubs, etc. to **discriminate** against women. But women still find it hard to advance beyond a certain point in their careers, the so-called **glass ceiling** that prevents them from having high-level jobs. Many women also face the problem of the **second shift**, i.e. the household chores.

In the 1980s feminism became less popular in the US and there was less interest in solving the remaining problems, such as the fact that most women still earn much less than men. But American women have more opportunities than anyone thought possible 30 years ago. One of the biggest changes is in how people think. Although there is still discrimination, the principle that it should not exist is widely accepted.

Feminism has brought about many changes in the English language. Many words for job titles that included 'man' have been replaced, for example 'police officer' is used instead of 'policeman' and 'chairperson' for 'chairman'. 'He' is now rarely used to refer to a person when the person could be either a man or a woman. Instead **he/she**, or sometimes **(s)he**, is preferred. The title **Ms** is used for women instead of 'Miss' or 'Mrs', since it does not show whether a woman is married or not.

ˈ**Fenian** /ˈfiːniən/ *n* a member of a revolutionary organization formed in the 1850s in the US and Ireland. Its aim was to end British rule in Ireland. The Fenians were involved in the *Easter Rising in 1916, and in forming the *IRA in 1919. Some people, especially *Protestants in Northern Ireland, use the word 'Fenian' as an offensive way of referring to Irish *Roman Catholics.

the **Fens** an area of low wet land in eastern England between *Lincoln and *Cambridge. Much of the land used to be covered by the sea, and it contains many drains and sluices (= sliding gates to control the flow of water) to prevent floods. It is a very rich agricultural area.

ˌEdna ˈ**Ferber** /ˈfɜːbə(r); *AmE* ˈfɜːrbər/ (1887–1968) a US writer of novels, short stories and plays. Her long novels often tell stories spread over many years. *So Big* (1924), about rich families in *Chicago, won the *Pulitzer Prize, *Giant* (1952) was about *Texas, and **Show Boat* (1926), about a Southern family, became a successful *Broadway musical play. All three were made into films. Ferber also wrote plays with George Kaufmann, including *Dinner at Eight* (1932).

ˌSarah ˈ**Ferguson** /ˈfɜːɡəsn; *AmE* ˈfɜːrɡəsn/ (*also infml* **Fergie**) (1959–) the English woman who became the Duchess of York when she married Prince *Andrew in 1986. She was well known for her informal and lively behaviour, which some people did not think was suitable for a member of the *royal family. She separated from Prince Andrew in 1992, and in the 1990s started writing children's books and appearing on US television programmes.

Ferˈmanagh /fəˈmænə; *AmE* fərˈmænə/ one of the historical *Six Counties of Northern Ireland. It is now a *local government district.

ˌGeraldine **Ferˈraro** /fəˈrɑːrəʊ/ (1935–) the only woman to be a candidate for US Vice-president for a major political party. The *Democratic Party chose her to join Walter Mondale in the 1984 election, but they lost to Ronald *Reagan and George *Bush. Ferraro was a lawyer from New York who was elected to the US *House of Representatives from 1979 to 1984. In 1993 she became a US representative on the Human Rights Commission of the *United Nations.

ˌKathleen ˈ**Ferrier** /ˌkæθliːn ˈferiə(r)/ (1912–53) an English singer who performed leading roles in many operas. She was best known for singing classical song cycles (= sets of songs) and English *folk songs.

the ˌ**Festival ˈHall** ⇨ ROYAL FESTIVAL HALL.

the ˌ**Festival of ˈBritain** an event consisting of exhibitions and celebrations that took place on the *South Bank of the Thames in London in 1951. The aim of the festival was to celebrate 100 years since the *Great Exhibition, and to show Britain's economic and technical progress after *World War II. It was the first time that the South Bank was used as a centre for the arts. Similar celebrations took place in other parts of Britain.

ˈ**Festival of ˈNine ˈLessons and ˈCarols** a Christian service that takes place in many British churches just before *Christmas. People sing *carols and appropriate sections of the Bible are read aloud.

festivals

Many branches of **the *arts** hold festivals each year in towns and cities throughout Britain and the US. Some larger festivals last several weeks and include music, drama, art and literature. People travel a long way to hear the top international performers that such festivals attract. Smaller festivals concentrate on one art form, such as poetry. Because the US is so large, most of its festivals are local, although a few famous ones, such as the ***Monterey Jazz Festival** in California, attract people from around the world. Americans most like summer festivals where they can enjoy art, music and food outdoors.

Many festivals try to obtain sponsorship money from local businesses to help cover the costs. In the US events are relatively cheap so the entire family can spend the day out. In Britain, however, tickets may be expensive. This tends to restrict the number and type of people who go to the main festivals, and many **festival-goers** are middle-aged, middle-class professional people. This in turn can affect the type of music or drama that the organizers to put on.

Some festivals, such as the ***Edinburgh Festival**, have been running for many years. A special feature of the Edinburgh Festival is the ***Fringe**. Fringe events are usually avant-garde (= new and experimental) and attract a wide audience. They also get a lot of attention from the critics, and this can help the careers of younger *performers. In Wales, several ***eisteddfods** celebrate Welsh culture and include competitions for composers and artists. In the US the ***Carmel Performing Arts Festival** in California offers a range of music, dance, theatre, stories and poetry.

Many festivals concentrate on music. In Britain, many people have heard of, if not been to, the ***Aldeburgh Festival** which was founded by Benjamin *Britten. The most famous British music festival, however, is **the *Proms**, held each summer at the

*Royal Albert Hall in London. Concerts contain a mixture of old favourites and new, specially commissioned pieces. Classical music is less popular in the US, but several festivals offer a mixture of concerts and classes, e.g. the ***Aspen Music Festival**.

Festivals of rock and pop music are often huge informal open-air events attended by thousands of young people, many of whom camp overnight in a nearby field. The biggest rock festivals in Britain include *Glastonbury, *Reading and Donnington. In the US the main events are the **Apple Rock Musical Festival**, held near Moderna, New York, and **Rock Fest**, held near Cadott, Wisconsin. The Southwest Louisiana Zydeco Music Festival celebrates the music (and *Cajun food) of Black French and *Creole peoples. The Beale Street Music Festival in *Memphis and the W C Handy Blues and Barbecue Festival in Henderson, *Kentucky, celebrate the *blues.

Film festivals are especially popular in the US. The best-known is the **Sundance Film Festival** organized by Robert *Redford's Sundance Institute in *Utah. The ***Hollywood Film Festival**, held each August, attracts big stars, but America's mix of people from different races and cultures has led to many smaller events such as the Boston Jewish Film Festival and the Los Angeles Asian-Pacific Film Festival. The main event in Britain is the London International Film Festival.

Fewer people generally attend literature festivals, but in the US the annual **Tennessee Williams/New Orleans Literary Festival** has become a major event. It includes performances of Williams's plays and a walking tour of 'Williams's New Orleans'. In Britain the village of Hay-on-Wye has a literary festival, and *Stratford-upon-Avon has a poetry festival.

In the US the most common festivals are arts, or arts and crafts, festivals. The **Utah Arts Festival**, mixes art with music, theatre and cooking.

---

fête *n* (*BrE*) (in Britain) an outdoor event that takes place in the summer. Fêtes usually consist of sports, children's games and competitions, with people selling things that they have made, such as jam and cakes. They are often used to raise money for a local *charity, church or school. In small towns they are important social events. Similar events in the US are usually called *bazaars*. Church and Christmas bazaars are traditional.

at a fête

ˌ**Fettes** ˈ**College** /ˌfetɪz/ a *public school(1) in *Edinburgh, Scotland. It was established in 1870 as a school for boys, and began to take girls in 1980. It is one of the best-known public schools in Scotland.

ˌRichard ˈ**Feynman** /ˈfaɪnmən/ (1918–88) a US physicist who began the first research into quantum electrodynamics. He shared the 1965 *Nobel Prize for physics for his work in this field. His 'Feynman diagrams' help to explain the behaviour of substances and light. During *World War II, Feynman worked on the *Manhattan Project. In 1986, he was a member of the committee that investigated the explosion of the **Challenger* spacecraft.

the **Ffeˌstiniog** ˈ**Railway** /feˌstɪniɒg; *AmE* feˌstmiɑːg/ a small railway line in north-west Wales which was used in the 19th century to carry slate (= a type of smooth grey stone used for covering roofs) down the Vale of Ffestiniog to the coast. The scenery is very beautiful and in the late 20th century the old steam trains were brought back into use and the railway became a tourist attraction.

the Ffestiniog Railway

the **FHA** /ˌef eɪtʃ ˈeɪ/ ⇨ FEDERAL HOUSING ADMINISTRATION.

ˌ**Fianna** ˈ**Fáil** /ˌfiːənə ˈfɔɪl/ an Irish political party, formed in 1926 by Eamon *de Valera and others who believed that the whole of Ireland should become one republic. It is one of the two main parties in the Republic of Ireland, and has been in power for most of the 20th century. Compare FINE GAEL.

FICA /ˈfaɪkə/ ⇨ FEDERAL INSURANCE CONTRIBUTIONS ACT.

FID DEF /ˌfɪd ˈdef/ (*also* **FD**) an abbreviation of the Latin phrase *Fidei Defensor*, which means 'Defender of the Faith', a title originally given to *Henry VIII for defending the *Roman Catholic religion. When he created the *Church of England he kept the title, referring to the new religion. The phrase appears on most British coins.

ˌ***Fiddler on the*** ˈ***Roof*** a musical play that ran for 3 242 performances on *Broadway (1964–72). It won several *Tony Awards in 1965, including ones for the leading actor Zero Mostel and the author Joseph Stein. The Israeli actor Chaim Topol played the main part on the London stage and in the film version (1971). The story is about the difficult life of a poor Jewish father in a Ukrainian village before the Russian Revolution. The songs include *If I Were a Rich Man*.

ˌArthur ˈ**Fiedler** /ˈfiːdlə(r)/ (1894–1979) a US conductor who began the *Boston Pops Orchestra in 1930 and led it for almost 50 years. Fiedler had joined the Boston Symphony Orchestra in 1916 and created the Boston Sinfonietta in 1924 to play music that was less well known.

The ***Field*** a British magazine, published every month, which contains articles about farming and the countryside, and in particular about horses and country sports such as shooting and fishing. Many people associate it with rich people who own land in the country.

ˌSally ˈ**Field** /ˈfiːld/ (1946–) a US actor who has won two *Oscars, the first for playing a poor factory worker in *Norma Rae* (1979) and the second as a *Texas farmer in *Places of the Heart* (1984). Her other films include *Steel Magnolias* (1989) and *Forrest Gump* (1994).

ˈ**field hockey** ⇨ note at HOCKEY.

ˌHenry ˈ**Fielding** /ˈfiːldɪŋ/ (1707–54) an English writer. In the 1730s he wrote political plays that made fun of the government, until the government became more strict about censoring (= removing or changing offensive parts in) plays. He then began writing novels. His most famous work, **Tom Jones*, has a long and complicated story and presents a strong, clear picture of English society at the time. It had an important influence on the development of the English novel. Fielding became a *Justice of the Peace in 1748 and was responsible for forming the *Bow Street Runners.

the ˈ**Field of ˌCloth of ˈGold** an event that took place near Calais in northern France in the summer of 1520 when the English king *Henry VIII met the French king Francis I. The meeting became famous for the beautiful tents the two kings stayed in, the grand meals they ate, and the sports that took place to mark the occasion.

ˌGracie ˈ**Fields**[1] /ˈfiːldz/ (1898–1979) an English singer, born in *Lancashire(1). She began her career as a *music-hall(1) performer and became famous when she sang in London in the 1920s. She appeared in several films, including *Sally in our Alley* (1931). The British people, who called her 'our Gracie', loved her friendly personality and the popular songs that she sang. She was made a *dame(1) in 1979.

ˌW C ˈ**Fields**[2] /ˈfiːldz/ (William Claude Fields 1879–1946) a US comic actor well known for his humorous remarks. He had a large nose and the characters he played often drank a lot of alcohol and hated children and dogs. He was in the Ziegfeld Follies on *Broadway (1915–21) and often on radio. His films, some of which he wrote, include *My Little Chickadee* (1940) with Mae *West, *The Bank Dick* (1940) and *Never Give a Sucker an Even Break* (1941).

field sports

The main field sports in Britain are **hunting**, **shooting** and **fishing**. They are often also called **blood sports** because they involve killing animals. All three sports were traditionally associated with the upper classes, although today they all, especially fishing, attract a much wider group of people.

Foxhunting is the most common form of hunting. Packs of **foxhounds** followed by horse riders wearing **pinks** (= red jackets), blowing **horns** and jumping hedges, are still a familiar sight. The most famous **hunts** (= clubs that hunt) include the Belvoir, and the Quorn. Foxhunting was once a popular subject for painting and some English country *pubs display sets of prints. **Staghunting** now takes place in only a few parts of Britain. **Hare coursing**, in which greyhounds are trained to chase a **hare**, is restricted mainly to northern England. Other traditional blood sports such as *badger-baiting and *cockfighting are now illegal. Because hunting involves chasing and killing animals it has many critics. **Hunt saboteurs** belonging to organizations such as the ***League Against Cruel Sports** often protest violently at meetings of hunts. People against hunting have also tried to persuade *Parliament to ban hunting with dogs. Supporters of hunting, who include many farmers, argue that hunting foxes with dogs is less cruel than shooting them.

Shooting **game birds**, such as pheasant and grouse, is a sport mainly of the upper and middle classes. Grouse shooting begins each year on 12 August, the ***Glorious Twelfth**, and takes place mainly in Scotland. The hunters often employ **beaters** to drive the birds towards their guns. Those who object to shooting at live birds for sport do **clay-pigeon shooting** (= shooting at clay discs fixed in the air).

Fishing, often called **angling**, is a very popular sport, mostly among men. Many belong to angling clubs. There are three main kinds of angling: ***fly-fishing**, **coarse fishing** and **sea-fishing**. Fly-fishing, which is expensive, is fishing for salmon, trout and other fish in fast-flowing rivers, using specially disguised hooks. Coarse fishing in rivers and lakes for fish other than salmon and trout, most of which are thrown back after being caught, is more widely popular. On the coast people may fish with a **rod and line** from a boat or from the shore.

The US probably has more hunting organizations than any other country. This is mainly because of two strong traditions: the *Constitution gives all Americans the right to own guns, and Americans have always hunted animals for food. The first Europeans who settled America hunted deer, bears, foxes, turkeys and ducks to survive, and many Americans still eat what they shoot. For these reasons, hunting is a sport for all classes and many people own **hunting rifles**. Americans do not use the name *field sports*. Instead they say **outdoor sports** or, because that can include camping, walking and boating, simply **hunting and fishing**. **Bird hunting** is often used instead of *shooting*, because that can also mean shooting at targets made of wood. People who enjoy these sports buy magazines like *Field & Stream* and *American Rifleman*. There are also many television programmes about hunting and fishing.

Many other Americans are against hunting, but animal rights groups have little power against organizations like the *National Rifle Association, which has more than 2.3 million members, and other politically active groups that support hunting and fishing. Conservation organizations like the Colorado Wildlife Conservation Coalition also use their influence to protect the rights of people to hunt and fish.

The first US hunting club, the Gloucester Fox Hunting Club, was established in 1766 in *Philadelphia. Foxhunting now only takes place in a few eastern states where it is associated with the upper class and has little opposition. Americans generally hunt deer, elk, bears, antelopes, mountain lions, raccoons and wild birds. Hunting licences may cost only $10 for one day's fishing but rise to $135 for a general hunting and fishing licence or $250 for hunting and **trapping** (= catching live animals). The **US Fish and Wildlife Service** is in charge of fishing and hunting laws. States have their own wildlife departments and sometimes both national and state permission is needed to hunt.

Fishing is the most popular outdoor sport in America. In *Florida alone over a million freshwater anglers each year pay $37 million in licence fees. Freshwater fish caught in the US include trout, bassand salmon. Saltwater fish include flounder, mackerel, shark, snapper and tuna.

ˌRanulph ˈ**Fiennes** /ˌrænəlf ˈfaɪnz/ (*full name* Ranulph Twisleton-Wykeham-Fiennes 1944–) an English explorer. He is well known for his trips to the North and South Poles. In 1993 he and his partner Michael Stroud became the first people to walk across Antarctica without help. He became a *baronet in 1944.

Fife a region of eastern central Scotland. Its administrative centre is Glenrothes.

the **Fifˈteen** (*also* the **'15 Rebellion**) an attempt in 1715 by the *Jacobite supporters of James *Stuart to defeat the forces of the House of *Hanover and make James king. By the time James arrived from France, the Jacobites had lost two important battles. James returned to France and the rebellion soon ended.

the ˌ**Fifth A'mendment** /ə'mendmənt/ one of the *amendments to the *American Constitution which is part of the *Bill of Rights. It states that people need not say anything against themselves in a court of law. However, when people 'take the Fifth' or 'plead the Fifth' in court, some people believe it is because they are guilty. The Fifth Amendment also protects individuals from *double jeopardy and requires *due process of law and fair payments in cases of *eminent domain.

ˌ**Fifth 'Avenue** a New York street famous for its expensive shops and department stores, especially between 47th Street and 59th Street. These include Saks Fifth Avenue, Bergdorf Goodman, *Tiffany's and *F A O Schwarz. Also on Fifth Avenue are the *Empire State Building *St Patrick's Cathedral, *Central Park, the *Metropolitan Museum of Art and the *Guggenheim Museum. The avenue divides the *East Side and *West Side of *Manhattan(1). On 17 March each year, the central line along it is painted green for the *St Patrick's Day parade.

F

the ˌ**Fifth of 'November** ⇨ BONFIRE NIGHT.

'**Fighter Comˌmand** a department of the *Royal Air Force set up in 1936 to be responsible for fighters. The aircraft of Fighter Command were very useful during the *Battle of Britain.

*The ˌ**Fighting Témé'raire*** /temə'reə(r); *AmE* temə'rer/ a famous painting (1838) by J M W *Turner. It is a picture of the *Téméraire*, an old military sailing ship, being pulled up the *Thames by a steamship, on its way to being destroyed. The subject of ships on the river and the colourful London sky are typical of Turner.

'**Fiji** /'fiːdʒiː/ a country in the southern Pacific Ocean, consisting of over 800 islands. The capital city is Suva, and the country's economy is based mainly on agriculture, fishing and tourism. Fiji was part of the *British Empire before becoming independent in 1970. In 1987 the armed forces took over the country, and Fiji left the *Commonwealth, though it has since joined it again. ▶ **Fijian** *adj, n.*

'**film cerˌtificate** (*BrE*) (*AmE* '**film ˌrating**) *n* a label that is put on films and videos, stating who can watch them legally. In Britain, films and videos are placed in one of five groups. Films marked U can be seen by anybody, films marked PG can only be seen by children if they are with an adult, films marked 12 can only be seen by people who are at least 12 years old, films marked 15 can only be seen by people who are at least 15, and films marked 18 can only be seen by people who are at least 18.

In the US, a film is given one of six labels by the Code and Rating Administration of the Motion Picture Association of America. These are: G for general audiences, PG for 'parental guidance' (meaning that parents decide whether to let their children see the film), PG–13 for parental guidance for children under 13, R for 'restricted' (meaning that children under 17 can only see the film with a parent or guardian (= an adult legally responsible for a child)), and NC–17 ('no children–17') and X for films which may not be seen by anyone under 17. The ratings are the same for videos of the films.

'**Filofax**™ *n* a book (sometimes called a 'personal organizer') in which people can write down addresses, appointments and other information, with loose pages that can be taken out or added. Filofaxes were especially popular in the 1980s, and some people make jokes about them because they were thought to be typically owned by yuppies.

The ***Fiˌnancial 'Times*** (*also* The ***FT***) Britain's most important financial newspaper. It is published every day except Sunday, and consists mostly of news about companies, stocks and shares. It is read mainly by business people and people who invest money in the financial markets. It is printed on pink paper and is sometimes called the 'pink 'un'. ⇨ article at NEWSPAPERS.

Fi'nancial 'Times 'Indices *n* [pl] different lists of share prices on the *London Stock Exchange that are published every day in *The *Financial Times*. They are used to show general trends in the British financial markets. The oldest of these is the **Financial Times Ordinary Share Index**, or **FT Index**, a list of the average prices of 30 industrial shares. The best known is the *FT-SE 100-Share Index, which gives the share values of the 100 largest British companies. The newspaper also publishes the **FT-Actuaries All-Share Index**, based on a wider range of share prices and giving the values of the top 250 and the top 350 shares in Britain.

ˌ**Fine 'Gael** /ˌfɪnə 'geɪl/ an Irish political party. It is one of the two main parties in the Republic of Ireland and is usually considered the more conservative. In 1985 the Fine Gael government signed the *Anglo-Irish Agreement with the British government. Compare FIANNA FÁIL.

ˌ**Fingal's 'Cave** /ˌfɪŋglz/ a large cave on the island of *Staffa in the *Hebrides, Scotland. It is well known for its large rock columns. Many poets and musicians have visited the cave and written about it, but it is best known as the subject of Mendelssohn's *Hebrides Overture* (1832), also called *Fingal's Cave*.

ˌHuckleberry '**Finn** /ˌhʌklberi 'fɪn/ a character created by Mark *Twain for his novel *The Adventures of Tom Sawyer* (1876) who he then made the main character in *The Adventures of Huckleberry Finn* (1885). Huckleberry, called Huck by his friends, is not educated but is an independent and happy boy. The second book is considered one of the greatest American novels. It is about Huck's trip down the *Mississippi River with a slave called Jim who has escaped.

ˌ***Finnegans 'Wake*** /ˌfɪnɪgənz/ a novel (1922) by James *Joyce. It describes in great detail one day in the lives and thoughts of a Dublin man, his wife and friends, and contains many references to history, mythology (= ancient stories) and literature. It was Joyce's last novel, and is well known for being difficult to read. It is a long book, written in an experimental style. Joyce made up his own grammar, and many of the words are invented or borrowed from other languages. The book was originally published in Paris and was not published in Britain until 1936.

ˌAlbert '**Finney**[1] /'fɪni/ (1936–) an English actor. He has been successful in the theatre and in films since the 1960s, when he became well known for playing young *working-class northern men, such as the main roles in *Billy Liar* (1959) and *Saturday Night and Sunday Morning* (1960).

ˌTom '**Finney**[2] /'fɪni/ (1922–) a British footballer who played for Preston North End (1937–59) and 76 times for England. He was considered one of the greatest attacking players of his time and was made a *knight in 1998.

the ˌ**Fire of 'London** (*also* the ˌ**Great 'Fire**, the **Great Fire of London**) a very large fire which lasted for two days in 1666 and destroyed many parts of London, including the old *St Paul's Cathedral. Many people remember that it is said to have started in a street called Pudding Lane and finished in another called Pie Corner.

ˌ**fireside 'chats** *n* [pl] the series of informal radio broadcasts that President Franklin D *Roosevelt made in 1932 to explain his *New Deal and the decisions of his government. He was the first president to use radio to talk directly to the people. He called them 'my fellow Americans' and spoke as if he was talking with friends.

'Firestone /'faɪəstəʊn; *AmE* 'faɪərstoʊn/ a large US tyre company, now owned by a Japanese company. The Firestone Tire and Rubber Company was established by Harvey S Firestone (1868-1938) in 1900 in Akron, *Ohio. It was bought in 1988 by the Bridgestone Company of Japan, and in 1990 the name was changed to Bridgestone/Firestone Inc.

the **ˌFirst A'mendment** /ə'mendmənt/ the first *amendment to the *American Constitution and part of the *Bill of Rights. It protects a person's freedom of religion (in the *Establishment Clause) as well as freedom of speech, the freedom of the press and the right to gather together in peaceful groups. It is often used by journalists to protect their sources and by the Supreme Court to explain why it cannot restrict offensive communications.

ˌfirst-class 'cricket *n* [U] the type of *cricket in which it takes three days or more to play a match. In Britain, first-class cricket refers to the *county championship and to international matches.

the **ˌFirst Di'vision** the second most important group of football teams in England, consisting of the top 24 teams in the *Football League. The top three teams in the First Division at the end of each season move up into the *Premier League for the following season. Until 1992 the First Division was the most important division in English football, but in that year the top clubs left to form the Premier League. ⇨ note at FOOTBALL – BRITISH STYLE.

the **ˌFirst 'Folio** the first collection of *Shakespeare's plays to be published. It consists of 36 plays and was published in 1623 by two actors who had worked with Shakespeare. Some of the individual plays had already been published, and were called *quartos*, but many of them contained mistakes. The First Folio is considered the first true and genuine written version of the plays. Copies of it are rare and very valuable.

ˌfirst-'footing *n* [U] the Scottish tradition of waiting for a new person to enter a house at *New Year before the celebrations can begin. Many people enjoy first-footing in Scotland by going to other people's houses. Traditionally, they take a piece of coal for the fire, some *whisky to drink, and sometimes something to eat.

the **ˌFirst 'Lady** *n* [usu sing] (in the US) the wife of the *President or the wife of a state governor. The President's family is also referred to as the **First Family**.

ˌfirst past the 'post a phrase describing the British election system, in which the person with the highest number of votes is the winner, even if he or she only has one vote more than the person who comes second. In the same way, the party with the most *MPs wins the election, even if they only have one more MP than the second party. Many people, particularly those in smaller parties, think that this system is unfair, and demand *proportional representation. ⇨ article at ELECTIONS TO PARLIAMENT.

ˌfirst 'reading *n* **1** (in Britain) the first time that a *bill(1) is discussed in the *House of Commons. Bills are formally announced at the first reading, and discussed in more detail in the *second reading and the *third reading. **2** (in the US) the introduction of a *bill(2) in the *House of Representatives or the *Senate, usually by reading out its name or number.

'first school *n* (*BrE*) a type of *primary school in some parts of Britain for children between five and eight years old. At the age of eight or nine they go on to a *middle school.

ˌBobby **'Fischer** /'fɪʃə(r)/ (1943–) a US chess player who became the youngest world champion when he defeated the Russian Boris Spassky in 1972. Fischer then stopped playing publicly and in 1975 he lost his title when he refused to play Anatoly Karpov. In 1992 he began again and defeated Spassky in Belgrade, but he has rarely competed since then.

ˌfish and 'chips a traditional British dish. It consists of fish (usually cod, plaice or haddock) which is covered in batter (= a mixture of flour and milk) and fried in deep fat. This is served with chips (= long thin pieces of fried potato). It is quite a cheap meal, which people usually buy at a **fish and chip shop** and take away wrapped in paper: *I didn't have time to cook anything so I went to the fish and chip shop.*

a fish and chip shop

'Fishbourne /'fɪʃbɔːn; *AmE* 'fɪʃbɔːrn/ the place near *Chichester in southern England where in 1960 parts of a large Roman building were found under the ground. It was probably built by the Romans in the 1st century for the leader of a local tribe. Much of it has been destroyed, but it is still possible to see that it was a very important house. It is open to the public. ⇨ article at ROMAN BRITAIN.

ˌFisherman's 'Friends™ *n* [pl] a British make of sweet that is small and hard and tastes very strong. Many people suck them when they have a cold or a cough because they help to clear the nose and throat.

'Fisons/'faɪsənz/ a large British company that produces medicines and products for gardens such as treatments to kill weeds. The company used to be well known for its agricultural products, but stopped making them in the 1980s.

ˌEdward **Fitz'gerald¹** /fɪts'dʒerəld/ (1809–83) an English writer and translator, best known for his English translation of the *Rubáiyát of Omar Khayyám*, a popular collection of 12th-century Persian poetry.

ˌElla **Fitz'gerald²** /fɪts'dʒerəld/ (1918–96) an *African-American singer of *jazz and popular songs. She had a clear, strong voice and was called 'the first lady of song'. She performed regularly with 'Duke' *Ellington, 'Count' *Basie and Louis *Armstrong, and later recorded many songs by George *Gershwin and Cole *Porter.

ˌF Scott **Fitz'gerald³** /skɒt fɪts'dʒerəld; *AmE* skɑːt/ (Francis Scott Key Fitzgerald 1896–1940) a US writer of novels and short stories about the *Jazz Age, a name he invented. The useless fun and immoral behaviour that were common in those years are described in his best-known novel, *The *Great Gatsby*. Fitzgerald and his wife Zelda (1901–48) lived a wild life themselves. She developed a mental illness, and he drank too much alcohol, experiences he used in **Tender is the Night* (1934). In 1936 Fitzgerald moved to Hollywood to write films. His last novel, *The Last Tycoon*, was not finished when he died.

ˌMrs **Fitzˈherbert** /fɪtsˈhɜːbət; *AmE* fɪtsˈhɜːbərt/ (Maria Anne Fitzherbert 1756–1837) the first wife of the British king *George IV. They were married secretly in 1785, before George became king, but the marriage was illegal because it did not have the king's official permission. Mrs Fitzherbert was a *Roman Catholic, and under British law a prince who married a Catholic could not become king.

ˌ**five-and-ˈten** (*also* ˌ**five-and-ˈten-cent ˈstore**, ˌ**five-and-ˈdime**, ˈ**dime store**) *n* [C] (*AmE old use*) a type of large shop/store in the US selling cheap goods. The first of them were opened in 1879 by F W *Woolworth and for many years they sold everything at a price of either five cents or ten cents. In 1997, the Woolworth Corporation closed its last 400 five-and-dimes in the US because they had lost customers to *Wal-Mart and other new companies.

F

the ˈ**Five ˈCivilized ˈTribes** the name used to refer to five groups of Native-American people in the *South: the *Cherokee, *Choctaw, Chickasaw, *Creek and *Seminole. The tribes were forced to leave their own lands and settle in the *Indian Territory, even though it was thought that they could be trusted because they had developed their own versions of the *American Constitution and US laws.

the ˌ**Five ˈNations** ⇨ IROQUOIS LEAGUE.

the ˈ**Five ˈNations ˈTournament** a *Rugby Union competition that takes place every year between the national teams of England, France, Ireland, Scotland and Wales. Each team plays each of the others once, and the winner is the team with the most points at the end.

fives *n* [U] a British game in which two or four players hit a small hard ball with their hands against any of three walls. The aim is to make the ball bounce in such a way that the next player makes a mistake. Most people think of it as a game typically played at *public schools such as *Eton and *Rugby, which each have their own particular versions of it.

the ˌ**Five ˈTowns** *n* [pl] five former towns in the *Potteries region of the English *Midlands. The towns were Tunstall, Burslem, Hanley, Stoke-upon-Trent and Longton. They were close to each other and were important centres of the pottery industry from the 17th century until in 1910 they joined together as one town, *Stoke-on-Trent. The Five Towns became well known as the setting for the novels of Arnold *Bennett.

ˈ**Flag Day** (in the US) 14 June, when people fly the US flag. It is the anniversary of the day in 1777 when the *Continental Congress passed a law making the *Stars and Stripes the official American flag.

ˌBud ˈ**Flanagan** /ˈflænəgən/ (1896–1968) a British *music-hall(1) singer and comedian who was a member of the *Crazy Gang. He and his partner Chesney Allen became famous during *World War II as **Flanagan and Allen** and made several successful films and records. Their best-known song is *Underneath the Arches.*

ˌ**Flanders and ˈSwann** /ˌflɑːndəz, ˈswɒn; *AmE* ˌflɑːndərz, ˈswɑːn/ a pair of English entertainers, **Michael Flanders** (1922–75) and **Donald Swann** (1923–94), who wrote and performed many humorous songs together. Flanders (who was unable to walk because of polio, a disease affecting the nervous system, and performed in a wheelchair) wrote the words and sang, and Swann wrote the music and played the piano. Their shows in London and New York were very successful in the 1950s and 1960s.

ˌ**Flanders ˈfields** /ˌflɑːndəz; *AmE* ˌflɑːndərz/ *n* [pl] a phrase used to refer to the areas of north-east France and Belgium where many soldiers from Britain and the *Commonwealth died and were buried in *World War I. The phrase comes from a poem, *In Flanders Fields* (1915) by John McCrae, which contains the lines:

In Flanders fields the poppies blow
Between the crosses, row on row,
That mark our place.

ˈ**flapper** *n* a fashionable and lively young woman of the 1920s. The typical flapper wore short skirts, had short hair, drank alcohol, and enjoyed smoking and dancing. At the time many people thought flappers were immoral, but they are now often regarded as the first modern, independent women.

flappers doing the Charleston

Flash™ /flæʃ/ *n* [U] a substance used for cleaning kitchens, bathrooms, floors, etc. It can be bought as a liquid or as a powder to be mixed with water.

ˌHarry ˈ**Flashman** /ˈflæʃmən/ a character in **Tom Brown's Schooldays*. He is a cruel older boy who is unkind to Tom and the other young boys. In the 20th century George MacDonald Fraser wrote a series of novels about Flashman's adventures as an adult.

the ˌ**Flat ˈEarth Soˌciety** an organization whose members claim that the Earth is flat, and refuse to believe in modern science. The society was established in America and has branches in Britain. Its members are called **flat-earthers**, and the expression is sometimes used to describe people who refuse to believe something that is clearly true.

ˌ***Flatford ˈMill*** /ˌflætfəd; *AmE* ˌflætfərd/ a painting (1817) by John *Constable of a water mill (= a building by a river that uses the water to turn a wheel and operate machinery) on the river Stour in south-east England. It is one of Constable's most famous paintings, and in 1928 the actual mill was given to the nation to be preserved in memory of the artist.

the ˈ**Flatiron ˌBuilding** /ˈflætaɪən; *AmE* ˈflætaɪərn/ a tall, thin office building that was New York's first *skyscraper. It was built in 1902 on *Fifth Avenue. The building has one thick end and one narrow, sharp end. It has 22 floors and is 285 feet (87 metres) tall. When it was completed, people said it was so tall it might fall over. It still stands today.

the ˌ**Fleet ˈAir Arm** the branch of the British *Royal Navy responsible for aircraft. Most of its planes are based on aircraft carriers, but some are also based on land. Compare RAF.

ˈ**Fleet Street** a street in central London, between the *City and the *West End, where most of Britain's major newspapers used to have their main offices. In the 1980s most of the newspapers moved to new buildings in different parts of London to use new printing technology, but many people still refer to the British press as 'Fleet Street': *Her defection to Labour took Fleet Street by surprise.*

ˌ**Fleetwood** ˈ**Mac** /ˌfli:twʊd ˈmæk/ a British pop group, formed in 1967, which plays a mixture of rock and *blues. The group's best-known songs include *Don't Stop* (1977) and *Little Lies* (1987).

ˌAlexander ˈ**Fleming**[1] /ˈflemɪŋ/ (1881–1955) a Scottish scientist who became well known for discovering penicillin, the first antibiotic that successfully killed bacteria and cured infections. He was made a *knight in 1944, and in 1945 shared the *Nobel Prize for medicine with two colleagues who helped him to develop the use of penicillin.

ˌIan ˈ**Fleming**[2] /ˈflemɪŋ/ (1908–64) an English writer, best known for creating the world's most famous secret agent, James *Bond. Fleming had some experience of the work of secret agents when he worked for the intelligence department of the *Royal Navy during *World War II. He used that experience, and his love of technology and foreign travel, to write his series of James Bond novels, which were later made into successful films.

ˌJohn ˈ**Fletcher** /ˈfletʃə(r)/ (1579–1625) an English writer of plays, many of which he wrote with Francis *Beaumont. He also worked with Ben *Jonson and possibly *Shakespeare.

ˌ**flexible** ˈ**friend** *n* (*BrE infml ironic*) a humorous way of referring to a *credit card after the phrase was used in British television advertisements for the former Access card in the 1980s.

ˌRussell ˈ**Flint** /ˈflɪnt/ (1880–1969) a Scottish painter, known for his landscapes (= pictures of the countryside) and his popular pictures of women with few clothes on. Many British people have copies of these in their homes. Flint was made a *knight in 1947.

The ˈ***Flintstones*** /ˈflɪntstəʊnz; *AmE* ˈflɪntstoʊnz/ a US comedy cartoon television series about a prehistoric family. The humour comes from the way they behave like modern Americans, using pieces of stone and wood as if they were cars, telephones, etc. The series began in 1960 and is still popular with children all around the world. A film version of *The Flintstones*, with real actors, appeared in 1994: *Their kitchen is like something out of the Flintstones.*

ˈ**Flodden** /ˈflɒdn; *AmE* ˈflɑ:dn/ a battle which took place in 1513 between the armies of England and Scotland on a hill in *Northumberland, near the border between the two countries. The English won the battle, and more than 10 000 Scots were killed, including their king, James IV.

ˈ**Flo-Jo** /ˈfləʊ dʒəʊ; *AmE* ˈfloʊ dʒoʊ/ the popular name for the US runner Florence Griffith *Joyner.

ˈ**floor** ˌ**leader** *n* a leader of the *Democratic Party or the *Republican Party in the US *Congress. There are four floor leaders because each of the two main parties chooses its own floor leader in both the *Senate and *House of Representatives. Their job is to speak for their party and work to pass their bills.

ˈ**Flora**™ /ˈflɔ:rə/ *n* [U] a British make of margarine (= a substance like butter, but usually made from vegetable oil). Flora is advertised as a healthy type of margarine because it does not contain much fat.

ˈ**Florida** /ˈflɒrɪdə; *AmE* ˈflɔ:rɪdə/ the most southern state in the US. It is internationally famous for its hot weather and white beaches. Florida's popular name is the Sunshine State. It forms a long, flat area of land in the south-east between the Atlantic Ocean and the *Gulf of Mexico. The largest city is *Miami and the capital city is Tallahassee. Florida was discovered in 1513 by Juan *Ponce de León. Its attractions include *Disney World, the *Everglades, *Cape Canaveral, the Gold Coast and the *Florida Keys.

the ˌ**Florida** ˈ**Keys** /ˌflɒrɪdə ; *AmE* ˌflɔ:rɪdə/ a line of about 20 islands to the west of the southern end of *Florida. The islands are connected by the world's longest road over water, the Overseas Highway that runs 160 miles (256 kilometres). The best-known Keys are *Key West and Key Largo. The islands are popular with tourists and people who like fishing.

ˈ**flower** ˌ**children** (*also* ˈ**flower** ˌ**people**) *n* [pl] young people in many countries in the 1960s who believed in peace and love, and were against war. They carried flowers or wore them in their hair as a symbol of their beliefs. They were part of the *hippie movement, and took part in many peaceful protests against wars, especially the *Vietnam War: *Thousands of flower children hitch-hiked to the festival.* See also FLOWER POWER.

F

ˈ**flower girl** *n* **1** (*AmE*) a very young girl who holds the end of the bride's dress at a wedding. In some weddings, she holds flowers or throws flower petals in front of the bride. She is usually a member of the family of one of the people who are being married. **2** (*BrE*) (especially formerly) a woman or girl who sells flowers in the street.

The ˌ***Flower of*** ˈ***Scotland*** /ˈskɒtlənd; *AmE* ˈskɑ:tlənd/ a song that was performed in the 1960s by the Corries, a Scottish pop group. In the 1980s it became the traditional song sung by Scottish supporters at international *football and *Rugby games.

ˈ**flower** ˌ**power** *n* [U] the beliefs of the *flower children in the 1960s that peace and love were more important than military and commercial activities, and that if enough people shared their ideas, wars would stop and the world would be a better place.

ˌKeith ˈ**Floyd**[1] /ˈflɔɪd/ (1943–) an English cook who appears on television. He has made many programmes about cooking, often travelling abroad to cook the food of a particular country. He is known for his energetic and amusing style, and is often seen drinking a glass of wine. He has also written several successful books about cooking.

ˈˌPretty Boy' ˈ**Floyd**[2] /ˌprɪti bɔɪ ˈflɔɪd/ (Charles Arthur Floyd 1901–34) a US criminal who robbed banks in the Midwest during the *Great Depression and was for a time 'Public Enemy Number One'. Some Americans admired him because he gave money to poor people, but he also murdered about ten men, including two *FBI officers. He was finally killed by the FBI in a field of corn in Ohio.

ˈ**fly-**ˌ**fishing** *n* [U] the sport of fishing in rivers or lakes using artificial flies of various types at the end of the line instead of live bait such as worms. The flies float on the surface of the water, instead of sinking like worms, and are attractive to salmon and trout. Fly-fishing requires a lot of skill, and it is considered a higher-class sport than using live bait.

artificial flies used for fly-fishing

ˌ**Flying** ˈ**Fortress** *n* the popular name for the B-17, a type of US plane that dropped bombs during *World War II.

the ˌ**Flying** ˈ**Scotsman** /ˈskɒtsmən; *AmE* ˈskɑ:tsmən/ a British steam railway engine, built in 1923, which was the fastest of its kind for many years. It was used mainly on trains travelling between London and Edinburgh until 1963. It is still driven on private railways by people who are interested in old trains.

the ˈ**Flying Squad** a department of the British *Metropolitan Police that deals with serious crimes, especially armed robbery. The name indicates that the department's officers are ready to move quickly to the scene of a crime. It is known officially as SO8, or branch 8 of the Specialist Operations Department, and informally as the *Sweeney: *He was arrested by armed Flying Squad officers in a raid this morning.*

ˌErrol ˈ**Flynn** /ˌerəl ˈflɪn/ (1909–59) an Australian actor who became famous as the strong and handsome hero of many *Hollywood adventure films. He is particularly remembered for roles that required him to run, jump, fight, etc., such as *The Adventures of Robin Hood* (1938). Flynn was also famous for his many affairs with women.

ˌMichael ˈ**Foale** /ˈfəʊl; *AmE* ˈfoʊl/ (1957–) a US astronaut, born in Britain. In 1997 he travelled on the space shuttle (= spacecraft that can be used again) *Atlantis* to join the Russian space station Mir, where he spent 145 days before returning to earth.

ˌ**Foggy** ˈ**Bottom** an area of low land in *Washington, DC, by the *Potomac River, on which the US *State Department buildings are situated. The name is also used to refer to the *State Department itself, and journalists often joke that this is a good name for the Department, because the information it gives them is 'foggy', i.e. not clear.

folk dancing

Folk dances are traditional dances in which everyone can take part. They are danced to folk tunes and have sequences of **steps** that are repeated several times. Dances are performed by pairs of dancers often arranged in **sets** (= groups of six or eight people). Dancers move up and down the set and change partners. The dancing is often very fast. A **caller** usually **calls** the steps during the dance. In England folk dances are now danced mainly by people who belong to a **country dancing** club, or at **barn dances** held in a village hall.

Many English villages have ***morris dancing** teams. Morris dancing is usually performed on *village greens or outside country *pubs on *May Day and throughout the summer. The dancers dress in white and wear sets of small bells at the knee. Dances consist of a series of jumps and hops. As they dance the dancers often wave handkerchiefs in the air. In some dances they carry a stick which they strike against that of their partner. Themes of the dances include death and rebirth in nature. In some dances mythological characters like the *Green Man appear. Sometimes dancers paint their faces black, perhaps reflecting the possible origin of morris dancing in Moorish dance. The music is provided by a fiddle (= violin) or accordion.

Another variety of English folk dance, also performed on May Day, is ***maypole dancing**. Children often take part. Each dancer holds the end of a long ribbon, which is attached to the top of a brightly painted maypole. The ribbons are woven round the maypole as the dancers dance round each other. Some towns have their own folk dance: for example, the **Furry Dance**, or **Floral Dance**, is danced through the streets of Helston in Cornwall.

Scottish dances are usually danced to the music of the *bagpipes or a fiddle at a **ceilidh** (= an evening of dancing, music and, formerly, story-telling). Traditionally they are performed in Scottish national dress, with men wearing kilts and women in plain dresses. Some people go to **Scottish dancing** classes as a hobby. The best-known Scottish dance is the ***Highland fling**, which is usually performed by one man alone. The **sword dance** is performed by one or two dancers over two crossed swords. Popular dances for groups of people are the **Gay Gordons** and the **Eightsome Reel**.

Ireland has a similar ceilidh tradition. In **Irish dancing** the dancers do not move the upper part of their body. In recent years there has been greater interest in Irish folk dancing resulting from the *Riverdance* stage show. In Irish **clog-dancing**, the dancers wear clogs (= heavy wooden shoes) with which they strike the floor.

***Line dancing**, which comes from the US, is also popular in Britain. In the US itself there are folk dances from many different countries, brought by people when they settled there. But the best-known kind of folk dancing is **square dancing**, which has its origins in various dances from Britain. Square dancing was an important part of social life in the days when people were moving west. On Saturday evenings people would gather in a barn for a dance. As in English country dancing there was a caller, and the dancers danced to the music of a fiddle. Most square dances start and finish with couples standing in a square, but some, like the **Virginia Reel**, involve people standing in two lines. American children still learn square dancing, but very few adults now do it.

ˈ**folk museum** *n* a museum that displays interesting or historical objects that were part of the local people's everyday lives, such as clothes and tools. Many British towns and cities have folk museums. Similar museums exist in the US but they are not often called folk museums.

folk music and songs

Traditional British folk music has many different forms, including songs and **ballads**. Many **folk songs** relate to the lives of ordinary people in past centuries; others tell of famous love stories or celebrate nature. The verses may be sung by one voice alone, with the choruses sung by everyone present. Some folk songs are learned at school and are familiar to everyone, e.g. **Greensleeves*, *The *Ash Grove*, **Green Grow the Rushes O* and **Auld Lang Syne*, which is always sung at *New Year. In Wales and Ireland a *harp may sometimes be used to accompany the singing, but most songs are now accompanied by a guitar or piano.

A lot of instrumental folk music comes from Scotland and Ireland and ranges from laments on the *bagpipes to lively dance tunes. Most dance music is traditionally played on the fiddle (= violin). Irish folk bands usually have flutes, tin whistles, string instruments, pipes and a bodhrán (= an Irish drum).

American folk music was created by the combination of many folk styles brought to America by immigrants. Music helped keep alive the traditions and memories of people's former homes.

From the late 19th century many songs and tunes that had been passed down orally were collected together and written down. In America more than 10 000 songs were collected by John and Alan Lomax, and in Britain Cecil Sharp (1859–1924) collected both songs and *folk dances. Such collections influenced major works by composers such as Vaughan *Williams and *Britten. Dvořák used American folk music in his symphony *From the New World* (1893), as did *Copland in *Appalachian Spring* (1944).

In the US the *Carter Family helped make folk music popular again in the 1920s. By the 1950s the recording industry had made folk music commercially successful. This interest in folk music also led to **folk clubs** being established all over the US.

In the 1960s other styles developed, including the ***bluegrass** of Bill Monroe and the ***country music** of Hank *Williams. The most important was ***folk rock** which combined traditional folk music with features of rock and pop. Popular folk-rock groups in Britain have included *Fairport Convention, the Spinners and Pentangle. The US created urban folk music which used the problems of cities as subjects for folk songs. By the 1960s, folk music was being used to encourage social change and it became the music of *hippies and the *civil rights movement. A new generation of singer-songwriters emerged, including Joan *Baez, Bob *Dylan, Richard Thompson and Dick Gaughan. **Folk festivals** were popular. In 1963, just before the *Vietnam War, performers at the Newport, Rhode Island festival included Bob Dylan, Pete *Seeger, and Peter, Paul and Mary. They attacked the prejudices of society and the violence of war in songs such as *Blowin' in the Wind*, *The Times They Are a Changin'* and *If I Had a Hammer*.

Folk music is still very popular. In Britain folk festivals are held regularly at Cropredy near *Banbury, and at *Warwick and *Cambridge. Many towns still have a folk club for amateur singers and musicians, which meets regularly in a local *pub.

ˌ**folk ˈrock** *n* [U] a type of *rock music in which groups with electric instruments perform traditional folk songs with a strong beat, sometimes also using traditional instruments such as flutes and violins. Folk rock was popular in Britain and America in the 1960s and 1970s. Many folk-rock songs by singers such as Bob *Dylan contained social and political comments about life in that period, such as protests against the *Vietnam War.

ˌ**follow-my-ˈleader** (*AmE* **follow-the-leader**) *n* [U] a children's game in which one player is the 'leader' and the others must do exactly what the leader does, such as jumping, holding out their hands, etc. The phrase is sometimes used to refer to people who do what they are told to do without thinking about it: *Most of them simply played follow-the-leader without adding anything to the debate.*

ˌHenry ˈ**Fonda**[1] /ˈfɒndə; *AmE* ˈfɑːndə/ (1905–82) a US actor who often played calm, honest characters. He was a *Hollywood star for more than 40 years in over 100 films, but won only one *Oscar, for his last film, *On Golden Pond*. His other successes included *The *Grapes of Wrath* (1939), *Mister Roberts* (1955) and *Twelve Angry Men* (1957).

ˌJane ˈ**Fonda**[2] /ˈfɒndə; *AmE* ˈfɑːndə/ (1937–) a US actor also known for her strong political opinions and her successful video of physical exercises for keeping fit. She won *Oscars for *Klute* (1971) and *Coming Home* (1978). Her other films include *Barbarella* (1968) and *On Golden Pond* (1981), the only film she made with her father Henry *Fonda. Fonda was once called 'Hanoi Jane' because of her long campaign against the *Vietnam War. She is married to Ted *Turner.

ˌPeter ˈ**Fonda**[3] /ˈfɒndə; *AmE* ˈfɑːndə/ (1939–) a US actor and director who is the son of Henry *Fonda and the brother of Jane *Fonda. His daughter Bridget Fonda (1964–) is also an actor. He became well known with the film **Easy Rider* but others, such as *Futureworld* (1976) and *The Hired Hand* (1978), were less successful. In 1997 he made *Ulee's Gold* about a man who keeps bees, as Fonda's own father did.

ˌ**F-1 ˈvisa** /ˌef wʌn/ *n* an official US government document that allows people from other countries to enter the US as students.

ˌMargot **Fonˈteyn** /ˌmɑːɡəʊ fɒnˈteɪn; *AmE* ˈmɑːrɡoʊ fɑːnˈteɪn/ (1919–91) a British ballet dancer who became internationally famous for the natural way in which she expressed emotions in her dancing. She is best remembered for her performances with Rudolf *Nureyev in the ballets directed by Frederick *Ashton in the 1960s.

Margot Fonteyn and Rudolf Nureyev in Giselle

Food ⇨ article.

the ˌ**Food and ˈDrug Adminiˌstration** ⇨ FDA.

The ˈ***Food ˌProgramme*** a *BBC radio programme about food. As well as discussing different dishes and styles of cooking, it also investigates the relationships between food and health, e.g. reporting on the dangers of some chemicals that are added to food. It has been broadcast regularly since 1979.

ˈ**food stamp** *n* [usu pl] (in the US) a small piece of printed paper that can be exchanged for food in shops. The government gives food stamps to people who are unemployed and have very little money: *Families receiving food stamps will not be affected by the cuts.*

ˌMichael ˈ**Foot** /ˈfʊt/ (1913–) a British *Labour politician. He was *Secretary of State for employment (1974–6), *Leader of the House of Commons (1976–9) and leader of the Labour Party from 1980 to 1983, when Labour lost a general election. He is well known for his left-wing views such as his opposition to nuclear weapons, but he is respected by both sides of British politics as a thinker, speaker and writer.

the ˈ**Football Assoc̩iˌation** (*abbr* the **FA**) a British organization that was established in 1863 to decide the rules of the game of *football. It is responsible for the *FA Cup competition, and for all English international and non-professional football. It also controls the *Premier League, which a group of top professional clubs joined in 1992.

the ˌ**Football ˈLeague** a British *football competition in which each team in a particular division plays each other team twice. At the end of the season, the team with the most points is the champion of the division. The League was established in 1888 because the *Football Association did not allow professionals to enter its competitions. It was the major competition in English football until the top clubs left to form the FA *Premier League in 1992.

football – American style

Football is one of the major sports in the US. In Britain and elsewhere the game is often called **American football** to distinguish it from soccer. American football developed from the games of football and *rugby. There is a lot of dangerous play, so **helmets** and thick **pads** must be worn. Each game has **cheerleaders** and bands of musicians who march on the field between the **halves** of the game. Whole families go to watch games, and there is almost no violence from supporters. Many games are shown live on US television. British television now also shows some games each week. In US *high schools, colleges and universities, football games are the centre of many social events, such as *homecoming.

The game is played by two teams of 11 players

each, with different players used for **defense**, **offense** and **kicks**. The field is 100 yards (91.5 metres) long and 53 yards 1 foot (49 metres) wide. It is sometimes called a **gridiron** because the lines across it that mark every 10 yards (9 metres) make it look like the metal tray on which meat is grilled or broiled. At each end of the field there is an extra 10 yards (9 metres), called the **end zone**, with a **goal post** in the shaped of an 'H'. The ball is oval-shaped and sometimes called a **pigskin** because the balls were formerly made from pig's skin.

A team scores when its players send the ball down the field and across the opponent's **goal line** for a **touchdown** of seven points. They can then add a **point after touchdown (PAT)** if they kick the ball through the goal posts. A team can get three points if the ball is kicked between the goal posts without a touchdown, and two points if their defense stops the opponents in their own end zone.

The team with the ball must move it 10 yards (9 metres) in four **downs** (= separate actions). This is done from behind **linemen** who face the defense's linemen. An action begins when the **quarterback** takes the ball from between the legs of the **center** and runs with it, hands it to another runner or **passes** (= throws) it to another player. Between actions, the team with the ball has a **huddle** so the quarterback can tell them what to do next. If 10 yards (9 metres) are not made in 4 downs, the team must **punt** (= kick the ball to the other team). The defense can also get the ball by an **interception** (= a catch of the opponent's pass) or a **fumble** (= a ball accidentally dropped).

The **National Football League (NFL)** has 30 professional teams. Six teams in the ***American Football Conference** and six in the ***National Football Conference** play against each other to decide the two that will meet in the ***Super Bowl**. The *Dallas Cowboys and San Francisco 49ers have won it the most, five times each. Other well-known teams include the Green Bay Packers, the Miami Dolphins, the Pittsburgh Steelers and the Chicago Bears.

The best college teams play in **bowl games**, e.g. the *Rose Bowl, Sugar Bowl, Orange Bowl and Cotton Bowl. The best college players are chosen as ***All-Americans**. Famous professional players almost always play in college teams first. They have included Jim *Brown, Jim *Thorpe, Joe *Namath, and O J *Simpson.

football – British style

Football is the most popular sport in Britain, particularly amongst men. It is played by boys in most schools. Most towns have an amateur football team which plays in a **minor league**. Football is also the most popular **spectator sport** in Britain. Many people go to see their favourite professional team playing **at home**, and some go to **away matches**. Many more people watch football on television.

The rules of football are relatively simple: two teams of 11 players try to get a round ball into the opposing team's **goal** and to prevent their opponents from scoring. The ball may be kicked or **headed**, but never handled, except by the **goalkeepers**. The *Football Association was founded in 1863 to decide the rules of football and the resulting game became known formally as **association football**. It is sometimes also called **soccer**. Many of today's leading **clubs** were established shortly afterwards.

Most professional clubs represent large cities, especially in the north of England, where interest in football is strongest, or parts of London. They include *Everton, Leeds United, Liverpool, *Manchester United, *Arsenal, *Chelsea and *Tottenham Hotspur. The most famous Scottish clubs include *Rangers and *Celtic. In 1992 football was reorganized so that the best 22 teams in England and Wales play in the ***Premier League**, while 70 other teams play in three **divisions**, run by the *Football League. Scotland has a *Premier Division and three lower divisions. At the end of each season, the top few teams in each division are **promoted** and the bottom teams are **relegated**. As well as the **Premiership**, the main competitions are the *FA Cup and the **League Cup**. A few of the most successful sides have won **the Double**, i.e. both titles in the same year. The biggest clubs are now run as major businesses, and top players earn large salaries. They are frequently **transferred** between clubs for millions of pounds. Many foreign stars also now play for British teams.

England, Wales, Scotland and Northern Ireland all have their own national sides. England won the World Cup in 1966, when its stars included Bobby *Charlton, Bobby *Moore and Geoff *Hurst.

The number of people attending football matches has fallen steadily since the 1940s. An increase in **football hooliganism** in the 1970s and 1980s frightened many people away. English fans got a bad reputation in Europe and football violence became known as 'the English disease'. Disasters such as that at *Hillsborough, in which many people died, also discouraged people from going to matches. Formerly, football grounds had **terraces**, where supporters stood packed close together, and **stands** containing rows of seats which were more expensive. These grounds have now been replaced by **all-seater stadiums**, but people complain about the rising cost of tickets and the lack of atmosphere. Despite efforts by many clubs to attract family support, relatively few women are interested in the game. Many clubs have their own **fanzine** (= a magazine about the club written and published by the fans). Some supporters also buy a copy of their team's **strip** (= shorts and shirt in team colours).

This type of football is known in the US as soccer to distinguish it from the American game, and has only become popular there in the last few years. Enthusiasm increased after 1994 when the World Cup was played for the first time in the US. In 1996 **Major League Soccer (MLS)** was established, and teams compete for the **MLS Cup**. Students in colleges and universities also play soccer in three *NCAA divisions. The nation's oldest tournament is the US Open Cup. The US also has national teams for both men and women. About 18 million American children now play regularly, and the expression *soccer mom* (= a mother who spends much of her time at games) has entered the language.

ˈ**Foot Guards** *n* [pl] (in Britain) five infantry regiments (= large military groups of soldiers who fight on foot) whose historical duty has been to protect the king or queen. They are the *Grenadier Guards, the *Coldstream Guards, the *Scots Guards, the Irish Guards and the *Welsh Guards. They are considered the best soldiers of their kind in the British Army.

ˈ**Footsie** /ˈfʊtsi/ an informal name for the *FT-SE 100-Share Index. It is the best known of the *Financial Times Indices, giving the share values of the 100 largest British companies every day. It is used to indicate the state of the British financial markets: *The Footsie closed three points higher today at 2 850.*

ˌAnna ˈ**Ford**[1] /ˈfɔːd; *AmE* ˈfɔːrd/ (1943–) a British television and radio presenter. In 1978 she became the first woman to read the news on *ITV. She later moved to the *BBC and to *TV-am. She has been a

Food

Visitors to the US often think either that there is no real American food, only dishes borrowed from other countries, or else that Americans eat only ***fast food**. While there is some truth in both these impressions, real American food does exist.

The British also have a poor reputation for food. Visitors to Britain often complain that food in restaurants is badly presented, overcooked and has no taste. But the best British food is not generally found in restaurants but in people's homes.

British cooking

Certain foods are considered essential to traditional British cooking and form the basis of most *meals. These include bread, pastry (for meat or fruit pies) and dairy products such as milk, cheese and eggs. Potatoes, especially **chips** (*AmE* **fries**), are eaten at lunch or dinner. They are an important part of the traditional meal of **meat and two veg** (= meat, potatoes and another vegetable). A **jacket potato** (= a potato baked whole in its skin) with cheese is a popular *pub lunch. Because of the increased cost of meat and various health scares many people now eat less meat. **Vegetarians** (= people who choose not to eat meat at all) and **vegans** (= people who eat no meat or animal products) are relatively few. After the main course, many families eat a **pudding**. This was traditionally sponge or pastry cooked with jam or fruit, usually served hot with *custard, but it may now be yogurt, fresh fruit or ice cream.

Good plain home cooking, i.e. food prepared without spicy or creamy sauces, used to be something to be proud of. Since the 1970s British people have become more adventurous in what they eat and often cook foreign dishes. Rice, pasta and noodles are regularly eaten instead of potatoes. Supermarkets offer an expanding range of foreign foods, including many **convenience foods** (= prepared meals that need only to be heated). **Takeaways** from Indian or Chinese restaurants are also popular.

People's interest in trying new **recipes** is encouraged by the many cookery programmes on television. Famous TV **chefs** include Delia *Smith and Ainsley Harriott. Few older men know how to cook, but many younger men share the cooking as well as other household chores.

Food in America

American dishes include many made from traditional foods. **Corn** is eaten as **corn on the cob**, which is boiled and eaten hot with butter, ground up into small pieces and cooked again to make **grits**, or baked to make **cornbread**. It can be dried and cooked with oil to make **popcorn**, which is eaten hot covered with melted butter and salt. **Turkey** was originally an American bird and is the most important dish at *Thanksgiving. It is served with a sauce made from an American plant, the **cranberry**, a small, red, sour berry, and is usually followed by **pumpkin pie**. The **hamburger** may also come from the US. The ***sandwich**, originally from Britain, is made with great variety in America.

Many of America's most popular dishes have been borrowed from other cultures. This **ethnic food** is not always the same in the US as in the country it comes from. Many popular dishes come from Italy, especially pasta dishes and pizza. From Mexico there are burritos, tacos and enchiladas; from China there are egg rolls, chop suey and egg foo yong; and from Japan sushi and teriyaki.

When Americans make food at home they rarely use basic **ingredients** (= raw foods). Cakes, for example, are often made from **cake mixes** bought in a box. They also use many **prepared foods** (= meals that need only to be heated). Americans also often **order in** (= have a meal delivered to their home by a restaurant).

In the 1980s younger people especially became more interested in food. These **foodies** helped to increase the variety of dishes and ingredients available in America. Olive oil became commonly used in cooking, and new sauces were developed for pasta. Many styles of real coffee also became popular.

Eating out

When British and American people eat out (= in a restaurant), they can choose from a wide range of eating places. The busiest tend to be **burger bars**, **pizzerias** and other **fast-food outlets** which are popular with young people and families. In Britain these have largely replaced traditional cafés selling meals like sausage, egg and chips, though most towns still have several ***fish and chip shops**. Many *pubs also serve reasonably priced meals.

Many people eat out at Italian, Mexican and Chinese restaurants and at **curry houses**. Fewer people go to smarter, more expensive restaurants. With the great variety of food available at relatively low prices, eating out is common.

Food and health

In Britain the government regularly gives advice about **healthy eating**. The main aim is to reduce the amount of fatty foods and sugar people eat, and to encourage them to eat more fruit and vegetables. Many people still enjoy a **fry-up** (= fried bacon, sausage and egg with fried bread) but there has been a gradual move towards eating healthier low-fat foods. Health risks connected with, for example, beef or eggs, are discussed by the media. People are also concerned about chemicals sprayed onto crops. Supermarkets sell **organic produce** (= cereals and vegetables grown without the use of chemicals), but few people are prepared to pay the higher prices for this.

Americans believe food has an important effect on their health but they do not always eat in a healthy way. Many eat **junk food**, including fast food, **snacks** like potato chips (*BrE* crisps) and cookies (*BrE* biscuits), fizzy drinks and ice cream. Some people eat mainly **health foods**. They take **vitamin** and **mineral supplements** and rush to eat the latest foods said to be healthy, like olive oil, oats and garlic. Americans always seem to be fighting a battle between what they want to eat and what is good for them. Most Americans weigh too much, so it seems that they still mostly eat what they want.

regular member of the team presenting **Today* on BBC radio.

ˌBetty ˈ**Ford**[2] /ˈfɔːd; *AmE* ˈfɔːrd/ (1919–) the wife of Gerald *Ford. She had an successful operation for breast cancer in 1974 and discussed it publicly to help people to understand the disease better. She also had problems with alcohol and medical drugs but was cured and later helped to establish the **Betty Ford Clinic** for people with similar problems. She received the *Presidential Medal of Freedom in 1991.

ˈFord ˈMadox ˈ**Ford**[3] /ˈfɔːd ˈmædəks ˈfɔːd; *AmE* ˈfɔːrd/ (1873–1939) an English writer. He wrote many novels, poems and critical studies (= books judging the qualities of works of literature, etc.), and worked with Joseph *Conrad on two novels, *The Inheritors* (1901) and *Romance* (1903). His best-known novels, *The Good Soldier* (1915) and the series of four *World War I novels together called *Parade's End* (1924–8), are carefully written studies of the English *upper classes in changing times.

ˌGerald ˈ**Ford**[4] /ˈfɔːd; *AmE* ˈfɔːrd/ (1913–) the 38th US *President. He was a *Republican(1) who was Vice-president under Richard *Nixon and replaced him in 1974, after *Watergate. Ford was criticized for giving Nixon a pardon (= official notice forgiving somebody) for Watergate. Ford could not change the poor economic condition of the US at that time, and he lost the next election in 1976 to Jimmy *Carter.

ˌHarrison ˈ**Ford**[5] /ˌhærɪsn ˈfɔːd; *AmE* ˈfɔːrd/ (1942–) a US actor whose films have earned more money (over $2 billion) than those of any other actor. The National Association of Theater Owners named him 'Star of the Century' in 1994, and in 1997 readers of *Empire* film magazine voted him Britain's favourite film star of all time. Ford often plays strong, calm characters, especially in adventure films. He first became well known as Han Solo in the **Star Wars* films and as *Indiana Jones. His other films have included *Witness* (1985), *The *Fugitive* and *Air Force One* (1997), in which he played a US president.

ˌHenry ˈ**Ford**[6] /ˈfɔːd; *AmE* ˈfɔːrd/ (1863–1947) the American who created the Ford car and changed the motor industry by introducing new ways of making cars in great numbers. He began the **Ford Motor Company** in 1903 and five years later produced the first *Model T. He became very rich and successful, and established the international *Ford Foundation. He is also famous for having said that 'history is bunk', meaning that it is not a true summary of what actually happened.

ˌJohn ˈ**Ford**[7] /ˈfɔːd; *AmE* ˈfɔːrd/ (1586–*c.* 1639) an English writer of plays and poems. His writing is well known for its strong descriptions of sadness and despair (= loss of hope). His best-known play is *'Tis Pity She's a Whore* (1633).

ˌJohn ˈ**Ford**[8] /ˈfɔːd; *AmE* ˈfɔːrd/ (1895–1973) a US film director, especially of *westerns. He received four *Oscars, for *The Informer* (1935), *The *Grapes of Wrath*, **How Green Was My Valley* (1941) and *The Quiet Man* (1953). Ford made about 125 films, many of them with his favourite actor John *Wayne. These included *Stagecoach* (1939), *Fort Apache* (1948) and *The Searchers* (1956).

the ˈ**Ford Foun**ˌ**dation** /ˈfɔːd; *AmE* ˈfɔːrd/ one of the world's largest public trusts (= organizations providing money for projects that help society). It was established in the US in 1936 by Henry *Ford and his son Edsel Ford for the state of *Michigan, and in 1950 it became a national and international organization. By 1997, it had given or lent over $8 billion, especially to projects for democracy, world peace and justice, education and the arts, science and communication. The Foundation also helped to establish the US *Public Broadcasting Service.

the ˌ**Ford** ˈ**Motor** ˌ**Company** /ˌfɔːd; *AmE* ˌfɔːrd/ a large US company that makes cars. It was established in *Detroit in 1903 by Henry *Ford, and the first *Model T was sold in 1908. The company has produced the Lincoln since 1922 and the Mercury since 1938. It became the main owner of *Aston Martin Lagonda in 1987 and bought *Jaguar Cars in 1990. It also owns the *Hertz Corporation, the world's largest company that rents cars. The Ford Motor Company had produced 250 million Ford cars by 1996.

the ˌ**Foreign and** ˈ**Commonwealth** ˌ**Office** the British government department responsible for relations with other countries. The Foreign Office and the Commonwealth Office used to be two different departments. They were joined together in 1968, but many people still refer to it as the Foreign Office. Compare HOME OFFICE.

the ˌ**Foreign Re**ˈ**lations Com**ˌ**mittee** a committee of the US *Senate that studies the American government's policy towards other countries, and offers advice and criticism.

the ˌ**Foreign** ˈ**Secretary** (*full title* **Secretary of State for Foreign and Commonwealth Affairs**) the British government minister in charge of the *Foreign and Commonwealth Office. It is one of the most important jobs in the government. The Foreign Secretary represents Britain at many international meetings, and discusses foreign policy with the *Prime Minister.

the ˈ**Foreign** ˌ**Service** all the officials who work in US embassies and consulates in other countries.

ˌGeorge ˈ**Foreman** /ˈfɔːmən; *AmE* ˈfɔːrmən/ (1949–) a US boxer who became the oldest heavyweight champion ever in 1994 at the age of 45 when he beat Michael Moorer. The next year, his title was taken away from him when he refused to fight Tony Tucker. Foreman was also champion from 1973 to 1974 and won a gold medal at the 1968 Olympics.

ˌC S ˈ**Forester** /ˈfɒrɪstə(r); *AmE* ˈfɔːrəstər/ (Cecil Scott Forester 1899–1966) an English writer, best known for his historical novels about life in the *Royal Navy. He created the famous character Horatio *Hornblower, and wrote 12 novels about his adventures at sea during the *Napoleonic Wars.

ˌ**Forest** ˈ**Lawn** a large US cemetery in Glendale, *California, near *Los Angeles. Its full name is Forest Lawn Memorial Park. Many *Hollywood stars are buried there. Copies of several famous British churches have also been built among the graves.

the ˌ**Forest of** ˈ**Arden** /ˈɑːdn; *AmE* ˈɑːrdn/ ⇨ ARDEN.

John Ford directing My Darling Clementine

the ˌ**Forest of ˈDean** /ˈdiːn/ a forest in south-west England containing many very old oak and beech trees. In 1938 it became Britain's first *forest park.

ˌ**forest ˈpark** *n* (*BrE*) an area of British forest that has been made into a park for the public to enjoy. Like *national parks, forest parks are usually large areas of attractive country with marked paths and special areas for camping.

the ˈ**Forestry Comˌmission** /ˈfɒrɪstri; *AmE* ˈfɔːrɪstri/ a British government organization that manages all the forests that are owned by the state. It is responsible for cutting down old trees, planting new ones, controlling diseases, and managing the *forest parks. It also gives help and advice to private owners of forest land.

For ˈHe's a ˈJolly Good ˈFellow a song that people sing to praise somebody who has done something that they admire. If the person is a woman, they sing *For She's a Jolly Good Fellow*. The song is usually sung without being planned or prepared, and the person is sometimes carried on the shoulders of the people singing. The words are:

For He's a jolly good fellow,
For He's a jolly good fellow,
For He's a jolly good fellow,
And so say all of us.

formal and informal dress

In general, people in Britain and the US dress fairly informally. Many wear **casual clothes** most of the time, not just when they are at home or on holiday. Men and women wear ***jeans** or **cords** (= corduroy trousers) with a shirt or T-shirt and a sweater to go shopping, meet friends, go to a pub or bar, or take their children out. **Leggings** (= women's trousers that stretch to fit tightly) or **jogging pants** are also popular. Older people are more likely to dress more smartly, with women wearing a dress or skirt and blouse, and men a shirt, jacket and trousers, when they go out. In summer younger people may wear shorts (= short trousers/pants), but some people think they are only appropriate on the beach. When the weather is hot some men take off their shirts, though some people do not like this.

Most people in Britain **dress up** (= put on smart clothes) to go to a party or restaurant. Some restaurants will not let in people who are wearing jeans, or men without a tie. People sometimes talk of **putting on their glad rags**, wearing **their Sunday best**, or being **dressed to the nines**. Many people do not now dress up to go to the theatre, as was once common, but prefer to wear casual or office clothes. Young people are most interested in following *fashion and regularly buy new clothes to wear when they go out with their friends.

Men wear **lounge suits**, and women wear suits or dresses, for formal occasions like funerals or interviews for jobs. Some wear suits or smart clothes every day because their employer expects it or because they think it makes them look more professional. In London many *City businessmen wear **pinstripe suits** made of dark cloth with narrow grey vertical lines. Most people prefer casual, comfortable clothes for work but some companies do not like people wearing jeans. Employees in banks and some shops have smart uniforms.

People tend to dress less formally in the US than in Britain. Americans believe that people should be judged according to how they behave, not how they dress. Jeans are worn on many occasions, including at dinner in a restaurant, and sometimes even to work. But many Americans wear formal clothes for work. Men wear dark suits and women wear skirts or dresses in brighter colours, or occasionally trouser suits. It is acceptable to wear informal clothes in very hot weather, and some employees are allowed to dress more informally on Fridays than during the rest of the week. People also dress more informally in the western US than in the east.

For formal occasions during the day, such as a wedding, men may wear **morning dress**. This includes a jacket with long 'tails' at the back, dark grey trousers and a grey top hat. Women wear a smart dress and often a hat. For formal events in the evening, men may wear **evening dress**, also called **white tie**, which consists of a black tailcoat, black trousers, a grey waistcoat, white shirt and white bow tie. Women usually wear a long evening dress or ball gown. For less formal evening events men wear **black tie**, consisting of a black dinner jacket, black trousers and a black bow tie.

ˌMilos ˈ**Forman** /ˌmiːlɒs ˈfɔːmən; *AmE* ˌmiːlɑːs ˈfɔːrmən/ (1932–) a US film director who was born in Czechoslovakia and moved to America in 1968. His films include *The Fireman's Ball* (1967), **One Flew Over the Cuckoo's Nest* (1975), *Ragtime* (1980) and *Amadeus* (1983), for which he won an *Oscar.

ˌGeorge ˈ**Formby** /ˈfɔːmbi; *AmE* ˈfɔːrmbi/ (1904–61) an English singer and comedy actor from *Lancashire. He began his career in *music-hall and later made many successful films. He always played a slightly silly character with a strong northern *accent and a big smile, and sang songs with sexual double meanings while playing the ukulele, an instrument like a small guitar.

ˈ**Formula** the word used to indicate different classes of cars that take part in international Grand Prix motor races. Formula One is the fastest class, Formula Two the second fastest, etc. The cars are built specially for these races, and the class that they are in is decided by factors such as the size of the engine and the weight of the car. Compare INDYCAR RACING.

ˌ***Forrest ˈGump*** /ˌfɒrɪst ˈɡʌmp; *AmE* ˌfɔːrɪst/ a US comedy film (1994), directed by Robert *Zemeckis, which won several *Oscars including Best Picture, Best Actor and Best Director. In its first year, it earned the third largest amount of any film ever ($330 million). Tom *Hanks plays Forrest, a mentally slow man from *Alabama who loves his mother, played by Sally *Field. He becomes successful because he speaks the truth. The film was especially popular because it showed that honesty and a simple life can bring happiness and other rewards.

ˌE M ˈ**Forster** /ˈfɔːstə(r); *AmE* ˈfɔːrstər/ (Edward Morgan Forster 1879–1970) an English writer of novels, short stories and essays. He is best known for his novels, which examine themes of understanding and friendship among the English *upper middle classes. His best-known works include **Howards End* (1910) and *A *Passage to India* (1924).

The ˈ***Forsyte ˌSaga*** /ˈfɔːsaɪt; *AmE* ˈfɔːrsaɪt/ a series of novels by John *Galsworthy, written between 1906 and 1921. They tell the story of Soames Forsyte, a lawyer, and his family from the 1880s to the 1920s. At the beginning they build a house in London, but after 40 years of difficult and complicated relationships there is nobody living in the house. The story was made into a successful television series in the 1960s.

ˌBruce ˈ**Forsyth**[1] /ˈfɔːsaɪθ; *AmE* ˈfɔːrsaɪθ/ (1928–) a English comedian and television presenter. He is best known for presenting game shows in which members of the public play games and win prizes, such as *The Generation Game*. He is also known for introducing his shows by saying, 'Nice to see you, to see you ... nice.' Another phrase he often uses is 'Didn't he (or she) do well?'

ˌFrederick **For'syth²** /fɔː'saɪθ; *AmE* fɔːr'saɪθ/ (1938–) an English writer of novels about international crime and politics, well known for their realistic details and exciting stories. They include *The Day of the Jackal* (1971) and *The Odessa File* (1972), both of which have been made into successful films.

Forth /fɔːθ; *AmE* fɔːrθ/ a river that flows through central Scotland into the North Sea. The long wide area of water where the Forth flows into the sea is called the **Firth of Forth**, and is well known for the *Forth Bridges.

the **ˌForth 'Bridge** /ˌfɔːθ; *AmE* ˌfɔːrθ/ **1** a railway bridge over the Firth of *Forth near *Edinburgh. It was built in 1890 and is considered one of the greatest engineering achievements of its period. Most British people know the story that it is always being painted, because when the painters have finished painting it from one end to the other, it is necessary to start at the beginning again: *Tidying up after the children is like painting the Forth Bridge.* **2** a road bridge that was built beside the Forth rail bridge in 1964. It is a suspension bridge (= a bridge hanging from cables supported by towers at each end) and one of the longest of its kind in the world.

the Forth Railway Bridge

ˌFort 'Knox /'nɒks; *AmE* 'nɑːks/ a military area in the state of *Kentucky where the US government keeps the nation's gold, in the US Gold Bullion Depository. It is famous for being impossible to enter because it has thick steel doors and is extremely well guarded: *The office security system is so complicated it's like trying to get into Fort Knox.*

ˌFortnum and 'Mason /ˌfɔːtnəm ənd 'meɪsn; *AmE* ˌfɔːrtnəm/ a large shop in *Piccadilly, London, which also contains a restaurant. It is famous for selling expensive and unusual food, and for its hampers, large boxes or baskets containing several different types of food and drink. The shop is considered one of the places in London where very rich people go. It is also popular with tourists.

ˌFort 'Sumter /'sʌmtə(r)/ the US fort on a small island in the harbour of *Charleston, *South Carolina, where the *Civil War began. Soldiers from South Carolina, led by General Beauregard, shot at the fort with cannons on 12 April 1861, and it surrendered the next day. The Union forces did not capture it again until 1865. Fort Sumter is now open to the public as a museum.

'Fort ˌTiconde'roga /ˌtɪkɒndə'rəʊgə; *AmE* ˌtɪkɑːndə'roʊgə/ an American fort built as Fort Carillon by the French in 1755 in north-east New York State. British forces captured it in 1759 in the *French and Indian War, and named it Fort Ticonderoga. During the *American Revolution, it was captured in 1775 by the Green Mountain Boys led by Benedict *Arnold and Ethan Allen, but the British under General John Burgoyne took it again in 1777. It is now a museum.

the **Fortune 500** /ˌfɔːtʃuːn faɪv 'hʌndrəd; *AmE* ˌfɔːrtjuːn/ a list showing the sales and profits of the 500 largest US companies which is published each year in the American business magazine *Fortune*. Companies want to be included because being a **Fortune 500 company** shows their importance.

ˌFort 'William /'wɪljəm/ a town in the southern *Highlands of Scotland. It takes its name from a fort built in 1655 and destroyed in 1866. It is now an important tourist centre.

ˌFort 'Worth /'wɜːθ; *AmE* 'wɜːrθ/ a city in the US state of *Texas. It is very close to *Dallas, and the Dallas-Fort Worth Airport is one of the largest in the world. Fort Worth contains the Texas Christian University, the Kimball Art Museum and the Cattleman's Museum, and its opera house and orchestra are well known. It is a centre for the oil, gas, electronics and aircraft industries. It was settled in 1843 and soon became the last stop for cattle being moved to *Kansas.

the **ˌForty-'Five** (*also* the **'45 Rebellion**) the second attempt by the Scottish *Jacobites to defeat the English and make the *Stuarts the kings of England and Scotland. This attempt, led by *Bonny Prince Charlie in 1745, was successful at first. The English forces were defeated at *Prestonpans and the Jacobites moved into England. They soon had to return to Scotland, however, and were finally defeated at *Culloden. See also FIFTEEN.

ˌforty-'niner *n* **1** any of the people who went to *California to look for gold during the *Gold Rush of 1849. **2 the Forty-Niners** [pl] the popular name for the *San Francisco professional football team.

42nd Street a *Hollywood musical film (1933) directed by Lloyd Bacon, with dances designed by Busby *Berkeley. A stage version opened on *Broadway in 1980. The film is about a Broadway producer whose musical star breaks an ankle. He has to use an unknown actor, but she is a great success. The title refers to a street in *Manhattan, New York City, in the heart of the city's theatre district.

For 'Whom the 'Bell 'Tolls a novel (1940) by Ernest *Hemingway. It is the story of a US volunteer who fights and dies in the Spanish Civil War. Before he dies he enjoys the love of a woman and the food, wine and friendship of the Spanish people, and considers that 'the world is a fine place and worth the fighting for'. A film version, with Gary *Cooper in the main part, appeared in 1943.

the **ˌFosbury 'flop** /ˌfɒzbri; *AmE* ˌfɑːzbri/ (in sport) a way of doing the high jump. The person jumps backwards over the bar with the legs following the upper body. It is named after the US athlete Dick Fosbury (1947–) who first used this method at the 1968 Olympics and won a gold medal. It is now widely used by other athletes.

ˌFosse 'Way (*also* the **Fosse Way**) /ˌfɒs; *AmE* ˌfɑːs/ a Roman road which crossed southern England from *Lincoln in the east to *Exeter in the south-west.

ˌJodie **'Foster¹** /'fɒstə(r); *AmE* 'fɑːstər/ (1962–) a US actor who has won *Oscars for *The Accused* (1988) and **Silence of the Lambs*. She was a child actor who became famous in **Taxi Driver*. Her more recent films have included *Sommersby* (1993) and *Contact* (1997), and she also directed *Home for the Holidays* (1995). She established her own production company, Egg Pictures, in 1990. When John Hinckley shot and wounded President Ronald *Reagan in 1981, he said he did it to impress Foster, because he loved her.

ˌNorman **'Foster²** /'fɒstə(r); *AmE* 'fɑːstər/ (1935–) an

English architect. He is well known for his 'high-tech' style (= using metal and glass to show the structure of a building instead of hiding it). His most famous buildings include the Sainsbury Centre for Visual Arts (1979) near Norwich, England, and the Hong Kong and Shanghai Bank (1986) in Hong Kong.

ˌStephen ˈ**Foster**[3] /ˈfɒstə(r); *AmE* ˈfɑːstər/ (1826–1864) a US writer of almost 200 popular songs, most of them about the US South. They are sometimes called *folk songs because they are so simple. Most were for *minstrel shows with words representing the speech of African Americans at that time. They include **Oh! Susanna*, **Old Folks at Home*, **Camptown Races*, **My Old Kentucky Home*, *Beautiful Dreamer* and *Old Black Joe*. Foster himself only visited the South once.

the ˌ**Founding ˈFathers** /ˌfaʊndɪŋ/ *n* [pl] the Americans who established the form of the US government at the Federal Constitutional Convention in *Philadelphia (1787) when they created and signed the *American Constitution. The best-known Founding Fathers are George *Washington, Thomas *Jefferson, Benjamin *Franklin, Alexander *Hamilton, John *Adams and James *Madison.

the ˌ**Fountain of ˈYouth** (in old stories) a spring of water that is believed to give youth to anyone who drinks it. In 1513, the Spanish explorer Juan *Ponce de León searched for it in America in an area that is now the state of *Florida. The city of Saint Augustine in that state has a 'Fountain of Youth' for tourists which, it is claimed, might have been the one he searched for.

ˌ**Fountains ˈAbbey** /ˌfaʊntənz/ a ruined abbey near Ripon in north-east England. It was built in 1132 and destroyed in the 16th century during the *Dissolution of the Monasteries. Many people visit the ruins, which have been well preserved in attractive countryside. They were made a *World Heritage Site in 1986.

Fountains Abbey

the ˌ**Four ˈFreedoms** four types of freedom that US President Franklin D *Roosevelt said were worth fighting for. They are freedom of speech and expression, freedom of worship, freedom from want (= the lack of basic needs) and freedom from fear. He said this during his *State of the Union Address to *Congress on 6 January 1941 nearly a year before the US entered *World War II. After the war, the Four Freedoms were included in the *United Nations Charter (= statement of the rights of people).

the ˌ**Four ˈHundred** the popular US name for members of high society in New York City. Other US cities also now use the expression.

ˌ***Four Quarˈtets*** a group of four poems by T S *Eliot, *Burnt Norton* (1935), *East Coker* (1940), *The Dry Salvages* (1941) and *Little Gidding* (1942). The poems contain Christian religious messages, and deal with themes such as time, nature, history and human experience. The titles refer to places that had a special meaning in Eliot's life or his Christian beliefs.

the ˌ**Fourteen ˈPoints** the 14 aims of the US at the end of *World War I, as presented by President Woodrow *Wilson to *Congress on 8 January 1918. They included a reduction in military weapons, freedom of the seas, free international trade and several land agreements, such as establishing an independent Poland. The Fourteen Points were used in preparing the *Treaty of Versailles. The *League of Nations was based on the last of them, which called for a general 'association of nations'.

the ˌ**Fourteenth Aˈmendment** /əˈmendmənt/ an *amendment to the *American Constitution, allowing former slaves to become US citizens. It also gave all Americans the right to 'due process of law' and to equal protection by the law. It was passed by *Congress in 1866 and received the approval of the states two years later.

the ˌ**Fourth of Juˈly** ⇨ INDEPENDENCE DAY.

ˈ***Four ˈWeddings and a ˈFuneral*** a British comedy film (1994) in which Hugh Grant plays a young man who falls in love with an American woman at a friend's wedding. They continue to meet at other weddings and social events, and although she marries somebody else, the film ends with them together. It was very popular in America, and made Hugh Grant famous there.

ˌJohn ˈ**Fowles** /ˈfaʊlz/ (1926–) an English writer who has written successful novels in a wide range of styles. These include *The Collector* (1963), a psychological crime novel, and *The Magus* (1966), a complicated and mysterious story about a young man on a Greek island. Fowles's best-known work is probably *The *French Lieutenant's Woman*.

ˈCharles ˈJames ˈ**Fox**[1] /ˈfɒks; *AmE* ˈfɑːks/ (1749–1806) an English *Whig(1) politician. For most of his career he was the *Leader of the Opposition, while *Pitt was *Prime Minister. He was a friend of the *Prince Regent and a supporter of ideas that shocked people at the time, such as the French Revolution, American independence and the ending of the slave trade. ⇨ article at SLAVERY.

ˌGeorge ˈ**Fox**[2] /ˈfɒks; *AmE* ˈfɑːks/ (1624–91) an English Christian religious leader. He established the *Society of Friends (the *Quakers) in the 1650s, after spending much of his life travelling and telling people about his belief that people should find God inside themselves. He was often put in prison for his beliefs.

ˌMichael J ˈ**Fox**[3] /ˈfɒks; *AmE* ˈfɑːks/ (1961–) a *Hollywood actor, born in Canada. He has often played teenage characters because he looks young. Fox was in the US television comedy series *Family Ties* (1982–9) before he became an international star in *Back to the Future, Parts 1, 2 and 3* (1985, 1989 and 1990). His later films have included *Doc Hollywood* (1991), *The American President* (1995) and *Mars Attacks!* (1996).

ˈ***Foxe's ˈBook of ˈMartyrs*** /ˈfɒksɪz ; *AmE* ˈfɑːksɪz/ (*also* ˈ***Acts and ˈMonuments of these ˈLatter and ˈPerilous ˈDays***) a book (1554) written by John Foxe (1516–87). It describes the deaths of the many British Protestants who were killed because of their religious beliefs when the Catholic *Mary I was queen. The book, with its frightening descriptions and illustrations, influenced many British people against *Roman Catholics.

Foyle's /fɔɪlz/ one of the largest bookshops in the world, on *Charing Cross Road, central London,

England. It was first established by the brothers William and Gilbert Foyle in 1906.

ˌA J ˈ**Foyt** /ˈfɔɪt/ (Anthony Joseph Foyt 1935–) a US driver of racing cars who has had great success in *IndyCar racing. He has won the *Indy 500 four times (1961, 1964, 1967 and 1977), a record shared only by Al *Unser. Foyt has been the US Auto Club Champion seven times.

FPO /ˌef piː ˈəʊ; *AmE* ˈoʊ/ (*in full* **Fleet Post Office**) the special post office system of the US Navy. Mail can be sent between navy bases and to ships quickly and at a reduced cost.

ˌClare ˈ**Francis** /ˈfrɑːnsɪs; *AmE* ˈfrænsɪs/ (1946–) an English writer and sailor, well known for sailing a yacht alone for long distances. In 1976 she became the fastest woman to sail across the Atlantic alone.

F

ˌJohn ˈ**Francome** /ˈfrænkəm/ (1952–) an English jockey. He was the most successful *National Hunt jockey in the early 1980s, and became *champion jockey seven times before retiring in 1985.

ˈ**franglais** /ˈfrɒŋgleɪ; *AmE* ˈfrɑːŋgleɪ/ *n* [U] (*humor*) a mixture of French and English words, from the French words *français* (French) and *anglais* (English). Many French people do not like franglais phrases such as 'le weekend' or 'le fair play' because they think that they are making the French language less pure, while other people have fun inventing new franglais phrases.

ˈ***Frankenstein*** /ˈfrænkənstaɪn/ a novel (1818) by Mary *Shelley. It is the story of a Swiss scientist, Dr Frankenstein, who makes a living creature from pieces of dead bodies. It is like a man, but stronger, and although it is gentle at first, it later attacks and kills Frankenstein. There have been many films based on the story and variations of it: *Everybody was dressed up as a ghost, a vampire or Frankenstein's monster.* See also KARLOFF.

Frankenstein's monster played by Boris Karloff

ˌFelix ˈ**Frankfurter** /ˈfræŋkfɜːtə(r); *AmE* ˈfræŋkfɜːrtər/ (1882–1965) a US Supreme Court judge (1939–62), born in Austria. He believed in 'judicial restraint', the idea that judges should not try to influence government policies through their decisions in courts of law. He helped to establish the *American Civil Liberties Union, taught at the Law School of *Harvard University (1914–39) and advised Presidents Woodrow *Wilson and Franklin D *Roosevelt. He received the *Presidential Medal of Freedom in 1963.

ˌ***Frankie and*** ˈ***Johnny*** an old US ballad about a woman who murders her lover and is hanged for the crime. In the story, Frankie sees Johnny with Alice Pry in a *Memphis hotel and shoots him three times. Most verses end with the line 'He was her man but he done her wrong.'

Aˌretha ˈ**Franklin[1]** /əˌriːθə ˈfræŋklɪn/ (1942–) an *African-American singer who has been called 'Lady Soul' and the 'Queen of Soul'. She won a *Grammy award every year from 1967 to 1974 and by 1997 had received 15, more than any other woman performer. Her best-known songs are *I Say a Little Prayer* (1967) and *Respect* (1968). In 1987 she was chosen for the Rock and Roll *Hall of Fame.

Benjamin Franklin, John Adams and Thomas Jefferson writing the Declaration of Independence, painted by Jean Ferris

ˌBenjamin ˈ**Franklin[2]** /ˈfræŋklɪn/ (1706–90) one of America's most famous *Founding Fathers. He was a wise and clever political leader, writer and printer, and a scientist who invented many things. Franklin helped to write the *Declaration of Independence, which he signed, and later the *American Constitution. In 1776 he went to France and persuaded the French to send money and military forces for the *American Revolution. Franklin proved that lightning is electricity by flying a kite in a storm, and his inventions included the Franklin Stove. He also published **Poor Richard's Almanack* (1732–57).

ˈ***Frasier*** /ˈfreɪʒə(r)/ a US television comedy series (1993–) on *NBC. It has won four *Emmy awards for the best comedy. The main character, Frasier Crane, is a psychologist who presents a radio advice programme. He first appeared as a character in the television comedy **Cheers*.

fraˈternity *n* a social organization for male students at many US colleges and universities. The members usually live in a house together and are called Greeks, because each fraternity takes as its name two or three Greek letters, such as Lambda Delta Chi. Fraternities do charity work but are sometimes criticized for their wild parties. Some fraternities are also concerned with academic achievement, such as *Phi Beta Kappa. Compare SORORITY.

the ˈ**Fraud Squad** a special British police department that investigates people who make money by deceiving other people: *The manager of the company is being questioned by Fraud Squad detectives.*

ˌJames ˈ**Frazer** /ˈfreɪzə(r)/ (1854–1941) a Scottish anthropologist. He is best known for writing *The *Golden Bough*, a study of many customs and religions. He had an important influence on the development of the science of anthropology in Britain, although most anthropologists now disagree with his ideas on the progress of human beliefs.

ˌ**Free** ˈ**Church** *n* any Christian religious group in Britain that is not part of the *Church of England or the *Roman Catholic Church. Such groups include the *Presbyterians, the *Baptists and the *Method-

Freedom and rights

Freedom of the individual is considered one of the essential features of western civilization, which is itself sometimes called the Free World. This freedom is often expressed in terms of rights to do certain things or to be treated in a particular way. When a person does something that others think strange, British and American people will often say, 'It's a free country,' meaning that although they disagree with the choice they recognize the other person's right to make it.

Americans sometimes call the US the 'land of the free', a phrase taken from its *national anthem. British people have always strongly defended their freedom and do not like being told what to do. The fear that they will lose the freedom to decide their own future is behind many people's lack of enthusiasm for European unity.

Constitutional rights

Many of the rights of US citizens are laid down in the ***Constitution** and the first ten *amendments to it, which are together called the ***Bill of Rights**. The Constitution was written in the late 1700s to explain not only how the US government would work, but also what limits there would be on its power. At that time, people were beginning to believe that the rights of individuals were important, and that the government was the main threat to those rights. Limiting the *federal government's power was also seen as necessary to protect the rights of states within the United States.

Britain does not have a written constitution or legal document describing the rights of individuals. Some legal experts believe that a bill of rights should be introduced. Without it, they argue, the rights of the individual will gradually be **eroded** (= reduced). To many British people, freedom to live without interference by the government is extremely important. Most take this freedom for granted and only realize how fortunate they are when they see people elsewhere being oppressed.

Personal freedoms

In Britain and the US the most basic rights include **freedom of expression** (= freedom to say or write anything), **freedom of choice** (= freedom to make decisions about your own life) and **freedom of worship** (= freedom to practise any religion).

Freedom of expression does not imply complete freedom for people to say what they like. In the US the *First Amendment protects freedom of speech and of the press but the courts, especially the *Supreme Court, decide how it should be applied. For instance, a newspaper is not allowed to print something bad about a person that is known not to be true: this is **libel**. The courts do not practise **prior restraint**, i.e. they cannot stop a newspaper from printing something, but they can punish the newspaper afterwards. However, in a few cases, e.g. when national security is involved, the courts may order newspapers not to print a report.

The right to free speech in the US has not always been respected. In the 1950s, when ***McCarthyism** was at its height, people who were suspected of being Communists were called before *Congress to answer questions. People who used their right to free speech and said they believed in Communism, or who ***took the Fifth**, i.e. used their right under the *Fifth Amendment not to give evidence against themselves, often lost their jobs or went to prison.

The Supreme Court has ruled that certain actions are **symbolic speech**. During the *Vietnam War some people burned the American flag to indicate their disagreement with the war. This was seen as symbolic speech and many Americans thought it should be limited.

Censorship of the press was ended in Britain in the 1960s, and newspapers and television companies are expected to behave responsibly. In 1988 the publication of Salman *Rushdie's novel *The Satanic Verses*, which was considered insulting by followers of Islam, led to a fierce debate about **freedom of artistic expression**. Some people thought the author had been foolish to write things which he knew would cause offence, but many strongly defended his right to free expression.

Legal rights

Many freedoms, such as freedom of choice, are linked with specific rights that can be enforced by law. These include the **right of equal opportunity** (= the right to be treated the same as others, regardless of race, sex, etc.). This right is enforced in Britain through *Race Relations Acts and the *Sex Discrimination Act. In the US the ***civil rights movement** of the 1960s influenced the making of new laws to protect the rights of minority groups, especially *African Americans. In 1972 an ***Equal Rights Amendment**, which would have given women the same rights and opportunities as men, failed to get the support of enough states to be passed. Later, however, several laws were passed making it illegal to discriminate against women.

People in Britain and the US have a much valued **right to privacy**. For instance, the police have to obtain permission to enter a person's house or stop them in the street without good cause. The US *Freedom of Information Act and the British *Data Protection Act allow a person access to information held about them on a computer and the opportunity to correct it if it is wrong.

If a person breaks the law he or she still has rights that the law is expected to defend. In the US several amendments to the Constitution deal specifically with the rights of people suspected or accused of a crime. In Britain, a person detained by the police has a right to be released if he or she is not charged within 24 hours. As in the US, people also have the **right to remain silent**. The police are heavily criticized if these rights are **infringed**.

In the US an individual's right to own weapons continues to cause disagreement. When this right was included in the Second Amendment, America had just finished fighting for independence. Since the US did not want to keep a permanent army its defence in the case of future attacks depended on ordinary people having weapons. Many people believe that since the US does now have a professional army individuals do not need guns, and that the interpretation of the amendment should take account of the modern situation. But others want to keep the right to have weapons and resist any changes to the law.

ists. Many people think of Free Church members as living strictly according to the rules of their church, e.g. not drinking alcohol and not working on Sundays.

the ˌ**Free Church of ˈScotland** /ˈskɒtlənd; *AmE* ˈskɑtlənd/ a large group of Scottish Protestants who left the *Church of Scotland in 1843 and established their own branch of the Christian religion because they did not agree with the way the Church of Scotland chose its priests. In 1929 most members of the Free Church joined the Church of Scotland again. Some members, especially in the *Highlands, remained independent, and they are often called the **Wee Frees**. (*Wee* is a Scottish word meaning small.).

Freedom and rights ⇨ article.

F

ˌ**freedom of asˈsembly** *n* [U] the right to have public meetings. This right became part of US law under the *First Amendment. In Britain, people are generally free to have public meetings but this freedom is not part of British law, and the government or the police can stop people from gathering if they wish.

ˌ**freedom of associˈation** *n* [U] the right to meet people and to form organizations without having to ask for permission from the government. People in America and Britain have this right.

ˌ**freedom of inforˈmation** *n* [U] the right to see any information that is held by the government. Under the *Freedom of Information Act, Americans are allowed to see government information about any person or organization. In Britain, the government can keep some information secret under the *Official Secrets Act, *D-notices and the *thirty-year rule. Many British people, and organizations such as Charter 88, demand more freedom of information.

the ˌ**Freedom of Inforˈmation Act** (*abbr* the **FOIA**) a US law that allows anyone to ask to see information kept by the government on a person or an organization. Such requests must be in writing and name specific documents. The law was passed in 1966 and strengthened in 1974, and journalists have often used it. Some personal files and information relating to national security (= the protection of the nation and its interests) are not included under the law. Individual states have similar laws. Compare OFFICIAL SECRETS ACT.

ˌ**freedom of reˈligion** *n* [U] the right to choose which religion to belong to, or to belong to no religion. This right became part of American law under the *First Amendment. In Britain, religious freedom was achieved gradually through a series of laws from the 17th century to the 19th century.

ˌ**freedom of ˈspeech** *n* [U] the right to express any opinions in public. This right became part of American law under the *First Amendment. If the opinions expressed are false or damage a person's reputation, however, that person can take legal action under US law. In Britain, people are free to express most opinions, but it is against the law to express some ideas, e.g. ideas that aim to cause racial hatred.

the ˌ**freedom of the ˈcity** *n* [U] an honour that a particular city gives to people. It is usually given to a famous person by the city that he or she lives in or was born in, or to a person who has done some good work for a city. It is a historical title, and does not give the person any special rights. In the US, a person who receives the freedom of the city is also given a large key as a symbol of the honour.

ˌ**freedom of the ˈpress** *n* [U] the right to publish news and opinions in the press without the government removing any of the information. This right became part of American law under the *First Amendment. In Britain the press is free to publish most types of information but the government can prevent newspapers and broadcasters from reporting some stories by using the *Official Secrets Act or *D-notices.

ˈ**freedom ˌriders** *n* [pl] (*AmE*) groups of black and white people from the northern US who in 1961 rode together in buses in the *Deep South as a protest against *segregation on public transport there. The first 'freedom rides' were organized by the *Congress of Racial Equality. The freedom riders were often attacked by angry crowds, but in November that year the *Interstate Commerce Commission legally ended segregation on buses.

ˈ**Freefone** /ˈfriːfəʊn; *AmE* ˈfriːfoʊn/ (in Britain) a special service provided by *BT which allows people to make free telephone calls to a company or organization. Freefone numbers begin with 0800. They are usually used by businesses to give people information or to sell their products on the telephone: *To place your order call Freefone 0800 567891.*

ˌ**free ˈhouse** *n* (in Britain) a pub that is not controlled by a particular beer company. Free houses are able to choose which beer they sell, and to sell more than one make of beer. Compare TIED HOUSE 1. ⇨ note at BEER.

Freemasonry

Freemasons, often called **Masons**, are members of a secret society for men, the **Free and Accepted Masons**, which is based on brotherly love, faith in the Supreme Being (= God) and good works.

Freemasonry, or **Masonry**, developed in Britain from *medieval **guilds** (= trade associations) of **masons** (= craftsmen) who travelled round the country. There was a guild for each craft. Its members were highly skilled master craftsmen and journeymen (= trained workers). Titles given to modern Masons reflect these origins. New members are admitted as **apprentices** and may go on to the higher rank of **fellowcraft** or **journeyman**, and finally **master mason**. Tools traditionally used by stonemasons are still used in the society's ceremonies.

During the 17th century the guilds became popular with rich gentlemen who gradually took them over. They developed into secret societies whose religious beliefs and practices provoked the hostility of many, including the *Roman Catholic Church. In 1717 the **Grand Lodge** was founded in London and became the most important branch of the society with authority over other branches or lodges. The Grand Lodge of Scotland was founded in 1736. There are now over 8 000 lodges in Britain, each in the charge of a **master**, with a total of about 750 000 Masons, and further branches in the US and other countries.

Most Masons today belong to the professional and middle classes and are lawyers, *civil servants, businessmen, etc., though members of the aristocracy and the royal family have also been Masons. The present Duke of *Kent is **Grand Master** of the Grand Lodge. In Britain, new members are only admitted at the invitation of existing Masons and have to go through a special **initiation** ceremony in which they promise not to tell anyone else the secrets of the society. It is commonly believed that they also learn special signs and words, and the Masons' **handshake**, which they can use in public to identify themselves to other Masons. In the US some of the details of Masonic practices are different: for example, people who wish to become Masons must ask to join, because Masons are not allowed to invite others to become Masons.

In Britain, because Masons keep their affairs secret, Freemasonry has often been viewed with suspicion. Many people believe that Masons in positions of power give other members of the society an unfair advantage. Masons themselves deny such practices and emphasize the social and charitable aspects of the movement. In the US there is a more tolerant attitude to Freemasonry. Perhaps the best known Freemasons in the US are a group called **Shriners**. Shriners are well known for their circuses which are held every year to raise money for charity work, including hospitals that the Shriners run.

Many other social clubs in the US which call themselves **fraternal organizations** have titles and ceremonies that are based on those of the Masons.

ˌ**free ˈpaper** *n* a free local newspaper that is delivered to people's homes every week. Most British and US towns and cities have free papers, which contain mostly advertisements and some local news. Many people dislike receiving them and ask for them not to be delivered to their homes.

ˈ**Freepost** /ˈfriːpəʊst; *AmE* ˈfriːpoʊst/ (in Britain) a special service provided by the *Post Office that allows people to post letters free to a company or organization. The company that receives the letter pays the cost.

ˌ**free ˈtrade** *n* [U] a system in which trade can take place between different countries without the payment of special taxes or other charges. After the end of the *Corn Laws in the 19th century Britain was in favour of free trade, but during the *Depression there were special charges on imports to protect local industry. In the late 20th century Britain joined free-trade organizations such as the *European Union.

During its history, the US has generally tried to protect its industries with charges on imports. Since *World War I, however, it has supported free trade, and in 1994 it began operating the *North American Free Trade Agreement with Canada and Mexico.

ˈ**freeway** *n* (*AmE*) a road for fast travel, with a limited number of places where drivers can join or leave it. ⇨ note at ROADS AND ROAD SIGNS.

ˌDawn ˈ**French** /ˈfrentʃ/ (1957–) an English comedy actor best known for appearing with Jennifer *Saunders in the television comedy series **French and Saunders*. She has also appeared in other television comedy series, including *Murder Most Horrid* (from 1991) and *The Vicar of Dibley* (from 1994). French is married to the comedy actor Lenny *Henry.

the ˈ**French and ˈIndian ˈWar** the part of the *Seven Years' War that was fought in America (1754–63). After a series of battles, the British forces defeated the French and Indians (*Native Americans), and the Treaty of Paris (1763) gave Britain all of Canada and much of the *Louisiana region that reached nearly to Canada. George *Washington was one of the British military leaders, and this war gave Americans the experience they needed to fight the *American Revolution.

ˌ***French and ˈSaunders*** /ˌfrentʃ ənd ˈsɔːndəz; *AmE* ˈsɔːndərz/ a series of popular British comedy television programmes written and performed by Dawn *French and Jennifer *Saunders in the 1980s and 1990s. The programmes consist of several short plays that make fun of modern life, films and other television programmes.

The ˈ***French Lieuˈtenant's ˈWoman*** a novel (1969) by John *Fowles. It is the story of a woman in a small town in England in the 19th century. She is not considered respectable because she has had a lover, a French soldier, who left her. A rich Englishman then falls in love with her. The book is written in a mixture of traditional and experimental styles, with a choice of two endings. It was made into a film in 1981, with Meryl *Streep and Jeremy *Irons.

the ˈ**French ˌQuarter** the old district of *New Orleans, *Louisiana. Local people sometimes call it the Vieux Carré (Old Square). It is next to the *Mississippi River and includes Bourbon Street, Rampart Street, Jackson Square and the French Market. The area is popular with tourists for its *jazz music, good food and buildings of Spanish and French architecture with decorative iron balconies.

ˈ**Fresno** /ˈfreznəʊ; *AmE* ˈfreznoʊ/ a city in the US state of *California. It is an international agricultural centre and produces many farm products, including grapes, wine, cotton, tomatoes and fruit. It also has oil and gas wells.

ˌLucien ˈ**Freud** /ˌluːsiən ˈfrɔɪd/ (1922–) a British artist, born in Germany. He is well known for his harshly realistic paintings of people which often make them look unpleasant. His grandfather was the Austrian psychiatrist (= specialist in the treatment of mental problems) Sigmund Freud.

ˈ**Friars Club** /ˈfraɪəz; *AmE* ˈfraɪərz/ a US club for people in the entertainment business. There are several around the country, but the most famous are in New York and *Los Angeles. They hold regular 'Stag Roasts', often on television, in which film or television stars sit among friends who make speeches with humorous insults about them.

ˌ**Friar ˈTuck** /ˌfraɪə ˈtʌk; *AmE* ˌfraɪər/ one of *Robin Hood's group of outlaws (= people who have broken the law and must hide to avoid being caught). According to the legend, he was a fat friar (= member of a Christian religious community) who enjoyed eating and drinking.

ˈ**Friday** (*also* ˌ**Man ˈFriday**) a character in Daniel *Defoe's novel **Robinson Crusoe*. He becomes Crusoe's faithful servant after Crusoe saves him from being eaten by cannibals. The phrase *Man Friday* or *Girl Friday* is sometimes used to describe an assistant who does many different jobs in an office.

ˌBetty ˈ**Friedan** /ˈfriːdən/ (1921–) a US writer and feminist (= a person who believes strongly that women should have the same rights and opportunities as men). She began the *National Organization for Women in 1966 and was its President until 1970. Her book *The Feminine Mystique* (1963) was an important influence on the *women's lib movement.

ˌMilton ˈ**Friedman** /ˌmɪltən ˈfriːdmən/ (1912–) a US economist who received the 1976 *Nobel Prize for Economic Science. He supports monetarism, the belief that a nation's economy is mostly affected by the control of the supply of money by its government. Friedman advised Presidents *Nixon and *Reagan.

ˈ**Friendly Soˌciety** (*also* **Provident Society**) (*BrE*) (*AmE* **benefit society**) *n* an association whose members regularly pay small amounts of money so that they can be cared for when they are ill or old. Friendly Societies first became common in Britain in the 18th century, and there are still several thousand of them in Britain and the US.

Friends a popular US television comedy series about six close friends in New York. It began in 1994. The characters are Monica, Rachel, Phoebe, Chandler, Ross and Joey. The stories are about the joys and problems of love, work and friendships.

ˌ**Friends' ˈMeeting House** (*also* **meeting house**) *n* a building where *Quakers have their religious meetings. Many Friends' Meeting Houses are also used for other functions such as public talks.

the ˌ**Friends of the ˈEarth** an international *pressure group which began in the US and aims to persuade people, companies and governments to do less damage to the environment. It has many members in America, Britain and other countries, and organizes a wide range of activities, from international campaigns to protect tropical forests to local communities' demands for clean water.

ˌFrigiˈdaire™ /ˌfrɪdʒɪˈdeə(r)/ *n* a US make of refrigerator. The name is sometimes used in America to refer to any kind of refrigerator, but there are also Frigidaire washing machines, dishwashers and other electrical household products.

the **Fringe** /frɪndʒ/ the performances at the *Edinburgh Festival that are not part of the official programme. These performances are usually more experimental than the official events, and are usually organized by small groups of people who are not well known, though some become famous after performing at the Fringe. See also *BEYOND THE FRINGE*.

F

EˌIisabeth **ˈFrink** /ˈfrɪŋk/ (1930–93) an English artist, well known for her sculptures in bronze, especially of the male figure and of birds and horses. She was made a *dame(2) in 1982.

Elisabeth Frink sculpting the head of Alec Guinness

ˈFrisco /ˈfrɪskəʊ; *AmE* ˈfrɪskoʊ/ a popular US name for *San Francisco.

ˌFrito-ˈLay™ /ˌfriːtəʊ ˈleɪ; *AmE* ˌfriːtoʊ/ a US company that makes a range of small potato and corn food products. They include Fritos, Doritos, Ruffles and Lay's.

From ˌHere to Eˈternity a novel (1951) by the US author James Jones (1921–77) about army life in *Pearl Harbor before the Japanese attack. It was made into a 1953 film which won *Oscars for Best Picture, Best Director (Fred *Zinnemann), Best Supporting Actress (Donna Reed) and Best Supporting Actor (Frank *Sinatra). The film is remembered especially because of a scene in which two of its other stars, Deborah Kerr and Burt *Lancaster, make love in the waves on a beach. This was regarded as rather shocking at the time.

ˈfrontiersman *n* (*pl* **frontiersmen**) a man who enters wild, unknown land or settles on the edge of it. In America, such people moved west in the 18th and 19th centuries and helped to increase the size of the United States. Famous frontiersmen include Davy *Crockett, Daniel *Boone, Kit *Carson and *Buffalo Bill.

ˌDavid **ˈFrost**[1] /ˈfrɒst; *AmE* ˈfrɑːst/ (1939–) an English television presenter. He first became famous during the 1960s when he presented the comedy news programme **That Was The Week That Was*. Since the 1960s he has had great success as a television journalist on both British and US television. He was made a *knight in 1993.

ˌRobert **ˈFrost**[2] /ˈfrɒst; *AmE* ˈfrɑːst/ (1874–1963) a US poet who won four *Pulitzer Prizes. He is best known for his poems about the countryside. From 1912 to 1915 Frost lived in England where he wrote *A Boy's Will* (1913). He then settled in the US state of *New Hampshire and wrote about *New England. His books of poetry include *A Witness Tree* (1942) and *In the Clearing* (1962).

ˈFrosties™ /ˈfrɒstiz; *AmE* ˈfrɑːstiz/ a well-known breakfast food, made by *Kellogg's and called Frosted Flakes in the US. It consists of small flat pieces of corn covered in sugar, and is eaten with milk. Its most famous advertising character is Tony the Tiger, who says, 'They're Gr-r-r-eat!'

FRS /ˌef ɑːr ˈes/ **1** ⇨ FEDERAL RESERVE SYSTEM. **2** ⇨ FELLOW OF THE ROYAL SOCIETY.

ˌFruit and ˈNut *n* [U] a popular British chocolate bar containing raisins and nuts, made by *Cadbury Schweppes: *Do you want a bit of Fruit and Nut?*

ˈfruit gum *n* [usu pl] (*BrE*) a small round British sweet/candy like a hard piece of jelly. Fruit gums are usually sold in a roll and have different fruit colours and flavours. They are especially popular with children. Older people remember the phrase 'Don't forget the fruit gums, mum!' which was used in advertisements.

ˌC B **ˈFry**[1] /ˈfraɪ/ (Charles Burgess Fry 1872–1956) one of the greatest English sportsmen of all time. He represented England in international *cricket, *football and athletics. He held the world record for the long jump for 21 years, and is one of only three people in the history of cricket to score 100 runs (= points) six times in a row.

ˌChristopher **ˈFry**[2] /ˈfraɪ/ (1907–) an English writer of plays in a form of poetry that is full of humour and rich language. They include *The Lady's Not For Burning* (1948) and *Venus Observed* (1950).

EˌIizabeth **ˈFry**[3] /ˈfraɪ/ (1780–1845) an English *Quaker who led many campaigns to improve the conditions of people in prison, especially women.

ˌStephen **ˈFry**[4] /ˈfraɪ/ (1957–) an English actor and writer who wrote and appeared in several British comedy television programmes in the 1980s and 1990s, often with Hugh Laurie as his partner. They became famous in 1989 with their own *BBC comedy series, *A Bit of Fry and Laurie*. Fry has also acted in films and written several novels, including *The Liar* (1991).

FT /ˌef ˈtiː/ ⇨ *FINANCIAL TIMES*.

the **FTC** /ˌef tiː ˈsiː/ (*in full* the **Federal Trade Commission**) an independent US government organization created in 1914 to protect free competition in business. It uses *antitrust legislation to prevent monopolies (= companies which are so large that no others can compete with them). It investigates unfair business practices and has the legal power to stop them and to take companies to a court of law. The FCT also controls labels on products and tries to stop false advertisements.

FT-SE 100-Share Index /ˌef tiː es ˈiː wʌn ˈhʌndrəd ˈʃeər ˌɪndeks/ ⇨ FOOTSIE.

The ***ˈFugitive*** a popular US television series (1963–7) on *ABC. The continuous story was about an innocent man, played by David Janssen, who is condemned to death for the murder of his wife, but escapes to find the person who killed her. The final show, in which the criminal is found, had the largest television audience in the 1960s. A film version was made in 1993, with Harrison *Ford in the main part.

ˈFulbright ˌscholarship /ˈfʊlbraɪt/ *n* any of a number of US scholarships (= awards of money for study) given for exchanges between US and foreign universities and colleges. Those who receive them are called **Fulbright scholars** and include students and teachers. The programme was established by the Fulbright Act (1946) of Senator J William Fulbright (1905–95), and it first used money from the sale of old US military equipment. About 200 000 scholarships had been awarded by 1997.

ˈ**Fulham** /ˈfʊləm/ **1** a district of west London on the north bank of the *Thames, west of *Chelsea, consisting mainly of houses. In the 1980s and 1990s it became a fashionable area to live in. **2** a football club whose ground is in the district of Fulham.

ˌ**Fulham** ˈ**Palace** /ˌfʊləm/ a large and grand house in *Fulham(1), London, built in the 16th century. It is the official home of the *Bishop of London.

ˈR ˈBuckminster ˈ**Fuller** /ˈɑː ˈbʌkmɪnstə ˈfʊlə(r); *AmE* ˈɑːr ˈbʌkmɪnstər ˈfʊlər/ (Richard Buckminster Fuller 1895–1983) a US engineer and inventor of devices and buildings that made the most efficient use of materials. His best-known inventions include the geodesic dome and the Dymaxion House. Fuller also created the idea of 'Spaceship Earth', which imagines all people on earth as travellers together through space. He was awarded the *Presidential Medal of Freedom in 1983.

Buckminster Fuller in front of a geodesic dome

The ˌ***Full*** ˈ***Monty*** /ˈmɒnti; *AmE* ˈmɑːnti/ a popular and successful British film (1997) about a group of unemployed working men in the north of England who get jobs as strippers (= performers who take their clothes off in front of an audience as a form of entertainment) because they cannot find any other work. *The full monty* is an informal phrase in British English meaning 'absolutely everything'.

ˌ**Fu Man**ˈ**chu** /ˌfuː mænˈtʃuː/ the main character in a series of novels by the British crime writer Sax Rohmer (*c.* 1883–1959), some of which were made into films in the 1930s. Dr Fu Manchu is an extremely clever Chinese criminal. He has a long moustache with ends that hang down, and long hair tied together at the back.

ˌ**funda**ˈ**mentalism** *n* [U] the belief, especially among some Protestant Christian groups in the US South and Midwest, that all statements in the Bible are true. **Fundamentalists** do not accept the theory of evolution. In recent years, the political Moral Majority led by Jerry *Falwell was based on fundamentalism. Compare EVANGELICAL, PENTECOSTALIST. See also SCOPES TRIAL.

ˈ**fundholding** /ˈfʌndhəʊldɪŋ; *AmE* ˈfʌndhoʊldɪŋ/ *n* [U] a system introduced in the British *National Health Service in 1991, in which doctors can choose to become **fundholders** and control their own budget (= amount of money available for a particular purpose). The money still comes from the *NHS, but fundholding doctors are more free to decide which medicines and treatments they spend it on. The government introduced fundholding in an attempt to save money by forming an '*internal market' inside the NHS. See also GP.

funk ⇨ JAZZ FUNK.

the ˈ**funnies** /ˈfʌniz/ (*also* the ˈ**funny** ˌ**papers**, the ˈ**funny** ˌ**pages**, the ˈ**comics**) *n* [pl] (*AmE*) the section of a newspaper containing *comic strips. US Sunday newspapers print colour sections with longer comic strips. Most are funny, like **Peanuts*, but some tell adventure or crime stories, like **Dick Tracy*. The funnies have been a US tradition since the early 20th century.

the ˈ**Furry Dance** /ˈfɜːri/ a traditional event that takes place in May each year in Helston, a small town in *Cornwall, England. People dance through the streets and some of the houses wearing formal clothes.

further education

Further education in Britain means education after *GCSE and *GNVQ exams taken around the age of 16. It includes courses of study leading to ***A levels** which students take at their school or **sixth-form college**. Some students go straight to a ***college of further education** which offers a wider range of full- and part-time courses. Further education also includes training for professional qualifications in nursing, accountancy and management, and in fields such as art and music. The term *higher education* is used to refer to degree courses at universities.

In the US *further education* usually means any education after secondary school. It can mean study at college or university, or any study towards a professional qualification. Americans may also use the term *higher education* to mean post-secondary education, and *further education* can have a meaning similar to that of ***adult education** or **continuing education**, i.e. something that people do after completing their main education, often for personal interest and satisfaction.

Many students in Britain take ***vocational training** courses in fields such as building, engineering, hairdressing or secretarial skills. Colleges of further education offer courses leading to ***NVQs** and other certificates and diplomas. **Work-related courses** are designed with advice from industry, with the aim of producing students who will have the skills employers require. On longer courses students may do **placements** (= periods of work) lasting several months with companies. On other courses, called **sandwich courses**, students divide their time between periods of paid work and periods of study. A common arrangement is for students to get **day release** from their work to attend college one or two days a week over several years. Some students do a formal **modern apprenticeship**, learning their skills on the job and attending college part-time.

The British government is keen to persuade more young people to remain in education as long as possible in order to build up a more highly skilled, better educated workforce. Over 700 000 people take part-time further education courses at around 500 institutions, while another 700 000 are accepted as full-time and sandwich course students.

ˈ**fusion** *n* [U] a type of music that is a mixture of *rock and *jazz styles. It was popular in the 1970s when groups such as Weather Report and jazz musicians such as Miles *Davis made fusion records.

F

Gg

ˌClark ˈ**Gable** /ˈgeɪbl/ (1901–60) a US film actor who was especially famous in the 1930s and 1940s. He was sometimes referred to as the 'King of Hollywood'. His best-known role was as Rhett *Butler in **Gone with the Wind*. Gable won an *Oscar for his part in the comedy **It Happened One Night*, and his other films included **Mutiny on the Bounty* (1935), *Mogambo* (1953) and *The Misfits* (1960) with Marilyn *Monroe. Gable was in the US Air Force during *World War II and received the Distinguished Flying Cross.

ˌPeter ˈ**Gabriel** /ˈgeɪbriəl/ (1950–) an English pop singer and writer. In the early 1970s he sang with the *rock group Genesis, but in 1975 he left the group to record and perform alone. In the 1980s he became interested in music from other cultures and made several records with musicians from Africa, Asia and the Caribbean. He also established WOMAD (World of Music, Arts and Dance), a festival that takes place every summer in Britain with performers from all around the world.

the ˌ**Gadsden** ˈ**Purchase** /ˌgædzdən/ an area in the south-west US that was bought from Mexico for $10 million in 1853. It was 29 640 square miles (76 768 square kilometres) and became part of the later states of *Arizona and *New Mexico. The agreement to buy the land was made by James Gadsden (1788–1858), the US ambassador in Mexico.

ˈ**Gaelic** *n* [U] the *Celtic language spoken in Ireland and Scotland. In Scotland it is only spoken by around 75 000 people in the *Highlands and on the west coast. Many more people speak Irish Gaelic, or **Erse**, in Ireland, where it is taught in schools as one of the country's two official languages.

ˌ**Gaelic** ˈ**football** *n* [U] a sport played by two teams of 15 players each. They play with a round ball that can be kicked, punched or bounced, but not carried. Points are scored either by kicking the ball into a net or by kicking it over the net between two tall posts. It is a popular game in Ireland, where it developed, and in some American cities.

the ˈ**Gaiety Girls** *n* [pl] the women who sang and danced in musical comedies at the Gaiety Theatre in London, England, in the 1890s. They were well known for their beauty, and many of them married members of the *peerage.

ˌThomas ˈ**Gainsborough** /ˈgeɪnzbrə/ (1727–88) an English artist. He was influenced by Dutch artists such as Rubens and Van Dyck, and became famous for his landscapes (= pictures of the countryside) and his portraits, usually of members of the *aristocracy. He often combined both skills and painted his portraits with outdoor country backgrounds, representing the effects of light on people's clothes or on trees, etc. His best-known painting is probably *The *Blue Boy*.

Mr and Mrs Andrews, painted by Thomas Gainsborough

ˌHugh ˈ**Gaitskell** /ˈgeɪtskɪl/ (1906–63) a British *Labour politician. He was the leader of the Labour Party from 1955 to 1963, and worked hard to unite the party at a time when there was a lot of disagreement among its members about nuclear weapons and other issues.

ˈ**Galahad** /ˈgæləhæd/ (*also* **Sir Galahad**) one of the *knights of King *Arthur's *Round Table(1). According to the legend he was the most innocent and morally good of all the knights, and because of this he succeeded in finding the *Holy Grail. Sometimes people are humorously called *Sir Galahad* if they have been very kind or polite to somebody: *He did his Sir Galahad act and carried her bag upstairs.*

ˈ**Galaxy**™ /ˈgæləksi/ *n* [C, U] a popular British make of chocolate bar.

ˈJohn ˈKenneth **Galˈbraith** /gælˈbreɪθ/ (1908–) a US economist, born in Canada. He advised President John F *Kennedy and was the US ambassador in India (1961–3). Galbraith has said that governments should spend more to help poor and unemployed people. He has criticized the power of international companies and the desire for continuous economic growth. His books include *The Affluent Society* (1958), *The New Industrial State* (1967) and *The Anatomy of Power* (1983).

ˌJohn **Galliˈano** /gæliˈɑːnəʊ; *AmE* gæliˈɑːnoʊ/ (1961–) a British fashion designer, born in *Gibraltar. He has worked with success in both Britain and France, and he became the main designer for the Christian Dior fashion company in 1996.

Galˈlipoli /gəˈlɪpəli/ a peninsula (= an area of land almost surrounded by water) in Turkey, which the armed forces of the *Allies tried to capture during *World War I. The Allies, including many soldiers from Australia and New Zealand, landed at Gallipoli and fought bravely, but they had little support and failed to capture the peninsula. More than 200 000 Allied soldiers died there.

ˈ**Gallup poll**™ /ˈgæləp/ *n* a way of estimating the public opinion in a country by selecting a group of people that represents the whole country and asking them questions. Gallup polls are often used in predicting the results of elections. They are named after G H Gallup, the US statistician (= expert on analysing information from numbers) who invented them. Compare MORI.

ˌJohn ˈ**Galsworthy** /ˈgɔːlzwɜːði; *AmE* ˈgɔːlzwɜːrði/ (1867–1933) an English writer of novels and plays. He wrote several successful plays that examine social and moral themes, including *Strife* (1909), about a strike, and *Justice* (1910), a criticism of the prison system, but he is best known for his series of novels *The *Forsyte Saga*. He was given the *Nobel Prize for literature in 1932.

ˌJames ˈ**Galway** /ˈgɔːlweɪ/ (1939–) a Northern Irish

musician who plays the flute. As well as playing and recording classical music with some of the world's leading orchestras, he has also made popular records and appeared on British television shows.

ˈ**Gambia** /ˈgæmbiə/ (*also* the **Gambia**) a country in West Africa where the official language is English. It is a long narrow country, on each bank of the Gambia river, surrounded by Senegal. Gambia was formed when Britain and France both had empires in the region, and could not agree on who should own this land. In the 19th century Britain took the banks of the river, and France the rest of the country. Gambia became independent in 1965, and is a member of the *Commonwealth. It now has an important tourist industry and many British people go there on holiday/vacation, especially in the winter. The capital city is Banjul. ▶ **Gambian** *adj, n.*

ˌMichael ˈ**Gambon** /ˈgæmbən/ (1940–) an English actor. He has acted in many successful plays and films, but is best known for playing the main character in *The Singing Detective*, a British television series by Dennis *Potter made in 1986. Gambon was made a *knight in 1998.

ˈ**gamesmanship** *n* [U] (*usu disapprov*) the practice of taking unfair advantage of opponents in order to win games without actually breaking the rules of the game, e.g. by upsetting somebody's confidence, or by taking their attention away from the game. The word *gamesmanship* was invented by the English writer Stephen Potter (1900–69), who in 1947 wrote a humorous book called *The Theory and Practice of Gamesmanship; or the Art of Winning Games without actually Cheating.*

the ˈ**Gaming Board for ˌGreat ˈBritain** the government organization that controls gambling in Britain. People or companies who want to run casinos (= gambling clubs), lotteries, *bingo or gambling machines must have a licence from the Gaming Board.

G and S /ˌdʒiː ənd ˈes/ an informal abbreviation of *Gilbert and *Sullivan, often used to refer to their operas: *I've never liked G and S.*

g and t /ˌdʒiː ənd ˈtiː/ *n* (*infml*) an abbreviation of gin and tonic, a popular alcoholic drink. In Britain, many people think of it as a drink for older *middle-class people.

ˈ***Gangbusters*** /ˈgæŋbʌstəz; *AmE* ˈgæŋbʌstərz/ a US radio programme each week on *CBS in the 1930s and 1940s. It was about police and criminals, and began with the noise of guns and police sirens (= devices that make a long, loud sound as a warning). This led to the US expression 'coming on like gangbusters', used to describe noisy, aggressive or successful activity.

the ˌ**Gang of ˈFour** the name given by the press to a group of four British politicians: Roy *Jenkins, David *Owen, William Rogers and Shirley *Williams. They left the *Labour Party in 1981 to form the *Social Democratic Party. The name is a humorous reference to four Chinese politicians who tried to take control of China in the 1970s.

gangs

In US history gangs are often associated with the Wild West, the western part of the US during the period when people were beginning to move there. People like Jesse *James became famous for leading gangs which committed crimes like robbing banks. People involved in organized crime, particularly during the 1920s and 1930s, were called **gangsters**. The word *gang* is no longer used to refer to the group known as the *Mafia, though members of the Mafia are often involved in **gangland killings**. Gangs involved in organized criminal activity have been less of a problem in Britain, though in the 1960s the *Kray twins ran a gang in east London.

In Britain and the US *gang* now usually means a **street gang**, a group of young people in an **inner city** area. Gangs have their own parts of the city and keep other gangs out of them. They may show which parts of the city they control by **tagging**, spraying paint in particular designs on the walls in the area. People who belong to such gangs are called **gang members**. Crimes commonly associated with street gangs include selling *drugs and, in the US, **drive-by shootings**, when they shoot a member of another gang while driving past, often injuring other people at the same time. In Britain in the 1960s and 1970s gangs of **skinheads** caused fear among ethnic minority groups, and more recently a number of Asian and West Indian gangs have been established in places such as Birmingham and Manchester. Many of these gangs were formed originally to defend the local community, but then became involved in criminal activity. There are also football gangs, groups of supporters who attack rival fans at big matches.

G

The **Gap** /gæp/ any of a group of fashionable US clothes shops. The first was opened in *San Francisco in 1969 and sold only *jeans. The company later started developing its own range of clothes and now has shops in several other countries, including Britain, where they are called simply Gap.

ˈ**garage** *n* [U] a type of dance music with strong, fast rhythms that became popular in nightclubs in America and Britain in the 1990s.

ˈ**garage sale** *n* (*esp AmE*) a sale of family possessions that are old or no longer wanted, usually held in or in front of the garage of a private house. People often have a garage sale before moving to a new house.

ˌGreta ˈ**Garbo** /ˌgretə ˈgɑːbəʊ; *AmE* ˈgɑːrboʊ/ (1905–90) a Swedish actor who moved to the US in 1925. Her beauty and acting skills made her one of the first famous *Hollywood stars, in silent as well as talking films. She is well known for saying 'I want to be alone,' and for retiring in 1941 to live a very quiet life alone in New York. Her films include *Queen Christina* (1933) and *Anna Karenina* (1935).

ˌ***Gardeners' ˈQuestion Time*** a popular British radio programme, broadcast once a week on *BBC *Radio 4 since 1947. It is recorded in different towns around the country, where local people ask a group of experts for advice about their gardens.

ˌ***Gardeners' ˈWorld*** a British television programme, broadcast on *BBC2 since 1968. It is filmed in a real garden, and usually gives advice on how to grow different types of flowers and plants.

the ˌ**garden of ˈEngland** a popular name for the county of *Kent in south-east England. Many different types of fruit and vegetables are grown there.

Gardens and yards ⇨ article.

ˈJohn ˈEliot ˈ**Gardiner** /ˈeliət ˈgɑːdnə(r); *AmE* ˈgɑːrdnər/ (1943–) an English conductor. He is best known for his performances of early music. He formed the Monteverdi Orchestra in 1968. He was made a *knight in 1998.

ˌAva ˈ**Gardner**[1] /ˌeɪvə ˈgɑːdnə(r); *AmE* ˈgɑːrdnər/ (1922–90) a US film actor who was once called 'the most beautiful woman in the world'. She was especially successful in the 1950s and 1960s. Her films included *Mogambo* (1953), *The Barefoot Contessa* (1954) and *55 Days at Peking* (1963). She was married three times: to the actor Mickey *Rooney, the band leader Artie *Shaw and the singer Frank *Sinatra.

ˈErle ˈStanley ˈ**Gardner**[2] /ˈɜːl, ˈgɑːdnə(r); *AmE* ˈɜːrl, ˈgɑːrdnər/ (1889–1970) a US author of over 140 crime

Gardens and yards

A private place

Most British people prefer to live in a house rather than a flat and one of the reasons for this is that houses usually have gardens. The garden is surrounded by a fence or hedge and is a place where people can be outside and yet private. It is somewhere to sit when the weather is sunny, and somewhere for children to play.

If a house has a front and back garden the front is likely to be formal and decorative, with a **lawn** (= an area of grass) or fancy paving and **flower borders**. In Britain people normally choose to sit in the back garden, out of view of other people. The back garden usually also has a lawn and **flower beds**, and sometimes a vegetable plot or fruit trees. There is often a **bird table** (= a raised platform on which food is put for birds) and a **shed** in which garden tools are kept.

British people spend quite a lot of money on their gardens and even the smallest may contain a variety of flowers and shrubs. In spring some people fix **window boxes** containing bulbs or other plants on their window sills, or attach a **hanging basket** containing ivy, lobelia, geraniums, etc. on the wall near the front door.

Some houses have only a very small back garden, mostly of concrete, called a backyard or, in more fashionable areas, a **patio**. People often decorate it with plants in **tubs**, or in pots or baskets fixed to the wall. For British people a garden is an extension of their home. They buy garden furniture – chairs, tables and sun loungers – so that they can sit outside in summer and relax.

In the US the area of grass in front of and behind most houses is called a **yard**. The word *garden* is used only for the areas where flowers and vegetables grow. Yards usually consist of a lawn and trees, flowers and bushes. They may have fences around them and, at the front of the house, a path going from the door of the house to the street. Many backyards have swings, slides or climbing frames for children. There may also be a patio or a **deck** (= a wooden platform attached to the house) where chairs and tables are kept in the summer. Garden decorations include **bird feeders** (= containers of food for birds) and lamps so that people can use the yard after dark.

During warm weather, Americans spend a lot of time in their yards, especially the backyard. Children play there and often have small pools of water or **sand boxes**. All the children living in an area go freely into each other's backyards. People like to eat outside, often preparing meals on a **barbecue**.

Gardening

Many British people make gardening one of their *hobbies and take great pride in their gardens, spending hours looking after them. Lawns are regularly **trimmed** or **mown**, and flower beds are **weeded** and tidied to keep them looking bright. Some towns and villages have competitions for the best kept small garden, the best hanging basket, etc. Keen gardeners may have a **greenhouse** in which to grow more delicate plants. People with a small garden, or no garden at all, can rent a piece of land, called an ***allotment**, from the local council. Most people grow vegetables on their allotments. Recently, people have shown interest in **wildlife gardening**: an area of garden is left uncultivated to encourage wild plants to grow which will attract butterflies and other insects.

There are **garden centres** near most towns, selling everything a gardener might need, from flowerpots to fishponds, and even the fish to go in them. They offer a huge range of plants, as well as **pot plants** for inside the house, and packets of flower and vegetable **seeds**. Garden centres are more than just shops: they have become places to take the family for a weekend outing. Some have display gardens, and many have a café.

The most enthusiastic gardeners can join a local **horticultural society** and take part in annual competitions and shows. National events such as the *Royal Horticultural Society Show and the *Chelsea Show in London attract many visitors. Thousands more people listen to radio shows such as **Gardeners' Question Time*, in which a panel of experts offer solutions to gardening problems. On television, **Gardeners' World* is equally popular.

Although many Americans enjoy gardening, it is not a national hobby as in Britain. But, as in any country, making a yard a nice place to sit takes a lot of work throughout the year.

Public gardens

The British interest in gardening affects the appearance of whole towns. Public parks and traffic roundabouts have bright displays of flowers in summer, public buildings have window boxes and hanging baskets, and offices and shops are encouraged to put up flower baskets. Many local councils enter their town or village for the annual *Britain in Bloom* competition.

At *weekends British people visit famous gardens, such as that at Stowe near Banbury, developed by William *Kent and 'Capability' *Brown in the 18th century. Other popular attractions include Vita *Sackville-West's garden at Sissinghurst, and the garden and **glasshouses** of the Royal Botanic Gardens at *Kew. Every summer the National Gardens Scheme publishes a booklet listing private gardens that are open to the public on a particular day. These gardens belong to ordinary people who are enthusiastic gardeners, and visitors like to look around and get ideas for their own gardens.

In the US parks and other public green spaces usually have paths for people to walk along, large areas of grass where children can play, and trees and flowers. There are some formal gardens in the US, but none is as famous as Kew or other well-known British gardens.

---

novels and short stories. His best-known character was Perry *Mason but he also wrote a series of novels about District Attorney Doug Selby.

ˈ**Garfield**[1] /ˈgɑːfiːld; *AmE* ˈgɑːrfiːld/ a character in humorous cartoons that appear in many US newspapers. Garfield is a cat, and is popular with children in America and Britain, where people buy Garfield toys, books, etc.: *She wore a Garfield T-shirt.*

ˌJames A ˈ**Garfield**[2] /ˈgɑːfiːld; *AmE* ˈgɑːrfiːld/ (James Abram Garfield 1831–81) the 20th US President, and a member of the *Republican Party. He had been a US Army general in the *Civil War. Four months after becoming President he was shot by a disappointed person who had wanted a government job.

ˌArt ˈ**Garfunkel** /ˌɑːt ˈɡɑːfʌŋkl; *AmE* ˌɑːrt ˈɡɑːrfʌŋkl/ ⇨ SIMON AND GARFUNKEL.

ˌ**Gariˈbaldi** /ˌɡærɪˈbɔːldi/ (*also* **Garibaldi biscuit**) *n* (*BrE*) a type of flat dry biscuit with a layer of currants (= dried grapes) in the middle. The humorous name for Garibaldis is 'squashed fly biscuits'.

ˌJudy ˈ**Garland** /ˈɡɑːlənd; *AmE* ˈɡɑːrlənd/ (1922–69) a US singer and actor. She began her acting career as a child actor at *MGM. She became famous as Dorothy in *The Wizard of Oz* (1944), in which she sang her best-known song, *Over the Rainbow*. She then made *Meet Me in St Louis* (1944), directed by Vincente Minnelli (1910–86), who married her the following year. Her other films included *A Star is Born* (1954) and *Judgment at Nuremberg* (1962). Garland had problems with drugs, and she died accidentally after taking too many. The singer and actor Liza *Minnelli is her daughter.

ˌErroll ˈ**Garner** /ˈɡɑːnə(r); *AmE* ˈɡɑːrnər/ (1921–77) an *African-American *jazz musician who played the piano and wrote more than 200 songs. The best-known of these include *Misty*, *Dreamy* and *Solitaire*. Garner often appeared on television and made many tours abroad.

ˌAlf ˈ**Garnett** /ˈɡɑːnɪt; *AmE* ˈɡɑːrnɪt/ a character in the *BBC television comedy series *Till Death Us Do Part*. He is proud to be British but is not well educated and has extreme right-wing opinions and prejudices, especially about black people and foreigners living in Britain. His name is often used when referring to someone who holds such opinions, which many people find offensive.

Warren Mitchell as Alf Garnett

ˌPat ˈ**Garrett** /ˈɡærət/ (1850–1908) a sheriff (= law officer) in the American *Wild West who arrested his former friend, the criminal *Billy the Kid, in 1880. When he escaped, Garrett chased him for months and finally shot him at Fort Sumter, *New Mexico.

ˌDavid ˈ**Garrick** /ˈɡærɪk/ (1717–79) an English actor. He changed the way plays were performed in Britain by introducing a more natural style of acting. His versions of Shakespeare's characters made Shakespeare popular again in the 18th century, and made Garrick the most famous actor of the period. He was also a theatre manager, and introduced many improvements to the way plays were shown.

the ˈ**Garrick Club** /ˈɡærɪk/ a club in central London, England. It was established in 1831 as a club for actors and gentlemen, and named after David *Garrick. Today many of its members are still connected with the theatre, television, etc. Women are not allowed to be members of the club. ⇨ article at CLUBS AND SOCIETIES.

ˌMarcus ˈ**Garvey** /ˌmɑːkəs ˈɡɑːvi; *AmE* ˌmɑːrkəs ˈɡɑːrvi/ (1887–1940) a US leader of the campaign for *African-American rights, born in Jamaica. After moving to the US in 1916 he began the Universal Negro Improvement Association. He also began a 'Back to Africa' campaign to encourage African Americans to move to Africa and establish a new nation there. In 1925 Garvey was sent to prison for illegal use of money. He was sent back to Jamaica and finally settled in Britain.

ˌBamber ˈ**Gascoigne**[1] /ˌbæmbə ˈɡæskɔɪn; *AmE* ˌbæmbər/ (1935–) an English writer and television presenter. He has written novels, an encyclopedia and several books about history, art and music, but is best known as the presenter of the television quiz show **University Challenge* from 1962 to 1987.

ˌPaul ˈ**Gascoigne**[2] /ˈɡæskɔɪn/ (*also infml* **Gazza**) (1967–) an English football player. In the 1980s and 1990s he played for Newcastle United, *Tottenham Hotspur, Glasgow *Rangers, the Italian club Lazio, and England. At his best he was regarded as one of the most skilful English players of his time. He is also known as a man who likes to enjoy himself and show his feelings. Many people remember him crying during a match in the 1990 World Cup.

G

ˌMrs ˈ**Gaskell** /ˈɡæskl/ (Elizabeth Gaskell 1810–65) an English writer of novels. Most of these are set in the north-west of England, including *Cranford* (1853), which is set in Knutsford, the town near *Manchester where she lived, and *Mary Barton* (1848), which is about the social conditions of *working-class people in Manchester. She also wrote a biography of her friend Charlotte *Brontë, published in 1857.

ˌBill ˈ**Gates** /ˈɡeɪts/ (1955–) the US businessman who, with Paul Allen, started the *Microsoft Corporation when he was only 19. He is now thought to be the richest person in the world. In 1997 Gates and his wife Melina gave $200 million to establish the Gates Library Foundation which gives computers to libraries in poor communities.

ˈ**Gateway** any of a group of British supermarkets selling mainly food.

ˈ**Gatorade**™ /ˈɡeɪtəreɪd/ a US drink intended for people who play a lot of sport. It replaces liquids in the body rapidly and adds carbohydrates. It was invented in 1965 at the University of Florida for its football team, who are called the Gators. It is now produced by the *Quaker Oats company.

ˌMike ˈ**Gatting** /ˈɡætɪŋ/ (1957–) an English cricket player. He was a successful batsman for *Middlesex and England in the 1970s and 1980s, and was captain of England from 1986 to 1988. He was criticized in 1988 for complaining about the umpires (= cricket referees) in Pakistan. One year later he was banned from playing for England for five years because he had gone to play in South Africa at a time when most countries refused to play against South Africa.

ˈ**Gatwick** /ˈɡætwɪk/ a major international airport, south of London. It is Britain's second largest airport.

Sir ˈ***Gawain and the*** ˌ***Green*** ˈ***Knight*** /ˈɡɑːweɪn/ a long English poem written in the 14th century by an unknown author. It is about Sir Gawain, a *knight at the court of King *Arthur, who is set various tasks to perform by the mysterious Green Knight as a test of his faith. The poem is much admired for its fine language and is regarded as one of the greatest poems of the period. Some people think it was written to celebrate the *Order of the Garter

ˌJohn ˈ**Gay** /ˈɡeɪ/ (1685–1732) an English writer of poems and plays. Most of his work was satirical, and his greatest success, *The *Beggar's Opera*, was banned from British theatres. He was a friend of Alexander *Pope and wrote the words for *Handel's *Acis and Galatea*.

ˌMarvin ˈ**Gaye** /ˌmɑːvɪn ˈɡeɪ; *AmE* ˌmɑːrvɪn/ (1939–84) an *African-American singer and writer of *soul music who was one of the stars of the *Motown(2) sound. His best-known songs include *How Sweet It Is* (1964), *Ain't that Peculiar* (1965) and *I Heard It Through the Grapevine* (1968). Gaye was killed when his father shot him during an argument.

ˌ***Gay*** ˈ***Times*** Britain's largest magazine for homosexuals, published once a month since 1984. It used to be called *Gay News*, but changed its name when *Gay News* went bankrupt after losing a case in a court of law against Mary *Whitehouse, who found some of the writing offensive.

ˈ**Gazza** /ˈɡæzə/ ⇨ GASCOIGNE.

GB plate /ˌdʒiː ˈbiː pleɪt/ *n* a white sign with the letters GB on it in black, attached to the back of a car to show that the car is from Great Britain. Many British people attach GB plates to their cars when they take them to other countries, although they are not required by law in the *European Union.

G

GCHQ /ˌdʒiː siː eɪtʃ ˈkjuː/ (*in full* **Government Communications Headquarters**) a British government centre in *Cheltenham, England. It was set up after *World War II to gather information about enemies of the government, and now employs many people to study radio, television, telephone and other communications from all around the world. Many people protested in 1984 when the government decided that GCHQ employees would no longer be allowed to be members of *trade unions. Since 1997 they have been allowed to do so again.

GCSE /ˌdʒiː siː es ˈiː/ (*in full* **General Certificate of Secondary Education**) *n* (in England and Wales) a school examination in any one of several subjects. Most students take GCSEs at the end of their fifth year of secondary school, around the age of 16. They are taken by students of all abilities, but those who want to continue studying for *A levels need to pass a certain number of GCSEs at a particular level.

GEC /ˌdʒiː iː ˈsiː/ (*in full* the **General Electric Company**) a large British company that produces a wide range of electrical and electronic goods, from household kitchen equipment to telecommunications systems and electronic systems for aircraft.

the ˈ**Geffrye Muˌseum** /ˈdʒefri/ a museum of furniture in east London, England. Most of the museum consists of a series of rooms, each one showing what a typical *middle-class English home would look like in various periods between 1600 and 1939.

ˌLou ˈ**Gehrig** /ˈɡerɪɡ/ (1903–41) a famous US *baseball player for the New York Yankees team. Gehrig was called 'the iron man' because he once played 2 130 games in a row, something that had never been done before. He died of a disease of the muscles which is now often called **Lou Gehrig's disease**.

ˌBob ˈ**Geldof** /ˈɡeldɒf; *AmE* ˈɡeldɔːf/ (1954–) an Irish pop singer who has raised large amounts of money for poor people without food or water in Ethiopia. He was the singer of the *punk(1) group the Boomtown Rats in the 1970s. In 1984 he heard about the problems in Ethiopia and brought together some of Britain's most famous pop stars to form a group called *Band Aid. Their record, *Do They Know It's Christmas?*, raised millions of pounds for Ethiopia. In 1985 even more money was raised when Geldof organized the *Live Aid concerts. He was made an honorary *knight by the British government in 1986.

the ˈ**Gemini ˌprogram** /ˈdʒemɪni/ a series of US space flights (1965–6) with two men in each. During the Gemini flights astronauts made space 'walks' and brought two spacecraft together in space for the first time. This was a preparation for the *Apollo program, and one of the Gemini astronauts was Neil *Armstrong, the first man on the moon.

General American English

General American English (GAE) is a term for the standard English of the US, though few Americans have heard of the name. GAE includes grammar and vocabulary as well as pronunciation. It can be compared in some respects to standard British English spoken with an RP (*Received Pronunciation) accent. GAE can be used as a standard of comparison for examining other **dialects** and ***accents**, though it does not imply that they are inferior or wrong.

GAE is especially common in the Midwestern part of the US, although speakers of GAE can be found all over the country. It is also the form of *American English that it is often heard on news programmes on national television. An important difference between GAE and standard English spoken with an RP accent is that GAE is connected more closely with certain geographical regions of the US than with a particular social class.

Sometimes, the term *General American* is used to refer only to a form of American pronunciation that does not have a strong regional accent.

---

the ˌ**General Asˈsembly** the main body of the *United Nations. It includes representatives of all the member nations of the UN, who discuss the problems of the world, including peace, human rights and health. They also give approval to the UN *budget. Each nation has one vote, and there must be a two-thirds approval on all important issues before any action can be taken.

the ˈ**General Asˈsembly of the ˈChurch of ˈScotland** /ˈskɒtlənd; *AmE* ˈskɑːtlənd/ the group of people governing the *Church of Scotland. It consists of ministers (= priests) and other officials who are elected by members of the Church. It is responsible for important decisions affecting the Church.

ˌ**General Eˈlectric** a US company that produces electrical products and aircraft engines, and owns *NBC. It was formed in 1892 when Thomas *Edison's company, Edison General Electric, joined with Thomson-Houston Electric. It broadcast the first dramatic play on television in 1928, and Ronald *Reagan presented *The General Electric Theater* on television in the 1950s.

the ˌ**General Eˈlectric ˌCompany** ⇨ GEC.

ˌ***General*** ˈ***Hospital*** a popular US television *soap opera on *ABC, set in a hospital. It began in 1963 and has won four *Emmy awards as the Best Daytime Drama Series (1981, 1984, 1994 and 1996).

ˌ**General ˈMotors Corpoˌration** (*also* **General Motors**) (*abbr* **GM**) the US car company that is the largest in the world, based in *Detroit. It produces *Chevrolet, *Oldsmobile, *Cadillac, *Buick and *Pontiac cars. The company was established in 1908 by William Durant. It is often said that 'what is good for General Motors is good for the USA'.

ˈ**General ˈNational Voˈcational Qualifiˈcation** ⇨ GNVQ.

the ˌ**General ˈPost Office** ⇨ GPO.

ˌ**general pracˈtitioner** ⇨ GP.

the ˌ**General ˈStrike** a strike by workers in all of Britain's important industries that took place in 1926. The coal miners were on strike because the owners of the mines wanted them to do more work for less money, and the *TUC advised all its members to go on strike in support of the miners. Over three million people joined the strike, which lasted for nine days until the TUC accepted a new offer for the miners. The miners did not accept the offer, and stayed on strike for six months. The strike had a great effect on people's attitudes in Britain. Many

a food convoy going from the London docks to Hyde Park during the General Strike

people were happy to see that workers could act together to improve their conditions, while others were afraid that it could lead to a revolution.

the ˌ**General** ˈ**Synod** the group of people governing the *Church of England. It consists of three levels: *bishops, clergy, and members of the church who are not clergy. The *Archbishop of Canterbury and the *Archbishop of York are in charge of the Synod, which is responsible for important decisions affecting the Church, such as educational policy, choosing the clergy and the care of church buildings.

ˈ**Genesis** /ˈdʒenəsɪs/ a British pop group, formed in 1967, whose albums included *Foxtrot* (1971), *Duke* (1980) and *We Can't Dance* (1991). Two of its members, Phil Collins and Peter *Gabriel, have also had successful careers outside the group.

ˈ**gentleman** *n* (*pl* **gentlemen**) **1** a formal or polite way of referring to a man. A common way to begin a speech, for example, is 'Ladies and gentlemen, ...'. **2** (*old-fash*) a man who is kind and polite and behaves with honour: *He behaved like a perfect gentleman.* **3** (formerly in Britain) a man who belonged to the gentry, a social class of the *aristocracy. They were considered well educated, and were generally so wealthy that they did not need to work.

ˌ**Gentleman** ˈ**Jim** ⇨ CORBETT.

ˌ**gentleman's** ˈ**gentleman** *n* (*rather old-fash*) a man's personal servant who looks after his clothes, answers his calls, and sometimes cooks his meals. The phrase is usually used to describe the servant of an *upper-class man.

gentlemen's clubs

The **gentlemen's club** is a British institution. Gentlemen's clubs are comfortable, private places with bars, a restaurant, a library and sometimes bedrooms. They attract as members businessmen, politicians and others from the *upper class and the *Establishment. Members use their club as a place to meet friends or take business contacts. Most are situated in London's *West End and many have large impressive buildings.

Membership is expensive and at most clubs is restricted to men, though the *Reform Club has had women members since 1981. Generally, women and other non-members are not allowed inside clubs except as guests of a member, and women are allowed only in certain rooms. Members must obey rules about dress and behaviour. People wanting to be members may have to wait a long time before they are admitted to the most popular clubs, and will only be allowed to join if an existing member **seconds** (= supports) them. Any member may object to membership being offered to a particular person by **blackballing** (= voting against) him.

Gentlemen's clubs developed in the mid 18th century. Men had previously met socially and to discuss business in coffee houses where coffee, tea and chocolate, all new drinks in Britain at the time, were available. *White's, the oldest London club, developed from a chocolate house. Some coffee houses, like the later clubs, were linked with particular professions. For instance, Lloyd's coffee house was associated with shipping and later became *Lloyd's of London. In the 18th century clubs were mainly used for drinking and gambling but later attracted members who shared more serious interests. People interested in science and literature joined the *Athenaeum, politicians went to the Reform, the *Carlton Club or Brooks's, and theatre people joined the *Garrick.

Today, the gentleman's club suggests to many people an old-fashioned world based on *class, where snobbery and prejudice still survive. There is now less interest among younger business people in joining clubs and several have had to close.

In the US there are not many institutions like the gentlemen's club. Private universities like *Harvard have *alumni associations for people who have studied there, and being a member of such clubs is associated with wealth and social status. The club building of the Harvard Club has in many ways the atmosphere of an English gentlemen's club.

ˈ**Geordie** /ˈdʒɔːdi; *AmE* ˈdʒɔːrdi/ *n* (*BrE infml*) a person from the *Newcastle area of north-east England. Geordies are well known in Britain for their friendly nature and sense of humour and for their *accent, which is very different from standard English. ▶ **Geordie** *adj*: *She has a strong Geordie accent.*

St ˈ**George** the national saint of England. Many people believe he was a Christian martyr (= a person who is killed because of his or her religious beliefs) in the third century. According to the legend, he killed a dragon to save a woman. He is often shown in pictures fighting the dragon.

George I /ˌdʒɔːdʒ ðə ˈfɜːst; *AmE* ˌdʒɔːrdʒ, ˈfɜːrst/ (1660–1727) king of Great Britain and Ireland (1714–27). He was the first of the *Hanoverian kings and came to Britain from Germany on the death of Queen *Anne. He was not popular in Britain, mainly because he did not learn to speak English, and because he arrived with two German lovers who the British people did not like. He did not get involved in British politics, leaving most decisions to the *Cabinet, which became much more important during his time as king.

George II /ˌdʒɔːdʒ ðə ˈsekənd; *AmE* ˌdʒɔːrdʒ/ (1660–1727) king of Great Britain and Ireland (1727–60). He was the only son of *George I and, like his father, was not very interested in the government of Britain, allowing the development of the *constitutional monarchy. He was, however, interested in the army, and fought against the French in the War of the Austrian Succession (1740–8). He was the last British king to lead his army into a battle.

George III /ˌdʒɔːdʒ ðə ˈθɜːd; *AmE* ˌdʒɔːrdʒ, ˈθɜːrd/ (1738–1820) king of Great Britain and Ireland (1760–1820). He was the grandson of King *George II. He was very interested in the government of Britain, and worked closely with *prime ministers such as Lord North and William *Pitt. He was strongly opposed to American independence, and was blamed by the public for losing the war of the *American Revolution. He suffered from mental illness for some periods of his life. In 1811 he became so ill that his son was made *Prince Regent.

a Georgian crescent in Bath

George IV /ˌdʒɔːdʒ ðə ˈfɔːθ; *AmE* ˌdʒɔːrdʒ ˈfɔːrθ/ (1762–1830) king of Great Britain and Ireland (1820–30). Before becoming king, he ruled as *Prince Regent because his father *George III was mentally ill. He had many lovers and shocked many people by the way he lived, spending a lot of time eating, drinking and gambling.

George V /ˌdʒɔːdʒ ðə ˈfɪfθ; *AmE* ˌdʒɔːrdʒ/ (1865–1936) king of Great Britain and Northern Ireland (1910–36). He was the son of *Edward VII. He became popular with the British people for supporting the British armed forces in *World War I. In 1917 he dropped all his German titles and changed the family name from *Saxe-Coburg-Gotha to *Windsor[1](2).

George VI /ˌdʒɔːdʒ ðə ˈsɪksθ; *AmE* ˌdʒɔːrdʒ/ (1894–1952) king of Great Britain and Northern Ireland (1910–36). He was the second son of *George V and became king after the abdication of his brother *Edward VIII. He was greatly admired by the British people during *World War II for staying in London when it was being bombed by German aircraft. He was the last British king to be called 'emperor' and the first head of the *Commonwealth of Nations.

the ˌ**George** ˈ**Cross** the highest award given to British civilians for doing something very brave, such as risking danger to help other people. It is a silver medal in the shape of a cross. The George Cross is not given to many people, and is considered a great honour. It was introduced by *George VI in 1940.

the ˌ**George** ˈ**Medal** an award given to British civilians for doing something brave. It is a round silver medal. The George Medal is considered a great honour, though not as great as the *George Cross. The two awards were introduced at the same time.

ˈ**Georgetown** /ˈdʒɔːdʒtaʊn; *AmE* ˈdʒɔːrdʒtaʊn/ a fashionable and expensive district of *Washington, DC. It is on the *Potomac River and is the oldest area of the city. Georgetown University, one of the best in the country, was established in 1789 and had more than 12 000 students in 1998.

the ˌ**George** ˈ**Washington Bridge** /ˈwɒʃɪŋtən; *AmE* ˈwɑʃɪŋtən/ a large US suspension bridge (= a bridge hanging from steel cables supported by towers at each end) across the *Hudson River from *Manhattan(1) in New York City to Fort Lee, *New Jersey. It is a 'double-decker', with one road above the other, and the length of the main section is 3 500 feet (1 068 metres). It was completed in 1931.

ˈ**Georgia** /ˈdʒɔːdʒə; *AmE* ˈdʒɔːrdʒə/ a US state in the *Deep South. It was named after King *George II of Great Britain and was one of the 13 original American states. It later joined the *Confederate States. Georgia's popular names are the Peach State and the Empire State of the South. The capital city is *Atlanta. It was a cotton state until the 20th century and now produces many paper and textile products.

ˈ**Georgian** /ˈdʒɔːdʒən; *AmE* ˈdʒɔːrdʒən/ *adj* of the period of the British kings *George I, II and III, most of the 18th century and the beginning of the 19th century. British architecture, furniture and silver of this period are considered particularly attractive. Many British towns and cities have areas of simple but elegant Georgian houses. Some people also refer to the time of *George IV as Georgian, while others call it *Regency: *They live in one of those big Georgian terraced houses near the park.*

the ˌ**Georgian** ˈ**poets** /ˌdʒɔːdʒən; *AmE* ˈdʒɔːrdʒən/ *n* [pl] a group of British poets who wrote and published poems together in the early part of the 20th century, when *George V was king. The group included Rupert *Brooke, Walter *de la Mare, A E *Housman and John *Masefield. They were influenced by *Wordsworth and wrote many poems about nature and country life.

ˌ***Georgie*** ˈ***Porgie*** /ˌdʒɔːdʒi ˈpɔːdʒi; *AmE* ˌdʒɔːrdʒi ˈpɔːrdʒi/ a boy in an old British *nursery rhyme with these words:

Georgie Porgie, pudding and pie,
Kissed the girls and made them cry;
When the boys came out to play,
Georgie Porgie ran away.

It is not known if the rhyme refers to a real historical person.

ˌRichard ˈ**Gere** /ˈɡɪə(r); *AmE* ˈɡɪr/ (1948–) a US film actor. His films have included *American Gigolo* (1980), *An Officer and a Gentleman* (1982), *Pretty Woman* (1990), *Primal Fear* (1996) and *Red Corner* (1998). Gere has been active in the campaign to protest against the treatment by China of the people of Tibet.

Geˈ**ronimo** /dʒəˈrɒnɪməʊ; *AmE* dʒəˈrɑːnɪmoʊ/ (*c.* 1829–1909) an *Apache who led his people in *Arizona against the US Army and the white people who settled there. After fighting for ten years (1876–86), Geronimo surrendered and finally settled in *Oklahoma as a farmer. In *World War II US military paratroopers used to shout his name as they jumped from their planes, to give themselves courage. Today, people often do this when jumping from a high place or doing something dangerous.

ˌGeorge ˈ**Gershwin** /ˈɡɜːʃwɪn; *AmE* ˈɡɜːrʃwɪn/ (1898–1937) a US composer who wrote many popular songs. He also wrote serious music in which he introduced elements of *jazz and other forms of popular music. His best-known works include *Rhapsody in Blue* (1924) and the *African-American opera *Porgy and Bess* (1935). He also wrote several musical comedy shows, including *Lady Be Good* (1924), *Strike up the Band* (1927) and *Of Thee I Sing* (1931), which won a *Pulitzer Prize. George Gershwin's brother Ira (1896–1983) wrote the words for many of his songs.

Gestures ⇨ article.

ˌJ Paul ˈ**Getty** /ˈɡeti/ (Jean Paul Getty 1892–1976) a US businessman who was one of the richest man in the world. He became President of the Getty Oil Company in 1947 and was estimated to be worth more than $1 billion by 1968. He collected art and established the J Paul Getty Museum in Malibu, *California, in 1954. He settled in Britain in the early

1950s. His son, **John Paul Getty Junior** (1932–), also lives in Britain and in 1984 gave £1 million to the *National Gallery in London to stop the J Paul Getty Museum buying one of its statues, *The Three Graces* by Canova. He became a British citizen in 1997.

the ˌBattle of ˈ**Gettysburg** /ˈgetizbɜːg; *AmE* ˈgetizbɜːrg/ a major battle (1–3 July 1863) during the American *Civil War which helped the US to win the war. More soldiers died than in any other battle in US history. It was fought in Gettysburg, *Pennsylvania, between the southern forces under General Robert E *Lee and the US soldiers led by General George Mead. Over 40 000 men on both sides were killed or wounded, and the battle ended as a major victory for the North.

the ˌ**Gettysburg Adˈdress** /ˌgetizbɜːg; *AmE* ˈgetizbɜːrg/ a short but very famous speech by US President Abraham *Lincoln on 19 November 1863 during the *Civil War. He was at the military cemetery at Gettysburg, *Pennsylvania, four months after the Battle of *Gettysburg. The speech consisted of only ten sentences, and Lincoln thought it was a 'flat failure' and would soon be forgotten. He said that the US was 'conceived in liberty and dedicated to the proposition that all men are created equal' and that 'government of the people, by the people, for the people shall not perish from the earth'.

ˌStan ˈ**Getz** /ˈgets/ (1927–91) a US *jazz musician who played the saxophone. He was a leader of the 'West Coast Cool' type of jazz, and his successes included *Early Autumn* (1948), *The Girl from Ipanema* (1963) and *I Remember You* (1991). Getz played with Benny *Goodman, Woody *Herman and other famous bands. He received three *Emmy awards (1962, 1964 and 1991) and was chosen for the Jazz *Hall of Fame in 1986.

ˈ**Ghana** /ˈgɑːnə/ a country in West Africa. It was part of the *British Empire from 1874, when it was called the Gold Coast, until 1957, when it was one of the first African countries to become independent. It is a member of the *Commonwealth, and many Ghanaian people now live in Britain. The capital city is Accra.
▶ **Ghanaian** *adj, n.*

a ghost shirt of the Arapaho

the ˈ**Ghost Dance** a *Native-American dance and religion that started among the *Paiute people in western *Nevada about 1870. The religion was based on a dance which lasted five days and which Native Americans believed would help them to get back their land. The *Sioux danced the Ghost Dance before the battle of *Wounded Knee. During the battle they wore 'ghost shirts' which they believed would stop bullets.

ˈ**ghost town** *n* a town with few or no remaining inhabitants. Most ghost towns were in the western US. They grew quickly because they were near gold and silver mines, but then soon became deserted when the mines closed.

GI /ˌdʒiː ˈaɪ/ (*also* ˌ**GI** ˈ**Joe**) *n* a name for a US soldier, used especially in *World War II. It came originally from the letters 'GI' (meaning 'government issue') stamped on military equipment.

the ˌ**Giant's** ˈ**Causeway** a group of several thousand columns of rock on the north-east coast of Northern Ireland. Most of the columns have five or six flat sides. According to the legend, it is one end of a road built by a giant across the sea to the island of *Staffa, where there is a similar group of rocks. It is an important tourist attraction and was made a *World Heritage Site in 1986.

the Giant's Causeway

ˌEdward ˈ**Gibbon** /ˈgɪbən/ (1737–94) an English historian and *Member of Parliament who spent much of his life writing his main work, *The *Decline and Fall of the Roman Empire*. He is regarded as one of the major thinkers and writers of the *Age of Enlightenment in Britain.

ˌGrinling ˈ**Gibbons**[1] /ˌgrɪnlɪŋ ˈgɪbənz/ (1648–1721) an English sculptor. He is well known for his realistic decorative wood carvings, some of which can be seen in *St Paul's Cathedral in London.

OrˌIando ˈ**Gibbons**[2] /ɔːˌlændəʊ ˈgɪbənz; *AmE* ɔːrˌlændoʊ/ (1583–1625) an English composer and musician. He was the greatest player of keyboard instruments of his time, and wrote many pieces of music for the *Church of England which are still used today.

the ˈ**GI** ˌ**Bill of** ˈ**Rights** (*also* the **GI Bill**) a US law passed in 1944 to give financial help to members of the armed forces when they returned from *World War II. This included money given to help pay for homes and education. By 1947, about 4 million people had benefited from the law. It now helps anyone leaving the US armed forces.

Giˈbraltar /dʒɪˈbrɔːltə(r)/ a large rock at the western end of the Mediterranean Sea, connected to the south coast of Spain. There is a small town and a large military base on Gibraltar, which is owned by Britain but claimed by Spain. It used to be an important centre for the *Royal Navy and the *RAF, guarding the area where the Mediterranean flows into the Atlantic, but many of the armed forces have left Gibraltar, and tourism is becoming a more important industry. Many monkeys, called Barbary apes, live on the Rock of Gibraltar, and there is a legend that the British will leave Gibraltar when the monkeys die or stop living there.

ˌMel ˈ**Gibson** /ˌmel ˈgɪbsn/ (1956–) an Australian actor who became a famous *Hollywood film star. His best-known films include the *Mad Max* series of films in the 1980s, the *Lethal Weapon* series in the 1980s and 1990s, and *Braveheart* (1995), which he also directed.

ˌ**Gideon** ˈ**Bible** /ˌgɪdiən/ *n* a copy of the Bible that has been left in a room in a hotel, hospital, etc. by the **Gideons**, a US Christian organization. They put Bibles in rooms in many countries around the world

Gestures

Some gestures are used by all British and American people. Many are appropriate only in informal situations; others are considered rude. Some people make many gestures when they speak, so they are sometimes said to **talk with their hands**. A **facial expression**, such as a smile or a frown, often makes it clear whether a gesture shows approval or disapproval, pleasure or impatience. Some gestures have several different meanings, depending on the context.

Head

People **nod** (= move the head gently down and up) to indicate 'yes'. Sometimes people nod repeatedly during a conversation to show that they agree with the speaker. Nodding at somebody can indicate that it is their turn to do something. You can also nod towards somebody or something instead of pointing with your finger. Nodding to somebody while you are talking to someone else shows that you have noticed them.

Shaking the head from side to side means 'no'. When somebody makes this gesture with their eyes wide open it indicates disbelief. If there is a slight smile then the person is also amused. If somebody shakes their head and keeps their mouth closed and pulled back it suggests that they are annoyed.

Fingers and thumbs

Thumbs up is a gesture showing approval or success. It is usually made with the thumb of only one hand. The thumb points straight up while the fingers are curled into the palm. The gesture is used to tell somebody that they can go ahead and do something, or to indicate that the person making the gesture has succeeded in something. To **give somebody the thumbs up** is to give them permission to do something. **Thumbs down** is a similar gesture but the thumb points down towards the ground. It is used by somebody to indicate they have failed to do or get something.

People **thumb a lift** (= try to get a ride in a passing vehicle) by holding their arm out with the thumb up and slightly forward. **Twiddling your thumbs** (= holding the hands loosely and letting the thumbs rub gently against each other) suggests boredom or impatience. The phrase is often used metaphorically to mean 'having nothing to do'.

Pointing with the forefinger (= first finger) at somebody or something shows which person or thing you want or are talking about. But in both Britain and the US it is considered rude to point.

People can indicate that they think somebody is mad by pointing one finger at the side of their forehead and turning it. If you hold two fingers at the side of your forehead like a gun you are pretending to shoot yourself for doing something silly. A finger held to the lips indicates 'Sh!' (= Be quiet!). If you **pinch your nose** you are indicating that there is a bad smell. If you **stick your fingers in your ears** you cannot stand the noise of something. If a child holds its thumb to its nose, with the fingers spread out and waving, they are making an insulting gesture called **cocking a snook**. American children move one forefinger down at right angles to the other to indicate somebody has done something bad.

Fingers crossed is a wish for good luck. The index finger is crossed over the forefinger of the same hand. In Britain people give a **V-sign** by holding the index finger and forefinger apart like a V and curling the other fingers and the thumb into the palm. If the palm is held outwards the sign means 'victory'; if the palm is turned inwards the gesture is rude and offensive. In the US people use the V-sign with the palm outwards to mean 'peace' but the rude version is not used. **Giving somebody the finger** (= holding the middle finger straight up and curling the other fingers into the palm) is used instead. Forming the thumb and forefinger into a

hoping that people will read them and learn about Christianity.

ˌJohn ˈ**Gielgud** /ˈgiːlgʊd/ (1904–) an English actor. He is well known for his fine voice and for the wide range of his acting. He first became famous for his stage performances in *Shakespeare plays with Laurence *Olivier in the 1930s, playing characters such as Romeo and Hamlet. He was also successful in comedy plays, and has appeared in many films. His role in the television version of **Brideshead Revisited* in the 1980s made him popular with a wider audience. He is considered one of the greatest actors of the 20th century. He was made a *knight in 1953.

John Gielgud in Prospero's Books

ˌRyan ˈ**Giggs** /ˌraɪən ˈgɪgz/ (1973–) a Welsh footballer who has played for *Manchester United and Wales since the early 1990s. He plays attacking football in the middle of the field or along the edges, and is well known as one of the most skilful players in Britain.

ˌW S ˈ**Gilbert** /ˈgɪlbət; *AmE* ˈgɪlbərt/ (William Schwenk Gilbert 1836–1911) an English writer of comedy plays and the words for comic operas. He is best known for the comic operas he wrote with Arthur *Sullivan, which show his skill at writing humorous songs and making fun of British life. **Gilbert and Sullivan** wrote 14 popular comic operas (sometimes called the *Savoy Operas), including *The *Mikado* and *The *Pirates of Penzance*. They are still performed regularly in Britain.

Giles /dʒaɪlz/ (Carl Ronald Giles 1916–95) an English cartoonist. His humorous cartoons were usually about current events and often involved a large family which was always in a state of disorder. They were published regularly in the **Daily Express* from the 1940s until his death.

ˌEric ˈ**Gill** /ˈgɪl/ (1882–1940) an English artist. He is well known for his sculptures, especially his bas-reliefs (= sculptures in which the design sticks out only slightly from its background) such as his *Stations of the Cross* (1914–18) in *Westminster Cathedral. He also created several new typefaces (= styles for printing letters in books, magazines, etc.).

ˈˌDizzy' **Gilˈlespie** /ˌdɪzi gɪˈlespi/ (1917–93) an *African-American *jazz musician who invented the name of *bebop and helped to develop that type of music. He played the trumpet in a wide range of groups and wrote several successful pieces, includ-

circle and moving the forefinger of the other hand in and out of it indicates the sex act.

Drumming your fingers, i.e. tapping them repeatedly on a desk or table, suggests impatience. **Scratching your head** suggests you are not sure what to do. These gestures may also be a sign that a person is nervous.

Hands and arms

People often **shake hands** when they are introduced to each other. Business people may shake hands when they make an agreement.

When somebody **waves**, one arm is raised and bent slightly and the wrist is shaken. We wave when saying goodbye to somebody. Waving is also used as a greeting, especially by somebody famous. In Britain children wave to trains, hoping that the driver will wave back. In the US children hold up their fist and move it down when a truck approaches, hoping the driver will sound the horn.

People **beckon** somebody to come over by holding the hand with the palm up and the fingers curled loosely in, and moving the forefinger backwards and forwards. If the person if further away the forearm is also moved.

Lifting the arm is used to attract attention. In schools teachers say '**Hands up**' when they ask a question, so that all the children get a chance to answer. Sometimes a vote can be taken by **a show of hands**, i.e. asking people who agree to **raise their hands**, and then, after they have lowered them, asking those who disagree to do the same. Adults also lift their arm to attract the attention of a waiter or a taxi driver. In Britain people stop a bus by holding one arm out at right angles while facing towards the bus.

If you stand with your hands on your hips it can suggest anger or defiance. If you **clench your fist** (= make the hand into a tight ball) you are angry.

People **clap their hands** to show they are pleased about something. After a concert, play, etc. they clap repeatedly to show they enjoyed it. The phrase **give somebody a** (**big**) **hand** means to clap to show pleasure at what they have done.

Shoulders

Shrugging your shoulders shows impatience or lack of interest. It can also be used to indicate that you do not mind which of several things is chosen. A person who stands with their elbows close to the body and forearms spread, with the palms of their hands upwards and their shoulders raised, does not know what is going to happen. Often, the head is held slightly to one side.

Feet

People sometimes **tap their feet** (usually only one foot) on the floor in time to music, but more often the gesture shows that they feel impatient. Children sometimes **stamp their feet** when they are angry.

Facial expressions

Winking at somebody reminds them of a shared secret or is used as a private signal. **Raising the eyebrows** with the eyes wide open, or **blinking** (= closing and opening both eyes very quickly) several times, expresses surprise, shock or sometimes disapproval. The phrase *eyebrows were raised* is often used metaphorically.

Frowning may suggest concentration, but is often a sign of disapproval or annoyance. **Wrinkling the nose** (= moving it up and to one side) suggests there is a bad smell, but if your nose **twitches** and you take a few quick breaths this means you can smell something nice, especially food cooking.

Children **stick their tongues out** to show they do not like somebody, but this is rude. **Pursing the lips**, making them very small and tight, is something people may do if they are concentrating hard. Sometimes, however, it shows a person is angry but trying hard to control their anger.

ing *Hot House* (1941) and *Groovin' High* (1944). He was chosen for the Jazz *Hall of Fame in 1960.

ˌ***Gilligan's*** ˈ***Island*** /ˌgɪlɪgənz/ a US television comedy series (1964–66) on *CBS. The old programmes have been shown on US television every week since the series finished. The story is about seven people trapped on an island after their boat has sunk. Bob Denver plays Willy Gilligan, a silly character who tries to help but ruins each new plan to escape.

ˌJames ˈ**Gillray** /ˈgɪlreɪ/ (1756–1815) an English caricaturist (= an artist who makes people appear ridiculous by exaggerating their characteristics). He often made fun of the government and the royal family and had a strong influence on the development of political cartoons in Britain. See also FARMER GEORGE.

ˌGary ˈ**Gilmore** /ˈgɪlmɔː(r)/ (1940–77) a US criminal who was executed for murder in January 1977. He is mainly remembered because he chose to be shot by a firing squad, as a condemned person is allowed to do in the state of *Utah, though no one else has chosen this form of death since.

ˈ**Gingerbread** a British charity that offers help and advice to single parents.

ˌNewt ˈ**Gingrich** /ˌnjuːt ˈgɪŋgrɪtʃ/ (1943–) a US *Republican politician. He was *Speaker of the House of Representatives from 1995 to 1998, when he resigned from the post. He is well known for his right-wing views, e.g. that Americans should pay less tax and that unemployed people should be given less money by the State. In 1995 he disagreed with President *Clinton about how to spend the government's money that year, and their disagreement led to many government departments closing temporarily because they did not have any money. In 1997 the House Ethics Committee found that Gingrich had used tax laws wrongly and lied to the committee.

ˌAllen ˈ**Ginsberg** /ˈgɪnzbɜːg; *AmE* ˈgɪnzbɜːrg/ (1926–97) a US poet of the *beat generation of the 1950s who was also closely associated with the *hippies of the 1960s. He supported illegal drugs and the rights of homosexuals, and protested against the *Vietnam War. Ginsberg's collections of poems included *Howl* (1956) which criticized American values, and *Kaddish and Other Poems* (1961).

ˌ**gin** ˈ**sling** *n* a drink consisting of a mixture of gin, sugar, water and lemon or lime juice, served with ice. Many people in Britain think of it as a typical *upper-middle-class drink, or as the typical drink of British people in tropical countries at the time of the *British Empire.

the ˌ**Girl** ˈ**Guides** ⇨ GUIDE.

ˌ**Girl** ˈ**Scout** *n* a member of the Girl Scouts of the USA, an organization for girls similar to the *Boy Scouts of America. It was established in 1912 and had about 3.5 million members in 1998. The main groups of Girl Scouts are Daisy Girl Scouts (for ages 5 to 6), Brownie Girl Scouts (6 to 8), Junior Girl Scouts (8 to 11), Cadette Girl Scouts (11 to 14) and Senior Girl Scouts (14 to 17). Compare GUIDE.

ˈ**Girobank** /ˈdʒaɪrəʊbæŋk; *AmE* ˈdʒaɪroʊbæŋk/ a British bank that has its branches in post offices. It used to belong to the *Post Office but it was sold in 1990 to the *Alliance and Leicester building society. Many people use the Girobank because they find it more convenient to use their local post office than to go to a bank.

ˌLillian ˈ**Gish** /ˈɡɪʃ/ (1893–1993) an US actor in silent and sound films, and on the stage. She was small and delicate, but her acting career lasted for nearly 90 years. She and her sister Dorothy Gish (1898–1968) were favourite actors of D W *Griffith, and Lillian became internationally famous in his **Birth of a Nation* (1915). Her sound films included *Night of the Hunter* (1955) and her last, *The Whales of August* (1987). She received a special *Oscar in 1970.

G

Gladiators

ˈ***Gladiators*** a popular British television programme in which members of the public take part in a series of difficult physical contests against the Gladiators, a group of very strong men and women with colourful names like Scorpio, Wolf and Cobra. Some of the Gladiators have became stars and appeared in other television programmes. *American Gladiators* is a similar programme on US television.

ˌWilliam ˈ**Gladstone** /ˈɡlædstən/ (1809–98) an English *Liberal politician who was *Prime Minister four times (1868–74, 1880–85, 1886 and 1892-4). He began as a *Tory *MP but left to form the Liberal Party, becoming its leader in 1867. He and his rival *Disraeli were the leading figures in British politics for over 30 years. Gladstone was responsible for many improvements to life in Britain: he made voting secret, gave most men the right to vote, and gave all children the right to an education. He also believed that the countries in the *British Empire should govern themselves and that Ireland should have *home rule(1), but he died before these aims could be achieved.

W E Gladstone in 1894

Glaˈ**morgan** /ɡləˈmɔːɡən; *AmE* ɡləˈmɔːrɡən/ a former county in south-east Wales. In 1974 it was divided into *Mid Glamorgan, *South Glamorgan and *West Glamorgan. Glamorgan County Cricket Club, whose ground is in *Cardiff, is the only Welsh club in the *county championship.

ˈ***Glamour*** a US women's magazine published by Condé Nast. It began in 1939 and now describes itself as 'the largest fashion, beauty and health magazine in the world'. In 1997 it had 10 million readers. It also has articles about other interests of women, such as business, politics, travel, food and relationships.

ˈ**Glasgow** /ˈɡlɑːzɡəʊ; *AmE* ˈɡlɑːsɡoʊ/ an industrial city in south-west Scotland. It is Scotland's largest city and a major port. It used to be an important centre for shipbuilding, and when this and several other industries closed down in the late 20th century it became well known for problems connected with unemployment, drugs and crime. Glasgow has many interesting and attractive buildings, as well as important schools, universities and museums, and in the 1990s it has developed into a major centre for culture, the arts and education. In 1990 it was named European City of Culture.

the ˌ**Glasgow** ˈ**Herald** /ˌɡlɑːzɡəʊ; *AmE* ˌɡlæsɡoʊ/ a Scottish daily newspaper. It is read mainly in the Glasgow area and the west of Scotland. It is one of Scotland's two main newspapers. Compare SCOTSMAN. ⇨ article at NEWSPAPERS.

ˌPhilip ˈ**Glass** /ˈɡlɑːs; *AmE* ˈɡlæs/ (1937–) a US composer. He is well known for developing a 'minimal' style of music based on repeated rhythms with slight changes of pattern. His best-known work is the opera *Einstein on the Beach* (1975).

ˈ**Glastonbury** /ˈɡlæstənbəri/ a town in south-west England. According to legend, *Joseph of Arimathea went there with the *Holy Grail. Another story states that King *Arthur and Queen *Guinevere are buried there, and that Glastonbury was originally *Avalon. Today it is famous for the **Glastonbury Festival**, a large pop concert that takes place in fields outside the town every summer.

Glasˈ**wegian** /ɡlæzˈwiːdʒn/ *n* a person who comes from or lives in *Glasgow. ▶ **Glaswegian** *adj*: *He had a strong Glaswegian accent.*

ˈ**Glaxo** /ˈɡlæksəʊ; *AmE* ˈɡlæksoʊ/ a large British company that produces many different types of drugs and medicines.

the **GLC** /ˌdʒiː el ˈsiː/ (*in full* the **Greater London Council**) the local authority that was in control of *Greater London from 1965 to 1983. It was popular with many *Londoners because it provided free entertainment, educational opportunities, etc., but many others thought that it wasted money on minority groups. Margaret *Thatcher found the GLC and its leader, Ken *Livingstone, too left-wing, and changed the system of local government so that after 1983 each *borough was responsible for itself, and no single authority was responsible for the whole of Greater London.

ˌJackie ˈ**Gleason** /ˈɡliːsn/ (1916–87) a US comic actor with a loud voice, sometimes called the 'Great One' because he was so fat. He had his own television show in the 1960s, and appeared in several films, including *Smokey and the Bandit* (1977).

Glenˈ**coe** /ɡlenˈkəʊ; *AmE* ɡlenˈkoʊ/ a valley in the Scottish *Highlands. In 1692 it was the scene of the **Glencoe Massacre**. About 40 members of the MacDonald *clan were killed by members of the Campbell clan and the soldiers of the English king, *William III. The MacDonalds were killed because they had supported the first *Jacobite rebellion and had been slow to recognize *William and Mary.

ˌOwen ˈ**Glendower** /ɡlenˈdaʊə(r)/ (*c.* 1355–*c.* 1417) a

Welsh military and political leader who led the Welsh forces resisting the English King *Henry IV in Wales. He had his own parliament in 1404 and was the last Welsh person to have the title of *Prince of Wales. He was defeated in battle by the son of Henry IV, who also claimed the title of Prince of Wales, but he was never captured. Many people know of him as a character in *Shakespeare's play *Henry IV*.

Glen'eagles /glen'i:glz/ a pair of famous golf courses (called the King's course and the Queen's course) belonging to a hotel in central Scotland. In 1977 the leaders of the *Commonwealth governments met there to sign the **Gleneagles Principle**, in which they agreed to have no contact in sport with South Africa because of the political situation there at the time.

glen'garry /glen'gæri/ *n* a type of Scottish cap, usually made of wool with a *tartan design. Glengarries have no brim and often have ribbons hanging at the back. They are worn by some regiments of Scottish soldiers.

ˌJohn **'Glenn** /'glen/ (1921–) a US astronaut and politician. He became the first American in space when in 20 February 1962 he made three orbits (= circular paths in space) around the earth in *Friendship 7*, a spacecraft of the *Mercury program. Glenn left *NASA two years later and has been elected a Senator from *Ohio for the *Democratic Party since 1974. He has twice tried but failed to become the Democratic candidate for US *President. In 1998 he again took part in a space flight, at the age of 77.

the **Globe** /gləʊb; *AmE* gloʊb/ the theatre in London where *Shakespeare's most famous plays were first performed. It was built in 1599 by the actor Richard Burbage on the south bank of the *Thames. It was a round, open-air building with a roof over the stage. It had three levels of seats and an area in front of the stage where some of the audience could stand. It was closed by the *Puritans in 1642. An exact copy of the Globe was built in the 1990s and plays are again performed there. Compare ROSE THEATRE.

the new Globe Theatre

the ˌ**Glorious Revo'lution** ⇨ BLOODLESS REVOLUTION.

the ˌ**Glorious 'Twelfth** **1** (*infml*) 12 August, the first day of the season for shooting grouse (= a fat bird which is shot for sport and food) in Britain. Grouse shooting is very popular with rich and *upper-class people in Britain. **2** 12 July, the anniversary of the *Battle of the Boyne, which is celebrated by many Protestants in Northern Ireland.

'Gloucester /'glɒstə(r); *AmE* 'glɑ:stər/ a city in south-east England, on the river *Severn. It was established as a Roman military camp in the first century. Its cathedral has fine examples of *Norman and *Perpendicular architecture. See also DOUBLE GLOUCESTER.

'Gloucestershire /'glɒstəʃə(r); *AmE* 'glɑ:stərʃər/ (*abbr* **Glos**) a county in south-west England, on the border with Wales. It contains part of the *Cotswolds. The administrative centre is *Gloucester.

'Glyndebourne /'glaɪndbɔ:n; *AmE* 'glaɪndbɔ:rn/ a large, grand house near *Brighton in southern England which is well known for the opera festival that takes place there every summer. A theatre was built in the garden for the first festival in 1934 and it was replaced by a larger theatre in 1994. The Glyndebourne opera has become one of the important social events of the English summer, particularly among *upper-middle-class people. The gardens are beautiful, and many members of the audience take their own food and drinks to enjoy there during the interval: *After a season at Glyndebourne she went on tour with a different company.*

GM /ˌdʒi: 'em/ ⇨ GENERAL MOTORS CORPORATION.

G-man /'dʒi: mæn/ *n* (*pl* **G-men**) (*AmE old-fash infml*) a man working for the *FBI. The word is an abbreviation of 'government man'.

GMAT /'dʒi:mæt/ (*in full* **Graduate Management Admission Test**) (in US *graduate schools) a standard test that students must take in order to be accepted to study for a degree in Business Administration.

GMB /ˌdʒi: em 'bi:/ a very large British *trade union. It was formed in 1989 when two large trade unions combined. The name GMB is partly an abbreviation of the name of one of these two (the General, Municipal, Boilermakers and Allied Trade Union), which represented mainly industrial and administrative workers. The new 'super union' represents people in most types of work.

GMT /ˌdʒi: em 'ti:/ (*in full* **Greenwich Mean Time**) the time of day on the line of 0° longitude (= a straight line between the North Pole and the South Pole), which goes through *Greenwich. It is the official time in Britain from October to March. Different time zones in other parts of the world are usually described with reference to GMT: *New York is five hours behind GMT so it's early morning there now.*

GNVQ /ˌdʒi: en vi: 'kju:/ (*in full* **General National Vocational Qualification**) *n* a type of qualification introduced in 1992 in England, Wales and Northern Ireland. It is designed to prepare students to do certain jobs, and is offered in subjects such as business management, teaching and computer skills. GNVQs can be taken at schools and colleges at the same time as (or instead of) *GCSEs or *A levels. ⇨ note at VOCATIONAL TRAINING. See also NVQ.

ˌ***God Bless A'merica*** a song praising America that was written by Irving *Berlin in 1939. It became the 'unofficial national anthem' for the US during the Second World War, when Kate *Smith regularly sang it. Some Americans still want it to replace *The *Star-Spangled Banner*.

The ***'Godfather*** a successful novel (1969) by Mario Puzo about the *Mafia(1). 'Godfather' is a popular name for a Mafia leader. The book became an equally successful 1972 film directed by Francis Ford *Coppola and won the *Oscar for Best Picture. An Oscar also went to Marlon *Brando who played the Mafia leader Don Corleone, though Brando refused the award as a protest against the treatment of *Native Americans. Al *Pacino played his son Michael, and was the star of two later films by Coppola which continued the story, *The Godfather II* (1974) and *The Godfather III* (1990). The three films won a total of 10 *Oscars.

ˌLady **Go'diva** /gə'daɪvə/ (11th century) the wife of an *earl(1) of *Mercia. According to legend, she asked her husband to lower the taxes on the people of *Coventry and he said that he would do so if she rode her horse naked through the town. She did this, and the taxes were lowered. See also PEEPING TOM.

ˌGod ˈRest You ˈMerry, ˈGentlemen a popular English *carol often sung at *Christmas. It is a happy song, telling the Bible story of the birth of Christ.

ˌGod Save the ˈQueen the British *national anthem. It is not known who wrote the words or the music, but it was already a traditional song in the 18th century. The song has several verses, but usually only the first verse is sung:

God save our gracious Queen,
Long live our noble Queen,
God Save the Queen.
Send her victorious,
Happy and glorious,
Long to reign over us;
God save the Queen.

If the country has a king at the time, the word 'Queen' is replaced by 'King'.

G

ˈGod's ˌcountry an expression used to describe a beautiful and greatly loved land. Americans use it to mean the US or regions of the country, especially the open areas of the western states.

ˈGod slot *n* [usu sing] (*BrE infml*) any religious television or radio programme that is broadcast at the same time every week. The traditional God slot on British television is early on Sunday evening.

ˌRube **ˈGoldberg¹** /ˌruːb ˈgəʊldbɜːg; *AmE* ˈgoʊldbɜːrg/ (1883–1970) a US cartoonist who drew complicated, ridiculous machines performing tasks that could be done more easily without them. The phrase 'Rube Goldberg' is still used to describe any complicated machine or plan with many parts. Goldberg was also a political cartoonist and won the *Pulitzer Prize in 1948 for his work. Compare HEATH ROBINSON.

ˌWhoopi **ˈGoldberg²** /ˌwʊpi ˈgəʊldbɜːg; *AmE* ˈgoʊldbɜːrg/ (1949–) an *African-American actor who usually makes comedy films. She won a *Golden Globe Award as Best Actress for a serious role in her first film, *The Color Purple* (1985), and received an *Oscar for Best Supporting Actress as a comic character in *Ghost* (1990). Her later films include *Sister Act* (1992) and *The Associate* (1996).

ˌGold ˈBlend™ *n* [U] a make of instant coffee, made by *Nescafé. Many people in Britain remember a series of television advertisements for Gold Blend in the 1990s in which a man and a woman gradually fell in love while drinking or talking about it.

the **ˌGolden ˈAge** (in Britain) a phrase used to describe the second half of the 16th century, when *Elizabeth I was queen. It was a time when Britain's military and economic influence on other countries became very strong, and many great works of art and literature were produced.

The ***ˌGolden ˈBough*** a book (1890) by James *Frazer. It is a long and detailed study of the history of people's religious beliefs and customs. A much longer version was published in 1915. It had a great influence on the development of the science of anthropology.

the **ˌGolden Gate ˈBridge** the famous US bridge that connects *San Francisco with Marin County, *California, to the north. It is the second longest US suspension bridge (= bridge hanging from cables supported by towers at each end). It is orange, not gold, in colour and crosses the Golden Gate, the water between San Francisco Bay and the Pacific Ocean. It was completed in 1937, and the length of the central section is 4 200 feet (1 281 metres). The bridge takes four years to paint, and the work of painting it never stops.

ˌGolden ˈGlobe Aˌward *n* any of several film and television awards given at a special ceremony each year since 1945 by the Hollywood Foreign Press Association. The film awards are similar to those of the *Oscars, and the television winners include various types of programme, such as Best Drama Series and Best Miniseries.

the ***ˌGolden ˈHind*** ⇨ DRAKE.

The ***ˌGolden ˈTreasury*** a book (1861) consisting of a collection of English poetry. The poems were chosen by Francis Turner *Palgrave with some help from his friend Lord *Tennyson. It had an important influence on future collections of poems, and on what the British public considered to be great poetry. Later, larger editions were published, and it is still in print today.

ˌGolden ˈWonder™ a popular British make of potato crisps/chips (= very thin slices of fried potato sold in small bags, often with salt or other flavours.

ˈGoldie /ˈgəʊldi; *AmE* ˈgoʊldi/ (1966–) a British pop musician known for his *jungle albums, including *Timeless* (1995) and *Saturnz Return* (1998). Earlier in his career he was a member of the group Metalheadz.

ˈGoldilocks and the ˌThree ˈBears /ˈgəʊldɪlɒks; *AmE* ˈgoʊldɪlɑːks/ a popular children's story. Goldilocks, a young girl with golden hair, goes to a house where three bears live (Mother Bear, Father Bear and Baby Bear). The bears are not at home, and Goldilocks eats some of their *porridge and tries all their beds before going to sleep in one of them. The bears return, see that someone has been there, and repeat phrases like 'Who's been eating my porridge?' until they find Goldilocks in bed and she escapes. The story is often used as the basis for a *pantomime in Britain.

ˌWilliam **ˈGolding** /ˈgəʊldɪŋ; *AmE* ˈgoʊldɪŋ/ (1911–93) an English writer of novels. He is best known for his first novel, *The *Lord of the Flies* (1954). Like many of his other works, it is concerned with human cruelty. He won the *Booker Prize for the novel *Rites of Passage* (1980), and the *Nobel Prize for literature in 1983. He was made a *knight in 1988.

the **ˈGold Rush** the rapid movement of about 40 000 people to the US state of *California in 1848–9 after gold was discovered there. They were called *forty-niners. The gold rush later spread to *Canada and *Alaska. See also JEANS. Compare KLONDIKE.

ˌOliver **ˈGoldsmith** /ˈgəʊldsmɪθ; *AmE* ˈgoʊldsmɪθ/ (*c.* 1730–74) an Irish writer of plays, novels and poetry. His best-known works are the play **She Stoops to Conquer* and the novel *The *Vicar of Wakefield*. He was a close friend of Samuel *Johnson and one of the group of writers living in 18th-century London known as the Club.

ˌSam **ˈGoldwyn** /ˈgəʊldwɪn; *AmE* ˈgoʊldwɪn/ (1882–1974) a US film producer, born in Poland. In 1916 he established Goldwyn Pictures, which later became part of *Metro-Goldwyn-Mayer. He received an *Oscar for *The Best Years of Our Lives* (1946), and his other films included **Wuthering Heights* (1939), **Guys and Dolls* (1955) and *Porgy and Bess* (1959). Goldwyn was famous for his strange and sometimes comic use of English, such as 'Gentlemen, kindly include me out' and 'In two words, im-possible'.

golf

Golf was first developed in Scotland in the 15th century but is now played all round the world by both professional and amateur players,.

The aim of golf is to hit a small ball from a **tee** (= a flat area of grass) into a hole on a **green** (= a very finely cut area of grass), which may be up to 600 yards (550 metres) away, using as few **shots** (= hits) as possible. Most **golf courses** consist of 18 **holes**. To make play more difficult they are often hilly and have various natural and man-made hazards such as lakes, bunkers (= pits filled with sand), and **rough**, long grass or trees on either side of the **fairway**.

Each player has his or her own ball and several different types of **club** (**woods**, **irons** and a **putter**) with which to hit it. The club chosen depends on the type of shot the player needs to make. In professional tournaments each player has a **caddie** to carry their bag of clubs from one hole to the next and to advise them on their play. Players try to finish each hole in a given number of shots, which is known as **par**. If they use one shot less than par they score a **birdie**; if they use two shots less they score an **eagle**; if they use three shots under par they score an **albatross**. If they manage to get the ball into the hole in a single shot they can claim a **hole in one**. If they use a shot more than par they score a **bogey**. Professional golfers have a handicap of zero. At the end of a **round** (= all 18 holes), the player with the lowest score is the winner. Professional matches may consist of several rounds. The result sometimes depends on the total number of shots players have taken (**strokeplay**), or else on the number of individual holes each player has won (**matchplay**).

Golf began as a sport of the upper classes and in Britain it continues to attract mainly people who work in business and the professions. The game is quite expensive to play and membership of the most popular **golf clubs** may cost a lot of money. The most famous British clubs include the *Royal and Ancient at *St Andrew's, where the first official rules of golf were agreed in 1754, *Muirfield and *Wentworth. Golf may have been taken to America by people from Scotland in the 17th century, but the first permanent club was not established there until 1888, in Yonkers, New York.

There are four important international competitions for professional golfers, known as the **majors**, three of them held in the US. The ***Masters Tournament** is always held at Augusta, Georgia. The others are the ***US Open** and the **US PGA Championship**. The ***British Open** is regarded as the world's top golf tournament. US and European teams also compete every two years in the *Ryder Cup. The major US competitions for women include the **US Women's Open** and the **du Maurier Classic**. Amateur events include the *Walker Cup and the *Curtis Cup. Television has helped to increase the popularity of the game, and many new golf courses have been created.

Many people who do not play golf enjoy a game of **crazy golf** in a local park. The idea is to hit a golf ball round a small grass and concrete course of nine holes, through tunnels, over bridges, round small pools, etc. Others enjoy **putting**, a miniature form of golf on a small grassy course.

ˈ**golliwog** (*AmE also* **golliwogg**, *BrE also* ˈ**golly**) *n* a soft, black doll with large white eyes and black hair that sticks out all around its head. Golliwogs were popular with British children for most of the 20th century, but since the 1980s they have become less common because many people regard them as offensive to black people.

The ˌ***Gondoˈliers*** a comic opera (1889) by *Gilbert and *Sullivan[1]. It is set in Venice, Italy, where a gondolier (= a person whose job is to carry passengers on a boat through the canals of Venice) is believed to be the prince of an imaginary country. A local aristocrat wants his daughter to marry the prince, but she loves a servant called Luiz. In the end, it is discovered that Luiz is the real prince.

ˌ***Gone with the ˈWind*** a popular US novel (1936) by Margaret Mitchell which won the *Pulitzer Prize. In 1939 it was made into one of the most successful films ever made, winning 10 *Oscars. The story is set in the state of *Georgia and follows the troubled love affair between Scarlett *O'Hara and Rhett *Butler during the *Civil War, which changes their lives.

a poster for the film of Gone with the Wind

ˌGraham ˈ**Gooch** /ˈguːtʃ/ (1953–) an English cricketer. He was a successful batsman for *Essex and England, and was captain of the England team from 1988 to 1993. He was banned from playing for England from 1982 to 1985 because he had gone to play in South Africa at a time when most countries were refusing to play any sport with South Africa.

The ˌ***Good ˈFood Guide*** a book giving information about many restaurants in Britain, and the writers' opinions about the quality of the food they offer. It is published every year by the *Consumers' Association, and contains many comments by members of the public.

ˌ**Good ˈFriday** the Friday before *Easter. In the Christian religion it represents the day on which Christ died. It is a *bank holiday in Britain. In the US, part of Good Friday is an official holiday in certain states. See also HOT CROSS BUN.

the ˌ**Good ˈFriday Aˌgreement** an agreement reached on *Good Friday 1998 between Irish political leaders and the British government. The agreement ended the violence of the *Troubles in Northern Ireland and established new Irish political institutions, including a new *Northern Ireland Assembly in *Belfast. Other parts of the agreement concerned the release of prisoners and the giving up of weapons. The agreement was the result of talks led by the US Senator George Mitchell between *Unionist and Republican groups, and was signed by politicians including Gerry *Adams, David *Trimble, John *Hume, Mo *Mowlam and Tony *Blair. Most of the people of Northern Ireland and the Irish Republic supported the agreement in a vote held in May 1998.

ˌ***Good ˈHousekeeping*** a magazine containing articles about houses, decoration, food and fashion. It is published once a month in different versions in America and Britain, and read mainly by women. It was first published in the US in 1885 and in Britain in 1922.

ˌ***Good King ˈWenceslas*** /ˈwensəslæs/ a Christmas *carol which is especially popular with children. Most British and US people know the first lines of the song:

Good King Wenceslas looked out
On the feast of Stephen,
When the snow lay round about,
Deep and crisp and even.

The ˈ***Good Life*** a British comedy television series which was popular in the 1970s. It is about a *middle-class couple who decide to convert their ordinary house in *suburbia into a farm where they grow all their own food, make their own clothes, etc.

ˌBenny ˈ**Goodman** /ˈgʊdmən/ (1909–86) a US musician

who played the clarinet and led a successful dance band in the 1930s and 1940s. He was called the 'King of Swing', and one of his hits was *Stompin' at the Savoy* (1936). Goodman was the first white band leader to use *African-American musicians. In 1938, his band played the first *jazz concert in *Carnegie Hall. He also played classical music written for him by Aaron *Copland, Béla Bartók and others.

ˌ**Good ˈNeighbor ˌPolicy** a friendly policy created by President Franklin D *Roosevelt for US dealings with Latin America. It was signed in 1933 at the Pan-American Conference. It encouraged good relations between the US and the other nations, and gave US financial support for Latin American programmes for agriculture, health, education and business.

The ˌ***Good ˈNews Bible*** a modern version of the Bible in simple English, published in 1976 by the American Bible Society. The 'good news' is from the word 'gospel', which means 'good message'.

G

ˌ**good old ˈboy** *n* (*AmE infml*) an expression used by white men in the southern US states to refer to a man they like and welcome into their group. He is usually a friendly person who has an easy manner and enjoys typically male activities.

The ˈ***Good Old Days*** a British television series consisting of old-fashioned *music-hall performances. The programmes are broadcast from a real music-hall, with members of the audience dressed in Victorian costume.

ˌ**Goodwill ˈIndustries** a major US charity, begun in 1910 by Edgar Helms, a Methodist minister. It operates in the US and in many other countries to provide training and employment for people who have physical or mental problems or who have committed crimes, etc. It collects money by asking people to give clothing and household items which are then sold in over 1 500 Goodwill shops.

ˌ**Goodwin ˈSands** /ˌgʊdwɪn/ a group of dangerous banks of sand just below the surface of the sea in the *English Channel near *Dover. Many ships have been damaged and sunk there. According to legend, they used to be an island belonging to an *earl(1) called Godwin which was washed away by the sea.

ˌ**Goodwood ˈHouse** /ˌgʊdwʊd/ a *stately home near *Chichester in southern England. It was first built in the 17th century, and rebuilt in the late 18th century. It contains many valuable pieces of furniture and works of art, especially from 18th-century France. It is best known for the horse races that take place near the house. The racecourse is often called 'Glorious Goodwood' because of the attractive scenery and the fashionable people who go there.

ˈ**Goodyear** /ˈgʊdjɪə(r)/ a large US company, established in 1898, which produces and sells tyres and other rubber products in many countries around the world. The company is also well known for its airships (= aircraft like large balloons filled with gas lighter than air and driven by engines). These regularly fly with television cameras over sports events.

The ˈ***Goon Show*** /ˈguːn/ a British comedy radio programme, broadcast by the *BBC in the 1950s. It consisted of jokes, songs and situations that were full of surprising and ridiculous humour, and had an important influence on the development of British comedy. The actors and writers, Michael Bentine (1922–97), Spike *Milligan, Harry *Secombe and Peter *Sellers, were called the **Goons**.

ˈ**Goosebumps** /ˈguːsbʌmps/ the title of a popular series of books for children by the US author R L Stine. They are horror stories, but are often humorous as well. Versions of the stories have appeared on children's television in Britain and the US.

GOP /ˈdʒiː əʊ ˈpiː; *AmE* oʊ/ (*in full* **Grand Old Party**) a popular name for the US *Republican Party.

the ˈ**Gorbals** /ˈgɔːblz; *AmE* ˈgɔːrblz/ a district of south *Glasgow. It used to be known for its bad slums (= streets of old buildings in a poor, dirty condition) where many unemployed people lived. Much of the area was rebuilt in the late 20th century, but many people still think of it as a dangerous place because of its former reputation: *He grew up in the Gorbals.*

ˌGeneral ˈ**Gordon** /ˈgɔːdn; *AmE* ˈgɔːrdn/ (Charles George Gordon 1833–85) an English military leader. He became known as 'Chinese Gordon' after defeating a rebellion against British rule in China in 1863. He was killed in a small military camp in Khartoum, Sudan, after resisting attacks from Sudanese forces for ten months with a small group of soldiers.

ˈ**Gordon's**™ /ˈgɔːdnz; *AmE* ˈgɔːrdnz/ a British company that produces a popular make of gin.

ˈ**Gordonstoun** /ˈgɔːdnstən; *AmE* ˈgɔːrdnstən/ a *public school(1) in north-east Scotland, established in 1934. It is well known for the importance it gives to developing students' physical as well as academic abilities. Several members of the British *royal family have been students there.

ˌAl ˈ**Gore** /ˈgɔː(r)/ (1948–) the 45th Vice-president of the US. He was elected with President Bill *Clinton in 1992 and 1996. Gore is from the *Democratic Party and first represented *Tennessee in the US House of Representatives (1977–85) and then the US Senate (1985–92). Among his other interests, he supports women's rights, the environment and international communications.

ˈ**gospel** *n* [U] religious music that is sung in a *blues style, especially by *African Americans. Mahalia *Jackson was a famous gospel singer, and Aretha *Franklin was strongly influenced by gospel music.

ˈ**Gotcha!** /ˈgɒtʃə; *AmE* ˈgɑːtʃə/ a humorous way of writing the phrase 'I've got you!', which a person says when they have found or caught somebody, or when they find themselves in a position to take advantage of somebody. It was used as the headline of the *Sun* newspaper with a picture of an Argentinian ship after it had been badly hit by guns fired from British ships during the *Falklands War. Many British people found this offensive and in very bad taste. See also BELGRANO.

ˈ**Gotham** /ˈgɒθəm; *AmE* ˈgɑːθəm/ a popular name for New York City. It comes from the name of an English village whose inhabitants were known to be very stupid.

ˈ**Gothic** *adj* of a style of architecture that was common in Western Europe from the 12th to the 16th

the Goons: Harry Secombe, Michael Bentine, Spike Milligan and Peter Sellers centuries. Gothic buildings can be recognized by their tall pointed arches and tall narrow windows and columns. Many British churches and cathedrals were built in this style. ⇨ article at CHURCHES AND CATHEDRALS.

ˌ**Gothic ˈnovel** *n* any of a class of English novels dealing with frightening or magic subjects. Most Gothic novels are set in ruined castles or large old houses with ghosts, and were written in the late 18th and early 19th centuries. The style was made popular by Horace *Walpole's *The Castle of Otranto* (1764), and influenced writers such as Mary *Shelley and Edgar Allan *Poe, as well as 20th-century horror stories and horror films.

the ˌ**Gothic Reˈvival** the return to a *Gothic style in British architecture that occurred between the middle of the 18th century and the middle of the 19th century. Many British churches were built in the new Gothic style, also called **neo-Gothic**, and are often more highly decorated than older Gothic churches. The style was also used for buildings such as hotels, railway stations and government buildings, including the *Houses of Parliament(2).

ˌStephen Jay ˈ**Gould** /ˈguːld/ (1941–) a US palaeontologist (= person who studies the remains of animals and plants hardened in rock as a guide to the history of life on earth). He is well known for his theory of 'punctuated equilibrium', which explains that forms of life developed through short periods of rapid change and long periods without change. He has written many popular books and articles about the history of life on earth.

ˌ**government ˈhealth ˌwarning** *n* (in Britain) a warning that must by law appear on all tobacco products and advertisements for them, to show that they are considered harmful to health.

ˌDavid ˈ**Gower** /ˈgaʊə(r)/ (1957–) an English cricketer. He was a successful batsman for *Leicestershire, *Hampshire and England from the 1970s to the 1990s. He was known for his relaxed and elegant style of play, and was captain of the England team from 1984 to 1985, and in 1989. Some people in Britain thought that he was not serious enough about cricket, and in 1991 he was criticized in the press when he hired a small plane and flew it low over a cricket match in Australia. He now appears regularly on television.

the ˌ**Gower Peˈninsula** /ˌgaʊə; *AmE* ˌgaʊər/ a peninsula (= an area of land almost surrounded by water) on the south coast of Wales, near *Swansea. It is well known for its attractive scenery and for the many remains of prehistoric people and animals that have been found there.

GP /ˌdʒiː ˈpiː/ (*in full* **general practitioner**) *n* (in Britain) a doctor who treats all types of illnesses within a community, sometimes called a **family doctor**. He or she can write prescriptions (= instructions that allow people to buy medicines), and may recommend that a person goes to see a specialist in a particular disease. Patients are usually treated at the doctor's surgery, and may also be visited at home. Since 1990 many GPs have chosen to become *fundholders, i.e. they receive a sum of money from the government and can make independent decisions about how to spend it on their patients. See also INTERNAL MARKET, NATIONAL HEALTH SERVICE.

GPA /ˌdʒiː piː ˈeɪ/ ⇨ GRADE POINT AVERAGE.

the **GPMU** /ˌdʒiː piː em ˈjuː/ (*in full* the ˈ**Graphical, ˈPaper and ˈMedia ˌUnion**) a British trade union, mainly representing workers in the printing, paper and design industries. It was formed in 1991.

the **GPO** /ˌdʒiː piː ˈəʊ; *AmE* ˈoʊ/ (*in full* the **General Post Office**) the former name for the British organization of post office services. In 1969 its name was changed to the *Post Office, but some people in Britain still refer to it as the GPO.

GQ /ˌdʒiː ˈkjuː/ a British magazine for men that contains articles on fashion, sport, sex, health and other subjects. The letters 'GQ' stand for 'Gentlemen's Quarterly'. It first appeared in 1988 and is published every month.

ˌBetty ˈ**Grable** /ˈgreɪbl/ (1916–73) a US actor, singer and dancer. She was especially popular during *World War II when US soldiers chose her as their favourite 'pin-up girl' (= attractive woman whose picture is displayed by men). She was known for her long fair hair and beautiful legs, which were insured for $1 million. Her films included *Mother Wore Tights* (1947) and *How to Marry a Millionaire* (1953).

ˌW G ˈ**Grace** /ˈgreɪs/ (William Gilbert Grace 1848–1915) an English cricketer. He was equally successful as a batsman and as a bowler, playing for *Gloucestershire and England from the 1860s to the beginning of the 20th century. He was one of the greatest cricket players of all time, and probably the most famous. He was also a qualified doctor. Most British people have heard of him, and recognize pictures of him because of his long beard.

W G Grace batting in his last match

ˌ**Grace and ˈFavour ˌresidence** *n* a house or flat/apartment owned by the British king or queen, in which people are invited to live without paying any rent. Among the best-known of these are the ones in *Kensington Palace and *Windsor Castle.

Gˈraceland /ˈgreɪslənd/ the large house in *Memphis, *Tennessee, where Elvis *Presley lived and died. It is now a popular museum. On 16 August 1997, about 75 000 people from around the world gathered there to celebrate the 20th anniversary of Presley's death.

ˈ**grade point ˌaverage** *n* (*abbr* **GPA**) (*AmE*) an average academic score for a student in a US *high school, college or university. The highest grade A receives 4 points, B is 3, C is 2, D is 1 and F is 0. Points received during an academic period of weeks or months are added together and the average calculated. A high GPA helps a high school student to get into a good college or university. High points received at a college or university can result in a student being named on the *dean's list and other honours. Students with low GPAs can be dismissed.

The ˈ***Graduate*** a US comedy film (1967) about an older woman who teaches sex to a young man who then realizes he loves her daughter. The film made a star of Dustin *Hoffman, and Mike Nichols won an *Oscar for directing it. *Simon and Garfunkel wrote the music, including the song *Mrs Robinson*.

ˈ**Graduate ˈManagement Adˈmission Test** ⇨ GMAT.

the ˌ**Graduate ˈRecord Examiˌnation** ⇨ GRE.

ˈ**graduate school** *n* (in the US) the department of a university or college for studies after the first degree is received. Students must do well in the *Graduate Record Examination to be accepted. Graduate school degrees include the *master's degree and PhD.

ˌBilly ˈ**Graham**[1] /ˈgreɪəm/ (1918–) a US *evangelist and minister in the Southern Baptist Church. He has led large religious meetings in many countries besides America, including Britain, Australia and Russia. During these dramatic 'Crusades for Christ', Graham asks people to come forward and give their lives to Christ, and millions have done so.

ˌKatherine ˈ**Graham²** /ˈgreɪəm/ (1917–) a US newspaper owner who has been one of America's most powerful women. She published the **Washington Post* from 1968 to 1978 (during the time it discovered *Watergate), and controlled the The Washington Post Company which owns **Newsweek* magazine. Graham won a *Pulitzer Prize in 1998 for her book about her life, *Personal History*.

ˌMartha ˈ**Graham³** /ˈgreɪəm/ (1894–1991) a US dancer and choreographer who helped to develop modern dance. She began her own dance company in 1929 and was the choreographer of more than 160 works including *Appalachian Spring* (1944) and *Seraphic Dialogue* (1955). Graham received the *Presidential Medal of Freedom in 1976.

G

ˈ**graham ˌcracker** /ˈgreɪəm/ *n* (*AmE*) a small, square, slightly sweet American biscuit made with wholemeal flour. Graham crackers are sometimes eaten with peanut butter spread on top and are often broken to form the bottom layer of pies. They are named after Sylvester Graham (1794–1851), an American who encouraged people to eat healthy foods.

ˌKenneth ˈ**Grahame** /ˈgreɪəm/ (1852–1932) a Scottish writer of children's books. He is best known for writing *The *Wind in the Willows*, which was based on bedtime stories he told to his son.

the **Grail** /greɪl/ ⇨ HOLY GRAIL.

ˈ**grammar school** *n* **1** (in Britain) a type of secondary school at which more academic subjects are studied than at *secondary modern or *comprehensive schools. Most British towns used to have at least one grammar school, which children could enter only if they passed examinations at the age of eleven. Many people thought that this system was unfair, and by the end of the 20th century most local education authorities had changed to the comprehensive system. Most of Britain's remaining grammar schools have now become independent of their local authorities. See also OPTING OUT. **2** (in the US) an *elementary school.

ˈ**Grammy** /ˈgræmi/ *n* any of the awards for special achievements in the recording industry presented each year since 1958 by the US National Academy of Recording Arts and Sciences. The name comes from the small model of a gramophone (= an old-fashioned machine for playing records) that is given to each winner.

ˈ**Grampian** /ˈgræmpiən/ (*also* ˈ**Grampian ˌRegion**) a *region in north-east Scotland. Its administrative centre is Aberdeen.

the ˈ**Grampians** /ˈgræmpiənz/ (*also* the ˌ**Grampian** ˈ**Mountains** /ˌgræmpiən/) *n* [pl] a range of mountains in central Scotland that includes the *Cairngorms and *Ben Nevis. They are popular with mountain climbers and hill walkers, and with people who like to shoot grouse (= birds that are shot for sport and food).

Graˈnada /grəˈnɑːdə/ (*also* **Graˌnada** ˈ**Television**) an independent British television company, based in *Manchester. It broadcasts programmes to north-west England, and produces programmes that are broadcast all over Britain on *ITV. It is the oldest commercial television station in Britain, and has a reputation for making programmes of high quality.

the ˌ**Grand** ˈ**Canyon** an extremely large gorge (= a valley with steep sides) in the US state of *Arizona. It is a major tourist attraction, visited by about 3 million people each year. The Canyon was created by the Colorado River and is about 1 mile (1.6 kilometres) deep, 200 miles (320 kilometres) long and 4–18 miles (6–29 kilometres) wide. It has colourful layers of rock, the oldest of which are about 2 billion years old. **Grand Canyon National Park** was opened in 1919 and made a *World Heritage Site in 1979.

ˈ**Grand** ˈ**Central** ˈ**Station** (*also* ˈ**Grand** ˈ**Central** ˈ**Terminal**) the best-known railway station in the US. It is on East 42nd Street in New York and was completed in 1913 in the American Beaux Arts style. The main area is very large, and the trains enter and leave the station on 123 tracks, arranged on two levels. The station is often very crowded: *You can't move in there – it's like Grand Central Station!*

Grand Central Station

ˈ**Grand** ˈ**Coulee** ˈ**Dam** /ˈkuːli/ a large dam on the Columbia River in the US state of *Washington. It was completed in 1942 and made larger in the 1980s. It was built to produce electricity from water power. The dam is 550 feet (168 metres) high and 4 173 feet (1 273 metres) long. It holds back the waters of Franklin D Roosevelt Lake, one of the largest US reservoirs (= places where water is stored for use).

the ˌ**Grand** ˈ**Lodge** the leading organization in British *Freemasonry, established in London in 1717. Many members of the British *royal family have been Grand Masters (= leaders) of the Grand Lodge.

ˌ**Grandma** ˈ**Moses** /ˈməʊzɪz/ (1860–1961) the popular name for the US painter Anna Mary Robertson Moses. She was a farmer's wife who did not paint until the age of 76 and then produced more than 1 200 works. Her colourful paintings are in the primitive style and show the countryside where she had lived in New York State and *Virginia. Her last paintings were done at the age of 101.

ˌ**Grand Metroˈpolitan** (*also infml* ˌ**Grand** ˈ**Met**) a large British company that owns hotels in many countries, and several famous food and drinks companies, including *Watney's and *Pillsbury.

the ˌ**Grand** ˈ**National** (*also infml* the **National**) the most famous and important horse race in Britain. It is a very long race, with many high fences for the horses to jump over, and it takes place every year in March or April at *Aintree, near *Liverpool. Many British people bet on the Grand National, even if they do not usually gamble on horse races.

The ˈ***Grand Old*** ˌ***Duke of*** ˈ***York*** /ˈjɔːk; *AmE* ˈjɔːrk/ a British *nursery rhyme. The first verse is:

Oh the Grand old Duke of York
He had ten thousand men,
He marched them up to the top of the hill
And he marched them down again.

It is sometimes used to refer to somebody who cannot decide what to do.

ˌ**Grand Old ˈMan** *n* [usu sing] (*sometimes humor*) a title used to describe a man who has been involved in a particular activity for a long time at a high level. It was originally used to refer to William *Gladstone, who spent many years in politics and was *Prime Minister four times: *He is very much the Grand Old Man of Canadian literature.*

The ˌ***Grand Ole ˈOpry*** /əʊl ˈɒpri; *AmE* oʊl ˈɔːpri/ (*also infml* The **Opry**) a US radio programme that has broadcast *country music from *Nashville, *Tennessee on Saturday nights since 1925. It has been running longer than any other radio programme in the world. Roy *Acuff was one of the first stars of the show, but all the most famous country singers and musicians have appeared on it.

the ˈ**Grand ˈOrder of ˈWater Rats** a British organization whose members are entertainers. They organize events to raise money for charity, including a comedy show that takes place every November.

ˌ**grand ˈslam** *n* **1** (in tennis and golf) a victory for a single player in all of the four most important competitions in a particular year (which are sometimes called **grand slam events**). **2** (in Rugby Union) a situation in which one country beats all four others in the *Five Nations Tournament. **3** (in baseball) a home run that is hit when three players are on the bases, so that four players each score a run (= point). **4** (in certain card games) a situation in which one player wins all 13 tricks (= rounds of cards) in a single game.

ˈ***Grandstand*** a popular *BBC sports television programme. It has been broadcast on Saturday afternoons since the 1950s and usually consists of some sports events shown as they happen, and recordings and reports of other events.

the ˌ**Grand ˈTour** (especially in the 18th century) a tour of Europe that was regarded as part of the education of wealthy young British people. The tour sometimes took several years, and usually included visits to Paris, the Alps, Florence and Rome.

the ˈ**Grand ˈUnion Caˈnal** a canal between London and *Birmingham. It is the longest canal in Britain, and used to be an important route for goods between the *Midlands and the south of England.

the ˌ**Grand ˈWizard** ⇨ KU KLUX KLAN.

ˌ***Grange ˈHill*** a British children's television programme that was popular in the 1970s and 1980s. It was set in a school in London, and was more realistic than many children's programmes, dealing with problems such as *bullying.

ˌ**Granny ˈSmith** *n* a type of apple with a green skin and hard sweet flesh. Granny Smiths are very popular in Britain.

ˌCary ˈ**Grant**[1] /ˌkeəri ˈɡrɑːnt; *AmE* ˌkeri ˈɡrænt/ (1904–86) a US film actor, born in England. He was known for his easy charm in romantic and comedy parts. His films included *The Philadelphia Story* (1940), *Mr Blandings Builds His Dream House* (1948), *To Catch a Thief* (1955), *Indiscrete* (1958) and *North by Northwest* (1959). He received a special *Oscar in 1969.

UˌIysses S ˈ**Grant**[2] /juˌlɪsiːz, ˈɡrɑːnt; *AmE* ˈɡrænt/ (Ulysses Simpson Grant 1822–85) the general who commanded the US Army during the *Civil War and later became the 18th *President of the US (1869–77). His greatest Civil War victory was at *Vicksburg, *Mississippi, and he accepted the surrender of Robert E *Lee at *Appomattox Court House. Grant was a *Republican. He was not a successful president because he failed to stop the illegal actions of friends he appointed. His two volumes of *Personal Memoirs* are among the best military books ever written.

ˈ**Granta** /ˈɡrɑːntə; *AmE* ˈɡræntə/ **1** the local name for the river Cam as it flows through *Cambridge, England. **2** ***Granta*** a British literary magazine, consisting mainly of short stories, poems, and parts of novels and travel books. It began as a *Cambridge University student magazine, but is now sold in many countries. It has a reputation for publishing the work of important new writers. There is now a Granta publishing house.

ˈ**Grantchester** /ˈɡrɑːntʃestə(r); *AmE* ˈɡræntʃestər/ a village near *Cambridge, England. It is well known because of a famous poem, *The Old Vicarage, Grantchester*, by Rupert *Brooke, who stayed there in 1910.

ˌ**grant-mainˈtained school** *n* a type of school in England and Wales which is controlled by a group of its own governors rather than a *Local Education Authority. Grant-maintained schools receive more money from the government than most other state schools, and are considered by some people to provide a better education. See also OPTING OUT. ⇨ article at EDUCATION IN BRITAIN.

ˌ**Grant's ˈTomb** /ˌɡrɑːnts; *AmE* ˌɡrænts/ the impressive stone building in which US President Ulysses S *Grant and his wife are buried, in Riverside Park, New York City. It was designed by John Duncan and completed in 1897. Its official name since 1958 has been the General Grant National Memorial.

ˈ**Grape Nuts**™ *n* [U] a breakfast food consisting of crisp pieces of cooked wheat, usually eaten with milk. It is made by a division of the US Kraft Foods company but is also sold in Britain.

The ˌ***Grapes of ˈWrath*** a novel (1939) by the US writer John *Steinbeck which won the *Pulitzer Prize. It tells the story of the Joad family, whose farm is ruined in the *Dust Bowl, and their journey to the 'promised land' of California. It is a sad story about the lack of government support for poor people. A film version in 1940 was directed by John *Ford[8], with Henry *Fonda as Tom Joad, the head of the family. The title of the book is a phrase from *The *Battle Hymn of the Republic*.

a scene from the film of The Grapes of Wrath

ˈ**Grasmere** /ˈɡrɑːsmɪə(r); *AmE* ˈɡræsmɪr/ a village in the English *Lake District where William *Wordsworth lived for much of his life, and where the *Lake Poets used to meet. Wordsworth's house, *Dove Cottage, and the churchyard where he is buried are popular with tourists. The village is by a small lake, also called Grasmere.

The ˌ**Grateful ˈDead** a US *rock band formed in 1965 in *San Francisco. They were known for their many stage performances and their willingness to change songs each time they played them. Their successful albums included *Grateful Dead* (1967) and *American Beauty* (1970). Their leader, Jerry Garcia

(1942–96), died at a drug treatment centre in California. In 1998 three other original members of the group formed a new group called The Other Ones.

ˈ**Grauman's** ˈ**Chinese** ˈ**Theater** /ˈgrɔːmənz/ the original name of a famous *Hollywood cinema, built in 1927 by Sid Grauman and designed like a Chinese pagoda (= religious building). Near its entrance there is a place where well-known film stars leave images of their hands or feet by pressing them into wet cement which then dries. It is now called Mann's Chinese Theater.

ˌRobert ˈ**Graves** /ˈgreɪvz/ (1895–1985) an English writer. He wrote many books of poetry, books about literature, and novels. He is now perhaps best known for his historical novels set in ancient Rome, *I, Claudius* (1934) and *Claudius the God* (1934), which were made into a *BBC television series in 1976. After fighting in *World War I, Graves left Britain and lived most of his life in Majorca.

ˌThomas ˈ**Gray** /ˈgreɪ/ (1716–1771) an English poet, best known for his **Elegy written in a Country Church Yard*. He was a friend of Horace *Walpole. The few poems that he wrote had a strong influence on the development of the *Romantic Movement.

ˌ***Gray's*** ˈ***Elegy*** /ˌgreɪz/ the name most people use to refer to the poem called *Elegy written in a Country Church Yard* (1751) by Thomas *Gray. It describes life in the country and the dignity of man, and was an early influence on the writers of the *Romantic Movement. It begins:

The curfew tolls the knell of parting day,
The lowing herd winds slowly o'er the lea,
The ploughman homeward plods his weary way,
And leaves the world to darkness and to me.

GRE /ˌdʒiː ɑːr ˈiː/ (*in full* **Graduate Record Examination**) a standard US examination taken to enter an American *graduate school.

Grease /griːs/ a US musical play that opened in 1972 in New York and had 3 388 performances. The story is about the love affairs of young people, especially Danny and Sandy, in a *high school in the early days of *rock and roll. The title refers to the hair oil used by the boys. In the successful film version (1978) John *Travolta and Olivia Newton-John played the main parts. There was also a *Grease 2* (1982) with different actors which was less successful.

the ˈ**Great** **A**ˈ**merican** ˈ**Desert** the area of desert in the south-west US and northern Mexico. It runs from southern *California north into *Idaho and *Oregon and east to the *Rocky Mountains. It includes the *Mojave Desert and the *Painted Desert.

the ˈ**great** **A**ˈ**merican** ˈ**novel** any novel that is regarded as having successfully represented an important time in US history or one that tells a story that is typical of America. Many US writers have tried to write such a book, though some people would say that none have yet succeeded. Others believe that some books do deserve to be called 'the great American novel', including **Gone with the Wind*, **Huckleberry Finn* and *The *Grapes of Wrath*.

Great Britain

Great Britain is, strictly, a geographical area consisting of the large island which is divided into England, Wales and Scotland. It is often called **Britain**. The name *Great Britain* was first used in a political sense after the *Act of Union between Scotland and England and Wales in 1707.

The British Isles describes the geographical area of Great Britain, all of Ireland (including the independent Republic of Ireland), and all the many smaller offshore islands, including the *Orkneys and the *Scilly Isles. It has a total area of 121 544 square miles (314 798 square kilometres).

The United Kingdom of Great Britain and Northern Ireland, called for short **the United Kingdom** or **the UK**, refers to the political state that includes the countries of England, Wales, Scotland and *Northern Ireland. It does not include the *Isle of Man or the *Channel Islands, which are **Crown dependencies**. The United Kingdom was formed in 1801 when the Irish parliament was joined with the parliament for England, Wales and Scotland in London, and the whole of the British Isles became a single state. However, in 1922 the south of Ireland became the Irish Free State and in 1949 an independent republic.

The names *Great Britain* and *United Kingdom* are now often used informally to mean the same thing. There are older names for parts of the United Kingdom, but these are found mostly in literature. ***Britannia** is the name the Romans gave to their province which covered most of England. ***Albion** was the original Roman name for England, **Caledonia** their name for Scotland, **Cambria** for Wales and **Hibernia** for Ireland.

The people of the United Kingdom are **British** and have British nationality. As a group they are usually referred to as **the British**, rather than as **Britons**, though this name is used in the media. **Ancient Britons** were the people who lived in Britain before the Romans came. Only people who come from England can be called **English**. People from Ireland are **Irish**, people from Wales **Welsh**, and people from Scotland **Scots** or **Scottish**, and they do not like being called English. The term **the Brits** is only used informally, often humorously. Many people from Scotland, Wales and Northern Ireland have stronger feelings of loyalty towards their own country than they do to the United Kingdom. British people who have come originally from Asia, Africa or the West Indies may also feel two sets of loyalties.

the ˌ***Great*** ˈ***Britain*** a large steamship, designed by *Brunel and built in 1843. It was the first of the large passenger ships that used to travel regularly between Europe and America.

the ˌ**Great De**ˈ**pression** (*also* the **Depression**) the period of severe economic failure in most countries of the world that lasted from 1929 until *World War II. It began in the US when the *New York Stock Exchange fell on 29 October 1929, known as *Black Tuesday. Many businesses and banks failed and millions of people lost their jobs. President Franklin D *Roosevelt improved the situation with his *New Deal policy, but the Great Depression was only ended by industrial production for the war.

the ˌ**Great Di**ˈ**vide** ⇨ CONTINENTAL DIVIDE.

ˌ**Greater** ˈ**London** /ˈlʌndən/ the area covered by the 32 *boroughs of London. It was established as a local government area in the 1960s when parts of the *counties closest to London became parts of London. It is a very large area, covering 610 square miles/ 1 580 square kilometres, with a population of around 6.7 million. It was governed by the *GLC until 1983.

the ˌ**Greater London** ˈ**Council** /lʌndən/ ⇨ GLC.

ˌ**Greater** ˈ**Manchester** /ˈmæntʃɪstə(r)/ a large area in north-west England consisting of *Manchester and parts of the towns and counties that surround it. It used to be a *metropolitan county until the system of local government was changed in the 1980s.

the ˌ**Great Exhi**ˈ**bition** an exhibition of products from many countries around the world that took place in London in 1851. It was the world's first international trade fair (= a large event where companies display their products in order to increase sales) and the *Crystal Palace was built to contain it.

ˌ***Great Expecˈtations*** a novel (1861) by Charles *Dickens. It is the story of a young man, Pip, who helped a prisoner to escape when he was a boy. Later, the man sends him money, but Pip thinks that it comes from the family of Estella, the girl he loves. He moves to London, expecting to become rich and to marry Estella. He is cruel to the people who looked after him as a child, because he is ashamed of their poverty, but when the money stops coming, and Estella marries somebody else, he goes back to them and learns to be a better person. See also HAVISHAM.

the ˌ**Great Fire of ˈLondon** ⇨ FIRE OF LONDON.

The ˌ***Great ˈGatsby*** /ˈgætsbi/ a novel (1925) by the US writer F Scott *Fitzgerald. The story is about Jay Gatsby, a man who has become very rich through illegal activities, and his attempts to win back his former lover Daisy Buchanan. The book is regarded as one of the best descriptions of the lives of rich, lazy people in the *Jazz Age. There have been three film versions.

the ˌ**Great ˈGlen** (*also* ˌ**Glen ˈMore** /ˈmɔː(r)/) a long valley running across the *Highlands of Scotland from the west coast near *Fort William to the east coast near Inverness. Loch *Ness fills part of it.

the ˌ**Great ˈLakes** a group of five large lakes along the central and eastern border between the US and Canada. They are connected and have a total area of 95 170 square miles (246 490 square kilometres), the largest area of fresh water in the world. They are Lake *Superior, Lake *Michigan (completely in the US), Lake *Huron, Lake *Erie and Lake *Ontario. Large ships use them to travel between the Atlantic Ocean and cities like *Chicago.

the ˌ**Great North ˈRoad** the name of the old road between London and *Edinburgh. It used to be the main road north from London, before it was replaced in the 20th century by more modern roads and *motorways. Some parts of the A1 road are still referred to as the Great North Road.

ˌ**Great ˈOrmond Street** /ˈɔːmənd; *AmE* ˈɔːrmənd/ a street in central London which contains the Hospital for Sick Children, which most people call the Great Ormond Street Hospital. It is the best-known children's hospital in Britain. Several television programmes have been made about it, and charities often collect money for it. Part of the profits from all sales and performances of **Peter Pan* go to the hospital: *She was transferred to Great Ormond Street for a life-saving operation yesterday.*

the ˌ**Great ˈPlague** the serious and widespread attack of bubonic plague (= a disease causing fever, swellings and death) in London in 1664–5. The disease was spread by the fleas (= insects that feed on blood) from rats and killed over 70 000 people. Most British people know about the plague from pictures, stories and films in which bodies are collected each morning in the streets.

London during the Great Plague

the ˌ**Great ˈPlains** a large area of the west central US where the land is high and flat. It includes the 10 *Plains States, stretching about 400 miles (644 kilometres) east from the *Rocky Mountains, and from Canada to southern *Texas. It was the home of the *Plains Indians and is also called the *Wheat Belt of America, although dry weather in the 1930s turned the southern part into the *Dust Bowl.

the ˌ**Great Salt ˈLake** a large shallow lake in the US state of *Utah whose water is more salty than sea water. It is the largest salt lake in North America, about 72 miles (116 kilometres) long and 30 miles (48 kilometres) wide. Industry takes salt and other minerals from it. Five miles south-east of the lake is *Salt Lake City. To the west is the Great Salt Lake Desert with the Bonneville Salt Flats where drivers have established the highest speeds on land.

the ˌ**Great ˈSeal** **1** the state seal (= a tool for putting a design in wax on a document to show that it is official) of the United Kingdom. It is kept by the *Lord Chancellor and used on documents of national importance. **2** the national seal of the US. It is kept by the *Secretary of State and used on documents of national importance.

the ˈ**Great ˈSmoky ˈMountains** (*also* the **Great Smokies**) a beautiful part of the *Appalachian Mountains which separates *Tennessee from *North Carolina. It gets its name from the thin clouds like smoke which often cover the valleys. The highest point is Clingman's Dome (6 642 feet/2 026 metres). Most of the area is within the **Great Smoky Mountains National Park** which was opened in 1934 and was made a *World Heritage Site in 1983.

the ˌ**Great Soˈciety** a phrase used by US President Lyndon *Johnson in 1964 to explain what his new social and economic programmes could achieve. He wanted to create a society in which all Americans were equal and there was no poverty. As part of this aim, Johnson's government created the *Medicare and *Medicaid medical programmes, the Head Start educational programme for poor children and the US Department of Housing and Urban Development. It also passed the *Voting Rights Act.

the ˌ**Great ˈSpirit** (in the religions of many *Native-American peoples) the father god who created everything.

the ˌ**Great ˈStorm** the name given to a storm with very strong winds that blew across much of southern England in October 1987. Several people were killed when buildings, cars and thousands of trees were blown over. Many people were surprised and angry because the *Meteorological Office gave no warning of the storm.

the ˌ**Great ˈTrain ˌRobbery** a robbery that took place in southern England in 1963. A group of men attacked a mail train and stole over £2 million. It is Britain's most famous robbery because little of the stolen money was ever found. Most of the robbers were caught and sent to prison, but one of them, Ronald Biggs, escaped from prison and still lives openly in Brazil.

The ˌ***Great ˈTrain ˌRobbery*** a 10-minute US silent film (1903) which has been called 'the first real movie', because it was the first to tell a story. It is a *western about criminals who rob a train and then celebrate in town.

ˈ**Great Uniˈversal ˈStores** (*abbr* **GUS**) a large British company which sells mainly clothes. It owns several *high-street shops, but most of its business is by mail order, selling goods through catalogues.

the ˌ**Great ˈWar** (*old-fash*) World War I.

the ˌ**Great White ˈFleet** a group of 16 US war ships sent on a tour around the world for 15 months (1907–9) by President Theodore *Roosevelt. His main aim was to show foreign countries, especially possible enemies, how powerful the US was.

ˌ**great white ˈhope** *n* (*AmE*) any white boxer who was thought to have a chance of beating Jack *Johnson, who was the first *African-American heavyweight champion and not popular with many white Americans. The expression is still sometimes used in the sport of boxing today, but usually in a humorous way.

the ˌ**Great White ˈWay** a popular name for the theatre district of *Broadway in New York, because of the many bright lights outside the theatres.

G

ˌJimmy ˈ**Greaves** /ˈgriːvz/ (1940–) an English footballer who played for *Chelsea, *Tottenham Hotspur and England in the 1950s and 1960s. He was an exciting attacking player who scored many goals. In the 1980s he became a television sports presenter, and is well known for his relaxed attitude and humorous comments about football. He is often referred to by the informal *nickname **Greavsie**.

ˌKate ˈ**Greenaway**[1] /ˈgriːnəweɪ/ (1846–1901) an English artist, well known for her illustrations for children's books. She developed her own style of drawing children, usually playing and dressed in early 19th-century clothes.

ˌPeter ˈ**Greenaway**[2] /ˈgriːnəweɪ/ (1942–) an English film director. His films make much use of colours and visual symbols, and are often compared with paintings. Some people find them difficult to understand. They include *The Draughtsman's Contract* (1982), *The Belly of an Architect* (1987) and *Prospero's Books* (1991).

ˌ**green ˈbelt** *n* [C, U] an area of countryside around a town. In Britain, building is strictly controlled in green belts to make sure that towns do not become too big and that there is some countryside for the people from the towns to enjoy. There are often strong protests when people are given permission to build on this land. In the US, a green belt is usually a nature area protected by a town or city. It is often a large park, with paths where people can walk: *The council rejected plans for a housing development on green belt land.*

the ˌ**Green ˈBerets** the popular name for the US Army Special Forces because of the green caps they wear. They fought a lot in the tropical forests of Vietnam during the *Vietnam War. *The Green Berets* (1968), with John *Wayne, was a film about that war.

the ˈ**Green Book** a US book containing the names of all the important people in Washington, DC, and its area. It includes members of the government, senior representatives of foreign countries and other people in Washington's high society.

ˌ**green ˈcard** *n* **1** (in Britain) a green document provided by British insurance companies to show that a person is insured to drive in other countries: *Are you sure you've got everything? Passport, road maps, green card?* **2** (in the US) an official document required by people who come from other countries to work in the US.

the ˌ**Green Cross ˈCode** a set of rules, first published in 1971, for teaching children how to cross roads safely in Britain. Children are reminded of the Green Cross Code through television advertisements and large illustrations on the walls of schools, doctors' waiting rooms, etc.

ˌGraham ˈ**Greene** /ˈgriːn/ (1904–91) a English writer of novels. He became a *Roman Catholic in 1926, and many of his books, such as *The *Power and the Glory*, have strong moral or religious themes. He travelled to many different parts of the world and many of his books are set in tropical countries. He divided his books into 'entertainments', such as *Our Man in Havana* (1958), and more serious novels, such as *The Heart of the Matter* (1948). Greene also wrote plays, travel books, essays and scripts for films,including *The *Third Man*.

ˌ**Green ˈGiant**™ a name used on its products by an international company that sells vegetables, either fresh or frozen or in cans. The advertisements describe the food as coming from 'the valley of the jolly Green Giant'. A giant is a creature in stories with a human form but great size and strength.

ˌ**green ˈgoddess** *n* the *nickname for a British military fire engine (= vehicle carrying equipment for putting out fires), which is green in colour. Green goddesses are used for fighting fires when the normal services for doing this are not available, e.g. during a strike.

ˌ***Green Grow the ˈRushes O*** an old English *folk song in which the line 'Green grow the rushes O' is repeated in every verse. Each verse names a number of people or things, mostly connected with the Bible, and repeats all the things named in the previous verses. The song is often sung by children in British schools.

ˌ**Greenham ˈCommon** /ˌgriːnəm/ a military air base in southern England. In the 1980s, when the British government agreed to keep US nuclear missiles there, the base became well known because a large group of women set up a camp around it to protest against the weapons. Many of the women were arrested several times, but they usually returned to the camp. Some stayed there until the weapons were taken away in 1991: *She's a veteran protester and was one of the original Greenham Common women.*

ˌ**Green ˈMan** *n* [usu sing] **1** a figure of a person that has a green light shining through it at traffic lights in Britain. The green man lights up when the traffic has stopped, to show people that it is safe to cross the road. **2** an image of a man surrounded by green plants, trees, etc. In Britain it is an old symbol of fertility (= the ability of people to have children, trees to produce fruit and the soil to produce crops). The Green Man is a common name for a pub.

the ˈ**Green ˌParty** a British political party that aims to protect the environment. It is against the use of nuclear power and other forms of industry and transport which it considers harmful. It was formed in 1973 as the Ecology Party, and changed its name to the Green Party in 1985. Many people voted for the party in the 1980s, particularly in elections for the *European Parliament, but it did not win enough votes in British elections to have any *MPs in the *House of Commons.

ˈ**Greenpeace** /ˈgriːnpiːs/ a large international *pressure group that aims to protect the environment. Its members are well known for taking direct action and putting their own lives in danger in order to stop people from harming the environment. For example, they often go out in small boats to stop people from killing whales or throwing poisonous material into the sea. See also RAINBOW WARRIOR.

ˈ***Greensleeves*** /ˈgriːnsliːvz/ a famous English song which has been popular since the 16th century. Its gentle tune has been arranged in many different musical styles. In the song a man sings sadly that he loves a woman, Lady Greensleeves, but she does not return his love. Some people believe that it was written by *Henry VIII, but there is no evidence for this.

the ˌ**green ˈwelly briˌgade** (*also* **wellie**) /ˈweli/ *n* [sing + sing/pl *v*] (*BrE humor disapprov*) a *nickname for *upper-class and *upper-middle-class British people who go to outdoor events in the countryside. The name comes from the green wellington boots (= rubber boots) that such people often wear: *There was a show-jumping competition in the village and the green welly brigade were out in force.*

ˈ**Greenwich** /ˈɡrenɪtʃ/ a district of south-east London, on the south bank of the *Thames, with many attractive old buildings and parks. The original *Royal Observatory was built there in the 17th century. Its buildings now form part of the *National Maritime Museum. The *Millennium Dome is being built in Greenwich as the main centre for Britain's celebrations for the year 2000. Maritime Greenwich was made a *World Heritage Site in 1997.

ˌ**Greenwich ˈMean Time** /ˌɡrenɪtʃ/ ⇨ GMT.

ˌ**Greenwich ˈVillage** /ˌɡrenɪtʃ/ a district of *Manhattan(1) where many artists, writers and students live, while others meet in the cafés, bars and clubs there. It was associated with the *beat generation. In the late 20th century it became a fashionable district for homosexuals: *She sings in jazz clubs and works as a waitress in Greenwich Village.*

Gerˌmaine ˈ**Greer** /dʒɜːˌmeɪn ˈɡriːə(r); *AmE* dʒɜːr ˌmeɪn ˈɡriːər/ (1939–) an Australian writer who has lived mainly in Britain since the 1960s. She became internationally famous as a feminist (= a person who believes strongly that women should have the same rights and opportunities as men) after writing *The Female Eunuch* (1970), one of the most popular books of the period about the position of women in society.

greetings cards

Specialist greetings card shops, newsagents and department stores sell millions of cards every year to help people celebrate important events in the lives of their friends and family. Most people send ***birthday cards**. They also send cards to celebrate engagements, weddings, births, moving to a new house, retirement from work, to wish somebody good luck, or to express sympathy when somebody has died. In addition, there are cards for *Christmas and *Easter, and other religious festivals.

Most greetings cards are folded and have a picture on the front and a verse or message inside. There are also many cards that are blank inside so that people can write their own message. Other cards say things like 'just because I was thinking about you', and are for people to send when there is no special occasion. There are also many postcards printed with simple pictures and messages such as 'Miss you' or 'Write to me'. Some cards show famous paintings, others have country scenes, flowers, animals, etc. on them. Children's birthday cards often have a number for the child's age, and sometimes a badge. Many cards for adults have cartoons or rude jokes about getting old, or humour with a strong sexual content.

The most popular time to send cards is at Christmas. **Christmas cards** often have pictures of *Santa Claus, reindeer, robins and snow on them, as well as scenes from the story of Christ's birth. Many families send over 100 Christmas cards each year. People send cards to neighbours or people they work with, as well as to friends they see less often. Sending a Christmas card is a way of keeping in touch. Many people like to send **charity cards**, cards sold in aid of a *charity, because they want to do some good for others at Christmastime. Business companies send cards to their main customers, and some have cards specially printed.

Some special days are thought to have been invented by greetings card manufacturers in order to increase their profits, e.g. **Father's Day**, when children are expected to send a card to their father, and **Grandparents' Day**. *Mother's Day is a much older festival which has its origins in the Christian Church. Another important date is *St Valentine's Day, when people send cards to the person they love. Each year, around £25 million-worth of cards are sold in Britain for this one day alone. Many people send **valentines** without signing them. Others are signed with phrases like 'from a secret admirer'. In the US, children give small Valentine's Day cards to everyone in their school class.

Greˈnada /ɡrəˈneɪdə/ a country consisting of the island of Grenada and a group of smaller islands in the *Caribbean. It has been an independent state and a member of the *Commonwealth since 1974. In 1983, after the *Prime Minister had been killed, Grenada was attacked and taken over by US armed forces, who set up a new government. Many people around the world protested against the US action. ▶ **Grenadian** *adj, n.*

the ˌ**Grenadier ˈGuards** /ˌɡrenədɪə; *AmE* ˌɡrenə dɪər/ one of the oldest regiments in the British army. It was the first regiment of *Foot Guards.

ˌJoyce ˈ**Grenfell** /ˈɡrenfəl/ (1910–79) an English entertainer who wrote and performed humorous songs and spoken pieces in which she made fun of different types of English women. She also appeared in many British films and television programmes.

ˌ**Gretna ˈGreen** /ˌɡretnə/ a village just north of the border between England and Scotland. It is famous as the place where English couples traditionally ran away to get married, usually without their parents' permission, which they would have needed to be married in England. The Scottish laws concerning marriage were much less strict, and many couples were married by the Gretna Green blacksmith (= a person whose job is making things out of iron). These marriages became illegal in Scotland in 1940.

ˌLady Jane ˈ**Grey**[1] /ˈɡreɪ/ (1537–54) queen of England for nine days in 1553. She was a great-granddaughter of *Henry VII and a *Protestant. She was 15 years old when the Duke of Northumberland persuaded her to marry his son and persuaded the king, *Edward VI, to name her as the next queen instead of his *Roman Catholic sister, *Mary I. Jane became queen when Edward died, but was soon put in prison by supporters of Mary, and was later killed in the *Tower of London.

ˌZane ˈ**Grey**[2] /ˌzeɪn ˈɡreɪ/ (1872–1939) a US author of *western novels which have sold millions of copies. They include *The Last of the Plainsmen* (1908) and his most famous, *Riders of the Purple Sage* (1912). See also ZANE GREY THEATER.

ˌ**Greyhound ˈbus** *n* any of the buses of the Greyhound Lines Company, the largest US bus company operating between towns and cities. It was established in 1914 and took its present name in 1930 because the buses were painted grey and had a smooth design. They have become a familiar part of US life.

the ˌ**Greyhound ˈDerby** one of the most important races in Britain for greyhounds (= dogs that can run very fast). It took place once a year at *White City until 1984, when it was moved to *Wimbledon. Many people bet on the race.

ˈ**greyhound ˌracing** *n* [U] a popular sport in Britain in which greyhounds (= large thin dogs) race around a circular track chasing an imitation hare. People make bets on the races, and refer to the sport informally as 'the dogs'. The two most important British races are the Greyhound Derby and the Grand National. The sport is also found in the US but is less popular there than in Britain.

ˌD W ˈ**Griffith** /ˈgrɪfɪθ/ (David Wark Griffith 1875–1948) the leading US director of silent films. He is remembered especially for making films on a large scale, using grand scenery and many actors. These included *The *Birth of a Nation*, *Intolerance* (1916) and *Broken Blossoms* (1919). In 1919 Griffith, together with Mary *Pickford, Douglas *Fairbanks[1] and Charlie *Chaplin, established the independent film production company *United Artists. He received a special *Oscar in 1936.

ˌJoseph **Griˈmaldi** /grɪˈmɔːldi/ (1779–1837) an English comedy actor who is regarded as the first British clown. He invented the style that is now typical of clowns in many countries, wearing strange, brightly-coloured clothes and white make-up on his face. Many clowns are still called 'Joey' after him.

ˌJohn ˈ**Grisham** /ˈgrɪʃəm/ (1955–) a US author of popular novels about lawyers. He was formerly a lawyer in a small town in *Mississippi. His books, many of which have become films, include *A Time to Kill* (1988), *The Firm* (1989), *The Chamber* (1994) and *The Partner* (1997).

ˌVirgil ˈ**Grissom** /ˌvɜːdʒɪl ˈgrɪsəm; *AmE* ˌvɜːrdʒɪl/ (1926–67) the second US astronaut to be sent into space (1961), and the first to make two space flights. He was killed with two other astronauts, Roger Chaffee and Edward White, in the Apollo 1 spacecraft when it was destroyed by fire during a test on the ground. See also APOLLO PROGRAM.

grits /grɪts/ *n* [U] (*AmE*) corn which has been partly crushed and then boiled. It is usually eaten warm, with butter, as part of breakfast in the southern US states. Compare HOMINY.

ˈGeorge and ˈWeedon ˈ**Grossmith** /ˈwiːdn ˈgrəʊsmɪθ; *AmE* ˈgroʊsmɪθ/ two English brothers (1847–1912 and 1854–1919), known for writing *The *Diary of a Nobody*. Weedon also illustrated the book.

ˌ**Grosvenor** ˈ**Square** /ˌgrəʊvnə; *AmE* ˈgroʊvnər/ a large square in central London, England. The US embassy is on one side of the square, and people have traditionally gone there to protest against US actions which they disapprove of, such as the *Vietnam War or the invasion of *Grenada.

ˈ**Groundhog Day** /ˈgraʊndhɒg; *AmE* ˈgraʊndhɔːg/ (in the US) 2 February. According to tradition, if the groundhog (= a small animal that lives under the ground) comes out of its hole after its winter sleep on that day and sees its own shadow, it is frightened by it and goes back down its hole. This means that there will be six more weeks of winter. If it sees no shadow, it is a sign that there will be an early spring. In many US communities people watch for the appearance of a groundhog on Groundhog Day. The best-known of these places is Punxsutawney, *Pennsylvania, where the groundhog is always called Phil.

ˌ**Group** ˈ**Four** a large British security company. It employs people to guard buildings, deliver money to banks, etc. There were many jokes about Group Four in the 1990s when the government used the company to take prisoners to and from prisons, and many of the prisoners escaped.

Grove /grəʊv/ (*full name* ***The*** ˈ***New Grove*** ˈ***Dictionary of*** ˈ***Music and*** ˈ***Musicians***) a large British dictionary in many volumes containing information about most types of serious music and musicians. It was originally written by George Grove (1820–1900). New editions have been published throughout the 20th century.

ˈ**Growmore**™ /ˈgrəʊmɔː(r); *AmE* ˈgroʊmɔːr/ *n* [U] a substance that people put on their gardens to make plants grow better.

ˈ**Grub Street** the former name of a street in London, England, which became famous as a place where you could find someone to write short books or articles on anything at all, though the quality would not be very good. The phrase 'Grub Street' is now used to refer to journalists and other writers who produce work of poor quality, simply to earn money: *It shows all the worst aspects of Grub Street journalism.*

grunge /grʌndʒ/ *n* [U] **1** (*also* **grunge rock**) a relaxed style of *rock music, with a harsh guitar sound. It was especially popular in the early 1990s. **2** a fashion associated with grunge music. It included untidy hair and torn clothes, especially *jeans.

the **G7** /ˌdʒiː ˈsevn/ (*in full* the **Group of Seven**) the seven richest industrial countries in the world: Britain, Canada, France, Germany, Italy, Japan and the US. Politicians from these countries have regular meetings, usually to discuss economic problems and policies: *The Prime Minister is urging the heads of the other G7 countries to come to an agreement.*

the ˈBattle of ˌ**Guadalcaˈnal** /ˌgwædlkəˈnæl/ the first major US military attack against the Japanese in *World War II. Guadalcanal, the largest of the Solomon Islands in the western Pacific Ocean, had been captured by the Japanese. An army of US Marines landed there on 7 August 1942 and, after a long campaign, defeated them on 13 November.

Guam /gwɑːm/ an independent US territory in the western Pacific Ocean. It is the largest and most southern of the Mariana Islands. Guam is popular with tourists, and there are large US Air Force and Navy bases there. In 1944, during *World War II, US forces landed in Guam and defeated the Japanese who occupied it.

Guanˌtánamo ˈ**Bay** /gwɑːnˌtɑːnəməʊ; *AmE* gwɑːnˌtɑːnəmoʊ/ a bay in Cuba where there is a US Navy base. The sailors call it 'Gitmo'. The base has been there since 1903, although President Castro of Cuba has often demanded that the Americans leave.

The ˈ***Guardian*** a British national newspaper. When it started in 1821 in *Manchester it was only published once a week, but since 1855 it has been published every day except Sunday. Until 1959 it was called *The Manchester Guardian*. The paper's political views are left-wing and it is regarded as one of the 'quality newspapers'. People sometimes joke about it because it used to contain a lot of printing errors. For this reason it is sometimes referred to as *The Grauniad* (i.e. *Guardian* with its letters in the wrong order).

the ˌ**Guardian** ˈ**Angels** a US organization of young people who work to protect people from crime in large US cities. They do not have weapons, and the police work with them. Members wear red caps, and shirts with 'Dare to Care' printed on them. The Guardian Angels formed in New York in 1979 to prevent crime on the underground trains. A London group was begun in 1989.

ˈ**Guardian** ˌ**reader** *n* an educated *middle-class British person who tolerates different opinions and behaviour, and who is therefore thought to be typical of the kind of people who regularly read *The *Guardian* newspaper: *It's a policy that is sure to be popular among Guardian readers, if no one else.*

the ˈ**Guards Di**ˌ**vision** the infantry division (= soldiers who fight on foot) in the British army. It consists of the *Coldstream Guards, the *Grenadier Guards, the *Irish Guards, the *Scots Guards, and the *Welsh Guards.

ˈ**Guernsey** /ˈgɜːnzi; *Am E* ˈgɜːrnzi/ the second largest of the *Channel Islands. It is famous for its milk products, as a tourist centre, and as a place where the people pay very little tax. Its capital city is St Peter Port. **Guernsey cattle** are a breed of cows that produce very rich milk.

the Guggenheim Museum

the **'Guggenheim Mu,seum** /ˌɡʊɡənhaɪm/ a museum of modern art in New York, built with money given by Solomon R Guggenheim (1861-1949), a rich businessman. The unusual circular building was designed by Frank Lloyd *Wright and opened in 1959. It is sometimes called the 'giant snail'.

Guide *n* a member of the **Guides Association**, especially one aged between 10 and 14. This organization for girls (formerly called the Girl Guides Association) was started in 1910 as an equivalent to the *Scouts (formerly called the Boy Scouts). It encourages practical skills and a helpful attitude to other people. In Britain, Guides are divided into four groups: Rainbow Guides (aged 5 to 7), Brownie Guides (aged 7 to 10), Guides (aged 10 to 14), and the Senior Section, consisting of Ranger Guides and Young Leaders (aged 14 to 25). Adult helpers in the Guides Association are called **Guiders**.

'Guide Dogs for the 'Blind Associ,ation a British charity, started in 1933, which trains dogs to lead blind people. The equivalent US organization is the Guide Dog Foundation for the Blind, started in 1946.

a guide dog with its owner

the **,Guildford 'Four** /ˌɡɪlfəd; *AmE* ˌɡɪlfərd/ four Irishmen who spent 18 years in prison because a court of law said they were members of the *IRA and found them guilty of putting bombs in pubs in Guildford and Woolwich, London, in 1974. They were released in 1989, when it was discovered that the police had made changes to their notes after questioning the four men. This was one of several similar cases at about this time which damaged the reputation of the British police and public confidence in them. See also BIRMINGHAM SIX, MAGUIRE SEVEN, TOTTENHAM THREE.

the **'Guildhall** the building that serves as the town hall (= local government offices) for the City of London. Grand meals and other events take place there on important occasions. The original building of 1411 was mostly destroyed in the *Fire of London (1666), and the one built in its place was badly damaged by bombs in *World War II.

'Guinevere /ˈɡwɪnəvɪə(r); *AmE* ˈɡwɪnəvɪr/ the wife of King *Arthur, who became the lover of *Lancelot, Arthur's friend and his best *knight.

'Guinness™1 /ˈɡɪnɪs/ **1** a large international company that makes alcoholic drinks, and has other interests, including publishing. It began in Dublin in 1759. **2** *n* [U, C] a type of stout (= dark strong beer) made by the Guinness company. It is very popular in Ireland, the only place where it was made between 1759 and 1936: *A pint of Guinness, please.*

,Alec 'Guinness2 /ˈɡɪnɪs/ (1914–) an English actor who has appeared in a wide variety of plays and films. Some of his best-remembered films were *Ealing Comedies, including *Kind Hearts and Coronets* (1949), in which he played eight parts, both male and female. He won an *Oscar in 1957 for his part in *The Bridge on the River Kwai*. He also played the part of George Smiley in television versions of novels by John *Le Carré. He was made a *knight in 1959.

the **'Guinness Af,fair** /ˈɡɪnɪs/ a series of events in 1990 which led to four men in high positions in British companies being punished for serious offences in connection with the takeover of the drinks company Distillers by *Guinness.

The ***,Guinness Book of 'Records*** /ˌɡɪnɪs/a book, published every year by a branch of the *Guinness company, which gives all the records achieved in a very wide range of fields and activities. For example, the names of the oldest, tallest, fattest, richest and fastest people in the world are all given. The book was first published in 1955 and is now so popular that it is available in nearly 40 languages. People sometimes talk of doing something that has never been done before just to 'get into' (= have their names mentioned in) *The Guinness Book of Records*.

the **,Gulf of 'Mexico** /ˈmeksɪkəʊ; *AmE* ˈmeksɪkoʊ/ part of the western Atlantic Ocean between the south-east coast of the US, Mexico and Cuba. At its northern edge are the US **Gulf States** of *Florida, *Alabama, *Mississippi, *Louisiana and *Texas. The Gulf has wide white beaches that attract many tourists, but it is also an area of hurricanes (= violent storms with strong winds). The **Gulf Stream** is a current of warm water that flows from the Gulf of Mexico across the Atlantic to north-west Europe, affecting the climate there.

the **'Gulf of 'Tonkin Reso,lution** /ˈtɒnkɪn; *AmE* ˈtɑːnkɪn/ a document produced by the US Congress in August 1964 which gave President Lyndon *Johnson extra powers to use military force for defence in areas near Vietnam. This was because two US Navy ships had been attacked by North Vietnamese ships in the Gulf of Tonkin next to Vietnam and China. The resolution led to the US becoming more deeply involved in the *Vietnam War.

the **,Gulf 'War** a war from 15 January to 28 February 1991 between Iraq and the United Nations Security Forces, which included British and US soldiers. The war started after Saddam Hussein had refused to take his soldiers out of Kuwait, which they had occupied illegally in August 1990. The UN troops forced the Iraqi army out of Kuwait and destroyed many of their military weapons, but not before the Iraqis had set fire to many Kuwaiti oil wells, causing great damage to the environment. See also DESERT SHIELD, DESERT STORM.

,Gulf 'War ,Syndrome *n* [U] a disease that has affected many of the soldiers who fought in the *Gulf War in 1991 though its cause is not fully known. Those with the disease feel very weak and tired all the time. Some people believe that it is connected with the use of chemicals during the war, but the governments of Britain and America have not been willing to accept that this is a cause, or even that the disease exists.

,Gulliver's 'Travels /ˌɡʌlɪvəz; *AmE* ˌɡʌlɪvərz/ a novel (1726) by Jonathan *Swift in which he attacked the British attitudes of his time towards religion, science, the law, etc, using satire. Lemuel Gulliver, an English traveller, visits strange lands, including *Lilliput, where the people are all tiny, *Brobdingnag, where the people are all giants, and the country of the *Houyhnhnms and the *Yahoos, where the horses are wise and the humans are stupid and cruel.

ˌ***Gunga*** ˈ***Din*** /ˌgʌŋgə ˈdɪn/ a poem (1892) by Rudyard *Kipling. It is written in the language of an ordinary British soldier praising a Hindu who carries water for the British army in India and dies taking water to a wounded soldier during a battle. Many people know the last line of the poem:

You're a better man than I am, Gunga Din.

ˈ**gun** ˌ**laws** *n* [pl] laws passed to restrict the sale of guns and to control their use. In the US many people feel strongly that ordinary people should not be allowed to own guns because of the large number of violent crimes in which they are used. Others argue that this would be against the US *Constitution which says that everyone has the 'right to bear arms'. The *National Rifle Association has opposed all gun laws, but in 1993 *Congress passed the 'Brady Bill' restricting the sale and use of some types of guns. In Britain, *Parliament passed a law in 1997 that forbids the ownership of handguns.

G

ˌSally ˈ**Gunnell** /ˈgʌnl/ (1966–) an English athlete who was the first woman to hold the world, Olympic, *Commonwealth and European titles in the women's 400-metre hurdles race all at the same time.

the ˈ**Gunpowder Plot** a secret plan by a group of Roman Catholics to blow up the *Houses of Parliament and kill King *James I in 1605. They put gunpowder (= an explosive powder) in the cellars before the opening of Parliament by the King on 5 November. The plan was discovered before the gunpowder could be exploded, and one of the group, Guy Fawkes, was arrested and forced to give the names of the others. His name has remained the only one most people know, although he was not the leader of the group. Every year, before the opening of Parliament, the cellars are searched in a special ceremony. ⇨ note at Bonfire Night.

ˌ**Guns N'**ˈ**Roses** a US *heavy metal band, formed in 1986, which was once called 'the most dangerous band in the world' because of the violent words of their songs. Their albums have included *Appetite for Destruction* (1987) and *Use Your Illusion I* (1991).

ˌWoody ˈ**Guthrie** /ˌwʊdi ˈgʌθri/ (1912–67) a US folk singer who played the guitar and wrote more than 1 000 songs. Many of his songs were written during the *Great Depression and were protests against poverty and war, but he also wrote many happy songs, including *This Land is Your Land* and *So Long, It's Been Good to Know Ya*. Guthrie was a big influence on popular musicians in the 1960s, especially Bob *Dylan and his own son, Arlo Guthrie.

Guyˈ**ana** /gaɪˈɑːnə/ a country on the north-east coast of South America, formerly called British Guiana. It was a British colony from 1796 until it became independent in 1966, since when it has been a member of the *Commonwealth. Guyana's official language is English and the capital city is Georgetown. More than half its population are descended from Indian workers brought in for the sugar industry after *slavery was ended there in 1838. ▶ **Guyanese** /ˌgaɪəˈniːz/ *adj, n* (*pl* **Guyanese**).

ˌ**Guy** ˈ**Fawkes Night** /ˈfɔːks/ ⇨ note at Bonfire Night.

ˌ***Guys and*** ˈ***Dolls*** a *Broadway comedy musical play (1950), based on stories by Damon *Runyon. It is about some New York criminals and the attempts of a woman in the *Salvation Army to convert them to Christianity. The songs in the show include *Luck Be A Lady* and *Sit Down, You're Rocking the Boat*. Marlon *Brando and Frank *Sinatra appeared in the later film version (1955).

ˌ**Guy's** ˈ**Hospital** /ˌgaɪz/ (*also infml* **Guy's**) a leading *teaching hospital in south London, England. It was started in 1721 by Thomas Guy, a man who had made a lot of money printing and selling books. John *Keats was at Guy's medical school in 1816.

Gwent /gwent/ (since 1974) a county in south Wales. Its administrative centre is Cwmbran.

ˌNell ˈ**Gwyn** /ˈgwɪn/ (1650–87) an English actor who was the lover of King *Charles II for many years. She came from a poor background and could not read or write, but she had two of Charles's sons. She is thought of as a lively, cheerful and attractive woman who at one time sold oranges in the theatre at *Covent Garden.

ˈ**Gwynedd** /ˈgwɪnəð/ (since 1974) a county in north Wales. Its administrative centre is *Caernarfon.

gypsies

Gypsies are a people scattered through many countries. The name *gypsy* comes from the word 'Egyptian' because gypsies were once thought to have come from Egypt. Some people now believe that they originally came from India. In the US gypsies are called **Roma**, and in Britain they are known as **Romanies** or **travellers**. In Scotland and Ireland they are sometimes also called **tinkers**. They do not live in settled communities but travel about from place to place living in caravans. Their traditional language is **Romany**.

There are about 50 000 gypsies in Britain. It is difficult to know how many there are in the US because records are not kept of people's ethnic group. Roma or Romanies, like many other minority groups, have a strong sense of pride in their identity. In Britain, they are often treated with fear and suspicion by the rest of the population and are forced to move on from places where they stop. There are now a few official campsites for them but groups of caravans are more often seen on waste ground beside a road. The campsites often look dirty and untidy because gypsies have different ideas about health and cleanliness from other people. They never keep rubbish/garbage in the caravans, and although some put it outside in containers, others throw it down anywhere. Gypsies are very concerned with personal cleanliness and use different bowls for washing themselves, their clothes and their dishes.

Gypsies usually make money by selling new and second-hand goods. Some collect and sell scrap metal, while others do agricultural work. A few make a living from entertainment and singing. The women are known for going from door to door selling clothes-pegs, 'lucky' white heather or bunches of flowers.

Gypsies have always been associated with **fortune-telling**. They can be found at fairgrounds predicting people's future by reading their palms (= examining their hands) or looking into a crystal ball. Because of the mystery associated with their origins and their magical powers, gypsies have a popular romantic image that conflicts with the reality of families living on dirty caravan sites and being moved on by council officials or the police. Americans have little contact with gypsies and think of the Roma only as exciting, mysterious people who wear brightly coloured clothes and gold jewellery and have unusual powers.

ˈ**Gypsy** ˈ**Rose** ˈ**Lee** ⇨ Lee.

Hh

ˌHäagen-ˈDazs™ /ˌhæɡən ˈdæs/ a US make of expensive ice cream which is sold in many countries around the world, often through its own shops. It is produced by the *Pillsbury company.

ˌhabeas ˈcorpus /ˌheɪbiəs ˈkɔːpəs; *AmE* ˈkɔːrpəs/ *n* a writ (= legal order) saying that a particular person who is being held by the police or in prison must be brought before a court of law so that the court can decide whether he or she is being held legally. Habeas corpus is one of the most important ways of protecting people's personal freedom. It formally became a part of the law in Britain in 1679. US procedure is also based on the Act of 1679. Article 1 of the *American Constitution says that a person's right to get a writ of habeas corpus can never be taken away except in cases of rebellion or invasion. 'Habeas corpus' is part of the Latin phrase *Habeas corpus ad subjiciendum*, which means 'You should have the body brought before the judge.'

ˈHabitat /ˈhæbɪtæt/ a group of shops selling furniture and other things for the home like cushions, curtains and lamps. It was started in Britain in 1964 by Terence *Conran, with some shops opening later in the US and France. In the 1980s Habitat joined with *Mothercare and then with British Home Stores to form the Storehouse group, but Habitat was later sold again. It was especially successful in the 1960s and 1970s when it was one of the first companies to sell original designs of furniture, etc. that most people could afford.

ˌHadrian's ˈWall /ˌheɪdriənz/ a wall in northern England built between 122 and 127 AD by the Roman emperor Hadrian, from Wallsend on the River *Tyne to Bowness on the *Solway Firth. It was the northern border of the Roman Empire, from which the Romans could keep back the *Picts. It was a major achievement, 73 miles (120 kilometres) long and 16 feet (4.9 metres) high, with forts every mile along its length. Long sections of the wall remain, and thousands of tourists visit it every year. It was made a *World Heritage Site in 1987. See also ANTONINE WALL.

Hadrian's Wall

ˌRider **ˈHaggard** /ˌraɪdə ˈhæɡəd; *AmE* ˌraɪdər ˈhæɡərd/ (1856–1925) an English writer of exciting adventure stories. The best-known of these, *King Solomon's Mines* (1885) and *She* (1887), are set in southern Africa, where Haggard worked for many years. He was made a *knight in 1912.

ˈhaggis *n* [C, U] a famous Scottish dish made mainly from a sheep's or calf's heart, lungs and liver and boiled in a bag made from part of a sheep's stomach. Haggis is traditionally eaten by the Scots on *Burns Night.

ˌWilliam **ˈHague** /ˈheɪɡ/ (1961–) an English *Conservative politician. He became a *Member of Parliament in 1989 and Secretary of State for Wales in 1995. In 1997, following the *Labour Party's victory in the general election, he replaced John *Major as leader of the Conservative Party.

ˌEarl **ˈHaig** /ˈheɪɡ/ (*born* Douglas Haig 1861–1928) a British soldier who commanded the British Army in France during *World War I. After the war he helped to start the *Royal British Legion and organized *Poppy Day. He was made an *earl(1) in 1919.

ˌHaight-ˈAshbury /ˌheɪt ˈæʃbri/ a small area of *San Francisco that became famous in the 1960s for the many *hippies who lived there. It is known today as a centre for homosexuals. Haight-Ashbury is two miles west of the business district of San Francisco and east of Golden Gate Park. It has beautiful Victorian houses and interesting shops.

ˌHail to the ˈChief the official song for welcoming the US *President. It is a march played by a band when he enters a room or an outdoor area for an official event. It was first played in 1815 to celebrate both the birthday of George *Washington and the end of the *War of 1812. The music was written about 1812 by James Sanderson, an Englishman, and the words are by Sir Walter *Scott.

Hair a 'rock musical' play (1967) about *hippies. It opened in New York and a year later in London. It was criticized (and attracted audiences) because in one scene the actors were naked and because the characters were against the *Vietnam War and thought that drugs were fun. The songs include *Let the Sunshine In* and *The Age of Aquarius*. A film version appeared in 1979.

ˌNathan **ˈHale** /ˈheɪl/ (1755–76) an American soldier who was hanged by the British during the *American Revolution for being a spy. He is remembered for saying 'I only regret that I have but one life to lose for my country,' just before he was killed.

ˌBill **ˈHaley** /ˈheɪli/ (1925–81) the US singer who, with his group the Comets, first made *rock and roll popular. They recorded *Shake, Rattle and Roll* and then *Rock Around the Clock*, which Haley wrote. It was used in the film *The Blackboard Jungle* (1955) and became an international hit, with 22.5 million copies sold.

ˌhalf-and-ˈhalf *n* [U] (*AmE*) a mixture of milk and cream: *I like half-and-half on my cereal.*

ˌhalf-ˈtimbered *adj* (of a building) having a visible wooden framework filled in with brick, stone or plaster. Half-timbered buildings were especially popular in England in the *Tudor(2) period, partly because there was already less good wood available for building by this time. See also BLACK-AND-WHITE.

Halifax[1] a large town in *West Yorkshire, in northern

England. In the past it was a centre of the wool industry.

the **Halifax²** the largest *building society in Britain, established in 1853. Since 1997 it has also operated as a bank. Its main offices are in *Halifax, England: *I'm with the Halifax.*

ˌPeter ˈ**Hall** /ˈhɔːl/ (1930–) an English theatre, opera and film director. He ran the *Royal Shakespeare Company (1960–68) and the *National Theatre (1973–88), and has also been involved with the opera at *Glyndebourne. He was made a *knight in 1977.

the ˌ**Hallelujah** ˈ**Chorus** /ˌhælɪluːjə/ a well-known chorus in the *Messiah* by George Frideric *Handel. The music expresses great joy. According to tradition, the audience always stands up while the Hallelujah Chorus is being sung, because King *George II did this at the first London performance of the *Messiah* in 1743.

the ˌ**Hallé** ˈ**Orchestra** /ˌhæleɪ/ a famous orchestra started in *Manchester, England, in 1858 by Sir Charles Hallé (1819–95), a German pianist and conductor. Other famous conductors of the orchestra have included Hamilton Harty and John *Barbirolli.

H

ˌEdmond ˈ**Halley** (*also* ˌEdmund ˈ**Halley**) /ˈhæli, ˈhɔːli/ (1656–1742) an English astronomer and mathematician who was a close friend of Isaac *Newton. He is best remembered for **Halley's comet**, which was named after him. A comet is a bright object that moves through space round the sun with a tail of gas and dust. Halley correctly predicted that this one would return regularly to be seen in the night sky about every 76 years. It was last visible in 1986.

ˈ**Hallmark card** *n* any of the *greetings cards made by the US company Hallmark Cards Inc, the biggest company of its kind in the world. It produces cards in 30 languages in more than 100 countries. Hallmark was established in 1910 by Joyce C Hall (a man), and it is now a $3 billion company. Its advertisements always include the sentence, 'When you care enough to send the very best.' Hallmark also sells Christmas ornaments, writing paper, paper for wrapping gifts, and other products. It produces the television show *The *Hallmark Hall of Fame*, and owns Hallmark Entertainment, a company that makes other television programmes.

The ˈ***Hallmark*** ˈ***Hall of*** ˈ***Fame*** the oldest dramatic series on US television, produced by the Hallmark Card company. It has won more *Emmy awards (76 by 1997) than any other series. It began in 1951 with *Amahl and the Night Visitors*, the first opera written for television. It has presented many performances of *Shakespeare, as well as other famous and original plays. It was first presented each week by Sarah Churchill, the daughter of Winston *Churchill. There are now four programmes a year.

hallmarks

Hallmarks are official marks that are stamped into articles made of gold, silver and platinum to prove their quality. Under British law all items made of these metals must be **hallmarked** before they are put on sale. The marks are very small and are usually placed where they will not spoil the appearance of an article.

Hallmarks were introduced in Britain in 1300. They are controlled in Britain by the *Assay **Office**.

lion mark for sterling silver

Assay Office marks for London, Birmingham, Sheffield and Edinburgh

Most modern hallmarks include four symbols: the **sponsor's mark** identifies the company which made the article; the **standard mark** describes the quality of the metal; the **Assay Office mark** indicates the city where the article was tested and marked. The **date letter** which indicates the year in which the article was stamped, is not compulsory.

The sponsor's mark used to be an emblem such as a bird, but now consists of the initials of the maker. The standard marks consist of a number which indicates the quality of the metal. The number 916, for example, indicates 22 carat (*AmE* karat) gold.Formerly gold items were marked with a crown. Any silver items are marked with a lion, as well as the number 925, to indicate **sterling silver**, which is 92.5% pure. Platinum items may be marked with an orb (= a decorated ball with a cross on top). The Assay Office mark was first added in 1478, when all items had to be tested for quality at Goldsmiths' Hall (hence the name *hallmark*) in London. Britain currently has Assay Offices in four cities: the symbol for London is a leopard, for Birmingham an anchor, for Sheffield a rose and for Edinburgh a castle. Date letters are in different styles of type and set inside a shield. Additional symbols may show that the article was made to celebrate a particular occasion such as a *coronation or the millennium.

In the late 18th and early 19th centuries a system of hallmarks similar to that used in Britain was introduced in the US. Items were stamped with a date letter, a **duty mark**, which indicated that tax had been paid, and a lion. The practice did not last long, and instead goldsmiths and silversmiths stamped their work with their initials or full name. Some added a date, but many items have no date, so their age can only be estimated by the style of the piece and its decoration. In 1868 *Baltimore silversmiths were the first to add below their names the **sterling standard** of 925/1000 (i.e. 92.5%). Silversmiths in *Boston and New York City had **guilds** which decided their own standards, and items were often marked with the name of the city in which they were made.

Items made in the US now must have on them the mark of the person or company that made them and a standard mark. Gold items are marked in karats, usually abbreviated to 'K'. Most gold jewellery in the US is 18 karat and marked '18K'. Silver items of sterling standard may be stamped 'silver', 'solid silver', 'sterling silver', 'sterling' or 'ster'.

The idea of a hallmark as a means of identifying the origin and quality of an item has a wider use in English. If something is *the hallmark of* or *has/bears all the hallmarks of* something, it has all the essential features associated with that thing. If somebody *leaves/stamps their hallmark on* something, they have a unique and lasting effect on it.

ˌ**Hall of** ˈ**Fame** *n* (in the US) a group of people who have been chosen for their special achievements in a particular activity or profession. New members of such groups are usually honoured at a ceremony after being chosen by special judges or by the public. Some Halls of Fame have their own museums, like the Baseball Hall of Fame and the Rock and Roll Hall of Fame. The original Hall of Fame was a building opened in 1900 in New York to honour famous Americans.

ˌ**Hallowˈe'en** (*also* **All Hallows Eve**) the night of 31 October, when people once believed that ghosts could be seen. Now, in Britain and America, it is a time when children have parties, dress up as *witches, make lanterns out of pumpkins (= large round vegetables) from which the inside has been removed, and play *trick or treat'.

Hallowe'en celebrations

ˌWilliam ˈ**Halsey** /ˈhɔːlsi / (1882–1959) a US admiral who won victories in the South Pacific during *World War II. He commanded the Allied Forces (1942–4) and the US Third Fleet (1944–5) from his ship, the *USS Missouri*. He defeated the Japanese at the Battle of Leyte Gulf (1944). Halsey's popular name was 'Bull'. In his early career, he was on the *Great White Fleet and commanded ships during *World War I.

ˌAlexander ˈ**Hamilton¹** /ˈhæməltən/ (*c.* 1757–1804) one of America's *Founding Fathers. He fought in the *American Revolution, was one of the writers of *The *Federalist Papers*, and established and led the *Federalist Party. Hamilton was the first US Secretary of the Treasury (1789–95) and established the central Bank of the United States. He died after Vice-president Aaron Burr wounded him in a duel.

ˌLady ˈEmma ˈ**Hamilton²** /ˈhæməltən/ (*born* Amy Lyon 1765–1815) a beautiful English woman from a poor family who became famous as the lover of Lord *Nelson and the mother of his child, although she was married to Sir William Hamilton, the British government's representative at the court of Naples. After her husband and Nelson died, Lady Hamilton was put in prison for debt.

ˈ**Hamlet** /ˈhæmlət/ the main character in the play of the same name by William *Shakespeare, written in about 1601. Many people consider it Shakespeare's finest play. Hamlet, the Prince of Denmark, becomes very sad when his father, the king, dies and his uncle, Claudius, becomes king. His father's ghost tells Hamlet that Claudius has killed him, and makes Hamlet promise to kill Claudius. Hamlet wants to do this but delays too long. The play is long and complicated, and all the main characters die in the end: Hamlet, his mother Gertrude, Claudius, Ophelia (the woman Hamlet loves), her father Polonius and her brother Laertes. The character of Hamlet has a lot of doubts about himself, and in his most famous speech considers killing himself. It begins:

To be or not to be: that is the question:
Whether 'tis nobler in the mind to suffer
The slings and arrows of outrageous fortune
Or to take arms against a sea of troubles,
And by opposing end them?

ˈ**Hamley's** /ˈhæmliz/ the best-known toy shop in Britain. When William Hamley started it in London in 1760, he called it 'Noah's Ark'. It became 'Hamley's' in 1906 when the shop moved to its present position in *Regent Street.

ˌArmand ˈ**Hammer¹** /ˌɑːmənd ˈhæmə(r); *AmE* ˌɑːrmənd ˈhæmər/ (1898–1990) a US businessman who traded with the Soviet Union from 1921 and had influence with Lenin and other Russian leaders. Because of this, he became an informal messenger between the two countries. Hammer was the head of the Occidental Petroleum company and gave money for many good causes. He took doctors to Russia after the Chernobyl disaster.

ˌMike ˈ**Hammer²** /ˈhæmə(r)/ the main character in the crime novels by Mickey *Spillane.

ˌOscar ˈ**Hammerstein** /ˈhæməstaɪn; *AmE* ˈhæmərstaɪn/ (1895–1960) a US writer of songs. He wrote the words for many famous *Broadway musical plays, most of which were also made into films. With Richard *Rodgers as his partner, his shows included **Oklahoma!* and *The *Sound of Music*. Earlier successes included the *The Desert Song* (1926) with Sigmund *Romberg, **Show Boat* (1927) with Jerome *Kern and *Carmen Jones* (1943).

ˌDashiell ˈ**Hammett** /ˌdæʃəl ˈhæmɪt/ (1894–1961) a US novelist who wrote tough crime stories of the kind that are sometimes referred to as 'hard-boiled fiction'. He had a great influence on Raymond *Chandler and other writers. Hammett created the character Sam *Spade in *The *Maltese Falcon* (1930) and the humorous couple Nick and Nora Charles in *The *Thin Man* (1932). These books and many of his others were made into films. Hammett was sent to prison in the 1950s when he refused to say if he was a Communist. See also McCARTHYISM.

ˌJohn ˈ**Hampden** /ˈhæmdən/ (1594–1643) an English politician who opposed King *Charles I by refusing to pay the tax called *ship money. He was one of the *Members of Parliament that the king tried to arrest in 1642, an action which started the *English Civil War. Hampden himself was killed in the war.

ˌ**Hampden ˈPark** /ˌhæmdən/ Scotland's national football ground, in *Glasgow.

ˈ**Hampshire** /ˈhæmpʃə(r)/ (*abbr* **Hants**) a county on the south coast of England. Its administrative centre is Winchester.

ˈ**Hampstead** /ˈhæmpstɪd/ an area of north London, since 1965 part of the *borough of *Camden. It is a fashionable place, with many elegant *Georgian houses, and still has the character of an attractive village, which it once was. Many writers and musicians live there. **Hampstead Heath** is a large area of open land where people enjoy walking.

ˌLionel ˈ**Hampton** /ˈhæmptən/ (1913–) an *African-American *jazz musician who plays the vibraphone (= an electric instrument with bars that are hit with a wooden hammer), piano and drums. He has also written music and led a big band (1941–65). In his early career Hampton played with Louis *Armstrong and Benny *Goodman. His hits included *Flyin' Home* (1939) and *Midnight Sun* (1947).

ˌ**Hampton ˈCourt** /ˌhæmptən/ a grand palace beside the River *Thames, 15 miles (24 kilometres) to the west of London. It was built by Cardinal *Wolsey in 1515 and given by him to King *Henry VIII so that he would remain in favour with the king. The house was made even bigger by King *William III in 1689,

the maze at Hampton Court

the additions being designed by Christopher *Wren. Hampton Court is now open to the public. As well as its fine buildings, it is famous for its gardens and maze (= an area of paths between high hedges designed as a puzzle through which people try to find their way).

ˌHerbie ˈ**Hancock**[1] /ˌhɜːbi ˈhænkɒk; *AmE* ˌhɜːrbi ˈhænkɑːk/ (1940–) a US *jazz musician who plays the piano and writes songs. He performed with the Chicago Symphony Orchestra at the age of 12. He began the Herbie Hancock Sextet in 1968. His successful albums have included *Headhunters* (1973), *Future Shock* (1983) and *The New Standard* (1996). Hancock won an *Oscar in 1986 for his music for the film *Round Midnight*.

ˌJohn ˈ**Hancock**[2] /ˈhænkɒk; *AmE* ˈhænkɑːk/ (1737–93) a leader of the *American Revolution who was President of the *Continental Congress (1775–77). He was the first to sign the *Declaration of Independence and wrote his signature very large so that King *George III could read it. Americans still refer to any signature as a 'John Hancock': *Just put your John Hancock on this letter.*

H

ˌTony ˈ**Hancock**[3] /ˈhænkɒk; *AmE* ˈhænkɑːk/ (1924–68) an English comedian who became famous between 1954 and 1961 in the programme *Hancock's Half Hour*, first on radio and then on television, written by Alan Simpson and Ray Galton. Hancock played an angry character upset by the little problems of life, such as a missing page in a library book. One of his most famous programmes (on television) was *The Blood Donor*, in which he caused a lot of trouble in a hospital trying to give blood. Hancock's best work was with a small team of other actors. When he tried performing on his own he was less successful and became very depressed. He killed himself in Australia in 1968.

ˈGeorge ˈFrideric ˈ**Handel** /ˈfrɪdrɪk ˈhændl/ (1685–1759) a German composer who came to live in London in 1712 and stayed until his death, becoming a British citizen in 1726. Handel's music has always been especially popular with British people. He wrote 40 operas but his best-known works are his 20 oratorios, musical dramas based on stories from the Bible, especially the **Messiah*, about the coming of Jesus Christ. He also wrote music for ceremonies at the court of King *George I, including **Water Music* (1717) and *Music for the Royal Fireworks* (1749). Handel stopped writing music in 1751 because he was going blind. He is buried in *Poets' Corner in *Westminster Abbey.

ˈ**Handi-Wrap**™ /ˈhændi/ *n* [U] a US make of cling film, thin transparent plastic material used for wrapping food, etc. It is produced by DowBrand, part of the Dow Chemical Company.

ˌW C ˈ**Handy** /ˈhændi/ (William Christopher Handy 1873–58) an *African-American musician who is often called 'the father of the blues'. He wrote *St Louis Blues* (1914) but failed to sell it, so he began to collect and publish traditional *blues music. His other songs included *Memphis Blues* (1912) and *Beale Street Blues* (1917). He also led a band (1903–21).

ˈ**hangman** /ˈhæŋmæn/ *n* [U] a children's game in which one person chooses a word and the others try to guess what it is. They do this by choosing letters which they think may be in the word. Each time they choose wrongly, the first person can draw one part of a man hanging by his neck from a rope on a frame (the way that people used to be officially killed in the past). If the people guessing do not get all the letters of the word before the drawing is complete, they lose and are 'hanged'.

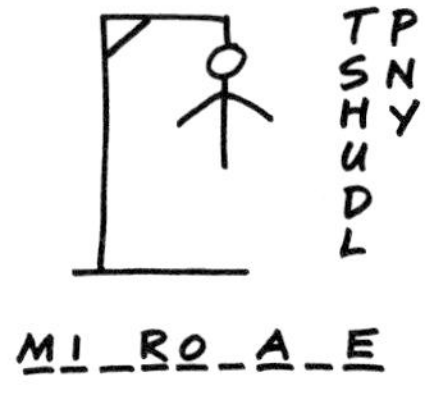

hangman

ˌTom ˈ**Hanks** /ˈhæŋks/ (1956–) a US actor who has won *Oscars for his parts in *Philadelphia* (1993) and **Forrest Gump*. He began in comedy films like *Big* (1988), and his other successes have included *Sleepless in Seattle* (1993) and *That Thing You Do* (1996), which he also directed. By 1997, he was being paid $20 million for each film he appeared in.

ˌ**Hanna and Barˈbera** /ˌhænə ənd bɑːˈbeərə; *AmE* bɑːrˈberə/ two US film cartoonists, **Bill Hanna** (1910–) and **Joe Barbera** (1911–), who have worked together for more than 50 years. They created the film characters of *Tom and Jerry for *MGM. They then set up Hanna-Barbera Productions in 1957 and made the popular television cartoon series *Huckleberry Hound* and *The *Flintstones*. See also SCOOBY DOO, YOGI BEAR.

the ˌHouse of ˈ**Hanover** /ˈhænəʊvə(r); *AmE* ˈhænoʊvər/ the British royal family between 1714, when George Louis, the leader of the German state of Hanover, became the king of Britain, and 1901, when Queen *Victoria died. George became the king because there was no heir to Queen *Anne, and the leaders of Hanover were related to King *James I through his granddaughter Sophia. Compare SAXE-COBURG-GOTHA.

ˌ**Hanoˈverian** /ˌhænəʊˈvɪəriən; *AmE* ˌhænoʊˈvɪriən/ *adj* of or relating to the British kings and queens from *George I to *Victoria (1714–1901): *the Hanoverian succession.*

ˈ**Hansard** /ˈhænsɑːd; *AmE* ˈhænsɑːrd/ the informal name for the *Official Report* of everything that is said in the British parliament, and in its committees. It is published every day. The name is also used for the reports of some of the *Commonwealth parliaments. It is probably named after Luke Hansard who first printed the *House of Commons *Journal* in 1774. Since 1909, every word has been printed exactly as it was spoken in the House of Commons: *I looked the debate up in Hansard.*

ˌ***Happy ˈBirthday to ˈYou*** a simple song which is traditionally sung for somebody on their birthday, especially before they blow out the candles on their birthday cake. If the person's name is Peter, the song goes:

Happy Birthday to you.
Happy Birthday to you.
Happy Birthday, dear Peter,
Happy Birthday to you!

ˌ**Happy ˈFamilies** a children's card-game played with a special pack of cards with pictures of members of various families on them. There are four members in each family: a man, his wife, their son and their daughter. The aim of the game is to collect as many complete families as possible. If you have one member of the family already, you can ask somebody if they have another member, e.g. 'Mr Bun, the Baker' or 'Miss Pill, the Doctor's daughter', and if they do, they have to give the card to you.

The ˌ**Happy ˈMondays** a British pop group (1984–93) whose best-known songs included *Kinky Afro* (1990) and the album *Pills 'n' Thrills 'n' Bellyaches* (1990). Two of the group's members later formed the group Black Grape.

ˈ**hardball** *n* [U] (*AmE*) another name for *baseball. The expression *to play hardball* can mean to use tough, aggressive methods in business, politics, etc.:

The police tried to negotiate with the protesters, but they wanted to play hardball. Compare SOFTBALL 1.

ˈ**hardcore** /ˈhɑːdkɔː(r); *AmE* ˈhɑːrdkɔːr/ *n* [U] a type of electronic pop music that became popular in Britain in the early 1990s. It is similar to *techno, with a very fast beat and few words.

ˌKeir ˈ**Hardie** /ˌkɪə ˈhɑːdi; *AmE* ˌkɪr ˈhɑːrdi/ (1856–1915) a Scottish miner who became a politician. He started the Scottish Parliamentary Labour Party in 1888, and the *Independent Labour Party in 1893, and then played a major part in creating the British *Labour Party, which he led from 1906 to 1908. He was proud of his *working-class origins, and became known as 'the member for the unemployed'.

ˌWarren G ˈ**Harding** /ˈhɑːdɪŋ; *AmE* ˈhɑːrdɪŋ/ (Warren Gamaliel Harding 1865–23) the 29th US *President (1921–23). Some members of his government were involved in illegal activities, including the *Teapot Dome scandal. Harding himself was opposed to the US becoming a member of the *League of Nations He was a member of the *Republican Party and had first been elected to the US Senate (1914–20) from *Ohio.

ˌ**Hard Rock** ˈ**Café** any of a group of *fast-food restaurants, started in 1971, with branches all over the world. The restaurants display objects from the history of pop music (e.g. guitars or clothing from famous musicians) on their walls, and are also famous because film actors and pop musicians sometimes go to them.

ˌ***Hard*** ˈ***Times*** a novel (1845) by Charles *Dickens. It tells how Thomas Gradgrind, a tough businessman, tries to bring up his children according to strict principles, and realizes too late that his very practical character has made their lives unhappy.

ˌAndy ˈ**Hardy**[1] /ˈhɑːdi; *AmE* ˈhɑːrdi/ a character in 15 *MGM films in the 1930s and 1940s. He was a boy who lived with his family in a small town, and Americans liked the happy, innocent stories. Mickey *Rooney played Andy, and Judy *Garland was his girlfriend. MGM won a special Oscar in 1942 because the series represented 'the American way of life'.

ˌOliver ˈ**Hardy**[2] /ˈhɑːdi; *AmE* ˈhɑːrdi/ ⇨ LAUREL AND HARDY.

ˌThomas ˈ**Hardy**[3] /ˈhɑːdi; *AmE* ˈhɑːrdi/ (1840–1928) an English writer of novels and poems. He was born in *Dorset and set most of his stories here, calling it 'Wessex' and its main town 'Casterbridge'. The region is still often called **Hardy country**. Many of his novels show how human life is often controlled by chance, which can be very cruel. His books often have an unhappy ending. The best-known include **Far from the Madding Crowd*, **Tess of the D'Urbervilles* and *Jude the Obscure* (1895). Many people in Victorian England did not like his books when they were first published, and for this reason Hardy stopped writing novels and wrote mostly poetry for the last part of his life.

the ˈ**Hardy Boys** /ˈhɑːdi; *AmE* ˈhɑːrdi/ two young brothers, Frank and Joe Hardy, who are characters in a US series of mystery adventure books for boys. They were created by Edward Stratemeyer, who also created Nancy *Drew, though the early books were mostly written by Franklin W Dixon. There have been more than 200 Hardy Boys books in all, and several television series.

The ˌ***Hare and the*** ˈ***Tortoise*** ⇨ *TORTOISE AND THE HARE*.

ˌLord ˈ**Harewood** /ˈhɑːwʊd; *AmE* ˈhɑːrwʊd/ (*born* George Lascelles 1923–) an English nobleman who is a cousin of Queen *Elizabeth II. For much of his life he has been closely involved with drama and music, especially opera, in Britain.

ˌ**Harewood** ˈ**House** /ˌhɑːwʊd; *AmE* ˌhɑːrwʊd/ a large, grand house to the north of *Leeds in England, built between 1759 and 1771. Much of the inside of the house was designed by Robert *Adam and the park around it was designed by 'Capability' *Brown.

ˈ***Hark! the*** ˈ***Herald*** ˈ***Angels*** ˈ***Sing*** the title and first line of a popular *carol sung at *Christmas. It was written by Charles *Wesley in the 18th century.

ˈ**Harlech** /ˈhɑːlək; *AmE* ˈhɑːrlək/ a town in *Gwynedd in Wales. It is famous for its castle, on a high rock above the town, built in 1289.

ˌ**Harlech** ˈ**Television** /ˌhɑːlək; *AmE* ˌhɑːrlək/ (*abbr* **HTV**) a commercial television channel that broadcasts programmes shown in Wales and south-west England.

ˈ**Harlem** /ˈhɑːləm; *AmE* ˈhɑːrləm/ a poor district of north *Manhattan(1) in New York that runs from 110th Street to 162nd Street. It was originally a Dutch village. Most of the people living there now are *African Americans, though there are many Puerto Ricans living in east Harlem, also called Spanish Harlem. All of Harlem is dangerous for tourists. Many African Americans moved there from the southern states in the 1920s and made it their cultural centre during the period called the *Harlem Renaissance. See also COTTON CLUB.

the ˌ**Harlem** ˈ**Globetrotters** /ˌhɑːləm ˈgləʊbtrɒtəz; *AmE* ˌhɑːrləm ˈgloʊbtrɑːtərz/ an *African-American *basketball team that plays exhibition games in the US and around the world to show their skills and make people laugh. In 1995 they lost their first game in 24 years, in Vienna. In the following year they had their 70th anniversary tour, and in 1998 they played their 20 000th game.

the ˌ**Harlem Re**ˈ**naissance** (*also* ˈ**Renaissance**) /ˌhɑːləm rɪˈneɪsns; *AmE* ˌhɑːrləm ˈrenəsɑːns/ a movement in *African-American culture in the 1920s which began in the New York district of *Harlem. Achievements were made in literature, music, art and the theatre. Among the writers involved were Countee Cullen, Jean Toomer and Zora Neale Hurston, and the musicians included 'Duke' *Ellington. The movement ended with the *Great Depression.

ˈ**Harlequins** /ˈhɑːləkwɪnz; *AmE* ˈhɑːrləkwɪnz/ (*also infml* **Quins**) *n* [pl] an English *Rugby Union club based in *Twickenham, south-west London. The team's shirt has many colours and it is has for many years been one of the most successful clubs in English Rugby: *He plays for Harlequins.*

ˌ**Harley-**ˈ**Davidson**™ /ˌhɑːli ˈdeɪvɪdsn; *AmE* ˌhɑːrli/ a large, heavy and expensive US motorcycle which has been very successful in races. William Harley and Arthur Davidson built the first three in 1903 in *Milwaukee, where the company's main office has always been. Popular models have included the 1936 Knucklehead, the 1957 Sportster 'super bike' and the 1995 Fat Boy.

ˈ**Harley Street** /ˈhɑːli; *AmE* ˈhɑːrli/ a street in central London, England, famous for the many private and expensive medical specialists who provide treatment there: *She couldn't afford to see a Harley Street doctor.*

ˌJean ˈ**Harlow** /ˈhɑːləʊ; *AmE* ˈhɑːrloʊ/ (1911–37) a US actor who was called the 'Blonde Bombshell'. She was a *Hollywood sex symbol in the 1930s, and often played aggressive but cheerful characters in comedy films. She had a love affair with Clark *Gable, and their films together included *China Seas* (1935) and *Saratoga* (1937).

ˈ**Harmsworth** /ˈhɑːmzwɜːθ; *AmE* ˈhɑːrmzwɜːrθ/ ⇨ NORTHCLIFFE, ROTHERMERE.

Harold II /ˌhærəld ðə ˈsekənd/ (*c.* 1019–66) the last

*Anglo-Saxon king of England. His army was defeated at the Battle of *Hastings on the south coast of England in 1066 by the army of *William the Conqueror from France. Harold died in the battle and William became King of England.

harp *n* a large upright musical instrument with many strings stretched across a frame that has three corners. There are various types of harp. One is sometimes used as a symbol representing Ireland, e.g. on coins, because it is an important instrument in traditional Irish music.

ˈ***Harper's*** /ˈhɑːpəz; *AmE* ˈhɑːrpərz/ an intellectual US magazine known for its news articles, essays and short stories. It was started in 1850 by Harper and Brothers (now HarperCollins), which also began the fashion magazine *Harper's Bazaar* in 1867. Since 1980, *Harper's* has been published by the Harper's Magazine Foundation.

ˌ***Harpers and*** ˈ***Queen*** /ˌhɑːpəz; *AmE* ˌhɑːrpərz/ a British magazine published once a month and written mainly for rich people, especially women. It contains articles about fashion and the social life of the upper classes.

ˌ**Harpers** ˈ**Ferry** /ˌhɑːpəz;; *AmE* ˌhɑːrpərz/ ⇨ BROWN.

ˈ**Harrier** /ˈhæriə(r)/ (*also* ˌ**Harrier** ˈ**jump jet**) *n* a British military aircraft which was the first to be able to take off and land with a vertical movement. The first model was made by the Hawker Siddeley company and the plane was first used by the *Royal Air Force in 1969.

ˌAverell ˈ**Harriman[1]** /ˌeɪvrəl ˈhærɪmən/ (1891–1986) a US diplomat. He was the US ambassador in the Soviet Union (1943–6) and in Britain (1946). He was also the US Secretary of Commerce (1946–8) and governor of New York (1954–8). Harriman helped to carry out the *Marshall Plan (1949–50) and to establish the Nuclear Test-Ban Treaty (1963). He was the main US representative at the Vietnam peace talks in Paris in 1968. His wife was Pamela *Harriman.

ˌPamela ˈ**Harriman[2]** /ˈhærɪmən/ (1920–97) a US ambassador in France (1993–7). She was born in Britain and was regarded as one of the most beautiful women of her day. She had many love affairs as well as three marriages. In 1936 she married Randolph Churchill, the son of Winston *Churchill. Her third husband was Averell *Harriman. After her death in France she was given the French Legion of Honour.

ˈˌBomber' ˈ**Harris[1]** /ˌbɒmə ˈhærɪs; *AmE* ˌbɑːmər/ (Arthur Harris 1892–1984) a British military leader in charge of the campaign carried out by *Bomber Command during *World War II. He was responsible for the success of this campaign, but has also been criticized for the number of civilian deaths it caused, e.g. in the *Dresden bombing. He was made a *knight in 1942 and a *baronet in 1953.

ˌRolf ˈ**Harris[2]** /ˌrɒlf ˈhærɪs; *AmE* ˌrɑːlf, ˈrɔːlf/ (1930–) an Australian entertainer who has been popular in Britain since the 1960s. He appears regularly on television and is especially popular with children. He is known for painting pictures very quickly on television, singing unusual songs and playing unusual musical instruments. He also presents a programme about animals.

ˌRex ˈ**Harrison** /ˈhærɪsn/ (1908–90) a English stage and film actor known mainly for playing light comic and romantic roles. His best-known part was that of Professor Higgins in the stage and film versions of **My Fair Lady*.

ˈ**Harris** ˌ**survey** /ˈhærɪs/ (*also* ˈ**Harris poll**) *n* any of the studies of public opinion carried out by the US company Harris Associates of New York.

ˌ**Harris** ˈ**tweed** /ˌhærɪs/ *n* [U] a type of thick woollen cloth for making coats, jackets, etc. It is woven on the island of Harris in the *Hebrides, off the west coast of Scotland: *a Harris tweed suit.*

ˈ**Harrods** /ˈhærədz/ a large, fashionable and expensive department store in the *Knightsbridge area of central London, England. It claims to be able to supply any article and provide any service. It began in 1861 as a small shop selling food, owned by Henry Harrod.

ˈ**Harrogate** /ˈhærəgət/ a spa town (= one where there are springs of mineral water considered healthy to drink) in *North Yorkshire, England. Many elderly and fairly rich people live there. It is also a conference centre.

ˈ**Harrow** /ˈhærəʊ; *AmE* ˈhæroʊ/ (*also* ˌ**Harrow** ˈ**School**) a well-known British *public school(1) for boys in north-west London, established in 1571. It is often considered to be one of the major boys' schools in Britain and many important people were educated there, including Winston *Churchill.

ˌLorenz ˈ**Hart** /ˌlɒrənz ˈhɑːt; *AmE* ˌlɔːrənz ˈhɑːrt/ (1895–1943) a US writer of songs who with Richard *Rodgers created 29 *Broadway musical plays, many of which became films. Hart wrote the words and Rodgers the music. Their plays included *Babes in Arms* (1937) and *Pal Joey* (1940), and among the songs they wrote were *The Lady is a Tramp* (1937) and *This Can't Be Love* (1938).

the ˌ**Harvard** ˈ**classics** /ˌhɑːvəd; *AmE* ˌhɑːrvərd/ *n* [pl] a series of 50 famous works of literature chosen and edited by Charles W Eliot (1834–1926), President of *Harvard University (1869–1909). He said they were 'all the books needed for a real education'. The series was published in 1909–10.

ˌ**Harvard Uni**ˈ**versity** /ˌhɑːvəd; *AmE* ˌhɑːrvərd/ the oldest US university and usually considered the best. Harvard is one of the *Ivy League universities. It was established as a college in 1636 in *Cambridge, *Massachusetts. Two years later, it was named after John Harvard, a *Puritan born in England who had given it money and books. Harvard is especially famous for its faculties (= departments) of law and business. Its library is the oldest in the US and one of the largest.

Harvard

ˌ**harvest** ˈ**festival** (*BrE*) *n* a Christian festival held each autumn to celebrate and give thanks for the gathering of crops. Fruit, vegetables, bread, etc. are taken to a church or school to decorate it, and a special service is held. Compare THANKSGIVING.

ˌWilliam ˈ**Harvey** /ˈhɑːvi; *AmE* ˈhɑːrvi/ (1578–1657) an English doctor who discovered how blood flows around the body.

ˈ**Harvey's**™ /ˈhɑːviz; *AmE* ˈhɑːrviz/ a British company based in *Bristol, England, which sells various types of sherry. The best known of these is Harvey's Bristol Cream.

ˌ**Harvey ˈWallbanger** /ˌhɑːvi ˈwɔːlbæŋə(r); *AmE* ˌhɑːrvi ˈwɔːlbæŋər/ *n* a US cocktail (= mixed alcoholic drink) made with vodka and orange juice, and with Galliano (= a strong, sweet Italian alcoholic drink) poured on top. It is served in a tall glass.

ˈ**Harwell** /ˈhɑːwel; *AmE* ˈhɑːrwel/ a British government research centre, near the village of Harwell in *Oxfordshire, England, where research is carried out into atomic energy.

ˌ**hash ˈbrowns** *n* [pl] (*AmE*) potatoes that have been cut into small pieces and fried. They are often eaten at breakfast.

the ˌBattle of ˈ**Hastings**[1] /ˈheɪstɪŋz/ a famous battle (1066) in English history at which *William the Conqueror defeated king *Harold II and became King of England. It was fought near Hastings on the south coast of England.

ˌWarren ˈ**Hastings**[2] /ˈheɪstɪŋz/ (1732–1818) the first British Governor-General of India. He was an important figure in the *East India Company. When he returned to Britain in 1785, he was accused of corruption but was found not guilty after a trial lasting seven years. ⇨ article at BRITISH EMPIRE.

ˌAnne ˈ**Hathaway** /ˈhæθəweɪ/ (1556–1623) the wife of William *Shakespeare. Her family home, **Anne Hathaway's Cottage**, is open to the public and is a popular tourist attraction in *Stratford-upon-Avon.

ˌRoy ˈ**Hattersley** /ˈhætəzli; *AmE* ˈhætərzli/ (1932–) a British politician who held a number of senior posts in the *Labour Party. He was a *Member of Parliament (1964–92) and deputy leader of the Labour Party (1988–92). He is now a journalist and author, and was made a *life peer in 1997.

ˌ**Hatton ˈGarden** /ˌhætn/ a street in central London, England, where a lot of jewellery companies have their offices.

ˈ**hat-trick** *n* (in sport) a series of three successes, e.g. scoring three goals in the same game or winning an event three times in a row. The expression was first used in cricket. A bowler who took three wickets in three balls was traditionally given a new hat by his club: *He completed his hat-trick with a wonderful third goal.* ○ *If she becomes champion again, it will be a hat-trick of victories for her in this tournament.*

Haˈwaii /həˈwaɪi/ the last state to join the US, in 1959, also known as the Aloha State. It consists of seven large islands and other smaller ones, in the north Pacific Ocean. The capital city *Honolulu and the port of *Pearl Harbor are on Oahu. The state attracts many tourists and produces pineapples, sugar, nuts and coffee. Captain James *Cook discovered the islands in 1778, and the US began to govern them in 1900.

Haˌwaiian ˈPunch /həˌwaɪən/ *n* [C, U] a US product name for a red fruit juice drink. It has been advertised on television for many years by a cartoon character called Punchy. Hawaiian Punch is especially popular with children, but adults also often drink it mixed with alcohol.

ˌLord ˈ**Haw-Haw** /ˈhɔː hɔː/ the name given to William Joyce (1906–46), who broadcast radio messages against Britain in an exaggerated English voice from Germany during *World War II. Although he was originally a US citizen he was hanged by the British as a traitor (= person who betrays his country) after the war.

ˌStephen ˈ**Hawking** /ˈhɔːkɪŋ/ (1942–) a British scientist who has greatly influenced people's ideas on the origins of the universe. His book on the subject, *A Brief History of Time* (1988), has sold millions of copies. He suffers from a serious disease which limits his ability to move and speak, so he communicates by means of a specially created computer which 'speaks' for him.

ˌHoward ˈ**Hawks** /ˈhɔːks/ (1896–1977) an American who directed, produced and wrote films in a *Hollywood career that lasted 52 years. The many famous stars he directed included Cary *Grant and Katherine *Hepburn in *Bringing Up Baby* (1938), Gary *Cooper in *Sergeant York* (1941), Humphrey *Bogart and Lauren *Bacall in *The Big Sleep* (1946), Marilyn *Monroe in *Gentlemen Prefer Blondes* (1953), and John *Wayne in *Rio Bravo* (1959). Hawks received a special *Oscar in 1974.

ˌNicholas ˈ**Hawksmoor** /ˈhɔːksmɔː(r)/ (1661–1736) an English architect who worked with Sir Christopher *Wren on the building of many churches in London, including *St Paul's Cathedral. He also worked with John *Vanbrugh on the building of *Blenheim Palace and *Castle Howard.

ˈ**Haworth** /ˈhaʊəθ; *AmE* ˈhaʊərθ/ a village in *West Yorkshire, England, where the *Brontë sisters lived and wrote their novels. It attracts many visitors, particularly because Emily Brontë's novel **Wuthering Heights* is set in the area.

H

Naˌthaniel ˈ**Hawthorne** /ˈhɔːθɔːn; *AmE* ˈhɔːθɔːrn/ (1804–64) a US writer of novels and short stories. He was born in Salem, *Massachusetts, and set his novels in *New England during the time of the *Puritans. The most famous are *The *Scarlet Letter* (1850) and *The House of the Seven Gables* (1851). His best-known collections of short stories are the two volumes of *Twice-Told Tales* (1837 and 1842).

ˌJoseph ˈ**Haydn** /ˈhaɪdn/ (1732–1809) an Austrian composer, known especially for his symphonies and choral music. His music was very popular in Britain while he was alive and is still performed regularly there. Haydn made two visits to England and his last 12 symphonies are called the London Symphonies because they were first performed in London. See also NELSON MASS.

ˌHelen ˈ**Hayes**[1] /ˈheɪz/ (1900–93) a US actor who was called the 'First Lady of the American Theater' and whose career on stage lasted 65 years. Her plays included *Dear Brutus* (1919) and *Victoria Regina* (1935). In films, she won *Oscars for *The Sin of Madelon Claudet* (1931) and *Airport* (1969).

ˌIsaac ˈ**Hayes**[2] /ˌaɪzək ˈheɪz/ (1942–) an *African-American singer of *rhythm and blues music. He also plays the saxophone and piano, and writes music. He won an *Oscar for his music for the film *Shaft* (1971). His successful albums have included *Black Moses* (1971), *Ike's Rap* (1986) and *Branded* (1995).

ˌRutherford B ˈ**Hayes**[3] /ˌrʌðəfəd biː ˈheɪz; *AmE* ˌrʌðərfərd/ (Rutherford Birchard Hayes 1822–93) the 19th US *President (1877–81). He was a Republican who ended *Reconstruction in the southern states. He had been a US officer in the *Civil War and a lawyer. Hayes was elected President by one vote of the *Electoral College. He had previously been elected to the US House of Representatives (1865–7) and was governor of Ohio (1867–71 and 1875–6). His wife was called 'Lemonade Lucy' because she would not allow alcohol in the *White House(1).

ˈ**Haymarket** /ˈheɪmɑːkɪt; *AmE* ˈheɪmɑːrkɪt/ (*also* **the Haymarket**) a street in the *West End of London, England, in which there is a famous theatre, also called the Haymarket.

the ˈ**Hays Office** /ˈheɪz/ the name more often used for the Motion Picture Producers and Distributors of America, because Will Hays (1879–1954) was its first president. The organization was established by the major US film companies to censor (= remove or change offensive parts in) their films. It published a Production Code (1930), usually called the **Hayes Code**, which contained rules on what films could show and say. These were followed until 1968.

The ˈ***Hay Wain*** /weɪn/ the best-known painting (1821) by the English artist John *Constable. It is in the *National Gallery in London, and shows a typical English countryside scene of the period, in summer. *Wain* is an old fashioned word meaning a farm cart.

the ˈ**Hayward ˌGallery** /ˈheɪwəd; *AmE* ˈheɪwərd/ an art gallery on the *South Bank in central London, England. It opened in 1968, mainly for exhibitions of 19th- and 20th-century art. There have also been displays of sculpture in the open air there.

ˌRita ˈ**Hayworth** /ˈheɪwɜːθ; *AmE* ˈheɪwɜːrθ/ (1918–87) a US actor and dancer known for her beauty. She was a major *Hollywood star, especially in the 1940s. She began in musical films, such as *You'll Never Get Rich* (1941) with Fred *Astaire, and then made a number of dramatic films. These included *The Lady from Shanghai* (1948), which was directed by Orson *Welles, one of her five husbands.

H

ˌWilliam ˈ**Hazlitt** /ˈhæzlɪt/ (1778–1830) an English writer and critic, best known for his essays and lectures. He expressed strong, often harsh opinions, especially about other writers. His best-known works include *Characters of Shakespeare's Plays* (1817–18) and *Table Talk* (1821).

ˈ**H-block** /ˈeɪtʃ/ *n* each of the buildings, built in the shape of an H, in which prisoners are kept in the *Maze prison near *Belfast in Northern Ireland.

HBO /ˌeɪtʃ biː ˈəʊ; *AmE* ˈoʊ/ ⇨ HOME BOX OFFICE.

ˌ**Head and ˈShoulders**™ *n* [U] a make of shampoo (= liquid soap for washing the hair) produced by the US company *Procter and Gamble. It is advertised as curing the problem of dandruff as well as making hair clean.

ˈ**Headingley** /ˈhedɪŋli/ a sports ground in *Leeds, *West Yorkshire, England, where Yorkshire County Cricket Club and Leeds Rugby League Club play their home matches. It was established in 1890 and since 1899 international cricket matches have been played there regularly. Headingley is also the name of an area of Leeds.

ˌDenis ˈ**Healey** /ˈhiːli/ (1917–) a leading British *Labour politician who held a number of senior government posts, including *Chancellor of the Exchequer (1974–9). He tried three times without success to become leader of the Labour Party, but was deputy leader from 1980 to 1983. When the *Conservative Party came to power Healey developed a reputation in parliament as a strong and effective opponent of their policies. In 1992, he retired from politics and was made a *life peer.

Heal's /hiːlz/ a fashionable furniture shop in central London, England, known especially for selling modern furniture. It was developed in its present building by Ambrose Heal (1872–1959), whose father had started the business.

the ˈ**Health and ˈSafety at ˈWork Act** a series of laws passed in Britain in 1974 which require employers to make sure that their employees are working in healthy and safe conditions.

the ˌ**Health and ˈSafety Eˌxecutive** a British government organization which recommends action concerning the standards of health and safety at places of work.

ˈ**health auˌthority** (*abbr* **HA**) *n* (in Britain) any of 100 local organizations within the *National Health Service responsible for health and health services in a particular area.

ˌ**health ˈmaintenance organiˌzation** ⇨ HMO.

ˌSeamus ˈ**Heaney** /ˈhiːni/ (1939–) a Northern Irish poet who won the *Nobel Prize for Literature in 1995. His work shows his concern both for the traditions of Irish culture and for the *Troubles in *Northern Ireland in recent times. His collections of poetry include *North* (1975), *Field Work* (1979), *The Haw Lantern* (1987), and *Seeing Things* (1991). In 1989 he became Professor of Poetry at *Oxford University.

ˈWilliam ˈRandolph ˈ**Hearst** /ˈhɜːst; *AmE* ˈhɜːrst/ (1863–1951) a very rich American who owned newspapers, magazines, radio stations and two film companies. He used *yellow journalism in his newspapers to increase their sales. His *New York Journal* competed fiercely in the 1890s with the *New York World*, owned by Joseph Pulitzer, and both encouraged the *Spanish-American War to help sales. Hearst built the castle of *San Simeon as his home in *California. Orson *Welles based his film **Citizen Kane* on Hearst's life.

The ˌ***Heart of ˈDarkness*** a long short story by Joseph *Conrad, published in 1902. The story is told by Marlow, a young man who travels up the Congo River in Africa to find Mr Kurtz, who works in the ivory trade. He discovers that Kurtz is worshipped by the local tribe and has fallen into a cruel and immoral way of life.

ˌ***Heart of ˈOak*** a British song written in 1770, with words by the English actor David *Garrick, which celebrates the qualities and achievements of British sailors. It contains the well-known lines:

Heart of oak are our ships,
Heart of oak are our men.

ˌEdward ˈ**Heath** /ˈhiːθ/ (1916–) a British *Conservative politician who became leader of the Conservative Party in 1965 and later *Prime Minister (1970–4). He is mainly remembered for taking Britain into the *European Union (then known as the *Common Market) in 1973. Faced with economic problems and strikes, he called a general election in 1974, which the Conservatives lost. In 1975 he was replaced as party leader by Margaret *Thatcher but he is still known as a firm supporter of the European Union and is highly critical of any opposition to it. He was made a *knight in 1992. When younger, Heath, who is often called Ted Heath, was also known as a keen sailor of yachts and as an organist and conductor.

ˈ**Heathcliff** /ˈhiːθklɪf/ a character in the novel **Wuthering Heights* by Emily *Brontë. He is found as a baby and brought up by the family of Catherine Earnshaw. He develops a strong love for her, but because of his wild nature and his background she cannot agree to marry him. He then leaves and Catherine marries. He returns three years later to take revenge on the people he blames for ruining his life.

ˈWilliam ˈ**Heath ˈRobinson** /ˈhiːθ ˈrɒbɪnsn; *AmE* ˈrɑːbɪnsn/ (1872–1944) a cartoonist and illustrator who was known especially for his comic drawings of strange and complicated machines for doing very simple tasks. As a result, any machine that appears strange and much more complicated than necessary is now often referred to as 'Heath Robinson': *He had rigged up a ridiculous Heath Robinson device to help him with the decorating.*

ˌ**Heathˈrow** /ˌhiːθˈrəʊ; *AmE* ˈhiːθroʊ/ the largest airport in Britain and the busiest airport for international flights in the world. It is 15 miles/24 kilometres west of London and was opened in 1946. By 1961 it had three terminals (= buildings for arrival and departure) and a fourth opened in 1986. There are plans to build a fifth, though many people are unhappy about the increased number of flights and passengers this would create. Heathrow is officially known as London Airport.

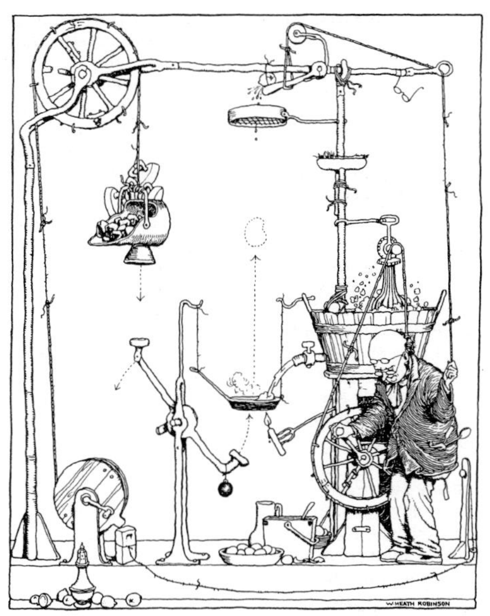

a pancake-making machine drawn by William Heath Robinson

ˌ**heavy** ˈ**metal** *n* [U] a kind of rock music, with very loud guitars, drums and singing. The term was first used of groups such as *Deep Purple and *Led Zeppelin in the early 1970s, when this kind of music first became popular. Other well-known heavy metal bands include Def Leppard and *Guns N' Roses. Heavy metal groups and their fans often have long hair, wear leather jackets and dance in a way that is known as 'headbanging' (= moving the head backwards and forwards very quickly to the rhythm of the music). In the US, people have expressed concern that the words of some heavy metal songs may have a disturbing effect on young people.

the ˈ**Hebrides** /ˈhebrɪdiːz/ a group of islands off the west coast of Scotland, consisting of the Inner Hebrides, which include *Skye and *Mull, and the Outer Hebrides, which include Harris and Lewis. All the islands are popular with tourists in the summer.

Uˌriah ˈ**Heep** /juˌraɪə ˈhiːp/ a character in the novel **David Copperfield* by Charles *Dickens. He is David's servant and, although he pretends to be anxious to serve him in any way, in reality he cheats him. His name is sometimes used to refer to someone who pretends to show great respect for a senior person but is not sincere.

ˌHugh ˈ**Hefner** /ˈhefnə(r)/ (1926–) the American who began **Playboy* magazine in 1953, and later created a larger company which included the Playboy Clubs.

ˈ**Hefty**™ /ˈhefti/ a US make of strong bags for putting rubbish in and for garden work, etc. There are also Hefty One-Zip bags for storing food.

ˈ**Heineken**™ /ˈhaɪnəkən/ a Dutch company that makes lager (= a type of pale light beer). It became famous in Britain for its humorous advertisements which ended with the words: 'Heineken reaches the parts other beers cannot reach.'

Heinz™ /haɪnz/ an international company that makes a large range of food in tins, including *baked beans, soup and baby food. Heinz tomato *ketchup (= sauce), sold in glass or plastic bottles, is also very popular in many countries. At one time the number 57 on Heinz tins was supposed to show the number of varieties of food produced by the company. It was never an accurate figure, however. The company now sells well over a thousand varieties of food, and the name Heinz is sometimes used in a humorous way to refer to something that has or consists of many varieties: *Our dog's a bit of a Heinz* (= a mixture of different breeds).

ˌLillian ˈ**Hellman** /ˈhelmən/ (1907–84) a US writer of plays. Her best known works were *The Children's Hour* (1934), *The Little Foxes* (1939), *Watch on the Rhine* (1941) and *Toys in the Attic* (1960). Her book about her own life, *An Unfinished Woman* (1969), won a *National Book Award. Hellman lived with the writer Dashiell *Hammett for more than 30 years. She had strong socialist opinions, and her career suffered in the 1950s because of *McCarthyism.

Helˈlo! a popular magazine published each week in Britain and read especially by women. It contains photographs of and articles about famous people, and is known for saying only positive things about them. It was first published in Britain in 1988 as a British version of the Spanish magazine *Hola!*, and quickly became very successful.

ˌ**Hell's** ˈ**Angel** *n* [usu pl] a member of a group of people who ride powerful motorcycles, wear leather clothes and have a reputation for wild and violent behaviour. Groups of Hell's Angels are called *chapters*, and they have their own rules which are different from those of the rest of society. The first groups were formed in *California in the 1950s but they now exist in several countries.

ˌRobert ˈ**Helpmann** /ˈhelpmæn/ (1909–86) an Australian ballet dancer, choreographer and actor, who came to Britain in 1933. He played a major part in the development of *Sadler's Wells in London in the 1930s and 1940s, dancing with Margot *Fonteyn and Alicia *Markova. In the 1950s he turned mainly to acting, especially with the *Royal Shakespeare Company. He was made a *knight in 1968.

ˌ**Help the** ˈ**Aged** a British charity that provides help for old people both in Britain and abroad. It was established in 1961.

ˌErnest ˈ**Hemingway** /ˈhemɪŋweɪ/ (1899–1961) a US writer of novels and short stories. He created a style of writing using short, simple sentences, and received the *Nobel Prize for literature in 1954. Hemingway drove an ambulance during *World War I and later worked in France and Spain as a journalist reporting on *World War II and the Spanish Civil War. His novels were about the loves and adventures of tough men. They included *The Sun Also Rises* (1926), *A Farewell to Arms* (1929), *For Whom the Bell Tolls* (1940) and *The Old Man and the Sea* (1952). Hemingway became ill and shot himself at his home in *Idaho.

Ernest Hemingway

the ˈ**Hemlock So**ˌ**ciety** a US organization that supports doctors who help people to end their own lives when they want to do so because they have a serious illness that cannot be cured. The organization was established in 1980 and in 1997 had 25 000 members in 80 local groups. Its slogan (= words that express an aim or belief) is 'Good Life, Good Death'.

ˌJimi ˈ**Hendrix** /ˈhendrɪks/ (1942–70) an *African-American pop singer who also wrote songs and played the guitar. His hit songs include *Hey Joe* (1967). He influenced many pop musicians and gave exciting stage performances, sometimes playing his guitar with his teeth or behind his back. He burned his guitar to end his performance at the 1969 Monterey Pop Festival. He moved to England in 1966 and formed a small band called the Jimi Hendrix Experience. He died there after taking too many drugs.

ˌStephen ˈ**Hendry** /ˈhendri/ (1969–) a Scottish *snooker player, the most successful in the history of the game. He was the youngest winner of the World Professional Championships in 1990 and became world champion for the sixth time in 1997.

ˈ**Henley** /ˈhenli/ a town on the River *Thames in *Oxfordshire, England. It is famous for the rowing races held there during the **Henley Regatta**, an event that takes place over five days every July. The Henley Regatta began in 1834. It is a fashionable event, attended by many rich and famous people, and is one of the sports and cultural events held every summer in Britain which together are known as the *Season.

ˌTim ˈ**Henman** /ˈhenmən/ (1974–) a leading English tennis player. He is especially popular with young people, whose enthusiasm for watching him play has been called **Henmania**.

ˌJohn ˈ**Henry**[1] ⇨ *JOHN HENRY*.

ˌLenny ˈ**Henry**[2] /ˈhenri/ (1958–) a well-known English comedy actor. His television shows include *The Lenny Henry Show* and *Chef!* He is married to the comedy actor Dawn *French.

ˌO ˈ**Henry**[3] /ˌəʊ ˈhenri; *AmE* ˌoʊ/ (1862–1910) a popular US writer of short stories who was born William Sydney Porter. He began to write in prison after being sent there for stealing money from the bank where he worked. O Henry's stories were simple and often humorous, and they usually ended with a surprise. More than 300 of them were collected in *Cabbages and Kings* (1904), *The Voice of the City* (1908) and other volumes.

ˌPatrick ˈ**Henry**[4] /ˈhenri/ (1736–99) a major political leader of the *American Revolution who is remembered for saying 'Give me liberty or give me death.' He was a member of the *Continental Congress (1774–6) and governor of *Virginia (1776–9 and 1784–6). Henry was at first opposed to the US *Constitution because he supported *states' rights, but he later helped to add the Bill of Rights to it.

ˌPrince ˈ**Henry**[5] (1984–) the second child of the *Prince and *Princess of Wales. He is usually called Prince Harry by the British press and public.

Henry I /ˌhenri ðə ˈfɜːst; *AmE* ˈfɜːrst/ (1068–1135) king of England (1100–35). The youngest of three sons of *William I, he became king when his eldest brother *William II died because his other brother Robert was out of the country on a *Crusade. Henry improved the administrative system of the country and established a system by which judges travelled around the country giving justice.

Henry II /ˌhenri ðə ˈsekənd/ (1133–89) king of England (1154–89). He was the grandson of *Henry I, succeeded King *Stephen and was the first *Plantagenet king. He reduced the power of the *barons and increased the power of the state. He wanted to reduce the power of the Church and this led to his dispute with the *Archbishop of Canterbury, Thomas *Becket, which ended in Becket's murder. During his rule England established control over Ireland. Henry also introduced various systems of justice which can be seen as the beginning of *common law.

Henry III /ˌhenri ðə ˈθɜːd; *AmE* ˈθɜːrd/ (1207–72) king of England (1216–72) and the son of King *John. He was not popular with the *barons, who disliked his use of foreign people to advise him and criticized him for having poor judgement in financial matters. In 1264, Simon de *Montfort led a rebellion of the barons and Henry was defeated and put in prison. He took back power in 1265 after a battle in which the rebels were defeated by an army led by Henry's son (later *Edward I).

Henry IV /ˌhenri ðə ˈfɔːθ; *AmE* ˈfɔːrθ/ (1366–1413) king of England (1399–1413) after his cousin *Richard II. He was born Henry Bolingbroke, the son of *John of Gaunt, and was a leading opponent of Richard's. In 1398 Richard sent him into exile, but in 1399 he returned to England, defeated Richard and was accepted as king by parliament. While he was king there were rebellions against him in Wales and the north of England. He was forced to accept the principle that the king should govern through parliament, and in 1407 parliament took control of the country's financial affairs.

***Henry IV**, Parts 1 and 2* /ˌhenri ðə ˈfɔːθ; *AmE* ˈfɔːrθ/ two plays (*c.* 1597–8) by *Shakespeare based on the period when *Henry IV was king of England. The play's main characters are Prince Hal (Henry IV's son and later *Henry V) and his friend *Falstaff. In *Part 1* Hal drinks and jokes with Falstaff and others in the Boar's Head, a London tavern (= old pub), and his father worries that he is not serious enough to become a king. However, at the end he accepts his responsibilities and fights in a battle to defeat a rebellion against his father. In *Part 2*, Hal is still friendly with Falstaff, but when Henry IV dies and Hal becomes king, he rejects him with the famous line: 'I know thee not, old man.'

Henry V /ˌhenri ðə ˈfɪfθ/ (1387–1422) king of England (1413–22) and son of *Henry. He is regarded as a symbol of English patriotism (= love of one's own country) and success in battle, especially because of *Shakespeare's play **Henry V*. He took an English army to France during the *Hundred Years War and defeated the French at the Battle of *Agincourt (1415), putting part of France under English control.

Henry V /ˌhenri ðə ˈfɪfθ/ a play (1599) by *Shakespeare which celebrates the military victories in France of King *Henry V. It contains several famous patriotic speeches. There have been two film versions, the first (1944) directed by Laurence *Olivier with himself as Henry, and the second (1989) directed by Kenneth *Branagh who also played the title role.

Henry VI /ˌhenri ðə ˈsɪksθ/ (1421–71) king of England (1422–61 and 1470–1) and son of *Henry V. He was not popular, mainly because England finally lost the *Hundred Years War while he was king. Opposition to him led to the *Wars of the Roses, in which the House of *Lancaster was defeated by the House of *York and Henry was put in prison. As a result of this, *Edward became king, but in 1470, with the help of the powerful Earl of Warwick, known as Warwick the Kingmaker, Henry became king again, though he was defeated once more in 1471. He was put in the *Tower of London, where he was murdered, and Edward became king again. Henry's greatest achievements were establishing *Eton College and *King's College, Cambridge.

***Henry VI**, Parts 1, 2 and 3* /ˌhenri ðə ˈsɪksθ/ three plays (*c.* 1590–92) by *Shakespeare, set during during the period of the *Wars of the Roses. They are among Shakespeare's earliest plays and some people believe that he may only have written parts of them.

Henry VII /ˌhenri ðə ˈsevnθ/ (1457–1509) king of England (1485–1509). He succeeded *Richard III (= followed him as king) and was the first *Tudor(1) king.

Born Henry Tudor, he was brought up in France. In 1485 he led a rebellion against Richard, defeated him at the Battle of *Bosworth Field and became king. In 1486 he married the daughter of *Edward, uniting the House of *Lancaster (to which he belonged) and the House of *York and so bringing the *Wars of the Roses to an end. Although there were rebellions during his rule, including those led by Lambert *Simnel and Perkin *Warbeck, Henry established greater order in the country, introduced a more modern system of government and greatly improved the country's financial position.

Henry VIII /ˌhenri ði ˈeɪtθ/ (1491–1547) king of England (1509–47) and son of *Henry VII. He is one of the most famous of all English kings, especially because he had six wives.

For political reasons, he married *Catherine of Aragon, the wife of his dead brother Arthur, just after he became king. They had a daughter, later *Mary I, but because they did not have a son who could be the future king, Henry decided to divorce her. However, the Pope refused to give the necessary permission for this, so Henry took England out of the Roman Catholic Church and made himself head of the Church in England. This act, together with others such as the *Dissolution of the Monasteries, were the beginning of the establishment of Protestantism in England.

Henry divorced Catherine of Aragon and married Anne *Boleyn in 1533. They had a daughter, later *Elizabeth I, but Henry had Anne executed for adultery. His third wife was Jane *Seymour, who died giving birth to a son (later *Edward VI). Henry married his fourth wife, *Anne of Cleves, for political reasons, but soon divorced her and in 1540 he married Catherine *Howard. She too was executed for adultery. Henry's sixth and last wife was Catherine Parr.

As a young man Henry was known for his love of hunting, sport and music, but he did not rule well and the country was in a weak and uncertain state when he died. See also CROMWELL, *GREENSLEEVES*, MORE, WOLSEY.

Henry VIII /ˌhenri ði ˈeɪtθ/ a play (1613) by *Shakespeare, possibly the last he wrote. Some people believe he wrote it with somebody else, perhaps John *Fletcher. It is about the events surrounding King *Henry VIII's divorce from *Catherine of Aragon.

ˌJim ˈ**Henson** /ˈhensn/ (1936–90) the American who created *The *Muppet Show*, as well as writing the words and speaking the lines of many of the characters in it. See also *SESAME STREET*.

ˌAudrey ˈ**Hepburn**[1] /ˈhepbɜːn; *AmE* ˈhepbɜːrn/ (1929–93) a British actor, born in Belgium. She appeared in many films, including *Roman Holiday* (1953), *Breakfast at Tiffany's* (1961), **My Fair Lady* (1964) and *Robin and Marian* (1976). She often played innocent, lively young women. After her film career ended she worked for UNICEF, visiting children in trouble all over the world.

ˌKatherine ˈ**Hepburn**[2] /ˈhepbɜːn; *AmE* ˈhepbɜːrn/ (1909–) a US actor, especially in films, who is best known for playing lively and forceful women, and for her clear, strong voice. She won *Oscars for her performances in *Morning Glory* (1933), *Guess Who's Coming to Dinner* (1967), *The Lion in Winter* (1968) and *On Golden Pond* (1981). Her other films include *The Philadelphia Story* (1940) and *The African Queen* (1951). She had a long love affair with Spencer *Tracy and made several films with him.

ˌGeorge ˈ**Hepplewhite** /ˈheplwaɪt/ (*died* 1786) an English maker of furniture noted for his simple and graceful style. His book *The Cabinet-maker and Upholsterer's Guide* (1788) had a great influence, but no piece of furniture that is known to be by him has survived.

ˌBarbara ˈ**Hepworth** /ˈhepwəθ; *AmE* ˈhepwərθ/ (1903–75) a English sculptor. Her work is mainly abstract and marked by strong curving lines. She was married for a time to the painter Ben *Nicholson and from 1939 lived in *St Ives, *Cornwall, a town still known for its many artists. She died in a fire at her home, which is now a museum.

the ˈ***Herald of*** ˌ***Free*** ˈ***Enterprise*** a car ferry (= boat) which turned over in the *English Channel near the Belgian port of Zeebrugge in 1987. Nearly 200 people died in the accident, which happened because the doors had not been properly closed.

heraldry

Heraldry is the design and study of **coats of arms**. Many British upper-class families, as well as thousands of public institutions such as city councils and universities have the right to their own coat of arms or shield. This is often printed on notepaper, used as a badge on uniforms and the sides of official vehicles, and put above the door of buildings. The **heraldic devices** (= designs) that can be used on a coat of arms are strictly controlled by the ***College of Arms** in England, and the ***Court of the Lord Lyon** in Scotland.

The origins of heraldry lie in the decorated shields that were carried into battle by *medieval knights. The designs painted on these shields were originally a means of identification. They then became much honoured family emblems which have changed little through the centuries. Sometimes the devices have been changed to combine the coats of arms of two families. A husband may **impale** his wife's family arms by dividing the shield vertically down the middle and putting his own arms on the **dexter** (= the wearer's right) side and his wife's on the **sinister** (= left) side.

Heraldry uses many technical terms, mostly derived from Old French. The background of a shield is known as the **field** and its main colour the **tincture**. The heraldic designs on the field are known as **charges**. They may include a simple **pale** (= broad vertical band) or a **fess** (= thin horizontal stripe), or a more elaborate device such as an animal, a cross or a castle. Shields are often **quartered**, with each quarter carrying a different design. On the *royal arms, the quarters represent different countries. The first and fourth **quarters** are **gules** (= red) and each contains three lions **passant** (= walking) shown in **or** (= gold) to represent England. The second quarter contains a red lion **rampant** (= standing upright), the symbol of Scotland, within a **tressure** (= border) on a gold background. The third quarter is **azure** (= blue) and contains a golden *harp with strings of **argent** (= silver) to represent Ireland. Wales is not included because it had its own heraldic device in the arms of the *Prince of Wales before the **quarterings** for Scotland and Ireland were added to the royal arms.

In most coats of arms the shield is surrounded by additional decorations, such as a pair of animal or human **supporters** (for instance, the lion and unicorn on the royal arms), a crown or helmet, and a **motto**. On the royal arms the motto is **Dieu et mon droit*, French for 'God and my right'.

Many Americans whose families came from Europe try to trace their origins and identify their ancestors' coat of arms. They may then use it on objects such as drinking glasses, or hang a drawing of the coat of arms in their house. For many people a coat of arms provides a connection with the past and a way of expressing family pride.

Herald-Tribune ⇨ INTERNATIONAL HERALD-TRIBUNE.

ˌA P ˈ**Herbert**[1] /ˈhɜːbət; *AmE* ˈhɜːrbərt/ (Alan Patrick Herbert 1890–1971) an English writer. He was best known for his humorous articles in the magazine *Punch, many of which made fun of the legal profession. He was made a *knight in 1945.

ˌGeorge ˈ**Herbert**[2] /ˈhɜːbət; *AmE* ˈhɜːrbərt/ (1593–1633) an English poet and priest. He was one of the *metaphysical poets and dealt with religious themes such as doubt, suffering and joy, using simple language.

ˌJames ˈ**Herbert**[3] /ˈhɜːbət; *AmE* ˈhɜːrbərt/ (1943–) an English writer of popular novels. His books are mainly horror stories, and include *The Rats* (1974), *The Fog* (1975), *Shrine* (1983) and *'48* (1996). Many of them have been made into films.

ˈ***Here*** ˈ***Comes the*** ˈ***Bride*** a piece of music which is often played at Christian weddings in church as the bride walks up to join the groom (= the man getting married) just before the marriage ceremony.

heˌreditary ˈpeer (in Britain) a male member of the *aristocracy who has received his title from his father and who has the right to vote in the *House of Lords. A small number of hereditary peers are women. Compare LIFE PEER. ⇨ note at PEERAGE.

ˈ**Hereford** /ˈherɪfəd; *AmE* ˈherɪfərd/ **1** a city on the River Wye in the west of England near the border with Wales. Its fine cathedral contains the **Mappa Mundi*, a very old map of the world. **2** *n* a common breed of cow bred for its meat. Hereford cattle are usually reddish in colour with a white head. They were originally developed around Hereford, England: *They farm Herefords and Jerseys.*

ˌ**Hereford and ˈWorcester** /ˌherɪfəd, ˈwʊstə(r); *AmE* ˌherɪfərd/ a county in the west of England on the border with Wales. It was created in 1974 by joining the former countries of Herefordshire and Worcestershire. Its administrative centre is *Worcester.

ˌ**Hereward the ˈWake** /ˌherɪwəd ðə ˈweɪk; *AmE* ˌherɪwərd/ (11th century) a British military leader who encouraged the *Anglo-Saxons to resist *William the Conqueror and the *Normans in 1070. His military base was the Isle of *Ely in *Cambridgeshire, and after the Normans had defeated him there he is said to have escaped. There are many stories about his adventures although few of them are based on historical fact.

ˌ**Heriot-ˈWatt Uniˌversity** /ˌheriət ˈwɒt; *AmE* ˈwɑːt/ a university in *Edinburgh, Scotland, established in 1966. It is known especially for teaching scientific subjects.

ˈ**heritage ˌcentre** *n* (in Britain) a place like a museum which people visit to learn about life in the past. Heritage centres often contain old buildings, machines, etc. which have been made to look as they did originally: *a railway heritage centre* ○ *There's a local heritage centre with some authentic fishermen's cottages.*. See also WORLD HERITAGE SITE.

ˌ**heritage ˈcoast** *n* [U, C] (in Britain) an attractive area of the coast which is protected by law. There are restrictions on building on heritage coasts and wildlife is preserved, but the public is free to walk on them. See also ENTERPRISE NEPTUNE.

Her ˌMajesty's ˈCoastguard the British government organization whose job is to watch the country's coast and help ships in trouble, prevent bringing goods being brought into the country illegally, etc.

Her ˈMajesty's ˈCustoms and ˈExcise (*also* **Customs and Excise**) a British government department that collects tax. Customs are the tax collected on certain imports, e.g. alcoholic drinks and perfume, and excise is the tax collected on certain goods made in Britain, e.g. beer and cigarettes. When people *go through customs* at an airport or port they must sometimes say whether they are carrying any of these goods, and officers from this department are allowed to search them. Her Majesty's Customs and Excise also collect *VAT and give licences (= official permission) to trade in certain things, e.g. alcoholic drinks.

Her ˌMajesty's ˈStationery ˌOffice (*abbr* **HMSO**) a British government organization responsible for publishing and controlling the copyright (= legal right of ownership) in certain important government documents. A large part of HMSO was sold to private owners in 1996 and now trades under the name of the *Stationery Office.

Her ˌMajesty's ˈTreasury ⇨ TREASURY.

ˌWoody ˈ**Herman** /ˌwʊdi ˈhɜːmən; *AmE* ˈhɜːrmən/ (1913–87) a US musician who played the clarinet, wrote music and from 1936 led a big band which came to be called the 'Thundering Herd'. Among the successful numbers Herman wrote and recorded was *Woodchoppers' Ball* (1939).

ˌRobert ˈ**Herrick** /ˈherɪk/ (1591–1674) an English poet and priest. He wrote many short, cheerful poems, including *Gather Ye Rosebuds While Ye May* and *Cherry Ripe.*

ˌJames ˈ**Herriot** /ˈheriət/ (1916–) an English writer, well known for his humorous books about the life of a country vet (= animal doctor). The books were made into a popular television series from 1977 called *All Creatures Great and Small.*

ˌWilliam ˈ**Herschel** /ˈhɜːʃəl; *AmE* ˈhɜːrʃəl/ (1738–1822) a British astronomer, born in Germany. He was originally a musician but became an astronomer by studying the sky through telescopes he made himself. He discovered Uranus, the first new planet to be identified since ancient times, and proved the existence of double stars. After becoming the official astronomer to King *George III, he was made a *knight in 1816.

ˈ**Hershey bar**™ /ˈhɜːʃi; *AmE* ˈhɜːrʃi/ *n* America's oldest chocolate sweet, sometimes called the 'Great American Chocolate Bar'. It was first produced by Milton Hershey in 1894. US soldiers kept Hershey bars to give to children in Europe during and after *World War II when sweets were scarce there. Hershey Foods Corporation in Hershey, Pennsylvania, now also makes many other sweets.

ˈ**Hertfordshire** /ˈhɑːtfədʃə(r); *AmE* ˈhɑːrtfərdʃər/ (*abbr* **Herts**) a *county in southern England, just to the north of London. Its administrative centre is the town of Hertford.

Hertz /hɜːts; *AmE* hɜːrts/ an international company that hires out cars and other vehicles. Branches of Hertz are often seen at airports.

ˌMichael ˈ**Heseltine** /ˈhesltaɪn/ (1933–) a British *Conservative politician. He went into politics in 1966 after establishing a successful publishing business, joined the *Cabinet in 1979, and by 1986 was *Secretary of State for Defence. However in that year he resigned his Cabinet post over the *Westland affair and in 1990 challenged Margaret *Thatcher in an attempt to become party leader. John *Major won the election that resulted and Heseltine was given a series of important posts in the new government. He shocked some people in 1976 when he picked up the *mace in the *House of Commons and shook it while making a speech. The popular newspapers often refer to him as 'Tarzan' (because of his hair) or 'Hezza'.

ˌCharlton ˈ**Heston** /ˌtʃɑːltən ˈhestən; *AmE* ˌtʃɑːrltən/ (1924–) a US actor famous for playing leading parts in big historical films. He was Moses in *The *Ten Commandments* and received an *Oscar for **Ben-Hur*. His other films include *El Cid* (1961), **Planet of the Apes* and *True Lies* (1994). He is known for his conservative views, and in 1997 he became First Vice-president of the *National Rifle Association.

ˌ**Hever ˈCastle** /ˌhiːvə; *AmE* ˌhiːvər/ a castle near Edenbridge in *Kent, England, where *Henry VIII is said to have stayed with Anne *Boleyn, his second wife, before they were married. The castle has a fine garden in the Italian style.

ˌ**Heysel ˈStadium** /ˌhaɪsl/ a football stadium in Brussels, the scene of a disaster on 29 May 1985 in which nearly 40 people died and many more were injured. It happened when British supporters of the *Liverpool football club attacked the supporters of the other team and a wall fell over, crushing people. After the disaster British teams were not allowed to play in Europe for five years.

the **HHS** /ˌeɪtʃ eɪtʃ ˈes/⇨ DEPARTMENT OF HEALTH AND HUMAN SERVICES.

ˌ**Hiaˈwatha** /ˌhaɪəˈwɒθə; *AmE* ˌhaɪəˈwɑːθə/ the main character in *The Song of Hiawatha* (1858), a long poem by Henry Wadsworth *Longfellow. The character is based on the *Native American who, according to ancient stories, established the *Iroquois League, and the poem describes his life and marriage to Minnehaha.

"Wild ˈBill' ˈ**Hickok** /ˈhɪkɒk; *AmE* ˈhɪkɑːk/ (1837–76) a famous *frontiersman in the American *Wild West. His real name was James Butler Hickok. He worked as a marshal (= law officer) in several *Kansas towns including *Abilene (1871–2) before joining *Buffalo Bill's *Wild West Show (1872–4) He then moved to Deadwood, *South Dakota, where he was shot in the back and killed while playing cards.

ˈ***Hickory, ˈDickory, ˈDock*** /ˈhɪkəri ˈdɪkəri ˈdɒk; *AmE* ˈdɑːk/ the title and first line of an old *nursery rhyme. The full song is:

Hickory, dickory, dock,
The mouse ran up the clock.
The clock struck one,
The mouse ran down,
Hickory, dickory, dock.

ˈ**Hickstead** /ˈhɪkstɪd/ a centre for showjumping (= the sport of riding over difficult barriers) in *Sussex, England. Many national and international competitions are held there.

ˌ**hide-and-ˈseek** (*AmE also* ˌ**hide-and-go-ˈseek**) *n* [U] a children's game in which one or more players hide and one or more of the others try to find them. ⇨ note at TOYS AND GAMES.

'ˌHurricane' ˈ**Higgins**[1] /ˈhɪgɪnz/ (Alex Higgins 1949–) a British *snooker player born in *Belfast, Northern Ireland. He was the youngest ever winner of the world snooker championship in 1972 and went on to win again in 1982. He was given the name 'Hurricane' (= a violent storm) because of the great speed at which he plays. He has sometimes been in trouble with the authorities because of his violent behaviour.

ˌJack ˈ**Higgins**[2] /ˈhɪgɪnz/ (1929–) an English author of thrillers (= exciting novels). His best-known book is *The Eagle has Landed* (1975), about an attempt to kill Winston *Churchill during *World War II. He has also written books under several other names, including his real name, Harry Patterson.

ˌ**High ˈChurch** *n* [U] the tradition within the Church of England that has the closest links with *Roman Catholic Christianity. High Church ceremonies are similar to Roman Catholic ones in the emphasis they place on the Virgin Mary, the burning of incense, etc. ▶ **High Church** *adj*: *My family have always been very High Church.* See also ANGLO-CATHOLICISM. Compare LOW CHURCH. ⇨ article at CHURCH OF ENGLAND.

the ˌ**High Court of ˈJustice** (*also* the **High Court**) the branch of the legal system in England and Wales that deals mainly with serious civil cases (= ones concerned with the private rights of citizens rather than with crimes). It is divided into the *Queen's Bench, the *Chancery Division and the *Family Division. Cases only go to the High Court if they cannot be dealt with in a lower court (e.g. a *county court). Some appeals are dealt with in the Queen's Bench Division of the High Court: *He was tried by a High Court judge.* ⇨ article at LEGAL SYSTEM IN BRITAIN.

the ˌ**High Court of Juˈsticiary** /dʒʌˈstɪʃəri/ (*also* the **High Court**) the court in Scotland that deals with the most serious criminal cases (e.g. murder). It also deals with appeals from lower courts. Compare SHERIFF COURT.

ˌ**higher deˈgree** *n* a degree taken after a first degree, at a more advanced level. Examples are an MA (Master of Arts), an MSc (Master of Science) or a PhD (Doctor of Philosophy). ⇨ note at FURTHER EDUCATION.

ˌ**Highgate ˈCemetery** /ˌhaɪgeɪt/ a burial ground in Highgate, a district of north London, England, where many famous people are buried, including Karl *Marx, George *Eliot and Michael *Faraday. Karl Marx's grave is famous for its large sculpture of his head.

ˌ**Highgrove ˈHouse** /ˌhaɪgrəʊv; *AmE* ˌhaɪgroʊv/ a house owned by the *Prince of Wales in *Gloucestershire, England. Its surrounding land includes a large organic farm (= one growing crops, etc. without the use of artificial chemicals).

ˈ**Highland** (*also* **Highland Region**) an administrative area of northern Scotland, to the north of the *Grampian mountains and including some of the Inner *Hebrides islands. It was created in 1975 and includes several former counties.

the ˌ**Highland ˈClearances** the forced removal of farmers from their small rented farms in the *Highlands of Scotland during the early 19th century. The owners of the land wanted to use it for sheep farming instead of growing crops, which meant that the farmers were no longer thought to be necessary. The Clearances caused great poverty and many farmers and their families left Scotland to live in the US.

ˌ**Highland ˈdress** *n* [U] the traditional costume worn by Scottish men on formal occasions or as a military uniform. Its main parts are a *tartan kilt (= a man's skirt with folds that reaches to the knees), a sporran (= a flat bag made of fur or leather hanging in front of the kilt), and a small knife which is stuck in the top of one of the stockings. ⇨ note at CLANS. See also SKEAN-DHU.

ˌ**Highland ˈfling** *n* a lively, traditional Scottish dance for one person, usually a man. In a Highland fling the dancer dances on the same spot, often with one arm above the head and the other resting on the hip, and makes quick arm and leg movements. It is often performed at *Highland Gatherings.

ˌ**Highland ˈGathering** *n* (*also* ˌ**Highland ˈGames**, *pl* **Highland Games**) a traditional Scottish outdoor festival which includes music, dancing and sports such as *tossing the caber* (= throwing a long wooden pole). Highland Gatherings are held each year in a number of places in Scotland, not only in the *Highlands. The most famous is the Braemar Gathering in north-east Scotland, held on the first Saturday in September.

the ˌ**Highlands** *n* [pl] the region of northern Scotland where there are many mountains. Compare LOWLANDS.

the ˌ**Highlands and** ˈ**Islands** *n* [pl] the whole of northern Scotland, including *Highland Region and the main island groups (the *Hebrides, the *Orkneys and the *Shetlands).

ˌ***High*** ˈ***Noon*** a US film (1952) which is considered by many people to be one of the best *westerns ever made. It was directed by Fred *Zinnemann. Gary *Cooper won an *Oscar in the role of Marshall Will Kane who finds out that nobody in the town will help him against four criminals who are coming to kill him. Grace *Kelly played his wife. Many Americans thought the film's story was meant as a criticism of people in the 1950s who failed to oppose *McCarthyism.

H

ˈ**high school** *n* (*esp AmE*) a secondary school, usually one for the last four years before college. Most US students complete high school at the age of 17 or 18.

ˌ**High** ˈ**Sheriff** *n* a representative of the king or queen in each of the *counties in England, Wales and Northern Ireland. The High Sheriff is appointed each year from among the local people and his or her duties include acting as the local *returning officer.

ˈ**high street** *n* (*BrE*) the main shopping street in the centre of a town or city. It is often used as part of a name: *Oxford High Street* ○ *I saw your sister in the high street.* ○ *high-street banks/shops*. Compare MAIN STREET 1.

ˌ**high** ˈ**tea** *n* [U] (*BrE*) an early evening meal, usually with a cooked dish and bread and butter. It used to be associated with the *upper classes but is now popular among ordinary people, especially in northern England and Scotland, and is often referred to simply as *tea*. The meal may not include the actual drinking of tea. Compare TEA 2. ⇨ note at MEALS.

the ˌ**Highway** ˈ**Code** *n* [sing] a set of official rules for British road users, published as a small book. Questions about the Highway Code are asked as part of a person's driving test.

ˌBenny ˈ**Hill**[1] /ˈhɪl/ (1925–92) an English comedy actor popular from the mid 1950s to the 1980s. His television series *The Benny Hill Show*, which he wrote himself, consisted mainly of clever visual humour and jokes about sex. It was popular both in Britain and abroad, although some people disapproved of its old-fashioned attitude towards women and sex.

ˌDamon ˈ**Hill**[2] /ˌdeɪmən ˈhɪl/ (1960–) an English racing driver, son of Graham *Hill. He became *Formula One world champion in 1996, driving a *Williams car.

ˈGeorge ˈRoy ˈ**Hill**[3] /ˈdʒɔːdʒ ˈrɔɪ ˈhɪl/ (1922–) a US film director. During his early career he directed plays and television programmes, and he was 40 before he made his first film. His best-known films include *Butch Cassidy and the Sundance Kid* (1969), *The Sting* (1973), for which he won an *Oscar, and *The World According to Garp* (1982).

ˌGraham ˈ**Hill**[4] /ˈhɪl/ (1929–75) a British racing driver. He won the *Formula One world championships in 1962 in a BRM car, and again in 1968 in a Lotus. He died in an air crash. His son Damon *Hill is also a racing driver.

ˌRowland ˈ**Hill**[5] /ˌrəʊlənd ˈhɪl; *AmE* ˌroʊlənd/ (1795–1897) a British *Post Office worker who invented the postage stamp, originally costing one penny (the *Penny Black, introduced in 1840). Before this, postage was paid by the person receiving a letter or parcel. Hill was made a *knight in 1860.

ˈ**hillbilly** /ˈhɪlbɪli/ *n* (*AmE*) a poor and often backward person living in *Appalachia. **Hillbilly music** is the *folk music of this region which became part of the more commercial *country music.

ˌNicholas ˈ**Hilliard** /ˈhɪliəd; *AmE* ˈhɪliərd/ (1547–1619) an English painter best known for his miniatures (= very small pictures of people), many of which are in the *Victoria and Albert Museum, London.

ˈ**Hillsborough** /ˈhɪlzbərə/ a football ground in *Sheffield, England. On 15 April 1989 it was the scene of the **Hillsborough disaster**, in which 96 people died and hundreds more were injured when they were crushed by other supporters trying to get into the ground. An official report criticized the police for not doing enough to prevent the disaster.

the ˈ**Hilton** /ˈhɪltən/ (*also* the ˌ**Hilton Ho**ˈ**tel**) any of a large group of modern, comfortable and expensive hotels in major cities around the world. The company that owns them was started by Conrad Hilton (1887–1979), who bought his first hotel in *Texas in 1919. The company now also owns many casinos (= gambling clubs).

ˌMyra ˈ**Hindley** /ˌmaɪrə ˈhɪndli/ (1942–) an Englishwoman who, together with Ian Brady, murdered four children in *Manchester in the early 1960s. The crimes are known as the *Moors murders because the bodies of two of the children were later found buried on Saddleworth Moor in the *Pennines. Hindley has been in prison since 1965 despite campaigns for her to be released.

ˈ**hip hop** *n* [U] a popular culture that developed among young black people in the US in the late 1970s, and is now also found in Europe and elsewhere. It is associated mainly with *rap music, as well as with 'break-dancing' (= fast dancing on the hands and feet, popular especially in the early 1980s), graffiti art (= decorative painting on the walls of buildings, etc) and fashion clothing.

ˈ**hippie** (*also* **hippy**) *n* a member of the movement of mainly young people in the 1960s and 1970s who rejected normal society and social habits. They dressed in unusual clothes, had long hair, often took illegal drugs, and believed in sexual freedom, sometimes living in large family groups called 'communes'. They were also called 'flower children' because they believed in peace and love. The *Haight-Ashbury district of *San Francisco became their centre, but there were hippies in all parts of the US and Western Europe. See also FLOWER POWER.

hippies in Hyde Park, London

the ˈ**Hippodrome** /ˈhɪpədrəʊm; *AmE* ˈhɪpədroʊm/ a name common to many places of public entertainment in Britain, especially theatres, cinemas and concert halls. The Hippodrome in *Leicester Square,

London, is a fashionable restaurant where well-known entertainers perform each night. Several theatres in the US have also had the name. The most famous was the New York Hippodrome (1905–39), where Harry *Houdini performed.

ˌThora ˈ**Hird** /ˌθɔːrə ˈhɜːd; *AmE* ˈhɜːrd/ (1911–) an English actor in theatre, films and television. She is best known for her many appearances in British television plays and comedy programmes, and won a *BAFTA award in 1988 for her part in Alan *Bennett's play *A Cream Cracker under the Settee.* She has presented several religious programmes on television, and was made a *dame(2) in 1993.

Hiˈroshima /hɪˈrɒʃɪmə; *AmE* hɪˈrɑːʃɪmə/ the Japanese city on which the first atomic bomb was dropped, on 6 August 1945. The city was destroyed and about 130 000 people were killed. Many who survived developed serious diseases. See also ENOLA GAY, NAGASAKI.

ˌDamien ˈ**Hirst** /ˌdeɪmiən ˈhɜːst; *AmE* ˈhɜːrst/ (1965–) an English artist. He became famous in the early 1990s with a series of works consisting of dead animals in glass cases full of formaldehyde (= a special liquid that preserves things). He won the *Turner Prize in 1995 with *Mother and Child Divided (Cow and Calf)*, a cow and calf each cut in half in a glass case. Although many people admire his work, others find it offensive or not serious enough.

His ˌMaster's ˈVoice ⇨ HMV.

Hiˈspanic *adj* of or from countries, especially in Latin America, in which Spanish is spoken: *They lived in a Hispanic neighbourhood of Los Angeles.*
▶ **Hispanic** *n* a person whose first language is Spanish, especially one from a Latin American country (or whose ancestors came from such a country) living in the US: *Hispanics are now the largest minority group in America.* Compare CHICANO, LATINO, TEX-MEX.

ˌAlger ˈ**Hiss** /ˌældʒə ˈhɪs; *AmE* ˌældʒər/ (1904–96) an American who advised the US *State Department and was accused in 1948 of giving information to the Russians. He denied it before a government committee but a court of law decided that he had lied, and he was sent to prison for 44 months. Many people still think he was an innocent victim of the strong public feeling against Communism at the time.

ˌAlfred ˈ**Hitchcock** /ˈhɪtʃkɒk; *AmE* ˈhɪtʃkɑːk/ (1899–1980) an English film director best known for his thrillers (= exciting films with a complicated story) and horror films. Following success with films such as *The Thirty-Nine Steps* (1935) and *The Lady Vanishes* (1938) he moved in 1940 to the US, where his films included *North by Northwest* (1959), **Psycho* (1963) and *The Birds* (1963). Hitchcock often made a brief appearance in his own films. He was made a *knight in 1980.

The ˈ***Hitch Hiker's*** ˈ***Guide to the*** ˈ***Galaxy*** a successful radio series (1978–80), book (1979) and television series (1981) written by Douglas *Adams. They are about Arthur Dent's comic adventures in space after the earth is destroyed by the Vogons. There were several further books, including *The Restaurant at the End of the Universe* (1980).

the ˈ**hit parade** *n* [sing] (*old-fash*) a list of pop records which changes regularly to show which song is selling the most copies. The list is now more often called 'the charts' or 'the pop charts', and the records in it 'the top ten', 'the top twenty', etc. See also *YOUR HIT PARADE.*

HMO /ˌeɪtʃ em ˈəʊ; *AmE* ˈoʊ/ (*in full* **health maintenance organization**) a US medical insurance system, with its own hospitals and doctors. Customers make regular payments each month or year and can then receive treatment from HMO doctors and hospitals. There were about 75 million HMO members in 1997. Compare PPO, BLUE CROSS 1.

HMSO /ˌeɪtʃ em es ˈəʊ; *AmE* ˈoʊ/ ⇨ HER MAJESTY'S STATIONERY OFFICE.

HMV™ /ˌeɪtʃ em ˈviː/ a former British company producing recordings of music, etc. HMV stands for 'His Master's Voice', and the company used on its record label a picture of a small dog listening to an old-fashioned gramophone (= a machine for playing records with a large horn to produce the sound). HMV is now part of *EMI and the name is used for a chain of record shops.

ˌThomas ˈ**Hobbes** /ˈhɒbz; *AmE* ˈhɑːbz/ (1588–1679) an English philosopher who developed a range of theories about nature, human behaviour and society. He did not believe in God and thought that the only way to hold society together was to have strong social institutions and a powerful ruler. His book *Leviathan* (1651) sets out these views.

Hobbies and leisure activities ⇨ article.

ˌJack ˈ**Hobbs** /ˈhɒbz; *AmE* ˈhɑːbz/ (1882–1963) one of the finest English cricketers, who established a number of records as a batsman. He played for *Surrey (1905–34) and England (1907–30), and was captain of the England team in 1926. He was made a *knight in 1953.

ˌ**Hobson's ˈchoice** /ˌhɒbsənz; *AmE* ˌhɑːbsənz/ *n* [U] a situation in which there is no choice, because only one course of action or result is possible. The expression comes from the name of Thomas Hobson, a 17th-century British horse dealer who would not allow his customers any choice when renting a horse: *It was Hobson's choice: I could either resign from the job or be fired.*

hockey

In Britain *hockey* refers to **field hockey**. Hockey played on ice is called **ice hockey**. In the US ice hockey is much more common and is called simply *hockey*.

Both men and women play field hockey. There are 11 players in each team, five **forwards**, three **half-backs**, two **full-backs** and a **goalkeeper**. A **hockey pitch** is 100 yards (91 metres) long and between 55 and 60 yards (50 and 55 metres) wide. There is a **goal** at each end. The aim of the game is to hit a small white ball into the other team's goal with wooden **hockey sticks**. A goal is worth one point. Each game has two halves of 35 minutes. A game begins with a **pass-back**: a forward hits the ball but it is not allowed to cross the centre line until another player from either team has also hit it.

The modern game of hockey developed in England in the mid 19th century, and the first hockey club was formed in 1849. The English Hockey League now organizes games in three divisions. Each year, the winners of the league competition qualify for the European Club Championship. The Scottish Hockey Union runs leagues in Scotland. The sport is not as popular as *cricket, *Rugby or *football. It is rarely shown on television, and most people could not name any famous hockey players. Hockey is traditionally also played by schoolgirls.

An English teacher visiting *Harvard introduced the sport to the US in 1901. Initially it was played only by women, and the first men's game was not until 1928. In the US the game is controlled by the USA Field Hockey Association. It is less popular than in Britain and there are no professional teams or national leagues. Teams of amateurs compete in local leagues.

Hobbies and leisure activities

Attitudes to leisure

Until the 20th century, Americans had little time for leisure activities and did not really approve of leisure. The *Puritan ideal of hard work remained strong, and leisure was associated with the 'idle rich', sometimes called **the leisure class**. In the 19th century one book warned: 'True recreation must not interfere with our duty; must not injure health; must not waste money; must not waste time.' At the end of that century, President James *Garfield said the question was: 'What shall we do with our leisure when we get it?' Modern Americans have not found this a problem and can choose from a wide range of leisure activities.

The British share the **Protestant work ethic** (= the belief that hard work is good for people) but have always believed that it is also good for people to have activities outside work. A traditional saying warns that 'all work and no play makes Jack a dull boy'. Many people now believe that making time for **relaxation** after work is also necessary for the sake of good mental health. Some people, however, think that leisure time should be spent on worthwhile activities and not just **frittered away** (= wasted). Children are often encouraged to develop an **interest** or **hobby** which they can pick up in their spare time. Many British people care more about their leisure time than their work which is, for some, simply a means of getting money to live on.

Hobbies

Traditional indoor hobbies or **pastimes** include **collecting** things, e.g. shells, model cars, dolls, comic books, stamps, coins or postcards. Children also collect sets of picture cards from packets of tea and small toys or models from packets of breakfast cereal. Many collect stickers (= pictures with glue on the back) of football or baseball players or pop stars. They buy packets of these and **trade** them with their friends, exchanging those they already have for the ones they need to complete the set. Many people continue to collect things as they get older. Formerly picture cards were given away in packets of cigarettes and many of these old cards are now valuable. Now people collect things like beer mats, concert programmes, decorated plates, and *antiques.

Many people like to do something creative, such as painting or drawing, playing music, knitting or sewing, *DIY, cooking, or doing *crossword puzzles. In 1996, 84% of US households contained one or more people with a hobby or **craft** (= an activity in which something is made) and over $10 million was spent on such activities.

Some people have hobbies which take them away from home. Birdwatching is especially popular. So too is flying model aircraft. Other people go to *public record offices and *churches to research their family history. One very British hobby is train-spotting, which involves visiting railway stations and recording the names or numbers of trains. The range of hobbies now popular is reflected in the number of specialist *magazines available in both Britain and the US.

Sports

Many people have a *sport as their hobby. The most popular sports that people play include *football, *basketball, *softball, *cricket and *tennis. Some people play informally with friends, others join a local team. Many companies also have teams which play against each other. Some people go regularly to a **sports centre** or **leisure centre**, which provides facilities for keep-fit classes and indoor sports such as squash and badminton, and usually has a swimming pool. Others join a sports club which caters for a particular sport, e.g. *golf or *snooker. Clubs usually also have a bar and organize social events for their members.

Sports such as football, basketball and swimming are cheap and attract a lot of people. Golf and sailing, which are more expensive, tend to attract wealthier people. Tenpin bowling and ice-skating are popular social activities among young people.

More unusual sports include orienteering (= running from place to place, following clues marked on a map), paragliding (= floating through the air attached to a canopy like a parachute) and hot-air ballooning.

A lot of people who are interested in sport prefer to watch others play, either at a stadium or on television, rather than play themselves. *Baseball, football, cricket, golf and also horse *racing are regularly broadcast on television.

Leisure activities

Television and videos provide easy indoor entertainment, and watching television is by far the most popular leisure activity. People also play computer games or use the Internet. Other home-based activities include reading and listening to music. Many people's social lives are closely bound up with their interests. Most towns in Britain and the US have a wide choice of *clubs and societies for people to join, including choirs, *amateur dramatics groups, film societies, dance clubs and special-interest societies for those interested in art, astronomy, local history, etc. There are usually also classes where people can learn a new skill.

A lot of people go out one or more evenings a week and at the *weekend. Children go to youth clubs or visit friends. Adults go to the cinema or theatre, eat out at a restaurant, or, very commonly, go to a *pub or bar.

At the weekend many people spend part of their time *shopping. For many, shopping for clothes and household goods is a pleasant activity, not a chore. People also visit relatives and friends or invite them to their house. They go to places of interest, such as *stately homes and *museums, to funfairs, boating lakes and safari parks, and to special events ranging from school fêtes to jazz festivals.

Some people like to go away for the weekend and turn it into a short *holiday/vacation. Many go to *national parks and other country areas, and go walking or fishing, or, in the US, hunting. Other people like to go to the *beach. In the US people own recreational vehicles, such as *Winnebagos, which they can live in during such trips. British people may have a camper van or caravan.

By contrast, ice hockey has long been popular in the US. It is a man's sport, and is fast and exciting. Each team has six players, a **centre**, two **forwards** and two **wingers**, all of whom try to score, and a **goalkeeper**. Players wear **skates**, and have **helmets**, **gloves** and **pads** for protection. They use long wooden **sticks** to hit the **puck**, a small, hard rubber disc, into the opponent's goal. If they succeed they score one point. The area of the **rink** is up to 67 yards (61 metres) long and 33 yards (30 metres) wide, and is divided into an attacking zone, a neutral zone and a defending zone.

A game has three 20-minute **periods**. Play begins with a **face-off** when the **referee** drops the puck between two opposing players. **Defenders** try to prevent the opposing team from scoring and can **check** (= crash into) another player with their bodies. Professional players often have fights on the ice, and the game has been criticized for being too violent. If a player commits an illegal action, he goes to the **penalty box**, informally called the **sin bin**, for a period of between 2 and 10 minutes and his team must continue without him.

The US **National Hockey League** has 26 teams, six of which are Canadian. The best teams in the **Eastern Conference** and the **Western Conference** play to decide which two will be in the ***Stanley Cup**. The Hart Memorial Trophy is given to the best player, and Wayne Gretzky, thought by many to be the greatest ice hockey player ever, won it eight times in the period 1980–7 and in 1989. Among the most successful teams have been the New York Islanders and the Detroit Red Wings. In the northern states college and university teams compete in three *NCAA divisions.

In Britain ice hockey attracts relatively little interest. This is despite the fact that the first game of ice hockey was played by Englishmen on the frozen waters of Kingston Harbour, Ontario, around 1860.

ˌDavid ˈ**Hockney** /ˈhɒkni; *AmE* ˈhɑːkni/ (1937–) an English painter associated with the *pop art movement. He has lived in the US since the 1960s, and is perhaps best known for his series of paintings of swimming pools done in *California, e.g. *A Bigger Splash* (1967). In the 1980s he created another series of pictures made of large numbers of photographs taken from slightly different angles. He was made a *Companion of Honour in 1997.

ˌJimmy ˈ**Hoffa** /ˈhɒfə; *AmE* ˈhɑːfə/ (1913–?1975) a US trade union leader. He was President of the International Brotherhood of *Teamsters (1957–71). Robert *Kennedy led an investigation into his connection with the *Mafia, and Hoffa was sent to prison from 1967 to 1971. He disappeared in 1975 and his body has never been found, though people assume he was murdered.

ˌDustin ˈ**Hoffman** /ˌdʌstɪn ˈhɒfmən; *AmE* ˈhɑːfmən/ (1937–) a US actor who is known for his close attention to details of character in a wide range of different roles. His first big success was in *The *Graduate*, and he won *Oscars for *Kramer vs Kramer* (1979) and **Rain Man*. His other films have included **Midnight Cowboy*, *All the President's Men* (1976), *Tootsie* (1982) and *Mad City* (1998).

ˌGerard ˈ**Hoffnung** /ˈhɒfnʊŋ; *AmE* ˌdʒerɑːrd ˈhɑːfnʊŋ/ (1925–59) a British cartoonist and musician, born in Germany. He established the Hoffnung Music Festivals at the *Royal Festival Hall, London, in which musicians often made fun of different musical styles. His humorous drawings, especially of musicians, are still popular on greetings cards, etc.

ˌBen ˈ**Hogan** /ˈhəʊgən; *AmE* ˈhoʊgən/ (1912–97) a US golf player who won more than 60 major competitions, including the US Open four times (1948, 1950, 1951 and 1953), the *PGA twice (1946 and 1948), the Masters twice (1951 and 1953) and the British Open once (1953). He was called 'Bantam Ben' because of his short height. (A bantam is a small hen.).

ˌWilliam ˈ**Hogarth** /ˈhəʊgɑːθ; *AmE* ˈhoʊgɑːrθ/ (1697–1764) an English painter and engraver (= person who cuts or carves designs in metal, stone, etc.), best known for his sets of paintings that tell a moral story, such as *The *Rake's Progress* (1733–5) and *Marriage à la Mode* (1743–5). His house in Chiswick, London, is now a museum.

ˈ**Hogmanay** the name in Scotland for *New Year's Eve (31 December) and the parties and celebrations traditionally held on that day. These include singing **Auld Lang Syne* at midnight and then going *first-footing (= visiting friends to bring good luck for the new year).

ˌHans ˈ**Holbein** /ˌhæns ˈhɒlbaɪn; *AmE* ˈhoʊlbaɪn/ (*also called* **Hans Holbein the Younger**) (1497/8–1543) a German painter who from 1526 lived and worked in England. He was made the official royal painter in 1536 and is best known for his paintings of King *Henry VIII and his court. One of his greatest paintings, *The Ambassadors* (1533), is in the *National Gallery, London.

ˈ**Holborn** /ˈhəʊbən; *AmE* ˈhoʊbən/ an area of central London, England, between *Westminster(1) and the City. Its important buildings include Lincoln's Inn and Gray's Inn. See also INNS OF COURT.

the ˌ**Hole-in-the-ˈWall Gang** (*also* the **Wild Bunch**) the group of *Wild West outlaws (= criminals) led by Butch *Cassidy.

ˌBillie ˈ**Holiday** /ˌbɪli ˈhɒlədeɪ; *AmE* ˈhɑːlədeɪ/ (1915–59) an *African-American singer of *jazz and the *blues whose popular name was 'Lady Day'. She recorded her first record in 1933 with Benny *Goodman, and later sang with 'Count' *Basie and Artie *Shaw. Her best-known songs include *The Very Thought of You* and *These Foolish Things*. She took drugs for most of her life and died young. Her autobiography, *Lady Sings the Blues* (1956), was made into a film (1972) with Diana *Ross.

ˌ**Holiday ˈInn**™ any of the hotels owned by the US company Holiday Inns, Inc, the largest of its kind in the world. It has more than 2 000 hotels in 60 countries.

holidays and vacations

Holiday in American English means a day that is special for some reason. Most people do not go to work on an important holiday, but may do so on a minor one. Few people have to work on federal (= national) holidays such as *New Year's Day or *Independence Day, though they may celebrate *St Valentine's Day or *Groundhog Day but still go to work or school. Apart from the main federal holidays each state decides its own holidays. In British English, special days like New Year's Day are called ***bank holidays** or **public holidays**.

Holiday in British English means a period of a week or more spent away from work or school. This is called a **vacation** in American English. So, the period of several weeks around Christmas when schools are closed is called the *Christmas holiday*, or the *Christmas holidays* in Britain and the *Christmas vacation* in the US.

Holiday and *vacation* are also used to refer to the period when people go away for a time to a beach resort or to the country, or go travelling. British people have about four weeks' paid **leave** from their jobs. Most take their main holiday in the summer. People without children of school age often **go on holiday** in the **off-season** when prices are lower and there are fewer other **holidaymakers**. Some people stay in Britain for their holiday, but many go to beach resorts in Europe for one or two weeks. Some travel to the US or visit India, the Far East and other parts of the world. Many British people going abroad buy **package holidays** sold by high-street **travel agents**, which include transport, accommodation and sometimes excursions in the price. Some people see their holidays as an opportunity to relax in the sun, but others prefer **activity holidays** during which they can visit famous buildings or go walking in the countryside. A few go to a **holiday camp**, such as *Butlin's or *Pontin's, which provides entertainment for all the family. People often arrange their holiday a long time in advance and look forward to it through the winter. Many people also have a **short break**, usually three or four days, e.g. at a country cottage in Britain or in a European city.

Americans have relatively short vacations, typically two weeks. People with important jobs or who have worked in their company for many years may have longer vacations. The many Americans with low paid jobs in shops, fast-food restaurants, etc, usually have no paid vacation at all. Not many Americans go abroad for their vacations and those who do generally go to Canada or Mexico.

The typical family vacation involves driving for many hours. Some people visit relatives or go **sightseeing** in cities like *Washington, DC or *New York. The *national parks, like *Yellowstone National Park or the *Grand Canyon, are also popular, and people sometimes rent a cabin (*BrE* cottage) in the country. Families often go to amusement parks like *Disney World in *Florida. People who do not drive usually fly to a place as air fares are relatively cheap. Package tours are not very common and most Americans arrange their transport and accommodation separately.

ˌJools ˈ**Holland** /ˌdʒuːlz ˈhɒlənd; *AmE* ˈhɑːlənd/ (1958–) a British musician and television personality. From 1974 to 1980 he played piano with the pop group Squeeze, and he is known for his skill in playing *jazz. He has presented television programmes including *The Tube* (1982–7), **Juke Box Jury* (1989–90) and *Later with Jools Holland* (1992–).

ˌDoc ˈ**Holliday** /ˌdɒk ˈhɒlədeɪ; *AmE* ˌdɑːk ˈhɑːlədeɪ/ (1852–87) a dentist who gambled and often fought with guns in the American *Wild West. He was born John Henry Holliday in *Georgia and moved west in the 1870s for his health. He helped Wyatt *Earp and his brothers in the famous gunfight at the *OK Corral in *Tombstone, *Arizona, but died six years later of tuberculosis (= a disease of the lungs).

ˈ**Holloway** /ˈhɒləweɪ; *AmE* ˈhɑːləweɪ/ (*also* **Holloway prison**) a large prison for women in north London, England.

ˌBuddy ˈ**Holly** /ˌbʌdi ˈhɒli; *AmE* ˈhɑːli/ (1936–59) a US singer in the early years of *rock and roll who played a guitar and wrote songs. He and his group, the Crickets, had a number of hits, including *That'll Be the Day* (1957) and *Peggy Sue* (1957). Although he died at the age of 22 in a plane crash, his music had a strong influence on other pop singers, especially in Britain.

The ˌ***Holly and the*** ˈ***Ivy*** the title and first line of a popular *Christmas carol (= religious song). ⇨ note at CAROLS AND CAROL-SINGING.

Hollywood

Hollywood, more than any other place in the world, represents the excitement and glamour of the **film industry**. The world's major film companies have studios in Hollywood and many famous **film/movie stars** live in its fashionable and expensive *Beverly Hills district. But Hollywood is also ***Tinseltown**, where money can buy an expensive lifestyle but the pressure to succeed can ruin lives, as in the case of Marilyn *Monroe and River *Phoenix. British people, and Americans too, have mixed feelings about Hollywood: they are fascinated by the excitement of the film world and by the lives of the stars, but also see Hollywood as a symbol of trashy, commercial culture.

Hollywood is now surrounded by *Los Angeles. In 1908, when film companies began moving west from New York, it was a small, unknown community. The companies were attracted to *California by its fine weather, which allowed them to film outside for most of the year, but they also wanted to avoid having to pay money to a group of studios led by Thomas *Edison which were trying to establish a monopoly. Most of the companies were run by Jews whose families came originally from Eastern Europe. By the 1920s, companies such as *Universal and *United Artists had set up studios around Hollywood. During this period Mary *Pickford, Douglas *Fairbanks[1] and John *Barrymore became famous in **silent films** (= films without sound). Mack *Sennett, a Canadian, began making comedy films, including those featuring the *Keystone Kops, in which Charlie *Chaplin and 'Fatty' *Arbuckle became stars. D W *Griffith directed expensive 'epic' films like *The *Birth of the Nation*, and William S *Hart made *westerns popular. Hollywood also created its first sex symbol, Theda Bara (1890–1955).

The 1920s saw big changes. The first film in *Technicolor was produced in 1922. *Warner Brothers was formed in 1923 and four years later produced Hollywood's first **talkie** (= film with spoken words), *The *Jazz Singer*. Middle-class Americans were now attracted to the **movies**. Stars like Pickford and Chaplin reached the height of their fame, and new stars were discovered, such as Rudolph *Valentino, *Laurel and Hardy, and Buster *Keaton.

The 1930s and 1940s were Hollywood's 'Golden Age' and films became popular around the world. Hollywood even made successes out of America's worst times: *Prohibition led to the gangster films of Edward G *Robinson and James *Cagney, and the *Great Depression to films like *The *Grapes of Wrath*. *World War II featured in successful films like **Casablanca*. The great Hollywood studios, *MGM, Warner Brothers, *20th Century Fox, *Paramount Pictures and *Columbia Pictures, controlled the careers of actors. Famous directors of the time included Orson *Welles and John *Ford. New screen stars included Clark *Gable, John *Wayne, Katharine *Hepburn, Errol *Flynn, Henry *Fonda, Humphrey *Bogart, Lauren *Bacall, Bette *Davis, Gregory *Peck, Kirk *Douglas and Robert *Mitchum.

New words were invented to keep up with Hollywood's development: *cliffhanger*, *tear-jerker*, *spine-chiller* and *western* describe types of film. Villains became *baddies*. As equipment became more sophisticated more people were needed to manage it. New jobs, still seen on lists of film credits today, included *gaffer* (= chief electrician) and *best boy*, his chief assistant.

In the 1950s large numbers of people abandoned the movies in order to watch television. The film industry needed something new to attract them back. This led to the development of **Cinerama** and ***3-D films**, which gave the audience the feeling of being part of the action. These proved too expensive but the wide screen of **CinemaScope** soon became standard throughout the world. The new stars of the 1950s, including Marilyn *Monroe, Rock *Hudson,

James *Dean and Steve *McQueen, also kept the film industry alive.

In the 1960s many companies began making films in other countries where costs were lower, and people said Hollywood would never again be the centre of the film industry. But the skills, equipment and money were still there, and Hollywood became important again in the 1980s. The old studios were bought by new media companies: 20th Century Fox was bought by Rupert *Murdoch, and Columbia by the Sony Corporation. New energy came from independent directors and producers like Steven *Spielberg, Robert *Redford and Martin *Scorsese. Rising stars included Meryl *Streep, Harrison *Ford, Arnold *Schwarzenegger, Kevin *Costner and Tom *Hanks.

Now, more than ever, Hollywood leads the world's film industry, producing the most expensive and successful films ever made, such as *Jurassic Park* (1993), **Forrest Gump* (1994), *Independence Day* (1996) and **Titanic* (1997). Companies like MGM own their own **movie theaters** in the US and elsewhere. Studios make additional profits from selling films to television companies and video producers. The ***Oscars**, presented by Hollywood's ***Academy of Motion Picture Arts and Sciences**, are the most valued prizes in the industry.

the ˌ**Hollywood** ˈ**Blacklist** /ˌhɒliwʊd; *AmE* ˌhɑːliwʊd/ a list of people in the US film industry who were refused work after being accused by the *House Un-American Activities Committee in the 1940s and 1950s of supporting Communism. They included actors and others who wrote, directed and produced films. Some of them took new names in order to be able to continue working. A small group of those on the Blacklist, called the **Hollywood Ten**, were sent to prison for about a year.

the ˌ**Hollywood** ˈ**Bowl** /ˌhɒliwʊd; *AmE* ˌhɑːliwʊd/ a large outdoor theatre in the natural curve of a hill in *Hollywood, *California. It was opened in 1919. The Bowl has 17 000 seats and presents concerts, operas, plays and other events.

the Hollywood Bowl

ˈOliver ˈWendell ˈ**Holmes**[1] /ˈwendəl ˈhəʊmz; *AmE* ˈhoʊmz/ (1809–94) a US doctor and writer of stories and poems. In 1857, they began to be published in the *The *Atlantic Monthly* magazine, and his famous 'Breakfast Table' conversations were later collected in several books. His poems include *The Chambered Nautilus* and *Old Ironsides*. Holmes also taught medicine at *Harvard University (1847–82).

Holmes's son, **Oliver Wendell Holmes Junior** (1841–1935), became one of the wisest and most respected judges on the US Supreme Court (1902–32). See also FALSELY SHOUTING FIRE IN A CROWDED THEATRE.

ˌSherlock ˈ**Holmes**[2] /ˌʃɜːlɒk ˈhəʊmz; *AmE* ˌʃɜːrlɑːk ˈhoʊmz/ a private *detective in the stories of Arthur *Conan Doyle. Holmes is able to solve crimes and mysteries using his powers of observation and deduction (= logical thought), sometimes without leaving his flat/apartment in *Baker Street, and often to the amazement of the police and his friend Dr *Watson. People often say, 'Elementary, my dear Watson,' when they think that a problem is easy to solve, although Holmes never actually says this in any of the stories. He is often shown wearing a special type of hat called a *deerstalker* and smoking a curved pipe. He also plays the violin and sometimes takes drugs. The Sherlock Holmes stories are still very popular and have been filmed many times: *I'm afraid I'm no Sherlock Holmes* (= I cannot solve the problem, etc.).

ˌGustav ˈ**Holst** /ˌgʊstɑːv ˈhəʊlst; *AmE* ˈhoʊlst/ (1874–1934) an English composer descended from Swedish and Russian ancestors. His best-known work is *The *Planets*.

Vicˌtoria ˈ**Holt** /ˈhəʊlt; *AmE* ˈhoʊlt/ a name under which the English author Eleanor Hibbert (1910–93) wrote some of her many historical, romantic or mystery novels. Another name she used was Jean Plaidy.

the ˌ**Holy** ˈ**Grail** (*also* the **Grail**) the plate or cup used by Jesus Christ at the Last Supper, in which some of his blood is said to have been collected after his death. There are many old stories about the Holy Grail. In the most famous of these King *Arthur's *Knights of the Round Table go to search for it, and it is finally found by Sir *Galahad, the only *knight who is completely pure. When Galahad dies, his men see the Grail rise into Heaven. The expression *Holy Grail* is sometimes used to mean something very valuable which is very hard to find: *A cure for cancer is the Holy Grail of medical researchers.*

ˈ**Holy Island** ⇨ LINDISFARNE.

ˌ**Holyrood** ˈ**House** (*also* **Holyroodhouse**) /ˌhɒliruːd; *AmE* ˌhɑːliruːd/ a royal palace in *Edinburgh, used by members of the British royal family when they visit Scotland and open to the public at other times. Most of the original early 16th-century palace burned down in 1544, and the present palace was built for King *Charles II in the 1670s.

ˌ***Home, Sweet*** ˈ***Home*** the title of a popular song 1923, with words by J H Payne, a US writer of plays. It contains the well-known line: 'Be it ever so humble, there's no place like home.' People often say 'Home sweet home' to show how pleased they are to be back in their own house or country again: *'At last, home sweet home!' he sighed, unlocking the front door.*

ˌ***Home A***ˈ***lone*** a US film (1990) which became the most successful comedy film ever made. It also made a child star of Macaulay Culkin. He plays Kevin, a young boy left at home by mistake when his family flies to Paris. Two further films, *Home Alone 2* and *Home Alone 3*, followed in 1992 and 1997.

ˌ**Home** ˈ**Box** ˌ**Office** (*abbr* **HBO**) a US cable television company which is the largest in the world. It operates two networks, HBO and Cinemax. Together in 1996 they had 2.7 million customers in the US and 5 million in other countries around the world. Cinemax shows films, and HBO presents films, sports, special programmes and series, such as *Tales from the Crypt* and the comedies *Dream On* and *The Larry Sanders Show*.

ˈ**homecoming** /ˈhəʊmkʌmɪŋ; *AmE* ˈhoʊmkʌmɪŋ/ *n* (in US colleges and universities) an event held each year, usually in the autumn, when former students return for special celebrations and social events. These include the **homecoming game** of football, the **homecoming parade** (= procession) and the **homecoming dance**. An attractive and popular girl is also elected as the **homecoming queen**.

at a homecoming

the ˌ**Home** ˈ**Counties** *n* [pl] (in Britain) the counties around London. People living in the Home Counties are generally regarded as being relatively wealthy, especially by those living in other parts of the country: *They enjoy a comfortable Home Counties lifestyle.*

ˌ**Home** ˈ**Depot**™ any of a large group of shops in the US and Canada that sell building materials for home improvement work, such as wood, paint and tools. The company was established in 1978, and the main office is in *Atlanta, *Georgia.

the ˌ**Home** ˈ**Guard** an army created during *World War II to defend Britain at home in case the enemy invaded the country. It consisted of older and younger men than those in the armed forces. They were originally called the Local Defence Volunteers. See also DAD'S ARMY.

homelessness

There is increasing concern about the number of people in Britain and the US who are **homeless**. Many are forced to **sleep on the streets** (*BrE also* **sleep rough**) because they have nowhere else to go. Formerly, people who had no permanent home were called **tramps** or **vagrants**. Most were older people. Now, many younger people are homeless. In the US the typical image of a homeless person is of a single man or an older woman. The women are sometimes called **bag ladies**, because they carry their things around in large bags. But many families with small children are also homeless.

Homeless people sleep in shop doorways, under bridges, or anywhere they can find away from the wind and rain. In major cities there are areas known as **cardboard cities**, where homeless people have built shelters out of cardboard and plastic. The alternative to sleeping rough may be to **live in a squat**. **Squatters** can only be **evicted** by the owner after a formal court order has been obtained.

It is estimated that there as many as half a million homeless people in Britain. Not all of these sleep rough or squat. Local councils are legally required to find somewhere for homeless people to live, and many are housed in **boarding houses** or **bed-and-breakfast accommodation**. *Charities such as *Shelter, *Centre Point and the *Salvation Army run **hostels** for the homeless. Each winter they also organize campaigns which raise money to provide extra **night shelters** and **soup kitchens** (= places giving free hot food).

In the US many towns have laws making it illegal to sleep on the streets, so the police may tell people to move during the night. The US also has shelters but it is not easy to get a bed in one. Many do not have enough space, or have only enough money to stay open for part of the year. They are often away from the centre of town, and people need to have money for the bus fare to get there. A recent study in New York showed that *African Americans are 17 times more likely than Whites to use such shelters.

For many people, homelessness begins when they lose their jobs and cannot pay their rent. Some become homeless as a result of family quarrels, broken relationships, violence, and mental illness. Some homeless people survive by **begging**. In Britain homeless people have an opportunity to help themselves selling *The *Big Issue* magazine: they buy copies of the magazine and sell them at a higher, fixed price to members of the public.

Many people give to charities, or to the homeless on the streets, but some think homeless people are wasters (= spend money carelessly), or are too lazy to work, and are responsible for their own situation. Americans generally believe that people should work hard to help themselves, instead of taking money from the government. For that reason, many Americans will give money to charities, but are opposed to a system of government benefits. But homeless people who have no address have difficulty getting even the limited kinds of help available from the government..

the ˈ**Home** ˌ**Office** the British government department dealing with many matters within the country, including law and order, the fire service, the control of people entering the country, political elections and broadcasting. The minister responsible for the Home Office is called the *Home Secretary. Compare FOREIGN AND COMMONWEALTH OFFICE.

ˌ***Home on the*** ˈ***Range*** a popular US song about the American West. It was first published in 1873 in the *Smith County Pioneer* newspaper in *Kansas, where it is now the official state song. It begins:

Oh give me a home where the buffalo roam,
Where the deer and the antelope play;
Where seldom is heard a discouraging word,
And the skies are not cloudy all day.

ˌ**home** ˈ**rule** *n* [U] **1 Home Rule** (in British and Irish history) the government of Ireland by the Irish. There was a strong political movement for this from the 1870s to 1914, when a Home Rule Bill was passed by the British parliament, but because of *World War I nothing was actually done about it. The *IRA was formed and began to use violent methods in order to get a greater degree of Home Rule than the Bill allowed. This led to a change in the situation when in 1920 Ireland was split into *Northern Ireland and the *Irish Free State (now the *Republic of Ireland). Most people in Northern Ireland are now strongly opposed to Home Rule. See also PARNELL. **2** the government of any country or region by its own citizens. In Britain, there are movements by Scottish and Welsh political groups to achieve Home Rule. See also DEVOLUTION.

ˌ**home** ˈ**run** *n* (in *baseball), the action of a player who hits the ball far enough, usually over the fence, to enable him to advance around all three bases and score a 'run'. See also GRAND SLAM 3.

ˌ***Homes and*** ˈ***Gardens*** a British magazine pub-

H

lished every month, which contains articles on house decorating, gardening and other subjects. It first appeared in 1919.

the ˌ**Home ˈSecretary** (in Britain) the minister responsible for the *Home Office. His or her full title is the Secretary of State for the Home Department.

the ˈ**Homestead Act** a law passed by the US Congress in 1862. It gave 160acres (65hectares) of government land in the west to anyone who would agree to live on it for five years. A small payment was required. A person who received any of this land was called a **homesteader**.

ˈ**hominy** /ˈhɒmɪni; *AmE* ˈhɑːmɪni/ *n* [U] (*AmE*) dry corn that is roughly ground. It is boiled with water or milk to produce a food called **hominy grits** which is often eaten at breakfast, especially in the southern states. Compare GRITS.

Hong Kong

Hong Kong, which means 'Fragrant Harbour' in Chinese, is a former British *Crown Colony off the south-east coast of China. The colony consisted of Hong Kong Island, many smaller islands, and the mainland areas of Kowloon ('Nine Dragons') and the New Territories. British opium traders working for the *East India Company began using Hong Kong Island's harbour in the 1820s. The island was occupied by the British during the first *Opium War and was given to them by China in 1842 at the end of the war. Kowloon was gained in 1860 following the second Opium War. In 1898 the colony again increased in size when the New Territories were leased to Britain for a period of 99 years. On 30 June 1997 the whole of Hong Kong, not just the New Territories, was handed over to China and it is now a Special Administrative Region of China.

Under British rule Hong Kong became a successful manufacturing, business and financial centre. The population of six million people, mostly Chinese, enjoyed a high standard of living and many made a lot of money. The wealth of Hong Kong and the relative freedom of its citizens attracted people from other countries in the Far East.

British control of Hong Kong became an embarrassment to China, and there were great celebrations in Beijing when the colony was returned to Chinese rule. In 1984 the British and Chinese negotiated an agreement to preserve the existing capitalist system and general way of life for at least 50 years after the handover. As a British dependency, Hong Kong was ruled by a governor appointed by the Queen, but in practice he agreed to all measures passed by the local, democratically elected, Legislative Council. A Chinese governor was appointed by the authorities in Beijing to take over from the British governor in 1997. The Legislative Council was to be retained but members of the Council in office in 1997 were not acceptable to the government in Beijing, and elections for a new Council were planned for the first year of Chinese rule.

Some people who left Hong Kong in the early 1990s fearing changes to the political and economic systems under Chinese rule have now returned. But others are still afraid that the government will become less democratic and that freedom of speech and of the press may gradually be removed.

ˈ**Honi ˈsoit qui ˈmal y ˈpense** /ˈɒni ˈswɑː kiː ˈmæl iː ˈpɒns; *AmE* ˈɑːni, ˈpɑːns/ ⇨ ORDER OF THE GARTER.

ˈ**honky-tonk** *n* (*AmE*) **1** [U] a type of *African-American *ragtime music played on a piano whose wires have been changed to give it a high sound. Honky-tonk music was first played at the beginning of the 20th century in the cheap bars or dance halls of *New Orleans. **2** [C] a cheap bar or dance hall.

ˌ**Honoˈlulu** /ˌhɒnəˈluːluː; *AmE* ˌhɑːnəˈluːluː/ the capital city of the US state of *Hawaii. It is a major port on the south-eastern coast of the island of Oahu, and sugar and pineapples are processed there. The University of Hawaii is in Honolulu, and so is *Pearl Harbor, the home of the US Pacific Fleet. The city is popular with tourists, especially *Waikiki beach.

ˈ**honor roll** *n* (*AmE*) (in US schools) a list of students who have achieved high grades in their work in a particular term or year. Compare DEAN'S LIST.

ˈ**honor soˌciety** (in US schools) an organization for students who have achieved high grades in their work. There are national and local honor societies, and many have Greek letter names, like the Beta Club. They can be for general academic achievement or for certain specific areas of study.

ˈ**Honourable** (*AmE* ˈ**Honorable**) **1 the Honourable** (*written abbr* **the Hon**) (in Britain) a title placed before the names of various members of the *peerage, including the children of *barons and *viscounts and the younger sons of *earls: *the Honourable Michael Stewart.* **2** (in Britain) a title used by *Members of Parliament when speaking to or about another member during a debate, even when they are criticizing one another: *I refer you to the answer given earlier by the Honourable Member for Chesterfield.* ○ *I disagree with my Honourable Friend the member for Bolsover.* **3** (in the US) a title of respect used before the names of certain important officials, but not when speaking to or about them. They include members of *Congress, the US *Attorney General, members of the *Supreme Court, other judges, members of the President's *Cabinet, US ambassadors, state governors and *mayors. See also RIGHT HONOURABLE.

the ˌ**Honourable Arˈtillery ˌCompany** the oldest regiment in the British army, started by King *Henry VIII in 1537. It is now part of the *Territorial Army.

honours

Twice a year several hundred British people who have distinguished themselves in some way, receive a variety of honours. A few are given **life *peerages**, some are made ***knights**, and many others are given lesser awards. The **honours lists** are published on *New Year's Day (**the New Year Honours**) and in mid June on the present Queen's official birthday (**the Birthday Honours**). At the end of each parliament before a general election, the *Prime Minister recommends a list of politicians for the **Dissolution Honours**.

For a long time honours were given almost automatically to senior members of the armed forces and the *civil service, and to those who had contributed to party political funds. In 1993 John *Major announced proposals to reduce the number of such honours and to give more awards to members of the public. People are nominated for honours by colleagues and friends, or by people who admire their achievements. The Office of Public Service receives nominations and draws up a final list which is approved by the Prime Minister. As well as the names of politicians and businessmen, it contains *charity workers, well-known sports and television personalities, actors, musicians, etc., and many ordinary people. Honours are awarded personally by the king or queen at *Buckingham Palace.

Many of the honours are associated with one of several **orders of chivalry**. Some of the orders have different grades of membership, ranging from 'knight' through 'commander' to 'officer' and 'member'. Many people are given awards in the **Order of the British Empire**. Famous people may be given a *CBE (commander rank) or *OBE (officer rank); people recommended by members of the public are usually given an *MBE (member rank). Some people think the Order of the British Empire should be renamed to get rid of the outdated reference to the Empire, and new names are being considered. Most honours allow a person to put the appropriate letters after their name. In addition to these honours there are many *medals and decorations for bravery, for civilians as well as for members of the police and the armed forces.

In the US there is no system of honours like that in Britain, though a number of medals are awarded for outstanding achievement or for bravery.

ˈJohn ˈLee ˈ**Hooker** /ˈhʊkə(r)/ (1917–) an *African-American singer and writer of *blues music who also plays the guitar. He won *Grammy awards for *I'm in the Mood* (1989) and *Chill Out* (1995). His other hits include *Boogie Chillen'* (1948), *Dimples* (1956) and *Boom Boom* (1962), and his albums include *The Healer* (1985) and *Don't Look Back* (1997), recorded when he was 79.

ˌ**Hooray** ˈ**Henry** *n* (*BrE infml disapprov*) a fashionable young *upper-class or *upper-middle-class man, especially one with a loud voice and cheerful manner who is regarded as rather stupid. The female equivalent of a Hooray Henry is sometimes referred to as a **Hooray Henrietta**. Compare SLOANE RANGER.

ˈ**hootenanny** /ˈhuːtənæni/ *n* (*AmE*) an informal performance of *folk music at which people come together to play, sing and sometimes dance for their own enjoyment. The word *hootenanny* was originally a nonsense name for a gadget (= small mechanical device).

ˌHerbert ˈ**Hoover**[1] /ˈhuːvə(r)/ (1874–1964) the 31st US *President (1929–33) and a member of the Republican Party. He had earlier been the US Secretary of Commerce (1921–9). A year after he became President, the *Great Depression began. Although it was not Hoover's fault, people blamed him because his government failed to stop it, and Franklin D *Roosevelt defeated him in the 1932 election. Hoover directed the European Food Program after *World War II.

ˈJ ˈEdgar ˈ**Hoover**[2] /ˈhuːvə(r)/ (John Edgar Hoover 1895–1972) the American who developed the *FBI into a successful and scientific national police organization. He directed it for almost 50 years, from 1924 until his death. He had great power and public support, and no president tried to replace him. Recently, however, it has been found that he kept illegal personal files on many people.

ˌ**Hoover** ˈ**Dam** /ˌhuːvə; *AmE* ˌhuːvər/ a large dam on the Colorado River on the border of *Nevada and *Arizona. It was completed in 1935 and originally called Boulder Dam. In 1947 the name was changed in honour of the US President Herbert *Hoover. It is 726 feet (221 metres) high and 1 244 feet (379 metres) wide, and it produces electricity for Arizona, Nevada and southern *California.

ˈ**Hooverville** /ˈhuːvəvɪl; *AmE* ˈhuːvərvɪl/ any collection of poor houses, usually at the edge of a city, that developed in the US during the *Great Depression. They were often temporary places for unemployed people and those without homes, and were named after Herbert *Hoover, the US President at that time.

ˌ**Hopalong** ˈ**Cassidy** ⇨ CASSIDY.

ˌBob ˈ**Hope**[2] /ˈhəʊp; *AmE* ˈhoʊp/ (1903–) a US comedian and comedy actor, born in Britain. He has performed for nearly 70 years and been a star of *vaudeville, radio, television and films. He is well known for his trips to entertain US soldiers around the world. His many films include the series of seven 'Road movies' (among them *The Road to Zanzibar* and *The Road to Morocco*), in which he appeared with Bing *Crosby and Dorothy Lamour. Hope presented the *Academy Awards television show for many years and has received several special *Oscars. He also received the *Presidential Medal of Freedom in 1969 and was made an honorary *knight by the British government in 1998.

HOPE /həʊp; *AmE* hoʊp/ (*in full* **Health Opportunity for People Everywhere**) (*also* ˌ**Project** ˈ**HOPE**) a US charity that provides medical help and training for poor countries. Doctors and nurses work without payment for the organization, which receives financial support from individuals, companies and governments. It began in 1958 with the *SS Hope*, a hospital ship that visited different countries from 1960 to 1973. Project HOPE has now trained more than 1.4 million professional health workers in 70 countries.

ˈ**Hopi** /ˈhəʊpi; *AmE* ˈhoʊpi/ *n* (*pl* **Hopis** *or* **Hopi**) a member of a *Pueblo *Native-American people living in north-east *Arizona. The Hopis are mostly farmers and very religious. Their god is Kachina, and their religious ceremonies include the snake dance. They have had a long dispute with the *Navajos about land on the border that separates them.

ˌAnthony ˈ**Hopkins**[1] /ˈhɒpkɪnz; *AmE* ˈhɑːpkɪnz/ (1937–) a Welsh stage and film actor. His theatre successes include *Pravda* (1985) and *King *Lear* (1986). He won an *Oscar for his role as the evil Hannibal Lecter in *The *Silence of the Lambs* (1991). His other films include *Shadowlands* (1993), *Remains of the Day* (1993), *Nixon* (1995) and *Amistad* (1997). He was made a *knight in 1993.

Anthony Hopkins with Debra Winger in Shadowlands

ˈGerard ˈManley ˈ**Hopkins**[2] /ˈmænli ˈhɒpkɪnz; *AmE* ˈhɑːpkɪnz/ (1844–89) an English Jesuit priest who wrote poems about religious ideas and the beauty of nature, using a form of verse which he called 'sprung rhythm'. His best-known works are *The Wreck of the Deutschland*, *Pied Beauty* and *Windhover*. None of his poems were published during his lifetime. They were first published by his friend Robert *Bridges in 1918 and influenced later poets, including W H *Auden and Dylan *Thomas.

ˌEdward ˈ**Hopper**[1] /ˈhɒpə(r); *AmE* ˈhɑːpər/ (1882–1967) a US artist best known for realistic pictures of American city scenes. These often showed lonely

Gas *by Edward Hopper, 1940 in the Museum of Modern Art, New York*

people in depressing streets or buildings. They include *Early Sunday Morning* (1930) and *Nighthawks* (1942).

ˌHedda ˈ**Hopper**[2] /ˌhedə ˈhɒpə(r); *AmE* ˈhɑːpər/ (1890–1966) a US journalist who wrote about the private lives of film stars. She was known for her unusual hats. Her great rival was Louella *Parsons.

ˈ**Horlicks**™ /ˈhɔːlɪks; *AmE* ˈhɔːrlɪks/ *n* [U] a British make of hot drink, usually taken before going to bed to make you sleep better. It is sold as a powder, which is mixed with hot milk or water before drinking: *Her words were as comforting as a cup of Horlicks.*

Hoˌratio ˈ**Hornblower** /həˌreɪʃiəʊ ˈhɔːnbləʊə(r); *AmE* həˌreɪʃioʊ ˈhɔːrnbloʊər/ the main character in a series of novels by the English writer C S *Forester. Hornblower is an officer in the British navy during the wars against Napoleon in the early 19th century.

ˌA S ˈ**Hornby** /ˈhɔːnbi; *AmE* ˈhɔːrnbi/ (Albert Sidney Hornby 1898–1978) an English teacher and writer of books for foreign learners of English. He is best known for the *Oxford Advanced Learner's Dictionary*, which was first published in Britain by *Oxford University Press in 1948 and is still bought in large numbers by students around the world. New editions of the dictionary are published regularly.

A S Hornby

ˌLena ˈ**Horne** /ˌliːnə ˈhɔːn; *AmE* ˈhɔːrn/ (1917–) an *African-American singer of the *blues who also acted in *Hollywood musical films. One of her most famous songs was *Stormy Weather* in the 1943 film of the same name.

ˌ***Horse and*** ˈ***Hound*** a British magazine containing news and information about sporting events involving horses, such as horse-racing and *hunting. It first appeared in 1884 and is published every week.

the ˈ**Horse Guards 1** (*also fml* the **Royal Horse Guards**) a group of cavalry soldiers (= soldiers who once fought on horses) in the British army. They were formed in 1661 and are now part of the Blues and Royals. **2** the building in *Whitehall in London where the ceremony of *Changing the Guard takes place.

ˌ**Horse Guards Pa**ˈ**rade** the open area behind the *Horse Guards(2) building in London, England, where the ceremony of *Trooping the Colour takes place every year on the queen's *Official Birthday.

the ˌ**Horse of the** ˈ**Year Show** (in Britain) a contest in showjumping (= the sport of riding horses over difficult barriers) which takes place every year in October, usually at *Wembley in London. It was first held in 1949.

the ˈ**Hospital for** ˈ**Sick** ˈ**Children** ⇨ GREAT ORMOND STREET.

the ˈ**hostage** ˌ**crisis** a dangerous international event in 1979–81, when Iranian students took 66 Americans from the US Embassy in Tehran and kept them as prisoners for more than 14 months. They demanded that the former Shah of Iran be sent back to Iran from the US for trial. The US President, Jimmy *Carter, ordered a small US military team to rescue the prisoners in April 1980, but it failed and eight American soldiers were killed. The hostage crisis was a major reason for Carter's losing the 1980 election to Ronald *Reagan. The prisoners were released on 20 January 1981, the day on which Reagan became President.

ˈ**Hostess** a US company, established in the 1920s, which makes many different types of cakes, including *Twinkies, HoHos and Ding-Dongs.

ˌ**hot cross** ˈ**bun** *n* a small sweet cake containing raisins and spices, and marked with the Christian symbol of the cross on the top. Hot cross buns are traditionally eaten hot, with butter on, on *Good Friday. People used to believe that hot cross buns could cure various illnesses. ⇨ note at EASTER.

ˈ**hot dog 1** a hot sausage served in a soft bread roll, often with onions, mustard, etc. In the US a hot dog is also sometimes called a *wiener*, a *frankfurter* or, more informally, a *weenie*. **2** (*AmE infml*) an enthusiastic person who tries too hard to impress others, especially in sport.

ˈ**hotline 1** a direct and private communication link between two heads of government, used especially in emergencies to reduce the risk of war. The first one was established in 1963 between the US President John F *Kennedy and Nikita Khrushchev of the USSR. **2** any direct telephone link for use in an emergency or to receive a special service: *Call the poison prevention hotline if your child accidentally swallows some dangerous liquid.*

ˈ**Hotpoint**™ /ˈhɒtpɔɪnt; *AmE* ˈhɑːtpɔɪnt/ a US company that makes electrical goods for the home: *a Hotpoint washing machine.*

ˌHarry **Hou**ˈ**dini** /huːˈdiːni/ (1874–1926) a US performer of magic, born in Hungary, who became famous for escaping from chains, locked boxes, etc. His name is often used to refer to a person or an animal that seems able to escape from any situation: *We try to keep our cat in the house but she's a real Houdini.*

ˈ**hound dog** *n* (*AmE*) (especially in the southern states) a dog trained to hunt. People joke in the South that hound dogs are often lazy and cannot be relied on.

house (*also* **house music**) *n* [U] a style of popular dance music that typically uses electronic drum sounds, a fast beat and a few words repeated many times.

the ˌ**Household** ˈ**Cavalry** a section of the of the British army consisting of two regiments, the *Life Guards and the Blues and Royals. Among other duties they ride horses to guard the king or queen at official ceremonies.

the ˌ**Household Di**ˈ**vision** (*also* the ˌ**Household** ˈ**Troops**) the soldiers of the *Household Cavalry of the British army. With some of the men of the *Guards Division, they carry out special duties for the king or queen.

the ˌ**House of** ˈ**Commons** (*also infml* the **House**, the **Commons**) the lower house of the British *Parliament, in which elected *Members of Parliament meet to discuss current political issues and vote on *Acts of Parliament. Compare HOUSE OF LORDS. See also STATE OPENING OF PARLIAMENT.

the ˌ**House of** ˈ**Lords** (*also infml* the **Lords**) the upper house of the British *Parliament, whose members are not elected. Its work consists mainly of examining and making changes to *Bills from the *House of Commons and discussing important matters which the House of Commons cannot find time to discuss. It also acts as a final *Court of Appeal. ⇨ article at PARLIAMENT. See also LAW LORDS, LORDS SPIRITUAL, LORDS TEMPORAL.

the ˌ**House of Repre**ˈ**sentatives** (*also* the **US House of Representatives**, the **House**) the lower and larger of the two houses of the US *Congress (the other being the *Senate). The *Speaker of the House is its leader. The House has 435 members, who are elected every two years. The states have different numbers of representatives according to the size of their population, so *Delaware has only two members while *California has 52. House members can introduce a proposal for a law and must approve any new law. If no candidate in an election for US President receives a majority of votes in the *Electoral College, the House chooses the President. This has only ever happened twice, in the cases of Thomas *Jefferson and John Quincy *Adams.

the ˌ**House of ˈWindsor** /ˈwɪnzə(r)/ the name of the British royal family since 1917.

the ˌ**Houses of ˈParliament** **1** the *House of Commons and the *House of Lords. **2** the group of buildings beside the River *Thames in central London where these two assemblies meet. It is also known as the *Palace of Westminster. The original 14th-century palace stood at this place until it was badly damaged by fire in 1834. Between 1840 and 1867, new buildings designed by Sir Charles *Barry and Augustus *Pugin were put up. In 1941 the *House of Commons was destroyed by German bombs, but it was built again after the war in exactly the same style. The Houses of Parliament are open to the public at certain times. See also BIG BEN.

the Houses of Parliament

The ˌ***House that ˈJack Built*** a traditional *nursery rhyme in which there are lots of verses, each one adding an extra line to the one before. It begins like this:

This is the house that Jack built.
This is the malt
That lay in the house that Jack built.
This is the rat,
That ate the malt
That lay in the house that Jack built.
This is the cat,
That killed the rat,
That ate the malt
That lay in the house that Jack built.

the ˈ**House Un-Aˈmerican Acˈtivities Comˌmittee** (*abbr* **HUAC**) a committee established in 1938 by the US *House of Representatives to investigate activities that might threaten the American government and people. It became famous in the 1950s when under the influence of Senator Joseph *McCarthy it accused many innocent people of supporting Communism. It was responsible for several of these being sent to prison. In 1969 the committee changed its name to the House Committee on Internal Security, and in 1975 it was brought to an end.

ˈ**housing associˌation** *n* (in Britain) a local organization that provides rented homes for poorer families, and especially for old, disabled and single people. It also shares the ownership of houses with people who cannot afford to buy a house on their own. There are about 2 800 housing associations in Britain. Similar organizations in the US are called **housing authorities**. There are about 3 100 of them, and they receive advice and financial help from the US Department of Housing and Urban Development.

ˈ**housing ˌbenefit** *n* [U] (in Britain) money given by the government to people who have a low income, to help them pay their rent or *rates. The amount varies according to people's family status and actual income: *Are you entitled to housing benefit?*

the ˈ**Housing Corpoˌration** a British government organization that provides money for English *housing associations. There are equivalent organizations in Scotland and Wales.

ˌA E ˈ**Housman** /ˈhaʊsmən/ (Alfred Edward Housman 1859–1936) an English writer of poetry who taught Latin at London and *Cambridge universities. His best-known work is *A *Shropshire Lad*, a collection of short poems.

ˈ**Houston[1]** /ˈhjuːstən/ the fourth largest US city and the largest in *Texas, named after Sam *Houston. It is a financial, commercial, cultural and industrial centre, especially for the oil industry. The city is also a major port connected to the *Gulf of Mexico by the Houston Ship Canal. It has two major universities, Rice University and the University of Houston, and the *Lyndon B Johnson Space Center is also there.

ˌSam ˈ**Houston[2]** /ˈhjuːstən/ (1793–1863) a US military and political leader. He helped *Texas gain its independence from Mexico, defeating the Mexican army at the Battle of *San Jacinto. Houston became the first *President of the Republic of Texas, and after Texas became a state he represented it as a US Senator (1846–59). He was also elected Governor of Texas but was forced to leave the job because he did not want Texas to join the *Confederate States.

ˌWhitney ˈ**Houston[3]** /ˌwɪtni ˈhuːstən/ (1963–) an *African-American singer of popular music and actor. She has won *Grammy awards for several songs, including *Saving All My Love for You* (1985), *I Wanna Dance with Somebody* (1987) and *I Will Always Love You* (1993). Her films include *The Bodyguard* (1993), *Waiting to Exhale* (1995) and *The Preacher's Wife* (1997).

ˈ**Houyhnhnm** /ˈhuːɪnɪm/ *n* a member of the race of kind and intelligent horses that Gulliver meets in **Gulliver's Travels* by Jonathan *Swift. They are completely different to the *Yahoos, who work for them. The Yahoos look like men but are stupid and cruel. Gulliver later returns to his own land and finds that he now dislikes men, having learned a lot from the Houyhnhnms. (Their name is intended to sound like the sound a horse makes.).

ˈ**Hovis**™ /ˈhəʊvɪs; *AmE* ˈhoʊvɪs/ a British make of brown bread, produced by the company *Rank Hovis McDougall. Each loaf has the word HOVIS along its side after baking: *I got a brown sliced Hovis.*

ˌCatherine ˈ**Howard[1]** /ˈhaʊəd; *AmE* ˈhaʊərd/ (*c.* 1521–42) the fifth wife of King *Henry VIII. He had her head cut off after they had been married for two years, when he found that she had had sexual relationships with other men.

ˌMichael ˈ**Howard[2]** /ˈhaʊəd; *AmE* ˈhaʊərd/ (1941–) a British *Conservative politician who held a number of senior government positions, including that of *Home Secretary in the 1990s.

ˌ**Howard ˈJohnson's** /ˌhaʊəd ˈdʒɒnsnz; *AmE* ˌhaʊərd ˈdʒɑːnsnz/ any of a group of US restaurants and hotels. The restaurants became famous for their red roofs and their 27 types of ice cream. The first of these was opened by Howard Deering Johnson in Quincy, *Massachusetts, in 1929. The company is now concerned mainly with developing its range of hotels. They include HoJo Inns, Park Square Inns, Howard Johnson Lodges and Howard Johnson Plazas.

the **ˈHoward ˈLeague for ˈPenal Reˈform** /ˈhaʊəd; *AmE* ˈhaʊərd/ a British organization that since 1866 has worked to improve conditions in prisons, and to help people who are in prison or leaving it. It is named after John Howard (1726–1790), a rich Englishman who spent all his money visiting prisons and making the public aware of the terrible conditions in them, until the government was forced to pass laws to improve these.

ˌ***Howards ˈEnd*** /ˌhaʊədz; *AmE* ˌhaʊərdz/ a novel (1910) by E M *Forster. It describes the relationships between two very different *middle-class families in *Edwardian England. *Howards End* is the name of the house in which one of the families lives. James *Ivory directed a successful film version in 1992.

ˌGeoffrey ˈ**Howe**[1] /ˈhaʊ/ (1926–) a British *Conservative politician who held senior positions in several governments during the 1980s. He resigned from the *Cabinet in 1990 because he was unhappy about Margaret *Thatcher's attitude to the *European Union. He made a strong speech attacking her in the *House of Commons, and this began the series of events that led to the *Conservative Party choosing a new leader, John *Major. Howe was made a *knight in 1970 and a *life peer in 1992.

ˈJulia ˈWard ˈ**Howe**[2] /ˈwɔːd ˈhaʊ; *AmE* ˈwɔːrd ˈhaʊ/ (1819–1910) the American who wrote *The *Battle Hymn of the Republic*. She was an *abolitionist and a writer, mostly of poetry. She also established the New England Woman Suffrage Association (1868) to support women's right to vote, and edited the abolitionist newspaper *Commonwealth* with her husband.

ˌFrankie ˈ**Howerd** /ˈhaʊəd; *AmE* ˈhaʊərd/ (1921–92) an English comedian and comedy actor who was famous for his exaggerated way of telling jokes and appearing to be shocked when the audience thought he was being funny in a rude way. He is probably best remembered for his performance in *Up Pompeii!* (1970–71), a television comedy series about the ancient Romans.

ˌFred ˈ**Hoyle** /ˈhɔɪl/ (1915–) an English astrophysicist (= scientist who studies the structure of stars, etc.). He has developed theories on the origins of stars and of life itself, and has written a number of works of popular science. He also writes science fiction. He was made a *knight in 1972.

ˌ**HP ˈSauce**™ /ˌeɪtʃ piː/ *n* [U] a popular British make of dark brown sauce sold in tall bottles. It is made with vegetables, vinegar and spices and is eaten with various different foods, especially meat, chips (= long thin pieces of fried potato), etc. The letters HP stand for *Houses of Parliament, and there is a picture of these on the label.

HSE /ˌeɪtʃ es ˈiː/ ⇨ HEALTH AND SAFETY EXECUTIVE.

HTV /ˌeɪtʃ ti ˈviː/ ⇨ HARLECH TELEVISION.

HUAC /ˌeɪtʃ juː eɪ ˈsiː, ˈhjuːæk/ ⇨ HOUSE UN-AMERICAN ACTIVITIES COMMITTEE.

ˈL ˈRon ˈ**Hubbard** /ˈhʌbəd; *AmE* ˈhʌbərd/ (Lafayette Ronald Hubbard 1911–86) a US writer of science fiction who established the Church of *Scientology in 1954. His novels included *Slaves of Sleep* (1939) and a series of 10 books with the general title of *Mission Earth* (1985–7).

ˌEdwin ˈ**Hubble** /ˈhʌbl/ (1889–1953) a US astronomer. He was the first to find evidence that the universe is becoming larger in size. He did this in 1929 when he discovered that galaxies (= very large groups of stars) move away from us in a regular way. This is now called Hubble's Law. In 1923, he had discovered that large galaxies exist beyond our own. His research was done at the Mount Wilson Observatory in *California.

the ˌ**Hubble ˈSpace ˌTelescope** /ˌhʌbl/ a large US telescope put into space in 1990 by *NASA. It is named after the US astronomer Edwin *Hubble and provides a much clearer view of the universe than could be obtained from the ground. Three months after it began to operate, it found a 'black hole' with a mass of 300 million suns.

the Hubble Space Telescope

ˌ**Huckleberry ˈFinn** ⇨ FINN.

HUD ⇨ DEPARTMENT OF HOUSING AND URBAN DEVELOPMENT.

ˌHenry ˈ**Hudson**[1] /ˈhʌdsn/ (*c.* 1550–*c.* 1611) an English explorer who, when he was looking for the *North-west Passage in 1609–1610, discovered what are now called the *Hudson River and **Hudson Bay**, a very large sea in north-eastern Canada connected with the North Atlantic by the **Hudson Strait**. In 1611 some of his men turned against him there, and put him in a small boat with his 12-year old son. They were never seen again.

ˌRock ˈ**Hudson**[2] /ˌrɒk ˈhʌdsn; *AmE* ˌrɑːk/ (1925–85) a US actor who became famous playing tough characters but later made several comedies. His films included *Magnificent Obsession* (1954), *Giant* (1956), *Pillow Talk* (1959) and *Send Me No Flowers* (1964). He also made a television series, *McMillan and Wife* (1971–5). Hudson was the first *Hollywood star who said publicly that he had AIDS, from which he died.

the ˌ**Hudson ˈRiver** /ˌhʌdsn/ a river in the US state of New York. It flows 315 miles (510 kilometres) from the *Adirondack Mountains to New York City where it joins the Atlantic Ocean. In 1825, it was connected to the *Great Lakes by the *Erie Canal. The river is named after Henry *Hudson who in 1609 was one of the first people to travel along its unknown areas.

ˌ**Hudson's ˈBay ˌCompany** /ˌhʌdsnz/ a British trading company set up in 1670 to buy and sell the products of northern Canada, such as furs. The company helped to make it easier for people to settle in Canada by establishing trading posts and transport routes all across the country. It owned very large areas of Canada, which it sold to the Canadian government in 1870. The company was run from England until 1931. It is still the world's largest company trading in furs, and it also has interests in oil and owns department stores.

ˌHoward ˈ**Hughes**[1] /ˈhjuːz/ (1905–76) a rich American who produced and directed films, and built planes. He owned an oil company and the Hughes Aircraft Company. His films included *Hell's Angels* (1930) and *The Outlaw* (1941). He established several fastest flights (1935–8) and designed the world's largest aircraft (1947). Hughes gained control of *RKO in (1948) and *TWA in 1959, and he helped to develop *Las Vegas in the 1960s. He hid from the public for the last 25 years of his life.

ˌLangston ˈ**Hughes**[2] /ˌlæŋstən ˈhjuːz/ (1902–67) an *African-American poet and writer who was a leading figure of the *Harlem Renaissance. He used African-American rhythms in his poems, most of which are about city life. They include *The Weary Blues* (1926), *Not Without Laughter* (1930) and *One-Way Ticket* (1949). He also wrote novels and plays.

ˌTed ˈ**Hughes**[3] /ˈhjuːz/ (1930–98) an English poet whose work gives a powerful picture of both the beauty and the violence of the natural world. His best-known collections of poetry included *The Hawk in the Rain* (1957) and *Crow* (1970). He also wrote books of poetry for children, including *The Iron Man* (1968) (*The Iron Giant* in the US). He was *Poet Laureate from 1984. His first wife was the US poet Sylvia *Plath.

ˈ**Huguenot** /ˈhjuːɡənəʊ; *AmE* ˈhjuːɡənɑːt/ a French Protestant in the 16th and 17th centuries. After 1685 the Huguenots were attacked by the Catholic majority. Thousands left France for other countries, including Britain and the US, where many became very successful, especially in the silver and textile industries.

Hull /hʌl/ (*also* ˌ**Kingston-upon-ˈHull**) a major port and industrial centre in *Humberside in north-eastern England. It is on the River *Humber.

the ˈ**Humber** /ˈhʌmbə(r)/ a major river in north-eastern England. A suspension bridge (= a bridge hanging from cables supported by towers at each end) across it, called the **Humber Bridge**, has the second longest span in the world.

ˈ**Humberside** /ˈhʌmbəsaɪd; *AmE* ˈhʌmbərsaɪd/ a *county of north-eastern England, formed in 1974. Its main town is *Hull, on the River *Humber, and its administrative centre is Beverley.

ˌCardinal ˈ**Hume**[1] /ˈhjuːm/ (George Basil Hume 1923–99) an English monk who was made *Archbishop of Westminster, the head of the Roman Catholic Church in Britain, in 1976. He became a cardinal (= one of the senior Roman Catholic priests who elect the Pope) in 1976.

ˌDavid ˈ**Hume**[2] /ˈhjuːm/ (1711–76) a Scottish philosopher and historian who is regarded as one of the greatest British thinkers. He said that people cannot be certain about anything that is not directly taken in through their senses. Hume was greatly respected during his lifetime, but was unable to get a university teaching job because he was an agnostic (= he could not say that he believed in God). His most important works include *A Treatise of Human Nature* (1739–40) and *History of England* (1754–62).

ˌJohn ˈ**Hume**[3] /ˈhjuːm/ (1937–) the Northern Irish leader of the *Social Democratic and Labour Party since 1979. With David *Trimble he received the *Nobel Peace Prize in 1998.

Humour ⇨ article.

ˌBarry ˈ**Humphries** /ˈhʌmpfriz/ (1934–) an Australian comedian who is well known in Britain for two characters he has created: 'housewife superstar' Dame Edna *Everage, for which Humphries wears women's clothes, and Sir Les Patterson, a disgusting man who is supposed to be a representative of the Australian government in London.

ˌ**Humpty ˈDumpty** /ˌhʌmpti ˈdʌmpti/ **1** a large egg-shaped character in a popular *nursery rhyme:

Humpty Dumpty sat on a wall.
Humpty Dumpty had a great fall.
All the king's horses,
And all the king's men,
Couldn't put Humpty together again.

2 a large egg-shaped character in **Through the Looking Glass* by Lewis *Carroll who has a strange and clever conversation with Alice. One of the things Humpty Dumpty says is, 'When I use a word, it means just what I choose it to mean, neither more nor less.'

the ˌ**Hundred Years ˈWar** a war between France and England that lasted, with long periods between battles, from the 1340s to the 1450s. The English were trying to get control of France, and won some major battles, including *Crécy (1346) and *Agincourt (1415), but by the end of the war they had only gained the area around Calais, which they kept until 1558.

the ˌ**Hungerford ˈmassacre** /ˌhʌŋɡəfəd; *AmE* ˌhʌŋɡərfərd/ an incident that took place in the town of Hungerford in *Berkshire, England, when in August 1987 a man called Michael Ryan shot and killed 15 people, including his mother, and wounded several others. He then shot himself. See also DUNBLANE.

ˌHolman ˈ**Hunt** /ˌhəʊlmən ˈhʌnt; *AmE* ˌhoʊlmən/ (1827–1910) an English *Pre-Raphaelite painter. His pictures are mostly scenes of the countryside or from the Bible, and many of them contain a moral message. Two of the best-known are *The *Light of the World* (1854) and *The Scapegoat* (1855).

ˈ**hunting** *n* [U] ⇨ note at FIELD SPORTS, article at ANIMALS.

The ˌ***Hunting of the ˈSnark*** /ˈsnɑːk; *AmE* ˈsnɑːrk/ a nonsense poem (1876) by Lewis *Carroll. Several characters go out in a boat to hunt the Snark, an imaginary creature, but in the end one of them meets the only dangerous kind of Snark, called a Boojum, and disappears.

ˌDouglas ˈ**Hurd** /ˈhɜːd; *AmE* ˈhɜːrd/ (1930–) a former British *Conservative politician. His early career was as a diplomat, but after he entered the *House of Commons in 1974 he became Secretary of State for Northern Ireland (1984–5), *Home Secretary (1986–9) and *Foreign Secretary (1989–95). He has also written several novels. He was made a *life peer in 1997.

the ˈ**Hurlingham** /ˈhɜːlɪŋəm; *AmE* ˈhɜːrlɪŋəm/ (*in full* the **Hurlingham Polo Association**) the organization in charge of the sport of polo in Britain. It is based at Cowdray Park in the county of *West Sussex, but was formed in 1886 at the **Hurlingham Club** in London, which is now a club for players of many sports.

ˌLake ˈ**Huron** /ˈhjʊərɒn; *AmE* ˈhjʊrɑːn/ one of the *Great Lakes on the border between the US and Canada. It is the second largest, and the fourth largest lake in the world. It covers 23 010 square miles (59 596 square kilometres) with a length of 206 miles (332 kilometres) and largest width of 183 miles (295 kilometres). Lake Huron separates the US state of *Michigan and the Canadian province of Ontario. Its ports include Alpena and Port Huron.

ˈ**Hurricane** *n* a type of British fighter plane, used successfully during the *Battle of Britain in *World War II. See also SPITFIRE.

ˌGeoff ˈ**Hurst** /ˈhɜːst; *AmE* ˈhɜːrst/ (1941–) an English football player. He was a member of the winning England team in the 1966 World Cup Final against West Germany. He scored three goals, the only player ever to do so in a World Cup Final. He was made a *knight in 1998.

Humour

A **sense of humour** (*AmE* **humor**), an ability to see the **funny side of life**, is considered essential by most British and American people. Everyone needs to be able to **laugh at themselves** sometimes, and to recognize that the situation they are in may look **funny** to others. If they can't people will say they have no sense of humour, which is a serious criticism.

The British sense of humour is very varied and what one British person finds very funny may not make another even smile. Some people have a **dry** sense of humour, and can **keep a straight face** (= not smile) and let their voice sound as though they are being serious when they are joking. Other people are said to be **witty** (= show a very clever type of humour), or to **have a quick wit**, and are never short of a **pithy** comment (= one that is short but full of meaning). American humour is usually more direct. But an individual's sense of humour is influenced by many things, including his or her family and social background and age.

Comedy shows

British and American humour on stage have some important differences, although the fact that some **comedy** television shows are popular in the other country shows that there is some common ground. American **sitcoms** or **situation comedies** (= shows in which the humour comes from situations that the characters get into) such as **Frasier*, **Friends* and **Seinfeld* are popular in Britain, together with Britain's own *Men Behaving Badly*. Sitcoms often have a **laugh track** (= a recording of people laughing), so that the audience at home will laugh in the right places. In many sitcoms gentle fun is made of ordinary life without the risk of causing anyone serious offence.

American stage humour is very direct, whereas a lot of British comedy is more sophisticated and subtle. In the American series **Cheers*, for instance, the humour comes from characters like Coach and Woody being more stupid than any real person could possibly be. But in the British comedy **Fawlty Towers* Basil Fawlty's funny characteristics are exaggerated versions of those found in the type of Englishman he represents. **Slapstick** comedy, which is based on people falling over, bumping into each other, etc., is now less popular in Britain.

British comedy makes frequent use of **irony**, humour which depends on a writer or performer suggesting the opposite of what is actually expressed. Many novels, films, stage plays, etc. use irony, even when discussing serious subjects such as death. The lack of irony in American comedy means that British people find some of it boring. Popular humour may sometimes rely on **double entendre** (= using a phrase that can be understood in two ways, one of which is usually sexual) or on **innuendo** (= making an indirect suggestion of something rude). These were both used a lot in the popular **Carry On* film series that began in the 1960s.

Satire (= making people or institutions appear ridiculous to show how foolish or bad they are) is an important element of popular British political comedy programmes such as **Yes, Minister* and **Spitting Image*. One of the most successful British comedy series, which also became popular in the US, was **Monty Python's Flying Circus*. It had a **zany** (= odd and silly) and **satirical** humour which appealed especially to young people.

*__Comic strips__ and **cartoons**, whether printed in newspapers, shown on television or the Internet or made into films, are popular in both the US and in Britain. The most famous include **Peanuts*, **Tom and Jerry* and *The *Simpsons*.

Comedians

Stand-up comedians like Bill *Cosby, Jerry Seinfeld and Joan *Rivers in the US and in Britain Ben *Elton, Eddy *Izzard and Lee Hurst, perform on television or in clubs, telling **gags** (= jokes) and funny stories which end with a **punch line**, the part where the audience is supposed to laugh. Many comedians **tell jokes** that are funny because of some racial or sexual innuendo, and this may be considered unacceptable for family audiences.

In Britain, common targets of comedians include mothers-in-law, foreigners and people from particular parts of Britain, especially Scotsmen (who are supposed to hate spending money) and Irishmen (who are supposed to be stupid). Many people find such jokes offensive, and the new generation of comedians has avoided making fun of people's race. A new form of comedy is for people from minority groups to make fun of their own customs and attitudes.

Jokes

Many people tell jokes at school, at home and at the office. People may start a speech with a joke or funny story to help **break the ice** (= make people feel more relaxed).

Children tell jokes that involve a play on words, such as *__knock-knock jokes__ or 'What do you call …' jokes, e.g. 'What do you call a man with a seagull on his head?' – 'Cliff.'

Adults sometimes tell what in the US are called **Polish jokes** because of an old idea that people from Poland were not very intelligent. These jokes are usually insulting and offensive to a particular race or group of people. Similar jokes are still told about blondes (= women with fair hair) because they are believed not to be very intelligent, and about lawyers because they are thought to have bad characters. For instance, 'Why do they do lab experiments on lawyers?' – 'Because there are some things that even a rat won't do.' **Light bulb jokes** make fun of the worst characteristic of any group of people, by suggesting mistakes they would make in trying to change a light bulb: 'How many psychologists does it take to change a light bulb?' – 'Just one, but it has to really *want* to change.'

Practical jokes involve tricking people, and are not usually very popular, but on *__April Fool's Day__ (1 April) people traditionally play practical jokes on each other. Newspapers often include a story that is not true hoping that some readers will believe it and then feel silly.

ˌ***Hush-a-bye, ˈBaby*** /ˌhʌʃ ə baɪ/ a popular old lullaby (= song sung to make a young child go to sleep). The words are:

Hush-a-bye, baby,
On the tree top.
When the wind blows,
The cradle will rock.
When the bough breaks,
The cradle will fall,
And down will come baby,
Cradle and all.

The tune is similar to *Lilliburlero.

ˈ**Hush ˌPuppies**™ *n* [pl] a British make of shoes made mostly of soft leather in various styles.

ˈ**hush ˌpuppy** *n* (*AmE*) a food eaten in the southern US, usually with fish. It is a round ball of corn flour that is fried. According to tradition, hush puppies were thrown to hungry dogs to keep them quiet, and this is the origin of their name.

ˌJohn ˈ**Huston** /ˈhjuːstən/ (1906–89) a US film director, actor and writer. He won an *Oscar for *The *Treasure of the Sierra Madre*, which he directed and wrote. He and his father, the actor Walter Huston, also acted in it. Other films that he directed included *The *Maltese Falcon*, *The African Queen* (1951), **Moby-Dick* and *Prizzi's Honor* (1985) for which his daughter, Anjelica Huston, won an Oscar as Best Actress.

ˈ**Hutterite** /ˈhʌtəraɪt/ *n* a member of a Protestant religious group living mainly in the US states of *South Dakota, *North Dakota and *Montana, and also in the Canadian province of Alberta. The Hutterites were established in 1533 in Moravia in Czechoslovakia as a division of the Anabaptists, and are named after Jacob Hutter. Their way of life is similar to that of the *Mennonites. It includes common ownership of property and a refusal to use violence.

ˌLen ˈ**Hutton** /ˈhʌtn/ (1916–90) an English cricketer and one of the best batsmen in the game. He played for *Yorkshire (1934–55) and England (1937–55), the last four years as captain. He was made a *knight in 1956, the year he left the sport.

ˈ**Huxley** /ˈhʌksli/ the name of an English family of scientists and writers. **Thomas Henry Huxley** (1825–95) was a biologist who publicly supported *Darwin's ideas about evolution, and became known as 'Darwin's bulldog'. He also invented the word *agnostic*, to describe a person who is not sure whether or not God exists. His son **Leonard Huxley** (1860–1933), a writer, had three famous sons. The first, **Julian Huxley** (1887–1975), was a biologist and writer who was well known for his appearances on the radio and television programme *The *Brains Trust* and later became director of UNESCO (1946–8). The second, **Aldous Huxley** (1894–1963), an author, is best known for his novel **Brave New World* (1932), which describes a future society in which people are born in factories and controlled by a continuous supply of drugs and sex. From 1937 Aldous Huxley lived in *California, where his experiences with drugs became the subject of a later book *The Doors of Perception* (1954). The third famous son, **Andrew Huxley** (1917–), is a scientist who received the *Nobel Prize in 1963 for his description of how animal muscles work.

ˌMr ˈ**Hyde** /ˈhaɪd/ ⇨ JEKYLL AND HYDE.

ˌ**Hyde ˈPark** /ˌhaɪd/ **1** a large public park in central London, England, next to *Kensington Gardens. It is famous for *Speakers' Corner, where people can make public speeches on any topic, *Rotten Row, a riding track for horses, and the *Serpentine lake. In 1851 the *Great Exhibition was held in Hyde Park, and it is today a centre for large public meetings and concerts. At the south-east corner of the park is **Hyde Park Corner**, a place where several busy streets meet. **2** a district to the south of central *Chicago, along the edge of Lake *Michigan. It includes the University of Chicago.

ˈ***Hymns ˈAncient and ˈModern*** a book of hymns used in *Church of England services. It was first published in 1861 and is still used today in many churches.

Ii

IBM /ˌaɪ biː ˈem/ (*in full* **International Business Machines**) a US company that was the first to develop computers successfully. IBM computers created an international system that most other computers now relate to. The company began in 1911 as the Computing-Tabulating-Recording Company. It developed the first electric typewriter in the 1930s, the first computer in the 1950s and the first personal computer (PC) in 1980. The company suffered big losses in the early 1990s because of strong competition: *an IBM-compatible machine.*

ˌIbrox ˈPark /ˌaɪbrɒks; *AmE* ˌaɪbrɑːks/ the football ground of *Rangers football club in *Glasgow, Scotland. In 1971 a serious accident happened there: 66 people were killed when part of the crowd became crushed in a narrow passage with stairs.

ICA /ˌaɪ siː ˈeɪ/ ⇨ INSTITUTE OF CONTEMPORARY ARTS.

ICC /ˌaɪ siː ˈsiː/ ⇨ INTERSTATE COMMERCE COMMISSION.

ˈice ˌhockey ⇨ note at HOCKEY.

ˌIch ˈdien /ˌɪx ˈdiːn/ the words that appear on the Prince of Wales's crest (= the design that represents his title). It was first used in 1346 and is German for 'I serve', indicating the Prince's loyalty to the king or queen.

ICI /ˌaɪ siː ˈaɪ/ (*in full* **Imperial Chemical Industries**) a very large British company, formed in 1926, which makes products such as paints, drugs, plastics and industrial chemicals.

the **ˌIcknield ˈWay** /ˌɪkniːld/ an ancient British path first used many thousands of years ago. It leads south-west from the *Wash to *Berkshire, often along the tops of hills. Modern roads now follow parts of it and other parts are used by people who enjoy walking in the countryside.

ˈIdaho /ˈaɪdəhəʊ; *AmE* ˈaɪdəhoʊ/ a state in the north-western US. Its popular name is the Gem State, because it has many minerals, including silver. It also produces a quarter of all the potatoes grown in the US. It was part of the *Louisiana Purchase and became a state in 1890. The capital city is Boise. Idaho's attractions include the *Rocky Mountains, Craters of the Moon National Monument and Hell's Canyon, which is the deepest gorge (= valley with steep sides) in North America.

ˌIdeal ˈHome a British magazine published every month for people who want to decorate or improve their homes.

the **ˌIdeal ˈHome Exhiˌbition** a popular exhibition of furniture and other products for the home, held every year in *Earl's Court, London, England. It was first held in 1908.

ˌIdylls of the ˈKing a series of 12 poems by Lord *Tennyson, published between 1842 and 1885. They tell the story of King *Arthur and the *Knights of the Round Table, and were very popular with *Victorian(1) readers.

If a poem published in 1910 by Rudyard *Kipling. It consists of a single long sentence beginning with the word 'if', giving advice to a boy on how to become a man. The author recommends firm control of mind, body and spirit in the *Victorian(2) tradition. This now seems rather old-fashioned, but the poem remains extremely popular and is often voted the favourite poem of British readers.

Ike /aɪk/ the popular name for the US President Dwight D *Eisenhower.

ˈIlkley /ˈɪlkli/ a town in *West Yorkshire, England. It is known mainly for **Ilkley Moor**, which appears in the popular folk song *On Ilkley Moor baht'at* (a local way of saying 'On Ilkley Moor without a hat').

ˌIlliˈnois /ˌɪlɪˈnɔɪ/ a state in the US *Midwest, also called the Prairie State. Its largest city is *Chicago and its capital city is Springfield. It has industry and produces coal and agricultural products such as corn and wheat. Illinois became a state in 1818 and is associated with Abraham *Lincoln, who was a lawyer in Springfield.

the ***ˈIllustrated ˈLondon ˈNews*** a British magazine, first published in 1842, which was especially successful in the 19th century with its combination of news stories and pictures, a new idea at the time. It originally appeared every week but is now published six times a year.

ˌI Love ˈLucy a very popular US television comedy series (1951–60) on *CBS with Lucille *Ball as the star. She played Lucy Ricardo and her real husband, Desi Arnez, played her husband Ricky. When Ball became pregnant and had a baby, this was written into the story of the shows, making them even more popular. The shows are still shown regularly around the world.

IMF /ˌaɪ em ˈef/ ⇨ INTERNATIONAL MONETARY FUND.

Immigration ⇨ article.

the **ˌImmiˈgration and ˌNaturaliˈzation ˌService** ⇨ INS.

imˈpeachment /ɪmˈpiːtʃmənt/ *n* [U, C] the procedure by which a public official in the US, including the President, is charged with acting illegally and may be forced to leave his or her job. President Richard *Nixon resigned after the House Judiciary Committee recommended that he should be impeached (= charged) for the crime of *Watergate. Only two presidents have been officially impeached. The first was Andrew Johnson in 1868, who remained President after the US Senate decided by one vote that he should do so. The second was Bill *Clinton in 1999, who was also judged not guilty of acting illegally.

Imˌperial ˈChemical ˌIndustries ⇨ ICI.

Imˈperial ˈCollege ˈLondon (*also* **Imperial College of Science and Technology**) a leading British college for the study of science, in *South Kensington, London. It was established in 1907 as part of *London University and offers courses in such subjects as science, medicine, engineering and mining, as well as providing opportunities for scientific research. It also has its own nuclear reactor at its research station at Silwood Park, near Ascot.

the **Imˌperial ˈWar Muˌseum** a large military museum in Lambeth, London, founded in 1917. It contains military equipment from the wars Britain has fought in since 1914, as well as a reference library of books, maps, photographs and films, and a large collection of work by war artists.

Immigration

An **immigrant** is somebody who goes to settle permanently in a different country.

The US – a nation of immigrants

Apart from *Native Americans who were living in North America when people first arrived there from Europe, all Americans have ancestors who were immigrants. In the US the word *immigrant* is often used with a positive meaning. People are proud to say that their ancestors were immigrants who came with very little and built a better life for themselves.

The English went to North America from the late 16th century; Spain sent people to the southern part of the region, and many Dutch and Germans also went over. When the US became independent, it was written into the *Constitution that there could be no limits on immigration until 1808.

The main period of immigration was between 1800 and 1917. Early in this period, many more immigrants arrrived from Britain and Germany, and many Chinese went to *California. Later, the main groups were Italians, Irish, Eastern Europeans and Scandinavians. Many Jews went from Germany and East Europe. Just before *World War I, there were nearly a million immigrants a year.

Most Americans have a clear idea of what life was like for the immigrants: they left home because they were poor and thought they would have better opportunities in the US. Most travelled in **steerage** (= the cheapest, least comfortable part of a ship). Because it was crowded, diseases spread quickly, so many arrived weak or ill. Many came to *New York and *Boston, and ***Ellis Island** near New York became famous as a **receiving station**. There they were asked questions and examined by a doctor before being allowed to enter the US. Once in the US, life was not easy. Many had to work in **sweatshops** (= factories where conditions were hard and dangerous) for little money and lived in **tenements**, crowded buildings where an entire family lived in one room. But slowly they improved their lives and many wrote home to encourage others to come.

The Immigration Act of 1917, and other laws that followed it, limited the number of immigrants who could settle in the US and the countries that they could come from. Since then, immigration has been limited to a few people who are selected for an **immigrant visa**, commonly called a ***green card**. *Hispanics and Asians now make up the largest groups of immigrants. The **Immigration and Naturalization Service** (***INS**) is responsible for issuing visas. It also tries to prevent people crossing the borders and entering the US illegally.

Immigration into Britain

People have been coming to Britain for centuries, but immigration only became an issue in the 1960s. After *World War II, Britain needed more workers and admitted citizens of *Commonwealth countries without restriction. Many came from the *Caribbean and from *India, *Pakistan and *Bangladesh. They found work in hospitals, in the textile industry and in the public transport system, though most jobs were poorly paid. Nearly 500 000 Commonwealth citizens came to Britain before 1962, many of whom were later joined by their wives and children. People from other countries were allowed in provided they had a **work permit** for a specific job.

When there were no longer enough jobs the Commonwealth Immigrants Act (1962) was passed to restrict the numbers entering Britain. The country was put under more pressure when many Asians arrived from East Africa in the late 1960s. Many had kept **British citizenship** after *Kenya and *Uganda became independent and were not subject to the restrictions of the 1962 Act. In the following years several more Acts were passed, further restricting the right to live in Britain.

Immigration is now strictly controlled. Normally, only people from the *European Union and certain Commonwealth citizens can get permission to live in Britain. The right to stay may also be given to people from other countries who have special skills, and to **asylum seekers** and **refugees**. Britain now accepts about 50 000 immigrants every year.

From time to time there are reports of immigrants entering the country illegally hidden in lorries or ships. Many are **deported** (= sent home), and though it is possible to appeal against **deportation** it may take several years for a case to be decided.

Attitudes to immigration

Americans are not very consistent in their attitudes towards immigration. They are proud of their own ancestors who were immigrants, but want to keep other people out. The **mainstream** culture is still that of white people whose ancestors came from northern Europe. There is a fear that people from other cultures may change America in ways that Americans do not want. Many people have believed that immigrants should not cling to their original culture but should become part of an American culture. The US has been likened to a ***melting pot** in which people from many cultures are 'melted' (= mixed) together.

But Americans continue to be proud of their ethnic backgrounds, and from the 1960s the melting pot image was partly replaced by **pluralism**, the idea that a variety of values, traditions and languages was good and a ***multicultural** society made the US stronger. Over time, immigrant families do **assimilate** (= change their lifestyle so it becomes more like that of the mainstream) to a certain extent. This can be seen in the lifestyles of second- and third-generation Americans (= the children of immigrants, and their children).

In Britain, black and Asian immigrants were at first welcomed. As more of them arrived and settled near people from the same country, whole areas of cities were taken over. This created fear and distrust among the rest of the population. In the 1960s the politician Enoch *Powell opposed further immigration and gained the support of many white people. Others thought he was exaggerating the problems and promoting **racism** (= hatred of people of a different race). About the same time the *National Front was formed, and in the 1970s it held demonstrations against black people and Asians, many of which resulted in violence.

More recently, there have been great efforts to **integrate** people from **ethnic minorities** into local communities and to develop a multicultural society based on equality and acceptance.

The Im'portance of 'Being 'Earnest a comedy play by Oscar *Wilde, first performed in 1895. A young man, Jack Worthing, wants to marry the daughter of Lady *Bracknell, but Lady Bracknell disapproves of him. It is later revealed, however, that his real name is Ernest John Moncrieff and he is from a good family. The play is often performed in Britain, especially by amateur actors, and is much loved for its clever humour and comic situations.

I,naugu'ration Day (in the US) the day every four years when the new *President, elected in November, officially takes power. The Inauguration ceremonies are always on 20 January in *Washington, DC. The President says the Oath of Office, and the Vice-president does the same. The President then gives the **Inaugural Address**, a speech about his plans. This is followed by a long parade along *Pennsylvania Avenue. In the evening there are official Inaugural balls (= formal events at which people dance).

In ,Cold 'Blood a US novel (1966) based on fact, written by Truman *Capote. It is about the murder in 1959 of four members of a farming family in *Kansas. Capote talked in prison to the men who killed them, and his book tells their story until they were hanged. It was the first major novel in which specific events were written as fiction in this way. A film version was made in 1967.

,income sup'port *n* [U] (in Britain) money given by the government's *Benefits Agency to help people with very low incomes, e.g. people without a job or single parents. It is available only to those who have not paid enough *National Insurance contributions to receive the *jobseeker's allowance.

'income tax *n* [U, C] a tax paid according to a person's level of income, with people on higher incomes paying higher rates of tax. It is used by the government to help pay for things like health care and education. It is collected in Britain by the *Inland Revenue and in the US (where it is used to pay for the armed forces) by the *Internal Revenue Service.

,Inde'pendence a US city in the state of *Missouri. President Harry S *Truman lived there, and his official library and museum can be visited. The international office of the Reorganized Church of Jesus Christ of Latter Day Saints is also there. In the 1830s and 1840s, people began their journeys west on the *Santa Fe Trail and the *Oregon Trail from Independence.

,Inde'pendence Day (*also* the **Fourth of July**) the official US holiday on 4 July that celebrates the nation's independence. On that day in 1776, the *Continental Congress gave its approval to the *Declaration of Independence. The day is celebrated with fireworks, outdoor meals, processions, flags and speeches.

,Independence 'Hall the building in the US city of *Philadelphia where the *Declaration of Independence was written and signed in 1776 by the *Continental Congress, and where the US Constitution was written and approved in 1787 by the Federal Constitution Convention. It is the most important building in America's history. It was built in 1732 as the Pennsylvania State House. The *Liberty Bell is also there. Independence Hall is on Chestnut Street in **Independence National Historic Park**. It was made a *World Heritage Site in 1979.

The ,Inde'pendent a British national daily newspaper, first published in 1986. It is a *broadsheet newspaper, which aims at political independence (i.e. it does not support any particular political party). Its success led to the publication in 1990 of a related *Sunday paper, *The Independent on Sunday*.

Independence Hall

the **,Independent 'Labour ,Party** (*abbr* the **ILP**) an early British socialist party formed in 1893 by Keir *Hardie. The British *Labour Party later developed from it.

,inde'pendent school *n* (in Britain) a school that does not receive money from the state and charges fees for teaching and other services. *Public schools and *preparatory schools are today often called independent schools, and the term also applies to other schools that offer various types of special education, e.g. for children with learning difficulties.

the **,Independent 'Television Com,mission** ⇨ ITC.

'India /'ɪndiə/ a country in southern Asia which used to be part of the *British Empire. It became independent and a member of the *Commonwealth in 1947. It is now the world's largest democracy, with a population of approximately 900 million. The official languages are Hindi and English, though over 200 other languages are spoken in different parts of the country. The capital city is New Delhi.

Britain became involved in India in the 17th century, with the *East India Company. The British government took control of India after the *Indian Mutiny, appointing a Viceroy as its ruler. A movement for independence began at this time, when the Indian National Congress Party (later the Congress Party) was formed in 1885. In the early 20th century, the leading figure in the movement for independence was Mahatma Gandhi, who led a campaign of peaceful protest against British rule. This led to India becoming independent in 1947, when it divided into two countries, India and *Pakistan. Since then, many Indian and Pakistani people have emigrated to Britain. ▶ **Indian** *adj*, *n*.

,Indi'ana /,ɪndi'ænə/ a US state in the *Middle West which is both agricultural and industrial. It became a state in 1816. Its popular name is the Hoosier State, but nobody knows why. People from Indiana are called Hoosiers, and Americans sometimes joke that they are innocent, old-fashioned farmers. *Indianapolis is the capital city and the largest in the state.

,Indiana 'Jones ⇨ JONES[3].

ˌ**Indiaˈnapolis** /ˌɪndiəˈnæpəlɪs/ the capital and largest city of the US state of *Indiana. It is in an agricultural region in the centre of the state on the White River. The city, which was settled in 1820, is a commercial centre with a large grain and cattle market. Its products include medical and electronic equipment, medicines and chemicals. It is known for the *Indianapolis 500 car race.

the **Indianapolis 500** /ˌɪndiəˈnæpəlɪs faɪv ˈhʌndrəd/ (*also infml* the **Indy 500**) the best-known US car race. The event (500 miles/805 kilometres) is held each year on *Memorial Day in *Indianapolis. It began in 1911 and has always been at the Indianapolis Speedway. Well-known winners have included Mario *Andretti, A J *Foyt and the *Unser brothers. The cars that compete are called *IndyCars.

the ˌ**Indian ˈMutiny** a serious revolt (1857–8) by the Indian army against British rule in India. It began in the north of India and in some places developed into a general protest. When it was defeated by the British, India was placed under the direct control of the British government, rather than the *East India Company which had previously governed it.

ˌ**Indian reserˈvation** *n* any of the areas of land given to *Native Americans by the US government. The US Bureau of Indian Affairs protects them and provides schools for them. There are 333 reservations in 33 states, with the majority of them in *California and *Oklahoma. Most Native Americans on reservations are poor and receive financial help from the government.

ˌ**Indian ˈTerritory** US land west of the *Mississippi River to which *Native Americans were forced to move in the 19th century. It was originally established for the *Five Civilized Tribes, but other Native Americans were sent there in 1866. The Indian Territory existed from 1834 to 1890, but many white people settled there, and in 1907 most of it became part of the new state of *Oklahoma.

the ˌ**Indian ˈwars** *n* [pl] the general name given to the various armed conflicts between *Native Americans and people who later settled in America, mostly from Europe, and those who were descended from them. These battles began at *Jamestown in 1622. The great Indian wars in the West were in the 1870s, with the final major battle in 1890 at *Wounded Knee in *South Dakota.

ˈ**indie ˌmusic** (*also* **indie**) *n* [U] certain kinds of pop or rock music in Britain, produced by small, independent record companies and played by groups with a relatively small but very enthusiastic number of fans. The expression was first used in the early 1980s, when a number of these companies were established. Indie music has its own 'chart' (= list of the most popular records), which is published regularly in some music papers.

ˌ**Indiˈvidual Reˈtirement Acˌcount** ⇨ IRA.

ˌ**Indiˈvidual ˈSavings Acˌcount** (*abbr* **ISA**) *n* a type of British savings account introduced in 1999, designed to replace *Tax-Exempt Special Savings Accounts and *Personal Equity Plans.

the **Inˌdustrial Revoˈlution** the phrase used to describe Britain's progress in the 18th and 19th century from being largely an agricultural country to being an industrial one. Britain was the first country to change in this way. During this time, many important machines were invented. These were mostly made possible by the discovery of steam power and the invention of the steam engine, which allowed one worker to do what before had required many workers. As a result, big factories were built which could produce a wide variety of goods in large quantities. New methods of transport, in particular canals and railways, were developed for transporting these goods from place to place. During the Industrial Revolution, the populations of cities grew rapidly as people moved from the countryside to work in factories. The same kind of development soon began in other countries in Europe and in the US.

inˌdustrial triˈbunal *n* (in Britain) a type of court that makes decisions about disputes between employees and employers, particularly when an individual believes they have been unfairly or illegally dismissed from their job.

Industry ⇨ article.

the **Indy 500** /ˌɪndi faɪv ˈhʌndrəd/ ⇨ INDIANAPOLIS 500.

IndyCar racing /ˈɪndikɑː; *AmE* ˈɪndikɑːr/ *n* [U] a popular type of car racing in the US. The cars are like those used for the *Indianapolis 500. They are very powerful and can go at more than 230 miles/370 kilometres per hour. Drivers compete in a season of 16 CART (Championship Auto Racing Teams) races between March and September to win the IndyCar World Series. The races are mostly in the US but some are also held in Canada, Australia and Brazil. The Championships were started in 1916 by the American Automobile Association.

IndyCars in the Indianapolis 500

ˈ**infant school** *n* (in Britain) a type of school for children from the age of five (when children are required by law to start school) until the age of seven or eight. Often an infant school forms, together with a *junior school, part of a primary school.

the ˌ**INˈF ˌTreaty** /ˌaɪ en ˈef/ (*in full* the **Intermediate Nuclear Forces Treaty**) an agreement reached in 1987 between the US and the USSR to destroy all nuclear missiles that could travel between 300 and 3 400 miles (483 and 5 471 kilometres). It was the first reduction in nuclear weapons that had ever taken place. The INF Treaty was signed in Washington, DC, by the US President Ronald *Reagan and the Soviet leader Mikhail Gorbachev. It involved 1 752 US missiles and 859 Soviet ones.

inˈheritance tax *n* [U] (since 1986) a British tax paid to the government if somebody dies and leaves more than a certain amount of wealth in their will. This tax also has to be paid if a person transfers more than a certain amount of wealth to somebody else up to 7 years before they die. Until 1975 it was called estate duty and from 1975 to 1986 capital transfer tax. In the past these taxes were also commonly referred to as death duties. With each change of name, there have been changes in the rules concerning the circumstances in which the tax has to be paid and how much has to be paid.

I-ˈ9 form /aɪ ˈnaɪn/ *n* (in the US) a form that a person must complete before beginning a job. It is required by the *INS from an employer as proof that the new employee is permitted to work in the US.

Industry

The Industrial Revolution

The *Industrial Revolution began in Britain in about 1750 and within 100 years the country developed from an agricultural society into an industrial nation with trading links across the world. Industry had a great effect on British social and economic life, as many people moved from the countryside to work in the rapidly growing towns.

In the US the Industrial Revolution brought similar changes. In 1790 only 5% of Americans lived in cities but by 1940 more than half had moved to urban areas. Starting a factory required a lot of money and a new class of rich people, called **capitalists**, began to appear.

British industry

British industry raises nearly £120 000 million each year. The most important products are food items, followed by transport equipment, machinery and motor vehicles. **Heavy industries** include *coal mining, engineering, manufacturing of cars, ships and aircraft, and steel and chemical production. **Light industries** include the manufacture of small electronic and household goods. Many privately-owned companies operate from **industrial estates** or **business parks** on the edge of towns.

The performance of heavy industry has declined since 1945 and many businesses have closed. This has resulted in high unemployment in northern England and in south Wales. The government designated these areas as **development areas**, and offered grants to new firms setting up business there. Hopes that the old industries would be replaced by **sunrise industries** (= industries making electronic equipment) in many cases proved false. Several foreign car manufacturers and electronics companies built factories in Britain in the 1980s, but some have since been forced to close because of world economic problems. In the 1990s British companies suffered because of the high value of the pound.

The government became closely involved in industry after *World War II when the *Labour Party nationalized (= transferred to state ownership) major industries. In the 1980s the *Conservatives privatized these industries again. Some industries, such as shipbuilding, survive with difficulty without government funding.

The ***Department of Trade and Industry** (**DTI**) is the government department dealing with industry. The ***CBI** (**Confederation of British Industry**) represents the interests of industry to the DTI.

Industry in the US

The *Founding Fathers believed that government should not interfere in industry and so it was allowed to develop freely. But in the early 1900s people realized that some control was necessary. Working conditions were very bad and people worked long hours for little money. Factories became known as **sweatshops**, and were dirty, noisy, dangerous places. Another problem was that there were few checks on a company's activities. Businessmen survived by driving their competitors out of business. The result was often a **monopoly**, an industry where competition no longer existed.

In the early 20th century laws were passed which limited the activities of industry. The first **labor union** (*BrE* ***trade union**), the ***Industrial Workers of the World**, was created in 1905 and soon after the ***Federal Reserve** was established, giving the government more control over the economy so that it did not depend on a few rich **industrialists**.

The US soon became the world's leading industrial nation. Most industry was originally in the north-east of the country, but *California and *Texas became important manufacturing centres. Products include chemicals, industrial machinery, food processing and electronic items. Mining for a variety of metals, including iron and gold, continues to be important. The US also produces very large quantities of oil, natural gas and coal. Since World War II there has been a huge growth in service industries, such as finance and insurance, and these now employ about 75% of the workforce.

Industrial wealth led to high *standards of living, but in many areas which were formerly centres of heavy industry, such as *Detroit and *Chicago, factories have now closed leaving many people unemployed.

Industrial relations

In the 1960s and 1970s Britain was well known for its bad **industrial relations**, relationships between management and workers. In the coal mining and car manufacturing industries there was frequent **industrial action** which took the form of a **strike** (= refusal to work) or a **work-to-rule** (= a way of working in which all the rules are followed exactly, making production less efficient). Since the 1980s there have been fewer strikes, partly because of restrictions placed on unions by the Conservative government of Margaret *Thatcher.

In the US there were many strikes after World War II, which caused *Congress to restrict the right of workers to strike. Strikers now risk being dismissed from their jobs, as happened to some air traffic controllers in 1981.

Problems and challenges

Computers and robots are increasingly important in production processes and factory workers need higher technical skills to operate equipment. Many managers now take business studies courses at university.

Efforts are being made to clean up industry. Many industries have caused damage to the environment, especially through **air pollution** and **acid rain**. Waste products may also be dangerous, and finding a safe place to **dump** (= leave) this **toxic waste** is a serious problem.

As international trade becomes easier because of associations like the *European Union and the *North American Free Trade Agreement, foreign companies and **multinationals** are keen to build factories in countries belonging to these groups to take advantage of the *free trade between them. These companies provide many new jobs but also enter into competition with existing companies and may eventually cause factories to close. In the future it seems likely that competition will become even fiercer and many companies will have to reduce costs still further and find new markets to survive.

the **I͵nitial ˈTeaching ͵Alphabet** (*abbr* **ITA**) a phonetic alphabet with 44 letters, each representing a sound in the English language. It was created to help people, especially children, learn how to read and write in English.

INLA /͵aɪ en el ˈeɪ/ ⇨ IRISH NATIONAL LIBERATION ARMY.

the **͵Inland ˈRevenue** (*in full* the **Board of Inland Revenue**) the government department in charge of the tax system in Britain. It collects *income tax, as well as other taxes including *capital gains tax, *corporation tax, *inheritance tax and *stamp duty. The US equivalent is the *Internal Revenue Service.

͵In Meˈmoriam /͵ɪn məˈmɔːriæm/ the most famous poem by Lord *Tennyson, published in 1850. It was written in memory of Tennyson's friend Arthur Henry Hallam, who died at the age of 22. The poem expresses Tennyson's sadness and his fears and doubt about life and death.

͵inner ˈcity *n* [often pl] a phrase first used in the early 1980s in Britain to describe the poorer areas in or near the centre of a large city (in contrast with the more prosperous suburbs). These areas often have high unemployment and crime, together with bad living conditions. They are also associated with tension between people of different races or between the police and the people living there. Sometimes these problems have led to a lot of violence, for example the 1981 riots in *Brixton in London and in *Toxteth in *Liverpool. The government reacted to this by establishing *enterprise zones, the *City Challenge, the *Urban Development Corporation and the *Urban Programme to improve conditions in inner cities.

͵Inner ˈWheel an international organization whose members are women, started in 1923 as a part of the *Rotary Club. It is now a separate organization, with branches that carry out work for charity and give practical help (such as *meals on wheels) in their local communities.

the **͵Inns of ˈCourt** four institutions in the *City of London, established in the Middle Ages, of which all *barristers are members and at which students of law are trained. They consist of Gray's Inn, Lincoln's Inn, the Inner Temple and the Middle Temple. It is thought that they began as hostels for people studying *common law during the Middle Ages, when it was not possible to study the subject at universities. The equivalent institution in Scotland is the Faculty of Advocates.

the **INS** /͵aɪ en ˈes/ (*in full* the **Immigration and Naturalization Service**) an organization that is part of the US Department of Justice. It is in charge of laws concerning people from other countries who want to move to the US (the process of immigration) and those who then want to become US citizens (naturalization).

In͵spector ˈMorse /ˈmɔːs; *AmE* ˈmɔːrs/ a popular television series in Britain during the 1980s and early 1990s, set in and around Oxford. The main character is a police *detective, Inspector Morse, who with his assistant, Sergeant Lewis, solves complicated murder cases. The series was originally based on the novels of Colin Dexter.

the **ˈInstitute for Adˈvanced ˈStudy** a private US centre for research in Princeton, *New Jersey. It was established in 1933 and has four departments: Historical Studies, Mathematics, Natural Sciences and Social Science. Each department has teachers and 'visiting members' from other research institutions or universities. About 160 financial awards for research work are given each year to members from many countries. Albert *Einstein was one of the first members. The Institute has a close but independent relationship with *Princeton University.

the **ˈInstitute of Conˈtemporary ˈArts** (*abbr* the **ICA**) an British institution in The *Mall(1) in central London that exists to encourage modern art, dance and film. It was established in 1947 and events held there have sometimes been controversial.

the **͵Institute of Diˈrectors** a British organization, like a club, for business people, especially company directors and senior people in industry. It was established in London in 1903.

͵institute of eduˈcation *n* (in England) a type of college for training teachers.

͵InterˈCity™ /͵ɪntəˈsɪti; *AmE* ͵ɪntərˈsɪti/ **1** any of the trains in Britain that travel quickly between the major towns and cities, without stopping at the smaller stations: *We took the InterCity from London to Glasgow.* **2** one of the five divisions of *British Rail, the national organization in charge of the British railway system, until it was privatized (= sold to private owners) in the mid 1990s.

the **in͵ternal ˈmarket** *n* [sing] (in Britain) a system of providing care under the *National Health Service, introduced in 1991. Doctors and hospitals are encouraged to operate as businesses, making independent decisions about how to spend government money on their patients. Most doctors and hospitals in Britain are now part of the internal market. Doctors who take part in the system are known as *fundholders, and hospitals that take part are known as NHS Trusts. In 1993 there were further changes, allowing more independence to institutions that care for old people, people with disabilities and people with learning difficulties.

the **In͵ternal ˈRevenue ͵Service** ⇨ IRS.

the ***͵Interˈnational ˈHerald-ˈTribune*** an international US newspaper known for its serious and thorough news items. It is based in Paris and published in 180 countries. It began in 1928 as the *Paris Herald*, but took its present name in 1966, when it was bought by the **New York Times* and the **Washington Post*.

the **ˈInternational ˈMonetary Fund** (*abbr* the **IMF**) an independent organization of the *United Nations, created by the *Bretton Woods Conference, which aims to encourage economic stability in countries all over the world. It provides financial help for member countries with large debts or other economic problems, although at the same time it demands that those countries take action to prevent such problems happening again. More than 150 countries are members. It was established in 1944 and is based in *Washington, DC.

Inspector Morse with Sergeant Lewis

the '**Internet** (*also infml* the **Net**) *n* [sing] an international computer network for the exchange of information. It was originally used mainly in the academic and military worlds but has since become available to the large and increasing number of people with personal computers. Other services, e.g. the World Wide Web, are available through it.

in'ternment *n* [U] the practice by which a government puts certain people in prison without trial because they are political opponents, because it is thought they may be involved in terrorism, or because they are from the country of an enemy during a war. In 1971, the government in *Northern Ireland, introduced internment and a number of people suspected of terrorism were put in prison. This led to an increase in terrorism in Northern Ireland and the policy was stopped in 1975.

'**interstate** (*also* ,**interstate 'highway**) *n* any of the national US roads that cross state borders. They have four lanes (= sections for single lines of traffic) and run for long distances. They are marked with red and blue signs, an 'I' and the road number. Interstates going east to west have even numbers and those going north to south have odd numbers. I-80 goes from New York to *California, and I-95 goes from *Maine to *Florida. They are usually referred to in this way: *They're building a new motel on I-10.*

the '**Interstate 'Commerce Com,mission** (*abbr* the **ICC**) the independent US government organization that controls transport and trade across the nation's state borders. This includes prices charged and equal rights. Since the 1980s, its control over lorries/trucks, buses and railways has been reduced. The ICC was established in 1887 and is the oldest organization created by the US government to establish rules and make sure they are obeyed.

'***In the 'Bleak Mid'winter*** the title and first line of a popular *Christmas carol (= religious song). The words are by Christina *Rossetti.

Inuits

Inuits are a related group of peoples found in *Alaska, and also in *Canada and Greenland. They are thought to have spread into North America from Siberia many thousands of years ago. In both the US and Britain these people are often called **Eskimos** but the name *Inuit* is now preferred by many of the people themselves and is becoming more widely used. The plural form is *Inuits* or *Inuit.* Although they live in small isolated communities, Inuits have a strong cultural identity and share the Inuit language. Other native peoples of Alaska include **Aleuts**, who come from the *Aleutian Islands to the west of Alaska, the **Tlingits** and the **Haida**. There are now under 60 000 Inuits in the US, and about 24 000 Aleuts.

Americans and British people still grow up thinking of Inuits as wearing animal skins and furs, living in **igloos** (= houses made of ice), and eating raw fish which they catch from a **kayak** or through a hole in the ice. The traditional life of Inuits involved travelling from place to place, fishing and hunting animals, including seals, whales and caribou (= a type of large deer).

As in the case of *Native-American peoples, the traditional way of life of the Inuit has been changed a great deal by the activities of other Americans. In particular, damage to the environment makes it hard for native Alaskans to find enough of their traditional foods. Many now live in permanent settlements which have schools and other facilities. They still live by hunting and fishing but instead of a **sledge** (*AmE* **sled**) pulled by dogs they may use a **snowmobile** (= a special car that can travel over snow) or a motor boat, and have guns and other modern equipment.

an Inuit driving a snowscooter

IOM /ˌaɪ əʊ 'em; *AmE* oʊ/ ⇨ ISLE OF MAN.

I'ona /aɪ'əʊnə; *AmE* aɪ'oʊnə/ a small island in the Inner *Hebrides, Scotland. It was a centre of early Christianity and a monastery (= Christian religious community) was established there by St Columba in 563. There are several early Christian monuments there and it is seen as a place of special religious importance, especially by Christian groups who go there in the summer to work and worship.

IOW /ˌaɪ əʊ 'dʌbljuː; *AmE* oʊ/ ⇨ ISLE OF WIGHT.

'**Iowa** /'aɪəʊə; *AmE* 'aɪoʊə/ a US agricultural state in the *Middle West. Its popular name is the Hawkeye State, and people from Iowa are called Hawkeyes, probably after Chief Black Hawk, a Native American leader. Iowa was part of the *Louisiana Purchase and became a state in 1846. Its products include corn, grain and farm animals. *Des Moines is the capital and largest city.

'**Ipswich** /'ɪpswɪtʃ/ the main town and administrative centre of *Suffolk in eastern England.

IRA[1] /ˌaɪ ɑːr 'eɪ/ (*in full* **Individual Retirement Account**) a US government plan that allows people to put part of their income into special bank accounts. No tax has to be paid on this money until they retire.

the **IRA**[2] /ˌaɪ ɑːr 'eɪ/ (*in full* the **Irish Republican Army**) an illegal Irish terrorist organization which believes that Northern Ireland and the Irish Republic should be united under one government. It was formed in 1919, but has become more active since 1968, when British soldiers began to be based permanently in Northern Ireland. During this period (sometimes called 'the *Troubles'), the IRA has committed many acts of violence in Northern Ireland, England and other countries, including the Birmingham and Guildford pub bombs (1974), the killing of Lord *Mountbatten (1979) and the *Enniskillen bomb (1987). In 1994 a ceasefire (= a period during which there is no fighting) was declared, which ended in 1996 but was declared again in 1997. The military part of the IRA is often referred to as the Provisional IRA (also called the *Provisionals or the Provos). *Sinn Fein is often called the 'political wing' of the IRA.

the **I,ran-'Contra af,fair** /ɪˌrɑːn 'kɒntrə; *AmE* 'kɑːntrə/ the name given to a series of secret and illegal actions by US government officials under President Ronald *Reagan. In 1985, officials in the *National Security Council sold military weapons to Iran so it would help in freeing US prisoners in Lebanon. The money received for these was then given to the Contras, military groups who wanted to defeat the Sandinista government in Nicaragua. The US Congress had forbidden this type of support. The deal was discovered in 1986 and several officials were charged with acting illegally. See also IRANGATE, NORTH.

I'rangate /ɪ'rɑːngeɪt/ another name, used especially by the media, for the *Iran-Contra affair. The word was invented to be similar to *Watergate.

the **I,ranian 'embassy siege** /ɪ,reɪmiən/ an incident in central London, England, in 1980, when six terrorists entered the Iranian embassy and held a number of people as hostages (= prisoners) for six days, killing two of them. The siege was ended when members of the *Special Air Service attacked the embassy, rescuing the hostages and killing five of the terrorists. This action was seen live on television in Britain and the skill, speed and success of the operation impressed the British public very much.

the **,Irish 'Free State** a state consisting of the whole of Ireland except *Northern Ireland. It was created by the Anglo-Irish Treaty of 1921, after the fighting called the *Troubles from 1919 to 1921. Its name was changed to Eire in 1937 and to the Republic of Ireland in 1949.

the **,Irish 'Guards** one of the *Guards regiments of the British army, formed in 1901.

the **'Irish 'National Libe'ration ,Army** (*abbr* the **INLA**) an Irish terrorist organization which believes that Northern Ireland and the Irish Republic should be united under one government. It was formed in 1974 by former members of the *IRA and was responsible in 1979 for killing the Conservative politician Airey Neave.

the **'Irish Re'publican 'Army** ⇨ IRA[2].

the **,Irish 'Sea** the area of sea between Britain and Ireland.

,Irish 'whiskey *n* [U, C] a type of *whisky produced in Ireland. The word is spelt 'whiskey' in Ireland and the US, and 'whisky' in Scotland.

Iron Age Britain

At the end of the Bronze Age iron began to be used instead of bronze for making tools and weapons. Iron tools were harder and more efficient, and also cheaper. Bronze became used only for decorated items such as bowls or brooches.

In Britain the Iron Age began about 500 BC. Some time before this, ***Celts** had begun arriving in the British Isles from Europe and had mixed with the people already living there. Some were farmers and grew wheat and beans, and kept animals. The Celts are best known for their metalwork, and there is archaeological evidence of metal workshops in southern England and near Grimsby on the east coast. There was a trading centre at Hengistbury Head near Bournemouth until the middle of the 1st century BC. Metal items such as weapons and jewellery were made near there and sold in Britain and abroad. Iron bars were used as currency before coins were introduced in the 1st century BC. Pieces of pottery indicate that at the same time food and wine were imported from France.

Hill forts such as that at *Maiden Castle in Dorset were the headquarters of local chiefs and centres of administration, craftwork and trade for their tribes, as well as being used for defence. Hill forts covered a large area of land, usually on top of a hill, and were surrounded by ditches and earth ramparts (= banks) with a wooden fence on top. Inside were round thatched houses, workshops and grain stores. Each hill fort also had a shrine or religious building.

The Celtic tribes, now often called the **ancient Britons**, were defeated by the *Julius Caesar in 55 BC and 54 BC, and again when the Romans invaded Britain in 43 BC. After peace was established the hill forts ceased to be used, though some were later repaired and used for defence against the *Anglo-Saxons in the late 5th century. In the Roman period new artistic influences came to southern Britain and many Celtic chiefs adopted Roman ways. Further north and west, the Celts fought to remain outside the Roman province of *Britannia. The Iron Age ended in England and Wales during Roman times, but little is known of the Celtic regions further north until their culture reached its highest point of achievement in the 7th and 8th centuries.

'Ironbridge /'aɪənbrɪdʒ; *AmE* 'aɪərnbrɪdʒ/ a town near *Telford in *Shropshire, England, which was an early centre of the *Industrial Revolution. It has the first major iron bridge in the world (opened in 1779) and several industrial museums.

the **,Iron 'Curtain** *n* [sing] (*becoming old-fash*) the name given to the border that once separated the former Communist countries of Eastern Europe from the West and made it difficult for people and information to pass from one side to the other. The phrase came into general use after Winston *Churchill used it in a political speech in 1946.

the **,Iron 'Lady** ⇨ THATCHER.

,Iron 'Maiden a British *heavy metal pop group formed in London in 1976. Their most successful songs include *Run to the Hills* (1982) and *Bring Your Daughter ... to the Slaughter* (1990).

,Jeremy **'Irons** /'aɪənz; *AmE* 'aɪərnz/ (1948–) an English actor best known for his appearances in films, including *The French Lieutenant's Woman* (1981), *Reversal of Fortune* (1990), for which he won an *Oscar, and *Lolita* (1997). He first became well known when he played a major part in the television version (1981) of Evelyn *Waugh's novel *Brideshead Revisited*.

the **'Iroquois League** /'ɪrəkwɔɪ/ (*also* the **,Iroquois Con'federacy**) a union of *Native-American peoples established about 1570. The groups involved, all in north-eastern America, were the Cayuga, the *Mohawk, the Oneida, the Onondaga and the *Seneca. The League was originally also called the Five Nations. When the Tuscarora joined in 1722, it became known as the Six Nations. Its members were farmers and hunters. They supported the British in the *French and Indian War and, except for the Oneida and Tuscarora, also in the *American Revolution.

the **IRS** /,aɪ ɑːr 'es/ (*in full* the **Internal Revenue Service**) the US government organization responsible for collecting taxes. These include income tax, company tax and taxes on gifts, goods, services and estates (= properties and other possessions left by people when they die). The IRS was created by the US Congress in 1789 and is part of the US Department of the Treasury.

,Lord **'Irvine** /'ɜːvɪn; *AmE* 'ɜːrvɪn/ (Alexander Andrew Mackay Irvine 1940–) a British *barrister and politician. He was given the title Lord Irvine of Lairg in 1987, and became *Lord Chancellor in 1997.

,Henry **'Irving[1]** /'ɜːvɪŋ; *AmE* 'ɜːrvɪŋ/ (1838–1905) an English actor who became famous in the late 19th century for his theatre performances in *Shakespeare plays. He often acted with Ellen *Terry. He was made a *knight in 1895, the first actor to receive this honour.

,Washington **'Irving[2]** /,wɒʃɪŋtən 'ɜːvɪŋ; *AmE* ,wɑːʃɪŋtən 'ɜːrvɪŋ/ (1783–1859) the first US writer to gain an international reputation. He is best known for two short stories, *The Legend of Sleepy Hollow* and **Rip Van Winkle*, which were published in *The Sketch Book of Geoffrey Crayon, Gent* (1820). He also wrote the comic *History of New York* (1809) under the name of Diedrich Knickerbocker. Irving was later the US ambassador to Spain (1842–6). See also CRANE[1], KNICKERBOCKER, RIP VAN WINKLE.

ISA /ˈaɪsə/ ⇨ INDIVIDUAL SAVINGS ACCOUNT.

ˌChristopher ˈ**Isherwood** /ˈɪʃəwʊd; *AmE* ˈɪʃərwʊd/ (1904–86) an English writer of novels and plays. The musical show *Cabaret* was based on a story in his 1939 collection *Goodbye to Berlin*, and much of his other writing is based on his experiences in Germany before *World War II. He also wrote three plays with W H *Auden. In 1939 he moved with Auden to the US and later became a US citizen.

the ˈ**Isis** /ˈaɪsɪs/ the name given to the River *Thames where it flows through *Oxford, England.

ˈ**islands** ˌ**area** *n* an administrative area of the Scottish islands. There are three islands areas: the *Western Isles (also known as the Outer *Hebrides), the *Orkneys and the *Shetlands.

the ˌ**Isle of** ˈ**Man** /ˈmæn/ (*abbr* **IOM**) a large island in the *Irish Sea which is a possession of the British crown but has its own parliament, the *Tynwald. The ancient language of the island is *Manx and the people are sometimes referred to as Manxmen and Manxwomen. The Manx cat, which has no tail, is native to the island. The Isle of Man is also famous for the TT (Tourist Trophy) races for motorcycles which are held there, and for the fact that *income tax is lower there than in other parts of Britain. The island's administrative centre is *Douglas.

the ˌ**Isle of** ˈ**Wight** /ˈwaɪt/ (*abbr* **IOW**) a large island off the coast of *Hampshire, in southern England. It has a warm climate which attracts tourists and people who enjoy sailing. The Isle of Wight has been an English county since 1974. Its administrative centre is Newport. See also COWES.

ˌ**iso**ˈ**lationism** *n* [U] the policy of not becoming involved in the affairs of other countries. The US has often followed this policy, especially before the mid 20th century. George *Washington, in his *Farewell Address, advised Americans to avoid strong connections with other nations. The US delayed entering both World Wars because of its isolationism.

ˌ**I-**ˈ**spy** *n* [U] a children's game in which one player gives the first letter of an object that he or she can see and the others try to guess what it is. For example, if the first letter is 'g', the player says, 'I spy, with my little eye, something beginning with "g".'

ITA /ˌaɪ tiː ˈeɪ/ ⇨ INITIAL TEACHING ALPHABET.

the **ITC** /ˌaɪ tiː ˈsiː/ (*in full* the **Independent Television Commission**) an organization established in Britain in 1990 to control the commercial television channels. Its functions include giving licences allowing companies to broadcast as commercial television channels.

It ˌ***Happened One*** ˈ***Night*** a US film (1934) which was the first comedy to win an *Oscar for Best Picture. Other Oscars went to Frank *Capra, who directed it, and to the actors Clark *Gable and Claudette Colbert. The story is about a journalist and a rich girl who has left her parents. He helps her hide, because he wants the news story. They argue a lot but then realize that they love each other.

It's a ˈ***Long*** ˈ***Way to*** ˌ***Tippe***ˈ***rary*** /ˌtɪpəˈreəri; *AmE* ˌtɪpəˈreri/ the title and first line of a *music-hall(1) song popular with British soldiers during *World War I. Tipperary is a town in southern Ireland, and the singer, an Irishman, wants very much to return there to see 'the sweetest girl I know'.

It's a ˈ***Wonderful*** ˈ***Life*** a US film (1946) about a man who wishes he had never been born, and the wish becomes real. Frank *Capra directed it, and the star was James *Stewart, who later chose it as his favourite of all the films he made. The story shows how the man's family would live if he had not been born. He realizes the importance of his life and is allowed to live again.

ITV /ˌaɪ tiː ˈviː/ (*in full* **Independent Television**) the commercial television companies that broadcast on Channel 3 in Britain. ITV is split into ten regions, each of which has its own programmes and news. Unlike the *BBC, ITV has advertising, and is controlled by the *ITC.

ˈ***Ivanhoe*** /ˈaɪvənhəʊ; *AmE* ˈaɪvənhoʊ/ a novel (1819) by Sir Walter *Scott. It is set in England after the *Norman Conquest and follows the adventures of Sir Wilfred of Ivanhoe, with appearances by such characters as *Robin Hood and King *Richard I.

ˌCharles ˈ**Ives** /ˈaɪvz/ (1874–1954) a US composer of modern classical music. His work introduced many new musical ideas but was not much played during his life. One of his best-known pieces is the *Concord* Piano Sonata (1915).

ˌJames ˈ**Ivory** /ˈaɪvəri/ (1928–) a US film director who has made many successful films with the producer Ismail *Merchant. These include *Shakespeare Wallah* (1965), *Heat and Dust* (1983), *Room with a View* (1986), *Howards End* (1992) and *Remains of the Day* (1994).

ˈ**Ivory soap** /ˈaɪvəri/ a popular US soap that floats, made by *Procter & Gamble since 1879. It is advertised as being '99 and 44/100 percent pure' and 'so pure it floats'. Ivory was created when a machine accidentally mixed bubbles into regular soap.

the **Ivy League**

US universities and colleges organize themselves into **conferences**, groups of institutions that are near each other and do certain activities, such as sports, together. The most highly respected of these groups is the **Ivy League** in the north-eastern US. Its most famous members are *Harvard and *Yale Universities, whose fierce rivalry in various sports is like that between *Oxford and *Cambridge Universities in Britain. The other members of the Ivy League are Columbia University, Cornell University, Dartmouth College, Brown University, Princeton University, and the University of Pennsylvania. The name Ivy League comes from the ivy that grows on the old buildings of the colleges.

Ivy League institutions have a very high academic reputation, and many more people want to attend them than are able to do so. They are very expensive, with tuition costing well over $20 000 at some universities, although **scholarships** are available to help students who cannot pay for themselves. People who are educated in the Ivy League have a good chance of finding a well-paid job, and many political leaders have been to Ivy League universities. Many other colleges and universities in the US offer a high standard of education but none has the status and prestige of the Ivy League institutions.

ˌ**Iwo** ˈ**Jima** /ˌiːwəʊ ˈdʒiːmə; *AmE* ˌiːwoʊ/ an island in the north-west Pacific Ocean that was captured by US Marines from Japan in 1945 during *World War II after a long and fierce battle. The US returned the island to Japan in 1968.

the **IWW** /ˌaɪ dʌbljuː ˈdʌbljuː/ (*in full* the **In**ˈ**dustrial** ˈ**Workers of the** ˈ**World**) a US trade union of 43 organizations, established in 1905 in *Chicago. Its leaders called for a workers' revolution. The IWW was most powerful from 1912 to 1917 when it had nearly 100 000 members (often called Wobblies). During World War I, its violent strikes were considered to be against the country's war effort. The leaders were put into prison, and the IWW soon ended.

I

Jj

ˈ***Jabberwocky*** /ˈdʒæbəwɒki; *AmE* ˈdʒæbərwɑːki/ a famous nonsense poem by Lewis *Carroll which first appeared in his book **Through the Looking Glass* (1872). It describes the hunt for a monster called the Jabberwock, using humorous invented words. Some of these words, including 'chortle' and 'galumph' are now part of the English language. The poem's first verse is:

'Twas brillig and the slithy toves
Did gyre and gimble in the wabe;
All mimsy were the borogoves
And the mome raths outgrabe.

ˌ***Jack and*** ˈ***Jill*** a traditional *nursery rhyme. The first verse is:

Jack and Jill went up the hill
To fetch a pail of water.
Jack fell down and broke his crown
And Jill came tumbling after.

ˌ***Jack and the*** ˈ***Beanstalk*** /ˈbiːnstɔːk/ a traditional story often told to children and used as a *pantomime. Jack is a boy who sells a cow for three magic beans. He plants these and they grow into a very tall beanstalk (= bean plant). He climbs up the beanstalk into the clouds where a giant lives, and steals a hen that lays golden eggs, some bags of money and a magic harp (= musical instrument). Jack escapes down the beanstalk and then cuts it down, so that the giant who is climbing down after him falls to the ground and is killed.

The details in the story are sometimes mixed with those of another old story, *Jack and the Giant Killer*. In it a boy called Jack travels around the country killing giants with his magic sword and wearing a coat that makes him invisible. In both stories the giants, trying to find Jack, repeat the rhyme:

Fee, fi, fo, fum,
I smell the blood of an Englishman.
Be he alive or be he dead,
I'll grind his bones to make my bread.

ˌ**Jack** ˈ**Daniels**™ /ˈdænjəlz/ a US 'bourbon' *whisky (= made from maize and rye) which is sold all over the world. It has been produced since 1866 at the Jack Daniels Distillery in Lynchburg, *Tennessee, the oldest in the US. It is now owned by the Brown-Forman Corporation of *Louisville, *Kentucky, which also makes *Southern Comfort.

ˌ**Jack** ˈ**Russell** /ˈrʌsl/ *n* a breed of small lively *terrier dog, named after the man who first developed the breed in the 19th century.

ˌAndrew ˈ**Jackson**[1] /ˈdʒæksn/ (1767–1845) the seventh US *President (1829–37) who was also a famous military officer. His popular name was Old Hickory. He won battles against *Native Americans and defeated the British at *New Orleans in the *War of 1812. As President, he began the *spoils system by giving political positions to his own supporters in the *Democratic Party. Jackson believed in the rights of the common man and was especially popular with ordinary people. 'Let the people rule' was a phrase he often used. His policies came to be known as **Jacksonian democracy**.

ˌGlenda ˈ**Jackson**[2] /ˈdʒæksn/ (1936–) an English actor who has worked in theatre, television and films, winning *Oscars for her parts in *Women in Love* (1969) and *A Touch of Class* (1973). She now works full-time in politics and since 1992 has been the *Labour *Member of Parliament for Hampstead and Highgate in London.

ˌJanet ˈ**Jackson**[3] /ˈdʒæksn/ (1966–) a US singer who is the sister of Michael *Jackson. Her most successful songs have included *When I Think of You* (1986) and *That's the Way Love Goes* (1993), which won a *Grammy award. She has also acted in two television series, *Good Times* and *Diff'rent Strokes*.

ˌJesse ˈ**Jackson**[4] /ˈdʒæksn/ (1941–) an *African-American leader and well-known *Democrat. He failed in his attempts to be chosen by the Democrats as their candidate for President in 1984 and 1988. Jackson is also a Baptist Church leader and is known as an excellent speaker.

ˌMahalia ˈ**Jackson**[5] /məˌheɪliə ˈdʒæksn/ (1911–72) an *African-American *gospel singer with a strong voice. Her successful songs included *Move On Up a Little Higher* and *Prayer Changes Things*. She was a supporter of the *civil rights movement in the 1960s and sang at the *Inauguration Day ceremony for President John F *Kennedy in 1961.

ˌMichael ˈ**Jackson**[6] /ˈdʒæksn/ (1958–) an *African-American pop singer, often called Jacko by the media. As a child he sang as the youngest of five brothers in The Jackson Five. His album *Thriller* (1983) sold more than 30 million copies, and he won eight *Grammy awards in 1984. He made a world tour in 1996 to advertise his album *HIStory*. His first wife was Lisa Marie Presley, the daughter of Elvis *Presley. Despite his great success Jackson is very shy about his private life. It is often said that he has had medical operations to change his appearance and the colour of his skin.

ˈˌStonewall' ˈ**Jackson**[7] /ˌstəʊnwɔːl ˈdʒæksn; *AmE* ˌstoʊnwɔːl/ (Thomas Jonathan Jackson 1824–63) an American military leader for the *Confederate States during the *Civil War. He fought at the Battles of *Bull Run and was given the popular name of 'Stonewall' during the first of these, because he stood like a stone wall as the enemy advanced. He was killed during the Battle of *Chancellorsville when his own soldiers shot him accidentally.

Jackˌsonian deˈmocracy /dʒækˌsəʊniən; *AmE* dʒækˌsoʊniən/ *n* [U] ⇨ JACKSON[1].

ˈ**Jacksonville** /ˈdʒæksənvɪl/ the largest city in the US state of *Florida, and the largest US city in area (759 square miles/1 966 square kilometres). It is a major port on the St Johns River and has a US Navy base. Jacksonville was first settled in 1816 and then named in 1822 after Andrew *Jackson.

ˌ***Jack*** ˈ***Sprat*** /ˈspræt/ a traditional *nursery rhyme. The words are:

Jack Sprat would eat no fat,
His wife would eat no lean.
And so between the two of them
They licked the platter clean.

ˌ***Jack the*** ˈ***Giant*** ˌ***Killer*** ⇨ JACK AND THE BEANSTALK.

ˌ**Jack the** ˈ**Ripper** /ˈrɪpə(r)/ the name given by the public to an unknown man who murdered and cut up several prostitutes in *Whitechapel, London, in

1888. People have tried ever since to find out who he was, but without success. There have been many books and films about the murders. See also YORKSHIRE RIPPER.

ˌ**Jacoˈbean** /ˌdʒækəˈbiːən/ *adj* of the period when *James I was king of England (1603–25). This followed the *Elizabethan period (1558–1603) and is noted for its writers (e.g. *Shakespeare, Ben *Jonson and the *metaphysical poets) as well as for its styles of architecture and furniture. The *King James Version of the Bible was also produced during the Jacobean period.

ˌDerek ˈ**Jacobi** /ˈdʒækəbi/ (1938–) an English actor on stage, in films and on television. He became famous after playing the Roman emperor Claudius in the television series *I, Claudius* (1976) and has since played the title part in the television series *Cadfael* (1994–), about a *medieval monk who solves crimes. Jacobi was made a *knight in 1994.

ˈ**Jacobite** /ˈdʒækəbaɪt/ (in 17th- and 18th-century Britain) a supporter of King *James II of England (James VII of Scotland) after he lost power to *William III in 1688, or, after James's death, a supporter of his son James Edward *Stuart (the *Old Pretender) and grandson Charles Edward Stuart (*Bonny Prince Charlie). James II and his son and grandson were members of a Scottish family, the House of Stuart, and most Jacobites were Scottish.

the ˌ**Jacobite reˈbellions** /ˌdʒækəbaɪt/ *n* [pl] a series of three rebellions which took place in Scotland after *James II lost power to *William III in 1688. In them the *Jacobites tried to return the *Stuarts to power in 1689, in 1715 (under the *Old Pretender, James II's son) and in 1745 (under *Bonny Prince Charlie, James II's grandson). After some success under Bonny Prince Charlie the Jacobites were finally defeated at the battle of *Culloden in 1746.

ˌHattie ˈ**Jacques** /ˌhæti ˈdʒeɪks/ (1924–80) an English comedy actor famous for her large figure. She appeared in many of the *Carry On films, and worked on television with Tony *Hancock and Eric *Sykes.

jaˈcuzzi™ /dʒəˈkuːzi/ *n* (*pl* **-is**) a type of bath with streams of warm water that come out below the surface. It is intended to make people feel relaxed, and was developed by the American Candido Jacuzzi to help his son, who had arthritis (= a painful disease in the joints of the body). Having a jacuzzi in the home is regarded as part of an expensive way of life.

ˈ**Jaffa cake**™ /ˈdʒæfə/ *n* a type of biscuit-shaped cake containing orange jelly and covered on one side with chocolate. Jaffa cakes are made by *McVitie's.

ˌMick ˈ**Jagger** /ˈdʒægə(r)/ (1943–) an English pop musician who is the singer for the *Rolling Stones. With Keith *Richard he has written many of the band's songs. He has also acted in a few films.

ˈ**Jaguar**™ /ˈdʒægjuə(r)/ a British car company or one of its cars. Jaguar is famous for its sports cars (e.g. the *E-type) and its larger cars of high quality. The company was bought by *Ford in 1989. The informal name often given to a Jaguar car is a **Jag**: *I like your new Jag.*

Jaˈmaica /dʒəˈmeɪkə/ an island in the *Caribbean Sea that is part of the *West Indies. It has been an independent country and a member of the *Commonwealth since 1962. Its capital city is Kingston and its official language English. It is popular with tourists. *Rastafarianism and *reggae music have their origins in Jamaica. After *World War II Jamaican people were encouraged by the British government to come to Britain to work, and Britain still has a large Jamaican community. ▶ **Jamaican** *adj, n.*

ˌClive ˈ**James**[1] /ˈdʒeɪmz/ (1939–) an Australian television personality and writer who lives and works in Britain. He is best known for humorous programmes such as *The Clive James Show* (1995–), in which he discusses news events with guests and introduces comedy acts, etc. He has also written novels, poetry and books about his own life.

ˌHenry ˈ**James**[2] /ˈdʒeɪmz/ (1843–1916) a US writer whose novels are often about Americans in Europe. They contrast the Americans' innocent ideas with the Europeans' understanding of the world. James settled in London in 1876 and became British in 1915. His novels included *The Turn of the Screw* (1898), *The Ambassadors* (1903) and *The Golden Bowl* (1904).

ˌJesse ˈ**James**[3] /ˈdʒeɪmz/ (1847–82) a US outlaw (= criminal) from the state of *Missouri. With his brother Frank (1843–1915) they led the 'James band', robbing banks and trains between 1866 and 1879. Jesse was finally shot in the back and killed by one of his former friends who wanted to collect the reward for his death offered by the state. Frank later lived on a farm. There have been many books and films about the James brothers.

ˌNaomi ˈ**James**[4] /ˈdʒeɪmz/ (1949–) an Englishwoman who became the first woman to sail alone around the world, in 1977–8. She was made a *dame(2) in 1979.

ˌP D ˈ**James**[5] /ˈdʒeɪmz/ (Phyllis Dorothy James 1920–) an English writer, mainly of *detective novels. Her main characters are the police officer Adam Dalgleish and the private detective Cordelia Gray. Many of her books have been filmed for television, including *Devices and Desires* (1989) and *Original Sin* (1997). She was made a *life peer in 1991.

ˌSid ˈ**James**[6] /ˈdʒeɪmz/ (1913–76) a British comedy actor, born in South Africa. He is best remembered for his parts in the *Carry On films, but he also appeared in television series such as *Citizen James* (1960–62) and *Bless This House* (1971–6). Much of his early work was with Tony *Hancock on both radio and television.

James I /ˌdʒeɪmz ðə ˈfɜːst; *AmE* ˈfɜːrst/ (1566–1625) the king of England from 1603 to 1625 and of Scotland (as James VI) from 1567 to 1625. His mother was *Mary Queen of Scots. As a relative of *Elizabeth I he became King of England after she died, uniting Scotland and England under one government. He was not a popular king, however, and Roman Catholic opposition led to the *Gunpowder Plot (1605). His son *Charles I became king after he died. James I is associated with the *Jacobean period in literature and the arts.

James II /ˌdʒeɪmz ðə ˈsekənd/ (1633–1701) the king of England and Scotland from 1685 to 1688. He was the son of *Charles I and the younger brother of *Charles II, becoming king after Charles II died. He faced a lot of opposition because he was a Roman Catholic, and in 1688 he was replaced by the Protestant *William III. James went to Ireland in 1689 to try to win back power, but was defeated at the *Battle of the Boyne. He lived the rest of his life in France.

ˈ**Jamestown** /ˈdʒeɪmztaʊn/ the first permanent community of English people in North America, in what is now *Virginia. It was established on 14 May 1607 by the London Company and named after King *James I. John *Smith[7] was an early leader. The first tobacco farms were begun here in 1612. The church tower and some graves remain, and are visited by many tourists. Jamestown is now part of Virginia's Colonial National Historic Park.

Jaˈmiroquai /dʒəˈmɪrəkwaɪ/ a British pop group formed in 1991. The group's style is influenced by *jazz funk, and its first album, *Emergency on Planet Earth* (1993), reached No. 1 in Britain.

Jane 1 a character in a strip cartoon in the British

J

*Daily Mirror newspaper from 1932 to 1959 and 1985 to 1990. Jane's habit of appearing in her underwear made her very popular with male readers, and during *World War II her cartoon adventures filled a whole page of the newspaper. **2** the female partner of *Tarzan in the books of Edgar Rice *Burroughs and the films later made from them.

ˌ**Jane ˈDoe** /ˈdəʊ; *AmE* ˈdoʊ/ a name used in the US to refer to a woman or girl whose identity is unknown or who does not want her real name to be made public. This is usually for cases in court and on legal papers. Compare JOHN DOE 1.

ˌ***Jane ˈEyre*** /ˈeə(r); *AmE* ˈer/ a novel (1847) by Charlotte *Brontë. Jane Eyre is a private teacher for the daughter of Edward Rochester. Jane and Mr Rochester fall in love and are about to marry when she discovers that he already has a wife, who is mentally ill. Years later the lovers meet again and marry, although Rochester has by this time been badly injured in a fire. The novel is still popular, mainly for the contrast in character between the shy Jane and the mysterious and violent Rochester.

ˈ**Jarrow** /ˈdʒærəʊ; *AmE* ˈdʒæroʊ/ a town in the county of *Tyne and Wear in north-east England. In the 1930s the local shipbuilding and steel industries in Jarrow were badly affected by the *Depression, making many workers unemployed. In 1936 about 200 unemployed workers walked 274 miles/441 kilometres from Jarrow to London on a 'hunger march' in an attempt to persuade the government do something about the problem. See also BEDE.

J

ˌDavid ˈ**Jason** /ˈdʒeɪsn/ (1940–) an English actor, especially on television. He became famous playing the part of *'Del Boy' Trotter in **Only Fools and Horses* and later that of Pop Larkin in *The Darling Buds of May*. He has also had success with serious acting, playing the police officer Jack Frost in the crime series *A Touch of Frost* from 1992.

Jaws /dʒɔːz/ a very successful film (1975) about a large shark (= dangerous fish) that attacks people. The film was directed by Stephen *Spielberg and was based on a novel of the same name by Peter Benchley. There have been several sequels (= later films that continue the original story and use some of the same characters).

ˈ**Jaycee** /ˈdʒeɪsiː/ *n* (*AmE infml*) a member of a junior *chamber of commerce. The name comes from the first letters of the words 'junior chamber'. The Jaycees are an organization of young business people in several countries involved in projects to support their local communities. The US Junior Chamber of Commerce was established in 1920 and its office is in *Tulsa, *Oklahoma.

jazz

Jazz is one of the greatest forms of music originating in the US. The names of its stars, who are mostly *African Americans, are known around the world. Most people have heard of stars like Ella *Fitzgerald, 'Count' *Basie, 'Duke' *Ellington and Louis *Armstrong. Wynton *Marsalis, who plays in the traditional style, is the best-known jazz musician today.

Jazz was begun in the *South by African Americans. Many of its rhythms came from the work songs and *spirituals (= religious songs) of black slaves. New Orleans street bands first made jazz popular. Early forms of jazz created at the beginning of the 20th century were ***ragtime** and the ***blues**. Ragtime musicians included the singer 'Jelly Roll' *Morton and the composer and piano player Scott *Joplin. Famous blues singers included Bessie *Smith and later Billie *Holiday. ***Dixieland** developed from ragtime and the blues and made a feature of improvisation (= making up the music as it is being played), especially on the trumpet and saxophone. Dixieland stars included Louis Armstrong and Sidney Bechet.

Miles Davis (trumpet) and Charlie 'Bird' Parker (saxophone) with Tommy Potter (double bass)

In the 1920s many African Americans moved north, taking jazz with them, and *Chicago and New York became centres for the music. This was the beginning of the **big band era**. In the 1930s swing music came into fashion and people danced to jazz. Radio and the new recording industry helped to make it even more popular. The big bands were led by Basie, Ellington, Woody *Herman, Glenn *Miller and 'the King of Swing', Benny *Goodman. In the 1940s there were new styles such as ***bebop**, developed by 'Dizzy' *Gillespie, Charlie 'Bird' *Parker and Thelonious *Monk. Freer forms like **progressive jazz** developed in the 1950s with stars including Stan *Getz and Dave *Brubeck. **Cool jazz** followed in the 1960s, led by Getz and Miles *Davis. More recent styles have included funky jazz, jazz-rock and hip-hop jazz. Many **jazz clubs**, like the *Cotton Club, have now closed but others, like Preservation Hall in *New Orleans, and Birdland in *Manhattan, remain.

In Britain jazz attracts a small but enthusiastic audience. The height of its popularity was in the 1940s and 1950s, when large crowds gathered to hear big bands. British jazz has always been heavily influenced by US jazz. In the 1960s pop and rock music replaced jazz as the music of the young generation. There are now few jazz bands, although smaller **combos** (= groups) continue to play a wide range of **trad** (= traditional), bebop, cool and avant-garde jazz. The most famous British jazz musicians have included Johnny *Dankworth and Cleo *Laine, George Melly, Humphrey *Lyttelton and Courtney *Pine. The home of jazz in Britain is Ronnie *Scott's club in London.

the ˈ**Jazz Age** a name for the 1920s, when *jazz music was especially popular. The name came from the book *Tales of the Jazz Age* (1922) by F Scott *Fitzgerald, who was called 'the spokesman of the Jazz Age'. See also ROARING TWENTIES.

ˌ**jazz ˈfunk** (*also* **funk**) *n* [U] a style of dance music that developed from the *soul music of James *Brown and others during the 1960s and 1970s. Famous jazz funk bands include Parliament and Funkadelic.

The ˈ***Jazz ˌSinger*** the first sound film. It was made in *Hollywood in 1927 by *Warner Brothers and was so successful that other companies soon changed to sound. Al *Jolson was the star and sang six songs, but only 354 words were actually spoken in the film, including his famous phrase, 'You ain't heard nothing yet.' The story is about the son of a Jewish rabbi

(= religious leader) who becomes a singer. Later versions of the film were made in 1953 and 1980.

JCB™ /ˌdʒeɪ siː ˈbiː/ *n* a large vehicle for moving earth, etc., with a large mechanical shovel at the front and a digging arm at the back. JCBs are made by the British company J C Bamford.

ˌ**J C ˈPenney** /ˌdʒeɪ siː ˈpeni/ any of a large group of US department stores. The company, also called Penney's, is known for low prices and its system of supplying goods ordered by mail. The shops/stores were begun in 1902 by James Cash Penney (1875–1971), who called them 'chain stores'.

ˈ**J Crew**™ any of a group of fashionable US clothes shops. The company also sells clothes through its well-known catalogues. J Crew is best known for its range of informal sports clothes.

jeans

Jeans, also called **blue jeans**, were first made in the US. They are now worn all over the world. Jeans were created during the *Gold Rush in the 1840s and 1850s, when many people went to the western US to search for gold. Miners often lived in tents made out of a strong fabric and, because they needed strong clothes, they began to wear trousers made from the same fabric. Many jeans were sold by Levi Strauss, who had a store in California, and today *Levi's are among the most famous jeans.

Traditionally, jeans are blue, but the fabric they are made of, **denim**, comes in many colours. Black jeans are fashionable, and also **stonewashed** jeans that are made from traditional blue denim which has been washed until it becomes light blue. Once it was fashionable to have **bell-bottoms** or **flares**, but today people prefer **straight-legs**. **Designer jeans** made by top fashion designers are sometimes worn by the rich.

For a long time jeans were worn only for physical work, but in the 1960s US society changed and young people questioned traditional attitudes to dress. Jeans were a symbol of these changes and became very popular. Now, people of any age wear jeans because they are comfortable, practical and cheap. In the US they can be appropriate for all but the most formal occasions. Many people wear jeans to work, to church or to go out in the evening. In Britain some restaurants and wine bars do not allow in people who are wearing jeans, and some companies do not like their staff to wear jeans for work.

Jeep™ (*also* **jeep**) *n* a small strong motor vehicle used for driving over rough ground or on mountain roads. The Jeep was first made for the US Army in *World War II. It was called a General Purpose vehicle, the short form of which was 'GP' or 'jeep'. Jeeps are now made by *Chrysler and sold around the world. Popular models include the Cherokee and the Wrangler.

Jeeves /dʒiːvz/ the male servant of Bertie *Wooster in the humorous stories of P G *Wodehouse. Jeeves is often seen as the perfect example of an intelligent and efficient servant who remains calm and can solve any problem.

ˌThomas ˈ**Jefferson** /ˈdʒefəsn/ (1743–1826) the third US *President (1801–9) and one of the nation's *Founding Fathers. He wrote most of the *Declaration of Independence but was opposed to a strong central government. As president, he supported the *Louisiana Purchase and the *Lewis and Clark Expedition. Jefferson helped design Washington, DC, and was the first president to have his *Inauguration Day there. He was also governor of *Virginia (1779–81) and US Secretary of State (1789–93). He established the University of Virginia (1819) and designed its buildings. He died on the 50th anniversary of the Declaration of Independence.

the ˌ**Jefferson Meˈmorial** /ˌdʒefəsn/ a building in Washington, DC, in memory of Thomas *Jefferson. It was opened in 1943 in East Potomac Park. John Russell Pope designed it like an ancient Greek building with a round roof, and it is made of white marble. Inside is a statue of Jefferson by Rudolph Evans.

ˌJudge ˈ**Jeffreys** /ˈdʒefriz/ (George Jeffreys *c.* 1648–89) a British judge who condemned to death many supporters of the Duke of *Monmouth at the *Bloody Assizes of 1685. He is often given as an example of a cruel and wicked judge. He was made a *baron in 1685 but later fell out of favour and died in prison.

Jeˌhovah's ˈWitness /dʒɪˌhəʊvəz; *AmE* dʒɪˌhoʊvəz/ *n* a member of a Christian organization started in the US in the 1870s. Jehovah's Witnesses believe that the end of the world is near and that when it comes everyone except them will be destroyed. They also refuse to do military service, do not celebrate birthdays or *Christmas, and believe in the absolute truth of the Bible. Members are encouraged to visit people in their homes and try to persuade them to join.

ˌ**Jekyll and ˈHyde** /ˌdʒekəl ənd ˈhaɪd/ a single person with two personalities, one good (Jekyll) and one bad (Hyde). The phrase comes from a character in Robert Louis *Stevenson's story *The Strange Case of Dr Jekyll and Mr Hyde* (1886) who can change into an evil person by drinking a special substance: *lead a Jekyll and Hyde existence* ○ *Her husband was a Jekyll and Hyde, first loving and then deceitful.*

ˈ**jello** (*also* ˈ**Jell-O**™) /ˈdʒeləʊ; *AmE* ˈdʒeloʊ/ *n* [U, C] (*AmE*) a popular US sweet dish of jelly/gelatin with a fruit flavour. It is eaten as a dessert or with salads. The word is often used in the US to refer to any jelly/gelatin dish.

ˈ**jelly ˌbaby** *n* [usu pl] (*BrE*) a small soft sweet shaped like baby. Jelly babies are sold in different colours and flavours, and are popular with children.

ˈ**jelly bean** *n* a small sweet/candy shaped like a bean. Jelly beans have centres of jelly/gelatin with hard sugar on the outside. They are sold in many different flavours and colours, and in the US they are traditionally put in children's Easter baskets.

ˌRoy ˈ**Jenkins** /ˈdʒenkɪnz/ (1920–) a British politician and author. He became *Home Secretary (1965–7 and 1974–6) and *Chancellor of the Exchequer (1967–70) in the *Labour governments of Harold *Wilson, and later, as a member of the *Gang of Four, established the *Social Democratic Party. From 1977 to 1981 he was President of the *European Commission. He has written several books about politics and politicians, and was made a *life peer in 1987.

ˌEdward ˈ**Jenner** /ˈdʒenə(r)/ (1749–1823) an English doctor who discovered vaccination. He found that by deliberately infecting people with cowpox (a disease of cows) he could prevent them from catching smallpox, a serious human disease.

ˈ***Jeopardy*** /ˈdʒepədi; *AmE* ˈdʒepərdi/ a popular US television quiz show. The competitors are given answers and have to guess what the questions are for each answer. The programme began in 1964, and Alex Trebek has presented it since 1984.

ˌJerome K ˈ**Jerome** /dʒəˈrəʊm; *AmE* dʒəˈroʊm/ (Jerome Klapka Jerome 1859–1927) an English writer, best known for his humorous novel **Three Men in a Boat* (1889).

ˈ**Jersey** /ˈdʒɜːzi; *AmE* ˈdʒɜːrzi/ **1** the largest of the *Channel Islands, off the north-west coast of France. The main town is St Helier. Jersey has its own government and tax system but has strong links with

Britain, and is popular with British tourists. Both English and French are spoken on the island. It is known for its fruit and vegetables (particularly tomatoes and Jersey Royal potatoes). The item of clothing called a *jersey* takes its name from a type of material originally made on the island. **2** (*also* **Jersey cow**) *n* a breed of cow originally from the *Channel Islands. Jersey cattle are light brown in colour and are known for their rich milk. **3** (in the US) another name for the state of *New Jersey.

ˌJersey ˈCity /ˌdʒɜːzi; *AmE* ˌdʒɜːrzi/ an industrial city in the US state of *New Jersey, across the *Hudson River from *Manhattan(1). It is a port with many factories. Many people who live there work in New York. Jersey City was settled in the middle of the 17th century and became a town in 1836.

the **ˌJersey ˈLily** /ˌdʒɜːzi; *AmE* dʒɜːrzi/ a name given to Lillie *Langtry (the lover of King *Edward VII), who was born on the island of *Jersey(1).

Jeˈrusalem /dʒəˈruːsələm/ a famous poem (1804) by William *Blake, later set to music by Hubert Parry (1848–1918). It expresses the hope for a future Christian society built in ‘England's green and pleasant land’, and contains several phrases that have become well known, including ‘dark Satanic mills’ and ‘chariot of fire’. It is traditionally sung at the *Last Night of the Proms as well as by *Women's Institutes and in churches.

J

ˈJesus ˈChrist ˈSuperstar a musical stage show about the life and death of Jesus Christ by Andrew *Lloyd Webber and Tim *Rice. It was very successful in Britain and the US in the 1970s and returned to the Lyceum Theatre, London from 1996. A film version was made in 1973.

ˌJewel in the ˈCrown a popular British television series, first broadcast in 1983, about the British in India just before it became an independent country. The series was adapted from the **Raj Quartet* novels of Paul *Scott. The phrase ‘the jewel in the crown’ was formerly used to describe India's place in the British Empire, and is used today to refer to something of great value among other valuable things: *Their new winger is the jewel in Newcastle's crown.*

JFK /ˌdʒeɪ ef ˈkeɪ/ **1** ⇨ KENNEDY. **2** (*also* **Kennedy**) a large international airport in New York, named after President John F *Kennedy. Its former name was Idlewild Airport.

ˈJiffy bag™ /ˈdʒɪfi/ *n* a type of padded envelope for protecting things that are being sent by post.

ˌJim ˈCrow /ˈkrəʊ; *AmE* ˈkroʊ/ (*also* **ˌJim ˈCrowism**) /ˈkrəʊɪzəm; *AmE* ˈkroʊɪzəm/ *n* [U] (*AmE offensive, rather old-fash*) the policy of *segregation or unfair treatment of *African Americans in hotels, restaurants, businesses, etc. The name came from the title of a song that was sung in *minstrel shows: *The South had many Jim-Crow laws.*

ˈJingle Bells a popular *Christmas song. It is sung by carol singers or at Christmas celebrations but not usually in church. ⇨ note at CAROLS AND CAROL-SINGING.

the **ˈjitterbug** /ˈdʒɪtəbʌg; *AmE* ˈdʒɪtərbʌg/ *n* [sing] a fast dance, originally from the US, which was popular in the 1940s. It involved wild movements, with the women being lifted in the air. A version popular with *African Americans was the Lindy or Lindy Hop.

jive *n* [U] **1** a lively style of dance, popular especially in the 1950s, performed to *jazz or *rock and roll music. **2** jive music. **3** (*AmE slang*) talk that is not sincere or is intended to deceive somebody: *Hey, man, don't give me that jive.*

▶ **jive** *v* [I] to dance jive or play jive music.

ˈJobcentre /ˈdʒɒbsentə(r); *AmE* ˈdʒɑːbsentər/ *n* (in Britain) a government office found in the centre of most towns, where local jobs are advertised. Jobcentres also offer advice on finding a job and help in arranging interviews with employers. They are run by the *Employment Service.

ˈJobclub /ˈdʒɒbklʌb; *AmE* ˈdʒɑːbklʌb/ *n* (in Britain) a local government centre where unemployed people can get advice and help in finding a job, with free use of telephones, office equipment, etc.

ˌjobseeker's alˈlowance /ˌdʒɒbsiːkəz; *AmE* ˌdʒɑːbsiːkərz/ *n* [U] (in Britain) money paid by the government to unemployed people. To claim the money, people must be capable of work and must prove that they are trying to find work.

Jock /dʒɒk; *AmE* dʒɑːk/ *n* (*BrE infml, sometimes disapprov or offensive*) a name used especially by English people to refer to a Scotsman: *I was talking to this Jock at the pub.* See also MICK, TAFFY.

the **ˈJockey Club** (in Britain) the organization formerly in charge of the sport of horse-racing. It is now controlled by the British Horseracing Board.

ˌJodrell ˈBank /ˌdʒɒdrəl; *AmE* ˌdʒɑːdrəl/ (*also* the **Nuffield Radio Astronomy Laboratories**) a place in *Cheshire north-west England, where there are several large radio telescopes (= devices for receiving radio waves from distant objects in the universe). The main one was designed by Sir Bernard *Lovell, and when it began operating in 1957 it was the largest of its kind in the world.

radio telescopes at Jodrell Bank

ˌJoe ˈBloggs /ˈblɒgz; *AmE* ˈblɑːgz/ (*also* **ˌJoe ˈSoap**) (*BrE*) (*AmE* **ˌJoe ˈBlow**, **ˌJoe ˈDoakes** /ˈdəʊks; *AmE* ˈdoʊks/) (*infml*) a name used to refer to an average or typical man: *Joe Bloggs is generally more interested in sport than in politics.* Compare JOHN Q PUBLIC.

ˌBilly **ˈJoel** /ˈdʒəʊl/ (1949–) a US pop singer who also writes songs and plays the piano. He has won many *Grammy awards for his songs, including *Just the Way You Are* (1978), *57th Street* (1979) and *Glass Houses* (1980). His other songs include *Back in the USSR* (1987), *River of Dreams* (1993) and *To Make You Feel My Love* (1997).

ˌJoe ˈSixpack /ˈsɪkspæk/ (*AmE infml*) a typical *working-class man. The phrase is often used as an insult. A sixpack is a pack of six cans of beer sold together, something that such a person is seen as buying regularly.

John[1] (1167–1216) the king of England from 1199 to 1216. He was the youngest son of *Henry II and became king after the death of his brother *Richard I, having previously tried to take power from him. He was not a popular or successful king. He lost most of the English land in France, quarrelled with the

Flags

the Stars and Stripes on a family's front porch, Delaware

The Stars and Stripes

The US flag is an important symbol to all Americans. During the revolution against Britain, George Washington asked Betsy Ross to make a flag as an encouragement for his soldiers. This flag had 13 stripes, seven red and six white, and in one corner 13 white stars on a blue background to represent the 13 states. On 14 June 1777 it became the flag of the independent US. As each new state became part of the US an extra star was added.

Today, the flag, called **Old Glory** or the **Stars and Stripes**, is widely seen in the US. Government offices and schools have flags flying from **flagpoles**, and many people have flags outside their houses, especially on Independence Day. Children start the school day by saying the Pledge of Allegiance, a promise to be loyal to the flag and to their country. When somebody important dies, flags are flown **at half mast** (*AmE also* **at half staff**). When a soldier dies his or her coffin is covered with a flag, and after the funeral the flag is given to the family. The flag has also been used as a symbol of protest, especially during the Vietnam War, when some people burnt the flag to show that they were ashamed of their country's actions.

Each of the US states also has its own flag. State flags may show the state flower or bird, or other emblem.

The Union Jack

The flag of the United Kingdom is commonly known as the **Union Jack**. (*Jack* is a sailing term for a flag.) It has been used as the British flag since 1603, when Scotland and England were united. The original design combined the red cross of England with the white diagonal cross on a blue background of Scotland. The red diagonal cross of Ireland was added in 1801, when Ireland became part of the United Kingdom. Wales is not represented on the Union Jack because it is a principality of England. The **red dragon of Cadwallader**, which is now often used as the national flag of Wales, dates from the 1950s.

The Union Jack is most often seen flying from public buildings or at sports events. Children may wave small Union Jacks when a member of the royal family visits their town. During national celebrations strings of small flags are hung across the street as **bunting**.

The Union Jack is less important to British people than the Stars and Stripes is to Americans. Many people feel a stronger loyalty to the national flags of England, Scotland, Wales or Northern Ireland. The flag of the European Union, a circle of gold stars on a blue background, is sometimes also seen in Britain, e.g. on car number plates.

football supporters holding up a Union Jack, London

The United States of America

Larger versions of these photographs, with captions, appear on other pages in the colour section.

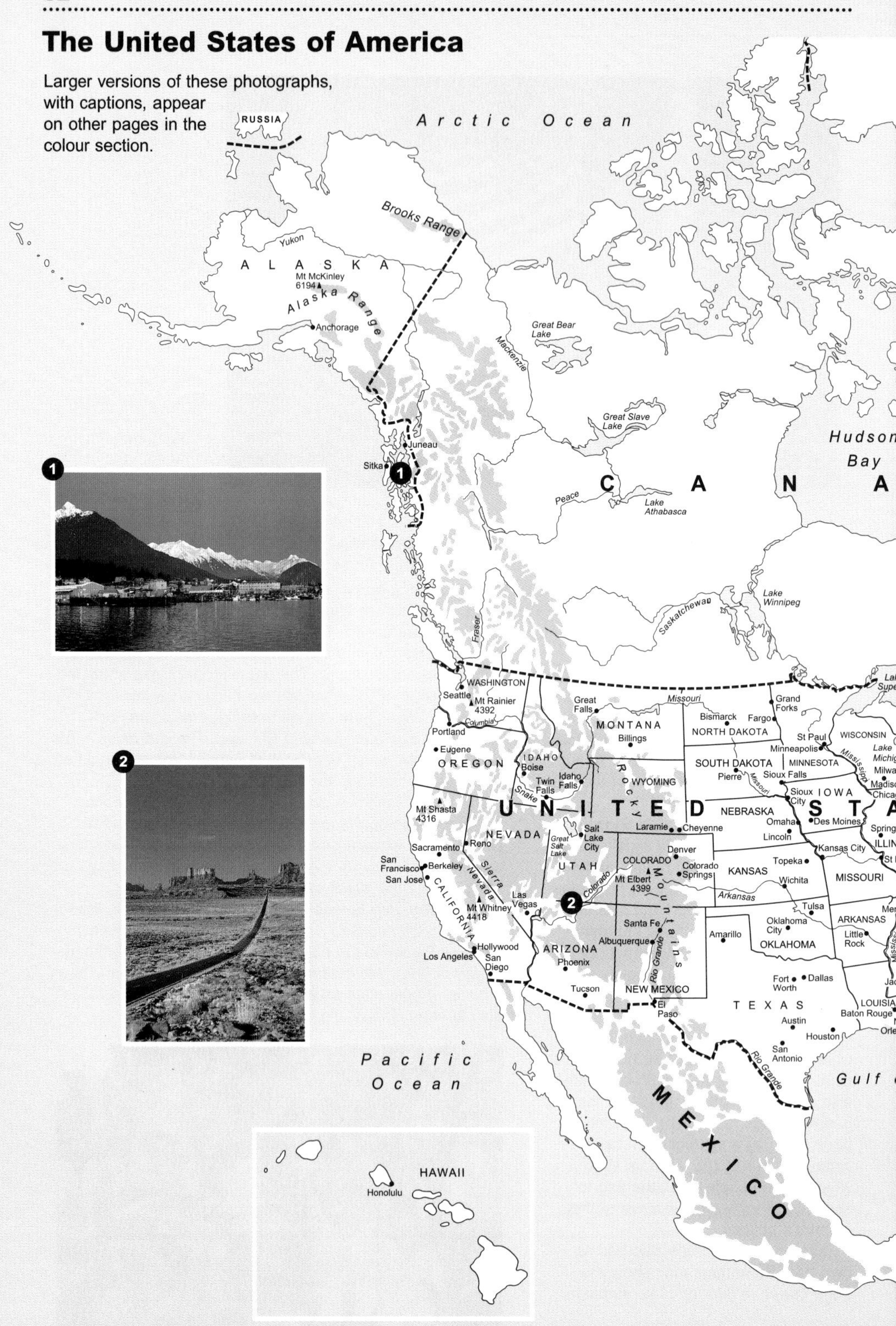

1

2

international boundary
state boundary
capital city
city
river
lake
peaks or highest points
land over 1500 metres
0
600
1200 km
GREENLAND
affin Bay
Labrador Basin
A
E
S
Great Lakes
Lake Huron
Lake Ontario
Lake Erie
St Lawrence
Hudson
MAINE
Augusta
NEW HAMPSHIRE
Manchester
VERMONT
Boston
MASSACHUSETTS
Providence
CONNECTICUT
RHODE ISLAND
NEW YORK
Long Island
New York
Newark
HIGAN
Detroit
PENNSYLVANIA
Philadelphia
OHIO
Columbus
Baltimore
NEW JERSEY
Dover
Washington DC
DELAWARE
MARYLAND
napolis
ANA
Ohio
WEST VIRGINIA
Richmond
Norfolk
VIRGINIA
Appalachian Mountains
NTUCKY
NORTH CAROLINA
shville
Charlotte
Raleigh
ESSEE
Tennessee
Columbia
SOUTH CAROLINA
Atlanta
Charleston
ngham
LABAMA
GEORGIA
Savannah
ontgomery
Jacksonville
Mobile
Tallahassee
FLORIDA
Orlando
Tampa
Miami
THE BAHAMAS
Atlantic Ocean
The West Indies
Mexico
DOMINICAN REPUBLIC
PUERTO RICO
CUBA
HAITI
JAMAICA
HONDURAS
ATEMALA
EL SALVADOR
NICARAGUA
COSTA RICA
PANAMA
3
4
5
6
7

The American land and people

wheat fields in the Midwest

autumn in Vermont

A big country

The US consists of 50 states and covers 3.7 million square miles (9.6 million square kilometres), making it the third largest country in the world. Flying is often the most practical way to travel between cities, but people who go by road get a better sense of the vastness of the country.

The country's size means that its climate and landscape are very varied. Florida and Hawaii have tropical heat and storms, while Alaska has an arctic climate. The South-west has deserts, while New England has green fields and forests. The **Rocky Mountains** running through the states of Montana, Wyoming, Utah and Colorado contrast with flat prairie grasslands and wheat fields to the east.

The population is not evenly distributed. The state of New Jersey has over 1 000 people per square mile, compared with only 4.9 per square mile in Wyoming and 1.1 in Alaska. In most states there is a racial mix, but California and Texas have more people of Hispanic origin and the southern states more African Americans than elsewhere.

The US is traditionally divided into five regions. **New England** in the North-east is the smallest region and has a cold climate. There are many small towns, and **Boston** is the only major city. New Englanders, sometimes called true Yankees, are proud of their history. The Pilgrim Fathers settled in the area, and the American Revolution began there.

The **Mid-Atlantic states** lie along the Atlantic Ocean to the south of New England. The region is also called the **East Coast**. Major cities include **New York**, **Philadelphia**, **Pittsburgh** and **Baltimore**, as well as **Washington, DC**, the capital city of the US. The East Coast is the country's main business area. To other Americans, East Coast people seem to have a fast and aggressive lifestyle.

The states of the **Middle West**, or **Midwest**, include the Wheat Belt and the Corn Belt. From here, pioneers set out to explore the West. The industrial cities of **Chicago** and **Detroit** are considered liberal, but most Midwesterners are thought to be conservative. People from the East Coast laugh about the old-fashioned ways of Midwesterners, but respect their concern for family values and religion.

The **South** has many poor areas. The people are traditionally very religious, and the region is often called the **Bible Belt**. The hot climate means that people have a slower lifestyle, so other Americans sometimes think Southerners are lazy. They also criticize the South for its past treatment of slaves. Much has now changed, with some African Americans having good jobs and with the growth of lively cities like **Atlanta**.

The **West** includes the cities of **Houston**, **Dallas** and **Los Angeles**, the entertainment centres of **Las Vegas** and **Hollywood**, and the religious town of **Salt Lake City**. Americans consider the West to be a place of new beginnings and opportunities. The Pacific Northwest has emerged recently as the most fashionable part of the US. It is in **Seattle**, after all, that Frasier sips his 'decaf skimmed milk caffe latte', and from where Bill Gates controls the electronic world.

Monument Valley, Utah/Arizona

moving a house, Kansas

students getting on a school bus, North Carolina

watching a football game, California

college graduates after receiving their degrees, Indiana

A young country

America is a young country. The year 1776 is usually considered to be the beginning of the country's independent history. Perhaps because the US has such a short a history, people put great value on historical places. Buildings like Ford's Theatre, where President Lincoln was killed, and open spaces like Valley Forge, which was important in the War of Independence, are protected so that people can visit them and learn about US history.

Youth and new things are also valued. To many people it is the future that matters, not the past. Young people are encouraged from an early age to make their own choices and to go out on their own and succeed.

Sport is an important part of American life. Young people do sports at school and college, and many people go to watch their favourite football or baseball team.

Change is a positive feature in the US. Americans change jobs and move house often, and a town may have a sudden period of rapid growth and change its character completely. To foreigners the US often seems an exciting, fast-moving, forward-looking place full of opportunity.

Four American cities

Most Americans now live in towns or cities. Foreigners tend to know the international cities, like New York, Washington, Miami and San Francisco. Other cities are very different.

Columbus, Ohio

Columbus, Ohio

Colombus, Ohio, for instance, in the Midwest is considered to be so typically American that new products are tested there before being sold elsewhere. It is believed that if the people of Columbus like something, then so will the rest of the country.

With almost 1.5 million people, Columbus is not sure whether it is a large town or a small city. It has museums, theatres and arts centres, a university, and companies such as Wendy's fast-food chain and the Limited clothing shops which help to give the city an international feel. Columbus is an easy place to live in. Jobs and houses are relatively easy to find, there are good shops and restaurants, and the cost of living is not too high.

But the people of Columbus worry that their city is not 'world class'. It is a pleasant, but very normal place. People from New York, Boston or Philadelphia do not need to say where their cities are. It bothers some people that it is not enough to say 'Columbus', they need to say 'Columbus, Ohio'.

Salt Lake City, Utah

Atlanta, Georgia

Until recently, many Americans knew more about the history of Atlanta, Georgia than about the city today. Atlanta was an important city during the period when the Deep South relied on slaves. Towards the end of the Civil War it was destroyed by the Northern army, and although the city was rebuilt and became the state capital, it attracted little attention. When the Olympic Games were held in Atlanta in 1996, people in the rest of the US were surprised to see a modern, international city. Atlanta has a population of over 3 million people and is the home of Coca Cola, Delta Airlines and the Turner news and entertainment business, which includes CNN.

The city is full of energy, but it does not attract visitors in the same way as New Orleans, which is famous for its Mardi Gras celebration, or Miami, where people from the North go to enjoy the sun during winter. Atlanta has worked hard to overcome its reputation for racism against African Americans and it is now proud of its ethnic diversity. But people say that there are still not enough opportunities for some sections of society.

Salt Lake City, Utah

Salt Lake City, Utah, is most famous for being the home of the Church of Jesus Christ of Latter-Day Saints, or Mormons. The population of Salt Lake City is 1.5 million, but there are only 2 million people in the whole state of Utah. The area is quite remote and the nearest large cities are Las Vegas, which is 420 miles (670 kilometres) away, and Denver, 530 miles (850 kilometres) away.

Salt Lake City is a quiet community surrounded by mountains and the Great Salt Lake. Nearly half of the land inside the city limits is empty. In winter nearby ski resorts attract visitors from all over the US. Although more than half of Utah's population is Mormon and believes that it is wrong to drink alcohol, Salt Lake City resembles Boulder, Colorado and other cities in the Rocky Mountains in having an active **alternative scene** (= a group of people who have a liberal, non-traditional lifestyle) based round several bars, restaurants and nightclubs.

Atlanta, Georgia

Sitka, Alaska

Sitka, Alaska

People wanting to go to Sitka, Alaska, have to go by sea or by air, because there are no roads into the town. Sitka was first established by the Tlingit native Alaskans. It then became the capital of Russian Alaska, before Alaska became a territory of the US in 1867. Russian influence can still be seen in the style of some buildings, and there are still Tlingits living there. About 20% of the population of 8 500 is Tlingit, Inuit, Haida or Aleut.

Sitka has a small hospital, seven schools, and a few restaurants and hotels. Shopping is very limited. Other communities of this size face similar problems in maintaining adequate services, but for the people of Sitka travelling to another city to shop or get medical attention is more difficult than just getting into a car and driving for an hour.

Tourists are one of Sitka's major sources of income, and many arrive on the cruise ships which sail along the Alaskan coast.

The British Isles

Larger versions of these photographs, with captions, appear on other pages in the colour section.

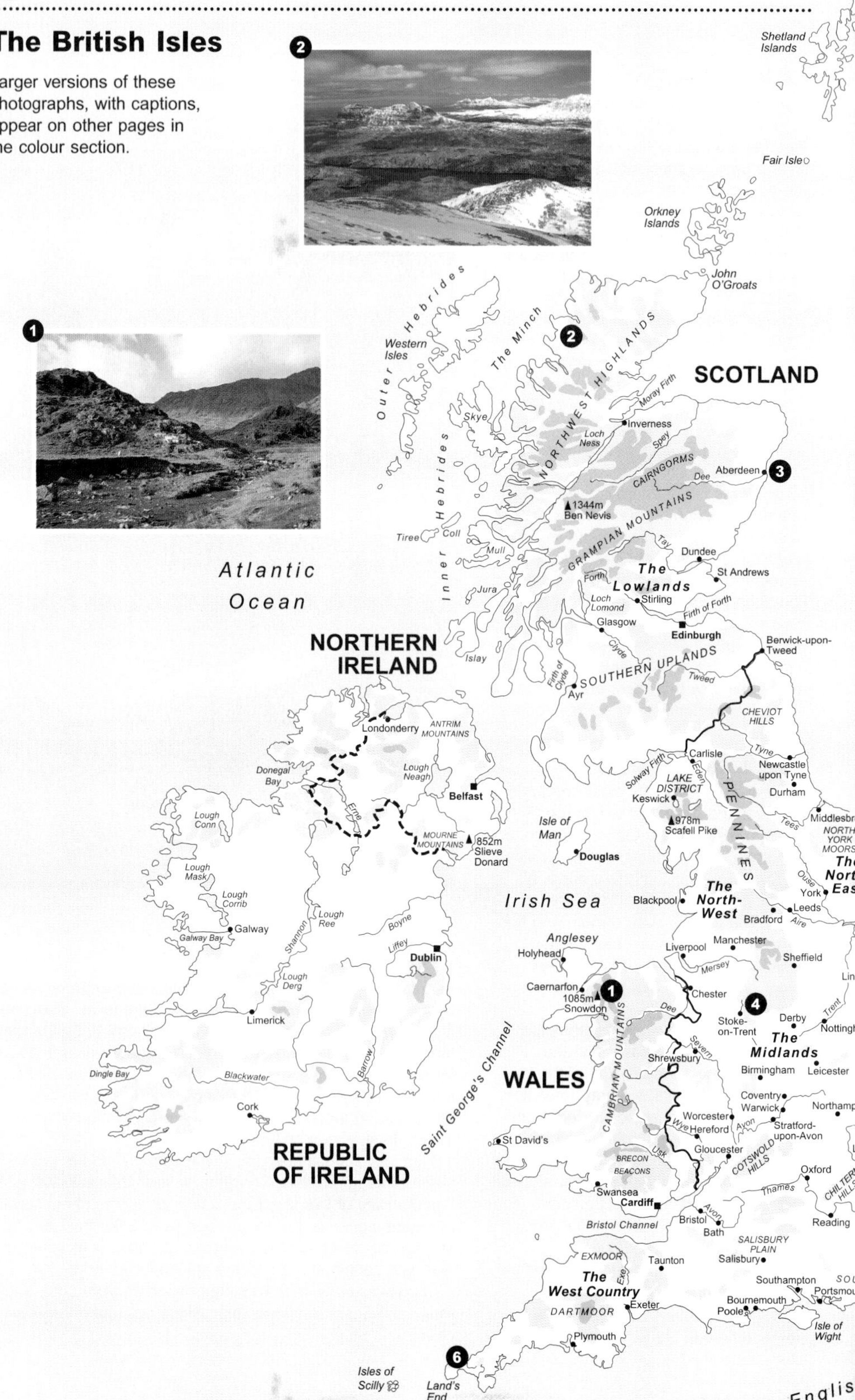

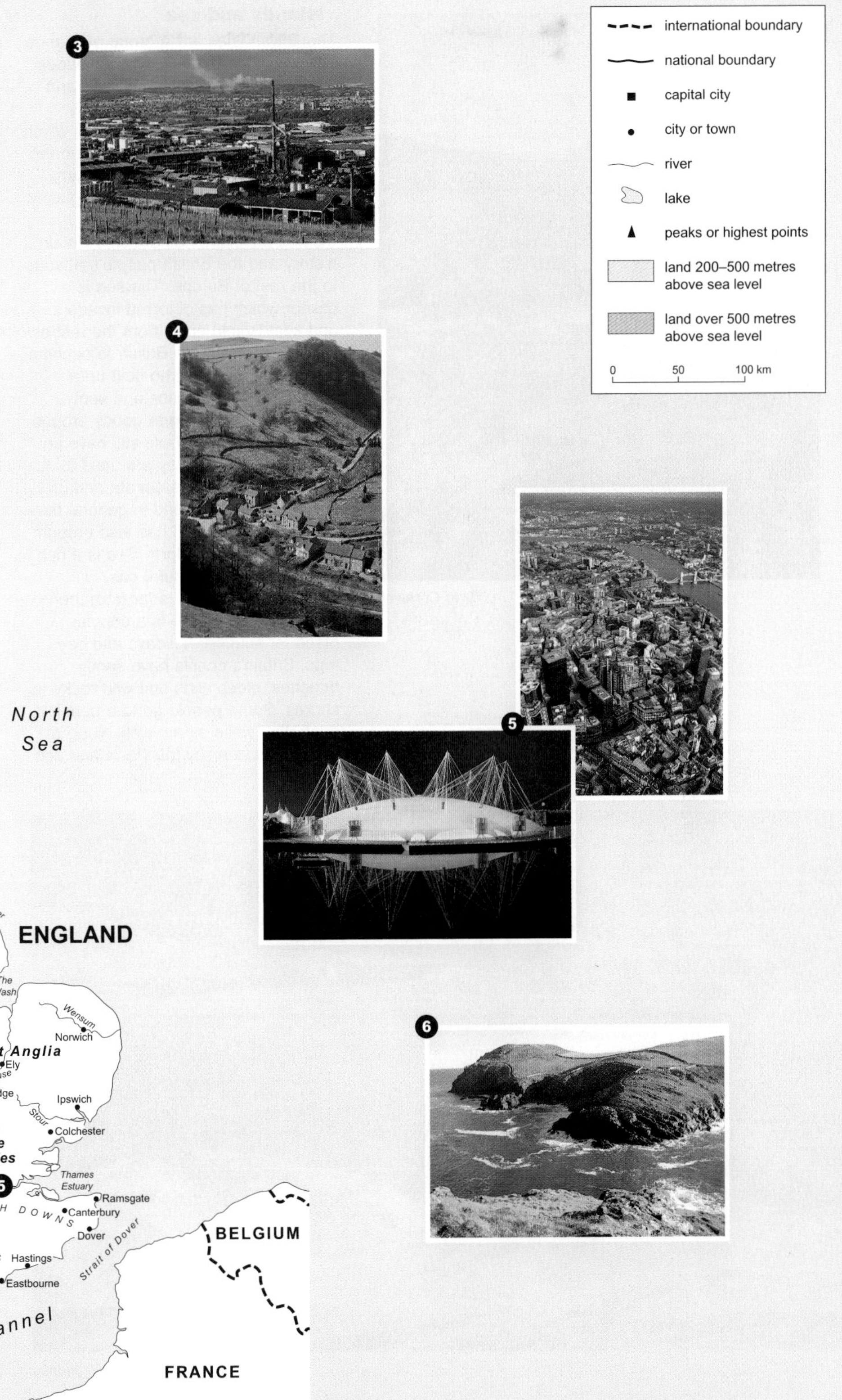

international boundary
national boundary
capital city
city or town
river
lake
peaks or highest points
land 200–500 metres above sea level
land over 500 metres above sea level
0
50
100 km
3
4
5
6
North Sea
ENGLAND
Humber
The Wash
Wensum
Norwich
East Anglia
Ely
Ipswich
Stour
Colchester
Thames Estuary
Ramsgate
Canterbury
Dover
Strait of Dover
Hastings
Eastbourne
Channel
BELGIUM
FRANCE

The British landscape

cliffs in Cornwall

Islands and sea

The British Isles are a group of islands. The largest is **Britain**, which includes the countries of England, Wales and Scotland. The island of **Ireland** is divided between Northern Ireland, which is part of the United Kingdom, and the Republic of Ireland. There are many smaller offshore islands, e.g. Anglesey, the Orkneys and the Scilly Isles.

Being an island has affected Britain's history and the British people's attitude to the rest of Europe. The sea is a barrier which has deterred invaders and kept Britain apart from the rest of Europe. It forced the British to become a seafaring people who built up a strong navy for defence and sent merchant ships to trade goods around the world. British people still have an **island mentality**: they are used to being independent, separate and on the edge of things, and in general they like this. The seabed has also brought Britain wealth: the North Sea is a rich source of oil and natural gas.

Nowhere in Britain is far from the sea, and the seaside is a popular place for summer holidays and day trips. Britain's coasts have sandy beaches, steep cliffs and wild rocky shores. Some people go to a beach to sunbathe, while others walk along a coast path to enjoy the views and sea breezes.

the Scottish Highlands

Country and climate

England has been called a 'green and pleasant land', and **Ireland** is known as 'the Emerald Isle'. The rain for which the British Isles are famous helps to keep the countryside fresh and green. On the Scottish mountains snow may last well into spring, and lower hills are often covered in mist even in summer.

Scotland has a romantic image of wild mountains, lochs (= lakes) and purple heather moors. The mainland is divided into two by the **Great Glen**, a series of valleys and lochs running south-west to north-east. It is in one of these lochs that the famous Loch Ness monster is supposed to live. North of the Great Glen are the **Highlands**, a mountainous and thinly populated region. This is the home of many of the Scottish clans that over the centuries resisted the influence of the Lowland Scots and the English. To the south are the hills of the **Lowlands** and the cities of Edinburgh and Glasgow. Off the west coast are the islands of the **Hebrides**.

North and central **Wales** are also mountainous, and there are few large towns. In the **Snowdonia National Park** Mount Snowdon rises to 3 560 feet (1 085 metres). The dark, jagged hillsides bear the scars of old slate quarries. In south Wales are the more rounded summits of the **Brecon Beacons** and the industrial valleys.

The beautiful and often romantic countryside of Ireland attracts many visitors from Britain. Areas popular with tourists include **Connemara** and **Killarney** in the Republic and the **Giant's Causeway** in Northern Ireland.

In England there are hills, rolling countryside and farmland. In summer the flatter land in the south and east turns yellow with oilseed rape flowers or ripening corn. The hills of the **Lake District** and the moors of North Yorkshire, celebrated in the writings of William Wordsworth and the Brontë sisters, are popular with walkers. Further south, chalk downs form sheer white cliffs where they meet the English Channel. The River Thames rises in the Cotswolds and flows east through Oxford to London and the sea. The **Norfolk Broads**, a large area of rivers and lagoons in East Anglia, are popular for boating and fishing trips.

the Outer Hebrides

Snowdonia

a Welsh slate mine

The British people

a Welsh woman playing a crwth

Orangemen marching through Belfast

Regional loyalties

The United Kingdom consists of four nations, England, Wales, Scotland and Northern Ireland, each with its own special character. Welsh and Scottish people feel their national identity very strongly, and value their cultural heritage. In Wales the Welsh language is used alongside English, and in Scotland over 75 000 people speak Gaelic. There are also many people of Asian, West Indian and African origin living in Britain, who retain some of their former loyalties and cultural traditions.

Until recently, British politics tended to be dominated by England, but both Wales and Scotland now have their own political assemblies, as well as continued representation in the British parliament. In Ireland nationalism has been complicated by religious and political loyalties. Pressure for Irish independence grew during the 19th century and finally led to independence for the south of Ireland in 1921. Northern Ireland remained part of the United Kingdom, a cause of the recent Troubles. After many years of violence a Northern Ireland Assembly was set up in 1998.

Although people move around the country to study or find work, national and regional rivalries based on traditional stereotypes can still be found. The most significant division in England is the **North–South Divide**. It is primarily an economic division between the richer south, particularly the area around London, and the poorer north. Some Londoners dismiss the whole of England north of London as **the provinces** where, they believe, there is little culture. The south likes to think that it is more sophisticated and more outward-looking. But the north can claim many positive things, such as beautiful countryside, a less pressured lifestyle and often cheaper housing. Northerners are also said to be more cheerful and friendly than southerners. Rural north Wales tends to be more traditional than the industrial south, where English influence is stronger. In Scotland, Highland people traditionally regarded people from the Lowlands as untrustworthy and weak. Lowlanders believed Highlanders were more aggressive and less civilized. Perhaps the greatest unifying factor between the two has been a dislike of 'Sassenachs' (= English people).

Life and work

For many British people the ideal place to live is a village set in attractive countryside. To those living in towns villages conjure up images of peace, a slow pace of life, pretty cottages and a country pub. But living in a village may be inconvenient, especially for people without a car, as many village shops have been forced to close and public transport services are limited. Most people now live in towns, in city suburbs or in larger villages which have become **dormitory communities** for nearby towns.

Some cities, such as Bath, Chester, York and London, are very old. Newcastle, Manchester and Birmingham are industrial towns which have had good and bad times according to the changing patterns of industry. New towns like Milton Keynes were built to relieve overcrowding in older cities. Aberdeen, Glasgow, Swansea, Bristol and Liverpool all developed as ports.

Important industries in Britain today include gas and oil production from the North Sea, engineering, pharmaceuticals, textile manufacture, food processing, electronics, tourism and insurance. Along the coasts fishing is an important source of income. Coal mining is now much less widespread than before. Much of the coal produced is used in power stations to generate electricity. The main centres of the steel industry are in south Wales, northern England and the Midlands. Factories are often located together on an industrial estate on the edge of a town. Many service industries are still based in or near London, but modern telecommunications have allowed companies to move to places where rents are cheaper and there are people needing jobs.

fishermen in Scotland

a coal-fired power station in Yorkshire

Milldale, a village in Staffordshire

a steelworks in Cleveland

an industrial estate near Aberdeen

New York

Manhattan

There is a great sense of excitement in New York and it has a reputation for being 'the city that never sleeps'. The '**Big Apple**', as it is sometimes called, feels alive, fast and at the centre of everything, with cars hooting, yellow taxis weaving through the traffic, brightly lit theatres, and restaurants busy late into the night. The city offers enormous contrasts. Some of the most expensive homes in the world are in New York City, but on the pavements outside are poor people without a home. It is possible to pay hundreds of dollars for a meal in a restaurant, or eat good, filling food for a couple of dollars from a street vendor.

Many Americans have never been to New York, but everyone knows something about the city. They are familiar with the tall **Manhattan skyline**, **Times Square** with its brightly lit advertisements, **Madison Square Gardens**, where many sports events take place, **Wall Street**, its financial heart, the **Empire State Building**, the **Statue of Liberty**, and **Ellis Island**, where many of their ancestors first arrived in the US.

The growth of the city

New York was founded in 1624 by the Dutch, who called it **New Amsterdam**. Its Dutch origins can be seen in the names of old New York families like Stuyvesant and Vanderbilt, and in place names such as Brooklyn (originally Breukelen) and Harlem. In 1664 the English gained control and changed the name to New York. In 1898 several towns were combined to make Greater New York City, which became the second largest city in the world, after London, though at the time part of it consisted of farms. Soon after, many new buildings were constructed, and in 1904 the New York **subway** was opened.

Many immigrants to the US stayed in New York, giving the city the variety of cultures it has today. During the 1920s New York had many speakeasies (= bars serving alcohol), which were illegal but very popular. This was also the time of the **Harlem Renaissance**, when Harlem became a centre for African-American arts and culture. In the latter half of the century wealthier people began moving out to the suburbs. Today there are about 7 million people in the city and 18 million in the area around it.

New Yorkers speak in a very direct way which can seem rude to people from other parts of the US. Some have little patience with visitors who are not used to the fast pace of the city. But for many visitors, meeting real, rude New Yorkers is part of the attraction of going to the city.

London

The capital city of England and the United Kingdom lies on the **River Thames**, which winds through the city. Its many bridges are a famous sight. The oldest is **London Bridge**, originally made of wood but rebuilt in stone in 1217. The most distinctive is **Tower Bridge**, which was designed to blend in with the nearby **Tower of London**.

The Tower, which is guarded by the Yeomen Warders, was built in the 11th century. In the medieval period London grew rapidly in size and importance. **Westminster Abbey** and the **Guildhall** date from this time, and the **Palace of Westminster** became the meeting place of Parliament. In 1666 many buildings were destroyed in the Fire of London. This provided an opportunity for architects like Christopher Wren to redesign much of the city. As London's population increased, new streets, squares and parks were added, and many public buildings. London was heavily bombed in World War II, after which a new cycle of rebuilding began.

Culture and commerce

London is a busy commercial and cultural centre. Many important financial organizations, including the Bank of England and the Stock Exchange, are located in the area called the **City**. Part of the old port in east London has been redeveloped as a business centre, called **Docklands**. In the **West End** there are theatres, cinemas, museums and shops. Many people who work in London commute by train or bus from the suburbs because buying a house or flat near the centre is very expensive. Different parts of the city are linked by the famous red London buses, black taxi cabs and the London Underground, often called '**the Tube**'.

People from all over the world have been attracted to London and it is now a cosmopolitan, multicultural city. People from other parts of Britain sometimes think that it is very noisy and dirty. Many go there only for the 'bright lights' – the theatres round **Shaftesbury Avenue** or the shops of **Oxford Street**. Others take their children to see the sights, such as **Buckingham Palace**, where the Queen lives, and the clock tower from which **Big Ben** sounds the hours. Young people are attracted to the bars and comedy clubs of **Covent Garden**, to live music concerts, and to the stalls of **Camden market**. In the year 2000 many people will visit the **Millennium Dome**.

the River Thames, Tower Bridge and part of London

The history of the US

Dawson City, Canada, a Klondike gold rush town, c. 1898

picking cotton, South Carolina

black soldiers of the Northern army attacking Fort Wagner in the Civil War

The beginning of a nation

Before the first Europeans came to North America Native Americans, sometimes called Indians, were living there. Modern America was created by the early European settlers and by the many immigrants who followed them.

The first colony in North America was founded in 1607 at Jamestown, Virginia, by the British. In 1620 the **Pilgrims** arrived at Plymouth, Massachusetts, on the ship *Mayflower*. By the late 18th century there were **13 colonies**. Over time the colonists were unhappy about having laws and taxes imposed by Britain and began to want more control over their affairs. The War of Revolution broke out in 1775, and the following year the colonists wrote the **Declaration of Independence**, which explained their reasons for wanting to be separate from Britain. At times it seemed likely that the colonies would lose the war, but in late 1781 the British surrendered.

Creating a single government for the 13 colonies was not easy, as each was afraid of giving the others too much power. A **Constitutional Convention** was held, and in 1787 the **Founding Fathers**, among them Thomas Jefferson, George Washington and Benjamin Franklin, wrote the **Constitution**, which set out how the new **United States** would be governed.

Changing borders

In the early days of the US many people believed in **manifest destiny**, the idea that the US was meant to extend its influence over the whole continent. Sometimes the US bought land, as with the **Louisiana Purchase** of 1803, when France sold its territory in North America. But the US fought a war against Mexico to win land in the South-west, and took land by force from Native Americans.

Pioneers moved west to find new land to farm and lived a hard life on the **frontier**. Away from centres of government, there was little law enforcement. This led to the famous image of the **Wild West** and stories of sheriffs involved in gun battles with violent criminals.

During the **gold rush**, many people moved to California and later to the **Klondike** in Canada. Some went as **prospectors**, but many others found that they could make smaller but safer profits selling supplies.

As new lands were settled and became states, the issue of slavery became important. In the southern states slaves worked on the **cotton plantations**. In the North slavery was illegal. Feelings about slavery grew stronger on both sides until, in 1861, the southern states withdrew from the US and formed the **Confederated States of America**. The South fought a long **Civil War** against the North, but in 1865 the North won. The South again became part of the US and slavery was made illegal everywhere. The bitter feelings that the war caused, especially in the South, were not easily overcome and may sometimes still be felt today.

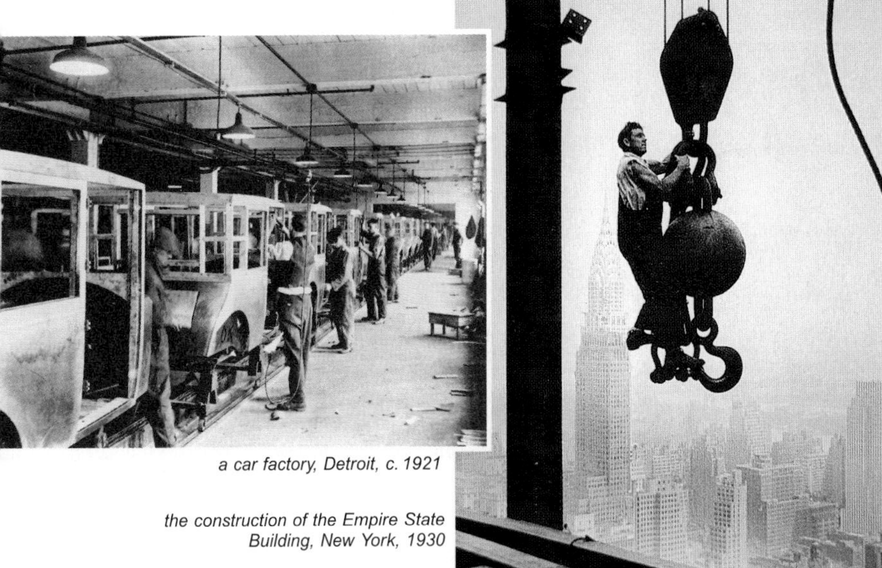

a car factory, Detroit, c. 1921

the construction of the Empire State Building, New York, 1930

The 20th century

Industrial development had helped the North to win the Civil War, and after the war industry continued to grow. Many factory workers were **immigrants** who came to the US looking for a better life. Working conditions were often hard and dangerous. In the early 1900s labor unions tried to change the law so that employers paid a decent wage and factories were safer.

The wealthy now had the opportunity to buy cars. There was a wide choice of makes by David Buick, Henry Ford and Walter Chrysler. The early 1900s was also a time of building. In Chicago and New York **skyscrapers** were constructed. The Chrysler corporation built its new headquarters, the now famous Chrysler Building, and soon after, in 1929, just before the beginning of the **Great Depression**, work began on the Empire State Building, for many years the tallest building in the world.

The next decades were difficult ones for the US. Americans had long believed they should not become involved in foreign wars, though they had entered World War I. As the Depression was ending, the US became involved in World War II. After the war, soldiers returned home to a very different America. Factories were producing many more goods to buy. Women who had worked during the war wanted to keep their jobs. African Americans and Native Americans, who had fought alongside white soldiers, began to demand equal rights. Soon, America was opposing the USSR in the **Cold War**. US soldiers were involved in restricting Soviet influence in Korea, and in 1962 the US had Soviet weapons removed from Cuba. America was also becoming involved in **Vietnam**. In 1963, however, the assassination of President Kennedy shocked the world. Under President Johnson, US troops were sent to Vietnam to push back the Communist forces. There was strong opposition to the Vietnam War, and as fighting continued protests became louder. Finally, in 1972 a ceasefire was negotiated, and the US pulled out of the war.

In the 1960s there were many social changes. Laws were introduced to end **segregation** and permit African Americans to use restaurants, schools, etc. previously reserved for Whites. Recreational drug use increased, and moral standards became more relaxed. Clothing also changed: women's skirts became very short, and both men and women began to wear jeans, once considered appropriate only for heavy work. In the 1980s there was a reaction to these liberal ideas, but the changes of the 1960s and 1970s have had a lasting effect, and as America enters the new millennium, almost everyone accepts the principles of equal rights and opportunity, and considerable personal freedom.

the assassination of President Kennedy in Dallas, Texas, 1963

The history of Britain

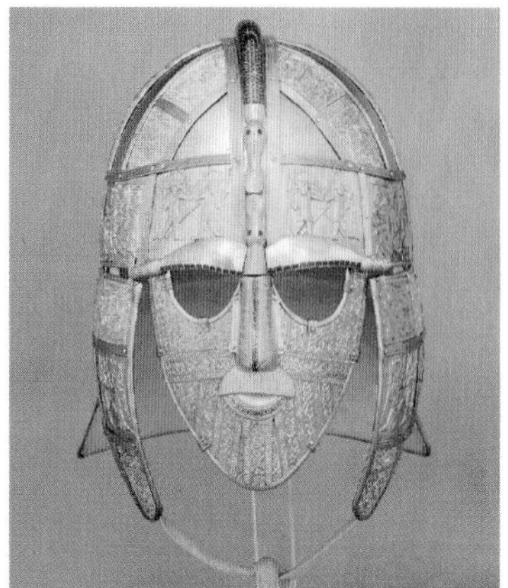

a 7th-century silver and gold helmet from Sutton Hoo

a man ploughing with oxen, from a 14th-century manuscript

Invaders and settlers

Archaeological evidence for British history dates back to the early Stone Age, before 12000 BC, though most evidence dates from 4000 BC. After the **Romans** came to Britain in 55 BC they defeated many of the Celtic tribes and created the province of **Britannia**. From this time archaeological evidence is supplemented by written evidence.

In the early 5th century **Anglo-Saxons** came from Germany and Scandinavia. They founded the kingdoms of East Anglia, Essex, Kent, Mercia, Northumbria, Sussex and Wessex, and confined the British tribes to Wales, the west of England and southern Scotland. Archaeological finds from Anglo-Saxon period include the treasures of **Sutton Hoo** in East Anglia.

From 800 AD the **Vikings** began to raid Britain. The Anglo-Saxons fought fiercely against them and they were confined to northern England, in an area that became known as the **Danelaw**. By the 10th century all of England, except the Danelaw, was one kingdom under the kings of Wessex. In 1066, one of the most famous dates in English history, England was again invaded, and **William the Conqueror**, a Norman duke, defeated King Harold II at the **Battle of Hastings** to become king. Shortly afterwards, a survey of land ownership was carried out in order to calculate the value of lands belonging to king and his barons (= lords), and the results were recorded in the **Domesday Book**.

Royalty, parliament and religion

Although the dates of kings and queens form a framework for British history, since the 13th century the powers of the monarch have been reduced. In 1215 King John was forced to sign the **Magna Carta**, a document giving the barons greater power. The word *parliament* was used to describe meetings of the king and the barons. The king had also to meet with representatives from the counties to raise taxes. The barons became known as the **House of Lords** and the people from the counties as the **House of Commons**.

During the medieval period monasteries were centres of learning. Monks prepared elaborately illustrated manuscripts, and in Jarrow **Bede** wrote a history of England.

One of the most famous English kings was Henry VIII. He divorced his first wife against the wishes of the Pope, and this led to a break with the Roman Catholic Church. Protestant ideas from central Europe influenced the founding of the **Church of England**, and monasteries were closed down. Henry's daughter, Elizabeth I, supported the Church of England, but her cousin, Mary, Queen of Scots, was executed for plotting with Spain to restore the Catholic church. This led to war with Spain, but the **Spanish Armada**, a fleet of ships sent to invade England, was defeated. Elizabeth's successor, James I, was hated by many Catholics, and on 5 November 1605 a group of them devised the **Gunpowder Plot**, an attempt to kill him while he was in Parliament.

James's son, Charles I, was often in conflict with Parliament, and after many disputes **civil war** broke out. The **royalists** were defeated and Charles was put on trial for waging war against his people. He was found guilty and beheaded. England was then ruled by a general, Oliver Cromwell, who dissolved Parliament and became **Lord Protector of England**. After his death the army invited Charles I's son, also called Charles, to return as king.

Religious conflict continued throughout the 17th century, but in 1689 the **Bill of Rights** laid down that only a Protestant could become king. This did not prevent the **Jacobites** trying to make the Catholic, James Stuart, king in 1715, and supporting Bonny Prince Charlie in 1745.

Henry VIII, painted by Hans Holbein

the Industrial Revolution, in a painting by W B Scott

In the early 18th century party politics became important. Later, there were attempts to rearrange parliamentary constituencies and to increase the number of people entitled to vote. In 1832 the first **Reform Act** was passed, but it took another hundred years before all adults were given the vote. At the end of the 20th century parliamentary reform continues to be an issue, as the House of Lords is being restructured.

A world power

In Elizabethan times the voyages of Francis Drake and Walter Raleigh encouraged people to set up trading posts and found colonies around the world. The earliest colonies were in North America and the Caribbean.

Although in 1783 Britain lost her American colonies she added India and Australia to the developing **British Empire**. In the 19th century several regions of Africa became part of the Empire, as European countries divided up the continent between them. The Empire was a source of pride and also wealth for Britain. The country was in the midst of the **industrial revolution**, and the colonies provided raw materials for the developing industries and were a market for the goods produced.

At the beginning of the 20th century there was fresh rivalry between Britain and Germany. This was one of many factors which led to the outbreak of **World War I**. Meanwhile, Ireland was demanding home rule, and other British territories began to seek independence. In the 1930s the Nazis became powerful in Germany, and Britain became involved in **World War II**.

In the 1950s and 1960s most of the remaining countries of the Empire became independent, but retained their links with Britain through the **Commonwealth**. In 1956 the **Suez crisis** showed how Britain's power had been reduced. She relied on support from the US, but also became involved in European affairs, and in 1973 joined the European Economic Community (now the European Union).

the peoples of the British Empire, painted by an unknown artist

Building styles and materials

Houses and public buildings in Britain and the US have been built in a range of styles and materials. Old and new stand side by side. In Britain there are timber-framed houses, buildings of brick or stone, and modern concrete and glass structures.

Many US architectural styles came originally from Europe. The South-west has many buildings in the Spanish **colonial** or **mission** style. The **federal** style borrowed elements from ancient Rome, and the façades and columns of **Greek revival** buildings are reminiscent of Greek temples.

a timber-framed Tudor house, Warwickshire

a clapboard house in Lexington, Massachusetts

Wooden buildings

In Britain most houses before the Norman Conquest had a timber frame filled in with **wattle and daub**, sticks plastered together with mud. The development of more sophisticated timber-framed houses became possible when brick and stone were used as **infilling** between the timber supports. This allowed the framework to be more open and decorative. Many Tudor and Elizabethan **timber-framed houses**, in which the wooden beams are visible from the outside, still stand. Glass was expensive, so only the rich could afford windows. In the 1980s there was a fashion for modern houses with wooden features in the Tudor style.

In pre-Columbian North America people used local timber to build houses, and settlers arriving from Europe copied them. Later, in New England especially, the heavy wooden framework of a house was covered with horizontal planking called **clapboarding** (*BrE* **weatherboarding**). Clapboard houses sometimes have a wood **shingle** (= tile) roof and brick chimneys. Inside the house the wood frame may be exposed. In the South **plantation houses** had wide verandahs supported on columns.

Wood has been used in church architecture for carved screens, elaborate roof supports, and sometimes for steeples.

Solid stone

In Britain, early structures like Stonehenge were built of massive blocks of stone. Later, stone was used to build city walls and castles. From the 13th century, **stonemasons** constructed increasingly ornate churches in the **English Gothic** style. The later, more **classical** style of architects like Wren and Gibbs was copied in churches in the US.

Many of the finest stone buildings in Britain were the homes of the aristocracy. These **stately homes** were designed for comfort as well as to impress. Bare stone walls were hidden behind wooden panelling, tapestries and paintings. The elegant **Palladian** style, influenced by the architecture of Greece, became fashionable in the 17th and 18th centuries and can be seen in the simple lines of houses like Holkham Hall. Castle Howard and Blenheim Palace were built in the more elaborate **baroque** style.

In the US stone was little used until the 19th century. In New York a local sandstone was widely used to build **brownstone** houses. The US Capitol and the Supreme Court building in Washington, DC are built with Pennsylvanian **marble**.

marble in the Greek style: the Supreme Court, Washington, DC

brick and stucco: a bank in Key West, Florida

brick, metal and glass: Liverpool Street Station, London

Decorated brickwork

Clay **bricks** were used for building early cliff houses in New Mexico and Colorado. More recently brick has been used for plantation houses and smaller homes, for public buildings such as banks, and for churches and factories. Brick buildings are sometimes decorated with bricks of a different colour or with **stucco** (= plaster). Independence Hall in Philadelphia is built of brick with white stone decoration.

In Britain the most impressive brick building is Hampton Court Palace, built in the early 16th century. Among its most striking features are the elaborately shaped and patterned chimneys. In Victorian times British towns grew rapidly in size, and brick was used for railway stations, town halls, factories and rows of terrace houses. Victorian universities, such as the University of Birmingham, have become known as 'red-brick universities'.

skyscrapers in Chicago, Illinois

The concrete age

Iron was used in the Middle Ages to strengthen stone structures, but in the 18th century it became an architectural material in its own right. The first iron bridge was built at Coalbrookdale in 1779, and iron was later used in the construction of factories. In structures such as Crystal Palace and the glasshouses at Kew Gardens an iron frame held in place the glass walls and roof. At Liverpool Street Station in London the iron and glass roof is supported by a brick end wall and decorated iron pillars.

Reinforced concrete, which is made of a mesh of steel with concrete over it, can be grey and monotonous, but it gives architects more scope to create curves. Columns of reinforced concrete can support ceilings from a central point, which means that walls no longer have to take the weight of the building and can be of lighter materials. This encouraged the development of **open-plan** buildings. In the US architects like Ludwig Mies van der Rohe and Frank Lloyd Wright designed open-plan houses with a steel frame and glass walls, which gave them a light and spacious feel.

Steel frames covered in concrete were used to build **skyscrapers**. Glass was used for the **curtain walls**. The invention of lifts/elevators made such tall buildings practicable.

Architects continue to experiment with new materials and techniques. London's **Millennium Dome**, for instance, is a circular canopy of steel netting covered with glass fibre and coated with Teflon, supported by 12 steel masts and cables.

a model of the Millennium Dome, London

Houses in the US

a ranch-style house, Rhode Island

American homes

In the US there is plenty of space, except in big cities, so many houses are large and have a lot of garden around them. Most are **detached** (= not joined to another house), but there are also **duplexes**, which are similar to British semi-detached houses. **Ranch-style** houses are built on one floor only. **Mansions** are very large houses where rich people live.

Some types of house are associated with certain parts of the country. New York City, for instance, is famous for its **brownstones**, tall, narrow buildings named after the material used to build them. New England has **clapboard** houses, and in some cities there are **row houses**, similar to British terraces. In the Midwest there are many wooden **frame houses** with pointed roofs. The South has large wooden houses built before the Civil War in the **antebellum** style. But all over the US houses are built in many different styles.

Many Americans prefer to live in **suburbs** rather than in a city centre, in order to have a pleasant environment and plenty of space. They often live on **housing developments**, areas where all the houses were built at the same time and are similar in style. Most of the 97 million households in the US have a home with at least five rooms and more than one bathroom. Most also have a **front yard** (= garden) and a **back yard**.

In the cities many people rent an **apartment** in an **apartment building**. Apartments usually have no more than three bedrooms, and are often rented furnished. An apartment with only one room may be called a **studio** or a **loft**. A building in which the apartments are owned by the people who live in them is called a **condominium** or, in some places, a **co-op**.

Poor people may live in apartments in **tenements** (= large old buildings) in the downtown area of a city, in small, very basic houses or in **mobile homes**. Despite the name, many people keep their mobile home in a **trailer park** and never move it.

Space for living

A typical US house has two **storeys** or **floors**. Upstairs there are several bedrooms and at least one bathroom. The parents share the **master bedroom**, which may have its own bathroom attached. Children often have their own bedrooms. Extra rooms are used as a study or playroom or as guest bedrooms. Downstairs there is a kitchen, a living room and a dining room. There is usually also a bathroom or a **half bath**, which has only a toilet and sink (*BrE* washbasin). Many houses have a **porch** (= covered area outside the house) where people sit when the weather is hot. Americans take pride in their homes and like to show visitors round.

a detached house, California

a suburban house, Florida

sitting on the porch, California

Bedrooms are usually considered the private space of the people who sleep in them, and children are allowed a great deal of freedom in their bedrooms. Parents usually knock before entering. Children are given the responsibility of cleaning their rooms, and the right to decide when that is necessary. This often leads to disagreement between parents and children.

In summer **screens** are put in doorways and windows, which allow fresh air to come in but keep insects out. Most houses have **air-conditioning**. In winter screens are replaced with glass **storm doors** and **storm windows** to keep the cold out. Central heating is standard, but many houses also have **fireplaces** where wood can be burned.

a group of mobile homes, California

To buy or to rent?

Americans often move home from one city to another. Finding a new place to live is not difficult, except when moving to a very large city. It is usually possible to find an apartment to rent one day and to move into it the next.

About 65% of US homes are owned by the people who live in them. The costs of buying and selling are relatively low. People thinking of buying a house ask a **real estate agent**, or **realtor**, to show them several houses. When they decide on one, they discuss the price with the people who are selling it, and then arrange a **mortgage** (= loan) with a bank.

People look for different kinds of homes at different points in their lives. Students and young professional people tend to live in apartments near city centres. When people get married and have children they often move out of the city and buy a house in a suburb. In most suburbs it is possible to tell how much money people have by the size of their houses and yards. In some parts of the US it is also possible to guess the racial background of the person living in a house. Although it is illegal to practise racial discrimination, there is still segregation in many cities since white people tend to live in some areas and black people in others.

Houses in Britain

a pair of semi-detached houses, Oxfordshire

terraced houses, South Wales

Choosing where to live

Towns and cities in Britain have grown a lot in size over the last two centuries. The oldest houses are usually those closest to the town centre. Many people live in the **suburbs**, areas on the edge of a town. Some suburbs consist of new **housing estates**, while others were originally villages that have become joined to the town as it has grown.

Some people prefer to live in a village and travel into the nearby town to work. Villages are considered to be pleasant places to live, as they are quieter and less polluted than towns and are closer to the countryside. They usually contain a range of houses, including old cottages and new houses and bungalows.

Many British people prefer to buy a house rather than renting one, because they can decorate or alter it to suit their own taste and because they believe they will have more privacy. Young people and those who cannot afford to buy a house live in rented accommodation. Some rent a furnished **bedsit** (or **bed-sitting room**), a combined bedroom and sitting room, and share washing and cooking facilities. Others rent a flat or house, often sharing the cost with friends.

Houses are bought and sold through **estate agents**. Few people can afford to buy a house outright, so they have to take out a **mortgage** (= loan) with a bank or building society.

Houses, bungalows and flats

Most houses are built of brick with a tiled roof, though some, especially in the country, are built of stone. The largest and most expensive type of house is a **detached** house, which is not joined to other houses and has a garden all round it. Detached houses have at least three bedrooms and one or two bathrooms upstairs, and one or more living rooms plus a separate dining room and kitchen downstairs. Many large Victorian houses with three or four **floors** or **storeys** have now been converted into several **flats**.

Semi-detached houses, or **semis**, are extremely common. They are built in pairs with one house joined to the other along one side. These houses usually have two or three bedrooms. There is a separate garden at the front and the back for each house.

Terraced houses date from Victorian and Edwardian times (the late 19th and early 20th century) and were built mainly for working-class people. Four or more houses are joined together in a row. There is little or no front garden, so the front door of each house opens onto the pavement. Access to the back garden is through the house. Terraced houses were originally quite small. They had two bedrooms, a sitting room and a kitchen/ dining room, an arrangement called 'two up, two down'. Most have now been extended and bathrooms added, and in some towns they have become fashionable with professional people.

a thatched cottage, Dorset

a bungalow, Oxfordshire

Cottages are small, very old village houses. Some have thatched roofs. Many have been modernized inside but still keep the wooden beams and other features that are thought to give them character. Some people think of a country cottage as their dream home. **Bungalows** have only one storey, and this makes them especially popular with older people. They are mostly found in villages or on housing estates.

High-rise **blocks of flats**, sometimes over 20 storeys high with several flats on each floor, were built in many towns in the mid 20th century. Many have since been pulled down because they needed a lot of repairs and because people did not like living in them.

Space for living

Houses in Britain often seem small for the number of people living in them. In some cities house prices are very high so people cannot afford to move to a larger house as the size of their family increases. In many families with more than two children some of the children have to share a bedroom and only get a room of their own when an older brother or sister leaves home. Very often all the family shares one bathroom. In many houses there is only one living room plus a kitchen with a dining area. Some houses have two small living rooms. Children often play and do homework in their bedrooms.

In order to overcome the problem of lack of space some people have a **loft conversion** to make a new bedroom in the roof space. Others add an extra room or bathroom downstairs. There is often not much space to extend because neighbours' houses are close. In warm weather people like to sit outside on the patio (= a small concreted area) or in the garden.

a family at home

Possessions

an American family with some of their possessions, Texas

In these two photographs the possessions of a white American family and a white British family are laid out for the photographer in front of their houses. It is interesting to see which possessions each family has chosen to display, and what item they treasure most. The possessions are a mixture of furniture and appliances considered essential for modern American or British life, and more personal things such as books, sports equipment and pictures.

The photographs are from a set of pictures taken in countries throughout the world to show differences in quantity and type of possessions between families typical of each country. They were taken in 1993–4 for the book *Material World* by Peter Menzel, published to celebrate the United Nations' International Year of the Family.

The American family

The American family consists of a mother and father and their two children, aged 7 and 10. They are dressed casually but well. They live in a suburban ranch-style house with a garden around it in a town in Texas. The US flag flies on the front of the double garage, between two deer heads, which are hunting trophies. The family owns two smart cars and also a dune buggy. They have a bicycle each.

There are comfortable beds, sofas and chairs, and matching wooden furniture from each room of the house. Kitchen appliances include a washing machine, a dryer and a dishwasher, and various electrical gadgets. There are two televisions and a stereo system. Personal possessions used for leisure activities include a piano and a guitar, and two sewing machines. There are various toys including balls and a doll's house (*AmE* dollhouse). A display of family photographs is very prominent. There are a number of books around, and more on a bookcase visible inside the house. The mother is holding the family's most valued possession, a Bible. Tied to a fire hydrant, one of the father's souvenirs, is the family's pet dog.

a British family with some of their possessions, Surrey

The British family

The British family also consists of two parents and their two children, aged 13 and 15. The parents are dressed in casual but good quality clothes and their children are in school uniform. They live in a suburban semi-detached house in a town in southern England. They have two cars, and each member of the family has a bicycle.

In the front garden and on the road there is a selection of furniture and kitchen appliances, and a television, stereo system and radio. There are also lamps, pictures, ornaments and vases of flowers. A traditional tea with crumpets is laid out on the table. The family has put out many personal possessions, which illustrate their hobbies and interests. The father is holding the tiller of his sailing dinghy, which is parked in front of the house next door. This is the family's most valued possession. Nearby there is gardening equipment and a barbecue. A cricket bat and pads and a boogie board are displayed in front of the garage. There is an exercise machine on the path and a squash racket leaning against the blanket chest. The elder daughter is holding her flute.

Clothes

a knight and his lady, 14th century

men's clothing, early 17th century

Medieval costume

For many years style and quality of clothing were dependent on social status and wealth. Before medieval times most people in Britain wore plain woollen clothes. The main garment was a long **tunic** fastened by a belt, and covered in cold weather by a **cloak**. In the 11th and 12th centuries differences in clothing between nobles and the common people became more noticeable. Women's dresses began to have more shape and style. They reached the ground and often had long hanging sleeves. Rich people lined their cloaks with fur. When knights returned from the Crusades they brought new fashions and materials from the Middle East. Men began to wear coloured tunics and **stockings**, and long pointed shoes.

Elaborate or plain?

During the 15th century noblemen wore fur-trimmed **gowns** over **doublet and hose** (= a short two-piece tunic with stockings). Pointed shoes were replaced by shoes with wide square toes. Men's clothing was often padded and made more splendid with embroidery and jewels. Slashes in the sleeves or bodice revealed a coloured silk lining beneath. Cloaks became shorter and hats were decorated with jewels and plumes. Noblewomen wore elaborate velvet gowns, split at the front to reveal an embroidered underskirt. A **farthingale** worn under the dress held out the wide skirt. Most women, and some men, wore **corsets** to control their figure, and women's dresses had a stiff central piece called a **stomacher**. Both men and women wore high collars and **ruffs**.

In the mid 17th century noblemen wore short jackets with slashed sleeves, knee-length trousers called **breeches** and high-heeled boots with spurs. To these they often added a lace collar and a broad-brimmed hat decorated with long plumes. Women's dresses became softer and more flowing.

The **Puritans** believed that people should dress simply, and they wore plain black and white clothing. Men wore tall black hats and white **stocks** (= neckbands). Puritans were among the early colonists of North America, so this style influenced American clothing.

At the end of the 17th century men began to wear the predecessor of the modern three-piece suit, a long collarless **coat**, a **waistcoat** and breeches, and a long wig. Women wore low necklines and looped back their dresses to reveal the underskirt. Cotton was used increasingly, especially for underclothes such as the **shift**, a long shirt worn by both sexes.

Puritan-style clothes, mid 17th century

a wealthy family, mid 18th century

A more casual age

During World War I many women had jobs, and their clothes needed to be more practical. They began wearing shorter skirts and bared their legs. Soon they began wearing trousers. The lively, outrageous **flapper style** of the 1920s included lower waistlines, long necklaces and short hair. Men's suits became looser and were worn with a long tie.

During the 1960s women wore **miniskirts**, and **jeans** and **T-shirts** became popular with both sexes. Women's shoes appeared in many colours and styles, including **sandals** and **platforms** (= shoes with a thick sole and high heel). Since then, fashions have continued to change rapidly, and young people, especially, are quick to wear the latest styles.

The 18th and 19th centuries

In the 18th century wealthy men wore waistcoats, breeches and **stockings** under long **frock coats** with deep cuffs, as well as plumed **tricorne** (= three-cornered) hats and buckled shoes. Women's dresses were worn over hoop **petticoats**, with a small **apron** and lace cap. Both sexes wore white powdered wigs and used make-up. Later, aristocratic women wore silk dresses with **sack-backs** (= lengths of material descending from the shoulders to the ground). Wigs disappeared after a tax was put on hair powder. Meanwhile, agricultural workers wore **smocks** (= loose shirts), while peasant women wore simple wool dresses.

In the early 19th century women wore low-necked, high-waisted Regency-style dresses made of muslin. Men wore close-fitting tailed **jackets** with padded shoulders and high collars. The **top hat** had by now replaced the tricorne, and by 1825 full-length **trousers** had replaced knee breeches and stockings. Breeches were still worn for country sports.

After the Revolutionary War people in America were able to get news of European fashions. **Fashion plates** (= pictures) and dolls showing the latest fashions were sent to the US, and American women began wearing large hoop skirts. Some people thought that heavy hoops and corsets were bad for the health, and encouraged women to wear looser clothes. Amelia Bloomer designed light frilled trousers, called **bloomers**, but many people laughed at them. Though bloomers were not popular, there was a fashion for smaller, lighter skirts. American men also followed fashion and began wearing long trousers (or **pants**) instead of breeches.

In the Victorian period men still wore frock coats but, for less formal occasions, changed into short **lounging jackets** worn with narrow trousers and a **bow tie**. For women, full dresses came back into fashion, held out from the body by a **crinoline** (= a frame worn under the skirt). These were later replaced by the **bustle**, a padded roll wrapped around the hips. Towards the end of the period women began wearing narrower skirts and two-piece **costumes** with corsets. They wore caps indoors and **bonnets** outside.

men's walking and sports clothes, late 19th century

women's fashions, 1933

Shops and shopping

a traditional grocer's shop on the Isle of Man

a street market in southern England

a supermarket, Florida

For many people in both Britain and the US shopping is a popular leisure activity. Women, especially, may let a shopping trip fill an entire day. People often go **window-shopping** without intending to buy anything, and may be tempted into buying goods that they do not really need. Other people, especially men, consider shopping tedious.

Two expressions, *the customer is king* and *the customer is always right*, show how Americans, and to a lesser extent British people, expect to be treated when they shop. People like to look around freely, touch things and try clothes on. Book stores have comfortable chairs where people can sit and read, and often also a café. People expect to have a wide choice of goods, and most stores have several different **makes** or **brands** of each item. Price is also important. People look for **special offers** or wait to buy something in a **sale**, when the prices of most goods are reduced. Some people cut **coupons** out of newspapers and magazines to get money off products. Most stores give a high priority to customers' comfort and convenience, because they want to make it easy and fun for them to spend their time and money in the store.

Shopping for food

Years ago, every British town had a range of small shops, including a **grocer**, a **butcher**, a **greengrocer** and a **newsagent**. Many of these specialist shops have gone out of business because large **supermarkets** or **superstores**, such as Sainsbury's and Tesco, can charge lower prices. Many supermarkets are on the edge of town and people need a car to get to them. People who do not own a car may find shopping difficult. Some villages still have a **post office and general store**, and in towns there are usually several **corner shops** and **mini-markets** selling food and other items. Petrol stations often have a small shop selling food.

In the US people may drive half an hour or more to a supermarket, and so buy food to last them a long time.

Mall of America, Minnesota

Quincy market in Boston, Massachusetts

Between trips, they buy food at small **grocery stores** or **convenience stores** close to where they live. Some are a part of big **chains**, some are **mom-and-pop stores** run by a family, others sell oriental or other foreign foods. Convenience stores are more expensive than supermarkets.

In the US many food stores are open 24 hours a day, every day of the week. Others are open until at least 11 p.m. In Britain supermarkets may stay open for 24 hours on some days, but most food shops close at 9 p.m. or earlier.

Many British people buy fruit and vegetables at a **market** because they are cheaper than in the supermarket. By contrast, food sold in markets in the US is usually more expensive. Many markets also sell clothes and household goods.

Town centres and shopping malls

In Britain town centre shops are busiest at weekday lunchtimes and on Saturdays. Most of the shops are **chain stores** or **department stores** which sell clothes, shoes and things for the home. Prices are fixed, and most items have a price tag attached. Many towns have a covered shopping **arcade** or **precinct**, or an **out-of-town shopping centre** with branches of all the major stores.

Americans used formerly to shop in the **downtown** areas of cities. In places like New York and Philadelphia there is still plenty of choice in downtown shopping, but elsewhere downtown shops have lost business to **shopping malls**, which people go to by car. A typical mall has one or more **anchor stores**, well-known stores which attract people in. The Mall of America in Minnesota is one of the largest, with 400 stores on four levels.

Outlet malls have stores selling products at lower prices than in ordinary stores. The goods may be **seconds** (= items with a slight fault), or have failed to sell during the previous season. In Britain outlet stores can usually be found in out-of-town **shopping villages**.

Second-hand shopping

Many people buy second-hand books, clothes, toys and household goods. Most towns have at least one **second-hand shop** run by a charity, to which people give things they no longer want so that they can be sold to raise money for the charity. Other second-hand shops sell things on behalf of people and give them part of the sale price. People also buy and sell things through the classified advertisements columns in newspapers.

In the US **garage sales** and **yard sales** also enable people to sell things they no longer want. Many people make a hobby out of going to garage sales to look for bargains. In Britain **car boot sales** are equally popular. Sometimes people organize a **jumble sale** (*AmE* **rummage sale**) to raise money for a school or charity.

Distance shopping

Mail-order shopping has a long tradition in the US. In the days when people were moving west many people lived a long way from any shops. The solution was the **Sears and Roebuck catalogue**, a thick book giving descriptions of every kind of product. People sent in their order by mail and the goods arrived the same way. Although Sears stopped producing its catalogue in the 1990s, mail-order shopping is still popular. People can now also browse the products of many companies on the Internet, place an order and pay by credit card. There are several mail-order services in Britain, and shopping on-line, especially for books, is becoming increasingly popular.

Christmas

Christmas decorations at a house in Arkansas

a nativity play in Britain

Christmas Day, 25 December, is celebrated by Christians as the day on which Jesus Christ was born. In Britain **carol services** take place in churches throughout December and children perform **nativity plays**, acting out the stories of Christ's birth. In the US some families have a model **nativity scene** in their house or garden. Many people go to **midnight mass** in church on **Christmas Eve**.

Christmas celebrations

Before Christmas, people send **Christmas cards** to their friends. These often show Santa Claus, angels, holly or snowmen, all traditional symbols of Christmas. People buy **Christmas presents** for their family and friends. Shopping malls are decorated for Christmas from September, though most people do not do their **Christmas shopping** until December. Most towns put up a **Christmas tree**, a fir tree decorated with coloured lights, **baubles** (= shiny balls), **tinsel** and **bows**, and put strings of lights across the streets. For children the highlight of this period is a visit to **Santa Claus**, to tell him what presents they would like.

A few days before Christmas families decorate a Christmas tree in their home. Some hang a **holly wreath** on their front door. Americans, especially, put lights and figures of Santa Claus and snowmen in their gardens.

Presents are wrapped in coloured paper and put under the Christmas tree. Small presents are put into a **stocking**, a long sock that each person hangs near the chimney or at the end of their bed. On Christmas Eve children go to bed full of excitement. On **Christmas morning** many families open their presents together round the Christmas tree.

Families try to get together at Christmas and in preparation most people rush to buy a lot of food and prepare special dishes. In Britain they make or buy **mince pies** and a **Christmas cake**; in the US they make **Christmas cookies**. In Britain **Christmas dinner** usually consists of turkey with many accompanying dishes, followed by **Christmas pudding** (= a rich fruit pudding) and brandy butter. Everyone pulls paper **crackers**, which make a loud bang and contain paper hats, jokes and small toys. In the US people have a special meal, though the dishes vary from family to family.

On the day after Christmas, called **Boxing Day** in Britain, many sports events take place, and in the US large shops begin their sales. Christmas decorations are taken down on **New Year's Day** or, in Britain, any time between New Year and 6 January, the festival of **Epiphany**.

a girl with Santa Claus at Macy's, New York

Church, and was forced by his *barons in 1215 to sign the *Magna Carta, which limited his royal powers. He is the subject of *King John*, an early play by *Shakespeare.

Auˌgustus ˈ**John**[2] /ɔːˌɡʌstəs ˈdʒɒn; *AmE* ˈdʒɑːn/ (1878–1961) a Welsh painter. He worked as an official war artist during *World War I and later became famous for his pictures of women. He also painted many of the leading writers of the time, including George Bernard *Shaw, Thomas *Hardy and W B *Yeats. His sister was Gwen *John.

ˌElton ˈ**John**[3] /ˌeltən ˈdʒɒn; *AmE* ˈdʒɑːn/ (1947–) an English pop singer and piano player, known for wearing unusual clothes and large colourful glasses. He has been popular since the 1970s and his most successful songs have included *Your Song* (1970), *Rocket Man* (1972), *Don't Go Breaking My Heart* (1976) and *Sacrifice* (1989). He was a friend of *Diana, Princess of Wales, and played and sang a special version of his song *Candle in the Wind* at her funeral service. This immediately became the most successful record of all time, with all the profits going to a special charity set up in memory of Princess Diana. Elton John was made a *knight in 1998.

Elton John

ˌGwen ˈ**John**[4] /ˈdʒɒn; *AmE* ˈdʒɑːn/ (1876–1939) a Welsh painter who lived in France for most of her life. She began as a pupil of James McNeill *Whistler and showed his influence by often painting single figures (especially girls) in quiet rooms. Augustus *John was her brother, and he is said to have predicted correctly that in the future she would be considered the better painter of the two.

ˌ***John Brown's*** ˈ***Body*** /braʊnz/ ⇨ BROWN.

ˌ**John** ˈ**Bull** /ˈbʊl/ the name given to an imaginary typical Englishman, representing English people as a whole. He is usually shown in pictures as a fat man with a red face, wearing a top hat, a waistcoat and high boots. He also often has a bulldog, suggesting that he is like the dog in having a brave, fierce and independent character. See also BULLDOG BREED.

John Bull with his bulldog

ˌ**John** ˈ**Deere**™ /ˈdɪə(r); *AmE* ˈdɪr/ a product name of US farm, building and garden vehicles made by Deere and Company. The company was established in 1837 and is now the biggest in the world producing agricultural equipment.

ˌ**John** ˈ**Doe** /ˈdəʊ; *AmE* ˈdoʊ/ **1** a name used in the US to refer to a man whose identity is unknown or who does not want his real name to be made public. This is usually for cases in court or on legal papers. Compare JANE DOE. **2** a name used in the US to refer to a typical ordinary man: *Any John Doe knows that.* Compare JOE BLOGGS.

ˌ**John** ˈ**Hancock** ⇨ HANCOCK.

ˌ**John** ˈ**Hancock** ˌ**Center** /ˈhænkɒk; *AmE* ˈhænkɑːk/ one of the tallest and most impressive buildings in the US, opened in 1969. It is in *Chicago on North Michigan Avenue. The building is of black steel, and the outside has lengths of steel that cross to support it. It is 1 127 feet/344 metres high and has 100 floors.

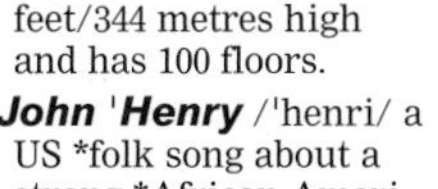

the John Hancock Center (centre back)

ˌ***John*** ˈ***Henry*** /ˈhenri/ a US *folk song about a strong *African American who built railway tracks. It was originally sung by African Americans. John Henry was 'a steel-driving man' who could crush more rocks than a machine. In part of the song

John Henry said to his captain,
'A man ain't nothin' but a man,
And before I'd let your steam drill beat me down,
I'd die with the hammer in my hand, Lord, Lord!
I'd die with the hammer in my hand.'

ˌ**John** ˈ**Lewis** /ˈluːɪs/ a British company that owns a chain of department stores. Employees receive a share of the profits made by the whole company. John Lewis also owns the supermarket chain *Waitrose. The original John Lewis started the company with a small shop in *Oxford Street in London in 1864.

ˌ**Johnnie** ˈ**Walker**™ /ˈwɔːkə(r)/ *n* [U] a make of Scotch *whisky. It is especially popular in the US and is available in several varieties, including Red Label and Black Label.

ˌ**Johnny** ˈ**Reb** /ˈreb/ (*also* **Johnny**) (*AmE infml old use*) any soldier in the *Confederate Army during the American *Civil War. 'Reb' is short for 'rebel'.

ˌ**John of** ˈ**Gaunt** /ˈɡɔːnt/ (1340–99) an English prince who was Duke of Lancaster from 1362. He was the son of *Edward II and acted as the head of government before *Richard II was old enough to be king. His son was *Henry IV. His name refers to his place of birth, which was Ghent, now in Belgium.

ˌ**John o'**ˈ**Groats** /əˈɡrəʊts; *AmE* əˈɡroʊts/ a village in north-east Scotland, traditionally thought of as the most northern point on the British mainland. The name may come from that of Jan de Groot, a Dutchman who is said to have lived there in the 15th century. Compare LAND'S END.

ˌ**John Q** ˈ**Public** (*AmE infml*) a name used to refer to any average person, especially when seen as representing typical public opinion: *What will John Q Public think of higher taxes?*

ˌJasper ˈ**Johns** /ˈdʒɒnz; *AmE* ˈdʒɑːnz/ (1930–) a US artist, known for his paintings of flags (especially the US flag), numbers and targets, done using thick paint textures. With Robert *Rauschenberg he was partly responsible for the move away from *abstract expressionism to *pop art in the late 1950s.

ˌAmy ˈ**Johnson**[1] /ˈdʒɒnsn; *AmE* ˈdʒɑːnsn/ (1903–41) an English pilot who became famous when she flew alone from London to Australia in 1930, winning a £10 000 prize. She followed this by flying alone to Japan in 1931 and to South Africa in 1932. She was killed when her plane crashed off the south-east coast of England.

ˌJack ˈ**Johnson**[2] /ˈdʒɒnsn; *AmE* ˈdʒɑːnsn/ (1878–1946) the first *African-American boxer to become World Heavyweight Champion, when he beat Tommy Burns in 1908 in Sydney, Australia. Johnson was disliked by many white people because he married three white women. He was accused of crimes and left America in 1912. He lost his championship to Jess Willard in 1915 in Havana, Cuba. He returned to the US in 1920 and was sent to prison for eight months. See also GREAT WHITE HOPE.

ˌLyndon B ˈ**Johnson**[3] /ˌlɪndən biː ˈdʒɒnsn; *AmE* ˈdʒɑːnsn/ (Lyndon Baines Johnson 1908–73) the 36th US *President (1963–69) and a member of the *Democratic Party, often referred to informally as LBJ. He was a teacher who was elected to the US Senate (1948–60) and was the Senate Majority Leader (1954–60). He was elected US Vice-president in 1960 and became President when John F *Kennedy was murdered. Johnson was elected again in 1964. As President, he introduced many social changes with his *Great Society programme, which gave special help to *African Americans and poor people. He decided not to stand again for election after increased protests about the *Vietnam War. His wife was Claudia 'Lady Bird' Johnson. See also WAR ON POVERTY.

ˈˌMagic' ˈ**Johnson**[4] /ˈdʒɒnsn; *AmE* ˈdʒɑːnsn/ (1959–) a famous US basketball player who played for the Los Angeles Lakers and was three times named the 'Most Valuable Player' in the National Basketball Association. In 1991 he announced publicly that he had the virus that causes the disease Aids. He has made many speeches about Aids and helped to raise a lot of money for research.

J

ˌMichael ˈ**Johnson**[5] /ˈdʒɒnsn; *AmE* ˈdʒɑːnsn/ (1967–) a US runner who was a star of the 1996 Olympics in *Atlanta. He won gold medals in the 200-metres race (in which he established a new world record) and in the 400-metres race.

ˌSamuel ˈ**Johnson**[6] /ˈdʒɒnsn; *AmE* ˈdʒɑːnsn/ (1709–84) an English writer and critic, often referred to as **Dr Johnson**. He is remembered for his many clever remarks (mostly recorded by his friend James *Boswell, who wrote his life story) and his *Dictionary of the English Language* (1755). Among his other important books are *Rasselas* (1759), which he wrote in a week to pay his mother's funeral expenses, and *The Lives of the Poets* (1779–81). He was an important figure in 18th-century London, and started a club (called simply The Club) with friends such as David *Garrick, Edward *Gibbon and Joshua *Reynolds. He remained poor all his life, but his great reputation as a writer and humorous speaker brought him the honorary title of Doctor from *Oxford University in 1775. His house in London is now a museum.

ˌ**Johns ˈHopkins Uniˌversity** /ˌdʒɒnz ˈhɒpkɪnz; *AmE* ˌdʒɑːnz ˈhɑːpkɪnz/ (*also* **Johns Hopkins**) a US university in *Baltimore, *Maryland. In 1997, it had about 5 000 students. It was established in 1867 with money given by Johns Hopkins, a Baltimore businessman, and opened in 1876.

ˌ**Johnson & ˈJohnson** /ˈdʒɒnsn; *AmE* ˈdʒɑːnsn/ a US company which is the world's largest producing health care products, with branches in 50 countries. Its many well-known products include *Band-Aid and *Tylenol. The company was first established in 1886 by Robert Wood Johnson.

ˌBrian ˈ**Johnston** /ˈdʒɒnstən; *AmE* ˈdʒɑnstən/ (1912–94) a popular English radio broadcaster, known informally as 'Johnners'. He was known for his cheerful good humour, especially as one of the presenters of the cricket programme *Test Match Special*. He also presented *Down Your Way* for many years.

ˈ**Joint ˈChiefs of ˈStaff** a US government committee which includes the Chiefs of Staff of the US Army, Navy and Air Force, and the Commandant of the US Marine Corps. It was established in 1942 and advises the US President, the *National Security Council and the Secretary of Defense. In 1989, General Colin *Powell became the first *African American to be the committee's chairperson (= person in charge of meetings).

ˌ**joint resoˈlution** *n* (in the US) a decision that has the approval of both the Senate and the House of Representatives. It becomes a law when signed by the US President or when Congress passes it if the President refuses to sign.

ˌ**Jolly ˈRoger** *n* [usu sing] (especially in former times) the flag of a pirate ship, showing a white skull and crossed bones on a black background. It is sometimes called the 'skull and crossbones'.

ˌAl ˈ**Jolson** /ˈdʒəʊlsn; *AmE* ˈdʒoʊlsn/ (1886–1950) a US singer and actor, born in Lithuania. He performed on *Broadway in the 1920s and painted his face black to pretend to be an *African American. He was in the first sound film, *The *Jazz Singer*. Jolson's sang with great emotion, and his most successful songs included *Swanee*, *Mammy*, *Sonny Boy* and *April Showers*. His story was told in two films, *the Jolson Story* (1946) and *Jolson Sings Again* (1949) with Larry Parks as Jolson.

ˌBobby ˈ**Jones**[1] /ˈdʒəʊnz; *AmE* ˈdʒoʊnz/ (1902–71) a US golf player. He was the most successful amateur player ever, and never became professional. He won the *US Open(1) four times (1923, 1926 and 1929–30). In 1930 he became the only person ever to win the four major competitions, the Amateur and *Open contests in both the US and Britain. Jones also helped to establish the *US Masters Tournament at Augusta, *Georgia.

ˌCasey ˈ**Jones**[2] ⇨ CASEY JONES.

ˌIndiana ˈ**Jones**[3] /ˌɪndiænə ˈdʒəʊnz; *AmE* ˈdʒoʊnz/ a character played by Harrison *Ford in three successful adventure films directed by Steven *Spielberg. They were *Raiders of the Lost Ark* (1981), *Indiana Jones and the Temple of Doom* (1984), and *Indiana Jones and the Last Crusade* (1989). Jones is an archaeologist and regularly gets into exciting, dangerous and sometimes humorous situations.

ˌInigo ˈ**Jones**[4] /ˌɪnɪgəʊ ˈdʒəʊnz; *AmE* ˌɪnɪgoʊ ˈdʒoʊnz/ (1573–1652) an English architect and stage designer who introduced *Palladianism (an Italian style) to Britain. Among his buildings are the Queen's House, *Greenwich, and the squares of *Covent Garden and Lincoln's Inn Fields in London. He also worked with Ben *Jonson to produce masques (= plays with music and dancing) for King *James I.

ˌJim ˈ**Jones**[5] /ˈdʒəʊnz; *AmE* ˈdʒoʊnz/ ⇨ JONESTOWN.

ˈJohn ˈPaul ˈ**Jones**[6] /ˈdʒəʊnz; *AmE* ˈdʒoʊnz/ (1747–92) an American navy officer during the *American Revolution, originally from Scotland. He was known for attacking British ships near the English coast. On one occasion in 1799, when his own ship was badly damaged and he was ordered by the British commander to surrender, he replied, 'Sir, I have not yet begun to fight!' He then captured the British ship before his own ship sank. After the war, Jones served in the Russian navy and then lived in Paris until his death.

ˌQuincy ˈ**Jones**[7] /ˌkwɪnsi ˈdʒəʊnz; *AmE* ˈdʒoʊnz/ (1933–) a US singer who writes music and plays the trumpet. Jones has won *Grammy awards for his albums *The Dude* (1981) and *Back on the Block* (1991). He produced the album *Thriller* (1983) for Michael *Jackson and has worked with such *jazz singers as Ella *Fitzgerald and Ray *Charles.

ˌTom ˈ**Jones**[8] /ˈdʒəʊnz; *AmE* ˈdʒoʊnz/ (1940–) a Welsh popular singer with a strong voice. His hits have included *It's Not Unusual* (1966), *Green Green Grass of Home* (1968) and *Kiss* (1988). In the 1970s he moved to the US where he performs regularly in clubs, though he remains popular in Britain.

ˈ**Jonestown** /ˈdʒəʊnztaʊn; *AmE* ˈdʒoʊnztaʊn/ an agricultural community in Guyana established in 1977 for a US religious group called the People's Temple of the Disciples of Christ by its leader Jim Jones (1933–78). After US Congressman Leo Ryan and four people with him were murdered while visiting Jonestown in 1978, Jones ordered the members of his community to kill themselves with a drink that contained poison. All 913 died, including more than 240 children, and Jones shot himself.

ˌBen ˈ**Jonson** /ˈdʒɒnsn; *AmE* ˈdʒɑːnsn/ (1572–1637) an English writer of plays and poetry. His most famous comedies are **Volpone*, *The *Alchemist* and *Bartholomew Fair* (1614), in which the characters are always trying to trick each other to gain advantage for themselves. Jonson is regarded as the first English *Poet Laureate. He was a friend of *Shakespeare, who acted in some of his plays.

ˌScott ˈ**Joplin** /ˈdʒɒplɪn; *AmE* ˈdʒɑːplɪn/ (1868–1917) an *African American piano player who wrote and helped to develop *ragtime music. His most popular tune was *Maple Leaf Rag* (1899). He also wrote the first African-American opera, *Treemonisha* (1911), but it was not successful. His music became popular again when some of his tunes, including *The Entertainer* (1902), were used in the film *The Sting* (1973).

ˌMichael ˈ**Jordan** /ˈdʒɔːdn; *AmE* ˈdʒɔːrdn/ (1963–) a US *basketball player with the Chicago Bulls team who is thought to be the richest athlete in the world. He has been named the *Most Valuable Player of the *National Basketball Association four times (1988, 1991–2 and 1996) and is the only player to have scored the most points in a season eight times (1987–93 and 1996). Jordan was in US Olympic basketball teams that won gold medals in 1984 and 1992. He changed to playing *baseball for two years in the early 1990s.

ˌChief ˈ**Joseph** /ˈdʒəʊzɪf; *AmE* ˈdʒoʊzɪf/ (*c.* 1840–1904) the leader of a group of *Nez Percé *Native Americans. When in 1877 they were told to move from *Oregon to a reservation (= land given and protected by the US government) in *Idaho, Chief Joseph's group killed 20 white people and tried to escape to Canada. They travelled over 1 000 miles (1 600 kilometres), but the US Army caught them 30 miles (48 kilometres) from Canada. Chief Joseph lived the rest of his life on a reservation in the state of *Washington.

ˌSt ˈ**Joseph of Arimaˈthea** /ærɪməˈθiːə/ (1st century AD) a rich supporter of Jesus who appears in the Bible. He asks for Jesus' body after he dies and puts it in his own tomb. In traditional English stories he is said to have visited *Glastonbury in Somerset, bringing the *Holy Grail with him, and to have started the first English church. A thorn tree at Glastonbury is said to have grown from the stick that he carried.

Joshua Fit the Battle of ˈJericho /ˈdʒɒʃuə, ˈdʒerɪkəʊ; *AmE* ˈdʒɑːʃuə, ˈdʒerɪkoʊ/ an old *African-American *spiritual based on the story of Joshua in the Bible. 'Fit' represents a way of saying 'fought'. The song tells how Joshua captured the city of Jericho when he ordered the Israelites to blow trumpets until the walls fell down. It begins:

Joshua fit the battle of Jericho,
Jericho, Jericho;
Joshua fit the battle of Jericho,
And the walls came tumbling down.

ˌJames ˈ**Joyce** /dʒɔɪs/ (1882–1941) an Irish author who is considered to be one of the greatest writers of the 20th century. He left Ireland in 1904 and spent the rest of his life abroad, in Trieste, Zürich and Paris. His novels **Ulysses* (1922) and **Finnegans Wake* (1939) introduced new ways of writing fiction, particularly the 'stream of consciousness' style, which presents a person's rapidly changing thoughts. He also made use of invented words and unusual sentence structures. His work was not well understood during his life and *Ulysses* was banned in Britain and the US until 1936 because it was considered offensive. Earlier books by him include *1914* (a collection of short stories) and *A Portrait of the Artist as a Young Man* (1914–15), which reflects Joyce's own experiences of growing up in Dublin.

ˈFlorence ˈGriffith ˈ**Joyner** /ˈɡrɪfɪθ ˈdʒɔɪnə(r)/ (1959–98) a US athlete, also known informally as 'Flo-Jo', who won three gold medals at the 1988 Olympic Games. They were in races of 100 metres, 200 metres (in which she ran the fastest time ever) and the 4 x 100 metres relay (= team race in which each member runs part of the distance). Joyner was the sister-in-law of Jackie *Joyner-Kersee.

ˈJackie ˈ**Joyner-ˈKersee** /ˈdʒɔɪnə ˈkɜːsi; *AmE* ˈdʒɔɪnər ˈkɜːrsi/ (1962–) an *African American who won three Olympic gold medals. Two were for the heptathlon (= an event involving seven separate contests) in 1988 and 1992. In the first of these she scored more points than any other competitor has ever done. Her third gold medal was for the long jump in 1988.

JP /ˌdʒeɪ ˈpiː/ ⇨ JUSTICE OF THE PEACE.

J17 /ˌdʒeɪ sevnˈtiːn/ a British magazine for teenage girls published every month and containing articles on fashion, beauty, entertainment, etc. The title stands for 'Just Seventeen'.

ˌ**Judge ˈDredd** /ˌdʒʌdʒ ˈdred/ the main character in *2000 AD*, a British *comic first published in 1977. The stories are set in the future in Mega City One, and Judge Dredd is a member of the police who is also a judge of criminals and executes them. *Hollywood based the film *Judge Dredd* (1997) on the character, which was played by Sylvester *Stallone.

juˌdicial ˈactivism *n* [U] (in the US legal system) the idea that the Supreme Court or other courts can approve new laws which do not follow the exact words of the *American Constitution but are based on changes in the nation's values and needs. This is also called a 'broad construction' of the Constitution. Judicial activism is the opposite of *judicial restraint.

the **Juˌdicial Comˈmittee** a committee of the British *Privy Council which acts as the highest court of appeal for the review of cases referred from courts in Commonwealth countries. Its members are the *Lord Chancellor and other senior judges.

juˌdicial reˈstraint *n* [U] (in the US legal system) the idea that judges of the Supreme Court or other courts should not try to change laws if they are consistent with the words of the *American Constitution. This is also called a 'narrow construction' of the Constitution. Judicial restraint is the opposite of *judicial activism.

juˌdicial reˈview *n* [U] (in the US legal system) the power of the US Supreme Court to decide if a state or national law or action is consistent with the *American Constitution. If the court states that a law or action is 'unconstitutional', it becomes illegal. See also CHECKS AND BALANCES.

the ˈ**Juilliard ˈSchool of ˈMusic** /ˈdʒuːliɑːd; *AmE* ˈdʒuːliɑːrd/ a US college established in 1905 for the study of classical music. It is now based at the *Lincoln Center for the Performing Arts, New York.

ˌ***Juke Box ˈJury*** a former British television series about pop music (1959–67, 1979 and 1989–90), in which a group of well-known people were chosen every week to listen to new pop records and judge whether the records would be 'hits' (= successes) or 'misses' (= failures). The series was originally presented by David Jacobs and later by Noel *Edmonds and Jools *Holland.

ˌJulius ˈCaesar /ˌdʒuːliəs ˈsiːzə(r)/ (100–44 BC) the best-known of all the ancient Roman leaders, and the first one to land in Britain with an army. He did this twice, in 55 and 54 BC, although Britain did not become part of the Roman empire until nearly a hundred years later.

ˌJulius ˈCaesar /ˌdʒuːliəs ˈsiːzə(r)/ a play written by William *Shakespeare in 1599. It is set mainly in Rome in AD 44, and tells how Brutus, Cassius and other Romans plan to kill Caesar because they think he wants to become king (rather than being the head of the republic). Caesar fails to listen to warnings to 'beware the Ides of March' (= 15 March) and is murdered by them. Later Mark Antony, in a skilful speech at Caesar's funeral, turns the Roman people against Brutus and Cassius, and a war begins. The army of Antony wins, and Brutus and Cassius kill themselves.

ˈjungle *n* [U] a style of dance music that developed in London in the early 1990s. It is a form of *house, and relies on very fast electronic drum beats and a strong bass part.

The ˈ***Jungle Book*** a collection of short stories for children by Rudyard *Kipling, published in 1894 and still popular today. They are about Mowgli, a young boy who grows up in the jungle and is taught how to survive by animals such as Mother Wolf, Baloo the bear and Bagheera the panther (= a large member of the cat family). *The Second Jungle Book* followed in 1895. The books were made into a successful Walt *Disney musical cartoon film in 1967.

ˌjunior ˈcollege *n* a US college for two years of study instead of the usual four years. Students receive an 'associate degree' when they successfully complete their studies. They can then move on to a four-year college or university for a *bachelor's degree. Junior colleges help many students who could not otherwise go to college, because they are cheaper than other colleges and accept students with fewer qualifications.

ˌjunior ˈhigh school (*also* **ˌjunior ˈhigh**) *n* (in the US) a school between the levels of *grammar school(2) and *high school. A junior high school is linked to a particular high school. If the high school has the usual four years of education, the junior high school will have two years, called seventh and eighth grades. In some systems each of the two offer three years of education, so the junior high school includes a ninth grade.

ˈjunior school *n* [C, U] (in Britain) a *state school for children aged between 7 and 11. Compare ELEMENTARY SCHOOL, INFANT SCHOOL. ⇨ article at EDUCATION IN BRITAIN.

ˌjunior ˈvarsity *n* a sports team at a US school, college or university for players who are not good enough for the school's regular *varsity(2) team. This is usually in American football and *basketball. The junior varsity competes against similar teams from other schools. ⇨ note at FOOTBALL – AMERICAN STYLE.

juries

Under the *legal systems of England and Wales, and also of Scotland, a person accused of a serious crime who pleads 'not guilty' to the crime will be **tried** by a jury. Juries also hear some civil cases (= disagreements between people about their rights) and decide whether a person is 'liable' (= required by law to do or pay something) or 'not liable'. In the US juries are also used in both criminal and civil cases, though the rules vary from state to state.

In Britain **jurors** (= jury members) are selected at random for each trial from lists of adults who have the right to vote. They must be between the ages of 18 and 70 and have lived in Britain for at least five years. Members of the armed forces, the legal profession and the police force are not allowed to **sit on** juries. Anybody **called for jury service** usually has to attend court for about two weeks, although some cases may go on for much longer. In England and Wales 12 people sit on a jury, in Scotland 15. Lawyers representing either side in a case have the right to object to a particular person being on the jury.

After the jury has heard the evidence presented by both sides, it **retires** to the **jury room**, a private room, to discuss the case. When all members of the jury agree they **return their verdict**, go back into court and say whether the accused is **guilty** or **not guilty**. In Scotland they can also return a verdict of **not proven**, which means the person is not proved guilty and can go free. The verdict is announced by the **foreman** (= the person chosen by the jury as their leader). Sometimes the jury cannot all agree and the judge may accept a **majority verdict**, provided that no more than two members of the jury disagree. If no verdict is reached the trial is abandoned and started again with a different jury. It is not the responsibility of the jury to decide *punishment .

In the US most juries have 12 members, though some have only six. Otherwise the system is very similar to that in England and Wales. When people are called for **jury duty** they must go, but people who cannot leave their jobs or homes can be excused. Before a trial begins lawyers ask questions to see if jurors are impartial, i.e. do not have strong opinions that would prevent them making a decision based on the facts. Lawyers can **challenge for cause**, if they can give the judge a good reason why somebody should not be a juror. They also have a number of **peremptory challenges** which means they can object to somebody without giving a reason. In some trials it can be difficult to find 12 people who are impartial, especially if a case has received a lot of publicity. In a criminal trial the jury decides whether the accused person is **guilty** or **innocent**, but does not decide on a punishment. In a civil trial they may decide how much money should be paid in compensation. A majority decision is usually acceptable.

ˌJustice of the ˈPeace (*abbr* **JP**) *n* (*pl* **Justices of the Peace**) a person who judges less serious cases in a local court. In England and Wales the title is given to a magistrate, while in Scotland it is given to a judge in a district court. In the US, Justices of the Peace are local judges who deal with minor legal matters, send cases to higher courts of law, and can also perform marriages. ⇨ article at LEGAL SYSTEM IN BRITAIN.

ˌJust ˈSo ˌStories a collection of stories and poems for children by Rudyard *Kipling, published in 1902. They give funny explanations for the features of different animals, and have titles such as 'How the Elephant got his Trunk' and 'How the Camel got his Hump'.

ˈjuvenile court (*also* **ˈyouth court**) *n* a court of law for the trials of young people under the age of 18. It uses special rules which are not as severe as adult courts, but in the US can take children from their parents if it believes that this would help them.

Kk

ˈ**kaffee klatsch** /ˈkæfeɪ klætʃ/ (*also* ˈ**coffee klatsch**) *n* (*AmE*) a social event at which people, especially women, meet for informal conversation. Coffee and small items of food and sweets are usually served.

ˈ**Kansas** /ˈkænzəs/ a US state in the *Middle West, the most central of all the states. It forms part of the *Great Plains and suffered badly during the *Dust Bowl. Its popular name is the Sunflower State. The capital city is Topeka, and the largest cities are Wichita and *Kansas City(2). Kansas was part of the *Louisiana Purchase and became a state in 1861. Its main products include wheat, corn, cattle, oil and salt. See also KANSAS-NEBRASKA ACT.

ˌ**Kansas** ˈ**City** /ˌkænzəs/ **1** the largest city in the US state of *Missouri. It is connected to Kansas City, *Kansas, and was established at the beginning of the *Santa Fe Trail. It is now a major industrial centre for the production of steel and vehicles. In the late 1920s, Kansas City became a centre for *jazz. 'Count' *Basie and 'Duke' *Ellington both began their careers there. **2** a city in eastern *Kansas. It is connected to Kansas City, *Missouri, but is only one third as large. The two cities are situated where the Missouri River and Kansas River meet. This smaller city was originally formed from eight separate towns.

the ˌ**Kansas-Ne**ˈ**braska Act** /ˌkænzəs nəˈbræskə/ a law passed by the US Congress in 1854 which was one of the causes of the *Civil War. It replaced the *Missouri Compromise and established the Kansas Territory and the Nebraska Territory as regions which could vote on whether to have slaves or not. This caused people to come from both the South and the North to fight about the issue, until 'bleeding Kansas' had two rival governments.

ˌ**Kao**ˈ**pectate**™ /ˌkeɪəʊˈpekteɪt; *AmE* ˌkeɪoʊˈpekteɪt/ a well-known US medicine for the treatment of diarrhoea (= an illness in which waste matter is emptied from the bowels frequently and in liquid form).

ˌBoris ˈ**Karloff** /ˈkɑːlɒf; *AmE* ˈkɑːrlɑːf/ (1887–1969) an English actor who began his career in silent films but became famous for appearing in many US horror films, especially as the monster in **Frankenstein*. His other films included *The Mummy* (1932), *The Bride of Frankenstein* (1935), *The Body Snatcher* (1945) and *The Raven* (1963).

ˌCasey ˈ**Kasem** /ˌkeɪsi ˈkeɪsəm/ (1932–) a US broadcaster who has presented a popular music programme, *Casey's Top 40*, on national radio every week since 1971. He also presents other shows, including *Casey's Countdown* and *Casey's Hot 20*, and has provided the voices for many characters in radio and television advertisements and cartoons, including Shaggy in **Scooby Doo*.

ˌDanny ˈ**Kaye** /ˈkeɪ/ (1913–87) a US comic actor and singer. He was a star of *vaudeville and *Broadway before he became an international success in films. These included *The Secret Life of Walter Mitty* (1947) and *Hans Christian Andersen* (1952). He received a special *Oscar in 1954. He later had his own show on television (1963–7).

ˌElia **Ka**ˈ**zan** /ˌiːljə kəˈzæn/ (1909–) a US director of films and plays, born in Turkey of Greek parents. He also wrote and produced films. He helped to set up the *Actors' Studio in New York and directed plays there, including *A *Streetcar Named Desire* (1947) and **Death of a Salesman* (1949). He won *Oscars for *Gentleman's Agreement* (1947) and *On the Waterfront* (1954). His other films include *A Streetcar Named Desire* (1951) and **East of Eden* (1955).

ˌEdmund ˈ**Kean** /ˈkiːn/ (*c.* 1789–1833) an English actor who was famous for playing the parts of evil characters in *Shakespeare plays, such as *Richard III, *Shylock and Iago.

ˌBuster ˈ**Keaton¹** /ˌbʌstə ˈkiːtn; *AmE* ˌbʌstər/ (1895–1966) one of the greatest US comic actors in silent films. His popular name was 'the Great Stoneface' because his expression never changed. His best-known films include *The Navigator* (1924) and *The General* (1926). He received a special *Oscar in 1959 and later made a few appearances on television and in sound films.

Buster Keaton in The General

Diˌane ˈ**Keaton²** /ˈkiːtn/ (1946–) a US actor who won an *Oscar for **Annie Hall*, directed by Woody *Allen. Keaton and Allen had a love affair and made several films together, including *Play It Again, Sam* (1972), *Sleeper* (1973) and *Manhattan* (1979). Among her other films are *Reds* (1981), *Crimes of the Heart* (1986) and *The First Wives Club* (1996).

ˌJohn ˈ**Keats** /ˈkiːts/ (1795–1821) an English poet. He is considered to be one of the greatest figures of the *Romantic Movement and was a friend of *Shelley², *Hazlitt and *Wordsworth. His best-known poems include **Ode on a Grecian Urn*, **Ode to a Nightingale*, **To Autumn* and *La *Belle Dame Sans Merci*, all written in 1819. Common themes in his poems are the beauty of nature and the short time available for human life and happiness. He asked that on his grave should be the words 'Here lies one whose name was writ (= written) in water'. He died in Rome of tuberculosis (= a disease of the lungs), aged only 26. His *Letters* were published in 1848.

Keds™ /kedz/ a popular US make of sports shoe for *basketball, tennis, etc. Keds are light, soft shoes with a rubber sole and a top usually made of cotton cloth. They were first produced by the United States

Rubber Company and are now made by the Stride Rite Corporation.

ˈ**Keebler** /ˈkiːblə(r)/ a US company that makes cookies and crackers (= thin, dry biscuits, typically eaten with cheese). Keebler biscuits were first made in 1853.

ˌKevin ˈ**Keegan** /ˈkiːgən/ (1951–) an English footballer who played for *Liverpool in the 1970s and was captain of the England team. Since then he has been manager of *Newcastle United and *Fulham, and from 1999 manager of the England team.

ˌHoward ˈ**Keel** /ˈkiːl/ (1917–) a US actor and singer, known especially for his roles in film *musicals. These include *Annie Get Your Gun* (1950), **Show Boat* (1951), *Kiss Me Kate* (1953) and *Seven Brides for Seven Brothers* (1954). Keel also played the role of Clayton Farlow in the television series **Dallas*.

ˈ**Keep** ˈ**Britain** ˈ**Tidy** a British campaign to persuade people not to leave rubbish in public places. The phrases is widely used on signs, etc. put up around the country.

ˌ**Keep it** ˈ**simple,** ˌ**stupid** (*abbr* **KISS**) (*esp AmE*) an informal phrase used to encourage people not to be too complicated in what they say or do. The 'KISS principle' is often used in business to remind employees to keep advertisements, designs, messages, etc. as simple as possible.

ˌGarrison ˈ**Keillor** /ˌgærɪsn ˈkiːlə(r)/ (1942–) a humorous US writer and broadcaster. He tells stories about the people of the imaginary town of Lake Wobegon, *Minnesota. His popular weekly radio programme, *A Prairie Home Companion*, began in 1974 and now has an audience of over 2 million. Keillor's books include *Lake Wobegon Days* (1985), *We Are Still Married* (1989) and a book for children, *The Old Man Who Loved Cheese* (1996).

Gene Kelly with Leslie Caron in An American in Paris

ˌHelen ˈ**Keller** /ˈkelə(r)/ (1880–1968) a US author and public speaker who became blind and deaf at the age of 19 months. Anne Sullivan became her teacher in 1887 and taught her to read, write, use sign language and speak. Keller received a degree from Radcliffe College in 1904 and spent the rest of her life encouraging others with difficulties like hers to overcome them. Her books include *The Story of My Life* (1902) and *Out of the Dark* (1913). Her life was the subject of the play *The Miracle Worker*.

the ˌ**Kellogg-**ˈ**Briand Pact** /ˌkelɒg ˈbriːɒ̃; *AmE* ˌkelɑːg ˈbriːɑːnd/ (*also* the **Kellogg Pact**, *fml* the **Pact of Paris**) an international agreement (1928) that nations would not use war to settle disputes. It was prepared by US Secretary of State Frank B Kellogg and French Foreign Minister Aristide Briand, and signed in Paris by 15 nations, and later by 62 others. The agreement failed because it lacked the power to prevent wars.

ˈ**Kellogg's**™ /ˈkelɒgz; *AmE* ˈkelɑːgz/ a large US company that sells its many breakfast cereals around the world. They include Kellogg's Corn Flakes, Rice Krispies, All Bran, Apple Jacks, Corn Pops and Cocoa Frosted Flakes. Other Kellogg's products include Pop Tarts and Eggo. The company was started in 1906 by Will Keith Kellogg (1860–1951) in *Battle Creek, Michigan.

ˌEmmett ˈ**Kelly**[1] /ˌemət ˈkeli/ (1898–1979) the best-known US clown (= a person with comic clothes and a painted face who does funny things). Kelly became famous as the character Weary Willie with the Ringling Brothers and Barnum and Bailey Circuses (1942–56). Willie's face was very sad, and everything seemed to defeat him.

Emmett Kelly

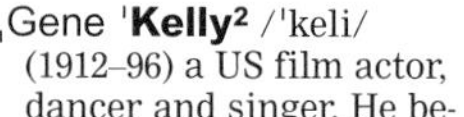

ˌGene ˈ**Kelly**[2] /ˈkeli/ (1912–96) a US film actor, dancer and singer. He became a star in the *Broadway musical show *Pal Joey* (1940). His film successes included *On the Town* (1949), *An American in Paris* (1951) and **Singin' in the Rain*. Kelly later directed films, including *Hello, Dolly!* (1969). He received a special *Oscar in 1951.

ˌGrace ˈ**Kelly**[3] /ˈkeli/ (1928–82) a US film star who became Princess Grace of Monaco. She was from a rich Irish-American family in*Philadelphia. She received an *Oscar for *The Country Girl* (1954), and her other films included **High Noon*, *Rear Window* (1954) and *High Society* (1956). Kelly made no more films after marrying Prince Rainier of Monaco in 1956. She died after a car crash.

the ˌ**Kelmscott** ˈ**Press** /ˌkelmskɒt; *AmE* ˌkelmskɑːt/ a printing business started by William *Morris at Hammersmith, London, England, in 1890. It produced fine editions of his own books and other works using traditional printing methods.

ˌFanny ˈ**Kemble** /ˌfæni ˈkembl/ (1809–93) an English actor who was famous for playing parts in Shakespeare plays. She was also known for her opposition to *slavery in the US, where she lived for a time as the wife of a US farmer. Her aunt was Mrs *Siddons.

ˌ**Kendal** ˈ**mint cake** /ˌkendl/ *n* [U] a sweet flavoured with mint and sold in hard, flat bars. It is often eaten by British people who walk or climb in the countryside, and is made in Kendal, *Cumbria.

ˌ**Kenilworth** ˈ**Castle** /ˌkenlwɜːθ; *AmE* ˌkenlwɜːrθ/ a castle near Coventry, England. It was owned by several kings, and the Earl of *Leicester entertained *Elizabeth I there in 1575. Parts of the castle were pulled down by Oliver *Cromwell's soldiers to sell as building materials.

ˈ**Kenmore**™ /ˈkenmɔː(r)/ a US product name for a range of popular household appliances, including refrigerators and washing machines.

ˈ**Kennedy**[1] /ˈkenədi/ ⇨ JFK 2.

ˌEdward ˈ**Kennedy**[2] /ˈkenədi/ (1932–) a US Senator from *Massachusetts since 1962, informally called Ted or Teddy Kennedy. He is the younger brother of John F *Kennedy and Robert *Kennedy. He is a *Democrat with liberal views and for many years has supported a national health programme. His career was damaged when a woman died in the car he was driving after an accident at *Chappaquiddick. In 1980, he tried but failed to be chosen as the Democrats' candidate for US President.

ˌJackie ˈ**Kennedy**[3] /ˈkenədi/ (*also* Jackie **Onassis**) (1929–94) the wife of President John F *Kennedy. She was born Jacqueline Bouvier and married him in 1953. She was an elegant US *First Lady who had the *White House rooms improved and in 1962 gave the first television tour of them. Americans admired her courage after her husband was murdered. Many, however, did not approve of her marriage to the rich Greek businessman Aristotle Onassis (1968–75). After his death she lived a very private life in New York, where she worked for the publishing company Doubleday.

ˌJohn F ˈ**Kennedy**[4] /ˈkenədi/ (John Fitzgerald Kennedy 1917–63) the 35th US *President (1961–3). He was the country's youngest president and the first Roman Catholic ever to be elected. He was also known informally as Jack Kennedy and JFK. His wife was Jackie *Kennedy. He won a medal for courage during *World War II, and after the war and was elected first to the US House of Representatives (1947–53) and then to the US Senate (1952–60).

Kennedy's greatest success as President was in dealing with the *Cuban missile crisis and his worst failure was over the *Bay of Pigs incident. He worked with his brother, US Attorney General Robert *Kennedy, to support the *civil rights movement. He was murdered in *Dallas, probably by Lee Harvey *Oswald, in one of the most shocking events in US history. Some people believe that others were responsible for his murder, but nothing has been definitely proved. See also WARREN.

the Kennedy family, 1960: (from left) Stephen Smith, Eunice Kennedy Shriver, Rose Kennedy, Jean Kennedy Smith, Joseph Kennedy, John F Kennedy, Jackie Kennedy, Robert F Kennedy, Edward Kennedy and Patricia Lawford

ˌJoseph ˈ**Kennedy**[5] /ˈkenədi/ (1888–1969) the father of US President John F *Kennedy. He was a rich businessman who became head of the *Securities and Exchange Commission (1934–5) and later the US Ambassador to Britain (1937–40). His oldest son Joe was killed in *World War II, and Kennedy successfully encouraged his other sons (John, Robert and Edward) to become politicians. His wife, Rose Kennedy, lived to the age of 104.

ˌLudovic ˈ**Kennedy**[6] /ˌluːdəvɪk ˈkenədi/ (1919–) a Scottish television presenter and author. In the 1960s he presented a number of news and current affairs programmes, including **Panorama* and *This Week*. He is well known for investigating of the cases of people wrongly put in prison, and also for his support for euthanasia (= allowing people the right to die when they want to do so because of serious illness, etc.) He was made a *knight in 1994.

ˌNigel ˈ**Kennedy**[7] /ˈkenədi/ (1959–) a English classical musician who plays the violin. He is well known for his unusual clothes and style of life. He recordings have been very successful, especially one of Vivaldi's *Four Seasons*. In 1992 he announced that he would not perform in public again, but he later changed his mind and is now performing again, preferring to call himself simply Kennedy.

Nigel Kennedy

ˌRobert F ˈ**Kennedy**[8] /ˈkenədi/ (Robert Francis Kennedy 1925–68) a US Attorney General (1961–4) appointed by his older brother, President John F *Kennedy. He was also informally called Bobby Kennedy or RFK. He strongly supported the *civil rights movement and better conditions for poor people. After his brother was murdered, Kennedy remained Attorney General under President *Johnson[3] until he was elected in 1964 to the US Senate. He wanted to be the Democratic candidate for President in 1968, but was murdered by Sirhan *Sirhan on the day he won the California *primary election.

the ˈ**Kennedy** ˌ**Center** /ˈkenədi/ (*also fml* the **John F Kennedy Center for the Performing Arts**) a US national cultural centre in Washington, DC, on the *Potomac River near the *Lincoln Memorial. It was opened in 1971 as a 'living memorial' to President *Kennedy. The main theatres are the Concert Hall, the Opera House and the Eisenhower Theater. Since 1978, Kennedy Center Honors have been awarded for special artistic achievements.

the ˈ**Kennel Club** an organization in London, England, that holds the official records relating to dog breeding in Britain. The records prove that particular dogs are 'pure' breeds, i.e. have the right features for their breed and are descended from a line of similar animals. The Kennel Club also organizes *Crufts dog show. The *American Kennel Club is a similar organization in the US.

ˈ**Kensington** /ˈkenzɪŋtən/ a district of south-west London, England, part of the *borough of Kensington and *Chelsea. It contains many of London's large museums, including the *Victoria and Albert Museum, the *Natural History Museum and the *Science Museum. It also contains the *Commonwealth Institute and *Imperial College London. Kensington has particular associations with the royal family, and was made a 'royal borough' by Queen *Victoria, who was born in *Kensington Palace. South Kensington in particular is a fashionable and expensive part of London.

ˌ**Kensington** ˈ**Gardens** /ˌkenzɪŋtən/ a park in south-west London, England, next to *Hyde Park(1). It was formerly the garden of *Kensington Palace, and was opened to the public in the 1830s. It contains the *Albert Memorial and a famous statue of *Peter Pan.

ˌ**Kensington** ˈ**Palace** /ˌkenzɪŋtən/ a 17th-century royal palace (= large, grand house) next to *Kensington Gardens in south-west London, England, designed partly by Christopher *Wren. Queen *Victoria was born there in 1819 and it has since been the main home for other members of the royal family. Parts of it are open to the public.

Kent[1] /kent/ a county in south-east England. Its main products are fruit and hops (= plants used in making beer), and it is known as the 'Garden of England'. Its administrative centre is Maidstone. See also KENTISHMAN, MAN OF KENT.

ˌClark ˈ**Kent**[2] /ˈkent/ ⇨ SUPERMAN.

the ˌDuke of ˈ**Kent**[3] /ˈkent/ (1935–) a British prince,

K

the grandson of King *George V. His brother is Prince Michael of *Kent and his sister is Princess Alexandra. He is the second Duke of Kent: the first *duke was his father George (1902–42), who was killed in a plane crash in *World War II.

Prince ˌMichael of ˈ**Kent**[4] /ˈkent/ (1942–) a British prince, the grandson of King *George V. His brother is the Duke of *Kent and his sister is Princess Alexandra. His wife, an Austrian Roman Catholic, is known as Princess Michael of Kent, but because of her religion Prince Michael no longer has the right to become king of England.

ˌWilliam ˈ**Kent**[5] /ˈkent/ (*c.* 1685–1748) an English painter and architect who also designed gardens and the insides of houses. He studied in Rome and helped to introduce *Palladianism (= an Italian style of architecture) to Britain. Several public buildings in London were designed by him, including the Royal Mews in *Trafalgar Square. In garden design he introduced more natural and informal styles. His interior designs can be seen at *Burlington House and at Holkham Hall, near *Norwich.

ˈ**Kentishman** /ˈkentɪʃmən/ *n* (*pl* **-men**) (*old-fash*) a name traditionally given to a man from the county of *Kent, England, especially one born west of the River *Medway. See also MAN OF KENT.

ˌStan ˈ**Kenton** /ˈkentən/ (1912–79) a US *jazz musician. He spent his early career as a bandleader in the *big band style of the 1940s and later became involved in the 'progressive' jazz style of the 1950s.

ˈ**Kent** ˈ**State Uni**ˈ**versity** /ˈkent/ (*also infml* **Kent State**) a US university in the town of Kent, *Ohio. It is mainly remembered for an incident there on 4 May 1970, when four students were shot and killed by members of the Ohio *National Guard as they protested against the *Vietnam War. Nine other students were wounded. As a result many people turned against the *Nixon government and the *Vietnam war.

Kenˈ**tucky** /kenˈtʌki/ a south-eastern US state, also called the Bluegrass State. The capital city is Frankfort, and the largest city is *Louisville. It became a state in 1792 and produces agricultural products and coal. It is well known for breeding horses for racing. Its tourist attractions include the place where Abraham *Lincoln was born (near the village of Hodgenville) and Mammoth Cave National Park, a *World Heritage Site since 1981.

Kenˌ**tucky** ˈ**Derby** /kenˌtʌki/ the most famous US horse-racing event. It is one of the *triple crown races and is run every year on the first Saturday in May in *Louisville, *Kentucky. The horses are all 3 years old, and the race is 1.25 miles/2 kilometres in length. The Kentucky Derby was begun in 1875 by Colonel M Lewis Clark and has become part of a social event that lasts several days. Compare DERBY[2].

Kenˌ**tucky Fried** ˈ**Chicken**™ /kenˌtʌki/ (*also* **KFC**) any of a group of US 'fast food' restaurants selling pieces of specially fried chicken and other dishes. Their food is advertised as being 'finger lickin' good'. Colonel Harland D Sanders opened the first restaurant in 1952. He sold the company in 1964 for $2 million and it was bought by PepsiCo in 1986 for $840 million. In 1994 KFC opened its 9 000th restaurant, in Shanghai, China.

ˌ**Kenwood** ˈ**House** /ˌkenwʊd/ a large 18th-century house in *Hampstead, north-west London, England, designed partly by Robert *Adam. It is open to the public and is known for its fine collection of pictures and its large park, where outdoor concerts are held.

ˈ**Kenya** /ˈkenjə, ˈkiːnjə/ a country in East Africa. Its capital city is Nairobi and its official languages are English and Swahili. It was a British colony between 1895 and 1964 and achieved independence after a campaign of violence by the Mau Mau and other groups. It is now a member of the Commonwealth. Major exports include tea and coffee, and it is popular with British and US tourists. ▶ **Kenyan** /ˈkenjən, ˈkiːnjən/ *adj, n.*

ˈ**Kermit** /ˈkɜːmɪt; *AmE* ˈkɜːrmɪt/ one of the main puppet characters in the **Muppet Show*. Kermit is a green frog who presents the show and is fond of making jokes.

Jeˌrome ˈ**Kern** /ˈkɜːn; *AmE* ˈkɜːrn/ (1885–1945) a US writer of many popular songs, especially for *Broadway musical shows and *Hollywood films. His best-known show was **Show Boat*, which included the song **Ol' Man River*. Kern won an *Oscar for the song *The Last Time I Saw Paris* in the film *Lady Be Good* (1941). His other songs include *Look for the Silver Lining* (1920) and *Smoke Gets in Your Eyes* (1933). Ira Gershwin and Oscar *Hammerstein were among the many people who wrote the words for Kern's songs. See also GERSHWIN.

ˌJack ˈ**Kerouac** /ˈkeruæk/ (1922–69) a US writer who has been called 'the spokesman for the *beat generation' of the 1950s. His best-known novel is *On the Road* (1957), about a journey across America by a young person who is opposed to traditional American values. His other novels included *The Subterraneans* (1958) and *Big Sur* (1962).

ˈ**ketchup** (*also BrE* **tomato sauce**, **tomato ketchup**, *esp AmE* **catsup**) *n* [U] a thick red sauce made with tomatoes, used cold to flavour food. People sometimes use the word in a humorous way to refer to artificial blood in films, etc.: *a bottle of ketchup* ○ *one of those gory films with tomato ketchup everywhere.*

ˈ**Kevin** a first name for a boy or a man. In Britain it is sometimes used as a typical name for a young man who is rude and not very well educated. See also SHARON AND TRACY.

ˌ**Kew** ˈ**Gardens** /ˌkjuː/ a park in west London, England, which contains a large collection of plants, trees, etc. from all over the world and is a major centre for the study of plants. Its official name is the Royal Botanic Gardens and it was opened to the public in 1840 by Queen *Victoria. It is very popular with tourists and British people, and among its famous buildings are the Chinese Pagoda (= a tall tower) and several very large greenhouses, including the Palm House (opened in 1848). See also BANKS.

the Palm House at Kew Gardens

ˈ**Kewpie doll**™ /ˈkjuːpi/ (*also* **Kewpie**) *n* a US make of child's doll with a fat, happy face, big eyes and a curl of hair on the top of its head. The name comes from Cupid, the god of love. Kewpie dolls are often given as prizes for games of skill at *fairs. The first were sold in 1913. The expression is also used in an informal way to describe a child or woman who looks like a doll because of their face and type of dress. If said about a woman, it is often an insult.

ˈFrancis ˈScott ˈ**Key** /ˈkiː/ (1779–1843) a US lawyer who wrote the words of the US *national anthem, *The *Star-Spangled Banner*.

ˌ**Key lime** ˈ**pie** /ˌkiː/ *n* [C, U] a light US pie made with the juice and skin of limes (= green fruit like lemons). It also contains sugar, beaten egg whites and sweet condensed (= thick) milk. The pie was first made in *Key West, *Florida, which has a well-known shop called The Key West Key Lime Shoppe.

ˈJohn ˈMaynard ˈ**Keynes** /ˈmeɪnɑːd ˈkeɪnz; *AmE* ˈmeɪnɑːrd/ (1883–1946) an English economist whose ideas have had a great influence on modern politics and economics. He argued that governments could deal with the problem of a failing economy by spending more money on public projects such as roads, schools, etc. This was popular until the 1980s when it was argued that such a policy would lead to inflation. Keynes also represented Britain in economic conferences after the two World Wars and helped to establish the *International Monetary Fund. He was a leading member of the *Bloomsbury Group and was made a *baron in 1942.

▶ **Keynesian** *n, adj* of or relating to the ideas of John Maynard Keynes, especially regarding government control of a country's economy through money and taxes: *Keynesian economics.*

the Keystone Kops

the ˌ**Keystone** ˈ**Kops** /ˌkiːstəʊn ˈkɒps; *AmE* ˌkiːstoʊn ˈkɑːps/ a team of actors who appeared as a group of comic police officers in a series of US silent films (1912–20) produced by Mack *Sennett and his Keystone Comedy Company. They had long and funny scenes in which they chased criminals or wrongly chased innocent citizens, often in cars.

ˌ**Key** ˈ**West** /ˌki; ˈwest/ the last island and town of the *Florida Keys. It is the most southern US town and is closer to Havana, Cuba, than to *Miami. Ernest *Hemingway and John James *Audubon lived there, and President *Truman had a 'summer White House' on Key West for holidays. People who live there are called 'conchs' after the local shellfish. It is the home of many artists and homosexuals.

KFC /ˌkeɪ ef ˈsiː/ ⇨ KENTUCKY FRIED CHICKEN.

KG /ˌkeɪ ˈdʒiː/ (in Britain) the abbreviation for Knight of the *Order of the Garter: *be made a KG* ○ *Sir Thomas Bell KG.*

ˌCaptain ˈ**Kidd** /ˈkɪd/ (William Kidd *c.* 1645–1701) a Scottish sea captain and pirate (= person on a ship who attacks and robs other ships). He was captured and hanged in London after attacking a number of ships in the Indian Ocean. It is said that he hid a large amount of stolen treasure which has never been found.

ˈ**Kidderminster** /ˈkɪdəmɪnstə(r); *AmE* ˈkɪdərmɪnstər/ a town in the county of *Hereford and Worcester, England. It is famous for producing carpets which are made of two cloths of different colours woven so that each carpet can be reversed.

ˈ***Kidnapped*** a novel (1886) by Robert Louis *Stevenson. It is about the adventures of David Balfour, a young man who is kidnapped (= taken away by force) from his home in Scotland and made to work as a slave. He escapes with the help of Alan Breck, a *Jacobite.

The ˈ***Killing Fields*** a well-known film (1984), directed by Roland Jaffe, about the war in Cambodia during the 1970s and the killing of many thousands of Cambodian people by the Khmer Rouge. The phrase 'the killing fields' is now often used to describe a place where many people are killed, e.g. in a war.

ˈ**Kilner jar**™ /ˈkɪlnə(r)/ *n* (*BrE*) a type of large jar which can be sealed tightly and is used for preserving fruit, etc. Compare MASON JAR.

ˈ**Kilroy was here** /ˈkɪlrɔɪ/ a phrase that people sometimes write on walls, etc. for no obvious reason. It was first used in *World War II, but it is not known who Kilroy was, or even if he was a real person.

Kim /kɪm/ a novel (1901) by Rudyard *Kipling. It is about the adventures of Kim, a young boy who becomes a spy for the British in India.

the **King**[1] a popular *nickname both for the actor Clark *Gable and for the singer Elvis *Presley. Gable was first called the King of Hollywood in the 1930s, and Presley was named the King of Rock and Roll in the 1950s.

ˌB B ˈ**King**[2] /ˌbiː biː ˈkɪŋ/ (1925–) an American *blues singer who plays the guitar. He was born Riley King. His early hits included *Three O'Clock Blues* (1950). He was an important influence on *rock and roll music. King made his first European tour in 1968 and played in *Carnegie Hall in 1970. He won *Emmy awards for *The Thrill is Gone* (1970) and the album *Blues 'n' Jazz* (1983). In 1997 he recorded the album *Deuces Wild* with the *Rolling Stones, Eric *Clapton, Willie *Nelson and others.

ˈBillie ˈJean ˈ**King**[3] /ˈkɪŋ/ (1943–) a US tennis player. She won the Women's Singles Championship at *Wimbledon six times (1966–8, 1972–3 and 1975) and 20 Wimbledon championships in all, more than any other player. She also won the *US Open(2) four times (1967, 1971–2 and 1974). King is a strong supporter of women's interests in sport.

ˌLarry ˈ**King**[4] /ˈkɪŋ/ (1933–) a US broadcaster who presents *Larry King Live*, a television talk show on *CNN. His guests include important politicians and other well-known people in the news.

ˈMartin ˈLuther ˈ**King**[5] /ˈluːθə ˈkɪŋ; *AmE* ˈluːθər/ (1929–68) the most important leader of the US *civil rights movement. King was an *African-American Baptist minister who led a series of peaceful cam-

Martin Luther King addressing a civil rights march at the Lincoln Memorial, 1963

K

paigns against *segregation in the southern states. In 1957 he established the *Southern Christian Leadership Conference. In 1963 he led about 250 000 people on a protest march to Washington, DC, where he made his famous 'I have a dream' speech at the *Lincoln Memorial. He was awarded the Nobel Peace Prize in 1964 and murdered four years later in *Memphis, *Tennessee by Earl Ray. King's wife, Coretta Scott King (1927–) has continued his work. His birthday, 15 January, is an official holiday in many states.

ˌRodney ˈ**King**[6] /ˈkɪŋ/ (1966–) an *African American who was severely beaten in 1991 by *Los Angeles police officers, an incident which led to America's worst race riots. The police stopped King for driving too fast and then hit and kicked him repeatedly. A person on the street made a video of the attack, and four of the police officers were put on trial. When they were judged innocent, African Americans reacted with violence in Los Angeles for four days, during which 52 people were killed and more than 600 buildings were burned. President *Clinton sent in US troops to deal with the trouble. The police officers were put on trial again in 1993, and two were given 2½ years in prison. Many Americans are still angry about the way King was treated.

ˌStephen ˈ**King**[7] /ˈkɪŋ/ (1946–) a very popular US writer, best known for his horror novels. About 20 of his books have been filmed, including *Carrie* (film date 1974), *The Shining* (1977), *Misery* (1987) and *The Shawshank Redemption* (1994).

the ˌ**King and ˈCountry deˌbate** a debate by students at Oxford University in 1933. It became famous because most of the students said that they would refuse to fight for their 'king and country' if there was a war. This shocked many people with traditional attitudes.

the ˌ**King ˈGeorge ˈV Gold ˈCup** /ˈdʒɔːdʒ ðə ˈfɪfθ; *AmE* ˈdʒɔːrdʒ/ a major British competition in show-jumping (= the sport of riding horses over difficult barriers) for men. It is held every year as part of the *Royal International Horse Show and was first held in 1911.

the ˌ**King ˈGeorge ˈVI and Queen Eˈlizabeth ˈDiamond ˈStakes** /ˈdʒɔːdʒ ðə ˈsɪksθ; *AmE* ˈdʒɔːrdʒ/ the main horse race at *Ascot, first run in 1951.

the ˌ**King ˈJames ˌVersion** ⇨ AUTHORIZED VERSION.

ˌ***King ˈKong*** /ˈkɒŋ; *AmE* ˈkɑːŋ/ a famous US film (1933) about a very large ape. In the story, King Kong captures Ann, played by Fay Wray, when she visits his island. She is rescued, and the ape is taken to New York to be presented as a show. He escapes and climbs to the top of the *Empire State Building, where he is killed by war planes. A second version of the film was made in 1976, with Jessica Lange as Fay Wray, and a further film, *King Kong Lives*, appeared in 1986.

King Kong on the Empire State Building

ˌ***King ˈLear*** /ˈlɪə(r); *AmE* ˈlɪr/ a play by William *Shakespeare first performed *c.* 1605. It is a tragedy about Lear, a British king who divides his land and possessions among his daughters. Lear foolishly gives a share each to the two older daughters, Regan and Goneril, who are greedy and cruel, but refuses to give anything to the youngest, Cordelia, who is honest and loyal. Regan and Goneril later treat Lear badly and Cordelia finally comes to rescue him with a French army. In the battle that follows, however, she is captured and killed. Lear dies too and the play ends. It is one of the most popular of Shakespeare's plays and is known for its speeches about the relationship between parents and children.

ˌ**king of the ˈcastle 1** a children's game in which one player stands on something and the others try to take his or her place. The traditional rhyme sung by the first player is:

I'm the king of the castle
And you're the dirty rascal!

2 (*infml*) a person in a position of advantage or control: *She'll be king of the castle when her boss retires.*

the ˌ**King's ˈBench** ⇨ QUEEN'S BENCH.

ˈ**King's ˈCollege, ˈCambridge** /ˈkeɪmbrɪdʒ/ a college established by King *Henry VI in 1441 as part of *Cambridge University in England. The college chapel is one of the most impressive buildings in Cambridge and known for its stained glass. A famous service of carols (= religious songs) is held there every *Christmas Eve and is broadcast on television.

ˈ**King's ˈCollege ˈHospital** a hospital in south-east London, England, which is part of *London University and is used to teach medical students.

ˌ**King's ˈCounsel** ⇨ QUEEN'S COUNSEL.

ˈ**King's ˈCross** an area of central London, England, that contains two large main line train stations (King's Cross and St Pancras) and a station on the *London Underground. A fire at the underground station in 1987 killed 31 people and led to attempts to improve safety generally on the London Underground. The area around King's Cross is also known for the prostitutes that work there.

the ˌ**King's ˈEnglish** ⇨ QUEEN'S ENGLISH.

ˌCharles ˈ**Kingsley** (1819–75) an English writer and priest. He is best known for the novel *Westward Ho!* (1855), about *Elizabethan England, and the children's book *The *Water-Babies*. He was also the chaplain (= private priest) to Queen *Victoria.

ˌ**King's ˈLynn** /ˈlɪn/ a port and market town in the county of *Norfolk, England. It is known for its many fine old buildings and for its Festival of Music and the Arts, held in July every year. The town was given its royal name by King *Henry VIII in 1537.

ˌ**King's ˈRoad** (*usually* **the King's Road**) the main street in the district of *Chelsea in central London, England. It is known for its many fashionable and colourful shops selling clothes, especially for young people. In the 1970s it was a centre of *punk fashion.

ˌNeil ˈ**Kinnock** /ˈkɪnək/ (1942–) a British politician who was leader of the *Labour Party and leader of the Opposition from 1983 to 1992. During this period he led the party away from extreme left-wing views and introduced more moderate policies, but he lost the general election to John *Major in 1992. He was then replaced as leader of the Labour Party by John *Smith[8]. Since 1995 he has been a *European Commissioner.

ˌAlfred ˈ**Kinsey** /ˈkɪnzi/ (1894–1956) a US scientist

K

Kings and Queens of England and Great Britain

871–99	Alfred (the Great)	1470–71	Henry VI
899–924	Edward (the Elder)	1471–83	Edward IV
924–39	Aethelstan (the Glorious)	1483	Edward V
939–46	Edmund I	1483–85	Richard III (Crookback)
946–55	Eadred	1485–1509	Henry VII
955–59	Eadwig (the Fair)	1509–47	Henry VIII
959–75	Edgar (the Peaceable)	1547–53	Edward VI
975–78	Edward (the Martyr)	1553	Jane
978–1016	Aethelred (the Unready)	1553–58	Mary I
1016	Edmund (Ironside)	1558–1603	Elizabeth I
1016–35	Canute	1603–25	James I (James VI of Scotland)
1035–40	Harold I (Harefoot)	1625–49	Charles I
1040–42	Harthacnut	1653–58	*Oliver Cromwell (Lord Protector)*
1042–66	Edward (the Confessor)	1658–59	*Richard Cromwell (Lord Protector)*
1066	Harold II	1660–85	Charles II
1066–87	William I (the Conqueror)	1685–88	James II
1087–1100	William II (Rufus)	1689–1702	William III
1100–35	Henry I	1689–94	Mary II
1135–54	Stephen	1702–14	Anne
1154–89	Henry II	1714–27	George I
1189–99	Richard I (the Lionheart)	1727–60	George II
1199–1216	John (Lackland)	1760–1820	George III
1216–72	Henry III	1820–30	George IV
1272–1307	Edward I (Longshanks)	1830–37	William IV
1307–27	Edward II	1837–1901	Victoria
1327–77	Edward III	1901–10	Edward VII
1377–99	Richard II	1910–36	George V
1399–1413	Henry IV	1936	Edward VIII
1413–22	Henry V	1936–52	George VI
1422–61	Henry VI	1952–	Elizabeth II
1461–70	Edward IV		

who published the first major scientific studies of human sexual behaviour. The results of his research, which shocked many people, came from answers to questions given by 10 000 people. His books were *Sexual Behavior in the Human Male* (1948) and *Sexual Behavior in the Human Female* (1953). Together they are called the **Kinsey Reports**. In 1942 he established the Institute for Sex Research at *Indiana University and directed it until his death.

ˌRudyard ˈ**Kipling** /ˌrʌdjɑːd ˈkɪplɪŋ; *AmE* ˌrʌdjɑːrd/ (1865–1936) an English writer. He was born in India, where many of his books are set (e.g. *The *Jungle Book* and **Kim*), and worked there as a journalist in the 1880s. He wrote in a wide range of forms, including novels, short stories and poems for adults and children. Many of his poems are still very popular, including **If*, **Gunga Din* and *Mandalay* (1892). The characters in his work are often soldiers in parts of the British Empire, and this has led some people to accuse him of taking too much pride in the British Empire and its use of military force. In 1907 Kipling became the first English writer to receive the *Nobel Prize for literature.

ˈ**kipper** *n* a herring (= type of fish) that has been split open, preserved with salt and then dried or smoked. In Britain kippers are often cooked and eaten for breakfast: *kipper fillets* (= pieces of kipper from which the bones have been removed) .

ˌ**Kiri**ˈ**bati** /ˌkɪrəˈbæs/ a country consisting of a group of 36 islands in the south-west Pacific Ocean. Its capital is Tarawa and its official languages are English and the local Melanesian language. Before 1975 it was part of the British colony of the Gilbert and Ellice Islands. It became fully independent in 1979 and is now a member of the Commonwealth.

KISS /kɪs/ a US *heavy metal band which formed in 1972. Members of the band painted their faces, coloured their hair and performed in a wild way on stage. This included destroying guitars, breathing fire and letting false blood come from their mouths. Their albums have included *KISS* (1974), *Unmasked* (1980) and *Carnival of Souls* (1997). The band was not very active after 1982 but in 1997 it had a 'reunion tour'. See also KEEP IT SIMPLE, STUPID.

ˌHenry ˈ**Kissinger** /ˈkɪsɪndʒə(r)/ (1923–) a US *Secretary of State (1973–7), born in Germany. After teaching at *Harvard University (1958–71) he became a special assistant to President *Nixon on National Security Affairs (1969–75). Kissinger was known especially for his 'shuttle diplomacy', in which he travelled regularly around the world to improve US relations with other countries and to find solutions to international conflicts. He helped to set up the *Strategic Arms Limitation Talks. In 1973 he helped to end both the Israeli-Arab War and the *Vietnam War, and was given the Nobel Peace Prize for his achievements.

ˌLord ˈ**Kitchener** /ˈkɪtʃənə(r)/ (Horatio Herbert Kitchener 1850–1916) a British soldier who commanded the army in the Sudan (1883–5), in South Africa during the *Boer War (1900–02) and in India (1902–9). At the beginning of *World War I he became Secretary of State for war and was responsible for encouraging

Lord Kitchener on a World War I recruiting poster

more men to join the army. He appeared on a famous poster telling people that they were needed to serve their country. He was made an *earl(1) in 1914 and died at sea during *World War I.

ˌ**kitchen-sink** ˈ**drama** *n* [C, U] (*sometimes disapprov*) a type of British play or plays of the 1950s and 1960s which showed the conflicts or unpleasant quality of home life in a realistic way. Typical examples are John *Osborne's **Look Back in Anger* and Arnold *Wesker's *Roots*.

ˈ**Kitemark** /ˈkaɪtmɑːk; *AmE* ˈkaɪtmɑːrk/ *n* (*BrE*) an official mark, in the form of a heart shape with an 'S' in the centre, which is put on products that are approved by the British Standards Institution (*BSI).

ˈ**KitKat**™ /ˈkɪtkæt/ *n* the most popular chocolate bar sold in Britain, often eaten as a snack (= quick meal). Each one consists of two or four strips of wafer (= layers of thin crisp biscuit) covered in chocolate. It first appeared in 1937 and is now made by *Nestlé. Most English people know the phrase often used to advertise KitKat: 'Have a break – have a KitKat.'

the ˈ**Kit Kat Club** /ˈkɪt kæt/ an early 18th-century club whose members included Joseph *Addison, Richard *Steele, William *Congreve and Robert *Walpole. The club was named after Christopher (Kit) Cat, a cook whose house was used as a meeting place. Pictures of the members were painted in a smaller size than usual to fit on the club walls, and pictures this size are still known as 'kit-cat portraits'.

Kiˈ**wanian** /kiˈwɑːniən/ *n* any member of the **Kiwanis Club**, formally called **Kiwanis International**, a US business club with branches all over the country which organize projects to help local communities. It was started in *Detroit in 1915 and in 1997 had about 325 000 members around the world.

KKK /ˌkeɪ keɪ ˈkeɪ/ ⇨ KU KLUX KLAN.

ˈ**Kleenex**™ /ˈkliːneks/ *n* [U, C] (*pl* **Kleenex** *or* **Kleenexes**) a type of soft paper tissue used for wiping the nose, face, etc. or cleaning things. In American English the word is often used to mean any type of paper tissue: *There's a box of Kleenex in the kitchen.* ○ *Could you pass me a/some Kleenex?*

ˌCalvin ˈ**Klein** /ˌkælvɪn ˈklaɪn/ (1942–) a US designer of casual (= informal) clothes. He began his company in 1968 making suits and coats, but changed to 'sportswear' in the 1970s. He is especially known for making fashionable *jeans, and also now sells other personal products, including Obsession perfume.

ˌFranz ˈ**Kline** /ˌfrænz ˈklaɪn/ (1910–62) a US painter who helped to develop *abstract expressionism. Before the 1950s he had painted realistic pictures of city life. He then became famous for his large paintings consisting of black lines with many angles. Kline later did works in colour, such as *Copper and Red* (1959).

the ˈ**Klondike** /ˈklɒndaɪk; *AmE* ˈklɑːndaɪk/ an area of the Yukon Territory of north-west Canada where gold was discovered in 1897. This led to the **Klondike gold rush**, in which about 30 000 people, many of them from the US, travelled to the Klondike in the hope of finding gold. Gold worth about $22 million was found in 1900, but the supply did not last long, and many people then moved on to *Alaska. Small amounts of gold are still found in the Klondike. Charlie *Chaplin's film *The Gold Rush* (1925), was based on this event. See also GOLD RUSH.

ˈ**Kmart** /ˈkeɪmɑːt; *AmE* ˈkeɪmɑːrt/ any of a group of large US shops that sell a variety of products at reduced prices. It began in 1899 as the S S Kresge Company.

ˈ**Knickerbocker** /ˈnɪkəbɒkə(r); *AmE* ˈnɪkərbɑːkər/ *n* (*AmE infml*) a person from New York. The word comes from the imaginary Dutch name of Diedrich Knickerbocker used by the writer Washington *Irving as the pretended author of his *History of New York* (1809). **Knickerbockers** (also called **knickers** in the US) are also a type of loose trousers/pants ending just below the knee where they fit closely.

ˌ**Knickerbocker** ˈ**Glory** /ˌnɪkəbɒkə; *AmE* ˌnɪkərbɑːkər/ *n* (*BrE*) a dish of ice cream served in a tall glass with other ingredients such as fruit, nuts and cream.

ˌGladys ˈ**Knight** /ˈnaɪt/ (1944–) an *African-American pop singer, especially popular in the 1960s and 1970s. She performed with her brother and two cousins as Gladys Knight and the Pips. Their best hit was *Midnight Train to Georgia* (1973), and the same year they won an *Emmy for *Neither One of Us*. Other successes included *I Heard It Through the Grapevine* (1967), *The Best Thing that Ever Happened to Me* (1974) and *The Way We Were* (1975).

knight (*also* ˌ**knight** ˈ**bachelor**) *n* (*abbr* **Kt**) a man with a rank of honour given to him by the king or queen for his services to the country. He has the title 'Sir' before his first name, used with or without his last name, and his wife has the title 'Lady'. The title cannot be passed on to his children. The equivalent title for women is *dame(2). Other types of knight are men who belong to an *order of chivalry.

▶ **knight** *v* [T] to make a man a knight: *He was knighted in the New Year Honours List.*

ˌ**Knight Com**ˈ**mander** a *knight who belongs to one of the higher *orders of chivalry. The equivalent title for women is *Dame Commander.

ˈ**Knight** ˈ**Grand Com**ˈ**mander** a *knight who belongs to one of the higher *orders of chivalry. There is no equivalent title for women.

ˈ**Knight** ˈ**Grand** ˈ**Cross** a *knight who belongs to one of the higher *orders of chivalry. The equivalent title for women is *Dame Grand Cross.

ˈ**Knightsbridge** /ˈnaɪtsbrɪdʒ/ a district of central London, England, between *Kensington and *Westminster(1). It is famous for its expensive shops, such as *Harrods, and its elegant houses.

the ˌ**Knights of Co**ˈ**lumbus** /kəˈlʌmbəs/ a US Roman Catholic organization with branches in other countries. It was established in 1881 in New Haven, *Connecticut, by Father Michael McGivney, and the main office is still there. Its aim is to help families of Catholics who die and also to create pride in the Catholic religion. The Knights of Columbus is now an important service organization and in 1997 had more than 1.5 million members.

the ˌ**Knights of the Round** ˈ**Table** (in British legend) the men of high rank who served King *Arthur. They are often shown in pictures wearing heavy armour and riding horses. They sat at a round table so that none of them would appear to have a higher rank than the others. The best-known Knights include Sir *Galahad, Sir *Gawain and Sir *Lancelot.

the ˌ**Knights** ˈ**Templars** /ˈtempləz; *AmE* ˈtemplərz/ (*also* the **Knights of the Temple of Solomon**) a religious and military organization formed in Jerusalem in 1119 to protect pilgrims (= people travelling to Jerusalem). In the 12th and 13th centuries they fought in the *Crusades.

ˌ**knock-**ˈ**knock joke** *n* a type of joke that depends on the way in which some words in English sound like other words. The person telling the joke says 'Knock-knock', someone answers 'Who's there?', and the first person says a name which isn't what it seems. A typical example might be: 'Knock-knock.' 'Who's there?' 'Lucy.' 'Lucy who?' 'Lucy Lastic (= loose elastic).'

the ˈ**Knowledge** detailed information about street names, famous buildings, etc. in London, England, which a taxi driver there must have before he or she can receive a licence. Anyone who wants to *do the Knowledge* must pass a series of examinations.

the ˌ**Know-ˈNothing** ˌ**Party** (*also* the ˌ**Know-ˈNothings**) the popular name for the American Republican Party. It was established in 1843 with the aim of restricting immigration and preventing Catholics from holding public office. They were called Know-Nothings because members of the party often refused to admit that they knew anything about it. They had some success in the 1850s, but were divided over the issue of slaves, and the party soon came to an end. The word *know-nothing* is still sometimes applied in the US to a person with political views which are too fixed and not reasonable.

ˌJohn ˈ**Knox** /ˈnɒks; *AmE* ˈnɑːks/ (*c.* 1514–72) a Scottish Protestant leader. He began his career as a *Roman Catholic priest but became a Protestant at the time of the *Reformation. Because of his beliefs he was forced to live abroad for much of his life, and he met John Calvin in Geneva. When he returned to Scotland in 1559 he led the opposition to the Roman Catholic *Mary Queen of Scots, and spent the rest of his life establishing the *Church of Scotland. See also *MONSTROUS REGIMENT OF WOMEN*.

ˈRobin ˈ**Knox-ˈJohnston** /ˈnɒks ˈdʒɒnstən; *AmE* ˈnɑːks ˈdʒɑːnstən/ (1939–) a British yachtsman who was the first man to sail alone around the world without stopping. The journey took ten months, from June 1968 to April 1969. In 1994 he was part of a team that sailed around the world in 74 days, then the fastest time ever. He was made a *knight in 1995.

ˌEd ˈ**Koch** /ˈkɒtʃ; *AmE* ˈkɑːtʃ/ (1924–) a popular former mayor of New York who was elected three times (1977–89) and was known for his lively style. He saved the city from severe financial problems by cutting costs while saving most public services.

ˈ**Kodak** /ˈkəʊdæk; *AmE* ˈkoʊdæk/ a US company which is the world's largest producer of cameras, film and other photographic equipment. It was started in 1892 by George *Eastman who created the name Kodak because he thought 'K' was a lucky letter. The company first sold its famous Brownie camera in 1900 with the advertising phrase, 'You push the button – we do the rest'. Its other products have included Kodachrome film (from 1935), the Instamatic Camera (from 1963) and the Panoramic 35 Camera (from 1990).

ˌArthur ˈ**Koestler** /ˈkɜːstlə(r)/ (1905–83) a British author, born in Hungary. His experiences as a Communist in the 1930s and later as a prisoner during the Spanish Civil War influenced his most famous novel, *Darkness at Noon* (1941). His other novels include *Arrival and Departure* (1943) and *The Call Girls* (1972). He also wrote many books about science, including *The Act of Creation* (1964), about the relationship between science and art. He killed himself in 1983 when suffering from a serious illness, and his wife Cynthia killed herself at the same time.

the ˈ**Kohinoor** /ˈkəʊɪnʊə(r); *AmE* ˈkoʊɪnʊr/ (*also* the **Kohinoor diamond**) a large diamond given to the British in 1849 by the ruler of the Punjab in India. It is now part of the *Crown Jewels.

ˈ***Kojak*** /ˈkəʊdʒæk; *AmE* ˈkoʊdʒæk/ a US television series (1973–8) about a tough New York police *detective, Lieutenant Theo Kojak, played by Telly Savalas. He wore fashionable clothes, was completely bald, and often sucked a lollipop (= small round sweet on a stick). One of his favourite expressions was 'Who loves ya, baby?'

ˈ**Kool-Aid**™ /ˈkuːl/ *n* [U, C] a US drink especially popular with children. It is sold as a powder in small paper packets and is available in several flavours.

ˌTed ˈ**Koppel** /ˈkɒpl; *AmE* ˈkɑːpl/ (1940–) a US television journalist, born in England. Since 1979 he has presented *Nightline*, a news programme on *ABC.

the **Korean War**

The Korean War began in 1950, during the ***Cold War**, a period when the US and the former Soviet Union were competing for power and influence but were trying to avoid a war which could lead to the use of nuclear weapons. On 25 June 1950 soldiers from Communist North Korea invaded South Korea, which had links with the US, and the *United Nations (UN) responded by sending soldiers to defend it.

The Soviet Union gave North Korea weapons, and almost certainly encouraged the invasion. The US persuaded the UN to act on behalf of South Korea and supplied many of the soldiers. General *MacArthur, an American, led the UN forces. But the US and the Soviet Union still tried to avoid war, the Soviet Union by denying it was involved, and the US by saying it was only taking part in a UN operation.

The North Koreans were pushed back above the **38th parallel** (= the imaginary line that divided the two Koreas) by the end of October 1950, and then the UN forces tried to take control of the North. At first they were successful, but as the soldiers got close to China's border China attacked and they were pushed back towards the 38th. After this, it seemed that either side could win only by taking control of all Korea, but to do so would have required more effort and resources. Both sides were afraid of **escalating** the situation (= making it more serious) in case that led to nuclear war. **Peace talks** made slow progress. Finally, on 27 July 1953, an agreement was reached at Panmunjom, ending the war and leaving Korea still divided.

The Korean War raised many questions which Americans found it difficult to answer. For example, why was the US fighting in a place so far away and so little connected with its own interests? Was it right to stop fighting without a clear result? If the US could not or would not use all its strength to win, was it better not to fight at all? And, above all, what was the right role for the country which, after *World War II, was the world's greatest power?

ˌDavid **Koˈresh** /kɒˈreʃ; *AmE* kɔːˈreʃ/ (1959–93) the leader of the religious group called the *Branch Davidians. He was born Vernon Wayne Howell in *Houston and became a member of the Church of *Seventh-Day Adventists but was forced to leave it for being a bad influence. He tried to become a pop singer in *Hollywood but failed. In 1981 he joined the Branch Davidians, later becoming their leader and changing his name. He died with most of the group's members during a battle with US government forces in Waco, *Texas in 1993.

KP /ˌkeɪ ˈpiː/ (*in full* **kitchen police**) *n* [U] (*AmE*) (in the US armed forces) work done in the military kitchens, in which soldiers help the regular cooks. Such work is often given as punishment. The soldiers doing it can also be called the 'kitchen police' but not the 'KP': *The sergeant assigned Brewster to KP for missing roll call.*

Kraft™ /krɑːft/ a US company best known for making various types of cheese, including Philadelphia cheese. Its other products include sauces and pickles.

ˌJudith ˈ**Krantz** /ˈkrænts/ (1928–) a US writer. Her

K

stories are about beautiful women and rich, powerful men. Her first and best-known novel was *Scruples* (1978). Others include *Princess Daisy* (1980), *I'll Take Manhattan* (1986), *Till We Meet Again* (1988) and *Spring Collection* (1997).

ˈ**K ˌrations** /ˈkeɪ/ *n* [pl] (*AmE*) special meals given to US soldiers during World War II. They were named after Dr Ancel Keys, the leader of the group that created them. The food was supplied in three boxes, one each for breakfast, lunch and dinner, and each contained a healthy number of calories (= units measuring energy value) and vitamins, as well as four cigarettes.

the ˈ**Kray twins** /ˈkreɪ/ two English brothers, **Ronnie Kray** (1934–95) and **Reggie Kray** (1934–), who led a group of criminals in the *East End of London in the 1960s. They were found guilty in 1969 of murdering two men and sent to prison for 30 years. Ronnie Kray died in prison in 1995. A third brother, Charlie Kray, was sent to prison in 1997 for selling drugs.

ˌ**Kriss** ˈ**Kringle** /ˌkrɪs ˈkrɪŋgl/ a US name for *Father Christmas. It comes from the German word *Christkindl*, meaning Christ child, because German children believe that the baby Jesus brings presents during the Christmas season.

ˌRay ˈ**Kroc** /ˈkrɒk; *AmE* ˈkrɑːk/ (1902–84) the American who developed *McDonald's into the biggest *fast-food restaurant company in the world. In 1955 he bought the company and its name from two brothers, Richard and Maurice McDonald, who had one restaurant in San Bernardino, *California. Kroc created the gold arches which are the McDonald's symbol, and established a Hamburger University to train the company's employees.

ˈ**Kroger** /ˈkrəʊgə(r); *AmE* ˈkroʊgər/ the largest US group of grocery stores. The company's first shop was opened by Barney Kroger in 1883 in Cincinnati, *Ohio, and its main office is still there. In 1994 Kroger introduced a system aimed at reducing violence in the US. They offered special tickets which could be exchanged for products in their shops to anyone owning a gun who gave it to the company.

the ˈ**Krogers** /ˈkrəʊgəz; *AmE* ˈkroʊgərz/ **Peter Kroger** (1910–95) and **Helen Kroger** (1913–92), a US married couple living in London, England, who were found guilty in 1961 of spying for the Russian government. They were sent to prison for 20 years.

ˈ**Krypton** /ˈkrɪptɒn; *AmE* ˈkrɪptɑːn/ the planet where *Superman was born, according to the original story. The people on Krypton were about to die, so his parents sent the baby Superman away in a spacecraft which later landed on Earth.

The ˈ***Krypton*** ˌ***Factor*** /ˈkrɪptɒn; *AmE* ˈkrɪptɑːn/ a popular British television series, first broadcast in 1977, in which people compete in contests that test their intelligence and physical strength.

ˈ**kryptonite** /ˈkrɪptənaɪt/ *n* [U] ⇨ SUPERMAN.

KT /ˌkeɪ ˈtiː/ (in Britain) the abbreviation for Knight of the *Order of the Thistle: *Sir Norman Smith KT.*

K-12 /ˌkeɪ ˈtwelv/ *adj* (*AmE*) (in the US education system) relating to the years from kindergarten (= school for very young children) to 12th grade: *The state pays for a K-12 education.*

ˌ***Kubla*** ˈ***Khan*** /ˌkuːblə ˈkɑːn/ a poem by Samuel Taylor *Coleridge written in 1797 but not published until 1816. It was written after the poet dreamed about a palace built by the Mongol ruler Kubla Khan. He was unable to finish the poem, however, because a 'person from Porlock' (a village in *Somerset) interrupted him while he was writing, and he forgot the dream. The poem begins with these well-known lines:

In Xanadu did Kubla Khan
A stately pleasure-dome decree:
Where Alph, the sacred river, ran
Through caverns measureless to man
Down to a sunless sea.

ˌStanley ˈ**Kubrick** /ˈkuːbrɪk/ (1928–99) a US film director, known for his great attention to detail. His best-known films include *Spartacus* (1960), *Lolita* (1962), *Dr Strangelove* (1963), **2001: A Space Odyssey*, *A Clockwork Orange* (1971) and *The Shining* (1980).

the ˌ**Ku Klux** ˈ**Klan** /ˌkuː klʌks ˈklæn/ (*abbr* the **KKK**) a secret US organization opposed to equal rights for *African Americans. The members wear long white robes and tall pointed hats to hide their identity. Their leader is called the Grand Wizard. They sometimes burn the Christian symbol of the cross in front of the houses of African Americans or people who support them. The organization was first formed in *Tennessee in 1866, to frighten African Americans after the *Civil War, but it was made illegal in 1871. It began again in 1915, attacking not only African Americans but also Jews, Roman Catholics and people from foreign countries. It had nearly 5 million members in the 1920s, including many outside the South. The Klan became strong again in the 1960s when it opposed the *civil rights movement, often with violence, but today it has less influence.

members of the Ku Klux Klan

ˌCharles **Ku**ˈ**ralt** /kəˈrɔː/ (1934–97) a US television journalist. He presented *Sunday Morning*, a news programme on *CBS from 1979 to 1994 and often travelled around America talking to ordinary people for special programmes called *On the Road*. His books include *A Life on the Road* (1991) and *Charles Kuralt's America* (1995).

ˈ**Kwanza** /ˈkwɑːnzə/ a cultural festival celebrated by some *African-American groups from 26 December to 1 January. The name comes from a Swahili phrase meaning 'first fruits'.

ˈ**Kwik-Fit**™ /ˈkwɪk/ a British company which owns garages where motor vehicles can be repaired or have parts replaced (especially tyres or exhausts).

ˈ**Kwik Save**™ /ˈkwɪk/ a British company which owns a chain of supermarkets selling food and household goods at low prices.

ˌ**KY** ˈ**jelly**™ /ˌkeɪ waɪ/ *n* [U] a make of soft jelly used to lubricate parts of the body, especially the vagina, before having sex.

Ll

LA /ˌel ˈeɪ/ ⇨ LOS ANGELES.

ˈ**Labor Day** /ˈleɪbə deɪ; *AmE* ˈleɪbər/ a US national holiday to honour workers, established in 1894. Labor Day is the first Monday in September and is the last big holiday before the school year begins.

ˈ**labor union** *n* ⇨ article at TRADE UNIONS AND LABOR UNIONS.

the ˈ**Labour ˌParty** (*also* **Labour**) one of the three main parties in British politics, established to represent the interests of workers, and traditionally supported by the *trade unions. It developed from the *Independent Labour Party and formed its first government in 1924 under Ramsay *MacDonald. Other Labour *prime ministers since then have been Clement *Attlee (1945–51), Harold *Wilson (1964–70), James *Callaghan (1974–9) and Tony *Blair (1997–). In the 1980s and 1990s the party moved away from traditional left-wing policies regarding public ownership of industry or giving up nuclear weapons. Because of these changes the party is now also known as **New Labour**. It was elected to government in 1997 under Tony Blair, with a large majority in the *House of Commons.

▶ **Labour** *adj* of or supporting the Labour Party: *a Labour minister* ○ *Is he Labour?* (= Does he support the Labour Party?)

ˈ**Labrador** (*also* ˌ**Labrador reˈtriever**) *n* a breed of dog with a smooth black or yellow coat, originally bred in Labrador, part of north-east Canada. See also RETRIEVER.

laˈcrosse *n* [U] a game similar to *field hockey, played on a field with a goal at each end between two teams of 10 or 12 players each. The players use sticks with nets at the end (called *crosses*) to catch, carry and throw a small rubber ball. In Britain it is popular in schools as a sport for girls.

lacrosse

ˈ**Ladbrokes** /ˈlædbrʊks/ a British company best known for its betting shops (= places in towns where people can bet on horse races, etc.). It also has interests in property and hotels.

ˌAlan ˈ**Ladd** /ˈlæd/ (1913–64) a US film actor who was popular in the 1940s and 1950s. He often played tough characters who showed little emotion. He is best remembered for the *western **Shane* (1953), and his other films included *This Gun for Hire* (1942) and *The Blue Dahlia* (1946). His son, Alan Ladd Junior (1937–), produces films and was at one time head of *20th Century Fox (1977–9).

ˈ**Ladies' Day** **1** (in Britain) the second day of horse-racing at *Ascot, when women traditionally wear elegant hats and fashionable clothes. **2** (in the US) a special day at a sports or other event when women are admitted free of for less than the normal price.

ˈ***Ladies*** ˈ***Home*** ˈ***Journal*** a US magazine for women, first published in 1883. It is sold in large food shops and in 1997 had more than 5 million subscribers (= people who pay to have a newspaper or magazine sent to them regularly).

ˈ**Ladybird** a British publisher of books for children. It is best known for its series of small books with hard covers, started in 1940, which are designed to help children to learn to read. The books have a picture of a ladybird (= a round, red insect with black spots) on the front.

ˌ**Lady** ˈ**Bountiful** (*BrE usu disapprov*) a woman, especially an *upper-class woman, who likes to appear generous with her money, time, etc. The name comes from a character in the play *The Beaux' Stratagem* (1707) by the Irish writer George Farquhar (1678–1707): *She likes to help out at the school and play Lady Bountiful.*

ˈ***Lady*** ˈ***Chatterley's*** ˈ***Lover*** /ˈtʃætəliz; *AmE* ˈtʃætərliz/ a novel by D H *Lawrence, first published in Italy in 1928. It is about an *upper-class married woman who has a sexual affair with her gamekeeper (= a servant who looks after the wild animals on her land). Lawrence was forbidden to publish the book in Britain until 1960 (1959 in the US) because of its detailed descriptions of sex and use of direct sexual language. However, in a famous British trial the publishers, *Penguin Books, were found not guilty of obscenity (= using offensive sexual language) and the book became an immediate success with the public.

ˈ**ladyfinger** /ˈleɪdifɪŋgə(r)/ *n* (*AmE*) a small, light cake, roughly like a finger in shape, made with eggs, sugar and flour.

The ˌ***Lady of Shaˈlott*** /ʃəˈlɒt; *AmE* ʃəˈlɑːt/ a poem by Lord *Tennyson, published in 1833. It tells the story of a mysterious woman living in a castle on an island. She follows Sir *Lancelot in a boat to the city of *Camelot and dies on the way.

the ˌ**Lady of the** ˈ**Lake** a character in stories about King *Arthur, who gives Arthur the sword *Excalibur by holding it above the surface of the lake in which she lives. *The Lady of the Lake* (1810) is also the title of a long romantic poem by Sir Walter *Scott. See also ARTHURIAN LEGEND.

the ˌ**Lady of the** ˈ**Lamp** a name given to Florence *Nightingale by wounded soldiers in the *Crimean War, because she carried a lamp with her as she walked around the hospital where she worked.

Marˌquis de **Lafayˈette** /mɑːˌkiː də læfaɪˈet; *AmE* mɑːrˌkiː/ (1757–1834) a French soldier and politician who helped the Americans during the *American Revolution and fought at the Battle of *Yorktown. He also persuaded the French king Louis XVI to send more soldiers to America to fight the British. This made him very popular in the US, and towns are named after him in several states, including *Indiana, *Louisiana and *Alabama. When the US sent armed forces to help France in *World War I, one American officer said, 'Lafayette, we are here.'

ˌFioˈrello **La** ˈ**Guardia** /ˌfiːəˈreləʊ lə ˈgwɑːdiə; *AmE* ˌfiːəˈreloʊ lə ˈgwɑːrdiə/ (1882–1947) a popular *mayor(2) of New York (1933–45). He was known as the 'Little Flower', which is what Fiorello means in Italian. He began his career as a *Republican(1) politician and was elected to the US Congress (1917–9 and 1923–33). As mayor, he introduced measures to deal with problems of health, housing, transport and crime. During a newspaper strike in 1937 he pleased children by reading *comic strips on the radio. *La Guardia Airport is named after him.

La ˌGuardia ˈAirport /lə ˌgwɑːdiə; *AmE* lə ˌgwɑːrdiə/ an airport in New York City used mostly for flights within the country. It is in north *Queens and is the closest to *Manhattan(1) of New York's three airports.

ˌCleo **ˈLaine**[1] /ˈleɪn/ (1927–) a British singer and actor who has appeared on stage, television and in films. She is married to the *jazz musician John *Dankworth and began her career performing with him, later achieving success with songs such as *You'll Answer to Me* (1961).

ˌFrankie **ˈLaine**[2] /ˈleɪn/ (1913–) a US singer with a strong voice who was especially popular in the 1950s, when 13 of his records each sold more than a million copies. They included *Jezebel* (1951), *Rawhide* (1952), *High Noon* (1952) and *I Believe* (1953).

ˌRicki **ˈLake** /ˌrɪki ˈleɪk/ (1968–) a US television presenter. Her show *Ricki Lake* (1993–) is popular in the US and Britain, and people appear on it to talk in front of an audience about their lives and problems.

the **ˈLake ˌDistrict** (*also* the **Lakes**) a region of lakes and mountains in Cumbria, north-west England. It contains the highest mountain in England, *Scafell Pike, and the largest lake, *Windermere(1). Other lakes include *Ullswater and *Derwentwater. The area is associated with the *Lake Poets, who lived there and wrote about it. It was later the home of the writers John *Ruskin and Beatrix *Potter. Its beautiful scenery is very popular with tourists, and it was made a *national park in 1951.

L

ˌLakeland ˈterrier /ˌleɪklənd/ *n* a type of small *terrier dog, originally bred in the *Lake District for use in hunting.

the **ˌLake ˈPoets** (*also* the **Lake School**) a group of English *Romantic poets who lived in the *Lake District. Its best-known members were William *Wordsworth, who was born in the Lake District and lived there for most of his life, and Samuel Taylor *Coleridge, who settled there in 1800. Others included Robert *Southey and Thomas *De Quincy.

ˌLake ˈPontchartrain ˈCauseway /ˈpɒntʃətreɪn; *AmE* ˈpɑːntʃərtreɪn/ a US *freeway in south-eastern *Louisiana which is the world's longest road built over water. It is 25 miles (40 kilometres) long and opened in 1957. *New Orleans is at its southern end. The shallow salt-water Lake Pontchartain is close to the *Gulf of Mexico and has an area of 625 square miles (1 619 square kilometres).

the **Lakes** ⇨ LAKE DISTRICT.

ˌLake ˈWobegon /ˈwəʊbɪgɒn; *AmE* ˈwoʊbɪgɔːn/ ⇨ KEILLOR.

ˈLallans /ˈlælənz/ (*also* **Lowland Scots**) *n* [U] a form of English traditionally spoken and written in the *Lowlands of Scotland. It was used by poets such as Robert *Burns and is still used by some Scottish writers today.

ˌCharles **ˈLamb**[1] /ˈlæm/ (1775–1834) an English writer. His best-known works are *Tales from Shakespeare* (1807), written for children with his sister Mary (1764–1847), and *Essays of Elia*, published in two collections in 1823 and 1833.

ˌLady ˈCaroline **ˈLamb**[2] /ˈlæm/ (1785–1828) an English author and the wife of William Lamb, who later became the British *Prime Minister Lord *Melbourne. She is best known for her sexual affair with the poet Lord *Byron, whom she described as 'mad, bad and dangerous to know', and who was the model for a character in her novel *Glenarvon* (1816).

the **ˌLambeth ˈConference** /ˌlæmbəθ/ a meeting of Anglican *Anglican *bishops from around the world. It was first held in 1876 at *Lambeth Palace and is now held every ten years.

ˌLambeth ˈPalace /ˌlæmbəθ/ the official home of the *Archbishop of Canterbury, the head of the *Church of England, in Lambeth, central London.

the ***ˌLambeth ˈWalk*** /ˌlæmbəθ/ a dance and a song named after Lambeth Walk, a street in central London, England. The dance involved dancers forming a long line, often in the street, and was popular in the 1930s and 1940s.

LAMDA /ˈlæmdə/ (*in full* the **London Academy of Music and Dramatic Art**) the oldest drama school in London, England, established in 1861. It no longer trains musicians.

ˌNorman **Laˈmont** /ləˈmɒnt; *AmE* ləˈmɑːnt/ (1942–) a former British *Conservative politician. He entered the *House of Commons in 1972 and became *Chancellor of the Exchequer in John *Major's government in 1990. Many people blamed him for the financial losses involved when Britain left the European *exchange-rate mechanism in 1992, and he left his post as Chancellor in 1993. He was made a *life peer in 1998.

ˌLouis **L'Aˈmour** /ləˈmʊə(r); *AmE* ləˈmʊr/ (1908–88) a US author of over a hundred books, most of them *westerns, which sold more than 200 million copies during his life. He is the only US writer to have received a gold medal from Congress (in 1983) and the *Presidential Medal of Freedom (in 1984). His first book, *Hondo* (1953), was made into a *3-D film with John *Wayne. Among his other books which also became films were *The Burning Hills* (1956) and *Heller in Pink Tights* (1960).

ˈLancashire /ˈlænkəʃə(r)/ **1** (*abbr* **Lancs**) a county in north-west England. It was one of the centres of the *Industrial Revolution, and was famous especially for its cotton mills and coal mines. In 1974 the county was reduced in size and it no longer includes the cities of *Liverpool and *Manchester. Its administrative centre is Preston. **2** (*also* **Lancashire cheese**) *n* [U] a type of mild white cheese that breaks easily into small pieces. It is traditionally made in Lancashire.

ˌLancashire ˈhotpot /ˌlæŋkəʃə; *AmE* ˌlæŋkəʃər/ *n* a dish, originally made in Lancashire, England, consisting of lamb and other ingredients covered with slices of potato and baked in an oven.

ˈLancaster[1] /ˈlæŋkəstə(r)/ **1** a city in *Lancashire(1), England, on the River Lune. *John of Gaunt became Duke of Lancaster in 1362, and since 1399 the *Duchy of Lancaster has been a possession of the British *Crown. The **Lancastrians** in the *Wars of the Roses were supporters of the royal house descended from John of Gaunt. **2** (*also* **ˌLancaster ˈbomber**) *n* a large British bomber during *World War II. Lancasters were introduced in 1942 and were used by the *Dam Busters. Compare BLENHEIM, WELLINGTON.

ˌBurt **ˈLancaster**[2] /ˌbɜːt ˈlæŋkəstə(r); *AmE* ˌbɜːrt ˈlæŋkəstər/ (1913–94) a US actor who was a *Hollywood star in the 1950s and 1960s. He began his career as a circus acrobat. He was known for playing strong characters and for his big smile. Lancaster won an *Oscar for **Elmer Gantry*. Among his other films were **From Here to Eternity*, *The Birdman of Alcatraz* (1962), *The Leopard* (1963) and *Field of Dreams* (1989).

the ˌHouse of **ˈLancaster**[3] /ˈlæŋkəstə(r)/ the English royal house (= family) descended from *John of Gaunt, Duke of Lancaster, which ruled England from 1399 to 1461. The three kings of the House of Lancaster were *Henry IV, *Henry V and *Henry VI. During the rule of Henry VI, the *Wars of the Roses began between the **Lancastrians** and the **Yorkists**, which resulted in the creation of a new royal house, the House of *York (1461–85).

ˌOsbert ˈ**Lancaster**[4] /ˌɒzbət ˈlæŋkəstə(r); *AmE* ˌɑːzbərt ˈlæŋkəstər/ (1908–86) an English cartoonist and writer. His 'pocket cartoons' (= small funny drawings) appeared in the **Daily Express* newspaper from 1939 onwards, and were popular for characters such as the *upper-class Lady Maudie Littlehampton. He also wrote books on architecture and designed scenery for the theatre. He was made a *knight in 1975.

ˌSir ˈ**Lancelot** /ˈlɑːnsəlɒt; *AmE* ˈlɑːnsəlɑːt/ the most famous of King *Arthur's *Knights of the Round Table, sometimes called Lancelot of the Lake. He was Arthur's favourite *knight, but deceived him by becoming the lover of Queen *Guinevere, Arthur's wife. Sir *Galahad was his son by Elaine, the daughter of King Pelles. ⇨ article at ARTHURIAN LEGEND.

The ˈ***Lancet*** a British magazine for doctors and other medical workers which first appeared in 1823. It is published every week by the *British Medical Association and contains articles on new medical procedures, drugs, etc. It has many readers in other countries.

ˌAnn ˈ**Landers** /ˈlændəz; *AmE* ˈlændərz/ (1918–) a US journalist who writes a national newspaper column giving advice on love and family problems. She began it in 1955 in the Chicago *Sun-Times*. Her twin sister, Abigail Van Buren, writes a similar column called **Dear Abby*.

ˈ**landlady** *n* **1** a woman who owns a guest house or boarding house and rents rooms to people. In the past British landladies had a reputation for being unfriendly and strict: *seaside landladies*. **2** a woman who rents a building, flat/apartment, etc. to somebody. **3** a woman who owns or manages a pub.

ˈ***Land of*** ˈ***Hope and*** ˈ***Glory*** the title and first line of a song by Edward *Elgar, originally part of his **Pomp and Circumstance* marches. The words (by A C Benson) are very patriotic (= expressing pride in Britain). The song is traditionally performed at the *Last Night of the Proms with the audience singing the words.

ˌ***Land of My*** ˈ***Fathers*** the title of the *national anthem of Wales.

the ˈ**Land** ˌ**Registry** a British government organization that keeps records of the owners of land, and must be informed whenever land is bought or sold.

ˈ**Land** ˌ**Rover**™ (*also* **Land-Rover**) /ˌrəʊvə(r); *AmE* ˌroʊvər/ a strong motor vehicle, first made by *Rover in 1949, and designed for use over rough ground or farm land. Compare JEEP.

ˌ**landscape** ˈ**gardening** *n* [U] the art of designing a garden, especially for the land around a large house, palace, etc. British landscape gardening developed in the 18th century under artists such as William *Kent who tried to create landscapes with a natural, informal effect similar to those seen in 17th-century Italian painting. Artificial lakes and buildings such as temples or 'ruins' were specially created for this purpose. The most famous figure in British landscape gardening was Lancelot 'Capability' *Brown, who designed the gardens at *Longleat House and *Blenheim Palace.

In the US, Frederick Law Olmstead (1822–1903) followed the British style when he created *Central Park in New York City. He was the first person to call himself a 'landscape architect'. In the 20th century, gardens and houses have often been designed together, e.g. by Frank Lloyd *Wright.

▶ **landscape gardener** *n* a person whose job is landscape gardening.

ˌEdwin ˈ**Landseer** /ˈlændsɪə(r)/ (1802–73) an English painter and sculptor best known for his paintings of animals. *Monarch of the Glen* (1850), one of his most famous paintings, shows a stag (= male deer) in a Scottish Highland scene. Landseer created the lions at the base of *Nelson's Column in *Trafalgar Square, and was Queen *Victoria's favourite painter. He was made a *knight in 1850.

ˌ**Land's** ˈ**End** the place in England that is furthest to the west, on the coast of *Cornwall. The point furthest to the south is the *Lizard. *John o'Groats is the point furthest to the north, and the phrase *from Land's End to John o'Groats* is used to mean 'all over Britain': *She's well known from Land's End to John o'Groats.*

ˌLois ˈ**Lane** /ˈleɪn/ ⇨ SUPERMAN.

ˌFritz ˈ**Lang** /ˌfrɪts ˈlæŋ/ (1890–1976) an Austrian film director who directed many *Hollywood films between 1936 and 1956. He began his film career in Germany, where he directed silent films, including *Metropolis* (1927) and *M* (1933). In America, he became known for his films about violence, including *Fury* (1936), *Hangmen Also Die* (1943) and *The Big Heat* (1953). After returning briefly to Germany, Lang finally settled in *Beverly Hills.

ˌWilliam ˈ**Langland** /ˈlæŋlənd/ (*c.* 1330–*c.* 1386) an English poet whose only known work is **Piers Plowman*, a poem describing a man's spiritual journey in search of the truth.

ˌLillie ˈ**Langtry** /ˌlɪli ˈlæŋtri/ (1853–1929) a British actor born in Jersey and known as the Jersey Lily. She was famous for her beauty and for being the lover of the Prince of Wales, later *Edward VII.

LAPD /ˌel eɪ piː ˈdiː/ ⇨ LOS ANGELES POLICE DEPARTMENT.

ˈ**lardy cake** /ˈlɑːdi; *AmE* ˈlɑːrdi/ *n* [C, U] a type of sweet cake traditionally made in the south of England. It is similar to bread but also has lard (= animal fat), sugar and dried fruit added.

ˌPhilip ˈ**Larkin** /ˈlɑːkɪn; *AmE* ˈlɑːrkɪn/ (1922–85) one of the best-known English poets of the second half of the 20th century. His work deals with subjects such as death, love, sex and the natural world, mixing humour with sadness. The poems in collections such as *The Whitsun Weddings* (1964) and *High Windows* (1974) are written in ordinary language but have traditional rhyme, rhythm and verse structure. Larkin also published two novels, *Jill* (1946) and *A Girl in Winter* (1947), as well as two collections of essays.

ˈ***Lark*** ˈ***Rise to*** ˈ***Candleford*** /ˈkændəlfəd; *AmE* ˈkændəlfərd/ a series of three books, *Lark Rise*, *Over to Candleford* and *Candleford Green*, published between 1939 and 1945 by Flora Thompson (1876–1947). They are about traditional village life in England just before the changes of the 20th century.

ˌGary ˈ**Larson** /ˈlɑːsn; *AmE* ˈlɑːrsn/ ⇨ *FAR SIDE*.

ˌHarold ˈ**Larwood** /ˈlɑːwʊd; *AmE* ˈlɑːrwʊd/ (1904–97) an English cricketer. He was one of the fastest bowlers in the game, playing for *Nottinghamshire (1924–38) and England (1926–33). He became involved in the *bodyline dispute during the 1932–3 series against Australia, and injured several players by bowling (= delivering the ball) directly at them. Shortly afterwards he retired from cricket and settled in Australia.

ˈ**Lassie** /ˈlæsi/ a dog that first appeared as a character in the film *Lassie Come Home* (1943), and went on to appear in several other films, a radio and television series, and a television cartoon, all mainly for children. Lassie is an intelligent dog that often rescues people from danger.

Andrew Davis conducting the Last Night of the Proms

the ˈ**Last** ˈ**Night of the** ˈ**Proms** /ˈprɒmz; *AmE* ˈprɑːmz/ the last performance of the *Proms, the series of concerts held every year at the *Albert Hall in London. The music in the second half traditionally consists of songs expressing pride in Britain, such as **Land of Hope and Glory*, **Rule, Britannia!* and **Jerusalem*. It is always a lively occasion, with the audience singing and waving British flags.

The ˌ***Last of*** ˈ***England*** the best-known painting (1855) by Ford Madox *Brown. It shows a young couple on a boat leaving England, and was painted at a time when many people were leaving the country to start a new life abroad. The young woman is holding the hand of a small child who is hidden under her coat.

L

The Last of England

The ˌ***Last of the Mo***ˈ***hicans*** /məʊˈhiːkənz; *AmE* moʊˈhiːkənz/ a famous novel (1826) by the US writer James Fenimore *Cooper. It was one of his **Leatherstocking Tales* about 18th-century life on the American frontier. It tells the story of Hawkeye who has grown up with *Native-American Mohican people after his European parents were killed. Film versions were made in 1936, with Randolph *Scott, and in 1992, with Daniel *Day-Lewis.

ˈ***Last of the*** ˈ***Summer*** ˈ***Wine*** a *BBC television comedy series about three old men (Compo, Clegg and Foggy) living in a Yorkshire village. It began in 1974 and has been running longer than any other comedy series on British television. See also BATTY.

ˌ**Las** ˈ**Vegas** /ˌlæs ˈveɪɡəs/ (*also infml* **Vegas**) a US city where many people go to gamble. It is the largest city in the state of *Nevada and one of the fastest growing cities in the US. It first became popular in the 1940s. Criminals once operated many of the hotels, nightclubs and casinos (= gambling clubs) on Las Vegas Bouvelard, known as 'the Strip', but this has changed and the city now offers much more family entertainment. Its many hotels and casinos include the MGM Grand, Caesar's Palace, Treasure Island and Luxor. Las Vegas is also a place where many couples go to get married quickly.

Las Vegas

ˈ**latchkey child** /ˈlætʃkiː/ *n* (*pl* ˈ**latchkey** ˌ**children**) a child who usually returns to an empty house or flat after school, because both his or her parents are out at work. The expression is used to show disapproval by people who think it is wrong for young children to be left at home alone.

ˌHugh ˈ**Latimer** /ˈlætɪmə; *AmE* ˈlætɪmər/ (*c.* 1485–1555) an English bishop who became one of the leading figures of the *Reformation in England. When *Mary I became queen he opposed her Catholic policies and was executed in Oxford by being burned, together with another bishop, Nicholas Ridley (*c.* 1500–55).

Laˈ**tino** /læˈtiːnəʊ; *AmE* læˈtiːnoʊ/ *n* (*pl* **-os**) a person from Latin America or descended from Latin Americans. Compare CHICANO, HISPANIC, TEX-MEX.

ˌEstée ˈ**Lauder**[1] /ˌesteɪ ˈlɔːdə(r)/ (1908–) a US businesswoman who established an international company selling cosmetics. She began it in 1946 with four products, and it remained a private company until 1996. In 1997 it had sales of over $3 billion around the world.

ˌHarry ˈ**Lauder**[2] /ˈlɔːdə(r)/ (1870–1950) a Scottish comic singer who wore *Highland dress on stage and became popular with songs such as *I Love a Lassie* and *Roamin' in the Gloamin'*. He was made a *knight in 1919 for his work entertaining soldiers during *World War I.

ˈ**Laugh-In** ⇨ ROWEN AND MARTIN'S LAUGH-IN.

The ˌ***Laughing Cava***ˈ***lier*** a well-known painting by the Dutch painter Frans Hals (*c.* 1580–1666) showing a smiling young man. It was painted in 1624 and is now in the *Wallace Collection, having become one of the most popular pictures in Britain.

ˌCharles ˈ**Laughton** /ˈlɔːtn/ (1899–1962) a British actor who became a US citizen in 1950. He worked in the theatre until the 1930s, when he began acting in films. These included *The Private Life of Henry VIII*

(1933), for which he won an *Oscar, and *The Hunchback of Notre Dame* (1939). He was not often given romantic parts, and described his own face as being 'like the behind of an elephant'. He settled in the US in 1940 and made several films for *Hollywood.

ˌ**Laura ˈAshley**™ /ˈæʃli/ a company started in 1953 by the Welsh designer Laura Ashley (1925–85) and her husband Bernard, which now owns a large number of shops in Britain and abroad. Its products are well known for their traditional country designs and soft colours, and include clothes, printed cotton fabrics, furniture and household goods.

ˌStan ˈ**Laurel** /ˈlɒrəl; *AmE* ˈlɔːrəl/ ⇨ LAUREL AND HARDY.

ˌ**Laurel and ˈHardy** /ˌlɒrəl, ˈhɑːdi; *AmE* ˈlɔːrəl, ˈhɑːrdi/ a pair of comedy film actors, **Stan Laurel** (1890–1965) and **Oliver Hardy** (1892–1957), who made over 100 long and short films together between 1926 and 1940 and formed the most successful comedy team in the history of *Hollywood. Laurel, born in Britain, was the thin one and Hardy was the fat one. In their films Laurel often caused the many accidents that happened to them both, after which Hardy would get angry and say, 'This is another fine mess you've gotten me into.' The Laurel and Hardy Museum is in Harlem, *Georgia, where Hardy was born.

Laurel and Hardy in Saps at Sea

ˌRalph ˈ**Lauren** /ˈlɔːrən/ (1939–) a US designer of informal clothes for men, women and children. He also produces many other products, such as bed sheets and luggage, and has designed costumes for films.

ˈ**laver bread** /ˈlɑːvə; *AmE* ˈlɑːvər/ *n* [U] a dish that is eaten mainly in Wales. It is made from laver, a type of seaweed, which is boiled, mixed with oatmeal (= a type of rough flour) and fried in flat cakes.

the ˈ**Law Comˌmission** a British government organization formed in 1965 to examine the nation's laws and publish proposals for changing them. Scotland has a separate Law Commission from England and Wales.

the ˈ**Law Courts** (*also* the **Royal Courts of Justice**) the building in central London, England, where most *High Court trials are held.

law enforcement

Britain has 52 regional **police forces**, which are responsible for maintaining **law and order** in their own area. London has two police forces, the ***Metropolitan Police**, often referred to as the **Met**, which covers *Greater London, and the smaller City of London Police.

Each regional police force is led by a Chief Constable. Police officers wear dark blue uniforms, and **constables** wear tall hard helmets. The British police force is relatively small, with one police officer to every 400 people. Some members of the public are trained as special constables and are available to help the police in an emergency.

British police officers

The **Criminal Investigation Department (CID)** is based at *New Scotland Yard and is sometimes referred to as 'Scotland Yard'. As well as operating in London, it provides **detectives** to help the regional forces solve more serious crimes. The CID is div-ided into several branches, including the ***Special Branch**, the ***Flying Squad**, the ***Fraud Squad**, the ***Vice Squad**, the **Criminal Record Office**, and **Traffic Control**. CID officers do not wear uniform.

Attitudes towards the police have changed in Britain over the years. The traditional image of the friendly **bobby on the beat**, a policeman going round his local area on foot or on a bicycle armed only with a whistle and a **truncheon** (= long club), is now out of date. The modern police officer, man or woman, is more likely to be **patrolling** in a **police car** and to have less contact with the public. Police officers generally still carry only truncheons as weapons, and though some are trained to use a gun they only carry one in special circumstances. Dishonesty, racial prejudice and excessive use of force by some officers have damaged the public image of the police. Insulting names such as *coppers*, *pigs*, *filth* and *the fuzz* are now common. In response, the police have tried to get rid of dishonest officers and build better relationships with local communities, a practice called **community policing**. More police now patrol on foot again, instead of in cars.

In the US, law enforcement is carried out by different organizations at the various levels of government. In all, there are about 17 000 **law enforcement agencies** and they employ more than 800 000 full-time officers. At national level, the ***FBI (Federal Bureau of Investigation)** has about 10 000 **special agents** who investigate crimes across the US. At state level, **state police departments** are responsible for **highway patrols** and their officers are called ***state troopers**. Each *county within a state has an elected **sheriff** and the people who work in the sheriff's office, **deputies**, are responsible for investigating crimes. Cities have their own police departments. They may be very large in cities like New York, but those in small towns have only a few officers. Most colleges and universities have their own small police forces.

The members of the US police force who have most contact with the public are **uniformed officers**, who patrol in cars and are the first to arrive when a

City of Pasadena police officers

L

crime is reported. More serious crimes are investigated by detectives, who usually wear **plain clothes** instead of a uniform. In spite of the fact that police officers in the US wear guns, they are seen by many Americans as being honest, helpful people who work hard at a dangerous job. This is the image that has been shown in popular television programmes such as **Columbo* and *Hill Street Blues*. But in recent years it has become clear that many police officers are prejudiced against *African Americans and *Hispanics and that in some polices forces, such as that in *Los Angeles, prejudice and even violence by the police have been common.

ˌSue **ˈLawley** /ˈlɔːli/ (1946–) a British television and radio broadcaster. She has presented current affairs programmes for television, including *Nationwide* (1972–83) and *Here and Now* (1994–7), and since 1988 she has presented the radio programme **Desert Island Discs*.

the **ˈLaw Lords** the eleven members of the *House of Lords in Britain who, together with the *Lord Chancellor, act as the highest *Court of Appeal in England and Wales. A Law Lord must have been a senior judge or a former Lord Chancellor.

Law-making in the US ⇨ article.

ˌ**lawn ˈtennis** ⇨ TENNIS.

ˌD H **ˈLawrence**[1] /ˈlɒrəns; *AmE* ˈlɔːrəns/ (David Herbert Lawrence 1885–1930) an English writer of novels, short stories and poetry. He came from a *working-class mining background which sometimes featured in his stories. His novels include **Sons and Lovers* (1913), *The Rainbow* (1915) and *Women in Love* (1920). A common theme in his writing is the importance of free emotional and sexual expression, and many of his books were originally considered to be obscene (= offensive or disgusting). His most famous novel, **Lady Chatterley's Lover*, was not published in full in Britain until 1960. Lawrence was also an important modern poet, and his collected poems were published in 1928.

L

ˌT E **ˈLawrence**[2] /ˈlɒrəns; *AmE* ˈlɔːrəns/ (Thomas Edward Lawrence 1888–1935) an English soldier and writer. He began his career as an archaeologist, but in 1916 went to Saudi Arabia to plan and lead a successful military campaign against Turkish rule in the Middle East, as a result of which he became known as Lawrence of Arabia. He described the campaign in his book **Seven Pillars of Wisdom* (1926). This brought him fame and a romantic reputation, but he disliked publicity and tried to escape it by twice changing his name. He died in a motorcycle accident in *Dorset, England. The film *Lawrence of Arabia* (1962) featured Peter O'Toole as Lawrence.

T E Lawrence

ˈ**law school** *n* a US college at which people study to become lawyers. It is usually part of a university, and students enter it after they have their first degree: *She's at Harvard Law School.* See also LSAT.

ˌ**Law School Adˈmission Test** ⇨ LSAT.

the **ˈLaw Soˌciety** the professional organization to which all solicitors in England and Wales belong. It holds examinations for those wishing to enter the profession, establishes rules for professional practice and deals with complaints against its members.

ˌNigel **ˈLawson** /ˈlɔːsn/ (1932–) an English *Conservative politician. He became a *Member of Parliament in 1974 and *Chancellor of the Exchequer in 1983. He left his job as Chancellor in 1989 after disagreements with the *Prime Minister, Margaret *Thatcher, and was replaced by John *Major. In 1992 he retired from Parliament, and was made a *life peer in the same year. He has worked as a journalist and published several books.

ˈ**layaway** /ˈleɪəweɪ/ *n* [U] (*AmE*) a special way of buying goods. A customer can pay a small part of the price of something, and the shop will keep the item for a period of time until the rest is paid. Layaway is commonly used for more expensive items, such as furniture: *I've put a winter coat on layaway.*

ˈ***Lays of ˈAncient ˈRome*** /ˈrəʊm; *AmE* ˈroʊm/ a series of four long poems by Thomas *Macaulay published in 1842. Each tells a story from early Roman history. The best-known of these is about how Horatius defended a bridge over the River Tiber against the Tuscan army. A later edition in 1848 added stories from modern times.

LBC /ˌel biː ˈsiː/ ⇨ LONDON BROADCASTING COMPANY.

LBJ /ˌel biː ˈdʒeɪ/ ⇨ JOHNSON[3].

LCC /ˌel siː ˈsiː/ ⇨ LONDON COUNTY COUNCIL.

L-driver /ˈel draɪvə(r)/ (*also* **learner driver**) *n* (in Britain) a person who is learning to drive and has not yet passed the driving test. L-drivers must display **L-plates**, square signs with a large red letter L on a white background, on the front and rear of the vehicle they are driving. L-plates on which the letter L is green are also available, to indicate a new learner driver.

LEA /ˌel iː ˈeɪ/ ⇨ LOCAL EDUCATION AUTHORITY.

ˌ**Lea and ˈPerrins** /ˌliː ənd ˈperɪnz/ the British company that makes *Worcester sauce.

'Leadbelly' /ˈledbeli/ (1888–1949) an *African-American singer of the *blues and *folk music who also played the guitar. His real name was Huddie Ledbetter. He was in prison three times between 1918 and 1939, once for murder, before achieving success as a singer. He had a powerful voice, and his hits included *Rock Island Line*, *How Long Blues* and *Goodnight, Irene*.

the ˌ**Leader of the ˈHouse** *n* a member of the government who is officially responsible for arranging and announcing the programme of business in the British parliament each week. There is a Leader of the *House of Commons and a separate Leader of the *House of Lords.

the ˌ**Leader of the Oppoˈsition** the leader of the largest political party opposing the government in the British *House of Commons, who is also in charge of the *Shadow Cabinet.

the ˈ**League Against ˈCruel ˈSports** a British organization formed in 1924 which opposes *hunting, shooting and other blood sports, and wants the government to make them illegal. ⇨ article at ANIMALS, note at PRESSURE GROUPS.

the ˌ**League of ˈNations** an international organization formed in 1920 to keep the peace after *World War I. Despite some successes it did little to oppose the rise of Fascism in Germany, Italy and Japan, and the US never became a member. It formed the basis for the *United Nations, which replaced it in 1946.

the ˈ**League of ˈWomen ˈVoters** an independent US organization of people interested in politics. It encourages citizens to take part in politics and to vote, and tries to influence the government on im-

Law-making in the US

How a law begins

The basic procedures involved in making laws in the US were first described in the *Constitution, though further stages have since been developed.

A proposal for a new law may come from the *President or from one or more members of *Congress. Sometimes the original idea for a law comes from a group of ordinary people who do the same job or who want to change a situation that they think is unjust. They use the process of ***lobbying** to try to convince members of Congress to help them make the law. In all cases a proposal must, in order to become a federal law (= one that applies throughout the US), go through Congress.

The role of Congress

A detailed proposal for law is called a ***bill**. A bill may be introduced first in either the House of Representatives or the Senate by a member of that house, who is called a **sponsor**. The more sponsors a bill has, and the more important and influential they are, the more likely it is to pass, especially if the sponsors come from different *political parties.

The bill is then **referred to committee**, i.e. it is examined by an appropriate committee in the house where it was introduced. A bill dealing with farming, for example, would go to the Agriculture Committee. The committee holds public **hearings** at which experts **testify** (= give their opinion of the bill). The committee members themselves then have a chance to give their opinion and to suggest changes. If the bill does not receive strong support, it may be **tabled**. (*Table* means here, in American English, 'to put aside or postpone', not, as in British English 'to bring forward for discussion'). In theory, this means that the committee can return to it later, but in practice it is often never considered again. Many bills **die in committee**.

If the members of a committee vote to approve the bill, they send it back for discussion to the house as a whole. After the debate members vote for or against it, either by a **voice vote**, when members say 'yea' or 'nay', or with a **recorded vote**, when an electronic system makes a record of how each member votes.

If a bill **passes** in the house where it began, it goes to the other house. There, a similar process of debate begins, first in committee and then by the whole house. If the bill passes, changes made in the second house mean that the bill is different from that passed by the first house, so the House of Representatives and the Senate together form a **conference committee** to create a final version. This version has to go back to both houses for another vote.

At all of these stages, where changes are made to a bill, lobbyists work hard to try to make it favourable to their interests. Sponsors of the bill try to convince other members of Congress to vote on it, sometimes by changing parts of the bill to make it more acceptable, sometimes by promising their support for other members' bills.

The role of the President

When both the House of Representatives and the Senate have passed the same version of a bill, they must ask for the President's approval. The President has three choices: to sign the bill, in which case it becomes the law; to do nothing, in which case the bill becomes law after ten days; or to **veto** the bill and send it back to Congress without his approval. If the President vetoes a bill, it still has one more chance: if two-thirds of the members of the House of Representatives and the Senate vote for the bill, they can **override** the veto and the bill becomes law.

Checks and balances

There are many stages in the law-making process at which a bill may be opposed and die. It may be that different parties hold the balance of power in the House of Representatives and in the Senate, or that Congress is controlled by one party while the President is from another. The people who wrote the Constitution intentionally made the law-making process long and complicated so that only those proposals which had wide support would become law. During the time that it takes to make a law, citizens have many opportunities to express their opinions about it and to convince their Senators and Representatives to vote for or against it.

If a law proves not to be successful, it can be **amended** (= changed) or **repealed** (= removed) by a process similar to that for making a new law. Sometimes a law is held to be **unconstitutional** (= goes against the principles of the Constitution) by the *Supreme Court, the highest court in the US. When a law is found to be unconstitutional, it can no longer be applied.

State and local law

At state level, two houses, often also called the Senate and the House of Representatives, form the **legislature**. State laws are made in a similar way to federal laws: they must be passed in both houses before being sent to the state governor for his or her signature. At local level, the process is usually simpler. Local laws, or **ordinances**, may be made by the city council, or possibly by voters at a **town meeting.**

In some states it is common for a few laws to be made directly by the people through a process called **initiative**. A group of people write a law and ask other people to sign a **petition** saying that they agree with it. With enough signatures, a petition can go on the **ballot** at the next election and people can vote for or against it. If enough people vote for it, it becomes a law. A **referendum** is similar to an initiative, but people vote only to show their opinion: if most people vote 'yes' to a proposal in a referendum, members of the legislature will probably decide to make it law.

portant issues. It does not support any particular political parties or candidates but arranges television debates between the candidates for US President. It was originally called the National American Women Suffrage Association and changed its name in 1920, the year in which American women won the right to vote. Men have been admitted as members since 1974.

ˌLeamington ˈSpa /ˌlemɪŋtən/ a spa town (= a town where there are springs of mineral water considered to be healthy to drink) in *Warwickshire, England. In the late 18th century it became a fashionable

L

place for *upper-class people to meet, and Queen *Victoria gave it the title of 'Royal Leamington Spa' in 1838.

ˌDavid ˈ**Lean** /ˈliːn/ (1908–91) an English film director. His early films included *Brief Encounter* (1946) and the *Dickens stories *Great Expectations* (1946) and *Oliver Twist* (1948). Lean's later films were on a larger scale, including *The Bridge on the River Kwai* (1957), *Lawrence of Arabia* (1962) and *Dr Zhivago* (1965). His last film was *A *Passage to India* (1984), based on the E M *Forster novel. He was made a *knight in 1984.

ˌEdward ˈ**Lear** /ˈlɪə(r); *AmE* ˈlɪr/ (1812–88) an English nonsense writer and painter. He spent his early career drawing and painting animals, and in 1832 began work as a painter for the Earl of Derby. He wrote *A Book of Nonsense* (1846) for the Earl's grandchildren, and it was the first of a series of books of nonsense poetry containing *limericks, drawings and longer poems such as *The *Owl and the Pussy-Cat* and *The *Dong with a Luminous Nose*. Lear travelled widely and is also remembered for his many paintings of Mediterranean and Middle Eastern scenes.

ˌ**learner** ˈ**driver** ⇨ L-DRIVER.

the ˌ***Leatherstocking*** ˈ***Tales*** /ˌleðəstɒkɪŋ; *AmE* ˌleðərstɑːkɪŋ/ a series of five novels by the US writer James Fenimore *Cooper. They follow the life of Natty Bumppo, an 18th-century *frontiersman. He first appears in *The Pioneers* (1823) and then (called Hawkeye) in *The *Last of the Mohicans* (1826) and (as the Old Trapper) in *The Prairie* (1827). The other two novels are *The Pathfinder* (1840) and *The Deerslayer* (1841).

L

ˌ***Leaves of*** ˈ***Grass*** the best-known collection of poems by the US poet Walt *Whitman. They praise America and the free American man. The collection was first published in 1855 with 12 poems, and then eight more times with poems added each time until there were more than 130. They were not very popular during Whitman's life, but are now considered to have had a great influence on later US poetry.

ˌF R ˈ**Leavis** /ˈliːvɪs/ (Frank Raymond Leavis 1895–1978) an English literary critic. He taught at *Cambridge University from 1936 to 1962 and started the magazine *Scrutiny* (1932–53). In his books *New Bearings on English Poetry* (1932) and *The Great Tradition* (1948) he helped to establish modern ideas on the work of such writers as Gerard Manley *Hopkins, T S *Eliot, Henry *James and D H *Lawrence.

ˌJohn **Le** ˈ**Carré** /lə ˈkæreɪ/ (1931–) an English author of novels about spies. The character George Smiley appears in many of these, including *The Spy Who Came in from the Cold* (1963) and *Tinker, Sailor, Soldier, Spy* (1974). Many of Le Carré's books have been made into films or television series.

ˌHuddie ˈ**Ledbetter** /ˌhʌdi ˈledbetə(r)/ ⇨ 'LEADBELLY'.

ˌ**Led** ˈ**Zeppelin** /ˌled ˈzepəlɪn/ a British pop group (1968–80). Their *heavy metal style was an important influence on later groups, and they were very popular in both Britain and the US. Their most famous song was *Stairway to Heaven* (1971).

ˌChristopher ˈ**Lee**[1] /ˈliː/ (1922–) an English actor who has appeared in over 120 films since 1948. He is best known for his parts in horror films such as *The Curse of Frankenstein* (1956) and *Dracula* (1958).

ˈGypsy ˈRose ˈ**Lee**[2] /ˈliː/ (1914–70) a US striptease artist (= entertainer who takes off her clothes for an audience), known for her elegant stage performances. She was a star of the *Ziegfeld Follies* in the 1930s, appeared in several films and became popular on television in the 1960s. Lee's book about her life, *Gypsy* (1957), became a *Broadway musical show (1959) and later a film (1962).

ˌLaurie ˈ**Lee**[3] /ˈliː/ (1914–97) an English writer best known for his book *Cider with Rosie* (1959), about his childhood in an English country village. He also published poetry and travel writing.

ˌPeggy ˈ**Lee**[4] /ˈliː/ (1920–) a US *jazz singer with a very soft voice who has also written songs and acted in films. Her successful songs have included *Why Don't You Do Right?* (1942), *Fever* (1958) and *Is That All There Is?* (1969). Her films include *Pete Kelly's Blues* (1955), and she wrote and recorded some of the songs in the *Disney film *Lady and the Tramp* (1955).

ˌRobert E ˈ**Lee**[5] /ˈliː/ (Robert Edward Lee 1807–70) the leader of the armies of the *Confederate States during the American *Civil War. He was respected for his honour and kindness. General Lee won many battles against the larger Union armies, including the second battle of *Bull Run and *Chancellorsville. He lost at *Gettysburg, however, and soon afterwards surrendered to General *Grant at *Appomattox Court House. Before the Civil War, Lee led US forces to arrest John *Brown at *Harpers Ferry. President *Lincoln[2] asked him to lead the US armies, but Lee was loyal to his state of *Virginia and joined the South. After the war, he became President of Washington College, later named Washington and Lee College.

'ˌSpike' ˈ**Lee**[6] /ˌspaɪk ˈliː/ (1957–) an *African American who directs, produces and writes films about African Americans and also acts in some of them. His films include *She's Gotta Have It* (1986), *Mo' Better Blues* (1990), *Malcolm X* (1992) and *Girl 6* (1996).

Leeds /liːdz/ a city in *West Yorkshire, England. In the 16th century it began to be an important centre for the production of cloth and clothing, and later became a centre of the *Industrial Revolution. It remains an important industrial city. Its famous buildings include the Town Hall (1853–8), the City Art Gallery (1888) and Armley Mills, a museum of local industrial history. The Royal Armouries opened there in 1996 and the Thackeray Medical Museum in 1997.

the ˈ**Leeds Inter**ˈ**national Pi**ˈ**ano Compe**ˌ**tition** a British competition for piano players, open to professional players under the age of 30 from around the world and held in Leeds, *West Yorkshire. It was established in 1963 and is held every three years.

leek *n* a vegetable related to the onion but with wider green leaves and a long white bulb. It is a Welsh national *emblem (= symbol for the country), possibly because Welsh soldiers used to wear a leek in their caps to recognize each other in battle. See also DAFFODIL. ⇨ note at EMBLEMS.

ˌ**legal** ˈ**aid** *n* [U] money available from the state to help people pay for legal expenses. Legal aid is only available to people whose income is below a certain level, and may not pay for all the expenses involved in a legal action. In the US, the Legal Services Corporation, a private organization that does not make a profit, gives financial support to local Legal Aid Society offices. In 1995 these offices completed 1.7 million court cases for people with low incomes: *They applied for and were granted legal aid.*

The **legal system in Britain** ⇨ article.

The **legal system in the US** ⇨ article.

ˈ**Legoland** /ˈlegəʊlænd; *AmE* ˈlegoʊlænd/ a place near Windsor, in Berkshire, England, popular for its displays of **Lego**™, small coloured plastic blocks, etc. that children can fit together to make into models. It was opened in 1996 and has other attractions such as

The legal system in Britain

For historical reasons a different system of law is used in Scotland from that in England and Wales. Northern Ireland law is similar to that in England.

Scots law was greatly influenced by Roman law. When making decisions Scottish courts look for an appropriate general principle and apply it to a particular situation. **English law** relies more on **case law**, a collection of previous decisions called **precedents**. English courts look at precedents for the **case** being tried and make a similar judgement.

English ***common law** developed in *Norman times when judges travelled round the country. Later, legal scholars collected together the most significant cases and they became part of case law. Another branch of law, **equity**, deals with cases involving rights and duties, e.g. in connection with contracts. These two branches were joined in 1873. A third branch of law, **statute law**, consists of laws made by *Acts of Parliament. It describes general principles and is superior to case law.

From 1536 Wales became subject to the same laws as England. Law in Northern Ireland is based on case law from England and Ireland, and on British and Irish statutes. By the time of the *Act of Union between England and Scotland in 1707, both countries had well-established legal systems. The Act allowed both systems to continue and this resulted in the different legal practices still in use.

Civil and criminal law

Civil law concerns disagreements between individuals over rights and responsibilities. Many civil cases relate to business contracts. The **plaintiff** (= the person who claims to have been wronged) **brings an action** against the **defendant** (= the person accused) in the hope of winning **damages** (= a financial payment) or an **injunction** (= a court order preventing the defendant from doing something that is causing harm). Taking a case to court is expensive, but people who do not have enough money may qualify for ***legal aid**.

Criminal law deals with offences that involve harm to a person resulting from somebody **breaking the law**. The most serious offences include murder, manslaughter and theft. Cases are brought against criminals by the state, in England and Wales through the ***Director of Public Prosecutions** and in Scotland through **procurators fiscal**.

A basic principle of law in Britain is that anyone accused is **innocent until proved guilty**, so it is the job of the **prosecution** to **prove beyond reasonable doubt** that the defendant has broken the law as stated in the **charge**. If this cannot be proved the accused person must be **acquitted** (= allowed to go free, with no blame attached).

Courts in England and Wales

Every town has a ***Magistrates' Court**, where minor cases are judged and more serious cases are examined briefly before being passed to higher courts. Cases are **heard** by three magistrates, called ***Justices of the Peace**, who are specially trained members of the public advised by a legally qualified **clerk**. Young people under 17 are sent to special **juvenile courts**.

More serious criminal cases are heard in the ***Crown Court**, which **sits** at a number of towns in England and Wales. Cases are heard by a **judge** and a ***jury**. At the end of a trial the jury decides whether the defendant is **guilty** or **not guilty**. If the **verdict** is 'guilty' the judge decides the punishment.

Minor civil cases, such as divorce and bankruptcy proceedings, are heard in the ***County Courts**. More serious cases are heard in the ***High Court of Justice**. This is divided into the *Chancery Division, the *Queen's Bench and the *Family Division. Cases are heard by one or more judges sitting together. **Appeals** against decisions of the County Courts also go to the High Court.

Appeals from the Crown Court or the High Court go to the ***Court of Appeal**. A few cases in which a question of law is in doubt are passed on to the *House of Lords. Here the *Lord Chancellor and Lords of Appeal, often called *Law Lords, make a final decision.

Courts in Scotland and Northern Ireland

Criminal cases in Scotland are heard in **District Courts** by members of the public called **lay justices**. More serious cases go to regional ***sheriff courts**, and are heard by the sheriff and a jury. Juries in Scotland can give a verdict of guilty or not guilty, or decide that a case is **not proven**. This verdict is given when there is not sufficient evidence to **convict** the accused but when it is probable that he or she is guilty. Appeals go to the ***High Court of Justiciary** in Edinburgh.

Civil cases begin in the sheriff court and may go **on appeal** to the ***Court of Session**. This is divided into two Houses. The **Inner House** hears appeals from the sheriff courts, while the **Outer House** hears cases that were too serious to go to the sheriff court.

In Northern Ireland minor cases are heard by magistrates. **County Courts** hear most civil cases, and **Crown Courts** most serious criminal cases. They also act as courts of appeal from the Magistrates' Courts. The higher court in Northern Ireland is the **Supreme Court of Judicature**.

The legal profession

A person who needs legal advice, e.g. when buying a house, usually goes to see a **solicitor**. Solicitors may represent their clients in Magistrates' Courts and, since 1994, in the higher courts. However, solicitors often use ***barristers** to represent their clients in the higher courts. Barristers are lawyers who have received special training at ***Inns of Court** and who have been **called to the *Bar**. They are not allowed to deal directly with the public and can only talk to their client if a solicitor is present. In court they wear a white curly wig and black robes. The most respected barristers hold the title ***QC** (Queen's Counsel). Barristers are called **advocates** in Scotland, and a solicitor or barrister representing a client in the English or Welsh courts is now often referred to as an advocate.

After many years in the courts barristers may be appointed as **judges**. Judges wear a white wig and red robes in court. They are highly paid and are sometimes accused of being remote from the rest of society.

The legal system in the US

The **judicial** system is one of the three branches of the US *federal government. But the legal system operates at many levels, since as well as federal courts there are state, county and city courts.

The courts

Each type of court has its own **jurisdiction**, i.e. it deals with certain kinds of **cases**. Some courts **hear** only **criminal** cases. Other courts are for **civil** cases, in which two people disagree over something. Cases are first heard in **trial courts**. The person accused in a criminal trial, and both sides involved in a civil trial, have the right to **appeal** against the court's decision, and if they do the case goes to a **court of appeals**.

Some trial courts have **limited jurisdiction**. Many states, for example, have **family courts** where people get divorced, and **small claims courts** which hear cases involving small sums of money. States have trial courts of **general jurisdiction** which can hear a wider range of cases. These are often called **courts of common pleas**. State courts of appeals are called **superior courts** or **district courts**, and most states have a **supreme court**. This is the highest court in the state and hears only the most serious appeals.

States have their own **criminal code**, but some crimes are **federal offences**, i.e. against federal law. Crimes may fall under **federal jurisdiction** if more than one state is involved, e.g. if cars are are stolen in one state and then sold in another.

The highest court is the ***Supreme Court** in *Washington, DC, which can hear almost any case on appeal. In fact, it hears only those cases that involve an important principle. When the Supreme Court decides such a case, it sets a **precedent** which lower courts will use to decide similar cases.

The people in a court

The most powerful person in court is the **judge**. Most courts have only one judge, but some higher courts have several. In the US Supreme Court, the nine judges are called **justices**, and the most senior is the **Chief Justice of the United States**. Many state judges are elected, but federal judges are appointed by the President.

The people on either side of a case are represented by **lawyers**, also called **attorneys-at-law**. In a criminal trial the **defendant** (= the person accused) is represented by a **defense attorney**. If he or she is too poor to pay a lawyer, the court will appoint a **public defender**. The **prosecution** is led by an **Assistant District Attorney** or, in a federal case, a **federal attorney**. In each county the people elect a ***District Attorney**, who hires other attorneys. In a civil trial the defendant and the **plaintiff** (= the person who claims to have been wronged) pay their own attorneys. When only a small amount of money is involved people go to a court of common pleas and represent themselves.

Witnesses go to court to **testify** (= tell what they know about the case). Sometimes one or both sides will pay **expert witnesses**. The **bailiff** calls witnesses when it is their turn to come into the courtroom. The **court reporter** keeps a record of everything that is said.

The court in action

At the beginning of a session, the bailiff calls out, 'All rise,' and everybody stands as the judge enters. Both attorneys make an **opening statement** to explain their case. Then each side calls witnesses and presents **evidence**. As each witness **takes the stand** (= goes and sits in a special place) the bailiff **swears them in**. Witnesses promise to tell 'the truth, the whole truth and nothing but the truth'.

Attorneys must not **lead the witness** by suggesting the answer they want to hear, and they must not keep repeating the question. When one attorney thinks another is breaking the rules he or she shouts 'Objection!' or 'Move to strike!' (= a request that words are deleted from the record).

At the end of a trial the jury **deliberate** together. In a case that gets a lot of media attention, the judge may **sequester** the jury (= send them to a hotel where they will not hear others' opinions). In a criminal trial the jury decide the **verdict** and if the verdict is guilty the judge gives the sentence. In a civil trial the jury decides who wins and may also decide the amount of **damages** (= money to be paid as compensation).

Problems in the system

Americans often **sue**, i.e. start a civil trial, for problems that might be solved in other ways. Large numbers of these **frivolous suits** may mean that people with genuine cases have to wait a long time. Although the *Constitution says that the law should protect everyone, rich people have an advantage: in civil cases both sides pay their own attorney, so a poor person who has a good reason to sue may not be able to. Some attorneys will work for a **contingency fee**, a proportion of the money that is awarded if they win the case, and nothing if they lose. A few lawyers, called **ambulance chasers**, encourage people hurt in accidents to sue because they think they can earn a large contingency fee.

The courts and society

Courts, especially the Supreme Court, are very powerful in the US. *Congress makes laws and the President approves them, but if the Supreme Court decides that a law is **unconstitutional** (= goes against the Constitution) it cannot be applied.

The Supreme Court has decided many important issues. For example, the case **Brown v Board of Education* helped to end separate schools for black and white children. For many years the police encouraged people they arrested to confess to a crime, even though they have the right not to. In **Miranda v Arizona* the Court said that the police had to tell people their rights, and now the police **Mirandize** people they arrest by reading them a formal statement saying that they have the right to remain silent and to see a lawyer.

Most Americans believe that their legal system is fair. The idea of **innocent until proven guilty** is especially important. Americans also want their legal system to be open. Members of the public can go into the courts, and real trials are shown on television. However, many African Americans think that the system is only fair and open for white Americans. This is a growing problem and one that seems likely remain as long as their is prejudice against African Americans in other areas of life.

fairground rides and restaurants: *The town looks from the air like a group of Legoland houses.*

ˌSimon **Le'gree** ⇨ SIMON LEGREE.

'Leicester[1] /'lestə(r)/ an English city, the administrative centre of *Leicestershire. Parts of the Roman city walls remain, as well as a ruined *medieval castle. Leicester became a centre of the wool trade in the 15th century and is today an important industrial city. The National Space Science Centre is due to open there in the year 2000.

the ˌEarl of **'Leicester**[2] /'lestə(r)/ (*born* Robert Dudley *c.* 1532–88) an English nobleman and soldier who was a close friend of Queen *Elizabeth I. He was suspected of murdering his wife Amy Robsart in 1560 in order to be free to marry the queen. He and Elizabeth did not marry, however, and she made him an *earl(1) in 1564. See also KENILWORTH CASTLE.

'Leicestershire /'lestəʃə(r); *AmE* 'lestərʃər/ (*written abbr* **Leics**) a *county in the English *Midlands. Its administrative centre is *Leicester.

ˌLeicester 'Square /ˌlestə; *AmE* ˌlestər/ a square in central London which is popular with tourists, and best known for its large cinemas. It became a public garden in 1874 and motor vehicles are not allowed in it. In its centre is a statue of William *Shakespeare, and to the north is a statue of Charlie *Chaplin.

ˌMike **'Leigh**[1] /'li:/ (1943–) an English film and theatre director. His work is mainly about people's ordinary lives, and is often funny and satirical. His films for television include *Nuts in May* (1976) and *Abigail's Party* (1977) and his cinema films include *High Hopes* (1988) and *Secrets and Lies* (1996).

ˌVivien **'Leigh**[2] /'li:/ (1913–67) an English actor, born in India. She achieved great success in the London theatre in the 1930s and in 1940 married Laurence *Olivier. They both moved to *Hollywood, where she won *Oscars for her parts in the films **Gone with the Wind* and *A *Streetcar Named Desire*.

ˌJack **'Lemmon** /'lemən/ (1925–) a US actor, mainly in comic roles. His best-known films include *Some Like It Hot* (1959), *The Apartment* (1960), *The Days of Wine and Roses* (1962) and *The Odd Couple* (1967), in which he appeared with Walter Matthau. Lemmon and Matthau also acted together in *Grumpy Old Men* (1993) and *Grumpier Old Men* (1995).

'Lend-Lease *n* [U] an arrangement during *World War II following the US Lend-Lease Act (1941). The US lent military and other equipment to countries at war with Germany, first to Britain and the Commonwealth and then to other nations. The programme cost the US $50 billion. Lend-Lease encouraged Americans to want to enter the war, and it marked the beginning of war production in the US. Countries paid back the loans (= sums of money lent) in various ways, e.g. by allowing the US to use military bases in Europe, etc.

ˌJohn **'Lennon** /'lenən/ (1940–80) an English singer and guitar player with the *Beatles pop group, who with Paul *McCartney wrote most of the group's songs. After the group broke up in 1970 Lennon began a new career with his wife Yoko Ono and the Plastic Ono Band, recording *Give Peace a Chance* in 1970 and the album *Imagine* in 1971. He was murdered in New York in 1980 by a mentally ill fan. Lennon's son Julian is also a pop musician.

ˌJay **'Leno** /ˌdʒeɪ 'lenəʊ; *AmE* 'lenoʊ/ (1950–) a US television personality who presents *The *Tonight Show*, having replaced Johnny *Carson in 1992. Leno first appeared on the show in 1977 as a comedian.

Lent *n* [U] the 40 days from *Ash Wednesday to *Easter, the most serious period in the Christian year. Traditionally, Christians did not eat meat or rich foods during Lent. Today some people stop doing something they enjoy, such as eating sweets or drinking alcohol, at this time.

ˌElmore **'Leonard**[1] /ˌelmɔː 'lenəd; *AmE* ˌelmɔːr 'lenərd/ (1925–) a US writer of crime novels. His books are known for their fast action, tough characters and their realistic language. His many novels include *Stick* (1983), *Freaky Deaky* (1988), *Rum Punch* (1992) and *Out of Sight* (1997). Several have been made into films, including *Get Shorty* (1995) with John *Travolta.

ˌ'Sugar' 'Ray **'Leonard**[2] /'ʃʊgə 'reɪ 'lenəd; *AmE* 'ʃʊgər, 'lenərd/ (1956–) a US boxer, the only one ever to have been world champion at different times in five different weight divisions. He also won an gold medal as the Light-Welterweight Champion at the 1976 Olympics.

ˌLeopold and 'Loeb /ˌliːəpəʊld, 'ləʊb; *AmE* ˌliːəpoʊld, 'loʊb/ two young US men, **Nathan Leopold Junior** (1904–71) and **Richard Loeb** (1905–31), who killed 14-year-old Bobby Franks in 1924. They were from rich *Chicago families and wanted to commit the perfect murder. This 'thrill killing' shocked America. Because of the skill of their lawyer, Clarence *Darrow, they were not condemned to death, but were sent to prison for 'life and 99 years'. Loeb was killed in prison but Leopold was released in 1958 and went to live in *Puerto Rico.

ˌLerner and 'Loewe /ˌlɜːnə(r), 'ləʊ; *AmE* ˌlɜːrnər, 'loʊ/ two Americans who wrote several successful *Broadway musical shows together. **Alan Jay Lerner** (1918–86) wrote the words and stories, and **Frederick Loewe** (1901–88), born in Austria, wrote the music. Their shows included *Brigadoon* (1947), *Paint Your Wagon* (1951), **My Fair Lady* (1964) and *Camelot* (1960). All of these were made into films, and Lerner and Loewe also wrote a musical film, *Gigi* (1958).

'Lerwick /'lɜːwɪk; *AmE* 'lɜːrwɪk/ a town in the *Shetlands, the islands to the far north of Scotland. It is a fishing port and the administrative centre of the islands. In January every year the festival of *Up-Helly-Aa is held in Lerwick to celebrate the islands' *Viking(1) past.

ˌDoris **'Lessing** /'lesɪŋ/ (1919–) a British writer, born in Iran. Her early novels, e.g. *The Grass is Singing* (1950), used the background of Southern Rhodesia (now *Zimbabwe), where she lived as a child. Later novels, including *The Golden Notebook* (1962), are concerned with social and political issues, especially relating to women. She has also written science fiction novels. In 1994 she published a book about her life, *Under My Skin*.

ˌLetter from A'merica /ə'merɪkə/ a British radio programme, broadcast every week since 1946 on *BBC *Radio 4 and presented by Alistair *Cooke. It was originally intended to 'discuss anything and everything American' for a British audience, but is now also broadcast on the *BBC World Service.

ˌDavid **'Letterman** /'letəmən; *AmE* 'letərmən/ (1947–) a US television personality who presents the chat show *The Late Show with David Letterman* on *CBS. He has won six *Emmy awards and is known for his unusual humour, which includes having animals do 'stupid pet tricks'. His show first followed *The Tonight Show* with Johnny *Carson, and when he was not chosen by *NBC to replace Carson he moved to *CBS. Compare LENO.

ˌLord **'Leverhulme** /'liːvəhjuːm; *AmE* 'liːvərhjuːm/ (*born* William Hesketh Lever 1851–1925) an English businessman. He became rich by making soap, and often gave his money to benefit others. One of his best-known projects was the establishment of a 'model industrial village', *Port Sunlight, near Liverpool. He was made a *viscount(1) in 1922. His company later became *Unilever.

Le'viathan /lə'vaɪəθən/ a book published by Thomas *Hobbes in 1651. It discusses human society and the relationship between rulers and people. Its conclusion is that a single powerful authority is necessary to prevent 'a war of every man against every man'. The book also contains the famous phrase describing a person's life as 'solitary, poor, nasty, brutish and short'.

ˌJames **Le'vine** /lə'vaɪn/ (1943–) the musical and artistic director of the *Metropolitan Opera in New York. He also plays the piano.

'**Levi's**™ /'liːvaɪz/ a popular type of *jeans produced by Levi Strauss Associates in *San Francisco. They were first made during the *Gold Rush by Levi Strauss (1829–1902) who was born in Germany. He had started a company making tents in 1853 and then began to produce tough work clothes in 1874. Levi's became fashionable in the 1960s and are now sold all over the world.

'**Levittown** /'levɪt-taʊn/ the name of three US towns designed and built by William Levitt soon after *World War II to meet the need for cheap houses for soldiers returning from the war. The first of the towns was built on *Long Island, New York, and the others are in *New Jersey and *Pennsylvania.

ˌCarl '**Lewis**[1] /'luːɪs/ (1961–) a US athlete who won eight Olympic gold medals. In the 1984 games, he won gold medals in the long jump and in the 100-metre, 200-metre and 400-metre relay races (= team races in which each member runs part of the distance). In the 1988 Olympics, Lewis won the long jump and 100-metre race and in 1992 he won two more gold medals, for the long jump and the 400-metre relay.

Carl Lewis

ˌC S '**Lewis**[2] /'luːɪs/ (Clive Staples Lewis 1898–1963) a British author, born in Northern Ireland. He is best remembered for his children's books about *Narnia, but he also wrote serious historical works and science fiction novels. His books on Christian themes are also well known, particularly *The Screwtape Letters*, a humorous collection of letters from a senior to a junior devil. Lewis' life was the subject of the film *Shadowlands* (1993).

'Jerry 'Lee '**Lewis**[3] /'luːɪs/ (1935–) a US singer of *rock and roll and *country music who plays the piano in a wild way, sometimes using his feet on the keys. He is sometimes known as 'the Killer'. His early hits included *Whole Lotta Shakin' Goin' On* (1957) and *Great Balls of Fire* (1957). His career was damaged when he married his cousin when she was only 13, but he returned in the 1960s as a country-music singer. Lewis is the cousin of the *evangelist Jimmy *Swaggert.

ˌJerry '**Lewis**[4] /'luːɪs/ (1926–) a US comic actor who also directs and produces films. He first became famous in the 1950s with Dean *Martin as his partner in a series of 16 comedy films. Lewis was the loud, crazy one and Martin was the calm, romantic one who also sang. Lewis's later films have included *The Nutty Professor* (1963). He became the star of the musical show *Damn Yankees* in which he appeared on *Broadway in 1995 and later in London, England.

ˌLennox '**Lewis**[5] /ˌlenəks 'luːɪs/ (1965–) a British heavyweight boxer. He spent his early years in Canada, where he achieved his first successes as a boxer, but returned to Britain to become European champion (1990), British champion (1991) and finally the world champion (1993–4).

ˌSinclair '**Lewis**[6] /ˌsɪŋkleə 'luːɪs; *AmE* ˌsɪŋkler/ (1885–1951) a US writer of novels which often deal with the more ridiculous aspects of American life. He was the first American to receive the *Nobel Prize (in 1930). His books include *Main Street* (1920), **Babbitt* (1922), *Arrowsmith* (1925) (which won the *Pulitzer Prize though Lewis refused it), **Elmer Gantry* (1927) and *Dodsworth* (1929).

ˌWyndham '**Lewis**[7] /ˌwɪndəm 'luːɪs/ (1882–1957) an English artist and writer who led the artistic movement known as *Vorticism. During *World War I he was a soldier and an official war artist, and his later paintings include several portraits of artistic figures of the time, including T S *Eliot and Ezra *Pound. He also wrote several novels.

ˌ**Lewis and 'Clark** /ˌluːɪs, 'klɑːk; *AmE* 'klɑːrk/ two US explorers who made the **Lewis and Clark Expedition** in 1804–5. President Thomas *Jefferson sent **Meriwether Lewis** (1774–1809) and **William Clark** (1770–1838) to lead an investigation of America's new *Louisiana Purchase and record what they saw. They left from *St Louis in 1804, reached the Pacific Ocean 18 months later, and then returned in 1806. Their journey encouraged many Americans to move to the West. The story of it was told in the film *The Far Horizons* (1955). See also SACAJAWEA.

the 'Battles of '**Lexington and 'Concord** /'leksɪŋtən, 'kɒŋkɔːd; *AmE* 'kɑːŋkɔːrd/ the first battles of the *American Revolution. On 19 April 1775, a British armed force of about 700 men marched from Boston to destroy American military weapons at the town of Concord, *Massachusetts. The British were stopped at Lexington by 70 *Minutemen, eight of whom were killed in the battle. They then marched to Concord for another battle in which they lost many more men than the Americans and were forced back. This greatly encouraged American hopes for the war.

ˌ**Libe'race** /ˌlɪbə'rɑːtʃi/ (1919–87) a US piano player who wore expensive and colourful clothes and performed in a very exaggerated style. He won an *Emmy for his popular television show (1952–7) and was a star in *Las Vegas for many years. Liberace played and sometimes sang romantic songs and always had candles on his piano. He died from an illness related to Aids. His full name was Wladziu Valentino Liberace.

the ˌ**Liberal Demo'cratic ˌParty** (*also* the **Liberal Democrats**, *infml* the **Lib Dems**) the third largest British political party. It was formed in 1988 when the *Liberal Party and the *Social Democratic Party joined together. In recent years it has been particularly successful in local government elections and in *by-elections. It argues in favour of *proportional representation and its leader from 1988 to 1999 has been Paddy *Ashdown.

▶ **Liberal Democrat** (*also infml* **Lib Dem**) *n* a member or supporter of the Liberal Democratic Party.

the '**Liberal ˌParty** (*also* the **Liberals**) a former British political party. It developed in the mid 19th century from the *Whigs, and under William *Gladstone and David *Lloyd George became the party of social and political reform. It lost support after the rise of the *Labour Party in the early 20th century. In the elections of 1983 and 1987 the Liberals achieved some success by joining with the *Social Democratic Party to form the Alliance, and the two parties were officially united in 1988. They are now called the *Liberal Democratic Party.

▶ **Liberal** *n* a member or supporter of the Liberal Party.

the **'Liberal-SD'P Al'liance** /es di: 'pi:/ ⇨ ALLIANCE.

'Liberty 1 an independent organization formed in 1934 to protect the legal rights of British citizens and to argue for greater freedom under the existing law. It has fought campaigns to defend the rights of women, homosexuals and people in prison. Until 1989 it was known as the National Council for Civil Liberties. ⇨ note at PRESSURE GROUPS. **2** (*also* **Liberty's**) a department store with branches in many cities in Britain. The first shop, started by Arthur Liberty, was opened in Regent Street, London, in 1875 and sold goods imported from countries such as India and Japan. It later became well known for its *Art Nouveau designs and its range of fabrics.

the **,Liberty 'Bell** a bell used by Americans during the *American Revolution. It is loved as a symbol of freedom and has these words from the Bible on it: 'Proclaim liberty throughout all the land unto all the inhabitants thereof.' It was made in London and taken to Philadelphia in 1752 where it cracked when it was first used. It was repaired and rung for such events as the *Boston Tea Party and when the *Declaration of Independence was first read to the public. It cracked again in 1835 and 1846. In 1976 it was placed in a special case of glass and steel behind *Independence Hall.

the Liberty Bell

'Liberty ,Bonds *n* [pl] a special issue of US government bonds (= official papers that are sold with the promise to pay the money back, with interest, on a certain date). Liberty Bonds were sold to raise money for *World War I. *Hollywood stars and other famous people attended large public meetings to encourage citizens to buy them, and John Philip *Sousa wrote a *Liberty Bond March*. The total amount of money raised was about $23 billion.

'Lib-Lab /'lɪblæb/ *adj* of any agreement between the *Liberal Party (or *Liberal Democratic Party) and the *Labour Party in Britain. The **Lib-Lab pact** (1977–8) was an agreement between David *Steel of the Liberal Party and James *Callaghan of the Labour government to work together to oppose the *Conservative Party in the *House of Commons: *a Lib-Lab deal/agreement/plan.*

libraries

Almost every town in Britain and the US has a **public library**. Many libraries were built in the 1800s with money given by Andrew *Carnegie, a US businessman originally from Scotland.

Public libraries are often open until late evening during the week, part of Saturday, and in the US even on Sunday. There are around 5 000 in Britain, with an average of 45 000 books in each. **Librarians** manage the libraries and advise people how to find the books or information they need.

Public libraries contain **fiction** (= story books), **non-fiction** (= books containing facts), children's books, and usually magazines, CDs and videos. Many now have a computer with access to the Internet. Every library has a **catalogue** which shows where books on a particular subject can be found. Many US libraries use the *Library of Congress system for arranging books in order on the shelves. In Britain the *Dewey decimal system is the most used.

Libraries are often divided into a **reference section** and a **lending section**. Books from the reference section, e.g. dictionaries and directories, as well as newspapers and magazines, can only be used in the library. Books from the lending section can be borrowed free of charge for a period of two or three weeks by people who are members of the library. Anyone living in the local area can join a library and obtain a **library card**. If a book is returned late, after the **due date**, the borrower has to pay a **fine**. Public libraries are also a source of local information and a centre for community activities. Many have special programmes for children to help them feel comfortable using a library. In school holidays they organize storytelling and other entertainments.

Travelling libraries (= libraries set up inside large vans) take books round country areas for people who cannot easily get to a town. In the US travelling libraries are called **bookmobiles**. Schools, colleges and universities have their own private libraries for the use of students and teachers.

In both Britain and the US public libraries receive money from local and national government but, increasingly, they do not receive enough for their needs. In Britain some smaller libraries have had to close. In the US people believe strongly that information and education should be freely available. Libraries are important in achieving this but, as in Britain, they do not get sufficient money and depend on the help of volunteers who work without pay.

The biggest library in Britain is the *British Library in London, which has over 18 million books, 1 million CDs and 55 000 hours of tape recordings. Other important libraries include the National Libraries of Scotland and Wales and the *Bodleian Library in Oxford. These libraries are called ***copyright libraries** and are entitled to receive a free copy of every book that is published in Britain. The largest library in the US is the ***Library of Congress** in Washington, DC, and it receives a copy of every book that is published in the US.

the **,Library of 'Congress** the national library of the US. It was established by the US Congress in 1800 and is on Independence Avenue in Washington, DC. It now has more than 80 million books and other items in 470 languages. The library receives two copies of every US work published with a copyright (= legal right of ownership).

licensing laws

The sale of alcohol in Britain is strictly controlled by licensing laws. These restrict where, when and by whom alcohol may be sold. In order to open a *pub or wine bar the owner must obtain the approval of the local magistrates, who must be satisfied that he or she is a suitable person to sell alcohol. If the application is approved the owner obtains a **licence** to sell alcohol and becomes the **licensee**. The name of the licensee is displayed above the front door. If magistrates are not happy with the way a pub is being run they can cancel the licence.

Many pubs are licensed to sell alcohol for drinking **on or off the premises** (= in the pub or somewhere else). However, most people buy alcohol for drinking at home in a supermarket or an **off-licence** (= a shop that sells mainly alcohol). Shops and supermarkets have to get a licence, called an off-licence, before they can sell alcohol. Nobody under 18 is allowed to buy alcohol, either in a pub or in a shop.

Pubs are only allowed to sell alcohol during official **opening hours**. Pubs are allowed to remain open all day from 11 a.m. to 11 p.m., though many close in afternoon, but if they wish to stay open after 11 p.m. they must obtain a special **late licence**. Pubs open for a shorter time on Sundays, and in some parts of Wales they are closed altogether.

In the US there are local laws about when and where alcohol can be sold. Some towns are **dry**, i.e. no alcohol can be sold there at all. In general, restaurants and bars need a licence to sell beer and wine. In some states alcohol for drinking at home is sold only in special **liquor stores**; in other places it is sold in any food shop. There are fewer restrictions on when alcohol can be sold than there are in Britain, and bars can stay open very late. The most common restriction is that alcohol may not be sold early on Sunday mornings.

The US has strict laws to attempt to keep young people from coming into contact with alcohol. The **drinking age** (= the age at which a person can buy alcohol) is 21, and bars and liquor stores often ask customers for proof of age. In many places, people below 21 cannot work in, or even enter, bars or restaurants that serve alcohol. College students, especially, try to drink in bars by pretending to be older than they are. Young people who work in food shops may have to ask an older employee to serve a customer who wants to buy a bottle of wine.

ˌRoy ˈ**Lichtenstein** /ˈlɪktənstaɪn/ (1923–97) a US painter who helped to establish *pop art. Many of his pictures, e.g. *Whaam!* (1963), are like large *comic strips, and are seen as comments on popular culture. His *Torpedo … Los Angeles* was bought for $5.5 million in 1989. Lichtenstein sometimes drew other artists' pictures again in his own style, such as his 1992 version of Vincent Van Gogh's *Bedroom at Arles*. He also made plastic and metal sculptures.

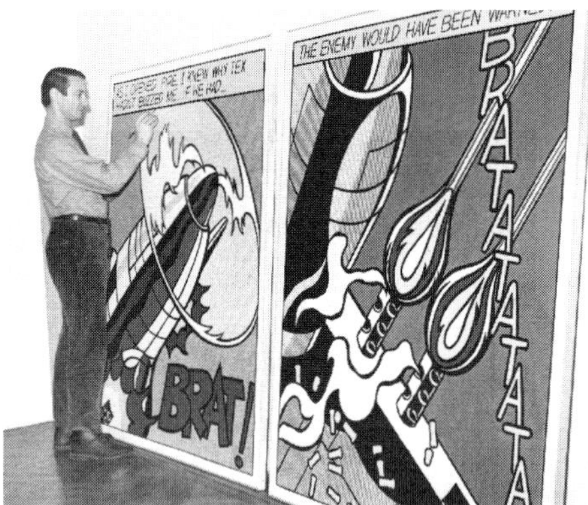

Roy Lichtenstein at work

Life a US magazine which is known especially for its photographs. It was first published in 1936 by Henry Luce who owned *Time* magazine. His aim was to enable readers 'to see life; to see the world; to witness great events'. After television became popular, *Life* went out of business in 1972, but it was brought back in 1978, appearing once a month. It is now published by Time Warner.

the ˈ**Life Guards** a regiment of the British royal *Household Cavalry, responsible for protecting the queen or king and appearing at state ceremonies. They also perform the ceremony of the *Changing the Guard. See also HORSE GUARDS 1.

ˌ***Life on ˈEarth*** a very successful British television series about the development of life on this planet, written and presented by David *Attenborough and broadcast on the *BBC in 1979. Four more series on natural history have followed it, all presented by Attenborough: *The Living Planet* (1984), *The Trials of Life* (1990), *The Private Life of Plants* (1995) and *The Life of Birds* (1998).

ˌ**life ˈpeer** *n* any of the members of the British *House of Lords who hold their position as a reward for public service but cannot pass their title on to their children. Male life peers are given the title of *baron and are addressed as 'Lord', and female life peers are given the title of *baroness or countess and are addressed as 'Lady', 'Baroness' or 'Countess'. **Life peerages** are given by the government, often to former *Members of Parliament. ⇨ note at PEERAGE.

ˈ**Life ˌSavers**™ *n* [pl] small, hard US sweets/candies which are round and have a hole in the middle. They are available in 25 different flavours and sold in tubes. They were invented in 1912.

ˌ***Lift ˈEvery ˈVoice and ˈSing*** a popular song that is often called the 'African-American National Anthem'. It was written in 1900 for *Lincoln's Birthday celebrations by James Weldon Johnson, a writer who was the first *African American to be leader of the *NAACP (1916–30), with music by his brother J Rosamond Johnson. The song begins:

Lift every voice and sing,
Till earth and heaven ring,
Ring with the harmonies of Liberty.
Let our rejoicing rise
High as the list'ning skies,
Let it resound loud as the rolling sea.

ˌ**light ˈale** *n* [U, C] (*BrE*) a type of pale *bitter beer which is quite low in alcohol and is often sold in bottles. ⇨ note at BEER. Compare PALE ALE.

The ˌ***Light of the ˈWorld*** a popular painting (1851–3) by Holman *Hunt, who did several versions of it. It shows Jesus Christ holding a lamp and knocking on the door of a house. It is widely used on greetings cards, etc.

ˌ***Li'l ˈAbner*** /ˌlɪl ˈæbnə(r)/ a popular US newspaper *comic strip (1934–77), drawn by Al Capp (1909–79) The stories were about *hillbillies who lived in Dogpatch, and the main characters were Li'l (Little) Abner, his beautiful girl friend Daisy Mae and his mother Mammy Yokum. The characters were used for a 1956 *Broadway musical show and later a film, both called *Li'l Abner*. See also SADIE HAWKINS DAY.

ˌ***Lili Marˈlene*** /ˌlɪli mɑːˈleɪn; *AmE* mɑːrˈleɪn/ a song that became popular with both British and German soldiers during *World War II, especially those fighting in North Africa. It is about a young woman waiting for a soldier outside the gate of the barracks where he is living. The most famous version was sung by Marlene *Dietrich.

ˌPeter ˈ**Lilley** /ˈlɪli/ (1943–) a British *Conservative politician. He became a *Member of Parliament in 1983 and held several senior government positions in the 1990s, including *Secretary of State for Social Security. He has written several books on politics.

ˌ***Lilliburˈlero*** (*also* ˌ***Lillibuˈlero***) /ˌlɪlibəˈleərəʊ; *AmE* ˌlɪlibərˈleroʊ, ˌlɪlibəˈleroʊ/ the signature tune (= tune played to identify a radio station) of the *BBC World Service. It was originally an extremely popular song of the 17th century with various words, often attacking Roman Catholics. The lullaby (= song sung to make a young child go to sleep) *Hush-a-bye, Baby* has a similar tune.

ˈ**Lilliput** /ˈlɪlɪpʊt/ a country visited by Gulliver in **Gulliver's Travels* by Jonathan *Swift. The **Lilliputians** are only six inches tall, and because of this their political disputes and wars with their neighbours are made to look ridiculous. See also BROBDINGNAG, YAHOOS.

▶ **ˌLilliˈputian** /ˌlɪlɪˈpjuːʃn/ *adj* very small: *From the plane the houses seemed Lilliputian.*

ˌRush **ˈLimbaugh** /ˌrʌʃ ˈlɪmbɔː/ (1951–) a US broadcaster. He has a popular radio talk show on which he expresses his strong right-wing opinions. Limbaugh also appears on television and has written several books.

ˈlimerick *n* a type of short funny poem with five lines, the first two rhyming with the last, and the third with the fourth. They are very popular in Britain and are sometimes quite rude. Limericks first appeared in print in 1820 and were later made famous by Edward *Lear in his *Book of Nonsense* (1846). Lear usually used the same word to end the first and last lines:

There was an Old Man of the the Border,
Who lived in the utmost disorder;
He danced with the Cat,
And made tea in his Hat,
Which vexed all the folks on the Border.

Modern limericks use a different rhyme at the end:

There was a young lady of Crewe,
Who dreamed she was eating her shoe.
She woke in the night,
In a terrible fright,
And found it was perfectly true.

ˈLimey /ˈlaɪmi/ *n* (*AmE slang offensive*) a British person. The word was used especially by US military forces during *World War II, often as an insult, to mean a British sailor or soldier. It refers to the old practice in the British navy of making sailors drink the juice of limes (= green fruit like lemons) to avoid getting the disease of scurvy.

ˈLincoln¹ /ˈlɪŋkən/ the administrative centre of *Lincolnshire, in the east of England. It was originally a Roman city and has several important Roman remains. It also contains many beautiful *medieval buildings, including a castle, begun in 1068, and a cathedral with three spires (= pointed towers), built mainly between the 11th and 14th centuries. The city has one of Britain's newest universities, the Lincolnshire and Humberside University, opened in 1996.

ˌAbraham **ˈLincoln²** /ˈlɪŋkən/ (1809–65) the 16th US *President (1861–5). He is regarded by many people as America's greatest president, because he served during the *Civil War, preserved the Union and freed the slaves. He is also often referred to as 'Honest Abe'. He was a lawyer who was elected to the US House of Representatives in 1846 and then elected President as a *Republican(1). Lincoln led the Union in the Civil War and in 1864 appointed Ulysses S *Grant to lead the Union armies. He announced his *Emancipation Proclamation in 1863 to free the slaves in the South. Lincoln was shot and killed by the actor John Wilkes *Booth. See also GETTYSBURG ADDRESS, LINCOLN MEMORIAL.

the **ˈLincoln ˈCenter for the Perˈforming ˈArts** (*also* the **ˈLincoln ˌCenter**) /ˈlɪŋkən/ a group of buildings that include theatres and concert halls in New York, west of *Central Park and *Broadway. They were built at various times between 1959 and 1991. The Center is the home of the *Metropolitan Opera, the *New York Philharmonic and the *Juilliard School of Music, as well as other organizations.

ˌLincoln ˈgreen /ˌlɪŋkən/ *n* [U] the colour of a type of green cloth originally made in Lincoln, England, or the cloth itself. It is traditionally said to have been worn by *Robin Hood and his men.

the **ˌLincoln Meˈmorial** /ˌlɪŋkən/ a large building in Washington, DC, in memory of President Abraham *Lincoln. It is made of marble and the design by Henry Bacon was based on the Parthenon in Athens, Greece. The Memorial is in West Potomac Park at one end of The Mall and was completed in 1922. Inside is a large statue of Lincoln sitting in a chair. The words of his *Gettysburg Address and his speech at his second *Inauguration Day are cut into stone inside the building.

Abraham Lincoln's statue in the Lincoln Memorial

ˌLincoln's ˈBirthday /ˌlɪŋkənz/ a US holiday on 12 February celebrating the birthday of President Abraham *Lincoln. It was first celebrated in 1866 in Washington, DC, and was declared a national holiday in 1892.

ˈLincolnshire /ˈlɪŋkənʃə(r)/ (*abbr* **Lincs**) a county in the east of England. Its administrative centre is *Lincoln.

ˌCharles **ˈLindbergh** /ˈlɪndbɜːg; *AmE* ˈlɪndbɜːrg/ (1902–74) a US pilot who became the first person to fly across the Atlantic Ocean alone. His popular name was Lindy, and he was also known as the 'Lone Eagle'. He flew from New York on 20 May 1927 and arrived in Paris 33½ hours later. His plane was called *Spirit of St Louis*. When he returned, he received the largest parade ever given in New York. In 1932, his baby child was stolen and killed in a case that shocked America. Lindbergh wrote the story of his life, called *The Spirit of St Louis*, which won the 1954 *Pulitzer Prize.

ˈLindisfarne /ˈlɪndɪsfɑːn; *AmE* ˈlɪndɪsfɑːrn/ (*also* **Holy Island**) a small island off the coast of *Northumberland in north-east England. A monastery was established there in the 7th century, although the ruined buildings that survive are from the early *Norman period. It also has a 16th-century castle.

the **ˌLindisfarne ˈGospels** /ˌlɪndɪsfɑːn; *AmE* ˌlɪndɪsfɑːrn/ a book containing the four Christian Gospels, produced on the island of *Lindisfarne around AD 700. It is written by hand, with many beautiful pictures and decorations, and contains early examples of the northern version of Old English. It is now kept in the *British Library, London.

ˈLindow Man /ˈlɪndəʊ; *AmE* ˈlɪndoʊ/ the body of a man found in 1984 preserved in Lindow Moss, an area of soft wet ground in *Cheshire, England. Scientists think that he was killed in a religious ceremony at some time between 300 BC and 300 AD, and may a page from the Lindisfarne Gospels

have been a local prince. The body can be seen in the *British Museum, London. See also PETE MARSH.

ˈ**line dancing** *n* [U] a style of dancing that became popular in the US in the early 1990s, and later in Britain. It involves dancing to *country music, with the dancers standing in lines and moving together with a series of the same steps, turns and kicks. Dancers often wear wide 'cowboy' hats and other clothing associated with country music.

ˌGary ˈ**Lineker** /ˈlɪnəkə(r)/ (1960–) an English football player. He began his career with Leicester City (1978–85) and then played for Everton and Barcelona before moving to *Tottenham Hotspur (1989–92). His 80 international games for England have included World Cup matches in 1986 and 1990. He stopped playing seriously in 1994 and now often appears on British radio and television.

Gary Lineker

the **Linˈnean Soˌciety** /lɪˈneɪən/ an organization established in 1788 at *Burlington House, London, England, for the scientific study of plants and animals. It was named after Carolus Linnaeus (1707–78), a Swedish scientist who invented a system for naming living things, and whose library and scientific collections are kept by the Society.

ˈ**Linus** /ˈlaɪnəs/ a characer in the cartoon **Peanuts*. He is a small boy who is usually seen holding a blanket for comfort. A **Linus blanket** is the name often given to the piece of material that a child uses in this way.

the ˌ**lion and the** ˈ**unicorn** two animals that appear on the British *royal arms (= a special royal symbol). The lion represents England, and the unicorn, an imaginary animal like a horse with a long horn on its forehead, represents Scotland. There is a traditional children's *nursery rhyme about the lion and the unicorn, which may have its origin in old conflicts between the two countries:

The lion and the unicorn
Were fighting for the crown;
The lion beat the unicorn
All round about the town.

the **Lions** ⇨ BRITISH LIONS.

the ˈ**Lions Club** a club of people who work together on projects to help their local communities. It has many branches around the world.
▶ **Lion** *n* a member of the Lions Club.

ˌWalter ˈ**Lippmann** /ˈlɪpmən/ (1889–1974) a US journalist. He wrote a regular political column called *Today and Tomorrow* which appeared in more than 250 newspapers around the world. He wrote for the *New York Herald-Tribune* (1931–62) and then for the **Washington Post* (1962–7), and won the *Pulitzer Prize twice. Lippman also helped to establish the magazine *New Republic* in 1914.

ˈ**Lipton** /ˈlɪptən/ a product name for the many varieties of tea sold by the Thomas J Lipton Company, part of *Unilever.

ˌ**Liquid** ˈ**Paper**™ *n* [U] a US make of liquid used for painting over written or typed mistakes on paper. It dries quickly and the correction can then be written or typed over it. It is sold in small bottles and is available in white and other pale colours. Compare TIPP-EX.

ˌ**liquorice** ˈ**allsorts** /ˈɔːlsɔːts; *AmE* ˈɔːlsɔːrts/ *n* [pl] (*esp BrE*) soft sweets made in a variety of colours and shapes, all containing liquorice (= a black substance obtained from a plant root). They are usually sold in packets.

ˌ**listed** ˈ**building** *n* (in Britain) a building that is protected by law because it is very old or has some other important feature. It appears on an official list and must not be pulled down or changed without special permission from a local government department.

ˌ***Listen with*** ˈ***Mother*** a *BBC radio programme (1950–82) for mothers to listen to with their small children. Each programme consisted of songs, rhymes and stories, and always began with these words: 'Are you sitting comfortably? Then I'll begin.'

ˌJoseph ˈ**Lister** /ˈlɪstə(r)/ (1827–1912) an English doctor who is best known for introducing the antiseptic system (= a way of preventing infection during medical operations by keeping things very clean and using a spray of a special acid). He was President of the *Royal Society (1895–1900) and was made a *baron in 1897.

ˈ**Listerine**™ /ˈlɪstəriːn/ *n* [U] a product name for a liquid for cleaning inside the mouth, sold in bottles. It is available in three different flavours and is produced by the US company Lambert-Warner.

the ˈBattle of ˈ**Little** ˈ**Bighorn** /ˈbɪɡhɔːn; *AmE* ˈbɪɡhɔːrn/ the battle (1876) in which George *Custer was killed with all 259 of his men of the Seventh Cavalry. This became known as Custer's Last Stand. The soldiers were surrounded near the Little Bighorn River in *Montana by a large force of *Cheyenne and *Sioux *Native Americans, led by *Crazy Horse and *Sitting Bull.

ˌ**Little Bo-**ˈ**Peep** /bəʊ ˈpiːp; *AmE* boʊ/ a girl in a traditional *nursery rhyme. The first verse is:

Little Bo-Peep has lost her sheep,
And doesn't know where to find them;
Leave them alone, and they'll come home,
Bringing their tails behind them.

In later verses the sheep lose their tails, but they are found 'hung on a tree to dry'.

ˌ**Little Boy ˈBlue** a boy in a traditional *nursery rhyme. The full poem is:

Little Boy Blue, come blow your horn,
The sheep's in the meadow, the cow's in the corn.
Where is the boy who looks after the sheep?
He's under a haycock fast asleep!

ˌ**Little ˈChef** a company with a number of restaurants by the sides of major roads in Britain, selling quick meals for travellers at low prices. The company is owned by *Trust House Forte: *There's a Little Chef in about five miles.*

ˌ***Little ˈDorrit*** /ˈdɒrɪt; *AmE* ˈdɔːrɪt/ a novel (1855–7) by Charles *Dickens. Little Dorrit (whose real name is Amy) is the main character. She is young woman whose father William Dorrit is in *Marshalsea prison for owing money. She falls in love with Arthur Clennam, a man who tries to help her father. The book is noted for its descriptions of Marshalsea, where Dickens's own father was a prisoner for a time.

ˌ**Little ˈItaly** /ˈɪtəli/ the Italian district of New York City. It is on the *Lower East Side of *Manhattan(1), and Mulberry Street is its lively centre. Little Italy is popular with tourists, especially for its many restaurants. The Feast of San Gennaro is celebrated on the streets in September.

ˌ**Little Jack ˈHorner** /ˈhɔːnə(r); *AmE* ˈhɔːrnər/ a boy in a traditional *nursery rhyme. The full poem is:

Little Jack Horner
Sat in a corner,
Eating a Christmas pie;
He put in his thumb
And pulled out a plum,
And said, What a good boy am I!

The poem may refer to a man called Jack Horner who was a servant of King *Henry VIII.

ˌ**Little ˈJohn** one of the companions of *Robin Hood. His name was a joke, because he was in fact very tall and strong.

ˌ***Little Lord ˈFauntleroy*** /ˈfɔːntlərɔɪ/ a children's book (1886) by Frances Hodgson *Burnett, about a young American boy who discovers that he is the son of a British *earl(1). He has long fair hair and is always well dressed and polite. The name is now sometimes used to describe a young boy who behaves badly because he is given everything that he wants and allowed to do what he likes.

ˌ**Little Miss ˈMuffet** /ˈmʌfɪt/ a girl in a traditional *nursery rhyme. The full poem is:

Little Miss Muffet
Sat on a tuffet,
Eating her curds and whey;
There came a great spider,
Who sat down beside her,
And frightened Miss Muffet away.

Miss Muffet, it is said, was the daughter of Dr Thomas Muffet, a famous 16th-century scientist who studied insects.

ˌ**Little ˈNell** a character in *The Old Curiosity Shop* (1841) by Charles *Dickens. The story is about a girl, Nell Trent, who together with her father is forced to leave her home. After many adventures and much suffering Nell finally dies. The scene describing her death is well known, and people sometimes criticize it as being too sentimental.

ˌ***Little Orphan ˈAnnie*** a popular US newspaper *comic strip. It was begun in 1924 by Harold Gray (1894–1968) and continued until 1979. The main characters are Annie, whose parents are dead, her dog Sandy, and rich 'Daddy' Warbucks who looks after her. They also appeared in a radio series and the *Broadway musical *Annie* (1977), which became a film (1982).

ˌ***Little Red ˈRiding Hood*** a traditional story found in many European countries. A girl called Little Red Riding Hood goes to visit her grandmother in the forest, but when she arrives a wolf has eaten her grandmother and put on her clothes. Little Red Riding Hood is surprised at the appearance of her grandmother and says, 'Grandmother, what big eyes you have!' 'All the better to see you with,' replies the wolf. 'Grandmother, what big teeth you have!' says the girl. 'All the better to eat you with,' replies the wolf, and eats her. Little Red Riding Hood and her grandmother are saved when a hunter cuts open the wolf's stomach and they escape.

ˌ**Little ˈRichard** (1935–) an *African-American singer of early *rock and roll who also played the piano. He was born Richard Wayne Penniman and was known for his wild, noisy style. His hits included *Tutti Frutti* (1956), *Lucille* (1957) and *Good Golly, Miss Molly* (1957). He stopped singing in 1957 to become a preacher (= religious leader) and said that rock and roll was 'the devil's music'. He began to sing again in 1964, mostly the *blues and *soul music.

ˈ**Little Rock** the capital and largest city of the US state of *Arkansas. It is an industrial centre on the Arkansas River. It became known around the world in 1957 when President *Eisenhower sent US Army forces there to protect *African Americans who wanted to attend city schools with white people. This caused a lot of violence. Bill *Clinton later lived in Little Rock as the governor of Arkansas (1978–80 and 1982–90) before he became President.

ˌ***Little ˈWomen*** a very popular US book (1868–9) written mainly for girls by Louisa May *Alcott. The story, based on that of her own family, is about the March family of four sisters, living in *New England in the 19th century. The girls are Meg, Jo, Beth and Amy. Film versions were made in 1933 with Katherine *Hepburn, 1949 with Elizabeth *Taylor, and 1994 with Winona Ryder. Alcott wrote two further books with the same characters: *Little Men* (1871) and *Jo's Boys* (1886).

ˌJoan ˈ**Littlewood** /ˈlɪtlwʊd/ (1914–91) an English theatre director. She began her career in the 1930s directing plays for *working-class audiences. She formed a group called Theatre Workshop in the *East End of London which developed new ways of presenting plays. Her productions there included *A Taste of Honey* (1959) and *Oh What a Lovely War* (1963).

ˈ**Littlewoods** /ˈlɪtlwʊdz/ a company that owns department stores with many branches around Britain, selling clothes, household goods and food.

ˌ**Littlewoods ˈPools** /ˌlɪtlwʊdz/ a part of the *Littlewoods company that organizes football *pools (= a form of gambling on the results of football games). ⇨ note at BETTING AND GAMBLING.

ˈ**Live Aid** two very large pop concerts held at the same time in London, England and Philadelphia, US, in 1985. The aim of the concerts was to encourage people to give money to help people dying of hunger in Africa. They were organized by Bob *Geldof and were broadcast in many countries around the world. The concerts followed the success of *Band Aid. See also COMIC RELIEF. ⇨ note at AID.

Peˌnelopeˈ**Lively** /ˈlaɪvli/ (1933–) a British writer,

born in Egypt, who has written novels and stories for adults and children. She won the *Booker Prize in 1987 for *Moon Tiger*, a novel set in Cairo during *World War II.

ˈ**liver bird** /ˈlaɪvə; *AmE* ˈlaɪvər/ *n* the name of an imaginary bird, from which the name 'Liverpool' is supposed to come. The liver bird is the symbol of Liverpool and can be seen on top of the two towers of the Royal Liver Building in Liverpool. *The Liver Birds* was also the name of a popular *BBC television comedy series (1969–79) about two young women living in Liverpool.

liver birds on top of the Royal Liver Building

ˈ**Liverpool** /ˈlɪvəpuːl; *AmE* ˈlɪvərpuːl/ a large city and port in north-west England, on the River Mersey. It first became important during the *Industrial Revolution, producing and exporting cotton goods. It was also an major port for the slave trade, receiving profits from the sale of slaves in America. In the 20th century the city became famous as the home of the *Beatles and for Liverpool and Everton football clubs. Among its many famous buildings are the Royal Liver Building with its two towers, the Anglican and Roman Catholic cathedrals, and the * Walker Art Gallery. See also ALBERT DOCK, MERSEY BEAT, TOXTETH.

the ˈ**Liverpool and** ˈ**Manchester** ˈ**Railway** /ˈlɪvəpuːl ənd ˈmæntʃəstə ˈreɪlweɪ; *AmE* ˈlɪvərpuːl ənd ˈmæntʃəstər/ a railway between Liverpool and Manchester in north-west England, opened in 1830. It was the first public railway in the world using steam trains for its whole length, and was built by George *Stephenson.

ˈ**Liverpool Street** /ˈlɪvəpuːl; *AmE* ˈlɪvərpuːl/ a train station in London, England, for trains to and from *East Anglia. It also has a station on the *London Underground.

ˌ**Liver**ˈ**pudlian** /ˌlɪvəˈpʌdliən; *AmE* ˌlɪvərˈpʌdliən/ *n* (*infml*) a person who was born in or who lives in *Liverpool (from a humorous use of 'puddle' instead of 'pool' at the end of the word 'Liverpool'). ▶ **Liverpudlian** *adj* (*infml*): *a Liverpudlian accent.*

ˈ**livery** ˌ**company** *n* any of the ancient City of London guilds (= associations of business people or skilled workers), each with their own special livery (= uniforms). Guilds of traders selling the same goods or services were once very powerful in London, and modern livery companies are descended from them. There are over a hundred of them, including the Grocers, the Drapers, the Fishmongers and the Goldsmiths. Members of each company meet together for social occasions and for charity work. See also GUILDHALL.

ˌDavid ˈ**Livingstone**¹ /ˈlɪvɪŋstən/ (1813–73) a Scottish explorer and missionary (= person sent to teach the Christian religion). He became famous through his travels in Africa, and was the first European to see the Victoria Falls in 1855. In the late 1860s he was thought to have died or become lost while trying to find the source of the River Nile. The journalist Henry Morton *Stanley went to look for him and found him at Ujiji in 1871. Stanley is said to have greeted him with the words 'Doctor Livingstone, I presume,' which people find funny because it shows so little emotion or excitement. Livingstone died in Africa but his body was brought back to England and buried in *Westminster Abbey.

ˌKen ˈ**Livingstone**² /ˈlɪvɪŋstən/ (1945–) a British *Labour politician. He was leader of the *Greater London Council (1981–6) and was known (especially in the newspapers) as 'Red Ken' because of his left-wing political views. After the Greater London Council was closed down in 1986 he became a *Member of Parliament. He is well known for his unusual hobby of keeping newts (= small animals with long tails that can live in water or on land).

the ˈ**Lizard** /ˈlɪzəd/ a piece of land that sticks out into the sea in southern *Cornwall, England. Its tip, **Lizard Point**, is the place on the British mainland that is furthest to the south. See also LAND'S END.

Llanˈ**gollen** /lænˈɡɒθlən; *AmE* lænˈɡɑːθlən/ a town in north Wales where the International Music *Eisteddfod is held every year.

ˌ**L L** ˈ**Bean** /ˌel el ˈbiːn/ any of a group of US shops selling a large range of equipment for outdoor activities, including boots, jackets, hats, tents, tools and fishing equipment. The company is known for its catalogues. It was established in 1912 by Leon Leonwood Bean in Freeport, *Maine, where the main office still is.

a contemporary lithograph showing Henry Morton Stanley meeting David Livingstone at Ujiji in 1871

Harold Lloyd in Safety Last

ˌHarold ˈ**Lloyd**[1] /ˈlɔɪd/ (1893–1971) a US comic actor in over 500 silent films. His typical character was shy and wore glasses, and often got into dangerous situations. The best-known of these was a scene in *Safety Last* (1923), in which Lloyd hangs by his hands from a large clock on the outside of a tall building. His other films included *The Freshman* (1925) and *The Kid Brother* (1927). He received a special *Oscar in 1952.

ˌMarie ˈ**Lloyd**[2] /ˌmɑːri ˈlɔɪd/ (1870–1922) one of the most popular of all English *music-hall(1) performers. She was famous for her *cockney humour and for comic songs such as *A Little of What You Fancy Does You Good* and *Oh, Mr Porter*, which shocked some people because they often referred to sex, though in a humorous way.

ˈDavid ˈ**Lloyd** ˈ**George** /ˈlɔɪd ˈdʒɔːdʒ; *AmE* ˈdʒɔːrdʒ/ (1863–1945) a British *Liberal politician of Welsh parentswho was *Prime Minister of Britain from 1916 to 1922. As *Chancellor of the Exchequer (1908–15) he introduced *pensions (1908) and *National Insurance (1911), two important elements of the modern *welfare state. He became Prime Minister during *World War I, but after the war *Conservative opposition to his policy of Irish independence forced him to resign. He remained in parliament for the rest of his life, but neither he nor the Liberal Party ever returned to power. He was made an *earl(1) shortly before his death in 1945.

ˌ**Lloyds** ˈ**Bank** /ˌlɔɪdz/ (*also* **Lloyds**) one of the largest British banks, established in 1765. Its symbol is a black horse on a green background. ⇨ article at BANKS AND BANKING.

ˌ**Lloyd's of** ˈ**London** /ˌlɔɪdz/ (*also* **Lloyd's**) an association of people in the City of London who provide insurance. These members, known as 'names', share the profits and also the risks involved. The first members used to meet at Edward Lloyd's coffee house (= a place like a café) in the late 17th century. They were originally concerned with insuring ships, but now deal with insurance of all kinds all over the world. In the early 1990s Lloyd's made a number of very large payments to people who were insured with them, with the result that the 'names' lost a lot of money. See also LUTINE BELL.

ˈ**Lloyd's** ˈ**Register of** ˈ**Shipping** /ˈlɔɪdz/ (*also* ˌ**Lloyd's** ˈ**Register**) a society, formed in 1760, which each year publishes **Lloyd's Register Book**, a detailed list of ships, boats, etc., for insurance purposes. The ships are listed according to their size, type and condition.

ˈAndrew ˈ**Lloyd** ˈ**Webber** /ˈlɔɪd ˈwebə(r)/ (1948–) a very successful English writer of *musicals. His early shows were 'rock operas' written with Tim Rice, including *Joseph and the Amazing Technicolour Dreamcoat* (1968), **Jesus Christ Superstar* and *Evita* (1976). Later successes include **Cats*, *The Phantom of the Opera* (1986) and *Sunset Boulevard* (1993). He was made a *knight in 1992.

lobbying

Lobbying is the practice of approaching politicians in order to persuade them to support a particular aim or cause, and then to speak about it and draw attention to it. In the US this means trying to obtain the support of members of *Congress or a state legislature (= people making laws at state level). In Britain lobbying involves persuading *MPs or members of the *House of Lords to speak in *Parliament.

Anyone can write to their MP or a member of Congress, or organize a petition about an issue, but most lobbying is now done by ***pressure groups** or by professional **lobbyists**. Pressure groups work on behalf of a particular section of society or for a specific issue or cause. Many employ full-time **liaison** officers to develop contacts with politicians who are likely to be sympathetic. In Britain some MPs are employed by pressure groups as **consultants**. They have to give details of such employment in a special **Register of Members' Interests**.

Large companies use professional lobbyists to keep them informed of what is being discussed in Congress or Parliament and to try to persuade politicians to put forward their point of view in debates. In the US lobbyists provide information to politicians, sometimes by testifying (= giving evidence) before Congress. They also try to influence the way members of Congress vote, for example by persuading them that a certain policy will be popular with the people they represent. Lobbyists may try to influence politicians by inviting them to an expensive lunch or dinner in a restaurant, or to a party. There are rules limiting what gifts politicians can accept and any gifts must be reported. Some organizations have many lobbyists who are very active. The tobacco industry, for example, has a strong lobby, and its representatives are good at getting what the industry wants from Congress and state legislatures.

In Britain the methods which lobbyists use to influence MPs, and the issue of whether MPs should be connected with lobbyists at all, came to public attention in 1996 when two MPs were found guilty of taking money in exchange for asking questions in Parliament. It became known as the ***cash for questions** affair.

ˌ**Local Edu**ˈ**cation Au**ˌ**thority** (*abbr* **LEA**) *n* a department of local government in Britain that provides money to run the schools and colleges in its area. A small number of the schools and colleges in the area of any Local Education Authority are given money directly by central government, for example the *City Technology Colleges. Compare SCHOOL DISTRICT. See also OPTING OUT. ⇨ article at EDUCATION IN BRITAIN.

Local government in Britain ⇨ article.

ˌ**local** ˈ**radio** *n* [U] the radio stations in Britain that broadcast to a local rather than a national audience, within a county or town. Local radio may be run by the *BBC or by a commercial company with a licence from the *Radio Authority. ⇨ note at RADIO.

ˌ***Loch*** ˈ***Lomond*** /ˌlɒx ˈləʊmənd, ˌlɒk; *AmE* ˌlɑːx ˈloʊmənd, ˌlɑːk/ a traditional Scottish song. It contains the well-known lines:

Oh, you'll take the high road,
And I'll take the low road,
And I'll be in Scotland before you;
But me and my true love will never meet again,
On the bonnie, bonnie banks of Loch Lomond.

L

Local government in Britain

Structure

For administrative purposes Britain is divided into small geographical areas. The oldest and largest divisions in England and Wales are called *__counties__. In Scotland, the largest divisions are **regions**. Counties and regions are further divided into **districts**. *__Parishes__, originally villages with a church, are the smallest units of local government in England. These are called **communities** in Scotland and Wales. Northern Ireland is sometimes known as the *Six Counties, but local government there is based on districts. *__Boroughs__ were originally towns large enough to be given their own local government. Now, only boroughs in London have political power, which they took over in 1985 when the *Greater London Council was abolished.

Counties and districts are run by **councils** which have powers given to them by central government. A system of local councils was first established in the 19th century, but since then there have been many changes to their structure and powers. During the 1970s, some counties were abolished and some new ones created, including new *__metropolitan counties__ around large cities. In 1992 a **Local Government Commission** was set up to consider whether counties should be replaced by *__unitary authorities__. Counties have a **two-tier** structure (= two levels of government), with both county and district councils. The county council is the more powerful. Unitary authorities have only one tier of government. The Commission recommended keeping a two-tier system in many places but suggested that some areas, especially large cities, should become unitary authorities. Local residents were given the opportunity to express their opinions. The first unitary authorities were created in 1995. Since then, all of Wales and Scotland and many parts of England have become unitary authorities.

Councils consist of elected representatives, called **councillors**. They are elected by the local people for a period of four years (in Scotland for three years). Counties, districts and parishes are divided into areas, often called **wards**, each ward electing one councillor or in some cases more. Most councillors belong to a *political party and, especially at county level, people vote for them as representatives of a party, not as individuals. County councils meet in a **council chamber** at the local **town hall** or **county hall**. Councillors elect a chairperson from amongst themselves. In cities, he or she is called the *__Lord Mayor__. Members of the public are allowed to attend council meetings.

In 1998 further changes to local government structure were proposed. The most widely discussed proposal is that mayors should be directly elected by the people. It has already been decided that the people of Greater London will elect their mayor.

Responsibilities

Councils make policies for their area. Decisions are made by the full council or in committees. Policy is carried out by **local government officers**, who have a similar role to that of *civil servants. **Local authorities** (= councils and committees) rather than central government are responsible for education, social services, housing, transport, the police and fire services, town planning, recreation facilities and other local services. In two-tier counties these responsibilities are divided between county and district authorities.

Councils employ about 1.4 million people. Formerly, staff employed by the council carried out most activities, but now councils often give contracts to private firms. Many local government functions, e.g. rubbish/garbage collection, must be **put out to tender** (= competed for by private companies). This procedure is called **compulsory competitive tendering** and is intended to save money. There is an increasing trend away from local authorities providing services directly. The social services department, for example, may decide who needs care and what sort of care they require, but the care itself is often provided by companies or voluntary organizations which are paid by the authority.

Finance

Central government provides a lot of the money spent by councils in the form of **grants**. It also collects taxes, called **business rates**, on commercial properties throughout the country and then shares the money out between local authorities according to their population.

Councils also charge local people a *__council tax__. This is the only tax that they are allowed to collect. The council tax has existed since 1993 and is based on the actual value of a person's house. A person living alone can claim a reduction of 25%. Previously, councils obtained money from the *__rates__, a tax based on the size of a house and its value if it were rented. Under this system, people living alone in a large property did badly. Rates varied a lot between councils, and in 1985 the government gave itself the power to set an upper limit on the amount that councils could raise from the rates. This was called **rate-capping**. In 1989–90 the rates were replaced by the *__community charge__ or 'poll tax'. Everyone paid the same, whether they owned or rented property. The community charge was very unpopular and many people refused to pay it. The government still has powers to limit or **cap** local authority budgets, and this is called **charge-capping**.

Loch Lomond is a lake surrounded by mountains in west Scotland.

ˌ**Loch** ˈ**Ness** /ˌlɒx ˈnes, ˌlɒk; *AmE* ˌlɑːx, ˌlɑːk/ a long, narrow and deep lake in the northern *Highlands of Scotland. It is famous for the **Loch Ness monster**, also known informally as **Nessie**. The monster is thought by some people to be a large animal like a dinosaur (= an animal that lived millions of years ago) that spends most of its time underwater. Many people claim to have seen it, and there is a special Loch Ness Monster Exhibition Centre for tourists on the edge of the lake. However several scientific investigations have failed to find any evidence that it exists.

ˌJohn ˈ**Locke** /ˈlɒk; *AmE* ˈlɑːk/ (1632–1704) an English philosopher. In his *Two Treatises of Government* (1690) he opposed the ideas of Thomas *Hobbes, arguing that governments should rule only if they are supported by the people. This was an important influence on the later revolutions in America and France, and on the development of Western democracy. Locke also wrote books on religion, education

L

a log cabin at Abraham Lincoln's birthplace

and economics. His most famous work of philosophy is *An Essay Concerning Human Understanding* (1690), an attempt to show what can and cannot be known.

'Lockerbie /'lɒkəbi; *AmE* 'lɑːkərbi/ a town in southern Scotland. It became famous in 1988 when a US plane exploded above it, killing all 259 people on board and 11 people on the ground. Authorities in Britain and the US believe the explosion was caused by a bomb placed on the plane by two Libyan men, although the men have never been arrested.

the **ˌLockheed 'Martin Corpoˌration** /ˌlɒkhiːd 'mɑːtɪn; *AmE* ˌlɑːkhiːd 'mɑːrtn/ a US company, formed in 1994 when the Lockheed Corporation and the Martin Marietta Corporation were joined together. It produces military aircraft, space rockets, satellites and other electronic equipment. Its F–22 Raptor aircraft for the US Air Force first flew in 1997. The company's main office is in Bethesda, *Maryland, and the Lockheed Martin Missiles and Space Corporation is in Sunnyvale, *California.

ˌDavid **'Lodge** /'lɒdʒ; *AmE* 'lɑːdʒ/ (1935–) an English author and critic. He is known especially for his humorous books about life in Britain's universities, such as *Changing Places* (1975) and *Small World* (1984), some of which have been made into successful television series. He has also written serious literary criticism.

ˌlog 'cabin *n* a small, simple house made of logs laid horizontally and joined without nails at the corners. Such houses were common in the frontier parts of America (= at the extreme limits of settled land) from the 17th century. President Abraham *Lincoln was born in one in *Kentucky. Many later politicians also claimed that they had been born in log cabins in order to persuade people that they came from poor, ordinary families and had become successful by hard work.

'logrolling /'lɒgrəʊlɪŋ; *AmE* 'lɑːgroʊlɪŋ/ *n* [U] (*AmE*) the practice among politicians of voting for each other's *bills. By giving support they expect to receive support in turn. The word comes from the early US custom by which friends helped each other to roll logs in order to clear land for farming, etc. Compare PORK BARREL.

Lo'lita /lə'liːtə/ a novel (1958) by Vladimir *Nabokov. The main character, Humbert Humbert, is sexually attracted to a girl called Lolita who is only 12 years old. There have been two film versions of the book (1962 and 1998), the first directed by Stanley *Kubrick. The name 'Lolita' is sometimes used to refer to a young girl who is regarded as sexually desirable or who shows interest in or enjoyment of sex.

ˌVince **Lom'bardi** /lɒm'bɑːdi; *AmE* lɑːm'bɑːrdi/ (1913–70) a US professional American football trainer, known for his tough methods. He was famous for saying, 'Winning isn't everything. It's the only thing.' He trained the Green Bay Packers of *Wisconsin from 1959 to 1967, during which time they won 141 games and lost only 39. His teams won the National Football League Championship five times (1961–2 and 1965–8) and the first two *Super Bowls (1967–8). The Vince Lombardi Trophy, given to the team that wins the Super Bowl, is named in memory of him.

'Lombard Street /'lɒmbɑːd; *AmE* 'lɑːmbɑːrd/ a street in the centre of London, England, which is the city's main financial district, containing branches of many of Britain's major banks. The street's name comes from Lombardy, the area in northern Italy from which many bankers came to settle in London in the late 13th century. Compare THREADNEEDLE STREET. ⇨ article at BANKS AND BANKING.

ˌJack **'London** /'lʌndən/ (1876–1916) a US writer of adventure novels and short stories. Before starting to write he worked as a sailor and went to the *Klondike to look for gold, both experiences which he later used in his books. His novels include *The Call of the Wild* (1903), *The Sea-Wolf* (1904) and *White Fang* (1906). His work influenced Ernest *Hemingway and other US writers.

ˌLondon 'Airport /ˌlʌndən/ another name for *Heathrow Airport.

ˌLondon 'Bridge /ˌlʌndən/ a bridge across the River *Thames in London, England, connecting the ancient centre of the city to the district of *Southwark. Until 1750 it was the only bridge crossing the Thames in London. The present bridge, built in 1973, replaced one that was sold to a US businessman and rebuilt in *Arizona.

London 'Bridge is 'Falling 'Down /'lʌndən/ the title and first line of an old children's song. In the song various materials are suggested for rebuilding the bridge, beginning with 'wood and clay' and ending with 'silver and gold'.

'London 'Central 'Mosque /'lʌndən/ a large mosque (= place of worship for Muslims) in *Regent's Park, London, England, completed in 1976 and serving as a community centre for Muslims living in London.

the London Central Mosque

'Londonderry /'lʌndənderi/ (*also* **'Derry**) **1** a city in the county of Londonderry, Northern Ireland, on the River Foyle. It is known as Londonderry because it was settled by English Protestants from London in 1611. Roman Catholics who live there call the city Derry, its original name. In 1689 the Protestant population were attacked by a Roman Catholic army, but survived because they had built strong walls around the city. This success is remembered every year with marches and celebrations, which often cause conflict with local Roman Catholics. The 17th-century city walls and many other old buildings still remain. **2** one of the *Six Counties of Northern Ireland.

the ***ˌLondonderry 'Air*** /ˌlʌndənderi/ a traditional tune from Northern Ireland, first published in 1855. Many different words have been set to it, the most famous being those of the Irish song *Danny Boy*.

'Londoner /'lʌndənə(r)/ *n* a person who lives in or comes from London, England.

The ˌ***London Ga***ˈ***zette*** /ˌlʌndən/ a newspaper that gives British government announcements, including information of interest to people in government departments and the legal profession, as well as lists of recent honours (= awards for services to the country). It first appeared in 1665 and is now published five times a week.

the ˌ**London** ˈ**Library** /ˌlʌndən/ a large private library in London, England, which members must pay to join. It was established in 1840 and contains over one million books. Compare BRITISH LIBRARY.

ˌ**London** ˈ**Lighthouse** /ˌlʌndən/ a British charity formed in 1986 to provide advice, information and medical care for people with the disease Aids.

the ˌ**London** ˈ**marathon** /ˌlʌndən/ a race for runners held every year in London, England, since 1981. The race is 26 miles (42 kilometres) long, starting at *Greenwich and ending at *Westminster Bridge. Thousands of runners take part, many of them to raise money for charity.

the London marathon

the ˌ**London Pal**ˈ**ladium** /ˌlʌndən pəˈleɪdiəm/ a large theatre in London, England, opened in 1910 and now used mainly for performances of *musicals.

L

the ˈ**London** ˈ**Philharmonic** ˈ**Orchestra** /ˈlʌndən/ (*abbr* the **LPO**) a leading British orchestra established in London in 1932 by Thomas *Beecham. Famous conductors of the orchestra have included Adrian *Boult (1951–7), Bernard Haitink (1967–79) and Georg *Solti (1979–83). It is based at the *Royal Festival Hall.

The ˈ***London Re***ˈ***view of*** ˈ***Books*** /ˈlʌndən/ a British newspaper containing reviews of new books, as well as essays on politics, literature and the arts. It was established in 1979 and appears every two weeks.

the ˈ**London** ˈ**School of Eco**ˈ**nomics** /ˈlʌndən/ (*abbr* the **LSE**) a famous college in London, England, offering courses in economics, politics, law and many other subjects. It was established in 1895 by Sidney *Webb and other members of the *Fabian Society and is part of *London University.

the ˌ**London** ˈ**Stock Ex**ˌ**change** /ˌlʌndən/ an institution in London, England, established in the 18th century, which allows trading in stocks and shares (= parts of the total value of a company). Since the *Big Bang in 1986 trading has taken place using computers and telephones, rather than in the offices of the Stock Exchange itself. See also NEW YORK STOCK EXCHANGE, STOCK EXCHANGE AUTOMATED QUOTATIONS.

the ˌ**London** ˈ**Symphony** ˌ**Orchestra** /ˌlʌndən/ (*abbr* the **LSO**) a leading British orchestra established in London in 1904. Famous conductors of the orchestra have included André *Previn (1968–79) and Claudio Abbado (1979–87), and its present main conductor is Colin *Davis (1993–). It is based at the *Barbican Centre.

the ˈ**London to** ˈ**Brighton** ˈ**Veteran** ˈ**Car Run** /ˈlʌndən, ˈbraɪtn/ a British race for old cars held in November every year. The race starts at *Hyde Park, London, and finishes at Brighton, *East Sussex, and is for cars built before 1904. It is a popular social occasion, with the drivers sometimes dressing in Victorian or Edwardian costumes, and is often shown on television.

ˌ**London** ˈ**Transport** /ˌlʌndən/ (*also* **London Regional Transport**) the British government organization responsible for public transport in London, including bus and underground train services.

ˌ**London** ˈ**Underground** the part of *London Transport that is responsible for London's underground train services. The first underground railways in London were begun in the 19th century, and were the first of their kind in the world. The 11 lines of the system (usually known as **the Underground** or informally as **the Tube**) are connected to *British Rail stations and extend out of the centre of London to surrounding regions. Not all of the lines are in fact underground. Recent additions to the system have included the Docklands Light Railway, a privately owned railway joined to the London Underground and providing services to London *Docklands.

ˌ**London Uni**ˈ**versity** /ˌlʌndən/ a university in London, England, established in 1836. It consists of a large number of colleges in different parts of the city, including *Imperial College London, the *London School of Economics and *University College, London. It also includes the *teaching hospitals *Bart's and *Guy's. About one fifth of London University students study abroad and take examinations in their own countries.

ˈ**London** ˈ**Weekend** ˈ**Television** /ˈlʌndən/ ⇨ LWT.

ˌ**London** ˈ**Zoo** /ˌlʌndən/ a zoo in *Regent's Park, London, England. It was established in 1826 by the Zoological Society of London. Today the zoo is an important centre for the study of animals, and breeds animals that are in danger of disappearing in their native environments. Another branch of the zoo is at *Whipsnade.

ˌ**lonely** ˈ**hearts** *n* [pl, usu before *n*] people who are seeking a friendship, especially one that will lead to marriage. A **lonely hearts advertisement** in a newspaper or magazine is one in which lonely people give details about themselves and the type of person they would like to meet. A typical advertisement might read: 'Female, 35, good sense of humour, non-smoker, would like to meet similar male for friendship or romance.' Replies are sent to the newspaper or magazine, who pass them on to the person who advertised: *a lonely hearts ad/club/column.* See also DATING AGENCY, *MISS LONELYHEARTS*.

the ˌ**Lone** ˈ**Ranger** a character of fiction in stories about the American *Wild West who spends his life preserving justice and fighting those who do wrong. He wears a mask and rides a white horse called Silver. His *Native-American friend Tonto calls him 'Kemo Sabe' (which means 'trusty scout'). Together they defeated many outlaws (= criminals). Fran Striker created the character for a US radio series (1933–54) and then wrote 17 Lone Ranger novels. *The Lone Ranger* was also a popular television series (1949–57), with Clayton Moore as the Lone Ranger.

ˌHuey ˈ**Long** /ˌhjuːi ˈlɒŋ; *AmE* ˈlɔːŋ/ (1893–1935) a powerful US politician in the state of *Louisiana, also known as 'Kingfish'. He used emotional speeches and a programme of taxes called Share the Wealth to get money from big businesses and win votes from poor people, while making himself very rich through dishonest deals. He became Governor of Louisiana (1928–31) and a US Senator (1930–5). He had hopes of standing for election as President but was murdered. *All the King's Men* was a novel (1946) by Robert Penn Warren and then a film (1949) based on Long's life.

ˈ**Long Beach** **1** a city near *Los Angeles in the US

state of *California. It is a popular holiday place and an industrial port that produces oil, and aircraft and electronic equipment. The British ship **Queen Mary* was moved there in 1967 as a hotel, museum and tourist attraction. **2** a US town on *Long Island, New York. It has a white beach which has attracted tourists since the 19th century.

ˈ***Long Day's*** ˈ***Journey into*** ˈ***Night*** a play by the US writer Eugene *O'Neill, written between 1939 and 1941. It was first performed in 1956 after O'Neill died, and won the *Pulitzer Prize. It is a sad story about the Tyrone family, based on O'Neill's own family. James Tyrone is a cruel father, his wife Mary takes drugs, one son Edmund has tuberculosis (= a disease of the lungs) and the other son Jamie is dependent on alcohol.

long-distance paths and national trails

Walking, taking long walks in the countryside for pleasure, is a popular *hobby in Britain, and many people go walking in *national parks and other country areas at weekends. *Walking* is also called **hiking**, especially in the US, and sometimes **rambling**. Many routes go along ***public footpaths**. These are **rights of way** (= paths across private land that the public has a legal right to use) which must be kept open and which are marked on *Ordnance Survey maps.

Keen walkers may walk one of Britain's many **long-distance footpaths** during their holiday/vacation. Leaflets and books describe the paths and the facilities available nearby. People doing long-distance walks camp out overnight or stay in bed-and-breakfast accommodation in nearby villages.

The first long-distance footpath, the *Pennine Way, which goes from Edale in Derbyshire to the Scottish border, was established in 1965 and was immediately popular. Other long-distance routes include the *Pembrokeshire Coast Path, *Offa's Dyke Path, the South-west Coast Path, and the West Highland Way. The use of the paths by many thousands of walkers, and now also people riding mountain bikes, has led to concern about vegetation being damaged or destroyed, and wide scars (= areas of bare rock or soil) being left on hillsides.

About half of the land of the US is open to the public, but there is no system equivalent to British public footpaths across private land. There are 19 **national trails** as well as many other paths and trails in national parks and other areas of natural beauty. Because the national trails are very long, few people walk their entire length.

The US National Park Service is in charge of the official trails and works with local organizations to keep them in good condition. There are 8 **national scenic trails** of which the Appalachian Trail is the best known and most popular. It was completed in 1937 and became an official trail in 1969. It begins at Mount Katahdin in *Maine and ends at Springer Mountain in *Georgia, running more than 2 000 miles (3 218 kilometres) and through 12 states over the tops of the *Appalachian Mountains. Other national trails include the Continental Divide National Scenic Trail running from the Canadian border over the *Rocky Mountains south to the Mexican border, and the *Natchez Trace from *Mississippi through *Alabama to *Tennessee. The Trace is in fact a road for cars and bicycles, but people can walk on some of the old *Native-American paths from which it was developed.

There are 11 **national historic trails**, including the Mormon Pioneer National Historic Trail from *Illinois to *Utah which connects places associated with the *American Revolution. The *Trail of Tears runs 2 000 miles (3 200 kilometres) on land and over water following the route used by *Cherokee Native Americans when they were forced to move west.

ˈHenry ˈWadsworth ˈ**Longfellow** /ˈwɒdzwəθ ˈlɒŋfeləʊ; *AmE* ˈwɑːdzwərθ ˈlɔːŋfeloʊ/ (1807–82) one of the most popular US poets. He wrote long poems which helped to create romantic American legends. They include *Evangeline* (1847), *The Song of Hiawatha* (1855), *The Courtship of Miles Standish* (1858) and **Paul Revere's Ride* (1861). Longfellow also taught modern languages at *Harvard University (1836–54). See also HIAWATHA.

ˌLord ˈ**Longford** /ˈlɒŋfəd; *AmE* ˈlɔːŋfərd/ (*born* Frank Pakenham 1905–) a British politician. He is the seventh *earl(1) of Longford and has held important posts as a *Labour member of the *House of Lords, including that of *Lord Privy Seal (1964–5 and 1966–8). He has written widely on subjects such as politics, law and the prison system, and is well known for his campaigns on behalf of prisoners, especially Myra *Hindley.

ˈ**longhorn** /ˈlɒŋhɔːn; *AmE* ˈlɔːŋhɔːrn/ *n* a breed of cattle with long horns, originally from Mexico, which was common in the US in the 19th century. **Texas longhorns** were usually the type taken along the *Chisholm Trail to *Abilene, *Kansas. Longhorns have now mostly been replaced by cows that have more meat.

ˌ**Long** ˈ**Island** an island off the southern end of the US state of New York. It is about 118 miles/190 kilometres long and 12–23 miles/19–37 kilometres wide and has an area of 1 400 square miles/3 627 square kilometres. Its western end includes the New York districts of *Brooklyn and *Queens, and the rest of the island has small towns and holiday places where mainly rich and *middle-class people live. Its beaches are very popular. During the *American Revolution, the army of General George *Washington lost the Battle of Long Island (August 1776) to the British forces of Sir William Howe. See also LONG BEACH.

ˌ**Long John** ˈ**Silver** /ˈsɪlvə(r)/ a character in **Treasure Island* by Robert Louis *Stevenson. Long John Silver is a pirate (= a person on a ship who attacks and robs other ships) with one leg and a parrot (= a colourful bird) which sits on his shoulder.

ˌ**Longleat** ˈ**House** /ˌlɒŋliːt; *AmE* ˌlɔːŋliːt/ a large Elizabethan house in *Wiltshire, England, owned by the Marquess of Bath. It was built in the late 16th century. It is now open to the public and has a safari park (= a park where people can drive round and see wild animals, e.g. lions) and gardens designed by 'Capability' *Brown. ⇨ note at STATELY HOMES.

the ˌ**Long** ˈ**Parliament** the English parliament first called to meet by King *Charles I in 1640. Its opposition to the king led to the *English Civil War between the **Parliamentarians** and the **Royalists**. Many of its members were dismissed in 1648 and it became known as the *Rump Parliament. This was itself dismissed in 1653. At the *Restoration in 1660 a new parliament was created.

ˌStuds ˈ**Lonigan** /ˌstʌdz ˈlɒnɪgən; *AmE* ˈlɑːnɪgən/ a character in three novels by the US writer James *Farrell. They are *Young Lonigan* (1932), *The Young Manhood of Studs Lonigan* (1934) and *Judgement Day* (1935). Lonigan is a good man who struggles to succeed in the 1920s in the poor Irish district of South Side, *Chicago.

ˌ**Lonsdale** ˈ**Belt** /ˌlɒnzdeɪl; *AmE* ˌlɑːnzdeɪl/ *n* a decorated belt given as a prize in British boxing to a boxer of any weight who wins a major professional competition. If a boxer wins such a competition three times in a row he is allowed to keep the belt.

ˌ***Look*** ˈ***Back in*** ˈ***Anger*** a play (1956) by John

L

*Osborne. Its main character, Jimmy Porter, is an '*angry young man' from a *working-class background who directs his anger about British society at his *upper-class wife Alison. The play was a great influence on other writers of the 1950s, and these writers and Osborne himself also became known as 'angry young men'. A film (1959) was later made, with Richard *Burton[3] as Jimmy Porter.

ˌ***Looney*** ˈ***Tunes*** /ˌluːni/ the general name for the US film cartoons produced by *Warner Brothers from the 1930s into the 1960s. The film characters included *Bugs Bunny, Porky Pig, *Daffy Duck, *Tweety Pie, Speedy Gonzales and Pepe le Pew. Tex *Avery drew many of them, and Mel Blanc supplied their voices. The characters also appeared in a Warner Brothers' series called *Merrie Melodies*. Every *Looney Tunes* film ends with the phrase 'That's all, folks' appearing on the screen.

the ˌ**loony** ˈ**left** *n* [U+sing/pl *v*] (*infml often offensive, becoming less frequent*) a name given, especially in some British newspapers, to the left wing of the British *Labour Party. The name was applied particularly to those Labour authorities in charge of local government during the *Conservative rule of the 1980s: *loony left councils/MPs/policies*. Compare MILITANT TENDENCY.

the **Loop** the central business district of the US city of *Chicago. It gets its name from the loop made by the *El railway/railroad that runs around its edges.

L

Lord 1 a title given to all members of the *House of Lords, including peers and *bishops. (*Dukes, although members of the House of Lords, are not addressed as 'Lord'.) It is also given as a *courtesy title to the children of some members of the House of Lords. The title is put before the last name or place where the Lord is from: *Baron Fleming of Rotherham can also be addressed as Lord Fleming.* ○ *Lord Derby* (= the title of the Earl of Derby) . **2** a title given to certain high officials: *Lord Lieutenant/Lord Chief Justice/Lord Chancellor*. **3 My Lord** a way of addressing judges, bishops and peers (except dukes), showing respect. ⇨ note at PEERAGE.

the ˌ**Lord** ˈ**Advocate** *n* the senior legal official in Scotland (equivalent to the *Attorney General in England, Wales and Northern Ireland) who is responsible for advising *Parliament on the law and who appears on behalf of the state in important cases. ⇨ article at LEGAL SYSTEM IN BRITAIN.

the ˌ**Lord** ˈ**Chamberlain** *n* (*in full* the ˌ**Lord** ˈ**Chamberlain of the** ˈ**Household**) (in Britain) the official who is in charge of the royal household and responsible for arranging royal ceremonies.

the ˌ**Lord** ˈ**Chancellor** (*also* the ˌ**Lord High** ˈ**Chancellor**) *n* the government minister who is head of the judiciary (= all the judges) in England and Wales. He is also the *Speaker of the *House of Lords, and sits on the *Woolsack. ⇨ article at LEGAL SYSTEM IN BRITAIN.

the ˌ**Lord Chief** ˈ**Justice** *n* (in British law) the President of the *Queen's Bench Division of the *High Court of Justice. He is next highest in rank to the *Lord Chancellor in the legal system of England and Wales. ⇨ article at LEGAL SYSTEM IN BRITAIN.

ˌ***Lord*** ˈ***Jim*** a novel (1900) by Joseph *Conrad. It tells the story of a young ship's officer who leaves a ship that appears to be sinking, ahead of all the other passengers on board. He later feels very ashamed of this act and goes to live abroad, where he finally wins back his honour.

the ˌ**Lord Lieu**ˈ**tenant** *n* (in Britain) a representative of the king or queen in a county, responsible for arranging royal ceremonies there when the king or queen visits. He is also the head of a county's magistrates. Compare HIGH SHERIFF.

the ˌ**Lord** ˈ**Mayor** *n* the *mayor of certain large cities in England and Wales. He or she is elected every year by the city council, and has mainly ceremonial duties. London has had a Lord Mayor since 1192, who during his or her period of office lives at the *Mansion House. In Scotland a similar post is held by the *Lord Provost.

the ˌ**Lord Mayor's** ˈ**Banquet** a large formal meal held every year at the *Guildhall, London, England, to mark the retirement of the previous year's *Lord Mayor of London. It is attended by the *Prime Minister, who traditionally makes a speech.

the ˌ**Lord Mayor's** ˈ**Show** a public procession held every year in London, England, when the new *Lord Mayor of London rides in a carriage to the *Law Courts to be presented to the *Lord Chief Justice. The carriage is joined by various other vehicles and people in colourful costumes. The ceremony takes place on the second Saturday in November.

the Lord Mayor's Show

ˌ***Lord of the*** ˈ***Flies*** a novel (1954) by William *Golding. It tells the story of a group of boys left on an island after a plane crash. At first they attempt to live together in a peaceful way but later become cruel to each other and worship an invented god, the 'Lord of the Flies' (a pig's head covered in flies). In writing the book Golding used some of the characters of an earlier children's story, *The Coral Island* (1858) by R M Ballantyne.

The ˌ***Lord of the*** ˈ***Rings*** a book in three parts (1954–5) by J R R *Tolkien. It features some of the characters from an earlier book, *The Hobbit* (1937), and tells of their long journey to a place where they can destroy a magic ring. It is set in the imaginary world of Middle-Earth. The book is popular with adults and children in many countries around the world.

the ˈ**Lord** ˈ**President of the** ˈ**Council** the title of the British government minister who is President of the *Privy Council. He or she is also either the *Leader of the House of Commons or the Leader of the House of Lords.

the ˈ**Lord** ˈ**Privy** ˈ**Seal** *n* the British government official who formerly kept the seal (= a piece of metal used to stamp wax to show that documents are genuine) of the king or queen. Today the Lord Privy Seal no longer has this responsibility, but is usually either the *Leader of the House of Commons or the Leader of the House of Lords.

ˌ**Lord Pro**ˈ**tector** (*also* **Protector**, ˌ**Lord Pro**ˈ**tector of the** ˈ**Commonwealth**) the title given to Oliver *Cromwell and later to his son Richard (1626–1712) during the period after the *English Civil War known as the *Protectorate (1653–9). During this time Cromwell and his son claimed greater powers to rule the country, including the power to rule independently of Parliament.

ˌ**Lord ˈProvost** *n* the Scottish equivalent of a *Lord Mayor.

Lord's a famous English cricket ground in St John's Wood, north London, where test matches (= international games) are regularly played. It is named after Thomas Lord (1755–1832), who established the ground in 1814. The *MCC and the *England and Wales Cricket Board are both based there, and it is the place where The *Ashes are kept. It is also the ground of Middlesex County Cricket Club. See also OVAL, SEASON.

The ˌ***Lord's My*** ˈ***Shepherd*** the title of a popular Christian hymn which uses the words of Psalm 23 in the Bible. The first verse is:

The Lord's my shepherd, I'll not want:
He makes me down to lie
In pastures green; he leadeth me
The quiet waters by.

the ˌ**Lord's ˈPrayer** (*also* **Our Father**) the prayer taught by Jesus in the Bible to his followers, beginning 'Our Father'. It is often used in Anglican church services and most Anglicans in Britain and the US know all the words.

the ˌ**Lords ˈSpiritual** *n* [pl] the 26 senior *bishops of the *Church of England who are members of the British *House of Lords.

the ˌ**Lord's ˈTaverners** /ˈtævənəz; *AmE* ˈtævərnərz/ a British cricket team made up of famous actors and entertainers, who play matches to raise money for charity. The team is named after the Tavern, a club at *Lord's cricket ground in London.

the ˌ**Lords ˈTemporal** *n* [pl] the members of the British *House of Lords who are not *bishops (i.e. who are members of the *peerage).

ˌ***Lorna*** ˈ***Doone*** /ˈduːn/ a romantic novel (1869) by the English author R D Blackmore (1825–1900). It is set on *Exmoor in *Devon in the 17th century, and tells the story of a young man who falls in love with a girl called Lorna Doone. Unfortunately she is from the family who murdered his father. Several historical events of the period form part of the story.

ˌ**Los ˈAlamos** /ˌlɒs ˈæləmɒs; *AmE* ˌlɔːs ˈæləmoːs/ a small US town in northern *New Mexico. The first atomic bomb and hydrogen bomb were developed there at the US government's nuclear research centre established in 1943, and the town grew around the centre. The Los Alamos National Laboratory is now operated by the University of California for the US Department of Energy, and its work in education and research includes a Neutron Science Center.

ˌ**Los ˈAngeles** /ˌlɒs ˈændʒəliːz; *AmE* ˌlɔːs/ (*also infml* **LA** /ˌel ˈeɪ/) the second largest city in the US and the largest in *California, with about 9 million people. Its greater area covers 34 000 square miles (more than 88 000 square kilometres) in the southern part of the state on the Pacific coast, and is connected by the world's largest road system. The city is famous for *Hollywood and *Beverly Hills and its tourist attractions include *Sunset Boulevard, the *Hollywood Bowl, *Universal Pictures and *Rodeo Drive. Local industry produces aircraft, chemicals, drugs and electronic products.

The US captured the town from the Mexicans in 1846, and oil was discovered there at the end of the 19th century. Americans think of Los Angeles as an exciting city with many opportunities. But it is also seen as a dangerous place because of its earthquakes, pollution, traffic problems and race riots (= violent conflicts between people of different races). See also KING, UCLA, WATTS RIOTS.

the ˌ**Los ˈAngeles ˈPolice Deˌpartment** /ˌlɒs ˈændʒəliːz; *AmE* ˌlɔːs/ (*abbr* **LAPD**) the large police department for the US city of *Los Angeles. It had 8 900 officers in 1997 and many divisions for crime and traffic, including the Air Support Division with two planes and 19 helicopters. The department has had problems with race prejudice by some of its officers, including the attack on Rodney *King and statements by one officer at the trial of O J *Simpson.

the ˌ***Los*** ˈ***Angeles*** ˈ***Times*** /ˌlɒs ˈændʒəliːz; *AmE* ˌlɔːs/ a newspaper for the US city of *Los Angeles. It has won more than 20 *Pulitzer Prizes and is considered to be one of America's best newspapers. It was first published in 1881 and now has more than 3 million readers each day. The *Los Angeles Times* Syndicate supplies special articles to about 3 000 newspapers and magazines in 120 countries, and the *Los Angeles Times-Washington Post* News Service sends news to about 650 newspapers, magazines, and radio and television stations around the world.

the ˌ**lost geneˈration** *n* [sing] **1** a generation (= group of people born at about the same time) with many of its young men killed in war, especially *World War I, or one which has suffered emotional damage by growing up during war. **2** a group of young US writers of the 1920s, among them Ernest *Hemingway, who were opposed to the moral values of US life in the period following *World War I and went to live abroad, especially in Paris.

ˈ**Lothian** /ˈləʊðiən; *AmE* ˈloʊðiən/ a *region of south-west Scotland. Its administrative centre is *Edinburgh.

lotteries

Britain did not have a national lottery until 1994 when the government finally approved the project despite strong opposition. The **National Lottery** is run by a private company, ***Camelot**, which was given the franchise (= licence) to run it until 2001. It is regulated (= supervised) by *OFLOT.

The lottery was an immediate success with the public and its 'crossed fingers' logo, a gesture supposed to bring luck, soon became familiar throughout Britain. Lottery **tickets** are sold at many shops and supermarkets. For £1.00 people choose a row of six numbers between 1 and 49, or take a **lucky dip** of random numbers. The **draw** ceremony is broadcast every Saturday night. Each week one of three machines containing 49 numbered balls is switched on and, after the balls have been turned, seven are tipped out. The first six are the winning numbers, the seventh is the **bonus ball**. Anyone who has chosen the six winning numbers wins or shares the **jackpot** (= the main prize), worth several million pounds. People with three, four or five matching numbers, or five plus the bonus ball, can also win prizes. If nobody wins the jackpot there is a **rollover** to the next draw. The success of the Saturday lottery led Camelot to introduce a second weekly draw on Wednesday, humorously called 'Winsday'. About 65% of adults play every week. Some also buy **Instants**, which show, when the surface is scratched off, if the buyer has won a prize.

Most of the money raised by the lottery is shared out by the **Lottery Commission** among a variety of **good causes**. These range from major arts institutions, such as the *Royal Opera House, to local sports, arts, conservation and *charity organizations. The lottery is not popular with everyone, and many charities complain that they have received less money from the public since the lottery began.

The amount of money Camelot itself keeps from the lottery is limited by the government, though many people feel that the company makes too much profit.

The US does not have a national lottery but by 1998 there were lotteries in 26 states. US lotteries date back to 1776 when the *Continental Congress gave its approval for lottery tickets to be sold to raise money for the *American Revolution. America's strong religious groups have always been against long-running lotteries, and lottery games did not become official until the 1970s. *New Jersey, which in 1969 became one of the first states to start a lottery, now sells more than $19-million worth of tickets each week, while the *Florida lottery sells over $23 million-worth. State lotteries often pay more than $20 million to the winner. Some games now give winners the choice of having the full amount of the prize paid over 20 to 25 years, or receiving a single payment of only about 50% of the amount.

Some games, such as Powerball and Cash-4-Life, can be played across several states. The US Lottery, run by the the Coeur d'Alene tribe in *Idaho, is played on the Internet.

ˌ**Lough ˈNeagh** /ˌlɒx ˈneɪ, ˌlɒk; *AmE* ˌlɑːx, ˌlɑːk/ the largest lake in the British Isles, near Belfast in Northern Ireland.

L

ˌJoe **ˈLouis** /ˈluːɪs/ (1914–81) an *African-American boxer, also known as the 'Brown Bomber', who was Heavyweight Champion of the World for 12 years (1937–49), longer than anyone else. He defended his title 25 times, also a record. Louis lost only three of his 71 fights, the last one to Rocky *Marciano.

Louˌisiˈana /luˌiːziˈænə/ a southern US state on the *Gulf of Mexico, also known as the Pelican State. It consists mainly of flat land and is separated from the state of *Mississippi by the *Mississippi River. The largest city is *New Orleans and the capital city is Baton Rouge. It was part of the *Louisiana Purchase, became a state in 1837, and was one of the *Confederate States. Louisiana is known for its *Cajun culture. The state produces oil, gas, salt, rice and sugar.

the **Louˌisiana ˈPurchase** /luˌiːziænə/ an area of US land bought from France in 1803 for $15 million, or less than 3 cents an acre. The area was about 828 000 square miles (more than 2 million square kilometres), and extended from the *Mississippi River to the *Rocky Mountains and from the *Gulf of Mexico to *Canada. It made the US more than twice as large as it had been, and encouraged Americans to move west. The French named the area after King Louis XIV.

ˈLouisville /ˈluːivɪl/ the largest city in the US state of *Kentucky, on the *Ohio River. It was settled in 1778 and named after King Louis XVI of France, and the University of Louisville was established in 1798. The US used the town as a military base during the *Civil War. The *Kentucky Derby is held in Louisville, and the city produces bourbon (= whisky made from corn grain), cigarettes, paint and household electrical items.

ˌRichard **ˈLovelace** /ˈlʌvleɪs/ (1618–58) an English poet. He was one of the '*Cavalier poets' who supported King *Charles I during the *English Civil War. He put in prison during the war and wrote some of his finest works there, including the poem *To Althea, from Prison*, which contains the famous lines:

Stone walls do not a prison make
Nor iron bars a cage.

ˌBernard **ˈLovell** /ˈlʌvl/ (1913–) an English astronomer. He helped to develop radar during *World War II and later established the famous radio telescope at *Jodrell Bank to study radio waves sent out by objects in other parts of the universe. He is the author of several books on science and astronomy, and was made a *knight in 1961.

ˈLove's ˈLabour's ˈLost a play (*c.* 1595) by William *Shakespeare. The story is about a king and three of his lords who decide to keep away from women for three years and spend the time studying. When the Princess of France arrives with three of her ladies, the four men forget their plans and fall in love. The play also contains the character Holofernes, a boring schoolteacher who is described as having been 'at a great feast of languages and stolen the scraps'.

ˈLow Church *n* [U] a tradition within the *Church of England that gives less importance to religious ceremonies and the authority of *bishops and priests, and more importance to faith and Bible study. Compare HIGH CHURCH. ▶ **Low Church** *adj*: *My family was very Low Church.*

ˌRobert **ˈLowell** /ˈləʊəl; *AmE* ˈloʊəl/ (1917–77) a US poet who won *Pulitzer Prizes for two books of poems, *Lord Weary's Castle* (1946) and *The Dolphin* (1973). His other collections included *Life Studies* (1959), *For the Union Dead* (1964) and *Day by Day* (1977). Lowell used 'confessional poetry' to write about his problems and his unhappy marriages. He also wrote plays and translated the work of European poets.

the ˌ**Lower ˈEast Side** a poor district of New York City in south-east *Manhattan(1). It includes *Little Italy around Mulberry Street, Chinatown, with Canal Street at its centre, and the Jewish area around Hester Street. Many people from *Puerto Rico have come to live there more recently. Much of the Lower East Side was built again in the 1930s under Mayor Fiorello *La Guardia.

the ˌ**lower middle ˈclass** *n* [sing+ sing/pl *v*] (*also* the **lower middle classes** [pl]) the class of people in British society between *working class and *middle class. Such people may be office workers or shopkeepers, but unlike the middle class they are not professional people or well educated. In modern Britain it is less common to refer to people as lower middle class, and it may be considered offensive. Compare WORKING CLASS, MIDDLE CLASS, UPPER MIDDLE CLASS. ⇨ article at CLASS. ▶ **lower-middle-class** *adj*: *lower-middle-class attitudes/lifestyle.*

ˈlower school *n* (in Britain) a name sometimes given to the classes for younger students (aged 11-14) at a secondary school (for children aged 11-18). ⇨ article at EDUCATION IN BRITAIN.

the **ˈLowlands** /ˈləʊləndz; *AmE* ˈloʊləndz/ *n* [pl] the region of Scotland south and east of the *Highlands. It has flatter countryside and a larger population. See also LALLANS.

ˌ**Lowland ˈScots** /ˈskɒts; *AmE* ˈskɑːts/ ⇨ LALLANS.

ˌL S **ˈLowry** /ˈlaʊri/ (Laurence Stephen Lowry 1887–1976) an English painter who is famous for his paintings of the industrial north of England, where he lived. They show buildings and factories with simple colours and forms, and crowds of 'matchstick' people represented in a few thin lines.

lox /lɒks; *AmE* lɑːks/ *n* [U] (*AmE*) a type of salty salmon (= large fish with pink flesh) that has been smoked. It is especially popular with Jewish people in New York, who often eat it with cream cheese on hard bread rolls called *bagels*.

ˈ**Loyalist** /ˈlɔɪəlɪst/ *n* any of the Protestants in *Northern Ireland who want it to stay part of the United Kingdom and not unite with the Irish Republic. Such people are also sometimes known as Unionists. Illegal Loyalist military groups such as the *Ulster Volunteer Force and the *Ulster Freedom Fighters have been responsible for acts of violence in Northern Ireland since the 1960s.

the ˌ**loyal** ˈ**toast** *n* [usu sing] (in Britain) a toast (= an act of raising one's glass and drinking at the same time as other people) at a formal dinner, to show loyalty to the queen or king. People say 'the Queen' or 'the King' and then drink. After the loyal toast people are traditionally allowed to smoke.

ˈ**loyalty card** *n* a small plastic card given by supermarkets and other shops to their customers in order to persuade them to continue to buy goods from them. Everything the customers buy is recorded, and the customers are given price reductions and other benefits according to the amount they spend.

LPO /ˌel piː ˈəʊ; *AmE* ˈoʊ/ ⇨ LONDON PHILHARMONIC ORCHESTRA.

LSAT /ˌel es eɪ ˈtiː/ (*in full* **Law School Admission Test**) (in US colleges and universities) a test taken by students wanting to be admitted to a *law school. It tests general academic knowledge and can be taken before or after the first degree is received.

LSD (*also* **£sd**) /ˌel es ˈdiː/ *n* [U] (*BrE old use infml*) an expression meaning money, from the pounds (£), shillings (s) and pence (d) used before the decimal system was introduced in Britain in 1971.

LSE /ˌel es ˈiː/ ⇨ LONDON SCHOOL OF ECONOMICS.

LSO /ˌel es ˈəʊ; *AmE* ˈoʊ/ ⇨ LONDON SYMPHONY ORCHESTRA.

ˌLord ˈ**Lucan** /ˈluːkən/ (*born* Richard John Bingham 1934–) an English peer who disappeared in 1974 after a female servant at his house was murdered. The police were never able to find him, and some people think he is still alive. People sometimes make jokes about his disappearance.

ˈClare ˈBooth ˈ**Luce** /ˈbuːð ˈluːs/ (1903–87) a US politician and journalist who also wrote plays. She was the managing editor of *Vanity Fair* magazine (1933–4). Her best-known plays include *The Women* (1936), which became a 1939 film with 135 female actors and no men, and *Kiss the Boys Goodbye* (1938). Luce was a *Republican(1) elected from *Connecticut to the US House of Representatives (1943–7), and she later became the US ambassador in Italy (1953–7). Her husband Henry Luce (1898–1967) started *Time* magazine.

Our Town, *painted by L S Lowry*

ˈˌLucky' **Luciˈano** /luːsiˈɑːnəʊ; *AmE* luːsiˈɑːnoʊ/ (1897–1962) a US criminal, born in Sicily. He became the head of a powerful criminal organization in New York in the 1920s and probably ordered the murder of his rival 'Dutch' Schultz in 1935. A year later he was sent to prison for controlling prostitutes. He continued to run his illegal activities from prison, but in 1946 he was sent back to Italy.

ˌ***Lucky*** ˈ***Jim*** a comic novel (1954) by Kingsley *Amis. The main character, Jim Dixon, is a young college teacher who dislikes his job and falls in love with another man's girlfriend. The funniest moments in the book are when Jim gets drunk and behaves badly in front of the senior teachers. The book was made into a film in 1957 by the *Boulting brothers.

ˌ**Lucky** ˈ**Strike**™ a US cigarette produced by the American Tobacco Company and first sold in 1916. Phrases used to advertise Lucky Strike cigarettes have included 'Reach for a Lucky', 'LS/MFT' (Lucky Strike Means Fine Tobacco) and 'Be Happy, Go Lucky'.

ˈ**Lucozade**™ /ˈluːkəzeɪd/ *n* [U] a sweet orange-coloured drink which is advertised as giving energy to people who take part in sports, etc. or helping people to get well after an illness. It is produced by *SmithKline Beecham.

ˈ**Luddite** *n* (*usu disapprov*) a person opposed to change in working methods or the introduction of new machines or technology. The original Luddites were early 19th-century workers who destroyed machinery because they thought it would threaten their jobs. Several of them were hanged for their crimes. ▶ **Luddite** *adj*: *Luddite attitudes to computers are all too common.*

L

ˌRobert ˈ**Ludlum** /ˈlʌdləm/ (1927–) a US author who has written more than 20 novels, with sales of over 200 million copies. The stories are about spies and international crime. They include *The Matlock Paper* (1973), *The Bourne Identity* (1980), *The Icarus Agenda* (1988) and *The Matarese Countdown* (1997).

ˈ**ludo** *n* [U] (*BrE*) a simple game played with dice and small coloured discs on a special board. A similar game popular in the US is called Parcheesi.

ˌBela **Luˈgosi** /ˌbelə luˈgəʊsi; *AmE* luˈgoʊsi/ (1884–1956) a US actor, born in Hungary. He appeared mainly in horror films, and is best remembered for playing the part of *Dracula, first in a *Broadway play (1927) and later in a film version (1931). His other films included *Mark of the Vampire* (1935) and *The Return of the Vampire* (1943). At his own request, Lugosi was buried in his Dracula costume.

the **lump** *n* [sing + sing/pl *v*] (*BrE infml*) workers in the British building industry who are employed on a temporary basis and do not usually pay tax or *National Insurance.

ˈ**Lundy** /ˈlʌndi/ a small island off the coast of *Devon, England, owned by the *National Trust. Its plants and animals are protected by law and it is a breeding ground for puffins (= black and white sea birds).

the ˌ***Lusiˈtania*** /ˌluːsɪˈteɪniə/ a British passenger ship of the *Cunard line that was attacked and sunk by a German submarine off the south coast of Ireland in 1915, killing about 1 200 people. They included 128 Americans, and this influenced the later US decision to enter *World War I against Germany.

the ˌ**Lutine** ˈ**bell** /ˌluːtiːn/ *n* [sing] a bell kept at *Lloyd's of London which is rung when important announcements are made. In former times it was rung to announce good or bad news for the company, such as the loss of a ship insured there, but today it is often rung to mark news of national importance, such as the death of a public figure. The bell was rescued from the *Lutine*, a ship insured at Lloyd's which sank in 1799 carrying a large amount of gold.

ˌ**Luton ˈHoo** /ˌluːtən ˈhuː/ a large, grand house near Luton in *Bedfordshire, England. It was originally designed by Robert *Adam in the late 18th century, with gardens by Lancelot 'Capability' *Brown, but was badly damaged by fire in 1843. In the early 20th century it was rebuilt and now contains an important collection of paintings.

ˌEdwin ˈ**Lutyens** /ˈlʌtjənz/ (1869–1944) an English architect. His early work on private houses was influenced by a wide range of English architecture, including *medieval styles and those of the *Arts and Crafts Movement. His later designs, as in the *Cenotaph, London, and the government buildings in New Delhi, show the influences of Greek and Roman architecture. He was made a *knight in 1918.

Folly Farm, designed by Edwin Lutyens

ˈ**luvvy** (*also* **luvvie**) /ˈlʌvi/ *n* [often pl] (*BrE infml, sometimes offensive*) an actor, especially one who behaves with exaggerated emotion. The word comes from the fact that many actors are thought to address each other as 'lovey': *Her friends are mainly luvvies and arty types.*

Lux™ /lʌks/ *n* [U] a popular make of soap sold in both Britain and the US. It is available in the form of bars or as packets of tiny thin flakes for washing clothes.

LWT /ˌel dʌbljuː ˈtiː/ (*in full* **London Weekend Television**) a British television company established in 1967. It broadcasts to a London audience on the *ITV channel from Friday evening to Sunday night. It produces many of its own programmes, including *The *South Bank Show*.

ˈ**Lycra**™ /ˈlaɪkrə/ *n* [U] an elastic material used especially for close-fitting sports clothing, or women's clothing such as tights and skirts: *Lycra shorts/leggings/tops.*

ˌ**Lyme ˈRegis** /ˌlaɪm ˈriːdʒɪs/ a popular holiday town in *Dorset on the south coast of England. It is famous for the fossils (= animals and plants preserved in rock) that can be found in its cliffs, and for the Cobb, a long stone wall stretching out into the sea, along which people can walk.

ˌDesmond ˈ**Lynam** /ˈlaɪnəm/ (1942–) a British television presenter, famous for his very relaxed style. He is best known for his sports programmes, including **Grandstand* and **Match of the Day*.

the ˈ**Lyndon B ˈJohnson ˈSpace ˌCenter** /ˈlɪndən biː ˈdʒɒnsn; *AmE* ˈdʒɑːnsn/ a US space centre at Clear Lake, *Texas, near *Houston. *NASA has its Mission Control there for space flights by astronauts. It was established in 1961 as the Manned Spacecraft Center, but the name was later changed to honour President Lyndon B *Johnson, who was from Texas.

Mission Control at the Lyndon B Johnson Space Center

Loˌretta ˈ**Lynn**¹ /ləˌretə ˈlɪn/ (1935–) a US singer of *country music. Her many hits include *Don't Come Home A Drinkin'* (1966) and, with Conway Twitty, *After the Fire Is Gone* (1971). Lynn was chosen for the Country Music *Hall of Fame in 1988. Her younger sister, Crystal Gayle (1951–), is also a country music singer, and so are her twin daughters Peggy and Patsy.

ˌVera ˈ**Lynn**² /ˈlɪn/ (1917–) an English singer. She was known as the 'Forces' Sweetheart' during *World War II and was very popular for her songs **We'll Meet Again* and *White Cliffs of Dover*. She was made a *dame(2) in 1975.

ˌ**Lyoˈnesse** /ˌlaɪəˈnes/ an imaginary land between *Cornwall, England, and the *Scilly Isles to the south-west, now said to be covered by sea. It is often connected with stories about King *Arthur. ⇨ article at ARTHURIAN LEGEND.

ˌ***Lyrical ˈBallads*** a book of poems (1798) by William *Wordsworth and Samuel Taylor *Coleridge. It was the first major work of *Romantic literature, and contained Wordsworth's **Tintern Abbey* and Coleridge's *The Rime of the *Ancient Mariner*. In the second edition (1800) Wordsworth added a famous introduction saying that poetry should be drawn from ordinary life and written in plain language.

ˌHumphrey ˈ**Lyttleton** /ˈlɪtltən/ (1921–) an English *jazz musician, broadcaster and author. He formed his own jazz band in 1948, playing the trumpet, and went on to present a number of jazz programmes on radio. He is also well known for presenting the *Radio 4 comedy show *I'm Sorry I Haven't a Clue*.

Mm

ˈ**Maastricht** /ˈmɑːstrɪkt, ˈmɑːstrɪxt/ a city in the Netherlands. The leaders of the 12 countries of the European Community met there in 1992 to sign the **Maastricht Treaty**, an agreement about closer union between European countries. This included plans to have a single currency, a shared defence force and a more powerful *European Parliament. Many people in Britain were opposed to the agreement, and there were disagreements about it within the British *Conservative government. Britain finally signed it in 1993, but the continued disagreements within the government were an important factor in their defeat at the election of 1997. A new version of the Treaty was signed in Amsterdam in 1997 by the British *Labour government. See also EUROSCEPTIC, EUROPEAN CURRENCY UNIT, SOCIAL CHAPTER. ⇨ article at EUROPEAN UNION.

Mac- Some names beginning with **Mac-** are spelt **Mc-** and appear as entries at that form, e.g. **McCarthy**, **McCartney**, etc.

ˌDouglas **MaˈcArthur** /məˈkɑːθə(r); *AmE* məˈkɑːrθər/ (1880–1964) a US military officer. In *World War II General MacArthur became Allied Supreme Commander of the Southwest Pacific Area. He left the Philippines when the Japanese were about to capture it, but promised: 'I shall return'. He did, two years later, and a famous photograph showed him walking up the beach. He accepted the Japanese surrender in 1945 and was head of the forces that occupied Japan. MacArthur also led the UN forces in Korea in 1950, but was ordered back to the US in 1951 because he wanted to attack China. MacArthur then made a speech in Congress, during which he said: 'Old soldiers never die, they only fade away,' a line from a song popular with British soldiers during *World War I.

ˌThomas **Maˈcaulay** /məˈkɔːli/ (1800–59) an English writer and politician. His best-known works are his unfinished *History of England*, which was a great influence on later writers of history, and *Lays of Ancient Rome*. He was a *Member of Parliament and Secretary of War (1839–41), and was made a *baron in 1857.

Macˈbeth /məkˈbeθ/ a play (1606) by William *Shakespeare telling the story of Macbeth, a figure from Scottish history. At the start he meets three witches who predict that he will one day become king. Lady Macbeth, Macbeth's ambitious wife, encourages him to murder the existing king, Duncan. He does so and takes Duncan's place, but finds he has to murder several more people to remain in power. Lady Macbeth goes crazy, imagining that her hands are covered with blood that cannot be washed off, and kills herself. Finally Macbeth is also killed. The play is one of Shakespeare's most popular works, and contains many famous lines. Actors traditionally consider it an unlucky play, and avoid mentioning it by name, calling it 'the Scottish play'.

ˌHugh **MacˈDiarmid** /məkˈdɜːmɪd; *AmE* məkˈdɜːrmɪd/ (1892–1978) a Scottish poet. He wrote in the Scottish dialect known as *Lallans and is best known for his poem *A Drunk Man Looks at the Thistle* (1926). He was a Communist and a supporter of Scottish independence, and was one of the first members of the *Scottish National Party.

ˌFlora **Macˈdonald**[1] /məkˈdɒnəld; *AmE* məkˈdɑːnəld/ (1722–90) a Scottish woman who helped *Bonny Prince Charlie to escape from Scotland in a small boat after his defeat by the English at the Battle of *Culloden.

ˌRamsay **MacˈDonald**[2] /ˌræmzi məkˈdɒnəld; *AmE* məkˈdɑːnəld/ (1866–1937) a British *prime minister. He was leader of the *Labour Party (1911–14 and 1922–31) and the first Labour prime minister (1924 and 1929–31). His second government failed to deal with economic difficulties, and was replaced by a coalition government (= one supported by all parties). MacDonald continued as prime minister (1931–5), but left the Labour Party, an act which made him unpopular with Labour supporters. In 1935 he resigned and was replaced by Stanley *Baldwin.

ˌRoss **Macˈdonald**[3] /ˌrɒs məkˈdɒnəld; *AmE* ˌrɔːs məkˈdɑːnəld/ (1915–83) a US writer of *detective stories. The main character in his books is Lew Archer, a tough but sympathetic detective. The books include *The Galton Case* (1959), *The Chill* (1964) and *Sleeping Beauty* (1973).

the **mace** /meɪs/ *n* [sing] a rod decorated with silver and gold, kept in the British *House of Commons as a symbol of the authority of the *Speaker. In 1976 Michael *Heseltine shocked some *Members of Parliament by picking up the mace and shaking it during a debate. In former times maces were large heavy clubs used as weapons in battle.

the mace and dispatch boxes

ˌCharles ˈ**Macintosh** /ˈmækɪntɒʃ; *AmE* ˈmækɪntɑːʃ/ (1766–1823) a Scottish inventor who developed a material made of rubber to keep out water. A 'mackintosh' is now a word for any coat made of a similar material for keeping off rain.

ˌCompton **Macˈkenzie** /ˌkɒmptən məˈkenzi; *AmE* ˌkɑːmptən/ (1883–1972) a British author. He is best known for his novel *Whisky Galore* (1947) about a boat carrying *whisky that gets stuck on the shore of a Scottish island. The people on the island keep the whisky but have to hide it from the authorities. It was later made into an *Ealing comedy. His many other books include *Sinister Street* (1913–4), based on his life in Oxford and London. He was made a *knight in 1952.

ˌCharles **Macˈkerras** /məˈkerəs/ (1925–) an Australian conductor who was born in America and has lived in Britain since the late 1940s. He has worked for the *English National Opera (1970–7), the *Welsh National Opera (1987–92) and many other groups. He was made a *knight in 1979.

ˈCharles ˈRennie ˈ**Mackintosh** /ˈreni ˈmækɪntɒʃ; *AmE* ˈmækɪntɑːʃ/ (1868–1928) a Scottish architect and designer who produced buildings, furniture and decorative objects in the *Art Nouveau style. His best-known building is the Glasgow School of Art (opened 1899). He is also known for his watercolour paintings, done mainly in France towards the end of his life.

a room designed by Charles Rennie Mackintosh

ˌShirley **Maˈclaine** /məˈkleɪn/ (1934–) a US film actor who began her career as a dancer on *Broadway. MacLaine won an *Oscar for *Terms of Endearment* (1983), and her other films include *The Apartment* (1960), *Sweet Charity* (1969), *The Turning Point* (1977) and *Steel Magnolias* (1989). She is the sister of the actor Warren *Beatty.

ˌAlistair **Maˈclean**[1] /məˈkleɪn/ (1922–87) a Scottish author of adventure novels. They include *The Guns of Navarone* (1957), *Ice Station Zebra* (1963) and *Where Eagles Dare* (1967), which have all been made into successful films. He also wrote books about T E *Lawrence and Captain James *Cook.

ˌDonald **Maˈclean**[2] /məˈkleɪn/ (1913–83) an English spy. He became a Communist as a young man at the same time as the other British spies Anthony *Blunt, Guy *Burgess and Kim *Philby, and from 1944 worked for the British Foreign Office while acting as a spy for the Russian government. In 1951 he learned of British suspicions against him, and escaped with Burgess to Russia, where he lived until his death.

ˌHarold **Macˈmillan**[1] /məkˈmɪlən/ (1894–1986) a British *Conservative politician. He entered Parliament in 1924 and was *Foreign Secretary (1955) and *Chancellor of the Exchequer (1955–7) before becoming *Prime Minister (1957–63). After gaining power he concentrated on improving Britain's international relations and encouraging economic growth, becoming known for his phrase 'You've never had it so good' (taken from a US election campaign). Because of his successes he was sometimes called 'Supermac' by the press. The *Profumo affair in 1963 damaged his party and he resigned later that year because of ill health, being replaced by Sir Alec *Douglas-Home. Macmillan was the author of several books, including *Winds of Change* (1966), the title of which refers to a famous phrase in his 1960 speech about African independence. He was made an *earl(1) in 1984. See also NIGHT OF THE LONG KNIVES.

ˌKenneth **MacˈMillan**[2] /məkˈmɪlən/ (1929–92) a Scottish choreographer. He was director of the *Royal Ballet (1970–77), and his work includes *Elite Syncopations* (1974) and *Mayerling* (1978). He was made a *knight in 1983.

ˌLouis **MacˈNeice** /məkˈniːs/ (1907–63) a Northern Irish poet. His books of verse include *Blind Fireworks* (1929) and *Autumn Journal* (1939), but he is perhaps best known for his radio play *The Dark Tower* (1947) and his friendship with the poet W H *Auden, with whom he wrote *Letters from Iceland* (1937). He also translated ancient Greek poetry.

ˈ**Macy's** /ˈmeɪsiz/ a famous shop in New York which calls itself 'the largest department store in the world' and has branches in other US cities. Each *Thanksgiving, it presents a colourful parade through New York which is shown on television.

Mad (*also* ***Mad Magazine***) a US humorous magazine, was first published in 1952. It now appears once a month and has had as many as 2.5 million readers. It uses an exaggerated cartoon style to make fun of films, advertisements, etc., and to make well-known people look foolish. It always has on its cover a picture of the imaginary character Alfred E Neuman, who has a wide face and a stupid smile and says 'What, me worry?'

ˌ**Madame Tusˈsaud's** /təˈsɔːdz/ a museum in London, England, started in 1835 by a Frenchwoman, Madame Marie Tussaud (1761–1850). It contains wax figures of famous people from past and present, and the *Chamber of Horrors, an exhibition of famous crimes and punishments.

ˌ**mad ˈcow diˌsease** ⇨ BSE.

the ˌ**Mad ˈHatter** a character in *Alice in Wonderland by Lewis *Carroll. The Mad Hatter, who wears a tall hat, holds a tea party with Alice, the March Hare and the Dormouse. The expression 'as mad as a hatter', meaning completely crazy, was already common when Carroll wrote the book.

ˌJames ˈ**Madison** /ˈmædɪsn/ (1751–1836) the fourth US *President (1809–17) and one of America's *Founding Fathers. He was called the *Father of the Constitution because of his important work on that document. He was *Secretary of State (1801–8) under President Thomas *Jefferson and was then elected President as a Democratic-Republican. He was in office during the *War of 1812 and when the British burned the *White House(1) in 1814. He later helped to establish the University of Virginia and was the last of the Founding Fathers to die. His wife, Dolly (or Dolley) Madison (1768–1849), was known for her charm and her social events.

ˌ**Madison ˈAvenue** /ˌmædɪsn/ a street in New York City where many advertising companies have their offices. The name 'Madison Avenue' has come to mean the US advertising industry itself, and the methods it uses, which many people regard as too aggressive and sometimes dishonest. The street also has several art galleries. In the past a number of rich families owned large houses on Madison Avenue.

ˈ**Madison ˈSquare ˈGarden** /ˈmædɪsn/ (*also* the **Garden**) a large building in New York City, opened in 1969, where major sports and cultural events are held. The main area has 20 000 seats.

ˈ**Madness** a British pop group formed in 1978, whose best-known songs have included *Baggy Trousers* (1980), *House of Fun* (1982) and *Our House* (1982). Many of the group's songs are influenced by *ska music.

Maˈdonna /məˈdɒnə; *AmE* məˈdɑːnə/ (1958–) a US pop singer and actor, born Madonna Louise Veronica Ciccone. She has emphasized sex in her music and stage performances, as well as in the clothes she wears for them. She appeared naked in a collection of photographs published in a book called *Sex* (1992). Her films include *Desperately Seeking Susan* (1985) and *Evita* (1996). Her song albums have included *Bedtime Stories* (1994) and *Ray of Light* (1998).

Madonna

ˌ**Mae ˈWest** /ˌmeɪ ˈwest/ *n* a popular name for a type of life jacket (= a jacket designed to keep a person floating in water) used especially during *World War II by British *Royal Air Force crews. It was named after the US actor Mae *West because the jacket reminded people of her large breasts.

MAFF /mæf/ ⇨ MINISTRY OF AGRICULTURE, FISHERIES AND FOOD.

ˈ**Mafia** *n* **1 the Mafia** [sing + sing/pl *v*] a secret organization of criminals, originally in Sicily. It is also sometimes called the Mob, the Syndicate or Cosa Nostra (Italian for 'our thing'), and is involved in all types of criminal activity, including drugs, gambling and prostitutes. The Italian-American Mafia began in the US in the late 19th century and became organized into powerful 'families'. They controlled the production of illegal alcohol during *Prohibition and only become weaker in the 1980s when several leaders, called 'godfathers', were sent to prison. Well-known members of the Mafia in the US have included Al *Capone and 'Lucky' *Luciano. There have been many books and films about the Mafia, including *The *Godfather*. **2 mafia** [C] (*disapprov or humor*) a group of people who have, or are thought to have, secret influence in society: *President Kennedy was supported by the Irish-American mafia.*

Magazines ⇨ article.

the ˌ**Magic ˈCircle** a British association for professional magicians (= people who entertain others with magic tricks) established in 1905. Only the best magicians can join, and members are not allowed to reveal their secrets to the public.

*The ˌ**Magic ˈRoundabout*** a British children's television programme (1965–77). The characters were all toys, including a little girl called Florence and a dog called Dougal. Each programme lasted five minutes. They were in fact made in France, with English words added later, and were very popular in Britain with both children and adults.

ˈ**magistrates' court** *n* a local court of law in England and Wales where magistrates judge minor criminal cases, and also decide whether more serious cases should be referred to a *Crown Court. Most criminal cases in England and Wales are judged in magistrates' courts. ⇨ article at LEGAL SYSTEM IN BRITAIN.

ˌ***Magna ˈCarta*** /ˌmægnə ˈkɑːtə; *AmE* ˈkɑːrtə/ (*also the **Magna Carta***) a document that King *John was forced to sign by the English *barons at *Runnymede in 1215. It restricted the king's power and gave new rights to the barons and the people. Some of these rights are basic to modern British law, e.g. the right to have a trial before being put in prison. Four of the original copies of the Magna Carta still exist, two in the *British Library and one each in the cathedrals of *Salisbury and *Lincoln.

ˌ**magna cum ˈlaude** /ˌmægnə kʊm ˈlaʊdeɪ/ (in the US) the Latin expression, meaning 'with great praise', used to indicate a high academic achievement of a college or university student who has completed his or her studies. It is the second of the three highest grades that can be achieved and is shown on the student's final diploma (= document awarded for completing a course of study): *Sally graduated magna cum laude.* Compare CUM LAUDE, SUMMA CUM LAUDE.

*The **Magˌnificent ˈSeven*** a US *western film (1960) about seven men who are hired by a Mexican village to protect them from bandits. It was based on Akira Kurosawa's Japanese film *The Seven Samurai* (1954). The music for the film was written by Elmer *Bernstein. Three later films used the same characters but different actors.

ˌMagnus ˈ**Magnusson** /ˌmægnəs ˈmægnəsən/ (1929–) a British broadcaster, writer and journalist, born of Icelandic parents. He presented the television quiz show *Mastermind* for 25 years (1972–97). He has also presented several other television programmes and written books on historical subjects.

the **Maˌguire ˈSeven** /məˌgwaɪə; *AmE* məˌgwaɪər/ seven people who were wrongly put in prison in 1976, after being accused of making bombs for the *IRA. Six of them were from the Maguire family, who were relatives of Gerry Conlon, one of the *Guildford Four. The Maguire Seven were officially declared innocent in 1991 after it was shown that false scientific evidence had been offered at their trial. The case was one of a number of similar cases in Britain in the 1980s and 1990s which led to demands for police and legal procedures to be changed. See also BIRMINGHAM SIX, BRIDGEWATER, GUILDFORD FOUR, TOTTENHAM THREE.

ˌ**Maiden ˈCastle** /ˌmeɪdn/ a very large ancient fort on a hill near *Dorchester, *Dorset, England. It was first occupied in about 2000 BC and was attacked and captured by the Romans in AD 43. Today only the impressive earth banks around it remain.

ˌ**Maid ˈMarian** (in old stories) the female companion of *Robin Hood. She also appears as a character in *morris dancing and as the *May Queen in the *May Day games.

ˌ**maid of ˈhonour** (*pl* **maids of honour**) (*AmE* **honor**) *n* **1** (*AmE*) the chief bridesmaid at a wedding. If she is a married woman she is called a **matron of honor**. **2** a woman who is not married and who is the companion of a princess or queen. **3** (*BrE*) a type of small cake flavoured with almonds.

the ***Mail*** ⇨ *DAILY MAIL*. See also *MAIL ON SUNDAY*. ⇨ article at NEWSPAPERS.

ˌNorman ˈ**Mailer** /ˈmeɪlə(r)/ (1923–) a US journalist and author who became famous with his first novel, *The Naked and the Dead*, about *World War II. He won *Pulitzer Prizes for *The Armies of the Night* (1968), about the 1967 peace march to Washington, DC, and *The Executioner's Song* (1979), a novel based on facts about Gary *Gilmore in prison. Mailer's other novels include *The Prisoner of Sex* (1971), *Ancient Evenings* (1983) and *Harlot's Ghost* (1991). He has been involved in a number of liberal protest movements, e.g. against the *Vietnam War.

*The ˌ**Mail on ˈSunday*** a British Sunday newspaper

Magazines

Many magazines are of general interest. Some of these are aimed specifically at women, men, or young people, while others cover a *hobby or leisure interest, e.g. sailing. Other magazines are for specialists in a particular field.

Most magazines contain news items, **features** (= articles), colour pictures, reviews and stories which establish an identity for the magazine. They also carry advertisements. Some have a page of readers' letters commenting on articles in a previous **issue** or asking for advice.

In Britain there are nearly 7 000 weekly and monthly magazines. The best-sellers are the **television guides**, such as **Radio Times*. Nearly as popular is the **Reader's Digest*, a collection of articles and short stories. In the US **TV Guide* and **People*, and **news magazines** such as **Time*, **Newsweek* and **US News and World Report*, are most popular. Magazines like **Ebony*, which are for people from a particular race or culture, have a smaller **circulation** (= number of readers).

Magazines with a **restricted circulation** (= available only to certain people) include **inflight magazines** published by airlines for people to read during a flight, and **store magazines** which customers can buy at a supermarket checkout. Special-interest *clubs and societies publish magazines for their members.

General-interest magazines

General-interest magazines, also called **consumer magazines**, concentrate on subjects of interest to many people. In Britain these include **Ideal Home*, *Garden News*, *BBC Good Food Magazine*, *Mother and Baby*. There are also magazines on *DIY, cars, sport, travel, films and music.

Music and film magazines cater for a wide range of tastes. *Q*, **Rolling Stone* and **New Musical Express* contain reviews of popular music and interviews with musicians. *Mixmag* covers dance culture. Classical music, opera, *jazz and *folk music have their own magazines, some of which give away free CDs. US film magazines include *Empire*, *Neon*, and *Sight and Sound*.

Sports magazines also attract many readers. US titles include *Total Sport* and, for individual sports, *Top Gear* and *Regatta*. In Britain some football clubs produce a club magazine. **Fanzines** are cheap magazines produced by fans (= supporters) of a singer, group or sports club.

Gossip magazines, also called **the gossips**, have stories about the rich and famous and range from the upmarket (= smart) **Hello!* to US supermarket tabloids like **National Enquirer*.

Some magazines are bought mainly for their **listings**, e.g. **Time Out*, which gives details of plays, concerts, etc. in London or New York. **Exchange & Mart* contains only advertisements of items for sale or wanted.

A few magazines have a more intellectual content. These include news and current affairs magazines, such as **Time*, **Life*, *The *Economist*, **Private Eye* and *The *Spectator*, as well as **New Scientist*, **Scientific American* and **National Geographic*.

Women's and men's magazines

Women generally buy more magazines than men. **Vogue* and **Harper's & Queen* are expensive, high-quality fashion magazines. Others have a more chatty style and contain stories, competitions, articles on fashion, make-up, food and fitness, and an agony (*AmE* advice) column (= replies to readers' letters on personal problems). One of the most popular magazines for younger women is **Cosmopolitan*, which also includes film and book reviews and advice on sex and careers. Other women's titles include **Good Housekeeping*, *She*, **Prima*, *Bella*, **Woman* and *Best*.

Teen mags have information and advice about clothes, school, friends and entertainment. *Mizz*, *Seventeen* and **J17* are written for older teenagers but often read by younger girls. Some parents disapprove of teen mags as they include stories about boys and sex.

Recently, more magazines have been produced specifically for men. Highly-illustrated magazines such as **Esquire*, *Arena* and *GQ* contain reviews and articles about cars, clothes, music and sport. In the US *Gentlemen's Quarterly* is famous. *Loaded* and *Sky* are based more on 'lad culture', where the emphasis is on sex, drink and music.

Most **pornographic magazines** (= magazines which contain photographs of people naked) are also aimed at men. Although British and American people believe in a **free press** (= the right to publish anything), there are limits in the case of magazines about sex.

Special-interest magazines

Special-interest magazines can be found on almost any subject including body-building, photography, fishing, electronics, computing and the paranormal. They contain detailed or technical information and are aimed at enthusiasts who do the activity.

Regional magazines in the US, e.g. *Alaska* and *New York Magazine*, contain articles about a particular state or city. In Britain county magazines describe mainly upper-class social events.

Trade magazines are aimed at people who work in various industries. Some, like **Billboard* for the music world, are famous, but most, like *Farmweek*, are known only to people in the trade.

Professional **journals** are for people working in a particular profession or academic field and contain articles about research or professional practice.

Buying magazines

Magazines can be bought in supermarkets and bookshops, at bookstalls and news stands, and in Britain at a newsagent's. But it is often cheaper to take out a **subscription** (= make a yearly payment) to a magazine and to have it sent by mail.

Many people do not buy magazines but read **back copies** (= old issues) put out in their doctor's or dentist's waiting room or at the hairdresser's. Libraries have a **periodicals** section containing *newspapers and a selection of more serious magazines which people can read in the library.

Magazines are now increasingly available on the Internet. Some, like *Wired* and *Toxic* (both about computers), and a few academic journals, are available only on the Internet.

published by the same group as the *Daily Mail*. It first appeared in 1982.

ˌ**main ˈdrag** *n* [usu sing] (*AmE infml*) the main street in a town or city. The phrase is also used by US students to refer to a busy street near their college or university.

Maine /meɪn/ the most northern of the *New England states in the US. Its popular name is the Pine Tree State, and people from Maine are called Down Easters. The capital city is Augusta and the largest city is Portland. Maine was separated from *Massachusetts in 1820 as a free state under the *Missouri Compromise. It is a popular area for outdoor holidays and sports, and the northern end of the Appalachian Trail begins there. Maine's products include paper, apples, lobsters and sardines (= small fish).

ˈ**main street** *n* (*esp AmE*) **1** [C] the most important street in a small town or city, especially in the business district. It is often called simply Main Street. Compare MAIN DRAG. **2 Main Street** [U] (*sometimes disapprov*) the attitudes and values thought to be typical of small US towns: *The government's new liberal policies will not go down well on Main Street.* See also LEWIS.

ˌJohn ˈ**Major** /ˈmeɪdʒə(r)/ (1943–) a British *Conservative politician. He became a *Member of Parliament in 1979 and was *Foreign Secretary and *Chancellor of the Exchequer before replacing Margaret *Thatcher as Prime Minister in 1990. Major was admired by some people for his *working-class background and for his aim to achieve a 'classless society', but others criticized him for being boring and 'grey' (= dull and ordinary). His period in power was marked by economic problems, and his party was divided over the issue of European union. In spite of this he won the general election of 1992, defeating the *Labour Party led by Neil *Kinnock. In 1995 he also won a leadership contest against John *Redwood, but the Conservatives were heavily defeated by the Labour Party in the 1997 general election, and Major was replaced as Conservative leader by William *Hague.

maˌjority ˈleader *n* the leader of the political party that has a majority in the US Senate or US House of Representatives. He or she organizes the party's members and their programme for new laws. In the House of Representatives, however, the majority leader is under the *Speaker of the House who is from the same party. Compare MINORITY LEADER, WHIP.

the ˈ**Majors** *n* [pl] the name given to the four most important tournaments (= sports competitions) in golf. They are the *British Open, the *US Open(1), the *US Masters Tournament and the US *PGA.

ˌBernard ˈ**Malamud** /ˈmæləmʊd/ (1914–86) a US writer whose novels and short stories were mostly about Jewish life in America. His novels include *The Natural* (1952), about a *baseball player. Malamud won a *National Book Award for *The Magic Barrel* (1958), a collection of short stories, and a *Pulitzer Prize for his novel *The Fixer* (1966).

ˌMrs ˈ**Malaprop** /ˈmæləprɒp; *AmE* ˈmæləprɑːp/ a character in *The *Rivals*, a comic play by Richard Brinsley *Sheridan. Mrs Malaprop is the aunt of Lydia Languish, and is noted for the way she confuses words that sound similar, e.g. saying 'the ineffectual (= useless) qualities of a woman' instead of 'the intellectual qualities of a woman'. Such a wrong use of words is called a **malapropism** after her.

Maˈlawi /məˈlɑːwi/ a country in southern central Africa, between Tanzania, Zambia and Mozambique. Its capital city is Lilongwe and its official languages are Chichewa and English. It was formerly a British colony called Nyasaland. It became independent in 1964 and is now a member of the *Commonwealth. Its main exports are tea and tobacco. ▶ **Malawian** *adj, n.*

Maˈlaysia /məˈleɪʒə, məˈleɪziə/ a country in south-east Asia. It consists of the area to the south of Thailand formerly known as Malaya, and the states of Sarawak and Sabah in the north-west of the island of Borneo. Its capital city is Kuala Lumpur and its official language is Malay. It was formed in 1963 from former British colonies in the area and is now a part of the *Commonwealth. Its main exports are rubber, tin, oil and electronic parts. *Singapore was a part of Malaysia until 1965. ▶ **Malaysian** *adj, n.*

ˌ**Malcolm ˈX** /ˈeks/ (1925–65) an *African-American leader, born Malcom Little. He joined the *Black Muslims in 1952, changed his 'slave name' to Malcolm X and became their leader in 1963. Their aim was to create a separate African-American nation, and he encouraged them to defend themselves in violent ways. In 1964, however, he left the Black Muslims to establish the Organization of Afro-American Unity, declaring that he was in favour of peace between the races. He was murdered, probably by Black Muslims, in *Harlem. He wrote *The Autobiography of Malxolm X* (1964), and 'Spike' *Lee directed a film, *Malcolm X* (1992), with Denzel Washington in the main role.

The ˈ**Maldives** /ˈmɔːldiːvz, ˈmɔːldaɪvz/ a country in the Indian Ocean, to the south-west of India, consisting of over 1 200 small islands. Its capital is Malé and its official language is Divehi. It was formerly a British colony, and became independent in 1965. It is now a member of the *Commonwealth. Its industries include fishing and tourism. ▶ **Malˈdivian** *adj, n.*

ˈ**Malibu** /ˈmælɪbuː/ a fashionable and expensive US town on the Pacific coast of *California, near *Los Angeles. It is known for its beaches, and is the home of several film stars.

The **Mall** /mæl/ **1** a straight road in central London, England, leading from *Buckingham Palace through *Admiralty Arch to *Trafalgar Square. It was first laid out in the 17th century and is used for royal processions. **2** a long park in *Washington, DC, covering about a mile (1.6 kilometres) between the *Capitol and the *Potomac River. The *White House(1) faces The Mall, which also includes the *Lincoln Memorial, the *Washington Monument and the *Vietnam Veterans Memorial.

mall /mɔːl, mæl/ ⇨ SHOPPING CENTRE.

ˈ***Mallard*** /ˈmælɑːd; *AmE* ˈmælɑːrd/ the name of a steam engine (= a type of early train) which set an unbeaten world record for a train of its type in 1938 by achieving a speed of 126 miles per hour (203 kilometres per hour). It is now kept at the *National Railway Museum in York.

ˌSeamus ˈ**Mallon** /ˌʃeɪməs ˈmælən/ (1936–) a British politician. He became Deputy Leader of the *Social Democratic and Labour Party in 1978 and a *Member of Parliament for the party in 1986. In 1998 he became Deputy First Minister of the *Northern Ireland Assembly.

ˌ**Mallory and ˈIrvine** /ˌmæləri, ˈɜːvɪn; *AmE* ˈɜːrvɪn/ two English climbers, **George Mallory** (1886–1924) and **Andrew Irvine** (1902–1924), who died while attempting to reach the top of Mount Everest. When Mallory was asked why he wanted to climb Everest, his famous reply was 'Because it is there'.

ˌThomas ˈ**Malory** /ˈmæləri/ an English author who wrote **Morte d'Arthur*, a collection of stories about King *Arthur and his *Knights of the Round Table. His identity is uncertain but he may have been Sir

Thomas Malory, a *Warwickshire *knight who died in prison in 1471.

ˈ**Malta** /ˈmɔːltə/ an island and country in the Mediterranean Sea, to the south of Sicily. Its capital is Valletta and its official languages are Maltese and English. From 1530 to 1798 it was ruled by the Knights of St John, a military and religious organization. In 1814 it was taken over by Britain and became an important navy base. In *World War II it was given the *George Cross for resisting heavy German air attacks. Together with the nearby islands of Gozo and Comino it became independent in 1964 and is now a member of the Commonwealth.Tourism is an important part of its economy, and many British people go there on holiday.

▶ ˌ**Malˈtese** /mɔːlˈtiːz/ *adj* of or from Malta.

ˌ**Malˈtese** *n* **1** [C] (*pl* **Maltese**) an inhabitant of Malta. **2** [U] the language of Malta.

The ˌ***Maltese*** ˈ***Falcon*** /ˌmɔːltiːz/ a novel (1930) by Dashiell *Hammett, in which he first used the character Sam *Spade, a private detective. The story is about people who commit murder to get a valuable statue called the Maltese Falcon. There have been two film versions, the first in 1931 with Ricardo Cortez as Sam Spade, the second (and more famous) in 1941 with Humphrey *Bogart.

Malˈtesers™ /mɔːlˈtiːzəz; *AmE* mɔːlˈtiːzərz/ *n* [pl] a British make of round chocolate sweets with light crisp centres.

ˌThomas ˈ**Malthus** /ˈmælθəs/ (1766–1834) an English economist and priest. In his *Essay on the Principle of Population* (1798) he suggested that human populations grow faster than the supply of food, and that unless population growth is artificially controlled, this leads to poverty and an increased death rate. His ideas were an important influence on Charles *Darwin.

▶ **Malthusian** /mælˈθuːziən/ *adj* of or similar to the ideas of Thomas Malthus.

the ˈ**Maltings** /ˈmɔːltɪŋz/ a concert hall in the village of Snape, near Aldeburgh, *Suffolk, England. The concerts that take place there are part of the international *Aldeburgh Festival. The building burnt down in 1969 but was quickly rebuilt.

the Malvern Hills

the ˈ**Malverns** /ˈmɔːlvənz; *AmE* ˈmɔːlvərnz/ the name of a group of five villages and a town (Great Malvern) in the **Malvern Hills**, *Hereford and Worcester, England. The hills are famous for their springs of pure water, sold under the name of **Malvern water**. Great Malvern is also famous for its festival of music and theatre, held every summer.

ˌDavid ˈ**Mamet** /ˈmæmɪt/ (1947–) a US writer of plays and films, which are often about human failure and disappointment. Many people have been offended by his use of language. His first successful play was *American Buffalo* (1977). He won the *Pulitzer Prize for *Glengarry Glen Ross* (1984). *Oleanna* (1992), a play about a woman who claims falsely that a man has sexually annoyed her, caused a lot of public discussion. Mamet's films include *The House of Games* (1987), which he also directed, *Hoffa* (1992) and *The Spanish Prisoner* (1998).

ˈ**Manchester** /ˈmæntʃəstə(r)/ a large city in north-west England, in the county of *Greater Manchester. It first became important as an industrial city during the 18th century, producing wool and cotton goods for sale in Britain and abroad. It was also a cultural and intellectual centre with a tradition of left-wing politics. In the 20th century it remains an important industrial city and has Britain's third largest airport. Its famous buildings include the Victorian Town Hall (1867–76), the G-Mex Centre for exhibitions and events, and the Bridgewater International Concert Hall (opened in 1996), where the *Hallé Orchestra is based. A new Millennium Stadium opens in 1999 and the *Commonwealth Games will be held there in 2002. Since the 1980s Manchester has also had a reputation for its pop groups, including *Oasis and The *Happy Mondays.

ˌ**Manchester** ˈ**City** /ˌmæntʃəstə; *AmE* ˌmæntʃəstər/ (*also infml* **Man City**) a football team from Manchester, England. It was formed in 1894 and has had several wins in the *FA Cup, as well as many other successes in Britain and Europe.

the ˌ**Manchester** ˈ**Ship Ca**ˌ**nal** /ˌmæntʃəstə; *AmE* ˌmæntʃəstər/ a canal completed in 1894 linking *Manchester with the River *Mersey and the sea. It can take very large ships and allowed Manchester to increase its level of exports in the late 19th and early 20th century.

ˌ**Manchester Uˈnited** /ˌmæntʃəstə; *AmE* ˌmæntʃəstər/ (*also infml* **Man United**) a football team from Manchester, England, with a ground at *Old Trafford(1). It was formed in 1902 and has won the *FA Cup more times than any other team, as well as having many other successes in Britain and Europe. In 1958 several of its players were killed in a plane crash in Munich. See also BUSBY.

ˌHenry **Manˈcini** /mænˈsiːni/ (1924–94) a US composer of music for films and writer of songs. After studying at the *Juilliard School of Music he won *Oscars for *Breakfast at Tiffany's* (1961), which included the song *Moon River*, and for *Victor/Victoria* (1982). His other films included the **Pink Panther* series, *Days of Wine and Roses* (1962), *Charade* (1963) and *10* (1979).

Manˈcunian /mænˈkjuːniən/ *n* a person who comes from *Manchester.

ˌPeter ˈ**Mandelson** /ˈmændlsn/ (1953–) a British *Labour politician. He became a *Member of Parliament in 1992, and was the Labour Party's Director of Campaigns and Communications from 1985 to 1990. He was later made Secretary of State for Trade and Industry, with responsibility for the *Millennium Dome project, but he resigned in 1998 after it became known that he had accepted a large personal loan from the *Paymaster General Geoffrey Robinson to buy a house. Mr Robinson also resigned.

M&M's™ /ˌem ənd ˈemz/ *n* [pl] small round chocolate sweets, brightly coloured and sometimes with peanuts inside, that are covered with hard sugar to stop them melting in a person's hand. They were first sold in 1941, and are named after the two Americans who originally made them, Forrest Mars and Bruce Murries.

M & S /ˌem ənd ˈes/ ⇨ MARKS & SPENCER.

ˌ**Man** ˈ**Friday** the name of the faithful servant and companion in Daniel *Defoe's novel **Robinson Crusoe*. Crusoe gives him this name after saving his life on a Friday. The phrase **man Friday** is now sometimes used to mean a trusted male assistant or servant. The female equivalent is a **girl Friday**.

Manˈ**hattan** /mænˈhætn/ **1** (*also* **Manhattan Island**) the island that forms the main *borough of New York City. It is 14 miles/23.5 kilometres long and 2.3 miles/3.7 kilometres wide, and is between the *Hudson River and the East River. It contains many of New York's most famous buildings, including the *Empire State Building and the *World Trade Center, and its streets include *Broadway and *Fifth Avenue. *Central Park and *Harlem are also in Manhattan. The island is named after a *Native-American people who once lived there. **2** *n* a US cocktail (= mixed alcoholic drink). It is made with *whisky, sweet vermouth (= a type of strong wine) and usually bitters, and is served with a maraschino cherry.

the **Man**ˈ**hattan** ˌ**Project** /mænˈhætən/ the secret US project to develop the atom bomb, begun in 1942. It involved a team of scientists led by J Robert Oppenheimer, first at Oak Ridge, *Tennessee, and later at *Los Alamos, *New Mexico, where the bomb was built. The first bomb was exploded as a test near Alamogordo, New Mexico, on 16 July 1945.

ˈ**Manic** ˈ**Street** ˈ**Preachers** a British pop group formed in 1988, whose best-known albums include *Generation Terrorists* (1992) and *This is My Truth, Tell Me Yours* (1998). Richey James, a guitar player in the group, disappeared in 1995, and it is believed that he may be dead.

ˌ**manifest** ˈ**destiny** *n* [U] a phrase much used in 19th-century America to mean the right of the US to own and occupy land across the continent to the Pacific Ocean. It was first used in 1845 by John L O'Sullivan, editor of the *United States Magazine and Democratic Review*. He wrote that the US should 'overspread the continent allotted by Providence for the free development of our yearly multiplying millions'. The idea of manifest destiny involved taking a lot of land belonging to *Native Americans, especially in *Oregon, and taking *California and *Texas from Mexico, which led to the *Mexican War.

ˌBarry ˈ**Manilow** /ˈmænələʊ; *AmE* ˈmænəloʊ/ (1946–) a US singer and writer of songs who plays the piano. His music is especially popular with older women. After studying at the New York College of Music and the *Juilliard School of Music Manilow received a *Grammy for his song *Copacabana* in 1978. His other hits have included *I Write the Songs* (1976) and *Looks Like We Made It* (1977), and his musical show *Harmony* opened in 1997.

Manners ⇨ article.

ˌ**Man of** ˈ**Kent** /ˈkent/ *n* (*pl* **Men of Kent**) a traditional name for an inhabitant of the eastern half of the English county of *Kent. Compare KENTISHMAN.

ˌ**man of the** ˈ**match** *n* [sing] a man who is chosen as having given the best performance in a game of football, cricket, etc. If officially chosen, he sometimes receives a prize: *They voted him man of the match.* ○ *My man of the match was definitely Giggs.*

ˌNigel ˈ**Mansell** /ˈmænsl/ (1954–) an English racing driver. After many Grand Prix successes in the 1980s and 1990s he became *Formula One world champion in 1992 in a *Williams car. He later had some success in *IndyCar racing.

ˌKatherine ˈ**Mansfield** /ˈmænsfiːld/ (1888–1923) a New Zealand writer who lived most of her life in England. Her collections of short stories, including *Bliss* (1920) and *The Garden Party* (1922), are full of intense feeling, often describing only a few hours in a person's life. Her poems and letters were published after her death.

ˌ***Mansfield*** ˈ***Park*** /ˌmænsfiːld/ a novel (1814) by Jane *Austen. It tells the story of Fanny Price, a young girl who goes to live with her rich uncle and his family at their country house, Mansfield Park. They treat her rather badly, but Edmund, the youngest son, recognizes her true worth and finally marries her.

ˈ**Mansion House** the official home of the *Lord Mayor of London, in the City of London. The building was completed in 1753 and contains the Egyptian Hall, where official dinners, etc. are held.

ˌCharles ˈ**Manson** /ˈmænsn/ (1934–) the leader of a group of *hippies, called his 'family', over whom he had a powerful influence, based on drugs and sex. In 1969 the group, acting on Manson's orders, murdered seven people near *Los Angeles, including the actor Sharon Tate with three of her friends. Manson and four of his followers were sent to prison for life. The murders shocked Americans and caused many to become hostile to hippies.

ˌMickey ˈ**Mantle** /ˈmæntl/ (1931–95) a US baseball player famous for his strong hitting. He played for the New York *Yankees (1951–68) and appeared with them in 12 *World Series. He was the *Most Valuable Player for the *American League three times (1956–7 and 1962). Mantle hit 536 home runs in his career, and was selected for the National Baseball *Hall of Fame in 1974.

Manx /mæŋks/ *n* [U] a *Gaelic language formerly spoken in the *Isle of Man, but now almost completely replaced by English.

▶ **Manx** *adj* of the *Isle of Man, its people or the language once spoken there.

the ˌ***Mappa*** ˈ***Mundi*** /ˌmæpə ˈmʊndiː/ a map of the world painted in the late 13th century and kept in Hereford Cathedral, England. It has a circular shape, with Jerusalem at the centre and the known continents of Europe, Africa and Asia placed around it. It is very valuable, and many British people were shocked when at one time the cathedral planned to raise money by selling it abroad. It later decided to keep it.

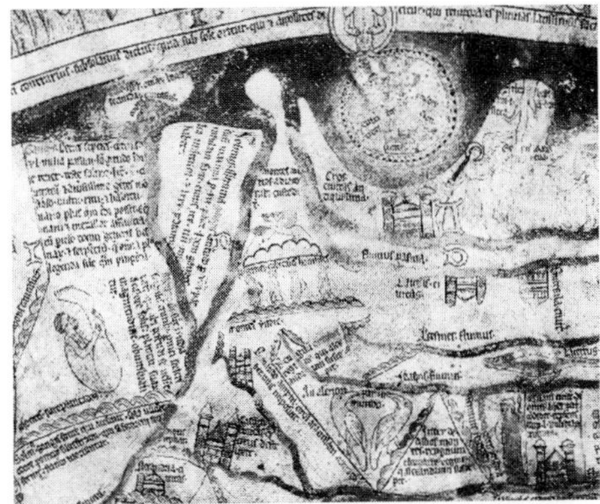

part of the Mappa Mundi

ˌRobert ˈ**Mapplethorpe** /ˈmeɪplθɔːp; *AmE* ˈmeɪplθɔːrp/ (1946–89) a US photographer of artistic pictures. Many people are offended by the sexual nature of his images, which often show the naked male body.

M

Manners

Children are taught **good manners**, or simply **manners** (= polite ways of behaving), so that when they are older they will automatically show respect and consideration for other people.

In Britain good manners were once seen as proof of a person's worth, as in the old saying 'manners maketh man'. Though attitudes have become more tolerant over the years, people still tend to judge others according to how they behave. People may be said to **have no manners** if they are rude or behave without thought for others. For instance, somebody who picks their nose in front of others, or belches (= lets out gas from the stomach through their mouth), or yawns without putting their hand in front of their mouth, or who speaks rudely to somebody, will attract criticism. On the other hand, a person who is **polite** and **courteous**, who is considerate towards other people, who says little about their own achievements and who respects the privacy of others, is much more likely to win approval and respect.

Ideas about appropriate personal behaviour vary from country to country, and it can be difficult in a foreign country to know what its people consider to be good manners.

Please and thank you

British and American parents often tell their children that 'please' is **the magic word**: if the children remember to say 'please', their parents are more likely to give them the things they ask for. 'Please' is used in many situations. People generally say 'please' whenever they ask for something, whether it is for goods in a shop, for help, for a favour or for information.

People are also taught to say 'thank you' or 'thanks' when somebody has given them something or done something for them. In a shop many British people say 'thank you' several times at the check-out, e.g. when the operator tells them the total cost of their goods, when he or she gives them their change or gives back their credit card, and sometimes again before they leave.

After receiving a present it is good manners to say 'thank you' and sound pleased. Some people add a specific comment, e.g. 'That's great – red's my favourite colour!' When a present is sent by mail it is polite to send a **thank-you note**, a short letter or card to thank the person who sent it and tell them how much you like it. It is also polite to write and say 'thank you' after you have been invited out for a meal or been to stay with somebody.

Table manners

Good manners are important at meal times, though people worry less about table manners than they once did now that many meals are less formal. When eating at a table with other people, it is considered polite to keep your napkin (= a piece of material or paper used to wipe your mouth) below the table on your lap, to chew with your mouth closed and not talk with food in your mouth, to keep your elbows off the table, and to eat fairly slowly. It is **bad manners** to take a lot of food all at once, or to take more until it is offered. It is also better to ask somebody to pass the salt, etc. rather than to reach across the table for it.

When invited to a meal at somebody else's house people often take a bottle of wine or chocolates or flowers, as a gift. Apart from this, it is not usual to give presents to people you do not know well. It is not considered polite to look round other people's houses without being invited to do so, and people usually ask where the toilet is rather than going to look for it. Many people do not smoke and visitors should ask permission before they smoke in somebody's house. Close friends are much less formal in each other's houses and may get their own drinks and help to clear away the meal.

Formal and informal manners

Good manners do not have to be formal. It is friendly as well as polite to say 'hello' or 'good morning' to somebody you meet, to say 'please' and 'thank you' to family and friends as well as to strangers, and to apologize if you hurt or upset somebody. A warm tone of voice and a smile are also important.

People shake hands when they are introduced to somebody for the first time but, except in business, rarely do so when they meet again. Nowadays, unless there is a great age difference, most adults use each other's first names straightaway. In shops and banks, on aircraft, etc. customers are often addressed respectfully as 'Sir' or 'Madam' to show that they are important to the company. People are expected to arrive on time for both business and social events and it is considered bad mannners to be late or not to telephone to let people know if you are delayed.

Manners are expected even in situations when it is impossible to talk. A well-mannered driver may, for instance, slow down to allow somebody to cross the road or make a gesture of thanks when another driver lets him or her pass. Airlines encourage passengers to consider others and to leave the washroom clean after use.

In the past but less commonly today, people often bought books on **etiquette** (= polite behaviour) to learn how to behave in **polite society**. Such books give suggestions for behaviour in very formal situations and do not help much with normal life. In Britain there are books on how to address members of the *royal family and the *aristocracy.

Formal manners are part of the British stereotype (= the typical characteristics of a person from a particular country). British people used to shake hands when meeting somebody, make polite conversation on general topics, but otherwise remain distant. Men used to take off their hat when a woman passed, walk on the outside of the pavement/sidewalk when with a woman so that she did not get splashed by traffic, and hold doors open for her. Keeping *feelings under control was also part of good manners, and it was not thought appropriate to show anger, affection, etc. in public. Now, fewer people **stand on ceremony** (= behave formally) and even in formal situations most people are friendly and relaxed and concerned to put others at their ease.

Marble Arch

ˌ**Marble ˈArch** a large stone arch with three gates, at the north-east corner of *Hyde Park(1) in central London. It was built in 1828 to a design by John *Nash as an entrance to *Buckingham Palace, but was later moved to its present position. At one time traffic drove through the central gate. Marble Arch is also the name of a nearby *London Underground station.

ˌ***Marbury v ˈMadison*** /ˌmɑːbri vɜːsəs ˈmædɪsn; *AmE* ˌmɑːrbri vɜːrsəs/ an important US Supreme Court case in 1803 which established its right to decide if a new law is illegal under the *American Constitution. William Marbury had taken Secretary of State James *Madison to court because he refused to keep an agreement that Marbury would become a judge. The court decided that Marbury was right, and established the principal of *judicial review.

ˈ**marching ˌseason** *n* the period in July and August every year when Protestant groups in Northern Ireland, especially the Order of *Orangemen, hold marches through the streets. These celebrate Protestant victories over Catholics in the 17th century, especially the *Battle of the Boyne. The marches are often the cause of conflict with Northern Ireland's Catholic population. In 1998 the Parades Commission was set up to decide where marches should be allowed to go and to make sure they caused no trouble. See also APPRENTICE BOYS' PARADE. ⇨ article at NORTHERN IRELAND.

ˌ***Marching Through ˈGeorgia*** /ˈdʒɔːdʒə; *AmE* ˈdʒɔːrdʒə/ a lively US song about the violent progress of General William Tecumseh *Sherman and his army through *Georgia during the *Civil War in November 1864. The words after each verse are:

'Hurrah! hurrah! we bring the Jubilee!
Hurrah! hurrah! the flag that makes you free!'
So we sang the chorus from Atlanta to the sea,
While we were marching through Georgia.

the ˌ**March of ˈDimes** a US charity that works to prevent the deaths of babies and to help young children born with physical problems. Its full name is the March of Dimes Birth Defects Foundation. President Franklin D *Roosevelt, who had polio (= a serious disease of the nervous system), started the charity in 1938 as the National Foundation for Infantile Paralysis. Among other activities it supported the research work which developed the *Salk vaccine. It has had its present name since 1979.

The ˌ***March of ˈTime*** a series of US news films shown in cinemas from 1935 to 1951. They were produced by the company that owned **Time* magazine and were one of the main sources of news on film before the days of television. There was a similar series with the same name on US radio.

ˈˌRocky' **Marciˈano** /ˌrɒki mɑːsiˈɑːnəʊ; *AmE* ˌrɑːki mɑːrsiˈænoʊ/ (1923–69) a US professional boxer. He won 49 fights and was the only World Heavyweight Champion (1952–6) never to be beaten. He died in a plane crash.

Guˌglielmo **Marˈconi** /guˌljelməʊ mɑːˈkəʊni; *AmE* guˌljelmoʊ mɑːrˈkoʊni/ (1874–1937) an Italian scientist and electrical engineer who lived for most of his life in Britain. Using the work of previous scientists he developed the practical use of radio, sending the first radio signals from England to France in 1898 and from England to America in 1901. He shared the *Nobel Prize for physics in 1909. He was also a successful businessman, establishing the Marconi Wireless Telegraph Company in London in 1899. In 1922 the company was in charge of the first broadcasts of the *BBC.

Marconi with some of his earliest apparatus, 1898

ˌHerbert **Marˈcuse** /mɑːˈkuːzə; *AmE* mɑːrˈkuːzə/ (1898–1979) a US political philosopher, born in Germany. He moved to America in 1934 and after working for the US government as an expert on Russian affairs, he taught at several universities, including *Harvard University from 1952 and the University of California at San Diego from 1965. Marcuse's ideas were strongly influenced by those of Marx and Freud. He was especially popular during the 1960s and supported the efforts of young people to change society. His books included *Eros and Civilization* (1955), *Soviet Marxism* (1958) and *One-Dimensional Man* (1964).

ˌ**Mardi ˈGras** /ˌmɑːdi ˈgrɑː; *AmE* ˌmɑːrdi/ a popular US carnival (= public festival) held in *New Orleans during the week before the first day of *Lent. Mardi Gras is French for 'Fat Tuesday', because it ends on Shrove Tuesday, a day when people traditionally eat a lot before the start of Lent. People come from around the world to see the parades, costumes, parties and decorations. Mardi Gras 'Kings' and 'Queens' are chosen by both the white and *African-American communities. A few other US cities celebrate Mardi Gras, and it is also celebrated in other Catholic countries.

Mardi Gras in New Orleans

M

ˌPrincess ˈ**Margaret** (1930–) the sister of Queen *Elizabeth II and the younger daughter of King *George VI. In 1960 she married the photographer Tony Armstrong-Jones, who was later given the title of Lord Snowdon, but they were divorced in 1978. Their two children are David, Viscount Linley (1961–) and Lady Sarah Armstrong-Jones (1964–).

ˈ**Margate** /ˈmɑːgeɪt; *AmE* ˈmɑːrgeɪt/ a town on the northern coast of *Kent, England. It is popular for its beaches, and is known especially as a place where people from London go for *bank holidays or family holidays.

the ˌ**Mariˈanas** /ˌmæriˈɑːnəz/ (*also* the ˌ**Mariˈana ˌIslands** /ˌmæriˈɑːnə/) a group of islands in the north-west Pacific Ocean. The US got them from Spain in 1898 after the *Spanish-American War. The most southern island is *Guam, where most of the inhabitants live.

ˌ***Marie ˈClaire*** a British magazine for women. It is published every month and contains articles on fashion, beauty, travel, the arts and other subjects.

the **Maˈrine Corps** ⇨ United States Marine Corps.

ˈ**Mariner** /ˈmærɪnə(r)/ the name of a series of flights of *NASA spacecraft that went past or around other planets. *Mariner 1* failed and was destroyed in flight in 1962, but in the same year *Mariner 2* flew past Venus. *Mariner 9* went into orbit around the planet Mars in 1971 and took more than 7 000 photographs. *Mariner 10* flew past Venus and Mercury in 1974 and again in 1975.

markets

Markets are very popular in Britain and sell a wide range of goods. Most are held in the open air, in town squares or **market places**. Goods for sale are piled up on **market stalls**, tables that are sheltered from bad weather by **awnings** (= sheets of cloth or plastic laid across poles to form a roof). Most markets are held only on **market day**, the same day each week, and sometimes on Saturdays, and the stalls are put up for each occasion. In small towns market day is often the busiest day of the week.

Permission to hold street markets in many **market towns** was given hundreds of years ago. Many towns still have a **market cross**, indicating where the market was originally held, or an old **market hall**, a covered area open at the sides. Today, street markets sell flowers, fruit and vegetables, fish and meat, clothes and household goods. Local *charities and branches of the *Women's Institute may have stalls selling cakes, jam and other goods. Prices are fixed by the **stallholders** and most accept only cash.

Some towns have a covered or indoor market. These markets are usually open every day except Sunday. **Sunday markets**, often at sites out of town, sell a wider range of goods and attract many people. Markets that sell cheap second-hand goods, including clothes, jewellery, books, pots and pans, are called **flea markets**.

The US used to have outdoor and covered markets like those in Britain. Today, however, shopping involves buying large quantities of things in tins and packets from a supermarket. There are a few markets, some in old market buildings, and other, newly created ones, e.g. *Philadelphia's Reading Terminal Market in a former rail station. But while many people like these markets, they are different from the traditional ones. Market **vendors** (= people who sell things) sell smaller quantities and so have to charge higher prices than large shops. As a result, only richer people shop in markets. Many markets sell more expensive things such as clothes, instead of food. The US also has flea markets but these are usually in buildings and open during normal shopping hours, so are more like shops than markets.

The word *market* is sometimes used in American English to refer to any food shop. Larger food shops in both America and Britain are called *supermarkets*. A hypermarket is a very large store or supermarket. In Britain small food shops are sometimes called *mini-markets*.

Aˌlicia **Marˈkova** /əˌlɪsiə mɑːˈkəʊvə; *AmE* mɑːrˈkoʊvə/ (1910–) an English ballet dancer. She was trained by Anna Pavlova, danced with Sergei Diaghilev's company (1925–9) and took leading parts in the first British productions of many classical ballets. After 1935 she worked mainly with Anton *Dolin, and was famous for her performance of *Giselle*. She retired from dancing in 1962 and became a ballet director for the *Royal Ballet and other companies. She was made a *dame(2) in 1963.

ˌ**Marks & ˈSpencer** /ˌmɑːks ənd ˈspensə(r); *AmE* ˌmɑːrks/ (*abbr* **M & S**) a well-known British department store, selling clothes, food and other products. The first shops were started by Michael Marks and Thomas Spencer in the late 19th century, and there are now about 700 shops in Britain and abroad. Marks and Spencer's is famous for its well made clothes at fairly low prices, and is where many people go to buy items such as underwear and socks rather than the latest fashions. The company is also known as **St Michael**, or informally as **Marks and Sparks** or simply **Marks**: *I buy my clothes at Marks.*

ˈ**Marlboro**™ /ˈmɔːlbərə; *AmE* ˈmɑːrlbəroʊ/ one of the most popular US cigarettes. It was first sold by the *Philip Morris company in the 1920s as a woman's cigarette, and advertised as being as 'Mild as May'. It was not available during *World War II, but returned in the early 1950s with 'filter, flavor, flip-top box'. Advertisements showing the **Marlboro Man** as a *cowboy began in 1957 with the words 'Come to Marlboro Country'.

the ˌDuke of ˈ**Marlborough** /ˈmɔːlbrə; *AmE* ˈmɑːrlbəroʊ/ (*born* John Churchill 1650–1722) one of Britain's greatest soldiers, who won important battles in the War of *Spanish Succession. These included *Blenheim (1704) and Malplaquet (1709). After his success at Blenheim, Queen *Anne gave him money to build *Blenheim Palace in *Oxfordshire, where his descendant Winston *Churchill was born in 1874. See also Marlborough House.

ˌ**Marlborough ˈHouse** /ˌmɔːlbrə; *AmE* ˈmɑːrlbəroʊ/ a large, grand house in *Pall Mall, London, England. It was designed by Christopher *Wren for the wife of the Duke of *Marlborough and built in 1709–11. After her death it was the home of various members of the royal family until 1962, when it became a centre for meetings of Commonwealth leaders.

ˌBob ˈ**Marley** /ˈmɑːli; *AmE* ˈmɑːrli/ (1945–81) a Jamaican singer and writer of reggae music who also played the guitar. He formed the Wailers group in 1965 and made reggae widely known around the world. His songs were influenced by his religious beliefs as a *Rastafarian and his support of *Black Power. His albums included *Burnin'* (1973), *Rastaman Vibration* (1976), *Exodus* (1977) and *Uprising* (1980). His early death was caused by cancer.

ˌChristopher ˈ**Marlowe**[1] /ˈmɑːləʊ; *AmE* ˈmɑːrloʊ/ (1564–93) an English writer of plays and poetry. He is considered the greatest English playwright of the period before William *Shakespeare, and was an important influence on Shakespeare's style. His best-known works are *Tamburlaine* (*c.* 1587), **Doctor Faustus*, *The Jew of Malta* (*c.* 1590) and *Edward II* (*c.* 1592). He may also have written parts of the Shakespeare plays **Titus Andronicus* and **Henry VI*. Marlowe led a wild and violent life, was put in prison briefly in 1589 on suspicion of murder, and was himself murdered in a fight at the age of 29.

ˌPhilip **ˈMarlowe²** /ˈmɑːləʊ; *AmE* ˈmɑːrloʊ/ a character created by the writer Raymond *Chandler. He is a tough but honest private detective and appears in seven Chandler novels, including *The Big Sleep* (1939).

ˈMarmite™ /ˈmɑːmaɪt; *AmE* ˈmɑːrmaɪt/ *n* [U] a soft black substance usually eaten on bread or toast. Marmite was first produced in 1902 and is made from yeast (= a natural substance used in making beer, wine and most types of bread). Marmite is thought of as a traditional British food, especially as a cheap and healthy filling for sandwiches or as a food for young children.

the ˌBattles of the **ˈMarne** /mɑːn; *AmE* mɑːrn/ two battles of *World War I around the River Marne in north-east France. In the first battle (1914) a German advance was stopped by British and French forces. In the second (1918) a similar advance was stopped by British, French and US forces, and was the beginning of a series of victories for the *Allies that led to the end of the war.

ˈMarplan /ˈmɑːplæn; *AmE* ˈmɑːrplæn/ a British organization established in 1959 that carries out opinion polls (= asks specially chosen groups of people certain questions, e.g. about political issues). The results are then published and appear in newspapers, on television, etc.

ˌMiss **ˈMarple** /ˈmɑːpl; *AmE* ˈmɑːrpl/ a character in several novels by Agatha *Christie. Miss Marple is a gentle, respectable old woman who has a remarkable ability to solve mysteries and crimes. She first appeared in the novel *The Murder in the Vicarage* (1930). There have been many film and television versions of the stories.

ˈmarquess (*also* **ˈmarquis**) /ˈmɑːkwɪs; *AmE* ˈmɑːrkwɪs/ *n* a British peer who is next in rank above an *earl(1) and next below a *duke. The wife of a marquess, or a woman with a similar title, is called a **marchioness**. ⇨ note at ARISTOCRACY.

ˌNeville **ˈMarriner** /ˌnevl ˈmærɪnə(r)/ (1924–) an English conductor, who established the *Academy of St Martin-in-the-Fields in 1959. He has also directed orchestras in the US. He was made a *knight in 1985.

ˌWynton **Marˈsalis** /ˌwɪntən mɑːˈseɪlɪs; *AmE* mɑːrˈseɪlɪs/ (1961–) an *African-American *jazz musician who plays the trumpet. He won a *Pulitzer Prize for Music in 1997 for *Blood on the Fields*. Earlier, he had become the first musician to receive Grammys for both jazz and classical works. He played with the New Orleans Philharmonic Orchestra at the age of 14, before forming his own jazz group in 1981.

Wynton Marsalis

ˈMars Bar™ /ˈmɑːz; *AmE* ˈmɑːrz/ (*also* **Mars**) *n* a popular British chocolate bar with a soft sweet filling, first sold in the 1930s and named after the American who originally made it, Forrest Mars. The advertisements for Mars Bars claim that 'A Mars a day helps you work, rest and play.'

the **ˈMarsden** /ˈmɑːzdən; *AmE* ˈmɑːrzdən/ (*in full* the **Royal Marsden Hospital**) a hospital in London, England, established in 1851 by William Marsden (1796–1867). It is a leading hospital for cancer treatment and research.

ˌNgaio **ˈMarsh¹** /ˌnaɪəʊ ˈmɑːʃ; *AmE* ˌnaɪoʊ ˈmɑːrʃ/ (1899–1982) a New Zealand writer of detective stories who lived in Britain from 1928. Her books include *A Man Lay Dead* (1934) and *Hand in Glove* (1962), and her most famous character is Chief Detective Inspector Roderick Alleyn. She was made a *dame(2) in 1948.

ˌPete **ˈMarsh²** /ˈmɑːʃ; *AmE* ˈmɑːrʃ/ a humorous name for *Lindow Man, the very old body of a man found in soft wet ground in *Cheshire, England in 1984. 'Pete Marsh' is an ordinary English name which also sounds like 'peat marsh' (= an area of soft wet earth formed from decayed plants).

ˌThurgood **ˈMarshall** /ˌθɜːɡʊd ˈmɑːʃl; *AmE* ˌθɜːrɡʊd ˈmɑːrʃl/ (1908–93) the first *African-American judge of the US Supreme Court (1967–91). He is remembered especially for winning the 1954 case before the Supreme Court which ended *segregation in public schools. He was later US Solicitor General (1965–7).

ˌMarshall ˈField's /ˌmɑːʃl; *AmE* ˌmɑːrʃl/ a well-known US department store in *Chicago. It was established on State Street in 1868 when Marshall Field moved his small shop there. He increased its size in 1907, and Marshall Field's became a place for social meetings, with a Ladies' Parlour and a Men's Reading and Writing Room. It has seven floors around a large central area which is open to the top of the building. There are now Marshall Field's stores in other US cities.

the **ˈMarshall Plan** /ˈmɑːʃl; *AmE* ˈmɑːrʃl/ a very large programme of US economic aid to 17 European countries after *World War II (1948–52). Its official title was the European Recovery Program. The plan was named after the person who set it up, US Secretary of State George C Marshall (1880–1959), and it was operated by the Organization for European Economic Cooperation. Marshall received the *Nobel Prize for peace in 1953.

ˈMarshalsea /ˈmɑːʃlsi; *AmE* ˈmɑːrʃlsi/ a prison in *Southwark, London, England, built around the 14th century and closed in 1842. It was used as a debtors' prison (= one for people who owed money) and is an important part of the story of **Little Dorrit* by Charles *Dickens. Dickens's own father was put in prison there in 1824.

ˌMarston ˈMoor /ˌmɑːstən; *AmE* ˌmɑːrstən/ a place near *York, northern England, where the largest battle of the *English Civil War took place in 1644. The Parliamentarians under Oliver *Cromwell defeated the Royalists under Prince *Rupert and gained control over the north of the country.

Marˌtello ˈtower /mɑːˌteləʊ; *AmE* mɑːrˌteloʊ/ *n* a type of circular stone tower, about 40 feet (12 metres) high, built in Britain in the early 19th century. The purpose of the towers was to defend the south coast of England against possible attack by the French during the *Napoleonic Wars, and each could contain a group of soldiers. About 25 of the towers still exist.

ˌMartha's ˈVineyard an island off the south-east coast of *Massachusetts, just south of *Cape Cod. Many writers and artists live there, and it is popular with tourists in summer. In the 18th and 19th centuries, the island was a centre for people who hunted whales.

ˌDean **ˈMartin¹** /ˈmɑːtɪn; *AmE* ˈmɑːrtn/ (1917–95) a US singer and actor, well known for his relaxed

M

charm. He and Jerry *Lewis made 16 comedy films together (1949–56). Martin's later films included *Rio Bravo* (1959) and *The Silencers* (1966). He had a popular music and comedy television series, *The Dean Martin Show*, on *NBC from 1965 into the 1970s. His song hits included *That's Amore* (1953) and his theme song *Everybody Loves Somebody* (1964).

ˌSteve ˈ**Martin²** /ˈmɑːtɪn; *AmE* ˈmɑːrtn/ (1945–) a US comic actor and writer who also produces films. He began his career in 1967 as a writer for *The Smothers Brothers Comedy Hour* and later performed in it. His films include *The Jerk* (1979), which he also wrote, *All of Me* (1985), *L A Story* (1991), which he also wrote, and *Sergeant Bilko* (1996).

ˌAndrew ˈ**Marvell** /ˈmɑːvl; *AmE* ˈmɑːrvl/ (1621–78) one of the English *metaphysical poets. Among his best-known poems is *To his Coy Mistress*, a clever and entertaining attempt to persuade a young woman to go to bed with him. It contains the famous lines:

But at my back I always hear
Time's wingèd chariot hurrying near.

During his life Marvell was better known as a *Member of Parliament (1659–78) and a supporter of Oliver *Cromwell.

ˌLee ˈ**Marvin** /ˌliː ˈmɑːvɪn; *AmE* ˈmɑːrvɪn/ (1924–87) a US actor who played mainly tough characters but won an *Oscar for a comic role in the *western *Cat Ballou* (1965). His other films included *The Killers* (1964), *The Dirty Dozen* (1967) and *Paint Your Wagon* (1969), in which he sang *I Was Born Under A Wandering Star* in a deep and not very musical voice.

ˌKarl ˈ**Marx** /ˌkɑːl ˈmɑːks; *AmE* ˌkɑːrl ˈmɑːrks/ (1818–83) a German writer on politics and economics. In 1848 he wrote the *Communist Manifesto* with Friedrich Engels (1820–95), and in the following year he came to live in London, England. He spent much of the rest of his life developing his theories, and published the results in *Das Kapital* (1867–95), the major work of Marxist economics. His theories about the need for a workers' socialist revolution had a very great influence on 20th-century history, especially in Russia, China and eastern Europe. Marx died in London and was buried in *Highgate Cemetery.

M

the ˈ**Marx ˌBrothers** /ˈmɑːks; *AmE* ˈmɑːrks/ a US comedy team of three brothers who made films full of crazy visual humour and quick, clever jokes. They were 'Groucho' (Julius) Marx (1890–1977), 'Chico' (Leonard) Marx (1886–1961) and 'Harpo' (Adolph) Marx (1888–1964). Their films included *Duck Soup* (1933) and *A Day at the Races* (1937). Groucho wore glasses and a large false moustache, walked in a funny way and smoked cigars. Chico played the piano, wore a pointed hat and spoke like an Italian-American. Harpo never spoke, played the harp and chased girls. Groucho later had his own comedy television quiz show, *You Bet Your Life* (1950–61).

the Marx Brothers

ˌQueen ˈ**Mary** (Mary of Teck 1867–1953) a British queen. In 1893 she married George, Duke of York, who in 1910 became King *George V. She was the mother of two kings, *Edward VIII and *George VI, and the grandmother of Queen *Elizabeth II.

Mary I /ˌmeəri ðə ˈfɜːst; *AmE* ˌmeri ðə ˈfɜːrst/ (Mary Tudor 1516–58) the queen of England and Ireland from 1553 to 1558. She was the daughter of King *Henry VIII and *Catherine of Aragon, and became queen after the death of King *Edward VI. Among her first acts as queen was the execution of Lady Jane *Grey, who also had a claim to be queen. Mary was determined to bring back *Roman Catholicism to England, and married the Catholic Philip II of Spain in 1554. Many Protestants opposed this, and she ordered hundreds of them to be burned to death, for which she became known as 'Bloody Mary'. Among those who died in this way were Thomas *Cranmer and Hugh *Latimer. Mary had no children, and after her death she was replaced by her half-sister (= sister by a different mother) *Elizabeth I.

Mary II /ˌmeəri ðə ˈsekənd; *AmE* ˌmeri/ (1662–94) the queen of England, Scotland and Ireland from 1688 to 1694. She was the elder daughter of King *James II, and married William of Orange (later King *William III), her Dutch cousin, in 1677. After James II was removed from power in the *Glorious Revolution of 1688 she and William ruled together until her early death at the age of 32.

the ˌ***Mary Ceˈleste*** /səˈlest/ a ship that was discovered empty in the North Atlantic Ocean in 1872, in perfect condition but with its crew all gone. What happened to them has never been explained.

ˈ***Mary ˈHad a ˈLittle ˈLamb*** the title and first line of a traditional *nursery rhyme. The first verse is:

Mary had a little lamb,
Its fleece was white as snow;
And everywhere that Mary went
The lamb was sure to go.

ˈ**Maryland** /ˈmeərilənd; *AmE* ˈmerilənd/ an eastern state of the US on the Atlantic Ocean. It is also known as the Old Lime State and the Free State. The largest city is *Baltimore, and the capital city is *Annapolis. Maryland was one of the original 13 states and gave some of its land to create Washington, DC. Tourists visit the Harpers Ferry National Historical Park and the Goddard Space Flight Center. Among the state's products are electrical equipment, wood and fish.

ˈ**Marylebone** /ˈmærələbən/ a district of central London in the *borough of *Westminster(1). It lies south of *Regent's Park and contains famous buildings such as the *Royal Academy of Music, *Madame Tussaud's and the *Wigmore Hall. Marylebone train station has train services to and from the west of England, and also has a station on the *London Underground.

ˌ**Marylebone ˈCricket Club** /ˌmærələbən/ (*abbr* the **MCC**) a cricket club, established in 1787, which used to be the main administrative organization for all cricket in England and Wales. It owns and has its headquarters at *Lord's in north London. The MCC is still responsible for the rules of cricket, wherever it is played. Many people consider the club and its members to be rather old-fashioned. Membership is limited and there is a long list of people waiting to join. Women members have only been allowed since 1998.

ˈ***Mary,*** ˈ***Mary,*** ˈ***Quite Con*ˈ*trary*** the title and first line of a traditional *nursery rhyme, sometimes set to music. The full poem is:

Mary, Mary, quite contrary,
How does your garden grow?
With silver bells and cockle-shells,
And pretty maids all in a row.

ˌ***Mary*** ˈ***Poppins*** /ˈpɒpɪnz; *AmE* ˈpɑːpɪnz/ a popular Walt *Disney film (1964), based on the character created by the Australian writer P L Travers. Mary is a nanny (= a woman who looks after young children) who can fly with an umbrella and do other magic things. Julie *Andrews played the part and won an *Oscar for it. The film's songs include *Chim-Chim-Cheree*, which won an Oscar, and *Supercalifragilistic-expialidocious*.

a scene from Mary Poppins

ˌ**Mary, Queen of** ˈ**Scots** (Mary Stuart 1542–87) the queen of Scotland from 1542 to 1567. She was the daughter of King James V of Scotland and the cousin of Queen *Elizabeth I, and became queen of Scotland shortly after her birth. She did not rule Scotland until 1561 and was instead brought up in France, where she was queen briefly in 1559. She was a Roman Catholic, and after her return to Scotland became involved in religious disputes with Scottish Protestants. In 1567 she was forced to give up power in favour of her son James VI (later King *James I of England), and moved to England where she was held as a prisoner. In the years that followed there were several attempts by Catholic groups to make her queen of England in place of Elizabeth I, and Elizabeth finally ordered Mary's head to be cut off. Her adventures, love affairs and three marriages have been the subject of many books, plays and films. See also Bothwell, Darnley.

the ˌ***Mary*** ˈ***Rose*** a ship built for King *Henry VIII in 1509–10 which sank off the south coast of England in 1545 and was brought up from the bottom of the sea in 1982. It can now be seen at the Royal Dockyards, *Portsmouth.

ˌJohn ˈ**Masefield** /ˈmeɪsfiːld/ (1878–1967) an English poet who often wrote about the sea. His best-known collections of poetry include *Sea Fever* (1902) and *The Everlasting Memory* (1911). He was *Poet Laureate from 1930 until his death. He also wrote children's books, novels and critical works.

M*A*S*H /mæʃ/ a US comic novel, film and television series about military doctors during the *Korean War. M*A*S*H is short for Mobile Army Surgical Hospital. Richard Hooker wrote the novel (1968) as a way of bringing the horrors of the *Vietnam War to people's attention. The film version (1970) was directed by Robert *Altman and won the prize for best film at the Cannes Film Festival. The television series on *CBS (1974–83) won several *Emmy awards, and the final programme was watched by more than 50 million people.

ˌPerry ˈ**Mason** /ˌperi ˈmeɪsn/ a character created by the US writer Erle Stanley *Gardner. He is a lawyer who appeared in 82 novels about court cases, none of which he ever lost. The first was *The Case of the Velvet Claws* (1933). Raymond Burr played the character in the popular television series *Perry Mason* (1957–66) on *NBC, with Barbara Hale as his secretary Della Street.

the ˌ**Mason-**ˈ**Dixon line** /ˌmeɪsn ˈdɪksn/ a boundary line between the US states of *Pennsylvania and *Maryland. It came to be seen as a symbol of the division between the free states of the North and those of the South which had slaves. The line was measured and drawn in 1763–7 by Charles Mason and Jeremiah Dixon, two British surveyors, in order to settle a dispute between the two states. Their story was used for the novel *Mason and Dixon* (1997) by Thomas *Pynchon. See also Dixie.

ˈ**Masonite**™ /ˈmeɪsənaɪt/ *n* [U] a US make of board or sheet consisting of small pieces of wood that have been pressed and stuck together. It is made to look like smooth sections of wood and is used to build doors, walls, roofs, etc.

ˈ**Mason jar** /ˈmeɪsn/ *n* (*AmE*) a glass container used for preserving food such as fruit, especially in the home. It has a wide opening and a metal lid that screws on tightly. It is named after John L Mason, who invented it in 1858. Compare Kilner jar.

masque *n* [C, U] a type of theatre which was especially popular with kings, queens and the *aristocracy in Britain in the 17th century. It involved actors in elaborate costumes, music and dancing. Many of the most popular masques were written by Ben *Jonson, with costumes and scenery designed by Inigo *Jones. Although masque died out after the *English Civil War, many of its features were used in later forms of theatre, opera and ballet.

ˌ**Massa**ˈ**chusetts** /ˌmæsəˈtʃuːsɪts/ a north-eastern US state in *New England, also known informally as the Bay State or the Old Colony. The capital and largest city is *Boston. The state was settled in 1620 by the *Pilgrim Fathers. It played an important part in the *American Revolution and was one of the original 13 states. It is largely industrial, but also produces a lot of vegetables and fruit, especially cranberries. Among its historical places visited by tourists are *Independence Hall, *Cape Cod and *Plymouth Rock.

ˌ**Massa**ˈ**chusetts** ˈ**Institute of** ˈ**Technology** /ˌmæsəˈtʃuːsɪts/ ⇨ MIT.

ˌ**Massive At**ˈ**tack** a British pop group, formed in 1988, whose music combines *dub, *rap and other styles. The group's most successful albums include *Blue Lines* (1991) and *Mezzanine* (1998).

ˈ***Mastermind*** a popular British television quiz programme from 1972 to 1997. The four people competing each week took turns to sit in a black chair and answer questions on a subject of their own choice and then general knowledge questions. The person with the most correct answers went on to the next round until the final winner became 'Mastermind' for the series. The questions were always asked by Magnus *Magnusson. Two phrases often used on the programme became widely used by British people in general. They were 'Pass', said when a person was unable to answer a question and wanted to move on to the next one, and 'I've started, so I'll finish', said by Magnus Magnusson if the time for questions ended while he was asking the last one.

M

ˈ**Master of the ˈQueen's ˈMusic** the title of the musician appointed to write and arrange music for certain British royal occasions, such as weddings. The post first came into existence in the 17th century. When a king is ruling the title is **Master of the King's Music**.

ˌ**Master of the ˈRolls** the most senior civil judge in the legal system in England and Wales. The Master of the Rolls is in charge of the *Court of Appeal and of keeping records at the *Public Record Office. He is also a member of the *Privy Council. His position is the third most important in the legal system in England and Wales, after the *Lord Chancellor and the *Lord Chief Justice.

ˌ***Masterpiece ˈTheater*** a US television series on *PBS which shows many of the best British programmes. It began in 1971 and was presented by Alistair *Cooke until 1994. The programmes have included **Upstairs, Downstairs* (1974–7), *The *Jewel in the Crown* (1984) and *The Buccaneers* (1997).

ˌ**Masters and ˈJohnson** /ˌmɑːstəz, ˈdʒɒnsn; *AmE* ˌmæstərz, ˈdʒɑːnsn/ **William Masters** (1915–) and **Virginia Johnson** (1925–), two US doctors who became well known for their study of human sexual behaviour. They discovered that women can enjoy sex as much as men, and this became the subject for many articles in women's magazines. They wrote several books about their research, including *Human Sexual Response* (1966), and started a programme in *St Louis in 1970 for training experts to help people with their sexual problems. Masters and Johnson were married to each other from 1971 to 1993.

ˈ**master's deˌgree** (*also* **master's**) *n* a higher degree in British and US universities, usually requiring one year of study. It is between a *bachelor's degree and *doctorate. Master's degrees include Master of Arts, Master of Science and Master of Business Administration: *She's doing her master's in computer studies.* See also GRADUATE SCHOOL.

the ˈ**Masters ˌTournament** /ˈmɑːstəz; *AmE* ˈmæstərz/ (*also* the **Masters**, the **US Masters**, the **US Masters Tournament**) a major international golf contest held each year in Augusta, *Georgia. It was established in 1934 by Bobby *Jones and is the only one of the four major golf tournaments (= sports competitions) that is always held on the same course. The winner receives a special green jacket as well as money. The most frequent winner has been Jack *Nicklaus with six victories.

ˌ***Match of the ˈDay*** a British television programme that shows details of the most important football matches of a particular day (usually a Saturday). It first appeared in 1964, and its presenters have included David *Coleman and Desmond *Lynam.

ˌCotton ˈ**Mather** /ˌkɒtn ˈmeɪθə(r); *AmE* ˌkɑːtn/ (1663–1728) an American Puritan minister (= church leader) in *Boston. He wrote more than 400 works on religion, history, science and other subjects. His writings led to an increased fear of witches and helped to cause the *Salem witch trials, although Mather himself was opposed to them. He also helped to establish *Yale University and was the first person born in America to be elected to the *Royal Society of London.

Maˈtilda /məˈtɪldə/ (1102–67) the queen of England for a short time in 1135. She was replaced by King *Stephen. Her father was *Henry I and her son became *Henry II in 1154..

ˌ**Matrix ˈChurchill** /ˌmeɪtrɪks ˈtʃɜːtʃɪl; *AmE* ˈtʃɜːrtʃɪl/ a British engineering company, based in *Coventry, which became well known in 1992 when three of its directors were accused of having sold military equipment to Iraq, against official British government policy. The case against the directors collapsed when Alan *Clark, who had been a government minister for trade, admitted in court that he had advised the company not to be completely honest about what they were exporting. This caused a big political scandal in Britain, since it appeared that members of the government were acting in a way that went against government policy. The directors were found not guilty and the matter became one of the subjects of the *Scott Inquiry. Soon after the court case, the company went bankrupt.

ˌStanley ˈ**Matthews** /ˈmæθjuːz/ (1915–) one of the most famous English football players of all time. He played on the wing (= as an attacking player along one side of the field) and was known for his skill at running past opponents with the ball and then passing it into the goal area. He is also remembered for having remained a professional player until the age of 50. He played for England 54 times and was the first football player to be made a *knight (in 1965).

ˌFrancis ˈ**Maude** /ˈmɔːd/ (1953–) a British *Conservative politician. He became a *Member of Parliament in 1983 and joined William *Hague's *Shadow Cabinet in 1997, becoming Shadow *Chancellor of the Exchequer in 1998.

the ˌ**Maudsley ˈHospital** /ˌmɔːdzli/ a psychiatric hospital (= one for the treatment of mental illness) in south-east London, established in 1916. It is the main centre for postgraduate education in psychiatry in Britain.

ˌSomerset ˈ**Maugham** /ˌsʌməset ˈmɔːm; *AmE* ˌsʌmərset / (1874–1965) an English writer considered to be one of the best writers of short stories in the English language. He also wrote plays and novels, including *Of Human Bondage* (1915) and *Cakes and Ale* (1930). Many of his stories are about human weakness.

ˈ**Maundy ˌmoney** /ˈmɔːndi/ *n* [U] specially produced silver coins given each year by the British king or queen to a selected group of poor people on **Maundy Thursday** (the Thursday before *Easter). The ceremony continues a tradition which began in the Middle Ages. At that time the king or queen washed the feet of the poor people, in memory of Christ's washing of his disciples' feet.

ˌArmistead ˈ**Maupin** /ˌɑːmɪstɪd ˈmɔːpɪn; *AmE* ˌɑːrmɪstɪd/ (1944–) a US writer and author of the popular 'Tales of the City' series of novels. The first of these, *Tales of the City* (1978), originally appeared in parts in the San Francisco *Chronicle* newspaper. Its characters live at 28 Barbary Lane in San Francisco. Like Maupin himself, several of them are homosexual. A British television series based on the novels caused arguments in the US when it was shown on *PBS in 1994. Although it had the largest ever audience for a PBS dramatic programme, several cities refused to show it.

Mauˈritius /məˈrɪʃəs/ an island in the Indian Ocean which is a member of the *Commonwealth. Before it became independent in 1968, it was at various times a colony of the Netherlands, France, and finally Britain. Its main industries are sugar and tourism. ▶ **Mauritian** *adj*, *n*.

ˌ**Max ˈFactor**™ /ˌmæks ˈfæktə(r)/ a company that makes a range of well-known cosmetics.

ˈJames ˈClerk ˈ**Maxwell**[1] /ˈklɑːk ˈmækswel; *AmE* ˈklɑːrk/ (1831–79) a Scottish scientist who made important contributions to many areas of physics, including gases, colour vision (= the power of sight), electricity and magnetism. His work also influenced the development of telephones and colour photography.

ˌRobert ˈ**Maxwell²** /ˈmækswel/ (1923–91) a British businessman, publisher and newspaper owner, born in Czechoslovakia. He came to Britain in 1940 and received the *Military Cross for his military achievements in *World War II. He first became rich through the company he owned, the Pergamon Press, which published scientific journals (= serious magazines). However, in 1969, an official investigation into the company decided that he was not a suitable person to run a company. He was also at this time a *Labour Party *Member of Parliament, a position he held from 1964 to 1970.

Despite doubts about some of his business methods, Maxwell built up a large business empire. In 1984 he bought *Mirror Group Newspapers and so became the owner of the **Daily Mirror*, the **Sunday Mirror* and *The *People*, all popular British newspapers. This made him one of the most powerful people in the newspaper industry.

Maxwell died when he fell from a boat and drowned. After his death it was discovered that he had illegally taken money from the *pension funds of Mirror Group employees to support other companies that he owned. His sons Kevin and Ian were prosecuted for financial crimes involving his companies but after long court cases they were found not guilty. Maxwell's reputation, however, was destroyed and he is now seen to have been a dishonest and cruel man.

ˈPeter ˈ**Maxwell** ˈ**Davies** /ˈmækswel ˈdeɪvɪs/ (1934–) an English composer of modern classical music, known mostly for his chamber music and operas, which include *The Lighthouse* (1979). He was made a *knight in 1987.

ˌ**Maxwell** ˈ**House**™ /ˌmækswel/ a popular make of instant coffee. It was first made in the US in 1886, and was often advertised as being 'good to the last drop'.

ˈ**May Day** the first day of May, which has been marked in Britain for many centuries by outdoor events held to celebrate the arrival of spring. In Britain, traditional events on or near May Day include dancing round the *maypole and choosing a *May Queen. May Day itself is not necessarily a holiday in Britain, but since 1978 there has been a *bank holiday on the Monday closest to 1 May, called the Early May Bank Holiday. In some countries, though not in Britain, May Day has been an occasion for socialist celebrations, often involving military parades.

ˌLouis B ˈ**Mayer** /ˈmeɪə(r)/ (Louis Burt Mayer 1885–1957) one of the people who established the US film company *MGM in 1924. As head of the company (until 1951) he became one of the most powerful men in *Hollywood. He also helped to create the *Academy of Motion Picture Arts and Sciences and received a special *Oscar in 1950. Mayer was born in Russia.

ˈ**Mayfair** /ˈmeɪfeə(r); *AmE* ˈmeɪfer/ a fashionable district in west central London where mostly rich and *upper-class people live or stay. As well as very expensive houses and flats, it contains many hotels, restaurants, shops and art galleries.

ˌCurtis ˈ**Mayfield** /ˌkɜːtɪs ˈmeɪfiːld; *AmE* ˌkɜːrtɪs/ (1942–) an *African-American singer of *soul music who has written songs, played the guitar, and produced records. He was the main singer for the group The Impressions, and their hit songs included *Gypsy Woman* (1961). After he left the group in 1970, Mayfield wrote the music for the film *Superfly* (1972) and produced several successful albums, including *Honesty* (1981). An accident on stage in 1990 left him paralysed (= unable to move his body).

The ˈ***Mayflower*** /ˈmeɪflaʊə(r)/ the ship in which the *Pilgrim Fathers sailed from *Plymouth in England to what is now the US, in 1620.

Mayflower II, a copy of the original ship

the ˈ**Mayo** ˌ**Clinic** /ˈmeɪəʊ; *AmE* ˈmeɪoʊ/ one of the largest medical centres in the world. It is in Rochester, New York, and was established in 1889 by William James Mayo (1861–1939) and his brother Charles Horace Mayo (1865–1939). It is famous for the high quality of treatment given there.

mayor *n* **1** (in England and Wales) a man or woman elected every year by other *councillors as head of the *council in a town, city or *borough. The mayor performs official duties, such as attending public ceremonies, entertaining visitors to the area or opening new buildings. He or she does not have much political power. The equivalent person in Scotland is called a *provost*. **2** (in the US) the head of the local government of a town or city, elected by the people living there. US mayors usually belong to one of the two main political parties and often have a lot of political power.

mayoˈress *n* the wife of a *mayor(1) or a woman who acts on behalf of a mayor on public occasions. The word is sometimes used to mean a female mayor.

ˈ**maypole** *n* a tall decorated pole which people dance around during traditional *May Day celebrations in Britain. The dancers, usually children, hold coloured ribbons attached to the top of the pole, which is fixed upright into the ground. Maypoles used to be common in villages on May Day but are now less often seen.

dancing round a maypole

ˈ**May Queen** (*also* ˌ**Queen of the** ˈ**May**) *n* a pretty girl who is chosen in a town or village to be the central figure of traditional *May Day celebrations in Britain. She wears a crown of flowers and may be driven through the streets on an open vehicle.

ˌWillie ˈ**Mays** /ˌwɪli ˈmeɪz/ (1931–) an *African-American *baseball player with the Giants in New

M

York (1951–7) and during their first years in *San Francisco (1958–72). His last year was with the New York Mets (1973). Mays hit 660 home runs during his career, the third most ever. He was twice named the *Most Valuable Player in the *National League (1954 and 1965), and was chosen for the National Baseball *Hall of Fame in 1979.

the **Maze** /meɪz/ a prison in Northern Ireland, just outside *Belfast, where people were kept under the policy of *internment. It opened in 1971, when it was called Long Kesh. The different sections of the prison are known as *H-blocks because each building is shaped like the letter H.

When internment ended in 1975, prisoners who had been found guilty of terrorism protested that they should be treated as political prisoners, which would have meant that they could wear their own clothes and not do prison work. Some of them went on hunger strike and several died, including Bobby Sands, who had been elected as a *Member of Parliament while in the prison.

There have been several riots (= violent protests) in the Maze, and in 1983 38 *IRA prisoners escaped together from it. There are plans to close the prison.

MBE /ˌem biː ˈiː/ (*in full* **Member of the Order of the British Empire**) an award given to people in Britain for public service. It given to people twice a year, in the *New Year Honours list and in the *Birthday Honours list. An MBE is the lowest grade of award of this kind.

In 1993, in response to the feeling that awards were not given often enough to ordinary people, the government changed the system so that people who are recommended by members of the public for the service they provide can receive the award.

MC /ˌem ˈsiː/ ⇨ MILITARY CROSS.

the **MCAT** /ˈemkæt/ (*in full* the **Medical College Admission Test**) (in the US) a standard test that students must normally take in order to be accepted into a medical college.

MCC /ˌem siː ˈsiː/ ⇨ MARYLEBONE CRICKET CLUB.

ˌJoseph **McˈCarthy**[1] /məˈkɑːθi; *AmE* məˈkɑːrθi/ (1908–57) a US politician. As a *Republican(1) *Senator from *Wisconsin he led a campaign against Communists in US society and government in the 1950s, during the Cold War. Important and well-known people were accused of being Communists or sympathetic to Communism, often without evidence, and forced to answer questions from the Senate Permanent Investigations Subcommittee, led by McCarthy. People were also encouraged to give information about their friends and those they worked with. Many people were forced from their jobs and 'blacklisted' (= prevented from getting jobs in future). In 1954 US Senate officially condemned McCarthy's activities and his influence decreased. Most Americans are now unhappy that the McCarthy trials were allowed to happen, and admire anyone who opposed them or refused to give evidence. Compare HOUSE UN-AMERICAN ACTIVITIES COMMITTEE.

▶ **McCarthyism** *n* [U] extreme opposition to Communism, as shown by Senator Joseph McCarthy in his campaign against people suspected of being Communists in the US. The word is also used more generally to mean the practice of investigating and accusing people who are thought to be opposed to the government, without sufficient evidence.

ˌMary **McˈCarthy**[2] /məˈkɑːθi; *AmE* məˈkɑːrθi/ (1912–89) a US writer whose intelligent novels made comments about American society. These include *The Groves of Academe* (1952), *The Group* (1963) and *Cannibals and Missionaries* (1979). She also wrote books about literature, travel books and *Memories of a Catholic Girlhood* (1957), about her own early life. She was married to the writer Edmund Wilson (1895–1972).

ˌPaul **McˈCartney** /məˈkɑːtni; *AmE* məˈkɑːrtni/ (1942–) an English musician and writer of songs who was a member of the *Beatles. In the 1960s, together with John *Lennon, he wrote and recorded some of the best-known pop songs of all time. When the Beatles split up in 1970, he formed a new group, Wings, whose successful records include *Mull of Kintyre* (1977).

Although remembered mainly for having been a member of the Beatles, McCartney is still very active as a musician. He has composed classical pieces, including *Liverpool Oratorio* (1991) and *Standing Stone* (1997), has established a college for the performing arts in *Liverpool, and continues to make successful pop records. He was made a *knight in 1997.

ˌLiz **McˈColgan** /məˈkɒlgən; *AmE* məˈkɔːlgən/ (1964–) a Scottish runner in long distance races. She won the gold medal for the 10 000 metres at the *Commonwealth Games in 1986 and 1990 and at the World Championships in 1991. She also won the silver medal in the same event at the Olympic Games in 1988. In 1991 she started to compete in marathon races (= ones run over a long distance) and won the first one she entered, the New York marathon. She has also won the *London marathon.

ˌCarson **McˈCullers** /ˌkɑːsn məˈkʌləz; *AmE* ˌkɑːrsn məˈkʌlərz/ (1917–67) a US writer from the state of *Georgia, where most of her novels and short stories were set. She said she wrote about 'spiritual isolation'. The novels included *The Heart is a Lonely Hunter* (1940), *Reflection in a Golden Eye* (1941), and *The Member of the Wedding* (1946), which she wrote again as a play in 1950. Her short stories were collected in *The Ballad of the Sad Café* (1951).

ˌTrevor **McˈDonald** /məkˈdɒnəld; *AmE* məkˈdɑːnəld/ (1939–) a British television newsreader, born in Trinidad. He joined Independent Television News in 1973 and was the main newsreader for **News at Ten* from 1992. He was made a *knight in 1999.

McˈDonald's™ /məkˈdɒnəldz; *AmE* məkˈdɑːnəldz/ any of a large group of US *fast-food restaurants in many countries of the world. The company, established in 1955 by Ray *Kroc, has become a symbol of US commercial success. McDonald's originally sold only hamburgers, such as the Big Mac, but now sells chicken, fish and breakfast foods as well. The restaurants are especially popular with children and are regarded as typical of the American way of life. In 1997 McDonald's won the longest trial in British legal history (over seven years) against two people who published claims that its food is not healthy and that to get the supply of meat it needs it causes damage to the environment.

ˌJohn **ˈMcEnroe** /ˈmækɪnrəʊ; *AmE* ˈmækɪnroʊ/ (1959–) a US tennis player who was especially successful in the early 1980s. He won the men's title at *Wimbledon three times (1981 and 1983–4) and at the *US Open(2) four times (1979–81 and 1984), but he had a reputation for losing his temper and behaving badly during games.

ˌIan **MˈcEwan** /məˈkjuːən/ (1948–) an English writer of short stories and novels, many of which are about the more strange and violent aspects of human nature. His novels include *The Child in Time* (1987), *The Innocent* (1990), *Enduring Love* (1997) and *Amsterdam* (1998), which won the *Booker Prize.

ˌDonald **McˈGill** /məˈgɪl/ (1875–1962) an English cartoonist famous for his *seaside postcards. These usu-

a Donald McGill postcard

ally showed fat people in humorous situations saying things that could have a rude meaning.

ˌWilliam **Mc'Gonagall** /mə'gɒnəgl; *AmE* mə'gɑːnəgl/ (1830–1902) a Scottish poet. His poems show no skill or understanding of poetry but are very popular and funny as a result. An example is his *Address to the Rev George Gilfillan*:

All hail to the Rev George Gilfillan of Dundee,
He is the greatest preacher I did ever hear or see ...
He has written the life of Sir Walter Scott,
And while he lives he will never be forgot,
Nor when he is dead,
Because by his admirers it will be often read.

His *Poetic Gems* were published in 1890.

McˌGuffey's 'Readers /məˌgʌfiz/ a series of six school books (1836–57) designed to teach American children to read. They were created by William McGuffey (1800–73), the President of Cincinnati College, who wrote the first four. He believed that they should also develop good character in children, so he included wise advice and sentences from great British writers such as *Shakespeare and *Shelley². About 122 million copies of the books were sold, and their moral stories influenced Americans for more than a century.

ˌMark **Mc'Gwire** /mə'gwaɪə(r)/ (1963–) a US *baseball player who in 1998 hit the most *home runs in a season (70) in the history of the game, beating the record of 61 set by Roger Maris in 1961. McGwire plays for the St Louis Cardinals in the *National League.

ˌIan **Mc'Kellen** /mə'kelən/ (1939–) a leading English actor known especially for his performances in *Shakespeare plays, although he has appeared in many other plays and in a number of films. He is also known for his efforts to raise money for the victims of the disease Aids and for his campaigns in support of equal rights for homosexuals. He was made a *knight in 1991.

ˌMount **Mc'Kinley¹** /mə'kɪnli/ the highest mountain in North America, with a height of 20 320 feet/6 198 metres. It is in *Denali National Park in southern central *Alaska, and is also called Denali in the Aleut language. The mountain was named after US President William *McKinley, and it was first climbed in 1913.

ˌWilliam **Mc'Kinley²** /mə'kɪnli/ (1843–1901) the 25th US *President (1897–1901). He was a US officer during the *Civil War and a *Republican(1) who served twice in the US House of Representatives (1877–83 and 1885–91) and as governor of *Ohio (1892–6). US power increased greatly during his time as President. He supported the *Spanish-American War and trade with China, and created the highest tariffs (= taxes on imports) in US history. He was murdered by an anarchist (= a person who believes there should be no laws or government).

M'cLaren¹ /mə'klærən/ one of the leading teams in *Formula One motor racing, with its main base in Britain. The company was established by Bruce McLaren (1937–70), a former racing driver from New Zealand. Its most successful period was from the mid 1980s to the early 1990s when its drivers Alain Prost and Ayrton Senna were world champions six times.

ˌMalcolm **M'cLaren²** /mə'klærən/ (1946–) an English pop group manager and businessman. He is best known for bringing together the *punk(1) group the *Sex Pistols in 1975, and later managing their career. Together with Vivienne *Westwood he also owned the clothes shop 'Sex' in the *King's Road, London, which became a centre of punk fashions.

ˌRobert **McNa'mara** /mæknə'mɑːrə/ (1916–) a US Secretary of Defense (1961–8) under President *Kennedy and President *Johnson. McNamara left this job because he had doubts about the *Vietnam War, and he later said publicly that it was wrong. When his political career ended, he became President of the World Bank (1968–81).

'Aimee 'Semple **Mc'Pherson** /'eɪmi 'sempl mək'fɜːsn; *AmE* mək'fɜːrsn/ (1890–1944) a US religious leader, born in Canada, who was especially popular in the 1920s. In 1923 she opened the Angelus Temple in *Los Angeles as the base for her International Church of Foursquare Gospel. She disappeared in 1926 and later said she had been kidnapped (= taken away by force), but it was discovered that she had been with a lover. She was taken to court for cheating some of her followers financially, but was judged innocent. She died when she accidentally took too much medicine to help her sleep.

ˌSteve **M'cQueen** /mə'kwiːn/ (1930–80) a US film actor who often played tough but honest characters. He first became well known in a television series, *Wanted – Dead or Alive* (1958). His films included *The *Magnificent Seven, The Great Escape* (1963), *Bullitt* (1968) and *The Towering Inferno* (1974).

Mc'Vitie's™ /mək'vɪtiz/ a British company that makes biscuits of different types. McVitie's Digestive Biscuits, made with wholemeal flour, are especially popular.

MDT /ˌem diː 'tiː/ ⇨ MOUNTAIN DAYLIGHT TIME..

ˌMargaret **'Mead** /'miːd/ (1901–78) a US anthropologist. She studied how children grow up in different cultures, especially in the Pacific islands, and argued that human behaviour is strongly affected by society. Some people criticized her research, but she made anthropology very popular. Her books included *Coming of Age in Samoa* (1928), *Growing Up in New Guinea* (1930), *Male and Female* (1949) and *Culture and Commitment* (1970).

ˌ**Meadowbank 'Stadium** /ˌmedəʊbæŋk; *AmE* ˌmedoʊbæŋk/ a sports stadium in *Edinburgh, Scotland, which was opened in 1970 to hold the *Commonwealth Games. The games were held there again in 1986. It has one large outdoor sports ground and several which are indoors.

meals

Americans and British people generally eat three meals a day though the names vary according to people's lifestyles and where they live.

The first meal of the day is **breakfast**. The traditional **full English breakfast** served in many British hotels may include fruit juice, cereal, bacon and eggs, often with sausages and tomatoes, toast and marmalade, and tea or coffee. Few people have time to prepare a cooked breakfast at home and most have only cereal or muesli (*AmE* granola) and/or toast with tea or coffee. Others buy coffee and a pastry on their way to work.

M

The traditional **American breakfast** includes eggs, some kind of meat and toast. Eggs may be fried, 'over easy', 'over hard' or 'sunny side up', or boiled, poached or in an omelette (= beaten together and fried). The meat may be bacon or sausage. People who do not have time for a large meal have toast or cereal and coffee. It is common for Americans to eat breakfast in a restaurant. On Saturday and Sunday many people eat **brunch** late in the morning. This consists of both breakfast and lunch dishes, including pancakes and waffles (= types of cooked batter) that are eaten with butter and maple syrup.

Lunch, which is eaten any time after midday, is the main meal of the day for some British people, though people out at work may have only *sandwiches. Some people also refer to the midday meal as **dinner**. Most workers are allowed about an hour off for it, called the **lunch hour**, and many also go shopping. Many schools offer a cooked lunch (**school lunch** or **school dinner**), though some students take a **packed lunch** of sandwiches, fruit, etc. **Sunday lunch** is special and is, for many families, the biggest meal of the week, consisting typically of roast meat and vegetables and a sweet course. In the US lunch is usually a quick meal, eaten around midday. Many workers have a half-hour break for lunch, and buy a sandwich near their place of work. Business people may sometimes eat a larger lunch and use the time to discuss business.

The main meal of the day for most people is the evening meal, called **supper**, **tea** or **dinner**. It is usually a cooked meal with meat or fish or a salad, followed by a sweet course. Some people have a **TV supper**, eaten on their knee while watching television. In Britain younger children may have tea when they get home from school. *Tea*, meaning a main meal for adults, is used especially in Scotland and Ireland; *supper* and *dinner* are more widely used in England and Wales. *Dinner* sounds more formal than *supper*, and guests generally receive invitations to 'dinner' rather than to 'supper'. In the US the evening meal is called *dinner*. It is usually eaten around 6 or 6.30 p.m and often consists of dishes bought ready-prepared that need only to be heated. In many families, both in Britain and in the US, family members eat at different times and rarely sit down at the table together. Unless it is a special occasion, few people drink wine with dinner.

Many people also eat **snacks** between meals. Most have tea or coffee at mid-morning, often called **coffee time** or the **coffee break**. In Britain this is sometimes also called **elevenses**. In the afternoon most British people have a **tea break**. Some hotels serve **afternoon tea** which consists of tea or coffee and a choice of sandwiches and cakes. When on holiday/vacation people sometimes have a ***cream tea** of scones, jam and cream. In addition many people eat chocolate bars, biscuits (*AmE* cookies) or crisps (*AmE* chips). Some British people have a snack, sometimes called supper, consisting of a milk drink and a biscuit before they go to bed. In the US children often have milk and cookies after school. Adults are especially likely to **snack** (= eat snacks) while watching television.

ˌmeals on ˈwheels *n* [U] a service in which meals are taken by car to old or sick people in their own homes. It is provided free in Britain by groups such as the *Women's Royal Voluntary Service, and in the US by various charities and service organizations.

ˈMean Streets a US film (1973) that made stars of Martin *Scorsese, who wrote and directed it, and the actor Robert *De Niro. It is about four youths who meet in Tony's Bar in the *Little Italy district of *Manhattan(1). De Niro plays Johnny Boy, a criminal who owes money to many people and creates trouble for others. By 1997 Scorsese and De Niro had made eight more films together.

ˌMeasure for ˈMeasure a play by *Shakespeare, thought to have been written in 1604 and often regarded as one of his comedies. It is about a *duke, Vincentio, who gives his power to his deputy (= assistant), Angelo, and then wears a disguise so that he can watch how Angelo behaves. Angelo behaves in an immoral and cruel way until the duke reveals who he really is and then there is a happy ending.

ˌmeat and two ˈveg (*BrE infml*) a meal consisting of some meat and two different vegetables, one of which is potato. It is regarded by many British people as a normal healthy meal, although in recent times British people in general have begun to enjoy a greater variety of foods, and 'meat and two veg' is now sometimes seen as old-fashioned and boring: *He does like his meat and two veg most days.*

ˈMeat Loaf (1951–) a US pop singer, known for his large size, whose real name is Marvin Lee Aday. His first album, *Bat Out of Hell* (1977), sold more than 12 million copies. He won a 1993 *Grammy award for his song *I'd Do Anything for Love (But I Won't Do That)*.

Mecˈcano™ /məˈkɑːnəʊ; *AmE* məˈkɑːnoʊ/ *n* [U] a toy in the form of a set of metal or plastic parts with which mechanical models can be built. It was invented by Frank Hornby in England in 1893 and has been popular in Britain for many years. Some modern Meccano sets also have electrical parts.

Meccano

meˈdallion man *n* (*pl* **medallion men**) (*BrE humor, often disapprov*) a man whose appearance suggests that he thinks he is very masculine and tough. Typically he has most of his shirt open and has a hairy chest with a large medallion (= round piece of metal jewellery) round his neck.

ˌMedal of ˈHonor ⇨ CONGRESSIONAL MEDAL OF HONOR.

medals

The highest **decoration** (= award) that can be awarded to a British person is the ***Victoria Cross (VC)**, which is given to members of the *armed forces 'for conspicuous bravery in the face of the enemy'. It is a bronze cross decorated with a lion and the words 'For Valour', which is hung from a crimson ribbon. The Victoria Cross was introduced by Queen *Victoria in 1856, during the *Crimean War. It is reserved for acts of the greatest courage and is often awarded **posthumously** (= to a person who died as a result of their brave action).

The highest decoration for members of the public is the ***George Cross (GC)**, which is also awarded for bravery in great danger. It is a silver cross decorated with St *George and the Dragon and the words 'For Gallantry', and is hung from a dark blue ribbon. It was introduced by *George VI in 1940, and was awarded to the island of *Malta for its heroic resistance during *World War II.

Other highly valued decorations include the the Distinguished Service Cross, the Military Cross and the George Medal. There are also medals for acts of bravery by police officers and by members of the fire-fighting, lifeboat and coastguard services.

The US also has many medals for military and civilian achievements. The ***Medal of Honor (MH)**, often called the Congressional Medal of Honor, is the highest military award and is given for 'the risk of life, above and beyond the call of duty'. It is a star that hangs from a blue ribbon which is decorated with 13 white stars. It was created in 1862 during the *Civil War, and by 1997 more than 3 400 had been awarded. Another well-known military medal is the ***Purple Heart (PH)** which is awarded to Americans wounded in wars. George *Washington introduced it in 1782 as the Badge of Military Merit, and the medal today has a ribbon above a purple heart with Washington's image on it. Other important military awards include the Distinguished Service Cross and the Bronze Star.

The highest US civilian award is the **Presidential Medal of Freedom**, established in 1945 as the Medal of Freedom. It was originally for military service, but President *Kennedy changed this and also its name. The **Congressional Gold Medal** is also now only for civilians. The first was awarded in 1776 to George Washington; in 1998 one was awarded to the entertainer Frank *Sinatra. The **Carnegie Medal**, another honour for civilians, is given to people who have saved, or tried to save, somebody's life. On the medal is a sentence from the Bible: 'Greater love hath no man than this, that a man lay down his life for his friends.'

ˈMedicaid the US government's medical programme for people under the age of 65 who have low incomes. It helps to pay the cost of doctors, dentists, hospitals, drugs, medicines and other items. Medicaid began in 1956, is operated by the individual states and is paid for by national, state and county governments. Compare MEDICARE.

the **ˈMedical ˈCollege Adˈmission Test** ⇨ MCAT.

the **ˌMedical Reˈsearch ˌCouncil** (*abbr* the **MRC**) a British government organization which gives government money to institutions doing medical research, usually universities and hospitals. It was established in 1920.

ˈMedicare the US government's medical programme for everyone over the age of 65. It began in 1965 and is part of the *Social Security system. It pays part of the costs of hospitals and offers additional medical insurance to people who pay an amount each month. Medicare costs the government more than was originally expected, but efforts by President *Clinton to increase the amount of money available have failed in Congress. Compare MEDICAID.

ˌmediˈeval (*also* **mediaeval**) *adj* of the *Middle Ages, the period in European history between about 1100 and about 1400. Things which are very old-fashioned, or are not comfortable or convenient, are sometimes described as medieval: *Conditions were pretty medieval – there were no toilets or running water, and no hot food.*

the **ˈMedway** /ˈmedweɪ/ a river in *Kent in south-east England which starts at the town of Rochester, flows through *Chatham and joins the River *Thames to the east of London.

ˌMeet the ˈPress a US television news programme, broadcast every Sunday, in which several journalists ask politicians questions. *Meet the Press* began on radio in 1945 and moved to television in 1947. It has been presented since 1991 by Tim Russert.

the **ˈme geneˌration** *n* [sing + sing/pl *v*] (*infml disapprov*) the name used to refer to young people in the 1970s and 1980s who were especially interested in money and success and cared more about themselves than about others: *The me generation was one of the legacies of Thatcherism in Britain.*

ˌLord **ˈMelbourne** /ˈmelbɔːn; *AmE* ˈmelbɔːrn/ (*born* William Lamb 1779–1848) a British *Whig(1) politician who was twice *Prime Minister (1834 and 1835–41). He is remembered especially for the good relationship he had with Queen *Victoria, who was young when he was in power and welcomed the advice he gave her, and for a very public scandal in 1812 when his wife, Lady Caroline *Lamb, had an affair with the poet Lord *Byron.

ˌVictor **ˈMeldrew** /ˈmeldruː/ the main character in the popular British television comedy series *One Foot in the Grave*, played by Richard Wilson. He is a retired man who is always bad-tempered, complains all the time, annoys people and often makes terrible mistakes. His name is often used in Britain to refer to somebody who behaves like this.

ˌAndrew **ˈMellon** /ˈmelən/ (1855–1937) a rich US businessman who also served in the US government. He was Secretary of the Treasury (1921–31) and then US Ambassador to Britain (1932–3). He gave large amounts of money to help charities, museums, etc., and he gave his large art collection to establish the *National Gallery of Art in Washington, DC.

ˈDavid **ˈMellor** /ˈmelə(r)/ (1949–) a former *Conservative politician in Britain. He held several important government positions in the 1990s, and was the first *Secretary of State at the Department of National Heritage, with responsibility for a wide range of British cultural matters. In 1992 there was a scandal in Mellor's private life when the press published stories about his affair with an actress. He remained in his job but was later forced to resign when he was involved in another scandal over air tickets given to him for a family holiday by a businessman. Since then, he has worked as a journalist and broadcaster, with a special interest in music and football. He presents a popular radio programme about football on *Radio 5 Live and also advises the *Labour government on the way football in England is run.

ˈMelody ˌMaker a British pop and rock music newspaper published once a week. It first appeared in 1926. Compare *NEW MUSICAL EXPRESS.*

the **ˈmelting pot** a phrase that has been used to describe the US, because it is a country in which people from many different races and cultures are 'melted' together, i.e. mixed, to form the US people. The British writer Israel Zangwill (1864–1926) wrote a play called *The Melting Pot* (1903) about Jewish immigrants in America.

ˌHerman **ˈMelville** /ˌhɜːmən ˈmelvɪl; *AmE* ˌhɜːrmən/ (1819–91) a US writer of novels whose early life as a sailor provided the material for many of his books, including his best-known novel, **Moby-Dick*. His other books include *Typee* (1846), *Omoo* (1847) and the short novel *Billy Budd* (1924), published after he died. Melville's books were not popular during his life, and he died in poverty. His importance as a writer was not recognized until the 1920s.

ˌMember of ˈParliament (*abbr* **MP**) *n* a member of the *House of Commons, elected in a general election or a *by-election. Each MP represents one of the 659 *constituencies into which England, Scotland, Wales and Northern Ireland are divided for these elections. The person elected to be a Member of Parliament in an election is the one who is given the most votes. ⇨ article at ELECTIONS TO PARLIAMENT.

ˈ**Member of the ˈEuropean ˈParliament** (*abbr* **MEP**) (*also* **Euro-MP**) *n* a person elected as the representative at the *European Parliament of any of the 81 *constituencies into which England, Scotland, Wales and Northern Ireland are divided in elections for this parliament. These elections are separate from general elections for the British *Parliament. They were first held in 1979 and take place every five years.

Meˈmorial Day (*also* ˌ**Decoˈration Day**) a US holiday to honour Americans killed in all wars. It is the last Monday in May, but a few states have it on 30 May. It began in the South during the *Civil War when flowers were placed on graves, and the North first celebrated it in 1868. Memorial Day traditionally begins the summer holiday from school. Southern states also celebrate **Confederate Memorial Day** on 26 April, 10 May or 3 June.

ˈ**Memphis** /ˈmemfɪs/ the largest city in the US state of *Tennessee. It is on the *Mississippi River in the extreme south-west of the state. Memphis is an agricultural and commercial centre established in 1819 and named after the ancient Egyptian city. It is called the 'home of the *blues' because W C *Handy lived there. Martin Luther *King was murdered in Memphis in 1968, and Elvis *Presley died there in 1977 at his home, *Graceland.

the ˌ**Menai ˈStrait** /ˌmenaɪ/ a channel that separates the island of *Anglesey from the north-west coast of Wales. The **Menai Bridge**, the road bridge that crosses it, was built by Thomas *Telford and was then the biggest suspension bridge (= bridge hanging from cables supported by towers at each end) of its kind in the world.

ˈ**Mencap** /ˈmenkæp/ (*in full* the **Royal Society for Mentally Handicapped Children and Adults**) a British charity which provides help, services and accommodation for mentally handicapped people. It was established in 1946.

ˈ**Mennonite** /ˈmenənaɪt/ *n* a member of a Protestant group, mostly in Canada and the US, who have a simple life and religion like the *Amish and the *Hutterites. Their rules come from the Bible, and they only baptize adults. They also refuse to hold public office or serve in the armed forces. The Mennonites came to the US from Switzerland in 1683 and settled mainly in *Pennsylvania and the *Middle West. They named themselves after Menno Simons, a 16th-century Dutch Anabaptist leader.

ˈ**Mensa** /ˈmensə/ a social organization for highly intelligent people. Established in Britain in 1946, it became an international organization in the 1960s. People wishing to join take special intelligence tests, and the results of these must show that they are among the 2% most intelligent people in their country.

Yeˌhudi ˈ**Menuhin** /jəˌhuːdi ˈmenjuɪn/ (1916–99) one of the greatest violinists of the 20th century. He was born in the US but settled permanently in England in the 1940s. He first achieved fame as a child violinist, giving his first public performance at the age of seven in *San Francisco. A number of works were later written specially for him by leading composers, including William *Walton. In 1963 Menuhin started a school for children with special musical ability. He was also a conductor and directed music festivals, as well as writing and broadcasting on humanitarian subjects. He was made a member of the *Order of Merit in 1987.

Yehudi Menuhin

MEP /ˌem iː ˈpiː/ ⇨ MEMBER OF THE EUROPEAN PARLIAMENT.

ˌJohnny ˈ**Mercer** /ˈmɜːsə(r)/ (1909–76) an American who wrote the words to more than 1 000 popular songs. They include *Jeepers Creepers* (1938), *That Old Black Magic* (1942), *Laura* (1945), *Come Rain or Come Shine* (1946), *Something's Gotta Give* (1955) and *Moon River* (1961). Mercer won four *Oscars.

ˌIsmail ˈ**Merchant** /ˌɪsmaɪl ˈmɜːtʃənt; *AmE* ˈmɜːrtʃənt/ (1936–) an Indian film producer who, together with his partner James *Ivory, has made a number of successful films, including *Heat and Dust* (1983) and *A Room with a View* (1986), which both won *Oscars. They are particularly associated with making romantic films set in a period of the past, with great attention to historical detail and the attitudes of the characters.

ˌ**merchant ˈnavy** (*also* ˌ**merchant maˈrine**) *n* the trading ships of a country and the sailors who work on them. The British merchant navy was very important during both world wars for the continued supply of goods to Britain from abroad, and many of its ships were sunk by enemy submarines. See also BATTLE OF THE ATLANTIC.

The ˌ***Merchant of ˈVenice*** a play by *Shakespeare, thought to have been written in 1596. It is about a merchant, Antonio, who borrows money from a Jew called *Shylock to help Bassanio marry Portia. According to their agreement, if Antonio fails to pay the money back, Shylock can claim a pound of Antonio's flesh. When Antonio is unable to pay the money back, Shylock demands that Antonio keeps to the agreement. However, he is defeated in a court case by Portia, disguised as a lawyer, who makes a powerful speech, wins the case and saves Antonio's life. The play is the origin of the expression *to demand, want, etc. your pound of flesh*, meaning to want or insist on getting what you have a legal right to, even when it is morally offensive to do so.

ˈ**Mercia** /ˈmɜːsiə; *AmE* ˈmɜːrsiə/ one of the *Anglo-Saxon regions of England, occupying a large area of central England. It was established in the 6th century and was very powerful during the 8th century, when it was ruled by Offa, who built *Offa's Dyke. Recently, the name Mercia has started to be used again in the names of organizations, buildings and companies in central England.

ˈ**Mercury**™ **1** a telecommunications company established in Britain in 1981, when the government ended the *Post Office's monopoly of the national telephone system to allow competition. Mercury was at first the only company to compete with *British Telecom, which had previously been part of the Post Office but was privatized (= sold to private owners) in 1981. In 1984, Mercury became part of *Cable and Wireless. In the late 1980s, it introduced its own public telephone boxes and in the early 1990s it started trying to attract private customers as well as businesses, which had previously been its only customers. It now also provides mobile phone services.

ˌFreddie ˈ**Mercury 2** /ˈmɜːkjəri; *AmE* ˈmɜːrkjəri/ (1946–91) the singer with the rock group *Queen. He was known particularly for his energetic performances at live concerts. He died of the disease Aids.

the ˈ**Mercury program** (*also* ˌ**Project ˈMercury**)

the US space programme (1961–3) to put a man into orbit around the earth. This was achieved when John *Glenn became the first person to go into orbit on 20 February 1962. See also SHEPARD.

ˈmerit badge any of several badges awarded in the *Boy Scouts of America for different achievements and sewn onto their uniforms. A certain number are needed before a Scout can move to a higher rank. Merit badges are awarded for skills and study in many areas, such as cooking, safety, communications, sports, computers, pets and family life.

ˈMerlin /ˈmɜːlɪn; *AmE* ˈmɜːrlɪn/ an important character in *Arthurian legend. He was a wizard (= a man with magic powers) who gave advice to King *Arthur and his father, Uther Pendragon. It was Merlin's idea that the man who could pull *Excalibur out of the stone should be king.

the ˌ**Mermaid** ˈ**Theatre** a theatre in London, England, which opened in 1959. Its building was converted from an old dock on the River *Thames, and it takes its name from the Mermaid Tavern, where *Shakespeare, Ben *Jonson and other great writers of the 16th and 17th centuries used to meet.

ˌEthel ˈ**Merman** /ˈmɜːmən; *AmE* ˈmɜːrmən/ (1909–84) a US singer and actor on stage and in films. She is remembered for her loud voice and lively performances. She appeared in many *Broadway musical shows, including *Anything Goes* (1934), **Annie Get Your Gun* (1946), *Call Me Madam* (1950) and *Gypsy* (1959). Several of her films were versions of her stage shows. She received a special *Tony award in 1972.

ˌ**Merry** ˈ**England** a phrase used to refer to England in the *Elizabethan period, which is often seen as a great period for the country, when it was powerful and prosperous, the people were happy and there was a lot of singing, dancing and happy music.

ˌ**Merry** ˈ**Men** the group of men who followed *Robin Hood, lived with him in *Sherwood Forest and joined him in his adventures: *the stories of Robin Hood and his Merry Men.*

The ˈ***Merry*** ˈ***Wives of*** ˈ***Windsor*** /ˈwɪnzə(r)/ a comedy play by *Shakespeare, thought to have been written in 1600. The main character is *Falstaff, who Shakespeare included again because he had been such a popular character in his earlier play **Henry IV*. In *The Merry Wives of Windsor* Falstaff tries to have affairs with two women at the same time. They realize what he is doing and play cruel tricks on him to cause him embarrassment.

the ˈ**Mersey** /ˈmɜːzi; *AmE* ˈmɜːrzi/ a river in north-west England which flows through *Greater Manchester and *Merseyside and into the *Irish Sea. It is usually associated with *Liverpool because it flows through that city and has played an important part in its history. There are three tunnels under it, one for the underground railway and two for roads.

the ˈ**Mersey beat** /ˈmɜːzi; *AmE* ˈmɜːrzi/ (*also* the **Mersey sound**) the name used to describe a style of pop music which was created and played by a number of groups from *Liverpool in the early and mid 1960s, and which became very popular all over the world. The most famous of these groups was The *Beatles.

ˈ**Merseyside** /ˈmɜːzisaɪd; *AmE* ˈmɜːrzisaɪd/ a county in north-west England. It was formed as a *metropolitan county in 1974. Its main city and administrative centre is *Liverpool.

ˈ**Mesa** ˈ**Verde** ˈ**National** ˈ**Park** /ˈmeɪsə ˈvɜːdi; *AmE* ˈvɜːrdi/ a US *national park in south-west *Colorado. It was established in 1906 and covers 52 122 acres (21 109 hectares). Tourists come to see the cliff houses of the *Pueblo *Native Americans which are more than

the cliff palace, Mesa Verde National Park

1 000 years old. The park includes mountains and deep valleys. It also has a museum. It was made a *World Heritage Site in 1978.

Mes*ˈ*siah (*also the* ***Messiah***) /məˈsaɪə/ a musical work by *Handel for voices and orchestra, with verses from the Bible. It was first performed in *Dublin in 1742 and has become one of the most popular pieces of classical music among British audiences. It is often sung around Christmas.

Meˈtallica /məˈtælɪkə/ a US pop band whose music combines *punk and *heavy metal. It was formed in 1981 by Lars Ulrich, who was born in Denmark. Their albums have included *Kill 'Em All* (1983) and *Metallica* (1991).

ˌ**metaphysical** ˈ**poets** *n* any of a group of 17th-century English poets, including John *Donne, George *Herbert and Andrew *Marvell. Their poetry was marked by a clever and complicated mixture of words and ideas, with each poem being based on a central idea, or 'conceit'. They gained a high reputation in the 20th century, mainly because of critical praise from T S *Eliot.

the ˌ**Meteoroˈlogical** ˌ**Office** (*also infml* the ˈ**Met** ˌ**Office**) a British government organization that collects and provides information on the weather. It was established in 1854 and its headquarters are in the town of Bracknell in *Berkshire. Most of the weather forecasts on radio and television are presented by people who work for the Met Office.

ˈ**method** ˌ**acting** *n* [U] a way of acting in which actors try to identify completely with the characters they are playing. It was based on the ideas of the Russian director Constantin Stanislavsky, and developed in the US by Lee *Strasberg at the *Actors' Studio in New York. Famous actors who have used 'the Method' include Marlon *Brando, Dustin *Hoffman and Robert *De Niro.

ˈ**Methodist** *n* a member of the **Methodist Church**, the largest of the Protestant *Free Churches in Britain and the US. It was established in 1739 by John *Wesley as part of the *Church of England but it became separate from it in 1795. It was introduced into the US in the 18th century and today has over 50 million members around the world. It emphasizes the importance of moral issues, both personal and social. ▶ **Methodism** *n* [U].

ˈ**Metro**-ˈ**Goldwyn**-ˈ**Mayer** /ˈmetrəʊ ˈɡəʊldwɪn ˈmeɪə(r); *AmE* ˈmetroʊ ˈɡoʊldwɪn ˈmeɪər/ ⇨ MGM.

ˌ**metroˈpolitan** ˈ**county** *n* each of six new administrative areas of Britain created in 1974. These were formed from large city areas which were separated from the counties they were formerly in. They were *Greater Manchester, *Merseyside, *Tyne and Wear, *West Midlands, *South Yorkshire and *West Yorkshire. Each one was divided into ten districts and there were two systems of local government, county councils and *district councils. In 1986, this system changed. County councils were abolished, leaving only district councils responsible for each district within the metropolitan counties. As far as local government is concerned, therefore, the metropolitan counties no longer exist, but they remain in existence as geographical areas and in postal addresses.

the ˌ**Metroˈpolitan Muˈseum of ˈArt** a famous US art museum in New York, first opened in 1880. The building has about 250 rooms and more than 3.5 million works of art from around the world, including the complete Temple of Dendur from Egypt. Much of the *medieval art is at the Cloisters, a separate building in Fort Tryon Park, opened in 1938.

the ˌ**Metroˈpolitan ˈOpera** (*also infml* the **Met**) the leading US opera company, and one of the best known in the world, based in New York at the *Lincoln Center for the Performing Arts. It was established in 1838. The company's most famous head was Rudolf Bing, between 1940 and 1972. Its conductors have included Gustav Mahler and Arturo Toscanini, and its singers have included Enrico Caruso, Maria *Callas, Joan Sutherland and Luciano Pavarotti.

the ˌ**Metroˈpolitan ˈPolice** (*also infml* the **Met**) the police force responsible for *Greater London (except for the *City, where the police force is the City of London Police). It was established in 1827 by Sir Robert *Peel. Its headquarters are at *New Scotland Yard in *Westminster(1). See also CID.

mews /mjuːz/ *n* (*pl* **mews**) (*esp BrE*) a street of buildings where horses used to be kept, but which have since been converted into homes. These homes are usually small but they are considered very fashionable and are therefore expensive to buy or rent, especially in parts of central London such as *Kensington and *Chelsea.

M

the ˌ**Mexican ˈWar** /ˌmeksɪkən/ a war (1846–8) fought between the US and Mexico. It began after *Texas became a state in 1845 and there was a dispute about where the border between Texas and Mexico should be. The war was won by the US forces under General Zachary *Taylor, who became President a year later. The Treaty of Guadalupe Hidalgo ended the war, and the US paid Mexico $15 million for land that is now in *California, *Arizona, *Colorado, *Nevada, *New Mexico and *Utah. Many people in the northern states worried that the victory would increase the number of the states with slaves, and this worry was one of the causes of the *Civil War.

MG™ /ˌem ˈdʒiː/ the name given to a series of popular and relatively cheap British sports cars, originally made by the *Morris company (MG is short for 'Morris Garages'). The first were made in the 1920s. MGs are now made by *Rover.

MGM /ˌem dʒiː ˈem/ (*in full* **Metro-Goldwyn-Mayer**) a well-known *Hollywood film company established in 1924. In its early days it was especially famous for its musical films, made with great style. The company employed many famous US actors. At the start of every MGM film there is a roaring lion and the words 'More stars than there are in the heavens'. The company has been sold several times since the 1970s. It owns a large group of cinemas and the MGM Grand Hotel and Theme Park, completed in 1993 in *Las Vegas. See also GOLDWYN, MAYER.

Miˈami /maɪˈæmi/ a US city and port in south-eastern *Florida on Biscayne Bay. It is a popular place for holidays because of the warm weather and **Miami Beach**, which is on an island three miles off the coast. The city is also an important financial and industrial centre. It became a town in 1892 and grew rapidly in the 1920s. Many immigrants live in the districts of 'Little Havana' and 'Little Haiti'. More than half of Miami's population are *Hispanic.

the ***Miˌami ˈHerald*** /maɪˌæmi/ a newspaper published every day in *Miami, *Florida. In 1997, it had about 500 000 readers on Sundays and nearly 400 000 on other days. It had also won 14 *Pulitzer Prizes. The *Herald* is known for its excellent news stories about Latin America.

ˌMr **Miˈcawber** /mɪˈkɔːbə(r)/ a character in the novel **David Copperfield* by Charles *Dickens. He is always in financial difficulties, but remains hopeful that 'something will turn up' to solve his problems without his having to make any effort himself. He is usually associated with this attitude to life and with his theory about income: if you spend a bit less than you earn, you will be happy; but if you spend a bit more than you earn, you will be unhappy.

ˌGeorge ˈ**Michael** /ˈmaɪkl/ (1963–) a popular British pop singer and song writer since the early 1980s. He was born in London and has a Greek Cypriot father and an English mother. He first became famous as a member of the group Wham!, and then began a successful career on his own in 1985. His albums have included *Faith* (1987) and *Listen Without Prejudice Volume 1* (1990). He lost a very expensive legal dispute with the record company Sony, which he claimed had not done enough to promote (= give publicity to) his records.

ˈ**Michaelmas** /ˈmɪklməs/ 29 September, the day celebrated by Christians as the festival of Saint Michael. It is not a *bank holiday in Britain.

ˈ**Michaelmas term** /ˈmɪklməs/ the name given to the autumn academic term in some British schools and universities.

ˌJames ˈ**Michener** /ˈmɪtʃənə(r)/ (1907–97) a US writer who won the *Pulitzer Prize for *Tales of the South Pacific* (1947) based on his experiences there. It was adapted as the musical play and film **South Pacific*. Michener then mainly wrote historical and adventure novels, most of them very long and based on careful research. They include *The Bridges of Toko-Ri* (1953), *Hawaii* (1959), *Centennial* (1974), *Chesapeake* (1978) and *Alaska* (1988). Several of his books were filmed.

ˈ**Michigan¹** /ˈmɪʃɪgən/ a northern US state, also called the Wolverine State and the Great Lakes State, because it is divided into two parts by Lake *Michigan and Lake *Huron, and also has borders with Lake *Superior and Lake *Erie. The largest city is *Detroit, and the capital city is Lansing. Michigan became a state in 1837. Its products include iron and other minerals, cars and breakfast cereals (= grains processed as food). Tourists visit the Henry Ford Museum in Dearborn, and Mackinac Island. People who live in the state are called **Michiganders**.

ˌLake ˈ**Michigan²** /ˈmɪʃɪgən/ one of the *Great Lakes, and the only one completely in the US. It is also the largest lake of fresh water in the US, having an area of 22 300 square miles (57 757 square kilometres). It is linked to Lake *Huron. The states around Lake Michigan are *Michigan, *Wisconsin, *Illinois and *Indiana. Cities on the lake include *Chicago and *Milwaukee. In 1997 oil was discovered under the lake.

Mick *n* (*infml, sometimes disapprov or offensive*) a name used to refer to an Irishman: *The pub was full of Micks.*

ˌ**Mickey ˈMouse** a famous cartoon character created by Walt *Disney, who called him 'the mouse that built an empire'. Mickey has become the symbol of the company and his high voice was spoken by Disney himself. He was first seen in *Steamboat Willie* (1928). Mickey's girlfriend is Minnie Mouse and his dog is Pluto. In 1929 Disney began Mickey Mouse Clubs in large shops and cinemas. *The Mickey Mouse Club* was also a popular Disney television programme (1955–9). The children on it wore mouse ears and were called Mouseketeers. In each programme they sang a song that spelled out Mickey's name.

Mickey Mouse and Minnie Mouse

ˈ**Microsoft** /ˈmaɪkrəsɒft; *AmE* ˈmaɪkrəsɔːft/ the US computer company that produces most of the computer software in the world. It was established in 1974 by Bill *Gates and Paul Allen. In 1980, the company adapted a system to operate personal computers made by *IBM, and in 1985 it developed the *Windows system. In 1997 the US Department of Justice accused Microsoft of forcing companies that make computers to use its *Internet browser (= system that finds information on the Internet).

the ˌ**Mid-Atˈlantic ˈstates** /ətˈlæntɪk/ the name given to five eastern US states between *New England and the South. They are *New York, *New Jersey, *Pennsylvania, *Delaware and *Maryland. All are on the Atlantic coast except Pennsylvania.

the ˌ**Middle ˈAges** *n* [pl] (in European history) the period between about 1100 and about 1400. It is associated with the *Crusades and *feudalism, and is thought of as a period when the Christian Church was very powerful. Some people also think of it as a period when there was little cultural or social development, but it produced important works of literature such as *Chaucer's **Canterbury Tales*, and many beautiful churches in the *Romanesque and *Gothic styles. Compare DARK AGES.

ˌ**Middle Aˈmerica** /əˈmerɪkə/ **1** *middle-class Americans, who usually have traditional values and are politically moderate or conservative. Compare MIDDLE ENGLAND. **2** another name for the *Middle West. **3** the part of North America south of the US, including Mexico, Central America and sometimes the West Indies.

the ˌ**middle ˈclass** *n* [C + sing/pl *v*] the social class between the *working class and the upper class. It consists of people who are generally regarded as having an average status, education, income, etc. in society. In Britain, the middle class is often divided into the upper middle class and the lower middle class. ⇨ article at CLASS. ▶ **middle-class** *adj*.

ˌ**Middle ˈEngland** *n* [U] British people who have traditional opinions about politics and society, especially *middle-class people living in the south of England: *The government needs to convince Middle England that its policies are working.* Compare MIDDLE AMERICA 1.

Middle English

From the 12th century Middle English replaced *Norman French as the most widely spoken language in England but, until the 14th century, French and Latin were used in government and law, and by writers of literature. Middle English developed from *Old English, the language used in England before the Norman Conquest and spoken by the common people throughout the Norman period.

By the time English reappeared as a literary language it had gone through various changes. The grammar was simpler, with fewer inflections, and the vocabulary had gained many French and Latin words. Some Old English words had disappeared, while others remained beside those of French or Latin origin, e.g. *freedom* and *liberty*. Compared with Old English, many more words of Middle English can be understood by speakers of modern English. However, the range of styles and spellings in surviving literature suggest that there was no single way of writing Middle English. The ancient letters, called *runes*, found in Old English soon ceased to be used, with only the thorn (þ) surviving into the 15th century. There were also changes to pronunciation, especially the pronunciation of vowels. Long, stressed vowels were formerly pronounced similarly to those in other European languages, for example the 'i' in *fine* was originally pronounced /iː/ but in late Middle English it became /aɪ/. This change came to be known as the **great vowel shift** and was a significant feature in the development of modern English.

The most important author who wrote in Middle English was Geoffrey *Chaucer. His most famous work, partly in verse and partly in prose, is *The *Canterbury Tales* (*c.* 1387) in which he introduces a varied group of people on a pilgrimage to *Canterbury. The following passage introduces the Miller:

The Miller was a stout carl, for the nones,
Ful big he was of braun, and eek of bones;
That proved wel, for over-al ther he cam,
At wrastling he wolde have alwey the ram.
He was short-sholdred, brood, a thikke knarre,
Ther nas no dore that he nolde heve of harre,
Or breke it, at a renning, with his heed.

(The Miller was a stout ruffian, believe me, very muscular and big-boned. That was well-tested because he towered over all present and in wrestling he would always win the ram. He was a short-necked, broad, thickset fellow and there was no door he couldn't take off its hinge or break with his head at a run.)

Other famous Middle English works include William Langland's **Piers Plowman*, and *Sir *Gawain and the Green Knight*, a poem by an unknown author about the adventures of one of King *Arthur's knights.

The first English printing press was set up in London by William *Caxton in 1476. One of the earliest books he printed was *The Canterbury Tales*. Caxton printed over 100 books, many of them by English authors, and so helped spread the literature of the period among a greater number of people.

ˈ***Middlemarch*** /ˈmɪdlmɑːtʃ; *AmE* ˈmɪdlmɑːrtʃ/ a novel (1871–2) by George *Eliot, widely considered to be one of the greatest English novels. Its subtitle is *A Study of Provincial Life* and it presents a detailed picture of the attitudes and behaviour of a number of people in the imaginary *middle-class town of Middlemarch.

the ˌ**middle ˈpassage** the journey across the Atlantic by ship as part of the slave trade. Ships travelled from Britain to Africa, where the slaves were bought and then taken to be sold in America or the West Indies. Conditions on the journey were terrible and many slaves died during it. ⇨ article at SLAVERY.

ˈ**middle school** *n* a type of state school in England and Wales for children aged 8-14. The name is also given to the classes for children aged 14-15 at a secondary school (for children aged 11-18). ⇨ article at EDUCATION IN BRITAIN.

ˈ**Middlesex** /ˈmɪdlseks/ a former county to the north-west of London until 1965, when it became part of *Greater London. The name is still used in postal addresses and in the names of organizations.

the ˌ**Middlesex** ˈ**Hospital** /ˌmɪdlseks/ a large *teaching hospital in central London, England. It was established in 1745.

the ˌ**Middle** ˈ**West** (*also* the **Mid**ˈ**west**) the northern central region of the US. It is considered to be between the *Rocky Mountains and the eastern borders of *Illinois or *Ohio, and from the *Great Lakes to the *Ohio River and the southern borders of *Kansas and *Missouri. It is rich farming land. People living in the Middle West are thought to be traditional and conservative. See also MIDDLE AMERICA 2.

ˌ**Mid Gla**ˈ**morgan** /glǝˈmɔːgǝn; *AmE* glǝˈmɔːrgǝn/ a county in south Wales. Its administrative centre is *Cardiff. Until the 1980s, it was known especially for its coal, iron and steel industries.

the ˌ**Midland** ˈ**Bank** /ˌmɪdlǝnd/ (*also* the **Midland**) one of the four big English *clearing banks, with branches in towns and cities all over the country. It was established in 1836 in *Birmingham. For many years the Midland described itself in its advertisements as 'the listening bank' to give the impression that it was always sympathetic towards its customers. In 1992 it became the first of the main English banks to operate a telephone banking service.

the ˈ**Midlands** /ˈmɪdlǝndz/ the central region of England, consisting of the counties of *Derbyshire, *Leicestershire, *Northamptonshire, *Nottinghamshire, *Staffordshire, *Warwickshire and *Hereford and Worcester, and the *metropolitan county *West Midlands. Its biggest cities are *Birmingham and *Coventry. In the 19th and 20th centuries it has been an important industrial region.

ˌBette ˈ**Midler** /ˌbet ˈmɪdlǝ(r)/ (1945–) a US singer and comic actor. She is small and enthusiastic and makes rude jokes about sex. She is sometimes called the Divine Miss M, which was the title of her first album (1973). Her films have included *Down and Out in Beverly Hills* (1986) and *The First Wives Club* (1996). She won a *Emmy in 1997 for her television programme *Bette Midler: Diva Las Vegas.*

ˌ***Midnight*** ˈ***Cowboy*** a US film (1969) that won an *Oscar as Best Picture. It was directed by the English director John Schlesinger (1926–), who also received an Oscar. The story is from a novel by James Leo Herlihy. It is about a young man from *Texas, played by John Voight, who goes to New York and becomes a male prostitute.

A ˌ***Midsummer Night's*** ˈ***Dream*** a comedy play by William *Shakespeare which takes place in a wood near Athens. The story involves three groups of characters in a mixture of magic and reality. *Oberon, the king of the fairies, is angry with his wife *Titania, and tells his servant *Puck to play a trick on her, so that she falls in love with *Bottom, one of a group of workers who are practising a play they are going to perform for the Athenian court. Bottom's head is changed into that of an ass. Puck also plays magic tricks on a group of young lovers with comic results, until everything is put right and the play ends with wedding celebrations and the performance of the workers' play.

ˈ**Midtown** /ˈmɪdtaʊn/ the centre or shopping area of a US city. The best-known is Midtown *Manhattan(1) in New York.

the ˌBattle of ˈ**Midway** /ˈmɪdweɪ/ an important US victory over Japanese forces in 1942 during *World War II. Japanese ships advanced on the US Navy base on Midway Island in the central Pacific Ocean, and the air and sea battle lasted from 3 to 6 June.

the **Mid**ˈ**west** ⇨ MIDDLE WEST.

ˈLudwig ˈ**Mies van der** ˈ**Rohe** /ˈlʊdvɪg ˈmiːs væn dǝ ˈrǝʊǝ; *AmE* dǝr ˈroʊǝ/ (1886–1969) a US architect, born in Germany, who was known for his glass and steel *skyscrapers. He helped to develop modern architecture and is considered one of the major architects of the 20th century. He used simple designs and said 'less is more'. The buildings in the US which he designed include the Lakeshore Drive Apartments in *Chicago (1948–51) and, with Philip Johnson, the Seagram Building in New York (1954–8). He also designed furniture.

MI5 /ˌem aɪ ˈfaɪv/ the former name (still used, though not officially) of the British government department responsible for state security within Britain. MI5 is short for Military Intelligence section 5. Its main activities used to involve protecting British military secrets and catching foreign spies. Since the early 1990s, it has been mainly responsible for collecting information about and dealing with terrorism, especially that involving the *IRA.

MI5 was a very secret organization until the early 1990s, when more information about its activities was made known to the public. It is now called the Security Service.

The ***Mi***ˈ***kado*** /mɪˈkɑːdǝʊ; *AmE* mɪˈkɑːdoʊ/ a comic opera (1885) by W S *Gilbert and Arthur *Sullivan, one of their *Savoy Operas. It takes place in a town in Japan called Titipu and contains many well-known songs, including *Three Little Maids from School* and *A Wandering Minstrel, I.* The Mikado himself is the emperor of Japan.

the Three Little Maids in The Mikado, *played by Thora Kerr, Vivian Tierney and Fiona O'Neill*

mild *n* [U] a type of English beer, darker and with a milder flavour than *bitter. Mild used to be very popular in pubs but is now less often drunk. ⇨ note at BEER.

ˌ**Milford** ˈ**Haven** /ˌmɪlfǝd; *AmE* ˌmɪlfǝrd/ a town on the south-west coast of Wales, in *Dyfed. It has a natural harbour and for many centuries was the place from which English armies crossed the *Irish Sea to Ireland. In the second half of the 20th century it became a port for oil because the deep waters there made it suitable for very large ships transporting oil. In 1995 one of these, the *Sea Empress,* crashed into the entrance to the harbour and the oil it was carrying poured out, causing serious damage to the environment.

the ˌ**Militant** ˈ**Tendency** an extreme left-wing group within the *Labour Party in Britain, formed in the 1960s with policies based on Trotskyism. It began to gain influence in some *constituencies and *trade unions in the early 1980s, when it also controlled the city council in *Liverpool. The group did a lot of damage to the reputation of the Labour Party, and in the mid 1980s the Labour leader Neil *Kinnock forced its members to leave the party. Since then it has had little real influence.

a milkman beside his milk float

the ˌ**Military** ˈ**Cross** (*abbr* **MC**) a medal given to British army officers for brave actions. It was created in 1914.

the ˌ**Military** ˈ**Medal** (*abbr* **MM**) a medal given to soldiers in the British army below the rank of officers, for brave actions. It was created in 1916.

ˈ**milkman** *n* (*pl* **milkmen**) (in Britain) a man who goes from house to house every day delivering milk. The milk is usually in bottles and is delivered early in the morning. In towns and cities milkmen travel in vehicles that use electrical power, called **milk floats**. Customers usually pay for their milk every week. In recent times, as more people have started buying milk from shops and supermarkets, there has been less demand for milkmen. As a result, they now often deliver other goods as well as milk, such as eggs, bread, potatoes and other drinks. Milkmen are generally thought of as cheerful, friendly people.

ˈ**Milk Marque** the independent organization that controls the supply, advertising and selling of milk in Britain. It was formerly called the Milk Marketing Board.

ˌ**Milk of Magˈnesia**™ /mæɡˈniːʃə/ *n* [U] (in Britain) a white medicine, in the form of tablets or liquid, for treating stomach problems such as indigestion and constipation. It can be bought at chemists and is widely used.

ˌ**Milky ˈWay**™ *n* **1** (in Britain) a chocolate bar with a soft, light centre. For many years it was advertised as 'the sweet you can eat between meals without ruining your appetite'. **2** (in the US) a chocolate bar with a soft, light centre and caramel inside it.

ˈJohn ˈStuart ˈ**Mill** /ˈmɪl/ (1806–73) an English philosopher whose ideas had a great influence on modern thought. His best-known works include *On Liberty* (1859), in which he argued that people should be free to do what they want if this does not harm others, and *Utilitarianism* (1863), in which he explained and supported the theory that actions are morally right if they lead to happiness.

ˈJohn ˈEverett ˈ**Millais** /ˈevərɪt ˈmɪleɪ; *AmE* mɪˈleɪ/ (1829–96) one of the original members of the group of British artists known as the *Pre-Raphaelites. His most famous paintings include *Christ in the House of His Parents* (1850), *Ophelia* (1852) and *The Blind Girl* (1856), all of which have the realistic detail characteristic of the Pre-Raphaelites. Later in life, he painted more sentimental pictures, such as **Bubbles*. He was the first painter to be made a *baronet, in 1885.

ˈEdna St ˈVincent **Milˈlay** /seɪnt ˈvɪnsnt mɪˈleɪ/ (1892–1950) a US poet who wrote romantic poems. Her collections include *The Harp-Weaver and Other Poems* (1922), which won the *Pulitzer Prize, and *Conversation at Midnight* (1937). She also wrote three verse plays.

ˈ**Millbank** /ˈmɪlbæŋk/ a road in central London along the north bank of the River *Thames. Part of the *Houses of Parliament(2) is at one end of it and the *Tate Gallery is towards the other end. **Millbank Tower**, a modern office building on Millbank, has been the headquarters of the British *Labour Party since 1998, and 'Millbank' is often used to refer to the Labour Party in general: *Millbank has been working on the image of New Labour.*

the **Milˈlennium Comˌmission** an independent organization set up by the British government to organize events to celebrate the end of the 20th century and the beginning of the 21st century. The Commission's plans include the building of the **Millennium Dome**, a very large structure with a round roof for exhibitions, etc. Some people in Britain think that the large amount of money this will cost to build would be better spent on more useful projects. A *millennium* is a period of 1 000 years.

ˌArthur ˈ**Miller**[1] /ˈmɪlə(r)/ (1915–) a US writer of plays. They include **Death of a Salesman* and *A View from the Bridge* (1955), both of which won the *Pulitzer Prize. In *The Crucible* (1953) he used the story of the *Salem witch trials as a symbol of *McCarthyism, which he strongly opposed. Miller was married to Marilyn *Monroe from 1955 to 1961 and wrote her last film, *The Misfits* (1961).

Arthur Miller with Marilyn Monroe

ˌGlenn ˈ**Miller**[2] /ˈmɪlə(r)/ (1904–44) the US leader of a popular *big band which played *swing music in the late 1930s and early 1940s. He also wrote music and played the trombone. His band's successes included his theme tune *Moonlight Serenade* (1938), which he wrote, and *In the Mood* (1939), *Pennsylvania 6-5000* (1940) and *Chattanooga Choo-Choo* (1941). Miller joined the US Army Air Force as its band leader during *World War II and was killed when the plane he was travelling in crashed on a flight from England to France.

ˌHenry ˈ**Miller**[3] /ˈmɪlə(r)/ (1891–1980) a US author whose work had an important influence on the writers of the *beat generation. His early books, *Tropic of Cancer* (1934) and *Tropic of Capricorn* (1939), published in Paris, were banned in Britain and the US for many years because of their detailed descriptions of sex. His other books included the series of three, together called *The Rosy Crucifixion* (1949–60).

ˌJonathan ˈ**Miller**[4] /ˈmɪlə(r)/ (1934–) a leading figure in the arts in Britain. He is now known mainly for directing plays and operas, but he first became famous as a performer in the satirical comedy show

**Beyond the Fringe* in the early 1960s. He originally trained as a doctor and used this knowledge to make the popular *BBC television series *The Body in Question* (1978), in which he explained medical matters in a way that ordinary people could understand.

ˌMax ˈ**Miller**[5] /ˈmɪlə(r)/ (1895–1963) an English comedian who was extremely popular in Britain, especially during the 1940s and 1950s. He was famous for telling rather rude jokes and was widely known by his *nickname, 'The Cheeky Chappie'.

ˌSpike ˈ**Milligan** /ˌspaɪk ˈmɪlɪɡən/ (1918–) a British comedian and writer, born in India. He first became famous as one of the stars of *The *Goon Show*, much of which he also wrote, in the 1950s. He later appeared in a number of television series of his own. Milligan has also written children's books, poetry, comic novels and humorous books based on his experiences in the British army in *World War II. His crazy and original style of humour has had a great influence on British comedy.

The ***ˌMill on the ˈFloss*** /ˈflɒs; *AmE* ˈflɔːs/ a novel (1860) by George *Eliot. It is mainly about the relationship between a brother and sister, Tom and Maggie Tulliver, who live in a mill (= a building where grain is ground into flour) on the river Floss. It describes their childhood and a dispute that causes them to separate. The book ends with them happily together again but they are both killed in a flood.

ˌ**Mills & ˈBoon** /ˌmɪlz, ˈbuːn/ the best-known British publishing company of romantic fiction, established in 1908. The stories are usually about a young woman who, after many problems, marries the man she considers perfect for her. People sometimes make fun of the books because the stories are very similar and characters in them seem very innocent, but they are extremely popular and sell in very large quantities: *The story of her youthful affair with a Russian prince reads like a Mills and Boon romance.*

ˌA A ˈ**Milne** /ˌeɪ eɪ ˈmɪln/ (Alan Alexander Milne 1882–1956) an English writer of children's books, known mainly as the person who created *Winnie-the-Pooh. The books in which Pooh appears, *Winnie-the-Pooh* (1926) and *The House at Pooh Corner* (1928), came from stories Milne invented for his son Christopher Robin. He also wrote collections of poetry for children, including *When We Were Very Young* (1924) and *Now We Are Six* (1927). All of these are still very popular with children today. Milne also wrote plays, including **Toad of Toad Hall* (1929), adapted from *The *Wind in the Willows* by Kenneth *Grahame.

ˌJohn ˈ**Milton** /ˈmɪltən/ (1608–74) one of the most famous of all English poets. He is best known for his great poem **Paradise Lost*, which he completed in 1667. This was based on the Old Testament story of the Garden of Eden, and its central character is Satan. It was followed by *Paradise Regained* and **Samson Agonistes*, published together in 1671. His earlier works of poetry included *L'Allegro* and *Il Penseroso* (both 1631) and *Lycidas* (1638), and he also wrote political articles supporting Parliament against the king, and the freedom of the press.

ˌ**Milton ˈKeynes** /ˌmɪltən ˈkiːnz/ the largest of Britain's *new towns, created in the 1960s in *Buckinghamshire. Many people and businesses were persuaded to move there and it has become a prosperous town. In spite of this, British people sometimes make fun of it as a town that has been artificially created. It also contains the headquarters of the *Open University.

Milˈwaukee /mɪlˈwɔːki/ the largest city in the US state of *Wisconsin. It is an industrial port on the western shore of Lake *Michigan. Many Germans settled there in the second half of the 19th century, and it is still well known for its beer and German foods. It also produces machinery and medical instruments.

MIND /maɪnd/ a British charity that works to help mentally ill people. It collects money for them, gives advice to them and their families, and aims to make people more aware of their problems. It was established in 1946 as the National Association for Mental Health, and changed its name in 1971.

ˈ***Minder*** /ˈmaɪndə(r)/ a popular British television comedy drama series (1979–94). Its main characters were Arthur *Daley, a middle-aged man who spends all his time finding ways, usually illegal, of making money and avoiding the police, and Terry, his 'minder' (= person employed to protect someone), who helps him, does jobs for him and often gets into trouble because of him.

ˈ**miners' strikes** occasions on which British coal miners have gone on strike, causing major problems for the government. There have been three main strikes. In 1972 the *National Union of Mineworkers called a strike for wage increases, after a vote by its members. There were power cuts (= interruptions in the supply of electricity) all over Britain, a state of emergency was announced, and the miners won, gaining a large pay increase. In 1974 the miners again voted for a national strike and the *Conservative *Prime Minister Edward *Heath called a general election on the issue of whether the government or the miners had more power in the country. The Conservatives lost the election, and the new *Labour government gave the miners a big pay increase, ending the strike.

In 1984–5 the miners went on strike again because the National Coal Board, which was in charge of all British mines at the time, planned to close several mines, with the loss of over 20 000 jobs. The strike was seen by the Conservative Prime Minister, Margaret *Thatcher, as a test of the new industrial relations laws, which were aimed at reducing the power of trade unions. There was a lot of violence between the miners and the police during the strike, but as it continued more and more miners returned to work, and finally it ended without any agreement being reached. The government therefore won and the National Union of Miners lost. Since then, the miners have had much less power than they used to have. See also SCARGILL.

ˌCharles ˈ**Mingus** /ˈmɪŋɡəs/ (1922–79) an *African-American *jazz musician. He played the bass and wrote music for it. His works included *Fables of Faubus* (1959) and *Epitaph* (1962). He was active in the *civil rights movement and wrote the story of his life, *Beneath the Underdog* (1971).

ˈ**Mini** *n* the name of a series of small and relatively cheap British cars. The Mini, which was designed by Alec Issigonis (1906–88) and first produced in 1959,

a Mini

became the most successful British car of all time. Minis were extremely popular during the 1960s, especially among young people, and are sometimes seen as symbols of that period in Britain.

the ˌ**Ministry of ˈAgriculture, ˈFisheries and ˈFood** (*abbr* **MAFF**) the British government department in charge of farming and food production, including food safety. It was established in 1954 and is in *Whitehall, central London. The title of its head is Minister of Agriculture, Fisheries and Food.

the ˌ**Ministry of Deˈfence** (*abbr* the **MOD**) the British government department in charge of the armed forces. It was established in 1964, when the *Admiralty, the *War Office and the Air Ministry were joined together. It is in *Whitehall and the title of its head is *Secretary of State for Defence.

the ˌ**Ministry of ˈTransport** (until 1997) the British government department responsible for road, rail, sea and air transport, including the building of new roads. In 1997 the Ministry of Transport and the Department of the Environment were joined together to form a new department, the Department of Environment and Transport. The title of the head of the new department is *Secretary of State for the Environment, Transport and the Regions.

the ˌ**Ministry of ˈTransport test** ⇨ MOT.

ˌ**Minneˈapolis** /ˌmɪniˈæpəlɪs/ the largest city in the US state of *Minnesota. It is an industrial port near the northern end of the *Mississippi River. The river separates it from *St Paul, Minnesota, and they are together called the 'twin cities'. Minneapolis was settled in 1847 and became a town in 1867. It is an agricultural centre for the northern *Middle West. Other companies there make computers and provide health services.

ˌLiza **Minˈnelli** /ˌlaɪzə mɪˈneli/ (1946–) a US singer, dancer and actor known for her energy and happy personality. She was especially popular in the 1970s. She won an *Oscar for her part in the film *Cabaret* (1972), and her other films have included *New York New York* (1977) and *Arthur* (1981). Minnelli is the daughter of Judy *Garland and the director Vincente Minnelli.

ˌ**Minneˈsota** /ˌmɪnɪˈsəʊtə; *AmE* ˌmɪnɪˈsoʊtə/ a state in the northern central US on the Canadian border. It has more than 10 000 lakes, and is also called the North Star State and the Gopher State. The largest city is *Minneapolis and the capital city is *St Paul. It became a state in 1858. Minnesota produces 75% of the country's iron ore (= rock), as well as agricultural products, chemicals and computers. The *Mayo Clinic, a famous medical centre, is in Rochester. Tourists visit Voyageurs National Park and the St Paul Winter Carnival.

ˈ**Minnesota ˈMining and Manuˈfacturing ˌCompany** /ˈmɪnɪsəʊtə; *AmE* ˈmɪnɪsoʊtə/ ⇨ 3M.

ˌ**Minnie ˈMouse** /ˌmɪni/ ⇨ MICKEY MOUSE.

miˌnority ˈleader the leader of the political party that has a minority (= fewer members than the largest party) in the US Senate or US House of Representatives. He or she organizes the party's members and their programme of new laws. Compare MAJORITY LEADER.

ˈ**minstrel show** *n* a show in which white entertainers wear black make-up to look like Negroes and perform songs and music in the style of Negro songs and music. In Britain a television show of this kind, the *Black and White Minstrels was popular for many years. Such shows no longer exist because they are now considered to be insulting to black people.

ˌ**mint ˈjulep** /ˈdʒuːlɪp/ (*also* **julep**) *n* a US alcoholic drink, especially popular during the summer in the southern states. It usually consists of bourbon (= whisky made from corn grain), sugar and crushed ice, served in a tall glass with peppermint leaves on top. A mint julep is the traditional drink at the *Kentucky Derby.

ˈ**Minton** /ˈmɪntən/ *n* [U] high-quality English pottery and china made at the factory in *Stoke-on-Trent established by Thomas Minton (1765–1836). The goods produced there are famous for the *willow pattern on them, which he is thought to have designed.

ˈ**Minuteman** *n* (*pl* **-men**) (*AmE*) **1** a member of a group of American citizens during the *American Revolution who fought when they were needed. They said they were ready to fight with only a minute's warning. Minutemen from *Massachusetts fought at the battles of *Lexington and Concord at the start of the war, and similar groups were also formed in *Connecticut, *New Hampshire and *Maryland. **2** a US nuclear missile, developed during the *Cold War.

ˈ**miracle play** (*also* ˈ**mystery play**) *n* any of a number of religious plays from the Middle Ages based on stories from the Bible or on the lives of saints. In Britain these were usually performed by guilds (= associations of skilled workers in Britain in the Middle Ages) in the streets of towns. Miracle plays are still performed today in the towns of *York, *Chester, *Coventry and Wakefield in West Yorkshire.

the **Miˈranda deˌcision** /mɪˈrændə/ an important decision reached in 1966 by the US Supreme Court, affecting police procedures. It said that people who are arrested for a crime must be informed of their rights under the US Constitution. These are the right to remain silent and the right to have a lawyer. They must also be told that anything they say can be used against them in court. The name comes from the court case of *Miranda v State of Arizona*. See also DUE PROCESS OF LAW, FIFTH AMENDMENT.

MIRAS /ˈmaɪræs/ (*in full* **mortgage interest relief at source**) a British government system which allows people who have *mortgages not to pay *income tax on the interest they pay to the *building society or bank that lent them the money.

The ˈ***Mirror*** one of Britain's national daily newspapers, formerly called the *Daily Mirror*. It was started in 1903 by Alfred *Harmsworth, who later became Lord *Northcliffe, as a newspaper for women. At first it was not a success, but it became very successful when it was made the world's first daily newspaper with pictures. It suffered badly after being bought in 1984 by Robert *Maxwell. It presents political views that are generally left-wing. The paper has a *tabloid format (= size of page), and is considered to be part of the 'popular press', not one of the 'quality papers'. See also *SUNDAY MIRROR*. ⇨ article at NEWSPAPERS.

ˌ**Mirror Group ˈNewspapers** (*also* the **Mirror Group**) a large newspaper company in Britain which publishes *The *Mirror*, the **Sunday Mirror*, *The *People* and *The *Sporting Life*. Its main offices are in central London. It used to be owned by Robert *Maxwell.

MI6 /ˌem aɪ ˈsɪks/ the former name (still used, though not officially) of the British government department which operates abroad to gather secret information about other countries. MI6 is an abbreviation of Military Intelligence section 6. Like *MI5, its role changed in the early 1990s and its activities became much less secret. It is now called the Secret Intelligence Service.

the ˌ**Miss Aˈmerica ˌPageant** /əˈmerɪkə/ a US contest held each September in *Atlantic City, *New Jersey, to choose the most beautiful American woman who can also sing, dance, act, etc. It was first held in 1922 and has been a popular television event since 1954. The pageant has sometimes been criticized as an insult to women.

ˈMission Conˌtrol ⇨ LYNDON B JOHNSON SPACE CENTER.

ˌMissisˈsippi /ˌmɪsɪˈsɪpi/ a southern US state, also called the Magnolia State. Jackson is the largest city and also the capital city. Mississippi became a state in 1817 and was one of the *Confederate States. It has had conflicts between the races, especially in the 1960s. Its main product is cotton, but other crops include corn, peanuts and rice. Tourists can visit the Vicksburg National Military Park and the historical buildings at *Natchez(2).

ˌMissisˈsippi mud ˈpie /ˌmɪsɪˈsɪpi/ *n* a US sweet dish that is especially popular with *Cajuns. It is made of chocolate ice cream that is frozen on pastry and covered with meringue (= a mixture of egg whites and sugar baked until crisp).

the **ˌMississippi ˈRiver** /ˌmɪsɪsɪpi/ a major river of North America that flows from the US state of *Minnesota to the *Gulf of Mexico. It was called the 'Father of Waters' by *Native Americans. It is 2 348 miles/3 778 kilometres long and passes the cities of *Minneapolis, *St Louis, *Memphis and *New Orleans. The Missouri River is connected to it, and together they form the third largest river system in the world (3 741 miles/6 019 kilometres long). The Mississippi is an important transport route and is known for its 19th-century river boats. See also *OL' MAN RIVER*.

ˌMiss ˈLonelyhearts /ˈləʊnlihɑːts; *AmE* ˈloʊnlihɑːrts/ a novel (1933) by the US writer Nathanael *West. It was written during the *Great Depression and is about human suffering. It is the story of a journalist who uses the name Miss Lonelyhearts as the writer of a newspaper column giving advice to readers with personal problems. When he becomes too involved with one of his readers, he is killed. The expression *a lonelyhearts column* is now used to mean a regular newspaper feature dealing with people's personal problems.

Misˈsouri /mɪˈzʊəri; *AmE* mɪˈzʊri/ a US state in the *Middle West, also called the Show Me State and, in former times, the Mother of the West. The largest city is *Kansas City(1) and the capital city is Jefferson City. Missouri was part of the *Louisiana Purchase and became a state in 1821 under the *Missouri Compromise. Its products include grain, beer, coal and aerospace equipment. Among places visited by tourists are the Gateway Arch at *St Louis and the homes of President Harry S *Truman at *Independence and Mark *Twain at Hannibal.

the **Misˌsouri ˈCompromise** /mɪˌzʊəri; *AmE* mɪˌzʊri/ the general name for several US laws passed in 1820–1 to end disputes between slave states and free states. Both groups wanted new states to follow their systems. According to the Compromise, *Missouri joined the Union as a slave state and *Maine as a free state. It also declared that slaves would not be allowed in the northern part of the *Louisiana Purchase. It was replaced in 1854 by the *Kansas-Nebraska Act.

MIT /ˌem aɪ ˈtiː/ (*in full* **Massachusetts Institute of Technology**) a US university known especially for its science courses. It was established in 1861 in *Boston and moved in 1916 to *Cambridge, *Massachusetts, close to *Harvard University. In 1997 MIT had about 10 000 students.

ˌRobert ˈ**Mitchum** /ˈmɪtʃəm/ (1917–97) a US actor who often played tough characters. He was noted for his relaxed style and for not taking his work too seriously. He made more than 125 films but once said, 'Movies bore me, especially my own.' His films include *The Story of GI Joe* (1945), *The Night of the Hunter* (1955), *Ryan's Daughter* (1971) and *Farewell My Lovely* (1975), in which he played the character Philip *Marlowe.

ˈMitford /ˈmɪtfəd; *AmE* ˈmɪtfərd/ the family name of six sisters, four of whom became famous for various reasons.

Nancy Mitford (1904–73) wrote humorous novels about girls in *upper-class families, including *The Pursuit of Love* (1945) and *Love in a Cold Climate* (1949). In 1956 she wrote an article in which she used the expressions *U and *non-U to describe language and behaviour that was or was not acceptable to upper-class people, and these expressions became part of the language.

Jessica Mitford (1917–96) also became a writer, well known for her extreme left-wing political views. She wrote *Hons and Rebels* (1960) about the lives of herself and her sisters as children. She later lived in the US, where her books included *The American Way of Death* (1963), about the US funeral industry.

Diana Mitford (1916–) and **Unity Mitford** (1914–48) became known for their fascist sympathies. Diana married the English fascist leader Oswald *Mosley in 1936 and Unity became a close friend of Adolf Hitler.

ˌWalter ˈ**Mitty** /ˈmɪti/ the main character in a well-known story by James *Thurber, *The Secret Life of Walter Mitty* (1942). He escapes from his sad, ordinary life by imagining that he is a much more interesting person than he really is and does much more exciting and important things than he actually does. The name is now sometimes used of a person who lives in an imaginary world like this: *He's a real Walter Mitty character, daydreaming the whole time.*

ˌTom ˈ**Mix** /ˈmɪks/ (1880–1940) a US actor in more than 400 silent *westerns. He was the first 'King of the Cowboys' and was one of *Hollywood's richest actors in the 1920s. He wore white clothes and a white hat, and was an excellent rider. His films included *Riders of the Purple Sage* (1925) and *The Last Trail* (1927). Mix toured the country with his own circus in the 1930s. He died in a car crash.

M'lud /məˈlʌd/ the way a judge is addressed in a British court of law. It is a form of 'My Lord': *I wish to call another witness, M'lud.*

MM /ˌem ˈem/ ⇨ MILITARY MEDAL.

the ˌBattle of **MoˈbileˈBay** /məʊˈbiːl; *AmE* moʊˈbiːl/ a US Navy victory on 5 August 1864 during the American *Civil War. The US sent 18 ships against 4 ships of the Confederate Navy in Mobile Bay at Mobile, *Alabama. The bay was also protected by three forts and by containers filled with explosive (called 'torpedoes') that floated in the water. Admiral David Farragut led the successful US attack with the famous remark: 'Damn the torpedoes! Full speed ahead!'

ˌMoby-ˈDick /ˌməʊbi ˈdɪk; *AmE* ˌmoʊbi/ a famous novel about the sea (1851) by the US writer Herman *Melville. It is the story of Captain Ahab's strong desire to find and kill Moby-Dick, a great white whale that had once bitten off his leg. Many people remember the book's first words: 'Call me Ishmael.' Film versions were made in 1926 and 1930, both with John *Barrymore as Ahab, and in 1956, with Gregory *Peck.

ˈmockingbird *n* a bird that lives mostly in the southern US. It can copy the calls of other birds and even the sounds made by people, dogs and chickens. Many people believe it is morally wrong to kill one, and this idea was used in the novel **To Kill a Mockingbird*. It is also mentioned in several traditional songs and is the official state bird of *Arkansas, *Florida, *Mississippi, *Tennessee and *Texas.

MOD /ˌem əʊ ˈdiː; *AmE* oʊ/ ⇨ MINISTRY OF DEFENCE.

mod *n* a young person, especially in Britain in the 1960s, of a group following a fashion of smart modern clothes. Mods had short, neat hair, rode scooters (= small motorcycles) and liked *soul music. Their rivals were the *rockers. Large groups of mods and rockers used to gather at seaside towns on *bank holidays and fight each other.

the ˌ**Model** ˈ**Parliament** the name later given to the English parliament set up in 1295 by King *Edward I. It was the first to include not only members of the clergy and the *aristocracy but also elected members to represent ordinary people. In this way it established the pattern for future parliaments.

ˌ**Model** ˈ**T** /ˈtiː/ the first car produced on an assembly line (= a line of workers who build something as it moves along on a large belt) and sold at a price that ordinary people could afford. Its popular name was the 'Tin Lizzie' and it was made by the Ford Motor Comany between 1908 and 1927. There is a joke that Henry *Ford told customers they could have the car in any colour as long as it was black. About 15 million Model Ts were produced before it was replaced by the Model A.

ˈ**Moderator of the** ˈ**Church of** ˈ**Scotland** /ˈskɒtlənd; *AmE* ˈskɑːtlənd/ the minister elected to be president for one year of the *General Assembly of the Church of Scotland.

ˌ***Modern*** ˈ***Times*** a comedy film (1936) which Charlie *Chaplin wrote and directed as well as acting the main part. It was the last time he used his 'Little Tramp' character. The film is an attack on the use of machines in modern factories and the bad treatment of factory workers.

ˈ**Mohawk** /ˈməʊhɔːk; *AmE* ˈmoʊhɔːk/ *n* (*pl* **Mohawks** *or* **Mohawk**) a member of a *Native-American people who live mostly in New York State and Ontario, Canada. They were part of the *Iroquois League, and tradition says that *Hiawatha was their leader. They originally lived in New York State in the Mohawk Valley along the Mohawk River, and they helped the British during the *American Revolution. Mohawks are known today as excellent steel workers who help to construct skyscrapers (= very tall buildings).

the **Moˌjave** ˈ**Desert** (*also* **Mohave Desert**) /məʊˌhɑːvi; *AmE* moʊˌhɑːvi/ a desert in south-eastern *California consisting of low, bare hills and wide, flat valleys. Its area is about 15 000 square miles/38 850 square kilometres. *Death Valley is at the northern end and the Joshua Tree National Monument at the southern end. The Mojave Desert is part of the Great Basin region that covers parts of California, *Nevada, *Utah, *Oregon and *Idaho.

ˌAdrian ˈ**Mole** /ˈməʊl; *AmE* ˈmoʊl/ the main character in a series of books by the English writer Sue Townsend. He is a teenage boy and the books are in the form of his diary, in which he describes his life, thoughts and problems. They became very popular because they describe in a humorous way the attitudes and worries typical of boys of that age. The books are *The Secret Diary of Adrian Mole – Aged 13¾* (1982), *The Growing Pains of Adrian Mole* (1984) and *The Wilderness Years* (1993), in which Adrian has become an adult. The original book was also made into a stage *musical.

ˌ***Moll*** ˈ***Flanders*** /ˌmɒl ˈflɑːndəz; *AmE* ˌmɑːl ˈflændərz/ a novel (1722) by Daniel *Defoe. The full title is *The Fortunes and Misfortunes of the Famous Moll Flanders*. It takes the form of an autobiography in which Moll Flanders looks back on a life full of adventures, with many marriages and love affairs, as well as time spent in prison for various crimes.

MOMA /ˈməʊmə; *AmE* ˈmoʊmə/ ⇨ MUSEUM OF MODERN ART.

ˌ**mom-and-**ˈ**pop** *adj* [only before *n*] (*AmE old-fash infml*) (of a small business, etc.) owned and operated by a small family, often just a married couple: *a mom-and-pop café/stand/store.*

MOMI /ˈməʊmi; *AmE* ˈmoʊmi/ ⇨ MUSEUM OF THE MOVING IMAGE.

The ˌ***Monarch of the*** ˈ***Glen*** (1851) the best-known painting by the English artist Edwin *Landseer. It is of an adult male deer in the Scottish countryside, and is often reproduced on cards and other products.

the ˈ**Monday Club** a club formed in 1961 by right-wing members of the British *Conservative Party. Some of its views, especially those concerning immigration into Britain, have been controversial. Its name comes from the fact that its meetings were originally held on Mondays.

ˈ**Monday** ˈ**morning** ˈ**quarterback** /ˈkwɔːtəbæk; *AmE* ˈkwɔːtərbæk/ *n* (*AmE rather disapprov*) a person who gives opinions and criticism about events, decisions, etc. only after they have happened. The expression comes from the fact that most US professional football games are on a Sunday, and people only get together to discuss them on the following day. A quarterback is the football player who makes decisions for his team during a game.

ˌ***Monday Night*** ˈ***Football*** a US television programme on *ABC which shows a professional football game each Monday night during the National Football League season. It began in 1970 and is the oldest evening sports programme on US television and the most popular, with an audience of 50 million.

Money ⇨ article.

ˌ***Monitor*** and ˈ***Merrimack*** /ˈmerimæk/ two ships during the American *Civil War that fought the first battle in history between 'ironclads' (= ships covered with iron). The battle was on 9 March 1862 at Hampton Roads, a channel of water in *Virginia. There was no clear result, showing that such ships were no longer useful in war.

TheˌIonious ˈ**Monk** /θəˌləʊniəs ˈmʌŋk; *AmE* θəˌloʊniəs/ (1917–82) an *African-American *jazz musician who played the piano and wrote music. He led a big band in the 1960s and helped to develop modern jazz. His albums include *Alone in San Francisco* (1959) and *Monk's Dream* (1962). He was chosen for the Jazz *Hall of Fame in 1963.

The ˈ***Monkees*** /ˈmʌŋkiːz/ a US television comedy and music series on *NBC (1966–70). The Monkees were a pop group created for television as a copy of the *Beatles. Their most successful records included *Last Train to Clarksville, I'm A Believer* and *Daydream Believer.*

the ˌDuke of ˈ**Monmouth** /ˈmɒnməθ; *AmE* ˈmɑːnməθ/ (*born* James Scott 1649–85) an illegitimate son of *Charles II who became a *duke in 1663. He was a Protestant, and powerful people who were against the idea of the Roman Catholic Duke of York (Charles II's brother and later King *James II) becoming king after Charles II supported him as Charles II's heir. Charles, however, wanted his brother to become king after him. A short time after James did become king, in 1685, the Duke of Monmouth started a rebellion but received little support. He was defeated at the Battle of *Sedgemoor and had his head cut off. His supporters were very harshly treated by Judge *Jeffreys at the *Bloody Assizes.

the **Moˌnopolies and** ˈ**Mergers Comˌmission**

Money

Dollars

The US **dollar** is made up of 100 **cents**. The *Department of the Treasury prints **bills** (= paper money) in various **denominations** (= values): $1, $2, $5, $10, $20, $50 and $100. US bills are all the same size, whatever their value, and measure about 2×6 inches (6.5×15.5 centimetres). All are green and so are sometimes called **greenbacks**. On the front, each has the picture of a famous American. The **dollar bill**, for instance, shows George *Washington, the first US president. An informal name for dollars is **bucks**, because in the early period of US history people traded the skins of bucks (= deer) and prices would sometimes be given as a number of buckskins. *Buck* refers to the dollar itself, and not to the bill. So although you can say: 'He earns 500 bucks a week', you have to say 'If I give you four quarters could you give me a dollar bill?'.

The Treasury also makes US coins: **pennies** which are worth .01 of a dollar, **nickels** (.05), **dimes** (.10) and **quarters** (.25). There are also **half-dollars** (.50) and **silver dollars** but these are not often seen. Pennies have a dark brown colour; all the other coins have a silver appearance.

When you write an amount in figures the **dollar sign ($)** goes to the left of the amount and a decimal point (.) is placed between the dollars and the **cents** (= hundredths of a dollar). If the amount is less than one dollar, the **cent sign (¢)** is put after the numbers. So you write $5, $5.62, and 62¢.

Pounds

Britain's currency is the **pound sterling**, written as **£** before a figure. A pound consists of 100 **pence**, written as **p** with figures. Pound coins are round and gold-coloured. They have the Queen's head on one side and one of four designs, English, Scottish, Welsh or Northern Irish, on the other. The £2 coin is silver-coloured with a gold edge. Coins of lower value are the silver-coloured 50p, 20p, 10p and 5p **pieces**, and the copper-coloured 2p and 1p pieces. All are round, except for the 50p and 20p pieces which have seven curved sides. Coins are made at the *Royal Mint. Paper **notes** (not *bills*), which have the Queen's head on one side and a famous person, e.g. Charles *Dickens, on the other, are worth £5, £10, £20 or £50.

A pound is informally called a **quid**, a £5 note is a **fiver**, and a £10 note is a **tenner**. Scottish **banknotes** have their own designs. They can be used anywhere in Britain, though shops can legally refuse to accept them. To prevent people **forging** (= making their own) paper money, designs are complicated and difficult to copy. To check that a note is genuine, a shop assistant may hold it up to the light to see if it has a narrow silver thread running through it.

The **decimal system** now in use in Britain replaced the old **pounds, shillings and pence**, or *LSD, system in 1971. Formerly there were 12 pence or **pennies** in a **shilling** and 20 shillings in a pound. Many people regretted the loss of the old system and for many years translated decimal prices into **old money**. The old coins included the **farthing** (= a quarter of a penny), the **halfpenny** or **ha'penny** (= half a penny), the **threepenny bit** (= threepence), the '**tanner**' (= sixpence), the '**bob**' (= one shilling), the **two-shilling piece**, or **florin**, and the **half-crown** (= two-and-a-half shillings). There were notes for 10 shillings, £1 and £5. Amounts were written as £2. 7s. 6d (*d* is the abbreviation of *denarius*, a small Roman coin), 5/- (or 5shs), and 3d.

Gold **guinea** coins were used in the 18th century and were worth 21 shillings. Until 1971 prices were often set in guineas instead of pounds for luxury items, such as fur coats, for the fees of doctors, lawyers, etc., and at auctions, though the guinea coin had long since gone **out of circulation**. Some racehorses are still auctioned in guineas.

On 1 January 1999 the ***euro** was introduced in the 11 countries of the *European Union which supported monetary union. Britain chose not to be part of this group. However, many British businesses which trade with countries in 'Euroland' have opened euro bank acounts so as to be able to pay for goods and be paid in euros. A euro is worth about 72p ($1.2). Euro banknotes and coins will not be in circulation until 2002.

Spending money

People now pay less often **in cash** or even **by cheque** for goods. Most use ***credit cards** or **debit cards**, informally called '**plastic**', for anything that costs more than a few dollars or pounds. Credit cards are **swiped** (= passed through an electronic device that reads them) if the owner is present. But people can also give their card details over the telephone or the Internet. Some people worry about this in case somebody finds out the number and uses it dishonestly. **Cash** or **change** is still needed to buy small items, put in parking meters, etc. A few older people prefer to keep money in their house, traditionally under the bed, rather than put it in a *bank.

British people rarely **haggle** (= negotiate the price of something) and almost always pay the full price. They find it embarrassing to haggle even when in a country where this custom is widely accepted. But some find it fun and, like all British people, love to believe they have bought a **bargain** (= something costing less than it is worth).

Americans like to choose how much to spend on things. They look for **discount stores** and **outlet malls** (= shops that have low prices all the time), wait to buy something until it is **on sale** (= the price is reduced for a period), or use **coupons** (= special advertisements that give money off products if they are handed over when the items are bought).

People have mixed feelings about money and its importance. Many older people, who had less money and fewer possessions when they were younger, believe that *society has become too materialistic (= attaching more value to money and possessions than to moral values). Younger people worry less about the negative influence of money and point out that, in the words of a popular song, 'Money makes the world go round'. Americans especially see money as powerful but dangerous and they believe the phrase 'money talks' (= if you have enough money, people pay attention to you), but also that 'the love of money is the root of all evil'.

an independent organization set up by the British government in 1948 to prevent unfair trading when single companies have so great a share of the supply of particular goods or services in Britain that there is little or no competition. The Commission investigates cases in which one company takes over another or when two companies join together. It then reports to the government, which may or may not do what it recommends.

Mo'nopoly™ one of the most popular and successful board games ever produced. Players throw dice and move their pieces round a board, buying and building houses on streets that are marked on it. They then charge the other players rent if they land on the streets that they have bought. Players use artificial money and the winner is the player who has all the money at the end.

The game was invented by Charles Darrow in the US in 1933 and the original version used the names of streets in *Atlantic City, *New Jersey. The British version uses London streets, and there are other versions of the game in other countries.

The expression *Monopoly money* is sometimes used to refer in a humorous way to a sum of money that is considered much too high: *Some football clubs pay Monopoly money for players.*

ˌJames **Mon'roe¹** /mən'rəʊ; *AmE* mən'roʊ/ (1758–1831) the fifth US *President. He is best remembered for the *Monroe Doctrine, which aimed to keep new European interests out of the Americas. He fought in the *American Revolution and helped to establish the Democratic Republican Party. He was elected as a US Senator (1790–4) and twice as governor of *Virginia (1799–1802 and 1811). His time as President was called the 'Era of Good Feeling'. He bought *Florida from Spain in 1819, settled a dispute with Britain over the US-Canadian border, and signed the *Missouri Compromise. See also DEMOCRATIC PARTY.

ˌMarilyn **Mon'roe²** /mən'rəʊ; *AmE* mən'roʊ/ (1926–62) a US actor who became *Hollywood's most famous sex symbol, though she was often unhappy. Her films include *Niagara* (1952), *Gentlemen Prefer Blondes* (1953), *The Seven Year Itch* (1954), *Bus Stop* (1956), *The Prince and the Showgirl* (1957), *Some Like It Hot* (1959) and *The Misfits* (1961). Her second and third husbands were the *baseball player Joe *DiMaggio and the writer Arthur *Miller. Many books and films have told her story, and the original version of Elton *John's song *Candle in the Wind* was about her. She died, perhaps accidentally, after taking too much medicine to help her sleep. Many people believe she had love affairs with President *Kennedy⁴ and his brother Robert *Kennedy.

the **Monˌroe 'Doctrine** /mənˌrəʊ; *AmE* mənˌroʊ/ a declaration of US foreign policy made in 1823 by President James *Monroe. It is one of the most important policies in US history. Monroe said the US would oppose any new European attempts to control countries in the Americas but it would not interfere with European interests already there. The British, who were well established in the New World, supported this. President Theodore *Roosevelt added in 1904 that the US might have to become involved in problems in other American nations. President Franklin *Roosevelt, however, introduced the *Good Neighbor Policy which said American nations should work together as equal partners. Though the US has been involved in some military and political actions in Latin America, this is still the official US policy.

the ˌBattle of '**Mons** /'mɒnz; *AmE* 'mɑːnz/ (1914) the first big battle of *World War I, fought in August 1914 near the Belgian town of Mons. The British soldiers managed to resist the attacks of much larger German forces for a time before being forced back.

the **'Monster 'Raving 'Loony ˌParty** a small and not serious political party established by *Screaming Lord Sutch in Britain in the 1960s. It has attracted a lot of publicity during elections because of its strange policies and the humorous appearance of its candidates. Before the general election of 1997 it had a candidate in every election and *by-election. Its policies originally concerned rights for young people and some young people have voted for it, either as a joke or because they did not support any of the main political parties. Its candidates have in fact won in some local elections.

Mon'tana¹ /mɒn'tænə; *AmE* mɑːn'tænə/ a large state in the north-western US, on the Canadian border. The capital city is Helena, and the largest city is Billings. Montana became a state in 1889, and is also called the Treasure State. It produces many minerals, and its mines once supplied half of all US copper. It also produces grain, potatoes, sheep and cattle. Montana's tourist attractions include the *Rocky Mountains, *Yellowstone National Park, the Glacier National Park and the Custer Battlefield National Monument.

ˌJoe **Mon'tana²** /mɒn'tænə; *AmE* mɑːn'tænə/ (1956–) a US professional football player with the San Francisco 49ers. He was captain of the team when they won four *Super Bowls (in 1982, 1985, 1989 and 1990). He was also the National Football League's *Most Valuable Player in 1989. After 16 years with San Francisco, Montana played briefly with the Kansas City Chiefs.

'Monterey /'mɒntəreɪ; *AmE* 'mɑːntəreɪ/ a US city on the coast of *California. It is one of the oldest cities in the state and was the Spanish capital of Alta California (1775–1846) until the US Navy captured it. The famous Monterey Jazz Festival has been held there every September since 1958. The Monterey area is popular with artists and attracts many tourists.

ˌSimon de **'Montfort** /də 'mɒntfət; *AmE* də 'mɑːntfərt/ (*c.* 1208–65) an English politician and soldier, the leader of the *barons who opposed *Henry III. After being defeated in battle in 1264, he lost the support of the other barons because he wanted to rule the country himself. In 1265, he appointed himself head of government and formed his own parliament in London. The same year he was killed when fighting at the Battle of Evesham against an army led by Henry III's son, who later became *Edward I.

Mont'gomery¹ /mənt'gʌməri/ the capital city of the US state of *Alabama. It is on the Alabama River, and is sometimes called the 'Cradle of the Confederacy' because the city was also the first capital of the *Confederate States. Martin Luther *King began the US *civil rights movement in Montgomery when he led an *African-American refusal to use the buses there. See also PARKS.

'Field ˌMarshal **Mont'gomery²** /mənt'gʌməri/ (Bernard Law Montgomery 1887–1976) perhaps the most well-known British military leader in *World War II, particularly because of his victory when leading the 8th Army against the German forces commanded by Rommel at the Battle of *El Alamein in 1942. The victory at El Alamein was the first major success for the *Allies in the war. It made Montgomery a national hero and did much to make the British forces and people believe that victory in the war as a whole was possible.

In 1944 Montgomery commanded the British forces in northern Europe after the *Normandy landings. However, the Allies at this time were commanded by General *Eisenhower, and Montgomery did not get on well with him or like the fact that Eisenhower was senior to him.

Montgomery was known by his men and the British public as 'Monty' and always recognized because he wore a beret (= military cap) with two badges on it. He had a strong personality and was very popular with his men. He was made a *knight in 1942 and a *viscount(1) in 1946.

ˌ**Monti'cello** /ˌmɒntɪ'tʃeləʊ; *AmE* ˌmɑːntɪ'tʃeloʊ/ the home of US President Thomas *Jefferson, on a hill near Charlottesville, *Virginia. Jefferson himself designed it in the *neoclassical style, and it was completed in 1809. He lived there for 56 years and is buried there. It became a National Shrine in 1926 and a *World Heritage Site in 1987. The image of Monticello is on one side of the US nickel (= 5-cent coin) and Jefferson's head is on the other side.

Thomas Jefferson's home at Monticello

'**Montserrat** /'mɒnsəræt; *AmE* 'mɑːnsəræt/ a small island in the *Caribbean Sea. It became a British colony in 1632 and is now a British *overseas territory. Its main town is Plymouth. The island has a volcano which in 1996–7 sent out clouds of ash and melted rock, forcing many people to leave their homes. Many of these people claimed that the British government had not done enough to help them after the disaster.

'***Monty*** '***Python's*** '***Flying*** '***Circus*** /'mɒnti 'paɪθənz; *AmE* 'mɑːnti/ a *BBC television comedy series (1969–74). It was extremely popular with young people, especially students, and its strange, wild and silly humour had a big influence on British comedy. It consisted of sketches (= short comic plays) with no logical connection. Among the most well-known of these are the *dead parrot sketch and the Ministry of Silly Walks. It was written and performed by a team of people who had met at Oxford or Cambridge Universities. Today the most famous of these are John *Cleese and Michael *Palin. After the television series, the team wrote and acted in several successful comedy films.

the '**Monument** a stone column in central London set up in memory of the *Great Fire of London in 1666. It was designed by Christopher *Wren and built in 1671–7. Its height (202 feet/61.5 metres) is believed to be the distance from the column to the place where the fire started. There are 311 steps up it, which visitors can climb.

'Helen 'Wills '**Moody** /'wɪlz 'muːdi/ (1906–98) a US tennis player in the 1920s and 1930s who was the best woman player of her time. Her popular name was 'Queen Helen'. She won eight *Wimbledon competitions (1927–30, 1932–3 and 1938), which remained a record for 52 years. Her total of 31 competition victories included the *US Open(2) seven times and the French Open four times. She also won a Gold Medal at the 1924 Olympics. Before she was married in 1929, she played as Helen Wills. She was chosen for the International Tennis *Hall of Fame in 1959.

'**Moonie** /'muːni/ *n* (*infml*) a member of the *Unification Church, a religious group started by the Korean businessman Sun Myung Moon. Many people are worried about the way in which Moonies are persuaded to leave their families to join the Church.

The '***Moonstone*** /'muːnstəʊn; *AmE* 'muːnstoʊn/ a novel (1868) by Wilkie *Collins. It is generally regarded one of the first English *detective novels. The moonstone of the title is a large diamond which disappears. The crime is solved by Sergeant Cuff.

ˌBobby '**Moore[1]** /'mɔː(r)/ (1941–93) one of the most famous English football players of all time, especially because he was captain of the England team which won the World Cup in 1966. For most of his career he played for the London club *West Ham (1958–74). In 1963, at the age of 22, he became the youngest ever England captain. In all he played for England 108 times.

DeˌmiˈMoore[2]** /dəˌmiː 'mɔː(r)/ (1962–) a US actor who became *Hollywood's highest paid female actor when she earned $12 million for *Striptease* (1996). Her other films include *Ghost* (1990), *Indecent Proposal* (1993) and *GI Jane* (1997). She was formerly married to the actor Bruce *Willis.

Demi Moore in Striptease

ˌDudley '**Moore[3]** /'mɔː(r)/ (1935–) an English comedian, actor and musician, now living in the US. He first became known as one of the performers in **Beyond the Fringe* and then as the partner of Peter *Cook in several popular television comedy series in the 1960s and 1970s, including *Not Only But Also* (1965–71). In the late 1970s he became a film star in comedy films such as *10* (1979) and *Arthur* (1980). He is also well-known as a pianist, playing *jazz and classical music in concerts and on television.

ˌHenry '**Moore[4]** /'mɔː(r)/ (1898–1986) an English sculptor with an international reputation. He was best-known for his very large sculptures, made from stone, wood or bronze (= a mixture of copper and tin) and with smooth curves. In these, the human figure is meant to be seen as part of the surroundings in which the sculpture is placed. Many of his sculptures are in public places.

a bronze sculpture by Henry Moore

ˌMarianne '**Moore[5]** /ˌmæriæn 'mɔː(r)/ (1887–1972) a US poet, known for her clever and intellectual poetry, who won the *Pulitzer Prize for *Collected Poems* (1952). Her other collections included *Poems* (1921), *Observations* (1924) and *Complete Poems* (1967).

ˈMary ˈTyler ˈ**Moore**[6] /ˈtaɪlə(r) ˈmɔː(r)/ (1936–) a US comic actor who had her own popular television series, *The Mary Tyler Moore Show*, on *CBS (1970–7). The show, in which she played a television journalist, won three *Emmy awards (1973–4 and 1976). She was later in the television series *Mary* (1986), *Annie McGuire* (1989) and *New York News* (1995). Moore's films include *Ordinary People* (1980) and *Flirting with Disaster* (1996).

ˌPatrick ˈ**Moore**[7] /ˈmɔː(r)/ (1923–) an English writer and broadcaster on astronomy He has presented every programme in the television series *The *Sky at Night* since it began in 1957. Moore is regarded with affection in Britain because of his rather strange manner. He speaks very fast, has untidy hair and often wears a monocle.

ˈ**Moorfields** /ˈmɔːfiːldz; *AmE* ˈmɔːrfiːldz/ a hospital in central London, England, which specializes in eye treatment. It opened in 1805.

the ˌ**Moors** ˈ**murders** /ˌmɔːz; *AmE* ˌmʊrz/ the name given to one of the most famous and terrible crimes in Britain in the 20th century. In the early 1960s Ian Brady and Myra *Hindley tortured and murdered several children, who they photographed and recorded while they were carrying out the crimes. They then buried the bodies on moors near *Manchester. In 1966 they were both sent to prison for life and they are still in prison.

ˌ**Moral Re-ˈArmament** (*abbr* **MRA**) a Christian movement begun in 1938 by the US *evangelist Frank Buchman (1878–1961). He developed it from his Oxford Group established during a visit to Britain in 1921. The movement, which was especially active in the 1950s and 1960s, aimed to encourage high moral standards of behaviour, based on God's will as interpreted by Buchman. It was strongly opposed to Communism and homosexuality.

ˌThomas ˈ**More** /ˈmɔː(r)/ (1478–1535) an English politician, author and scholar. He became a friend of King *Henry VIII,who first employed him as a representative in foreign countries. In 1518 More became a member of the *Privy Council, in 1521 he was made a *knight, and in 1529 he became *Lord Chancellor after Cardinal *Wolsey. However, when the king decided that he, and not the Pope, was the head of the Church in England, More refused to accept this decision. For this he was put in prison and then executed. He was made a saint in 1935.

Thomas More was also the author of *Utopia* (1516), in which he described his ideas of a perfect society. It was very successful all over Europe.

ˌ**Morecambe and ˈWise** /ˌmɔːkəm, ˈwaɪz; *AmE* ˌmɔːrkəm/ **Eric Morecambe** (1926–84) and **Ernie Wise** (1925–99), a pair of English television comedians who were very popular in the 1960s and 1970s. Their shows attracted extremely large audiences, particularly on Christmas Day, and they were popular with all sections of the public. Well-known people often appeared on the shows as guests and were made to look ridiculous. Eric made the jokes and Ernie was the serious one who the jokes were often about. Several of their catchphrases became widely used in Britain and their shows are often repeated on British television.

ˈ**Morgan**™[1] /ˈmɔːgən; *AmE* ˈmɔːrgən/ a type of sports car made by the small British car company Morgan and first produced in 1935. All models have a wooden frame and each car takes a long time to make. As a result, customers have to wait for as long as 4 years to receive cars they have ordered.

ˌHenry ˈ**Morgan**[2] /ˈmɔːgən; *AmE* ˈmɔːrgən/ (*c.* 1635–88) a Welsh sailor and pirate who operated mainly in the *Caribbean. In 1671 he fought against the Spanish and in 1674 he captured Panama. The same year he was made a *knight.

ˌJ ˈPierpoint ˈ**Morgan**[3] /ˈpɪəpɔɪnt ˈmɔːgən; *AmE* ˈpɪərpɔɪnt ˈmɔːrgən/ (John Pierpoint Morgan 1837–1913) a powerful US industrial leader and financier who established the United States Steel Corporation and had interests in many other areas of business, including railways and shipping. Morgan had become a partner in his father's bank in 1871 and in 1895 he named it J P Morgan and Company. He gave his large art collection to New York's *Museum of Modern Art.

MORI /ˈmɒri; *AmE* ˈmɔːri/ (*in full* **Market and Opinion Research International**) a British/US organization that carries out public opinion polls (= asks specially chosen groups of people certain questions, e.g. about political issues). It was established in 1969.

Proˌfessor **Moriˈarty** /mɒriˈɑːti; *AmE* mɔːriˈɑːrti/ a character in the Sherlock *Holmes stories by Arthur *Conan Doyle. He is the clever but evil enemy of Sherlock Holmes. In a story published in 1894 both of them fall to their deaths after a fight on a cliff path, though Conan Doyle later brought Holmes 'back to life' by writing that he had survived the fall. This was because the public was so keen for more Holmes stories.

ˈ**Mormon** /ˈmɔːmən; *AmE* ˈmɔːrmən/ *n* a member of the Christian religion called the *Church of Jesus Christ of Latter-Day Saints. It was established in the US in New York State in 1830 by Joseph *Smith. Its members later moved west, led by Brigham *Young, to establish *Salt Lake City and the state of *Utah. Their centre is still in Salt Lake City, and most people in Utah are Mormons. The church has about 10 million members, and they are well known in many countries for visiting people in their homes to talk about their religion. Mormons have strict moral rules and do not drink alcohol or even coffee. At one time Mormon men were allowed to have more than one wife, but the Church stopped this in 1890.

the ˌ***Morning*** ˈ***Star*** ⇨ *DAILY WORKER*.

ˈ**Morris**™[1] /ˈmɒrɪs; *AmE* ˈmɔːrɪs/ a British car company started in 1912 near Oxford by William Morris, later Lord *Nuffield. The first car it produced was the Morris Oxford, which was very popular. It also produced *MG cars. In 1949 the company began production of the *Morris Minor, which became one of the most popular cars in Britain for many years. In 1959 it began producing the *Mini, with even greater success. In the 1950s the company combined with *Austin to form the British Motor Corporation, which later became part of *British Leyland.

ˌDesmond ˈ**Morris**[2] /ˈmɒrɪs; *AmE* ˈmɔːrɪs/ (1928–) an English zoologist (= person who studies animals) and anthropologist. He has written several very successful books of popular science, including *The *Naked Ape* (1967) and *The Human Zoo* (1968). In these he argues that the behaviour of animals is similar to that of human beings. Some of his more recent work has been about body language (= the way in which people's movements indicate something about their personalities and feelings). Several of his books have been made into television series.

ˌWilliam ˈ**Morris**[3] /ˈmɒrɪs; *AmE* ˈmɔːrɪs/ (1834–96) an English designer, artist, poet, businessman and socialist. As an artist and poet he was influenced by the *Pre-Raphaelites but he is best known as a designer of furniture and decoration for houses. He disliked the mass production methods of his time and wanted the role of the traditional craftsman to continue. He established his own company which produced hand-made furniture and interior decoration using traditional methods. Many of these designs, especially for wallpaper and fabrics, are still used today. His belief in traditional methods led to Morris to become much involved in the *Arts and Crafts Movement. He also started the *Kelmscott Press to continue traditional methods of printing.

As one of the early socialists in Britain, Morris was a supporter of social change and formed his own Socialist League in 1884. He led his own campaigns on the streets against what he saw as the terrible effects of the *Industrial Revolution on workers.

The Strawberry Thief, a design by William Morris

ˈmorris dance /ˈmɒrɪs; *AmE* ˈmɔːrɪs/ *n* a type of old English dance traditionally performed by men wearing special (usually white) costumes, often with small bells around their legs below the knee. Dances from some parts of Britain involve waving handkerchiefs, and in others the dancers knock sticks together. Morris dances are usually performed outdoors in the summer. Women now also sometimes take part. ⇨ note at FOLK DANCING. ▶ **morris dancer** *n*, **morris dancing** *n* [U].

morris dancers

ˌ**Morris ˈMinor**™ /ˈmɒrɪs ˈmaɪnə(r); *AmE* ˈmɔːrɪs ˈmaɪnər/ a popular small British car designed by Alec Issigonis (1906–88) and produced by the *Morris company from 1949. The **Morris Minor Traveller** model had a partly wooden frame, an unusual feature in a relatively cheap car. Morris Minors are no longer produced but old ones are often carefully looked after by their owners and can be valuable.

ˌHerbert ˈ**Morrison**¹ /ˈmɒrɪsn; *AmE* ˈmɔːrɪsn/ (1888–1965) a British *Labour Party politician who held several senior government positions. As Minister of Transport, he established *London Transport in 1931. During *World War II, he was *Home Secretary and from 1945 to 1951 he was *Leader of the House of Commons. He was *Foreign Secretary for a short period in 1951 and deputy leader of the Party from 1951 to 1955.

ˌJim ˈ**Morrison**² /ˈmɒrɪsn; *AmE* ˈmɔːrɪsn/ (1943–71) a US singer who led the rock group The *Doors. He led a wild life involving too much sex, drugs and alcohol, and was arrested several times. He left the band in 1971 to live in Paris and died there in his bath, though some people believe he is still alive.

ˌToni ˈ**Morrison**³ /ˌtəʊni ˈmɒrɪsn; *AmE* ˌtoʊni ˈmɔːrɪsn/ (1931–) an *African-American woman writer, the first to win a *Nobel Prize (in 1993). She studied at *Harvard University and has taught there as well as at *Princeton and *Yale Universities. Her novels are mostly about African-American life in the southern countryside. They include *The Bluest Eye* (1970), *Song of Solomon* (1977), *Beloved* (1987), which won the *Pulitzer Prize, *Jazz* (1992) and *Paradise* (1998).

ˌVan ˈ**Morrison**⁴ /ˌvæn ˈmɒrɪsn; *AmE* ˌvæn ˈmɔːrɪsn/ (1945–) a Northern Irish singer and writer of songs who has been popular since the 1960s. His first album, *Astral Weeks* (1968), is still regarded as a one of the best popular music albums ever produced. His music has used influences from *Celtic culture, *blues, *gospel music, *jazz and *country music, and he is considered to have a very individual style.

ˈ**Morrissey** /ˈmɒrɪsi; *AmE* ˈmɔːrɪsi/ (Steven Morrissey 1959–) ⇨ SMITHS.

Inˌspector ˈ**Morse**¹ ⇨ INSPECTOR MORSE.

ˌSamuel ˈ**Morse**² /ˈmɔːs; *AmE* ˈmɔːrs/ (1791–1872) an American who invented the telegraph (= a device for sending messages on electric wires) and **Morse code**, a special 'alphabet' in which letters are represented by a series of short and long radio signals or flashes of light (*dots* and *dashes*). His first public message, sent in Morse code from *Baltimore to *Washington, DC on 24 May 1844, was 'What hath God wrought!' His inventions were important to communication during the *Civil War.

Le ˌ***Morte*** ˈ***d'Arthur*** /lə ˌmɔːt ˈdɑːθə(r); *AmE* lə ˌmɔːrt ˈdɑːrθər/ stories from *Arthurian legend, written by Thomas *Malory around 1470 when he was in prison, and printed by *Caxton in 1485. It is considered to be the first great work of English prose.

mortgages

Houses are expensive to buy and few people have enough money of their own. Most people have to **take out a mortgage**, a type of loan. In Britain people usually get a mortgage from a **bank** or a ***building society**; in the US they get one from a bank or a ***savings and loan association**. People borrow as much as 95% of the total price of the house and pay the rest themselves. Mortgages are paid back in fixed monthly payments over a period ranging from 15 to 30 years. The person borrowing the money has to pay **interest** on the loan, so that the final amount paid is considerably more than the amount of the loan itself. The **security** for the loan is the house itself. If a borrower fails to **keep up payments**, the house may be **repossessed** by the bank or building society and sold so that the bank can get its money back. In Britain over 30 000 houses were repossessed in 1997.

There are several kinds of mortgage. With a **repayment mortgage** the borrower's monthly payments go partly towards paying back the loan and partly towards the interest on it. In an **endowment mortgage**, borrowers pay interest on the loan to the bank or building society and a fixed sum towards an endowment policy, a type of insurance policy which will pay a large sum of money at a future date and will be used to repay the loan. Banks, building societies and savings and loan associations offer a range of special deals to attract customers. In Britain borrowers who pay income tax are entitled to **mortgage interest relief**, a scheme whereby they pay less income tax on the interest paid for the money they borrowed.

For many people, paying back a mortgage is their greatest financial burden. People talk of being 'mortgaged up to the hilt', meaning that their mortgage payments leave them with little money for anything else. If the owner of a house needs to borrow money he or she may decide to take out a **second mortgage** on the house, a practice also called **remortgaging**. This mortgage is usually much more expensive than the first. The organization lending the money is given certain rights over the property until the mortgage is **redeemed** (= paid off).

In Britain in the 1980s house prices rose very fast and then fell again. Some people who had bought a house when prices were high became victims of **negative equity**. *Equity* means the actual value of a house, and *negative equity* means a situation in which the value of a house falls below the amount borrowed as a mortgage. This makes it impossible to sell the house without making a loss.

When Americans finish paying their mortgage they may celebrate with a **mortgage-burning party**.

ˌ'Jelly Roll' '**Morton** /ˌdʒeli rəʊl 'mɔːtn; *AmE* roʊl 'mɔːrtn/ (1885–1941) a US *jazz piano player who is regarded as the first great writer of jazz music. He helped to develop *ragtime into New Orleans jazz. He was born Ferdinand Joseph La Menthe Morton in *New Orleans. He formed a band, the Red Hot Peppers, in 1926 and made many recordings with them. His works include *Jelly Roll Blues* (1905) and *Black Bottom Stomp* (1925). In 1998 Morton was chosen for the Rock and Roll *Hall of Fame as a person who had influenced that type of music.

ˌGrandma '**Moses** ⇨ GRANDMA MOSES.

ˌOswald '**Mosley** /'məʊzli; *AmE* 'moʊzli/ (1896–1980) an English politician who left the *Labour Party in 1931 to form and lead the British Union of Fascists. (He had previously also been a *Conservative and an Independent *Member of Parliament.) The policies of his own party reflected his admiration of the Nazis, and its members became increasingly violent and anti-Semitic. In 1936 Mosley married Diana *Mitford. They were both kept in prison between 1940 and 1943, during *World War II. Mosley himself had become a *baronet in 1928.

Oswald Mosley speaking at a meeting in Hyde Park

Mos'quito /mə'skiːtəʊ; *AmE* mə'skiːtoʊ/ *n* (*pl* **-toes**) a British plane used by the *Royal Air Force between 1941 and 1955. It was used both for dropping bombs and for fighting enemy aircraft during *World War II. It could fly more than 1 500 miles/2 412 kilometres without needing more fuel.

ˌStirling '**Moss** /ˌstɜːlɪŋ 'mɒs; *AmE* ˌstɜːrlɪŋ 'mɔːs/ (1929–) a very successful English racing driver. Although he never became world champion, he won 16 Grand Prix races before an accident ended his career in 1962. His name is still the one many older British people think of first when asked to mention a famous racing driver.

'**Moss Bros**™ /'mɒs; *AmE* 'mɔːs/ a British clothing company that is famous for hiring formal clothes to men for weddings, etc. It started in 1881: *I've taken the suit back to Moss Bros.*

ˌ**Moss 'Side** /ˌmɒs; *AmE* ˌmɔːs/ an area of *Manchester, England, which was badly affected by the high level of unemployment in Britain in the 1970s and 1980s. It is still a violent area with a lot of crime, much of it related to drugs.

ˌ**Most 'Valuable 'Player** (*abbr* **MVP**) (in some US sports) the award and name given to the best player in a game or series of games or during a particular season. The best known are in *football, *baseball and *basketball. The players given the award are usually chosen by sports journalists: *Larry Brown was the MVP for the 1996 Super Bowl.* Compare MAN OF THE MATCH.

MOT /ˌem əʊ 'tiː; *AmE* oʊ/ *n* (*infml*) (*in full* the **Ministry of Transport test**) (in Britain) an official test carried out on a car to make sure that it is safe to drive. Any car over three years old must have the test once a year. If the car passes the test, a certificate is given; if not, repairs must be carried out. It is illegal to drive a car without a valid certificate. The tests are done by private garages. The abbreviation MOT is used both for the test and for the certificate: *I need to take my car in for its MOT.* ○ *Make sure you see the MOT before you buy the car.*

'**Mothercare**™ /'mʌðəkeə(r); *AmE* 'mʌðərker/ any of a group of British shops that sell clothes and equipment for babies and children up to the age of eight, and clothes for women who are pregnant. The first Mothercare shop was opened in 1961.

ˌ**Mother 'Goose** an old woman who is supposed to have written *nursery rhymes. She is shown in pictures as a woman with a pointed nose and chin riding on the back of a flying goose. She first appeared in English in two books published in London, *Mother Goose's Tales* (1768) and *Mother Goose's Melody; or Sonnets for the Cradle* (1781), some of which was probably written by Oliver *Goldsmith. The name 'Mother Goose' comes from part of a French expression which means 'old wives' tales'.

ˌ**Mother 'Hubbard** /'hʌbəd; *AmE* 'hʌbərd/ ⇨ OLD MOTHER HUBBARD.

'**Mother's Day** **1** (*BrE also* '**Mothering ˌSunday**) (in Britain) the fourth Sunday in Lent (around the middle of March), when mothers traditionally receive gifts and cards from their children. It was originally a day when servants were given a holiday to visit their families, taking gifts of flowers or a cake. **2** (in the US) the second Sunday in May, when mothers traditionally receive gifts, etc. from their children and are taken by their family for a meal at a restaurant. Many Americans wear a carnation (= a flower with a pleasant smell) on Mother's Day, a coloured one if their mother is alive and a white one if she is dead. Compare FATHER'S DAY.

the ˌ**Mothers' 'Union** an international organization for women, started by the *Church of England in 1876 but now open to women of other Christian groups. It is intended to make family life stronger.

'**motor inn** (*also* '**motor lodge**, '**motor court**) *n*

M

(*AmE*) a motel (= hotel, often near a motorway/freeway, for people driving cars, with space for parking cars near the rooms). Many US companies owning them now use the names *motor inn/lodge/court* instead of *motel*.

the ˈ**Motor Show** a large international exhibition of new cars, held in October every two years at the *National Exhibition Centre in *Birmingham, England. It started in 1903, in London.

ˈ**motorway** *n* (*BrE*) a major road for fast travel between cities, usually with three lanes (= sections for single lines of traffic) in each direction. The names of British motorways all begin with 'M' – the M1, the M2, etc. Drivers join or leave motorways at **motorway junctions**. People can stop at **motorway service areas** for petrol, food, etc.: *We joined the motorway at Junction 7.* ○ *I don't like motorway driving.* Compare EXPRESSWAY. ⇨ note at ROADS AND ROAD SIGNS.

ˈ**Motown** /ˈməʊtaʊn; *AmE* ˈmoʊtaʊn/ **1** the popular US name for *Detroit, *Michigan, because it is the 'motor town', i.e. the centre of the US car industry. **2** a type of *African-American *soul music. Motown Records, established in 1959, became famous for this type of music, sometimes called the **Motown sound**. Its recording stars included the *Supremes and Stevie *Wonder.

the ˈ**Moundbuilders** /ˈmaʊndbɪldəz; *AmE* ˈmaʊndbɪldərz/ *n* [pl] early *Native-American groups who built mounds (= raised masses of earth). These were used for graves and as the bases for religious temples and other important buildings. Well-known mounds that survive include those at Moundville, *Alabama, and the Serpent Mound in Adams County, *Ohio.

M

Serpent Mound

ˌ**Mountain** ˈ**Daylight Time** (*abbr* **MDT**) (in the US), the time used between early April and late October in the *Rocky Mountain States. It is one hour later than *Mountain Standard Time.

ˈ**mountain man** *n* (*pl* **mountain men**) (*AmE*) a man who lives in the mountains, often alone and far from other people. The term was often applied to trappers (= people who catch animals in traps, usually for their fur).

ˌ**Mountain** ˈ**Standard Time** (*abbr* **MST**) (*also* **Mountain Time**) (in the US) the time used between late October and early April in the *Rocky Mountain States. It is seven hours earlier than *Greenwich Mean Time.

the ˈ**Mountain States** ⇨ ROCKY MOUNTAIN STATES.

ˌLord **Mount**ˈ**batten** /maʊntˈbætn/ (*born* Louis Mountbatten 1900–79) a British admiral who during *World War II commanded the Allied forces in South-East Asia, defeating the Japanese in Burma and the Indian Ocean. He was the last viceroy of India before it became independent, and remained there for a year as its first Governor-General. He was killed while sailing off the west coast of Ireland by a bomb put on his boat by the *IRA. Lord Mountbatten was a great-grandson of Queen *Victoria, and the uncle of Prince *Charles. He became an *earl(1) in 1947. See also ALLIES.

ˌ**Mount** ˈ**Vernon** /ˈvɜːnən; *AmE* ˈvɜːrnən/ the home of US President George *Washington in *Virginia. It is on the *Potomac River about 15 miles/24 kilometres south of Washington, DC. It was built in 1743 in the *Georgian style. Washington lived at Mount Vernon from 1747 until his death in 1799, and he and his wife Martha are buried there.

The ˈ***Mousetrap*** a mystery play by Agatha *Christie which has been running continuously in the *West End of London since its first performance in 1952. No other play has ever been performed for so long anywhere in the world. *The Mousetrap* is also the title of the play performed to the court in *Shakespeare's play **Hamlet*.

ˈ**Mowgli** /ˈməʊgli; *AmE* ˈmoʊgli/ the main human character in *The *Jungle Book* by Rudyard *Kipling. As a baby, Mowgli is found in the forest by wolves which look after him until he grows up.

ˌMo ˈ**Mowlam** /ˌməʊ ˈməʊləm; *AmE* ˌmoʊ ˈmoʊləm/ (Marjorie Mowlam 1949–) a British *Labour politician. She became a *Member of Parliament in 1987 and held several important positions in the Labour *Shadow Cabinet before becoming *Secretary of State for Northern Ireland in the Labour government of 1997. She is well known for taking part in the peace talks in Northern Ireland which led to the *Good Friday Agreement of 1998.

ˈ**moxie** /ˈmɒksi; *AmE* ˈmɑːksi/ *n* [U] (*AmE infml*) courage, energy or an aggressive attitude. The word comes from the name of a former US soft drink (= a drink containing no alcohol) which was advertised with the phrase: 'What this country needs is plenty of Moxie': *She had the moxie to ask him to marry her.*

MP /ˌem ˈpiː/ ⇨ MEMBER OF PARLIAMENT.

MRA ⇨ MORAL RE-ARMAMENT.

ˌ**Mr** ˈ**Bean** /ˈbiːn/ a comedy character played in a British television series by the actor Rowan *Atkinson. The programmes have very few spoken words and show Mr Bean in funny or embarrassing situations: *Well, say something! Don't just stand there like Mr Bean.*

Mr Bean

MRC ⇨ MEDICAL RESEARCH COUNCIL.

ˌ**Mr** ˈ**Charlie** (*AmE slang*) an informal name used by *African Americans for a white man or for white men in general. It is often meant as an insult.

ˌ**Mr** ˈ**Chips** /ˈtʃɪps/ an expression sometimes used to refer to a male teacher, especially one who is loved by his students. It comes from the main character in the novel *Goodbye Mr Chips* by James Hilton.

ˌ**Mr** ˈ**Clean** (*AmE infml*) a man who is considered to be very honest and good. It is especially used in politics for a candidate or elected politician who has done nothing morally wrong in his personal or political life: *Many people voted for Jimmy Carter because he was the Mr Clean of US politics.*

ˌ**Mr** ˈ**Fixit** /ˈfɪksɪt/ (*BrE infml, sometimes disapprov*) a name for a person who organizes things and solves problems for other people. It is sometimes used to refer to criminals or to show disapproval when referring to other people: *He is getting a reputation as the government's Mr Fixit.*

ˌMr ˈKipling™ /ˈkɪplɪŋ/ a British make of cakes of various kinds. They are well known for the advertisements, which say that Mr Kipling makes 'exceedingly good cakes'.

ˌMr Maˈgoo /məˈguː/ a character in a series of US cartoon films (1949–65). He is old and cannot see very well, so he talks to objects and walks into dangerous situations. A Walt *Disney film, *Mr Magoo* (1997), used real actors, with Leslie Nielsen as Magoo.

ˈMr ˈRogers' ˈNeighborhood a popular US television series on *PBS for young children which began in 1966. It is presented by Fred Rogers (1928–), who always tells children, 'You are special. I like you just the way you are.'

ˌMrs ˈMop /ˈmɒp; *AmE* ˈmɑːp/ (*BrE humor*) a typical cleaning woman, thought of as looking untidy, wearing a scarf on her head, and smoking a cigarette while she carries her bucket and mop (= tool for cleaning floors) around: *Their firm provides Mrs Mops for local offices.*

ˈMrs OˈˈLeary's ˈcow /əʊˈlɪəriz; *AmE* oʊˈlɪriz/ the cow that is traditionally blamed for the great Chicago fire in October 1871. Mrs O'Leary lived in the west part of Chicago on De Koven Street. People there claimed that her cow kicked over an oil lamp, though Mrs O'Leary herself denied it. The fire burned for nearly a week, killing 250 people and destroying 7 450 buildings.

MSF /ˌem es ˈef/ (*in full* the **Manufacturing, Science and Finance Union**) a British trade union for professional and skilled workers in areas such as science, finance, business and the health service. It is Britain's fifth largest union and was formed in 1988.

MST /ˌem es ˈtiː/ ⇨ MOUNTAIN STANDARD TIME.

MTV /ˌem tiː ˈviː/ a US television company that broadcasts music videos and programmes about the music industry all round the world by satellite, 24 hours a day. It began in 1981.

the **M25** /ˌem twentiˈfaɪv/ a British motorway that runs in a circle around London. It was completed in 1986, but since then has become quite crowded, and traffic on it often moves very slowly. People often complain or make jokes about the difficulties of driving on the M25.

ˈMuch Aˈdo About ˈNothing a play (*c.* 1598) by William *Shakespeare. It is a comedy about two love affairs, one between Beatrice and Benedick and the other between Hero and Claudio.

ˈmuckraker /ˈmʌkreɪkə(r)/ *n* any of a group of US writers in the early 1900s who wrote criticizing aspects of US life, such as dishonest behaviour in business and government, companies making children work long hours, and unfair treatment of black people. President Theodore *Roosevelt gave them the name 'muckrakers' in 1906, suggesting that they were only interested in finding bad things to write about. However, their work increased public knowledge and led to a lot of social changes. One example of a muckraker was Upton *Sinclair, whose book *The Jungle* (1906) led to the US *Pure Food and Drug Act.

ˈmuffin (*AmE also* **English muffin**) *n* a soft, round, flat cake made with yeast dough and usually eaten hot with butter.

ˈmugwump /ˈmʌɡwʌmp/ *n* (*AmE often disapprov*) a person who cannot decide how to vote on a political issue, or who prefers not to become involved in party politics. The word was first applied in US politics to a group of *Republicans who in 1884 supported the *Democrats' candidate Grover *Cleveland for US President. It comes from the *Native-American Algonquian language and means 'great man' or 'chief'.

Muˌhammad Aˈli ⇨ ALI.

ˌFrank **ˈMuir**[1] /ˈmjʊə(r); *AmE* ˈmjʊr/ (1920–98) an English broadcaster and writer of comedy who with Denis *Norden wrote several successful comedy series for radio and television, including *Take It From Here* (1947–58). He appeared regularly on a number of popular panel games and quiz shows and was well known for his clever and intelligent humour. He also wrote a novel and a series of children's books.

ˌJohn **ˈMuir**[2] /ˈmjʊə(r); *AmE* ˈmjʊr/ (1838–1914) an American, born in Scotland, who was one of the first conservationists (= people who work to preserve the natural environment). He helped to establish *Yosemite National Park and Sequoia National Park in *California. Muir Woods National Monument in California and Muir Glacier in *Alaska were named after him. His books include *The Mountains of California* (1894) and *Our National Parks* (1901). The John Muir Trust was established in 1984 to protect land in Britain.

ˈMuirfield /ˈmjʊəfiːld; *AmE* ˈmjʊrfiːld/ a golf course on the east coast of Scotland near *Edinburgh, one of the courses on which the *British Open is regularly played.

the **ˌMulberry ˈharbours** two very large artificial harbours that were built in Britain and then pulled across the *Channel to the French coast so that supplies could be provided for the Allied soldiers who landed in Normandy on *D-Day in June 1944. See also ALLIES.

Mull /mʌl/ a large island of the Inner *Hebrides in Scotland. It is known for its high cliffs and beautiful scenery, and is popular with tourists.

Multicultural Britain and the US ⇨ article.

ˈmummer *n* an actor in a traditional English play without words in which the actors wear masks covering their faces. The story involves a fight between St *George and a Turkish *knight. One of them is killed, but a doctor brings him back to life. The idea behind the play, which was performed especially at Christmas, is the earth's death in winter and return to life in the spring. It is occasionally still performed.

ˈMummerset /ˈmʌməset; *AmE* ˈmʌmərset/ *n* [U] (*humor*) an invented word meaning the strong *accent sometimes used by English actors when they are playing characters from the *West Country, including *Somerset: *It's one of those plays in which everyone speaks a variety of broad Mummerset.*

the **ˌMunich Aˈgreement** /ˌmjuːnɪk/ (*also* the **ˌMunich ˈPact** /ˌmjuːnɪk/) an agreement signed in Munich in September 1938 between Britain, France, Germany and Italy. It allowed Germany to take control of a part of Czechoslavakia. The British Prime Minister, Neville *Chamberlain, said that the agreement represented 'peace in our time', and at the time many people believed that it had saved Europe from war. However, in March 1939 Hitler took all of Czechoslovakia and in September *World War II began. Now people sometimes call an agreement that has no value 'another Munich'. See also APPEASEMENT.

ˌAlfred **ˈMunnings** /ˈmʌnɪŋz/ (1878–1959) an English painter known especially for his pictures of horses and horse-racing, and for criticizing a lot of modern art. He was made a *knight in 1944.

the **Munˈros** /mʌnˈrəʊz; *AmE* mʌnˈroʊz/ the 277 mountains in Scotland which are all over 3 000 feet

Multicultural Britain and the US

Both Britain and the US are multicultural societies, i.e. they are made up of people from many different racial and cultural backgrounds. The biggest group in *society is often called the **mainstream**. In the US, it is white people whose ancestors came from Europe, especially northern Europe. In Britain the mainstream is the white population from England, Wales, Scotland and Ireland. Both mainstream groups are of mixed origin, but consist entirely of white people. Other racial or cultural groups that are present in smaller numbers are often called **ethnic minorities**. In the US *Native Americans, *African Americans and *Hispanics are the main ethnic minorities. In Britain ethnic minorities include the families of former **immigrants** from South Asia and the *Caribbean, as well as people from China, Italy and many other countries.

The terms *mainstream* and *ethnic minority* point out and reinforce divisions in society, whereas the phrase *multicultural society* suggests that the different groups are part of a whole. In both Britain and the US society is still divided, with some groups receiving better treatment or having more opportunities than others, but many attempts have been made to reduce **discrimination** (= different treatment on account of a person's race, colour, etc.) and to increase harmony and understanding between people from all cultural backgrounds.

A history of discrimination

Throughout the history of the US, minority groups have faced **prejudice**. During the main period of ***immigration**, each new group of immigrants was treated with suspicion by those already there. The groups that suffered most were those whose colour or physical features were most distinctive. Black people, now widely called African Americans, who had been brought to the US as *slaves, suffered both on account of their colour and because of their former status. American Indians, now often called Native Americans, who were the **aboriginal population** of the US (= the people living there before settlers arrived), and Hispanics have also suffered. These groups are still **discriminated against** (= treated worse than other people) and may be **under-represented** (= found in smaller numbers compared with other ethnic groups) in certain jobs.

When slavery was ended in the US, many white people could not accept that black people should have the same status as Whites, and the ***Ku Klux Klan** (**KKK**) was formed to fight against equal treatment for Blacks. For a long time ***segregation** was practised in the *South: black people were not allowed to go to the same schools, churches or restaurants as Whites, and they had to sit in different areas on buses.

Native Americans were given no rights under the *Constitution and have been frequently attacked and forced to give up their lands. Now, most live on special **reservations** and struggle to preserve their culture, religion and political independence.

Social division in Britain

Many immigrants came to Britain from *Jamaica and other *Caribbean countries and from South Asia after 1945. These countries were formerly part of the *British Empire, and when the people came to Britain they were often treated as inferior to white people. They tended to live close to each other in a particular part of a town and often married within their own community. In this way cultural traditions were preserved and **social divisions** reinforced. There was discrimination against ethnic minorities in housing, *social welfare and employment. Few white people were interested in getting to know the immigrants as individuals, and there was general ignorance and lack of cultural sensitivity. The immigrants were distrusted and thought by some people to be more likely to commit a crime than white people. Younger Blacks are still more likely to be arrested by the police than white youths.

By the 1960s increasing numbers of immigrants had caused fear among the white population that there would be serious unemployment and poverty. Prejudice increased and sometimes turned into **racism** (= hatred of people of a different race). The *National Front organized demonstrations in areas with a large black or Asian population. Then in 1962 a law was passed restricting immigration.

Mass demonstrations are now rare, but **racially-motivated attacks** on individuals continue. In 1993, for instance, a black teenager, Stephen Lawrence, was murdered by a group of white youths, though no one was convicted of the murder. Generally, there is less racism in Britain than in other European countries. Most white people live in harmony with Blacks and Asians, but often because they have little social contact with them, not because of any very positive feelings.

Civil rights and equal opportunities

After *World War II, considerable progress was made in the US to improve the position of minorities. The ***civil rights movement** of the 1950s and 1960s brought about changes in the law that improved social conditions for minority groups, especially black people. Demonstrations led by people like Martin Luther *King drew attention to their problems and helped change people's attitudes. The *Supreme Court in the case **Brown v Board of Education* decided that black children should be allowed to attend the same schools as white children. The army was needed in order to enforce the law, but it succeeded. Later, ***Civil Rights Acts** made segregation illegal in public places such as restaurants. Civil rights laws also apply to Native Americans, though most have never wanted to be part of American society.

The US ***Equal Employment Opportunity Commission** was created in 1965 to make employers follow laws forbidding discrimination at work. Many people felt that getting rid of discrimination was not enough, and this led to a policy of ***affirmative action** (= preferential treatment towards members of particular groups). However, the policy did little to help less well-educated and unskilled black people. Affirmative action also caused a lot of disagreement. Some people say that giving extra opportunities to minorities is just another form of discrimination. Some black people do not want special as distinct from fair treatment. In response, educational institutions and employers are now changing the way they practise affirmative action, and its future is not clear.

Minorities in the US are in a much better position now than at the beginning of this century. There is also respect among many white people for the good things that **cultural diversity** has brought. But discrimination is still present. Black Americans earn less money, on average, than Whites, and have shorter lives. The KKK still exists. Black people are still attacked by Whites. There are clubs which have no black or Jewish members, and others which have a **token** minority member (= just one person from a minority group) to show that they are not racist.

In Britain it is government policy to promote **equality of opportunity**, and to make improvements in social conditions, employment, etc. that will benefit everyone. In 1965 and 1968 legislation (= laws) made discrimination in housing, employment and education illegal. The law was further strengthened in 1976 when **indirect discrimination** (= the practice of suggesting, e.g. in an advertisement, that people from minority groups are less important, less suitable, etc.) was made illegal. Affirmative action, also called **reverse discrimination**, is not allowed in Britain, though some forms of **positive action**, such as providing training and encouraging people to apply for jobs in areas of work in which their group is under-represented, are permitted. The*__Commission for Racial Equality__ helps to enforce the law and tries to promote good **race relations**.

In the 1980s black people in Britain protested against continued discrimination and the lack of houses and job opportunities in a campaign that resulted in the *Brixton riots. Since then, the government has provided more money for social, economic and educational programmes to combat inequality. Local community associations, ethnic arts groups and sports clubs have also received money. Since 1986 it has been an offence to use language or publish material likely to stir up racial hatred. Radio and television programmes now reflect the diversity of culture in Britain. The police have tried to improve their relationship with minority groups by recruiting officers from among them, but in 1999 a report on the handling of the Stephen Lawrence case accused the police of **institutional racism** (= having policies which result in people of a particular race or colour being treated worse than those of another race or colour).

Future prospects

The balance of America's multicultural society is changing. The African-American and Hispanic populations are growing faster than the white population. Soon, white non-Hispanics will be less than 50% of the population. Fear of immigrant communities gaining in importance has led to the ***English Only Movement**, a campaign by people who see other cultures and languages as a threat to the US. They want to make English the official language of the US and are opposed, for example, to allowing students to be taught in other languages or letting people vote using forms printed in another language. Their ideas are based on the *melting pot, the idea that immigrants should change to fit into society. As the numbers of people making up the traditional mainstream get smaller, attitudes toward minorities will have to change.

In Britain, most members of ethnic minority groups now think of themselves as British and take pride in this description. But many also feel considerable pride in their cultural origins and keep alive their traditional festivals and practices. Many people from the mainstream also enjoy cultural events such as the *Notting Hill Carnival, and this has helped promote tolerance. But there is still need for greater acceptance. Organizations like the National Front continue to attract support and there are still attacks on black people and Asians. In a recent survey 80% of 18–34-year-olds from ethnic minorities thought that racism had got worse. But, provided that there is no serious decline in the country's economy, racial harmony amongst the majority of the population seems likely to continue.

(913 metres) high. In 1891 a man called Hugh Munro published a list of them, and since then people have had the aim of climbing all of them. Munro himself died with only one of them left to climb.

The ***ˈMuppet Show*** /ˈmʌpɪt/ a popular British television comedy series (1976–81) with a range of puppet characters, including *Kermit the frog, Miss Piggy and Fozzy Bear. The Muppets were created in the US in the 1950s by Jim *Henson and Frank Oz, and first became popular in the US children's series **Sesame Street*.

ˌ**Murder, ˈInc** /ˈɪŋk/ an informal US name for the *Mafia(1) or other powerful criminal groups. It was first used to refer to a criminal organization run by Albert Anastasia and Louis 'Lepke' Buchalter in *Brooklyn, New York, during the *Great Depression.

the ˈ**Murder Squad** an informal name for the *CID, the *detective branch of the British police force.

ˌIris ˈ**Murdoch**[1] /ˈmɜːdɒk; *AmE* ˈmɜːrdɑːk/ (1919–99) a British writer, born in Dublin. Her clever novels explore complicated human and sexual relationships among 20th-century *middle-class people, often with great humour. Among the best-known are *The Sandcastle*, (1957) *A Severed Head* (1961) and *The Sea, The Sea* (1978), which won the *Booker Prize. Iris Murdoch was made a *dame(2) in 1987.

ˌRupert ˈ**Murdoch**[2] /ˈmɜːdɒk; *AmE* ˈmɜːrdɑːk/ (1931–) a very rich businessman who owns an international group of newspaper and broadcasting companies. He was born in Australia but is now a US citizen. In Britain he owns News International, a group which

the Muppets

M

includes the *News of the World*, the **Sun*, *The *Times*, and the **Sunday Times*, and half of the satellite television company *BSkyB. In the US Murdoch also owns the film company *20th Century Fox, the Fox Television Network and the Los Angeles Dodgers baseball team.

ˌEddie ˈ**Murphy** /ˈmɜːfi; *AmE* ˈmɜːrfi/ (1961–) a US comic actor who usually plays lively, confident characters. He began his career on the television programme **Saturday Night Live* (1981–4). His films include *48 Hours* (1982), *Trading Places* (1983), *Beverly Hills Cop* (1984), *Coming to America* (1988), *Harlem Nights* (1989), which he wrote and directed, *The Nutty Professor* (1996) and *Doctor Dolittle* (1998).

ˌJames ˈ**Murray** /ˈmʌri/ (1837–1915) a Scottish lexicographer (= writer of dictionaries) who is mainly remembered as the first editor of *The New Oxford English Dictionary* (later called *The *Oxford English Dictionary*), published between 1884 and 1933. He was made a *knight in 1908.

James Murray

ˈ**Murrayfield** /ˈmʌrifiːld/ the Scottish national Rugby Union ground in *Edinburgh, where all Scotland's home international matches are played.

ˌEdward R ˈ**Murrow** /ˈmʌrəʊ; *AmE* ˈmʌroʊ/ (Edward Roscoe Murrow 1908–65) a US radio and television journalist who has been called 'the father of television journalism'. He was head of the *CBS radio European Bureau during *World War II. In the 1950s, he had two programmes on CBS television, *See It Now* and *Person to Person*. In the first he examined current affairs, and in the second he talked to famous people in their homes. Murrow later became head of the *United States Information Agency (1961–3).

the **Muˌseum of ˈChildhood** a British museum in *Bethnal Green, London, which shows what children's lives were like at different periods in history.

the **Muˌseum of Manˈkind** a British museum that shows how peoples from Africa, America and the Pacific live, mainly today rather than in the past. It opened in central London in 1970, when this part of the collection of the *British Museum was moved there.

the **Muˈseum of ˌModern ˈArt** (*abbr* **MOMA**) the largest museum of modern art and photography in the world. The collection starts with works from 1880. It opened in *New York in 1939.

the **Muˈseum of the ˈMoving ˈImage** (*abbr* **MOMI**) a British museum that shows how film, television, video and other ways of showing moving images developed. It opened on the *South Bank in London in 1988, next to the *National Film Theatre.

museums

Many people have a *hobby that involves collecting things, e.g. stamps, postcards or *antiques. In the 18th and 19th centuries wealthy people travelled and collected plants, animal skins, historical objects and works of art. They kept their collection at home until it got too big or until they died, and then it was given to a museum. The 80 000 objects collected by Sir Hans Sloane, for example, formed the core collection of the *British Museum which opened in 1759.

The parts of a museum open to the public are called **galleries** or **rooms**. Often, only a small proportion of a museum's collection is on display. Most of it is stored away or used for research. A person in charge of a department of a museum is called a **keeper**. Museum staff involved in the care and conservation of items are sometimes called **curators**.

Many museums are lively places and they attract a lot of visitors. As well as looking at **exhibits**, visitors can play with computer simulations and imagine themselves living at a different time in history or walking through a rainforest. At the Jorvik Centre in *York, the city's *Viking settlement is recreated, and people experience the sights, sounds and smells of the old town. Historical accuracy is important but so also is entertainment. Museums must compete for people's leisure time and money with other amusements. Most museums also welcome school groups and arrange special activities for children.

In Britain, the largest museums are the *British Museum, the *Science Museum, the *Natural History Museum and the *Victoria and Albert Museum. Museums outside London also cover every subject and period. Homes of famous people sometimes become museums, such as the house where *Shakespeare was born in *Stratford-upon-Avon.

The first public museum in the US was the Charlestown Museum in South Carolina, founded in 1773. The largest is the *Smithsonian Institution in Washington, DC, a group of 14 museums. The most popular of these is the *National Air and Space Museum. Some US museums are art museums. Many describe a period of history. In *Gettysburg, Pennsylvania, for example, a museum explains the *Civil War and gives details of the battle of Gettysburg. ***Halls of Fame** are museums that honour people who have been outstanding in a certain field, e.g. baseball or rock music.

National museums receive money from the government but not enough to cover their costs, and visitors to museums usually have to pay to go in. Some people believe that this is wrong, because a museum's exhibits belong to the nation. Museum's usually have a shop selling books, postcards and gifts, and often a café. Their profits help to fund the museum. Some museums have the support of a commercial sponsor. In small museums only a few people have paid jobs, and the rest are volunteers, called **docents** in the US, who lead tours and answer visitors' questions.

ˌStan ˈ**Musial** /ˈmjuːziəl/ (1920–) a famous US *baseball player with the St Louis Cardinals team (1941–63), often known informally as 'Stan the Man'. He was chosen as the *Most Valuable Player in the *National League three times (1943, 1946 and 1948) and was its most successful batter seven times. He was chosen for the Baseball *Hall of Fame in 1969.

ˈ**musical** (*also* **musical comedy**) *n* an amusing play or film with songs and usually dancing. Musicals started to develop in the early 20th century, combining features of comic opera and the British *music-hall tradition. The modern *Broadway musical began with **Show Boat*, and others have included **Oklahoma!*, **My Fair Lady*, **West Side Story*, **Hair* and **Sunset Boulevard*. Most later became films. Musicals written originally as films include **Singin' in the Rain* and *Gigi* (1958). US writers of musicals have included Irving *Berlin, George and Ira *Gershwin, Jerome *Kern, Cole *Porter, Richard *Rodgers, Lorenz *Hart, Oscar *Hammerstein and *Lerner and Loewe. The best-known British composer of musicals is Andrew *Lloyd Webber, whose work includes *Jesus Christ Superstar* and *Cats*.

ˌ**musical ˈchairs** *n* [U] **1** a game, played e.g. at children's parties, in which people run around a group of chairs while music is played. The number of chairs is always one fewer than the number of people, so that when the music stops the person who cannot find a chair has to leave the game. The winner is the one who manages to sit on the last remaining chair. ⇨ note at TOYS AND GAMES. **2** (*fig, often disapprov*) a situation in which people or things often change places, or take turns to do something: *Government ministers are expected to engage in musical chairs, moving from one department to another.*

ˈ**music-hall** *n* **1** [U] a type of popular entertainment in Britain in the late 19th and early 20th centuries. Performers sang cheerful, sometimes rather rude, songs and danced in bright costumes, or performed acts of skill. Some of them, such as Marie *Lloyd and George *Robey, became very famous: *the great music-hall entertainers.* **2** [C] a theatre in which music-hall was performed. Music-halls were often called 'the Palladium', 'the Palace', 'the Hippodrome', or 'the Empire', names which were kept later when many of them became cinemas. See also GOOD OLD DAYS. Compare VAUDEVILLE.

ˌ***Mutiny on the ˈBounty*** the name of two films about a famous historical incident which occurred in 1789. The sailors on the British ship *HMS Bounty* took control of it by force and put the captain and some senior officers in a small boat on the open sea. In the first film (1935), which won an *Oscar as Best Picture, Clark *Gable played Fletcher *Christian, the leader of the mutiny, and Charles *Laughton played Captain *Bligh. In the second (1962), Marlon *Brando took the part of Christian and Trevor Howard that of Bligh. See also PITCAIRN ISLANDS.

ˌEadweard ˈ**Muybridge** /ˌedwəd ˈmaɪbrɪdʒ; *AmE* ˌedwərd/ (1830–1904) a US photographer, born in England, who used a series of cameras to study the way both animals and humans move. He developed a way of showing series of pictures quickly one after the other to give the impression of continuous movement. He presented these to the public in a theatre in *Chicago, which some people therefore regard as the first cinema.

ˈ**Muzak**™ *n* [U] a system that plays continuous recorded light music in public places, e.g. in restaurants, shops and airports. It was first produced in 1922 by the US Muzak Corporation for use in lifts/elevators to help people to stay calm. Many people dislike it and use the name Muzak to refer to music that is boring or that no one listens to.

MVP /ˌem viː ˈpiː/ ⇨ MOST VALUABLE PLAYER.

ˌ***My Fair ˈLady*** a successful musical version of the play *Pygmalion*, by George Bernard *Shaw. It was written by *Lerner and Loewe, and opened on *Broadway in 1956, with Rex *Harrison as Professor Higgins and Julie *Andrews as Eliza Doolittle. Harrison was also in the film version (1964), with Audrey *Hepburn as Eliza. The film won three *Oscars.

the ˌ**My Lai ˈmassacre** /ˌmiː laɪ/ an incident that occurred during the *Vietnam War on 16 March 1968. A group of US soldiers killed 347 ordinary people, including women and children, in the Vietnamese village of My Lai. In 1971, the officer who ordered the attack, Lieutenant William Calley, was sent to prison for life, but this was later reduced to 10 years and he was in fact released in 1974. Many Americans were shocked by the incident, and as a result protests against the war increased.

ˌ***My ˈOld Kenˈtucky ˈHome*** /kenˈtʌki/ a popular US song written in 1853 by Stephen *Foster. It became the official song of the state of *Kentucky and is played at each *Kentucky Derby when the horses come out. It contains the well-known lines:

Oh the sun shines bright on my old Kentucky home,
My old Kentucky home far away.

ˈ**mystery play** ⇨ MIRACLE PLAY.

Nn

the **NAACP** /ˈen dʌbl ˈeɪ siː ˈpiː/ (*in full* the **National Association for the Advancement of Colored People**) a US organization that supports the rights of *African Americans. It was formed in 1909 and played an important part in the *civil rights movement. One of its major achievements was to bring a legal case which led to the US Supreme Court's decision in 1954 against *segregation in schools. In recent years, other African-American groups have accused the NAACP of not being aggressive enough. Its main office is in *Baltimore, *Maryland, and it had more than 500 000 members in 1997. See also *Brown v Board of Education*.

the **NAAFI** /ˈnæfi/ (*in full* the **Navy, Army and Air Force Institutes**) a British organization that provides shops and places to eat for members of the armed services in Britain and abroad. Compare PX.

Naˈbisco /nəˈbɪskəʊ; *AmE* nəˈbɪskoʊ/ a large US food company. Its products include *Oreo biscuits, *Ritz Crackers and Planters nuts.

ˌVladimir **Naˈbokov** /ˌvlædɪmɪə nəˈbəʊkɒf; *AmE* ˌvlædɪmɪr nəˈboʊkɔːf/ (1899–1977) a US writer of novels and short stories, born in Russia, who is much admired for his skilful use of language. He is best known for his novel **Lolita*. His other novels include *Pnin* (1957), *Pale Fire* (1962) and *Ada* (1969). Nabokov taught poetry at Cornell University from 1948 to 1959 before settling in Switzerland.

ˌRalph **ˈNader** /ˌrælf ˈneɪdə(r)/ (1934–) a US lawyer who became famous for representing the rights of consumers (= people who buy goods or use services) and led many important campaigns against big companies. In his book *Unsafe at Any Speed* (1965) he attacked the car industry for producing dangerous cars, and this led to new safety laws for cars being passed. The assistants who helped him in his investigations became known as Nader's Raiders.

ˈNAFTA /ˈnæftə/ (*in full* the **North American Free Trade Agreement**) an agreement signed in 1989 between the US, Canada and Mexico to allow goods to be transported and sold more easily over their borders. It also makes it easier for business and professional people to move between the three countries. The agreement began to operate in 1994.

ˌNagaˈsaki /ˌnægəˈsɑːki/ a city and port in south-west Japan. It was, after *Hiroshima, the second city to be destroyed by an atom bomb at the end of *World War II. The bomb was dropped from a US plane on 9 August 1945, killing about 75 000 people immediately and another 75 000 who died later.

ˌV S **ˈNaipaul** /ˈnaɪpɔːl/ (Vidiadhar Surajprasad Naipaul 1932–) a writer of novels, short stories and travel books, born in *Trinidad, who has lived in Britain since 1950. He is perhaps best known for his comic novels, many of them set in the *West Indies, including *A House for Mr Biswas* (1961).

NALGO /ˈnælgəʊ; *AmE* ˈnælgoʊ/ (*in full* the **National and Local Government Officers' Association**) ⇨ Unison.

Nam /næm/ (*AmE infml*) a short name for Vietnam, first used by US soldiers during the *Vietnam War.

names

Apart from their *surname or last name, most British and American children are given two personal names by their parents, a **first name** and a **middle name**. These names are sometimes called **Christian** names or **given** names. Some people have only one given name, a few have three or more. Friends and members of a family who are of similar age usually call one another by their first names. In some families young people now also call their aunts and uncles and even their parents by their first names. Outside the family, the expression *be on first name terms* suggests that the people concerned have a friendly, informal relationship

When writing their name Americans commonly give their first name and their **middle initial**, e.g. *George M Cohan*. Both given names are used in full only on formal occasions, e.g. when people get married. In Britain many people **sign their name** on cheques using the initials of both their given names and their surname, e.g. *J E Brooks*, but may write *Joanna Brooks* at the end of a letter. The **full name** (= all given names and surname) is usually only required on official forms.

Parents usually decide on given names for their children before they are born. In some families the oldest boy is given the same name as his father. In the US the word **junior** or **senior**, or a number, is added after the name and surname to make it clear which person is being referred to. For example, the son of *William Jones Sr* (Senior) would be called *William Jones Jr* (Junior), and *his* son would be called *William Jones III* ('William Jones the third').

Many popular names come from the Bible, e.g. *Jacob*, *Joshua* and *Matthew*, *Mary*, *Rebecca* and *Sarah*, though this does not imply that the people who choose them are religious. Other people give their children the name of somebody they admire, such as a famous sports personality, or a film or pop star. In Britain the names *William* and *Harry* have become common again since the sons of Prince *Charles were given these names. In the US *Chelsea* was not a common name for a girl until President Bill *Clinton's daughter Chelsea came to public attention.

Names such as *David*, *Michael*, *Paul* and *Robert* for boys and *Helen*, *Jane* and *Susan* for girls remain popular for many years. Others, e.g. *Darrell*, *Darren*, *Wayne*, *Tracey*, *Jade* and *Zara*, are fashionable for only a short period. Names such as *Albert*, *Herbert*, *Wilfrid*, *Doris*, *Gladys* and *Joyce* are now out of fashion and are found mainly among older people. Some older names come back into fashion and there are now many young women called *Amy*, *Emma*, *Harriet*, *Laura* and *Sophie*. The birth announcements columns in *newspapers give an indication of the names which are currently popular.

People from Wales, Scotland or Ireland, or those who have a cultural background from outside Britain, may choose from an additional set of names. In the US Jews, *African Americans or people of Latin American origin may also choose different names.

Naˈmibia /nəˈmɪbiə/ a country in south-west Africa which joined the *Commonwealth when it became independent from South Africa in 1990, although it had never been a British colony. The capital city is Windhoek. ▶ **Namibian** *adj, n.*

nannies and nannying

A nanny is a woman who is paid to look after children in their own home. In 19th- and early 20th-century Britain, nannies worked for *upper-class families. They lived in the family house and cared for all the children's needs. Now, a few British *middle-class families also have a nanny. A popular modern alternative is an **au pair**, a young person, often a foreign student. Unlike professionally trained nannies, au pairs are usually expected to do some housework as well as look after the children.

Americans who want somebody to **live in** and look after their children are much more likely to employ an au pair than a nanny because they are less expensive. Often, however, an au pair is loosely referred to as a nanny. In 1997 the Louise Woodward case, in which an English au pair was accused of killing the American child in her care, caused intense public debate about whether parents should leave young children with a stranger who has little experience or formal training.

When people talk of somebody being **nannied** they mean that they are being looked after too carefully and are overprotected, as if they were a young child. Some people believe Britain has become a **nanny state** in which the government goes too far in its efforts to look after people's interests and does not allow them to make decisions for themselves. British people are used to having a *National Health Service and a range of social welfare benefits, but they like to be free to make choices in their personal lives. Examples of state interference have included the proposed banning of unpasteurized milk, the banning of the sale of beef on the bone, and campaigns to reduce smoking. Other examples of nannying or **mollycoddling** include 'weather advisories' from the *Meteorological Office. These may suggest when frost is forecast, for example, that roads may be icy so people should drive carefully.

Some people in the US are also worried about the government making too many rules, although this is not referred to as the nanny state and has not produced the same amount of public annoyance as in Britain. But some businesses are so afraid of being sued and having to pay heavy costs that they limit their own activities without waiting for the government to make laws. For example, some restaurants refuse to serve alcoholic drinks to women who are pregnant, since alcohol could hurt the baby and they could then be sued as a result.

Nan'tucket /næn'tʌkɪt/ a US island off the south-east coast of *Massachusetts, near *Cape Cod and *Martha's Vineyard. The island is separated from the coast by **Nantucket Sound**. It is 15 miles/24 kilometres long and has a small town also called Nantucket. It attracts summer tourists, and many rich people have homes there.

ˌNapa 'Valley /ˌnæpə/ a valley in the US state of *California which is the centre of the US wine industry. It is north of *Oakland, and its largest town is Napa.

the **Naˌpoleonic 'Wars** /nəˌpəʊliɒnɪk; *AmE* nəˌpoʊliɑːnɪk/ a conflict (1802–1815) in which the French Emperor Napoleon Bonaparte tried to gain control of the whole of Europe. He had great success against all his enemies except Britain, whose navy under *Nelson defeated the French navy at the Battle of *Trafalgar (1805), and whose army fought the *Peninsular War against him from 1808 to 1814, making him weaker in his other campaigns. In 1812 Napoleon lost half a million men when he invaded Russia in winter, and in 1814 the British, Russians, Prussians and Austrians entered Paris. They sent Napoleon to rule the island of Elba in the Mediterranean, but he collected an army around him and returned to Paris. He was soon defeated again, at the Battle of *Waterloo (1815), and was sent to the island of St Helena in the south Atlantic, where he died in 1821.

'Narnia /'nɑːniə; *AmE* 'nɑːrniə/ an imaginary land of strange people and talking animals in a series of seven children's books (sometimes called the **Narnia Chronicles**) by C S *Lewis. In the first of these, *The Lion, the Witch and the Wardrobe* (1950), four children get into Narnia through an old wardrobe (= a large cupboard for clothes).

NASA /'næsə/ (*in full* the **National Aeronautics and Space Administration**) the US government organization responsible for research into space and space travel. Its office is in Washington, DC, and the main centres include the John F Kennedy Space Center at *Cape Canaveral, *Florida, the *Lyndon B Johnson Space Center near *Houston, *Texas, and the Jet Propulsion Laboratory at the California Institute of Technology in Pasadena. NASA was established in 1958 by President *Eisenhower to replace the National Advisory Committee for Aeronautics (NACA). See also APOLLO PROGRAM, *CHALLENGER*, SKYLAB, SPACE SHUTTLE.

NASCAR /'næskɑː(r)/ (*in full* the **National Association for Stock Car Auto Racing**) the US organization for the sport of racing stock cars (= ordinary cars fitted with especially powerful engines). It was established in 1948 at Daytona Beach, *Florida, and the NASCAR office is still there. The *Daytona 500 is the most famous of its races.

the ˌBattle of **'Naseby** /'neɪzbi/ an important battle (1645) of the *English Civil War, fought in *Northamptonshire. The Parliament's *New Model Army defeated the supporters of the King, and they never became strong again.

ˌBeau **'Nash**[1] /ˌbəʊ 'næʃ; *AmE* ˌboʊ/ (1674–1762) the name by which Richard Nash is usually known. He was a Welshman who became a leading figure in fashionable English society in the 18th century. He helped to make the English towns of *Bath and *Tunbridge Wells into fashionable holiday centres.

ˌJohn **'Nash**[2] /'næʃ/ (1752–1835) an English architect. He planned *Regent's Park in London, and the area around it, between 1811 and 1825 for the *Prince Regent, who later became King *George IV. He also designed *Trafalgar Square, *Saint James's Park and the *Marble Arch in London, and the *Brighton Pavilion on the south coast of England.

ˌOgden **'Nash**[3] /ˌɒgdən 'næʃ; *AmE* ˌɑːgdən/ (1902–71) a US writer of humorous verse. Many of his poems were first published in *The *New Yorker* magazine. He was known especially for his clever rhymes. His 20 collections of verse include *You Can't Get There from Here* (1957) and *Bed Riddence* (1970).

ˌPaul **'Nash**[4] /'næʃ/ (1899–1946) an English painter who did many types of work, including theatre and book design, but who is remembered especially for the pictures he painted as an official war artist in both world wars.

'Nashville /'næʃvɪl/ the capital city of the US state of *Tennessee, in the northern central part of the state. It was settled on the Cumberland River in 1779 as Fort Nashborough and its name was changed in 1784. It is the centre of the *country music industry and among its attractions are the *Grand Ole Opry. It is also known as a centre for religious education and for Vanderbilt University.

The Mule Track, *painted by Paul Nash*

the **NASUWT** /ˌen eɪ ˈes ˌjuː dʌbljuː ˈtiː/ (*in full* the **National Association of Schoolmasters/Union of Women Teachers**) a British trade union for teachers, formed in 1975. ⇨ article at TRADE UNIONS AND LABOR UNIONS. Compare NUT.

ˈ**Natchez** /ˈnætʃiz/ **1** *n* (*pl* **Natchez**) a member of a former *Native-American agricultural people who lived on the *Mississippi River near the modern city of Natchez, *Mississippi. They spoke the Muskogean language and worshipped the sun. About 400 Natchez were captured by the French in 1729 and sold as slaves in the West Indies. The rest joined the Chickasaw, *Creek and *Cherokee peoples, and some then went to *Oklahoma. **2** a city in the US state of *Mississippi. It is the oldest city on the *Mississippi River and is famous for its beautiful homes built before the *Civil War. Natchez was settled in 1716 by the French who defeated the Natchez people. It was then controlled in turn by Britain, Spain and the US. For a short time (1817–21) it was the state capital. The **Natchez Trace National Parkway** runs from Natchez to *Nashville, *Tennessee.

N

ˌCarry ˈ**Nation** /ˌkæri ˈneɪʃn/ (1846–1911) an American woman who tried to improve society. She is best remembered for her campaign against alcohol during which she often entered bars to destroy bottles and barrels containing alcoholic drink. She was arrested many times, especially in the 1890s. She also destroyed tobacco, foreign food and paintings of naked women. She published a paper called *Smasher's Mail*.

The ˈ***Nation*** a left-wing US magazine, published each week since 1865. It contains articles on politics, society and the arts.

the ˈ**National** (*BrE infml*) **1** the *Grand National horse race. **2** the Royal *National Theatre.

the ˈ**National** ˈ**Air and** ˈ**Space Mu**ˌ**seum** a US museum of air and space travel which is part of the *Smithsonian Institution in Washington, DC. Its displays include the Wright Flyer (the first aircraft to fly successfully), Charles *Lindbergh's plane **Spirit of St Louis*, **Enola Gay* (the US plane that dropped the first atom bomb), and the only surviving section of Apollo 11, which made the first space flight to the moon.

national anthems

Britain's official national anthem is *God Save the Queen* (or *God Save the King* if the ruler is a man). It is not known who wrote the words, but it seems that the song, said to be the oldest national anthem in the world, was written many years before it was chosen as an official national song in the 18th century. It was first performed in public in 1745, during the *Jacobite Rebellion, to a musical arrangement by Thomas Arne (1710–78). The first verse is played or sung on formal occasions, especially if the Queen or another member of the *royal family is present:

God save our gracious Queen,
Long live our noble Queen,
God save the Queen.
Send her victorious,
Happy and glorious,
Long to reign over us,
God save the Queen.

Everybody stands while it is being played, as a mark of respect.

Many British people think *God Save the Queen* is too slow and solemn, and would prefer a more lively national song such as **Land of Hope and Glory* or **Rule, Britannia!* Both express pride in Britain's achievements but were perhaps more appropriate in the days when Britain had an empire.

Wales has its own national anthem, *Hen Wlad fy Nhadau* (**Land of My Fathers*). It celebrates the survival of Welsh traditions, language and scenery and is often sung at concerts and at major sports events in which Wales is taking part. Scotland does not have an official national anthem, though **Scotland the Brave* is often sung at public gatherings. *The *Flower of Scotland* is played and sung as an anthem before international *Rugby games in which the Scottish team is playing.

The national anthem of the US is The **Star-Spangled Banner*, referring to the US flag. The words were written in 1814 and set to the music of a popular song. It became the national anthem in 1931. Every American knows the story of how *The Star-Spangled Banner* was written during a war between the US and Britain. Its author, Francis Scott *Key, was a prisoner on a British ship off the coast of *Baltimore. From there he could watch the battle for control of Fort McHenry. The song tells how he watched as the sun went down. He could no longer see the fighting, but since bombs were still exploding he knew that the British had not won. When the morning came he could see the American flag still flying over the fort.

The Star-Spangled Banner is played at official ceremonies and sung at public events. On these occasions everyone present is expected to stand up and sing. Although there are three verses only the first is normally used:

Oh, say, can you see by the dawn's early light,
What so proudly we hailed at the twilight's last
  gleaming?
Whose broad stripes and bright stars, thro' the
  perilous fight,
O'er the ramparts we watched were so gallantly
  streaming?
And the rockets' red glare, the bombs bursting
  in air,
Gave proof thro' the night that our flag was still
  there.
Oh, say does that star-spangled banner yet wave
O'er the land of the free and home of the brave?

---

the ˌ**National** ˈ**Archives** the US government's official collection of historical records, documents, papers, films, maps, etc. They include the original *Declaration of Independence, the *American Constitution and the *Bill of Rights. The National Archives Building is in Washington, DC, on Constitution Avenue.

the ˌ**National** ˈ**Art Col**ˈ**lections Fund** a British charity that tries to keep great works of art in Britain. Since it was started in 1903, it has saved more than 10 000 important art objects from being sold abroad.

the **ˈNational Asˈsembly for ˈWales** /ˈweɪlz/ ⇨ WELSH ASSEMBLY.

the **ˈNational Associˈation for the Adˈvancement of ˈColored ˌPeople** ⇨ NAACP.

the **ˌNational ˈBasketball Associˌation** ⇨ NBA.

the **ˌNational ˈBook Aˌward** one of several US awards given each year by the Association of American Publishers. Each winner receives $10 000, and the awards include those for the best works of Fiction, Non-fiction, Poetry and Young People's Literature. They were first presented in 1950.

the **ˌNational ˈBook Critics ˌCircle** a US organization for book reviewers. It has about 700 members and was established in 1974. In the same year it started presenting the **National Book Critics Circle Awards**. These are chosen by a group of book reviewers and authors, and given to writers of Fiction, Non-fiction, Biography or Autobiography, Poetry and Criticism.

the **ˌNational ˈBroadcasting ˌCompany** ⇨ NBC.

the **ˈNational ˈChildbirth ˈTrust** (*abbr* the **NCT**) a British organization that aims to teach people about the process of having babies and about looking after them. People who are having their first child can go to NCT classes, often in the teacher's home. A woman may learn, for example, the best way of breathing to help her to relax when the baby is actually being born.

the **ˈNational Colˈlegiate Athˈletic Associˌation** ⇨ NCAA.

the **ˌNational Conˈsumer ˌCouncil** an independent organization started by the British government in 1975 to work on behalf of the public who pay for goods and services. It aims to improve companies and products which are not satisfactory, but in a general way. It does not deal with people's individual problems.

ˌNational Conˈsumers League (*abbr* **NCL**) a US organization, established in 1899, which influences the government to pass laws to protect people who buy goods or use services. It is private and does not make a profit. It also informs consumers of their rights, has a National Fraud Information Center and publishes several magazines.

the **National Curriculum**

The National Curriculum was introduced in all *state schools in England and Wales in 1988. Children's education from 5 to 16 is divided into four **key stages**. Key stage 1 covers ages 5–7, key stage 2 ages 7–11, key stage 3 ages 11–14 and key stage 4 ages 14–16. At key stages 1 and 2 pupils study English, mathematics, science, technology, history, geography, art, music and physical education. A modern foreign language is added at key stage 3. Pupils at key stage 4 must study English, mathematics, science, physical education, technology and a modern foreign language and may take several other subjects. In Wales the Welsh language is also studied. Detailed guidance about what children should be taught is given in official **programmes of study**. A disadvantage for teachers has been the increase in the number of documents they are expected to read and the reports they have to write. The National Curriculum does not apply in Scotland, where individual schools decide which subjects and topics to teach.

Attainment targets are set within each subject and pupils' progress is checked at the ages of 7, 11 and 14 when they complete **standard assessment tasks (SATs)**. Pupils are graded into eight levels for all subjects except art, music and physical education. At the age of 16, at the end of key stage 4, pupils take ***GCSE** exams, which are also based on material covered in the National Curriculum. Some children struggle to reach the required standard. If they have learning difficulties, and their parents may ask for them to be **statemented**, i.e. given an official document saying that they have **special educational needs**.

The SATs allow education authorities, in theory at least, to compare standards between different schools. Since the National Curriculum was introduced many people have expressed doubts about the publication in the press of **school league tables** showing the relative performance of schools and about the increased competition.

There is no national curriculum in the US. State governments are responsible for deciding the curriculum for primary and secondary schools. The curriculum is often the cause of debate between people who want to emphasize basic skills, such as reading, writing and mathematics, and others who see the curriculum as a political issue and want schools to teach respect for other cultures or history from the point of view of African Americans, or to offer less traditional topics.

the **ˌNational ˈDebt** *n* [sing] the total amount of money that has been borrowed by a government to help pay for *public spending. In Britain, the amount borrowed every year is known as the *Public Sector Borrowing Requirement, and is added to the National Debt.

the **ˌNational Eduˈcation Associˌation** ⇨ NEA.

The ***ˌNational Enˈquirer*** a popular US *tabloid newspaper, first published in 1952. It contains articles which are often difficult to believe about the private lives of famous people, creatures from space, ghosts, etc. It sells about 2.5 million copies a day, mostly in supermarkets and other public places.

the **ˌNational Eˈxecutive Comˌmittee** a committee elected by the British *Labour Party and *trade unions to make decisions about the policy of the Labour Party.

the **ˌNational Exhiˈbition ˌCentre** (*abbr* the **NEC**) a large centre for exhibitions and conferences near *Birmingham in England, opened in 1976. It holds over 100 exhibitions a year. An example is the *Motor Show.

the **ˌNational ˈFarmers' ˌUnion** (*abbr* the **NFU**) an organization for farmers in England and Wales. It is not a *trade union but exists to give practical advice and support to farmers. There is a separate **National Farmers' Union of Scotland**.

the **ˌNational ˈFilm ˌTheatre** (*abbr* the **NFT**) a cinema on the *South Bank in London, run by the *British Film Institute. It shows the best British and foreign films from all periods, and films of special historical interest. The London Film Festival is held there every year. The NFT has existed since the 1950s, and in 1988 the *Museum of the Moving Image was opened next to it.

the **ˌNational ˈFootball ˌConference** (*abbr* the **NFC**) (in American football) one of two groups of teams in the *National Football League (NFL). The NFC has an Eastern Division, a Central Division and a Western Division, and there are five teams in each division. The other NFL group is the *American Football Conference (AFC).

the **ˌNational ˈFootball League** (*abbr* the **NFL**) the organization for professional American football teams. It is divided into the *American Football Conference and the *National Football Conference and both have Eastern, Central and Western Divisions, with five teams in each. After the regular season, the best six teams in each conference play to decide which two will go to the *Super Bowl. The NFL began in 1933.

the ˌ**National** ˈ**Front** an extreme right-wing political party in Britain. It was formed in 1966 and caused some street violence in the 1970s, mainly because of its campaign against black and Asian people. In 1980 the party split, and some of its members formed the new *British National Party. The National Front has put forward many candidates for election to parliament but none of them has received more than a few hundred votes.

the ˌ**National** ˈ**Gallery** (in Britain) the buildings in *Trafalgar Square, London, which contain the largest collection of paintings belonging to the nation. The paintings represent every period and style in western art from the 14th to the early 20th century. The main building was completed in 1838, and a new building, the Sainsbury Wing, paid for by members of the family that owns *Sainsbury's and designed by the US architect Robert *Venturi, was added in 1991. More modern paintings are held at the *Tate Gallery.

the ˈ**National** ˈ**Gallery of** ˈ**Art** a US museum of art owned by the nation and supported by the government. It is part of the *Smithsonian Institution in Washington, DC, and was established in 1937, when Andrew *Mellon died and left his collection of art to the nation. The West Building opened in 1941 and contains works by such great artists as Raphael, Reubens, Rembrandt and El Greco. The East Building for 20th-century art was opened in 1978.

the ˈ**National** ˈ**Gallery of** ˈ**Scotland** /ˈskɒtlənd; *AmE* ˈskɑːtlənd/ a building in Edinburgh which contains an important collection of European and Scottish paintings from the 14th to the early 20th century. It was opened in 1859.

N

ˌ***National Geo*****ˈ*graphic*** a US magazine published each month by the National Geographic Society. It has about 9 million readers and is famous for its beautiful photographs and maps as well as its articles about different countries, societies and animals. US readers must join the Society in order to receive the magazine, but in Britain it can be bought in shops. The Society also publishes books and other magazines, and has a television series.

the ˌ**national** ˈ**grid** *n* [sing] **1** the network of wires, pipes and other equipment that supply electricity, gas and water all over England, Scotland and Wales. **2** the system of horizontal and vertical lines that is used on British *Ordnance Survey maps to divide the country into squares so that the position of a place on the map can be referred to easily.

the ˌ**National** ˈ**Guard** a military force of volunteers in each US state. The total force is about 500 000. **National Guardsmen** can be called to service by the nation or by a state, often after destruction caused by violent weather. They were used by the southern states to oppose the *civil rights movement and by the US government to support it. The Ohio National Guard killed four *Kent State University students during *Vietnam War protests there in 1970. Some National Guard groups took part in the *Gulf War (1990–1).

the ˌ**National** ˈ**Health** ˌ**Service** (*abbr* **NHS**) the British public service providing medical care that is paid for mainly by the government. British people have strong feelings about its importance, and it became one of the top political issues in the 1990s. The National Health Service was introduced in 1946 by the *Labour government as part of the *welfare state system recommended in the *Beveridge Report, and it came into operation in 1948. At first it provided free medical, dental and hospital services for everyone, but in the 1960s charges for medicines and dental services were introduced. Since then the cost of the NHS has continued to rise and governments have been forced to find new ways of paying for it. The Conservative government under Margaret *Thatcher was accused of trying to privatize (= sell to private owners) the NHS after introducing *trust status for hospitals and *fundholding for doctors, and encouraging the growth of private medical services and private medical insurance. There are now fewer NHS dentists, but doctors and hospitals are still free of charge. See also PRIVATE PATIENT.

the ˈ**National** ˈ**Heritage Me**ˈ**morial Fund** a fund (= money for a special purpose) set up by the British parliament in 1980 for buying and preserving buildings, works of art and other objects that are seen as part of Britain's history. The money for the fund comes mainly from the government and, since 1995, from the *National Lottery. It is called a Memorial Fund because it is intended to honour the memory of people who have died for Britain.

the ˌ**National** ˈ**Hunt** the British name for professional horse racing over jumps, also called *steeplechasing*. It comes from the name of the organization that is responsible for the sport in Britain, the National Hunt Committee. Compare JOCKEY CLUB.

ˌ**National In**ˈ**surance** *n* [U] (*abbr* **NI**) (in Britain) a system of payments, called **National Insurance contributions**, that all working people and employers have to make. The money is used by the government for payments to unemployed people and others in need, and also to help pay for the *National Health Service. National Insurance is therefore an important part of the *welfare state. Every adult has a **National Insurance number** and this number is used by the *Department of Social Security to identify people.

the ˈ**National** ˈ**Labor Re**ˌ**lations Board** (*abbr* the **NLRB**) an independent US government organization responsible for preventing illegal practices in industrial relations and settling disputes between workers and managers. It was established by the National Labor Relations Act (1935) to direct trade elections and to protect unions from companies that tried to interfere with their organization and members.

the ˈ**National League** (*abbr* the **NL**) the older of America's two professional *baseball associations. It was established in 1876 as the National League of Professional Baseball Clubs. It now has 14 teams with five in the Eastern Division, five in the Central Division and four in the Western Division. The National League offices are in New York.

the ˌ**National** ˈ**Lottery** (in Britain) a lottery which raises money for the arts, sports, charities, the *National Heritage Memorial Fund, and other projects. The lottery was introduced by the government in 1994 and is run by the company *Camelot. See also OFLOT, SCRATCHCARD.

the ˌ**National** ˈ**Maritime Mu**ˌ**seum** a museum in *Greenwich, London, with a collection of paintings, boats and other historical items connected with the sea.

the ˌ**National** ˈ**Motor Mu**ˌ**seum** a museum at *Beaulieu near *Southampton, England, with a large collection of motor vehicles from every period from the late 19th century to the present day. It is one of Britain's most popular tourist attractions.

the ˌ**National** ˈ**Motto** the official US motto since 1956: 'In God We Trust.' It is based on a line from *The *Star-Spangled Banner*: 'And this be our motto: "In God is our trust".' The motto has appeared on all US paper money and coins since 1955. All US states have their own individual mottos, often in Latin.

the ˈ**National Muˈseum of ˈWales** a museum in *Cardiff, Wales, with exhibitions of archaeology, nature, art, and industrial and social history, mainly but not only connected with Wales.

ˌ**National ˈNature Reˌserve** *n* any of several areas of land in Britain that are protected by law in order to preserve the plants and animals that live there, or to preserve other features of the environment. Marine Nature Reserves in Britain also give protection to plants and animals living in sea areas. ⇨ note at NATIONAL PARKS.

ˌ**National Oˈpinion Polls** (*abbr* **NOP**) a British organization that interviews people from all sections of society to find out their opinions on various subjects. The results help organizations like newspapers, businesses and political parties to understand public opinion and to predict events such as the results of elections.

the ˈ**National Organiˈzation for ˈWomen** (*abbr* **NOW**) a large US organization that works for women's rights. It was established in 1966 by Betty *Friedan, who was its first president. It supported the *Equal Rights Amendment that failed. In 1997 NOW had about 250 000 members.

national parks and protected areas

The idea of **national parks** began in the US, which now has 54 of them, covering over 80 000 square miles (200 000 square kilometres). The great majority are in western states. The **National Park Service** is responsible for protecting the natural state of the parks for the benefit of the public. America's parks are so popular that they are being harmed by the number of visitors and their cars. To try to stop this, the National Park Service announced in 1997 that people would only be able to visit some parks using public transport.

The oldest national park in the world is *Yellowstone National Park, established in 1872. The largest US park is Wrangell–St Elias in *Alaska with 13 000 square miles (34 000 square kilometres). It has few visitors because it is very remote. The most popular park is the *Great Smoky Mountains. Many parks are well known for some special feature, such as the *Grand Canyon, the *Everglades and the *Petrified Forest.

There are many other sites run by the National Park Service. The most visited area is the Blue Ridge Parkway in *Virginia and *North Carolina which received more than 17 million visits in 1996. (Parkways are roads with parkland either side). **National recreation areas** such as the Golden Gate in *California also receive many visitors. Most have water sports and other activities. **National preserves** are similar to national parks but are not as well protected. Companies can even search for oil and gas on them. Ten of the 16 national preserves are in *Alaska, including the oldest, *Denali, established in 1917.

The US Bureau of Land Management is in charge of **wilderness areas** created by *Congress. Visitors can camp in wilderness areas if they follow the 'leave no trace' policy. *Native Americans are allowed to use them for religious ceremonies.

National parks are also important as recreation areas in Britain. In 1949 10 national parks were established and they continue to attract thousands of visitors each year. The aim is to keep them as far as possible in their natural state, while balancing the different needs of agriculture, industry, housing and tourism. Many of the people who live in national parks depend on tourists for their living and are used to crowded roads in summer. A more serious problem is that some visitors who go regularly to the national park buy cottages in the area as second homes. This means there is less property for local people to buy and many are forced to move.

National parks cover 5 250 square miles (13 600 square kilometres), 9% of England and Wales. They include the *Lake District, *Dartmoor, and *Snowdonia. Each is managed by a *National Park Authority, responsible in England to the *Countryside Commission and in Wales to the Countryside Council for Wales. The government provides 75% of the money to run the parks. National Park Authorities control development within each park, look after *public footpaths and run information and study centres. Some of the land in national parks is owned by the *National Trust but a lot is privately owned.

Some areas, such as the *Gower Peninsula and the *Malvern Hills, are officially protected as **areas of outstanding natural beauty (AONBs)**. They tend to be less developed than national parks but still attract many visitors. There are 41 AONBs in England and Wales, and another nine in Northern Ireland. Scotland has 40 ***national scenic areas**, including the *Cairngorm Mountains and *Loch Lomond.

---

the ˌ**National ˈPortrait ˌGallery** a building in London containing thousands of paintings and photographs of famous people from British history. It is next to the *National Gallery and was opened in 1896.

ˌ**National ˈPower** the larger of the two companies that have made most of the electricity used in England and Wales since 1991, when the *Central Electricity Generating Board, which was owned by the State, was sold to private owners. See also NATIONAL GRID 1, OFFER, POWERGEN.

the ˌ**National ˈRailway Muˌseum** a museum in *York which contains a large collection of old railway carriages and steam locomotives, including the world speed record holder for steam engines, the *Mallard. The museum is a branch of the *Science Museum in London and was opened in 1975.

the ˌ**National ˈRifle Associˌation** (*abbr* the **NRA**) a US organization, established in 1871, which supports the use of guns for hunting, sport and self-defence. Its 3.4 million members argue that according to the US *Constitution people have a right to own guns, and they form a powerful group trying to prevent *Congress passing new laws restricting the use of guns.

the ˌ**National ˈRivers Auˌthority** a British government organization that is responsible for the country's rivers and other water resources. It investigates pollution, and manages flood control and the use of rivers for fishing and sailing.

ˌ**National ˈSavings** (in Britain) a system that encourages people to save some of their money and enables the government to borrow money from the people. The system is managed by the government's **Department of National Savings**. This department runs the **National Savings Bank**, which operates mainly through post offices all over Britain and by mail. The bank offers various ways of saving and investing money, including *National Savings Certificates and *Premium Bonds. About half the people in Britain have some money in National Savings, which raises billions of pounds for the government's *Public Sector Borrowing Requirement.

ˌ**National ˈSavings Cerˌtificate** *n* (in Britain) one of the types of investment (= plan for investing money) offered by the government's *National Savings Bank. People buy the Certificates for a fixed period, usually five years, and at the end of the period receive the amount paid plus interest, which is not taxed. National Savings Certificates were introduced in 1916 as a way for the government to borrow extra money during *World War I.

ˈnational ˈscenic ˈarea *n* (in Scotland) an area of natural beauty which is protected and preserved, and which people can visit and enjoy. These areas cover about 15% of Scotland and are similar to *national parks in England and Wales.

the **ˌNational Seˈcurity ˌCouncil** (*abbr* the **NSC**) a committee responsible for advising the US *President on matters of national security (= the protection of the nation and its interests) and defence policies. It was established by *Congress in 1947. The President leads the committee's meetings, and other NSC members are the Vice-president, the *Secretary of State and the Secretary of Defense. They are advised by the Chairman of the *Joint Chiefs of Staff and the Director of the *CIA.

national service

Conscription (= compulsory service in the armed forces) was introduced in Britain in *World War I and again in 1939. It continued long after the end of *World War II under the name **national service**. During wartime, all men between the ages of 18 and 41 were likely to be **called up** to join the *armed forces, unless they were medically unfit or were working in a **reserved occupation**. Many women were called up to serve in industry or as *land girls in the Women's Land Army. **Conscientious objectors** (= people who did not want to join the armed forces for moral or religious reasons) were at first the target of public insults, but later established a role for themselves in caring for the wounded.

After 1948 men between the ages of 19 and 25 were expected to serve 21 months (later increased to two years) in the services, and were often based outside Britain. This was very unpopular with most young men, and national service was ended in 1960. Since then, Britain has depended on **volunteers** to join the services and runs recruiting offices in many towns. Some young people join an ***Officers' Training Corps** while at school or university, or become members of the *Territorial Army. From time to time politicians and others call for national service to be introduced again, believing that military life is a good way to encourage discipline among young people.

In the US national service is called **selective service** or conscription, but its popular name is **the draft**. It was first introduced during the *Civil War by both the North and the *Confederate States, and was very unpopular. One reason for this was that anyone could avoid service if he paid money ($300 in the North), or hired somebody to replace him. This led to **draft riots** by poor people in New York City, and almost 1 000 *African Americans and others were killed.

The US next used conscription during World War I. Some called it 'another name for slavery', but 10 million men put their names on the draft list. America's first conscription in peacetime began in 1940 when Europe was at war. A man could receive an **exemption** if he was in the '4-F' group for physical or mental reasons, or had an important job. There were also some conscientious objectors who had to take jobs provided by the government.

The draft was stopped in 1947 but begun again a year later, and men aged 18–25 had to serve 21 months. This supplied soldiers for the *Korean War and the *Vietnam War. Many young men were unwilling to fight in Vietnam and some tried to stay in college and university where they could have a '2-S deferment' from the war. **Draft dodgers** sometimes burned their **draft cards** or went abroad. Conscription was finally ended in 1973, and two years later President *Ford offered to forgive draft dodgers, but only 22 000 of the 125 000 accepted. In 1977 President *Carter officially forgave all of them, provided that they had not committed any violence. Although the draft has ended, all men must put their names on the draft list when they become 18 in case there is a national emergency. Few seem to object to this.

---

the **ˈNational Soˈciety for the Preˈvention of ˈCruelty to ˈChildren** ⇨ NSPCC.

the ˈRoyal **ˈNational ˈTheatre** (*usu* the **National Theatre**, *also infml* the **National**) a modern building containing three theatres on London's *South Bank, and the theatre company that performs there. The National Theatre company was started in 1963. Its home was the *Old Vic until the new National Theatre building was opened in 1976. In 1988 the title *Royal* was officially added to the company's name to mark its 25th anniversary. However, most people call the company and the building by their original name. The three theatres at the National are the Lyttelton, the Olivier (named after the company's first artistic director, Lawrence *Olivier) and the Cottesloe. The directors since Olivier have been Peter *Hall, Richard *Eyre and Trevor *Nunn. The theatre has presented a wide range of old and new plays and is known for the high quality of its productions.

the **ˌNational ˈTrust** (*abbr* the **NT**) a British organization for preserving old buildings and beautiful *countryside so that people can visit and enjoy them. Its full name is the National Trust for Places of Historic Interest and Natural Beauty. It began as a small private organization in 1895 but is now the largest private owner of land in Britain, having bought or been given historic houses, whole villages, *stately homes, gardens and many areas of land. The Trust has more than two million members, which makes it one of the most popular membership groups in Britain. Compare ENGLISH HERITAGE.

the **ˈNational ˈUrban ˈLeague** a US organization, established in 1910, which supports the rights of *African Americans and other minority groups. Its main offices are in New York and it has branches in 34 states.

ˌNational Voˈcational Qualifiˌcation ⇨ NVQ.

the **ˌNational ˈWar ˌCollege** the US government's college for training future leaders of the armed forces, the *State Department and other organizations. It was established in 1946 to replace the Army-Navy Staff College and is at Fort Lesley J McNair in Washington, DC.

the **ˈNational ˈWestminster ˈBank** /ˈwestmɪnstə; *AmE* ˈwestmɪnstər/ (*also* **NatWest**) one of the four main *clearing banks in England and Wales with branches in most towns and cities. Its head offices are in London's National Westminster Tower, one of the tallest buildings in the city.

the **ˌNational ˈYouth ˌOrchestra** a British orchestra for musicians under 20 years old. It gives performances during the school holidays, including one every year at the *Proms.

Native Americans ⇨ article.

ˌ*Native* ˈ*Son* a novel (1940) by the *African-American writer Richard *Wright. It is about a young and poor African-American man in *Chicago who is badly treated because of his colour. He kills a white girl and is condemned to death. The book is a strong attack on racism and was a major influence on other writers.

Native Americans

Native Americans were living in North America for many hundreds of years before Europeans reached the continent. For a long time white people called them **Indians**. Today, many people do not like this name since it is based on a mistake: it was given to the people living in the Americas by Christopher *Columbus who, when he arrived there, thought he had discovered India. Instead, people prefer to use the term **Native Americans**. There are also native peoples living in *Alaska and Canada, e.g. ***Inuits** and **Aleuts**, but they are separate groups and are not called Native Americans.

Early contact with Europeans

In *Pre-Columbian North America there were many **tribes** who lived by hunting animals and gathering plants. Many of the tribes moved from one place to another according to the season and what food was available. Most of what is known about Native Americans dates from the time when they came into contact with Europeans.

The first place in the US where Europeans settled permanently was *Jamestown, Virginia, founded in 1607. At first Native Americans were positive about the Europeans and were happy to have the many new things they brought, e.g. metal cooking pots, cloth and guns. But the Europeans also introduced diseases that Native Americans had no resistance to, so many became ill and died. They also brought alcohol, the effects of which Native Americans did not know. Some Europeans took advantage of this by getting them drunk and then paying low prices for their goods.

The worst problem for Native Americans, which lasted into the late 20th century, was that the new settlers wanted their land. To native Americans owning land was a strange idea. Tribes moved around as they pleased and shared land with any other tribe that was friendly. They did not understand that a person might believe a piece of land was theirs, or that they would try to keep others from using it. The settlers, on the other hand, assumed that they would take control of North America and used all means to do this, including making agreements, which they usually did not keep, tricking Native Americans into selling land cheaply, and taking it by military force. Native American chiefs like *Sitting Bull, *Tecumseh and *Geronimo fought against the settlers.

As Whites began moving west, Native American tribes had to be moved on. Some were forced to go to other parts of North America, to areas very different from the ones they were used to. The ***Trail of Tears** was one of many terrible examples: in the cold winter of 1838–9 17 000 *Cherokees had to move from their land in the south-east to what is now *Oklahoma and more than 4 000 died. The government promised tribes that if they agreed to stay in one part of the country they could keep that land forever. But the promises lasted only until Americans discovered that the land they had given them was good for farming or had gold.

Whites have explained this behaviour in different ways. When the Indians fought and killed white people they said that this proved that Native Americans were wild and had to be controlled. People also believed that the Native Americans were wasting good land by not developing it. In the 19th century Americans believed in ***manifest destiny**, meaning that they thought God wanted them to occupy the whole continent. They also believed that it was better for the Native Americans to learn to live like white people and tried to teach them Christianity. Many Native American children, including the athlete Jim *Thorpe, were taken away from their tribe and sent to schools where they were not allowed to speak their own language.

Native American languages

Before Europeans arrived in North America there were over 300 Native American languages. Some have now died out, and of the 250 or so remaining many are spoken only by a few older people. Other languages, like Cherokee, are more widely spoken. Most Native Americans speak English, some as their first language and others as their second.

Native American languages have added many words to English, though the meaning of a word has often been changed. **Teepees** are a kind of tent, ***wampum** belts were made of beads and since the belts had great value Europeans used *wampum* to mean ‘money’. **Moccasins**, a kind of shoe, are today worn by people all over the world. Many Native American words describe the things they name. For example, the Asakiwaki tribe’s name means ‘people of the yellow earth’, and the Cherokees’ name for themselves, Ani-Yun’wiya, means ‘the leading people’. Indian names for Whites included ‘people greedily grasping for land’.

Many American place names have their roots in Native American languages. *Ohio, for instance, is a Native American name, and the names of many of its towns and cities, such as Chillicothe and Sandusky, and the lakes Scioto and Olentangy, are of Native American origin.

Native Americans today

According to the **Bureau of Indian Affairs**, a part of the US government, there are now about 550 tribes. These include well-known groups like the ***Navajo** and ***Sioux**, and less famous tribes like the **Cayuse**. The number of Native Americans living in the US is about 1.2 million.

Almost a million live on **reservations**, areas of land that the government has allowed them to keep as their own. Native Americans are US citizens, and have the rights and responsibilities of any US citizen. However, reservations have their own governments and police forces and Native Americans pay different taxes. They also have the right to hunt and fish where and when they like, while other Americans have to get a licence.

On or off the reservations Native Americans find it difficult to live the traditional life. Activities of other Americans affect the way they live. Building dams across a river, for example, can affect the numbers of fish living there, so that even though Native Americans have the right to fish they may not be able to catch anything. Away from the reservations, many Native Americans find that their culture is very different from that of white people and have difficulty adapting.

Poverty is a serious problem. About 37% of people who live on reservations are unemployed, compared with 6% of the general population. Many tribes try to bring in money from outside. Some sell rights to search for oil on their reservation, others use the fact that the reservation makes its own rules to open casinos where people from outside can come and gamble. Gambling is illegal in most parts of the US and many Americans want it to remain so, but it makes a lot of money for the tribes. This brings Native Americans, once again, into conflict with white Americans.

Native Americans in the popular imagination

An American tradition dating back to early times is ***Thanksgiving**. When the English arrived in Jamestown many died during the long cold winter, but in the following spring Native Americans showed them what local foods they could eat. In the autumn, well-prepared for the winter, settlers and Native Americans had a special dinner together, the first Thanksgiving, to thank God and the Native Americans for all the food they had.

Another story describes how the Native American princess ***Pocahontas** saved the life of John *Smith, the leader in Jamestown, when her father, ***Powhatan**, wanted to kill him. She later married another Englishman, John Rolfe, and went to England with him. The story of Pocahontas is widely known and many Americans are proud to have her as an ancestor.

But Native Americans were more often seen by white settlers as the enemy. *Westerns, i.e. films and books about the ***Wild West**, use the threat from Indians as their central theme. In this context Native Americans are still called 'Indians'. Children often play 'cowboys and Indians' and pretend to kill each other. When *Buffalo Bill, began touring the US with his Wild West show, the chief Sitting Bull was one of many Native Americans in it, and many people went to see this former great enemy.

Many Americans have an image of a 'typical Indian', a chief who lived in a teepee with his **squaw** (= wife), smoked a **peace pipe** after signing a treaty with the white man (whom he called **pale face**), sent **smoke signals** to communicate with people far away, and spoke broken English full of colourful expressions such as 'big heap wampum' (a lot of money) and 'speaks with forked tongue' (is lying). Most of these ideas have some basis in Native American culture, but it is wrong to put them all together and believe that that was how Native Americans lived.

Americans make such mistakes because they have little interest in Native Americans. Having succeeded in pushing them out of the way onto reservations, most Americans ignore them. This may be because the Native Americans who are left are living proof of a hard truth: America wants to be, and often is, a land where everyone has a chance and where the government behaves fairly and honestly to all, but this America is built on land stolen from the people who lived there first.

N

NATO /ˈneɪtəʊ; *AmE* ˈneɪtoʊ/ (*in full* the **North Atlantic Treaty Organization**) an organization originally formed by 12 countries in 1949 to defend Europe and North America against what was seen as the threat of Soviet attack after *World War II. They agreed that an armed attack against one or more of them should be considered an attack against them all, and set up military bases all over Europe to protect themselves against the Communists. Since the end of the *cold war in the late 1980s, and the joining of East and West Germany in 1990, it has been suggested that NATO should become a political organization rather than a military one. In 1995 NATO started a major new approach called Partnership for Peace, which tries to make political and military links stronger between NATO and the central and eastern European countries. NATO's main offices are in Brussels, and its members now include Belgium, Britain, Canada, Denmark, France, Germany, Greece, Iceland, Italy, Luxembourg, the Netherlands, Norway, Portugal, Spain, Turkey and the US.

the **ˌNatural ˈHistory Muˌseum** a big museum in London, England, with displays and information about plants, animals, insects, fossils (= animals and plants preserved in rock) and minerals. The museum's collections are so large that the discovery of previously unknown insects in the collections is not uncommon. It was originally part of the *British Museum but has been independently run since 1963.

the **ˌNature Conˈservancy ˌCouncil** a British government organization which chooses and manages national nature reserves and other *conservation areas, and provides information and advice on these to the government.

nature reserves

Nature **conservation areas** are areas of the countryside which have special protection under law because they have interesting or unusual wild plants or animals in them.

In Britain there are now about 350 **national nature reserves**, 600 **local nature reserves**, **forest** and **marine nature reserves**. Many contain species that are protected under the Wildlife and Countryside Act (1981). In addition, some relatively small pieces of land get special protection as **sites of special scientific interest** (**SSSIs**) because rare or **endangered** plants or animals are to be found there, or because they have special geological (= rock) features. There are over 6 000 SSSIs in Britain, many of which are not open to the public. In theory, SSSIs are safe from the threat of commercial development, but this is not always the case. Despite protests, several SSSIs have been lost in recent years to make way for new roads.

Nature conservation areas in Britain are managed by English Nature, Scottish Natural Heritage, the Countryside Council for Wales and the Department of the Environment for Northern Ireland, with the help of local naturalists' trusts and natural history societies.

The US also has many **nature preserves**. People can visit them for enjoyment or to do scientific research, but must stay on paths and cannot disturb or remove anything. They are not allowed to drive vehicles, camp, hunt or start fires. *Indiana has 151 nature preserves, more than 20 000 acres (8 100 hectares) in total. A popular type of nature preserve is the **wildlife refuge**, such as Lake Woodruff Natural Wildlife Refuge in Florida, where John James *Audubon once watched and drew birds.

There are also many national forests, rivers and seashores, and scenic trails. Many **national monuments** are also natural areas. They include the Great Sand Dunes in *Colorado, Lava Beds in *California and Organ Pipe Cactus in *Arizona. The US National Park Service is in charge of all of these and cares for the plants, animals and scenery so that they can be enjoyed by the public.

ˌ**Nat'West** /ˌnæt'west/ the banking group that owns Britain's *National Westminster Bank (also called NatWest) and *Coutts Bank, as well as other financial services.

the ˌ**NatWest 'Trophy** /ˌnætwest/ a British *cricket competition organized with financial help from the *National Westminster Bank. It involves teams from *counties in England and Wales and national teams from Scotland, Ireland and Holland: a total of 32 teams. There are cash prizes for the four best teams and for the 'man of the match' in each of the five rounds.

'**Naugahyde**™ /'nɔːgəhaɪd/ *n* [U] a type of artificial leather used for covering furniture, etc. and for making gloves. It can be cleaned with soap and water. Some people think that Naugahyde products show bad taste.

'**Nauru** /'naʊruː/ a small island and country in the Pacific Ocean north-east of Australia. It became independent in 1968 and is one of the smallest members of the *Commonwealth, with a population of under 10 000. ▶ **Nauruan** *adj*, *n*.

'**Navajo** (*also* '**Navaho**) /'nævəhəʊ; *AmE* 'nævəhoʊ/ *n* (*pl* **-o** *or* **-os**) a member of the largest group of *Native-American people, related to the *Apache. There are about 100 000 Navajo, and they live mostly in *Arizona, *New Mexico and *Utah on reservations (= lands given and protected by the US government). They work mainly as farmers and raising sheep. They have also earned money from oil and other minerals on their land. The Navajo are known for weaving carpets and blankets and for making silver jewellery.

Mar'tina ˌ**Navrati'lova** /mɑː'tiːnə ˌnævrætɪ'ləʊvə; *AmE* mɑːr'tiːnə ˌnævrætɪ'loʊvə/ (1956–) a US tennis player, born in Czechoslovakia. She was one of the most successful women players in the history of the game, winning *Wimbledon nine times (1978–9, 1982–7 and 1990), more than any other player, and the *US Open(2) four times (1983–4 and 1986–7), as well as many other competitions.

Martina Navratilova with the Wimbledon women's singles trophy

navy ⇨ articles at ARMED FORCES.

the **NBA** /ˌen biː 'eɪ/ (*in full* the **National Basketball Association**) the US organization in charge of professional *basketball. It was established in 1949, and its office is in New York. There are 29 NBA teams divided between the Eastern Conference (with an Atlantic Division and a Central Division) and the Western Conference (with a Midwest Division and a Pacific Division). At the end of each season, the best teams play to produce the NBA Champion.

NBC /ˌen biː 'siː/ (*in full* the **National Broadcasting Company**) the first of the original three US national broadcasting companies. It was established in 1926 by *RCA as two groups of radio stations. The first NBC television channel opened in 1940. The company is now owned by *General Electric. Its main offices are at *Rockefeller Center in New York.

the **NCAA** /ˌen siː dʌbl 'eɪ/ (*in full* the **National Collegiate Athletic Association**) an organization in charge of US college sports. It establishes rules for sports competitions between colleges and universities. The NCAA was established in 1906, and more than 1 000 colleges and universities are now members. It also publishes information about players, games and seasons. Its offices are at Overland Park, *Kansas.

NCT /ˌen siː 'tiː/ ⇨ NATIONAL CHILDBIRTH TRUST.

the **NEA** /ˌen iː 'eɪ/ (*in full* the **National Education Association**) a US trade union that aims to improve the school system, conditions for teachers, etc. In 1997 it had more than 2.3 million members, mostly teachers. Its head offices are in *Washington, DC.

ˌLough '**Neagh** ⇨ LOUGH NEAGH.

Ne'braska /nə'bræskə/ a US state in the western part of the *Middle West, also called the Cornhusker State. The Missouri River forms its eastern border. The largest city is *Omaha, and the capital city is Lincoln. It was part of the *Louisiana Purchase and explored by *Lewis and Clark. Nebraska produces corn, beans, wheat, potatoes and other crops. It also makes industrial machinery and electronic equipment. Its tourist attractions include Scotts Bluff National Monument and Chimney Rock National Historic Site.

NEC /ˌen iː 'siː/ ⇨ NATIONAL EXHIBITION CENTRE.

the '**Needles** /'niːdlz/ three tall pointed rocks sticking out of the sea near the *Isle of Wight. They are among the best-known and most unusual features of the British coast.

a Neighbourhood Watch sign

ˌ**Neighbourhood 'Watch** (in Britain) an arrangement by which people who live in a particular street or area watch each other's houses and tell the police if they see anything suspicious. Many people have formed local Neighbourhood Watch groups to try to prevent crime, but others have refused to join them because they do not like the idea of being watched by their neighbours: *It was one of those streets of semi-detached houses with shiny cars parked outside and Neighbourhood Watch stickers in the windows.*

'***Neighbours*** an Australian *soap opera that is very popular in Britain. It is about the lives and relationships of the people living on an imaginary street in Melbourne. It has been broadcast five times a week by the *BBC since 1986.

ˌ**Neiman 'Marcus** /ˌniːmən 'mɑːkəs; *AmE* 'mɑːrkəs/ (*also* '**Neiman's** /'niːmənz/) a very expensive department store with branches in many major US cities. The original shop was opened in *Dallas, *Texas in 1907 by Carrie Neiman and her brother Herbert Marcus. The company's Christmas Catalog is famous for containing many expensive items which only rich people have enough money to buy.

ˈˌBaby Face' ˈ**Nelson**[1] /ˈnelsn/ (1908–34) a US criminal, born Lester Gillis in *Chicago. He worked for a time with Al Capone and later robbed banks with John *Dillinger and 'Pretty Boy' *Floyd. He was named '*Public Enemy No. 1' by the *FBI in 1934 after killing several people. Soon afterwards he was shot dead by FBI men during a gun battle in Barrington, *Illinois.

ˌLord ˈ**Nelson**[2] /ˈnelsn/ (*born* Horatio Nelson 1758–1805) an English admiral who became famous for winning a number of sea battles against the French in the 1790s. These victories strengthened British military power at sea, and prevented Napoleon's forces attacking Britain. Many people know that Nelson lost his right arm and his right eye in different battles, and there is a famous story that he said 'Kiss me, Hardy' to another officer just before dying at *Trafalgar. He was made a *viscount(1) in 1801.

ˌRick ˈ**Nelson**[3] /ˈnelsn/ (1940–85) a US pop singer who was especially popular in the 1950s. He was the son of Ossie and Harriet Nelson and began singing (as Ricky Nelson) at the age of 16 on their television comedy show *The Adventures of *Ozzie and Harriet*. His hits included *Poor Little Fool* (1958), *Travellin' Man* (1960) and *Hello, Mary Lou* (1961). He later changed to *country music and had a hit with *Garden Party* (1972). He died in a plane crash.

ˌWillie ˈ**Nelson**[4] /ˈnelsn/ (1933–) a US *country music singer and writer of songs. He was very popular in the 1970s and his most successful songs included *On the Road Again* and *Blue Eyes Crying in the Rain*.

ˌ**Nelson's** ˈ**Column** /ˌnelsnz/ a tall column in the middle of *Trafalgar Square, London, which was built in memory of Lord *Nelson between 1839 and 1843. It has a statue of Nelson on top, and four bronze lions round its base. It is one of London's most famous tourist sights.

ˌ**neo**ˈ**classicism** /ˌniːəʊˈklæsɪsɪzəm; *AmE* ˌniːoʊˈklæsɪsɪzəm/ *n* [U] a style of art, architecture and design that is strongly influenced by the styles of ancient Greece and Rome. It became popular in Europe and North America in the second half of the 18th century, when many buildings were designed with geometrical forms, straight lines and Greek columns. ▶ **neoclassical** *adj*.

ˌE ˈ**Nesbit** /ˈnezbɪt/ (Edith Nesbit 1858–1924) an English writer of children's stories. She wrote several books about the children of the imaginary Bastable family that are still popular with British children today. Her best-known book, *The Railway Children* (1906), was made into a film in 1970.

ˈ**Nescafé**™ /ˈneskæfeɪ/ *n* [U] a popular make of instant coffee. Some people refer to any type of instant coffee as Nescafé: *It'll have to be Nescafé, I'm afraid – we've run out of real coffee.*

ˌEliot ˈ**Ness** /ˌeliət ˈnes/ (1902–57) an officer with the US Justice Department during *Prohibition. With a team of men called the 'Untouchables' he led surprise attacks on illegal alcohol operations run by Al *Capone in *Chicago, and helped to end Capone's criminal career. The US television series and film, both called *The *Untouchables*, were based on Ness's work.

ˈ**Nessie** /ˈnesi/ an informal name for the *Loch Ness monster.

ˈ**Nestlé** /ˈnesl, ˈnesleɪ/ a large international company that produces many types of food and drink, including *Nescafé, powdered milk and many popular makes of chocolate. Since the 1980s many people in Europe and America have refused to buy any Nestlé products as a protest against the way the company sells powdered milk for babies in poor countries.

ˈ**netball** *n* [U] a game based on *basketball that is played mainly by women and is very popular with British schoolgirls. It is played by two teams who score points by throwing the ball through a net with an open bottom at the opponents' end of the court. The rules are similar to those in basketball except that in netball the player holding the ball is not allowed to move.

playing netball

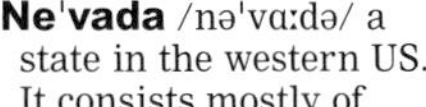

Neˈ**vada** /nəˈvɑːdə/ a state in the western US. It consists mostly of desert and mountains. It attracts many visitors from other US states to cities such as *Las Vegas and *Reno because of its relaxed laws which allow gambling and easy divorces.

the ˌ**Never** ˈ**Never Land** the imaginary place in **Peter Pan* where Peter and the children have adventures with pirates and animals. It is a magic world where children can fly, and never grow up. It is sometimes used to refer to an imaginary perfect place: *He talks about Scotland as if it was the Never Never Land.*

the **New Age**

People have often questioned the accepted philosophies of the modern western **materialist** society, and have looked to much older traditions for an increased spiritual awareness. Since the 1980s this movement, and the ideas behind it, have been given the name *New Age*. The movement started in *California but quickly spread throughout the US and northern Europe. It attracts young people, people who were ***hippies** in the 1960s and 1970s, and some older people. **New Age people** believe that a more **holistic** approach to life, which takes account of the whole of personal experience and of the cycles of nature, can help to restore the spiritual balance within themselves and harmony in the environment.

The New Age movement has been especially involved in religion, philosophy, medicine, and a broad area of study called **earth mysteries** which includes astrology and people's relationship with the environment. Some people have turned to religions that combine elements of Christianity with the worship of nature, or to eastern religions, such as Buddhism, that emphasize the personal development of the individual. There has also been a fascination with the **occult** and **parapsychology**, including telepathy, the mental communication of thoughts and feelings. **Crystals** (= pieces of special kinds of stone) are used for a type of healing. **Meditation** is used as a way to gain greater self-awareness. **New Age music**, which is usually soft and slow is supposed to make it easier to meditate. **Incense** helps promote a good atmosphere. Some people also use **psychedelic drugs**, though they are illegal. In Britain, ancient sites are thought to have special powers. Each year, on Midsummer's Day, large crowds attempt to reach *Stonehenge to celebrate the summer solstice, because they believe that it is one of the most magical places in Britain.

The New Age interest in nature has led to greater concern for environmental issues among the wider public. New Age people are often involved in protests at the sites of new roads or other projects that threaten to destroy the countryside. They are often prepared to take extreme measures and may be regarded by others as cranks (= people obsessed with a particular idea), though they are respected for their commitment.

New Age people tend to be regarded with suspicion by the rest of society. This is partly because people believe New Age people are involved in *drug abuse, and also, in Britain, because of the bad publicity given to **New Age travellers**. In the late 1980s several thousand young people chose to live in old buses or vans and to travel round Britain. Other people generally ignored them until they arrived in their local area, when they tried to have them moved on. There were complaints of vehicles holding up traffic, loud music, litter, etc. Now, the name *New Age traveller* is less common and they are usually called **travellers** or the **travelling community**.

New Age can also be used to describe people who have relatively modern opinions. The American phrase **sensitive new-age guy** (SNAG), for example, means a man who believes that it is his responsibility to help with the housework.

ˌNew Amsterˈdam /æmstəˈdæm; *AmE* æmstərˈdæm/ the name of what is now New York City when it was the Dutch capital of New Netherlands in the 17th century. It was a small town at the southern end of *Manhattan(1). The British captured it in 1664 and named it New York. Dutch forces took it again in 1673 for 15 months and called it New Orange.

ˈNewark /ˈnjuːək; *AmE* ˈnuːərk/ the largest city in the US state of *New Jersey. It is an industrial port on the Passaic River and has one of the three airports used for New York City, which is only 8 miles (13 kilometres) away. The city produces chemicals, beer, paint, leather goods and electronic equipment.

the **ˈNewbery ˌMedal** /ˈnjuːbəri; *AmE* ˈnuːberi/ a US award presented each year to the author of the best US children's book. It was established in 1922 and is presented by the Association for Library Service to Children, a division of the American Library Association. It is named after John Newbery (1713–67), an Englishman who published children's books.

ˌNewcastle-upon-ˈTyne /ˌnjuːkɑːsl, ˈtaɪn; *AmE* ˌnuːkæsl/ (*also* **ˈNewcastle**) an industrial city and port on the river *Tyne in north-east England. It used to be an important centre for *coal mining and shipbuilding, and many people became unemployed in the region when these industries became less active in the 1980s. It is now an important commercial, cultural and administrative centre, and is attracting new industries, with several foreign companies opening new factories in the area.

ˌNew ˈCovent ˈGarden ˈMarket /ˈkɒvənt; *AmE* ˈkɑːvənt/ (*also* **New Covent Garden**) London's main market selling fruit, vegetables and flowers in large quantities to people who then sell them to the public. It has been in *Vauxhall on the south bank of the *Thames since it was moved from *Covent Garden in 1973.

the **ˌNew ˈDeal** the programme begun by US President Franklin D *Roosevelt in the 1930s to end the *Great Depression. It introduced new economic and social measures, and made the national government more powerful. New organizations were created to manage it, including the *Securities and Exchange Commission, the *Works Progress Administration and the *Tennessee Valley Authority. Some people criticized the New Deal for being too expensive and for giving too much power to the government. Compare SQUARE DEAL.

ˌNew ˈEngland an area of the north-eastern US which includes the states of *Maine, *New Hampshire, *Vermont, *Massachusetts, *Rhode Island and *Connecticut. It is known for its beautiful small towns which are popular with visitors, especially in the autumn. **New Englanders**, a large number of whom have Irish ancestors, are often called the real Yankees. Other Americans consider them to be very independent, clever, practical and suspicious of people they do not know. The English explorer Captain John Smith named the area in 1614, and the *American Revolution began there.

the ***ˌNew English ˈBible*** a version of the Bible that was translated into modern English by a group of British *Protestant writers. It was published in two sections, the Old Testament in 1961 and the New Testament in 1970.

the **ˌNew ˈForest** an attractive area of countryside in southern England consisting of forest and open wild land covered with rough grass. It has belonged to the *royal family since *William the Conqueror began hunting there in 1079. It is a popular tourist centre, and especially well known for the **New Forest ponies**, a breed of small horses living there in almost wild conditions.

the **ˌNew ˈFrontier** a phrase used by John F *Kennedy to describe his aims and policies. In 1960 he said that the US was on 'the edge of a new frontier', and asked Americans to join together for new achievements in space, science, education and social conditions. This was said during the speech in which he accepted his nomination as the *Democratic Party's candidate for President. Compare NEW DEAL.

ˈNewgate /ˈnjuːgeɪt; *AmE* ˈnuːgeɪt/ (*also* **ˌNewgate ˈprison**, **ˌNewgate ˈgaol**) a prison in London which was first built in the 12th century on land where the *Old Bailey now stands. It was rebuilt several times before it was finally destroyed in 1902. In the 18th century it became famous for the very bad conditions in which the prisoners were kept. It is mentioned in many 18th- and 19th-century novels.

ˌNew ˈHampshire /ˈhæmpʃə(r)/ a north-eastern US state in *New England, also called the Granite State. The largest city is Manchester, and the capital city is Concord. New Hampshire was the first independent English colony (from 1776) and one of the original 13 states. It produces many crops, maple syrup, plastics, paper and electrical goods. Popular tourist attractions include the White Mountain National Forest and Lake Winnipesaukee.

ˌNew ˈJersey /ˈdʒɜːzi; *AmE* ˈdʒɜːrzi/ a north-eastern US state on the Atlantic Ocean. Local people often call it Jersey, and it is also known as the Garden State. The largest city is Newark, and the capital city is Trenton. New Jersey was settled by the Dutch, became British in 1664, and was one of the original 13 states. It produces vegetables, chemicals, medicines and clothing. *Atlantic City and *Princeton University are both in New Jersey.

ˌNew ˈLabour a phrase used by Tony *Blair in the 1990s to refer to his aim of making the British *Labour Party more modern. New Labour became more attractive to the British public, for example, when the party voted to change *Clause 4 and be less influenced by the *trade unions. A phrase used often by Blair in the campaign to win the general election in 1997 was 'New Labour, new Britain!'.

the **ˌNew ˈLeft** a group of people who developed left-wing political ideas in many countries, especially the US, in the 1960s. They protested against the conditions of poor people in society, and against the *Vietnam War, but they did not support the Soviet Union. The New Left included many students and writers.

ˌCardinal ˈ**Newman**[1] /ˈnjuːmən; *AmE* ˈnuːmən/ (John Henry Newman 1801–90) an English priest and poet. When he was the vicar (= priest) of the Anglican University Church in *Oxford he shocked many people because his opinions seemed closer to those of the *Roman Catholic Church than the *Church of England. He became a Roman Catholic in 1845, and a Catholic priest the next year. In 1879 he was made a cardinal (= a senior Roman Catholic priest). His writing had a wide influence on religious thought, and some of his poems are still sung as hymns.

ˌPaul ˈ**Newman**[2] /ˈnjuːmən; *AmE* ˈnuːmən/ (1925–) a US actor who has also produced and directed films. He is perhaps best remembered for his part in *Butch Cassidy and the Sundance Kid* (1969). His other films include *Cat on a Hot Tin Roof* (1958), *The Hustler* (1961), *Cool Hand Luke* (1967), *The Sting* (1973), *Nobody's Fool* (1994) and *Twinkle* (1998). He received a special *Oscar in 1985 and an Oscar for *The Color of Money* (1986). Newman is married to the actor Joanne Woodward, with whom he has often appeared in films. He has also been a *NASCAR racing driver and he owns a food company called Newman's Own.

ˈ**Newmarket** /ˈnjuːmɑːkɪt; *AmE* ˈnuːmɑːrkɪt/ a town in *Suffolk, south-east England, which has been a major horse-racing centre for more than 300 years. It has two famous racecourses where some of Britain's most important races take place each year. It is also the home of the *Jockey Club, the National Stud (= centre for breeding horses) and the National Horseracing Museum.

ˌ**New ˈMexico** /ˈmeksɪkəʊ; *AmE* ˈmeksɪkoʊ/ a south-western US state on the Mexican border, also called the Land of Enchantment. The largest city is Albuquerque, and the capital city is *Santa Fe. It became part of the US in 1848 after the *Mexican War, and a state in 1912. The first atom bomb was exploded at Alamogordo, New Mexico, in 1945. The state produces many minerals, including uranium, gold and silver, as well as oil and gas. Its tourist attractions include *Carlsbad Caverns and White Sands National Monument.

N

the ˈ**New ˈModel ˈArmy** the army organized by Oliver *Cromwell in 1645 to fight the supporters of *Charles I in the *English Civil War. It was Britain's first professional army, and its discipline and training were important factors in winning the war. See also FAIRFAX.

ˈ***New ˈMusical Exˈpress*** (*abbr* ***NME***) a British newspaper, published every Saturday, that consists mainly of articles about pop music. It has a reputation for recognizing new groups and musical styles before they become fashionable. It is especially popular with students.

ˌ**New ˈOrder** a British pop group formed in 1980 by members of the group *Joy Division after the death of their singer, Ian Curtis (1957–80). The group's best-known songs include *Blue Monday* (1983) and *Thieves Like Us* (1984).

ˌ**New Orˈleans** /ɔːˈliənz; *AmE* ɔːrˈliənz/ the largest city in the US state of *Louisiana. It is on the *Mississippi River and *Gulf of Mexico, and is the second largest US port. Its popular name is the Big Easy. The city is famous for its *French Quarter, *jazz and food, and millions of tourists visit it each year. The French established it in 1718, and it was part of the *Louisiana Purchase. Andrew *Jackson won the Battle of New Orleans against the British, the last battle of the *War of 1812. See also MARDI GRAS.

ˈ**Newport** /ˈnjuːpɔːt; *AmE* ˈnuːpɔːrt/ a city in the US state of *Rhode Island. It is on Aquidneck Island on the Atlantic coast. It was famous for the Newport Jazz Festival each year from 1954 until the festival moved to New York in 1972. Newport was settled in 1639 and became a place of safety for *Quakers and Jews. It was one of the state's two capitals until 1900. It contains many large houses built by rich people in the 19th century. The *America's Cup races were held there from 1851 to 1953.

The ˌ***New Reˈpublic*** a US political and cultural magazine known for its liberal opinions. It was established in 1914 and is published each week. People who have written for the magazine include John *Steinbeck, Thomas *Wolfe and Mary *McCarthy. Its editors have included Walter *Lippmann and Joyce Carol Oates.

the ˌ**New ˈRight** a general name for US right-wing politicians since the 1980s who have been in favour of a return to *states' rights and traditional family values, and against abortion and equal rights for homosexuals. Their views have been supported by the Moral Majority of Jerry *Falwell and other religious groups based on *fundamentalism. They helped to elect both Ronald *Reagan and George *Bush as *President.

ˌ***News at ˈTen*** a British television news programme that was broadcast for many years on *ITV at 10 o'clock every evening from Monday to Friday. It was well known for announcing the main points of the news between the chimes (= sounds of the bells) of *Big Ben, and for ending the programme with an amusing or unusual news story.

The ˌ***New ˈScientist*** a British magazine containing news and opinions about new developments in science and technology and their effects on society and the environment. It has been published every week since 1956.

ˈ**New ˈScotland ˈYard** /ˈskɒtlənd; *AmE* ˈskɑːtlənd/ the main offices in London, England, of most departments of the *Metropolitan Police. The original offices were in a street off *Whitehall called Scotland Yard. They were moved to a new building near *Victoria Station in 1966, but many people still refer to it as **Scotland Yard** or simply **the Yard**.

ˈ***Newsnight*** /ˈnjuːznaɪt; *AmE* ˈnuːznaɪt/ a television news programme that is broadcast in Britain on *BBC2 late every evening from Monday to Friday. It usually includes a serious discussion about an important news item. Some of its presenters, especially Jeremy *Paxman, are well known for asking politicians difficult questions.

the ˌ***News of the ˈWorld*** a British *tabloid Sunday newspaper, owned by Rupert *Murdoch. It is Britain's best-selling newspaper, and consists mainly of news about sport, crime and famous people such as film and television actors or members of the *royal family. It was first published in 1843.

Newspapers ⇨ article.

The ˌ***New ˈStatesman*** a British magazine published each week, containing articles about politics, society and the arts, usually written from a left-wing point of view. Established in 1913, it is Britain's oldest and best-known left-wing magazine, and has a reputation for independence and for criticizing the government.

ˈ***Newsweek*** /ˈnjuːzwiːk; *AmE* ˈnuːzwiːk/ a US news magazine published each week in New York. It contains articles on politics, science, society, culture and other subjects. It was first published in 1933 and is now owned by the **Washington Post*. In 1997, the magazine had more than 3 million readers.

Newspapers

Many British families buy a **national** or **local** newspaper every day. Some have it delivered to their home by a **paper boy** or **paper girl**; others buy it from a **newsagent** (= a shop selling *magazines, sweets, etc.) or a **bookstall**. National **dailies** are published each morning except Sunday. Competition between them is fierce. Local daily papers, which are written for people in a particular city or region, are sometimes published in the morning but more often in the early evening.

The US has only one national newspaper, **USA Today*. The rest are local. A few newspapers from large cities, such as the **New York Times* and *The *Washington Post*, are read all over the country. The **International Herald-Tribune* is published outside the US and is read by Americans abroad. Many Americans **subscribe** to a newspaper which is delivered to their house. This costs less than buying it in a shop. Papers can also be bought in bookshops and supermarkets. Large cities have **news stands**, small covered areas on the street, and smaller towns have **vending machines** from which people take a paper after putting in money.

Many newspapers are now available on the Internet. This is useful for checking the **headlines**, but most people prefer to read the printed version.

British newspapers

Britain has two kinds of national newspaper: the **quality papers** and the ***tabloids**. The qualities, often called ***broadsheets** because they are printed on large pages, report national and international news and are serious in tone. They have **editorials** which comment on important issues and reflect the political views of the paper's **editor**. They also contain financial and sports news, **features** (= articles), **obituaries** (= life histories of famous people who have just died), **listings** of television and *radio programmes, theatre and cinema shows, a *crossword, *comic strips, *advertisements and the weather forecast.

The main quality dailies are *The *Times* and the **Daily Telegraph*, which support the political right, *The *Guardian*, which is on the political left, *The *Independent*, and the **Financial Times*. People choose a paper that reflects their own political opinions. Sunday papers include the **Sunday Times*, *The *Observer* and *The *Independent on Sunday*. They have more pages than the dailies, **supplements** (= extra sections) on, for example, motoring and the arts, and a colour magazine.

The tabloids have a smaller page size and report news in less depth. They concentrate on **human-interest stories** (= stories about people), and often discuss the personal lives of famous people. Some have *page-three girls, photographs of half-naked young women. Many people disapprove of the tabloids, and they are sometimes called **the gutter press**. The most popular are *The *Sun*, *The *Mirror*, *The *Express* and the **Daily Mail*. The **News of the World*, a Sunday tabloid, sells more copies than any other newspaper in Britain.

There are about 1 500 local papers, many of which are **weeklies** (= published once a week). They contain news of local events and sport, carry advertisements for local businesses, and give details of houses, cars and other items for sale. Some are paid for by the advertisements they contain and are delivered free to people's homes. A few people do not like them and put up a notice on their door saying 'No free papers, thank you'.

Newspapers in the US

A daily newspaper from a medium-sized US city has between 50 and 75 pages, divided into different sections. The most important stories, whether international, national or local, are printed on the front page, which usually has the beginnings of four or five articles, and colour photographs. The articles continue inside. The rest of the first section contains news stories, an **opinion page** with editorials, and **letters to the editor**, written by people who read the paper. Another section contains local news. The sport section is near the end of the paper, with the features section. This contains comics and also **advice columns**, such as **Dear Abby*. There are advertisements throughout the paper.

Tabloids contain articles about famous people but do not report the news. They are displayed in supermarkets, and many people read them while they are waiting to pay but do not buy them.

On Sundays newspapers are thicker. There are usually fewer news stories but more articles analysing the news of the past week and many more features, including a colour section of comics.

America has many papers in languages other than English for people from various ethnic backgrounds.

The Press

In Britain, the newspaper industry, often called ***Fleet Street**, has a major influence on public opinion and is a strong force in political life. The ***freedom of the press** to publish whatever it wants, without the government interfering, is considered important. The tabloids often rely on **cheque-book journalism** (= paying people large amounts of money for their story) in order to be the first to publish a human-interest story. Many people do not like this approach. Recently, there has been concern about people's rights to privacy and now a voluntary **press code** gives guidelines on, amongst other things, photographing famous people.

In the US **journalists** try be objective and report facts, but financial pressures can work against this. Most of a paper's profits come from advertising, and if a company is offended by something the paper writes, it may decide not to advertise there again.

Newspapers get material from several sources. **Staff reporters** write about national or local news. Major newspapers also have their own **foreign correspondents** throughout the world. Others get foreign news from **press agencies** or **wire services,** such as *Associated Press or *Reuters. Some papers have their own **features writers**. In the US features are usually **syndicated**, which means that one newspaper in each area can buy the right to print them. The editor decides what stories to include each day but the **publisher** or owner has control over general policy. Newspaper owners are very powerful and are sometimes called **press barons**. The most famous in recent years have been Robert *Maxwell and Rupert *Murdoch.

ˌIsaac ˈ**Newton** /ˈnjuːtn; AmE ˈnuːtn/ (1642–1727) an English scientist. He is well known for discovering **Newton's Laws**, which explained the relationships between force, mass and movement. Many people know the story that he discovered the idea of gravity (= the force that attracts things towards the centre of the planet) when he saw an apple fall from a tree in his garden. He also discovered differential calculus, a branch of mathematics, at the same time as Leibniz discovered it in Germany, and made important discoveries about the nature of light and colour. He was made a *knight in 1705.

ˈ**new town** *n* any of the 32 towns that were planned and built in Britain in the second half of the 20th century. They were established by the government to encourage people, businesses and industries to move out of the crowded cities. Some, such as *Milton Keynes, became large successful towns, but not all of them attracted as many people or businesses as they expected. Many British people think that new towns are ugly, boring places because they do not have many interesting old buildings or streets: *The company is relocating to Glenrothes, a new town to the north of Edinburgh.*

ˌ**New ˈYear** *n* [U] the first few days of January. In Britain and America many people have parties on **New Year's Eve** (= 31 December). At midnight it is traditional for everybody to sing **Auld Lang Syne*, to wish each other 'Happy New Year', and often to kiss each other. In large cities many people gather in public places on New Year's Eve, such as *Trafalgar Square in London or George Square in *Glasgow. In Scotland the celebration of the New Year is called *Hogmanay. **New Year's Day** (= 1 January) is a *bank holiday in Britain.

the ˌ**New Year ˈHonours** the aristocratic titles and other awards given to people by the British king or queen on New Year's Day (= 1 January) each year: *She got an OBE in the New Year Honours list.*

the ˌ***New ˈYork Daily ˈNews*** /ˈjɔːk; *AmE* ˈjɔːrk/ a popular tabloid newspaper published in New York every day. It was established in 1919 and is known for its large headlines, large photographs and short articles. In 1991, after a long labour dispute, it was bought by the British publisher Robert *Maxwell, but he died later that year. It is now owned by Mortimer Zuckerman and Fred Drasner.

the ˌ**New ˈYork ˈDrama ˌCritics ˌCircle AˌwardDrama** any of several awards given each year by New York theatre critics (= newspaper and magazine writers who give their opinions about plays performed). The awards were first given for the 1935–6 season by members of the New York Drama Critics Circle. Recent winners have included *Three Tall Women* (1993–4) by Edward *Albee and *Arcadia* (1994–5) by Tom *Stoppard.

The ˌ***New ˈYorker*** /ˈjɔːkə(r); *AmE* ˈjɔːrkər/ a famous US magazine published each week in New York. It is known for its long articles, fiction, humour and comic drawings. It was established in 1925 by Harold Ross, and its writers have included Ogden *Nash, Dorothy *Parker, James *Thurber and S J Perelman. The English journalist Tina Brown was the magazine's editor from 1992 to 1998, and some readers have complained about the new, more lively style she introduced. It had about 850 000 readers in 1997.

the ˌ***New ˈYork ˈHerald-ˈTribune*** /ˈjɔːk; *AmE* ˈjɔːrk/ ⇨ INTERNATIONAL HERALD-TRIBUNE.

the ˌ**New ˈYork Philharˈmonic** /ˈjɔːk; *AmE* ˈjɔːrk/ the oldest orchestra in the US. It was established in 1842 and gave its 12 000th concert in 1993. It has more than 100 musicians and performs in the Avery Fisher Hall, completed in 1962 as part of the *Lincoln Center for the Performing Arts. The orchestra's free concert given in *Central Park in 1986 had an audience of about 800 000, the largest ever in the world for a concert of classical music. Musical directors of the Philharmonic have included Gustav Mahler (1909–11), Arturo Toscanini (1928–36), Leonard *Bernstein (1958–69), Zubin Mehta (1978–91) and Kurt Masur (1991–).

the New York Stock Exchange

the ˌ**New ˈYork ˈPublic ˈLibrary** /ˈjɔːk; *AmE* ˈjɔːrk/ the largest research library in the world that lends books to the public. The main building in New York is on *Fifth Avenue and *42nd Street, but it includes 87 other local libraries in Manhattan, the *Bronx and *Staten Island. Together they hold over 50 million books, etc. and about 10 000 new ones are added every week.

The ˌ***New ˈYork Reˈview of ˈBooks*** /ˈjɔːk; *AmE* ˈjɔːrk/ a US magazine, started in 1963 and published every two weeks, which contains articles about new books and also science, politics, US culture and the arts. It is respected for the high quality of its writing, and had more than 115 000 readers in 1997.

the ˌ**New York ˈSchool** /jɔːk; *AmE* jɔːrk/ the name given to a group of US abstract painters (= artists whose works are not realistic) who worked in New York in the 1940s and 1950s. Leading members of the group included Willem *de Kooning, Jackson *Pollock and Mark *Rothko.

ˌ**New York ˈState** /jɔːk; *AmE* jɔːrk/ a north-eastern US state which was one of the 13 original states. It is also known as the Empire State. It has the second largest population of any state, after *California. The largest city is New York, and the capital city is Albany. Henry *Hudson visited the area in 1609, and the first people to settle there permanently were the Dutch in 1624. Tourist attractions include the *Statue of Liberty, *Niagara Falls, the *Adirondack Mountains and the *Catskill Mountains. See also FIVE NATIONS.

the ˌ**New York ˈStock ExˌChange** /jɔːk; *AmE* jɔːrk/ (*abbr* **NYSE**) the largest US stock exchange and one of the largest in the world. It is on *Wall Street in New York City and has about 1 350 members. It was first established in 1792.

the ˌ***New York ˈTimes*** /jɔːk; *AmE* jɔːrk/ a famous US newspaper read mainly by people who are well educated. Its well-known motto is 'All the News That's Fit to Print'. The paper is published each morning in New York and can also be bought all round the world. It has more than 1 million readers. There is also a large Sunday issue. The *Times* first appeared in 1851 (as the *New York Daily Times*) and has won the most *Pulitzer Prizes of any newspaper, including one for the *Pentagon Papers. The New York Times Company also owns radio and television stations, magazines and other newspapers, including the **International Herald-Tribune* and the **Washington Post*.

ˌ**New ˈYork Uniˈversity** /ˈjɔːk; *AmE* ˈjɔːrk/ (*abbr* **NYU**) a private university in New York City. Its main buildings are in *Greenwich Village, with some also in the *Bronx. It was established in 1831 and is now one of the largest private universities in the world, with more than 36 000 students in 1998.

ˌ**New ˈZealand** /ˈziːlənd/ a country in the southern Pacific Ocean consisting of two large islands and several small islands. The capital city is Wellington. Most of the population is of British origin, people whose ancestors went there to be farmers. There are also many Maoris, who are descended from the original inhabitants of New Zealand and are now demanding some of the rights and areas of land that they believe were unfairly taken from their ancestors in the 19th century. New Zealand became a British colony in 1841, and an independent country in 1907. It is a member of the *Commonwealth. Tourism and agriculture are its main industries. New Zealand lamb and butter are sold in Britain and many other countries. ▶ **New Zealander** *n.*

Next /nekst/ any of a group of *high-street shops in Britain selling fashionable clothes.

ˌ**Nez ˈPercé** /ˌnez ˈpɜːs; *AmE* ˈpɜːrs/ *n* (*pl* **Nez Percés** *or* **Nez Percé**) a member of a *Native-American people who now live in the state of *Idaho on a reservation (= land given and protected by the US government). Their name means 'pierced nose' in French. They bred excellent horses and originally lived in west Idaho. Although they gave most of their land to the US in 1855, later land disputes led to a war in 1877 in which Chief *Joseph and his people were defeated.

NFC /ˌen ef ˈsiː/ ⇨ NATIONAL FOOTBALL CONFERENCE.

NFL /ˌen ef ˈel/ ⇨ NATIONAL FOOTBALL LEAGUE.

NFT /ˌen ef ˈtiː/ ⇨ NATIONAL FILM THEATRE.

NHS /ˌen eɪtʃ ˈes/ ⇨ NATIONAL HEALTH SERVICE.

NI /ˌen ˈaɪ/ ⇨ NATIONAL INSURANCE.

Niˌagara ˈFalls /naɪˌægrə ˈfɔːlz/ a famous American waterfall on the Niagara River that joins Lake *Erie to Lake * Ontario on the US-Canadian border. It actually consists of two waterfalls (the American Falls and the Horseshoe Falls), separated by Goat Island. They are a very popular tourist attraction, especially with honeymooners (= people who are just married), and are also used to produce electricity. Both the US and Canada have cities called Niagara Falls, and they are joined by Rainbow Bridge.

Niagara Falls

ˌ***Nicholas ˈNickleby*** /ˈnɪklbi/ a novel (1839) by Charles *Dickens. Nicholas Nickleby is a young man who has to make enough money to support his mother and sister after his father dies. He first goes to work as a teacher at *Dotheboys Hall, a school run by the evil Wackford Squeers. Nicholas is shocked by the conditions there, and by their cruel treatment of a poor boy called Smike. Nicholas and Smike escape from the school together and later work in a theatre company run by Vincent Crummles. There are many other linked stories in the novel, but its main importance is that it showed *Victorian(1) society how terrible conditions in many of its schools were, and in fact led to a lot of them being closed or improved.

ˌBen ˈ**Nicholson**[1] /ˈnɪkəlsn/ (1894–1982) an English artist who was one of the first in Britain to produce abstract paintings. His second wife was Barbara *Hepworth.

ˌJack ˈ**Nicholson**[2] /ˈnɪkəlsn/ (1937–) a US actor known for playing attractive but dangerous characters. He won *Oscars for **One Flew Over the Cuckoo's Nest*, *Terms of Endearment* (1983) and *As Good as it Gets* (1998). He first became internationally known in **Easy Rider*, and his other films include *Five Easy Pieces* (1970), *Chinatown* (1974), *The Shining* (1980), *A Few Good Men* (1993) and *Mars Attacks!* (1996).

ˌ**Nickelˈodeon** /ˌnɪklˈəʊdiən; *AmE* ˌnɪklˈoʊdiən/ a US television channel that broadcasts programmes for children during the day. In the evening it changes its name to Nick at Nite and shows old 'television classics'.

ˌJack ˈ**Nicklaus** /ˈnɪkləs/ (1940–) a US golfer who won twenty major tournaments (= competitions) between 1962 and 1986, a world record. These included the British *Open three times, the *US Open(1) four times and the *US Masters Tournament six times, more than any other golfer. The popular name for him is the 'Golden Bear' and in 1988 he was voted the 'Golfer of the Century'. He now mainly designs golf courses.

nicknames

Nicknames are informal, sometimes humorous names that are based on a person's real name or on an obvious characteristic or habit. Nicknames were in use before *surnames became widespread in the 13th century and were a means of identifying a person. Some nicknames, such as 'Russell' meaning 'red-haired' and 'Brown' referring to brown hair or skin, later developed into surnames.

Nicknames reduce the level of formality in a relationship and may suggest a close friendship. Many people are given a nickname while they are still children and may keep it throughout their life, whether they like the name or not. Nicknames may also be given to politicians and other public figures, especially by the press. This makes famous people seem more ordinary, and also leads to shorter, eye-catching headlines.

There are several kinds of nickname in common use. The most popular are **short forms**, shortened versions of a person's first name. Some common short forms include: Bob or Rob for Robert, Ted or Ed for Edward, Dick or Rick for Richard, Meg or Maggie for Margaret, Beth, Liz or Lizzie for Elizabeth, and Kathy, Kate or Katie for Katherine.

Nicknames may also be derived from surnames. Nicknames for famous people that have been much used by the British media include 'Fergie' for Sarah *Ferguson and 'Gazza' for the footballer Paul *Gascoigne.

Other nicknames, like the original ones, reflect a personal characteristic. 'Ginger' or 'Carrot-top' are now commonly used for people with red hair. 'Shorty', or even teasingly 'Lofty', is used for short people. Names like 'Fatty', 'Tubby' or 'Skinny' that refer to a person's weight are rude and generally used only as insults. Nicknames based on skin colour are offensive and should not be used. 'Brains' is used for somebody who is very intelligent, and 'Tiger' for someone who is brave or aggressive. The Duke of *Wellington has frequently been called 'The Iron Duke' and more recently Margaret *Thatcher was called 'The Iron Lady' because of her strength and determination. These more descriptive nicknames are less common in the US.

Nicknames based on a person's race or country can still be heard but are often highly offensive. In England, for instance, men from Scotland used to be addressed as 'Jock' or 'Mac', people from Ireland were 'Paddy' or 'Mick', and people from Wales 'Dai' or 'Taffy'. Members of *immigrant groups in both Britain and the US have had to suffer rude names from the native or mainstream population. Nicknames for people in foreign countries are also usually offensive, e.g. 'Yanks' or 'Yankees' for Americans, 'Frogs' for the French, and 'Jerries' for Germans.

The British have nicknames for many other things: a 'Roller' is a Rolls-Royce car and 'Marks and Sparks' is *Marks and Spencers. 'The Hammers' and 'Spurs' are both football teams, West Ham United and *Tottenham Hotspur. In the US all states have nicknames: *California is 'The Golden State', *Texas is 'The Lone Star State', and *Wyoming is 'The Equality State'.

N

ˌHarold ˈ**Nicolson** /ˈnɪkəlsn/ (1886–1968) a British diplomat and the writer of 125 books, of which his *Diaries and Letters* (1968) is the best-known. He was a *Member of Parliament from 1935 to 1945, and was made a *knight in 1953. He married Vita *Sackville-West in 1913, and their marriage survived, in spite of both of them having homosexual affairs, until her death in 1962.

ˈ**Nielson ˌrating** /ˈniːlsn/ *n* a figure produced by the A C Nielson Company in the US to indicate how many people watch a particular television programme. The figures are used by television companies in deciding how much to charge for advertising on different programmes.

Niˈgeria /naɪˈdʒɪəriə; *AmE* naɪˈdʒɪriə/ a large country on the west coast of Africa. It was a British colony from 1914 and has been a member of the *Commonwealth since becoming independent in 1960, although in 1995 its membership was stopped temporarily after a dispute over the execution of nine men. The capital city of Nigeria is Abuja, in the middle of the country, although its biggest city is Lagos, on the coast. The official language is English.
▶ **Nigerian** *adj, n.*

The ˌ***Night Before*** ˈ***Christmas*** a poem (1823) by Clement Moore (1779–1863) which is well known to many American children. It presents the traditional image of Santa Claus as a cheerful fat man who travels through the sky at Christmas bringing gifts. It begins:

'Twas the night before Christmas, when all through the house
Not a creature was stirring, not even a mouse;
The stockings were hung by the chimney with care,
In hopes that St Nicholas soon would be there.

Florence Nightingale working in a hospital at Scutari

ˌFlorence ˈ**Nightingale** /ˈnaɪtɪŋɡeɪl; *AmE* naɪtŋɡeɪl/ (1820–1910) an English nurse who became famous for her work during the *Crimean War. In spite of a lot of opposition from army officials, she greatly improved the conditions of military hospitals and reduced the numbers of soldiers dying of disease. She used to walk round the hospital beds at night with her lamp, comforting the patients, and so became known as the 'Lady of the Lamp'. Later she ran a campaign to change the British hospital system and improve the training of nurses. She never married. In 1907, she became the first woman to receive the *Order of Merit.

nightlife

What people do in the evening depends very much on where they live as well as on their tastes. In Britain Friday and Saturday evenings in most city centres are busy, with crowds of mainly young people moving between cinemas, pubs, clubs and wine bars. In the country people often go to the local pub but if they want more choice of entertainment they have to travel to a town. Similarly in the US, people living in New York City have very different possibilities for a good **night out** compared with those living in small towns.

***Pubs** in Britain attract a wide range of age groups. Older people tend to choose quieter pubs where conversation is easier than in the pubs popular among younger people, where loud music is played. The main activity is drinking, usually beer or lager. People have to be over 18 to drink alcohol. Some pubs also have live music. **Pub crawls**, in which several pubs are visited in one evening, are popular with younger people. Pubs close at 11 p.m. and after this people may look for something to eat or go to a **club**.

Wine bars sell mainly wine. They are usually smarter than pubs and more expensive. In the US **bars** range from those popular with students, where the beer is cheap and the floor is dirty, to those in hotels where customers must dress smartly. **Bartenders** make hundreds of different drinks by combining various kinds of alcohol. The British custom of buying a round, when each person in a group takes a turn to buy a drink for everyone else, is not always the rule in the US. Sometimes each person pays for his or her own drinks, or a group might **run a tab** (= the bartender writes down what they have) and then everyone pays part of the bill when they leave. Some bars provide free snacks, especially during **happy hour** (= a time around 5 p.m. when drinks cost less). In the US people must be over 21 to drink alcohol. There are special alcohol-free bars for teenagers.

A popular activity among young people is to **go clubbing**, i.e. go to clubs where they can drink, dance and meet members of the opposite sex. Admission charges are high, but drinks are fairly cheap. Cities like New York and London are famous for their clubs. The music is usually modern dance music but some play *soul, *jazz or pop. In Britain there are also smaller, sometimes illegal, clubs on the 'underground' club scene, where people dance to the latest music, often while taking drugs such as Ecstasy. Occasionally, illegal **raves** (= dance parties) are held at secret locations.

People living in or near a city can go to the **cinema** (*AmE* **movie theater**) or **theatre** or to a concert. The biggest concert venues in Britain, where international rock and pop stars perform, include the *Wembley Arena in London and the *National Exhibition Centre in Birmingham. In the US people occasionally go to **dinner theater**: they sit at tables in a theatre for a meal and stay there afterwards to watch a play. Other places to go include comedy clubs, where comedians perform live, cybercafés (cafés where people can use the Internet) and sports events.

Gambling is illegal in most parts of the US but in *Las Vegas and *Atlantic City there are many casinos where people can gamble. Some communities run **bingo** games for low stakes (= bets). Britain has some casinos but relatively few people go there. Bingo is popular, but mainly among elderly people.

Going out for dinner in a restaurant is a very popular activity. Many people also enjoy entertaining at home. They may have a **dinner party** for a few friends and cook an elaborate meal, or have a **party** with drinks and snacks to which many people are invited.

ˈNike™ /ˈnaɪki/ a US company that makes sports clothes. Its trainers (= sports shoes) are very fashionable among young people, who often wear them when not playing sport. (Nike was the ancient Greek goddess of victory, who had wings.).

the ˌBattle of the **ˈNile** /ˈnaɪl/ a sea battle fought in 1798 between the British and the French near Alexandria in Egypt. The British under *Nelson won an important victory, trapping the army of Napoleon in Egypt and gaining control of the Mediterranean for Britain.

ˌChester **ˈNimitz** /ˌtʃestə ˈnɪmɪts; *AmE* ˌtʃestər/ (1885–1966) the admiral who commanded the US Pacific Fleet during *World War II. The Japanese surrender was signed on his ship, the *USS Missouri*. He later served as Chief of Naval Operations (1945–7).

900 number /naɪn ˈhʌndrəd ˌnʌmbə(r)/ *n* (in the US) a telephone number that begins with 900. A call to it is more expensive than those to ordinary numbers. 900 numbers are used by companies who have 'chat lines', operate competitions, etc., and they usually allow people who call to record messages or answers and their phone numbers and addresses.

ˌ**Nine Inch ˈNails** a US rock band formed by Trent Reznor (1965–), who often performs alone. His style is known as 'industrial music' and his songs are often about sex, suffering and violence. The group's most successful albums have included *The Downward Spiral* (1994) and *The Perfect Drug* (1997).

999 /ˌnaɪn naɪn ˈnaɪn/ the telephone number used in Britain for calling the police, fire or ambulance services in an emergency: *Quick! Dial 999!*

The ˌ***Nine O'Clock*** ˈ***News*** a news programme on *BBC1 at 9 o'clock every night from Monday to Friday. It started in 1963.

the ˌ**nine o'clock ˈwatershed** (in Britain) 9 o'clock at night, thought of as the time before which scenes of sex and violent behaviour should not be broadcast on television because they are not suitable for children to watch. The British television companies have said that this is their policy 'under normal circumstances', but there is no law that requires them to do this: *Many people rang in to complain that the programme should not have been shown before the nine o'clock watershed.*

911 /ˌnaɪn wʌn ˈwʌn/ the telephone number used in the US for calling the police, fire or ambulance services in an emergency: *a 911 call.*

ˌ***Nineteen Eighty-ˈFour*** a novel about the future, written in 1948 by George *Orwell. The main character, Winston Smith, dares to think his own thoughts and fall in love in a society ruled by 'the Party', which tells everyone what they must think and do. The Party is led by Big Brother, who may not even exist, and everywhere there are pictures of him, with the words 'Big Brother is watching you'. The book is a satire on life in Russia under Stalin. It was very successful, and introduced several new ideas and words into the language, including *Big Brother*, the *Thought Police, Newspeak* and *doublethink*. Although 1984 is now in the past, it is still sometimes used to refer to some frightening future world.

the **1922 Committee** /ˌnaɪntiːn twentiˈtuː kəˌmɪti/ (*also* the **Conservative and Unionist Members' Committee**) (in Britain) the group of *Conservative *Members of Parliament that includes all the party's *backbenchers. Its name comes from a meeting of Conservative MPs in the *Carlton Club, London, in October 1922, when the need for an organization through which backbenchers could have more influence was discussed. Members of the Committee now meet regularly and its opinions are passed on to the party leader.

ˈNirex /ˈnaɪreks/ a British company whose business is storing radioactive waste (= the dangerous material left over after nuclear energy has been produced). The company's full name is UK Nirex Limited, and Nirex stands for Nuclear Industry Radioactive Waste Executive.

Nirˈvana /nɜːˈvɑːnə; *AmE* nɜːrˈvɑːnə/ a US rock band in the 1980s and 1990s, known for the harsh words of their songs and their wild stage performances. Their main singer was Kurt *Cobain and their albums included *Nevermind* (1991), *Incesticide* (1992) and *In Utero* (1993).

ˈNissen hut /ˈnɪsn/ *n* a large hut shaped like a tunnel, made of curved sheets of metal covering a concrete floor. They were used in Britain, especially during *World War II, to store equipment or as temporary shelters for soldiers. They were named after the man who originally designed them. Compare ANDERSON SHELTER, QUONSET HUT.

ˈNivea™ /ˈnɪviə/ *n* [U] a range of products for skin care, made by the British company Smith and Nephew: *If you have rough skin, put some Nivea cream on it.*

ˌDavid **ˈNiven** /ˈnɪvən/ (1910–1983) an English film actor well known for playing pleasant, gently comic roles, usually as an elegant English gentleman. His many films included *Wuthering Heights* (1939), *Around the World in Eighty Days* (1956), *The Pink Panther* (1964) and *Death on the Nile* (1978). He also wrote two humorous books about his own life.

ˌRichard **ˈNixon** /ˈnɪksn/ (1913–94) the 37th US *President (1969–74) and the only one to resign. He was elected to the US House of Representatives in 1946, where he was on the *House Un-American Activities Committee, and then to the US Senate in 1950. He was Vice-president under President *Eisenhower (1953–61) but was defeated by John F *Kennedy in the 1960 election for President. As President, Nixon was successful in ending the *Vietnam War and for establishing a closer relationship between the US and China, but he is mainly remembered for having to leave office because of the *Watergate scandal. He was given the *nickname 'Tricky Dick' because he was often not direct or honest in his dealings with people.

NLRB /ˌen el ɑː ˈbiː; *AmE* ɑːr/ ⇨ NATIONAL LABOR RELATIONS BOARD.

NME /ˌen em ˈiː/ ⇨ *NEW MUSICAL EXPRESS*.

ˌ**Nobel ˈPrize** /ˌnəʊbel; *AmE* ˌnoʊbel/ *n* each of six international prizes given each year since 1901 for the highest achievement in physics, chemistry, medicine, literature, economics and work towards world peace. Winners of the prizes are called **Nobel laureates**. The prizes are named after the Swedish scientist Alfred Nobel (1833–96), who invented dynamite: *He won a/the Nobel Prize for his work.*

ˌ**Nob ˈHill** /ˌnɒb; *AmE* ˌnɑːb/ a fashionable district of *San Francisco, *California. It includes Grace Cathedral and two famous hotels, the Fairmont and the Mark Hopkins. Many of the large Victorian houses originally built there by rich people, or 'nobs', were destroyed by the 1906 earthquake.

ˈ**Noddy** /ˈnɒdi; *AmE* ˈnɑːdi/ a character in a series of young children's books by Enid *Blyton, the first of which was published in 1949. Noddy is a small boy with a large head on which he wears a long blue cap with a bell on the end of it. He lives in Toytown and drives a small red and yellow car. His best friend is an old man called Big Ears. The local policeman is Mr Plod. The Noddy books have sometimes been criticized by adults for being old-fashioned and even racist but they are still very popular with children.

the ˈ**Nolan Comˌmittee** /ˈnəʊlən; *AmE* ˈnoʊlən/ a committee set up by the British government in 1994 to examine standards of behaviour among people who have a responsibility to the public to behave in an honest and respectable way, such as *Members of Parliament. Its full title is the Nolan Committee on Standards in Public Life, and it is led by Lord Nolan.

ˌ**Nonconˈformist** *n* (in England and Wales) any member of a Protestant Church which does not follow the beliefs and practices of the *Church of England. For example, members of the *Baptist, *Methodist, and *Presbyterian Churches, or of the *United Reformed Church, are all Nonconformists. Members of independent groups such as the *Quakers, the *Plymouth Brethren, and the *Salvation Army are also referred to as Nonconformists. In Scotland, where the *Presbyterian Church is the official one, members of any other church, including members of the *Church of England, are considered Nonconformists. Compare FREE CHURCH. ▶ **Nonconformist** *adj*.

ˌ**non-ˈU** /ˌnɒn ˈjuː; *AmE* ˌnɑːn ˈjuː/ *adj* (*BrE humor disapprov*) (of a word or an action) not showing the correct manners that are typical of someone who has been properly educated or an *upper-class person. The term was invented by an English professor in 1954 to discuss the speaking habits of English people, but it was made popular and its meaning was extended by Nancy *Mitford: *It's terribly non-U to eat your peas with a knife.* See also U 1.

NOP /ˌen əʊ ˈpiː; *AmE* oʊ/ ⇨ NATIONAL OPINION POLLS.

NORAD /ˈnɔːræd/ ⇨ NORTH AMERICAN AIR DEFENSE COMMAND.

ˌDenis ˈ**Norden** /ˈnɔːdn; *AmE* ˈnɔːrdn/ (1922–) an English broadcaster and writer of comedy whose clever humour has been popular for many years. With Frank *Muir he wrote many successful radio and television series. In recent years he has presented television shows showing humorous accidents that have occurred while people were making television programmes.

ˈ**Norfolk** /ˈnɔːfək; *AmE* ˈnɔːrfək/ a county in the east of England, part of *East Anglia. It is known for the Norfolk *Broads and for being very flat. Its administrative centre is *Norwich.

the ˌ**Norfolk ˈBroads** /ˌnɔːfək; *AmE* ˌnɔːrfək/ ⇨ BROADS.

ˈ**Norman**[1] /ˈnɔːmən; *AmE* ˈnɔːrmən/ *n* any of the people from Normandy in northern France who settled in England after their leader William defeated the English king at the Battle of *Hastings in 1066. The Normans took control of the country, a process known as the **Norman Conquest**. They used many of the existing *Anglo-Saxon methods of government of the state and the church, but added important aspects of their own and made government much more effective. The language of government became first Latin, and then Norman French, and this caused many new words to be added to the existing English language. The name 'Norman' comes from the Old French for 'Northman', as the Normans originally came from Denmark, Norway and Iceland. See also WILLIAM I.

▶ **Norman** *adj* **1** of the Normans: *a Norman castle.* **2** of the style of *Romanesque architecture used in Britain from the Norman Conquest to the early 13th century. Its features included round arches and heavy pillars, and often roofs made of wood. The cathedrals at *Ely, *Norwich, Peterborough and *Durham are in the Norman style.

ˌJessye ˈ**Norman**[2] /ˌdʒesi ˈnɔːmən; *AmE* ˈnɔːrmən/ (1945–) a US opera singer known for her strong, clear soprano (= highest female) voice. She began her career with the German Opera in Berlin, and first sang in New York with the *Metropolitan Opera in 1973. She is also known for her performances of songs by Wagner and Richard Strauss.

the ˌ**Norman ˈConquest** /ˌnɔːmən; *AmE* ˌnɔːrmən/ ⇨ CONQUEST.

the ˌ**Normandy ˈlandings** /ˌnɔːməndi; *AmE* ˌnɔːrməndi/ the military operation, beginning on 6 June 1944 (*D-Day) during which large numbers of British, US and Canadian soldiers landed in Normandy in northern France, and began the campaign to drive the Germans out of France.

ˌOliver ˈ**North** /ˈnɔːθ; *AmE* ˈnɔːrθ/ (1943–) a US Marine officer who was a member of the *National Security Council under President Ronald *Reagan. He was charged with being involved in the illegal operations of the *Iran-Contra affair, but the legal case against him was dropped in 1991. Many Americans regarded him as a good soldier who obeyed orders and was blamed for crimes committed by politicians. In 1994, he lost an election for the US Senate as a *Republican Party candidate from *Virginia.

the ˈ**North Aˈmerican ˈAir Deˈfense Comˌmand** /əˈmerɪkən/ (*abbr* **NORAD**) a military defence organization established in 1957 by the US and Canadian air forces. It has a large underground base in Cheyenne Mountain near Colorado Springs, *Colorado, to provide early warning of air attacks.

the ˈ**North Aˈmerican ˈFree ˈTrade Aˌgreement** /əˈmerɪkən/ ⇨ NAFTA.

Norˈthampton /nɔːˈθæmptən; *AmE* nɔːrˈθæmptən/ a large town in *Northamptonshire, in the area of England known as the *Midlands. Northampton has some buildings of historical importance, but it is now largely a *new town. Its main industry is making shoes.

Norˈthamptonshire /ˌnɔːˈθæmptənʃə(r); *AmE* nɔːrˈθæmptənʃə(r)/ (*abbr* **Northants**) an English *county in the *Midlands. Its administrative centre is *Northampton.

ˌNorthanger ˈAbbey /ˌnɔːθæŋgər; *AmE* ˌnɔːrθæŋgər/ a novel (1818) by Jane *Austen in which a romantic young woman, Catherine Morland, falls in love with a young priest, Henry Tilney. His father believes she is rich and invites her to the family's home, Northanger Abbey. Catherine imagines that the house contains all kinds of terrible secrets. The father discovers that she has no money, and orders her to leave, but she marries Henry in the end. The book was written as a satire on the type of *Gothic novel that was popular at the time.

the **ˈNorth Atˈlantic ˈTreaty ˌOrganization** /ətˈlæntɪk/ ⇨ NATO.

ˌNorth Caroˈlina /kærəˈlaɪnə/ a southern US state on the Atlantic Ocean, also called the Tarheel State and the Old North State. The largest city is Charlotte, and the capital city is Raleigh. The state was settled by the English and named after King *Charles I. It was one of the original 13 states and later one of the *Confederate States. Its products include tobacco, corn, furniture, paper and chemicals. Its tourist attractions include the *Great Smoky Mountains, the Blue Ridge National Parkway and the Wright Brothers National Memorial at *Kitty Hawk.

the **ˌNorth ˈCircular** a series of roads that join together and pass through many areas of North London. They join the *South Circular at the *Thames, east and west of London. Until the *M25 was built they formed the main road round London. They still carry a lot of traffic, which often moves very slowly.

ˌLord **ˈNorthcliffe** /ˈnɔːθklɪf; *AmE* ˈnɔːrθklɪf/ (*born* Alfred Charles William Harmsworth 1865–1922) a British newspaper publisher, born in Ireland. He started the **Daily Mail* in 1896 and the **Daily Mirror* in 1903, introducing a style of journalism that was then new to Britain. Articles were short and lively, with some written specially for women, and more headlines were used. Northcliffe was also the owner of *The *Times* from 1908 to 1922. He helped the British government with their propaganda (= information published to influence public opinion) during *World War I, and in 1917 was made a *viscount. He was a very strong character who liked power. His younger brother Harold (later Lord *Rothermere) was his partner in his early career.

ˌNorth Daˈkota /dəˈkəʊtə; *AmE* dəˈkoʊtə/ a northern central US state on the Canadian border, also called the Sioux State and the Peace Garden State. The largest city is Fargo, and the capital city is Bismarck. Most of North Dakota was in the *Louisiana Purchase, and Britain gave the rest in 1818. The land is mostly used for agriculture, with crops like wheat and beans. It also produces coal, oil and gas. Its tourist attractions include the Theodore Roosevelt National Park.

Northern Ireland ⇨ article.

the **ˈNorthern ˈIreland Asˈsembly** /ˈaɪələnd; *AmE* ˈaɪərlənd/ the name of the governing body in *Northern Ireland from 1973 to 1975 and again from 1982. In 1986, the majority party in it, the *Ulster Unionist Party, stopped supporting it in protest at the *Anglo-Irish Agreement, and the British government decided to close it.

However in 1998 the Labour government under Tony *Blair created a new Northern Ireland Assembly, based in *Belfast, as a separate parliament for Northern Ireland, giving it greater political independence from the British parliament. The First Minister in the new Assembly is David *Trimble and the majority party is the Ulster Unionist Party.

the **ˌNorthern ˈIreland ˌOffice** /ˈaɪələnd; *AmE* ˈaɪərlənd/ the British government department responsible for *Northern Ireland since 1972, when *direct rule was introduced. It is run by the *Secretary of State for Northern Ireland. Its responsibilities are likely to change following the establishment of the new *Northern Ireland Assembly.

the **ˌNorth ˈSea** a part of the north-eastern Atlantic Ocean. The North Sea has the *Shetlands to the north of it, the United Kingdom and the *Orkneys to the west, Norway and Denmark to the east, and France, Belgium, Holland and Germany to the south. It covers about 220 000 square miles (570 000 square kilometres), and is relatively shallow, mostly less than 300 feet (90 metres) deep. It has less salt in it than the North Atlantic, partly because a lot of fresh water flows into it from the *Thames, the Rhine, the Elbe and other large rivers. There are large amounts of oil and gas under it which are being taken out for commercial use.

ˌNorth Sea ˈgas (in Britain) natural gas obtained from under the *North Sea, mainly off the east coast of Scotland and the coast of *East Anglia. Britain's gas supply was formerly produced from coal, but since the late 1960s the North Sea has been the only source of the country's gas.

ˌNorth Sea ˈoil (in Britain) oil obtained from under the *North Sea, mainly from the area around the east coast of Scotland and the north-east coast of England. The oil was discovered in 1969 and first brought out in 1975. By 1994, Britain had become the world's eighth largest producer. North Sea oil has been a major political issue between the British government and the Scottish people, many of whom have felt that Scotland should benefit more from the great wealth that lies under the sea off its coast.

the **ˌNorth-South Diˈvide** (in Britain) the economic and social differences between the North and the South of England, shown by things like house prices, crime figures and rates of pay.

Norˈthumberland /nɔːˈθʌmbələnd; *AmE* nɔːrˈθʌmbərlənd/ (*written abbr* **Northd**) a *county in north-east England, on the Scottish border. It has a number of castles and Roman remains, including *Hadrian's Wall. Its administrative centre is *Newcastle-upon-Tyne.

Norˈthumbria /nɔːˈθʌmbriə; *AmE* nɔːrˈθʌmbriə/ an area of northern Britain ruled by kings from the 7th to the 9th centuries AD. It was famous at that time for its monasteries. The name Northumbria is still sometimes used to mean north-east England and south-east Scotland, especially in books, etc. written for tourists.

the **ˌNorthwest ˈOrdinance** a US law, passed by *Congress in 1787, which established the Northwest Territory, the area from the *Great Lakes south to the *Ohio River. It was the country's first official addition of western lands. The law said that the region could become a state when its population reached 60 000.

the **ˌNorth-west ˈPassage** a sea route along the northern coast of the US between the Atlantic and Pacific Oceans. From the end of the 15th century, many explorers looking for an easy route to Asia tried to find the North-west Passage, including Sir Francis *Drake and Captain *Cook. But it was not until 1906 that the first journey through, taking three years, was made by the Norwegian explorer Roald Amundsen. The Canadian government claims the Northwest Passage as part of Canada, but the US government regards it as an international area of water. For various reasons, including the ice, it is not regularly used by commercial ships. See also HUDSON.

ˌNorth ˈYorkshire /ˈjɔːkʃə(r); *AmE* ˈjɔːrkʃər/

N

Northern Ireland

Northern Ireland is a province (= an administrative region) of the United Kingdom (UK). It is sometimes referred to as *Ulster, which was one of the ancient kingdoms of Ireland, or as **the *Six Counties**, after the counties which remained part of the UK in 1921 when the rest of Ireland became the *Irish Free State. The capital city is ***Belfast**.

The Troubles

Northern Ireland has had a troubled history as a result of deep cultural and religious divisions within its population. The province's relationship with the British mainland has always been difficult. The majority of the population are *Protestants, who are descended from English and Scottish settlers. Protestants are mainly **unionist** or **loyalist**, and want Northern Ireland to remain part of the UK. Some of them are ***Orangemen**. A minority of the population are *Roman Catholics. Catholics tend to be **nationalist** or **republican**, and support the idea of a single Irish nation with a republican government. For many years Catholics were not allowed to hold public office in the province and may still suffer discrimination. The two communities each have their own political parties, as well as schools, pubs, etc.

From 1921 Northern Ireland was governed by a parliament at ***Stormont**. Protestant unionists held both political and economic power, and in 1949, when southern Ireland became a republic, the north remained part of the UK. The situation became unacceptable to Catholics, and in the 1960s there were violent demonstrations. This was the start of the most recent period of ***Troubles**. British forces were sent to keep order. After acts of terrorism (= murders and bombings) committed by the *IRA and by Protestant **paramilitary** groups, the Stormont government introduced ***internment** (= imprisonment without trial). This increased hostility and there were more acts of violence. In 1972, the year of ***Bloody Sunday**, the province was placed under ***direct rule** from London, and the Stormont parliament was abolished. Northern Ireland was controlled by a Secretary of State for Northern Ireland at the ***Northern Ireland Office**.

Working for peace

Acts of terrorism continued in Northern Ireland despite various attempts to establish peace. There were also bombings in towns on the British mainland. Although these shocked and frightened the public, most people agreed that the government should not surrender to the terrorists. In 1985 the ***Anglo-Irish Agreement** set up talks between Britain and the Republic of Ireland. In 1993 the ***Downing Street Declaration** by the British and Irish Prime Ministers followed meetings between John *Hume of the republican *SDLP and Gerry *Adams of *Sinn Fein, the political branch of the IRA. The declaration explored ways to peace and, most importantly, said that Sinn Fein would be welcome at future peace talks if the IRA ended violence. The following year the IRA announced 'a complete cessation of military operations'. By this time over 3 000 people had been killed.

Many Americans have Irish ancestors and some have given money to the IRA. But Americans also believe that US politicians can help bring peace

a peace rally in Belfast, February 1996

to Northern Ireland. In 1996 US Senator George Mitchell, who was advising on setting up peace talks, announced the **Mitchell Principles**. These said that all parties taking part in talks should give up violence, hand in their weapons and use only peaceful means to resolve disagreements. But soon after, the IRA bombed *Canary Wharf in London and the 1994 ceasefire was ended.

Following a new ceasefire in 1997 talks began again at Stormont, chaired by Senator Mitchell. Sinn Fein entered the talks despite the IRA's rejection of the Mitchell Principles. In early 1998 there was fresh violence. Despite various other setbacks the talks continued, and a deadline of 9 April was set to reach agreement.

The Good Friday Agreement

After a period of hard bargaining the ***Good Friday Agreement** was reached on 10 April. Its terms included setting up a new political assembly for Northern Ireland. The UK agreed to amend its claim to supreme authority over Northern Ireland in return for the Republic giving up its claim to the Six Counties. Prisoners belonging to paramilitary groups would be released provided that the groups gave up their weapons. The Agreement was to be ratified (= confirmed) by referendums in Northern Ireland and the Republic.

Ian *Paisley's *Ulster Democratic Unionist Party rejected the Agreement outright, and it split the *Ulster Unionist Party. On the republican side it caused disagreement in Sinn Fein and the IRA, and led to some people joining extremist groups. But in the referendum 71% of people in Northern Ireland voted for the agreement.

Elections for the new ***Northern Ireland Assembly** were held in June 1998. The two main republican parties, Sinn Fein and the SDLP, were very successful. The Ulster Unionist Party did less well than it hoped but got more votes than unionists opposed to the Agreement. David *Trimble, leader of the Ulster Unionists, became Chief Minister, and the SDLP's Seamus *Mallon his deputy.

Problems and prospects

There are still many problems facing Northern Ireland. Many terrorists have not handed in their weapons. Extremist groups on both sides oppose the Agreement and are committed to violence. The issue of religious **parades**, which increase tension during the ***marching season**, also remains a problem. But many people feel that despite these problems there is a strong desire to end the conflict and hope of peaceful cooperation between all parties.

(*written abbr* **N Yorks**) a *county in north-east England, formed in 1974 from parts of the former county of *Yorkshire. Its administrative centre is Northallerton.

ˈ**Norwich** /ˈnɒrɪdʒ, ˈnɒrɪtʃ; *AmE* ˈnɔːrɪdʒ, ˈnɔːrɪtʃ/ the administrative centre of the English *county of *Norfolk. It has a *Norman castle and cathedral. The University of East Anglia is in Norwich.

No. 10 ⇨ NUMBER TEN.

the ˌUniˈversity of ˌ**Notre ˈDame** /ˌnɒtrə ˈdɑːm; *AmE* ˌnoʊtər ˈdeɪm/ the most famous Catholic university in the US. It is in South Bend, *Indiana, where it was established in 1842. In 1997 it had more than 10 000 students. Notre Dame has America's best-known college football team, sometimes called 'the fighting Irish'.

ˈ**Nottingham** /ˈnɒtɪŋəm; *AmE* ˈnɑːtɪŋəm/ a large town in the *county of *Nottinghamshire, on the River Trent. It is known for its lace industry and has a fine *Roman Catholic cathedral. See also SHERIFF OF NOTTINGHAM.

ˌ**Nottingham ˈForest** /ˌnɒtɪŋəm; *AmE* ˌnɑːtɪŋəm/ one of the two football clubs of *Nottingham. The other is *Notts County.

ˈ**Nottinghamshire** /ˈnɒtɪŋəmʃə(r); *AmE* ˈnɑːtɪŋəmʃə(r)/ (*abbr* **Notts** /nɒts; *AmE* nɑːts/) a county in the *Midlands of England, famous (especially formerly) as a centre of the coal-mining industry. Its administrative centre is *Nottingham.

ˌ**Notting ˈHill** /ˌnɒtɪŋ; *AmE* ˌnɑːtɪŋ/ an area of west London, England, where many West Indians live. It is especially famous for the **Notting Hill Carnival**, a colourful street festival held there every year on *Summer Bank Holiday.

the Notting Hill Carnival

ˌ**Notts ˈCounty** /ˌnɒts; *AmE* ˌnɑːts/ one of the two football clubs of *Nottingham. The other is *Nottingham Forest. Notts County is the oldest professional football club in Britain, started in 1864.

ˌIvor **Noˈvello** /nəˈveləʊ; *AmE* nəˈveloʊ/ (1893–1951) a Welsh composer, actor and writer of plays. He wrote many successful songs and musical plays, in some of which he also acted. Two of the best-known are *Glamorous Night* (1935) and *King's Rhapsody* (1949), and his songs include *Keep the Home Fires Burning*, which was very popular during *World War I.

NOW /naʊ/ ⇨ NATIONAL ORGANIZATION FOR WOMEN.

NSC /ˌen es ˈsiː/ ⇨ NATIONAL SECURITY COUNCIL.

the **NSPCC** /ˈen es ˈpiː siː ˈsiː/ (*in full* the **National Society for the Prevention of Cruelty to Children**) a British charity that has worked to prevent child abuse of all kinds since 1884. It now operates a 24-hour national telephone helpline and has about 50 000 *voluntary workers who investigate reports of children in danger. They give help and advice to children and parents, and often work closely with professional social workers, doctors and police officers. The British public gives between 30 and 40 million pounds a year to help with this work.

NT /ˌen ˈtiː/ ⇨ NATIONAL TRUST.

ˌ**Nuclear Eˈlectric** a company, owned by the British government, which operates several power stations to produce electricity in England and Wales. It was formed in 1991. Compare NATIONAL POWER, POWERGEN. See also BRITISH NUCLEAR FUELS.

ˌLord ˈ**Nuffield** /ˈnʌfiːld/ (*born* William Richard Morris 1877–1963) an English businessman who was the first person in Britain to mass-produce cars (= make them in large quantities by mechanical processes). He started his business repairing bicycles in *Oxford, and soon moved into making bicycles and then cars. The *Morris car company was very successful and Morris himself became very rich. He gave a lot of his money to hospitals and charities and also to *Oxford University, where Nuffield College was named after him. See also MG, MORRIS MINOR.

the **NUJ** /ˌen juː ˈdʒeɪ/ (*in full* the **National Union of Journalists**) (in Britain) the main *trade union for people who work in newspaper and magazine journalism, publishing and broadcasting.

the **NUM** /ˌen juː ˈem/ (*in full* the **National Union of Mineworkers**) (in Britain) the main *trade union for people who work in coal mines. For most of the 20th century, the production of coal was very important for Britain's economy, so the NUM was in a powerful position. However, since the 1980s most of Britain's coal mines have been closed down and the power of the unions has been greatly reduced. Compare UNION OF DEMOCRATIC MINEWORKERS. ⇨ note at COAL MINING. See also MINERS' STRIKES.

ˌ**Number ˈTen** (*also* **No. 10**) **1** the house at 10 *Downing Street, the official London home of the British *Prime Minister (although Tony *Blair and his family in fact live next door at No. 11, which is usually the official home of the *Chancellor of the Exchequer). The Prime Minister usually has another home that he or she owns privately: *There has been a stream of visitors to Number Ten today.* See also CHEQUERS. **2** the British *Prime Minister and the people who advise him or her: *The paper got its story from sources close to Number Ten.*

ˌTrevor ˈ**Nunn** /ˈnʌn/ (1940–) an English theatre director who helped to run the *Royal Shakespeare Company from 1968 to 1987. He has also produced three of Andrew *Lloyd Webber's *musicals in London and some opera at *Glyndebourne. He was appointed director of the *National Theatre in 1996.

NUPE /ˈnjuːpiː/ ⇨ UNISON.

the **NUR** /ˌen juː ˈɑː(r)/ (until 1990) a British trade union for people who worked in the rail industry. Its full title was the National Union of Railwaymen. In 1990 it joined with the National Union of Seamen to form the *RMT.

ˌRudolf ˈ**Nureyev** /ˌruːdɒlf ˈnjʊəriefˌ *AmE* ˌruːdɑːlf ˈnjʊrief/ (1939–93) a Russian ballet dancer and choreographer who came to live in the West in 1961. At first he worked mainly with the *Royal Ballet in London, and became famous as the favourite partner of Margot *Fonteyn. In 1982 he became an Austrian citizen, and from 1983 to 1989 he was a director of the Paris Opéra Ballet.

nursery rhymes

Nursery rhymes are short verses and songs for children. Some are more than 200 years old. An early collection of rhymes, *Mother Goose's Melody*, was published in England in about 1780 and in America five years later. *Mother Goose is herself a traditional figure and teller of tales who was later included in *pantomime. Her name is still associated with books of nursery rhymes, especially in America.

Parents sing nursery rhymes to their children while they are still babies, and children soon learn the words themselves. The rhymes are popular because they are short, easy to say, and tell simple, often funny stories. For instance, *The *Queen of Hearts* is about a queen who makes some tarts for the king, but somebody steals them and the king punishes the thief.

Some nursery rhymes may refer to people or events in history. *The *Grand Old Duke of York*, for instance, is supposed to be about the Duke of *Cumberland, a famous army commander, while **Mary, Mary, Quite Contrary* may describe *Mary Queen of Scots. **Ring a Ring o' Roses* may refer to the *Great Plague: the roses are red spots on the skin and the last line, 'We all fall down', refers to people dying. Other rhymes are about country life and farm animals, such as sheep or mice. They include **Baa, Baa, Black Sheep*, **Little Miss Muffet*, **Sing a Song of Sixpence* and **Three Blind Mice*.

Rhymes such as **Hush-a-bye, Baby* are popular **lullabies**, songs that are sung to send children to sleep. Others are old **riddles**: *Humpty Dumpty, for example, is an oval-shaped figure who breaks after falling off a wall and cannot be mended – the answer to the riddle is 'egg'. Some rhymes have simple actions that go with them. Parents say the rhyme **This little pig went to market* while pulling their children's toes. *Pat-a-Cake, Pat-a-Cake, Baker's Man*, **Oranges and Lemons* and *Ring-a-Ring o' Roses* are all associated with simple games. Children use **Eeny Meeny Miney Mo* to choose somebody for a role in a game or to count the seconds to the start of a game.

Most nursery rhymes told in the US come from Britain, though **Mary Had a Little Lamb* was written by an American, Sara Hale. Since rhymes are usually spoken or sung there are often small differences in the words. For example, Americans say *Ring Around the Rosie* and *Pattie Cake, Pattie Cake, Baker's Man*. Nursery rhymes describe things that are unknown to most American children. They refer to places in Britain e.g. **London Bridge* or *Banbury Cross*, and talk about country life, whereas the majority of Americans live in cities. Some rhymes use old or unusual language. For instance, Little Miss Muffet eats 'curds and whey', and few people know that this is a kind of cheese. But none of these things really matter and nursery rhymes continue to be popular with young children everywhere.

ˈ**nursery school** *n* [C, U] a school for children aged between 2 and 5. Children are not required by law to go to nursery school, and may go instead to other groups such as **playgroups** or **crèches**. ⇨ note at EDUCATION.

the **NUS** /ˌen juː ˈes/ (*in full* the **National Union of Students**) (in Britain) an organization for students in universities and *colleges of further education, where it organizes entertainments and represents students' interests. It also represents students generally and organizes national campaigns against any threat to their interests.

the **NUT** /ˌen juː ˈtiː/ (*in full* the **National Union of Teachers**) (in England and Wales) the main *trade union for teachers. Most of its members work in *state schools but there are some in *independent schools also.

NVQ /ˌen viː ˈkjuː/ (*in full* **National Vocational Qualification**) (in Britain) a system of grades for people in work who acquire technical and other skills through *vocational training. It was started in the late 1980s to establish national standards. The training can be done at people's place of work or at special colleges or schools. The qualifications are awarded by organizations such as the *Royal Society of Arts, the *City and Guilds Institute and BTEC (the Business and Technology Education Council). See also GNVQ.

NWA /ˌen dʌbljuː ˈeɪ/ an *African-American *rap group formed in 1986. The letters NWA stood for 'Niggas With Attitude'. Many people thought their music was dangerous, because the words encouraged violence. After the group split up in 1991, the main singer, Ice Cube, developed his own career. See also EAZY-E.

ˌ***NYPD*** ˈ***Blue*** /ˌen waɪ piː diː/ a US television series on *ABC about police *detectives in the imaginary 15th Precinct of New York City. It began in 1993 and won 16 *Emmy awards in its first four years, including Best Drama (1994). Some Americans were offended by its bad language and scenes of naked people.

NYSE /ˌen waɪ es ˈiː/ ⇨ NEW YORK STOCK EXCHANGE.

NYU /ˌen waɪ ˈjuː/ ⇨ NEW YORK UNIVERSITY.

Oo

ˈOakland /ˈəʊklənd; *AmE* ˈoʊklənd/ an industrial city and port in the US state of *California. It is on the east side of San Francisco Bay and connected to *San Francisco by the Bay Bridge, the largest and busiest bridge in the US. Oakland companies build ships and cars, make electronic equipment and chemicals, and process food and oil.

ˌAnnie ˈ**Oakley** /ˈəʊkli; *AmE* ˈoʊkli/ (1860–1926) a famous US sharpshooter (= expert at shooting accurately). Her popular name was 'Little Sure Shot', because she was less than 5 feet (153 centimetres) tall. She and her husband Frank Butler, also a sharpshooter, worked as entertainers in *Buffalo Bill's *Wild West Show. The musical play and film **Annie Get Your Gun* was based on her life.

the **Oaks** /əʊks; *AmE* oʊks/ a major English horse race without jumps run every year at *Epsom. It was first run in 1779.

OAP /ˌəʊ eɪ ˈpiː; *AmE* oʊ/ ⇨ OLD AGE PENSIONER.

Oˈasis /əʊˈeɪsɪs; *AmE* oʊˈeɪsɪs/ a British pop group from Manchester, formed in 1993. The best-known members are Noel and Liam Gallagher, two brothers who often argue with each other. Liam is the band's singer, and Noel writes songs and plays the guitar. The group is known for its bad behaviour, often related to drugs and alcohol, but its records have been extremely successful. They include the albums *Definitely Maybe* (1994), *(What's the Story) Morning Glory?* (1995) and *Be Here Now* (1997), and the single records *Live Forever*, *Cigarettes and Alcohol* and *Wonderwall*.

ˈ**oast house** /ˈəʊst; *AmE* ˈoʊst/ *n* (*esp BrE*) a building containing a special oven for drying hops (= plants used for giving a special flavour to beer). It has an unusual shape, with a round pointed roof. There are a lot of oast houses in the county of *Kent, many of which have been converted into private houses.

oast houses

ˈ**oater** /ˈəʊtə(r); *AmE* ˈoʊtər/ *n* (*AmE slang*) a *western film or television programme. The word comes from the fact that horses, which appear in most *westerns, eat oats (= a type of grain). Compare HORSE OPERA.

ˌCaptain ˈ**Oates**[1] /ˈəʊts; *AmE* ˈoʊts/ (Lawrence Oates 1880–1912) an English explorer who went to the South Pole with Captain *Scott. He is remembered for the brave way in which he died on the journey back. He was very ill and did not want to delay the rest of the party. So he walked out of the tent and into the snow, saying, 'I am just going outside and may be some time.' People sometimes use this last phrase as a joke when they leave to do something dangerous or difficult.

ˌTitus ˈ**Oates**[2] /ˌtaɪtəs ˈəʊts; *AmE* ˈoʊts/ (1649–1705) an English Protestant priest. He wanted people to turn against the Roman Catholics, so he invented the *Popish Plot of 1678, a story that the Catholics were planning to kill King *Charles II and make his brother James king. Oates was regarded as a hero, and many people were put to death because of him. Seven years later he was found guilty of lying and sent to prison.

OBE /ˌəʊ biː ˈiː; *AmE* ˌoʊ/ (*in full* **Officer of the Order of the British Empire**) a British honour that is given by the queen or king to people who have done something special for their country in any activity, including sport, entertainment, politics and business. People who receive it may put the letters OBE after their name. It is the fourth highest honour within the *Order of the British Empire, above an *MBE but below a CBE (Commander of the British Empire): *Peter Martin OBE* ○ *She got an OBE in the New Year Honours.* ⇨ note at HONOURS.

ˈ**Oberon** /ˈəʊbərɒn; *AmE* ˈoʊbərɑːn/ the king of the fairies in stories of the Middle Ages. He is best known as a character in *Shakespeare's play *A *Midsummer Night's Dream*, in which he is the husband of *Titania.

ˈ**Obie** /ˈəʊbi; *AmE* ˈoʊbi/ *n* (*AmE*) any of several US awards given each year for the best plays performed off-Broadway (= not in one of the main *Broadway theatres). They were established in 1955 by *The *Village Voice* newspaper. The name comes from 'OB', the first letters in 'off-Broadway'.

The ***Obˈserver*** a British Sunday newspaper, regarded as one of the 'quality papers'. First published in 1791, it is the oldest national newspaper in Britain. Its political views are 'left of centre'. It was bought in 1993 by *The *Guardian*.

the ˈ**Occupational** ˈ**Safety and** ˈ**Health Adminiˌstration** (*abbr* **OHSA**) a US government organization that protects the safety and health of workers. Its officers visit work places and can punish companies for bad standards. It also informs the public about possible risks at work, such as the use of dangerous materials. OHSA was set up in 1970 and is part of the US Department of Labor.

O ˌCome, All Ye ˈFaithful ⇨ *ADESTE FIDELES.*

ˌDes **OˈˈConnor** /əʊˈkɒnə(r); *AmE* oʊˈkɑːnər/ (1932–) an English singer and television personality, popular especially with older people. He has his own television show in which he sings, tells jokes and talks to other entertainers. Other performers often make jokes about his singing.

ˈ**Odeon** /ˈəʊdiən; *AmE* ˈoʊdiən/ *n* (in Britain) any of a group of cinemas owned by the *Rank Organization. There is an Odeon in most British towns and cities, usually showing popular *Hollywood films: *They went to see 'Batman Returns' at the Odeon.*

ˈ***Ode on a ˈGrecian ˈUrn*** /ˈgriːʃn/ a long poem (1820) by John *Keats which describes how perfect art is when compared with natural things that change and grow old.

ˌ***Ode to a ˈNightingale*** a long poem (1820) by John *Keats which describes how he feels as he listens to the beautiful song of a nightingale (a small bird).

ˈ***Ode to the ˈWest ˈWind*** a poem (1820) by *Shelley[2]. The poet describes the violence of the 'wild West Wind' and of nature itself, causing so much destruction in the autumn, but at the same time he finds it good because it prepares the way for new life in the spring.

OECD /ˌəʊ iː siː ˈdiː; *AmE* ˌoʊ/ ⇨ ORGANIZATION FOR ECONOMIC COOPERATION AND DEVELOPMENT.

OED /ˌəʊ iː ˈdiː; *AmE* ˌoʊ/ ⇨ OXFORD ENGLISH DICTIONARY.

ˌ**Offa's ˈDyke** /ˌɒfəz; *AmE* ˌɔːfəz/ a large bank of earth along the border between England and Wales. It was built in the 8th century by Offa, a king of *Mercia, as a protection against the *Britons who lived to the west of it. Later, it became the border between the two countries. Today people enjoy walking along it, or parts of it.

OFFER /ˈɒfə(r); *AmE* ˈɔːfər/ (*in full* the **Office of Electricity Regulation**) the British government organization responsible for making sure that the private electricity companies treat their customers fairly.

the ˌ**Office of Fair ˈTrading** the British government department that is responsible for making sure that businesses treat their customers fairly, that their advertising is honest and that their products follow the *Trade Descriptions Act.

the ˈ**Office of ˈManagement and ˈBudget** a US government department that helps the *President prepare each year's national *budget. It also helps to manage government spending. The department was established in 1970 and is part of the Executive Office of the President.

the ˈ**Office of ˈPublic ˈService** a major department of the British *Cabinet Office, formed in 1992. It is responsible for large parts of the *Civil Service and is in charge of the *Citizen's Charter.

ˌ**office ˈparty** *n* a party, usually just before *Christmas, for the people who work in a particular office or company. Office parties usually take place in the office or in a club or restaurant near it. Most people drink alcohol and behave in a more relaxed way than they usually do at the office. There are many jokes about office parties because people sometimes get drunk or have sex with others from their office.

the **Ofˌficial ˈBirthday** the second Saturday in June, the date on which the birthday of the British king or queen is officially celebrated, though it is not his or her real birthday. It is marked by *Trooping the Colour and the announcement of the *Birthday Honours.

the **Ofˌficial ˈSecrets Act** a British law that aims to prevent important government information from being passed to enemies. People who work for many government departments must 'sign the Official Secrets Act', i.e. sign a document saying that they will not discuss their work with anybody who has not also signed the Act. People who break this rule may be sent to prison.

the **Ofˌficial ˈUnionist ˌParty** /ˈjuːniənɪst/ a name sometimes used to refer to the *Ulster Unionist Party to distinguish it from the other political parties in Northern Ireland which have the word 'Unionist' in their titles. Compare ULSTER DEMOCRATIC UNIONIST PARTY.

ˈ**Ofgas** /ˈɒfgæs; *AmE* ˈɔːfgæs/ (*in full* the **Office of Gas Supply**) the British government organization responsible for making sure that the private gas companies treat their customers fairly.

ˈ**Oflot** /ˈɒflɒt; *AmE* ˈɔːflɑːt/ (*in full* the **Office of the National Lottery**) a British government department, established in 1993, which is in charge of the *National Lottery.

OFSTED /ˈɒfsted; *AmE* ˈɔːfsted/ (*in full* the **Office for Standards in Education**) a British government department, established in 1972, which employs independent inspectors to visit schools and make sure that the standards of education are as high as they should be.

ˈ**Oftel** /ˈɒftel; *AmE* ˈɔːftel/ (*in full* the **Office of Telecommunications**) the British government organization responsible for making sure that the private telephone companies treat their customers fairly. In the 1990s Oftel forced *British Telecom to reduce its prices every year for four years.

ˈ**Ofwat** /ˈɒfwɒt; *AmE* ˈɔːfwɑːt/ (*in full* the **Office of Water Services**) the British government organization responsible for making sure that the private water companies treat their customers fairly.

ˌScarlett **O'ˈHara** /ˌskɑːlət əʊˈhɑːrə; *AmE* ˌskɑːrlət oʊˈhærə/ the main female character in the novel **Gone with the Wind* by Margaret Mitchell. Scarlett is a lively woman who uses her charm to get what she wants. She loves Ashley Wilkes, who rejects her because he is already married, so she marries the charming but immoral Rhett *Butler, who finally leaves her. In the 1939 film version of the book, Scarlett was played by the English actor Vivien *Leigh.

O'Hare /əʊˈheə(r); *AmE* oʊˈher/ (*also* **O'Hare International Airport**) the airport for the US city of *Chicago. It is the busiest airport in the world, with about 70 million passengers using it each year.

Oˈhio /əʊˈhaɪəʊ; *AmE* oʊˈhaɪoʊ/ a north-eastern US state, also called the Buckeye State (and its people Buckeyes). The capital and largest city is Columbus. It is an industrial state that produces cars, steel and rubber, as well as corn, grapes and minerals, including coal and oil.

the **Oˌhio ˈRiver** /əʊˌhaɪəʊ; *AmE* oʊˌhaɪoʊ/ a major river in the eastern central US. It begins at *Pittsburgh, *Pennsylvania, where the Allegheny River and Monongahela River come together, and flows 981 miles/1 578 kilometres past Cincinnati and into the *Mississippi River at Cairo, *Illinois. The Ohio was the main route to the West in the late 18th and early 19th centuries.

OHMS /ˌəʊ eɪtʃ em ˈes; *AmE* ˌoʊ/ (*in full* **On Her/His Majesty's Service**) the abbreviation printed on official documents, envelopes, etc. of British government departments and the armed forces.

OHSA /ˌəʊ eɪtʃ es ˈeɪ; *AmE* ˌoʊ/ ⇨ OCCUPATIONAL SAFETY AND HEALTH ADMINISTRATION.

ˌ***Oh! Suˈsanna*** a well-known US song written in 1848 by Stephen *Foster. It became especially popular with the *forty-niners who sang it on their way to look for gold in *California. It ends:

Oh! Susanna, oh don't you cry for me;
For I come from Alabama with my banjo on
my knee.

Oˈjibwa /əʊˈdʒɪbwɑː; *AmE* oʊˈdʒɪbwɑː/ (*also* **Oˈjibway** /əʊˈdʒɪbweɪ; *AmE* oʊˈdʒɪbweɪ/, ˈ**Chippawa** /ˈtʃɪpəwɑː/, ˈ**Chippaway** /ˈtʃɪpəweɪ/) *n* (*pl* **-was**/**-ways** *or* **-wa**/**-way**) a member of a *Native-American people who speak the Algonquin language. About 100 000 live on reservations (= land given and protected by the government) in the US states of *Michigan, *Wisconsin and *Minnesota, and in Ontario, Canada.

O

They once lived mostly around Lake *Superior and Lake *Huron, where they were farmers who also hunted. The Ojibwas often fought with the *Sioux.

the ˌ**OK Cor'ral** /ˌəʊkeɪ; *AmE* ˌoʊkeɪ/ a corral (= place where horses or cows are enclosed within fences) in *Tombstone, *Arizona. It was the scene of a famous fight with guns on 26 October 1881, in which Deputy Marshal Wyatt *Earp, with his brothers Virgil and Morgan and their friend Doc *Holliday, killed three members of the Clanton gang. The Earps were arrested for murder, but then released. The incident has been the subject of many films, including *Gunfight at the OK Corral* (1957) with Burt *Lancaster as Wyatt Earp.

ˌGeorgia **O'ˈKeeffe** /əʊ'kiːf; *AmE* oʊ'kiːf/ (1887–1986) a US artist known for her colourful abstract images from nature and her pictures of the south-western US countryside. She was married to the photographer Alfred *Stieglitz.

the ˌ**Okefe'nokee 'Swamp** /ˌəʊkəfə'nəʊki; *AmE* ˌoʊkəfə'noʊki/ a large area of land full of water in the US states of *Georgia and *Florida. It covers 600 square miles/1 554 square kilometres and is part of Georgia's **Okefenokee National Wildlife Refuge**. The animals there include alligators, bears, deer, raccoons and many types of birds and fish.

'**Okie** /'əʊki; *AmE* 'oʊki/ *n* (*AmE infml*) **1** a person who moves from farm to farm looking for work. The original Okies were farmers who had to leave Oklahoma in the 1930s because dry weather had created the *Dust Bowl. **2** (*sometimes offensive*) a person who lives in Oklahoma.

ˌ**Okla'homa** /ˌəʊklə'həʊmə; *AmE* ˌoʊklə'hoʊmə/ a southern central state of the US. It is also called the Sooner State and people from Oklahoma are called Sooners. The capital and largest city is Oklahoma City. The area was part of the *Louisiana Purchase, and the *Five Civilized Tribes were forced to settle there in the 19th century. Oklahoma became a state in 1907. It produces oil, gas, coal, wheat and cotton. Its places of interest include the Cherokee Cultural Center in Tahlequah and the National Cowboy *Hall of Fame in Oklahoma City.

ˌ***Okla'homa!*** /ˌəʊklə'həʊmə; *AmE* ˌoʊklə'hoʊmə/ a musical play (1943) by Richard *Rodgers and Oscar *Hammerstein. It ran for 2 212 performances on *Broadway and was one of the first modern musical plays to combine a strong story with songs. It is about the love between the *cowboy Curly and the farmer's daughter Laurie. The songs included *Oklahoma!* and *Oh, What a Beautiful Mornin'*. A film version appeared in 1955.

the ˌ**Okla'homa 'City 'bombing** /ˌəʊklə'həʊmə; *AmE* ˌoʊklə'hoʊmə/ the occasion on 19 April 1995 when a car bomb exploded in Oklahoma City, *Oklahoma, killing 168 people and injuring more than 400. It was the worst terrorist act ever carried out in the US. The bomb destroyed the city's Federal Building. After investigating the crime, the FBI arrested Timothy McVeigh and Terry Nichols, members of a group who were prepared to use violence to protest against actions by the government. McVeigh was condemned to death. The bombing made Americans aware of new dangerous groups within the country.

damage resulting from the Oklahoma City bombing

old age

Society is getting older. In 1990 about 14% of the population of the US was over 60; in 2020 it will be about 20%. In Britain the figures are similar. With further developments in medicine more and more people can expect to live a long time. This means that **senior citizens** (= people over about 65) may become a more powerful group, but it also means that services for them will need to improve.

For people who have enough money from their ***pension** and who are in good health, the years of **retirement** may be an opportunity to do some of the things they did not have time for when they were working and bringing up a family. Some people take courses, some go on more holidays/vacations, others do *voluntary work and continue to use the skills they learned for their job. Public transport, theatres, and sometimes restaurants give discounts to retired people to encourage them to go out. In Britain some go to play *bingo or to a tea dance (= a dance held in the afternoon). In the US senior citizens are expected to be active, if their health permits, and the sight of a 70-year-old lifting weights in a gym is not uncommon. Many elderly people, however, have a more difficult old age. Those who rely on the British state pension or US *social security have to spend most of their money on food and heating and have little left for luxuries (= expensive pleasures). Others have poor health and cannot move around easily. Some are afraid to go out in case they are attacked and robbed. Many are lonely.

Older Americans who can afford a comfortable retirement may move to states like *Florida and *Arizona where the weather is warm all year. Many get an apartment in a **retirement community**, where they are near people of their own age and where there is somebody nearby to provide help if they need it. If they become ill they may need to move into a **nursing home** where they can get special medical care. Often the patient's husband or wife can live there too. The cost of nursing homes is very high, and while many are excellent, others are not good. A few older people live with their children, but Americans do not usually feel that it is the responsibility of children to take care of their parents.

In Britain too, elderly people also like to be independent and to live in their own home for as long as possible. Those who find it difficult to look after themselves may have a **home help** for a few hours each week. Some may use a ***meals on wheels** service. Some towns have **pensioners' clubs** which serve cheap meals. People who are less able to get about may be taken each day to a **day centre** where they can sit with others. As in the US, some elderly people move into **sheltered accommodation** or **warden housing**. Others go to live with one of their children. Many families, however, do not have room for their elderly relatives or do not want them to live with them. When these people can no longer care for themselves they have to move into an **old people's home**, run by the local council

In Britain especially, old people get less respect than they do in many other societies. They are often thought by younger people to have little to contribute to society and to be a burden on the rest of the population. They used to be referred to as **old age pensioners** or **OAPs** but the name 'senior citizens' was introduced as part of a campaign to give the elderly a more positive image. Many, however, still feel that they are powerless, unwanted and have no role in society.

ˌold age ˈpensioner (*also* **OAP**) *n* (*BrE old-fash*) a person who is old enough to receive a *pension from the state. In Britain, men over 65 and women over 60 can receive state pensions. Some people find the phrase 'old age pensioner' offensive, and prefer phrases such as 'senior citizen', 'retired person' or simply 'pensioner'.

the **ˌOld ˈBailey** /ˈbeɪli/ the popular name for the Central Criminal Court in London, England, where serious cases are tried. It is built on the place where *Newgate prison used to be. There have been many famous trials at the Old Bailey. On top of the building is a well-known statue of Justice holding a sword in one hand and a pair of scales (= a weighing instrument) in the other.

Justice on top of the Old Bailey

ˌOld ˈBlood and Guts ⇨ PATTON.

ˌOld ˈBlue Eyes ⇨ SINATRA.

the **ˌold ˈboy ˌnetwork** *n* [sing] (*BrE infml, often disapprov*) the situation in many British companies, government departments and branches of the armed forces where people give jobs and other privileges to 'old boys' (= former students) of the *public school(1) or university that they went to: *Most of the managers were chosen by the old boy network and many of them turned out to be incompetent.*

the **ˌOld Conˈtemptibles** *n* [pl] a *nickname for the *British Expeditionary Force in *World War I. The soldiers who survived chose the name for themselves when they heard that the German Kaiser (= ruler) had called them 'a contemptible (= worthless) little army'.

ˌClaes **ˈOldenburg** /ˌklɔːs ˈəʊldənbɜːɡ; *AmE* ˈoʊldənbɜːrɡ/ (1929–) a US sculptor, born in Sweden. He was a leading figure in the *pop art movement and used soft materials to make large models of ordinary objects, such as his *Soft Telephone* (1963) and *Lipstick Monument* (1969).

Old English

Old English, sometimes called ***Anglo-Saxon**, was the language of the German peoples who settled in England from around 400 AD. It had three main **dialects**: Kentish, Saxon and Anglian. Saxon was the language spoken at the court of King *Alfred, who encouraged people to translate Latin books into English, and so it became the main language of literature. Modern standard English, however, developed from Mercian, a variety of Anglian which was spoken in the Midlands. Relatively few Latin words dating back to the Roman occupation of England survived into Old English. After the arrival of the *Vikings from the 8th century onwards, many Norse words, e.g. *dirt, blunder* and *squeak*, were added to the language.

Several written works have survived from the Old English period. Most of these are short religious writings or poems about great heroes. The most famous of these is **Beowulf*, composed by an unknown author and written down in the 8th or 9th century.

To modern readers Old English looks at first like a foreign language. It was originally written in **runes** or **runic letters**, an ancient alphabet of 24 angular letters, and then in a form of the Roman alphabet that included several of these letters, such as the thorn (þ) for 'th', both voiced /ð/ and voiceless /θ/, and the ash (æ). Some Old English words, such as *dead, is, brother* and *and* in the following passage from *Beowulf*, have survived with little change into modern English. Some words become easier to recognize when they are translated, e.g. *yldra* meaning 'older' and *min* for 'my', whereas others are completely foreign to us. Word order is also different from modern English.

Hroðgar maþelode, helm Scyldinga:
'Ne frin þu æfter sælum! Sorh is geniwod
Denigea leodum. Dead is Æschere,
Yrmenlafes yldra broþer,
min runwita and min rædbora,
eaxlgestealla ...'

(Hrothgar, protector of the Danes, spoke: 'Do not ask about it! There is more sorrow for the Danish people. Aeschere, Yrmenlaf's older brother, my trusted friend and my adviser, my close companion, is dead ...')

Several shorter poems written in Old English have also survived. These include *The Seafarer*, *The Wanderer* and *The Dream of the Rood*, which all have a Christian message. Few authors are known by name, apart from *Caedmon, a 7th-century monk, and the 9th-century Northumbrian or Mercian poet Cynewulf. Other authors of the period wrote in Latin.

The **Anglo-Saxon Chronicle*, a history of England beginning with the arrival of Christianity, was probably begun in the court of King Alfred in 891 and was continued in monasteries until 1154. The writers used a wide range of sources for the *Chronicle* and it is thought to be the first original prose text in English.

Old English was replaced by *Norman French as the official language of England after the Norman Conquest of 1066, but it continued to be spoken by the ordinary people and, influenced by French and Latin, developed into *Middle English, the language of the 12th to the 15th centuries.

Balancing Tools *by Claes Oldenburg*

ˌOld English ˈsheepdog *n* a breed of very large dog with long thick grey and white hair, often covering its eyes. In former times these dogs were used by farmers in Britain to control sheep. They are now popular as pets.

Old Faithful

ˌOld ˈFaithful a famous US geyser (= an underground hot spring that shoots water or steam up into the air) in *Yellowstone National Park. It is a popular tourist attraction. Approximately once an hour it shoots hot water and steam into the air to a height of about 150 feet (46 metres).

ˌOld Folks at ˈHome a popular US song written in 1851 by Stephen *Foster. It is now the official state song of Florida, and it begins:

Way down upon the Swanee River,
Far, far away,
There's where my heart is turning ever,
There's where the old folks stay.

ˌOld ˈGlory a popular name for the US flag, first used by William Driver, a ship's captain from *Massachusetts, in 1831. See also STARS AND STRIPES, STAR-SPANGLED BANNER.

ˌOld ˈIronsides /ˈaɪənsaɪdz; *AmE* ˈaɪərnsaɪdz/ the popular name for the famous old American ship the *USS *Constitution*.

ˌOld King ˈCole /ˈkəʊl; *AmE* ˈkoʊl/ a *nursery rhyme which may refer to a legendary king of England in ancient times, or to an old man who enjoyed drinking, smoking and music. The full rhyme is:

Old King Cole was a merry old soul,
And a merry old soul was he.
He called for his pipe
And he called for his bowl
And he called for his fiddlers three.

the **ˈOld ˈLady of Threadˈneedle Street** /θredˈniːdl/ a *nickname for the *Bank of England, which is in Threadneedle Street in the *City of London.

ˈOld Macˈdonald ˈHad a ˈFarm /məkˈdɒnəld; *AmE* məkˈdɑːnəld/ an old children's song. Each verse refers to a different animal on Old Macdonald's farm and repeats the sound made by that animal and all the previous ones, so that the verses get longer and longer.

ˌOld Moore's ˈAlmanack /mɔːz; *AmE* mɔːrz/ a book published once a year in Britain which claims to predict the important events of the next year. It was first published in 1700 by Francis Moore, a London doctor and astrologer. It is a very popular book, and refers to people and events in such a general way that some people believe that it can really predict the future.

ˌOld Mother ˈHubbard /ˈhʌbəd; *AmE* ˈhʌbərd/ a *nursery rhyme about an old woman trying to feed her dog. Many people know the first verse:

Old Mother Hubbard, she went to the cupboard
To get her poor dog a bone;
But when she got there, the cupboard was bare,
And so the poor dog had none.

the **ˌOld North ˈChurch** the popular name for Christ Church, built in *Boston, *Massachusetts, in 1723. On 19 April 1775 Paul *Revere waited for a signal in its tower to tell him the British army had been seen. Henry Wadsworth *Longfellow made the church famous in his poem *Paul Revere's Ride* (1861), which includes the line: 'Hang a lantern in the belfry arch of the North Church tower.' The tower, which has the first bells ever made in America, was blown down by strong winds in 1954 and built again to its former condition.

the Old North Church

the **ˌOld Preˈtender** a *nickname for James *Stuart, who claimed the right to be the British king. A pretender is a person who claims something, usually the right to be a king or queen, although not everybody agrees that the claim is just. See also FIFTEEN, YOUNG PRETENDER.

ˌold school ˈtie *n* (*esp BrE*) **1** a tie worn by former students of a particular school, usually a British *public school(1). **2** the school tie used as a symbol of the attitudes considered typical of people who were educated at *public schools. They are usually thought to be old-fashioned, *upper-class, opposed to social or political change, and proud of their country and their old school. **3** another name for the *old boy network: *Too many civil servants rely on the old school tie to open doors for them.*

ˈOldsmobile /ˈəʊldzməbiːl; *AmE* ˈoʊldzməbiːl/ a large, expensive US make of car. The company that makes Oldsmobiles began in 1897 and is now part of the *General Motors Corporation.

ˌOld ˈTrafford /ˈtræfəd; *AmE* ˈtræfərd/ **1** a well-known football stadium in south-west *Manchester. It is the club ground of *Manchester United and is sometimes used for important international matches. **2** a well-known cricket ground in south-west *Manchester, near the football stadium. It is the main ground of *Lancashire(2) County Cricket Club, and test matches (= international matches) take place there when foreign teams tour England.

O

the **ˌOld ˈVic** /ˈvɪk/ a famous theatre in south London, built in 1818. It was officially named the Royal Victoria Theatre in 1833, and was given the *nickname the 'Old Vic' later in the century. It became well known in the early 20th century when Lilian *Baylis began producing *Shakespeare's plays there. The *National Theatre was based there from 1963 until its own building was completed in 1976.

the **ˌOld ˈWest** a phrase used to refer to the western parts of America in the 19th century when white people first settled there. Compare WILD WEST.

The ***ˈOld ˈWoman Who ˈLived in a ˈShoe*** a traditional *nursery rhyme about a poor woman who has many children:

There was an old woman who lived in a shoe,
She had so many children she didn't know what
  to do.
She gave them some broth without any bread;
And whipped them all soundly and put them to bed.

O ˈLittle ˈTown of ˈBethlehem /ˈbeθlɪhem/ the title and first line of a popular Christmas *carol.

ˌOliver ˈTwist /ˈtwɪst/ a novel (1838) by Charles *Dickens, well known for its realistic descriptions of London's poor districts and criminals. Oliver is a poor orphan (= child whose parents are dead) who

Oliver Twist, *illustrated by George Cruikshank*

runs away to London. There he joins a group of criminals, including *Fagin, the *Artful Dodger and Bill Sikes, who try to turn him into a thief. He is rescued by a good man, Mr Brownlow, but captured again by the criminals. Nancy, Sikes's girlfriend, tries to help Oliver and is killed by Sikes, who dies while trying to escape from the police. The criminals are all arrested and Oliver goes to live with Mr Brownlow. It is one of Dickens's most famous books, and has been made into a successful film (1948) and a musical show called *Oliver!* (1960).

ˌLaurence **Oˈlivier** /əˈlɪvieɪ/ (1907–89) an English theatre, film and television actor and director. He first became famous for his Shakespearian roles in the theatre in the 1930s, and was considered the greatest English actor of the time. He performed many Shakespearian roles in films, many of them directed by himself, as well as acting in more modern plays such as *The Entertainer* (1957) by John *Osborne, and films such as *Sleuth* (1972). He was the first director of the *National Theatre (1963–73). He was made a *knight in 1947 and a *life peer in 1970.

Laurence Olivier as Richard III

ˌ***Ol' Man ˈRiver*** a song about the *Mississippi River from the musical play **Show Boat*. The best-known performance of it was by Paul *Robeson, who joined the show after it moved to London in 1928. It is sung by the character Joe and is a sad song about the hard life of African Americans in the South. They are soon forgotten, it says, 'But Ol' man river, he just keeps rollin' along'.

Oˈlympia /əˈlɪmpiə/ a group of large buildings in west London where many exhibitions and shows take place.

OM /ˌəʊ ˈem; *AmE* ˌoʊ/ ⇨ ORDER OF MERIT.

ˈ**Omaha** /ˈəʊməhɑː; *AmE* ˈoʊməhɑː/ the largest city in the US state of *Nebraska. It is on the Missouri River on the border of *Iowa. *Lewis and Clark visited the area in 1804, and it was settled in 1854, being named after a local *Native-American people. It is a centre for insurance companies and companies that process food.

ˈ**ombudsman** *n* (*pl* **-men**) ⇨ PARLIAMENTARY COMMISSIONER FOR ADMINISTRATION.

ˈ***Omnibus*** /ˈɒmnɪbəs; *AmE* ˈɑːmnɪbəs/ **1** a British television programme about the arts. It has been broadcast by the *BBC since 1967. Each programme is usually about one particular artist. **2** a US cultural television programme broadcast on *CBS on Sunday afternoons from 1952 to 1961. It was presented by Alistair *Cooke and offered a mixture of plays, music, talks with artistic people, and even comedy.

ˌJackie **Oˈnassis** /əʊˈnæsɪs; *AmE* oʊˈnæsɪs/ ⇨ KENNEDY³.

ˈ***Once in ˈRoyal ˈDavid's ˈCity*** the title and first line of a Christian hymn about the birth of Christ. It is often sung as a *carol at *Christmas.

ˌ**one-day ˈcricket** *n* [U] a version of *cricket in which each team bats once, within a limited period, so that the match finishes in one day. One-day matches were introduced in the 1960s to try to make cricket a more exciting game. There are two popular one-day competitions for professional teams in Britain, the *NatWest Trophy and the *Benson and Hedges Cup. There are also many one-day international matches.

ˈ***One Flew ˈOver the ˈCuckoo's Nest*** a US novel (1962) by Ken Kesey that became a successful *Broadway play (1963) and film (1975). It is about a man with mental problems who tries to resist the harsh discipline of the hospital where he is a patient. The film, directed by Milos *Forman with Jack *Nicholson in the main part, won four *Oscars.

ˈ***One ˈFoot in the ˈGrave*** ⇨ MELDREW.

ˌEugene **O'ˈNeill** /əʊˈniːl; *AmE* oʊˈniːl/ (1888–1953) a US writer of plays who received the 1936 *Nobel Prize for literature. He won *Pulitzer Prizes for his best-known play, **Long Day's Journey into Night*, and for *Beyond the Horizon* (1920), *Anna Christie* (1922) and *Strange Interlude* (1928). O'Neill's other works include *The Emperor Jones* (1920), *Mourning Becomes Electra* (1931) and *The Iceman Cometh* (1946). His daughter Oona married Charlie *Chaplin.

the **1 000 Guineas** ⇨ THOUSAND GUINEAS.

ˌ**On Her ˈMajesty's ˈService** ⇨ OHMS.

ˈ***Only ˈFools and ˈHorses*** a *BBC television comedy series about two brothers living in south London. Most of the humour comes from their attempts to make money without actually working. In the 1980s it was one of the most popular programmes in Britain. See also DEL BOY.

ˌLake **Onˈtario** /ɒnˈteəriəʊ; *AmE* ɑːnˈterioʊ/ the smallest and most eastern of the *Great Lakes. It has an area of 7 340 square miles (19 011 square kilometres) and is linked to Lake *Erie by the Niagara River. Lake Ontario separates the state of New York from the Canadian province of Ontario. Cities on it include Toronto, Canada, and Rochester, New York.

ˈ***On ˈTop of Old ˈSmoky*** /ˈsməʊki; *AmE* ˈsmoʊki/ a traditional US song which has been recorded by several performers. It begins:

On top of old Smoky,
All covered with snow,
I lost my true lover,
By a-courting too slow.

ˈ***Onward, ˈChristian ˈSoldiers*** a popular Christian hymn with a strong rhythm that is often sung in British schools. The music was written by Arthur *Sullivan.

007 /ˌdʌbl əʊ ˈsevn/ the British Secret Service codename of James *Bond in the novels by Ian *Fleming and in the films based on them. According to the stories, numbers beginning '00' are given to Secret Service agents who are 'licensed to kill'.

the ˈ**Open** ⇨ BRITISH OPEN.

open learning

Some adults who do not go to college or university when they leave school may wish to do so later in life but find they cannot because of work or family commitments or lack of money. Open learning schemes enable people to take educational courses at any level through part-time study at home when it is convenient for them. Open learning is sometimes called **distance learning**, because most students do not go to an educational institution for classes but study in their own home.

At an informal level, open learning may include learning a language through watching television programmes and studying an associated coursebook. Open learning leading to *A levels, professional qualifications and degrees, is often based on **correspondence courses**, though such courses existed before the term *open learning* became popular in the 1970s. Students taking correspondence courses receive printed materials through the post and send essays to a **tutor** to be marked. On other postal courses students receive all the course material at once and work through it entirely by themselves. Some courses are now offered through the Internet or by subscription to a series of television programmes. Although students have to pay to do the courses the total cost is much less than if they were to give up work to study full-time.

The best-known open learning institution is the **Open University (OU)**, which was founded in 1969. It accepts students from Britain and from other countries in the *European Union. Students can be of any age and, if they do not have the standard qualifications for entering university, they take an **access course** before starting their degree. Teaching is by a mixture of printed materials, and television and radio programmes. Students study at home and post their work to their tutors. Many go to monthly **tutorials** at **study centres** in their home town, and they may also attend **summer schools**. Most students take part-time degree courses lasting four or five years, though there is no time limit. Postgraduate and professional courses are also offered. By the mid 1990s the OU had around 200 000 students and its success has led to similar organizations being set up in other parts of the world.

Although the US has no national institution like the Open University, the principle that *further education should be open to everyone is widely accepted and there are many opportunities. Many universities and colleges operate correspondence courses, and most, especially those run by state governments, have some means by which interested people can study at the university.

ˌ**open ˈshop** *n* a business, factory, etc. where people can work without being members of a *trade union. Many British factories and other places of work used to be *closed shops, where everybody had to belong to a particular trade union, until the 1980s when the laws affecting the unions were changed, and the unions became less powerful. In the US most companies operate as open shops though there is no longer a law requiring them to do so.

the ˌ**Open Uniˈversity** ⇨ note at OPEN LEARNING.

ˌ**Operation ˈDrake** /ˈdreɪk/ a series of scientific and other projects in 16 countries involving 400 young people from 27 countries and a British sailing ship, *Eye of the Wind*, as a floating base. It was started by Prince *Charles and lasted for two years (1978–80), during which the ship sailed completely round the world, as Sir Francis *Drake had done 400 years before. It was followed in 1980 by Operation Raleigh, which then developed into a regular international event for young people. The events and the charity that organizes them are now known as *Raleigh International.

ˈJ ˈRobert ˈ**Oppenheimer** /ˈɒpənhaɪmə(r); *AmE* ˈɑːpənhaɪmər/ (Julius Robert Oppenheimer 1904–67) the scientist in charge of the US *Manhattan Project (1942–5) which built the first atom bomb. After *World War II, Oppenheimer directed the *Institute for Advanced Study. In the 1950s he opposed the creation of the hydrogen bomb, and because he was thought to hold left-wing opinions he was not allowed to work on government research projects for a time.

ˌ**opting ˈout** *n* [U] (in Britain) the process of choosing to leave the previous system in order to become more independent. The *Conservative government in the 1990s encouraged many secondary *state schools to 'opt out' of *Local Education Authority control and receive money directly from the central government so that they could operate more like independent businesses. Hospitals were also encouraged to opt out and apply for *trust status.

ˈ**Optrex**™ /ˈɒptreks; *AmE* ˈɑːptreks/ *n* [U] a liquid for washing sore eyes. A bottle of Optrex can be bought with or without an eye bath (= a small container for the liquid which is held against the eye to wash it).

ˈ**Orange** /ˈɒrɪndʒ; *AmE* ˈɔːrɪndʒ/ a British mobile phone service.

ˌ**orange ˈbadge** *n* (in Britain) a small orange sign with a picture of a wheelchair which can be displayed in the window of a car. It shows that the driver is officially recognized as a disabled person and is allowed to park in certain places where other drivers may not park.

ˈ**Orangeman** /ˈɒrɪndʒmən; *AmE* ˈɔːrɪndʒmən/ *n* (*pl* **-men**) a member of the Northern Irish **Orange Society** (also known as the **Orange Order**), a political society that aims to preserve Protestant power in Northern Ireland. The Orangemen march through the streets every year on 12 July to celebrate the victory of the Protestant king *William III of Britain, also known as William of Orange, over the *Roman Catholic *James II at the *Battle of the Boyne in 1690. See also APPRENTICE BOYS' PARADE, MARCHING SEASON.

the ˈ**Orange Prize** /ˈɒrɪndʒ; *AmE* ˈɔːrɪndʒ/ *n* a British prize given every year for the best novel written in English by a woman from any part of the world. The money for this large prize is provided by *Orange, and the competition is organized by Book Trust. The prize was first given in 1996.

ˌ***Oranges and ˈLemons*** an old English children's song about the sounds of church bells in various parts of London. It is often part of a game that young children play: two of them form an arch with their arms and the rest take turns to run under the arch until one of them is caught when the arch falls at the end of the song.

O

'Oranges and Lemons'
  say the bells of St Clements.
'You owe me five farthings'
  say the bells of St Martins.
'When will you pay me?'
  say the bells of Old Bailey.
'When I grow rich'
  say the bells of Shoreditch.
'When will that be?'
  say the bells of Stepney.
'I do not know'
  says the great bell at Bow.
Here comes a candle to light you to bed.
Here comes a chopper to chop off your head.
Chip, chop, chip, chop; the last man's DEAD!

A similar game is played with *London Bridge is Falling Down*. ⇨ note at NURSERY RHYMES.

ˌRoy ˈ**Orbison** /ˈɔːbɪsn; *AmE* ˈɔːrbɪsn/ (1936–88) a US singer and writer of pop songs who was very successful in the early 1960s. He was sometimes called the 'Big O'. His voice had a sad and emotional quality and he always wore dark glasses while performing. His best-known songs include *Only the Lonely* (1960), *Cryin'* (1961) and *Pretty Woman* (1964). Orbison was chosen for the Rock and Roll *Hall of Fame in 1987.

ˈ**Orchard Street** a well-known New York shopping street in the *Lower East Side of *Manhattan(1). It is in the old Jewish district where many Puerto Ricans and other racial groups also now live. Many shops close on Saturdays, but on Sunday mornings clothes and other items are sold at reduced prices in and outside the shops.

ˌ**order of ˈchivalry** *n* (in Britain) any of several special honours given to people as a reward for doing something good or serving the country. They include the *Order of Merit, the *Order of the Bath, the *Order of the British Empire, the *Order of the Garter, the *Order of the Thistle, the *Distinguished Service Order, the Royal Victorian Order and the Order of the *Companions of Honour. ⇨ note at HONOURS.

the ˌ**Order of ˈMerit** (*abbr* **OM**) *n* one of the British *orders of chivalry and the name of the honour that a person receives when he or she is appointed to this Order. The Order of Merit, which is limited to 24 British people and one foreigner, was created in 1902 by King *Edward VII for men and women who have achieved great things, especially in the arts, literature and science. Early members included Joseph *Lister and Florence *Nightingale. Current members include Margaret *Thatcher and Lucian *Freud. People who are appointed to this order may place the letters OM after their name.

the ˌ**Order of the ˈBath** one of the British *orders of chivalry. People who are appointed to this order receive one of three ranks within it: *Knight Grand Cross (or *Dame Grand Cross for a woman), *Knight Commander (or *Dame Commander) or Companion. The full name of the order is the Most Honourable Order of the Bath. It may have been started as early as 1399, but it later disappeared and was started again in 1725. Originally, people receiving the order washed in a bath as part of the ceremony. ⇨ notes at ARISTOCRACY, HONOURS.

the ˈ**Order of the ˈBritish ˈEmpire** one of the British *orders of chivalry. People who are appointed to this order receive one of five ranks within it: *Knight Grand Cross (or *Dame Grand Cross for a woman), *Knight Commander (or *Dame Commander), Commander, Officer or Member, and may put the appropriate letters after their name, such as CBE, *OBE or *MBE. The Order was started in 1917. Its full title is the Most Excellent Order of the British Empire. ⇨ notes at ARISTOCRACY, HONOURS.

the ˌ**Order of the ˈGarter** the oldest and highest of the British *orders of chivalry. It includes members of the British and other royal families and a maximum of 24 other people, who receive the rank of Knight Companion when they are appointed to the order, and may put the letters KG after their names. It was probably started in 1348 by King *Edward III. According to tradition, it was named after an occasion when a woman in the presence of the king dropped a garter (= a band worn around the leg to hold up a sock). The king saved her from embarrassment by picking up the garter and fixing it to his own leg, saying 'Honi soit qui mal y pense', French for 'Shame on anyone who thinks badly of this'. This phrase became the motto of the order, whose full name is the Most Noble Order of the Garter. ⇨ notes at ARISTOCRACY, HONOURS.

the ˌ**Order of the ˈThistle** one of the highest British *orders of chivalry. Its full name is the Most Ancient and Most Noble Order of the Thistle. People who are appointed to the order may put the letters KT (meaning *Knight of the Thistle*) after their names. The order was started in 1687 and is mainly for members of the Scottish *peerage. The thistle, a prickly plant, is the national *emblem of Scotland. ⇨ notes at ARISTOCRACY, HONOURS.

the ˌ**ordination of ˈwomen** *n* [U] the process of admitting women as priests in the Church. The *Roman Catholic Church does not allow women to be priests, but the *Church of England and the rest of the *Anglican Communion around the world now do. The first women were ordained in 1974 as priests in the *Episcopal Church in the US, where there has also been a female *bishop since 1989. In Britain, the *Church of England decided at a meeting of the *General Synod in 1985 to allow women to become deacons (= junior priests). Full ordination was allowed from 1992, and the first women were ordained in 1994. These decisions were strongly opposed by many people, especially *Anglo-Catholics and *evangelicals.

the ˌ**Ordnance ˈSurvey** (*abbr* the **OS**) the British government organization responsible for making maps of Britain. These are available in a range of different scales, some of which are very detailed. They are especially popular with people who enjoy walking in the countryside. The OS was started in 1791 to make maps for the army. It also produces historical maps. See also NATIONAL GRID 2.

ˈ**Oregon** /ˈɒrɪgən; *AmE* ˈɔːrɪgən/ a state in the northwestern US, also called the Beaver State. The largest city is *Portland(1), and the capital city is Salem. Captain James *Cook sailed along its coast in 1778, and *Lewis and Clark visited the area in 1805. Oregon became a state in 1859. Its products include salmon and other fish, wood, paper and fruit. Tourists can visit Crater Lake National Park, the Oregon Dunes National Recreation Area and the John Day Fossil Beds National Monument.

the ˌ**Oregon ˈTrail** /ˌɒrɪgən; *AmE* ˌɔːrɪgən/ a US route used in the 19th century by people travelling west to settle new lands. About 10 000 people travelled along it in the 1840s. It was about 2 000 miles (3 218 kilometres) long and the journey took about six months in *covered wagons. It went from *Independence, *Missouri, through *Nebraska and *Wyoming and over the *Rocky Mountains to the Columbia River. The route became the **Oregon National Historic Trail** in 1978. Compare OVERLAND TRAIL, SANTA FE TRAIL.

ˈ**Oreo**™ /ˈɔːriəʊ; *AmE* ˈɔːrioʊ/ *n* (*pl* **Oreos**) a popular

US cookie. Oreos have two hard, round chocolate sides stuck together by a sweet white filling, and children often open them to eat the white part first.

the ˌ**Organiˈzation for Ecoˈnomic Coopeˈration and Deˈvelopment** (*abbr* the **OECD**) an international organization set up in 1961 with the aim of helping member countries to work together in areas of economic and social policy. There are 24 members, including Britain and the US. The main offices are in Paris.

the ˌ**Organiˈzation of Aˈmerican ˈStates** (*abbr* the **OAS**) an international organization of 35 American nations established in 1948 in Bogotá, Columbia. OAS members work together to settle disputes in a peaceful manner, as well as discussing political, economic, social and cultural issues. Compare ALLIANCE FOR PROGRESS, MONROE DOCTRINE.

The ˌ***Origin of ˈSpecies*** the short title which many people use to refer to *On the Origin of Species by Means of Natural Selection* (1859) by Charles *Darwin. In it he explained his theory of evolution (= the development of different life forms over millions of years). When it was published, all the copies were sold on the first day. His theory caused a lot of anger at that time, but its main ideas now form the basis of scientific understanding of the subject.

the ˈ**Orkneys** /ˈɔːkniz; *AmE* ˈɔːrkniz/ (*also* the **Orkney Islands**) a group of more than 70 islands off the north-east coast of Scotland. The largest island, called Mainland, has a number of prehistoric structures such as *Skara Brae. The Orkneys and the *Shetlands belonged to Norway and Denmark until the 15th century, when they were given to Scotland. Fishing and farming are two of the main industries on the islands. They are also popular with tourists.

Orˈlando /ɔːˈlændəʊ; *AmE* ɔːrˈlændoʊ/ a US city in central *Florida, known as an international entertainment centre. It was a quiet farming town until the 1970s but its attractions now include *Disney World, Sea World, Universal Studios and Disney-MGM Studios. Orlando is the centre of an agricultural area which produces a lot of fruit.

ˌJoe ˈ**Orton** /ˈɔːtn; *AmE* ˈɔːrtn/ (1933–67) an English writer of plays that are full of wild and often shocking humour, including *Entertaining Mr Sloane* (1964), *Loot* (1965) and *What the Butler Saw* (1967). He was murdered by his jealous male lover.

ˌGeorge ˈ**Orwell** /ˈɔːwel; *AmE* ˈɔːrwel/ (1903–50) an English writer of essays and novels. He was born in India and educated at *Eton. His first job was with the British police in Burma (1922–7), but he reacted against his background and spent the next few years living with very little money in Paris and London. He wrote about his experiences among poor people there in *Down and Out in Paris and London* (1933). His next book, *The Road to Wigan Pier* (1937), described *working-class life in Britain during the *Depression. He joined the Republican side in the Spanish Civil War and wrote about this in *Homage to Catalonia* (1938). His two best-known novels, **Animal Farm* and **Nineteen Eighty-Four*, were written in the 1940s. In their different ways, they both show his disappointment with the results of socialist revolutions, especially in the Soviet Union.

OS /ˌəʊ ˈes; *AmE* ˌoʊ/ ⇨ ORDNANCE SURVEY.

Oˈsage /əʊˈseɪdʒ; *AmE* oʊˈseɪdʒ/ *n* (*pl* **Osages** *or* **Osage**) a member of a *Native-American people in the US state of *Oklahoma. Many of them have become very rich since oil was discovered on their reservation (= land given and protected by the US government) at the beginning of the 20th century. The Osage had earlier lived in the *Ohio River valley and then along the Osage River in *Missouri. The US government moved them to the Oklahoma reservation in 1872.

ˌJohn ˈ**Osborne** /ˈɒzbɔːn; *AmE* ˈɑːzbɔːrn/ (1929–94) an English writer of realistic plays about *working-class life, including **Look Back in Anger* and *The Entertainer* (1957). This type of play was new and shocking in the 1950s when they were written, and Osborne and similar writers became known as *angry young men.

ˌ**Osborne ˈHouse** /ˌɒzbɔːn; *AmE* ˌɑːzbɔːrn/ a house on the *Isle of Wight which was built for Queen *Victoria in 1851 as a quiet and private place for herself and her family. The house has been kept as it was when they lived there. It is open to the public at certain times of the year.

O

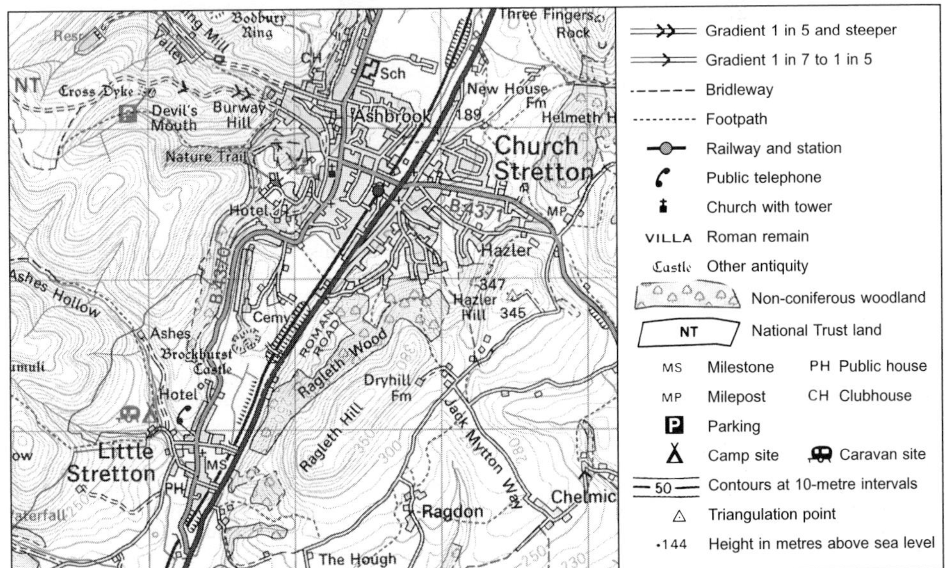

part of an Ordnance Survey 1:50 000 map and some of the symbols used

ˌOzzy ˈ**Osbourne** /ˌɒzi ˈɒzbɔːn; *AmE* ˌɑːzi ˈɑːzbɔːrn/ (1948–) a British *heavy metal musician. He was the singer for the group Black Sabbath (1969–79), and later formed his own Ozzy Osbourne group, which achieved success in the 1980s and 1990s with such albums as *Talk of the Devil* (1982).

ˈ**Oscar** /ˈɒskə(r); *AmE* ˈɑːskər/ *n* another name for a US *Academy Award. The awards, which are in the form of small metal statues, are presented each year at a special ceremony. The ceremony itself is sometimes called the Oscars: *He won the Oscar for Best Supporting Actor.* ○ *The film won four Oscars.*

Anthony Minghella and Saul Zaentz holding their Oscars for The English Patient

the ˈ**Osmonds** /ˈɒzməndz; *AmE* ˈɑːzməndz/ a US group of popular singers who were all members of the same family. They included six brothers and one sister. The most famous were Donny Osmond (1957–) and Marie Osmond (1959–). The Osmonds were *Mormons and had a reputation for being very religious and morally good. Their hits included *One Bad Apple* (1971). Donny and Marie later had separate careers on their own, as well as recording several songs together, including *I'm Leaving It Up to You* (1974) and other hits.

ˈLee ˈHarvey ˈ**Oswald** /ˈliː ˈhɑːvi ˈɒzwəld; *AmE* ˈhɑːrvi ˈɑːzwəld/ (1939–63) the man who was arrested for the murder of US President John F *Kennedy in 1963. He said he was innocent but was never tried, because he was killed by Jack *Ruby two days after being arrested. The official *Warren Report stated that Oswald was the only person who shot Kennedy, but many people still believe that others were involved.

O'thello /əˈθeləʊ; *AmE* əˈθeloʊ/ a play (*c.* 1603) by William *Shakespeare The story is about a great man who is destroyed by jealousy. Othello is a Moor (= North African) who is a powerful and respected commander in the navy of Venice. He is gradually persuaded by the evil officer Iago that his wife, Desdemona, and another officer, Cassio, are lovers. Othello kills his wife but then discovers that she was innocent and kills himself.

OUP /ˌəʊ juː ˈpiː; *AmE* ˌoʊ/ ⇨ OXFORD UNIVERSITY PRESS.

ˌ**Our** ˈ**Father** ⇨ LORD'S PRAYER.

ˈ***Our*** ˈ***Mutual*** ˈ***Friend*** the last complete novel (1864–5) by Charles *Dickens. Like his previous novel, **Little Dorrit*, it is full of comedy and social comment about how wealth can destroy people.

ˌ***Our*** ˈ***Town*** a play (1938) by the US writer Thornton *Wilder which won a *Pulitzer Prize. It is set in the imaginary small town of Grover's Corners and is about the simple lives of ordinary people. A character called the Stage Manager makes comments on the story directly to the audience. The play is still often performed by amateur groups.

Ouse /uːz/ the name of several English rivers. The longest, the Great Ouse, is in the east of England and flows from *Northamptonshire through the *Fens and out into the *Wash at *King's Lynn. Another Ouse is in the north-east and flows through *York to the *Humber. A third Ouse begins halfway between London and the south coast and flows into the *English Channel at Newhaven.

ˈ**OutRage!** /ˈaʊtreɪdʒ/ a British organization that works for the rights of homosexual men and women and to encourage public discussion of the issue. OutRage! started in 1990 and quickly became well known for its use of direct action which it often combines with humour, as in the Queer *St Valentine's Day Carnival.

the ˈ**Outward** ˈ**Bound** ˈ**Trust** (*also* **Outward Bound**) an international organization with its base in Britain which arranges outdoor adventure training for young people. Its activities include sailing and rock climbing. The Trust was set up in 1941 by Kurt Hahn, the man who started *Gordonstoun school. ⇨ article at YOUTH ORGANIZATIONS. Compare DUKE OF EDINBURGH'S AWARD SCHEME, RALEIGH INTERNATIONAL.

the ˈ**Oval** a *cricket ground in south-east London, England. It has been the home of the Surrey County Cricket Club since 1845 and international cricket matches are regularly played there.

the ˌ**Oval** ˈ**Office** the office of the US *President in the *White House(1). It has this name because of its shape. The phrase is sometimes also used to mean the President himself: *Congress is waiting to see how the Oval Office will react.*

the Oval Office

ˈ**Ovaltine**™ /ˈəʊvltiːn; *AmE* ˈoʊvltiːn/ *n* [U, C] a hot drink made from a sweet brown powder mixed with water and milk, or the name of the powder itself, which contains dried milk, dried egg and malt (= grain that has been soaked in water and dried). Ovaltine is usually drunk just before going to bed at night. It was first sold in Britain in the early 20th century and is now popular around the world, though many young people regard it as rather boring and old-fashioned: *Have a nice cup of Ovaltine – it'll help you to sleep.*

the ˌ**Overland** ˈ**Trail** any of several different routes taken by people travelling to the US West in the 19th century, including the main route to the California goldfields (= areas where gold was found as a mineral). Compare OREGON TRAIL, SANTA FE TRAIL.

ˌ**overseas** ˈ**territory** (*also* **dependent territory**, **Crown Colony**) *n* any of several small territories (mainly islands or groups of islands) which have a governor appointed by the British government. Examples include the *Falkland Islands, *Gibraltar and *St Helena. Britain is responsible for their defence and other aspects of their government, e.g. their police and *Civil Service.

ˌ***Over ˈThere*** a lively song written by George M *Cohan to praise US soldiers serving abroad in *World War I. He wrote it on 6 April 1917, the day on which the US entered the war, and it includes the words: 'The Yanks are coming! And we won't come home 'til it's over over there.' The song was also popular during *World War II.

ˌDavid **ˈOwen**[1] /ˈəʊɪn; *AmE* ˈoʊɪn/ (1938–) a British politician who became *Foreign Secretary in the *Labour government in 1977, but left the Labour Party in 1981 and, with three other politicians, started the *SDP (Social Democratic Party). He was leader of the SDP from 1983 to 1990. In 1992 Owen was made a *life peer, and in the same year he was appointed with Cyrus *Vance to lead the international effort to end the war in former Yugoslavia.

ˌRobert **ˈOwen**[2] /ˈəʊɪn; *AmE* ˈoʊɪn/ (1771–1858) a Welsh industrialist whose ideas on social reform influenced the development of the *Co-operative Movement and *trade unions in Britain. He bought some cotton mills (= factories) in Scotland and created a model industrial community for his workers, providing them with good housing and education. The factories made a good profit and his ideas were admired even among the upper classes, though they were less enthusiastic when he argued that workers should share the ownership of factories. He started several other communities, including New Harmony in the US, but these were less successful.

ˌWilfred **ˈOwen**[3] /ˈəʊɪn; *AmE* ˈoʊɪn/ (1893–1918) an English poet who fought in *World War I and whose poems are about the horrors of war and the waste of life it causes. He was killed a week before the end of the war, and his poems were published two years later by his friend Siegfried *Sassoon. Six of them were set to music in Benjamin *Britten's *War Requiem* (1962).

ˌJesse **ˈOwens** /ˈəʊɪnz; *AmE* ˈoʊɪnz/ (1913–80) an *African-American athlete who won four gold medals (for running and the long jump) at the 1936 Olympic Games in Germany. This annoyed Adolf Hitler, who wanted to show that the white Aryan race was best. Owens later received the *Presidential Medal of Freedom for his achievements.

The ˌ***Owl and the ˈPussy-Cat*** a well-known nonsense poem (1871) by Edward *Lear. It tells the story of the adventures of an owl and a cat and is very popular with children. Many people know the first few lines:

The owl and the pussy-cat went to sea
In a beautiful pea-green boat.
They took some honey and plenty of money
Wrapped up in a five-pound note.

the Owl and the Pussy-Cat, drawn by Edward Lear

Oxbridge

Oxbridge is a word made from the names *Oxford and *Cambridge and is used to refer informally to the universities of Oxford and Cambridge together, especially when they are being distinguished from other universities.

Oxford and Cambridge are the oldest universities in Britain. They are generally also thought to be the best universities to get a place at. An Oxbridge degree makes a good impression with many employers, and graduates of these universities may have an advantage when applying for jobs, e.g. in the *Civil Service. Although efforts are being made to attract more students from state schools, many of the 14 000 **undergraduates** at each university have been educated at *public schools. The upper class have traditionally sent their children to Oxbridge, and many *prime ministers and politicians went there. To many people, Oxford and Cambridge seem very remote places where only the very privileged can go.

Students at Oxford and Cambridge must be accepted at one of the 30 semi-independent **colleges**. They used to have to sit an **entrance exam** and many still take an exam if they want to get a **scholarship** or an **exhibition**. Others have to sit special exams in addition to *A levels. Each college has its own teaching and research staff, called **fellows**, and its own buildings, including **hall** (= a dining hall), a library, a chapel, and rooms for students to live in during the term. The buildings are often arranged round a **quad** (= square). Until the 1970s colleges were single-sex, but now almost all are mixed. The universities provide other facilities centrally, including laboratories, lecture rooms and libraries.

The teaching system is different from that at most other universities. Students have **tutorials**, called **supervisions** at Cambridge, at which they read their essays to their **tutor**, a fellow who is a specialist in what they are studying. There are usually no more than two or three students at a tutorial. Students also go to lectures that are arranged by the university and open to all students. Final examinations at Oxford are called **schools**, and at Cambridge **the tripos**. Undergraduates at Oxford and Cambridge study for a BA degree, but after a period of time graduates can convert their BA to an **MA (Oxon)** or an **MA (Cantab)** without doing any further study. *Oxon* is short for *Oxoniensis*, and *Cantab* for *Cantabrigiensis*, Latin for 'of Oxford' and 'of Cambridge'.

At Oxford students sometimes have to wear **gowns**, e.g. when they go to see the college principal. When they sit examinations or go to a degree ceremony they have to wear **academic dress**. This consists of **subfusc**, a black suit or skirt, black shoes and socks or tights, a white shirt or blouse and a black tie. Women also have to wear a tie or ribbon. On top they wear their gown and a **mortar board** (= a black hat with a flat, square top) and, when they graduate, a **hood** that shows their status. At Cambridge students only have to wear gowns when they **matriculate** (= become members of the university) and at **graduation**.

The two universities are academic rivals, and rivals also in debating and sport. The ***Boat Race**, held each year around Easter, attracts national attention. *Rugby and *cricket teams play against each other in **varsity** matches, as well as against professional sides.

ˈOxfam /ˈɒksfæm; *AmE* ˈɑːksfæm/ Britain's largest and best-known aid agency (= a charity that helps people in poor countries). It was set up in 1942 (as the Oxford Committee for Famine Relief) to send food to people with very little food in other European countries. It now works mainly in developing countries, sending help when there is an emergency, and working with governments on projects to help poor people. Oxfam runs **Oxfam shops** in most British towns and cities, where new and second-hand clothes, books, etc. are sold to raise money for the charity: *The shoes are new but everything else came from Oxfam shops.*

'Oxford /'ɒksfəd; *AmE* 'ɑːksfərd/ a city in southern England, west of London, and the administrative centre of *Oxfordshire. Oxford is famous for its university, the oldest in Britain, established in the mid 12th century. The buildings of its many colleges are a major feature of the city, which is a tourist centre as well as an important centre of academic research. It is also an industrial city, and had one of the main factories producing British cars for much of the 20th century. ⇨ note at OXBRIDGE.

Oxford

The ***'Oxford 'Book of 'English 'Verse*** /'ɒksfəd; *AmE* 'ɑːksfərd/ a collection of English poetry that was first published in 1900 and has appeared in several new editions since then. It is one of the most popular books of poetry in Britain, and has had an important influence on which English poems became well known.

O

the ***'Oxford 'English 'Dictionary*** /'ɒksfəd; *AmE* 'ɑːksfərd/ (*also* the **OED**) a very large historical dictionary of the English language, published by *Oxford University Press. It is one of the most famous dictionaries in the world, well known for including many different meanings of words, and for giving real examples to show how each word was originally used and how its meaning has changed through time. Work on it began in 1858 and the final volume (= separate book) was published in 1928. The second edition, with many new words, was published in 1989. See also MURRAY.

the **'Oxford Group** /'ɒksfəd; *AmE* 'ɑːksfərd/ ⇨ MORAL RE-ARMAMENT.

the **'Oxford ˌMovement** /'ɒksfəd ; *AmE* 'ɑːksfərd/ a group of people based in *Oxford in the 1830s and 1840s who believed that many of the *Roman Catholic ideas and ceremonies should be introduced into the *Church of England. The group included Cardinal *Newman, Edward *Pusey and John Keble, and had an important influence on the development of the Church of England, which became more *High Church in the 19th century.

'Oxfordshire /'ɒksfədʃə(r); *AmE* 'ɑːksfərdʃər/ (*abbr* **Oxon**) a county in central southern England. It contains the city of Oxford and some attractive countryside, and the River *Thames runs through it.

'Oxford Street /'ɒksfəd; *AmE* 'ɑːksfərd/ a popular shopping street in the *West End of London. It is one of London's best-known streets, containing a number of famous department stores as well as large branches of all the *high-street shops.

ˌOxford Uni'versity /ˌɒksfəd; *AmE* ˌɑːksfərd/ the oldest university in Britain, established in the mid 12th century in the town of Oxford, England. It has a high reputation for academic achievement. The university consists of a number of separate colleges, the earliest of which is University College (established 1249). Other famous colleges include All Souls, Balliol, Christ Church, Magdalen, New College, St John's and Trinity. There is one college for women only. All the rest take both male and female students. Among the university's famous buildings are the *Bodleian Library and the *Sheldonian Theatre. See also EIGHTS. Compare CAMBRIDGE UNIVERSITY. ⇨ note at OXBRIDGE.

'Oxford Uni'versity 'Press /'ɒksfəd; *AmE* 'ɑːksfərd/ (*abbr* **OUP**) a large publishing company which is part of *Oxford University and has been publishing books since the late 17th century. It is an important publisher of academic and school books, as well as famous dictionaries, such as the **Oxford English Dictionary* and the *Oxford Advanced Learner's Dictionary*, and reference books such as the *Oxford Companion to English Literature.*

'Oxo™ /'ɒksəʊ; *AmE* 'ɑːksoʊ/ *n* [U] a popular British make of stock cube (= a small square piece of dried stock made by cooking meat, bones, fish or vegetables very slowly). Oxo is used for adding flavour to sauces, soups, etc.: *The gravy was thin and watery so he crumbled another Oxo cube into it.*

'Oxon /'ɒksn; *AmE* 'ɑːksn/ **1** an abbreviation for *Oxfordshire, usually written in addresses. **2** an abbreviation for *Oxford University, usually written after a person's degree title: *Peter Smith MA (Oxon).*

o'yez! /əʊ'jez, əʊ'jeɪ; *AmE* oʊ'jez, oʊ'jeɪ/ (*old use*) an old word meaning 'listen'. It is traditionally shouted, usually three times, to get people's attention by officials in courts of law and by town criers (= people whose job is to walk through the streets of towns and shout official announcements and other news).

Oz /ɒz; *AmE* ɑːz/ **1** an informal word for *Australia, used mainly by Australians. **2** the imaginary magic place where Dorothy is carried by a storm in the children's book *The *Wizard of Oz.*

the **ˌOzark 'Mountains** /ˌəʊzɑːk; *AmE* ˌoʊzɑːrk/ (*also* the **'Ozarks**) a US area of high land and mountains mostly in southern *Missouri and northern *Arkansas. Its large forests and grand views make it popular with tourists. Parts of it are very remote, and Americans sometimes make jokes about the simple culture of the people who live there.

ˌOzy'mandias /ˌɒzɪ'mændiəs; *AmE* ˌɑːzɪ'mændiəs/ a well-known poem (1818) by *Shelley[2]. It describes a broken statue of a legendary king of ancient times, lying forgotten in the desert, with these words carved on its base:

'My name is Ozymandias, king of kings:
Look on my works, ye Mighty, and despair!'

ˌOzzie and 'Harriet Ozzie Nelson (1906–75) and his wife Harriet Nelson (1914–94), a popular couple on US radio and television. They used their real names and the names of their sons, Ricky *Nelson and David Nelson, as characters in their comedy series about family life, *The Adventures of Ozzie and Harriet* (1952–66). The Nelsons were regarded by many Americans as the perfect family because they appeared so happy and pleasant.

Pp

the **PA** /ˌpiː ˈeɪ/ ⇨ PRESS ASSOCIATION.

PAC /ˌpiː eɪ ˈsiː/ ⇨ POLITICAL ACTION COMMITTEE.

Paˌcific ˈDaylight Time /pəˌsɪfɪk/ (*abbr* **PDT**) (in the US) the time used between early April and late October in the far western states, but not *Alaska or *Hawaii. It is an hour earlier than *Pacific Standard Time.

Paˌcific ˈStandard Time /pəˌsɪfɪk/ (*abbr* **PST**) (*also* **Pacific Time**) (in the US) the time used between late October and early April in the far western states, but not *Alaska or *Hawaii. It is eight hours earlier than *Greenwich Mean Time.

ˌAl **Paˈcino** /pəˈtʃiːnəʊ; *AmE* pəˈtʃiːnoʊ/ (1940–) a US actor who usually plays tough characters. He won an *Oscar for his part in *Scent of a Woman* (1992). He began his career on stage before becoming famous for his performances as Michael Corleone in the three **Godfather* films. His other films have included *Serpico* (1973), *Dog Day Afternoon* (1975), *Scarface* (1983), *Dick Tracy* (1990), *Glengarry Glen Ross* (1992), *Looking for Richard* (1996), which he also produced and directed, and *Devil's Advocate* (1997).

ˈPaddington /ˈpædɪŋtən/ a train station in west London for trains to and from west and south-west England and Wales. It is a large station, built in the 1850s with a glass and iron roof designed by *Brunel. It also has a station on the *London Underground.

ˌPaddington ˈBear /ˌpædɪŋtən/ the main character in a series of children's books by Michael Bond (1926–). Paddington is a toy bear, usually wearing a large hat and coat. He was found at *Paddington station and taken home by an English family. Many of his adventures have been made into children's television programmes.

ˌpage-ˈthree girl *n* a young woman, usually one with large breasts, who appears naked or partly naked on the third page of some British *tabloid newspapers. The first of these photographs appeared in the **Sun* in 1970, and several other tabloids published similar pictures in the 1970s and 1980s. They became less popular in the 1990s, and now even the **Sun* does not have a page-three girl every day: *The newspapers don't influence the way he votes – he only gets them for the football and the page-three girls.*

ˌThomas **ˈPaine** /ˈpeɪn/ (1737–1809) an English writer and politician who wrote and spoke in favour of freedom and democracy. He moved to America in 1774 and wrote *Common Sense* (1776), a short book proposing American independence from Britain. When he returned to England he wrote *The *Rights of Man* in support of the French Revolution, and had to escape to France to avoid being arrested for treason. In France he became a member of the revolutionary government, but was put in prison because he was opposed to killing the king. There he wrote the last of his famous books, *The Age of Reason* (1794–5), which attacked many Christian beliefs and practices.

the **ˌPainted ˈDesert** a beautiful region in the northern part of the US state of *Arizona, near the *Petrified Forest. It is a tourist attraction east of the Little Colorado River and is about 150 miles (240 kilometres) long. It is a high, flat area covered with red, purple, grey and brown rocks whose colours change slightly through the day.

ˈpairing /ˈpeərɪŋ; *AmE* ˈperɪŋ/ *n* [U] the practice in the British *Parliament in which two *MPs from opposing parties agree that neither of them will vote on a particular question in parliament, so neither needs to attend the debate on it. MPs who have made such agreements are called **pairs**.

ˈPaisley¹ /ˈpeɪzli/ a town in western Scotland, near *Glasgow, with a long tradition of producing clothes and fabrics in wool and cotton. It became well known in the 19th century when the **paisley pattern** was introduced. It is a design like a feather or teardrop (= a single tear) with a curved end which originally came from India, but which became popular around the world after it was used in Paisley: *You can't wear a paisley tie with a striped shirt!*

a paisley tie

ˌIan **ˈPaisley²** /ˈpeɪzli/ (1926–) a Northern Irish religious and political leader, well known for his strong views against the *IRA, the Republic of Ireland and the *Roman Catholic Church. He was made a *Presbyterian minister (= priest) in 1946 and established his own religious group, the Free Presbyterian Church of Ulster, in 1951. He established the *Ulster Democratic Unionist Party in 1971, and has been its leader since 1974. He has been an *MP since 1970 and an *MEP since 1979. He often appears on British television expressing his opinion that Northern Ireland should remain part of the *United Kingdom.

ˈPaiute /ˈpaɪuːt/ *n* (*pl* **Paiutes** *or* **Paiute**) a member of a *Native-American people in the south-western US. There are now only about 4 000 of them and they live mostly on reservations (= land given and protected by the US government) in *Nevada, *California, *Utah and *Arizona. They began the *Ghost Dance and its religion. In earlier times the northern Paiutes attacked white people who settled in their areas, and the southern Paiutes were called Digger Indians because they ate roots.

ˈPaki /ˈpæki/ *n* (*pl* **-is**) (*BrE infml offensive*) a person from *Pakistan living in Britain, or one whose ancestors came from Pakistan. It is sometimes used to refer to anybody in Britain whose ancestors came from other south Asian countries such as *India or *Bangladesh.

ˌPakiˈstan /ˌpækɪˈstɑːn, ˌpɑːkɪˈstɑːn, ˌpækɪˈstæn/ a country in southern Asia, west of India. During the time of the *British Empire it was part of India. When India became independent in 1947, Pakistan became a separate state consisting of the two areas where most of India's Muslims lived: West Pakistan to the west, and East Pakistan to the east. In 1971 there was a civil war between the two parts of the country and East Pakistan became the independent country of *Bangladesh. West Pakistan became Pakistan and left the *Commonwealth in protest against Bangladesh becoming a member. Pakistan joined the Commonwealth again in 1989. Its capital city is Islamabad and its official language is Urdu. Many **Pakistanis** now live in Britain. ▶ **Pakistani** /ˌpækɪ'stɑːni, ˌpɑːkɪ'stɑːni, ˌpækɪ'stæni/ *adj, n.*

Pal™ /pæl/ *n* [U] a British make of food for dogs. The advertisements claim that it 'prolongs active life'.

the **'Palace** *n* **1** (*infml*) *Buckingham Palace. **2** a way of referring to the British king or queen and their advisers: *The Palace will not be pleased by the revelations in the new book.*

the **ˌPalace of 'Westminster** /'westmɪnstə(r)/ the official name of the British *Houses of Parliament. Its full name is the **New Palace of Westminster**, since it was built after the **Old Palace of Westminster** was destroyed in a fire in 1834. *Parliament used to meet in the Old Palace, which was first built for *Edward the Confessor in the 11th century. The Palace of Westminster was made a *World Heritage Site in 1987.

ˌpale 'ale *n* [U, C] (*BrE*) a type of pale *bitter beer, often sold in British pubs under the name 'India Pale Ale' or 'IPA'. ⇨ note at BEER.

ˌFrancis **'Palgrave** /'pælgreɪv/ (1824–97) an English writer and teacher. He was professor of poetry at *Oxford University from 1885 to 1895. He is best remembered for his selection of English poems, published as *The *Golden Treasury* and often referred to as *Palgrave's Treasury*. He also wrote several books of his own poetry.

ˌMichael **'Palin** /'peɪlɪn/ (1943–) an English actor and writer. He first became famous in the 1970s as one of the team of comedy actors and writers of **Monty Python's Flying Circus*. He has acted in a wide variety of films and television programmes, and in the 1990s he began presenting programmes for the *BBC in which he travels around the world and gives his own views of the places he visits. He has also written a novel.

Pal'ladianism /pə'leɪdiənɪzəm/ *n* [U] a style of architecture based on the work of Andrea Palladio, a 16th-century Italian architect who was influenced by the buildings of ancient Greece and Rome. Buildings in the **Palladian** style often have a pediment (= a large triangle above the entrance) and many columns. The style became fashionable in Britain in the 18th century after it was introduced by Inigo *Jones, and led to the development of *neoclassicism.

the **Pal'ladium** /pə'leɪdiəm/ (*also* the **London Palladium**) a well-known theatre in central London. It is used mainly for *musicals, comedies and *music-hall performances.

ˌPall 'Mall /ˌpæl 'mæl/ a street in central London, running west from *Trafalgar Square. It is known for its many *clubs, including the *Athenaeum and the *Reform Club. Pall mall is the name of an old game like *croquet that used to be played there.

ˌPalm 'Beach a city on a long island off the south-east coast of *Florida. It is one of the richest communities in the US, with many large private houses, including the Kennedy family home bought in 1933 by Joseph *Kennedy. The main shopping street, with many expensive shops, is Worth Avenue.

ˌArnold **'Palmer** /'pɑːmə(r)/ (1929–) a US golf player who was especially successful in the 1960s. He was the first person to earn $1 million from golf. He won the *Masters Tournament four times (1958, 1960, 1962 and 1964), a US Open (1960) and the *British Open twice (1961–2). The many people who came to support him as he played were often referred to as 'Arnie's Army'.

ˌLord **'Palmerston** /'pɑːməstən; *AmE* 'pɑːmərstən/ (Henry John Temple, 3rd Viscount Palmerston 1784–1865) an English *prime minister (1855–58 and 1859–65). He began his career as a *Tory, but in 1830 he became *Foreign Secretary for the *Whig(1) government. He was well known for using the armed forces to protect British interests in other countries. He was Prime Minister during the *Crimean War, the *Indian Mutiny and the second *Opium War, and nearly involved Britain in the American *Civil War.

ˌPalm 'Springs a rich and fashionable city in a desert area of southern *California. It is about 120 miles (193 kilometres) east of *Los Angeles and is very popular with *Hollywood stars. Palm Springs has the Betty Ford Center, which helps people with alcohol and drug problems, and there is a large community of homosexuals.

ˌPalm 'Sunday (in the Christian Church) the Sunday before *Easter. In many Christian churches people who come to church on Palm Sunday are given a leaf of the palm tree folded in the shape of a cross. This tradition comes from the Bible story that people put palm leaves on the ground in front of Christ as he entered Jerusalem.

ˌMount **'Palomar** /'pæləmɑː(r)/ a mountain in southern *California, north-east of *San Diego. It is 6 126 feet/1 868 metres high. It is the site of the Hale Observatory, which has one of the world's largest telescopes (= instruments for looking at the stars, planets, etc.).

ˌpalo'mino /ˌpælə'miːnəʊ; *AmE* ˌpælə'miːnoʊ/ *n* (*pl* **-os**) a breed of horse with a yellowish or pale brown colour and a white tail and mane (= hair on the neck). Palominos were first bred in the south-western US, and the name in Spanish means 'young pigeon'.

the **ˌPanama Ca'nal** /ˌpænəmɑː/ a canal through Panama which connects the Atlantic and Pacific Oceans and is of great importance to world trade. It is owned and operated by the US government. The canal is 51 miles/82 kilometres long and was completed by the US in 1914. The area on both sides of it, the **Panama Canal Zone**, was controlled by the US until 1979, when it was returned to Panama. The US also plans to return the canal to Panama in 1999.

the **ˌPan 'Am ˌBuilding** /ˌpæn 'æm/ one of the best-known buildings in New York, near *Grand Central Station, built by *Pan American World Airways and completed in 1963. It has the shape of a plane wing and has more office space than the *Empire State Building. Helicopters used to land on its roof, but this was stopped after an accident killed five people in 1977. The building was sold to an insurance company in 1991 and is now officially the Met Life Building, though many people still use its original name.

the **ˌPan A'merican 'Games** /ˌpæn/ a sports competition between countries of North and South America, held every four years. It began in 1951, and the different sports are similar to those in the Olympic Games.

ˌPan A'merican 'World 'Airways /ˌpæn/ (*also* **ˌPan 'Am**) /ˌpæn 'æm/ a large US company, established in 1927, which called itself 'the World's Most Experienced Airline'. It was one of the first to use jet passenger planes (in 1958) and the first to use *Boeing 747 'jumbo jets' regularly. One of these crashed in 1988 at *Lockerbie, Scotland, after a bomb on board exploded. Because of this and financial problems, Pan Am went out of business in 1991.

'pancake *n* a type of soft, thin, flat cake made from a mixture of flour, eggs and milk which is quickly fried on both sides in a little hot fat. In Britain, pancakes are traditionally eaten hot, served with lemon and sugar and often rolled up. In the US they are a traditional breakfast food, usually eaten with butter and maple syrup (= a thick, sweet, sticky substance obtained from a type of maple tree). They are also sometimes eaten wrapped round sausages, a dish called 'pigs in a blanket'.

ˈ**Pancake Day** (*also* ˌ**Pancake** ˈ**Tuesday**) (*BrE*) another name for *Shrove Tuesday, when many people eat pancakes in Britain. Traditionally, this was the last day when people could enjoy rich food before *Lent.

ˈ**pancake race** *n* (in Britain) a race in which people carry pancakes in frying pans and repeatedly toss them (= throw them into the air so that they land the other way up in the pan) as they run. Tossing pancakes is the traditional way of cooking them on both sides. Pancake races take place in many parts of Britain on *Shrove Tuesday.

P & O /ˌpiː ənd ˈəʊ; *AmE* ˈoʊ/ a British shipping company, well known for its large cruise liners (= ships on which people spend their holidays/vacations, sailing from place to place). The company was established in 1837, when it was called the Peninsular and Oriental Steam Navigation Company, and sailed mainly to Spain and Portugal, but it soon became the most important company sailing between Britain and India and Hong Kong. In the late 20th century it also became one of the largest companies sailing across the *English Channel between *Dover and *Calais and Newhaven and Dieppe, forming a company with Stena Sealink called P & O Stena Line.

panˈ**dowdy** /pænˈdaʊdi/ (*also* ˌ**apple pan**ˈ**dowdy**) *n* [C, U] (*AmE*) a deep pie or pudding (= a cooked sweet dish) made with apples. Its name may come from an old English word meaning 'custard'.

ˈ**panhandle** *n* (*AmE*) a narrow piece of land that sticks out from the main part of a state, like the handle of a pan. Two well-known examples are the Florida panhandle and the Texas panhandle, both of which stick out to the north-east of their states.

▶ **panhandle** *v* [I] (*AmE*) to beg for money, especially in the street, e.g. by holding out a pan by its handle. A person who begs is called a **panhandler**.

ˌEmmeline ˈ**Pankhurst** /ˌeməliːn ˈpæŋkhɜːst; *AmE* ˈpæŋkhɜːrst/ (1858–1928) an English *suffragette leader. She established a political group, the Women's Social and Political Union, in 1903. Her influence on the campaign for women's right to vote made it more active and determined, and made her the most famous of the British suffragettes. She and her daughter Christabel (1880–1958) were often put in prison for their actions.

Emmeline Pankhurst being arrested in 1914

ˌ***Pano***ˈ***rama*** /ˌpænəˈrɑːmə/ a British television documentary programme (= one that presents facts about real life). It has been broadcast by the *BBC once a week since 1957. It usually examines social or political issues that are in the news.

pantomime

Pantomimes, also called **pantos**, are traditionally put on in theatres throughout Britain for several weeks before and after *Christmas. Most are intended for children. They are a British tradition which has developed over several centuries. A pantomime combines a fairy tale with comedy, music and singing, acrobatics and verse. Among the most popular stories are **Aladdin*, **Babes in the Wood*, **Cinderella*, *Dick *Whittington* and, **Jack and the Beanstalk*.

the Ugly Sisters in Cinderella

The audience usually takes an active part in a performance: characters on stage speak to the audience directly and they shout back their answer. Sometimes they have noisy arguments, exchanging shouts of 'Oh yes, it is' and 'Oh no, it isn't'. Audiences are often encouraged to join in the singing, and to **boo** loudly whenever a bad character appears. Other pantomime traditions include that of the hero, called the **principal boy**, being played by a young woman, and a comic old woman, called a ***dame**, being played by a male comedian. Pantomimes often also include several animal characters played by actors in animal costume.

Many of the most successful pantomimes performed in professional theatres have well-known television or sports personalities playing leading roles. Hundreds of amateur pantomimes are also put on each year.

Pantomimes of this kind do not exist in the US where the word *pantomime* means a play or entertainment performed without words.

Edˌuardo **Pao**ˈ**lozzi** /edˌwɑːdəʊ paʊˈlɒtsi; *AmE* edˌwɑːrdoʊ paʊˈlɑːtsi/ (1924–) a Scottish sculptor, the son of Italian parents. He was influenced especially by Paul Klee and the Surrealists, and much of his work is constructed from pieces of metal from machines, etc. He has also made prints and textile designs. He was made a *knight in 1989.

ˌ**Papua New** ˈ**Guinea** /ˌpæpuə njuː ˈgɪni/ a part of the former country of New Guinea in east Asia. The British and Australian governments had colonial interests there from 1888. Papua New Guinea has been a member of the *Commonwealth since it became fully independent in 1975. Its official language is English and its capital city is Port Moresby. ▶ **Papua New Guinean** *adj*, *n*.

ˌ**Papworth** ˈ**Hospital** /ˌpæpwəθ; *AmE* ˌpæpwərθ/ a hospital near *Cambridge, England, which is especially known for carrying out heart operations.

the ˈ**Parachute** ˌ**Regiment** (*also infml* the **Paras**) a section of the British army, started in 1940, which is trained in the use of parachutes. They are known for being a very strong and controlled fighting force, and for the red berets (= military caps) they wear. See also RED DEVILS.

ˌ***Paradise*** ˈ***Lost*** a very long poem (1667) by John *Milton. It tells the story of Adam and Eve and how they are driven out of the Garden of Eden by God because they do not obey him. In 1671 Milton published *Paradise Regained*, about how Jesus was sent to get Paradise back again for Man.

ˌ**Paramount** ˈ**Pictures** /ˌpærəmaʊnt/ a major *Hollywood film company. It originally owned cinemas and began producing films in the 1920s. The company was bought by Gulf & Western Industries in 1966 and by Viacom, Inc in 1994.

the ˈ**Paras** /ˈpærəz/ ⇨ PARACHUTE REGIMENT.

ˈ**parish** *n* **1** (in Britain) an area with its own church and priest. It is a part of a diocese (= a district for which a *bishop is responsible). People go to their **parish church**, and all the details of local births, marriages and deaths are put down in a special book called the **parish register**. In the US, a parish can mean a church, its administrative area, its members, or the area where they live. **2** (*also* **civil parish**) the smallest unit of *local government in England. Since 1894, a parish of more than a certain size has had to elect a *parish council. **3** (in the US state of *Louisiana) a *county.

ˌ**parish** ˈ**council** *n* [C + sing/pl *v*] (in England) the administrative body of a civil *parish(2). Most of its members are elected by members of the parish.

P

ˌ**parish** ˈ**pump** *n* (*BrE*) a symbol of local affairs and a restricted attitude to wider issues. In the past, the parish pump was the source of water in a village, and so it became the place where people gathered to discuss problems, exchange news, etc.: *parish pump gossip*.

a parish pump

ˌ**Park** ˈ**Avenue** a street in *Manhattan(1), New York, known for its rich, fashionable homes. At one point it runs under *Grand Central Station and the *Pan Am Building. See also WALDORF-ASTORIA.

ˈCharlie ˈˈBird' ˈ**Parker**[1] /ˈpɑːkə(r); *AmE* ˈpɑːrkər/ (1920–55) an *African American who greatly influenced modern *jazz and helped to create the style of *bebop. He played the saxophone and also wrote music. In the 1940s, he played with such musicians as Miles *Davis, Thelonious *Monk and 'Dizzy' *Gillespie. His problems with drugs and alcohol led to his early death.

ˌDorothy ˈ**Parker**[2] /ˈpɑːkə(r); *AmE* ˈpɑːrkər/ (1893–1967) a US writer of humorous poems and short stories. She was also a critic for *The *New Yorker* (1927–33), and a member of the *Algonquin Round Table. Parker's best-known short story was *Big Blonde* (1933). Her short clever comments included 'Men seldom make passes at girls who wear glasses', and she described the Alps as 'beautiful but dumb'.

Caˈmilla ˈ**Parker-**ˈ**Bowles** /kəˈmɪlə ˈpɑːkə ˈbəʊlz; *AmE* ˈpɑːrkər ˈboʊlz/ (1947–) an Englishwoman who is known to be having a relationship with Prince *Charles, and to have had this relationship during his marriage to *Diana, Princess of Wales. There has been a lot of discussion in the media about whether Prince Charles might marry Mrs Parker-Bowles.

Camilla Parker-Bowles

ˈ**Parkhurst** /ˈpɑːkhɜːst; *AmE* ˈpɑːrkhɜːrst/ a British prison on the *Isle of Wight for men who have to stay in prison for a long time. It has been a prison since 1838.

ˌCecil ˈ**Parkinson**[1] /ˈpɑːkɪnsn; *AmE* ˈpɑːrkɪnsn/ (1932–) a British *Conservative politician who held several senior government positions in the 1980s. He left his *Cabinet job in 1984 because of public reaction to his personal life. He was married but had been having a relationship with his former secretary Sara Keays, and she became pregnant. In 1987 Parkinson returned to the Cabinet, and in 1997 he was chosen by the new Conservative leader William *Hague to try to unite the party after it lost the election. He was made a *life peer in 1992.

ˌMichael ˈ**Parkinson**[2] /ˈpɑːkɪnsn; *AmE* ˈpɑːrkɪnsn/ (1935–) an English journalist and television presenter, best known for the programme *Parkinson* (1971–82 and 1998–), a popular Saturday night *chat show. Parkinson often writes and talks about *Yorkshire and especially the town of Barnsley, where he was born. He is sometimes referred to informally as 'Parky'.

ˌ**Park** ˈ**Lane** a street in the centre of London, England, along the eastern side of *Hyde Park(1), near *Mayfair. It is known for its very expensive houses and hotels, including the *Dorchester.

ˌRosa ˈ**Parks** /ˌrəʊzə ˈpɑːks; *AmE* ˌroʊzə ˈpɑːrks/ (1913–) an *African-American woman who is associated with the start of the *civil rights movement in the US. In 1955 she refused to sit in the back of a bus in *Montgomery, *Alabama, as the local law required. She was arrested, and Martin Luther *King then organized African Americans in a refusal to use the buses. This forced the city to change the law. See also SEGREGATION.

parks

British towns and cities have at least one **municipal park**, where people go to relax, lie in the sun, have picnics, walk their dogs and play games. Most US city and town governments also provide parks. They are open to anybody free of charge. The most famous parks in Britain include *Hyde Park and *Regent's Park in London. In the US, New York's *Central Park is the best known. Open-air events, such as plays and concerts, are sometimes held in these parks. At night, however, many people are afraid to go into parks in case they are attacked.

Most British parks were created in the 19th century, when more people moved into the towns. Some still have a rather old-fashioned, formal atmosphere, with paths to walk on, seats or **benches**, tidy **lawns**, flower beds and trees. There are often signs that say: 'Keep off the grass'. A few parks have a **bandstand**, a raised platform on which *brass bands play occasionally during the summer. Most parks are protected by iron railings and gates which are locked by the **park keeper** each evening.

Many parks have a **children's playground** with swings and roundabouts. Larger parks have a sports field, tennis courts and sometimes a boating lake. In the US *softball diamonds are marked on the grass and in Britain there are goalposts for *football. Large parks may have **picnic benches** and, in the US, **barbecues**. In the US it is usually illegal to drink alcohol in a park. In many parks dog excrement is now a serious problem.

In Britain there are ***country parks**, large areas of grass and woodland, where people can go for long walks. Some charge an admission fee. Many have **nature trails** where people can see interesting plants, birds or animals. ***National parks**, such as *Snowdonia, are areas of great beauty protected by the government. In the US there are both **state parks** and **national parks**. Many provide a safe place for wild animals to live.

Parliament ⇨ article.

the ˌ**Parliaˈmentary Comˈmissioner for Adminiˈstration** *n* the official title of the British Parliamentary Ombudsman, an important official who examines complaints from members of the public about government departments or organizations. The Parliamentary Ombudsman is independent of government and has the right to look at any documents or ask any government employee questions. He or she can order the government to pay money to the person making the complaint, or to put things right in some other way.

ˌ**Parliaˈmentary ˈPrivate ˈSecretary** (*abbr* **PPS**) *n* (in Britain) a *Member of Parliament who works for a government minister as his or her personal secretary and who also gives the minister advice on political matters. Compare PARLIAMENTARY SECRETARY.

ˌ**parliamentary ˈprivilege** *n* [U] (in Britain) certain special rights given to *Members of Parliament, especially the right to say something in either of the *Houses of Parliament that attacks somebody else without the fear of being taken to a court of law by that person. The *House of Lords has more such rights than the *House of Commons. Both Houses can, however, punish their own members for 'a breach of privilege' (= unsatisfactory behaviour in Parliament, or behaviour that makes Parliament look bad to the public): *She was accused of hiding behind parliamentary privilege.*

ˌ**parliamentary ˈsecretary** *n* (in Britain) a *Member of Parliament working in a government job immediately below a minister who is not a *Secretary of State. Compare PARLIAMENTARY PRIVATE SECRETARY, PARLIAMENTARY UNDER-SECRETARY OF STATE.

ˌ**parliaˈmentary under-ˈsecretary of ˈstate** *n* (in Britain) a *Member of Parliament working in a government job immediately below a minister who is a *Secretary of State. Compare PARLIAMENTARY SECRETARY.

ˈCharles ˈStewart **Parˈnell** /pɑːˈnel, ˈpɑːnl; *AmE* pɑːrˈnel, ˈpɑːrnl/ (1846–91) an Irish politician who led the campaign for *Home Rule in Ireland from 1877 to 1890. He then suddenly lost all his public support because it was revealed that he had been having a sexual relationship with another man's wife for ten years. He was known by his supporters as 'the uncrowned king of Ireland'. Parnell is often mentioned in the books of James *Joyce, who admired him greatly.

paˈrochial ˈchurch ˈcouncil *n* ⇨ PCC. Compare PARISH COUNCIL.

Louˌella **ˈParsons** /luˌelə ˈpɑːsnz; *AmE* ˈpɑːrsnz/ (1880–1972) a US journalist who wrote about the private life of *Hollywood stars for the newspapers of William Randolph *Hearst. Her great rival was Hedda *Hopper.

Parˈtition the division of British *India into the independent countries of India and *Pakistan in August 1947. This was one of the conditions under which India was given independence, though it led to much violence between Hindus and Muslims.

ˌDolly **ˈParton** /ˈpɑːtn; *AmE* ˈpɑːrtn/ (1946–) a US *country music singer and writer of songs who has also acted in films. She is known for her cheerful personality, large breasts and blonde (= very fair) hair. She has received *Grammy awards for *Here You Come Again* (1978) and *Nine to Five* (1981). In 1987 she opened Dollywood, an entertainment park named after her, in Pigeon Forge, *Tennessee.

ˈ**party poˈlitical ˈbroadcast** *n* (in Britain) a short broadcast on radio or television made by a political party to try to persuade people to vote for it, e.g. in a general election. There are special rules to make sure that each party is allowed the same amount of time for such broadcasts.

Such broadcasts in the US are called **paid political broadcasts**, or, more generally, 'political advertising'. The *FCC requires television companies to give political parties and candidates 'reasonable access' but does not say how many advertisements are allowed.

A ˌ***Passage to ˈIndia*** /ˈɪndiə/ a novel (1924) by E M *Forster which examines the cultural differences between the British and the Indians in India when it was under British rule. A film version (1984) was directed by David *Lean.

ˈ**Passchendaele** /ˈpæʃəndeɪl/ a series of *World War I battles (1917) fought near the small town of Passchendaele in Belgium. About 300 000 Allied soldiers and a similar number of Germans died, in terrible conditions. See also ALLIES, YPRES.

the ˌ**Patent and ˈTrademark ˌOffice** the US government department that decides who should be given patents (= official documents that give people the right to make, use or sell an invention, and stop other people from copying them).

the ˈ**Patent ˌOffice** the British government department that decides who should be given patents (= official documents that give people the right to make, use or sell an invention, and stop other people from copying them).

ˈ***Pathfinder*** /ˈpɑːθfaɪndə(r); *AmE* ˈpæθfaɪndər/ a US spacecraft that landed on the planet Mars in July 1997 and sent back to Earth many pictures of the planet's surface. This was the first trip to Mars since the two **Viking* spacecraft landed there in 1976. See also *SOJOURNER*.

the ˌ**Patient's ˈCharter** a statement of the rights of people who use the *National Health Service in Britain. It was first produced by the government in 1992, and is changed as circumstances within the Health Service change. Compare CITIZEN'S CHARTER.

St ˈ**Patrick** (*c.* 389–*c.* 461) the national saint of Ireland. He was not Irish, but was probably born in Wales, the son of a Roman father. Patrick became a monk in Gaul (= France) and went to Ireland in 432. He converted many people to Christianity, and there are many stories about his great powers, including one which explains why there are no snakes in Ireland. Patrick is said to have tricked them all so that they went into the sea and drowned. He is also said

Parliament

In the United Kingdom the institution responsible for making laws, discussing major issues affecting the country and raising taxes is called **Parliament**. The three parts of Parliament, the **sovereign** (= the king or queen), the ***House of Lords** and the ***House of Commons**, meet together only on special occasions. Although the agreement of all three is required for laws to be passed, that of the king or queen is now given without question.

Parliament comes from 'parley', a discussion. The word was first used in the 13th century to describe meetings between *Henry III and his noblemen in the Great Council. At that time, the king used his and his noblemen's money to pay for government and war. Several kings found that they did not have enough money, and so they called together representatives from the *counties and towns of England to ask them to approve increased taxes. Over time, the Great Council became the House of Lords, and the people from the counties and towns became the House of Commons. Originally, the king needed only the support of his councillors to pass a law, but by the end of the 15th century members of the House of Commons were taking part in the law-making process.

Control of the money supply by the House of Lords and the House of Commons made it difficult for the sovereign to ignore Parliament's wishes. Ministers were appointed by the sovereign but they needed support in the House of Commons to be able to pass laws and raise taxes. The rise of ***political parties** during the 18th century gave them the means to obtain that support. The involvement of the sovereign in policy-making and administration was gradually reduced, leaving government in the hands of a ***cabinet**, presided over by a ***prime minister**. Since the 19th century, the **Government** has been the party with the most members in the House of Commons, and the leader of that party has been the Prime Minister.

The House of Commons

The House of Commons, often called simply **the Commons** or **the House**, is elected by the adult population of Britain and is responsible to them. Members of the House of Commons are known as ***Members of Parliament**, or **MPs**. There are currently 659 MPs representing **constituencies** (= special districts) in England, Wales, Scotland and *Northern Ireland. ***Elections** must be held every five years, but if an MP resigns or dies there is a ***by-election** in that constituency.

Until the 20th century MPs did not receive a salary, so that only rich people could afford to be MPs. Most MPs are now full-time politicians but the hours of business of the Commons reflect a time when MPs had other jobs. The House does not **sit** in the mornings, except on Fridays, but starts at 2.30 p.m and does not finish until 10.30 p.m., and sometimes much later. On Fridays, they finish early for the weekend. MPs spend their mornings on committee work, preparing speeches and dealing with problems from their constituency.

The House of Commons has several rows of seats facing each other (⇨ picture). MPs who belong to the Government sit on one side and those from the **Opposition** sit on the other. There are no **cross-benches** (= seats for MPs who do not support the main parties). ***Ministers** and members of the ***Shadow Cabinet** (= leaders of the Opposition) sit on the **front benches**. Other MPs sit behind and are called ***backbenchers**. On the table between them are two wooden ***dispatch boxes**. Ministers and **shadow ministers** stand beside them when making a speech. **The *Speaker**, who is chosen by MPs from amongst themselves to preside over debates, sits on a raised chair at the top end of the table. MPs sit wherever they can find room on their side of the House. There are only about 400 seats, not enough for all MPs to sit down at once. The press and members of the public can listen to debates from the ***Strangers' Gallery**.

The House of Lords

The House of Lords consists of ***Lords Spiritual**, i.e. the *Archbishops of Canterbury and York and senior *bishops, and ***Lords Temporal**, i.e. all **hereditary peers** and **life peers** (⇨ note at PEERAGE). The total number of people eligible to attend **the Lords** is about 1 200 but some get permission to be absent. The *Lord Chancellor presides over debates from the ***Woolsack**.

The power of the House of Lords has been reduced over time. Since 1911 the Lords have had no control over financial matters, and since 1949 they have not been able to reject legislation (= laws) passed by the Commons, though they may suggest **amendments**. At various times people have suggested that the House of Lords should be abolished (= got rid of), or that its composition and functions should be changed. In 1998 the *Labour government announced that it would abolish the right of hereditary peers to sit in the Lords, and also that it would create new life peers to take their place. It is not yet clear how they will be chosen.

The sovereign

The United Kingdom is officially governed by **Her Majesty's Government** in the name of the Queen (or by His Majesty's Government when there is a king). The Queen is involved in some acts of government, including **summoning** and **dissolving** (= ending) Parliament, and giving the ***royal assent** to new laws. She also formally appoints the Prime Minister, senior ministers, judges and diplomats. She is expected to be completely impartial and not to support any political party.

Meetings of Parliament

The word *parliament* is also used to mean a period of government. Each parliament lasts a maximum of five years and is divided into shorter **sessions** lasting one year, beginning in October. There are **adjournments** at night and for holidays.

The ***State Opening of Parliament** takes place at the beginning of each session. *Black Rod, a servant of the Queen, knocks on the door of the House of Commons and demands that MPs allow the Queen to come inside and tell them what her Government is planning to do in the next year. The Commons always refuse to let her in because in the 17th century *Charles I once burst in and tried to arrest some MPs. Instead, MPs agree to go to the House of Lords and listen to the ***Queen's**

the House of Commons

speech there. By tradition, they enter in pairs with an MP from a different party. Parliament is then **prorogued** (= told not to meet) for a week.

Parliament works in the ***Palace of Westminster**, often called the ***Houses of Parliament**. As well as the two **chambers** where the House of Commons and the House of Lords meet, there are committee rooms, libraries, offices and restaurants.

Parliamentary procedure

The party system is essential to the way Parliament works. The Government proposes new laws in accordance with its policies, and the Opposition opposes or tries to amend them, and puts forward its own policies. Detailed arrangements of parliamentary business are settled by the ***Chief Whips**. The Whips then inform party members, and make sure that enough of them attend and vote in important debates. The Whips also pass on the opinions of backbenchers to the party leaders.

Both Houses have a similar system of debate. Each debate starts with a proposal or **motion** by a minister or a member of the house. This may be about a new law or tax, or about plans for spending money. A proposal for a new law or ***Act of Parliament** is called a ***bill**. Bills introduced in the House of Commons go through several **readings** and are then passed to the Lords, referred to by MPs as '**another place**'. Likewise, bills that have their first reading in the Lords are passed to the Commons. MPs or Lords may speak only once in a debate. They stand up and speak from wherever they are sitting. MPs do not use personal names but refer to another MP as '**my right honourable friend**' or '**the honourable Member for ...**'. This practice was originally intended to prevent MPs getting too angry with each other.

After a debate the Speaker **puts the question** whether to agree with the motion or not. This may be decided without voting or by a simple majority vote. If there is a vote this is carried out by a **division**: MPs vote for or against the proposal by walking through one of two **division lobbies** (= corridors), one for those in favour (**the Ayes**) and one for those against (**the Noes**). The Whips tell members of their party which way they should vote but sometimes people defy their Whip and vote in the opposite way or **abstain**. If the Government loses a vote on an important issue it has to resign. Sometimes there is a **free vote** so that MPs can vote according to their beliefs and not according to party policy, e.g. on issues such as the death penalty. The Speaker announces the result of a vote and says either '**The ayes have it**' or '**The noes have it**'. If the number of votes cast is equal, he or she gives a **casting vote**. Speeches and minutes of debates are published daily in ***Hansard** and may be broadcast on television or radio.

One of the liveliest, noisiest times in the House of Commons is ***Question Time**. For an hour each day MPs may ask ministers questions. Questions have to be **tabled** (= put on the table of the House) two days in advance so that ministers have time to prepare answers. The Government can therefore usually avoid major embarrassment. The trick is to ask a **supplementary question**: after the minister has answered the original question, the MP who asked may ask a further question relating to the minister's answer. It is then possible to catch a minister unprepared. On Wednesdays ***Prime Minister's Questions** lasts for 30 minutes. MPs no longer have to ask a standard question about the Prime Minister's official engagements but can immediately ask their 'supplementary' question.

to have used the *shamrock plant to explain the Christian idea of the Trinity, because it has three leaves on one stem. That is why it is traditional for Irish people to wear a shamrock on **St Patrick's Day**, 17 March.

ˌChristopher ˈ**Patten** /ˈpætn/ (1944–) a British *Conservative politician who held various important government posts before losing his seat in Parliament in 1992. He spent five years as the governor of *Hong Kong, before it was returned to Chinese rule in 1997.

ˌGeorge ˈ**Patton** (1885–1945) a senior US Army officer during *World War II. His popular name was 'Old Blood and Guts'. After *D-day General Patton led the US 3rd Army rapidly through France and into Germany. He was a tough man who demanded strict discipline and was either loved or hated by his soldiers. His story was told in the film *Patton* (1970) with George C Scott, which won three *Oscars.

ˌLinus ˈ**Pauling** /ˌlaɪnəs ˈpɔːlɪŋ/ (1901–94) a US scientist who won the 1954 *Nobel Prize for his discoveries about how chemicals join together. He was known for his opposition to the testing of nuclear weapons and for his campaigns to have all such weapons destroyed. For this, he won the 1962 Nobel Peace Prize. He also believed that people should take large amounts of vitamin C to prevent colds and other illnesses.

ˌ**Paul** ˈ**Jones** /ˈdʒəʊnz; *AmE* ˈdʒoʊnz/ *n* [usu sing] a traditional dance in which the people dancing change partners repeatedly each time the music stops. It is sometimes used at parties as a way of introducing a lot of guests who do not know each other. It was named after John Paul *Jones.

ˈ***Paul Re*ˈ*vere's* ˈ*Ride*** /rɪˈvɪəz; *AmE* rɪˈvɪrz/ a poem (1861) by Henry Wadsworth *Longfellow. It was about the ride of Paul *Revere to warn Americans that British soldiers were coming. The poem helped make the ride one of the best-known events in American history. See also OLD NORTH CHURCH.

ˈ**Pawnee** /ˈpɔːniː/ *n* (*pl* **Pawnees** *or* **Pawnee**) a member of a *Native-American people of whom only about 3 000 survive. Some live in northern *Oklahoma on a reservation (= land given and protected by the US government). They originally lived on the *Great Plains of *Kansas and *Nebraska as farmers who also hunted buffalo. They helped white people who came into their land, and often fought the *Sioux. The Pawnee were moved to the reservation in 1876.

P

ˌJeremy ˈ**Paxman** /ˈpæksmən/ (1950–) an English journalist and television presenter. He has presented *Newsnight* since 1989 and is known for his sometimes aggressive questions, especially to politicians. He also presents **University Challenge* (1994–).

PAYE /ˌpiː eɪ waɪ ˈiː/ (in Britain) the arrangement by which an employee's *income tax and *National Insurance is taken directly from his or her pay by the employer and sent to the government. The letters PAYE stand for 'pay as you earn'.

the ˌ**Paymaster** ˈ**General** the British government minister in charge of the department of the *Treasury which provides bank services for all departments except the *Inland Revenue and *Customs and Excise. Payments of *pensions to civil servants, teachers, the armed forces and workers in the *National Health Service are also made by the Paymaster General's office.

ˈ**pay** ˌ**television** (*also* **pay-TV**) ⇨ SUBSCRIPTION TELEVISION.

PBS /ˌpiː biː ˈes/ (*in full* the **Public Broadcasting Service**) (in the US) a television system that broadcasts programmes to an association of local stations which use no television advertisements and do not make a profit. It was established by the Public Broadcasting Act (1967) and is supported by money from the US government, large companies and the public. PBS is known for broadcasting programmes of good quality, such as **Sesame Street* and the National Geographic Special series. Many of the best British programmes are shown on **Masterpiece Theater*.

ˌ**p**ˈ**c** /ˌpiː ˈsiː/ ⇨ POLITICAL CORRECTNESS.

PCC /ˌpiː siː ˈsiː/ (*in full* **parochial church council**) *n* [C + sing/pl *v*] the administrative body of a *parish(2) church. Its members are usually people who go to church regularly and most of them are elected by members of the parish.

ˌ**PC** ˈ**Plod** /ˌpiː siː ˈplɒd; *AmE* ˈplɑːd/ (*BrE*) a name used to refer in a humorous way to a policeman, suggesting that he is not very intelligent. 'PC' stands for 'Police Constable' and to 'plod' means to walk slowly, with heavy steps.

PDSA /ˌpiː diː es ˈeɪ/ ⇨ PEOPLE'S DISPENSARY FOR SICK ANIMALS.

PDT /ˌpiː diː ˈtiː/ ⇨ PACIFIC DAYLIGHT TIME.

the ˈ**Peace Corps** an independent US government organization that sends Americans, usually young adults, to work without pay in poorer countries. President John F *Kennedy began it in 1961 with the aim of helping other countries in the fields of health, education, farming, etc. and so developing international friendship.

ˌ**peace in our** ˈ**time** a phrase used by the British *Prime Minister Neville *Chamberlain in 1938 after signing the *Munich Agreement by which Britain, France and Italy allowed Hitler to take control of a part of Czechoslovakia. Chamberlain got off the plane from Munich holding up a piece of paper which, he said, represented 'peace in our time' and 'peace with honour'. At the time many people believed that he was right, and that the Munich Agreement had saved Europe from war, but in March 1939 Hitler took all of Czechoslavakia and in September *World War II began. Now people remember these two phrases with rather bitter feelings.

ˈ**peace pipe** *n* a type of traditional tobacco pipe with a long stem once smoked by most *Native Americans to celebrate a peace discussion or agreement. The pipe was decorated and was respected as a symbol of its owner's power. To 'smoke the peace pipe' is a phrase used in American English meaning to end a

a chief smoking a peace pipe, painted by George Catlin

dispute or argument: *After much squabbling Linda and Rick finally decided to smoke the peace pipe.*

ˈThomas ˈLove ˈ**Peacock** /ˈlʌv ˈpiːkɒk; *AmE* ˈpiːkɑːk/ (1785–1866) an English writer of novels and poetry. He used satire to attack the attitudes of well-known people of his time. For example, in *Nightmare Abbey* (1818) he makes fun of *Coleridge, *Shelley[2] and *Byron, among others.

the ˈ**Peak ˌDistrict** /ˈpiːk/ an area of hills, valleys, moors and caves, mostly in north *Derbyshire, England. It has been a *national park since 1951 and is very popular with people who enjoy walking and climbing.

ˈNorman ˈVincent ˈ**Peale** /ˈpiːl/ (1898–1993) a US religious leader who wrote *The Power of Positive Thinking* (1952), one of the most successful 'self-help' books, advising people how to improve the quality of their lives. He also had radio and television programmes, and wrote regularly in newspapers and magazines. He was the leader of the Marble Collegiate Reformed Church in New York (1932–84). His other books include *The Art of Living* (1948) and *Power of the Positive Factor* (1987).

ˈ***Peanuts*** /ˈpiːnʌts/ a very popular US *comic strip which also appears in many newspapers all over the world. It is drawn by Charles *Schulz and was first published in 1950. It is about children who talk like adults, and the characters include Charlie *Brown, his dog *Snoopy, his aggressive friend Lucy and her nervous little brother *Linus.

a Peanuts *comic strip*

ˌ**Pearl ˈHarbor** /ˌpɜːl ˈhɑːbə(r); *AmE* ˌpɜːrl ˈhɑːrbər/ a harbour on the island of Oahu in *Hawaii. It is the US Navy's main Pacific base. A surprise attack by the Japanese on the navy ships there on 7 December 1941 brought the US into *World War II. The attack killed 2 403 people, injured 1 178 and destroyed 19 ships and 188 planes. The phrase 'Remember Pearl Harbor' came to be used to encourage Americans to support the war.

ˌ**pearly ˈking** *n* (*BrE*) (in London) a man who on special occasions wears dark clothes covered in thousands of small shiny buttons. A **pearly queen** is a woman who does the same. This is a tradition among the people who sell fruit and vegetables from carts in the streets, but is now only done for tourists and to collect money for charities.

pearly kings and queens

ˌPeter ˈ**Pears** /ˈpɪəz; *AmE* ˈpɪrz/ (1910–86) an English singer with a tenor voice who worked a lot with Benjamin *Britten. In 1948 they started the *Aldeburgh Festival together. Pears was made a *knight in 1978.

ˌRobert E ˈ**Peary** /ˈpɪəri; *AmE* ˈpɪri/ (Robert Edwin Peary 1856–20) a US Navy officer and explorer. After two earlier attempts which failed, he became the first man to reach the North Pole, on 6 April 1909.

the ˌ**Peasants' Reˈvolt** an incident in 1381 when the peasants (= poor farmers) of *Kent and *Essex marched to *Canterbury and then to London to protest at their conditions of life and the harsh taxes they had to pay. They occupied several major buildings, including the *Tower of London. The young king, *Richard II, talked to their leader, Wat *Tyler, and promised to help them. Many of them then went home, but Tyler was killed and the Revolt ended in complete failure, gaining nothing for the peasants.

ˌGregory ˈ**Peck** /ˈpek/ (1916–) a US actor with a pleasant deep voice who usually plays honest, good men. He won an *Oscar playing the part of a southern lawyer in **To Kill a Mockingbird*. His other films include *Spellbound* (1945), *Duel in the Sun* (1946), *Gentleman's Agreement* (1947), *The Man in the Gray Flannel Suit* (1956), **Moby-Dick* (1956), *The Omen* (1976) and *Other People's Money* (1991).

ˌSam ˈ**Peckinpah** /ˈpekɪnpɑː/ (1925–85) a US film director who was sometimes criticized for the amount of realistic violence shown in his films. These include *Major Dundee* (1965), *The *Wild Bunch*, *Straw Dogs* (1971), *Pat Garrett and Billy the Kid* (1973) and *The Osterman Weekend* (1983).

ˌ**Pecos ˈBill** /ˌpeɪkəs/ a popular *cowboy character in US legends, about whom many wild stories are told. For example, one says that he dug the *Rio Grande River when he dragged his pickaxe (= heavy tool with a metal point) behind him. Bill's girlfriend was called Slue Foot Sue and his horse was called Widowmaker. Compare BUNYAN[2].

ˌJohn ˈ**Peel[1]** /ˈpiːl/ (1939–) an English disc jockey and broadcaster who has worked for *Radio 1 since it started in 1967. He encourages good bands which are not well known by playing their records. He also presents the *BBC radio programme about family life called *Home Truths*.

ˌJohn ˈ**Peel[2]** /ˈpiːl/ ⇨ *D'YE KEN JOHN PEEL?*

ˌRobert ˈ**Peel[3]** /ˈpiːl/ (1788–1850) one of the most important British politicians of the early 19th century and one of the people who started the modern *Conservative Party. As *Home Secretary (1822–30), Peel was responsible for giving Catholics the right to hold jobs in public life and for the organization of the *Metropolitan Police. (British police officers are still sometimes called *bobbies* from Bobby, the short form of Robert. They were once also called *peelers*.) He was *Prime Minister twice (1834–5 and 1841–6) and his government passed a number of major new laws, especially in relation to British trade. He was made a *baronet in 1830. See also CORN LAWS.

ˌ**Peeping ˈTom** *n* a person who likes to watch other people when they are doing something private, for example when they are taking their clothes off or kissing someone. The phrase 'Peeping Tom' comes from the story of Lady *Godiva, who rode through the streets naked. Everyone was told not to look at her, but one man, 'Peeping Tom of Coventry', did and he went blind: *He realized that he was watching the lovers like a common Peeping Tom.*

the **peerage**

Peers of the realm are people who hold the highest ranks in the British ***aristocracy**. As a group, they are sometimes referred to as **the peerage**. There are

P

two main types of peers: **hereditary peers** hold **titles** that are passed from one generation to the next, while life peers have a personal title which lasts for their own lifetime but is not passed on to their children.

The peerage is divided into five main ranks. The most senior rank is that of **duke** (for a man) or **duchess** (for a woman), a hereditary title which was created in *Norman times. There are five royal Dukes, including the Duke of *Edinburgh, and 24 other dukes. The second most senior rank is that of **marquess** (man) or **marchioness** (woman), of which there are under 40. The third rank is that of **earl** (man) or **countess** (woman), of which there are nearly 200. This is the oldest title of all. Next in rank is a **viscount** (man) or **viscountess** (woman). The fifth and lowest rank of the peerage is that of **baron** (man) or **baroness** (woman), of which there are around 500 with hereditary titles. At present, about two thirds of all peers hold hereditary titles, many of which were originally given by the reigning king or queen to close friends or in return for some service. Senior titles often include the name of the place where the family comes from, e.g. the Duke of Devonshire, the Marquess of Normanby. A woman may be a duchess, marchioness, etc. in her own right or receive the title when she marries a duke, etc.

Life peers include the **Lords of Appeal in Ordinary**, usually referred to as ***Law Lords**, who are the most senior judges in the land, the ***Lords Spiritual**, who are the *archbishops of Canterbury and York and 24 *bishops of the *Church of England and, since 1958, many other men and women who have been **given a peerage** in recognition of their public service. Most of these are given the rank of baron or baroness.

There are complicated rules for how to address and refer to members of the peerage. Dukes, for instance, are addressed formally as 'Your Grace', marquesses and earls as 'My Lord', and viscounts and barons as 'Lord X'. There are also rules for addressing members of their families. Most British people know that such complicated forms of address exist but many would not be able to use them correctly, and would probably think that they are rather strange and old-fashioned.

Peers cannot be elected to the *House of Commons as *Members of Parliament unless they have first **disclaimed** their title. Tony *Benn campaigned for members of the peerage to have this right and was himself the first to give up his title and become an MP. Former members of the *House of Commons who have been **elevated to the peerage** as a reward for their service are sometimes said to have been 'kicked upstairs'.

At present, all hereditary and life peers may take part in the government of Britain by **taking their seat** in the *House of Lords, though many do not attend regularly. There has for a long time been talk of changing this right, which many people consider undemocratic, and even of abolishing the House of Lords. At the end of 1997 there were about 650 hereditary peers compared with 500 life peers. About 500 of the total were *Conservative peers, most of whom were hereditary. This means that the *Labour government is heavily outnumbered in the Lords, which causes problems in getting new laws passed. In 1998 the Labour party announced that it would introduce laws to abolish the right of hereditary peers to sit in the House of Lords, and also that it would create about 600 new life peers to take their place. It is not yet clear how they will be chosen.

ˈ**penalty points** *n* [pl] a system used by the government to control drivers on Britain's roads. If, for example, somebody is stopped by the police for driving too fast or in a dangerous way, they get a number of penalty points on their driving licence. After a certain amount of time, the points are removed from the licence. However, if at any time somebody has 12 penalty points, they are not allowed to drive at all for a period of time decided by a court of law: *I've still got six penalty points on my licence.* ⇨ note at DRIVING.

ˈ**Penguin**™ *n* **1** a book published by *Penguin Books: *her collection of battered Penguins.* **2** a British make of chocolate biscuit: *a packet of Penguins.*

ˌ**Penguin** ˈ**Books** a British company that publishes paperback books (= books with paper covers). It was started in 1935 and was the first to publish books of good quality in this way at reasonable prices. See also PUFFIN BOOKS.

the **Peˌninsular** ˈ**War** /pəˌnɪnsjələ; *AmE* pəˌnɪnsjələr/ a war (1808–14) fought in Spain and Portugal, in which British, Spanish and Portuguese soldiers defeated the armies of the French Emperor Napoleon Bonaparte. The Peninsular War was one of the *Napoleonic Wars.

ˌSean ˈ**Penn**[1] /ˈpen/ (1960–) a US actor and writer who also directs. He is known for his independent and sometimes violent style of life. His films include *At Close Range* (1985), *The Indian Runner* (1991), which he also wrote and directed, and *Dead Man Walking* (1996). He was married to the singer and actor *Madonna from 1985 to 1989.

ˌWilliam ˈ**Penn**[2] /ˈpen/ (1644–1718) an English *Quaker who established the American colony of *Pennsylvania on land given to him by King *Charles II. He made it a place of safety for Quakers and all other religious groups, and called this a 'holy experiment'. He also helped to create the city of *Philadelphia.

the ˈ**Pennines** /ˈpenaɪnz/ a series of hills in northern England that run from the *Peak District to the Scottish border, a distance of about 250 miles/400 kilometres. They are sometimes called 'the backbone of England'. See also PENNINE WAY.

the ˌ**Pennine** ˈ**Way** /ˌpenaɪn/ a path along the *Pennines in northern England, used by people who like walking as a hobby. It is about 250 miles/400 kilometres long and passes through three *national parks, including the *Peak District. It was opened in 1965.

ˌ**Penn** ˈ**Station** /ˌpen/ (*also fml* ˌ**Pennsylvania** ˈ**Station**) /ˌpenslveɪniə/ a railway station in New York City. It is under *Madison Square Garden at 34th Street and Eighth Avenue. It is used by trains going to and from *Long Island and *New Jersey, as well as such major cities as *Boston and *Washington, DC.

ˌ**Pennsylˈvania** /ˌpenslˈveɪniə/ a state in the north-eastern US, also called the Keystone State for its central position among the 13 original states. The largest city is *Philadelphia, and the capital city is Harrisburg. The area was established for *Quakers in 1681 by William *Penn, who named it Pennsylvania ('Penn's small forest') for his father. The Battle of *Gettysburg was fought there during the *Civil War. The state produces chemicals, electrical machinery and farm products. Tourist attractions include *Valley Forge and the *Pennsylvania Dutch region.

ˌ**Pennsylvania** ˈ**Avenue** /ˌpenslveɪniə/ a famous broad street in *Washington, DC. It is 1.3 miles (2 kilometres) long and connects the *White House(1) and the *Capitol. Along the way are other government buildings, including the offices of the *FBI, the *FTC, the Commerce Department and the Treasury Department.

ˌ**Pennsylvania** ˈ**Dutch** /ˌpenslveɪniə/ *n* **1** [pl] a group of people who live in the US state of *Pennsylvania, west of *Philadelphia. They are descended from German (not Dutch) Protestant religious groups who settled there in the 17th and 18th centuries. They include the *Amish, *Mennonites and Moravians. They have a strict, simple way of life, wear plain black clothes and do not use machines, including cars. They are known for making beautiful furniture which is carved or painted with designs of flowers, birds, etc. **2** [U] the language of the Pennsylvania Dutch people. It is a form of German.

ˌ**Penny** ˈ**Black** *n* a British stamp first produced in 1840. It cost one penny and had a picture of Queen *Victoria on it. Because it was the first stamp in the world there was no need to print the word 'Britain' on it, and even today British stamps do not have the country's name on them. Penny Blacks are now quite rare and highly valued.

ˌ**penny-**ˈ**farthing** *n* an old type of bicycle, popular in the late 19th century, with a very large wheel at the front and a much smaller one at the back (similar to the old British penny and farthing coins).

a penny-farthing

pensions

Pensions are regular payments made to people who have **retired**. Most people retire and start to receive a pension when they are about 60 or 65. The amount of money they receive depends on how much they have paid into their **pension scheme** and also on the type of scheme.

In Britain, a basic **state pension** has been provided by the government since 1908 for those who paid ***National Insurance contributions** while they were working, or whose husband or wife paid contributions. Pensions for each generation are paid for out of the contributions of people still working. A problem arising from this arrangement is that more people now live longer but the number of younger people in work has fallen, so that there is less money to pay for pensions.

Many **pensioners** (= old people receiving a pension) collect their pension each week from the local post office, using a **pension book**. Some complain that the state pension does not provide enough money for them to have a reasonable standard of living. People who do not qualify for a state pension, e.g. because they have not paid enough National Insurance, may receive ***income support** if they have no other source of money. **War pensions** for soldiers injured on duty are also paid by the government.

There are several other kinds of pension which pay larger amounts of money, though people have to pay more towards them. There are many **company pension schemes**, into which both workers and their employers pay certain amounts. A similar scheme, ***SERPS**, was started by the government in 1978 for people who could not join a company scheme. Some people, especially those who are self-employed, belong to **private pension schemes** arranged through insurance companies. The money paid into company or private pension schemes is invested in the stock market and the **pension funds**, the organizations that manage this money, are among the most important investors in the *City. However, many people who, encouraged by the government, left SERPS and company schemes in the 1980s and took out private pensions, were badly advised by financial organizations and lost money.

In the US there are three main types of pension. The US government operates a programme called ***social security**, and people who work have to pay into this programme. The amount of money they get when they retire depends on how much they earned when they were working, but it is never a lot. It would be difficult to live only on social security payments, and so people also arrange to receive a pension from another source.

Many employers and unions operate pension programmes for their workers. As in Britain both employers and workers put money into these private pension funds and the money is invested. By law, pension funds must report to the government and to their members about the way they manage the money. Many people who want to be sure of having enough money when they retire also make their own personal arrangements. One common way of doing this is by opening a special bank account called an ***IRA**, or **Individual Retirement Account**. With this kind of account people pay less tax than normal, but must agree to leave the money in the bank until they retire.

the ˈ**Pentagon** **1** the building in Arlington, *Virginia, completed in 1943, which contains the administrative offices of the US Department of Defense and divisions of the US armed forces. It has five sides and is the largest office building in the world. **2** (*infml*) the military leaders of the US: *The Pentagon says more spy planes are needed.*

the Pentagon

the ˈ**Pentagon** ˌ**Papers** secret papers from the *Pentagon(1) which were printed in the **New York Times* in 1971. The papers had been taken by Daniel Ellsberg, a government employee, and given to the newspaper. They were about a government study of the *Vietnam War, and they revealed military actions about which the public had not been told. The US Justice Department tried to stop them being published, but the *Supreme Court decided that the newspaper had the right to publish them under the *First Amendment. The Pentagon Papers helped to turn public opinion against the war and also strengthened the freedom of the press.

ˌ**Pente**ˈ**costalist** /ˌpentɪˈkɒstəlɪst; *AmE* ˌpentɪˈkɑːstəlɪst/ *n* a member of any of the Protestant **Pentecostal** religious groups or churches. They believe that illnesses can be healed by faith and in 'baptism in the spirit' in which a person 'speaks in tongues' with unknown words that come from the Holy Spirit. Pentecostalism began in the US at the beginning of the 20th century and now has support in other major Christian Churches. The largest Pentacostal church in the US is the Church of God in Christ, with more than 5.5 million members. ▶ **Pentecostalism** *n* [U]. **Pentecostalist** *adj.*

ˈ***Penthouse*** a US magazine for men. It is known for

P

its pictures of almost naked women and articles about sex, though it also includes articles on other subjects. It was started by Bob Guccione (1930–) who first published it in London, England, in 1965.

ˈ**Pentonville** /ˈpentənvɪl/ a large prison for men in north London, England, opened in 1842.

Penˈzance /penˈzæns/ a port in *Cornwall in south-west England, near *Land's End. It is a popular place for holidays/vacations.

ˈ***People*** a popular US magazine published each week. It contains photographs of and articles about film and television stars, as well as news stories. It was begun in 1974 by the Time-Life Company, now *Time Warner.

The ˈ***People*** one of Britain's national *Sunday papers, started in 1881. It is not regarded as one of the 'quality papers'. ⇨ article at NEWSPAPERS.

the ˈ**People's Diˈspensary for ˈSick ˈAnimals** (*abbr* the **PDSA**) a British charity that gives free treatment to sick animals and encourages people to look after their pets properly. It was started in 1917.

Peˈoria /piˈɔːriə/ a small city in the US state of *Illinois. It is considered a typical US city, and people living there are thought to have opinions which in general represent the opinions of the whole country: *Before you go ahead with a new product you must ask yourself what the folks in Peoria will think of it.*

PEP /pep/ *n* ⇨ PERSONAL EQUITY PLAN.

ˌ**Pepsi-ˈCola**™ /ˌpepsi ˈkəʊlə; *AmE* ˈkoʊlə/ (*also* ˈ**Pepsi**™) *n* [U, C] a US sweet fizzy drink (= one containing many bubbles). It is, after its great rival *Coca-Cola, the second most popular drink of this type in the world. The company that makes it, PepsiCo Inc, also owns *Pizza Hut, *Taco Bell and *Kentucky Fried Chicken.

ˌSamuel ˈ**Pepys** /ˈpiːps/ (1633–1703) an Englishman known today because of his detailed diaries, written between 1660 and 1669 but not published until the 19th century. He was a senior government officer in the service of two kings, *Charles II and *James II, and he wrote about court and social life in the 17th century, as well as recording major events such as the *Great Fire of London. He also included many private details about his own life. He knew many of the most important figures of his day, including Sir Christopher *Wren and Sir Isaac *Newton. Pepys often ended his writing for the day with the phrase 'And so to bed', which people sometimes use in a humorous way today.

The ˌ***Perils of*** ˈ***Pauline*** a very popular series of early US silent films telling a continuous story, released in 1914. At the end of each film the main character Pauline, played by Pearl White, was shown in great danger, so people went to see the next one to find out how she escaped. After its success, many other similar series were made.

ˌCarl ˈ**Perkins** /ˈpɜːkɪnz; *AmE* ˈpɜːrkɪnz/ (1932–98) a US singer and writer of *rockabilly songs which combined *country music with *rock and roll. His first hit, *Blue Suede Shoes* (1956), was later recorded by Elvis *Presley. His songs have also been recorded by country music singers like Johnny *Cash and by various pop groups, including the *Beatles. He was chosen for the Rock and Roll *Hall of Fame in 1987.

ˌ**Permanent ˈSecretary** *n* a senior officer in the British *civil service who often has the job of advising a government minister: *the Permanent Secretary at the Foreign Office.* Compare PARLIAMENTARY SECRETARY.

perˌmissive soˈciety (*usu* **the permissive society**) *n* [sing] (*often disapprov*) the social conditions and attitudes in countries such as Britain and the US in the 1960s and 1970s, when there was a new freedom of sexual behaviour and a greater willingness to tolerate different ways of living. These changes were originally made by younger people, and developed from ideas such as *flower power and the *hippie culture. Some people blame the permissive society for modern problems like the use of illegal drugs, lack of respect for authority and low moral standards.

ˈH ˈRoss **Peˈrot** /ˈrɒs pəˈrəʊ; *AmE* ˌrɔːs pəˈroʊ/ (Henry Ross Perot 1930–) a rich US businessman who stood without success as an independent candidate for US President in the 1992 and 1996 elections. He argued that the government should reduce the amount of money it spends. Perot had started the Electronic Data Systems Corporation in 1962.

ˌ**Perpenˈdicular** /ˌpɜːpənˈdɪkjələ(r); *AmE* ˌpɜːrpənˈdɪkjələr/ *n* [U] a style of *Gothic architecture used in England during the 14th and 15th centuries. It was marked by large windows, vertical lines, and ceiling patterns in stone called *fan vaulting*. An example of this style is the chapel of *King's College, Cambridge. Compare EARLY ENGLISH, DECORATED STYLE.

Perpendicular architecture in the chapel of King's College, Cambridge

ˌFred ˈ**Perry** /ˈperi/ (1909–97) an English tennis player who won the *Wimbledon men's championship three years in a row (1934–36). No Englishman has won it since then. Before his tennis career, Perry had been the men's world champion at *table tennis in 1929. He later started a company making sports clothes.

ˌJohn ˈ**Pershing** /ˈpɜːʃɪŋ; *AmE* ˈpɜːrʃɪŋ/ (1860–1948) the army officer who commanded the US Expeditionary Force in France in *World War I. General Pershing's popular name was 'Black Jack' because of his tough discipline. He had earlier served in the *Indian wars and the *Spanish-American War. He received the *Pulitzer Prize for his book *My Experiences in the World War* (1931). The US nuclear weapon called the **Pershing missile** is named after him.

ˈ**Persil**™ /ˈpɜːsɪl; *AmE* ˈpɜːrsɪl/ *n* [U] a British make of powder or liquid for washing clothes. Its advertisements claim that 'Persil washes whiter'.

ˌ**Personal ˈEquity Plan** (*abbr* **PEP**) *n* a system started by the *Conservative government in Britain in 1987 to encourage people to save their money. People who bought a Personal Equity Plan could invest a limited amount of money in companies and did not have to pay any tax on the profits they made. The system was replaced by a new one, the *Individual Savings Account, which was announced by the *Labour government in 1998.

personal space

Personal space can be imagined as a kind of bubble surrounding a person that protects his or her *privacy and which other people may not normally enter. The amount of space people need to feel around them is different in every culture, though British and American people have similar ideas about how much it should be. People from cultures that like a lot of personal space feel awkward and embarrassed when somebody comes too close to them and try to move away; people who need less personal space are often offended when others seem to want to keep them at a distance.

The amount of personal space people need also depends on several other factors. People of the same sex may sit or stand closer to each other than to somebody of the opposite sex. Strangers and casual acquaintances usually need more space than friends and members of the same family who know each other well. But in a noisy street people may need to stand closer than they would normally, simply in order to hear each other. Strangers try to respect each other's space and not stand too close even in busy places. Some British people avoid sitting next to strangers on buses and if there are lots of empty seats they choose one by itself.

For a private conversation Americans need at least a foot (30 centimetres) between each other, and British people more. Distances as great as 5 feet (1.5 metres) may also seem comfortable. People who are enjoying talking to each other may move in closer during the conversation. Allowing somebody to get very close and enter your personal space may be a sign of trust or love.

British people tend to avoid touching or being physically close to people outside their own family. Americans are only a little more comfortable about touching each other. When people meet for the first time they shake hands and let go quickly and move back. In formal situations they may also shake hands when they say goodbye though they often avoid doing this. Women often greet members of their family with a hug or kiss on one cheek, and may also greet friends in this way. They also hug and kiss each other when saying goodbye. But they do not hold hands or link arms with each other when walking along. Men are often embarrassed about kissing female members of the family or children in public, and never kiss men. They may shake hands but often simply nod and smile. Men rarely touch their friends unless to shake hands or slap them on the back in congratulation.

Kissing on the mouth, holding hands and other sorts of touching usually only take place between people who have a romantic relationship.

Perˈsuasion a romantic novel (1818) by Jane *Austen, the last book she wrote. The main character is Anne Elliot, who refuses Frederick Wentworth's offer of marriage but regrets doing so and accepts when he asks her again several years later.

ˌ**Pete ˈMarsh** ⇨ MARSH².

part of the Petrified Forest, Arizona

ˌ**Peter ˈJones** /ˈdʒəʊnz; *AmE* ˈdʒoʊnz/ a fashionable department store in *Sloane Square, London. It is one of the *John Lewis group of shops.

ˌ**Peterˈloo** /ˌpiːtəˈluː; *AmE* ˌpiːtərˈluː/ (*also* the ˌ**Peterloo ˈMassacre**) the name given to an incident that took place in *Manchester, England, in 1819. A group of people gathered in St Peter's Fields in central Manchester to demand political change. The crowd was large, but peaceful and not armed. It was attacked by the army, who killed eleven people and injured about 500. The name Peterloo is a mixture of St Peter's Fields and *Waterloo, the battle at which many people had recently died.

ˌ***Peter ˈPan*** /ˈpæn/ a children's play (1904) by J M *Barrie. Peter Pan is a boy who lives in a magic place called *Never Never Land where he never grows up. One night he visits three children in London and takes them to Never Never Land. They have a series of adventures with Peter, a fairy called Tinkerbell, a group of pirates and a crocodile. It is a very popular play, and is traditionally performed every *Christmas in London. It was made into a successful Walt *Disney film in 1953. It is so well known to most people that a person who seems never to grow any older is sometimes called a 'Peter Pan': *Still winning matches at 35, he's the Peter Pan of the tennis world.* See also CAPTAIN HOOK.

ˌ**Peter ˈRabbit** /ˈræbɪt/ a character in several of Beatrix *Potter's stories for children, including her first, *The Tale of Peter Rabbit.* He is a young rabbit who often gets into trouble.

Ellis **Peters** /ˌelɪs ˈpiːtəz; *AmE* ˈpiːtərz/ (1913–1995) an English writer best known for her series of *detective novels set in the *Middle Ages, in which the main character is the monk Brother Cadfael.

the ˌ**Petrified ˈForest** /ˌpetrɪfaɪd/ a large area in the US state of *Arizona where ancient trees have turned into stone. It has been a *national park since 1962 and includes part of the *Painted Desert.

pets

Over half of all British and US families keep an animal as a pet. Families with children are most likely to havepets, but other people, especially old people, often keep a pet for company. Some animals belong

P

to a group of people: for example, many British railway stations, old people's homes and even offices have a resident cat.

The most popular pets for children include cats, dogs, birds, fish, rabbits, guinea pigs, hamsters and mice, and children are usually expected to help take care of their pet. Older people are more likely to have a cat or dog, or perhaps a budgerigar. Since dogs and cats have different characters and needs, many people have a strong preference for one or the other. People who say that they are **dog people** like the fact that dogs like to go for walks, enjoy being touched and need lots of attention. **Cat people** like cats because they are independent. Other people prefer **exotic pets**, such as snakes, spiders, iguanas and stick insects. Many pets can be bought at a **pet shop**, though people often buy dogs and cats direct from breeders or from homes for stray (= lost) animals.

Most pets are treated as members of the family. People buy special pet food and biscuits, or sometimes fresh fish or meat. Pets have their own place to sleep, bowls to eat from and toys to play with. There are even clothes for pets, and **salons** where their fur is washed and cut.

Pets are a responsibility which must be taken seriously. Dog owners in the US have to buy a **dog licence** (*AmE* **dog license**) which allows them to keep a dog. This was formerly also the case in Britain. Pure-bred dogs may also be taken to local and national **shows** where there are prizes for the best of each breed. But many people are not bothered about having a pure-bred dog and are happy with a **mongrel** (*AmE* **mutt**).

A few dogs are kept outside and sleep in a **kennel** (*AmE* **doghouse**). Most, however, like cats, are allowed to go where they like inside the house. Most dogs wear a **collar**, with a small metal disc attached giving the dog's name and address. In the US there are laws in most places requiring dogs to be kept on a **leash** (*BrE* **lead**). People teach their dogs to **walk to heel** (*AmE* **heeling**) and not to jump up at people. Some also teach them to do tricks like **fetching** or **begging**. Some people take their dog to **obedience school** (*BrE* **obedience classes**) for training. There is now pressure for dog-owners to clear up any mess left by their dog, and people can be fined for not doing so.

Cats are less trouble to look after. They can often enter or leave their house as they please through a **cat flap**. If they are kept inside they are trained to urinate in a litter tray filled with **cat litter** (= a special absorbent material). Many cat-owners give their cats a **flea collar** and a disc with their name and address on it in case they get lost.

Looking after a pet properly can be quite expensive. In 1996 Americans spent $22.7 billion on their pets. Many animals, especially dogs, go on holiday with their owners, but if British people go abroad they leave their pets at home as there would be a problem bringing them home again because of **quarantine regulations**. Many pay for their dog to stay at a local **kennels**, or their cat at a **cattery**. In the US there are **pet motels**. Many people take out insurance to cover medical treatment by a **vet**. In the US animals with emotional problems can be taken to a **pet psychologist**. When a pet dies many people bury it in their garden, but others arrange for it to be buried in a special **pet cemetery**.

If people do not want a pet of their own they can sponsor an animal through a charity and receive regular information about it. Many people also put out bird tables containing food for wild birds.

ˌ**Petticoat ˈLane** a street in the *East End of London, England, where a famous market takes place every Sunday, selling a wide variety of goods. The name of the street was officially changed to Middlesex Street in the 19th century, but people still refer to the market as Petticoat Lane.

ˌ**Petworth ˈHouse** /ˌpetwəθ; *AmE* ˌpetwərθ/ a *stately home near *Chichester in southern England. It was first built in the Middle Ages but most of it was rebuilt in the 17th and 18th centuries. It is well known for its collection of paintings by *Turner[2], who used to stay there as a guest, and for its garden, designed by 'Capability' *Brown.

ˌNikolaus ˈ**Pevsner** /ˌnɪkələs ˈpevznə(r)/ (1902–83) a British architectural historian, born in Germany. His best-known work, *The Buildings of England* (1941–74), describes every important building in England. It is a large book, published in 46 volumes, and is often referred to simply as 'Pevsner'. He was made a *knight in 1969.

ˌ***Peyton ˈPlace*** /ˌpeɪtn/ a novel (1956) by the US writer Grace Metalious which shocked many people when it was first published but still sold millions of copies. It is about the sexual relationships and often dishonest behaviour of people living in a small *New England town. There was a film version in 1957, and it later became the basis for the first evening *soap opera on US television.

PG /ˌpiː ˈdʒiː/ (*in full* **parental guidance**) a British *film certificate indicating that some scenes in the film may not be suitable for young children, and that an adult must be present if they wish to watch it.

the **PGA** /ˌpiː giː ˈeɪ/ (*in full* the **Professional Golfers' Association**) the US association for men who play or are involved in professional golf, established in 1916. It is in charge of the major tournaments (= competitions) during the golf season and has its own **PGA Tournament** each year. The equivalent women's organization is the Ladies Professional Golfers' Association (LPGA).

ˈ**Phi ˈBeta ˈKappa** /ˈfaɪ ˈbiːtə ˈkæpə/ the most famous *honor society for US college and university students in the arts and sciences. It is the oldest organization with Greek letters in the US, having been established in 1776 at the College of William and Mary in *Virginia. Students with high academic grades can be chosen in their third or fourth years.

ˌ**Philaˈdelphia** /ˌfɪləˈdelfiə/ the fifth largest city in the US and the largest in *Pennsylvania. It is a major port on the Delaware River and was established by William *Penn. Philadelphia is one of America's most historical cities. It is the place where the *Declaration of Independence was signed and the *American Constitution was written. *Independence Hall and the *Liberty Bell are also there.

ˌKim ˈ**Philby** /ˈfɪlbi/ (1912–88) a British spy who gave British secrets to the Soviet Union. He was a member of a group called the *Cambridge spies, and continued as the 'third man' after the first two, Guy *Burgess and Donald *Maclean were discovered. Later, like them, Philby, escaped to the USSR and became a Soviet citizen.

the ˌ**Philharˈmonia** /ˌfɪlɑːˈməʊniə; *AmE* ˌfɪlɑːrˈmoʊniə/ (*also* the ˌ**Philharˈmonia ˌOrchestra**) a well-known British orchestra which is based in London but regularly performs abroad. It was established in 1945 and has had a number of famous foreign conductors.

ˌPrince ˈ**Philip** ⇨ DUKE OF EDINBURGH.

ˌ**Philip ˈMorris** /ˈmɒrɪs; *AmE* ˈmɔːrɪs/ a large US company that originally produced only cigarettes but now sells a wide range of products. It makes *Marlboro, America's most popular cigarettes, and *Virginia Slims. In 1997, the head of the company became the first leader in the industry to admit that smoking cigarettes has killed many people. The company's other products include *Maxwell House coffee, *Kool-Aid, Jell-O, *Kraft cheese, Post cereals and Miller beer.

ˌ**Phillips**™ ˈ**screwdriver** /ˌfɪlɪps/ *n* a type of screwdriver (= tool that turns a screw) with two small blades on the end shaped like a cross. It is named after the American H F Phillips who invented it, and is used with a **Phillips screw**.

ˈ**Phoenix**[1] /ˈfiːnɪks/ **1** the capital and largest city in the US state of *Arizona. It is on the Salt River in central Arizona and has a warm, dry climate that attracts tourists. It is a centre for agricultural products and information technology. Phoenix became a city in 1881 and the capital of the Arizona Territory in 1889. **2** the *nickname of the British Criminal Justice Record Service, a computer system which allows any police force in England or Wales to look up national records of everyone who has been arrested for a crime, found guilty in a court of law, etc.

ˌRiver ˈ**Phoenix**[2] /ˌrɪvə ˈfiːnɪks; *AmE* ˌrɪvər/ (1970–93) a US actor who became a cult figure (= a person who is fashionable with a particular group) among young people after he accidentally took too many drugs and died at the age of 23. He played sensitive characters, and his films include *Stand By Me* (1986), *Running on Empty* (1988), *My Own Private Idaho* (1991) and *Sneakers* (1992).

ˌ**phony** ˈ**war** (*also* **phoney war**) *n* a situation in which two or more countries have officially declared war but have not yet started to fight. The best-known phony war was the first six months of *World War II. Britain and France declared war against Germany in September 1939, but did not send any soldiers to fight until Germany attacked Denmark and Norway in April 1940: (*fig*) *The President spoke of the need for a real war, not a phony war, against drugs.*

ˌ**Picca**ˈ**dilly** /ˌpɪkəˈdɪli/ a famous street in London's *West End, between *Piccadilly Circus and Hyde Park Corner. Some of London's most expensive hotels, shops and clubs are on Piccadilly. The origin of the name is not known.

Piccadilly Circus

ˌ**Piccadilly** ˈ**Circus** /ˌpɪkədɪli/ a place in the *West End of London, England, where several famous streets meet, including *Piccadilly, *Regent Street and *Shaftesbury Avenue. Many tourists go there to see the statue of *Eros and the brightly-lit advertisements on the sides of the buildings. There is also a Piccadilly Circus station on the *London Underground. Noisy, crowded places are sometimes compared to Piccadilly Circus: *I can't get any work done, it's like Piccadilly Circus in here.*

ˌWilson ˈ**Pickett** /ˌwɪlsn ˈpɪkɪt/ (1941–) an *African-American singer and writer of songs, mostly of *soul music. They include *In the Midnight Hour* (1965), *Mustang Sally* (1966) and *Don't Let the Green Grass Fool You* (1971). He was chosen for the Rock and Roll *Hall of Fame in 1991, and that year appeared in the film *The Commitments*. He still performs on tours.

ˌMary ˈ**Pickford** /ˈpɪkfəd; *AmE* ˈpɪkfərd/ (1893–1979) one of the most famous actors in US silent films, born in Canada, who became known as 'America's Sweetheart'. She had long curls and played innocent characters. In 1919, she joined Douglas *Fairbanks[1] (her husband from 1920 to 1936), Charlie *Chaplin and D W *Griffith to establish the film company *United Artists. Her films included *Rebecca of Sunnybrook Farm* (1917) and **Pollyanna* (1920). In 1976, she received a special *Oscar for her services to the film industry.

ˈ**Pickford's** /ˈpɪkfədz; *AmE* ˈpɪkfərdz/ a well-known British company that transports people's furniture and other possessions in large vans when they move to a new home.

The ˌ***Pickwick*** ˈ***Papers*** /ˌpɪkwɪk/ a novel (1837) by Charles *Dickens, the full title of which is *The Posthumous Papers of the Pickwick Club*. It was originally written as a series of stories, published each month, about the amusing adventures of the members of the club established by Samuel Pickwick. Pickwick is a kind, friendly, fat man who often gets into difficult situations caused by misunderstandings or by his own good nature.

Pict /pɪkt/ *n* a member of an ancient British people. They lived in northern Scotland between the first and 9th centuries AD, when they became united with the *Scots. Little is known about the Picts, but they are famous for their stone carvings decorated with mysterious symbols.

The ˈ***Pied*** ˈ***Piper of*** ˈ***Hamelin*** /ˈhæmlɪn/ a poem (1842) by Robert *Browning. It tells the story of an old European legend about a man who gets rid of all the rats in the German town of Hamelin by playing his pipe. The rats follow the music and the piper leads them out of the town. When the people of Hamelin refuse to pay him for getting rid of the rats, he plays his pipe again and leads their children away.

pier *n* a long structure, usually made of wood and iron, built out into the sea or a lake or river. Piers were originally built so that people could walk along them to get onto boats at the end, or load or unload goods, but in the 19th century many British seaside towns built large piers for pleasure, often with theatres, restaurants and entertainments on them. The piers at towns such as *Blackpool and *Brighton are still popular tourist attractions.

the Palace Pier at Brighton

ˌ***Piers*** ˈ***Plowman*** /ˌpɪəz ˈplaʊmən; *AmE* ˌpɪrz/ a long poem written in the late 14th century by William Langland. The poem describes a vision (= a religious experience like a dream) in which different objects represent good and evil, and how Piers helps a group of people to search for truth through Christianity. It describes the life of ordinary people in great detail, and criticizes the social and moral evils of the time. See also MIDDLE ENGLISH.

ˌLester ˈ**Piggott** /ˌlestə ˈpɪɡət; *AmE* ˌlestər/ (1935–) a famous English jockey. He has won more races than anybody in the history of horse racing, including the *Derby nine times. He was *champion jockey eight times. He was sent to prison in 1987 for not paying tax, but started racing again in 1990.

ˈ**Piglet** a character in A A *Milne's children's stories about *Winnie-the-Pooh. Piglet, a cheerful young pig, is one of *Pooh's friends.

ˌ**Pike's** ˈ**Peak** /ˌpaɪks/ a US mountain in the *Rocky Mountains near Colorado Springs, *Colorado. 'Pike's Peak or Bust' was the cry of people who rushed to that area when gold was discovered in 1859 and of later people who used the mountain as a place to aim for as they travelled west. It is 14 110 feet/4 304 metres high and named after Zebulon Pike, who discovered it in 1806.

the ˌ**Pilgrim** ˈ**Fathers** (*also* the ˈ**Pilgrims**) the 102 English people who sailed to America on the *Mayflower* in 1620. Their group included 35 *Puritans whose aim was to create a safe religious community in the New World. The Pilgrims probably landed at *Plymouth Rock, and they established *Plymouth Colony. Compare FOUNDING FATHERS.

The ˌ***Pilgrim's*** ˈ***Progress*** a religious novel written between 1678 and 1684 by John *Bunyan. It is an allegory (= a story in which the characters and events are symbols representing other things, such as truths, fears and human qualities) about a man's journey through life to heaven. The man, whose name is Christian, meets many symbolic difficulties on the way, including the *Slough of Despond, Vanity Fair and Giant Despair. He finally reaches heaven, and his wife and children follow him.

ˈ**Pilkington** /ˈpɪlkɪŋtən/ a British company that makes many different types of glass. The company has produced glass since the early 19th century, but it became well known in 1959 when Alastair Pilkington invented a new way of making flat glass by floating it on metal that has been heated until it becomes liquid.

ˈ**pillar box** *n* (*BrE*) a tall iron box in the shape of a pillar for posting letters, etc. Pillar boxes stand in the street and are painted bright red. The letters in them are usually collected several times each day: *I'll post it for you, there's a pillar box on the way to the shops.* ○ *She painted her nails pillar-box red.*

a Victorian pillar box

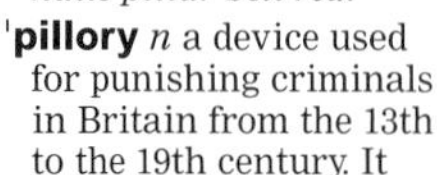

ˈ**pillory** *n* a device used for punishing criminals in Britain from the 13th to the 19th century. It was a wooden framework with holes for the head and hands. Criminals were locked into pillories in public places so that people could laugh at them, insult them and sometimes throw things at them. Compare STOCKS.

ˈ**Pillsbury** /ˈpɪlzbri/ a large US food company. It is known especially for using the **Pillsbury Doughboy** in its advertisements for bread and other baked products. He is a small, fat, white boy called Poppin Fresh who is shy and wears a baker's cap.

ˌ**Piltdown** ˈ**man** /ˌpɪltdaʊn/ a type of prehistoric human being that was believed to exist in ancient times. Piltdown man was 'discovered' when some bones were found in 1912 on Piltdown Common in southern England. It was later proved to be a trick, perhaps meant as a joke, when scientific tests showed that they were a mixture of modern human and ape bones that had been treated to look ancient.

ˈ**Pima** /ˈpiːmə/ *n* (*pl* **Pimas** *or* **Pima**) a member of a *Native-American people who live in southern *Arizona on two reservations (= lands given and protected by the US government). They are agricultural people known for their beautiful baskets. They fought against the *Apache and were friendly to Europeans who settled in their areas.

Pimm's™ /pɪmz/ *n* [U, C] a fashionable British alcoholic drink, made with gin. Its full name is **Pimm's Number One Cup** and it is usually drunk mixed with lemonade, ice and pieces of fresh fruit at summer parties and outdoor events. It is considered a typical *upper-class drink: *They were all drinking Pimm's on the lawn.* ○ *Would you like a Pimm's?*

ˌCourtney ˈ**Pine** /ˌkɔːtni ˈpaɪn; *AmE* ˌkɔːrtni/ (1964–) an English *jazz a musician who plays the saxophone. In the 1990s he became known for mixing jazz with other popular musical forms such as *reggae and *hip hop.

ˌ**Pinewood** ˈ**Studios** /ˌpaɪnwʊd/ a place in *Buckinghamshire, England, where cinema films are made. It was established in 1936 and is owned by the *Rank Organization.

ˌAllan ˈ**Pinkerton** /ˈpɪŋkətən; *AmE* ˈpɪŋkərtən/ (1819–84) an American, born in Scotland, who established the first US company of private detectives. He began the Pinkerton National Detective Agency in 1850 in *Chicago. Its advertisements showed a large eye, with the words 'We never sleep'. Pinkerton also established a US organization during the *Civil War which later became the US *Secret Service. The company today operates in 20 countries and provides protection for large companies.

ˌ**Pink** ˈ**Floyd** /ˈflɔɪd/ one of the most popular British *rock music groups, formed in 1965. The group's most successful albums include *The Dark Side of the Moon* (1973) and *The Wall* (1979). The group is particularly well known for its exciting live performances involving lights and screen images as well as music.

The ˌ***Pink*** ˈ***Panther*** a comedy film (1963) directed by Blake *Edwards in which Peter *Sellers first played the ridiculous French Inspector Clouseau. The Pink Panther is the *nickname of the criminal he is trying to catch. There were several later films about Clouseau and the Panther. There was also a series of television *Pink Panther* cartoon films in which the main character is a pink panther (= large member of the cat family). All the films and cartoons had music by Henry *Mancini.

Piˈ***nocchio*** /pɪˈnəʊkiəʊ; *AmE* pɪˈnoʊkioʊ/ a full-length Walt *Disney cartoon film (1940). It is based on an Italian story about a wooden puppet that becomes a real boy. The story is told by the character Jiminy Cricket, who sings *When You Wish Upon a Star*, a song that won an *Oscar and later became the theme song for a Disney television series.

ˌHarold ˈ**Pinter** /ˈpɪntə(r)/ (1930–) an English writer of plays who has had a major influence on modern British theatre. His characters are often ordinary, unimportant people who find it difficult to communicate properly with each other, and his plays combine humour with an atmosphere of danger and unhappiness. The word **Pinteresque** is sometimes used to describe these qualities. Pinter's best-known plays include *The Birthday Party* (1958), *The Caretaker* (1960), *The Homecoming* (1965), *Old Times* (1971), *No Man's Land* (1975) and *Betrayal* (1978). He has also written many film scripts, including those for *The Go-Between* (1969), *The French Lieutenant's Woman* (1982) and *The Comfort of Strangers* (1983).

ˌJohn ˈ**Piper** /ˈpaɪpə(r)/ (1903–92) an English artist and designer. His work includes paintings of buildings damaged in *World War II, stained glass for church windows (especially one in *Coventry Cathedral), and stage designs for the operas of Benjamin *Britten.

ˌ**Piper** ˈ**Alpha** /ˌpaɪpər ˈælfə/ an oil rig (= platform) in the *North Sea which exploded and caught fire in 1988, causing the deaths of 167 people. As a result of this disaster, rules concerning safety on oil rigs were changed.

pipes ⇨ BAGPIPES.

The ˌ***Pirates of Pen*ˈ*zance*** /penˈzæns/ a comic opera (1880) by W S *Gilbert and Arthur *Sullivan, one of their *Savoy Operas. It is about a group of pirates who are all in fact of noble birth and a group of policemen who are not very brave. One of the best-known songs in the opera is *A Policeman's Lot is Not a Happy One*.

ˌ**pit bull** ˈ**terrier** (*also* ˈ**pit bull**) *n* a fierce breed of dog, originally bred in the US for fighting. In the 1980s a number of people were attacked and badly injured by pit bull terriers and other dogs. As a result a law was passed in Britain in 1991 requiring owners to register them with a special government department. It also stated that the dogs must wear a muzzle (= a covering over the mouth) in public places.

the ˈ**Pitcairn** ˌ**Islands** /ˈpɪtkeən; *AmE* ˈpɪtkern/ a group of small islands under British rule in the southern Pacific Ocean, only one of which, Pitcairn Island, has people living on it. They are mostly descended from the sailors who took part in the *Mutiny on the Bounty and who then occupied the island in 1789.

ˌBrad ˈ**Pitt**[1] /ˈpɪt/ (1964–) a US film actor who became a major star in the 1990s. His films include *Thelma and Louise* (1991), *Interview with the Vampire* (1994), *Seven* (1995) and *Seven Years in Tibet* (1997). He is widely considered to be one of the most physically attractive film stars in the world.

ˌWilliam ˈ**Pitt**[2] /ˈpɪt/ (1759–1806) the youngest man ever to become *Prime Minister of Britain (at the age of 24). He was Prime Minister from 1783 to 1801 and again from 1804 to 1806. His achievements included removing much of the corruption from British politics and improving the financial position of the country. He also introduced *income tax and was responsible for the *Act of Union (1800), by which Ireland became part of the United Kingdom. He is often referred to as **Pitt the Younger**. His father was the Earl of *Chatham, also known as **Pitt the Elder**.

ˈ**Pittsburgh** /ˈpɪtsbɜːg; *AmE* ˈpɪtsbɜːrg/ a US industrial city in western *Pennsylvania where the Allegheny and Monongahela rivers come together to form the *Ohio River. It began in 1758 as Fort Pitt, named after William *Pitt. For a century until the 1980s, it was a centre for iron and steel production. Pittsburgh now produces high technology products and leads the world in medical operations for replacing body organs.

ˈ**Pizza Hut** a US company, owned by PepsiCo Inc, with a large number of restaurants in the US, Britain and other countries that serve pizzas and other food.

PLA /ˌpiː el ˈeɪ/ ⇨ PORT OF LONDON AUTHORITY.

Place names ⇨ article.

ˌ**Plaid** ˈ**Cymru** /ˌplaɪd ˈkʌmri/ the Welsh nationalist political party, started in 1925 with the aim of making Wales an independent country, separate from the rest of the United Kingdom. It carries out campaigns to preserve the individual culture of Wales and the *Welsh language. One of its campaigns led to the creation of the television station *S4C, which broadcasts programmes in Welsh. In 1966, a Plaid Cymru candidate was elected as a *Member of Parliament for the first time.

the ˌ**Plains** ˈ**Indians** *n* the traditional name for the *Native-American peoples who once lived on the *Great Plains in the western central US. They often fought each other and the white people who settled on their land. They include the *Arapaho, *Blackfoot, *Cheyenne, *Comanche, *Crow and *Sioux. Many now live on western reservations (= land given and protected by the US government).

the ˌ**Plains** ˈ**States** the 10 states in the *Great Plains region of the western central US. They are, from north to south, *Montana, *North Dakota, *South Dakota, *Wyoming, *Iowa, *Nebraska, *Colorado, *Kansas, *Oklahoma and *Texas.

ˌ**Planet** ˈ**Hollywood**™ /ˈhɒliwʊd; *AmE* ˈhɑliwʊd/ an international chain of fashionable restaurants partly owned by the US film stars Demi *Moore, Arnold *Schwarzenegger, Sylvester *Stallone and Bruce *Willis. The first was opened in the US in 1991. The restaurants are decorated with objects connected with films and film stars. Some also have shops selling clothes and other goods connected with films.

ˌ***Planet of the*** ˈ***Apes*** a US film (1968) about a planet on which apes are the rulers and humans have become like animals. Several later films continued the story. There was also a television series in 1974 and a television cartoon series the following year.

The ˈ***Planets*** a popular piece of music for orchestra by the British composer Gustav *Holst, which had its first complete public performance in 1920. Each of its seven sections has the name of one of the major planets.

ˈ**Planned** ˈ**Parenthood Fede**ˈ**ration of A**ˈ**merica** a private US organization that gives free information and advice on planning a family. It was established in 1916 and has more than 150 local branches, with its main office in New York.

Planˈ**tagenet** /plænˈtædʒənət/ the name of the family to which all the kings of England from 1154 to 1485 belonged. The first Plantagenet king was *Henry II and the last was *Richard III. The name was originally a *nickname of Geoffrey, Count of Anjou in France (1113–51), who was the father of *Henry II.

the ˌBattle of ˈ**Plassey** /ˈplæsi/ a battle (1757) fought near Calcutta in north-east India. The British army, led by Robert *Clive, defeated the much larger army of the Indian ruler of Bengal, and the victory established British rule in the region.

ˌSylvia ˈ**Plath** /ˈplæθ/ (1932–63) a US writer who came to Britain after marrying the English poet Ted *Hughes. Her novel *The Bell Jar* (1963) was based on her own life and is about a young woman's unhappiness. She also wrote poems, many of them about illness and death. She killed herself in 1963. After her death, collections of her poems were published, including *Ariel* (1965) and *Collected Poems* (1981), which won the *Pulitzer Prize.

ˈ***Playboy*** a US magazine for men known especially for its pictures of nearly naked women. It was started by Hugh *Hefner in 1953, when it was seen as part of the 'sexual revolution' of that time. In 1997 it had more than 3 million readers. The magazine also includes serious articles, short stories, etc., as well as Hefner's own writing on the history and importance

Place names

Britain and the US have a rich variety of place names. Some names are derived from a feature of the local countryside. Others are named after a church or fort. Some honour famous people, while others have been brought from abroad.

Many names reflect the history of an area and of the people who once lived there. Some of the oldest place names in Wales and Scotland date back to the time when Britain was occupied by the *Celts. Some towns in southern England have Latin names dating from *Roman times. Other names are of *Anglo-Saxon or Danish origin and date from the period when these peoples invaded Britain. Later, the *Normans introduced some French names.

In the US many place names are derived from *Native-American words: Chicago, for example, means 'place of the onion', Seattle is named after a chief, and Natchez after a tribe. Sometimes the names were translated, sometimes not: the Black Warrior River in Alabama runs through the city of Tuscaloosa, which was named after a Native-American whose name means 'Black Warrior'. Names of Spanish origin are found mainly in the south-western US. They include San Francisco, San Diego, Las Vegas and Los Angeles. A few names are of French origin, e.g. Baton Rouge and La Crosse. Some names are derived from more than one culture: Anaheim combines the Spanish name 'Ana' with the German 'heim' (= home).

Names based on natural features

Many British towns take their name from a river. In Wales and Scotland many towns have names beginning with *Aber-*, which means 'river mouth', e.g. Aberystwyth, Aberdeen. In England towns close to a river mouth often end with *-mouth*, e.g. Weymouth. The name of the river forms the rest of the name. Names ending in *-ford* (Oxford) suggest a place where a river is shallow enough to cross. A town beside a lake may, in Scotland, contain *loch-* or, in England, *-mere*, e.g. Lochinver, Windermere.

In Scotland, there are several place names beginning with *Dun-*, meaning 'hill', e.g. Dunbar. Any place whose name ends with *-don* (Swindon), *-hurst* (Sandhurst), *-head* (Gateshead) or, in Wales, begins with *pen-* (Penarth), probably stands on or near a hill. Towns near passes may end in *-gate*, e.g. Harrogate, or, in Scotland, begin with *Glen-*, e.g. Glencoe. Names ending with *-combe* (Ilfracombe) or *-dale* (Rochdale), or, in Wales, beginning with *cwm-* (Cwmbran) suggest that the town is in a valley.

American place names based on natural features are easier to recognize. Examples include Two Rivers, River Edge, Mirror Lake, Ocean City, Gulf Breeze, Seven Hills, Shady Valley, Twentynine Palms, Lookout, Little Rock, Round Rock, White Rock and Slippery Rock. French names include La Fontaine and Eau Claire. Some place names describe a product, e.g. Bean City, Copper City.

Buildings in place names

Many British towns developed around an early fort or castle. This may be indicated by a name ending in *-burgh* (Edinburgh), *-bury* (Salisbury), *-caster* or *-cester* (Doncaster, Gloucester) or *-chester* (Dorchester), or beginning or ending with *castle* (Newcastle). A Welsh variant is *Caer-* (Caernarfon).

Names that include *church-*, *kirk-* or, in Wales, *llan-* refer to a church (Offchurch, Kirkby, Llandaff). Towns where there was a monastery may have names ending in *-minster* (Kidderminster).

Names ending with *-ham* (Evesham), *-hampton* (Southampton), *-ington* (Workington), *-stock* or *-stoke* (Woodstock, Basingstoke), *-thorpe* (Scunthorpe), *-wich* or *-wick* (Norwich, Warwick) mean that there was a village or farm there.

In the US place names that refer to buildings include House, Brick Church and High Bridge. Atlanta, Georgia is named after a railway/railroad.

Places named after people

Some British place names refer to ancient tribes. The elements *-ing* and *-ingham* at the end of a name mean 'people of' and 'home of the people of', as in Reading ('Read's people') and Birmingham ('home of Beorma's people'). Places with names ending in *-by* were the homes of Danish invaders, e.g. Grimsby ('Grim's village').

Some towns take their name from Christian saints, particularly if they had local connections. These include St Albans, St Andrews and St David's. Towns named after people who lived in more recent times are rare in Britain. They include Nelson, named after Lord *Nelson, and Telford, named after the engineer Thomas *Telford.

By contrast, many towns in the US honour famous Americans, especially presidents. Abraham *Lincoln is honoured in towns named Lincoln, Lincolnville, Lincolnwood, etc., Andrew *Jackson at Jackson and Jacksonville, and Thomas *Jefferson at Jefferson, Jeffersonville and Jefferson City

Other towns named after famous Americans include Houston, Texas, named after Sam *Houston; Cody, Wyoming, after *Buffalo Bill; Boone, Tennessee, after Daniel *Boone; and Custer, Montana, after General George *Custer. Often the person is now little heard of, e.g. H M Shreve, a 19th century boat captain on the *Mississippi River, whose name was used for Shreveport, Louisiana. A few towns are named after companies, e.g. *Hershey, Pennsylvania.

Towns named after foreign places

Many American towns are named after a place in Britain or another country from which settlers in the US originally came. British names are found especially in *New England. They include Boston, Cambridge, Gloucester, Manchester-by-the-Sea, New Bedford, Greenwich, Norwich and Stafford. British names used in other parts of the US include New York and Birmingham, both large cities, and Glasgow, a small town in Montana.

Names from other countries include New Orleans, Moscow, Athens, Paris, Naples and New Holland.

More unusual names

Americans enjoy creating unusual or humorous names, such as Tombstone in Arizona. Truth or Consequences in New Mexico is named after a radio quiz show. Other names include Cannon Ball, Hot Coffee, Waterproof, Pie Town, Smackover, Humble City, High Lonesome, Orderville, Cut and Shoot, Happy Jack, and Monkey's Eyebrow.

of sex. Some people joke that they only buy the magazine for the articles.

ˈplay dough™ (*also* **ˈPlay-Doh**™) *n* [U] a soft substance, similar to clay, which is sold in a range of bright colours for children to play with by shaping it. It was first invented in the US in 1955 by Joseph McVicker.

ˈPlaytex™ /ˈpleɪteks/ the product name of a range of women's underwear, including *Wonderbra.

plc (*also* **PLC**) /ˌpiː el ˈsiː/ ⇨ PUBLIC LIMITED COMPANY.

the **ˌPledge of Alˈlegiance** a promise of loyalty made by Americans to their flag and country. The words are: 'I pledge allegiance to the flag of the United States of America and to the republic for which it stands, one nation under God, indivisible, with liberty and justice for all.' It was first published in 1892 in the magazine *Youth's Companion* and written by the journalist Francis Bellamy. Congress added the words 'under God' in 1954 and this caused a lot of argument. Many American children say the Pledge each morning at school as they face the flag and put their right hands over their hearts. Adults also often do this on formal public occasions.

ˌPlessy v ˈFerguson /ˌplesi vɜːsəs ˈfɜːɡəsn; *AmE* vɜːrsəs ˈfɜːrɡəsn/ a court case in 1896 which was decided by the US *Supreme Court. It stated that *segregation on trains was legal if black and white people received equal services. Southern states soon also used this idea of '*separate but equal' in schools, public buildings, etc. The ruling (= decision) was replaced in 1954 by the Supreme Court's decision in the case of **Brown v Board of Education* of Topeka, which stated that segregation in schools was illegal.

ˈPlexiglas™ /ˈpleksiɡlɑːs; *AmE* ˈpleksiɡlæs/ *n* [U] a US make of strong transparent plastic that looks like glass. It is used in many products, e.g. car windows.

ˈPlimsoll line /ˈplɪmsəl/ *n* [usu sing] a mark on the side of a ship which shows how far down in the water (because of the weight of its cargo) it can legally be. It was named after the English politician Samuel Plimsoll (1824–98), who did a lot to improve the rules about safety at sea.

Plod ⇨ PC PLOD.

ˌploughman's ˈlunch (*also infml* **ˈploughman's**) *n* (*BrE*) a light meal often served in pubs and usually eaten in the middle of the day. It consists of cheese (or sometimes cold cooked meat), bread and butter, salad and pickles (= a mixture of fruit and vegetables preserved in vinegar). Its name was invented in the early 1970s to suggest the sort of food traditionally eaten by people working the fields: *I'll have a Cheddar ploughman's, please.*

PLR /ˌpiː el ˈɑː(r)/ ⇨ PUBLIC LENDING RIGHT.

ˈPlymouth /ˈplɪməθ/ a city and port on the coast of *Devon in south-west England. It has long been associated with ships and the sea. The *Royal Navy has an important base there. In 1588 English ships waited for the *Spanish Armada at Plymouth, and while they were waiting Sir Francis *Drake is said to have played a game of *bowls on Plymouth Hoe, a piece of flat high ground above the sea. In 1620 the *Pilgrim Fathers sailed from Plymouth across the Atlantic.

the **ˌPlymouth ˈBrethren** /ˌplɪməθ/ (*also* the **Brethren**) *n* [pl] a Christian religious group established in *Plymouth, England, in 1830 by people who did not agree with the ideas and ceremonies of the *High Church. The Brethren have no priests, and live according to a set of strict moral rules that they have taken from the Bible. They believe that Jesus Christ will soon return to judge people.

ˌPlymouth ˈColony /ˌplɪməθ/ the American community in *Massachusetts established in 1620 by the *Pilgrim Fathers. Half of the people died during the first harsh winter, but good crops the next year led to the first *Thanksgiving. Plymouth Colony joined the New England Confederation in 1643 and became part of the colony of Massachusetts in 1691.

ˌPlymouth ˈRock /ˌplɪməθ/ a large rock on the coast of Plymouth, *Massachusetts, where the *Pilgrim Fathers probably landed in 1620, although there is no proof. In 1774, the rock split while it was being dragged into the town of Plymouth as a symbol of freedom from the British. It is now back in its original position, under a protective roof. Next to it is the *Mayflower II*, a copy of the Pilgrims' original ship that was sent as a gift from Britain in 1957. See also *MAYFLOWER*.

PM /ˌpiː ˈem/ ⇨ PRIME MINISTER.

ˌPocaˈhontas /ˌpəʊkəˈhɒntəs; *AmE* ˌpoʊkəˈhɑːntəs/ (*c.* 1595–1617) a *Native-American girl who in 1607 saved the life of Captain John *Smith[7] when he was about to be killed by her father, Chief Powhatan. She became a Christian in 1613 and changed her name to Rebecca. A year later, she married the English colonist John Rolfe and in 1616 went to England, where she created a lot of interest. She became ill and died on the way home. Her story was told in the Walt *Disney cartoon film *Pocahontas* (1995).

ˈPodunk /ˈpəʊdʌŋk; *AmE* ˈpoʊdʌŋk/ (*AmE infml disapprov*) any small town that is regarded as dull, remote and not important. There are two actual US towns called Podunk, one in *Connecticut and one in *Massachusetts: *He grew up in Podunk and feels lost in the big city.*

ˈEdgar ˈAllan **ˈPoe** /ˈpəʊ; *AmE* ˈpoʊ/ (1809–49) a US writer of short stories and poems. His best remembered works are frightening stories of mystery and death, including *The Fall of the House of Usher* (1839) and *The Pit and the Pendulum* (1843). He is also regarded as having invented the modern *detective story on the basis of such stories as *The Murders in the Rue Morgue* (1841). His poems include *The *Raven* (1845) and *Annabel Lee* (1849). Poe drank too much alcohol and died young. There have been film versions of many of his stories.

ˌPoet ˈLaureate *n* (*pl* **Poets Laureate**) (in Britain) a poet officially chosen to write poems on special state occasions such as royal weddings, births and funerals. The first Poet Laureate was Ben *Jonson (from 1616). Others have included *Dryden, *Wordsworth and *Tennyson, and more recently *Masefield, *Day-Lewis, *Betjeman and Ted *Hughes.

The US has had Poets Laureate since 1986 when Robert Penn *Warren became the first. They are appointed by the *Library of Congress but only serve for one or two years.

ˌPoets' ˈCorner a part of *Westminster Abbey where many famous English writers and poets are buried or where there are memorials to them. The writers and poets buried there include *Chaucer, *Browning, *Tennyson, *Dickens, *Hardy and *Kipling. There are also memorials to *Shakespeare, *Milton, *Byron, *Shelley[2] and many others.

The **Pogues** /pəʊɡz; *AmE* poʊɡz/ a British pop group formed in 1983, whose style mixes Irish folk music with *punk. The group's best-known recordings include *Dirty Old Town* (1985) and *The Irish Rover* (1987).

Hercule **Poirot** /ˌeəkjuːl ˈpwɑːrəʊ; *AmE* erˈkjuːl pwɑːˈroʊ/ a Belgian *detective who appears as a character in many of the mystery novels by Agatha *Christie. He has a very neat appearance and a neat pointed moustache. He often considers English people strange and English people in the books are

P

amused by his *accent. He is extremely clever and uses his intelligence, or what he calls his 'little grey cells', to solve every crime. Many of the stories were adapted for a popular British television series called *Poirot* in the 1980s and 1990s.

ˌSydney ˈ**Poitier** /ˈpwɑːtieɪ/ (1927–) one of the first *African-American actors to play important film roles. He won an *Oscar for his part in *Lilies of the Field* (1963). His other films have included *Blackboard Jungle* (1955), *Porgie and Bess* (1959), *Guess Who's Coming to Dinner* (1967), *In the Heat of the Night* (1967), *The Wilby Conspiracy* (1975) and *The Day of the Jackal* (1997).

ˈ**Polack** /ˈpəʊlæk; *AmE* ˈpoʊlæk/ *n* [C] (*AmE sl offensive*) a person from Poland. 'Polack jokes' are told in the US about Polish people being stupid, but many people regard them as insulting.

ˈ**Polaroid**™ /ˈpəʊlərɔɪd; *AmE* ˈpoʊlərɔɪd/ *n* a type of camera that produces a completed print of a photograph immediately after the photograph is taken. It was invented in the US in 1947 by Edwin Land.

poˈlice ⇨ LAW ENFORCEMENT.

poˌlitical ˈaction comˌmittee (*abbr* **PAC**) *n* (in the US) any group formed to raise money for candidates in elections who support their views and agree to protect their interests.

political correctness

Political correctness, often called simply **PC**, is concerned with avoiding certain attitudes, actions and, above all, forms of expression which suggest prejudice and are likely to cause offence. This may be against men or women, against older people, or against people with a particular skin colour, racial background or physical disability.

Political correctness developed in the 1980s and 1990s as an ideal of intellectuals and *feminists in the US and later in Britain. Now the phrase is often used in a negative way to refer to the more extreme ideas and especially the attempt to change the language by replacing words said to have negative associations with new, often clumsy phrases that, to many people, seem just as negative. Many people are also doubtful whether changing words will remove prejudice in people's minds or in the social system.

In the 1960s and 1970s public debate caused many people to accept the principle that discrimination (= treating some people worse than others) is wrong. Changes of many kinds have happened in schools and offices. Where once schoolchildren celebrated only Christian holidays such as *Christmas, they now often learn about the holidays of other religious and ethnic groups. History was traditionally taught from the point of view of white people, but now more children learn about the history and culture of other groups in the community. In offices sexual and racial **harassment** (= comments or behaviour intended to worry or upset somebody) are not allowed. The PC movement has also been against **stereotyping** (= having fixed ideas about people), especially of women and black people, and making jokes against minority groups. Politicians, public relations officers and others became afraid of being accused of being **politically incorrect**.

A major concern of political correctness has been to avoid racist or sexist language that will offend particular groups. However some language changes are much older than the PC movement. *Ms* has been used for a long time as a title for women who do not wish to identify themselves as being either married (*Mrs*) or single (*Miss*). A few other PC phrases, notably *chair* or *chairperson* instead of *chairman*, are also fairly common. More recent changes in the US include saying *African American* instead of *Black*, and *Native American* instead of *Indian*.

Other changes have been less widely accepted. For example, the words *blind* and *deaf* were felt to suggest something negative, so people began using *visually impaired* and *hearing impaired*, which, they believed, did not carry the same negative associations. Other examples of less acceptable PC terms include *vertically challenged* (short), *differently sized* (fat), *physically challenged* (disabled), *economically exploited* (poor), *involuntarily leisured* (unemployed), and *domestic operative* (housewife). As a result, many people came to the conclusion that, although political correctness might in itself be desirable, some of the language associated with it is ridiculous.

Political parties in Britain ⇨ article.

Political parties in the US ⇨ article.

Politics and politicians ⇨ article.

ˌJames K ˈ**Polk** /ˈpəʊk; *AmE* ˈpoʊk/ (James Knox Polk 1795–1849) the 11th US *President (1845–9) and a member of the *Democratic Party. He had earlier been in the US House of Representatives (1825–39), the last four years as the *Speaker of the House, and was then Governor of *Tennessee (1839–41). During his time as President, the US added *Texas to the Union and fought the *Mexican War which also added *California and most of the South-West.

ˌJackson ˈ**Pollock** /ˌdʒæksn ˈpɒlək; *AmE* ˈpɑːlək/ (1912–56) a US artist who was a leader of *abstract expressionism. He developed a style of 'action painting', in which paint is dropped or thrown onto a large canvas placed on the floor or on a wall. He sometimes used sticks and knives instead of brushes. Pollock drank too much, had severe mental problems and was killed in a car crash.

ˈ**poll tax** ⇨ COMMUNITY CHARGE.

ˌ**Pollyˈanna** /ˌpɒliˈænə; *AmE* ˌpɑːliˈænə/ *n* (*AmE*) a girl or woman who is always cheerful and expects good things to happen. The name comes from the character in the novels *Pollyanna* (1913) and *Pollyanna Grows Up* (1915) by the US writer Eleanor H Porter (1868–1920). *Pollyanna* was later a silent film (1920) with Mary *Pickford and a Walt *Disney film (1960) with Hayley Mills.

ˈ**Polo**™ /ˈpəʊləʊ; *AmE* ˈpoʊloʊ/ *n* a popular British peppermint sweet, sold in tubes and made by *Nestlé. Polo mints are round with a hole in the middle. They are advertised as 'the mint with the hole'. Polos are also made with fruit flavours.

ˌ***Pomp and ˈCircumstance*** a set of five marches by the English composer Edward Elgar, written between 1901 and 1930. A version of one of them later had words written for it and was given the title **Land of Hope and Glory*. This is played every year at the *Last Night of the Proms, with the audience singing the words.

ˌJuan ˈ**Ponce de Leˈón** /ˈhwɑːn ˈpɒnθeɪ deɪ leɪˈɒn, ˈpɒnseɪ; *AmE* ˈpɑːnθeɪ, ˈpɑːnseɪ, leɪˈɑːn/ (1460–1521) a Spanish explorer who discovered *Florida in 1513 while searching for the *Fountain of Youth. He had captured *Puerto Rico in 1508 and become governor there (1509–12).

Pond's™ /pɒndz; *AmE* pɑːndz/ a product name for a range of creams for cleaning and softening the skin. They are produced by Chesebrough-Pond's. The best known is Pond's Cold Cream, which is often used to remove make-up from the face.

ˈ**Pontiac** /ˈpɒntiæk; *AmE* ˈpɑːntiæk/ *n* a US car made by the *General Motors Corporation, named after a 18th-century Native-American leader. The company advertises Pontiacs with the phrase 'We are driving

Political parties in Britain

The party system

The British political system relies on having at least two parties in the *House of Commons able to form a government. Historically, the main parties were the ***Tories** and the ***Whigs**. More recently these parties became known as the ***Conservative Party** and the ***Liberal Party**. The Conservative Party's main rival is now the ***Labour Party**, but there are several other smaller parties. The most important is the ***Liberal Democratic Party**, which developed from the old Liberal Party and the newer *Social Democratic Party. Wales and Scotland have their own nationalist parties, *Plaid Cymru (The Party of Wales) and the *Scottish National Party. Northern Ireland has several parties, including the *Ulster Unionist Party, the *Ulster Democratic Unionist Party and the *Social Democratic and Labour Party.

Party support

The Conservative Party is on the political right and the Labour Party on the left. The Liberal Democrats are generally closer to Labour in their opinions than to the Conservatives. Each party has its own *emblem and colour: the Conservatives have a blue torch, Labour a red rose, and Liberal Democrats a yellow bird.

In order to have closer contact with the electorate (= people who have the right to vote in elections), the Conservative Party set up **constituency associations**, local party offices coordinated by Conservative Central Office. These raise money for the party and promote its policies. By contrast, the Labour Party began outside *Parliament amongst *trade unions and socialist organizations, and tried to get representatives into Parliament to achieve its aims. Both parties now have many local branches which are responsible for choosing candidates for parliamentary and *local government elections.

Conservative supporters are traditionally from the richer sections of society, especially landowners and business people. The Labour Party originally drew its support from the *working classes and from people wanting social reform. It has always had support from the trade unions, but recently has tried to appeal to a wider group, especially well-educated and professional people. The Liberal Democratic Party draws most of its votes from those people who are unwilling to vote Labour.

Support for the main parties is not distributed evenly throughout Britain. In England, the south has traditionally been Conservative, together with the more rural areas, while the north and inner cities have been Labour. In Scotland, Wales and Northern Ireland the situation is complicated by the existence of the nationalist parties. Wales is traditionally a Labour region, though Plaid Cymru is strong. Scotland, formerly a Conservative area, is now also overwhelmingly Labour, though many people support the Scottish Nationalist Party. After the 1997 election the Conservative Party had no MPs representing Welsh or Scottish constituencies. Support for the Liberal Democratic Party is not concentrated in any one area. In a *first-past-the-post system, where the winner in an election is the candidate with the most votes in each constituency, a strong geographical base is important. In the 1992 election, over 17% of all the votes cast were for the Liberal Democratic Party but these were spread too thinly and the party won only 3% of the seats in Parliament.

At present, political parties do not have to say where they obtain their money. The Labour Party receives a lot of its money from trade unions, whereas the Conservative Party receives gifts from individuals, especially businessmen, and sometimes from people living outside Britain. The Labour Party would like to have a law passed that forced parties to reveal the source of large donations and to prevent money being sent from abroad.

Party conferences

A **party conference** is organized each year by the national office of each party, to which constituency offices send representatives. Prominent members of the party give speeches, and representatives debate party policy. Conferences are usually lively events and receive a lot of attention from the media. They also give party leaders the opportunity to hear the opinions of ordinary party members. Before an election, each party prepares a detailed account of its ideas and intended policies and presents them to the electorate in an **election manifesto**.

The Labour leader is elected at the party conference by representatives of trade unions, individual members of the party and Labour MPs. The Liberal Democrats' leader is also elected by party members but by a postal vote. But the Conservative leader is elected only by Conservative MPs in a secret ballot.

The parties in Parliament

In debates in Parliament, MPs from different parties argue fiercely against each other. However, representatives of all parties cooperate in arranging the order of business so that there is enough time for different points of view to be expressed. Another example of cooperation between parties is the ***pairing** system. An MP of one party is **paired** with an MP of another party, and when there is to be a vote and the two MPs know that they would vote on opposite sides, neither of them will be present to vote. In this way, the difference in numbers between the two sides is maintained while MPs are free to do other parliamentary work.

The parties are managed by several ***Whips**, MPs or peers (= members of the House of Lords) chosen from within their party. The **Government *Chief Whip** and the **Opposition Chief Whip** meet frequently and are '**the usual channels**' through which arrangements for debates are made. Junior whips act as links between the Chief Whips and party members.

The main parties hold regular meetings at which party policy is discussed. Conservative MPs belong to the ***1922 Committee** which meets once week and provides an opportunity for MPs to give their opinions on current issues. Meetings of the **Parliamentary Labour Party** are generally held twice a week and are open to all Labour MPs and Labour members of the House of Lords. Liberal Democrat MPs and peers also meet regularly. In addition, the parties have their own specialist committees that deal with different areas of policy.

Political parties in the US

The growth of the party system

The US has two main political parties, the *Democratic Party and the *Republican Party. There are other, smaller parties but they rarely win elections, and then usually only at the local level.

The first political party was the *Federalist Party, which was begun while George *Washington was President. Soon after, a group of people led by Thomas *Jefferson formed a faction (= rival group) within the Federalist Party called the **Democratic Republican Party**. The Democratic Party grew out of this party in the 1820s. The ***Whigs** were formed in the 1830s to oppose the Democratic Party. They borrowed their name from a British political party. The Republican Party began in 1854 with members from both the Democratic Party and the Whigs.

The way politicians are elected in the US makes it difficult for more than two main parties to exist at one time. When a third party appears, it disappears again quite soon or replaces one of the other parties. This often happens when a particular issue becomes important. During the 1850s, for instance, many Americans wanted to make *slavery illegal and started the Republican Party. As it gained support, it took the place of the Whig Party. This process is called **realignment**.

The role of the parties

Party organizations are less important in the US than in countries like Britain which have a parliament. This is partly because, due to the *separation of powers between the executive, legislative and judicial branches of government, a political party is not so closely identified with government. In addition, candidates for many offices are chosen by voters in ***primary elections** rather than by the party.

The national organization for each of the main parties is called the **National Committee**, and its head is the **National Chairman**. This person is appointed by the party's candidate for President. The head of a US political party is not, as in Britain, the head of the **administration** (= people running the government at a particular time).

An important job of the national party is to organize the party **convention** (= meeting), which is held every four years in the summer before the *elections for President. The convention decides who will be the party's candidates for President and Vice-president, as well as the **platform**, the ideas and opinions of the party and the policies it will introduce if it wins the election.

The national parties raise money for election campaigns and provide other kinds of help to their candidates. They may, for example, help them make television advertisements.

In the *House of Representatives and the *Senate the **majority party** controls the most powerful committees, the groups that decide what laws are made and how the administration spends its money. Members of *Congress are allowed more independence from their parties than British *Members of Parliament. They aim to appear loyal first of all to the people they represent. But to other politicians from their party they want to be seen as loyal party members, so that they will have the chance of sitting on important committees and build up support for any proposals they may introduce.

Americans hope that politicians will devote themselves more to their country than to their own careers. They do not want politicians to appear too **partisan** (= strongly attached to their party) but to show a **bipartisan** (= cooperative) spirit and work together for the good of the country.

What are the parties like?

There is less difference between the two main US parties than there is between parties in some other countries. Both parties are moderate and close to **the political centre**, but the Republicans are to the **right** and the Democrats are to the **left** of centre. Typically, the Democrats support government spending on social welfare programmes, while the Republicans are against this. The Republicans are usually in favour of spending money on the armed forces and believe there should be few laws restricting business and trade. Republicans are sometimes called the *GOP, or Grand Old Party, and have an elephant as their symbol. The Democrats' symbol is a donkey.

Traditionally, the Democratic Party has drawn its support from poor people, workers with low-paid jobs, *African Americans, and many people in the southern states. People with more money and jobs in the professions, and those who live in the central parts of the US, have tended to vote for the Republicans. Many white southerners are closer in their political beliefs to the Republicans but do not want to vote for them because it was a Republican president, Abraham *Lincoln, who fought the *Civil War against the South. As a compromise, they elect politicians who are on the right of the Democratic party, sometimes called 'Dixiecrats'.

In the 20th century the Republicans have elected presidents such as Richard *Nixon, Ronald *Reagan and George* Bush. Democratic presidents have included Franklin D *Roosevelt, John F *Kennedy and Bill *Clinton.

Party membership

If somebody becomes a member of a political party it does not mean that they remain committed to it. Americans believe that the personal qualities of a candidate for office are more important than the party he or she belongs to, and they do not stay loyal to one party. Every four years each party holds primary elections to decide who will be the party's candidate for President. People who vote in a party's primary must be members of that party. Many people change their party membership often, in some cases every four or eight years. Some people even vote in one party's primary, and then vote for the candidate from the other party in the general election.

Very few party members take part in party political activities. Local branches of the parties support candidates running for local offices and people who are active in a party are involved at this level. The branches use members to distribute information before an election or to telephone people to remind them to vote.

Politics and politicians

What Americans think ...

American political life is relatively honest compared with that in many countries. But there have been famous cases of **corruption** (= dishonest use of political power, especially to make money) and **scandals**, such as *Watergate. In New York in the 1800s, a group of politicians became known for their corrupt behaviour, and the name of the building where they met, ***Tammany Hall**, became a general expression for political corruption. Some cities still have a **political machine**, which means that the people who manage the city government use their power to prevent other people taking part.

Americans generally have little trust in politicians and little interest in politics. Many people do not like either of the two main *political parties, the *Republicans and the *Democrats. This lack of interest is slowly changing the political system. The number of people who vote in *elections keeps going down, and in elections for President only about half of the people who could vote actually do so. This means that a candidate getting only 25% of all possible votes can be elected. There is also a problem of **fall-off**, i.e. people vote for candidates for important positions, like President or State Governor, but not for lower positions, like city judge.

Every two years, when there are elections for *Congress, many people change the party they vote for. This happens even if there have been no economic problems or major events such as a war. The explanation is that once a party has been elected it is associated with government, and this makes Americans suspicious of it. Some people think there should be **term limitation**, a limit to the number of years a person can serve in Congress so that he or she does not have time to become dishonest. Others say that such a rule would mean that the country lost honest politicians, and that people should make more effort to find out which politicians are dishonest and not vote for them.

Americans like to choose candidates for political office because of their character, not for their policies, so in election campaigns politicians have to be careful not to seem **partisan** (= strongly attached to a political party). They avoid discussing political issues and what they would do if elected, and talk instead about their beliefs and values, such as the importance of family and religion. Since television is important in American politics, candidates try to think of good **soundbites** (= short, meaningful phrases) that will be repeated in news bulletins and make a strong impression on voters. This rather empty style of communication has led to the rise of **spin doctors**, whose job is to present political ideas in a way that makes them look good.

When Americans have a serious complaint about something they may say, 'I'll write a letter to my Congressman.' In fact many cannot name their Congressman or Congresswoman, and many would not know where to find that information.

Although the political system has many strengths, Americans mostly see only its problems. Their response is to avoid getting involved in politics, but this has the effect of making the problems worse.

What the British think ...

A street survey in Britain would reveal that not many people know who their *Member of Parliament (MP) is. Even fewer could name their *Euro-MP or any of their local councillors. British people vote at general elections but show little interest in politics at other times. Only if there is a local issue that affects them personally will they bother to write to their MP or attend a **surgery** (= a session when people can talk to their MP). Even then, many people prefer to write to a newspaper or organize a protest campaign because they think that this has more chance of achieving results.

At election time there are ***party political broadcasts** on radio and television, in which leading politicians say what their party will do if it wins the election and try to persuade people to vote for them. Many people do not listen. By contrast, special broadcasts on election night are popular, and people stay up late to listen to the election results as they are announced. Experts make predictions throughout the night about the final overall result. As the 'swing' or change of support from one party to another becomes clearer, the experts calculate and recalculate the likely number of seats that each party will win, and display the information on a *swingometer.

Political parties try to persuade their supporters to become party members so that they can keep in contact with them between elections. However, only a small percentage of the population belongs to a party and takes part in any political activity.

During sessions of *Parliament, members of the public may go and sit in the ***Strangers' Gallery** at the *House of Commons or the *House of Lords. Few people, however, have the time for this. Parts of debates are broadcast on radio and television, but not many people listen regularly. Most rely on news and current affairs programmes, such as the **Today* programme on *Radio 4, to find out what is happening. Newspapers summarize parliamentary affairs in varying amounts of detail. Different papers support different parties, and this affects how they report political policy and events.

The media concentrate more on political personalities than on issues because they know that this is what many people like to hear and read about. The main parties employ advertising consultants to improve their image. Party leaders are often photographed with their families to show how ordinary and respectable they are. Cartoonists care little for a politician's image, and in their drawings they emphasize a prominent physical feature or well-known gesture and add a humorous comment relating to current events.

British people would like to think that politicians deserve respect, but they know that they cannot trust the image. Newspapers are full of stories of scandal and **sleaze**. For instance, MPs have been accused of taking bribes to ask questions in Parliament, and there are **dirty tricks** and **smear campaigns** (= false accusations intended to damage an MP's reputation). MPs' private lives are often shown to be less than perfect. So it is perhaps not surprising that many people find it difficult to take politics seriously.

excitement', and the models include the Firebird, Bonneville, Grand Am, Grand Prix and Sunfire.

ˈ**Pontin's** /ˈpɒntɪnz; *AmE* ˈpɑːntɪnz/ any of a group of British holiday camps, the first of which was opened by Fred Pontin in 1946. These camps, offering cheap family holidays/vacations, were very popular in the years after *World War II, but became less so towards the end of the 20th century: *We used to go to Pontin's every summer when I was young.* Compare BUTLIN'S.

the ˈ**Pony Club** a British club for children who ride ponies. It was started in 1929 and now has many branches, mainly in country areas, which organize competitions, shows and other activities. It is considered a typically *middle-class institution: *Edward is a prominent member of the local golf club and his daughters are all Pony Club members.*

the ˌ**Pony Ex**ˈ**press** a US mail service in the *Old West, using riders and horses (not ponies). It operated from April 1860 to October 1861, between St Joseph, *Missouri and Sacramento, *California, a distance of 1 966 miles (3 163 kilometres), which the riders could complete in 10 days by changing horses at regular stations along the way. *Buffalo Bill was one of the riders. The service came to an end when a telegraph line (= a device for sending messages on electric wires) was completed. The **Pony Express National Historic Trail** was established in 1992.

Pooh /puː/ (*also* ˌ**Winnie-the-**ˈ**Pooh**, ˌ**Pooh** ˈ**Bear**) the main character in A A *Milne's children's stories, *Winnie-the-Pooh* (1926) and *The House at Pooh Corner* (1928). Pooh is a bear who is not very intelligent but very friendly. He enjoys eating, singing songs, and playing with his friends, including *Christopher Robin, *Piglet and *Eeyore.

Winnie-the-Pooh with Christopher Robin and friends

ˈ**Poohsticks** /ˈpuːstɪks/ *n* [U] a simple children's game, first described in A A *Milne's stories about *Winnie-the-Pooh. A group of people throw sticks off a bridge into a stream, then watch to see whose stick appears first on the other side of the bridge.

the **pools** (*also* the ˈ**football pools**) *n* [pl] a British gambling competition in which people try to predict the results of football matches. Every week people taking part fill in **pools coupons** (= special documents for marking the results of the matches that will take place on Saturday) and send these with the money they wish to bet to one of the pools companies. Those who predict the results most accurately receive the most prize money. It was the most popular form of gambling in Britain before the *National Lottery was introduced in the 1990s: *I'd buy a big house like that if I won the pools.*

the ˈ**Poor Laws** *n* [pl] a series of British laws that were concerned with helping poor people. The first Poor Law (1601) stated that the poor were the responsibility of the *parish(1), and that local people should be taxed to provide food for the poor. These taxes became too high when the number of poor people increased in the early 19th century, and in 1834 a new Poor Law stated that the poor should be made to work in *workhouses. This system was very unpopular, but it was not officially changed until the 1930 Poor Law introduced a national system of social welfare.

ˈ***Poor*** ˈ***Richard's*** ˈ***Almanack*** a book published each year in the US between 1733 and 1758. It was written by Benjamin *Franklin under the name of Richard Saunders. It contained useful information on important dates, anniversaries, etc., as well as wise advice in the form of short sayings and verses. Many of these are still repeated, such as 'A penny earned is a penny saved,' and

Early to bed and early to rise
Makes a man healthy, wealthy and wise.

ˌMr ˈ**Pooter** /ˈpuːtə(r)/ the main character in *The *Diary of a Nobody*. Mr Charles Pooter is a simple and rather boring man who gets into amusing and embarrassing difficulties in his social, family and business life. Awkward social situations, or people who find themselves in them, are sometimes described as **Pooterish**.

ˌ**pop** ˈ**art** *n* [U] a style of art that represents objects or people from everyday life, often using materials and techniques from popular culture, such as advertisements and *comics. Pop art was developed in the 1950s by artists such as Eduardo *Paolozzi in Britain and Jasper *Johns in the US. It became well known in the 1960s through the work of **pop artists** such as David *Hockney, Andy *Warhol and Roy *Lichtenstein.

ˌAlexander ˈ**Pope** /ˈpəʊp; *AmE* ˈpoʊp/ (1688–1744) an English poet, well known for his humour and intelligence. He is considered the greatest poet of the *Augustan Age. He gained his reputation as a major writer by translating Homer's *Iliad* (1715–20) and *Odyssey* (1725–6), but is now better known for his satirical poems such as *The *Rape of the Lock* and *An Epistle to Dr Arbuthnot* (1735) which made fun of the writers and fashionable people of the period. See also *DUNCIAD*.

ˈ**Popeye** /ˈpɒpaɪ; *AmE* ˈpɑːpaɪ/ a popular US cartoon character first created for a comic strip in 1929 by E C Segar. Popeye is a sailor who has a kind nature but loves fighting and becomes especially strong when he eats spinach (= a green vegetable). He has a very thin girlfriend called Olive Oyl and his main rival is the big, bad Bluto. A film version of *Popeye* with real actors appeared in 1980, directed by Robert *Altman, with Robin *Williams in the main part.

ˌ***Pop Goes the*** ˈ***Weasel*** a popular British song in the 19th century, still sung today though mainly by children. Nobody is sure what the title means, and it may be simply a nonsense phrase. The first verse is:

Half a pound of twopenny rice,
Half a pound of treacle;
That's the way the money goes,
Pop goes the weasel!

the ˌ**Popish** ˈ**Plot** /ˌpəʊpɪʃ; *AmE* ˌpoʊpɪʃ/ ⇨ OATES.

ˌKarl ˈ**Popper** /ˌkɑːl ˈpɒpə(r); *AmE* ˌkɑːrl ˈpɑːpər/ (1902–94) a British philosopher, born in Austria. He wrote mainly about science, and argued that scientific ideas cannot be proved to be true, so that the closest thing to a true idea is one that has not been proved false. His books include *The Logic of Scientific Discovery* (1934) and *The Open Society and its Enemies* (1945). He was made a *knight in 1965.

ˈ**Poppy Day** the popular name for *Remembrance Sunday, when many people in Britain wear plastic or paper poppies (= red flowers) in memory of the people who died in the two world wars. The poppies represent the real flowers that grew in the fields of France and Belgium, where many soldiers died. See also BRITISH LEGION.

ˈ**Popsicle**™ /ˈpɒpsɪkl; *AmE* ˈpɑːpsɪkl/ *n* a popular US make of sweet flavoured ice on a flat stick, called an *ice lolly* in British English. Children often use the sticks to build things.

population

In 1995 the United Kingdom had a total population of just over 58 million people. About 80% of the people (49 million) live in England, nearly 10% (5 million) in Scotland, 6% (3 million) are Welsh and 3% (1.5 million) are from Northern Ireland. Around 3.5 million of these belong to **ethnic minorities**, of which the largest groups are Indian (1 million), Caribbean (0.5 million) and Pakistani (0.5 million) in origin. Many people from *Commonwealth countries came to Britain during the 1960s. Since then ***immigration** regulations have made it much more difficult to settle in Britain and the population has changed little in size since the 1970s. It is expected to rise very little until the year 2025, when it might even start to fall.

The situation is very different in the United States. In 1997 the US had a population of about 267 million people, of which about 72% (195 million) were white, 12% (33.8 million) were black, 11% (29 million) were *Hispanic (= from Central and South America), 4% (10 million) were Asians and Pacific island peoples and under 1% (2.3 million) were *Native Americans. The US Census Bureau predicts that the nation will have about 323 million people by 2020 and 394 million by 2050. In 1996, a total of 24.6 million Americans (9.3% of the population) had been born outside the US, and immigration is currently at about 900 000 per year. Most come from Mexico (6.7 million), the Philippines (1.2 million) and China (800 000), and the only Europeans to arrive in large numbers are from Germany (515 000). Some Americans are worried that this new pattern will change the country's traditional Anglo-American culture.

Each year in Britain there around 730 000 babies born, a **birth rate** of about 13 for every 1 000 of the population. In 1997, the US had more than 3.9 million births but the birth rate of 14.6 for each 1 000 people was the same as for 1976, the lowest ever. The birth rate in the US has decreased by 38% since 1960. On average, males born in the 1990s in both Britain and the US can expect to live 73 years and females 79 years. The main causes of death are heart disease and cancer. About 12 in every 100 000 people died from Aids or other HIV-related causes.

Around 75% of the population of the UK live in cities, so that although people think of the British Isles as being crowded compared to some other parts of the world, much of the countryside is relatively empty. The most densely populated regions are the south-east, especially London, which has a population of nearly 7 million, and the regions around the industrial cities of *Birmingham, *Liverpool, *Manchester and *Newcastle. Most of the population of Scotland lives in the lowlands, where the cities of *Glasgow and *Edinburgh are located.

In the US about 80% of the population lives in cities. The largest are New York with nearly 8 million people, *Los Angeles and *Chicago. The states with the largest populations are *California with 32 million people, *Texas with more than 19 million and New York with 18 million. Some large states have very few people: *Wyoming has the fewest, 482 000, or about 5 people for every square mile.

ˌ***Porgy and*** ˈ***Bess*** /ˌpɔːgi ənd ˈbes; *AmE* ˌpɔːrgi/ a musical play (1935) by George and Ira *Gershwin which has been called 'America's first folk opera'. It was based on the 1925 novel *Porgy* by Dubose Heyward, and is about poor *African Americans in *Charleston, *South Carolina. The main characters are the lovers Porgy, who lives by begging, and Bess. Its best-known songs are *Summertime, I Got Plenty o' Nothing* and *It Ain't Necessarily So*. Sidney *Poitier and Dorothy Dandridge were the stars of the film version (1959).

ˈ**pork** ˌ**barrel** *n* (*AmE infml*) a source of government money for projects which are designed to win votes and not necessarily for the public good: *The new road was a pork barrel that nobody needed.* ○ *pork-barrel politics*. Compare LOGROLLING.

ˌ**Porky** ˈ**Pig** a US film cartoon character. He is a pig that stutters (= speaks with a fault so that he repeats the beginning of some words) and was created by *Warner Brothers for the **Looney Tunes* series. All **Looney Tunes* and *Merry Melodies* cartoons end with Porky saying 'Tha-tha-tha-that's all folks!'

ˈ**porridge** *n* [U] a type of soft food made by boiling oats (= grains from a plant that grows in cool countries) in water or milk and eaten hot, usually for breakfast. It is a traditional Scottish food, eaten with salt, but it is now eaten in many countries with sugar. In Britain generally it is less often eaten for breakfast than it used to be.

ˈ***Porridge*** a British comedy television series set in a prison, broadcast by the *BBC from 1974 to 1977. Ronnie *Barker played the role of an experienced prisoner, and much of the humour came from the clever ways in which he influenced the prison officers and the other prisoners to his advantage. *Porridge* is a British *slang word for time spent in prison.

ˌCole ˈ**Porter** /ˌkəʊl ˈpɔːtə(r); *AmE* ˌkoʊl ˈpɔːrtər/ (1892–1964) a US writer of popular songs with clever words for *Broadway musical shows and *Hollywood films. His shows included *Anything Goes* (1934) and *Kiss Me, Kate* (1948), and his films included *High Society* (1956). Among his best-known songs are *Let's Do It* (1928), *I Get A Kick Out of You* (1934), *Night and Day* (1932), *Begin the Beguine* (1935) and *True Love* (1956).

ˈ**Portishead** /ˈpɔːtɪshed; *AmE* ˈpɔːrtɪshed/ a British pop group formed in 1993. Their songs are particularly slow and sad, dealing with pain and loss, as on their first album, *Dummy* (1994).

ˈ**Portland** /ˈpɔːtlənd; *AmE* ˈpɔːrtlənd/ **1** the largest city in the US state of *Oregon. It is on the Williamette River. *Lewis and Clark camped there in 1805, and it was settled in 1851. It is an industrial port and a centre for car imports and companies that build ships. The city was named after Portland, *Maine. **2** the largest city in the US state of *Maine. It is on Casco Bay, and many imports for Montreal, Canada, land there. Portland has companies that build ships and sell fish. It was settled about 1632 and was the state capital from 1820 to 1832.

ˌ**Portland ce**ˈ**ment** /ˌpɔːtlənd; *AmE* ˌpɔːrtlənd/ *n* [U] the most common type of cement used today, made from chalk and clay. It was invented in England in the early 19th century. When it is hard its colour is like that of **Portland stone**, a type of stone from the Isle of Portland in *Dorset used to make grand buildings such as *St Paul's Cathedral.

ˌ**Portobello** ˈ**Road** /ˌpɔːtəbeləʊ; *AmE* ˌpɔːrtəbeloʊ/ a street in the *Notting Hill district of west London. It is well known for its market, which sells food, clothes and second-hand goods. On Saturdays the second-hand area of the market attracts many tourists. In the late 20th century it became a very fashionable street, and many cafés, restaurants and antique shops opened beside the market: *I bought this old lampshade in the Portobello Road.*

the ˈ**Port of ˈLondon Auˈthority** /ˈlʌndən/ (*also* the **PLA**) the organization that operates the port of London. It controls all business on the *Thames between west London and the sea, but is mainly concerned with the docks at Tilbury, east of London. The authority used to be a trust (= a public organization that is independent of the government) but it was sold to private owners in the 1990s.

ˌ**Porton ˈDown** /ˌpɔːtn; *AmE* ˌpɔːrtn/ the usual name for the Centre for Applied Microbiology and Research at Porton, near *Salisbury in southern England. It is a British government centre for studying chemical and biological weapons. In the late 20th century many people protested against the government being involved in this type of research, and against the experiments on live animals that take place there.

ˈ**Portsmouth** /ˈpɔːtsməθ; *AmE* ˈpɔːrtsməθ/ a city and port on the south coast of England. It is the main base of the *Royal Navy and contains the Royal Naval Museum which has several famous old ships including the **Mary Rose* and the **Victory*.

ˌ**Port ˈSunlight** a small town near *Liverpool, England, built by Lord *Leverhulme at the end of the 19th century for the people working in his soap factory. It was a 'model village', designed and built to high standards, and meant to be copied by others.

ˌEmily ˈ**Post**[1] /ˈpəʊst; *AmE* ˈpoʊst/ (1873–1960) a US expert on manners and correct social behaviour. Americans still use her best-known book, *Etiquette* (1922). Post also had a radio programme and wrote a regular newspaper column which was printed each day in more than 200 newspapers.

ˌWiley ˈ**Post**[2] /ˌwaɪli ˈpəʊst; *AmE* ˈpoʊst/ (1899–1935) a US pilot of early aircraft. He was the first person to fly around the world alone, in 1933. He died with a famous passenger, Will *Rogers, when their plane crashed near Point Barrow, *Alaska.

ˈ**postal ˌdistrict** *n* a district of a British town or city that has been given a particular code by the *Post Office. Most postal districts have one or two letters for the town, and a number for the district. For example, the districts of Oxford are OX1, OX2, etc. In London, the letters represent an area. N1, for example, is in north London and SW8 is in south-west London.

P

postal services

Most letters and packages **posted** in Britain are dealt with by the ***Post Office**, a public authority. It is divided into three parts, the ***Royal Mail**, which delivers letters, **Parcelforce** and **Datapost**, which deliver larger packages, and ***Post Office Counters**, which manages the country's many **post offices**. As well as selling stamps, post offices take in letters and packages that are to be sent by special delivery. Post offices also sell vehicle and television licences, pay out pensions and child benefit money, and sell greetings cards and stationery. In villages they are often combined with a newsagent's and general store. In recent years, many smaller post offices have been closed because they do not make a profit, though this often led to protests from local people.

Mail (= letters, bills, etc.) is often called *post* in British English. When sending a letter, people can choose between two levels of service, **first class** or the cheaper **second class**. Normally, first-class mail is delivered the day after it is posted and second-class mail within two or three days. Letters are posted in red **postboxes**, also called **letter boxes**. Each has a sign giving times of **collections**. Postmen also deliver mail each morning direct to homes and businesses. They put the mail through a flap in the door, which is also called a *letter box*. In the country they travel round in red vans, but in towns and villages it is common to see a postman on a bicycle.

The system that deals with mail in the US, the **US Postal Service (USPS)**, is an independent part of the government. Its head is the **Postmaster General**. **Mail carriers**, sometimes called **mailmen** though many are women, deliver mail to homes and businesses once a day. Most homes have **mailboxes** fixed outside, near the door. People whose houses are a long way from the road have a special **rural mailbox** by the road. This has a flag which the mail carrier raises so that the people in the house can see when they have mail. To mail (= send) a letter, people leave it on top of their own mailbox or put it in one of the many blue mailboxes in cities and towns. Every address in the US includes an abbreviation for the name of the state and a **ZIP code**, which is used to help sort the mail. Post offices sell stamps and deal with mail that has to be insured. Most cities have one post office which stays open until late. Americans complain about the Postal Service, but it usually does an efficient job at a reasonable price.

In both Britain and the US only the Post Office or Postal Service can deliver mail, though private **couriers**, are allowed to offer **express** services. This competition has hurt the postal services. They have lost further business as electronic communication, such as e-mail, has become more common.

ˌ**post exˈchange** ⇨ PX.

ˈ**Post-it**™ /ˈpəʊst; *AmE* ˈpoʊst/ a product name for small pads of paper with a strip of special glue on the back of each piece which allows it to be stuck to something and later removed easily. Post-its can have many uses, e.g. for writing notes or marking a place in a book, etc. They are available in different colours and sizes and are made by the *3M Company.

ˌ**Postman ˈPat** a toy character in a series of children's books and *BBC television programmes written by Ivor Wood (1932–) and John Cunliffe (1933–). He is a postman (= a person whose job is delivering letters) in a village in the English countryside, who is very friendly to everybody he meets. He also has a black and white cat called Jess.

ˌ**postman's ˈknock** (*AmE* **post office**) *n* [U] a traditional children's game, played e.g. at parties, in which one player pretends to be a postman delivering a letter, knocks on a door, and kisses the player who opens it.

ˌ**postmaster ˈgeneral** (*pl* **postmasters general**) *n* [usu sing] **1** the person in charge of the British *Post Office. **2** the person in charge of the US Postal Service.

the ˈ**Post ˌOffice** the organization responsible for post office services in Britain. It has more than 20 000 branches, from large post offices in cities to **sub-post offices** in small towns, which are sometimes part of a shop selling other goods. British people use their local post office to send letters and parcels, and also to pay bills, collect their *pensions and pay for official documents such as *tax discs and *television licences. ⇨ note at POSTAL SERVICES. See also GPO.

ˌ**Post Office ˈCounters** the department of the British *Post Office that manages individual post offices, sells stamps, issues official documents and licences, and acts as an agent for *National Savings and *Girobank. ⇨ note at POSTAL SERVICES. See also PARCELFORCE, ROYAL MAIL.

the **poˈtato ˌfamine** a disaster that happened in Ireland between 1845 and 1847 when most of the potato crop was destroyed by a plant disease. Potatoes were the main food in Ireland then, and about a million people died for lack of food. At least another million people left Ireland for Britain and America because of the famine.

ˌ**Pot ˈNoodle**™ *n* a type of food, usually sold in plastic cups, which consists of dried noodles (= long thin strips of mixed flour and water that become soft when cooked), meat and vegetables, with different flavours. Pot Noodles are cheap and quick to prepare, simply by adding hot water.

the ˌ**Potomac ˈRiver** /pəˌtəʊmæk; *AmE* pəˌtoʊmæk/ a river in the eastern US. It begins in the *Appalachian Mountains in *West Virginia and flows 285 miles/459 kilometres past *Harpers Ferry, *Mount Vernon and Washington, DC, into Chesapeake Bay on the Atlantic coast.

ˌBeatrix ˈ**Potter¹** /ˌbɪətrɪks ˈpɒtə(r); *AmE* ˌbɪrtrɪks ˈpɑːtər/ (1866–1943) an English writer of children's books about the adventures of animals, including *Peter Rabbit, Tom Kitten, Benjamin Bunny, Jemima Puddle-Duck, and many others. She also painted the illustrations for the books, which are still popular with children today. Though born in London, she spent most of her later life in the *Lake District.

FIRST he ate some lettuces and some French beans; and then he ate some radishes;

a page from Beatrix Potter's The Tale of Peter Rabbit

ˌDennis ˈ**Potter²** /ˈpɒtə(r); *AmE* ˈpɑːtər/ (1935–94) an English writer of television plays, many of them broadcast in several parts. He is well known for writing dramatic stories about relationships, often set in the recent past, in which the characters often sing popular songs of the period. He is considered one of the most important television writers of his time. His best-known plays include *Pennies from Heaven* (1978), *The Singing Detective* (1986) and *Lipstick on Your Collar* (1993).

the ˈ**Potteries** the area of the English *Midlands around *Stoke-on-Trent. It has been an important centre of the pottery industry since the 17th century. See also FIVE TOWNS.

ˌEzra ˈ**Pound** /ˌezrə ˈpaʊnd/ (1885–1972) a US poet who had a great influence on other modern poets, including T S *Eliot, Robert *Frost, W B *Yeats and James *Joyce. He moved to Britain in 1907 and then lived in France and Italy. He made broadcasts praising Fascist ideas during *World War II and was accused of helping the enemy. After the war, he was kept in a US mental hospital from 1946 to 1958 and then returned to Italy. Pound's best-known poems are the *Cantos* (1925–60).

ˌColin ˈ**Powell¹** /ˌkəʊlɪn ˈpaʊəl; *AmE* ˌkoʊlɪn/ (1937–) a senior *African-American soldier who became head of the *Joint Chiefs of Staff (1989–93) and directed policy for the Allied Forces during the *Gulf War. General Powell held the highest rank of any African-American officer in history. He had earlier fought in the *Vietnam War and been a member of the *National Security Council (1987–9). Many Americans wanted him to stand as a candidate for US *President in 1996, but Powell refused, saying he was not a politician.

Colin Powell

ˌEnoch ˈ**Powell²** /ˈpaʊəl/ (1912–98) an English politician. He is mainly remembered for his opposition to the government policy in the late 1960s of allowing people who were not white to come from other countries to live and work in Britain. One of his speeches came to be known as the 'rivers of blood' speech because he predicted violent fights in the streets between different races (though he did not actually use the words 'rivers of blood'). Powell was a *Conservative *Member of Parliament from 1950 to 1974 and an *Ulster Unionist *Member of Parliament from 1974 to 1987.

ˌMichael ˈ**Powell³** /ˈpaʊəl/ (1905–90) an English film director. He is best known for the films he made with his partner Emeric Pressburger in the 1940s and 1950s. Films such as *The Life and Death of Colonel Blimp* (1943) and *Black Narcissus* (1946) are considered among the greatest British films of the period.

The ˌ***Power and the*** ˈ***Glory*** a novel (1940) by Graham *Greene. It tells the story of a *Roman Catholic priest trying to escape from Mexico at a time when his religion has been made illegal. He is caught and killed when he returns to help a dying man. The novel, considered by many people to be Greene's best, examines his usual themes of religion, moral choices and human weakness.

ˈ**PowerGen** /ˈpaʊədʒen; *AmE* ˈpaʊərdʒen/ the smaller of the two companies that began supplying electricity in England and Wales in 1991 when the electricity industry was sold to private owners. Compare NATIONAL POWER.

ˈ**Powhatan** /ˈpaʊətæn/ (*c.* 1550–1618) the *Native-American leader of the Powhatan people and the Powhatan Confederacy of 30 groups in *Virginia and part of *Maryland. He was the father of *Pocahontas, and after she married an Englishman Powhatan made peace with the *Jamestown community.

ˈ**Powys** /ˈpaʊɪs/ a large region in central Wales, on the border with England. It was a county from 1974 to 1996, and is now the *unitary authority responsible for local government and public services.

PPO /ˌpiː piː ˈəʊ; *AmE* ˈoʊ/ ⇨ PREFERRED PROVIDER ORGANIZATION.

PPS /ˌpiː piː ˈes/ ⇨ PARLIAMENTARY PRIVATE SECRETARY: *the Prime Minister's PPS.*

ˈ**prairie dog** *n* a small animal found mainly in the western US and northern Mexico. It makes a harsh sound like a dog's bark. Large family groups live underground but come out for the sun and to eat. They stand upright on their back legs to look for danger.

a prairie dog

P

ˈPraise the ˈLord and ˈPass the Ammuˈnition a popular US song during *World War II, written in 1942 by Frank Loesser. It was based on words said by a US Navy chaplain (= priest) during the Japanese attack on *Pearl Harbor.

ˌTerry ˈ**Pratchett** /ˈprætʃɪt/ (1948–) an English author. His best-known books are humorous novels about Discworld, a strange, flat planet inhabited by imaginary beings such as witches and dragons. They include *The Colour of Magic* (1983) and *Small Gods* (1992).

Pre-Columbian North America

Pre-Columbian means 'before the time of *Columbus', and refers to the period of North American history before the region was discovered by Christopher Columbus at the end of the 15th century.

The first people to arrive in America crossed over a strip of land, known as Beringia, between America and Eurasia about 40 000 years ago. It is now covered by the *Bering Strait. The people were **nomads** who hunted large animals such as mammoths and bison. They had only basic tools made of stone.

About 6000 BC some groups of people began to rely more on gathering wild fruits, nuts and vegetables for food. They also began to settle in permanent villages. They made a wider range of tools, from stone and animal bone, simple copper items, and baskets and nets from wild plants. This period, which is known as the **archaic period**, lasted from *c.* 6000 to 1000 BC, though in some parts of North America, especially the desert regions of *California, people had a similar lifestyle until the arrival of the first Europeans.

Elsewhere, a major change in society began from about 1000 BC. Although **hunting and gathering** were still the main source of food, agriculture began about this time. Goods were taken long distances across the country to be traded. Society became much more complex and developed differently in different regions. The people buried their dead in earth mounds, similar to the *barrows of *Stone Age Britain, and often put precious objects in the mounds with them. These developments are known as the **Woodland tradition**.

The period from 800 AD until the arrival of European settlers was one of even greater change. More widespread agriculture, and the growing of crops such as corn, beans and squashes, allowed the development of much larger villages and towns. Cahokia, *Illinois, may have had a population of up to 30 000 people. In these settlements temples were built on top of earth mounds. More than 120 temples were built at Cahokia alone. The style may have been influenced by temples in Central America. Large circles of wooden posts have also been found, which may have acted as a calendar, similar to *Stonehenge in England. Another important site is Moundville, *Alabama, built by people now known as the ***moundbuilders**. About 3 000 people were buried at this site, many with pottery and copper axes.

In *Colorado and *Arizona people began to live in houses built with adobe (= mud bricks) in the sides of cliffs. The best preserved of these can still be seen at ***Mesa Verde**. Canals and ditches were dug to take water into the desert so that corn, vegetables and also cotton could be grown there. They made baskets and sandals, and elaborate painted pottery. The Anasazi were the most developed people and traded their goods as far away as Mexico for feathers and copper. They were the ancestors of the modern *Pueblo people. In the 16th century the Athabaskan tribes moved down from Canada. These were the ancestors of the modern *Navajo and *Apache tribes.

Although *Columbus is traditionally believed to have been the first European to discover America there is good evidence that *Vikings had settled in Canada long before. The remains of a Viking settlement have been found at L'Anse aux Meadows, in Newfoundland, Canada. The Viking stories say that while they were in America they met 'Skraelings', probably *Inuit peoples.

The arrival of people from Europe caused serious problems to the pre-Columbian peoples. The Europeans took their land in order to build settlements, and over time they controlled almost all of North America, putting the native peoples on a few **reservations**. In addition, the Europeans brought diseases that the Native Americans could not overcome, and many died.

White Americans today know about Native-American peoples, or Indians as many still call them, from the time when they came into contact with Europeans. Most know little about, and have little interest in, the Americans of the pre-Columbian period.

---

preˌferred proˈvider organiˌzation *n* (*abbr* **PPO**) (in the US) a special type of *health maintenance organization (HMO) which provides health insurance for groups. Companies often pay most of the cost for their employees.

Preˈliminary Schoˈlastic ˈAptitude Test ⇨ PSAT.

the ˈ**Premier Diˌvision** the top ten teams in Scottish football, run by the Scottish Football League. There are three divisions below it, also run by the League. ⇨ note at FOOTBALL – BRITISH STYLE.

the ˈ**Premier League** the top 20 teams in English and Welsh football, run by the *Football Association. There are three divisions below it, run by the *Football League. The Premier League, which was formerly Division 1 of the Football League, took the name in 1992. ⇨ note at FOOTBALL – BRITISH STYLE.

ˈ**Premium Bond** (*also* ˌ**Premium ˈSavings Bond**) *n* (in Britain) a document with a number on it which can be bought from the government and which offers a chance of winning money as a prize every month. Unlike *National Lottery tickets the Premium Bonds can be sold back to the government at any time. They were introduced in 1956 as a way of encouraging people to save money. See also ERNIE.

preˈparatory school (*also* ˈ**prep school**) *n* **1** (in Britain) a private school for students aged between 7 and 13, whose parents pay for their education. Preparatory schools prepare their students for the *Common Entrance exam, which allows them (if they pass) to go on to a *public school(1). Most preparatory schools are for either boys or girls, and some students may live at the school rather than at home. **2** (in the US) a private school that prepares students for college.

ˈ**preppy** (*also* ˈ**preppie**) /ˈprepi/ *n* [C] (*AmE infml*) a person who attends an expensive private school or looks like such a person (e.g. has short hair, dresses neatly, etc.).

▶ **preppy** *adj* typical of or looking like a preppy; neat and fashionable: *the preppy look* ◦ *preppy clothes.*

ˈ**prep school** ⇨ PREPARATORY SCHOOL.

ˌ**Pre-ˈRaphaelite** /ˌpriːˈræfəlaɪt/ *n* any one of a group of late 19th-century British painters who worked in a style influenced by Italian painting of the period before Raphael. The group included John Everett *Millais, Dante Gabriel *Rossetti and Holman *Hunt (who formed what they called the **Pre-Raphaelite Brotherhood**). Other artists associated with the group included William *Morris and Edward *Burne-Jones. Their subjects were usually

Presidents of the United States

1	1789–97	George Washington	*Federalist*	**20**	1881	James A Garfield	*Republican*
2	1797–1801	John Adams	*Federalist*	**21**	1881–85	Chester A Arthur	*Republican*
3	1801–09	Thomas Jefferson	*Democratic Republican*	**22**	1885–89	Grover Cleveland	*Democrat*
4	1809–17	James Madison	*Democratic Republican*	**23**	1889–93	Benjamin Harrison	*Republican*
5	1817–25	James Monroe	*Democratic Republican*	**24**	1893–97	Grover Cleveland	*Democrat*
6	1825–29	John Quincy Adams	*Democratic Republican*	**25**	1897–1901	William McKinley	*Republican*
7	1829–37	Andrew Jackson	*Democrat*	**26**	1901–09	Theodore Roosevelt	*Republican*
8	1837–41	Martin Van Buren	*Democrat*	**27**	1909–13	William H Taft	*Republican*
9	1841	William H Harrison	*Whig*	**28**	1913–21	Woodrow Wilson	*Democrat*
10	1841–45	John Tyler	*Whig, then Democrat*	**29**	1921–23	Warren G Harding	*Republican*
11	1845–49	James K Polk	*Democrat*	**30**	1923–29	Calvin Coolidge	*Republican*
12	1849–50	Zachary Taylor	*Whig*	**31**	1929–33	Herbert Hoover	*Republican*
13	1850–53	Millard Fillmore	*Whig*	**32**	1933–45	Franklin D Roosevelt	*Democrat*
14	1853–57	Franklin Pierce	*Democrat*	**33**	1945–53	Harry S Truman	*Democrat*
15	1857–61	James Buchanan	*Democrat*	**34**	1953–61	Dwight D Eisenhower	*Republican*
16	1861–65	Abraham Lincoln	*Republican*	**35**	1961–63	John F Kennedy	*Democrat*
17	1865–69	Andrew Johnson	*Democrat*	**36**	1963–69	Lyndon B Johnson	*Democrat*
18	1869–77	Ulysses S Grant	*Republican*	**37**	1969–74	Richard M Nixon	*Republican*
19	1877–81	Rutherford B Hayes	*Republican*	**38**	1974–77	Gerald R Ford	*Republican*
				39	1977–81	James Earl Carter	*Democrat*
				40	1981–89	Ronald W Reagan	*Republican*
				41	1989–93	George Bush	*Republican*
				42	1993–	Bill Clinton	*Democrat*

from literature or the Bible, and were painted in bright colours with realistic detail.

▶ **ˌPre-ˈRaphaelite** /ˌpriːˈræfəlaɪt/ *adj* of or in the style of the Pre-Raphaelites: *She had a certain Pre-Raphaelite beauty.*

ˌPresbyˈterian *adj* (of a Protestant Church, especially the national Church of Scotland) governed by senior members (**elders** or **presbyters**) who are all equal in rank. The Presbyterian Church in Scotland has been the established Protestant Church since 1690. In England the *United Reformed Church is a Presbyterian Church, and there are other Presbyterian Churches in the US, Ireland, Wales, Switzerland and elsewhere. Compare EPISCOPAL CHURCH.

▶ **Presbyterian** *n* a member of a Presbyterian Church.

Presbyterianism *n* [U] Presbyterian beliefs, or the Presbyterian system of Church government.

ˌJohn ˈ**Prescott** /ˈpreskɒt; *AmE* ˈpreskɑːt/ (1938–) a British *Labour politician. He began his career in the *merchant navy before becoming a *Member of Parliament in 1970. From 1994 to 1997 he was deputy leader of the Labour Party under Tony *Blair, and became deputy *Prime Minister after Labour's victory in the 1997 general election. He is now also Minister for the Environment, Transport and the Regions.

preˈscription charge *n* [usu pl] (in Britain) money paid (usually to a chemist) for medicine supplied on the *National Health Service. The amount paid is the same for any medicine, and is usually less than its actual cost. Some groups, e.g. old people, children, pregnant women and the unemployed, do not have to pay prescription charges.

president

The President is the **head of state** of the US and is part of the ***executive branch** of government. He (the President has so far always been a man) decides US policy on foreign affairs and is the **commander-in-chief** of the armed forces. He can appoint heads of government *departments and federal judges. *Congress must ask the President to approve new laws, although it is possible to pass a law without the President's approval. Each year, the President gives a *State of the Union Address to Congress. The President works in what may be the most famous office in the world, the *Oval Office in the ***White House** in Washington, DC.

The *Constitution requires that a president should be at least 35 years old, and have been born in the US. It is often said that the President is **directly elected** by the people, and this is true in comparison with countries like Britain where the *Prime Minister is selected by *Members of Parliament. In fact, although people vote for one of the candidates for President, an *electoral college makes the final choice (⇨ article at ELECTIONS IN THE US). A president can serve a maximum of two **terms** (four years each).

Americans have a lot of respect for the office of President, and they are shocked when the president is believed to have done something wrong or illegal. In such a case it is possible for Congress to **impeach** the President (= remove him from his job). Congress attempted to impeach President Richard *Nixon during the *Watergate scandal of the 1970s but he decided to resign before the impeachment process was completed. In 1999 President Bill *Clinton was tried by the Senate after admitting that he had had a sexual relationship with Monica Lewinsky, having earlier denied it. Many Americans continued to support him and the Senate decided that he was not guilty of 'high crimes and misdemeanours' (= offences for which a person can be impeached).

the ˌ**Presiˈdential ˈMedal of ˈFreedom** the highest US award given to a person who is not in the armed forces. It was established as the Medal of Freedom in 1945 and was given its new name in 1963 by President *Kennedy[4]. People who have received the award in recent years include Colin *Powell, Thurgood *Marshall and Arthur *Ashe.

ˈ**Presidents' Day** (in the US) a holiday on the third Monday in February. It celebrates the birthdays of both George *Washington (22 February) and Abraham *Lincoln (12 February). Some states celebrate the two birthdays separately.

pre,siding 'officer /prɪ,zaɪdɪŋ/ *n* (in Britain) an official in charge of a polling station (= place where people go to vote) during an election. ⇨ article at ELECTIONS TO PARLIAMENT.

,Elvis **'Presley** /,elvɪs 'prezli/ (1935–77) a US pop singer and guitar player, sometimes called the 'King of Rock and Roll'. In the late 1950s and the 1960s he was probably the most successful popular singer in the world. He helped to make *African-American music popular with young white people and was an influence on many popular singers, including the *Beatles and the *Rolling Stones. He was also known as 'Elvis the Pelvis' because of the way he moved his lower body when he sang. His songs included *Hound Dog* (1956), *All Shook Up* (1957), *It's Now or Never* (1960) and *Good Luck Charm* (1962). He appeared in several films, including *Jailhouse Rock* (1957), *Girls! Girls! Girls!* (1962) and *Viva Las Vegas* (1964). Presley died at his home, *Graceland, after accidentally taking too many drugs, though many people claim or pretend that he is still alive. In 1998 he was chosen for the Country Music *Hall of fame.

the **'Press Associ,ation** (*abbr* the **PA**) a leading British news organization, established in 1868. Its job is to gather news about Britain and supply it, together with photographs, to newspapers, television stations and radio stations in Britain and abroad.

the **,Press Com'plaints Com,mission** a British organization formed in 1991 to deal with complaints about the behaviour of the press, especially its attempts to find out about people's private lives. It replaced a similar organization, the Press Council.

pressure groups

Pressure groups work on behalf of a particular section of society, e.g. children or nurses, or for a particular issue or cause, e.g. banning the use of landmines. Groups that work on behalf of a section of society are sometimes called **interest groups**. Those that work for a particular cause are known as **promotional groups** or simply pressure groups. These pressure groups operate in a similar way in Britain and in the US.

There are several types of interest groups. ***Trade unions** and **labor unions** represent workers in industry and are mostly concerned with their wages and welfare. **Professional bodies** such as the *British Medical Association are similar to trade unions. In Britain several ***watchdogs** have been established by Act of Parliament to monitor (= check the performance of) certain industries, e.g. *OFGAS, which oversees the gas industry on behalf of gas users. Many promotional groups are linked to ***charities**. Since charities are not allowed to take part in party political activity, many set up a related organization to act as a pressure group. In the US many pressure groups form ***political action committees** which are allowed to give money to political campaigns. Well-known promotional groups include *Friends of the Earth and *Amnesty International. There are also many smaller groups, usually less permanent, which are formed to protest about local issues.

Pressure groups aim to influence the government to the benefit of their members or the cause they support. They may draw attention to problems by asking people to sign a petition (= a formal request signed by many people), by giving media interviews, or by organizing demonstrations that will attract public and media attention. Many groups try to get the support of well-known people such as pop stars. They also try to persuade politicians to support their cause and to speak about it in *Parliament or *Congress, a practice known as ***lobbying**. More established pressure groups may be consulted by a government department or take part in working groups when changes to the law are being considered.

the 'Battle of **,Preston'pans** /,prestən'pænz/ a battle fought in 1745 during the *Forty-Five Rebellion, in which the army of *Bonny Prince Charlie defeated the English at Prestonpans, near Edinburgh, Scotland.

'Prestwick /'prestwɪk/ a town in *Strathclyde region, south-west Scotland. It has an international airport and port, and is famous for its golf course, where the *Open was held for many years until 1924.

the **Pre,vention of 'Terrorism Act** a British *Act of Parliament introduced on a temporary basis in 1984 to prevent terrorism in Northern Ireland. It gives the police power to arrest anyone suspected of terrorist activities (especially members of the *IRA) and to hold them for 48 hours without giving a reason. It may also be used to make certain kinds of political or military group illegal.

,André **'Previn** /,ɑːndreɪ 'prevɪn/ (1929–) a US conductor, born in Germany, who also plays the piano and writes music. He has directed orchestras in London, Houston, Los Angeles and Pittsburgh, and has done a lot to make classical music more popular. He has also written film music, winning *Oscars for his work on *Gigi* (1958), **Porgy and Bess*, *Irma La Douce* (1963) and **My Fair Lady*. Previn was formerly married to the actor Mia *Farrow.

,Leontyne **'Price** /,liːɒntiːn 'praɪs; *AmE* ,liːɑːntiːn/ (1927–) an *African-American opera singer known for the great range of her voice. She was the first African American to sing with the La Scala Opera Company of Milan (in 1959) and then became a leading singer with the *Metropolitan Opera (1961–85). Price was known especially for her performances in operas by Verdi.

*The **,Price is 'Right*** a television game show in which competitors try to guess the price of products, and the one with the closest guess wins. It began in the US in 1956 and is now called *The New Price is Right*, presented on *NBC by Bob Barker. Other countries, including Britain, have their own versions. The British one is now called *Bruce's Price is Right* (1995–) and is presented by Bruce Forsyth.

,Pride and 'Prejudice a novel (1813) by Jane *Austen. Its main characters are the sensible and intelligent Elizabeth Bennet and the rich and handsome Fitzwilliam Darcy. Elizabeth at first dislikes Darcy because of his pride, but they finally recognize each other's good qualities and fall in love. The book ends with their marriage and that of another couple, Elizabeth's sister Jane and Darcy's friend Charles Bingley. It is one of Austen's most popular books and has been filmed several times.

,J B **'Priestley**[1] /'priːstli/ (John Boynton Priestley 1894–1984) an English writer. His best-known works are probably the novel *The Good Companions* (1929) about a small theatre company, and his play *An Inspector Calls* (1947), but he wrote many other popular novels and plays, often comedies about English life and society. He was also known for his critical writings on English literature and his radio broadcasts during *World War II.

,Joseph **'Priestley**[2] /'priːstli/ (1733–1804) an English scientist, priest and writer. His most famous achievement was the discovery of the chemical element oxygen (which he called 'dephlogisticated air'). He attacked the established Church, and was one of the founders of Unitarianism (= a form of Christianity). His support for the American and French Revolutions led to protests in which his house was

Prime Ministers of Great Britain

1721–42	Sir Robert Walpole	*Whig*
1742–43	Earl of Wilmington	*Whig*
1743–54	Henry Pelham	*Whig*
1754–56	Duke of Newcastle	*Whig*
1756–57	Duke of Devonshire	*Whig*
1757–62	Duke of Newcastle	*Whig*
1762–63	Earl of Bute	*Tory*
1763–65	George Grenville	*Whig*
1765–66	Marquis of Rockingham	*Whig*
1766–68	Earl of Chatham	*Whig*
1768–70	Duke of Grafton	*Whig*
1770–82	Lord North	*Tory*
1782	Marquis of Rockingham	*Whig*
1782–83	Earl of Shelburne	*Whig*
1783	Duke of Portland	*(coalition)*
1783–1801	William Pitt	*Tory*
1801–04	Henry Addington	*Tory*
1804–06	William Pitt	*Tory*
1806–07	Lord William Grenville	*Whig*
1807–09	Duke of Portland	*Tory*
1809–12	Spencer Perceval	*Tory*
1812–27	Earl of Liverpool	*Tory*
1827	George Canning	*Tory*
1827–28	Viscount Goderich	*Tory*
1828–30	Duke of Wellington	*Tory*
1830–34	Earl Grey	*Whig*
1834	Viscount Melbourne	*Whig*
1834	Duke of Wellington	*Tory*
1834–35	Sir Robert Peel	*Conservative*
1835–41	Viscount Melbourne	*Whig*
1841–46	Sir Robert Peel	*Conservative*
1846–52	Lord John Russell	*Whig*
1852	Earl of Derby	*Conservative*
1852–55	Earl of Aberdeen	*(coalition)*
1855–58	Viscount Palmerston	*Liberal*
1858–59	Earl of Derby	*Conservative*
1859–65	Viscount Palmerston	*Liberal*
1865–66	Earl Russell	*Liberal*
1866–68	Earl of Derby	*Conservative*
1868	Benjamin Disraeli	*Conservative*
1868–74	William Ewart Gladstone	*Liberal*
1874–80	Benjamin Disraeli	*Conservative*
1880–85	William Ewart Gladstone	*Liberal*
1885–86	Marquis of Salisbury	*Conservative*
1886	William Ewart Gladstone	*Liberal*
1886–92	Marquis of Salisbury	*Conservative*
1892–94	William Ewart Gladstone	*Liberal*
1894–95	Earl of Rosebery	*Liberal*
1895–1902	Marquis of Salisbury	*Conservative*
1902–05	Arthur James Balfour	*Conservative*
1905–08	Sir Henry Campbell-Bannerman	*Liberal*
1908–16	Herbert Henry Asquith	*Liberal*
1916–22	David Lloyd George	*(coalition)*
1922–23	Andrew Bonar Law	*Conservative*
1923–24	Stanley Baldwin	*Conservative*
1924	James Ramsay MacDonald	*Labour*
1924–29	Stanley Baldwin	*Conservative*
1929–35	James Ramsay MacDonald	*(coalition)*
1935–37	Stanley Baldwin	*(coalition)*
1937–40	Neville Chamberlain	*(coalition)*
1940–45	Winston Churchill	*(coalition)*
1945–51	Clement Attlee	*Labour*
1951–55	Sir Winston Churchill	*Conservative*
1955–57	Sir Anthony Eden	*Conservative*
1957–63	Harold Macmillan	*Conservative*
1963–64	Sir Alexander Douglas-Home	*Conservative*
1964–70	Harold Wilson	*Labour*
1970–74	Edward Heath	*Conservative*
1974–76	Harold Wilson	*Labour*
1976–79	James Callaghan	*Labour*
1979–90	Margaret Thatcher	*Conservative*
1990–97	John Major	*Conservative*
1997–	Tony Blair	*Labour*

burned down, and he left England in 1794 to settle in the US.

ˈ**primary** (*also* ˌ**primary eˈlection**) *n* (in the US) an election in a state to appoint representatives of a political party who will attend the party conference, or to select party candidates for a future election. Candidates for US President are chosen after a long series of state primaries: *Bobby Kennedy was assassinated after he won the California primary.* ⇨ article at ELECTIONS IN THE US.

ˈ**primary school** *n* [C, U] (in Britain) a *state school for children aged between 5 and 11. Primary schools often consist of a separate *infant school and *junior school. *First schools are a type of primary school for children aged between 5 and 10. ⇨ article at EDUCATION IN BRITAIN.

the ˌ**Primate of All ˈEngland** the official title of the *Archbishop of Canterbury in the *Church of England.

the ˌ**Primate of All ˈIreland** /ˈaɪələnd; *AmE* ˈaɪərlənd/ the official title of each of the two Archbishops of Armagh in Northern Ireland. One is the *Roman Catholic Archbishop and the other is the Anglican (*Church of England) Archbishop, and each is head of their Church in the whole of Ireland.

the ˌ**Primate of ˈEngland** the official title of the *Archbishop of York in the *Church of England.

prime minister

Originally, the king or queen could choose anyone they liked to be chief or 'Prime' Minister, and for a long time the prime minister could come from either the *House of Lords or the *House of Commons. In recent years the Prime Minister has always come from the Commons and the king or queen gives the job to the leader of the party with the largest number of *MPs. Lord Home, who became leader of the Conservative Party in 1963, was the first politician to be allowed to renounce a *peerage (= give up an inherited title and status) to become Prime Minister (as Sir Alec *Douglas-Home).

The Prime Minister is by tradition *First Lord of the Treasury and Minister for the Civil Service. He or she chooses and presides over the ***Cabinet** and heads the government. The Prime Minister also chooses senior ministers and recommends their appointment to the king or queen. While other ministers are responsible for particular government *departments, the prime minister is concerned with policy as a whole. Cabinet committees usually report directly to him or her. The Prime Minister has regular meetings with the sovereign to inform him or her of the activities of the government.

The face and voice of the Prime Minister, informally called the PM, are familiar to everyone in the country through television, radio and newspapers. Public image is now very important, and specialist advisers are employed to make sure that the Prime Minister's appearance, manner and tone of voice show qualities that they think will appeal to the public. The prime minister usually lives at 10 *Downing Street, above the offices used by the Cabinet, and is often photographed outside the front door.

ˌPrime ˈMinister's ˈQuestions questions put to the British *Prime Minister in the *House of Commons for half an hour each week, on Wednesday afternoons. The questions are from both government and Opposition *Members of Parliament and are not known by the Prime Minister in advance. His answers often lead to noisy disagreement between members of parliament in different parties. The occasion is often broadcast on radio or television.

Prince /prɪns/ (1958–) a US pop singer and actor. In 1993 he changed his name into a symbol that nobody can pronounce, so many people now call him 'formerly Prince'. He was born Prince Rogers Nelson in Minneapolis. He has shocked a lot of people with his sexual songs and performances on stage. He was the star of the film *Purple Rain* (1984) and won an *Oscar for its music. He also wrote the music for *Batman* (1989).

ˌPrince ˈConsort a title sometimes given by a British queen to her husband during her rule. Prince *Albert, the husband of Queen *Victoria, was the most recent person to be given the title.

ˌPrince of ˈWales /ˈweɪlz/ a title given to the eldest son of a British king or queen, who becomes king after them. The title was first used in 1301 and is traditionally given together with the titles of Duke of *Cornwall and Earl of Chester. The present Prince of Wales is Prince *Charles. See also ICH DIEN.

ˌPrince ˈRegent the title of George, *Prince of Wales (later King *George IV), who ruled Britain from 1811 to 1820 while his father, King *George III, was mentally ill. *Regent Street and *Regent's Park in London are named after him, and the period 1811–20 is known as the *Regency.

the **ˌPrinces in the ˈTower** a name given to the two young sons of King *Edward IV, i.e. the boy king *Edward V and his brother Richard, Duke of *York[3](3) (1472–83), who went to live in the royal apartments (= private rooms) in the *Tower of London in 1483 after their father died. They disappeared, and some people believe they were murdered either by *Richard III, who had become king, or by *Henry VII. The bones of two young children found in the Tower and tested in 1933 are believed to be theirs. See also WHITE TOWER.

ˌPrincess of ˈWales /ˈweɪlz/ the title given to the wife of the British *Prince of Wales. Until her death in 1997 the title was held by Princess Diana, who married Prince *Charles (the Prince of Wales) in 1981.

ˌPrincess ˈRoyal the title usually given to the eldest daughter of a British king or queen. The present Princess Royal is Princess *Anne.

ˈPrinces Street the main street in *Edinburgh, Scotland, named after the princes who were sons of King *George III. On its north side it has shops and restaurants and on its south side there are large sloping gardens. Also on the south side is the Scott Monument, a very large *Gothic structure built in 1840–4 in memory of Sir Walter *Scott.

the **ˌPrince's ˈTrust** an organization established by Prince *Charles in 1976. It aims to help young people to develop their skills through programmes of training and employment, and gives grants of money to groups and individuals. It includes a number of other organizations doing similar work, such as the Queen's Silver Jubilee Trust and the Prince's Youth Business Trust, and it operates in several countries around the world.

ˌPrinceton Uniˈversity /ˌprɪnstən/ one of the oldest and most respected universities in the US. It was established in 1746 and is in Princeton, *New Jersey. Its presidents have included Jonathan *Edwards (1757–8) and Woodrow *Wilson (1902–10). Princeton is known for its studies in international affairs, and it has a special relationship with the *Institute for Advanced Study. See also IVY LEAGUE.

ˌprincipal ˈboy *n* the leading male part in a *pantomime, traditionally played by a young female actor. For example, Prince Charming is the principal boy in the pantomime **Cinderella*.

ˈPrinny /ˈprɪni/ a humorous name given to *George IV before he became king. The name comes from 'prince', since his title was *Prince of Wales.

prisons

Britain's system of justice relies heavily on **imprisonment** as a form of *punishment. Until the late 18th century conditions in prisons such as *Newgate were dirty and violent. In the 19th century conditions improved, thanks to the work of reformers like Elizabeth *Fry. New prisons were built, in which most prisoners had their own **cell** facing into a large central area. Many of these prisons, such as *Pentonville and *Strangeways, are still used today.

The type of prison in which criminals **serve their sentence** depends on their **category**. Category A prisoners are considered dangerous and are held in high-security closed prisons, such as *Wormwood Scrubs. Prisoners may be kept in **solitary confinement** if they are likely to harm others. Category B and C prisoners are also held in closed prisons. Category D prisoners are trusted not to escape and are sent to low-security **open prisons**. Prisoners **on remand** (= waiting for their trial) are held in **remand centres**, but problems of overcrowding have resulted in many of them being kept in prisons or police stations. Young people aged 15–20 are normally sent to ***young offender institutions**, sometimes called detention centres or youth custody centres. These have replaced the old *Borstals. However, if space is not available, young people are sometimes sent to adult prisons. A prison is run by a **governor** who is responsible to the *Home Office, and the prisoners are guarded by **warders**.

There is not enough space available in prisons for the number of people being given **custodial sentences**. Cells intended for one person now contain two or three. In the 1990s there were riots at several prisons because of poor living conditions. Despite this, some people think life in Britain's prisons is not hard enough. Some prisons are described as 'universities of crime', where prisoners gain new skills in breaking the law and have access to drugs.

In the US the federal and state governments have **prisons**, sometimes called **penitentiaries** or **correctional facilities**. *Counties and cities have **jails**. There are 92 federal prisons classified as minimum, low, medium or high security. There are about 100 000 **inmates** (= prisoners), and all who can must work. People are sent to a prison if their sentence is for several years. If the sentence is a year or less they are sent to jail. Some prisoners on **work release** are allowed to leave jail during the day to go to a job. Prisoners often spend the last few months of their sentence in a **halfway house** where they are helped to prepare for life outside prison.

There are more than 1.5 million people in US prisons and jails, about twice as many as ten years ago. The increased use of drugs may be partly responsible for this. Other problems include overcrowding, and the fact that the racial mix of people in prison does not reflect the population. Over 40% of prisoners are black, compared with 12% of the general population. Many people see this as evidence that African Americans are treated unfairly by the justice system and are more likely than white Americans to be sent to prison.

In the US people who are awaiting trial often do not go to prison but instead **make bail** (= pay money to the court) as a guarantee that they will return for the trial. People sent to prison as punishment rarely serve their full sentence but after some time are released **on parole**, which means they must report regularly to a government official. It is possible that two people who have committed the same crime may receive different punishments. To stop this happening some states have introduced **mandatory sentencing**, which means that the punishment for a crime is fixed by law.

ˌV S **ˈPritchett** /ˈprɪtʃɪt/ (Victor Sawdon Pritchett 1900–97) an English author. He is best remembered for his short stories, which are full of humorous criticism of British life, and for his writings about literature, e.g. *The Living Novel* (1946). He also wrote the life stories of several authors, including Chekhov, Turgenev and Balzac. He was made a *knight in 1975.

privacy

The British value their privacy (= having a part of their life that is not known to other people) and believe that everyone has a right to a **private life**. Most British people like to 'keep themselves to themselves' and do not discuss their private affairs. Things people like to keep private vary but may include personal relationships, family problems, how much they earn, their health, their political opinions, and sometimes what they do in their free time. It is considered rude to ask somebody about their private life, even if you know them well.

There is a traditional saying: 'an Englishman's home is his castle', i.e. a private place where he can behave as he wishes. People hang lace curtains or blinds in their windows, or plant bushes in their gardens, to prevent others from seeing inside. However, some people are very curious about other people's lives. Nosy neighbours, sometimes called **Nosy Parkers**, peep out from behind their own curtains to see what others are doing. When several people share a house, each person's room is considered their own private place, and anyone else is expected to knock before entering. A person's private space often includes their car, and because of this people often do not like to give lifts to others.

In the US the *Constitution protects people's right to privacy. A police officer has no power to stop people and ask them what they are doing unless they have committed a crime. Information about people can be shown to others only under special circumstances, and usually only with their permission. When newspapers print details about the family life of a politician or film actor they are often criticized for **invasion of privacy**. On the other hand, actors and politicians tell the press about their family life for publicity reasons, and ordinary Americans appear on television talk shows where they discuss their bad marriages, health problems and how they cannot control their children. The apparent contradiction in attitudes may be explained by the fact that Americans believe strongly in the right to privacy, but as long as that right is respected, they are happy to give it up. They believe it is better to be open and honest than to have secrets. The British may be less willing than Americans to talk about their own lives but they have an equally strong desire to know about the private lives of famous people. There is a constant argument, for instance, about the extent to which the media should be allowed to report the private lives of members of the *royal family.

Not all Americans tell the world everything about their lives. Money and sex are rarely discussed. Husbands and wives usually know how much each other earns, but other family members do not. People may say how much they paid for something, especially if the price was low, but asking somebody else how much they paid is acceptable only for small things, not a house or a car. In general people are happier offering information than being asked for it.

Being given advice can also disturb an American's sense of privacy. If somebody gives them advice it suggests that that person can solve their problem better than they can themselves. When offering advice, people use indirect language, and instead of saying, 'You should do this,' they may say, 'I tried doing this, and it worked for me.'

ˌ**private ˈbill** *n* a *bill(1) (= the proposal for a new law in the British Parliament) that affects a person or group rather than the whole country. Compare PRIVATE MEMBER'S BILL, PUBLIC BILL.

ˌ***Private ˈEye*** a British satirical magazine first published in 1961 and now appearing twice a month. It contains humorous articles and cartoons, but also investigates dishonest behaviour in politics and business. The magazine's editors have appeared many times in courts of law, charged with falsely accusing people and damaging people's reputations.

ˈ**private ˈlimited ˈcompany** *n* (in Britain) a type of company, usually small, that does not issue shares to the public. The company's name is usually followed by 'Ltd', short for 'Limited'. Compare PUBLIC LIMITED COMPANY.

ˌ**private ˈmember's bill** *n* a *bill(1) (= proposal for a new law) presented to the British *House of Commons by a private member (= a *Member of Parliament who is not a minister). Few private member's bills become law because they usually lack support and receive little time for debate. Compare PRIVATE BILL, PUBLIC BILL.

ˌ**private ˈpatient** *n* (in the British health system) a patient who pays for medical care rather than receiving it free from the *National Health Service. People choose to do this because they believe they will receive better care and will not have to wait. Some private patients make regular insurance payments to companies such as *BUPA, which then provide care when the patient needs it.

ˌ**private ˈroad** *n* (in Britain) a road that crosses the private property of a person or group of people and is owned by them. Private roads are usually open to the public for them to reach the house or houses that they lead to, but they must be closed at least once a year in order to remain private.

the ˌ**Privy ˈCouncil** a group of people appointed to advise the British king or queen. It is made up of politicians and other important people in the legal profession, the Church and the Commonwealth, and its head is the *Lord President of the Council. At present it has over 400 members, who are given the position for life. The Privy Council first became powerful in the 14th century, but was replaced in 1688 by the *Cabinet. It now has few functions in government, and is mainly important as a personal honour for its members.

▶ **Privy Councillor** (*also* **Privy Counsellor**) *n* a

member of the Privy Council. Privy Councillors are formally addressed as ‘the Right Honourable Mr/Mrs Smith’, etc. and have the letters ‘PC’ after their name.

the ˌ**Privy** ˈ**Purse** a payment made every year to the British king or queen from the government, for official expenses and some private expenses. The money comes mainly from the income of the *Duchy of Lancaster. The Privy Purse is separate from the *Civil List, which pays for other official expenses of the whole royal family.

ˌ**Procter &** ˈ**Gamble** /ˌprɒktər, ˈɡæmbl; *AmE* ˌprɑːktər/ a large US international company that produces a wide range of household goods. It was established in 1837 by William Procter and James Gamble as a soap and candle business in Cincinnati, *Ohio, where the main offices still are. The company’s products include *Ivory soap, Crest toothpaste, Tide soap for clothes, Mr Clean for bathroom and kitchen surfaces, Oil of Olay (Ulay in Europe) personal cream, Folger’s coffee, Hawaiian Punch juice and Duncan Hines cakes.

The ˈ**Prodigy** a British pop group formed in 1991 and known for their fast, aggressive dance music. Their albums include *Music for the Jilted Generation* (1994) and *The Fat of the Land* (1997), and their song *Firestarter* reached Number One in Britain in 1996.

the ˌ**Professional** ˈ**Golfers’ Associˌation** ⇨ PGA.

ˌJohn **Proˈfumo** /prəˈfjuːməʊ; *AmE* prəˈfjuːmoʊ/ (1915–) a minister in the Conservative government of Harold *Macmillan, who admitted in 1963 that he had had a sexual affair with a prostitute called Christine Keeler. Keeler was also having an affair with a Russian navy officer, and this was felt to threaten national safety. Profumo resigned, and at the court trial of Christine Keeler shocking details were reported about the behaviour of top government figures, involving prostitutes and criminals. The matter became known as the **Profumo Affair**, and severely damaged public trust in the government. Profumo left politics but later followed a new career in social work and adult education.

proˌgressive eduˈcation *n* [U] an important movement in US education which began at the end of the 19th century, when it was mainly associated with the ideas of John Dewey (1859–1952). It placed emphasis on developing students’ practical and social skills in addition to purely academic subjects. Progressive education was popular in US schools in the first half of the 20th century and its influence is still found, though in recent years there has been a return to more basic teaching and learning methods.

the **Proˈgressive ˌParty** the name taken at different times by three separate US political parties in opposition to the two major parties. **Progressivists** wanted social and economic changes to make society fairer, including higher taxes for rich people. Each had a candidate in one election for *President. The first, with the popular name of the Bull Moose Party, chose former President Theodore *Roosevelt as its candidate in 1912, and he gained more than 4 million votes. The second party, established by farm and trade-union leaders, was led by Robert La Follette, who won about 5 million votes. Henry A Wallace was the candidate for the last party in 1948 and received more than 1 million votes.

ˌ**Prohiˈbition** (in the US) the period from 1919 to 1933 when it was illegal by national law to make or sell alcohol and alcoholic drinks. Prohibition was not popular, and it was too expensive to make sure that the law was obeyed. It also produced criminals like Al *Capone who made and sold alcohol. A few states kept prohibition laws for several years, and some counties in certain states still have them.

pumping wine into the street during Prohibition

ˈ**Promise ˌKeepers** a US organization of *evangelical Christian men who promise to worship God, preserve the family and support the nation. They have been criticized by some women who believe they want men to control families. The organization was started in 1990 by Bill McCartney, and holds regular large meetings for men around the US.

the **Proms** /prɒmz; *AmE* prɑːmz/ *n* [pl] a series of concerts started by Henry *Wood in 1895 and now held every year at the *Albert Hall, London. The name is short for ‘promenade concerts’, i.e. concerts in which there are no seats in parts of the hall and members of the audience stand up or sit on the floor during the performance. The series lasts for eight weeks, and most of the concerts are broadcast on the *BBC. The *Last Night of the Proms is an occasion for special celebration, when several well-known songs are performed, with the audience joining in. The Proms are particularly popular with young people.

proˌportional represenˈtation *n* [U] a system used in political elections, in which the number of candidates elected for each party is decided according to the number of votes the party receives as a whole. This system is not used in Britain or the US, which both operate a *first-past-the-post system, in which candidates are elected who receive the most votes in a particular area. Proportional representation is generally thought to benefit smaller parties, and is favoured by the British *Liberal Democratic Party but not by the larger *Conservative or *Labour Parties.

ˈ**Prospero** /ˈprɒspərəʊ; *AmE* ˈprɑːspəroʊ/ the leading character in *Shakespeare’s play *The *Tempest*.

the **Proˈtectorate** the period from 1653 to 1658 when Oliver *Cromwell ruled Britain with the title of *Lord Protector, and from 1658 to 1659 when his son Richard (1626–1712) ruled with the same title. During this time they claimed greater powers, often ruling alone without a parliament. In 1659 the *Long Parliament was established again, which voted for the return of King *Charles II.

ˈ**Protestant** *n* a member of any of the Christian groups that separated from the *Roman Catholic Church in the 16th century, or of their branches formed later. Protestant Churches usually have simpler ceremonies than Roman Catholic Churches, with more emphasis on preaching (= teaching about religion) and the authority of the Bible. Most Christians in the US and Britain are Protestants, and the *Church of England and *Church of Scotland are Protestant Churches. Other Protestant Churches include the *Methodists, the *Baptists, the *Presbyterians and the *Quakers. Disagreements between Protestants and Roman Catholics in Northern Ireland have led to the conflict known as the *Troubles. ⇨ article at RELIGION. See also REFORMATION.

▶ **Protestant** *adj*.

Protestantism *n* [U] the beliefs and teachings of Protestants, or Protestants as a group.

the ˈ**Protestant Eˈpiscopal ˈChurch** ⇨ EPISCOPAL CHURCH.

ˈ**Providence** /ˈprɒvɪdəns; *AmE* ˈprɑːvɪdəns/ the capital and largest city of the US state of *Rhode Island. It is on the Providence River and Narragansett Bay. Roger Williams established it in 1636 as a safe place for people of all religions. It is known for its silver products and jewellery. Brown University was established there in 1764.

ˈ**Provident Soˌciety** ⇨ FRIENDLY SOCIETY.

the **Proˈvisionals** /prəˈvɪʒənls/ (*also infml* the **Provos**) another name for the Provisional *IRA, the part of the IRA that commits acts of violence for political purposes (as opposed to its official part, *Sinn Fein).

ˈ**Prozac**™ /ˈprəʊzæk; *AmE* ˈproʊzæk/ *n* [U] a drug used for treating people who are depressed. It first became available in 1987 and many users claimed it increased their confidence and helped them in their daily lives. It soon became very popular for general use, especially in the US. In recent years some people have become worried about possible unpleasant secondary effects of the drug.

Pruˈdential /pruˈdenʃl/ (*also* the **Prudential**, *infml* the **Pru** /pruː/) an international company, formed in Britain in 1848, dealing in insurance, property and financial services. It is Britain's largest insurance company and the third largest property owner in Britain after the Crown and the Church of England.

PSAT /ˌpiː es eɪ ˈtiː/ (*in full* **Preliminary Scholastic Aptitude Test**) (in the US) an examination that *high school students take, mostly to practise for the *SAT examination. It is sometimes called the PSAT/NMSQT (Preliminary Scholastic Aptitude Test/National Merit Scholarship Qualifying Test), because students who do well can receive money from the National Merit Scholarship Corporation to attend a college or university.

PSBR /ˌpiː es biː ˈɑː(r)/ ⇨ PUBLIC SECTOR BORROWING REQUIREMENT.

PST /ˌpiː es ˈtiː/ ⇨ PACIFIC STANDARD TIME.

ˈ***Psycho*** /ˈsaɪkəʊ; *AmE* ˈsaɪkoʊ/ a US film (1960) directed by Alfred *Hitchcock. Anthony Perkins plays Norman Bates, a man with mental problems who owns a hotel and kills people who stay there. The scene in which he kills a woman in a shower is considered one of the most frightening ever filmed. Perkins later played Bates in three more films.

PT /ˌpiː ˈtiː/ ⇨ PACIFIC TIME.

PT boat /ˌpiː ˈtiː/ (*in full* **patrol torpedo boat**) *n* a small, fast US Navy boat that carries torpedoes (= tube-shaped bombs that are fired under water). PT boats were used especially during *World War II, and John F *Kennedy commanded one. It was sunk by the Japanese, and Kennedy helped his men to survive until they were rescued. The story was told in the film *PT 109* (1963).

ˌ**public ˈaccess ˌchannel** *n* (in the US) a cable television channel reserved for broadcasts by people and organizations that do not make a profit. The Cable Act (1984) requires private cable companies to provide equipment and time for such broadcasts. Compare CATV.

ˌ**public ˈbill** *n* a *bill(2) (= a proposal for a new law in the British Parliament) that affects the whole country rather than one person or group. Compare PRIVATE BILL, PRIVATE MEMBER'S BILL.

the ˌ**Public ˈBroadcasting ˌService** ⇨ PBS.

ˌ**Public ˈEnemy** a US *rap music group. They began in 1987 as the Black Panthers of Rap. Their songs, known for their aggressive ideas and words, include *Don't Believe the Hype* (1988) and *Fear of a Black Planet* (1990). Among their albums are *It Takes a Nation of Millions to Hold Us Back* (1988) and *Give It Up* (1994).

ˈ**Public ˈEnemy ˈNo. ˈ1** /ˈnʌmbə ˈwʌn; *AmE* ˈnʌmbər/ the title used by the *FBI in the 1930s to refer to the criminal they considered the most dangerous and the one they most wanted to arrest at any particular time. In 1934 both John *Dillinger and 'Baby Face' *Nelson were named as 'Public Enemy No. 1'. The FBI now names the 'Ten Most Wanted Fugitives'.

ˌ**public ˈfootpath** *n* (*BrE*) a way or track along which people walk, especially in country areas. In England and Wales public footpaths are marked on *Ordnance Survey maps and are legal rights of way. They are often very old and people have the right to use them even if they cross private land. They allow people to discover the countryside, and organizations like the *Rambler's Association try to make sure that they are kept open and are well looked after.

a public footpath

ˌ**Public ˈLending Right** (*abbr* **PLR**) the system by which authors in Britain receive payment when their books are borrowed from public libraries. It was introduced in 1984 and the money is provided by the British government.

ˈ**public ˈlimited ˈcompany** (*abbrs* **plc**, **PLC**) *n* a type of British company, usually large, that issues shares to the public, and allows the public to examine its accounts. A public limited company must have the letters 'plc' after its name. Compare PRIVATE LIMITED COMPANY. ⇨ note at COMPANIES.

the ˌ**Public ˈOrder Act** a British *Act of Parliament which replaced the old *Riot Act in 1986. It was introduced in response to the riots in *Toxteth, *Brixton and other places in the early 1980s, and gave the police new powers to control crowds and arrest people who they thought threatened public order. The Act also created several new offences under the law, including 'violent disorder', 'threatening behaviour' and 'disorderly conduct'.

the ˌ**Public ˈRecord ˌOffice** the name of two offices in London where government records for England and Wales are kept. These are made available to the public, without charge, under the *thirty-year rule, which allows most official records to be seen by the public after 30 years. Among the important historical documents kept at the Public Record Office is the *Domesday Book of 1086. The equivalent office in Scotland is the Scottish Record Office.

public schools

Public schools are, in most of Britain, **independent schools** and, despite their name, are not part of the state education system. Schools run by the state are called *state schools. In Scotland however, which has a separate education system from the rest of Britain, the term *public school* refers to a state school. Only about 10% of children attend independent public schools, and their parents have to pay **fees** that may amount to several thousand pounds a year. A small number of children from less wealthy families win **scholarships**, in which case their fees are paid for them.

Many of Britain's 200 public schools are very old. They include *Eton, *Harrow, *Winchester and, for girls, *Cheltenham Ladies' College and *Roedean. Public schools were originally *grammar schools which offered free education to the public and were under public management. This was in contrast to private schools which were privately owned by the teachers. Since the 19th century, the term *public school* has been applied to grammar schools that began taking fee-paying pupils as well as children paid for from public funds.

Most pupils go to public school at the age of 13, after attending private **prep schools**. The majority of public schools are **boarding schools** where students live during term-time. Most have a **house system**, with **boarders** living in one of several **houses** under the charge of a **housemaster**. In a few schools younger pupils have to do small jobs for the senior pupils. This is sometimes called *fagging*.

Public schools aim for high academic standards and to provide pupils with the right social background for top jobs in the *Establishment. A much higher proportion of students from public schools win university places, especially to *Oxford and *Cambridge Universities, than from state schools. Former public school students may also have an advantage when applying for jobs because of the '**old school tie**', the **old boy network** through which a former public school pupil is more likely to give a job to somebody from a public school, especially his own public school, than to someone from a school in the state system. Some people send their children to public school mainly for this reason; others believe public schools provide a better education than state schools. Public schools have at various times also been associated with strict discipline, *bullying and occasionally homosexuality.

In the US a *public school* is a school run by the government. Schools that students have to pay to attend are called **private schools**. There are many private schools in the US, some of which are boarding schools. Some, like Phillips Exeter Academy and the Bath Academy, are very similar to Britain's public schools. They are very expensive, have a high reputation, and many of their students come from rich and well-known families. Children often go to the same school as their parents. Many of the most famous schools of this sort are in *New England.

Some US private schools give special attention to a particular area of study. There are, for example, schools for people who are good at music or art. Military schools are often chosen by parents who are in the armed forces, or who think their children need a lot of discipline. Religious groups also run private schools, although not all of the students who attend practise that religion. Schools run by the Catholic church are called **parochial schools**.

Private schools in the US are often single-sex and their students usually wear a uniform. This is unusual in public schools. Parents choose a private school for their children for a number of reasons, but in general they believe that the quality of education is higher in private schools, and there is some evidence to support this. Most private schools offer scholarships to students from poorer families, and in some parts of the US the government may under certain circumstances pay for children to attend a private school.

---

the **ˈPublic ˈSector ˈBorrowing Reˌquirement** (*abbr* **PSBR**) the amount of money the government needs to borrow every year to pay for public spending, if money from taxes is not enough. It is borrowed from the banking system and other sources, and is considered an addition to the *national debt.

ˌpublic ˈservice ˌbroadcasting *n* [U] (in Britain) radio or television broadcasting by the *BBC. The aim of public service broadcasting is to make programmes of a high standard that educate, inform and entertain, and the BBC received a *royal charter to do this in 1927. Anyone who owns a television must pay a licence fee, which pays for the service. Compare PUBLIC ACCESS CHANNEL, PUBLIC BROADCASTING SERVICE.

ˌpublic ˈspending round *n* [usu sing] the arrangement made every year by the British government in which different government departments are given money for the year. The public spending round is announced in the *budget, together with details about how taxes will be collected.

ˌpublish and be ˈdamned a phrase meaning 'you can publish if you like, I don't care'. It is thought to have been used by the Duke of Wellington when he received threats that private details about him were going to be published. It is now used more often when someone wants to publish something offensive or unpopular, and must therefore face public criticism: *A lot of people will disagree with what I've written – I'll just have to publish and be damned.*

ˌpublish or ˈperish a phrase used to express the idea that it is important for teachers in US colleges and universities to publish books, etc. about their research, and that if they fail to do so it will have a bad effect on their career. The idea is sometimes criticized because teachers are seen to be spending more time on their writing than on their teaching.

Pubs and pub names ⇨ article.

Puck /pʌk/ (*also* **ˌRobin ˈGoodfellow**) (in English legend) a spirit who lives in the English countryside and plays tricks on people. He appears as a character in *Shakespeare's *A Midsummer Night's Dream.*

ˈPueblo /ˈpwebləʊ; *AmE* ˈpwebloʊ/ *n* (*pl* **Pueblos** *or* **Pueblo**) a member of one of the groups of *Native-American people who live in the US states of *Arizona and *New Mexico. The groups include the *Hopi and the *Zuñi. They are descended from people who lived in cliff houses, some of which can be seen in the *Mesa Verde National Park. They now live in communities called *pueblos* and build their houses of dried clay, called *adobe.*

ˌPuerto ˈRico /ˌpwɜːtəʊ ˈriːkəʊ; *AmE* ˌpwɜːrtoʊ ˈriːkoʊ/ an island in the West Indies, south-east of *Florida. The capital and largest city is San Juan. **Puerto Ricans** are US citizens but govern themselves, pay no US taxes and cannot vote in US elections. The island produces metals, chemicals and sugar and tobacco products. It was discovered by Christopher *Columbus in 1493, captured by Juan *Ponce de León in 1508, passed to the US in 1898 after the *Spanish-American War, and became the Commonwealth of Puerto Rico in 1952. Some Puerto

Pubs and pub names

The British pub

Pubs are important in the social life of many British people. The word *pub* is short for **public house**, but the full name is rarely used. Pubs serve a range of alcoholic drinks, and also low-alcohol and soft drinks. They used to be visited mainly by men but now women also go, though usually with friends or with their partner. Some pubs are called **inns**. These were originally hotels and some still offer accommodation.

Most pubs have a choice of **bars** (= rooms to drink in). Drinks are sold from a counter in each room, also called a **bar**. The **public bar** is a fairly plain room with **bar stools** beside the bar itself and often a pool table and dartboard. The **saloon bar** has more comfortable seats and is usually quieter. The most popular drinks are *beer, lager and, in some areas, cider. **Tied houses** (= pubs owned by breweries, companies that make beer) sell beers made by the company and sometimes **guest beers** from other breweries. **Free houses**, pubs not owned by a brewery, offer beers made by several companies, including **real ales** made using traditional methods. A few **brewery pubs** brew their own beer at the pub. Pubs usually also sell crisps and nuts, and many do simple **pub meals** like scampi and chips or a ***ploughman's lunch**. Others offer more elaborate meals.

Under Britain's **licensing laws** alcohol can only be sold to people over 18. Children under 14 are not allowed in pubs unless there is a **family room**, a room without a bar.

People often choose a pub near where they live as their **local** and go there as **regulars** several times a week. At lunchtime people may go to a pub with colleagues from work, and in the evening they go with friends. Younger people sometimes go on a **pub crawl**, visiting several pubs in the same evening. Now that there are tougher laws on **drink-driving** (= driving after drinking alcohol) many people prefer to walk to a pub near their home.

Pubs have their own character and atmosphere. Some attract young people by playing loud music or inviting live bands to perform. Others have televisions in the bars and show sports games. Some **landlords** (= pub managers) organize teams to play *darts or take part in quiz nights. **Theme pubs** are decorated in a particular style. The most popular is the Irish pub, which sells Irish beers and plays Irish music. Many village pubs are very old and are the centre of village life. For much of the year they rely on local customers but in the summer they attract people from nearby towns. Pubs with a garden or situated by a river or canal are especially popular.

a pub sign: The Blue Boar

Before 1988, pubs were only allowed to open at lunchtime and in the evenings, but since then the law has been changed to allow greater flexibility in **opening hours** and pubs can remain open all day. Most, however, continue to open only at lunchtime and in the evening, closing finally at 11 p.m. When **closing time** approaches, the **barman** or **barmaid** rings a bell and calls out 'Last orders!', to give customers time to order one more drink. After the bar person has called 'Time!' customers are allowed ten minutes **drinking-up time** to finish their drinks and leave.

Pub names and signs

Pubs always have a name, often hundreds of years old. Originally, because few people could read, pubs were identified by the picture on a sign hanging outside them. Today, in addition to a picture, pub signs often give the name of the pub and the brewery that owns it. The signs are brightly painted and attractive. As the signs are easy to see from a distance many people use the names of pubs when giving directions, saying for example: 'Turn left at *The Red Lion*'.

Some names have their roots in legend or history, e.g. *St *George and the Dragon*, *The *Robin Hood* and *The *Green Man*. *The Rose and Crown* refers to the *Wars of the Roses. Names like *The Queen's Head*, *The George* and *The Duke of *Wellington* refer to kings and queens or national heroes, and *The *Victoria Arms*, *The *Unicorn*, *The Blue Boar* and *The Star and Garter* refer to their coats of arms. Names taken from country life include *The Bull*, *The Plough* and *The Fox and Hounds*. A pub called *The Coach and Horses* was probably once a **coaching inn**, where horse-drawn coaches stopped on their journey. More unusual names include *The World Turned Upside Down*, *The Case is Altered* and *The Gate Hangs Well*. Modern pubs sometimes make up a humorous name, e.g. *The Frog and Lettuce*.

The Victoria

The oldest pub in England is said to be *The Trip to Jerusalem* in *Nottingham. Its name is supposed to refer to a tradition that the *Crusaders set off from there for the Holy Land.

American pubs?

Americans have nothing exactly like the pub and are a little jealous of it. Formerly, working men went to the **corner bar and grill** near where they lived, but now that Americans have moved out of city centres few people have a local bar. The television programme **Cheers*, set in a friendly bar, showed how popular the idea of a pub is with Americans.

In the past 20 years some Americans have taken part in the **microbrewery** movement and become interested in high-quality beer made in small quantities, often in the **brewpub** where it is served. But most brewpubs are in city centres where few people live, and they do not have traditional names like British pubs.

P

Ricans want it to become a US state, and many have moved to New York.

ˌ**puffed** ˈ**wheat** *n* [U] (*BrE*) grains of wheat which have been artificially swollen. They are sold in packets and eaten with milk and sugar as a breakfast food, especially by children.

ˌ**Puffin** ˈ**Books** /ˌpʌfɪn/ a British company that publishes children's paperback books (= books with paper covers). It was formed in 1941 as part of *Penguin Books.

ˌ***Puffing*** ˈ***Billy*** the name of one of the earliest British steam trains, first used in 1813 and now kept in the *Science Museum, London.

Auˌgustus ˈ**Pugin** /ɔːˌgʌstəs ˈpjuːdʒɪn/ (1812–52) an English architect and designer. He was a leading figure in the English *Gothic Revival, and had an important influence on the *Arts and Crafts Movement. Pugin was a Roman Catholic, and designed several Catholic churches and cathedrals, but is best remembered for his work with Charles *Barry on the decoration inside the *Houses of Parliament.

ˈ**Pulitzer Prize** /ˈpʊlɪtsə; *AmE* ˈpʊlɪtsər/ *n* any of about 30 US awards given each May for achievements in journalism, literature, music and other fields. The prizes began in 1917 after Joseph Pulitzer (1847–1911), the owner of the *New York World*, died and left money to *Columbia University to establish a School of Journalism and be in charge of the awards.

ˈ**Pullman**™ /ˈpʊlmən/ (*pl* **-mans**) *n* (especially formerly) a comfortable railway carriage, often with beds for passengers to sleep in during journeys at night. It was developed by George Pullman (1831–1901) who built the Pioneer Sleeping Car in 1863 and formed the Pullman Palace Car Company in 1867. From 1985, *British Rail applied the name 'Pullman' to its first-class carriages serving meals, drinks, etc.

Pulp /pʌlp/ a British pop group formed in 1981 and led by the singer Jarvis Cocker (1962–). The group's songs are often about the experiences and problems of ordinary life, and they include *Do You Remember the First Time?* (1994) and *Sorted for E's and Wizz* (1995).

P

Punch /pʌntʃ/ a British humorous magazine, established in 1841, which took its name from the character Punch in *Punch and Judy shows. It became Britain's leading magazine for humorous political and social comment, and included drawings by famous artists such as John *Tenniel. It was originally published every week. In the 1980s it began losing readers to other magazines such as *Private Eye*, and a common joke was that it was only read in dentist's waiting rooms. It stopped appearing in 1992 but started again in 1996, with an issue every two weeks.

ˌ**Punch and** ˈ**Judy** the name of a traditional British puppet play, also called a **Punch and Judy show**. Punch (also called **Mr Punch**) is a character with a long curved nose and a big chin who argues with his wife Judy and the other characters (including the policeman and the doctor), shouting in a high voice and hitting them with his stick. He also has a dog called Toby. The characters are glove puppets (= small figures worn over the hand and moved by the fingers) and the show is presented in a special tent, often at the seaside or at parties for children.

a Punch and Judy show

punctuality

Most Americans and British people would agree that it is good *manners to be **punctual** (= to arrive at the right time) for an appointment. Arriving **on time** for formal events such as a business meeting or an interview is considered important. If somebody arrives late for a job interview it may suggest that they are not reliable or not interested in the job. Many people try to arrive a few minutes early for an appointment to avoid the risk of rushing in at the last minute. Even in less formal situations people are generally expected to think about the person they are meeting and not to keep them waiting unnecessarily.

People are also expected to arrive on time for social events, especially weddings. Traditionally, only the bride is allowed to be late. People are generally more relaxed about the time they arrive for more informal social occasions. When meeting a friend for lunch at a restaurant people try to arrive at the time arranged, or no more than five minutes late. If they are later than this the person they are meeting will start to think they are not going to come at all. However, when invited to dinner in somebody's home it is actually considered polite to arrive a few minutes late. Under no circumstances should guests arrive early. Some formal invitations to dinner may say 'seven for seven-thirty', meaning that guests should arrive any time after 7 p.m. in order to be ready to eat at 7.30 p.m. At a party, however, people may arrive an hour or more after the start time written on the invitation.

If somebody does arrive late, they are expected to apologize. Depending on the circumstances and how late they are, people may say, 'I'm sorry I'm late' or 'Sorry to keep you waiting'. If they are very late they may feel obliged to give an explanation as well, e.g. 'I'm sorry I'm so late, but the traffic was bad.'

People expect concerts, plays etc. to start at the time advertised, and if they are kept waiting a long time they may start a slow handclap to show that they are impatient. But anyone who arrives late for a show may not be allowed in until there is a convenient break in the performance. People also expect public transport to depart and arrive on time and get very frustrated if delays are frequent.

punishment

Punishment for people who break the law is decided in a court of law. In the US federal, state and local governments each have their own systems of law and of punishment. The *Constitution forbids 'cruel and unusual punishment', but it is the responsibility of the *Supreme Court to decide whether a punishment is 'cruel and unusual'. In Britain, the Scottish legal system is different from that in England and Wales, but methods of punishment are similar throughout Britain.

When an accused person is found guilty of a crime the judge decides what punishment he or she should suffer. In both Britain and the US the least serious offences are punished by **fines** which must be paid to the court. Fines or **fixed penalties** (= fines at a level decided in advance) are often **imposed** for minor traffic offences such as parking illegally.

If a fine is not considered adequate, a person may be **sentenced** to do *community service (= work without pay in hospitals, homes for old people, etc.) or be put **on probation** (= required to have regular meetings with a social worker over a set period). When the crime committed is more serious, the **convicted** person is likely to be given a prison sentence. If it is their **first offence** the sentence may be **suspended** (= only carried out if the person is found guilty of another crime) and the person is allowed to remain free on a **conditional discharge**.

If a person is given a prison sentence its length depends on how serious their crime is and on their past **record**. If a person thinks the sentence is too severe he or she has the right to **appeal** against it in a higher court, which has the power to reduce the sentence. As a reward for good behaviour prisoners are often given **remission** (= are released early). Others get **parole**, which means that they can go free as long as they do not commit any further crimes. In the US the number of people on probation has increased in recent years, as there is not always room in prisons for all those given a prison sentence. A variety of **non-custodial punishments** (= ones not requiring time in prison) have been tried in both Britain and the US, including **electronic tagging**. This punishment requires people to stay in their homes and wear a device that informs the police if they leave.

In Britain the maximum sentence that can be **handed down** by a judge is a **life sentence**, which in fact usually means spending about 20–25 years in prison. Convicted murderers are given life sentences. The most serious punishment in the US is the **death penalty**. Not all states allow ***capital punishment**, and in those that do there may be many years of appeals before it is carried out.

---

punk *n* **1** [U] a movement in music and fashion that became popular, mainly in Britain, in the late 1970s, with groups such as The *Sex Pistols and The Clash. The music they played, called **punk** or **punk rock**, was usually loud, fast and violent, and expressed anger against society. Punk fashions, introduced by Vivienne *Westwood and others, included torn clothes, safety pins, and brightly coloured hair. **2** (*also* **punk rocker**) [C] a person who dresses in punk fashions and likes punk music.

'punting /ˈpʌntɪŋ/ *n* [U] the activity of going along a river in a punt (= a long boat with a flat bottom that is moved by pushing against the bottom of the river with a long pole). People go punting for pleasure rather than sport, and punting is especially popular in the British university towns of *Oxford and *Cambridge.

ˌHenry **'Purcell** /ˈpɜːsl; *AmE* ˈpɜːrsl/ (1659–95) an English *baroque composer. Many people regard him as the greatest English composer of the period. He wrote many different types of music, including songs, church music and theatre music, and his *Dido and Aeneas* (1689) is considered the first English opera. He was an important influence on later composers, especially *Handel.

the ˌ**Pure Food and 'Drug Act** a US law passed on 30 June 1906 with the support of President Theodore *Roosevelt. It stated that labels on food and drugs should say exactly what they contain and that no other substances should be added to them. See also MUCKRAKER.

'Puritan *n* a member of an English Protestant group of the 16th and 17th centuries. Puritans believed in simple forms of church ceremony and strict moral behaviour, and were associated with the Parliamentary party during the *Commonwealth of Oliver *Cromwell. Because of this they were treated badly after the *Restoration of King *Charles II, and many left Britain to settle in the US, where their simple way of life and religious discipline became an important influence on American culture.

the ˌ**Purple 'Heart** *n* a US medal given to members of the armed forces who are wounded in battle. It was established by George *Washington on 7 August 1782 as the Badge of Military Merit, but was immediately called the Purple Heart. It is in the form of a purple heart with an image of Washington on it. Compare CONGRESSIONAL MEDAL OF HONOR.

ˌEdward **'Pusey** /ˈpjuːzi/ (1800–82) an English *Church of England priest. He was a supporter of *Anglo-Catholicism and became the leader of the *Oxford Movement after John Henry *Newman converted to *Roman Catholicism.

ˌPuss in 'Boots an old children's story that is often used for a *pantomime. It is about a poor young man who owns a cat that can talk and wears boots. By playing a series of tricks on people, the cat makes his owner rich and helps him to marry a princess.

'Pussy Cat, 'Pussy Cat, 'Where Have You 'Been? the title and first line of a traditional children's *nursery rhyme. The full poem is:

Pussy cat, pussy cat, where have you been?
I've been up to London to look at the queen.
Pussy cat, pussy cat, what did you there?
I frightened a little mouse under her chair.

ˌDavid **'Puttnam** /ˈpʌtnəm/ (1941–) an English film producer who played a major part in the success of the British film industry in the 1980s. His films include *Midnight Express* (1978), **Chariots of Fire* and *The *Killing Fields*. In 1986–8 he was head of the US film company *Columbia Pictures. He was made a *life peer in 1997.

PX /ˌpiː ˈeks/ (*pl* **PXs** /ˌpiː ˈeksɪz/) (*in full* **post exchange**) *n* [usu sing] (*AmE*) a general shop on a US army base for members of the armed forces and their families. It sells a wide range of goods, such as clothes, gifts, food, etc. Prices are cheaper than in regular shops because there are no taxes and the PX does not make a profit. Such a shop on a US Air Force base is called a **BX** (base exchange) and on a US Navy base or ship it is called a **commissary**.

Pyg'malion /pɪɡˈmeɪliən/ a comic play (1913) by George Bernard *Shaw about a professor, Henry Higgins, who teaches a young *cockney *flower girl, Eliza Doolittle, how to speak in an *upper-class way. She becomes a success in society and falls in love with Higgins. The play was made into a successful musical comedy and film called **My Fair Lady*. Shaw took his title from an ancient Greek story about Pygmalion, an artist who falls in love with a statue he has created.

ˌJohn **'Pym** /ˈpɪm/ (1584–1643) an English politician who led the *Long Parliament against King *Charles I and helped to start the *English Civil War in 1642.

ˌThomas **'Pynchon** /ˈpɪntʃən/ (1937–) a US writer of complicated novels. He uses words in humorous ways and often refers to literature and technology. His books include *V* (1963), *The Crying of Lot 49* (1966), *Gravity's Rainbow* (1972), *Vineyard* (1990) and *Mason & Dixon* (1997). Pynchon avoids publicity and is rarely seen in public.

PYO /ˌpiː waɪ ˈəʊ; *AmE* ˈoʊ/ ⇨ PICK YOUR OWN.

Qq

the ***QE2*** /ˌkjuː iː ˈtuː/ a British passenger ship built by *Cunard. The name is an abbreviation for 'Queen Elizabeth II', who launched the ship in 1967. It was the second ship of that name to be built by Cunard, the earlier being the **Queen Elizabeth*. In 1982 the *QE2* was used to carry soldiers to the *Falklands War.

QPR /ˌkjuː piː ˈɑː(r)/ ⇨ QUEEN'S PARK RANGERS.

Q-Tip™ *n* a US make of small plastic stick with a pad of soft cotton on each end. Q-Tips are often used for cleaning the ears but they have many other uses.

ˈ**Quaker** *n* any member of the *Society of Friends, a religious group established in England in the 1650s by George *Fox. They were originally called Quakers because members were thought to 'quake' or shake with religious excitement. Quakers worship Christ without any formal ceremony or fixed beliefs, and their meetings often involve silent thought or prayer. They are strongly opposed to violence and war, and are active in education and charity work.

ˌ**Quaker** ˈ**Oats**™ a popular US breakfast cereal. The Quaker Oats Company, whose main office is in *Chicago, also makes a range of other food products.

ˈ**quango** /ˈkwæŋɡəʊ; *AmE* ˈkwæŋɡoʊ/ *n* (*pl* **-os**) (in Britain) any independent organization established to manage a particular area of public life, with financial support from the government. Examples are the *Arts Councils and the *Equal Opportunities Commission. Some people criticize quangos because they think the people who run them are paid too much or are not directly elected by the public. (The word *quango* comes from the first letters of 'quasi-autonomous non-governmental organization'.)

ˌMary ˈ**Quant** /ˈkwɒnt; *AmE* ˈkwɑːnt/ (1934–) an English fashion designer. Her shop Bazaar in *King's Road, *Chelsea, London, became famous in the 1960s, and her style included short skirts, short hair and strong make-up. Her company is now an international success, selling make-up, textiles and other fashion items.

Mary Quant pinning up one of her designs

the ˈ**Quantocks** /ˈkwɒntɒks; *AmE* ˈkwɑːntɑːks/ (*also* the ˌ**Quantock** ˈ**hills**) a range of hills in Somerset, England, well known for their attractive scenery.

ˌ**Quantrill's** ˈ**Raiders** /ˌkwɒntrɪlz; *AmE* ˌkwɑːntrɪlz/ *n* [pl] a small independent military group that fought for the *Confederate States in *Missouri and *Kansas during the American *Civil War. It was led by Captain William Quantrill (1837–65), a former criminal, and included Jesse and Frank *James and the *Younger brothers. The Raiders attacked the town of Lawrence, Kansas, on 21 August 1863, and murdered 150 men and boys who were not soldiers. Quantrill was later killed in a gun fight with US soldiers in *Kentucky.

quarter days

In Britain, quarter days have since the Middle Ages marked the beginning of each new **quarter** (= period of three months) of the year. Rent and interest payments are often made on quarter days, and many contracts, especially concerning property, begin or end then. In former times quarter days were often celebrated with big *fairs. Agricultural workers and servants who wanted to change their jobs went to the fair to try to find a new employer.

The names of quarter days are taken from the calendar of the *medieval Church. In England and Wales the quarter days are: 25 March (**Lady Day**, marking the Annunciation of the Blessed Virgin Mary), 24 June (**Midsummer Day** or St John the Baptist's Day), 29 September (**Michaelmas Day** or St Michael and All Angels' Day) and 25 December (**Christmas Day**).

In Scotland quarter days are known as **term days**. They formerly followed the Christian calendar and were: 2 February (**Candlemas**), 15 May (**Whit Sunday**), 1 August (**Lammas Day**) and 11 November (**Martinmas**). Since 1991 the dates have been changed, although the traditional names have been kept. The dates are now 28 February, 28 May, 28 August and 28 November.

There are no quarter days in the US.

ˌDan ˈ**Quayle** /ˈkweɪl/ (1947–) the US Vice-president under George *Bush (1989–93). Some people criticized him because they said he joined the *National Guard to avoid the *Vietnam War. Americans also made jokes about his mistakes as Vice-president and his lack of experience. Quayle was a *Republican(1) from *Indiana.

Queen¹ a successful British pop group formed in 1971. Its singer was Freddie *Mercury and the group's albums include *A Night at the Opera* (1975), *The Game* (1980) and *Innuendo* (1991), all of which were No. 1 in Britain. Their song *Bohemian Rhapsody* (1975) was No. 1 in Britain for nine weeks.

ˌEllery ˈ**Queen**² /ˌeləri ˈkwiːn/ a *detective in many US novels and short stories written between 1929 and 1971 by Frederic Dannay (1905–82) and Manfred B Lee (1905–71) under the same name of Ellery Queen. There were also radio, television and film series, and Dannay and Lee also started *Ellery Queen's Mystery Magazine* in 1941.

ˌ**Queen** ˈ**Anne** a style of architecture and furniture popular in England in the early 18th century, during the rule of Queen *Anne. In furniture its main features were curved legs and simple elegant designs. A later style in architecture, known as Queen Anne or Queen Anne Revival, was popular in England from the 1860s, and used elements such as red brick, high narrow windows and tall chimneys. Its best-known architect was Norman Shaw (1831–1912).

the ˌ***Queen E***ˈ***lizabeth*** a British passenger ship built by *Cunard, the largest of its type ever built. It was named after Queen Elizabeth, now the *Queen Mother(2), and was launched by her in 1938. It was first used in *World War II to carry soldiers, and after the war carried passengers between England

and the US. In 1972 it was destroyed by a fire. See also *QE2*.

the ˌ***Queen*** ˈ***Mary*** a British passenger ship built by *Cunard and named after Queen *Mary, the wife of King *George V. It was launched by her in 1934 and won the *Blue Riband in 1938, sailing between England and the US in just under four days.

ˌ**Queen** ˈ**Mother** **1** a title sometimes used by the wife of a British king after his death, if she is the mother of the next king or queen. **2** Queen Elizabeth (1900–), the widow (= woman whose husband has died) of King *George VI. She was born Elizabeth Bowes-Lyon, the youngest daughter of the Earl of Strathmore, and married George in 1923, becoming the Duchess of York. He became king in 1936, so she then became known as Queen Elizabeth. When her daughter became Queen *Elizabeth II, she became known as the Queen Mother. She is very popular with the people of Britain.

The ˌ***Queen of*** ˈ***Hearts*** the title and first line of a traditional *nursery rhyme. The first verse is:

The Queen of Hearts
She made some tarts,
All on a summer's day;
The Knave of Hearts
He stole the tarts,
And took them clean away.

Characters from the poem appear in **Alice in Wonderland*, where a trial is held at which the knave (= the jack in a pack of cards) is accused of stealing the tarts (= pastries with jam inside).

ˌ**queen of** ˈ**puddings** (*also* ˈ**queen's** ˌ**pudding**) *n* [U] a traditional English pudding (= cooked sweet dish) made from bread, jam, lemons, sugar and meringue (= a mixture of egg whites and sugar).

Queens /kwiːnz/ the largest of the five *boroughs of New York City. It has a border with *Long Island. It was named after the wife of *Charles II. The area of Queens called Astoria is known for its large Greek community.

ˈ**Queen's A**ˌ**ward** *n* any of a number of awards given to British companies who have achieved success in any of three areas: exports, technology or the environment. Over 100 awards are given each year. A company that wins an award may use a special symbol for five years.

Queen's Award emblems

the ˌ**Queen's** ˈ**Bench** (*also* the ˌ**Queen's** ˈ**Bench Di**ˌ**vision**) one of the three divisions of the *High Court of Justice in Wales. When a king is ruling it is called the **King's Bench (Division)**. Its head was formerly the king or queen, but today it is the *Lord Chief Justice. It deals mainly with civil cases, e.g. ones in which money is claimed because of loss or damage, but it may also deal with appeals in criminal cases. See also FAMILY DIVISION, CHANCERY DIVISION. ⇨ article at LEGAL SYSTEM IN BRITAIN.

the ˈ**Queensberry Rules** /ˈkwiːnzbəri/ *n* [pl] the standard rules for the sport of boxing, named in 1867 in honour of the Marquess of Queensberry (1844–1900). The use of gloves and shorter rounds were among the rules first introduced at that time.

the ˌ**Queen's** ˈ**Birthday** either the real birthday (21 April) or the *Official Birthday of the present British queen, *Elizabeth II.

ˈ**Queen's Club** a sports club in Hammersmith, London, England, established in 1886. It is famous as a centre for *real tennis and *rackets, and the London Grass Court Tennis Championships are held there every year.

ˌ**Queen's** ˈ**Counsel** *n* (*abbr* **QC**) (in Britain) a senior *barrister who is appointed by the *Lord Chancellor. He or she wears a silk gown (= a long loose piece of clothing worn over other clothes) and is also known as a 'silk'. Other barristers are known as 'juniors'. When a king is ruling the title becomes a **King's Counsel (KC)**: *Sir Rodney Fisher QC* ○ *He was made a QC last year.* ⇨ article at LEGAL SYSTEM IN BRITAIN.

the ˌ**Queen's** ˈ**English** the English language as it is correctly written or spoken in Britain. It is called the **King's English** when a king is ruling.

ˌ**Queen's Park** ˈ**Rangers** (*abbr* **QPR**) an English football club formed in 1885. Its ground is in Loftus Road, near White City, west London.

the ˌ**Queen's Regu**ˈ**lations** a set of rules governing the behaviour of the British armed forces, issued as a book. When a king is ruling it becomes the **King's Regulations**.

the ˌ**Queen's** ˈ**Speech** a speech made by the Queen at the *State Opening of Parliament in the *House of Lords. In it she reads out the government's plans for the coming year. The speech is written for her by members of the government. It is an important occasion and is broadcast on television and radio. When a king is ruling it becomes the **King's Speech**.

ˈ**Queen's Uni**ˈ**versity,** ˈ**Belfast** /ˈbelfɑːst/ a university in *Belfast, Northern Ireland, established in 1845. It is Northern Ireland's oldest university and was known as Queen's College until 1908.

A ˌ***Question of*** ˈ***Sport*** a popular *BBC television quiz show about sport, first shown in 1970, with teams of famous sports stars. From 1979 to 1997 the questions were asked by David *Coleman and since then they have been asked by Sue *Barker.

ˈ**Question Time** (in the British parliament) a period between 2.30 and 3.30 p.m. from Monday to Thursday in which *Members of Parliament can put questions to government ministers in the *House of Commons. Each question is in two parts, the first known to the minister in advance and the second not known. Many of the questions are also answered in writing. See also PRIME MINISTER'S QUESTIONS.

ˈ***Question Time*** a *BBC television series first shown in 1979 and based on the radio series **Any Questions?* In it a group of four public figures (usually politicians) answer questions on political subjects from an audience. The original chairman was Robin *Day. It is now David *Dimbleby.

ˈ**Quonset hut**™ /ˈkwɒnset; *AmE* ˈkwɑːnset/ *n* a US military shelter. It is a long metal building with a round roof, like a tunnel above ground. The huts are made in sections which can be put together for soldiers to live in. They were first made for the US Navy in 1941 in Quonset Point, *Rhode Island. Compare NISSEN HUT.

the **Quorn** /kwɔːn; *AmE* kwɔːrn/ one of Britain's best-known fox-hunts (= groups of people who hunt foxes), established in Leicestershire in 1698. In 1991 a film was secretly made showing a fox being torn apart by the Quorn's hounds (= dogs trained to hunt), which shocked many people when it was shown on television. ⇨ note at FIELD SPORTS.

Rr

RA /ˌɑːr ˈeɪ/ ⇨ ROYAL ARTILLERY.

RAC /ˌɑːr eɪ ˈsiː/ **1** ⇨ ROYAL ARMOURED CORPS. **2** ⇨ ROYAL AUTOMOBILE CLUB.

ˈRacal /ˈreɪkl/ a British company that makes electronic equipment, formed in London in 1950. Its most famous product is the Vodafone mobile telephone.

the **ˌRace Reˈlations Acts** three British *Acts of Parliament (1965, 1968 and 1976) designed to protect the rights of *ethnic minorities living in Britain, and making it illegal to treat people differently because of their race. The 1976 Act established the *Commission for Racial Equality to investigate complaints and improve relations between the races. ⇨ article at IMMIGRATION.

racing

Horse racing has been popular as a **spectator sport** throughout the British Isles for hundreds of years. It was also the first sport organized in the American colonies. This was in 1664 on *Long Island, New York. Four years later the first American sports trophy, a silver bowl, was presented there.

There are two main types of horse racing. In **flat racing** horses run against each other over a set distance. In ***National Hunt** racing, also called **steeplechasing**, horses jump over fences and ditches round a course. The main **flat races** in Britain each year are the English Classics, five races for three-year-old horses. These are the ***Derby** and the ***Oaks** (both run at *Epsom), the ***One Thousand Guineas** and the ***Two Thousand Guineas** (run at *Newmarket) and the ***St Leger** (run at *Doncaster). The four-day *Royal Ascot meeting is an important social occasion, attended by members of the *royal family. The most famous **steeplechase** is the ***Grand National**, which was first run in 1836 and which takes place each spring at *Aintree. Many people who take no interest in horse racing have a bet on this race. Racing attracts people from all levels of British society but only the rich can afford to own and train a **racehorse**.

In the US flat racing is called **thoroughbred racing** or just racing; **steeplechasing** is not often seen. The most famous race is the ***Kentucky Derby**, which began in 1875 and is run each year at *Louisville, Kentucky. This is a big event on national television, and informal bets are made in offices and homes, even in states where gambling is illegal. Other important races are the **Preakness** at *Baltimore, Maryland, and the ***Belmont Stakes** at Elmont, New York. The three together are called the ***triple crown**. Only 11 horses have won the triple crown since 1919, and none since 1978. The most famous was Citation.

Famous British and US jockeys have included Willie *Carson, Pat *Eddery, Lester *Piggott, Peter *Scudamore, Willie *Shoemaker, Laffit Pincay, Angel Cordero and Steve *Cauthen. Horses famous in Britain have included Arkle, Desert Orchid, Nijinsky, *Red Rum and *Shergar, and in the US Galant Fox, Secretariat, Affirmed, Man o' War, Native Dancer and Cigar, which was chosen **Horse of the Year** in 1995 and 1996.

A type of race popular in America is **harness racing**, in which a horse pulls a small two-wheeled cart called a **sulky** with its driver. The most famous race is the Hambletonian, popularly called the 'Hambo', at the Meadowlands Racetrack in *New Jersey. Harness racing's triple crown is the Hambletonian, the Kentucky Futurity, and the Yonkers Trot.

***Betting** on the result of a race is for many British people an important part of the sport and contributes to the atmosphere of excitement and tension at a **racecourse**. Before a race starts **bookmakers** take bets, calculate **the odds** and say which horse is the **favourite**. People can also bet on a race at a **bookmaker's** or **betting shop**. Betting shops show live television broadcasts of races.

Americans also like to **play the ponies**. People can bet beside the track or **off-track**. Telephone bets can be made in some states. Even though many Americans do not approve of betting, most have accepted horse racing as an exciting sport and a US tradition. This is reflected in popular culture. **Camptown Races* is one of Stephen *Foster's most popular songs. Damon *Runyon set many of his short stories at race tracks, and *Hollywood has produced popular films about racing such as *National Velvet* (1945) and *The Black Stallion* (1980). See also GREYHOUND RACING.

ˈrackets *n* [U] a ball game for two or four people played with rackets and a small hard ball in an enclosed court. It first became popular in the 18th century in England, and is now played mainly at boys' *public schools. *Squash is a similar game that developed from rackets, and is played in a smaller court with a softer ball.

ˌArthur **ˈRackham** /ˈrækəm/ (1867–1939) an English artist. He is famous for his highly detailed illustrations of children's books, drawing a world of strange imaginary creatures for books such as *Fairy Tales of the Brothers Grimm* (1900) and **Peter Pan* (1906).

ˈracquetball /ˈrækɪtbɔːl/ *n* [U] a game played by two or four players using rackets with short handles and a small ball. The court for play has four walls, and the ball can be hit against them or the ceiling. The sport began in the US in the 1960s and is now played in several countries.

RADA /ˈrɑːdə/ ⇨ ROYAL ACADEMY OF DRAMATIC ART.

radio

People in Britain listen to the radio a lot, especially in the morning and the early evening or while they are in their cars. Many people rely on the radio to hear the latest news. Later in the evening television attracts larger audiences. Radio is sometimes still called **the wireless**, especially by older people.

Around 50% of the British radio audience listen to the ***BBC**; the rest listen to independent **commercial radio**, which has *advertising. There are five national BBC **radio stations**: *Radio 1 plays rock and pop music, Radio 2 broadcasts popular music, comedy and entertainment programmes, *Radio 3 offers classical music and arts programmes, *Radio 4 broadcasts popular news and current affairs programmes such as **Today*, drama and arts programmes, and *Radio 5 Live has sport. The BBC also operates the ***World Service**, which broadcasts to most parts of the world. Independent radio stations which broadcast in competition with the BBC include *Classic FM, Virgin Radio and Talk Radio UK. Programmes broadcast by the BBC and the main independent stations are listed in the **Radio Times* and **TV Times* and in national newspapers.

Many people also listen to **local radio**. Local radio stations concentrate on local news, traffic reports and pop music. Smaller stations are run by students or by hospitals for their patients. The ***Radio Authority** issues licences to commercial broadcasters.

In the US there are more than 10 000 radio stations. Many people listen to the radio during **drive time**, the time when they are travelling to or from work. There are no national radio stations, but there are **networks**, groups of stations that are associated with each other. The network **affiliates** (= stations in the group) use some of the same programmes.

The ***Federal Communications Commission** (FCC), a part of the US government, issues licences to radio stations and says what **frequency** they can use. The FCC also gives a station its **call letters**, the letters that it uses to identify itself. Many stations make their name from their call letters or frequency, e.g. *Sunny 95*.

Each station has a specific **format** (= style of programmes), which it hopes will be popular with its **listenership** (*AmE* for 'audience'). Some stations play a particular kind of music, such as 'top 40' (= popular songs), *country music or *golden oldies. Other stations have **talk radio** and **phone-in programmes**, in which radio **presenters** discuss an issue and invite people listening to telephone the station and take part in the discussion. Ethnic radio stations operated by people from particular cultural groups offer programmes in languages other than English. Some stations broadcast religious **programming**.

Many towns also have a **public radio station**, which is part of the **National Public Radio** network. Public radio stations often have public affairs programming and classical music, which is not common on commercial radio. The *United States Information Agency, part of the US government, operates the ***Voice of America**, which brings information about the US, its culture and language to people around the world.

---

the **ˈRadio Auˌthority** a British organization established by the government in 1991 to control independent commercial radio stations and issue licences to broadcast. ⇨ note at RADIO.

ˌRadio ˈCaroline a British pirate radio station (= an illegal station), started in 1964, which broadcast pop music from a ship at sea. It was extremely successful and led to the forming of Britain's first official pop music station, *Radio 1, in 1967. Radio Caroline continued broadcasting until 1990.

ˈRadio ˈCity ˈMusic Hall the largest cinema and theatre in the world, with more than 6 000 seats. It is in *Rockefeller Center in New York. It combines films with stage performances by the famous dancers, the *Rockettes. Radio City Music Hall opened in 1932. It was due to close in 1979 but stayed open because of public demand.

the **ˈRadio Corpoˈration of Aˈmerica** ⇨ RCA.

ˌRadio 5 ˈLive /ˌreɪdiəʊ faɪv ˈlaɪv; *AmE* ˌreɪdioʊ/ a British national radio station of the *BBC that broadcasts mainly sport, music and talk programmes. It was established in 1990 and broadcasts 24 hours a day.

Radio 4 /ˌreɪdiəʊ ˈfɔː(r); *AmE* ˌreɪdioʊ ˈfɔːr/ a British national radio station of the *BBC. It broadcasts regular news and weather reports as well as plays, comedy shows, live broadcasts of important events, and other programmes. It was established in 1967 and before that was known as the Home Service. It broadcasts from 6 a.m. to 1 a.m.

ˈRadio ˈFree ˈEurope/ˌRadio ˈLiberty a private US radio company that broadcasts to central and eastern Europe and the former Soviet Union. It is supported financially by the US government. The main office is in Munich, Germany, and it broadcasts each day in 23 languages to an audience of 20 million. Radio Free Europe was established in 1950 for the European audience, and Radio Liberty began in 1951 for the Soviet one. They joined together in 1976. The programmes have always been about US and world news and subjects, including the arts, but they were more political before the end of Communism. Compare VOICE OF AMERICA.

ˈRadiohead /ˈreɪdiəʊhed/ a British pop group formed in 1988. Their most successful albums include *Pablo Honey* (1993) and *OK Computer* (1997).

Radio 1 /ˌreɪdiəʊ ˈwʌn; *AmE* ˌreɪdioʊ/ a British national radio station of the *BBC that broadcasts pop music and news, and is listened to mainly by young people. It was established in 1967 and broadcasts 24 hours a day.

ˈRadio Shack™ any of a US group of about 6 800 shops that sell a wide range of electrical goods, including computers and video and sound equipment.

Radio 3 /ˌreɪdiəʊ ˈθriː; *AmE* ˌreɪdioʊ/ a British national radio station of the *BBC that broadcasts mainly classical music, but also presents plays, talks and readings of short stories and poetry. It was established in 1967 and before that was known as the Third Programme. It broadcasts 24 hours a day.

the ***ˌRadio ˈTimes*** a British magazine published every week by the *BBC. It gives details of the week's radio and television programmes on both BBC and commercial stations, and also contains articles relating to the week's broadcasts. It first appeared in 1923. Compare *TV TIMES*.

Radio 2 /ˌreɪdiəʊ ˈtuː; *AmE* ˌreɪdioʊ/ a British national radio station of the *BBC that broadcasts popular music, *jazz, news and sport, and is listened to mainly by older people. It was established in 1967 and before that was known as the Light Programme. It broadcasts 24 hours a day.

ˌRadley ˈCollege /ˌrædli/ a *public school(1) for boys aged between 13 and 18 near Abingdon, Oxfordshire, England, established in 1847 as St Peter's College, Radley. It is a boarding school (= a school where the pupils live).

ˌHenry **ˈRaeburn** /ˈreɪbɜːn; *AmE* ˈreɪbɜːrn/ (1756–1823) a Scottish painter. He worked in Edinburgh and produced many pictures of important Scottish figures of the time, often in *Highland dress. His best-known painting is probably *The Reverend Robert Walker Skating on Duddingston Loch* (1784). He was made a *knight in 1822.

RAF /ˌɑːr eɪ ˈef; *also infml* ræf/ ⇨ ROYAL AIR FORCE.

ˌStamford **ˈRaffles** /ˌstæmfəd ˈræflz; *AmE* ˌstæmfərd/ (1781–1826) an English politician. He is best known for buying *Singapore for the *East India Company in 1819 and for developing the island as a commercial centre. The famous Raffles Hotel there is named after him. He was also the governor of Java (1815–17) and Sumatra (1818–23) and wrote a *History of Java* (1817). In 1826 Raffles became the first President of *London Zoo. He was made a *knight in 1817.

ˈragga /ˈrægə/ (*also* **dance-hall reggae**) *n* [U] a type of pop music that developed from *reggae in *Jamaica in the early 1980s, using fast electronic drum and bass sounds, and a singing style similar to *rap. It is now popular in many countries.

The **'Ragged 'Trousered Phi'lanthropists** /ˈtraʊzəd; *AmE* ˈtraʊzərd/ a novel by Robert Tressall (*c.* 1870–1911) about the harsh lives of working people in the early 20th century. It was published after his death, in 1918, and is still highly regarded for its comments on industrial relations.

'ragtime *n* [U] a style of music developed by *African Americans in the 1890s and played especially on the piano. It led to the development of traditional *jazz. Ragtime is played with a strong rhythm which is 'ragged', i.e. not regular. Pieces of ragtime music are often called **rags**. The most famous ragtime musicians were 'Jelly Roll' *Morton and Scott *Joplin.

'Railcard /ˈreɪlkɑːd; *AmE* ˈreɪlkɑːrd/ *n* a card that can be bought at train stations in Britain by students, people over 60, disabled people and other groups. It allows them to buy cheaper train tickets for a period of one year.

'Railtrack /ˈreɪltræk/ a company formed in 1994 as part of the privatization of British railways. It owns all of Britain's railways and train stations, and is responsible for signals and train schedules (= times of running). Smaller companies then rent the track and stations from Railtrack and provide the train services.

railways and railroads

The world's first railway along which passengers travelled on trains pulled by **steam locomotives** was opened in 1825 between *Stockton and Darlington in north-east England. By the early 1900s, when railways reached the height of their popularity, there were about 23 000 miles (37 000 kilometres) of railway **track**. *Victorian engineers such as Isambard Kingdom *Brunel designed bridges for the railway, and architects designed elaborate station buildings such as St *Pancras in London.

The railways played a vital role in Britain's industrial development during the 19th and early 20th centuries. Later, with the invention of the internal combustion engine (= the type of engine used in cars), *road transport became more popular for both goods and passengers. In 1947 regional railway companies were *nationalized and became *British Rail (later BR), but following the Beeching report many **lines** (= routes) were closed in order to save money. In 1994 the government decided that BR should be returned to private ownership. Tracks and stations were made the responsibility of a company called *Railtrack, while trains were once again operated by several companies on a regional basis. People have been encouraged to use trains and other forms of public transport to help reduce fuel consumption and pollution.

The railway network connects all the major towns in Britain, and now, via the ***Shuttle**, links Britain with France and Belgium. Railways are used for both short and long journeys, for *commuting to work each day, and for transporting **freight**. Some routes are now electrified and have high-speed trains. Others still rely on diesel-powered locomotives. Some trains are old, dirty and overcrowded. They also have the reputation for being late, and jokes are often made about the excuses given for delays. These have included 'leaves on the line' in autumn, and 'the wrong kind of snow'. Tickets are quite expensive, although students and the elderly can get **railcards** which entitle them to cheaper fares.

Most Americans have never been on a train. This is sad because the **railroads**, as they are generally called in the US, were the means by which the *Old West was settled. Passenger trains today mainly serve commuters around large cities. The only major long-distance railway business is done by **freight trains** (*BrE also* **goods trains**).

The first US rail company was the Baltimore & Ohio Railroad in 1828, but its **cars** (*BrE* **carriages**) were pulled by horses. Steam power was used by the 1830s, and the *Pullman car was invented in 1856. The *Civil War led to the rapid development of railroads, and the nation was connected from east to west in 1869 when the *Union Pacific Railroad and Central Pacific joined their tracks in *Utah. The 20th century brought more powerful locomotives and huge stations, like *Grand Central in New York. The greatest period of US railroads began in the middle of the 19th century and lasted about 100 years. This time has been celebrated with popular songs like *I've Been Working on the Railroad*, *Freight Train Blues*, **John Henry*, **Chattanooga Choo-Choo*, *Orange Blossom Special* and **Casey Jones*. Trains and railroad workers were also the subjects of many films and novels.

After *World War II car ownership greatly increased and people no longer used trains as a means of transport. Union Pacific, once known for its two-level 'dome lounge cars' from which passengers could see the scenery, stopped long-distance passenger services in 1971. *Amtrak, a public company, now runs the California Zephyr, the Texas Eagle and other trains but it is not very successful in attracting passengers.

Some Americans are **train buffs** and take special steam locomotive trips. Americans also collect model trains, some of which, including the heavy Lionel sets from the 1940s, are now valuable. In Britain old and young alike visit railway museums, e.g. at Didcot and *York. **Trainspotting** (= recording the names and registration numbers of locomotives) used to be a popular *hobby, especially for boys, but is less common now.

,Rainbow 'Bridge the largest natural bridge of rock in the world. It is on Lake Powell in the US state of *Utah, near the border with *Arizona. It is 278 feet/85 metres long, and it curves upward to a height of 309 feet/94 metres. It has always been an important place for the *Navajo people and was made a US national monument in 1916.

,Rainbow 'Warrior a ship owned by the organization *Greenpeace, used by them in protests against damage done to the environment at sea. In 1985 it was sunk by French soldiers as it took part in protests against French nuclear testing in the South Pacific Ocean. One member of the crew was killed. A new ship, *Rainbow Warrior II*, replaced it in 1989.

Rainbow Warrior

R

ˈrain dance *n* a dance performed by many *Native-American groups to create rain. Rain dances sometimes last several days.

ˌMount **ˈRainier** /ˈreɪnɪə(r)/ the highest mountain in the Cascade Range of the US state of *Washington. It is 14 410 feet/4 395 metres high and is a volcano that is no longer active (= a mountain from the top of which melted rock and gases once exploded with great force). It is in **Mount Rainier National Park**.

ˈRain Man a US film (1988) which won four *Oscars, directed by Barry Levinson. It is about the relationship between two brothers, one of whom is autistic (= suffering from a serious mental condition which makes him unable to communicate properly). The two brothers are played by Dustin *Hoffman (who won an Oscar) and Tom *Cruise.

the **Raj** /rɑːdʒ/ (*also* the **ˌBritish ˈRaj**) *n* [U] the period of British rule in India. It is often used to refer to the styles of dress, furniture, architecture, etc. and social attitudes of the British in India in the first half of the 20th century: *The food is excellent, and the decor and service are straight out of the Raj.*

The ***ˌRaj Quarˈtet*** /ˌrɑːdʒ/ a series of four novels (1966–75) by Paul *Scott about the last years of British rule (= the Raj) in India. In 1983 a popular television version of the novels was made under the title **Jewel in the Crown*.

A ***ˌRake's ˈProgress*** a series of eight paintings (1733–5) by William *Hogarth telling the story of a rake (= a fashionable young man who leads a wild and immoral life) who finally dies in *Bedlam (= a hospital in London for the mentally ill). Hogarth later made the paintings into a popular series of engravings (= cheap printed copies). The phrase 'rake's progress' is still used about somebody ruining their life by wild and immoral behaviour.

ˈRaleigh¹ /ˈræli/ a British company that makes bicycles, established in Nottingham in 1890: *My first bike was a Raleigh.*

ˌWalter **ˈRaleigh²** (*also* **Ralegh**) /ˈræli, ˈrɑːli, ˈrɔːli/ (*c.* 1552–1618) an English explorer, politician and soldier. He began his career fighting the Spanish and the Irish, and was made a *knight in 1584 by Queen *Elizabeth I. With her support he made several journeys to North America (1584–9) and South America (1595), bringing back tobacco and the potato, but failed to establish a permanent base there. After the death of Elizabeth he was put in prison for treason for 13 years, during which he wrote his *History of the World* (1614). In 1616 he was released by King *James I to look for gold in South America. He was not successful in this, and when he returned he was punished by having his head cut off. One of the most popular stories about Raleigh describes how he once spread his coat over a piece of wet ground so that Queen Elizabeth could walk over it.

ˌRaleigh Interˈnational /ˌræli/ an international organization based in Britain for young people between 17 and 25. It organizes journeys, usually of 10 weeks, to distant countries for a combination of adventure and useful environmental and community projects. It began as Operation Raleigh in 1980, following the success of *Operation Drake.

ˌRalston Puˈrina /ˌrɔːlstən pjuˈriːnə/ a large US company that sells a variety of products, including batteries and pet food. It was established in 1902, and uses the phrase 'Where purity is paramount' in its advertisements.

ˌMarie **ˈRambert** /ˈrɑːmbeə(r); *AmE* ˈrɑːmber/ (1888–1982) a British ballet dancer and director, born in Poland. After dancing with Sergei Diaghilev's company (1912–13) she opened a ballet school in London (1920) which developed into the *Rambert Dance Company. She was made a *dame(2) in 1962. See also ASHTON.

the **ˌRambert ˈDance ˌCompany** /ˌrɑːmbeə; *AmE* ˌrɑːmber/ a British dance company, based in London, which developed out of the ballet school started by Marie *Rambert in 1920. From 1926, the school's students gave regular public performances, and in 1934 a dance company was officially formed, then called the Ballet Rambert. It was directed by Marie Rambert until 1966. It then began to perform mostly modern dance and has performed all over the world. It took its present name in 1987.

the **ˈRambler's Assocіˌation** a British association formed in 1935 to keep *public footpaths open for ramblers (= people who enjoy walking in the countryside), and to make sure that the countryside is protected. ⇨ note at LONG DISTANCE PATHS AND NATIONAL TRAILS.

ˈRambo /ˈræmbəʊ; *AmE* ˈræmboʊ/ a US film character played by Sylvester *Stallone in three popular films. Rambo is a powerful and violent man with big muscles who fights against evil forces threatening the world. The films were *First Blood* (1982), *Rambo: First Blood Part II* (1985) and *Rambo III* (1988). The name Rambo is sometimes used humorously when referring to a tough person or way of behaving: *The senator used Rambo methods to get his bill passed.*

Rambo

ˌRampton ˈHospital /ˌræmptən/ a special hospital near Retford in *Nottinghamshire, England, for men and women who are mentally ill and are considered to be dangerous. Many of them have committed violent crimes and are carefully guarded.

ˌAlf **ˈRamsey¹** /ˈræmzi/ (1920–99) an English football player and manager. He was manager of the England team that won the World Cup in 1966, and was made a *knight in the following year. His career as a player with Southampton and *Tottenham Hotspur was also highly successful, and he played for the England team 32 times.

ˌMichael **ˈRamsey²** /ˈræmzi/ (1904–88) an English *Archbishop of Canterbury (1961–74). He was the author of several books on religious subjects and was made a *life peer in 1974.

ˈranch house *n* (*AmE*) a type of house on one level with a central room and other rooms connected to it on all sides, sometimes by passages. It copies the style of houses on western ranches (= large farms), and is now common in town suburbs (= outer areas).

ˌR and ˈR /ˌɑːr ənd ˈɑː(r)/ **1** an abbreviation for 'rest and recreation' (or 'rest and relaxation' or 'rest and recuperation'). It is now generally used to mean any holiday/vacation, but was originally a US military expression for a time when soldiers were allowed to relax during a war or after very hard work. **2** an abbreviation for *rock and roll.

ˈRange ˌRover™ /ˌrəʊvə(r); *AmE* ˌroʊvər/ a make of car produced by *Rover since 1970. It is a large, high vehicle, designed for use over rough ground and especially popular with wealthy country people. Range Rovers are sometimes associated with an *upper-class way of life. See also LAND ROVER.

a Range Rover

ˈ**Rangers** /ˈreɪndʒəz; *AmE* ˈreɪndʒərz/ a football team from *Glasgow, Scotland, with a ground at *Ibrox Park. It was established in 1873 and has had many successes in Scottish football, including several wins in the *Scottish FA Cup. Its traditional rival in Glasgow is *Celtic, which has mainly Roman Catholic supporters, while Rangers has mainly Protestant supporters.

ˌJ Arthur ˈ**Rank** /ˈræŋk/ (1882–1972) an English businessman who established two highly successful companies, the *Rank Organization and *Rank Hovis McDougall. He was a *Methodist and became involved in films in 1933 as a way of spreading religious ideas. In 1935 Rank helped to establish *Pinewood Studios and in 1941 he gained control of Gaumont and the *Odeon Theatre group, which all became part of the Rank Organization. He was made a *life peer in 1957.

ˈ**Rank** ˈ**Hovis McˈDougall** /ˈræŋk ˈhəʊvɪs məkˈduːgl; *AmE* ˈhoʊvɪs/ a large British company that makes food products, including bread, cakes and sauces. It was formed by J Arthur *Rank, who bought *Hovis and McDougall in 1962.

the ˈ**Rank Organiˌzation** /ˈræŋk/ a large British company, established by J Arthur *Rank, best known for making films. Its symbol, often seen at the beginning of films, is a man striking a large gong (= a metal disc that makes a loud noise when struck). The Rank Organization also owns several other entertainment companies, including *Odeon, *Butlin's and *Pinewood Studios.

R

ˌArthur ˈ**Ransome** /ˈrænsəm/ (1884–1967) an English author of children's books. He is best known for his adventure story **Swallows and Amazons*, the first of 12 books with the same characters, mostly set in the *Lake District. He also worked as a journalist in Russia during *World War I.

ˌEsther ˈ**Rantzen** /ˌestə ˈræntsən; *AmE* ˌestər/ (1940–) an English television presenter and producer, best known from the programme **That's Life!* She has also presented programmes about child abuse, including *Childwatch* (1987), and established the charity *ChildLine. Since 1994 she has presented the discussion show *Esther*.

rap *n* [U] a style of *African-American popular music with a strong beat to which words are spoken rather than sung. It first became popular in the 1980s, and well-known performers include Hammer, the Beastie Boys and Salt-N-Pepa.

▶ **rap** *v* [I] (**-pp-**) to perform rap music or speak in the style of rap.

*The ˌ**Rape of the ˈLock*** a long humorous poem (1712) by Alexander *Pope, about a man who cuts off a small piece of a woman's hair (= a lock). Pope describes this rather unimportant act in grand and elegant language, which gives the poem its humour.

ˌ**Rapid DeˈPloyment Force** /dɪˈplɔɪmənt/ a special US military unit, based in Tampa, *Florida, which moves quickly to meet international problems. It was established in 1980 to protect oil supplies in the Middle East. It took part in Operation *Desert Shield and Operation *Desert Storm, and helped to protect food supplies to Somalia in 1992.

a Rastafarian

ˌ**Rastaˈfarian** /ˌræstəˈfeəriən; *AmE* ˌræstəˈferiən/ (*also infml* **Rasta**) *n* a person who believes in **Rastafarianism**, a religion that began in *Jamaica in the 1930s. It is based on the ideas of Marcus *Garvey, who taught that black people around the world would one day return to Africa, and that they should worship the ruler of Ethiopia, Haile Selassie (1892–1975). Rastafarians wear their hair in long twisted pieces, called *dreadlocks*, sometimes with red, gold, black and green hats. They also often smoke the drug marijuana, which they call *ganja*. Many *reggae musicians are Rastafarians.

the **rates** /reɪts/ *n* [pl] a tax which was formerly paid in Britain by owners of houses and used to provide money for local services. It was replaced in 1989–90 by the *community charge, also known as the *poll tax, which taxed everyone registered to vote in a particular area. This was very unpopular and caused widespread protests until it was itself replaced in 1993 by the *council tax, a compromise between the rates and the poll tax. ⇨ article at LOCAL GOVERNMENT IN BRITAIN.

ˌDan ˈ**Rather** /ˈræðə(r)/ (1931–) a US television journalist who has presented *CBS Evening News* since 1981, when he replaced Walter *Cronkite. He has won several Emmy awards, including three for his reports on the war in Afghanistan. Compare BROKAW.

ˈ**rationing** /ˈræʃənɪŋ/ *n* [U] a system of limiting and sharing food, clothing, fuel, etc., especially in times of war. Rationing was introduced in Britain and the US during both world wars, and continued after World War II in Britain for several years. People were given **ration books** which showed how much food, etc. they were allowed to buy each week. Many people grew extra food to feed their families and there was a black market (= illegal trade) in many goods.

ˈ**Ratners** /ˈrætnəz; *AmE* ˈrætnərz/ a group of British shops formerly known for selling jewellery at low prices. In 1991 the company's director, Gerald Ratner, made a joke describing one of its products as 'crap' (= worthless), which received wide publicity. People stopped buying the jewellery, and Ratner was forced to leave the company, which later changed its name to Signet.

ˌTerence ˈ**Rattigan** /ˈrætɪgən/ (1911–77) an English writer of plays, including the comedy *French Without Tears* (1936) and more serious works such as *The Winslow Boy* (1946) and *The Browning Version* (1948). Several of them were made into films. Rattigan was made a *knight in 1971.

ˌSimon ˈ**Rattle** /ˈrætl/ (1955–) an English conductor. He joined the *City of Birmingham Symphony

Orchestra in 1980 and became well known for conducting both modern and traditional classical music. Since 1981 he has been a conductor of the Los Angeles Philharmonic. He was made a *knight in 1994.

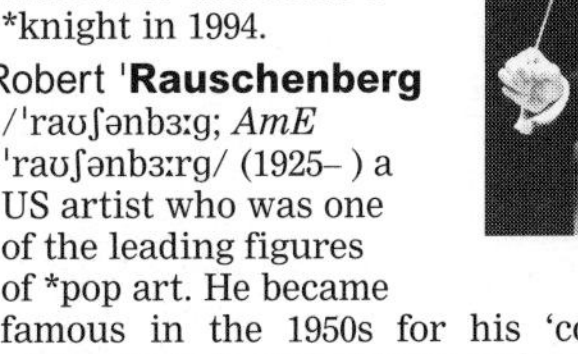

Simon Rattle

ˌRobert ˈ**Rauschenberg** /ˈraʊʃənbɜːg; *AmE* ˈraʊʃənbɜːrg/ (1925–) a US artist who was one of the leading figures of *pop art. He became famous in the 1950s for his 'combine' paintings which include real objects such as bottles, nails and news photographs.

rave *n* a large party for young people, with dancing to loud, fast electronic music such as *house or *techno. Raves were popular in Britain in the late 1980s and early 1990s, and were often held illegally, in large buildings or outdoors, with the police trying to prevent them. They were especially associated with the use of the drug Ecstasy: *all-night raves* ○ *the rave scene.*

The ˈ***Raven*** the best-known poem by Edgar Allan *Poe, first published in 1845. In it a man is visited by a raven (= a large black bird) and asks it when he will see his lost lover again. The bird repeatedly answers 'Nevermore'.

ˈ**Rawlplug**™ /ˈrɔːlplʌg/ *n* a British make of small hollow plastic tube that can be placed into a hole to allow a screw to be fixed firmly in position, e.g. in a wall.

ˈ**Ray-Bans**™ *n* [pl] /ˈreɪ bænz/ a popular US make of sunglasses (= spectacles with dark glass to protect the eyes from the sun). They were originally developed for use by US air force pilots but are now regarded as very fashionable.

ˌClaire ˈ**Rayner** /ˈreɪnə(r)/ (1931–) an English agony aunt (= journalist who replies to people's letters about their personal problems). She has worked for newspapers, radio and television, appearing in the *TV-am Advice Spot* (1985–92) and presenting programmes such as *Medical Matters* (1997). She has also published many books giving medical and personal advice, and is the author of several novels.

RCA /ˌɑː siː ˈeɪ; *AmE* ˌɑːr/ (*in full* the **Radio Corporation of America**) a large US company producing electronic equipment, especially for radio, television and music. It is owned by *General Electric and was started in 1919 It began the *RKO film company in 1921, sent the first photographs by radio (from London to New York) in 1924, and established *NBC in 1926.

RE /ˌɑːr ˈiː/ ⇨ ROYAL ENGINEERS.

ˌ***Reader's*** ˈ***Digest*** a US magazine, published each month, which is one of the most popular in the world. It was started in 1922 by DeWitt and Lila Wallace and is now read in 19 languages by more than 100 million people. It originally contained short versions of articles already published, but now has many written by its own journalists. The Reader's Digest Association also sells books, music and other products.

ˈ**Reading** /ˈredɪŋ/ a large town in *Berkshire in southern England, and the administrative centre of the county. It is famous for its music festivals, especially the Reading Rock Festival. Oscar *Wilde spent two years in Reading prison (1895–7), and he wrote his **Ballad of Reading Gaol* there.

ˌRonald ˈ**Reagan** /ˈreɪgən/ (1911–) a US film actor and later *Republican(1) politician who became the 40th US *President (1981–9). He was also governor of *California (1966–74). He was a popular president, especially because of his ability to explain the government's plans and problems in a simple way to ordinary people. He reduced taxes and increased government spending on defence. He was strongly opposed to Communism but reached agreements with the Soviet Union to reduce the number of nuclear weapons in the two countries. In 1981 Reagan was shot and wounded by a person who was mentally ill. In his last years as President, he was criticized for the *Iran-Contra affair. Some people also said that his wife Nancy had too much power. See also INF TREATY, REAGANOMICS.

ˌ**Reagaˈnomics** /ˌreɪgəˈnɒmɪks; *AmE* ˌreɪgəˈnɑːmɪks/ *n* [U] the economic policies of US President Ronald *Reagan. They involved reducing taxes for companies to help them increase production and create jobs. Government spending was also cut, mainly in the area of social welfare. This made the economy strong but greatly increased the *national debt.

ˌ**real** ˈ**tennis** /ˌrɪəl/ *n* [U] a very old form of tennis, played by two or four people in a large indoor court with rackets, a hard ball and a net. It was originally played by British kings and noblemen ('real' is an old form of the word *royal*), and lawn *tennis developed from it. Real tennis has complicated rules. There are very few courts, so not many people play the game.

ˌ***Rebel Without a*** ˈ***Cause*** the US film (1955) which made James *Dean famous. He plays a young person who resists his parents' authority and gets into trouble with the police. Many US parents were shocked by the film because it showed children from good families who were not satisfied with their comfortable and respectable style of life.

Received Pronunciation

Received Pronunciation, often called **RP**, is the *accent that is widely accepted as the standard accent for both native and foreign speakers of *British English. Although only about 5% of British people speak with an RP accent, it is considered the correct form of speech. Pronunciations given in most dictionaries are RP, or an adapted form of it.

RP is a social accent not linked to any particular region of Britain, though it developed originally from the form of *Middle English spoken around London. At that time London was the economic centre of England and the place where people were trained for professions such as the law. From the 15th century it became a centre for publishing. RP was the accent of upper-class people, and of the most highly educated people. The connection between RP and education was important in establishing the accent.

People became increasingly conscious of accent and by the late 19th century it was considered necessary to adopt RP and lose any trace of a regional accent in order to have a successful career, especially in the army or government. RP was spread among children of the upper and upper middle classes through the ***public school** system. Others took elocution lessons in order to learn to speak 'properly'. Later, RP was taught in state schools. The *public school accent and the **Oxford accent**, the accent adopted by some members of *Oxford University, which many former public school pupils attended, are now considered by many to be rather artificial.

The RP spoken by members of the upper class, including the *royal family, is called **advanced RP** or **marked RP**. Many people think that, like the Oxford accent, it sounds affected. It may be described as 'clipped' if it is spoken with a tight mouth, or 'plummy' if it sounds as though the speaker had a plum in his or her mouth. The vowel sounds of marked RP are distinctive, for example the 'a' in *sat* sounds more like the 'e' in *set*, the short 'o' in *cost* sounds like the long 'o' in *for*, and *really* and *rarely* sound the same.

The status of RP was strengthened in the 1920s after the *BBC began radio broadcasts. For a long time announcers spoke with RP accents, and the accent became known as the **BBC accent**. Standard English, the form of English grammar considered correct, is, when spoken with an RP accent, sometimes called **BBC English**, **Oxford English**, or **the Queen's/King's English**.

Only relatively recently did the BBC begin accepting announcers with regional or other social accents. Even now a strong regional accent may be considered inferior to ordinary or **unmarked** RP, though some regional accents are much liked. Many younger people dislike RP because of its associations with class and privilege, and most educated people now speak a modified, less extreme form or use a modified regional accent.

ˌ**Reckitt and ˈColman** /ˌrekɪt, ˈkəʊlmən; *AmE* ˈkoʊlmən/ a British company that makes cleaning products, including *Brasso and *Dettol, as well as food products such as Colman's English Mustard. It was formed in 1954 from the companies of Isaac Reckitt (1792–1862) and Jeremiah Colman (1777–1855).

ˌ**recomˈmended ˈretail ˈprice** *n* (*abbr* **RRP**) (in Britain) a price that a company recommends for one of its products. Shops may then sell the product at this price, but are not legally required to do so.

ˌ**Reconˈstruction** *n* [U] the period of about ten years after the American *Civil War during which the *Confederate States were brought back into the US. US political and military forces controlled and punished the southern states. Laws were passed making *slavery illegal and giving African Americans the right to vote and hold public office. White Southerners were upset by many Reconstruction practices, such as unusual elections that put former slaves in state governments. This was one cause of the growth of the *Ku Klux Klan.

the ˌ**Red ˈArrows** *n* [pl] a team of planes from the British *Royal Air Force which is famous for its skilful flying displays. The planes are red, and let out long streams of coloured smoke.

R

the ˌ**Red ˈBerets** a popular name for the British Army's *Parachute Regiment. Compare GREEN BERETS, RED DEVILS.

ˈ**redcoat** /ˈredkəʊt; *AmE* ˈredkoʊt/ *n* **1** a name for a British soldier in the 17th, 18th and 19th centuries, when red uniforms were worn. **2** a name for a worker at a *Butlin's holiday camp, who wears a red jacket and whose job is to help and entertain guests.

the ˌ**Red ˈCross** the short name used in non-Muslim countries for the International Movement of the Red Cross and the Red Crescent, an international organization formed in 1864 which works to relieve suffering caused by wars and natural disasters. In Muslim countries it is known as the **Red Crescent**. The symbol of the Red Cross is a red cross on a white background. There are Red Cross Societies in many countries around the world, including Britain and the US. They provide food, clothing, equipment and other services to countries in need.

the ˌ**Red ˈDevils** a team from the British *Parachute Regiment who are famous for their skilful skydiving displays, in which they jump from planes and let out streams of coloured smoke as they fall.

ˌOtis ˈ**Redding** /ˌəʊtɪs ˈredɪŋ; *AmE* ˌoʊtɪs/ (1941–67) an *African-American singer of *soul music. His successful records included *I've Been Loving You Too Long* (1965) and *My Girl* (1966). The magazine **Melody Maker* chose him as the 'World No. 1 Male Singer' in 1967 just before he died in a plane crash. The year after his death, he won a *Grammy award for *Dock of the Bay*.

ˌ**red ˈensign** (*also infml* **red duster**) *n* [usu sing] the flag of the British *merchant navy, first used in 1674. It is red with a *Union Jack in the top left quarter: *The ship was flying the red ensign.*

*The ˌ**Red ˈFlag*** the official song of the British *Labour Party, written in 1889 by James Connell (1853–1929) and usually sung at the end of large party meetings. The red flag is the international symbol of revolution and socialism. The song ends with its best-known line, 'We'll keep the red flag flying here.'

ˌRobert ˈ**Redford** /ˈredfəd; *AmE* ˈredfərd/ (1936–) a US actor who also directs and produces films. His acting roles include parts in *Butch Cassidy and the Sundance Kid* (1969), *The Sting* (1973), *All the President's Men* (1976), *Out of Africa* (1986), *Indecent Proposal* (1993) and *Up Close and Personal* (1996). He won an *Oscar as Best Director for *Ordinary People* (1980). Redford established the Sundance Film Festival in 1978 at his Sundance Institute in Park City, *Utah. He also leads campaigns for a cleaner environment.

ˌMichael ˈ**Redgrave**[1] /ˈredgreɪv/ (1908–85) an English actor. He is especially remembered for his stage roles in plays by *Shakespeare and Chekhov, but he also acted in many films, including *The Lady Vanishes* (1938) and *The Browning Version* (1950). He was made a *knight in 1959. Vanessa *Redgrave is his daughter.

ˌSteve ˈ**Redgrave**[2] /ˈredgreɪv/ (1962–) an English sportsman who has won gold medals in four Olympic Games (1984, 1988, 1992 and 1996) in the sport of rowing, as well as many other international competitions.

Vaˌnessa ˈ**Redgrave**[3] /ˈredgreɪv/ (1937–) an English actor on stage, on television and in films. She began acting with her father, Michael *Redgrave, in 1958, and became well known for her stage performances in *Shakespeare plays. Her films include *Blow-Up* (1967), *Julia* (1977) and **Howards End* (1991). She is also known for her involvement in left-wing politics, e.g. opposing nuclear weapons.

the ˈ**Red ˈHand of ˈUlster** /ˈʌlstə(r)/ the symbol of *Ulster (= Northern Ireland), shown as a red upright hand cut off at the wrist. It was originally the symbol of one of Ulster's ruling families, the O'Neills. ⇨ note at NORTHERN IRELAND.

ˌ**Red ˈHot Organiˌzation** (*abbr* **RHO**) a charity set up in 1989 to raise money for the treatment of the disease Aids around the world. It mostly receives money from the sale of pop music albums.

ˌ**Red ˈNose Day** (in Britain) a day of events and activities organized every two years by *Comic Relief to collect money for charity. Performances by famous comedians are shown during the day on television, and people can also buy and wear red plastic noses, or buy larger noses to put on the fronts of cars, to show their support. The first Red Nose Day was in 1988. Most of the money raised goes to African countries.

Little ˌ**Red ˈRiding Hood** ⇨ LITTLE RED RIDING HOOD.

ˌ***Red River ˈValley*** a traditional US song, sung especially by *cowboys. It is about a man who is told that the woman he loves is going to move away. It begins with the line 'From this valley they say you are going' and ends:

Come and sit by my side, if you love me.
Do not hasten to bid me adieu.
Just remember the Red River Valley
And the cowboy who loved you so true.

ˌ**Red ˈRum** a famous British racehorse that won the *Grand National three times, and was second twice, in the 1970s. There is now a statue of him at *Aintree.

ˌJohn ˈ**Redwood** /ˈredwʊd/ (1951–) a British *Conservative politician and leading *Eurosceptic. He became Secretary of State for Wales in 1993, and in 1995 lost a contest against John *Major for the leadership of the Conservative Party. When Major resigned as leader of the party after losing the 1997 election, Redwood again tried without success to become leader.

ˈ**redwood** (*also* **seˈquoia**) /sɪˈkwɔɪə/ *n* a very tall tree with reddish wood, found mainly near the US coasts of *California and southern *Oregon. The **giant redwood** (or **giant sequoia**) is the tallest tree in the world. It can grow to more than 300 feet (92 metres) tall and live more than 2 000 years. Many redwoods grow in the **Redwood National Park**, a *World Heritage Site in north-western California, and in the **Sequoia National Park** in southern central California.

a giant redwood

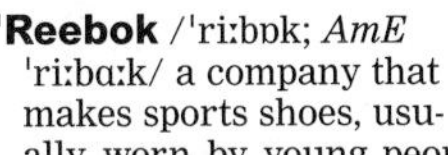

ˈ**Reebok** /ˈriːbɒk; *AmE* ˈriːbɑːk/ a company that makes sports shoes, usually worn by young people for fashion rather than sport: *a pair of Reeboks*.

ˌCarol ˈ**Reed**[1] /ˈriːd/ (1906–76) an English film director best remembered for his film of the Graham *Greene novel *The *Third Man*. His other films include *Our Man in Havana* (1959) and *Oliver!* (1968), a *musical version of **Oliver Twist* by Charles *Dickens, for which Reed won an *Oscar. He was made a *knight in 1952.

ˌLou ˈ**Reed**[2] /ˈriːd/ (1943–) a US pop singer who plays the guitar and writes songs, many of which have serious or disturbing themes. He began in 1967 with the *Velvet Underground pop group before following a career on his own. His successful albums have included *Transformer* (1972), *New York* (1989), *Songs for Drella* (1990), *Magic and Loss* (1992) and *Set the Twilight Reeling* (1996).

ˌ**Reed Interˈnational** /ˌriːd/ a large British company best known for publishing magazines and books, as well as information about science, business and travel. It became a public company in 1903.

ˌMartin ˈ**Rees** /ˈriːs/ (1942–) an English astronomer whose work has been important for the study of galaxies (= very large groups of stars). He was made a *knight in 1992 and became *Astronomer Royal in 1995.

ˌChristopher ˈ**Reeve** /ˈriːv/ (1952–) a US actor best known for his role as *Superman in four films. His other films have included *The Bostonians* (1984) and *Remains of the Day* (1993). Reeve fell from his horse while riding in 1995 and has been paralysed (= unable to move his body) ever since. In 1996 he established a charity which has given a lot of money for research into such injuries.

ˌJim ˈ**Reeves**[1] /ˈriːvz/ (1924–64) a US singer of *country music, known for his smooth voice. His popular name was 'Gentleman Jim'. He joined the *Grand Ole Opry in 1955, and his successful records included *Four Walls* (1957), *He'll Have to Go* (1959) and *Distant Drums* (1966). Reeves was killed in a plane crash. In 1967 he was chosen for the Country Music *Hall of Fame.

ˌKeanu ˈ**Reeves**[2] /ˌkiːənuː ˈriːvz/ (1964–) a US stage and film actor, born in Lebanon of a Canadian mother and Chinese-Hawaiian father. 'Keanu' means 'Cool breeze over the mountains' in the Hawaiian language. His films include *Bill and Ted's Excellent Adventure* (1989), *My Own Private Idaho* (1991), *Speed* (1994) and *Devil's Advocate* (1997).

the **Reˈform Acts** three British *Acts of Parliament passed during the 19th century to change the way *Members of Parliament were elected and to allow more people to vote. The first Reform Act (1832) got rid of the *rotten boroughs, created more seats in parliament and increased the number of men able to vote. The second and third Acts (1867 and 1884) created new seats for city and county areas and increased the number able to vote to about 5 million.

the ˌ**Reforˈmation** the 16th-century European movement, led by Martin Luther and others, to reform the *Roman Catholic Church. Supporters of the Reformation opposed the political powers of the Pope and argued for a simpler religion with less ceremony and more emphasis on the authority of the Bible. In England, King *Henry VIII appointed himself head of a new Protestant *Church of England in 1534, mainly so that he could get divorced from his first wife and marry again. The new Church was supported by bishops such as Thomas *Cranmer and Hugh *Latimer, and became firmly established under Queen *Elizabeth I. In Scotland, the strict Protestant views of John *Knox and others led to the creation in 1690 of the *Presbyterian *Church of Scotland. See also ACT OF SUPREMACY, DISSOLUTION OF THE MONASTERIES. ⇨ article at CHURCH OF ENGLAND.

the **Reˈform Club** a club in *Pall Mall, London, England, established in 1832 by supporters of the first *Reform Act. Its later members were mainly supporters of the *Liberal Party. In modern times it was the first of the traditional London clubs to allow women to become members. ⇨ article at CLUBS AND SOCIETIES.

the ˈ**Regency** the period from 1811 to 1820 when the *Prince of Wales (later King *George IV) ruled Britain as *Prince Regent in place of his father, King *George III, who was mentally ill. The architecture and design of the period is in a simple elegant style based on ancient classical models. The best-known Regency architect is John *Nash, who designed *Regent Street and *Regent's Park.

▶ **Regency** *adj* in the style of the Regency period: *Regency furniture*.

ˌ**Regent's ˈPark** a park in central London, England, designed by John *Nash for the *Prince Regent and completed in 1828. It contains an outdoor theatre, flower gardens, sports fields and a large lake, and *London Zoo is on its north side. The park is surrounded by several grand buildings in the *Regency style, known as the Terraces.

ˈ**Regent Street** a main street in central London, England, designed in 1813–23 by John *Nash and named after the *Prince Regent. It joins Oxford Circus to *Piccadilly Circus and contains several famous shops, including *Liberty's and *Hamley's, and restaurants such as the *Café Royal.

ˈ**reggae** *n* [U] a type of pop music that began in *Jamaica in the 1960s and is now well known in Britain, the US and other countries. Reggae songs often have a *Rastafarian message, and the musicians often wear their hair in long tight curls called *dreadlocks*. Famous reggae groups have included Bob *Marley and the Wailers, Aswad, and Burning Spear.

Reˈgina /rɪˈdʒaɪnə/ a Latin word meaning the ruling queen. It is used in official documents or announcements after a queen's name, e.g. *Elizabeth Regina*. In British law it is also used in the titles of court cases involving the government, e.g. *Regina v Jones*, where *Regina* stands for the government. Compare REX.

ˈ**region** *n* an administrative area in Scotland. The nine regions are *Borders, *Central, *Dumfries and Galloway, *Fife, *Grampian, *Highland, *Lothian, *Strathclyde and *Tayside. There are also three *islands areas: the *Orkneys, the *Shetlands and the *Western Isles.

ˈ**Registered** ˈ**General** ˈ**Nurse** *n* (*abbr* **RGN**) (in Britain) a nurse who is qualified to care for patients in hospitals, schools and elsewhere, after a training period of three years.

ˌWilliam H ˈ**Rehnquist** /ˈrenkwɪst/ (William Hubbs Rehnquist 1924–) the Chief Justice of the US *Supreme Court since 1986. Before that he was the Chief Legal Counsel for the US Department of Justice (1969–71) and a judge on the Supreme Court (1971–86). He was appointed Chief Justice by Ronald *Reagan, and under his leadership the court has become more conservative.

ˌLord ˈ**Reith** /ˈriːθ/ (John Reith 1889–1971) a Scottish broadcaster who became the first general manager of the *BBC. He began his career in industry, but joined the BBC in 1922. During his period as general manager (1927–38) he set high standards in *public service broadcasting, believing that the BBC had a responsibility to inform, educate and entertain the public. He also helped to keep it free from government control. Reith was a government minister during *World War II and was made a *life peer in 1940.

the ˈ**Reith** ˌ**lectures** /ˌriːθ / a series of talks given each year in Britain on *BBC radio. The talks are on serious subjects, e.g. politics, history or economics, and are given by a leading figure in the subject. They were established in 1948 in honour of Lord *Reith, the first head of the BBC.

R

Reˈlate /rɪˈleɪt/ a British organization that gives advice to people who are having difficulties in a marriage or other relationship, and has a number of centres around the country where couples can talk with trained staff. It was formed in 1938 as the Marriage Guidance Council and changed its name in 1988.

Relationships ⇨ article.

Religion ⇨ article.

REM /ˌɑːr iː ˈem/ a US pop group established in 1980. Their records have included *The One I Love* (1987), *Stand* (1988), *Losing My Religion* (1990) and the album *New Adventures in Hi-Fi* (1996).

Reˈmembrance ˌ**Sunday** the nearest Sunday to 11 November (*Armistice Day), on which ceremonies are held in Britain to remember the people killed during the two world wars and other conflicts. The largest ceremony is held in London, when politicians, Commonwealth figures and members of the royal family lay flowers at the *Cenotaph in Whitehall. People traditionally wear a paper or plastic poppy (= a red flower) on Remembrance Sunday and the days leading up to it, and the day is also called *Poppy Day. See also VETERANS' DAY, TWO-MINUTE SILENCE.

ˌFrederic ˈ**Remington** /ˈremɪŋtən/ (1861–1909) a US artist and writer, best known for his realistic paintings, drawings and sculptures of the American West. His subjects were usually *cowboys, *Native Americans, and soldiers and horses in scenes of action. His books include *Pony Tracks* (1895).

ˈ**Remploy** /ˈremplɔɪ/ a British company formed in 1945 which employs about 11 000 people with physical handicaps (= conditions that affect their ability to walk, see, speak, etc.). It has many factories producing goods such as furniture, textiles, electrical goods and musical instruments. The company receives money from the government.

ˌ**Ren and** ˈ**Stimpy** /ˌren, ˈstɪmpi/ a US television cartoon series on the *Nickelodeon channel. It began in 1991 and has been criticized because the characters have disgusting personal habits. They are the 'asthma-hound' Chihuahua dog Ren Höek and his stupid friend Stimpson J Cat.

ˌRuth ˈ**Rendell** /ˈrendl/ (1930–) an English author of *detective and mystery novels. Her main character is Chief Inspector Wexford, and her books include *Wolf to the Slaughter* (1967), *Shake Hands Forever* (1975) and *Road Rage* (1997). She also writes under the name of Barbara Vine. Many of her books have been made into successful television series. She was made a *life peer in 1977.

ˈ**Reno**[1] /ˈriːnəʊ; *AmE* ˈriːnoʊ/ a city in the US state of *Nevada near the border with *California. Because of its easy laws, people can gamble there and get married and divorced quickly. It also has legal prostitutes. Reno is on the Truckee River. It was settled in 1859 and named after General Jesse Reno, a US officer in the *Civil War.

ˌJanet ˈ**Reno**[2] /ˈriːnəʊ; *AmE* ˈriːnoʊ/ (1938–) the first woman to become the US Attorney General, in 1993. She gave approval for the attack that year on the Branch Davidians led by David *Koresh in Waco, *Texas.

the ˈ**Rent Act** a British *Act of Parliament of 1977 that gave new rights to people living in rented accommodation, including the right to a fair rent fixed at a particular amount, and protection from eviction (= removal from a property).

ˈ**Rentokil**™ /ˈrentəkɪl/ a British company that can be employed to kill insects, rats, birds and other animals that cause damage to buildings. Since 1996 the company has been called Rentokil Initial and now also provides other services such as office cleaning and property care.

reˈport stage *n* [sing] (*BrE*) one of the stages that a *bill(1) must go through in order to become an *Act of Parliament. It follows the *committee stage, and takes the form of a debate in the *House of Commons. After passing the report stage the bill then goes to the *third reading.

ˌ**Repreˈsentative** *n* a member of the US *House of Representatives.

Reˈpublican *n* **1** a member or supporter of the US *Republican Party. **2** a person in Northern Ireland who believes that that country should be a part of the Republic of Ireland and not be ruled by Great Britain.

the **Reˈpublican** ˌ**Party** one of the two main political parties in the US, sometimes called the Grand Old Party. It receives more support from rich people and is more conservative than its rival the *Democratic Party. It was established in 1854 by people who wanted to free the slaves. Abraham *Lincoln was the first Republican *President, and others have included Theodore *Roosevelt, Dwight D *Eisenhower,

Relationships

Family and friends

Many British and American people feel closer to their friends than to their *family. In the US especially this is often because members of a family live far apart. It is also because people are able to choose their friends. But in the southern US family ties are strong and **reunions** (= social gatherings) may attract 40 or more family members from all over the country.

In Britain many adults live quite near their family and continue to have close relationships with their parents and brothers and sisters. Some rely on family members to help look after their *children. People who have moved away from home spend more time with their friends, though they may turn to their family for help in a crisis.

Making friends

Many people are too shy to introduce themselves to people they do not know and start a conversation. British people usually feel uncomfortable if a stranger starts to talk to them, even while they are waiting in a queue or standing at a bar when they know they can get away. But in the US to be **outgoing** (= eager to talk to others) is considered a positive quality.

Americans can be quick to make friends with people, but then may have so many friends that they cannot spend much time with them. Foreigners find Americans **friendly** but discover that it is difficult to develop close **friendships** with them. British people, on the other hand, may seem **reserved** (= rather shy and distant) at first but as they get to know somebody they become more relaxed and a friendship may develop.

Americans get on a **first-name basis** (= use each others' given names) easily. Nearly all Americans under 50 – friends, neighbours, co-workers, and business people – use each other's first name. In the US people are afraid of being too formal, whereas in Britain, if people are not sure how to address somebody they call them 'Mr Richards', 'Mrs Davies', etc. rather than risk offence by using their first name.

People often distinguish between **acquaintances**, people they know, and friends, people that they have something in common with and like to spend time with. But people who become close friends at school or college may remain friends for life, even if they no longer see each other very often. Many people have a **best friend**, a friend to whom they feel particularly close. Though it is possible to have friends of either sex, it is most common for men to be friends with other men, and women with women. Some Americans are very **open** and tell others a great deal about their private lives. Though people are not embarrassed to hear private things, they like to choose whether or not to give private information, so it is not polite to ask personal questions. The British are generally less willing to talk about personal matters except to close friends.

Many people who work for the same company take part in social activities together. These may include going to a bar after work, going to parties and attending sports events. In the US people may work long hours because they are afraid of losing their jobs and have little time for a **social life**. In Britain, some people become close friends with people they work with, while others prefer to keep their work and their personal life separate.

Love and romance

Young people generally start to have romantic relationships at school or college. In the US this is called **dating**, and in Britain **going out together** or **seeing** somebody. It is common for young people to hold hands with their **boyfriend** or **girlfriend** and to kiss in public. People who find it difficult to get a boyfriend or girlfriend may use a **dating agency** or advertise in the **personal column** of a newspaper.

If a relationship becomes serious the two people may **get engaged** and then **get married**. But it is also common for a couple to decide they want to have a permanent relationship and to **live together** without getting married. In Britain and the US this is now socially acceptable, though in the US living together is generally seen as a step towards marriage. Marriage has some economic benefits. In Britain, for example, there are tax advantages and in the US only a **spouse** (= a husband or wife) can be covered by a health insurance policy. Whether a couple are married or are living together, they normally expect each other to be loyal and not to **have an affair** or **sleep with** (= have sex with) anyone else.

In Britain people who are in a long-term relationship often refer to their boyfriend or girlfriend as their **partner**, but the word can also refer to a business partner. In the US the term *boyfriend* or *girlfriend* is preferred. Other terms occasionally used include **significant other**, a person who is special and important, and also **POSSLQ**. This humorous name comes from the way the government refers to people living together as 'persons of the opposite sex sharing living quarters'.

In Britain and the US there is no longer a generally accepted moral code about sex. Ideas of when sex is appropriate are based on an individual's own standards and are very varied. Sex is not necessarily linked to marriage or a long-term commitment and is now part of most romantic relationships. This is due not only to a change in attitudes but also to the wide availability of contraception (= means of preventing a woman from becoming pregnant). Sleeping around (= having sex with many people), and having sex for money are, however, generally disapproved of. People now talk about sexual relationships more easily, though many prefer to talk to a doctor or counsellor rather than their friends, or write to an **agony aunt** or **advice columnist** in a magazine.

Homosexual relationships (= relationships between two men or two women) are now heard of and talked about more frequently. Formerly, many people in Britain and the US were hostile to homosexuals but they are now more widely tolerated, though many people do not approve. In the 1990s many **gay** men and **lesbians** (= homosexual women) have **come out** (= said publicly that they are homosexuals) and talk freely about their partner. Their interests and rights are now increasingly being protected by law, though in the US in some states the opposite is true.

Religion

Religious freedom

Modern Britain is a **multi-faith** community, in which many religions are practised, but the main religion is Christianity. *Freedom of worship is generally accepted, though in *Northern Ireland religious tensions contributed greatly to the *Troubles. It is said that as many as 75% of adults believe in God, though only about 4% **go to church** regularly. Many people are *christened, some get married in church, and many have a Christian funeral service, but otherwise they have little interest in religion. White British people rarely discuss religion and feel that a person's religious beliefs are a private matter.

The US is well known for its many traditional churches and less formal religions, though almost all are Christian. Freedom of worship is a result of the separation of Church and State that is written into the *First Amendment of the *Constitution. This happened because many people, including the *Pilgrim Fathers, went to America to avoid religious persecution in Europe.

American *Protestants are very religious, though the *Catholic Church has more members than any one Protestant group. Religious beliefs are strong: it is said that 96% of Americans believe in God, 90% pray and 41% go to church regularly. Churches are centres of social events and business activities, as well as places of worship. Prayers are said at *football games, and some teams kneel together on the field before a game.

Church and State

The **established** (= official) church in England is the *Church of England. In Scotland it is the *Presbyterian Church of Scotland, known by Scots as 'the kirk'. Over 60% of English people describe themselves as 'C of E', even if they never go to church. Many national and local events include prayers. The Church is also involved to some extent in political life as *archbishops and some *bishops sit in the *House of Lords. Some people believe that politics and religion should be kept apart, but others believe that the Church should be much more active in demanding social justice. Christian religious education is provided in all British *state schools, though it is not compulsory.

Despite the fact that only 10% of the population are *Roman Catholic, they make up the biggest active **congregation** (= group of worshippers). The most important Catholic church is *Westminster Cathedral in London.

There is no established religion in the US but Christianity is built into some important aspects of American life. The *Pledge of Allegiance includes the phrase 'one nation under God', and the official US motto is 'In God We Trust'. US presidents always attend church regularly, but they may come from any **denomination** (= religious group).

Since the 1960s some Americans have tried to stop government support of religion. In 1963 the *Supreme Court decided it was 'unconstitutional' for students to say the *Lord's Prayer or to read the Bible in class. Many schools have ignored this ruling. In 1997 a judge in Alabama was ordered to remove a list of the Ten Commandments from the wall of his court, but he refused.

Christian churches

Protestant groups in Britain other than the Church of England are called ***Free** or ***Nonconformist Churches**. Most consider high moral standards to be important and discourage drinking alcohol, gambling, and sex outside marriage. The Free Churches include the *United Reformed Church, the *Baptist Church, which is particularly strong in Wales, and the *Methodist Church. Members of these churches worship in a ***chapel**.

A growing **ecumenical movement** has tried to remove barriers between the established and free churches, and in many places there are ecumenical services at which members from all **faiths** are welcome. Hopes that the Church of England and the Roman Catholic Church might be reunited were dashed in the 1990s when the Church of England began admitting women priests.

In the US the Catholic Church has over 60 million members. The largest Protestant group are the Baptists, with nearly 37 million members. Other Protestant groups include Methodists, *Lutherans and Presbyterians. Episcopalians, who are part of the *Anglican Communion, number only 2.5 million. Part of the *Deep South is called the ***Bible Belt** because Protestants there are **fundamentalists** (= believe the exact words of the Bible). Their **preaching** (= teaching) is sometimes rudely called 'Bible-bashing'.

People who have not found spiritual satisfaction within the traditional churches may join a **sect** such as the *Jehovah's Witnesses, the *Christian Scientists, the *Mormons or the *Seventh-Day Adventists. Others join a **charismatic** church, such as the Pentecostal Church, where emotions are freely expressed and **spiritual healing** is practised. In the US there are over 10 million Pentecostalists. Smaller churches in the US include the *Shakers, the *Amish, the *Mennonites and the *Hutterites. America also has strong religious groups that are not churches, for example the *Promise Keepers.

The US has many *evangelical churches, which believe that Christians should help others find God. ***Evangelists** such as Billy *Sunday, Aimee Semple *McPherson and Billy *Graham have gathered groups of followers through the strength of their personalities. But some, including *televangelists Jim *Bakker and Jimmy *Swaggert, have shown that they care more about money and other pleasures than about God.

America also has many religious **cults**. They include the *Moonies and the large and financially successful *Scientology organization. Other groups have shown themselves to be fanatical (= obsessed with certain ideas) and dangerous, as seen in the violent deaths in 1993 of more than 70 people at the *Branch Davidians' house in Waco, Texas.

Cults have gained a bad reputation in Britain too, mainly because of widely-publicized stories about **brainwashing** (= replacing an individual's ideas with a new set of rules and attitudes) and the requirement that members of cults break off all contact with their families.

Other faiths

The main non-Christian faiths in Britain and the US are Judaism and Islam, though in Britain especially there are also many Sikhs and Hindus, and some Buddhists. Many members of these religions came originally from *India, *Pakistan, *Bangladesh or the Middle East and have brought up their families in their traditional faith.

Britain's relatively small Jewish community enjoys more freedom from religious prejudice than Jews in many other countries. The US has about 6 million Jews and there are **synagogues** (= buildings where Jews worship) in many towns and cities. Jewish men may be recognized in the street if they are wearing a skullcap (= a small circle of cloth on the head). Men from some branches of Judaism wear long black coats and black hats.

Both Britain and the US now have large numbers of Muslims. In general, people outside Islam know little about Muslim beliefs and practices and are sometimes excessively influenced by media reports. There are many **mosques** (= buildings where Moslems worship) in areas where Muslims have settled, though sometimes the building does not look like a traditional mosque. In Britain Muslims fought for the right to have Islamic state schools, similar to those for Jews and Roman Catholics.

Most Hindu **temples** in Britain are in London, *Bradford, *Leicester and *Birmingham, where Hindus originally settled when they came to Britain. The largest Sikh communities are in London, *Manchester and *Leeds. Worship may take place in a private house or a **gurdwara**. There are about 25 000 Buddhists in Britain, and some 20 Buddhist temples and **monasteries**. Most people know little about these religions but in general respect their religious and social practices.

Richard M *Nixon, Ronald *Reagan and George *Bush.

the **Re,public of 'Ireland** /'aɪələnd; *AmE* 'aɪərlənd/ the official name for Ireland since 1949. See also EIRE, IRISH FREE STATE.

re'search ,council *n* any of several government organizations in Britain that support and carry out scientific research, and also provide scientific advice and information to the public and to professional groups. Among the largest research councils are the *Medical Research Council, the Natural Environment Research Council and the Particle Physics and Astronomy Research Council.

Re'serve 'Officer 'Training Corps ⇨ ROTC.

'Restart /'riːstɑːt; *AmE* 'riːstɑːrt/ a British government programme which provides advice and training to people who have been unemployed for six months or more, in order to help them get a job.

the **,Resto'ration** the return of the British monarchy in 1660, when *Charles II became king after the rule of Oliver *Cromwell. 'The Restoration' refers to this event and the period after it, which is known for its lively developments in the arts, particularly in the theatre. The Earl of Rochester (1648–80) was the period's most famous poet, and other artists included the painter Peter Lely (1618–80) and the playwright William *Wycherley: *a Restoration play*.

,Restoration 'comedy *n* [C, U] a type of comedy play written during and after the *Restoration in Britain. Restoration comedies often deal with the sexual adventures of the upper classes, and show characters behaving in a foolish or wicked way. Examples include *The Country Wife* (1675) by William *Wycherley, *Love for Love* (1695) by William *Congreve and *The Beaux' Stratagem* (1707) by George Farquhar. They were also the first plays in the British theatre in which women appeared as actors.

the **,Retail 'Price ,Index** (*abbr* the **RPI**) a figure published by the British government every month which shows the change in the overall cost of goods and services bought by an average household. It is used to calculate the rate of inflation.

re,turning 'officer *n* (in Britain) an official who arranges an election in a *constituency and announces the result. Compare PRESIDING OFFICER.

,Reuben 'sandwich /,ruːbən/ *n* (in the US) a popular sandwich made with corned beef (= cow meat preserved in salt), Swiss cheese and sauerkraut on rye bread which is then grilled.

'Reuters /'rɔɪtəz; *AmE* 'rɔɪtərz/ a British company which employs journalists all over the world and sells news to newspapers, television and radio. It also provides stock exchange information and various other business services. The company was formed in 1851 by Paul Julius Reuter (1816–99).

,*HMS* *Re'venge* /,eɪtʃ em es/ a ship commanded by Francis *Drake and used in the battle against the *Armada in 1588. It was later commanded by Richard Grenville (1542–91) and captured by the Spanish in 1591 after a fierce battle. Lord *Tennyson's poem *The Revenge* (1880) tells the story of the incident, in which Grenville and many of his crew died.

,Paul Re'vere /rɪ'vɪə(r); *AmE* rɪ'vɪr/ (1735–1818) a US hero of the *American Revolution. He is remembered for his horse ride at night from *Boston to Lexington on 19 April 1775 to warn people that British armed forces had landed. This is described in *Longfellow's well-known poem **Paul Revere's Ride*. Revere had earlier been one of the people involved in the *Boston Tea Party. He was an artist who designed and made silver products, and his illustrations of the *Boston Massacre helped to encourage the *American Revolution. See also OLD NORTH CHURCH.

an engraving of the Boston Massacre by Paul Revere

re,verse discrimi'nation *n* [U] (in the US) the action of favouring members of minority groups for jobs, entry to college, etc., over equally or better qualified white people, in order to increase their numbers. This was regarded by many white people as an unfair aspect of the US government's policy of *affirmative action.

the Re,vised 'Standard ,Version (*abbr* the **RSV**) a modern version of the Bible produced by the British and Foreign Bible Society in 1946–57. It is based on the *Authorized Version. See also AMERICAN STANDARD VERSION.

the **Re'vised ,Version** (*abbr* the **RV**) a version of the Bible produced in Britain in 1881–95, based on the *Authorized Version but using more modern language.

Rex /reks/ a Latin word meaning the ruling king. It is used in official documents or announcements after a king's name, e.g. *George Rex*. It is also used in British law in the titles of court cases, e.g. *Rex v Jones*, where *Rex* stands for the government. Compare REGINA.

,Burt '**Reynolds**[1] /ˌbɜːt 'renldz; *AmE* ˌbɜːrt/ (1936–) a US film actor known especially for appearing in adventure films and romantic comedies. His films have included *Deliverance* (1972), *Smokey and the Bandit* (1977), *Switching Channels* (1988), *Striptease* (1996) and *Boogie Nights* (1998). He was the first man to appear naked in **Cosmopolitan* magazine (in 1972). He has had serious financial problems in recent years.

,Debbie '**Reynolds**[2] /'renldz/ (1932–) a US actor, singer and dancer known for her energy and bright personality. Her films include **Singin' in the Rain*, *Tammy and the Bachelor* (1957), *The Unsinkable Molly Brown* (1964) and *Mother* (1996). She now performs in a *Las Vegas hotel which she owns. She was formerly married to the singer Eddie Fisher (1928–), and their daughter is the actor Carrie Fisher (1956–).

,Joshua '**Reynolds**[3] /ˌdʒɒʃjuə 'renldz; *AmE* ˌdʒɑːʃuə/ (1723–92) an English painter. He was the most successful artist of his time, and painted pictures of many important people, including his friend Samuel *Johnson. He was the first President of the *Royal Academy (1768) and used his lectures, called the *Discourses on Art* (1769–91), to express his views on the importance of the 'grand manner' in art and the high status of the artist. He was made a *knight in 1769.

RFC /ˌɑːr ef 'siː/ ⇨ ROYAL FLYING CORPS.

RFK /ˌɑːr ef 'keɪ/ ⇨ KENNEDY[8].

RGN /ˌɑː dʒiː 'en; *AmE* ˌɑːr/ ⇨ REGISTERED GENERAL NURSE.

,Rhapsody in 'Blue a popular musical work (1924) for piano and orchestra by George *Gershwin. It combines *jazz and classical music, and was first performed by the band of Paul *Whiteman, with Gershwin at the piano. The film *Rhapsody in Blue* (1945) was about Gershwin's life.

R

,Rhode 'Island /ˌrəʊd; *AmE* ˌroʊd/ the smallest US state, also called the Ocean State. It is in the northeast of the country on the Atlantic coast. It was named after the Greek island of Rhodes and was one of the original 13 states. *Providence is the capital and largest city. Rhode Island has a fish industry and produces jewellery, electronic equipment, potatoes and apples. Popular tourist attractions include *Newport and Samuel Slater's Mill in Pawtucket.

,Cecil '**Rhodes** /'rəʊdz; *AmE* 'roʊdz/ (1853–1902) a British politician and businessman. He went to South Africa in 1870 and made a lot of money from diamond and gold mining, forming the De Beers Mining Company in 1880. His ambition was to bring the whole of Africa under British control, and he took an active part in opposing Britain's rivals in South Africa, the Boers. In 1889 he formed the British South Africa Company, which owned land later known as Rhodesia (now *Zimbabwe and *Zambia), and became the President of Cape Colony in 1890.

,Rhodes 'scholar /ˌrəʊdz; *AmE* ˌroʊdz/ *n* a student from the US, Germany or the Commonwealth who has received an award to study at Oxford University. The money for these awards was originally provided by Cecil *Rhodes.

the **,Rhondda 'Valley** /ˌrɒndə; *AmE* ˌrɑːndə/ (*also* the '**Rhondda**) an area in south Wales famous for its coal-mining industry in the 19th and early 20th centuries. The last mine closed in 1990, and the area now has a much smaller population.

coal mining in the Rhondda Valley c. 1960

RHS /ˌɑːr eɪtʃ 'es/ ⇨ ROYAL HORTICULTURAL SOCIETY.

rhyming slang

Rhyming slang is a form of *slang in which a word is replaced by a phrase that **rhymes** with it, and is often humorous. Rhyming slang is closely associated with the ***cockney** working-class population of London, though some phrases are more widely heard. It may have developed in the late 18th century as a private language used by thieves or as part of the patter (= talk) of street traders.

Examples of rhyming slang which are familiar to most British people are *apples and pears* (stairs), *trouble and strife* (wife), *plates of meat* (feet) and *dicky dirt* (shirt). Sometimes the rhyming part of the phrase has been dropped. Somebody may say, for instance, that they are going to *take a butcher's* (have a look at something). The original expression was *take a butcher's hook* which rhymed with *look*. Similarly, a person may say *use your loaf* (think about something). Originally the rhyming phrase was *use your loaf of bread*, which rhymed with *head*.

Rhyming slang tends to be thought of as old-fashioned by younger people and phrases like *take a butcher's* and *use your loaf* are now less often heard. But some words that originated in rhyming slang have become part of the regular language. For instance, *raspberry* in the sense of a disapproving sound made with the tongue and lips, comes from *raspberry tart*, the rhyming slang for 'fart'.

,rhythm and 'blues (*abbr* **R and B**) a style of popular music of the 1950s and 1960s played especially by *African Americans. It developed out of the *blues, with added rhythms associated with *jazz and rock and roll. Leading R and B stars included 'Muddy' *Waters, Joe Turner, B B *King and 'Fats' *Domino.

RIBA /ˌɑːr aɪ biː 'eɪ/ ⇨ ROYAL INSTITUTE OF BRITISH ARCHITECTS.

,Tim '**Rice** /'raɪs/ (1944–) an English writer and performer. He is best known for his work with Andrew *Lloyd Webber, writing words for the *musicals *Joseph and the Amazing Technicolour Dreamcoat* (1968), **Jesus Christ Superstar* and *Evita* (1976). He has also written words for songs in films, including

The Lion King (1994), and appears regularly on radio and television. He was made a *knight in 1994.

ˌ**Rice 'Krispies**™ /'krɪspiz/ *n* [pl] a well-known breakfast food consisting of small pieces of crisp rice. They are usually eaten with milk and sugar. The famous advertising phrase 'snap, crackle and pop' represents the noise they make when milk is poured onto them.

ˌ**rice 'pudding** *n* [C, U] a traditional English pudding (= cooked sweet dish) made with rice, sugar and milk. If you say that somebody 'couldn't knock the skin off a rice pudding' you mean that they are very weak or unable to defend themselves in a fight. This is an informal British expression.

ˌCliff '**Richard** /'rɪtʃəd; *AmE* 'rɪtʃərd/ (1940–) an English pop singer. He began his career singing with The Shadows group in 1958, achieving success with *Living Doll* (1959). A series of musical films followed, including *Summer Holiday* (1962). He continues to produce popular records, e.g. *Saviour's Day* (1990), and was made a *knight in 1995. He is well known for his Christian beliefs.

Richard I /ˌrɪtʃəd ðə 'fɜːst; *AmE* ˌrɪtʃərd ðə 'fɜːrst/ (1157–99) the king of England from 1189 to 1199, following his father King *Henry II. He is often called **Richard the Lionheart** or **Richard, Coeur de Lion** because of his courage in battle. He spent the first part of his rule abroad fighting in the Third *Crusade, at the end of which he reached a peace agreement with Saladin in 1191. On his journey home he was captured and held as a prisoner by the Austrian emperor Henry VI, until a large amount of money was paid for releasing him. He spent his later years fighting against the French, and after his death in battle in 1199 he was replaced as king by his brother *John.

Richard II /ˌrɪtʃəd ðə 'sekənd; *AmE* ˌrɪtʃərd/ (1367–1400) the king of England from 1377 to 1399, following his grandfather King *Edward III. He became king at the age of 10, relying on his uncle *John of Gaunt to help rule the country, and was successful in defeating the *Peasants' Revolt of 1381. The rest of his rule was spent trying to control the other powerful men of the country, particularly Henry of Bolingbroke, John of Gaunt's son. In 1398 Richard sent Henry abroad, but he returned the following year and seized power, ruling as King *Henry IV. Richard was put in prison, where he died, possibly murdered.

Richard II /ˌrɪtʃəd ðə 'sekənd; *AmE* ˌrɪtʃərd/ a play (1595) by William *Shakespeare. It tells the story of the final years of King *Richard II's life, presenting him as a weak man who cannot control the powerful men of the time.

Richard III /ˌrɪtʃəd ðə 'θɜːd; *AmE* ˌrɪtʃərd ðə 'θɜːrd/ (1452–85) the king of England from 1483 to 1485, following his nephew King *Edward V. He is often thought of as a cruel and violent king, who probably ordered the murder of the *Princes in the Tower, but not all historians accept this view. He was killed at the battle of *Bosworth Field by Henry Tudor, who became King *Henry VII.

Richard III /ˌrɪtʃəd ðə 'θɜːd; *AmE* ˌrɪtʃərd ðə 'θɜːrd/ an early play (*c*. 1592) by William *Shakespeare. It presents King *Richard III of England as a cruel and violent man who murders several people to become king, and is killed at the battle of *Bosworth Field. During the battle Richard is forced to fight on foot, and shouts the famous line: 'A horse! A horse! My kingdom for a horse!' At the start of the play he delivers the famous speech that begins:

Now is the winter of our discontent
Made glorious summer by this sun of York.

ˌGordon '**Richards**[1] /'rɪtʃədz; *AmE* 'rɪtʃərdz/ (1904–86) an English jockey. He was *champion jockey 26 times during his career (1920–54), winning 4 870 races. He was made a *knight in 1953.

ˌI A '**Richards**[2] /'rɪtʃədz; *AmE* 'rɪtʃərdz/ (Ivor Armstrong Richards 1893–1979) an English writer and critic of literature. He was a professor at *Cambridge and *Harvard universities, and with C K Ogden (1889–1957) developed the idea of *basic English. His best-known book is *Principles of Literary Criticism* (1924). He also published several collections of poetry.

ˌRalph '**Richardson**[1] /ˌræːlf 'rɪtʃədsn; *AmE* 'rɪtʃərdsn/ (1902–83) an English actor on stage, in films and on television. His early career was spent in the theatre, playing leading parts in plays by Chekhov, Ibsen and *Shakespeare, and he was made a *knight in 1947. Later he appeared in works by modern writers, including J B *Priestley and Harold *Pinter. His many films included *Richard III* (1956), *The Bed Sitting Room* (1969) and *O Lucky Man!* (1973).

ˌSamuel '**Richardson**[2] /'rɪtʃədsn; *AmE* 'rɪtʃərdsn/ (1689–1761) an English author best known for his novels *Pamela* (1740) and *Clarissa* (1748). They are among the first novels in English literature, and are written in the form of letters between the characters. Both novels contain strong messages about the importance of sexual morals, and were extremely successful when first published.

ˌLionel '**Richie** /'rɪtʃi/ (1949–) an *African-American singer and writer of *soul music whose records have sold more than 50 million copies. He helped to form the Commodores group in 1967, and their hits included *Three Times a Lady* (1978). Richie left the group in 1982, the year he won a *Grammy as Best Male Vocal. He won another in 1984 for Album of the Year, *Can't Slow Down*. In 1986 he wrote with Michael *Jackson *We Are the World* for *Live Aid. His later albums have included *Louder then Words* (1996).

'**Richmond** /'rɪtʃmənd/ **1** a town in North Yorkshire, England. It is famous for its castle, built in the late 11th century on a hill above the town, and its theatre, opened in 1788. **2** a town on the River *Thames in the *borough of Richmond-upon-Thames in London, England. It is close to two large parks, *Richmond Great Park and *Kew Gardens. King *Henry VII built a palace at Richmond in the late 15th century, but only a small part of the building now remains. **3** the capital city of the US state of *Virginia. It is a port on the James River. Patrick *Henry made his famous 'liberty or death' speech there. Richmond was the capital city of the *Confederate States during the *Civil War and was destroyed by US soldiers in 1865. Its products include machinery and processed tobacco, food and wood.

ˌ**Richmond Great 'Park** /ˌrɪtʃmənd/ a large public park in *Richmond(2), south-west London, England, created in 1637 for King *Charles I as a place for hunting deer. It is the largest of the royal parks, and still contains large numbers of deer.

ˌ**Rich 'Tea**™ *n* a popular British make of round, thin, sweet biscuits with a yellowish colour. They are made by *McVitie's.

ˌSally '**Ride** /'raɪd/ (1951–) the first US woman in space. She went on two flights made by *Challenger* *space shuttles in 1983 and 1984. Ride left *NASA in 1987 to teach and do research. She now directs the California Space Institute.

'***Ride a Cock-'horse to 'Banbury 'Cross*** /'bænbəri/ a traditional *nursery rhyme, often said by mothers to their babies as they bounce them on their knee. A 'cock-horse' is a male horse. The words are:

Ride a cock-horse to Banbury Cross,
To see a fine lady upon a white horse;
Rings on her fingers and bells on her toes,
And she shall have music wherever she goes.

the '**Ridgeway** /'rɪdʒweɪ/ an ancient path in southern England that leads from *Avebury along the Berkshire Downs to Streatley, a distance of 85 miles/137 kilometres. It was once used as a trade route, and passes several places of importance in ancient times, including the Uffington *White Horse. ⇨ note at IRON AGE BRITAIN.

'**riding** /'raɪdɪŋ/ *n* each of the three administrative divisions of *Yorkshire, England, until 1974. Their names were **East Riding**, **North Riding** and **West Riding**. The word *riding* comes from an Anglo-Saxon word meaning a third part of something.

Di,ana '**Rigg** /'rɪg/ (1938–) an English actor who first became well known playing the part of Emma Peel in the television series *The *Avengers* (1965–8). She also worked with the *Royal Shakespeare Company (1959–64) and has appeared in many films. Her recent stage work has included a part in **Who's Afraid of Virginia Woolf?* (1996–7). She was made a *dame(2) in 1994.

the ,**Right** '**Honourable** (*written abbr* **Rt Hon**) (in Britain) the formal title of *Cabinet ministers, *Privy Councillors, certain members of the *peerage, and others: *the Right Honourable Jack Straw MP* ○ *the Right Honourable Member for Brent East.* Compare HONOURABLE 2.

the ,**Right** '**Reverend** (*written abbrs* the **Rt Rev**, the **Rt Revd**) the formal title of *bishops in the *Church of England: *the Right Reverend the Lord Bishop of Winchester.*

*The ,**Rights of** '**Man*** a book (1791–2) by Thomas *Paine. It explained his ideas for a fair society, and supported free education, *pensions for old people, greater rights for women, a fairer tax system, and the right to vote. It also supported the revolutions in America and France, and criticized the British government. Because of this, Paine was accused of treason by the British government, and was forced to leave Britain.

the ,**right to** '**buy** (in Britain) the legal right of people renting *council houses to buy them cheaply, introduced by the *Conservative government in the 1980 Housing Act. Over 1 million people bought their houses, although opponents of the idea claimed that it reduced the amount of cheaper property available to poorer families.

,Bridget '**Riley** /'raɪli/ (1931–) a leading English painter in the style known as *op art*. Her early paintings featured black, white and grey shapes in repeated patterns, creating effects of movement. She introduced colour into her work from the late 1960s.

Ring a Ring o' Roses /,rɪŋ ə rɪŋ ə 'rəʊzɪz; *AmE* 'roʊzɪz/ a traditional children's song and game in which the players join hands and dance in a circle singing, then pretend to sneeze, and fall down on the last line. The words are:

Ring a ring o' roses,
A pocket full of posies,
A-tishoo! A-tishoo!
We all fall down.

'**Ringling** '**Brothers,** '**Barnum and** '**Bailey** /'rɪŋlɪŋ, 'bɑːnəm, 'beɪli; *AmE* 'bɑːrnəm/ the most famous US circus. It calls itself 'the Big One' and has three 'ring' areas where people perform at the same time. Two separate circus groups tour around the country and are seen by about 25 million people each year. The five original Ringling brothers started a circus in 1884 and bought their great rival, the *Barnum and Bailey Circus, in 1907. See also KELLY.

,**Rin Tin** '**Tin** /,rɪn tɪn 'tɪn/ the name of the German shepherd dog that was the popular animal star in many US silent adventure films of the 1920s. His popular name was 'Rinty'. The first Rin Tin Tin was found on the field of battle during *World War I by US Captain Lee Duncan, who made more than $5 million from the dog's *Hollywood career. Compare LASSIE.

the ,**Rio** '**Grande** /,riːəʊ 'grænd; *AmE* ,riːoʊ 'grændi/ the river that forms the border between Mexico and the US state of *Texas. Its Mexican name is the Rio Bravo del Norte. A dispute over this border caused the *Mexican War. The Rio Grande begins in the *Rocky Mountains in south-west *Colorado and flows about 1 885 miles (3 033 kilometres) to the *Gulf of Mexico. See also WETBACK.

the '**Riot Act** a British *Act of Parliament, passed in 1715, which allowed the government to use force to control public protest or disorder. During any such disturbance an official could read part of the Act ordering people to leave a place. To *read the riot act* is an expression which means to warn someone forcefully to stop doing something: (*humor*) *If she comes home late again I'm going to read (her) the riot act.* Compare PUBLIC ORDER ACT.

RIP /,ɑːr aɪ 'piː/ an abbreviation for the Latin phrase *requiescat/requiescant in pace*, meaning 'may he (or she or they) rest in peace'. It is sometimes seen on people's graves. The letters RIP are often used in cartoons or other jokes to show that somebody has died.

'***Ripley's Be'lieve It or* '*Not*** /'rɪpliz/ a US newspaper feature created in 1918 by Robert Ripley (1893–1949) who also drew cartoons. It brings together strange facts and customs from around the world. It is still published and appears in many different newspapers. Ripley also used the title for a museum of strange things, and there are now 27 such museums in the US and other countries.

,**Rip Van** '**Winkle** /,rɪp væn 'wɪŋkl/ a character in a short story by the US writer Washington *Irving. Rip Van Winkle is a man who sleeps for 20 years under a tree and is amazed to wake up and find how much the world has changed.

,**ritual a'buse** ⇨ SATANIC ABUSE.

the **Ritz** /rɪts/ (*also* the **Ritz Hotel**) any of a number of hotels around the world established by or named after the Swiss businessman César Ritz (1850–1918). They are famous for being very comfortable and expensive. The first Ritz Hotel was opened in London, England, in 1906. The word *ritzy*, meaning expensive and elegant, was formed from the name of the Ritz Hotels.

,**Ritz** '**Crackers**™ /,rɪts/ *n* [pl] small thin round biscuits with a salty flavour, often eaten with cheese or other foods, and made by *Nabisco.

The '***Rivals*** a comic play (1775) by Richard Brinsley *Sheridan, in which two young men are rivals for the love of the same young woman, Lydia Languish. The play's most famous character is Mrs *Malaprop, who is known for her tendency to confuse words that sound similar.

the ,**River** '**Café** a fashionable restaurant by the River *Thames in Hammersmith, London, established in 1987. It is famous for its Italian food and has produced two popular cookery books.

,Joan '**Rivers** /'rɪvəz; *AmE* 'rɪvərz/ (1937–) a US comedian, known especially for her jokes about sex. She presents a television *talk show and won an *Emmy award in 1990 as 'Best Host of a Talk Show'.

,Brian '**Rix** /'rɪks/ (1924–) an English theatre actor

R

and manager. He was closely involved with the *Whitehall Theatre for many years, and later became known for his work for the British charity *Mencap, of which he was made director in 1988. Rix was made a *knight in 1986 and a *life peer in 1992.

RKO /ˌɑː keɪ ˈəʊ; *AmE* ˌɑːr, ˈoʊ/ a major *Hollywood film company in the 1930s and 1940s. It was established in 1921 as RKO Radio Pictures. Its successful films include **King Kong*, *Flying Down to Rio* (1933) and other musical films with Fred *Astaire and Ginger *Rogers, **Citizen Kane* and *Suspicion* (1941). Howard *Hughes took control of the company in 1948, five years before it made its last film.

the **RMT** /ˌɑːr em ˈtiː/ (*in full* the **National Union of Rail, Maritime and Transport Workers**) a British trade union formed in 1990 from the combination of the National Union of Railwaymen and the National Union of Seamen.

RNLI /ˌɑːr en el ˈaɪ/ ⇨ ROYAL NATIONAL LIFEBOAT INSTITUTION.

ˌHal ˈ**Roach** /ˈrəʊtʃ; *AmE* ˈroʊtʃ/ (1892–1992) a US director, producer and writer of early films, mostly comedies. He developed the careers of Harold *Lloyd and *Laurel and Hardy, and received a special Oscar in 1983.

ˈ**road fund ˌlicence** *n* (*BrE*) ⇨ CAR TAX.

ˈ**road ˌmovie** *n* (*esp AmE*) a type of film in which one or more characters travel across the country by road, often to escape the police. The journeys often involve violence. Well-known road movies have included **Easy Rider*, *Badlands* (1973), *Smokey and the Bandit* (1977), *Thelma and Louise* (1991) and *Natural Born Killers* (1994).

roads and road signs

The US road system is the largest in the world, mainly because of the long distances between cities. The distance between *Boston and *San Francisco, for instance, is more than 3 000 miles (4 827 kilometres). The US began to build the ***interstate** highway system in 1956. By 1998 it had more than 42 000 miles (67 578 kilometres) of road and carried 21% of America's traffic. The interstate system greatly helped the country's economy, but it also hurt the economies of many small towns not on an interstate. Interstates running north to south have odd numbers and those going from east to west have even numbers. They often have only two or three **lanes** in each direction through the countryside but may have eight or more each way through cities. The New Jersey Turnpike, for instance, has 12 lanes each way near New York City.

Other major roads in the US are called **superhighways**, **freeways**, **expressways**, **thruways** or **parkways**. There are also many *county and local roads, called variously **arterial roads**, **feeder roads** or **farm roads**. Some states have **tollways** or **turnpikes**, on which drivers must pay a toll.

Interstate highways are marked with red and blue signs showing an 'I' followed by the road's number. Other US highways have red, white and blue signs. Some state roads, like those in *Louisiana and *Texas, have signs in the shape of the state. Since 1995 states have been able to set their own speed limits. This is usually 65 or 70 mph (105 or 112 kph) on interstate roads but lower on other main roads.

In Britain the fastest and most direct routes between major cities are by **motorways**, which usually have three lanes of traffic in each direction and a speed limit of 70 mph (112 kph). Each motorway is identified by the letter 'M' and a number. Main roads other than motorways are called **A-roads** and are numbered A6, A34, etc. Some A-roads are **dual carriageways** with two or more lanes each way. Most A-roads now follow a **bypass** round towns. Narrower roads which have only one lane in each direction are called **B-roads**. Most roads have **white lines** and **cats'-eyes** (= lights sunk into the ground) down the middle. Only a very few roads have tolls. Narrow country roads below B-road standard may be known locally by the name of the place they go to, e.g. Orston Lane.

In Britain the ***Highway Code** describes the many signs placed beside roads. Red circular signs give instructions that must by law be obeyed. These include 'no overtaking' signs and signs about speed limits. Red triangular signs give warnings about possible dangers ahead, e.g. slippery roads. Direction signs to major towns are blue on motorways and green on other roads; signs to smaller places are white. Old-fashioned **signposts** can still be seen in many country areas.

In the US red road signs, like 'Stop', must be obeyed. Signs that indicate danger, as in areas where rocks might fall, have a yellow diamond shape. Arrows indicating bends in the road are shown in green circles on white signs. Many other US road signs are now similar to those in Europe.

In Britain there is pressure from both business and private road users for more and better roads, despite the damage to the environment and increase in pollution that this may cause. People who are against the building of new roads regularly challenge proposed routes of new motorways or bypasses. If they fail, environmentalists set up protest camps along the route of the new road. Recently, experts too have cast doubt on the wisdom of building more roads, saying it simply encourages greater use of cars. In the US there are few protests against road-building. People generally want more roads to make their journeys faster and more convenient.

ˈ**road tax** ⇨ CAR TAX.

the ˌ**Roaring ˈTwenties** (*infml*) a name given to the 1920s, when there were exciting new developments in fashion, music and art, and when *Prohibition and *flappers appeared in the US.

ˌ**robber ˈbaron** *n* (*AmE*) a person in business who becomes very rich, often by illegal means and without caring about other people. The term was applied especially to a number of leading US businessmen in the late 19th century, including John D *Rockefeller and Cornelius *Vanderbilt.

ˌHarold ˈ**Robbins**[1] /ˈrɒbɪnz; *AmE* ˈrɑːbɪnz/ (1916–97) a US author of popular novels that contain a lot of sex and violence. Many of them were made into films. The best known is *The Carpetbaggers* (1961), which sold more than 6 million copies. Others include *Never Love a Stranger* (1948), *A Stone for Danny Fisher* (1952), *The Betsy* (1971), *Piranha* (1986) and *The Stallion* (1996).

Jeˌromeˈ**Robbins**[2] /ˈrɒbɪnz; *AmE* ˈrɑːbɪnz/ (1918–98) a US dancer and choreographer. He joined the New York City Ballet in 1949 and was later one of its Ballet Masters-in-Chief (1983–9). His ballets included *Fancy Free* (1944), which he helped to adapt for the film *On the Town* (1949). He was the choreographer for several *Broadway musical plays, including *The King and I* (1951), **West Side Story* (1957) and *Fiddler on the Roof* (1964).

ˌJulia ˈ**Roberts**[1] /ˈrɒbəts; *AmE* ˈrɑːbərts/ (1967–) one of the highest paid US actors. Her films have included *Steel Magnolias* (1989), *Pretty Woman* (1990), *Sleeping with the Enemy* (1990), *The Pelican Brief* (1993) and *My Best Friend's Wedding* (1997).

ˌOral ˈ**Roberts**[2] /ˌɔːrəl ˈrɒbəts; *AmE* ˈrɑːbərts/ (1918–)

a US *televangelist who broadcasts regularly on radio and television. He claims to cure people's illnesses through the power of prayer. In 1963 he established Oral Roberts University in Tulsa, *Oklahoma.

ˌGeorge ˈ**Robertson**[1] /ˈrɒbətsn; *AmE* ˈrɑːbərtsn/ (1946–) a British *Labour politician. He became a *Member of Parliament in 1978 and held several important positions in the Labour *Shadow Cabinet before becoming *Secretary of State for Defence in the Labour government of 1997.

ˌPat ˈ**Robertson**[2] /ˈrɒbətsn; *AmE* ˈrɑːbərtsn/ (1930–) a US *televangelist. He is President of the Christian Coalition. In 1959, he bought a television station in Portsmouth, *Virginia, and a year later began the Christian Broadcasting Network (CBN) which now reaches 90 countries in 46 languages. Robertson tried without success to become the *Republican Party candidate for US President in 1988.

ˈ***Robert's*** ˈ***Rules of*** ˈ***Order*** /ˈrɒbəts; *AmE* ˈrɑːbərts/ a small US book containing rules for running formal meetings, based on the procedures used in the British Parliament. It was first published in 1876 and has appeared since then in several new versions. It is used by the US Congress, businesses and even small clubs.

ˌ**Robert the** ˈ**Bruce** /ˈbruːs/ (*also* ˌ**Robert** ˈ**Bruce**, **Robert I**) (1274–1329) the king of Scotland from 1306 until his death. He joined William *Wallace in trying to take power from the English in Scotland, but was defeated several times by the army of King *Edward I. He finally defeated the English at *Bannockburn in 1314, and England recognized Scotland as an independent country in 1328. After his death Robert's son, David II, ruled Scotland from 1329 to 1371. There is a popular story about how Robert the Bruce, when he was hiding in a cave from the English, watched a spider repeatedly trying to attach its web to a rock until it finally succeeded. This made him determined to keep trying to defeat the English.

ˌPaul ˈ**Robeson** /ˈrəʊbsn; *AmE* ˈroʊbsn/ (1898–1976) an *African-American singer and actor famous for his rich, deep voice. He appeared in the London production of **Show Boat* (1928), in which he sang **Ol' Man River*. His other stage successes included *Emperor Jones* (1925) in New York and **Othello* in both London (1930) and New York (1943). Because he expressed political views in support of Communism and criticized the US government's treatment of African Americans, his passport was taken away for several years. He later lived in Europe (1958–63) before returning to New York.

ˌGeorge ˈ**Robey** /ˈrəʊbi; *AmE* ˈroʊbi/ (1869–1954) an English *music-hall performer best known for the song *If You Were the Only Girl in the World* (1916). He was made a *knight in 1954.

ˌ**Robin** ˈ**Goodfellow** /ˈɡʊdfeləʊ; *AmE* ˈɡʊdfeloʊ/ ⇨ PUCK.

ˌ**Robin** ˈ**Hood** /ˈhʊd/ a character in traditional British stories, who is said to have lived in *Sherwood Forest near *Nottingham during the rule of King *Richard I (1189–99). His companions (usually called his *Merry Men) included *Friar Tuck, *Little John and Will Scarlet, and his lover was *Maid Marian. Together they robbed rich people and gave money to poor people, and their enemy was the *Sheriff of Nottingham. There is no evidence that Robin Hood ever existed but there are many stories about him and many films have been made about his adventures. In these he is often shown wearing clothes made of a material called *Lincoln green, and holding a bow.

the statue of Robin Hood in Nottingham

ˈBill "Bojangles' ˈ**Robinson**[1] /ˈbəʊdʒæŋɡlz ˈrɒbmsn; *AmE* ˈboʊdʒæŋɡlz ˈrɑːbmsn/ (1878–1949) an *African-American actor and tap-dancer (= a dancer who wears special shoes to beat out the rhythm on the floor). He is best remembered for appearing in films with Shirley *Temple, including *The Little Colonel* (1935), *The Littlest Rebel* (1935) and *Rebecca of Sunnybrook Farm* (1938).

ˌEdward G ˈ**Robinson**[2] /ˈrɒbmsn; *AmE* ˈrɑːbmsn/ (1893–1973) a US actor, born in Romania, who was best known for playing tough criminals in films. His films include *Little Caesar* (1930), *The Last Gangster* (1938), *Double Indemnity* (1944), *All My Sons* (1948), *The Cincinnati Kid* (1965) and *Solvent Green* (1973). Robinson received a special *Oscar in 1972.

ˌJackie ˈ**Robinson**[3] /ˈrɒbmsn; *AmE* ˈrɑːbmsn/ (1919–1972) the first *African-American baseball player in either of the two US major leagues (= associations of teams). He played for the Brooklyn Dodgers (1947–56) and was *Most Valuable Player for the *National League in 1949. In 1962 he became the first African American to be chosen for the National Baseball *Hall of Fame.

ˌRobert ˈ**Robinson**[4] /ˈrɒbmsn; *AmE* ˈrɑːbmsn/ (1927–) an English radio and television presenter, especially of quiz shows. His programmes for television have included *Ask the Family* (1967–84) and *Call My Bluff* (1967–88), and his programmes for radio have included *Stop the Week* (1974–92) and **Brain of Britain* (1973–).

ˈˌSmokey' ˈ**Robinson**[5] /ˌsməʊki ˈrɒbmsn; *AmE* ˌsmoʊki ˈrɑːbmsn/ (1940–) an *African-American singer and writer of songs, born William Robinson. His pop group, 'Smokey' Robinson and The Miracles (1957–72), had hits with *Shop Around* (1960), *You've Really Got a Hold of Me* (1962) and *The Tears of a Clown* (1970). He then began singing alone, and had success with *Cruisin'* (1979), *Being with You* (1981) and *One Heartbeat* (1987). Robinson later became Vice-president of Motown Records.

ˈ'Sugar' ˈRay ˈ**Robinson**[6] /ˈʃʊɡə, ˈrɒbmsn; *AmE* ˈʃʊɡər, ˈrɑːbmsn/ (1920–89) an *African-American boxer who many people regard as the greatest of all time. He was the World Welterweight Champion (1946) and then the only person to become World Middleweight Champion five times. During his career, he lost only 19 of his 202 professional fights.

ˈWilliam ˈHeath ˈ**Robinson**[7] ⇨ HEATH ROBINSON.

ˌ**Robinson** ˈ**Crusoe** /ˌrɒbmsn ˈkruːsəʊ; *AmE* ˌrɑːbmsn ˈkruːsoʊ/ a character in a book of the same name by Daniel *Defoe, published in 1719. Crusoe is left alone on an island after his ship sinks, and uses his few possessions to survive there. He is helped by *Man Friday, a man who becomes Crusoe's faithful servant after Crusoe saves him from death. The book was based on a true story and is often considered to be the first English novel. See also SELKIRK.

ˌ**Rob** ˈ**Roy** (1671–1734) the popular name for Robert MacGregor, a Scottish *Jacobite outlaw (= a person who has broken the law and who must hide to avoid being caught). After his land and property were taken by the English, he lived by stealing cows and forcing people to pay him money for protection. He

R

is the main character in Sir Walter *Scott's romantic novel *Rob Roy* (1817).

ˌBobby ˈ**Robson**[1] /ˈrɒbsn; *AmE* ˈrɑːbsn/ (1933–) an English football player and manager. After playing for Fulham (1950–6 and 1962–7) and West Bromwich Albion (1956–62), he became manager of Ipswich Town (1969–82) and later of England (1982–90).

ˌFlora ˈ**Robson**[2] /ˈrɒbsn; *AmE* ˈrɑːbsn/ (1902–84) an English actor remembered especially for her historical films, including *Fire Over England* (1931), in which she played the part of Queen *Elizabeth I, and for stage appearances in plays by Ibsen and *Shaw[2]. She was made a *dame(2) in 1960.

rock *n* [U] **1** (*also* **rock and roll**) a type of modern popular music with a strong beat, played with electric guitars, drums, etc. It developed in the 1960s from *rock and roll. Famous rock groups include the *Rolling Stones, *Genesis and *KISS. Rock later developed into forms such as *folk rock and *heavy metal. **2** (*BrE*) a type of hard sugar sweet, usually made in long sticks which are flavoured with peppermint and brightly coloured on the outside. In Britain, rock is sold especially in seaside towns, and has the name of the town all through the length of the stick on the inside: *He bought her a stick of Brighton rock as a present.* See also EDINBURGH ROCK.

ˈ**rockabilly** *n* [U] a type of US popular music. It combines rock and roll with *country music, which was originally called '*hillbilly music'. Rockabilly was especially popular in the mid 1950s, and was sung by Elvis *Presley, Conway *Twitty, Carl *Perkins, the *Everly Brothers, Brenda Lee and other early rock and roll stars.

ˌ***Rock-a-bye,*** ˈ***Baby*** /ˌrɒk ə baɪ; *AmE* ˌrɑːk ə baɪ/ an alternative to the first line of the children's song **Hush-a-bye, Baby*.

ˌ**rock and** ˈ**roll** (*also* **rock 'n' roll**) *n* [U] **1** a type of popular music played with electric guitars, drums, etc., that first appeared in the 1950s. It developed from *jazz and *country and western music, and was played by such performers as Bill *Haley, Elvis *Presley, Chuck *Berry and Buddy *Holly. **2** ⇨ ROCK 1.

ˈ**rock cake** *n* a type of small sweet cake traditional in Britain, with a hard rough surface and usually containing currants (= dried grapes).

ˌ**rock** ˈ**candy** *n* [U] (*AmE*) a type of sweet/candy, often made by children. It consists of sugar which has been left in water until it forms large, hard crystals that stick together. Artificial flavours and food colours are often added.

ˌJohn D ˈ**Rockefeller**[1] /ˈrɒkəfelə(r); *AmE* ˈrɑːkəfelər/ (John Davison Rockefeller 1839–1937) a US businessman who became very rich as the owner and President of the Standard Oil Company in 1870. He gave the business to his only son, John D Rockefeller Junior (1874–1960), in 1911 and then gave about $500 million of his own money for good causes. He established the *Rockefeller Foundation and the University of Chicago (1892).

ˌNelson ˈ**Rockefeller**[2] /ˌnelsn ˈrɒkəfelə(r); *AmE* ˈrɑːkəfelər/ (1908–79) the 41st Vice-President of the US (1974–7) and only the second not to be elected. Gerald *Ford chose him after replacing Richard *Nixon as President. Rockefeller had earlier been Governor of New York (1959–73). He tried and failed three times to be the *Republican Party candidate for President. He was the second son of John D Rockefeller Junior.

ˈ**Rockefeller** ˌ**Center** /ˈrɒkəfelə; *AmE* ˈrɑːkəfelər/ a group of 19 buildings in *Manhattan(1), New York, used for offices and various kinds of entertainment. They were mostly built between 1931 and 1939, in the *art deco style, by John D Rockefeller Junior, on land owned by *Columbia University. The buildings are connected by underground passages containing shops. They include *Radio City Music Hall and the central General Electric Building (former RCA Building) which contains the offices of *NBC.

ˈ**Rockefeller Foun**ˌ**dation** /ˈrɒkəfelə; *AmE* ˈrɑːkəfelər/ a large US public trust (= organization providing money for projects that help society). It was established in 1913 by John D *Rockefeller and supports research in medical science, agriculture and social issues. These includes problems of hunger, education, social equality and the environment.

ˈ**rocker** *n* a member of a group of young people in Britain, especially in the 1960s, who listened to *rock and roll music, wore leather jackets and rode motorcycles. The rockers were rivals of the *mods and often fought with them.

ˈ***Rocket*** /ˈrɒkɪt; *AmE* ˈrɑːkɪt/ the name of an early steam engine (= type of train) designed in the 1820s by Robert *Stephenson. It was the first engine to be used regularly on the *Liverpool and Manchester Railway, and the original version of it is now in the *Science Museum, London, England.

Rocket

the **Roc**ˈ**kettes** /rɒˈkets; *AmE* rɑːˈkets/ *n* a well-known group of female dancers at the *Radio City Music Hall in New York. They dance in a long line, kicking their legs in the air at the same time and in time to the music. The Rockettes perform all year between the films being shown there, and they also present special shows at Easter and Christmas.

ˌ***Rock of*** ˈ***Ages*** the title of a well-known Christian hymn first published in 1775. The phrase 'Rock of Ages' refers to Jesus Christ, and the first words are:

Rock of ages, cleft for me,
Let me hide myself in thee.

the ˌ**Rock of Gi**ˈ**braltar** /dʒɪˈbrɔːltə(r)/ a high cliff in southern Spain, at the south-western edge of the Mediterranean Sea, near the town and port of *Gibraltar. When people say that something is like the Rock of Gibraltar, they mean it is very safe or solid: *When I invested my money with the company I was told it was as safe as the Rock of Gibraltar.*

ˌNorman ˈ**Rockwell** /ˈrɒkwel; *AmE* ˈrɑːkwel/ (1894–1978) a US magazine artist who drew over 300 covers for the **Saturday Evening Post* between 1916 and 1963. His pictures, done in a realistic style, were full of warmth and humour and very popular with most Americans. They showed people in small towns and in the country engaged in ordinary activities at home and at work. Although some people criticized his work for presenting life as happier than it really is, Rockwell said, 'I paint life as I would like it to be.'

Thanksgiving Day Turkey, *painted by Norman Rockwell*

ˈ**Rocky** /ˈrɒki; *AmE* ˈrɑːki/ a film character created and played by Sylvester *Stallone. He wrote and acted in five successful films about Rocky Balboa, a boxer who overcomes difficulties to defeat strong opponents. The first, *Rocky* (1976), made him famous and won two *Oscars. Stallone himself directed *Rocky II* (1979), *Rocky III* (1981) and *Rocky IV* (1985).

The ˈ***Rocky*** ˈ***Horror*** ˈ***Picture Show*** /ˈrɒki; *AmE* ˈrɑːki/ a US comedy musical film (1975) which makes fun of *Hollywood *musicals, horror films and sex. The story is about a nice couple who visit a castle in *Ohio and meet Transylvanians who dress and act in a strange way. It has become a cult film (= one that is fashionable among a particular group). People who go to the film often dress as the characters and say or sing the actors' lines.

R

the ˌ**Rocky** ˈ**Mountains** /ˌrɒki; *AmE* ˌrɑːki/ (*also* the ˈ**Rockies** /ˈrɒkiz; *AmE* ˈrɑːkiz/) the largest mountain range in North America. They form the *Continental Divide and were a major barrier for people crossing the country to settle in the *Far West. The range covers more than 3 000 miles/4 800 kilometres from the Yukon Territory in *Canada through the US *Rocky Mountain States to the Mexican border. The highest mountain is Mount Elbert in *Colorado, which is 14 433 feet/4 402 metres high.

the ˌ**Rocky Mountain** ˈ**States** /ˌrɒki; *AmE* ˌrɑːki/ the eight US states covered by the *Rocky Mountains. From north to south they are *Montana, *Idaho, *Wyoming, *Colorado, *Utah, *Nevada, *Arizona and *New Mexico.

Aˌnita ˈ**Roddick** /ˈrɒdɪk; *AmE* ˈrɑːdɪk/ (1942–) an English businesswoman who formed the *Body Shop group in 1976, selling beauty products made from natural materials. She is well known for her campaign to end the testing of these types of products on animals, and for her interest in the environment.

ˈ**rodeo** /ˈrəʊdiəʊ, rəʊˈdeɪəʊ; *AmE* ˈroʊdioʊ, roʊˈdeɪoʊ/ *n* (*pl* **-os**) (in the US and Canada) a popular entertainment in which *cowboys compete for prizes by showing their skills in various events. These include riding dangerous horses and bulls, pulling down young bulls by their horns and catching cows with ropes. The first official rodeo was held in 1888 in Prescott, *Arizona.

a rodeo

Roˌdeo ˈ**Drive** /rəʊˌdeɪəʊ; *AmE* roʊˌdeɪoʊ/ a famous street in *Beverly Hills, *California, which is popular with rich tourists, film stars, etc. It has a lot of expensive shops selling clothes, jewellery, leather goods, etc.

ˌJimmie ˈ**Rodgers¹** /ˌdʒɪmi ˈrɒdʒəz; *AmE* ˈrɑːdʒərz/ (1897–1933) a US singer who became an early star of *country music, selling over 20 million records between 1928 and 1933. He was sometimes called the 'Blue Yodeler' because of his ability to yodel (= sing in the traditional Swiss manner with sudden changes of note). He was the first person chosen for the Country Music *Hall of Fame, in 1961.

ˌRichard ˈ**Rodgers²** /ˈrɒdʒəz; *AmE* ˈrɑːdʒərz/ (1902–79) an American who wrote the music for many *Broadway musical shows. He and Lorenz *Hart, who wrote the words, produced 29 such shows, including *Babes in Arms* (1937) and *Pal Joey* (1940). He then joined Oscar *Hammerstein to write many more, including **Oklahoma!*, *Carousel* (1945), **South Pacific*, *The King and I* (1951) and *The *Sound of Music*. Many of these shows became films. Rodgers also wrote the music for the television series **Victory at Sea*.

ˌ**Roedean** ˈ**School** /ˌrəʊdiːn; *AmE* ˌroʊdiːn/ a leading British *public school(1) for girls near *Brighton, *East Sussex. It was established in 1885 and takes girls between the ages of 10 and 18. ⇨ note at PUBLIC SCHOOLS.

ˌ***Roe v*** ˈ***Wade*** /ˌrəʊ vɜːsəs ˈweɪd; *AmE* ˌroʊ vɜːrsəs/ a US *Supreme Court case (1973) which ended in a decision making it legal to have an abortion. The judges said that a state must allow any woman, if she wishes, to have an abortion within the first three months after she becomes pregnant. The decision divided US society and caused a lot of discussion all over the country. See also PRO-CHOICE.

Roˈgation Days /rəʊˈgeɪʃn; *AmE* roʊˈgeɪʃn/ *n* [pl] the three days before *Ascension Day in the *Church of England, during which people traditionally pray for a good harvest. The ceremony of *beating the bounds is sometimes held at this time. The Sunday before Ascension Day is also called **Rogation Sunday**.

Sir ˌ**Roger de** ˈ**Coverley** /də ˈkʌvəli; *AmE* ˈkʌvərli/ the name of an old English country dance. In early issues of *The *Spectator*(2) magazine, Richard *Steele and Joseph *Addison wrote under the name 'Roger de Coverley', presenting him as a typical English country *gentleman.

ˌBuck ˈ**Rogers¹** /ˌbʌk ˈrɒdʒəz; *AmE* ˈrɑːdʒərz/ a character in popular US stories. He was a traveller in space in the 25th century and fought criminals, such as Killer Kane. His world capital was Niagra, and he was helped by Wilma Deering, Dr Huer and, from Mars, Black Barney. The Rogers character appeared first in a novel in the 1920s and was then in films, a *comic strip and comic books, and on radio and television. ⇨ note at COMICS AND COMIC STRIPS.

ˌGinger ˈ**Rogers²** /ˌdʒɪndʒə ˈrɒdʒəz; *AmE* ˌdʒɪndʒər

ˈrɑːdʒərz/ (1911–95) a US actor, singer and dancer. She is best remembered as the partner of Fred *Astaire in several musical films, including *Flying Down to Rio* (1933), *Top Hat* (1935) and *Swing Time* (1936). She was later appeared on stage in *Hello Dolly* (1966) in New York and *Mame* (1969) in London. She married five times.

ˌRichard ˈ**Rogers³** /ˈrɒdʒəz; *AmE* ˈrɑːdʒərz/ (1933–) a British architect, born in Italy. His buildings include the Pompidou Centre (1971–9, with Renzo Piano) in Paris and the Lloyd's Building (1979–85) in London, both of which are famous for having large tubes for water, air and electricity showing on the outside. He was made a *knight in 1991 and was chosen to design the *Millennium Dome at *Greenwich, London.

ˌRoy ˈ**Rogers⁴** /ˈrɒdʒəz; *AmE* ˈrɑːdʒərz/ (1912–98) a US singer and actor. He was the most popular *Hollywood *cowboy star of the 1940s and was called the 'King of the Cowboys'. He and his famous horse Trigger appeared in about 100 films, including *Under Western Skies* (1938) and *Night Time in Nevada* (1949). His wife, the actor Dale Evans (1912–), often acted with him. He made many records and was chosen for the Country Music *Hall of Fame in 1988. After his acting career ended he also owned a chain of *fast-food restaurants.

ˌWill ˈ**Rogers⁵** /ˈrɒdʒəz; *AmE* ˈrɑːdʒərz/ (1897–1935) a US entertainer, sometimes called the 'cowboy philosopher'. He was famous for his sharp but humorous comments about politicians and news events, but is best remembered for two remarks: 'All I know is what I read in the papers,' and 'I never met a man I didn't like.' He first became well known in 1916 in the *Ziegfeld Follies and later made many films, including *State Fair* (1933) and *Steamboat Round the Bend* (1935). He also wrote a humorous column which appeared in many newspapers. He died in a plane crash with the pilot Wiley *Post.

ˌ***Roget's The*ˈ*saurus*** /ˌrɒʒeɪz; *AmE* roʊˌʒeɪz/ (*also infml* ***Roget***) a popular reference book, originally written by Peter Mark Roget (1779–1869) and first published in 1852. It contains English words or phrases arranged together in groups according to their meaning, and is still used today by people looking for the most appropriate word or phrase to use in a piece of writing. New editions of *Roget* are published regularly.

ˈ**Rolex**™ /ˈrəʊleks; *AmE* ˈroʊleks/ a type of expensive watch of high quality, first made in 1908 by the Swiss company Montres-Rolex. Rolex watches are often regarded as a sign of success or wealth: *They beat him up and stole his Rolex.*

ˌ***Rolling*** ˈ***Stone*** a US *rock music magazine, known especially for its interviews with famous singers and musicians. It began in 1967 in *San Francisco. Its name came from the words of a Bob *Dylan song.

The ˌ**Rolling** ˈ**Stones** (*also infml* The **Stones**) a British pop group formed in 1962. Its original members were Mick *Jagger, Brian Jones (1941–69) and Keith Richard (later Richards) (1943–), who were later joined by Bill Wyman (1936–) and Charlie Watts (1941–). Their music was influenced by US *blues and their most successful early records were *(I Can't Get No) Satisfaction* (1965) and *Jumpin' Jack Flash* (1968), with albums including *Sticky Fingers* (1971) and *Exile on Main Street* (1972). They were known for their noisy and aggressive performances, and they shocked many people by behaving badly in public and taking drugs. Brian Jones died when he accidentally drowned while under the influence of drugs in 1969. His place in the group was taken by Mick Taylor (1948–), who was later replaced by Ron Wood (1942–). The group still play together and make records. Their more recent albums have included *Voodoo Lounge* (1994).

ˌSonny ˈ**Rollins** /ˌsʌni ˈrɒlɪnz; *AmE* ˈrɑːlɪnz/ (1930–) an *African-American saxophone player who helped to develop the 'hard-bop' style of *jazz. In his early career he was influenced by Thelonious *Monk. His albums include *Bebop Professors* (1949), *Sonny Meets Hawk* (1963), *Nucleus* (1975) and *Plus 3* (1995). Rollins was chosen for the Jazz *Hall of Fame in 1973.

ˌ**Rolls-**ˈ**Royce**™ /ˌrəʊlz ˈrɔɪs; *AmE* ˌroʊlz/ (*also infml* **Rolls**, ˈ**Roller** /ˈrəʊlə(r); *AmE* ˈroʊlər/) *n* any of the large, expensive, comfortable cars made by the British company Rolls-Royce. Many people recognize them by the small metal statue (representing the 'Spirit of Ecstasy') on the front of every Rolls-Royce car. The company was formed in 1905–6 by Charles Rolls (1877–1910) and Henry Royce (1863–1933) and also produces aircraft engines, e.g. for the *Spitfire during *World War II and later for *Boeing. In 1980 the part of the company that makes cars joined with another British company, *Vickers. The Rolls-Royce company was bought by the German company Volkswagen in 1998. The name Rolls-Royce is also used informally to refer to the best product of a particular type: *This is the Rolls-Royce of electric guitars – it costs £5 000.*

Roman Britain ⇨ article.

ˌ**Roman** ˈ**Catholic** (*also* ˈ**Catholic**) *n* a member of the Christian Church that recognizes the Pope as its head. It was the established Church in Britain until the *Reformation of the 16th century, when it was replaced by the Protestant *Church of England and *Church of Scotland. After this Roman Catholics were forbidden to hold public positions or receive university education. In the 19th century the *Emancipation Act led to greater religious freedom, but Roman Catholics still cannot be appointed to some high positions in public life, including that of *Lord Chancellor, and the king or queen may not practise the religion or marry a Catholic. The Catholic religion is still strong in the Republic of Ireland, and there is violent conflict between Protestants and Catholics in *Northern Ireland. The Roman Catholic Church in Britain is led by the *archbishops of *Westminster(1), *Glasgow and *Armagh. ▶ **Roman Catholic** (*also* **Catholic**) *adj*. **Roman Catholicism** (*also* **Catholicism**) *n* [U].

ˌ**Roma**ˈ**nesque** *adj* of the style of architecture that developed in Europe from about 900 to 1200, with round arches, high ceilings and thick walls. English Romanesque architecture, which developed from about 1150, is usually called *Norman architecture, and one of the finest examples is *Durham cathedral. Romanesque architecture was replaced by the *Gothic style.

▶ **Romanesque** *n* [U] the Romanesque style.

Roˈ**manticism** *n* [U] (*also* the **Ro**ˈ**mantic** ˌ**Movement**) a movement in European literature, art and music that began in the late 18th century. It was partly influenced by the American and French revolutions, and its main themes were the importance of imagination and feeling, the love of nature, and an interest in the past. In Britain, its greatest achievements were in poetry, especially that of *Wordsworth, *Coleridge, *Keats, *Shelley², *Blake⁴ and *Byron. Romantic novels produced during this period include **Wuthering Heights* and **Frankenstein*. In painting, Romantic artists included *Constable and *Turner².

▶ **Romantic** *adj* of or relating to the Romantic movement. **Romantic** *n* a person who writes, paints, etc. in the Romantic style.

ˈ**Romany** *n* **1** [C] a *gypsy. Gypsies are a travelling

Roman Britain

There are many traces of the Roman occupation of Britain visible today. Many archaeological sites are open to the public, and Roman roads and walls stretch across the countryside.

The province of Britannia

Julius *Caesar came to Britain in 55 BC and 54 BC and defeated some of the local *Celtic tribes. He introduced taxes and established trade in corn, leather, iron and lead. When, in AD 43, this was under threat, the emperor Claudius ordered an invasion. Togodumnus and Caractacus of the Catuvellauni tribe led the Celtic resistance but they were driven back to Wales. *Maiden Castle in Dorset and other hill forts were destroyed and southern Britain became **Britannia**, a province of the Roman Empire. In AD 60 Queen *Boudicca, leader of the Iceni tribe, tried again to drive the Romans from Britain but failed.

Britannia was ruled by a Roman **governor**. Another Roman official was responsible for taxation and for exploiting Britain's mineral wealth. Celtic chiefs were used to keep order. Many of them became Roman citizens and adopted Roman ways.

In AD 78 the governor Agricola brought Wales under Roman control. Afterwards he went north to try to conquer the *Picts and other Scottish tribes, but did not succeed. He then built a line of forts marking the northern frontier of the province.

The emperor Hadrian visited Britain in AD 122 and after that ***Hadrian's Wall** was built between *Newcastle-upon-Tyne and Bowness. It was 73 miles (117 kilometres) long and 22 feet (6.7 metres) high. There was a path along the top and ditches on both sides. Small forts to contain 30 to 50 men were built at every Roman mile (= 1 000 paces, shorter than a modern mile), with larger forts every four or five miles. Long stretches of wall can still be seen, as well as the remains of forts at Chesters and Housesteads. The wall was guarded by soldiers from all parts of the Empire. Legions composed of Roman citizens were based in more luxurious accommodation at *York, called *Eboracum* by the Romans.

After AD 138 the frontier was moved further north and a new wall, the ***Antonine Wall**, was built between the *Forth and *Clyde rivers. Hadrian's Wall became the frontier again later in the century.

Towns and roads

The Romans founded over 20 large towns called *coloniae*. *Colchester (*Camulodunum*) was built by Claudius as the new capital. It was followed by *Gloucester (*Glevum*) and *Lincoln (*Lindum*). Some *coloniae* were built to provide homes for retired soldiers. It often took many years before a town had all the amenities that Roman citizens expected: a forum (= meeting place) with shops and a town hall, and baths and theatres. Buildings were decorated with painted walls, plaster mouldings (= raised decorations) and mosaic floors (= floors made of many small coloured stones arranged to form a picture or a pattern).

Many smaller towns including *St Albans (*Verulamium*) were formerly tribal centres. Under the Romans, they grew in importance and became centres of local government called *municipia*.

London (*Londinium*) developed first as a trading centre and became the focus of several roads. It soon replaced Colchester as the capital. Walls were built round the town in the 2nd century. By the 3rd century coins were being minted there and it became the financial centre of the province.

Roads were needed to transport soldiers to border areas and, later, for travel between towns. They were made of layers of gravel on a stone foundation and are famous for being very straight. The most famous Roman roads are ***Watling Street**, which ran from *Dover to London and then on to St Albans and *Chester, ***Ermine Street** between London and York, and the ***Fosse Way**, which ran from *Exeter to Lincoln. Roman routes are marked on *Ordnance Survey maps, and several modern roads follow their course.

Country villas

During the Roman occupation most of the native population continued to live in the countryside. After peace was established, Romans also began to live there. Some may have been local government officials; many were farmers. An increased demand for food in the new towns made improvements in agriculture necessary. A wider variety of fruit and vegetables was grown, and there were attempts to cultivate vines.

Villas were built from the 1st century onwards. *Fishbourne in Sussex is one of the largest and may have been built for the Celtic chief Cogidubnus who was put in charge of southern Britannia. Other villas were more like farmhouses and had workshops and barns nearby. Many, including Chedworth and Woodchester, were built near the towns of *Bath (*Aquae Sulis*) and Cirencester (*Corinium*). Most villas had central heating, glass windows and mosaic floors. Some also had their own baths. The remains of Chedworth and many other villas can be visited by the public.

Religion

The *druids, influential Celtic priests, were banned by the Romans, but otherwise people were free to worship as they wished. Worship of the old Celtic gods continued alongside that of Roman gods. The goddess Sulis-Minerva, worshipped at Bath, was a combination of the Celtic goddess Sul and Roman Minerva. Soldiers brought their own gods with them, and a temple to Mithras, whose cult originated in Persia, has been found near Hadrian's Wall. After the emperor Constantine became a Christian in AD 313, Christianity became the state religion throughout the Empire, though there is little evidence of it in Britain until the 4th century.

The end of Roman rule

By AD 410, when Roman officials left Britain, the country had already been attacked by the Picts and invaded by Germanic tribes from northern Europe. The invaders caused great destruction and more soldiers were sent to defend the province. When part of the army was withdrawn to deal with trouble elsewhere, the British rebelled against Roman rule. After this, Roman influence declined. Germanic settlers, the Angles, *Saxons and *Jutes, began arriving in Britain from about AD 430 and took over much of the south and east of the country.

people, usually living in caravans, who arrived in Britain around 1500 and are now found in both Britain and the US. **2** [U] the language of the gypsy people.

▶ **Romany** *adj* of the gypsy people or their language.

ˌSigmund ˈ**Romberg** /ˌsɪɡmənd ˈrɒmbɜːɡ; *AmE* ˈrɑːmbɜːrɡ/ (1887–1951) a US composer, born in Hungary, who wrote more than 70 *Broadway musical plays and light operas. They included *Maytime* (1917), *The Student Prince* (1924) and *The Desert Song* (1926). Several became films with Nelson *Eddy and Jeanette MacDonald.

ˌ***Romeo and ˈJuliet*** /ˌrəʊmiəʊ; *AmE* ˌroʊmioʊ/ a play (*c.* 1595) by *Shakespeare. It is set in Verona in Italy, and tells the story of two young people, Romeo and Juliet, who fall in love although they are from families who are enemies. They marry secretly but are unable to live together and finally kill themselves. The play is famous for its beautiful poetry and for the *balcony scene*, during which Juliet says 'O Romeo, Romeo! Wherefore art thou Romeo?' and 'What's in a name? That which we call a rose/By any other name would smell as sweet.' The ballet *Romeo and Juliet* (1938) by Prokoviev and the musical show **West Side Story* were both based on the play.

ˌGeorge ˈ**Romney** /ˈrɒmni; *AmE* ˈrɑːmni/ (1734–1802) an English painter. He was one of the most fashionable portrait painters of the late 18th century and was famous for his use of bright colours. He painted many pictures using Lady Emma *Hamilton as his model.

ˌEgon ˈ**Ronay** /ˌeɡɒn ˈrəʊneɪ, *also* ˌiːɡɒn; *AmE* ˌeɡɑːn ˈroʊneɪ, *also* ˌiːɡɑːn/ (1920–) a British writer about food and restaurants, born in Hungary, who began his career as a professional cook. His books, which include *Egon Ronay's Guide to Hotels and Restaurants*, give information for travellers and tourists in Britain and abroad.

ˌ***Room at the ˈTop*** a novel (1957) by John *Braine about Joe Lampton, a young man who leaves the woman he loves and marries another one who has more money. The book, which became very popular, established Braine as one of the *angry young men of the period. It was made into a film in 1958, and Braine later wrote a sequel (= a book continuing the original story), *Life at the Top* (1962).

ˌMickey ˈ**Rooney** /ˈruːni/ (1920–) a US actor known for his cheerful personality. He began as a child actor and first became famous in the late 1930s as the film character Andy *Hardy. He then made several films with Judy *Garland. His film successes included *Babes in Arms* (1939), *The Human Comedy* (1943), *The Bold and the Brave* (1956) and *The Black Stallion* (1979). Rooney later had more success in the *Broadway musical play *Sugar Babies* (1978–81). He received a special *Oscar in 1983. He has been married eight times.

ˌEleanor ˈ**Roosevelt**[1] /ˈrəʊzəvelt; *AmE* ˈroʊzəvelt/ (1884–1962) the wife of US President Franklin D *Roosevelt, whom she married in 1905. She was also the niece of President Theodore *Roosevelt. She was known for supporting the rights of women and minority groups. After her husband's death, she became a US representative at the *United Nations and helped to write the Universal Declaration of Human Rights (1948).

ˌFranklin D ˈ**Roosevelt**[2] /ˌfræŋklɪn, ˈrəʊzəvelt; *AmE* ˈroʊzəvelt/ (Franklin Delano Roosevelt 1882–1945) a *Democratic politician who became the 32nd US *President (1933–45), also known informally as FDR, and the only one to be elected four times. From 1921 he suffered from polio (= a serious disease affecting the nervous system) and could hardly walk without help. Before becoming President he was Governor of New York (1929–33). As President, he introduced his *New Deal programme which helped the US to recover from the *Great Depression. Roosevelt was a cheerful man who gave Americans confidence with his *fireside chats on radio. Before the US entered *World War II, he supported Britain with the *Lend-Lease plan. He died while President just before the war ended. See also FOUR FREEDOMS, MANHATTAN PROJECT, YALTA.

ˌTheodore ˈ**Roosevelt**[3] /ˈrəʊzəvelt; *AmE* ˈroʊzəvelt/ (1858–1919) the 26th US *President (1901–9) and a member of the *Republican Party. His popular name was Teddy. He led the *Rough Riders in the *Spanish-American War. He became Vice-president in 1900 and replaced William *McKinley as President when McKinley was murdered a year later. As President, Roosevelt introduced his *Square Deal programme, began to build the *Panama Canal, created the *Great White Fleet, and used the *big stick military policy. He won the 1906 *Nobel Prize for peace after helping to end the Russo-Japanese War. Roosevelt enjoyed the outdoor life and was keen on hunting.

ˈ**root beer** *n* [U, C] a sweet fizzy drink (= one containing many bubbles) popular in the US. It is made from the juices of different roots, barks and herbs.

Roots /ruːts/ a long US novel (1976) by the *African-American writer Alex Haley, for which he received a special *Pulitzer Prize. The story, based on Haley's research into his own family's history, is about an African-American family of slaves. A television version (1977) ran for eight nights on *ABC and had an audience of about 100 million, the largest ever. It received nine *Emmy awards.

Roˈseanne /rəʊˈzæn; *AmE* roʊˈzæn/ (1953–) the main character in the popular US television comedy series on *ABC of the same name (1988–97). She was played by Roseanne (originally Roseanne Barr, later Roseanne Arnold), a US comedy actor with a large figure and a loud voice. The series is about a family which is loving but always arguing.

the ˈ**Rose Bowl** (in the US) the oldest and best-known of the college football *bowl games. It is played on New Year's Day in Pasadena, *California, in the Rose Bowl stadium which has 102 000 seats. The game follows the **Rose Bowl Parade**, in which many vehicles decorated with flowers take part.

ˈ**Rosenberg**[1] /ˈrəʊzənbɜːɡ; *AmE* ˈroʊzənbɜːrɡ/ the name of a US married couple, **Julius Rosenberg** (1918–53) and his wife **Ethel Rosenberg** (1915–53), who were executed in 1953 for giving the Soviet Union secret US nuclear information during *World War II. Many people thought they were innocent and there are still doubts about the evidence.

ˌIsaac ˈ**Rosenberg**[2] /ˈrəʊzənbɜːɡ; *AmE* ˈroʊzənbɜːrɡ/ (1890–1918) an English poet and artist who was killed during *World War I. Many of his poems are about the horror of war. His collections of poetry include *Night and Day* (1912) and *Youth* (1915).

ˌ**Rosencrantz and ˈGuildenstern** /ˌrəʊzənkrænts, ˈɡɪldənstɜːn; *AmE* ˌroʊzənkrænts, ˈɡɪldənstɜːrn/ two minor characters in the play *Hamlet* by *Shakespeare. They appear as the main characters in *Rosencrantz and Guildenstern are Dead* (1966), a comedy play by Tom *Stoppard which tells the story of *Hamlet* from their point of view.

the ˌWars of the ˈ**Roses** ⇨ WARS OF THE ROSES.

the ˌ**Rose ˈTheatre** a theatre built in 1586–7 near *Southwark Bridge in central London, England, where many of *Shakespeare's plays were performed and where Edward *Alleyn acted. Surviving parts of the theatre were discovered in 1989 during work on a new office building. Compare GLOBE.

the **Ro'setta ,Stone** /rəʊ'zetə; *AmE* roʊ'zetə/ a large, flat, black stone which was discovered in Egypt in 1799 and is now in the *British Museum, London. The same text is written on it three times in three different types of writing, including hieroglyphics (= Egyptian writing). This enabled the French language expert Jean-François Champollion (1790–1832) to read hieroglyphics for the first time.

,Rosie the 'Riveter /'rɪvətə(r)/ the name used in the US to refer to any American woman who worked in factories to help the war effort during World War II. A riveter fixes sheets of metal together with thick metal pins. The name was used as the title of a popular song, and a real riveter, called Rose Monroe, was chosen for a famous poster which showed a woman worker saying, 'We can do it!'

,Betsy **'Ross¹** /'rɒs; *AmE* 'rɔːs/ (1752–1836) the *Philadelphia woman who, according to tradition, sewed the first US flag in 1776. No evidence for this exists, but she did sew early flags. George *Washington designed the first flag, which had a circle of stars.

Di,ana **'Ross²** /'rɒs; *AmE* 'rɔːs/ (1944–) an *African-American singer and actor who began her career as the main singer with the *Supremes. She later left the group to sing alone and her hits have included *Ain't No Mountain High Enough* (1970) and *Endless Love* (1982). She also played the part of Billie *Holiday in the film *Lady Sings the Blues* (1970). Among her other films are *The Wiz* (1978) and, on television, *Out of Darkness* (1994).

Chri,stina **Ros'setti¹** /rə'zeti/ (1830–94) an English poet, the sister of Dante Gabriel *Rossetti. Her poetry shows her religious faith and a romantic sadness, and she is best known for the collection *The Goblin Market and Other Poems* (1862). She also wrote poems for children, and the words to the religious song *In the Bleak Midwinter*.

'Dante 'Gabriel **Ros'setti²** /'dænti, rə'zeti/ (1828–82) an English painter and poet. In 1848 he formed the *Pre-Raphaelite Brotherhood with John Everett *Millais and Holman *Hunt. His earliest work includes *The Girlhood of Mary Virgin* (1849), with his sister Christina *Rossetti as the model. Rossetti's best-known paintings, e.g. *The Daydream* (1880), are of tall, thin women with pale skin and sad expressions, and they are now considered to be typical of the Pre-Raphaelite style. For many of them his model was Elizabeth Siddal, who became his wife before her early death. Rossetti also published several collections of poetry and translated the work of Dante and other poets.

La Ghirlandata *by Dante Gabriel Rossetti*

Ro'tarian /rəʊ'teəriən; *AmE* roʊ'teriən/ *n* a member of a *Rotary Club.

'Rotary Club /'rəʊtəri; *AmE* 'roʊtəri/ *n* a branch of an international organization of businessmen (called **Rotary International**) who meet for social reasons and to collect money for charity. The first Rotary Club was formed in 1905 by the US lawyer Paul Harris (1878–1947).

ROTC /'rɒtsi; *AmE* 'rɑːtsi/ (*in full* **Reserve Officers' Training Corps**) (in the US) a group of students who train to be military officers while at college or university. The army pays for most or all of the education for many ROTC students, who must then spend at least four years in the army. The US Navy and Air Force have similar programmes.

,Philip **'Roth** /'rɒθ; *AmE* 'rɑːθ/ (1933–) a US writer of novels and short stories, mostly about Jewish-American life. His best-known novel is *Portnoy's Complaint* (1969). The short novel *Goodbye Columbus* (1959) won a *National Book Award and became a successful film (1969). His other novels include *My Life as a Man* (1974), *Zukerman Bound* (1985), *Sabbath's Theater* (1995), which won a National Book Award, and *American Pastoral* (1997), which won the *Pulitzer Prize.

,Lord **'Rothermere** /'rɒðəmɪə(r); *AmE* 'rɑːðərmɪr/ (*born* Harold Sydney Harmsworth 1868–1940) an English businessman who owned several newspapers, including the **Daily Mirror* and **Daily Mail*. His brother was Lord *Northcliffe.

,Mark **'Rothko** /'rɒθkəʊ; *AmE* 'rɑːθkoʊ/ (1903–70) a US painter, born in Russia, who was a leading figure in the *abstract expressionism movement. He was known for producing very large pictures in which bands of strong colour with soft edges are arranged in a vertical pattern, creating a calm effect.

'Rothmans /'rɒθmənz; *AmE* 'rɑːθmənz/ a British company that makes cigarettes. In 1999 it joined with British American Tobacco to form one of the world's largest tobacco companies.

'Rothschild /'rɒθstʃaɪld; *AmE* 'rɔːθstʃaɪld/ the name of a British family of businessmen and politicians, originally from Germany. **Nathan Mayer Rothschild** (1777–1836) opened the bank of N M Rothschild and Sons in London in 1798, and became a British citizen in 1804. His son **Lionel Nathan Rothschild** (1808–79) became the first Jewish *Member of Parliament in 1858 and worked to achieve new legal freedoms for British Jews. Lionel's son **Nathaniel Mayer Rothschild** (1840–1915) became the first Jew to be made a *life peer, in 1885. **Miriam Rothschild** (1908–), the granddaughter of Nathaniel, is a noted scientist.

,Rotten 'Row /,rɒtn 'rəʊ; *AmE* ,rɑːtn 'roʊ/ a wide track for riders of horses that runs along the south side of *Hyde Park(1), London, England.

'Rottweiler *n* a breed of large, strong, fierce dog with a short black and brown coat. A number of attacks on children by Rottweilers and other dogs were reported in Britain in the late 1980s and early 1990s, and many people consider them to be dangerous.

the **'Rough ,Riders** *n* [pl] the popular name for the First Regiment of US Cavalry Volunteers in the

*Spanish-American War. They included many *cowboys and were led by Colonel Leonard Wood and Lieutenant Colonel (later President) Theodore *Roosevelt. They became famous for their part in the victory at San Juan Hill in Cuba (1898), led by Roosevelt on his horse Little Texas.

ˈ***Round*** ˈ***Britain*** ˈ***Quiz*** a quiz programme on *BBC *Radio 4, in which two teams from different parts of the country are asked difficult questions to test their knowledge. It was first broadcast in 1947. In 1997 the BBC decided to end the programme but so many people protested that the decision was changed.

ˈ**rounders** *n* [U] (*BrE*) a children's game for two teams, played with a bat and a ball, in which players have to run round four bases. It has been played in Britain since at least the beginning of the 18th century, and is the origin of modern *baseball.

ˈ**Roundhead** *n* a supporter of Parliament against King *Charles I in the *English Civil War. Roundheads were given the name because of their short hair. Their opponents were the *Cavaliers.

the ˌ**Round** ˈ**Table 1** the circular table at which the *Knights of the Round Table sat. Its shape meant that none of the knights appeared to be more important than any of the others. ⇨ article at ARTHURIAN LEGEND. **2** an organization for young business and professional people, with clubs in Britain, the US and many other countries, who work together on projects to help their local communities and to improve international understanding. It was started in 1927: *He's a member of the local Round Table.*

Route 128 /ˌruːt ˈwʌntwentiˈeɪt/ a circular road around *Boston and *Cambridge in the US state of *Massachusetts. Its name has become a symbol for information technology because the technical research done at the local universities of *Harvard and *MIT has created many computer and electronic companies along the Route.

Route 66 /ˈruːt sɪkstiˈsɪks/ the main road from *Chicago to *Los Angeles between 1926 and the 1960s. Its popular name was the 'Mother Road'. It was 2 448 miles/3 940 kilometres long, passing through eight states, and became a symbol of Americans' freedom of movement. Parts of Route 66 still exist, but it was officially replaced by *interstate motorways/freeways in the 1980s. It gave its name to the *CBS television series *Route 66* (1960–3), whose popular theme song ended: 'Get your kicks on Route 66.'

ˈ**Rover** /ˈrəʊvə(r); *AmE* ˈroʊvər/ a company that makes cars, especially large, expensive ones. Two of its best-known cars are the *Land Rover and *Range Rover. It started in Coventry, England, in 1904, and was taken over by the German company BMW in 1994. See also BRITISH LEYLAND.

the ˌ**Rovers Reˈturn** /ˌrəʊvəz; *AmE* ˌroʊvərz/ a pub in the British television *soap opera **Coronation Street* where the characters often meet.

ˈ***Rowan and*** ˈ***Martin's*** ˈ***Laugh-In*** /ˈrəʊən, ˈmɑːtɪnz; *AmE* ˈroʊən, ˈmɑːrtɪnz/ (*also infml* ***Laugh-In***) a popular US comedy television series (1968–73) on *NBC. It was presented by Dan Rowan (1922–87) and Dick Martin (1923–), with a regular team of actors, and used short, fast jokes and comedy situations, a new idea at the time. Certain phrases were also used regularly each week, such as 'Sock it to me!' and 'Tell it to the judge!'

ˌThomas ˈ**Rowlandson** /ˈrəʊləndsn; *AmE* ˈroʊləndsn/ (1756–1827) an English artist. He is famous for his caricatures (= exaggerated humorous drawings) showing the society and politics of the time, e.g. the series *The English Dance of Death* (1814–16). He also painted portraits and drew illustrations for books by Tobias *Smollett and Laurence *Sterne.

ˌ**Rowntree** ˈ**Mackintosh** /ˌraʊntriː ˈmækɪntɒʃ; *AmE* ˈmækɪntɑːʃ/ a British company that makes many well-known types of sweets, including *KitKat, *Smarties and *Black Magic. It is now owned by *Nestlé.

the ˌ**Royal Aˈcademy** (*also* the ˈ**Royal Aˈcademy of ˈArts**) an organization formed in 1768 to encourage the arts of painting, sculpture and architecture in Britain. Its first president was Joshua *Reynolds. The Academy's buildings at *Burlington House, London, contain an art school and a number of galleries, where a popular exhibition is held every summer showing work sent in by the public. Members of the Academy are often famous artists, and are allowed to put the letters RA after their names. See also ROYAL COLLEGE OF ART, ROYAL SCOTTISH ACADEMY, ROYAL SOCIETY OF ARTS.

the ˈ**Royal Aˈcademy of Draˈmatic ˈArt** (*abbr* **RADA**) a college in central London, England, for training professional actors. It was established in 1904 by the actor Sir Herbert Beerbohm Tree, and contains the Vanbrugh Theatre, where students perform plays.

the ˈ**Royal Aˈcademy of ˈMusic** a college for the study of music in Marylebone, London, England. It was established in 1822 and is London's oldest music college. Compare ROYAL COLLEGE OF MUSIC.

the ˌ**Royal ˈAir Force** (*abbr* the **RAF**) ⇨ article at ARMED FORCES IN BRITAIN.

the ˈ**Royal ˈAlbert ˈHall** ⇨ ALBERT HALL.

the ˌ**Royal and ˈAncient** a golf club established in 1754 at St Andrews, Scotland. It is recognized as the world's leading authority on the rules of golf (except in the US). It also organizes The *Open golf competition, which is sometimes played on the course there.

the ˌ**Royal ˈArmoured Corps** (*abbr* the **RAC**) a division of the British Army formed in 1939 to combine all the units using armoured vehicles (= tanks or other heavily protected and armed vehicles). It also includes all the old cavalry regiments (= soldiers who fought on horses) except the *Household Cavalry.

the ˌ**royal ˈarms** *n* [pl] the personal symbol of the British king or queen, consisting of a *lion and a unicorn holding a shield, on which other symbols represent England, Scotland and Ireland. The words **Honi soit qui mal y pense* (the motto of the Order of the *Garter) are written on a belt around the shield. Underneath are the words **Dieu et mon droit* (the personal motto of the king or queen). Companies with a *royal warrant to supply goods to members of the *royal family may use the royal arms on their products, etc.

the royal arms

the ˌ**Royal Arˈtillery** (*abbr* the **RA**) a division of the British Army, formed in 1716, whose main weapons are large guns and missiles for shooting at enemy soldiers, aircraft, etc.

ˌ**Royal ˈAscot** /ˈæskət/ (*also* **Ascot**) a fashionable British horse-racing event held at *Ascot each year in June. Members of the *royal family attend some of the races, and many people go there for social reasons

fashion at Royal Ascot

rather than sport. The third day of Royal Ascot is usually *Ladies' Day(1), for which many of the women present wear large and elegant hats. See also ROYAL ENCLOSURE, SEASON.

the ˌ**royal as'sent** *n* [sing] the final stage that a British *Act of Parliament must go through to become law, when it is signed by the king or queen.

the ˌ**Royal 'Automobile Club** (*abbr* the **RAC**) a British club for drivers of motor vehicles. It offers various services to its members, especially help when their vehicles break down. It developed from a club established in London in 1897. Compare AUTOMOBILE ASSOCIATION.

the ˌ**Royal 'Ballet** the national ballet company of Britain. It was formed from a company started in 1931 by Ninette *de Valois and became the Royal Ballet in 1956. Its famous dancers in the years before *World War II included Alicia *Markova, Anton *Dolin and Robert *Helpmann, and after the war Margot *Fonteyn and Rudolf *Nureyev. It performs both modern and traditional works. Its main base until 1997 was the *Royal Opera House, *Covent Garden, London, after which it began a period of two years performing in other theatres in Britain and abroad. See also SADLER'S WELLS.

the **'Royal 'Bank of 'Scotland** /'skɒtlənd; *AmE* 'skɑtlənd/ the largest Scottish bank, established in 1727, with many branches in Scotland and England. Compare BANK OF SCOTLAND.

the **'Royal 'British 'Legion** ⇨ BRITISH LEGION.

ˌ**royal 'charter** *n* an award given by the British *Privy Council to certain organizations or institutions which are recognized as the leading authorities in their field. Organizations with royal charters include the *BBC, the *British Academy and some British universities.

the **'Royal 'College of 'Art** a college for the study of art, in central London, England, established in 1837. Many famous British artists studied there in the 1950s and 1960s, including David *Hockney and Bridget *Riley. It now only offers postgraduate courses (= courses above ordinary degree level). See also ROYAL ACADEMY OF ARTS, ROYAL SOCIETY OF ARTS.

the **'Royal 'College of 'Music** a college for the study of music in *Kensington, London, England, established in 1883. The college has a museum of musical instruments. Compare ROYAL ACADEMY OF MUSIC.

the **'Royal 'College of 'Nursing** Britain's largest trade union for nurses, which also provides education for its members at the Royal College of Nursing Institute in London.

the **'Royal 'College of Phy'sicians** a professional organization for doctors in England, Wales and Northern Ireland, first formed in 1518. Its equivalents in Scotland are the Royal College of Physicians of Edinburgh and the Royal College of Physicians and Surgeons of Glasgow.

ˌ**Royal Com'mission** *n* a group of people appointed by the British government to investigate and report on a particular matter. For example, the Royal Commission on Criminal Justice (1993) recommended changes to police and legal procedures after the cases of the *Guildford Four and *Birmingham Six.

the **'Royal 'Courts of 'Justice** ⇨ LAW COURTS.

the **'Royal 'Court 'Theatre** a theatre in south-west London, England, established in 1870. It is known for its performances of modern plays, particularly by the *English Stage Company.

the ˌ**Royal 'Crescent** a long curved street in the town of *Bath, south-west England, with a continuous row of houses on one side and a large open area on the other. It was designed in 1767–75 by John Wood the younger (1728–81), and is admired as a fine example of *Georgian architecture.

ˌ**Royal 'Doulton**™ /'dəʊltən; *AmE* 'doʊltən/ an English company that makes pottery and porcelain (= hard, white, shiny material made by baking a type of fine clay). It was started in London in the early 19th century by John Doulton and his son Henry. The company's factory is now at Burslem near *Stoke-on-Trent, and there is a Doulton museum nearby.

the ˌ**Royal En'closure** a special area of the grounds at *Royal Ascot, a famous British horse-racing event. People are only allowed in if they have a ticket, and there are strict rules about dress. Men must wear very formal suits and women must wear skirts that reach below the knee.

the ˌ**Royal Engi'neers** (*abbr* the **RE**) a division of the British Army, formed in 1717, which deals with engineering tasks such as building bridges, etc.

the ˌ**Royal Ex'change** a theatre in *Manchester, England, built in the city's old cotton exchange (= a large circular trading hall). The theatre was badly damaged by an *IRA bomb in 1996.

The **royal family** ⇨ article.

the **'Royal 'Festival 'Hall** (*also* the ˌ**Festival 'Hall**) a large concert hall on the *South Bank of the *Thames in London. It was opened in 1951 as part of the *Festival of Britain. Since then various other concert halls and theatres have been built around it. The *London Philharmonic Orchestra has performed there regularly since 1992.

the ˌ**Royal 'Film Perˌformance** an event held each year in London, England, in which a new British film is shown for the first time before an audience including members of the *royal family. Money from the event goes to charity. Its former name was the Royal Command Performance. Compare ROYAL VARIETY PERFORMANCE.

the ˌ**Royal 'Flying Corps** (*abbr* the **RFC**) the name of the first British air force, formed in 1912. It became the *Royal Air Force in 1918.

the ˌ**Royal 'Free ˌHospital** a hospital in *Hampstead, London, England, established in 1828 by Wil-

R

The royal family

When British people talk about the royal family they usually mean the present Queen and her family: her husband, Prince *Philip, and their children, Prince *Charles, Princess *Anne, Prince *Andrew and Prince *Edward, together with their wives or husbands and their children, including Princes *William and *Henry. The *Queen Mother, and the Queen's sister, Princess *Margaret, and her children are usually also included. The wider family, who gather on ceremonial occasions, includes the Queen's cousins and their children.

The present **royal house** (= ruling family) is the House of *Windsor, popularly known as 'the Windsors'. *Elizabeth II is descended from *William I (1066–87), and before that from Egbert, King of *Wessex 802–39. The ruling house has changed several times over the centuries.

The role of the monarchy

The **monarch** or **sovereign** (= king or queen) originally had sole power. Over time, the sovereign's powers have been reduced and, though the present Queen is still **head of state** and Commander-in-Chief of the armed forces, she 'acts on the advice of her ministers', and Britain is in practice governed by 'Her Majesty's Government'. The Queen has various duties connected with government, such as formally opening a new session of *parliament and giving the *royal assent to new laws. She is also Supreme Governor of the *Church of England.

The main role of the Queen is as a representative of Britain and the British people. She is a symbol of the unity of the nation beyond party politics. She is also head of the *Commonwealth and works to strengthen the links between member countries. Other members of the royal family assist the Queen in her duties, often in less formal ways. They act as patrons of British cultural organizations and support the work of *charities and good causes.

Changing public attitudes

During *World War II, when London was bombed, *George VI and his queen (the present Queen Mother) won great public admiration by staying in London throughout the war. The present Queen has also been much respected and her concern for the Commonwealth has strengthened the monarchy.

For many years, people expected the royal family to have high moral standards and to display all the ideals of family life, an attitude which developed in the time of Queen *Victoria. Until recently, the public rarely saw the royal family except on formal occasions. They remained aloof (= distant) and dignified, and any family problems were kept private. The younger **royals**, however, have lived more public lives and attracted enormous media interest. Royal marriage problems and love affairs became headline news. Alongside a hunger for yet more revelations, traditional respect for the royal family began to decline. The reported treatment of *Diana, Princess of Wales and Sarah, Duchess of *York, especially after the breakdown of their marriages, brought criticism on the Queen and older members of the family. The family were again criticized for their apparent reluctance to share in the public's grief after the death of Princess Diana.

members of the British royal family

All this caused people to question the role of the monarchy. Many people began to think that the royal family was out of touch with modern attitudes. Some felt that they should be more open about their problems and not try to be different. Others thought that the royal family should express the nation's feelings, that in effect they should become a **people's monarchy**. Many people liked the combination of glamour and human concern that Princess Diana brought to the royal family and did not want this human touch to be lost.

In response to the criticism the royal family is trying to be more open and the Queen wants to meet a wider range of people. The royal family had already established its own **Way Ahead** group to consider the monarchy's future. It also has its own Internet site. Since 1993, the Queen has paid *income tax on her private wealth and on the part of the *Privy Purse used for personal expenses. Her official expenses and the upkeep of the royal palaces are paid for through the *Civil List.

The future of the monarchy

The constitutional position of the monarchy has also suffered. It has been suggested that the monarchy is undemocratic and unnecessary. Legal experts argue that getting rid of the monarchy would create serious constitutional difficulties. Defenders of the monarchy claim that the royal family, nicknamed 'the firm', pays for itself because it attracts tourists and business to Britain. Others say it is an expensive luxury. Many people have no strong feelings. They are used to the present system and, though they might like some aspects of the monarchy to be more modern, they would be reluctant to see any radical changes.

At present, the **heir to the throne** is the sovereign's eldest son, even if his or her first child is a daughter. Other sons **take precedence** in the **order of succession** before any daughters. There has been talk of this being changed so that the eldest child, male or female, would **succeed to the throne** and the others would follow in order of age. The present order of succession is as follows:

1. The Prince of Wales
2. Prince William of Wales
3. Prince Henry of Wales
4. The Duke of York
5. Princess Beatrice of York
6. Princess Eugenie of York
7. Prince Edward
8. The Princess Royal (Princess Anne)
9. Peter Phillips (Princess Anne's children)
10. Zara Phillips

liam Marsden (1796–1867), who also established London's *Marsden Hospital. It was one of the first hospitals to treat patients free of charge.

the ˌ**Royal Geoˈgraphical Soˌciety** an organization formed in London, England, in 1830 to provide money and support for journeys of discovery abroad, especially in Africa. Among the first journeys were those of David *Livingstone and Richard *Burton². Its main work today is in scientific publishing and education.

the ˈ**Royal ˈGreenwich Obˈservatory** /ˈgrenɪtʃ/ ⇨ ROYAL OBSERVATORY.

the ˌ**Royal ˈHighland ˌRegiment** ⇨ BLACK WATCH.

the ˌ**Royal Hortiˈcultural Soˌciety** (*abbr* the **RHS**) a British society of gardeners, started in 1804 by Joseph *Banks and others, which holds the *Chelsea Flower Show each year. The Society owns various gardens around Britain, including the garden at *Wisley where research into horticulture (= growing flowers, fruit and vegetables) is carried out.

the ˌ**royal ˈhousehold** *n* the staff of a British king or queen. Its senior members include the *Lord Chamberlain, and it also includes representatives of the armed forces and the church, medical staff and various other officials. Other members of the *royal family have their own smaller households.

the ˈ**Royal ˈInstitute of ˈBritish ˈArchitects** (*abbr* the **RIBA**) a British organization, started in 1834, that aims to encourage the understanding, study and practice of architecture. Its members are architects and other people with an interest in *architecture, and it arranges various exhibitions, events and talks at its centre in London.

the ˌ**Royal Instiˈtution** a British organization established in 1799 with the aim of teaching science to the public through talks and experiments. Its past directors have included Michael *Faraday and Humphrey *Davy, and Faraday's scientific equipment is kept at the Institution's buildings in London. The most famous of its public talks is the Christmas Lecture for Young People, started in 1826 and now shown every Christmas on British television.

the ˈ**Royal Interˈnational Agriˈcultural Show** (*also* the **Royal Show**) an exhibition of farming methods, machinery, animals, etc. held every year at Kenilworth, *Warwickshire, England.

the ˈ**Royal Interˈnational ˈHorse Show** an international competition of showjumping (= the sport of riding horses over difficult barriers) held every year at *Hickstead, *Sussex, England.

the ˈ**Royal ˈLiverpool Philharˈmonic ˌOrchestra** /ˈlɪvəpuːl; *AmE* ˈlɪvərpuːl/ (*abbr* the **RLPO**) a leading British orchestra established in Liverpool in 1840. Famous conductors of the orchestra have included Thomas *Beecham and Malcolm *Sargent.

the ˌ**Royal ˈMail** the department of the British *Post Office that collects and delivers letters. Larger items are dealt with by another department, called Parcelforce. See also POST OFFICE. ⇨ note at POSTAL SERVICES.

the ˌ**Royal Maˈrines** /məˈriːnz/ a branch of the British *Royal Navy that can fight on land as well as at sea. It was formed in 1664 and is best known for its divisions of *Commandos who are trained to operate in difficult environments (e.g. in extreme cold). Compare MARINE CORPS.

the ˈ**Royal ˈMarsden ˈHospital** /ˈmɑːzdən; *AmE* ˈmɑːrzdən/ ⇨ MARSDEN.

the ˌ**Royal ˈMile** the line of three streets in *Edinburgh, leading down the hill from Edinburgh Castle to *Holyrood House.

the ˌ**Royal ˈMilitary Aˌcademy** ⇨ SANDHURST.

the ˌ**Royal ˈMint** the British government organization responsible for making all the coins used in Britain. It also makes coins for other countries, and produces military and prize medals. Paper money is made by the *Bank of England. Since 1968 the Royal Mint has been based at Llantrisant in South Wales.

the Royal Mint

the ˈ**Royal ˈNational Eiˈsteddfod of ˈWales** /aɪˈsteðvɒd, ˈweɪlz; *AmE* aɪˈsteðvɑːd/ ⇨ EISTEDDFOD.

the ˈ**Royal ˈNational ˈInstitute for ˈDeaf ˌPeople** a British organization that helps people who are deaf or cannot hear very well. It was formed in 1911, and provides services such as special employment and housing.

the ˈ**Royal ˈNational ˈInstitute for the ˈBlind** a British organization that helps people who are blind or cannot see very well. It was formed in 1868. Among its activities it publishes books in Braille (= a system of reading and writing for blind people) and runs schools for blind children.

the ˈ**Royal ˈNational ˈLifeboat Instiˌtution** (*abbr* the **RNLI**) a popular British charity, formed in 1824, which provides boats to rescue people at sea around the coasts of Britain and Ireland. Small models of these boats are found in many shops and pubs, with a hole in the top for people to put money in. The people who work in the rescue service, which is available at all times, do so without pay.

a lifeboat

the ˈ**Royal ˈNational ˈTheatre** ⇨ NATIONAL THEATRE.

the ˌ**Royal ˈNaval ˌCollege** ⇨ BRITANNIA ROYAL NAVAL COLLEGE.

the ˈ**Royal ˈNaval Reˈserve** a branch of the British *Volunteer Reserve Forces which works with the *Royal Navy. Its members are volunteers who train in their spare time to do jobs at sea or on land that would be important in time of war or emergency.

the ˌ**Royal ˈNavy** (*abbr* the **RN**) ⇨ ARMED FORCES IN BRITAIN.

the ˌ**Royal Obˈservatory** (*also* the **Royal Greenwich Observatory**) an observatory (= a building from which to study the stars, weather, etc.) at *Greenwich, London, England. Its original purpose was to study the stars in order to help sailors find their position at sea, and its work led to the widespread use of *Greenwich Mean Time and the Greenwich Meridian, an imaginary line running through Greenwich from north to south around the earth. International time zones are still measured from the Greenwich Meridian. In 1990 the scientific work of

the Greenwich Meridian at the Royal Observatory

the observatory was moved to *Cambridge University, and the building in Greenwich is now part of the *National Maritime Museum. See also ASTRONOMER ROYAL.

the ˌ**Royal ˈOpera House** a large theatre in London, England, where performances are given by the Royal Opera and the *Royal Ballet. The present building was opened in 1858. The theatre is also known as 'Covent Garden' after the area in London in which it stands.

ˌ**royal ˈpark** *n* any of the nine parks in London, England, originally owned by the king or queen and now managed by the government. They include the large central London parks of Green Park, *Regent's Park, *St James's Park, *Kensington Gardens and *Hyde Park(1), as well as *Richmond Great Park, *Hampton Court Park, Bushey Park and Greenwich Park.

the ˌ**Royal Paˈvilion** (*also* the **Brighton Pavilion**) a famous building in *Brighton, England, designed in an Indian style by John *Nash. It was completed in 1820 and was a favourite building of the *Prince Regent, later King *George IV. The rooms are mainly in a Chinese style. It is now kept as a museum.

the Royal Pavilion

the ˈ**Royal ˈPhilharmonic ˈOrchestra** a leading British orchestra established in London in 1946 by Thomas *Beecham. Since 1996 its musical director has been Daniele Gatti (1962–).

ˌ**royal saˈlute** *n* (in Britain) the firing of cannons to mark certain royal or state occasions. These include the *Queen's Birthday, the opening of Parliament, and the visits of foreign heads of state. The guns are normally fired near the *Tower of London or in one of the *royal parks. The number fired varies according to the occasion. For example, 41 guns are fired when a child is born to a member of the *royal family.

the ˌ**Royal ˈScots** /ˈskɒts; *AmE* ˈskɑːts/ the oldest division of the British Army, formed in Scotland in 1633. It is also known as the Royal Regiment.

the ˈ**Royal ˈScottish Aˈcademy** /ˈskɒtɪʃ; *AmE* ˈskɑːtɪʃ/ an organization formed in 1826 to encourage painting, sculpture and architecture in Scotland, similar to the *Royal Academy in London. Its buildings are in *Princes Street, *Edinburgh.

the ˌ**Royal ˈShakespeare ˌCompany** /ˈʃeɪkspɪə; *AmE* ˈʃeɪkspɪr/ (*abbr* the **RSC**) a leading British theatre company that performs plays by *Shakespeare and other writers. It was formed in 1961 and its first director was Peter *Hall. The company performs regularly at theatres in London, *Stratford-upon-Avon, *Newcastle and *Plymouth, and its present director is Adrian Noble.

the ˌ**Royal ˈShakespeare ˌTheatre** /ˈʃeɪkspɪə; *AmE* ˈʃeɪkspɪr/ a theatre in *Stratford-upon-Avon, England, where the *Royal Shakespeare Company regularly performs. It opened in 1879 as the Shakespeare Memorial Theatre.

the Royal Shakespeare Theatre

the ˌ**Royal ˈShow** ⇨ ROYAL INTERNATIONAL AGRICULTURAL SHOW.

the ˌ**Royal Soˈciety** the oldest and most important scientific organization in Britain, formed in 1660. Among its first members were Robert *Boyle and Christopher *Wren, and its presidents have included Isaac *Newton and Ernest *Rutherford. Its work now includes scientific publishing and giving awards. Being elected as a *fellow* (= member) of the Royal Society is one of the highest honours in British science. The Society's main buildings are at *Burlington House in London.

the ˈ**Royal Soˈciety for the Preˈvention of ˈCruelty to ˈAnimals** (*abbr* the **RSPCA**) a well-known British charity, formed in 1824, which aims to make sure that the laws about protecting animals are being followed. It also tries to get new laws introduced and gives medical care to animals that need it. In the past it has helped to end many forms of cruel treatment, and one of its present concerns is to end *hunting.

the ˈ**Royal Soˈciety for the Proˈtection of ˈBirds** (*abbr* the **RSPB**) a well-known British charity formed in 1889 with the aim of protecting wild birds. It owns over 100 special areas of land in Britain where birds can breed.

the ˈ**Royal Soˈciety of ˈArts** (*abbr* the **RSA**) a British organization formed in 1754 to encourage high standards in the arts, industry and business. Its full name is the Royal Society for the Encouragement of Arts, Manufactures and Commerce. It is best known today for holding examinations and giving qualifications in various subjects, including *TEFL (= Teaching English as a Foreign Language): *an RSA Preparatory Certificate in TEFL.*

the ˌ**Royal** ˈ**Tournament** an event held every year at *Earl's Court, London, England, in which teams from the British army, navy and air force show their skill in various physical exercises, displays of motorcycle riding, etc.

the ˈ**Royal** ˈ**Ulster Con**ˈ**stabulary** /ˈʌlstə; *AmE* ˈʌlstər/ (*abbr* the **RUC**) the police force of *Northern Ireland, formed in the early 19th century. It now works closely with the British army in trying to stop political violence in Northern Ireland.

the ˌ**Royal Va**ˈ**riety Per**ˌ**formance** a show held every year at a leading theatre in London, England, attended by members of the *royal family and shown on television, in which various entertainers perform for charity. Compare ROYAL FILM PERFORMANCE.

ˌ**royal** ˈ**warrant** *n* the right given to some British companies to display the personal symbol of the Queen, the *Duke of Edinburgh, the *Queen Mother(2) or the *Prince of Wales on their products, etc. The warrant indicates a company that supplies goods or services to these members of the *royal family.

the ˌ**royal** ˈ**we** *n* [sing] the use of 'we' instead of 'I' by British kings or queens in former times. Although this is no longer done, people still sometimes make jokes about it. The most famous example of its use was by Queen *Victoria, who is supposed to have said 'We are not amused' about something that annoyed her.

ˌ**Royal** ˈ**Worcester** /ˈwʊstə(r)/ an English company that has been making china of high quality since the 18th century. Its factory is in the city of *Worcester.

ˌ**royal** ˈ**yacht** *n* a ship that was used by members of the British *royal family when making trips abroad. The last royal yacht, **Britannia*, was first used in 1953 and was taken out of service in 1997. There are no plans to replace it.

the ˌ**Royal** ˈ**Yacht** ˌ**Squadron** a British club for people who own and sail yachts. Its base is at *Cowes on the *Isle of Wight and was established in 1815.

RP /ˌɑː ˈpiː; *AmE* ˌɑːr/ ⇨ RECEIVED PRONUNCIATION.

RPI /ˌɑː piː ˈaɪ; *AmE* ˌɑːr/ ⇨ RETAIL PRICE INDEX.

RRP /ˌɑːr ɑː ˈpiː; *AmE* ɑːr/ ⇨ RECOMMENDED RETAIL PRICE.

RSA /ˌɑːr es ˈeɪ/ ⇨ ROYAL SOCIETY OF ARTS.

RSC /ˌɑːr es ˈsiː/ ⇨ ROYAL SHAKESPEARE COMPANY.

RSPB /ˌɑːr es piː ˈbiː/ ⇨ ROYAL SOCIETY FOR THE PROTECTION OF BIRDS.

RSPCA /ˈɑːr es ˈpiː siː ˈeɪ/ ⇨ ROYAL SOCIETY FOR THE PREVENTION OF CRUELTY TO ANIMALS.

RSV /ˌɑːr es ˈviː/ ⇨ REVISED STANDARD VERSION.

ˌ**Rube** ˈ**Goldberg** ⇨ GOLDBERG.

ˌArthur ˈ**Rubinstein**[1] /ˈruːbɪnstaɪn/ (1888–1982) a US piano player of classical music, born in Poland. He first played in public at the age of 12, and continued performing until he was 90. He became a US citizen in 1946. Rubinstein made many recordings, including the complete works of Chopin and many by Beethoven and Brahms.

ˌHelena ˈ**Rubinstein**[2] /ˌhelənə ˈruːbɪnstaɪn/ (1882–1965) a US businesswoman, born in Poland, who created the famous cosmetics company that carries her name. She began her business in 1902 in Australia and later opened salons (= places for beauty treatments) in London, Paris and New York. Her business became a large international company after *World War I.

ˌJack ˈ**Ruby** /ˈruːbi/ (1911–67) the man who shot and killed Lee Harvey *Oswald in 1963. Oswald had been arrested two days before for the murder of President John F *Kennedy and was being taken by the police to a prison in *Dallas. Ruby pushed through the crowd who were watching and shot Oswald at close range in front of television cameras. Some people thought he did this because there had been a secret plan to kill Kennedy and Ruby was told to stop Oswald revealing it, but this was never proved. Ruby was sent to prison and died there.

the **RUC** /ˌɑː juː ˈsiː; *AmE* ˌɑːr/ ⇨ ROYAL ULSTER CONSTABULARY.

ˈ**Rudolph, the** ˈ**Red-nosed** ˈ**Reindeer** a reindeer (= type of deer) in a children's Christmas song. In the song Rudolph has a shiny red nose, and the other reindeer laugh at him because they think it looks ridiculous. In spite of this *Santa Claus chooses him to pull his sleigh on Christmas Eve.

Rugby

Rugby is a fast, rough team game that is played throughout the British Isles. The game split off from British *football in the mid 19th century when the *Football Association forbade players to handle the ball. There are two **codes** of Rugby football, **Rugby Union** and **Rugby League**, which have slightly different rules and scoring systems. In Rugby League each team has 13 players, compared with 15 in Rugby Union. Players sometimes change from one code to the other during their careers.

In Rugby teams try to **win possession** of a large oval-shaped ball and carry or kick it towards the opposing team's **goal line**, the line at each end of the **pitch** where the H-shaped **goalposts** are. If the ball is **touched down** (= put down by hand) on the grass beyond the touchline a **try** (worth five points in Rugby Union, four points in Rugby League) is scored. A further two points are scored if the try is **converted** (= kicked between the goalposts, above the horizontal crossbar). Points can also be obtained from **penalty goals** scored as a result of **free kicks**, and from **drop goals** (= kicks at the goal during play). Players try to stop opponents carrying and passing the ball by **tackling** them. When a minor rule is broken players restart play by forming a **scrum** (= linking together in a group) or by taking a free kick.

Rugby Union, also called **rugger**, is the older of the two Rugby codes. It is said to have begun at *Rugby School in 1823. Rugby Union has always had strong upper-class and middle-class associations, except in Wales, and is the main winter sport of most English *public schools. It is played mainly by men, though there are now some women's teams. The most important national competitions include the *County Championship, the Pilkington Cup and the Schweppes Welsh Cup.

Rugby League broke away from Rugby Union in the 1890s. Rugby had become popular among *working-class people in northern England and many could not afford to take time off work to play in matches without being paid. The Northern Union, later called the **Rugby League**, was formed in 1895 and soon had many full-time paid professional players. The most important competitions include the Challenge Cup and the League Championship. The two codes may reunite in the future, particularly since in 1995 the International Rugby Board allowed Rugby Union players to become paid professionals.

National Rugby Union teams from England, Wales, Scotland and Ireland play against each other for the *triple crown. The teams also play with France in the annual ***Five Nations' Championship**, and against Australia, New Zealand, South Africa and other countries. Major international grounds include *Twickenham and *Murrayfield.

Most Americans have little knowledge of Rugby and in the US it is mostly played by amateur players in colleges and universities. Rugby was first played in the US in 1874 at *Harvard University, but after the development of American football in about 1880 it almost disappeared. It continued to be played in *California, but it was not until 1975 that the *USA Rugby Football Union was established in *Denver. By 1998, 1 420 clubs were associated with the organization. Competitions include the Saint Patrick's Day Tournament in El Paso, Texas, the Aspen Ruggerfest in *Aspen, Colorado, and, for women, the Mardi Gras Tournament in *New Orleans.

ˌ**Rugby** ˈ**School** /ˌrʌgbi/ a leading English *public school(1) in the town of Rugby, *Warwickshire, established in 1567. Its headmaster from 1827 to 1842 was Thomas *Arnold, and it is the school where the book **Tom Brown's Schooldays* is set. *Rugby football was first played at the school and is named after it.

ˌ***Rule, Bri*ˈ*tannia!*** /brɪˈtænjə/ a British patriotic song (= one expressing pride in Britain) written in 1740 by Thomas Arne (1710–78) with words by James Thomson (1700–48). It is sung at the *Last Night of the Proms. Its last words, which most British people know, are:

Rule, Britannia! Britannia rules the waves;
Britons never, never, never shall be slaves.

ˈ**Rumpole** /ˈrʌmpəʊl; *AmE* ˈrʌmpoʊl/ a character who appears in various books and television programmes by the English writer John Mortimer. Rumpole is a bad-tempered old *barrister (= an English lawyer) who helps people with their legal cases, especially difficult ones. He is best known from the television series *Rumpole of the Bailey* (1978–92), in which the actor Leo McKern played Rumpole.

the ˌ**Rump** ˈ**Parliament** a name given to the parliament that governed Britain from 1648 to 1653 and from 1659 to 1660, after the *Long Parliament had been reduced in size. (The *rump* of something is a small part left from something that was much bigger.) It voted for the trial and execution of King *Charles I and ended just before the *Restoration.

ˌRobert ˈ**Runcie** /ˈrʌnsi/ (1921–) an English *Archbishop of Canterbury (1980–91). During his time as Archbishop he became known for criticizing the government on its social policies, and dealt with other difficult issues such as the place of women priests in the Church. He was made a *life peer in 1991.

ˈ**Runnymede** /ˈrʌnimiːd/ a field beside the River *Thames near *Windsor[1](1), famous as the place where King *John of England agreed to sign the *Magna Carta.

ˌDamon ˈ**Runyon** /ˌdeɪmən ˈrʌnjən/ (1884–1946) a US author and sports journalist. He is known for his humorous short stories about unusual and colourful New York characters, including criminals, sports people and actors. They are written in the sort of *slang that is typically used by such people. The *Broadway musical play **Guys and Dolls* and its film version were based on Runyon's 1932 collection of stories by that name.

ˌPrince ˈ**Rupert** (1619–82) an English soldier. He was the grandson of King *James I and is best remembered for commanding the Royalist cavalry (= soldiers on horses) during the *English Civil War. He was defeated at the battles of *Marston Moor and *Naseby, but escaped abroad, returning to England after the *Restoration. He later helped to form the *Hudson's Bay Company and the *Royal Society.

ˌ**Rupert the** ˈ**Bear** (*also* ˌ**Rupert** ˈ**Bear**) a character in the British children's stories by Mary Tourtel (1874–1948). Rupert is a bear who wears a red top, yellow checked trousers and a yellow checked scarf. He appeared first in 1920 in a regular cartoon strip in the **Daily Express* newspaper, and later in several books and television series.

ˌ***Rural*** ˈ***Rides*** ⇨ COBBETT.

ˌGreg **Ru**ˈ**sedski** /ruˈzedski/ (1973–) a British tennis player, born in Canada. He began playing for Britain in 1995 and has won several international competitions.

ˌSalman ˈ**Rushdie** /ˌsælmən ˈrʌʃdi/ (1947–) a British writer, born in India. His first successful novel was *Midnight's Children* (1981), which won the *Booker Prize. It was followed by *Shame* (1983). A later novel, *The *Satanic Verses* (1988), was about the religion of Islam, and was thought by some Muslims to be very offensive. The Ayatollah Khomeini of Iran declared that Rushdie should be killed, and copies of the book were burned in the streets of Bradford, England. As a result Rushdie lived under police protection at a secret address for many years. He continues to publish novels, among them *The Moor's Last Sigh* (1995), and often appears on British television.

ˌMount ˈ**Rushmore** /ˈrʌʃmɔː(r)/ a high rock cliff in the Black Hills of the US state of *South Dakota. It is famous for the very large heads of four US presidents carved in the rock: George *Washington, Thomas *Jefferson, Abraham *Lincoln and Theodore *Roosevelt. The heads are each about 60 feet/18 metres high and were designed and carved by Gutzon Borglum between 1867 and 1941.

Mount Rushmore

ˌJohn ˈ**Ruskin** /ˈrʌskɪn/ (1819–1900) an English writer and artist. He supported the work of J M W *Turner and the *Pre-Raphaelites and was a leading figure in the *Gothic Revival. In 1869 he became the first Professor of Art at *Oxford University, and his books about art included *Modern Painters* (1843–60) and *The Stones of Venice* (1851–3). He also wrote about social justice and was in favour of education for working people. Ruskin College, Oxford, is named after him. His house in the *Lake District, Cumbria, is kept as a museum.

ˌBertrand ˈ**Russell**[1] /ˌbɜːtrənd ˈrʌsl; *AmE* ˌbɜːrtrənd/ (1872–1970) an English philosopher and writer. His began his career as a writer on mathematics and logic, and his best-known early book was *Principia Mathematica* (1910–13). He also taught philosophy, and in 1912–13 Ludwig *Wittgenstein was one of his students at *Cambridge University. In 1931 he became the 3rd Earl Russell. Among his other works are popular books on philosophy, education and social

R

Bertrand Russell (left) with Lady Russell and other protesters against nuclear weapons

issues, and his *History of Western Philosophy* (1945) was particularly successful. He won the *Nobel Prize for literature in 1950. In the later years of his life he was famous for his strong political opinions. He became the first president of the *Campaign for Nuclear Disarmament in 1958.

ˌJane ˈ**Russell**[2] /ˈrʌsl/ (1921–) a US film actor who became a sex symbol. She was discovered by Howard *Hughes, who made her a star in *The Outlaw* (1943). The *Hays Office refused to give it their approval because she showed too much of her breasts in it. Her other films included *The Paleface* (1948), *Gentlemen Prefer Blondes* (1953) and *The Tall Men* (1955).

ˌKen ˈ**Russell**[3] /ˈrʌsl/ (1927–) an English film director. He began his career producing films for television about the lives of poets and composers, but is best known for his cinema films. These include *Women in Love* (1969), *The Music Lovers* (1971), *Mahler* (1974) and **Tommy* (1975). He has also made a television version of **Lady Chatterley's Lover* (1993). Some people criticize his films for including too much sex and violence, but others admire his lively and imaginative style.

ˈWilliam ˈHoward ˈ**Russell**[4] /ˈrʌsl/ (1820–1907) an English journalist. He wrote mainly about foreign wars for *The *Times* newspaper, and his reports on the suffering of British soldiers in the *Crimean War (1954–6) helped to bring about improved conditions in the armed forces. He later reported on the *Zulu War. He was made a *baron in 1894.

the ˈ**Rust Belt** an informal name for the *Middle West and north-eastern states of the US. This is because many of the large factories in these areas are old or have closed. Some former industries there, such as steel, have now almost gone, and many workers have moved to the *Sunbelt.

ˌ**Rutgers Uniˈversity** /ˌrʌtgəz; *AmE* ˌrʌtgərz/ the famous university of the US state of *New Jersey. It was established as Queens College in 1766 at New Brunswick and changed its name in 1825. In 1997 it had more than 9 000 students.

ˈˌBabeˈ ˈ**Ruth** /ˌbeɪb ˈruːθ/ (1895–1948) the most famous US *baseball player in the history of the game. He was born George Herman Ruth, and his popular name was the 'Bambino'. He played for the New York *Yankees (1919–35), and Yankee Stadium is sometimes called 'the house that Ruth built'. He had 60 home runs in 1927, the most ever for a baseball season until 1961, and 714 during his career, the most until 1974. He was chosen for the National Baseball *Hall of Fame in 1936.

ˌErnest ˈ**Rutherford**[1] /ˈrʌðəfəd; *AmE* ˈrʌðərfərd/ (1871–1937) a British scientist, born in New Zealand. His main interest was in the structure of the atom, and he worked for much of his career at the *Cavendish Laboratory at *Cambridge University. In 1902 he explained the process of radioactive decay, in which one chemical element can turn into another, and he received the *Nobel Prize for this work in 1908. Later work identified alpha, beta and gamma rays, and he discovered and named the proton (= part of the atom) in 1919. His work was of great importance in the later development of nuclear technology. He was made a *life peer in 1931.

ˌMargaret ˈ**Rutherford**[2] /ˈrʌðəfəd; *AmE* ˈrʌðərfərd/ (1892–1972) an English comedy actor. She is best remembered for playing rather eccentric older women, e.g. in the film versions of *Blithe Spirit* (1945) and *The *Importance of Being Earnest* (1952). She also played the part of Miss *Marple in several film versions of the novels of Agatha *Christie. She was made a *dame(2) in 1967.

ˈ**Rutland** /ˈrʌtlənd/ a former *county in eastern central England. It was England's smallest county, but became part of *Leicestershire in 1974. Many local people opposed this and in 1996 the people of Rutland chose to have their own separate *unitary authority.

RV /ˌɑː ˈviː; *AmE* ˌɑːr/ **1** ⇨ RECREATIONAL VEHICLE. **2** ⇨ REVISED VERSION.

ˌNolan ˈ**Ryan** /ˌnəʊlən ˈraɪən; *AmE* ˌnoʊlən/ (1947–) a US baseball pitcher (= player who throws the ball to be hit). He has made more opponents strike out (= fail to hit the ball three times and be dismissed) than anyone in a single baseball season (383 in 1973) and during a career (5 714). He played with the New York Mets (1967–70), the California Angels (1971–8), the Houston Astros (1979–87) and the Texas Rangers (1988–93).

ˌSue ˈ**Ryder** /ˈraɪdə(r)/ (1923–) an English charity worker. In 1953 she started the Sue Ryder Foundation, which gives care to sick or disabled people in about 80 centres around the world. She had earlier played an important part in *World War II, working with people who resisted the Nazis in Europe. In 1959 she married Leonard *Cheshire, who had done a lot of charity work similar to hers.

the ˌ**Ryder** ˈ**Cup** /ˌraɪdə; *AmE* ˌraɪdər/ a professional golf competition for men held every two years between teams of US and European players. From 1927, when it was first held, to 1977 it was played between US and British teams. ⇨ note at GOLF.

ˌMartin ˈ**Ryle** /ˈraɪl/ (1918–84) an English astronomer. His work helped to establish the 'big bang' theory, which argues that all the matter in the universe exploded from a tiny point many millions of years ago. (This was opposed to the 'steady state' theory of Fred *Hoyle and others.) Ryle was made a *knight in 1966 and given the *Nobel Prize in 1974.

'Babe' Ruth

R

Ss

ˌ**Saatchi & ˈSaatchi** /ˈsɑːtʃi/ a British advertising company started in 1970 by two brothers, **Charles Saatchi** (1943–) and **Maurice Saatchi** (1946–). It was very successful during the 1980s, and was known especially for its work for the British *Conservative Party. Charles Saatchi is now better known for collecting work by young British artists such as Damien *Hirst, and he owns the Saatchi Gallery in west London.

ˌ**Sacajaˈwea** /ˌsækədʒəˈwiːə/ (*c.* 1784–*c.* 1884) a *Shoshone *Native American who guided *Lewis and Clark in 1805 when they investigated the *Louisiana Purchase. She was the wife of the French *frontiersman Toussaint Charbonneau, who also travelled with them and interpreted for them. Sacajawea was especially helpful when they reached her home region around the Missouri River.

ˌ**Sacco and Vanˈzetti** /ˌsækəʊ ənd vænˈzeti; *AmE* ˌsækoʊ/ two Italian-Americans, born in Italy, who were executed in the US in 1927 for the murder of two workers during a robbery at a *Massachusetts factory, although the evidence against them was not very strong. **Nicola Sacco** (1891–1927) and **Bartolomeo Vanzetti** (1888–1927) were anarchists (= people who believe there should be no laws or government). Many people thought that they were found guilty because of their political views and there were strong protests. The city of *Boston decided in 1997 to honour Sacco and Vanzetti with a statue.

ˌOliver ˈ**Sacks** /ˈsæks/ (1933–) an English neurologist (= doctor who studies the nerves and their diseases). He has written more than 30 books about unusual mental conditions. He has lived in the US since 1960 and has been Professor of Clinical Neurology at New York's Albert Einstein College of Medicine since 1965. His book *Awakenings* (1973) about a 'sleeping sickness' was made into a 1990 film with Robin *Williams. His other books include *The Man Who Mistook His Wife for a Hat* (1985) and *An Anthropologist on Mars* (1995).

ˈVita ˈ**Sackville-ˈWest** /ˈviːtə ˈsækvɪl ˈwest/ (1892–1962) an English writer who published several novels, collections of poetry and other books. She married the writer Harold *Nicolson, but also had sexual affairs with women, including Virginia *Woolf. The gardens she created around her home at Sissinghurst in *Kent are now owned by the *National Trust.

ˌ**Sadie ˈHawkins Day** /ˌseɪdi ˈhɔːkɪnz/ (in the US) a day on which women invite men to a social event, especially a **Sadie Hawkins Day dance**. This is often done by students in a *high school, college or university. The custom takes its name from a character in the **Li'l Abner* *comic strip. Sadie Hawkins is a woman who is not married and is very anxious to have affairs with men.

ˌ**Sadler's ˈWells** /ˌsædləz ˈwelz; *AmE* ˌsædlərz/ a theatre in north-east London, England. It became famous as the home of three important national companies: the *Royal Ballet, the Sadler's Wells Theatre Ballet (now the Birmingham Royal Ballet) and *English National Opera. All three have since moved to other theatres. Sadler's Wells continues to present a variety of theatre, music and dance.

ˈ**Safeway** /ˈseɪfweɪ/ any of a group of supermarkets in the US and Britain: *We've got a Safeway just down the road.*

SAG /ˌes eɪ ˈdʒiː/ ⇨ SCREEN ACTORS GUILD.

saˈguaro /səˈgwɑːrəʊ; *AmE* səˈgwɑːroʊ/ *n* (*pl* **-os**) a very large US cactus (= plant with thick, usually prickly stems that grows in hot, dry regions). Saguaros are found mainly in the US states of *Arizona and *California and in northern Mexico. They can grow to 50 feet/15 metres tall and live for more than 200 years old. The **Saguaro National Park** is in Arizona, and the white flower of the saguaro is Arizona's state flower.

a saguaro

ˈ**Sainsbury's** /ˈseɪnzbriz/ a large group of British supermarkets. The first Sainsbury's was a small shop in London, opened in 1869 by John James Sainsbury (1844–1928) and Mary Ann Sainsbury (1849–1927). The company developed steadily and opened its first supermarket in *Southampton in 1954. Since then many more have opened all over England. The Sainsbury family are now also known for supporting the arts and charities in Britain: *I always buy my food at Sainsbury's.* ○ *Have you got a Sainsbury's near you?* See also NATIONAL GALLERY.

Saint For entries beginning with the word 'Saint', see **St** (the usual form in written English), e.g. **St Albans**, **St Andrews**, etc. The names of individual saints are shown under the names themselves, not at 'St', e.g. the entry for St George is at **George**.

ˈ**Saki** /ˈsɑːki/ the name under which the English author Hector Hugh Munro (1870–1916) wrote his short stories. These are often about *upper-class English life, and are humorous in a clever and sometimes cruel way. His collections of short stories include *Beasts and Superbeasts* (1914), and he also wrote three novels. He was killed in *World War I.

the ˌ**Salem ˈwitch trials** /ˌseɪləm/ a series of trials in 1692 in Salem, *Massachusetts, of people accused of being witches. They began after a group of young girls started behaving in a crazy way and saying that they were 'possessed'. People in the town were quick to accuse each other, and the trials ended with 20 people being executed, on very little evidence. Arthur *Miller used the trials as the basis for his play *The Crucible* (1953).

ˌJ D ˈ**Salinger** /ˈsælɪndʒə(r)/ (Jerome David Salinger 1919–) a US writer of novels and short stories which were especially popular with college and university students in the 1950s and 1960s. His best-known novel is *The *Catcher in the Rye*. Many of Salinger's short stories were published in *The *New Yorker*. He is famous for his dislike of appearing in public.

ˈ**Salisbury**[1] /ˈsɔːlzbri/ a town in *Wiltshire, southern England, on the River *Avon. It is famous for its cathedral, which has the highest spire (= pointed tower) in Britain, and for the ancient remains at Old Sarum, the original place where the town was built, to the north of the present town. Salisbury and its cathedral appear in many of the paintings of John *Constable.

ˌLord ˈ**Salisbury**[2] /ˈsɔːlzbri/ (*born* Robert Gascoyne-Cecil) 1830–1903 a British *Conservative *Prime Minister (1885–6, 1886–92 and 1895-1902). He helped to increase the power of the *British Empire, especially in Africa, and supported the activities of Cecil *Rhodes and others. During his final period in power he led Britain in the *Boer Wars.

ˌ**Salisbury ˈPlain** /ˌsɔːlzbri/ a large area of open land to the north and west of *Salisbury in southern England. It is used by the British Army as a training ground, and also contains *Stonehenge, an ancient circle of stones.

ˌ**Salisbury ˈsteak** /ˌsɔːlzbri/ *n* (*AmE*) a dish consisting of finely chopped meat mixed with egg and onions and fried, baked or cooked under a strong heat. It was named after J H Salisbury, a 19th-century English expert on diet.

the ˈ**Salk ˌvaccine** /ˈsɔːlk/ *n* [sing] a medicine used to prevent polio (= a serious disease affecting the nervous system), developed in 1954 by the US scientist Jonas Salk (1914–95).

ˈ**Salop** /ˈsæləp/ an old name for the English county of *Shropshire, used as its official name from 1974 to 1980.

Saˈlopian /səˈləʊpiən; *AmE* səˈloʊpiən/ *n* **1** a person from the English *county of *Shropshire. **2** a person from the town of *Shrewsbury in Shropshire. **3** a pupil or former pupil of *Shrewsbury School. ▶ **Salopian** *adj.*

ˈ**salsa** *n* [U] a type of Latin American dance music popular in Britain and the US. It is played especially by big bands with many brass instruments.

SALT /sɔːlt/ ⇨ STRATEGIC ARMS LIMITATION TALKS.

ˌ**Salt Lake ˈCity** the capital and largest city of the US state of *Utah, on the Jordan River near the *Great Salt Lake. It was established in 1847 by Brigham *Young for his *Mormon group, and is still the home of that religion and its very large temple. Its original name was Great Salt Lake City and it was also called the 'New Jerusalem'. Local companies now produce processed food, computers and other electronic equipment.

S

the **Salˌvation ˈArmy** (*also infml* the ˌ**Sally ˈArmy**) a Christian organization started by William Booth (1829–1912) in the *East End of London, England, in 1865. It does a wide range of charity work, and is especially known for providing centres for old people and people without homes. It holds religious services in public with music from *brass bands, and its members wear military uniforms and have military ranks. They are sometimes seen in British pubs collecting money for their work. The organization's magazine, *The War Cry*, has appeared every week since 1879. Branches of the Salvation Army now exist in many countries around the world. ▶ **Salˈvationist** *n* a member of the Salvation Army.

a Salvation Army band

the **Saˈmaritans** a British charity, started in 1953 by Chad Varah (1911–), which gives free help and advice to people who are very depressed or thinking of killing themselves. People can call the Samaritans on the telephone and discuss their problems, and members of the staff work without payment. There are now over 80 local branches of the charity, with other branches abroad.

ˈ**sambo** /ˈsæmbəʊ; *AmE* ˈsæmboʊ/ (*pl* **-os**) *n* [C] (*sl offensive*) a black man. The children's book *The Story of Little Black Sambo* (1899) by the English author Helen Bannerman was originally very popular both in Britain and the US but is now regarded as insulting to black people. The US group of Sambo's Restaurants is named after the main character in the book and has been criticized for this by African Americans and the *Equal Employment Opportunity Commission.

ˌ**Sam ˈBrowne** /ˈbraʊn/ (*also* ˌ**Sam Browne ˈbelt**) *n* (*BrE*) a type of leather belt with a strap that passes from the left side over the right shoulder, worn by British army officers, certain police officers, etc.

ˌPete ˈ**Sampras** /ˈsæmprəs/ (1971–) a US tennis player, thought by many people to be the greatest in the history of the game. By 1998 he had won ten *grand slam(1) titles, including *Wimbledon five times (1993–5 and 1997–8) and the *US Open three times (1993 and 1995–6).

ˌ***Samson Agoˈnistes*** /ˌsæmsən ægəˈnɪstiz/ a play in verse by John *Milton, telling the story of the Bible character Samson. Its style is based on ancient Greek plays and it was published in 1671 in the same book as *Paradise Regained.*

ˌ**Samuel ˈFrench** /ˈfrentʃ/ a publishing company that produces versions of plays for use by actors. As well as suggesting where and when actors should move on stage, they include information on lighting and sound effects. The company was formed in 1830 and has branches in both Britain and the US.

ˌ**San Anˈdreas ˈFault** /ˌsæn ænˈdreɪəs/ a break in the layers of rock forming the earth's surface that runs about 600 miles/965 kilometres north to south through the US state of *California. It causes earthquakes, such as those in *San Francisco (1906 and 1989) and *Los Angeles (1994).

ˌ**San Anˈtonio** /ˌsæn ænˈtəʊniəʊ; *AmE* ænˈtoʊnioʊ/ a city in the US state of *Texas on the San Antonio River. The *Alamo was built there in 1781 and can still be visited. The city attracts many tourists because of its attractive shops and restaurants along the river. It also has five large US military bases.

ˌCarl ˈ**Sandburg** /ˈsændbɜːg; *AmE* ˈsændbɜːrg/ (1878–1967) a US poet, writer and singer of *folk songs. He first worked on farms, and his poems are about ordinary life. He twice won the *Pulitzer Prize, for *Complete Poems* (1951) and for *Abraham Lincoln: The War Years* (1939), part of his long biography of *Lincoln.

ˌColonel ˈ**Sanders** /ˈsɑːndəz; *AmE* ˈsændərz/ the man who began the *Kentucky Fried Chicken restaurants.

ˈ**Sandhurst** /ˈsændhɜːst; *AmE* ˈsændhɜːrst/ (*also fml* the **Royal Military Academy**) a training college for British Army officers near the village of Sandhurst,

*Berkshire, established in 1799. In the past it was known as the place where *upper-class young men could receive a military education, although this is less true today. Compare WEST POINT.

ˌ**San Di'ego** /ˌsæn dɪ'eɪgəʊ; *AmE* dɪ'eɪgoʊ/ the second largest city in the US state of *California. It is on **San Diego Bay** on the Pacific coast near the Mexican border, and has a large US Navy base. Tourists are attracted to its beaches and historical buildings. The city is also known for its electronics and aerospace industries.

S & L /ˌes ənd 'el / ⇨ SAVINGS AND LOAN ASSOCIATION. ⇨ note at BUILDING SOCIETIES.

ˌ**Sandringham 'House** /ˌsændrɪŋəm/ a country house owned by the British *royal family, near *King's Lynn in *Norfolk. It was built in 1870 for the *Prince of Wales (later King *Edward VII), and is traditionally the place where the royal family spend Christmas. It is open to the public in the summer.

'**Sandwich** /'sændwɪdʒ/ a town on the south coast of *Kent, England, which was one of the original *Cinque Ports. It is now especially famous for its golf course, also called the Royal St George's golf course, where the *Open golf competition is regularly held.

'**sandwich** (*also BrE infml* **sarnie**) *n* two or more slices of bread and butter with meat, cheese, etc. between, eaten with the hands. Sandwiches are popular as a light midday meal, and are often bought from **sandwich bars**, shops selling a wide range of different sandwiches. The 4th Earl of Sandwich (1718–92) is said to have invented them as a quick and easy meal to eat while gambling: *a tomato sandwich* ○ *a lunch of beer and sandwiches*. See also DAGWOOD, REUBEN SANDWICH.

'**sandwich board** *n* either of a pair of connected boards with advertisements on them which are hung over the front and back of a person (called a **sandwich man**) who walks about the streets to display them. They are no longer very common, but often appear in cartoons, etc., especially with the words 'The end is nigh' written on them, because religious people sometimes wore them to warn others that they believed the world was about to end.

sandwich boards

ˌ**San Fran'cisco** /ˌsæn frən'sɪskəʊ; *AmE* frən'sɪskoʊ/ a city in the US state of California, on **San Francisco Bay**. It is built on hills and is known for its beautiful views and Victorian houses. It was established by the Spanish in 1776 as Yerba Buena, taken by the US in 1846 and given its present name the following year. It grew rapidly after the *Gold Rush but was badly damaged by an earthquake in 1906. Its many tourist attractions include the cable cars (= public vehicles that carry passengers up and down the steep hills), *Golden Gate Bridge, the restaurants along Fisherman's Wharf, *Nob Hill, *Haight-Ashbury, *Alcatraz and *Chinatown. San Francisco is a financial and communications centre and a centre for trade with Asia. It is also known for its many homosexuals. See also FRISCO.

ˌFrederick '**Sanger** /'sæŋə(r)/ (1918–) an English scientist. He is the first scientist to have received two *Nobel Prizes for chemistry (in 1956 and 1980), and his work has been important for the development of genetic engineering (= the deliberate changing of small parts of the cells of plants or animals in order to change the way they grow). He became a member of the *Order of Merit in 1986.

the 'Battle of '**San Ja'cinto** /'sæn dʒə'sɪntəʊ; *AmE* dʒə'sɪntoʊ/ the battle in 1836 that gained *Texas its independence from Mexico. The US forces led by Sam *Houston defeated a larger Mexican army led by General *Santa Anna. The battle was fought near the San Jacinto River in south-east Texas, and a tall monument was later built there.

'**San Joa'quin 'Valley** /'sæn wɑː'kiːn/ a central valley in the US state of *California, around the **San Joaquin River**. It is considered to be one of the best agricultural regions in the US. Farmers there produce such crops as cotton, wheat, nuts, grapes and vegetables.

ˌ**San Jo'se** /ˌsæn həʊ'zeɪ; *AmE* hoʊ'zeɪ/ a city in western *California, in the Santa Clara Valley. Because of the many computer and electronics companies there, the area is often called *Silicon Valley. San Jose also produces fruit and wine. It was the capital of California from 1849 to 1851. An earthquake in 1989 caused some damage.

'**Sanka**™ /'sæŋkə/ *n* [U] a make of 'instant' decaffeinated coffee. It was originally made in Germany but is now produced by *Kellogg's.

ˌ**San 'Quentin** /ˌsæn 'kwentɪn; *AmE* 'kwentn/ a large prison near *San Francisco, *California, established in 1852. It is a 'maximum security' prison, and many of America's most violent criminals are sent there.

ˌ**San 'Simeon** /ˌsæn 'sɪmiən/ the very expensive 'dream castle' built by the rich US newspaper owner William Randolph *Hearst on the Pacific coast between *San Francisco and *Los Angeles. He began it in 1919 and continued to make additions to it until he died in 1951. It combines Greek, Roman and Gothic architecture and has many original items from the ancient world. More than a million tourists now visit it every year.

An'tonio 'López de **Santa 'Anna** /æn'təʊniəʊ 'ləʊpez də sæntə 'ænə; *AmE* æn'toʊnioʊ 'loʊpez/ (1794–1876) the Mexican army officer who in 1836 led the attack on the *Alamo. Texas became independent of Mexico when his forces were defeated at the Battle of *San Jacinto in the same year. General Santa Anna later became Mexico's president and lost the *Mexican War in 1848.

San Francisco and Alcatraz

S

Santa Claus

Santa Claus, also called simply **Santa** or, in Britain, **Father Christmas**, is a fat, cheerful old man with a long white beard who brings children their presents on *Christmas Eve. Traditionally, he wears a bright red suit, a red hat lined with white fur and shiny black boots. Santa Claus is said to live at the North Pole and to have a workshop there where he and his elves makes toys. Santa Claus is also called **St Nick** and identified with St Nicholas, who lived in the 4th century AD and is the patron saint of children

In the period before Christmas children write letters to Santa telling him what gifts they would like. In Britain these letters are 'posted' up the chimney or sent to local newspapers, which arrange for Santa to send a reply. Children are careful to behave well, because Santa only brings toys to good children.

During this time Santa can also be found visiting many large shops, so that children can sit on his knee and tell him what presents they would like. In Britain children have to pay to enter Santa's **grotto** and in return receive a small gift from him; in America visiting Santa is free.

On 24 December, the night before Christmas, children hang **stockings** (= long socks) at the end of their beds. Santa leaves the North Pole with a **sled** or **sleigh**. Santa's sled is pulled by **reindeer** called Dasher, Dancer, Prancer, Vixen, Comet, Cupid, Donner, Blitzen and Rudolph, who know how to fly. They travel through the air stopping on the roof of every house where a child is sleeping. Santa slides down the chimney and leaves big presents under the Christmas tree and small ones in the stockings. He usually finds that the children have left him a plate of **Christmas cookies** or, in Britain, a **mince pie** (= a small pastry containing dried fruits), and possibly salt or a carrot for his reindeer.

Santa Claus is an important symbol of Christmas, and pictures of him appear on Christmas cards and decorations. He is mentioned in poems and Christmas *carols such as *The *Night Before Christmas* and **Rudolph, the Red-nosed Reindeer*. As children get older they realize that Santa Claus cannot be real and stop believing in him.

ˌSanta ˈFe /ˌsæntə ˈfeɪ/ the capital of the US state of *New Mexico. It is in the northern part of the state, close to the Sangre de Cristo Mountains. The Spanish established it in 1610 and built its Palace of Governors, the oldest public building in the US. About 1.5 million tourists visit the city each year.

ˌSanta Fe ˈTrail /ˌsæntə feɪ/ an important US trade route in the 19th century. It was about 780 miles/ 1 255 kilometres long and went from *Independence, *Missouri, to *Santa Fe, *New Mexico. Factory products were sent along it from east to west, and furs and gold went in the opposite direction. It stopped being used for trade when the Santa Fe Railroad was opened. Since 1987 it has been the **Sante Fe National Historic Trail**. See also COVERED WAGON.

ˌSara ˈLee™ /ˌseərə ˈliː; *AmE* ˌserə/ a large US food company best known for its frozen sweet dishes. According to its advertisements, 'Everybody doesn't like something, but nobody doesn't like Sara Lee.' It also owns companies that make meat products, frozen fruit and vegetables, and underwear.

Saˈran Wrap™ /səˈræn/ *n* [U] a US make of cling film, thin transparent plastic material used for wrapping food, etc. It is produced by DowBrands, part of the Dow Chemical Company.

ˌSaraˈtoga /ˌsærəˈtəʊgə; *AmE* ˌsærəˈtoʊgə/ the original name of Schuylerville, *New York. The Americans won two important victories over British forces there in October 1777, during the *American Revolution. The battles have been called the 'turning point' of the war, because the French then decided to give military support to the Americans. **Saratoga National Historical Park** was established in 1938.

ˌSaratoga ˈSprings /ˌsærətəʊgə; *AmE* ˌsærətoʊgə/ a city in north-eastern New York State which is an international centre for horse-racing. It was settled in 1773 around 122 natural mineral springs and became popular as the 'Queen of Spas' during the 19th century. The two battles of *Saratoga were fought not far away.

ˈJohn ˈSinger **ˈSargent**[1] /ˈsɪŋə ˈsɑːdʒənt; *AmE* ˈsɪŋər ˈsɑːrdʒənt/ (1856–1925) a US artist known for painting rich and famous people. They included President Theodore *Roosevelt and the author Robert Louis *Stevenson. Sargent was born in Florence, Italy, of US parents. He studied and painted in Paris (1874–84) but his career was damaged when his painting *Madame X* (1884) was considered too sexual. He then settled in London, though he remained a US citizen.

Mrs Carl Meyer and her children, *painted by John Singer Sargent*

ˌMalcolm **ˈSargent**[2] /ˈsɑːdʒənt; *AmE* ˈsɑːrdʒənt/ (1895–1967) an English conductor. He worked with several orchestras and is best remembered as a conductor of the *Proms. He was made a *knight in 1947.

Sark /sɑːk; *AmE* sɑːrk/ a part of the British *Channel Islands, consisting of two islands, Great Sark and Little Sark, which are joined by a narrow strip of land. Sark has its own parliament, and a leader called the Seigneur (if a man) or the Dame (if a woman), who passes the title on to his or her children. The islands are popular with tourists.

ˌWilliam **Saˈroyan** /səˈrɔɪən/ (1908–81) a US author of novels, plays and more than 400 short stories. He wrote about ordinary people and refused the *Pulitzer Prize for his play *The Time of Your Life* (1939) because he did not want rich people to support the arts. Saroyan's best-known novel is *The Human Comedy* (1943).

the **SAS** /ˌes eɪ ˈes/ (*in full* the **Special Air Service**) a branch of the British army consisting of a small group of soldiers who are specially trained to fight terrorists. Members of the SAS have many skills such as parachuting, climbing and fighting. They are well known for their ability to surprise groups of terrorists by attacking them very quickly.

ˈ**Sasquatch** /ˈsæskwɒtʃ; *AmE* ˈsæskwɑːtʃ/ (*also* ˈ**Bigfoot** /ˈbɪgfʊt/) *n* a large hairy creature like a human with big feet and long arms that is believed by some people to live in the north-west mountains of North America. Although reports that such a creature has been seen appear occasionally in popular newspapers, most people regard them as a joke.

ˌSiegfried **Sasˈsoon** /ˌsiːgfriːd səˈsuːn/ (1886–1967) an English poet and author. He served as a soldier in *World War I and is best known for his poems about the horror of war. He was awarded the *Military Cross for his courage in battle but later rejected it because of his opposition to war. His collections of poetry include *Counterattack* (1918), and he wrote a series of books about his life, including *The Memoirs of a Fox-Hunting Man* (1928).

SAT /ˌes eɪ ˈtiː/ **1** (*in full* **Scholastic Aptitude Test**) (in the US) a standard test which students must pass in order to be accepted by most colleges and universities. It tests abilities in language and mathematics and is usually taken during the last year of *high school. Compare ACT, PSAT. **2** ⇨ STANDARD ASSESSMENT TASK.

The ***Saˌtanic ˈVerses*** a novel (1988) by Salman *Rushdie about the religion of Islam. Some Muslims found it very offensive. The Ayatollah Khomeini of Iran declared that Rushdie should be killed, and copies of the book were burned on the streets of Bradford, England. Public protests also took place in many other countries, during which some people were killed. As a result Rushdie was forced to live for ten years under police protection at a secret address.

ˈ**Satchmo** /ˈsætʃməʊ; *AmE* ˈsætʃmoʊ/ the popular name of the *jazz musician Louis *Armstrong. It was short for 'satchel mouth', because he had a very large mouth. A satchel is a type of large bag.

The ***ˈSaturday ˈEvening ˈPost*** a US magazine established in 1821 and published each week. It became one of America's most popular general magazines from the 1920s to the 1960s and was known especially for its covers painted by Norman *Rockwell and its fiction by such writers as William *Faulkner and Agatha *Christie. It stopped being published in 1969 but began again in 1971 and is now published six times a year.

ˈSaturday ˈNight ˈLive the longest running US television comedy series, which started in 1975 on *NBC. The careers of many comic actors have begun on the programme. The original group included Chevy Chase, John Belushi and Dan Aykroyd. Later members included Eddie *Murphy, Billy Crystal and Bill Murray. Each show is presented by a different guest, and they have included New York Mayor Ed *Koch and the comic actors Robin *Williams and Steve *Martin.

ˈ**Saturn 1** a US rocket used in the 1960s and 1970s to send spacecraft and satellites into space. The original Saturn was developed in 1958 by Wernher *von Braun, and it had two rockets used in sequence. Saturn 5 had three rockets and carried 12 million US gallons (45.6 million litres) of fuel. It was used for the *Apollo Project to send men to the moon. **2** a popular make of small US car that is cheap to run, produced by *General Motors since 1990.

ˌJennifer ˈ**Saunders** /ˈsɔːndəz; *AmE* ˈsɔːndərz/ (1958–) an English comedy actor best known for appearing with Dawn *French in the television comedy series **French and Saunders* and for playing the part of Edina Monsoon in the television comedy series **Absolutely Fabulous*.

ˌLily ˈ**Savage** /ˈsævɪdʒ/ (1955–) an English comedy performer. Lily Savage is a man who dresses as a woman (real name Paul Grady) and has appeared on television programmes including *The Lily Savage Show* (1997) and *Blankety Blank* (1998–).

the ˌ**Save the ˈChildren Fund** (*also* **Save the Children**) a large international charity that helps children. It was started in London in 1919 and provides services such as education, health care and emergency relief in many of the the world's poorer countries. It also works to help children in Britain. Its president is Princess *Anne.

ˌJimmy ˈ**Savile** /ˈsævl/ (1926–) an English radio and television personality and charity worker. He began his career as a disc jockey and later became well known as the presenter of the television series *Jim'll Fix It* (1975–94), in which he arranged for children to do things they specially wanted to do. Savile also works to collect money for British hospitals, and often appears on television wearing heavy gold jewellery and smoking a cigar. He was made a *knight in 1990.

ˌ**Savile ˈRow** /ˌsævl ˈrəʊ; *AmE* ˈroʊ/ a street in London, England, which is famous for its tailors (= people who make clothes for individual customers). It is considered the centre of high-quality men's fashions in Britain: *He was wearing an expensive Savile Row suit.*

ˌ**savings and ˈloan associˌation** (*abbr* **S & L**) *n* (*AmE*) ⇨ note at BUILDING SOCIETIES.

the **Saˌvoy Hoˈtel** /səˌvɔɪ/ a very comfortable and expensive hotel near the *Strand, London, England. It was built in 1884–9 by Richard *D'Oyly Carte, who owned the Savoy Theatre nearby, and has a famous restaurant, the Savoy Grill.

the **Saˌvoy ˈOperas** /səˌvɔɪ/ a name for the operas of *Gilbert and *Sullivan[1], performed from the 1880s until the 1960s mainly at the Savoy Theatre in London, England. They include *The *Pirates of Penzance*, *The *Mikado* and *The *Gondoliers*.

ˌTom ˈ**Sawyer** /ˈsɔːjə(r)/ the main character in *The Adventures of Tom Sawyer* (1876), a novel by Mark *Twain which is especially popular with children. Tom is a lively and clever boy who lives with his Aunt Polly in St Petersburg, *Missouri. He has an exciting life and many adventures on the *Mississippi River with his friends Huckleberry *Finn and Becky Thatcher.

ˌ**Saxe-ˈCoburg-ˈGotha** /ˌsæks ˈkəʊbɜːg ˈgəʊθə; *AmE* ˈkoʊbɜːrg ˈgoʊθə/ the name of the British *royal family from the beginning of the rule of King *Edward VIII in 1901. The name originally belonged to Edward VII's father, the German Prince *Albert. Public dislike of Germany caused King *George V to change it to Windsor in 1917.

ˈ**Saxon** *n* a member of a people from north-west Germany who settled in England in the 5th and 6th centuries. Together with the Angles and the *Jutes they formed the group known as the *Anglo-Saxons. Saxon architecture is Britain's earliest style of architecture, with round arches, small windows and thick stone walls.

ˌDorothy ˈ**Sayers** /ˈseɪəz; *AmE* ˈseɪərz/ (1893–1957) an English writer. She is famous for her detective stories, such as *Strong Poison* (1930), in which the main character is Lord Peter *Wimsey. She also wrote plays on religious subjects and translated the poetry of Dante into English.

ˌ**Scafell ˈPike** /ˌskɔːfel/ the highest mountain in England, in the *Lake District in *Cumbria. It is 3 210 feet/978 metres high.

Pruˌnella ˈ**Scales** /pruːˌnelə ˈskeɪlz/ (1932–) an English actor, especially in comedy parts. She is best known for playing the part of Sybil Fawlty in the television comedy series *Fawlty Towers*. She is married to the actor Timothy West.

ˌ**Scapa** ˈ**Flow** /ˌskɑːpə ˈfləʊ; *AmE* ˈfloʊ/ an area of the *North Sea surrounded by several of the *Orkney Islands and used as a base by the British navy until 1956. Two famous incidents happened there: in 1919 a number of captured German ships were sunk by their own crews, and in 1939 a German submarine sank a British ship, the *Royal Oak*, killing over 800 men.

ˈ**Scarborough** /ˈskɑːbrə/ a town on the coast of *North Yorkshire, England. It was popular in the past as a spa town (= one where there are springs of mineral water considered to be healthy to drink) and is now known for its parks, theatres and beaches.

ˌArthur ˈ**Scargill** /ˈskɑːɡɪl; *AmE* ˈskɑːrɡɪl/ (1938–) an English trade union leader and politician. In 1981 he became the President of the *National Union of Mineworkers and in 1984–5 he led the *miners' strike in protest against the *Conservative government's plans to close several mines. In 1996 he formed a new political party, the Socialist Labour Party, which he considered to be closer to the original principles of the Labour Party.

The ˌ***Scarlet*** ˈ***Letter*** a novel (1850) by the US writer Nathaniel *Hawthorne. The story is about *Puritans in 17th-century *New England. Hester Prynne is found guilty of adultery and is made to wear a scarlet (= red) letter A on her dress. There have been three film versions, including one in 1995 with Demi *Moore as Hester.

The ˌ***Scarlet*** ˈ***Pimpernel*** /ˈpɪmpənel; *AmE* ˈpɪmpərnel/ a novel (1905) by Baroness Orczy (1865–1947). It is about a group of Englishmen who rescue *upper-class French people from being killed during the French Revolution. The main character is Sir Percy Blakeney, also known as the Scarlet Pimpernel, who dresses in various disguises to avoid being captured by the French.

ˌ**scepter'd** ˈ**isle** /ˌseptəd; *AmE* ˌseptərd/ a phrase describing England, which appears in *Shakespeare's play *Richard II*, in a speech by the character *John of Gaunt. It is part of a long list of well-known phrases in praise of England, beginning:

This royal throne of kings, this scepter'd isle,
This earth of majesty, this seat of Mars,
This other Eden, demi-Paradise ...

ˌ***Schindler's*** ˈ***List*** /ˌʃɪndləz; *AmE* ˌʃɪndlərz/ a US film (1993), directed by Stephen *Spielberg, which won seven *Oscars, including Best Picture and Best Director. It was based on the novel *Schindler's Ark* (1982) by the Australian writer Thomas Keneally, which won the *Booker Prize. The story is about a real person, Oskar Schindler, a German who risked his own life during *World War II to save Polish Jews sent to work in his factory. The Irish actor Liam Neeson played the part of Schindler in the film.

Schlitz™ /ʃlɪts/ *n* [U, C] a popular US beer, advertised as 'the beer that made Milwaukee famous'. It was produced from 1874 to 1982 by the Joseph Schlitz Brewing Company in *Milwaukee, *Wisconsin, and has since been made by the Stroh Brewing Company of *Detroit, *Michigan.

Schoˌlastic ˈ**Aptitude Test**™ ⇨ SAT.

ˌ**school** ˈ**district** *n* (in US education) an area containing several *grammar schools and *high schools run by the same administrative **school board**. The board's members are usually elected. A city school district may only cover part of a large city, but one in the countryside may include several towns.

The ˌ***School for*** ˈ***Scandal*** a comedy play (1777) by Richard Brinsley *Sheridan about two brothers who both want to marry the same young woman.

Schools in Britain ⇨ article.

Schools in the US ⇨ article.

ˌCharles ˈ**Schulz** /ˈʃʊlts/ (1922–) the US artist who created and draws the popular *comic strip *Peanuts*. He based the character of Charlie *Brown on himself.

ˌArnold ˈ**Schwarzenegger** /ˈʃwɔːtsənegə(r); *AmE* ˈʃwɔːrtsənegər/ (1947–) a US actor with large muscles, known especially for his parts in violent action films. He was born in Austria and won several competitions for muscle development, including 'Mr Universe'. His films include *Conan the Barbarian* (1982), the *Terminator* films (1984 and 1991), *True Lies* (1994) and *Eraser* (1996). See also PLANET HOLLYWOOD.

Arnold Schwarzenegger and Danny DeVito in Twins

Schweppes /ʃweps/ ⇨ CADBURY SCHWEPPES.

the ˈ**Science Muˌseum** Britain's largest museum of science and technology, in South *Kensington, London, established in 1909. It contains many objects from the history of science, and has a large number of displays which the public can touch and operate. A new section with a large cinema and other attractions will open in the year 2000.

ˌ***Scienˈtific Aˈmerican*** a US magazine published each month about scientific research and discoveries. The articles are more technical than those in a general magazine. The company owning the magazine also has a television series on *PBS, called *Scientific American Frontiers*. It began in 1990 and is presented by the actor Alan Alda.

ˌ**Scienˈtology** /ˌsaɪənˈtɒlədʒi; *AmE* ˌsaɪənˈtɑːlədʒi/ an international religious philosophy established in 1954 by the US writer of science fiction L Ron *Hubbard. It is based on his book *Dianetics* (1950) and officially became the Church of Scientology in 1965. It believes in a 'life energy' and encourages its members to improve themselves in a spiritual way by a greater understanding of themselves. The organization has been criticized for the methods it uses to attract and keep members. They include several well-known actors, including Tom *Cruise and John *Travolta. ▶ **Scientologist** *n*.

the ˈ**Scilly Isles** /ˈsɪli/ (*also* the ˈ**Scillies** /ˈsɪliz/ the **Isles of Scilly**) a group of about 140 small islands about 28 miles/45 kilometres off the south-west coast of England. Five of the larger islands have people living on them, and the capital is Hugh Town on the island of St Mary's. The Scillies have a mild climate and are popular for holidays/vacations.

SCLC /ˌes siː el ˈsiː/ ⇨ SOUTHERN CHRISTIAN LEADERSHIP CONFERENCE.

Schools in Britain

British law requires all children to be in full-time *education from the age of 5 to 16, but parents like, if possible, to send younger children to a **nursery school** or **playschool** from the age of 2 or 3.

Most children go to ***state schools** near their home. Britain has several different school systems. Depending on where they live, children may go to an ***infant school** from age 5 to 7 and then a ***junior school** until they are 11. Others attend a ***primary school** from age 5 to 11. They enter the **reception class** as 'rising fives', just before their fifth birthday. Most primary schools are **mixed**, taking both boys and girls.

At 11 children begin their **secondary education**. They go to a ***grammar school**, ***comprehensive school** or **high school**, depending on their ability, their parents' wishes, and what schools there are nearby. Some are **single-sex** schools. In a few cities children can go to a *city technology college, a school partly funded by industry. Some students leave school at 16 but many stay on for a further two years in the ***sixth form**.

In a few areas children go to a ***first school** at the age of 5, a ***middle school** at 8 and an ***upper school** from 13 onwards.

***Special schools** cater for people with **special educational needs**, though many parents of disabled children prefer them to attend an ordinary school. Some primary and a few secondary schools are supported by the *Church of England or the *Roman Catholic Church. There are also some Islamic schools. A small number of children attend **music schools** or **language schools** where academic studies are combined with special music or language lessons.

Children of richer parents may be sent to a private ***preparatory school**, often called a **prep school**, for which they pay high fees, and then to an ***independent school** or a ***public school**. Many public schools are boarding schools.

School organization

The **academic year** starts in September and is divided into three **terms**. Pupils have holidays at Christmas and Easter and during the summer, and short breaks at **half-term**. National ***GCSE** and ***A level** *exams take place in May and June.

Most schools have a five-day week, from Monday to Friday. The school day begins around 9 a.m. and ends around 3 p.m. for the youngest children, and 4 p.m. for older ones. There is a **break** of 15 or 20 minutes in the morning and sometimes also in the afternoon. Many children take a packed lunch from home; others have **school dinner**, a cooked meal at the school for which parents have to pay.

Parents may support their children's school by joining the **PTA** (**Parents' and Teachers' Association**). They meet teachers at regular **parents' evenings** to discuss their child's progress.

Life at primary school

After teachers have **marked the register** most schools start the day with **assembly**, a religious service. Parents may have their child excused from this service.

Pupils are divided into classes according to age. Formerly, individual schools decided how much time they would give to each subject, but in 1988 the ***National Curriculum** was introduced which set programmes of study in a range of subjects for all state schools in England and Wales. It does not apply in Scotland, and independent schools do not have to follow it, though many do. In primary schools a class teacher teaches most subjects, but some schools have specialist teachers for music or technology. Pupils at primary schools do not usually have **homework** but may take part in after-school clubs. Their progress is tested by their teacher through **standard assessment tests** (SATs) set nationally at the ages of 7 and 11.

Secondary schools

Secondary education used to be **selective**, i.e. secondary schools accepted children based on their performance in an exam called the ***eleven-plus**. Grammar schools and high schools, which concentrated on academic subjects, **creamed off** the best pupils. Those who failed the exam went to ***secondary modern schools** which taught more practical subjects. In the 1960s it was thought that 11 was too young an age for a child's future to be decided in this way. It was also clear that the eleven-plus reinforced social divisions, as most childen who passed the exam were *middle-class. As a result **selective education**, and with it the eleven-plus, was ended in many areas. Secondary moderns and many grammar schools became comprehensive schools offering a broad education to students with a wide range of abilities. Some grammar schools and high schools became independent. A few areas kept a selective system based on an eleven- or twelve-plus exam.

Many schools are under the control of a ***Local Education Authority** (LEA). ***Grant-maintained schools** are run entirely by **governors**, parents of pupils and members of the local community, and are responsible to central government. Grant-maintained schools are free to change their status, so a comprehensive school may choose to become a grammar school and admit only brighter students, as under the old system.

Secondary schools are much larger than primary schools and students may have to travel longer distances by school bus or public transport. Most secondary school students wear **school uniform**. Students in each year may be divided into groups based on ability. Classes are taught by teachers who have specialist knowledge of a particular subject. Students continue to study subjects in the National Curriculum and take SATs at 14, and then work towards ***GCSEs** in as many subjects as they can manage, often eight or ten. Students who hope to go to *university stay on at school or go to a **sixth-form college** to study for ***A levels** in two, three or four subjects. Some secondary schools now offer more practical courses leading to ***GNVQs** as an introduction to work-related skills.

In Scotland students take the ***Scottish Certificate of Education** (**SCE**). The standard grade, which is roughly equivalent to GCSE, is taken at 16 at one of three levels, and the higher grade is taken at 17. Students take five or six subjects as **Highers** and may then take A levels.

Schools in the US

School usually means the same in American English as in British English, but sometimes it can also mean 'university'. If a parent says 'I work during the mornings when the children are at school', it means that the children are young and are probably at ***elementary school**. But 'My youngest son is away at school now' almost certainly means that he has started university in another city.

Many Americans send their children to a **nursery school**, or to **day care** or **pre-school** at an early age. At 5 children go to **kindergarten** and begin their formal ***K–12** education. As in Britain, US schools are divided into primary and secondary, but these words are rarely used. It is more common to talk about *elementary school, ***junior high school** and ***high school**, and the **grade**, or year group, students are in. Elementary schools teach children from kindergarten till the end of sixth grade. Grades seven and eight are taken at junior high school, and the ninth to the twelfth grades at high school.

Life in elementary school

The school year runs from early September to the following June. Students attend daily from Monday to Friday. The school day in elementary school usually lasts from about 8.30 a.m. to 3.30 p.m., though kindergarten children usually attend for only half the day.

Students spend most of the day with their **class**. The class is taught most of the time by the same teacher. A few times each week they will have a gym class or do music or art with another teacher. Students rarely have **homework** until they reach the final grades of elementary school, and even then there is very little.

The school day is divided into various sections and in the morning and the afternoon students have **recess**, a time when they can go outside and play, for about 15 minutes. Schools usually have a **playground** attached, a large area outside with equipment for playing different games. In the middle of the day students eat lunch, either a meal prepared by their parents or a hot meal which they buy from the school. The rest of the **lunch period** is free and spent playing.

The traditional subjects for elementary school students are called **the three Rs**: *r*eading, w*r*iting, and a*r*ithmetic. In addition, the students study other subjects, such as history and geography, and are given a chance to do creative activities and sports. It is thought to be important to give children the chance to study as many subjects as possible, so that whatever their natural skills are they will have the chance to develop them.

Teachers are rather relaxed about the kind of behaviour they expect from students at elementary school. Children should be fairly quiet during lessons but they are not punished unless their behaviour is out of control and could hurt other students. Punishments include making the student stay behind for a few minutes when others have left for the day, or sending him or her to the principal's office. Teachers in elementary school are usually called by their title and surname, e.g. Mr Johnson.

Students at public schools (= those run by the state) do not usually have a school uniform. Students who attend private and **parochial** (= religious) schools do wear uniform.

Junior high school and high school

Students at junior high school take different lessons from different teachers who are specialists in their subjects. Students are required to study certain subjects, but they can choose which classes they take. For example, students may be required to study a science for three years, but they can choose whether to take chemistry, physics or biology. There are also many subjects that students can choose to do or to drop, without any limits at all.

At high school, students may take technical subjects such as computer programming alongside academic subjects. As in elementary school the aim is to help children develop their natural potential. Additional summer sessions enable students to catch up with work they have missed or to take a course they did not have time for during the year. When students **graduate** from high school they receive a **diploma**, a document to say that they have finished their courses.

An important part of junior high school and high school is, for many students, the increasing amount of independence and responsibility they are given. Students in high school have special names: ninth-grade students are called **freshmen**; tenth-graders are **sophomores**; students in the eleventh grade are **juniors**, and those in the twelfth grade are **seniors**. As students go through these levels, they expect to have more and more freedom.

Part of the independence of secondary education comes from being away from home for longer, and having to travel further to school. Many students go to school in a **school bus** which picks them up near their homes and takes them back again in the evening. '**Busing**' students for long distances became necessary in some cities in order to keep a mix of white and black students in each school. At the age of 16, when most Americans learn to drive, students often go to school in their own car or borrow that of their parents.

After school, students can choose from many **extra-curricular activities**. These include joining clubs based on a particular interest, e.g. chess, computers, acting or cooking, working on the school newspaper or playing in a sports team. A teacher from the school spends time with each group, but as students get older they are expected to organize and run things themselves.

During the school year there are important social activities. In the autumn ***homecoming**, the day when former students return to the school, is celebrated with a big football game and a dance. Other dances are held during the year. The most important of these is the **Prom** which is held near the end of the school year. Students take special care to find the right clothes for this event, which is usually limited to juniors and seniors. Younger students are very pleased if they have the chance to go as the guest of an older student.

scone *n* (*BrE*) a small round cake made of flour, fat and milk, sometimes containing sultanas (= a type of dried fruit). Scones are usually eaten with butter or cream and jam for the afternoon meal of tea. Compare DROP SCONE. See also CREAM TEA.

ˌ**Scooby 'Doo** /ˌsku:bi 'du:/ a character in US television cartoons. He is a Great Dane dog who helps to solve mysteries with his human friends Fred, clever Velma, pretty Daphne and the *hippie 'Shaggy'. *Scooby Doo* began on *CBS in 1969.

SCOPE /skəʊp; *AmE* skoʊp/ a British charity which helps people with cerebral palsy (= a condition caused by brain damage before or at birth, which makes people lose control of their movements). It was formed in 1952 as the Spastics Society, and has several schools and other centres in Britain.

the '**Scopes trial** /'skəʊps/ a famous US court case in 1925 in Dayton, *Tennessee. A teacher, John Scopes, was put on trial because he taught Charles *Darwin's theory of evolution, which was illegal under local law. The case was informally called the 'monkey trial'. The *American Civil Liberties Union got Clarence *Darrow to defend Scopes, and William Jennings *Bryan helped to argue the case against him. Scopes was judged guilty but freed for technical reasons. The law was only changed in 1967.

ˌMartin **Scor'sese** /skɔ:'seɪzi; *AmE* skɔ:r'seɪzi/ (1942–) a US director of films, many of them with the actor Robert *De Niro, including **Mean Streets*, **Taxi Driver*, *Raging Bull* (1980), *GoodFellas* (1990) and *Casino* (1995). Scorsese's other films include *The Last Temptation of Christ* (1988), which was criticized by some religious groups, *The Age of Innocence* (1993) and *Kundun* (1997).

Scot /skɒt; *AmE* skɑ:t/ *n* **1** a member of a Celtic people from Northern Ireland who moved into and controlled the west coast of Scotland in the 6th century. Their enemies in Scotland were the *Picts. **2** a person who comes from Scotland.

Scotch *n* [U, C] *whisky (= a strong alcoholic drink) produced in Scotland.

The adjective **Scotch** was used in former times to describe the people and things of Scotland, but it is now only used of products like whisky and wool. The adjective **Scottish** is now used to describe the people and things of Scotland, and **Scots** is used to describe its people, its law and its language: *Scotch beef* ○ *Scottish dancing* ○ *a Scots accent.*

'**Scotchgard**™ /'skɒtʃgɑ:d; *AmE* 'skɑ:tʃgɑ:rd/ *n* [U] a chemical, produced by the *3M company, which protects cloth and material from water, oil and other substances that make marks. It is often used for carpets.

ˌ**Scotch 'pancake** ⇨ DROP SCONE.

'**Scotch tape**™ *n* [U] (*AmE*) a make of transparent sticky tape used for sticking paper together, mending things, etc.

ˌ**Scotch 'terrier** (*also infml* **Scottie**, **Scottie dog**) *n* a breed of small dog with rough, usually black hair and short legs, originally bred in Scotland. See also TERRIER.

ˌ***Scotland the 'Brave*** /ˌskɒtlənd; *AmE* ˌskɑ:tlənd/ a traditional patriotic Scottish song (= one expressing pride in Scotland), sung (especially formerly) at sports matches. Compare *FLOWER OF SCOTLAND*.

ˌ**Scotland 'Yard** /ˌskɒtlənd; *AmE* ˌskɑ:tlənd/ the main office of the British *Metropolitan Police, now officially called *New Scotland Yard. Its original office was in a building in London that once belonged to the royal family of Scotland: *Scotland Yard detectives have been investigating the crime.*

ˌ**Scots, wha 'hae** /ˌskɒts wæ 'heɪ; *AmE* ˌskɑ:ts/ the first words of a traditional Scottish song, taken from a poem by Robert *Burns celebrating the victory of the Scots over the English at *Bannockburn. The first line in full is 'Scots, wha hae wi' Wallace bled' (Scots, who have with Wallace bled), referring to the Scottish soldiers who fought with William *Wallace.

the ˌ**Scots 'Guards** /ˌskɒts; *AmE* ˌskɑ:ts/ one of the *Guards regiments of the British army, established in Scotland in 1660. Compare ROYAL SCOTS.

The '***Scotsman*** /'skɒtsmən; *AmE* 'skɑ:tsmən/ a leading Scottish newspaper, published every day. It first appeared in 1817.

ˌCaptain '**Scott**¹ /skɒt; *AmE* skɑ:t/ (Robert Falcon Scott 1868–1912) an English explorer and navy officer, often referred to as Scott of the Antarctic. He became widely known and admired in Britain as a result of his two journeys to the Antarctic. On the second journey (1910–12) he reached the South Pole a month after the Norwegian explorer Roald Amundsen (1872–1928) had become the first man ever to reach it. Scott and his four companions died of cold on the journey back. His records of the journey were found in 1912 and published in 1913. His son was Peter *Scott. See also OATES¹.

Scott's team at the South Pole: Edward Wilson, Captain Scott, Edgar Evans, Lawrence Oates and H R Bowers

'George 'Gilbert '**Scott**² /skɒt; *AmE* 'skɑ:t/ (1811–78) an English architect. He was one of the leading figures of the *Gothic Revival in England, and designed *St Pancras station and the *Albert Memorial in London, as well as restoring (= repairing) many old churches. He was made a *knight in 1872.

'Giles 'Gilbert '**Scott**³ /skɒt; *AmE* 'skɑ:t/ (1880–1960) an English architect, the grandson of George Gilbert *Scott. His best-known buildings include *Battersea Power Station and the Anglican cathedral at Liverpool (completed in 1978). He was made a *knight in 1924.

ˌPaul '**Scott**⁴ /'skɒt; *AmE* 'skɑ:t/ (1920–78) an English author. He served as a soldier in India during *World War II, and is best known for *The *Raj Quartet*, a series of four novels set in India during the final years of British rule there (= the Raj). A popular television version of the novels was made under the title **Jewel in the Crown*. A further novel by Scott about India, *Staying On*, won the *Booker Prize in 1977.

ˌPeter '**Scott**⁵ /'skɒt; *AmE* 'skɑ:t/ (1909–89) an English artist and writer, the son of Captain Robert *Scott¹. He started the Wildfowl Trust at *Slimbridge in 1946 and was made a *knight in 1973 for his work in protecting plants and animals, especially birds. His paintings of birds are well known. He also appeared in several television programmes about the natural world.

ˌRandolph '**Scott**⁶ /'skɒt; *AmE* 'skɑ:t/ (1903–87) a US actor who appeared mainly in *westerns from the 1930s to 1950s. His films included **Last of the Mohi-*

cans (1936), *Western Union* (1941), *Santa Fe* (1951) and *Ride Lonesome* (1958).

ˌRonnie ˈ**Scott**[7] /ˈskɒt; *AmE* ˈskɑːt/ (1927–96) an English musician and club owner. He played the saxophone in several *jazz bands, starting his own band in 1953, and opened the leading London jazz club, Ronnie Scott's, in 1959.

ˌSheila ˈ**Scott**[8] /ˈskɒt; *AmE* ˈskɑːt/ (1927–88) an English pilot. She flew alone round the world three times, and in 1971 was the first to do this over the North Pole in a light aircraft.

ˌWalter ˈ**Scott**[9] /ˈskɒt; *AmE* ˈskɑːt/ (1771–1832) a Scottish author and poet. Most of his poetry and his historical novels are based on the traditions and history of Scotland, especially the border region. His most famous poems include *The Lay of the Last Minstrel* and *The *Lady of the Lake*, and his best-known novels include **Waverley*, **Rob Roy* and **Ivanhoe*. All were extremely popular during his life and influenced writers in Britain and Europe. Scott was made a *baronet in 1820. See also WAVERLEY NOVELS.

ˈ**Scottie** /ˈskɒti; *AmE* ˈskɑːti/ (*also* ˈ**Scottie dog**) ⇨ SCOTCH TERRIER.

the ˈ**Scott Inˌquiry** /ˈskɒt; *AmE* ˈskɑːt/ a British government committee formed in 1993 to investigate illegal sales of weapons to Iraq by British companies. It followed the *Matrix Churchill trial of 1992 and was led by Sir Richard Scott (1934–). In its report, published in 1996, it said that government ministers had known that illegal sales of weapons were taking place, but had failed to inform Parliament. It especially criticized the actions of the Foreign Office minister William Waldegrave.

the ˈ**Scottish Cerˈtificate of Eduˈcation** /ˈskɒtɪʃ; *AmE* ˈskɑːtɪʃ/ *n* an examination in Scottish schools. The Standard grade of the examination is taken at the age of 16 and is equivalent to *GCSE in England and Wales. The Higher grade is taken at the age of 17 and is equivalent to *A level. ⇨ article at EDUCATION IN BRITAIN.

the ˈ**Scottish** ˈ**FA** ˈ**Cup** /ˈskɒtɪʃ ˈef eɪ; *AmE* ˈskɑːtɪʃ/ the series of matches in which Scottish football teams compete to win the Scottish Football Association cup (= a prize in the form of a cup). The first series was held in 1873. The final match, which decides the winner, is played every year at *Hampden Park, Glasgow. Compare FA CUP.

ˌ**Scottish** ˈ**law** /ˌskɒtɪʃ; *AmE* ˌskɑːtɪʃ/ ⇨ article at LEGAL SYSTEM IN BRITAIN.

S

the ˌ**Scottish** ˈ**National** ˌ**Party** /ˌskɒtɪʃ; *AmE* ˌskɑːtɪʃ/ (*abbr* the **SNP**) a political party formed in 1934 whose aim is to achieve independent government for Scotland (not simply a separate Scottish parliament within the UK). Its leader since 1990 has been Alex Salmond (1954–), and six of its candidates were elected as *Members of Parliament in the 1997 general election in Britain.

the ˈ**Scottish** ˈ**National** ˈ**Portrait** ˌ**Gallery** /ˈskɒtɪʃ; *AmE* ˈskɑːtɪʃ/ an art gallery in *Edinburgh, established in 1882, which shows paintings and photographs of people. Compare NATIONAL PORTRAIT GALLERY.

the ˈ**Scottish** ˌ**Office** /ˈskɒtɪʃ; *AmE* ˈskɑːtɪʃ/ a British government department responsible for a wide range of Scottish affairs, including education, the environment, farming, industry and health. It is led by the Secretary of State for Scotland and is based mainly in *Edinburgh. The Scottish Office will cease to exist after the new *Scottish Parliament is established.

ˌ**Scottish** ˈ**Opera** /ˌskɒtɪʃ; *AmE* ˌskɑːtɪʃ/ Scotland's national opera company, formed in *Glasgow in 1962 and based at the Theatre Royal, Glasgow. The company has regular tours in Scotland and England.

the ˌ**Scottish** ˈ**Parliament** /ˌskɒtɪʃ; *AmE* ˌskɑːtɪʃ/ a separate parliament for Scotland, based in *Edinburgh. It began work in 1999, and gives Scotland greater political independence from the British parliament in London. Compare NORTHERN IRELAND ASSEMBLY, WELSH ASSEMBLY. See also DEVOLUTION.

the ˈ**Scottish play** /ˈskɒtɪʃ; *AmE* ˈskɑːtɪʃ/ ⇨ MACBETH.

Scottish TV /ˌskɒtɪʃ tiː ˈviː; *AmE* ˌskɑːtɪʃ/ (*abbr* **STV**) an independent television company, started in 1957, which broadcasts to central Scotland as part of *ITV.

ˌ***Scott v*** ˈ***Sandford*** /ˌskɒt vɜːsəs ˈsændfəd; *AmE* ˌskɑːt vɜːrsəs ˈsændfərd/ the official legal name for the *Dred Scott Case.

Scouse /skaʊs/ *adj* (*BrE infml*) of the people living in and around *Liverpool, north-west England, and their way of speaking, etc.: *Scouse words/humour/pop stars.*

▶ **Scouse** *n* **1** [U] the way of speaking of the people of *Liverpool: *They were talking broad Scouse.* **2** (*also* ˈ**Scouser** /ˈskaʊsə(r)/) [C] a person who was born in Liverpool.

the **Scouts** (*also fml* the ˈ**Scout Associˌation**) an international association formed in Britain in 1908 by Lord Robert *Baden-Powell. It organizes outdoor activities for boys, e.g. camping, and aims to teach them practical skills, discipline and social responsibility. Members wear uniforms, and their motto is 'Be prepared'. The four main groups are *Beaver Scouts (for ages 6–8), *Cub Scouts (8–10½), Scouts (10½–15½) and *Venture Scouts (15½–20). Girls were admitted to the Scouts for the first time in Britain in 1990. See also BOY SCOUTS OF AMERICA. Compare GUIDES.

ˈ**Scrabble**™ /ˈskræbl/ a popular board game in which players try to build words on a board marked with squares, using letters printed on small square blocks. The words must be arranged to fit together like a *crossword puzzle. Scrabble was invented in the US in the 1930s by Alfred Butts, who first called it 'Criss Cross'. It became very popular in the 1960s, and there are now many Scrabble clubs and national competitions in both Britain and the US.

ˈ**scratchcard** /ˈskrætʃkɑːd; *AmE* ˈskrætʃkɑːrd/ *n* (in Britain) a small paper card which can be bought from shops as a form of gambling. A covering on parts of the card can be scratched off to reveal whether or not you have won a cash prize. Although scratchcards have been legal in Britain since 1976 they became especially popular in 1995 as part of the *National Lottery. Scratchcard prizes are generally smaller than the major national Lottery prizes. Scratchcards have also been part of state lotteries in the US since the 1980s.

ˌ**Screaming Lord** ˈ**Sutch** /ˈsʌtʃ/ the name used by an Englishman, David Sutch (1942–99), who began his career as a pop singer but was best known as the leader of the *Monster Raving Loony Party. He often appeared on television dressed in strange and colourful clothing and a tall hat.

Screaming Lord Sutch

ˈScreen ˌActors Guild the US trade union for film and television actors, established in 1933.

Scrooge /skruːdʒ/ *n* (*disapprov*) a person who is mean with money or does not care about others, similar to the character Ebenezer Scrooge in the book *A *Christmas Carol* by Charles *Dickens: *He's a bit of a Scrooge when it comes to lending money.*

the **Scrubs** /skrʌbz/ ⇨ WORMWOOD SCRUBS.

ˈscrumpy /ˈskrʌmpi/ *n* [U] (*BrE*) a type of strong cider (= an alcoholic drink made from apples), especially as made in the *West Country of England.

ˌPeter **ˈScudamore** /ˈskuːdəmɔː(r)/ (1958–) an English jockey. He was the *National Hunt *champion jockey every year from 1986 to 1992 and set several records in the sport. His racing career ended in 1993 and he now trains horses.

SDI /ˌes diː ˈaɪ/ ⇨ STRATEGIC DEFENSE INITIATIVE.

the **SDLP** /ˌes diː el ˈpiː/ (*in full* the **Social Democratic and Labour Party**) a Northern Irish political party, formed in 1970 by a group of *MPs in favour of equal rights for *Roman Catholics. The party, supported mainly by Catholics, would like Northern Ireland and the Republic of Ireland to be united as one country, but does not approve of the violent methods of the *IRA. Its MPs in the *House of Commons vote the same way as the *Labour Party on most issues.

the **SDP** /ˌes diː ˈpiː/ (*in full* the **Social Democratic Party**) a British political party formed in 1981 by a group of *MPs who left the *Labour Party to start a new 'middle party' in British politics. In 1987 it combined with the *Liberal Party to form the *Liberal Democratic Party. A small group led by David *Owen continued to call themselves the SDP until 1990.

SDS /ˌes diː ˈes/ ⇨ STUDENTS FOR A DEMOCRATIC SOCIETY.

the ˌ**Sealed ˈKnot Soˌciety** a British society, formed in 1968, which performs historical scenes, especially from battles of the *English Civil War. Members dress as soldiers of the period and usually perform where the original battles took place. The organization also works as an educational charity in schools.

members of the Sealed Knot Society taking part in a mock battle

ˈSea Lord *n* either of two senior admirals (the First and Second Sea Lords) who are responsible for the training, equipment, etc. of the British *Royal Navy.

ˈSealy™ /ˈsiːli/ a US make of mattress for beds, first produced in 1950. The advertisements claim that 'Sleeping on a Sealy is like sleeping on a cloud.'

SEAQ /ˌes iː eɪ ˈkjuː/ (*in full* **Stock Exchange Automated Quotations**) an electronic system for buying and selling shares in companies on the *London Stock Exchange. It was introduced in 1986 as part of the *Big Bang, and allows people to receive information about the Stock Exchange much more quickly than before. It also makes it possible for people to buy or sell shares by computer or telephone from anywhere in the world.

ˌRonald **ˈSearle** /ˈsɜːl; *AmE* ˈsɜːrl/ (1920–) an English artist. He is best known for his humorous drawings of the schoolgirls of *St Trinian's, and his work has appeared in many magazines and books. His work as a serious artist includes drawings done while he was a prisoner of the Japanese during *World War II.

ˌ**Sears, ˈRoebuck and ˌCompany** /ˌsɪəz ˈrəʊbʌk; *AmE* ˌsɪrz ˈroʊbʌk/ (*also* **Sears and Roebuck**, **Sears**) any of a very large group of US department stores selling a wide range of products for the family. The company was begun in 1886 in *Minneapolis by Richard Sears. He was then joined by Alvah Roebuck when he moved the company to *Chicago in 1887. In 1891, they began the company's famous mail-order catalogue (= book showing items that can be ordered by post). See also SEARS TOWER.

the ˌ**Sears ˈTower** /ˌsɪəz; *AmE* ˌsɪrz/ the tallest building in the US and (from 1974 to 1996) the tallest in the world. It is in *Chicago and was built by *Sears, Roebuck and Company. It is 1 454 feet/443 metres high, with 110 floors.

seaside and beach

In the 18th century British people started going to the **seaside** for pleasure and for their health. Seaside towns such as *Brighton, *Lyme Regis and *Scarborough became fashionable with the upper class. **Bathing** in the sea became popular and *bathing machines were invented for people to get changed in. Later, towns like *Blackpool, Clacton-on-Sea and Margate, which were close to industrial areas or to London, developed into large **seaside resorts** to which workers went for a day out or for their *holiday. Long *piers were built stretching out to sea and soon a wide range of amusements were built on them. **Promenades** were built along the shore for people to walk along. Rows of **beach huts** and **chalets** (= buildings where people could get changed or sit and have tea) took the place of bathing machines, and **deckchairs** were for hire on the beach. There were ice cream sellers, *whelk stalls, stalls selling buckets and spades for children to build sandcastles, and the occasional *Punch and Judy show. In the early 1900s it became popular to send *seaside postcards to friends. Children bought seaside **rock**, a long sugary sweet with the name of the place printed through it.

Most British people like to go to the sea for a day out or for a weekend. Resorts like Blackpool are still popular, but others are run-down and rather quiet. British people now prefer to go on holiday to **beach resorts** in Spain, Greece or the *Caribbean because the weather is more likely to be sunny and warm. About a quarter of all beaches in Britain fail standards set by the *European Union because they are not clean enough or because the water quality is poor.

Americans talk of going to the **ocean** or the **beach**, rather than the seaside. Some places, especially on the East coast, have very popular beaches and people travel long distances to go there. *Florida is especially popular and in spring when it is full of students.

Beach activities include swimming, **surfing** and **windsurfing**, also called sailboarding. Many people go to the beach but never go into the water. They spend their time playing games like **volleyball** and **frisbee** (= throwing a flat plastic disc). Other people go to the beach to get a **tan** and spend all their time **sunbathing**. Except on a very few **nudist beaches** women wear **bathing suits** (*BrE* **bathing costumes**) or **bikinis** and men wear **trunks** or **shorts**. Many people worry about getting skin cancer if they get burnt by the sun and so put on **sun cream** or **sun block** to protect their skin. A day at the beach also involves a picnic meal or, especially in the US, a **barbecue** (= meat cooked over an open fire).

ˌseaside ˈpostcard *n* a postcard (= a card for sending messages by post without an envelope) traditionally sent while on holiday at a British seaside town. Seaside postcards have brightly coloured comic drawings on one side, often with a mild sexual humour. The best-known artist of postcards of this type was Donald *McGill.

the **ˈSeason** *n* [sing] (*BrE*) the name given to a number of fashionable sports and cultural events held in Britain every summer and attended by many rich, famous or *upper-class people. The main events are *Glyndebourne, *Derby Day, the *Royal Academy Summer Exhibition, *Royal Ascot, *Wimbledon, *Henley Royal Regatta, International Polo Day (held by the Guards Polo Club at *Windsor[1](1)), *Goodwood, *Cowes Week and the *Lord's test match (= international cricket match). Members of the *royal family attend some of the events, and tickets are often expensive and difficult to get.

Seˈattle /siˈætl/ the largest city in the north-western US, also known as the 'Emerald City'. It is in the state of *Washington and is a Pacific port on Elliott Bay. It was settled in 1852 and named after a *Native-American leader. It is the home of the *Boeing aircraft company and other industries, but tourists are attracted by its clean air and beautiful scenery.

SEC /ˌes iː ˈsiː/ ⇨ SECURITIES AND EXCHANGE COMMISSION.

ˌHarry **ˈSecombe** /ˈsiːkəm/ (1921–) a Welsh comic performer and singer. He is best known for having appeared in the radio comedy series *The *Goon Show*. He has also presented religious programmes on television. He was made a *knight in 1981.

secondary modern *n* a type of secondary school (= for children aged 11–18) in England, providing a general education with an emphasis on practical or technical skills. There are now only a small number of such schools. ⇨ article at EDUCATION IN BRITAIN.

ˌsecond ˈreading *n* the second stage in presenting a *bill(1) (= proposal for a new law) to the British parliament, usually followed by a debate. ⇨ article at ACT OF PARLIAMENT.

the **ˈSecond ˈWorld ˈWar** ⇨ WORLD WAR II.

the **ˌSecretary of ˈState 1** (in Britain) the head of a major government department. **2** (in the US) the head of the Department of State. The person holding the office is the most important member of the President's *Cabinet and has an important role in the creation of US foreign policy. Well-known Secretaries of State have included John Foster *Dulles, Henry *Kissinger and Madeleine *Albright.

the **ˌSecret ˈService** (*in full* the **United States Secret Service**) a division of the US Treasury Department responsible for protecting the President and his family. It also guards the Vice-president, former Presidents and major political candidates for President. It was originally set up to investigate and arrest people who printed false money. Its present duties began in 1901 after President William *McKinley was murdered. See also PINKERTON.

ˌSection ˈEight *n* (*AmE*) **1** the action of dismissing somebody from the US armed forces because they are not fit enough physically or mentally. It takes its name from a section of US Army rules in force between 1922 and 1944. **2** a member of the US armed forces who is dismissed under Section Eight: *He said he would never employ a Section Eight.*

seˌcure ˈtraining ˌcentre *n* a centre in Britain for children aged between 12 and 14 who repeatedly break the law. The children are kept within the centre and are given education and training. The first centre opened in 1998 and several more are planned. Compare YOUNG OFFENDER INSTITUTION.

Seˈcuricor™ /sɪˈkjʊərɪkɔː(r); *AmE* sɪˈkjʊrɪkɔːr/ a British company best known for guarding and transporting cash or valuable objects, e.g. from shops to banks. Securicor guards wear uniforms and helmets and drive large blue vehicles.

the **Seˌcurities and Exˈchange Comˌmission** (*abbr* the **SEC**) an independent US government organization responsible for controlling the financial markets and making sure that people and companies that deal on the stock exchange do not break the law. It investigates complaints and can take people to court for illegal operations. The SEC was established in 1934 and its five members are appointed by the US President.

ˌNeil **Seˈdaka** /səˈdɑːkə/ (1939–) a US pop singer who has written more than 500 songs. His first hit was *Stupid Cupid* (1958), sung by Connie Francis. He then made several successful records of his own, including *Happy Birthday, Sweet Sixteen* (1961), *Breaking Up Is Hard to Do* (1962) and *Laughter in the Rain* (1974).

the ˌBattle of **ˈSedgemoor** /ˈsedʒmɔː(r)/ a battle (1685) at Sedgemoor in *Somerset, England, in which a Protestant army led by the Duke of *Monmouth was defeated by an army led by the *Roman Catholic King *James II. See also BLOODY ASSIZES.

ˌPete **ˈSeeger** /ˈsiːgə(r)/ (1919–) a US singer who has been called 'the father of the American folk revival'. He plays the guitar and banjo and has written many folk songs. He formed and sang with the Weavers (1949–52). Seeger's successful songs of protest have included *If I Had a Hammer* (1949), *Where Have All the Flowers Gone* (1956) and **We Shall Overcome*.

ˌsegreˈgation *n* [U] the policy of separating certain groups from the rest of the community, especially because of their race. In the US, the policy of segregation, especially in the southern states, denied African Americans their rights and forced them to use separate schools, restaurants, hotels, cinemas, etc. from those used by white people. As a result of the *civil rights movement laws were passed in the 1950s and 1960s which greatly reduced segregation in US society. This process is called **desegregation** or 'integration'. See also BUSSING, SEPARATE BUT EQUAL.

ˈSeinfeld /ˈsamfeld/ a popular US comedy series (1990–8) on *NBC, in which Jerry Seinfeld plays himself, a New York stage comedian. The stories are about humorous situations involving him and his friends Cosmo Kramer, George Costanza and Elaine Benes.

seˌlect comˈmittee *n* a small committee, usually consisting of 10–15 members of the British *Parliament, which is formed to investigate a particular matter or to examine the activities of a particular government department.

the **Seˌlective ˈService ˌSystem** ⇨ DRAFT.

ˌMonica **ˈSeles** /ˈseles/ (1973–) a US tennis player, born in Yugoslavia. In 1991 she became the youngest woman ever to hold the position of Number 1 in international tennis. She has won the French Open three times (1990–2), the Australian Open four times (1991–3 and 1996) and the US Open twice (1991–2). Her career was interrupted for two years after she was attacked with a knife by a supporter of the German player Steffi Graf during a match in Hamburg, Germany, in 1993.

ˈ**Selfridges** /ˈselfrɪdʒɪz/ a famous department store on *Oxford Street, London. It is one of the oldest and largest department stores in Britain, and is particularly well known for its food department. See also MISS SELFRIDGE.

ˈ**Sellafield** /ˈseləfiːld/ a nuclear power station (= a building where electricity is produced) on the coast of north-west Britain, near the *Lake District. It is the only centre in Britain for reprocessing the nuclear waste from other power stations (= making it into a form that can be used again). Most of the waste is converted into nuclear fuel, but some of it is stored at Sellafield. Local people are worried about this, since there are often reports of dangerous nuclear waste being allowed to escape into the environment: *The statistics on childhood leukemia have put the government under renewed pressure to close the Sellafield plant.* See also WINDSCALE.

ˌPeter ˈ**Sellers** /ˈseləz; *AmE* ˈselərz/ (1925–80) an English comedy actor. His skill at copying other people's voices in an amusing way first became well known through the radio programme *The *Goon Show*. By the 1960s he had become a major comedy film star, best known for playing three different roles in *Dr Strangelove* (1963) and for playing Inspector *Clouseau in the **Pink Panther* series of films.

ˌDavid O ˈ**Selznick** /ˈselznɪk/ (David Oliver Selznick 1902–65) a successful US film producer. His films included **King Kong* for *RKO and *Anna Karenina* (1935) for *MGM. After forming his own company, Selznick International Pictures, in 1936, he produced *A *Star is Born*, **Gone with the Wind* and *Rebecca* (1940). The last two won *Oscars as Best Picture.

ˈ**Seminole** /ˈsemɪnəʊl; *AmE* ˈsemɪnoʊl/ *n* (*pl* **Seminoles** *or* **Seminole**) a member of the last *Native-American people to make peace with the US government. In 1817–8 they defended their land in *Florida against soldiers led by Andrew *Jackson, and then fought another war against white people in 1835–42. They were moved to *Indian Territory in *Oklahoma and became one of the *Five Civilized Tribes. Some who escaped to the *Everglades did not agree to peace until 1934, and many Seminoles are still there today. See also TRAIL OF TEARS.

the ˈ**Senate** ⇨ UNITED STATES SENATE.

ˈ**Senator** *n* a member of the US *Senate.

ˈ**Seneca** /ˈsenəkə/ *n* (*pl* **Senecas** *or* **Seneca**) a member of a *Native-American people who formed the largest group in the *Iroquois League. They supported the British during the *American Revolution, which led to their villages being destroyed by US troops. Senecas now live mainly on four reservations (= lands given and protected by the US government) in western New York and eastern *Ohio.

ˌ**senior** ˈ**citizen** *n* a phrase used to refer to an old person, especially one over the age of 60. Some old people prefer it to the less gentle phrase '*old age pensioner', but others find it patronizing (= treating them as if they were less important or intelligent than other people).

the ˌ**senior** ˈ**service** *n* [sing + sing/pl *v*] (*BrE*) a name for the *Royal Navy, the oldest of Britain's armed forces.

ˌMack ˈ**Sennett** /ˌmæk ˈsenɪt/ (1880–1960) a US producer and director of silent comedy films, born in Canada. He established the Keystone Company in 1912 and made the first long comedy, *Tilly's Punctured Romance* (1914). Sennett created the *Keystone Kops and brought Charlie *Chaplin to *Hollywood. He received a special *Oscar in 1937.

ˌ***Sense and Sensi*ˈ*bility*** the first novel (1811) by Jane *Austen, in which she creates a clever comedy about the importance of money and marriage to the English *upper middle class. It is the story of two sisters, Elinor, who is very sensible, and Marianne, who is much more emotional. They fall in love with two men but discover that they are both engaged to be married to other women. When Edward, the man loved by Elinor, loses his wealth and the woman he is engaged to marry, he is happy to marry Elinor, the woman he really loves. John, however, the man loved by Marianne, leaves her to marry a rich woman. She is sad for a time, but finally marries somebody else.

ˌ**separate but** ˈ**equal** the phrase used to support the principle of *segregation in the southern US. It was based on a US *Supreme Court decision in 1896 which said that segregation was legal provided that the separate facilities for black people were equal to those for white people. It was also used as an excuse for segregation in schools, restaurants, etc., where conditions for black people were usually much worse than those for white people. The Supreme Court case of **Brown v Board of Education* in 1954 resulted in a decision which ended the principle of 'separate but equal'.

the ˌ**sepa**ˈ**ration of** ˈ**church and** ˈ**state** (in the US) the principle that the government must not interfere in matters of religion. This is written into the *First Amendment of the *American Constitution. Since the 1960s, it has been used in court cases to stop prayers in public schools, but many schools continue to allow time for private prayers.

the ˌ**sepa**ˈ**ration of** ˈ**powers** a basic principle in the *American Constitution which separates national political power into three 'branches' or divisions of government. They are the executive branch under the *President, the legislative branch (i.e. *Congress) and the judicial branch (i.e. the *Supreme Court). The arrangement is intended to make sure that no one branch has too much power, and this is achieved by a system of '*checks and balances'.

Seˈ**quoyah** (*also* **Se**ˈ**quoya**) /sɪˈkwɔɪə/ (*c.* 1765–1843) a *Cherokee Native American who created an alphabet of 86 syllables for his people's language in the early 19th century. He is the only person known to have invented a whole alphabet. The Cherokees used it to communicate in writing, and he also recorded their history. Sequoyah had a Cherokee mother and European father. The sequoia tree is named after him. See also REDWOOD.

ˌ***Sergeant*** ˈ***Pepper*** /ˈpepə(r)/ (*also* ˈ***Sergeant*** ˈ***Pepper's*** ˈ***Lonely*** ˈ***Hearts Club*** ˈ***Band*** /ˈpepəz; *AmE* ˈpepərz/) an album (1967) by the *Beatles. Many people consider it to be the record on which the Beatles stopped producing the simple love songs that had made them pop stars, and began to create new themes and new forms of music. It contains some of their most famous songs, including *Lucy in the Sky with Diamonds*. It is one of the Beatles' best-known records, and one of the most successful albums of all time.

the ˌ**Serious** ˈ**Fraud** ˌ**Office** (*abbr* the **SFO**) a British government agency set up in 1987 to investigate cases of fraud (= deceiving people in order to obtain money or goods) which are too large or complicated for the police *Fraud Squad to deal with. The office was criticized in the 1990s for spending large amounts of money investigating frauds but failing to prosecute anybody in a court of law: *The government confirmed that the Serious Fraud Office was investigating the bank's activities.*

the ˈ**Serpentine** /ˈsɜːpəntaɪn; *AmE* ˈsɜːrpəntaɪn/ the lake in London's *Hyde Park(1). It is mainly used by people sailing small boats, but there is a tradition of swimming in it on *Christmas Day.

SERPS /sɜːps; *AmE* sɜːrps/ (*in full* the **State Earnings-Related Pension Scheme**) the British government *pension system in which people who have retired are paid a basic amount of money every week, and an extra amount of money that depends on how much they earned when they were working.

ˈ***Sesame Street*** /ˈsesəmi/ a popular US television series for young children on *PBS. The programmes, which combine education and social values with entertainment, began in 1969 and are now shown in more than 50 countries. They include real actors and the **Muppet Show* characters created by Jim *Henson, such as Bert and Ernie, Big Bird, the Cookie Monster, Kermit the Frog and Oscar the Grouch.

the ˌ**seven ages of ˈman** a seven periods into which a human life can be divided, i.e. those of the baby, the child, the lover, the soldier, the middle-aged person, the old person, and second childhood. The seven ages are best known through the description of them in the speech by Jaques in *Shakespeare's **As You Like It* which begins: 'All the world's a stage, and all the men and women merely players.'

747 /ˌsevn fɔː ˈsevn; *AmE* ˌsevn fɔːr ˈsevn/ (*also* **Boeing 747**) *n* [C] the largest passenger aircraft in the world, also called informally the 'jumbo jet'. It was first made by the US *Boeing Company in 1969. Each plane can carry more than 400 passengers. The 747–400 model is the longest, at more than 231 feet (70 metres). The safety of 747s was investigated after one exploded and crashed in 1996 off *Long Island, New York, killing all 230 passengers and crew.

ˈ***Seven ˈPillars of ˈWisdom*** a book (1926) by T E *Lawrence. It describes his experiences in the Arabian desert during *World War I when he went to help the Arabs in their fight against Turkey.

the ˌ**Seven ˈSisters** the seven oldest and most respected US women's colleges. They are: Barnard in New York City (associated with *Columbia University), Bryn Mawr in Bryn Mawr, *Pennsylvania, Mount Holyoke in South Hadley, *Massachusetts, Radcliffe in *Cambridge, Massachusetts (associated with *Harvard University), Smith in Northampton, Massachusetts, Vassar (which now also has male students) in Poughkeepsie, New York, and Wellesley in Wellesley, Massachusetts. Compare IVY LEAGUE.

ˌ**Seventh-Day ˈAdventist** /ˈædvəntɪst/ *n* a member of a Christian religious group that was established in 1860. They have their sabbath (= the day of the week when they rest and worship God) on Saturday instead of Sunday, and they believe that Christ will soon return to earth. They are well known for their strict religious rules.

737 /ˌsevn θriː ˈsevn/ (*also* **Boeing 737**) *n* [C] the most widely used passenger aircraft in the world, first made by the US *Boeing Company in 1967. Since then there have been several different models, the latest and longest of which is the 737–900.

7UP™ /ˈsevnʌp/ *n* [C, U] a sweet, clear, fizzy drink (= one containing many bubbles) without alcohol, similar to lemonade and sold in cans or bottles. It was first produced in the US in 1929 and for many years was advertised as 'the Uncola'.

the ˌ**Seven Years ˈWar** a war (1756–63) between Britain, Prussia and Hanover on one side and Austria, France, Russia, Saxony and Sweden on the other. Its main causes were the struggle between Britain and France to be the most important imperial power (= country in control of an empire), and the struggle between Austria and Prussia to be the most important country in central Europe. The British and Prussian side won, and France had to give most of its land in America, Canada and India to Britain, while Prussia began to be one of the most powerful countries in Europe.

S

the ˈ**Severn** /ˈsevən; *AmE* ˈsevərn/ the second longest river in Britain. It starts in Wales and flows through western England and into the *Bristol Channel. It is well known for the **Severn Bore**, a tall wave of water that regularly flows up the river from the sea.

the ˌ**Severn ˈBridge** /ˌsevən; *AmE* ˌsevərn/ a high suspension bridge (= a bridge that hangs from cables supported by towers at each end) which carries the M4 motorway over the river *Severn between south-west England and south Wales. It was built near *Bristol in the 1960s. A second motorway bridge was built over the Severn in the 1990s.

the ˌ**Severn ˈTunnel** /ˌsevən; *AmE* ˌsevərn/ a rail tunnel under the river *Severn between south-west England and south Wales. It was built near *Bristol between 1873 and 1886 and is 4.35 miles/7 kilometres long, the longest tunnel in Britain.

ˌWilliam H ˈ**Seward** /ˈsuːəd; *AmE* ˈsuːərd/ (William Henry Seward 1801–72) the US *Secretary of State who persuaded the government to buy *Alaska from Russia in 1867 for $7.2 million. It became known as **Seward's Folly** because many people thought it was foolish to pay so much for such an empty, frozen region. Seward was Secretary of State under Abraham *Lincoln (1861–5) and survived a murder attempt when Lincoln was killed. He then became Secretary of State under Andrew *Jackson (1865–9). A town in Alaska is named after him.

the ˌ**Sex Discrimiˈnation Act** a British *Act of Parliament which became a law in 1975. Under the Act, people of both sexes have the right to equal opportunities in education and employment, and to be paid the same amount for doing the same work. People who break this law, for example by paying women less than men, can be put on trial and punished in a court of law.

the ˈ**Sex ˌPistols** a British *punk(1) group. They were one of the first groups to play punk music in Britain, and became famous in the 1970s for their lack of respect for anybody. Some people were offended by the words of their songs, including *Anarchy in the UK* (1976) and *God Save the Queen* (1977), and others were offended by their behaviour, which included spitting and swearing in public and on television. The best-known members of the group were Johnny Rotten and Sid Vicious.

the **Seyˈchelles** /seɪˈʃelz/ a country in the Indian Ocean consisting of over 100 islands. It was part of the French empire until the late 18th century, when it became part of the *British Empire. It has been an independent republic and a member of the *Commonwealth since 1976. Tourism is an important industry in the Seychelles. In Britain it is thought of as a place where rich people go for expensive holidays. ▶ **Seychellois** /ˌseɪʃelˈwɑː/ *adj*, *n* (*pl* **Seychellois**).

ˌJane ˈ**Seymour** /ˈsiːmɔː(r)/ (*c.* 1509–37) the third wife of King *Henry VIII. She married him in 1536, but died soon after the birth of their son Edward, who became King *Edward VI.

SFO /ˌes ef ˈəʊ; *AmE* ˈoʊ/ ⇨ SERIOUS FRAUD OFFICE.

S4C /ˌes fɔː ˈsi; *AmE* fɔːr/ (*in full* **Sianel Pedwar Cymru**) the Welsh television channel. It broadcasts a mixture of programmes in Welsh and *Channel Four programmes seen in the rest of Britain.

ˌErnest ˈ**Shackleton** /ˈʃækltən/ (1874–1922) an Irish explorer. He went to the Antarctic as a member of Captain *Scott's group from 1901 to 1904, and later led three more trips to the Antarctic. He died on the fourth journey. He was made a *knight in 1909.

the ˌ**Shadow ˈCabinet** the group of British *MPs from the Opposition (= the main party opposing the government) who would probably form the *Cabinet if their party were in power. Each member of the Shadow Cabinet speaks on behalf of his party on matters for which he or she would be responsible.

ˌPeter ˈ**Shaffer** /ˈʃæfə(r)/ (1926–) an English writer of plays, several of which have been very successful in *West End and *Broadway theatres. His best-known works are *Equus* (1973) and *Amadeus* (1979), both of which were made into films.

ˌ**Shaftesbury ˈAvenue** /ˌʃɑːftsbri; *AmE* ˌʃæftsbri/ a street in central London, running north-east from *Piccadilly Circus. It is famous for the many *West End theatres on it.

the ˈ**Shakers** /ˈʃeɪkəz; *AmE* ˈʃeɪkərz/ the popular name for the United Society of Believers in Christ's Second Appearing, a Christian religious group that separated from the *Quakers in England and moved to the US in 1774. They were called Shakers because they shook with emotion when they worshipped. Strict Shakers believe people should not have sex, so few children were born, and now only a few live in *New Hampshire and *Maine. Shakers are well known for the simple, elegant furniture they made.

a Shaker home

Shakespeare ⇨ article.

ˌTupac **Shaˈkur** /ˌtuːpæk ʃəˈkʊə(r); *AmE* ʃəˈkʊr/ (1971–96) an *African-American singer of *rap music, also known as 2Pac. His album *All Eyez on Me* (1996) had sold more than 7 million copies by 1998. Shakur led a criminal and violent life which ended when he was murdered in *Las Vegas.

ˈ**shamrock** *n* [C, U] a plant with three small leaves on each stem. It is well known as the national symbol of Ireland. Many Irish people wear a piece of shamrock attached to their clothes on special occasions such as *St Patrick's Day.

Shane /ʃeɪn/ a US film (1953) which many people consider one of the best *westerns ever made. It was directed by George Stevens, with Alan *Ladd in the main role. He plays Shane, a lonely man who visits a farmer and his family and helps them against violent *cowboys who want their land.

the ˌ**Shankhill ˈRoad** /ˌʃæŋkɪl/ a street in a Protestant area of *Belfast, Northern Ireland, where there have been many violent disturbances between *Roman Catholics, Protestants and British soldiers during the *Troubles.

ˈ**sharecropper** /ˈʃeəkrɒpə(r); *AmE* ˈʃerkrɑːpər/ *n* [C] (*esp AmE*) (in the southern US) a poor farmer who rents land and gives part (i.e. a share) of his crops to the owner as payment. This is usually 50% to pay for his house, equipment, seeds and land. The system, which is widely regarded as unfair, was common after the *Civil War, and many sharecroppers were poor slaves who had been freed. ▶ **sharecropping** *n* [U].

ˌHelen ˈ**Sharman** /ˈʃɑːmən; *AmE* ˈʃɑːrmən/ (1963–) an Englishwoman who became the first British astronaut in 1989 when she spent eight days in space in a Soviet spacecraft.

ˌ**Sharon and ˈTracy** (*humor disapprov*) (in Britain) two women's names that are sometimes used to represent a type of young woman who is not well educated. The names were used by the writer Keith *Waterhouse in a series of newspaper articles in the 1980s to refer to women with poor taste who speak English badly and are not very polite. Sharon and Tracy are also the names of the two main characters in the British television comedy series *Birds of a Feather*, who are both women of this type: *We're not going there! It's the sort of place that Sharon and Tracy go to.*

ˌArtie ˈ**Shaw**[1] /ˌɑːti ˈʃɔː; *AmE* ˌɑːrti/ (1910–) a US musician who led big bands in the 1930s and 1940s. He also played the clarinet and wrote music. One of his best-known tunes was *Begin the Beguine* (1938). Shaw also led a US Navy band during *World War II. He married eight times and his wives included the actors Lana Turner and Ava *Gardner.

ˈGeorge ˈBernard ˈ**Shaw**[2] /ˈʃɔː/ (1856–1950) an Irish writer of plays, novels and articles about music and literature who lived in England for much of his life. He is best known for his plays, which are full of intelligent and amusing remarks and criticisms of society. He is also famous for his campaigns for social change. He was one of the earliest members of the *Fabian Society and a supporter of feminism (= women's rights) and vegetarianism (= not eating meat). His best-known works include *The Devil's Disciple* (1897), *Major Barbara* (1905) and **Pygmalion* (1913). He was given the *Nobel Prize for literature in 1925. When he died he left money for making the English spelling system simpler.

ˈ**Shawnee** /ˈʃɔːniː/ *n* (*pl* **Shawnees** *or* **Shawnee**) a member of a *Native-American people living mostly in *Oklahoma. They first settled in the Ohio Valley as farmers who also hunted. *Tecumseh tried to unite them to defend their land against white people but failed. The Shawnees were then moved to the *Indian Territory.

She /ʃi/ a British magazine for women that contains articles on health, fashion, sex, food and other subjects. It first appeared in 1955 and is published every month.

ˌAlan ˈ**Shearer** /ˈʃɪərə(r); *AmE* ˈʃɪrər/ (1970–) an English football player known for his strength and speed and his ability to score goals. He has played for Southampton (1988–92) and Blackburn Rovers (1992–6), and in 1996 he was bought by Newcastle United for £15 million, the largest sum ever paid for a player at the time. He has played regularly for the England team since 1992.

ˌGeorge ˈ**Shearing** /ˈʃɪərɪŋ; *AmE* ˈʃɪrɪŋ/ (1919–) an English *jazz pianist and composer who was born blind. He has written many popular pieces of music, including *Lullaby in Birdland* (1952). He moved to the US in 1947.

ˌMartin ˈ**Sheen** /ˈʃiːn/ (1940–) a US actor whose sons Emilio Estevez (1962–) and Charlie Sheen (1965–) are also actors. Martin Sheen was born Ramon Estevez. In 1964 he appeared in the *Broadway play *The Subject of Roses* and later made the 1968 film version. His other films include *Badlands* (1973), *Apocalypse Now* (1979) and *The American President* (1995). Emilio Estevez's films include *Stakeout* (1987), *Men*

Shakespeare

Shakespeare's life

William Shakespeare

The English poet and playwright (= writer of plays) William Shakespeare is often described as the greatest writer in the English language.

Shakespeare was born in *Stratford-upon-Avon on 23 April 1564. He was the eldest son of a wealthy glove maker and wool merchant. Little is known about his childhood, but he probably attended the local grammar school. In 1582 he married Anne *Hathaway, and they had three children.

In 1588 Shakespeare moved to London and joined a leading theatre company called the *Chamberlain's Men. He quickly established a reputation as a writer of plays for the company and appeared in his own dramas at the *Globe Theatre. He also wrote many poems, the best known of which are *The *Sonnets*, a series of love poems addressed to an unknown man and a *dark lady. The poems are famous for their beautiful language and strong emotions.

Shakespeare returned to Stratford-upon-Avon in about 1611 and died there in 1616. Ben *Jonson, a playwright and friend of Shakespeare, wrote of him: 'He was not of an age, but for all time.'

The plays

Shakespeare's most famous works are the 36 plays he wrote for the London stage. The **comedies** include *The *Comedy of Errors*, *A *Midsummer Night's Dream*, **As You Like It* and **Twelfth Night*. The most famous **history plays** are **Richard II* and **Richard III*, **Henry IV* (*Parts 1 and 2*) and **Henry V*. Perhaps his greatest works are the **tragedies**, which include **Hamlet*, **Othello*, **King Lear*, **Macbeth*, **Romeo and Juliet* and **Antony and Cleopatra*. Shakespeare's career as a playwright ended with two **romances**, *The *Winter's Tale* and *The *Tempest*. Some plays, such as *The *Merchant of Venice* and **Measure for Measure*, do not fit easily into any group.

The plays are written mainly in verse and are greatly admired for their poetic language, dramatic technique and literary style. Many people in Britain and the US study Shakespeare at school and learn whole speeches by heart. Among the most well-known lines are:

> 'To be, or not to be: that is the question:
> Whether 'tis nobler in the mind to suffer
> The slings and arrows of outrageous fortune,
> Or to take arms against a sea of troubles,
> And by opposing end them? To die: to sleep;
> No more; and, by a sleep to say we end
> The heartache and the thousand natural shocks
> That flesh is heir to, 'tis a consummation
> Devoutly to be wish'd. To die, to sleep;
> To sleep: perchance to dream: ay, there's the rub;
> For in that sleep of death what dreams may come
> When we have shuffled off this mortal coil,
> Must give us pause ...'
>
> *Hamlet*, Act III, Scene i

Some scholars have developed theories that the plays were created not by Shakespeare but by writers such as Francis *Bacon and Christopher *Marlowe. These theories generally attract little support, though it is possible that other writers may have contributed to some of the plays.

Shakespeare on the stage

Shakespeare's plays are regularly staged all over the world. In Britain they are often performed by the *Royal Shakespeare Company and the Royal *National Theatre. At the new Globe Theatre, recently rebuilt near the site of the original theatre, plays are presented in conditions similar to those experienced by audiences in Shakespeare's time.

Many actors consider performing major roles such as Hamlet, Othello and Lady Macbeth to be the height of their stage careers. Among the greatest Shakespearean actors have been David *Garrick, Edmund *Kean, and Henry *Irving and, more recently, Laurence *Olivier, John *Gielgud, Sybil *Thorndike, Peggy *Ashcroft, Ian *McKellen, Antony *Sher and Kenneth *Branagh.

The plays of Shakespeare are constantly being reinterpreted by new generations of theatre directors, who find different ways of making them relevant to modern audiences. It is common for the plays to be set in different historical periods, even though the actors continue to speak their lines in the original Elizabethan English. Some plays have been made into operas, musicals and films.

Shakespeare's plays and their dates

1589–90	*Henry VI, Part 1*
1590–92	*Henry VI, Parts 2 and 3*
1590–94	*The Comedy of Errors* *Titus Andronicus* *Love's Labour's Lost*
1592	*The Taming of the Shrew*
1592–93	*Richard III* *The Two Gentlemen of Verona*
1595	*A Midsummer Night's Dream* *Richard II*
1595–96	*Romeo and Juliet*
1595–97	*King John*
1596	*Henry IV, Part 1*
1596–98	*The Merchant of Venice*
1597	*The Merry Wives of Windsor* *Henry IV, Part 2*
1598	*Much Ado About Nothing*
1599	*Julius Caesar* *Henry V* *As You Like It*
1600–01	*Hamlet*
1600–02	*Twelfth Night*
1601–02	*Troilus and Cressida*
1602–03	*All's Well That Ends Well*
1604	*Othello*
1604–05	*Measure for Measure*
1605–06	*King Lear* *Macbeth*
1605–09	*Timon of Athens*
1606–07	*Antony and Cleopatra*
1607–08	*Coriolanus* *Pericles, Prince of Tyre*
1609–10	*Cymbeline*
1611	*The Winter's Tale*
1613	*Henry VIII* *The Tempest*

at Work (1990), which he wrote and directed, and *Mission: Impossible* (1996). Charlie Sheen, born Carlos Estevez, has appeared in *Platoon* (1986), *Wall Street* (1987), *Major League* (1989), *Hot Shots!* (1991) and *The Arrival* (1996).

ˈ**Sheffield** /ˈʃefiːld/ a large industrial city in *South Yorkshire, England. It is the historical centre of the British steel industry. There has been an important iron industry there since the 12th century, and by the time of the *Industrial Revolution the high quality of **Sheffield steel** was famous around the world. Many steel items are still produced in Sheffield, particularly cutlery (= knives, forks, etc.) and special tools, but several local factories closed down in the late 20th century, leaving many people unemployed.

ˌ**Sheffield ˈplate** /ˌʃefiːld/ *n* [U] a type of metal consisting of copper covered with a thin layer of silver. The method of covering copper objects with silver and then heating them to keep it in place was discovered by Thomas Boulsover in *Sheffield in the 1740s. It became an important industry because objects such as pots and plates could be made of Sheffield plate much more cheaply than solid silver ones.

ˌ**Sheffield ˈWednesday** /ˌʃefiːld/ an English football club based at *Hillsborough in north-west *Sheffield. The club was established in 1867 and originally played its matches on Wednesdays. It has been in the highest division of English football for most of its history, although most of its successes in the *Football League and the *FA Cup were in the first part of the 20th century.

ˌSidney ˈ**Sheldon** /ˈʃeldən/ (1917–) a US writer of books, films, plays and television series. Several of his novels have been made into films, including *The Other Side of Midnight* (1977). His other books include *Windmills of the Gods* (1987) and *Morning, Noon and Night* (1995). He has written six *Broadway plays and won a 1959 *Tony award for *Redhead*. His 23 films include *The Bachelor and the Bobby Soxer* (1947), for which he won an *Oscar, and **Annie Get Your Gun*. Sheldon also wrote the successful television shows *I Dream of Jeannie* and *Hart to Hart* (1979).

the Sheldonian Theatre

the **Shelˌdonian ˈTheatre** /ʃelˌdəʊniən; *AmE* ʃelˌdoʊniən/ (*also* the **Sheldonian**) a large theatre that is part of *Oxford University. It was designed by Christopher *Wren and built in 1663. Graduates of the university are given their degrees there. It is also used for concerts (not plays) and for other university ceremonies.

Shell /ʃel/ a large international oil company that was formed when the British company Shell combined with the Dutch company Royal Dutch in the 1890s. It is now involved in producing oil and gas in Asia, the Middle East, the *North Sea and South America. It also owns petrol/gasoline stations in many countries.

ˌMary ˈ**Shelley¹** /ˈʃeli/ (1797–1851) an English writer, best known as the author of **Frankenstein*. She was the daughter of Mary *Wollstonecraft, and is also remembered for having run away with the poet *Shelley² at the age of 16. She became Shelley's second wife after his first killed herself in 1816.

ˈPercy ˈBysshe ˈ**Shelley²** /ˈbɪʃ ˈʃeli/ (1792–1822) one of the major poets of the English *Romantic Movement. He is well known for the beauty of his verse. He was an atheist (= a person who believes that there is no God) and an anarchist (= a person who believes there should be no laws or government) whose love of freedom and left-wing political opinions influenced poems such as *Prometheus Unbound* (1820). He ran away twice with young women, and lived the last few years of his life with his second wife Mary in Italy, where he died in an accident at sea. His best-known poems include **Ode to the West Wind* and **To a Skylark*.

ˈ**shell game** *n* [C] (*AmE*) **1** (*also* **thimblerig** [U]) a game in which one person tries to trick the other players. The first person places a small object under one of three upside-down cups, nut shells, etc. He or she then quickly moves the cups around, and the others try to guess which contains the object, sometimes betting on their choice. **2** any action that is intended to cheat or deceive somebody: *She promised to double my money, but it was just a shell game.*

ˈ**Shelter** /ˈʃeltə(r)/ a British charity established in 1966 to help people who have nowhere to live, either by finding homes for them or by providing places in cities where they can sleep at night. It also acts as a *pressure group to try to influence the government to do more to help people without homes.

ˌ**sheltered ˈhousing** *n* [U] (in Britain) houses or flats/apartments that are specially designed and built for old or disabled people so that they can live in the local community instead of in hospitals. Sheltered housing is usually arranged in small blocks, with a person in each block whose job is to help the people living there. The term is less often used in the US for this type of housing, though the state of *Maryland has a large Accessory, Shared and Sheltered Housing Program (ACCESS): *The new sheltered housing project will be built close to the shops and main bus routes.*

the ˌ**Shenandoah ˈValley** /ˌʃenəndəʊə; *AmE* ˌʃenəndoʊə/ a large, beautiful valley in the northern part of the US state of *Virginia, between the *Allegheny Mountains and the Blue Ridge Mountains. It was used by many Americans when they moved west, and several *Civil War battles were fought there because it supplied food for the Confederate forces. The **Shenandoah River** flows through it and is the subject of the folk song *Shenandoah*, which begins: 'Oh Shenandoah, I long to see you, Far away, you rolling river.' The **Shenandoah National Park** was established in 1926.

ˌAlan ˈ**Shepard¹** /ˈʃepəd; *AmE* ˈʃepərd/ (1923–98) the first American in space. He made a short sub-orbital flight (= one that does not go completely round the earth in space) in 1961 as part of the *Mercury programme. He became the fifth man on the moon when he commanded Apollo 14 in 1971.

ˌE H ˈ**Shepard²** /ˈʃepəd; *AmE* ˈʃepərd/ (Ernest Howard Shepard 1879–1976) an English artist, best remembered for his illustrations for **Winnie-the-Pooh* and other books and poems by A A *Milne, and for

*The *Wind in the Willows*. He also drew many cartoons for **Punch* magazine.

ˌSam ˈ**Shephard** /ˈʃepəd; *AmE* ˈʃepərd/ (1943–) a US actor who also writes and directs plays and films. His play *Buried Child* (1978) won a *Pulitzer Prize, and he wrote such films as *Paris, Texas* (1984) and *Silent Tongue* (1994). His films as an actor include *Crimes of the Heart* (1986), *The Right Stuff* (1983) and *The Pelican Brief* (1993).

ˌ**Shepherd's ˈBush** an area of west London, England, consisting mainly of houses and flats/apartments and a busy market and shopping centre.

ˌ**shepherd's ˈpie** (*BrE also* ˌ**cottage ˈpie**) *n* [C, U] a dish consisting of minced meat with mashed potato on top. It is then baked until the top of the potato turns brown. Traditionally, shepherd's pie is made with lamb or mutton (= sheep's meat) and cottage pie is made with beef.

ˌ**Shepperton ˈStudios** /ˌʃepətən; *AmE* ˌʃepərtən/ a large film studio near *London, England. Since the 1930s it has been one of the two major British centres of film production. Many famous films have been made there, including *The African Queen* (1951) and *The *Third Man*. Compare PINEWOOD STUDIOS.

ˌAntony ˈ**Sher** /ˈʃeə(r); *AmE* ˈʃer/ (1949–) a British actor and writer, born in South Africa. He is best known for his theatre performances in plays by *Shakespeare, but he has also worked in films and television. He has written several novels.

ˈ**Sheraton**[1] /ˈʃerətən/ *n* any of a large international group of US hotels owned by the ITT Corporation of New York. They include hotels in the major cities and in unusual places, such as The Great Wall Sheraton Hotel in China and the Sheraton Casablanca in Morocco. There are also special Sheraton Four Points Hotels at less expensive prices.

ˌThomas ˈ**Sheraton**[2] /ˈʃerətən/ (1751–1806) an English furniture designer. His book *The Cabinet-Maker and Upholsterer's Drawing Book* (1791–4) was an important influence on the development of *neoclassical furniture, and his designs are typically delicate and graceful: *a beautiful Sheraton chair/table*.

ˈ**Shergar** /ˈʃɜːgɑː(r); *AmE* ˈʃɜːrgɑːr/ a very successful racehorse. It won many important races, including the *Derby in 1981, but in 1983 it was stolen from a farm in Ireland by a group of armed men, and never seen again. Most people believe that it was taken and killed by the *IRA.

ˈPhilip ˈHenry ˈ**Sheridan**[1] /ˈʃerɪdən/ (1831–1888) a US military leader in the *Civil War. General Sheridan commanded the Army of the Shenandoah Valley in *Virginia and defeated the Confederate army there in 1864. He later forced the army of General Robert E *Lee to surrender near *Appomattox Court House (1865).

S

ˈRichard ˈBrinsley ˈ**Sheridan**[2] /ˈʃerɪdən/ (1751–1816) a British writer of plays, born in Ireland. He wrote a series of popular comedies, including *The *Rivals* and **School for Scandal*, and was well known in London for his quick and intelligent humour. He became a friend of the *Prince of Wales and several important politicians. In 1780 he became a *Whig(1) *MP, and held several important government positions. Although he had successful careers in politics and the theatre, he had many debts, and died in poverty.

ˈ**sheriff court** *n* (in Scotland) a type of court of law where the sheriff (= a Scottish title for a judge) deals with less serious criminal and civil cases. Serious crimes such as murder are dealt with in the *High Court of Justiciary and serious civil cases go to the *Court of Session.

the ˌ**Sheriff of ˈNottingham** /ˈnɒtɪŋəm; *AmE* ˈnɑːtɪŋəm/ (in old stories) the main enemy of *Robin Hood. He was a cruel and dishonest government official responsible for the town of *Nottingham and the area around it.

ˈWilliam Teˈcumseh ˈ**Sherman** /təˈkʌmsə ˈʃɜːmən; *AmE* ˈʃɜːrmən/ (1820–91) a US military leader during the *Civil War. General Sherman commanded the US Army in the West (1864–5). He is best remembered for his march through *Georgia with 60 000 soldiers, destroying anything that might be useful to the South in the war, including military equipment, factories, railways, homes and farm animals. After the war, in 1879, he made his famous statement that 'War is hell'.

ˌ**Sherwood ˈForest** /ˌʃɜːwʊd; *AmE* ˌʃɜːrwʊd/ a forest in the English *Midlands, famous in old stories as the place where *Robin Hood's *Merry Men lived and fought against the forces of the *Sheriff of Nottingham. It used to be a very large forest, but only a small part of it still remains. It is preserved as a *country park near *Nottingham.

ˌ***She ˈStoops to ˈConquer*** the best-known play (1773) by Oliver *Goldsmith. It is a comedy based on a misunderstanding. Marlow, a shy young man, goes with a friend to visit the Hardcastle family because their parents hope that he will marry Miss Hardcastle. The friends get lost on the way and look for an inn (= a pub that is also a small hotel) but actually arrive at the Hardcastles' house. Most of the humour comes from the way Marlow treats the family when he thinks that their house is an inn and that Miss Hardcastle is a servant.

ˌ**Shetland ˈpony** /ˌʃetlənd/ *n* a breed of small, strong pony with long, rough hair and a long tail. Shetland ponies were originally bred in the *Shetlands and used for work, but they are now popular for children to ride because of their small size.

a girl riding a Shetland pony

the ˈ**Shetlands** /ˈʃetləndz/ (*also* ˈ**Shetland** /ˈʃetlənd/, the ˈ**Shetland ˌIslands**) a group of over 100 islands north of Scotland. The main industries are farming, fishing and making clothes out of the famous **Shetland wool** from local sheep. Since the 1970s the islands have become an important centre of the *North Sea oil industry.

the ˌBattle of ˈ**Shiloh** /ˈʃaɪləʊ; *AmE* ˈʃaɪloʊ/ a major battle of the American *Civil War, fought on 6–7 April 1862 at Pittsburgh Landing, *Tennessee. It was won by the US Army, led by General Ulysses S *Grant, after they had been forced back on the first day. More than 10 000 soldiers were killed or wounded on both sides. The victory helped Grant to take control of the *Mississippi River. The battle was named after Shiloh Church, a small Methodist church near where it was fought.

ˌPeter ˈ**Shilton** /ˈʃɪltən/ (1949–) an English football

player. He was the England national team's main goalkeeper (= player who defends the goal) in the 1970s and 1980s and played for several major English clubs. He has played more *Football League games and appeared more times for England than any other player, and is considered one of England's greatest goalkeepers.

'shinty /'ʃɪnti/ *n* [U] a traditional Scottish game, similar to *field hockey. The sticks used (also called **shinties**) are shorter and thicker than those used in hockey, and the game is faster, since the ball is often hit when it is in the air. It is mainly played in the Scottish *Highlands. A related form of shinty, called *hurling*, is played in Ireland.

'ship ˌmoney *n* [U] a tax that English kings and queens traditionally collected from people living on the coast in times of war. In the 1630s *Charles I used the tax to collect money without involving *Parliament, at first on the coast and then all over England, by saying that there was a possibility of war. A group of people led by John *Hampden refused to pay the tax, and in 1640 the *Long Parliament made it illegal.

the **'shipping ˌforecast** a detailed report on the weather conditions at sea, prepared by the *Meteorological Office and broadcast four times a day on *BBC *Radio 4. The seas around the British Isles and northern and western Europe are divided into 31 areas, and information is given on the speed of the wind and how far it is possible to see in each area.

the **shires** /ʃaɪəz; *AmE* ʃaɪərz/ *n* [pl] a traditional name for the *counties in the English *Midlands which have names ending in *-shire* (= an old word for county). Originally they were called this by people from southern counties which did not have *-shire* in their names. In modern times the shires refer mainly to counties famous for *hunting, especially *Northamptonshire and *Leicestershire, where people have been using dogs to hunt foxes since the 17th century. Many British people think of the shires as an area where *upper-class people with old-fashioned attitudes live: *Gay MPs may win votes in London but they wouldn't stand a chance in the shires.*

ˌShirley 'Temple /'templ/ *n* a US drink that contains no alcohol but looks like a cocktail (= mixed alcoholic drink). It is usually made with lemon juice and grenadine (= a thick, sweet, red liquid made from fruit juice). Ice is added and often a cherry on top. It is popular with children and was named after the former child actor Shirley *Temple.

ˌWillie **'Shoemaker** /ˌwɪli 'ʃuːmeɪkə(r)/ (1931–) the most successful US professional jockey ever. His popular name is 'the Shoe'. Between 1949 and 1990 he won 8 833 of his 40 351 races, including victories in four *Kentucky Derby races. A car crash in 1991 left him unable to walk.

ˌshoofly 'pie /ˌʃuːflaɪ/ *n* (*AmE*) an open pie filled with a mixture of brown sugar and molasses (= a dark, sweet, thick liquid obtained from sugar). It takes its name from the fact that people have to shoo (= frighten away) flies that are attracted to it.

'shopping ˌcentre (*also esp AmE* **'shopping ˌmall, mall**) *n* a large building or covered area containing many different shops. Shopping centres may also have their own car parks, restaurants, banks and other services.

ˌshopping days to 'Christmas a phrase used to explain how many days are left on which the shops will be open between the present time and *Christmas. It is written in the windows of some shops to encourage people to buy their Christmas presents before it is too late: *I can't believe there are only fifteen shopping days to Christmas.*

'shopping ˌprecinct *n* (*BrE*) an area of a town or city where cars are not allowed, so that it is easy for people to walk between the many shops, banks, restaurants, etc. in the precinct.

ˌClare **'Short**[1] /'ʃɔːt; *AmE* 'ʃɔːrt/ (1946–) a British *Labour politician. She became a *Member of Parliament in 1983 and held several important positions in the *Shadow Cabinet before being appointed International Development Secretary in the Labour government of 1997. She is well known for her support for women's rights, especially for her opposition to the use of *page-three girls in British newspapers.

ˌNigel **'Short**[2] /'ʃɔːt; *AmE* 'ʃɔːrt/ (1965–) an English chess player. He became a grandmaster (= a chess player of the highest class) at the age of 19. In 1993 he played at the highest level of chess that a British player had ever reached when he lost the final match of the world championship against Garry Kasparov.

'shortbread (*also* **'shortcake**) *n* [U] a type of rich sweet biscuit made with flour, sugar and a lot of butter. It is associated especially with Scotland.

'Shortnin' Bread /'ʃɔːtnɪn; *AmE* 'ʃɔːrtnɪn/ a traditional African-American children's song about home-made 'shortening bread', bread or pastry made with cheap fat. It includes the lines:

Two little children lying in bed;
One turned over, and the other one said,
'Mammy's little baby loves shortnin', shortnin',
Mammy's little baby loves shortnin' bread.

ˌshort-order 'cook *n* (*AmE*) a professional cook who prepares quick dishes ordered by customers, especially at a *fast-food restaurant, café, etc.

the **'Short ˌParliament** the first of two parliaments set up by the English king *Charles I in 1640 when he needed the legal power of Parliament to raise money for a war against Scotland. When the *MPs refused to support the king he dismissed the parliament. It was replaced later in the same year by the *Long Parliament.

Sho'shone /ʃəʊ'ʃəʊni; *AmE* ʃoʊ'ʃoʊni/ *n* (*pl* **Shoshones** *or* **Shoshone**) a member of a *Native-American people who originally lived as hunters in an area stretching from south-eastern *California to western *Wyoming. About 8 000 still live there on reservations (= lands given and protected by the US government). The *Comanche people separated from the Wyoming group.

'Show Boat a famous *Broadway musical play (1927) by Jerome *Kern and Oscar *Hammerstein. It was based on a novel (1926) by Edna *Ferber about people on the *Cotton Blossom*, a *showboat on the *Mississippi River. It includes the songs *Ol' Man River* and *Only Make Believe*. There have been three film versions (1929, 1936 and 1951).

'showboat /'ʃəʊbəʊt; *AmE* 'ʃoʊboʊt/ *n* (*AmE*) (in the 19th and early 20th centuries) a large river boat driven by steam, on which plays and other shows were performed for people living in towns along the rivers, especially the *Mississippi. Well-known showboats included the *Water Queen*, the *Cotton Blossom* and the *Floating Circus Palace*. Ships built to look like showboats now take tourists for rides from *New Orleans.

ˌShredded 'Wheat /ˌʃredɪd/ *n* [U] a type of breakfast food consisting of thin crisp strips of wheat shaped into larger pieces. It is eaten with milk and sometimes sugar. It is well known in Britain because of its television advertising, which sometimes shows sports stars giving it to their children, or humorous situations suggesting that it is difficult to eat more than two pieces of Shredded Wheat.

'Shrewsbury /'ʃrəʊzbri; *AmE* 'ʃruːzberi/ a town in

*Shropshire, England, near the border with Wales. It is the administrative centre for Shropshire and was important in history as a military centre between England and Wales. It has a *Norman castle and many attractive old churches and other buildings.

ˌ**Shrewsbury** ˈ**School** /ˌʃrəʊzbri; *AmE* ˈʃruːzberi/ (*also* ˈ**Shrewsbury**) a well-known English *public school(1), established in 1552 in the town of *Shrewsbury.

ˈ**Shropshire** /ˈʃrɒpʃə(r); *AmE* ˈʃrɑːpʃər/ a county in the west *Midlands of England, on the Welsh border. It consists mainly of agricultural land. Its administrative centre is *Shrewsbury.

A ˌ***Shropshire*** ˌ***Lad*** /ˌʃrɒpʃə; *AmE* ˌʃrɑːpʃər/ a collection of poems (1896) by A E *Housman. The poems are short and easy to read. They express love for the people and countryside of Housman's home in *Shropshire, and sadness to be away from that home. They became especially popular during *World War I, and are still widely read.

ˌ**Shrove** ˈ**Tuesday** /ˌʃrəʊv/ the day before *Ash Wednesday. In the Christian religion it is traditionally the last day on which people can enjoy rich food before *Lent, and it is celebrated in different ways in different countries. In Britain it is often called *Pancake Day and in America it is called *Mardi Gras.

the ˈ**Shuttle** /ˈʃʌtl/ *n* [U] the train service that takes cars and their passengers through the *Channel Tunnel between England and France. The French name for it is 'le Shuttle'. People drive their cars onto special trains near the entrance to the tunnel, and drive off at the other end: *We usually take the ferry but we're going to try the Shuttle this time.* Compare EUROSTAR.

ˈ**Shylock** /ˈʃaɪlɒk; *AmE* ˈʃaɪlɑːk/ a character in *Shakespeare's play *The *Merchant of Venice.* He is a Jewish moneylender who demands a pound of flesh from somebody who cannot pay back the money that he borrowed. Although the play shows him as a person who is treated badly as well as a person who treats others badly, his name is sometimes used to describe people who are greedy for money.

ˈ**Sianel** ˈ**Pedwar** ˈ**Cymru** /ˈʃænel ˈpedwɑːr ˈkʌmri/ ⇨ S4C.

ˌWalter ˈ**Sickert** /ˈsɪkət; *AmE* ˈsɪkərt/ (1860–1942) an English artist. He was the most important painter of the *Camden Town Group, and was influenced by the French Impressionists and by *Whistler. He is famous for his paintings of life in the theatre, and for his later paintings of dull rooms, often with a naked model.

S

ˌMrs ˈ**Siddons** /ˈsɪdənz/ (Sarah Siddons 1755–1831) an English actor. She is considered to have been one of the greatest actors in tragedies (= serious plays with sad endings) and was especially famous for playing the role of Lady *Macbeth.

ˈ**sidewinder** /ˈsaɪdwaɪndə(r)/ *n* **1** a dangerous North American snake that lives in the desert. It moves sideways by throwing its body in S-shaped curves. **2** (*AmE*) a hard blow with the closed hand swung from the side. **3 Sidewinder** a US weapon, fired from an aircraft, that can find and destroy enemy aircraft.

ˌPhilip ˈ**Sidney** /ˈsɪdni/ (1554–86) an English poet and soldier who is considered one of the greatest Englishmen of the *Elizabethan period. His best-known works are *Arcadia* (1590) and *Astrophel and Stella* (1591). He was made a *knight in 1583 and died of wounds received while fighting the Spanish in the Netherlands. There is a popular story that as he lay dying he refused a drink of water and passed it to another wounded soldier who he said needed it more.

the ˌ**Sidney Street** ˈ**siege** /ˌsɪdni/ an incident that took place in the *East End of London in 1911. Two anarchists (= people who believe there should be no laws or government) were trapped and finally killed in a house surrounded by police officers and soldiers. It is mainly remembered because Winston *Churchill, who was then *Home Secretary, directed the operation personally, and was much criticized for doing this.

the ˈ**Siegfried Line** /ˈsiːɡfriːd/ **1** (in *World War I) a line of military defence set up by the Germans in Belgium and France. **2** (in *World War II) the name given by the *Allies to the German line of military defence between France and Germany. A song that was popular with British soldiers at the time began with the line, 'We're going to hang out our washing on the Siegfried Line.'

Siˌ**erra Le**ˈ**one** /siˌerə liˈəʊn; *AmE* liˈoʊn/ a country on the west coast of Africa which is a member of the *Commonwealth. The capital city, Freetown, was established in 1787 by British people who were against the slave trade, as a place where former slaves could start new lives. There have been several conflicts between the descendants of these people and those of the original population. Sierra Leone became part of the *British Empire in the 19th century, and an independent country in 1961. ⇨ article at SLAVERY. ▶ **Sierra Leonian** *adj, n.*

the **Si**ˌ**erra Ne**ˈ**vada** /siˌerə nəˈvɑːdə/ (*also* the **Si**ˈ**erras** /siˈerəz/) a mountain range in the US state of *California. It is 420 miles/673 kilometres long, and the highest point is Mount *Whitney. It includes *Yosemite National Park and two other national parks, Sequoia and Kings Canyon.

ˌ**Silbury** ˈ**Hill** /ˌsɪlbri/ a prehistoric mound (= raised mass of earth) near *Avebury in south-west England, built before 2000 BC. It is the largest of these mounds in Europe, and unlike most of the others there is nobody buried in it. Nobody knows what it was built for.

ˈ**Silchester** /ˈsɪltʃestə(r)/ the site of an ancient Roman town near *Reading in southern England. It was an important regional centre from the second to the fourth century, and contains the remains of many Roman temples.

The ˌ***Silence of the*** ˈ***Lambs*** a US film (1991) in which Anthony *Hopkins plays Hannibal Lecter, a violent murderer who eats the people he kills. Jodie *Foster plays the police officer who needs his help to catch another murderer. Some people were shocked by the violence of the film when it was first shown.

the ˌ**silent ma**ˈ**jority** *n* [pl] the majority of people in a country, who do not have extreme opinions about political or moral matters, and who do not express their opinions in public. Many people think of the silent majority as being old-fashioned and opposed to change: *She claims to speak for the silent majority who have always wanted peace in the province.*

ˌ***Silent*** ˈ***Night*** a popular *Christmas *carol about Christ when he was a baby with his mother.

ˌ**Silicon** ˈ**Valley** the name given to an area in the Santa Clara Valley of *California where there are many computer and electronics companies. It is near the cities of *San Francisco and *San Jose. Silicon is an important chemical element used in computers and electronic equipment. Compare ROUTE 128.

ˌBeverly ˈ**Sills** /ˌbevəli ˈsɪlz; *AmE* ˌbevərli/ (1929–) a leading US opera singer with a soprano (= highest female) voice. Her first major performance was in 1947 with the Philadelphia Civic Opera. She was later General Director of the New York City Opera (1979–84), and she has been Chairwoman of the *Lincoln Center for the Performing Arts since 1994.

ˌPhil ˈ**Silvers** /ˈsɪlvəz; *AmE* ˈsɪlvərz/ (1912–85) a US

comic actor best known as the television character Sergeant Ernie *Bilko. Silvers also won a *Tony award in 1972 for his part in the play *A Funny Thing Happened on the Way to the Forum.*

ˈSilverstone /ˈsɪlvəstəʊn; *AmE* ˈsɪlvərstoʊn/ Britain's main motor racing track, near *Northampton in southern England. The *British Grand Prix car and motorcycle races take place there every year.

ˌVictor **Silˈvester** /sɪlˈvestə(r)/ (1900–78) an English popular music band leader in the 1930s and 1940s. He later became famous on radio for playing dance tunes requested by people in countries all round the world. The Victor Silvester Television Dancing Club ran for 17 years and his orchestra appeared in more than 6 500 broadcasts for *BBC radio.

ˌLambert **ˈSimnel** /ˌlæmbət ˈsɪmnəl; *AmE* ˌlæmbərt/ (*c.* 1475–1525) a man who pretended that he had the right to be the king of England during the *Wars of the Roses. He was persuaded by supporters of the House of *York to pretend to be the Earl of Warwick, whose uncle was *Richard III. Simnel was crowned king in 1487 in Ireland, and then invaded England with a small army. They were defeated by the forces of *Henry VII, who pardoned (= decided not to punish) Simnel and gave him a job in the royal kitchen.

ˈsimnel cake /ˈsɪmnəl/ *n* (*BrE*) a rich fruit cake with a layer of marzipan (= a soft mixture of sugar, eggs and almonds) inside or on top. It is traditionally eaten in Britain at *Easter or on *Mother's Day(1).

ˌNeil **ˈSimon** /ˈsaɪmən/ (1927–) a US writer of mainly comedy plays, many of which have also appeared as films. He began in the 1950s as a writer for Sid *Caesar, an experience he used for *Laughter on the 23rd Floor* (1993). He has won *Tony awards for *The Odd Couple* (1965), *Biloxi Blues* (1985) and *Lost in Yonkers* (1991), which also won a *Pulitzer Prize. His 30th play, written at the age of 70, was the serious *Proposals* (1997). Simon owns the Eugene O'Neill Theatre in New York.

ˌSimon and ˈGarfunkel /ˌsaɪmən, ˈɡɑːfʌŋkl; *AmE* ˈɡɑːrfʌŋkl/ **Paul Simon** (1942–) and **Art Garfunkel** (1941–), US popular singers who performed together with great success in the 1960s. Their songs included *Sounds of Silence* (1966), *Scarborough Fair* (1966), *Mrs Robinson* and other music for the film *The *Graduate*, and *Bridge Over Troubled Water* (1970), which won three *Emmy awards. They started separate careers in 1970. Simon has since had success with *Mother and Child Reunion* (1972), *Graceland* (1986), which won a Grammy, and songs with South African musicians. He produced his first *Broadway musical play, the *The Capeman* in 1998, but it was an expensive failure. Garfunkel continues to tour and perform.

ˌNina **Siˈmone** /ˌniːnə sɪˈməʊn; *AmE* sɪˈmoʊn/ (1933–) an *African-American *jazz singer who also plays the piano. Her early hits included *I Loves You Porgy* (1959). Simone's career suffered when she became involved in *black power activities in the 1960s and 1970s. She has since become popular again, however, and her songs were used in the British film *The Crying Game* (1992).

ˌSimon Leˈgree /ləˈɡriː/ (in the US) a name applied to somebody who forces others to work very hard and is often cruel to them. It comes from the character in the novel **Uncle Tom's Cabin* who beats Uncle Tom so badly that he dies: *Charlie said his history teacher was a real Simon Legree.*

ˌSimon ˈSays *n* [U] a children's game in which a leader gives a series of commands, such as 'Simon says put your hands in the air'. The players must do everything that Simon says, but when the leader gives a command without saying 'Simon says ...', they must not do it.

ˌSimple ˈSimon a name used to refer to a foolish man or boy. Originally it was the name of a foolish boy in a *nursery rhyme which begins:

Simple Simon met a pieman
Going to the fair.

ˌSimply ˈRed an English pop group formed in 1985. The style of their songs, like the voice of their singer Mick Hucknall, is a mixture of pop and *soul. Their best-known records include *Holding Back the Years* (1985) and *Stars* (1991).

ˌO J **ˈSimpson**[1] /ˈsɪmpsn/ (Orenthal James Simpson 1947–) a US football player who was accused of murdering his wife Nicole and her friend Ronald Goldman. Simpson was judged innocent in 1995 after the longest trial ever shown on television. The result divided white and black Americans. He was later accused again in a civil court (= one concerned with private, not criminal, cases) by the families of those killed. This time he was judged guilty and ordered to pay $8.5 million. During his career as a football player Simpson established many records playing for the University of Southern California and the professional Buffalo Bills. He also acted in a few films.

ˌWallis **ˈSimpson**[2] /ˌwɒlɪs ˈsɪmpsn; *AmE* ˌwɑːlɪs/ (1896–1986) an American woman who became the Duchess of *Windsor when she married her second husband, Edward, Duke of *Windsor. He had been King *Edward VIII but abdicated (= gave up his position as king) in order to marry her because kings were not allowed to marry divorced women. See also ABDICATION CRISIS.

The ***ˈSimpsons*** /ˈsɪmpsnz/ a popular US television cartoon series on the Fox Television Network since 1990. The characters are a family of yellow people with big eyes whose attitudes and language are offensive to some people. Bart Simpson is a boy of 10 who hates school and has problems with his stupid father Homer and his sisters Lisa and Maggie.

ˌFrank **Siˈnatra** /sɪˈnɑːtrə/ (1915–98) one of the most popular US singers from the 1940s to the 1960s, who continued performing into the 1980s. He also acted in many films. His popular name was 'Old Blue Eyes', and he was known for his romantic voice. He became famous in the 1940s with the big band of Tommy Dorsey and was especially popular with young women. His many successful records included *All the Way* (1957), *Witchcraft* (1958), *Strangers in the Night* (1966) and *My Way* (1968). His films included *On the Town* (1949), **From Here to Eternity* (1953), in which he won an *Oscar, and *High Society* (1956). Two of his four marriages were to the actors Ava *Gardner and Mia *Farrow.

ˌClive **ˈSinclair**[1] /ˈsɪŋkleə(r); *AmE* ˈsɪŋkler/ (1940–) an English inventor and businessman. He became successful in 1972 when he produced Britain's first pocket calculator. He has developed many other successful electronic products including computers, televisions and the Zike (a new type of bicycle), but his most famous invention was his first failure, the **Sinclair C5**, a small electric vehicle with three wheels. It was introduced in 1985 but very few people bought it. Sinclair was made a *knight in 1983.

Clive Sinclair on his Zike

ˌUpton ˈ**Sinclair**² /ˌʌptən ˈsɪŋkleə(r); *AmE* ˈsɪŋkler/ (1878–1968) a US writer of novels and other books intended to improve conditions in society. The first and best-known of these, *The Jungle* (1906), was about the terrible conditions in the *Chicago meat industry, and it resulted in new laws being passed. One of his later novels, *Dragon's Teeth* (1942), won the *Pulitzer Prize.

ˈ**Sindbad** /ˈsɪndbæd/ (*also* ˌ**Sinbad the** ˈ**Sailor**) a character in one of the stories in the **Arabian Nights*. He is a sailor who has unusual and dangerous adventures each time he goes to sea. In the 19th century the story of his seven journeys became a popular subject for *pantomimes in Britain.

ˌ**Singa**ˈ**pore** /ˌsɪŋəˈpɔː(r), ˌsɪŋgəˈpɔː(r)/ a small country in south-east Asia, consisting of the island of Singapore and 54 smaller islands near the end of the Malay Peninsula. It has been a republic and a member of the *Commonwealth since 1965. The first town there was established by Stamford *Raffles in 1819, and it soon became an important port for ships travelling between Europe, India and China. It was part of the *British Empire until it became independent in 1963. Singapore is well known for its political and economic stability. It is still one of the world's most important ports, and has successful banking and high technology industries. ▶ **Singaporean** /ˌsɪŋəˈpɔːriən, ˌsɪŋəˈpɔːriən/ *adj, n.*

ˈ***Sing a*** ˈ***Song of*** ˈ***Sixpence*** /ˈsɪkspəns/ an old English children's song, which may refer to the life of *Henry VIII. Some people think that the birds in the song represent the *Roman Catholic choirs after the *Dissolution of the Monasteries. Most people in Britain know the first verse:

Sing a song of sixpence, a pocket full of rye,
Four and twenty blackbirds baked in a pie.
When the pie was opened, the birds began to sing,
Wasn't that a dainty dish to set before the king?

ˌIsaac ˈ**Singer**¹ /ˈsɪŋə(r)/ (1811–75) an American who in 1851 designed and built the first sewing machine to be sold successfully. Today Singer sewing machines are the best-known make in the world.

ˈIsaac Baˈshevis ˈ**Singer**² /bɑːˈʃevɪs ˈsɪŋə(r)/ (1904–91) a Jewish-American writer, born in Poland, who won the 1978 *Nobel Prize for literature. He is best known for his short stories, in collections which include *Gimpel the Fool* (1957) and *The Death of Methuselah and Other Stories* (1988). His novels include *The Family Moskat* (1950) and *Shosha* (1978).

ˌ***Singin' in the*** ˈ***Rain*** an *MGM film (1952) which many people think is the best musical comedy film ever made. The stars were Gene *Kelly, Debbie *Reynolds and Donald O'Connor. The story is about the troubles that stars of silent films had when sound films began. The songs include *Singin' in the Rain*, *Good Morning* and *Make 'Em Laugh*. In 1983 Tommy *Steele directed and was the star of a stage version in London.

S

the ˈ**single** ˈ**European** ˈ**currency** *n* [sing] the currency of the *European Union, called the *euro (formerly the *ecu). It became Europe's official currency on 1 January 1999 as part of *European Monetary Union, and will be available as coins and paper money from 1 January 2002. It will then be used in addition to the existing national currencies of some European countries for a period of six months. After this the national currencies will no longer be used. Britain does not plan to join the single European currency immediately, partly because some *Eurosceptics in Britain fear that doing so will lead to a loss of economic power and political control for Britain.

ˈ**Sing Sing** /ˈsɪŋ sɪŋ/ a US prison for the state of New York. It is in Ossining, New York, and its first building was completed in 1925 by prisoners used as workers. Many of the state's most dangerous criminals have been sent to Sing Sing because of its strong discipline. Its name was officially changed to Ossining State Correctional Facility in 1969, but most people still use the old name.

ˌ**Sinn** ˈ**Fein** /ˌʃɪn ˈfeɪn/ an Irish political party. It was established in 1902 with the aim of making Ireland independent. Many of its members left to join *Fianna Fáil when it was formed in 1926. Those who stayed in Sinn Fein became the political branch of the *IRA, an organization which believes that Northern Ireland should become part of the Republic of Ireland, and has often used violence to try to achieve its political goal. Sinn Fein has been criticized for being connected to a terrorist organization, and some of its members have been put in prison in Northern Ireland, or refused permission to enter Britain. In the 1990s Sinn Fein was one of the groups responsible for the IRA ceasefire (= a period during which there is no fighting) and the peace discussions between the governments involved. The name means 'we ourselves' in Irish *Gaelic. See also ADAMS.

Sioux /suː/ *n* (*pl* **Sioux**) a member of a *Native-American people, also called the Dakota people, many of whom live in *South Dakota on reservations (= land given and protected by the US government). The Sioux were originally an association of seven groups on the *Great Plains where, led by *Sitting Bull and *Crazy Horse, they fought the US Army. They defeated General George *Custer at the Battle of *Little Bighorn but lost their final battle at *Wounded Knee.

Sir the title used before the first name of a *knight or *baronet: *Sir Cliff Richard* ○ *Sir John is in a meeting – would you like to wait?* ⇨ note at ARISTOCRACY.

Sirˌhan **Sir**ˈ**han** /sɜːˌhɑːn sɜːˈhɑːn; *AmE* sɜːrˌhɑːn sɜːrˈhɑːn/ (1944–) the man who murdered Robert F *Kennedy on 6 June 1968 in *Los Angeles, as well as shooting and wounding eight other people. Sirhan was a Jordanian who had moved to the US and disliked Kennedy's policy of support for Israel. He was captured immediately and is still in prison.

ˌ**site of** ˈ**special scien**ˈ**tific** ˈ**interest** *n* (*abbr* **SSSI**) any of the places or areas of Britain in which the wild animals or plants are considered rare or of scientific importance. There are over 6 000 SSSIs in Britain, and they are protected by the government against damage caused by farming or building.

ˌ**Sitting** ˈ**Bull** /ˌsɪtɪŋ ˈbʊl/ (*c.* 1831–90) a leader of one of the *Sioux peoples. He and *Crazy Horse defeated General George *Custer at the Battle of *Little Bighorn. He then lived for a short time in Canada but agreed in 1881 to settle with his people on the Standing Rock Reservation in *North Dakota, and in 1885 appeared in *Buffalo Bill's *Wild West Show. Because he encouraged the Sioux to keep the *Ghost Dance religion, US soldiers and Native-American police tried to arrest him and he was killed.

Sitting Bull

ˈ**Sitwell** /ˈsɪtwel/ the name of a sister and two brothers of an aristocratic English family, all three of whom became writers. **Edith Sitwell**

(1887–1964) was a poet, best known for writing the series of poems *Façade* (1923). She was also known for her unusual clothes and appearance. She was made a *dame(2) in 1954. Her brother **Osbert Sitwell** (1892–1969) wrote poems and novels, but is best known for his autobiography, published in five books. The youngest, **Sacheverell Sitwell** (1897–1988), wrote poetry and books about the history of art.

Edith and Osbert Sitwell

the ˌ**Six ˈCounties** *n* [pl] the six counties that make up Northern Ireland. They are Antrim, *Armagh, Down, *Fermanagh, *Londonderry(1) and Tyrone. Historically, the ancient Irish kingdom of *Ulster was divided into nine counties. Six of these counties remained part of the *United Kingdom in 1921. People sometimes refer to Northern Ireland as 'the Six Counties'.

ˈ**sixth form** *n* the classes that make up the last two years in British secondary schools, often divided into the **upper sixth** and **lower sixth**, and consisting mainly of students between 16 and 18 who are studying for the *A level examination. Some students leave their secondary schools after taking the *GCSE examination and go to a **sixth-form college**, a separate school where students study for A level.

*The **$64 000 Question*** /ˈsɪksti fɔː ˈθaʊsənd dɒlə ˈkwestʃn; *AmE* fɔːr, ˈdɑːlər/ a popular US television game show in the 1950s, presented by Hal March. It offered the largest prizes ever given, and even people who lost received cars for competing. It was later copied by other shows.

60 Minutes /ˌsɪksti ˈmɪnɪts/ a US television news programme which has been broadcast each week since 1968 on *CBS. By 1997, it had won 63 *Emmy awards, more than any other news programme, and had been voted one of the 10 most popular programmes on US television every year for 20 years.

ˈ**Sizewell** /ˈsaɪzwel/ a group of nuclear power stations (= buildings where electricity is produced) on the east coast of England, in *Suffolk. The first one, **Sizewell A**, was built in 1966. **Sizewell B**, a much larger power station, began producing electricity in 1995. The company *Nuclear Electric plans to build two more power stations there, called **Sizewell C**.

ska /skɑː/ *n* [U] a type of popular music similar to *reggae but with a faster beat, and often using brass instruments. It developed in *Jamaica in the 1960s and was also popular in Britain in the late 1970s and early 1980s. Well-known ska bands included Madness and The Specials.

ˌ**Skara ˈBrae** /ˌskærə ˈbreɪ/ a *Stone Age village on Mainland, the largest island of the *Orkneys. It is the best preserved village of its period in Europe, because it was covered in sand for almost 3 000 years.

ˈˌRed' ˈ**Skelton** /ˌred ˈskeltən/ (1913–97) a US comic actor in *vaudeville, in films and on radio and television. *The Red Skelton Show* (1953–64) and *The Red Skelton Hour* (1964–70) were on *CBS. His films included *Whistling in the Dark* (1941) and *Three Little Words* (1950). Skelton was chosen for the Comedy *Hall of Fame in 1993.

ˈ**skiffle** *n* [U] **1** (in Britain) a style of 1950s pop music. It was a mixture of *jazz and *folk music, and usually played by small groups, sometimes on instruments they had made themselves. One of the most popular British skiffle musicians was Lonnie Donegan (1931–). **2** (in the US) a style of 1920s and 1930s jazz which included elements of *blues, *ragtime and folk music. It was played on normal instruments and also on instruments made by the players themselves.

ˈ**skinhead** *n* a young person, usually a man, with a shaved head and often wearing braces and heavy boots, especially *Doc Martens. Skinheads first appeared in Britain in the 1960s and are known for their violent behaviour and their support for right-wing political groups such as the *British National Party.

ˌB F ˈ**Skinner** /ˈskɪnə(r)/ (Burrhus Frederic Skinner 1904–90) a US psychologist who believed that the learning processes in humans and animals were very similar, and that behaviour could be predicted and controlled. He taught at *Harvard University and created the **Skinner Box** to measure how much animals could learn if given rewards. His books included *Science and Human Behavior* (1953) and *About Behaviorism* (1974).

Sky /skaɪ/ Britain's first satellite television company, owned by Rupert *Murdoch. It began broadcasting in 1989 but combined with another company the following year and changed its name to *BSkyB. BSkyB still uses Sky as the name of several television channels broadcast in Europe, which can only be seen by people who have satellite dishes or special cable connections. Most of the channels broadcast one particular type of programme and have names like 'Sky Sports' and 'Sky Movies'.

*The ˌ**Sky at ˈNight*** a popular British television programme about the stars and planets, broadcast every month by the *BBC since 1957. It is well known for the way in which its presenter, Patrick *Moore, gives scientific information in an entertaining way.

Skye /skaɪ/ the largest island in the Inner *Hebrides, off the coast of north-west Scotland. Its attractive lakes and mountains make it a popular tourist centre. It is famous as the island to which *Bonny Prince Charlie escaped in a boat after the battle of *Culloden. A bridge, built in the 1990s, now connects Skye to the mainland of Scotland.

the ˌ***Skye ˈBoat Song*** /ˌskaɪ/ a popular Scottish song about how Flora *MacDonald helped *Bonny Prince Charlie escape to Skye. The sad, slow music is sometimes used to represent Scotland in films and television programmes. Many people in Britain know the first verse:

Speed, bonnie boat, like a bird on the wing;
Onward, the sailors cry:
Carry the lad that's born to be king
Over the sea to Skye.

ˌ**Skye ˈterrier** /ˌskaɪ/ *n* a breed of *terrier with short legs and long hair. They were originally bred as working dogs on the island of *Skye.

ˈ***Skylab*** /ˈskaɪlæb/ the first US space station. It was used in the early 1970s for scientific research by three different groups of three astronauts. In 1979 *Skylab* fell to earth in pieces which landed in the Indian Ocean and Australia without causing any damage.

skyscrapers

Skyscrapers are very tall buildings that contain offices or places to live. The first were built in *Chicago in the late 1880s but they have since been copied all over the world. After 1913 the top few storeys of skyscrapers were often stepped back (= built gradually narrower, floor by floor) to allow more light to reach street level.

Many of the most famous skyscrapers are in New York City. The ***Chrysler Building**, at 1 047 feet (319 metres), was by far the tallest building in the world in 1930 when it was built. The taller ***Empire State Building**, 1 250 feet (381 metres) high, was finished the following year. The ***World Trade Center**, built in the early 1970s, is about 1 350 feet (412 metres) tall. Many visitors to New York take the ferry to *Staten Island so that they can see the **Manhattan skyline**, the outline of all the tallest buildings in New York.

The ***Sears Tower** in Chicago, built shortly after the World Trade Center, is said to be 1 454 feet (443 metres) high and is currently the tallest building in the US. The Petronas Towers, built in 1996 in Malaysia, are about 1 483 feet (452 metres) tall, though some people in Chicago disagree with the way they were measured and say that the Sears Tower is really taller. But in 2001 the Shanghai World Financial Center in China will become the world's tallest building at 1 510 feet (460 metres) high.

By comparison with skyscrapers in the US, those in Britain are rather small. ***Canary Wharf**, an office building in London's *Docklands, stands only 800 feet (244 metres) high but it replaced the **National Westminster Tower**, also in London, as Britain's tallest building in 1986. Other skyscrapers in the *City of London include the Lloyds Building, designed by Richard *Rogers.

Skyscrapers which contain people's homes are, in Britain, usually called **high-rises** or **tower blocks**. They became a common feature of British cities when hundreds of them were built to replace slums in the 1950s and 1960s. Many are 20 or 30 storeys high, and have several flats on each floor. The tallest residential block in Britain is the Shakespeare Tower, part of the *Barbican complex in London, which is 419 feet (128 metres) high. At first, high-rises were welcomed because they provided cheap, modern housing. Now, they are no longer considered desirable places to live. Many suffered from lack of repair and have been pulled down. People who live in high-rises often complain that they are not private enough, that there is nowhere for children to play, and that they feel cut off from life in the street.

S

the ˈ**Slade** ˈ**School of** ˈ**Fine** ˈ**Art** /ˈsleɪd/ a famous art school in London. It is a part of *University College, London, and different from most of London's other art schools because its students study only fine art such as painting and sculpture rather than design.

slang

Slang words are very informal words. They may be new, or existing words used in a new sense and context. As time goes by, some are used more widely and are no longer thought of as slang. *Clever* and *naughty*, for instance, were both formerly slang words that are now accepted as standard. Many slang words die out after a few years or sooner. The regular introduction of new words to replace them helps keep the language alive.

A lot of slang words are restricted to a particular social group. Use of slang suggests an easy, informal relationship between people and helps reinforce social identity. In the 18th century the word *slang* described the language of criminals, but since then every group in society has developed its own slang terms. The groups that use most slang are still those closest to the edge of society: criminals, prisoners and drug users. Young people also develop slang expressions to distance themselves from older people.

The **street language** of young people changes fast. Street slang includes words relating to young people's attitudes. Young people today may describe something exciting as *cool*, *massive*, *wicked*, *wild* or *storming*. If something is old-fashioned or undesirable it is *naff*. Anything bad is *rank*. A *nerd*, a *prat* or an *anorak*, or in the US a *dweeb* or a *geek*, is somebody who seems rather stupid. Going out and having a good time is *larging it* or *chilling*. As people get older they sometimes keep on using the same slang words and in this way slang may indicate a person's age. The parents of today's young people used *great*, *super*, *fab* or *smashing*, *square* or *old hat*, and *berk* and *clot*, when they were young, and many of them still use these words. Some older people try to use current street slang in order not to seem old-fashioned, though in many cases it sounds odd and inappropriate.

A lot of street slang refers to drink, *drugs and sex. Many of these words and phrases are not socially acceptable and are widely considered rude and offensive. The expressions *get pissed*, *get smashed* and be *off your face* relate to getting drunk. There are many expressions for vomiting after drinking too much, e.g. *blowing chunks*, *chundering* or (*AmE*) *praying to the porcelain god*. Slang words for drugs include *smack* (heroin) and *crack* (cocaine). Expressions connected with drug-taking include *chasing the dragon* (= smoking heroin in tinfoil) and *jacking/banging up* (= injecting drugs). Some of these terms have become more widely known through films like **Trainspotting*. *Shagging*, *screwing* and *getting your leg over* all refer to sex. Other common slang expressions refer to the body's waste functions, e.g. *piss*, *take a leak*, *have a shit* and (*AmE*) *take a dump*. Some words, such as *fuck* and *shit*, have become *swear words.

Slang words are also widely used for things found in everyday life. The television, for instance, can be called the *box* and the remote control the *clicker* or *flicker*. The *blower* or the *horn* is the telephone. A *dive* or a *hole* is a cheap restaurant, bar or nightclub. Money can be referred to as *dough*, *dosh*, *dollars* (whatever the currency), *wonga* or *moolah*.

Some slang expressions are **euphemisms**. Many older people use euphemisms for bodily functions, e.g. *spend a penny*, *powder your nose*, *visit the bathroom*, meaning 'to go the toilet'. Some common serious diseases have slang names which are lighter in tone than the formal name, e.g. *the big C* for cancer. Somebody with a bad heart has a *dicky ticker*. People use expressions like *pass away* or *pop your clogs* to refer to dying. In business, some companies, instead of sacking or firing an employee, may speak of *letting them go* or (*AmE*) *dehiring them*. Job titles can make a job sound more important than it is. In the US a person who takes away rubbish used to be called a garbage man, but now may be called a *sanitary engineer*.

Some professions and areas of work have their own terms, often called **jargon**, which are different from slang. Many people learn bits of the jargon of other groups through television programmes and films about hospitals, law courts, etc. Some of the jargon used by people who work with computers has also become well known. Most people know, for instance, that a *hacker* is somebody who gets into other people's computers without permission.

Slavery ⇨ article.

ˈ**slave state** *n* (in the US) any state that had slaves before and during the *Civil War. The term was especially important when new states were established as either free states or slave states, as in the *Missouri Compromise. Most slave states were in the South, but several northern states had slaves early in their history.

ˌWayne ˈ**Sleep** /ˈsliːp/ (1948–) an English dancer. He was a member of the *Royal Ballet before forming his own dance company, Dash, in 1980. In the 1980s he danced in **Cats* and often appeared on British television.

*The ˌ**Sleeping** ˈ**Beauty*** a traditional children's story about a princess who falls asleep and cannot wake up because a witch has put a spell (= a condition caused by magic) on her. A hundred years later, a prince finds her and kisses her. The kiss breaks the spell and she wakes up. The story is often used in British *pantomimes.

ˈ**Slimbridge** /ˈslɪmbrɪdʒ/ a bird sanctuary (= a place where birds are protected and encouraged to breed) on the river *Severn in south-west England. It has many varieties of birds, and is the main centre of the *Wildfowl and Wetlands Trust.

ˌ**Sloane** ˈ**Ranger** /ˌsləʊn; *AmE* ˌsloʊn/ (*also infml* **Sloane**) *n* (*humor*) an expression used to refer to a type of *upper-class or *upper-middle-class young person, usually a woman. Sloane Rangers typically live in fashionable areas of London such as *Chelsea, wear expensive clothes (often ones designed to be worn in the country), and have loud voices and old-fashioned ideas about politics and society. The phrase, invented by a journalist in the 1970s, is a mixture of *Sloane Square and the *Lone Ranger: *I could tell by the address on the invitation that the party would be full of Sloane Rangers.* See also GREEN WELLY BRIGADE.

ˌ**Sloane** ˈ**Square** /ˌsləʊn; *AmE* ˌsloʊn/ a square in a very fashionable and expensive part of *Chelsea, London. It is connected to *Knightsbridge by **Sloane Street**.

the ˌ**Slough of De**ˈ**spond** /ˌslaʊ əv dɪˈspɒnd; *AmE* dɪˈspɑːnd/ a place in *The *Pilgrim's Progress*. It is a slough (= an area of soft, wet ground) that is full of fears and doubts. It is sometimes used to refer to the mental condition of a person with many doubts and fears: *While he was in that Slough of Despond his agent rang, and suddenly everything seemed all right.*

ˈ**Sly and the** ˈ**Family** ˈ**Stone** /ˈslaɪ, ˈstəʊn; *AmE* ˈstoʊn/ a US pop group which was especially popular with *hippies. It was formed in 1967 by Sly Stone, who was born Sylvester Stewart. The next year they had a hit with their song *Dance to the Music*. Among their most successful albums were *Stand!* (1969) and *There's a Riot Goin' On* (1971).

ˌ**small** ˈ**claims court** *n* a type of court of law dealing with cases in which one person has a small claim against another person or a company. This is usually less than £1 000 in Britain and $5 000 in the US. It is much cheaper to use small claims courts than any other type of court, and they are usually used by customers who feel that they have been treated dishonestly. In the US the court cost is usually only about $10–20 for a case, and people often act as their own lawyers. The court can also decide personal disputes that do not involve money, e.g. forcing somebody to return property to its owner.

ˈ**Smarties**™ /ˈsmɑːtiz; *AmE* ˈsmɑːrtiz/ *n* [pl] small sweets that are hard on the outside with chocolate inside. They are in several different colours and are very popular in Britain, especially with children: *She bought her a comic and a tube of Smarties.*

ˌSamuel ˈ**Smiles** /ˈsmaɪlz/ (1812–1904) a Scottish writer and teacher. He believed that people could improve themselves and have better lives, and wrote books about people who had done this, including *Lives of the Engineers* (1861–2). He also wrote several books explaining how people could improve their lives. The most famous of these was *Self-help* (1859).

Smith[1] /smɪθ/ a very common family name in Britain and the US. It is sometimes used by people who do not want their real names to be known: *They had registered at the motel in the names of Mr and Mrs Smith.*

ˌAdam ˈ**Smith**[2] /ˈsmɪθ/ (1723–90) a Scottish philosopher and economist. He believed in *free trade and private enterprise (= the idea that business and industry should be controlled by private individuals or companies, not by the state). His book, *The *Wealth of Nations*, is regarded as the first major work in the modern science of economics. His ideas have influenced several 20th-century politicians, including Margaret *Thatcher.

ˌBessie ˈ**Smith**[3] /ˈsmɪθ/ (1895–1937) the leading *African-American *blues singer of her time. Her popular name was 'Empress of the Blues'. During her career, she performed with such musicians as Benny *Goodman, Louis *Armstrong and Fletcher Henderson. Her hits included *Downhearted Blues* (1923). She died after a car crash.

ˌChris ˈ**Smith**[4] /ˈsmɪθ/ (1951–) a British *Labour politician. He became a *Member of Parliament in 1983, and held several important positions in the Labour *Shadow Cabinet before becoming *Secretary of State for Culture, Media and Sport in the Labour government of 1997.

ˌDelia ˈ**Smith**[5] /ˈsmɪθ/ an English presenter of popular television programmes on cooking. She is also the author of several cookery books which have sold in very large numbers.

ˌIan ˈ**Smith**[6] /ˈsmɪθ/ (1919–) the last *prime minister of Rhodesia, the country now called Zimbabwe. In 1965 he declared Rhodesia to be an independent African country ruled by white people. Although very few countries recognized Rhodesia, Smith stayed in charge until the country became Zimbabwe in 1979.

ˌJohn ˈ**Smith**[7] /ˈsmɪθ/ (*c.* 1579–1631) an English colonist (= a person who establishes a colony, an area settled and controlled by people from another country) in America. He was one of the early colonists in Virginia, and was president of the North American colony from 1608 to 1609. In 1614 he explored New England, and gave it its name. He traded goods with Native Americans, and is best known for the story that his life was saved by the Native-American princess *Pocahontas.

ˌJohn ˈ**Smith**[8] /ˈsmɪθ/ (1938–94) a Scottish *Labour politician. He had several positions in the *Shadow Cabinet before becoming the *Leader of the Opposition in 1992. In 1993 he was responsible for changing the way decisions are made in the Labour Party by giving each party member and *trade union member one vote. Before that, the unions had always voted on behalf of all their members.

ˌJoseph ˈ**Smith**[9] /ˈsmɪθ/ (1805–44) the US religious leader who started the *Mormon Church of Jesus Christ of Latter-Day Saints and published *The Book of Mormon* (1830) containing their basic beliefs. After some of his followers burnt down the offices of a Mormon newspaper that had criticized him, Smith was arrested with his brother Hyrum and taken to a prison at Carthage, *Illinois, where an angry crowd shot and killed them.

ˌKate ˈ**Smith**[10] /ˈsmɪθ/ (1909–86) a US singer. She

Slavery

A **slave** is considered to be the property of another person and to have no rights of their own. Slavery has been practised in many countries, but played a particularly important role in the history of the US.

The development of slavery

The first slaves were taken to North America from Africa by the Dutch in 1619. By the time of the *American Revolution (1775) there were 500 000 slaves, mostly in the South. After the Revolution the northern states made slavery illegal but the *South needed cheap labour for the cotton plantations. Gradually, the South's economy became dependent on slaves and by 1860, the year before the *Civil War, there were about 4 million.

Conditions on ships bringing slaves from Africa were very bad. People were packed in tightly and there was little to eat and drink. Many died during the trip. Those who reached America were put up for sale and buyers had a chance to look at them and feel them as if they were animals. In 1808 it became illegal to bring slaves into the US, but by then many were being born there, so the slave markets continued.

The quality of life for slaves depended on the treatment they received from their **master** and on the kind of work they did. Those working on the cotton plantations of the *Deep South suffered most. Families were regularly broken up and sent to different plantations. The worst situation was to be sold further down the *Mississippi River. The expression *to sell somebody down the river* means to betray their trust and leave them in difficulties.

Opposition to slavery

It is hard to understand how slavery was allowed to continue in a country that thought of itself as the 'land of the free'. But people found ways to explain it. They said, for example, that Blacks were lazy and needed discipline. Some people pointed out the benefits for slaves who had a good master: housing, food and clothing were provided, and they did not have to worry about getting money to buy these things as poor Whites did. Many people believed that the two races were different, and so treatment that would not be good for Whites was all right for Blacks.

Not everyone shared these beliefs, and in the 1830s opposition to slavery grew. Leaders of the **abolition movement** included William Lloyd *Garrison, publisher of an anti-slavery newspaper, *The Liberator*, and Harriet Beecher *Stowe who wrote **Uncle Tom's Cabin*, a novel about a slave who was badly treated. Former slaves Frederick *Douglass and Sojourner *Truth described the evils of slavery from their own experience.

Some ***abolitionists** took direct action. In 1831 a former slave, Nat *Turner, organized an **uprising** of slaves in *Virginia. In 1859 a white man, John *Brown, tried to free some slaves. The work of the ***Underground Railroad**, a group of people who helped slaves to escape to the North, had more impact. One of its most famous workers was Harriet *Tubman. Other people hoped to end slavery by sending Blacks back to Africa and in 1822 created the new country of Liberia.

Laws were made to restrict the growth of slavery. In 1787 the North-West Ordinance said that slavery would not be allowed in newly developed regions in the west. But the South wanted slavery to expand westward, and politicians found it increasingly difficult to reach agreement. In 1820 the *Missouri Compromise said that *Missouri would be admitted to the US as a **slave state** (= one where slavery was allowed) and *Maine as a **free state** (= one where it was not). The Compromise of 1850 made *California a free state and let the people in *New Mexico and *Utah make their own choice. The *Kansas-Nebraska Act also let the people decide.

Some laws made conditions worse for slaves. A few states made it illegal for people to **manumit** (= free) their slaves. The Fugitive Slave Law of 1850 made it illegal to help slaves escape.

Conflict between the North and South increased, and it became clear that supporters and opponents of slavery could not continue to be part of the same country. In 1861 the slave states left the US and formed their own government. This was the beginning of the Civil War.

The end of slavery

After the North won the Civil War and brought the southern states back into the US, slavery was ended. But little changed for former slaves. Some moved to the North but there were not enough jobs there and many suffered prejudice from Whites. Those that stayed in the South often worked on the plantations where they had been slaves. They were paid for their work, but had to buy food and clothes. Wages were low and they got into debt, which meant they had to stay there trying to pay off debts which became larger each year.

The North hoped quickly to forget the Civil War but did little to help the Blacks. The effects of this are still felt today, and black Americans have fewer advantages than Whites. On average they get less education, earn less money, have less respect and die younger. Blacks and Whites often find it difficult to trust each other, and many people think that this problem is getting worse rather than better.

The British and slavery

During the 17th century many slaves were taken from Africa to British colonies in the *Caribbean to work on sugar plantations. Many businessmen made fortunes from the **triangular trade** that grew up between Britain, Africa and the *West Indies. They transported cloth and iron goods to West Africa. These were exchanged for slaves which were then taken to the West Indies and exchanged for sugar. The sugar was taken back to Bristol and other British ports for sale in Europe.

The *Quakers were among the first people in Britain to demand an end to slavery and it was declared illegal in Britain as early as 1772. The campaign for total abolition grew with the formation of the Society for the Abolition of the Slave Trade, whose members included the politician William *Wilberforce, but it was not until 1807 that *Parliament passed an act making it illegal for British ships to carry slaves and for British colonies to import them. Slavery was not finally abolished in the *British Empire until 1833, when all slaves were set free and their owners compensated.

became famous during *World War II for her version of **God Bless America* and for travelling thousands of miles to entertain the military forces. Smith recorded about 3 000 songs including her theme song, *When the Moon Comes Over the Mountain*, which began her radio shows in the 1930s and the 1940s. She later had her own television series (1950–6).

ˌMaggie **'Smith¹¹** /'smɪθ/ (1934–) an English actor well known for the quality of her many theatre and film performances. She was one of the original members of the *National Theatre company in the 1960s, and in 1969 she won an *Oscar for her part in the film *The Prime of Miss Jean Brodie* (1969). She was made a *dame(2) in 1990.

'Margaret 'Chase **'Smith¹²** /'tʃeɪs 'smɪθ/ (1897–1995) the first US woman elected to both the US House of Representatives (1940–9) and the US Senate (1949–73). She was also, in 1964, the first woman to be named by a major political party as a possible candidate for US President. Smith was a member of the *Republican Party from *Maine.

ˌStevie **'Smith¹³** /ˌstiːvi 'smɪθ/ (1902–71) an English writer of poems and novels. She wrote three novels but is best known for the harsh and intelligent humour of her poetry. Her most famous poem is *Not Waving but Drowning* (1957).

ˌSydney **'Smith¹⁴** /'smɪθ/ (1771–1845) an English writer and *Church of England priest. He played an important role in social and political campaigns such as Catholic emancipation and the abolition of *slavery. He was also famous for making remarks full of clever humour.

ˌW H **'Smith¹⁵** /'smɪθ/ (*also infml* **Smith's**) any of a large group of British shops selling newspapers, magazines, books, cards, etc. Most British *high streets and many train stations and airports have a branch of Smith's.

ˌSmith & 'Wesson /ˌsmɪθ ənd 'wesn/ a company that makes guns, and also knives and bicycles. It was established in 1852 in Springfield, *Massachusetts, by Horace Smith and Daniel B Wesson, and is now owned by a British firm: *He had been shot at close range by a Smith & Wesson handgun.*

ˌSmithfield 'Market /ˌsmɪθfiːld/ London's main meat market. There has been a meat market at Smithfield, on the edge of the *City, since the 12th century. The glass buildings of today's market were built in 1868.

ˌSmithKline 'Beecham /ˌsmɪθklaɪn 'biːtʃəm/ a very large international drug company. It was formed in 1989 when the US company SmithKline combined with the Beecham Group, the British makers of *Beecham's pills.

Smith's /smɪθs/ ⇨ SMITH¹⁵.

The **Smiths** /smɪθs/ a British pop group formed in Manchester in 1982. The group made several successful albums in the 1980s, including *The Smiths* (1984) and *Meat is Murder* (1985). Their best-known songs include *This Charming Man* (1983) and *Shoplifters of the World Unite* (1987). The group's singer Morrissey began a successful career on his own in 1987.

the **Smithˌsonian Insti'tution** /smɪθˌsəʊniən; *AmE* smɪθˌsoʊniən/ (*also* the **Smith'sonian**) a US national institution that consists of several museums and centres for scientific research in Washington, DC. It was established in 1846 by the US Congress with money given by James Smithson (1765–1829), an English scientist. Its popular name is 'the nation's attic'. The 12 major museums, most of which are situated along the Mall, include the *National Air and Space Museum, the *National Gallery of Art, the National Museum of American Art, the National Portrait Gallery and the National Museum of American History. The *Kennedy Center is an independent part of the Smithsonian.

ˌSmith 'Square /ˌsmɪθ/ a square in central London, near the *Houses of Parliament. It is well known as the address of the main offices of the *Conservative Party. People sometimes use 'Smith Square' to refer to the party's central office: *Many Tories in the country are unhappy with the decisions made in Smith Square.*

ˌSmokey the 'Bear /ˌsməʊki; *AmE* ˌsmoʊki/ **1** the symbol used by the US Forest Service to help prevent forest fires. He is a friendly bear wearing a Forest Service hat and is used on posters and television advertisements with the message 'Only you can prevent forest fires.' **2** (*also* **Smokey Bear**, **Smokey**) an informal US name for a member of the motorway/freeway police, so called because the hats they wear in some states are similar to the one worn by Smokey the Bear.

smoking

Tobacco was taken to Europe from America in the 16th century by Sir Walter *Raleigh. Today, smoking is popular all over the world and tobacco plays an important role in the US economy.

About 25% of Americans smoke. This figure is much lower than in the past, although the number of people under 18 who smoke is high, about 20%. In Britain, ASH (Action on Smoking and Health) was set up in 1971 to reduce smoking. About 28% of men and 26% of women now smoke, compared with 52% and 41% in 1972. Men are more likely to be **heavy smokers** (= people who smoke 20 or more cigarettes a day) than women. There is growing concern about the number of children who smoke.

Most people who smoke buy commercially made **cigarettes**. Some people **roll their own**, using loose tobacco and cigarette papers. **Roll-ups** are less popular in the US. A few people, especially men, smoke **cigars**. Some smoke **pipes**. In the US some people in the country use **chewing tobacco**. Hardly anyone now takes **snuff** (= tobacco sniffed up the nose). The smoking of **cannabis** and other drugs is illegal.

Every pack of cigarettes and every advertisement for tobacco products must have a **government health warning** printed on it. A few people deny that smoking damages health, but most now recognize that there is a link with lung cancer and other health problems. People trying to **give up smoking** may use **nicotine patches** stuck to their skin or attend a special course. Smokers may find they are at a disadvantage when applying for insurance and they may have to pay more than **non-smokers**. Many people are also concerned about the dangers of **passive smoking** caused by breathing in smoke from other people's cigarettes.

Various measures have been taken to discourage smoking. Cigarettes and tobacco can no longer be advertised on television. Tobacco companies used to advertise at sports events, but in Britain this is now also forbidden. There are high taxes on tobacco, and laws preventing the sale of cigarettes to young people below the age of 16. Smoking is no longer allowed in many public places, including public transport and restaurants. Some airlines do not allow smoking on their flights. Office workers often have to stand outside if they wish to smoke.

A few people find it impossible to give up smoking and some poorer people consider smoking one of the few luxuries they can afford. Others believe that the freedom to smoke is a right. But the main opposition to laws against smoking comes from people who have a financial interest in it, such as the states of

*Kentucky and *Virginia where it is grown, and the tobacco industry. The industry has been badly hit recently by court decisions saying that cigarette companies hid evidence about how dangerous their product was. A number of people have gone to court and won money from tobacco companies because their health was harmed by cigarettes.

the ˌ**Smoky** ˈ**Mountains** /ˌsməʊki; *AmE* ˌsmoʊki/ (*also* the ˈ**Smokies** /ˈsməʊkiz; *AmE* ˈsmoʊkiz/) another name for the *Great Smoky Mountains.

Toˌbias ˈ**Smollett** /təˌbaɪəs ˈsmɒlɪt; *AmE* ˈsmɑːlɪt/ (1721–71) a Scottish writer of novels. His early books, *The Adventures of Roderick Random* (1748) and *The Adventures of Peregrine Pickle* (1751) describe the travels and often rough adventures of characters who are not always honest but are easy to like. Smollett's other major work, *The Expedition of Humphry Clinker* (1771), is in the form of letters.

the ˈ**Smothers** ˌ**Brothers** /ˈsmʌðəz; *AmE* ˈsmʌðərz/ **Tom Smothers** (1937–) and **Dick Smothers** (1939–), two brothers who entertain with jokes and humorous songs. Tom often reminds Dick, 'Mother always liked you best.' Their television series, *The Smothers Brothers Comedy Hour* (1966–9), was stopped by *CBS because of their jokes about religion, drugs and sex, as well as their songs and comments against the *Vietnam War. They returned with another television series in the late 1980s and they still do tours.

ˌ**snakes and** ˈ**ladders** a popular children's game. It is played with a dice on a board marked with squares, and with pictures of snakes and ladders that go over more than one square. To win the game, a player must reach the top of the board by moving along the squares. A player who arrives on a square where there is the bottom of a ladder can move straight to the top of the ladder, but one arriving at the head of a snake has to move back down to its tail.

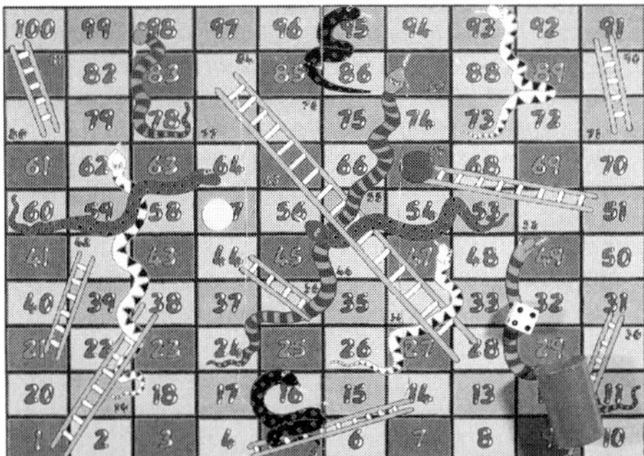

snakes and ladders

snap *n* [U] (*BrE*) a card game, often played by children, in which players lay down cards at the same time, and shout 'Snap!' when two similar cards are laid down. The player who calls first wins the cards already laid down. The winner of the game is the player who wins all the cards in this way. People sometimes say 'Snap!' when they notice that two things are similar: *Snap! You've got the same shoes as me!*

SNCC /snɪk/ ⇨ STUDENT NONVIOLENT COORDINATING COMMITTEE.

ˌSam ˈ**Snead** /ˈsniːd/ (1912–) one of the most successful US golf players in the 1940s and 1950s, also known as 'Slammin' Sam' because he hit the ball so far. He won the *PGA Championship three times (1942, 1949 and 1951) and the *Masters Tournament three times (1949, 1952 and 1954).

ˈ**snooker** *n* [U] a game for two, played on a large table with fifteen red balls and seven balls of different colours. The players use long sticks (called *cues*) to hit the white ball across the table, trying to make it knock one of the other balls into any of six holes (called *pockets*) round the edge of the table. Points are scored according to the colour of the ball that is hit into a pocket. A red ball, worth one point, must be hit into a pocket first, to allow the player who hit it to try a ball of higher value. Snooker used to be considered a *working-class game, but since it became popular on British television in the 1970s it is now enjoyed by people of all types in Britain and several other countries.

ˈ**Snoop** ˈ**Doggy** ˈ**Dogg** /ˈsnuːp ˈdɒgi ˈdɒg; *AmE* ˈdɔːgi ˈdɔːg/ (1971–) an *African-American singer of *rap music. He was born Calvin Broadus. His albums include *Doggystyle* (1993), which sold more than 4 million copies, and *Tha Doggfather* (1996). In 1993, he was accused of a murder but was judged innocent.

ˈ**Snoopy** /ˈsnuːpi/ the dog owned by Charlie *Brown in the comic strip **Peanuts*. Snoopy sleeps on the roof of his kennel and has human thoughts and ideas. He tries to write novels and has imaginary adventures, such as being a *World War I pilot who has battles with Germany's famous 'Red Baron'.

ˌC P ˈ**Snow** /ˈsnəʊ; *AmE* ˈsnoʊ/ (Charles Percy Snow 1905–80) an English writer of novels and scientist. He worked as a scientist for the British government during *World War II, and at *Cambridge University. He used these experiences to write his best-known work, *Strangers and Brothers*, a series of novels (1940–1970) describing British life in that period, particularly in scientific, academic and government fields. He was also well known for speaking and writing about the lack of communication between the 'two cultures' of scientific and artistic life. He was made a *knight in 1957 and a *life peer in 1964.

the ˈ**Snow Belt** (*also* the ˈ**Snowbelt**) (*infml*) the north-eastern US states and those in the *Middle West that have cold winters with snow. Compare RUST BELT, SUNBELT.

ˈ**Snowdon** /ˈsnəʊdn; *AmE* ˈsnoʊdn/ a mountain in north-west Wales, in *Snowdonia *national park. It is the highest mountain in England and Wales, and has a railway to the top which was built in the 19th century and is very popular with tourists.

Snowˈ**donia** /snəʊˈdəʊniə; *AmE* snoʊˈdoʊniə/ a *national park around *Snowdon in north-west Wales. It is an important tourist centre, famous for its attractive mountain scenery.

The ˈ***Snowman*** a children's book (1978) written and illustrated by Raymond *Briggs. It is the story of a small boy's adventures with a snowman (= a figure of a man made with snow). A film version made for television is usually shown on British television each year around Christmas.

ˌ***Snow*** ˈ***White*** a traditional children's story. Snow White is a beautiful princess. Her stepmother (= the woman who married her father after her mother died) is jealous of her beauty and orders a man to kill her. He takes pity on her and leaves her alive in a forest, where she lives happily with seven dwarfs (= very small people). The stepmother discovers that Snow White is alive, and gives her an apple full of poison. Snow White falls asleep after eating it and does not wake up until a prince kisses her, and all ends happily. The story was made into a successful Walt *Disney film in 1937, and is a popular subject for *pantomimes in Britain. In the film the seven dwarfs are called Dopey, Doc, Sneezy, Bashful, Sleepy, Grumpy and Happy.

SNP /ˌes en ˈpiː/ ⇨ SCOTTISH NATIONAL PARTY.

ˌJohn ˈ**Soane** /ˈsəʊn; *AmE* ˈsoʊn/ (1753–1837) an English architect whose work was influenced by *neo-classicism. His best-known buildings are the *Bank of England and his own house in central London, which is now a museum called **Sir John Soane's Museum**, filled with the works of art and other interesting objects that he collected. He was made a *knight in 1831.

soap operas

Soap operas, also called **soaps**, are amongst the most popular television programmes. They are stories about the lives of ordinary people that are broadcast, usually in half-hour **episodes**, three times or more each week. Episodes broadcast during the week are often repeated in a single **omnibus** programme at the weekend. They are called *soap operas* because in the US they were first paid for by companies who made soap. Some people buy books about their favourite soap and visit the places where the stories are supposed to happen.

Most soap operas describe the daily lives of a small group of people who live in the same street or town and go to the same pub, shops, etc. The most successful soaps reflect the worries and hopes of real people, though the central **characters** frequently have exaggerated personal problems in order to make the programmes more exciting. Some **storylines** deal with sensitive social issues, such as alcoholism, homosexuality and racism.

In Britain soaps operas are broadcast in the early evening. The longest-running soap opera in the world is *The *Archers*, 'an everyday story of country folk', which began on *BBC radio in the 1950s. The most popular of the television soaps is ITV's **Coronation Street*, first broadcast in 1960. Its main rival is the BBC's **EastEnders*. Other popular soaps include *Channel Four's **Brookside* and ITV's **Emmerdale*. **Neighbours* and *Home and Away*, both from Australia, are aimed at younger audiences. Older US soaps such as **Dallas* and **Dynasty*, are occasionally repeated on satellite television.

In the US, soap operas are also called **daytime dramas**. A few, like *Dynasty* and *Dallas*, have been successful in the evenings, but most soaps are broadcast during the afternoon. The main audience for them is housewives. Though soaps have a limited audience, the names of many of the long-running ones, e.g. *Days of Our Lives*, **General Hospital* and *The Young and the Restless*, are well-known. US soaps are often criticized for having plots which are not realistic and move too slowly: it is possible to miss many **instalments** and still understand the story. In spite of this, people who watch soaps usually have one or two favourites which they try never to miss. There are special telephone numbers for people who do miss instalments to hear a recording that tells them what has been happening.

People who do not like soaps criticize them for being boring and predictable. In the US especially, soap operas get little respect. Many people are embarrassed to admit that they watch them.

the ˌ**Social** ˈ**Chapter** a section of the *Maastricht Treaty that deals with people's rights. It is a long document that proposes European laws to protect the rights of employees to be paid fairly and to work in safe conditions, the rights of old people and children to be treated fairly, the rights of men and women to have equal opportunities, and the rights of people to move freely between *European Union countries. Every European Union country except Britain signed the document in 1992, when the British Conservative government argued that it would be too expensive for British business and industry. In 1997 the new British Labour government stated that it would sign the Social Chapter.

the ˈ**Social Demo**ˈ**cratic and** ˈ**Labour** ˌ**Party** ⇨ SDLP.

the ˌ**Social Demo**ˈ**cratic Party** ⇨ SDP.

the ˌ***Socialist*** ˈ***Worker*** a British newspaper produced by the **Socialist Workers Party**, a left-wing political party. It consists mainly of political articles and is sold on the street in many towns and cities by members of the party.

ˌ**social se**ˈ**curity** *n* [U] government payments to help people who are unemployed, poor or old, or who cannot work because they are ill or injured. In the US, these payments are made by the government's **Social Security Administration**, established in 1935 as part of the government's *New Deal. Money for the payments (called *welfare*) is provided by taxes on employers and workers. In Britain, payments (called *benefits*) are made by the *Department of Social Security and the *Department for Education and Employment, with money from *National Insurance and other taxes. Payments in Britain include the *jobseeker's allowance, *income support, *family credit, *statutory sick pay and *housing benefit. See also BENEFITS AGENCY, BEVERIDGE REPORT, EMPLOYMENT SERVICE, MEDICARE, NATIONAL HEALTH SERVICE, WELFARE STATE.

ˌ**social se**ˈ**curity** ˌ**number** *n* (in the US) an identity number that everyone must have. It was originally a qualification for work and *social security, but in 1987 the US government decided that children should also be given numbers. The number is now also used in other ways, e.g. on bank cheques and driving licences and as a student's number at college or university.

Society ⇨ article.

the **So**ˈ**ciety for Pro**ˈ**moting** ˈ**Christian** ˈ**Knowledge** ⇨ SPCK.

the **So**ˌ**ciety of** ˈ**Friends** the formal name for the *Quakers.

ˈ**softball** *n* **1** [U] a form of *baseball played on a smaller area with a larger, softer ball and easier to play. Softball is especially popular with children, but many adult competitions are organized, e.g. between company teams. **2** [C] the ball used in the game of softball. Compare HARDBALL.

ˈ**Soho** /ˈsəʊhəʊ; *AmE* ˈsoʊhoʊ/ a district in the *West End of London, between *Oxford Street, *Piccadilly Circus and *Leicester Square. It is famous for its lively atmosphere and its many cafés, nightclubs, theatres and restaurants. It also has many sex shops, strip clubs (= places where people pay to watch other people take their clothes off) and prostitutes. Since the 1980s it has also been the favourite part of London for film, television, music and advertising com-panies to have their offices: *Before they became famous they used to perform in a tiny basement club in Soho.*

ˈ**SoHo** /ˈsəʊhəʊ; *AmE* ˈsoʊhoʊ/ a small fashionable area of *Manhattan(1) in New York City. SoHo is short for 'South of Houston', because it is south of West Houston Street which separates it from *Greenwich Village. Many artists live in SoHo in old industrial buildings which have been made

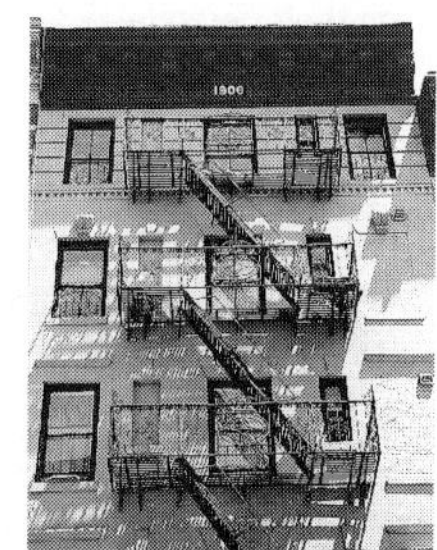

SoHo

S

Society

The word *society* can be used to mean what people also call **high society**, the activities of very rich and famous people, the clothes they wear, the parties they go to, etc. A **society wedding** means a wedding at which everyone is well-known.

But when people speak of British or American society they mean the whole population, the way people live together and the institutions they develop in order to do so.

Society and the individual

America is often said to be an **individualistic society**, i.e. the needs and desires of individuals are put before those of society as a whole. In many ways this is true. Americans strongly support the rights of individuals, and most would agree that people should be free to make their own choices and do what they want, provided that they do not hurt other people. Americans also believe that individuals should take responsibility for their own situation and not expect society as a whole, through the government, to take care of them.

It is said that, since the 1980s, British society has become more selfish and individualistic, and that people try to improve their own position at the expense of others. Britain is still a *class-based society, but now *education, *employment and *money matter as much in determining people's opportunities and place in society as their *family background. There is also a belief that personal morality is a matter for the individual, and that society should not expect everyone to have the same values. Most British people, however, believe that society has a moral responsibility to care for those in need, even though they are afraid that they will have to pay higher *taxes to pay for *social welfare benefits.

Before the 18th century, membership of a particular social *class defined an individual's status and determined the level of education they got, the work they could do, and who they might marry. The idea of an individual having personal *freedom and equality of opportunity is relatively new. The challenge facing modern society is to balance an individual's freedom of expression and choice with the need to maintain basic social structures and processes for the benefit of society as a whole.

S

Society's values

American society is often associated with ***Middle America** (= people who live in the central part of the US, who are *middle-class and neither very rich nor very poor). In the US a person's class or social status depends not on their family background but on their personal achievements and wealth.

Some of the things that Middle America believes to be important include traditional **institutions** like government, *religion and family values. Democracy (= a system of government through representatives elected by the people) is fundamental (= very important) to American society. Americans follow different religions, but many people believe that this does not matter, only that religion makes society stronger. Americans believe that family relationships should be close, that couples should get married and not get divorced if they can avoid it, and that children should grow up with both parents. In fact, although these values are thought to be important, they do not reflect the way many Americans live. Most people do not bother to vote in elections, some are not religious, and many married couples split up, so that single-parent families are becoming more common. Many people see in these facts a great threat to American society.

Many British people believe that they live in a civilized, liberal society in which individuals have the freedom to live as they wish, to be treated fairly, and to be respected. Others believe that British society is still firmly based on the class system, and that though politicians often talk about working towards a **classless society**, this will never be achieved. The ***Establishment**, which consists of the major institutions in British society – the *royal family, the *House of Lords, the *civil service, the law, the *Church of England, and the *armed forces – is still mainly *upper-class and white, and is not representative of the modern multiracial society.

Most people in Britain still have a sense of what class they belong to and of their **place in society**, though education has cut across the boundaries. At the same time there has been in recent years a breakdown of traditional **class barriers** and a marked increase in **social mobility**, the ability and readiness of people to change their social status (⇨ articles at CLASS and MULTICULTURAL BRITAIN AND THE US).

It is important to almost everyone in Britain that they live in a democracy, though after a government has been elected many people take little interest in *politics. As in Middle America, the people of ***Middle England** still believe in marriage and think that a couple should stay together. Some politicians actively promote traditional family values, but most people realize that society has changed and that other lifestyles should be accepted. People now expect to be allowed to live as they wish, and are no longer willing to have a moral or social code (= set of rules) forced on them.

Society in Britain and the US is faced with many moral dilemmas and decisions about its future. Many people welcome the chance to discuss moral and social issues such as access to healthcare, fertility treatment for older women, and assisted suicide (*BrE* euthanasia), and are not content to leave it to politicians or philosophers. In Britain the *Radio 4 programme *The Moral Maze* discusses the moral issues behind a topic in the news. Many other programmes on *radio and television question society's attitudes and values.

Social change

America is a ***multicultural society**. Some have likened it to a ***melting pot**, in which people from different cultures eventually become part of a single American culture. Others believe that a continuing variety of values and traditions is good, and support a **pluralist** view of society. In the US the white **mainstream** (= the largest group in society) is now only about 50% of the total population, and some members of this group are worried that their position is under threat. Language is an important social bond, and many Americans believe that encouraging *Hispanic immigrants to continue to speak Spanish, e.g. by providing road signs and school lessons in Spanish, rather than making them use English, will reinforce social divisions and weaken traditional American institutions.

In Britain's multicultural society, different social traditions and sets of values exist together and are generally respected. The white mainstream is much stronger than in the US and, although lack of tolerance has sometimes led to social unrest, the mainstream has not felt seriously threatened.

The roles of men and women in Britain and the US have changed enormously during the 20th century, and women now expect and have the right to similar treatment and opportunities as men. Many women work full time, leaving their *children in the care of others. Some people question whether this is good for the children and, at a wider level, for the institution of the family. Women have moved into many areas of employment which were traditionally male-only, e.g. the law and engineering, and men have to compete with them for jobs at all levels. At home, a man is no longer automatically considered the head of the household. Men are expected to share decision-making, do some of the housework and help look after the children. While women have gained in confidence and status, some men feel uncomfortable and unsure about their role in society.

Britain and the US are both ageing societies. Many more people now reach *old age, and society has had to to take account of this and provide for their needs. Old people in Britain and the US sometimes receive less respect than they deserve from younger people, and may be considered a burden by their families. Unlike in some countries, many old people do not live with their grown-up children and do not want to de dependent on them.

Young people regularly challenge traditional values and rebel against social **norms** (= standards of behaviour). In the US especially, young people are encouraged to become independent and question everything from an early age. In Britain, young people were formerly expected to obey their parents and had little chance to express themselves. Many parents are now less strict and think that children should be encouraged to develop their own ideas. Many young people have a strong social conscience and work to change things that seem unfair, but some become cynical (= believe that people will do things only for their own benefit) and **opt out** of society and look for an alternative lifestyle.

modern. They have iron fronts and large windows. The buildings were to be destroyed in the 1960s but were saved when the city made SoHo an official historical district.

ˈ***Sojourner*** /ˈsɒdʒənə(r); *AmE* ˈsoʊdʒərnər/ the small vehicle sent by *NASA on the *Pathfinder* space trip to Mars in 1997. It weighed 25 pounds (11 kilograms), had six wheels and was controlled from earth. It moved on the surface of Mars, taking many photographs and measurements and analysing the rocks, etc. It was named after Sojourner *Truth.

Sojourner *examining a rock on Mars*

the ˈ**Solent** /ˈsəʊlənt; *AmE* ˈsoʊlənt/ the area of sea between the *Isle of Wight and the south coast of England, where many sailing events take place.

the **Soˌlicitor ˈGeneral** *n* (*pl* **Solicitors General**) **1** (in Britain) a government law officer who acts as the *Attorney General's main assistant. The Solicitor General is a lawyer and an *MP belonging to the ruling party, who advises the government on legal matters. **2** (in the US government) the law officer who is next in rank to the US *Attorney General. Some states also have a Solicitor General as the main assistant to the state Attorney General.

the ˈ**Solomon ˌIslands** /ˈsɒləmən; *AmE* ˈsɑːləmən/ a country consisting of a group of islands in the south-west Pacific. The islands became a British protectorate (= a country controlled and protected by Britain) in the 1890s, and an independent member of the *Commonwealth in 1978. The main island, *Guadalcanal, is well known because of the battle that took place there in *World War II.

ˌGeorg ˈ**Solti** /ˌdʒɔːdʒ ˈʃɒlti; *AmE* ˌdʒɔːrdʒ ˈʃɑːlti/ (1912–97) a British conductor, born in Hungary. He was in charge of many famous orchestras, including the Chicago Symphony Orchestra and the orchestra of the *Royal Opera House, and was considered one of the leading conductors of his time. He was made a *knight in 1971.

the ˌ**Solway ˈFirth** /ˌsɒlweɪ ˈfɜːθ; *AmE* ˌsɑːlweɪ ˈfɜːrθ/ the part of the *Irish Sea that separates north-west England from south-west Scotland.

ˈ**Somerset** /ˈsʌməset; *AmE* ˈsʌmərset/ a county in south-west England. It consists mainly of agricultural land, and is well known for its cider (= an alcoholic drink made from apples). Its administrative centre is *Taunton.

ˌ**Somerset ˈHouse** /ˌsʌməset; *AmE* ˌsʌmərset/ a large, grand 18th-century building in central London, between the *Strand and the River *Thames. It is now an art gallery, but from the 1830s to the 1970s it contained the main offices of the *Inland Revenue and the General Register Office, where records of all births, marriages and deaths in the country were kept. Some people still refer to the new General Register Office as Somerset House.

S

the ˌBattles of the ˈ**Somme** /ˈsɒm; *AmE* ˈsɑːm/ two long battles that took place in the valley of the river Somme in northern France during *World War II. In the first battle, which lasted from July to November 1916, more than a million British, French and German soldiers died. The second battle lasted two weeks in the spring of 1918, and almost half a million soldiers died. Very little ground or any other advantage was won by either side in these battles, which are considered among the most terrible in history.

ˌStephen ˈ**Sondheim** /ˈsɒndhaɪm; *AmE* ˈsɑːndhaɪm/ (1930–) a US writer of *Broadway musical plays, many of which have been made into films. He wrote the words for **West Side Story* and *Gypsy* (1959), and the words and music for *A Funny Thing Happened on the Way to the Forum* (1962), *Company* (1970), *A Little Night Music* (1973) and *Sweeney Todd* (1979). *Sunday in the Park with George* (1984) won the *Pulitzer Prize. His best-known song is probably *Send in the Clowns* from *A Little Night Music*.

ˌ***Songs of ˈInnocence and of Exˈperience*** a collection of poems (1794) by William *Blake. He had published a group of poems in 1789 called *Songs of Innocence*, expressing the idea that God's love and sympathy is in everything on Earth. Five years later he added the *Songs of Experience* to the collection. The new poems express the power of evil as well as the power of love, and include some of Blake's most famous poems, including *The Tyger*.

ˌ***Songs of ˈPraise*** a regular *BBC television programme in which people sing hymns, usually in a church, and some of them talk about their faith. It is broadcast from a different place each Sunday.

The ˈ***Sonnets*** the sonnets (= poems of 14 lines) of William *Shakespeare, which were probably written in the 1590s. Many of them are addressed to a young man, expressing the poet's affection for him and giving him advice. Others are written to a beautiful *dark lady. The sonnets are famous for the beauty of their language, but also because no one has discovered for sure who the young man and the dark lady really were. The sonnets are dedicated to 'Mr W H', and his identity is also a mystery.

ˌ***Sons and ˈLovers*** a novel (1913) by D H *Lawrence. It is one of Lawrence's best-known books and is about a young man and his relationships with his mother (a teacher), his father (a coal miner), and the two women he loves. It is partly based on Lawrence's own life.

the ˌ**Sons of ˈLiberty** a number of secret organizations formed in the American colonies in 1765 to protest against the *Stamp Act. They were strongest in Boston and New York, where a group of them attacked British soldiers in 1770, one of the first serious actions that led to the *American Revolution.

soˈrority *n* (*AmE*) a social organization for women students at many US colleges and universities. Members often live together in a **sorority house**. They are called 'Greeks', because each sorority's name consists of two or three Greek letters, such as Chi Omega or Kappa Kappa Gamma. They also help charities and do community work. A few student sororities are academic or professional organizations. Compare FRATERNITY.

SOS pad™ /ˌes əʊ ˈes pæd; *AmE* ˌes oʊ ˈes/ *n* a US product like a rough metal ball for cleaning surfaces and kitchen pans, etc.

ˈ**Sotheby's** /ˈsʌðəbiz/ a leading London firm of auctioneers. Sotheby's is famous for dealing in works of art and antiques, and has a particularly strong reputation for selling old books. The company was established in 1744. It also has a branch in New York. Compare CHRISTIE'S.

an auction at Sotheby's

soul (*also* **soul music**) *n* [U] a type of emotional *African-American music that developed out of *gospel and *rhythm and blues in the 1950s and 1960s. The most famous form of soul music was *Motown(2). Well-known soul singers include James *Brown, Ray *Charles, Marvin *Gaye, The *Supremes, Aretha *Franklin, Otis *Redding, Roberta Flack and Stevie *Wonder. *Harlem has been called 'Soul City'.

The ˌ***Sound of ˈMusic*** a *Broadway musical play (1959) by Richard *Rodgers and Oscar *Hammerstein. It is based on the true story of the Austrian Trapp family who sang together and escaped to Switzerland from the Nazis. The film version, in which Julie *Andrews plays Maria Trapp, won six *Oscars. The songs include *The Sound of Music*, *Maria*, *Do Re Mi* and *Climb Every Mountain*.

ˈ**sourdough** *n* [U] (*AmE*) dough (= a mixture for making bread, etc.) which is kept from a previous time when something was baked and is later used instead of dry ingredients to make the bread rise. Sourdough breads were first made in the *Old West and are now especially popular in *San Francisco.

ˈJohn ˈPhilip ˈ**Sousa** /ˈsuːzə/ (1854–1932) a US composer, also known as the 'March King'. He wrote about 140 works of music for military marches, including *Semper Fidelis* (1888), *The Washington Post* (1889) and *The Stars and Stripes Forever* (1897). He led the US Marine Band (1880–92) and then formed his own band which made tours of Europe and around the world. The *sousaphone*, a large brass musical instrument, was named after him.

the **South** (*also* the ˌ**southern ˈstates**) the south-east and south-central US states, regarded as beginning to the south of the *Mason-Dixon Line. Their region is part of the *Sunbelt. The 14 states are *Maryland, *Virginia, *West Virginia, *Kentucky, *Tennessee, *North Carolina, *South Carolina, *Georgia, *Florida, *Alabama, *Mississippi, *Arkansas, *Louisiana and *Texas, especially its eastern part. All were *Confederate States except Maryland, West Virginia and Kentucky.

The South has sometimes seemed a mysterious region to Americans who live outside it and who associate it with a mixture of romantic charm, traditional family values, dangerous independence and violent prejudice. These ideas have been supported by the works of southern writers such as William *Faulkner and Tennessee *Williams and by the real conflicts of the *civil rights movement. Today, however, a 'New South' has been recognized. *Atlanta and other modern cities have developed, many companies from other parts of the US have moved to the *Sunbelt, and African Americans now serve as *mayors and community leaders. Two US Presidents (*Carter and *Clinton) have come from the South, and the US government has even developed the southern idea of *states' rights. In spite of these changes, however, many people still believe that the South is a region that wants to keep its strong separate character. Compare DEEP SOUTH.

ˌ**South ˈAfrica** /ˈæfrɪkə/ the country at the southern tip of Africa. Its capital city is Cape Town. In the 17th and 18th centuries different areas of the country were settled by the Dutch and the British, who fought each other in the *Boer Wars. South Africa became part of the *British Empire in the late 18th century. In 1909 it became an independent member of the *Commonwealth, but left in 1961 after establishing the policy of apartheid (= trying to keep the races of the country separate, with the white people in control). Most other countries disapproved of this policy, and many countries refused to trade with South Africa or to take part in sporting events with it. In 1994, after years of international pressure, the South African government allowed everybody the same voting rights and Nelson Mandela became the country's first black president. South Africa is the richest country in Africa, and is one of the world's largest producers of diamonds, gold and other valuable metals. Its official languages are English and Afrikaans. ▶ **South African** *adj, n.*

Sou'thampton /saʊˈθæmptən/ a city on the south coast of England. It is one of Britain's most important ports. For much of the 20th century it was the main port for passenger ships crossing the Atlantic. Some passenger ships still use the port of Southampton, but it now deals mainly with container ships (= ships that carry goods in large metal boxes).

the **ˌSouth ˈBank** an area of the south bank of the River *Thames around Waterloo Bridge which is London's main cultural centre. Most of the centre was built in the 1950s and 1960s. It includes the *Hayward Gallery, the *Museum of the Moving Image, the *National Film Theatre, the Purcell Room concert hall, the *Royal Festival Hall and the Royal *National Theatre, as well as gardens and areas where people can walk by the river and see outdoor concerts and exhibitions.

*The **ˌSouth ˈBank Show*** a popular British television programme about the arts. It has been presented by Melvyn *Bragg and broadcast on Sunday evenings by *ITV since 1978. The programmes usually include reports and comments on several different artists or artistic events, but they sometimes deal with one particular artist.

ˌSouth Caroˈlina /kærəˈlaɪnə/ a south-eastern US state on the Atlantic Ocean, also called the Palmetto State. The capital and largest city is Columbia. The state was named after the English king *Charles I and was one of the original *thirteen colonies. It attracts many tourists and produces tobacco, corn, cotton and fruit.

the **ˌSouth ˈCircular** a series of roads that join together and pass through many areas of South London. They join the *North Circular at the *Thames, east and west of London, to form a full circle around London. Until the *M25 was built they formed the main road round London. They still carry a lot of traffic, which often moves very slowly.

ˌSouth Daˈkota /dəˈkəʊtə; *AmE* dəˈkoʊtə/ a northern central US state, also called the Coyote State and the Mount Rushmore State. The capital city is Pierre and the largest city is Sioux Falls. It was part of the *Louisiana Purchase, and gold was discovered there in 1874. The *Sioux fought white people who settled there, until they were defeated at *Wounded Knee. The state grows corn and wheat, and produces machinery and electronic equipment. Many tourists visit Mount *Rushmore and the *Badlands National Park.

the **ˌSouth ˈDowns** a range of hills across southern *Hampshire and *Sussex near the south coast of England. They are popular with people who enjoy walking.

the **ˌSouth-ˈEast** the south-eastern region of England that includes London and the *Home Counties. More people live there than in any other part of Britain. Many rich people live there, and most businesses and industries have their main offices in the South-East, which does not have the same economic problems as Britain's other areas of high population: *House prices are rising faster in the South-East than in the rest of the country.*

Southˈend /saʊθˈend/ (*also* **Southˌend-on-ˈSea** /saʊˌθend/) a town on the south-east coast of England, east of London. It has the world's longest *pier and is traditionally the place where *Londoners, particularly from the *East End, go for day trips and summer holidays.

ˌsouthern ˈbelle *n* (*AmE*) a woman from the southern US who is young and attractive. The term was used especially in the 19th century when it also meant a young woman who belonged to one of the best families. Scarlett *O'Hara was a famous southern belle in fiction.

the **ˈSouthern ˈChristian ˈLeadership ˌConference** (*abbr* **SCLC**) a US organization started by Martin Luther *King in 1957 at the beginning of the *civil rights movement. Its members were mostly *African-American church leaders. They supported peaceful protests and organized the large 1963 march on Washington, DC. After King was murdered, Ralph Abernathy became the head of SCLC (1968–77). It has less influence and importance today.

ˌSouthern ˈComfort™ *n* [U, C] a sweet alcoholic drink which is especially popular in the southern US. It is produced by the Brown-Forman Corporation in *Louisville, *Kentucky.

ˌRobert **ˈSouthey** /ˈsaʊði, ˈsʌði/ (1774–1843) an English poet who also wrote histories and biographies. He was a friend of *Coleridge and *Wordsworth and was one of the *Lake Poets. He was made *Poet Laureate in 1813.

ˌSouth Glaˈmorgan /gləˈmɔːgən; *AmE* gləˈmɔːrgən/ a *county in South Wales. Its administrative centre is *Cardiff.

ˌSouth ˈKensington /ˈkenzɪŋtən/ (*also infml* **ˌSouth ˈKen** /ˈken/) a district in west London that contains several museums and foreign embassies (= buildings where people who represent foreign governments work). It is well known for its fashionable and expensive houses, shops and restaurants. There is a South Kensington station on the *London Underground.

ˌSouth Paˈcific /pəˈsɪfɪk/ a Broadway musical play (1949) and film (1958) by Richard *Rodgers and Oscar *Hammerstein. It was based on *Tales of the South Pacific* by James *Michener and is a love story about Nellie Forbush, a US Navy nurse working on a Pacific island during *World War II. The songs include *Some Enchanted Evening, There Is Nothing Like a Dame* and *I'm Gonna Wash That Man Right Outa My Hair.*

ˈSouthwark /ˈsʌðək; *AmE* ˈsʌðərk/ a *borough of South London, on the opposite side of the *Thames from the *City. Historically it was one of London's main centres for entertainment. It included Shakespeare's *Globe and many other theatres. Today it is a mainly *working-class area of houses and flats/apartments, with its own cathedral.

S

ˌSouth ˈYorkshire /ˈjɔːkʃə(r); *AmE* ˈjɔːrkʃər/ (*written abbr* **S Yorks**) the southern part of *Yorkshire, in northern England, where there are many industrial towns. It was made into a separate county in 1974. Its administrative centre is *Sheffield.

ˈsovereignty *n* [U] the condition of being an independent country with the power to govern itself. The British government has always had the authority to make and change laws, but as a member of the *European Union, Britain now has to respect some European laws that cannot be changed by the government. In the 1980s and 1990s some British people though that this was a serious loss of sovereignty. *Eurosceptics said that there would be more losses of sovereignty, and that Britain should leave the EU, but most people agreed with the idea of 'subsidiarity', i.e.

that most local decisions should be made by individual countries or regions, unless there is an important reason for deciding something at a European court.

the ˈ**space race** *n* [sing] the competition between the US and the former USSR to develop spacecraft and send them successfully into space. The USSR was the early leader in 1957 with the Sputnik satellite, but the Americans were ahead by 1969 when the *Apollo Project landed men on the moon. The space race was once thought to have military importance, but the US and Russia now work together, e.g. in developing future space stations. See also STRATEGIC DEFENSE INITIATIVE.

ˈ**space ˌshuttle** *n* a spacecraft developed by the US to take a crew and cargo into space and then return to the earth for future flights. Space shuttles are part of the US Space Transportation System (STS), and the flights began in 1981. The first four were **Columbia*, **Challenger*, *Discovery* and *Atlantis*. When *Challenger* exploded in 1986 killing all seven of its crew, all flights were stopped for more than two years. **Endeavor* replaced *Challenger* in 1992.

Space travel ⇨ article.

ˌSam ˈ**Spade** /ˈspeɪd/ a character created in 1930 by the US writer Dashiell *Hammett in his book *The *Maltese Falcon*. Spade is a tough but honest private detective. Hammett also wrote Sam Spade stories for *Black Mask* magazine. Compare MARLOWE.

spaˌghetti ˈjunction *n* a place where many roads join or pass over or under each other, so that from the air they look a little like spaghetti (= Italian food consisting of many long thin pieces that become soft when cooked). There are many spaghetti junctions in the US, but in Britain the expression is mainly used as the name for a major road link near Birmingham: *There are so many cables behind your computer it looks like Spaghetti Junction.*

spaˌghetti ˈwestern *n* any of the *western films made by Italian film companies in the 1960s and 1970s. They often had complicated stories and contained a lot of violence. The first were directed by Sergio Leone, including *A Fistful of Dollars* (1964). Several US actors, especially Clint *Eastwood, first became famous by appearing in spaghetti westerns.

Spam™ /spæm/ *n* [U] a US make of processed meat, sold in tins and usually eaten cold. It is made mainly from ham and was widely used to feed US soldiers during *World War II, when it also became popular in Britain. It is still popular in the US today but less so in Britain. Because it is a simple and cheap food, people often make jokes about it. It is made by the Hormel Foods Corporation of Austin, *Minnesota, and the city is sometimes called **Spamtown**.

the ˈ**Spanish-Aˈmerican ˈWar** a war fought between the US and Spain in 1898. The US had promised to recognize the right of Cubans to be independent from Spain. When in 1898 the US warship *Maine* exploded in Havana harbour and sank with 260 deaths, the US blamed Spain and both nations soon declared war. The US won easily, and the Treaty of Paris ended Spanish rule in Cuba, giving the US *Puerto Rico, *Guam and the Philippines. After this victory, the US came to be recognized by other countries as a world power. See also ROUGH RIDERS.

the ˌ**Spanish Arˈmada** ⇨ ARMADA.

the ˌ**Spanish ˈMain** /ˈmeɪn/ a former name for the *Caribbean Sea and the north-east coast of South America. In the 16th and 17th centuries many Spanish ships sailed through this area, carrying gold back to Spain. They were often attacked by pirates and there are many stories and films about the adventures that people had there in this period.

the ˈWar of the ˈ**Spanish Sucˈcession** a war (1701–14) between Britain, Austria, the Netherlands, Portugal and Denmark on one side, and France and Spain on the other side. It started when the king of Spain died leaving no children, and Philip, the grandson of the king of France, became the next king of Spain. The Austrians believed that an Austrian had the right to be the king of Spain, and the British supported them because they did not want France to become too strong. This aim was mainly achieved. At the end of the war, although Britain recognized Philip as the king of Spain, it received large areas of Canada from the French, and *Gibraltar and Minorca from the Spanish.

ˌMuriel ˈ**Spark** /ˈspɑːk; *AmE* ˈspɑːrk/ (1918–) a Scottish writer whose novels are well known for their intelligent humour. Her best-known work is *The Prime of Miss Jean Brodie* (1961). She has also written poetry and short stories. She was made a *dame(2) in 1993.

the **SPCK** /ˌes piː siː ˈkeɪ/ (*in full* the **Society for Promoting Christian Knowledge**) a British organization that was established in 1698 to provide religious education for children in Britain and for people in the *British Empire. Today it is mainly concerned with publishing the Bible and other religious books, and selling them in its own shops in Britain. The SPCK still sends people to some African and Asian countries to teach Christianity.

the ˈ**Speaker** *n* the person who is in charge of debates in the *House of Commons. The Speaker decides who speaks in a debate, calls for a vote at the end, and keeps order. He or she is elected by *MPs of all the political parties, and must treat all parties fairly during debates. When MPs address the Speaker during a debate, they say 'Mr Speaker' or 'Madam Speaker'.

the Speaker, Betty Boothroyd, in the Speaker's Chair

the ˌ**Speaker of the ˈHouse** *n* the person who is in charge of most of the activities of the *House of Representatives. He is responsible for keeping order in debates, for naming the members of committees, and for referring *bills to committees. The Speaker of the House is chosen by the party with the majority in the House and is one of their leaders. He is addressed as 'Mr Speaker'.

ˌ**Speakers' ˈCorner** the north-east corner of *Hyde Park(1) in London, England. Since the 19th century people have been allowed to make speeches to the public there about any subject they choose. At weekends there are usually several people standing on

Space travel

The space race

For years people dreamt of travel in **outer space** (= the region beyond the earth's atmosphere). **Science fiction** (= imaginary stories based on developments in science and technology) often had space travel as a theme, but many people said that it was impossible. Then in 1957 the USSR took the first big step in space travel by sending up *Sputnik*, the first **satellite**, a device that **orbits** (= goes around) the earth.

Sputnik was **launched** (= sent up) during the *Cold War, when the US and the USSR were competing for world power. Before *Sputnik* was launched, Americans believed that their country was much more advanced than the USSR. The US government immediately began spending a lot of money on research into space travel and this was the beginning of the ***space race**.

In 1958 the US government created the **National Aeronautics and Space Administration** (***NASA**) and launched its own satellite. The following year both the US and the USSR sent **probes** (= vehicles to find out about space) to the moon but both missed the moon and **went into orbit** around the sun. In the early 1960s the US launched several more satellites to help with telecommunications, navigation and predicting the weather.

In 1961 the USSR sent the first person into space, the **cosmonaut** Yuri Gagarin. In the same year, American **astronauts** Alan *Shepard and Virgil *Grissom took part in separate space flights, *Mercury 3* and *4*, and in 1962 John *Glenn became the first American to orbit the earth. In the 1960s and 1970s, America sent up a series of **spacecraft** under the *Gemini and *Apollo programs. In 1969 *Apollo 11* became the first vehicle to land on the moon with people on board, and Neil *Armstrong became the first person to walk on the moon.

During this period there was strong support for space exploration among the American people, and television programmes such as *I Dream of Jeanie* made space seem exciting. *Cape Canaveral in Florida, for a while renamed *Cape Kennedy, where the launches took place, became well known.

Science in space

Once people had reached the moon, there was a desire to find out more about space, and both the US and the USSR built **space stations** (= vehicles which remain in space), **Skylab* and *Salyut*, which allowed scientists to do long-term research.

From 1981 the US used **space shuttles**, vehicles that could return to earth and be used again, to launch satellites. Several **unmanned spacecraft** were sent out to other planets. In 1971 **Mariner 9* took photographs while in orbit round Mars, and *Pioneer 10* went past Jupiter. **Voyager 1* and *2* were launched in 1977 and *Voyager 2* reached Neptune in 1989 before passing out of the **solar system**, still sending back information.

The Cold War made the US and USSR rivals in space but over time, as the relationship between them improved, competition became less intense. More recently NASA has been required to produce results at lower cost. In 1997 **Pathfinder* reached Mars, and its small **rover** (= a vehicle that moves across the ground) **Sojourner* took photographs of the planet's landscape and of individual rocks. The *Pathfinder* **mission** cost much less than previous projects, and some people believe that the limited money available forced scientists to think harder about what they were doing.

Not all space research has been successful. In 1990 the US sent up the *Hubble Space Telescope but there were problems with its lenses and scientists had to try and repair it. In the mid 1990s problems with *Mir*, a Soviet space station, led to US and Russian scientists working on *Mir* together.

A growing problem is that, after 40 years of activity in space, there are many old satellites, space stations, and other objects in orbit around the earth, creating the risk of an accident every time a vehicle goes into space.

Space travel has cost lives. Perhaps the most famous disaster was that involving the space shuttle **Challenger*, which exploded in 1986 as it was being launched, killing seven people. One of them was a school teacher, Christa McAuliffe, who was part of a plan to allow ordinary people to travel in space. In the early days, all the astronauts were white and male. Sally *Ride became the first US woman in space in 1983, and in the same year Guion Bluford became the first African-American astronaut.

Benefits from the space programme

Satellites now enable people to speak easily by telephone, to watch television programmes from all over the world, and to get advance information about the weather. Space technology has also produced new fabrics and many small things that make life easier, such as *Velcro, strips of material that stick tightly to each other but open easily. Velcro was invented because astronauts needed something to fasten their clothing which would not be affected by extreme temperatures and which they could open with gloves on.

The space programme has given English many new expressions. *Astronauts* wear a *spacesuit* and may do a *space walk* outside their *spacecraft*. *Blast-off* or *lift-off* is when a spacecraft leaves the earth; *touchdown* is when it lands, or *splashdown* if it lands in the sea. *Mission Control* is the centre on earth that manages the space flight. Some words, like *space-age*, meaning 'very modern', are used outside the context of space travel.

Europe in space

European countries including Britain work together within the ***European Space Agency** (**ESA**) which in 1984 launched the world's largest satellite. ESA also launched the European Spacelab in 1983 and the Giotto probe which entered the tail of *Halley's comet in 1986, both of which used European-made Ariane rockets. ESA contributed towards the Hubble telescope, and British scientists provide some of the instruments and experiments that are carried on board US shuttle missions. An ESA space shuttle, *Eureca*, was first launched in 1992.

It was not until 1991 that the first Briton, Helen *Sharman, went into space, working on board *Mir* for one week. British-born Michael *Foale travelled on board a US space shuttle in 1992 and later worked on *Mir*.

Speakers' Corner

boxes, making speeches about politics, religion or other subjects. Sometimes members of the public argue with them.

the ˌ**speaking** ˈ**clock** *n* [sing] a telephone service in Britain in which a recorded voice gives the correct time to anyone who rings a special number.

the ˌ**Special** ˈ**Air** ˌ**Service** ⇨ SAS.

the ˈ**Special Branch** the department of the British police force that deals with political crimes. It used to be responsible for fighting terrorist groups such as the *IRA, but *MI5 took over this work in 1992. The Special Branch is now mostly involved in protecting government ministers and foreign politicians in Britain, and investigating people who break the *Official Secrets Act.

ˌ**special** ˈ**prosecutor** *n* (in the US) a special official who can be appointed by the US *Attorney General to investigate illegal activities by politicians and government officials. In 1973, Congress began to consider the *impeachment of President *Nixon after he ordered the Attorney General to dismiss the special prosecutor for *Watergate. In 1998 the special prosecutor Kenneth Starr published the results of his investigation into the relationship between President *Clinton and a member of the *White House staff, Monica Lewinsky, which led to the President's impeachment.

the ˌ**special re**ˈ**lationship** *n* [sing] ⇨ note at BRITAIN AND THE US.

The Spec*ˈ*tator **1** a British magazine, published each week and containing articles on politics, society and the arts which are usually written from a right-wing point of view. It was first published in 1828. **2** a non-political magazine written by Joseph *Addison and Richard *Steele between 1711 and 1714. It appeared every day, and each issue contained a single long essay.

S

ˌPhil ˈ**Spector** /ˈspektə(r)/ (1940–) a US pop record producer best known for creating the 'wall of sound' in the 1960s, in which songs were recorded with music played by many instruments. This idea influenced many other recording companies. Spector produced records for such groups as the Righteous Brothers, the Crystals and the Ronettes.

ˌStanley ˈ**Spencer** /ˈspensə(r)/ (1891–1959) an English artist. He is most famous for his unusual religious paintings, especially the series of pictures of Christ appearing at Cookham, the small town on the River *Thames west of London where he was born. His style has been described as 'primitive realism', because many of his paintings look like the work of an artist who has had no formal training and has tried to paint in a realistic style. He was made a *knight in 1958.

ˌStephen ˈ**Spender** /ˈspendə(r)/ (1909–95) an English poet and critic. He was a friend of W H *Auden and Louis *MacNeice, and many of his poems contain left-wing political and social comments, although his style can also be very personal. He was made a *knight in 1983.

ˌEdmund ˈ**Spenser** /ˈspensə(r)/ (*c.* 1552–99) an English poet. His first important work was *The Shepheardes Calendar* (1579), a group of twelve poems about the countryside, one for each month of the year. He is best known for his long poem *The *Faerie Queene*. He invented a new form of verse for this poem, which became known as the **Spenserian stanza** and was used by many later poets. Several important English poets were strongly influenced by Spenser, especially *Milton and *Keats.

the **Spey** /speɪ/ a river in the *Highlands of Scotland. It flows north-east through the *Grampian Mountains to the Moray Firth (a narrow area of water stretching from the *North Sea into north-east Scotland), and is famous for its salmon fishing.

the ˈ**Spice Girls** /ˈspaɪs/ an English pop group consisting of young women who sing and dance. The media often distinguish between them by using a different adjective for each, e.g. 'Sporty Spice' and 'Posh Spice'. The group's first five records, released in 1996 and 1997, were all No. 1 hits, including *Wannabe*, *Say You'll Be There* and *2 Become 1*. They often appear in British *tabloid newspapers and on television, sometimes talking about their philosophy of 'girl power', the idea that women should have a strong attitude about their identity, support each other and enjoy themselves. One of the five original Spice Girls, Geri Halliwell (known as 'Ginger Spice'), left the group in 1998.

the original Spice Girls

ˈ**Spider-Man** a US cartoon character in Marvel Comics, created in 1962 by Stan Lee and Steve Ditko. He is Peter Parker, a newspaper photographer who changes into Spider-Man to fight criminals. He has great strength and can climb buildings. He has also appeared in films and television cartoons.

ˌSteven ˈ**Spielberg** /ˈspiːlbɜːg; *AmE* ˈspiːlbɜːrg/ (1947–) a US film director and producer. Most of his films have been very successful financially. They include *Jaws* (1975), **ET*, the Indiana *Jones films, *The Color Purple* (1985), *Jurassic Park* (1993), **Schindler's List* and *Saving Private Ryan* (1998). In 1994 he established his own film company, *DreamWorks SKG, with two partners.

ˌMickey **Spil**ˈ**lane** /spɪˈleɪn/ (1918–) a US writer of crime stories who created the tough private detective Mike Hammer. When the stories first appeared in the late 1940s many people were shocked by the amount of sex and violence in them, but they have been very successful and many have been made into films. They include *I, the Jury* (1947), *My Gun Is Quick* (1950) and *Kiss Me Deadly* (1952).

ˌ**spinning ˈjenny** /ˈdʒeni/ *n* an early machine that could spin many threads of wool at the same time. It was invented by James Hargreaves in *Lancashire(1), England, in the 1760s. It caused a revolution in the wool industry because previously it had only been possible for a person to spin one thread at a time.

the ˌ***Spirit of St ˈLouis*** /snt ˈluːɪs/ the name of the small plane in which Charles *Lindbergh made his famous flight across the Atlantic in 1927. The name was also used for a 1957 *Hollywood film about the flight, in which James *Stewart played Lindbergh.

Charles Lindbergh standing beside the Spirit of St Louis

ˈ**spiritual** *n* a type of religious song traditionally sung by African Americans in the southern US. Spirituals began in the 18th century when American slaves combined African rhythms with Protestant European hymns. Famous spirituals include *Swing Low, Sweet Chariot*, *Steal Away* and *Nobody Knows the Trouble I've Seen*. Well-known singers of spirituals have included Paul *Robeson and Marian *Anderson. See also GOSPEL.

ˈ**Spitalfields** /ˈspɪtlfiːldz/ a district of east London, England, east of the *City. It used to be famous for its large fruit and vegetable market, which was moved to north-east London in 1991. Spitalfields still has Brick Lane, one of London's largest flea markets (= markets selling old clothes, books, furniture, etc., usually at low prices). It is also the centre of one of the largest *Bangladeshi communities in Britain.

ˈ**Spitfire** /ˈspɪtfaɪə(r)/ *n* a British fighter plane that became famous during *World War II. It was one of the fastest aircraft of its time, and could be moved easily and quickly into different positions in the air. Spitfires played an important role in the *Battle of Britain.

ˌ***Spitting ˈImage*** a British comedy television series (1984–96) that used large rubber models to make fun of famous people (such as politicians, film stars and even members of the royal family) by making them do and say ridiculous things.

Spitting Image: *the Queen and Prince Edward*

ˌMark ˈ**Spitz** /ˈspɪts/ (1950–) a US swimmer who won seven gold medals at the 1972 Olympic Games, the most ever won by one person on one such occasion. He had also won two gold medals at the 1968 games. During his career, Spitz set 35 world records.

ˌ**split ˈticket** *n* (in US elections) a vote in which a person votes for candidates from more than one political party. This happens, for example, when somebody chooses to vote for Congressmen from the party they usually support but votes for a popular candidate for US President from the other party. Compare STRAIGHT TICKET.

ˌBenjamin ˈ**Spock**[1] /ˈspɒk; *AmE* ˈspɑːk/ (*also* ˌ**Dr ˈSpock**) (1903–98) a US doctor whose book *The Common Sense Book of Baby and Child Care* (1946) has sold more copies than any book by an American and has had a great influence on parents all over the world. He advised them to use less discipline on children and to understand their needs. Although many people have welcomed his ideas, some think they have led to children being more badly behaved and hard to control. Dr Spock protested against the *Vietnam War and in 1972 was a candidate for US President for the People's Party.

ˌMr ˈ**Spock**[2] /ˈspɒk; *AmE* ˈspɑːk/ a character played by Leonard Nimoy in the US television series **Star Trek*. Spock is the First Officer of the *Starship Enterprise* spacecraft. He is from the planet Vulcan (though one of his parents was from Earth) and has large pointed ears. He thinks in a very logical way and does not show or understand normal human emotions.

Spode /spəʊd; *AmE* spoʊd/ *n* [U] pottery and porcelain (= hard, white, shiny material made by baking a type of fine clay) made at the Spode factory in *Stoke-on-Trent, England. The factory was established by Josiah Spode (1733–97) in 1770 and soon became famous for the quality of its products, which included *willow-pattern plates. The company combined with *Wedgwood in the 1960s but the name Spode is still used for its products.

the ˈ**spoils ˌsystem** /ˈspɔɪlz/ *n* [sing] (in US politics) the system in which the winner of an election gives government jobs to his or her party workers and supporters. The tradition was begun by President Andrew *Jackson and is followed by each new US president.

ˌWilliam ˈ**Spooner** /ˈspuːnə(r)/ (1844–1930) an English clergyman and teacher at *Oxford University. He was well known for his habit of accidentally changing round the first sounds of two or more words when he spoke, so that he might say 'the wrong liver' instead of 'the long river'. This type of phrase, which is often humorous, is called a **spoonerism**.

sport and fitness

The British are very fond of sport, but many people prefer to watch rather than take part. Many go to watch *football, *cricket, etc. at the ground, but many more sit at home and watch sport on television.

Most people today take relatively little general **exercise**. Over the last 30 or 40 years lifestyles have changed considerably and many people now travel even the shortest distances by car or bus. Lack of exercise combined with eating too many fatty and sugary foods has meant that many people are becoming too fat. Experts are particularly concerned that children spend a lot of their free time watching television or playing computer games instead of being physically active. In the 1980s and 1990s, however, there has been a growing interest in fitness among young adults and many belong to a **sports club** or do sport as their main *leisure activity.

In Britain most towns have an amateur football and cricket team, and people also have opportunities to play sports such as tennis and *golf. Older people may play *bowls. Some people go regularly to a **sports centre** or **leisure centre** where there are facilities for playing badminton and squash, and also a swimming pool. Some sports centres arrange classes in **aerobics**, **step** and **keep-fit**. Some people **work out** (= train hard) regularly at a local gym and do **weight training** and **circuit training**. A few people do judo or other **martial arts**. Others **go running** or **jogging** in their local area. For enthusiastic runners there are opportunities to take part in long-distance runs, such as the *London marathon. Other people keep themselves fit by walking or cycling. Many people now go abroad on a *skiing holiday each year and there are several dry slopes in Britain where they can practise.

Membership of a sports club or gym can be expensive and not everyone can afford the subscription. Local sports centres are generally cheaper. **Evening classes** are also cheap and offer a wide variety of fitness activities ranging from yoga to jazz dancing. Some companies now provide sports facilities for their employees or contribute to the cost of joining a gym.

Sports play an important part in American life. Professional *baseball and football games attract large crowds, and many people watch games on television. Although many parents complain about their children being **couch potatoes** (= people who spend a lot of time watching television), there are sports sessions at school for all ages. College students are usually also required to take physical education classes to complete their studies. But an official report published in 1996 said that more than 60% of adults in the US were not regularly physically active.

Many popular keep-fit activities began in the US. Charles *Atlas, Arnold *Schwarzenegger and others have inspired people to take up **body-building** (= strengthening and shaping the muscles). Many women joined the 'fitness craze' as a result of **video workouts** produced by stars such as Jane *Fonda and Cindy Crawford which they could watch and take part in at home. New fitness books are continually being published and these create fashions for new types of exercise, such as **wave aerobics**, which is done in a swimming pool, and **cardio kick-boxing**, a form of aerobics which involves punching and kicking a punchbag. There is even a 'dancing through pregnancy' programme. Many richer Americans employ their own **personal trainer**, either at home or at a **fitness centre**, to direct their exercise programme. Local *YMCAs offer programmes which include aerobics, gym, running, weights, treadmills and rowing machines, as well as steam rooms and swimming. But many people just walk or jog in the local park or play informal games of baseball or football.

The ˌ***Sporting*** ˈ***Life*** a British daily newspaper that consists mainly of articles and information about horse-racing and other sports that people bet on. It was first published in 1859.

ˈ**Sports** ˌ**Council** *n* each of four British government organizations that aim to encourage sport in England, Northern Ireland, Scotland and Wales. They advise the government on matters relating to sport, give money to sports organizations, local authorities and schools, and run Britain's National Sports Centres, where the highest levels of training and equipment are available to national sports teams.

ˈ**sports day** *n* (*BrE*) (*AmE* ˈ**field day**) one day each

a sack race at a children's sports day

year when most of the children at a school take part in outdoor sports competitions. In Britain, it usually takes place in the summer. There are no lessons for the day, and parents are invited to watch the sports and sometimes take part.

ˌ***Sports*** ˈ***Illustrated*** a popular US sports magazine published each week by Time Inc, part of *Time Warner. It first appeared in 1954, and is read mainly by men. The magazine also publishes the *Sports Illustrated Sports Almanac* every year.

ˌ**spotted** ˈ**dick** /ˈdɪk/ (*also* ˌ**spotted** ˈ**dog**) *n* [C, U] (*BrE*) a traditional British sweet dish. It consists of a pudding (= a dish made of flour and fat) in the shape of a roll, with fruit such as currants (= dried grapes) mixed into it.

ˌ**Spring Bank** ˈ**Holiday** *n* [C, U] the *bank holiday that takes place each year on the last Monday in May in England, Northern Ireland and Wales.

ˌDusty ˈ**Springfield** /ˌdʌsti ˈsprɪŋfiːld/ (1939–99) an English pop singer with a rich, strong voice whose style was much influenced by *soul music. She was especially successful in the 1960s when her many hit records included *You Don't Have to Say You Love Me* (1966) and *Son of a Preacher Man* (1969).

ˌBruce ˈ**Springsteen** /ˈsprɪŋstiːn/ (1949–) a US rock singer and writer of songs whose popular name is 'the Boss'. He is known for his powerful live performances. He formed the E Street Band in 1973, and their No. 1 albums have included *Born in the USA* (1984) and *Tunnel of Love* (1987). His song *Streets of Philadelphia* (1994) for the film *Philadelphia* won an *Oscar, a *Golden Globe Award and four *Emmy awards. By 1998, Springsteen had also won eight Grammys.

Spurs /spɜːz; *AmE* spɜːrz/ the popular name for *Tottenham Hotspur football club.

ˈ***Spycatcher*** /ˈspaɪkætʃə(r)/ a book (1987) by Peter Wright, a former member of *MI5. It describes his life as a spy and reveals many of the secrets of the way MI5 works. It was originally banned in Britain.

ˈ**Squanto** /ˈskwɒntəʊ; *AmE* ˈskwɑːntoʊ/ (*c.* 1585–1622) a *Native American who helped the Pilgrims to survive when they landed in America in 1621. He taught them to plant corn and to hunt and fish. He had been taken to England by sailors in 1605 and had learned to speak English.

ˈ**square dance** *n* (*esp AmE*) a dance in which four couples dance together. They usually start in a square, facing inwards. A 'caller' tells them what steps to do. Square dances are popular in all parts of the US, but are especially associated with *Appalachia and the western states.

the ˌ**Square** ˈ**Deal** the political programme of US President Theodore *Roosevelt. He wanted to give fair treatment to all Americans, and a main part of this was his *antitrust legislation. Compare FAIR DEAL, NEW DEAL.

the ˌ**Square** ˈ**Mile** (*BrE infml*) another name for the *City of London, which covers an area of roughly one square mile. The phrase is often used to refer to the City's financial institutions.

squash (*also fml* ˈ**squash** ˌ**rackets**) *n* [U] a sport for two players using rackets and a small hollow rubber ball, played in an indoor court with high walls. One player must hit the ball against the front wall, after which it can bounce against other walls and/or the floor before the other player hits it. It is a very fast game, which many people play as a way of keeping fit. It developed from the game of *rackets but is now played by many more people. In the US form of the game, the ball is harder and the regular court smaller than in Britain. There are also larger courts for games of 'doubles' (involving four players), which are more popular than in Britain.

ˌ**squashed** ˈ**fly** ˌ**biscuit** *n* (*BrE humor*) ⇨ GARIBALDI.

ˌ**Sri** ˈ**Lanka** /ˌʃri ˈlæŋkə/ an island off the southern tip of *India Its capital city is Colombo and its official language is Sinhalese. When it was part of the *British Empire (1802–1948) it was called **Ceylon**. It is a member of the *Commonwealth and one of the world's most important tea producers. In Britain, many people still refer to **Ceylon tea**. ▶ **Sri Lankan** *adj, n*.

SSP /ˌes es ˈpiː/ ⇨ STATUTORY SICK PAY.

SSSI /ˌes es es ˈaɪ/ ⇨ SITE OF SPECIAL SCIENTIFIC INTEREST.

St ⇨ SAINT.

St ˌ**Abb's** ˈ**Head** /ˌæbz/ a high cliff in south-east Scotland which is well known for the large numbers of sea birds that gather and breed there. It is a National Nature Reserve.

ˈ**Staffa** /ˈstæfə/ an island in the *Hebrides, Scotland, close to *Mull. Nobody lives there but many people visit the island to see *Fingal's Cave and the rocks there, which are well known for their unusual shapes. See also GIANT'S CAUSEWAY.

ˈ**Stafford** /ˈstæfəd; *AmE* ˈstæfərd/ a town in western central England. It is the administrative centre of *Staffordshire and a traditional centre of the shoe-making industry.

ˈ**Staffordshire** /ˈstæfədʃə(r); *AmE* ˈstæfərdʃər/ (*abbr* **Staffs**) a county in western central England. It consists mainly of agricultural land and also contains the *Potteries.

ˌ**Staffordshire bull** ˈ**terrier** /ˌstæfədʃə; *AmE* ˌstæfərdʃər/ *n* a small, strong breed of dog. It was originally bred in *Staffordshire for dog fights (= events in which two dogs fight and people bet on which one will win) in the early 19th century. In the 1980s it was fashionable in Britain to have these dogs as pets, particularly among people in cities who wanted to appear strong or dangerous. In the 1990s more people bought them after a new law made it difficult to own the larger and more violent US *pit bull terriers.

ˌ**Staffordshire** ˈ**pottery** /ˌstæfədʃə; *AmE* ˌstæfərdʃər/ *n* [U] pottery made in *Staffordshire, the traditional centre of the pottery industry in England. The most famous makes of English pottery, including *Minton, *Spode and *Wedgwood, are all produced in or near *Stoke-on-Trent in Staffordshire.

ˈ**stagecoach** (*also* **stage**) *n* (in former times) a public vehicle pulled by two to six horses along a regular route. Each place where it stopped was called a *stage*. Stagecoaches usually carried up to eight passengers and sometimes also mail, etc. The driver sat outside. In the US West, stagecoaches were sometimes attacked by *Native Americans or robbers. For this reason, a man with a gun often sat next to the driver. This was called 'riding shotgun', and Americans still sometimes call the front passenger's seat in a car the 'shotgun seat'. Compare CONESTOGA WAGON, PRAIRIE SCHOONER.

St ˈ**Albans** /ˈɔːlbənz/ a town in *Hertfordshire, southern England, built near the old Roman town of Verulamium. Its cathedral (11th–14th centuries) is in honour of St Alban, a Roman soldier who was the first person in Britain to be killed for his Christian beliefs. Two battles (1455 and 1461) were fought at St Albans during the *Wars of the Roses.

Sylˌvester **Stalˈlone** /sɪlˌvestə stəˈləʊn; *AmE* sɪlˌvestər stəˈloʊn/ (1946–) a US actor who also writes and directs films. His popular name is 'Sly'. He is best known for playing the characters *Rocky and *Rambo. His other films include *Demolition Man* (1993), *Judge Dredd* (1995), *Daylight* (1996) and *Cop Land* (1998). Stallone also paints and is one of the owners of the restaurant group *Planet Hollywood.

ˌ**Stamford** ˈ**Bridge** /ˌstæmfəd; *AmE* ˌstæmfərd/ **1** a village in north-east England. A famous battle took place there in 1066, when the forces of King *Harold II defeated the invading army of King Harald Hardraade of Norway, three weeks before the Battle of *Hastings. **2** a well-known football stadium in *Fulham(1), west London. It is the home ground of *Chelsea football club.

the ˈ**Stamp Act** a British *Act of Parliament in 1765. It stated that all publications and legal documents in British colonies (= parts of the empire) in America must have official stamps, sold by the British government. Many people in America thought that this was an unfair tax. They refused to use the stamps and prevented British ships from entering or leaving their ports. The Stamp Act was removed in 1766 but the tax, and the people's protests against it, are among the important events that led to the *American Revolution.

ˈ**stamp** ˌ**duty** *n* [U] a tax that must be paid on some legal documents in Britain. The most common type of stamp duty is paid when people buy or sell houses or flats/apartments. In the 1990s it is one per cent of the price of any property that costs more than £60 000: *After we'd paid the solicitors' fees and the stamp duty we had no money left for furniture.*

the ˈ***Standard*** ⇨ *EVENING STANDARD*.

ˌ**Standard Asˈsessment Task** (*abbr* **SAT**) (*also* **Standard Assessment Test**, **Standard Task**, **Standard Test**) *n* a test taken by British schoolchildren to check their progress in the subjects of the *National Curriculum. ⇨ note at EDUCATION IN BRITAIN. Compare SCHOLASTIC APTITUDE TEST.

ˌ**Standard** ˈ**Oil** a large US oil company established in 1870 by John D *Rockefeller. In 1911 the US *Supreme Court decided it restricted trade and divided it into 34 individual companies. Rockefeller's original company became Standard Oil (Ohio). It was bought by *British Petroleum in 1987 and named BP America. The Standard Oil Company (Indiana) became Amoco in 1985. The Amoco Building, opened in 1973 in *Chicago as the Standard Oil Building, is one of the tallest in the world. Compare EXXON.

standards of living

The British enjoy the high standard of living of an industrialized western country. However, people living in Britain are less well off than people in most other countries in the *European Union and living standards have not risen as fast as, for instance, in France and Germany Most British people tend not to

S

judge **quality of life** by money alone, and would point out benefits such as a stable political situation, freedom of speech and choice, and relatively little official interference in their lives.

Disposable income (= the amount of money people have to spend after paying taxes) is commonly used to measure the standard of living. This has risen steadily since the 1960s. People with low wages or who are unemployed, and people who have retired, have less income and a lower standard of living. Between 1970 and 1994 disposable income rose by nearly 50% but the gap between rich and poor grew wider. People from ethnic minority groups are among the poorer sections of society. Standards of living also vary from region to region. The wealthiest region is the south-east. The poorest areas include the north-east and parts of Wales, where many traditional industries such as coal mining and shipbuilding have closed down.

The **cost of living** in Britain is relatively high, due partly to **inflation** (= a general increase in prices and reduction in the value of money) and high interest rates. Britain also has high indirect *taxes. The **inflation rate** is measured by the **retail price index** which monitors changes in the price of a 'shopping basket' of goods bought by a typical family. Since 1992 the government has aimed to keep inflation below 4%.

Household expenditure (= the normal living expenses of a family) increased by over 70% between 1970 and 1995. During this time the amount spent on food fell by a third but the amount spent on education, entertainment and leisure activities rose by over 60%. Since 1971 there has also been an increase in the ownership of **consumer durables**, e.g. CD players, microwaves and home computers. Household expenditure, like disposable income, was highest in the south-east of Britain. People's standard of living is also linked to government expenditure. The amount spent by the government on goods, services, social security benefits, etc. has fallen for several years.

In the 1920s people in the US began to believe in the ***American dream**, the idea that anyone who worked hard could have material goods as a reward. Having such goods proves that a person is hard-working, so many people try to have everything their neighbours have, a practice called 'keeping up with the Joneses'. As a result, America is often said to be a **consumer society**. The material standard of living is very high and the cost of living relatively low.

S

Since the early 1980s inflation, as shown by the **consumer price indexes**, similar to Britain's retail price index, has generally remained under 5% and is now about 3%. Many Americans have large **discretionary incomes** (= money which people do not need for food and clothing and can spend as they choose) and can therefore buy many consumer goods. Almost all American households have a refrigerator, a colour television, a video cassette recorder and at least one telephone and car. Most have two or more cars, air conditioning, dishwashers and microwaves. But many people achieve a high standard of living by spending more time at work. Since the 1970s, free time has fallen by 40%, to an average of 17 hours per week. People often say that they are always in a hurry and under pressure.

As in Britain, there is a large and increasing gap between rich and poor. Although many people eat very well and weigh too much, about 13% of Americans say they sometimes do not have enough money for food. About 14% live below the **poverty line**. Some ethnic groups and areas suffer more than others. The average income for a family of four is $49 687, but *Connecticut in the north-east has an average of $62 157 while *Mississippi in the poorer South has an average of only $37 328. A higher proportion of African Americans and Hispanics live below the poverty line. Women earn much less than men, so women living alone, or families in which a woman is the only person with a job, are also more likely to be poor.

ˈ**standing stone** *n* a large stone placed in an upright position during the *Stone Age or the *Bronze Age. There are many of these stones in Britain, often arranged in circles as at *Stonehenge and *Avebury. Nobody knows exactly why they were put there, though many people think it was for religious reasons, or to study the stars and planets.

St ˈAndrews /ˈændruːz/ a town in *Fife, Scotland. It is named after St *Andrew, whose bones are said to have been brought here in the 4th century, and it was an early centre of the Christian Church. Its university, established in 1412, is the oldest in Scotland. The town is also famous for the *Royal and Ancient golf club, which is recognized as an international authority on the rules of golf.

St ˌAndrew's ˈCross /ˌændruːz/ the national flag of Scotland, consisting of an X-shaped white cross on a blue background. The cross also forms part of the British *Union Jack flag. St *Andrew is Scotland's national saint. Compare ST GEORGE'S CROSS.

St ˈAndrew's Day /ˈændruːz/ 30 November, the day celebrated as the national day of Scotland (although not a public holiday). St *Andrew is Scotland's national saint.

ˌ**Stanford-Biˈnet test** /ˌstænfəd bɪˈneɪ; *AmE* ˌstænfərd/ *n* a US test used to measure intelligence, especially in children. It was developed at *Stanford University in 1916.

ˌ**Stanford Uniˈversity** /ˌstænfəd; *AmE* ˌstænfərd/ a major private university in Stanford, *California, near Palo Alto. It was established in 1885 by Leland Stanford and his wife. In 1998 it had about 14 000 students.

ˈHenry ˈMorton ˈ**Stanley** /ˈmɔːtn ˈstænli; *AmE* ˈmɔːrtn/ (1841–1904) a Welsh journalist and explorer. He went to live in the US in 1859, and worked as a journalist for the *New York Herald*. In 1869 he was sent by his newspaper to find the explorer David *Livingstone, who was thought to have become lost in Africa. Stanley found him at Ujiji in 1871, and is said to have greeted him with the words 'Dr Livingstone, I presume?' Stanley continued to explore Africa until the early 1890s, and returned to live in Britain in 1892. He became a *Member of Parliament (1895–1900) and was made a *knight in 1899.

the ˌ**Stanley ˈCup** /ˌstænli/ a competition to decide the best team in the National Hockey League in America, first held in 1893. It consists of a series of games between the winners of the Eastern Conference and the winners of the Western Conference. The first of the two teams to win four games in the series becomes the Stanley Cup Champion.

ˌ**Stanley ˈGibbons** /ˈɡɪbənz/ a large British company that sells stamps to people who collect them. It has the world's largest stamp shop in the *Strand, London, and organizes auctions of stamps. It also publishes well-known stamp catalogues.

ˌ**Stanley ˈKaplan** /ˈkæplən/ a US company that prepares students for examinations which they need to pass in order to enter American colleges or universities. These include the *SAT and *GRE. In 1997 there were more than 1 200 Stanley Kaplan Educational Centers in the US and many other countries, including Russia and China. Kaplan, a teacher from *Brooklyn, began the first one in the 1930s. The centres are now owned by the Washington Post Company, which also publishes Stanley Kaplan books.

ˌ**Stansted ˈAirport** /ˌstænsted/ (*also* ˈ**Stansted**) an airport in *Essex, north-east of London. It was a very small airport until the 1990s, when it became London's third airport. An impressive modern airport building, designed by Norman *Foster, was completed in 1991, and in 1997 *British Airways announced plans to use Stansted for many of its European flights.

ˌBarbara ˈ**Stanwyck** /ˈstænwɪk/ (1907–90) a US film actor known for playing strong characters. Her films include *Double Indemnity* (1944), *Sorry, Wrong Number* (1948) and *Executive Suite* (1954). She was also a star of the television *western series *The Big Valley* (1965–9). Stanwyck received a special *Oscar in 1982.

the ***Star*** ⇨ DAILY STAR. ⇨ article at NEWSPAPERS.

ˈ**Starbucks**™ /ˈstɑːbʌks; *AmE* ˈstɑːrbʌks/ a popular US make of coffee sold by the Starbucks Coffee Company in its restaurants and shops around North America, especially in the Pacific states. The company's main office is in *Seattle.

the ˌ**Star ˈChamber** (*also* the **Court of Star Chamber**) a British court of law that was first used in the 14th century. It consisted of the members of the *Privy Council, and had no jury. It was often used in the *Tudor(1) and *Stuart periods to deal with cases affecting the state or the *royal family. It already had a reputation for treating people unfairly when *Charles I used it to punish people who refused to do what he wanted. It was closed down by the *Long Parliament in 1641. The phrase is sometimes used to refer to any group of people that makes unfair decisions: *This is not a star chamber, you will be given a fair hearing.*

A ˌ***Star is*** ˈ***Born*** the title of three US films about an old actor who helps a young woman with her career, marries her and then kills himself. The best-known version (1954) was a *musical with Judy *Garland and James *Mason. It was made again in 1976 with Barbra *Streisand and Kris Kristofferson, and its song *Evergreen* won an *Oscar. The first version of the film was made in 1932.

ˌFreya ˈ**Stark** /ˌfreɪə ˈstɑːk; *AmE* ˈstɑːrk/ (1893–1993) an English traveller and writer. Her best-known books were about her travels in the Middle East, including *The Valley of the Assassins* (1934) and *The Southern Gates of Arabia* (1936). She was made a *dame(2) in 1972.

ˌBelle ˈ**Starr** /ˌbel ˈstɑː(r)/ (*c.* 1848–89) a US outlaw (= criminal) in the *Wild West. She was a friend of Jesse and Frank *James and let outlaws stay at her home in *Oklahoma. She was sent to prison for nine months in 1883 for stealing horses. Starr died after being shot by an unknown person.

the ˌ**Stars and ˈBars** the flag of the *Confederate States during the *Civil War.

the ˌ**Stars and ˈStripes** (*also* **Old Glory**, the **Star-Spangled Banner**) the US flag.

ˌ***Starship ˈEnterprise*** /ˌstɑːʃɪp; *AmE* ˌstɑːrʃɪp/ ⇨ STAR TREK.

The ˌ***Star-Spangled*** ˈ***Banner*** /spæŋgld/ the US *national anthem. It was written in 1814 by Francis Scott *Key, an American lawyer, as he watched British ships trying without success to capture Fort McHenry in *Maryland during the *War of 1812. He wrote the words and added the music of an old British song. The US Congress officially made it the country's national anthem in 1931. It ends:

And the star-spangled banner in triumph shall wave
O'er the land of the free and the home of the brave!

START /stɑːt; *AmE* stɑːrt/ ⇨ STRATEGIC ARMS REDUCTION TALKS.

ˈ***Star Trek*** a US television series first shown on *NBC in the 1960s which later became a cult programme (= very fashionable with a particular group). It is about the spacecraft **Starship Enterprise* whose crew includes Captain James *Kirk, Mr *Spock, 'Bones' McCoy and 'Scotty' Scott. They made six *Star Trek* films between 1979 to 1991. A later television series with different actors, *Star Trek: the Next Generation*, began in 1988, and there have been three further films. See also TREKKIE.

Captain Kirk (William Shatner), Mr Spock (Leonard Nimoy) and 'Bones' McCoy (DeForest Kelley) in Star Trek

ˌ***Start the*** ˈ***Week*** a British radio programme, broadcast on *BBC *Radio 4 every Monday morning. It consists of a discussion between the presenter, Jeremy *Paxman, and his guests, who are usually well-known politicians, entertainers or experts on a particular subject in the news.

ˈ***Star Wars*** a very successful US film (1977), directed by George Lucas, about a war in space. The story is about Luke Skywalker and Han Solo who fight the evil *Darth Vader to rescue Princess Leia. The same characters appeared in two further films, *The Empire Strikes Back* (1980) and *Return of the Jedi* (1983). The term 'Star Wars' was later used by President Ronald *Reagan for his *Strategic Defense Initiative, and he also called the USSR 'the evil empire', a phrase taken from the film.

State and local government in the US ⇨ article.

the ˈ**State Deˌpartment** (*also* the **Department of State**) the US government department responsible for international affairs. It is directed by the *Secretary of State. It advises the president on foreign policy and makes agreements and treaties (= formal agreements) with other countries.

the ˈ**State ˈEarnings-ReˈIated ˈPension Scheme** /ˈɜːnɪŋz rɪˈleɪtɪd; *AmE* ˈɜːrnɪŋz/ ⇨ SERPS.

stately homes

In Britain there are many large stately homes that belong or used to belong to *upper-class aristocratic families. The houses are called *stately homes* from the opening lines of a poem by Felicia Hemans (1793–1835):

The stately homes of England
How beautiful they stand!
Amidst their tall ancestral trees,
O'er all the pleasant land.

They are sometimes also called **country houses** because most of them are in the countryside. They may be approached through large iron gates down a long drive. Many have formal gardens and are surrounded by a large private **park**, often with a lake.

Stately homes range from small **manor houses** to **palaces**. Manor houses date from the 14th century and are often square stone buildings with a central **courtyard**, and are entered by crossing a moat which was originally a means of defence. Some larger houses were built in the 16th century, including *Hampton Court in south-west London, *Burghley House near Peterborough and Hardwick Hall near Derby.

Many stately homes date from the 18th century, and are associated with famous architects. *Blenheim Palace near Oxford was designed in the *baroque style by *Vanbrugh and *Hawksmoor. Holkham

State and local government in the US

State government

State government is similar in its organization to *federal, or national, government. In most states, a **state constitution** explains the powers of the three branches of state government. These are the **executive**, the **legislative** and the **judicial**, as in the federal government. In a state, the executive branch is headed by a **governor**, and the person beneath him or her is the **lieutenant governor**. State laws are made by a **legislature**, which usually has two houses, a **Senate** and a **House of Representatives**, though the names of the houses may be different in some states. The judicial branch usually consists of a state supreme court and several lower courts.

US states have traditionally had many powers and considerable direct influence on the lives of their citizens. State governments organize their own system of courts and set local income tax and sales tax. They decide at what age residents can, for example, drink alcohol or get married, and what students must study in school. Even actions that are illegal in all or most states are the subject of laws at the state rather than the federal level. For example, murder is illegal everywhere in the US but every state has its own law against murder, and the punishment for this crime is different in every state.

County government

States are divided into ***counties**. Most counties include several towns, although a large city might occupy a whole county, or even lie across the border between two or more counties. The county government is located in a town or city called the **county seat**. The structure of county government varies from state to state, but most have a **Board of Commissioners**, sometimes called a **Board of Supervisors**. The Board and other county officials are usually elected.

Services provided by a county government depend on whether the county is urban, consisting mainly of a large city or several towns, or rural, consisting of a few small towns and areas of country. In urban areas, city and county governments may work together to provide services for the area. In rural counties, the county government may provide some services, e.g. schools, that would in an urban county be the responsibility of the city. County governments are responsible for repairing country roads.

Counties usually have a **sheriff's department**, a kind of police department. Its officers are called **sheriff's deputies**. People who are accused of a crime are **prosecuted** in county courts by the **district attorney**.

Towns and cities

America's cities, towns, villages and other **municipalities** vary greatly. They range from small towns of a few hundred people to cities of millions. For that reason there is no single model of local government; every municipal area decides for itself the form its government should have. Most towns and cities have an elected **mayor** as their head. A **city council** is made up of members elected from different areas of the city and makes **ordinances** (= local laws).

A municipal government usually has its own police force and courts, runs local schools, takes care of the roads, and may also provide services like public transport, water and electricity. There is often a separate elected body called the **school board**, which controls the way schools are run.

As there are so many offices in local government it is fairly easy to become an elected official at this level. Although many ambitious politicians see local office as the first step towards a more important position, many ordinary people get involved in local politics because they want to contribute to their community. Only a few places now maintain the custom of a **town meeting**, a chance for everyone in the town to meet once a year to talk about matters of concern to the community. But most city council and school board meetings are open to the public and the meetings are often well attended.

Since laws are made at several different levels of government they vary greatly across the country. A person who moves to a new state, or even to a new town in the same state, will have a different amount of income tax taken out of his or her pay. In some towns it is illegal to sell alcohol, and so there may be a restaurant on one side of the road that serves wine and another across the street, across the **city limits**, that is not allowed to do so. People who like to gamble take trips to *Nevada or *New Jersey because gambling is legal there but illegal in many other states. Although these differences can be confusing they rarely cause serious difficulty. Americans place great value on the fact that they can decide the rules they live by.

S

Hall in Norfolk, designed only a few years later by William *Kent, is in the *Palladian style. Kedleston Hall near Derby, the home of the *Curzon family, was mainly the work of Robert *Adam. The large estates attached to stately homes attracted *landscape gardeners such as 'Capability' *Brown, who laid out the gardens at Burghley, Blenheim and *Chatsworth.

Stately homes are very expensive to look after and, in order to get enough money to do this, some owners open their houses to the public. They charge visitors an **admission fee**. Many stately homes have been given by their owners to the *National Trust, an organization which raises the money to look after them from gifts, membership fees and admission charges. In many cases, the former owners continue to live in part of the house. This arrangement means that the house is well cared for, and the family does not have to pay *inheritance tax when the owner dies.

Visitors go to stately homes to admire their architecture, and to walk round the gardens. They also go

visiting a stately home

to see valuable furniture, paintings, tapestries and china that have been collected over a long period. Sometimes, documents about the family or about historical events are also displayed. There is generally a café and a shop selling souvenirs. During the summer concerts or plays may be performed in the house or gardens. Some owners have added other attractions: at *Longleat House, for example, there is a safari park.

ˌStaten ˈIsland /ˈstætn/ an island which is one of the *boroughs of New York City. Its former name was Richmond. It is connected to *Brooklyn by the Verrazano-Narrows Bridge. The **Staten Island Ferry** goes to *Battery Park in *Manhattan(1) and provides good views of the city.

President Clinton giving the State of the Union Address to Congress

the **ˈState of the ˈUnion Adˈdress** a speech given each year by the US President to Congress. He is required by the *American Constitution to give 'information on the State of the Union', and he also talks about his government's successes, plans and policies. The speech is shown on national television.

the **ˈState ˈOpening of ˈParliament** the official opening of each session (= series of meetings) of the British *Parliament. The ceremony takes place each year in October or November, and after a change of government. The queen or king travels in a special coach to the *Houses of Parliament(2), and makes the *Queen's Speech (or King's Speech) to members of both Houses in the *House of Lords.

the State Opening of Parliament

ˈstate school (in Britain) a school that offers free education and receives money from a *Local Education Authority or directly from the government. Most schools in Britain are state schools. Some church schools also receive money from the government and offer free education. ⇨ note at PUBLIC SCHOOLS. ⇨ articles at EDUCATION IN BRITAIN, SCHOOLS IN BRITAIN.

ˌstates' ˈrights *n* [pl] (in the US) the rights held by individual states under the 10th Amendment to the *American Constitution. These include the right to have their own criminal laws, laws regarding commerce and taxes, and laws on education, health and social welfare, and also the right to have their own police force. The principle of states' rights is supported by those who think that the central government should not interfere too much in state affairs. It has been supported especially by the states in the *South, five of which voted for the States' Rights Party in the 1948 election for President. There has been much argument in US history over the division of responsibility between state and national governments. In recent years the national government has given more rights to the states.

ˌstate ˈtrooper /ˈtruːpə(r)/ *n* (*AmE*) a US state police officer, especially a member of the highway patrol (= police officers who travel along motorways/freeways to stop dangerous drivers): *He was stopped for speeding by a Mississippi state trooper.*

ˌstate uniˈversity *n* (in the US) a public university run by an individual state and supported by state taxes. Every state has a main university, usually with the state's name, such as the University of Alabama or the University of Colorado. Most states also have other state universities, and all have several state colleges.

the **ˈState Uniˈversity of New ˈYork** /njuː ˈjɔːk; *AmE* ˈjɔːrk/ (*abbr* **SUNY**) the large *state university system of New York State in the US. It is in the six cities of Albany, Binghamton, Buffalo, New Paltz, Oswego and Stony Brook. In 1998 they had a total of about 83 000 students. There are also SUNY colleges in 11 cities.

the **ˈStationery ˌOffice** a private British organization that publishes and prints official government documents and books. It also has bookshops in London and some other cities. See also HER MAJESTY'S STATIONERY OFFICE.

the **ˌStatue of ˈLiberty** the famous US statue on Liberty Island in New York harbour. It is a woman holding the torch (= burning light) of liberty (= freedom), and its official name is the 'Statue of Liberty Enlightening the World'. It has become a symbol of freedom and was the first American sight seen by many people who went to the US for a better life. It was designed by Frederic Auguste Bartoldie and given to the US people by France in 1884. The poem

The Statue of Liberty with Ellis Island behind

by Emma Lazarus on the base of the statue includes the lines: 'Give me your tired, your poor, Your huddled masses yearning to breathe free.' The statue was made a *World Heritage Site in 1984.

ˌ**statutory** ˈ**sick pay** *n* [U] (*abbr* **SSP**) (in Britain) money that employers must pay their employees when they cannot work because of illness. Employers must pay this, by law, for up to 28 weeks. If the employee is still ill after this time, he or she then receives money from the government, called *incapacity benefit.*

St Barˌ**tholomew's** ˈ**Hospital** /bɑːˌθɒləmjuːz; *AmE* bɑːrˌθɑːləmjuːz/ ⇨ BART'S.

St ˌ**Clement** ˈ**Danes** /ˌclemənt ˈdeɪnz/ a church in central London, England, designed by Christopher *Wren in 1682 at a place where a group of Danes are thought to have settled in the 9th century. It was partly destroyed by bombs in *World War II and was built again as a special church of the *Royal Air Force. It is probably the church mentioned in the children's song **Oranges and Lemons*, although there is another church called St Clement's in Eastcheap, London.

St ˈ**David's** /ˈdeɪvɪdz/ a very small town on the west coast of Wales. It is known as the home of St *David, and its 12th-century cathedral is the largest in Wales.

St David's

St ˈ**David's Day** /ˈdeɪvɪdz/ 1 March, the day celebrated as the national day of Wales (although not a public holiday). St *David is the national saint of Wales. Many Welsh people wear a *daffodil (= a yellow spring flower) on St David's Day.

St ˈ**Dunstan's** /ˈdʌnstənz/ a charity providing training and accommodation for people who have become blind while serving in the British or Commonwealth armed forces. It was started in 1915 by the newspaper owner Arthur Pearson (1866–1921), who was blind himself.

ˌ**steak and kidney** ˈ**pie** *n* [U, C] a traditional British dish made with pieces of beef and kidneys (= organs that remove waste from the body) baked in pastry. It is regarded as a typical British dish and is often served in pubs.

ˌ**steak and kidney** ˈ**pudding** *n* [U, C] a traditional British dish made with pieces of beef and kidneys (= organs that remove waste from the body) covered in suet (= a mixture of flour and fat) and cooked by steaming.

ˌDavid ˈ**Steel** /ˈstiːl/ (1938–) a Scottish politician and the last leader of the *Liberal Party. He became an *MP in 1965, and was made leader of the party in 1976. During his time as leader, the Liberals began to work closely with the *SDP, and he was partly responsible for the two parties combining to form the *Liberal Democratic Party in 1988. He was made a *life peer in 1997.

The states of the United States
(with postal abbreviations)

Alabama	AL	Montana	MT
Alaska	AK	Nebraska	NE
Arizona	AZ	Nevada	NV
Arkansas	AR	New Hampshire	NH
California	CA	New Jersey	NJ
Colorado	CO	New Mexico	NM
Connecticut	CT	New York	NY
Delaware	DE	North Carolina	NC
Florida	FL	North Dakota	ND
Georgia	GA	Ohio	OH
Hawaii	HI	Oklahoma	OK
Idaho	ID	Oregon	OR
Illinois	IL	Pennsylvania	PA
Indiana	IN	Rhode Island	RI
Iowa	IA	South Carolina	SC
Kansas	KS	South Dakota	SD
Kentucky	KY	Tennessee	TN
Louisiana	LA	Texas	TX
Maine	ME	Utah	UT
Maryland	MD	Vermont	VT
Massachusetts	MA	Virginia	VA
Michigan	MI	Washington	WA
Minnesota	MN	West Virginia	WV
Mississippi	MS	Wisconsin	WI
Missouri	MO	Wyoming	WY

ˌRichard ˈ**Steele**[1] /ˈstiːl/ (1672–1729) an Irish writer of plays and essays. He moved to London as a young man, and wrote several comedy plays. They contained more social and moral comments than the popular *Restoration comedies, and were not very successful. He is best remembered for starting two magazines, *The *Tatler*(2) and *The *Spectator*(2), for which he wrote essays about literature and moral questions. See also ADDISON.

ˌTommy ˈ**Steele**[2] /ˈstiːl/ (1936–) an English actor and singer, known for his lively and cheerful personality. He began his career as a pop star in the late 1950s and later appeared in many *West End musical shows (including *Half a Sixpence*) as well as films and television programmes.

ˌRod ˈ**Steiger** /ˈstaɪɡə(r)/ (1925–) a US actor who often plays tough characters. His films include *The Pawnbroker* (1965), *Doctor Zhivago* (1965), *In the Heat of the Night* (1967), for which he won an *Oscar, *Waterloo* (1970) in which he played Napoleon, *The Amityville Horror* (1979) and *Mars Attacks!* (1996).

ˌGertrude ˈ**Stein** /ˈstaɪn/ (1874–1946) a US writer who lived mainly in Paris after 1903. Her home there became a centre for writers, including Ernest *Hemingway and Ford Madox *Ford, and artists such as Picasso and Matisse. She wrote in an unusual style, often repeating words and using no punctuation. Her best-known work is *The Autobiography of Alice B Toklas* (1933), which is really an account of her own life. She also wrote poetry, including the famous line: 'A rose is a rose is a rose.'

ˌJohn ˈ**Steinbeck** /ˈstaɪnbek/ (1902–68) a US author who received the 1962 *Nobel Prize for literature. He often wrote about poor farmers in California. His best-known books include *Of Mice and Men* (1937), *The *Grapes of Wrath*, *Cannery Row* (1945) and **East of Eden*. Many of his books were made into films.

ˌGloria ˈ**Steinem** /ˈstaɪnəm/ (1934–) a US journalist

and author who has been a leading figure in the campaign for women's rights since the 1960s. She helped to establish the Women's Action Alliance (1971), the National Women's Political Caucus (1971) and *Ms* magazine (1972), which she edited until 1987. Her own articles were collected in *Outrageous Acts and Everyday Rebellions* (1983).

Stephen (*c.* 1097–1154) the king of England from 1135 to 1154. He was the grandson of *William the Conqueror and became king even though he had agreed that his cousin *Matilda had the right to the throne. He spent much of his period as king resisting her attempts to become queen, and finally agreed that her son *Henry II would become king when he died.

ˌGeorge ˈ**Stephenson**[1] /ˈstiːvnsn/ (1781–1848) an English engineer. He designed some of the first steam trains and railways in Britain, including the engines for the first passenger trains for the *Stockton and Darlington Railway in 1825, and the *Liverpool and Manchester Railway in 1826.

ˌRobert ˈ**Stephenson**[2] /ˈstiːvnsn/ (1803–59) an English engineer, the son of George *Stephenson. He helped his father on the *Liverpool and Manchester Railway, for which he designed and built **Rocket*, before becoming the engineer on the London and Birmingham Railway. He also designed many important bridges and was a *Conservative *Member of Parliament for the last 12 years of his life.

ˈ***Steptoe and Son*** /ˈsteptəʊ; *AmE* ˈsteptoʊ/ a *BBC comedy television series, broadcast between 1964 and 1973. It is about a father and son who are rag-and-bone men (= people who collect old clothes, furniture, etc. to sell again) in London. Much of the humour comes from the characters of the two people, who often argue and trick each other. It is considered one of the best British comedies of all time: *Look at all the stuff in this office – it's like Steptoe's back yard!*

ˌIsaac ˈ**Stern** /ˈstɜːn; *AmE* ˈstɜːrn/ (1920–) a US violin player. He was born in Russia, went to the US as a baby with his family, and first played in public at the age of 11. His many successful world tours began in 1937. In the late 1950s he organized a successful campaign to save *Carnegie Hall from being destroyed.

ˌLaurence ˈ**Sterne** /ˈstɜːn; *AmE* ˈstɜːrn/ (1713–68) a British author, born in Ireland. He spent most of his life as a *Church of England priest in *Yorkshire. He is best known for his novel **Tristram Shandy*, one of the most unusual and humorous books in English literature.

ˈ**Stetson**™ *n* a type of tall hat with a wide brim worn especially by *cowboys and other people in the western US states. It was invented by John B Stetson (1830–1906).

a cowboy wearing a Stetson

ˌWallace ˈ**Stevens** /ˌwɒlɪs ˈstiːvnz/ (1879–1955) a US writer of elegant and imaginative poetry. His *Collected Poems* (1954) won the *Pulitzer Prize. His other collections included *Harmonium* (1923), *The Man with the Blue Guitar* (1937) and *Transport to Summer* (1947).

ˌAdlai ˈ**Stevenson**[1] /ˌædleɪ ˈstiːvnsn/ (1900–65) a US *Democratic politician who was defeated by Dwight D *Eisenhower in the 1952 and 1956 elections for US President. Stevenson was a lawyer known for his clever remarks and fine mind. He was Governor of *Illinois (1949–53) and later US Ambassador to the *United Nations (1961–5).

ˈRobert ˈLouis ˈ**Stevenson**[2] /ˈluːɪs ˈstiːvnsn/ (1850–94) a Scottish writer of novels. He is best known for his famous children's adventure stories **Treasure Island* and **Kidnapped*, but he also wrote poetry for children and the well-known adult psychological novel *The Strange Case of Dr Jekyll and Mr Hyde*. Because of poor health Stevenson went to live on the island of Samoa in the Pacific for the last few years of his life. See also JEKYLL AND HYDE.

ˌJackie ˈ**Stewart**[1] /ˈstjuːət; *AmE* ˈstuːərt/ (1939–) a Scottish racing driver who was very successful in the 1960s and 1970s. He won 27 Grand Prix races and was *Formula One world champion three times. He now owns a team of racing cars together with his son and the *Ford Motor Company.

ˌJames ˈ**Stewart**[2] /ˈstjuːət; *AmE* ˈstuːərt/ (1908–97) a popular US actor who usually played good, honest characters. He was a tall man, known for speaking in a slow and hesitating way. He won an *Oscar for *The Philadelphia Story* (1940) and a special Oscar in 1984 for his contribution to the film industry. His other films include **It's a Wonderful Life*, *Rear Window* (1954), *The Glenn Miller Story* (1954), *The Man from Laramie* (1955), *The Spirit of St Louis* (1957) and *The Shootist* (1986). Stewart was awarded the Distinguished Flying Cross in *World War II and was later a Brigadier General in the US Air Force Reserve.

ˌRod ˈ**Stewart**[3] /ˈstjuːət; *AmE* ˈstuːərt/ (1945–) an English pop singer. He is well known for his rough voice and for his love of Scotland, from where his family originally came. He has made many successful records, including *Maggie May* (1971) and *Sailing* (1975). Since the 1970s he has lived mainly in the US.

St ˌGeorge's ˈCross /ˌdʒɔːdʒɪz/ the national flag of England, consisting of an upright red cross on a white background. The cross also forms part of the British *Union Jack flag. St *George is England's national saint. Compare ST ANDREW'S CROSS.

ˌ**St Heˈlena** /həˈliːnə/ a small island in the southern Atlantic Ocean. It is famous as the place where Napoleon was kept as a prisoner by the British from 1815 until his death in 1821. It was owned by the British *East India Company from 1659, and became a possession of the British Crown in 1834. The island's capital is Jamestown. The Governor of Saint Helena is also responsible for *Tristan da Cunha and Ascension Island.

ˌMount **St ˈHelens** /ˈhelənz/ a volcano in the Cascade Range of the US state of *Washington. It exploded in 1980 for the first time in 120 years, killing about 60 people and caused damage to the surrounding area. The explosion also reduced the height of the mountain by over 1 000 feet (300 metres). There have been several weaker explosions since.

ˌAlfred ˈ**Stieglitz** /ˈstiːɡlɪts/ (1864–1946) a US photographer who developed photography into a fine art. He managed several New York galleries where he presented exhibitions of photographs and modern art. He was married to the artist Georgia *O'Keeffe and often photographed her.

ˈ**Stilton** /ˈstɪltən/ *n* [U] a white English cheese with greenish-blue lines running through it and a strong flavour. It is often eaten at the end of a meal, and traditionally it is eaten with port (= strong sweet wine from Portugal) after large meals on special occasions such as *Christmas. It was originally made in various places in the *county of Leicestershire (though not the village of Stilton, now in *Cambridgeshire, where it was first sold).

ˈJoseph ˈWarren ˈ**Stilwell** /ˈstɪlwel/ (1883–1946) a senior US military officer during *World War II. General Stilwell's popular name was 'Vinegar Joe'. He commanded US forces in China, Burma and India but was sent back to the US in 1944 because of disagreements with Chiang Kai-shek. He later commanded US forces on the Japanese island of Okinawa.

Sting /stɪŋ/ an English pop singer whose real name is Gordon Sumner (1951–). He first became famous in the 1970s as the singer of the group The Police. In 1985 he left the group and began to make pop records with a *jazz influence. He had several successful records in the 1980s and 1990s, including *All This Time* (1991) and *Fields of Gold* (1993). He is also well known for his campaigns to protect the environment, especially in South America.

Sting

ˈ**Stirling**[1] /ˈstɜːlɪŋ; *AmE* ˈstɜːrlɪŋ/ a town in central Scotland. It is the administrative centre of the Central Region, and has an important place in Scottish history. It has a very old castle where the kings and queens of Scotland used to live. Scottish forces defeated the English in two important battles, Stirling Bridge (1297) and *Bannockburn, for control of the castle and the bridge across the *Forth river.

ˌJames ˈ**Stirling**[2] /ˈstɜːlɪŋ; *AmE* ˈstɜːrlɪŋ/ (1926–92) an English architect. He is well known for designing modern buildings with many straight lines and bright colours. Some people with traditional ideas about architecture do not approve of his work. He has designed buildings for the universities of *Oxford, *Cambridge and *Leicester, and his best-known buildings include a new part of the *Tate Gallery, the Clore Gallery, and the art gallery in Stuttgart, Germany. He was made a *knight in 1992.

St ˈIves /ˈaɪvz/ a town on the coast of *Cornwall in south-west England. It is popular with tourists, and several well-known artists have lived there, including Bernard Leach (1887–1979), Barbara *Hepworth, Ben *Nicholson and Patrick Heron (1920–99). A branch of the *Tate Gallery opened in St Ives in 1993. The town is also mentioned in a traditional *nursery rhyme:

As I was going to St Ives,
I met a man with seven wives.
Each wife had seven sacks,
Each sack had seven cats,
Each cat had seven kits;
Kits, cats, sacks and wives,
How many were going to Saint Ives?

(The answer is one, since the man and his wives, etc. were going the other way.)

St ˌJames's ˈPalace /ˌdʒeɪmzɪz/ a large, grand house built by King *Henry VIII in 1552 at the edge of *Saint James's Park in London. It was the main London home of the king or queen from 1697 to 1837. See also COURT OF ST JAMES'S.

St ˌJames's ˈPark /ˌdʒeɪmzɪz/ a park in central London, England, in front of *Buckingham Palace. It is the oldest of London's *royal parks, and contains a long lake with an island where birds can breed.

St ˌJohn ˈAmbulance Briˌgade a British charity. Its staff work without payment to provide medical care at public events, e.g. concerts or football matches. They also run medical centres and homes for sick people. It was started in 1887 and is named after the Order of the Hospital of St John of Jerusalem, an ancient military organization that cared for the sick.

St ˈKilda /ˈkɪldə/ a group of four islands off the west coast of Scotland, at the most western point in Britain. Nobody has lived there since 1930. Their high mountains and cliffs are the home of many different sea birds. St Kilda became a *World Heritage Site in 1986.

St ˌKitts-ˈNevis /ˌkɪts ˈniːvɪs/ (*also fml* **St Christopher and Nevis**) a country consisting of two islands in the eastern Caribbean Sea. It was claimed by Britain in 1623, and the island of Anguilla was part of it until 1967. In 1983 it became an independent member of the Commonwealth. Its capital town is Basseterre.

St ˌLawrence ˈSeaway a major water transport system for the US and Canada. It was built by the two countries and opened in 1959. It connects the St Lawrence River with Lake *Ontario and then, with the Great Lakes system, forms a channel 2 342 miles/3 768 kilometres long. Large ships use it to travel between the Atlantic Ocean and the Great Lakes.

the ˌ**St ˈLeger** /ˈledʒə(r)/ a race held every September at *Doncaster, *South Yorkshire, England, for horses that are three years old. It was first held in 1776.

St ˈLouis /ˈluːɪs, ˈluːi/ a city on the *Mississippi River in the US state of *Missouri. It was established in 1764 by the French, who named it after King Louis IX. It was part of the *Louisiana Purchase and became a major port for steamboats (= river boats driven by steam) in the 19th century. It now produces cars, aircraft, metal and chemicals. The city was known as the 'Gateway to the West', and its Gateway Arch (630 feet/192 metres high) is a symbol of this.

St ˈLucia /ˈluːʃə/ an island in the Caribbean Sea. It was claimed by Britain in 1814 and has been an independent member of the *Commonwealth since 1979. Its capital town is Castries. ▶ **St Lucian** *adj, n.*

St ˌMartin-in-the-ˈFields a church in central London, England, designed by James Gibbs and completed in 1726. The *Academy of St Martin-in-the-Fields was originally based there, and performances by other musical groups are still given there. The church also started an art college in 1854, now called the Central St Martin's College of Art and Design in *Bloomsbury.

the ˈ**stockbroker belt** *n* [usu sing] (*BrE*) an area outside a city, where rich people live in large expensive houses. Many of them work in the city as highly paid professional people, e.g.stockbrokers (= people who buy and sell shares in companies on behalf of other people). Most people think of the typical stockbroker belt as *Surrey, south-west of London, but the phrase can be used to refer to any expensive area outside a city: *They bought a large detached house in the heart of the stockbroker belt.*

ˈ**stock ˌcompany** *n* (*AmE*) a US company of actors, usually at one theatre, who present a variety of plays. **Summer stock** is the traditional production of plays by stock companies in small American towns during the summer.

ˈ**Stock Exˌchange ˈAutomated Quoˈtations** ⇨ SEAQ.

the **stocks** /stɒks/ *n* [pl] a device used for punishing criminals in Britain from the 13th century to the 19th century. It was a wooden framework with holes for the feet, and sometimes also for the hands. Criminals were locked into the stocks in public places so that people could laugh at them, insult them and sometimes throw things at them. Compare PILLORY.

the ˈ**Stockton and ˈDarlington ˈRailway** /ˈstɒktən, ˈdɑːlɪŋtən; *AmE* ˈstɑːktən, ˈdɑːrlɪŋtən/ the world's first railway on which passengers were carried on steam trains. It was built by George *Stephenson in the 1820s between Stockton, a port on the River *Tees in north-east England, and Darlington, an industrial town ten miles away.

ˌ**Stoke ˈMandeville** /ˌstəʊk ˈmændəvɪl; *AmE* ˌstoʊk/ a hospital near the village of Stoke Mandeville in *Buckinghamshire, England. It is well known for its department that deals with injuries and diseases of the spine (= the row of bones along the back). The official name for this department is the National Spinal Injuries Unit.

ˌ**Stoke-on-ˈTrent** /ˌstəʊk, ˈtrent; *AmE* ˌstoʊk/ an industrial city on the River Trent in *Staffordshire, England. It was formed in 1910 when the *Five Towns combined, and is the main centre of the *Potteries. Most of the famous *Staffordshire pottery companies have their factories in Stoke-on-Trent.

ˌLeopold **Stoˈkowski** /ˌliːəpəʊld stəˈkɒfski; *AmE* ˌliːəpoʊld stəˈkɑːfski/ (1887–1977) a US conductor who did a lot to make classical music more popular in America. He was born in London, England, and was known for his dramatic style. He directed the Philadelphia Orchestra (1912–36) and they played the music for the Walt *Disney film **Fantasia*. Stokowski established the American Symphony Orchestra in 1962.

ˌOliver ˈ**Stone¹** /ˈstəʊn; *AmE* ˈstoʊn/ (1946–) a US director, producer and writer of films. His films have been very successful but sometimes criticized for containing too much violence. They include *Platoon* (1986), *Born on the Fourth of July* (1989) for which he won an *Oscar as Best Director, *The *Doors* (1991), *JFK* (1991), *Natural Born Killers* (1994) and *Nixon* (1995).

ˌSharon ˈ**Stone²** /ˈstəʊn; *AmE* ˈstoʊn/ (1958–) a US film actor who had her first major success as an attractive but dangerous woman in *Basic Instinct* (1992). Her other films include *Total Recall* (1990), *Casino* (1995), *Diabolique* (1996) and *Last Dance* (1996).

Stone Age Britain

The earliest **archaeological remains** found in Britain are tools thought to have been made before 12000 BC, when Britain was still attached to the rest of Europe. No human bones from this period were found until 1912 when a skull that had characteristics of both humans and apes was found in a gravel pit in Sussex. The skull became known as ***Piltdown man**. From geological evidence it was calculated that the skull belonged to somebody who lived more than two million years ago. Later scientific tests showed that it was not genuine and that the jaw of an ape had been attached with glue to a human skull and then treated to make it look very old. The earliest genuine human bones found in Britain are those of a woman from Swanscombe, Kent, who lived about 325 000 years ago.

Most Stone Age remains in Britain are much later and date from after 4000 BC, the Neolithic period. There is evidence of woodland being cleared for farming, and polished stone axes and fragments of pottery have been found. The remains of a Stone Age village built about 3100 BC can be seen at *Skara Brae in the Orkneys. The houses were buried in sand after a storm in about 2000 BC and only found when another storm in 1850 blew the sand away.

Other Stone Age remains include **long *barrows**, piles of earth up to 300 feet long, found mainly in England and Wales. They were used as burial mounds and sometimes have several rooms inside containing human and animal remains and pottery. **Henges**, circular areas surrounded by a ditch and a bank, may have been built as meeting places. One of the most impressive is at *Avebury. It is large enough to contain the modern village of Avebury. A **stone circle** made of upright **megaliths** (= very large stones) up to 20 feet (6 metres) high was added inside the henge in about 2400 BC, at the end of the Stone Age. The henge at Britain's best-known **prehistoric monument**, *Stonehenge on *Salisbury Plain, also dates from the Stone Age, though the circles of huge stones inside it date from about 2100 BC, the beginning of the *Bronze Age.

Stoneˈhenge /stəʊnˈhendʒ; *AmE* stoʊnˈhendʒ/ Britain's most famous prehistoric monument, on *Salisbury Plain in southern England. It consists of two circles of large *standing stones, one inside the other. The inner circle consisted of arches made by laying one stone across the tops of two others. Some of these have fallen, but some are still in position. Stonehenge was built between 3000 and 1500 BC. Nobody knows why it was built, but many people think it was to study the stars and planets or to worship the sun, because a line through its centre would point directly to the position of the rising sun on Midsummer's Day. Since the 1980s young people, including many *hippies and *New Age Travellers, have been going there for their own midsummer celebrations, but the police usually prevent them from getting near the stones. Stonehenge was made a *World Heritage Site in 1986.

Stonehenge

the ˌ**Stone of ˈScone** /ˈskuːn/ a large stone that was the traditional seat on which the ancient kings of Scotland were crowned. It was used until 1296, when *Edward I had it brought to London and made into part of the *Coronation Chair. For many Scottish people it is an important national symbol, and they asked repeatedly for it to be returned. It was removed from *Westminster Abbey several times by Scottish people who thought that it should be kept in Scotland. In 1996 the government finally agreed to return it to Scotland.

The ˌ**Stone ˈRoses** a British pop/*rock group formed in 1984. Their best-known songs include *Elephant Stone* (1988) and *Fool's Gold* (1989).

The **Stones** /stəʊnz; *AmE* stoʊnz/ ⇨ ROLLING STONES.

ˌMarie ˈ**Stopes** /ˌmɑːri ˈstəʊps; *AmE* ˈstoʊps/ (1880–1958) a Scottish scientist who was one of the first people to write and teach people about sex and contraception (= ways of preventing a woman from becoming pregnant). She wrote two important books on the subject in 1918, *Married Love* and *Wise Parent-*

ˌTom ˈ**Stoppard** /ˈstɒpɑːd; *AmE* ˈstɑːpɑːrd/ (1937–) a British writer of plays, born in Czechoslovakia. His plays are noted for discussing philosophical questions in a clever and humorous way. They include *Rosencrantz and Guildenstern are Dead* (1967), *Jumpers* (1972), *Travesties* (1974) and *Arcadia* (1993). Stoppard was made a *knight in 1997.

Stork™ /stɔːk; *AmE* stɔːrk/ *n* [U] a British make of margarine (= a substance like butter, but usually made from vegetable oil). It became well known in the 1960s and 1970s when many television advertisements claimed that people could not tell the difference between Stork and butter.

ˈ**Stormont** /ˈstɔːmɒnt; *AmE* ˈstɔːrmɑːnt/ **1** a district of eastern *Belfast, in which **Stormont Castle** was built. **2** the usual name for **Stormont Castle**, a large administrative building which was built in the 1920s for the Northern Ireland parliament. The parliament met there until 1972, when *direct rule was introduced, and it is now the home of the Northern Ireland Assembly.

ˈ**Stornoway** /ˈstɔːnəweɪ; *AmE* ˈstɔːrnəweɪ/ a port on the east coast of Lewis with Harris, an island in the Outer *Hebrides. It is the administrative centre of the Western Isles region of Scotland and an important centre of the *Harris tweed industry.

ˌRex ˈ**Stout** /ˈstaʊt/ (1896–1975) a US writer of more than 70 popular mystery stories. Most of them were about Nero Wolfe, a fat *detective and his assistant Archie Godwin. They include *Malice in Wonderland* (1940), *Royal Flush* (1965) and *Three Aces* (1971).

stout *n* [U] a strong, dark type of beer. See also GUINNESS.

ˈHarriet ˈBeecher ˈ**Stowe** /ˈbiːtʃə ˈstəʊ; *AmE* ˈbiːtʃər ˈstoʊ/ (1811–96) a US writer whose best-known work, **Uncle Tom's Cabin*, increased support in the northern states for the movement to free the slaves in the South. She wrote 16 books, including several about life in *New England, such as *The Minister's Wooing* (1859) and *Old Town Folks* (1869).

St ˈ**Pancras** /ˈpæŋkrəs/ a large train station in central London, England, for trains to and from the *Midlands. The station building was originally a hotel, designed in a *Gothic style by George Gilbert *Scott and completed in 1872. St Pancras also has a *London Underground station which it shares with *King's Cross.

St ˌ**Patrick's Ca**ˈ**thedral** /ˌpætrɪks/ the largest Roman Catholic church in the US, on *Fifth Avenue, New York. It was designed by James Renwick (1818–95) in a mixture of French and English *Gothic styles, and completed in 1879.

S

St ˈ**Patrick's Day** /ˈpætrɪks/ 17 March, the day celebrated as the national day of Ireland. It is named after St *Patrick, and is a public holiday in Northern Ireland. Many Irish people wear a *shamrock on St Patrick's Day. In the US there are St Patrick's Day parades in *Boston, *Chicago and *New York.

St ˈ**Paul** the capital city of the US state of *Minnesota. It is on the *Mississippi River which separates it from *Minneapolis, and the two are known as the 'twin cities'. St Paul was first established in 1840, when it was called Pig's Eye Landing. It became the capital of the Minnesota Territory in 1849. Today it produces computers and other electronic equipment and cars. It has a famous Winter Carnival each year.

St ˌ**Paul's Ca**ˈ**thedral** /ˌpɔːlz/ (*also* **St** ˈ**Paul's**) a large cathedral in London, England. It was designed in the late 17th century by Sir Christopher *Wren to replace a previous cathedral destroyed in the *Fire of London, and was completed in 1710. It has a large dome, inside which is the famous *Whispering Gallery. The cathedral contains the graves of many famous people, including Lord *Nelson, the Duke of *Wellington and Christopher Wren himself.

St Paul's Cathedral

ˌLytton ˈ**Strachey** /ˌlɪtn ˈstreɪtʃi/ (1880–1932) an English writer and one of the most famous members of the *Bloomsbury Group. He was noted for his intelligent humour, and for creating a new style of biography full of amusing remarks and without too much respect for the subject of the book. His best-known work is **Eminent Victorians*. He also wrote about Queen *Elizabeth I and Queen *Victoria.

ˈ**straight glass** *n* a plain glass with no handle that holds one pint of beer. Most pubs in Britain serve beer in these glasses and also in 'pint pots' which have handles and are made of thicker glass, and many beer drinkers prefer their beer in one type of glass or the other: *Would you like a straight glass or a handle?*

a straight glass and a 'pint pot' on a bar counter

ˌ**straight** ˈ**ticket** *n* (in US elections) a vote in which a person votes for candidates who are all from the same political party. Compare SPLIT TICKET.

the ˈ**Strand** /ˈstrænd/ a street in central London, England, between *Charing Cross and *Fleet Street. It has many famous theatres, shops and hotels, including the *Savoy Hotel.

the ˈ**Strangers'** ˌ**Gallery** either of two raised areas of seats in the *House of Commons and the *House of Lords where members of the public can sit and watch the debates.

ˈ**Strangeways** /ˈstreɪndʒweɪz/ a prison in central *Manchester, England. It was in the news in 1990, when many of the prisoners took part in violent protests against the poor conditions there. One person died and the prison was so badly damaged that it had to be rebuilt. A report on the events recommended major improvements to Britain's prisons.

ˌLee ˈ**Strasberg** /ˈstræzbɜːg; *AmE* ˈstræzbɜːrg/ (1901–82) a US actor and stage director, born in Austria. He directed the *Actors' Studio in New York City from 1948 to 1982 and is remembered for training actors in *method acting. His many students included Marlon *Brando, James *Dean, Marilyn *Monroe, Al *Pacino, Robert *De Niro, Dustin *Hoffman, Jack *Nicholson and Jane *Fonda.

the **Straˈtegic ˈArms Limiˈtation Talks** (*abbr* **SALT**) talks between the US and the USSR to limit their nuclear weapons. The first agreement was signed in 1972 by President *Nixon and the Soviet leader Leonid Brezhnev and was known as the SALT I Treaty. In the SALT II talks in 1979, President *Carter[2] and Brezhnev agreed to more limits, but they were not approved by the US Senate because Soviet forces entered Afghanistan.

the **Straˈtegic ˈArms Reˈduction Talks** (*abbr* **START**) talks between the US and the USSR to reduce the number of their nuclear weapons. Reductions were made after President *Reagan and the Soviet leader Mikhail Gorbachev signed the *INF Treaty in 1987 and President *Bush and Gorbachev signed the START Treaty in 1991.

the **Straˌtegic Deˈfense Iˌnitiative** (*abbr* **SDI**) the plan by US President *Reagan to build a defence in space against nuclear weapons. Its popular name was 'Star Wars'. He announced this in 1983, but it was never built because of the expense and the end of the *Cold War. SDI was cancelled in 1993.

ˌ**Stratford-upon-ˈAvon** /ˌstrætfəd; *AmE* ˌstrætfərd/ (*also* ˈ**Stratford**) the town in *Warwickshire where William *Shakespeare was born. Tourists from all over the world come to see plays at the *Royal Shakespeare Theatre and to visit places associated with Shakespeare, including the house where he was born, the church where he is buried, and Anne *Hathaway's Cottage.

Strathˈclyde /stræθˈklaɪd/ a *region in south-west Scotland. Its main city and administrative centre is *Glasgow.

ˌIgor **Straˈvinsky** /ˌiːgɔː strəˈvɪnski; *AmE* ˌiːgɔːr/ (1882–1971) a US composer best known for his ballet music. He was born in Russia and studied with Nikolai Rimsky-Korsakov. He settled in France in 1934 and became a US citizen in 1945. Much of his music was not immediately popular but he is now regarded as one of the greatest 20th-century composers. His best-known works include *The Firebird* (1910), *The Rite of Spring* (1913) and the opera *The Rake's Progress* (1951).

ˌJack ˈ**Straw** /ˈstrɔː/ (1946–) a British *Labour politician. He became a *Member of Parliament in 1979, and held several important positions in the Labour *Shadow Cabinet before becoming *Home Secretary in the Labour government of 1997. He is known to favour harsh punishments for people who commit crimes or use illegal drugs. In 1997 it was found that his son William Straw (1980–) had tried to sell the illegal drug cannabis to a journalist.

ˌ**Strawberry ˈHill** a large house by the River *Thames, west of London, well known for its *Gothic architecture. Horace *Walpole bought the house in 1749 and added several towers and detailed and complicated decorations. It is one of the earliest examples of the *Gothic Revival, and the style of architecture which it influenced is sometimes referred to as 'Strawberry Hill Gothic'.

ˌMeryl ˈ**Streep** /ˌmerəl ˈstriːp/ (1949–) a US actor known for her ability to play a wide range of different characters. She won *Oscars for her parts in *Kramer versus Kramer* (1979) and *Sophie's Choice* (1982). Her other films include *The French Lieutenant's Woman* (1981), *Out of Africa* (1986), *The Bridges of Madison County* (1995) and *Before and After* (1996).

The ***Street*** (*infml*) a popular name for the British television *soap opera **Coronation Street*.

A ˌ***Streetcar Named*** ˈ***Desire*** a powerful play (1947) by the US writer Tennessee *Williams which won the *Pulitzer Prize. The main characters are a rough and aggressive man called Stanley Kowalski and his wife's delicate sister Blanche DuBois who is driven mad by Kowalski when she visits them in *New Orleans. A film version (1951) directed by Elia *Kazan, with Marlon *Brando and Vivien *Leigh, won four *Oscars.

street names

In Britain, main *roads outside towns and cities are known by numbers rather than names. An exception is the A1 from London to north-eastern England, which is often called the Great North Road. Roads that follow the line of former *Roman roads also have names, e.g. the *Fosse Way. If a main road passes through a town, that part of it usually has a name, often that of the place which the road goes to, e.g. London Road.

The main shopping street in a town is often called High Street, or sometimes Market Street. Many streets take their name from a local feature or building. The most common include Bridge Street, Castle Street, Church Street, Mill Street, School Lane and Station Road. Some names indicate the trade that was formerly carried on in that area. Examples are Candlemaker's Row, Cornmarket, Petticoat Lane and Sheep Street. Many streets laid out in the 19th century were named after famous people or events. These include Albert Street, Cromwell Road, Shakespeare Street, Wellington Street, Trafalgar Road and Waterloo Street. When housing estates are built, the names of the new roads in them are usually all on the same theme. Names of birds or animals are popular. Others are based on the old names for the fields that the houses were built on, e.g. Tenacres Road, The Slade and Meadow Walk. The name of a road is written on signs at each end of it, sometimes together with the local postcode.

Some streets have become so closely identified with people of a particular profession that the street name itself is immediately associated with them. In London, *Harley Street is associated with private doctors and *Fleet Street with newspapers.

In the US main roads such as interstates and highways are known by numbers. Most towns and cities are laid out on a **grid** pattern and have long **streets** with **avenues** crossing them. Each has a number, e.g. 7th Avenue, 42nd Street. The roads are often straight and have square **blocks** of buildings between them. This makes it easier to find an address and also helps people to judge distance. In *Manhattan, for example, *Tiffany's is described as being at East 57th Street and Fifth Avenue, i.e. on the corner of those two streets. The distance between West 90th Street and West 60th Street is 30 blocks.

As well as having numbers, many streets are named after people, places, local features, history and nature. In Manhattan there is *Washington Street, *Lexington Avenue, Liberty Street, Church Street and Cedar Street. Some streets are named after the town to which they lead. The most important street is often called *Main Street, and one that is especially busy and lively often has the informal name of **the drag** or **the strip**. A **suburb** or **subdivision** of a city may have streets with similar names. In a subdivision of Baton Rouge, *Louisiana, all the names end in 'wood', e.g. Balsawood Drive, Limewood Drive and Aspenwood Drive.

ant street is often called *Main Street, and one that is especially busy and lively often has the informal name of **the drag** or **the strip**. A **suburb** or **subdivision** of a city may have streets with similar names. In a subdivision of Baton Rouge, *Louisiana, all the names end in 'wood', e.g. Balsawood Drive, Limewood Drive and Aspenwood Drive.

Some roads are called boulevards, with *Hollywood's *Sunset Boulevard and *Miami's Biscayne Boulevard among the best known. Avenues sometimes cross streets, as in New York, but often the word is chosen as part of a name for no particular reason. *Avenue* and *boulevard* once indicated roads with trees along each side, but few have trees today. A *road* in the US is usually found outside cities, though Chicago uses the name for some central streets.

Some street names have particular associations: Grant Avenue in *San Francisco is associated with *Chinatown, *Beale Street in *Memphis with the *blues, and Bourbon Street in New Orleans with *jazz. In New York *Wall Street is associated with the financial world, Madison Avenue with *advertising and *Broadway with theatres.

ˈJanet ˈ**Street-ˈPorter** /ˈstriːt ˈpɔːtə(r)/ (1946–) an English television presenter and producer. In the 1980s she was in charge of a wide range of *BBC programmes for young people, often humorously referred to as *yoof programmes, and became well known for her strong *cockney *accent and unusual clothes.

ˌBarbra ˈ**Streisand** /ˈstraɪsænd/ (1942–) a US actor and singer known for her clear, strong voice. She became a star in the *Broadway musical play *Funny Girl* (1964) and won an *Oscar for its film version (1968). She won another for *Evergreen*, the song she wrote for her film *A *Star is Born* (1976). Her many successful songs include *People* (1964) and *The Way We Were* (1973).

the **Strip** **1** the popular name for part of Las Vegas Boulevard, a long street in the centre of *Las Vegas in the US. It has bright, colourful signs at night. Many of the hotels on the Strip have casinos (= gambling clubs). They include Caesar's Palace, Excalibur, Luxor, Treasure Island, the Tropicana and the MGM Grand Hotel and Theme Park. **2** the popular name for *Sunset Boulevard in *Hollywood.

ˈ**strip-ˌfarming** *n* [U] a system of farming (sometimes called the **open field system**) which was common in *Anglo-Saxon Britain and lasted until the *common land began to be enclosed by fences in the 13th century. Different fields were divided into long strips in which farmers could grow food for their families. Each farmer had several strips of land in different fields, so that the good and bad areas of soil were shared among the community.

ˈ**strip ˌmining** (*esp AmE*) (*BrE also* ˈ**opencast ˌmining**) *n* [U] a method of mining coal that is at or near the earth's surface. The surface is removed and the coal is taken from above, instead of digging a deep mine. People sometimes organize campaigns against this type of mining in their area because it leaves the countryside looking very ugly.

St ˈ**Swithin's Day** /ˈswɪðɪnz/ the Christian church festival of St Swithin, held on 15 July. According to traditional belief in Britain, if it rains on this day it will continue to rain for 40 days afterwards.

St ˌ**Thomas's** ˈ**Hospital** /ˌtɒməsɪz/ a large *teaching hospital in central London, England, established in the early 12th century and later named after St Thomas *Becket. It moved to its present buildings opposite the *Houses of Parliament(2) in 1871.

St ˈ**Trinian's** /ˈtrɪniənz/ an imaginary *public school(1) for girls in the humorous drawings of Ronald *Searle. The girls are famous for their bad behaviour, and have appeared in several books and films, e.g. *The Belles of Saint Trinian's* (1954).

ˈCharles ˈEdward ˈ**Stuart**[1] /ˈstjuːət; *AmE* ˈstuːərt/ ⇨ BONNY PRINCE CHARLIE.

the ˌHouse of ˈ**Stuart**[2] /ˈstjuːət; *AmE* ˈstuːərt/ the name of the family who were kings and queens of Scotland from 1371 to 1714. When *Elizabeth I of England died without any children in 1603, her relative James VI of Scotland became also *James I of England. The Stuarts continued to be kings and queens of England and Scotland until 1714, when the *Act of Settlement made the House of *Hanover the British royal family. See also JACOBITE.

ˌJames ˈ**Stuart**[3] /ˈstjuːət; *AmE* ˈstuːərt/ (1688–1766) the son of *James II, also called the *Old Pretender. His supporters, the *Jacobites, referred to him as James VIII of Scotland and III of England. He lived in France and Italy for most of his life, and claimed that he had a right to be the king of Britain. He came to Scotland in 1715 to lead the *Fifteen rebellion, but was defeated by the English.

ˌGeorge ˈ**Stubbs** /ˈstʌbz/ (1724–1806) an English artist. He is famous for his paintings of horses, which show the animals in realistic detail, often with their owners, and sometimes in imaginary situations.

student life

The popular image of student life is of young people with few responsibilities enjoying themselves and doing very little work. This is often not true. Many older people now study at college or university, sometimes on a part-time basis while having a job and looking after a family. These students are often highly motivated and work very hard.

Younger students are often thought to be lazy and careless about money but this situation is changing. In Britain reduced government support for higher education means that students can no longer rely on having their expenses paid for them. Formerly, students received a **grant** towards their living expenses. Now most can only get a **loan** which has to be paid back. From 1999 they will also have to pay £1 000 towards **tuition fees**. In the US students already have to pay for **tuition** and **room and board**. Many get a **financial aid package** which may include grants, scholarships and loans. The fear of having large debts places considerable pressure on students and many take part-time jobs during the term and work full-time in the vacations.

Many students in Britain go to a university away from their home town. They usually live in a **hall of residence** for their first year, and then move into **digs** (= a rented room in a private house) or share a house with other students. They may go back home during vacations, but after they graduate most leave home for good. In the US too, many students attend colleges some distance from where their parents live. They may live **on campus** in one of the **dorms** (= halls), or **off campus** in apartments and houses which they share with **housemates**. Some students, especially at larger universities, join a ***fraternity** or ***sorority**, a social group usually with its own house near the campus. Fraternities and sororities often have names which are combinations of two or three letters of the Greek alphabet. Some people do not have a good opinion of them because they think that students who are members spend too much time having parties. Many US colleges and universities encourage an atmosphere of ***political correctness** to try to help students get on together.

In Britain the interests of students are represented

range of societies, clubs and social activities including sports, drama and politics. One of the highlights (= main events) of the year is **rag week**, a week of parties and fund-raising activities in support of various *charities.

Especially in their first year, US students spend a lot of time on social activities. One of the most important celebrations, especially at universities which place a lot of emphasis on sports, is ***homecoming**. Many **alumni** (= former students) return to their **alma mater** (= college) for a weekend in the autumn to watch a *football game. During homecoming weekend there are also parties and dances, and usually a parade.

When social activities take up too much time, students **skip lectures** (= miss them) or **cut class** (*AmE*) and **take incompletes** (*AmE*), which means they have to finish their work after the vacation. In the US this has the effect of lowering their course grades, but most US universities expect this behaviour from students and do little to stop it. Students are thought to be old enough to make their own decisions about how hard they work and to accept the consequences. A few students **drop out** (*AmE* **flunk out**) but the majority try hard to get good grades and a good degree.

ˈStudent Nonˈviolent Coˈordinating Comˌmittee (*abbr* **SNCC**) one of the active *African-American organizations during the *civil rights movement. It was begun in 1960 by black and white students in Raleigh, *North Carolina. SNCC was against the use of violence until Stokely *Carmichael became its leader in 1966. It ended three years later.

ˈStudents for a Demoˈcratic Soˈciety (*abbr* **SDS**) an extreme US student political organization in the 1960s which opposed the *Vietnam War. It was begun in 1960 and spread to many colleges and universities. Its members organized street protests which led to violence outside the Democratic National Convention in *Chicago in 1968. A year later, it divided into smaller groups.

STV /ˌes tiː ˈviː/ ⇨ SCOTTISH TV.

St ˈValentine's Day /ˈvæləntaɪnz/ (*also* **ˈValentine's Day**) 14 February, the day on which lovers traditionally send one another *greetings cards called **Valentine cards** or **Valentines**. The cards usually have designs of hearts, etc. on them and often contain a sentimental or funny message. People sending Valentine cards do not usually sign their name. Sometimes people have a similar short message printed in a newspaper or magazine, and may also give each other gifts such as flowers or chocolates. The people who send or receive gifts, etc. in this way are also known as **Valentines**.

a shop window display for St Valentine's Day

the **St ˌValentine's Day ˈMassacre** /ˌvæləntaɪnz/ the murder of seven US criminals in *Chicago on 14 February 1929. The men killed were members of 'Bugs' Moran's 'North Side gang' and were shot by a group of Al *Capone's men dressed as police officers. The murders shocked Americans and caused the Chicago police to increase their efforts against Capone. The incident has occurred in many films.

St ˌVincent and the ˈGrenadines /ˈgrenədiːnz/ a country consisting of a group of islands in the Caribbean Sea. It was claimed by Britain in 1783 and became an independent member of the Commonwealth in 1979. Its capital town is Kingstown.

ˈStyrofoam™ /ˈstaɪrəfəʊm; *AmE* ˈstaɪrəfoʊm/ *n* [U] a type of very light plastic material, also called 'expanded polystyrene', made by the US Dow Chemical Company. It is used as protective material for packing things in, and for making many products, e.g. coffee cups which can be thrown away after use.

ˌWilliam **ˈStyron** /ˈstaɪrən/ (1925–) a US writer of powerful novels. He received the *Pulitzer Prize for *The Confessions of Nat Turner* (1967), which some people criticized for its violent story based on the murders committed by the *African-American slave Nat *Turner. Styron's other novels include *Lie Down in Darkness* (1951) and *Sophie's Choice* (1979), which became a successful film (1982).

subˈscription ˌtelevision (*also* **subscription TV**, **pay television**, **pay-TV**) *n* [U] (in the US) a commercial television service that is regularly paid for by people who receive it.

suˈburbia *n* [U] (*often disapprov*) the suburbs (= areas of towns and cities that are outside the centre, and consist mainly of houses and flats/apartments). Suburbia is also used to refer to the people who live in the suburbs and their way of life. They are seen as being typically white, *middle-class and opposed to change. Life in suburbia, both in Britain and in the US, is usually considered rather boring: *The former revolutionary settled for a steady job and a house in suburbia.*

ˈsuccotash /ˈsʌkətæʃ/ *n* [U] (*AmE*) a dish of corn and beans cooked together, often with green and red peppers. See also SYLVESTER.

the **ˈSuez ˌCrisis** /ˈsuːɪz/ a series of events that took place in 1956 when the Egyptian government nationalized the Suez Canal. The two main owners of the canal, Britain and France, attacked Egypt by air and sent groups of soldiers to attack on land. This caused many arguments in Britain. Some people thought that the government was right to use the armed forces and show that Britain was still a strong country, but many people were shocked and angry at the use of force, and believed that the government was wrong. The *United Nations was opposed to the British and French action, and after less than two months the soldiers left Egypt. These events made many people realize that European countries such as Britain and France now had much less influence than in the first half of the 20th century, when they still had large empires. See also EDEN.

ˈSuffolk /ˈsʌfək/ a county in *East Anglia, eastern England. It consists mainly of agricultural land. The administrative centre is *Ipswich.

ˌSuffolk ˈPunch /ˌsʌfək ˈpʌntʃ/ *n* a breed of British carthorse (= a large strong horse, bred for pulling heavy carts and farm equipment). It is smaller than other carthorses, and usually a reddish-brown colour.

suffragettes

The US has had major campaigns to win **suffrage** (= the right to vote in political elections) for two groups of people: women and *African Americans. But the word *suffrage* is more closely associated with women's voting rights, and the women who took part in the movement were often called **suffragettes**. Today, most people in the US use the word **suffragists**, as it also includes the men who supported the movement.

The suffrage movement became important in the US in the second half of the 19th century. As early as

1848 an meeting was held in *Seneca Falls, New York, to discuss the issue. But only in 1920 was the US *Constitution changed to give women the right to vote. The **Nineteenth Amendment** to the Constitution is sometimes called the **Anthony Amendment**, after Susan B *Anthony, who was an important suffragist.

In the late 19th and early 20th century women in Britain also began to demand the right to vote. After several bills promising them suffrage were defeated in *Parliament, British suffragettes turned to violent protest. As well as holding noisy public meetings they chained themselves to iron railings and broke windows of government buildings. One suffragette, Emily Davison, threw herself in front of the king's horse during a race at *Epsom and died from her injuries. When suffragettes were put in prison many of them went on hunger strike (= refused to eat anything), so that the authorities had to force food into them to keep them alive. Leaders of the campaign, such as Emmeline *Pankhurst, the head of the Women's Social and Political Union, and her daughter Christabel, were imprisoned on many occasions under the terms of the so-called **Cat and Mouse Act** of 1913 which allowed the women out of prison just long enough for them to get well before taking them back in again.The campaign was interrupted in 1914 at the start of *World War I, so that women could contribute to the war effort. When the war ended in 1918 the government at last agreed to give the vote to women over 30, partly in recognition of their role in the war effort. Finally, in 1928, women won equal voting rights with men and were allowed to vote from the age of 21.

ˈ**Sugar Puffs**™ *n* [pl] a well-known breakfast food, made by the Quaker Oats Company. It consists of small pieces of crisp wheat covered in sugar, and is eaten with milk. Its most famous advertising character is a large furry yellow creature called the Honey Monster.

ˌArthur ˈ**Sullivan**[1] /ˈsʌlɪvən/ (1842–1900) an English composer. He is best known for the *Savoy Operas, a series of operettas (= light comic operas) he wrote with W S *Gilbert, which show his skill for writing light, often humorous music. **Gilbert and Sullivan** wrote 14 popular operettas, including *The *Mikado* and *The *Pirates of Penzance*, which are still performed regularly in Britain. He also wrote serious operas and other pieces of classical music, but they are less well known than the Savoy Operas. He was made a *knight in 1883. See also *LOST CHORD*, *ONWARD, CHRISTIAN SOLDIERS*.

ˌEd ˈ**Sullivan**[2] /ˈsʌlɪvən/ (1902–74) a US television personality. He is best remembered as the presenter of *Toast of the Town* (1948–55), later called *The Ed Sullivan Show* (1948–71), a popular Sunday variety programme on *CBS.

ˌJohn L ˈ**Sullivan**[3] /ˈsʌlɪvən/ (John Lawrence Sullivan 1858–1918) a US boxer who became the World Heavyweight Champion (1882–92), the last to fight without gloves. His popular name was the 'Boston Strong Boy'. The first time Sullivan wore gloves under the *Queensberry Rules, in 1892, he was beaten by 'Gentleman Jim' *Corbett.

ˌ**Sullom** ˈ**Voe** /ˌsʌləm ˈvəʊ; *AmE* ˈvoʊ/ Britain's largest *North Sea oil terminal (= place where an oil pipeline arrives on land), in the *Shetlands. It is also a major port for exporting oil.

ˌ**summa cum** ˈ**laude** /ˌsʊmə kʊm ˈlaʊdeɪ/ (in the US) the Latin phrase, meaning 'with highest praise', used to indicate the highest academic achievement of a college or university student who has completed his or her studies. It is written on the student's diploma (= document awarded for completing a course of study). Compare CUM LAUDE, MAGNA CUM LAUDE.

ˌ**Summer Bank** ˈ**Holiday** ⇨ AUGUST BANK HOLIDAY.

ˈ**summer camp** *n* (especially in the US) a camp where young people go for sports and other outdoor activities for several weeks in the summer. Summer camps are usually private and expensive. They have been a strong tradition in the US since the early 20th century.

ˌ**summer** ˈ**pudding** *n* [C, U] a traditional British sweet dish. It consists of summer fruit, usually berries such as raspberries and blackcurrants, pressed into a case of bread in a bowl. It is then left so that the fruit juice soaks into and colours the bread, and the pudding becomes the shape of the bowl. Summer pudding is eaten cold, often with cream.

The ***Sun*** a British *tabloid newspaper, published every day except Sunday. It is owned by Rupert *Murdoch and is well known for its *page-three girls and its stories about scandals (= things that people have done that are considered wrong and shocking). It expresses right-wing opinions and has been the best-selling daily newspaper in Britain since the 1970s. The phrase **Sun readers** is sometimes used to refer to British people with little education who hold right-wing opinions and prejudices about women and people from other countries.

the ˈ**Sunbelt** /ˈsʌnbelt/ an informal name for the southern and south-western US states, usually from *Virginia to *California. Their economic and political power has grown since the 1960s as more people move from the *Snow Belt and *Rust Belt to the warm climate and new job opportunities of the Sunbelt.

ˌ**Sun** ˈ**City** a community in the US state of *Arizona for people of 55 and older. It organizes special activities for its members and provides them with police protection and medical services. It was established by Del Webb in 1960 because of the dry, warm climate of the area. The Del Webb Corporation now has eight Sun City communities in five states, and more than 90 000 people live in them.

the ˌ**Sundance** ˈ**Kid** /ˌsʌndɑːns; *AmE* ˌsʌndæns/ (1860–1909) the popular name of the US criminal Harry Longbaugh. He got the name after robbing a bank in Sundance, *Nevada. He was associated for a long time with Butch *Cassidy.

the ˌ***Sunday Ex'press*** a British *Sunday paper, published by the same company as *The *Express*. Like *The Express*, it is a *tabloid newspaper that puts forward moderate right-wing opinions. It has a *colour supplement called the *Sunday Express Magazine*.

the ˌ***Sunday*** ˈ***Mirror*** a British *Sunday paper, published by the same company as *The *Mirror*. Like *The Mirror*, it is a *tabloid newspaper that puts forward moderate left-wing opinions. It has a *colour supplement called the *Sunday Mirror Magazine*.

the ˌ**Sunday** ˈ**papers** *n* [pl] (in Britain) newspapers that are sold only on Sundays. Most are published by companies which also publish daily newspapers on the other days of the week, and they usually have the same style, opinions and type of stories as their equivalent daily papers. For example, *The Independent on Sunday* is similar to *The *Independent*. Sunday papers have more pages than daily newspapers, and are usually divided into several sections, such as sport, news and the arts. Many of them also have *colour supplements: *We spent the whole afternoon in the garden reading the Sunday papers.*

The ˌ***Sunday*** ˈ***Post*** a Scottish *Sunday paper, first published in 1914. It is Scotland's best-selling news-

S

paper and its traditional Scottish opinions and moral values make it popular with many Scottish people living in other countries.

ˌ**Sunday ˈroast** (*also* ˌ**Sunday ˈjoint**) *n* a large piece of meat, usually beef or lamb, cooked in an oven. The Sunday roast/joint is the main part of the traditional lunch that many British families eat on Sundays, usually with potatoes, vegetables and gravy (= sauce made from the juice of cooked meat). See also YORKSHIRE PUDDING.

ˈ**Sunday school** *n* [U, C] religious education classes for children held on Sundays. They are usually given in a church building by a priest or an adult member of the church. The first Sunday schools were held in Britain in the 1780s. In the US they are also called **Sabbath schools**.

the ˌ***Sunday ˈSport*** a British *tabloid newspaper sold on Sundays and first published in 1986. It consists mainly of photographs of naked or nearly naked women, sports news and ridiculous 'news' articles that are invented by the writers. Although many people buy it, it is not generally considered a serious newspaper. See also DAILY SPORT.

the ˌ***Sunday ˈTelegraph*** a British *Sunday paper, published by the same company as the **Daily Telegraph*. Like the *Daily Telegraph*, it is a *broadsheet newspaper that expresses right-wing opinions and traditional, *Conservative attitudes. It has a *colour supplement and is well known for its detailed news and sports reports. It was first published in 1961.

the ˌ***Sunday ˈTimes*** a British *Sunday paper, published by the same company as *The *Times*. Like *The Times*, it is a *broadsheet newspaper that expresses moderate right-wing opinions. It is Britain's best-selling Sunday paper, and was the first British newspaper to introduce a *colour supplement in the 1960s. The *Sunday Times* was first published in 1822.

ˌ**Sunday ˈtrading** *n* [U] the practice of opening shops for business on Sundays. Traditionally, most British shops do not open on Sundays except for newsagents and some *corner shops. In the past, even *pubs could only open for a few hours on Sunday afternoon and evening. In the 1980s and 1990s the government made the laws on Sunday trading less strict, allowing pubs and small shops to open all day, and large shops such as supermarkets to open for six hours. Now major shopping centres such as *Oxford Street in London are busy seven days a week. Some religious groups are still opposed to all forms of Sunday trading.

In the US, individual states and sometimes counties make the laws on Sunday trading. Some businesses, such as restaurants and petrol/gasoline stations, have opened on Sunday through most of the 20th century. Many other businesses started to open on Sunday in the 1960s, though religious groups have opposed this. In some parts of the country it is illegal to sell alcohol on Sunday.

ˈ**Sunderland** /ˈsʌndələnd; *AmE* ˈsʌndərlənd/ a city and port in north-east England. In the *Industrial Revolution it was an important centre for the coal and shipbuilding industries, and many people lost their jobs in the region when these industries became less active in the 1980s. It is now an *assisted area.

ˌ**Sunset ˈBoulevard** a famous street in *Hollywood, also called 'the Strip' or 'Sunset Strip', where many early film companies had their offices. Charlie *Chaplin also lived there. The Boulevard now has expensive shops and restaurants as well as cheap businesses. *Sunset Boulevard* was the title of a famous film (1950) about an old film star, and of a *musical (1994) based on it by Andrew *Lloyd Webber.

SUNY /ˈsuːni/ ⇨ STATE UNIVERSITY OF NEW YORK.

the ˈ**Super Bowl** the US football game that decides the *National Football League Championship. It is played each January between the winners of the *American Football Conference and the *National Football Conference. The first Super Bowl was played in 1967. The 1998 game was seen by nearly 800 million people in 188 countries.

ˈ**Superglue**™ /ˈsuːpəgluː; *AmE* ˈsuːpərgluː/ *n* [U] a make of very strong liquid glue that sticks things together very quickly. It is sold in small tubes: *You can mend it with Superglue but be careful not to get any on your fingers.*

ˈ**superhighway** ⇨ EXPRESSWAY.

ˌLake **Suˈperior** /suˈpɪəriə(r), *also* sju-; *AmE* suˈpɪriər/ the largest of the *Great Lakes, and the world's largest lake of fresh water. Its area is 31 820 square miles (82 414 square kilometres). It is the most western of the Great Lakes and is connected to Lake *Huron by the Sault Sainte Marie Canals. It is surrounded by the states of *Michigan, *Wisconsin and *Minnesota and by Ontario in Canada. The main port is Duluth, *Minnesota.

ˈ**Superliner** /ˈsuːpəlamə(r), *also* ˈsjuː-; *AmE* ˈsuːpərlamər/ *n* a type of US train run by *Amtrak. It is mainly used over long distances west of *Chicago. Superliner carriages have two levels with large windows for passengers to watch the scenery, and there are also Superliner Sleeping Cars.

ˈ**Superman** /ˈsuːpəmæn, *also* ˈsjuː-; *AmE* ˈsuːpərmæn/ the best-known hero of US comic books. He was created by the writer Jerry Siegel and the artist Joseph Shuster, and first appeared in 1938 in *Action Comics*. The character began in newspapers a year later and has been used for novels, radio and television programmes and several films, including four with Christopher *Reeve (the first of them in 1978). Superman has special powers, including great strength and the ability to fly. He uses these powers to fight evil and danger. He only appears when he is needed. For the rest of the time he is Clark Kent, a rather dull and timid journalist. His girlfriend is Lois Lane but she is in love with Superman, not knowing his other identity. One of Superman's regular enemies is Lex Luther. The only thing that can harm Superman is a green mineral called *kryptonite which makes him lose all his powers. ⇨ note at COMICS AND COMIC STRIPS.

Superstitions ⇨ article.

the **Supreme Court**

The **judicial** branch is one of the three branches of US *federal government and operates the system of law courts. The Supreme Court in *Washington, DC is the highest court in the US, and is very powerful. It has nine judges, called **justices**. Traditionally, they are called the **nine old men**, although there has been one woman justice. The head of the court has the title of **Chief Justice of the United States**. Justices are appointed by the *President, although the *Senate must confirm (= give its approval to) the choice. There has been only one African-American justice.

Some of the power of the Supreme Court was given to it in the ***Constitution**. In 1803, in a famous case called **Marbury v Madison*, the Court gave itself the additional power of **judicial review**. This means that it has the power to decide if a law is constitutional (= follows the principles of the Constitution). If a law is said to be **unconstitutional** it cannot be put into effect unless it is added to the Constitution, a long and difficult process that has succeeded only 27 times in more than 200 years. In this way the Supreme

Superstitions

Superstitions are beliefs that certain things or events will bring good or bad **luck**. Many people believe that luck plays an important part in their lives, and they **wish somebody luck** (= good luck) in many situations, e.g. before an exam or when they get married. People learn superstitions while they are children, and though few adults will admit to being **superstitious**, many act on superstitions out of habit. Most superstitions are centuries old, and British and American people have many in common.

People are also interested in **fate** (= a power that controls everything) and in knowing what will happen to them in the future. Most people know which **sign of the zodiac** they were born under, and read their **horoscope** or '**stars**' in *magazines, though only a few take what is said seriously. People may **thank their lucky stars** for a piece of **good fortune**. When things go wrong they may say '**Just my luck!**', blaming their own bad luck, or look back on an **unlucky** act that has, in some unexplained way, caused their current problem.

Omens of bad luck

There are many well-known **omens** (= signs) of bad luck, some of which have a religious origin. The number 13 is considered unlucky because there were 13 people at the Last Supper. Tall buildings often do not have a 13th floor; instead the numbers jump from 12 to 14. Many people believe they will have a bad day when the 13th day of the month falls on a Friday (**Friday the 13th**). In Britain the **magpie** is widely considered an unlucky bird and has been associated with the Devil. The number of magpies seen is important: 'One for sorrow, two for joy, three for a girl, four for a boy.'

A well-known cause of bad luck is to **walk under a ladder** leaning against a wall. This idea may have developed out of the practice in *medieval times of hanging criminals from ladders. **Treading on cracks** between paving slabs is also bad luck, and it is unwise to **cross on the stairs** (= pass somebody going in the opposition direction). A person who **breaks a mirror** will have seven years' bad luck, but an old, little-known solution is to put the pieces under running water in order to wash away the bad luck. It is unlucky to **spill salt**, but bad luck can be avoided by throwing a little of it over the left shoulder with the right hand. People should not **open an umbrella indoors** as this will annoy the sun. Some people think it is bad luck to let a **black cat** cross in front of them; others think black cats bring good luck, and they give paper black cats as tokens at *weddings.

A person, place or event that often experiences bad luck is said to be **jinxed**.

Lucky charms

There are various ways in which people try to ensure good luck. Some people carry a **lucky charm**, such as a rabbit's foot or a special coin. Finding a **four-leaf clover** (= a clover plant with four leaves instead of the usual three) is also lucky. People sometimes place an old **horseshoe** over the front door of their house. It must be hung with both ends pointing upwards; if it is hung upside down the luck will run out through the gap. Sports teams and military regiments often have a lucky **mascot**, usually an animal or a model of an animal, which travels with them.

Rituals are actions that people believe are necessary in order to have good luck. When people talk about something that they hope will **come true** (= happen) they may touch something made of wood and say '**touch wood**' (*AmE* '**knock on wood**'). If something goes badly for somebody on two occasions people may say '**third time lucky**' (*AmE* '**third time's charm**'). If people fear that they have **tempted fate** (= assumed too confidently that everything will go well) they may **cross their fingers** to protect their good luck. Actors believe that wishing somebody good luck will bring them the opposite, and often say '**break a leg**' instead.

Predicting the future

There are many other ways, apart from reading a horoscope, of finding out what will happen in the future. **Fortune-tellers** at fairs use a **crystal ball** or **read a palm** (= look at the lines on a person's hand) to **foretell** the future. Other people use **tarot cards** (= special cards with pictures on) or **read tea leaves** (= look at the size and arrangement of tea leaves left after a cup of tea). Some people take all this seriously but many treat it as fun.

Children, especially girls, have games that they believe will tell them whom they will marry. In Britain on *Hallowe'en, a girl can find out the first letter of her future husband's name by peeling an apple in one long piece and then dropping it to see what letter the peel forms. A woman can check if her lover is faithful by picking the petals one by one from a flower while saying alternately '**he loves me**' and '**he loves me not**' until there are no petals left.

Other superstitions apply to the weather. A well-known rhyme is 'Red sky at night, shepherd's delight; red sky in the morning, shepherd's warning'. In the US *sailor's* replaces *shepherd's*. (A red sky in the evening means good weather ahead, while a red sky in the morning means storms are coming). British people believe that if it rains on 15 July (St Swithin's Day) it will rain every day for the next 40 days. On ***Groundhog Day**, 2 February, Americans look for a groundhog coming out of its hole. If it sees its shadow (i.e. if it is sunny) then winter will last a lot longer, but if it sees no shadow, winter is almost over.

Folk medicine

Many superstitions are related to health, though few are now taken seriously. It is still very common for people to say '**bless you**' or '**gesundheit**' (German for 'good health') when somebody sneezes. This was originally said in order to prevent a person's soul being sneezed out of their body.

Folk remedies have been used to cure many common problems. For hiccups (= sudden sharp sounds in the throat) remedies include dropping a cold key down the person's back or getting them to hold their breath and count to ten. To get rid of a sty (= a swelling on the eyelid) it is necessary to rub it with a gold ring. Warts will disappear if a piece of wool is tied in the same number of knots as there are warts and buried in the garden. As the wool rots the warts will disappear.

S

Court has the power to block laws made by the US government and state and local laws.

The Supreme Court is a court of appeal and hears cases on appeal that were first heard in the lower courts. It can hear only a small number of appeals and so tries to choose cases that involve important principles of law. Once the Court has decided a case, lower courts use it as a **precedent**, i.e. they follow the Supreme Court's decision in similar cases.

Many of the Supreme Court's decisions are famous because they changed some aspect of US life. For instance, in the cases **Scott v Sandford* (1857), **Plessy v Ferguson* (1896) and **Brown v Board of Education* (1954) the Court made important decisions about the rights of African Americans. In *Miranda v Arizona* (1966) the Court said that police officers must inform the people they arrest of their constitutional rights. In 1978, the decision in *Regents of the University of California v *Bakke* upheld (= supported) *affirmative action but made *reverse discrimination illegal. This means that, when trying to give more opportunities to women, African Americans and minority groups, people cannot deny members of other groups fair treatment. The **Roe v Wade* decision of 1973 gave women across the US the right to abortion. The decision in *US v Nixon* (1974) required President *Nixon to hand over evidence that later led to his having to resign.

---

the **Su,preme Court 'Building** /su,pri:m kɔ:t 'bɪldɪŋ; *BrE also* sju-/ the building in Washington, DC, on *Capitol Hill, where the US *Supreme Court meets. It was built in 1935 is the last of the national government buildings in the Greek style. Visitors can tour the building when the court is not sitting.

The **Su'premes** /su'pri:mz; *BrE also* sju-/ a female *African-American pop group. They formed in 1959 in *Detroit as The Primettes. The original members were Diana *Ross, Mary Wilson (1944–) and Florence Ballard (1943–76). They joined *Motown(2) Records in 1960, became The Supremes, and had such hits as *Baby Love* (1964) and *Stop! In the Name of Love* (1965). Ross left in 1970 and the group continued with different singers until 1976.

Surf™ /sɜ:f; *AmE* sɜ:rf/ *n* [U] a make of soap powder for washing clothes. It is made by Lever Brothers.

,Surgeon 'General *n* the head of the US Public Health Service and the senior medical officer in the US. The Surgeon General is responsible for protecting people's health, and his warnings about the dangers of smoking are printed on every cigarette packet.

surnames

In Britain and the US surnames, also called **last names** or **family names**, pass from fathers to their children. Traditionally, women change their surname when they marry, replacing their **maiden name**, the surname they had from birth, with the surname of their husband. In the US especially, some women keep their maiden name as a middle name. Others choose to keep their maiden name as their surname after they are married. A few create a **double-barrelled** name (*AmE* **hyphenated name**) from the two surnames, such as Johnson-Brown. In a few cases the husband and children may also take this name. In Britain a double-barrelled surname used to suggest an upper-class background, but this is no longer always so.

In the US, laws about changing a last name, whether after marriage or for some other reason, vary from state to state, but it is usually a simple process and in some states people can just begin to use a new name if they want to. In Britain a woman can change her surname automatically after marriage. If people wish to change their name for any other reason they can do so by **deed poll**, a simple legal procedure.

In fact people rarely change their surname except after marriage, and many people are able to research their family history over many centuries. Most families were known by surnames by 1300 and many of the old names are still common. Sometimes the names reflected the place where the family lived, such as the name of their village or a reference to a feature of the local countryside, e.g. *Ford*, *Hill* or *Wood*. Other surnames refer to the original occupation or trade of the family, e.g. *Baker*, *Miller*, *Shepherd* and *Smith*. Sometimes the surname began as a *nickname. For instance, someone with dark hair or a dark skin might be called *Black*, *Blake* or *Brown*. Some surnames were taken from personal names, as in *Andrews*, *Martin* and *Roberts*. Others were based on French names that came to Britain during the *Norman Conquest, e.g. *Sinclair* from the French 'Saint-Clair'.

Many surnames occur throughout Britain, but others suggest a particular regional origin. Many Scottish names begin with *Mc-* or *Mac-*, meaning 'son of', e.g. *McDonald* and *MacGregor*. Members of a *clan added this prefix to their father's name. Irish surnames often begin with *O'*, meaning 'descended from', e.g. *O'Brien*. Many Irish surnames are derived from ancient *Celtic names. Common Welsh surnames include *Evans*, *Morgan*, *Price*, *Rees* and *Williams*. The most common surname in England and Scotland is *Smith*, closely followed by *Jones*, a name also widely found in Wales. Other surnames were brought to Britain by families from India, Pakistan, Bangladesh and China. These include *Ahmed*, *Hussain*, *Khan*, *Patel*, *Singh* and *Tsang*.

All the surnames found in Britain are also found in the US, together with many others from all over the world. Some people wanted to sound more American when they arrived in the US and so took English last names. Sometimes government officials could not understand the names of new arrivals and wrote similar English names on their documents. Many Americans of German origin changed their names during the two world wars. *African Americans whose ancestors were slaves do not know what last names their families originally had. Most have English or Irish names, because slaves had to take the names of their owners.

When British and US people introduce themselves they give their **first name** and then their surname, e.g. Michael Johnson, Linda Johnson. The opposite order 'Johnson, Michael' is used only in alphabetical lists. When people are addressed formally a title is put before their last name, usually **Mr** for men and **Mrs**, **Miss** or **Ms** for women. Married women used always to be called Mrs Johnson, etc. In formal situations they used to be referred to as e.g. Mrs Michael Johnson, using their husband's first name rather than their own, but this is now much less common. Unmarried women were known as Miss Johnson, etc. Many women now prefer the title *Ms* because, like *Mr*, it does not give any information about whether the person is married. Other titles include **Dr** for medical doctors and people with a doctorate and **General**, **Colonel**, etc. for people holding military ranks. Men especially may be referred to simply by their last name, e.g. *the previous Democratic president was Carter*, but addressing somebody in this way may cause offence.

'Surrey /'sʌri/ a county in south-east England, south-west of London. It consists of some agricultural land and many small towns in the *stockbroker belt for people who work in London. The administrative centre is Kingston upon Thames.

Sur'vival a popular British television series about nature, made by *Anglia TV. Each programme usually describes the life of a particular wild animal. It has been broadcast on *ITV since 1960.

'Sussex /'sʌsɪks/ a former county on the coast of south-east England. In 1974 it was divided into the smaller administrative counties of *East Sussex and *West Sussex, but many people still refer to the whole area as Sussex.

'Screaming 'Lord **'Sutch** ⇨ SCREAMING LORD SUTCH.

ˌRosemary **'Sutcliff** /'sʌtklɪf/ (1920–92) an English writer of novels. She wrote both adults' and children's literature, mostly set in *Roman Britain, but is best known for her books for older children, including *The Eagle of the Ninth* (1954).

ˌPeter **'Sutcliffe** /'sʌtklɪf/ ⇨ YORKSHIRE RIPPER.

ˌGraham **'Sutherland** /'sʌðələnd; *AmE* 'sʌðərlənd/ (1903–80) an English artist. He is well known for his portraits, landscapes and religious art. He painted many pictures of *World War II and the Welsh countryside, but his best-known works are a tapestry (= a picture made by sewing coloured threads on a cloth) of Christ in *Coventry Cathedral, and a portrait of Winston *Churchill which was later destroyed by his wife because he did not like it.

ˌSutton 'Hoo /ˌsʌtn 'huː/ an area of *Suffolk, England, where an *Anglo-Saxon ship was found buried in 1939. It was full of treasure and many people think that a 7th-century king was buried there. The treasure is now in the *British Museum.

Sven'gali /sven'gɑːli/ *n* (*pl* **Svengalis**) a person who controls what another person does in a mysterious way that is hard to resist, usually for dishonest or evil reasons. The original Svengali is a character in *Trilby*, a novel by George *du Maurier: *Her manager, a Svengali figure rarely in the public eye, was the main influence in her career.*

ˌJimmy **'Swaggert** /'swægət; *AmE* 'swægərt/ (1935–) a well-known US *televangelist who lost many supporters in 1988 when it became known that he had visited a prostitute. Swaggert appeared on television asking to be forgiven, and he still broadcasts from his church in Baton Rouge, *Louisiana. He is the cousin of the singer Jerry Lee *Lewis.

ˌSwallows and 'Amazons /ˌswɒləʊz ənd 'æməzənz; *AmE* ˌswɑːloʊz/ the first in a series of children's books (1930) by Arthur *Ransome. It describes the adventures of four children sailing small boats in the *Lake District, and is still popular among British children.

S

'Swanee /'swɒni; *AmE* 'swɑːni/ a song made popular by Al *Jolson. It was written by George *Gershwin and Irving Caesar for the *Broadway musical play *The Capitol Revue* (1919). Jolson added it later that year to a play he was appearing in, called *Sinbad*.

ˌSwanee 'River ⇨ *OLD FOLKS AT HOME*.

ˌDonald **'Swann** /'swɒn; *AmE* 'swɑːn/ ⇨ FLANDERS AND SWANN.

the **ˌSwan of 'Avon** /'eɪvn/ a *nickname for William *Shakespeare. It was invented by Ben *Jonson in a poem he wrote in the *First Folio. The phrase refers to the swans (= large white water birds with long necks) on the River *Avon at *Stratford, where Shakespeare was born, and also to the ancient Greek belief that the souls of poets pass into swans.

'Swansea /'swɒnzi; *AmE* 'swɑːnzi/ a city and port on the south coast of Wales. It used to be an important port and a major centre of the Welsh coal, metal and shipbuilding industries. As these industries became less important towards the end of the 20th century the city was developed as a tourist centre. It is the nearest city to the *Gower Peninsula and the *Brecon Beacons. See also DVLC.

'Swanson™ /'swɒnsn; *AmE* 'swɑːnsn/ the name used for a range of frozen food dinners produced by the Campbell Soup Company. The first were made in 1954 by C A Swanson & Sons, and Campbell's bought the company a year later. The original '*TV dinners' were frozen on metal trays which could be quickly heated.

ˌGloria **'Swanson** /'swɒnsn; *AmE* 'swɑːnsn/ (1897–1983) a US actor who was a leading star of silent films in the 1920s. She is best remembered, however, for her part as an old film star in *Sunset Boulevard* (1950). She was married six times.

the **ˌSwan 'Theatre** a small theatre in *Stratford-upon-Avon which was built in the 1980s for the *Royal Shakespeare Company. It is next to the company's main theatre and was designed to be like the theatres of *Jacobean times.

ˌswan-'upping /'ʌpɪŋ/ *n* [U] a ceremony that takes place every summer on the River *Thames, in which groups of people in boats mark swans (= large white water birds with long necks) to show who owns them. Most swans in Britain belong to the queen, but in the 15th century a few groups of swans on the Thames were given to two of the City of London *livery companies. The young birds descended from these groups are marked each year to distinguish them from the royal swans.

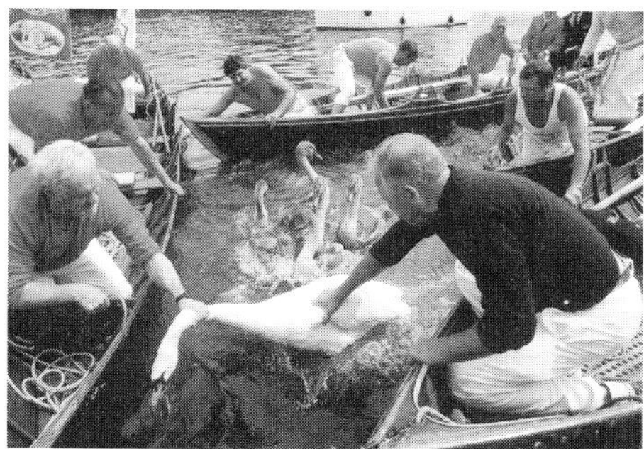

swan-upping

Swar'fega™ /swɔː'fiːgə; *AmE* swɔːr'fiːgə/ *n* [U] a thick, soft, green substance that is used for cleaning oil, paint and similar materials from the skin.

'Swaziland /'swɑːzɪlænd/ a small country in south-east Africa, between *South Africa and Mozambique. It was under the control of the Boers until the *Boer War, when it became a British protectorate (= a country controlled and protected by Britain). It became an independent member of the *Commonwealth in 1968. Swaziland is ruled by a king who chooses the Prime Minister and the Cabinet. It has many cultural and economic links with South Africa. Its capital city is Mbabane and its official languages are Swazi and English.

swear words

Many people find **swearing** offensive and it is best avoided. Swear words are used mainly in two situations: to relieve feelings of anger and frustration when something bad happens, and to show your anger to somebody who has upset you. The words used often lose their normal meaning and act simply as a way of expressing feelings. Swear words are usually short and have a strong sound that can be spat out. Since many swear words have four letters they are sometimes called **four-letter words**.

Like *slang expressions, swear words come in and out of fashion and over time often lose their capacity to shock. They are replaced by new, stronger words, though the outdated words may continue to be used by older people. Exclamations such as *Drat!*, *Blow!* and *Blast!*, for instance, are now rarely heard among young people, although the older generation still use them.

Swear words are also called **bad language**, **dirty language** or **obscene language** and many refer to sex or to bodily functions. Other swear words have a religious origin and are sometimes called **oaths**. Many were used for **cursing** (= asking for the help of a supernatural power to punish somebody). Often, obscene and religious language are combined, as in the expression *Fucking hell!* A person who is very angry and using a lot of swear words may be said to be **cursing and swearing** or **effing and blinding**.

The most common oaths include *Heavens above!* and *Oh, Lord!*, and the stronger *Damn!*, *God!* and *Jesus Christ!* They cause offence mainly to Christians. Many people are upset when they hear obscene language. The strongest swear words include *Fuck!* and *Shit!* Swear words used to insult people include *Bastard!*, *Bitch!*, *Son of a bitch!*, *Asshole!*, *Cunt!* and, especially in the US, *Motherfucker!*

Expressions with 'it' added such as in *Damn it!* and *Fuck it!* are used as alternatives to the single word. When 'off' is added, as in *Fuck off!*, its derivative *Eff off!*, *Piss off!* and *Bog off!*, the expressions take on the meaning of 'Go away!'

The words *fucking*, *frigging* (*BrE*) and *bleeding* are used as intensifiers (= words that strengthen the meaning of a word) in expressions like *Fucking hell!* and *You're a bleeding liar! Damn*, and the stronger *bloody* (*BrE*), are used before nouns, as in *a damn nuisance* and *You bloody fool!*

Some people feel strongly that it is always wrong to swear and do not like to hear others swearing. The angrier the tone of voice, the more unpleasant and frightening it is likely to be. Other people swear only when a situation makes them very upset. But some people use swear words in almost every sentence. Using a lot of swear words may suggest low intelligence or lack of self-control. People may apologize if they use a swear word in front of somebody who does not approve of swearing, possibly by saying 'Pardon my French'. Some people may use an ordinary word or a mild swear word in place of the stronger one they would really like to say. People may say *Sugar!*, for example, instead of *Shit!*, though this is now rather old-fashioned. Children are usually not allowed by their parents to swear, and so often find bad words especially interesting.

When strong swear words are spoken on television they may be **bleeped out** (= replaced by a high-pitched noise) to avoid causing offence. Some words may not be used during times when children might hear them. Film classifications are based partly on the language used in them. Newspapers and books may leave out some of the letters in swear words, for example printing *fuck* as f***. As a result this is sometimes known as 'the f-word'.

The '**Sweeney** /'swi:ni/ one of the most popular British television series of the 1970s, broadcast on *ITV. It was about a group of police officers in the *Flying Squad. Its name comes from *Sweeney Todd*, which is *rhyming slang for 'Flying Squad'. The series was more violent and realistic than any other programme about the police at the time.

ˌ**Sweeney 'Todd** /ˌswi:ni 'tɒd; *AmE* 'tɑ:d/ an imaginary character, also known as the 'demon barber of Fleet Street', who first appeared in 18th-century English cheap magazines and plays. He is a London barber (= a person whose job is to cut men's hair and shave them) who kills his customers by cutting their throats and then sells their bodies to be made into meat pies. *Sweeney Todd*, a musical show with words and music by Stephen *Sondheim, opened on *Broadway in 1979.

ˌ**Sweet 'N 'Low**™ /ˌswi:t ən 'ləʊ; *AmE* 'loʊ/ *n* [U] a US product name for an artificial sweet substance used instead of sugar in drinks and foods. It is made in *Brooklyn by the Cumberland Packing Company.

ˌJonathan '**Swift** /'swɪft/ (1667–1745) an Irish writer, best known as the author of **Gulliver's Travels*. He was the dean (= priest in charge of the other priests) of St Patrick's Cathedral in *Dublin, but also spent much time in London, where he knew many important writers and politicians. He is considered one of the greatest satirists (= writers who use humour to criticize people and things such as the social and political systems) in Englsh literature. He also wrote poetry.

ˌAlgernon '**Swinburne** /ˌældʒənən 'swɪnbɜ:n; *AmE* ˌældʒərnən 'swɪnbɜ:rn/ (1837–1909) an English poet and critic. He was a very skilful writer, but his lack of respect for the Christian religion and the sexual themes in his poetry shocked many people in *Victorian(1) Britain. His best-known work includes three plays about *Mary Queen of Scots and the poem *Tristram of Lyonesse* (1882). He was a close friend of Dante Gabriel *Rossetti and the other *Pre-Raphaelites.

swing *n* [U] a type of US *jazz dance music played especially by big bands in the 1930s and 1940s. The band leader Benny *Goodman was called 'the King of Swing', and other swing bands included those of Glenn *Miller and Jimmy and Tommy *Dorsey. The word *swing* had been used to refer to all *jazz music in the early 1930s.

ˌ***Swing 'Low, Sweet 'Chariot*** a US *spiritual. It is well known in Britain, where it is often sung at matches by supporters of the English national *Rugby Union team.

Switch™ /swɪtʃ/ *n* [U] a make of British *debit card: *Can I pay by Switch?*

the ˌ**sword in the 'stone** (in *Arthurian legend) the magic sword *Excalibur, which Arthur as a boy is able to pull out of the large stone in which it is fixed. By doing this he shows that he will be the next king of England.

ˌEric '**Sykes** /'saɪks/ (1923–) an English comedian. He is a tall thin man with a funny sad expression who has written and appeared in many films and television programmes. He is best known for his work with Hattie *Jacques.

Syl'vester /sɪl'vestə(r)/ a character in *Warner Brothers cartoons from the 1940s to the 1960s. He is a cat who keeps trying to catch a small bird called *Tweety Pie, but never succeeds. He spits when he talks and often says 'Sufferin' succotash!' when he is surprised or angry.

ˌJ M '**Synge** /'sɪŋ/ (John Millington Synge 1871–1909) an Irish writer of plays. W B *Yeats persuaded him to write about the life of Irish peasants (= poor farmers). His plays use the language of ordinary country people in a dramatic way. His best-known work, *The Playboy of the Western World* (1907), is the story of a man who arrives in a small community and pretends that he has killed his father. Many Irish people were angry at the idea that Irish peasants would welcome a murderer and treat him with respect. There were protests when the play was first performed at the Abbey Theatre in *Dublin, but it is now considered one of the greatest plays in Irish literature.

Tt

TA /ˌtiː ˈeɪ/ ⇨ TERRITORIAL ARMY.

Ta'basco™ (*also* **ˌTabasco 'sauce**) *n* [U] a very spicy sauce made from red peppers,vinegar and salt. It is used to flavour food and often *Bloody Mary drinks.

The **'*Tablet*** a British *Roman Catholic newspaper, published once a week. It was first published in 1840 and consists mainly of news and articles about the Catholic Church and religion.

'table ˌtennis (*also* **'ping-pong**) *n* [U] a game like tennis that is played with small hard bats and a small plastic ball on a table with a net across it. It is a popular children's game, but is also played seriously as an international sport. It was invented in Britain in the mid 19th century.

'tabloid *n* (*sometimes disapprov*) a newspaper with pages that are half the size of those of larger newspapers (called *broadsheets*). Most of Britain's most popular newspapers are tabloids. These include *The *Sun*, *The *Mirror*, *The *Express* and the *Daily Mail*. Although some tabloids are serious newspapers, many people talk about **tabloid journalism** or the **tabloid press** to refer to a type of newspaper that contains many articles about sex, sport and famous people, and little serious news, and is often insulting to women and people from other countries. The word *tabloid* is less widely used in the US, where most of the important national newspapers are of a regular size. The best-known US tabloid, which uses short articles and large photographs, is the *New York Daily News*. Serious tabloids include the *Chicago Sun-Times*: *The tabloids are full of photographs of the couple on holiday.* Compare BROADSHEET. ⇨ article at NEWSPAPERS.

ˌTaco 'Bell™ /ˌtɑːkəʊ; *AmE* ˌtɑːkoʊ/ any of a large group of US *fast-food restaurants serving Mexican food, both in the US and in many other countries. The first was opened in 1962 in Downey, *California.

'Taffy /ˈtæfi/ *n* (*humor, sometimes offensive*) an English *nickname for a Welshman. The name comes from the Welsh pronunciation of *Dafydd*, the Welsh form of *David*, which is a popular name in Wales: *The bar was full of Taffies singing patriotic songs.*

'William 'Howard **'Taft** /ˈtæft/ (1857–1930) the 27th US *President (1909–13). He was a *Republican(1) who had earlier been the US Secretary of War (1904). As President, he created the Department of Labor and continued the foreign policies of President Theodore *Roosevelt. He was later Chief Justice of the *Supreme Court (1921–30), and is the only person to have been the head of two different divisions of the US government.

the **ˌTaft-'Hartley Act** /ˌtæft ˈhɑːtli; *AmE* ˈhɑːrtli/ an important US law passed in 1947 to restrict strikes. It gave the US President the power to stop strikes for 80 days if they represented a national emergency. It also set up a special committee to settle labour disputes. The bill, which was opposed by President *Truman, was introduced by Senator Robert A Taft and Representative Fred Hartley.

ˌtake the 'Fifth ⇨ FIFTH AMENDMENT.

A **ˌ*Tale of Two* '*Cities*** a novel (1859) by Charles *Dickens, set in London and Paris at the time of the French Revolution. Charles Darnay is a young French aristocrat who disagrees with the cruel way his family has been treating poor people. He moves to London and falls in love with Lucie, the daughter of an old doctor who had been put in prison by Darnay's family. Darnay marries Lucie before going back to France to rescue an old servant, but he is arrested there and condemned to death. He is saved by an Englishman, Sidney Carton, who is also in love with Lucie. The two men look very similar, and Sidney takes Charles's place on the scaffold (= the structure on which people are killed in public). The book ends with his thoughts as he walks to his death, which form one of the most famous sentences in English literature: 'It is a far, far better thing that I do, than I have ever done; it is a far, far better rest that I go to than I have ever known.'

ˌTalking 'Heads a US pop group formed in 1975 and known for the unusual words of their songs. David Byrne was the group's singer. Their albums included *Fear of Music* (1979), *Remain in Light* (1980) and *Naked* (1988).

'talk show *n* (*esp AmE*) **1** a television programme in which people, often ordinary members of the public, appear in front of an audience to talk about a particular topic, or about their lives and problems. The audience are encouraged to ask questions and make comments. Talk shows are often broadcast in the morning or afternoon. **2** a *chat show.

ˌThomas **'Tallis** /ˈtælɪs/ (*c.* 1505–85) an English composer. He wrote mainly religious music, and was one of the official musicians and composers of the royal family. He is best known now through a piece of his music that was adapted by Ralph *Vaughan Williams: *Fantasia on a Theme by Thomas Tallis* (1910).

the **'Tamar** /ˈteɪmɑː(r)/ a river in south-west England. Most of it forms the border between *Cornwall and *Devon. The *Royal Navy keeps ships in the part of the river where it flows into the *English Channel near *Plymouth.

The **ˌ*Taming of the* '*Shrew*** /ˌteɪmɪŋ/ a comedy play (*c.* 1594) by *Shakespeare. It is about Petruchio, a young Italian man who wants to marry Katharina, a rich but unfriendly woman. (*Shrew* is an old-fashioned word for a bad-tempered woman.) She behaves unpleasantly to him but he pretends not to notice. In the end he marries her and 'tames' her by treating her roughly until she becomes as easy to control as wives were expected to be at that time.

The musical comedy *Kiss Me Kate* (1948) by Cole *Porter was based on *The Taming of the Shrew*.

ˌTammany 'Hall /ˌtæməni/ the popular name for the powerful but often dishonest Tammany Society, the *Democratic Party organization that ruled New York City from the 1830s to the 1930s. They bought votes and made illegal agreements. The organization was named after the building in which they met. The name Tammany Hall is now used to refer to any dishonest political or other group: *Gloria turned the club's financial committee into Tammany Hall.* See also TWEED.

ˌ*Tam o'* '*Shanter* /ˌtæm ə ˈʃæntə(r)/ a poem (1790) by Robert *Burns. Tam o' Shanter, a Scottish farmer,

Tam o' Shanter's Ride, *an engraving*

gets drunk one night, and when he is riding home he sees three witches and they begin to follow him. He rides away as fast as possible and escapes by crossing a bridge over a river that the witches cannot cross. One of the witches pulls off his horse's tail before it crosses the bridge. The hat which Tam wears in many illustrations of the poem, a traditional round Scottish cap made of wool, is now called a **tam o' shanter**.

ˈ**Tampax**™ /ˈtæmpæks/ *n* a popular make of tampon (= a piece of soft material that is put into a woman's vagina to absorb blood during menstruation).

ˌ**T and ˈG** /ˌtiː ənd ˈdʒiː/ a short name for the *TGWU.

TANF /ˌtiː eɪ en ˈef/ ⇨ TEMPORARY ASSISTANCE TO NEEDY FAMILIES.

ˌ**Tanzaˈnia** /ˌtænzəˈniːə/ a country in East Africa which is a member of the *Commonwealth. It was formed in 1964 when two other Commonwealth countries, Tanganyika and Zanzibar, combined. Its capital city is Dodoma and its official languages are Swahili and English. It is a mainly agricultural country, with an important tourist industry. Many people visit Tanzania to see the wide variety of wild animals living there. ▶ **Tanzanian** *adj, n*.

ˌQuentin **Taranˈtino** /ˌtærənˈtiːnəʊ; *AmE* ˌtærənˈtiːnoʊ/ (1963–) a US film director and actor who also writes films. He has been criticized for the violence in such films as *Reservoir Dogs* (1991) and *Pulp Fiction* (1994), for which he won an *Oscar for Best Original Screenplay. It was also chosen as the best film at the 1994 Cannes Film Festival. Other films written by Tarantino include *True Romance* (1993) and *Natural Born Killers* (1994).

the ˈ***Tardis*** /ˈtɑːdɪs; *AmE* ˈtɑːrdɪs/ the vehicle in which *Doctor Who travels through time and space in the British children's television series. Outside, it looks like an old-fashioned British police telephone box. Inside, it is much larger than outside, and looks like a modern spacecraft: *It's not a very big bag, but it's like the Tardis, I can fit everything I need in it.*

ˌ***Tarka the ˈOtter*** /ˌtɑːkə; *AmE* ˌtɑːrkə/ a novel (1927) by Henry Williamson (1895–1977). It is a very realistic story about an otter (= a small animal with thick brown fur that lives in rivers), which dies after being hunted for a long time by men and dogs.

ˈ**Tarmac** /ˈtɑːmæk; *AmE* ˈtɑːrmæk/ a large British company that builds roads and large buildings. The company was established in the early 20th century by the inventor of **tarmac**™, a material for making road surfaces.

tartan

Tartan is a traditional woollen cloth from Scotland that has patterns of squares and lines woven in various colours. Patterns depended originally on dyes available from local plants, so each area developed its own tartan. Tartans were not at first associated with a particular *clan. From the late 18th century, Scottish regiments wore different tartans as an identifying feature, and the design of an individual tartan for each clan followed soon afterwards. The most famous tartans include 'Black Watch', the tartan of the *Royal Highland Regiment, which is black and dark green, and 'Royal Stuart', the mainly red tartan of the *royal family.

Now Scotsmen may wear a kilt (= a man's skirt with pleats that reaches to the knees) and sometimes a **plaid** (= cloak), or simply a tie, in their clan's tartan. Apart from those who work in the tourist industry, few Scots wear tartan as part of their ordinary clothing. Men wear kilts when taking part in Scottish dancing displays or for formal occasions such as weddings.

Many Scots consider it wrong to wear the tartan of a clan to which they do not belong, but this has not prevented tartan, or tartan-like patterns, becoming fashionable in Britain and abroad. For some people tartan has romantic associations with Scotland's history and its wild and beautiful countryside. Women's kilts, skirts and dresses, as well as scarves, bags, travelling rugs, and many other articles, are made in tartan patterns. Goods sold to tourists, such as tins of *shortbread biscuits, are decorated with tartan patterns to indicate their origin.

ˈ**Tarzan** /ˈtɑːzæn; *AmE* ˈtɑːrzæn/ a character in a series of novels by Edgar Rice *Burroughs, the first of which was *Tarzan of the Apes* (1914). Tarzan is an English nobleman who has grown up with apes in Africa after his parents died there. He is friendly with the animals and uses his great strength to swing quickly through the trees. There have been many Tarzan films, including several with Johnny *Weissmuller as Tarzan and Maureen O'Sullivan as his partner Jane. Tarzan speaks poor English. Many people know that in one of the films he says 'Me Tarzan, you Jane' to Jane, and make jokes about it. The most recent Tarzan film was *Greystoke* (1984). There have also been radio and television programmes and newspaper *comic strips about him. See also HESELTINE.

ˌ**Tate and ˈLyle** /ˌteɪt ənd ˈlaɪl/ a large British company that makes sugar. In the 19th century it was one of the first companies to produce sugar in cubes, and became very successful as a result. One of its original owners, Henry Tate (1819–99), used some of his wealth to build the *Tate Gallery.

the ˈ**Tate ˌGallery** /ˈteɪt/ an important art gallery on the north bank of the River *Thames in central London. It contains the main national collections of British art and international modern art. It is especially well known for its collection of works by *Turner[2]. These are kept in the Clore Gallery, a new building at the side of the Tate Gallery which opened in 1987. In 1988 a second Tate Gallery opened in *Liverpool, and in 1993 a third opened in *St Ives. In the early 21st century the modern art collection will move to a new building on the south side of the Thames, leaving the original Tate Gallery with the national collection of British art.

The ˈ***Tatler*** /ˈtætlə(r)/ **1** a British magazine, published once a month and containing articles about *upper-class and *upper-middle-class social events, fashion and the arts. It was first published in 1901. **2** a magazine written by Richard *Steele and Joseph *Addison from 1709 to 1711. It was published three times a week and consisted of long articles about a wide range of subjects, written with intelligence and humour, and usually from a *Whig(1) point of view.

T

ˈ**Tattersall's** /ˈtætəsɔːlz; *AmE* ˈtætərsɔːlz/ a well-known British company of racehorse auctioneers. Tattersall's organizes important auctions once a year at *Newmarket.

ˌArt ˈ**Tatum** /ˌɑːt ˈteɪtəm; *AmE* ˌɑːrt/ (1910–56) a US musician considered one of the greatest *jazz piano players. He was nearly blind all his life.

ˈ**Taunton** /ˈtɔːntən/ a town in south-west England. It is the administrative centre of *Somerset, and is well known for its attractive old buildings, and for the cider (= an alcoholic drink made from apples) produced there.

ˌJohn ˈ**Tavener** /ˈtævənə(r)/ (1944–) an English composer. He became well known after writing *The Whale* (1968), an unusual piece of music for singers, orchestra, people speaking and recorded sounds. His more recent music has been religious in character.

ˈ**tax disc** *n* (in Britain) a round piece of paper which must be displayed on the front window of a vehicle to show that the owner has paid his or her road tax (= a tax on all vehicles that use public roads). People usually pay their road tax and get their tax discs at a post office. They may cover periods of three months, six months or one year.

a tax disc

ˌ**Tax-Eˈxempt ˈSpecial ˈSavings Acˌcount** ⇨ TESSA.

ˈ**taxi ˌdancer** *n* (*AmE*) a woman employed at a dance hall to dance with customers who pay for each dance or a period of time. Taxi dancers are called this because they are hired like a taxi.

ˈ***Taxi ˌDriver*** a US film (1976) which was the first big success for Martin *Scorsese, who directed it, and the actor Robert *De Niro. It won the prize for the best film at the Cannes Film Festival. De Niro plays Travis Bickle, an ordinary New York taxi driver who becomes depressed by all the evil and crime he sees and tries to fight it in a violent way. Jodie Foster plays a very young prostitute whom he tries to rescue.

the **Tay** /teɪ/ the longest river in Scotland, 120 miles/193 kilometres long. From its source in the *Grampians it flows through central Scotland and into the **Firth of Tay**, a narrow strip of sea that runs a long way into the land near Perth.

the ˌ**Tay ˈBridge** /ˌteɪ/ **1** a rail bridge over the River *Tay near *Dundee in Scotland. It was completed in 1878 and collapsed in 1879 when a train was crossing. It was one of Britain's first serious rail disasters. **2** a second rail bridge over the River *Tay near *Dundee. It was completed in 1888 and is still in use. A road bridge was built near the rail bridge in the 1960s.

ˌA J P ˈ**Taylor**[1] /ˈteɪlə(r)/ (Alan John Percivale Taylor 1906–90) a leading English historian. He wrote many books and newspaper articles about the history of Europe in the 19th and 20th centuries, and became famous in Britain when he appeared on television to explain events such as the Russian revolution.

Eˌlizabeth ˈ**Taylor**[2] /ˈteɪlə(r)/ (1932–) a US actor, born in England. She began her career as a child star in films that included *National Velvet* (1944). Two of her eight marriages were to Richard *Burton[3], and their films together included **Cleopatra* and **Who's Afraid of Virginia Woolf?*, for which she received an *Oscar. They also acted together in the *Broadway play *The Little Foxes* (1981). Taylor's other films include *Cat on a Hot Tin Roof* (1958) and *Butterfield 8* (1960), for which she won another *Oscar.

ˌJames ˈ**Taylor**[3] /ˈteɪlə(r)/ (1948–) a US singer with a soft voice who plays the guitar and writes songs. He was especially popular in the 1970s. His best-known songs include *Fire and Rain* (1970), *You've Got a Friend* (1972), *How Sweet It Is* (1975) and *Handy Man* (1977). Later albums have included *Never Die Young* (1988) and *Hourglass* (1998).

ˌZachary ˈ**Taylor**[4] /ˌzækəri ˈteɪlə(r)/ (1784–1850) the 12th US *President (1849–50). He was an army officer known as 'Old Rough and Ready' who fought in the *War of 1812 and in the *Mexican War, in which he defeated General *Santa Anna. Taylor owned slaves but as President supported *California as a new state without slaves.

ˈ**Tayside** /ˈteɪsaɪd/ a *region in eastern Scotland. Its administrative centre is *Dundee.

ˈ**T-bill** /ˈtiː bɪl/ *n* (*AmE*) ⇨ TREASURY BILL.

T-Bird /ˈtiː bɜːd; *AmE* ˈti bɜːrd/ *n* ⇨ THUNDERBIRD.

TBS /ˌtiː biː ˈes/ ⇨ TURNER BROADCASTING SYSTEM.

tea *n* **1** [U] a drink made by adding hot water to the dried leaves of a plant. It is very popular in Britain, where it is usually drunk hot, with milk, and sometimes sugar. Many British people have a cup of tea in the morning, and several more during the day. Some people stop work for a few minutes to have a **tea break**. Most people in Britain offer a cup of tea to anybody visiting their home or office. Tea also suggests comfort and warmth, and sitting down with a 'nice cup of tea' is a common response to problems and worries: *Mr Lewis will be with you in a minute. Would you like a cup of tea or coffee while you are waiting?* **2** [U, C] (in Britain) a light meal eaten in the late afternoon. It usually consists of tea and cakes, biscuits or sandwiches: *Mary has invited us to tea.* ○ *The hotel serves afternoon teas.* **3** [U] (in Britain) the word used by some older people to refer to their main evening meal. It usually consists of cooked food and is eaten early in the evening, when the family arrives home from work, school, etc: *What's for tea tonight, mum?* Compare HIGH TEA. ⇨ note at MEALS.

ˈ**teaching ˌhospital** *n* a hospital where medical students are taught. Many of Britain's largest and best-known hospitals are teaching hospitals. As well as having medical students, they also have some of the best doctors and equipment in the country. Teaching hospitals in the US are often part of medical schools or associated with them.

the ˈ**Teamsters** /ˈtiːmstəz; *AmE* ˈtiːmstərz/ (*also* the ˈ**Teamsters ˌUnion**) the largest US trade union. It was established in 1903 and in 1997 had about 1.4 million members. A teamster is a person who drives a lorry/truck, but the union now includes many other professions. Its full official name is the International Brotherhood of Teamsters, Chauffeurs, Warehousemen and Helpers of America. Because of illegal activities within the union, the Teamsters were put out of the *AFL-CIO from 1957 to 1987. See also HOFFA.

ˈ**Teapot ˌDome** a US political scandal in 1922 in the government of President Warren G *Harding. Secretary of the Interior Albert Fall secretly accepted money from the Mammoth Oil Company to let them develop oil lands at Teapot Dome, *Wyoming, and Elks Hill, *California. The Senate investigated, and Fall left the government in 1923. He was later sent to prison.

ˌNorman ˈ**Tebbit** /ˈtebɪt/ (1931–) an English *Conservative politician who held several important govern-

T

ment posts under Margaret *Thatcher. He is known for his right-wing opinions. In the 1980s he was well known for using the phrase 'on your bike' to suggest that unemployed people should get on their bicycles and look for work, rather than expecting the state to help them. In the 1990s he used the phrase 'the cricket test' to suggest that people in Britain whose families came originally from other countries could not be regarded as British if they still supported the sports teams of their original countries. He was made a *life peer in 1992.

'techno /'teknəʊ; *AmE* 'teknoʊ/ *n* [U] a type of loud, fast dance music that is a mixture of electronic music and 'samples' (= short pieces of music recorded from other records). It became very popular in Britain and America in the 1990s, especially among young people who go to nightclubs.

Te'cumseh /tə'kʌmsə/ (*c.* 1768–1813) a leader of the *Shawnee *Native-American people. He tried to unite them to defend their lands against white people. His efforts failed when his brother, Tenskwatawa 'the Prophet', was defeated at the Battle of Tippecanoe (1811). Tecumseh later supported the British in the *War of 1812 and was killed during a battle.

'teddy bear *n* a soft toy bear. In Britain and America, teddy bears are typically given to babies and very young children. Some older children, and even some adults, still have the teddy bears that they were fond of when they were younger. The first teddy bears were made in the US, where they were named after President Theodore (Teddy) *Roosevelt, because he was thought to have saved a very young bear while hunting one day.

teddy bears

'teddy boy (*also* **ted**) *n* (in Britain, especially in the 1950s) a young man following a popular fashion in clothing and music. Teddy boys wore long, loose jackets, called *drape coats*, very narrow trousers, called *drainpipes*, and leather shoes with narrow points at the end, called *winkle-pickers*, or soft shoes with thick rubber soles, called *brothel creepers*. They put special oil on their hair and arranged it so that it stood up at the front. Teddy boys were strongly associated with *rock and roll music. They were seen as being rebellious and were sometimes involved in violence. Their style of clothing was intended to be similar to that of certain fashionable young men in Britain during the *Edwardian period in the early 20th century. (Ted is a short form of Edward.).

ˌ*Te 'Deum* /ˌtiː 'diːəm/ an ancient Latin hymn, praising God. It is traditionally sung on special occasions in morning church services, in Latin in the *Roman Catholic church and in English in the *Church of England. In Latin it begins with the words *Te Deum laudamus*, meaning 'We praise you, O God'.

the **Tees** /tiːz/ a river in north-east England that flows from the *Pennines through the *Teesside region and into the *North Sea at the port of Middlesborough.

'Teesside /'tiːzsaɪd/ an industrial area within the county of *Cleveland(1) in north-east England, consisting mainly of the port of Middlesborough and its surrounding areas. Its main industries have been steel and chemicals, although in recent times its industries have suffered and many local workers have become unemployed.

TEFL /'tefl/ (*in full* the **Teaching of English as a Foreign Language**) the practice or business of teaching the English language to people for whom English is a foreign language. Both in Britain and in other countries, this often takes place in private language schools and in Britain courses are usually taught completely in English. TEFL began to grow into what is now a major industry in the 1970s.

'Teflon™ *n* [U] a substance used to form a surface on e.g. cooking implements and pans to stop food, etc. sticking to them and so making them easier to clean. It was invented in 1938 by the US company *DuPont. The name is now used to describe politicians and others who make mistakes or act illegally but manage to avoid being blamed or charged. Ronald *Reagan was often called the 'Teflon President'.

the **ˌTelecom 'Tower** /ˌtelɪkɒm; *AmE* ˌtelɪkɑːm/ a very tall tower in central London which is one of the city's best-known landmarks. It is 620 feet/189 metres high and was completed in 1966. It is a communications centre for telephone, television and radio communications. It was originally called the Post Office Tower until the *Post Office and *British Telecom became separate organizations, and British Telecom has an office there. There was originally a restaurant at the top of the Tower which moved round continuously and gave excellent views over London, but this was closed in 1971 after a bomb attack on the Tower.

the **'*Telegraph*** ⇨ *DAILY TELEGRAPH*. See also SUNDAY TELEGRAPH. ⇨ article at NEWSPAPERS.

'Teletext a British television information service provided on *ITV and *Channel Four. It offers many different types of information, e.g. weather reports, sports results, financial news and advertisements, and the information is shown without sound. It is available by use of a remote control device on most modern televisions. Compare CEEFAX.

'*Teletubbies* /'telitʌbiz/ a popular British television series (1997–) for young children. Its main characters are Tinky Winky, Dipsy, Laa-Laa and Po, four large creatures covered in brightly coloured fur, with television screens on their stomachs, who talk a simple language like that of very young children. In 1997 the characters appeared on a successful pop record, *Teletubbies Say Eh-Oh!*

the Teletubbies

ˌtele'vangelist /ˌtelɪ'vændʒəlɪst/ *n* (*esp AmE*) an *evangelist who has a series of religious programmes on television. Many have become very rich from money sent in by supporters. Well-known US televangelists include Jerry *Falwell, Oral *Roberts and Pat *Robertson. Such programmes lost supporters in the 1980s after Jim *Bakker was sent to prison for financial crimes and Jimmy *Swaggert admitted that he had visited a prostitute. ▶ **televangelism** *n* [U].

'television ˌlicence (*also* **'TV ˌlicence**) *n* (in Britain) an official piece of paper giving permission to own a television. The cost of this (the **licence fee**) is set every year by the government, with one price for colour televisions and a lower price for black-and-white televisions. A licence lasts for one year. The money collected in this way is used to pay for *BBC television and radio programmes.

ˌThomas ˈ**Telford** /ˈtelfəd; *AmE* ˈtelfərd/ (1757–1834) a Scottish engineer who designed many bridges, canals and roads in Britain. Among his best-known achievements are the *Caledonian Canal in northern Scotland and the *Menai Bridge in north Wales. Many of his bridges are still in use.

ˌEdward ˈ**Teller** /ˈtelə(r)/ (1908–) a US scientist who has been called the 'father of the hydrogen bomb'. He was born in Hungary and became a US citizen in 1941. He worked on the first atom bomb during the *Manhattan Project and then led the team of scientists who created the first hydrogen bomb, which was exploded in 1952.

the ˈ**temperance ˌmovement** a movement involving organized campaigns by various groups in the US, Britain and some other countries in the 19th century to persuade people to drink little or no alcohol. These groups believed that the effects of alcohol were bad both for individual people and for society in general.

The ˈ***Tempest*** a play by William *Shakespeare, probably written in 1611 and generally thought to be the last play he wrote. It takes place on an island and its central character is Prospero, who lives there with his daughter Miranda. Prospero, who has magic powers, has been illegally replaced as duke of Milan by his brother Antonio and uses his magic powers to create a storm. In the storm, his brother's ship is wrecked and his brother and others come onto the island. With the help of Ariel, a magical creature, Prospero then gets back his position as duke.

the ˈ**Temple**[1] a group of buildings in the *City of London, England, which contain two of the *Inns of Court, the Inner Temple and the Middle Temple. Lawyers work and are trained there.

ˌShirley ˈ**Temple**[2] /ˈtempl/ (1928–) the most famous and popular child star in the history of *Hollywood. She was known for the curls in her hair and the dimples (= hollow places) in her cheeks. Her many films, in which also danced and sang, included *Curly Top* (1935), *Heidi* (1937) and *Rebecca of Sunnybrook Farm* (1938). She was later, under her married name of Shirley Temple Black, an active *Republican(1) politician. She was appointed as a US representative to the *United Nations (1969) and as ambassador to Ghana (1974–6) and Czechoslovakia (1989–92).

ˈ**Temporary Asˈsistance to ˈNeedy ˈFamilies** (*abbr* **TANF**) a US government programme that provides financial help for poor families with children. It is run by the US Department of Health and Human Services, and each state receives a certain amount of money. It provided more than $20 billion in 1996.

The ˌ***Ten Comˈmandments*** a US film (1956) which at the time was the most expensive ever made. It was directed by Cecil B *De Mille, who had made a silent version of it in 1923. It tells the Bible story of Moses and was filmed in Egypt with Charlton *Heston as Moses and Yul Brynner as the Egyptian king Rameses II.

ˌ***Tender is the ˈNight*** a novel (1934) by the US writer F Scott *Fitzgerald. It is about the unhappy marriage of a rich American couple, Dick and Nicole Diver, living on the French Riviera in the 1920s. The story was based on the Fitzgerald's own marriage problems. A film version was made in 1962.

1040 form /ten ˈfɔːti fɔːm; *AmE* ˈfɔːrti fɔːrm/ *n* (in the US) the main official income tax document that people must complete and send to the *IRS each year by 15 April. It contains questions to show whether a person owes tax or has paid too much. There are shorter versions of the document for people whose income is below a certain amount.

ˌ**ten-gallon ˈhat** *n* a tall hat with a wide brim worn, especially by US *cowboys, to protect the face against the bright sun. Compare STETSON.

ˌ***Ten Green ˈBottles*** a traditional song, sung especially by children. It is about ten bottles falling off a wall one by one and many of the words are repeated many times. The song begins:

Ten green bottles hanging on the wall.
Ten green bottles hanging on the wall.
And if one green bottle should accidentally fall,
There'll be nine green bottles hanging on the wall.
Nine green bottles hanging on the wall.
Nine green bottles ...

ˌ**Tennesˈsee** /ˌtenəˈsiː/ a south-eastern US state, also called the Volunteer State. It became a state in 1796 and later joined the *Confederate States. Many *Civil War battles were fought there. The largest city is *Memphis and the capital city is *Nashville. Tourist attractions include the *Great Smoky Mountains, *Graceland and the *Grand Ole Opry. Its products include corn, tobacco, cotton, chemicals and electrical goods. See also SHILOH, TENNESSEE VALLEY AUTHORITY.

ˌ**Tennessee ˈValley Auˌthority** /ˌtenəsiː/ (*abbr* **TVA**) an independent US government organization that provides cheap electricity to seven southern states. TVA was established in 1933 by President Franklin D *Roosevelt, as part of his *New Deal, to encourage the economic development of the area around the Tennessee River. As well as providing electricity it builds and operates dams, controls floods and protects the soil.

ˌJohn ˈ**Tenniel** /ˈteniəl/ (1820–1914) an English artist and cartoonist, best known for his illustrations of Lewis *Carroll's books **Alice in Wonderland* and **Through the Looking Glass*. These still appear in versions of the books produced today and most people identify them closely with the original stories. Tenniel was also for many years a political cartoonist for the magazine **Punch*. He was made a *knight in 1893.

ˈ**tennis** (*also* ˌ**lawn ˈtennis**) *n* [U] a game for two or four players, who hit a small soft ball backwards and forwards over a low net using rackets. It is often played on a grass court but can also be played on harder surfaces. See also DAVIS CUP, GRAND SLAM 1, REAL TENNIS, US OPEN 2, WIGHTMAN CUP, WIMBLEDON.

ˌLord ˈ**Tennyson** /ˈtenɪsn/ (Alfred Tennyson 1809–92) an English poet known especially for his long narrative poems (= ones that tell a story). He made his reputation with the poem **In Memoriam*, which he wrote after the sudden death of his close friend Arthur Hallam and published in 1850. The same year he was made a *Poet Laureate. His other well-known poems include *The *Lady of Shalott*, *Maud*, **Idylls of the King* and *The *Charge of the Light Brigade*. He was made a *baron in 1884.

1066 /ˌten sɪksti ˈsɪks/ the year when the Battle of *Hastings took place, and the *Normans gained control of England. It is one of the few dates that most British people remember, because it was the last time that Britain was successfully invaded by the forces of another country.

1066 And All That /ˌten sɪksti ˈsɪks ənd ɔːl ˈðæt/ a humorous book (1930) about the history of Britain which also makes fun of the way in which it was taught in schools. The two authors, Walter Sellar and Robert Yeatman, were themselves teachers.

ˈˌStuds' ˈ**Terkel** /ˌstʌdz ˈtɜːkl; *AmE* ˈtɜːrkl/ (1912–) a US writer, born Louis Terkel. He is known for his 'oral histories' of Americans in which he records conversations with different groups within US society. His books include *Hard Times: An Oral History* *of the Great Depression in America* (1970), *The Good War: An Oral History of World War II* (1986), which won a *Pulitzer Prize, and *My American Century* (1997) which marked the end of his 52 years of broadcasting on radio.

the ˈ**Terrence** ˈ**Higgins** ˈ**Trust** /ˈhɪgɪnz/ a British charity whose activities are concerned with the disease Aids. It was established in 1982, when the first cases of Aids were beginning to appear in Britain, and took its name from one of the first people in Britain to die of the disease. It aims to provide care and support for people suffering from Aids, to give information and advice to prevent the disease from spreading, and to make the general public more aware of the issues surrounding Aids.

ˈ**terrier** *n* any of several breeds of small, lively and intelligent dogs. They were originally bred for hunting, during which they were often sent underground to chase out animals being hunted. Common types of terrier include the *Airedale terrier, the *cairn terrier, the *Jack Russell, the *Lakeland terrier, the *Scottie, the *Skye terrier and the *Yorkshire terrier.

the ˌ**Territorial** ˈ**Army** (*abbr* the **TA**) (*also infml* **Terriers**) a British military force of part-time voluntary soldiers who are trained to join with the professional British Army to defend the country in an emergency. It joined together with the British Army to fight in *World War II. The TA was established in 1908 and now has about 59 000 members as part of the *Volunteer Reserve Forces.

ˌEllen ˈ**Terry** /ˈteri/ (1847–1928) an English actor famous for her performances with Henry *Irving in plays by *Shakespeare. She was also known for the clever and amusing letters she and George Bernard *Shaw exchanged in the 1890s, which were published in 1931. She was made a *dame(2) in 1925.

TES /ˌtiː iː ˈes/ ⇨ *TIMES EDUCATIONAL SUPPLEMENT*.

ˈ**Tesco** /ˈteskəʊ; *AmE* ˈteskoʊ/ (*also* ˈ**Tesco's**) one of Britain's largest chains of supermarkets. It was started by Jack Cohen (1898–1979), a Jewish immigrant who started selling tea in a market in the *East End of London just after *World War I. In 1931 he opened two food shops in London, and by the beginning of *World War II there were about 100 Tesco shops in or near London. In the 1970s, Tesco 'superstores' began to appear and there are now hundreds all over Britain, in or just outside most towns and cities. The largest ones sell not only food but also clothes and household goods, as well as providing other services. In 1997, Tesco started its own bank: *I buy most of my food at Tesco.* ○ *There's a new Tesco's opening near us.*

TESSA /ˈtesə/ (*in full* **Tax-Exempt Special Savings Account**) *n* a type of account available in most British banks and *building societies People with these accounts do not have to pay any income tax on the interest that they earn, as long as they leave the money in the account for five years. TESSAs were introduced by the *Conservative government in 1991 to encourage people to save money.

ˌ***Tess of the*** ˈ***D'Urbervilles*** /ˈdɜːbəvɪlz; *AmE* ˈdɜːrbərvɪlz/ a novel (1891) by Thomas *Hardy. It tells the sad story of a young woman, Tess, and the troubles she has in her relationships with two men. She marries one and kills the other, for which she is *hanged. Many readers were shocked by the book's unhappy ending when it was first published.

the ˈ**Test Act** a law passed in England in 1673 which prevented *Roman Catholics from holding any official public position, including becoming *Members of Parliament, studying at a university or joining military forces. The law stated that people had to be members of the *Church of England to do any of these things. It was not cancelled until 1828.

ˌ***Test Match*** ˈ***Special*** a *BBC radio programme which provides complete commentary on every cricket test match (= international match) played in England and some test matches involving the England team in other countries. It began in 1957 and has become almost a national institution. It is known for the humorous style of the commentators when describing each game. Listeners regularly send them cakes and other food, which they also describe. The two most famous commentators have been John *Arlott and Brian *Johnston.

ˈ**Texaco** /ˈteksəkəʊ; *AmE* ˈteksəkoʊ/ a large US oil company that owns petrol/gasoline stations in many countries of the world. It was established in 1902 in Beaumont, *Texas, as The Texas Company, and the main offices are now in White Plains, New York.

ˈ**Texas** /ˈteksəs/ a large south-western US state, also called the Lone Star State because it was once an independent republic. The largest cities are *Houston and *Dallas, and the capital city is Austin. Texas became independent of Mexico in 1836 and a US state in 1845. It was also one of the *Confederate States. It has been well known for its *cowboys and now produces a lot of oil and gas as well as beef and many agricultural products. Tourists visit the *Alamo, Big Bend National Park and the *Lyndon B Johnson Space Center.

the ˌ**Texas** ˈ**Rangers** /ˌteksəs/ a division of the Texas state police. They were originally formed in 1823 as a small group of men who offered to protect communities from attacks by *Native Americans and Mexican criminals. The Rangers became a much larger group of law officers during the days of the *Wild West, and in 1935 they became part of the Texas Highway Patrol.

ˈ**Tex-Mex** /ˈteks meks/ *n* [U] (*AmE*) the Texan or other southern US variety of Mexican food, music, architecture, etc. ▶ **Tex-Mex** *adj*: *Anna took classes in Tex-Mex cooking.*

the **TGWU** /ˌtiː dʒiː dʌbljuː ˈjuː/ (*in full* the **Transport and General Workers' Union**) one of Britain's most important *trade unions, both in size and influence. It represents several different groups of workers, including transport workers, engineers, and factory and office workers. It was established in 1922, when 14 separate trade unions joined together. The TGWU has traditionally had strong links with the *Labour Party. See also TRANSPORT HOUSE.

ˈWilliam ˈMakepeace ˈ**Thackeray** /ˈmeɪkpiːs ˈθækəri/ (1811–63) an English writer best known for his long historical novel **Vanity Fair*(1). He was also a journalist, writing regularly for **Punch* and other magazines under many different names. His other successful novels include *The History of Pendennis* (1848–50) and *The Virginians* (1858–9).

ˌIrving ˈ**Thalberg** /ˌɜːvɪŋ ˈθɔːlbɜːg; *AmE* ˌɜːrvɪŋ ˈθɔːlbɜːrg/ (1899–1936) a US businessman who became head of film production at *Universal Pictures at the age of 20 and then at *MGM when he was 25. He was known as the 'boy wonder'. He produced such films as **Ben-Hur*, **Mutiny on the Bounty* and *The Good Earth* (1937). Thalberg was married to the actor Norma Shearer.

the **Thames** /temz/ the longest and best-known river in Britain. It is 210 miles/338 kilometres long and flows from the *Cotswolds in central England to the *North Sea after passing through the centre of London. Other famous towns on the river include *Oxford, *Windsor[1](1), *Henley and *Greenwich. Well-known bridges across the Thames in London include *London Bridge, *Tower Bridge and *Westminster Bridge. Large ships can sail up the Thames as far as London and smaller ones a further 86 miles (138 kilometres). A large area to the east of London was formerly a major port on the river, but in recent times this area has been turned into *Docklands.

the ˌ**Thames** ˈ**Barrier** /ˌtemz/ a large barrier built across the River *Thames at *Woolwich(1), east of London, to prevent London from being flooded. It was completed in 1982 and officially opened in 1984. It consists of ten gates, which lie on the bottom of the river when the barrier is not required. If there is a danger of flooding, the gates rise to form a solid wall 50 feet (15 metres) high.

Thanksgiving

Thanksgiving is celebrated in the US on the fourth Thursday in November. For many Americans it is the most important holiday apart from *Christmas. Schools, offices and most businesses close for Thanksgiving, and many people make the whole weekend a vacation.

Thanksgiving is associated with the time when Europeans first came to North America. In 1620 the ship the **Mayflower* arrived, bringing about 150 people who today are usually called ***Pilgrims**. They arrived at the beginning of a very hard winter and could not find enough to eat, so many of them died. But in the following summer *Native Americans showed them what foods were safe to eat, so that they could save food for the next winter. They held a big celebration to thank God and the Native Americans for the fact that they had survived.

Today people celebrate Thanksgiving to remember these early days. The most important part of the celebration is a traditional dinner with foods that come from North America. The meal includes **turkey**, **sweet potatoes** (also called **yams**) and **cranberries**, which are made into a kind of sauce or jelly. The turkey is filled with **stuffing** or **dressing**, and many families have their own special recipe. Dessert is **pumpkin** made into a pie.

On Thanksgiving there are special television programmes and sports events. In New York there is the ***Macy's Thanksgiving Day Parade**, when a long line of people wearing fancy costumes march through the streets with large balloons in the shape of imaginary characters. Thanksgiving is considered the beginning of the Christmas period, and the next day many people go out to shop for Christmas presents.

ˌTwyla ˈ**Tharp** /ˌtwaɪlə ˈθɑːp; *AmE* ˈθɑːrp/ (1942–) a US dancer and choreographer. She has created more than 80 dances, including *Push Comes to Shove* (1976) for Mikhail Baryshnikov. She also designed the dances for several films, including **Hair* and *Amadeus* (1984). Tharp has worked with the American Ballet Theatre, the Joffrey Ballet, New York City Ballet, the Paris Opera Ballet and the Martha Graham Dance Company.

T

ˌMargaret ˈ**Thatcher** /ˈθætʃə(r)/ (*also* ˌ**Mrs** ˈ**Thatcher**, ˈ**Maggie**, *now* **Lady Thatcher**) (1925–) a British *Conservative politician who became Britain's first female *prime minister and was one of the longest serving British prime ministers of the 20th century. She became a *Member of Parliament in 1959 and a member of the *Cabinet in 1970 when she was made *Secretary of State for education and science. In 1975 she defeated Edward *Heath in a party election, and became leader of the Conservative Party and Prime Minister in 1979 when the party won the general election. She believed that the state should not interfere in business, and privatized many industries that had been owned by the state. She reduced the power of the *trade unions by a series of laws, and defeated the miners in the *miners' strike in 1985. She also encouraged people not to rely on the *welfare state, and instead to pay for their own health care, education and pensions.

Margaret Thatcher

People were often critical of Mrs Thatcher's policies, and blamed her for the decline of many British industries and high unemployment. However she was seen as a very determined and patriotic prime minister, and she became especially popular after the *Falklands War. Because of this she was often referred to as the 'Iron Lady'.

After winning three general elections, she was forced to resign in 1991 by members of her own party who criticized her attitude to the *European Union. She was succeeded as Prime Minister by John *Major. She was made a *life peer in 1992 and is still a well-known public figure. See also POLL TAX, WESTLAND, WET.

ˈ**Thatcherism** /ˈθætʃərɪzəm/ *n* [U] the political and economic policies of Margaret *Thatcher when she was Britain's *Prime Minister. It is therefore especially associated with the 1980s in Britain. Some British people think that Thatcherism was good for the British economy because of the emphasis it placed on private enterprise (= the idea that business and industry should be controlled by private individuals or companies, not by the state), privatization, a reduction in inflation and government spending, and the idea that people should help themselves rather than relying on the state to help them. An opposite view is that Thatcherism led to the loss of Britain's traditional industries, a greater gap between the rich and the poor, more people without jobs, and a period in which many British people came to care less about each other than about making money.

ˈ**Thatcherite** /ˈθætʃəraɪt/ *n* a person, especially a *Conservative Party politician, who agreed completely with the policies of Margaret *Thatcher and supported them publicly.

▶ **Thatcherite** *adj* associated with or agreeing with the policies of Margaret *Thatcher: *a politician who showed Thatcherite tendencies in his early career.*

ˌ***That's*** ˈ***Life!*** a popular *BBC television programme (1973–94), presented by Esther *Rantzen. It combined serious items, e.g. investigations of companies treating members of the public badly or behaving illegally, with amusing items, such as comic songs, interviews in the street and strange stories involving members of the public.

ˈ***That Was The*** ˈ***Week That*** ˈ***Was*** (*also infml* **TW3**) a popular satirical programme on British television (1962–3). It was broadcast live late on Saturday nights on *BBC, and was presented by David *Frost. It was the first British television programme to make fun of the *Establishment and to make jokes that were critical of politicians. It caused much public debate and was criticized by several leading politicians. Later satirical programmes were influenced by its style.

the ˌ**Theatre** ˈ**Royal** a famous theatre in *Drury Lane in central London. It opened in 1812 and is the oldest theatre still in use in London. It is known mostly for presenting *musicals.

ˌ***There*** ˈ***is a*** ˈ***green hill*** ˈ***far a***ˈ***way*** the first line of a well-known Christian hymn traditionally sung at *Easter.

ˌ***There*** ˈ***was an old*** ˈ***woman*** a the first line of a well-known children's *nursery rhyme. The full rhyme is:

There was an old woman who lived in a shoe.
She had so many children she didn't know
what to do.
She gave them some broth without any bread,
Then scolded them soundly and sent them to bed

THES /ˌtiː eɪtʃ iː ˈes/ ⇨ *TIMES HIGHER EDUCATIONAL SUPPLEMENT*.

The ˌ***Thin*** ˈ***Man*** a crime novel (1932) by the US writer Dashiell *Hammett in which he created the married couple of Nick and Nora Charles. They solved crimes together and often discussed them in a humorous way. It was made into a film (1934) with William Powell and Myrna Loy, which was so successful that five more were made. Although the 'thin man' of the original book title was murdered, most people assumed from the titles of the films that it referred to Nick Charles.

The ˌ***Third*** ˈ***Man*** a story written by Graham *Greene for a successful film (1949), directed by Carol *Reed, and later published as a short novel. The story takes place in Vienna just after the end of *World War II and is about a US journalist's search for his friend Harry Lime. Lime has made it appear that he died in a road accident but in fact he is involved in selling harmful drugs. The star of the film is Orson *Welles as Lime, although he appears in very few scenes. Many people remember the film's music, which is played on a zither, an instrument with many strings stretched over a flat wooden box, played with the fingers.

ˌ**third** ˈ**reading** *n* [C] the third and last discussion about a *bill(1) (= a possible new law) in the British parliament. If agreement is reached, the bill later officially becomes a law.

the ˌ**thirteen** ˈ**colonies** the original 13 areas controlled by Britain in what is now the eastern US. They joined together to fight the *American Revolution and became the first 13 states. The colonies were, from north to south, *New Hampshire, *Massachusetts, *Rhode Island, *Connecticut, *New York, *New Jersey, *Pennsylvania, *Delaware, *Maryland, *Virginia, *North Carolina, *South Carolina and *Georgia.

ˌ***Thirty*** ˈ***days hath Sep***ˈ***tember*** the first line of a traditional rhyme which helps people to remember how many days there are in each month. The words are:

Thirty days hath September,
April, June and November.
All the rest have thirty-one
Excepting February alone.

the **38th parallel** /ˌθɜːtiəɪtθ ˈpærəlel / the line on the map that marks the border between North Korea and South Korea, established in 1945 after *World War II. When US troops crossed it during the *Korean War in 1950 this caused the Chinese to enter the war. It was again used as the border when peace was signed in 1953.

the ˌ**Thirty-nine** ˈ**Articles** the set of religious principles that form the basic beliefs of the *Church of England. They were agreed upon in 1571 and were based on an earlier set produced by Thomas *Cranmer in 1563. Traditionally they are printed at the end of *The *Book of Common Prayer* and anyone becoming a minister in the Church of England has to agree with them.

the ˌ**thirty-**ˈ**year rule** *n* [sing] a British government rule which prevents certain official documents from being made public until a period of thirty years has passed.

ˌ***This Is Your*** ˈ***Life*** a popular British television programme, broadcast regularly since 1955. Each programme tells the story of the life of a famous person or one who has helped others. They do not know about it in advance, and the presenter surprises them at the beginning of the programme. They are then taken to a television studio where their friends, family and other people who have been important in their lives appear as guests and tell stories about them. All the details of their life are collected in a big red book, which is given to them at the end of the programme. The programme was presented until 1987 by Eamonn *Andrews and since then it has been presented by Michael Aspel (1933–). A similar programme, with the same title, was broadcast on US television from 1952 to 1961.

ˈ***This little*** ˈ***pig went to*** ˈ***market*** the first line of a traditional *nursery rhyme which parents say to small children when counting their toes to amuse them. Each 'pig' is a toe, starting with the biggest. The full rhyme is:

This little pig went to market,
This little pig stayed at home,
This little pig had roast beef,
This little pig had none,
And this little pig cried, Wee-wee-wee-wee-wee,
I can't find my way home.

ˌDylan ˈ**Thomas** /ˌdɪlən ˈtɒməs; *AmE* ˈtɑːməs/ (1914–53) a Welsh writer. He is known especially for his radio play **Under Milk Wood* (1953) and for his poems, the best-known of which were published in two collections, *Deaths and Entrances* (1946) and *Collected Poems* (1952). His collection of short stories, *Portrait of the Artist as a Young Dog*, was published in 1940. Thomas had a reputation for often getting drunk and he died in the US as a result of drinking too much alcohol.

Dylan Thomas

ˌ**Thomas à** ˈ**Becket** /ə ˈbekɪt/ ⇨ BECKET.

ˌ**Thomas** ˈ**Cook** /ˈkʊk/ ⇨ COOK.

ˌ**Thomas, the** ˈ**Tank** ˌ**Engine** the best-known character in a popular series of British children's stories about railways (1945–72) written by the Rev Wilbert *Awdry and later by his son Christopher. Thomas and the other trains in the books have faces and human characteristics and can speak. The books have been made into television programmes and videos for children.

ˌDaley ˈ**Thompson**[1] /ˌdeɪli ˈtɒmpsn; *AmE* ˈtɑːmpsn/ (1958–) a British athlete, the son of a Nigerian father and a Scottish mother. He was the greatest athlete of all time in the decathlon, a contest involving ten different events. He won gold medals in the Olympic Games in 1980 and 1984, in the World Championships in 1983, in the European Championships in 1982, and in the *Commonwealth Games in 1978, 1982 and 1986. He also broke the world record four times.

ˌEmma ˈ**Thompson**[2] /ˈtɒmpsn; *AmE* ˈtɑːmpsn/ (1959–) an English actor. After early work on television she won an *Oscar for her performance in the film **Howards End* (1992) and in 1995 directed her own version of Jane *Austen's **Sense and Sensibility*.

T

Her other films have included *The Remains of the Day* (1993), *Carrington* (1995) and *Primary Colors* (1998). She has often acted with Kenneth *Branagh, to whom she was formerly married.

ˌJ J ˈ**Thomson**[1] /ˈtɒmsn; *AmE* ˈtɑːmsn/ (Joseph John Thomson 1856–1940) an English physicist who won the *Nobel Prize for physics in 1906 for discovering the electron. He was also responsible for running the *Cavendish Laboratory in Cambridge, England, which became the world's leading centre for research into atomic physics. His son George Thomson (1892–1975) and seven of his assistants all won Nobel Prizes. He was made a *knight in 1908.

ˌRoy ˈ**Thomson**[2] /ˈtɒmsn; *AmE* ˈtɑːmsn/ (1884–1976) a Canadian newspaper owner who created an international business empire based in Britain. The **Thomson Organization** includes publishing, travel, printing, radio and television companies all over the world. At one time Thomson was the owner of two British national newspapers, the **Sunday Times*, which he bought in 1959, and *The *Times*, which he bought in 1966. He was made a *life peer in 1964.

ˌWilliam ˈ**Thomson**[3] /ˈtɒmsn; *AmE* ˈtɑːmsn/ (1824–1907) a British physicist and inventor. He did much work on the laws of thermodynamics and in 1848 produced a temperature scale that later became known as the Kelvin Scale. He also did important work in the areas of magnetism and electricity. He invented many scientific instruments, especially for use at sea, and was involved in the laying of the first cable under the Atlantic. He was made a *knight in 1866 and a *baron in 1892.

The ˈ***Thomson Diˌrectory*** /ˈtɒmsn; *AmE* ˈtɑːmsn/ (in Britain) a book containing the names, addresses and telephone numbers of businesses in a particular area. Copies of the book are delivered free to every house and business, and there are different versions for each area of the country.

ˈHenry ˈDavid ˈ**Thoreau** /ˈθɔːrəʊ; *AmE* ˈθɔːroʊ/ (1817–62) a US writer and poet who believed strongly in the rights of individual people. As an experiment he lived a simple life for two years (1845–7) in a small wooden house near *Concord, *Massachusetts, and then wrote about this in *Walden, or Life in the Woods* (1854). He also wrote the essay *Civil Disobedience* (1849), a work that influenced such leaders as Mahatma Gandhi and Martin Luther *King to protest in a peaceful way. See also TRANSCENDENTALISM.

ˌSybil ˈ**Thorndike** /ˈθɔːndaɪk; *AmE* ˈθɔːrndaɪk/ (1882–1976) an English actor best-known for her performances in the plays of *Shakespeare, especially at the *Old Vic theatre in London. She also appeared in several films and continuing acting until she was 87 years old. She was made a *dame(2) in 1931.

T

ˌ**Thorn-EMˈI** /ˌθɔːn iː em ˈaɪ; *AmE* ˈθɔːrn/ a large British company involved in music recording and selling, music publishing, and the renting and selling of electrical equipment.

ˌJeremy ˈ**Thorpe**[1] /ˈθɔːp; *AmE* ˈθɔːrp/ (1929–) a British politician who was the leader of the *Liberal Party (now called the *Liberal Democratic Party) from 1967 to 1976. He resigned when a former male model called Norman Scott claimed in public that they had had a homosexual relationship. In 1979 Thorpe and three others were tried and found not guilty of having planned to murder Scott, but the scandal ended his political career. He was a *Member of Parliament from 1959 to 1979.

ˌJim ˈ**Thorpe**[2] /ˈθɔːp; *AmE* ˈθɔːrp/ (1888–1953) a US athlete who is widely regarded as the greatest of the century. He was the first to win both the decathlon and pentathlon events at the Olympic Games (in 1912). He later played professional baseball (1913–9) and professional football (1917–29). He was chosen for the Football *Hall of Fame in 1963.

the ˌ**Thousand** ˈ**Guineas** (*also* the **1 000 Guineas** /ˌwʌn θaʊznd ˈɡɪniz/) a horse race that takes place at *Newmarket in eastern England every year in April or May. It is a flat race (= one without jumps) for female horses that are three years old, and the course is 1 mile/1.6 kilometres long. It is one of the most important horse races in Britain and was first run in 1814.

ˈ**Thousand** ˈ**Island** ˈ**dressing** *n* [U] a US sauce for salads. It is made with mayonnaise, *ketchup, eggs, red peppers, pickles, etc.

Threadˈneedle Street /θredˈniːdl/ a street in the *City of London where the *Bank of England has been situated since 1734. The Bank is sometimes referred to as the *Old Lady of Threadneedle Street.

the ˌ**Three** ˈ**As** /ˈeɪz/ the informal name for the *Amateur Athletic Association (AAA), the organization in charge of amateur athletics in Britain, which was established in 1880. It is also the name of the national competition the AAA organizes every year and which was first held in 1886. Since athletics became a professional sport, both the organization and the event have become less important.

ˌ***Three Blind*** ˈ***Mice*** a well-known *nursery rhyme which tells a rather unpleasant story. The words are:

Three blind mice, see how they run!
They all ran after the farmer's wife,
Who cut off their tails with a carving knife
Did you ever see such a thing in your life,
As three blind mice?

the ˌ**Three** ˈ**Choirs** ˌ**Festival** a British music festival which is held every year in either *Gloucester, *Hereford(1) or *Worcester. The three cities take turns to hold the event. Much of the music is performed by their cathedral choirs, though visiting choirs also take part. Most of the performances also take place in the cathedrals. The festival was first held in 1724.

3-D (*also* **three-D**) *n* [U] (in films) the quality of appearing to have three dimensions, i.e. depth as well as length and width. Audiences for 3-D films have to wear special glasses to get the proper effect. The process for making such films was invented in 1936 but not used by *Hollywood until the 1950s. Popular 3-D films included *House of Wax* (1953) and *Hondo* (1953). Only a few films were made after the 1950s, but a new 3-D cinema opened in 1997 in London, England.

ˌ**three-day eˈvent** *n* a type of horse-riding competition that lasts for three days. On the first day there is a dressage contest, in which judges decide how well riders can control their horses when performing certain movements. On the second day, there is cross-country riding, when the horses are ridden through the countryside. On the third day, there is show-jumping, when the horses have to jump over high barriers in a specially constructed area. The riders must ride the same horse on all three days. The two most important three-day events in Britain are held at *Badminton and *Burghley every year. They are less common in the US.

ˌ**three-line** ˈ**whip** *n* a written notice sent by the *Whips in the main British political parties to tell their *Members of Parliament that they must attend a particular debate and vote according to the wishes of their party leader. The instructions have three lines marked under them to show that they are very urgent. ⇨ article at PARLIAMENT.

ˌ***Three Little*** ˈ***Pigs*** a well-known children's story. It is about three little pigs and a wolf. The pigs each build their houses from different materials and the 'big bad wolf' tries to destroy their houses by blowing on them. Only the pig whose house is built with bricks remains safe.

3M /ˌθriː ˈem/ (*in full* **Minnesota Mining and Manufacturing Company**) a large US company best known for its *Scotch tape, *Scotchgard Fabric Protection and *Post-it Notes. It actually produces about 50 000 products, including household items, electrical equipment and chemicals. The company was established in 1902 and has its main office is in *St Paul, *Minnesota.

ˌThree ˈMen in a ˈBoat a humorous novel (1899) by Jerome K *Jerome. It tells the story of a journey taken by three men and a dog along the River *Thames in a rowing boat, and the many accidents that happen to them.

ˌThree Mile ˈIsland an US island south of Harrisburg, *Pennsylvania, where there was an accident in a nuclear power station on 28 March 1979. Some radiation got into the air, causing great fear among local people. This led to a lot of criticism of the national programme for producing nuclear power.

ˈThriller an album by Michael *Jackson that has sold more than any other in the history of music. It appeared in 1982 and by 1997 more than 25 million copies had been bought. Five of its songs became No. 1 hits, including *Beat It* and *Billie Jean*. Jackson later made a video, *The Making of Thriller*, which sold over a million copies.

ˌThrough the ˈLooking Glass a well-known children's book by Lewis *Carroll, first published in 1872 with illustrations by John *Tenniel. It is about the adventures in a strange world of Alice, a little girl who was also the subject of Carroll's earlier book **Alice in Wonderland*. These include meeting *Tweedledum and Tweedledee, *Humpty Dumpty(2) and the *lion and the unicorn. See also *JABBERWOCKY*, *WALRUS AND THE CARPENTER*.

Thrust SSC /ˌθrʌst es es ˈsiː/ a British vehicle which in 1997 broke the world land speed record in the Black Rock Desert, *Nevada. It was driven by Andy Green. SSC stands for 'supersonic car'.

Thrust SSC

ˈThunderbird /ˈθʌndəbɜːd; *AmE* ˈθʌndərbɜːrd/ (*also infml* **T-Bird**) *n* a popular US sports car, produced since 1954 by the *Ford Motor Company. Thunderbirds have become a familiar part of American life.

ˈThunderbirds /ˈθʌndəbɜːdz; *AmE* ˈθʌndərbɜːrdz/ a popular British television series for children, first shown in the 1960s. The puppet characters included Lady Penelope and the scientist Brains. The stories were about the Thunderbirds International Rescue Service which rescues people in space using special aircraft, vehicles and technical inventions.

ˌJames **ˈThurber** /ˈθɜːbə(r); *AmE* ˈθɜːrbər/ (1894–1961) a US writer of humorous stories who also drew comic drawings for them. They are often about men and women defeated by the ordinary problems of life. From 1927, most of his best work was published in the *The *New Yorker* magazine. His collections of stories include *My World and Welcome to It* (1942), which contains his best-known story, *The Secret Life of Walter Mitty*. See also MITTY.

ˈJ ˈStrom **ˈThurmond** /ˈstrɒm ˈθɜːmənd; *AmE* ˈstrɔːm ˈθɜːrmənd/ (James Strom Thurmond 1902–) a US Senator who has served longer than any other in the history of the *Senate. He has represented *South Carolina since 1954. He was also a candidate for President in 1948 for the States' Rights Party and was Governor of South Carolina (1947–51). Thurmond began as a *Democrat but later changed to the *Republican Party.

ˈticker-tape paˌrade *n* a traditional parade in US cities, especially New York, during which people throw many small bits of paper from the tall buildings onto the parade as it passes in the street. Such parades are held to honour famous people, such as Charles *Lindbergh after his famous flight. Ticker tape is paper in a thin strip from a machine used for receiving and recording telegraph messages, but the paper used in ticker-tape parades today is usually confetti (= tiny pieces of coloured paper traditionally thrown at weddings).

a ticker-tape parade in New York in honour of Charles Lindbergh, 1927

ˈtick-tack man /ˈtɪk tæk/ *n* (*pl* **men**) (*BrE*) a bookmaker (= a man who takes bets) at a horse-racing course, who communicates betting information to other bookmakers there by means of **tick-tack**, a special language of signals involving movements of the hands and arms.

ˌtied ˈhouse *n* (*BrE*) **1** a pub which is owned or controlled by a particular company and sells the beer produced by that company. Compare FREE HOUSE. **2** (*also* **tied cottage**) a home rented to somebody, especially a farm worker, by their employer, who owns it. The person can only continue to live there if he or she continues to be employed by the owner.

ˈTiffany's /ˈtɪfəniz/ a well-known jewellery shop on *Fifth Avenue in New York. It was established in 1839 by Charles Tiffany (1812–1902), and the shop now has branches in London, Paris and other cities.

ˌBill **ˈTilden** /ˈtɪldən/ (1893–1953) a US tennis player who was the leading player in the world during the

T

1920s. His popular name was 'Big Bill'. In 1920 he became the first American to win at *Wimbledon, and he also won there in 1921 and 1930. He won the *US Open(1) seven times (1920–5 and 1929) and played in 11 *Davis Cup teams.

ˌ***Till ˈDeath Us Do ˈPart*** a popular *BBC television comedy series (1965–75). The main character, Alf *Garnett, is not well educated and has extreme right-wing opinions, especially about black people and foreigners living in Britain. He argues all the time with his wife, his daughter and her husband, who all make fun of him. A US television series based on *Till Death Us Do Part*, called *All in the Family*, was broadcast on *CBS in the 1970s and 1980s. See also BUNKER.

ˌVesta **ˈTilley** /ˌvestə ˈtɪli/ (1864–1952) a famous male impersonator (= a woman pretending to be a man when performing on stage) in British *music-hall(1). Her most famous song was *Burlington Bertie*.

Time a popular US news magazine, published every week. It was started in 1923 by Henry Luce, the husband of Clare Booth *Luce, and Briton Hadden. It created offices for its journalists around the world and has developed a particular style of writing which has come to be called 'Timese'. It now has four different international versions. People consider it a great honour to have their picture on the cover of the magazine, and as a special feature every year it chooses a man or woman of the year. Its company, Time Inc, is part of *Time Warner.

ˌ***Time ˈOut*** a magazine published each week in London, England, and read mainly by young people. It gives details of the entertainment available in London each week (cinema, theatre, music, etc.) and information about exhibitions, museums, sports, special activities, etc. It also contains reviews and other articles. It was first published in 1968.

The ***Times*** a British national daily newspaper, the oldest in England. It was first published (as the *Daily Universal Register*) in 1785 and is generally regarded as having a lot of influence on public opinion. Though politically independent, it is seen as representing the attitudes and opinions of the *Establishment, and many of its readers support the *Conservative Party.

The newspaper went through a difficult period in the 1970s, when there were a number of industrial disputes involving *trade unions representing workers in the printing industry. A strike began in 1978 and the paper was not published for nearly a year. In 1981 Rupert *Murdoch became the owner and in 1986 he moved the paper's offices and printing works to a new building in *Wapping, east London.

The Times is noted for the quality and extent of its news reporting, for its editorials, in which the paper's own views on issues in the news are given, for the letters from readers, for the announcements of births, deaths and marriages, and for its *crossword. See also SUNDAY TIMES, THOMSON.

T

the ˌ***Times Eduˈcational ˌSupplement*** (*also infml* the ˌ***Times ˈEd***) (*abbr* the ***TES***) a British newspaper published each week by company that owns *The *Times*. It is for teachers and other people involved in education, and contains articles on education issues and advertisements for jobs in the teaching profession. It was first published in 1910.

the ˈ***Times ˈHigher Eduˈcational ˌSupplement*** (*abbr* the ***THES***) a British newspaper published each week by the company that owns *The *Times*. It is similar to the **Times Educational Supplement* but it is for teachers and other people involved in higher education (= education at colleges and universities rather than at schools). It was first published in 1972.

the ˌ***Times ˈLiterary ˌSupplement*** (*abbr* the ***TLS***) a British newspaper published each week by the company that owns *The *Times*. It consists mainly of reviews of new books and also includes articles on literature. It was first published in 1902.

ˌ**Times ˈSquare** a busy square in central *Manhattan(1), New York City. It is known for its bright lights and many theatres and cinemas. On New Year's Eve, thousands of people gather there to watch a ball move down the side of the No. 1 Times Square building as the new year approaches. The square is named after the Times Tower, once the offices of the **New York Times*.

Times Square

ˌ**Time ˈWarner** /ˌtaɪm ˈwɔːnə(r); *AmE* ˈwɔːrnər/ a very large US media and entertainment company that sells magazines, films, television programmes and videos all over the world. It was formed in 1989 when the magazine company Time Inc joined with the film company *Warner Brothers. It now operates in more than 100 countries. In 1996 it bought the *Turner Broadcasting System which owns *CNN. Time Warner's 30 magazines include **Time*, **People*, **Life* and **Sports Illustrated*.

ˈ***Tinker, ˈtailor, ...*** the first words of an old children's rhyme. It is usually said when counting things, such as the stones from fruit that has just been eaten, in order to see what the child will be when he or she grows up. The full version is:

Tinker, tailor, soldier, sailor,
Rich man, poor man, beggar man, thief.

ˌ**Tin ˈLizzie** (*also* ˌ**tin ˈlizzie**) /ˈlɪzi/ *n* (*AmE old-fash slang*) a popular name for the *Model T car. It is sometimes still used to mean any old or cheap car: *He was very rich but drove a tin lizzie all his life.*

ˌ**Tin Pan ˈAlley** (*becoming old-fash*) an informal name for the popular music industry, especially the people who write and publish songs. The name originally referred to an area of New York where such people worked.

ˈ**Tinseltown** /ˈtɪnsltaʊn/ an informal name for *Hollywood. Tinsel is a collection of bright shiny metal strips often used to decorate Christmas trees. It is cheap and does not last, which led to the comparison with Hollywood's false scenery and most actors' brief fame.

Tinˈtagel /tɪnˈtædʒəl/ a ruined castle and a village on the north coast of *Cornwall in south-west England. It is supposed to be the place where King *Arthur was born and is very popular with tourists.

ˌ**Tintern ˈAbbey** /ˌtɪntən; *AmE* ˌtɪntərn/ a beautiful ruined abbey by the River *Wye, near the border between England and Wales. It was originally built in the 12th century. It has been painted by many artists, including *Turner[2], and *Wordsworth wrote a romantic poem about it in his **Lyrical Ballads*.

ˌ**Tiny ˈTim** a character in the story *A *Christmas Carol* by Charles *Dickens. He is a disabled little boy, the son of Bob Cratchit who works for *Scrooge. Tiny Tim speaks the famous last words at the happy ending of the story: 'God bless Us, Every One.'

Diˌmitri ˈ**Tiomkin** /dɪˌmiːtri ˈtjɒmkɪn; *AmE* ˈtjɑːmkɪn/ (1894–1979) a US composer of film music. He was born in Russia and moved to the US in 1925. He won *Oscars for **High Noon*, *The High and the Mighty* (1954) and *The Old Man and the Sea* (1958). His other films included **It's a Wonderful Life*, *Friendly Persuasion* (1956) and *Giant* (1956).

ˌMichael ˈ**Tippett** /ˈtɪpɪt/ (1905–98) an English composer of classical music, much of which shows his strong concern for the suffering of human beings. He established his reputation in 1941 with the oratorio (= large piece of music for voices and orchestra) *A Child of Our Time*. He also wrote several operas, including *The Midsummer Marriage* (1955), *The Knot Garden* (1970), *The Ice Break* (1977) and *New Year* (1989). His other works include four symphonies and various songs and piano works. During *World War II he was sent to prison for a short time for refusing to fight. He was made a *knight in 1966 and a member of the *Order of Merit in 1983.

ˈ**Tipp-Ex**™ /ˈtɪp eks/ *n* [U] a liquid used for painting over written or typed mistakes on paper. It dries quickly and the correction can then be written or typed over it. Tipp-Ex is sold in small bottles with a small brush attached to the top on the inside. It is available in white and some other pale colours.

▶ **Tipp-Ex** *v* [T] to remove a mistake made on paper using Tipp-Ex or a similar product: *You'll have to Tippex the mistakes (out).*

Tiˈtania /tɪˈtɑːniə/ a character in *Shakespeare's play *A *Midsummer Night's Dream*. She is the queen of the fairies and the wife of *Oberon.

the ***Tiˈtanic*** /taɪˈtænɪk/ a very large British passenger ship which in 1912 sank on its first voyage across the Atlantic after hitting an iceberg (= a large mass of floating ice), although its owners had claimed that it could never sink. There were not enough lifeboats for all the passengers and over 1 500 people died. As a result of this disaster, new laws were introduced concerning safety at sea. The wreck of the ship was found at the bottom of the sea in 1985 and there have been several attempts to raise it to the surface, though without success. The disaster has been the subject of several films. The most recent of these, *Titanic* (1997), won 11 *Oscars and is the most financially successful film ever made.

the Titanic

ˌ***Titus Anˈdronicus*** /ˌtaɪtəs ænˈdrɒnɪkəs; *AmE* ænˈdrɑːnɪkəs/ a play by William *Shakespeare and possibly another writer, written about 1591. It is a tragedy that takes place in ancient Rome and there are many murders in it.

ˈ**Tlingit** /ˈtlɪŋɡɪt/ *n* (*pl* **Tlingits** *or* **Tlingit**) a member of the largest group of *Native Americans in *Alaska. There are about 14 000 Tlingits, and most live along the coast. They have kept many of their traditional skills and live by catching fish, making baskets, carving wood, and weaving.

TLS /ˌtiː el ˈes / ⇨ *Times Literary Supplement*.

Toad one of the main characters in *The *Wind in the Willows* by Kenneth *Grahame. Toad (an animal like a frog) is a very lively character who owns a big house. He becomes very enthusiastic about cars but is sent to prison for driving in a dangerous way. He escapes dressed as a woman and is then helped by his friends to get back into his home, which has been captured by his enemies.

ˌ***Toad of Toad ˈHall*** a play (1929) by A A *Milne, based on the children's story *The *Wind in the Willows* by Kenneth *Grahame. It is still regularly performed in Britain.

ˌ***To a ˈSkylark*** one of the best-known short poems by Percy Bysshe *Shelley. It was inspired by the song of a bird he heard when in Italy and begins with the famous lines:

Hail to thee, blithe Spirit!
Bird thou never wert.

ˌ***To ˈAutumn*** a poem (1819) by *Keats that celebrates the autumn season. It is sometimes referred to as *Ode to Autumn*. It is one of Keats's best-known poems, enjoyed by many people for the musical sounds of lines such as the famous opening:

Season of mists and mellow fruitfulness,
Close bosom-friend of the maturing sun.

ˈ**toby jug** /ˈtəʊbi; *AmE* ˈtoʊbi/ *n* a traditional type of large pottery container with a handle, for drinking beer, etc. from. It is usually in the form of a fat old man who is sitting, smoking a pipe and wearing a hat with three corners. Some people collect toby jugs and old ones can be quite valuable.

toby jugs made c. 1785

Toc H /ˌtɒk ˈeɪtʃ; *AmE* ˌtɑːk/ a British Christian organization formed after *World War I to encourage friendship and kindness in society. It developed from a club formed by a group of British soldiers in Belgium in 1915, in a building they called Talbot House, after Gordon Talbot, who was killed that year and was the brother of one of the members. The name Toc H comes from the former code in telegraphy for the letters T and H, standing for Talbot House.

Toˈday **1** a *BBC radio news programme, broadcast on *Radio 4 in the early morning from Monday to Saturday. Many people listen to it while they are getting up and having breakfast. It consists mainly of discussions about important matters in the news, especially politics. It was first broadcast in 1958. **2** a US national television news programme broadcast every day in the early morning on *NBC. It consists of a mixture of news, interviews, special features and informal discussion. People presenting the show have included Dave Garroway, Barbara *Walters, Tom *Brokaw, Jane Pauley and Bryant Gumbel. **3** a former British national newspaper which was established in 1986 but closed because of poor sales in 1995. It was the first British national newspaper to have colour photographs. *Today* was popular especially with *middle-class readers and was similar in style to *The *Express* and the **Daily Mail*.

ˌSweeney ˈ**Todd** ⇨ SWEENEY TODD.

TOEFL /ˈtəʊfl; *AmE* ˈtoʊfl/ (*in full* **Test of English as a Foreign Language**) an examination for students whose first language is not English and who wish to enter a university in the US.

ˌAlvin ˈ**Toffler** /ˌælvɪn ˈtɒflə(r); *AmE* ˈtɔːflə(r)/ (1928–) a US writer known for his books about future societies, written with his wife Heidi. *Future Shock* (1970) is about the anxiety felt by people who do not understand new technology. *The Third Wave* (1980) divides history into three periods of great change: the beginning of agriculture, the *Industrial Revolution and the present Information Age. *War and Anti-War* (1990) describes how companies can survive in the 21st century.

To ˌKill a ˈMockingbird the only novel (1960) by the US writer Harper Lee (1926–). It won the *Pulitzer Prize and is thought by many people to be the best US novel of the 20th century. The story is about Scout Finch, a young girl in *Alabama who learns about prejudice when her father, a lawyer, defends an *African American in a court case. Gregory *Peck won an *Oscar for his performance in the film version (1962).

ˌ**Tokyo** ˈ**Rose** /ˌtəʊkiəʊ ˈrəʊz; *AmE* ˌtoʊkioʊ ˈroʊz/ the name given by US soldiers during *World War II to Iva Ikuko Toguri d'Aquino (1916–). She was an American citizen who broadcast on a Japanese radio programme telling US soldiers to refuse to fight. After the war, she was sent to a US prison until 1956, and President *Ford gave her a pardon (= official notice forgiving somebody) in 1977. Compare HAW-HAW.

ˌJ R R ˈ**Tolkien** /ˈtɒlkiːn; *AmE* ˈtɔːlkiːn/ (John Ronald Reuel Tolkien 1882–1973) an English writer, best known as the author of *The Hobbit* (1937) and *The *Lord of the Rings* (1954–5). Tolkein was also a professor at *Oxford University.

ˌ**toll-ˈfree** *adj* (*AmE*) (of telephone calls) without cost. A person can make a toll-free call by using a company's toll-free number, e.g. one beginning with 1-800. The cost is paid by the company as a service to customers.

ˌ**tollhouse** ˈ**cookie** /ˌtəʊlhaʊs; *AmE* ˌtoʊlhaʊs/ *n* (*AmE*) a crisp sweet biscuit that contains small pieces of chocolate and sometimes pieces of nuts. The biscuits were first made in the 1930s at the Toll House restaurant in Whitman, *Massachusetts.

T

ˈ**tollroad** /ˈtəʊlrəʊd; *AmE* ˈtoʊlrəʊd/ (*also* ˈ**toll road**, *AmE* ˈ**tollway**, ˈ**turnpike**) *n* a road that drivers must pay to use. In the US such roads are now mostly motorways/freeways. The money may be collected from drivers as they join or leave them.

the ˌ**Tolpuddle** ˈ**Martyrs** /ˌtɒlpʌdl; *AmE* ˌtɔːlpʌdl/ the name given to six farm workers from the village of Tolpuddle in *Dorset, England, when they were found guilty in 1834 of illegal *trade union activity. They were punished by being sent to Australia for seven years. There were many protests about this, and in 1836 the decision was changed and they were brought back to England as free men.

ˌ**Tom and** ˈ**Jerry** characters in a popular US series of cartoon films. Tom, the cat, is always trying to catch Jerry, the mouse, but Jerry is too clever for him.

toˌmato ˈ**ketchup** ⇨ KETCHUP.

toˌmato ˈ**sauce** ⇨ KETCHUP.

the ˈ**Tomb of the** ˈ**Unknown** ˈ**Warrior** (*also* the ˈ**Tomb of the** ˈ**Unknown** ˈ**Soldier**) ⇨ UNKNOWN WARRIOR.

ˌTom Brown's ˈSchooldays /braʊnz/ a novel (1857) by the English author Thomas Hughes (1822–96) about a young boy growing up at *Rugby School, where Hughes himself was a pupil. A real headmaster of Rugby, Dr Thomas *Arnold, appears as a character in the book and has a great influence on Tom, but many of Tom's experiences are unhappy ones and he is often badly treated by a cruel older boy called *Flashman.

ˈ**Tombstone** /ˈtuːmstəʊn; *AmE* ˈtuːmstoʊn/ a town in the US state of *Arizona known for its violent history. It was established in 1879 for workers in the local silver mines, and the famous gun fight at the *OK Corral happened there in 1881. It nearly became a *ghost town, but tourists now come to see the OK Corral, *Boot Hill and other *Wild West places of interest.

ˌ**Tom** ˈ**Collins** /ˈkɒlɪnz; *AmE* ˈkɑːlɪnz/ *n* a drink made with gin, lemon or lime juice, fizzy water (= water containing bubbles of gas) and sugar, with ice added. Other versions can be made with different types of alcohol.

ˌTom ˈJones /ˈdʒəʊnz; *AmE* ˈdʒoʊnz/ a well-known novel (1749) by Henry *Fielding. It describes the complicated adventures of a young man called Tom Jones. Tom is found as a baby and brought up as his own son by Squire Allworthy, a wealthy landowner. He falls in love with Sophie Western, the daughter of another landowner, but is unfairly forced to leave home. Tom then travels around England, often getting into trouble, especially because of his affairs with a number of women. Tom has a good nature but is often not careful in his actions. The novel has many comic scenes and a happy ending, when Tom marries Sophie. The book has been made into a film (1963), with Albert *Finney as Tom, and into a *BBC television series (1997).

ˈ**Tommy** /ˈtɒmi; *AmE* ˈtɑːmi/ *n* (*infml, becoming old-fash*) a British soldier of the lowest rank. It is short for **Tommy (Thomas) Atkins**, the name formerly used as that of a typical soldier on official army documents, to show how these should be completed.

ˈTommy /ˈtɒmi; *AmE* ˈtɑːmi/ a rock opera (= a story told through a series of rock music songs), written by Pete Townshend of the group The *Who and originally recorded and performed by the group in 1969. It tells the story of a boy called Tommy who cannot hear, speak or see but who becomes very good at the game of pinball. It was made into a film (1974) directed by Ken *Russell, and later into a stage show.

ˌ**Tom** ˈ**Sawyer** ⇨ SAWYER.

ˌ**Tom** ˈ**Thumb** /ˈθʌm/ a tiny boy (no bigger than a thumb) who appears in many traditional British children's stories, as well as those of other countries.

ˈ**Tonga** /ˈtɒŋə; *AmE* ˈtɑːŋə/ a country in the south-west Pacific, consisting of over 150 small islands, many of them without inhabitants. Its former name was the Friendly Islands. It was part of the *British Empire from 1900 until 1970, when it became independent and a member of the *Commonwealth. It is ruled by a king or queen. Its capital city is Nuku'alofa and its official language is English. ► **Tongan** *adj, n.*

The ***Toˈnight Show*** a popular US television *chat show which has been running since 1954. Johnny *Carson presented it for 30 years (1962–92). He was replaced by Jay *Leno who has continued the tradition of a telling a few jokes before talking with guests and introducing music by the show's band.

ˈ**Tonka**™ /ˈtɒŋkə; *AmE* ˈtɑːŋkə/ a product name for a range of toy lorries/trucks produced by the US company Hasbro, Inc. They have been made for more than 50 years, first in metal and later in plastic, and are often collected.

the ˌ**Tonkin ˈGulf ˌincident** /ˌtɒnkɪn; *AmE* ˌtɑːnkɪn/ the incident which led to the *Gulf of Tonkin Resolution.

ˈ**Tonto** /ˈtɒntəʊ; *AmE* ˈtɑːntoʊ/ the *Native-American friend of the *Lone Ranger.

ˈ**Tony** /ˈtəʊni; *AmE* ˈtoʊni/ *n* (*pl* **Tonys**) any of the awards given in the US each spring by the American Theater Wing to the best *Broadway plays, actors and other professional theatre people. The Tonys began in 1947 and are named after Antoinette ('Tony') Perry (1888–1946) who produced and directed Broadway plays, and established the American Theater Wing in 1941.

ˈ**tooth ˌfairy** *n* [usu sing] an imaginary creature that some parents tell their children about. The children are told that, when one of their teeth falls out, the tooth fairy will leave a coin under their pillow if they leave the tooth there while they are asleep.

ˈ**Tootsie Roll**™ /ˈtʊtsi/ *n* a US chocolate candy bar that takes several minutes to chew. It was created in 1896 by Leo Hirshfield, an Austrian who had settled in New York, and named after his daughter. During *World War II, Tootsie Rolls were included in the meal boxes of US soldiers. They are now produced by Tootsie Roll Industries in *Chicago, whose other products include Tootsie Pops, Charms and Junior Mints.

ˈ***Top Gun*** the US film (1986) that made Tom *Cruise an international star. He plays the part of an aggressive student pilot at Top Gun, the US Navy Fighter Weapons School at *San Diego, *California. The film contains exciting scenes of air battles, and its song, *Take My Breath Away*, won an *Oscar.

ˌ**Top ˈMan** a chain of shops in Britain, selling fashionable clothes for boys and young men. They are owned by the company that also owns *Top Shop.

ˌ***Top of the ˈPops*** (*abbr* ***TOTP***) a British pop music programme, shown every week on *BBC television. Singers and groups that have made new records perform on the programme and videos are shown. The programme also includes a list of the top 30 most popular records of the week and ends with the No. 1 record of the week. *Top of the Pops* was first broadcast in 1964.

ˈ**Top Shop** a chain of shops in Britain selling fashionable clothes for girls and young women. They are owned by the company that also owns *Top Man.

ˈ**Topsy** /ˈtɒpsi; *AmE* ˈtɑːpsi/ the character of a young black slave girl in the novel **Uncle Tom's Cabin* by Harriet Beecher *Stowe. Topsy has no parents and, when asked to explain this, she answers, 'I 'spect I growed (= I expect I grew).' People often mention Topsy when they are talking about something that seems to have grown quickly without being noticed: *Once the arms race began, it just grew, like Topsy.*

Torˈnado /tɔːˈneɪdəʊ; *AmE* tɔːrˈneɪdoʊ/ *n* (*pl* **-oes**) a British military aircraft, used by the *Royal Air Force. The Tornado is both a fighter and a bomber.

Torˈquay /tɔːˈkiː; *AmE* tɔːrˈkiː/ a town by the sea in south *Devon, England. It has an unusually mild climate and this has made it a popular place for holidays since the early 19th century. In 1968 Torquay joined together with the small towns of Paignton and Brixham, which are close to it, to form a district called Torbay. This is advertised as 'The English Riviera' because of its warm weather.

The ˌ***Tortoise and the ˈHare*** one of the best known of **Aesop's Fables*. It tells the story of a race between a tortoise (= a creature that moves very slowly) and a hare. The hare is very confident of winning, so it stops during the race and falls asleep. The tortoise continues to move very slowly but without stopping and finally it wins the race. The moral lesson of the story is that you can be more successful by doing things slowly and steadily than by acting quickly and carelessly.

Aesop's Fables: The Tortoise and the Hare, *illustrated by Charles Folkard*

ˌ**Torvill and ˈDean** /ˌtɔːvɪl ənd ˈdiːn; *AmE* ˌtɔːrvɪl/ **Jayne Torvill** (1957–) and **Christopher Dean** (1958–), a pair of English ice dancers who together won many international competitions in the 1980s. They were the Olympic champions in 1984 and the world champions every year from 1981 to 1984. They were known for their exciting, dramatic performances and for the number of times they were given maximum points by judges. Later, they became professional and performed in specially created shows on ice.

Torvill and Dean

ˈ**Tory** *n* a member of one of the two main political parties in Britain from the 1670s until the 1830s. The Tories were originally a group of politicians who wanted the *Roman Catholic James, Duke of York (later *James II) to be allowed to become king of England. They were powerful for various periods during the 18th and 19th centuries. In the 1830s, the Tories developed into the *Conservative Party and the name is widely used as an informal alternative name for the Conservative Party.

ˈ**Total**™ /ˈtəʊtl; *AmE* ˈtoʊtl/ a British oil company which also operates petrol/gasoline stations.

the **Tote** /təʊt; *AmE* toʊt/ the informal short name

for the Horserace Totalisator Board, a British government organization, established in 1929, which operates a system of betting on all British racecourses and owns a chain of more than 100 betting shops. Its profits are put back into the sport of horse-racing.

ˌ**Tottenham Court ˈRoad** /ˌtɒtnəm; *AmE* ˌtɑːtnəm/ one of the main streets in central London. It is known for the large number of shops there selling radio, television and video equipment and home computers. The furniture shop *Heal's is also on Tottenham Court Road.

ˌ**Tottenham ˈHotspur** /ˌtɒtnəm ˈhɒtspɜː(r); *AmE* ˌtɑːtnəm ˈhɑːtspɜːr/ (*also infml* **Spurs** /spɜːz; *AmE* spɜːrz/) an English football club whose home ground is at White Hart Lane in the north London district of Tottenham. It was established in 1882 and has had many successes. In 1961 it became the first club in the 20th century to win both the League Championship and the *FA Cup in the same season. It has won the FA Cup eight times and the League Championship twice. Famous players who have played for the club in recent years include Paul *Gascoigne and Gary *Lineker.

the ˌ**Tottenham ˈThree** /ˌtɒtnəm; *AmE* ˌtɑːtnəm/ the name given to three young men who in 1987 were sent to prison for life for having taken part in the murder of a policeman during violent events on the *Broadwater Farm Estate in Tottenham, north London. After a campaign of protest, they were officially declared innocent of the crime in 1991, when it was shown that some of the police evidence against them had been false. Together with similar cases at the time, this caused some concern in Britain about dishonest behaviour by the police and about whether the legal system was always fair. See also BIRMINGHAM SIX, GUILDFORD FOUR, MAGUIRE SEVEN.

ˈ**tourist ˌoffice** (*also* ˌ**tourist inforˈmation ˌoffice**) *n* (in Britain) an office in many towns and cities where tourists can get information on interesting things to see and do in the local area, help with finding somewhere to stay, and advice on travel. Tourist offices often also sell postcards, souvenirs, etc.

the ˌ**Tourist ˈTrophy** (*abbr* the **TT**) Britain's most important event for motor cycles, consisting of a series of races held every year on the *Isle of Man. It was first held in 1907 and takes place on ordinary roads. It can be dangerous and a number of riders have been killed taking part in it.

the ˌ**Tour of ˈBritain** the most important international bicycle race in Britain. It takes place every year and was first held in 1951. It lasts for 12 days, takes place on roads all over Britain, and covers a total distance of approximately 1 000 miles (1 600 kilometres). Since 1987 the race has been sponsored (= paid for) by *Kellogg's. In previous years, when it was sponsored by the *Milk Marque, it was often called the Milk Race.

T

ˌ**Tower ˈBridge** a bridge across the River *Thames and one of the most famous structures in London. It was built between 1886 and 1894 and is close to *London Bridge and the *Tower of London. Its towers are in the *Gothic style and the part of the bridge with the road on it can be raised to allow ships to pass through.

ˌ**Tower ˈHamlets** /ˈhæmləts/ a *borough of London, England, on the east side of the city and north of the River *Thames. It includes the *Docklands area.

ˌ**Tower ˈHill** an area of high ground close to the *Tower of London where in former times certain prisoners held in the Tower, especially the most famous and important ones, were executed by having their heads cut off.

the ˌ**Tower of ˈLondon** /ˈlʌndən/ one of the oldest and most famous buildings in London, England. It is an ancient fortress (= strong castle) on the north bank of the River *Thames to the east of the city, and is a popular tourist attraction. It was made a *World Heritage Site in 1988.

The building of the Tower was begun in the 11th century by *William the Conqueror, and completed in the 13th century. At various times it was a royal palace, the last monarch to live there being *James I in the early 17th century. It is best known, however, as a prison in which many famous people accused of crimes against the king or queen were kept. These included *Mary Queen of Scots, Anne *Boleyn and Thomas *More.

The Tower of London has many well-known features. These include the *White Tower, which is the oldest part, the *Bloody Tower, where some prisoners were kept, and *Traitor's Gate, an entrance for prisoners on the bank of the river. The *Crown Jewels have been kept there since 1303 and are on public display. Perhaps the most famous image associated with the Tower is that of the *Yeomen Warders, the official guards, who are also known as *beefeaters. They were established in the 16th century and still wear costume of the *Tudor(1) period.

ˌ**town and ˈgown** a phrase used about certain towns and cities where there are universities, especially *Oxford and *Cambridge, to describe the contrast between the two kinds of people who live there. 'Town' refers to the people who live and work there permanently and who are not 'gown', i.e. students or members of the academic staff of the university. The phrase is often used to indicate that there is tension between the two groups because of their different backgrounds and interests: *a town-and-gown incident involving students and local youths.*

ˌ**Townswomen's ˈGuild** /ˌtaʊnzwɪmɪnz/ *n* any of over 2 000 branches of a society for women in British towns and cities. The Townswomen's Guilds were established to encourage friendship between women. They hold social events, organize activities to benefit the community and represent the views of women on issues that affect them. They were formed in 1929 and developed from earlier groups which had been involved in trying to change the law so that women could vote. Compare WOMEN'S INSTITUTE.

ˈ**Toxteth** /ˈtɒkstəθ; *AmE* ˈtɑːkstəθ/ an area in central *Liverpool, which became famous in Britain in 1981 when there were a number of riots on the streets there. It was an area with many poor, black and unemployed people, and there was a lot of tension between the local people and the police. The violence attracted attention to the problems of people living in Britain's *inner cities, especially problems related to racial issues, poverty and unemployment.

Tower Bridge

toys and games

Most young children are given toys for their *birthday or at *Christmas. Many regularly spend their pocket money or allowance on smaller toys. Toys that have always been popular include building bricks such as *Lego, plastic farm animals, toy cars, model railways and dressing-up costumes. Girls especially have **dolls**, and several sets of clothes to dress them in. *Action Man figures are mainly for boys and *Barbie dolls for girls. Babies are given **rattles**, soft **cuddly toys** and a ***teddy bear**. **Action figures**, small plastic models of characters from television shows or films, are also popular. Some parents do not allow their children to have guns or other 'violent' toys because they do not want them to think it is fun to kill people.

Among traditional games that are still popular are marbles, which is played with small, coloured glass balls, **board games** such as *snakes and ladders and *ludo, **card games** such as *Happy Families, and **word games** such as *hangman. Board and card games are played with family or friends, but increasingly children play alone with **computer games**, such as Tetris and Minesweeper.

Many children collect things like shells, model animals, stamps or picture cards. In the US baseball cards, cards with a picture of a baseball player on them, are sold with bubblegum. In Britain picture cards are often given free in packets of tea or breakfast cereal.

Children play outside with skipping ropes, bicycles, skateboards and Rollerblades. In **playgrounds** there are often swings, a slide, a see-saw and a climbing frame (*AmE* jungle gym) to climb on. Traditional games played outside include hopscotch, a game in which children hop over squares drawn on the ground to try to pick up a stone, and tag, in which one child chases the others until he or she catches one of them and then that child has to chase the rest.

Toys are often expensive and even if they can afford them many parents are unwilling to spend a lot of money on something that they know their children will soon get bored with. Children want toys they see advertised on television or in *comics, or toys that their friends already have. There are sometimes crazes for toys connected with characters from a film. Some people believe that it is wrong to give children too many toys because they will become spoilt.

Few people give up toys and games completely when they become adults. Many keep their old teddy bear for sentimental reasons. There are now also **executive toys**, made specially for adults to keep on their desks. Many people play card games like bridge and poker, and board games such as **Monopoly, Trivial Pursuit*, backgammon and chess.

ˌToys 'R' ˈUs /ɑːr/ a large US company producing children's toys and clothes. In 1997 it had about 1 500 shops. The main office is in Paramus, *New Jersey.

ˈ*Toy ˌStory* a US film (1995) by the Walt Disney Company. It was the first film in which all the movements of the cartoon characters were created by computer. It is about a toy *cowboy who becomes jealous when his boy owner gets a toy astronaut.

ˌDick **ˈTracy**[1] ⇨ *DICK TRACY*.

ˌSpencer **ˈTracy**[2] /ˌspensə ˈtreɪsi; *AmE* ˌspensər/ (1900–67) a US actor, known for playing calm, reliable characters. He won *Oscars for his parts in *Captains Courageous* (1937) and *Boys Town* (1938). He had a long relationship with Katherine *Hepburn, and they made nine films together, including *Adam's Rib* (1949), *Pat and Mike* (1952) and his last, *Guess Who's Coming to Dinner* (1967). His other films include *Father of the Bride* (1950), *Bad Day at Black Rock* (1955), *The Old Man and the Sea* (1958) and *Inherit the Wind* (1960).

the ˌ**Trade Deˈscriptions Act** a British law, passed in 1968. It states that all goods and services offered to customers must be described in a way that is completely accurate and honest, and that it is illegal to make false claims about goods or services in advertising or in any other attempt to sell them: *They could be charged under the Trade Descriptions Act.*

the ˌ**Trades Union ˈCongress** ⇨ TUC.

Trade unions and labor unions ⇨ article.

the ˌBattle of **Traˈfalgar** /trəˈfælgə(r)/ an important sea battle (1805) in which the English, commanded by Lord *Nelson, defeated both the French and the Spanish. It was fought near Cape Trafalgar, in south-west Spain, during the *Napoleonic Wars. During the battle Nelson was badly wounded on his ship, *HMS *Victory*. As he lay dying he made the famous request to one of his senior officers: 'Kiss me, Hardy.' The victory established Britain as the world's leading power at sea for many years. See also ENGLAND EXPECTS.

Traˌfalgar ˈSquare /trəˌfælgə; *AmE* trəˌfælgər/ a large square in central London, England. It was created in 1830–41 and named in honour of Lord *Nelson's victory at the Battle of *Trafalgar. In the centre of the square is *Nelson's Column and on one side of it is the *National Gallery. It is one of London's most popular tourist attractions. It is also a place where political protests and other demonstrations are often held and very large numbers of people gather there every year to celebrate *New Year. See also ST MARTIN-IN-THE-FIELD.

ˈtraffic ˌwarden *n* (*BrE*) an official who is employed to make sure that parking laws are obeyed by drivers. Traffic wardens wear special uniforms and each of them is responsible for a particular area in a town, etc. If they find a car parked illegally, they can give a ticket which requires the driver to pay a fine.

the ˌ**Trail of ˈTears** the name given to the long journey from *Georgia to *Oklahoma made in 1838 by the *Cherokee and other *Native Americans. They were being forced by the US government to move to the *Indian Territory, and thousands died on the way. ⇨ note at LONG-DISTANCE PATHS AND NATIONAL TRAILS.

ˈTrailways /ˈtreɪlweɪz/ ⇨ CONTINENTAL TRAILWAYS.

ˈ*Trainspotting* a British film (1996) about a group of young people living in *Edinburgh who spend their time taking illegal drugs and committing crimes. The film was popular for its humour and realistic scenes, and was based on a novel by Irvine Welsh.

ˈtrain-ˌspotting *n* [U] (*BrE*) a hobby in Britain, popular mainly with boys but also with some adult men. It involves going to places where trains can be seen, especially railway stations, and collecting the numbers of railway engines they see by writing them down. People sometimes make fun of this hobby and the people who do it because they think it is a boring and ridiculous thing to do: *John goes train-spotting every weekend.*

▶ **train-spotter** *n* a person whose hobby is train-spotting.

ˌTraitor's ˈGate the main entrance to the *Tower of London from the River *Thames. It is a wide, low arch through which prisoners accused of crimes against the king or queen were taken on their way to being kept in the Tower.

ˈTranscash™ /ˈtrænzkæʃ/ a service offered by the *Post Office in Britain for people who want to make payments to charity or pay bills through *Girobank.

T

Trade unions and labor unions

The British trade union movement

The trade union movement was founded in the 19th century. Following the *Industrial Revolution workers began to form ***pressure groups**, often called **unions**, to defend their interests and to argue for improved working conditions and pay. Each **trade** (= type of work) formed its own **trade union** but, over the years, some combined with the unions of related trades to form larger, more powerful groups.

Among the best known and most influential unions are the *TGWU (Transport and General Workers' Union), the *AEEU (Amalgamated Engineering and Electrical Union), the *NUM (National Union of Mineworkers) and *UNISON.

Workers belonging to a union elect fellow-workers as **shop stewards** to negotiate on their behalf with the management. Union members are represented nationally by a local **chapel**. Many unions are **affiliated** (= linked) to the ***TUC** (**Trades Union Congress**), which represents the trade union movement as a whole. Representatives gather each September for the annual **congress** (= meeting). The Scottish TUC represents unions in Scotland.

Trade union influence in politics

At first, the interests of the unions were social and economic, but in 1900 the Labour Representation Committee was founded to enable the unions to enter politics. This later became the *Labour Party. Unions began sponsoring Labour *MPs, and many unions now have a **political fund** from which such money is taken. Members can choose not to give contributions to this fund.

By 1926 45% of the workforce were members of a union, and the ***General Strike** showed there was nationwide support for the union movement. After World War II union membership continued to grow. The political influence of the unions also increased as union leaders, particularly the General Secretary of the TUC, had high-level discussions with the Prime Minister. Membership of the unions reached a peak in 1979, with a total of 13.5 million members.

Throughout the 1960s and 1970s **industrial relations** (= relationships between workers and managers) were bad. Workers did not produce as many goods as workers in other countries, and the there were a lot of **strikes**. This condition came to be known as the *English disease. To try to avoid future strikes the independent organization ***ACAS** was set up to **mediate** (= try to get agreement) between workers and their employers.

In 1979, after the '*winter of discontent' when **industrial unrest** was particularly bad, the *Conservative government introduced a series of reforms to control the activities of the unions: a union was no longer allowed to send members to support strike action by another union (a practice called **secondary picketing**); union leaders could not declare a strike unless they had the support of a majority of their members in a secret ballot; the ***closed shop**, which required all employees in an industry to join a union, was ended.

In 1984 the NUM held a long and bitter strike to fight these reforms. Anyone who refused to **go on strike** or who joined the rival *UDM was called a **blackleg** and risked physical attack. The failure of the *miners' strike, after months of suffering, proved to many people that the days when union leaders could influence political thinking were over. In the 1990s the Labour Party tried to show that it is no longer greatly influenced by the unions and, as *New Labour, to gain wider popular support.

The US labor unions

In the US most unions are **labor unions**. Those that represent a particular trade or **craft**, e.g. the Union of Needletrades, Industrial, and Textile Employees may be called trade unions. The early unions were mostly crafts unions, but in 1905 the ***IWW** (**Industrial Workers of the World**) united miners and textile workers and became the first labor union. It demanded far-reaching social changes and was responsible for a lot of social unrest. Modern labor unions, which are concerned mainly with improving pay and conditions for their members, began as a result of Franklin D *Roosevelt's *New Deal. The Wagner Act of 1935 gave workers the right to **collective bargaining** (= negotiation by a group of people) for pay increases, and this led to many new unions being formed.

Most labor unions belong to the ***AFL-CIO**, which was created in 1955 when the American Federation of Labor joined with the Congress of Industrial Organizations. In 1998 there were 75 unions in the AFL-CIO, with a total of 13 million members. The larger ones included the International Brotherhood of *Teamsters, the American Federation of State, County and Municipal Employees, and the United Food and Commercial Workers' International Union. However, the largest union in the US, the *NEA (National Education Association), which has over 2.3 million members, is independent.

The activities of the labor unions

The reputation of the labor unions has been damaged by their history of violence, and by the activities of some union leaders. Many people were killed during workers' protests in *Chicago in the late 19th century and during a strike at the Carnegie Steelworks in *Pennsylvania in 1922. In the 1960s, two presidents of the Teamsters, Jimmy *Hoffa and Dave Beck, were sent to prison, and in 1997 the election for union president was found to have involved illegal campaign money.

The Department of Labor is responsible for seeing that laws concerning workers' pay and conditions are obeyed. The government supports the right of workers to belong to unions, but is opposed to strikes. The many strikes immediately after World War II caused *Congress to pass the *Taft-Hartley Act which restricted the right of workers to strike and also made the closed shop illegal. In 1981 air traffic controllers began an illegal strike and President *Reagan had most of them dismissed. A strike in 1997 by 185 000 Teamsters against United Parcel Service (UPS) had better results: workers received a pay increase and more jobs were created, which cost UPS $600 million.

Fewer people are now joining the unions, only about 14% of the workforce. The old struggles for fair pay, shorter hours and decent treatment have been won, and the emphasis is now on pay rises, job protection, equal rights and political influence.

The name Transcash was formerly used for a *Post Office system for sending money to and receiving money from other countries.

ˌ**transcenˈdentalism** *n* [U] a philosophy, influenced by the Hindu religion, which emphasizes the spiritual benefits to people of periods of deep thought instead of action. It involves **Transcendental Meditation**, a way of relaxing by sitting quietly and repeating to oneself a special phrase over and over again. It was first introduced into Britain by Maharishi Mahesh Yogi and attracted much publicity when the *Beatles practised it for a short period. Many people still practise it today, both in Britain and in the US, especially *California.

ˈ**Transit**™ (*also* ˌ**Ford** ˈ**Transit**, ˈ**Transit van**) a well-known model of van made by the *Ford Motor Company. It is widely used by companies and individual people whose work involves manual labour, such as builders, plumbers and decorators, because it is the right size for transporting the equipment they need in their work.

transport

Most journeys in Britain and the US are made by *road. Some of these are made on **public transport** (*AmE* **public transportation**) but most are by private car.

In Britain many people rely on their car for daily local activities, e.g. getting to work, doing the shopping, and visiting friends. People living in urban areas may use buses, trains or, in London, the *Underground, to get to city centres, mainly because traffic is often heavy and it is difficult to find anywhere to park a car. Some places in the country may have a bus only two or three times a week so people living there have no choice but to rely on their cars.

In the US large cities have good public transportation systems. The *El railroad in Chicago and the underground systems of New York, *Boston, *San Francisco and *Washington, DC are heavily used. Elsewhere, most Americans prefer to use their cars. Families often have two cars and, outside major cities, have to drive fairly long distances to schools, offices, shops, banks, etc. Many college and even *high-school students have their own cars.

Long-distance travel in Britain is also mainly by road, though ***railways** link most towns and cities. Most places are linked by *motorways or other fast roads and many people prefer to drive at their own convenience rather than use a train, even though they may get stuck in a traffic jam. Long-distance **coach/bus** services are usually a cheaper alternative to trains, but they take longer and may be less comfortable. Some long-distance travel, especially that undertaken for business reasons, may be by air. There are regular flights between regional airports, as well as to and from London. A lot of freight is also distributed by road, though heavier items and raw materials often go by rail.

In the US much long-distance travel is by air. America has two main long-distance bus companies, *Greyhound and Trailways. *Amtrak, the national network, provides rail services for passengers. Private railway companies such as *Union Pacific now carry only freight, though in fact over 70% of freight goes by road.

The main problems associated with road transport in both Britain and the US are **traffic congestion** and **pollution**. It is predicted that the number of cars on British roads will increase by a third within a few years, making both these problems worse. The British government would like more people to use public transport, but so far they have had little success in persuading people to give up their cars or to share rides with neighbours. Most people say that public transport is simply not good enough. Americans too have resisted government requests to share cars because it is less convenient and restricts their freedom. Petrol/gasolene is relatively cheap in the US and outside the major cities public transport is bad, so they see no reason to use their cars less.

Despite the use of unleaded petrol/gasolene, exhaust emissions (= gases) from vehicles still cause air pollution which can have serious effects on health. The US was the first nation to require cars to be fitted with catalytic converters (= devices that reduce the amount of dangerous gases given off). Emissions are required to be below a certain level, and devices have been developed to check at the roadside that vehicles meet the requirement. Stricter controls are also being applied to lorries/trucks. Car manufacturers are now developing electric cars which will cause less pollution.

The cheapest and most environmentally-friendly ways to travel are to walk or ride a bicycle. In *Oxford and *Cambridge bicycles are common, and many other cities now have special **cycle routes** or **cycle lanes** beside the main road. Elsewhere, there are so many cars on the roads that cycling can be dangerous. In the US bicycles are used mostly for fun or sport.

ˌ**Transport** ˈ**House** the building in central London, England, which is the main office of the *Transport and General Workers' Union. It was also the headquarters of the *Labour Party until 1980.

ˌ**Trans World** ˈ**Airlines** ⇨ TWA.

ˈ**Travelcard** /ˈtrævlkɑːd; *AmE* ˈtrævlkɑːrd/ *n* (in Britain) a special ticket which allows passengers to travel on underground trains, ordinary trains and buses in Greater London at a reduced cost for a period of one day or one week. Passengers with these tickets can make as many journeys as they want during that period.

ˌBen ˈ**Travers** /ˈtrævəz; *AmE* ˈtrævərz/ (1886–1980) an English writer of farces (= comedy plays in which characters are often in embarrassing situations and many ridiculous things happen). His plays were especially popular in Britain in the 1920s and 1930s and are still regularly performed. They were originally known as the 'Aldwych farces' because they were first produced at the *Aldwych Theatre in London. They include *A Cuckoo in the Nest* (1925), *Rookery Nook* (1926) and *Thark* (1927).

ˌJohn **Traˈvolta** /trəˈvɒltə; *AmE* trəˈvoːltə/ (1954–) a US actor who began on television in the 1970s and became a major star after appearing in two musical films, *Saturday Night Fever* (1977) and **Grease*. His more recent films have included *Pulp Fiction* (1994), *Get Shorty* (1995) and *Primary Colors* (1998).

ˌ***Treasure*** ˈ***Island*** an adventure story by Robert Louis *Stevenson, popular especially with children and published in 1883. The hero of the book is Jim Hawkins, a boy who finds a map of an island where some treasure is buried. He joins a group of sailors on a ship called *Hispaniola* and they set off to search for it. One of the best-known characters in the book is *Long John Silver, a pirate (= a person who robs ships at sea) with one leg, and a parrot (= a colourful bird) that sits on his shoulder. The story has been adapted for the stage and television, and there have been several film versions.

ˈ***Treasure of the Siˈerra*** ˈ***Madre*** /siˈerə ˈmɑːdreɪ/ a US film (1948) that won three *Oscars. It was directed and written by John *Huston. It is about three American friends who become enemies after finding gold in Mexico. The main actors were Walter Huston, Humphrey *Bogart and Tim Holt.

ˈ**treasure trove** *n* [U] valuable objects, such as gold, silver, jewellery, coins and pots, which are found buried in the ground or in a building and have no known owner. According to British law, such objects belong to the king or queen and are offered first to the *British Museum. The person finding them is given money equal to the full value of the objects if they were sold at their modern value.

the ˈ**Treasury** the British government department in charge of the country's financial affairs. One of its main responsibilities is deciding how much money should be spent on various aspects of national life, such as education, health care, defence, etc., and providing such money to the appropriate authorities. The department is in *Westminster(1) in central London. Three of its senior officials are also members of the *Cabinet: the First Lord of the Treasury (which is one of the titles of the *Prime Minister), the *Chancellor of the Exchequer, who is really the head of the Treasury, and the *Chief Secretary to the Treasury.

the ˈ**Treasury bench** the front row of seats on the government side of the *House of Commons in the British parliament. It is where the most important government ministers sit, including the *Prime Minister and the *Chancellor of the Exchequer.

ˈ**treasury bill** (*also infml* **T-bill**) *n* a type of US government bond (= official paper sold with the promise to pay the money back on a certain date). Treasury bills are sold by the US Department of the Treasury to raise money for the government. They are bought for less money than their value, kept for a fixed time, and then sold back to the government for their full value. No interest is paid.

the ˌ**Treaty of U**ˈ**trecht** /juːˈtrekt/ the agreement in 1713 which marked the end of the War of *Spanish Succession. As part of the agreement, France gave Britain various parts of Canada and accepted Queen *Anne rather than James *Stuart as the British monarch. Britain also received possession of *Gibraltar and Minorca from Spain.

the ˌ**Treaty of Ver**ˈ**sailles** /veəˈsaɪ; *AmE* verˈsaɪ/ the agreement, made in 1919 between the *Allies and Germany, which officially ended *World War I and established the *League of Nations. According to the agreement, Germany was severely punished. It was forced to pay large amounts of money for damage done during the war, tight restrictions were placed on the number of armed forces it was allowed to have, and it lost possession of large areas of territory. This helped to cause poverty and disorder in Germany, and many people believe that the Treaty of Versailles created the circumstances which led to the Nazis coming to power and therefore to *World War II.

T

ˈ**Trekkie** /ˈtreki/ *n* a person who is very keen on following the television science fiction series **Star Trek*. Serious Trekkies attend special conferences to share their enthusiasm and discuss the series in great detail.

ˌ**Trent** ˈ**Bridge** /ˌtrent/ a cricket ground in *Nottingham, England, where Nottinghamshire County Cricket Club play and where test matches (= international matches) are regularly held.

ˌG M **Tre**ˈ**velyan** /trɪˈveljən/ (George Macaulay Trevelyan 1876–1962) an English historian best known for his *History of England* (1926) and *English Social History* (1942). His uncle was the historian Thomas *Macaulay. Trevelyan was made a member of the *Order of Merit in 1930.

ˌRichard **Tre**ˈ**vithick** /trɪˈvɪθɪk/ (1771–1833) an English engineer who was the first man to develop steam engines into vehicles carrying passengers. The first of these were for use on roads, but in 1804 he built the first steam engine that moved on rails.

ˈ***Tribune*** /ˈtrɪbjuːn/ an independent British left-wing political newspaper which represents the views of some members of the *Labour Party. It was established in 1937 and is published every week. It traditionally supported very left-wing policies but in recent times has become more moderate.

the ˈ**Tribune group** /ˈtrɪbjuːn/ a group of *Labour Party *Members of Parliament who support left-wing policies. It was formed in 1966.

ˌ**trick or** ˈ**treat** a traditional activity at *Hallowe'en, in which children dress in costumes and visit houses. At each house they say 'Trick or treat'. This means that they will play a 'trick', or joke, on the people in the house unless they are given a 'treat', e.g. sweets or money. Most people prefer to give treats rather than having tricks played on them. The practice of 'trick or treat' began in the US in the 1930s but is now common in Britain also.

Tricky (1969–) a British pop musician (real name Adrian Thawes). His best-known albums include *Maxinquaye* (1995) and *Angels with Dirty Faces* (1998), which combine styles of music such as *rap, *trip-hop and *dub.

ˈ**Trident** /ˈtraɪdnt/ a US missile designed to be fired over long distances from a submarine and able to carry a nuclear bomb. The British *Royal Navy has built several submarines to carry Trident missiles, although many people in Britain are against such weapons and regard them as unnecessary and too expensive.

ˌDavid ˈ**Trimble** /ˈtrɪmbl/ (1944–) a British politician who has been the leader of the *Ulster Unionist Party since 1995. In 1998 he became First Minister of the new *Northern Ireland Assembly, and later in the same year he received the *Nobel Peace Prize with John *Hume.

ˌ**Trinidad and To**ˈ**bago** /ˌtrɪnɪdæd ənd təˈbeɪgəʊ; *AmE* təˈbeɪgoʊ/ an independent country, consisting of two islands in the *Caribbean near the coast of Venezuela. Trinidad and Tobago was part of the *British Empire until 1962, when it became independent and joined the *Commonwealth. Its capital city is Port of Spain and its official language is English. People from Trinidad are called **Trinidadians** and people from Tobago are called **Tobagans** or **Tobagonians**.

ˌ**Trinity** ˈ**House** the British organization responsible for lighthouses, buoys and beacons (= buildings and objects in the sea which warn ships of the danger of rocks) around the coasts of England and Wales. It was established in 1514 and is also a charity, providing homes and financial support for retired sailors and their families.

ˌ**Trinity** ˈ**Sunday** the Sunday after *Whit Sunday and an important Christian festival every year.

ˈ**Trinity term** the name given to the summer academic term in some British colleges and universities.

ˌ**triple** ˈ**crown** *n* [usu sing] the achievement of winning three important victories in certain sports. It originally meant winning three important horse races: the *Derby[2], the *St Leger and the *Two Thousand Guineas. It is also used in *Rugby Union, where it refers to one of the four British countries (England, Ireland, Scotland and Wales) defeating the other three in the same season. In the US, the phrase refers to victories in the country's three most important horse races: the Preakness Stakes, the *Belmont Stakes and the *Kentucky Derby: *win/take the triple crown.*

ˈ**tripos** /ˈtraɪpɒs; *AmE* ˈtraɪpɑːs/ *n* [usu sing] (*pl*

ˈ**triposes** /ˈtraɪpɒsɪz; *AmE* ˈtraɪpɑːsɪz/) the examinations for a BA (Bachelor of Arts) degree in certain subjects at *Cambridge University. The name is also given to the course of study for the BA degree in these subjects.

ˌ**Tristan da ˈCunha** /ˌtrɪstən də ˈkuːnjə/ the largest of a small group of islands in the south Atlantic which has historical links with Britain. In 1961 the volcano on the island erupted (= exploded, throwing out melted rock and gases) and all the inhabitants were brought to Britain. They returned to the island in 1963.

ˌ***Tristram ˈShandy*** /ˌtrɪstrəm ˈʃændi/ a novel (1759–67) by Laurence *Sterne, considered to be one of the first novels in English. Although it sets out to be about the life of Tristram Shandy, there is no clear structure to the way the story is told and the reader is introduced to many other strange and amusing characters.

ˈ**Triumph** a former British company, established in 1902, which made motor cycles and (later) cars. Triumph motor cycles were popular both in Britain and abroad from the 1920s until the 1960s. The company then went through a period of financial difficulty and closed for a time. It is now owned by the Japanese company Honda. The original Triumph company began making cars in 1923. It became part of the Standard Motor Company after *World War II and then part of *British Leyland in 1968. Its most successful models were the TR series of sports cars and the small, relatively cheap, Triumph Herald. These cars are no longer produced.

Trog /trɒg; *AmE* trɔːg/ the name used by the British cartoonist Wally Fawkes (1924–). He has drawn political cartoons for several newspapers, including the **Observer*, but is perhaps best known for creating the humorous cartoon series *Flook*, which appeared for many years in the **Daily Mail* newspaper.

ˌ***Troilus and ˈCressida*** /ˌtrɔɪləs ənd ˈkresɪdə/ a play by William *Shakespeare, probably written in 1602. It tells the unhappy story of two young lovers in Troy at the time of the Trojan War.

ˌAnthony ˈ**Trollope** /ˈtrɒləp; *AmE* ˈtrɑːləp/ (1815–82) an English author of many novels, mainly about *middle-class society in *Victorian(1) England. His series of six novels (1855–67) set in the imaginary county of *Barsetshire are mainly about the priests and other church officials connected with a cathedral, and include the novel **Barchester Towers*. Another series of six novels (1864–80) involves the Palliser family and is mainly about politics and society in London. Some of Trollope's novels were made into popular television series by the *BBC in the 1970s and 1980s.

ˌ**Trooping the ˈColour** /ˌtruːpɪŋ/ (*also* **the ˌTrooping of the ˈColour**) a colourful ceremony that takes place every year on *Horse Guards Parade in central London, England, on the *Queen's Birthday. Soldiers on foot and on horses parade in front of the queen, carrying the flags that represent their regiments. These include the *Household Cavalry and the *Foot Guards. The ceremony is popular with tourists and is also shown on television.

Trooping the Colour

the ˈ**Trossachs** /ˈtrɒsəks; *AmE* ˈtrɑːsəks/ an attractive area of countryside in central Scotland, north-east of *Glasgow.

ˌ**trouble at ˈt' mill** /ˌtrʌbl ət ˈtmɪl/ a humorous phrase sometimes used by British people to refer to a problem somewhere, especially at home or at work. It is said in the *accent of the people of northern England, especially *Yorkshire or *Lancashire(1), where there used to be many mills (= factories where certain materials were processed), and where the word 'the' is often not fully pronounced. The phrase suggests the idea that there were regular disputes between the workers in these mills and their owners.

the ˈ**Troubles** the name given to periods of political and social disturbance in Ireland, especially in the 20th century. The expression is now often used to refer to the period of violence and terrorist activity between Catholics and Protestants in Northern Ireland since 1968, but it has also been applied to events such as the *Easter Rising (1916) and the *Anglo-Irish War (1919–21). Thousands of people have been killed in the Troubles. ⇨ article at NORTHERN IRELAND.

ˌ***True Conˈfessions*** a US magazine containing articles which are supposed to be true stories written by ordinary people about their love and marriage problems. They are written in a very romantic and emotional way and are especially popular with young women.

ˌFred ˈ**Trueman** /ˈtruːmən/ (1931–) a famous English cricket player. He was a fast bowler who played for Yorkshire (1949–68) and for England (1952–65). He was known for his aggressive attitude as a player, as a result of which he was sometimes called 'Fiery Fred' and he was often in trouble with the cricket authorities. He was the first bowler in the history of the game to take 300 wickets in test matches (= international matches). Since he stopped being a player he has appeared regularly on the radio programme **Test Match Special*. His honest views often involve criticizing players and those in charge of the game, and he is regarded both with affection and amusement by people who follow cricket in Britain.

ˌHarry S ˈ**Truman** /ˈtruːmən/ (1884–1972) the 33rd US *President (1945–53). He was Vice-president under Franklin D *Roosevelt, replaced him when he died in 1945, and then won the 1948 election. He gave permission for the first atom bombs to be dropped on Japan. His government began the *Marshall Plan and helped to establish the *United Nations and *NATO. Truman was strongly opposed to Communism. He began the *Truman Doctrine and involved the US in the *Korean War. He also began the *Fair Deal programme which made him popular with ordinary people. Before becoming President, he represented *Missouri in the US *Senate as a Democrat.

the ˈ**Truman ˌDoctrine** /ˈtruːmən/ a policy announced in 1947 by President Harry *Truman in which he promised US financial and military help for Greece, Turkey and other countries threatened by Communism.

ˌDonald ˈ**Trump** /ˈtrʌmp/ (1946–) a very rich US property owner. He built Trump Tower (a large office building) and the Trump International Hotel in New York, and he owns the Trump Castle and Taj Mahal casinos (= gambling clubs) in *Atlantic City,

*New Jersey. Trump also bought the famous Plaza Hotel in New York in 1983.

the ˌ***Trumpet*** ˈ***Voluntary*** a popular piece of music for the trumpet by Henry *Wood which is often played at ceremonies. Wood adapted it from a piece originally written for the harpsichord by Jeremiah Clarke in 1700, called *The Prince of Denmark's March*.

ˈ**Truro** /ˈtrʊərəʊ; *AmE* ˈtrʊroʊ/ the administrative centre of the county of *Cornwall in south-west England. It has a cathedral.

the ˌ**Trustee** ˈ**Savings Bank** (*abbr* the **TSB**) one of the major British banks, with branches all over the country. It was formed in 1986 from a number of smaller local banks originally established to help people in industrial areas to save money. In 1995 the TSB joined together with *Lloyds Bank.

ˌ**Trust House** ˈ**Forte**™ /ˈfɔːteɪ; *AmE* ˈfɔːrteɪ/ a large British company that owns a chain of hotels and restaurants in many towns and cities. It was formed in 1970, when the hotel group Trust Houses joined together with various companies owned by Charles Forte, who had built up a large group of hotels and restaurants.

ˈ**trust** ˌ**status** *n* [U] the status given by the British government since 1990 to a number of hospitals which are part of the *National Health Service. These hospitals become responsible for their own administrative and financial affairs, rather than being governed by a central authority. The idea is that they should be run on a more commercial basis, with less waste of money and resources, but some people are worried that this can lead to a reduction in essential services.

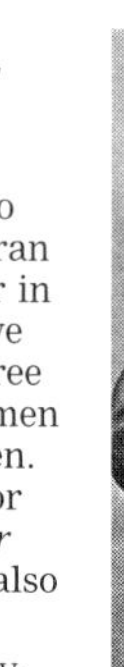

ˌSojourner ˈ**Truth** /ˌsɒdʒənə ˈtruːθ; *AmE* ˈsoʊdʒərnər/ (*c.* 1797–1883) an *African-American woman who was born a slave but ran away from her master in 1827 and became active in the campaigns to free slaves and to give women the same rights as men. Her name was used for the *NASA **Sojourner* vehicle on Mars. See also ABOLITIONISM.

Sojourner Truth

the **TSB** ⇨ TRUSTEE SAVINGS BANK.

TT /ˌtiː ˈtiː/ ⇨ TOURIST TROPHY.

the **Tube** /tjuːb; *AmE* tuːb/ an informal name for the *London Underground.

ˌHarriet ˈ**Tubman** /ˈtʌbmən/ (1821–1913) an African-American woman who was born a slave but escaped in 1849 and became active in the campaign to free slaves. She was given the *nickname Moses because she helped more than 300 slaves to escape by the *Underground Railroad. She also worked as a spy for the US Army during the *Civil War. See also ABOLITIONISM.

the **TUC** /ˌtiː juː ˈsiː/ (*in full* the **Trades Union Congress**) the association of English trade unions. It was established in 1868 and its main function is to protect the interests of trade union members in the country as a whole in matters such as pay and conditions of work. The TUC meets every year for four days at the beginning of September, when representatives from all the trade unions gather to discuss various issues that affect them. The head of the TUC is called the General Secretary and its members elect the General Council every year to represent it. Its headquarters are at *Congress House in central London. The Scottish TUC was established in 1897 and meets in *Glasgow every April.

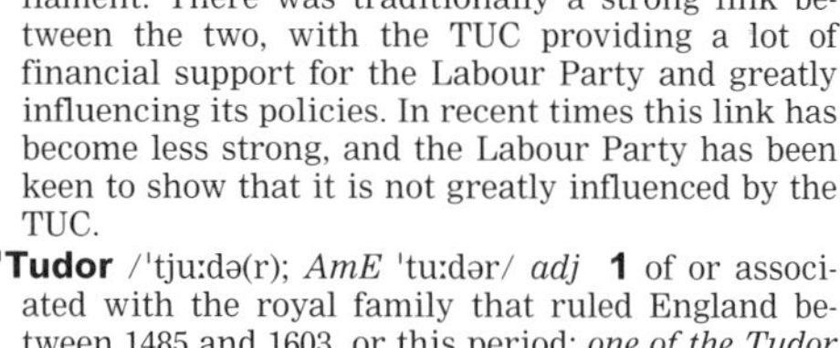

The TUC established the *Labour Party in 1906 and paid the wages of the first Labour *Members of Parliament. There was traditionally a strong link between the two, with the TUC providing a lot of financial support for the Labour Party and greatly influencing its policies. In recent times this link has become less strong, and the Labour Party has been keen to show that it is not greatly influenced by the TUC.

ˈ**Tudor** /ˈtjuːdə(r); *AmE* ˈtuːdər/ *adj* **1** of or associated with the royal family that ruled England between 1485 and 1603, or this period: *one of the Tudor kings.* **2** of the style of architecture common during the 16th century in England. A characteristic feature of Tudor buildings is the use of black wooden frames surrounding white outer walls. See also HALF-TIMBERED.

ˌ**Tudor** ˈ**rose** /ˌtjuːdə; *AmE* ˌtuːdər/ *n* the symbol of the *Tudor(1) family when its members were the kings and queens of England (1485–1603). It was introduced by *Henry VII when he became the first Tudor monarch, and was a combination of the white rose (the symbol of the House of *York) and the red rose (the symbol of the House of *Lancaster).

ˌJethro ˈ**Tull** /ˌdʒeθrəʊ ˈtʌl; *AmE* ˌdʒeθroʊ/ (1674–1741) an English farmer who invented the 'seed drill', a piece of agricultural equipment that made it possible for agricultural production to become mechanical. It was pulled by a horse, sowed (= planted) three rows of seed at the same time and removed weeds. It represented a major advance in agricultural methods, both in England and other countries.

ˈ**Tulsa** /ˈtʌlsə/ the second largest city in the US state of *Oklahoma. It is a port on the Arkansas River which connects it to the *Gulf of Mexico. It was settled and named Tulsy in the 1830s by *Native Americans forced to leave *Alabama. Oil was discovered there in 1901, and the city remains a centre for the oil industry.

ˌ**Tunbridge** ˈ**Wells** /ˌtʌnbrɪdʒ ˈwelz/ a town in *Kent, southern England, which in the 17th and 18th centuries was an important spa town (= one where there are springs of mineral water considered to be healthy to drink). It has a reputation for being a place where many older, *middle-class, right-wing people live. See also DISGUSTED, TUNBRIDGE WELLS.

ˌGene ˈ**Tunney** /ˈtʌni/ (1898–1978) a US boxer who became World Heavyweight Champion when he defeated Jack *Dempsey in 1926. He beat Dempsey again in the famous 'long count' contest (1927) when Tunney was knocked down but got up to win after the referee delayed.

ˈ**Tupperware**™ /ˈtʌpəweə(r); *AmE* ˈtʌpərwer/ *n* [U] a make of plastic containers for storing food in, widely used in Britain. When it was first introduced in the 1960s, the company paid people to hold **Tupperware parties** in their homes, to which they invited friends and offered to sell them Tupperware goods. Tupperware is now sold in many shops.

ˌEva ˈ**Turner**[1] /ˈtɜːnə(r); *AmE* ˈtɜːrnər/ (1892–1990) an English opera singer. She was known for her performances of operas by Puccini, Wagner and Verdi, and spent much of her career with the Chicago Opera Company. She retired in 1948 and was made a *dame(2) in 1962.

ˈJ M ˈW ˈ**Turner**[2] /ˈtɜːnə(r); *AmE* ˈtɜːrnər/ (Joseph Mallord William Turner 1775–1851) a major English artist, famous for his landscape and seascape paintings (= scenes of the countryside and of the sea). A characteristic feature of his work is his original treatment of light and weather conditions. His style had a great influence on later artistic movements, especially Impressionism and *abstract expressionism. Turner spent much of his life travelling widely in Britain and Europe, doing drawings for his paintings. His best-known paintings include *The *Fighting Téméraire* (1838) and *Rain, Steam and Speed* (1844), both of which are in the *National Gallery in London. Many of his paintings became the property of the British nation after his death and are in the *Tate Gallery in London. In 1987 the Clore Gallery was added to the Tate especially to display Turner's works.

The Fighting Téméraire *by J M W Turner*

ˌNat **'Turner³** /ˌnæt 'tɜːnə(r); *AmE* 'tɜːrnər/ (1800–1831) a US slave who in 1831 led a group of slaves to murder over 50 white people in Southampton County, *Virginia. This was called the Southampton Insurrection. Turner and 16 other slaves were hanged. The murders almost ended *abolitionism in the South and led to strict new laws to control slaves. See also STYRON.

ˌTed **'Turner⁴** /'tɜːnə(r); *AmE* 'tɜːrnər/ (1938–) a successful US businessman who established the *Turner Broadcasting System and *CNN. In 1996 he sold his company to *Time Warner. He also won the 1977 *America's Cup. In 1997, Turner announced that he would give $1 million to the *United Nations. He is married to the actor Jane *Fonda.

ˌTina **'Turner⁵** /ˌtiːnə 'tɜːnə(r); *AmE* 'tɜːrnər/ (1939–) an *African-American singer whose early successes were with her husband Ike. Their records together included *River Deep, Mountain High* (1966) and *Proud Mary* (1972), which won two *Grammy awards. Their marriage ended in 1976. Tina has since then won five more Grammys and is famous for her live performances. She was chosen for the Rock and Roll *Hall of Fame in 1991.

the **'Turner 'Broadcasting ˌSystem** /'tɜːnə; *AmE* 'tɜːrnər/ (*abbr* **TBS**) the television system created by Ted *Turner from the single station he bought in *Atlanta in 1976. He began *CNN in 1980 as part of TBS, which also now includes the TBS SuperStation, Turner Network Television, the Cartoon Network, the Atlanta Braves *baseball team and the Atlanta Hawks *basketball team. TBS became part of *Time Warner in 1996.

the **'Turner Prize** /'tɜːnə; *AmE* 'tɜːrnər/ a prize of £20 000 given every year by the *Tate Gallery to a British artist under the age of 50 for a work of modern art. Winners in the past have included Howard Hodgkin (1985) and Damien *Hirst (1995). The prize is an important cultural event in Britain, and a special exhibition of work by the four leading competitors is held at the Tate Gallery before the winner is announced.

ˌDick **'Turpin** /'tɜːpɪn; *AmE* 'tɜːrpɪn/ (1706–39) a famous English highwayman (= a criminal who robbed travellers in former times). He was captured and hanged in York, possibly for murder or for stealing horses. After his death many romantic stories were told about him, especially one about his ride from London to York on his horse Black Bess.

'Turtle Wax™ /'tɜːtl; *AmE* 'tɜːrtl/ *n* [U] a US make of wax polish for cars which is sold in many countries around the world. In 1983, the company also began to sell products to clean shoes and household items.

TusˌkegeeUni'versity /tʌsˌkiːgiː/ a university in Tuskegee, *Alabama, mainly for *African Americans. It was first established in 1881 by Booker T *Washington to educate freed slaves. The university has a large library of books on African-American history and a museum. See also CARVER.

MaˌrieTus'saud /məˌriː tʊ'sɔːd/ ⇨ MADAME TUSSAUD'S.

ˌTuva'lu /ˌtuːvɑː'luː/ a country consisting of nine islands in the south-west Pacific Ocean. Its capital city is Fongafale and its official languages are Tuvaluan and English. It was formerly a British colony called the Ellice Islands and became an independent member of the *Commonwealth in 1978.

▶ **Tuvaluan** *n* **1** [C] a native or inhabitant of Tuvalu. **2** [U] the language of Tuvalu. **Tuvaluan** *adj.*

TVA /ˌtiː viː 'eɪ/ ⇨ TENNESSEE VALLEY AUTHORITY.

TV-am /ˌtiː viː eɪ 'em/ a British company broadcasting *breakfast television (= early morning programmes). It started in 1983 and ended in 1992. Its best-known presenter was David *Frost.

the **TV Code** /ˌtiːviː 'kəʊd/ (in the US) a list of rules designed to restrict the amount of sex, violence and bad language on television programmes. The National Association of Broadcasters began it in 1952 so that the industry could control itself. The Code also states that advertisements should not make false claims. Television companies are not forced to follow the TV Code, but most do. There is also a Radio Code.

TV Guide /ˌtiː viː 'gaɪd/ the most popular television magazine in the US, with more than 13 million readers in 1997. It began in 1953 and is published each week. It gives details of the times and channels for programmes but also has stories about stars and shows, and more serious articles about television.

TV licence /ˌtiː 'viː ˌlaɪsns/ ⇨ TELEVISION LICENCE.

TV Times /ˌtiː viː 'taɪmz/ a British magazine that gives details of the week's radio and television programmes, and also includes articles about television actors, etc. It first appeared in 1968 and is published every week. Compare *RADIO TIMES*.

TWA /ˌtiː dʌbljuː 'eɪ/ (*in full* **Trans World Airlines**) a US airline. It was established in 1930, and made its first international flight (to Paris) in 1946. It was the first airline to show films on its planes (in 1961). It went bankrupt in 1992 but now has a new organization in which its employees own 45% of the company. In 1996 a TWA flight exploded over *Long Island and all 230 people on board were killed. The cause has not been found.

ˌMark **'Twain** /'tweɪn/ (1835–1910) the leading US humorous writer of the 19th century. His real name was Samuel Langhorne Clemens. He is best known for the novels *The Adventures of Tom Sawyer* (1876) and *The Adventures of Huckleberry Finn* (1885), but he also wrote travel books and essays, many of them based on his experiences of life on the *Mississippi River. His other books include the historical novels *The Prince and the Pauper* (1882) and *A Connecticut Yankee in King Arthur's Court* (1889), and *Life on the Mississippi* (1889), an account of his early life. See also FINN, SAWYER.

ˈWilliam ˈMarcy ˈ**Tweed** /ˈmɑːsi ˈtwiːd; *AmE* ˈmɑːrsi/ (1823–78) a New York City political leader, known as 'Boss' Tweed, who became a symbol for dishonest behaviour in city politics. In the 1860s he was the leader of *Tammany Hall and ran the 'Tweed Ring', which accepted millions of dollars illegally from companies wanting to do business with the city authorities. He was finally removed from office and died in prison.

ˌ**Tweedleˈdum and ˌTweedleˈdee** /ˌtwiːdlˈdʌm ənd ˌtwiːdlˈdiː/ two characters in the children's book **Through the Looking Glass* by Lewis *Carroll. They are both fat and are dressed in exactly the same way, and their names are sometimes used to describe two people who look or behave like one another: *Two bald politicians in suits appeared, looking exactly like Tweedledum and Tweedledee.*

ˈ**Tweety Pie** /ˈtwiːti paɪ/ a canary (= a small yellow bird) in *Warner Brothers cartoons from the 1940s to the 1960s. He first appeared in 1941 and was joined by his enemy *Sylvester the cat in 1947. Tweety Pie speaks in a high voice rather like a baby, and when Sylvester is near often says, 'I tawt I taw a puddy tat.' ('I thought I saw a pussy cat.')

ˌ**Twelfth ˈNight** the night of 5/6 January, formerly celebrated as the last night of *Christmas, and the night before the church festival of Epiphany. It is the time when many people take down their Christmas decorations.

ˌ***Twelfth ˈNight*** a comedy play (*c.* 1601) by William *Shakespeare. It is set in the court of Orsino, Duke of Illyria, and is a complicated love story. The humour of the play is provided mainly by the characters Malvolio, Sir Toby Belch and Sir Andrew Aguecheek. The play begins with one of Shakespeare's best-known lines: 'If music be the food of love, play on.'

The ˌ***Twelve Days of ˈChristmas*** a traditional song often sung at *Christmas. It is about a person who receives a gift for each of the twelve days of Christmas. The song begins: 'On the first day of Christmas, my true love sent to me/A partridge in a pear tree.' Finally, on the 12th and last day, the person receives 'twelve lords a-leaping'.

ˈ**20th ˈCentury ˈFox** a major *Hollywood film company. It was established in 1935, with Darryl F *Zanuck as head of production until 1956. Its many successful films have included *The *Grapes of Wrath*, **Cleopatra*, *The *Sound of Music*, **Star Wars*, **Home Alone* and *Independence Day*. The company was bought by Rupert *Murdoch in 1985.

ˈ**Twickenham** /ˈtwɪkənəm/ an area of the *borough of Richmond-upon-Thames in south-west London, England. Twickenham Stadium, also known informally as 'Twickers', is the national ground for *Rugby Union football, where *Five Nations matches and other Rugby Union games are played. It is also the home ground of the *Harlequins club.

ˈ**Twiggy** /ˈtwɪgi/ (1949–) an English fashion model who became famous in the 1960s. She was known for being very thin, with short hair, and often wore very short skirts. She later became an actor, and appeared in the film of *The Boy Friend*. Her real name is Lesley Hornby.

The ***Twilight Zone*** a US television series (1959–65) which each week had a different strange story with a surprising ending. There was also a film (1983), and another television series, *The New Twilight Zone* (1985–9). The phrase 'in the twilight zone' is still used in American English to describe something mysterious.

the ˌ**Twin ˈCities** a popular name for *Minneapolis and *St Paul, *Minnesota, because they are next to each other, separated only by the *Mississippi River. They share the Twin Cities International Airport and the Mall of America, the largest shopping area in the US.

ˈ**Twinkie**™ /ˈtwɪŋki/ *n* a small, sweet yellow cake with a soft filling like cream, sold in the US. It is regarded as typical of foods that are very popular but not very good for you.

ˈ***Twinkle, ˈTwinkle, ˈLittle ˈStar*** the title and first line of a traditional *nursery rhyme. The words are:

Twinkle, twinkle, little star,
How I wonder what you are.
Up above the world so high,
Like a diamond in the sky

ˌOliver ˈ**Twist** /ˈtwɪst/ ⇨ *OLIVER TWIST*.

ˌConway ˈ**Twitty** /ˌkɒnweɪ ˈtwɪti; *AmE* ˌkɑːnweɪ/ (1933–93) a US singer, mainly of country music. He often sang with Loretta *Lynn and they had five No. 1 hits in a row, including *After the Fire Is Gone* (1971). He also opened a tourist attraction, Twitty City, in Hendersonville, *Tennessee.

the ˌ**two ˈcultures** a phrase made popular by the author C P *Snow in 1959. He used it to describe the division between the arts and the sciences in Britain, and argued that people trained in the arts did not understand or appreciate people trained in the sciences.

The ˈ***Two ˈGentlemen of Veˈrona*** /vəˈrəʊnə; *AmE* vəˈroʊnə/ a comedy play (*c.* 1593) by William *Shakespeare. It is about two friends, Valentine and Proteus, who both fall in love with the same young woman, Silvia. Another young woman, Julia, is in love with Proteus, and a complicated love story follows. It is one of Shakespeare's less well-known plays.

ˌ**two-minute ˈsilence** *n* (in Britain) a silence lasting two minutes, held every year at 11 a.m. on *Remembrance Sunday, in memory of the people who died during the two world wars and other conflicts. The silence is usually held at public ceremonies such as the one at the *Cenotaph in London.

2001: A Space Odyssey a film (1968) about future travel in space, written by Arthur C *Clarke and Stanley *Kubrick, who also directed it. The story is about a long trip taken in a spacecraft by two astronauts with an intelligent computer called HAL. It raised interesting questions about the influence of computers and the possibility of life on other planets. The film won an *Oscar for its special visual effects. Clarke later wrote the novel *2010: Odyssey Two* (1982) which was also made into a film (1984).

the ˌ**Two Thousand ˈGuineas** (*also* the **2 000 Guineas**) /ˌtuː θaʊzənd/ a well-known British horse race run every year at *Newmarket in late April or early May. It was first held in 1809.

ˈ**Tyburn** /ˈtaɪbɜːn; *AmE* ˈtaɪbɜːrn/ a place in London, England, near the present *Marble Arch, where people were hanged in public between about 1300 and 1783. After this the hangings took place outside *Newgate Prison.

an engraving of a hanging at Tyburn

ˈ**Tylenol**™ /ˈtaɪlənɒl; *AmE* ˈtaɪlənɑːl/ *n* [U] a US medicine that relieves pain and does not contain aspirin. The drug it contains is called *paracetamol* in Britain.

ˌAnne ˈ**Tyler**[1] /ˈtaɪlə(r)/ (1941–) a US writer of popular novels that are intelligent and humorous. She received the *National Book Critics Circle award for *The Accidental Tourist* (1985) and the *Pulitzer Prize for *Breathing Lessons* (1988). Her other books include *If Morning Ever Comes* (1964), *Ladder of Years* (1995) and *A Slipping-Down Life* (1997).

ˌWat ˈ**Tyler**[2] /ˌwɒt ˈtaɪlə(r); *AmE* ˌwɑːt/ (*died* 1381) an English leader of the *Peasants' Revolt of 1381. He brought his army from *Kent to London, where he met and talked with King *Richard II. During the meeting he was injured in a fight, and he was later murdered.

ˌKenneth ˈ**Tynan** /ˈtaɪnən/ (1927–80) an English journalist. He wrote mainly about the theatre, and was a strong supporter of the work of John *Osborne. Tynan's stage show *Oh, Calcutta!* shocked some people with its sexual humour, and he is also remembered as the first person to say the word 'fuck' on British television (in 1965). From 1963 to 1969 he was literary manager of the *National Theatre.

ˌWilliam ˈ**Tyndale** /ˈtɪndeɪl/ (*c.* 1494–1536) an English writer who translated the Bible. His work as a translator was opposed in England and he was forced to live in Germany, where he produced the first English version of the Bible between 1525 and 1531. This later became the basis for the *King James Version of 1611. He was burnt alive in Belgium as a punishment.

the **Tyne** /taɪn/ a river in north-eastern England which passes through *Newcastle-upon-Tyne and reaches the *North Sea between Tynemouth and South Shields.

ˌ**Tyne and** ˈ**Wear** /ˌtaɪn ənd ˈwɪə(r)/ a small county in north-east England, formed in 1974 from parts of *Durham and *Northumberland.

ˈ**Tyneside** /ˈtaɪnsaɪd/ an area of north-east England around the River *Tyne, including *Newcastle-upon-Tyne, Gateshead and South Shields. Tyneside was formerly an important centre for the shipbuilding and *coal-mining industries, but the area now has a lot of unemployment. People from Tyneside are informally called *Geordies.

Tyne Tees TV /ˌtaɪn ˈtiːz tiː ˈviː/ a British independent television company, formed in 1959, which broadcasts to the north-east of England. In 1993 it joined with *Yorkshire TV to form a single company.

the ˈ**Tynwald** /ˈtɪnwəld/ the parliament of the *Isle of Man, based in the island's capital, *Douglas. It is one of the oldest parliaments in the world, originally formed in the 10th century. In 1881 it became the first parliament to allow women to vote. See also HOUSE OF KEYS.

ˌ**Typhoid** ˈ**Mary** (1868–1938) the *nickname given to Mary Mallon, the first person known to carry typhoid fever (= a serious disease caused by infected food or water) in the US (though she did not suffer from the disease herself). She was an Irish woman who settled in New York City as a cook and is believed to have infected 25 people in 1906–7. She refused treatment but was kept in New York's Sloane Hospital where she gave more people the disease before dying there. Americans call somebody Typhoid Mary in a humorous way if they think they should be avoided because they bring bad luck or are dangerous in some way.

Tyˈ**phoo**™ /taɪˈfuː/ a popular British make of tea.

ˌMike ˈ**Tyson** /ˈtaɪsn/ (1966–) a US boxer who became the World Heavyweight Champion (1987–90 and 1996). He was sent to prison (1992–5) for rape (= the sex act forced on somebody). In 1996 he was defeated by Evander Holyfield, and when they fought again in 1997, Tyson bit off part of his opponent's ear, and Holyfield was automatically declared the winner. Tyson was made to pay $3 million and not allowed to fight in the US for a year.

Uu

U2 /ˌjuː ˈtuː/ a British pop group formed in Dublin in 1977. Their successful albums include *Boy* (1980), *The Joshua Tree* (1987) and *Zooropa* (1993). The group's main singer is Bono (real name Paul Hewson).

UA /ˌjuː ˈeɪ/ ⇨ UNITED ARTISTS.

UAW /ˌjuː eɪ ˈdʌbljuː/ (*in full* **United Automobile Workers**, *also* **United Auto Workers**) a large US trade union for workers in the car, aerospace and metal industries. Its full name is the United International Union of the Automobile, Aerospace & Agricultural Implement Workers of America. It was established in 1935 and had 1.3 million members in 1997. It left the *AFL-CIO in 1968.

UB40 /ˌjuː biː ˈfɔːti; *AmE* ˈfɔːrti/ (in Britain) a card formerly given to people claiming money from the government for being unemployed. In 1996 it was replaced by a similar card, the ES40, for people claiming the *jobseeker's allowance.

UCAS /ˈjuːkæs/ ⇨ UNIVERSITIES AND COLLEGES ADMISSIONS SERVICE.

UCATT /ˈjuːkæt/ (*in full* the **Union of Construction, Allied Trades and Technicians**) a British *trade union for workers in the building trades, formed by joining several other trade unions in 1970.

UCL /ˌjuː siː ˈel/ ⇨ UNIVERSITY COLLEGE, LONDON.

UCLA /ˌjuː siː el ˈeɪ/ (*in full* the **University of California at Los Angeles**) the largest of the eight branches of the University of *California. It was established in 1919 and in 1998 had about 35 000 students. UCLA is known especially for its film studies. It also has a strong sports programme and has won the *NCAA National Basketball Championship 11 times.

UDA /ˌjuː diː ˈeɪ/ ⇨ ULSTER DEFENCE ASSOCIATION.

the **UDM** /ˌjuː diː ˈem/ (*in full* the **Union of Democratic Mineworkers**) a British *trade union for coal miners. It was formed in 1985 as a protest against the actions of the *National Union of Mineworkers, which had failed to hold an election among its members before the *miners' strike in the previous year.

UDR /ˌjuː diː ˈɑː(r)/ ⇨ ULSTER DEFENCE REGIMENT.

the **UEFA Cup** /juːˌeɪfə ˈkʌp/ a football competition organized by UEFA (the Union of European Football Associations). It is played between European teams who have not qualified for the *European Cup or *European Cup-Winners' Cup, and was started in 1958.

UFF /ˌjuː ef ˈef/ ⇨ ULSTER FREEDOM FIGHTERS.

Uˈganda /juːˈgændə/ a country in eastern central Africa. Its capital city is Kampala and its official language is English. The economy is based mainly on farming, and its main exports are cotton and coffee. From 1894 to 1962 Uganda was a British protectorate (= a country controlled and protected by Britain), and it then became an independent member of the *Commonwealth. In the 1970s the country suffered under the violent rule of Idi Amin. One of his acts was to force Ugandan Asians to leave the country, and many of them settled in Britain. ▶ **Ugandan** *adj, n.*

the **ˌUgly ˈSisters** the two older sisters of *Cinderella in the traditional children's story. In *pantomimes the Ugly Sisters are usually played by men dressed as women.

UK /ˌjuː ˈkeɪ/ ⇨ UNITED KINGDOM.

UKAEA /ˈjuː keɪ ˈeɪ iː ˈeɪ/ ⇨ UNITED KINGDOM ATOMIC ENERGY AUTHORITY.

ˈUllswater /ˈʌlzwɔːtə(r)/ one of the largest lakes of the English *Lake District. It is 7.5 miles/12 kilometres long.

ˈUlster /ˈʌlstə(r)/ another name for *Northern Ireland, consisting of the *Six Counties (Antrim, Armagh, Down, Fermanagh, Londonderry and Tyrone). When politicians or journalists refer to Ulster they usually mean these six counties, although there is also a province of Ulster in the Republic of Ireland, consisting of three counties (Cavan, Donegal and Monaghan).

the **ˌUlster DeˈfenceAssociˌation** /ˌʌlstə; *AmE* ˌʌlstər/ (*abbr* the **UDA**) an illegal Protestant military group in *Ulster (= Northern Ireland). The group wants Ulster to remain a part of the United Kingdom, and uses violence to oppose the *IRA. It was formed as a legal political organization in 1971, but was made illegal in 1992 after committing acts of violence against *Roman Catholics. Other similar groups include the *Ulster Freedom Fighters and the *Ulster Volunteer Force.

the **ˌUlster DeˈfenceˌRegiment** /ˌʌlstə; *AmE* ˌʌlstər/ (*abbr* the **UDR**) a branch of the British army operating in Northern Ireland. It was formed in 1970 to help to control the violence there, and is made up mainly of Irish soldiers. In 1992 it became a part of the Royal Irish Regiment.

the **ˈUlster Demoˈcratic ˈUnionist ˌParty** /ˌʌlstə; *AmE* ˌʌlstər/ a political party in Northern Ireland. It is supported mainly by Protestants, and wants Northern Ireland to remain a part of the United Kingdom. It is regarded as having more extreme policies than the *Ulster Unionist Party, and has been led since 1971 by Ian *Paisley. In 1998 it had two *MPs in the *House of Commons.

the **ˌUlster ˈFreedom ˌFighters** /ˌʌlstə; *AmE* ˌʌlstər/ (*abbr* the **UFF**) an illegal Protestant military group in *Ulster (= Northern Ireland), formed in 1973. The group wants Ulster to remain a part of the United Kingdom, and uses violence to oppose the *IRA. Other similar groups include the *Ulster Defence Association and the *Ulster Volunteer Force.

the **ˌUlster ˈUnionist ˌParty** /ˌʌlstə; *AmE* ˌʌlstər/ a political party in Northern Ireland, formed in 1905. It is the main political party that wants Northern Ireland to remain a part of the United Kingdom. In 1998 it had 10 *Members of Parliament in the *House of Commons and its leader since 1995 has been David *Trimble.

the **ˌUlster Volunˈteer Force** /ˌʌlstə; *AmE* ˌʌlstər/ (*abbr* the **UVF**) a Protestant military group in *Ulster (= Northern Ireland). The group wants Ulster to remain a part of the United Kingdom, and opposes the *IRA. The present group was formed in 1966, but an earlier group with the same name was formed in

1913. Other similar groups include the *Ulster Freedom Fighters and the *Ulster Defence Association.

Ulysses /ˈjuːlɪsiːz, juːˈlɪsiːz/ a novel (1922) by James *Joyce. It is considered by many people to be one of the greatest novels of the 20th century, although it was not published in Britain and the US until the 1930s because it was thought to be too offensive. It is written in a wide variety of styles, and deals with the events of one day through the experiences of three main characters, Stephen Dedalus, Leopold Bloom and Molly Bloom.

UMIST /ˈjuːmɪst/ ⇨ UNIVERSITY OF MANCHESTER INSTITUTE OF SCIENCE AND TECHNOLOGY.

UN /ˌjuː ˈen/ ⇨ UNITED NATIONS.

the ˈ**Unabomber** /ˈjuːnəbɒmə(r); *AmE* ˈjuːnəbɑːmər/ the name used especially by the press and the police to refer to a person in the US who for 17 years (1978–95) sent bombs to people in universities and airline companies who he thought supported modern technology. The bombs killed three and injured 23. Theodore Kaczynski, a former mathematics teacher at the University of California at *Berkeley, was arrested in 1996 and charged with being the Unabomber. He was found guilty and sent to prison for life in 1998.

ˌ**Uncle ˈBen's**™ a US product name for rice produced by the Uncle Ben's Converted Brand Rice Company. The original Uncle Ben was a farmer in *Texas who supplied rice to the Converted Rice Company.

ˌ**Uncle ˈRemus** /ˈriːməs/ the character who tells the stories in several books by Joel Chandler Harris (1848–1908). Uncle Remus is a former slave whose stories include Brer (Brother) Rabbit, Brer Fox and Brer Bear. Among the books are *Uncle Remus, His Songs and His Sayings* (1881), *The Tar Baby* (1904) and *Uncle Remus and Brer Rabbit* (1906). He was also the main character in the Walt *Disney film *Song of the South* (1946).

ˌ**Uncle ˈSam** the imaginary person who represents the US and its government. He became an official symbol in 1961. Uncle Sam has a white beard and wears red, white and blue clothes, with stars on his tall hat. He was probably named after 'Uncle' Sam Wilson (1766–1854) who examined army supplies for the US government during the *War of 1812. During both world wars, a picture of Uncle Sam appeared on posters telling young men that they should join the armed forces.

Uncle Sam on a World War II recruiting poster

ˌ**Uncle Tom ˈCobbleigh** /ˈkɒbli; *AmE* ˈkɑːbli/ a character from the traditional English song **Widdicombe Fair*. The song includes a long list of people who go to the *fair, ending with the line 'Old Uncle Tom Cobbleigh and all'. People sometimes use this phrase to mean that a large group of people are present in a place, including everyone that one might expect or imagine: *Everyone turned up at the party – Jack, Ella, Steve, Roger, old Uncle Tom Cobbleigh and all!*

ˌ***Uncle Tom's ˈCabin*** a novel (1852) by the US writer Harriet Beecher *Stowe which increased support for the movement to free slaves. It is about a kind slave called Tom who is badly treated and finally killed by Simon *Legree. Tom's daughter Little Eva also dies, and another well-known character in the novel is the slave child *Topsy. The name 'Uncle Tom' is sometimes used as an insult to describe an African American who has too much respect for white people.

the ˈ**Underground** ⇨ LONDON UNDERGROUND.

the ˌ**Underground ˈRailroad** a secret system used in the US before the *Civil War for helping thousands of slaves to escape to the free northern states or Canada. The slaves were called 'passengers', the people who helped them were 'conductors', and the slaves hid in 'stations' (safe houses) along the way.

ˌ***Under Milk ˈWood*** a play (1953) by Dylan *Thomas about a day in the life of a Welsh village by the sea. It was originally written for radio, and is still very popular because of its rich language and its range of humorous characters.

ˈ**unicorn** *n* an imaginary animal like a horse with a single straight horn growing from its forehead. It appears in many traditional stories, and can be seen on the *royal arms, where it represents Scotland. See also LION AND THE UNICORN.

the ˌ**Unifiˈcation ˈChurch** a religious organization begun in Korea in 1954 by the businessman Sun Myung Moon (1920–) and now established in many other countries, including the US (where its main offices now are), Britain and Australia. Members of the organization are called *Moonies. Sun Myung Moon was sent to prison in 1984–5 for failing to pay enough US income tax.

ˈ**Unilever** /ˈjuːnɪliːvə(r)/ a large British and Dutch company that makes food, drink and soap products. It was formed in 1930 by joining two companies, Lever Brothers (established by Lord *Leverhulme) and the Dutch company Margarine Unie. Its best known products include *Birdseye, *Brooke Bond, *Lux, *Persil and *Wall's.

the ˈ**Union** another name for the United States. It was used especially during the *Civil War in which 'the Union' fought the Confederate States: *The Union forces captured Atlanta in 1864.*

ˌ**Union ˈCarbide** /ˈkɑːbaɪd; *AmE* ˈkɑːrbaɪd/ a large US chemicals company whose main office is in Danbury, *Connecticut. In December 1984, there was a serious accident at the Union Carbide factory in Bhopal, India. Poisonous gases were released into the air, killing more than 2 000 people. Many relatives brought legal cases against Union Carbide, and the disaster caused a lot of public discussion about the responsibilities of international companies operating in poorer countries.

ˈ**Unionist** *n* a person who favours political union between Britain and Northern Ireland, and opposes union between Northern Ireland and the Irish Republic. The main Unionist parties in Northern Ireland are the *Ulster Unionist Party and the *Ulster Democratic Unionist Party. Compare LOYALIST. See also ACT OF UNION, HOME RULE, MARCHING SEASON, ORANGEMEN. ⇨ article at NORTHERN IRELAND.

the ˌ**Union ˈJack** /ˈdʒæk/ (*also* the **Union Flag**) *n* the national *flag of the United Kingdom. It is made up of the designs of three different flags: the *St George's Cross of England, the *St Andrew's Cross of Scotland and the St Patrick's Cross of Northern Ireland. Wales, although part of the United Kingdom, has its own national flag.

ˈ**Union Paˈcific ˈRailroad** /pəˈsɪfɪk/ a US rail line built in the 1860s, consisting of 1 086 miles/1 747 kilometres of track stretching west from *Omaha, *Nebraska. On 10 May 1869, at Promontory Point, *Utah, it met the Central Pacific Railroad, 690 miles/1 110 kilometres of track stretching east from Sacramento,

*California. There was a special ceremony in which a large gold nail was hit with a silver hammer to mark the first complete railway running all the way from the east to the west of America.

ˌUnion ˈSquare a park in *Manhattan(1), New York City. It is between *Broadway and *Park Avenue and between East 17th Street and East 14th Street. Rich people lived in the area before the *Civil War. In the 1960s Union Square became associated with illegal drugs and violence but since then the city authorities have made it a more modern and pleasant place.

ˈUnison /ˈjuːnɪsn/ Britain's largest *trade union, formed in 1993 by combining three existing unions (NALGO, NUPE and COHSE). Its members work mainly in local government, the health service and other industries serving the public.

ˌunitary auˈthority /ˌjuːnɪtri; *AmE* ˌjuːnɪteri/ (*also* **ˌunitary ˈcouncil**) *n* (in Britain) a type of local *council introduced in 1995. Unitary authorities replaced the old system of county and district councils, providing a single level of local government. They are now found in all areas of Wales and Scotland, and in some areas of England.

Uˈnited an informal name for any British football club with 'United' in its name, e.g. *Manchester United: *United have won all their matches this season.*

Uˌnited ˈArtists (*abbr* **UA**) a US film company started in 1919 by Mary *Pickford, Douglas *Fairbanks[1], Charlie *Chaplin and D W *Griffith. It was the first *Hollywood company to allow actors to be independent. Its successful films included *The *Gold Rush*, *Scarface* (1932), *The African Queen* (1951), **High Noon*, *Some Like It Hot* (1959), *The *Magnificent Seven*, the James *Bond films of the 1960s, **One Flew Over the Cuckoo's Nest*, *Rocky* (1976) and **Rain Man*.

the **Uˌnited ˈKingdom** (*abbr* the **UK**) (*in full* the **United Kingdom of Great Britain and Northern Ireland**) a country made up of England, Wales, Scotland and Northern Ireland. It is a member of the *Commonwealth and the *European Union and its capital is *London. The name United Kingdom is found mainly in formal and official use. In more general use the country is referred to as Britain. See also ACT OF UNION. ⇨ note at GREAT BRITAIN.

the **Uˈnited ˈKingdom Aˈtomic ˈEnergy Auˌthority** (*abbr* **UKAEA**) a British government organization formed in 1954 to develop Britain's nuclear power programme and produce electricity. Today its main task is to manage the older nuclear power stations and carry out nuclear research.

the **Uˈnited ˈKingdom ˈUnionist ˌParty** a British political party. It is supported mainly by Protestants in Northern Ireland who want Northern Ireland to remain a part of the United Kingdom.

U

the **Uˌnited ˈNations** (*also* the **ˌUnited ˈNations Organiˌzation**) (*abbrs* the **UN**, **UNO**) an international organization, based in New York, which aims to preserve peace around the world and solve international problems. It was formed in 1945, and replaced the *League of Nations. Most of the world's independent states are members, and each has one vote in the *General Assembly. The *United Nations Security Council has the power to take military or economic action to settle international disputes. Other branches of the United Nations include the World Bank, the International Court of Justice in The Netherlands, and the United Nations Children's Fund (UNICEF). The Secretary General of the United Nations is Kofi Annan.

the **Uˈnited ˈNations Seˈcurity ˌCouncil** (*also* the **UN Security Council**) the part of the *United Nations which has the power to take political, economic or military action to settle international disputes and preserve world peace. It has 15 members, of which five are permanent (Britain, China, France, the Russian Federation and the US). Any decisions it makes must be agreed by a majority of its members, including all five of the permanent members.

the **Uˈnited ˈNegro ˈCollege Fund** a US charity, established in 1944, which raises money to support private colleges and universities with mostly *African-American students. It also helps individual students.

Uˈnited ˈPress Interˈnational (*abbr* **UPI**) a US company that collects news items and sells them to newspapers and radio and television stations. It was established in 1958 when United Press and the International News Service joined together. Compare ASSOCIATED PRESS.

the **Uˈnited Reˈformed ˈChurch** a Christian Church formed in Britain in 1972 when the *Presbyterian Church in England joined with the *Congregationalist Church in England and Wales.

the **Uˈnited ˈStates ˈAir Force Aˌcademy** the university that trains officers for the US Air Force. It was established in 1954 in Colorado Springs, *Colorado, and is the newest of the US military colleges. It had about 4 300 students in 1997. They receive a *bachelor's degree in science when they complete their four years of studies.

the **Uˈnited ˈStates ˈCoast Guard** the US military service that is controlled by the US Department of Transportation but becomes part of the US Navy during a war. It was established in 1915. The Coast Guard stops ships suspected of carrying drugs and other illegal goods, and can make arrests. It also keeps watch to see that other laws of the sea are obeyed, rescues ships in danger and has a weather service.

the **Uˈnited ˈStates ˈForest ˌService** the organization controlled by the US Department of Agriculture which protects and manages America's forests. It was established in 1905. It does research and provides educational programmes and advice to individual states and private forest owners. It is also responsible for 31 Special Recreation Areas.

the **Uˈnited ˈStates Inforˈmation ˌAgency** (*abbr* the **USIA**) a US government organization responsible for providing information about the US to other countries of the world, e.g. through libraries and cultural programmes. It also runs the *Fulbright scholarship programme and advises the *National Security Council on what other countries think of US policies. The USIA was established in 1948. See also VOICE OF AMERICA.

the **Uˈnited ˈStates Maˈrine Corps** (*also* the **United States Marines**) a US armed service that is part of the US Navy. It was established by *Congress in 1798 as the only service trained to fight on the sea, on land and in the air. The Marines became well known during *World War II when they successfully attacked the Pacific islands occupied by the Japanese. They were also active in the *Korean War and the *Vietnam War. See also LEATHERNECK.

the **Uˈnited ˈStates ˈMilitary Aˌcademy** (*also* **ˌWest ˈPoint**) the military school that trains officers for the US Army. It is at West Point, New York, and was established by Congress in 1802. In 1998, it had about 4 000 students, who are called *cadets*. Famous US generals who were trained there include Robert E *Lee, Ulysses S *Grant, John *Pershing, Dwight D *Eisenhower, George *Patton, Douglas *MacArthur and Norman Schwartzkopf.

the **U'nited 'States 'Naval A,cademy** (*also* **Annapolis**) the military school that trains officers for the US Navy and the US Marine Corps. It was established in 1845 at *Annapolis, *Maryland. In 1998, it had about 4 000 students, called *midshipmen*.

the **U'nited 'States 'Senate** (*also* the **Senate**) the upper house of the US *Congress. There are 100 **Senators** (two from each state), and they are elected for periods of six years. Laws must be passed by both houses (i.e. the Senate and the *House of Representatives), but the Senate has special responsibility in matters to do with foreign policy, and it also has the power to 'advise and consent' on appointments made by the President. The Vice-president is the senior officer in the Congress.

the **U'nited 'Way of A'merica** a large US charity, established in 1918, with branches in nearly 2 000 cities and towns. It has campaigns once a year to collect money which is then divided among local charities and organizations. The main office is in Alexandria, *Virginia.

,Universal 'Pictures (*also* **Universal**) a *Hollywood film company, established in 1912. The large area where many of its films are made is called **Universal City** and attracts many tourists. Steven *Spielberg has made several of his films there, including **Jaws*, *ET* and *Jurassic Park*. The company opened a second Universal City at *Orlando, *Florida, in 1990.

The ***'Universe*** a leading newspaper for *Roman Catholics in Britain. It appears every week and was first published in 1860.

Universities and colleges ⇨ article.

the **,Uni'versities and 'Colleges Ad'missions ,Service** (*abbr* **UCAS**) the organization that deals with students wanting to apply to study at British universities and colleges. Students must complete a special form, and may apply to a maximum of eight institutions. Each institution then considers the requests and may offer students places. The organization also publishes the UCAS Handbook, which lists all the courses available at British universities and colleges, and gives information about them. The only university that does not take part in the UCAS service is the *Open University. ⇨ article at UNIVERSITIES AND COLLEGES.

,Uni'versity 'Challenge a British television quiz show in which teams of students from different universities compete to answer difficult questions on a wide range of subjects. It was presented from 1962 to 1987 by Bamber *Gascoigne and since 1994 it has been presented by Jeremy *Paxman. A phrase often used in the programme is 'Your starter for ten' to introduce a first question worth ten points.

,Uni'versity 'College, 'London /ˈlʌndən/ (*abbr* **UCL**) a college of *London University, established in 1826. It was the first college to be established in England apart from the colleges of *Oxford and *Cambridge, and was originally for students who were *Nonconformists (= Christians who did not belong to the *Church of England), Catholics and Jews.

,Uni'versity 'College 'Hospital (*abbr* **UCH**) a *teaching hospital in London, England, opened in 1833 as part of *University College, London.

the **,Uni'versity of Cali'fornia at Los 'Angeles** /kælɪˈfɔːniə, lɒs ˈændʒəliːz; *AmE* kælɪˈfɔːrniə, lɔːs/ ⇨ UCLA.

the **,Uni'versity of 'Manchester 'Institute of 'Science and Tech'nology** /ˈmæntʃəstə(r)/ (*abbr* **UMIST**) a university in Manchester, north-west England. It was established in 1824 to provide training in engineering and other practical subjects, and is now well known for its scientific research. It is independent from the two other universities in Manchester. Over 20% of its students are from foreign countries.

the 'Tomb of the **'Unknown 'Warrior** (*also* the 'Tomb of the **'Unknown 'Soldier**) a grave inside *Westminster Abbey, London, England, which contains the body of an unknown British soldier who died in *World War I. The grave represents the many other soldiers who died, especially those whose bodies were never identified. There is a similar grave at the *Arlington National Cemetery, Virginia, US, now called officially the **Tomb of the Unknowns**, where unknown US soldiers from both world wars, the *Korean War and the *Vietnam War are buried.

the Tomb of the Unknowns in Arlington National Cemetery

UNO /ˌjuː en ˈəʊ; *AmE* ˈoʊ/ ⇨ UNITED NATIONS.

'Unser /ˈʌnsə(r)/ the name of three successful US racing car drivers. They are the brothers **Bobby Unser** (1934–) and **Al Unser** (1939–), and Al's son, **Al Unser Junior** (1962–). Bobby won the *Indianapolis 500 race three times (1968, 1975 and 1981), Al won it four times (1970, 1971, 1978 and 1987) and his son has won it twice (1992, 1994).

the **Un'touchables** the popular name for the team of US Justice Department officers led by Eliot *Ness. They were given the name because people believed that they were too honest ever to accept illegal payments.

,John **'Updike** /ˈʌpdaɪk/ (1932–) a US writer of novels about the hopes, worries and fears of modern *middle-class Americans. He is best known for his four novels about a former *basketball player, Harry 'Rabbit' Angstrom. They are *Rabbit, Run* (1960), *Rabbit Redux* (1971), *Rabbit is Rich* (1981) and *Rabbit at Rest* (1990). The last two each won the *Pulitzer Prize. His other novels include *The Witches of Eastwick* (1984) and *Toward the End of Time* (1997).

,Up-Helly-'Aa /ˌʌp heli ˈɑː/ a festival held every January in *Lerwick, in the *Shetlands, to mark the islands' historical links with the *Vikings. In the main ceremony a model of a Viking long ship (= a type of long narrow warship) is burned in the middle of the town.

Up-Helly-Aa

UPI /ˌjuː piː ˈaɪ/ ⇨ UNITED PRESS INTERNATIONAL.

the **,upper 'class** *n* [sing + sing/pl *v*] (*also* the **upper classes** [pl]) the highest class of people in society. In Britain the upper class are usually from rich families who own land and property. They may have noble titles such as 'Lord' or 'Lady', and they typically send their children to *public schools. Many people also think of them as having a particular way of speaking. Because of their connection with the land and the countryside, they are often associated with country sports such as *hunting and horse riding. ⇨ article at CLASS. ▶ **upper-class** *adj*: *an upper-class accent/education/family*.

the ˌ**upper middle** ˈ**class** *n* [sing + sing/pl *v*] (*also* the **upper middle classes** [pl]) the class of people in British society between the *middle class and the *upper class. Its members include people such as company directors, professors or *barristers, who have a high social status and may earn a lot of money. In modern Britain, however, it is less common to identify people in this way. ⇨ article at CLASS. ▶ **upper-middle-class** *adj*: *an upper-middle-class lifestyle/background*.

ˈ**upper school** *n* (in Britain) the name given to the classes for older children (aged 14–18) in a secondary school (for children aged 11–18). It may also include a *sixth form. ⇨ article at EDUCATION IN BRITAIN.

ˌ***Upstairs,*** ˈ***Downstairs*** a very successful British television series (1971–5) about the life of a rich London family and their servants in the early years of the 20th century. It was common in the houses of such families for the servants to live in rooms below the ground floor level, i.e. 'downstairs'.

ˈ**Uptown** /ˈʌptaʊn/ **1** the part of *Manhattan(1) in New York City which is north of 59th Street. It includes *Central Park and areas on both sides of it. The Upper East Side includes the *Metropolitan Museum of Art, the *Guggenheim Museum and *Bloomingdale's. The Upper West Side has the *Lincoln Center for the Performing Arts and Fordham University. Compare DOWNTOWN. **2 uptown** *n* (*AmE*) the outer districts of a city or large town, where its people mostly live.
▶ **uptown** *adj*, *adv* (*AmE*) to or in the outer districts of a large city or town: *an uptown residential area* ○ *go/drive uptown*.

ˌ**Urban De**ˈ**velopment Corpo**ˌ**ration** any of several organizations started by the British government to develop and improve areas of the *inner cities. The first two were started in 1981 in London's *Docklands and in *Merseyside, and created new offices, houses and industries. The Corporations especially encouraged businesses from abroad to come to the areas.

the ˌ**Urban** ˈ**League** (*also* the ˈ**National** ˈ**Urban** ˈ**League**) a US organization of people who work without pay to help *African Americans and other minority groups to gain equal rights. It was established in 1910 and now has more than 100 local groups that train minorities for jobs and help them to receive health care and other support.

USA for Africa /ˌjuː es ˈeɪ fər ˈæfrɪkə/ a US charity that collected money from sales of its very popular album *We Are the World* (1985) to buy food for Africans who might die without such help. The album received an *Emmy award, and the *MTV gave an award to its video. Many famous singers and musicians performed the songs, including Ray *Charles, Diana *Ross, Bob *Dylan, Michael *Jackson, Bette *Midler and Bruce *Springsteen. USA for Africa ended its work after six years. Compare BAND AID, LIVE AID.

USAID /ˌjuː es ˈeɪd/ (*in full* the **US Agency for International Development**) an independent US government organization that works to provide help for poor countries. It was established in 1961 by President John F *Kennedy and gives financial, technical and medical assistance in such areas as economic development and birth control.

ˌ**USA** ˈ**Networks** /ˌjuː es eɪ/ a US cable television company. It owns the USA Network, which in 1997 had 73 million subscribers (= people who pay to receive programmes), and the Sci-Fi Channel with 46 million subscribers. It recently began a USA Latin America Network (1994), Sci-Fi Channel Europe (1995) and USA Brazil Network (1996). The USA Network has major sports events, and original and older films and programmes. Series include *Duckman*, *Gargoyles* and *Pacific Blue*. The Seagram Company bought USA Networks in 1997.

USA Today /ˌjuː es ˈeɪ təˈdeɪ/ a national US newspaper read by more people than any other. It sells about 2.2 million copies each day. The Gannett Company began *USA Today* in 1979, and it is now published around the world by satellite. It has colourful pictures, short news summaries and longer articles.

USDAW /ˈʌzdɔː/ (*in full* the **Union of Shop, Distributive and Allied Workers**) a British *trade union for people who work in shops, factories, restaurants and other trades serving the public. It was formed in 1891.

ˌ**used-**ˈ**car** ˌ**salesman** *n* (*pl* **-men**) (*BrE*) a man whose job is selling cars that have already had one or more owners. Used-car salesmen are often presented in jokes, cartoons, etc. as not very honest or reliable. The British television character Arthur *Daley is regarded as a typical used-car salesman, i.e confident and friendly, but dishonest and not very successful. Opponents of US President Richard *Nixon used to show his picture with the words, 'Would you buy a used car from this man?', suggesting that he could not be trusted.

USIA /ˌjuː es aɪ ˈeɪ/ ⇨ UNITED STATES INFORMATION AGENCY.

the ˌ**US** ˈ**Masters** ˌ**Tournament** /ˌjuː es/ (*also* the **US Masters**) ⇨ MASTERS TOURNAMENT.

ˈ***US*** ˈ***News and*** ˈ***World Re***ˈ***port*** /ˈjuː es/ a popular US news magazine published each week. It is often referred to simply as *US News* and is known for its conservative opinions. It contains many articles on business and economic affairs, and also news about political, social and cultural matters.

the ˌ**US** ˈ**Open** /ˌjuː es/ **1** a major US golf competition held each year at different places. It was first held in 1895. The most wins by a single player have been four. Four players have achieved this: Willie Anderson, Bobby *Jones, Ben *Hogan and Jack *Nicklaus. Compare MASTERS TOURNAMENT, BRITISH OPEN. **2** a US tennis competition each year which is one of the sport's *grand slam(1) events. It was first played in 1968 in Forest Hills, New York, and moved in 1978 to Flushing Meadow, New York. Jimmy *Connors has won the men's competition the most times (5), and Chris *Evert has won the most women's events (6). Compare WIMBLEDON.

ˌPeter ˈ**Ustinov** /ˈjuːstɪnɒf; *AmE* ˈjuːstɪnɑːf/ (1921–) an English actor, writer and film director. He is best known for playing unusual characters, e.g. in *Death on the Nile* (1978), in which he played the *detective Hercule *Poirot. He is also admired for telling funny stories on stage and television and for his ability to copy many different foreign *accents. Ustinov has written several plays and novels. He was made a *knight in 1990.

USWA /ˌjuː es dʌbljuː ˈeɪ/ (*also* **USW**) (*in full* the **United Steel Workers of America**) one of the largest US *trade unions. It was established in 1936 as the Steel Workers' Organizing Committee for steel, iron and tin workers, and took its present name in 1942. It now includes workers in other industries, such as rubber and plastics. In 1998 it had about 550 000 members.

US West /ˌjuː es ˈwest/ a large US telephone and cable television company. In 1997 it provided tele-

Universities and colleges

Going to university in Britain

After *school many British students go to university. They apply to several universities through ***UCAS** (Universities and Colleges Admission Service) and receive **offers** of a place on condition that they achieve certain grades in their *A levels.

Most universities receive some money from the state. The oldest and most famous are *Oxford and *Cambridge. Other much respected universities include London, Durham and St Andrew's. Some universities such as Birmingham and Manchester are called **redbrick universities** because they were built in the 19th century with brick rather than stone. The newer universities have their buildings grouped together on a **campus**.

A **first degree**, which is usually an **honours degree**, generally takes three years. Most courses end with exams called **finals**. Results are given as **classes** (= grades): a first is the highest class, seconds are often split between upper second and lower second, and below that is a third. **Graduates** may add the letters **BA** (Bachelor of Arts) or **BSc** (Bachelor of Science) after their name. Some graduates go on to study for a further degree, often a **master's degree** or a **doctorate**.

Students in Britain formerly had their **tuition fees** paid by the state and received a government **grant** to help pay their living expenses. Now, they receive only a loan towards their expenses, and from 1999 most will also have to pay £1 000 a year towards tuition fees. The new arrangements have caused a great deal of concern both among students and among members of the public who believe that education should be free.

Going to college in the US

Americans talk about 'going to college' even if the institution they attend is a university. To Americans the phrase 'going to university' sounds pretentious. Most colleges offer classes only for **undergraduate** students studying for a **bachelor's degree**. ***Community colleges** offer two-year courses leading to an **associate's degree**, and afterwards students transfer to a different college or university to continue their studies. Universities are larger than colleges and also offer courses for **graduate students** who study in **graduate school**. Many universities also have separate professional schools, e.g. a **medical school** or a **law school**.

American *high school students who want to study at a college or university have to take a **standardized test**, e.g. the ***SAT** (Scholastic Aptitude Test) or the ***ACT** (American College Test). Students from countries outside the US who are not native speakers of English must also take the ***TOEFL** (Test of English as a Foreign Language). Each college or university decides on the minimum **score** it will accept, though test scores are never the only factor taken into account. Students apply direct to between three and six colleges in their last year of high school. Each college has its own **application form** and most include a question for which the student must write an essay. The student also has to send a **transcript** (= an official list of all the subjects studied and the grades received) and letters of reference.

There are many private colleges and universities but most students choose a public institution because the costs are lower. All universities charge **tuition**, and students pay extra for **room and board**. Prices range from a few hundred dollars a year to well over $25 000 at some private colleges. Students whose families cannot afford to pay the full amount apply for **financial aid**. Many students receive a **financial aid package** which may be a combination of **grants** from the government, a **scholarship**, a **student loan** and **work-study** (= a part-time job at the college).

The most famous universities are those in the ***Ivy League**, including *Harvard and *Yale, but many others have good reputations. Large universities often put most emphasis on research. Smaller colleges tend to concentrate on teaching undergraduates, and many students prefer these colleges because they offer smaller classes and more personal attention from teachers (⇨ note at STUDENT LIFE).

Teaching and learning

The US academic year may be divided into two **semesters** of about 15 weeks or three **quarters** of about 10 weeks each. Students take courses in a variety of subjects, regardless of their main subject, because the aim of the **liberal arts** curriculum is to produce well-rounded people with good critical skills. At the end of their **sophomore** (= second) year students choose a **major** (= main subject) and sometimes a **minor** (= additional subject) which they study for the next two years. Students take four or five courses each semester from the **course catalog**. Courses may consist mainly of **lectures** or may include **discussion sections** or **lab sessions**.

Students are given **grades** at the end of each course. The highest grade is A; the lowest is F, which means that the student has failed the course and will not get **credit** for taking it. To check a student's overall progress, the university calculates a ***grade point average** (**GPA**). Students who finish their degree with a high GPA may be awarded **Latin honours**, of which the highest is **summa cum laude*.

At most British universities the academic year is divided into three **terms**. Students study a main subject throughout their degree course, which is usually a mix of compulsory courses and **electives**. Teaching methods vary between universities. Most students have lectures and **seminars** (= discussion groups) and there are **practicals** for those doing a science subject. At some universities students have individual **tutorials** or **supervisions**.

In Britain a **professor** is the person in charge of a department or a senior member of staff. Other teaching and research staff are called **lecturers**. Junior academic staff may be called **research associates**. In the US most people who teach at colleges or universities and have a doctorate are addressed as *professor*. **Full professors** are senior to **associate professors**, **assistant professors** and **instructors**. Graduate students working towards a higher degree may teach undergraduate courses at larger universities. These **grad students** are called **TAs** (teaching assistants). In return, TAs do not have to pay for their own tuition and get a small amount of money to live on.

phone services to 25 million people in 14 states in the *Middle West and West. It is also involved in British telephone and cable television services.

ˈ**Utah** /ˈjuːtɑː/ a western US state which is one of the *Rocky Mountain States. About two-thirds of the population are *Mormons. It was named after the *Ute *Native-American people, and its popular name is the Beehive State. Other Native Americans, such as the *Navajo, lived in the area when the Mormons began to settle there in 1847. It became a state in 1896. Products include corn, apples, potatoes, copper, gold, silver, steel and medical instruments. Tourist attractions include the *Great Salt Lake, the *Rainbow Bridge and *Zion National Park.

Ute /juːt/ *n* a member of a *Native-American people who mostly live in *Colorado and *Utah on reservations (= land given and protected by the US government). They are farmers and make money from oil and gas on their lands. Their name means 'people of the mountains', and they were originally the same people as the southern *Paiutes. The Utes became excellent fighters after they received Spanish horses in the early 19th century. They were placed on reservations in 1868.

Uˌtiliˈtarianism /juːˌtɪlɪˈteəriənɪzəm; *AmE* juːˌtɪlɪˈteriənɪzəm/ *n* [U] a system of ideas based on the work of Jeremy *Bentham and John Stuart *Mill. It argues that actions can be considered good if they produce happiness, and that governments should try to produce 'the greatest happiness for the greatest number' of people.

Uˈtopia (*also* **uˈtopia**) *n* [C, U] an imaginary place or state of things in which everything is perfect. The original Utopia was an imaginary island described by Thomas *More in a book of the same name which appeared in 1516. He criticized the political systems of France and England and went on to describe life in Utopia, where everyone shared their possessions and led a happy life.

▶ **Uˈtopian** (*also* **uˈtopian**) *adj* (*usu disapprov*) having a perfect society; aiming for a perfect society, which may be impossible to achieve: *Her political beliefs are just Utopian fantasies.*

U /juː/ *adj* (*BrE*) **1** (*approv humor*) typical of the dress, behaviour, speech, etc. of the *upper class; showing good taste: *It's a very grand house – all the furnishings are terribly U.* ○ *Darts is not considered a very U sort of game.* Compare NON-U. **2** (of films) officially judged to be suitable for anyone, including children; not containing violence, sex or bad language: *a U film/certificate.*

the **U-2 incident** /ˌjuː ˈtuː ˌɪnsɪdənt/ an incident in May 1960 when an US U-2 spy plane (= aircraft that takes secret photographs of enemy places) was shot down over the USSR. The pilot Gary Powers survived. The Russian leader Nikita Khrushchev ended a meeting in Paris with US President *Eisenhower 11 days later when Eisenhower refused to say he was sorry. Powers was exchanged for the Soviet spy Rudolf Abel in 1962.

UVF /ˌjuː viː ˈef/ ⇨ ULSTER VOLUNTEER FORCE.

Vv

VA /ˌviː ˈeɪ/ ⇨ DEPARTMENT OF VETERANS AFFAIRS.

Vail /veɪl/ a town in the US state of *Colorado that is an expensive centre for skiing. It is near the White River National Forest 122 miles (196 kilometres) west of *Denver. Its special holiday buildings, opened in 1952, are in the Tyrolean style. Tennis and golf are available in the summer.

ˌ**valedicˈtorian** /ˌvælɪdɪkˈtɔːriən/ *n* (*AmE*) a student in a *high school, college or university who gives the valedictory (= goodbye speech) on the day when degrees are presented. The valedictorian is traditionally the student with the highest grades. Most schools also have a 'salutatorian', who has the next highest grades and gives the salutatory (= speech of welcome to the event).

ˌRudolph **Valenˈtino** /vælənˈtiːnəʊ; *AmE* vælənˈtiːnoʊ/ (1895–1926) one of the most successful US stars in silent films. He was born in Italy and went to America in 1913. He played romantic roles and is best remembered for his part in *The Sheik* (1921). His other films included *The Four Horsemen of the Apocalypse* (1921), *Blood and Sand* (1922) and *The Son of the Sheik* (1926). When Valentino died young, over 100 000 people attended his funeral.

ˌ**Valley ˈForge** an area in the US state of *Pennsylvania where General George *Washington and his Continental Army spent the severe winter of 1777–8 during the *American Revolution. Hundreds died of cold and lack of food, but the army remained loyal.

ˈ**valley girl** *n* (*AmE*) a girl from a rich family who is not very intelligent and only interested in things like shopping, typically one of those living in the San Fernando Valley of *California in the 1980s.

ˌFrankie ˈ**Valli** /ˈvæli/ (1937–) a US pop singer with a high voice. His group, The Four Seasons, formed in 1956 and still sing together. They were chosen for the Rock and Roll *Hall of Fame in 1990. They had hits in the 1960s with *Sherry* and *Big Girls Don't Cry*. Valli has also had hits singing alone with *Can't Take My Eyes Off You* (1967) and the title song for the film **Grease*.

ˌ**Value ˈAdded Tax** *n* [U] (*abbr* **VAT**) (in Britain) a tax of 17.5% which is added to the price of certain goods when they are sold. The money from the tax is collected by the person selling the goods and must then be paid to the government. Many types of goods are free from the tax, including food, books and children's clothes. VAT has existed in Britain since 1971 and there are similar taxes in many European countries.

ˌJohn ˈ**Vanbrugh** /ˈvænbrə/ (1664–1726) an English architect and writer of plays. His plays, which are late *Restoration comedies, include *The Relapse* (1696) and *The Provok'd Wife* (1697). In his mid 30s he began a second career as an architect, working with Nicholas *Hawksmoor. Together they designed several grand houses and other buildings, including *Castle Howard and *Blenheim Palace. He was made a *knight in 1714.

ˌAbigail **Van ˈBuren**[1] /væn ˈbjʊərən; *AmE* ˈbjʊrən/ the writer of the US newspaper column **Dear Abby*.

ˌMartin **Van ˈBuren**[2] /væn ˈbjʊərən; *AmE* ˈbjʊrən/ (1782–1862) the eighth US *President (1837–41). His popular name was the 'Little Magician' because of his political skills. He was a lawyer and a *Democrat who first served under Andrew *Jackson as *Secretary of State (1829–31) and Vice-president (1832–6). He is remembered especially for establishing the Independent Treasury System to deal with the country's financial difficulties.

ˌCyrus ˈ**Vance** /ˌsaɪrəs ˈvæns/ (1917–) the US *Secretary of State under President *Carter[2] (1977–80). He left the post because he disagreed with Carter's decision to try to rescue the Americans kept as prisoners in Iran during the *hostage crisis. In 1992, Vance and the British politician David *Owen represented the *United Nations and the European Community in trying to bring peace to Bosnia-Herzegovina.

ˌ**Van ˈCliburn** ⇨ CLIBURN.

the **V and A** /ˌviː ənd ˈeɪ/ ⇨ VICTORIA AND ALBERT MUSEUM.

Corˌnelius ˈ**Vanderbilt**[1] /kɔːˈniːliəs ˈvændəbɪlt; *AmE* kɔːrˈniːliəs ˈvændərbɪlt/ (1794–1877) a US businessman who became very rich from his shipping and railway companies, and gave a lot of his money to support good causes. He established Vanderbilt University in *Nashville, *Tennessee, in 1873. His sons, especially the oldest, William Henry Vanderbilt (1821–85), increased the family's wealth and continued its financial gifts.

ˌGloria ˈ**Vanderbilt**[2] /ˈvændəbɪlt; *AmE* ˈvændərbɪlt/ (1924–) a US businesswoman who designs women's products, including *jeans and perfume. Cornelius *Vanderbilt was her father's grandfather. She was called the 'poor little rich girl' after her mother, who had left her, and her aunt had a legal dispute, and a court decided in 1934 that she should live with her aunt. She received $4 million at the age of 21. Leopold *Stokowski was one of her four husbands.

ˌAnthony **van ˈDyck** ⇨ DYCK.

ˌDick **Van ˈDyke** /væn ˈdaɪk/ (1925–) a US comedy actor, singer and dancer. He had his own television series, *The Dick Van Dyke Show* (1961–6), which won three Emmys (1963, 1964 and 1966), and *The New Dick Van Dyke Show* (1971–2). He later played Dr Mark Sloan in the *CBS television series *Diagnosis Murder* (1993–). His films include *Bye Bye Birdie* (1963), **Mary Poppins*, *Chitty Chitty Bang Bang* (1968) and *Dick Tracy* (1990).

ˌ***Vanity ˈFair*** **1** a novel by William Makepeace *Thackeray. It contrasts the lives of two characters who first meet at school: Becky Sharp, who is intelligent, ambitious and poor, and Amelia Sedley, who is gentle, pretty and rich. The book contains many humorous characters and was published in parts between 1847 and 1848. **2** a magazine published every month both in Britain and the US, with articles about politics, society, culture and other subjects.

ˌ**Vanuˈatu** /ˌvænuˈɑːtuː/ a group of 13 large and about 70 small islands in the south-west Pacific Ocean. Its capital is Port Vila and its official languages are French, English and Bislama. The country was formerly owned by the British and French and known as the New Hebrides, but it became an independent member of the *Commonwealth in 1980.

Vaˈriety a US newspaper of the entertainment industry, published each week in New York. It includes reviews of plays, films, etc. and special articles about the entertainment world, and is known for its colourful and informal style of language. It was first published in 1905.

the **Va'riety Club** an international charity that helps children. Its members are famous actors and entertainers who collect money by organizing shows and concerts. The first Variety Club was started in the US in 1927 and the charity now has branches in many countries of the world, including Britain.

'varsity /ˈvɑːsəti; *AmE* ˈvɑːrsəti/ *n* **1** [sing, usu before *n*] (*BrE*) (usually with reference to sports) a university, especially *Oxford or *Cambridge: *the varsity football match* (= between Oxford and Cambridge). **2** (*AmE*) a main team representing a university, college or school, especially in sports.

'Vaseline™ /ˈvæsəliːn/ *n* [U] a thick, soft, yellowish substance used to treat dry skin, or to put on sore parts of the body, etc.

ˌVassar 'College /ˌvæsə; *AmE* ˌvæsər/ (*also* **'Vassar**) a private US college in Poughkeepsie, New York. It had about 2 330 students in 1998. It was established by Matthew Vassar in 1861 as a woman's college and became one of America's best. Vassar now accepts some male students.

VAT /ˌviː eɪ ˈtiː/ ⇨ VALUE ADDED TAX.

'vaudeville *n* [U] (*AmE*) a type of entertainment on stage, especially popular in the US between the 1840s and the 1930s. A typical vaudeville show included a variety of performers, including singers, dancers, comedians and sometimes animals. The best-known vaudeville theatre was the Palace in New York. US stars who began in vaudeville included Will *Rogers, Al *Jolson, the *Marx Brothers and W C *Fields. Compare MUSIC-HALL 1.

ˌSarah **'Vaughan** /ˈvɔːn/ (1924–90) a US *jazz singer noted for her great range. She sang many songs by 'Duke' *Ellington and George *Gershwin, and she recorded with 'Dizzy' *Gillespie, 'Cannonball' Adderley and many other jazz musicians. Her most successful songs included *Mr Wonderful* (1956) and *Broken-Hearted Melody* (1959).

'Ralph **'Vaughan 'Williams** /ˈreɪf ˈvɔːn ˈwɪljəmz/ (1872–1958) a popular English composer. He was influenced mainly by traditional English music, especially of the *Tudor(1) period, and his work often suggests English life and traditions and the English countryside. His best-known short pieces include *Fantasia on a Theme by Thomas Tallis* (1910) and *The Lark Ascending* (1914). He also wrote several works for orchestra, as well as songs, operas and film music. He was made a member of the *Order of Merit in 1935.

'Vauxhall /ˈvɒksɔːl; *AmE* ˈvɑːksɔːl/ a company that produces many different makes of cars, mostly of medium price. It was formed in Britain in 1903 and bought by the *General Motors Corporation in 1925.

VC /ˌviː ˈsiː/ **1** ⇨ VICTORIA CROSS. **2 the VC** an informal name used by US soldiers during the *Vietnam War to refer to the enemy Viet Cong soldiers. They also called them Victor Charlie, the communication words for VC, or simply Charlie.

V-chip /ˈviː tʃɪp/ *n* an electronic device in a television set which parents can use to block programmes they do not want their children to see, e.g. ones containing a lot of sex or violence. According to the 1996 Telecommunications Act all new television sets in the US must contain a V-chip. Some Americans have criticized this because they believe it stops free speech. Others would like all computers to be fitted with V-chips as well as televisions.

VC10 /ˌviː siː ˈten/ a British passenger aircraft of the 1960s and 1970s, made by *Vickers.

V-E Day /ˌviː ˈiː deɪ/ Victory in Europe Day, 8 May 1945. The day marked the end of fighting in Europe during *World War II, and there were public celebrations in London and many other places. The 50th anniversary of V-E Day, 8 May 1995, was celebrated in many European cities by soldiers and others who had lived through the war.

'Vegas /ˈveɪɡəs/ ⇨ LAS VEGAS.

V8™ /ˌviː ˈeɪt/ *n* [U, C] a juice made from eight different vegetables. It has been produced by the Campbell Soup Company since 1948, and its advertisements often used the phrase, 'Wow, I could have had a V8!'

Vel'veeta™ /velˈviːtə/ *n* [U] a popular US make of processed cheese, made by *Kraft.

the **ˌVelvet 'Underground** a US rock group that had no big commercial hits but influenced many later groups and singers, including David *Bowie. Their albums included *The Velvet Underground and Nico* (1967), *White Light/White Heat* (1967), *The Velvet Underground* (1969) and *Loaded* (1970). The group broke up in 1971 and formed again for a short time in the 1990s. See also REED.

'Veni, 'vidi, 'vici /ˈveni ˈviːdi ˈviːki/ a Latin phrase meaning 'I came, I saw, I conquered'. It was first said by *Julius Caesar after winning a battle in Asia Minor (now Turkey). Many people, especially in Britain, wrongly think he said it after defeating the *Britons.

ˌRobert **Ven'turi** /venˈtjʊəri; *AmE* venˈtʊri/ (1925–) a US architect who developed the Post-Modernist style. Venturi's buildings include the Humanities Classroom Building at the *State University of New York (1973) and the *Sainsbury Wing of the *National Gallery (1991) in London. His books include *Complexity and Contradiction in Architecture* (1966).

Ver'mont /vɜːˈmɒnt; *AmE* vɜːrˈmɑːnt/ a *New England state in the US, on the border with Canada. It is also known as the Green Mountain State. The largest city is Burlington and the capital city is Montpelier. The French settled there first in the 17th century, and Vermont became a state in 1791. Its produces different types of stone, including granite and marble, and other products include wood, furniture, machine tools and maple syrup (= a sweet, sticky sauce produced from a type of maple tree). Tourist attractions in Vermont include the Green Mountain National Forest.

the **ˌVerra'zano-'Narrows 'Bridge** /ˌverəˈzɑːnəʊ ˈnærəʊz; *AmE* ˌverəˈzɑːnoʊ ˈnæroʊz/ the longest bridge in the US. It is in New York City and connects *Staten Island to *Brooklyn. It is 4 260 feet/1 300 metres long, and one of the world's longest suspension bridges (= bridges that hang from steel cables supported by towers at each end). It is named after Giovanni da Verrazano, an Italian who in 1524 was the first European to land on Staten Island. After the bridge was opened in 1964, many people began to buy homes on the island. Compare GEORGE WASHINGTON BRIDGE, BROOKLYN BRIDGE, GOLDEN GATE BRIDGE.

the **ˌVery 'Reverend** (*written abbrs* the **Very Rev**, the **Very Revd**) a title used before the name of certain senior priests, especially a dean or provost of the *Church of England, or a former *Moderator of the Church of Scotland: *the Very Reverend William Wallis.* Compare RIGHT REVEREND.

Aˌmerigo **Ves'pucci** /əˌmerɪɡəʊ veˈspuːtʃi; *AmE* əˌmerɪɡoʊ/ (1454–1512) an Italian sailor and explorer. He made several journeys across the Atlantic and claimed to have been the first to have seen South America (in 1497). The name America is said to have been based on his first name, but other origins of the name have been suggested.

ˈVeterans' Day (in the US and Canada) a holiday on 11 November to honour all men and women who have served in the armed forces. People hang flags outside their homes, and many cities celebrate with parades. It began in 1926 as *Armistice Day in memory of the end of *World War I. Its present name was established in 1954. Compare MEMORIAL DAY.

the **ˈVeterans of ˈForeign ˈWars** (*abbr* **VFW**) a large organization for former members of the US armed forces who fought in wars abroad. It helps those in need, has campaigns to influence the government on military matters, and does community service. It was established in 1899 and has more than 2.8 million members. Compare AMERICAN LEGION.

Viˈagra™ /vaɪˈægrə/ the commercial name of a drug used to cure impotence (= the condition of a man who is unable to have full sex). It is produced in the US by Pfizer Inc, and is the treatment for this condition in the form of pills. It can be bought only with a doctor's written instruction. When it first became available in 1998 it received a lot of publicity because many people said it had improved their sex life.

the **ˌVicar of ˈBray** /ˈbreɪ/ a vicar (= a *Church of England priest) in a traditional English song. He changes his religious and political beliefs according to the beliefs of the ruling king or queen, and is concerned only with keeping his job. The name 'Vicar of Bray' is sometimes used to describe somebody who is prepared to change their beliefs to gain some advantage.

The ***ˌVicar of ˈWakefield*** /ˈweɪkfiːld/ a novel (1766) by Oliver *Goldsmith. It is about a vicar (= a *Church of England priest) who is kind and honest but experiences several disasters in his life, such as his house burning down and his son being put in prison. After many complicated adventures the book ends happily.

le ***ˌvice anˈglais*** /lə ˌviːs ɒŋˈgleɪ; *AmE* ɑːŋˈgleɪ/ *n* [sing] a French phrase meaning 'the English vice'. It sometimes refers to the practice of gaining sexual pleasure by beating or whipping people, thought to be characteristic of the English, but is often used to mean any typically English fault or weakness.

ˌvice-ˈchancellor *n* (in Britain) the most senior official in a university. The vice-chancellor of a British university is responsible for its administration, in contrast to the chancellor, who is given the title as an honour and has only a few formal duties, such as attending ceremonies, etc. In the US, a vice-chancellor is the assistant to the chancellor, who is the senior university official, with the most responsibility and power. Many US universities, however, use the titles 'president' and 'vice-president' instead of 'chancellor' and 'vice-chancellor'.

ˈvice squad *n* [C + sing/pl *v*] a police department in Britain or the US that tries to prevent prostitution, gambling, drug dealing and similar offences.

ˈVickers /ˈvɪkəz; *AmE* ˈvɪkərz/ a British company known for making military equipment, especially weapons and aircraft. Among the best-known are the Vickers-Maxim machine-gun, the *Spitfire and *Wellington aircraft, the Challenger tank and the *Trident submarine. The branch of the company that made aircraft now forms part of *British Aerospace, and the rest of it joined with *Rolls-Royce in 1980.

Vicks™ /vɪks/ the name of a range of products for treating coughs produced by the US company Richardson-Vicks Inc (part of Procter and Gamble) and available without a doctor's written permission. They include Vicks Cough Drops, Vicks Formula 44, Vicks VapoRub and Vicks VapoSteam.

ˈVicksburg /ˈvɪksbɜːg; *AmE* ˈvɪksbɜːrg/ a city on the *Mississippi River in the US state of *Mississippi. During the *Civil War it was captured after the US army of General *Grant had surrounded it for seven months. This gave the *Union control of the river and split the *Confederate States. The **Vicksburg National Military Park** is a popular tourist attraction.

Vicˈtoria[1] /vɪkˈtɔːriə/ a major train station in London for trains to and from the south of England. It also has a station on the *London Underground.

Queen **Victoria**[2] (1819–1901) a British queen who ruled from 1837 to 1901. She was the granddaughter of King *George III and became queen after the death of King *William IV. Her rule was the longest of any British king or queen, and happened at the same time as Britain's greatest period of world power and industrial development. In 1840 she married her cousin Prince *Albert of *Saxe-Coburg-Gotha. They had nine children. After Albert's death Victoria took no further part in public affairs, but was persuaded to return by her *prime minister Benjamin *Disraeli, who gained for her the title Empress of India. She is often remembered as a bad-tempered old woman who once said, 'We are not amused.' However in her early life she was a happy and enthusiastic queen who was very popular with ordinary people.

Queen Victoria (centre) with her family, 1898

the **Vicˈtoria and ˈAlbert Muˈseum** (*abbr* the **V and A**) Britain's national museum of art and design, in *South Kensington, London, established in 1852. It contains over 4 million objects, including important collections of painting, sculpture, textiles, furniture and other objects from around the world, and is one of London's most popular museums.

Vicˌtoria ˈCross *n* (*abbr* **VC**) the highest British military award for courage in war. It was first given by Queen *Victoria in 1856, and has the form of a cross with a crown and a lion in the centre and the words 'For Valour': *Leonard Cheshire VC.*

the **Vicˌtoria Meˈmorial** a large sculpture in front of *Buckingham Palace, London, England. It was made in 1911 in memory of Queen *Victoria, and shows her sitting with several other figures under a gold statue representing Victory.

Vicˈtorian /vɪkˈtɔːriən/ *adj* **1** of, living in or made during the rule of Queen *Victoria (1837–1901): *The square is dominated by the huge red-brick Victorian town hall.* **2** having the qualities associated with *middle-class people of the 19th century. These qualities are sometimes called **Victorian values**. Some people think they are mainly good, and see them as including loyalty, self-control and the willingness to work hard. Others think they are mainly bad, and see them as including sexual hypocrisy, lack of concern for the poor, and lack of a sense of humour: *My* *mother's attitude to sex was rather Victorian – she thought it was dirty and refused to talk about it.*

▶ **Victorian** *n* a person living during the rule of Queen Victoria (1837–1901): *The programmes are about famous Victorians like Brunel and Disraeli.*

Vic,tori'ana *n* [U] objects made during the rule of Queen *Victoria (1837–1901), especially when they are for sale or as part of a collection: *She runs a stall selling old dolls, china plates and other Victoriana.*

the **'*Victory*** /'vɪktəri/ Lord *Nelson's ship at the Battle of *Trafalgar. It is now on display at the Royal Dockyard at *Portsmouth in southern England.

,*Victory at 'Sea* a US television series in 26 parts first shown on *NBC (1952–3). It told the story of the battles fought at sea in the Pacific during *World War II, using real film. The music for the series was written by Richard *Rodgers. The series was later reduced to 97 minutes for a film (1954) shown in cinemas.

,Gore **Vi'dal** /ˌɡɔː vɪ'dɑːl; *AmE* ˌɡɔːr/ (1925–) a US writer known for his intelligent criticism of American politics and culture. His best-known works are the novel *Myra Breckinridge* (1968) and the play *Suddenly Last Summer* (1958) which was made into a film (1959) with Elizabeth *Taylor. Vidal has acted in a few films, including *The Eighth Day* (1997) and *Gattaca* (1997). He is critical of people who disagree with him and has had arguments for years with the writer Norman *Mailer.

the **'Vietnam 'Veterans Me'morial** /'viətnæm/ a long wall built in memory of Americans who were killed or lost in the *Vietnam War. It is in Washington, DC, near the *Lincoln Memorial. The wall is V-shaped and made of black polished stone. It has more than 58 000 names on it. The Memorial was designed by Maya Ying Lin, an architecture student at *Yale University, and was dedicated in 1982. It has become an emotional place for former Vietnam soldiers and their families.

the Vietnam Veterans Memorial

the **Vietnam War**

Like the war in *Korea, the Vietnam War was a result of US policy during the ***Cold War**, a period when Americans believed that **Communism**, the political system in the Soviet Union and China, was a threat to their security and power.

Vietnam, a colony of France, wanted to become independent, but the US believed that Communists were behind the independence movement, and so opposed it. The US became involved in Vietnam only gradually. At first, under President *Eisenhower, it provided the French with supplies. In 1954 the **Geneva Accords** divided Vietnam into the Communist North and the anti-Communist South. Under President *Kennedy, in the early 1960s, many US soldiers were sent to the South as advisers. In 1964, after an attack on US ships, *Congress passed the ***Gulf of Tonkin Resolution** which gave President *Johnson greater powers to fight a war, and in the spring of 1965 **Marines** were sent to South Vietnam.

It was easy to keep the Communist forces, called the **National Liberation Front** or the **Viet Cong**, out of South Vietnam, but much harder to defeat them permanently. The US used bombs against the Vietnamese troops, and chemicals to destroy crops, which had a terrible effect on people as well as on the land. There were also reports of atrocities (= acts of extreme violence and cruelty) committed by both sides. In 1968 the *My Lai massacre, in which over 300 civilians were killed by US soldiers, shocked Americans at home. Many US soldiers were not sure why they were fighting the war and became traumatized (= mentally disturbed) by the violence around them. Discipline became a problem, and the use of *drugs was common. Soldiers were accused of committing acts of violence against each other and against Vietnamese civilians.

In 1968 the Viet Cong started a major attack known as the **Tet Offensive**, and the US position in South Vietnam was threatened. As the war **escalated** (= became more intense) it lost support at home and also in other countries. When Richard *Nixon became President he at first tried to attack hard and force the Viet Cong to come to an agreement. The war then spread to Vietnam's neighbour, Cambodia. Finally, in 1972, Nixon sent Henry *Kissinger to negotiate a **ceasefire**, and afterwards the US was no longer directly involved in the war, though it continued to provide supplies. In 1975 the government of South Vietnam fell and the country was taken over by the Communist forces.

The Vietnam War divided US society. Opposition to it was led mainly by university students, many of whom were young men facing the ***draft** (= compulsory service in the armed forces). They said they should not be forced to fight a war that they believed was wrong. As a protest, many burned their **draft cards**. Some became **draft dodgers** by remaining students as long as possible, or by going to Canada. Others took their case to court on the grounds that they were **conscientious objectors** and had moral or religious reasons for not fighting a war. These protests resulted in violent conflicts between police and students. In the summer of 1968, during a protest in *Chicago, people saw on television the violent way in which the police behaved. In 1970, during another protest, the *National Guard shot and killed four American students at Kent State University in *Ohio. After this, many of the ***silent majority**, people whom Nixon thought supported the government, believed that things had gone too far and began to question government policy and the reasons for US involvement in the war. But others continued to accuse the students of being unpatriotic.

When Vietnam **veterans** returned home they found that, instead of receiving the respect normally given to war veterans, they were the object of public anger. They had to cope with this in addition to the mental stress caused by the violence they had seen and taken part in. In the years since the war, films such as **The Deer Hunter*, *Born on the Fourth of July* and *Good Morning, Vietnam* have shown the war from different angles and helped Americans understand and come to terms with their anger and hurt.

The war in Vietnam taught the US that there are limits to its military strength, and showed that the American people were not willing to pay the high cost in money and in lives for a war away from home. The strong desire to avoid another Vietnam has played an important role in deciding subsequent US foreign policy.

---

the ˌ**Vieux Car'ré** /ˌvjɜː kə'reɪ/ the old name for the *French Quarter in the US city of *New Orleans in the US. It means 'Old Square' in French.

'**Viking** /'vaɪkɪŋ/ *n* a member of a people from Scandinavia who attacked parts of northern and western Europe, including Britain and Ireland, in the 8th-11th centuries. In Britain they were also known as Danes or Norsemen. They settled in the Scottish islands and in areas of eastern England, and the Danish king *Canute (often also spelt Cnut) ruled England from 1016. The Vikings were feared as violent and cruel, but they were also noted for their skill in building ships and as sailors. They travelled in their long ships (= long narrow warships) to Iceland, Greenland and North America. They had an important influence on English culture and the English language, and their achievements are still celebrated in festivals such as *Up-Helly-Aa. See also DANEGELD, DANELAW, ERICSSON, VINLAND.

Viking the name of two *NASA spacecraft that left Earth in 1975 and landed on the planet Mars in the following year. They analysed the surface of the planet for evidence of life but found nothing very important. They also sent the first television pictures of the surface of Mars back to earth.

the '**Village** a short name for *Greenwich Village in New York. See also *VILLAGE VOICE*.

The ˌ***Village*** '***Blacksmith*** a popular poem by the US poet Henry Wadsworth *Longfellow about the simple, healthy life of a country blacksmith (= a person whose job is making things out of iron, especially 'shoes' for horses). American children often have to learn it in school. It begins:

Under the spreading chestnut tree
The village smithy stands.
The smith, a mighty man is he,
With large and sinewy hands.

ˌ**village** '**green** *n* (in Britain) an area of grass in the centre of a village. It is one of the traditional centres of village life, used for games, *fêtes and other public events: *Traditional English pastimes like cricket on the village green seem to be disappearing.*

The ˌ***Village*** '***Voice*** (*also The* ***Voice***) a US newspaper published each week in *Greenwich Village in New York, known especially for its articles on entertainment and the arts. It first appeared in 1955 as a newspaper for *hippies and others with an 'alternative' culture, but is now more traditional. In 1997 it had about 223 000 readers. See also OBIE.

ˌ**vinda'loo** /ˌvɪndə'luː/ *n* [U, C] a type of Indian curry dish, popular in Britain. It contains very hot spices and is usually made with meat or fish: *He needed three pints of lager after his prawn vindaloo!*

ˌBarbara '**Vine** /'vaɪn/ ⇨ RENDELL.

'**Vinland** /'vɪnlənd/ a *Viking(1) name for an area on the east coast of North America which was visited by the Norwegian explorer Lief Ericsson around the year 1000, and possibly named by him. The exact area is not known, and it may have been named after the grape vines (= climbing plants) found growing there.

Viˌ**rago** '**Press** /vɪˌrɑːgəʊ; *AmE* vɪˌrɑːgoʊ/ a British company, formed in 1973, that publishes books by and about women. It is especially known for publishing books by female authors of the past.

'**Virgin** /'vɜːdʒɪn; *AmE* 'vɜːrdʒɪn/ a British company formed in 1970 by Richard *Branson. It began as a record company, producing and selling records through its own shops. In 1984 it introduced an airline service, Virgin Atlantic, with flights to and from the US. The company now offers many other products and services, including clothing, video games and financial services, and has extended its air service to other parts of the world. Since 1996 it has also operated some train services in Britain.

Vir'ginia /və'dʒɪniə; *AmE* vər'dʒɪniə/ a US state on the Atlantic coast, also called the Old Dominion. Its largest city is Virginia Beach, and the capital city is *Richmond(3). It was the first permanent English colony in North America and was named after the 'Virgin Queen', *Elizabeth I. It was one of the original *thirteen colonies, and the *American Revolution was ended by the Battle of *Yorktown in Virginia. Richmond became the capital of the *Confederate States and the *Civil War ended at *Appomattox Court House. Eight presidents were born in Virginia, including George *Washington, Thomas *Jefferson and Woodrow *Wilson. Local products include tobacco and electrical equipment. Among the tourist attractions are *Williamsburg, *Mount Vernon and *Monticello.

The ***Vir'ginian*** /və'dʒɪniən; *AmE* vər'dʒɪniən/ a US television *western series each week on *NBC (1962–71). The Virginian is a mysterious man with no name who visits the Shiloh Ranch in Medicine Bow, *Wyoming, in the 1880s. The series was based on a 1902 novel of the same name by Owen Wister, the first western novel in American literature, and there had been film versions in 1929 (with Gary *Cooper) and 1946.

Virˌ**ginia** '**Slims**™ /vəˌdʒɪniə; *AmE* vərˌdʒɪniə/ a make of cigarettes produced by *Philip Morris, especially for women. A well-known advertisement for them showed photographs of modern, independent women next to photographs of women in old-fashioned clothes, with the phrase, 'You've Come A Long Way, Baby.' For many years until 1993 there were Virginia Slims Tennis Tournaments for women.

the '**Virgin** ˌ**Islands** /'vɜːdʒɪn; *AmE* 'vɜːrdʒɪn/ a group of over 90 islands in the Caribbean. The western ones have belonged to the US since 1917 and the eastern ones to Britain since 1666. Christopher *Columbus was the first European to visit them, in 1493, and they have long been a popular place for tourists. The **US Virgin Islands** cover 133 square miles/344 square kilometres, with a population of more than 97 000. The capital is Charlotte Amalie. The **British Virgin Islands** cover 59 square miles/153 square kilometres, with a population of more than 13 000. The capital is Road Town.

the ˌ**Virgin** '**Queen** a name given to the British queen *Elizabeth I, because she did not marry and may never have had sex.

'**Visa** /'viːzə/ (*also* '**Visa card**) *n* a type of *credit card, a small plastic card which allows a person to buy goods and services, the cost of which is paid for later from his or her bank account: *We take MasterCard, Visa and Switch* (= accept them as forms of payment).

viscount *n* **1** a member of the British *peerage who is next in rank above a *baron and next below an *earl(1). The wife of a viscount, or a female viscount, is called a **viscountess**. A viscount has the title 'Lord' and a viscountess 'Lady'. **2** a *courtesy title given to the eldest son of an *earl(1). ⇨ notes at ARISTOCRACY, PEERAGE.

'**Vitagraph** /'vaɪtəgrɑːf; *AmE* 'vaɪtəgræf/ the most successful US film company in the early years of the film industry. It was established in 1896 in New York by two men born in Britain, Alfred E Smith and J Stuart Blackton. Its stars included Rudolph *Valentino and Norma Talmadge. Vitagraph moved to

*Hollywood in 1911 and was bought by *Warner Brothers in 1925.

Vi'yella™ /vaɪ'elə/ *n* [U] the name of a mixture of wool and cotton used in knitting, as well as a type of cloth. Both have been made for many years by Coats Viyella, one of Britain's largest clothing and textile companies. The company also owns a chain of *high-street shops in Britain selling fashionable clothes: *a Viyella shirt/dress/blouse.*

Viz /vɪz/ a British humorous magazine known for its rude humour. It contains *comic strips with characters like 'The Fat Slags' and 'Billy the Fish', which often show scenes of sex and violence or are funny in a strange, silly way. It first appeared in 1979 and is published every two weeks.

V-J Day /ˌviː 'dʒeɪ deɪ/ Victory in Japan Day, 15 August 1945, when fighting with Japan ended in *World War II.

VOA /ˌviː əʊ 'eɪ; *AmE* oʊ/ ⇨ VOICE OF AMERICA.

vo'cational school *n* (in US education) a school, especially a *high school, which teaches students practical skills to prepare them for a particular type of work, such as photography, cooking, etc. **Vocational education** classes are also taught in regular high schools.

vocational training

Vocational training is intended to give people the skills and knowledge they need to perform a particular job, and involves practical instruction as well as theory. In Britain most vocational training takes place not in universities but in ***colleges of further education** and in colleges specializing in art, accountancy, etc. Some secondary schools now also offer an introduction to vocational training.

***NVQs (National Vocational Qualifications)** are qualifications that can be obtained by people already working in a particular industry. Colleges of further education run courses to provide a theoretical background. NVQs are awarded on the basis of practical work, spoken and written tests, and coursework. There are five levels, from Foundation to Management. Since 1992 many students in schools and colleges have been working for ***GNVQs (General National Vocational Qualifications)**, as an alternative to *GCSEs and *A levels. GNVQs cover similar areas to NVQs and are intended as introductions to a particular field of work and the skills required. Students can choose from over 500 subjects. At the lowest of its three levels, Foundation, a GNVQ is equivalent to a GCSE.

In the US there are no national qualifications like GNVQs and NVQs, though some professional organizations decide on their own qualifications and some of these have become widely accepted. Much vocational training is done by private institutions which are sometimes called **proprietary schools**. Although many of these are good, in general they have a bad reputation. This is partly because there are no controls over who can operate such a school. Some proprietary schools try to get as many students as possible, including some who will probably not be able to complete their training.

Most US secondary schools programmes do not provide a choice between an academic and a practical track (= programme of study), but give students an opportunity to take some practical or vocational classes. Large school districts may have **magnet schools**, schools that attract students with certain interests, and some of these may have a larger choice of vocational courses.

'Vodafone™ /'vəʊdəfəʊn; *AmE* 'voʊdəfoʊn/ *n* a make of mobile phone, originally made by the British company *Racal.

Vogue /vəʊg; *AmE* voʊg/ a magazine for women published every month in Britain and the US, which contains articles about fashion, beauty, the arts and other subjects. It first appeared in the US in 1892 and in Britain in 1916.

the **ˌVoice of A'merica** (*abbr* the **VOA**) the official radio station of the *United States Information Agency (USIA). It broadcasts news and other programmes to other countries from Washington, DC, in over 50 different languages. It was established in 1942 to broadcast to Germany during *World War II. The USIA has run it since 1953 and it began a new television station called Worldnet in 1996 in Washington. Compare RADIO FREE EUROPE/RADIO LIBERTY.

Vol'pone /vɒl'pəʊneɪ; *AmE* vɔːl'poʊneɪ/ a comedy play (1606) by Ben *Jonson. The main character, Volpone, is a rich Italian businessman who pretends that he is dying so that people give him gifts. Finally he is betrayed by his closest friend and punished. All the characters in the play are named after animals, and Volpone means 'fox'.

the **'Volstead Act** /'vɒlsted; *AmE* 'vɑːlsted/ the name usually used to refer to the United States National Prohibition Act passed by the US Congress in 1919 to introduce the laws relating to *Prohibition. It was named after US Congressman Andrew Volstead of *Minnesota who began it. The Act and Prohibition were ended in 1933.

'voluntary school *n* a type of British school run by a religious group or other independent organization. Voluntary schools receive money from the *Local Education Authority in the same way as other state schools, but may provide the school buildings. Most voluntary schools are run by Christian or Jewish groups, and the first Muslim voluntary school in Britain was created in 1998. ⇨ article at EDUCATION IN BRITAIN.

'Voluntary 'Service Over'seas (*abbr* **VSO**) a British charity, established in 1958, which sends doctors, teachers, engineers and other skilled people to live and work in poorer countries. They usually stay and help local people for two years, and are paid only a small amount. Compare PEACE CORPS.

voluntary work

Voluntary work is work that you do not get paid for and usually involves doing things to help other people, especially the elderly or the sick, or working on behalf of a ***charity** or similar organization. Most charitable organizations rely on unpaid **volunteers**, and thousands of Americans and British people give many hours of their time to doing some form of social work or organizing fund-raising events to support the work. **Volunteering** is especially popular in the US and the reasons for this may be found in basic American values such as the Protestant work ethic, the idea that work improves the person who does it, and the belief that people can change their condition if they try hard enough.

Volunteering is usually enjoyable, as people choose jobs close to their personal interests. For instance, people who like animals may volunteer in an animal shelter, a place for animals which have been treated cruelly. Some voluntary work is short-term, e.g. when people from a community get together to create a park. Other work is longer term, such as that of the US organization Habitat for Humanity which builds houses for poor people. Parents often volunteer at their children's schools, and do things like building a play area or raising money for new equipment. Young people are also encouraged to do voluntary work. Schoolchildren visit old people in hospitals or homes, and students at college often raise money for charities. In the US young people over 18 can take part in ***AmeriCorps**, a government programme that encourages them to work as volunteers for a period of time, with the promise of help in paying for their education later. Older Americans who do not work may spend much of their free time volunteering.

In Britain a lot voluntary work is directed towards supporting the country's social services. The ***WRVS** runs a ***meals-on-wheels** service in many parts of Britain, providing hot food for old people who are unable to cook for themselves. The organization is also involved in other kinds of welfare work, such as arranging holidays for needy children. The nationwide ***Citizens' Advice Bureau**, which offers free advice to the public on a wide range of issues, is run mainly by volunteers, and the Blood Transfusion Service relies on voluntary blood donors to give blood for use in hospitals. *Political parties use volunteers at election time, and Churches depend on volunteers to keep buildings clean.

Both Britain and the US have organizations dedicated to helping people overseas. Britain's ***Voluntary Service Overseas** sends people to work in developing countries for up to two years to share their skills with the local population. The US ***Peace Corps** has similar aims and programmes.

---

the ˌ**Volunteer Re'serve ˌForces** the branches of the British armed forces that are made up of volunteers (= people who train in their spare time to do various jobs that would be important in times of war or emergency, including fighting). The branches include the *Territorial Army, the *Royal Naval Reserve and the Royal Air Force Volunteer Reserve.

ˌWernher **von 'Braun** /ˌveənə fɒn 'braʊn, ˌwɜːnə vɒn 'brɔːn; *AmE* ˌvernər fɑːn; ˌwɜːrnər vɑːn/ (1912–77) a US expert on rockets, born in Germany. He designed Germany's *V2 rocket during *World War II. In 1945, von Braun and his German team went to the US where he became head of the Marshall Space Flight Center at Huntsville, *Alabama. He developed the first US satellite, the *Saturn(1) rocket used for the *NASA *Apollo program flights to the moon, and the idea of the *space shuttle.

V1 /ˌviː 'wʌn/ (*also infml* **doodlebug**) *n* a type of flying bomb used by Germany against southern England during the later part of *World War II. It was slower than the *V2 and its engine made a loud noise, which stopped suddenly before it was about to fall to earth and explode.

'Kurt '**Vonnegut** 'Jr /'kɜːt 'vɒnɪgət; *AmE* 'kɜːrt 'vɑːnɪgət/ (1922–) a US writer of novels and short stories, known for his dark humour. He was especially popular among American college and university students in the 1960s and 1970s. His best-known novel is *Slaughterhouse Five* (1969), about the bombing of Dresden, Germany, during *World War II, which Vonnegut saw as a prisoner of war there. His other books include *Cat's Cradle* (1963), *Galapagos* (1985), *Hocus Pocus* (1990) and *Timequake* (1997).

ˌCarol '**Vorderman** /'vɔːdəmən; *AmE* 'vɔːrdərmən/ (1960–) an English television personality. She has appeared on **Countdown* since 1982 and is famous for her skill at mathematics. She has also presented a number of other programmes, including **Tomorrow's World* (1994–5) and *Mysteries* (1997–8).

'**Vorticism** /'vɔːtɪsɪzəm; *AmE* 'vɔːrtɪsɪzəm/ *n* [U] a movement in British art and literature that began in 1913 and lasted through the early years of *World War I. Its main figure was Wyndham *Lewis, and other artists associated with the group were Jacob *Epstein and Ezra *Pound. The paintings of the group were influenced by Cubism and Futurism, and dealt with such themes as energy, violence and machines.

the **Voting Rights Act of 1965** /'vəʊtɪŋ raɪts 'ækt əv 'naɪntiːn sɪksti 'faɪv; *AmE* 'voʊtɪŋ/ a US law passed during the *civil rights movement, signed by President *Johnson. It made illegal a number of restrictions that had been used, mostly in the South, to keep *African Americans from voting. These restrictions included a test of people's ability to read and write.

'**Voyager** /'vɔɪɪdʒə(r)/ the *NASA programme which in 1977 sent two spacecraft into space to investigate certain planets. *Voyager 1* discovered rings around the planet Jupiter in 1979 and flew past Saturn the following year. It sent back to earth the first close photographs of both planets. *Voyager 2* has had the longest journey in the history of spacecraft. It passed Jupiter in 1979, Saturn in 1981, Uranus in 1986 and Neptune in 1989.

'**V-sign** /'viː/ *n* the act of holding up the first and second fingers of the hand so they are spread to form a V. With the back of the hand towards the body this expresses 'victory' (as used by Winston *Churchill during *World War II), or peace (as used by *hippies and others during the 1960s). In Britain, however, when it is made with the back of the hand towards another person and an upward movement of the fingers, this sign is very offensive, showing extreme anger and dislike.

VSO /ˌviː es 'əʊ; *AmE* 'oʊ/ ⇨ VOLUNTARY SERVICE OVERSEAS.

V2 /ˌviː 'tuː/ *n* a type of flying bomb used by Germany against southern England during *World War II. It was larger and faster than the *V1 and was the first modern rocket. About 1 300 V2s were fired, causing a lot of damage.

Ww

W-2 form /ˌdʌbljuː ˈtuː fɔːm; *AmE* fɔːrm/ *n* (in the US) an official document prepared each year by employers for their employees, for tax purposes. It shows how much an employee has earned and how much tax the employer has taken from his or her pay to send to the government. When employees send in their *1040 forms or other tax documents, the W-2 form must be included.

Wac /wæk/ *n* (*AmE*) a member of the Women's Army Corps (*WAC) in the US army: *She's joined the Wacs.*

the **WAC** /wæk/ (*in full* the **Women's Army Corps**) a branch of the US army for women soldiers.

Virˌginia ˈ**Wade** (1945–) an English tennis player who won the Women's Singles title at *Wimbledon in 1977, and was successful in several other international competitions. In 1980 she became a tennis commentator on television.

ˈ**wagon train** *n* a long line of *covered wagons used for journeys in the US *Old West. They often carried families going to settle in the West but were also used to move military and other supplies. *Wagon Train* was a popular *NBC television series (1957–65) about people making such a journey. See also CONESTOGA WAGON, PRAIRIE SCHOONER.

Waiˈkiki /waɪˈkiːkiː/ a holiday beach and area of *Honolulu, *Hawaii. Tourists stay in tall hotels on the beach, shop on Kalakaua Avenue and enjoy the area's many entertainments.

ˌAlfred ˈ**Wainwright** /ˈweɪnraɪt/ (1907–91) an English author of books that give information to people walking for pleasure in the north of England, e.g. in the *Lake District. The books also contain his own illustrations.

a drawing from Wainwright's Pictorial Guide to the Lakeland Fells

ˌTerry ˈ**Waite** /ˈweɪt/ (1939–) an English representative of the *Church of England who was held in the Middle East as a hostage (= a person kept as a prisoner until certain demands are satisfied). He was captured by an Islamic group in Beirut, Lebanon, while trying to get some other hostages released, and held from 1987 to 1991. He later wrote a book about this experience, *Taken on Trust* (1993).

ˌ***Waiting for*** ˈ***Godot*** /ˈɡɒdəʊ; *AmE* ˈɡɑːdoʊ/ a play (1952) by Samuel *Beckett, originally written in French. It is about two men, Vladimir and Estragon, who are waiting for a third, Godot, to arrive. Very little happens, and during their long wait the men talk about their lives. Godot never comes, and the play suggests that life has no meaning and is full of suffering. It is probably Beckett's best-known play and is often performed in the theatre.

ˈ**Waitrose** /ˈweɪtrəʊz; *AmE* ˈweɪtroʊz/ any of a large group of British supermarkets. They were started in 1908 and are now owned by *John Lewis: *I do most of my shopping at Waitrose.* ○ *They're opening a new Waitrose near the town centre.*

ˌTom ˈ**Waits** /ˈweɪts/ (1949–) a US musician and singer with a rough voice, whose songs are often about the more depressing and violent aspects of life in modern cities. He has written music for films, including *One from the Heart* (1982) and *Night on Earth* (1992), and has also acted in several films. His albums include *Heartattack and Vine* (1980) and *Asylum Years* (1985).

ˈ***Walden*** /ˈwɔːldən/ the best-known book by the US writer Henry David *Thoreau. Its full title is *Walden, or Life in the Woods.*

the Waldorf-Astoria Hotel

the ˌ**Waldorf-Aˈstoria** /ˌwɔːldɔːf æˈstɔːriə; *AmE* ˌwɔːldɔːrf/ a famous New York hotel on *Park Avenue. Every US President has stayed there since Herbert *Hoover in 1931. The Waldorf Hotel and the Astor Hotel, situated where the *Empire State Building now stands, were opened separately by different members of the rich Astor family in the late 19th century. They combined in 1931 in the present building, designed in the *art deco style.

ˌ**Waldorf** ˈ**salad** /ˌwɔːldɔːf; *AmE* ˌwɔːldɔːrf/ *n* [C, U] a salad made with chopped apples and celery, nuts and mayonnaise (= sauce made of eggs). It was created by a cook at the *Waldorf-Astoria Hotel.

ˌAlice ˈ**Walker** /ˈwɔːkə(r)/ (1944–) an *African-American writer. She won the *Pulitzer Prize and the *National Book Award for *The Color Purple* (1982). Her other works include the novel *Possessing the Secret of Joy* (1992), a book about her early life, *The Same River Twice* (1996), and several collections of poems.

the ˌ**Walker** ˈ**Art** ˌ**Gallery** /ˌwɔːkər/ an art museum in Liverpool, north-west England. It was opened in

1877 and contains one of Britain's largest collections of European painting.

the ˌ**Walker** ˈ**Cup** /ˌwɔːkə; *AmE* ˌwɔːkər/ a golf competition for men who are not professional players, held every two years between a US team and a mixed British and Irish team. It was first held in 1922 and named after George Herbert Walker, President of the US Golf Association.

ˌEdgar ˈ**Wallace**[1] /ˈwɒlɪs; *AmE* ˈwɑːlɪs/ (1875–1932) an English author. His most popular books are stories about crime and adventure, such as *The Four Just Men* (1905) and *The Ringer* (1926). He was also a successful writer of plays and films, including the film **King Kong*.

ˌGeorge ˈ**Wallace**[2] /ˈwɒlɪs; *AmE* ˈwɑːlɪs/ (1919–98) a US politician. He was governor of the state of *Alabama and tried to keep *segregation in public schools there in the 1960s. He supported *states' rights as a candidate for US President for the American Independent Party in 1968, when he received 13% of the vote. In 1972 he was shot and became paralysed (= unable to move his body) for the rest of his life. Wallace was elected governor of Alabama four times (1963–7, 1971–9 and 1983–7), the last time with the support of *African Americans. His wife Lurleen (1926–68) was also governor of Alabama for a time (1967–71).

ˌLew ˈ**Wallace**[3] /ˌluː ˈwɒlɪs; *AmE* ˈwɑːlɪs/ (1827–1905) a US writer best known for his novel *Ben-Hur*. He wrote other historical novels, including *The Fair God* (1873) and *Prince of India* (1893). Wallace was also a lawyer, a soldier, governor of the New Mexico Territory (1878–81) and a US government representative in Turkey (1881–5).

ˌWilliam ˈ**Wallace**[4] /ˈwɒlɪs; *AmE* ˈwɑːlɪs/ (*c.* 1270–1305) a Scottish soldier. He led an army against the English forces of King *Edward I, who had occupied Scotland, and defeated them at Stirling Bridge in 1297. The following year Wallace was defeated by Edward at Falkirk, and was later captured and hanged. The film *Braveheart* (1995) was made about his life.

ˌ**Wallace and** ˈ**Gromit**™ /ˌwɒlɪs ənd ˈgrɒmɪt; *AmE* ˌwɑːlɪs, ˈgrɔːmɪt/ two characters, a man and his dog, who appear in the short animated films made by Nick Park (1958–). In the first film, *A Grand Day Out* (1989), Wallace builds a rocket and takes Gromit to the moon. Two later films, *The Wrong Trousers* (1993) and *A Close Shave* (1995), both won *Oscars.

Wallace and Gromit in The Wrong Trousers™
©Aardman/Wallace & Gromit Ltd, 1993

the ˈ**Wallace Col**ˌ**lection** /ˈwɒlɪs; *AmE* ˈwɑːlɪs/ a museum of art in London, England. It was opened in 1900 and contains a large collection of 18th-century French paintings and furniture, as well as other paintings, sculpture, decorative objects and weapons from Europe and around the world.

ˌFats' ˈ**Waller** /ˌfæts ˈwɒlə(r); *AmE* ˈwɑːlər/ (1904–43) an *African-American *jazz musician who sang, played the piano and wrote popular songs. His real name was Thomas Waller. His humorous style influenced many later jazz performers. His hits included *Ain't Misbehavin'* (1928) and *Honeysuckle Rose* (1929), and he wrote the African-American musical shows *Keep Shufflin'* (1928) and *Hot Chocolates* (1929). He later led the group Fats Waller and His Rhythm, whose songs included *The Joint Is Jumpin'* (1937) and *Honey Hush* (1939).

ˌBarnes ˈ**Wallis** /ˌbɑːnz ˈwɒlɪs; *AmE* ˌbɑːrnz ˈwɑːlɪs/ (1887–1979) an English engineer. He designed some of the most important aircraft and weapons of *World War II, including the *Wellington and Wellesley bombers and the 'bouncing' bomb used by the *Dam Busters. After the war he invented the 'swing-wing' aircraft and helped to design *Concorde. He was made a *knight in 1968.

Wall's /wɔːlz/ a British company known for making ice cream and also for meat products such as pies and sausages. It is owned by *Unilever.

ˈ**Wall Street** /ˈwɔːl/ the street which is the centre of New York's financial district, where the *New York Stock Exchange is situated. The street name is often used to refer to the stock exchange itself: *Wall Street has reacted positively to the change in interest rates.*

The ˌ***Wall Street*** ˈ***Journal*** /ˌwɔːl/ the leading financial newspaper in the US. It was first published in 1889 by Charles H Dow and Edward D Jones and is still owned by Dow Jones & Company, which also publishes the *Dow Jones Average. Although it emphasizes business and economic news, the *Journal* also has long articles about political and general news. Compare *FINANCIAL TIMES*.

ˈ**Wal-Mart** /ˈwɔːl mɑːt; *AmE* mɑːrt/ any of a very large group of shops in the US selling a wide range of goods at low prices. The first Wal-Mart Discount City was opened in 1962 by Sam Walton, who became one of the richest people in the US.

ˌHorace ˈ**Walpole**[1] /ˈwɔːlpəʊl; *AmE* ˈwɔːlpoʊl/ (1717–97) an English author, the son of Robert *Walpole. His best-known book is *The Castle of Otranto* (1764), an early *Gothic novel set in the 12th–13th centuries. Walpole is also famous for his house, *Strawberry Hill, which he designed as a *Gothic castle.

ˌRobert ˈ**Walpole**[2] /ˈwɔːlpəʊl; *AmE* ˈwɔːlpoʊl/ (1676–1745) a British *Whig(1) politician who was Britain's first *prime minister (1715–17 and 1721–42). He also served the longest time of any prime minister and was the first to live at *Number Ten, *Downing Street. His periods in power were times of peace and economic success for the country, although Walpole himself was accused of dishonest behaviour in government. He was made an *earl(1) in 1742.

The ˌ***Walrus and the*** ˈ***Carpenter*** a famous nonsense poem in the children's book **Through the Looking Glass* by Lewis Carroll. It describes how the walrus and the carpenter persuade some young oysters (= a type of shellfish) to come with them, and then eat them. The poem's best-known lines are:

'The time has come', the walrus said,
'To talk of many things:
Of shoes – and ships – and sealing-wax –
Of cabbages – and kings.'

ˌFrancis ˈ**Walsingham** /ˈwɔːlsɪŋəm/ (*c.* 1532–90) an English politician. He was a close adviser to Queen *Elizabeth I and was made a *knight in 1577. By creating an organization of spies he helped to reveal the

Babington Plot against the queen, and in 1587 was able to warn the government just before the arrival of the *Spanish Armada.

ˈ**Walter** ˈ**Reed** ˈ**Army** ˈ**Medical** ˌ**Center** /ˈriːd/ a large hospital and medical centre in Washington, DC, that provides medical care for members of the US armed forces and their families. The US President often goes there for medical checks. The Center, which also does research, opened as a hospital in 1909 and is named after Major Walter Reed (1851–1902), a US Army doctor who discovered that mosquitoes (= small insects that suck blood) cause the tropical disease yellow fever.

ˌBarbara ˈ**Walters** /ˈwɔːltəz; *AmE* ˈwɔːltərz/ (1931–) a US television journalist known especially for her series *Barbara Walters Special*, in which she has conversations with famous people. She began on **Today*(2) and in 1976 became the first woman to present a major news programme, the *ABC Evening News*, and the first journalist to earn $1 million a year. She won an Emmy in 1982 for *The Barbara Walters Show* and has presented the news programme *20/20* since 1984. She was chosen for the Television *Hall of Fame in 1990.

ˌIzaak ˈ**Walton**[1] /ˌaɪzək ˈwɔːltən/ (1593–1683) an English writer. He is best known for *The Compleat Angler* (1653), a book of advice on fishing which also includes poems, philosophy and descriptions of the English countryside.

ˌWilliam ˈ**Walton**[2] /ˈwɔːltən/ (1902–83) an English composer. He best-known works include *Façade* (1923) and the oratorio (= large piece of music for voices and orchestra) *Belshazzar's Feast* (1931), both of which have words written by members of the *Sitwell family. Walton also wrote operas, pieces for orchestra and music for films, including *Henry V* (1944) and *Hamlet* (1948). He was made a *knight in 1951.

The ˈ***Waltons*** /ˈwɔːltənz/ a US television series (1972–81) about a large family in the Blue Ridge Mountains of *Virginia during the *Great Depression. It was very popular, but some people made jokes about the simple stories of honesty, love and family values. Compare *LITTLE HOUSE ON THE PRAIRIE*.

ˌSam ˈ**Wanamaker** /ˈwɒnəmeɪkə(r); *AmE* ˈwɑːnəmeɪkər/ (1919–93) a US actor who also directed films and plays. He settled in England in 1951 and worked for the last 24 years of his life on his plan to build a copy of the *Globe theatre in London. It was completed after his death. His daughter is the actor Zoe Wanamaker.

ˈ**Wapping** /ˈwɒpɪŋ; *AmE* ˈwɑːpɪŋ/ an area of *Docklands in London, England. It is known especially as the British base of News International, the newspaper company owned by Rupert *Murdoch. Soon after the company moved there in 1986 it was the scene of violent conflicts between the police and trade union members, who were protesting about the introduction of new computer technology.

ˌPerkin ˈ**Warbeck** /ˌpɜːkɪn ˈwɔːbek; *AmE* ˌpɜːrkɪn ˈwɔːrbek/ (*c.* 1474–99) a man who claimed that he should be made the king of England because he was really Richard, Duke of York, brother of *Edward V and the younger of the two *Princes in the Tower. He was supported against the king at the time, *Henry VII, by the House of *York and by the king of France. He made several attempts to start rebellions against Henry VII but in 1497 he was captured, kept for a time in the *Tower of London and later executed.

ˈ**Wardour Street** /ˈwɔːdə; *AmE* ˈwɔːrdər/ a street in the *Soho district of central London, England, known mainly as the place where a lot of film companies have their offices. The name Wardour Street is sometimes used to refer to the British film industry in general.

the ˈ**War Graves Com**ˌ**mission** an organization, started in 1917, that cares for the graves of members of the British and Commonwealth armed forces who died in both world wars. It looks after over a million graves and other monuments around the world. Its full name is the Commonwealth War Graves Commission.

ˌAndy ˈ**Warhol** /ˈwɔːhəʊl; *AmE* ˈwɔːrhoʊl/ (1928–87) a US artist who was a leading figure in the *pop art movement in the 1960s. He painted such familiar objects as Campbell's Soup cans and dollar bills. Another famous picture consisted of several similar images of Marilyn *Monroe. Warhol made a number of long films in which little happened, including *Chelsea Girls* (1966). His most famous statement was: 'In the future, everyone will be famous for fifteen minutes.'

Self-portrait *by Andy Warhol*

ˈ**Warner** ˌ**Brothers** /ˈwɔːnə; *AmE* ˈwɔːrnər/ a major *Hollywood film company established in 1923 by four brothers, **Harry Warner** (1881-1958), **Albert Warner** (1884-1967), **Sam Warner** (1888-1927) and **Jack Warner** (1892-1978). It produced the first sound film, *The *Jazz Singer*, in 1927. Other Warner Brothers films have included **Casablanca*, **Yankee Doodle Dandy*, **My Fair Lady*, *The Exorcist* (1973), **Superman*, *Driving Miss Daisy* (1989), **Batman*, *Unforgiven* (1992), *The *Fugitive* and *Fallen* (1998). The company also makes the television series **ER* and **Friends*. Warner Brothers Records produces music by such singers as *Madonna and Rod *Stewart. Warner Brothers combined with Time, Inc in 1989 to form *Time Warner.

the **War of 1812** /ˈwɔːr əv ˈeɪtiːn ˈtwelv/ a war (1812–15) fought between Britain and the US. One of the main causes was the British action of forcing American sailors to serve on British ships. During the war, US soldiers attacked Canada, but without success. The British captured Washington, DC, in 1814 and burned the *Capitol and the *White House(1). American successes, however, led to the Treaty of Ghent (1814) which ended the war. General Andrew *Jackson, not aware of the Treaty, defeated the British three weeks later at the battle of *New Orleans (1815). The war made Americans more united and less willing to become involved in European affairs. See also ISOLATIONISM, *STAR-SPANGLED BANNER*.

the ˈ**War Office** the former name of the British government department in charge of the Army, established during the *Crimean War. In 1964 it became the army department of the *Ministry of Defence.

ˌ***War of the*** ˈ***Worlds*** a science fiction novel (1898) by H G *Wells. It is about an attack on Earth by creatures from the planet Mars. The creatures have powerful weapons and technology, but are finally killed by Earth's bacteria. A famous US radio version of the story, broadcast in 1938 by Orson *Welles, caused great fear because people thought that the attack was actually happening.

ˌ**War on** ˈ**Want** a British charity, established in 1951, which collects money, clothes, etc. to help poor people in many countries of the world.

the ˈ**War Powers Act** a US law passed in 1973 which allows *Congress to limit the President's use of military forces. It states that the President must tell Congress within 48 hours if he sends armed forces anywhere, and Congress must give approval for them to stay there for more than 90 days. The Act was passed in spite of a veto (= refusal to sign a law) by President Richard *Nixon.

ˌEarl ˈ**Warren**[1] /ˌɜːl ˈwɒrən; *AmE* ˌɜːrl ˈwɔːrən/ (1891–1974) a Chief Justice of the US *Supreme Court (1953–69). He was a strong supporter of the *civil rights movement and his court decided against *segregation in public schools in the famous **Brown v Board of Education* case (1954). Warren led the **Warren Commission**, a committee formed to investigate the murder of President *Kennedy. It published the **Warren Report** (1964) which said that Kennedy had been killed by Lee Harvey *Oswald, acting alone.

ˈRobert ˈPenn ˈ**Warren**[2] /ˈpen ˈwɒrən; *AmE* ˈwɔːrən/ (1905–89) a US writer who was the country's first *Poet Laureate and the only American to receive the *Pulitzer Prize for both fiction and poetry. He wrote mostly about the *South. His Pulitzer Prizes were for the novel *All the King's Men* (1946) and his poetry collections *Promises* (1957) and *Now and Then* (1979). Warren was also a well-known critic.

the ˌ**Wars of the ˈRoses** the name now used for the period of fighting (1455–85) in England between the supporters of the two most powerful families in the country at the time, the House of *Lancaster, whose symbol was a red rose, and the House of *York, whose symbol was a white rose. The aim of each side was to make a member of their family the king of England. Each side was successful at different times and the wars only ended when Henry *Tudor (House of Lancaster) defeated *Richard III (House of York) and became King *Henry VII. His marriage to Elizabeth of York united the two sides and ended the fighting. See also BOSWORTH FIELD, TUDOR ROSE.

ˈ**Warwick** /ˈwɒrɪk; *AmE* ˈwɔːrɪk/ an ancient town on the River *Avon in central England. It is the administrative centre of the county of *Warwickshire. It contains **Warwick Castle**, a very popular tourist attraction, the earliest parts of which were built in the 14th century. The town also has other buildings from the Middle Ages, although many of these were destroyed in a fire in 1694.

Warwick Castle

ˈ**Warwickshire** /ˈwɒrɪkʃə(r); *AmE* ˈwɔːrɪkʃər/ (*written abbr* **Warks**) a county in central England, with the town of *Warwick as its administrative centre. It was reduced in size when part of it, including the city of *Coventry, became part of the *West Midlands, one of the *metropolitan counties created in 1974.

the **Wash** /wɒʃ; *AmE* wɑːʃ/ a large, shallow bay on the east coast of England, where the *North Sea separates the counties of *Norfolk to the south and *Lincolnshire to the north. Many English people know the story of how in 1216 King *John lost his luggage and some of his men when they tried to cross the Wash where the water was shallow, during a military campaign.

ˈ**Washington**[1] /ˈwɒʃɪŋtən; *AmE* ˈwɑːʃɪŋtən/ a northwestern state of the US, also called the Evergreen State. The largest city is *Seattle and the capital city is Olympia. Both Britain and the US occupied the land in the first half of the 19th century. Washington became part of the Oregon Territory in 1848 and a state in 1889. Its products include wood, paper, apples and fish, and it has a large aerospace industry. Tourist attractions include Mount *Rainier, Mount *St Helens and Seattle's Pacific Science Center and Space Needle.

ˌBooker T ˈ**Washington**[2] /ˌbʊkə tiː ˈwɒʃɪŋtən; *AmE* ˌbʊkər, ˈwɑːʃɪŋtən/ (Booker Taliaferro Washington 1856–1915) an *African-American teacher, born into a slave family in *Virginia. In 1881 he started Tuskegee Institute (now *Tuskegee University) for black students. He encouraged African Americans to achieve economic independence before fighting for equal rights, and for this he was sometimes criticized. The best-known of his many books is *Up from Slavery* (1901), the story of his own life.

Washington Crossing the Delaware, *painted by E G Leutze*

ˌGeorge ˈ**Washington**[3] /ˈwɒʃɪŋtən; *AmE* ˈwɑːʃɪŋtən/ (1732–99) the first US *President (1789–97), who had led its army to success in the *American Revolution. He is called 'the Father of His Country'. The *Continental Congress placed him in charge of the American forces in 1775. Although his army had a difficult and dangerous winter at *Valley Forge, General Washington led them to several victories, including the final Battle of *Yorktown. He later gave his important approval for the *American Constitution and was elected in 1789 as the country's first president. He supported a strong central government but disliked political party arguments. He was elected a second time, but refused to stand as a candidate for a third time and returned to his home at *Mount Vernon.

Americans have always admired Washington as one of their best and most moral presidents. He is considered by many to have been the country's greatest leader and perhaps the only one who could have united the colonists during the American Revolution. Most people know the story of how as a boy he cut down his father's cherry tree and then admitted what he had done, saying, 'I cannot tell a lie.' The story may not be true but it is seen as a symbol of his honesty. Washington's fine personal qualities and fair politics were recognized during his life, and they seem even more impressive today. His memory is honoured by the *Washington Monument and the names of the country's capital city, a state, many *counties, government buildings, schools, streets, mountains, etc., and his image appears on the dollar note and the 25-cent coin.

ˌ**Washington, DˈC** /ˌwɒʃɪŋtən diː ˈsiː; *AmE* ˌwɑːʃɪŋtən/ (Washington, District of Columbia) the capital city of the US, whose area covers the *District of Columbia. The place was chosen by George *Washington in 1790, and since 1800 the main departments of the US government have been there. It is known for its historical monuments and important buildings, including the *Capitol, the *White House(1), the *Supreme Court, the *National Archives, the *Library of Congress, the *Smithsonian Institution, the *National Gallery of Art and the *Kennedy Center. About 66% of Washington's population are *African Americans. See also ARLINGTON NATIONAL CEMETERY, LINCOLN MEMORIAL, JEFFERSON MEMORIAL, PENTAGON 1, VIETNAM VETERANS MEMORIAL, WASHINGTON MONUMENT.

the ˌ**Washington ˈMonument** /ˌwɒʃɪŋtən; *AmE* ˌwɑːʃɪŋtən/ a tall, thin monument on The *Mall(2) in *Washington, DC, built to honour the memory of George *Washington. It is 555 feet/169 metres high and made of white marble. Tourists can climb the 898 steps to the top, from which there are fine views of the city. The Monument took 40 years to build and was completed in 1888.

The ˌ***Washington ˈPost*** /ˌwɒʃɪŋtən; *AmE* ˌwɑːʃɪŋtən/ (*also infml The* ***Post***) a US national newspaper, published in Washington, DC and known for its liberal opinions. It was the first newspaper to investigate the full *Watergate story, and for this it won a *Pulitzer Prize (1973). It was first published in 1877, and now owns other newspapers, magazines and several television stations.

Wasp (*also* **WASP**) /wɒsp; *AmE* wɑːsp/ (*in full* **white Anglo-Saxon Protestant**) *n* (*AmE, sometimes disapprov*) a white person in the US whose family came originally from Britain or northern Europe and whose religion is Protestant. Wasps are considered to have the best social status and the most political power. People in all social classes who are white have sometimes been called Wasps, especially if they have prejudices against other races. ▶ **Waspy** (*also* **WASPy**) *adj.*

The ˈ***Waste Land*** a poem (1922) by T S *Eliot, which has been seen as an expression of the depressed mood and sense of disorder after *World War I. Many of its lines refer to other works of literature and to cultural matters, and these are explained in notes at the bottom of each page. The style of the poem, involving short sections that do not at first seem to be closely connected, has had a great influence on modern poetry.

ˈ**watchdog** *n* a person or organization that exists to protect people's rights and to check on the behaviour of others, especially that of big companies and institutions. In Britain the word is often used of organizations set up by the government to make sure that the actions of former public companies and institutions which became privately owned in the 1980s and 1990s are both legal and fair. Such organizations include *OFFER, *Ofgas, *Oftel and *Ofwat.

The ˈ***Watchtower*** /ˈwɒtʃtaʊə(r); *AmE* ˈwɑːtʃtaʊər/ the magazine produced by the religious group the *Jehovah's Witnesses. Members often try to interest people in it and in their beliefs by going from house to house offering it to them and trying to discuss matters in it.

W

The ˈ***Water-ˌBabies*** a children's book (1863) by Charles *Kingsley. It is about a small boy who works cleaning chimneys, escapes from his cruel employer and falls into a stream, where he meets the little creatures who live there, the water-babies. It is a moral story about good and evil. Many people remember the names of two of its characters especially: Mrs Bedonebyasyoudid, who is fierce, and Mrs Doasyouwouldbedoneby, who is very kind.

ˈ**Watergate** /ˈwɔːtəgeɪt; *AmE* ˈwɔːtərgeɪt/ the US political scandal that forced President Richand *Nixon to leave office in 1974. It involved *Republican Party members who in 1972 tried to steal information from the offices of the *Democratic Party in the Watergate building in Washington, DC. Nixon said he did not know about this, but *The *Washington Post* and tapes of his telephone conversations proved he did. He resigned as *Congress was about to begin *impeachment, and several important government officials were sent to prison for illegally trying to keep the affair secret. The Watergate incident made the role of the President weaker for several years and many people were shocked that people in power had behaved so badly. The word ending *-gate* has since been used to create names for other scandals, e.g. *Irangate.

ˌKeith ˈ**Waterhouse** /ˈwɔːtəhaʊs; *AmE* ˈwɔːtərhaʊs/ (1929–) an English journalist and writer of novels and plays. He first became well known with his novel *Billy Liar* (1959), which was later adapted as a play, a film, and a musical. With Willis Hall (1929–) he wrote a number of successful television series, including *Budgie* (1971–3) and *Worzel Gummidge*. Waterhouse's other plays have included *Jeffrey Bernard is Unwell* (1991). He also writes a regular humorous newspaper column for the **Daily Mail*.

ˌ**Waterˈloo**[1] /ˌwɔːtəˈluː; *AmE* ˌwɔːtərˈluː/ one of London's main train stations, for trains to and from the south, south-east and south-west of England. In 1993 a new part was added to the building for trains travelling to and from the rest of Europe through the *Channel Tunnel. Waterloo also has a station on the *London Underground station, and it is one end of the **Waterloo and City Link**, a special underground railway service that transports people who arrive from outside London to the *City for work each day.

the ˌBattle of **Waterˈloo**[2] /wɔːtəˈluː; *AmE* wɔːtərˈluː/ a battle fought on 18 June 1815 in which the British, led by the Duke of *Wellington, and the Prussians defeated the French army of Napoleon. It was the last battle of the *Napoleonic Wars and took place near the village of Waterloo, not far from Brussels in Belgium. It is seen as one of the most important victories in British history and it made Wellington a national hero. The phrase *to meet one's Waterloo* means to suffer a serious defeat.

ˈ***Water ˌMusic*** a popular piece of music for orchestra by the composer George Frideric *Handel. It was written and first performed in 1717, probably for a party held by King *George I on a boat on the River *Thames.

ˈˌMuddy' ˈ**Waters** /ˌmʌdi ˈwɔːtəz; *AmE* ˈwɔːtərz/ (1915–83) a US *blues singer who played the guitar and wrote songs, often with a sexual theme. His powerful style influenced many other rock musicians. He first became famous with his song *Rollin' Stone* (1950), a name later taken by the *Rolling Stones group and the music magazine **Rolling Stone*. Waters formed a band in 1950, and his later hits included *I'm Your Hoochie Coochie Man* (1954) and *Got My Mojo Working* (1957).

the ˈ**watershed** /ˈwɔːtəʃed; *AmE* ˈwɔːtərʃed/ (*also* the **nine o'clock watershed**) *n* [sing] (in Britain) 9.00 p.m., the time before which the main television stations agree not to broadcast programmes that are not suitable for children, e.g. because they include too much sex, violence or bad language. If this rule is broken, complaints can be made to an official organization, the *Broadcasting Complaints Commission.

ˌ***Watership*** **ˈ*Down*** /ˌwɔːtəʃɪp; *AmE* ˌwɔːtərʃɪp/ a very successful novel for children (1972) by Richard Adams. It tells the story of a group of rabbits who are forced to leave the place where they live and go to live in an area called Watership Down. The book was also very popular with adults and was made into a cartoon film.

ˈ**Watford** /ˈwɒtfəd; *AmE* ˈwɑːtfərd/ a town in *Hertfordshire, just to the north of London. The phrase 'north of Watford' is sometimes used in a humorous way to suggest that any part of England north of the London area is less important, interesting and sophisticated (= knowing about fashion, culture, new ideas, etc.) than London and the south of England: *He seems to think that everywhere north of Watford is uncivilized.*

ˈ**Watling Street** /ˈwɒtlɪŋ; *AmE* ˈwɑːtlɪŋ/ a road in England, originally built by the Romans and still in use today under various different names. It runs from Dover, on the south-east coast of England, through London and *St Albans to Wroxeter, a small town in *Shropshire. Its name comes from the *Anglo-Saxon name for St Albans.

ˈ**Watney's** /ˈwɒtniz; *AmE* ˈwɑːtniz/ a British company that makes various types of beer and also owns many pubs in Britain.

ˌDr ˈ**Watson[1]** /ˈwɒtsn; *AmE* ˈwɑːtsn/ the companion of Sherlock *Holmes in the stories by Arthur *Conan Doyle. He is the narrator of most of the stories and his simple, pleasant attitude to life and events contrasts with the complicated thought processes of Sherlock Holmes. In the stories, he lives with Holmes at 221B *Baker Street.

ˌJames D ˈ**Watson[2]** /ˈwɒtsn; *AmE* ˈwɑːtsn/ (James Dewey Watson 1928–) a US scientist who did important work on DNA (= the substance in the human body that passes from parents to children and makes it possible to identify every individual human being). He worked mainly at the *Cavendish Laboratory in Cambridge, England, and in 1962, with Francis *Crick and Maurice Wilkins, he won the *Nobel Prize for medicine for his work.

ˌTom ˈ**Watson[3]** /ˈwɒtsn; *AmE* ˈwɑːtsn/ (1949–) a US golf player who was especially successful in the 1970s and 1980s. He won the *British Open(1) five times (1975, 1977, 1980 and 1982–3), the *Masters Tournament twice (1977 and 1981) and the *US Open (1982). He has won more *PGA competitions (33) than any other player.

ˌJames ˈ**Watt** /ˈwɒt; *AmE* ˈwɑːt/ (1736–1819) a Scottish inventor whose work played an important part in the development of the steam engine. His designs for engines improved on those in existence at the time because they used much less fuel. Watt's engines were the first to be suitable for use in factories and were therefore one of the major advances in industry that led to the *Industrial Revolution.

the ˌ**Watts** ˈ**riots** /ˌwɒts; *AmE* ˌwɑːts/ a number of violent disturbances between black people and the police in August 1965 in the poor *African-American district of Watts in *Los Angeles. More than 30 people were killed and a large amount of damage was done. The *National Guard sent 12 000 soldiers to control the riots, and the police arrested over 4 000 people. An investigation by the state decided that the riots had happened because 30% of the people in Watts were unemployed.

ˌEvelyn ˈ**Waugh** /ˌiːvlɪn ˈwɔː/ (1903–66) an English writer of novels which are greatly admired for their elegant style and humour. In novels such as *Decline and Fall* (1928) and *A Handful of Dust* (1934), he made fun of the upper class and *upper middle class in England in the 1920s and 1930s. His travels in Africa provided the ideas for novels such as *Black Mischief* (1932) and *Scoop* (1938). In 1930 he became a *Roman Catholic and his interest in Catholic beliefs is shown in the more serious novel **Brideshead Revisited* (1945), about an upper-class English Roman Catholic family. Waugh's other books include a series of three with the title *Sword of Honour* (1952–61), based on his experiences as a soldier in *World War II. He had a reputation as a rude, bad-tempered man with fixed, rather right-wing views.

ˌLord ˈ**Wavell** /ˈweɪvəl/ (*born* Archibald Percival Wavell 1883–1950) a senior military officer in charge of British forces in the Middle East from 1939 to 1941, during *World War II. He later commanded British forces in India and from 1943 to 1947 he was Viceroy of India (= the representative of the British government ruling India when it was part of the British Empire). He was made an *earl(1) in 1947.

ˈ**Waverley** /ˈweɪvəli; *AmE* ˈweɪvərli/ the main railway station in *Edinburgh, Scotland, at the eastern end of *Princes Street. It was opened in 1846, when it was called the General Station, but in 1854 it was named after the *Waverley novels by Sir Walter *Scott.

the ˈ**Waverley** ˌ**novels** /ˈweɪvəli; *AmE* ˈweɪvərli/ the name given to the novels of Sir Walter *Scott because he said at the beginning of them that they were written 'by the author of Waverley' and did not give his name. The first of them (itself called *Waverley*) was published in 1814, and it was not until 1827 that Scott announced publicly that he was in fact the author of the novels.

ˌRuby ˈ**Wax** /ˌruːbi ˈwæks/ (1953–) a US television presenter who appears mainly on British television. She is known for programmes such as *The Full Wax* (1991–4) and *Ruby Wax Meets …* (1996–8), in which she meets famous people and asks them questions in a funny and energetic way.

ˌJohn ˈ**Wayne** /ˈweɪn/ (1907–79) a US actor who made more than 200 films, many of which were *westerns. His popular name was 'the Duke' or 'Duke', and he came to represent the image of the strong, independent American character. John *Ford[8] directed many of his films, including *Stagecoach* (1939) which made him famous. His other films included *Fort Apache* (1948), *The Searchers* (1956), *The Alamo* (1960), which he also directed and produced, and *True Grit* (1969), for which he won an *Oscar. Wayne was criticized by some people for his support of the *Vietnam War.

John Wayne

the ˌ**Ways and** ˈ**Means Com**ˌ**mittee** a permanent committee of members of the US *House of Representatives which makes suggestions about laws for raising money for the US government. It suggests new laws or changes to existing ones affecting things such as taxes and trade agreements with other countries.

the **Weald** /wiːld/ an area of attractive countryside in south-east England which includes parts of the counties of *Kent, *Surrey and *Sussex. It is known especially as an area where many fruit and vegetables are grown. It was formerly covered by woods, and *weald* is an old-fashioned word meaning wild, i.e. not cultivated.

The ˌ**Wealth of** ˈ**Nations** an important work of economic and social theory by Adam *Smith, published in 1776. Its full title was *Inquiry into the Nature and Causes of the Wealth of Nations*. In it he analysed the relationship between work and the production of a nation's wealth. His conclusion was that the best economic situation results from encouraging free enterprise (= an economic system in which there is open competition in business and trade, and no government control). This idea has had a great influence on economic theories since and it formed the basis of the economic policies of the *Conservative government in Britain in the 1980s.

weather

The popular view of the British weather is that it rains all the time. This is not true and Britain gets no more rain in an average year than several other European countries. In some summers the country goes for weeks with nothing more than a **shower**. Perhaps the main characteristic of Britain's weather is that it is hard to predict. This is probably why people regularly listen to **weather forecasts** on radio and television. However, the **weathermen** (= people who present the forecasts) are sometimes wrong. Many people remember especially their failure to predict the *Great Storm of 1987 which caused a lot of damage.

The British are not used to extremes. In summer the temperature rarely goes higher than 30° C (86° F). **Heatwaves** are greeted with newspaper headlines such as 'Phew! What a scorcher!' In winter the south and west are fairly **mild**. The east and north get much colder, with **hard frosts** and snow. A **cold snap** (= period of very cold weather) or heavy falls of snow can bring transport to a halt.

Samuel *Johnson observed that 'when two Englishmen meet their first talk is of the weather', and this is still true. The weather is a safe, polite and impersonal topic of conversation. Most British people would agree that bright sunny weather, not too hot and with enough rain to water their *gardens, is good. Bad weather usually means dull days with a lot of cloud and rain or, in winter, fog or snow. The British tend to expect the worst as far as the weather is concerned and it is part of national folklore that summer *bank holidays will be wet. It may be *pouring with rain*, *teeming down*, *bucketing*, or even just *drizzling* or *spitting*, but it will be wet.

The US is large enough to have several different **climates**, and so the weather varies between regions. In winter the temperature in *New York state is often –8° C (17° F), or lower; in the summer in *Arizona it is often above 40° C (104° F). Arizona gets less than an inch (2.5 centimetres) of rain most months; the state of *Washington, DC can get 6 inches (15 centimetres). The North-east and Midwest have cold winters with a lot of snow, and summers that are very hot and humid. The South has hot, humid summers but moderate winters. The South-west, including Arizona and *New Mexico, is dry and warm in the winter and very hot in the summer. Some parts of the US suffer tornadoes (= strong circular winds) and hurricanes.

In autumn people put **storm doors** and **windows** on their houses, an extra layer of glass to keep out the cold wind. Cities in the **snow belt** have several **snow days** each winter, days when people do not go to school or work. But then **snow ploughs** clear the roads and life goes on, even when the weather is bad.

In the US it is considered boring to talk about the weather, but some phrases are often heard. In the

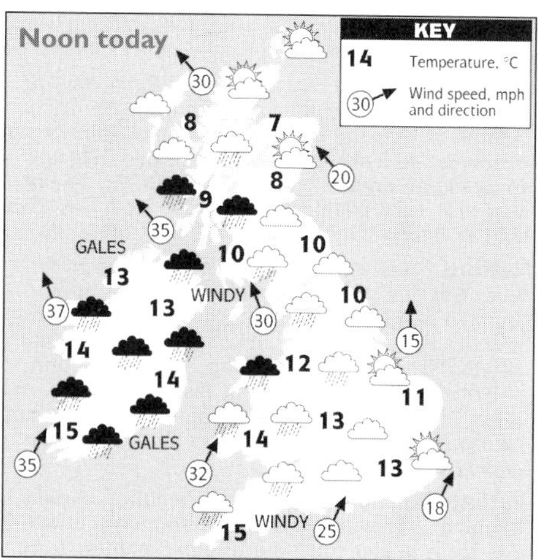

a weather map from The Independent

summer people ask, 'Is it hot enough for you?' or say that the street is 'hot enough to fry an egg'. When it rains they say 'Nice day if you're a duck', or that they do not mind the rain because 'the farmers need it'.

Many people in Britain and the US, as elsewhere, are worried about **global warming** due to emissions from vehicles and factories of **greenhouse gases** such as carbon dioxide (CO_2) and nitrous oxide (N_2O) and any **climatic changes** this may cause. There are also fears that global warming is affecting **El Niño**, a weather pattern associated with a warm Pacific Ocean current, resulting in more frequent storms and floods in *California and Central and South America, and droughts (= long periods of dry weather) in other parts of the world.

Webb /web/ the name of a married couple who were important figures in socialist politics in Britain during the late 19th and early 20th century. **Sidney Webb** (1859–1947) and his wife **Beatrice Webb** (1858–1943) wrote several books together which had a great influence on political thought at the time. These included *The History of Trade Unionism* (1894) and *Industrial Democracy* (1897). Together they helped to establish the *London School of Economics and the **New Statesman* magazine. Sidney was made a *baron in 1929.

ˌJohn ˈ**Webster**[1] /ˈwebstə(r)/ (*c.* 1578–*c.* 1632) an English writer of plays. The best-known of these are *The White Devil* (*c.* 1608) and *The Duchess of Malfi* (*c.* 1614), which are full of violence and strong emotions. Little is known about his life, but he is now considered to be one of the greatest *Jacobean writers.

ˌNoah ˈ**Webster**[2] /ˌnəʊə ˈwebstə(r); *AmE* ˌnoʊə/ (1758–1843) a US teacher and author, best known for his *American Dictionary of the English Language* (1828). He also helped to establish a standard American spelling of English with *The Elementary Spelling Book* (1783). His name is now used on many dictionaries published by different US companies.

ˈ**wedding march** *n* a piece of music traditionally played at wedding ceremonies in church in Britain, either when the bride enters the church or while the couple who have just been married walk down the aisle before leaving the church. The most popular piece for the entry of the bride is from Wagner's opera *Lohengrin*, and the most popular piece for the end of the ceremony is from Mendelssohn's music for *A Midsummer Night's Dream*.

Weddings ⇨ article.

a Wedgwood teapot made in 1785

ˈ**Wedgwood**™ /ˈwedʒwʊd/ *n* [U] fine English pottery and china made by the company established in 1759 by Josiah Wedgwood (1730–95) near *Stoke-on-Trent in *Staffordshire. Its most characteristic design uses raised white patterns or figures on a blue background. This design was influenced by *neoclassicism and became very fashionable when first produced. Wedgwood products remain popular in Britain today.

weekends

The weekend lasts from the end of working hours or school hours on Friday until Monday morning. For most people it is a chance to be at home with their family, do their *hobby or go out somewhere. Both adults and children look forward to the freedom of the weekend and to having time to please themselves. On Friday people with jobs may say '**TGIF**' (Thank God it's Friday) and may go to a bar together after work. People who work in factories, shops and restaurants and on buses often have to work at weekends and instead get time off during the week. Sometimes people take an extra day off on Friday or Monday to make a **long weekend**, especially if they want to have a short holiday/vacation. Several holidays, such as *Memorial Day in the US and *Spring Bank Holiday in Britain, are on a Monday in order to create a long weekend.

At the weekend (*AmE* **On the weekend**) people may do jobs around the house, look after their garden, wash the car, play sport or watch television. On Saturday mornings many US television channels show *cartoons. The weekend is also the busiest time of the week for shopping. Shops are open on both Saturday and Sunday. For a long time many British people opposed **Sunday trading** and wanted to 'keep Sunday special', but there was pressure from some of the larger stores and *DIY shops to be allowed to open, and now many people like shopping on a Sunday because it is less busy.

Friday and Saturday nights are popular, especially among young people, for parties and visits to clubs and *pubs. People also go to the theatre or cinema, eat out at a restaurant, or invite friends to their house for dinner or a barbecue.

On Sundays many people have a **lie-in** (= stay in bed longer than usual). Some people go to church on Sunday morning. In the US many adults enjoy reading the newspaper while eating **brunch**, a combination of breakfast and lunch that includes dishes from both. Brunch is eaten between about 10 and 12 in the morning and, unusually for an American meal, is enjoyed slowly, in a relaxed atmosphere. In Britain some people sit around and read the Sunday papers. They may have other members of the family round for **Sunday lunch**. Many people go out for a walk or visit a theme park, *stately home or other attraction, depending on their interests. In summer many families go out for the day to the countryside.

In general people are very busy at the weekend and often finish it more tired than they began it, so for many Monday morning is the least pleasant part of the week.

ˈ**Weetabix**™ /ˈwiːtəbɪks/ *n* [U, C] (*pl* **Weetabix**) a popular breakfast cereal made from processed wheat formed into blocks. These are usually eaten with milk and sugar: *Would you like some Weetabix?* ○ *I always have a couple of Weetabix for breakfast.*

ˌ**Wee Willie ˈWinkie** /ˌwiː wɪli ˈwɪŋki/ a character in a traditional *nursery rhyme. The words are:

Wee Willie Winkie runs through the town,
Upstairs and downstairs in his nightgown,
Rapping at the window, crying through the lock,
Are the children all in bed, for now it's eight o'clock?

Weights and measures ⇨ article.

ˈ**Weight ˌWatchers**™ an organization in both Britain and the US that gives advice and special classes for people who are worried that they are too fat and want to lose weight. It advises customers on what foods to eat and produces a range of its own foods.

ˌKurt ˈ**Weill** /ˌkɜːt ˈvaɪl; *AmE* ˌkɜːrt ˈwaɪl/ (1900–50) a US composer, born in Germany. He is best known for *Die Dreigroschenoper* (in English *The Threepenny Opera*) (1928). He moved to the US in 1935 to escape from the Nazis, and wrote the music for several *Broadway musical plays, including *Knickerbocker Holiday* (1938), *Lady in the Dark* (1941) and *Street Scene* (1947). His music was used by Woody *Allen in his film *Shadows and Fog* (1992).

ˌJohnny ˈ**Weissmuller** /ˈwaɪsmʊlə(r)/ (1909–84) a US swimmer who later became a film actor. As a swimmer, he established 28 world records in various events and won a total of five gold medals at the Olympic Games of 1924 and 1928. He then played the role of *Tarzan in several popular films of the 1930s and 1940s.

ˌRacquel ˈ**Welch** /ˌrækel ˈweltʃ/ (1940–) a US film actor who was one of the most sexually attractive stars of the 1960s and 1970s. Her physical beauty is emphasized in the films she has appeared in. These include *One Million Years BC* (1963), *Myra Breckinridge* (1970) and *The Three Musketeers* (1974).

the ˌ**welfare ˈstate** *n* [sing] the system by which the government of a country cares for its citizens through a range of services provided and paid for by the State, including medical care, financial help for poor people and homes for old people. In Britain the term applies mainly to the *National Health Service, *National Insurance and *social security. The US does not consider itself a true welfare state, but Americans use the terms 'welfare' and 'welfare programmes' for the various ways the national, state and local governments help people who are poor, sick, old, unemployed, etc. The national programmes include *Medicare, *Medicaid and *Aid to Families with Dependent Children. See also Beveridge Report.

ˌ**Welfare to ˈWork** a phrase used by the *Labour Party in the British general election of 1997 to promote (= give publicity to) their policy of reducing the number of people who are unemployed and receiving money from the State, by creating jobs for them or training them for work. The phrase had earlier been used by the US *Democratic Party during the campaign that resulted in the election of Bill *Clinton as President in 1992.

ˈ**Wellcome** /ˈwelkəm/ a large British company producing drugs and other medicines. It was started in 1880 by two US chemists, Henry Wellcome (1853–1936) and Silas Burroughs (1846–95). When Henry Wellcome died, he left the whole company to the **Wellcome Trust**, a charity formed to provide money for medical research projects.

ˈ**well-ˌdressing** *n* [U] a traditional English custom, especially in the towns and villages of *Derbyshire. It involves decorating wells (= places where water

Weddings

A *wedding* is the occasion when people **get married**. *Marriage* is the state of being married, though the word can also mean the wedding ceremony.

Attitudes to marriage have changed a lot over the last 50 years. Many people in Britain and the US now **live together** without getting married. This was once called 'living in sin' and was not socially acceptable. Marriage is still popular, though people tend to be older when they get married. People can marry at 18, or at 16 if their parents agree, but the average age is, in the US, 23 for women and 26 for men, and in Britain 26 and 28 respectively.

In past times, if parents did not approve of a marriage, the couple **eloped** (= went away and got married secretly).

Planning to get married

Before getting married a couple **get engaged**. It is traditional for the man to **propose** (= ask his girlfriend to marry him) and, if she accepts, to give his new **fiancée** an **engagement ring**. Today many couples decide together to get married.

The couple then **set a date** and decide who will perform the marriage ceremony and where it will be held. In the US judges and religious leaders can perform weddings. Religious weddings are often held in a *church or chapel, but the ceremony can take place anywhere and couples often choose somewhere that is special to them. In Britain many couples still prefer to be married in church, even if they are not religious. Others choose a **civil ceremony** at a **registry office** or a hotel.

Traditionally, the family of the **bride** (= the woman who is to be married) paid for the wedding, but today the couple usually pay part of the cost. A traditional wedding with a hundred or more **guests** is expensive. Before the wedding, the couple send out printed **invitations** and guests buy a gift for them, usually something for their home. In the US couples **register** at a store by leaving there a list of presents they would like. Guests go to the store to look at the list and buy a present. In Britain couples send a **wedding list** to guests or, as in America, open a **bride's book** in a large store.

Before a wedding can take place in a church it must be announced there on three occasions. This is called **the reading of the banns**. Some religious groups refuse to allow a couple to marry in church if either of them has been divorced, but they may agree to **bless** the marriage after a civil ceremony.

The night before the wedding the bride and **bridegroom** or **groom** (= her future husband) often go to separate parties given for them by friends. At the groom's **stag party** guests drink alcohol, joke about how the groom is going to lose his freedom, and may watch a stripper (= a woman who takes her clothes off). The **hen party** for the bride, called in the US a **bachelorette party**, is usually quieter.

The wedding

Some people play a special role as part of the **wedding party**. The groom's closest male friend acts as the **best man** and stands next to him during the ceremony. Other friends act as **ushers** and show guests where to sit. The bride's closest woman friend is **chief bridesmaid** (*AmE* **maid of honour**), or **matron of honour** if she is married, and other friends and children are **bridesmaids**.

a white wedding

Many women choose to have a **white wedding**, so called because the bride wears a long white **wedding dress**, with a **veil** (= a piece of thin white material) covering her face. Her wedding clothes should include 'something old, something new, something borrowed, something blue', to bring luck. The bridesmaids wear matching dresses specially made for the occasion and, like the bride, carry **bouquets** of flowers. The bridegroom, the best man and other men may wear **morning dress** (= a long-tailed jacket, dark trousers and a top hat) or, in the US, a **tuxedo** (= a black suit with a white shirt). Women guests dress smartly and often wear hats.

On the **wedding day** the bride traditionally arrives at the church a few minutes late and enters with her father who will **give her away** to her husband. Some brides today find this offensive. A *wedding march is played as the bride enters. Typically, the person performing the ceremony talks about the importance of marriage, and a friend of the couple may read a poem. Then the bride and groom **exchange vows** (= promise to stay together and support each other). The groom places a **wedding ring** on the third finger of the bride's left hand, and sometimes the bride gives him a ring too. The couple are then declared **man and wife**. They **sign the register** (= the official record of marriages) and as they leave the church guests throw rice or **confetti** (= small pieces of coloured paper in lucky shapes, such as horseshoes and bells) over them.

The '**happy couple**' and their guests then go to the bride's home or a hotel for the **wedding reception**. This may be a formal meal or a party. The bride and groom and their parents greet the guests, who, in the US, say '**congratulations**' to the groom and '**felicitations**' to the bride. There are often speeches by the best man, the bride's father and the bridegroom. The bride and groom together cut a **wedding cake**, which usually has several tiers (= layers), each covered with white icing (*AmE* frosting), with figures of a bride and groom on the top one. Before the **newly-weds** leave for their **honeymoon** (= a holiday to celebrate their marriage) the bride throws her bouquet in the air: there is a belief that the woman who catches it will soon be married herself. The car the couple leave in has usually been decorated by their friends with the words '**just married**' and with old tin cans or shoes tied to the back.

can be taken from under the ground) with pictures made from flowers, leaves and other natural materials in early summer, especially around the time of *Whit.

well-dressing

ˌOrson ˈ**Welles** /ˌɔːsən ˈwelz; *AmE* ˌɔːrsən/ (1915–85) a US actor who also wrote, directed and produced films and plays. He became famous in 1938 when his radio production of H G *Wells's *The War of the Worlds* frightened many people who thought it was a real attack by Martians. Welles's most famous film was his first, **Citizen Kane*. Others included **Jane Eyre* (1944), *The Lady from Shanghai* (1948) with his wife Rita *Hayworth, *The *Third Man*, **Othello* (1952) and *Touch of Evil* (1958). For the last 30 years of his life he worked mainly in Europe.

ˈ**Wellington[1]** /ˈwelɪŋtən/ *n* a British bomber much used in *World War II. It was made by the *Vickers company and was the main aircraft used by *Bomber Command for night attacks until 1943, when it was mostly replaced by the *Lancaster[1](2), which could carry heavier bombs.

the ˌDuke of ˈ**Wellington[2]** /ˈwelɪŋtən/ (*born* Arthur Wellesley 1769–1852) an English soldier and politician, sometimes called the Iron Duke. He was made a *duke in 1814 as a reward for his victories against the French general Napoleon in the *Peninsular War. The next year Wellington's army, with the Prussians, completely defeated Napoleon at the Battle of *Waterloo. The Duke then began an active political career and in 1828 became leader of the *Tories and *Prime Minister of Britain. He made a lot of enemies in only two years. First he supported the *Emancipation Act, giving Roman Catholics the right to vote. This was unpopular in his own party. Then he opposed the *Reform Act, which was popular in the country. In 1830 he was forced to resign, although he returned to the government in 1834. He is buried in *St Paul's Cathedral, beside *Nelson. See also APSLEY HOUSE.

a painting on a vase showing the Duke of Wellington going into battle

ˌ***We'll Meet Aˈgain*** one of the best-known songs in Britain during *World War II, originally sung by Vera *Lynn and still popular today. The sentimental words express hope for the future at a time of trouble.

Wells[1] /welz/ a town in *Somerset in the west of England. It is famous for its fine cathedral, built in the 13th and 14th centuries, and its many other old buildings.

ˌH G ˈ**Wells[2]** /ˈwelz/ (Herbert George Wells 1866–1946) an English author known especially as a writer of early science fiction novels. These include *The Time Machine* (1895), *The Invisible Man* (1897) and *The War of the Worlds* (1898). He also wrote successful comic novels about *lower-middle-class life in Britain, including *Kipps* (1905) and *The History of Mr Polly* (1910). Wells believed strongly in the importance of science and the need for social change and world peace.

ˌ**Wells ˈFargo** /ˌwelz ˈfɑːgəʊ; *AmE* ˈfɑːrgoʊ/ a US company that became famous in the *Old West for carrying goods and passengers between *San Francisco and New York. Their *stagecoaches also carried gold, money and mail and were often attacked by thieves. The company was established as a bank in 1852 by Henry Wells and William G Fargo. In 1861 they bought the *Pony Express. In 1918 Wells Fargo combined with several other companies to form the American Railway Express Company.

Welsh /welʃ/ *n* [U] the ancient Celtic language of Wales. It is still spoken today as their first language by about 20% of the population of Wales, mainly in the north and west of the country. Groups like the Welsh Language Society try to encourage its use, and in 1988 the British government established the Welsh Language Board to help in this by giving Welsh equal status with English. Welsh is the first language in many schools in Wales and is taught in most. Road signs, etc. in Wales are in both Welsh and English. There are also programmes in Welsh on the Welsh radio station, Radio Cymru, and on the television station *S4C.

the ˌ**Welsh Asˌsembly** /ˌwelʃ/ (*also fml* the **National Assembly for Wales**) a separate parliament for Wales, based in *Cardiff. It began work in 1999, and gives Wales greater political independence from the British parliament in London. Compare NORTHERN IRELAND ASSEMBLY, SCOTTISH PARLIAMENT. ⇨ note at DEVOLUTION.

the ˌ**Welsh ˈdragon** /ˌwelʃ/ a red dragon which is the official symbol of Wales and appears on the Welsh flag.

the ˌ**Welsh ˈGuards** /ˌwelʃ/ a regiment in the British Army. It is one of the *Guards regiments and was established in 1915 from a group of Welshmen in the *Grenadier Guards.

ˈ**Welsh ˈNational ˈOpera** /ˈwelʃ/ an opera company based in *Cardiff. It first performed in *Cardiff in 1946 and became fully professional in the 1970s. The company makes regular tours in Wales and parts of England. See also OPERA NORTH, SCOTTISH OPERA.

the ˈ**Welsh ˌOffice** /ˈwelʃ/ a British government department in charge of Welsh affairs in certain areas, including health, social services and education. It was established in *Cardiff in 1964. It has limited powers, with many decisions concerning Wales being made by the central government in London. The Welsh Office will no longer exist after the *Welsh Assembly is created.

ˌ**Welsh ˈrabbit** /ˌwelʃ/ (*also* **Welsh rarebit** /ˈreəbɪt; *AmE* ˈrerbɪt/) a dish eaten as a small meal or as part of a meal, consisting of bread with cheese on it cooked under heat until the cheese melts. The origin of its name is not clear, and it is often simply called 'cheese on toast'.

the ˌ**Welsh ˈvalleys** /ˌwelʃ/ (*also infml* the **valleys**)

Weights and measures

Imperial or metric?

The **imperial system** of weights and measures is gradually being replaced in Britain by the **metric system**, which is used in most other countries in the *European Union. Though it makes sense for Britain to use the same system of measurement as other EU countries, many British people have resisted the idea of change and the introduction of the metric system has been slow. But by 1999 most imperial measures will have gone out of use. The measurement which it is most difficult to change is the **mile**. Road signs still give distances in miles and British people still think in miles.

US **customary measure** is similar to imperial measure. The metric system is used only in a limited way in the US. Measurements in scientific research are usually made using the metric system, although not all laboratory instruments use it. Pressure, for example, may be measured in pounds per square inch. Distances in the US are generally given in miles, but in areas that receive many foreign tourists road signs may give distances in kilometres. In the 1970s Americans were encouraged to use the metric system and children were taught it in school, but it proved unpopular and is now rarely used. Some Americans believe that it is time to change but, since relatively few Americans are involved in foreign trade or travel abroad, many people feel that the limited rewards would not be worth the effort.

The imperial system

The imperial system was developed in the 19th century to replace many local standards of measurement. It was first used in the measurement of liquids, when the imperial **gallon** replaced the ale gallon and the wine gallon. The wine gallon was smaller than the new imperial gallon but the same as the gallon measure still used in the US.

The names of imperial measures give a fascinating insight into their origins. **Length** is measured in **yards**, **feet** and **inches**. *Yard* comes from a word meaning a stick or rod, and *foot* was based on the length of a man's foot. *Inch* comes from the *Old English *ynce* meaning one twelfth. There are 12 inches in a foot. Longer distances are measured in miles. The expression *give him an inch and he'll take a mile* (= give way a little to somebody and they will demand a lot more) is still in common use. The **furlong**, a distance of an eighth of a mile, is now only used in horse-racing. It was originally the length of a ploughed furrow.

Some measures such as a **perch**, also called a **pole** or **rod**, have not been used for a long time. A perch was a measure for land, equal to 5.5 yards. A **chain** was 22 yards, i.e. four perches, and was originally a measuring line made of metal rods joined together. Cricket pitches are a chain long.

The **fathom**, equal to 6 feet, was used at sea and on charts to measure **depth**. It was the length of both arms stretched out, from fingertip to fingertip.

The imperial unit of **area** is the **acre**, an Old English word meaning field. It consists of 4 840 square yards. The acre is still used in Britain in preference to the metric **hectare**.

Weight is measured in **pounds** and **ounces**. Many people say their own weight in **stones** and pounds (a stone is 14 pounds). The **avoirdupois** weight is based on 16 ounces in one pound. The smallest unit of weight is a **grain**. Jewellers still use the older system of **troy weights** in which there are 12 ounces to the pound. *Ounce*, like *inch*, comes from *ynce*, meaning one twelfth. Measures formerly used by apothecaries (= chemists) include scruples, drachms and minims.

Larger quantities are weighed in **hundredweights** and **tons**. Britain used the full hundredweight which consists of 112 pounds, and the full ton of 2 240 pounds. In the US the standard unit is the 'short' hundredweight, which is 100 pounds, and the 'short' ton, 2 000 pounds. The name *hundredweight* suggests that it was originally 100 pounds.

Volume is measured in litres, e.g. at petrol stations, but the imperial measures of a **pint** and half-pint are used in pubs for beer and cider. Spirits (= strong alcohol) used to be sold in measures of a sixth of a **gill** (a gill is a quarter of a pint). **Fluid ounces** are often used in cooking.

Large quantities of corn and fruit were originally measured in **pecks** and **bushels**. A bushel is equal to 8 imperial or 8 US gallons and a peck is a quarter of a bushel. These measures are not often used, but many people know the tongue-twister (= a group of words that is difficult to pronounce): 'Peter Piper picked a peck of pickled peppers.'

Weather forecasters in Britain now describe **temperature** in degrees Celsius or Centigrade with freezing point at 0° and boiling point at 100°. They often then convert it into the Fahrenheit scale, where freezing point is 32° and boiling point 212°, for the benefit of older viewers and listeners. The Fahrenheit scale is still used in the US.

US customary measure

Most of the units used in US customary measure are the same as in imperial measure, but there are a few differences in measuring volume. Liquids are measured in the same units (2 pints to a quart, 4 quarts to a gallon) but the US gallon is smaller than the imperial gallon. Cookery recipes use a different set of volume measures, a **cup** and a quarter-, third-, and half-cup, and also **spoons**, called tablespoon, teaspoon, half- and quarter-teaspoon. A cup is equal to 8 fluid ounces; a tablespoon is equal to half a fluid ounce.

The metric system

The metric system is sometimes also called the **International System** or **Système International**, and the units of measurement are called **SI units**. Measurements of length, weight and volume are each derived from a single base unit, the **metre**, the **gram** and the **litre**. From these are derived other units of measurement that are 10, 100 or 1 000 times small or larger, e.g. one metre consists of 100 centimetres or 1 000 millimetres. The metre was originally defined as one ten-millionth of the distance from the equator to the North Pole.

Some metric units of measure are spelt differently in British and American English: words ending in *-metre* in British English are spelled *-meter* in American English, likewise *-litre* and *-liter*.

the industrial region of south Wales, especially the *Rhondda Valley. The main industries there were coal and steel, and coal mines were first established there in the early 19th century. For many years these industries employed most of the men in the region but the coal industry has now disappeared and the steel industry has become much smaller.

Eu,dora '**Welty** /ju,dɔːrə 'welti/ (1909–) a US writer of novels and short stories about her home state of *Mississippi and the US *South. She won the *Pulitzer Prize for her novel *The Optimist's Daughter* (1972) and her collections of stories include *The Golden Apples* (1949).

'**Wembley** /'wembli/ (*also* ,**Wembley** '**Stadium**) a famous sports stadium in the district of north-west London of the same name, generally considered to be England's national sports stadium. It opened in 1923 and the Olympic Games were held there in 1948. The most important sports event held there every year is the football *FA *Cup Final and England's national football team plays its home games there. Important *Rugby League and *hockey matches are also played at Wembley, and big rock music concerts are often held there. Next to it is a separate building, the **Wembley Arena**, where rock concerts, shows (especially on ice) and sports events, especially competitions in showjumping (= the sport of riding horses over difficult barriers), regularly take place. Wembley Arena was built in 1934 and was originally called the Empire Pool because it contained a big swimming pool. Close to both of these buildings is the large Wembley Conference Centre, which opened in 1977.

'**Wendy** /'wendi/ a character in the children's story **Peter Pan* by J M *Barrie. She is one of the children of the Darling family who are taken by Peter Pan to the *Never Never Land, where they have many adventures. Barrie invented the name Wendy, which has since become a popular name for girls.

'**Wendy's**™ /'wendiz/ any of a group of US *fast-food restaurants that serve mostly hamburgers. The company has nearly 5 000 restaurants around the world. It was established in 1969 by Dave Thomas who named it after one of his daughters.

'**Wensleydale** /'wenzlideɪl/ *n* [U] a type of English cheese which is mild and white and easily breaks into pieces. It was originally made in the valley of Wensleydale in *Yorkshire.

'**Wentworth** /'wentwəθ; *AmE* 'wentwərθ/ a famous golf course in *Surrey in southern England. A number of important competitions are held there, including the World Matchplay Championship, which has taken place there every year since it began in 1964.

,***We Shall Over'come*** a song used during the *civil rights movement by *African Americans and their supporters to show that they intended to overcome prejudice and *segregation. Mahalia *Jackson often sang it at their meetings. It was originally a *gospel song, and includes the lines:

Deep in my heart, I do believe
We shall overcome some day.

,Arnold '**Wesker** /'weskə(r)/ (1932–) an English writer of plays. He grew up in a left-wing Jewish family in London and many of his plays reflect this background and the problems created by class divisions in Britain. They include *Chicken Soup with Barley* (1957), *Roots* (1959), *I'm Talking about Jerusalem* (1960), *Chips with Everything* (1962) and *Annie Wobbler* (1983).

,Charles '**Wesley**[1] /'wezli/ (1707–88) one of the people who helped to establish the *Methodist Church in Britain, with his brother John *Wesley. He is mainly known as the writer of over 7 000 hymns, many of which are still popular today. These include *Love Divine, All Loves Excelling* and the Christmas *carol **Hark! the Herald Angels Sing*.

,John '**Wesley**[2] /'wezli/ (1703–91) the person mainly responsible for establishing the *Methodist Church in Britain. He became a priest in the *Church of England in 1725 and in 1729 joined a religious group started by his brother Charles *Wesley in *Oxford. People called the group 'Methodists' because of their fixed methods of praying and studying. They were known for the very personal and intense style of their preaching (= speaking about religion) during church services and for the highly emotional response of those who heard them. When the Church of England decided not to allow the Methodists to continue preaching in its churches, John Wesley spent the next 50 years travelling around Britain on a horse preaching to people, mostly outdoors. As a result, the number of people following his religious beliefs greatly increased.

The Methodist Church remained part of the Church of England until after Wesley's death, when it became a separate Church following a disagreement with the Church of England.

'**Wessex** /'wesɪks/ a region of southern England in *Anglo-Saxon times. Originally part of what is now *Hampshire and *Oxfordshire, it grew to include most of southern England by the 9th century. The name Wessex was used by Thomas *Hardy for the area of south-west England (especially Dorset) where his novels are set. It is also used today in the names of certain local authorities and companies in the region.

'Frederick and 'Rosemary **West**[1] /'west/ a married couple at the centre of one of the most famous and terrible criminal cases in Britain in the 20th century. Over a number of years they together murdered a number of young women and buried them in the garden and cellar of their house in Cromwell Street in *Gloucester. The bodies were discovered in 1994 and the house became known as the 'House of Horror'. The Wests were charged with the murders and Frederick (commonly known as Fred) was also charged with the murders of several other women whose bodies were found in other places. Before the trial, he killed himself in prison. Rosemary was later found guilty and sent to prison for life.

,Mae '**West**[2] /,meɪ 'west/ (1892–1980) a US actor who became a sex symbol in the 1930s and was famous for her humorous remarks suggesting sex. Her best-known line in films was 'Come up and see me some time,' which she said to Cary *Grant in *She Done Him Wrong* (1933). Her other films include *My Little Chickadee* (1940) and *Myra Breckinridge* (1970). See also MAE WEST.

Na,thanael '**West**[3] /nə,θænjəl 'west/ (1903–40) a US author. His novels, which did not become well known until after his death, were strongly critical of American society. They include **Miss Lonelyhearts* and *The Day of the Locust* (1939), based on his experiences as a *Hollywood writer. West was killed in a car crash.

Re,becca '**West**[4] /'west/ (1892–1983) an English writer and journalist. She wrote many novels, including *The Thinking Reed* (1936), *The Fountain Overflows* (1956) and *The Birds Fall Down* (1966), but is best remembered for the books she wrote as a result of her work as a journalist. These include *The Meaning of Treason* (1949), about the spies *Burgess[2] and *Maclean[2], and *A Train of Powder* (1955) about the Nuremberg trials. West had a long love affair with the writer H G *Wells. She was made a *dame(2) in 1959.

the ˌ**West** ˈ**Coast** the name commonly used for the states on the west coast of the US, especially *California. To many people the West Coast suggests a place that has sunny weather most of the time, where the people have a relaxed way of life and often invent or follow new fashions, particularly those involving physical fitness or psychological help.

the ˈ**West** ˌ**Country** the name often used to refer to the south-west of Britain, particularly the counties of *Cornwall, *Devon, *Somerset and *Dorset.

the ˌ**West** ˈ**End** the area of west central London that contains the city's most famous streets for shopping, theatres and cinemas, as well as many restaurants and other forms of entertainment. It includes such places as *Soho, *Oxford Street, *Shaftesbury Avenue, *Chinatown, *Leicester Square, *Regent Street and *Piccadilly Circus.

ˈ**western** *n* a book or film that tells a story about *cowboys in the *Wild West. Westerns involve guns, horses and often Indians (*Native Americans). They are popular because they represent the traditional struggle between good and bad, often in a simple but exciting way. Famous western films include **High Noon* and **Shane*. Western television series have included **Gunsmoke* and **Bonanza*. See also COWBOYS AND INDIANS, L'AMOUR, SPAGHETTI WESTERN.

the ˈ**Western** ˈ**European** ˈ**Union** (*abbr* the **WEU**) a defence alliance between countries which are members of the *European Union. It was established in 1948 and its original members were Belgium, France, Holland, Luxembourg and Britain. West Germany and Italy joined in 1954 and Spain and Portugal joined in 1988. The organization makes decisions on military matters affecting western European countries. In the agreement signed at *Maastricht in 1991, it was decided to establish the WEU as a formal European defence force which can send armed forces to other European countries if they are needed.

the ˌ**Western** ˈ**Isles** the region of north-west Scotland which consists of the islands of the Outer *Hebrides: Lewis with Harris, North Uist, South Uist and Barra. Its administrative centre is *Stornoway. The Western Isles is also sometimes used to mean all the islands in the Hebrides.

ˌ**Western Sa**ˈ**moa** /səˈməʊə; *AmE* səˈmoʊə/ a group of islands in the southern Pacific which has been an independent country since 1962 and a full member of the *Commonwealth since 1970. It is ruled by a king and its official languages are English and Samoan. The main exports are bananas, cocoa and copra (= the dried inner part of coconut). ▶ **Western Samoan** *adj, n.*

ˌ**Western** ˈ**Union** a US telegraph company (= one offering a service of sending people's messages by the use of electric current along wires). It was established in 1851 and used during the *Civil War. Since it could deliver written messages quickly in an emergency, people often feared it was bad news when one arrived. The company became Western Union Corporation in 1970 and now send messages by computers and satellites.

ˌ**West Gla**ˈ**morgan** /gləˈmɔːgən; *AmE* gləˈmɔːrgən/ a county in south Wales which was created in 1974 from an area that was part of the former county of *Glamorgan. Its administrative centre is the city of *Swansea.

ˌ**West** ˈ**Ham** /ˈhæm/ (*also* **West Ham United**) an English football club whose home ground is Upton Park in the West Ham area of east London. Its most successful period was in the 1960s when players such as Bobby *Moore and Geoff *Hurst played for it. It was established in 1900 and its informal name is the Hammers. It has won the *FA Cup three times and the *European Cup-Winners' Cup once. It has not had any major success in recent years.

the ˌ**West** ˈ**Indies** /ˈɪndiz/ several groups of islands between the south coast of the US and the north coast of South America, forming a line which encloses the *Caribbean Sea. There are about 1 200 islands in all. They include Cuba, *Jamaica, Hispaniola, *Puerto Rico, *Dominica, *Saint Lucia, *Barbados, *Grenada, and *Trinidad and Tobago. Many of the islands in the West Indies formerly belonged to Britain and are now members of the *Commonwealth. ▶ **West Indian** *adj, n.* ⇨ article at MULTICULTURAL BRITAIN AND THE US.

ˈ**Westinghouse** /ˈwestɪŋhaʊs/ a large US television company which also makes electronic goods and supplies nuclear and electrical power. It was established in 1886 by George Westinghouse and was mostly responsible for the US decision to use AC (= alternating current) instead of DC (= direct current) electricity. Its main office is in *Pittsburgh, *Pennsylvania.

ˈ**Westland** /ˈwestlənd/ a British company making helicopters which was at the centre of a major public disagreement between senior politicians in the *Conservative government led by Margaret *Thatcher in 1986. Westland was in serious financial difficulties. Michael *Heseltine, the minister of defence, wanted it to be sold to a group of European companies, but Leon *Brittan, the secretary of state for trade and industry, and other senior politicians, wanted it to be sold to the US company Sikorski. Michael Heseltine resigned from the *Cabinet when he was told that he could not make any public statements on the matter without Mrs Thatcher's approval. Leon Brittan later resigned when he was forced to admit that he had allowed a secret letter criticizing Michael Heseltine to be made public. Westland was sold to Sikorski.

the ˌ**West** ˈ**Midlands** /ˈmɪdləndz/ a *metropolitan county in central England, created in 1974 and consisting of seven districts which were previously parts of the counties of *Warwickshire, Worcestershire and *Staffordshire, including the cities of *Birmingham and *Coventry.

ˈ**Westminster** /ˈwestmɪnstə(r)/ **1** a *borough of central London which contains many important government buildings, including the Houses of Parliament, the offices in *Whitehall and *Downing Street, and the royal palaces, *Buckingham Palace and *St James's Palace. Other well-known places there include *Westminster Abbey, *St James's Park, The *Mall(1) and *Victoria station. The River *Thames flows on one side of it. **2** the British *Houses of Parliament(2) and British politics in general: *There was a heated debate at Westminster today.*

ˌ**Westminster** ˈ**Abbey** /ˌwestmɪnstər/ a very big church in *Westminster(1), London, which is one of the most famous buildings in Britain. Most of the present building, which replaced an earlier one, was built in the 13th and 14th centuries, in the *Gothic style. Every English king and queen has been crowned there since *William the Conqueror in 1066. Many famous English people are buried in the Abbey or have memorials in it, and it contains *Poets' Corner and the *Tomb of the Unknown Soldier. In 1997, the funeral of *Diana, Princess of Wales, took place there. The Abbey was made a *World Heritage Site in 1987. See also CORONATION CHAIR.

Westminster Abbey

ˌ**Westminster ˈBridge** /ˌwestmɪnstə; *AmE* ˌwestmɪnstər/ one of the best-known bridges over the River *Thames in central London. The *Houses of Parliament(2) are close to the north end of the bridge, and the south side leads to County Hall and the *South Bank. It is popular with tourists, who like to take photographs of each other with the *Houses of Parliament(2) in the background. *Wordsworth's poem *On Westminster Bridge* begins with the famous line: 'Earth has not anything to show more fair.'

ˌ**Westminster CaˈthedraI** /ˌwestmɪnstə; *AmE* ˌwestmɪnstər/ the main *Roman Catholic church in England. It was built in neo-Byzantine style (= like the architecture of ancient Turkey) at the end of the 19th century near *Victoria Station in central London, and was still being decorated at the end of the 20th century.

the ˈ**Westminster ˈKennel Club ˈDog Show** /ˈwestmɪnstə; *AmE* ˈwestmɪnstər/ the oldest and most important dog show in the US. It began in 1877 and is now held every February in *Madison Square Garden with more than 150 breeds of dogs competing. Compare CRUFTS.

ˌ**Westminster ˈSchool** /ˌwestmɪnstə; *AmE* ˌwestmɪnstər/ a well-known British *public school near *Westminster Abbey. It began as a *Roman Catholic school in the 12th century, and became a *Church of England school at the *Reformation. Traditionally it only accepted boys as students, but in the late 20th century it began to take girls in the *sixth form.

ˈ**Westmorland** /ˈwestmələnd; *AmE* ˈwestmərlənd/ a former county in north-west England. In 1974 it was combined with *Cumberland and part of *Lancashire(1) to form *Cumbria.

ˌ**West ˈPoint** ⇨ UNITED STATES MILITARY ACADEMY.

the ˈ**West Side** the western part of *Manhattan(1) in New York City, from *Fifth Avenue to the *Hudson River. It contains *Rockefeller Center, *Times Square, *Madison Square Garden, *Macy's, *Carnegie Hall and the theatre district, as well as some poor and violent areas, in which the musical show **West Side Story* is set. The Upper West Side has the *Lincoln Center for the Performing Arts and *Columbia University.

ˌ***West Side ˈStory*** a *Broadway musical play (1957) with music by Leonard *Bernstein and words by Stephen *Sondheim. The film version (1961) won several *Oscars, including Best Picture. The story is a modern version of Shakespeare's play **Romeo and Juliet* set in the tough West Side of New York's *Manhattan(1). The songs include *Maria, Tonight* and *There's a Place for Us*.

ˌ**West ˈSussex** /ˈsʌsɪks/ a county in southern England created when the former county of *Sussex was divided into two separate counties in 1974. Its administrative centre is the town of *Chichester.

ˌ**West VirˈginIa** /vəˈdʒɪniə; *AmE* vərˈdʒɪniə/ a central eastern state of the US, also called the Mountain State. The capital and largest city is Charleston. West Virginia separated from *Virginia in 1861 because its people did not want to join the *Confederate States, and became a US state two years later. It produces apples, tobacco, corn, coal, gas, steel, glass and chemicals. Tourist attractions include Harpers Ferry National Historic Park and Monongahela National Forest. Nearly 75% of the state is covered by forests. See also HARPERS FERRY.

ˌVivienne ˈ**Westwood** /ˈwestwʊd/ (1941–) an English fashion designer, well known for her unusual clothes based on historical themes. She first became famous in the 1970s by selling her *punk(1) designs in a shop on *King's Road, London, with her partner Malcolm *McLaren, who became the manager of the *Sex Pistols. In recent years, Westwood's designs have become more traditional.

Vivienne Westwood (right) with one of her models

ˌ**West ˈYorkshire** /ˈjɔːkʃə(r); *AmE* ˈjɔːrkʃər/ (*written abbr* **W Yorks**) a *metropolitan county in the north of England, created in 1974 and consisting of five districts which were previously part of the West *Riding of *Yorkshire.

wet *n* (in Britain) a politician who believes in moderate rather than extreme policies. The word was used by Margaret *Thatcher in the 1980s to insult the members of her own party who did not agree with some of her more right-wing policies. Later, moderate members of the *Conservative Party began to refer to themselves as wets: *She easily fended off the challenge from the Tory wets.*

ˈ**wetback** /ˈwetbæk/ *n* (*AmE infml disapprov, often offensive*) a Mexican worker who enters the US illegally, often by swimming across the *Rio Grande river.

WEU /ˌdʌbljuː iː ˈjuː/ ⇨ WESTERN EUROPEAN UNION.

Mr **W H** /ˌmɪstə ˈdʌbljuː ˈeɪtʃ/ an unknown man for whom William *Shakespeare said he had written his **Sonnets* at the beginning of the first published version of the poems. Shakespeare was in love with a young man when he wrote them and this has led many people to think that Mr W H and the young man were the same person, but nobody knows this for certain. There have been many different theories about the identity of Mr W H.

Wham! /wæm/ a British pop group formed in 1982. The group was very successful in the 1980s, with songs including *Wake Me Up Before You Go Go* (1984) and *I'm Your Man* (1985). Its main singer was George

*Michael, who left the group to begin a career on his own in 1986.

ˌEdith ˈ**Wharton** /ˈwɔːtn; *AmE* ˈwɔːrtn/ (1862–1937) a US writer of novels and short stories, many of which are about high society in New York. Her best-known novel is *The Age of Innocence* (1920), which won a *Pulitzer Prize and became a film (1993) directed by Martin *Scorsese. Wharton's other novels include *The House of Mirth* (1905) and *Ethan Frome* (1911). She lived in France after 1913.

ˌ***What's My*** ˈ***Line?*** **1** a British television programme that was popular in the 1950s. Each programme consisted of a game in which a group of famous people had to guess a person's job by asking him or her questions about it. It was presented by Eamonn *Andrews. **2** a similar programme on US television which ran from 1950 to 1972, presented by John Daly, followed by Wally Brunner and Larry Blyden.

ˌ***What the*** ˈ***Papers Say*** a British television programme that examines the different ways in which the news is reported in different newspapers. Each week it is presented by a different journalist, who shows and makes comments on a range of news reports. It was first broadcast in 1956 on *ITV, and then moved to *Channel Four in the 1980s and to *BBC2 in the 1990s.

the ˈ**Wheat Belt** the western central region of the US, where most of the country's wheat is grown. It includes the *Great Plains.

ˈ**Wheaties**™ /ˈwiːtiz/ *n* [pl] a popular US breakfast cereal made of wheat. There are three varieties: Wheaties, Honey Frosted Wheaties and Crispy Wheaties N Raisins. It is advertised as 'The Breakfast of Champions'. The packets carry pictures of successful sports people and teams, which young people save and exchange. Wheaties were first produced in 1924 and are made by the General Mills company.

ˌCharles ˈ**Wheatstone** /ˈwiːtstəʊn; *AmE* ˈwiːstoʊn/ (1802–75) an English scientist and inventor. He invented many things, including the kaleidoscope (= a toy consisting of a tube containing pieces of coloured glass and mirrors which reflect these to form changing patterns when the tube is turned), the electric clock and the **Wheatstone bridge**, a device for measuring electrical resistance. He taught physics at *London University, and was made a *knight in 1868.

ˌ***Wheel of*** ˈ***Fortune*** a popular US television game show, first broadcast in the 1970s. It has been presented for many years by Pat Sajak and his assistant Vanna White, and in 1998 it was watched regularly by 100 million people around the world. The game involves competitors trying to guess popular expressions. Other countries, including Britain, have their own versions of the show.

a whelk-stall

ˈ**whelk-stall** *n* (in Britain) a small covered stand from which whelks (= small sea animals in shells) and other types of cheap seafood are sold. Whelk-stalls are traditionally found on the streets of the *East End of London, and in British seaside towns. They are sometimes used as an example of a very small and simple business: *I can't believe they made him manager – he couldn't run a whelk-stall.*

ˌ***When*** ˈ***Johnny Comes*** ˈ***Marching*** ˈ***Home*** a song from the American *Civil War which was popular with both sides. It was written in 1863 by Patrick Gilmore (1829–92) who was born in Ireland. The first verse is:

When Johnny comes marching home again, hurrah!
  Hurrah!
We'll give him a hearty welcome then, hurrah!
  Hurrah!
The men will cheer, the boys will shout,
The ladies, they will all turn out,
And we'll all feel gay, when Johnny comes
  marching home.

ˌ***When the*** ˈ***Saints Go*** ˈ***Marching*** ˈ***In*** one of the best-known traditional *Dixieland songs in the US. It is played every day in the *French Quarter of *New Orleans. The first verse is:

Oh, when the saints go marching in,
Oh, when the saints go marching in,
Oh, Lord, I want to be in that number,
When the saints go marching in.

Which? a magazine produced each month by the *Consumers' Association in Britain. It consists of reports comparing different makes of similar products and services, to help people to decide which one to buy. It is only available to members of the Consumers' Association, but many people who are not members go to public libraries to study the old copy of *Which?* that deals with the product they want to buy. *Which?* was first published in 1957.

Whig /wɪg/ *n* **1** a member of a British political party established in the late 17th century. The Whigs believed that *Parliament should have more power than the king or queen, and supported the *Hanoverian kings and queens against the *Stuarts. They believed in religious freedom and political reforms. The Whigs, who were mainly rich businessmen and people who owned land in the country, were in power for the first half of the 18th century. In the 19th century they changed into the *Liberal Party. Compare Tory. **2** a member of an American political party, established in 1834 to oppose the *Democrats. In the 1850s the party broke up and many of its members joined the new *Republican Party.

ˌ***While*** ˈ***Shepherds*** ˈ***Watched Their*** ˈ***Flocks by*** ˈ***Night*** a popular *carol often sung at Christmas.

Whip *n* (in Britain) any of several *MPs who are responsible for keeping discipline among the MPs belonging to their party, making sure that they go to debates and advising them how to vote. In the US *Congress there are also Whips for each party. The *House of Representatives has a Democratic Whip and a Republican Whip, and each has 19 assistants. The *Senate Whips are called Assistant Majority Leader and Assistant Minority Leader, and each is assisted by four *senators.

ˈ**Whipsnade** /ˈwɪpsneɪd/ a zoo in southern England, north-west of London. When it opened in 1931 it was one of the first zoos in the world to breed animals that were in danger of dying out, and to allow them to live freely in natural surroundings, rather than in cages.

ˈ**whisky** (*also* ˈ**whiskey**) *n* [U] a strong alcoholic drink made from cereals. The best-known whisky, made in Scotland, is often called 'Scotch', and the best quality of Scotch whisky is 'single malt', made in the *Highlands from a single type of grain. Many people drink it mixed with water, soda water or soft drinks (= drinks containing no alcohol) such as ginger ale or *Coca-Cola, while others prefer to drink it with nothing added or just ice. **Whiskey** is the usual spelling for the drink made in Ireland and America.

the **'Whispering ˌGallery** the famous gallery (= a raised platform along the inner wall of a building) that goes all the way round the inside of the dome of *St Paul's Cathedral in London. It is well known for the way it carries sounds: if a person whispers close to the wall on one side of the gallery, they can be heard by another person close to the wall on the other side of the gallery, 107 feet/32 metres away.

'James Mc'Neill **'Whistler** /mək'ni:l 'wɪslə(r)/ (1834–1903) a US artist who was educated in France and lived mostly in London, England, after 1859. His best-known painting is usually called **Whistler's Mother*. In a famous legal case he took John *Ruskin to court for publicly criticizing his painting *Nocturne in Black and Gold*. Whistler won the case but was awarded only a quarter of one penny.

ˌWhistler's 'Mother /ˌwɪsləz; *AmE* ˌwɪslərz/ the popular title of the painting *Arrangement in Grey and Black* (1872) by the US artist James *Whistler. It is a picture of his mother, Mrs George Washington Whistler, sitting in an upright chair and painted from the side. It is now in the Louvre in Paris.

ˌwhistle-stop cam'paign *n* a political campaign in which a politician makes short stops at many different towns. The expression was first used in the US, where small American towns were called 'whistle-stops' because trains only stopped at them if a whistle signal was given. President *Truman was well known for his whistle-stop campaigns, during which he made speeches in many small towns from the platform on the end of a train.

Whit (*also* **'Whitsun**) the seventh Sunday after Easter (also called **Whit Sunday**) and the days close to it. Whit Sunday is an important Christian religious festival which celebrates the Holy Ghost coming down from Heaven to the apostles (= the twelve people sent out by Christ to spread his teaching). See also WHIT MONDAY.

ˌWhitaker's 'Almanack /ˌwɪtɪkəz; *AmE* ˌwɪtɪkərz/ a well-known British reference book. It is published in December every year and consists of a wide range of information about Britain and other countries, including lists of organizations and officials, details of important events in the previous year, and information about the positions of the planets and stars. It was first published in 1868.

'Whitbread /'wɪtbred/ a large British company that makes several types of *beer and owns many *pubs.

'Whitbread 'Book of the 'Year /'wɪtbred/ a major British literary prize, organized and paid for by *Whitbread. At the beginning of January each year, four new British or Irish books are chosen as the best book of their type: best novel, best first novel, best book of poems and best biography. At the end of the month, one of the five is chosen as the book of the year. There is also a separate **Whitbread Children's Book of the Year Award**, which is the largest prize offered to writers of children's literature in Britain.

the **'Whitbread 'Round the 'World Race** /'wɪtbred/ a major international race for sailing boats. They start and finish in *Portsmouth or *Southampton, England, and race in stages to different ports around the world. The race takes place every four years and is sponsored (= paid for) by *Whitbread.

ˌE B **'White¹** /'waɪt/ (Elwyn Brooks White 1899–1985) a US author known for his humorous pieces about American society in *The *New Yorker* magazine. He received a special *Pullitzer Prize in 1978. His books included *Is Sex Necessary?* (1929), written with James *Thurber, and the children's book *Charlotte's Web* (1952). His introduction to the art of writing, *The Elements of Style*, first published in 1959, is a standard book in US schools.

ˌGilbert **'White²** /'waɪt/ (1720–93) an English naturalist (= a person who studies animals, birds, plants, etc.). He spent most of his life working as an assistant to a Church of England priest in Selborne, a village near *Winchester(1) in southern England, and wrote in great detail about the natural life of the countryside there. His best-known work is *The Natural History and Antiquities of Selborne* (1789).

'Whitechapel /'waɪttʃæpl/ a district in the *East End of London. It has a reputation as one of the poorest areas of central London, and one where many immigrants have settled. In the late 19th and early 20th centuries many Jewish people came to live in Whitechapel, and it still has many Jewish shops and businesses. It is also well known as the area where *Jack the Ripper committed his murders.

ˌWhite 'Christmas a song by Irving *Berlin. It has become a traditional song for Christmas, when many people hope that there will be snow. The song was first written for the film *Holiday Inn* (1942) and won an *Oscar. Bing *Crosby sang it in the film and his recording has sold more than 40 million copies, the most for any recording until recent years. He was also in a second version of the film, made in 1954 with the new title *White Christmas*.

ˌWhite 'City an area of north-west London, England, where there used to be a famous sports stadium. The Olympic Games took place there in 1908, and for most of the 20th century it was a well-known stadium for *greyhound racing. It was destroyed in the 1980s.

the **ˌwhite cliffs of 'Dover** /'dəʊvə(r); *AmE* 'doʊvər/ *n* [pl] the tall chalk cliffs on the south-eastern coast of England, around the port of *Dover. They can be seen from several miles away at sea, so they are the first part of England that people see as they approach Dover by ship. To many British people in other countries, they represent the idea of going home. One of the most popular songs of *World War II, sung by Vera *Lynn, begins with the lines:

There'll be bluebirds over
The white cliffs of Dover
Tomorrow, just you wait and see.

ˌwhite 'ensign *n* a flag used only by ships of the British *Royal Navy and members of the *Royal Yacht Squadron. It is white with an upright red cross and a small British flag in the top left quarter. Compare BLUE ENSIGN, RED ENSIGN.

ˌwhite 'flight *n* [U] (*AmE*) (in the US) the movement of *middle-class white people away from the centre of cities into the suburbs (= outer areas). It began in the 1950s and was caused by the increase in crime in city centres and the rise in the number of African Americans living there.

'Whitehall /'waɪthɔ:l/ a street in central London, between *Trafalgar Square and the *Houses of Parliament(1). Most of the buildings in it are government offices, so that 'Whitehall' is often used to refer to the government: *Whitehall is extremely embarrassed about the leaked memo.*

the **ˌWhitehall 'Theatre** /ˌwaɪthɔ:l/ a theatre on *Whitehall, London. It is famous for its farces (= light comedy plays based on ridiculous situations). See also RIX.

ˌwhite 'horse *n* any of several large figures of white

horses in the English countryside, mainly in southern England. Most of them were made in prehistoric times, by cutting the grass away from the surface of chalk hills. They probably had a religious meaning for the people who made them, but some of them are believed to be more recent. The best-known white horses are at Uffington in Oxfordshire and at Westbury in Wiltshire.

ˌMary ˈ**Whitehouse** /ˈwaɪthaʊs/ (1910–) an Englishwoman who became famous in the 1960s and 1970s for her campaigns against sex, violence and bad language on British television and radio and in the theatre and cinema. In 1965 she formed the National Viewers' and Listeners' Association, a *pressure group which has had some influence on the British media by stopping some performances and publications and taking the companies responsible to courts of law. Some British people make jokes about Whitehouse. Many consider her old-fashioned, and believe that she has no right to decide what other people can see or hear.

the ˈ**White House** **1** the home and office of the US President, at 1600 *Pennsylvania Avenue in Washington, DC. It is built of stone painted white and was designed in 1800 by James Hoban, who was born in Ireland. The building was burned by British troops during the *War of 1812 and later built again. Tourists can visit parts of it, including the Blue Room and the State Dining Room. See also OVAL OFFICE. **2** [sing + sing/pl *v*] the US President and his advisers: *The White House has refused to comment on the allegations.*

ˌWilliam ˈ**Whitelaw** /ˈwaɪtlɔː/ (1918–99) an English *Conservative politician who held many important positions in Conservative governments in the 1970s and 1980s. He was made a *viscount(1) in 1983.

ˌPaul ˈ**Whiteman** /ˈwaɪtmən/ (1890–1967) a US musician, also known as the 'King of Jazz', who led bands and orchestras playing 'symphonic jazz', a mixture of *jazz and classical music. George *Gershwin wrote *Rhapsody in Blue* for Whiteman's orchestra, and they were the first to play it in 1924. The orchestra made a European tour in 1926 and played at the *Albert Hall in London.

the ˌ**white man's ˈburden** (*old use, rather offensive*) a phrase that was used mainly in the 19th century to express the idea that European countries had a duty to run the countries and organizations of people in other parts of the world with less money, education or technology than the Europeans. The phrase was first used in a poem by Rudyard *Kipling.

ˌ**White ˈPaper** *n* (in Britain) an official report presenting the government's policy on a particular question to be discussed in *Parliament.

the ˌ**White ˈRabbit** a character in Lewis *Carroll's **Alice in Wonderland*. He is the white rabbit that Alice follows down a hole at the beginning of the story. He is worried that he is late for something and keeps looking at his watch.

White's /waɪts/ the oldest and one of the most famous of London's clubs. It first opened in 1693 as a place where famous and fashionable people went to drink chocolate and gamble. In the late 18th century it began to be connected with the *Tory Party. ⇨ note at GENTLEMEN'S CLUBS.

the ˌ**White ˈTower** the oldest part of the *Tower of London. It is a large *Norman keep (= an ancient castle, built to be very strong) made of white stone at the centre of the group of buildings. In the 17th century the bones of two children were found there, and many people believe that they are the bones of the *Princes in the Tower.

the ˈ**Whitewater afˌfair** /ˈwaɪtwɔːtər/ the name used by the press, etc. to refer to the illegal sale of property in *Arkansas by the Whitewater Development Corporation, a company that had connections with US President Bill *Clinton and his wife Hillary. Investigations into the affair, begun in 1994 by *Congress and the Independent Counsel Kenneth Starr, are still continuing. Some people have been sent to prison for their part in it.

ˌWalt ˈ**Whitman** /ˌwɔːlt ˈwɪtmən/ (1819–92) a major US poet who wrote about individual freedom, equal rights and sexual love, as well as about his love for America. Though many readers thought his poems were immoral, he had a strong influence on later American poets, especially the *beat generation. He used the new form of 'free verse', in which lines do not rhyme. His best-known works are **Leaves of Grass*, *Drum Taps* (1865) and a collection of writings, *Democratic Vistas* (1871).

ˌ**Whit ˈMonday** the day after *Whit Sunday. It used to be a popular *bank holiday in Britain. In the 1960s it was replaced by the *Spring Bank Holiday, which some people still call Whit Monday.

ˌEli ˈ**Whitney**[1] /ˌiːlaɪ ˈwɪtni/ (1765–1825) an American who in 1793 invented the cotton gin, a machine for separating cotton from its seeds which greatly helped the development of the cotton industry in the *South. He was also the first person to produce large numbers of small parts for guns which could be changed without replacing the whole gun.

ˌMount ˈ**Whitney**[2] /ˈwɪtni/ a mountain in the *Sierra Nevada range in central *California. It is 14 494 feet/4 421 metres high and was named after Josiah Whitney (1819–96), the first head of the California State Geological Service, who measured it in 1864.

ˈJohn ˈGreenleaf ˈ**Whittier** /ˈɡriːnliːf ˈwɪtiə(r)/ (1807–92) a US *poet and journalist who supported the campaign to free American slaves. Whittier's work, most of which is about *New England, includes *Legends of New England* (1831) and *In War Time and Other Poems* (1864). Among his best-known poems is *Snow-bound* (1866).

ˌDick ˈ**Whittington** /ˈwɪtɪŋtən/ (*died* 1423) *Lord Mayor or London three times (1397–98, 1406–07 and 1419-20). Most British people known the stories about him: that he was running away from London when he was a boy, but thought he heard the church bells telling him to 'Turn again, Whittington, Lord Mayor of London', and that he became rich by selling his cat to a foreign king. The story of his life is a popular subject for *pantomimes.

ˌFrank ˈ**Whittle** /ˈwɪtl/ (1907–96) an English engineer, best known for inventing the jet engine, the type of engine now used in most aircraft, which gives forward movement by releasing a stream of gases at high speed behind it. He was made a *knight in 1948.

the **Who** a British pop group. It began as a *mod group in the 1960s, and by the early 1970s was one of the most popular *rock groups in the world. They were known for behaving wildly and sometimes destroying their equipment during their performances. The Who's best-known records include *My Generation* (1965) and two rock operas (= stories told through a series of *rock music songs), *Tommy* (1969) and *Quadraphenia* (1973).

ˌ***Who Killed Cock ˈRobin?*** an old English *nursery rhyme in which a group of animals talk about the death of a robin (= a small bird) and offer to help at his funeral. It may refer to the loss of political power of Robert *Walpole in 1742.

ˈ***Who's Aˈfraid of Virˈginia ˈWoolf?*** /ˈwʊlf/ the best-known play (1962) by the US writer Edward *Albee. It is about a college teacher and his wife who constantly argue and play cruel games with each other and a younger couple who visit them. In the film version (1966) the older couple were played by Elizabeth *Taylor and Richard *Burton[3].

ˌ***Who's*** ˈ***Who*** a British book, published every year, which gives the personal details of important, rich or famous people. The details are written by the people themselves, and some of them write amusing things about their hobbies and interests. It was first published in 1849.

WI /ˌdʌbljuː ˈaɪ/ ⇨ WOMEN'S INSTITUTE.

ˌ***Widdicombe*** ˈ***Fair*** /ˌwɪdɪkəm/ a popular old English song about a group of people who borrow a horse to go to a horse *fair in Widdicombe, a village in *Devon. Each verse of the song ends with the names of the people in the group: Bill Brewer, Jan Stewer, Peter Gurney, Peter Davy, Dan'l (Daniel) Whiddon, Harry Hawk and old *Uncle Tom Cobbleigh.

the ˌ**Wife of** ˈ**Bath** /ˈbɑːθ; *AmE* ˈbæθ/ one of the best-known characters in *Chaucer's **Canterbury Tales*. She is a lively woman who has been married five times and makes many humorous remarks about sex. The story she tells, the **Wife of Bath's Tale**, is about one of King *Arthur's *knights. He has to find the answer to the question 'What do women love most?' to avoid being killed. An ugly old woman says that she will tell him the answer, but only if he marries her. He agrees, and she becomes a beautiful young woman.

ˈ**Wigan** /ˈwɪɡən/ an industrial town in *Greater Manchester, England. In the *Industrial Revolution it had important coal-mining and cotton industries. It is famous today for its *Rugby League club, one of the oldest in England and the most successful in the history of the sport.

the ˌ**Wightman** ˈ**Cup** /ˌwaɪtmən/ a women's tennis competition between British and US players which took place every year from 1923 to 1989. It was then stopped because the British players were not good enough to compete with the US players, who almost always won easily.

the ˌ**Wigmore** ˈ**Hall** /ˌwɪɡmɔː; *AmE* ˌwɪɡmɔːr/ a hall for concerts in the *West End of London. It is used mainly for the performance of classical songs and chamber music (= music written for a small orchestra).

ˌWilliam ˈ**Wilberforce** /ˈwɪlbəfɔːs; *AmE* ˈwɪlbərfɔːrs/ (1759–1833) an English politician, best known for his successful campaigns to stop the slave trade and to make *slavery illegal in the *British Empire.

the ˈ**Wild Bunch** ⇨ HOLE-IN-THE-WALL GANG.

The ˈ***Wild Bunch*** a violent *western film (1969), directed by Sam *Peckinpah, about a group of outlaws (= criminals) who become involved in the Mexican Revolution. Some people consider it to be one of the best *westerns ever made.

ˌOscar ˈ**Wilde** /ˈwaɪld/ (1854–1900) an Irish writer of plays, poetry and one novel, *The Picture of Dorian Gray* (1891). He became famous after moving to London, where he wrote his most successful comedy plays, including *Lady Windermere's Fan* (1892) and *The *Importance of Being Earnest*. He is also well known for his humorous and intelligent remarks, and for being homosexual. In 1895 he was sent to prison for his homosexuality, which was illegal at the time. He described his prison experience in the poem *The *Ballad of Reading Gaol*. After he was released he lived the rest of his life in France and Italy. Many of his clever and amusing remarks are still repeated today: *As Wilde said to the customs officer, 'I have nothing to declare but my genius.'*

Oscar Wilde

▶ ˈ**Wildean** /ˈwaɪldiən/ *adj* of or typical of Oscar Wilde: *Wildean wit.*

ˌBilly ˈ**Wilder**[1] /ˈwaɪldə(r)/ (1906–) a US writer, director and producer of films, born in Austria. His many successful films, some of which he also wrote or helped to write, include *Double Indemnity* (1944), *The Lost Weekend* (1945), **Sunset Boulevard, The Seven Year Itch* (1955), *Some Like It Hot* (1959) and *The Apartment* (1960). He has won a total of five *Oscars.

ˌThornton ˈ**Wilder**[2] /ˌθɔːntən ˈwaɪldə(r); *AmE* ˌθɔːrntən ˈwaɪldər/ (1897–1975) a US writer of novels and plays. He won *Pulitzer Prizes for the novel *The Bridge of San Luis Rey* (1927) and the plays **Our Town* and *The Skin of Our Teeth* (1942). His comedy play *The Matchmaker* (1954) was used as the basis for the *Broadway musical play *Hello, Dolly!* (1964).

the ˈ**Wildfowl and** ˈ**Wetlands** ˈ**Trust** a British organization, set up in 1946 by Peter *Scott to study and protect wildfowl (= wild birds that live on or near water, such as ducks and geese). See also SLIMBRIDGE.

the ˌ**Wild** ˈ**West** the western US during the later part of the 19th century, when communities were settled but there was not much law and order. This is the period shown in *westerns, though the picture they present of the Wild West is not often very accurate. Towns that were known for their outlaws (= criminals) and violence included *Tombstone, *Arizona, and *Dodge City, *Kansas. Famous outlaws included Jesse and Frank *James, *Billy the Kid and the *Younger brothers. Compare OLD WEST.

ˌ**Wild** ˈ**West show** *n* (in the US) a show in which performers create the atmosphere and characters of the *Wild West, with *cowboys and *Native Americans. They ride horses, shoot at objects and demonstrate other western skills. Such shows were especially popular at the end of the 19th century, when they were often performed in large tents. The most famous was *Buffalo Bill's Wild West Show, which he took to many US cities and also to Europe. See also OAKLEY.

ˈ**William**[1] the main character in a series of children's stories by Richmal *Crompton. He is a *middle-class English schoolboy and the leader of the Outlaws, a group of children who have amusing adventures and often get into trouble.

ˌPrince ˈ**William**[2] (1982–) the first child of the *Prince and *Princess of Wales. He is sometimes called Wills informally by his family and in the press.

William I /ˌwɪljəm ðə ˈfɜːst; *AmE* ˈfɜːrst/ (*also* ˌ**William the** ˈ**Conqueror**) (*c.* 1027–87) the king of England from 1066 to 1087. He was the Duke of Normandy, in northern France, when the English king *Edward the Confessor died, and claimed that Edward had promised him the right to be the next king of England. He invaded England and defeated King *Harold II at the Battle of *Hastings in 1066. Later that year he became king. He gave power and land in England to other *Normans, and built many castles to control the English people.

William II /ˌwɪljəm ðə ˈsekənd/ (*also* ˌ**William** ˈ**Rufus**) (*c.* 1056–1100) the king of England from 1087 to 1100. He became king when his father *William I died. He was a skilful leader but his attempts to take money from his *barons and the church made him unpopular. He died in an accident while hunting, but many people think he was murdered so that his brother *Henry I could be king. He was called Rufus, meaning red, because of the colour of his hair.

William III /ˌwɪljəm ðə ˈθɜːd; *AmE* ˈθɜːrd/ (*also* ˌ**William of ˈOrange** /ˈɒrɪndʒ; *AmE* ˈɔːrɪndʒ/) (1650–1702) the king of Great Britain and Ireland from 1688 to 1702. He was a Dutch prince, married to Mary, the daughter of *James II. They were invited by British *Protestants to be the king and queen of Britain in order to prevent the *Roman Catholic James II from being king. William became king in the *Bloodless Revolution and defeated the forces of James II in Ireland at the *Battle of the Boyne. He is remembered by a group of Protestants in Northern Ireland who are opposed to Ireland becoming one republic, and call themselves *Orangemen. See also WILLIAM AND MARY.

William IV /ˌwɪljəm ðə ˈfɔːθ; *AmE* ˈfɔːrθ/ (1765–1837) the king of Great Britain and Ireland from 1830 to 1837. He was the son of *George III and spent many years in the *Royal Navy. He is also remembered for having had ten illegitimate children (= ones born outside marriage) with a female actor. His most important action was to create 50 new *Whig(1) peers to vote for the *Reform Act against the *Tories in *Parliament who were opposed to it.

ˌ**William and ˈMary** *n* [U] a style of furniture that was popular in Britain at the end of the 17th century, during the reign of King *William III and Queen *Mary. Elegant tables, chairs and cupboards with designs carved into the wood are typical of the style.

ˌ**William of ˈOckham** (*also* **Occam**) ⇨ OCKHAM.

ˌ**William of ˈWykeham** /ˈwɪkəm/ (1324–1404) the *bishop of *Winchester(1) from 1367 to 1404. He is best remembered for establishing *Winchester(2) College, whose pupils are still called Wykehamists.

ˈ**Williams**[1] /ˈwɪljəmz/ a British company that makes racing cars and organizes teams of drivers, mechanics (= people skilled in working on engines), etc. to enter competitions. It was established in 1967 by Frank Williams (1942–), and in the 1980s and 1990s it was one of the most successful teams in motor racing.

ˌAndy ˈ**Williams**[2] /ˈwɪljəmz/ (1930–) a US popular singer, especially of love songs. His hits include *Moon River* (1963) and *Born Free* (1967). He had his own television series, *The Andy Williams Show* (1970–1), on which the *Osmonds first became famous.

ˌHank ˈ**Williams**[3] /ˌhæŋk ˈwɪljəmz/ (1923–53) the most important early singer and writer of US *country music. His sad voice and simple songs influenced many later singers. His best-known songs include *Lovesick Blues* (1949), *Your Cheatin' Heart* (1953) and *Take These Chains from My Heart* (1953). Williams drank too much alcohol and died young. He was chosen for the Country Music *Hall of Fame in 1961. In a film about his life, *Your Cheatin' Heart* (1964), his songs were sung by his son Hank Williams, Junior (1949–).

W

ˌJ P R ˈ**Williams**[4] /ˈwɪljəmz/ (John Peter Rhys Williams 1949–) a famous Welsh *Rugby Union player. He was a skilful defensive player, and played 55 times for Wales between 1969 and 1981, more than any other player in the history of Welsh Rugby. He also played eight times for the *British Lions.

ˌKenneth ˈ**Williams**[5] /ˈwɪljəmz/ (1926–88) an English actor, well known for his funny, exaggerated way of speaking. He appeared in several popular radio comedy programmes, but is perhaps best remembered for acting in the *Carry On films.

ˌRobbie ˈ**Williams**[6] /ˌrɒbi ˈwɪljəmz; *AmE* ˌrɑːbi/ (1974–) a British pop singer. He began his career as a member of the group Take That but left them in 1995 to perform on his own. His successful records have included *Angels* and *No Regrets*, and the album *Life Thru a Lens*.

ˌRobin ˈ**Williams**[7] /ˈwɪljəmz/ (1952–) a US actor known for his energy and wild humour. He began his career on the television comedy series *Mork and Mindy* (1978–82). He has won an *Oscar for *Good Will Hunting* (1998) and *Golden Globe Awards for *Good Morning, Vietnam* (1987), *The Fisher King* (1991) and *Mrs Doubtfire* (1993). His other films include *Dead Poets Society* (1989), *The Bird Cage* (1996) and *Flubber* (1997).

ˌShirley ˈ**Williams**[8] /ˈwɪljəmz/ (1930–) an English politician. She began her career in the *Labour Party and was a member of the *Cabinet in the 1970s. In 1981 she was one of the *Gang of Four who left Labour to set up the *SDP. She was made a *life peer in 1993.

ˌTennessee ˈ**Williams**[9] /ˌtenəsiː ˈwɪljəmz/ (1914–83) a major US writer of plays. These were often set in the *South and about people with emotional and sexual problems, which many people found shocking when the plays were first performed. Two of his 24 plays, *A *Streetcar Named Desire* and *Cat on a Hot Tin Roof* (1955), won *Pulitzer Prizes. Others included *The Glass Menagerie* (1945), *Sweet Bird of Youth* (1959) and *Night of the Iguana* (1961). There were film versions of many of them.

ˈ**Williamsburg** /ˈwɪljəmzbɜːg; *AmE* ˈwɪljəmzbɜːrg/ a historic US town in south-eastern *Virginia. It was settled in 1633 as Middle Plantation but soon named after the English king *William III. It was the capital of the colony from 1699 to 1779. The College of William and Mary was established there in 1693. The 18th-century town was built again in the 1930s as Colonial Williamsburg and is now very popular with tourists.

ˌ**William the ˈConqueror** ⇨ WILLIAM I.

ˌBruce ˈ**Willis** /ˈwɪlɪs/ (1955–) a US actor, especially in action films. His career began with the television series *Moonlighting* (1985–9). His films include *Die Hard* (1988), *Pulp Fiction* (1994), *Day of the Jackal* (1997) and *Armageddon* (1998). Willis was formerly married to the actor Demi *Moore. He is one of the owners of the restaurant group *Planet Hollywood.

ˈ**willow ˌpattern** *n* [U] a design that is often seen on English pottery. It consists of a blue and white picture, in traditional Chinese style, which usually includes people on a bridge over a river, near a willow (= a tree with long thin branches that grows near water). It was first used in *Staffordshire pottery in the late 18th century, and is still popular today.

a willow-pattern plate

ˌHelen ˈ**Wills** ⇨ MOODY.

ˌAngus ˈ**Wilson**[1] /ˈwɪlsn/ (1913–91) a British writer of novels and short stories, born in South Africa. His books, including *Hemlock and After* (1952) and *Anglo-Saxon Attitudes* (1956), are known for their humorous descriptions of unusual characters in the different social *classes. He was made a *knight in 1980.

ˌHarold ˈ**Wilson**[2] /ˈwɪlsn/ (1916–95) an English *Labour politician who was twice *Prime Minister (1964–70 and 1974–6). His government aimed to make Britain a more modern country, encouraging more people to be involved in science and technology, but the country also had economic problems at the time, which forced Wilson to devalue the pound (= reduce its value compared with foreign currencies). Many people were surprised when he resigned in 1976. It was later discovered that *MI5 had been dishonestly trying to bring down Wilson's government during the 1960s and 1970s. He was made a *knight in 1976 and a *life peer in 1983. See also POUND IN YOUR POCKET.

ˌWoodrow ˈ**Wilson**[3] /ˌwʊdrəʊ ˈwɪlsn; *AmE* ˌwʊdroʊ/ (1856–1924) the 28th US *President (1913–21). He was a Democrat and is remembered as an honest man who worked hard for world peace. Earlier in his career he had been President of *Princeton University (1902–10) and Governor of *New Jersey (1911–3) As US President, he tried to keep the US out of *World War I, but he finally sent US soldiers to join the Allied forces in 1917, saying that 'the world must be made safe for democracy'. After the war Wilson's *Fourteen Points were used as the basis for the peace agreement, and he was given the Nobel Peace Prize in 1919. He also created the idea for the *League of Nations and was greatly disappointed when *Congress decided that the US should not join it. Wilson's government also established the *Federal Reserve System and the *Federal Trade Commission.

ˈ**Wilton** /ˈwɪltn/ *n* [C, U] a type of carpet made of loops of wool which are cut to produce a thick, even surface. Wilton carpets are usually plain, but some have patterns of different colours. They were first made in Wilton, a town in *Wiltshire, England.

ˈ**Wiltshire** /ˈwɪltʃə(r)/ (*abbr* **Wilts**) a county in south-west England. It consists mainly of agricultural land. Its administrative centre is Trowbridge.

ˈ**Wimbledon** /ˈwɪmbldən/ a district of south-west London, consisting mainly of houses. It is well known around the world as the home of the *All England Club. Many people refer to the major international tennis competition which takes place there each year simply as Wimbledon. It was first held in 1877: *She became Wimbledon champion for the fourth time.*

ˈ**Wimpy**™ /ˈwɪmpi/ *n* a hamburger sold at a **Wimpy Bar**, any of a group of British *fast-food restaurants. Wimpy Bars were the most popular restaurants of this type in Britain in the 1950s and 1960s. In 1989 many of them were sold to the *Burger King company: *He bought me a Wimpy and chips.*

ˈLord ˈPeter ˈ**Wimsey** /ˈwɪmzi/ a character in several crime novels by Dorothy *Sayers. He is an English *lord who is a very good amateur detective.

ˌWalter ˈ**Winchell** /ˈwɪntʃəl/ (1897–1972) a popular US radio and newspaper journalist in the 1930s and 1940s. He began his radio broadcasts with the phrase 'Good evening, Mr and Mrs America and all the ships at sea'. His style of reading the news was very dramatic and he was one of the first journalists to add his own comments to news stories. From 1929 to 1969 he wrote a regular column about politicians and entertainers for *The Mirror* in New York.

ˈ**Winchester** /ˈwɪntʃɪste(r); *AmE* ˈwɪntʃester/ **1** a city in southern England. It is the administrative centre of *Hampshire and until *Norman times was the capital of England. It is well known for its cathedral, which was begun in the 11th century, and other very old buildings. **2** (*also* **Winchester College**) a well-known *public school(1) in Winchester. It was established by *William of Wykeham in 1382 and was the first of its kind. **3** (*also* **Winchester rifle**) *n* a type of rifle developed in the US by Oliver F Winchester and first produced in 1860 by the Volcanic Repeating Arms Company. It was especially successful because it could be fired repeatedly without the need to put bullets in each time. Winchesters were widely used in the *Civil War and are often seen in *western films.

ˈ**Windermere** /ˈwɪndəmɪə(r); *AmE* ˈwɪndərmɪr/ **1** the largest lake in England (10.5 miles/17 kilometres long), in the *Lake District. It is known for the natural beauty of its scenery, and for water sports such as sailing and fishing. **2** a town on the eastern edge of Lake Windermere, in the county of *Cumbria. It is one of the main tourist centres in the *Lake District.

The ˌ***Wind in the*** ˈ***Willows*** a children's novel (1908) by Kenneth *Grahame. It describes the adventures and relationships of a group of small animals, including a mole, a rat, a toad and a badger, who live by a river. It is one of the most popular British children's books of the 20th century. A version of it for the stage, called *Toad of Toad Hall*, was written in 1929 by A A *Milne.

Toad, Mole, Ratty and Badger from The Wind in the Willows, *illustrated by E H Shepard*

the ˌ**Windmill** ˈ**Theatre** a small theatre in the *West End of London. It is well known for its shows of dancing by naked or almost naked women. Until the 1960s comedians used to tell jokes between the dancing shows, and many famous performers (including Tony *Hancock and Peter *Sellers) started their careers there. It was the only theatre that stayed open when bombs were being dropped on London during *World War II.

ˈ**Windows**™ /ˈwɪndəʊz; *AmE* ˈwɪndoʊz/ a system developed by the US company *Microsoft to operate computer programs. Each program has its own window on the screen. There have been several versions of the system since it was first produced in 1990. Microsoft have also produced Windows NT for large computers and Windows CE for small computers held in the hands.

ˈ**window tax** *n* [U] a historical tax that British people had to pay according to how many windows they had in their houses. It was in use between 1675 and 1851. It is still possible to see old houses in Britain that had their windows filled in with bricks, etc. in order to save tax.

ˈ**Windsor**[1] /ˈwɪnzə(r)/ **1** a town in southern England on the River *Thames, west of London. It is famous for its castle. **2** the family name of the British *royal family since 1917. It was changed from the German *Saxe-Coburg-Gotha by *George V because of strong British feelings against Germany during *World War I.

the ˌDuke of ˈ**Windsor**[2] /ˈwɪnzə(r)/ the title given to *Edward VIII after he abdicated (= gave up his right to be king). His wife was given the title of the **Duchess of Windsor**. See also ABDICATION CRISIS.

ˌ**Windsor** ˈ**Castle** /ˌwɪnzə; *AmE* ˌwɪnzər/ a castle in *Windsor[1](1). It is one of the official homes of the

Windsor Castle

British king or queen. It was started by *William I in the 11th century, and parts were added to it by several later kings and queens. Most of the present castle was either built or decorated in the early 19th century. Some of the rooms are open to the public when the king or queen is not staying there. In 1992 some parts of the castle were badly damaged by a fire, but these have now been repaired.

the ˌ**Windy** ˈ**City** a popular name for the city of *Chicago in the US, because of the strong winds that blow there from across Lake *Michigan.

ˌOprah ˈ**Winfrey** /ˌəʊprə ˈwɪnfri; *AmE* ˌoʊprə/ (1954–) an *African-American entertainer who presents *The Oprah Winfrey Show*, the most popular US television *chat show. She has won six *Emmy awards as 'Best Host of a Talk Show' (1986 and 1990–4). The show began in 1986 and includes ordinary people talking about their personal problems, often in a very emotional way. In 1996 Winfrey was paid more than any other US entertainer. In 1998 she won a court case after *Texas cattle farmers accused her of harming their business by discussing on her show the existence in the US of BSE, a disease that kills cows.

Oprah Winfrey

ˌ**Winne**ˈ**bago**™ /ˌwɪnɪˈbeɪɡəʊ; *AmE* ˌwɪnɪˈbeɪɡoʊ/ *n* (*pl* **-gos**) a popular US make of motor home (= a large motor vehicle fitted as a home and used for holidays, etc.). The first Winnebago was made in 1966 at Forest City, *Iowa, where Winnebago Industries still is. The company is named after a *Native-American people.

ˌ**Winnie-the-**ˈ**Pooh** /ˌwɪni ðə ˈpuː/ ⇨ POOH.

ˌ**winter of discon**ˈ**tent** a phrase first used by some British newspapers and politicians to describe the winter of 1978–9 in Britain, when there were many strikes and economic problems. The phrase was taken from the opening lines of *Shakespeare's play *Richard III*: 'Now is the winter of our discontent/Made glorious summer …' It was used to suggest that people were not happy with the way the *Labour government was running the country. The same phrase is now used to refer to any difficult political situation that occurs during the months of winter: *The government will have to settle the miners' pay dispute soon if they are to avoid another winter of discontent.*

The ˌ***Winter's*** ˈ***Tale*** a play (*c.* 1610) by William *Shakespeare. It begins sadly and ends happily. Leontes, king of Sicilia, thinks that his wife is not faithful. He puts her in prison and orders his baby daughter to be left on a 'desert shore'. He believes that they are both dead, and feels very sorry for what he has done. His daughter, however, is found by a shepherd (= a person whose job is to look after sheep), and grows up to become a shepherd herself. When she falls in love with a prince they run away together to Sicilia. There, Leontes recognizes his daughter and finds out that his wife is also alive. The young lovers are married and the king and queen are united again.

Wiˈ**sconsin** /wɪˈskɒnsɪn; *AmE* wɪˈskɑːnsɪn/ a northern US state which has borders with Lake *Michigan and Lake *Superior. Its popular name is the Badger State. The largest city is *Milwaukee and the capital city is Madison. The US won the land from Britain in the *American Revolution, but the British did not leave until after the *War of 1812. Wisconsin became a state in 1848. Its farm products include cheese, milk and corn, and it also produces beer, cars and machinery. The state has more than 14 000 lakes, many of which are popular with tourists.

ˈ***Wisden*** /ˈwɪzdən/ (*full title* ˈ***Wisden*** ˈ***Cricketers'*** ˈ***Almanack*** /ˈwɪzdən/) a British book of information about cricket. It has been published each year since 1864 and contains details such as the results of all the previous year's matches and the achievements of individual players. It also contains a lot of historical information and essays on various aspects of the game. Many lovers of cricket collect copies of *Wisden* from different years.

ˌErnie ˈ**Wise** /ˌɜːni ˈwaɪz; *AmE* ˌɜːrni/ ⇨ MORECAMBE AND WISE.

ˈ**Wisley** /ˈwɪzli/ the main public garden of the *Royal Horticultural Society in *Surrey, south of London. It consists of a large and attractive garden and several smaller areas which are designed to show people how to grow different types of plant or arrange different types of garden.

witch *n* a person, usually a woman, who is believed to have or use magic powers. Witches are often shown in pictures and described in old stories as ugly old women with black clothes and pointed hats. They were typically believed to be able to fly on broomsticks. Witches used to be considered evil and dangerous in Britain and America, but in the late 20th century many young people began to call themselves witches as part of the *New Age interest in ancient beliefs and cultures: *The witch made her sleep for many years but she woke up when the handsome prince kissed her.*

ˌLudwig ˈ**Wittgenstein** /ˌlʊdvɪɡ ˈvɪtɡənstaɪn/ (1889–1951) an Austrian philosopher. He studied in Britain under Bertrand *Russell before *World War I. After the war he moved back to Britain, becoming a British citizen in 1938. He worked on theories of language and philosophy. In his *Tractatus Logico-Philosophicus* (1922) he suggested the theory that language represents pictures of things according to established conventions (= general agreement). Later, he decided that this was wrong, and worked on the theory that usage was more important.

The ˌ***Wizard of*** ˈ***Oz*** /ˈɒz; *AmE* ˈɑːz/ a very popular US film (1939) based on the children's book *The Wonderful Wizard of Oz* (1900) by Frank Baum (1856–1919). In the film a little girl called Dorothy, played by Judy *Garland, is blown by a strong wind from her home in *Kansas to the strange land of Oz. She has to defeat the Wicked Witch of the West in order to return home, and she does this with the help of the Scarecrow, the Tin Woodman, the Cowardly Lion and the Wizard of Oz himself. The film's best-known

a scene from The Wizard of Oz

songs include *Over the Rainbow, We're Off to See the Wizard* and *Follow the Yellow Brick Road.*

the '**Wobblies** /ˈwɒbliz; *AmE* ˈwɑːbliz/ *n* [pl] an informal name for the members of the US trade union *IWW.

ˌ**Woburn 'Abbey** /ˌwəʊbɜːn; *AmE* ˌwoʊbɜːrn/ a *stately home near the town of Bedford in southern England. It was built in the 18th century on land where an abbey had once been. It is open to the public, who come to see the many works of art in the house, and the deer and birds in the attractive gardens.

ˌP G '**Wodehouse** /ˈwʊdhaʊs/ (Pelham Grenville Wodehouse 1881–1975) an English writer of humorous novels and short stories. He is best known for his books about *Jeeves and Bertie *Wooster, but he wrote many other stories of life among the English *aristocracy. He also wrote the words for several successful American musical comedies. He became a US citizen in 1955, and was made a *knight in 1975: *We went to her great aunt's country house, which was just like something out of P G Wodehouse.*

ˌTerry '**Wogan** /ˈwəʊgən; *AmE* ˈwoʊgən/ (1938–) an Irish radio and television presenter. He was one of the first disc jockeys on *Radio 1 when it opened in 1967, and later had his own *chat show on *BBC television (1984–92). He is now perhaps best known as the presenter on British television of the *Eurovision Song Contest, in which he gently makes fun of the whole event.

the **Wolds** /wəʊldz; *AmE* woʊldz/ *n* [pl] two ranges of hills in north-east England. The range to the north of the River *Humber used to be called the **Yorkshire Wolds**, and is now simply called the Wolds. The range to the south of the Humber is known as the **Lincolnshire Wolds**.

'General 'James '**Wolfe**[1] /ˈwʊlf/ (1726–59) an English soldier. He is remembered in history for leading the attack on Quebec, Canada, in 1759, and for dying during the battle. His victory there led to France giving up Canada to Britain at the end of the *Seven Years' War.

ˌNero '**Wolfe**[2] /ˌnɪərəʊ ˈwʊlf; *AmE* ˌnɪroʊ/ the *detective created by the US writer Rex *Stout.

ˌThomas '**Wolfe**[3] /ˈwʊlf/ (1900–38) a US writer whose four long and powerful novels are set in the *South and are based on his own life. They are *Look Homeward Angel* (1929), *Of Time and the River* (1935), and two published after he died, *The Web and the Rock* (1939) and *You Can't Go Home Again* (1940). Wolfe also wrote short stories.

ˌTom '**Wolfe**[4] /ˈwʊlf/ (1931–) a US writer, many of whose books are about US popular culture and social life. They include *The Electric Kool-Aid Acid Test* (1968) and the novels *The Bonfire of the Vanities* (1988) and *A Man in Full* (1998). Earlier in the 1960s, Wolfe was a leading figure in the 'New Journalism' movement, in which facts were written about in the style of fiction. He was a journalist for *The *Washington Post* (1959–62) and *The New York Herald-Tribune* (1962–6).

the '**Wolfenden Reˌport** /ˈwʊlfəndən/ a British government report, completed in 1957, on homosexuality. It was responsible for homosexual acts between consenting (= agreeing) adults becoming legal in Britain. All homosexual acts had been illegal until then.

ˌMary '**Wollstonecraft** /ˈwʊlstənkrɑːft; *AmE* ˈwʊlstənkræft/ (1759–97) an English writer and feminist (= person who believes strongly that women should have the same rights and opportunities as men). She led a campaign for equal opportunities in education for women, and wrote books on the subject, including *A Vindication of the Rights of Woman* (1792). Her daughter was Mary *Shelley.

'**Wolseley** /ˈwʊlzli/ *n* a former make of British car. The first Wolseleys were made in the late 19th century, but the company was bought by *Morris in 1927 and later became part of *British Leyland. The name was still used for some cars until the 1960s.

ˌCardinal '**Wolsey** /ˈwʊlzi/ (Thomas Wolsey *c.* 1474–1530) an English *cardinal (= very senior Roman Catholic priest), who was *Henry VIII's most important political adviser in the first half of his reign. Wolsey became very powerful, but was dismissed by Henry when he failed to get the Pope's permission for the king to divorce *Catherine of Aragon.

ˌ**Wolver'hampton** /ˌwʊlvəˈhæmptən; *AmE* ˌwʊlvərˈhæmptən/ an industrial town in the English *Midlands. It was an important centre of the iron industry in the 18th century, and now has several industries, including metals, chemicals and vehicles.

'***Woman*** a popular British women's magazine. It has been published once a week since 1937 and contains a wide range of articles. It is read mainly by older women.

ˌ***Woman and 'Home*** a British women's magazine. It has been published once a month since 1926 and contains articles on subjects such as fashion, homes, cooking and travel. It is read mainly by older women.

'***Woman's Hour*** a British radio programme consisting of a wide range of reports, talks and fiction by, for and about women. It has been broadcast every weekday on *Radio 4 since 1946.

ˌ***Woman's 'Own*** a popular British women's magazine. It has been published once a week since 1932 and contains short stories, usually about love, as well as articles on subjects like fashion and cooking. It is read mainly by older women.

ˌ***Woman's 'Realm*** a British women's magazine. It has been published once a week since 1958 and contains a wide range of true and fictional stories. It is read mainly by older women.

ˌ***Woman's 'Weekly*** a popular British women's magazine. It has been published once a week since 1911 and consists of a mixture of true stories about people's lives, fictional love stories, articles about famous people such as film stars, and articles about practical subjects such as homes and cooking. It is read mainly by older women.

'**Womble** /ˈwɒmbl; *AmE* ˈwɑːmbl/ *n* any of a group of imaginary animals with long fur and long noses. They live underground in a large London park and at night they come out to collect the rubbish that people have left behind. They were invented by the children's writer Elizabeth Beresford in her book *The Wombles* (1968), and became very popular when the children's television series *The Wombles* was broadcast in the 1970s.

the ˌ**Women's** ˈ**Army Corps** ⇨ WAC.

ˌ**Women's** ˈ**Institute** (*abbr* **WI**) *n* (in Britain) any of the local branches of the **National Federation of Women's Institutes** (itself sometimes referred to as the Women's Institute). This organization was started in 1915 with the aim of improving and developing the lives of women living in country areas. Each branch organizes social, cultural and charity events, and holds meetings where members can learn skills connected with the home, such as cooking. Most small towns and country areas have a Women's Institute. People generally associate the organization with older *middle-class women: *There's a jumble sale at the Women's Institute this Saturday.*

ˌ**women's** ˈ**lib** /ˈlɪb/ (*in full* ˌ**women's libe**ˈ**ration**) *n* [U] (*becoming old-fash*) the name that most people used to refer to feminism in the 1960s. At that time, many women in Britain and America began to demand the same rights and opportunities as men. They were sometimes called **women's libbers**.

the ˈ**Women's** ˈ**Royal** ˈ**Air Force** ⇨ WRAF.

the ˈ**Women's** ˈ**Royal** ˈ**Army Corps** (*abbr* the **WRAC**) the women's section of the British Army for most of the 20th century. In 1992 it combined with the rest of the army.

the ˈ**Women's** ˈ**Royal** ˈ**Voluntary** ˌ**Service** (*abbr* the **WRVS**) a large organization of British women who do voluntary work (= without pay) in their communities. For example, they deliver *meals on wheels and visit people in hospitals and prisons.

ˌStevie ˈ**Wonder** /ˌstiːvi ˈwʌndə(r)/ (1950–) an *African-American singer and writer of *soul and *rock music who also plays the piano. Wonder, who was born blind, has won 10 *Grammy awards, including ones for *You Are the Sunshine of My Life* (1973) and *For Your Love* (1995). His other hits have included *For Once in My Life* (1968), *Yester-me, Yester-you, Yester-day* (1969), *Superstition* (1973) and *Happy Birthday* (1981). His albums include *Innervisions* (1973) and *Songs in the Key of Life* (1976).

ˈ**Wonderbra**™ /ˈwʌndəbrɑː; *AmE* ˈwʌndərbrɑː/ *n* a popular make of bra (= an item of underwear that women wear to support their breasts). Wonderbras, which were introduced in 1968, make the breasts appear larger. They became very well known in Britain in the 1990s after a major advertising campaign showing attractive women wearing them.

ˈ**Wonder Bread**™ *n* [U] a popular US make of soft white bread produced by the Interstate Bakeries Corporation, the largest company of its kind in the US. It has been advertised on television by Fresh Guy, a character in the form of a face on a packet of bread.

ˌHenry ˈ**Wood**[1] /ˈwʊd/ (1869–1944) an English conductor, best known for establishing the *Proms. He was one of the greatest conductors of his time, and did much to improve the standard of music in Britain. He introduced the work of many new foreign composers, and allowed women to play in orchestras for the first time. He was made a *knight in 1911.

Vicˌtoria ˈ**Wood**[2] /ˈwʊd/ (1953–) an English comedy entertainer and writer. She wrote and appeared in many British television programmes in the 1980s and 1990s, and is well known for her intelligent humour and clever songs.

ˌJohn ˈ**Wooden** /ˈwuːdn/ (1910–) a successful US university *basketball manager at *UCLA (1948–75). His teams were US National Champions 10 times (1964–5, 1967–73 and 1975), and he was chosen Coach of the Year seven times. The US Basketball Writers Association each year presents the John R Wooden Award to the best US college or university basketball player.

ˌParson ˈ**Woodforde** /ˈwʊdfəd; *AmE* ˈwʊdfərd/ (James Woodforde 1740–1803) an English parson (= a priest of the *Church of England). He wrote a diary that describes his life over many years in a village in *Norfolk. It was published later (1924–31) as *The *Diary of a Country Parson*.

ˌTiger ˈ**Woods** /ˌtaɪgə ˈwʊdz; *AmE* ˌtaɪgər/ (1975–) an *African-American golf player. Before he became a professional, he was the US Junior Amateur Champion for three years running (1991–3). Woods won six of his first 21 *PGA competitions. One was the 1997 *US Masters Tournament, in which at 21 he was the youngest winner ever and achieved the lowest score (270) in the competition's history.

ˈ**Woodstock** /ˈwʊdstɒk; *AmE* ˈwʊdstɑːk/ a very large *rock music festival held in August 1969 near Bethel, New York, 60 miles/97 kilometres south-west of Woodstock, the place originally planned for it. Many famous singers and groups performed, including Jimi *Hendrix and Jefferson Airplane. The festival was attended by hundreds of thousands of young people, many of whom took drugs, but there was no violence. It became a symbol of the new youth culture of the *hippies.

ˌ**Wookey** ˈ**Hole** /ˌwʊki / a group of caves in south-west England. In prehistoric times people lived in the caves, and there is a local story that a *witch used to live there. They are now a tourist attraction.

Virˌginia ˈ**Woolf** /ˈwʊlf/ (1882–1941) an English writer of novels. She is well known for the experimental style of many of her books. She was one of the first writers to use the 'stream of consciousness', a way of describing a person's thoughts and feelings as a flow of ideas as the person would have experienced them, without using the usual methods of description. She was a member of the *Bloomsbury Group and is considered an important early writer about feminism (= the idea that women should have the same rights and opportunities as men). Her best-known novels include *Mrs Dalloway* (1925), *To the Lighthouse* (1927) and *Orlando* (1928).

Virginia Woolf

ˈ**Woolite**™ /ˈwʊlaɪt/ *n* [U] a US make of soap for washing delicate clothes and fabrics.

the ˈ**Woolsack** /ˈwʊlsæk/ the seat on which the *Lord Chancellor sits in the *House of Lords in the British parliament. It is a large square cushion filled with wool and covered with red cloth, and it has no back, arms or legs.

ˈ**Woolwich** /ˈwʊlɪtʃ/ **1** a district of London in the south-east of the city. It was once a separate town with an important dockyard (= place for building ships) on the River *Thames, which closed in 1869, and the Woolwich Arsenal, for many years Britain's biggest arms factory. The *Arsenal football club was established there in 1886 and named after the factory. It later moved to the north London district of Highbury. **2 the Woolwich** one of Britain's biggest *building societies, established in 1847. It was the first building society to advertise on television in Britain, which it began doing in the 1970s, and is often associated with the phrase it has always used in its advertisements: 'We're (or I'm) with the Woolwich.'

ˌF W ˈ**Woolworth** /ˈwʊlwəθ; *AmE* ˈwʊlwərθ/ (Frank Winfield Woolworth 1852–1919) a US businessman, the son of a poor farmer, who began the group of *five-and-ten shops/stores named after him. The first was opened in 1879 in Lancaster, *Pennsylvania, and when he died, there were more than 1 000. The first British *Woolworth's stores opened in 1909. The Woolworth Corporation today owns many other groups, such as Kinney Shoes, Champs Sporting Goods and the Foot Locker. It closed the last 400 *five-and-ten stores in 1997. See also WOOLWORTH BUILDING.

the ˈ**Woolworth ˌBuilding** /ˈwʊlwəθ; *AmE* ˈwʊlwərθ/ a New York building which was the tallest in the world when it was completed in 1913. It is on *Broadway and is 792 feet/242 metres high. It cost $13.5 million and was built by F W *Woolworth for his company. The *Chrysler Building replaced it in 1930 as the world's tallest.

ˈ**Woolworth's** /ˈwʊlwəθs; *AmE* ˈwʊlwərθs/ (*BrE also infml* **Woollie's**) a chain of large shops in the US, Canada, Britain, Ireland and other countries, selling a wide variety of goods at low prices. It has branches in many British towns and cities and for many years was Britain's leading chain of retail shops. The first shop was established in the US in 1879 by F W *Woolworth (1852–1919) and the first British shop opened in *Liverpool in 1909. In 1982 the company in Britain was bought by the Kingfisher company and it remains successful today.

ˌBertie ˈ**Wooster** /ˌbɜːti ˈwʊstə(r); *AmE* ˌbɜːrti ˈwʊstər/ one of the main characters in many humorous stories by P G *Wodehouse. He is a young *upper-class man who often gets into difficult situations because he is rather foolish and relies on his servant *Jeeves to solve all his problems for him. Wooster and his friends are members of the Drones Club in London.

ˈ**Worcester**[1] /ˈwʊstə(r)/ a city in west central England, on the River *Severn. It is the administrative centre of the county of *Hereford and Worcester. It was an *Anglo-Saxon town and has a famous cathedral, which was mostly built in the 14th century. The city is known as the place where Royal Worcester porcelain is produced and it is also one of the cities where the *Three Choirs Festival is held.

the ˌBattle of ˈ**Worcester**[2] /ˈwʊstə(r)/ a battle (1651) in which *Charles II was defeated by Oliver *Cromwell. Charles was trying to establish himself as the king of England after the execution of his father *Charles I. His attempt failed and the *Commonwealth, led by Cromwell, continued. Charles escaped by hiding in a tree when the battle was lost.

ˌ**Worcester ˈsauce** /ˌwʊstə; *AmE* ˌwʊstər/ (*also fml and AmE* **Worcestershire Sauce**) *n* [U] a very popular dark sauce with a strong flavour made in *Worcester by the *Lea and Perrins company. It was originally created in 1835 by two chemists, Lea and Perrins, in Worcester and they began commercial production of it in 1837. How it is made and exactly what it contains has always been kept a secret but it is known to contain vinegar and spices. It is widely used in cooking and often added to tomato juice as a drink. See also BLOODY MARY.

ˌWilliam ˈ**Wordsworth** /ˈwɜːdzwəθ; *AmE* ˈwɜːrdzwərθ/ (1770–1850) one of the most popular of all English poets who, together with Samuel Taylor *Coleridge, started the *Romantic Movement in English poetry. His poems are mainly about the beauty of nature and its relationship with all human beings. Many of them describe the countryside of the *Lake District in north-west England, where he was born and spent most of his life. His best-known works include *Lyrical Ballads* (1798), a collection of poems by himself and Coleridge, *Poems* (1807), which includes the poems *Daffodils* and *Intimations of Mortality*, and *The Prelude*, a long poem about his early life and his intense experiences of nature then, which was published in 1850 after his death. For much of his life he lived in the Lake District with his sister Dorothy (1771–1855), who had a great influence on him and kept a journal (= written record) about their life together. He wrote many of his best-known poems while they were living in *Dove Cottage in *Grasmere. The house is now a museum and a popular tourist attraction.

ˈ**workhouse** *n* [C] (*often* **the workhouse** [sing]) (in Britain in the 19th century) a place where very poor people were sent by the authorities to live and work. Conditions in these places were very bad and the people living there had to work very hard and obey strict rules. As a result, poor people were frightened of being sent there. Life in the workhouse is described in some of the novels of Charles *Dickens.

the ˌ**working ˈclass** *n* [C + sing/pl *v*] the social class consisting mainly of people who do physical jobs and their families. It has traditionally been regarded as below the *middle class in education, background and culture, but many working-class people, including those who rise to a higher social status, are proud to be so. Members of the working class may in fact have more money than members of the middle class. ⇨ article at CLASS.

ˌ**working men's ˈclub** *n* (in Britain, especially in the industrial areas of the *Midlands and northern England) a club where people go after work to meet each other, drink in the bar, play games such as *darts, cards and *bingo, and watch entertainments including singing, dancing and comedy. Since the 1960s, many famous British entertainers have started their careers performing in these clubs. They were established in the 1850s by the church and grew in number after a central organization, the Working Men's Club and Institute Union (WMCIU), was established in 1862.

ˌ**workmen's compenˈsation** (*also infml* ˌ**workmen's ˈcomp** /ˈkɒmp; *AmE* ˈkɑːmp/) *n* [U] (in the US) payments made to a person who is injured while at work or who becomes ill because of his work. To protect their workers, employers are required by law to pay money into a workmen's compensation insurance scheme run by the US government. The system began in 1908: *Sam had to spend a week in bed, but workmen's comp covered it.*

the ˌ**Works ˈProgress Adminiˌstration** (*abbr* the **WPA**) a US government programme (1935–43) established by President Franklin D *Roosevelt as part of his *New Deal. Its name was later changed to the Works Projects Administration. It created millions of jobs for unemployed people during the *Great Depression, mainly in building and the arts.

The ˌ***World ˈAlmanac*** the oldest US almanac (= book of facts on many subjects) still published. The New York *World* newspaper began it in 1868. It is now published regularly by K-III Reference Corporation, which also publishes *The World Almanac for Kids.*

The ˌ***World at ˈOne*** a well-known British national radio news programme, broadcast on *Radio 4 every day from Monday to Friday at 1 p.m. It contains reports and comments on the important news events of the day. It was first broadcast in 1965.

World English

English is the most widely spoken language in the world. It is the **first language**, or **mother tongue**, of around 400 million people living in Britain, Ireland, the US, Australia, New Zealand, Canada and South Africa, and it is spoken as a **second language** by another 300 million people. English is learned by many more people worldwide as a **foreign language**. Altogether about 1.3 billion (= 1 300 million) people speak English, and the number is increasing. English has become a **global language** or **international language**, used by people who speak different **native languages** to communicate with each other.

English has achieved the status of a world language over a long period of time, and for various historical and cultural reasons. In the 17th century English was spread by settlers going from Britain to America, and in the 18th and 19th centuries by the expansion of the *British Empire. Many countries which were part of the empire kept English as their official language after independence. This avoided their having to choose between competing local languages. As an official language, English is generally used in government, public administration and the law, and children may be taught in English. Some countries feel that using English gives them an advantage in international affairs. More recently, the military and political power of the US has contributed to the spread of English. People in many countries who have had contact with these great powers have been expected to learn English. Since the middle of the 20th century, English has been an official language of international organizations such as the *United Nations.

Economic factors are also important. Britain and the US are both major business and financial centres, and many multinational corporations started in these countries. Elsewhere, a knowledge of English is often seen as necessary for success in business, and in countries which have become tourist destinations English has been chosen as the main foreign language used in hotels and at tourist attractions.

Advances in technology and telecommunications have also helped to establish English as a global language. Many inventions important to modern life, e.g. electricity, radio, the car and the telephone, were developed in Britain or the US. English became the language for international communications in air traffic control and shipping. Now, major computer systems and software developers are based in the US, and English is the **lingua franca** (= common language) of the Internet. English is also spread through leisure activities. The US is the home of the cinema, and English language films are shown throughout the world.

Britain and the US have invested a lot of money in **English Language Teaching** (**ELT**). The *British Council has offices worldwide which promote British culture and support the teaching of English. The *United States Information Agency also has libraries and cultural programmes in many countries. English language broadcasts of *BBC World Service, *Voice of America and other services are widely popular, and many people listen to their news broadcasts in order to get an independent account of events in their own region. They also broadcast study programmes for learners of English. ELT has become a growth industry. Language schools have been established throughout the world and publishers bring out many new books for students.

As an international language, English continues to develop. People who speak English as a first or second language have their own variety of the language, each of which is changing independently of other varieties. There are many differences, for instance, between *British English and *American English, and between Australian, South African, Indian, African and Jamaican English, though all can be understood, more or less, by speakers of other varieties. Foreign learners of English learn one of the major varieties, usually British or American English, or some sort of international English. As a global language, English can no longer be thought of as belonging only to British or American people, or to anyone else. This loss of ownership is often uncomfortable, especially in Britain. As the number of people using English as a second or foreign language is increasing faster than the number who speak it as a first language, further drifts away from a British or American standard are likely.

The status of English as a global language has unfortunately tended to mean that British and American people assume everyone speaks English, so they do not bother to learn foreign languages. However, better language teaching, and an awareness of the advantages of speaking another language, are slowly changing this situation.

ˌWorld ˈHeritage Site *n* a place or structure included on an official list produced by the World Heritage Committee of the *United Nations. Places are chosen for the list because they are considered to be 'of outstanding universal value', often for historical reasons, and are therefore preserved. There are several in Britain, including *Hadrian's Wall, *Stonehenge, the *Tower of London and *Westminster Abbey. World Heritage Sites in the US include *Grand Canyon National Park, *Independence Hall and the *Statue of Liberty.

ˌWorld in ˈAction a well-known television programme shown on British independent television, in which situations and problems of interest to the British public are investigated. It was first broadcast in 1963 and is usually shown on Monday evenings.

the **ˌWorld ˈSeries** a series of games each year to decide the best US professional *baseball team. It began in 1903 and is between the *American League and *National League. The four best teams in each have a short series, and the two winners then play in the World Series. The first team to win four World Series games become the World Champions.

the **ˌWorld ˈService** ⇨ BBC WORLD SERVICE.

the **ˌWorld ˈTrade ˌCenter** two very tall office buildings in *Manhattan(1), New York City, built by the Port Authority of New York and New Jersey in 1972–3. For a short time they were the tallest buildings in the world. Each is 1 350 feet/412 metres high and has 110 floors. A terrorist bomb exploded in the Center in 1993 killing six people and injuring more than a thousand.

World War I /ˌwɜːld wɔː ˈwʌn; *AmE* ˌwɜːrld wɔːr/ (*also* the **First World War**, *old-fash* the **Great War**) a war (1914–8) between the Central Powers (Germany, Austria-Hungary and Turkey) and the *Allies (Britain, France, Russia, Italy and the US). Most of the fighting took place in Europe, around the borders of Eastern Germany, Poland and Russia, and in north-east France and Belgium, where millions of soldiers died in long battles between armies in trenches (= long narrow holes dug in the ground). For many people these battles represent the essential horror and waste of war. The Germans agreed to stop fighting in 1918, after more then 10 million people had been killed.

World War II /ˌwɜːld wɔː ˈtuː; *AmE* ˌwɜːrld wɔːr/

(*also* the **Second World War**) a war (1939–45) between the Axis powers (Germany, Italy and Japan) and the *Allies (Britain and the countries in the *British Empire, France, and later the USSR and the US). Many other countries were also involved both directly and indirectly.

The war started when Germany, under Adolf Hitler and the Nazis, invaded and took control of other countries and the Allies wanted to prevent German power growing in this way. Britain declared war on Germany in September 1939 when German troops entered Poland, and soon afterwards Winston *Churchill, who in Britain is closely associated with the Allies' victory in the war, became the British *prime minister.

In 1940 Germany attacked Britain but was not successful, mainly because of the British victory in the *Battle of Britain. In 1941 Germany invaded Russia and Japan attacked *Pearl Harbor, an action which brought the US into the war. In 1942 Japan increased its control over several countries in Asia but was checked by US forces in the Pacific. In the same year, at the Battle of *El Alamein, Allied forces began to defeat Germany and Italy in northern Africa. In 1943 the Allies took Italy and Russian forces began to advance on Germany from the east. In 1944 the Allies invaded northern Europe with the *Normandy landings and began to defeat Germany in Europe. The war ended in 1945 when the Allies took control of Germany, Hitler killed himself, and Japan was defeated as a result of the atom bombs being dropped on the cities of *Hiroshima and *Nagasaki. Germany and Japan surrendered separately in 1945.

Over 50 million people were killed in the war, more than 20 million of them Russians. World War II is also remembered for the very large number of Jewish and other people killed in German concentration camps and the harsh treatment of prisoners of war captured by the Japanese. See also D-DAY, DUNKIRK, MIDWAY.

World Wars I and II – the legacy ⇨ article.

ˌ**Wormwood** ˈ**Scrubs** /ˌwɜːmwʊd ˈskrʌbz; *AmE* ˌwɜːrmwʊd/ (*also infml* **the Scrubs**) a prison for male prisoners in west London. It was built in 1874–90, partly by prisoners being kept there.

ˈ**Worship** /ˈwɜːʃɪp; *AmE* ˈwɜːrʃɪp/ **Your/His/Her Worship** (in Britain) the title used when speaking or referring to certain important officials, particularly magistrates and *mayors: *May I say something, Your Worship?*

ˌ**Wounded** ˈ**Knee** /ˌwuːndɪd ˈniː/ a small river in the US state of *South Dakota where US soldiers killed more than 200 *Native-American men, women and children of the *Sioux people on 29 December 1890. This was the final major battle of the *Indian wars. In 1973 members of the American Indian Movement occupied a community there for over two months, demanding that the US Senate take action to help Native Americans.

WRAC /ræk/ ⇨ WOMEN'S ROYAL ARMY CORPS.

the **WRAF** /ræf/ (*in full* the **Women's Royal Air Force**) the women's section of the *RAF for most of the 20th century. In 1992 it combined with the RAF.

ˈ**Wranglers**™ /ˈræŋgləz; *AmE* ˈræŋglərz/ a make of *jeans which is popular in Britain and the US, made by the Wrangler company: *a new pair of Wranglers.*

The ˌ***Wreck of the*** ˈ***Hesperus*** /ˈhespərəs/ a poem by the US poet Henry Wadsworth *Longfellow. It was in his collection *Ballads and Other Poems* (1841), which also included *The *Village Blacksmith.* It tells the story of a father and his small daughter who die when their ship hits rocks during a storm. It includes these lines:

'O father! I see a gleaming light.
Oh, say, what may it be?'
But the father answered never a word,
A frozen corpse was he.

The phrase *like the wreck of the Hesperus* is may be used to mean 'very untidy' or 'in a ruined state'.

Wren[1] /ren/ *n* a member of the *WRNS.

ˌChristopher ˈ**Wren**[2] /ˈren/ (1632–1723) one of the most famous English architects, known especially for designing the present *St Paul's Cathedral (where he is buried) and other churches in London that replaced those destroyed in the *Great Fire of London. Among other buildings he designed are *Chelsea Hospital, *Marlborough House, the *Royal Naval College and parts of *Hampton Court. His buildings combined the *baroque style with the classical style. He was also a scientist and astronomer and one of the group of people who established the *Royal Society. He was made a *knight in 1673.

ˈ**wrestling** *n* [U] a sport in which two people (usually men) fight, each trying to force the other onto the ground, using a variety of holds. The popular variety of it is more of an entertainment than a serious sport, with the competitors wearing colourful costumes and crowds being encouraged to cheer or insult them. Many people think that the fights are merely a performance, with the results arranged before they start.

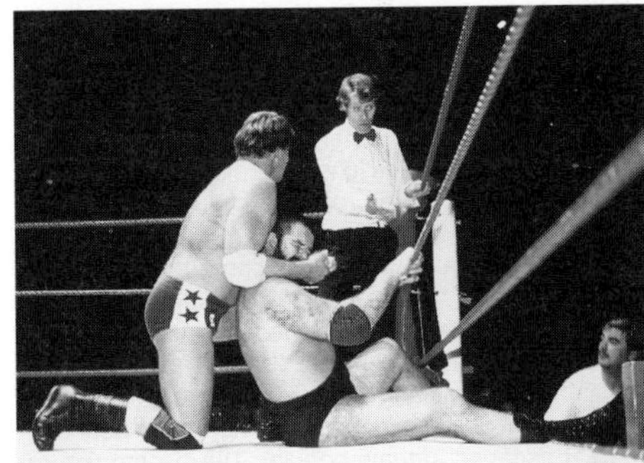

wrestling

ˈFrank ˈLloyd ˈ**Wright**[1] /ˈlɔɪd ˈraɪt/ (1869–1959) a leading US architect who helped to develop modern architecture. His 'prairie-style' houses used long, low lines and open spaces inside, and his 'organic' buildings were designed to match their natural surroundings and often used their materials. One of Wright's best-known buildings is the *Guggenheim Museum.

ˌRichard ˈ**Wright**[2] /ˈraɪt/ (1908–60) an *African-American writer whose best-known books are the novel **Native Son* and his own life story, *Black Boy* (1945). He also wrote a collection of stories, *Uncle Tom's Children* (1938). Wright was a Communist for many years. He lived in Paris after *World War II and died there.

the ˈ**Wright** ˌ**brothers** /ˈraɪt/ **Wilbur Wright** (1867–1912) and **Orville Wright** (1871–1948), US engineers who built the first successful aircraft that used an engine and was heavier than air. They first flew their aircraft, called Flyer, on four successful flights on 17 December 1903 near Kitty Hawk, *North Carolina. Their longest flight was 852 feet/260 metres, and lasted 59 seconds.

ˈ**Wrigley's**™ /ˈrɪgliz/ *n* [U] chewing gum made by the US William Wrigley Jr Company of *Chicago. It is available in several different flavours, including Wrigley's Peppermint, Spearmint, Doublemint,

World Wars I and II – the legacy

Memories of war

Few soldiers who fought in *World War I (1914–8) are still alive, but many people have heard stories of the war from parents and grandparents and most have seen old films of the fighting. The victory of Britain and her *Allies in what used to be called the *Great War is remembered mainly for the horror of trench warfare (= fighting by soldiers sheltering in deep ditches) and for the millions who were killed. Poems by Rupert *Brooke and Wilfred *Owen, both of whom died in the war, and by Siegfried *Sassoon, describe the different moods of war and the feeling of tragic waste.

One of the few positive results was a growing confidence among women, many of whom worked in factories or on farms in the place of men who had gone to fight. Shortly after the war ended women gained the right to vote.

British people who remember *World War II (1939–45) often think of it with pride. Unlike the earlier war, it was fought to defend clear moral and national values. The whole population was also more directly involved. Stories of the *Blitz, when London and other British cities were bombed by German aircraft and people took shelter together, and of the escape from *Dunkirk, when many small boats sailed across the Channel to rescue trapped soldiers, bring back memories of a time when everyone 'pulled together'.

News of the war reached people far more quickly through *BBC *radio broadcasts. The BBC also provided a light entertainment programme for the forces which, after the war, became the Light Programme, later *Radio 2. Many books have been written about the war, and the paintings of Paul *Nash and other war artists are displayed in art galleries. Television films and documentaries about the war, especially those featuring heroic acts or great escapes, remain popular. The *Home Guard, which trained men who were not part of the regular forces to defend the country, has been the subject of an often repeated comedy series, **Dad's Army*.*

Recrimination and remembrance

After the war Nazis were tried for war crimes at the *Nuremberg Trials. Some veterans still feel hatred towards the Germans. Former prisoners-of-war of the Japanese continue to demand compensation for their sufferings, and many Jews are trying to reclaim money taken from them by the Nazis.

Many people who lived through World War II worry that young people are ignorant of what happened and must be reminded of the suffering, particularly that of the Jews in concentration camps, in order to make sure that a similar thing does not happen again. Others think that it is better now to put the past aside. But each year, on ***Remembrance Sunday***, British people remember the dead of both wars in religious services and parades. People wear red paper poppies as a symbol of the poppies that grew on the fields of *Flanders and lay poppy wreaths at hundreds of **war memorials** where the names of those who died are listed. Remembrance Sunday is important to many people, especially since people who died in more recent conflicts are also remembered then.

The rise of America

The wars changed America's opinion of itself and its role in the world. George *Washington had warned his country not to become involved in the affairs of other nations, and for a long time the US followed a policy of *isolationism. Since Americans came from a variety of national backgrounds, there was in any case a confusion of old loyalties. But the predominantly Anglo-American culture and attacks by German submarines on ships like the **Lusitania* carrying American passengers convinced America to support the Allies and send its first force ever to Europe in 1918. 'The Yanks are coming!' warned America's favourite song, **Over There*.

This was the beginning of a new closeness between the US and Britain. Americans bought *Liberty Bonds to support the war effort and had 'heatless Mondays' to save coal. There were also more jobs and better pay, and women began to do jobs traditionally done by men. *African Americans moved from the agricultural South to factories in the North, an event which was to change the character of both regions.

Americans were proud of the part they played in World War I, but many were still uncertain that the problems of distant countries were worth American lives. They hesitated to send armed forces back to Europe, even against Hitler. America only joined in the fighting after Japan attacked its base at *Pearl Harbor. The dropping of atom bombs on *Hiroshima and *Nagasaki by US planes ended the war in the east but showed the horrors of a new kind of war.

As in Britain, the war brought people closer together. *Hollywood films praised the soldiers, and songs like *Boogie Woogie Bugle Boy* were popular for years. Americans who died are remembered on *Memorial Day and *Veterans' Day, and many people visit *Arlington National Cemetery and the Tomb of the *Unknowns. In many ways the war was good for the US. It ended the *Great Depression and led to many technological developments.

World War II also forced the US into becoming a world power, a position it soon grew to like. Its new role as 'the world's policeman' led America into the disaster of the *Vietnam War but also helped bring freedom to South Korea and Kuwait. The continued presence of US forces in Europe and the Far East after the war also helped spread American culture.

Post-war politics

The two world wars led to some important political changes. In 1920 the *League of Nations was set up. Over 40 nations became founder members, agreeing to take disputes to the League before declaring war, but despite the fact that it was the idea of Woodrow *Wilson, the US did not join it. The League was too weak to prevent another war but in 1945 it was the basis for a new international peace-keeping organization, the *United Nations.

In Europe, increasingly tight Russian control over East Germany after 1945 led to greater cooperation between the countries of western Europe and the US. This resulted in 1949 in the founding of *NATO. In the same year the *Council of Europe was founded to encourage cooperation between European governments, and in 1951 the Treaty of Paris led to the setting up of a trade organization which later became the *European Union.

Juicy Fruit, Freedent and Big Red, as well as Hubba Bubba bubble gum.

ˈ**write-in ˌcandidate** *n* (*AmE*) a candidate in an election for public office whose name is not printed on the official list of candidates, usually because he or she has not been selected by a political party. People voting for such a candidate must therefore write his or her name on the voting paper. Some use this **write-in vote**, or **write-in**, as a form of protest by writing ridiculous names on the voting paper.

the **WRNS** /ˌdʌblju: ɑ:r en ˈes/ (*in full* the **Women's Royal Naval Service**) (*also* the **Wrens**) the female section of the British *Royal Navy. It was established in 1917 and until 1990 its members could not serve on ships. In 1993 the WRNS became officially part of the Royal Navy and ceased to exist as a separate section.

WRVS /ˌdʌblju: ɑ: vi: ˈes; *AmE* ɑ:r/ ⇨ WOMEN'S ROYAL VOLUNTARY SERVICE.

ˌ***Wuthering*** ˈ***Heights*** /ˌwʌðərɪŋ/ the only novel (1847) by Emily *Brontë. The story is set on the *Yorkshire Moors and is about the intense relationship between Catherine Earnshaw and *Heathcliff, which leads to many problems and sad events. Laurence *Olivier played Heathcliff in the 1939 film version, directed by William *Wyler. In the 1978 it was the subject of a successful pop song by Kate Bush, and in the 1990s it was made into a musical show, with Cliff *Richard as Heathcliff.

ˌWilliam ˈ**Wycherley** /ˈwɪtʃəli; *AmE* ˈwɪtʃərli/ (1640–1716) an English writer of *Restoration comedy plays. His best-known play is *The Country Wife* (1675), which is still performed today and which has as its theme the immoral behaviour of a section of the society of his time.

ˌJohn ˈ**Wycliffe** /ˈwɪklɪf/ (*c.* 1330–84) an English writer on religion who criticized various bad practices that were common in the Church at that time. He said that the Bible, not the Church, was the most important religious authority, and was involved in translating the Bible into English. The group who supported his beliefs were called *Lollards.

the **Wye** /waɪ/ a river that flows from *Powys in central Wales, passes through the city of *Hereford(1) in England and forms, in one section, the border between Wales and England. It is 130 miles/210 kilometres long and flows into the sea in the *Bristol Channel.

ˌAndrew ˈ**Wyeth** /ˈwaɪəθ/ (1917–) a US painter whose realistic pictures often show the people or lonely countryside of *Pennsylvania and *Maine. His best-known work is probably *Christina's World* (1948).

ˈ**Wykehamist** /ˈwɪkəmɪst/ *n* a pupil or former pupil at *Winchester(2) College school. Wykehamists are named after the man who established the school, *William of Wykeham.

ˌWilliam ˈ**Wyler** /ˈwaɪlə(r)/ (1902–81) a US film director, born in Germany and known for his great attention to detail. He won *Oscars for directing *Mrs Miniver* (1942), *The Best Years of Our Lives* (1946) and **Ben-Hur* (1959). His other films include **Wuthering Heights* (1939), *Roman Holiday* (1953), *The Big Country* (1958) and *Funny Girl* (1968).

ˌJane ˈ**Wyman** /ˈwaɪmən/ (1914–) a US actor who was the first wife of Ronald *Reagan. She won an *Oscar for her role as a girl who could not speak or hear in *Johnny Belinda* (1948). Her other films include *The Lost Weekend* (1945), *The Yearling* (1946) and *Magnificent Obsession* (1954).

ˌJohn ˈ**Wyndham** /ˈwɪndəm/ (1903–69) an English writer of science fiction novels, including *The Day of the Triffids* (1951), *The Chrysalids* (1955) and *The Midwich Cuckoos* (1957). His books are often about how people deal with disasters, both natural ones and those created by humans.

ˌTammy **Wy**ˈ**nette** /ˌtæmi wɪˈnet/ (1942–98) a popular US *country music singer with a strong, sad voice. Her best-known song was *Stand By Your Man* (1968). She was married for a time to the singer George Jones, and they often sang songs together about their difficult marriage, including *D-I-V-O-R-C-E* (1969), *We're Gonna Hold On* (1973) and *Golden Rings* (1976). Wynette was chosen for the Country Music *Hall of Fame in 1998.

Wyˈ**oming** /waɪˈəʊmɪŋ; *AmE* waɪˈoʊmɪŋ/ one of the *Rocky Mountain States in the western central US. It is also called the Equality State because it was the first state to give women the right to vote (in 1869). Although is the 10th largest state it has the smallest population (about 481 000 in 1996). The capital and largest city is Cheyenne. Wyoming was part of the *Louisiana Purchase and became a state in 1890. Its products now include wheat, wool, oil, gas, wood and stone. Tourist attractions include *Yellowstone National Park, Grand Teton National Park, Fort Laramie National Historic Site and the Cheyenne Frontier Days celebration.

Xx Yy Zz

X-Acto™ /ɪɡˈzæktəʊ; *AmE* ɪɡˈzæktoʊ/ *n* (*pl* **-os**) a US make of knife with thin steel blades which can be changed. It is used for delicate work, e.g. by artists to cut paper accurately and by people building model aircraft.

ˈ**X certificate** /ˈeks/ a label formerly given to certain cinema films in Britain by the British Board of Film Censors (now called the *British Board of Film Classification). Films were given an X certificate if they were considered to be not suitable for people under 18, usually because they contained violence, sex or bad language. Young people under 18 were not allowed to go into cinemas to see such films. In 1982, the label 'X certificate' was changed to '18', but people still sometimes use the old name informally.

ˈ**Xerox**™ /ˈzɪərɒks; *AmE* ˈzɪrɑːks/ a large US company that produces copying and printing machines, as well as scanners (= devices that copy documents, etc. onto a computer screen) and faxes. Its name is based on the process of 'xerography' (meaning 'dry writing') which the company developed. Xerox's international companies include Rank Xerox in Europe and Fuji Xerox in Japan. People sometimes use the word 'xerox' as a noun meaning any photographic copy and the verb 'to xerox' meaning 'to make a photographic copy of something'.

The ˈ***X-files*** /ˈeks/ a popular US television series that began in 1993 and is widely shown in other countries. It is about two members of the FBI, Agent Mulder (David Duchovny) and Agent Scully (Gillian Anderson), who investigate mysterious events suggesting other forms of life in space. There has also been a film, *The X-Files* (1998).

the **Y** /waɪ/ (*AmE*) an informal short form for the *YMCA(1) or the *YWCA(1).

Yaˈ**hoo** /jɑːˈhuː/ *n* any of an imaginary race of creatures in **Gulliver's Travels* by Jonathan *Swift. The Yahoos are animals with human form who behave in a rude, aggressive manner. The word *yahoo* is now used to mean a rude, violent and aggressive person.

ˌ**Yale Uni**ˈ**versity** /ˌjeɪl/ a major US university, often seen as a rival of *Harvard University. It is in New Haven, *Connecticut, and is known for its large library, the Yale Art Gallery and the Peabody Museum of Natural History. Yale was established (originally as Yale College) in 1701 and was named after Elihu Yale (1649–1721) who gave it books and other items. See also IVY LEAGUE.

ˈ**Yalta** /ˈjæltə/ a holiday town by the sea in the Ukraine in the former USSR, where the **Yalta Conference** took place in February 1945. The leaders of the *Allies, Winston *Churchill, Franklin D *Roosevelt and Joseph Stalin, met to agree on plans to defeat Germany in *World War II, to decide on what the borders of various countries in Europe would be after the war ended, and to make plans for setting up the *United Nations.

ˈ**Yankee** /ˈjæŋki/ **1** (*also* **Yank**) (*BrE infml, sometimes disapprov*) a person from the US; an American. **2** (*often disapprov*) (in the southern US) a person from the northern states. US soldiers and people from the North were called Yankees during the *Civil War. **3** (in the US, especially the northern states) a person from *New England.

ˌ***Yankee*** ˈ***Doodle*** /ˌjæŋki ˈduːdl/ a popular 18th-century marching song which has become almost a national song in the US. It was first sung by British soldiers to make fun of Americans during the *American Revolution, but then became popular with George *Washington's soldiers.'Yankee' probably comes from 'Janke', the Dutch for 'Johnny' and a common name in early New York. 'Doodle' is an old-fashioned English word meaning a stupid person. The song begins:

Yankee Doodle came to town:
Riding on a pony;
He stuck a feather in his cap
And called it macaroni.

ˌ***Yankee Doodle*** ˈ***Dandy*** /ˌjæŋki ˌduːdl ˈdændi/ a lively song written by George M *Cohan for his *Broadway musical play *Little Johnny Jones* (1904). It became a favourite American song for *Independence Day and during the world wars. The song begins:

I'm a Yankee Doodle Dandy,
A Yankee Doodle, do or die,
A real live nephew of my Uncle Sam,
Born on the Fourth of July.

the ˈ**Yankees** /ˈjæŋkiz/ the New York City professional baseball team. It has won 23 *World Series, more than any other team. Famous Yankee players have included 'Babe' *Ruth, Lou *Gehrig and Joe *DiMaggio. The team plays its home games in the famous **Yankee Stadium** in the *Bronx.

The **Yard** an informal name for *Scotland Yard or *New Scotland Yard, referring both to the *Metropolitan Police and to its head offices in central London.

ˌW B ˈ**Yeats** /ˈjeɪts/ (William Butler Yeats 1865–1939) a leading Irish writer of poetry, plays and stories. His best-known works of poetry include *The Wild Swans at Coole* (1917), *The Winding Stair* (1933) and *Collected Poems* (1933). His plays include *The Land of Heart's Desire* (1894) and *The Green Helmet* (1910), and several were written to be performed at the Abbey Theatre in Dublin, which he helped to establish. His book of stories, *The Celtic Twilight*, created a lot of interest in traditional Irish stories. Yeats was also much involved in politics as a nationalist and became a *Senator in the Irish parliament (1922–8). He received the *Nobel Prize for literature in 1923.

the ˌ**Yellow Brick** ˈ**Road** a course of action that a person takes believing that it will lead to good things. It comes from the Yellow Brick Road in *The *Wizard of Oz* which Dorothy and her friends follow to the Emerald City.

ˌ**yellow** ˈ**journalism** *n* [U] a type of journalism that exaggerates news stories and deliberately includes exciting or shocking material in order to attract readers. The name comes from the *Yellow Kid* *comic strip which began in the New York *World* in 1895 and used yellow ink to attract readers' attention. Newspapers that include yellow journalism are often called the **yellow press**.

the ˌ***Yellow*** ˈ***Pages***™ a book (or in the US sometimes part of a book) printed on yellow paper and containing the telephone numbers and addresses of companies, arranged in alphabetical order according to the kind of business they are involved in. There are different versions for each area of the country. In Britain the *Yellow Pages* are published by *British Telecom and sent to every home, office, etc. with a telephone in the country. In the US, where the *Yellow Pages* began, the books are published by regional telephone companies and sent to their customers. A well-known advertisement for the *Yellow Pages* uses the phrase 'Let your fingers do the walking': *If you need a local builder, try looking in the Yellow Pages.*

ˌyellow ˈribbon *n* (in the US) a piece of yellow ribbon used as a sign to show that people, especially those in the armed forces, are not forgotten while they are away from home. Yellow ribbons are often tied round trees. The practice began during the *Vietnam War and was later used during the Iranian *hostage crisis and the *Gulf War. *Tie A Yellow Ribbon Round the Ole* (= Old) *Oak Tree* was a very popular song in 1973.

ˈYellowstone ˈNational ˈPark /ˈjeləʊstəʊn; *AmE* ˈjeloʊstoʊn/ the first US national park, established in 1872, and one of the largest. It covers about 3 500 square miles/9 065 square kilometres in north-west *Wyoming and parts of *Idaho and *Montana. It has many wild animals, including bears and buffalo, and is famous for its fine scenery, hot springs and geysers (= underground hot springs that shoot hot water or steam up into the air). The park has about 3 million visitors a year. It was made a *World Heritage Site in 1978. See also OLD FAITHFUL.

ye ˈolde /jiː ˈəʊld; *AmE* ˈoʊld/ a phrase meaning 'the old' in an old form of English. (The old letter 'y' represented what is now written as 'th'.) The phrase is now sometimes used in the names of restaurants, shops, pubs or hotels in Britain to show or pretend that they are very old: *Ye Olde Tea Shoppe.*

Yeomen Warders

ˌYeoman ˈWarder *n* (*pl* **ˌYeomen ˈWarders**) any of the group of men who guard the *Tower of London. They are thought to have existed since the *White Tower was built in the 11th century. They wear a red uniform from the *Tudor(1) period similar to that worn by the *Yeomen of the Guard and are also called *beefeaters. For visitors to London, they are often seen as one of the symbols of the city.

the **ˌYeomen of the ˈGuard** *n* [pl] a military unit of men who traditionally guard the British king or queen at certain ceremonies. It was created in 1485 for the ceremony in which *Henry VII became king. Its members still wear a red uniform in the *Tudor(1) style of that period, similar to that worn by *Yeomen Warders, though the two groups are quite separate.

The ***ˌYeomen of the ˈGuard*** one of the operas by *Gilbert and *Sullivan[1]. It is about a man who gets married just before he is to be executed in the *Tower of London and is then told that he has been forgiven and will not be *executed after all.

ˌYerkes Obˈservatory /ˌjɜːkiːz; *AmE* ˌjɜːrkiːz/ the observatory (= a building from which to study the stars, weather, etc.) of the University of Chicago in the US. It was built in 1892 at Lake Geneva, *Wisconsin, with money given by Charles Yerkes. It contains the world's largest refracting telescope (= an instrument that uses light rays to make distant objects appear much larger).

ˈYes, ˌMinister a popular *BBC television comedy series (1980–5), which made fun of those involved in politics. The main characters are a government minister who is often not sure how to solve problems affecting his work and career, and a senior member of the *Civil Service, whose job is to advise him and who creates complicated plans for solving these problems and protecting his own position. In a later series, *Yes, Prime Minister* (1986–7), the minister had become *prime minister.

YHA /ˌwaɪ eɪtʃ ˈeɪ/ ⇨ YOUTH HOSTELS ASSOCIATION.

the **YMCA** /ˌwaɪ em siː ˈeɪ/ **1** (*in full* the **Young Men's Christian Association**) a Christian organization that offers a wide range of religious, educational, sports and social activities to young men of all races, religions and social backgrounds. It was established in Britain in 1844 and now operates in many countries around the world. It is known especially for its hostels (= places offering cheap food and accommodation). **2** *n* a building owned and run by the YMCA: *I stayed in a YMCA in London for two weeks.* See also Y.

ˌYogi ˈBear /ˌjəʊgi; *AmE* ˌjoʊgi/ a US television cartoon character created in 1958 by *Hanna and Barbera. Yogi is a cheerful bear who wears a flat hat and white collar and lives in Jellystone National Park with his small bear friend Boo Boo. He is always trying to steal food. See also BERRA.

yoof /juːf/ *n* [U] (*BrE infml humor, usu disapprov*) young people in general, especially when seen as a group for whom a particular product or type of entertainment is designed. The word was invented in the 1980s as a deliberate wrong spelling of *youth.* It implies that much of what is produced for young people assumes that they are not very intelligent: *I find the whole notion of yoof culture pretty depressing.*

ˈYorick /ˈjɒrɪk; *AmE* ˈjɔːrɪk/ a former court jester (= a man employed to amuse the king in the *Middle Ages) whose skull is found by the men digging Ophelia's grave in the *Shakespeare's play **Hamlet.* Hamlet picks up the skull and makes a famous speech, which begins:

Alas, poor Yorick. I knew him, Horatio;
A fellow of infinite jest ...

York[1] /jɔːk; *AmE* jɔːrk/ a city in the English county of *North Yorkshire, on the River *Ouse, known especially for its ancient buildings, including *York Minster. It was an important city in Roman times and in the *Middle Ages, and it was the most important city in the *Anglo-Saxon region of *Northumbria. The city has many visitors and its attractions include the *National Railway Museum and the Jorvik Viking Centre, which has exhibitions about the period when people from Scandinavia invaded Britain.

the ˌDuchess of ˈ**York**[2] /ˈjɔːk; *AmE* ˈjɔːrk/ (1959–) the title given to Sarah *Ferguson after her marriage in 1986 to Prince *Andrew, Duke of *York[3](1). The royal couple had two children, Princess Beatrice and Princess Eugenie, but separated in 1992. The Duchess is often referred to informally as 'Fergie'.

the Duchess of York

the ˌDuke of ˈ**York**[3] /jɔːk; *AmE* ˈjɔːrk/ **1** (1960–) Andrew, the third child of Queen *Elizabeth II. He was educated at *Gordonstoun in Scotland, a college in Ontario, Canada, and the *Royal Naval College, Dartmouth. He became a helicopter pilot in the *Royal Navy, and took part in the *Falklands War. He used to be known as 'Prince Andrew', but in 1986 the Queen made him the Duke of York. He married Sarah *Ferguson in that year, and she therefore became the Duchess of York. They had two daughters, Princess Beatrice, born in 1988, and Princess Eugenie, born in 1990. In 1992 the Duke and Duchess separated, though they still remain friends. ⇨ article at ROYAL FAMILY. **2** (1763–1827) the second son of King *George III, who was a soldier. There is a well-known *nursery rhyme about him that begins:

Oh, the grand old Duke of York,
He had ten thousand men;
He marched them up to the top of the hill,
And he marched them down again.

3 a title given to various second sons of kings and queens of Britain since 1474, when King *Edward IV gave it to his son Richard. King *Henry VIII held the title of Duke of York before he became king.

the ˌHouse of ˈ**York**[4] /ˈjɔːk; *AmE* ˈjɔːrk/ the English royal house (= family) to which the kings of England between 1461 and 1485 belonged. They were *Edward IV, *Edward V and *Richard III, and were descended from the first Duke of York, Edmund of Langley (1341–1402). See also WARS OF THE ROSES.

ˈ**Yorkist** /ˈjɔːkɪst; *AmE* ˈjɔːrkɪst/ *n* a member or supporter of the House of *York. ▶ **Yorkist** *adj.*

ˌ**York** ˈ**Minster** /ˌjɔːk; *AmE* ˌjɔːrk/ the cathedral in the city of *York[1] and one of the largest and best-known in Britain. It was built during the 13th, 14th and 15th centuries and is famous for its beautiful stained glass windows. A serious fire in 1984 damaged parts of the building, but it has since been repaired.

ˈ**Yorkshire** /ˈjɔːkʃə(r); *AmE* ˈjɔːrkʃər/ a former county in north-east England. In 1974 it was divided into two new counties, *North Yorkshire and *Humberside, and two *metropolitan counties, *West Yorkshire and *South Yorkshire. The two metropolitan counties are now ordinary counties. See also RIDING.

the ˌ**Yorkshire** ˈ**Dales** /ˌjɔːkʃə; *AmE* ˌjɔːrkʃər/ *n* [pl] an area of countryside, valleys and villages in the north of England. They are mainly in the county of *North Yorkshire but also partly in *Cumbria. The area became a *national park in 1954. It is considered one of the most beautiful areas in England and is especially popular with British people on walking holidays or making tours around it by car.

the ˌ**Yorkshire** ˈ**Moors** /ˌjɔːkʃə; *AmE* ˌjɔːrkʃər/ *n* [pl] areas of high, open land with few trees in *North Yorkshire, England. They include the area known as the North York Moors.

ˌ**Yorkshire** ˈ**pudding** /ˌjɔːkʃə; *AmE* ˌjɔːrkʃər/ *n* [C, U] a British dish made by baking a mixture of flour, eggs and milk, usually in separate pieces like small cakes. Yorkshire pudding is usually eaten with roast beef as part of a traditional Sunday lunch. See also SUNDAY ROAST.

the ˌ**Yorkshire** ˈ**Ripper** /ˌjɔːkʃə ˈrɪpə(r); *AmE* ˌjɔːrkʃər/ the name given by the press to Peter Sutcliffe, an Englishman who murdered thirteen women and tried to kill several more in the north of England in the 1970s, before he was caught in 1981. The name was meant to suggest that his crimes were similar to those of *Jack the Ripper.

ˌ**Yorkshire** ˈ**terrier** /ˌjɔːkʃə; *AmE* ˌjɔːrkʃər/ *n* a breed of small *terrier dog with long, straight, shiny hair that is dark grey or brown. It was originally bred in *Yorkshire.

Yorkshire TV /ˌjɔːkʃə tiː ˈviː; *AmE* ˌjɔːrkʃər/ an independent television company, based in *Leeds, which broadcasts programmes shown in the area in the north-east of England formerly called *Yorkshire. In 1993 it joined with *Tyne Tees Television to form a single company.

ˈ**Yorktown** /ˈjɔːktaʊn; *AmE* ˈjɔːrktaʊn/ the town in south-east *Virginia where the final military campaign of the *American Revolution took place. The British army, led by General Charles *Cornwallis, were surrounded there in 1781 by 16 000 American and French soldiers. The surrender of Cornwallis to General George *Washington ended the war.

Yoˈ**semite** ˈ**National** ˈ**Park** /jəʊˈseməti; *AmE* joʊˈseməti/ a US national park in the *Sierra Nevada mountains of eastern *California. It was established in 1890 and covers 1 189 square miles/3 080 square kilometres. It was named after the **Yosemite River** that runs through it and contains **Yosemite Falls**, the highest waterfall in the US (2 425 feet/740 metres). The park is also famous for its many giant *sequoia trees. It was made a *World Heritage Site in 1984. See also REDWOOD.

Yoˌ**semite** ˈ**Sam** /jəʊˌseməti; *AmE* jəʊˌseməti/ a US cartoon character created for *Warner Brothers in 1948. He is a very short *cowboy with guns, a long red moustache and a bad temper. His regular opponent is *Bugs Bunny.

ˌAndrew ˈ**Young**[1] /ˈjʌŋ/ (1932–) a leader in the US *civil rights movement. He was a member of the US House of Representatives (1973–7) and the first African-American representative to the *United Nations (1977–9) where he was known for his strong, open comments. He later became *mayor of Atlanta (1982–9).

ˌBrigham ˈ**Young**[2] /ˌbrɪgəm ˈjʌŋ/ (1801–77) the US leader of the *Mormons who brought them to *Utah in 1846–7 and established *Salt Lake City. He became the first Governor of the Utah Territory in 1850. He is believed to have had 27 wives. See also SMITH[9].

ˈˌCy' ˈ**Young**[3] /ˌsaɪ ˈjʌŋ/ (1867–1955) a famous US *baseball player (1890–1911). He was a pitcher (= player who throws the ball to be hit) who played in more games (906) and had more wins (511) than any other player in the history of the game. His real name was Denton True Young. He played for the Cleveland Indians, the St Louis Cardinals, the Boston Red Sox and the Boston Braves. He was chosen for the National Baseball *Hall of Fame in 1937.

ˌJimmy ˈ**Young**[4] /ˈjʌŋ/ (1923–) a popular British radio broadcaster who has had his own programme every morning from Monday to Friday on *Radio 2 since 1973. It combines popular music and other entertainment with more serious parts, including discussion of news items and interviews with politicians. Young began his career as a singer and he was also one of the original disc jockeys on *Radio 1 when it was established in 1967.

ˌWhitney ˈ**Young**[5] /ˌwɪtni ˈjʌŋ/ (1921–71) an *African-American leader during the *civil rights movement. He was head of the *National Urban League (1961–70). Young was criticized by some African Americans because he made compromises with white political leaders, but he had great influence.

the ˈ**Younger ˌbrothers** /ˈjʌŋgə; *AmE* ˈjʌŋgər/ four US outlaws (= criminals) in the *Wild West. The best-known of the four brothers were **Cole Younger** (1844–1916) and **Jim Younger** (1848–1902). They were cousins of Jesse and Frank *James, and the group was sometimes called the James-Younger Gang. Three of the brothers were captured and sent to prison after trying to rob a bank in Northfield, *Minnesota in 1876. There have been several films about them. See also QUANTRILL'S RAIDERS.

the ˌ**Young Men's ˈChristian Assoˌciˌation** ⇨ YMCA.

ˌ**young ofˈfender instiˌtution** *n* a type of prison in Britain for young people who have committed crimes. Young offender institutions contain people aged 15–17 who have been found guilty in *youth courts and people aged 18–20 who have been found guilty in ordinary courts for adults. They were called *Borstals until 1983.

the ˌ**Young Preˈtender** a *nickname of Charles Edward *Stuart (1720–88), also known as *Bonny Prince Charlie. A pretender is a person who claims something, usually the right to be a king or queen, although not everyone agrees that the claim is just. See also FORTY-FIVE, OLD PRETENDER.

ˌ**Young Women's ˈChristian Assoˌciˌation** ⇨ YWCA.

ˈ**youth court** *n* (in England and Wales) a court of law for young people aged 10–17 accused of committing crimes. Three magistrates (at least one of whom is always a woman) decide whether the accused person is guilty or not. The cases are held privately and the names of those accused are usually not published. Young people aged 10–14 can only be found guilty if it is proved that they knew that what they were doing was legally and morally wrong. Youth courts were formerly known as *juvenile courts. See also ATTENDANCE CENTRE, COMMUNITY SERVICE, YOUNG OFFENDER INSTITUTION.

the ˈ**Youth Hostels Assoˌciˌation** (*abbr* the **YHA**) an organization that provides cheap accommodation (called **youth hostels**) for people who are travelling from place to place, usually on holiday, and who are members of the organization. It was established in Britain in 1930 and now operates in many countries around the world. Although mostly young people stay in youth hostels, people of any age can become members.

Youth organizations ⇨ article.

ˌ**Youth ˈTraining** (*abbr* **YT**) a British government system, introduced in the 1980s, by which young people, especially those who have just left school and have no job, are given training and other help so that they can gain qualifications that will help them to get jobs. The system has been criticized by some people as a waste of time and an attempt by the government to reduce the number of people who are officially unemployed. The system is run by the *Training and Enterprise Councils.

ˈ**Ypres** /ˈiːprə/ a town in Belgium near which three separate battles (1914, 1915 and 1917) were fought in *World War I. In the first the *British Expeditionary Force suffered terrible losses, the second involved the first use of poisonous gas as a weapon by the Germans, and the third resulted in the deaths of over half a million men.

the **YWCA** /ˌwaɪ dʌbljuː siː ˈeɪ/ **1** (*in full* the **Young Women's Christian Association**) a Christian organization, similar to but separate from the *YMCA(1), which provides accommodation for young women living away from home. It was established in Britain in 1855 and now operates in many countries around the world. **2** *n* a building owned and run by the YWCA: *When I first moved to the city, I lived in a YWCA.* See also Y.

ˈˈBabe' ˈDidrikson **Zaˈharias** /ˈbeɪb ˈdɪdrɪksn zəˈhæriəs/ ⇨ DIDRIKSON.

ˈ**Zambia** /ˈzæmbiə/ a country in southern central Africa. As Northern Rhodesia it was formerly part of the *British Empire and became independent and a member of the *Commonwealth in 1964. Zambia has many minerals and produces a large amount of the world's copper. Its official language is English and its capital city is Lusaka. ▶ **Zambian** *adj, n.*

ˌDarryl F ˈ**Zanuck** /ˌdærəl, ˈzænək/ (Darryl Francis Zanuck 1902–79) a US film producer. After working for *Warner Brothers he formed his own company, which became *20th Century Fox. Darryl Zanuck's successful films included *The *Grapes of Wrath, The Longest Day* (1962), *How Green Was My Valley* (1941), *The *Sound of Music* and *Patton* (1970). He won a special *Oscar in 1937.

ˌFrank ˈ**Zappa** /ˈzæpə/ (1940–93) a US singer and writer of *rock music who was especially popular with *hippies. He joined the Soul Giants group in 1964 and a year later changed their name to the Mothers of Invention. They were known for 'psychedelic rock', wild stage performances and songs which were deliberately shocking. Their albums included *Freak Out* (1966). Zappa later made the album *Hot Rats* (1970) without the group.

ˈ***Z Cars*** /ˈzed/ a popular *BBC television series (1960–78) about a group of fictional police officers in *Liverpool. It dealt with the problems of ordinary police work in a realistic way and strongly influenced later programmes of this type.

ˌ**zebra ˈcrossing** *n* (*BrE*) (in Britain) an area of road with broad white lines painted on it, at which vehicles must stop if people on foot wish to walk across. Zebra crossings are indicated by *Belisha beacons on each side of the road to warn approaching drivers. The name comes from the zebra, a wild animal similar to a horse with black and white lines on its body.

a zebra crossing

ˈ**Zeebrugge** /ˈzeɪbrʊgə/ ⇨ *HERALD OF FREE ENTERPRISE.*

ˌRobert **Zeˈmeckis** /zəˈmekɪs/ (1952–) a US director and writer of films. He won the *Oscar as 'Best

Z

Youth organizations

Young people in Britain and the US have a wide choice of *clubs and organizations to join. Some clubs concentrate mainly on sports or public service or are connected with a particular religion, though most provide a range of activities. Parents are often keen to support local clubs because they believe they will keep their children off the streets (= stop them from hanging around doing nothing in particular) and out of trouble. But although many children like to go to clubs, older teenagers are often less interested in organized activities and prefer to go to the cinema or a sports centre, or to a club (= nightclub) or bar, when they feel like it.

Scouts and Guides

Among the best-known youth organizations in Britain are the **Scout Association** and the **Guide Association**. They have a total of about 1.5 million British members. In the ***Scouts** boys and girls have an opportunity to learn practical outdoor skills such as map-reading and camping. In the ***Guides**, which is only for girls, the main focus is on practical and social skills. Both associations encourage young people to become responsible citizens.

The equivalent American organizations are called the ***Boy Scouts of America** and the **Girl Scouts of the USA**. Between them, Boy and Girl Scout groups have over 8 million members. Scouts in the US can join special troops that learn about different careers such as medicine and communications.

Religious groups

In the US many churches have youth groups that meet to discuss religion. There are also religious organizations not associated with a particular church. These are usually established so that young Christians can meet together and encourage each other, and also take along their friends and encourage them to become Christians. Examples include **Youth for Christ**, whose first paid member was the *evangelist Billy *Graham, and **Young Life**, which has groups in schools and organizes camps. Many towns also have branches of the ***YMCA** and ***YWCA** (Young Men's and Women's Christian Associations). The **Campus Crusade for Christ** has branches at universities and colleges.

In Britain young children may go to a ***Sunday school** where they learn about the Bible. Older children may join a church youth group. These offer sports and social activities, as well as discussion of religious and moral issues. The ***Boys' Brigade** and **Girls' Brigade** encourage Christian values and their members do *voluntary work in the community. Most British universities have a **Christian Union**.

In both countries there are Muslim and Jewish youth groups, and groups linked to other religions.

Service organizations

Some American service clubs are involved in community projects. The *Kiwanians operate **Key Clubs** for young people and members visit old people and help with collections for charities. Members of the **Big Brothers** and **Big Sisters** clubs spend time with a Little Brother or Little Sister from a disadvantaged family. They become their friend and give help and advice like a real elder brother or sister. In 1998 there were around 500 local groups helping 100 000 children. Many young people from disadvantaged homes belong to the **Boys and Girls Clubs of America**.

In Britain a lot of community work done by young people is organized through schools, and students visit elderly or disadvantaged people on a regular basis. Some children join the **Junior Red Cross** or the **Badgers**, the junior branch of the *St John Ambulance Brigade, and learn first-aid skills.

School and college clubs

Schools have lunchtime and after-school clubs for a range of subjects. Many schools also have student bands, choirs and sports teams. Universities and colleges have subject-based societies to help students on the same course get to know each other. In the US many *high-school and college students also join social *fraternities and *sororities.

American high schools have **school professional clubs**, student organizations associated with various careers. Junior Achievement, for example, helps students learn about economics and business, and students can own small businesses through their schools. Other such clubs include Future Teachers of America and Future Business Leaders of America.

The US Army, Navy and Air Force all have ***ROTC** (Reserve Officers Training Corps) groups at colleges. In Britain there are **CCF** (Combined Cadet Forces) groups at some secondary schools, and **OTC** (Officers' Training Corps) groups at most universities. Members of these groups are given basic military training and are encouraged to consider a career in the armed forces.

Special interest groups

Many towns have clubs for young people interested in dance, drama and music. Some activities, such as youth orchestras, are supported by grants of money from local or national government. Many organizations in Britain now apply for National *Lottery money to buy equipment or pay for a hall.

National societies for people interested in archaeology, natural history, astronomy, etc. have sections for young people. Members of these groups receive magazines and also have a chance to go on field trips or visit museums.

Sports and social activities

In the US many children go to ***summer camp** during school vacation and take part in sports, craftwork and social activites. In Britain local **youth clubs** offer social activities ranging from *snooker and discos to visits to the theatre. Many towns also have leisure centres which run sports programmes for young people in school holidays. ***Outward Bound** centres offer adventure sports such as rock-climbing and canoeing.

Some young people have the opportunity to take part in environmental projects combined with travel and adventure through ***Raleigh International**. The ***Youth Hostels Association**, which has branches in many countries, encourages young people to travel by offering them cheap accommodation.

Members of many youth organizations take part in the ***Duke of Edinburgh's Award Scheme**, which offers medals for achievement in community service and physical recreation.

Director' for **Forrest Gump*. His other films include *Romancing the Stone* (1984), *Back to the Future* (1985), which he wrote, *Who Framed Roger Rabbit* (1988), *Death Becomes Her* (1992) and *Contact* (1997).

ˈ**Zenith** /ˈzenɪθ; *AmE* ˈziːnɪθ/ a leading US company in the production of radio and television equipment, first established in 1918. Its full name is the Zenith Electronics Corporation. For many years it has used the advertising phrase, 'the quality goes in before the name goes on'. It made the world's first portable radio (= one that is easy to carry) and the first practical television remote control device (= one that operates a television from a distance, using electronic signals).

ˌ**zero** ˈ**tolerance** *n* [U] the policy of catching and taking to court people who commit any crime, however minor. It was followed by the police in both Britain and the US in the 1990s as part of a campaign to reduce crime generally.

ˌFlorenz ˈ**Ziegfeld** /ˌflɒrəns ˈziːgfeld; *AmE* ˌflɔːrəns/ (1869–1932) a US theatre manager who produced *Broadway shows. He is remembered especially for the **Ziegfeld Follies**, variety shows which he put on each year from 1907 until his death. They included the beautiful 'Ziegfeld Girls' who danced in a long line. Ziegfeld helped the early careers of many performers, including Fred *Astaire, Will *Rogers and W C *Fields. He also produced **Show Boat*.

Zimˈ**babwe** /zɪmˈbɑːbwi/ a country in southern Africa, formerly called Rhodesia and earlier Southern Rhodesia. It was part of the *British Empire and became independent and a member of the *Commonwealth in 1980. From 1964 until it became independent, Zimbabwe was ruled by a white minority government led by Ian *Smith, who announced a Unilateral Declaration of Independence (UDI) from Britain. After many discussions with the British government, the country became fully independent, with a black majority government led by Robert Mugabe. Its capital city is Harare and its main products include minerals, tobacco and coal. The official language is English. ▶ **Zimbabwean** *adj, n.*

ˌFred ˈ**Zinnemann** /ˈzɪnəmən/ (1907–97) a US film director who won *Oscars for **From Here to Eternity* and *A Man for All Seasons* (1966) but not for his best-known film, **High Noon*. He was born in Austria and went to *Hollywood in 1929. His other films include **Oklahoma!*, *The Nun's Story* (1959) and *The Day of the Jackal* (1973).

ˈ**Zion** ˈ**National** ˈ**Park** /ˈzaɪən/ a US national park in the state of *Utah, established in 1919. It is known for its canyons (= deep, narrow valleys) with rocks of many beautiful colours and unusual shapes.

ˈ**ZIP code** /ˈzɪp/ *n* (*AmE*) a string of numbers following the name of a state at the end of a postal address in the US. 'ZIP' is an abbreviation for the Zone Improvement Plan, a system introduced by the US Postal Service in 1963. The word 'zip' also suggests speed, because the numbers help mail to be delivered quickly. Most ZIP codes have five numbers, but some have nine with a hyphen after the fifth, e.g. NY 10016-4314. Compare POSTAL DISTRICT.

ˈ**Ziploc**™ /ˈzɪplɒk; *AmE* ˈzɪplɑːk/ a US product name for a make of plastic bags with edges that close tightly. Ziploc bags are mostly used for storing food and are made by the Dow Chemical Company.

ˈ**zoning** /ˈzəʊnɪŋ; *AmE* ˈzoʊnɪŋ/ *n* [U] (in US town planning) the process of dividing parts of a town or city into **zones**, areas reserved for either houses, businesses or industries.

ˈ**Zorro** /ˈzɒrəʊ; *AmE* ˈzɔːroʊ/ a character in US *westerns who first appeared in a *comic strip in 1919. Zorro (which means 'the Fox' in Spanish) wears a black mask to hide his real identity when fighting evil. He fights with a sword and sometimes makes a sign like the letter 'Z' with it in the air or even on an enemy's shirt. There have been many Zorro films and a Walt *Disney television series.

ˌAdolph ˈ**Zukor** /ˌædɒlf ˈzuːkə(r); *AmE* ˌædɑːlf ˈzuːkər/ (1873–1976) a US film producer. He was born in Hungary and moved to the US in 1888. In 1912 he began the Famous Players film company which later became *Paramount Pictures. He received a special *Oscar in 1949 for his services to the film industry.

the ˌ**Zulu** ˈ**War** /ˌzuːluː/ a war in South Africa (1879) between Zulu tribes and British armed forces. After several battles the Zulus were finally defeated at Ulundi. See also RORKE'S DRIFT.

ˈ**Zuni** (*also* ˈ**Zuñi**) /ˈzuːni, ˈzuːnji/ *n* (*pl* **Zunis** *or* **Zuni**) a member of a *Native-American *Pueblo people in western *New Mexico. Nearly 6 000 live in the town of Zuni Pueblo, which was established about 1695. The Zunis are now mostly farmers. They are known for making jewellery and for their religious dance ceremonies and colourful costumes.

ˈ**zwieback** /ˈzwiːbæk/ *n* [U] (*AmE*) a type of dry, hard biscuit or sweet cake that is cut into slices and baked. The word means 'twice baked' in German. Zwieback is often given to babies to chew when their teeth are starting to appear.

Pronunciation and phonetic symbols

Stress

The mark /ˈ/ shows a strong (primary) stress. For example, in the word **ˈOxford** the first syllable has a primary stress and the second syllable is unstressed. Unstressed syllables are shown without a mark. A stressed syllable is relatively loud, long in duration, said clearly and distinctly, and made noticeable by the pitch of the voice.

The mark /ˌ/ shows a secondary stress, which is felt to be weaker than a strong stress nearby. For example, in **ˌOxford Uniˈversity** there are two stresses, but the stress on **University** seems stronger because that word carries the main change of pitch (this will generally be a falling pitch when the phrase is said on its own). Many examples with two important words (including names of people such as **ˌJohn ˈBrown**, **ˌJane ˈAusten**) have the same secondary-plus-primary stress pattern.

Sometimes the main stress is not on the last word of a phrase. In this case you must look for the last (or only) primary stress-mark earlier in the phrase. For example, in **ˈOxford Street** the main stress (pitch change) is on **Oxford**, with **Street** said on a low-level pitch. Where they are necessary to show the rhythm, secondary stress marks are put after the main stress as in **ˈOxford ˌMovement** but they do not affect the position of the main stress – again, the main stress is on **Oxford**.

Longer phrases, with more than two important words, are generally shown with several primary stresses. Here the last one should always be made the main stress. For example, in **ˈOxford Uniˈversity ˈPress** there are three fairly equal beats in the rhythm, but the main fall in pitch should come on **Press**.

Pronunciation

Phonetic symbols are used in the dictionary to show pronunciations (both British and American) for uncommon or difficult words. The pronunciations include stress marks which match those shown on the entry words themselves. If there is a difference between British and American pronunciations, the British one is given first, with *AmE* before the American pronunciation. For example, **ˈOxford** /ˈɒksfəd; *AmE* ˈɑːksfərd/. Pronunciations are not shown for ordinary common words (such as **university**, **street**, **movement**) or for common first names (such as **John** or **Jane**). The British pronunciations given are those of younger speakers of General British, which includes RP (Received Pronunciation) and a range of similar accents which are not strongly regional. The American pronunciations chosen are also as far as possible the most general (not associated with any particular region).

Many British speakers use /ɔː/ instead of the diphthong /ʊə/, especially in common words, so that **pure** becomes /ˈpjɔː(r)/, etc.

(r) indicates that British pronunciation will have /r/ only if a vowel sound follows directly at the beginning of the next word as in **far away**; otherwise the /r/ is omitted. For American English, all the /r/ sounds should be pronounced.

The mark /˜/ over a vowel indicates a nasal quality. Nasalized vowels are often retained in certain words or names taken from French.

Consonants

p	pen	/pen/
b	bad	/bæd/
t	tea	/tiː/
d	did	/dɪd/
k	cat	/kæt/
ɡ	get	/ɡet/
tʃ	chin	/tʃɪn/
dʒ	jam	/dʒæm/
f	fall	/fɔːl/
v	van	/væn/
θ	thin	/θɪn/
ð	this	/ðɪs/
s	see	/siː/
z	zoo	/zuː/
ʃ	shoe	/ʃuː/
ʒ	vision	/ˈvɪʒn/
h	hat	/hæt/
m	man	/mæn/
n	now	/naʊ/
ŋ	sing	/sɪŋ/
l	leg	/leɡ/
r	red	/red/
j	yes	/jes/
w	wet	/wet/
x	loch	/lɒx/

Vowels and diphthongs

iː	see	/siː/
i	happy	/ˈhæpi/
ɪ	sit	/sɪt/
e	ten	/ten/
æ	cat	/kæt/
ɑː	father	/ˈfɑːðə(r)/
ɒ	hot	/hɒt/ (*BrE*)
ɔː	saw	/sɔː/
ʊ	put	/pʊt/
u	actual	/ˈæktʃuəl/
uː	too	/tuː/
ʌ	cup	/kʌp/
ɜː	fur	/fɜː(r)/
ə	about	/əˈbaʊt/
eɪ	say	/seɪ/
əʊ	go	/ɡəʊ/ (*BrE*)
oʊ	go	/ɡoʊ/ (*AmE*)
aɪ	five	/faɪv/
aʊ	now	/naʊ/
ɔɪ	boy	/bɔɪ/
ɪə	near	/nɪə(r)/ (*BrE*)
eə	hair	/heə(r)/ (*BrE*)
ʊə	pure	/pjʊə(r)/ (*BrE*)